Court of Protection Practice 2011

Court of Protection Practice 2011

JORDANS

Published by
Jordan Publishing Limited
21 St Thomas Street
Bristol BS1 6JS

British Library Cataloguing-in-Publication Data
A catalogue record for this book is available from the British Library.

ISSN   2040-2627

ISBN   978 1 84661 266 4

Whilst the publishers and the authors have taken every care in preparing the material included in this work, any statements made as to the legal or other implications of particular transactions are made in good faith purely for general guidance and cannot be regarded as a substitute for professional advice. Consequently, no liability can be accepted for loss or expense incurred as a result of relying in particular circumstances on statements made in this work.

Crown Copyright material is reproduced with kind permission of the Controller of Her Majesty's Stationery Office.

This volume is typeset by Letterpart Ltd, Reigate, Surrey

LEGAL EDITOR: Juliet Smith BA (Hons) Law

COMMISSIONING EDITOR: Greg Woodgate LLB, LLM, Barrister

PUBLISHER: Caroline Vandridge-Ames LLM

The Tables and Index are researched and compiled by Josephine Joyce

The Directories appearing in Section XI of this work are researched and compiled by Sally Drever.

Printed in Great Britain by CPI Antony Rowe, Chippenham, Wiltshire

GENERAL EDITOR AND CONTRIBUTOR
District Judge Gordon Ashton, OBE
Nominated Judge of the Court of Protection
Visiting Professor in Law at Northumbria University

PRESENT CONTRIBUTORS
Penny Letts, OBE
Policy Consultant, Editor of Elder Law Journal

District Judge Marc Marin
Nominated Judge of the Court of Protection

Martin Terrell
Partner, Thomson Snell & Passmore

Adrian D Ward, MBE
Partner, Turnbull & Ward, Scotland

Richard Frimston
Partner, Russell-Cooke LLP

Alex Ruck Keene
Barrister, 39 Essex Street

PAST CONTRIBUTOR
Laurence Oates
Official Solicitor to the Supreme Court 1999–2006

Foreword to the First Edition

Practitioners in the Court of Protection will be familiar both with the previous work of the authors, *Mental Capacity: The New Law*, and with the reputation of the authors as expert and experienced practitioners themselves.

The authors have developed their previous book into this practice volume with the objective of providing all who work in the Court of Protection with easily accessible guidance to the principles, law and practice to be followed when considering how to proceed in mental capacity cases.

The resulting *Court of Protection Practice* usefully brings together statutory materials and key forms, and case-law supporting practice and procedures in the Court of Protection, together with authoritative comment from the authors. It is laid out in a logical manner, easy to follow, and will be invaluable both to those who are already familiar with mental capacity work and those who are new to this area of the law.

The law is stated as at 1 February 2009, but the authors have also included a helpful chapter on the Deprivation of Liberty Safeguarding provisions which will come into effect in April 2009. It is likely that the law governing Mental Capacity issues will continue to develop apace; I therefore welcome the authors' intention to update at regular intervals what will surely prove to be an essential volume for those who work in or appear before the Court of Protection.

Mark Potter.

Sir Mark Potter
President of the Family Division and of the Court of Protection
December 2008

Preface to the First Edition

Some 20 years ago the Law Society's Mental Health Sub-Committee drew attention to the legal vacuum in which people who lacked mental capacity were obliged to exist. This provoked the Law Commission to take the topic on board and, after several years of consultation, recommendations were made for a statutory mental incapacity jurisdiction. Different governments then pursued further consultation whilst lacking the will to introduce legislation, but pressures to do so became overwhelming with the introduction of community care policies, disability discrimination laws and ultimately human rights legislation. The Mental Capacity Act 2005 is the result, but a consequence of the changed climate is that it must meet higher standards than were expected when the need was first identified.

In addition to making provision for delegated decision-making and setting out the principles to be applied for assessment of capacity and a best interests approach, the Act establishes a new Court of Protection, with nominated judges and a regional presence. As a contributor on disability issues to Jordans' *The Family Court Practice* (the 'Red Book') and *Civil Court Service* (the 'Brown Book'), I perceived the need for a similar volume for those who practice in the new Court of Protection. So with the small team of 'experts' who wrote *Mental Capacity: The New Law*[1] as an introduction to this legislation, and joined by District Judge Marc Marin who sits in the Court of Protection at Archway, we have launched this further volume with the support of Jordans. In addition to the updated chapters from our previous work, it contains the Act, Regulations, Court Rules and Practice Directions (with our annotations where appropriate), together with the Code of Practice, Lasting Power of Attorney and Court Forms and some Procedural Guides. We hope that the *Court of Protection Practice 2009* will assist in the development and growth of this new jurisdiction and provide in a single handy volume all that those who work in or appear before the Court routinely need to accomplish their roles.

I wish to thank my co-authors for their dedicated contributions, each being highly experienced in the topics that they have covered. We have endeavoured to state the law as at 1 February 2009 whilst anticipating prospective changes coming into effect in April 2009. But this is an evolving area with new Lasting Power of Attorney forms, changes to the supervisory regime and a review of the working of the Rules all expected in 2009. It is hoped that, once this work is established, it will be updated at intervals so as to remain a reliable practice book, perhaps also identified by its colour!

Gordon R Ashton
Grange-over-Sands
December 2008

---

[1]   G Ashton, P Letts, L Oates and M Terrell *Mental Capacity: The New Law*, New Law Series (Jordans, 2006).

Introduction

The *new* Court of Protection continues to grow and mature, and in the process is involving a wider range of lawyers throughout the country. The regional presence is not only being felt but also providing a valuable service to those individuals and families who become involved in the uncertainty or disputes that can arise from adult incapacity. Many judges are also involved and developing new skills, especially in assessing capacity and determining best interests for those who cannot make their own decisions. This is surely to the benefit of society at large, but care must be taken to justify all advice that is given and all decisions that are taken so as not to appear out of step with public expectations.

We are fortunate to have the resources of the Office of the Public Guardian to support the new jurisdiction and provide supervision and support for decision-makers, whether they be deputies appointed by the Court or attorneys appointed by the individual. In Japan the courts were given this task and have become so overwhelmed that they now propose that funds be placed in private trusts where there may be no oversight. There is little point in having a statutory jurisdiction and then seeking to avoid it.

We continue our efforts to make this work of real value to practitioners and others who are involved with the Court. There has been little change to the legislative material or Rules and Practice Directions during 2010, but case law has continued to develop and thrown up a few surprises which are covered in the narrative, annotations and case summaries. The ad hoc Rules Committee worked hard to prepare and deliver in 2010 a set of proposals to streamline the procedures of the court and simplify the forms used, but we have yet to see these proposals implemented. To make access easier we have retained in Part IV the Court of Protection Rules 1998 and Practice Directions but moved the other statutory instruments and PDs into a new Part V, re-numbering the subsequent Parts. A new Part XI under the supervision of an experienced editor, Sally Drever, contains useful addresses and websites.

The major development for 2011 is the introduction of a new Part X *International*. The updated narrative chapter on Scottish law and procedure has been moved into this Part along with the former material on the International Protection of Adults but that is not all. Questionnaires have been sent to experienced lawyers in many other jurisdictions which are designed to identify how an adult from England or Wales who becomes incapacitated whilst living or owning property abroad may be dealt with. This is an increasing problem for lawyers called upon to advise families, and it is a maze if not a jungle 'out there'. We hope that this initiative will provide the guidance and support that readers may on occasions need, and intend to develop the scope of this coverage in future editions.

We have said goodbye to Laurence Oates, the former Official Solicitor, whose contributions to the first two editions proved invaluable. He has been succeeded by Alex Ruck Keene from Thirty Nine Essex Street Chambers who practices extensively in this area and was on the ad hoc Rules Committee. We also welcome Richard Frimston from Russell-Cooke LLP who has taken responsibility for the International content along with Adrian Ward from Scotland. I also wish to thank James Beck from the Office of the Official

Solicitor for continuing to support this work, and Joan Goulbourn from the Office of the Public Guardian for her oversight of relevant material.

We have endeavoured to state the law as at 1 February 2011. Constructive comment on the development of this volume would be welcome and should be sent to the publishers.

Gordon R Ashton
Grange-over-Sands
February 2011

Contents

Foreword	vii
Preface	ix
Introduction	xi
Table of Statutes	xxxix
Table of Statutory Instruments	xlix
Table of Cases	lix
Table of Practice Directions	lxv
Table of Codes of Practice	lxix
Table of EC and International Regulations	lxxi
List of Abbreviations	lxxiii

PART I: Narrative

CHAPTER 1
Background	**19**
Preliminary	19
Overview	19
Issues	19
Capacity	19
Decision-making	20
Communication	20
Conclusion	21
Legal competence	21
Tests of mental capacity	22
Assessment of mental capacity	22
Incapacitated people	23
Decision-making	23
Delegated decision-making	24
Decision-makers	24
Best interests	25
A special jurisdiction	25
Confidentiality	26
Undue influence	27
Assisted decision-making	27
The legal position	28
Legal background	29
Historical	29
Parens patriae	29
The declaratory jurisdiction	29
Terminology	30
Incapacity	31
Legislation	31
Mental Health Acts	31

Enduring Powers of Attorney Act 1985   31

The new climate   32
  The social climate   32
    General   32
      Community care   32
    Discrimination   32
      Attitudes to disability   33
      Terminology   34
      Attitudes of minority ethnic communities   35
    Role of the law   35
      Support   36
      Protection   36
      Empowerment   37
      Problems   37
    Role of lawyers   37
      Who is the client?   38
  The legal climate   38
    General   38
      Legal publishing   38
      Elderly client practices   39
    Community Care   39
      Background   39
      Reports   39
      Legislation   40
      Circulars and directions   42
    Equality and discrimination   42
      Background   42
      Equality Act 2010   43
      Prohibited conduct   44
      Direct discrimination   44
      Discrimination arising from disability   44
      Indirect discrimination   45
      Duty to make adjustments   45
      Harassment   46
      Victimisation   46
      Implications of conduct   46
      Premises   47
      Associations   47
    Human Rights Act 1998   48
      The Convention   48
      The legislation   48
      Interpretation   49
      Remedies   50
      New concepts   50
      Application to the Court of Protection and Public Guardian   51
      Comment   51
    Civil Partnership Act 2004   52
      Background   52
      The legislation   52

Incapacity issues 53
Access to justice 54
Background 54
A change of culture 54
Discrimination 54
Unrepresented parties 55
Disadvantages 55
Personal assistance 56
Physical and sensory impairments 57
Hearings 57
Interpreters 57

The (former) Court of Protection 58
Origins of the jurisdiction 58
Practice and procedure 58
General 58
Applications 59
Short orders 59
Persons under disability 60
Service 60
Evidence 60
Hearings 61
Conduct 61
Reviews and appeals 61
Fees and costs 61
Court fees 61
Legal costs 61
Venue 62
Background 62
Regional hearings 63
An evaluation of the Court of Protection 64
Court Rules 64
Contested hearings 65
Other hearings 65

Law reform 66
Origins 66
The Law Commission 66
Consultation 66
Report 67
The Government's response 68
'Who Decides?' 68
'Making decisions' 68
Legislation 68
Adults with Incapacity (Scotland) Act 2000 68
Mental Incapacity Bill 69
Mental Capacity Act 2005 69
Human rights compatibility 70
Conclusion 72

CHAPTER 2
The Mental Capacity Jurisdiction   **77**

Introduction   77

Part 1: Overview   77
  Key elements   77
    General   77
    Essential provisions   78
    The public bodies   79
  The Code of Practice   79
    Application   80
    Legal effect   81
      Sanctions for non-compliance   82
    Creation   83
      Consultation   83
      Procedure for approval   83
      Publication   84

Part 2: Principles and concepts   84
  The principles   84
    Background   84
      The statement of principles   85
    Presumption of capacity   86
      Law Commission proposals   87
      The legislation   87
      The Code of Practice   87
    Practicable steps to help decision-making   88
      Law Commission proposals   88
      The legislation   88
      The Code of Practice   88
    Unwise decisions   89
      The legislation   89
      Law Commission proposals   89
      Evidence before the Joint Committee   90
    Best interests   91
      The Law Commission proposals   91
      The Joint Committee's view   92
      The legislation   92
    Less restrictive alternative   92
      The Law Commission proposals   92
      The legislation   92
      The Scottish approach   93
    Application to the Court of Protection   93
  Defining lack of capacity   94
    The functional approach   94
    People who lack capacity   94
      The two-stage test of capacity   95
      A diagnostic threshold   95
      Principle of 'equal consideration'   96
      Qualifying age   96

Inability to make decisions 98
  Understand the information relevant to the decision 98
  Retain the information 100
  Use or weigh the information 100
  Unable to communicate 102
Common law tests of capacity 102
Reasonable belief of lack of capacity 103
Competence and capacity: children and young people 104
  Children under 16: '*Gillick* competence' 104
  Young people aged 16 or 17: Capacity or competence? 105
The assessment of capacity 106
  Background 106
  When should capacity be assessed? 106
  Who should assess capacity? 107
  The need for formal assessment 108
    Legal or professional requirements 109
    The 'Golden Rule' 109
    Other expert assessments 110
  How capacity is assessed 111
    Confidentiality 112
    Refusal to be assessed 113
  Recording assessments of capacity 113
    Professional records 113
    Formal reports or certificates of capacity 114
Determining best interests 114
  Background 114
  The best interests checklist 115
    Principle of equal consideration 116
    All relevant circumstances 117
    Regaining capacity 117
    Permitting and encouraging participation 118
    Life-sustaining treatment 118
    The person's wishes and feelings, beliefs and values 120
    The weight to be given to P's wishes and feelings 122
    The views of other people 123
    Duty to apply the best interests principle 124
    Reasonable belief 124

Part 3: General powers and duties 125
Acts in connection with care or treatment – background 125
  The problem 125
  The Law Commission proposal 126
    The general authority 126
  The views of the Joint Committee 126
Acts in connection with care or treatment – the legislation 127
  Protection from liability 127
    Section 5 acts 128
  Serious acts relating to medical treatment or welfare 129
    Who can act in connection with care or treatment? 131
    No protection in cases of negligence 132

Effect on advance decisions to refuse treatment   132
Limitations on permitted acts   132
    Restraint   132
    Decisions of donees or deputies   135
Paying for goods, services and other expenditure   136
    Background   136
    The legislation   136
        Responsibility to pay for necessary goods and services 137
        Expenditure   138
Excluded decisions   139
    Background   139
    The legislation   139
        Family relationships etc   139
        Mental Health Act matters   140
        Voting rights   141
Ill-treatment or neglect   142
    Background   142
    The new offence   142
        Scope of the offence   143
        Person who lacks capacity   143
        Ill-treatment   144
        Wilful neglect   144

CHAPTER 3
Lasting Powers of Attorney   **145**

Background   145
    Powers of attorney   145
        Limitations   145
        The incapable donor   147
    Statutory powers of attorney   147
        Enduring powers of attorney   147
            Success of enduring powers   150
            Problems with enduring powers   150
            Abolition of enduring powers   153
        Lasting Powers of Attorney   154

Nature of lasting power of attorney   154
    Character of lasting power of attorney   154
        Problems in practice   156
    Scope of lasting power of attorney   157
        Property and affairs   158
        Acting in the best interests of the donor   159
            Power to maintain others   160
            Limited power to make gifts   161
            The donor as trustee   163
            The donor as a litigant   163
        Welfare matters   164
            Limits on welfare matters   164
        Alternatives to welfare lasting powers of attorney   168

Form of lasting power of attorney   169
  Who can give a lasting power of attorney?   169
    Prescribed forms   169
      Use of different prescribed forms   169
      Defective forms   170
  Content of LPA   173
    Part A – the Donor's Statement   174
      Choice of attorney   174
      More than one attorney   174
      Replacement attorneys   176
      Restrictions and conditions   178
      Welfare restrictions   180
      Life-sustaining treatment   180
      Named persons to be notified   181
    Part B – the Certificate Provider's Statement   184
    Part C – the Attorney's Statement   188

Creation of lasting power of attorney   190
  A lasting power of attorney is created in two stages   190

The first stage: completing the instrument   190
  Capacity to create a power   191

The second stage: registration   192
  The requirement of registration   192
    Problems with capacity not being relevant to registration 193
    Problems with early registration   193
    Procedure for registration   194
    Status of attorney prior to registration   195
    Notices   196
      Service of notices   196
      Dispensing with notice   197
    Completion of registration   197
  Objections to registration   197
    The role of the Public Guardian   197
      Objections made to the Public Guardian 198
    The role of the Court of Protection   199
      Whether the requirements for the creation of the power have
        been met   200
      Whether the power has been revoked   200
      That fraud or undue pressure was used to induce the donor to
        create the power   201
      That the donee has behaved, is behaving or proposes to
        behave in a way that contravenes his or her authority or
        contrary to the donor's best interests 201
    Procedure   203

Enduring powers of attorney   203
  The future of existing powers   203

CHAPTER 4
Powers of the Court   205

Preliminary   205

Declarations   206
  Background   206
  General powers of the Court   207
    Declarations as to capacity   207
    Declarations as to medical treatment   208

Making decisions and appointing deputies   208
  Powers of the Court   208
  Making decisions   209
    General   209
      Children   209
    Personal welfare   209
    Property and affairs   210
      Wills   210
      Settlements   211
      Miscellaneous   212
  Deputies   212
    Appointment   212
      Who may be appointed?   213
      Control of the deputy   213
    Powers   213
      Conditional on lack of capacity   214
      Powers that cannot be given   214
      Medical treatment   214
      Conflict with an attorney   214
      Restraint   214
    Revocation of appointment   215
  How will the Court exercise these powers?   215
    The new approach   215
    What happens to receiverships?   216
      The past regime   216
      The new regime   216

Control of lasting powers of attorney   217
  Court's powers to intervene   217
    General   217
    Specific powers   218
      Creation and revocation   218
      Capacity   219
      Registration   219
      Meaning and effect of the power   220
      Directions to the attorney   221
      Rendering accounts etc   221
      Relieving the attorney of liability   221
      Gifts   222
    Applying to the Court   222

The role of the Public Guardian   223

Living with the new jurisdiction   224
  Overview   224
    Property and affairs   225
    Personal welfare   225
      Health care   225
      Personal care   226

CHAPTER 5
Welfare and Health Care, Advance Decisions and Research   **229**

Preliminary   229

The pre-existing common law   229
  The three bases for medical treatment   229
  Court's power to authorise treatment   229
    The demise of parens patriae   229
    The declaratory jurisdiction   230
    Emerging principles   230
  The development of the jurisdiction   231
    Welfare   231
    Power to grant injunctions   231
    Test of capacity   232
    Best interests   232
  Practice and procedure at common law   232
  Impact of the European Convention on Human Rights   233
    Relevant Convention rights   233
    The need for references to the High Court   234
    The background to reform   235

The position under the Mental Capacity Act 2005   235
  General   235
    Principles (s 1) and Codes of Practice (s 42)   236
    Capacity (s 2)   236
    Inability to make decisions (s 3)   237
    Best interests (s 4)   237
    'Acts in connection with care or treatment' (ss 5–6)   239
    The powers of the Court of Protection   239
  Practice and procedure under the Mental Capacity Act 2005   240
    Court Rules and Practice Directions   240
    Permission   240
    Serious medical treatment cases   241
    When should cases be brought to Court?   242
    Welfare or less serious medical treatment cases   244
  Withholding or withdrawing life-sustaining treatment   244
    Intolerability   246
    Best interests under the Mental Capacity Act 2005   246
  An exclusive jurisdiction   247
    Overlap with judicial review   248

Independent mental capacity advocates   248
  Establishment   248
    Appointment, functions and role   249
  The duty to instruct   250
    NHS bodies   250
    Local authorities   251
    Expansion of role   251
  Powers of the advocate   251
  Comment   252

The competent adult – advance decisions   252
  Preliminary   252

Advance directives at common law   253
  Refusal of treatment   253
    Essential features   253
    The relationship with suicide   253
  Requests for treatment   254

Advance decisions under the Mental Capacity Act 2005   254
  Recognition   254
    Advance refusals of treatment   254
    Advance requests for treatment   255
  Conditions for validity   255
    Applicability   255
    Life-sustaining treatment   255
  Implications of an advance decision   256
    Effect   256
    Doubt or disagreement   256
  The Code of Practice   256
  Comment   257
    Striking a balance   257
    The alternative of a lasting power of attorney   257
    Decisions by health care professionals   257
    References to the Court of Protection   258

Medical research   258
  Common law position   258
    The regulation of research   258
      General principles   259
      Clinical Trials Regulations   259
  Research authorised by the Mental Capacity Act 2005   260
    Background   260
    Application of the Act   261
      Pre-condition to authorisation   261
      Pre-conditions relating to the individual   261
    Comment   262

CHAPTER 6
Deprivation of Liberty Safeguards   **265**

Background   265

The Mental Health Act 1983, as amended by the Mental Health
    Act 2007   265
  Powers of admission, detention and treatment   265
  Review and appeals   266
  Purpose   267

Comparisons   267
  Differences   267
  Overlaps   268

The Deprivation of liberty safeguards   268
  The 'Bournewood Gap'   268
  The decisions of the domestic courts   269
  European Court of Human Rights   269

The MCA solution   270
  Meaning of deprivation of liberty   270
  Court of Protection powers   274
  Deprivation of liberty in a hospital or care home   274
  The age requirement   275
  The mental health requirement   275
  The mental capacity requirement   275
  The best interests requirement   275
  The eligibility requirement   275
  The no refusals requirement   276

Standard authorisations   276
  Urgent authorisations   278
  The Standard Authorisations, Assessments and Ordinary
    Residence Regulations   279
  The Appointment of Relevant Person's Representative Regulations   281

Review by the Court of Protection   282

Monitoring   282

Comment   283

CHAPTER 7
Court Practice and Procedure   **285**

Preliminary   285
  Role of the Lord Chancellor   285
  Judiciary   286
  Rules and Practice Directions   286

Status of the Court of Protection   286
  Preliminary   286
  The Court   287
    Name and venue   287

Administration	287
Forms	287
Judges	288
Regional judges	288
Allocation of cases	289
Transfer of cases	289
Powers	290
General	290
Interim orders and directions	290
Reports	291
The Court Rules	291
Court of Protection Rules 2007 (COPR 2007)	291
Practice Directions	293
The overriding objective	293
General	293
Duties of the Court and parties	293
Interpretation	294
Case management powers	294
General	294
Security for costs	295
Court's own initiative	295
Human rights	295
Practice and procedure	295
Court documents	295
Statements of truth	296
Personal details	296
Access to documents	296
Service of documents	296
Who serves?	297
How is service effected?	297
Notifying the incapacitated person	297
Permission to apply	298
Who may apply?	298
Applications for permission	299
Starting proceedings	299
Initial steps	299
Responding to an application	300
Parties	300
Applications within proceedings	301
Applications without notice	302
Interim remedies	302
Dealing with applications	302
Directions	303
Allocation	303
Disputing the Court's jurisdiction	303
Hearing the incapacitated person	303
Reconsideration	303

Hearings   304
  Types of case   304
Evidence   305
  Admissions   306
  Witnesses' evidence   306
  Depositions   307
  Reports   307
Experts   307
Disclosure   308
  Inspection   309
Litigation friends   309
Representation   310
Costs   310
  The general rule   311
  Assessment   311
  Public funding   312
Fees   313
Appeals   314
  Permission to appeal   315
Enforcement   315
Transitional provisions   316
Miscellaneous provisions   316

Practical points   316
The workload   316
  Volume of cases   316
  Cases under the new jurisdiction   317
Integration with other courts   318
  Judicial support   318
  Dual jurisdiction   319

CHAPTER 8
The Public Guardian and Supporting Services   **321**

Background   321
The administration   321
The Public Trust Office   322
  Nature   322
  Quinquennial Review   322
The Public Guardianship Office   324
  Launch of the PGO   324
  Progress   325
    The Mission statement   325
    The Consultative Forum   326
    National Audit Office Report   326
    A critical analysis   327
  Other jurisdictions   328
    Scotland   328
    Northern Ireland   329
    Ireland   329

The Public Guardian   329
  Office of the Public Guardian   330
  Functions   330
    Powers   331
    Fees   332
    Annual Report   332
  Public Guardian Board   332
    Annual Report   333
  Challenges ahead   333
    The new role   333
    Dispute resolution   334
    Investigating abuse   334
    Use of technology   335
    Partnerships   335
    Funding   335
    Relationship with the Court of Protection   335

Court of Protection Visitors   337
  Background   337
    Historical   337
    Types of Visitor   338
      Medical Visitors   338
      Legal Visitor   339
      General Visitors   339
      Enduring powers of attorney   340
    Recommendations for change   341
      Confidentiality of reports   341
      National Audit Office   342
      Interim reform   343
      Purpose of visits   344
  The new regime   345
    Appointment   345
      General Visitors   345
      Special Visitors   346
    Reports by Visitors   347
    Powers   347
    The changed climate   348
    Association of Independent Visitors   348

The Official Solicitor   348
  Status and function   348
  Background   349
  The present office   350
    Vision Statement   351
    Acceptance policy   351
    The incapacity work of the Official Solicitor   351
      Giving advice   351
      Representing adults who lack capacity   351
      Assisting the civil and family courts   352
      Assisting the Court of Protection   353

Adult medical and welfare declarations 353
Other jurisdictions 353
Scotland 354
Northern Ireland 354
Ireland 354
The future 354

CHAPTER 9
Miscellaneous **357**

Enduring powers – transitional (Mental Capacity Act 2005, Sch 4) 357

Transitional provisions (Mental Capacity Act 2005, Sch 5) 358
Mental Health Act 1983, Part VII 358
Enduring Powers of Attorney Act 1985 358

International Protection of Adults 359
The position in Non-Convention Countries 359
Scotland 359

Consequential amendments and repeals (Mental Capacity Act 2005, Sch 6) 359

PART II: Procedural Guides

Procedural Guide 1: Application to Register an Enduring Power of Attorney 365

Procedural Guide 2: Application to Register a Lasting Power of Attorney 366

Procedural Guide 3: Application for Appointment of a Deputy Relating to Property and Financial Affairs 367

Procedural Guide 4: Applications Relating to Personal Welfare 369

Procedural Guide 5: Proceedings in the High Court or a County Court Involving a Protected Party 370

Procedural Guide 6: Resolving doubt about capacity under the Civil Procedure Rules 1998 382

PART III: Mental Capacity Act 2005

Mental Capacity Act 2005 393

PART IV: Court of Protection Rules 2007 and Practice Directions

Court of Protection Rules 2007 573

Practice Direction – General provisions 680

Practice Direction A – Court documents (PD4A) 680

Practice Direction B – Statements of truth (PD4B) 682

Practice Direction – Service of documents 685

Practice Direction A – Service (PD6A) 685

Practice Direction – Notifying P 688

Practice Direction A – Notifying P (PD7A) 688

Practice Direction – Permission 690

Practice Direction A – Permission (PD8A) 690

Practice Direction – How to start proceedings 692

Practice Direction A – The application form (PD9A) 692

Practice Direction B – Notification of other persons that an application form has been issued (PD9B) 695

Practice Direction C – Responding to an application (PD9C) 697

Practice Direction D – Applications by currently appointed deputies, attorneys and donees in relation to P's property and affairs (PD9D) 699

Practice Direction E – Applications relating to serious medical treatment (PD9E) 702

Practice Direction F – Applications relating to statutory wills, codicils, settlements and other dealings with P's property (PD9F) 706

Practice Direction G – Applications to appoint or discharge a trustee (PD9G) 709

Practice Direction H – Applications relating to the registration of enduring powers of attorney (PD9H) 712

Practice Direction – Applications within proceedings 714

Practice Direction A – Applications within proceedings (PD10A) 714

Practice Direction B – Urgent and interim applications (PD10B) 717

Practice Direction – Deprivation of liberty applications 720

Practice Direction – Human Rights 726

Practice Direction A – Human Rights Act 1998 (PD11A) 726

Practice Direction – Dealing with applications 728

Practice Direction A – Court's jurisdiction to be exercised by certain judges (PD12A) 728

Practice Direction B – Procedure for disputing the court's jurisdiction (PD12B) 730

Practice Direction – Hearings 731

Practice Direction A – Hearings (including reporting restrictions) (PD13A) 731

Practice Direction – Admissions, evidence and depositions 736

Practice Direction A – Written evidence (PD14A) 736

Practice Direction B – Depositions (PD14B) 746

Practice Direction C – Fees for examiners of the court (PD14C) 751

Practice Direction D – Witness summons (PD14D) 753

Practice Direction E – Section 49 reports (PD14E) 754

Practice Direction – Experts 759

Practice Direction A – Expert evidence (PD15A) 759

Practice Direction – Litigation friend 761

Practice Direction A – Litigation friend (PD17A) 761

Practice Direction – Change of solicitor 764

Practice Direction A – Change of solicitor (PD18A) 764

Practice Direction – Costs 765

Practice Direction A – Costs in the Court of Protection (PD19A) 765

Practice Direction – Fixed Costs 767

Practice Direction B – Fixed costs in the Court of Protection (PD19B) 767

Practice Direction – Solicitors' and other professionals' fixed costs 772

Practice Direction B – Fixed costs in the Court of Protection (PD19B) 772

Practice Direction – Appeals 776

Practice Direction A – Appeals (PD20A) 776

Practice Direction – Enforcement 782

Practice Direction A – Contempt of court (PD21A) 782

Practice Direction – Transitory and transitional provisions 784

Practice Direction A – Transitional provisions (PD22A) 784

Practice Direction B – Transitory provisions (PD22B) 786

Practice Direction C – Appeals against decisions made under Part 7 of the Mental Health Act 1983 or under the Enduring Powers of Attorney Act 1985 which are brought on or after commencement (PD22C)   789

Practice Direction – Miscellaneous   791

Practice Direction A – Request for directions where notice of objection prevents public guardian from registering enduring power of attorney (PD23A)   791

Practice Direction B – Where P ceases to lack capacity or dies (PD23B)   793

PART V: Other Statutory Instruments and Practice Directions

Lasting Powers of Attorney, Enduring Powers of Attorney and Public Guardian Regulations 2007   799

Public Guardian (Fees, etc) Regulations 2007   822

Court of Protection Fees Order 2007   827

Mental Capacity Act 2005 (Transitional and Consequential Provisions) Order 2007   831

Mental Capacity Act 2005 (Transfer of Proceedings) Order 2007   851

Mental Capacity (Deprivation of Liberty: Appointment of Relevant Person's Representative) Regulations 2008   854

Mental Capacity (Deprivation of Liberty: Standard Authorisations, Assessments and Ordinary Residence) Regulations 2008   859

Civil Procedure Rules 1998   868

Practice Direction – Children and Protected Parties (PD21)   891

Practice Direction – About Costs (PDCosts)   920

Family Procedure (Adoption) Rules 2005   1005

Practice Direction – Service out of the Jurisdiction   1009

Guidance in cases involving protected parties in which the Official Solicitor is being invited to act as guardian ad litem or litigation friend   1026

PART VI: Codes of Practice

Mental Capacity Act 2005: Code of Practice   1033

Mental Capacity Act 2005: Deprivation of Liberty Safeguards Code of Practice   1272

PART VII: Forms

Court of Protection Forms 1369
  Form COP1 – Application 1369
  COP1A – Annex A: Supporting information for property and
    affairs applications 1382
  COP1B – Annex B: Supporting information for personal welfare
    applications 1400
  Form COP2 – Permission 1407
  Form COP3 – Assessment of capacity 1411
  Form COP4 – Deputy's declaration 1423
  Form COP5 – Acknowledgment of service/notification 1431
  Form COP7 – Application to object to the registration of a Lasting
    Power of Attorney 1437
  Form COP8 – Application relating to the registration of an
    Enduring Power of Attorney 1443
  Form COP9 – Application notice 1449
  Form COP10 – Application notice for applications to be joined as
    a party 1454
  Form COP12 – Special undertaking by trustees 1459
  Form COP14 – Proceedings about you in the Court of Protection 1463
  Form COP15 – Notice that an application form has been issued 1465
  Form COP20A – Certificate of notification/non-notification of the
    person to whom proceedings relate 1467
  COP 21A – Guidance notes on completing form COP20A 1471
  Form COP20B – Certificate of service/non-service
    notification/non-notification 1472
  COP 21B – Guidance notes on completing form COP20B 1476
  Form COP22 – Certificate of suitability of litigation friend 1477
  Form COP23 Certificate of failure or refusal of witness to attend
    before an examiner 1481
  Form COP24 – Witness statement 1485
  Form COP25 – Affidavit 1489
  Form COP29 – Notice of hearing for committal order 1493
  Form COP30 – Notice of change of solicitor 1494
  Form COP31 – Notice of intention to file evidence by deposition 1497
  Form COP35 – Appellant's notice 1499
  Form COP36 – Respondent's notice 1510
  Form COP37 – Skeleton argument 1520
  COP37 – Guidance notes 1522

Lasting Powers of Attorney Forms 1523
  Form LPA PFA and LPA HW – Form for Instrument Intended to
    Create a Lasting Power of Attorney 1524
  Form LPA 001 – Notice of Intention to Apply for Registration of a
    Lasting Power of Attorney 1559
  Form LPA 002 – Application to Register a Lasting Power of
    Attorney 1563
  Forms LPA 003A and LPA 003B – Notice of Receipt of an
    Application to Register a Lasting Power of Attorney 1577

Form LPA 004 – Notice of Registration of a Lasting Power of
    Attorney   1580
Form LPA 005 – Disclaimer by Donee of a Lasting Power of
    Attorney   1581
Enduring Power of Attorney Forms   1583
    Form EPI PG – Notice of Intention to Apply for Registration of an
        Enduring Power of Attorney   1583
    Form EP2 PG – Application to Register an Enduring Power of
        Attorney   1585
Deprivation of Liberty Forms   1597
    DLA – Deprivation of Liberty Application Form   1597
    DLB – Deprivation of Liberty Declaration of Exceptional Urgency   1606
    DLC – Deprivation of Liberty Permission Form   1608
    DLD – Deprivation of Liberty Certificate of Service/Non-service;
        Certificate of Notification/Non-notification   1610
    DLE – Deprivation of Liberty Acknowledgment of
        Service/Notification   1612

PART VIII: Precedent Orders

Section A: Standard Orders   **1619**

A 1 – GENERAL TITLE   1619

A 2 – ORDER appointing a deputy for property and affairs   1619

A 3 – ORDER appointing local authority as deputy for property and
    affairs   1622

A 4 – INTERIM ORDER for sale of property   1624

A 5 – INTERIM ORDER to investigate and report   1625

A 6 – ORDER discharging a property and affairs deputy where
    capacity is regained   1625

A 7 – ORDER refusing permission to be appointed as deputy for
    personal welfare   1626

A 8 – ORDER appointing a deputy for personal welfare   1627

Section B: Directions Orders   **1630**

B 1 – CASE MANAGEMENT CHECKLIST   1630

B 2 – MULTI-PURPOSE DIRECTIONS ORDER   1632

B 3 – FIRST DIRECTIONS ORDER family dispute as to residence
    and contact   1637

B 4 – DIRECTIONS ORDER 'adult care' case   1640

B 5 – DIRECTIONS ORDER local authority personal welfare application   1644

Section C: Final Orders   **1649**

C 1 – ORDER Capacity: financial affairs   1649

C 2 – ORDER EPA or Deputy   1650

C 3 – ORDER Discharge from the jurisdiction   1651

C 4 – ORDER Change of financial Deputy   1653

C 5 – ORDER Cancellation of EPA and appointment of financial Deputy   1654

C 6 – ORDER Appointment of financial Deputy in respect of large brain injury award   1657

PART IX: Case Summaries

Assessment of capacity   1667
  Enduring power of attorney   1667
    Duty of solicitor when carrying out an assessment of capacity to execute an EPA   1667
      Re AS and DS   1667
      Re HW   1668

Best interests   1670
  Deputy   1670
    Appointment – choice – wishes of 'P' – whether joint attorney should be appointed   1670
      Re: S and S (Protected Persons)   1670
  Statutory will   1673
    Approach to be adopted under MCA – interpretation of 'best Interests'   1673
      In the Matter of P   1673
  Lifetime gifts   1674
    Approach to be adopted under MCA – interpretation of 'best interests'   1674
      Re G (TJ)   1674

Capacity to litigate   1677
  Civil proceedings – assessment of capacity   1677
    Did a party to a settlement lack capacity? – implications   1677
      Martin Masterman-Lister v Brutton & Co and Jewell & Home Counties Dairies   1677
  Civil proceedings – implications of lack of capacity   1679
    Did a party to a settlement lack capacity? – implications   1679
      Bailey v Warren   1679
  Civil proceedings – assessment of capacity   1680

Capacity to litigate – factors of relevance for MCA 1680
   D v R (Deputy of S) and S 1680
Civil proceedings – protected party – protected beneficiary 1682
   CPR Pt 21 – how a civil court may resolve uncertainty as to
      capacity 1682
   In the matter of AKP 1682
   Approach of the court to assessment of capacity – CPR Pt 21 –
      implications of MCA 1683
   Saulle v Nouvet 1683
   CPR Pt 21 – how a civil court may resolve uncertainty as to
      capacity 1685
   In the matter of GS 1685

Court of Protection 1687
   Jurisdiction – test of capacity – powers of the court 1687
   Test of capacity to be satisfied for the court to assume
      jurisdiction under s 48 MCA to make Interim orders and
      directions 1687
   Re F 1687
   Principles to be adopted in health and welfare applications 1688
   Justification for the interference in the private family life of P 1688
   Re GC 1688
   Costs 1689
   Guidance for award of costs following cancellation of health
      and welfare LPA 1689
   Re RC 1689
   Costs 1691
   Guidance for award of costs – circumstances under which
      professional should not advance themselves as deputy 1691
   EG v RS, JS and BEN PCT 1691
   Evidence 1692
   Admissibility of hearsay evidence – Disclosure of police
      interviews 1692
   London Borough of Enfield v SA 1692
   Public hearings 1695
   Basis upon which the Court of Protection should hear matters
      in public or private 1695
   A v Independent News and Media Limited 1695
   Public hearings 1696
   Reporting of the names of parties 1696
   G v E & Ors 1696
   Schedule 3 – international jurisdiction of the Court 1697
   Basis upon which Court of Protection is to exercise jurisdiction
      under Schedule 3 – whether required to consider s.1(5) in
      so doing 1697
   Re MN 1697

Deprivation of liberty safeguards 1700
   Meaning of deprivation of liberty 1700

Circumstances under which there will be a deprivation of
    liberty – placement in residential home and foster
    placement   1700
    Re MIG and MEG   1700
Meaning of deprivation of liberty   1701
    Circumstances under which there will be a deprivation of
        liberty – obligations upon local authority   1701
    Re A (child) and Re C (adult)   1701
Meaning of deprivation of liberty   1702
    Circumstances under which there will be a deprivation of
        liberty – 16 and 17 year olds   1702
    Re RK   1702
Eligibility to be deprived of liberty when the purpose of the
    treatment to be provided relates to mental disorder   1704
    Placement in a residential home not registered as an
        independent hospital – to be assessed for treatment
        relating to mental disorder – authority under s 4A MCA –
        whether Case E, para 2, Sch 1A rendering person
        ineligible to be deprived of liberty under MCA applies to
        detention in a care home   1704
    *W PCT v (1) TB (2) V (3) S MBC (4) C&W Partnership NHS
        Trust and (5) W MBC*   1704
Ineligible to be deprived of liberty by MCA as being subject to the
    Mental Health Act 1983   1705
    Jurisdictional basis of a person being not ineligible to be
        deprived of liberty under MCA – tests or gateways for
        when ineligible under Sch 1A – general points and points
        of statutory construction.   1705
    *GJ v (1) The Foundation Trust (2) The PCT and (3) The
        Secretary of State for Health*   1705
Schedule A1   1707
    Interaction of urgent and standard authorisations – whether
        second urgent authorisation can be used   1707
    Re MB   1707
Schedule A1   1709
    Compatibility of DOLS safeguards with Article 5 ECHR   1709
    G v E   1709

Deputies   1710
Civil proceedings – damages   1710
    Need for a professional deputy to administer a brain injury
        award   1710
    Eagle v Chambers   1710
Deputy for property and affairs – Security Bond   1711
Professional deputy – size of security bond   1711
    In the Matter of H (a minor and an incapacitated person)   1711
When required   1713
    When the Court should appoint a deputy for P – construction of
        s 16(4) MCA   1713
    Re P   1713

When required   1714
  When the Court should appoint a deputy for P – construction of
      s 16(4) MCA   1714
    G v E   1714

Enduring Powers of Attorney   1715
  Enduring power of attorney – validity   1715
    Lack of capacity – standard of proof   1715
      Re K, Re F   1715
    Lack of capacity – burden of proof   1716
      Re W (Enduring Power of Attorney)   1716
    Lack of capacity – burden of proof – costs   1717
      In the Matter of C   1717
    Appointment of substitute attorney – whether valid   1718
      In the Matter of J (Enduring Power of Attorney)   1718

Inherent jurisdiction   1720
  Survival of jurisdiction following the MCA   1720
    Scope of declaratory jurisdiction of the High Court   1720
      LBL v RYJ and VJ   1720

Inherent jurisdiction   1721
  Survival of jurisdiction following the MCA   1721
    Scope of declaratory jurisdiction of the High Court   1721
      A v DL, RL and ML   1721

Wills   1723
  Statutory will   1723
    Approach to be adopted under MCA   1723
      In the Matter of P   1723
    Approach to be adopted under MCA – exclusion of individual –
      benefitting charity   1725
      In the Matter of M   1725
  Statutory will   1726
    Approach to be adopted under MCA – interpretation of 'best
      Interests'   1726
      Re D (Statutory Will)   1726

PART X: International Protection of Adults

CHAPTER 1
Introduction and Overview   1733

Introduction   1733

Private International Law   1734

CHAPTER 2
The Convention on the International Protection of Adults   **1735**

Introduction   1735

Mental Capacity Act 2005, Sch 3   1736

Jurisdiction and Habitual residence   1737

Applicable Law   1737

Recognition and Enforcement   1738

Protective Measures   1738

Within the United Kingdom   1738

The position in Non-Convention Countries   1739

CHAPTER 3
Northern Ireland   **1741**

CHAPTER 4
Scotland   **1743**

Background   1743

Adults with Incapacity (Scotland) Act 2000   1747

Measures outwith the Incapacity Act   1764

APPENDIX 1
Adults with incapacity   **1765**

International questionnaire on cross border recognition and
    enforcement   1765

APPENDIX 2
Completed questionnaires   **1773**

Australia: NSW   1773

Australia: Victoria   1781

Belgium   1786

Canada: Alberta   1793

Canada: Manitoba   1800

Canada: Nova Scotia   1806

Canada: Ontario   1811

Canada: Saskatchewan   1816

Denmark   1821

Finland   1826

France 1831
Germany 1837
Iceland 1849
Japan 1854
Serbia 1859
Slovenia 1869
Spain 1878
Switzerland 1884
USA: Florida 1890

PART XI: Directories

Organisations 1901

Websites 1914

Useful publications 1922

Index 1927

Table of Statutes

References are to page numbers.

Abortion Act 1967
  s 1 — 243
Access to Justice Act 1999
  s 6(8) — 312
Administration of Estates Act 1925 — 359
Administration of Justice Act 1960 — 359
Adoption and Children Act 2002 — 360
  s 1 — 1726
  s 52 — 140
Adult Support and Protection (Scotland) Act
    2007 — 21, 329, 1744, 1746, 1747
Adults with Incapacity (Scotland) Act
    2000 — 21, 53, 68, 85, 87, 91, 328,
        329, 354, 1744, 1745, 1747,
        1748, 1749, 1750, 1755, 1757,
        1761, 1763, 1764
  Pt 2 — 1754
  Pt 3 — 1750, 1755, 1758, 1760, 1763
  Pt 4 — 1760, 1761
  Pt 5 — 1761
  Pt 6 — 1758, 1759, 1760, 1761, 1762, 1763
  s 1 — 85, 1744, 1754, 1764
  s 1(1)–(5) — 1752
  s 1(2) — 93
  s 1(3) — 93
  s 1(4)(a) — 1754
  s 1(4)(b) — 53
  s 1(6) — 1753
  s 1(7) — 1753
  s 3(5A) — 1753
  s 3(5A), (5B) — 1751
  s 4 — 1751
  s 6 — 1750
  s 6(2)(da) — 1745
  s 7 — 1750
  s 9 — 1751
  s 10 — 1751
  s 16(6) — 1755
  s 20 — 1757
  s 24A — 1759
  s 27A(1)(b) — 1759
  s 27C — 1759
  s 27F — 1758
  s 32 — 1758
  s 51 — 1752
  s 53(3) — 1751
  s 57(2) — 1751
  s 58(1)(b) — 1758
  s 64(1) — 1763
  s 64(2) — 1763
  s 66 — 1752
  s 67(3) — 1764

Adults with Incapacity (Scotland) Act
    2000—*continued*
  s 67(4) — 1764
  s 70 — 1764
  s 71 — 1764
  s 77 — 1764
  s 79A — 1747
  s 82 — 1752
  s 83 — 1752
  s 87(1) — 1751
  s 87(2) — 53
  Sch 3 — 1735, 1748
    para 2(1) — 1748
    para 2(2) — 1748
    para 2(3) — 1748
    para 3(3) — 1757
    para 4 — 1757
Age of Legal Capacity (Scotland) Act
    1991 — 1747
Autism Act 2009 — 41

Care Standards Act 2000 — 41, 291, 1041, 1232
  Pt 2 — 331, 348
Carers (Equal Opportunities) Act 2004 — 41
Carers (Recognition and Services) Act
    1995 — 41
Carers and Disabled Children Act 2000 — 41
Charging Orders Act 1979
  s 5 — 672
Child Support Act 1991 — 360
Children Act 1989 — 23, 36, 96, 97, 104, 140,
        209, 227, 231, 233, 235, 289,
        298, 300, 317, 319, 415, 425,
        851, 853, 1141, 1202, 1204,
        1209, 1255, 1640, 1694
  Pt V — 1187
  s 1 — 1726
  s 47 — 1187
Children and Young Persons Act 1933
  s 1 — 144, 442
Chronically Sick and Disabled Persons Act
    1970 — 40
Civil Evidence Act 1995
  s 5 — 1693
  s 11 — 306, 1693
Civil Partnership Act 2004 — 52, 53
  s 1 — 52, 425
Community Care (Delayed Discharge, etc)
    Act 2003 — 41
Compulsory Purchase Act 1965 — 359

Constitutional Reform Act 2005	285, 333
s 59(5)	563, 565, 917, 919, 983
Sch 1	349
Pt 1	611
Sch 11	
para 1(2)	563, 565
Pt 1	
para 1(2)	917, 919, 983
Consumer Credit Act 1974	360
Courts Act 2003	285
Courts and Legal Services Act 1990	
s 27	450
s 27(2)(c)	56
s 28	450
s 71	339
Data Protection Act 1998	26, 263, 1041,
	1244, 1246, 1247, 1248, 1256,
	1260
s 7	1245, 1246
Disability Discrimination Act 1995	42, 55,
	360, 881, 1041
s 1	312
Disabled Persons Act 1981	40
Disabled Persons (Services Consultation and	
Representation) Act 1986	41
Enduring Powers of Attorney Act 1985	58,
	147, 148, 153, 160, 162, 182,
	202, 203, 341, 357, 358, 359,
	360, 458, 532, 533, 1120, 1258,
	1718, 1719
s 1(1)(a)	148
s 2(1)(a)	149
s 3(4)	160
s 4(1)	149, 152
s 5	149
s 6(4)(a)	149
s 6(5)	149, 1716
s 6(6)	200, 1716
s 8	149
s 8(2)	150
s 8(2)(c)	221
s 8(4)	149
s 9	413
s 9(3)	148
s 10(1)(a)	340
s 10(2)	340
s 11(1)	175
s 13	153
s 48	154
Sch 1	
para 2(1)	149, 181
para 2(2)	197
para 4(1)	149
Equality Act 2006	42
Equality Act 2010	43, 44
s 5	43
s 6	43
s 7	43

Equality Act 2010—*continued*	
s 8	43
s 9	43
s 10	43
s 11	43
s 12	43
s 13	44
s 15	43, 44
s 16	43
s 19	45
s 20	45, 46
s 21	45
s 26	46
s 27	46
s 29	46
ss 32–35	47
ss 100–103	47
Sch 1	43
Family Law Act 1996	53
Family Law Reform Act 1969	359
s 8	229
s 8(1)	105, 1205
Fatal Accidents Act 1976	53
Fines and Recoveries Act 1833	359
Fraud Act 2006	1226
Health Act 1999	41
Health Act 2009	41
Health and Social Care Act 2001	
Pt 4	41
s 60	1193
s 61	1194
Health and Social Care Act 2008	41, 82
Health and Social Care (Community Health	
and Standards) Act 2003	
s 148	291
Health and Social Services and Social	
Security Adjudications Act 1983	40
Health Services and Public Health Act	
1968	40
Housing Act 1985	40, 41
Housing Act 1996	
Pt VII	41
Human Fertilisation and Embryology Act	
1990	140, 1040
Human Fertilisation and Embryology Act	
2008	
s 56	424
s 65	427
Sch 6	
Pt 1	
para 40	424
Sch 7	
para 25	427
Human Rights Act 1998	42, 48, 51, 58, 75,
	106, 134, 233, 295, 632, 881,
	1041, 1114, 1246, 1259
s 1	48
s 2(1)	49

Human Rights Act 1998—*continued*
s 3 49
s 4 .... 242, 295
s 6 51
s 7 51
s 8(1) 50
s 10 49
s 19 48
Sch 1 48
Human Tissue Act 2004 ...... 263, 1041, 1193,
                                        1200, 1259
s 1(9) 1193, 1200

Industrial and Provident Societies Act
    1965 359
Inheritance (Provisions for Family and
    Dependents) Act 1975 619
Insolvency Act 1986 360
Interpretation Act 1978
s 7 538
Intestates' Estates Act 1952 359

Judicature (Northern Ireland) Act 1978
s 28(1) 329

Law of Property Act 1925 359
s 204 290
Law of Property (Miscellaneous Provisions)
    Act 1989
s 1 .... 145, 190
Law Reform (Miscellaneous Provisions)
    (Scotland) Act 1990
s 71 1746
Leasehold Reform Act 1967 359
Leasehold Reform, Housing and Urban
    Development Act 1993 360
Legal Services Act 2007
s 194(3) 929
s 210 563
Sch 23 563
Licensing Act 2003 360
Limitation Act 1980
s 38 360
Local Authority Social Services Act
    1970 359
s 1A 446
s 7 .... 42, 1187
Local Government Act 1972 360
Lunacy Act 1890 58
Lunacy Regulation Act 1853 337
Lunacy Regulation Act 1862 337
Lunatics' Visitors Act 1833 337

Matrimonial Causes Act 1973 360
s 25 .... 1725, 1726
Medicines Act 1968 359
Mental Capacity Act 2005 ...... 21, 25, 26, 30,
    34, 37, 53, 67, 69, 70, 73, 75, 77,
    78, 79, 80, 81, 82, 83, 84, 85, 89,
    92, 93, 94, 95, 100, 103, 104,

Mental Capacity Act 2005—*continued*
    105, 106, 114, 119, 123, 127,
    130, 133, 136, 142, 147, 149,
    150, 152, 153, 154, 157, 158,
    160, 161, 163, 165, 166, 167,
    168, 170, 174, 178, 180, 181,
    182, 183, 184, 185, 187, 188,
    190, 191, 192, 193, 195, 197,
    198, 199, 202, 203, 204, 205,
    206, 208, 212, 214, 217, 225,
    226, 227, 229, 235, 239, 244,
    249, 252, 263, 265, 267, 268,
    270, 285, 286, 287, 288, 289,
    293, 306, 313, 316, 336, 351,
    353, 354, 356, 357, 370, 372,
    396, 463, 582, 583, 584, 607,
    611, 673, 853, 872, 873, 878,
    880, 1033, 1036, 1039, 1041,
    1204, 1209, 1266, 1619, 1622,
    1624, 1625, 1627, 1632, 1638,
    1641, 1644, 1649, 1650, 1651,
    1653, 1655, 1678, 1680, 1682,
    1683, 1686, 1719, 1723, 1747
s 1 ... 70, 72, 93, 131, 155, 189, 208, 214,
    236, 275, 404, 406, 408, 445,
    533, 583, 1042, 1108, 1124,
    1132, 1139, 1142, 1151, 1177,
    1620, 1623, 1628, 1655, 1670
ss 1–4 873
s 1(1)–(6) 85
s 1(2) 87, 252, 396, 1043, 1670
s 1(3) 88, 117, 396, 401, 1044, 1671
s 1(4) 89, 397, 1046, 1671
s 1(5) .. 92, 114, 124, 165, 397, 402, 1048,
                                        1080, 1096
s 1(6) 92, 160, 397, 404, 1048, 1671,
                                        1673
s 1(7) 71, 1672
s 1(8) 71
s 2 ... 70, 94, 155, 236, 275, 396, 398, 404,
    406, 408, 413, 445, 462, 653,
    1254, 1265, 1630, 1670
ss 2–5 235
s 2(1) ... 94, 102, 191, 370, 397, 398, 873,
    1059, 1202, 1203, 1206, 1208,
                                        1684
s 2(2) 95, 398, 1060
s 2(3) 96, 116, 398, 400, 1060
s 2(4) 398, 1061
s 2(5) 97, 398, 1203
s 2(6) 97, 398, 1203
s 3 ... 94, 98, 237, 275, 396, 397, 404, 406,
    408, 445, 462, 1060, 1265, 1670
s 3(1) 98, 371, 874, 1062
s 3(1)(a) 399
s 3(1)(b) 399
s 3(1)(c) 101, 399
s 3(1)(d) 98, 102, 167, 399
s 3(2) 98, 237, 399, 1049, 1063
s 3(3) 100, 237, 399, 1064

Mental Capacity Act 2005—*continued*

s 3(4)	98, 399, 1063
s 4	70, 92, 114, 115, 154, 155, 158, 165, 189, 202, 212, 214, 237, 239, 397, 408, 414, 445, 463, 656, 884, 1048, 1081, 1084, 1096, 1124, 1132, 1151, 1670
s 4(1)	116, 398, 400, 1085
s 4(2)	117, 246, 400
s 4(3)	117, 401, 1088
s 4(4)	118, 401, 1087, 1671
s 4(5)	118, 119, 165, 238, 246, 401, 1089, 1090
s 4(6)	120, 246, 255, 258, 401, 1090, 1671
s 4(6)(a)	401, 1092
s 4(6)(b)	401
s 4(6)(c)	121, 401, 1093
s 4(7)	53, 123, 158, 164, 168, 401, 1094, 1190, 1671
s 4(7)(b)	402
s 4(8)	103, 107, 124, 402
s 4(9)	124, 125, 167, 402, 404, 442, 1096
s 4(10)	118, 401, 405, 410, 1163, 1261
s 4(11)	117, 400, 1086
s 4A	274, 405, 415, 520, 1704
s 4A(3)	402
s 4A(5)	402
s 4B	274, 405, 520
s 5	70, 113, 125, 128, 129, 130, 131, 132, 134, 135, 137, 139, 140, 141, 164, 168, 239, 244, 265, 268, 274, 317, 355, 404, 405, 406, 425, 426, 1091, 1100, 1102, 1104, 1105, 1106, 1107, 1108, 1111, 1114, 1115, 1116, 1117, 1163, 1164, 1203, 1206, 1207, 1211, 1626, 1764
s 5(1)	87, 103, 107, 222, 404, 442, 1070, 1102
s 5(1)(a)	131, 404, 1108
s 5(1)(b)	404
s 5(1)(b)(ii)	131, 404
s 5(2)	127, 404
s 5(3)	132, 404
s 5(4)	132, 404
s 6	70, 132, 265, 268, 1104
s 6(1)	132, 405
s 6(2)	132, 133, 405
s 6(3)	133, 405
s 6(3)(a)	1150
s 6(4)	133, 405, 1112, 1265
s 6(4)(b)	405
s 6(5)	134, 135, 1104, 1114
s 6(6)	135, 139, 405, 407, 1116, 1119
s 6(6)(a)	164
s 6(7)	71, 135, 405
s 7	136, 195, 1117
ss 7–9	70

Mental Capacity Act 2005—*continued*

s 7(1)	137, 406
s 7(2)	136, 406, 1117
s 8	138, 195, 406, 1117
s 8(1)(a)	138, 406
s 8(1)(b)	138, 406, 407
s 8(2)	138
s 8(2)(a)	406, 407
s 8(2)(b)	407
s 8(3)	138, 407
s 9	70, 154, 217
ss 9–14	407, 423
s 9(1)	155, 158, 407, 408, 1260
s 9(1)(a)	408
s 9(1)(b)	408
s 9(2)	190
s 9(2)(b)	191, 192, 195
s 9(2)(c)	219, 1205
s 9(3)	170
s 9(4)	158, 408, 1124
s 9(4)(b)	157, 178, 1132
s 10	175
s 10(1)	174
s 10(1)(b)	409
s 10(2)	70
s 10(4)	174, 1122
s 10(4)–(7)	409
s 10(5)	409, 1123
s 10(6)	175, 219
s 10(8)	1123
s 10(8)(a)	176
s 10(8)(b)	177, 409
s 11	70
s 11(1)–(5)	410
s 11(1)–(6)	408
s 11(3)	165
s 11(4)	165
s 11(4)(a)	1150
s 11(6)	165
s 11(7)	410
s 11(7)(a)	156, 165, 169, 192, 1126
s 11(7)(b)	165, 1126
s 11(7)(c)	164, 1126
s 11(8)	165, 180, 410
s 12	70, 160, 161, 162, 179, 1130
s 12(2)	161, 222, 411, 1131
s 12(2)(b)	1129
s 12(3)	161
s 12(3)(b)	1129
s 12(4)	411
s 13	412
s 13 (6)(b)	199
s 13(2)	412
s 13(3)	198, 199
s 13(6)	146, 412
s 13(6)(a)–(d)	176, 198, 409
s 13(6)(c)	412
s 13(8)	70, 146
s 13(9)	70
s 13(11)	412

Mental Capacity Act 2005—*continued*

s 15   207, 217, 239, 1142, 1143, 1257,
             1685, 1687
ss 15–17   157
ss 15–21   71
ss 15–23   443
s 15(1)   109
s 16   208, 240, 612, 1145, 1171, 1670,
             1705
ss 16–20   534
s 16(1)   109, 197
s 16(1)(b)   422
s 16(2)   70, 1258
s 16(2)(a)   165, 274, 355, 402, 515, 722,
             1706
s 16(3)   93
s 16(4)   93, 240, 1626
s 16A   274
s 17   209, 217, 414, 1171
s 17(1)(d)   240
s 17(1)(e)   1170
s 17A   426
s 18   195, 210, 217, 414, 612
s 18(1)(b)   162, 611
s 18(1)(h)   611
s 18(1)(i)   416, 611
s 18(1)(j)   612, 773
s 18(1)(k)   163
s 18(2)   1205
s 18(3)   97, 398, 416, 851, 1202
s 19   212, 414
s 19(1)   1148
s 19(1)(b)   417
s 19(2)   174
s 19(4)(c)   1149
s 19(5)   417
s 19(6)   417, 1152
s 19(7)   213
s 19(8)   213
s 19(9)   677
s 19(9)(a)   1150
s 19(13)   215
s 20   70, 213, 240, 414, 415, 416, 1150
s 20(7)–(11)   214
s 20(11)(a)   1150
s 21   97, 209, 235, 289, 1141, 1208
s 21A   282, 720, 722
s 21A(1)(a)   420
s 21A(1)(b)   420
s 21A(3)(b)   420
s 21A(5)(b)   420
s 22   199, 617, 1135
s 22(1)(a)   421
s 22(2)   196, 200, 218
s 22(3)   192, 198
s 22(3)(a)   219
s 22(3)(b)   219, 220, 421
s 22(4)   200
s 22(5)   219
s 23   157, 162, 617, 1135

Mental Capacity Act 2005—*continued*

s 23(1)   220
s 23(2)   221
s 23(3)   453
s 23(3)(a)   178, 223
s 23(3)(a)–(c)   221
s 23(3)(d)   222
s 23(4)   160, 162, 222, 422
s 24   132, 254, 404, 1092, 1157
ss 24–26   168
s 24(1)(a)   254
s 24(2)   254
s 24(3)   1164
s 24(5)   254, 422
s 25   132, 165, 254, 404, 1157, 1165
s 25(1)   1158
s 25(2)   255
s 25(2)(b)   164, 423
s 25(3)   1166
s 25(3), (4)   255
s 25(4)   1166
s 25(5)   71, 181
s 25(5), (6)   255
s 25(6)   168, 181
s 26   132, 254, 404, 1157, 1169
s 26(1)   424
s 26(2)   256, 1111, 1169
s 26(3)   256, 1170
s 26(4)   256
s 26(5)   71, 256, 424
s 27   139, 146, 166, 408, 414, 1040
ss 27–29   157, 1040
s 27(1)(a)   425
s 27(1)(b)   318, 425
s 27(1)(c)   425
s 27(1)(d)   425
s 27(1)(f)   425
s 27(1)(g)   425
s 27(2)   425
s 28   139, 140, 166, 268, 408, 414, 1041,
       1126, 1222
s 28(1)   425
s 28(1A)   141, 425
s 28(1B)   141, 426
s 29   139, 141, 146, 166, 408, 414, 1041
s 30   260, 261
ss 30–33   1201
s 30(1)   427, 428
s 30(5)   427
s 30(6)   427
s 31   260, 261
ss 31–34   427
s 31(1)   428
s 32   260, 262, 1197, 1207
s 32(3)   262, 429
s 33   260, 262
s 33(2)(b)   429
s 34   260, 262
s 34(2)   430
s 35   248, 1260

Mental Capacity Act 2005—*continued*

ss 35–39	71
ss 35–41	130, 1173
s 35(1)	431
s 35(2)	431
s 35(4)	248
s 35(6)	70, 251, 1177, 1179
s 35(6)(b)	1176
s 36	249, 1260
s 37	250, 1183, 1187
s 37(2)	432
s 37(6)	432, 434
s 37(7)	432, 434
s 38	250, 1187
s 38(2)	434, 435
s 38(4)	251
s 38(6)	434
s 38(7)	434
s 38(8)	434
s 39	251, 1187
s 39(2)	435
s 39(3)	435
s 39(3), (4)	251
s 39A	436
s 39A(5)	436
s 39C(1)(b)	437
s 40	250
s 40(1)	439
s 41(1)	439
s 42	79, 236, 1033, 1034
s 42(1)	80
s 42(2)	80
s 42(3)	80, 441
s 42(4)	81, 441, 1042
s 42(5)	82, 441, 1042
s 43	83, 1033, 1034
s 43(1)	83
s 43(1)(a)	441
s 43(1)(b)	441
s 43(2)	83
s 43(2)(b)	441
s 43(3)	84, 442
s 43(4)	83, 441
s 43(5)	83, 441
s 44	142, 201, 1137, 1202, 1204, 1224, 1230, 1259, 1265
s 44(1)(a)	143, 442
s 44(1)(b)	143
s 44(1)(c)	143
s 44(2)	442
s 44(3)(b)	142, 442
s 45	1139
ss 45–56	71, 286
s 46	247, 288
s 47	244
s 47(1)	290, 315, 445
s 47(3)	290
s 48	87, 208, 290, 396, 1687
s 48(a)	445
s 48(c)	445

Mental Capacity Act 2005—*continued*

s 49	291, 307, 347, 622, 644, 1687
s 49(2)	223, 455
s 49(5)	581, 934, 1034
s 49(7)–(9)	70
s 50	71, 298, 367, 369, 609, 1141
s 50(1)	609
s 50(1)(b)	164
s 50(1)(c)	222
s 50(2)	199, 609
s 50(3)	93, 241
s 50(3)(b)	1627
s 50(3)(c)	1627
s 51	291, 581
s 51(1)	1693
s 51(2)	1693
s 51(2)(d)	71, 314
s 51(2)(i)	1693
s 51(3)	448
s 52	240, 293, 448
s 53	314, 666, 1242
s 53(2)	449, 581
s 53(4)	449, 581
s 54	71, 314
s 54(1)	450
s 55	310
s 55(1)	450
s 55(5)	450
s 56	310
s 57	329, 425, 446, 1226, 1262
s 57(4), (5)	330
s 58	223, 330, 425, 446
s 58(1)(c)	453
s 58(1)(d)	347, 453, 455, 1256
s 58(1)(e)	418
s 58(1)(f)	418, 453
s 58(1)(h)	222
s 58(3)(b)	453
s 58(3), (4)	331
s 58(4)	453
s 58(5)	70
s 58(5), (6)	331
s 58(6)	70
s 58A	425
s 59	332, 1227
s 59(6)	333, 454
s 59(9)	333
s 60	332
s 61	446, 1256
s 61(1)–(4)	345
s 61(5)	70, 348
s 61(6)	348
s 62	119, 165, 247, 401, 1040, 1041, 1158
s 63	1735
s 64(1)	404, 409, 416, 417, 446, 1102
s 65(1)	581
s 66(1)(b)	154, 532
s 66(4)	358
s 67(4)(b)	581

Mental Capacity Act 2005—*continued*

Sch A1	270, 402, 436, 460, 507, 520,	
		720, 1705, 1706
	para 2	1705
	para 12(1)(a), (b)	1707
	para 14(1)	462
	para 14(2)	462
	para 16(1)	463, 492
	para 16(5)	463
	para 17	515
	para 33(4)	468
	para 42(2)(b)	470
	para 47(1)	471
	para 70(1)	477
	para 70(2)	477
	para 129(3)	477, 491
	para 130(2)	492
	para 130(5)	492
	para 139	281
	para 146	470
	para 161	436
	para 176	420, 464
	para 177	420, 464
	para 179	420, 464
	para 180	464
	paras 180–182	420
	para 181	464
	para 182	464
	para 182(2)	281
	para 183(6)	504
	Pt 1 (paras 1–4)	274
	Pt 3 (paras 12–20)	275
	Pt 4	420
	Pt 4 (paras 21–73)	276
	Pt 5	420
	Pt 5 (paras 74–90)	278
	Pt 6 (paras 91–97)	276
	Pt 7 (paras 98–100)	276
	Pt 8 (paras 101–125)	276
	Pt 9 (paras 126–136)	276
	Pt 10	437, 438
	Pt 10 (paras 137–153)	276
	Pt 11 (paras 154–161)	276
Sch 1	145, 146, 150, 170, 192, 196, 220,	
		407
	para 1	409
	para 1(2)	169, 508
	para 1(3)	508
	para 1(e)	187
	para 2(1)(c)	181, 182
	para 2(1)(d)	188, 191
	para 2(1)(e)	184, 191
	para 2(2)(a)	509
	para 2(2)(b)	182, 188
	para 2(3)	177, 509
	para 2(b)	184
	para 3(1)	509
	para 3(2)	218, 509
	para 4(1)	194
	para 4(1)(a)	510

Mental Capacity Act 2005—*continued*

Sch 1—*continued*		
	para 4(3)	195
	para 5	192, 197
	para 6	196
	para 7	196, 510
	para 8	510
	para 8(1)	196
	para 8(2)	177, 196
	para 10	183, 197
	para 11(1)	170, 198, 511
	para 11(2)	198, 511
	para 11(3)	198
	para 12	198
	para 13(1)	198
	para 13(1)(b)	512
	para 13(2)	198
	para 13(3)	198, 199
	para 13(3)(b)(i)	512
	para 13(3)(b)(ii)	512
	para 13(4)	198
	para 14	199
	para 14(1)(b)	512
	para 17(1)	513
	para 18	200
	para 18(b)	194
	Pt 1	169
Sch 1A	165, 276, 415, 507, 515, 520,	
		1647
	para 2	
	Case E	1705, 1706, 1707
	Cases A–D	1707
	para 5(3)	1707
	para 5(4)	1707
Sch 2		211, 416
	para 5	211
	para 6	211
	para 7	211
	para 8–9	212
	para 13(4)	199
Sch 3		1735, 1736, 1748
	para 19	530
	para 20(2)	298, 609
	para 35	529, 1735
	Pt 3	365
Sch 4	145, 148, 153, 202, 204, 357, 359,	
		365, 458, 532, 618, 1142, 1258
	para 1	148, 149, 542
	para 1(1)	357, 533
	para 1(1)(c)	533
	para 1(2)	158, 195
	para 2	148, 533
	para 2(1)	149
	para 2(3)	534, 542
	para 2(9)	534, 618
	para 2(10)	534
	para 3	148
	para 3(1)	158
	para 3(2)	158, 160
	para 3(2)(a)	534

Mental Capacity Act 2005—*continued*
Sch 4—*continued*

para 3(3)	158, 222
para 4(1)	152, 535
para 4(2)	223
para 4(4)	535
para 4(5)(a), (b)	618
para 4(6)	534
para 4(8)	535
para 5	149
para 6	149, 181
para 6(2)	177
para 6(3)	183
para 7(2)	618
para 8	149
para 9	149
para 9(e)	202
para 10(c)	618
para 13	618
para 13(3)	203
para 13(4)	149
para 13(9)(e)	220
para 14	330
para 15(1)	534
para 15(4)	540
para 16	413
para 16(2)	221, 618
para 16(2)(a)	149
para 16(2)(e)	150, 222
para 16(2)(f)	222
para 16(3)	618
para 16(4)	149, 618
para 16(4)(g)	421
para 16(6)	618
para 18(3)	148
para 20(1)	409
para 23	149
para 23(1)	153, 535, 545
Sch 5	316, 358, 458
para 1(2)(a)	1625, 1652
para 5	582
para 12	582
Sch 6	102, 397, 1067
para 20	1067
para 22	563
para 28	563
Sch 7	203, 357, 359, 360
para 4(1)	357
Sch 8	365
Sch 9(2)	190

Mental Deficiency Act 1913	19, 34

Mental Health (Care and Treatment)
(Scotland) Act 2003   21, 1744, 1761

s 254	1751
s 259(1)	1751
s 328	1754
s 329	1751

Mental Health Act 1959   31, 58, 63, 147,
230, 1723

Mental Health Act 1983   22, 31, 40, 58, 67,
140, 141, 147, 149, 232, 236,
250, 251, 265, 266, 267, 268,
269, 275, 341, 358, 360, 415,
434, 463, 872, 874, 1037, 1041,
1076, 1105, 1115, 1116, 1126,
1130, 1157, 1184, 1186, 1187,
1204, 1208, 1209, 1211, 1214,
1216, 1217, 1223, 1239, 1252,
1254, 1262, 1686, 1704, 1705,
1723, 1746

Pt 3	1213
Pt 4 432, 1041, 1165, 1217, 1218, 1219,	
	1220, 1221
Pt 7	458, 872, 876, 1685
s 1(2) 24, 166, 265, 426, 462, 535, 872	
s 1(2A)	462
s 1(3)	24, 872
s 1(4)	462
s 2	113, 1211, 1218, 1706, 1707
s 2(2)	265
s 3 113, 1212, 1213, 1216, 1218, 1706,	
	1707
s 3(2)	266
s 4(4)(a)	1218
s 5	1218
s 7	1213
s 12	279, 280
s 17	1706
ss 17A–17G	141
s 17A(5)	266
s 17A(7)	141
s 25A	1216
s 26	1213
s 35	1218
s 37(4)	1218
s 57	140, 1222
s 58	140
s 58A	140
s 64B(3)(b)(ii)	141
ss 93–111	872
s 93(4)	58, 63
s 94(1)	58
s 94(2)	58
s 98	339
s 99	1625, 1652
s 102	337
s 102(3)(a)	338
s 102(3)(b)	339
s 103	337
s 103(3)	338
s 103(5)	338
s 103(6)	339
s 103(7)	337
s 103(8)	341
s 106	58
s 114(1)	280
s 117	251, 435, 1185, 1186, 1221
s 129	337
s 131	268

Mental Health Act 1983—*continued*
s 135	1076, 1218
s 136	1218
s 145	426

Mental Health Act 2007   78, 80, 140, 165,
232, 239, 252, 265, 266, 268,
270, 402, 535, 1704
s 1(2)	426
s 1(4)	545
s 7	426
s 27	425
s 28(6)	140
s 28(10)	141, 425
s 32	426
s 32(1), (2)	141
s 35(4)	141, 425, 432
s 35(5)	141, 425
s 35(6)	432
s 49	439
s 50	135, 270, 274
s 50(1)	402, 405, 410, 415, 419
s 50(1), (2)	403
s 50(2)	274, 402
s 50(3)	274, 415
s 50(4)(a)	405
s 50(4)(b)	410
s 50(4)(c)	419
s 50(5)	460, 507
s 50(6)	515, 520
s 50(7)	80, 81, 419, 420, 431, 434, 435, 436, 437, 438, 439, 440, 447, 457, 458
s 51	419
s 55	215, 405, 410, 415, 419, 545

Sch 1
para 23(1)–(3)	545

Sch 3
para 3(5)	266
Sch 7	270, 274, 460, 507
Sch 8	270, 276, 515, 520
para 2	282

Sch 9
para 1	80, 81, 419, 420, 431, 434, 435, 436, 437, 438, 439, 440, 447, 457, 458
para 2	419, 420
para 3	431
para 4(1)–(3)	434
para 5(1)–(3)	435
para 6	435, 436, 437, 438, 439
paras 7(1)–(4)	439
para 8(1)–(3)	440
para 8(1), (2)	80
para 8(3)	81
para 9	447
para 10(1)–(4)	457
para 11	458

Sch 11
Pt 1	545
Pt 10	215, 405, 410

Mental Health (Scotland) Act 1984	1746
National Assistance Act 1948	40
s 21	251
s 29	251
s 49	359
National Health Service Act 1977	40
National Health Service Act 2006	41
s 251	1193
s 252	1194

National Health Service (Consequential
Provisions) Act 2006
s 2	434

Sch 1
paras 277, 278	434

National Health Service and Community
Care Act 1990   39, 40, 41, 1041,
1175
s 47	435, 1185, 1186

National Health Service Reform and Health
Care Professions Act 2002
Pt 1	41

New Zealand Protection of Personal and
Property Rights Act 1988
s 1(3)	89

Offences Against the Person Act 1861   143, 443

Personal Care at Home Act 2010	41

Police and Criminal Evidence Act 1984
s 2	142, 442
Powers of Attorney Act 1971	145, 147
s 1	145, 190
s 3	540
s 5	145, 413, 533, 542
s 10	195
Prosecution of Offenders Act 1985	639
Public Interest Disclosure Act 1998	1233
Public Trustee Act 1906	349
s 4(3)	409

Public Trustee and Administration of
Funds Act 1986   322, 360

Race Relations Act 1976	42

Regulation of Care (Scotland) Act
2001   1744

Safeguarding Vulnerable Groups Act
2006   41, 1177, 1231
Sale of Goods Act 1979	136, 360
s 3(2)	405
s 3(3)	136, 406
Scotland Act 1998	1744
Senior Courts Act 1981	349
s 1(1)	58
s 9	289
s 90	348
s 91	63
s 144	337

Sex Discrimination Act 1975   42, 53
Sexual Offences Act 2003   425
Smoking, Health and Social Care (Scotland)
     Act 2005   1744
Social Security Administration Act
     1992   360
Social Work (Scotland) Act 1968   1743
Statute de Prerogativa Regis, 17 Edw II
     (1339) St I cc 9, 10   29, 58
Suicide Act 1961
     s 2   455
Supreme Court Act 1981   59, 349
     s 1(1)   58
     s 9   289
     s 90   348
     s 91   63
     s 144   337
Supreme Court of Judicature Act 1873
     s 84   349

Tribunals, Courts and Enforcement Act 2007
     Pt 1   266
Trustee Act 1925   30, 59, 359
     s 25   163

Trustee Act 1925—*continued*
     s 36   163
     s 36(1)   611
     s 36(6A)   163
     s 36(6C)   163
     s 36(9)   611, 773
     s 54   773
     s 54(1)   610
     s 54(2)   610
     s 68(1)   409, 417
Trusts of Land and Appointment of
     Trustees Act 1996   360
     s 20   611, 773

Variation of Trusts Act 1958   359

Wills Act 1837   211, 412
     s 9   146, 211
     s 20   146
Work and Families Act 2006   41

Youth Justice and Criminal Evidence Act
     1999   57

Table of Statutory Instruments

References are to page numbers.

A chronological list of statutory instruments referred to in this work appears at the end of the alphabetical list below.

Allocation and Transfer of
    Proceedings Order 2008, SI 2008/
    2836   845

Civil Procedure (Amendment) Rules 1999,
    SI 1999/1008   910, 912, 913, 917,
                                            919
Civil Procedure (Amendment) Rules 2001,
    SI 2001/256   900, 906, 919, 996
Civil Procedure (Amendment) Rules 2002,
    SI 2002/2058   906, 912, 915, 918,
                                    919, 978, 980
Civil Procedure (Amendment) Rules 2006,
    SI 2006/1689   994
Civil Procedure (Amendment) Rules 2007,
    SI 2007/2204   872, 877, 879, 880,
            882, 883, 884, 885, 886, 888,
                    890, 907, 916, 917
Civil Procedure (Amendment) Rules 2008,
    SI 2008/2178   872, 882, 884, 900,
            902, 905, 908, 911, 913, 915
Civil Procedure (Amendment) Rules 2009,
    SI 2009/2092   900, 902, 907, 910,
                                            1002
Civil Procedure (Amendment) Rules 2010,
    SI 2010/621   886
Civil Procedure (Amendment No 2)
    Rules 2000, SI 2000/940   915, 916
Civil Procedure (Amendment No 2)
    Rules 2003, SI 2003/1242   900
Civil Procedure (Amendment No 2)
    Rules 2009, SI 2009/3390   902, 906,
            907, 908, 910, 911, 912, 913,
            915, 917, 918, 978, 980, 981,
            984, 988, 991, 993, 994, 995,
                                    999, 1002
Civil Procedure (Amendment No 3)
    Rules 2000, SI 2000/1317   900, 901,
            902, 903, 904, 905, 906, 909,
            910, 911, 914, 915, 916, 919
Civil Procedure (Amendment No 3)
    Rules 2003, SI 2003/1329   900
Civil Procedure (Amendment No 3)
    Rules 2005, SI 2005/2292   905, 917
Civil Procedure (Amendment No 3)
    Rules 2006, SI 2006/3435   901
Civil Procedure (Amendment No 3)
    Rules 2008, SI 2008/3327   980
Civil Procedure (Amendment No 4)
    Rules 2000, SI 2000/2092   914

Civil Procedure (Amendment No 4)
    Rules 2001, SI 2001/2792   978, 979,
            980, 981, 982, 983, 984, 985,
            986, 987, 988, 989, 990, 991,
                    992, 993, 994, 995
Civil Procedure (Amendment No 4)
    Rules 2003, SI 2003/2113   900, 980
Civil Procedure (Amendment No 4)
    Rules 2004, SI 2004/3419   886, 917
Civil Procedure (Amendment No 4)
    Rules 2005, SI 2005/3515   906
Civil Procedure (Amendment No 5)
    Rules 2001, SI 2001/4015   905, 917,
                    980, 982, 983, 985
Civil Procedure (Amendment No 5)
    Rules 2003, SI 2003/3361   872, 995,
                999, 1002, 1004, 1005
Civil Procedure Rules 1998, SI 1998/
    3132   24, 58, 60, 103, 147, 163, 233,
            293, 294, 309, 311, 315, 360,
            398, 416, 582, 590, 636, 638,
            639, 662, 671, 672, 877, 878
    r 2.7   875
    r 3.1(7)   888
    r 3.3   884
    r 3.9   902
    Pt 5   594
    Pt 6   882
    r 6.13   374, 884
    r 6.13(2)   376
    r 6.13(4)   376
    r 6.13(6)   376
    r 6.25(2)   376
    r 6.25(3)   377
    r 6.25(5)   377
    Pt 8   379, 659, 887
    r 12.10(a)(i)   377
    r 12.11(3)   377
    Pt 14   1693
    r 14.1(4)   378
    Pt 20   877
    r 20.2(2)(a)   880
    r 20.3   377
    r 20.3(1)   373, 877, 880
    Pt 21   370, 653, 872, 873, 880, 1677,
                        1678, 1680, 1686
    r 21.1   109, 372, 877, 1075
    r 21.1(1)(b)   873
    r 21.1(1)(c)   872

Civil Procedure Rules 1998, SI 1998/
    3132—*continued*
r 21.1(2)(a)	873
r 21.1(2)(d)	370, 873
r 21.1(2)(e)	379, 873, 889
r 21.1(d)	1682, 1683, 1685
r 21.1(e)	1682, 1684, 1685
r 21.2	883, 885
r 21.2(1)	371
r 21.2(3)	873, 878
r 21.2(5)	873
r 21.3	654, 878
r 21.3(2)	371, 879
r 21.3(3)	371, 879
r 21.3(4)	371, 879, 1679
r 21.4	882, 883, 884
rr 21.4–21.7	350
r 21.4(1)	883, 884
r 21.4(2)	372
r 21.4(3)	372, 373, 374, 375, 878, 880, 882, 883, 884, 885
r 21.4(3)(c)	880, 885
r 21.4(7)	375
r 21.5	373, 883, 884
r 21.5(3)	882
r 21.5(4)(a)	373
r 21.5(4)(b)	374
r 21.5(6)(b)	882
r 21.6	371, 374, 884
r 21.6(4)	374
r 21.6(5)	374
r 21.7	880
r 21.7(1)(c)	878
r 21.8	377
r 21.8(1)	377, 883, 884
r 21.8(2)	377, 883
r 21.8(3)	377, 884
r 21.8(4)	375, 883, 884
r 21.9(1)	878
r 21.9(2)	375, 878
r 21.9(3)	375, 878, 885
r 21.9(4)	375, 885
r 21.9(5)	376, 885
r 21.9(6)	381, 886
r 21.9(6)(b)	885
r 21.10	878, 1679
r 21.10(1)	378, 379, 1679
r 21.10(2)	379, 887
r 21.11	380, 878
r 21.11(1)(b)	379
r 21.11(2)	380
Pt 22	878, 892
r 22.1(5)	377, 878
r 22.1(6)	377, 878
r 25.1(1)(b)	233
rr 25.12–25.15	295, 598
r 30.7	380
r 31(3)	652
r 31(4)	650
r 32.1(1)–(3)	1693

Civil Procedure Rules 1998, SI 1998/
    3132—*continued*
r 32.13(3)(e)	378
r 35.4(4)	904
Pt 36	887
r 39.2(3)(d)	378, 887, 889
Pt 43	898, 906
Pt 44	898
r 44.3B	906
r 44.5	903
Pt 45	888, 898
Pt 46	898
r 46(1)(2)(c)(ii)	381
Pt 47	898, 904
r 47.3(1)(b)	381
Pt 48	898
r 48.2	881
r 48.3	903
r 48.5	381, 887
r 48.5(2)	887, 891
Pt 67	659
Pt 70	671
Pt 71	671, 672
Pt 72	672
Pt 73	672
Pt 75	872
r 95(b)	1693
r 95(d)	1693
r 133(2)(b)	1694
r 133(3)	1695

Companies (Tables A to F)
    Regulations 1985, SI 1985/805
Table A, art 71	146

Costs in Criminal Cases (General)
    Regulations 1986, SI 1986/1335   639

County Court Rules 1981, SI 1981/
    1687   672

Court of Protection (Amendment)
    Rules 2009, SI 2009/582   282, 588, 610, 627

Court of Protection (Enduring Power of
    Attorney) (Amendment) Rules 2005,
    SI 2005/668   150

Court of Protection (Enduring Power of
    Attorney) Rules 2001, SI 2001/
    825   292, 582
r 15(1)	149
reg 15	196
reg 16	196

Court of Protection Fees (Amendment)
    Order 2009, SI 2009/513   450, 829, 830

Court of Protection Fees Order 2007,
    SI 2007/1745   314, 450, 827

Court of Protection Rules 2001, SI 2001/
    824   58, 59, 60, 64, 292, 582
Pt 10A	282
r 8	59
r 11	353
r 13	353

Court of Protection Rules 2001, SI 2001/
   824—*continued*
  r 29   341
  r 67   338
Court of Protection Rules 2007, SI 2007/
   1744   114, 203, 205, 222, 223, 240,
        241, 288, 291, 292, 293, 294,
        295, 296, 297, 298, 301, 302,
        304, 306, 307, 310, 311, 314,
        315, 349, 350, 446, 448, 529,
      605, 612, 881, 1634, 1638, 1649
  Pt 2   1630
  Pt 4   295, 1630
  Pt 6   605
  Pt 7   297, 300, 605, 679, 1631
  Pt 8   299, 367, 369, 447, 614, 1630
  Pt 9   295, 299, 367, 369, 1630, 1631
  Pt 10   295, 301, 369, 606, 621, 635, 671,
         1630
  Pt 11   628
  Pt 13   1632
  Pt 14   305, 1631, 1693
  Pt 15   307, 645, 1631
  Pt 16   308, 1631
  Pt 17   309, 1630, 1631
  Pt 19   450
  Pt 20   314, 367, 449, 666
  Pt 22   316, 581, 589, 666
  Pt 23   316
  r 3   608
  r 3(1)   584
  r 3(3)   630
  r 3(3)(b)   583, 605
  r 3(3)(c)   629
  r 5(2)   630
  r 5(2)(a)   649
  r 5(2)(b)(i)   586
  r 5(2)(b)(ii)   605, 621
  r 5(2)(g)   647
  r 6   294, 645, 653, 673
  r 7   294
  r 8   294
  r 10   616
  r 10(3)(a)   589
  r 11   350
  rr 11–14   296
  r 11(2)   591
  r 13   350, 621
  r 14   647
  r 15   296, 616
  r 15(4)   593
  r 16   594, 616
  rr 16–19   296
  r 16(b)   593
  r 17   594, 616
  r 17(1)   593
  r 18   616
  r 19   594
  r 20   296
  r 20(6)   594

Court of Protection Rules 2007, SI 2007/
   1744—*continued*
  r 21   296
  r 23   296
  r 24   296
  rr 25–28   294
  r 25(2)(a)   617
  r 25(2)(h)   635
  r 25(3)   630
  r 25(7)   647
  r 26   617
  r 27   1627, 1637
  rr 29–39   296
  r 31(5)   600
  r 37   608
  rr 40–49   297
  r 40(2)   605
  r 41(1)(c)   606
  r 42   297
  r 42(2)   606
  r 42(4)   606
  r 43(4)   606
  r 44(2)   607
  r 49   605
  r 49(2)   350
  rr 50–53   298, 605
  rr 50–60   447
  r 51   241, 609
  r 51(2)(b)   366
  r 51(4)   621
  r 52   299
  r 52(2)   611
  r 52(3)   611
  r 52(4)   611
  r 52(5)   611
  r 53   299
  r 54   307, 612, 616
  r 55   367, 617
  rr 55–60   299
  r 55(a)   612
  r 56   367, 612
  r 57   367
  r 57(6)   613
  r 58   613
  r 59(b)   612
  rr 61–76   299
  rr 62–64   367, 369
  r 64   366, 612
  r 64(a)   307
  r 65   368, 612, 614
  r 66   368, 617
  rr 66–70   619
  r 67   350
  r 68   350
  r 68(4)   365, 368
  r 69   368, 605
  r 70   368, 616
  r 70(3)   368
  r 71   619
  r 72   365, 368, 584, 597, 617

Court of Protection Rules 2007, SI 2007/
    1744—*continued*
r 72(5)   621
r 72(6)   621
r 73   226, 621, 1631
r 73(1)(b)   621
r 73(2)   630
r 73(4)   622
r 74   605
rr 77–82   301
r 83   295
r 84   368, 369
rr 84–89   302
r 84(3)   630
r 85   368, 1631
r 85(2)(a)   644
r 85(c)   605
r 86   130, 598
r 87   1630
r 89   314, 367, 612, 666, 678, 1627, 1637
r 89(4)   612
r 89(5)   612
r 89(8)   612
r 90   593, 633, 634, 635, 724
rr 90–93   304
r 90(1)   634
r 90(2)   632
r 91   633, 634, 635
r 92   633, 634, 635, 724
r 93   724
rr 94–118   305
r 95   1693
r 95(a)–(c)   1693
r 95(d)   1693
r 97   621
r 99   637
r 99(1)   621
r 100   621
r 107   650
r 116   643
r 117   644
rr 119–131   307
r 123(2)(d)   647
r 125(7)   647
r 126   647
r 130   646
rr 132–139   308
r 140   656
rr 140–149   309
r 140(1)   654, 655
r 141(4)   654
r 141(6)   654
r 142(3)(a)   655
r 144(1)   654
r 148   631
rr 150–154   310
r 152(2)(b)   660
rr 155–168   311, 450
r 156   584, 586, 772
r 157   584, 586, 724

Court of Protection Rules 2007, SI 2007/
    1744—*continued*
r 159   585, 662
r 160   662
r 167   772
r 168   772
rr 169–182   314, 449
r 172   725
r 172(6)   670
r 172(7)   670
r 173   725
r 180(a)   670
r 180(b)   670
r 182(3)   670
rr 183–194   315
r 184   672
rr 195–199   316
rr 200–202   316
r 202   1625

Employment Equality (Age)
    Regulations 2006, SI 2006/1031   42
Enduring Powers of Attorney Act 1985
    (Commencement Order) 1986,
    SI 1986/125   147
European Communities (Quality System
    for Blood Establishments)
    Regulations 2006, SI 2006/562   427
European Qualifications (Health and Social
    Care Professions) Regulations 2007,
    SI 2007/3101   427
European Qualifications (Pharmacy)
    Regulations (Northern Ireland) 2008,
    SR 2008/192   427

Family Procedure (Adoption) Rules 2005,
    SI 2005/2795   583, 584, 1005
Pt 6
    Section 2   604
Family Proceedings Rules 1991, SI 1991/
    1247   24, 140, 233, 300, 360, 416,
                                               425
Pt IX   653, 873
r 9.5(1)(a)   350
r 10(3)   592

Health and Social Care Act 2008
    (Consequential Amendments No 2)
    Order 2010, SI 2010/813   431, 434,
                        446, 452, 455, 493, 502
Health Care and Associated
    Profes-
    sions (Miscellane-
    ous Amendments and
    Practitioner Psychologists)
    Order 2009 (Commencement No 1
    and Transitional Provisions) Order of
    Council 2009, SI 2009/1357   862
Health Service (Control of Patient
    Information) Regulations 2002,
    SI 2002/1438   1193

Insolvency Rules 1986, SI 1986/1925   360

Lasting Powers of Attorney, Enduring
    Powers of Attorney and Public
    Guardian (Amendment)
    Regulations 2007, SI 2007/2161   453,
        535, 545, 806, 807
Lasting Powers of Attorney, Enduring
    Powers of Attorney and Public
    Guardian (Amendment)
    Regulations 2009, SI 2009/1884   169,
        453, 508, 535, 545, 808, 813,
            820, 1523
Lasting Powers of Attorney, Enduring
    Powers of Attorney and Public
    Guardian Regulations 2007, SI 2007/
    1253   153, 169, 203, 204, 331, 453,
        508, 535, 545, 582, 801, 1523
    reg 5   169
    reg 6   509
    reg 8(1)   185
    reg 8(2)   186
    reg 8(3)   186
    reg 9(1)   190
    reg 9(4)   184
    reg 9(5)   188
    reg 9(9)   190
    reg 10   196, 366
    reg 11   366
    reg 12   197, 366, 510
    reg 13   366
    reg 14   199
    reg 14(2)   366
    reg 14(4)   366
    reg 15(3)   366
    reg 17   366
    reg 17(5)   197
    reg 21   194, 200, 412, 513
    reg 23   365
    reg 23(3)   196
    reg 24   365
    reg 26   365
    reg 33   677
    reg 43   331
    reg 46   453
    reg 47   453
    Sch 2   196, 366, 510
    Sch 3   194, 366, 614
    Sch 4   510
    Sch 5   197, 513
    Sch 7   149, 365, 537
    Sch 8   535, 614
Lay Representatives (Right of Audience)
    Order 1999, SI 1999/1225   56
Legal Services Act 2007 (Consequential
    Amendments) Order 2009, SI 2009/
    3348   588

Lord Chancellor (Transfer of Functions and
    Supplementary Provisions) (No 2)
    Order 2006, SI 2006/1016   419, 443,
        444, 448, 454, 458

Medicines (Advisory Bodies) (No 2)
    Regulations 2005, SI 2005/2754   427
Medicines for Human Use (Clinical Trials)
    Amendment (No 2)
    Regulations 2006, SI 2006/2984   427
Medicines for Human Use (Clinical Trials)
    Amendment Regulations 2006,
    SI 2006/1928   427
Medicines for Human Use (Clinical Trials)
    and Blood Safety and Quality
    (Amendment) Regulations 2008,
    SI 2008/941   427
Medicines for Human Use (Clinical Trials)
    Regulations 2004, SI 2004/1031 259,
        260, 261, 262, 427, 1192, 1193,
            1200
Medicines for Human Use
    (Miscellaneous Amendments)
    Regulations 2009, SI 2009/1164   427
Medicines (Marketing Authorisations and
    Miscellaneous Amendments)
    Regulations 2004, SI 2004/3224   427
Medicines (Marketing Authorisations Etc)
    Amendment Regulations 2005,
    SI 2005/2759   427
Mental Capacity Act 2005 (Appropriate
    Body) (England) Regulations 2006,
    SI 2006/2810   427, 1194
Mental Capacity Act 2005 (Appropriate
    Body) (Wales) Regulations 2007,
    SI 2007/833   427
Mental Capacity Act 2005 (Commencement
    No 1) (Amendment) Order 2006,
    SI 2006/3473   459
Mental Capacity Act 2005 (Commencement
    No 1) (England and Wales)
    Order 2007, SI 2007/563   459
Mental Capacity Act 2005 (Commencement
    No 1) Order 2006, SI 2006/2814   459
Mental Capacity Act 2005 (Commencement
    No 2) Order 2007, SI 2007/1897   459
Mental Capacity Act 2005 (Commencement)
    (Wales) Order 2007, SI 2007/
    856   459
Mental Capacity Act 2005 (Independent
    Mental Capacity Advocates)
    (Expansion of Roles)
    Regulations 2006, SI 2006/2883   251,
        439, 1174
Mental Capacity Act 2005 (Independent
    Mental Capacity Advocates)
    (General) Regulations 2006, SI 2006/
    1832   249, 431, 1174
    reg 4(2)   432

Mental Capacity Act 2005 (Independent
    Mental Capacity Advocates) (Wales)
    Regulations 2007, SI 2007/852   431,
                            432, 439, 1174
Mental Capacity Act 2005 (Loss of Capacity
    During Research Project) (England)
    Regulations 2007, SI 2007/679   262,
                            430, 1200
Mental Capacity Act 2005 (Loss of Capacity
    During Research Project) (Wales)
    Regulations 2007, SI 2007/837   430
Mental Capacity Act 2005 (Transfer of
    Proceedings) Order 2007, SI 2007/
    1899   235, 289, 419, 851
  art 2   853
  art 2(2)   97
  art 2(3)   852
  art 2(3)(a)   852
  art 2(3)(b)   852
  art 2(3)(c)   853
  art 2(3)(d)   853
  art 3(2)   97
  art 3(3)(c)   97
Mental Capacity Act 2005 (Transitional and
    Consequential Provisions)
    Order 2007, SI 2007/1898   360, 831
  Sch 1   360
Mental Capacity (Deprivation of Liberty:
    Appointment of Relevant
    Person's Representative)
    (Amendment) Regulations 2008,
    SI 2008/2368   278, 281, 470, 496
Mental Capacity (Deprivation of Liberty:
    Appointment of Relevant
    Person's Representative)
    Regulations 2008, SI 2008/1315   278,
                    281, 470, 494, 854
  Pt 1   496
  reg 3   281
  reg 4   281
  reg 5   281, 438
  reg 6   281
  reg 7   281
  reg 8   281
  reg 9   281
  reg 10   281, 495
  reg 12   496
  regs 12–14   281
  reg 13   437, 497
  reg 14   437, 497
  reg 15   281, 497
Mental Capacity (Deprivation of Liberty:
    Appointment of Relevant
    Person's Representative) (Wales)
    Regulations 2009, SI 2009/266 (W
    29)   431, 467, 470
  reg 15   496

Mental Capacity (Deprivation of Liberty:
    Assessments, Standard
    Authorisations and Disputes about
    Residence) (Wales) Regulations 2009,
    SI 2009/783   477, 492
Mental Capacity (Deprivation of Liberty:
    Monitoring and Reporting; and
    Assessments – Amendment)
    Regulations 2009, SI 2009/827   276,
            279, 282, 477, 491, 492, 499,
                        504, 861, 868
Mental Capacity (Deprivation of Liberty:
    Standard Authorisations,
    Assessments and Ordinary
    Residence) Regulations 2008,
    SI 2008/1858   276, 279, 477
  Pt 2   492
  Pt 3   492
  Pt 6   504
  reg 2   492
  reg 3   279
  reg 4   280
  reg 5   280
  reg 6   280
  reg 7   280
  reg 8   280
  reg 9   280
  reg 10   280
  reg 11   280
  reg 12   280
  reg 13   280
  reg 14   280
  reg 15   280
  reg 16   280, 467
Mental Health Act 2007 (Commencement
    No 7 and Transitional Provisions)
    Order 2008, SI 2008/1900   425
Mental Health Act 2007 (Commencement
    No 10 and Transitional Provisions)
    Order 2009, SI 2009/139   270
Mental Health Act 2007 (Commencement
    No 10 and Transitional Provisions)
    Order 2009, SI 2009/139 (C.9)   460,
                                507
Mental Health and Mental Capacity
    (Advocacy) Amendment (England)
    Regulations 2009, SI 2009/2376   431
Mental Health Review Tribunal Rules 1983,
    SI 1983/942   360
Motor Vehicles (Tests) Regulations 1981,
    SI 1981/1694   360

National Savings Bank Regulations 1972,
    SI 1972/764   360
National Savings Stock
    Register Regulations 1976, SI 1976/
    2012   360
Non-contentious Probate Rules 1987,
    SI 1987/2024   360

Pharmacists and Pharmacy
    Technicians Order 2007, SI 2007/
    289   427
Premium Savings Bond Regulations 1972,
    SI 1972/765   360
Public Guardian Board Regulations 2007,
    SI 2007/1770   454
Public Guardian (Fees etc) (Amendment)
    Regulations 2007, SI 2007/2616   332
Public Guardian (Fees etc)
    Regulations 2007, SI 2007/2051   332
Public Guardian (Fees, etc) (Amendment)
    Regulations 2007, SI 2007/2616   453
Public Guardian (Fees, etc) (Amendment)
    Regulations 2009, SI 2009/514   453,
        822

Public Guardian (Fees, etc)
    Regulations 2007, SI 2007/2051   150,
        195, 453, 535, 537, 545, 822,
        823, 824, 825, 826, 827

Road Vehicles (Construction and Use)
    Regulations 1986, SI 1986/1078   360

Savings Certificates Regulations 1991,
    SI 1991/1031   360
Supreme Court Rules 1965, SI 1965/
    1776   60, 315, 672
    Ord 45   672
    Ord 46   672
    Ord 80
      r 10 1677

Chronological List of Statutory Instruments

1965 Supreme Court Rules 1965, SI 1965/1776

1972 National Savings Bank Regulations 1972, SI 1972/764
Premium Savings Bond Regulations 1972, SI 1972/765

1976 National Savings Stock Register Regulations 1976, SI 1976/2012

1981 County Court Rules 1981, SI 1981/1687
Motor Vehicles (Tests) Regulations 1981, SI 1981/1694

1983 Mental Health Review Tribunal Rules 1983, SI 1983/942

1985 Companies (Tables A to F) Regulations 1985, SI 1985/805

1986 Enduring Powers of Attorney Act 1985 (Commencement Order) 1986, SI 1986/125
Road Vehicles (Construction and Use) Regulations 1986, SI 1986/1078
Costs in Criminal Cases (General) Regulations 1986, SI 1986/1335
Insolvency Rules 1986, SI 1986/1925

1987 Non-contentious Probate Rules 1987, SI 1987/2024

1991 Savings Certificates Regulations 1991, SI 1991/1031
Family Proceedings Rules 1991, SI 1991/1247

1998 Civil Procedure Rules 1998, SI 1998/3132

1999 Civil Procedure (Amendment) Rules 1999, SI 1999/1008
Lay Representatives (Right of Audience) Order 1999, SI 1999/1225

2000 Civil Procedure (Amendment No 2) Rules 2000, SI 2000/940
Civil Procedure (Amendment No 3) Rules 2000, SI 2000/1317
Civil Procedure (Amendment No 4) Rules 2000, SI 2000/2092

2001 Civil Procedure (Amendment) Rules 2001, SI 2001/256
Court of Protection Rules 2001, SI 2001/824
Court of Protection (Enduring Power of Attorney) Rules 2001, SI 2001/825
Civil Procedure (Amendment No 4) Rules 2001, SI 2001/2792
Civil Procedure (Amendment No 5) Rules 2001, SI 2001/4015

2002 Health Service (Control of Patient Information) Regulations 2002, SI 2002/1438
Civil Procedure (Amendment) Rules 2002, SI 2002/2058

2003 Civil Procedure (Amendment No 2) Rules 2003, SI 2003/1242
Civil Procedure (Amendment No 3) Rules 2003, SI 2003/1329
Civil Procedure (Amendment No 4) Rules 2003, SI 2003/2113
Civil Procedure (Amendment No 5) Rules 2003, SI 2003/3361

2004 Medicines for Human Use (Clinical Trials) Regulations 2004, SI 2004/1031
Medicines (Marketing Authorisations and Miscellaneous Amendments) Regulations 2004, SI 2004/3224
Civil Procedure (Amendment No 4) Rules 2004, SI 2004/3419

2005 Court of Protection (Enduring Power of Attorney) (Amendment) Rules 2005, SI 2005/668
Civil Procedure (Amendment No 3) Rules 2005, SI 2005/2292
Medicines (Advisory Bodies) (No 2) Regulations 2005, SI 2005/2754
Medicines (Marketing Authorisations Etc) Amendment Regulations 2005, SI 2005/2759
Family Procedure (Adoption) Rules 2005, SI 2005/2795
Civil Procedure (Amendment No 4) Rules 2005, SI 2005/3515

2006 European Communities (Quality System for Blood Establishments) Regulations 2006, SI 2006/562
Lord Chancellor (Transfer of Functions and Supplementary Provisions) (No 2) Order 2006, SI 2006/1016
Employment Equality (Age) Regulations 2006, SI 2006/1031
Civil Procedure (Amendment) Rules 2006, SI 2006/1689
Mental Capacity Act 2005 (Independent Mental Capacity Advocates) (General) Regulations 2006, SI 2006/1832
Medicines for Human Use (Clinical Trials) Amendment Regulations 2006, SI 2006/1928
Mental Capacity Act 2005 (Appropriate Body) (England) Regulations 2006, SI 2006/2810

Mental Capacity Act 2005
(Commencement No 1)
Order 2006, SI 2006/2814
Mental Capacity Act 2005
(Independent Mental Capacity
Advocates) (Expansion of Roles)
Regulations 2006, SI 2006/2883
Medicines for Human Use (Clinical
Trials) Amendment (No 2)
Regulations 2006, SI 2006/2984
Civil Procedure (Amendment No 3)
Rules 2006, SI 2006/3435
Mental Capacity Act 2005
(Commencement No 1)
(Amendment) Order 2006, SI
2006/3473
2007 Pharmacists and Pharmacy
Technicians Order 2007, SI 2007/
289
Mental Capacity Act 2005
(Commencement No 1) (England
and Wales) Order 2007, SI 2007/
563
Mental Capacity Act 2005 (Loss of
Capacity During Research
Project) (England)
Regulations 2007, SI 2007/679
Mental Capacity Act 2005
(Appropriate Body) (Wales)
Regulations 2007, SI 2007/833
Mental Capacity Act 2005 (Loss of
Capacity During Research
Project) (Wales)
Regulations 2007, SI 2007/837
Mental Capacity Act 2005
(Independent Mental Capacity
Advocates) (Wales)
Regulations 2007, SI 2007/852
Mental Capacity Act 2005
(Commencement) (Wales)
Order 2007, SI 2007/856
Lasting Powers of Attorney,
Enduring Powers of Attorney
and Public Guardian
Regulations 2007, SI 2007/1253
Court of Protection Rules 2007, SI
2007/1744
Court of Protection
Fees Order 2007, SI 2007/1745
Public Guardian Board
Regulations 2007, SI 2007/1770
Mental Capacity Act 2005
(Commencement No 2)
Order 2007, SI 2007/1897
Mental Capacity Act 2005
(Transitional and Consequential
Provisions) Order 2007, SI 2007/
1898
Mental Capacity Act 2005
(Transfer of Proceedings)
Order 2007, SI 2007/1899
Public Guardian (Fees etc)
Regulations 2007, SI 2007/2051

Public Guardian (Fees, etc)
Regulations 2007, SI 2007/2051
Lasting Powers of Attorney,
Enduring Powers of Attorney
and Public Guardian
(Amendment) Regulations 2007,
SI 2007/2161
Civil Procedure (Amendment)
Rules 2007, SI 2007/2204
Public Guardian (Fees etc)
(Amendment) Regulations 2007,
SI 2007/2616
Public Guardian (Fees, etc)
(Amendment) Regulations 2007,
SI 2007/2616
European Qualifications (Health
and Social Care Professions)
Regulations 2007, SI 2007/3101
2008 European
Qualifications (Pharmacy)
Regulations (Northern Ireland)
2008, SR 2008/192
Medicines for Human Use (Clinical
Trials) and Blood Safety and
Quality (Amendment)
Regulations 2008, SI 2008/941
Mental Capacity (Deprivation of
Liberty: Appointment of
Relevant Person's Representative)
Regulations 2008, SI 2008/1315
Mental Capacity (Deprivation of
Liberty: Standard Authorisations,
Assessments and Ordinary
Residence) Regulations 2008, SI
2008/1858
Mental Health Act 2007
(Commencement No 7 and
Transitional Provisions)
Order 2008, SI 2008/1900
Civil Procedure (Amendment)
Rules 2008, SI 2008/2178
Mental Capacity (Deprivation of
Liberty: Appointment of
Relevant Person's Representative)
(Amendment) Regulations 2008,
SI 2008/2368
Allocation and Transfer of
Proceedings Order 2008, SI 2008/
2836
Civil Procedure (Amendment No 3)
Rules 2008, SI 2008/3327
2009 Mental Health Act 2007
(Commencement No 10 and
Transitional Provisions)
Order 2009, SI 2009/139
Mental Health Act 2007
(Commencement No 10 and
Transitional Provisions)
Order 2009, SI 2009/139 (C.9)
Mental Capacity (Deprivation of
Liberty: Appointment of

Relevant Person's Representative) (Wales) Regulations 2009, SI 2009/266 (W 29)

Court of Protection Fees (Amendment) Order 2009, SI 2009/513

Public Guardian (Fees, etc) (Amendment) Regulations 2009, SI 2009/514

Court of Protection (Amendment) Rules 2009, SI 2009/582

Mental Capacity (Deprivation of Liberty: Assessments, Standard Authorisations and Disputes about Residence) (Wales) Regulations 2009, SI 2009/783

Mental Capacity (Deprivation of Liberty: Monitoring and Reporting; and Assessments – Amendment) Regulations 2009, SI 2009/827

Medicines for Human Use (Miscellaneous Amendments) Regulations 2009, SI 2009/1164

Health Care and Associated Profes-sions (Miscellane-ous Amendments and Practitioner Psychologists) Order 2009 (Commencement No 1 and Transitional Provisions) Order of Council 2009, SI 2009/1357

Lasting Powers of Attorney, Enduring Powers of Attorney and Public Guardian (Amendment) Regulations 2009, SI 2009/1884

Civil Procedure (Amendment) Rules 2009, SI 2009/2092

Mental Health and Mental Capacity (Advocacy) Amendment (England) Regulations 2009, SI 2009/2376

Legal Services Act 2007 (Consequential Amendments) Order 2009, SI 2009/3348

Civil Procedure (Amendment No 2) Rules 2009, SI 2009/3390

2010 Civil Procedure (Amendment) Rules 2010, SI 2010/621

Health and Social Care Act 2008 (Consequential Amendments No 2) Order 2010, SI 2010/813

Table of Cases

References are to page numbers.

A (Conjoined Twins: Medical Treatment) (No 2), Re [2001] 1 FLR 267, [2001]
  Fam Law 100, (2000) *The Times*, November 15, CA   656, 884, 888
A (Male Sterilisation), Re [2000] 1 FLR 549, [2000] Lloyd's Rep Med 87,
  (2000) 53 BMLR 66, CA   114, 121, 230, 232, 1048, 1094, 1097, 1144
A Local Authority v A Health Authority [2003] EWHC 2746 (Fam), [2004] 2
  WLR 926, [2004] 1 All ER 480, 76 BMLR 210, FD   231
A Local Authority v Mrs A [2010] EWHC 1549 (Fam), [2011] All ER (D) 205
  (Jan)   99
A v A Health Authority, Re J (a child), R (on the application of S) v Secretary
  of State for the Home Department [2002] EWHC 18 (Fam/Admin)
  [2002] Fam 213, [2002] 3 WLR 24, [2002] 1 FLR 845   231, 248
Airedale NHS Trust v Bland [1993] AC 789, [1993] 2 WLR 316, [1993] 1 FLR
  1026, [1993] 1 All ER 821, HL 29, 230, 231, 234, 239, 243, 244, 245, 247, 313, 1143
AK (Medical Treatment: Consent), Re [2001] 1 FLR 129, [2000] Fam Law
  885, 58 BMLR 151, FD   98, 102, 253, 399, 1065
AKP, In the Matter of (2007) 1 November, CoP Case No 10185666, Ct of
  Protection   1682, 1685
Albon v Naza Motor Trading Sdn Bhd [2007] EWHC 2613 (Ch), [2008] 1 All
  ER 995, [2008] 2 All ER (Comm) 280, [2008] 1 WLR 2380   584
Allen, Re [2009] (CoP No 11661992) (2009) 21 July (unreported), Ct of
  Protection   123, 402
An NHS Trust v Miss T [2004] EWHC 1279 (Fam), [2005] 1 All ER 387,
  [2004] 3 FCR 297, 80 BMLR 184   233
An NHS Trust v S [2003] EWHC 365 (Fam)   1086
Artico v Italy A/37 (1980) 3 EHRR 1, ECHR   52
AS and DS, Re (2004) Case No 2120091/2, Ct of Protection   1667
Ashingdale v UK (1985) 7 EHRR 528, ECHR   270
Austin v Metropolitan Police Commissioner [2009] UKHL 9, [2009] AC 564,
  [2009] 2 WLR 372, (2009) 26 BHRC 642   272

B (Consent to Treatment: Capacity), Re [2002] EWHC 429 (Fam), [2002] 2 All
  ER 449, [2002] 1 FLR 1090, [2002] Lloyd's Rep Med 265, FD   232, 252, 1170
B (Court of Protection: Notice of Proceedings), Re [1987] 2 All ER 475, [1987]
  1 WLR 552, [1987] Fam Law 242, ChD   619
B, Applicant 2005 SLT (Sh Ct) 95, 2005 GWD 19–334   1764
Bailey v Warren [2006] EWCA Civ 51, [2006] CP Rep 26, [2006] WTLR 753,
  [2006] All ER (D) 78, (2006) *The Times*, 20 February   108, 876, 1679
Banks v Goodfellow (1870) LR 5 QB 549, [1861–73] All ER Rep 47, 39 LJQB
  237   102, 103, 397, 1067
Beaney (deceased), Re [1978] 1 WLR 770, [1978] 2 All ER 595, 121 SJ 832,
  ChD   102, 153, 1067
Beatham v Carlisle Hospitals NHS Trust (1999) *The Times*, May 20, QBD   888, 889
Bird v Luckie (1850) 8 Hare 301, 14 Jur 1015   89, 397
Birkin v Wing (1890) 63 LT 80   109
Black v Yates [1992] QB 526, [1991] 3 WLR 90, [1991] 4 All ER 722   887
Boughton v Knight (1873) LR 3 PD 64, [1861–73] All ER Rep 40, 42 LJ P&M
  25   102, 1067
Bratt, Re (2009) 14 September, Ct of Protection   175
Britton v Britton's curator bonis 1992 SCLR 947   1746
Buckenham v Dickinson [2000] WTLR 1083, [1997] CLY 661   109
Burridge v Stafford; Khan v Ali [2000] 1 WLR 927, [1999] 4 All ER 660, CA   945

C (2009) 23 Sept, Kilmarnock Sh Ct   1743
C (Adult: Refusal of Treatment), Re [1994] 1 WLR 290, [1994] 1 All ER 819,
    [1994] 1 FLR 31, FD   232, 236, 267, 874
C (Mental Patient: Contact), Re [1993] 1 FLR 940, [1993] Fam Law 404, FD   231
C (Power of Attorney), Re [2000] 2 FLR 1, CA   221
C v V, S and S (Protected Persons), Re [2008] EWHC B16 (Fam), [2009]
    WTLR 315   118, 122, 159, 401, 1670, 1673, 1724
C, In the Matter of [2008] EWHC 1869 (Ch)   1717
Cameron, Re [1999] Ch 386, [1999] 2 All ER 924, [1999] 3 WLR 394   148, 160
Cathcart, Re [1893] 1 Ch 466, 62 LJ Ch 320, 68 LT 358, CA   62
Cattermole v Prisk [2006] 1 FLR 693, ChD   109
Chan U Seek v Alvis Vehicles Ltd and Guardian Newspapers [2004] EWHC
    3092 (Ch), [2005] 1 WLR 2965, [2005] 3 All ER 155, [2004] All ER
    (D) 114 (Dec)   594
Chaudhry v Prabhakar [1988] 3 All ER 718, (1988) 138 NLJ 172, CA   146
CIBC Mortgages plc v Pitt [1994] 1 AC 200, [1993] 3 WLR 802, [1993] 4 All
    ER 433, HL   29
City of Westminster v IC, KC and NNC [2007] EWHC 3096 (Fam)   247
Clarkson v Gilbert [2000] 2 FLR 839, [2000] Fam Law 809, (2000) *The Times*,
    4 July, CA   56, 451
Clauss v Pir [1988] 1 Ch 267, [1987] 3 WLR 493, [1987] 2 All ER 752   146
Crossley v Crossley [2007] EWCA Civ 1491, [2008] 1 FLR 1467   1725

D (J), Re [1982] 2 WLR 373, [1982] 2 All ER 37   121, 210, 1723
D v An NHS Trust (Medical Treatment: Consent: Termination) [2003] EWHC
    2793 (Fam), [2004] 1 FLR 1110, [2004] Fam Law 415   243, 313, 1144
Davey (Deceased), Re [1980] 3 All ER 342, [1981] 1 WLR 164, ChD   619
Dian AO v Davis Frankel and Mead [2004] EWHC 2662 (Comm), [2005] 1
    WLR 2951, [2005] 1 All ER 1074, [2005] 1 All ER (Comm) 482   594
Drew v Nunn (1879) 4 QBD 661, 48 LJQB 591, [1874–80] All ER Rep 1144,
    CA   147
Drinkall v Whitwood [2003] EWCA Civ 1547, [2004] 1 WLR 462, [2004] 4
    All ER 378, [2003] TLR 622, CA   887
Dunnett v Railtrack Plc [2002] EWCA Civ 303   586

E (By her litigation friend the Official Solicitor) v Channel Four;
    News International Ltd and St Helens Borough Council [2005] EWHC
    1144 (Fam), [2005] 2 FLR 913, [2005] EMLR 709, [2005] UKHRR
    789, FD   231
E (Enduring Power of Attorney), Re [2001] Ch 364, [2000] 3 WLR 1974, *sub
    nom* E, Re, X v Y [2000] 3 All ER 1004   175
E (Mental Health Patient), Re [1985] 1 WLR 245, [1985] 1 All ER 609, CA   651
Eagle v Chambers [2004] EWCA Civ 1033, [2005] 1 WLR 3081, [2005] 1 All
    ER 136, 82 BMLR 22   1710

F (Adult: Court's Jurisdiction), Re [2000] Fam 38, [2000] 3 WLR 1740, [2000]
    2 FLR 512, CA   231
F (Mental Patient: Sterilisation), Re [1990] 2 AC 1, [1989] 2 WLR 1025,
    [1989] 2 All ER 545, [1989] 2 FLR 376, HL   1100
F v West Berkshire Health Authority; *sub nom* F (Mental Patient: Sterilisation),
    Re [1990] 2 AC 1, [198] 2 WLR 1025, [1989] 2 All ER 545, [1989] 2
    FLR 376, CA   29, 125, 230, 231
F, Re (2009) 28 May, CoP Case No 11649371, Ct of Protection   1687
F, Re [2009] EWHC B30 (Fam)   87, 396
Findlay v Barrington Jones & MIB [2009] EWHC 90130 (Costs), SCCO   891
Folks v Faizey [2006] EWCA Civ 381, [2006] CP Rep 30, (2006) *Independent*,
    April 12   877

G (TJ), Re [2010] EWHC 3005 (COP), [2010] All ER (D) 218 (Nov)   401
G, Applicant 2009 SLT (Sh Ct) 122   1764
GC, Re [2008] EWHC 3402 (Fam)   122, 401

Gillick v West Norfolk & Wisbech Area Health Authority [1986] AC 112,
    [1985] 3 WLR 830, [1985] 3 All ER 402, [1986] 1 FLR 224, HL   104, 105, 654, 878,
        1206
GJ v The Foundation Trust [2009] EWHC 2972 (Fam)   274, 275, 463, 515, 1705
Glass v UK [2004] 1 FLR 1019, 77 BMLR 120, [2004] Lloyd's Rep Med 76,
    ECHR   234
Gorjat v Gorjat [2010] EWHC 1537 (Ch), [2010] All ER (D) 247 (Jun)   100
Great Ormond Street Hospital v Pauline Rushie (unreported) 19 April 2000   109
Greensill v Greensill [2007] EWCA Civ 680; *sub nom* G v G [2007] 2 FLR
    1127, [2007] Fam Law 899   673
Gregory v Turner [2003] EWCA Civ 183, [2003] 1 WLR 1149, [2003] 2 All
    ER 1114, [2003] CP Rep 40   147, 164, 880
GS, In the Matter of (2008) 10 July, CoP Case No 11582024, Ct of Protection   1685
Guzzardi v Italy (1980) 3 EHRR 333, ECHR   270

H (A Minor and an Incapacitated Person), In the Matter of (2009) 15 October,
    CoP Case No 11461874, Ct of Protection   1711
H (Minors) (Sexual Abuse: Standard of Proof), Re [1996] AC 563, [1996] 2
    WLR 8, [1996] 1 All ER 1, [1996] 1 FLR 80, HL   398
H, (2008) 6 May, Dunoon Sh Ct   1743
H, Applicant 2007 SLT (Sh Ct) 5, 2006 GWD 21–447   1743, 1762
H, In the Matter of (Court of Protection No 11649371)   208, 290
Hale v Tanner [2000] 1 WLR 2377, [2000] 2 FLR 879, CA   674
Hammerton v Hammerton [2007] EWCA Civ 248, [2007] 2 FLR 1133, [2007]
    3 FCR 107, [2007] Fam Law 798   673
Harbin v Masterman [1896] 1 Ch 351, [1895–9] All ER Rep 695, 65 LJ Ch
    195, CA   352, 876
HE v A Hospital NHS Trust [2003] EWHC 1017 (Fam), [2003] 2 FLR 408,
    [2003] Fam Law 733   230, 253, 255
Henry v Hammond [1913] 2 KB 515, 82 LJKB 575, 108 LT 729, KBD   146
HL v The United Kingdom (Application No 45508/99) (2004) 40 EHRR 761,
    [2004] 1 FLR 1019, 81 BMLR 131, ECHR   134, 141, 165, 269, 270, 271, 1115, 1223
HM v Switzerland (2002) 38 EHRR 314, ECHR   270, 271
HMF (Mental Patient: Will), Re [1976] Ch 33, [1975] 3 WLR 395, [1975] 2 All
    ER 795, ChD   622
Hoff v Atherton [2004] EWCA Civ 1554, [2005] WTLR 99, [2004] All ER (D)
    314 (Nov)   109
Howarth, Re (2008) 29 July, Ct of Protection   177
HW, Re (2005) Case No 2122208, Ct of Protection   1668

Imperial Loan Company v Stone [1892] 1 QB 599, 61 LJQB 449, 56 JP 436,
    CA   136, 406
Independent News and Media Ltd v A [2009] EWHC 2858 (Fam), [2009] WLR
    (D) 332   634
ITW v Z [2009] EWHC 2525 (Fam); *sub nom* M (Vulnerable Adult)
    (Testamentary Capacity), Re [2009] All ER (D) 314 (Oct)   210, 400, 1725
Izzo v Phillip Ross & Co [2002] BPIR 310, [2001] All ER (D) 464 (Jul),
    (2001) *The Times*, August 9, ChD   56

J (A Minor) (Medical Treatment) [1993] Fam 15, [1992] 3 WLR 507, [1992] 4
    All ER 614, [1992] 2 FLR 165, CA   232
J (A Minor) (Wardship: Medical Treatment), Re [1991] Fam 33, [1991] 2 WLR
    140, [1990] 3 All ER 930, [1991] 1 FLR 366, CA   245
J (Enduring Power of Attorney), Re [2009] EWHC 436 (Ch)   176, 1718
JE v DE, Surrey CC and EW; *sub nom* DE, Re [2006] EWHC 3459 (Fam),
    [2007] 2 FLR 1150, (2007) 10 CCL Rep 149, [2007] MHLR 39   270, 271, 272

K, Re F [1988] Ch 310, [1988] 1 All ER 358, [1988] 2 WLR 781   191, 875, 1715, 1717
KC and Anor v City of Westminster Social and Community
    Services Department and Anor [2008] EWCA Civ 198, [2009] Fam 11,
    [2008] 2 FLR 267   30

Kenward v Adams (1975) *The Times*, November 29, [1975] CLY 3591   109, 1075

Law Hospital NHS Trust v Lord Advocate 1996 SC 301, 1996 SLT 848, [1996]
     2 FLR 407, (1998) 39 BMLR 166, [1996] Fam Law 670, Ct of Sess (IH)   1745, 1746
LBL v RYJ and VJ [2010] EWHC 2665 (COP)   30
Leather v Kirby [1965] 1 WLR 1489, [1965] 3 All ER 927, (1965) 109 SJ 936,
     HL   889
Lilly Icos Ltd v Pfizer (No 2) [2002] EWCA Civ 2, [2002] 1 WLR 2253,
     [2002] 1 All ER 842, [2002] FSR 54   594
Lindsay v Wood [2006] EWHC 2895 (QB), [2006] MHLR 341, (2006) *The
     Times*, 8 December   875, 876
London Borough of Enfield v SA [2010] EWHC 196 (Admin)   306, 1692
London Borough of Lewisham v Malcolm [2008] UKHL 43, [2008] 1 AC
     1399, [2008] 3 WLR 194, [2008] 4 All ER 525, 102 BMLR 170   44, 45

M, Applicant 2007 SLT (Sh Ct) 24, 2006 GWD 19–418   1755, 1764
Masterman-Lister v Jewell [2002] EWCA Civ 1889, [2003] 3 All ER 162,
     [2003] 1 WLR 1511, CA; [2002] EWHC 417 (QB), [2002] All ER (D)
     247 (Mar)   22, 73, 102, 109, 163, 874, 875, 876, 877, 878, 879, 881, 882, 1068, 1075,
      1677
MB (Medical Treatment), Re [1997] 2 FLR 426, [1997] Fam Law 542, CA   100, 232, 399,
      874, 875, 1048, 1065
McDowall's Executors v Inland Revenue Commissioners [2003] UKSC
     SPC00382, [2004] STC (SCD) 22, [2004] WTLR 221, [2004] STI 146,
     Sp Comm   148, 1755
Mitchell v Alasia [2005] EWHC 11 (QB), [2005] All ER (D) 07 (Jan)   875
MM (An Adult), Re; A Local Authority v MM and another; *sub nom* Local
     Authority X v M [2007] EWHC 2003 (Fam), [2008] 3 FCR 788, (2008)
     11 CCL Rep 119, [2008] Fam Law 213   103
Morris, Petitioner 1986, Ct of Sess (IH)   1745, 1746
Muldoon, Applicant 2005 SLT (Sh Ct) 52, 2005 SCLR 611, 2005 GWD 5–57   1744

National Westminster Bank v Morgan [1985] 1 AC 686, [1985] 2 WLR 588,
     [1985] 1 All ER 821, HL   29
NHS Trust A v H [2001] 2 FLR 501, [2001] Fam Law 664, FD   245
Niall Baker v H and the Official Solicitor (unreported, 15 October 2009) Case
     No 11461874, Ct of Protection   677
Nielson v Denmark (1988) 11 EHRR 175, ECHR   270
North Ayrshire Council v JM 2004 SCLR 956, Sh Ct   1744

P, In the Matter of [2009] EWHC 163 (Ch), [2009] All ER (D) 160 (Feb)   121, 122, 210,
      1723, 1725
P, Re (2009) 9 June, Ct of Protection   179
P, Re [2009] EWHC 163 (Ch), [2009] All ER (D) 160 (Feb)   159, 202, 1673
PCT v P, AH & The Local Authority [2009] EW Misc 10 (EWCOP)   101
Pretty v UK (2002) 35 EHRR 1, [2002] 2 FLR 45, (2002) 12 BHRC 149,
     ECHR   245, 254
PS (Incapacitated or Vulnerable Adult), Re; *sub nom* Sunderland City Council v
     P; Sunderland City Council v PS [2007] EWHC 623 (Fam), [2007] 2
     FLR 1083, (2007) 10 CCL Rep 295, [2007] LS Law Med 507, [2007]
     Fam Law 695   30, 265

R (A Minor) (Wardship: Consent to Medical Treatment), Re [1992] Fam 11,
     [1991] 3 WLR 592, [1992] 1 FLR 190, [1992] 4 All ER 177, CA   104
R (Burke) v General Medical Council and Others [2005] EWCA Civ 1003,
     [2006] QB 273, [2005] 3 WLR 1132, [2005] 2 FLR 1223, 85 BMLR 1,
     CA; [2005] QB 424, [2004] 2 FLR 1121, [2004] All ER (D) 588 (Jul),
     QBD   168, 232, 234, 243, 244, 245, 246, 252, 254, 313
R (Enduring Power of Attorney), Re [1990] Ch 647, [1990] 2 All ER 893,
     [1990] 2 WLR 1219   162

R (Hussain) v Birmingham City Council [2002] EWHC 949 (Admin), [2002]
     CP Rep 54, QBD   880, 881
R (S) v Plymouth City Council and C [2002] EWCA Civ 388, [2002] 1 WLR
     2583, [2002] 1 FLR 1177, CA   26, 112, 124, 1076
R v Bournewood Community and Mental Health NHS Trust ex p L [1999] AC
     458, [1998] 3 WLR 107, [1998] 3 All ER 289, [1998] 2 FLR 550, HL;
     [1998] 2 WLR 764, [1998] 1 All ER 634, [1998] COD 35, CA   165, 269
R v Bow County Court ex parte Pelling (No 2) [2001] EWCA Civ 122   632
R v C [2009] UKHL 42, [2009] 1 WLR 1786   425
R v Collins and Ashworth Hospital Authority ex parte Brady [2001] 58 BMLR
     173, [2000] Lloyd's Rep Med 355   100, 399, 1065
R v Holmes (1979) 1 Cr App R (S) 233, [1979] Crim LR 52, Bodmin Cty Ct   144, 442
R v Newington (1990) 91 Cr App R 247, 6 BMLR 99, [1990] Crim LR 593,
     CA   144, 442, 1230
R v North Yorkshire CC, ex p Hargreaves (1994) *The Times*, November 9   42
R v Portsmouth Hospitals NHS Trust ex parte Glass [1999] 2 FLR 905, [1999]
     Lloyd's Rep Med 367, (1999) 50 BMLR 269, CA   234
R v Sheppard [1981] AC 394, [1980] 3 WLR 960, [1980] 3 All ER 899, HL   144, 442
Richmond v Richmond (1914) 111 LT 273   109
Roult (by his mother and litigation friend) v North West Strategic Health
     Authority [2009] EWCA Civ 444, [2009] PIQR P18, [2009] LS Law
     Med 383, (2009) 106(22) LSG 25, [2009] All ER (D) 173 (May)   888
Royal Bank of Scotland v Etridge (No 2) [2001] UKHL 44, [2002] 2 AC 773,
     [2001] 3 WLR 1021, [2001] 4 All ER 449, [2001] 2 FLR 1364, HL   29, 1045
RP v Nottingham City Council & the Official Solicitor (Mental Capacity of
     Parent) [2008] EWCA Civ 462, [2008] 2 FLR 1516, [2008] All ER (D)
     102 (May)   653, 875

S (A Child) (Identification: Restrictions on Publication), Re [2004] UKHL 47,
     [2005] 1 AC 593, [2004] 3 WLR 1129, [2005] 1 FLR 591, [2004] 4 All
     ER 683   634
S (Adult Patient: Sterilisation), Re [2001] Fam 15, [2000] 3 WLR 1288; *sub
     nom* S (Sterilisation: Patient's Best Interests), Re [2000] 2 FLR 389, CA 114, 230,
                                                                            313, 1048
S (Hospital Patient: Court's Jurisdiction), Re [1996] Fam 1, [1995] 3 WLR 78,
     [1995] 3 All ER 290, [1995] 1 FLR 1075; [1995] Fam 26, [1995] 2
     WLR 38, [1995] 1 All ER 449, [1995] 1 FLR 302, FD   29, 30
S, Re: D v R (Deputy of S) and S [2010] EWHC 2405 (COP)   99
SA (Vulnerable Adult With Capacity: Marriage), Re [2005] EWHC 2942
     (Fam), [2006] 1 FLR 867, [2006] Fam Law 268, FD   231, 247
Salford City Council v BJ [2009] EWHC 3310 (Fam)   355
Salford City Council v GJ, NJ and BJ (by their Litigation Friends); *sub nom* GJ
     (Incapacitated Adults), Re; BJ, Re [2008] EWHC 1097 (Fam), [2008] 2
     FLR 1295, (2008) 11 CCL Rep 467, [2008] MHLR 274   265, 721
Saulle v Nouvet [2007] EWHC 2902 (QB), [2008] LS Law Med 201, [2008]
     MHLR 59, [2008] WTLR 729, [2007] All ER (D) 08 (Dec)   103, 398, 875, 886, 1683,
                                                                               1686
Scammell and Scammell v Farmer [2008] EWHC 1100 (Ch), [2008] WTLR
     1261, [2008] All ER (D) 296 (May)   103, 109, 398
Sheffield City Council v E [2004] EWHC 2808 (Fam), [2005] Fam 326, [2005]
     2 WLR 953; *sub nom* E (An Alleged Patient), Re: Sheffield City Council
     v E & S [2005] 1 FLR 965, FD   102, 397, 1068
Shtukaturov v Russia, Application no 44009/05, 27/06/2008, ECHR   72
Simms v Simms; A v A (a child) [2002] EWHC 2734 (Fam), [2003] Fam 83,
     [2003] 2 WLR 1465, [2003] 1 All ER 669, FD   248, 259
Simpson (Deceased), Re, Schaniel v Simpson (1977) 121 SJ 224   109
SK (Proposed Plaintiff) (An adult by way of her litigation Friend), Re [2004]
     EWHC 3202 (Fam), [2005] 2 FLR 230, [2005] 3 All ER 421, [2005]
     Fam Law 460, FD   247
St George's Healthcare NHS Trust v S; R v Collins and Others [1999] Fam 26,
     [1998] 3 WLR 936, [1998] 3 All ER 673, [1998] 2 FLR 728, CA   118, 230

Storck v Germany (2005) 43 EHRR 96, ECHR   270, 271
Swain v Hillman [2001] 1 All ER 91, [2001] CP Rep 16, [1999] CPLR 779,
     CA   667

T (A Minor) (Wardship: Medical Treatment), Re [1997] 1 WLR 242, [1997] 1
     All ER 906, [1997] 1 FLR 502, CA   230
T (Adult: Refusal of Treatment), Re [1993] Fam 95, [1992] 3 WLR 782, [1992]
     4 All ER 649, [1992] 2 FLR 458, CA   253, 1045
T, Applicant 2005 SLT (Sh Ct) 97, 2005 GWD 26–501   1764
Trust A and Trust B v H (an Adult Patient); *sub nom* v H (Adult Patient)
     (Medical Treatment), Re [2006] EWHC 1230 (Fam) [2006] 2 FLR 958
     (2006) 9 CCL Rep 474, [2006] Fam Law 842, [2006] All ER (D) 372
     (May), FD   233

V (Declaration against Parents), Re [1995] 2 FLR 1003, [1996] Fam Law 76,
     FD   30

W (Enduring Power of Attorney), Re [2001] Ch 609, [2001] 2 WLR 957,
     [2001] 4 All ER 88, [2001] 1 FLR 832, CA; [2000] Ch 343, [2000] 3
     WLR 45, [2000] 1 All ER 175, [1999] 2 FLR 1163   152, 162, 188, 192, 200, 1716
W Healthcare NHS Trust v KH [2004] EWCA Civ 1324, [2005] 1 WLR 834,
     (2004) *The Times*, December 9   246
W PCT v TB (an adult by her litigation friend the Official Solicitor) [2009]
     EWHC 1737 (Fam)   274, 275, 463, 515, 1704
W v Egdell [1990] Ch 359, [1990] 2 WLR 471, [1990] 1 All ER 835, CA;
     [1990] Ch 359, [1989] 2 WLR 689, [1989] 1 All ER 1089, ChD   26, 112, 1076
W v UK Series A No 121, (1987) 10 EHRR 29, ECHR   51
White v Fell (1987) 12 November (unreported)   875, 876
White v White [2001] 1 AC 596, [2000] 3 WLR 1571, [2000] 1 All ER 43,
     [2000] 2 FLR 981, HL; [1999] Fam 304, [1999] 2 WLR 1213, [1998] 4
     All ER 659, [1998] 2 FLR 310, CA   1725
WLW, Re [1972] 1 Ch 456, [1972] 2 WLR 1207, [1972] 2 All ER 433   341, 651

X NHS Trust v J (by her litigation friend the Official Solicitor) [2005] EWHC
     1273 (Fam), [2006] Lloyd's Rep Med 151   353

Y (Mental Patient: Bone Marrow Donation), Re [1997] Fam 110, [1997] 2
     WLR 556; *sub nom* Y (Mental Incapacity: Bone Marrow Transplant), Re
     [1996] 2 FLR 787, FD   121, 259, 1094, 1144
Yonge v Toynbee [1910] 1 KB 215, 79 LJKB 208, [1908–10] All ER Rep 204,
     CA   147, 881

Z (An Adult: Capacity), Re [2004] EWHC 2817 (Fam), [2005] 1 WLR 959,
     [2005] 3 All ER 280, [2005] 1 FLR 740, FD   252

Table of Practice Directions

References are to page numbers.

Civil Procedure Rules 1998, SI 1998/3132
    Practice Direction – About Costs   906, 907, 920
        para 50.2   887
        para 51.1   887
    Practice Direction 2B – Allocation of Cases to Levels of Judiciary
        para 5.1(a)   379
    Practice Direction 12 – Default Judgment
        para 2.3(1)   377
        para 4.2   377
    Practice Direction 21 – Children and Protected Parties   872, 877, 882, 883, 885, 887, 888, 890, 891
        para 1.1   372
        para 2.1   878, 880
        para 2.2   373
        para 2.2(2)(e)   880
        para 2.3   877
        para 2.3(4)   880
        para 2.4   878, 882
        para 3.4   375, 883
        para 3.6   883
        para 4.5   375
        para 4.6   375
        para 4.7   375
        para 5.5   381
        para 5.6   887, 889
        para 6.5   887, 889
        para 8.2(3)   380
        para 10.2   890
        para 13   380
        para 13.3   381
        paras 3.1–3.4   374
        paras 5.1–5.3   379
        paras 8–12   889
        paras 8.1–8.5   380
        paras 8.1(2)   380
        paras 9.1–9.8   380
        paras 10.1–10.7   380
    Practice Direction 22 – Statements of Truth
        para 3.1(1)   377
        para 3.7   377
    Practice Direction 23 – Applications
        para 6   1636
    Practice Direction 37 – Miscellaneous provisions about payments into court   898
    Practice Direction 39 – Miscellaneous provisions relating to hearings
        para 1.4A   887
        para 1.6   378
    Practice Direction 40C   379
    Practice Direction 41 – Provisional Damages   888
Court of Protection Rules 2007
    Practice Direction – Deprivation of Liberty Applications   282, 627

Court of Protection Rules 2007—*continued*
   Practice Direction 4A – Court Documents 240, 295
      para 7 .... 589, 590
      para 7(c) 589, 590
   Practice Direction 4B – Statements of Truth 240, 296, 304, 591
      para 16 591
      paras 7–16 591
      paras 17–20 591
   Practice Direction 6A – Service 240, 296, 604
      para 3 606
      para 5(a) 601
      para 13 600
      para 15 600
      para 17 604
      paras 1–8 601
      paras 4–8 587
   Practice Direction 7A – Notifying P 240, 297
   Practice Direction 8A – Permission 240, 299, 447, 609
      para 3 614
      para 4 614
      para 7 612
      paras 2–4 612
   Practice Direction 9A – The Application form 240, 299, 366, 367, 369
      para 14 616
      paras 2–8 615
      paras 9–12 616
   Practice Direction 9B – Notification of other persons that an application
      form has been issued 240, 299, 367, 619
      para 6 619
      para 7 619
      para 9 619
      para 10 619
      para 11 619
   Practice Direction 9C – Responding to an application 240, 299
      para 3 621
      para 4 621
      para 6–13 621
      para 14 621
   Practice Direction 9D – Application by currently appointed Deputies,
      Attorneys, and Donees in relation to P's property and affairs 223, 367, 620
      para 8 615
      paras 4, 5 615
   Practice Direction 9D – Applications by currently appointed Deputies,
      Attorneys, and Donees in relation to P's property and affairs 299
   Practice Direction 9E – Applications relating to serious medical treatment 130, 240, 299, 369, 620, 630
      paras 11, 12 598
      paras 13–15 630
   Practice Direction 9F – Applications relating to statutory wills, codicils,
      settlementsand other dealings with P's property 299, 620
      para 6 616
      paras 2–4 616
   Practice Direction 9G – Applications to appoint or discharge a trustee 240, 299
      para 5 616
      paras 2, 3 616
      paras 8, 9 616
   Practice Direction 9H – Applications relating to the registration of Enduring
      Powers of Attorney 299, 620, 679
      para 2 616
      paras 6–8 616

Court of Protection Rules 2007—*continued*
    Practice Direction 9H – Applications relating to the registration of Enduring Powers of
        Attorney—*continued*
        paras 6–10   365
    Practice Direction 10A – Applications within proceedings   240, 301, 369, 624
        para 4   625
        para 7   625
        para 9   626
        para 10   626
        para 11   626
        para 13   626
        para 21   597
        paras 18–20   587, 597
        paras 18–21   624
        paras 22, 23   624
    Practice Direction 10B – Urgent and interim applications   240, 242, 243, 301, 369, 624,
         627
        para 5   627
        para 6   627
        para 7   587, 627
        para 9   627
        para 11   627
        para 12   587
        para 16   627
    Practice Direction 11A – Human Rights   240, 295, 628
        para 9   628
    Practice Direction 12A – Court's jurisdiction to be exercised by Certain
        Judges   130, 240, 302
        para 3(b)   628
        paras 2, 3   598, 630
    Practice Direction 12B – Process for disputing the Court's jurisdiction   240, 302, 631
    Practice Direction 13A – Hearings (including reporting restrictions)   240
        para 6   635
        para 27   635
        para 29   635
        paras 7, 8   633
        Pt 2   635
    Practice Direction 14A – Written evidence   240, 305
        Annex   587
        Annex 2   597, 637
        para 21   587
        para 32   638
        para 35   638
        para 42   638
        para 54   640
        paras 1–19   638
        paras 20–31   638
        paras 33–45   638
        paras 33–50   621
    Practice Direction 14B – Depositions   240, 305, 307, 640, 643
    Practice Direction 14C – Fee for examiners of the Court   240, 305, 641
    Practice Direction 14D – Witness summons   240, 305, 639
        para 9   639
    Practice Direction 14E – Section 49 reports   240, 305, 307, 644, 1631
        Annex   644
        paras 11–16   644
    Practice Direction 15A – expert evidence   240, 307
        para 1   646, 649
        para 6(a)   646
        paras 2–7   646

Court of Protection Rules 2007—*continued*
    Practice Direction 15A – expert evidence—*continued*
        paras 3, 4   645
        paras 8–12   648
    Practice Direction 17A – Litigation friend   240, 309, 653, 659
    Practice Direction 18A – Change of solicitor   240, 310, 659
    Practice Direction 19A – Costs in the Court of Protection   240, 311, 450, 662
        para 20   664
    Practice Direction 19B – Fixed costs in the Court of Protection   311, 772
    Practice Direction 20A – Appeals   240, 314, 449, 666
    Practice Direction 21A – Contempt of Court   240, 315, 671
        para 9   673
        paras 4–6   673
    Practice Direction 22A – Transitional provisions   316, 582
    Practice Direction 22B – Transitory provisions   316, 582
    Practice Direction 22C – Appeals against decisions made under Pt 7 of
        MHA 1983 or the EPA 1985 which are brought on
        or after commencement   316, 582
    Practice Direction 23A – Request for directions where notice of objection
        prevents the Public Guardian from registering an Enduring Power of
        Attorney   316, 679
    Practice Direction 23B – Where P ceases to lack capacity or dies   240, 316, 679, 1625

Family Procedure (Adoption) Rules 2005, SI 2005/2795
    Practice Direction – Service out of the Jurisdiction   1009

Practice Note (Official Solicitor: Declaratory Proceedings: Medical and Welfare
    Decisions for Adults Who Lack Capacity) [2006] 2 FLR 373   233
Practice Note (Official Solicitor: Medical and Welfare Decisions for Adults who Lack
    Capacity) [2001] 2 FLR 158   350
Practice Note: Family Division: Incapacitated Adults (2002) *The Times*, 4 January   350
Practice Note: PVS Cases [2001] 2 FLR 155   351
Practice Note: Sterilisation Cases [2001] 2 FLR 155   350
President's Direction 'Applications Relating to Serious Medical Treatment'   241, 250
President's Practice Direction Declaratory Proceedings concerning Incapacitated Adults:
    Medical and Welfare Decisions of 14 December 2001   233

Table of Codes of Practice

References are to page numbers.

Code of Practice Access to Funds (Revised) 1760
Code of Practice to supplement the main Mental Capacity Act 2005 – Deprivation of Liberty
    Safeguards 2008 79, 80, 270, 440
  para 2.6 273
  paras 2.17–2.24 272
Code of Practice under the Mental Capacity Act 2005 77, 79, 80, 81, 82, 83, 84, 87, 102,
    104, 106, 153, 155, 208, 212, 236, 396, 440, 441, 1620, 1623, 1628,
    1655, 1670
  Ch 3 88, 111, 396, 401
  Ch 9 256
  Ch 11 260
  Ch 16 112
  para 2 441
  para 2.5 87
  para 2.11 91
  para 4.20 100
  para 4.24 102
  para 4.45 104, 404
  para 5.11 108
  para 5.28 118
  para 5.31 167
  paras 5.37–5.48 122
  para 5.38 401
  para 5.47 121
  para 5.51 123
  para 5.68 244
  para 6.5 128, 404
  paras 6.7–6.19 129
  para 6.18 130
  paras 6.49–6.53 134
  para 6.58 406
  para 9.19 256
  para 9.51 258
  para 10.69 250
  para 12.13 105

Table of EC and International Regulations

References are to page numbers.

Convention on the International Protection
    of Adults 2000   456, 524, 532, 1735,
                   1743, 1748
    Art 4   531
    Art 7   525
    Art 8   525
    Art 12   526
    Arts 28–36   530
    Art 33   529, 530
    Art 38   531
Council of Europe Convention on Human
    Rights and Biomedicine   261
Council Regulation (EC) No 1348/2000 of
    29 May 2000 on the service in the
    Member States of judicial and
    extrajudicial documents in civil
    or commercial matters   1016

European Convention on Human Rights 48,
    49, 50, 55, 68, 165, 233, 245,
    877, 1257, 1259, 1744
    Art 2   48, 71, 233

European Convention on Human
    Rights—*continued*
    Art 3   48, 71, 233
    Art 5   48, 272
    Art 5(1)   133, 134, 165, 215, 269, 270,
               405, 1114
    Art 5(4)   269, 420
    Art 6   48, 51, 71, 632
    Art 6(1)   887
    Art 8 26, 48, 70, 71, 233, 234, 634, 1246
    Art 10   46, 634
    Art 14   42, 49, 71
    First Protocol
        Art 1   70
        Art 2   49
European Union Directive on Good Clinical
    Practice in Clinical Trials, Directive
    2001/20/EC   259

Helsinki Declaration 1964   261

List of Abbreviations

Statutes

AWI(S)A 2000	Adults with Incapacity (Scotland) Act 2000
CPA 2004	Civil Partnership Act 2004
DDA 1995	Disability Discrimination Act 1995
EPAA 1985	Enduring Powers of Attorney Act 1985
HRA 1998	Human Rights Act 1998
MCA 2005	Mental Capacity Act 2005
MHA 1983/2007	Mental Health Act 1983/2007
SGA 1979	Sale of Goods Act 1979

Statutory instruments

2007 Regs	Lasting Powers of Attorney, Enduring Powers of Attorney and Public Guardian Regulations 2007
COPR 2001/2007	Court of Protection Rules 2001/2007
CPR	Civil Procedure Rules 1998

International Conventions

ECHR	European Convention on Human Rights and Fundamental Freedoms 1950

General

ADR	Alternative dispute resolution
ANH	Nutrition and hydration supplied by artificial means
CAFCASS	Children and Family Court Advisory and Support Service
CLS	Community Legal Service
Convention rights	ECHR rights
CTO	Community treatment order
DCA	Department for Constitutional Affairs
DHSS	Department of Health and Social Security
DSS	Department of Social Security
DWP	Department for Work and Pensions
ECT	Electro-convulsive therapy
EPA	Enduring power of attorney
FDR	Financial dispute resolution
GMC	General Medical Council
IMCA	Independent mental capacity advocate
JAC	Judicial Appointments Commission
JCHR	Joint Committee on Human Rights
JSB	Judicial Studies Board
LPA	Lasting power of attorney
MCIP	Mental Capacity Implementation Programme
MHRT	Mental health review tribunal
NHS	National Health Service
OPG	Office of the Public Guardian

PGO	(Old) Public Guardianship Office
PTO	Public Trust Office
PVS	persistent vegetative state
SDD	Social services departments of local authorities
section 5 act	Act which may be carried out with protection from liability under MCA 2005, s 5
SFE	Solicitors for the Elderly Limited

PART I

Narrative

PART I: Narrative

Contents

CHAPTER 1
Background 19

Preliminary 19
  Overview 19
    Issues 19
      Capacity 19
      Decision-making 20
      Communication 20
      Conclusion 21
    Legal competence 21
      Tests of mental capacity 22
      Assessment of mental capacity 22
      Incapacitated people 23
    Decision-making 23
      Delegated decision-making 24
      Decision-makers 24
      Best interests 25
    A special jurisdiction 25
    Confidentiality 26
    Undue influence 27
      Assisted decision-making 27
      The legal position 28
  Legal background 29
    Historical 29
      Parens patriae 29
      The declaratory jurisdiction 29
      Terminology 30
      Incapacity 31
    Legislation 31
      Mental Health Acts 31
      Enduring Powers of Attorney Act 1985 31

The new climate 32
  The social climate 32
    General 32
      Community care 32
    Discrimination 32
      Attitudes to disability 33
      Terminology 34
      Attitudes of minority ethnic communities 35
    Role of the law 35
      Support 36
      Protection 36

Empowerment   37
Problems   37
Role of lawyers   37
Who is the client?   38
The legal climate   38
General   38
Legal publishing   38
Elderly client practices   39
Community Care   39
Background   39
Reports   39
Legislation   40
Circulars and directions   42
Equality and discrimination   42
Background   42
Equality Act 2010   43
Prohibited conduct   44
Direct discrimination   44
Discrimination arising from disability   44
Indirect discrimination   45
Duty to make adjustments   45
Harassment   46
Victimisation   46
Implications of conduct   46
Premises   47
Associations   47
Human Rights Act 1998   48
The Convention   48
The legislation   48
Interpretation   49
Remedies   50
New concepts   50
Application to the Court of Protection and Public Guardian   51
Comment   51
Civil Partnership Act 2004   52
Background   52
The legislation   52
Incapacity issues   53
Access to justice   54
Background   54
A change of culture   54
Discrimination   54
Unrepresented parties   55
Disadvantages   55
Personal assistance   56
Physical and sensory impairments   57
Hearings   57
Interpreters   57

The (former) Court of Protection   58
  Origins of the jurisdiction   58
  Practice and procedure   58
    General   58
      Applications   59
      Short orders   59
      Persons under disability   60
      Service   60
      Evidence   60
    Hearings   61
      Conduct   61
      Reviews and appeals   61
    Fees and costs   61
      Court fees   61
      Legal costs   61
    Venue   62
      Background   62
      Regional hearings   63
    An evaluation of the Court of Protection   64
      Court Rules   64
      Contested hearings   65
      Other hearings   65

Law reform   66
  Origins   66
  The Law Commission   66
    Consultation   66
    Report   67
  The Government's response   68
    'Who Decides?'   68
    'Making decisions'   68
  Legislation   68
    Adults with Incapacity (Scotland) Act 2000   68
    Mental Incapacity Bill   69
    Mental Capacity Act 2005   69
      Human rights compatibility   70
  Conclusion   72

CHAPTER 2
The Mental Capacity Jurisdiction   **77**

Introduction   77

Part 1: Overview   77
  Key elements   77
    General   77
    Essential provisions   78
    The public bodies   79
  The Code of Practice   79
    Application   80

Legal effect   81
    Sanctions for non-compliance   82
Creation   83
    Consultation   83
    Procedure for approval   83
    Publication   84

Part 2: Principles and concepts   84
  The principles   84
    Background   84
      The statement of principles   85
    Presumption of capacity   86
      Law Commission proposals   87
      The legislation   87
      The Code of Practice   87
    Practicable steps to help decision-making   88
      Law Commission proposals   88
      The legislation   88
      The Code of Practice   88
    Unwise decisions   89
      The legislation   89
      Law Commission proposals   89
      Evidence before the Joint Committee   90
    Best interests   91
      The Law Commission proposals   91
      The Joint Committee's view   92
      The legislation   92
    Less restrictive alternative   92
      The Law Commission proposals   92
      The legislation   92
      The Scottish approach   93
    Application to the Court of Protection   93
  Defining lack of capacity   94
    The functional approach   94
    People who lack capacity   94
      The two-stage test of capacity   95
      A diagnostic threshold   95
      Principle of 'equal consideration'   96
      Qualifying age   96
    Inability to make decisions   98
      Understand the information relevant to the decision   98
      Retain the information   100
      Use or weigh the information   100
      Unable to communicate   102
    Common law tests of capacity   102
    Reasonable belief of lack of capacity   103
    Competence and capacity: children and young people   104
      Children under 16: 'Gillick competence'   104
      Young people aged 16 or 17: Capacity or competence?   105

The assessment of capacity   106
  Background   106
  When should capacity be assessed?   106
  Who should assess capacity?   107
  The need for formal assessment   108
    Legal or professional requirements   109
    The 'Golden Rule'   109
    Other expert assessments   110
  How capacity is assessed   111
    Confidentiality   112
    Refusal to be assessed   113
  Recording assessments of capacity   113
    Professional records   113
    Formal reports or certificates of capacity   114
Determining best interests   114
  Background   114
  The best interests checklist   115
    Principle of equal consideration   116
    All relevant circumstances   117
    Regaining capacity   117
    Permitting and encouraging participation   118
    Life-sustaining treatment   118
    The person's wishes and feelings, beliefs and values   120
    The weight to be given to P's wishes and feelings   122
    The views of other people   123
    Duty to apply the best interests principle   124
    Reasonable belief   124

Part 3: General powers and duties   125
  Acts in connection with care or treatment – background   125
    The problem   125
    The Law Commission proposal   126
    The general authority   126
    The views of the Joint Committee   126
  Acts in connection with care or treatment – the legislation   127
    Protection from liability   127
    Section 5 acts   128
    Serious acts relating to medical treatment or welfare   129
    Who can act in connection with care or treatment?   131
    No protection in cases of negligence   132
    Effect on advance decisions to refuse treatment   132
    Limitations on permitted acts   132
    Restraint   132
    Decisions of donees or deputies   135
  Paying for goods, services and other expenditure   136
    Background   136
    The legislation   136
    Responsibility to pay for necessary goods and services   137
    Expenditure   138

PART I

Excluded decisions   139
    Background   139
    The legislation   139
        Family relationships etc   139
        Mental Health Act matters   140
        Voting rights   141
Ill-treatment or neglect   142
    Background   142
    The new offence   142
        Scope of the offence   143
        Person who lacks capacity   143
        Ill-treatment   144
        Wilful neglect   144

CHAPTER 3
Lasting Powers of Attorney   **145**

Background   145
    Powers of attorney   145
        Limitations   145
        The incapable donor   147
    Statutory powers of attorney   147
        Enduring powers of attorney   147
            Success of enduring powers   150
            Problems with enduring powers   150
            Abolition of enduring powers   153
        Lasting Powers of Attorney   154

Nature of lasting power of attorney   154
    Character of lasting power of attorney   154
        Problems in practice   156
    Scope of lasting power of attorney   157
        Property and affairs   158
        Acting in the best interests of the donor   159
            Power to maintain others   160
            Limited power to make gifts   161
            The donor as trustee   163
            The donor as a litigant   163
        Welfare matters   164
            Limits on welfare matters   164
        Alternatives to welfare lasting powers of attorney 168

Form of lasting power of attorney   169
    Who can give a lasting power of attorney?   169
        Prescribed forms   169
            Use of different prescribed forms   169
            Defective forms   170
    Content of LPA   173
        Part A – the Donor's Statement   174
            Choice of attorney   174

More than one attorney 174
Replacement attorneys 176
Restrictions and conditions 178
Welfare restrictions 180
Life-sustaining treatment 180
Named persons to be notified 181
Part B – the Certificate Provider's Statement 184
Part C – the Attorney's Statement 188

Creation of lasting power of attorney 190
A lasting power of attorney is created in two stages 190

The first stage: completing the instrument 190
Capacity to create a power 191

The second stage: registration 192
The requirement of registration 192
Problems with capacity not being relevant to registration 193
Problems with early registration 193
Procedure for registration 194
Status of attorney prior to registration 195
Notices 196
Service of notices 196
Dispensing with notice 197
Completion of registration 197
Objections to registration 197
The role of the Public Guardian 197
Objections made to the Public Guardian 198
The role of the Court of Protection 199
Whether the requirements for the creation of the power have
been met 200
Whether the power has been revoked 200
That fraud or undue pressure was used to induce the donor to
create the power 201
That the donee has behaved, is behaving or proposes to
behave in a way that contravenes his or her authority or
contrary to the donor's best interests 201
Procedure 203

Enduring powers of attorney 203
The future of existing powers 203

CHAPTER 4
Powers of the Court 205

Preliminary 205

Declarations 206
Background 206
General powers of the Court 207
Declarations as to capacity 207
Declarations as to medical treatment 208

Making decisions and appointing deputies   208
  Powers of the Court   208
  Making decisions   209
    General   209
      Children   209
    Personal welfare   209
    Property and affairs   210
      Wills   210
      Settlements   211
      Miscellaneous   212
  Deputies   212
    Appointment   212
      Who may be appointed?   213
      Control of the deputy   213
    Powers   213
      Conditional on lack of capacity   214
      Powers that cannot be given   214
      Medical treatment   214
      Conflict with an attorney   214
      Restraint   214
    Revocation of appointment   215
  How will the Court exercise these powers?   215
    The new approach   215
    What happens to receiverships?   216
      The past regime   216
      The new regime   216

Control of lasting powers of attorney   217
  Court's powers to intervene   217
    General   217
    Specific powers   218
      Creation and revocation   218
      Capacity   219
      Registration   219
      Meaning and effect of the power   220
      Directions to the attorney   221
      Rendering accounts etc   221
      Relieving the attorney of liability   221
      Gifts   222
    Applying to the Court   222
  The role of the Public Guardian   223

Living with the new jurisdiction   224
  Overview   224
    Property and affairs   225
    Personal welfare   225
      Health care   225
      Personal care   226

CHAPTER 5
Welfare and Health Care, Advance Decisions and Research 229

Preliminary 229

The pre-existing common law 229
  The three bases for medical treatment 229
  Court's power to authorise treatment 229
    The demise of parens patriae 229
    The declaratory jurisdiction 230
    Emerging principles 230
  The development of the jurisdiction 231
    Welfare 231
    Power to grant injunctions 231
    Test of capacity 232
    Best interests 232
  Practice and procedure at common law 232
  Impact of the European Convention on Human Rights 233
    Relevant Convention rights 233
    The need for references to the High Court 234
    The background to reform 235

The position under the Mental Capacity Act 2005 235
  General 235
    Principles (s 1) and Codes of Practice (s 42) 236
    Capacity (s 2) 236
    Inability to make decisions (s 3) 237
    Best interests (s 4) 237
    'Acts in connection with care or treatment' (ss 5–6) 239
    The powers of the Court of Protection 239
  Practice and procedure under the Mental Capacity Act 2005 240
    Court Rules and Practice Directions 240
    Permission 240
    Serious medical treatment cases 241
    When should cases be brought to Court? 242
    Welfare or less serious medical treatment cases 244
  Withholding or withdrawing life-sustaining treatment 244
    Intolerability 246
    Best interests under the Mental Capacity Act 2005 246
  An exclusive jurisdiction 247
    Overlap with judicial review 248

Independent mental capacity advocates 248
  Establishment 248
    Appointment, functions and role 249
  The duty to instruct 250
    NHS bodies 250
    Local authorities 251
    Expansion of role 251
  Powers of the advocate 251
  Comment 252

PART I

The competent adult – advance decisions   252
    Preliminary   252

Advance directives at common law   253
    Refusal of treatment   253
        Essential features   253
        The relationship with suicide   253
    Requests for treatment   254

Advance decisions under the Mental Capacity Act 2005   254
    Recognition   254
        Advance refusals of treatment   254
        Advance requests for treatment   255
    Conditions for validity   255
        Applicability   255
        Life-sustaining treatment   255
    Implications of an advance decision   256
        Effect   256
        Doubt or disagreement   256
    The Code of Practice   256
    Comment   257
        Striking a balance   257
        The alternative of a lasting power of attorney   257
        Decisions by health care professionals   257
        References to the Court of Protection   258

Medical research   258
    Common law position   258
        The regulation of research   258
            General principles   259
            Clinical Trials Regulations   259
    Research authorised by the Mental Capacity Act 2005   260
        Background   260
        Application of the Act   261
            Pre-condition to authorisation   261
            Pre-conditions relating to the individual   261
        Comment   262

CHAPTER 6
Deprivation of Liberty Safeguards   265

Background   265

The Mental Health Act 1983, as amended by the Mental Health
    Act 2007   265
    Powers of admission, detention and treatment   265
    Review and appeals   266
    Purpose   267

Comparisons   267
    Differences   267
    Overlaps   268

The Deprivation of liberty safeguards   268
   The 'Bournewood Gap'   268
   The decisions of the domestic courts   269
   European Court of Human Rights   269

The MCA solution   270
   Meaning of deprivation of liberty   270
   Court of Protection powers   274
   Deprivation of liberty in a hospital or care home   274
   The age requirement   275
   The mental health requirement   275
   The mental capacity requirement   275
   The best interests requirement   275
   The eligibility requirement   275
   The no refusals requirement   276

Standard authorisations   276
   Urgent authorisations   278
   The Standard Authorisations, Assessments and Ordinary
      Residence Regulations   279
   The Appointment of Relevant Person's Representative Regulations 281

Review by the Court of Protection   282

Monitoring   282

Comment   283

CHAPTER 7
Court Practice and Procedure   **285**

Preliminary   285
   Role of the Lord Chancellor   285
   Judiciary   286
   Rules and Practice Directions   286

Status of the Court of Protection   286
   Preliminary   286
   The Court   287
      Name and venue   287
      Administration   287
      Forms   287
   Judges   288
      Regional judges   288
      Allocation of cases   289
      Transfer of cases   289
   Powers   290
      General   290
      Interim orders and directions   290
      Reports   291

PART I

The Court Rules   291
   Court of Protection Rules 2007 (COPR 2007)   291
     Practice Directions   293
   The overriding objective   293
     General   293
     Duties of the Court and parties   293
     Interpretation   294
   Case management powers   294
     General   294
     Security for costs   295
     Court's own initiative   295
     Human rights   295

Practice and procedure   295
   Court documents   295
     Statements of truth   296
     Personal details   296
     Access to documents   296
   Service of documents   296
     Who serves?   297
     How is service effected?   297
   Notifying the incapacitated person   297
   Permission to apply   298
     Who may apply?   298
     Applications for permission   299
   Starting proceedings   299
     Initial steps   299
     Responding to an application   300
     Parties   300
   Applications within proceedings   301
     Applications without notice   302
     Interim remedies   302
   Dealing with applications   302
     Directions   303
     Allocation   303
     Disputing the Court's jurisdiction   303
     Hearing the incapacitated person   303
     Reconsideration   303
   Hearings   304
     Types of case   304
   Evidence   305
     Admissions   306
     Witnesses' evidence   306
     Depositions   307
     Reports   307
   Experts   307
   Disclosure   308
     Inspection   309
   Litigation friends   309
   Representation   310

Costs   310
  The general rule   311
  Assessment   311
  Public funding   312
Fees   313
Appeals   314
  Permission to appeal   315
Enforcement   315
Transitional provisions   316
Miscellaneous provisions   316

Practical points   316
  The workload   316
    Volume of cases   316
    Cases under the new jurisdiction   317
  Integration with other courts   318
    Judicial support   318
    Dual jurisdiction   319

CHAPTER 8
The Public Guardian and Supporting Services   **321**

Background   321
  The administration   321
  The Public Trust Office   322
    Nature   322
    Quinquennial Review   322
  The Public Guardianship Office   324
    Launch of the PGO   324
    Progress   325
      The Mission statement   325
      The Consultative Forum   326
      National Audit Office Report 326
      A critical analysis   327
    Other jurisdictions   328
      Scotland   328
      Northern Ireland   329
      Ireland   329

The Public Guardian   329
  Office of the Public Guardian   330
  Functions   330
    Powers   331
    Fees   332
    Annual Report   332
  Public Guardian Board   332
    Annual Report   333
  Challenges ahead   333
    The new role   333
    Dispute resolution   334

PART I

Investigating abuse   334
Use of technology   335
Partnerships   335
Funding   335
Relationship with the Court of Protection   335

Court of Protection Visitors   337
  Background   337
    Historical   337
    Types of Visitor   338
      Medical Visitors   338
      Legal Visitor   339
      General Visitors   339
      Enduring powers of attorney   340
    Recommendations for change   341
      Confidentiality of reports   341
      National Audit Office   342
      Interim reform   343
      Purpose of visits   344
  The new regime   345
    Appointment   345
      General Visitors   345
      Special Visitors   346
    Reports by Visitors   347
    Powers   347
    The changed climate   348
    Association of Independent Visitors   348

The Official Solicitor   348
  Status and function   348
  Background   349
  The present office   350
    Vision Statement   351
    Acceptance policy   351
    The incapacity work of the Official Solicitor   351
      Giving advice   351
      Representing adults who lack capacity   351
      Assisting the civil and family courts   352
      Assisting the Court of Protection   353
      Adult medical and welfare declarations   353
    Other jurisdictions   353
      Scotland   354
      Northern Ireland   354
      Ireland   354
  The future   354

CHAPTER 9
Miscellaneous   **357**

Enduring powers – transitional (Mental Capacity Act 2005, Sch 4)   357

Transitional provisions (Mental Capacity Act 2005, Sch 5)   358
    Mental Health Act 1983, Part VII   358
    Enduring Powers of Attorney Act 1985   358

International Protection of Adults   359
    The position in Non-Convention Countries   359
    Scotland   359

Consequential amendments and repeals (Mental Capacity Act 2005,
    Sch 6)   359

PART I

Chapter 1

Background

PRELIMINARY

Overview

Issues

1.1 The *Concise Oxford Dictionary* defines a decision as 'a conclusion or resolution reached after consideration', and we all assume that fellow citizens are able to make their own decisions. Those who cannot do so depend upon the support of others and are vulnerable to abuse or neglect. A civilised society must make provision for such people in its laws, but this assumes that they can be properly identified.

Capacity

1.2 The assessment of capacity is not an easy matter for society. To deprive people who are capable of making their own decisions of the right to do so would be an abuse, yet failure to recognise lack of capacity results in continuing vulnerability. It is possible to stigmatise a person as lacking capacity for a variety of reasons and our history provides many examples of this.[1] Is the objective to protect the individual or society? Is it to afford power to one section of society over another by categorising some people as being unable to make decisions? We accept that children may be denied capacity, especially during their formative years, but the age at which capacity becomes recognised by the law has progressively reduced during recent years. It is only within the past century that all people in our society have been recognised as equals, and this means that some objective justification must exist before personal capacity is denied to an adult. That justification is generally to be found in the diagnosis of some form of mental impairment.

1.3 Legal incompetence is thus to be found when there is lack of capacity due to a mental disability. It may arise for a variety or reasons and may be merely temporary or may be a permanent condition. The lack of capacity may be partial or total. Insofar as an individual does have capacity, any decisions that are made should be recognised and an 'all or nothing' approach should not be adopted. Some decisions require little thought and may be identified from a mere assent or even body language. Others require knowledge and understanding and need to be communicated in a reasoned manner.

---

[1] Women, felons and lunatics have all at some time been treated as incompetent. The Mental Deficiency Act 1913 extended to 'moral imbeciles' and thus unmarried mothers could be deprived of their liberty.

Decision-making

1.4 When lack of capacity is temporary it may be possible to defer decisions until capacity is restored. But if it is of lasting duration or permanent, or if an urgent decision otherwise needs to be made, there must be some legally recognised procedure whereby necessary decisions can be made by some other person or body. The decision-maker must be identified so that any decision that is made will be recognised by others.

1.5 There are different types of decision that we all make. We have to manage our financial affairs, and those who enter into transactions with us must be satisfied that these are enforceable and not likely to be set aside due to lack of competence on our part or lack of authority on the part of the person who transacts them for us. Decisions about medical treatment may also need to be made and should not simply be left to doctors, especially if they could have a serious effect upon the rest of our lives. Many personal welfare decisions are trivial, but some may have implications for other persons and lead to disputes within families.[2] Each of these three types of decision-making needs to come within any jurisdiction afforded by the law.

1.6 If personal choices are to be made for us then there must be a recognised basis on which this should be done. Is the decision-maker free to make whatever decisions he or she thinks best, which might be subjective and influenced by personal interests, or is an objective basis to be adopted? What might that basis be? There seems to be general acceptance that the paternalistic approach adopted in respect of children is not appropriate for an adult.

1.7 It is not acceptable for one person to assume dominion over another without the facility for this to be questioned and it is a function of the law to provide this facility. Although various procedures may be devised to resolve disputes, as a last resort it is the courts that are usually relied upon to undertake this task. They need to be legally empowered to do so, but it is not only disputes that may need to be referred to the courts: where there is uncertainty as to what may be done or what would be lawful, the courts are usually expected to determine this.

Communication

1.8 There is no magic about decision-making: it merely means making a choice, but this does require the ability to identify the range of possible choices and the implications of each. It also requires the ability to communicate the choice once this has been made. Communication is a two-way process: it is as important to ensure that the person understands what is being said to them as that their attempts to respond are understood.

---

2   Compare decisions about what to wear and what to eat with decisions about where to live or with whom.

Impairment of communication does not necessarily indicate lack of mental capacity and, where there is doubt, a medical report may establish the capacity of the individual.

1.9 If we are to empower people we must not rely solely upon normal methods of communication, but should explore and adopt any method that will achieve effective communication.[3] This may involve using available aids or an interpreter where this will assist. If verbal dialogue is not possible, written notes or sign language may facilitate communication. A simple response to questions, such as movement of a finger, may be found reliable but in that event questions must be phrased so as to facilitate a range of responses.

Conclusion

1.10 These are the fundamental issues that should be addressed by any legal system, and other countries including Germany, the provinces in Canada and the states of the USA, Australia and New Zealand have through their legislation over the years developed an adult guardianship law. The Mental Capacity Act 2005 is the first attempt to remedy this shortcoming in England and Wales and it contains some innovative features.[4] A slightly different approach has already been adopted in Scotland.[5]

Legal competence

1.11 The law assumes that an adult has the capacity to make and the ability to communicate personal decisions so there is a vacuum if someone is not able to do this. Concerns may also arise as to whether an individual is competent to make a particular decision or acquiesce in the decisions of others, even though he or she purports to do so. In a legal context we are assessing whether the choice would be recognised by the law.

1.12 When talking about competence we are considering the ability to understand, make a choice and then make this clear to others, even though assistance may be needed to carry the choice into effect. It follows that neither age nor physical or sensory impairment should by itself affect competence. Lack of legal competence may arise through mental incapacity, an inability to communicate or a combination of the two, but every effort should be made to overcome communication difficulties.

---

[3] The phrase 'locked in syndrome' is used to describe a person who can reason and make decisions but is unable to communicate.

[4] The implementation date was 1 October 2007 for England and Wales and it could be adopted in Northern Ireland by regulations.

[5] Adults with Incapacity (Scotland) Act 2000; Mental Health (Care and Treatment) (Scotland) Act 2003; and Adult Support and Protection (Scotland) Act 2007. See Chapter 10.

Tests of mental capacity

1.13 Although the term 'mental incapacity' conveys a fairly consistent impression to most people it does not have a precise meaning. It would be convenient if there were a universal definition, so that we could readily identify those members of society who are eligible for special treatment, but this could never be the case because very few people are incapable in all things. Legal tests of capacity must vary according to the circumstances.

1.14 The classic definition of a 'patient' which is found in the Mental Health Act 1983 and elsewhere has only recently been interpreted by the appeal courts.[6] In some situations specific tests have been developed by case-law, so textbooks are able to identify testamentary capacity and the capacity required to sign an enduring power of attorney, conduct civil proceedings in the courts, enter into a marriage or make a gift. Otherwise general principles must be relied upon, and these are now based upon function rather than status or the outcome of decisions. Furthermore, it is the individual's understanding rather than judgment that is relevant – we are all entitled to make unwise decisions.

Assessment of mental capacity

1.15 Doubts about capacity may arise for several reasons but these should not be confused with tests of capacity. Thus the status of the individual (such as being elderly and living in a nursing home), the outcome of a decision (viewed by others as illogical) or the appearance or behaviour of the individual may cause capacity to be questioned. Yet it is not unusual for outward appearances to create a false impression of incapacity and, conversely, the absence of any of these indications does not mean that the individual is capable. In all these situations a proper assessment should be made according to appropriate criteria.

1.16 One of the difficulties is that the various professionals who may be involved approach the question of capacity from different standpoints so often reach different conclusions. In case of dispute, capacity is a question of fact for the Court to decide on the balance of probabilities with a presumption of capacity. The opinions of professionals will be admitted as 'expert' evidence but considered alongside factual evidence from those who know the individual and will only be persuasive if the experts have been given all relevant information and applied the appropriate legal test.

1.17 The medical profession tends to be concerned with diagnosis and prognosis rather than the severity and implications of mental disability. The doctor may well be able to identify the cause of the disability and indicate its likely future consequences, but what is in issue to the lawyer is the effect on the individual at this moment in time.[7] Care workers classify people

---

6   *Masterman-Lister v Brutton & Co and Jewell & Home Counties Dairies* [2002] EWCA Civ
         1889, [2002] All ER (D) 297 (Dec).
7   The Law Society and the British Medical Association have produced guidance in a book

according to their degree of independence, which involves consideration of levels of competence in performing skills such as eating, dressing, communication and social skills. These skills may be affected by mental or physical causes. An assessment based upon a medical diagnosis is of little use to the care worker other than to explain the reason for the present impairment and indicate whether improvement or deterioration is to be expected. The carer may become concerned as to the vulnerability of the person cared for and the entitlement of others to take decisions on that person's behalf.

1.18 The lawyer wishes to establish whether the individual is capable of making a reasoned and informed decision, although there may be a need to assess the degree of dependence, for example, when considering what financial provision should be made for the individual. There can be no universally applied test because the capacity required will depend upon the nature of the decision to be made, but the medical diagnosis will be largely irrelevant except insofar as it points to the degree of capacity that may be anticipated and the carer's view may be helpful but will not be based on any particular legal test. Thus the lawyer may need to consult the doctor and carer (or social worker) but their views merely form part of the evidence when considering the question of legal capacity. Having gathered this evidence the lawyer is in the best position to form a considered view as to legal capacity or to refer the issue to the Court for determination.

Incapacitated people

1.19 Children are adequately catered for under the law of England and Wales.[8] Those adults who may lack capacity fall into four main groups. The largest group comprises elderly people who are deprived of their capacity by senile dementia but have previously been able to manage their own affairs. At the other extreme are those with learning disabilities which may be so severe that they have never been able to enjoy personal autonomy. In between are those who encounter a period of mental illness or suffer brain damage rendering them incapable of making decisions that others should recognise. The situation is made more complicated by the fact that for some capacity may fluctuate and in every instance there is the potential for partial capacity.

Decision-making

1.20 Decisions fall into three broad categories: financial, personal welfare and health care. When an adult is incapable of making decisions special procedures should be available for these to be taken on his or her behalf if that is appropriate. This raises the questions of when decision-making

---

entitled *Assessment of Mental Capacity: Guidance for Doctors and Lawyers* (BMA, 1995; BMJ Books, 2nd edn, 2004; Law Society Publishing, 3rd edn, 2009).

8   The Children Act 1989 contains the necessary powers for intervention by the courts and the High Court wardship jurisdiction remains.

powers should be delegated, who should then be empowered to take the decisions and the basis on which they should be taken.

Delegated decision-making

1.21 Although under general legal principles a specific decision may be held to be invalid due to lack of competence this may be merely a 'one-off' situation[9] and something more is needed if decision-making powers are to be delegated. This was in the past the existence of a 'mental disorder' which caused the lack of capacity. It was then clear that an ongoing problem needed to be addressed.

1.22 'Mental disorder' was defined in the Mental Health Act 1983 as: 'mental illness, arrested or incomplete development of mind, psychopathic disorder and any other disorder or disability of mind' but did not include the effect of alcohol or drugs.[10] This definition is extremely wide but provided a useful screening process because merely being eccentric should not be a basis for being deprived of one's rights.

Decision-makers

1.23 There have in the past been various persons who might represent the interests of a mentally disabled individual to a greater or lesser extent. These included:[11]

- appointee for state benefits;
- receiver appointed by the former Court of Protection for financial affairs;
- attorney under an enduring power for financial affairs;
- trustees for financial affairs;
- litigation friend for civil proceedings;[12]
- next friend or guardian ad litem for family proceedings;[13]
- personal advocate – used in practice but not recognised in law.

Most of these roles still exist, but despite the length of this list the authority of such representatives extended to very few ordinary decisions for the individual and there were large gaps where no one had any power to make such decisions.

1.24 In a climate where many marriages end in separation or divorce and 'living together relationships' have become almost the norm, it would no longer be acceptable for a spouse or designated blood relative to be given special status by the law as decision-maker. Preserving personal autonomy requires that the incapacitated individual has the opportunity to make the

---

[9] The individual may be under the influence of alcohol or drugs at the time.
[10] Mental Health Act 1983, s 1(2) and (3).
[11] This list applies to England and Wales. A different list could be produced for Scotland.
[12] Civil Procedure Rules 1998, SI 1998/3132, Part 21.
[13] Family Proceedings Rules 1991, SI 1991/1247, Part IX.

choice of decision-maker in advance (if then capable) and to influence that choice even after losing mental capacity to the extent that wishes can be ascertained. Introducing such flexibility creates its own problems but there must be a procedure whereby the appointment of a nominee can be challenged on established principles.

Best interests

1.25 There has been much debate about the basis on which delegated decisions are to be made. Should this be what the decision-maker thinks best or what the incapacitated individual would have decided had he or she been capable? The former is too paternalistic for contemporary society whereas the latter is not feasible for those who have never been able to express their own wishes. The concept of best interests has emerged, which is an attempt to combine respect for the wishes of the individual with the views of others in a climate of minimum intervention. But what exactly does this mean in practice?

A special jurisdiction

1.26 There is an increasing number of adults who lack mental capacity and have property or financial affairs that need to be dealt with. This is partly because the population is living longer with greater home ownership, and partly because more brain-damaged children survive – some with substantial damages awards. Existing procedures allow these affairs to be dealt with but there is a vacuum in our law for other forms of decision-making.

1.27 It is a nonsense that financial management should control personal welfare: none of us run our own lives in that way. We each decide what we wish to do and how we wish to conduct our lives and then temper this according to what we can afford. It is also unacceptable that uncertainty prevails on issues such as where the individual should live, with whom he or she should have contact and what medical treatment should be given. It was inevitable that sooner or later legislation would have to be introduced to tackle this issue. The Mental Capacity Act 2005 superimposes a procedure for decision-making on our existing law.

1.28 It has to be acknowledged that any jurisdiction whose role is to address the needs of 'adults with incapacity'[14] has little relevance to the work of most lawyers and, apart from an occasional high-profile case, is of little interest to the public at large. But to anyone who encounters a decline in the mental capacity of a loved one, and to the professionals involved, the manner in which issues that arise are addressed is seen as a test of the integrity of the legal system. No one can afford to ignore reform in this area,

---

[14] This is the terminology now creeping into use, based on the title to the Scottish legislation, but it is questionable. It may be thought that referring to those who 'lack capacity' is demeaning and to be discouraged, but it is illogical to refer to someone as being with something that they are without.

because this is not a 'them and us' situation. Any of us may encounter a period when we lack capacity whether temporary, progressive or permanent, especially as we grow older. We and our loved ones will then depend on the new jurisdiction established by the Mental Capacity Act 2005.

1.29 The new jurisdiction must also set standards for others to follow in the field of disability. Disabled people must be assured of equal access to justice and that the discrimination they still encounter in society will not be reproduced within the system of justice. This applies to the legal principles that are applied, the procedures that are followed, the facilities available and the attitudes of those involved. There will be many lessons to be learnt by the Public Guardian and the new Court of Protection, but hopefully these will be well learned and thereafter permeate throughout the legal system.[15]

Confidentiality

1.30 Doctors, lawyers, social workers and professional persons generally owe a duty of confidentiality to their patients or clients, which means that personal information should only be revealed to others with the consent of the patient or client.[16] This duty is not absolute and may be overridden where there is a stronger public interest in disclosure.[17] Where the individual lacks the mental capacity to consent to (or refuse) disclosure, it may be desirable to permit disclosure in certain circumstances. This has been expressed as follows:[18]

> 'C's interest in protecting the confidentiality of personal information about himself must not be underestimated. It is all too easy for professionals and parents to regard … incapacitated adults as having no independent interests of their own: as objects rather than subjects. But we are not concerned here with the publication of information to the whole wide world. There is a clear distinction between disclosure to the media with a view to publication to all and sundry and disclosure in confidence to those with a proper interests in having the information in question.'

1.31 During an assessment as to mental capacity it is essential that information is shared by the professionals involved. The patient's consent to this should be obtained wherever possible, but in the absence of this relevant disclosure may be permitted. However, this does not extend to confidential information about the patient unrelated to the assessment. Disclosure will be based on a need-to-know and the overall test will be the best interests of the patient.

---

15   Guidance to judges is available from the Judicial Studies Board in the *Equal Treatment Bench Book*, which can be accessed at www.jsboard.co.uk/etac/etbb/index.htm.
     A summary in PDF format can be downloaded at www.jsboard.co.uk/downloads/fairness_guide_final.pdf.
16   This may be imposed by codes of professional conduct or by the law, eg Data Protection Act 1998 or European Convention on Human Rights, Art 8.
17   *W v Egdell* [1990] Ch 359, at 419.
18   *R (on the application of Ann Stevens) v Plymouth City Council and C* [2002] EWCA Civ 388, per Hale LJ.

1.32 Similar principles must apply in a family context. Parents may choose not to reveal their financial affairs to their children and the situation does not change simply because a parent ceases to be mentally capable. This can cause suspicion when one of the children is appointed to deal with those affairs, but the duty of confidentiality will apply to such child whether acting as attorney or receiver (henceforth deputy) appointed by the Court of Protection.

Undue influence

Assisted decision-making

1.33 One of the problems when dealing with individuals who are frail or of borderline mental capacity is undue influence. Some adults prefer to have many of their decisions made by others and tests of capacity encourage the acceptance of support from others even though this may amount to influence.[19] But there may be cause for concern if an individual is too easily influenced or becomes too much under the influence of another person. Also, understanding of relevant factors may be corrupted by the manner and selectivity in which information is provided. A person who is constantly given incomplete or even incorrect information is likely to make choices that they would not otherwise have made. The ability to make a choice may also be affected by threats, perceived or actual. Thus a decision which appears to have been competently made could be the outcome of at best a limited perception of the choices available or at worst fear of the consequences of making a different decision.

1.34 This problem is magnified by the fact that those seeking to challenge a decision may themselves be seeking to exert an influence over the individual. All too often these situations of conflict develop from a power struggle between otherwise concerned relatives with the vulnerable person becoming a pawn in the game. A tendency by this person to agree with the party who presently has their audience either because of a short-term desire for peace or the strength of that party's personality merely provides evidence which fuels the problem. Experience in the Court of Protection demonstrates that many of the disputes arise from the abuse of power or desire of another individual for control over the vulnerable individual.

1.35 Perhaps of more concern is the situation where undue influence is not recognised and financial or emotional abuse is taking place. An individual who needs assistance from others before making significant personal decisions is vulnerable. There is a tendency to delegate decisions to others who demonstrate a willingness to take them over, and when those others are influenced by personal gain or improper motives there is likely to be abuse. The courts are prepared to set aside transactions adverse to an individual when these are the result of undue influence, but these matters can be

---

[19] Under the new decision-making jurisdiction the real problem is likely to become undue influence of those whose capacity is impaired but not lacking.

expensive to litigate and the interaction between improper influence and
mental capacity has yet to be fully developed.

The legal position

1.36 People may not be saved from their own foolishness but will be
protected from being victimised by other people. The common law
developed a principle of duress but equity supplemented this by enabling
gifts and other transactions to be set aside if procured by undue influence or
if they are otherwise unconscionable. The manner in which the intention to
enter into the transaction was secured may be investigated and if produced
by unacceptable means, the law will not permit the transaction to stand.
There are thus three situations where transactions may be set aside:

- where duress or undue influence has been expressly used for the
  purpose of achieving a gift or benefit – the burden of proof is on the
  party alleging this;
- where undue influence is presumed – the burden is then on the other
  party to justify the transaction; and
- where a contract of an improvident nature has been made by a poor
  and ignorant person acting without independent advice, and the
  other party cannot show that it was fair and reasonable – this is a
  fall-back remedy for unconscionable conduct.

1.37 The law has appeared to approach the issue of undue influence
according to the specific relationship between the parties but the question is
whether one party has placed sufficient trust and confidence in the other,
rather than whether the relationship between the parties is of a particular
type.[20] However, a presumption may arise in two ways:

(1) *The type of relationship*: where there is a recognised relationship in
which one party acquires influence over another who is vulnerable
(eg client and solicitor, patient and doctor, beneficiary and trustee).
There is then an irrebuttable presumption of influence and it is not
necessary to establish that the relationship was based upon trust and
confidence. If it appears that this influence has been inappropriately
exercised then the party with influence must prove that this was not
the case.
(2) *The evidential presumption*: where there is evidence that the
relationship was based on trust and confidence in relation to the
management of the complainant's financial affairs, coupled with a
transaction giving rise to suspicions which must be addressed.
There may then be a rebuttable presumption of undue influence and
it is for the other party to produce evidence to counter the inference
which otherwise should be drawn.

1.38 There are thus two prerequisites to the burden of proof shifting to the
other party. First, that trust and confidence was placed in the other party, or

---

[20]   GH Treitel *The Law of Contract* (Sweet & Maxwell, 10th edn, 1999), at pp 380–381.

that party was in a position of dominance or control. Secondly, that the transaction is not readily explicable by the relationship of the parties. The mere existence of influence is not enough, but it is not essential that the transaction should be disadvantageous to the pressurised or influenced person, either in financial terms or in any other way.[21] However, questions of undue influence will not usually arise where the transaction is innocuous.[22]

Legal background

Historical

Parens patriae

1.39   Until 1959 the High Court and its predecessors had jurisdiction over the lives of incompetent adults pursuant to the rights of the Crown, known as the Royal Prerogative or parens patriae jurisdiction which was given statutory recognition in 1339.[23] This arose from concern about the seizure by the sovereign of the lands of 'idiots' ('fools from birth') and 'lunatics' ('sometimes of good and sound memory and understanding and sometimes not'). The King was to take custody of the property of idiots and provide any necessary care to them whilst keeping any profits, but after death he must 'render it to their heirs'. In the case of lunatics, the King had to 'provide for their custody and sustenance' and preserve their lands for their use when 'they come to their right mind', taking nothing for his own use. However, the care provided might be brutal.[24]

The declaratory jurisdiction

1.40   Nevertheless, the High Court found it necessary to facilitate decisions in extreme cases for incompetent adults (ie. where the individual lacked capacity) and did so by making *declarations* as to best interests, relying on its inherent jurisdction. This was initially in respect of serious health care decisions[25] but subsequently this remedy was extended to personal welfare decisions. In 1995 Mrs Justice Hale not only applied the procedure to a personal welfare decision[26] but also backed it up with an injunction and this

---

21   The label 'manifest disadvantage' adopted by Lord Scarman in *Morgan's Case* [1985] 1 All ER 821 can give rise to misunderstanding and should no longer be adopted – see the judgment of Lord Nicholls in *Bank of Scotland plc v Etridge (No 2)* [2001] UKHL 44, [2001] 4 All ER 430.

22   *CIBC Mortgages plc v Pitt* [1993] 4 All ER 433, [1994] 1 AC 200, HL.

23   Statute de Prerogativa Regis, 17 Edw II (1339) St I cc 9, 10. The earliest reference is to be found in a semi-official tract known as the *De Praerogativa Regis* ('On the King's Prerogative') dating from the reign of Edward 1 (1272-1307).

24   See the history of Bedlam Hospital, established 1329, which began to admit idiots and lunatics in 1377.

25   This power was first recognised by the House of Lords in *F v West Berkshire Health Authority* [1989] 2 All ER 545 and confirmed in *Airedale NHS Trust v Bland* [1993] 2 WLR 316. See generally Chapter 5.

26   *Re S (Adult Patient: Jurisdiction)* [1995] 1 FLR 302. An injunction was granted to stop the wife of an elderly, infirm man taking him abroad out of the care of his mistress.

was upheld by the Court of Appeal.[27] In that same year the High Court held that the Court had jurisdiction to grant a declaration that a child with cerebral palsy and learning difficulties was upon attaining majority entitled to choose where to live and with whom to associate, and to restrain the parents by injunction from interfering.[28] However, it should be noted that the making of a declaration or an injunction is a discretionary remedy and this procedure is inordinately expensive and scarcely available for everyday situations even though these do arise.

1.41 More recently the High Court has extended this power beyond incompetent adults to those who were vulnerable for other reasons. Thus it has been stated:[29]

'... there is no doubt that the court has jurisdiction to grant whatever relief in declaratory form is necessary to safeguard and promote the vulnerable adult's welfare and interests.'

and subsequently:[30]

'... the inherent jurisdiction remains alive, in appropriate cases, to meet circumstances unmet by the scope of the legislation'

So, it appears that the inherent jurisdiction may continue notwithstanding that the Mental Capacity Act 2005 now provides a statutory decision-making jurisdiction for those who lack capacity.[31]

Terminology

1.42 Even if there was no need for decisions to be made on behalf of those who lacked capacity, it was necessary for the courts to decide whether decisions could be made by the individual or whether those purported to have been made were effective. There was confusion in the legal terms found in statutes and law reports well into the twentieth century which pointed to a general condition but did not assist in determining the specific implications. Undefined and stigmatising phrases such as 'of unsound mind',[32] 'mentally defective' and 'mentally disordered' were sometimes used with little attempt to define or assess the implications in any particular case. These terms reflected the period when used rather than the interpretation that should now be placed on the words chosen.

---

[27]   *Re S (Hospital Patient: Court's Jurisdiction)* [1996] Fam 1, [1995] 1 FLR 1075.

[28]   *Re V (Declaration against Parents)* [1995] 2 FLR 1003, Johnson J.

[29]   *Re PS* [2007] EWHC 623 (Fam), [2007] 2 FLR 1083, Munby J. at para 13.

[30]   *KC and Anor v City of Westminster Social and Community Services Department and Anor* [2008] EWCA Civ 198, [2009] Fam 11, Roderic Wood J. at para 56.

[31]   For a contrary view see Macur J. in LBL v RYJ and VJ [2010] EWHC 2665 (COP): 'I reject what appears to have been the initial contention of this local authority that the inherent jurisdiction of the court may be used in the case of a capacitous adult to impose a decision upon him/her whether as to welfare or finance ... the relevant case law establishes the ability of the court, via its inherent jurisdiction, to facilitate the process of unencumbered decision-making by those who they have determined have capacity free of external pressure or physical restraint in making those decisions.'

[32]   This phrase is actually defined in the Trustee Act 1925 as 'incapable from infirmity of mind of managing his own affairs'. Typical of the 1925 property legislation this has stood the test of time.

Incapacity

1.43 Lawyers too frequently failed to distinguish mental illness, mental handicap (now know as learning disability) and brain injury or to realise that although any of these conditions may result in lack of mental capacity they did not inevitably do so. Their approach tended to concentrate upon the nature of the condition rather than its effect on the individual. Unless a status test applied lawyers relied on doctors to assess capacity and little guidance was given as to the specific test to be applied. An 'all or nothing' approach tended to be adopted rather than asking whether the individual was capable of making the particular decision in question. Thus there were people who were without doubt capable and those who clearly lacked capacity, but between these extremes was a grey area for the most part avoided by lawyers.

Legislation

Mental Health Acts

1.44 The Lunacy Act 1890 gave various powers to the Office of the Master in Lunacy (which was not renamed the Court of Protection until 1947) and these were the basis of the provisions contained in the Mental Health Act 1983, Part VII.[33] This former Court of Protection had powers over the property and affairs of an individual who was 'incapable, by reason of mental disorder, of managing and administering his property and affairs'. Usually someone would be appointed as a *receiver* to handle those affairs under the supervision of the Court, but a *short order* was available for small or straightforward cases.

Enduring Powers of Attorney Act 1985

1.45 Demand for a less expensive and simpler procedure of choice[34] coupled with the inability of the Court of Protection to cope with the financial affairs of all mentally incapacitated persons resulted in recommendations by the Law Commission in 1983[35] and the passing of the Enduring Powers of Attorney Act 1985. This overcame the problem with ordinary powers of attorney that they were revoked by the subsequent mental incapacity of the donor[36] under normal agency principles. Some formality was introduced into the documentation and an application had to be made to the Public Guardianship Office for the power to be registered with the Court of Protection upon the donor becoming mentally incapable but there was no supervision although the Court had power to intervene.

1.46 Enduring powers have proved to be a great success but they have their limitations (only financial decisions can be dealt with in this way) and leave

---

[33]   These largely re-enact the Mental Health Act 1959, Part VIII.
[34]   Ie the choice of the person whose affairs are to be dealt with.
[35]   *The Incapacitated Principal*, Law Com No 122, Cmnd 8977 (HMSO, 1983).
[36]   Ie the person who granted the power.

scope for financial abuse. In terms of numbers they far surpassed receivership orders. The development of enduring powers into lasting powers dealing with a wider range of decision-making is considered in Chapter 3, but enduring powers that existed in October 2007 when the new jurisdiction was introduced remain valid under the former principles.

THE NEW CLIMATE

The social climate

General

1.47 There is now a new social and legal climate that emphasises personal autonomy, favours community care and disapproves of discrimination in any form. It should not be overlooked that those who lack mental capacity frequently have other physical or mental impairments as well, so the combined implications of mental and physical disabilities have to be considered.

Community care

1.48 New community care policies were introduced in 1993. There are many facets to community care, but of particular relevance to disabled people are the requirement for their needs to be assessed, the duty placed upon the social services departments of local authorities (subject to available funding) to ensure that these needs are met rather than expecting the individual to cope with whatever services are available and the move away from institutional care to care in the community. The consequence is that people with disabilities are more visible in society and both they and their family/carers have greater expectations as to how they will be treated. Their rights are increasingly being recognised and enforced, by others if not by themselves.

Discrimination

1.49 Discrimination is not always intentional. It may be due to pure ignorance or mere thoughtlessness (ie treating people in an insensitive way) but stereotyping and prejudice also give rise to discrimination. Unwitting or unconscious prejudice – demonstrating prejudice without realising it – is difficult to tackle. Ignorance of the cultures, beliefs and disadvantages of others encourages prejudices and these are best dispelled by greater awareness. For people with disabilities it is not just a question of avoiding these forms of discrimination because any special needs also have to be addressed. Providing equal treatment may involve different treatment so as to ensure equal opportunity.

1.50 Discrimination takes many forms: it may be actual or perceived and it may be direct or indirect. *Direct* discrimination occurs where a person is treated less favourably on grounds of race, colour, religion, gender, ethnic or national origin or disability than others would be in similar circumstance.

Indirect discrimination occurs where a requirement is applied equally to all groups, but has a disproportionate effect on the members of one group because a considerably smaller number of members of that group can comply with it.

1.51 Discrimination may also be found in an entire organisation through its processes, attitudes and behaviour.[37] A culture of prejudice may have grown up within an organisation which is seen as acceptable by those involved and results in unquestioning behaviour that disadvantages a section of the community.[38] If this arises in the legal system or in any environment it should be addressed in an appropriate way.

1.52 Discrimination in any form is now disapproved of as it means being treated unfairly or denied opportunities. It should be avoided even if not intended. Indirect discrimination should not be tolerated unless it can be objectively justified by a legitimate aim and the means of achieving that aim are appropriate and necessary. Even if there is no discrimination every effort should be made to avoid the perception that there has been.

Attitudes to disability

1.53 Attitudes to disability in general have also changed in three significant respects:

(1) We have moved away from the medical model of disability which concentrates on the limitations of the individual to a social model which identifies the barriers created in society. Thus lack of access to a building is not seen as being due to the fact that the individual is a wheelchair user but rather that the building has been constructed with steps but no ramp. In other words, don't blame the individual but blame the way society is structured. It is the barriers that should be removed (or not put there in the first place) rather than the individual that should be given special treatment.

(2) Stereotyping has been recognised as the most significant form of discrimination that affects people with disabilities. This is exhibited in the unjustified assumption that people who meet particular criteria will behave in a particular way. In other words, we must be careful not to apply labels to people, often unconsciously, and then make assumptions based thereon. People who have a specific condition should not all be assumed to have the same limitations or approach to life – they should be treated as 'people first' rather than identified by their perceived disability.

(3) There is a greater awareness of mental health problems and arguably less social stigma involved although it is still prevalent in

---

[37] This was one of the conclusions of *The Stephen Lawrence Inquiry – Report by Sir William Macpherson*, Cmnd 4264-1 (1999). 'Institutional racism' was identified in the police force.
[38] Eg failure to provide assistance to wheelchair users or to communicate in a friendly manner with people from ethnic minorities.

PART I

certain sections of the community.[39] There are many myths about people with mental health problems, in particular that they are dangerous and violent, can't work and are incapable of making their own decisions. Contrary to popular belief, mental health problems are not rare and unusual. However, there remains a tension, reflected in the debate about the new Mental Health Act, between the need to protect society and the best interests of the individual. Society and politicians still tend to be obsessed with those few cases where the individual has become a public danger when in the vast majority of cases any risk is purely to the individual.

Terminology

1.54 How we refer to people is important. Use of inappropriate terms can cause great offence to the individual and also demonstrates prejudicial attitudes towards disabled people. Also, if we attach labels to people there is a danger that we then use these, however inadvertently, to take away their rights by making assumptions that are not in fact justified. Comparisons should never be made with 'normal'[40] and we should not refer to 'the disabled' or 'the handicapped' as if these are a class of person.[41] Terminology that suggests a value judgment should also be avoided.[42] One of the difficulties is that defined medical or legal terms have over the years tended to become used in a derogatory manner[43] and then new neutral terms have to be found. Thus 'mental handicap' has been replaced by 'learning disability' and efforts are being made to find a new term for 'mentally ill'.[44]

1.55 Use of appropriate terminology is not just political correctness but is also an attitude of mind: we should recognise the person rather than any disability. Organisations such as People First prefer that we state 'people with disabilities' for this reason. More recently the Disability Rights Commission opted for 'disabled people' because this emphasises that the individual is disabled by society (the social model of disability).[45]

---

[39]   Stigma arises from negative stereotypes associated with the symptoms or diagnosis of mental health problems.

[40]   Instead refer to non-disabled or able bodied.

[41]   These terms are grammatically incorrect! Similarly 'the blind' or 'the deaf' – instead use 'people with impaired sight' or 'people with impaired hearing'.

[42]   Eg referring to someone as 'a victim of ...', 'suffering from ...', 'afflicted by ...' or 'wheelchair bound'.

[43]   Eg the terms *idiot, imbecile, lunatic, cretin, moron*, all of which have appeared in earlier legislation or medical textbooks. The Mental Deficiency Act 1913 used the defined terms 'idiot' and 'imbecile'.

[44]   MIND, the national organisation, tends to use 'people who experience mental distress' or 'people with mental health problems' but at one time the expression 'mentally challenged' was advocated.

[45]   The Disability Rights Commission has now become part of the Equality and Human Rights Commission. The website is www.equalityhumanrights.com.

Attitudes of minority ethnic communities

1.56 It has become apparent that some minority ethnic communities have a distrust of mental health authorities, try to deal with problems within the family and viewed the former Public Guardianship Office as 'interfering'. It is essential that our new mental capacity jurisdiction reaches out to such communities and recognises cultural norms. The problems that are faced may be illustrated by reference to two communities.

1.57 Asian communities in the UK have tended to be young, with the men mainly working and in consequence controlling the finances. This is changing as they move into the second and third generation, and as members become older more are presenting with senile dementia. There is a stigma associated with mental health problems which tend to be concealed with a consequent delay in accessing services. Many unwritten transactions take place within the community so incapacity issues are not being faced up to. There is a need to raise awareness of the legal position because families react with disbelief when told that they have no authority over the finances of an incapacitated member.

1.58 The Jewish community ranges across a religious spectrum from liberal to ultra-orthodox and increased numbers come from a range of racial groups, mainly Asian and African. They generally live in urban areas situated around local and regional centres close to religious, education and cultural venues. Some are assimilated into the general community but others lead segregated lives. Parents tend to request the continuation of a Jewish life and value base for their children, of whom they have high expectations. Jews have a different experience, both historically and culturally, from the mainstream population. They would define themselves as an ethnic minority and carry a shared past and present experience of persecution and discrimination.

1.59 National statistics tend to show a higher than average incidence of mental health problems in the Jewish community, especially in students and young people. This is coupled with a lack of knowledge and awareness of mental health issues and a feeling of stigma within families who have difficulty in accepting problems. In consequence these are often concealed and not regularly acknowledged as a Jewish issue. There are a large number of Jewish social care agencies and care tends to be segregated in the Jewish community with culturally specific services – kosher food, prayer facilities and religious activities.

Role of the law

1.60 People with disabilities are vulnerable to neglect, abuse and exploitation and may need support, protection and empowerment.

Support

1.61   There are three sources of support, all regulated by the law:

(1)   DWP – the Department for Work and Pensions,[46] which through the *Benefits Agency* provided state benefits, generally on a weekly basis. These may be contributory, non-contributory[47] or a means-tested top-up to ensure that everybody has a minimum income to meet their requirements.[48] The Benefits Agency has since been replaced by *Job Centre Plus* (for adults of working age), the *Disability and Carers Service* (for disability-related benefits) and the *Pensions Service* (for people over pension age);

(2)   SSD – the social services departments of local authorities,[49] which are responsible for providing or arranging community care services and services for disabled persons. These must generally be paid for, subject to a means test;

(3)   NHS – the National Health Service which, largely now through NHS Trusts, provides free hospital and nursing care and general medical services.[50]

1.62   The respective roles of these providers are changing and overlapping, with social services applying means tests which may take away state benefit yet now providing cash to pay for services, whilst state benefits are withdrawn from those in 'hospital'.[51] In some areas, Care Trusts provide both health and social care services, particularly mental health and learning disability services and care for older people.

Protection

1.63   The law must also ensure protection and has done so by providing a representative in the form of an *appropriate adult* for police interviews and a *statutory guardian* or *nearest relative* for Mental Health Act functions. The authorities should investigate and intervene where there is a suspicion of abuse but their powers are limited at present when compared with those under the Children Act 1989 and there is no duty to act – which means that often they do not do so despite conflict or perceived abuse. Some local authorities have set up adult protection procedures under the *No Secrets* guidance.[52]

---

[46]   Formerly known as the Department of Social Security (DSS), and previously the Department of Health and Social Security (DHSS).

[47]   Eg disability benefits. Contributory benefits are generally for earnings replacement, e g retirement pension and incapacity benefit.

[48]   Often referred to as 'welfare benefits'.

[49]   Not all local authorities have such departments and reference is often now made to 'local authorities with social services responsibilities'.

[50]   Older readers will remember the DHSS, when health and social security came within the same government department.

[51]   The definition of 'hospital' for benefits purposes is wider than the generally recognised meaning.

[52]   Department of Health and Home Office *No secrets: guidance on developing and implementing multi-agency policies and procedures to protect vulnerable adults from abuse*, 20 March 2000. Available on the website at www.dh.gov.uk.

Empowerment

1.64 Empowerment means enabling individuals to take decisions for which they are competent. There must be a proper assessment of capacity and any communication difficulties should be overcome. A suitable person should be empowered to take decisions for individuals who are not competent. At present we have a number of potential representatives but coverage is not comprehensive.

Problems

1.65 There have been four significant problems in our present law and procedures:

(1) A lack of adequate public funding to cover the needs of disabled people and a lack of ring-fencing of the funds that could be available.

(2) Buck-passing between the DWP, local authorities and health authorities with the disabled individual becoming a pawn in the funding game, and money that could have been expended on unquestionable needs being wasted on the argument over which funder must provide. In recent years many appeal decisions have sought to define responsibilities but to some extent the problem has been alleviated by the introduction of joint commissioning of services by health and social services.

(3) The delicate balance between protection and empowerment, because protection involves taking away the personal autonomy it is desired to preserve. This dilemma is frequently encountered in our courts when dealing with vulnerable persons and is especially apparent when seeking to identify the best interests of an incapacitated individual.

(4) No adequate legally authorised representative in many situations because of the piecemeal nature of our legal system, in particular the lack of procedures for personal and medical decision-making.

The new jurisdiction introduced by the Mental Capacity Act 2005 has addressed the third and fourth of these problems and assists family and carers to address the second, but will not assist where there is inadequate funding for care needs.

Role of lawyers

1.66 Lawyers have developed considerable skills in negotiating on behalf of, and promoting the rights of, individuals who for one reason or another are at a disadvantage in looking after their own interests. The lawyer can also act as a whistle-blower to draw attention to situations where the rights of a vulnerable person are being overlooked or abuse is taking place.

Who is the client?

1.67 It is essential for any adviser in these situations to start by identifying the client. The identity of the client does not change just because of communication difficulties or even lack of capacity. Undue reliance should not be placed on relatives or carers in identifying the wishes of the client especially where these persons may be affected by the outcome of any decision. Any potential conflicts of interest should be identified at an early stage and if appropriate independent legal advice recommended either for the would-be client or for the relatives or carers.

1.68 A solicitor receiving instructions from a third party on behalf of an individual who is or may become mentally incapacitated should at all times remember that this individual is the client, not the third party. This is so even if the third party has legal authority to represent the individual, whether as deputy appointed by the Court of Protection, attorney acting under a registered enduring power of attorney or donee of a lasting power of attorney. The third party is merely an agent with a duty to act in the best interests of the incapacitated principal, and any solicitor who accepts instructions shares this duty even if it brings them into conflict with the agent through whom they receive instructions.

The legal climate

General

1.69 Driven by these social forces the legal climate has changed too over the past decade. Lawyers and the courts are having to cope with the needs of infirm elderly and disabled people. Some practitioners concentrate upon this aspect of the law and have developed considerable expertise. There have also been significant legislative initiatives which provide the basis for the growth of legal activity and a wide range of new outcomes from the courts.

Legal publishing

1.70 A new approach to legal publishing and the practice of the law was also developing. In July 1992 *Mental Handicap and the Law*[53] was published with the aim of addressing the needs of people with learning disabilities and their families and carers. This was followed by further books by the same author relating to elderly people[54] which represented a radical new approach to the law based on the needs of client groups rather than the coverage of legal topics as hitherto favoured by practitioners, authors and academics.

---

[53]   GR Ashton and AD Ward *Mental Handicap and the Law* (Sweet & Maxwell, 1992).
[54]   C Bielanska and M Terrell (general eds), GR Ashton (consultant ed) *The Elderly Client Handbook* (The Law Society, 1994; 3rd edn, 2004); GR Ashton *Elderly People and the Law* (Butterworths, 1995); GR Ashton *Butterworths Older Client Law Service* (Butterworths, looseleaf, 1997). Further books have followed by other authors.

Elderly client practices

1.71 With the encouragement of the Law Society, solicitors have developed 'elderly client practices' providing a full range of services targeting the needs of older clients that go beyond the traditional wills and enduring powers of attorney.[55] These developments have resulted in a wider range of legal services being available to the public thereby increasing expectations and creating a greater awareness of the weaknesses of our existing legal system in regard to incapacitated people.

Community Care

Background

1.72 Care in the community is not a new concept. For many it had been the reality for years, but meant living alone or being cared for by family with little support from the state in an indifferent society. The need became apparent to reduce institutional care and provide alternative services in a community setting, and increasing pressure from concerned people and organisations to recognise the rights and freedoms of people who need care or support found expression in policies which have become known as *community care*.

1.73 It was also recognised that this meant more than just the provision of a home in the community for former hospital patients: a whole range of support and services had to be provided for all persons needing care, including those already living in their own family homes. The emphasis should be upon enabling them to remain in their own homes or otherwise in the community when they, their family and friends could no longer cope without support. In the absence of a suitable range of services the only alternative had been long-term care in a residential home or hospital.

Reports

1.74 In 1986 the Audit Commission carried out a review of community-based care services and identified many problems which needed to be tackled. Resources, staffing and training were all directed towards the more institutional forms of care, organisation was fragmented and there was a lack of effective joint working and planning between the different agencies involved in the provision of services. The Commission regarded community care as providing clients with a full range of services, and a wide range of options; bringing services to people, rather than people to services; the adjustment of services to meet the needs of people, rather than the adjustment of people to meet the needs of services.[56]

---

[55] First advocated by this author at the Annual Conference of the Law Society in 1992. A new professional body, Solicitors for the Elderly Limited (SFE), now has several hundred members, runs conferences and has a website at www.solicitorsfortheelderly.com.

[56] Audit Commission Report *Making a Reality of Community Care* (1986).

PART I

1.75   A further review, *Community Care: Agenda for Action*, was published in 1988.[57] It acknowledged the need to promote 'the provision of services to individuals, developed from a multi-disciplinary assessment of their needs and made with proper participation of the individuals concerned, their families and other carers'. This was followed in 1989 by the publication of a White Paper *Caring for People: Community Care in the Next Decade and Beyond* in which it was stated:

> 'Community care means providing the services and support which people who are affected by problems of ageing, mental illness, mental handicap or physical or sensory disability need to be able to live as independently as possible in their own homes, or in homely settings in the community.'

1.76   Since the introduction of the new community care policies further changes have been implemented within social services and the NHS.[58] There have been many consultation papers and policy initiatives reflecting the need for fundamental change in the provision and funding of services. It has been recognised that people want greater control and choice over the services and support they receive and this has led to the introduction of direct payments and personal budgets. Following consultation two Green Papers were published: *Shaping the Future of Care Together* (Cm7673) and *Paying for Care in Wales*, identifying the need to provide early intervention or prevention services to avoid the need for more intensive care.[59]

Legislation

1.77   Although the legislation seen as introducing community care policies and procedures is the National Health Service and Community Care Act 1990, this devotes only nine sections[60] to the topic in England. The Act does not create new rights to new services, and although it imposes a new duty upon local authorities to assess anyone who appears to them to need a community care service which they may provide, it relied heavily on the following earlier legislation some of which had existed for many years:

- National Assistance Act 1948, Part III;
- Health Services and Public Health Act 1968;
- Chronically Sick and Disabled Persons Act 1970;
- Housing Act 1985;
- National Health Service Act 1977;
- Disabled Persons Act 1981;
- Mental Health Act 1983;
- Health and Social Services and Social Security Adjudications Act 1983;[61] and

---

[57]   Report to the Secretary of State for Social Services by Sir Roy Griffiths (the *Griffiths Report*).
[58]   See in particular the White Paper *Modernising Social Services* 1998, *The NHS Plan* (Cmd4818-I) July 2000 and subsequent reports.
[59]   The DoH White Paper *Building the National Care Service* (Cm7854) 2010 promoted joined up services with a national and portable needs assessment.
[60]   See National Health Service and Community Care Act 1990, Part III.
[61]   Known as the HASSASSA Act.

- Disabled Persons (Services Consultation and Representation) Act 1986.

1.78 The National Health Service and Community Care Act 1990 extended the role of local authorities in the provision of residential accommodation and welfare services, enabling them to make agency arrangements with other organisations and persons whilst restricting their powers to provide accommodation. It amended the provisions as to charges for residential accommodation and other community care services and dealt with recovery of such charges. Local authorities were required following consultation with health and housing authorities to prepare and publish a community care plan. They had to assess the care needs of any person who might appear to them to require community care services and decide what services needed to be provided. Disabled individuals were given a right to an assessment. Further provisions dealt with the inspection of certain premises used for community care services, access to information and the transfer of staff from health authorities to local authorities. Finally, local authorities had to provide a complaints procedure and comply with directions from the Secretary of State in carrying out their social services functions failing which default powers became available.

1.79 Further legislation has followed (including a plethora of Directions, Circulars and Guidance) and this has proved a prolific area for litigation with many appeal cases contributing to the implementation of the policy. In particular the following legislation should be considered:[62]

- Carers (Recognition and Services) Act 1995;
- Housing Act 1996 Part VII (replacing the 1985 Act);
- Health Act 1999;
- Carers and Disabled Children Act 2000;
- Care Standards Act 2000 (to be replaced);
- Health and Social Care Act 2001, Part 4;
- National Health Service Reform and Health Care Professions Act 2002 Part 1;
- Community Care (Delayed Discharge, etc.) Act 2003;
- Carers (Equal Opportunities) Act 2004;
- National Health Service Act 2006;
- Work and Families Act 2006;
- Safeguarding Vulnerable Groups Act 2006;
- Health and Social Care Act 2008;
- Autism Act 2009;
- Health Act 2009;
- Personal Care at Home Act 2010.

---

[62] For a useful introduction to this complex area see C Bielanska and M Terrell (general eds), GR Ashton (consultant ed) *The Elderly Client Handbook* (The Law Society, 1994; 4th edn, 2010).

PART I

Circulars and directions

1.80 The legislation is supplemented by government guidance and circulars, and by directions issued by the Secretary of State. A local authority may only be obliged to take account of advice contained in circulars and having done so may not be under a duty to comply,[63] though where an appeal to the Secretary of State is provided for it may be expected that he or she will follow his or her own advice. The policy documents of a local authority (including its community care plan) should reflect any directions and guidance in circulars and these are likely to be quoted in Court proceedings and could form the basis for a legal challenge of an authority's action or inaction. The Secretary of State is empowered to issue directions to local authorities in regard to the exercise of their social services functions, and these must be observed with the sanction being the use of default powers.

Equality and discrimination

Background

1.81 People with impaired capacity are particularly susceptible to discrimination on account of their age or disabilities. During recent years certain forms of discrimination have been made unlawful and statutory remedies provided for a breach, more recently fuelled by European Directives. Standards have been set in these areas and enforced through the courts and tribunals. Failure to comply could lead to an expensive lesson but, whilst a few test cases achieved a high profile, discrimination remained rife in society without effective sanction. Article 14 of the European Convention on Human Rights, now part of UK law,[64] is particularly relevant because it provides:

> 'Prohibition of discrimination: the enjoyment of the rights and freedoms set forth in this Convention shall be secured without discrimination on any ground such as sex, race, colour, language, religion, political or other opinion, national or social origin, association with a national minority, property, birth or other status.'

This provision is not, however, freestanding and has to be joined to other Articles.

1.82 Until recently we had a plethora of inconsistent yet overlapping legislation dealing with substantive law on discrimination.[65] The Equality Act 2006 established from October 2007 a new *Equality and Human Rights Commission* (EHRC)[66] which merged the three existing commissions.[67] The

---

[63]	Local Authority Social Services Act 1970, s 7. In this respect there may be a difference between general guidance and a direction, but the other view is that guidance is instruction that must be followed – see *R v North Yorkshire CC, ex p Hargreaves* (1994) *The Times*, November 9.

[64]	Under the Human Rights Act 1998.

[65]	Sex Discrimination Act 1975, Race Relations Act 1976, Disability Discrimination Act 1995 and Employment Equality (Age) Regulations 2006.

[66]	The website is: www.equalityhumanrights.com.

EHRC can tackle prejudice based on race, gender and sexual orientation and disability as well as human rights, and has wide powers to enforce legislation.

In February 2005, the Government set up the Discrimination Law Review to address long-term concerns about inconsistencies in the current discrimination law framework, and this was followed by consultation[68] and further papers.

Equality Act 2010

1.83 The outcome is this Act whose purpose is to harmonise discrimination law and strengthen the law to support progress on equality. It brings together and re-states all the existing anti-discrimination legislation and a number of other related provisions and most provisions were brought into effect from October 2010. It also extends the categories by identifying the following 'protected characteristics':

- age (section 5)
- disability (sections 6 and 15, and Schedule 1)
- gender reassignment (sections 7 and 16)
- marriage and civil partnership (section 8)
- race (section 9)
- religion or belief (section 10)
- sex (ie gender) (section 11)
- sexual orientation (section 12)

1.84 The definitions are similar to those that applied before,[69] but the application of disability discrimination is brought into line with the other categories. The Act also strengthens the law in a number of areas by:

- placing a new duty on certain public bodies to consider socio-economic disadvantage when making strategic decisions about how to exercise their functions;
- extending the circumstances in which a person is protected against discrimination, harassment or victimisation because of a protected characteristic;
- making it unlawful to discriminate against, harass or victimise a person when (a) providing a service (which includes the provision of goods or facilities), (b) exercising a public function or (c) disposing of (for example, by selling or letting) or managing premises;

---

[67] Equal Opportunities Commission, Commission for Racial Equality and Disability Rights Commission.

[68] *A Framework for Fairness – Proposals for a Single Equality Bill for Great Britain* – a consultation paper, June 2007.

[69] The definition of a disabled person is complex but extends to mental impairments and includes an adult who lacks capacity.

- making it unlawful for associations (for example, private clubs) to discriminate against, harass or victimise members, associates or guests.
- requiring taxis, other private hire vehicles, public service vehicles (such as buses) and rail vehicles to be accessible to disabled people and to allow them to travel in reasonable comfort.

1.85 The Act creates a duty on listed public bodies when carrying out their functions and on other persons when carrying out public functions to have due regard to the need to:

- eliminate conduct which the Act prohibits;
- advance equality of opportunity between persons who share a relevant protected characteristic and those who do not; and
- foster good relations between people who share a relevant protected characteristic and people who do not.

Prohibited conduct

1.86 Several forms of conduct are now defined for the purpose of prohibition. Enforcement continues to be through the county courts (in relation to services and public functions) and employment tribunals (in relation to work and related areas, and equal pay).

Direct discrimination

1.87 This occurs where the reason for a person being treated less favourably than another is a protected characteristic.[70] This definition is broad enough to cover cases where the treatment is because of the victim's association with someone who has that characteristic (for example, is disabled). For age, different treatment that is justified as a proportionate means of meeting a legitimate aim is not direct discrimination. In relation to disability it is not discrimination to treat a disabled person more favourably than a person who is not disabled.

Discrimination arising from disability

1.88 It is discrimination to treat a disabled person unfavourably not because of the person's disability itself but because of something arising from, or in consequence of, his or her disability.[71] The perpetrator must know, or reasonably be expected to know, of the disability, and it is possible to justify such treatment if it can be shown to be a proportionate means of achieving a legitimate aim.[72]

---

[70]   Equality Act 2010, s 13. Thus excluding old people would be discrimination.
[71]   Equality Act 2010, s 15. This would cover the need to have a guide dog.
[72]   This is a new provision designed to overcome the problem caused by *London Borough of Lewisham v Malcolm [2008] UKHL 43* explained above.

Indirect discrimination

1.89 This would occur when a policy which applies in the same way for everybody has an effect which particularly disadvantages people with a protected characteristic.[73] Where a particular group is disadvantaged in this way, a person in that group is indirectly discriminated against if he or she is put at that disadvantage, unless the person applying the policy can justify it. Indirect discrimination can also occur when a policy would put a person at a disadvantage if it were applied and thus acts as a deterrent.[74]

The treatment of the claimant must be compared with that of an actual or a hypothetical person – the comparator – who does not share the same protected characteristic as the claimant but who is (or is assumed to be) in not materially different circumstances from the claimant.

Duty to make adjustments

1.90 Section 20 defines what is meant by the duty to make reasonable adjustments to the 'provision, criterion or practice' whereby things are done.[75] The duty comprises three requirements which apply where a disabled person is placed at a substantial disadvantage in comparison to non-disabled people:

- the first covers changing the way things are done (such as changing a practice);
- the second covers making changes to the built environment (such as providing access to a building); and
- the third covers providing auxiliary aids and services (such as providing special computer software or providing a different service).

For the second requirement, taking steps to avoid the disadvantage would include removing or altering the physical feature where it would be reasonable to do so. For the first and third a reasonable step might include providing information in an accessible format). Except where the Act states otherwise, it would never be reasonable for a person bound by the duty to pass on the costs of complying with it to an individual disabled person.

1.91 A failure to comply with any one of the reasonable adjustment requirements amounts to discrimination against a disabled person to whom the duty is owed.[76]

---

[73]   Equality Act 2010, s 19. This would cover the need to have a guide dog.
[74]   The extension of indirect discrimination to disability is new, coming after consultation following *London Borough of Lewisham v Malcolm* [2008] UKHL 43.
[75]   This replaces with some changes provisions in the Disability Discrimination Acts.
[76]   Equality Act 2010, s 21. This replaces comparable provisions in the Disability Discrimination Acts.

PART I

Harassment

1.92 There are three types of harassment, but the one which applies to disability and age involves unwanted conduct which is related to the characteristic and has the purpose or effect of creating an intimidating, hostile, degrading humiliating or offensive environment for the complainant or violating the complainant's dignity.[77] There may be a need to balance the right of freedom of expression (as set out in Article 10 of the European Convention on Human Rights) against the right not to be offended in deciding whether a person has been harassed.

Victimisation

1.93 Victimisation takes place where one person treats another badly because he or she in good faith has done a "protected act" or is suspected of having done so or intending to do so.[78] This might include taking or supporting any action taken in relation to any alleged breach of the Act. Only an individual can bring a claim for victimisation and a person is not protected from victimisation where he or she maliciously makes or supports an untrue complaint.

Implications of conduct

1.94 Previous legislation provided some protection from discrimination, harassment and victimisation in the provision of services and the exercise of public functions. However, the protection was not uniform for the different protected characteristics. For example, there was no protection for discrimination because of age, either in the provision of services or in the exercise of public functions. Section 29 replaces the provisions in previous legislation and extends protection so that it is generally uniform across all the protected characteristics.

It unlawful to discriminate against or harass a person because of a protected characteristic, or victimise someone when providing services (which includes goods and facilities). The person is protected both when requesting a service and during the course of being provided with a service. It is also unlawful to discriminate against, harass or victimise a person when exercising a public function which does not involve the provision of a service. Examples of such public functions include law enforcement and revenue raising and collection. Public functions which involve the provision of a service, for example, medical treatment on the NHS, are covered by the provisions dealing with services. This section also imposes the section 20 duty to make reasonable adjustments in relation to providing services and exercising public functions.

---

[77]   Equality Act 2010, s 26.
[78]   Equality Act 2010, s 27. This is not really a form of discrimination.

Premises

1.95 There is protection from discrimination in the disposal and management of premises across all the protected characteristics with the exception of age and marriage and civil partnership, although other provisions MAY be relied on where they apply.[79] It is unlawful for a person who has the authority to dispose of premises (for example, by selling, letting or subletting a property) to discriminate against or victimise someone else in a number of ways including by offering the premises to them on less favourable terms; by not letting or selling the premises to them or by treating them less favourably. It is also unlawful for a person whose permission is needed to dispose of premises to discriminate against or victimise someone else by withholding that permission.

It is unlawful for a person who manages premises to discriminate against or victimise someone who occupies the property in the way he or she allows the person to use a benefit or facility associated with the property, by evicting the person or by otherwise treating the person unfavourably.

Associations

1.96 It is unlawful for an association to discriminate against, harass or victimise an existing or potential member, or an associate. This means that an association cannot refuse membership to a potential member or grant it on less favourable terms because of a protected characteristic. It does not, however, prevent associations restricting their membership to people who share a protected characteristic.[80] It is also unlawful to discriminate against, harass or victimise existing or potential guests. In particular, an association cannot refuse to invite a person as a guest because of a particular characteristic or invite that person on certain conditions which the association would not apply to other would-be guests. There is also a duty to make reasonable adjustments for disabled members and guests.

1.97 The courts are not exempted from these provisions: they provide legal services and may be in breach of this legislation if they do not take into account the needs of disabled people.[81] The Office of the Public Guardian and the Court of Protection must be fully conversant with these provisions both as regards the manner in which they deal with disabled people and the expectations that they have for incapacitated persons when dealing with their financial, social welfare and health care decisions.

---

[79]   Equality Act 2010, s 32-35. Similar protection was available in the previous legislation.
[80]   Equality Act 2010, ss 100–103. Similar protection was available in the previous legislation.
[81]   HM Courts Service has already found itself having to admit liability in a claim involving access to the courts for a hearing impaired person.

Human Rights Act 1998

The Convention

1.98 The European Convention on Human Rights[82] (ECHR) is a treaty of the Council of Europe.[83] It was signed in 1950 and ratified by the UK in 1951, which means that under international law the UK became obliged to abide by its terms, although the right of individual petition was only afforded in 1966. But this did not mean that Convention rights could be relied upon in proceedings in our courts. The treaty has subsequently been amended by Protocols which are either mandatory or optional, the latter only binding states that choose to ratify them.

The legislation

1.99 The long title to the Human Rights Act 1998 (HRA 1998) states that it is 'to give further effect to' the Convention rights and it was said to be 'bringing rights home' on the basis that individuals within the UK would be enabled to rely on their rights in their home courts,[84] although the right to bring a case in Strasbourg is not prevented. The Act is a compromise, representing an attempt to incorporate the ECHR into our law whilst still recognising the traditions of the common law and the sovereignty of Parliament. Every new Bill must, when introduced, be supported by a *statement of compatibility* by the Minister responsible.[85]

1.100 Only certain of the rights contained in the ECHR have been designated as 'Convention rights' for the purpose of HRA 1998,[86] but those omitted must no doubt be 'taken into account'. Those of particular relevance in the present context are:

- Article 2 – the right to life, which has implications for the health services and especially decisions as to whether to treat those who would otherwise die.
- Article 3 – the prohibition of inhuman or degrading treatment, which is of particular relevance to the abuse and neglect of vulnerable people.
- Article 5 – the protection of liberty, which may affect detention in a care home or hospital.
- Article 6 – the right to a fair trial, which concerns participation and ensuring an independent and impartial tribunal.
- Article 8 – respect for private and family life, home and correspondence, which extends to bodily integrity, access to information, confidentiality and sexual relations.

---

[82]   The full title is *Convention for the Protection of Human Rights and Fundamental Freedoms*.
[83]   This is a separate organisation from the European Union and now comprises more than 40 member states. For further information see www.coe.int.
[84]   See the White Paper *Bringing Rights Home*, Cm 3782 (1997).
[85]   HRA 1998, s 19.
[86]   HRA 1998, s 1. The text of these Articles is set out in HRA 1998, Sch 1.

- First Protocol, Art 2 – protection of property, which has implications for ownership, access to and control of property.

Some of these are 'absolute' in the sense that they do not include any qualification or allow for any derogation[87] by a ratifying country and others are qualified by some limitation or restriction.[88] Non-discrimination operates within all other rights pursuant to Art 14.[89]

Interpretation

1.101 The courts must interpret our primary and secondary legislation 'so far as it is possible to do so' in a way which is not incompatible with the ECHR whilst not having power to overrule any such legislation.[90] Where this cannot be done a *declaration of incompatibility* may be made[91] and it then becomes a matter for Parliament (which has a fast-track procedure for remedying the incompatibility[92]), although in the meanwhile the legislation must still be applied.[93] So legislation must henceforth be interpreted so as to give effect, if possible, to Convention rights.

1.102 It has been stated that an Act must receive a 'generous and purposive' interpretation to ensure that Convention rights are effective rather than illusory. Techniques may include 'reading down' (choosing between two possible interpretations and opting for the narrower) and 'reading in' (inserting words to make the statute compatible). Strasbourg jurisprudence must be 'taken into account' by our courts and tribunals,[94] which means that decisions of the European Court of Human Rights now become part of our case-law.

1.103 The European Court has recognised that the obligations of states under the ECHR are not limited to refraining from interfering with individual human rights. There is a positive obligation to ensure that one person's rights are protected from violation by another person and this has led to five duties being imposed on states in relation to Convention rights:

(1) to have a legal framework providing effective protection;
(2) to prevent breaches;
(3) to provide information and advice;

---

87 An exceptional limitation imposed by the ratifying country on a particular right in specified circumstances. It must be in accordance with the law, directed to a 'particular purpose' and 'necessary in a democratic society'.

88 This relates to some existing law of the country concerned which is not to be affected.

89 A breach of another Convention right does not need to be established, but the circumstances must fall within the ambit of an ECHR provision.

90 HRA 1998, s 3.

91 HRA 1998, s 4. This power is restricted to the High Court, Court of Appeal and House of Lords and the Crown is entitled to make representations.

92 HRA 1998, s 10. This procedure will also be appropriate when a finding of the European Court in proceedings against the UK renders a provision incompatible.

93 If subordinate legislation (e g a statutory instrument) is incompatible with Convention rights, and the incompatibility is not required by primary legislation, either the courts will find ways of interpreting it so as to be compatible or will set it aside.

94 HRA 1998, s 2(1).

(4)   to respond to breaches; and

(5)   to provide resources to individuals to prevent breaches.

Remedies

1.104   When a Convention right is found to have been breached (or is about
to be breached) the Court may grant such relief or remedy, or make such
order, within its powers as it considers 'just and appropriate'.[95] The Act does
not give additional powers and the normal routes of an appeal or judicial
review apply. There can be no claim for damages in respect of a judicial act
done in good faith except in the case of a breach of liberty.

New concepts

1.105   It follows that each branch of government (legislature, executive and
judicial) is responsible for giving effect to Convention rights when
exercising public powers. However, various concepts apply in the
interpretation and application of Convention rights which will not be
familiar to lawyers brought up on the common law and statute law:

(1)   Not only can proceedings be brought against a public authority in
relation to Convention rights (the 'vertical' effect), but as the courts
are public authorities they must apply Convention rights when
adjudicating on proceedings between private individuals (the
'horizontal' effect). So litigants can argue their human rights in the
courts and these must be respected.

(2)   To some extent the European Court adopts a hands-off approach to
the way that individual countries apply Convention rights, although
this 'margin of appreciation' has no application to national courts.
This reflects the fact that those courts are in a better position to
assess the needs and standards of their own society and the national
authorities should be deferred to (especially in moral matters and
social policy) as long as the whole process is fair and the outcome is
true to the Convention.

(3)   Where a state interferes with a Convention right, the means ('the
limitation') must be balanced against the end ('the permitted
purpose') and shown to be necessary. There must be a reasonable
relationship between the goal pursued and the means employed.
This follows from the fact that any limitation on a Convention right
must be in accordance with law and 'necessary in a democratic
society',[96] and has become the principle of 'proportionality'.

(4)   A 'principle of legality' is derived from the use by the ECHR of the
phrases 'in accordance with the law' and 'prescribed by law' and the
use of the word 'lawful'. It has been stated to mean:[97]

---

[95]   HRA 1998, s 8(1).

[96]   A 'democratic society' means a society which is pluralistic and tolerant. The interests of
minorities and individuals must be carefully considered.

[97]   K Starmer *European Human Rights Law* (Legal Action Group, 1999), at para 4.29.

(a) the legal basis for any restriction on Convention rights must be identified and established by the domestic law;

(b) that law must be accessible and not interpreted according to unpublished criteria; and

(c) the law must be clear to those affected by it so that they can understand it, although it may allow some discretion as long as the limits are clear.

Application to the Court of Protection and Public Guardian

1.106 Not only must the courts apply Convention rights but rather than giving individuals personal rights HRA 1998 also imposes a new statutory duty on 'public authorities' not to act in contravention thereof. This term is not defined but a function based test is to be applied. Courts and tribunals are expressly included, as is 'any person certain of whose functions are functions of a public nature' which would include the Public Guardian. It is 'unlawful for a public authority to act in a way which is incompatible with a Convention right'[98] and even a failure to act would be construed as non-compliance. An individual who claims that a public authority has acted in an incompatible way may bring proceedings against that authority either directly or within the context of other proceedings.[99]

1.107 Where the public body determining the civil rights or obligations is not a court or tribunal[100] a two-limbed test is applied: either that body must comply with the right to a fair hearing under ECHR, Art 6 or there must be a right of appeal or review from that body to a court or tribunal which fully complies. The previous right to apply for judicial review is not sufficient because the Administrative Court cannot make findings of fact.[101]

Comment

1.108 People who lack capacity do not lose their human rights, but the rights of others must also be respected. In delivering its services the new jurisdiction must not overlook the human rights of anyone, but there will be many situations when there is a conflict between the rights of those involved, whether it be the incapacitated individual, family members or others. An appropriate balance must then be achieved.

1.109 The ECHR is a living instrument so, unlike the common law where previous decisions of higher courts create precedents, it must be interpreted in accordance with present-day conditions. This means that what was decided yesterday may be decided differently tomorrow, although this may be a whole generation later. The difficulty lies in determining what the

---

[98] HRA 1998, s 6.
[99] HRA 1998, s 7.
[100] Eg a local housing authority, a health authority, social services and probably the Public Guardian.
[101] *W v UK* (1987) 10 EHRR 29, at para 82.

contemporary standards are which merit protection. However, the ECHR is intended to guarantee rights that are practical and effective rather than theoretical and illusory.[102]

Civil Partnership Act 2004

Background

1.110   This recent legislation reflects more liberal social attitudes. It has become widely accepted that it is both logically and morally indefensible to prevent homosexual couples from access to formal recognition of their relationships and to the 'next of kin' rights and the tax, pension and other advantages that flow from marriage. Encouraging stability in relationships, whether heterosexual or homosexual, should involve the same sorts of protections as come with marriage, and the Civil Partnership Act 2004 (CPA 2004) addresses these issues in considerable detail.

The legislation

1.111   CPA 2004[103] introduces greater recognition for same-sex relationships in England and Wales, Scotland and Northern Ireland by an option of registration as 'civil partners'. A 'civil partnership' is defined as:[104]

'... a relationship between two people of the same sex ... which is formed when they register as civil partners of each other ...'

It ends only on death, dissolution or annulment. Heterosexual couples are specifically excluded because they have the option of marriage. The general approach is to make detailed provision for the formation and ending of civil partnerships, and for the consequences that flow from them. It deals with these matters by treating civil partners in very much the same way as married couples.

1.112   To create a civil partnership a specific document is required, signed in the presence of each other and of a civil partnership registrar and two witnesses. No religious service is to be used during the registration formalities, and it cannot take place on religious premises. A couple cannot register if one is already married or a civil partner of someone else, nor if either is under 16 or within prohibited degrees of relationship.

1.113   The provisions for court proceedings to end partnerships[105] and as to children and finances in most cases mirror existing provisions for married couples. In the case of disputes about property either civil partner may apply to the county court, and the court may make such order with respect to the

---

102	*Artico v Italy* A/37 (1980) 3 EHRR 1.
103	It has 196 sections arranged in 8 Parts and there are 22 Schedules.
104	CPA 2004, s 1.
105	Including nullity, presumption of death and separation orders.

property as it thinks fit, including an order for sale. Contributions to property improvement if substantial and in money or money's worth are recognised.

1.114 Other amendments align civil partners with married persons, for example, in certain parts of the law relating to housing and tenancies, in domestic violence proceedings[106] and under the Fatal Accidents Act 1976. Interpretation of statutory references to step-relationships (eg stepson, stepmother etc), and the terms 'in-law' (eg brother-in-law and daughter-in-law) are amended to apply in civil partnerships. There are amendments to the sex discrimination, social security, child support and tax credits legislation. Civil partners will have an insurable interest in each other.

1.115 Implementation involves significant changes in many areas, for example, in court rules, the registration service, training and guidance for employers. CPA 2004 does not address the problems in the legal treatment of those cohabiting without registration by marriage or by civil partnership.

Incapacity issues

1.116 Civil partnership is not merely a matter of contract but affects status and creates a completely new legal relationship. Clearly this has implications for a mental capacity jurisdiction. The civil partner must be recognised to the same extent as a spouse when decisions are to be made, whether relating to financial matters, personal welfare or health care. Comparable duties and responsibilities may also arise on the part of the civil partner.

1.117 The civil partner must also be afforded the same status as a spouse as regards participation in any of the procedures. This is not as radical as it may seem, because the new social attitudes have already resulted in domestic partners being involved in many situations, and this has included same-sex partners even in the absence of a civil partnership. To this extent there has been a move away from relationships of blood and marriage to de facto relationships. The Adults with Incapacity (Scotland) Act 2000 provided 'next of kin' rights to same-sex partners by including them within the definition of nearest relative whose views must be taken into account,[107] and the equivalent provision under the Mental Capacity Act 2005 includes 'anyone engaged in caring for the person or interested in his welfare' as well as 'anyone named by the person as someone to be consulted on the matter in question or matters of that kind'.[108]

---

[106] Under Family Law Act 1996, Part IV.
[107] Adults with Incapacity (Scotland) Act 2000, ss 1(4)(b) and 87(2).
[108] Mental Capacity Act 2005, s 4(7).

Access to justice

Background

1.118 Any court that seeks to protect and empower those who have mental impairments must set a good example to other courts and tribunals in ensuring equal access to justice, and the establishment of a new Court of Protection is an opportunity to get things right from the start.[109]

A change of culture

1.119 There has been a change of culture in the civil and family courts during the past decade. Proceedings not only have to be fair, but also have to be seen as fair and it is the view of the public that is relevant rather than that of lawyers. No longer are litigants expected to cope with the court process and denied access to justice if unable to do so. There is an expectation, in a diverse and multi-cultural society, that judges will ensure that there is effective communication with all manner of persons and take into account their personal attributes and beliefs. This is the art of *Judgecraft* on which judges receive training through the Judicial Studies Board (JSB).

1.120 An Equal Treatment Advisory Committee of the JSB[110] ensures that all training courses include this topic and has produced an *Equal Treatment Bench Book* which is supplied to all judges and tribunal chairmen.[111] This identifies potential problem areas, offers information and guidance, and then concentrates upon the following areas of particular concern:

(1) minority ethnic communities;
(2) belief systems (different religions);
(3) gender issues;
(4) disability;
(5) children; and
(6) sexual orientation.

The issues of unrepresented parties and social exclusion are also addressed. Equal access to justice is not assured if people are too frightened to attend a hearing or unable to cope when they get there.

Discrimination

1.121 There must be no discrimination in the delivery of legal services. A person who cannot cope with the facilities and procedures of the courts and the administration is as entitled to justice as those who have no such difficulty. It is fundamental to the delivery of justice that those involved are

---

[109] The Mental Capacity Bill team set the standard for the Department for Constitutional Affairs by producing various documents in easy read format for their stakeholders with learning difficulties prior to Royal Assent. It also worked closely with the Disability Rights Commission and various representative disability groups.

[110] The author of this chapter was a member of that Committee.

[111] This is available on the JSB website: www.jsboard.co.uk/etac/etbb/index.htm.

able to appear before and communicate with the relevant court or tribunal. It is equally important that judges understand what those who appear before them are endeavouring to say and that they in turn understand what the judge and any advocates are saying and have an adequate opportunity to consider this. Any misunderstanding may impair justice and it is not sufficient to say that this is the failing of the individual who must take the consequences – it is the responsibility of the court to ensure that communication is effective.

1.122 A further development is that those who appear before the courts are no longer expected to cope with whatever facilities happen to be available. The special needs of those with disabilities must be addressed in an effective way both by the administration in regard to the facilities made available and by the judge in the manner in which hearings are conducted. All courts and tribunals must comply with DDA 1995 and also ensure that the human rights of those who become involved in the justice system are respected.[112]

1.123 It follows that courts and tribunals must be accessible to those who appear before them. This is not merely a question of access to the building or the provision of disabled facilities within the courtroom, but also of proximity.

Unrepresented parties

1.124 Some litigants seek to represent themselves rather than instruct a lawyer[113] and everybody of full age and capacity is entitled to do so. This may be because they cannot afford a solicitor, distrust lawyers or believe that they will be better at putting their case across.

Disadvantages

1.125 Those who do exercise this right find that they are operating in an alien environment because the courts have not traditionally been receptive to their needs:[114]

> 'All too often the litigant in person is regarded as a problem for judges and for the court system rather than a person for whom the system of civil justice exists.'

They are likely to experience feelings of fear, ignorance, anger, frustration and bewilderment. Their cases will tend to dominate their thoughts and they will feel at a disadvantage. The aim of the judge should be to ensure that the parties leave with the sense that they have been listened to and have had a fair hearing – whatever the outcome.

---

[112] Before the ECHR became enforceable it was the principles of 'natural justice' that were invoked.

[113] Traditionally known as 'litigants in person'.

[114] Lord Woolf *Access to Justice*: Interim Report (June 1995).

1.126 Disadvantages stem from a lack of knowledge of the law and court procedure. For many their perception of the court environment will based on what they have seen on the television and in films. They:

- are likely to be unfamiliar with the language and specialist vocabulary of legal proceedings;
- have little knowledge of the procedures involved and find it difficult to apply the rules even if they do read them;
- tend to lack objectivity and emotional distance from their case;
- may not be skilled in advocacy and are unlikely to be able to undertake cross-examination or to test the evidence of an opponent;
- may be confused about the presentation of evidence; and
- are unlikely to understand the relevance of law and regulations to their own problem, or to know how to challenge a decision that they believe to be wrong.

1.127 The aim must be to ensure that unrepresented parties understand what is going on and what is expected of them at all stages of the proceedings. The Court is therefore under an obligation to ensure that:

(1) the process is (or has been) explained to them in a manner that they can understand;
(2) they have access to appropriate information through books or websites;
(3) they are informed about what is expected of them in ample time for them to comply; and
(4) wherever possible they are given sufficient time according to their needs.

Personal assistance

1.128 A litigant who cannot arrange legal representation may request that someone be permitted to 'quietly assist' at the hearing (the role of the *McKenzie friend*). The Court can refuse this and will do so if the friend is unsuitable.[115] Such assistance is less likely to be needed at a hearing in the Court of Protection because a more informal approach is adopted and the judge is more likely to provide explanations and assistance.

1.129 Alternatively the litigant may request that someone speak for him or her (known as a *lay representative*). There is no right of audience but the Court has a discretion to allow such representation and it may be in the interests of justice to do so.[116] The litigant should normally justify the request and be present in court when personal interests are involved.[117] The

---

[115] The 'friend' may be seeking to provide general advocacy services or pursuing a separate agenda the pursuit of which is not in the best interests of the litigant.
[116] Advocacy rights may be granted under the Courts and Legal Services Act 1990, s 27(2)(c) – see also Civil Procedure Rules 1998, SI 1998/3132, PD 27, para 3.2; Lay Representatives (Right of Audience) Order 1999, SI 1999/1225.
[117] *Clarkson v Gilbert & ors* [2000] 2 FLR 839, CA; *Izzo v Phillip Ross & Co* [2002] BPIR 310.

doubt about the status of an attorney under a power of attorney has recently been resolved – there is still no right of audience.[118]

Physical and sensory impairments

Hearings

1.130   There is a Directory of courts with disabled facilities and when it is known that a party or witness has a physical impairment, arrangements should be made for any hearing to take place where there are appropriate facilities. These may extend beyond wheelchair access to the existence of disabled toilets and the loop system for those with hearing impairments. Ideally every regional venue of the Court of Protection will have suitable facilities but if these are inadequate for a particular hearing consideration should be given to conducting the hearing at a more suitable venue. When necessary justice should be taken to those who are unable to come to the Court and the examination of a witness or even part of a hearing may take place elsewhere, for example, in a residential care home or mental hospital. A video link may assist where an infirm party cannot travel far.[119]

1.131   It may be appropriate to arrange hearings at particular times, keep them shorter or take more frequent breaks. Allowance should be made for the need to attend a toilet, take medication or otherwise recover concentration. This may result in a longer time estimate for the hearing.

Interpreters

1.132   Interpreters are provided for a party or witness who does not speak the language of the Court or has a hearing impairment, and the Court must arrange one if the party cannot. Other communication difficulties may need to be addressed in a similar manner.[120] The interpreter should not be simply a relative or friend but needs to be independent and fully conversant with the individual's preferred method of communication. A witness will only need an interpreter whilst giving evidence but a party may need one before, during and after the hearing. The interpreter should be provided with breaks at regular intervals.

---

[118]   If this is an enduring power of attorney inquiry should be made as to whether it has been registered with the Public Guardianship Office, because if it has the litigant may be a patient who needs a litigation friend.

[119]   The President of the Family Division adopted both these procedures in the *Re B* case when she attended at the hospital and then continued by video-link.

[120]   The special measures directions introduced by the Youth Justice and Criminal Evidence Act 1999, Part II to assist vulnerable and intimidated witnesses to give evidence in criminal proceedings refer to communicators rather than just language interpreters. These include the use of *intermediaries* and *communication aids*.

THE (FORMER) COURT OF PROTECTION

Origins of the jurisdiction

1.133 The former Court of Protection existed to protect and manage the property and financial affairs of people in England and Wales (known as 'patients') who were incapable, by reason of mental disorder, of managing and administering their own affairs.[121] The origins of state involvement in the financial affairs of the mentally incapacitated citizen go back a long way.[122] Until 1960 the jurisdiction 'in Lunacy' was in part statutory and in part dependent on the inherent jurisdiction of the Court derived from the Royal Prerogative which is often referred to as the parens patriae jurisdiction. Under the Lunacy Act 1890 the jurisdiction relating to the administration and management of patients' affairs was assigned to a Master in Lunacy, who operated under different titles[123] until 1947 when the term Court of Protection was established. The Mental Health Act 1959, Part VIII re-established the Court of Protection and its continuing existence was confirmed by the Mental Health Act 1983, Part VII. Further jurisdiction was conferred on the Court by the Enduring Powers of Attorney Act 1985.

1.134 This was not a court as such but an office of the Supreme Court of Judicature (as it then was),[124] although in practice this was of little significance and some High Court judges were nominated to conduct its work. Headed by the Master and situated in London, much of the work was delegated to nominated officers appointed by the Lord Chancellor. The three senior ones adopted the courtesy title of Assistant Master and were given more authority including the conduct of hearings.[125] The Public Guardianship Office provided administrative support for the Court and had a staff of several hundred, including those in the Judicial Support Unit who processed formal applications and appeals.[126]

Practice and procedure

General

1.135 The procedure of the Court was governed by the Court of Protection Rules 2001 (COPR 2001),[127] which were brief compared with the Civil

---

[121]   Mental Health Act 1983, s 94(2).

[122]   The earliest reference is to be found in a semi-official tract known as the *De Praerogativa Regis* ('On the King's Prerogative') dating from the reign of Edward 1 (1272-1307). For a history of the jurisdiction see G Ashton, P Letts, L Oates and M Terrell *Mental Capacity: The New Law* (Jordans, 2006).

[123]   Initially the 'Office of the Master in Lunacy' but this was changed to the 'Management and Administration Department' in 1934 (note the abbreviation MAD).

[124]   Supreme Court Act 1981, s 1(1) – now the Senior Courts Act 1981.

[125]   Mental Health Act 1983, ss 93(4) and 94(1). It is questionable whether and to what extent judicial powers should have been delegated in this way following the Human Rights Act 1998.

[126]   Refer to Chapter 8 for the historical background to the Public Guardianship Office.

[127]   SI 2001/824. This update to the existing Rules was required following the demise of the Public Trust Office and the creation of the Public Guardianship Office from 1 April 2001. The authority for the rules is to be found in Mental Health Act 1983, s 106.

Procedure Rules 1998 (CPR).[128] Instead of a statement of objectives they started with an Interpretation clause in which reference was made to the Supreme Court Act 1981 for the meaning of expressions used: a 'direction' meant a direction or authority given under the seal of the Court and an 'order' included a certificate, direction or authority of the Court under the official seal of the Court. A 'patient' was a person who was alleged to be or who the Court had reason to believe might be 'incapable by reason of mental disorder of managing and administering his property and affairs'.

1.136 Any function of the Court could be exercised by a nominated judge of the High Court, the Master or (to the extent authorised) a nominated officer and this might, except where COPR 2001 provided otherwise, be:

(1) without an appointment for a hearing;
(2) by the Court of its own motion or at the instance or on the application of a person concerned;
(3) whether or not proceedings have been commenced with respect to the patient.

COPR 2001 then dealt with applications and hearings.

Applications

1.137 Provision was made as to the form of applications, but apart from those for the first appointment of a receiver there was considerable informality and a letter might be sufficient. The Court could allow applications to be amended at any stage, and where it was urgent could dispense with an application in writing. Hearings were notified by letter and might be dispensed with where it was considered that the application could properly be dealt with without one. Special rules dealt with applications under the Trustee Act 1925, for settlement or a gift of a patient's property and for the execution of a will for a patient.

Short orders

1.138 COPR 2001, r 8 provided that where the property of the patient did not exceed a specified value[129] or it was otherwise considered appropriate, the Court might instead of appointing a receiver make a short order or direction which authorised some suitable person to deal with the patient's property or affairs in the manner specified. This power came to be used increasingly where it was felt that intrusive supervision was not necessary. Not only might small estates be dealt with in this summary way but, for example, a tenancy could be authorised.

---

[128]   SI 1998/3132.
[129]   Latterly £16,000.

Persons under disability

1.139   Relatives or other persons associated with a patient may themselves lack capacity. The rules dealt with applications involving 'persons under a disability'[130] and were modelled on the former Rules of the Supreme Court. The person had to be represented by a 'next friend' if bringing the application or by a 'guardian ad litem' if responding.[131] An order making the appointment was not necessary unless an existing representative was to be replaced. A written consent of the person to be appointed had to be filed, and also a certificate by a solicitor acting for the person under a disability that this person was a minor or a patient and that the person to be appointed had no adverse interest. It followed that a person under a disability must, through his or her representative, initially instruct a solicitor but there were no further safeguards.

Service

1.140   COPR 2001 specified the persons who should be given notice, who included 'such other persons who appear to the Court to be interested as the Court may specify'. The mode of service was prescribed and far from antiquated, being personal service, first class post or document exchange and even fax or 'other electronic means'. Service on a solicitor and substituted service were provided for, and service on a person under a disability was to be on the parent or guardian (for a minor) and the receiver, registered attorney or 'person with whom he resides or in whose care he is' (for a patient).

Evidence

1.141   Except where COPR 2001 otherwise provided evidence was by affidavit.[132] However, the Court might accept such oral or written evidence as it considered sufficient even if not on oath. The Court could give directions as to how any such evidence was to be given but in general it was to be dated, signed and have numbered paragraphs. Persons who gave written evidence could be ordered by the Court to attend and the oath might then be administered. Any such evidence could be used in other proceedings in the Court relating to the same patient and, if authorised by the Court, in proceedings in other specified courts.

---

[130]   These are minors (ie persons under 18 years of age) and 'patients' who could themselves potentially be within the jurisdiction of the Court.

[131]   CPR Part 21 now uses the term 'litigation friend' for both.

[132]   COPR 2001 did not introduce the concept of a statement containing a certificate of truth that now applies under the CPR.

Hearings

Conduct

1.142   Where appropriate the Master referred matters to a High Court judge who might refer any question back to the Master for inquiry and report.[133] Applications were heard in chambers (ie in private) unless, in the case of an application before a judge, the judge otherwise directed.[134] The Master and Assistant Masters had their own private hearing rooms.

1.143   The Court decided who attended any part of a hearing, although obviously certain persons needed to attend although they might be excluded for part of a hearing. A witness summons could be issued to require a person to attend and give oral evidence or produce any document.

1.144   The Court had wide powers to require persons having conduct of proceedings to explain delay or other causes of dissatisfaction and to make orders for expediting proceedings. It could direct any person to make an application or carry out directions and even appoint the Official Solicitor (with his or her consent) to act as solicitor for a patient. There was also a valuable power to require a patient to attend at a specified time and place for examination by the Master, a Visitor or any medical practitioner.

Reviews and appeals

1.145   Where a decision was made without an attended hearing, any aggrieved person could apply to have the decision reviewed and if still not satisfied apply for an attended hearing. Appeals from decisions made at attended hearing were heard by High Court judges of the Chancery or Family Division.

Fees and costs

Court fees

1.146   The Court charged fees which were usually paid out of the estate of the patient, or by the donor in the case of a registered enduring power of attorney. A policy of full costs recovery applied and the fees were intended to reflect the actual cost of the service provided. There was power to remit or postpone the payment of the whole or part of any fee on grounds of hardship.

Legal costs

1.147   All costs incurred in relation to proceedings were at the discretion of the Court, which could order them to be paid out of the estate of the patient

---

[133]   This mirrors the procedure in Chancery and insolvency proceedings in the High Court.
[134]   This inevitably means a High Court judge.

(or donor in the case of an enduring power of attorney), or by an applicant, objector or any other person attending or taking part in the proceedings. Unlike proceedings in the civil courts, costs did not automatically follow the event and the Court had an unlimited discretion to make whatever order it considered that the justice of the case required. In exercising its discretion the Court had regard to all the circumstances of the case, including the relationship between the parties, their conduct, their respective means and the amount of costs involved.

1.148 Where an application was made in good faith, supported by medical evidence, in the best interests of the donor and without any personal motive, the applicant was generally awarded his or her costs, even if unsuccessful. However, in cases where the Court considered an objection or application to have been made in bad faith, frivolous, malicious, vexatious or motivated by self-interest, it might order the applicant or objector to pay some or all of the costs. Similarly, where a person placed him- or herself in a hostile position to the donor, or where his or her conduct resulted in the costs of the proceedings being more expensive than they might otherwise have been, the Court might consider it appropriate to penalise him or her as to costs.[135]

1.149 There was a range of procedures available to approve the costs including fixed costs, agreed costs and assessment of costs. The costs actually charged by solicitors had to be approved by the Court before being paid from the funds of a patient and although summary assessment was not allowed the Court sometimes ordered the patient to pay a fixed contribution towards the costs of a party.

Venue

Background

1.150 Although in the early days inquisitions took place throughout the country and involved local people who knew the alleged patient, since its creation the Court of Protection sat in London despite having a jurisdiction extending to England and Wales. Following an extensive consultation[136] the Law Commission proposed that a reconstituted Court of Protection with jurisdiction over incapacity matters should have a regional presence, with designated judges throughout the country dealing with hearings locally. After further consultation the Lord Chancellor published the Government's proposals in October 1999 in the Report *Making Decisions* and these included a new Court of Protection with a regional presence. It thus became current policy to make the Court of Protection more accessible to the public by providing it with a regional presence.

1.151 The Court of Protection was not readily accessible to those in the North of England and other parts of the country. The cost to parties of

---

[135]   *Re Cathcart* [1893] 1 Ch 466.
[136]   This is outlined below. The proposal of a tribunal for some types of case was rejected.

travelling to and staying in London for a hearing was prohibitive and represented a denial of justice to those involved. In addition, solicitors in the provinces were discouraged from gaining 'hands-on' experience of the work of the Court by attending hearings and therefore less able to give well-informed advice to their clients. Concerns were also expressed that the Master was the only human rights-compliant judge of the Court, as the Assistant Masters did not have a judicial appointment.[137]

1.152 In consequence it was proposed that even before the implementation of a new mental incapacity jurisdiction a few district judges based at carefully selected locations (eg one on each circuit) should be appointed as Deputy Masters to hear locally cases that were referred to them by the Master.[138]

Regional hearings

1.153 On 1 October 2001 District Judge Ashton was appointed a part-time Deputy Master of the Court of Protection to hear any case where it was more convenient for the parties to attend at Preston in Lancashire. Thereafter the 'Northern Court of Protection' operated as a 'satellite' of the central Court in London and on certain days in each month hearings took place at Preston Combined Court Centre. These were generally contested hearings (mainly disputes over enduring powers of attorney and the choice of receiver) and fund management hearings for large damages awards, but also hearings of applications for gifts, statutory wills and to be discharged from the jurisdiction due to recovery.

1.154 This link with the civil and family courts led to the cross-fertilisation of ideas and resulted in more local practitioners becoming familiar with the work of this specialised but nonetheless essential jurisdiction. Based on experience at Preston the Court of Protection in London then introduced the recording of hearings, telephone conferences and attendance by video link.

1.155 The selection of venues and judges is crucial to the success of a regionalised Court of Protection. Having a centralised administration with satellite courts raises many problems. To a large extent these were tackled in the Preston pilot and workable solutions devised. Communication by e-mail proved effective and the main problems proved to be access to the case file,[139] uncertainty amongst parties and solicitors as to where to send documents and delay in receiving documents sent at a late stage to the Public Guardianship Office. There was a lack of administrative support

---

[137] The term Assistant Master was a courtesy title and they were in reality legally qualified civil servants in the Department of Constitutional Affairs who were 'nominated officers' under the Mental Health Act 1983, s 93(4). The post of Deputy Master of the Court of Protection had been created by the Mental Health Act 1959, but ceased to exist on the retirement of the then Deputy Master in 1982, and was not mentioned in the Mental Health Act 1983.

[138] Supreme Court Act 1981, s 91 permitted the Lord Chancellor to appoint deputy judges if he considered that it was expedient to do so in order to facilitate the disposal of the business of the court. This has now been renamed the Senior Courts Act 1981.

[139] A courier service has been established.

because HM Courts Service staff had no involvement with the Public Guardianship Office. Experience showed that these difficulties could be overcome.

An evaluation of the Court of Protection

1.156 Hitherto the Court of Protection has been the Cinderella of the judicial system, underfunded, unrecognised and only appreciated by those who knew it well. This has changed with generic judges becoming involved, a regional structure and the acquisition of jurisdiction for declarations previously dealt with by the High Court. There will be more inter-dependence between the civil and family courts and the Court of Protection now it is no longer restricted to financial affairs.

1.157 How different is the Court of Protection from other courts? Which functions are truly judicial? How many judges should be nominated to the Court and where should they be deployed? On what basis should the different levels of the judiciary be allocated cases? What procedural rules are appropriate? How should hearings be conducted and what human rights issues arise? To what extent and in what manner should judgments be reported? What right should individuals have to disclosure of information held about them by the Court? What should be the relationship between the new Court of Protection and the Public Guardian? To what extent may the legal profession become involved and who funds the non-money cases? When should cases be publicly funded? These are all questions that are now being faced.

Court Rules

1.158 It will be seen from the above outline that COPR 2001 provided only the most basic structure for the conduct of applications and hearings, and much was left to the discretion of the Master, Deputy Master or Assistant Master dealing with the case. The lack of guidance to practitioners or the parties themselves as to the submission of applications and preparation for or conduct of hearings coupled with no requirement for active case management might be seen as an obstacle to justice.

1.159 However, the issues that have to be tackled are very different from those in the civil courts, although a parallel may be drawn with proceedings relating to the welfare of children. Whilst a paternalistic approach is acceptable when considering the best interests of children, it must be avoided for adults. A Court of Protection is concerned to identify and safeguard the best interests of incapacitated adults rather than to impose what other persons think is best for them, and will be influenced more by the previous lifestyle and any expressed wishes of the individual. However, the former Court only had power to do this through the management and administration of the individual's property and financial affairs.

Contested hearings

1.160   It is only when there is disagreement or conflict resulting in the need for an attended hearing that more prescriptive Rules are required to regulate the conduct of the parties involved. Under the former regime this might arise in the following situations, namely where:

(1) there was uncertainty as to whether an individual was a patient within the jurisdiction of the Court and this had to be resolved;

(2) there was a dispute as to who should be appointed to act as receiver;

(3) there was an unresolved challenge to the registration of an enduring power of attorney;

(4) a receiver or registered attorney was not satisfied with the extent of any authority given or restriction imposed;

(5) family, carers or other persons concerned with the welfare of the patient were in dispute; or

(6) an application was made for a statutory will, gift or settlement.

Other hearings

1.161   Attended hearings were also required for the setting of broad policy where substantial compensation had been awarded for brain injury, typically following a clinical negligence claim. The family, who may have been the carers to date and contemplate the continued provision of a care environment, would be anxious to have authoritative guidance as to how they should handle the funding. There might be an enhancement in their own standard of living and judicial approval assuaged any feeling of guilt in a context where earning capacity was otherwise impaired.

1.162   These hearings or 'attendances' were generally friendly and constructive. The Master would look to the heads of loss in the civil claim as pointers to what should be considered but would not seek to impose these on the family. It was more appropriate to concentrate upon what was achievable with the personal and financial resources available whilst keeping an eye on the future when intensive family care may no longer be available. Headings that were discussed included:

(1) the provision of a suitable home and modifications to meet disability needs;

(2) transport (usually a personal vehicle which can accommodate any disability needs);

(3) the monthly personal and household budget;

(4) care provision and funding;

(5) holidays;

(6) disability aids and appliances (including computers); and

(7) the retention by the parents or family carers of a personal stake in the housing market where the shared home is purchased by the patient.

Investment policy then had to be determined for the contingency fund available after the provision of a home, although in some cases there would be an index-linked tax-free annuity for the life of the patient from a structured settlement. It seems that this type of support may no longer be forthcoming under the new jurisdiction because there is more delegation to deputies.

LAW REFORM

Origins

1.163 During the 1980s it became apparent that the law and procedures in England and Wales failed to address in a comprehensive manner the problems raised by those who were incompetent in the sense that they could not make their own decisions. The courts did not have adequate powers to fill the vacuum and such legislation as there had been was piecemeal and not based upon an underlying philosophy. Comprehensive reform became essential. This was first highlighted in a paper produced by the Law Society in 1989[140] which was followed by a conference when the speakers included Professor Brenda Hoggett who had recently been appointed as a Law Commissioner.[141]

The Law Commission

1.164 Prompted by this initiative the Law Commission of England and Wales embarked upon a consideration of the whole question of decision-making and mental incapacity.[142] Serious deficiencies were identified during a protracted consultation and it became clear that reform was badly needed.[143]

Consultation

1.165 The first consultation paper in March 1991[144] provided an invaluable overview of the present state of the law and its procedures. It recognised that the existing law was inadequate to cope with the range of decisions that needed to be made on behalf of mentally incapable people but that the issue was large and complex. Further consultation followed.

1.166 The second consultation paper in December 1992[145] dealt with private law aspects and proposed procedures whereby decisions relating to the personal care and financial affairs of incapacitated people could be

---

[140]   *Decision-making and Mental Incapacity: A Discussion Document*: Memorandum by the Law Society's Mental Health Sub-Committee, January 1989.
[141]   *Decision-making and Mental Incapacity*, The Law Society, 5 May 1989.
[142]   A similar review was undertaken by the Law Commission of Scotland.
[143]   Professor Brenda Hoggett, the Law Commissioner responsible, later became Mrs Justice Hale and rapidly progressed through the Court of Appeal to become the first lady to sit in the House of Lords. In these capacities she has had the opportunity to shape the law in accordance with her previous thinking.
[144]   *Mentally Incapacitated Adults and Decision-Making: An Overview*, Law Com No 119.
[145]   *Mentally Incapacitated Adults and Decision-Making: A New Jurisdiction*, Law Com No 128.

made. A third consultation paper in March 1993[146] explored legal procedures whereby substitute decisions about medical treatment could be authorised at an appropriate level. The fourth consultation paper in April 1993[147] considered the powers of public authorities and was expanded to cover vulnerable as well as mentally incapacitated people.

Report

1.167 The Law Commission published its final Report in March 1995[148] with the almost unanimous support of charities and others concerned with the welfare of mentally incapacitated people. This set out comprehensive recommendations and included a draft Mental Incapacity Bill. It was recommended that there should be a single comprehensive piece of legislation[149] to make new provision for people who lack mental capacity. This should provide a coherent statutory scheme to which recourse could be had when any decision (whether personal, medical or financial) needed to be made for a person aged 16 or over who lacked capacity. Two concepts were identified as being fundamental to any new decision-making jurisdiction, namely capacity and best interests.[150]

1.168 The proposals included:

(1) a general authority to act reasonably;

(2) living wills to be given statutory authority subject to safeguards;

(3) the appointment of someone to take treatment decisions;

(4) independent supervision of certain medical and research procedures;

(5) 'continuing power of attorney' which could extend to a donor's personal welfare, health care and property and affairs;

(6) decision-making by the Court and power to make declarations and one-off orders or appoint a manager with substitute decision-making powers;

(7) a new Court of Protection with a central registry in London and regional hearing centres;

(8) a code of practice; and

(9) public law protection of vulnerable adults.[151]

---

[146] *Mentally Incapacitated Adults and Decision-Making: Medical Treatment and Research*, Law Com No 129.

[147] *Mentally Incapacitated and Other Vulnerable Adults: Public Law Protection*, Law Com No 130.

[148] *Mental Incapacity*, Law Com No 231.

[149] This would move these problems away from the Mental Health Act 1983 and facilitate a different approach to the needs of incapacitated persons from that of mental health professionals.

[150] These concepts have been further developed in the Mental Capacity Act 2005.

[151] These proposals, which went beyond the initial Law Commission brief, have not been adopted.

The Government's response

1.169   The Government announced that it did not intend to proceed with legislation 'in its present form' but would undertake further consultation on the Report. That consultation did not materialise until October 1997 when the new Lord Chancellor, Lord Irvine of Lairg, announced that he intended to issue a consultation paper seeking views on the Report.

'Who Decides?'

1.170   In December 1997 the Lord Chancellor's consultation document *Who Decides? Making Decisions on Behalf of Mentally Incapacitated Adults*[152] was published with a relatively short period for consultation. This was in addition to an ambitious programme of law reform which included a Human Rights Bill to give effect to the ECHR in the UK and the continuance of civil justice reforms following Lord Woolf's Report *Access to Justice.*

1.171   This Green Paper was structured to follow the Law Commission's Report *Mental Incapacity*. The Government accepted that there was a clear need for law reform in this area and contemplated that there would be codes of practice dealing with specific areas. Whilst emphasising that there would be no move towards euthanasia (which is illegal) the Government supported many of the Law Commission's recommendations and expressed the wish to consult further on how they might best be implemented and those that might be controversial.[153] Inevitably the issue of resources arose.

'Making decisions'

1.172   In October 1999 the Government's proposals were published in the Report *Making Decisions*. Much, but not all, of the Law Commission's recommendations survived.[154] The Lord Chancellor announced in November 1999 that there would be legislation 'when Parliamentary time allows' but much of the detail had still to be worked out. In the meanwhile some of the recommendations of the Law Commission were already finding their way into our law through decisions of the courts.

Legislation

Adults with Incapacity (Scotland) Act 2000

1.173   Scotland achieved legislation first. The Adults with Incapacity (Scotland) Act 2000, which followed recommendations of the Scottish Law Commission[155] and was widely welcomed as a significant and much-needed

---

[152]   Cm 3803, issued by the Lord Chancellor's Department.
[153]   These included advance statements about health care and non-therapeutic research.
[154]   In particular the proposals for public law protection have not been followed up.
[155]   *Report on Incapable Adults*, Scot Law Com No 151 (July 1995).

reform of the law, received Royal Assent on 16 May 2000 and came into force in stages.[156] It protects the rights and interests of adults in Scotland who are incapable of managing their own affairs, acknowledged to be one of the most vulnerable groups in society. There are regulations under the Act and codes of practice which provide guidance on the legislation itself and offer further practical information for those people and organisations that have functions given to them by the Act.

1.174   A number of different agencies are involved in supervising those who take decisions on behalf of the adult:

(1)   the Public Guardian has a supervisory role and keeps registers of attorneys, people who can access an adult's funds, guardians and intervention orders;

(2)   local authorities look after the welfare of adults who lack capacity; and

(3)   the Mental Welfare Commission protects the interests of adults who lack capacity as a result of mental disorder.

Mental Incapacity Bill

1.175   On 27 June 2003 the Government published a draft Mental Incapacity Bill which was then scrutinised by a joint committee of both Houses of Parliament which published its response in November 2003.[157] The Government commented on some of those recommendations.[158] The title was to be changed to the *Mental Capacity Bill* and it was considered that draft *Codes of Practice* should be available before the Bill was passed. The joint committee considered that priority should be given to the Bill so that account could be taken of its provisions when framing new mental health legislation.

Mental Capacity Act 2005

1.176   A Bill, duly called the Mental Capacity Bill and incorporating the desired changes to the draft Bill, was introduced in Parliament in June 2004. This Bill (as amended) was finally passed in April 2005 and extends to England and Wales only. It was intended to come into force on 1 April 2007 but this date was postponed to 1 October 2007 due to delays in the implementation process. The Mental Capacity Act 2005 (MCA 2005) does not provide all the answers but lays down the principles, creates a statutory framework and authorises rules, practice directions and codes of practice to

---

[156]   Available at www.opsi.gov.uk/legislation/scotland/s-acts.htm and also accessible through the Office of Public Sector Information website: www.opsi.gov.uk. Information about implementation, which is updated at intervals, is to be found on the Scottish Executive website: www.scotland.gov.uk.

[157]   *Report of the Joint Committee on the Draft Mental Incapacity Bill*, HL Papers 189-1 and 189-II, HC 1083-1 and 1083-II) (TSO, 2003), vols I and II.

[158]   *The Government's Response to the Scrutiny Committee's Report on the draft Mental Incapacity Bill*, Cm 6121 (TSO, 2004).

be made. Much now depends upon the manner in which these are implemented. The new social and legal climate will dictate the content, but this will change over the years.

Human rights compatibility

1.177   Explanatory notes[159] prepared by the Department for Constitutional Affairs and the Department of Health state that MCA 2005 meets the state's positive obligation under ECHR, Art 8 to ensure respect for private life. Issues are acknowledged to arise in relation to the following provisions:

- *Article 8 – private life*
  This Article is engaged in connection with MCA 2005, ss 5, 6, 9 and 11 and could also be engaged as a result of s 20 and a court order made under s 16(2). Any interference pursues the legitimate aim of protecting the health and well-being of the person lacking capacity and ensures that those who care for and treat persons who lack capacity are protected from certain liabilities where appropriate. The principles in s 1, the criteria for lack of capacity (s 2), the checklist as to best interests (s 4) and the safeguards within the sections themselves create a framework within which any interference will be proportionate to this legitimate aim. MCA 2005, s 49(7)–(9) allows the Court to direct a medical examination or interview of the person concerned and the examination of his or her health and social services records although the Court is bound by the principles in s 1 and the best interests checklist. MCA 2005, ss 35(6), 58(5) and (6) and 61(5) and (6) also make provision whereby particular persons may interview the person concerned and examine relevant records. Again, any interference is justified as being for the protection of that person's own health and welfare and proportionate to that aim. The powers are given to the relevant officials for the purpose of enabling them to carry out their functions, which are directed to the protection of the interests of the person who lacks capacity.

- *Article 1 of the First Protocol – protection of property*
  These rights may be engaged in connection with MCA 2005, ss 7–9 and 12 which provide for the control of a person's property and affairs and payment on his or her behalf for necessary goods and services. The statutory rules are intended to be clear and precise and are designed to strike a fair balance between the property interests of the person lacking capacity, his or her own wider welfare interests and the interests of others (persons supplying necessary goods and services to the person lacking capacity, anyone bearing the cost and, in the case of s 12, persons related to or connected with that person). MCA 2005, ss 10(2) and 13(8) and (9) prevent a bankrupt from acting as a donee of a lasting power of attorney (LPA) where the power covers property and affairs and suspend that

---

[159]   These do not form part of MCA 2005 and have not been endorsed by Parliament.

power where there is an interim bankruptcy restrictions order. Article 8 and Art 14 rights may be engaged but any difference of treatment has the legitimate aim of protecting an incapacitated donor from the possibility of financial abuse and is proportionate to that end.

- *Articles 2 and 3 – right to life and prohibition from torture*
  A donee of an LPA can be given power to refuse to give consent to life-sustaining treatment on behalf of the donor (see MCA 2005, s 1(7) and (8)). A person can also make an advance decision to refuse treatment, including life-sustaining treatment. MCA 2005, s 25(5) provides that an advance decision will not apply to any treatment necessary to sustain life unless the advance decision is in writing and is signed and the signature is witnessed. Further, there must be a statement that the decision stands even if life is at risk (and this statement must also be in writing and be signed and the signature must be witnessed). MCA 2005, ss 6(7) and 26(5) provide that action can be taken to preserve life or prevent serious deterioration while the Court resolves any dispute or difficulty. These provisions are designed to protect a person's Art 2 and 3 rights, while also discharging the obligation to respect the Art 8 rights of those who choose to give powers to a donee under an LPA or to make an advance decision.

- *Article 14 – prohibition of discrimination*
  MCA 2005, ss 35–39 may engage these rights in connection with Art 8 by providing for an independent mental capacity advocate to represent and support people who lack capacity where they are being treated and cared for by the NHS or a local authority and there is no one who could be consulted about that treatment or care. Any relevant difference in treatment which there might be would have the legitimate aim of protecting the Art 8 rights of incapacitated persons.

- *Article 6 – right to a fair trial*
  The comprehensive jurisdiction of the new Court of Protection (MCA 2005, ss 15–21 and 45–56) ensures protection for any rights engaged in connection with the provisions of the Act. The Government is satisfied that MCA 2005, ss 50 (certain applicants to obtain permission to apply), 51(2)(d) (exercise of jurisdiction by officers or staff) and 54 (court fees) do not breach Art 6 rights.

1.178 The European Court of Human Rights has made it clear that there must be adequate involvement of the individual in the court process. A person of unsound mind must be allowed to be heard either in person or, where necessary, through some form of representation. He will play a double role in the proceedings: as an interested party, and, at the same time, the main object of the court's examination. Participation is therefore necessary not only to enable him to present his own case, but also to allow the judge to form a personal opinion about mental capacity. In one case it was held that despite the applicant's mental illness he had been a relatively autonomous person. In such circumstances it was indispensable for the judge to have at least a brief visual contact with the applicant, and preferably to question him. The decision of the judge to decide the case on the basis of documentary evidence, without seeing or hearing the applicant, was unreasonable and in breach of the principle of adversarial proceedings enshrined in Article 6.[160]

1.179 This analysis concentrates upon the rights of the incapacitated person. Procedures for decisions to be made on behalf of such persons may also have an impact upon the human rights of other persons, and especially members of the family. Experience of the former Court of Protection shows that there may be strong sibling rivalry for control over the financial affairs of a parent and that the person in control of the finances, although not legally empowered to make personal welfare decisions, has a strong influence over such decisions. This may impact upon the human rights of other members of the family to respect for family life. The new jurisdiction will be better able to tackle these issues but must do so in a way that is human rights compliant for all concerned.

Conclusion

1.180 At last we are to have in England and Wales a statutory jurisdiction for decision-making in respect of mentally incapacitated adults. The need for this has been clearly demonstrated and the legislation is overdue, but will it fill the vacuum in our legal system? The general principles contained in MCA 2005, s 1 are relatively innovative so far as UK legislation is concerned and have been much praised. However, there have also been complaints that the system is 'a legal and bureaucratic minefield' and that 'a secret court is seizing the assets of thousands of elderly and mentally impaired people and turning control of their lives over to the State – against the wishes of their relatives'.[161]

1.181 Of key importance are the statutory formulae for assessing a lack of capacity and determining best interests. We now have a benchmark against which people with a mental impairment are to be assessed and interventions must be justified. This should apply beyond the specialist jurisdiction of the Court of Protection and be adopted by all courts and tribunals when they encounter people with impaired capacity. There is now the potential for the specialist judges to sit in a dual jurisdiction but the benchmark should become second nature to all professionals working in this field. There is also a developing awareness of the need to identify incapacity as a discrete area of law divorced from provisions that deal with the treatment of those who are mentally ill.

---

[160]   *Shtukaturov v Russia*, Application no 44009/05, 27/06/2008.
[161]   *The Mail on Sunday* (25 October 2009). The editorial comments that the system assumes individuals have suspect motives and treats them as potential thieves, and that this tendency should be reversed.

1.182 The new procedures to implement decision-making over a wider range of content are intended to empower those members of our families and society who lack capacity, but must also ensure that they are protected from abuse. This is a delicate balance and where that balance should be struck depends upon one's viewpoint and how one interprets the statistics. It should not be assumed that everyone is satisfied with the present balance.[162] There is a range of diversity within mental incapacity and a 'one size fits all' approach cannot be adopted. There is a world of difference between the needs of a wealthy senior citizen who develops Alzheimer's, an autistic young person dependent on means-tested benefits and a brain-injured individual who has recovered compensation of several million pounds. There is also a difference between the incapacitated adult with dedicated family carers and the similarly incapacitated adult who has been abandoned by family.

1.183 Those working in this field become concerned about vulnerability, but of course this does not feature in the test of mental capacity. In a recent decision of the Court of Appeal it was stated:[163]

> '... the courts have ample powers to protect those who are vulnerable to exploitation from being exploited; it is unnecessary to deny them the opportunity to take their own decisions if they are not being exploited. It is not the task of the courts to prevent those who have the mental capacity to make rational decisions from making decisions which others may regard as rash or irresponsible.'

1.184 Many practitioners working in this field would question the suggestion that the courts have ample powers to protect those who are vulnerable. However, where vulnerability is perceived it becomes appropriate to inquire why this should be so and a thorough investigation may reveal that the underlying cause is a mental impairment. Although there may be sufficient understanding, resulting personal qualities such as impulsiveness, recklessness and being easily manipulated may mean that there is an inability to make and implement decisions based on that understanding.

1.185 The procedures need to be publicly known and accessible. There is a role for the new Office of the Public Guardian in this respect, but that role should extend to resolving uncertainties where these exist and assisting in facilitating the resolution of disputes as to best interests. We also have a specialist Court charged with the responsibility of interpreting the statutory criteria and exercising the new jurisdiction. But although empowering a new court to make all types of decisions or to authorise other persons to do so is a sine qua non, delivering that which is needed depends upon those called upon to implement the new jurisdiction at all levels. Where will these people come from and how will they be trained? The success or failure of this much

---

[162] The Law Society paper of 1989 was concerned about protection and the Law Commission proposals were perhaps the high point of empowerment. The continuing consultation appeared to swing back towards protection but the emphasis in MCA 2005 appears to be empowerment.

[163] Chadwick LJ in *Masterman-Lister v Brutton & Co and Jewell & Home Counties Dairies* [2002] EWCA Civ 1889, [2003] 3 All ER 162.

needed initiative depends on the guidance that is produced and the availability of professionals who are familiar with the new law and procedures.

1.186 Any new court or administrative body that is established to implement the new mental capacity jurisdiction will be judged by people whose needs have for too long been overlooked but who have now become vocal in support of their increased expectations of the legal system. It must not only be compatible with the new social and legal climate but also set a good example to other courts and bodies.

1.187 The following pages address the manner in which these issues have been addressed. It is too much to expect that all of the objectives will be met initially, and in response to public criticisms and concerns expressed by practitioners an *ad hoc* Rules Committee was set up early in 2010 to consider what improvements could be made. The following recommendations were made:[164]

1   The procedure and practice of the court should reflect the differences in the nature of the following categories of its work, namely (a) non-contentious property and affairs applications, (b) contentious property and affairs applications and (c) health and welfare applications.

2   This change should be implemented by (a) the introduction of new forms, and (b) relevant changes in the rules and practice directions.

3   The distinction between serving and notifying people who are or may be interested in making representations to the court should be preserved. But it should be better explained and some amendments to the present provisions relating to this process should be made.

4   The present position relating to the notification and participation of P should be retained (with some minor amendments).

5   Strictly defined and limited non-contentious property and affairs applications should be dealt with by court officers (e.g. applications for a property and affairs deputy by local authorities and in respect of small estates that do not include defined types of property). The provisions will also have to provide for an automatic right to refer any such decision to a judge and internal monitoring and review by the judges.

6   Separate applications for permission should be abandoned and the application for permission should be incorporated into the main application form.

7   The detailed and minor changes set out in annex 1 [to the Report] should be considered. It is recognised that on a detailed consideration some may be rejected and others added and this recommendation and annex is included to assist those who are performing that detailed exercise.

---

[164]   The full Report is available at: www.judiciary.gov.uk/publications-and-reports/reports/family/court-of-protection

8   Issues as to whether and when the court should sit in public or permit its proceedings to be made public should be dealt with by the courts through decisions rather than any rule change.

9   The proposed new forms prepared by members of this committee should be "tested" with a range of potential users before they are finalised and the relevant rules and practice directions are altered.

A Committee should be established to review and make recommendations relating to the procedure and practice of the Court of Protection.

1.188   Within the framework established by MCA 2005 there is the prospect of a ground-breaking improvement in the lives of those who have the misfortune to be unable to structure these for themselves. Whether that improvement actually takes place may depend upon those involved adopting a pragmatic approach rather than becoming rule-bound. The following questions remain and will only be answered as the new jurisdiction reaches maturity:

- Is a decision-specific assessment of capacity viable?
- Does a test based on understanding protect those who are mentally unstable or vulnerable to influence?
- Does the 'best interest' approach involving the need to consult create too much opportunity for disputes?
- Does a 'best interest' test for the incapacitated person infringe the human rights of others?
- Will the Court be accessible and affordable to those who need it?
- Will the Court become a battleground between families/carers and social services/health authorities?
- Will the Court resolve disputes or address best interests?
- Will the new jurisdiction achieve the right balance between empowerment and protection?
- Is the new jurisdiction too complex and theoretical?
- Will HRA 1998, which made the new jurisdiction inevitable, now render it illusory?

Chapter 2

The Mental Capacity Jurisdiction

INTRODUCTION

2.1 The Mental Capacity Act 2005 (MCA 2005) establishes a comprehensive statutory framework setting out how decisions should be made by and on behalf of adults whose capacity to make specific decisions is in doubt. It also clarifies what actions can be taken by others involved in the care or medical treatment of people lacking capacity to consent. The framework provides a hierarchy of processes, extending from informal day-to-day care and treatment, to decision-making requiring formal powers and ultimately to court decisions and judgments. The full range of processes is intended to govern the circumstances in which necessary acts of caring can be carried out, and necessary decisions taken, on behalf of those lacking capacity to consent to such acts or make their own decisions.

2.2 This chapter is in three parts:

- Part 1 gives a brief overview of the jurisdiction created by MCA 2005 and discusses the role and status of the Code of Practice which provides statutory guidance on its operation.
- Part 2 looks in detail at the guiding statutory principles that underpin MCA 2005's key messages and govern how the Act is to be interpreted and implemented. The two fundamental concepts – capacity and best interests, which form the basis of the statutory framework – are discussed and their definitions explained.
- Part 3 looks at the provisions in MCA 2005 which permit actions to be taken in relation to the care and treatment of people lacking capacity to consent to those actions. Some types of decisions are excluded from the Act's provisions and these are explored. Finally, an explanation is given of the criminal offence created under the Act to deal with cases of ill-treatment or wilful neglect of people lacking capacity to protect themselves from such abuse.

PART 1: OVERVIEW

Key elements

General

2.3 MCA 2005 sets out a comprehensive integrated jurisdiction for the making of personal welfare decisions, health care decisions and financial decisions on behalf of people who may lack capacity to make specific decisions for themselves. The Act's starting point is to enshrine in statute thepresumption at common law that an adult has full legal capacity unless it is established that he or she does not. It also includes provisions to ensure that people are given all appropriate help and support to enable them to make their own decisions or to maximise their participation in the decision-making process.

2.4   MCA 2005 also enshrines in statute current best practice and former common law principles concerning people who lack capacity and those who take decisions on their behalf. The statutory framework is based on two fundamental concepts:[1] lack of capacity and best interests. For those who lack capacity to make particular decisions, the Act provides a range of processes, extending from informal arrangements to court-based powers, to govern the circumstances in which necessary decisions can be taken on their behalf and in their best interests.

Essential provisions

2.5   The essential provisions of MCA 2005 are intended to:

- set out five guiding principles to underpin the Act's fundamental concepts and to govern its implementation and operation;
- define people who lack decision-making capacity;
- set out a single clear test for assessing whether a person lacks capacity to take a particular decision at a particular time;
- establish a single criterion (best interests) for carrying out acts or taking decisions on behalf of people who lack capacity to consent to such acts or take those specific decisions for themselves;
- clarify the law when acts in connection with the care or treatment of people lacking capacity to consent are carried out in their best interests, without formal procedures or judicial intervention, but with clear restrictions on the use of restraint and, in particular, acts resulting in deprivation of liberty; [2]
- extend the provisions for making powers of attorney which outlast capacity (lasting powers of attorney (LPA)) covering health and welfare decisions as well as financial affairs, with improved safeguards against abuse and exploitation;
- provide for a decision to be made, or a decision-maker (deputy) to be appointed, by a specialist Court of Protection;
- make statutory rules, with clear safeguards, for the making of advance decisions to refuse medical treatment;
- set out specific parameters for research involving, or in relation to, people lacking capacity to consent to their involvement;
- provide for the appointment of independent mental capacity advocates (IMCAs) to support people with no one to speak for them who lack capacity to make important decisions about serious medical treatment and changes of accommodation, and in some circumstances to support those lacking capacity who are involved in safeguarding adult procedures; and

---

[1]   A full discussion of the meaning of these concepts is set out in the Law Commission Report, *Mental Incapacity*, Law Com No 231 (HMSO, 1995), Part III. See also Part 2 of this chapter below.

[2]   MCA 2005 has subsequently been amended by the Mental Health Act 2007 to provide procedural safeguards in cases where someone lacking capacity may be deprived of their liberty in their best interests – see Chapter 6.

- provide statutory guidance, in the form of a code (or codes) of
practice, setting good practice standards for the guidance of people
using the Act's provisions.

The public bodies

2.6 MCA 2005 also created two public bodies to support and implement
the statutory framework:

(1) a superior court of record, the Court of Protection, with jurisdiction
relating to the whole of MCA 2005 and its own procedures and
nominated judges; and

(2) a Public Guardian, whose office is the registering authority for
LPAs and deputies, with responsibility to supervise deputies and
respond to any concerns raised about donees or deputies.

The Code of Practice

2.7 It has long been recognised that complex legislation of this sort will
require an accompanying code (or codes) of practice for the guidance of
practitioners using MCA 2005 and those affected by its provisions, and also
to assist with interpretation and implementation of the Act.[3] Provision for
such statutory guidance is made in the Act.[4] Following parliamentary
pre-legislative scrutiny of the Draft Mental Incapacity Bill in 2003, the Joint
Scrutiny Committee specifically recommended that the Bill should not be
introduced into Parliament unless it could be considered alongside a draft
code of practice.[5]

2.8 A draft Code was placed in the libraries of both Houses of Parliament
on 8 September 2004 and was made available on the Department for
Constitutional Affairs (DCA) website. Members of both the House of
Commons and the House of Lords were able to refer extensively to the draft
Code during debates on the passage of the Bill.

2.9 Following Royal Assent of MCA 2005, a revised version of the draft
Code was issued for formal public consultation during 2006. It was further
revised in the light of responses to the consultation and the final version was
laid before Parliament in February 2007. The Code of Practice[6] was
formally issued in April 2007 and came fully into effect on 1 October 2007
as the statutory guidance for the entire MCA 2005 as originally enacted. A
supplement to the Code[7] has since been issued separately to deal with the

---

3   Law Com No 231, n 1 above, at para 2.53.
4   MCA 2005, s 42.
5   *Report of the Joint Committee on the Draft Mental Incapacity Bill, Vol 1*, HL 189-1, HC
     1083-1 (TSO, 2003), at para 229.
6   Mental Capacity Act 2005: Code of Practice (TSO, 2007). The Code is reproduced in Part V
     of this book and is also available online at www.publicguardian.gov.uk/mca/code-of-
     practice.htm.
7   Mental Capacity Act 2005: Deprivation of Liberty Safeguards – Code of Practice to
     supplement the main Mental Capacity Act 2005 Code of Practice (TSO, 2008). Also

deprivation of liberty provisions inserted into MCA 2005 by the Mental Health Act 2007, which came into effect in April 2009 (see Chapter 6).

Application

2.10   The Lord Chancellor is required to prepare and issue one or more codes of practice and MCA 2005 specified the particular issues, as well as particular categories of people, that guidance in the Code(s) must address.[8] These are:

- persons involved in assessing capacity;
- persons acting in connection with the care or treatment of a person lacking capacity;
- donees of LPAs;
- deputies appointed by the Court of Protection;
- persons carrying out research involving people lacking capacity;
- independent mental capacity advocates (IMCAs);
- persons involved in using the deprivation of liberty procedures;
- representatives appointed for people deprived of their liberty;
- the provisions in the Act covering advance decisions to refuse treatment;
- any other matters concerned with the Act as the Lord Chancellor thinks fit.

2.11   The Government originally decided to issue one Code of Practice (sometimes referred to as the main Code) to include guidance on the whole of the MCA jurisdiction. However, the deprivation of liberty provisions subsequently inserted into MCA 2005 (which came into effect in 2009) are dealt with in a separate supplement.[9] The main Code is intended to give practical guidance and examples to illustrate the provisions of MCA 2005, rather than imposing any new legal or formal requirements. It is intended that the Code will be revised as and when required[10] and the Lord Chancellor may delegate the preparation or revision of the whole or any part of the Code as he considers expedient.[11]

2.12   Responsibility for the dissemination of the Code of Practice has now passed from the Ministry of Justice (formerly the Department for Constitutional Affairs, which published the Code) to the Office of the Public Guardian (OPG). Apart from the Code appearing on the OPG's website,[12] it appears that little effort has been made to promote the Code or to make sure that the people required by MCA 2005 to 'have regard' to it have it drawn to their attention.

---

reproduced in Part V of this book and available online at www.dh.gov.uk/en/
Publicationsandstatistics/Publications/PublicationsPolicyAndGuidance/DH_085476.

[8]   MCA 2005, s 42(1), as amended by the Mental Health Act 2007, s 50(7), Sch 9, Part 1, paras 1, 8(1), (2).

[9]   See n 7 above.

[10]   MCA 2005, s 42(2).

[11]   MCA 2005, s 42(3).

[12]   See www.publicguardian.gov.uk/mca/code-of-practice.htm.

2.13   In October 2008, the Public Guardian announced the first stage of a wider review of the implementation of MCA 2005[13] with later stages intended, amongst other issues, to review and improve the Code of Practice and other guidance on MCA 2005.[14] No further details were announced until October 2010, when the Ministry of Justice published a Memorandum to the Justice Select Committee, providing a preliminary assessment of the Mental Capacity Act 2005 following its implementation in October 2007.[15] The Memorandum recognised the importance of the Code of Practice not just in the precise area of MCA 2005 but also in offering guidance whenever mental capacity is a consideration. It referred to the Code as "a living document that develops over time to reflect changes in policy, practice and jurisprudence". The Memorandum indicated that the Government expects to review the Code within the next two years to ensure it remains fit for purpose.

PART I

Legal effect

2.14   The Code of Practice is statutory guidance in that MCA 2005 imposes a duty on certain people to 'have regard to any relevant Code' when acting in relation to a person lacking capacity.[16] The specified people are those acting in one or more of the following ways:

(1) as a donee of a LPA;
(2) as a deputy appointed by the Court;
(3) as a person carrying out research under the Act;
(4) as an IMCA;
(5) in exercising the procedures authorising deprivation of liberty;
(6) as a representative of someone deprived of their liberty;
(7) in a professional capacity; and/or
(8) for remuneration.

2.15   The statutory duty to have regard to the Code therefore applies to those exercising formal powers or duties under MCA 2005, and to professionals (including lawyers, health and social care professionals) and others acting for remuneration (such as paid carers). The position of informal carers, such as family members, was considered by the Joint Committee on the Draft Bill:[17]

> 'The position is different with regard to guidance issued to assist non-professional or informal decision-makers, such as family members and unpaid carers acting under the general authority. It is essential that family members and carers carrying out such responsibilities are provided with appropriate guidance and assistance, both to

13   Office of the Public Guardian (2008) *Reviewing the Mental Capacity Act 2005: Forms, supervision and fees* – Consultation Paper CP26/08 (London: Ministry of Justice).
14   Office of the Public Guardian (2009) *Business Plan 2009–2010*, p 10. Available online at http://www.publicguardian.gov.uk/docs/opg-business-plan-2009-10.pdf
15   Ministry of Justice (2010) *Memorandum to the Justice Select Committee: Post-Legislative Assessment of the Mental Capacity Act 2005* (Cm 7955), paras 19–27. Available online at www.justice.gov.uk/memorandum-mental-capacity-act.htm.
16   MCA 2005, s 42(4), as amended by the Mental Health Act 2007, s 50(7), Sch 9, Part 1, paras 1, 8(3).
17   Joint Committee Report, Vol I, n 5 above, at para 232.

promote good practice and also to impress upon them the seriousness of their actions
and the need to be accountable for them. However, we accept that it would be
inappropriate to impose on them a strict requirement to act in accordance with the
codes of practice.'

Sanctions for non-compliance

2.16   MCA 2005 provides that a provision of a code of practice, or a failure
to comply with the guidance set out in a code, can be taken into account by
a court or tribunal where it appears relevant to a question arising in any
criminal or civil proceedings.[18] There is no liability for breach of the Code
itself, but compliance or non-compliance may be an element in deciding the
issue of liability for breach of some other statutory or common law duty. For
example, the need to have regard to the Code is highly likely to be relevant
to a question of whether someone has acted or behaved in a way which is
contrary to the best interests of a person lacking capacity. Breach of the
Code might also be relevant to an action in negligence or to a criminal
prosecution.

2.17   This applies not only to those categories of people who have a duty to
have regard to the Code of Practice, but also to those who are not under a
duty. This is because informal carers still have an obligation to act in
accordance with the principles of MCA 2005 and in the best interests of a
person lacking capacity.[19] The provision therefore remains applicable where
any such person is facing civil or criminal proceedings and the court or
tribunal considers the Code to be relevant.

2.18   As no arrangements have been made to monitor compliance with the
Code of Practice,[20] it is impossible to gauge how it is being used in practice.
The Care Quality Commission (CQC)[21] has issued guidance on MCA 2005
for providers of registered care, treatment and support services indicating
the action the CQC may take if, during inspections and monitoring of health
and social care services, it finds that MCA 2005 and its Codes of Practice
are not being complied with.[22] Other professionals (such as lawyers) must
monitor their own compliance with the Code.

---

[18]   MCA 2005, s 42(5).
[19]   See Part 2 at **2.23**ff below.
[20]   By way of comparison, the Secretary of State for Health delegated to the Mental Health Act
Commission (which in April 2009 became part of the Care Quality Commission)
responsibility to monitor compliance with the Code of Practice to the Mental Health
Act 1983 and to advise Ministers of any changes to the Code which the Commission feels
might be appropriate.
[21]   Health and Social Care Act 2008, Part 1.
[22]   Care Quality Commission (2009) *Guidance for CQC staff and providers of registered care,
treatment and support services: The Mental Capacity Act 2005.* Available at
www.cqc.org.uk/guidanceforprofessionals/socialcare/careproviders/guidance.
cfm?widCall1=customWidgets.content_view_1&cit_id=34918

Creation

Consultation

2.19 MCA 2005 sets out the procedures required for the preparation or revision of the Code(s) and for parliamentary approval.[23] In particular, there must be formal consultation with anyone whom the Lord Chancellor considers appropriate before a Code is prepared or revised.[24] Since health and social care responsibilities are devolved in relation to Wales, the National Assembly for Wales must specifically be consulted and involved in the preparation of the Codes. During the parliamentary debates, the Government committed itself to wide consultation:[25]

> 'By the time the code is published it will have undergone a long process of formal and informal consultation. That is important; the more collaborative and informed the process, the better the code ... I also want to make sure the code speaks to all the different groups of people that it needs to address, and that they clearly understand it, and we can only do that if we get input from those people. This process will take many months and the draft that is finally laid before Parliament will have been informed and improved by both laymen and experts.'

It remains to be seen what arrangements are made to consult on the need for revision of the Code or how any revisions will be carried out.

Procedure for approval

2.20 A draft of the Code(s) must be laid before Parliament.[26] The Code takes effect after 40 days unless, within that time, either House has resolved not to approve it (known as the 'negative resolution' procedure).[27] Neither the Law Commission nor the Joint Committee on the Draft Mental Incapacity Bill suggested that any procedure, other than laying the Code before Parliament, was in fact necessary. However, the Government decided that some form of parliamentary scrutiny was desirable in view of the importance and scope of the statutory guidance provided in the Code(s). Parliament's Delegated Powers and Regulatory Reform Committee accepted that the negative resolution procedure was appropriate.[28]

2.21 Several amendments were proposed to the Bill, suggesting that closer parliamentary scrutiny was required, for example, through the affirmative resolution procedure requiring Parliament to debate and approve the Codes and any changes made to them. This was rejected by the Government as too cumbersome and unnecessary, not least because it would be very difficult to

---

[23] MCA 2005, s 43.
[24] MCA 2005, s 43(1).
[25] *Hansard*, HC Official Report, SC A (Draft Mental Incapacity Bill), 4 November 2004, col 375.
[26] MCA 2005, s 43(2). The draft Code was laid before both Houses of Parliament on 23 February 2007.
[27] The 40-day period is defined in MCA 2005, s 43(4)–(5).
[28] *Hansard*, HL Deb, vol 669, ser 5, col 220 (1 February 2005).

find the necessary parliamentary time. The Under Secretary of State for Constitutional Affairs, Baroness Ashton said:[29]

'So my issue with the amendment is not that I object to coming to your Lordship's House and debating the matter. The negative procedure enables the House to debate the matter if someone feels strongly that we have got it wrong. But I do not accept the idea that the code will have validity only when it goes through the affirmative process.'

Publication

2.22 The Lord Chancellor is allowed considerable flexibility in arranging for the Codes to be produced in the most appropriate format and for bringing the guidance to the attention of everyone who needs to know about it.[30] It has been suggested that separate Codes should be produced for different types of decisions or aimed at different decision-makers. The Mental Capacity Implementation Programme[31] (MCIP) produced a range of booklets to explain aspects of MCA 2005 from different perspectives and for people in different situations,[32] but these do not form part of the Code. Instead the Code suggests that professional organisations may themselves wish to produce specialist information and guidance for their members.[33]

2.23 The Government also made a commitment to publish accessible versions of the Codes in various formats, and in particular to make the Code available to people who may lack capacity.[34] The 'easyread' version of the Code issued for consultation in 2006 was criticised for being too lengthy and complex,[35] so efforts to produce a final version were abandoned. Instead, an 'easyread' booklet describing the main provisions of MCA 2005 has been produced.[36]

PART 2: PRINCIPLES AND CONCEPTS

The principles

Background

2.24 Much of the evidence submitted to the Joint Committee undertaking pre-legislative scrutiny of the Draft Mental Incapacity Bill was concerned with the principles said to underlie the provisions of the Bill. In particular,

---

29   *Hansard*, HL Deb, vol 670, ser 5, col 1533 (17 March 2005).
30   MCA 2005, s 43(3).
31   A joint government programme between the Ministry of Justice, the Office of the Public Guardian, the Department of Health and the Welsh Assembly Government established to implement the organisation, processes and procedures needed to launch MCA 2005.
32   MCIP *Mental Capacity Act: Making Decisions booklets* (OPG601-606). These are only available online at www.publicguardian.gov.uk/forms/additional-publicationsa-newsletters.htm.
33   Mental Capacity Act 2005: Code of Practice, at p 5
34   *Hansard*, HL Deb, vol 669, ser 5, cols 217–218 (1 February 2005).
35   Department for Constitutional Affairs *Mental Capacity Act Code of Practice: Response to Consultation* (September 2006), at p 68.
36   MCIP *The Mental Capacity Act – Easyread* (OPG605), available online at www.publicguardian.gov.uk/docs/making-decisions-opg605-1207.pdf.

commentators stressed the need for a clear statement of those principles to be set out on the face of the legislation.[37] Comparisons were made with s 1 of the Adults with Incapacity (Scotland) Act 2000 (AWI(S)A 2000), which sets out five general principles to govern all 'interventions' in the affairs of an adult taken under or in pursuance of AWI(S)A 2000.[38]

2.25 It is important to note that while some of the specific provisions of AWI(S)A 2000 and the draft Bill (and subsequently MCA 2005) are similar, there are significant differences in the underlying intentions and operation of both pieces of legislation as well as in the respective jurisdictions. Both are based on the recommendations of the respective Law Commissions, each of which adopted a different approach as a result of their separate consultation exercises. There are also differences in drafting styles.

2.26 The Joint Committee examined these differences in approach, and was persuaded that the statement of principles in AWI(S)A 2000 provided not only necessary protection for people with impaired capacity and a framework for ensuring that appropriate action is taken in individual cases, but also that the specified principles were extremely helpful in pointing the way to solutions in difficult or uncertain situations.[39] In conclusion, the Joint Committee commented:[40]

'... we were struck by the absence of a specific statement of principles on the face of the Bill as an initial point of reference, as had been done in the Scottish Act. Although the principles of the draft Bill may be discernible to lawyers from the opening clauses of the draft Bill, they may not be so obvious to the majority of non-legal persons who will have to deal with the Bill in practice.'

The statement of principles

2.27 The Joint Committee's strong recommendations[41] that a statement of principles be incorporated on the face of MCA 2005 were accepted by the Government. As a result, MCA 2005, s 1 now sets out five guiding principles designed to emphasise the underlying ethos of the Act, which is not only to protect people who lack capacity to make specific decisions, but also to maximise their ability to participate in decision-making. This section provides as follows:

'(1) The following principles apply for the purposes of this Act.
(2) A person must be assumed to have capacity unless it is established that he lacks capacity.
(3) A person is not to be treated as unable to make a decision unless all practicable steps to help him to do so have been taken without success.
(4) A person is not to be treated as unable to make a decision merely because he makes an unwise decision.

---

[37] See in particular the evidence submitted by the Making Decisions Alliance, Joint Committee Report, Vol II, HL 198-II, HC 1083-II (TSO, 2003), at Ev 85.
[38] AWI(S)A 2000, s 1.
[39] *Evidence for the Law Society of Scotland*, Joint Committee Report, Vol II, n 34 above, at Ev 2.
[40] Joint Committee Report, Vol I, n 5 above, at para 39.
[41] Joint Committee Report, Vol I, n 5 above, Recommendations 4 and 5.

(5)   An act done, or decision made, under this Act for or on behalf of a person who lacks capacity must be done, or made, in his best interests.

(6)   Before the act is done, or the decision is made, regard must be had to whether the purpose for which it is needed can be as effectively achieved in a way that is less restrictive of the person's rights and freedom of action.'

2.28 In his ministerial statement announcing the publication of the Mental Capacity Bill and its introduction into Parliament, David Lammy, the then Parliamentary Under Secretary of State for Constitutional Affairs said:[42]

'The overriding aim of the Bill is to improve the lives of vulnerable adults, their carers, families and professionals. It provides a statutory framework for decision making for people who lack capacity, making clear who can take decisions, in which situations and how they should go about this.

The Bill is based on clearly defined principles. Its starting point is that everyone has the right to make his or her own decisions, and must be assumed to have capacity to do so unless it is proved otherwise. No-one should be labelled as incapable – each decision should be considered individually and everyone should be helped to make or contribute to making decisions about their lives. The Bill sets out clear guidelines for, and limits on, other people's role in decision making.'

2.29 The statement of principles was warmly welcomed, not only by voluntary and professional organisations involved with people who lack capacity,[43] but also by MPs and Peers commenting on the principles during the parliamentary debates. In particular, during the Bill's second reading in the House of Lords, the Lord Bishop of Worcester said:[44]

'The result is not just a Bill with important protections for vulnerable people; Clause 1 contains a statement about a vision of humanity and how humanity is to be regarded. I hope children in generations to come will study that as one of the clearest and most eloquent expressions of what we think a human being is and how a human being is to be treated …

I believe that [the Bill] states what is fundamentally right. In the course of Committee we shall no doubt improve and tighten some of the wording, but we shall never take away the powerful and eloquent statement in Clause 1. That should underlie our treatment of one another in all circumstances and for all purposes.'

2.30 The following paragraphs consider the origins of each of the key principles and their operation in practice.

Presumption of capacity

2.31 Practitioners will have been familiar with the presumption, at common law, that an adult has full legal capacity unless it is established that he or she does not. If a question of capacity comes before a court, the burden of proof is generally on the person who is seeking to establish a lack of capacity and the matter is decided according to the usual civil standard, the balance of probabilities.

---

42   *Hansard*, HC Deb, vol 422 ser 6, col 67WS (18 June 2004).
43   See e g Making Decisions Alliance *Briefing for 2nd Reading debate in House of Commons* (11 October 2004), at pp 7–9.
44   *Hansard*, HL Deb, vol 668, ser 5, cols 53–54, 55 (10 January 2005).

Law Commission proposals

2.32 Taking account of responses to consultation and in keeping with its proposal to establish a single comprehensive jurisdiction, the Law Commission recommended that the new statutory provisions should expressly include and re-state both the common law principle of presumption of capacity and the relevant standard of proof.[45]

The legislation

2.33 The Joint Committee also supported the principle of presumption of capacity and recommended that this principle should be given primacy of place in the legislation:[46]

> 'This is because it better reflects the positive nature of the Bill's purpose and will increase confidence in the operation of this legislation.'

The presumption of capacity therefore appears in MCA 2005, s 1(2) as the first principle relating to the Act.

The Code of Practice

2.34 The Code of Practice stresses that the starting point for assessing someone's capacity to make a particular decision is always the assumption that the individual does have capacity:[47]

> 'Some people may need help to be able to make a decision or to communicate their decision. However, this does not necessarily mean that they cannot make that decision – unless there is proof that they do lack capacity to do so.'

2.35 Capacity must then be judged in relation to the particular decision at the time that decision needs to be made, and the presumption of capacity may only be rebutted if there is acceptable evidence that the person is incapable of making the decision in question. In relation to most decisions in connection with the person's care and treatment, a 'reasonable belief' that the person lacks capacity is sufficient, so long as reasonable steps have been taken to establish this.[48] Where the question of capacity is to be decided in proceedings before the Court of Protection, it has been held that the threshold for engagement of the court's powers (under MCA 2005, s 48) is lower than that of evidence sufficient in itself to rebut the presumption of capacity. The proper test in such circumstances is whether there is evidence giving good cause for concern that the person may lack capacity in some relevant regard.[49]

---

[45]   Law Com No 231, n 1 above, at para 3.2. In Scotland, the presumption of capacity is established under common law and is not re-stated in AWI(S)A 2000.

[46]   Joint Committee Report, Vol I, n 5 above, at paras 66–67.

[47]   Mental Capacity Act 2005: Code of Practice, at para 2.5.

[48]   MCA 2005, s 5(1). See **2.81–2.84**.

[49]   *Re F* [2009] EWHC B30 (Fam) at 44.

Practicable steps to help decision-making

2.36 The second of MCA 2005's key principles[50] clarifies that a person should not be treated as unable to make a decision until everything practicable has been done to help the person make his or her own decision. All practicable steps to enable decision-making must first be shown to be unsuccessful before the person can be assessed as lacking capacity.

Law Commission proposals

2.37 The Law Commission had originally proposed that it would only be necessary for 'reasonable attempts' to be made to understand a person who has difficulty in communicating a decision.[51] However, many respondents to the consultation paper made the point that the reference to 'reasonable attempts' was too weak and, for people who are not simply unconscious, 'strenuous steps must be taken to assist and facilitate communication before any finding of incapacity is made'.[52] Other respondents stressed the need for help and support to maximise a person's potential to make their own decisions, not just those with communication difficulties.

The legislation

2.38 This requirement has now been translated into MCA 2005's guiding principles in s 1(3). There are a number of ways in which people can be given help and support to enable them to make their own decisions, and these will vary depending on the decision to be made, the timescale for making the decision and the individual circumstances of the person wishing to make it. The practicable steps to be taken might include using specific communication strategies, providing information in an accessible form or treating an underlying medical condition to enable the person to regain capacity.

The Code of Practice

2.39 The main Code of Practice devotes a whole chapter to provide guidance and prompt consideration of a range of practicable steps which may assist decision-making, although the relevance of the various factors will vary depending on each particular situation.[53] As a minimum, the following steps should be considered:

(1) Try to minimise anxiety or stress by making the person feel at ease. Choose the best location where the client feels most comfortable and the time of day when the client is most alert.

---

[50]   MCA 2005, s 1(3).
[51]   *Mentally Incapacitated Adults and Decision-Making: A New Jurisdiction*, Law Com Consultation Paper No 128 (HMSO, 1993), at para 3.41.
[52]   Law Com No 231, n 1 above, at para 3.21.
[53]   Mental Capacity Act 2005: Code of Practice, chapter 3.

(2) If the person's capacity is likely to improve, wait until it has improved (unless the decision is urgent). If the cause of the incapacity can be treated, it may be possible to delay the decision until treatment has taken place.

(3) If there are communication or language problems, consider using a speech and language therapist or interpreter, or consult family members on the best methods of communication.

(4) Be aware of any cultural, ethnic or religious factors which may have a bearing on the person's way of thinking, behaviour or communication.

(5) Consider whether or not a friend or family member should be present to help reduce anxiety. But in some cases the presence of others may be intrusive.

Unwise decisions

The legislation

2.40   The third principle underlying the Act, set out in MCA 2005, s 1(4), confirms that a person should not be treated as lacking capacity merely because he or she makes a decision that others consider to be unwise. The intention here is to reflect the nature of human decision-making. Different people will make different decisions because they give greater weight to some factors than to others, taking account of their own values and preferences. Some people are keen to express their own individuality or may be more willing to take risks than others. The diagnostic threshold requiring evidence of some mental impairment or disturbance[54] will to some extent ensure that the capacity of those who are merely eccentric is not challenged unnecessarily. However, people who have mental disabilities which could affect their decision-making capacity should not be expected to make 'better' or 'wiser' decisions than anyone else. What matters is the ability to make a decision – not the outcome.

Law Commission proposals

2.41   Originally, the Law Commission had suggested that it was unnecessary to make such provision in MCA 2005. The right to make unwise decisions has been part of the common law since at least 1850.[55] In a consultation paper the Law Commission argued:[56]

> 'If it is feared that a function test along these lines is not strong enough, interference in the lives of the merely deviant or eccentric could be expressly excluded. New Zealand law (Protection of Personal and Property Rights Act 1988, s 1(3)) provides that the fact that the client "has made or is intending to make any decision that a person exercising ordinary prudence would not have made or would not make is not in itself sufficient ground for the exercise of its jurisdiction by the court." A similar

---

[54]   See **2.59–2.60**.
[55]   *Bird v Luckie* (1850) 8 Hare 301.
[56]   Law Com Consultation Paper No 128, n 47 above, at para 3.25.

safeguard is proposed by the Scottish Law Commission, with a stipulation that "the fact that the person has acted or intends to act in a way an ordinary prudent person would not should not by itself be evidence of lack of capacity" (Discussion Paper No 94, para 4.40). We, however, doubt the need for any such stipulation, in the light of the definition we have proposed, which clearly directs an assessor to the decision-making process, rather than its outcome. We invite views on this.'

2.42 The views received by the Law Commission were strongly in favour of explicit provision being made in the legislation:[57]

'Those we consulted, however, overwhelmingly urged upon us the importance of making such an express stipulation. This would recognise that the "outcome" approach to capacity has been rejected, while recognising that it is almost certainly in daily use. We recommend that a person should not be regarded as unable to make a decision by reason of mental disability merely because he or she makes a decision which would not be made by a person of ordinary prudence.'

Evidence before the Joint Committee

2.43 During pre-legislative scrutiny of the draft Bill, the Joint Committee received evidence from some witnesses expressing concern that a person with apparent capacity may be able to make repeatedly unwise decisions that put him or her at risk or result in preventable suffering or disadvantage.[58] Particular concerns were raised by Denzil Lush, then Master of the Court of Protection (now Senior Judge of the Court of Protection), who drew attention to the distinction between decision-specific capacity and more general ongoing incapacity. He gave examples of cases where people had made unwise decisions, each of which they appeared capable of making, but where they in fact lacked an overall awareness or understanding of the implications of those decisions.[59] Master Lush has explained his concerns as follows:[60]

'Even though they may be suffering from a condition that restricts their ability to govern their life and make independent choices, so long as they have the basic ability to consider the options and make choices, we must not intervene against their will. By intervening against their will, even for their own good, we show less respect for them than if we had allowed them to go ahead and make a mistake. This lack of inter-personal respect is potentially a more serious infringement of their rights and freedoms than allowing them to make an unwise decision.'

2.44 Some caution may therefore need to be applied in operating this principle in practice. Although as a general rule, capacity should be assessed in relation to each particular decision or specific issue, there may be circumstances where a person has an ongoing condition which affects his or her capacity to make a range of interrelated or sequential decisions. One decision on its own may make sense but the combination of decisions may

---

57   Law Com No 231, n 1 above, at para 3.19.
58   Joint Committee Report, Vol I, n 5 above, at paras 72, 78.
59   Joint Committee Report, Vol II, n 34 above, at Ev 184, Q495–Q496.
60   Denzil Lush 'The Mental Capacity Act and the new Court of Protection' (2005) *Journal of Mental Health Law* 12, at p 34.

raise doubts as to the person's capacity or at least prompt the need for a proper assessment. The Code of Practice suggests that further investigation may be needed if somebody:[61]

> '... repeatedly makes unwise decisions that put them at significant risk of harm or exploitation; or makes a particular unwise decision that is obviously irrational or out of character.'

But equally, an unwise decision should not, by itself, be sufficient to indicate lack of capacity.

Best interests

The Law Commission proposals

2.45 In seeking to establish a clear legal framework for making decisions with, or on behalf of people who lack capacity, the Law Commission proposed a single criterion to govern all decision-making:[62]

> 'Although decisions are to be taken by a variety of people with varying degrees of formality, a single criterion to govern any substitute decision can be established. Whatever the answer to the question "who decides?", there should only be one answer to the subsequent question "on what basis?".
>
> We explained in our overview paper that two criteria for making substitute decisions for another adult have been developed in the literature in this field: "best interests", on the one hand, and "substituted judgment", on the other. In Consultation Paper No 128 we argued that the two were not in fact mutually exclusive and we provisionally favoured a "best interests" criterion which would contain a strong element of "substituted judgment". It had been widely accepted by respondents to the overview paper that, where a person has never had capacity, there is no viable alternative to the "best interests" criterion. We were pleased to find that our arguments in favour of a "best interests" criterion found favour with almost all our respondents, with the Law Society emphasising that the criterion as defined in the consultation papers was in fact "an excellent compromise" between the best interests and substituted judgment approaches. We recommend that anything done for, and any decision made on behalf of a person without capacity should be done or made in the best interests of that person.'

2.46 It is notable that the Scottish Law Commission took a different approach in formulating proposals which led to AWI(S)A 2000:[63]

> 'We consider that "best interests" by itself is too vague and would require to be supplemented by further factors which have to be taken into account. We also consider that "best interests" does not give due weight to the views of the adult, particularly to wishes and feeling which he or she had expressed while capable of doing so. The concept of best interests was developed in the context of child law where a child's level of understanding may not be high and will usually have been lowered in the past. Incapable adults such as those who are mentally ill, head injured or suffering from dementia at the time when a decision has to be made in connection with them, will have possessed full mental powers before their present incapacity. We think it is wrong to equate such adults with children and for that reason would

---

[61]   Mental Capacity Act 2005: Code of Practice, at para 2.11.
[62]   Law Com No 231, n 1 above, at paras 3.24–3.25.
[63]   *Report on Incapable Adults*, Scot Law Com No 151 (Scottish Executive, 1995) para 2.50.

avoid extending child law concepts to them. Accordingly, the general principles [of AWI(S)A 2000] are framed without express reference to best interests.'

The Joint Committee's view

2.47   The Joint Committee on the draft Bill compared the two approaches and came down in favour of including the concept of best interests within the Act's key principles:[64]

> 'We heard evidence that the concept of best interests has been usefully developed by the courts and that its inclusion in statute would assist in promoting awareness and good practice, thereby ensuring some consistency in approach.'

The legislation

2.48   MCA 2005, s 1(5) establishes in statute the former common law principle that any act done, or any decision made, under MCA 2005 for or on behalf of a person who lacks capacity must be done, or made, in that person's best interests. This establishes 'best interests' as the single criterion to govern all decision making affecting people who lack capacity to make their own decisions. Further details on the meaning and determination of best interests are set out in the Act.[65]

Less restrictive alternative

The Law Commission proposals

2.49   The Law Commission originally proposed that the 'least restrictive alternative' principle should be included in the new legislation as one of the factors to be taken into account in determining the best interests of a person who lacks capacity.[66] The Commission considered that the principle had been developed over many years by experts in the field so as to become widely recognised and accepted.[67] The Draft Mental Incapacity Bill therefore included this principle in the proposed statutory checklist for best interests.[68]

The legislation

2.50   However, in response to the Joint Committee's recommendation[69] the Government agreed to incorporate in MCA 2005, s 1(6) the principle that, where possible, a less restrictive option should be chosen. This became the

---

[64]   Joint Committee Report, Vol I, n 5 above, at para 82.
[65]   MCA 2005, s 4, and see **2.118–2.141**.
[66]   Law Com No 231, n 1 above, at paras 3.28, 3.37.
[67]   For a discussion of the origins and development of the principle of least restrictive alternative, see Denzil Lush 'The Mental Capacity Act and the new Court of Protection', n 56 above, at pp 37–38.
[68]   Draft Mental Incapacity Bill, Cm 5859-I (TSO, 2003) cl 4(2)(e).
[69]   Joint Committee Report, Vol I, n 5 above, at para 44.

fifth key principle to guide the use of MCA 2005 generally, rather than just one factor in the best interests checklist.

2.51 Before any action is taken, or any decision is made under MCA 2005 in relation to a person lacking capacity, the person taking the action or making the decision must consider whether it is possible to act or decide in a way that is less restrictive of the person's rights and freedom of action. Where there is more than one course of action or a choice of decisions to be made, all possible options or alternatives should be explored (including whether there is a need for any action or decision at all) in order to consider which option would be less restrictive or intrusive. However, other options need only be considered so long as the desired purpose of the action or decision can still be achieved. In any event, the option chosen must be in the person's best interests, which may not in fact be the least restrictive.

The Scottish approach

2.52 This formulation differs from the principles set out in AWI(S)A 2000, which starts with a specific 'no intervention' provision[70] – that there shall be no intervention in the affairs of an adult unless the intervention will benefit the adult and that such benefit cannot reasonably be achieved in any other way. This is then followed by the 'least restrictive option' principle.[71] The Joint Committee considered this approach, but took the view that the less restrictive alternative principle would involve decision-makers in having to consider whether any intervention at all was in fact necessary.[72]

Application to the Court of Protection

2.53 Although the Court of Protection is subject to the principles set out in MCA 2005, s 1,[73] including best interests and the less restrictive alternative, specific provision is made to limit the scope of any intervention where court proceedings are contemplated. MCA 2005 requires the Court, in deciding whether to grant permission for an application to it, to consider the reasons for the application, the benefit to the person lacking capacity and whether the benefit can be achieved in any other way.[74] In addition, the Act imposes an obligation on the Court to make a single order in preference to appointing a deputy, and where the appointment of a deputy is considered necessary, that the powers conferred on the deputy should be as limited in scope and duration as possible.[75]

---

[70]   AWI(S)A 2000, s 1(2).
[71]   AWI(S)A 2000, s 1(3).
[72]   Joint Committee Report, Vol I, n 5 above, at para 96.
[73]   MCA 2005, s 16(3).
[74]   MCA 2005, s 50(3).
[75]   MCA 2005, s 16(4). See Chapter 4.

Defining lack of capacity

The functional approach

2.54 Before MCA 2005 came into effect, the lack of a clear statutory definition of capacity (or lack of capacity) caused confusion and difficulty for all concerned, not least for professionals called on to assess someone's decision-making capacity. There were also significant differences in approach between legal and medical or psychological concepts of capacity.[76] Case-law offered a number of tests of capacity depending on the type of decision in issue.[77] The Law Commission recommended that, in order to provide certainty and clarity in using the new jurisdiction, a single statutory definition of capacity should be adopted.[78] Therefore, having set out the key principles governing its operation, MCA 2005 goes on to define the people affected by its provisions.

2.55 MCA 2005, s 2 sets out the definition of a person who lacks capacity. MCA 2005, s 3 sets out the test for assessing whether a person is unable to make a decision and therefore lacks capacity. By applying these together, MCA 2005 adopts a functional approach to defining capacity, requiring capacity to be assessed in relation to each particular decision at the time the decision needs to be made, and not the person's ability to make decisions generally. This means that individuals should not be labelled 'incapable' simply on the basis that they have been diagnosed with a particular condition, or because of any preconceived ideas or assumptions about their abilities due, for example, to their age, appearance or behaviour. Rather, it must be shown that they lack capacity for each specific decision, or type of decision, at the time the particular decision needs to be made. The following paragraphs consider in turn each element of the Act's definition and test of capacity.

People who lack capacity

2.56 MCA 2005, s 2(1) sets out the definition of a person who lacks capacity as follows:

> 'For the purposes of this Act, a person lacks capacity in relation to a matter if at the material time he is unable to make a decision for himself in relation to the matter because of an impairment of, or a disturbance in the functioning of, the mind or brain.'

2.57 Capacity is therefore both decision-specific and time-specific. The inability to make the particular decision in question must be *because of* 'an impairment of, or a disturbance in the functioning of, the mind or brain' (ie a mental disability or disorder). It does not matter whether the

---

[76] The Law Society and British Medical Association attempted to address this problem by providing much needed guidance in *Assessment of Mental Capacity: Guidance for Doctors and Lawyers* (BMA, 1995; BMJ Books, 2nd edn, 2004; Law Society Publishing, 3rd edn, 2010).

[77] See **2.79–2.80**.

[78] Law Com No 231, n 1 above, at para 3.7.

impairment or disturbance is permanent or temporary.[79] A person can lack capacity to make a decision even if the loss of capacity is partial or temporary or if his or her capacity fluctuates. In particular, a person may lack capacity in relation to one matter but not in relation to others.

The two-stage test of capacity

2.58 In order to decide whether an individual has capacity to make a particular decision, a two-stage procedure must be applied:

(1) it must be established that there is an impairment of, or disturbance in the functioning of, the person's mind or brain; and

(2) it must be established that the impairment or disturbance is sufficient to render the person unable to make that particular decision at the relevant time.

2.59 If there is no indication of impairment or disturbance, the individual should be presumed to have capacity and his or her ability to make decisions should not be questioned.

A diagnostic threshold

2.60 During its consultation processes, the Law Commission considered the finely balanced arguments for and against having a diagnostic threshold, requiring a 'mental disability' to be established before someone is deemed to lack capacity.[80] The Commission concluded that a diagnostic 'hurdle' would serve a useful gate-keeping function, to ensure that decision-making rights are not taken over prematurely or unnecessarily and to make the test of capacity stringent enough *not* to catch large numbers of people who make unusual or unwise decisions. It was felt that the protection offered by a diagnostic threshold outweighs any risk of prejudice or stigma affecting those who need help with decision-making.[81]

2.61 Instead of using the term 'mental disability', MCA 2005 refers to 'an impairment of, or a disturbance in the functioning of, the mind or brain'. This covers a wide range of conditions. For example, people taken to casualty requiring treatment for a physical disorder who are incapacitated in the short term through alcohol or drug misuse, delirium or following head injury may need urgent attention which cannot wait until their capacity has been restored. People in such situations are entitled to the protections and safeguards offered by the Act in the same way as those found to lack the capacity to make specific financial, health or welfare decisions as a result, for example, of mental illness, dementia, learning disabilities or the long-term effects of brain damage.

PART I

---

[79] MCA 2005, s 2(2).
[80] The arguments are set out in Law Com Consultation Paper No 128, n 47 above, at paras 3.10–3.14.
[81] Law Com No 231, n 1 above, at para 3.8.

Principle of 'equal consideration'

2.62 During the Bill's Report stage in the House of Lords, an amendment was passed to make it clear that lack of capacity cannot be established merely by reference to a person's age or appearance, or any condition or aspect of his or her behaviour which might lead others to make unjustified assumptions about the person's capacity.[82] This amendment was originally proposed by the Making Decisions Alliance[83] as a 'principle of non-discrimination and equal consideration' which the Alliance sought to have included in MCA 2005's statement of principles, in order to ensure that people with impaired capacity are treated no less favourably than people with capacity:[84]

> 'Our concerns stem from evidence, anecdotal and otherwise, that prejudices and attitudes about the quality of life of a person with serious learning disabilities, mental health problem or a head injury or other condition that leads to loss of capacity can get in the way of supporting that person and how they are, what they want and what they need.'

2.63 While the Government was sympathetic to these concerns, the drafting of a broad 'equal consideration' principle proved unworkable. Instead the Government put forward two amendments, one relating to the definition of capacity and the second concerning best interests determinations[85] in order to:[86]

> '... reinforce the belief, shared across the House, that no-one should be assumed to lack capacity, excluded from decision-making, discriminated against or given substandard care and treatment simply, for example, as a result of disability.'

2.64 The amendment therefore ensures that individuals should not be labelled 'incapable' because of their age or appearance, or because of any preconceived ideas or prejudicial assumptions about their abilities due to their particular condition or behaviour. The reference to 'condition' covers a range of factors, including both mental or physical disabilities, age-related illness and temporary conditions such as drunkenness. 'Appearance' is also deliberately broad, covering all aspects of physical appearance, visible medical problems or disfiguring scars, disabilities, skin colour, religious dress or simply being unkempt or dishevelled. 'Behaviour' relates to ways of behaving that might seem unusual or odd to others, such as failing to make eye contact, talking to oneself or laughing inappropriately.

Qualifying age

2.65 It has always been the intention that the new jurisdiction should apply only to *adults* who lack capacity, leaving disputes about the care and welfare of children and young people to be resolved under the Children Act 1989.

---

[82]   MCA 2005, s 2(3)
[83]   A coalition of around 40 charities that campaigned for MCA 2005.
[84]   Making Decisions Alliance *House of Lords Briefing*, Second Reading (10 January 2005), at p 3.
[85]   See **2.120–2.121**.
[86]   *Hansard*, HL Deb, vol 670, ser 5, col 1318 (15 March 2005).

However, the Law Commission commented that a number of the statutory provisions in the Children Act 1989 do not apply to 16–18-year-olds or only in 'exceptional' circumstances. The Law Commission concluded that:[87]

> 'If continuing substitute decision-making arrangements are needed for someone aged 16 or 17, this is likely to be because the young person lacks mental capacity and not because he or she is under the age of legal majority.'

2.66 It followed that the provisions of the new jurisdiction, rather than the Children Act 1989, should apply in those circumstances for young people aged 16 or 17, and not just where there is no one available to exercise parental responsibility. For example, there may be circumstances where it is in the young person's best interests for someone other than a person with parental responsibility to be appointed as deputy to make financial or property decisions. Or it may be appropriate for the Court of Protection to make personal decisions, for example, where the young person should live, or medical treatment decisions concerning a young person lacking capacity where it is considered that those with parental responsibility are not acting in the young person's best interests. It was suggested that the resultant overlap would pose no great problems in practice.

2.67 MCA 2005, s 2(5) therefore makes it clear that the powers exercisable under MCA 2005 apply in general only to people lacking capacity who are aged 16 years or over. However, as was the case under the previous law, MCA 2005's powers to deal with property and financial affairs might be exercised in relation to a child whose disabilities will cause a lack of capacity to manage those affairs to continue into adulthood.[88]

2.68 In cases where legal proceedings are required to resolve disputes or make legally effective arrangements for someone aged 16 or 17, the Law Commission pointed out that it would not make sense to require two sets of legal proceedings to be conducted within a short period of time where the problems arising from the young person's incapacity are likely to continue after the age of 18. MCA 2005, therefore, makes provision for transfer from the Court of Protection to the family courts, and vice versa.[89] The choice of court will depend on what is 'just and convenient' in the particular circumstances of the case.[90] In particular, in considering whether to transfer a case from a court having jurisdiction under the Children Act 1989 to the Court of Protection, the court must consider:[91]

> 'The extent to which any order made as respects a person who lacks capacity is likely to continue to have effect when that person reaches 18.'

---

[87]   Law Com No 231, n 1 above, at para 2.52.
[88]   MCA 2005, ss 2(6) and 18(3).
[89]   MCA 2005, s 21.
[90]   Mental Capacity Act 2005 (Transfer of Proceedings) Order 2007, SI 2007/1899, arts 2(2) and 3(2).
[91]   Ibid, art 3(3)(c).

The different concepts of 'competence' in relation to children under 16 years and 'capacity' applying to young people aged 16-17 are considered further below.[92]

Inability to make decisions

2.69 The second stage of the test of capacity[93] requires it to be shown that an impairment of, or disturbance in the functioning of, the person's mind or brain is sufficient to make the person unable to make the decision in question. The impairment or disturbance must be shown to cause the person to be unable to make that decision at the relevant time. MCA 2005, s 3 sets out the test for assessing whether a person is unable to make a decision for him or herself. This is a 'functional' test, focusing on the personal ability of the individual concerned to make a particular decision and the processes followed by the person in arriving at the decision – not on the outcome. A person is unable to make a decision if he or she is unable:[94]

'(a) to understand the information relevant to the decision,
(b) to retain that information,
(c) to use or weigh that information as part of the process of making the decision, or
(d) to communicate his decision (whether by talking, using sign language or any other means).'

2.70 If someone cannot undertake one of the first three aspects of the decision-making process, then he or she is unable to make the decision. The fourth criterion in MCA 2005, s 3(1)(d) relates only to a residual category of people who are totally unable to communicate.[95]

Understand the information relevant to the decision

2.71 Information relevant to the decision includes the particular nature of the decision in question, the purpose for which the decision is needed and the likely effects of making the decision. It must also include the reasonably foreseeable consequences of deciding one way or another or of making no decision at all.[96]

2.72 Following lobbying by the Making Decisions Alliance, amendments were made to the Bill in both Houses of Parliament to require communication support, as is *appropriate* to meet individual needs, to be provided to help people with impaired capacity to express their views and, wherever possible, to make their own decisions.[97] As a result, MCA 2005[98]

---

92 See **2.85–2.88**.
93 See **2.57**.
94 MCA 2005, s 3(1).
95 See **2.77–2.78**.
96 MCA 2005, s 3(4).
97 See e g *Re AK (Medical Treatment: Consent)* [2001] 1 FLR 129, where strenuous efforts were made to communicate with someone able only to move one eyelid.
98 MCA 2005, s 3(2).

requires every effort to be made to provide an explanation of information relevant to the decision in question in a way that is appropriate to the circumstances of the person concerned and using the most effective means of communication (such as simple language, visual aids or any other means) to assist their understanding. Cursory or inadequate explanations are not acceptable unless the situation is urgent.

2.73 The threshold of understanding is quite low, requiring an ability to understand an explanation of what is proposed and any possible consequences given in broad terms and simple language – it is not always necessary to understand all the details. This approach is consistent with the desire to enable people to take as many decisions as possible for themselves, while also ensuring that the more serious the consequences of any decision, the greater the degree of understanding required.

2.74 However, identifying what is the specific decision in question, and the information relevant to the decision, is not always straightforward. For example, in *Re S: D v R (Deputy of S) and S* [2010] EWHC 2405 (COP),[99] in the context of assessing whether S had capacity to continue litigation commenced in his name by his property and affairs deputy, his daughter, to set aside gifts he had made to Mrs D, Mr Justice Henderson commented[100]:

> 'At a superficial level, the nature of the decision may be simply stated… it is whether to discontinue, or to continue to prosecute, the Chancery proceedings. But that decision cannot be taken, it seems to me, without at least a basic understanding of the nature of the claim, of the legal issues involved, and of the circumstances which have given rise to the claim. It would be an over-simplification to say that the claim is just a claim to set aside or reverse the gifts which Mr S made to Mrs D, because in the ordinary way a gift is irrevocable once it has been made and perfected by delivery or transfer of the relevant assets. If a gift is to be set aside or recovered, some vitiating factor such as fraud, misrepresentation or undue influence has to be established; and if the donor is to decide whether or not to pursue a claim, he needs to understand, at least in general terms, the nature of the vitiating factor upon which he may be able to rely, and to weigh up the arguments for and against pursuing the claim. Provided that the donor is equipped with this information, and provided that he understands it and takes it into account in reaching his decision, it will not matter if his decision is an imprudent one, or one which would fail to satisfy the 'best interests' test in section 4. But if the donor is unable to assimilate, retain and evaluate the relevant information, he lacks the capacity to make the decision, however clearly he may articulate it.'

In this case, the decision was held to be "a complex one which requires a good deal of detailed information and self-awareness".[101]

2.75 Similarly, it may not always be easy to identify the 'reasonably foreseeable consequences' of deciding one way or another or making no decision at all, particularly in relation to a personal welfare decision. In *A Local Authority v Mrs A* [2010] EWHC 1549, concerning the capacity of a woman to make decisions about contraceptive treatment, the local authority argued that 'the reasonably foreseeable consequences' included the ability to

---

[99]   For case summary, see Part IX of this work.
[100]   *Re S: D v R (Deputy of S) and S* [2010] EWHC 2405 (COP) at para 43.
[101]   Ibid, at para 144.

understand and envisage what would actually be involved in caring for and committing to a child, but this argument was rejected by the court:[102]

> 'Although in theory the 'reasonably foreseeable consequences' of not taking contraception involve possible conception, a birth and the parenting of a child, there should be some limit in practice on what needs to be envisaged, if only for public policy reasons. I accept the submission that it is unrealistic to require consideration of a woman's ability to foresee the realities of parenthood, or to expect her to be able to envisage the fact-specific demands of caring for a particular child not yet conceived (let alone born) with unpredictable levels of third-party support. I do not think such matters *are* reasonably foreseeable: or, to borrow an expression from elsewhere, I think they are too remote from the medical issue of contraception. To apply the wider test would be to 'set the bar too high' and would risk a move away from personal autonomy in the direction of social engineering. Further, if one were to admit of a requirement to be able to foresee things beyond a child's birth, then drawing a line on into the child's life would be nigh impossible.'

However, in financial trasactions dealing with significant amounts of money, the reasonably foreseeable consequences may be more clearly identified.[103]

Retain the information

2.76 The ability to retain information for a short period only should not automatically disqualify the person from making the decision.[104] The person must be able to retain the information for long enough to make a choice or take an effective decision and the length of time will therefore depend on what is necessary for the decision in question. The Code of Practice suggests that items such as notebooks, photographs, videos and voice recorders could be used to assist retention and recording of information.[105]

2.77 It has been suggested that MCA 2005's failure to define for how long the information must be retained may cause confusion for those seeking to assess a person's capacity, particularly, for example, a person suffering from dementia or other condition affecting his or her short-term memory. However, as yet, no applications have been made to the Court of Protection to provide clarification on this point.

Use or weigh the information

2.78 Prior to MCA 2005 coming into effect, a number of cases came before the courts where the person concerned had the ability to understand information but where the effects of a mental health problem or disability prevented him or her from using that information in the decision-making process.[106] The Law Commission gave examples of certain compulsive conditions (such as anorexia) which cause people, who are quite able to

---

[102] *A Local Authority v Mrs A* [2010] EWHC 1549 at para 63.
[103] See for example, *Gorjat v Gorjat* [2010] EWHC 1537 (Ch)
[104] MCA 2005, s 3(3).
[105] Mental Capacity Act 2005: Code of Practice, at para 4.20.
[106] See e g *Re MB* [1997] 2 FLR 426; *R v Collins and Ashworth Hospital Authority ex parte Brady* [2001] 58 BMLR 173.

absorb information, to make decisions which are inevitable (e g not to eat) regardless of the information and their understanding of it. To reflect these concerns, the Law Commission originally proposed that in order to have capacity, a person must be able to make a 'true choice'.[107] However, in its final report, the Commission recognised that:[108]

> 'Common to all these cases is the fact that the person's eventual decision is divorced from his or her ability to understand the relevant information. Emphasising that the person must be able to use the information which he or she has successfully understood in the decision-making process deflects the complications of asking whether a person needs to "appreciate" information as well as understand it. A decision based on a compulsion, the overpowering will of a third party or any other inability to act on relevant information as a result of mental disability is not a decision made by a person with decision-making capacity.'

2.79   The courts have further defined the process as the ability to weigh all relevant information in the balance as part of the process of making a decision and then to use the information in order to arrive at a decision. MCA 2005, s 3(1)(c) translates this former common law provision into statute.

2.80   Further guidance on applying this element of the capacity test is given in *The PCT v P, AH & The Local Authority* [2009] EW Misc 10 (EWCOP) where Mr Justice Hedley described it as 'the capacity actually to engage in the decision-making process itself and to be able to see the various parts of the argument and to relate the one to another'.[109] In assessing P's capacity to make a range of decisions concerning his care, residence and medical treatment, the judge concluded that, in addition to his disabilities, P's relationship with his adoptive mother hindered his ability to 'use or weigh' information which conflicted in any way with his mother's views:[110]

> 'The reasons that I am persuaded that he lacks that capacity are the cumulative force of the following: (a) his epilepsy and its impact on his functioning, (b) his learning disability which is at the lower end of mild, (c) the enmeshed relationship that he has with AH [his adoptive mother] which severely restricts his perspective in terms of being able to think about his future, (d) his inability, frequently articulated by him to those who have interviewed him, to visualise any prospect of having a different view to his mother on any subject that matters and his inability to understand what the other aspects of the argument may be in relation to his expressed wishes simply to return and live undisturbed with his mother. Finally, I have regard to that which has emerged more recently ... namely some disparity between his words on the one hand and his actions and attitudes in his dealings with staff on the other ...
>
> No one of those matters by themselves would justify a finding of disability, but the cumulative effect of all of them is to satisfy me beyond a preadventure that at the present time he wants capacity to deal with the matters to which I have related.'

[107]   Law Com Consultation Paper No 128, n 47 above, at paras 3.31–3.35.
[108]   Law Com No 231, n 1 above, at para 3.17.
[109]   *The PCT v P, AH & The Local Authority* [2009] EW Misc 10 (COP) at para 35
[110]   Ibid, at paras 37–38.

Unable to communicate

2.81 The final criterion which would indicate an inability to make a decision is the fact that the person is *unable to communicate the decision* by any possible means.[111] There are obvious situations, such as unconsciousness, which would result in a person being unable to communicate a decision. Other types of cases may include people in a persistent vegetative state or with the condition sometimes known as 'locked-in syndrome'. The Law Commission intended this to be very much a residual category affecting a minority of people:[112]

> 'This test will have no relevance if the person is known to be incapable of deciding (even if also unable to communicate) but will be available if the assessor does not know, one way or the other, whether the person is capable of deciding or not.'

2.82 Strenuous efforts must first be made to assist and facilitate communication before any finding of incapacity is made. Communication by simple muscle movements, such as blinking an eye or squeezing a hand, to indicate 'yes' or 'no', can be sufficient to indicate that the person has the ability to communicate and therefore may have capacity.[113] The Code of Practice recommends that in cases of this sort, the involvement of speech and language therapists or professionals with specialist skills in verbal and non-verbal communication may be required to assist in the assessment.[114]

Common law tests of capacity

2.83 The definition and two-stage test of capacity set out in MCA 2005 are expressed to apply 'for the purposes of this Act'[115] and MCA 2005, Sch 6 makes consequential amendments to existing statutes, inserting the new statutory definition. There are also several *common law* tests of capacity set out in case-law before MCA 2005 came into effect.[116] Examples given in the Code of Practice are as follows:

- capacity to make a will;[117]
- capacity to enter into marriage;[118]
- capacity to make a gift;[119]
- contractual capacity;[120] and
- capacity to litigate.[121]

---

[111] MCA 2005, s 3(1)(d).
[112] Law Com No 231, n 1 above, at para 3.20.
[113] *Re AK (Adult Patient) (Medical Treatment: Consent)* [2001] 2 FCR 35, [2001] 1 FLR 129.
[114] Mental Capacity Act 2005: Code of Practice, at para 4.24.
[115] MCA 2005, s 2(1).
[116] Details of the relevant common law tests of capacity can be found in BMA/Law Society *Assessment of Mental Capacity: Guidance for Doctors and Lawyers* (BMA, 1995; BMJ Books, 2nd edn, 2004; Law Society Publishing, 3rd edn, 2010).
[117] *Banks v Goodfellow* (1870) LR 5 QB 549.
[118] *Sheffield City Council v E & S* [2005] 1 FLR 965.
[119] *Re Beaney (deceased)* [1978] 2 All ER 595.
[120] *Boughton v Knight* (1873) LR 3 PD 64.
[121] *Masterman-Lister v Brutton & Co and Jewell & Home Counties Dairies* [2003] 3 All ER 162, CA.

2.84 MCA 2005's definition of capacity is intended to build on, rather than contradict, the terms of pre-existing common law tests.[122] The Code of Practice suggests that, as cases come before the Court, judges may adopt the statutory definition if they see fit and use it to develop common law rules in particular cases.[123] For example, the High Court has confirmed that the correct approach is to apply the MCA test for capacity in deciding whether a person has capacity to conduct litigation in proceedings to which the Civil Procedure Rules apply,[124] since those Rules have subsequently been amended to conform with changes brought about by MCA 2005. In relation to testamentary capacity, the Court has confirmed that in respect of wills made before MCA 2005 came into effect on October 2007, the question of capacity should be based on the common law test, without reference to the Act, while assessment of testamentary capacity subsequent to October 2007 should have regard to the MCA test of capacity, informed by the common law test.[125] However, it remains uncertain the extent to which the statutory test of capacity set out in MCA 2005 will replace common law tests, particularly in areas beyond the scope of the Act.[126]

PART I

Reasonable belief of lack of capacity

2.85 In most day-to-day decisions or actions involved in caring for someone, it will not be appropriate or necessary to carry out a formal assessment of the person's capacity. Indeed many informal carers or others exercising powers under MCA 2005 will not be equipped to carry out a detailed assessment. Rather, it is sufficient that they 'reasonably believe' that the person lacks capacity to make the decision or consent to the action in question,[127] but they must be able to point to objective reasons to justify why they hold that belief.

2.86 This is based on the Law Commission's explanation that:[128]

'It would be out of step with our aims of policy, and with the views of the vast majority of the respondents to our overview paper, to have any general system of certifying people as "incapacitated" and then identifying a substitute decision-maker for them, regardless of whether there is any real need for one. In the absence of certifications or authorisations, persons acting informally can only be expected to have reasonable grounds to believe that (1) the other person lacks capacity in relation to the matter in hand and (2) they are acting in the best interests of that person.'

---

[122] Law Com No 231, n 1 above, at para 3.23.
[123] Mental Capacity Act 2005: Code of Practice at para 4.33
[124] See *Saulle v Nouvet* [2007] EWHC 2902 (QB), [2008] WTLR 729 for an early decision under the new jurisdiction on capacity to litigate in regard to a brain-injured claimant. For case summary, see Part IX of this work.
[125] *Scammell and Scammell v Farmer* [2008] EWHC 1100 (Ch), [2008] WTLR 1261 at 24–29. In this case, Mr Stephen Smith QC held that in most respects, the MCA test of capacity is a 'modern restatement' of the test in *Banks v Goodfellow*.
[126] See eg *MM (An Adult), Re; Local Authority X v MM and KM* [2007] EWHC 2003 (Fam), [2008] 3 FCR 788.
[127] MCA 2005, ss 4(8) and 5(1).
[128] Law Com No 231, n 1 above, at para 4.5.

2.87 Reasonable steps must be taken to establish the person's lack of capacity to make a particular decision. Responses to the consultation on the draft Code of Practice requested additional guidance on what might be considered 'reasonable'. The Code confirms that:[129]

'... the steps that are accepted as "reasonable" will depend on individual circumstances and the urgency of the decision. Professionals who are qualified in their particular field are normally expected to undertake a fuller assessment, reflecting their higher degree of knowledge and experience, than family members or other carers who have no formal qualifications.'

2.88 It goes on to suggest a number of steps that may be helpful in establishing a 'reasonable belief' of lack of capacity:

'• Start by assuming the person has capacity to make the specific decision. Is there anything to prove otherwise?
• Does the person have a previous diagnosis of disability or mental disorder? Does that condition now affect their capacity to make this decision? If there has been no previous diagnosis, it may be best to get a medical opinion.
• Make every effort to communicate with the person to explain what is happening.
• Make every effort to try to help the person make the decision in question.
• See if there is a way to explain or present information about the decision in a way that makes it easier to understand. If the person has a choice, do they have information about all the options?
• Can the decision be delayed to take time to help the person make the decision, or to give the person time to regain the capacity to make the decision for themselves?
• Does the person understand what decision they need to make and why they need to make it?
• Can they understand information about the decision? Can they retain it, use it and weigh it to make the decision?
• Be aware that the fact that a person agrees with you or assents to what is proposed does not necessarily mean that they have capacity to make the decision.'

Competence and capacity: children and young people

Children under 16: 'Gillick competence'

2.89 MCA 2005 generally applies only to people aged 16 years and over.[130] Where welfare or healthcare decisions are required of a child aged under 16, any disputes may be resolved by the family courts under the Children Act 1989. In such cases, the common law test of *Gillick* competence applies: whether the child has sufficient maturity and intelligence to understand the nature and implications of the proposed treatment.[131] *Gillick* competence is a developmental concept and will not be lost or acquired on a day-to-day or week-by-week basis.[132] The

---

[129] Mental Capacity Act 2005: Code of Practice, at para 4.45.
[130] See **2.64–2.67**.
[131] *Gillick v West Norfolk and Wisbech Area Health Authority* [1986] 1 AC 112.
[132] *Re R (A Minor) (Wardship: Consent to medical treatment)* [1992] 1 FLR 190 at 200.

understanding required for different treatments or decisions may vary, depending on the nature of the decision in question.

Young people aged 16 or 17: Capacity or competence?

2.90 The main provisions of MCA 2005 apply to adults, which includes young people aged 16 years or over. The starting point for assessing whether a young person aged 16 or 17 has capacity to make a specific decision is therefore the test of capacity in MCA 2005, having regard to the MCA principles. However, there may be circumstances where 16-17 year olds who are unable to make a decision for themselves will not be covered by the provisions of MCA 2005. A young person may be unable to make a decision either:

- because of an impairment of, or disturbance in the functioning of, their mind or brain (they lack capacity within the meaning of the MCA); or
- for reasons of immaturity (due to the person's age, they are unable to make the decision in question).

2.91 Young people aged 16 and 17 are presumed to have capacity in relation to any surgical, dental or medical treatment.[133] If a young person suffers from an impairment of, or a disturbance in the functioning of, the mind or brain which may affect their ability to make a particular healthcare decision, an assessment of capacity under MCA 2005 will be required, notwithstanding the presumption that the young person has capacity. However, if there is no such impairment or disturbance, MCA 2005 will not apply if it can be established that the young person's inability to make a decision is because:

- they do not have the maturity to understand fully what is involved in making the decision (ie they lack *Gillick* competence); or
- the lack of maturity means that they feel unable to make the decision for themselves (for example, where particularly complex or risky treatment is proposed, they may be overwhelmed by the implications of the decision).[134]

2.92 In cases where MCA 2005 applies, decisions about a young person's care or treatment may be made under the provisions of the MCA in the person's best interests (see below and Chapter 5), without the need to obtain parental consent, although those with parental responsibility for the young person should generally be consulted.[135]

---

[133] Family Law Reform Act 1969, s 8(1).
[134] Mental Capacity Act 2005: Code of Practice, at para 12.13. Specific guidance on assessing the ability of children and young people to make treatment decisions is given in National Institute for Mental Health in England (2009) *The Legal Aspects of the Care and Treatment of Children and Young People with Mental Disorder: A guide for professionals* (National Mental Health Development Unit), Chapter 2 (available online at www.nmhdu.org.uk).
[135] MCA 2005, s 4(7)(b).

The assessment of capacity

Background

2.93   By making a judgment on an individual's decision-making capacity, anyone with authority over that person can deprive him or her of civil rights and liberties enjoyed by most adults and now safeguarded by the Human Rights Act 1998. Alternatively, such a judgment could permit a person lacking capacity to do something, or carry on doing something, whereby serious prejudice could result, either putting that person at risk or causing harm or inconvenience to others. It is therefore essential that anyone called upon to assess another person's capacity must understand what they are being asked to judge and be prepared to justify their findings.

2.94   The Joint Committee on the Draft Mental Incapacity Bill received evidence from a number of organisations expressing concern that the Bill made no specific provisions for the assessment of capacity, despite the far-reaching implications of the outcome of assessment.[136] These concerns were discussed during the Bill's Committee stage in the House of Lords, when Lord Carter put forward a probing amendment, seeking to impose a statutory duty on public bodies to carry out a formal assessment of a person's capacity where it may be relevant in the context of any assessment of needs or the provision of services to meet those needs. The Minister responded:[137]

> 'This is important – I recognise that – but I am not sure that is something I want to see covered in primary legislation. The purpose of the Bill is to set out the broad principles and absolutes ... to be followed, but we cannot lay out on the face of the Bill the practical detail of how professionals should operate ... The details of the assessment procedure must be a matter for professional judgement in relation to the case, with support from the code of practice in training and guidance.'

2.95   The following sections draw on the guidance given in the Code of Practice and on the professional guidance for doctors and lawyers on assessment of mental capacity issued jointly by the BMA and the Law Society.[138]

When should capacity be assessed?

2.96   According to the principles of MCA 2005, the starting point should be the presumption of capacity. Doubts as to a person's capacity may arise for a number of reasons, either because of the person's behaviour or circumstances, or through concerns raised by someone else, but any concerns must be considered specifically in relation to the particular decision which needs to be made. Where doubts are raised about a person's decision-making abilities, the following questions should first be considered:

---

[136]   Joint Committee Report, Vol I, n 5 above, at para 242.
[137]   *Hansard*, HL Deb, vol 668, ser 5, col 1230 (25 January 2005).
[138]   BMA/Law Society *Assessment of Mental Capacity: Guidance for Doctors and Lawyers* (BMA, 1995; BMJ Books, 2nd edn, 2004; Law Society Publishing, 3rd edn, 2010).

(1) Does the person have all the relevant information needed to make the decision in question? If there is a choice, has information been given on any alternatives?

(2) Could the information be explained or presented in a way that is easier for the person to understand?

(3) Are there particular times of day when the person's understanding is better, or particular locations where they may feel more at ease? Can the decision be put off until the circumstances are right for the person concerned?

(4) Can anyone else help or support the person to make a choice or express a view, such as an advocate or someone to assist communication?

2.97 If all these steps have been taken without success in helping the person make a decision, an assessment of their capacity to make the decision in question should be made.

Who should assess capacity?

2.98 In keeping with the functional approach, the question of who assesses an individual's capacity will depend on the particular decision to be made, but will in general be the person who needs the decision to be made. For most day-to-day decisions in connection with the person's care or treatment, the carer most directly involved with the person at the time the decision has to be made assesses his or her capacity to make the decision in question. Carers acting informally are not expected to be experts in assessing capacity, but they must be able to show they have reasonable grounds for believing that the person lacks capacity to make the decision or do the act in question, at that particular time.[139] Formal processes are rarely required unless the assessment is challenged, for example, by the person whose capacity is being assessed or by another family member. In such circumstances, the assessor must be able to point to objective reasons as to why they believe the person lacks capacity to make the decision in question.

2.99 Where consent to medical treatment or examination is required, the doctor or healthcare professional proposing the treatment must decide whether the patient has capacity to consent and should record the assessment process and findings in the person's medical notes. Where a legal transaction is involved, such as making a will or a power of attorney, the solicitor handling the transaction will need to assess whether the client has capacity to give instructions – this requires the solicitor to assess whether the client has the required capacity to satisfy the relevant legal test, perhaps assisted by an opinion from a doctor. The position is less clear where the decision relates to the provision of social care services – the

---

[139]   MCA 2005, ss 4(8) and 5(1). See **2.81–2.84**.

assessment of capacity may be carried out by a social worker or care manager, depending on the particular circumstances. The Code of Practice advises:[140]

> 'There are also times when a joint decision might be made by a number of people. For example, when a care plan for a person who lacks capacity to make relevant decisions is being put together, different healthcare or social care staff might be involved in making decisions or recommendations about the person's care package. Sometimes these decisions will be made by a team of healthcare or social care staff as a whole. At other times, the decision will be made by a specific individual within the team.'

2.100   The more serious the decision, the more formal the assessment of capacity may need to be, but whoever assesses capacity must be prepared to justify their findings. Ultimately, if a person's capacity to do something is disputed, it is a question for the Court to decide. Cases referred to the Court of Protection will require formal evidence of the assessment of capacity, either to enable the Court to make a declaration as to whether the person has or lacks capacity to make a specific decision or to confirm that the Court has jurisdiction to deal with the matter in question.[141]

The need for formal assessment

2.101   For certain more complex or serious decisions, a formal assessment of capacity may be required, sometimes involving different professionals. Doctors are generally regarded as experts in the assessment of capacity, and in many cases all that may be needed is an opinion from the person's GP or family doctor. Where the person has been diagnosed with a particular condition or disorder, it may be more appropriate to seek an opinion from a specialist, such as a consultant psychiatrist or psychologist who has extensive clinical experience of the disorder and is familiar with caring for patients with that condition. In some cases, a multi-disciplinary approach is best, using the skills and expertise of different professionals. A professional opinion may help to justify a finding about capacity, but the decision as to whether someone has or lacks capacity must be taken by the potential decision-maker, and not the professional who is merely there to advise.[142]

2.102   Doctors or other experts should never express an opinion without first conducting a proper assessment of the person's capacity to make the decision in question and applying the appropriate test of capacity. Solicitors requesting a professional opinion should send full letters of instruction, setting out details of the requisite test of capacity and how this should be applied in relation to the client's particular circumstances.[143] However, a doctor's opinion may not necessarily be given greater weight than other

---

[140]   Mental Capacity Act 2005: Code of Practice, para 5.11
[141]   See Chapters 4 and 6.
[142]   *Bailey v Warren* [2006] EWCA Civ 51, [2006] WTLR 753 at [87]. For case summary see Part IX of this work.
[143]   Sample letters have been provided in BMA/Law Society *Assessment of Mental Capacity* (BMJ Books, 2004) and Denzil Lush *Elderly Clients: A Precedent Manual* (Jordans, 2nd edn, 2005).

relevant evidence, such as the views of a solicitor where capacity to undertake a legal transaction is involved.[144]

Legal or professional requirements

2.103 In some cases it is a requirement of the law, or good professional practice, that a formal assessment of capacity be carried out. These include the following situations:

(1) where a doctor or other expert witness certifies a legal document (such as a will) signed by someone whose capacity could be challenged (the so-called 'golden rule' established in *Kenward v Adams*[145] – see below);

(2) to establish that a particular person requires the assistance of the Official Solicitor or other litigation friend;[146]

(3) to establish that a particular person comes within the jurisdiction of the Court of Protection;[147]

(4) where the Court is required to determine a person's capacity to make a particular decision;[148] and

(5) if there may be legal consequences of a finding of capacity (e g in the settlement of damages following a claim for personal injury).

The 'Golden Rule'

2.104 There are particular circumstances where the courts have strongly advised that a doctor should witness a person's signature on a legal document such as a will, thereby providing medical evidence as to the person's capacity. In *Kenward* v *Adams* Templeman J. set out what he called 'the golden if tactless rule' that, where a will has been drawn up for an elderly person or for someone who is seriously ill, it should be witnessed or approved by a medical practitioner, who should make a formal assessment of capacity and fully record the examination and findings. The need to observe this 'golden rule' was restated in subsequent cases.[149] However, it

---

[144] *Richmond v Richmond* (1914) 111 LT 273; *Birkin v Wing* (1890) 63 LT 80.

[145] (1975) *The Times*, November 29. The advice to observe this 'golden rule' was repeated in *Re Simpson (Deceased), Schaniel v Simpson* (1977) 121 SJ 224; *Buckenham v Dickinson* [1997] CLY 661; and more forcefully in *Great Ormond Street Hospital v Pauline Rushie* (unreported) 19 April 2000, in which the solicitor was strongly criticised for failing to follow the 'golden rule'. However, it has also been acknowledged that failure to observe the 'golden rule' would not invalidate the will: *Buckenham v Dickinson* [1997] CLY 661; *Hoff v Atherton* [2005] WTLR 99; *Cattermole v Prisk* [2006] 1 FLR 693. The 'golden rule' was also considered in some detail in *Scammell and Scammell v Farmer* [2008] EWHC 1100 (Ch), [2008] WTLR 1261 at 117–123.

[146] Civil Procedure Rules 1998, SI 1998/3132, r 21.1.

[147] MCA 2005, ss 15(1), 16(1). See Form COP3 – *Assessment of Capacity* reproduced in Part VI of this book.

[148] *Masterman-Lister v Brutton & Co and Jewell & Home Counties Dairies* [2002] EWCA Civ 1889, [2003] 3 All ER 162, at [54].

[149] The advice to observe the 'golden rule' was repeated in *Re Simpson (Deceased), Schaniel v Simpson* (1977) 121 SJ 224; *Buckenham v Dickinson* [1997] CLY 661; and more forcefully in *Great Ormond Street Hospital v Pauline Rushie* (unreported) 19 April 2000, in which the solicitor was strongly criticised for failing to follow the 'golden rule'.

has also been acknowledged that failure to observe the 'golden rule' would not invalidate the will.[150] Most recently in *Key* v *Key*, the 'golden rule' was again reinforced and the solicitor involved strongly criticised for failing to follow it:[151]

> '[The solicitor's] failure to comply with what has come to be well known in the profession as the Golden Rule has greatly increased the difficulties to which this dispute has given rise and aggravated the depths of mistrust into which his client's children have subsequently fallen ...
>
> Compliance with the Golden Rule does not, of course, operate as a touchstone of the validity of a will, nor does non-compliance demonstrate its invalidity. Its purpose, as has repeatedly been emphasised, is to assist in the avoidance of disputes, or at least in the minimisation of their scope. As the expert evidence in the present case confirms, persons with failing or impaired mental faculties may, for perfectly understandable reasons, seek to conceal what they regard as their embarrassing shortcomings from persons with whom they deal, so that a friend or professional person such as a solicitor may fail to detect defects in mental capacity which would be or become apparent to a trained and experienced medical examiner, to whom a proper description of the legal test for testamentary capacity had first been provided.'

Some commentators have argued that attempted compliance with the golden rule will in fact cause more practical problems than non-compliance, because of the practical difficulties, consequent delay and increased costs that may be involved in obtaining an in-depth specialist assessment of capacity before accepting instructions even for a straightforward will or gift.[152] Ultimately, the onus is on the solicitor taking the client's instructions to satisfy themselves as to the person's capacity and understanding of the decision in question, and to keep a proper record and attendance notes of the steps taken and the evidence on which they base their conclusions.

Other expert assessments

2.105 In other cases, a judgment will need to be made as to whether the particular circumstances make it appropriate or necessary to seek a formal assessment of capacity by obtaining a professional opinion from a doctor or other expert. The Code of Practice suggests that any of the following factors might indicate the need for a professional to be involved in the assessment:[153]

- the decision that needs to be made is complicated or has serious consequences;
- an assessor concludes a person lacks capacity, and the person challenges the finding;

---

[150] *Buckenham v Dickinson* [1997] CLY 661; *Hoff v Atherton* [2005] WTLR 99; *Cattermole v Prisk* [2006] 1 FLR 693. The 'golden rule' was also considered in some detail in *Scammell and Scammell v Farmer* [2008] EWHC 1100 at 117–123.

[151] [2010] EWHC 408 (Ch) at paras 6, 8.

[152] See for example, Stephen Lawson, 'The Golden Rule: Time to move on' in *Trusts Quarterly Review* (TQR, Vol 8, Issue 3), (STEP, Sept 2010) and Barbara Rich 'The Assessment of Mental Capacity for Legal Purposes' in *Elder Law Journal* (EldLJ, Issue 1) (Jordans, Jan 2011). See also *Re S* [2010] EWHC 2405 (COP) for an illustration of the costs and complexity that may be involved.

[153] Mental Capacity Act 2005: Code of Practice, at para 4.53.

- family members, carers and/or professionals disagree about a person's capacity;
- there is a conflict of interest between the assessor and the person being assessed;
- the person being assessed is expressing different views to different people – they may be trying to please everyone or telling people what they think they want to hear;
- somebody might challenge the person's capacity to make the decision – either at the time of the decision or later (eg a family member might challenge a will after a person has died on the basis that the person lacked capacity when they made the will);
- somebody has been accused of abusing a vulnerable adult who may lack capacity to make decisions that protect them;
- a person repeatedly makes decisions that put them at risk or could result in suffering or damage.

How capacity is assessed

2.106 Where there are doubts about capacity, it is important that people are assessed when they are at their highest level of functioning because this is the only realistic way of determining what they may or may not be capable of doing. Many of the practicable steps which can be taken to enable a person to make his or her own decisions[154] may also be helpful in creating the best environment for capacity to be assessed. Once this has been done, the two-stage test of capacity[155] must then be applied, ie:

(1) Is there an impairment of or disturbance in the functioning of the person's mind or brain? If so,

(2) Is the impairment or disturbance sufficient to render the person unable to make that particular decision?

2.107 In many cases, it may be obvious whether there is any impairment or disturbance which could affect the person's ability to make a decision. For example, there may have been a previous diagnosis of an ongoing mental illness or learning disability, or recognisable symptoms to indicate the recurrence of illness or the disabling effects of a head injury. However, in other cases, such as dementia, the onset of debilitating illness is gradual and the point at which capacity is affected is hard to define. During the period when capacity is borderline, a medical opinion may be required.

2.108 People should not be considered 'incapable' simply on the basis that they have a particular diagnosis or condition, but this must be shown to affect their ability to make a decision at the time the decision needs to be made. The following questions must be considered:

(1) Does the person have a general understanding of what the decision is and why he or she is being asked to make it?

---

[154] Mental Capacity Act 2005: Code of Practice, chapter 3. See **2.35–2.38**.
[155] See **2.57–2.58**.

111

(2) Does the person have a general understanding of the consequences of making, or not making, this decision?

(3) Is the person able to understand and weigh up the information relevant to the decision as part of the process of arriving at it?

2.109 In borderline cases, or where there is any element of doubt, the person doing the assessment must be able to show that it is more likely than not that the answer to the above questions is 'No'.

Confidentiality

2.110 Carrying out an assessment of capacity requires the sharing of information about the personal circumstances of the person being assessed. Yet doctors, lawyers and other professionals are bound by a duty of confidentiality towards their clients, imposed through their professional ethical codes and reinforced by law. As a general principle, personal information may only be disclosed with the client's consent, even to close relatives. However, there are circumstances when disclosure is necessary in the absence of consent.[156]

2.111 In relation to people who lack capacity to consent (or refuse) disclosure, a balance must be struck between the public and private interests in maintaining confidentiality and the public and private interest in permitting, and occasionally requiring, disclosure for certain purposes. Some guidance has been offered in the case of *S v Plymouth City Council and C*, which established:[157]

> '... a clear distinction between disclosure to the media with a view to publication to all and sundry and disclosure in confidence to those with a proper interest in having the information in question.'

2.112 A similar balancing act must be carried out by professionals seeking or undertaking assessments of capacity. It is essential that information concerning the person being assessed which is directly relevant to the decision in question is made available to ensure that an accurate and focused assessment can take place. Every effort must first be made to obtain the person's consent to disclosure by providing a full explanation as to why this is necessary and the risks and consequences involved. If the person is unable to consent, relevant disclosure – that is the minimum necessary to achieve the objective of assessing capacity – may be permitted where this is in the person's best interests.[158] However, this does not mean that everyone has to know everything.

---

[156]   *W v Egdell and others* [1990] 1 All ER 835, at p 848.
[157]   [2002] EWCA Civ 388, at [49].
[158]   Further guidance is given in the Code of Practice, chapter 16.

Refusal to be assessed

2.113   There may be circumstances in which a person whose capacity is in doubt refuses to undergo an assessment of capacity or refuses to be examined by a doctor. It will usually be possible to persuade someone to agree to an assessment if the consequences of refusal are carefully explained. For example, it should be explained to people wishing to make a will that the will could be challenged and held to be invalid after their death, while evidence of their capacity to make a will would prevent this from happening.

2.114   If the person lacks capacity to consent to or refuse assessment, it will normally be possible for an assessment to proceed so long as the person is compliant and this is considered to be in the person's best interests. In many situations, a 'reasonable belief' of lack of capacity will be sufficient.[159] However, where a formal assessment is needed, no one can be forced to undergo an assessment of capacity in the face of an outright refusal. For example, entry to a person's home cannot be forced and a refusal to open the door to the doctor may be the end of the matter. Where there are serious concerns about the person's mental health, an assessment under mental health legislation may be warranted, but only so long as the statutory grounds are fulfilled.[160]

Recording assessments of capacity

2.115   The majority of decisions made on behalf of people lacking capacity will be informal day-to-day decisions and, as such, those caring for them on a daily basis will be able to assess their capacity and carry out acts in connection with their care and treatment in accordance with MCA 2005, s 5.[161] No formal assessment procedures or recorded documentation will be required. However, if the carer's assessment is challenged, they must be able to point to the steps they have taken to establish the person's capacity to make the decision in question and the grounds which justified a reasonable belief of lack of capacity.[162]

Professional records

2.116   Where professionals are involved, it is a matter of good practice that a proper assessment of capacity is made and the findings recorded in the relevant professional records. This includes, for example:

> (1)   an assessment of a patient's capacity to consent to medical treatment made by the doctor proposing the treatment and recorded in the patient's clinical notes;

---

[159]   See **2.81–2.84**.
[160]   Mental Health Act 1983, ss 2, 3. A refusal to be assessed is in no way sufficient grounds for assessment under the Mental Health Act 1983.
[161]   See **2.154–2.166**.
[162]   See **2.81–2.84**.

(2) an assessment of a client's capacity to instruct a solicitor to carry out a legal transaction (where necessary supported by a medical opinion) made by the solicitor and recorded on the client's file; and

(3) an assessment of a person's capacity to consent to or agree the provision of services should be made as part of the care planning processes for health or social care needs and should be recorded in the relevant documentation.

Formal reports or certificates of capacity

2.117 In some cases, a more detailed report or certificate will be required, for example:

(1) for use in court or other legal proceedings;
(2) as required by regulations made under MCA 2005;
(3) as required by the Court of Protection Rules.

Determining best interests

Background

2.118 Before MCA 2005 came into effect, the principle of acting in the best interests of a person who lacks capacity has become well established in the common law and the concept has been developed by the courts in cases relating to incapacitated adults, mainly those concerned with the provision of medical treatment.[163] MCA 2005, s 1(5) enshrines this principle in statute as the overriding principle that must guide all actions done for, or all decisions made on behalf of, someone lacking capacity.[164] MCA 2005, s 4 goes on to describe, for the purposes of this Act, the steps that must be taken in determining what is in a person's best interests.

2.119 Given the wide range of decisions and acts covered by this legislation and the varied circumstances of the people affected by its provisions, the concept of best interests is not defined in MCA 2005. In considering the need for a definition, the Law Commission acknowledged that:[165]

'... no statutory guidance could offer an exhaustive account of what is in a person's best interests, the intention being that the individual person and his or her individual circumstances should always determine the result.'

2.120 Instead, the Law Commission recommended that statute should set out a checklist of common factors which should always be taken into account. It also set out some important considerations as to how a statutory checklist should be framed:[166]

---

[163] See eg *Re A (Male Sterilisation)* [2000] 1 FLR 549; *Re S (Sterilisation: Patient's Best Interests)* [2000] 2 FLR 389; *Re F (Adult Patient: Sterilisation)* [2001] Fam 15.
[164] See **2.44–2.47**.
[165] Law Com No 231, n 1 above, at para 3.26.
[166] Ibid, at para 3.28.

'First, a checklist must not unduly burden any decision-maker or encourage unnecessary intervention; secondly it must not be applied too rigidly and should leave room for all considerations relevant to the particular case; thirdly, it should be confined to major points, so that it can adapt to changing views and attitudes.'

2.121 The Joint Committee on the Draft Mental Incapacity Bill agreed with this approach:[167]

'We agree that no list of "best interest" factors can ever be comprehensive or applicable in all situations. We therefore endorse the approach recommended by the Law Commission that a checklist of common factors to be considered in all cases should be set out in statute. However, it should be made clearer in the Bill that in addition to these common factors, all other matters relevant to the incapacitated individual and the decision in question must also be considered.'

2.122 Both as a result of recommendations made by the Joint Committee and amendments made during the parliamentary process, the best interests checklist contained in MCA 2005, s 4 has been extended and made more prescriptive in relation to certain types of decisions, in particular, those involving end-of-life decisions. The specific requirements for determining best interests are considered in detail in the following paragraphs.

The best interests checklist

2.123 Under MCA 2005, a person's capacity to make the decision or take the action in question must first be assessed. MCA 2005, s 4 only comes into play once it has been established (or there are reasonable grounds for believing) that the person lacks capacity to make the decision in question and needs someone else to decide or act on his or her behalf. It then sets out a checklist of factors which must be considered in deciding what is in a person's best interests aimed at identifying those issues most relevant to the individual who lacks capacity (as opposed to the decision-maker or any other persons). The particular factors in the checklist can be broadly summarised as follows:

- equal consideration and non-discrimination;
- considering all relevant circumstances;
- regaining capacity;
- permitting and encouraging participation;
- special considerations for life-sustaining treatment;
- the person's wishes and feelings, beliefs and values;
- the views of other people.

Not all the factors in the checklist will be relevant to all types of decisions or actions, but they must still be considered if only to be disregarded as irrelevant to that particular situation.

2.124 The serious nature of this task of determining best interests was recognised by the Joint Committee:[168]

---

[167] Joint Committee Report, Vol I, n 5 above, at para 85.
[168] Ibid, at para 89.

'We acknowledge that consideration of best interests requires flexibility, by allowing and encouraging the person [lacking capacity] to be involved to the fullest possible extent but also enabling the decision-maker to take account of a variety of circumstances, views and attitudes which may have a bearing on the decision in question. This flexibility is particularly important in cases of partial or fluctuating capacity. Determining best interests is a judgement, requiring consideration of what will often be conflicting or competing concerns, while seeking to achieve a consensus approach to decision-making.'

2.125 The Court of Protection has subsequently confirmed that there is no hierarchy in the checklist – the weight to be attached to the various factors will depend on the specific circumstances. In *Re M, ITW v Z*, applying the statutory scheme under MCA 2005 ss 1 and 4, Mr Justice Munby (as he then was) summarised three points derived from experience in other jurisdictions:[169]

'(i) The first is that the statute lays down no hierarchy as between the various factors which have to be borne in mind, beyond the overarching principle that what is determinative is the judicial evaluation of what is in P's "best interests".

(ii) The second is that the weight to be attached to the various factors will, inevitably, differ depending upon the individual circumstances of the particular case. A feature or factor which in one case may carry great, possibly even preponderant, weight may in another, superficially similar, case carry much less, or even very little, weight.

(iii) The third, following on from the others, is that there may, in the particular case, be one or more features or factors which, as Thorpe LJ has frequently put it, are of "magnetic importance" in influencing or even determining the outcome: see, for example, *Crossley v Crossley*,[170] at para [15] (contrasting "the peripheral factors in the case" with the "factor of magnetic importance") and *White v White*[171] where at page 314 he said "Although there is no ranking of the criteria to be found in the statute, there is as it were a magnetism that draws the individual case to attach to one, two, or several factors as having decisive influence on its determination." Now that was said in the context of section 25 of the Matrimonial Causes Act 1973 but the principle, as it seems to me, is of more general application.'

Principle of equal consideration

2.126 Similar to the 'equal consideration' requirement imposed as an amendment to the definition of people who lack capacity,[172] MCA 2005, s 4(1) begins with a clear statement that a determination of someone's best interests must not be based merely on the person's age or appearance, or any condition or aspect of his or her behaviour which might lead others to make unjustified assumptions about the person's best interests. As in MCA 2005, s 2(3), the reference here to 'condition' covers a range of factors, including both mental or physical disabilities and age-related illness as well as temporary conditions, such as drunkenness. 'Appearance' is also deliberately broad, covering all aspects of physical appearance, visible

---

[169]   *Re M, ITW v Z & Ors* [2009] EWHC 2525 (Fam) at 32. For case summary, see Part IX of this work.
[170]   *Crossley v Crossley* [2007] EWCA Civ 1491, [2008] 1 FLR 1467.
[171]   [2007] EWCA Civ 1491.
[172]   Fam 304 (affirmed, [2001] 1 AC 596.

medical problems or disfiguring scars, disabilities, skin colour, religious dress and so on. 'Behaviour' relates to ways of behaving that might seem unusual or odd to others, such as failing to make eye contact or laughing inappropriately.

2.127   This is intended to ensure that people with impaired capacity are treated no less favourably than people with capacity. Thus, decisions about best interests must not be based on any preconceived ideas or negative assumptions, for example, about the value or quality of life experienced by older people or people with mental or physical disabilities who now lack capacity to make decisions for themselves.

All relevant circumstances

2.128   A determination of a person's best interests involves identifying those issues most relevant to the individual who lacks capacity in the context of the decision in question. The statutory checklist sets out the minimum necessary considerations but all other matters relevant in the particular situation must also be taken into account. MCA 2005, s 4(2) therefore requires the person making the determination to consider 'all the relevant circumstances' as well as following the steps set out in the checklist.

2.129   It is recognised that the person making the determination may not be in a position to make exhaustive inquiries to investigate every issue which may have some relevance to the incapacitated person or the decision in question. Therefore relevant circumstances are defined in MCA 2005 as those:[173]

(a)   of which the person making the determination is aware; and

(b)   which it would be reasonable to regard as relevant.

Regaining capacity

2.130   Following further consultation on the checklist suggested by the Law Commission for the determination of best interests, the Government proposed an additional factor – whether the person is likely to regain capacity.[174] One of MCA 2005's key principles is that before a person is found to be incapable of making a decision, all practicable steps must be taken to help the person make that decision.[175]

2.131   In keeping with this approach, when looking at best interests, it is important to consider whether the individual concerned is likely to have capacity to make that particular decision in the future and, if so, when that is likely to be.[176] It may be possible to put off the decision until the person can make it him or herself. This delay may allow further time for additional

---

[173]   MCA 2005, s 4(11).
[174]   Lord Chancellor's Department *Making Decisions*, Cm 4465 (TSO, 1999), at para 1.12.
[175]   MCA 2005, s 1(3). See **2.35–2.38**.
[176]   MCA 2005, s 4(3).

steps to be taken to restore the person's capacity or to provide support and assistance which would enable the person to make the decision.

2.132 The Code of Practice suggests some factors which may indicate that a person may regain capacity:[177]

'• the cause of the lack of capacity can be treated, either by medication or some other form of treatment or therapy;
• the lack of capacity is likely to decrease in time (for example, where it is caused by the effects of medication or alcohol, or following a sudden shock);
• a person with learning disabilities may learn new skills or be subject to new experiences which increase their understanding and ability to make certain decisions;
• the person may have a condition which causes capacity to come and go (such as some forms of mental illness) so it may be possible to arrange for the decision to be made during a time when they do have capacity;
• a person previously unable to communicate may learn a new form of communication.'

Permitting and encouraging participation

2.133 MCA 2005, s 4(4) requires that, even where a person does not have capacity to make an effective decision, he or she should be both permitted and encouraged to participate, or to improve his or her ability to participate as fully as possible, in the decision-making process or in relation to any act done for him or her. It will always be important to consult the person on the particular act or decision to be made and to try to seek their views, not only to encourage the development of decision-making skills, but also as an important contribution in determining best interests. The practicable steps to enable decision-making will also be relevant here.[178] The importance of involving the person in the decision-making process has been reinforced by the Court of Protection (*C v V, Re S and S (Protected Persons)*).[179]

Life-sustaining treatment

2.134 A specific best interests factor relates to decisions concerning the provision (or withdrawal) of life-sustaining treatment, which is defined as treatment which a person providing health care regards as necessary to sustain life, usually the life of a person lacking capacity to consent to that treatment.[180] MCA 2005, s 4(5) clarifies that in determining whether the

---

[177] Mental Capacity Act 2005: Code of Practice, at para 5.28.
[178] See **2.35–2.38**.
[179] [2008] EWHC B16 (Fam) at 54–55. A copy of the judgment is available on the OPG website at www.publicguardian.gov.uk/forms/other-orders-cop.htm.
[180] MCA 2005, s 4(10). In parliamentary debate, it was also clarified that 'in the case of a pregnant woman we want to ensure that the life of the baby, not only the life of the mother, must be considered': *Hansard*, HL Deb, vol 668, ser 5, col 1184 (25 January 2005). However, an unborn child does not have an independent set of interests to be weighed against the mother's best interests (*St George's Healthcare NHS Trust v S* [1998] 3 All ER 673).

treatment is in the best interests of someone who lacks capacity to consent to it, the person making the determination must not be motivated by a desire to bring about the individual's death.

2.135 A great deal of the debate in both Houses of Parliament concerned life and death decisions affecting people who lack capacity to make those decisions for themselves. In order to provide clarity and reassurance on these very difficult issues, the Government agreed to a number of amendments introducing specific statements in the legislation. In particular, MCA 2005, s 62 confirms that the Act does not have the effect of authorising or permitting unlawful killing (including euthanasia) or assisted suicide. Secondly, in relation to decisions about whether the provision or continuance of life-sustaining treatment would be in a person's best interests, MCA 2005, s 4(5) clarifies that the decision-maker must not be motivated by a desire to bring about the person's death.

2.136 This particular factor was introduced as an amendment in the House of Lords after an undertaking was given in correspondence between the Lord Chancellor and the Roman Catholic Archbishop of Cardiff, Peter Smith, that MCA 2005 would make this point absolutely clear. Commenting on a situation where no advance decision has been made about whether treatment should be continued or refused, the Lord Chancellor said:[181]

> 'The decision about whether to continue to give life-sustaining treatment will then fall to be taken by the doctor, acting with an attorney who has relevant powers ... In some cases a decision ... will still be taken by the court. The Bill preserves the jurisdiction exercised in the Tony Bland case and restates the principles applied in that case. These are very difficult decisions, even for a court. In making them the decision-maker must act in the best interests of the patient. Above all, he must make an objective assessment. The decision cannot simply be the personal value judgement of the decision-maker – the decision-maker cannot say "If I were in the patient's position, I would want to die" – nor can it be motivated by the desire to bring about the death of the patient.'

2.137 Any decision about life-sustaining treatment for a person lacking capacity will take as its starting point the assumption that it is in the person's best interests for life to continue. However, there will be some cases, for example, in the final stages of terminal illness or for some patients in a permanent vegetative state, where treatment is futile, overly burdensome or intolerable for the patient or where there is no prospect of recovery, where it may be in the best interests of the patient to withdraw or withhold treatment or to give palliative care that might incidentally shorten life.[182] All the factors in the best interests checklist must be considered, but the person determining best interests must not be motivated in any way by the desire to bring about the person's death.

---

[181] *Hansard*, HL Deb, vol 668, ser 5, cols 14–15 (10 January 2005).
[182] See Chapter 5.

The person's wishes and feelings, beliefs and values

2.138   A particularly important element of the best interests checklist is the consideration, so far as these can be ascertained, of:[183]

'(a)   the person's past and present wishes and feelings (and in particular, any relevant written statements made by him when he had capacity),

(b)   the beliefs and values that would be likely to influence his decision if he had capacity, and

(c)   the other factors that he would be likely to consider if he were able to do so.'

This places the focus firmly on the person lacking capacity, taking into account the issues most important to him or her and what he or she would have wanted to achieve. It also reflects the need to make every effort to find out whether the person has expressed any relevant views in the past, whether verbally, in writing or through behaviour or habits, as well as trying to seek his or her current views.

2.139   The reference to written statements was included as a Government amendment in the House of Lords in response to lobbying by the Making Decisions Alliance and other stakeholder organisations. Those organisations had requested that advance statements, particularly those expressing wishes about medical treatment, should be given some form of statutory recognition and should specifically be taken into account in determining a person's best interests. The Minister for Constitutional Affairs, Baroness Ashton confirmed:[184]

'... the purpose of this amendment is to clarify that if someone with capacity has written down their wishes and feelings in respect of a matter, including positive preferences, those must be explicitly taken into account in a best interests determination.

Patients do not have a right to demand and receive treatment, so advance requests cannot have the same legal effect as advance decisions to refuse treatment. However, the amendment makes clear that preferences about any aspect of a person's life, including treatment, should be respected and taken into account ... The more specific and well thought out the statement, the more likely it will be persuasive in determining best interests.'

2.140   The Draft Mental Incapacity Bill published in 2003 made no mention of the person's 'beliefs and values' but this was added to the Bill in response to a recommendation of the Joint Committee:[185]

'The Medical Ethics Alliance suggested to us that the factor involving the need to consider the incapacitated person's "past and present wishes and feelings" should also contain reference to that person's values. Others suggested that specific reference should be made to social, psychological, cultural, spiritual and religious issues. It is anticipated that the need to consider a wide range of issues, in particular religious and cultural concerns, will be spelt out in the Code of Practice. We seek reassurance that the form of words used in the Bill will require a person's values to be given due weight.'

---

[183]   MCA 2005, s 4(6).
[184]   *Hansard*, HL Deb, vol 670, ser 5, cols 1441–1442 (17 March 2005).
[185]   Joint Committee Report, Vol I, n 5 above, at para 90.

2.141 The reference to factors the person 'would be likely to consider' if able to do so provides the 'substituted judgment' element of the best interests checklist, as previously reflected in case-law in relation to the powers exercised by the previous Court of Protection to make a statutory will, where:[186]

> '... subject to all due allowances ... the court must seek to make the will which the actual patient, acting reasonably, would have made if notionally restored to full mental capacity, memory and foresight.'

2.142 MCA 2005, s 4(6)(c) extends this notion as a factor to consider for all decisions or actions, whether or not the person concerned ever had capacity in relation to the matter in question. Prior to implementation of MCA 2005, the courts had held that the possible wider benefits to a person lacking capacity, arising for example from emotional support from close relationships, are important factors which the person would be likely to consider if able to do so, and are therefore relevant in determining the person's own best interests.[187] The Code of Practice suggests that such factors might include altruistic motives, such as 'the effect of the decision on other people, obligations to dependants or the duties of a responsible citizen'.[188]

2.143 In the case of *Re G (TJ)*, Mr Justice Morgan considered whether it was in Mrs G's best interests to continue to pay a regular sum for the maintenance of her adult daughter. In considering the difference between substituted judgement and best interests, he reviewed the relevant cases (summarised below) and reached the following conclusions:[189]

> 'The best interests test involves identifying a number of relevant factors. The actual wishes of P can be a relevant factor: section 4(6)(a) says so. The beliefs and values which would be likely to influence P's decision, if he had capacity to make the relevant decision, are a relevant factor: section 4(6)(b) says so. The other factors which P would be likely to consider, if he had the capacity to consider them, are a relevant factor: section 4(6)(c) says so. Accordingly, the balance sheet of factors which P would draw up, if he had capacity to make the decision, is a relevant factor for the court's decision. Further, in most cases the court will be able to determine what decision it is likely that P would have made, if he had capacity. In such a case, in my judgment, P's balance sheet of factors and P's likely decision can be taken into account by the court. This involves an element of substituted judgment being taken into account, together with anything else which is relevant. However, it is absolutely clear that the ultimate test for the court is the test of best interests and not the test of substituted judgment. Nonetheless, the substituted judgment can be relevant and is not excluded from consideration. As Hoffmann LJ said in the *Bland* case, the substituted judgment can be subsumed within the concept of best interests. That appeared to be the view of the Law Commission also.

---

[186]   *Re D (J)* [1982] 2 All ER 37, at p 43. It has since been held that the approach in making a statutory will is now the best interests of the testator, rather than what the testator 'might be expected to have done', but such considerations are important factors to be taken into account in determining best interests – see *In the Matter of P* [2009] EWHC 163 (Ch) (for case summary, see Part IX of this work).

[187]   See e g *Re Y (Mental Incapacity: Bone marrow transplant)* [1996] 2 FLR 787; *Re A (Male Sterilisation)* [2000] 1 FLR 549.

[188]   Mental Capacity Act 2005: Code of Practice, at para 5.47.

[189]   *In the Matter of G (TJ)* [2010] EWHC 3005 (COP) at paras 55-56.

Further, the word 'interest' in the best interests test does not confine the court to considering the self interest of P. The actual wishes of P, which are altruistic and not in any way, directly or indirectly self-interested, can be a relevant factor. Further, the wishes which P would have formed, if P had capacity, which may be altruistic wishes, can be a relevant factor. It is not necessary to establish that P would have been aware of the fact that P's wishes were carried into effect. Respect for P's wishes, actual or putative, can be a relevant factor even where P has no awareness of, and no reaction to, the fact that such wishes are being respected.'

The weight to be given to P's wishes and feelings

2.144 The Code of Practice acknowledges that while this checklist factor establishes the importance of the individual views of the person lacking capacity (P), those views will not automatically determine the outcome.[190] Indeed, in some cases, there may be a conflict between the person's past and present wishes, so that these must be weighed against each other and considered alongside other factors in the checklist. In *Re GC,* Mr Justice Hedley suggested:[191]

'Where a person is in a position to express views, however limited their horizons, those are views which carry weight. The greater their appreciation of the horizons, the greater the weight those views must carry and they can, of course, by definition never be decisive.'

The importance of taking account of the person's past and present wishes and feelings was reinforced in a judgment in the Court of Protection (*C v V, Re S and S (Protected Persons)*) when HHJ Hazel Marshall QC held that there is a presumption in favour of implementing the person's wishes unless they are irrational, impractical, or irresponsible (with reference to resources), or there is a sufficiently countervailing consideration.[192] In the later case of *Re P*, in the context of a statutory will application, Mr Justice Lewison complimented Judge Marshall QC for considering the MCA 2005 "in a most impressive and sensitive judgment", the broad thrust of which he agreed with, but he thought she "may have slightly overstated the importance to be given to P's wishes" and he preferred "not to speak in terms of presumptions".[193]

2.145 In *Re M, ITW v Z and others,* Mr Justice Munby considered a statutory will application in a case in which an elderly woman had been the victim of financial abuse by a neighbour. When considering the weight and importance to be attached to the person's (P's) wishes and feelings, he stated that the court must have regard, amongst other relevant considerations, to:[194]

'(a)   the degree of P's incapacity, for the nearer to the borderline the more weight must in principle be attached to P's wishes and feelings: *Re MM; Local Authority X v MM (by the Official Solicitor) and KM*,[195] at para [124];

---

[190]   Mental Capacity Act 2005: Code of Practice, at paras 5.37–5.48.
[191]   [2008] EWHC 3402 (Fam) at 23.
[192]   [2008] EWHC B16 (Fam) at 57–58, 87. A copy of the judgment is available on the OPG website at www.publicguardian.gov.uk/forms/other-orders-cop.htm.
[193]   *In the matter of P* [2009] EWHC 163 (Ch) at paras 40 and 41.
[194]   Re M, *ITW v Z & Ors* [2009] EWHC 2525 (Fam) at para 35(iii).
[195]   [2007] EWHC 2003 (Fam), [2009] 1 FLR 443.

(b)   the strength and consistency of the views being expressed by P;

(c)   the possible impact on P of knowledge that her wishes and feelings are not being given effect to: see again *Re MM; Local Authority X v MM (by the Official Solicitor) and KM*,[196] at para [124];

(d)   the extent to which P's wishes and feelings are, or are not, rational, sensible, responsible and pragmatically capable of sensible implementation in the particular circumstances; and

(e)   crucially, the extent to which P's wishes and feelings, if given effect to, can properly be accommodated within the court's overall assessment of what is in her best interests.'

The views of other people

2.146   For the first time, MCA 2005 ensures that carers, family members and other relevant people are consulted on decisions affecting the person lacking capacity to make those decisions for themselves. People who must be consulted include anyone previously named by the person who now lacks capacity as someone they would wish to be consulted, carers and anyone interested in the person's welfare, donees and deputies.[197] Any person who is determining the best interests of someone lacking capacity is required to take into account the views of these key people, but only if it is 'practicable and appropriate' to consult them. The Senior Judge of the Court of Protection has held that where consultation is likely to be unduly onerous, contentious, futile or serve no useful purpose, it is not 'practicable or appropriate'.[198]

2.147   The Code of Practice suggests:[199]

'Decision-makers must show they have thought carefully about who to speak to. If it is practical and appropriate to speak to the above people, they must do so and must take their views into account. They must be able to explain why they did not speak to a particular person – it is good practice to have a clear record of their reasons.'

2.148   The consultation is limited to two matters – first, what those people consider to be in the person's best interests on the matter in question and, secondly, whether they can provide any information on the wishes, feelings, values or beliefs of the person lacking capacity. If, prior to losing capacity, the person concerned has nominated someone whom he or she would like to be consulted, the named person is more likely to have that information. People who are close to the person lacking capacity, such as relatives, partners and other carers, may also be able to assist with communication or interpret signs which give an indication of the person's present wishes and feelings.In *Re M, ITW v Z* Mr Justice Munby suggested that in determining

---

[196]   [2007] EWHC 2003 (Fam), [2009] 1 FLR 443.
[197]   MCA 2005, s 4(7).
[198]   *Re Allen* [2009] (CoP No 11661992) (unreported). A copy of the judgment is available on the OPG website at www.publicguardian.gov.uk/forms/other-orders-cop.htm.
[199]   Mental Capacity Act 2005: Code of Practice, at para 5.51.

best interests, it may be appropriate to consult with former carers and to take into account oral statements made to them by the person who lacks capacity.[200]

2.149 The requirement for consultation must be balanced against the right to confidentiality of the person lacking capacity. That right should be protected so that consultation only takes place where relevant and with people whom it is appropriate to consult. For example, it is unlikely to be appropriate to consult anyone whom the person had previously indicated should not be involved. However, there may be occasions where it is in the person's best interests for specific information to be disclosed, or where the public interest in disclosure may override the person's private interest in maintaining confidentiality.[201] If professionals are involved in the determination of best interests, they will also need to comply with their own duties of confidentiality in accordance with their professional codes of conduct.

Duty to apply the best interests principle

2.150 The principle set out in MCA 2005, s 1(5) confirms that any act done, or any decision made, on behalf of a person lacking capacity must be done in his or her best interests. MCA 2005, s 4(8) confirms that the best interests principle, and the duties to be carried out in determining best interests, also apply in certain circumstances where the person concerned may not in fact lack capacity in relation to the act or decision in question. This applies in relation to any powers which:

(1) are exercisable under a lasting power of attorney;
(2) are exercisable by a person under MCA 2005 where he or she 'reasonably believes' that another person lacks capacity.

Reasonable belief

2.151 The second situation reflects the position that in most day-to-day decisions or actions involved in caring for someone, it will not be appropriate or necessary to carry out a formal assessment of the person's capacity. Rather, it is sufficient for there to be a 'reasonable belief' that the person lacks capacity to make the decision or consent to the action in question.[202]

2.152 Similarly, MCA 2005, s 4(9) confirms that, in cases where the Court is not involved, carers (both professionals and family members) and others who are acting informally can only be expected to have reasonable grounds for believing that what they are doing or deciding is in the best interests of

---

[200] *Re M, ITW v Z and Ors* [2009] EWHC 2525 (Fam) at para 36.
[201] *S v Plymouth City Council and C* [2002] EWCA Civ 388, at [49]. See **2.105–2.107**.
[202] See **2.81–2.84**.

the person concerned, but they must still, so far as possible, apply the best interests checklist and therefore be able to point to objective reasons to justify why they hold that belief.

2.153 MCA 2005, s 4(9) also applies to donees and deputies appointed to make welfare or financial decisions, as well as to those carrying out acts in connection with the care and treatment of a person lacking capacity. In deciding what is 'reasonable' in any particular case, higher expectations are likely to be placed on those appointed to act under formal powers and those acting in a professional capacity than on family members and friends who are caring for a person lacking capacity without any formal authority.

PART 3: GENERAL POWERS AND DUTIES

Acts in connection with care or treatment – background

The problem

2.154 Until MCA 2005 came into effect, legislation has been silent about what actions could lawfully be taken by carers in looking after the day-to-day personal or health care needs of people who lack capacity to consent to those actions. These actions may include helping individuals to wash, dress and attend to their personal hygiene, feeding them, taking them out for walks and leisure activities, taking them to the doctor or dentist or providing necessary treatment.

2.155 In consequence, doctors, dentists and other health care professionals were hesitant about carrying out examinations, treatment or nursing care on patients unable to consent to those medical procedures. In the absence of any clear statutory provision, it was left to the courts to establish the former common law 'principle of necessity', setting out the circumstances in which actions and decisions could lawfully be taken on behalf of adults who lack capacity.[203]

2.156 The courts confirmed that where the principle of necessity applied (ie that it was necessary to act in relation to the well-being of a person lacking capacity to consent), and the action taken was reasonable and in the person's best interests, that action which would otherwise amount to a civil wrong, or even a crime (eg of battery or assault) would in fact be lawful. The principle of necessity is *not* equivalent to having consent but may constitute a defence if an action is subsequently challenged.

2.157 Such actions might involve touching or interfering with the person's bodily integrity, or using or interfering with the person's property or possessions. In such cases, the lack of capacity of the people concerned means that they cannot give their informed consent and therefore the proposed actions, if they were to take place, could potentially be unlawful unless the principle of necessity applied.

---

[203] *Re F (Mental Patient: Sterilisation)* [1990] 2 AC 1, at p 75.

The Law Commission proposal

2.158 The Law Commission acknowledged that within the new jurisdiction it proposed, there should remain scope for caring actions to take place, and for some informal decision-making 'without certifications, documentation or judicial determinations'.[204] However, the Commission recognised that the common law 'principle of necessity' was not widely understood and there was therefore a need to clarify the confused state of the law governing such actions:[205]

> 'We suggested in our consultation papers that there was a strong case for clarifying in statute the circumstances in which decisions can be taken for people who lack capacity, but without anyone having to apply for formal authorisation. We did not envisage this as conferring any new power on anyone, but rather as a clarification of the uncertain "necessity" principle. Respondents gave an enthusiastic welcome to our provisional proposals. There was very broad agreement that a statutory provision would be invaluable in dispelling doubt and confusion and setting firm and appropriate limits to informal action.'

The general authority

2.159 The Law Commission proposed a new statutory authority, which it called the 'general authority to act reasonably', to codify in statute what had become practice under common law and to clarify the 'principle of necessity'. It was intended that the general authority would provide legal authorisation for acts connected with the personal welfare or health care of a person lacking capacity to consent if it is reasonable in the particular circumstances for the act to be done by the person who does it. The legal authorisation would apply to different people acting at different times, so long as it was appropriate for them to do the act in question and they were acting reasonably and in the best interests of the person lacking capacity.

The views of the Joint Committee

2.160 However, the clauses in the Draft Mental Incapacity Bill making provision for the 'general authority'[206] caused significant concerns and confusion to a number of witnesses giving evidence to the Joint Committee on the Bill:[207]

> 'A number of the concerns which have been brought to our attention seem to be premised on a misunderstanding of the general authority as it is set out in the draft Bill. The extent of the misunderstandings apparent in the evidence we have received suggests that the drafting of this provision is not sufficiently clear. Many interested parties appear to be under the erroneous impression that the general authority would be assumed by a single individual who would then take all decisions on behalf of an incapacitated individual. In fact the general authority is for the relevant person, in the context of a specific decision or action, at a particular point in time, so long as it is reasonable for that person to act. Others have suggested that the general authority

---

[204] Law Com No 231, n 1 above, at para 4.1.
[205] Ibid, at para 4.2.
[206] Draft Mental Incapacity Bill, cls 6–7.
[207] Joint Committee Report, Vol I, n 5 above, at paras 109–110.

may be used by carers to justify taking decisions for which they would otherwise need formal authorisation. In fact the general authority is not intended to convey any new powers on anyone but rather to clarify the uncertain principle of "necessity".

We have come to the conclusion that the term "general authority" itself has contributed to the misinterpretations apparent within the evidence we have received. The word "authority" implies an imposition of decision making upon an incapacitated individual rather than an enabling process designed to enact decisions taken in their best interests. This may have contributed to perceptions of the general authority as likely to promote "over-paternalistic attitudes" towards incapacitated individuals. We are convinced that semantic issues are important in affecting public perceptions of the draft Bill as well as in determining legal interpretations of the provisions it contains.'

2.161 The Joint Committee recommended radical redrafting to clarify the legislative intent of the 'general authority' and the use of alternative terminology to avoid its misleading connotations. The Government's response was to recast the provisions to allow for a limitation of liability for people who need to act in connection with the care or treatment of a person lacking capacity to consent. Offering protection from liability is intended to enable caring actions to take place in the absence of consent, but also to make clear that anyone acting unreasonably, negligently or not in the person's best interests would forfeit that protection.

Acts in connection with care or treatment – the legislation

Protection from liability

2.162 MCA 2005, s 5 makes provision to allow carers (both informal carers, such as family members, and paid carers) and health and social care professionals to carry out certain acts in connection with the personal care, health care or treatment of a person lacking capacity to consent to those acts. These provisions are intended to give legal backing, in the form of protection from liability, for actions which are essential for the personal welfare or health of people lacking capacity to consent to having things done to or for them. Such actions can be performed as if the person concerned had capacity and had given consent.[208] There is no need to obtain any formal powers or authority to act.

2.163 In introducing the Bill into the House of Commons, the Under Secretary of State for Constitutional Affairs, David Lammy explained:[209]

'Clause 5, entitled "Acts in connection with care and treatment", is an important clarification of the law surrounding what someone can do to or for a person lacking mental capacity who is unable to give consent. The current law is based on the poorly understood and obscure "doctrine of necessity". Hon. Members will know of constituents who are worried and uncertain about what they are allowed to do, because they do not understand the law. For example, a nurse may want to restrain someone who is having an epileptic fit. Someone caring for an elderly patient at

---
[208] MCA 2005, s 5(2).
[209] *Hansard*, HC Deb, vol 425, ser 6, col 29 (11 October 2004).

home may need to help them to use the toilet. Someone whose daughter suffers from bipolar disease may want to go to her house to cook for her and to help her to eat because she is in too much distress.

It is not right that people in such situations should have to rely on what seems to them to be an outdated and obscure legal concept. Clause 5 explains what they can do. It provides that one is protected from liability when the person cannot consent, provided that one takes reasonable steps to establish whether that person lacks mental capacity in relation to the matter in question, that one reasonably believes that the person lacks capacity in relation to the matter, and that what one does is in the person's best interests.'

Section 5 acts

2.164   The types of acts which may be carried out with protection from liability under MCA 2005, s 5 (sometimes referred to as 'section 5 acts') are those carried out *in connection with the care or treatment* of a person who is believed to lack capacity in relation to the matter in question, at the time the act needs to be carried out. The Code of Practice provides examples (but not an exhaustive list) as follows:[210]

'Personal care

- helping with washing, dressing or personal hygiene
- helping with eating and drinking
- helping with communication
- helping with mobility (moving around)
- helping someone take part in education, social or leisure activities
- going into a person's home to drop off shopping or to see if they are alright
- doing the shopping or buying necessary goods with the person's money
- arranging household services (for example, arranging repairs or maintenance for gas and electricity supplies)
- providing services that help around the home (such as homecare or meals on wheels)
- undertaking actions related to community care services (for example, day care, residential accommodation or nursing care)
- helping someone to move home (including moving property and clearing the former home)

Healthcare and treatment

- carrying out diagnostic examinations and tests (to identify an illness, condition or other problem)
- providing professional medical, dental and similar treatment
- giving medication
- taking someone to hospital for assessment or treatment
- providing nursing care (whether in hospital or in the community)
- carrying out any other necessary medical procedures (for example, taking a blood sample) or therapies (for example, physiotherapy or chiropody)
- providing care in an emergency.'

As a general rule, a 'section 5 act' is one where consent (either explicit or implied) would normally be required from a person of full capacity for the particular act to be carried out. Only acts or arrangements involving

---

[210]   Mental Capacity Act 2005: Code of Practice, at para 6.5.

minimum legal formality are covered, since more formal legal transactions (particularly those requiring written documentation) would require more than the person's 'consent'.

Serious acts relating to medical treatment or welfare

2.165 In a briefing on the Mental Capacity Bill, the Making Decisions Alliance expressed concern that the scope of MCA 2005, s 5 'remains unclear and is too wide'. It argued that the legislation should:[211]

> '… establish a clear hierarchy of safeguards which reflect the seriousness of the action taken and the consequences for that individual. The MDA recommends that some actions taken under section 5 require additional safeguards to counter against its inappropriate use. For example, we think it is important that a person has the support of an independent advocate when moving home which would involve a change of carer. Similarly, we think that there should be an independent second medical opinion, in relation to serious medical treatment.'

2.166 The Government recognised that some acts in connection with care or treatment may cause major life changes with significant consequences for the person concerned, particularly those involving a change of residence (eg into a care home or nursing home) or major decisions about medical treatment. The Code of Practice, therefore, gives detailed guidance aimed at ensuring that the decision in question is made in accordance with the principles of MCA 2005 and is in the person's best interests.[212] The best interests checklist must therefore be carefully applied and particular consideration must be given to whether there is any other choice that would be less restrictive of the person's rights and freedom of action (under MCA 2005, s 1(6)). The Act itself also imposes some limitations on the scope of MCA 2005, s 5, described below.[213]

2.167 If a proposed move to a hospital or care home would have the effect of depriving the person of their liberty, the protection afforded by section 5 will not be available.[214] Instead, authorisation for the deprivation of liberty will be required using the deprivation of liberty safeguards (DOLS) (see Chapter 6) or by order of the Court of Protection. In *A Local Authority v A (Re A (Adult) and Re C (Child))*, Munby LJ gave guidance to local authorities as to the exercise of their powers in respect of the welfare of adults lacking capacity to consent. He stressed that:[215]

> 'People in the situation of A and C, together with their carers, look to the State – to a local authority – for the support, the assistance and the provision of the services to which the law, giving effect to the underlying principles of the Welfare State, entitles them. They do not seek to be "controlled" by the State or by the local authority. And

---

[211] Making Decisions Alliance *Mental Capacity Bill: Briefing for 2nd Reading* (11 October 2004).
[212] Mental Capacity Act 2005: Code of Practice, at paras 6.7-6.19.
[213] See **2.165**ff.
[214] See **2.172–2.176** below and Chapter 6.
[215] [2010] EWHC 978 (Fam) at para 52.

it is not for the State in the guise of a local authority to seek to exercise such control. The State, the local authority, is the servant of those in need of its support and assistance, not their master.'

He warned against the 'mindset' of some local authorities seeking to exercise control, citing examples of the removal of incapacitated adults from the care of their relatives into residential accommodation, without the sanction of the court and, therefore in some cases, without any legal authority.

2.168 In relation to serious medical treatment, the Code of Practice confirms that the previous case-law requirement to seek a declaration from the Court in cases where particularly serious forms of medical treatment are proposed, is unaffected by MCA 2005.[216] The Court of Protection Rules, supplemented by Practice Directions, confirm that such cases must always be heard before the President of the Court of Protection or another High Court judge nominated by him or her.[217] This includes the withdrawal or withholding of life-sustaining treatment from patients in a permanent vegetative state (PVS), the proposed non-therapeutic sterilisation of a person lacking capacity or other cases involving an ethical dilemma in an untested area which may well involve doubts as to the person's best interests and such cases should therefore continue to be referred to the Court.[218] One such case *DH NHS Foundation Trust v PS* came before Sir Nicholas Wall, President of the Court of Protection, who held that it was in the best interests of PS, who lacked capacity to agree to medical treatment due to her learning difficulties and her phobia of needles and hospitals, to undergo treatment for cancer. Since she had previously both failed and refused to attend hospital for treatment, the President authorised the use of force if necessary to sedate her and convey her to hospital and to detain her in hospital during the period of post-operative recovery.[219]

2.169 An additional safeguard is provided where serious medical treatment or a change of residence is proposed for a person lacking capacity, but *only* where the person concerned has no family or friends available to be consulted or to speak up on his or her behalf. In such cases, MCA 2005 makes provision for an independent mental capacity advocate (IMCA) to be appointed to support and represent the person.[220] In these and any other cases where there is a doubt or dispute about whether a particular section 5 act is in the person's best interests, and the matter cannot be resolved through negotiation or other means of dispute resolution, the Court of Protection has ultimate jurisdiction to resolve the matter.

---

[216]   Mental Capacity Act 2005: Code of Practice, at para 6.18.
[217]   Court of Protection Rules 2007, SI 2007/1744, r 86, supplemented by Practice Direction 12A *Court's Jurisdiction to be exercised by Certain Judges.*
[218]   Ibid. See also Practice Direction 9E *Applications relating to Serious Medical Treatment.*
[219]   *DH NHS Foundation Trust v PS* [2010] EWHC 1217 (Fam).
[220]   MCA 2005, ss 35–41. See Chapter 5.

Who can act in connection with care or treatment?

2.170   There is no intention that MCA 2005, s 5 applies to a single identifiable person involved in the care or treatment of a person lacking capacity, nor does it convey any powers on anyone to make substitute decisions or to give consent on behalf of the person lacking capacity. The intention is to allow carers, health and social care professionals to do whatever is necessary to safeguard and promote the welfare and health of individuals who lack capacity to consent, so long as it is appropriate for the particular carer or professional to take the action in question and the act is in the best interests of the incapacitated person.

2.171   Before doing anything, the person wishing to take action in connection with the care or treatment of another person must take 'reasonable steps' to establish whether the person concerned has capacity in relation to the matter in question.[221] This does not necessarily require a formal assessment of capacity, although professional practice may require this, for example, in respect of medical treatment. In any event, steps must be taken to look for objective reasons which would justify a reasonable belief of lack of capacity.[222] If it is found that the person has capacity, his or her consent to the action will be required to provide protection from liability.

2.172   Anyone proposing to carry out an act under MCA 2005, s 5 must also take account of the MCA 2005's key principles set out in s 1.[223] This includes starting with the presumption of capacity and taking all practicable steps to enable the person to express a view about the proposed action. If it is believed the person lacks capacity, the 'less restrictive alternative' principle requires consideration of whether the act is needed at all and if so, whether the purpose for which the act is needed can be achieved in a way less restrictive of the person's future choices or would allow him or her the most freedom.

2.173   In addition, the person wishing to act must 'reasonably believe' that what they are doing is in the best interests of the person lacking capacity.[224] Again, they must be able to point to objective reasons to justify that belief. They must be able to show that they have taken account of all relevant circumstances, including those set out in the best interests checklist.[225] If their judgment of best interests is challenged, they will be protected if they can show that it was reasonable in all the circumstances of that particular case for them to have arrived at that judgment. Where professionals are involved, their professional skills and levels of competence will be taken into account in determining what would be considered 'reasonable'.

---

[221]   MCA 2005, s 5(1)(a).
[222]   See **2.81–2.84**.
[223]   See **2.23–2.52**.
[224]   MCA 2005, s 5(1)(b)(ii).
[225]   See **2.118–2.141**.

No protection in cases of negligence

2.174 Professionals and other carers may have duties of care which, if breached, give rise to liability in the tort of negligence. Consent is not a defence to a claim of negligence. Similarly in relation to people who lack capacity to consent, MCA 2005, s 5(3) clarifies that protection from liability does not extend to situations where the person taking the action has acted negligently, whether in carrying out the act or by failing to act in breach of duty. Therefore, there is no protection excluding a person's civil liability for any loss or damage, or his or her criminal liability, resulting from his or her negligence in carrying out or failing to do an act.

Effect on advance decisions to refuse treatment

2.175 In cases where anadvance decision to refuse treatment is known to exist, is clear and unambiguous and is valid and applicable in the circumstances which have arisen, any health professionals who knowingly provide treatment contrary to the terms of the decision may be liable to legal action for battery or assault, or for breach of the patient's human rights.[226] The provisions of MCA 2005, s 5 do not provide protection from liability in these circumstances, since s 5(4) specifically excludes the operation of advance decisions to refuse treatment.

Limitations on permitted acts

2.176 MCA 2005, s 6 imposes two important limitations on the acts which can be carried out with protection from liability under s 5. The first relates to acts intended to restrain a person who lacks capacity and the second to situations where the act might conflict with a decision made by a donee of a lasting power of attorney or a deputy appointed by the Court.

Restraint

2.177 As a general rule, any act that is intended to restrain a person lacking capacity will not attract protection from liability[227] and any carer or professional using restraint could be liable to legal action and will be personally accountable for their actions. In particular, no protection from liability is offered to people who use or threaten violence in order to carry out any action in connection with the care or treatment of a person lacking capacity or to force that person to comply with the carers' actions. However, the practicalities of caring for and providing protection for people who are unable to protect themselves are also recognised. MCA 2005 therefore permits the use of some form of restraint or physical intervention in limited circumstances in order to protect the person from harm.[228]

---

[226] MCA 2005, ss 24–26. See also Chapter 5.
[227] MCA 2005, s 6(1).
[228] MCA 2005, s 6(2).

2.178 An individual restrains a person lacking capacity if he or she (a) uses, or threatens to use, force to secure the doing of an act which the person resists or (b) restricts that person's liberty of movement, whether or not there is resistance.[229] Restraint may take many forms. It may be verbal or physical and may vary from shouting at someone, to holding them down, to locking them in a room. It may also include the prescribing of a sedative or other chemical restraint which restricts liberty of movement.

2.179 MCA 2005 permits restraint to be used *only* where two conditions are satisfied:[230]

(1) the person using it must reasonably believe that it is necessary to do the act in order to prevent harm to the person lacking capacity; and

(2) the restraint used must be a proportionate response both to the likelihood of the person suffering harm and the seriousness of that harm.

2.180 MCA 2005 does not define 'harm', since this will vary according to individual circumstances. The restraining act must be 'necessary' to avert harm – not simply to enable the carer or professional to do something more quickly or easily. Similarly, what is likely to be a 'proportionate response' to harm, both in scale and nature, will depend on the seriousness of the particular circumstances and the desired outcome. However, where there are objective reasons for believing that restraint is necessary to prevent the person from coming to any harm, only the minimum necessary force or intervention may be used and for the shortest possible duration.

2.181 These provisions attracted some criticism from the Joint Committee on Human Rights (JCHR) in two of its reports on the human rights implications of the Mental Capacity Bill.[231] The Committee was concerned that use of these provisions could lead to deprivations of liberty which are not compatible with Art 5(1) of the European Convention on Human Rights, and in particular could lead to involuntary placement in hospital of a person lacking capacity and thereby deprive them of the procedural safeguards available if they had been detained under Mental Health Act powers:[232]

'Although clauses 5 and 6 contain important safeguards against the inappropriate use of restraint ... the combined effect of the two clauses appears to be to authorise (in the sense of protect against liability for) the use of force or the threat of force to overcome an incapacitated person's resistance in certain circumstances, or restrict their liberty of movement, in order to avert a risk of harm. For example, the power in clause 5 could be used to secure the admission into hospital of a person lacking capacity who is resisting such admission, where the person using or threatening force reasonably believes that the person lacks capacity in relation to his treatment, that it is in his best interests for him to be admitted to hospital for treatment and that it is necessary to admit the person in order to prevent harm to himself.

---

[229] MCA 2005, s 6(4).
[230] MCA 2005, s 6(2) and (3).
[231] JCHR, Twenty-third Report of Session 2003–04 *Scrutiny of Bills: Final Progress Report*, HL Paper 210, HC 1282, Part 2; JCHR, Fourth Report of Session 2004–05 *Scrutiny: First Progress Report*, HL Paper 26, HC 224, Part 4.
[232] JCHR, Twenty-third Report of Session 2003–04, at paras 2.22–2.23. See also Chapter 6.

We have written to the minister asking why the Government has not adopted the recommendation of the Joint Committee [on the Draft Mental Incapacity Bill] that the use or threat of force or other restriction of liberty of movement be expressly confined to emergency situations. Without such an express limitation on the face of the Bill, it appears to us that these provisions are likely to lead to deprivations of liberty which are not compatible with Article 5(1) ECHR, because they do not satisfy the Winterwerp requirements that deprivations of liberty be based on objective medical expertise and are necessary in the sense of being the least restrictive alternative. The Bill as drafted therefore does not appear to contain sufficient safeguards against arbitrary deprivation of liberty.'

2.182 The response from the Under Secretary of State, Baroness Ashton, confirmed that: 'It has never been the Government's policy that acts in connection with care and treatment in clause 5 might amount to a deprivation of liberty.'[233] The Government therefore moved a series of amendments in the House of Lords to address the Committee's concerns:[234]

'The committee wanted the Bill to confirm expressly that actions amounting to deprivation of liberty do not fall within the definition of "restraint" used in the Bill. The amendments achieve this ... This means that no-one acting in connection with care or treatment under Clause 5, nor an attorney or deputy, may deprive a person who lacks capacity of his liberty. "Restraint" includes only restrictions of liberty.'

2.183 One amendment introduced by the Government (previously MCA 2005, s 6(5)) expressly confirmed that someone carrying out an act under MCA 2005, s 5 will do more than 'merely restrain' a person lacking capacity if he or she deprives that person of liberty within the meaning of Art 5(1). This applied not only to public authorities covered by the Human Rights Act 1998 but to anyone carrying out acts in connection with care or treatment under s 5. Subsequent amendments to the Act introducing the new 'deprivation of liberty safeguards' made these provisions redundant, but confirm that specific authorisation is required to deprive someone of their liberty.[235]

2.184 There is clearly a fine line to be drawn between *restriction* of liberty, permitted under the definition of restraint, and *deprivation* of liberty under Art 5(1).[236] This was considered by the European Court of Human Rights in *HL v The United Kingdom* (the so-called *Bournewood* case) which said:[237]

'... in order to determine whether there has been a deprivation of liberty, the starting point must be the specific situation of the individual concerned and account must be taken of a whole range of factors arising in the particular case such as the type, duration, effects and manner of implementation of the measure in question. The

---

[233]   JCHR, Fourth Report of Session 2004–05, Appendix 4, at para 11.
[234]   *Hansard*, HL Deb, vol 670, ser 5, col 1468 (17 March 2005).
[235]   Under the MCA 2005 Deprivation of Liberty Safeguards (see Chapter 6) or by authorisation of the court – see for example *DH NHS Foundation Trust v PS* [2010] EWHC 1217 (Fam)), in which the President of the Court of Protection authorised the use of force if necessary to sedate PS and convey her to hospital for cancer treatment and to detain her in hospital during the period of post-operative recovery.
[236]   Some guidance is given in the Mental Capacity Act 2005: Code of Practice, at paras 6.49–6.53.
[237]   *HL v The United Kingdom* (Application No 45508/99), judgment of 5 October 2004, at paras 89 and 91.

distinction between a deprivation of, and restriction upon, liberty is merely one of degree or intensity and not one of nature or substance ...

... the Court considers the key factor in the present case to be that the health care professionals treating and managing the applicant exercised complete and effective control over his care and movements ...'

2.185 The judgment in this case was delivered at a very late stage in the parliamentary passage of the Mental Capacity Bill. It identified serious deficiencies (known as the '*Bournewood* gap') in that the law provided insufficient safeguards against unlawful deprivation of liberty of people lacking capacity to consent. The Government promised further safeguards, which have now been introduced into MCA 2005 by the Mental Health Act 2007 (MHA 2007). MHA 2007, s 50 has repealed MCA 2005, s 6(5) and substituted complex provisions and procedures allowing for the lawful deprivation of liberty of a person with mental disorder who lacks capacity to consent, where that is in the person's best interests.[238] The interface between MCA 2005 and mental health legislation, and the Deprivation of Liberty safeguards introduced in response to the European Court judgment, are considered in more detail in Chapter 6.

Decisions of donees or deputies

2.186 The provisions of MCA 2005, s 5 provide protection from liability to carers and professionals in circumstances where no formal decision-making powers are required. However, where formal powers already exist, for example, under a lasting power of attorney or through an order made by the Court of Protection, these formal decision-making powers will take precedence. Thus, MCA 2005, s 6(6) confirms that the provisions of s 5 do not authorise a person to do an act which conflicts with a decision made by a donee of a lasting power of attorney previously granted by the person lacking capacity, or by a deputy appointed by the Court, so long as the donee or deputy is acting within the scope of their authority. Anyone acting contrary to a decision of a donee or deputy will not have protection from liability.

2.187 In cases of dispute, for example, when carers or health professionals feel that a donee or deputy is acting outside the scope of his or her authority, or contrary to the incapacitated person's best interests, an application may be made for permission to apply to the Court of Protection to resolve the matter. Where the dispute involves serious health care decisions, MCA 2005, s 6(7) clarifies that life-sustaining treatment, or treatment necessary to prevent a serious deterioration in the person's condition, can be given pending a ruling from the Court.[239]

---

[238] These provisions and procedures were implemented in April 2009 accompanied by guidance in a supplement to the Code of Practice.

[239] Issues around life-sustaining treatment are dealt with in Chapter 5.

Paying for goods, services and other expenditure

Background

2.188 Before implementation of MCA 2005, the law already made provision for the enforceability of contracts, including contracts to purchase goods, which were made 'with' a person who lacked capacity or whose mental capacity was in doubt. In such cases, the courts have had to counterbalance two important policy considerations. One is a duty to protect those who are incapable of looking after themselves, and the other is to ensure that other people are not prejudiced by the actions of persons who lack capacity to contract but who appear to have full capacity. So, people without contractual capacity are bound by the terms of a contract they have entered into, even if it was unfair, unless it can be shown that the other party to the contract was aware of their mental inlack of capacity or should have been aware of this.[240] If the other party knows, or must be taken to have known, of the lack of capacity the contract is voidable.

2.189 The Sale of Goods Act 1979 (SGA 1979) modified this rule when applied to contracts for 'necessaries'. A person without mental capacity who agrees to pay for goods which are necessaries is legally obliged to pay a reasonable price for them. Although SGA 1979 applies to goods, similar common law rules were believed to apply to essential services.

The legislation

2.190 These rules are now brought together and given statutory force under MCA 2005, s 7. This clarifies that the obligation to pay a reasonable price applies to both the supply of necessary goods and the provision of necessary services to a person without capacity to contract for them, and it is the person who lacks capacity who must pay.

2.191 The definition of 'necessary' set out in MCA 2005, s 7(2) is based on that in SGA 1979,[241] meaning goods and services which are suitable to the person's condition in life (ie his or her place in society, rather than any mental or physical condition) and his or her actual requirements at the time of sale and delivery (eg ordinary drink, food and clothing or the provision of domiciliary or residential care services).

2.192 During parliamentary debate of these provisions, Lord Goodhart put forward some probing amendments to try to protect people with impaired capacity from entering into contracts which may be disadvantageous to them, for example, through abusive doorstep selling:[242]

'These amendments have been proposed by the CAB [Citizens Advice Bureau] which is concerned with the number of cases in which businesses have entered into contracts with people who lack capacity, and those contracts were unduly

---

[240]   *Imperial Loan Company v Stone* [1892] 1 QB 599.
[241]   SGA 1979, s 3(3).
[242]   *Hansard*, HL Deb, vol 668, ser 5, col 1396 (27 January 2005). See also HL Deb, vol 670, ser 5, cols 1469–1472 (17 March 2005).

disadvantageous to those people. At present under English law, though not under the law of Scotland, a contract entered into by a person lacking capacity can be set aside only if the other party to that contract was aware of the incapacity. The CAB amendment alters this, and it wants to apply to England the rule in Scotland which is that a contract can be set aside on grounds of incapacity even if the other party was not aware of the incapacity.'

The amendments were resisted by the Government on the ground that they may have unintended consequences, either by disempowering people with impaired capacity with whom traders may be reluctant to contract, or by allowing the possibility of abuse by people claiming incapacity in order to avoid being bound by a contract. However, the Minister committed the Government to further work during implementation of the Act to ensure that 'policy development ... on consumer strategy, credit and indebtedness is sensitive to the needs of consumers who lack capacity'.[243]

Responsibility to pay for necessary goods and services

2.193   MCA 2005 therefore confirms that the legal responsibility for paying for necessary goods and services lies with the person for whom they are supplied even though that person lacks the capacity to contract for them. The obligation is to pay 'a reasonable price' for them[244] so this provision cannot be used to enforce a contract which involves gross overcharging for goods or services.

2.194   Where the person also lacks the capacity to arrange for payment to be made, the carer who has arranged for the provision of goods and services necessary for the person's care or treatment may also have to arrange settlement of the bill. The Law Commission described the problem as follows:[245]

'We are not here concerned with ways in which a person may gain access to another person's income or assets. Where assets are held by a bank or other institution, specific authority will certainly be required before they can be transferred to anyone other than the legal owner. We are concerned, rather, with the situation where a carer arranges for something which will cost money to be done for a person without capacity. Family members often arrange for milk to be delivered, or for a hairdresser, gardener or chiropodist to call. More costly arrangements might be roof repairs, or for an excursion or holiday. In many cases it may be reasonable for a family member to arrange such matters, if it is done in the best interests of the person without capacity. Such actions could therefore fall within the confines of the general authority to provide for the person's welfare and care recommended above. Who, however, is to pay the provider of the goods or services supplied?'

2.195   Where it is appropriate for carers to arrange such matters, and so long as the arrangements made are in the best interests of the person lacking capacity, the carers' actions are therefore likely to be considered 'acts in connection with care or treatment' under MCA 2005, s 5, providing them with some protection from liability if their actions were to be challenged.

---

[243]   *Hansard*, HL Deb, vol 670, ser 5, col 1472 (17 March 2005).
[244]   MCA 2005, s 7(1).
[245]   Law Com No 231, n 1 above, at para 4.7.

However, some further arrangements may need to be made to meet the costs involved or to pay the provider of the goods or services supplied.

Expenditure

2.196 In such cases where necessary goods or services must be paid for, provision is made under MCA 2005, s 8 to meet the expenditure involved. This may be done in any one of three ways, described in the Code of Practice as follows (with footnotes added):[246]

- '• If neither the carer nor the person who lacks capacity can produce the necessary funds, the carer may promise that the person who lacks capacity will pay.[247] A supplier may not be happy with this, or the carer may be worried they may be held responsible for any debt. In such cases the carer must follow the formal steps ... below.
- If the person who lacks capacity has cash, the carer may use that money to pay for goods or services[248] (for example, to pay the milkman or the hairdresser).
- The carer may choose to pay for the goods or services with their own money. The person who lacks capacity must pay them back.[249] This may involve using cash in the person's possession or running up an IOU. (This is not appropriate for paid care workers, whose contracts might stop them handling their clients' money.) The carer must follow formal steps to get money held in a bank or building society account.'

2.197 The intention of these provisions is to make it possible for ordinary but necessary goods and services to be provided for people who lack the capacity to organise and pay for them, but without requiring carers to invoke expensive and time-consuming court proceedings to obtain authority to do so. However, MCA 2005, s 8 does not give any authorisation to a carer to gain access to the incapacitated person's income or assets or to sell the person's property. A distinction is drawn between the use of available cash already in the possession of the person lacking capacity, on the one hand, and the removal of money from a bank account or selling valuable items of property, on the other. Where a carer has promised that the person lacking capacity will pay for the goods or services supplied (ie has pledged the person's credit), formal authority may then need to be obtained before that promise can be put into effect. Similarly, formal arrangements may need to be made before a carer can be reimbursed if a large amount of expenditure is involved.

2.198 Some carers (such as family members) may already have such formal authority, for example, under an enduring or lasting power of attorney, as a deputy appointed by the Court of Protection or as a social security 'appointee'. MCA 2005, s 8(3) makes clear that these arrangements are not affected or changed by the above provisions allowing carers to arrange and pay for necessary goods and services on behalf of a person lacking capacity to make their own arrangements. However, as confirmed by

---

[246]   Mental Capacity Act 2005: Code of Practice, at para 6.61
[247]   'The carer may pledge the credit of the person who lacks capacity': MCA 2005, s 8(1)(a).
[248]   MCA 2005, s 8(1)(b).
[249]   MCA 2005, s 8(2).

s 6(6), an informal carer cannot make arrangements for goods or services to be provided for someone lacking capacity if this conflicts with a decision made by a donee or deputy acting within the scope of their authority.

Excluded decisions

Background

2.199   The Law Commission recognised the need to place some restrictions on carers and others acting under its proposed 'general authority' (now section 5 acts) without the need to apply for formal powers:[250]

> 'One benefit of setting out a clear general authority in statute is that the statute can then specify which matters fall outside the scope of that general authority. The general law already provides that certain acts can only be effected by a person acting for himself or herself. Examples would be entering into marriage or casting a vote in a public election. For the avoidance of doubt, our draft Bill lists certain matters which must be done by a person acting for him or herself … In many areas, however, it is at present quite unclear whether action may be lawfully taken on behalf of a person without capacity. If no-one is sure what can lawfully be done, then no-one can be sure what must and must not be done.'

The legislation

2.200   MCA 2005 therefore seeks to make clear what can and cannot be done by someone else in relation to a person lacking capacity. There are certain acts which cannot be done and certain decisions which can never be made on behalf of a person who lacks capacity to consent to those actions or to make those decisions for him or herself, either because they are so personal to the individual concerned or because they are governed by other legislation. In ss 27–29, the Act lists those specific decisions which are excluded and cannot be made under MCA 2005, whether by a carer or professional acting under MCA 2005, s 5, a donee under a lasting power of attorney, a deputy or by the Court of Protection itself.

Family relationships etc

2.201   MCA 2005, s 27 excludes the following decisions on family relationships from being taken on behalf of a person lacking capacity to make the decision:

'(a)   consenting to marriage or civil partnership,
(b)   consenting to have sexual relationships,
(c)   consenting to a decree of divorce being granted on the basis of two years' separation,
(d)   consenting to a dissolution order being made in relation to a civil partnership on the basis of two years' separation,
(e)   consenting to a child's being placed for adoption by an adoption agency,
(f)   consenting to the making of an adoption order,

---

[250]   Law Com No 231, n 1 above, at para 4.29.

(g)   discharging parental responsibilities in matters not relating to a child's property,

(h)   giving a consent under the Human Fertilisation and Embryology Act 1990.'

2.202   Where a person lacking capacity becomes involved in divorce or dissolution proceedings on any basis other than 2 years' separation, or where someone loses capacity during the course of such proceedings, a litigation friend (previously referred to as a next friend or guardian ad litem) will be appointed under the Family Proceedings Rules 1991 to give instructions and otherwise act on their behalf in relation to the proceedings.[251] Where a decision needs to be made about placing a baby for adoption, if the birth parent lacks capacity to consent to an adoption order, the rules relating to dispensing with consent in adoption legislation apply.[252] Matters concerned with the discharging of parental responsibilities not related to a child's property are dealt with under the Children Act 1989.

Mental Health Act matters

2.203   MCA 2005, s 28 states that the Act's decision-making powers cannot be used to give or to consent to treatment for mental disorder if the treatment is regulated by the Mental Health Act (MHA) 1983, Part 4. The purpose of Part 4 is to clarify the extent to which treatment for mental disorder can be imposed on detained patients in hospital and to provide specific statutory safeguards concerning the provision of treatment without consent.[253] Section 28 ensures that where a person lacking capacity to consent to treatment is detained in hospital under MHA 1983, the powers available under Part 4 would 'trump' the decision-making powers under MCA 2005 in relation to treatment for mental disorder.

2.204   This means that the safeguards and procedures of MHA 1983 (as amended by MHA 2007) relating to treatment for the person's mental disorder cannot be avoided by reference to MCA 2005, s 5 or by the consent or refusal of treatment by a donee or deputy. However, depending on the scope of their authority, a welfare attorney or deputy may apply to a mental health tribunal, or to the hospital managers, for the patient's discharge where the patient lacks capacity to make the application. For all other decisions affecting that person, the principles and provisions of MCA 2005 would apply.

2.205   Provisions in the Mental Health Act 2007 (which came into effect on 3 November 2008) amended MCA 2005, s 28 to take account of the new provisions in the amended Mental Health Act 1983 relating to the use of electro-convulsive therapy (ECT)[254] and those introducing compulsory community treatment orders (CTOs – also referred to as supervised

---

[251]   Family Proceedings Rules 1991, SI 1991/1247, Part IX. New Family Proceedings Rules are due to come into effect in 2010.

[252]   Adoption and Children Act 2002, s 52.

[253]   MHA 1983, ss 57–58.

[254]   MHA 1983, s 58A, inserted by MHA 2007, s 28(6).

community treatment) for patients previously detained in hospital who are now living in the community, but who continue to need treatment for their mental disorder. [255] The new s 28(1A)[256] removes the exclusion in relation to patients aged 16-17 years who lack capacity to consent to ECT, thus allowing ECT to be given to informal patients aged 16-17 under MCA 2005, s 5 rather than under the amended provisions of MHA 1983, where such patients lack capacity to consent, so long as the treatment is in their best interests, it is being given in circumstances that do not amount to a deprivation of their liberty and a Second Opinion Appointed Doctor considers ECT to be appropriate. Where a patient subject to a CTO (known as a 'community patient'[257]) is being treated under Part 4A of the amended 1983 Act, MCA 2005, s 28(1B) [258] prohibits that treatment being given under s 5, so that powers under the 1983 Act must be used. However, MHA 1983, Part 4A provides authority for attorneys or deputies with relevant powers to consent to treatment on behalf of a community patient.[259]

2.206 During the two pre-legislative scrutiny exercises carried out – on the draft Mental Incapacity Bill in 2003 and on the draft Mental Health Bill in 2004–05, both Joint Committees expressed concern about the interrelation between the two pieces of legislation and the potential for overlap and confusion between them.[260] These concerns were also raised frequently during the parliamentary debates on the Mental Capacity Bill. Of particular concern were the need to:

(1) provide appropriate safeguards in relation to the treatment of adults lacking capacity who are compliant with their care and treatment as required by the European Court judgment in *HL v The United Kingdom*;[261] and

(2) ensure that health professionals are clear about which law should be used to provide treatment for serious mental disorder for those lacking capacity to consent.

These matters are considered further in Chapter 6.

Voting rights

2.207 The final category of excluded decisions concerns voting rights. MCA 2005, s 29 confirms that no one can make a decision on voting or cast a vote at an election or a referendum on behalf of a person lacking capacity to vote.

---

[255] MHA 1983, ss 17A–17G, inserted by MHA 2007, s 32(1), (2).
[256] Inserted by MHA 2007, s 28(10).
[257] MHA 1983, s 17A(7).
[258] Inserted by MHA 2007, s 35(4), (5).
[259] MHA 1983, s 64B(3)(b)(ii).
[260] Joint Committee on the Draft Mental Incapacity Bill, Vol I, HL Paper 189-I, HC 1083-I, chapter 12; Joint Committee on the Draft Mental Health Bill, Vol I, HL Paper 79-I, HC 95-I, chapter 4.
[261] *HL v The United Kingdom* (Application No 45508/99), judgment of 5 October 2004.

Ill-treatment or neglect

Background

2.208   MCA 2005 created a number of ways in which someone can acquire powers over another person who lacks some decision-making capacity. For this reason the Law Commission concluded that:[262]

> 'It is right that a person with such powers should be subject to criminal sanction for ill-treating or wilfully neglecting the other person concerned.'

2.209   The Government was not at first 'persuaded that the creation of a new offence would be the best way of tackling abuse'.[263] However, a number of high-profile cases concerning abuse and ill-treatment of vulnerable people resulted in such an offence being included in the Draft Mental Incapacity Bill. This proposed the creation of an offence of ill-treatment or neglect with a maximum penalty of two years' imprisonment.[264]

2.210   The original impetus for the creation of a specific offence was the *Longcare* case, in which more than 50 adults with learning difficulties were abused at two care homes in South Buckinghamshire between 1983 and 1993. Despite the severity of abuse (which included rape, assault, over-sedation, starvation and neglect over a period of 10 years) existing law meant those responsible only received light sentences. The *Independent Longcare Inquiry*, the report of which was published in 1998,[265] recommended that the Government introduce a new, arrestable offence of harming or exploiting a vulnerable adult, with a maximum penalty of 10 years in prison. Lack of action in implementing any changes led to a campaign called 'Justice for Survivors' launched in 2003 by the journal *Disability Now* and supported by leading disability organisations and charities.

The new offence

2.211   MCA 2005, s 44 addressed some of these concerns by creating a new criminal offence of ill-treatment or wilful neglect of a person who lacks, or is believed to lack, capacity by any person involved in caring for that person or in a position of trust or power over the person. The penalty will vary according to the seriousness of the offence, ranging from a fine to a term of imprisonment, but the maximum penalty has been increased to 5 years' imprisonment.[266] This has the effect of making it an 'arrestable offence' under the Police and Criminal Evidence Act 1984, s 2. It also reflects the potential severity of the crime, with sentences in parallel with those for serious assaults on individuals, including the offences of inflicting

---

262   Law Com No 231, n 1 above, at para 4.38.
263   Lord Chancellor's Department *Making Decisions*, Cm 4465 (1999), at para 1.37.
264   Draft Mental Incapacity Bill, cl 31.
265   Tom Burgner *Independent Longcare Inquiry* (Buckingham County Council, 1998).
266   MCA 2005, s 44(3)(b).

grievous bodily harm and assault occasioning actual bodily harm under the Offences Against the Person Act 1861, which both carry maximum sentences of 5 years.

Scope of the offence

2.212 The criminal offence has a wide application to 'anyone who has the care of' a person who lacks, or is reasonably believed to lack, capacity.[267] This includes not only family carers, but also health and social care staff in hospital or care homes or providing domiciliary care. It also applies to donees of a lasting power of attorney or attorneys of an enduring power of attorney previously made by the person now lacking capacity[268] and to any deputy appointed by the Court of Protection for that person.[269] No lower age limit is specified, so the offence also applies to the ill-treatment or wilful neglect of children under 16 whose lack of capacity is caused by an impairment of, or disturbance in the functioning of, the mind or brain, not solely by the immaturity of youth.

2.213 During the parliamentary stages, amendments were put aimed at extending the application of the new offence to appointees, appointed by the Department for Work and Pensions (DWP) to collect and manage social security benefits on behalf of claimants unable to do so for themselves. The Minister clarified that:[270]

> '... it is clear that noble Lords are still concerned that because DWP appointees are handling only financial matters they might not be considered as having "care of the person" and, as such, would fall outside the scope of the offence. Again, we made clear during the Report stage in the other place that, in the majority of cases, the appointee will have care of the person and will therefore be covered by the offence.'

2.214 The Minister also confirmed that DWP officials were considering ways of introducing more effective monitoring of appointees.

Person who lacks capacity

2.215 In *R v Dunn*[271], the court considered the meaning of 'a person who lacks capacity' since this is not defined further within MCA 2005, s 44. Dunn had been convicted of four counts of ill-treating a person without capacity contrary to MCA 2005 s44 against three victims at the residential care home of which she was manageress. The judge in the Crown Court had directed that 'a person without capacity' meant a person unable to make decisions for himself because of a disturbance or impairment of function of the mind or brain, that a diagnosis of dementia was not enough, that 'impairment' could be permanent or temporary, that capacity was presumed

---

[267] MCA 2005, s 44(1)(a). The section does not specify which particular decision the person lacks capacity to make and it is not yet known how this will be interpreted by the courts.
[268] MCA 2005, s 44(1)(b).
[269] MCA 2005, s 44(1)(c).
[270] *Hansard*, HL Deb, vol 669, ser 5, col 746 (8 February 2005).
[271] R v Dunn (2010) All ER (D) 250 (Nov).

unless disproved on the balance of probabilities, and that this direction applied to all three victims. The defendant appealed on the basis that the direction on 'a person without capacity' was inadequate, failed to focus on the capacity of each victim to make a decision at the relevant time, and failed to identify the questions required by MCA 2005, s 3. The appeal was dismissed on the following grounds:[272]

> '(1) The legislation, including MCA, 2005 s 2, was convoluted and did not appropriately define the elements of the offence (including 'matter' and 'disturbance or impairment').
>
> (2) Lack of capacity had to be decided on the balance of probabilities.
>
> (3) There was a disconnect between MCA 2005, s 44 (referring to 'persons without capacity') and the elaborate definition sections (MCA 2005, ss 2 and 3), but it was open for the jury to conclude that the decisions regarding care (the 'matter') had been made because the victims lacked capacity.
>
> (4) It was unnecessary for the judge to complicate matters by referring to MCA 2005 s 3, and the conviction was safe.'

Ill-treatment

2.216   A single act is sufficient to show ill-treatment.[273] For a conviction of ill-treatment, it is necessary to show deliberate conduct by the accused which could properly be described as ill-treatment, whether or not it had caused or was likely to cause harm. The accused must either realise that he or she is inexcusably ill-treating the other person or be reckless as to whether he or she is doing so.[274]

Wilful neglect

2.217   Ill-treatment and neglect are separate offences.[275] In the context of the offence of wilfully neglecting a child in a manner likely to cause unnecessary suffering or injury to health (under the Children and Young Persons Act 1933, s 1), it has been held that neglect cannot be described as *wilful* unless the person:[276]

- either had directed his or her mind to whether there was some risk (although it might fall far short of a probability) that the child's health might suffer from the neglect, and had made a conscious decision to refrain from acting; or
- had so refrained because he or she did not care whether the child might be at risk or not.

2.218   Similar considerations are likely to apply in cases of wilful neglect of an adult lacking capacity.

---

[272]   Based on the All ER (D) summary in the absence of a transcript.
[273]   *R v Holmes* [1979] Crim LR 52.
[274]   *R v Newington* (1990) 91 Cr App R 247, CA.
[275]   *R v Newington* (1990) 91 Cr App R 247, CA.
[276]   *R v Sheppard* [1981] AC 394, [1980] 3 All ER 899, HL.

Chapter 3

Lasting Powers of Attorney

BACKGROUND

Powers of attorney

3.1   A power of attorney is simply a formal arrangement, undertaken by deed, whereby one person ('the donor') entrusts to another person ('the attorney' or 'the donee') authority to act in his or her name and on his or her behalf. A power of attorney is a form of agency which has been recognised at common law and used for centuries to enable the affairs of the donor (the principal) to be conducted on his or her behalf by an attorney (the agent) while the donor is away on business, overseas or physically unwell.

3.2   Common law principles of agency apply to powers of attorney, although the law relating to powers of attorney has been developed by statute, beginning with the Powers of Attorney Act 1971.[1] This short statute confirmed that a power of attorney must be made by deed[2] and provided for the protection of the attorney and a third person where they act in good faith without knowledge of revocation of the power.[3]

3.3   Notwithstanding the introduction of statutory rules governing their operation, common law principles concerning the creation, operation and revocation continue to apply, and in particular the principle that a power of attorney is revoked by the supervening incapacity of the donor. The rationale behind this principle is quite straightforward. An act carried out by an attorney is treated in law as an act carried out by the donor. The attorney can only do what the donor can give authority for him or her to do and if the donor lacks capacity then he or she cannot give that authority. The attorney and any third party dealing with the attorney can therefore assume, in the absence of any evidence to the contrary, that the donor is able to know and approve of what is being done on his or her behalf. The only exception to this cardinal rule is where the power of attorney is made in a prescribed statutory form that complies with the Mental Capacity Act 2005 (MCA 2005), Sch 1 (Lasting Powers of Attorney) or Sch 4 (Enduring Powers of Attorney) which provide for the power to continue notwithstanding the supervening incapacity of the donor.

Limitations

3.4   Any power of attorney has to be understood in the context of the common law principles of agency and their limitations. A power of attorney

---

[1]   This implemented the recommendations of the Law Commission's report *Powers of Attorney (1970)* Law Com No 30 (HMSO, 1970).
[2]   Law of Property (Miscellaneous Provisions) Act 1989, s 1.
[3]   Powers of Attorney Act 1971, ss 1 and 5.

confers rights on the attorney as well as responsibilities. And while an attorney may, if authorised, do anything that can lawfully be done by the donor, this is not an open-ended right to deal with the donor's property as he or she wishes. In particular:

- an attorney owes a fiduciary duty to the donor and cannot act so as to benefit him or herself or any other person to the detriment of the donor or the donor's estate. The attorney must act in good faith, keep accounts and disclose any conflict of interest;

- an attorney contracts in the name of the donor and while not personally liable under the contract, any property acquired or money held as attorney should be kept in the donor's name and must be kept separate from the attorney's own estate;[4]

- an attorney owes a duty of skill and care commensurate with the degree of expertise offered by him or her and whether he or she is acting gratuitously or for reward;[5]

- an attorney owes a duty of confidentiality to the donor and cannot disclose information unless authorised or to the extent required by the agency. This duty survives the operation of the power;

- an attorney cannot generally delegate his or her authority to another person;[6]

- an attorney is chosen to exercise personal skill and cannot appoint a successor in the same way as a trustee can appoint a new or replacement trustee;

- a power of attorney may be revoked by the donor by a deed or other act inconsistent with the continued operation of the power, which must include the giving of notice to the attorney;[7]

- the authority of the attorney is revoked by the death, incapacity or bankruptcy of the attorney;[8]

- the attorney may disclaim the power at any time;

- the attorney may only do such things as may lawfully be done by an attorney. Thus an attorney cannot perform an act which can only be performed personally, such as swearing an affidavit[9] or executing a will.[10] Neither can an attorney perform an act arising by virtue of the donor's office[11] or which is of a personal nature;[12]

---

[4] If the attorney holds property of the donor then he or she holds it as trustee. See *Henry v Hammond* [1913] 2 KB 515.

[5] See e g *Chaudhry v Prabhakar* [1988] 3 All ER 718.

[6] Delegation may be permitted if authorised by the instrument or by statute, if it is purely administrative, it is usual practice in the business of the donor or the attorney or if it is due to necessity. For example, directors of a company may delegate powers to an attorney or agent who may in turn delegate all or any of his or her powers (Art 71 of Table A).

[7] Thus the creation of a new power does not operate to revoke an earlier one, in contrast to a will under the Wills Act 1837, s 20.

[8] In respect of lasting powers of attorney, see MCA 2005, s 13(6). A welfare lasting power of attorney is not, however, revoked by the bankruptcy of the donee: s 13(8).

[9] *Clauss v Pir* [1988] 1 Ch 267.

[10] Wills Act 1837, s 9.

[11] The attorney of a judge cannot pass a sentence nor the attorney of a bishop ordain a priest.

[12] Thus an attorney cannot e g sit an exam, drive a car, marry or vote on behalf of the donor. These last two circumstances are specifically excluded from the scope of an attorney's authority under a lasting power of attorney by MCA 2005, ss 27 and 29.

- Rules of Court do not permit an attorney, in that role, to conduct legal proceedings in the name of the donor;[13] and
- a power of attorney is revoked by the incapacity of the donor.[14]

The incapable donor

3.5 It is the last limitation that has been regarded as having the largest impact for most people. A power of attorney made using common law principles or under the Powers of Attorney Act 1971 was adequate for businessmen or families going abroad leaving a relative or solicitor to manage their property. It would also help where a donor was physically unable to manage his or her affairs.[15] However, it was of no assistance in the increasingly frequent cases where a person had become incapable and had property and affairs that required administration. There were three solutions to that situation. Either the person's affairs were neglected, were dealt with under a potentially invalid power of attorney or the Court of Protection would appoint a receiver to manage that person's property and affairs.[16]

3.6 The traditional power of the Court to appoint a receiver was reviewed by the Law Commission in its report *The Incapacitated Principal* (1983).[17] This drew attention to the fact that the slow and bureaucratic jurisdiction of the Court of Protection and the Public Trust Office might not be necessary or appropriate in every situation where an incapable person's property and affairs needed to be administered. Surely if a person could plan ahead and choose who would administer their property and affairs in the event of their incapacity, that person should be allowed to do just that without having to undergo a formal judicial process. In such cases a loving spouse or mature and sensible children could look after the affairs of the incapable person without having to go to the expense and indignity of accounting for their conduct. It was also assumed that the existing judicial and administrative framework would not be able to cope with the increasing demands placed upon it by an ageing population.

Statutory powers of attorney

Enduring powers of attorney

3.7 In response to the Law Commission report *The Incapacitated Principal*, Parliament enacted the Enduring Powers of Attorney Act 1985 (EPAA 1985) which came into force on 10 March 1986.[18] This created a new type of power of attorney, enduring powers of attorney (EPA), which

---

[13]   See *Gregory v Turner* [2003] EWCA Civ 183. The appointment of a litigation friend for a 'protected party' is dealt with by the Civil Procedure Rules 1998, SI 1998/3132, Part 21.
[14]   See *Drew v Nunn* (1879) 4 QBD 661, CA; *Yonge v Toynbee* [1910] 1 KB 215, CA.
[15]   Such powers of attorney can still be made and are often used for those specific situations.
[16]   First under the Mental Health Act 1959 and then under the Mental Health Act 1983. Under MCA 2005, the Court has power to appoint a deputy.
[17]   Law Com No 122.
[18]   Enduring Powers of Attorney Act 1985 (Commencement Order) 1986, SI 1986/125.

would function in the same way as a conventional power of attorney but which, subject to a basic registration process, would continue or 'endure' beyond the onset of incapacity.[19] So long as that formality was complied with, a third party dealing with the attorney could assume that the attorney had a valid form of authority from the donor.[20]

3.8   An attorney acting under an EPA would still be subject to the laws and principles governing the relationship between the donor and the attorney. However, EPAA 1985 also provided some practical extension to the attorney's authority under a conventional power. Thus an attorney would be able to make gifts or provide for the needs of someone the donor might be expected to provide for.[21] For example, a husband looking after an incapable wife would be able to make gifts at Christmas to grandchildren on behalf of their grandmother and an attorney could use the donor's estate to maintain a disabled child or pay a grandchild's school fees.[22]

3.9   EPAA 1985 further provided a number of safeguards for the protection of donors of EPAs and placed the EPA jurisdiction under the authority of the Court of Protection. However, such safeguards were the result of a compromise between two competing objectives: on the one hand, individuals should be able to entrust their affairs to someone with as little interference from the state as possible; on the other, the vulnerable would need protection from the unscrupulous as well as the inefficient. Any system of protection would also have to be simple to operate, cost effective and largely self-financing.

3.10   The result of this tension was a simple system of protection which would operate on two levels. On the first level, there would be an administrative process of registration which would involve the donor and his or her next of kin being notified of an intention to register the EPA and therefore having an opportunity to object. The onus would be on the donor and his or her family to alert the Court of Protection in the event of misuse. On the second level, the civil law would apply to acts carried out by an attorney who was acting beyond the scope of his or her authority, particularly if the donor were incapable and the power was not registered. Acts carried out by an attorney would be invalid and provide the donor or his or her estate with a form of redress.[23]

3.11   The level of protection offered by an EPA, reflecting two opposing ideals, represented an imperfect compromise.[24] EPAA 1985 (which is largely incorporated in MCA 2005, Sch 4 insofar as existing EPAs are concerned) provided the following safeguards:

---

[19]   EPAA 1985, s 1(1)(a); MCA 2005, Sch 4, para 1.
[20]   EPAA 1985, s 9(3); MCA 2005, Sch 4, para 18(3).
[21]   EPAA 1985, s 3(4), (5); MCA 2005, Sch 4, paras 2, 3.
[22]   *Re Cameron* [1999] Ch 386, [1999] 2 All ER 924, [1999] 3 WLR 394.
[23]   Although a Scottish case and not directly involving EPAs, this principle was applied in *McDowall v Inland Revenue* [2003] UKSC SPC00382 (26 June 2003). Ironically the beneficiary of this case was not the donor's estate but the Inland Revenue.
[24]   Problems with the EPA jurisdiction are considered in more detail at **3.15**.

- The power of attorney must be in a prescribed form[25] and must be executed by the donor and attorney and attorneys.
- The prescribed form contains a brief explanation of the nature and effect of the power.
- The attorney or attorneys must undertake a process of official validation or registration when they believe that the donor is or is becoming mentally incapable of managing their property and affairs.[26] The EPA is registered by the Public Guardian, the registration providing a degree of protection for the donor and for third parties dealing with the attorney.
- Before applying for registration the attorney or attorneys must notify the donor of their intention and also at least three relatives in a prescribed order of classes of relatives.[27] All the members of a class must be notified, even if there are more than three persons, so that if a donor has one child, one sibling and six grandchildren all eight relatives must be notified.
- The donor must be given notice personally of the intention to register.[28]
- Any notices must be in a prescribed form and provide the recipient with details of the applicant and the grounds on which an objection can be made.[29]
- Any person notified of an application to register an EPA, and any other person at any other time (with the leave of the Court), may apply to the Court to refuse registration or to revoke the EPA.
- The Court shall refuse to register a power or cancel the registration of a power if satisfied that the donor has revoked the power, the donor remains capable, the donor has died or become bankrupt, that fraud or undue influence was used to create the power or 'having regard to all the circumstances and in particular the attorney's relationship or connection with the donor, the attorney is unsuitable to be the donor's attorney'.[30]
- If no valid notice of objection is received within five weeks of the last notice being given, the EPA is registered.[31]
- The Court of Protection has powers to intervene generally on behalf of the incapable or potentially incapable donor of the EPA. Thus the Court may exercise its powers to determine whether the EPA is effective,[32] and give directions as to the management of the donor's

[25] EPAA 1985, s 2(1)(a); MCA 2005, Sch 4, para 2(1).
[26] EPAA 1985, s 4(1); MCA 2005, Sch 4, paras 4(1) and 23. Notwithstanding the implementation of MCA 2005, the Mental Health Act 1983 definition of 'mental disorder' is preserved in relation to existing EPAs.
[27] EPAA 1985, Sch 1, para 2(1); MCA 2005, Sch 4, paras 5 and 6.
[28] EPAA 1985, Sch 1, para 4(1) and Court of Protection (Enduring Power of Attorney) Rules 2001, SI 2001/825, r 15(1); MCA 2005, Sch 4, para 8.
[29] The current notices are set out in the Lasting Powers of Attorney, Enduring Powers of Attorney and Public Guardian Regulations 2007, SI 2007/1253, Sch 7.
[30] EPAA 1985, ss 6(5) and 8(4); MCA 2005, Sch 4, paras 9 and 16(4).
[31] EPAA 1985, s 6(4)(a); MCA 2005, Sch 4, para 13(4).
[32] EPAA 1985, ss 5 and 8; MCA 2005, Sch 4, para 16(2)(a).

affairs and the rendering of accounts or the making of gifts.[33] In addition the Court retains its powers under MCA 2005 to intervene in the affairs of a person who lacks capacity so that there is an overlap between the two jurisdictions.

Success of enduring powers

3.12   That the EPA responded to a legal and social need is evident from the substantial number of EPAs in place. Because EPAs were often made for use prior to the onset of incapacity or as an insurance against incapacity, there remains no reliable method of knowing how many EPAs have been created. Those that can be measured are those which are registered with the Court of Protection or Office of Public Guardian and the number of registrations has increased steadily each year since the first such powers were registered in 1986. In 2004, 16,314 EPAs were registered.[34] In 2009/2010 over 21,000 EPAs were registered by the Public Guardian.[35]

3.13   While the number of registered EPAs has increased, the number of incapable persons whose affairs are subject to the traditional jurisdiction of the Court of Protection has remained stable, at around 32,000. Thus, without the introduction of EPAs, it would not have been possible for the existing judicial and administrative system to manage without a significant increase in resources.

3.14   There is no doubt that EPAs have, by the measure of their popularity alone, proved useful. They were seen as simple documents and therefore inexpensive to create.[36] The registration process is also easy to operate, with registration forms available from the Office of Public Guardian and a one-off fee of £120 payable on registration.[37]

Problems with enduring powers

3.15   Despite the widespread acceptance and use of EPAs, the EPA jurisdiction had several clear drawbacks, principally:

- An EPA relates only to the property and affairs of the donor. The attorney therefore has no authority over the personal welfare of the incapable donor, covering matters such as where the donor should

---

[33]   EPAA 1985, s 8(2); MCA 2005, Sch 4, para 16(2)(e).

[34]   National Audit Office *Protecting and promoting the financial affairs of people who lose capacity*, HC 27 (Session 2005–6). Under MCA 2005, the Public Guardian is the registration authority for EPAs: see Sch 1.

[35]   The number of registrations will reduce slowly as no new EPAs can be created under MCA 2005. It is impossible to compare with number of incapable persons with LPAs as these are often registered before the donor loses capacity.

[36]   The prescribed form was readily available, including on the Office of the Public Guardian website.

[37]   Court of Protection (Enduring Power of Attorney) (Amendment) Rules 2005, SI 2005/668; from 1 October 2007 dealt with by the Public Guardian (Fees, etc) Regulations 2007, SI 2007/2051.

live, what care he or she should receive or whether a particular treatment can be given or withheld. This is despite the fact that an attorney acting in the best interests of the incapable donor needs to take account of the welfare of the donor. The donor's estate cannot, in practice, be dealt with in isolation from the actual needs of the donor.

- The EPA jurisdiction rests on the principle that the donor's autonomy and right to choose the person to manage his or her affairs needs to be respected, so that the attorney can operate with as little official intervention as possible. This avoids the point of such official intervention, which is to protect the incapable person who is by the nature of his or her situation vulnerable and at risk from abuse. The Senior Judge of the Court of Protection has estimated that financial abuse takes place in about 10–15% of cases.[38] This substantial proportion includes not just cases of actual fraud but also cases of misuse where, for instance, an attorney is acting beyond the scope of his or her authority, and may be overly optimistic in view of the extent to which unregistered EPAs are used beyond the onset of incapacity. An attorney might therefore dispose of an asset belonging to an incapable donor using an unregistered EPA or make gifts which are beyond the scope of his or her authority as an attorney.

- That fraud or misuse takes place so extensively is due to the very limited degree of official supervision provided. There is no means of knowing that a particular EPA is being used, let alone that it is being used correctly. The Court of Protection relies on misuse being notified to it, but this in turn presupposes that an attorney who registers an EPA correctly notifies relatives and they in turn file an objection with the Court of Protection. In one recent instance the manager of a nursing home was attorney for several residents and systematically defrauded them of their savings over a couple of years. The residents had no relatives and, in any event, the EPAs were not registered. An improper benefit claim brought the fraud to light. Although the Court of Protection revoked the EPA, the civil and criminal laws offered little recompense for the victims. Recovery of the stolen assets was impossible as these had been dissipated and a criminal prosecution was made difficult by the fact that the witnesses could not give evidence for themselves.[39] The

---

[38] This bold assertion was first made by Denzil Lush in 'Taking Liberties: Enduring Powers of Attorney and financial abuse' (1998) *Solicitors Journal*, 11 September, at p 808 but has been restated by Denzil Lush in *Cretney & Lush on Enduring Powers of Attorney* (Jordans, 5th edn, 2001) at p 133 and see also oral evidence given by Master Lush to the Joint Committee on the Draft Mental Incapacity Bill, HL Paper 189-11, HC 1083-11, at p 188.

[39] In this tragic example, although the Crown prosecuted the former manager, it accepted an admission of liability in respect of only certain counts where the victims were capable of giving evidence. Where the victims were incapable or had subsequently died, there was no conviction in their individual cases, making civil recovery very difficult to pursue.

failure of the system to protect vulnerable adults was recognised officially in 1999 by the Quinquennial Review of the then Public Trust Office:[40]

> 'An EPA bestows virtually unfettered control of someone's finances once it is brought into force. While its objective (to put someone's financial affairs into the hands of an individual they have pre-selected, rather than surrendering to the Court of Protection) fits entirely with the objective of keeping the state out of family affairs unless there is no alternative, if an EPA goes wrong the results can be catastrophic for the person concerned. Although comparatively rare, there are plenty of instances where the system has been deliberately or accidentally abused and getting the position rectified through the Court is a long and difficult process ...'

- In view of these difficulties, the choice of attorney is crucial to the success or failure of a person's EPA. Unfortunately, many EPAs are made long before they are needed and the donor is unable to foresee changes in his or her circumstances that might otherwise have led him or her to choose a different attorney. The knowledge of the donor and the advice he or she receives at the time the EPA is made is therefore of utmost importance. However, the prescribed form of EPA is easy to obtain and complete and offers little effective protection. The form only requires a signature by the donor and one witness whereupon it is presumed to have been validly executed.[41] There is furthermore no requirement that the donor has any form of legal or independent advice or that there be any assessment of the donor's capacity to create the power. Thus the ability to misuse the EPA is instituted quite easily at the time the form is created.

- EPAs have proved a victim of their own success. They were designed to be simple to complete and the forms could be obtained from stationers or from the internet. Many solicitors prepared EPAs for a nominal cost, often in connection with another matter such as a will. The problem, however, was that many such EPAs were prepared too quickly, without proper care, and without proper thought being given to problems that might arise in the future. A carefully prepared EPA would take account of family dynamics, the donor's capacity, conditions and restrictions available to the donor and the nature of his or her estate: in too many cases advice on such matters was not available.[42]

- An attorney is required to register an EPA once he or she 'has reason to believe that the donor is or is becoming mentally incapable'.[43] Therefore once the EPA has been registered, it appears to anyone dealing with the attorney that the donor is mentally incapable and thereby incapable, by reason of mental disorder, of

---

[40]   Ann Chant CB *The Public Trust Office of the Lord Chancellor's Department: A Quinquennial Review* (November 1999), at para 47.

[41]   *Re W (enduring power of attorney)* [2001] Ch 609, [2001] 4 All ER 88, [2001] 2 WLR 957.

[42]   The Law Society published detailed Guidance in 1995 (revised in 1995) on EPAs and while this was very detailed and encouraged best practice among solicitors, it was not always followed and of course not all EPAs were professionally prepared.

[43]   EPAA 1985, s 4(1). Notwithstanding the implementation of MCA 2005, this is still the case for existing EPAs; see MCA 2005, Sch 4, para 4(1).

managing and administering his or her property and affairs.[44] The presumption arises therefore that once the EPA is registered, the donor is unable to manage or administer the full extent of his or her property and affairs. This sits uneasily with the principle, now enshrined in MCA 2005, that capacity is function specific and that a person may have capacity or lack capacity in respect of different functions.[45] Thus a donor could be prevented from making decisions in respect of which he or she had capacity. For example, a donor might be able to manage small amounts of money or collect his pension, but his bank or pension administrator would assume, from the fact that the EPA had been registered, that he could not and would therefore deny him any rights whatsoever over his own estate.

Abolition of enduring powers

3.16 The Law Commission considered these inherent failings in the EPA jurisdiction in the context of a review of the law relating to mental incapacity in its report *Mental Incapacity* (1995).[46] This review of the law, considered in more detail in Chapter 1, led to the passing of MCA 2005 in April 2005 which came into force on 1 October 2007.

3.17 Although no new EPAs may be made after 1 October 2007, all existing EPAs will continue to remain effective. The Law Commission had proposed converting all existing EPAs to new-style powers of attorney. However, EPAs have been made in good faith to comply with a different statutory framework and for many of those powers there is no means for the persons who made them to change them. Therefore instead of cancelling or converting existing EPAs into new lasting powers of attorney (LPAs), MCA 2005 provides for existing EPAs to continue to operate under the same legal basis as they were created, but within the framework of the new 2005 Act. MCA 2005 does, however, impose one further set of obligations on an attorney making decisions for a donor who lacks capacity. The attorney must act in the donor's best interests within the meaning of MCA 2005, s 4 and must also comply with the statutory Code of Practice.[47]

3.18 The provisions of the new Act relating to existing EPAs are contained in MCA 2005, Sch 4. Apart from a few small changes, Sch 4 incorporates the provisions of EPAA 1985 into the new Act.[48]

---

[44] EPAA 1985, s 13. This is now set out in MCA 2005, Sch 4, para 23(1).

[45] *Re Beaney* (deceased)[1978] 2 All ER 595, [1978] 1 WLR 770 and see generally Chapter 2.

[46] Law Com No 231.

[47] The 'best interests' requirements are dealt with at **2.113–2.145** and the Code of Practice is dealt with at **2.7–2.22**.

[48] Forms and procedures are dealt with by provisions issued under MCA 2005, such as the Lasting Powers of Attorney, Enduring Powers of Attorney and Public Guardian Regulations 2007, SI 2007/1253.

Lasting Powers of Attorney

3.19 MCA 2005 provides expressly for the revocation of the EPAA 1985,[49] and for the creation of a new type of power of attorney, a LPA.[50]

3.20 LPAs and MCA 2005 jurisdiction cannot, however, be comprehended without reference to EPAs:

- EPAs made before MCA 2005 came into force will continue to operate in accordance with the same legal principles as existed as when they were made, although within the framework of the 2005 Act.[51] Thus different procedures as well as laws will operate side by side for many years to come.
- The Public Guardian and the Court of Protection will be responsible for administering the two sets of procedures and laws.
- A LPA, like an EPA, is a statutory form of power of attorney that builds on existing common law and statutory principles. Thus decisions of the courts affecting EPAs as well as practical and professional experience gained in their use will have a bearing on the use and understanding of LPAs.
- Attorneys acting under LPAs and EPAs are, where the donor lacks capacity, bound by the same requirements to act in the donor's best interests under MCA 2005, s 4.
- The principle requirement of the LPA is to address problems inherent in the EPA jurisdiction. It therefore needs to be measured against that standard.

NATURE OF LASTING POWER OF ATTORNEY

Character of lasting power of attorney

3.21 A LPA is defined by MCA 2005, s 9 as 'a power of attorney' under which one party (the donor) confers on another (the donee) authority to make certain decisions.[52] A LPA is therefore at heart 'a power of attorney' so that the principles governing the relationship in law between principal and agent apply to it. However, the scope of such a power is both restricted and extended by statute.

3.22 Under a LPA the donor may confer authority on the attorney to make decisions, including decisions in circumstances where the donor no longer has capacity in relation to all or any of:

- the donor's personal welfare or specified matters concerning the donor's personal welfare; and

---

49   MCA 2005, s 66(1)(b).
50   MCA 2005, s 9.
51   See **3.132**.
52   MCA 2005 generally refers to a 'donee' in the context of LPAs and an 'attorney' in the context of EPAs. The author has used the term 'attorney' as a generic term that applies to a person to whom authority has been delegated under a power of attorney, whether it be an ordinary, enduring or lasting power.

- the donor's property and affairs or specified matters concerning the donor's property and affairs.[53]

3.23 The essential character of the LPA is that it respects the presumption contained in MCA 2005, ss 1 and 2, that a person must be assumed to have capacity unless it can be established that he or she lacks capacity and that capacity is only relative to the matter and at the time that capacity needs to be determined. The LPA of itself is silent as to the capacity of the donor.[54] The LPA therefore must work in tandem with the ability of the donor to make decisions for him or herself over a range or spectrum of matters for which decisions might be made. At one end of the spectrum, the donor continues to make all decisions for him or herself, with the attorney having no role to play (waiting in the background to be called upon to act); further into the spectrum, the donee carries out specific functions such as the sale of a property and the investment of the proceeds. At the other end of the spectrum, the attorney makes all the decisions the donor cannot make for him or herself.

3.24 A LPA therefore functions at several different levels, applying different principles according to the circumstances in which the power is being operated. Thus:
- the LPA operates, in respect of property and affairs, as an ordinary power of attorney so that the attorney acts with the implied knowledge and approval of the donor;
- the LPA operates, in respect of property and affairs, in relation to matters which the donor lacks capacity to determine for him or herself;
- in respect of welfare decisions, the LPA only operates where the donor lacks capacity to make decisions; and
- where the attorney makes decisions on behalf of the donor which the donor lacks capacity to make, the attorney must also act in the donor's best interests, applying the criteria laid down in MCA 2005, s 4 as well as the Code of Practice.

3.25 This holistic approach to the requirements of the donor obviates the need for an attorney to register the LPA specifically on the onset of incapacity. Although registration might be delayed until that point is reached, the lack of capacity of itself does not require the attorney to take any action to validate the power. The existence of a LPA thereby avoids a presumption, as is the case with an EPA, that the donor is incapable of managing the full extent of his or her property and affairs.[55] The criterion for registration is not 'does the donor lack capacity?', but 'does the power need to be used?'. If it needs to be used, the power can be registered by the donor or the donee. To any third party dealing with the attorney (where the

---

[53] MCA 2005, s 9(1).
[54] By contrast with EPAs whose registration is triggered by a defined medical state which therefore creates a presumption that the donor lacks capacity (see **3.15**).
[55] This follows the recommendation of the Law Commission, see Law Com No 231 (see **3.16**), at para 7.31.

property and affairs of the donor are concerned), the state of mind of the donor is irrelevant and the donor is not labelled or stigmatised as being incapable.

3.26 This approach is not followed where the power relates to welfare matters. Although the LPA can be registered at any time irrespective of the capacity of the donor, when the LPA comes to be used, it can only be used where the donor lacks capacity to make the decision in question..[56] For obvious reasons, the donor's right to make decisions over his or her own welfare takes precedence. A doctor or other person treating the donor and seeking to rely on the authority of the donee to make a decision must ensure that:

- there is a valid (ie registered) LPA in place; and
- the donor lacks capacity to make the decision.

Problems in practice

3.27 While it is obviously sensible to allow a person autonomy over his own affairs to the extent possible without making presumptions about capacity, this can cause practical difficulties. Any third party dealing with the attorney acting under a registered LPA is not 'on notice' that the donor lacks capacity. This may cause problems if there are conflicting instructions or the LPA is being used fraudulently. It may, for instance, be possible for the attorney to arrange the sale of the donor's property against the donor's wishes. Will anyone check with the donor that the donor wants the property sold? Or take the case of a donor who makes regular withdrawals from his account to pay a friendly tradesman, even though there is a LPA in place and registered with the bank. In both cases the status of the LPA does not of itself provide any greater degree of protection for either party than an ordinary power of attorney.

3.28 The protection afforded by the LPA is in the making and registration of the power. Once those steps have been taken and the LPA is in place, there is no further formal protection for the donor. The status of the LPA and the statutory presumption of capacity may well make it easier for the confused and the vulnerable to make mistakes which will be harder to detect in practice. Although LPAs may be drafted to ensure that they will only operate on the onset of incapacity (in the same way as an EPA), this does not appear to be common in practice.[57] Where a LPA is restricted in this way, the donor will end up reversing the statutory presumption in favour of capacity intended by Parliament to benefit the donor. Restrictions also cause their own difficulties in terms of drafting, evidence and defining the actual trigger for registration. Should for instance the LPA be used if the donor is physically incapable but mentally capable? Should it be used if the donor needs his attorneys to act (in relation to property and affairs) while he has

---

[56]   MCA 2005, s 11(7)(a).
[57]   See **3.78**. Problems caused by the policy of early registration are considered in more detail at **3.117**.

capacity? There is also a danger in delaying registration until a triggering condition has arisen as the registration process takes time and the LPA may need to be used at short notice.[58] Experience suggests that most LPAs are drafted on the basis that there should be flexibility to make decisions for the donor when they need to be taken and the donees should be trusted to act accordingly.

Scope of lasting power of attorney

3.29   The scope of the attorney's authority is very extensive. Legislation and cases concerning powers of attorney tend to emphasise what an attorney cannot do rather than what an attorney can do. However, the starting point is the principle that an attorney stands in the place of the donor and can do whatever the donor could do for him or herself. That seemingly limitless power is then restricted in one of four ways:

(1) *By the terms of the power itself.* The donor may limit the authority of the attorney so that the power relates only to specified matters or operates in certain circumstances.[59] For example, a power may provide that it only relates to property and affairs or that it will only operate if the donor becomes incapable. Limitations in the form of the power are considered in more detail at **3.76**.

(2) *By common law.* There are certain personal acts that cannot be delegated to an attorney and an attorney cannot act to benefit him or herself or delegate his or her authority. These and other restrictions, including duties imposed on the attorney by law, such as a duty of care and a duty not to benefit, are considered in more detail at **3.4**.

(3) *By statute.* MCA 2005 includes some crucial extensions to these restrictions. Subject to the formalities of the Act being complied with, a LPA is not revoked by the lack of capacity of the donor and in certain circumstances a power can be used to make gifts, delegate trustee functions and make decisions concerning personal welfare matters. MCA 2005 also sets out limits on the scope of the 2005 Act itself and limits on the attorney's authority.[60]

(4) *By the Court.* The Court of Protection has powers to intervene in the operation of the power. The Court can cancel the power in favour of an attorney, attach conditions to the power or provide the attorney with authority to make a decision which is beyond the scope of the attorney's authority within the LPA.[61] The Court can also make decisions of its own concerning the property and affairs and welfare of the donor.[62]

---

[58]   The prescribed period which must expire before the Public Guardian can register an LPA where there are no objections is six weeks (Lasting Powers of Attorney, Enduring Powers of Attorney and Public Guardian Regulations 2007, SI 2007/1253, reg 12).

[59]   MCA 2005, s 9(4)(b) and see **3.77**.

[60]   MCA 2005, ss 27–29.

[61]   MCA 2005, s 23.

[62]   MCA 2005, ss 15–17.

Property and affairs

3.30 MCA 2005 does not specify the extent or scope of an attorney's powers over a person's property and affairs. MCA 2005, s 9(1) describes a LPA as 'a power of attorney' which confers authority on a donee to make decisions about 'all or any of' the donor's property and affairs or specified matters concerning the donor's property and affairs. What is peculiar to a LPA (as opposed to an ordinary power of attorney) is that the LPA includes authority to make such decisions in circumstances where the donor no longer has capacity.

3.31 The actual authority granted to an attorney is similar, if more clearly defined in relation to EPAs. Where a donor grants general authority in an EPA, the power 'operates to confer, subject to the restriction imposed ... and to any conditions or restrictions contained in the instrument, authority to do on behalf of the donor anything which the donor can lawfully do by an attorney'.[63] Thus the EPA also refers back to the common law principles. MCA 2005, Sch 4, para 1(2) also provides a description of an attorney's limited authority to 'maintain the donor or prevent loss to his estate' which is the very least an attorney can and should do when an application for registration has been made and the power has not been registered. As well as his or her common law powers, the attorney acting under an EPA also has authority to make gifts and provide for the needs of any other person if the donor might be expected to provide for that person's needs.[64]

3.32 MCA 2005 provides less assistance in understanding the attorney's core authority so that a LPA must also be understood in terms of the common law relationship between principal and agent. In practice, an attorney will have access to the full extent of the donor's property and affairs. Unless the donor expressly limits the scope of the attorney's authority, the attorney has authority to administer such property and affairs. Clearly the attorney also has a fiduciary duty to the donor and the donor's estate. But MCA 2005 takes the attorney into a new area of responsibility. As we have seen, an attorney is acting at different levels: at one level he or she is acting as the donor's agent, in a fiduciary role; but the 2005 Act also requires the attorney to make decisions on the donor's behalf where the donor lacks capacity and when a decision made at that level is also subject to MCA 2005, s 4 and therefore to the best interests criteria laid down by the 2005 Act.[65] The donor must therefore take into account matters such as the donor's past and present wishes and feelings, beliefs and values, the views of anyone specified as a person to be consulted or caring for the donor or interested in the welfare of the donor as well as the other factors the donor would be likely to consider if he or she had capacity.

---

[63] MCA 2005, Sch 4, para 3(1).
[64] MCA 2005, Sch 4, para 3(2) and (3). Curiously, the specific reference to a power to provide for another person's needs is not repeated in the provisions of the MCA 2005 dealing with LPAs. See 3.35 below.
[65] MCA 2005, s 4(7) and also s 9(4).

Acting in the best interests of the donor

3.33   The importance of the application of 'best interests' to the attorney's role is more than a restatement of the common law duty of an agent to act in the best interests of his or her principal. Neither is the attorney necessarily doing what the donor would have done and making a substituted decision on his behalf. The attorney must act in the best interests of the donor, taking account of a whole range of factors, only one of which might be the actual or likely wishes of the donor.

3.34   The extended test of best interests requires an attorney to possess an appropriate understanding of the character and circumstances of the donor. It may though be difficult to reconcile this with an objective responsibility towards the donor's estate. For example, a donor may have been determined to live in his own home, notwithstanding a worrying degree of self-neglect. Or a donor may have been profligate or lived beyond his means. An attorney may have to make a tactful compromise between these personal circumstances and his or her responsibilities to the estate (and its preservation for the long-term benefit of the donor). The attorney may have to assume that the donor would appreciate his predicament as one of the 'other factors he would be likely to consider if he were able to do so'. Where there is a conflict between these two objectives, it is clear that an attorney should not expose himself to liability and the objective best interests of the donor should prevail. This potential dilemma was addressed by Her Honour Judge Marshall QC in the case of *Re S and S*.[66] Although this case related to the wishes of a donor of an EPA whose wishes (that the attorneys should act jointly and if they could not act jointly a professional deputy should be appointed), the judge explained that the donor's wishes should have priority. But such priority is not an absolute requirement, rather a practical presumption. But although the donor's wishes in this case could be adhered to, the donor's wishes are not paramount. They are a factor that must be considered, and one to which a great deal of weight must be given. But they remain just one of several factors in the balancing act that the attorney must perform when acting in the donor's best interests. As the judge pointed out (at paras 57 and 58):[67]

> '... where P can and does express a wish or view which is not irrational (in the sense of being a wish which a person with full capacity might reasonably have), is not impracticable as far as its physical implementation is concerned, and is not irresponsible having regard to the extent of P's resources (ie whether a responsible person of full capacity who had such resources might reasonably consider it worth using the necessary resources to implement his wish) then that situation carries great weight, and effectively gives rise to a presumption in favour of implementing those wishes, unless there is some potential sufficiently detrimental effect for P of doing so which outweighs this.
>
> That might be some extraneous consequence, or some other unforeseen, unknown or unappreciated factor. Whether this further consideration actually should

---

[66]   [2008] EWHC B16 (Fam).

[67]   This approach was followed in the High Court decision of Lewison J in the case of *Re P* [2009] EWHC 163 (Ch) and by Morgan J in the case of *Re G (TJ)* [2010] EWHC 3005 (CoP).

justify overriding P's wishes might then be tested by asking whether, had he known of this further consideration, it appears (from what is known of P) that he would have changed his wishes. It might be further tested by asking whether the seriousness of this countervailing factor in terms of detriment to P is such that it must outweigh the detriment to an adult of having one's wishes overruled, and the sense of impotence, and the frustration and anger, which living with that awareness (insofar as P appreciates it) will cause to P. Given the policy of the Act to empower people to make their own decisions wherever possible, justification for overruling P and "saving him from himself" must, in my judgment be strong and cogent. Otherwise, taking a different course from that which P wishes would be likely to infringe the statutory direction in s 1(6) of the Act, that one must achieve any desired objective by the route which least restricts P's own rights and freedom of actions.'

Power to maintain others

3.35 The EPA jurisdiction refers expressly to the maintenance of others.[68] Thus the attorney 'may so act in relation to himself or in relation to any other person if the donor might be expected to provide for his or that person's needs respectively; and ... may do whatever the donor might be expected to do to meet those needs'. By contrast, where LPAs are concerned, MCA 2005 makes no reference to the maintenance of anyone else.[69] It is arguable that the attorney under a LPA has no authority to maintain anyone apart from the donor. There is no express power for the attorney to act upon any moral obligation the donor might have to maintain another person, for instance, a spouse or a disabled child.

3.36 The Law Commission report *Mental Incapacity* took the view that the power to act in a donor's 'best interests' was more flexible and wider than the power of an attorney at common law, because:[70]

'... it requires the attorney to consider the wishes and feelings of the donor and the factors he or she would have taken into account, the attorney would in appropriate cases be quite able to meet another person's needs (including the attorney's own needs) or make seasonal or charitable gifts, while still acting within the best interests duty.'

However, this rather sweeping assumption is implicitly contradicted by MCA 2005, s 12, which sets out the attorney's authority to make gifts. This is further emphasised by s 23(4), which provides that any gifts not within the scope of that section must be authorised by the Court of Protection. If the attorney had such wide powers on a general interpretation of the Act then there would be no need for such an express provision.[71] There is no corresponding provision addressing maintenance and, while it can be argued that maintenance is not the same as a gift, there must be some uncertainty as to whether the attorney can – or the extent to which the attorney should – act

---

[68]   MCA 2005, Sch 4, para 3(2); formerly covered by EPAA 1985, s 3(4).
[69]   The extent of the EPAA 1985 power was illustrated in the case of *Re Cameron (deceased), Phillips v Cameron* [1999] Ch 386, [1999] 2 All ER 924, [1999] 3 WLR 394.
[70]   Law Com No 231, at para 7.11.
[71]   MCA 2005, s 12 and see **3.37–3.43**. The draft Bill prepared by the Law Commission made no reference to gifts or to maintenance.

on this without the sanction of the Court of Protection.[72] Where the attorney is the person whom the donor might be expected to provide for there is a further conflict of interest which the attorney, as a fiduciary, cannot resolve in that role.

Limited power to make gifts

3.37 MCA 2005, s 12 restates the principle that an attorney cannot make gifts, but allows gifts to be made in certain limited circumstances. The donor can limit this authority, but cannot extend it.[73] Subject to any limitation contained in the power, the donee may make gifts:[74]

> '(a) on customary occasions to persons (including himself) who are related to or connected with the donor, or
>
> (b) to any charity to whom the donor made or might have been expected to make gifts,
>
> if the value of each such gift is not unreasonable having regard to all the circumstances and, in particular, the size of the donor's estate.'

3.38 MCA 2005 therefore imposes four basic conditions on an attorney before a gift can be made:

(1) there must be no restriction in the power itself which prevents the gift from being made;

(2) the gift must be made on a 'customary occasion';

(3) an individual must be related to or connected with the donor, while a charity must be one which has benefited or might be expected to benefit from the donor; and

(4) the value of any gift must not be unreasonable having regard to all the circumstances and especially to the value of the donor's estate.

3.39 'Customary occasion' is defined by MCA 2005, to allow for all types of family, seasonal or religious events which justify the making of a gift, as:[75]

> '(a) the occasion or anniversary of a birth, a marriage or the formation of a civil partnership, or
>
> (b) any other occasion on which presents are customarily given within families or among friends or associates.'

---

[72] It might be argued that maintenance in return for consideration such as the care of the donor is not a gift. But there is bound to be some uncertainty as to what is bounty and what is value and until the matter has been judicially considered, an attorney would be acting appropriately in referring such a matter to the Court of Protection.

[73] See the decision in the case of *Re Baker* (an order of the Senior Judge made on 12 November 2010). An LPA included the following provision: "I authorise my Attorneys to make gifts from my assets on such terms and conditions as they think fit, for the purposes of inheritance tax planning, including but not restricted to the making of gifts in line with the annual lifetime gift allowance." On the application of the Public Guardian the provision was severed on the grounds that it contravened section 12 of the MCA 2005.

[74] MCA 2005, s 12(2).

[75] MCA 2005, s 12(3).

3.40 The attorney cannot therefore make a gift at a time that is not a 'customary occasion' such as the beginning or end of a tax year. For the attorney to make a valid gift as part of a tax-planning exercise, it must also be of a 'customary occasion'.

3.41 In determining whether an attorney can make a gift, MCA 2005, s 12 requires the attorney to take account of the donor's history and likely wishes where a gift is made to charity. This would, for instance, allow an attorney to continue an established pattern of giving, for example, maintaining standing orders to charities. However, regardless of whether gifts are made to a charity or to an individual, the attorney cannot avoid the overriding duty to act in the donor's 'best interests' and take account of matters such as the donor's past and present wishes and feelings or factors that he or she would consider if he or she had capacity.

3.42 A consideration of the donor's best interests is consistent with an attorney's responsibilities to act prudently in relation to the management of the donor's estate. A donor who had in the past been very generous may now have a commitment to funding long term care costs. This is a factor that he would consider if he had capacity. The attorney furthermore cannot avoid his or her fiduciary duty to the donor's estate and could not make a gift which the donor could not afford to make. The gift must in any event be reasonable having regard to the circumstances and the size of the donor's estate. It is for the attorney to exercise his or her judgment in measuring the appropriate value of a gift. There is no fixed limit as to what is reasonable or not. Different recipients may have greater or lesser needs or be more or less deserving of a gift. A wealthy donor may be able to afford a gift of several thousand pounds, although a gift of £20,000 has been treated as beyond the scope of an attorney's authority under an EPA. [76] A donor with limited capital and in receipt of benefits may, by contrast, only be able to afford a gift of a few pounds.

3.43 Where there is any doubt about the attorney's authority to make the gift or it is clear that a proposed gift goes exceeds the attorney's authority under the LPA, the Court of Protection can authorise the gift under MCA 2005, s 23, which deals with the Court's powers in relation to the operation of LPAs. The Court cannot, however, ignore an express limitation in the power itself and allow the attorney to exceed his or her authority under the power.[77] In this situation, the attorney or any other person who may apply, may request the Court to authorise a gift under either MCA 2005, s 23(4) or under MCA 2005, s 18(1)(b).[78]

---

[76] See *Re W (enduring power of attorney)* [2001] 4 All ER 88, [2001] 2 WLR 957 and in particular the comments of the judge at first instance, Jules Sher QC [2000] 1 All ER 175, at p 181 and [2000] 3 WLR 45, at p 51.

[77] See *Re R (enduring power of attorney)* [1990] Ch 647, [1990] 2 All ER 893, [1990] 2 WLR 1219. This does not prevent a person applying to the Court of Protection for an order for a gift under MCA 2005, s 18.

[78] There are therefore two similar provisions that can be used. This may be due to the fact that EPAA 1985 provided its own basis for the Court to authorise gifts and a similar power has

The donor as trustee

3.44 A LPA confers the same rights as an EPA in favour of an attorney who is a trustee of land. An attorney acting under a LPA has no power to act as a trustee unless the power complies with the Trustee Act 1925, s 25 or the provisions of the Trustee Act 1925, s 36 apply. This latter provision saves most domestic situations where a property is owned by husband and wife under a trust for land. One of the owners, who is also a trustee for land becomes incapable. To fulfil the 'two trustee' rule, the attorney of the incapable trustee – acting under a registered power[79] – can appoint a new trustee to act on the sale and give a valid receipt for capital monies.[80]

The donor as a litigant

3.45 A person's right or standing to conduct proceedings is governed by the relevant Rules of Court in which those proceedings take place. Civil proceedings in the High Court and county court are governed by the Civil Procedure Rules 1998 (CPR).[81] The issue of whether a person has capacity to conduct or settle proceedings is the very matter for which capacity is required. A person may therefore have capacity to issue and then settle proceedings even though he or she might otherwise be unable to administer his or her property and affairs.[82] CPR Part 21 therefore distinguishes between the person conducting proceedings who is the 'protected party' and the person who is in receipt of a damages award who is the 'protected beneficiary'.

3.46 The litigation friend can be appointed to act by the Court of Protection[83] but if the Court of Protection is not involved in the affairs of the person who lacks capacity, a suitable representative can nominate him or herself as litigation friend. The litigation friend must be someone capable of acting in the protected party's best interests with no conflict of interest in the matter and whose role is limited to the proceedings in question.

3.47 An attorney acting under a LPA has no standing as an attorney to bring or defend proceedings on behalf of the donor.[84] There is no reference in the CPR to an attorney. There is therefore no change to the established procedure whereby if the donor lacks capacity, the attorney – if he or she

---

been incorporated into MCA 2005 to distinguish applications made by attorneys as opposed to applications made by deputies or other parties.

[79] 'Registered power' is defined as an 'Enduring Power of Attorney or Lasting Power of Attorney registered under the Mental Capacity Act 2005' (Trustee Act 1925, s 36(6C)).

[80] Trustee Act 1925, s 36(6A).

[81] SI 1998/3132.

[82] *Masterman-Lister v Jewell* [2002] EWHC 417 (QB), [2002] All ER 247 (Mar); on appeal sub nom *Masterman-Lister v Jewell* [2002] EWCA Civ 1889, [2003] 3 All ER 162, [2003] 1 WLR 1511.

[83] MCA 2005, s 18(1)(k).

[84] The Law Commission's draft Bill proposed giving the attorney power over 'all matters relating to the donor's property or affairs, including the conduct of legal proceedings' (clause 16(1) of the draft Bill set out as Appendix A to Law Com No 231 (see **3.16**)). There is no corresponding reference in MCA 2005.

wishes to act in the proceedings – must demonstrate his or her suitability to act as a litigation friend or obtain the express authority of the Court of Protection to conduct the proceedings.[85]

Welfare matters

3.48   The donor of a LPA may authorise the attorney to make decisions on his or her behalf about his or her personal welfare or specified matters concerning personal welfare. This appears at first sight an extensive power to direct matters such as where and how the donor shall live and to give or refuse consent to treatment.[86] In certain circumstances, the attorney's authority may even extend to giving or refusing consent to life-sustaining treatment.

3.49   The principle application of this authority is to enable those providing health care or treatment for a person who lacks capacity to obtain consent to what they propose to do in that person's best interests. A doctor performing a hip replacement or a dentist fitting a denture can be assured of having formal consent to an invasive treatment rather than having to rely on his or her own judgment about the necessity of the treatment and whether it is covered by MCA 2005, s 5.[87] A LPA also gives an attorney certain rights, in particular:

- a person or body determining whether a proposed act is in the best interests of the incapable person must take into account the views of, and if possible consult, the donee of the LPA (MCA 2005, s 4(7));
- an act performed in connection with 'care or treatment' under MCA 2005, s 5 is not authorised by that section if it conflicts with a decision of an attorney acting within the scope of his or her power (MCA 2005, s 6(6)(a));
- a LPA made after an advance decision conferring authority in respect of treatment to which the advance decision relates takes precedence over the refusal of consent contained in the advance decision (MCA 2005, s 25(2)(b)); and
- the attorney may apply to the Court of Protection for the exercise of any of its powers under MCA 2005 without seeking prior permission (MCA 2005, s 50(1)(b)).

Limits on welfare matters

3.50   The scope of an attorney's authority in welfare matters is more limited than may at first be apparent. The principal limitations are as follows:

---

[85]   See *Gregory v Turner* [2003] EWCA Civ 183. Although this case concerned an action conducted by an attorney acting under an EPA, the principle will be the same where a LPA is concerned.

[86]   MCA 2005, s 11(7)(c).

[87]   Acts in connection with care or treatment are dealt with at **2.146**ff.

- Any act performed by an attorney must be in accordance with the donor's best interests (MCA 2005, ss 1(5) and 4)).

- There is no power to make decisions if the donor has capacity to make decisions for him or herself (MCA 2005, s 11(7)(a)). The fact that there is a valid registered LPA in place does not of itself authorise the person treating the donor to take instructions directly from the attorney. The carer or clinician must also be satisfied that the donor lacks capacity.

- A LPA does not authorise the attorney to restrain the donor unless the attorney reasonably believes that it is necessary to prevent harm to the donor and the act of restraint is a proportionate response to the likelihood of the donor suffering harm and the seriousness of that harm (MCA 2005, s 11(3) and (4)).

- Any restraint of the donor cannot deprive the donor of his or her liberty within the meaning of Art 5(1) of the European Convention on Human Rights (MCA 2005, s 11(6)). This may be at odds with the power to restrain the donor which by its nature deprives the donor of his or her liberty. In the light of the Bournewood case, it is likely that the power to 'restrain' under MCA 2005 will be interpreted narrowly, for use in emergencies or as a very temporary measure.[88] A longer-term detention of a person who cannot consent to it or detention for the purposes of treatment, must either be authorised by the Court of Protection under MCA 2005, s 16(2)(a) or by one of the bodies empowered by MCA 2005, Sch 1A.[89]

- The donor's authority to consent to care or treatment is subject to a valid and applicable advance decision made after the LPA.[90]

- The attorney only has authority to give or refuse consent to life-sustaining treatment if this is expressly allowed by the LPA and this authority is furthermore subject to any restrictions or conditions in the power.[91] This power of 'life and death' is considered in more detail below, but is in its turn subject to two further safeguards:

  - a person considering whether a life-sustaining treatment is in a person's best interests must not be motivated by a desire to bring about that person's death;[92] and

  - the declaration in MCA 2005, s 62 that the existing law relating to murder or manslaughter is not affected by anything contained in MCA 2005.

---

[88]   *HL v United Kingdom* (2004) 5 October (the Strasbourg proceedings arising out of the decision of the House of Lords in *R v Bournewood Community and Mental Health NHS Trust ex p L* [1999] 1 AC 458, [1998] All ER 303).

[89]   For a more detailed consideration of the powers of restraint in MCA 2005 in the light of the European Convention on Human Rights, see **2.168–2.176**. The Act has been considerably amended by the Mental Health Act 2007 which introduced new safeguards for the deprivation of liberty: see Chapter 6.

[90]   MCA 2005, ss 11(7)(b) and 25(7).

[91]   MCA 2005, s 11(8).

[92]   MCA 2005, s 4(5). This was a late amendment to the Mental Capacity Bill, first referred to in a letter from the Lord Chancellor to Archbishop Smith on 14 December 2004 and subsequently incorporated in an amendment introduced in the House of Lords by Baroness Ashton of Upholland.

- An attorney acting under a welfare LPA cannot compel the carrying out of a particular treatment or decision. An attorney may give or refuse consent to treatment, but if a doctor is unwilling to carry out a treatment, the attorney cannot force another person to make a decision which he or she believes is contrary to rhe donor's best interests.[93]
- MCA 2005 confers no authority on any person or body to make decisions in respect of:
    - family relations, including consent to a marriage or civil partnership, sexual relations, divorce (based on 2 years' separation) and parental responsibilities relating to a child's welfare;[94]
    - MCA 2005 matters, where medical treatment is required for mental disorder as defined by the Mental Health Act 1983;[95] and
    - voting rights where the election is for any public office or at a referendum.[96]

3.51 It is unclear therefore how useful or widespread welfare LPAs are going to be. It may be that they will serve little practical purpose beyond giving the person named by the donor an authority to act as a 'consultee' or 'advocate' for the incapable donor, thus someone who can speak for the donor when he or she can no longer speak for him or herself. It is also possible that LPAs will become widely used (and abused) and carers will defer to attorneys making life and death decisions on behalf of incapable donors. Early experience of the operation of the new LPA forms indicates that they are of limited popularity or applicability. The length and complexity of the statutory forms acts as a deterrent to all but the most determined of donors.

3.52 The provisions of MCA 2005 relating to LPAs and life-sustaining treatment are both confusing and controversial.[97] How, for instance, is the authority of an attorney to refuse consent to 'life-sustaining treatment' reconciled with the requirement that 'best interests' cannot include a desire to bring about the death of the donor? These provisions of the Act appear mutually inconsistent, but the Act does clearly allow the donor to authorise the attorney to make these decisions on his or her behalf. The only way of giving effect to this requirement is to ensure that a decision to withhold treatment can be made on the basis that it is unduly burdensome or futile and it is not in the best interests of the donor to continue treatment. The motive

---

93   See AVS v a NHS Foundation Trust [2011] EWCA Civ 7.
94   MCA 2005, s 27.
95   MCA 2005, s 28 and see also Mental Health Act 1983, s 1(2), which defines 'mental disorder' as 'mental illness, arrested or incomplete development of mind, psychopathic disorder and any other disorder or disability of mind'.
96   MCA 2005, s 29. The Act makes no reference to voting as a member of any other association such as a political party or unincorporated association.
97   An article in the *Daily Mail* of 8 December 2004 by Melanie Philips, headed 'A barbaric Bill that would destroy the value of life', was not untypical of some of the press coverage of the Bill at the time of its passage in the House of Commons.

of the attorney is to relieve pain and suffering and not primarily or exclusively to bring about the death of the patient.[98]

3.53 The problem remains therefore that LPAs may be easy to abuse.[99] The attorney may well end up as sole arbiter of whether a refusal of a treatment is in the donor's 'best interests'. This gives rise to several potential problems:

- MCA 2005 does not address the fundamental question of who is making the decision. The attorney is still exercising his or her judgment as to what is in the donor's best interests;[100]

- doctors and other carers may find that the permission of an attorney to withdraw life-sustaining treatment avoids the inconvenience of a more detailed or independent assessment of the donor's best wishes;

- the fiduciary character of a power of attorney is more difficult to apply to a power which relates to welfare. Many attorneys will have an obvious conflict of interest as potential beneficiaries of the donor's estate. While an attorney (who is a beneficiary) should not benefit from his or her dealings with the property and affairs of the donor, there is no equivalent safeguard to dealings with the welfare of the donor;

- a person may be deemed to lack capacity because he or she is unable to communicate a decision;[101]

- an attorney acting in respect of a donor's welfare will generally be a relative or friend, and is unlikely to be a professional person with a professional duty of care. It is unclear therefore what skill or judgment a lay attorney may be expected to exercise in making welfare decisions;

- an attorney acting in the best interests of the donor must take account of the views of anyone caring for the donor, so may be expected to act on medical advice where this is appropriate. But a decision to treat or not to treat can only be informed by medical advice – the actual decision remains with the attorney. The attorney makes what he or she believes to be the right decision and is protected by MCA 2005 so long as he or she 'reasonably believes that what he does or decides is in the best interests of the person concerned'.[102]

3.54 Although LPAs will be of use to some people in some circumstances, these concerns and the extent of the attorney's powers will need to be addressed carefully by donors when executing LPAs. The drafting and execution of LPAs will therefore be a relatively painstaking process,

---

[98] See Mental Capacity Act 2005: Code of Practice, at para 5.31.
[99] The scope for abuse in the creation of LPAs is considered at **3.84**.
[100] Much of the controversy around this question is based on the assumption that the attorney will bring about the death of the donor when the donor might not have wished that outcome. But the reverse scenario is equally valid, where the attorney refuses consent to the withdrawal of treatment which prolongs the life of a donor who has no desire to go on living.
[101] MCA 2005, s 3(1)(d).
[102] MCA 2005, s 4(9).

involving clear professional advice from solicitors and doctors. This will affect the costs involved and either deter potential donors from making LPAs or encourage the making of such powers without proper advice or assistance.

Alternatives to welfare lasting powers of attorney

3.55 While there are situations in which LPAs are necessary and useful, many people who might benefit from their provision will be put off by the length and complexity of the forms. If they seek professional assistance, they may be further deterred by the costs involved. They may therefore consider whether a LPA is really necessary and whether their objectives can be achieved in other ways:

- MCA 2005, s 5 provides a defence for a person who carries out an act in connection with the care or treatment of a person lacking capacity so long as the act carried out is in that person's best interests. Most day-to-day acts of care and treatment of persons who lack capacity are carried out by carers and doctors without the permission of an attorney or deputy or order of the Court of Protection, relying on this provision.

- Any determination of another person's best interests requires the person making the determination to take into account the views of 'anyone named as someone to be consulted' as well as the views of anyone engaged in caring for the person or interested in his or her welfare.[103] Many people worry that when they lack capacity their loved ones will have no rights and that they will be abandoned to painful and pointless treatment. Although in practice it would be unethical for a physician to treat a patient lacking capacity without consulting the views of family and carers, MCA 2005 gives carers rights to be consulted.[104]

- MCA 2005 gives statutory recognition to an advance refusal of treatment.[105] The difference between an advance refusal and a LPA is that the former represents the decision of the person made at a time when he or she has capacity for use when he or she subsequently lacks capacity; the LPA, by contrast, requires the attorney to make the decision at the relevant time. While the LPA has the benefit of being a flexible document, an advance directive is easier to complete. So long as it is clear in its purpose, there is no prescribed form. Only an advance refusal of life-sustaining treatment must be in writing and witnessed.[106] It may well be that many individuals who are primarily concerned at being over-treated will find that a simple advance refusal of treatment will meet those concerns.

---

[103]   MCA 2005, s 4(7).
[104]   See e g the General Medical Council Guidelines considered in the case of *R (on the application of Burke) v General Medical Council* [2005] EWCA Civ 1003.
[105]   MCA 2005, ss 24–26.
[106]   MCA 2005, s 25(6).

FORM OF LASTING POWER OF ATTORNEY

Who can give a lasting power of attorney?

3.56   Any person who has reached the age of 18 and who has capacity to do so, may grant a LPA.[107] For a LPA to be effective, it must be made in a prescribed form and in a prescribed manner, must comply with certain requirements as to the appointment of an attorney and must be registered.

Prescribed forms

3.57   No instrument can be effective as a LPA unless it is in the prescribed form.[108] The actual forms that must be used are prescribed by the Lasting Powers of Attorney, Enduring Powers of Attorney and Public Guardian Regulations 2007.[109] The principle of using a standard statutory form is the same that applied to EPA made prior to 1 October 2007. However, the 2007 Regulations provide for two different prescribed forms depending on whether the power relates to personal welfare or property and affairs.

Use of different prescribed forms

3.58   The same donor may give two LPAs dealing with personal welfare matters and property and affairs respectively. Different considerations apply to the requirements and content of each power, different attorneys may be appointed for different purposes and the powers may be registered at different times. For instance, a donor may want a solicitor to act as an attorney in respect of property and affairs but a relative to act in respect of personal welfare matters. The former power can also be used at any time after it has been registered and without reference to the capacity of the donor; a power dealing with personal welfare matters only extends to making decisions in circumstances where the donor lacks capacity.[110] The LPAs may also be made at different times. A donor may create a LPA when he or she has capacity and requires assistance and then makes a welfare power later to anticipate medical treatment. The donor may already have made an EPA and now requires a separate welfare LPA.

3.59   Because different powers may be given for different purposes, there are two prescribed forms, one for personal welfare matters and one for property and affairs.[111]

---

[107]   For capacity to grant a LPA, see **3.109–3.110**.

[108]   MCA 2005, Sch 1, Part 1.

[109]   SI 2007/1253. New prescribed forms were introduced from 1 October 2009 by the Lasting Powers of Attorney, Enduring Powers of Attorney and Public Guardian (Amendment) Regulations 2009, SI 2009/1884 (reproduced in Part VI). Prescribed forms issued under the 2007 Regulations can be used until 1 April 2011.

[110]   MCA 2005, s 11(7)(a).

[111]   Although MCA 2005, Sch 1, Part 1, para 1(2) allows for an instrument dealing with *both* welfare matters and property and affairs, a hybrid form has not been prescribed. The measure requiring the prescribed forms is contained in the Lasting Powers of Attorney, Enduring Powers of Attorney and Public Guardian Regulations 2007, SI 2007/1253, reg 5.

Defective forms

3.60 At first sight, MCA 2005 appears unequivocal about a LPA being in the prescribed form. Thus, s 9(3) clearly states that an instrument which does not comply with the relevant sections 'confers no authority'. When it comes to registration, Sch 1, para 11(1) states that the Public Guardian must not register an instrument (unless directed to do so by the Court) if it appears to him that the instrument is not made in accordance with Sch 1. The role of the Public Guardian is to register the instrument and act as the gatekeeper or guardian of the system. Registration confers formal validity on the power. It is therefore vital for the integrity of the system that a defective form is not registered and therefore the Public Guardian is obliged to refuse registration of a defective instrument, 'if it appears to the Public Guardian' that the instrument has not been made in accordance with schedule 1 of the Act.[112]

On receipt of an application to register an instrument that is potentially defective, the Public Guardian has a limited number of options. He may:

- Reject the application and return the papers to the applicant. The applicant may then either correct the LPA or apply to the Court of Protection to exercise its powers relating to the validity of the LPA.
- The Public Guardian has a limited power to register a LPA if there is a minor error or 'slip'. Sch 1, para 3(1) 'if an instrument differs in an immaterial respect in form or mode of expression from the prescribed form, it is to be treated by the Public Guardian as sufficient in point of form and expression.[113]
- Apply to the Court to exercise its powers. Under Sch 1, para 11(2) the Public Guardian must refer to the Court an instrument which contains a provision which prevents it from operating as an LPA, for the Court to sever the provision. If it appears to the Public Guardian that the LPA may be valid but there is a doubt for instance over the capacity of the donor, then the Public Guardian will refer it to the Court.

3.61 The Court of Protection has a number of powers under MCA 2005 to determine questions relating to the validity or form of a LPA:

- Under s 23(1) the Court may 'may determine any question as to the meaning or effect of a lasting power of attorney or an instrument purporting to create one.'
- Under Sch 1, para 3(2) the Court may '… declare that an instrument which is not in the prescribed form is to be treated as if it were, if it

---

[112]   MCA 2005, Sch 1, para 11(1).
[113]   This might be used where there is a clerical error where the content or meaning in the power can be readily inferred from other evidence. For example, an inconsistency in an address, a crossing out and correction or a box has been ticked incorrectly or not ticked. For example, the pre 2009 forms required a certificate provider to tick the box marked 'I am 18 or over'. Where the certificate provider also states his qualification as a consultant psychiatrist or solicitor, ticking this box might be considered immaterial.

is satisfied that the persons executing the instrument intended it to create a lasting power of attorney.'

- Under s 23(1) and Sch 1, para 11(4) the Court may sever a provision from an instrument which prevents it operating as a valid LPA.

3.62 The interaction of the Public Guardian's responsibility to register an LPA and the Court's authority to determine the validity of the power, whether by a declaration or severance of a provision which would otherwise invalidate the power is illustrated by a number of cases reported by way of short summaries on the website of the Public Guardian.[114] Many of these cases relate to restrictions or conditions that are inconsistent either with the status of an attorney or the appointment of more than one attorney. For example:

- In the case of *Re Davies* (an order of the Senior Judge made on 5 July 2010), the donor appointed two attorneys, A and B, to act jointly and severally. He then imposed the following restriction: "If in the unlikely event of A and B not being wholly in agreement, B is to defer to the wishes of A." On the application of the Public Guardian the Court severed the restriction as being incompatible with a joint and several appointment.
- In the case of *Re Clarke* (an order of the Senior Judge made on 18 November 2009) the donor appointed three attorneys, A (his wife), B, and C, to be his attorneys. They were appointed to act jointly in some matters and jointly and severally in others. He then stated that the attorneys were to act independently for transactions not exceeding £5,000 "but together in respect of all other decisions subject to my wife A's opinion prevailing in the event that my attorneys are not unanimous in any decision involving property or expenditure exceeding £5,000". On the application of the Public Guardian, the words "subject to my wife A's opinion ..." onwards were severed on the ground that they purported to allow one of the three attorneys to act independently in relation to matters that had been specified as subject to the joint decision making powers of the attorneys.
- In the case of *Re Moore* (an order of the Senior Judge made on 26 October 2010) the donor appointed three attorneys to act jointly. She then imposed the following restriction: "At least two attorneys to act on any transactions". On the application of the Public Guardian the Court severed the restriction as being incompatible with a joint appointment.
- In the case of *Re Weyell* (an order of the senior Judge made on 2 December 2010) the donor appointed three attorneys, A, B and C, to act jointly for some decisions and jointly and severally for others. He then imposed the following restrictions:

---

[114]   At www.publicguardian.gov.uk/information-professionals.htm

(a) "Two out of three of my attorneys must act jointly in relation to any transaction with a value in excess of £5,000 and my attorneys may act jointly and severally in relation to everything else."

(b) I direct that when acting jointly and severally where possible my attorneys are to act in the following order of priority: firstly A, then B and then C."

On the application of the Public Guardian the first restriction was severed as being incompatible with the joint aspect of the appointment. As to the second restriction, the Public Guardian submitted that a direction that attorneys appointed to act jointly and severally must act in an order of priority would normally be regarded as incompatible with a joint and several appointment, the addition of the words "where possible" made the direction in effect a statement of wishes only. The Court accepted this submission and did not sever the second restriction.

- In the case of *Re Sykes* (an order of the Senior Judge made on 9 July 2009), the donor of a property and affairs LPA imposed a restriction stating that no gifts of any of her assets should be made other than "annual or monthly gifts already being made by me at the date of my signing this LPA by regular bank standing orders or direct debits". On the application of the Public Guardian the Court severed this restriction on the ground that the gifts envisaged by the donor exceeded the attorney's authority to make gifts as set out in section 12 of the MCA 2005.[115]

- In the case of *Re Begum* (an order of the Senior Judge made on 24 April 2008), the Court directed the severance from a Property and Affairs LPA instrument of the following clauses, on the ground that they were ineffective as part of an LPA:

    (a) "All decisions about the use or disposal of my property and financial resources must be driven by what my Personal Welfare Lasting Power of Attorney(s) believe will support my long term interests.

    (b) Any decisions affecting assets (individually or together) worth more than £5,000 at any one time must be discussed and agreed with Dr X.

    (c) In the event of there being any disagreement between my Personal Welfare Lasting Power of Attorney(s) and/or Dr X this should be resolved by these parties appointing an independent advocate to adjudicate."

- In the case of *Re Kittle* (a judgment of the Senior Judge given on 1 December 2009), the Court was asked to consider whether a first cousin was prevented from acting as a certificate provider. Regulation 8(3) of the LPA, EPA and PG Regulations 2007 sets out categories of persons who cannot act in this role, who include "a family member" of the donor or of the attorney (or of the owner, director, manager or employee of any care home in which the donor

---

[115]   The clearly defined and limited authority of a donor to make gifts is dealt with at **3.37** above.

is living when the instrument is executed). The Public Guardian declined to register the instrument on the ground that a first cousin was a family member of the donor. The Court ruled that a first cousin is not a family member, and so the LPA was valid.[116]

3.63 It is not, however, always for the Court to remedy a failing on the part of the donor or a solicitor and there is a limit as to how far the Court will go in assisting a party in these circumstances. It is likely that the circumstances will determine the outcome. There will for instance be cases where the donor no longer has capacity and there is no possibility of a new LPA being prepared. In general, the Public Guardian and the Court will assist where possible, especially where the LPA was prepared without professional support or there is a disproportionate burden on the parties to complete a new LPA. In the case of Re Nazran, the certificate provider had not completed the first two boxes in Part B of the instrument to confirm that he was acting independently of the donor, was not ineligible to provide a certificate, and was aged 18 or over.[117] The Public Guardian refused to register the instrument. As the donor was suffering a wasting illness and could not make a new LPA, the attorneys applied to the Court for a declaration that the instrument was a valid LPA or, alternatively, that the instrument was to be treated as valid under MCA 2005 Sch 1, para 3(2). The Court, in the exercise of its discretion under Sch 1 para 3(2), declared that the instrument was to be treated as if it were an LPA and registered accordingly.

Content of LPA

3.64 The prescribed forms are at least 11 pages long and at first sight somewhat daunting.[118] Large parts of the forms do, however, consist of boxes and fields which may or may not be relevant. The forms can also be broken down into their component parts, there being four main parts, reflecting the three stages in their completion and the prescribed information. The forms are divided as follows:

- The Prescribed Information – set out in pages 1–2, which the donor, certificate provider(s) and any attorney(s) are required to read or have read or have read to them;
- Part A – the Donor's Statement – setting out the powers granted by the donor;
- Part B – the Certificate Provider's Statement; and
- Part C – the Attorney's Statement.

---

[116] A full decision of the case is published on the Public Guardian's website under the heading 'other orders of interest' at www.publicguardian.gov.uk/forms/other-orders-cop.htm

[117] An order of the Senior Judge made on 27 June 2008, reported on the Public Guardian website. This related to a LPA made using the 2007 prescribed form.

[118] As prescribed by the the Lasting Powers of Attorney, Enduring Powers of Attorney and Public Guardian (Amendment) Regulations 2009, SI 2009/1884. These forms are half the length of the forms originally prescribed by the 2007 Regulations.

Part A – the Donor's Statement

3.65 The prescribed form provides space for the donor to write or print his or her name and address, date of birth and contact details and is followed by the essential wording that makes the form a power of attorney: 'I appoint the following attorney(s) in accordance with the provisions of the Mental Capacity Act 2005.' There is then space for the names of the attorney(s) and the basis of their appointment and to set out any special conditions or restrictions in the power. The oversight in the 2007 prescribed forms that omitted any space for the attorneys to complete their addresses has been rectified in the 2009 forms.[119]

Choice of attorney

3.66 A donor may appoint any person or, in the case of a power relating to property and affairs, a trust corporation, to act as his or her attorney. Apart from where a trust corporation is appointed, the appointment of an attorney is personal and an attorney cannot be appointed by reference to an office or title.[120]

3.67 Where an individual is appointed then he or she must have reached 18 and must not be a bankrupt.[121] If the attorney subsequently becomes bankrupt, then his or her appointment as an attorney is terminated.

3.68 Clearly the choice of attorney is essential to the effective operation of a LPA. And because a LPA may be made many years before it is used, the donor may need some insurance against the risk of an attorney becoming unable to act due to death, divorce, bankruptcy, incapacity or disclaimer. MCA 2005 therefore allows the donor to appoint two or more attorneys and also allows for the appointment of successive attorneys.

More than one attorney

3.69 MCA 2005, s 10(4) allows the donor to appoint more than one attorney provided that the attorneys are appointed to act 'jointly' or 'jointly and severally'. The Act uses the terms 'jointly' or 'jointly and severally' whereas the original prescribed forms use the terms 'together' or 'together and separately' – presumably to make the terms comprehensible to non-lawyers.[122] However, if the language is clear there is still scope for

---

[119]   In the 2007 forms the the Attorney's Statement (Part C) provides fields for a telephone number, mobile and e-mail address but not a residential address.

[120]   The Law Commission assumed that an officeholder could be appointed under existing law (Law Com No 231 (see **3.16**), at para 7.21) but recommended a specific provision authorising an attorney to be described as 'the holder for the time being or a specified office or position'. This provision was not included in MCA 2005, and contrasts with the power of the Court to appoint 'the holder for the time being or a specified office or position' as a deputy (MCA 2005, s 19(2)).

[121]   MCA 2005, s 10(1).

[122]   The prescribed forms introduced on 1 October 2007 use the statutory terminology 'jointly' and 'jointly and severally.'

further complication as s 10 also permits attorneys to be appointed jointly in respect of some matters and jointly and severally in respect of others. Thus a donor is able to appoint attorneys to act jointly and severally in respect of his or her investments but require them to act jointly where a major decision was required, for instance, to sell the donor's home or, in a welfare power, to withhold consent to life-sustaining treatment. If it is unclear whether attorneys are appointed jointly or jointly and severally, the appointment is construed in favour of their being appointed jointly.[123]

3.70　A joint appointment of attorneys clearly provides a greater degree of protection, as the attorneys must act unanimously in any act carried out under the power. For example, a contract for a care home or even a cheque drawn on the donor's bank account must be signed by both attorneys. The disadvantages are that the LPA may be cumbersome to operate in practice and that the LPA is terminated if the appointment of either attorney fails.[124] These difficulties inherent in a joint appointment can be remedied by limiting the scope of the joint appointment to certain decisions and by appointing a replacement attorney to act on the failure of the joint appointment. Where these issues are addressed, careful drafting is required.

3.71　Where two or more attorneys are appointed *jointly and severally*, each attorney may act independently of the other. Most EPAs which appoint more than one attorney to deal with a person's property and affairs provide for the attorneys being appointed jointly and severally. It is simply more practical for attorneys to work separately, either with a clear division of responsibility between them or on the understanding that one will take a lead role and another will act as a spare or default attorney. However, any potential conflict or discord between the attorneys will make the power extremely difficult to operate in practice. Care must be taken to address the issue of how they are to act at the time the instrument is made, rather than leave matters to wishful thinking. If the authority of one attorney to act independently of another is limited, there is a danger that the 'joint and several' nature of the appointment will be fatally compromised.[125] Where one of the attorneys is a professional attorney, it will also be important for the donor to define the extent to which the professional attorney is expected to be actively involved in the administration of the donor's affairs or the supervision of the other attorney.

---

[123]　This avoids the problem created by EPAA 1985, s 11(1), where an EPA had to be joint or jointly and severally to be valid as an EPA. An instrument that was unclear might therefore be defective. See also *Re E (enduring power of attorney)* [2001] Ch 364, [2000] 3 WLR 1974, sub nom *Re E, X v Y* [2000] 3 All ER 1004.

[124]　MCA 2005, s 10(6).

[125]　For instance in the case of *Re Bratt* (an order made by the Senior Judge on 14 September 2009) the donor appointed two attorneys, A and B, to act jointly and severally, and directed that 'B is only to act as attorney in the event of A being physically or mentally incapable of acting in this capacity'. On the application of the Public Guardian this provision was severed as being inconsistent with a joint and several appointment. See also the cases referred to at **3.62** above and the website of the Public Guardian under 'Information for Professionals.'

Replacement attorneys

3.72   The appointment of a replacement attorney is often desirable. Attorneys cannot appoint their own successors in the same way that trustees can.[126] This preserves the distinction between an attorney and a trustee in that the attorney is the agent of the donor and is appointed personally in his or her own right.[127] MCA 2005 does provide expressly for the appointment of a replacement attorney, so that a new attorney, who has also been chosen by the donor, may replace the old attorneys on the failure of the earlier appointment on one of the grounds mentioned in s 13(6)(a)–(d). Thus if the choice of the first attorney should fail on the death, divorce, bankruptcy or incapacity of that attorney, a new attorney or new attorneys can be appointed, within the same instrument, to act in that event. However, the replacement attorney can only be appointed to act on the failure of the first appointment on the grounds mentioned. If the first appointed attorney, for example, refuses to act or is removed by the Court for failure to act in the donor's best interests then the provision in favour of the replacement attorney cannot operate.

3.73   A replacement attorney will often be appointed to cover the failure of a joint appointment of attorneys. Thus, for example, a donor may appoint his son and daughter to act jointly, with his solicitor as a replacement. If the son dies or becomes bankrupt then the appointment of both attorneys would appear to fail. The solicitor will then be appointed as sole attorney. Care therefore needs to be taken in drafting as, in this scenario, the donor may well have preferred to have the solicitor act with his daughter. The donor therefore needs to appoint two replacement attorneys. Unfortunately the prescribed form only allows space for one attorney to be appointed and additional copies of the relevant pages need to be added to the form.[128]

3.74   While it makes sense for a donor to cover as many eventualities as possible within the same instrument, this can give rise to unexpected complications. The practice with EPAs had been for a donor to create separate instruments, with the replacement power taking effect on the failure of the first. In this way, if the first power failed, the attorneys under the second or replacement power would apply to register that instrument. As the new EPA could only take effect on the failure of the first, evidence of its failure would need to be produced to register the new EPA and once it was registered, no further explanation would be needed. The protection afforded by the registration process would come into play, even if the first EPA had been registered previously. It was, however, cumbersome to prepare two instruments for use in situations that might not arise and the practice arose of appointing successor attorneys within the same instrument.[129] This

---

[126]   MCA 2005, s 10(8)(a).

[127]   A trust by contrast is a distinct legal entity that may need to be administered for much longer and the trustees owe their primary duty to the beneficiaries.

[128]   There is some uncertainty on this point which has yet to be considered judicially. A prudent donor may be advised to create separate LPAs for use in these different situations.

[129]   The practice was shown in *Elderly Clients: A Precedent Manual* (Jordans, 2005) edited by the Master (now Senior Judge) of the Court of Protection, Denzil Lush, and is based on a

would, after all, only reflect the practice used in will drafting. However, as EPAs were usually made long before they would be used, it was anticipated that registration would be effected by the first attorney or the successor. It was never established what would happen if the EPA was registered by the first attorney who died or became unable to act, leaving the successor attorney appointed on the face of the instrument.

3.75 MCA 2005, s 10(8)(b) makes it clear that a replacement attorney can be appointed in the same instrument. A potential complication arises, however, where the original attorney registers the instrument. The attorney (or donor) sends out the notices in the usual way and the named persons are satisfied that the attorney is acting in the donor's best interests.[130] Subsequently the authority of the first attorney is terminated. If the replacement attorney is appointed by the instrument no new registration is required. No one is notified of the existence of a different attorney who unlike the first attorney may be wholly unsuitable for the role.[131] The named person will have no knowledge that a replacement attorney has been appointed, let alone of that attorney's identity. Moreover, the effectiveness of the named person as a safeguard is further undermined by the fact that the replacement attorney cannot be a named person.[132] While it makes sense to separate the roles of attorney and named person, this in turn causes its own problems and removes a potentially important level of protection. In many cases, the replacement attorney is also someone who will be concerned for the best interests of the donor. A donor may, for instance, appoint one person as attorney in the first instance and another person as a replacement attorney. The replacement attorney is not given notice by the Public Guardian and may be unaware that the instrument is being registered.[133] In contrast, a co-attorney who did not join in making the application for the purposes of the notification requirements is notified.[134]

---

simple application of existing legal principles. See also Law Com No 231 (see **3.16**), at p 114. This approach was approved in the decision of Lewison J in the case of *Re J (Enduring Power of Attorney)* [2009] EWHC 436 (Ch).

[130] Persons named as persons t o be notified are considered at **3.82ff**.

[131] It is of course open to a donor to create two LPAs with separate appointments, the second taking effect on the failure of the first. But given the complexity of the forms, it is unlikely that many donors will realistically complete two LPAs to deal with their property and affairs.

[132] MCA 2005, Sch 1, para 2(3). There was initially some confusion over whether a replacement attorney was appointed as a donee when the event triggering his or her appointment has not occurred. The Public Guardian has refused to register instruments in such cases. In the case of *Re Howarth*, the Court of Protection severed the appointment of a replacement attorney as one of the notified persons (see the website of the Public Guardian under 'Information for Professionals'. If the replacement attorney was the only named person then the instrument would not be effective as a LPA.

[133] This also contrasts with the principle applied in the registration of EPAs where a class of relatives is notified, and a replacement attorney would be notified if within the prescribed class. See MCA 2005, Sch 4, Part 3, para 6(2). The inclusion of named persons and the problems associated with their role is dealt with in more detail at **3.82ff**.

[134] MCA 2005, Sch 1, para 8(2).

Restrictions and conditions

3.76 The authority of an attorney is not only subject to the limitations imposed by MCA 2005 but also any conditions or restrictions specified in the instrument.[135] In view of the wide-ranging scope of a LPA, the donor needs to consider very carefully how the LPA can be 'tailored' to meet his or her requirements and provide the right level of compromise between function and protection. Although the forms are designed with plenty of space for donors to insert their own conditions, there is a danger that conditions made without proper advice will prove unworkable in practice.[136]

3.77 Special conditions that a donor might add, in respect of property and affairs, to the prescribed form include:

- A right to remuneration by a professional attorney. An attorney acts as a fiduciary role and should not benefit from his or her so acting without the consent of the donor. It is therefore advisable for this to be expressly provided for in the instrument.
- Authority for the delegation of investment powers to a professional fund manager. An attorney cannot generally delegate his or her functions except where he or she cannot be expected to attend to them personally.
- Authorising disclosure or safe custody of the donor's will. A solicitor holding a will owes a duty of confidentiality to the donor and would not normally release documents without the consent of the donor (if capable) or the Court (if incapable). An attorney may, however, need to know the contents of the will, especially if a property is to be sold or gifts made.
- Requiring the attorney to keep accounts or to render an account to a co-attorney or to a third party such as another member of the family, a solicitor or accountant. Although an attorney has a common law duty to keep accounts, this is not always followed in practice. The Court of Protection has authority to require an attorney to deliver an account, but it is unlikely that this authority will be widely exercised.[137] Many of the disputes that EPAs (and, by implication, LPAs) have given rise to have been caused by a lack of awareness of what an attorney is doing: a duty to disclose information and/or account to another party or to an independent professional often provides an adequate degree of reassurance in such cases.
- Restricting the operation of the LPA to use in specified circumstances. The LPA can be used – subject to registration – at any time by the attorney. Many donors will be unhappy with going through the formalities and expense of registration when the power

---

135   MCA 2005, s 9(4)(b).
136   Although the forms are intended for completion without professional help, not every donor will be able to deal with this unaided. The Guidance Booklet LPA103 provides some assistance but not every donor will work through the 60 pages of notes to find the right advice and even this concludes: 'we are not able to provide you with wording for restrictions or conditions. In any particular situation, you may want to seek further advice from a legal or financial professional such as a solicitor or accountant' (at p 38).
137   MCA 2005, s 23(3)(a).

only needs to be used for a limited time or function. They may also be unhappy with the prospect of the LPA being used while they are still capable. They may therefore restrict the creation of the LPA to, for example, such time as they become mentally incapable of managing their property and affairs. Although this is suggested in the prescribed form, such a condition does contradict the spirit of a property and affairs LPA which is that the LPA itself is neutral as to the donor's capacity.[138]

- Requiring medical evidence to be supplied on an application to register the LPA. Many donors will be uncomfortable with the idea of the attorney registering and using the power without any formal medical evidence being supplied.

- Restricting the power to make gifts under MCA 2005, s 12 by setting a maximum amount for gifts or prohibiting the making of gifts without the consent of the Court or a third party.

- Restricting the amount of capital which can be applied or limiting the value of transactions that may be entered into by the attorney.

- Confirming the revocation of an earlier LPA or EPA. One power of attorney does not automatically revoke an earlier power and there must be a clear act of revocation and the attorney under the earlier power must be notified. However, as a LPA is not created until it is registered, it is not clear whether this formality would be required where the instrument has not yet been registered. However, it must be good practice to ensure that there is a clear record of revocation of an earlier instrument.

- Requiring the consent of a third party to the disposal of a particular asset, such as the family home, heirlooms or shares in a family company.[139]

- Restricting the scope of the LPA so that it does not apply to a particular asset, for instance, that it should not apply to the sale of the family home.

Great care needs to be taken in drafting restrictions and conditions, as there is a danger in making the power unworkable in practice or even invalidating it. Cases that have come before the Court dealing with these issues are summarized on the Office of the Public Guardian website at: www.publicguardian.gov.uk/information-professionals.htm.[140]

---

[138] Page 9 of the 2007 edition of the prescribed form suggested as follows: 'You can use this section to specify that your LPA is only to be used when you lack capacity. If you decide to do this, you should specify anything you want the attorney(s) to do to confirm that you lack capacity to make the decision in question.' This issue is further considered at **3.28** above.

[139] Care needs to be taken to prevent rendering a joint and several appointment ineffective. See for instance the decision of the Senior Judge in the case of *Re P (an order of the Senior Judge made on 9 June 2009)* where the donor appointed three attorneys to act jointly and severally, and imposed the following restriction: 'I require that two attorneys must act at any one time so that no attorney may act alone.' On the application of the Public Guardian the Court severed the restriction on the ground that it was ineffective as part of an LPA. See the website of the Public Guardian under 'Information for Professionals.' See also the case of *Re Moore* described at **3.62** above.

[140] See also a series of articles published by Senior Judge Lush in *Trusts & Estates Law & Tax Journal* numbers 102 and 103.

Welfare restrictions

3.78 Where the welfare of the donor is concerned, the same restrictions as to when and with what evidence the LPA is created may be applicable. A welfare LPA is perhaps a more personal and subjective instrument than its financial counterpart. It may need careful consideration and discussions with the attorneys, family members, carers and doctors. The donor may need to address a particular set of circumstances the LPA is required to address, such as a terminal illness. The donor may have strong views as to how he or she should be treated and whether or not the LPA extends to the giving or refusing of consent to life-sustaining treatment. Special conditions might include:

- requiring decisions to be taken in consultation with or subject to the agreement of a named individual or subject to medical evidence or advice;
- restricting the right to 'give or refuse consent to life-sustaining treatment' so that the attorney may only give such consent; or
- qualifying the right to refuse consent to life-sustaining treatment so that it does not include the right to refuse artificial nutrition and hydration or that such a decision should be subject to the consent of other relatives or medical experts.

3.79 The danger of placing too many restrictions in a LPA is that it may make the power inflexible in practice and lead to the expense and inconvenience of involving the Court of Protection. For instance, a LPA may give effect to the sensibilities of an elderly donor who is determined to stay in his own home and restrict the power accordingly. The attorney then finds he or she lacks authority to sell the property when inevitably the donor needs to go into a care home. Preparing a LPA does therefore impose a burden on a professional adviser who must have sufficient knowledge of the donor's circumstances to be able both to address the donor's concerns without making the power unduly prescriptive.

Life-sustaining treatment

3.80 The authority of an attorney under a welfare LPA does not extend to 'giving or refusing of consent to the carrying out or continuation of life-sustaining treatment' unless the instrument so permits.[141] MCA 2005 does therefore contain a default provision so that a LPA should not deal with issues of life-sustaining treatment unless this is positively specified. The prescribed form departs from this presumption by setting out two choices and requiring the donor to specify one of them. Thus the donor must sign the box beside Option A or Option B specifying as follows:

- A   I want to give my attorney(s) authority to give or refuse consent to life-sustaining treatment;
- B   I **do not** want to give my attorney(s) authority to give or refuse consent to life-sustaining treatment.

---

[141]   MCA 2005, s 11(8).

3.81 As a further safeguard and to prevent the donor signing the wrong box in error, the signature beside the chosen box must be signed in the presence of a witness, who must sign and complete the boxes at the foot of the same page. The form does not specify who can witness this statement. The guidance notes merely state that 'your witness must be at least 18 years of age and must not be your attorney(s). Your witness can be your Part B certificate provider'.[142]

Named persons to be notified

3.82 LPAs, in the same way as EPAs, are designed as a simple and accessible means of providing a legal basis for future decision-making on behalf of a person who lacks capacity. By exercising a choice over the attorney, the donor of a power of attorney obviates the need for a formal court-based process or future supervision. This does not, however, mean that there is no protection available to a donor and there are in effect three levels of protection:

- the creation of the power of attorney;
- the notification of specified persons on registration; and
- the registration process which allows time for objections to be made by persons notified as well as allowing the registration authority to ensure that the documentation is all correct.

3.83 MCA 2005 introduced a further safeguard to the first of these levels, as a LPA requires a certificate of capacity from an independent person who can confirm that the donor understands the scope and purpose of the power. The notification procedure has, however, been altered rather than replaced or supplemented with a further degree of protection. On registration of an EPA, the attorney must notify prescribed members of a class of relatives.[143] By contrast, the donor of a LPA may specify in the instrument the persons to be notified of an application to register the LPA. This follows on from the principle that the donor should be free to make his or her own choice of persons to be notified. That principle is taken a stage further, as the donor is also free to specify that there should be no such persons to be notified.[144] The only limits on the donor's freedom of choice are that a named person cannot be a donee of the power (including a replacement donee), there is a maximum of five named persons and that if there are no named persons then

---

[142]   The declaration concerning life-sustaining treatment is in effect a separate advance statement within the LPA and complies with MCA 2005, s 25(5) and (6).

[143]   EPAA 1985, Sch 1, Part 1, para 2(1). The same provisions apply to EPAs registered after 1 October 2007: MCA 2005, Sch 4, Part 3, para 6. Safeguards in the EPA jurisdiction are considered at **3.11**.

[144]   MCA 2005, Sch 1, Part 1, para 2(1)(c).

two certificates of capacity must be given.[145] The persons named by the donor must be named as individuals rather than as a class or by reference to a relationship.[146]

3.84 The right of the donor to choose the persons to be notified of the application to register the LPA differs significantly from the requirements of EPAA 1985, which requires prescribed members of a class of relatives to be notified. This has proved controversial, but embodies a recommendation of the Law Commission,[147] which was critical of the statutory list of notifiable relatives which:

'... makes no acknowledgement that close and important relationships may exist outside of legal marriage and blood ties. It conflicts with the autonomy principle to require, regardless of the donor's wishes, that certain relatives must be notified of a private arrangement to govern future decision making.'

3.85 This approach was actively supported by the Government in the long legislative process that led to the passing of MCA 2005. In the Report Stage of the Bill in the House of Lords, the Minister of State, Baroness Ashton made the following comments:[148]

'I said that families are different. I did not say that they were not very important. I simply said that families are not what they used to be. We have lots of different kinds of families. People have many strong relationships – for example, half-siblings, step-children, and different situations within families ...

I am also very clear that this provision is about the donor making a choice. Ultimately, the donor should say who they would like to have notified. It could be a relative, but there may not be any relatives around or the donor may be estranged from his or her family – so there would be little point in notifying a relative. Just because someone is related does not necessarily mean that he will care anything for the donor. He may even have his own selfish motives for showing an interest in trying to object to the donor's chosen attorney.

So the Bill provides freedom of choice, but it does not lose sight of protection. My noble friend has made it clear that he is worried about the coercion or pressure that could be put on someone to give a decision-making power to a person through a lasting power of attorney.

That is why the Bill provides that all applications to register a lasting power of attorney must be accompanied by a certificate from a person of prescribed description that, in his opinion, the donor understands what he is doing and that no fraud or undue pressure is being used to induce the donor to create that lasting power of attorney. It goes one step further than that. Where there is no named person, regulations may require two certificates of that kind to be provided. This is the balance that I feel we have struck within the Bill: freedom and protection working in tandem.'

3.86 The obligation to give notice of an intention to register the power is therefore a key safeguard against abuse. But the Government's approach is

---

[145]   MCA 2005, Sch 1, Part 1, para 2(2)(b). The certificate of capacity is considered in more detail at **3.60**ff.

[146]   MCA 2005, Sch 1, para 2(1)(c) refers to the donor 'naming a person or persons'. The donor cannot therefore refer to a description of a person or class of persons.

[147]   Law Com No 231 (see **3.16**), at para 7.37.

[148]   *Hansard*, HL Deb, vol 670, ser 5, col 1316 (15 March 2005).

political as much as functional, as concerned with reflecting its particular view of society as protecting the donor. However well-intentioned is this approach, it assumes that the competent donor putting his or her affairs in order is acting with a complete understanding of all the relevant factors will choose sensibly those persons who might actually be in a position to protect his or her interests in the event of abuse or a future change in circumstances. The benefit inherent in a prescribed list of relatives is lost. Disputes concerning EPAs often come to light when relatives are notified. Sometimes relatives will conduct their own disputes with each other at the expense of the donor, but there are also many cases where the attorney was in a position of trust and confidence at the time the power was made. The attorney may have abused that position of trust to influence a power of attorney in his or her favour; but there are other more innocent but equally difficult cases where at the time the power was made, the choice of attorney seemed sensible. The trusted friend may subsequently have had financial difficulties or have fallen out with the donor; or the favourite nephew may have moved away and become less helpful. When preparing a LPA a donor will be under the influence of the circumstances that exist at that time and the persons named will reflect that.

3.87 It is also common for many elderly people who live alone to find that the people they trust and would like to be notified are of a similar age. No allowance is made for the passage of time and the donor's own choice may well be out of date by the time the power comes to be registered several years later. MCA 2005 assumes that a LPA will be registered shortly after the instrument is prepared, and while this seems to happen in the majority of cases, this cannot be relied upon. Persons must be named in the instrument at the time it is made, but they are notified when the power is registered, which may be several months or even years afterwards.[149] No provision is made for such persons having died, lost contact or themselves become incapable. The person registering the power must either send out notices to the last address shown on the power or apply to the Court to exercise its powers under MCA 2005, Sch 1, para 10 to dispense with the requirement to notify.[150]

3.88 MCA 2005 therefore replaces one flawed safeguard with another flawed safeguard. This will impose a greater burden on professional advisers to ensure that the donor makes an informed choice about the persons to be notified. If close relatives are excluded, then it may be that there are suspicious grounds for doing so. If there is no one the potential donor might wish to be notified then at the very least the donor's adviser or doctor might be named as a person to be notified. It would be unusual, if not suspicious,

---

[149] In the majority of cases where the LPA is registered shortly afer the instrument has been executed, the donor is fully aware of the procedure of taking place and notifying named persons adds no benefit to the procedure.

[150] This will involve a formal application to the Court of Protection. By contrast a relative is not entitled to receive notice of registration of an EPA if his or her 'name or address is not known to the attorney and cannot be reasonably ascertained by him or the attorney has reason to believe that he has not reached 18 or is mentally incapable'. See MCA 2005, Sch 4, para 6(3).

for a donor not to name anyone, even though the Act provides for this by requiring two certificates of capacity in such a situation.[151] However, even this safeguard can be avoided by naming someone as a person to be notified; there is no requirement that such person be capable of responding or willing to take an interest.[152]

Part B – the Certificate Provider's Statement

3.89 One of the principal objections to EPAs was that they were completed too readily, without the extent of the donor's capacity being addressed. The presumption would then arise that the EPA had been validly executed and as it might be several years before the problem came to light, there was no contemporaneous evidence to address the issue one way or the other. To address this particular problem and to add a further safeguard, the LPA must also contain a certificate of capacity. This added level of protection is all the more important where the LPA relates to welfare decisions, which may include decisions concerning life-sustaining treatment.

3.90 The LPA instrument therefore requires a certificate to be given by a person of a prescribed description, who is not a donee of the power, stating that in his or her opinion, at the time the donor executes the instrument:[153]

   (a) the donor understands the purpose of the instrument and the scope of the authority given under it;

   (b) no fraud or undue pressure is being used to induce the donor to create a LPA; and

   (c) there is nothing else which would prevent a LPA from being created.[154]

3.91 The certificate provider's statement constitutes Part B of the prescribed form. There is no time-limit in which the certificate must be completed, although the instrument cannot be registered until it has been completed. Clearly, the longer the gap between execution and the giving of the certificate, the harder it is for the certificate provider to be able to certify the facts required by MCA 2005. All that the legislation actually requires is that the certificate of capacity is completed 'as soon as reasonably practicable' after the preceding steps (the execution of the instrument) have been carried out.[155] However, it can be argued that any gap between the two events makes it impossible for the certificate to be given, as the certificate provider is addressing a prior event of which he or she had no actual

---

[151]   MCA 2005, Sch 1, para 2(b).

[152]   It is quite possible for a donor to name anyone as a person to be notified; that person could be someone who is terminally ill, mentally incapable or completely unconnected to the donor. It has been suggested that public figures or even politicians such as Baroness Ashton could be named persons.

[153]   The giving of the certificate is a separate act to the execution of the instrument and does not need to be contemporaneous with execution.

[154]   MCA 2005, Sch 1, Part 1, para 2(1)(e).

[155]   Lasting Powers of Attorney, Enduring Powers of Attorney and Public Guardian Regulations 2007, SI 2007/1253, reg 9(4).

knowledge. To address this difficulty, the certificate provider should be if at all possible be a witness to the LPA or be present when the LPA is executed.

3.92 The prescribed forms do not prevent the witness to the donor's signature also completing the certificate of capacity. This should therefore reflect best practice among solicitors, where the LPA is professionally prepared. Any professional who was accustomed to witnessing a client's EPA would in effect be certifying his or her understanding that in his or her opinion the client had capacity to grant the EPA.[156] Where there was doubt about a donor's capacity then a doctor might be asked to confirm that the client had capacity. The certificate of capacity in an LPA would simply serve as a record of the donor's capacity on the face of the document.

3.93 The certificate of capacity is an important safeguard provided by MCA 2005; but it is not intended to be so onerous that it deters potential donors from making LPAs. To encourage completion of LPAs, the certificate can be given by a wide class of persons, who need not necessarily be professionally qualified. A certificate may therefore be given by:[157]

'(a) someone the donor has known personally for two years;

[OR]

(b) someone who because of their relevant professional skills and expertise, considers themselves able to provide the certificate.'

3.94 The prescribed forms therefore provide for a 'lay' certificate provider or a 'professional' certificate provider. There is no requirement for the lay certificate provider to show any particular expertise or experience. The Regulations refer to "a person chosen by the donor as being someone who has known him personally for the period of at least two years which ends immediately before the date on which that person signs the LPA certificate."[158] The prescribed form contains the declaration that "I have known the donor for at least two years and as more than an acquaintance. My personal knowledge of the donor is ..." There is then a box for the certificate provider to complete, showing how he knows and has known the donor. There is no way of showing or indeed requiring the friend to show that he understands the concept of capacity in the light of MCA 2005 as well as the nature and effect of the form. The onus is on the donor to choose – and the Regulations deliberately use the words 'chosen by the donor' – a suitable certificate provider who can if called upon to do so, show that he understood what he was doing and more importantly, that he understood what the donor was doing at the relevant time. It is then for the certificate provider to subscribe to the wording in the prescribed form: "I understand my role and responsibilities as a certificate provider."

---

156 The problem was that many EPAs were created too quickly without sufficient attention to the donor's capacity. See further **3.15**.
157 Lasting Powers of Attorney, Enduring Powers of Attorney and Public Guardian Regulations 2007, SI 2007/1253, reg 8(1).
158 Lasting Powers of Attorney, Enduring Powers of Attorney and Public Guardian Regulations 2007, SI 2007/1253, reg 8(1).

3.95 There is no prescriptive definition of who can be a professional certificate provider. The Regulations refer to "a person chosen by the donor who, on account of his professional skills and expertise, reasonably considers that he is competent to make the judgments necessary to certify the matters set out in paragraph (2)(1)(e) of Schedule 1 to the Act." As with choosing a lay certificate provider, the onus is on the donor to choose a suitable certificate provider but it also rests on the certificate provider to consider that he is competent. It is for the certificate provider to certify that "I understand my role and responsibilities as a certificate provider." As to who may or may not be competent, the Regulations merely provide the following examples of persons who can act as certificate providers, namely:[159]

- a registered health care professional;
- a barrister, solicitor or advocate called or admitted in any part of the United Kingdom;
- a registered social worker; or
- an independent mental capacity advocate.

3.96 This list is not, however, exhaustive, and the defined skills are provided as examples only. Although the Regulations refer to the 'professional skills' of the certificate provider, the prescribed form requires the certificate provider to complete two tests. He must state his profession and then state his particular skills. Clearly a certificate provider acting in a professional capacity must have a profession; it must also be a relevant profession. A solicitor may for instance be a professional person but may specialise in commercial litigation and have no experience of assessing capacity and understanding the nature and effect of the LPA. A solicitor experienced in this area of law should state this in the box in provided for the certificate provider to place this information on record.[160]

3.97 There are, however, some persons who cannot provide a certificate.[161] A certificate provider must be over 18.[162] A donee of a power – including the donee of another LPA or EPA given by the same donor – cannot be a certificate provider. A certificate provider must be acting 'independently' and must not be a relative of the donor or the attorney, a business partner or paid employee, or anyone involved in the care home in which the donor lives.[163] This may cause difficulties where the donor wishes to appoint a

---

[159]   Lasting Powers of Attorney, Enduring Powers of Attorney and Public Guardian Regulations 2007, SI 2007/1253, reg 8(2).

[160]   The prescribed form refers to a consultant specializing in geriatric care as an example of the particular skills of a professional certificate provider.

[161]   Lasting Powers of Attorney, Enduring Powers of Attorney and Public Guardian Regulations 2007, SI 2007/1253, reg 8(3).

[162]   The forms prescribed by the 2007 Regulations contained a box requiring the certificate provider to confirm that he or she was over 18. Failure to tick the box 'I am aged 18 or over' would in theory prevent the Public Guardian from registering the instrument – even though the certificate provider is a solicitor or doctor who could be expected to be over 18. See also **3.63** above.

[163]   In the case of *Re Kittle* referred to at **3.62** above and reported on the Public Guardian's website, it was held that a first cousin was not a 'relative' for the purposes of preventing a person from acting as a certificate provider.

professional attorney. A donor appointing a professional attorney will not be able to have the certificate given by a partner or employee of the attorney's firm. The donor will need to find someone else to complete the certificate or else take it to a doctor or another solicitor. By contrast, however, the certificate provider can be an employer of the donee. There is also nothing to prevent a named person or the witness to the donor's signature being a certificate provider.[164]

3.98 A professional certificate provider will furthermore need to consider carefully matter such as:[165]

- the extent of his or her instructions or retainer;[166]
- whether the donor(s) should provide proof of their identity;
- the time that has passed between execution of the instrument and the certificate of capacity;
- whether the contents of the instrument give rise to any queries or concerns;
- whether, if he or she is not medically qualified, medical advice is required;
- whether, if he or she is not legally qualified, legal advice is required;
- what records should be kept and for how long; and
- that if the power is given by one spouse (or civil partner) to the other, the donor in each case must be interviewed separately.

3.99 Notwithstanding these considerations, the three tests set out in MCA 2005, Sch 1, para 1(e) are ostensibly quite limited. It should quickly be established that there is no fraud or undue pressure and that there is nothing else to prevent the instrument taking effect as a LPA. It is the first of the statutory requirements – that 'the donor understands the purpose of the instrument and the scope of the authority given under it' – that in practice requires the greatest degree of attention. But the certificate provider is not primarily concerned with the content of the instrument or the wisdom or lack of wisdom in the decisions being made by the donor, or even the capacity of the donor to make his own decisions. All the Act requires is an assessment that the donor understands the purpose of the instrument – that it is a power of attorney, who the attorneys are and when they may act and the scope of the power – that it extends to property and affairs or welfare matters.[167] Clearly the certificate provider should be alert to a lack of

---

[164] It may in fact be good practice for a doctor or solicitor who knows the donor sufficiently well to give a certificate of capacity and also to act as a named person, especially if the donor has few close friends or relatives.

[165] It is unclear what responsibility or duty a non-professional person has in giving a certificate of capacity. However, there is no doubt that a professional person will have a greater responsibility and this will be reflected in the fee he or she will be obliged to charge, thereby making it more likely that LPAs will not be certified appropriately.

[166] A solicitor who prepared an EPA for a client needed to be satisfied that on the balance of probabilities the client has the mental capacity to make an EPA (see *Enduring Power of Attorney Guidelines for Solicitors* prepared by the Law Society's Mental Health and Disability Committee). A validly executed document endorsed by a solicitor should therefore provide clear evidence of the donor's capacity.

[167] The donor must show that he or she understands the 'purpose' and 'scope' of the instrument. Most definitions of capacity to perform a legal act refer to 'nature' and 'effect' and it is

understanding of the proposed LPA, but neither is he or she conducting a separate examination on the subject, or expecting the donor to go through the same set of instructions twice.

3.100 The certificate of capacity is intended to provide an important safeguard, to protect the donor from undue influence of abuse and also to avoid subsequent doubts about the validity of the power. This will therefore reinforce the presumption that already exists in the due execution of an EPA, that a LPA which has been properly executed and contains such a certificate is a valid power.[168] A certificate of capacity will, to most persons dealing with the LPA, serve as a badge of authenticity that will make it that much harder to query or object to the power. This will widen the scope for abuse where a certificate of capacity is procured fraudulently or without proper consideration for the importance of the subject matter. Only when the validity of the LPA or the conduct of the attorneys is queried and addressed by the Court of Protection will it become obvious that the certificate of capacity is only as good as the person giving the certificate.

3.101 In the event that the donor does not require any person to be notified of registration of the instrument, the instrument must contain two such certificates.[169] The prescribed forms therefore have space for two certificates to be given.

Part C – the Attorney's Statement

3.102 The final section of the form is the Attorney's Statement, which must be completed after the Donor and the Certificate Provider have completed their respective parts of the form.[170] As with the prescribed form of EPA, the prescribed form must also contain a statement by the attorney that he or she is prepared to take on the role of attorney and understands his or her obligations. To act as an attorney under a LPA, MCA 2005 requires from the attorney a statement in the following terms:[171]

'(i) I have read the prescribed information (the section called 'information you must read on page 2), and

(ii) I understand the role and responsibilities under this lasting power of attorney, in particular'

---

arguable that the former requires a lesser degree of understanding. See the decision of the Senior Judge of the Court of Protection in the case of *Re Collis* reported on the website of the Public Guardian at: www.publicguardian.gov.uk/information-professionals under the heading 'other orders of interest made by the Court of Protection since 1 October 2007.'

[168] *Re W (enduring power of attorney)* [2001] Ch 609, [2001] 4 All ER 88, [2001] 2 WLR 957.

[169] MCA 2005, Sch 1, Part 1, para 2(2)(b). The space for two certificates adds to the length and complexity of the form. There can be no demand for two certificates as it is hardly a hindrance to name at least one person to be notified on registration, especially as the persons named can be complete strangers.

[170] Lasting Powers of Attorney, Enduring Powers of Attorney and Public Guardian Regulations 2007, SI 2007/1253, reg 9(5).

[171] MCA 2005, Sch 1, Part 1, para 2(1)(d).

- I have a duty to act based on the principles of the Mental Capacity Act 2005 and have regard to the Mental Capacity Act Code of Practice
- I can make decisions and act only when this lasting power of attorney has been registered
- I must make decisions and act in the best interests of the person who is giving me this lasting power of attorney
- I can spend money to make gifts but only to charities or on customary occasions and for reasonable amounts [property and affairs power only]
- I have a duty to keep accounts and financial records and produce them to the Office of the Public Guardian and/or the Court of Protection on request [property and affairs power only]

3.103 The same form is used for a replacement attorney and should be completed in the same way and annexed to the form after the Part C form(s) completed by the first attorney(s) As we have seen, it is easy for the appointment of a replacement attorney to be overlooked on registration and subsequently when he is called upon to act.[172] The prescribed form therefore includes a declaration (which the replacement attorney is assumed to agree to) that in the event of a triggering event arising – namely the the disclaimer, death, divorce, bankruptcy or incapacity of the first attorney – the replacement attorney will notify the Public Guardian and return the original LPA to the Public Guardian. This serves two important purposes:

- The Public Guardian has notice of an event that has occurred which not only triggers the appointment of the replacement attorney but which also allows him to update his records.
- The original LPA can be endorsed so that the replacement attorney can produce this (or a certified copy) of his authority to act.

3.104 Under a welfare LPA the second of the above statements is modified to make it clear that the attorney understands that he or she can only act where the power has been registered and the donor lacks mental capacity.

3.105 MCA 2005 refers to the duties imposed on an attorney under sections 1 (the principles) and 4 (best interests) in the same way as they are imposed on any person or body who makes decisions which another person lacks capacity to make. This is however a minimum requirement, as the attorney may well have other duties. A donee, for instance, has other common law or fiduciary obligations when dealing with property and affairs.[173] The sensible aim of the forms is to ensure that an attorney makes a positive commitment to his or her legal obligations (and provides a measure against which his or her performance can be judged in the future). No attorney should undertake the role without careful consideration. It is likely that many attorneys will sign a form without thinking too carefully about what they are signing, but at least there is a record of what they should be thinking about when signing the forms.

---

[172] See **3.72**.
[173] See **3.4**.

CREATION OF LASTING POWER OF ATTORNEY

A lasting power of attorney is created in two stages

3.106   A power of attorney intended to be a LPA for the purposes of MCA 2005 must be made in two stages for it to be valid as a LPA: the drawing up and execution of the instrument followed by its formal registration by the Public Guardian. The terminology can cause some confusion. Until both stages have been completed, a properly completed and duly executed instrument has no legal effect.[174] A completed document headed 'Lasting Power of Attorney' is not therefore a LPA until both stages have been completed. Until that has been done, the document is a worthless piece of paper, of no legal effect whatsoever. MCA 2005, s 9(2) describes the unregistered form somewhat clumsily as 'an instrument conferring authority of the kind mentioned in subsection (1)'; thereafter it is referred to as an instrument 'intended to create a lasting power of attorney' or, more commonly, simply as an 'instrument'.

THE FIRST STAGE: COMPLETING THE INSTRUMENT

3.107   The first stage is the completion and execution of the prescribed form. This involves a number of steps, which may or may not be taken at some distance in time from each other, although the Regulations assume that each step will be taken 'as soon as reasonably practicable' after the previous step.[175] The steps must however be taken in the correct sequence. Thus:

(1)   The donor reads the prescribed information.

(2)   The donor completes the provisions of the instrument that pertain to him or her (Part A) and executes the instrument, by signing it in the presence of a witness. Once Part A has been completed, the witness must sign the instrument and give his or her full name and address.[176] Although MCA 2005 refers to the time when the donor 'executes the instrument' there is no mention in the Act to execution as a deed.[177] A power of attorney, however, is regarded as a deed and a LPA complies with the Law of Property (Miscellaneous Provisions) Act 1989, s 1.[178] The original prescribed forms introduced by the 2007 Regulations made no reference to the document being a deed; this is now made clear in the 2009 forms.

(3)   A welfare LPA also requires the page dealing with life-sustaining treatment to be completed and that page must therefore be signed separately in the presence of a witness.

---

[174]   MCA 2005, s 9(2).
[175]   Lasting Powers of Attorney, Enduring Powers of Attorney and Public Guardian Regulations 2007, SI 2007/1253, reg 9(1).
[176]   Lasting Powers of Attorney, Enduring Powers of Attorney and Public Guardian Regulations 2007, SI 2007/1253, reg 9(9).
[177]   MCA 2005, s 9(2)(c).
[178]   Powers of Attorney Act 1971, s 1.

(4) The Certificate of Capacity (Part B) is signed by a person of a prescribed description confirming that in his or her opinion, at the time the donor executes the instrument:[179]

'(i) the donor understands the purpose of the instrument and the scope of the authority conferred under it,

(ii) no fraud or undue pressure is being used to induce the donor to create a lasting power of attorney, and

(iii) there is nothing else which would prevent a lasting power of attorney from being created by the instrument.'

(5) A statement (Part C) is made by the donee or by each donee to the effect that he or she:[180]

'(i) I have read the prescribed information (the section called 'information you must read on page 2), and

(ii) I understand the role and responsibilities under this lasting power of attorney ...'

3.108 Only when all these steps have been completed can the instrument be registered by the Public Guardian. It is this second stage which 'creates' the power in its registration with the Public Guardian and until the instrument is actually registered, it is ineffective as a power of attorney.[181] The registration procedure is described in more detail below.

Capacity to create a power

3.109 A person's capacity to execute a LPA is specific to that matter at the material time.[182] Although MCA 2005 sets out a framework for assessing capacity, and expects a person to certify that the donor 'understands the purpose of the instrument and the scope of the authority conferred under it', it is likely that the existing case-law will assist in determining questions concerning capacity to grant a LPA.

3.110 The principle that capacity to create an EPA required a different test to that of managing property and affairs was considered in the case of *Re K, Re F*.[183] Registration of an EPA was objected to on the grounds that the power had been made immediately before an application was made for its registration – on the basis that the donor lacked capacity to manage her property and affairs. Hoffman J confirmed the validity of the power, it being a specific legal act at the time it was made and therefore distinct from the donor's ability to manage or not manage her property and affairs. He set out four basic requirements as to what the donor should understand:[184]

'... first, if such be the terms of the power, that the attorney will be able to assume complete authority over the donor's affairs; second, if such be the terms of the power, that the attorney will in general be able to do anything with the donor's property

---

[179] MCA 2005, Sch 1, para 2(1)(e). The Certificate of Capacity is dealt with at **3.89**ff.
[180] MCA 2005, Sch 1, para 2(1)(d). See **3.102** above for the complete declaration.
[181] MCA 2005, s 9(2)(b).
[182] MCA 2005, s 2(1).
[183] [1988] Ch 310, [1988] 1 All ER 358, [1988] 2 WLR 781.
[184] [1988] 1 All ER 358, at p 363. This approach was followed by the Senior Judge of the Court of Protection in the case of *Re Collis*, reported on the website of the Public Guardian. See **3.99**.

which the donor could have done; third, that the authority will continue if the donor should be or become mentally incapable; fourth, that if he should be or become mentally incapable, the power will be irrevocable without confirmation by the court.'

3.111 As with EPAs, a properly executed LPA will create a presumption of due execution. The certificate of capacity alone places a very strong burden on anyone objecting to registration on the grounds that the power is invalid. The Public Guardian furthermore has a positive duty to register a LPA unless he receives a valid objection to registration within the prescribed period or an objection is made to the Court.[185] The Court can only revoke the power if it is satisfied that one of the limited grounds allowed by MCA 2005 has been established.[186] Thus, unless the Court is satisfied that the ground for revocation has been established, it cannot prevent the LPA from being registered.

3.112 This approach is the same applied by the Court of Protection in the context of registration of EPAs.[187] The evidential burden is weighted against the objector, which in practice makes it very difficult for the Court to revoke an EPA on the grounds of its invalidity. Unless there is clear and compelling evidence that the donor lacked capacity at the time of execution or that there was fraud or undue influence, the Court must register the EPA. An even greater burden of proof will apply on anyone seeking to challenge the validity of the LPA.

THE SECOND STAGE: REGISTRATION

The requirement of registration

3.113 A LPA is not effective as a power of attorney unless and until it is registered with the Public Guardian in accordance with MCA 2005, Sch 1.[188] The aim of the Act is to encourage early registration of LPAs, so that the process of validation and supervision is started as soon as the power is used. However, a welfare power – which has in any event already been registered – can only operate in respect of those decisions which the donor lacks capacity to make.[189]

3.114 An attorney operating a welfare power must therefore pass two separate thresholds before he or she can make a decision: the first is that the power must be registered; the second is that the donor lacks capacity. Any clinician or other person treating or caring for a person and seeking to take instructions from the attorney must likewise ensure that the two thresholds are passed, checking that there is a registered LPA in place and also verifying that the donor lacks capacity.

---

[185] MCA 2005, Sch 1, Part 2, para 5.
[186] MCA 2005, s 22(3).
[187] *Re W* [2001] Ch 609, [2001] 4 All ER 88, [2001] 2 WLR 957, [2001] 1 FLR 832.
[188] MCA 2005, s 9(2)(b).
[189] MCA 2005, s 11(7)(a).

3.115 A property and affairs LPA is by contrast more straightforward as it can operate notwithstanding the capacity of the donor. This has three practical benefits:

(1) It avoids misuse of the power where the attorney continues to act notwithstanding the revocation of the power on the incapacity of the donor. As often happens with EPAs the power is used by an attorney where it should be registered with the result that the donor's interests are not protected and the attorney (even though he or she may be acting in good faith) is acting beyond the scope of his or her authority.

(2) The attorney is not required to conduct a medical assessment of the donor's capacity. He or she does not need to take responsibility for or undergo the awkwardness of asserting that the donor is mentally incapable.

(3) No other person is entitled to make an assessment based on the fact, that by virtue of registration, the donor is incapable of managing all his or her property and affairs. Thus the fact of registration does not give rise to a presumption of incapacity.

Problems with capacity not being relevant to registration

3.116 While the benefits of avoiding the issue of capacity on registration of a LPA are self-evident, there are also several disadvantages. A third party dealing directly with the donor of the LPA cannot make any assumption as to the donor's lack of capacity, but must make his or her own assessment of the donor's capacity at the relevant time. While this respects the integrity of the donor, the third party's position is less clear. A bank, for example, cannot rely on the fact of registration to prevent the donor from using his or her account, where, for instance, there are large or frequent withdrawals from the account. Likewise a solicitor selling a property on the authority of the attorney of a LPA cannot assume that the donor is incapable and the property is being sold to pay for nursing care. The donor therefore may have less protection against financial abuse than the donor of an EPA.

Problems with early registration

3.117 Although the aim of MCA 2005 is to encourage early registration of LPAs, it is likely that over time many donors and attorneys will not follow this in practice. A capable donor may well feel stigmatised by the fact of registration but is more likely to resent the expense and inconvenience of registration as well as the sense that this restricts his or her freedom. Of course the donor can revoke the LPA but he or she must still go through the process of having the registration cancelled. There is no prescribed form or procedure for a donor who has revoked a LPA to cancel registration. A donor who has capacity or who recovered capacity and wishes to revoke the LPA needs to provide the Public Guardian with sufficient evidence to cancel the registration.[190] This may cause not only inconvenience, expense, embarrassment or family discord, but also force the donor to demonstrate to the Public Guardian that he or she is capable of revoking the power. Moreover if the revocation is contested or the donor's evidence of revocation is contested, then the matter must be referred to the Court of Protection for determination.[191]

3.118 In the first two years of their operation and while LPAs have a novelty value and there is uncertainty over their formal validity, instruments are being registered even though there is no intention to use them.[192] With time it is likely that in the majority of cases, LPAs will not be used (whether or not they have been registered) unless and until the donor lacks capacity to manage his or her property and affairs. It is also likely that some LPAs will contain special conditions to this effect. Thus, if most LPAs are registered on incapacity, many third parties dealing with the attorney will associate registration with a lack of capacity and in practice make assumptions to that effect.

3.119 If, however, registration is delayed, the benefits of early registration are also lost. Thus, if there is a dispute or query, the evidence of the donor and the certificate provider will not be as fresh and the notified persons may not be available to object to an inappropriate registration.[193]

Procedure for registration

3.120 The procedure for registration of a LPA is relatively straightforward, and should not therefore deter attorneys from taking on their responsibilities to register and act under the LPA. In contrast to the procedure for registration of an EPA, the application may be made by the donor as well as by the attorney.

3.121 Application to register a LPA can be made by the donor or donee or by one of two or more donees appointed to act jointly and severally. Application must be made in the prescribed form, LPA002, which contains the prescribed information.[194] The application form contains sufficient information about the donor, the donee or donees and service of notices to

---

190   Lasting Powers of Attorney, Enduring Powers of Attorney and Public Guardian Regulations 2007, SI 2007/1253, reg 21.
191   MCA 2005, Sch 1, para 18(b).
192   This does perhaps explain why applications for registration, which amounted to 7,500 in September 2008 (Bridget Prentice MP, addressing the Public Guardian Board General Meeting, 7 October 2008). This is more than double the level predicted and may account in part for some of the administrative problems faced by the Public Guardian in the first year of operating the new regime.
193   See **3.87**.
194   MCA 2005, Sch 1, para 4(1). The form is set out as Schedule 3 to the Lasting Powers of Attorney, Enduring Powers of Attorney and Public Guardian Regulations 2007, SI 2007/1253.

enable the Public Guardian to deal with the registration process. The applicant for registration will also need to submit the original LPA and the prescribed fee of £120.[195]

3.122 Where the donor has created separate LPAs in respect of property and affairs and welfare matters, then they will need to be registered separately. It will often be the case that different attorneys are appointed for different purposes or the powers need to be registered at different times. There is therefore no obvious mechanism for registering the two powers by the same process. An attorney registering welfare and financial powers for his elderly parents will therefore have to make four applications and pay four separate fees of £120. It is therefore possible that a separate fee for each process may deter attorneys from registering LPAs – especially welfare powers – until the last moment.[196]

Status of attorney prior to registration

3.123 A LPA has no legal effect until it is registered.[197] As the document is not a power of attorney, there is no legal basis on which an attorney can act or the Court of Protection can assist. MCA 2005 does not therefore provide any interim or limited authority for the attorney to act after the application has been made but before the power has been registered.[198] Where a donor has become incapable of carrying out an act for which authority is urgently required by the donee, the donee has no ability to act under the LPA, even though an application to register the power has been made.

3.124 This omission from MCA 2005 may cause difficulties for an attorney who needs to administer the donor's affairs while the power is being registered. It may be that a short delay will not prejudice the donor's interests, but the situation is more complicated if registration is delayed for perhaps several months while there is a dispute over the validity of the power or the conduct of the attorney. If the attorney requires authority in this period, he or she must either apply to the Court for a specific order under MCA 2005, s 18 or rely on the provisions of MCA 2005, ss 7 and 8. Thus an attorney who needs to access the donor's bank account to pay for nursing home fees must either apply to the Court of Protection for an order or spend his or her own money and be reimbursed by the donor subsequently.[199]

---

[195] MCA 2005, Sch 1, para 4(3). The actual fees prescribed are set out in the Public Guardian (Fees, etc) Regulations 2007, SI 2007/2051.

[196] The unintended consequence may prove positive: a welfare LPA is only intended as a 'last resort' and may well not need to be registered. Many donors whose property and affairs are dealt with by an attorney will carry on being cared for informally without the need for intervention by an attorney. Thus a welfare power will not be registered as a matter of course on incapacity, but may be held back until there is a dispute or contentious treatment that requires the authority of an attorney to resolve. This should not, however, be used to overlook the risk of the power being needed urgently and its use is delayed by registration.

[197] MCA 2005, s 9(2)(b).

[198] Compare the provisions of MCA 2005, Sch 4, para 1(2). An EPA is already a power of attorney when it is made.

[199] It has therefore been suggested by some practitioners that a donor who does not want his or

3.125 Where the donee wishes to resolve any queries concerning the validity of the power, he or she can apply to the Court of Protection for a determination under MCA 2005, s 22(2).

Notices

3.126 The person applying to register the LPA (who may be the donor or the donee) must notify any person named in the LPA for that purpose of his or her intention to register the power.[200] Notification is made in the prescribed form LPA001.[201]

3.127 The applicant is only obliged to notify the persons named in the LPA for that purpose of his or her intention to register the power. The Public Guardian is responsible for notifying:

- the donee or donees where the application is made by the donor, using form LPA003A;[202]
- the donor where the application is made by the donee or donees, using form LPA003B;[203] and
- a donee where two or more donees have been appointed jointly and severally and who has not applied to register the power (using form LPA003A).[204]

Service of notices

3.128 MCA 2005, Sch 1 refers to the applicant having to 'notify' a person; the Lasting Powers of Attorney, Enduring Powers of Attorney and Public Guardian Regulations 2007, reg 10 refers to notices being 'given'. Even form LPA003B must be 'given' by the Public Guardian. There is, however, no reference in the legislation to the mode of service of documents.[205] Only form LPA001 refers to the forms being 'sent'.

---

her LPA used immediately should also complete a simple power of attorney in accordance with the Powers of Attorney Act 1971, s 10 to operate while the donor has capacity and before the LPA is registered.

[200] MCA 2005, Sch 1, para 6. The rationale for notifying only named persons is dealt with at **3.84–3.85**. There is no requirement for the donee to notify any close relatives or persons involved in the care and welfare of the donor unless they have been actually named by the donor for this purpose.

[201] Lasting Powers of Attorney, Enduring Powers of Attorney and Public Guardian Regulations 2007, SI 2007/1253, reg 10 and Sch 2.

[202] MCA 2005, Sch 1, para 7.

[203] MCA 2005, Sch 1, para 8(1).

[204] MCA 2005, Sch 1, para 8(2).

[205] Compare the Court of Protection (Enduring Power of Attorney) Rules 2001, SI 2001/825, rr 15 and 16 which applied to the registration of EPAs prior to 1 October 2007. A notice of intention to register an EPA must also be served personally on the donor: Lasting Powers of Attorney, Enduring Powers of Attorney and Public Guardian Regulations 2007, SI 2007/1253, reg 23(3). It is difficult to see how the sending of a form by post to a donor will provide a greater degree of protection.

Dispensing with notice

3.129   Only the Court can direct that service of a notice on a named person be dispensed with.[206] However, the Court must first be satisfied that no useful purpose would be served by giving notice. There is no corresponding power for the Court to dispense with the requirement for the Public Guardian to notify the donor.

3.130   There is no provision in MCA 2005 or regulations which allows the person who is applying to register the LPA to dispense with the service of notice without reference to the Court. Thus if the named person cannot be located or is him or herself incapable, the Court must first agree to notice being dispensed with before the application to register the power is made.[207] If that is the approach of the Court, and a formal application needs to be made to dispense with notice, then it is likely that applicants in such cases will simply send the notice to the address on the form. He or she can claim to have 'notified' the named persons at their last known address.

Completion of registration

3.131   Unless there is a valid objection to registration of the LPA, the Public Guardian must register the power at the end of the prescribed period.[208] There is therefore a positive duty on the Public Guardian to register the power unless there is a defect in the power or a valid objection is received.

3.132   Once the LPA is registered, the Public Guardian must notify the donor and attorney(s) of the fact of registration in form LPA004.[209] While the original LPA will be sealed and endorsed with details of the registration and returned to the applicant or his or her solicitor, MCA 2005, s 16(1) provides authority for office copies to be conclusive evidence of the fact of registration and the contents of the power.

Objections to registration

The role of the Public Guardian

3.133   The registration authority is the Public Guardian who must register the LPA unless:

---

[206]   MCA 2005, Sch 1, para 10.

[207]   In contrast to the donee of an EPA who does not need to notify a relative if his or her name or address is not known to the attorney and cannot reasonably be ascertained or the attorney believes that the relative is aged under 18 or mentally incapable (EPAA 1985, Sch 1, para 2(2)).

[208]   MCA 2005, Sch 1, para 5. The Lasting Powers of Attorney, Enduring Powers of Attorney and Public Guardian Regulations 2007, SI 2007/1253, reg 12 specifies a period of 6 weeks, from the date of the last notice given to a person required to be notified.

[209]   Lasting Powers of Attorney, Enduring Powers of Attorney and Public Guardian Regulations 2007, SI 2007/1253, reg 17(5) and Sch 5.

- it appears to the Public Guardian that the LPA is not a valid power, in which case the power cannot be registered unless directed by the Court;[210]
- the Court of Protection has already appointed a deputy and it appears to the Public Guardian that the powers conferred on the deputy would conflict with the powers conferred on the attorney, in which case the power cannot be registered unless directed by the Court;[211]
- it appears to the Public Guardian that there is a provision in the instrument which would be ineffective as part of a LPA or which would prevent the power from operating as a LPA, in which case the power must be referred to the Court for determination;[212]
- the Public Guardian receives a notice of objection from the donee or named person on one of the specified grounds and it appears to the Public Guardian that the ground for making the objection is satisfied, in which case the Public Guardian must not register the power unless directed by the Court;[213] or
- the Court of Protection receives a notice of objection from the donee or named person on one of the prescribed grounds, in which case the Public Guardian must not register the power unless directed by the Court.[214]

Objections made to the Public Guardian

3.134 The Public Guardian's authority to refuse registration of the LPA is limited to cases where there is a defect in the power, which is either apparent from the facts or which is brought to the Public Guardian's attention by a named person who is objecting to registration of the power. Although MCA 2005 provides for the Public Guardian to be notified by means of an objection, it would be more appropriate to describe this process as a technical or procedural notice. The notice form given to a named person (LPA001) or by the Public Guardian to a co-attorney who is not applying to register the LPA (LPA003A) refer to these grounds as the 'factual grounds'.

3.135 An objection to proposed registration on one of the 'factual' grounds can only be made to the Public Guardian by the donor, an attorney or named person, before the expiry of the period of 5 weeks beginning with the date

---

[210] MCA 2005, Sch 1, para 11(1). For example, where the power was made using the incorrect form or there was a technical defect in the form which prevented it from operating as a valid LPA.
[211] MCA 2005, Sch 1, para 12.
[212] MCA 2005, Sch 1, para 11(2) and (3).
[213] MCA 2005, Sch 1, para 13(1) and (2). These are the narrow or factual grounds defined in s 13(3) and (6)(a)–(d) on which the Public Guardian can refuse to register the power without reference to the Court. See **3.134**.
[214] MCA 2005, Sch 1, para 13(3) and (4). This part of the Act refers to prescribed grounds and these are not defined. It can be assumed that these are the wider or substantive grounds defined in s 22(3) whereby the Court can direct that the power is not to be registered or revoke the power.

on which the notice is given.[215] An attorney or named person must file their objection with the Public Guardian using form LPA007. The 'factual' grounds on which a named person or a donee (where the application is made by the donor or the other donee) can 'object' in this way are limited to the following cases:

- insofar as the LPA relates to the property and affairs of the donor, the bankruptcy of the donor or the donee or, where the donee is a trust corporation, its winding up or dissolution;[216]
- the LPA has been disclaimed by the attorney;
- the death of the attorney;
- the dissolution or annulment of the donor's marriage or civil partnership between the donor and the donee (unless the power excludes revocation in these circumstances); or
- the attorney lacks capacity.

3.136 On receipt of an objection on the factual grounds, the Public Guardian will simply stop the registration process. It is then for the applicant to accept the situation or apply to the Court of Protection to consider the matter and to require the Public Guardian to register the power.

3.137 If the donor objects to registration, he or she simply gives notice to the Public Guardian in form LPA006. The Public Guardian must refuse to register the LPA unless the Court of Protection is satisfied that the donor lacks capacity to object to the registration.[217] However, it would be unlikely for the Public Guardian to refer the case immediately to the Court of Protection and it will be for the attorneys – if they wish – to persist with their application and refer the matter to the Court

The role of the Court of Protection

3.138 Where a donee or a named person receives a notice of registration and objects on one of the 'prescribed grounds' the Public Guardian cannot register the LPA until directed to do so by the Court of Protection.[218] The 'prescribed grounds' on which a person can object to registration are not defined by MCA 2005 but will mirror the grounds on which the Court can revoke a power under MCA 2005, s 22.

3.139 The Court's powers are not limited to the period of registration, but can be exercised at any time after a person has executed a power or a power has been registered as a LPA. However, an objection to registration made after the power has been registered will require the leave of the Court.[219]

---

[215] Lasting Powers of Attorney, Enduring Powers of Attorney and Public Guardian Regulations 2007, SI 2007/1253, reg 14.
[216] MCA 2005, s 13(3) and (6)(b).
[217] MCA 2005, Sch 1, para 14.
[218] MCA 2005, Sch 1, para 13(3) and (4).
[219] MCA 2005, s 50(2).

3.140   The Court may in such cases either refuse to register the LPA or, if the donor lacks capacity, revoke the LPA.[220] MCA 2005 does not, however, allow the Court to revoke the LPA if the donor retains capacity, although registration can be refused or cancelled. Thus if the power has already been registered where the donor has capacity and the Court is satisfied that undue pressure was used to create the power, it appears that the Court cannot interfere with the donor's choice of attorney.

Whether the requirements for the creation of the power have been met

3.141   The Court can determine any question relating to whether or not any of the requirements for creating or revoking a lasting power have been met.[221] This power covers not just the formal requirements of completing and executing the power, but also covers the ability or capacity of the donor to grant the power.

3.142   Although the Court may determine any question relating to the validity of the power, where an application to register is made, the Public Guardian is obliged to register the power unless one of the grounds for objection exists. This is consistent with EPAA 1985, which imposes a positive obligation to register an EPA unless a valid ground for objection is established to the satisfaction of the Court, thereby placing the evidential burden of proof on the objector.[222] The Court will assume that a LPA which has been correctly executed and which contains a certificate of capacity has been validly executed and that alone will place a strong burden of proof on the objector seeking to establish that the donor lacked capacity.

Whether the power has been revoked

3.143   The Court may determine any question relating to whether the power has been revoked or otherwise come to an end.[223] This power enables the Court to determine whether the power has been revoked by the donor. The donor must not only demonstrate capacity to revoke the instrument, but must also communicate to the donee an intention to revoke the power. If the Court determines the power has been revoked, it will direct the Public Guardian to cancel registration of the power.

3.144   The role of the Court to determine such matters is in addition to a separate power of the Public Guardian to cancel registration if he or she receives notice of revocation and is satisfied 'that the donor has taken such steps as are necessary in law to revoke it'.[224]

---

[220]   MCA 2005, s 22(4). The power to refuse registration or revoke the power is without prejudice to the Court's powers to give directions under s 22.
[221]   MCA 2005, s 22(2).
[222]   EPAA 1985, s 6(6) and see *Re W* [2001] 1 FLR 832.
[223]   MCA 2005, Sch 1, para 18.
[224]   Lasting Powers of Attorney, Enduring Powers of Attorney and Public Guardian

That fraud or undue pressure was used to induce the donor to create the power

3.145 If fraud pressure is alleged, the objection will be considered very carefully with the Court expecting all available evidence to be placed before it. Although the Court of Protection has wide powers to summon witnesses and cross-examine them, it is not an appropriate venue for a detailed investigation into an alleged fraud. If the LPA has been used improperly to commit a fraud then the police should be notified and the Court may revoke the power. If fraud is merely alleged, this may merely indicate a breakdown in relations between relatives or other concerned persons.

3.146 Similar considerations arise where 'undue pressure' is alleged. Pressure may be brought which is not 'undue pressure', for instance, where an elderly client is regularly advised by a solicitor or concerned relative that he or she should make a power of attorney. 'Undue pressure' is a matter of degree and requires a subjective assessment of whether the pressure was extreme or disproportionate to the extent that the donor could not have executed the power of his or her own free will.

That the donee has behaved, is behaving or proposes to behave in a way that contravenes his or her authority or contrary to the donor's best interests

3.147 The Court's power to intervene in the absence of fraud or undue influence and where the power is otherwise valid is limited to two grounds only:

(1) the donee has behaved, is behaving or proposes to behave in a way that contravenes his or her authority; or
(2) the donee has behaved, is behaving or proposes to behave in a way that is not or would not be in the donor's best interests.

3.148 These two grounds represent a limitation in the Court's powers to intervene in the conduct of an attorney. The first ground, where the donor contravenes his or her authority, can only cover acts which are illegal or in breach of the attorney's fiduciary duty to the donor. Thus they are acts which are actionable in their own right and for which there would be a civil or criminal remedy. For instance, an attorney who causes loss to the donor's estate may be liable to remedy the loss and an attorney who ill-treats or neglects the donor may be guilty of an offence under MCA 2005, s 44.

3.149 It is the second of these two grounds that may be problematic in practice. The difficulty for the Court is that the Court must impose its own view of what is in the donor's 'best interests' when there is no objective measure of a person's best interests. If the attorney takes account of the

---

Regulations 2007, SI 2007/1253, reg 21. This does appear to confer on the Public Guardian a judicial discretion to consider evidence and either cancel or refuse to cancel registration of the LPA.

factors and consults with the persons referred to in MCA 2005, s 4, then he or she has complied with the requirements of MCA 2005 if he or she 'reasonably believes that what he does or decides is in the best interests of the person concerned'. It will take time and no doubt several cases to establish the extent of the Court's power to impose its judgment as to a person's best interests and whether it can do this without finding that the attorney has in any event exceeded the scope of his or her authority.[225]

3.150 A person challenging a LPA on this ground also has to cross a very high evidential threshold in showing that an action (let alone a proposed action) is contrary to a person's 'best interests'. It is likely that such cases will centre around a simple argument over 'best interests' and may involve the Court being asked to make a welfare decision on a matter such as where the donor should live rather than on the operation of the LPA.

3.151 By contrast with EPAA 1985 and MCA 2005, Sch 4, the Court may refuse to register an enduring power or cancel such a power if satisfied that:[226]

> '... having regard to all the circumstances and in particular the attorney's relationship to or connection with the donor, the attorney is unsuitable to be the donor's attorney.'

3.152 The 'unsuitability' ground gives the Court more discretion to intervene in cases where it might be difficult to prove, on the balance of probabilities, that an act or proposed act is not in a person's best interests. There are also cases where an attorney is unsuitable despite ostensibly acting in the donor's best interests. For example:

- two attorneys are in conflict and both claim to be acting in the donor's best interests;
- the attorney's financial dealings with the donor's estate give rise to a potential conflict of interest or require further investigation, even though there is no evidence or it is very difficult to prove any actual wrongdoing.

3.153 The reason for changing the basis on which the Court of Protection can intervene is that the Court's powers should be consistent with MCA 2005 generally and applied in the context of the attorney's duty to act in the best interests of the donor.[227] The Court should be reluctant to dispute the donor's choice of attorney who in turn represents the donor's judgment as to who should interpret his or her best interests.

---

[225] More than two years after the MCA 2005 came into force, there has yet to be a case heard by the Court of Protection on these grounds. However, for an analysis of how best interests should be interpreted generally, see *Re P* [2009] EWHC 163 (Ch) which implies that the Court should take a robust or objective view of what is in a person's best interests.

[226] MCA 2005, Sch 4, Part 4, para 9(e).

[227] This follows the recommendation of the Law Commission: see Law Com No 231 (at **3.16**), at para 7.58.

Procedure

3.154 The process for objection is not defined by MCA 2005. The separate roles of the Public Guardian as the registration authority and the Court of Protection as the judicial authority cause some confusion and the procedure for dealing with objections and further proceedings falls between the Lasting Powers of Attorney, Enduring Powers of Attorney and Public Guardian Regulations 2007[228] and the Court of Protection Rules 2007.[229] A person who has been notified of an application and who wishes to object on one of the substantive grounds therefore has quite an arduous responsibility. It is not possible for a concerned relative to write to the Public Guardian setting out his or her concerns. Not only must a formal application be made to the Court of Protection, but the Public Guardian must also be notified so that the application for registration is suspended.[230] The objector must, within the prescribed period of 5 weeks (beginning with the date on which the notice is given):

- file a formal application for objection in form COP7 with the Court of Protection; and
- notify the Public Guardian in form LPA008.

3.155 Form COP7 serves as the formal application to the Court of Protection (instead of form COP1). This form is issued by the Court and must be served on the donor and attorneys as practicable and in any event within 21 days of issue. Each application form must be accompanied by a form for acknowledging service (COP5) and a certificate of service (COP20) must be filed with the Court within 7 days of service.

3.156 A person who is not a person named for notification and who wishes to object to registration of the LPA or who if the LPA has already been registered wishes to apply to have power cancelled must apply directly to the Court of Protection in form COP1, paying an application fee and using the procedure under the Court of Protection Rules, Part 9. Applications to the Court of Protection and its procedures are dealt with in more detail in Chapter 4. An attorney also has standing to make applications to the Court of Protection where the donor lacks capacity and will use the same procedures as any other person who has standing to make an application. These are also dealt with in Chapter 4.

ENDURING POWERS OF ATTORNEY

The future of existing powers

3.157 MCA 2005 repeals EPAA 1985 and provides for a new type of power of attorney, the LPA. No new EPAs can therefore be created.[231] There will, however, remain in place countless numbers of EPAs.[232] There is no

---

[228] SI 2007/1253.
[229] SI 2007/1744.
[230] MCA 2005, Sch 4, Part 2, para 13(3).
[231] MCA 2005, Sch 7.
[232] There is no reliable record of how many EPAs have actually been created. Probably tens if

reliable record of how many EPAs have been made and what proportion of them should be registered or might in future need to be registered on the grounds that the donor lacks capacity. Those EPAs which are registrable as well as the thousands which have already been registered cannot be replaced by new powers of attorney. Not only does the donor lack capacity to grant a new power, but it would be contrary to public policy to require donors – who have in good faith provided for the management of their property and affairs in the event of incapacity – to go to the effort and expense of making new powers of attorney. Neither was it considered appropriate to alter the terms on which a person was appointed to act.[233] MCA 2005 therefore addresses the status of those EPAs, registered and unregistered, made before its commencement. These transitional provisions are considered in Chapter 9.[234] The procedure for registering EPAs is set out in the Lasting Powers of Attorney, Enduring Powers of Attorney and Public Guardian Regulations 2007[235] and the prescribed forms set out in the Schedules thereto.

3.158   EPAs are dealt with in more detail above and a detailed account of the rules and principles applicable to their operation is beyond the scope of this work.[236] However, practitioners will need to be able to advise on and administer two distinct types of statutory power of attorney and apply different principles and procedures to each one. There will no doubt be endless debate over whether one is better than the other, but the inevitable result will be the complexity of two different jurisdictions applicable to persons in identical circumstances. Given the difficulties faced by the Court of Protection and Public Guardianship Office in operating one jurisdiction, it must be hoped that the new Court of Protection and Public Guardian will fare better than its predecessor in the operation of two jurisdictions.

---

not hundreds of thousands have been created as 'insurance policies' and remain in deed boxes and solicitors' offices across the country.

[233]   The Law Commission had proposed that unregistered EPAs could be converted to new-style powers of attorney, but that the expectations of donors should continue to be met. See Law Com No 231 (at **3.16**), at para 7.59.

[234]   See MCA 2005, Sch 4.

[235]   SI 2007/1253.

[236]   See **3.7–3.18**. The topic is covered in greater and better detail in *Cretney & Lush on Enduring Powers of Attorney* (Jordans, 5th edn, 2001) which will remain the definitive work on the subject. See also *Heywood & Massey: Court of Protection Practice* (Sweet & Maxwell). The same law and procedure will apply to existing EPAs, only different statutory provisions will apply to their operation.

Chapter 4

Powers of the Court

PRELIMINARY

4.1 The Mental Capacity Act 2005 (MCA 2005) only sets out the basic powers of the new Court of Protection and one must look at the Court of Protection Rules 2007[1] and Practice Directions to see how these are to be implemented. In addition to explaining the Court's jurisdiction an attempt is made here to address some of the issues that must be faced. The manner in which the Court conducts its business is dealt with in Chapter 7.

4.2 A helpful summary of the Court's approach to the exercise of its powers is to be found in *G v E and others*.[2] The following extracts from the judgment of Mr Justice Baker are worth setting out as an introduction to this Chapter:

'(i) The vast majority of decisions about incapacitated adults are taken by carers and others without any formal general authority. That was the position prior to the passing of the MCA under the principle of necessity … In passing the MCA, Parliament ultimately rejected the Law Commission's proposal of a statutory general authority and opted for the same approach as under the previous law by creating in section 5 a statutory defence to protect all persons who carry out acts in connection with the care or treatment of an incapacitated adult, provided they reasonably believe that it will be in that person's best interests for the act to be done. Crucially, however, all persons who provide such care and treatment are expected to look to the Code …

(ii) The Act and Code are therefore constructed on the basis that the vast majority of decisions concerning incapacitated adults are taken informally and collaboratively by individuals or groups of people consulting and working together. It is emphatically not part of the scheme underpinning the Act that there should be one individual who as a matter of course is given a special legal status to make decisions about incapacitated persons.

(iii) it will usually be the case that decisions about complex and serious issues are taken by a court rather than any individual. In certain cases, as explained in paragraphs 8.38 and 8.39 of the Code, it will be more appropriate to appoint a deputy or deputies to make these decisions. But because it is important that such decisions should wherever possible be taken collaboratively and informally, the appointments must be as limited in scope and duration as is reasonably practicable in the circumstances. … the appointment of deputies is likely to be more common for property and affairs than for personal welfare.

(iv) It is axiomatic that the family is the cornerstone of our society and a person who lacks capacity should wherever possible be cared for by members of his natural family, provided that such a course is in his best interests and assuming that they are able and willing to take on what is often an enormous and challenging task. That does not, however, justify the appointment of family members as deputies simply because they are able and willing to serve in that capacity.'

---

[1] SI 2007/1744.

[2] [2010] EWHC 2042 (COP) (Fam). For case summary, see Part IX of this work, but the entire judgment is worth reading. An earlier judgment on an emergency application in this case was reported as *G v E and others* [2010] EWHC 621 (Fam).

4.3 Applying this approach to the facts of the particular case Baker J. stated:

'(v) … the application for the appointment of F and G as personal welfare deputies is, in my judgment, misconceived. The routine decisions concerning E's day-to-day care, including decisions about holidays and respite care can be taken by F as his carer. Decisions about his education should be taken collaboratively by F, G, his teacher, and other relevant professionals. Decisions about possible medical treatment should be taken by his treating clinicians, who will doubtless consult both F and G and others as appropriate. If there is any disagreement about any of these matters, an application can be made to the Court of Protection. Decisions about who should look after E in the event that F is no longer able to do so should equally be considered (when the need arises) in a collaborative way and only referred to the court for endorsement if required or if there is any disagreement. That is an issue for the very long term and it would be wholly inappropriate to appoint a deputy or deputies now to make that decision …

(v) I am also unpersuaded that the appointment of deputies for property and affairs is justified at this point. Currently, E's income consists of state benefits alone and his savings are less than one thousand pounds. … the management of his independent budget … do not justify the appointment of a financial deputy. I recognise that an appointment of a deputy for property and affairs would become appropriate were E to acquire assets of a size that required the sort of management decisions described in section 18. That might occur, for example, were he to be awarded a significant sum of damages as a result of his forthcoming claim …'

DECLARATIONS

Background

4.4 In regard toserious medical treatment and, more recently, welfare decisions the High Court found it necessary to make declarations as to both capacity and then best interests when there was uncertainty or dispute over these issues in relation to an individual.[3] The High Court then enforced these declarations when necessary. The court had to do this under its inherent powers because the courts did not have power to make decisions on behalf of those who lacked capacity.

4.5 This vacuum in the law has now been resolved by MCA 2005, which not only puts declarations on a statutory basis but also enables decisions to be made.

4.6 The civil and family courts in general struggle when doubt is raised as to the mental capacity of a party because generic judges have little experience in this area. Nevertheless, these courts must then decide whether the party is a 'protected party' (formerly a 'patient') who needs to be represented by a suitable person, and if so the implications of the lack of capacity.[4]

---

[3]   For the case-law and a further explanation reference should be made to Chapter 5.
[4]   This topic is covered in Chapter 1.

General powers of the Court

4.7 The new Court of Protection may make declarations as to:

(1) whether a person has or lacks capacity to make a decision specified in the declaration;

(2) whether a person has or lacks capacity to make decisions on such matters as are described in the declaration;

(3) the lawfulness or otherwise of any act done, or yet to be done, in relation to that person.

In this respect an 'act' includes an omission and a course of conduct.[5] There is a clear distinction here, which has always applied at common law, between a declaration as to capacity and a declaration as to the lawfulness of an act. But one follows from the other – if the person does not lack capacity it will not be appropriate for the Court to make a declaration as to the lawfulness of an act. What is lawful will generally be what is in the best interests of the individual applying the statutory criteria.

Declarations as to capacity

4.8 The previous jurisdiction under the Mental Health Acts required the former Court of Protection to make an initial decision as to whether the individual was a patient and thus within its jurisdiction. That decision was seldom reconsidered thereafter and usually a receiver would be appointed to manage the patient's property and financial affairs under fairly close supervision unless there was so little involved that a short order could be made delegating everything to a suitable person without continuing supervision. The emphasis was thus on protection.

4.9 Under the new jurisdiction there will be a constant need to reassess capacity in regard to different decisions and at different times. The emphasis becomes empowerment, with protection when necessary. This power to make declarations as to capacity in regard to a particular decision or range of decisions will therefore be of considerable importance. In every case the Court will need to make a decision about capacity before it exercises its jurisdiction although it may not need to make a declaration in each instance.[6]

4.10 As the judges of the Court of Protection either sit full-time in the Court at Archway or are nominated from amongst circuit and district judges and sit on a regional basis, it will become possible for them to be treated as specialists in capacity issues. Colleagues may refer to the regional judges for guidance or even transfer cases to them when difficult issues as to capacity arise. This may be helpful not only for case management but also for substantive decisions. There is the potential for these judges not only to

---

5 MCA 2005, s 15.
6 Refer to **4.12** for an elaboration of this.

make declarations as to capacity in the Court of Protection (which may be treated as binding within particular proceedings in another court) but also to sit in a dual jurisdiction.

Declarations as to medical treatment

4.11   The Code of Practice provides that certain types of medical decision should be brought before the Court.[7] Although the Court may actually make decisions concerning medical treatment under its new statutory powers, it is likely that in serious or developing situations a declaration as to the lawfulness of treatment will be preferred because this delegates to the medical profession the decision as to whether treatment is appropriate in the circumstances.

4.12   For situations where the treatment will definitely be provided if it is authorised (e g non-therapeutic dental treatment or cosmetic surgery for a learning disabled adult) there is no reason why the Court should not exercise its power to make the treatment decision.

MAKING DECISIONS AND APPOINTING DEPUTIES

Powers of the Court

4.13   If a person ('P') lacks capacity in relation to a matter or matters concerning his or her personal welfare, or his or her property and affairs, the Court is given certain powers, but these are subject to the provisions of MCA 2005 and, in particular, to s 1 (the principles) and s 4 (best interests).[8] In these situations the Court may:[9]

(1)   by making an order, make the decision or decisions on P's behalf in relation to the matter or matters; or

(2)   appoint a person (a 'deputy') to make decisions on P's behalf in relation to the matter or matters.

An order of the Court may be varied or discharged by a subsequent order.

4.14   It is a pre-requisite of the jurisdiction of the Court that the person to whom the proceedings relate (now referred to as 'P') lacks capacity. In an early case a District Judge at Archway held that since the Act laid down that mental capacity was to be presumed, she had no jurisdiction to make an order (for directions) unless and until this presumption was rebutted.[10] This therefore raised issues of the correct test to be applied for the Court to assume jurisdiction under s 48 of the MCA, to make 'Interim orders and directions'. On appeal it was held that the 'gateway' test for the engagement of the Court's powers under s 48 must be lower than that of evidence

---

7   See paras 8.18–8.24 of the Code.
8   These are dealt with in Chapter 2.
9   MCA 2005, s 16.
10   *In the matter of H* (Court of Protection No 11649371), HHJ Hazel Marshall QC (see Case Summaries).

sufficient, in itself, to rebut the presumption of capacity. It was held that the proper test for the engagement of s 48 in the first instance is whether there is evidence giving good cause for concern that P may lack capacity in some relevant regard. Once that is raised as a serious possibility, the court then moves on to the second stage to decide what action, if any, it is in P's best interests to take before a final determination of his capacity can be made.

Making decisions

General

4.15 Instead of making the decision in question the Court may decide to appoint a deputy with powers to make decisions both now and in the future. The appointment of deputies is dealt with below.[11]

Children

4.16 Some flexibility has been provided in regard to people under the age of 18 years. The Lord Chancellor may by order make provision as to the transfer of proceedings relating to a person under 18, in such circumstances as are specified in the order:

(1) from the Court of Protection to a court having jurisdiction under the Children Act 1989; or

(2) from a court having jurisdiction under that Act to the Court of Protection.[12]

Personal welfare

4.17 The powers as respects P's personal welfare extend in particular to:[13]

(1) deciding where P is to live;

(2) deciding what contact, if any, P is to have with any specified persons;

(3) making an order prohibiting a named person from having contact with P;

(4) giving or refusing consent to the carrying out or continuation of a treatment by a person providing health care for P; and

(5) giving a direction that a person responsible for P's health care allows a different person to take over that responsibility,

but this is subject to the restrictions on deputies set out at **4.25**ff.

---

[11]   See **4.25** *et seq*.
[12]   MCA 2005, s 21. See the Mental Capacity Act 2005 (Transfer of Proceedings) Order 2007, SI 2007/1899 reproduced in Part IV of this work.
[13]   MCA 2005, s 17.

Property and affairs

4.18   The powers as respects P's property and affairs extend in particular to:[14]

(1) the control and management of P's property;
(2) the sale, exchange, charging, gift or other disposition of P's property;
(3) the acquisition of property in P's name or on P's behalf;
(4) the carrying on, on P's behalf, of any profession, trade or business;
(5) the taking of a decision which will have the effect of dissolving a partnership of which P is a member;
(6) the carrying out of any contract entered into by P;
(7) the discharge of P's debts and of any of P's obligations, whether legally enforceable or not;
(8) the settlement of any of P's property, whether for P's benefit or for the benefit of others;
(9) the execution for P of a will;
(10) the exercise of any power (including a power to consent) vested in P whether beneficially or as trustee or otherwise; and
(11) the conduct of legal proceedings in P's name or on P's behalf.

4.19   The powers as respects matters relating to P's property and affairs may be exercised even though P has not reached 16, if the Court considers it likely that P will still lack capacity to make decisions in respect of that matter when he or she reaches 18. Once again restrictions apply to deputies as set out at **4.25**ff.

Wills

4.20   The Court can thus, if P is an adult, make an order or give directions requiring or authorising a person (the 'authorised person') to execute a will on behalf of P. The restrictions prevent this being done by a deputy or if P has not reached 18.[15] However, the approach of the Court to the terms of the will has changed. It is no longer a question of seeking to make the will that the testator would have made if acting reasonably on competent legal advice and notionally restored to full mental capacity, memory and foresight.[16] The Court must now act in the best interests of the testator in accordance with the statutory formula, and this will include consideration of how the testator would be remembered after his death.[17] It seems that the best interests approach may justify the Court authorising a statutory will when there is doubt as to the validity of the last will due to concerns as to testamentary

---

[14]   MCA 2005, s 18.
[15]   It has been held that the approach is the best interests of the testator, which is different from the enquiry as to what the testator 'might be expected to have done' under the former jurisdiction – see *In the Matter of P* [2009] EWCH 163 (Ch).
[16]   The test expounded by Megarry J in *Re D (J)* [1982] 2 All ER 37.
[17]   *In the Matter of P* [2009] EWHC 163 (Ch), Lewison J; *In the Matter of M* [2009] EWHC 2525 (Fam), Munby J.

capacity or undue influence.[18] It remains to be seen whether this opens the floodgates for statutory will applications where there is discord within families, as the outcome may be different provision from that intended by the testator.

4.21 There are further provisions in respect of wills in MCA 2005, Sch 2. The will may make any provision (whether by disposing of property or exercising a power or otherwise) which could be made by a will executed by P if he or she had capacity to make it. The will must:

(1) state that it is signed by P acting by the authorised person;

(2) be signed by the authorised person with the name of P and his or her own name in the presence of two or more witnesses present at the same time;

(3) be attested and subscribed by those witnesses in the presence of the authorised person; and

(4) be sealed with the official seal of the Court.

4.22 If a will has been so executed the Wills Act 1837 has effect in relation to the will as if it were signed by P by his or her own hand, except that the Wills Act 1837, s 9 (requirements as to signing and attestation) does not apply, and in the subsequent provisions of the Act any reference to execution in the manner required by the previous provisions is to be read as a reference to execution as stated above.

4.23 The will then has the same effect for all purposes as if P had had the capacity to make a valid will, and the will had been executed by him or her in the manner required by the Wills Act 1837. But this does not apply in relation to the will insofar as:

(1) it disposes of immovable property outside England and Wales; or

(2) it relates to any other property or matter if, when the will is executed, P is domiciled outside England and Wales, and under the law of P's domicile, any question of his or her testamentary capacity would fall to be determined in accordance with the law of a place outside England and Wales.

Settlements

4.24 Special provisions in regard to settlements are also to be found in MCA 2005, Sch 2. The Court may make vesting or other orders as required, and may vary or revoke a settlement in certain circumstances. The Court may also order that investments be vested in a suitable curator outside England and Wales.[19] This provision is sometimes used to facilitate personal injury settlements in the case of brain injury awards, thereby by-passing the statutory procedures for the management of financial affairs where there is a lack of capacity. Such settlements were common under the former regime,

---

[18] *Re D (Statutory Will)* [2010] EWHC 2159 (Ch), HHJ Hodge QC sitting as a nominated Judge (for case summary, see Part IX of this work).

[19] MCA 2005, Sch 2, paras 5, 6 and 7.

but it remains to be seen whether the new best interests approach now supports this outcome. Supervision and intervention is more difficult in the cases of a settlement and would involve expensive Chancery proceedings, whereas the decisions of a deputy can readily be examined by the Court of Protection and costs are more closely monitored.

Miscellaneous

4.25   Further provisions enable the Court to preserve the interests of others (eg under a will or in intestacy) in property disposed of on behalf of the person lacking capacity. This might involve transferring the interest to a replacement property. There can also be a charge imposed for P's benefit on property that has been improved at P's expense.[20]

Deputies

Appointment

4.26   As stated above, instead of making decisions itself the Court may appoint a person (a 'deputy') to make decisions on P's behalf in relation to matters concerning P's personal welfare, or P's property and affairs, or both.[21] A deputy is to be treated as P's agent in relation to anything done or decided by the deputy within the scope of his or her appointment and in accordance with MCA 2005.

4.27   When deciding whether it is in P's best interests to appoint a deputy, the Court must have regard (in addition to the matters mentioned in MCA 2005, s 4[22]) to the principles that:

(1)   a decision by the Court is to be preferred to the appointment of a deputy to make a decision; and

(2)   the powers conferred on a deputy should be as limited in scope and duration as is reasonably practicable in the circumstances.

The Code of Practice gives examples of decisions that it may be appropriate for the Court to make[23] and also of situations where it may be appropriate to appoint a welfare deputy.[24]

4.28   The Court may make such further orders or give such directions, and confer on a deputy such powers or impose on him or her such duties, as it thinks necessary or expedient for giving effect to, or otherwise in connection with, an order or appointment made by it. The Court may make the order, give the directions or make the appointment on such terms as it considers

---

[20]   MCA 2005, Sch 2, paras 8 and 9.
[21]   MCA 2005, s 19.
[22]   This defines the concept of best interests – see generally Chapter 2.
[23]   See paras 8.27–8.28 of the Code.
[24]   See paras 8.38–8.39 of the Code. For different views as to whether a personal welfare deputy should be appointed see *Re P* [2010] EWHC 1592 (Fam), Hedley J. and *G v E* [2010] EWHC 2512 (COP) (Fam), Baker J. These cases are summarised in Part IX of this work.

are in P's best interests, even though no application is before the Court for an order, directions or an appointment on those terms.Who may be appointed?

Who may be appointed?

4.29 A deputy appointed by the Court must be an individual who has reached 18, but for powers in relation to property and affairs the deputy could be a trust corporation. A person may not be appointed as a deputy without his or her consent, but the Court may appoint an individual by appointing the holder for the time being of a specified office or position.

4.30 The Court may appoint two or more deputies to act jointly, jointly and severally, or jointly in respect of some matters and jointly and severally in respect of others. The Court may also appoint one or more other persons to succeed the existing deputy or deputies in such circumstances, or on the happening of such events, as may be specified by the Court and for such period as may be so specified.[25]

Control of the deputy

4.31 The Court may require a deputy:

    (1) to give to the Public Guardian such security as the Court thinks fit for the due discharge of his or her functions; and

    (2) to submit to the Public Guardian such reports at such times or at such intervals as the Court may direct.

4.32 The levels of supervision by the Public Guardian are considered in Chapter 8.

Powers

4.33 The Court may confer on a deputy powers to take possession or control of all or any specified part of P's property and to exercise all or any specified powers in respect of it, including such powers of investment as the Court may determine.[26]

4.34 The deputy is entitled to be reimbursed out of P's property for his or her reasonable expenses in discharging his or her functions and, if the Court so directs when appointing him or her, to remuneration out of P's property.[27]

4.35 There are various restrictions on the powers of deputies appointed by the Court and indeed of the powers that the Court may give to deputies[28] and

---

[25]   For guidance as to the appointment of family members see *Re P* [2010] EWHC 1592 (Fam), Hedley J. For case summary, see Part IX of this work.

[26]   MCA 2005, s 19(8).

[27]   MCA 2005, s 19(7).

[28]   See MCA 2005, s 20.

these are dealt with under the following headings. The authority conferred on a deputy is always subject to the provisions of MCA 2005 and, in particular, s 1 (the principles) and s 4 (best interests).[29]

Conditional on lack of capacity

4.36 A deputy does not have power to make a decision on behalf of P in relation to a matter if he or she knows or has reasonable grounds for believing that P has capacity in relation to the matter.

Powers that cannot be given

4.37 A deputy may not be given power:
  (1) to prohibit a named person from having contact with P;
  (2) to direct a person responsible for P's health care to allow a different person to take over that responsibility;
  (3) with respect to the settlement of any of P's property, whether for P's benefit or for the benefit of others;
  (4) with respect to the execution for P of a will; or
  (5) with respect to the exercise of any power (including a power to consent) vested in P whether beneficially or as trustee or otherwise.

Medical treatment

4.38 A deputy may not refuse consent to the carrying out or continuation of life-sustaining treatment in relation to P.

Conflict with an attorney

4.39 A deputy may not be given power to make a decision on behalf of P which is inconsistent with a decision made, within the scope of his or her authority and in accordance with MCA 2005, by the donee of a lasting power of attorney granted by P (or, if there is more than one donee, by any of them).

Restraint

4.40 A deputy may not do an act that is intended to restrain P unless the following four conditions are satisfied:[30]
  (1) in doing the act, the deputy is acting within the scope of an authority expressly conferred on him or her by the Court;
  (2) P lacks, or the deputy reasonably believes that P lacks, capacity in relation to the matter in question;

---

[29]   These are dealt with in Chapter 2.
[30]   MCA 2005, s 20(7)–(11).

(3) the deputy reasonably believes that it is necessary to do the act in order to prevent harm to P; and

(4) the act is a proportionate response to the likelihood of P's suffering harm, or the seriousness of that harm.

4.41 A deputy will be treated as having restrained P if he or she uses, or threatens to use, force to secure the doing of an act which P resists, or restricts P's liberty of movement, whether or not P resists, or if he or she authorises another person to do any of those things. But a deputy does more than merely restrain P if he or she deprives P of his or her liberty within the meaning of Art 5(1) of the European Convention on Human Rights (whether or not the deputy is a public authority).[31]

Revocation of appointment

4.42 The Court may revoke the appointment of a deputy or vary the powers conferred on him or her if it is satisfied that the deputy:

(1) has behaved, or is behaving, in a way that contravenes the authority conferred on him or her by the Court or is not in P's best interests; or

(2) proposes to behave in a way that would contravene that authority or would not be in P's best interests.

How will the Court exercise these powers?

The new approach

4.43 The Court thus has a wide range of options for decision-making on behalf of the incapacitated person ('P'). It may make supervised or non-supervised single orders, or may appoint a deputy to make all decisions or a specified range of decisions in regard to personal welfare matters and/or financial affairs. The Court has a duty to take into account P's best interests as now defined but also to act in a way that is least restrictive of P's rights and freedom of action. The all-or-nothing approach of the past will no longer be appropriate.

4.44 There will be a desire to deal with matters so that they do not need to be repeatedly referred back to the Court, and in cases where this would be likely the appointment of a deputy may be appropriate. Conversely, if only a one-off decision is needed, perhaps about the grant of a tenancy or minor medical treatment for a person with learning disabilities, it would be unduly restrictive to appoint a deputy.

4.45 The administration has endeavoured to anticipate the types of orders that judges will make and the frequency with which they will make different orders so that it can plan its procedures and allocate resources for the future.

---

[31] MCA 2005, s 19(13). This provision has been repealed by the Mental Health Act 2007, s 55, Sch 11, Pt 10 upon the introduction of the deprivation of liberty safeguards.

PART I

But whilst the Court administration and the Public Guardian can indicate the types of outcome that it can best cope with, these bodies are not in a position to dictate to judges the types of order that should be made and in what circumstances. Nevertheless, continued training of those nominated to sit in this jurisdiction is essential, and an attempt will inevitably be made to discuss and achieve some consistency of approach.[32]

4.46 The bulk of this work relates to the management of financial affairs and in considering the range of orders that should be made it may be instructive to consider the terms of the previous receiverships which inevitably continue in one form or another.

What happens to receiverships?

The past regime

4.47 Unless a short order was appropriate, the standard outcome had been to appoint a receiver who administered the financial affairs of the patient under the supervision of the Court. This was costly and bureaucratic, and although control over day-to-day finances might be delegated to the patient there was a reluctance by receivers to allow this in case they were later criticised. Latterly there had been a tendency for the Court to adopt a less interventionist approach. The following case is an example.

> The patient, who had recovered significant damages for a brain injury, fell out with his solicitor receiver so the Public Trustee (later the Chief Executive of the Public Guardianship Office) was appointed. The patient was frustrated by the control over his spending and applied to be released from the jurisdiction. Instead the Master approved an order discharging the receiver and retaining the fund in Court whilst mandating the interest to the patient and giving him the right to receive all his state benefits. The home that had been purchased for him was vested under the control of the Court.
>
> On transfer of the file from the receivership division to the 'short order section' this arrangement was questioned as not meeting normal criteria. The patient then complained when he was not given access to the fund to cover debts which he had incurred. The case was referred to the regional hearing centre for resolution at an attended hearing. The Deputy Master explained to the patient how the procedure was intended to operate and that he should manage his budget so that the fund was not prematurely exhausted. The procedure was commended as being the least restrictive option and the patient was satisfied that it empowered him whilst providing necessary protection with minimum supervision. He was permitted to make infrequent applications for release of capital for specific purposes.

The new regime

4.48 In many cases, the existing receiver has simply been replaced by a deputy, but with wider delegated powers. Where appropriate, arrangements such as that set out above are likely to be more frequent under the new

---

[32] The initial training was carried out by judges through the Judicial Studies Board and took into account the needs of the Public Guardian, who then provided the administration to implement the orders were made.

jurisdiction. The Court may also be inclined, especially in the case of professional deputies, to give them powers similar to those exercisable by donees under lasting powers of attorney dealing with financial affairs. There may even be a greater willingness to approve settlements rather than retain funds, although the statutory jurisdiction of the Court of Protection may be preferred for substantial brain injury awards.

4.49 The key criteria will be whether the continued involvement of the Office of the Public Guardian provides added value. This may depend upon an assessment of the family and other persons involved and of the risks involved in permitting more delegation. To some extent this risk can be minimised by requiring insurance bonds to be in place. The levels of supervision by the Public Guardian are considered in Chapter 8.

4.50 The approach to investment of funds has also changed, with the deputy being expected to seek advice from an independent financial adviser, and the special account which for many years has provided a high interest return but now provides interest below market rates may ultimately cease to be available.

CONTROL OF LASTING POWERS OF ATTORNEY

Court's powers to intervene

General

4.51 Lasting powers of attorney (LPAs) introduced by MCA 2005, s 9 are dealt with in more detail in Chapter 3. Until the registration of a LPA is revoked by a donor with capacity or by the Court on any of the specified grounds, the attorney (in MCA 2005 referred to as 'the donee') can continue to act with all the powers of an attorney subject to any restrictions and conditions contained in the power.[33] The Court, however, retains the following powers which are exercisable at any time, not just to revoke or cancel the power or attach conditions to the donee's conduct, but also to guide the donee or provide authority where the donee requires this to carry out his or her duties under the power.[34]

4.52 All these powers which are specific to the operation of LPAs are in addition to the Court's general powers which are exercisable in respect of any matter in which a person lacks capacity, whether or not the donee has authority to act in respect of the same matter. Thus the Court has power to make a declaration of capacity under MCA 2005, s 15, decisions in respect of personal welfare under s 17 and decisions concerning a person's property and affairs under s 18.

4.53 In most cases, the Court will be required to exercise its powers where these are needed to supplement the donee's powers under the LPA. For example, if the power is restricted to property and affairs the donee may

---

[33] See generally Chapter 3.
[34] These matters are considered in greater detail in Chapter 3.

apply to the Court of Protection for a decision concerning medical treatment or personal welfare. A LPA furthermore does not authorise the donee to make a will or settlement. Equally the Court may need to supplement the powers of an attorney under a registered enduring power of attorney.

4.54 Conflicts between the authority of the Court and the authority of the donee should be rare. If the donee has authority to carry out an act under the LPA then there is no need for the Court to intervene unless there are grounds for overruling the donee, for instance, if the donee is acting contrary to the best interests of the donor. There may also be cases where the donee simply requires the assistance of the Court to confirm that a proposed act may be carried out.

Specific powers

Creation and revocation

4.55 The Court may determine any question relating to whether the requirements for the creation of the power have been met or the power has been revoked or come to an end.[35] There is concern that although there is a prescribed form which must be adopted, the Public Guardian is to ignore an immaterial difference and the Court:[36]

> '... may declare that an instrument which is not in the prescribed form is to be treated as if it were, if it is satisfied that the persons executing the instrument intended it to create a lasting power of attorney.'

4.56 It is feared that the Office of the Public Guardian and the Court will be faced with numerous applications to permit registration of otherwise defective forms. A relaxed response would encourage a sloppy approach to these important documents, whereas refusal to register will generally result in an application for the appointment of a deputy.

4.57 Unless a hearing is needed these applications are likely to be dealt with 'on paper' by one of the nominated district judges based at Archway rather than sent to regional judges.[37] Whilst the view may be taken that in the absence of objections it is preferable to empower the donor by registering the power, how will the intention of the donor be known? Defective forms are most likely to arise where there has been no proper professional advice and these are the very situations where lack of capacity or undue pressure tends to arise. To some extent the certificate of capacity on the form provides a safeguard, but at this stage this will merely be a signature on the form. The absence of such a certificate would be a fatal defect and the Court may adopt a policy of requiring further information from the maker of the certificate before accepting a defective form.

---

[35] MCA 2005, s 22(2).
[36] MCA 2005, Sch 1, Part 1, para 3(2).
[37] Significant decisions are reported on the Office of the Public Guardian website – commence a search at: www.publicguardian.gov.uk/information-professionals.htm .

Capacity

4.58   The Court's power to determine any question relating to whether the requirements for the creation of the power have been met extends to whether the donor had the capacity to execute it.[38] Lack of capacity at the time of execution is often alleged in dysfunctional family cases, but the onus is on an objector to establish this and it is difficult to do so retrospectively in the absence of contemporary medical evidence. The objectors must therefore turn to one of the grounds on which registration of the power may be refused.

Registration

4.59   The Court may refuse registration or revoke an otherwise valid lasting power if satisfied that:

(1)   fraud or undue pressure was used to induce the donor to create the power;[39] or

(2)   the donee (or, if more than one, any of them) has behaved, is behaving or proposes to behave in a way that contravenes his or her authority or is not in the donor's best interests.[40]

4.60   If there is more than one donee the Court may revoke the power so far as it relates to any of them thus allowing it to be registered as regards another.[41] Presumably if fraud or undue pressure is established the whole power must fail (although MCA 2005 appears to provide otherwise), but it is not clear whether the Court is empowered to remove one misbehaving donee under a joint power (as distinct from a joint and several power).[42]

4.61   The approach to fraud or undue pressure is unlikely to differ from that previously adopted in relation to enduring powers of attorney. Fraud does not require further comment, but in the case of dysfunctional families (and even where a solicitor has been involved) there is generally an objection on the basis of undue pressure in the execution of the power. There can be no objection to mere influence – it is undue pressure that is objectionable, but the boundaries may be difficult to define.[43]

4.62   The new certificate of capacity on the LPA form should assist in these cases. It will be interesting to see if the makers of these certificates attend hearings to give evidence as to the manner in which they have formed their opinion that the donor understood the purpose of the instrument and the scope of the authority given under it, and that execution was not induced by

---

[38]   MCA 2005, s 9(2)(c).
[39]   MCA 2005, s 22(3)(a).
[40]   MCA 2005, s 22(3)(b). The criteria for refusing to register or revoking an enduring power of attorney are slightly different – see Chapter 3.
[41]   MCA 2005, s 22(5).
[42]   Reference should be made to MCA 2005, s 10(6) in this context.
[43]   There may be no difference between 'undue pressure' as now defined and the previous term 'undue influence' in respect of which there is considerable case-law.

fraud or undue pressure.[44] If the maker is a practising solicitor it would be preferable to have taken instructions from and acted for the donor rather than simply to have provided the certificate.

4.63 In these dysfunctional family cases it will generally also be necessary for the Court to decide whether one or more of the attorneys has behaved, is behaving or intends to behave in a way that contravenes his or her authority or is not in the donor's best interests. [45]

4.64 Even if such a finding is made there will be a discretion on the part of the Court to overlook the behaviour, taking into account all the circumstances. This differs from the equivalent ground under enduring powers of attorney, which is (and remains for those powers yet to be registered):[46]

> '... that, having regard to all the circumstances and in particular the attorney's relationship to or connection with the donor, the attorney is unsuitable to be the donor's attorney.'

4.65 A test based on behaviour is very different from one based upon suitability, and it will be interesting to see how this change affects the conduct and outcome of these cases especially where there is implacable hostility within the family. More findings of fact may be needed and this will affect the length of hearings. If past behaviour is relied upon and the donor knew about this when the LPA was executed, it may be difficult to argue that such behaviour, or the propensity for such behaviour in the future, is not in the donor's best interests. This change demonstrates a move away from a paternalistic approach towards empowerment of the donor, whose choice of donee must be respected. It will shift the emphasis when objections are raised from suitability of the donees to the validity of the power and the presumption of validity may dictate the outcome in many cases. There will be cases where, despite genuine concerns as to the manner in which an LPA was procured and the intentions of the donee, family members cannot establish an objection to registration and bringing an application to revoke the power when there has been actual misbehaviour may prove to be 'closing the stable door after the horse has bolted'.

Meaning and effect of the power

4.66 The Court may determine any question as to the meaning or the effect of the LPA (or an instrument purporting to create a LPA). The Court may therefore clarify any uncertainty as to the form of the power or the scope of the donee's authority.[47]

---

[44]   The limited extent to which solicitors who have acted in the preparation of enduring powers of attorney are presently called to give evidence in support of the power does not provide an encouraging precedent.

[45]   See MCA 2005, s 22(3)(b) and also Sch 1, Part 3.

[46]   See MCA 2005, Sch 4, Part 4, para 13(9)(e).

[47]   MCA 2005, s 23(1).

Directions to the attorney

4.67 The Court may, if the donor lacks capacity, give directions with respect to decisions the donee has authority to make or give any consent or authorisation to act which the donee would have to obtain from a mentally capable donor.[48] Thus a donee who is unsure about whether he or she has authority to act can obtain prior approval from the Court before acting. A donee who might otherwise need to obtain the consent of the donor to a proposed act, where, for instance, he or she may benefit from the act or the act is subject to the express agreement of the donor, can also obtain the prior approval of the Court.

PART I

Rendering accounts etc

4.68 The Court may, if the donor lacks capacity, give directions to the donee with respect to the rendering of accounts or production of records, require the donee to supply information or produce documents,[49] and give directions with regard to remuneration or expenses.[50] These are useful powers and mirror those for enduring powers of attorney.[51]

4.69 It may be rare in practice for the Court to authorise the production of accounts, whether to the Court or to a third party,[52] but the power can be useful to dispel mistrust and suspicion within families in regard to financial management. An objection to registration may be withdrawn if the Court is prepared to require basic financial disclosure to an objector whose intervention might be justifiable, and the power must then be registered. This was sometimes viewed as preferable to revocation of an enduring power and the imposition of a professional receiver under the former jurisdiction and a similar approach is likely to be adopted towards the appointment of a deputy as an alternative to registration of a lasting power. There is a difficult balance to be achieved between maintaining confidentiality in regard to the donor's financial affairs, which should not automatically be disclosed to family members on the onset of mental incapacity, and avoiding the suspicion and mistrust that arises when a financial manager is unduly secretive, especially when all involved are potential beneficiaries of the donor's estate.

Relieving the attorney of liability

4.70 The Court has power, if the donor lacks capacity, to relieve the donee wholly or partly from any liability which he or she has or may have incurred

---

[48]   MCA 2005, s 23(2).
[49]   For example, the deeds to a property or a testamentary document where it is a confidential document.
[50]   MCA 2005, s 23(3)(a), (b) and (c).
[51]   Cf Enduring Powers of Attorney Act 1985, s 8(2)(c), now reproduced in MCA 2005, Sch 4, para 16(2).
[52]   Re *C (Power of Attorney)* [2000] 2 FLR 1 provides one example of an account being required.

on account of a breach of his or her duties as attorney.[53] Although this power is included in MCA 2005 with those set out under the above heading it is fundamentally different in nature, being retrospective in nature. Where financial shortcomings are involved it may be difficult to find that relief for the attorney is in the best interests of the donor. Where a liability has been incurred to a third party, which could presumably be for breach of contract or negligence, relieving the attorney of liability would presumably involve requiring the donor to provide an indemnity because this provision is not intended to take away the rights of third parties. Nevertheless, this provision enables the Court to provide relief where the donor would have so done if capable.

Gifts

4.71 The Court may authorise the making of any gift which is beyond the scope of the donor's limited authority under MCA 2005, s 12(2).[54]

Applying to the Court

4.72 Following creation by registration, any person who wishes to apply to the Court to invoke its powers dealing with the validity and operation of a LPA must apply directly to the Court in form COP1. A donee or other party who wishes to apply for an order for a gift or authority for any decision not within the scope of the donee's authority must use the same formal procedure. The formalities of an application are governed by Court of Protection Rules 2007[55] made pursuant to MCA 2005, s 51(1), as supplemented by Practice Directions.

4.73 A donor or donee under a LPA does not require permission from the Court to make an application for the exercise of any of its powers.[56] Neither does MCA 2005 appear to prevent the Court from exercising its powers of its own volition, for instance, in response to a report made to it by the Public Guardian or a Visitor. Although permission may be required for another person to make an application to the Court, this does not apply in respect of disputes about enduring or lasting powers of attorney.[57]

4.74 Instead of applying to the Court directly a concerned relative or other body may make a complaint to the Public Guardian about the conduct of the donee and then leave the Public Guardian to make inquiries or take action directly or through the Court of Protection.[58]

---

[53]   MCA 2005, s 23(3)(d). For enduring powers see MCA 2005, Sch 4, para 16(2)(f).
[54]   MCA 2005, s 23(4). For enduring powers see MCA 2005, Sch 4, paras 3(3) and 16(2)(e).
[55]   SI 2007/1744.
[56]   MCA 2005, s 50(1)(c).
[57]   See Court of Protection Rules 2007, SI 2007/1744, Part 8 and in particular r 51.
[58]   MCA 2005, s 58(1)(h).

4.75 If the applicant knows or has reasonable grounds for believing that the donor lacks capacity, then the procedure for notifying P under the Court of Protection Rules 2007, Part 7 applies to the donor. Any person making such an application must proceed on the basis that the Court has no existing record of the case and cannot assume that P lacks capacity. Clearly the fact that the LPA is operational does not in any way indicate that the donor lacks capacity. Each application must stand alone and be justified on its own merits and with its own evidence, including medical evidence. Only in very straightforward cases covered by Practice Direction 9D is this procedural burden relaxed.

The role of the Public Guardian

4.76 The role of the Public Guardian has been considered in more detail in Chapter 3 in the context of his or her principle role of registering LPAs. The Public Guardian is also responsible for registering enduring powers of attorney (EPAs) created before the coming into force of MCA 2005.[59] However, the Public Guardian has a distinct legal personality as well as an important administrative role, dealing with most routine applications to the Court of Protection.[60]

4.77 Where LPAs are concerned, the Public Guardian is the main administrative focus for all applications and inquiries, whether contentious or non-contentious. Thus the Public Guardian will be able to determine whether applications need to be forwarded to the Court or can be addressed through correspondence by the Public Guardian.

4.78 The Public Guardian therefore has the following statutory functions:[61]

(1) establishing and maintaining registers of LPAs and EPAs;

(2) directing Court of Protection Visitors to visit the donee of a LPA and making reports on such matters as the Public Guardian may direct;

(3) receiving reports from donees of LPAs;[62]

(4) reporting to the Court of Protection on such matters as the Court requires; and

(5) dealing with representations (including complaints) about the way in which a donee is exercising his or her powers.

4.79 The Secretary of State may by regulations confer other functions in connection with MCA 2005 upon the Public Guardian or make provision in connection with the discharge of his functions.[63] It is therefore likely that the Public Guardian's role will be developed beyond the scope of the former

---

[59] MCA 2005, Sch 4, para 4(2). See Chapter 8.

[60] The powers and responsibilities of the Public Guardian are considered in more detail in Chapter 7.

[61] MCA 2005, s 58.

[62] The Public Guardian receives the report but only the Court can direct a report: see MCA 2005, ss 23(3)(a) and 49(2).

[63] MCA 2005, s 58.

Public Guardianship Office, so that through his office he can take a more proactive role in monitoring the operation of LPAs. In view of the likely volume of transactions it is unlikely that there will be much scope for routine investigation, but where there are complaints or concerns are expressed about the conduct of a donee (or an attorney), the Public Guardian will be able to respond and make inquiries. In most cases a call for a report from a public body such as the Public Guardian and some discrete correspondence or negotiation may be sufficient to address the particular concern. In other cases the Public Guardian will be expected to advise and involve the Court to ensure that action is taken.

LIVING WITH THE NEW JURISDICTION

Overview

4.80 People who lack mental capacity fall into four broad groups:

(1) The largest group comprises elderly people who are deprived of capacity due to senile dementia, a condition that tends to be irreversible. They have enjoyed personal autonomy in the past and may have a personal income and savings that require management, but are no longer able to conduct their own lives.

(2) People with learning disabilities[64] form the second distinct group. They may never have matured to the stage where they can live a totally independent and self-supporting life, and in consequence do not have significant savings or income unless they have come into an inheritance.

(3) Some people are deprived of mental capacity for a period or periods of their lives due to a mental illness which might be treatable. They will need to be supported and protected when the illness is acute but at other times can make their own decisions and may be financially successful.

(4) The fourth group comprises people who have had an acquired brain injury which affects their ability to make decisions. This is seldom treatable and may be linked with physical disabilities. Large sums of compensation may need to be managed to finance a comprehensive care plan.

4.78 Each of these groups presents different challenges as regards both financial and care management, and some people overlap these groups. Those working in the new jurisdiction must be sensitive to this diversity and there can be no standard approach.

4.81 In the past the Court of Protection was only concerned with financial management, but the new Court has to contend with a mixture of financial and welfare issues. A nominated judge of the new Court of Protection will not be able to state, as did the Masters of the former Court, that they do not have jurisdiction over personal welfare except insofar as it is influenced by

---

64   In an educational context referred to as 'learning difficulties' and previously known as 'mental handicap'.

financial decisions. A single issue may be brought to the Court where there is uncertainty that must be resolved or a decision is needed to authorise some action, but any conflict over control of the individual will inevitably extend to both financial and welfare decisions.

4.82   The Law Commission identified three types of decision that may need to be made or delegated. These relate respectively to property and affairs, personal welfare and health care. MCA 2005 merely adopts the first two categories, with health care falling within personal welfare. The significance of this is that it may be appropriate for these two categories to be delegated to different persons.

Property and affairs

4.83   The management of financial affairs is not a new concept for a Court of Protection and, although new statutory criteria have been imposed, and in particular a 'best interests' approach, in most respects these do not depart from the approach that has developed over recent years. The Court will still need to adjudicate on struggles for control, whether this be the appointment of a donee or a deputy, to approve gifts and wills and to make policy decisions in regard to large damages awards. The change is the availability of a wider range of possible outcomes and the requirement for minimum intervention. A more personalised regime is likely to be established, with more input where possible from the incapacitated individual and greater integration with welfare decisions. The pendulum has swung from protection to empowerment, but time will tell whether this creates unacceptable vulnerability.

Personal welfare

4.84   What is untried and untested is the making of personal welfare decisions, especially when the need for these arises through conflict within families or between families, carers and professionals. A simple decision may have wider implications. The issue is always the best interests of the incapacitated individual, but the process whereby this is addressed may differ according to whether the Court is required to resolve a dispute or an uncertainty. The Official Solicitor will generally be involved to represent the incapacitated individual.

Health care

4.85   The Family Division of the High Court has become accustomed to identifying best interests in regard to serious medical treatment, often in controversial and high-profile situations. Little changes following the transfer of this work to the new Court of Protection. The same judges will be nominated to hear these cases, but instead of doing so under the inherent jurisdiction they do so under a statutory framework. Their approach has already been influenced by the Law Commission proposals and the public debate leading up to MCA 2005 so the substantive law that is applied may not be radically different.[65]

4.86 Applications relating to less serious medical treatment and health care issues that do not need to be dealt with by High Court judges will tend to be resolved in the same way as other personal welfare issues, although expert medical evidence will be required. These applications do not necessarily result from disputes but may arise due to uncertainty, such as a proposal for non-therapeutic dental treatment or cosmetic surgery.

Personal care

4.87 The issues arising under this heading encompass the full range of decisions, from where to live and with whom to have contact down to holiday arrangements, mode of dress and choice of diet. Any issue that parents cannot agree in respect of their adult child with severe learning disabilities or siblings cannot agree in respect of their parent with senile dementia has the potential to be referred to the Court. Professional carers may also wish to validate their plans for vulnerable individuals, such as participation in adventure holidays that carry some degree of risk.

4.88 'Adult contact' disputes are becoming more common and previously could only be resolved in the High Court at disproportionate expense, but the seniority of that court discouraged the type of application that is now becoming the norm for the new Court of Protection. There will therefore be more of these applications now that a regional Court is able to deal with them, and there is no reason why a nominated district judge who spends much of his or her time deciding such issues in respect of children should not have jurisdiction, although this may be shared with nominated circuit judges.

4.89 These cases cannot all be treated as litigation to be resolved on an adversarial basis. In some instances findings of fact are required, but otherwise the hearing will be more of an inquiry with input from family, friends, carers and professionals – and, of course, the incapacitated person to the extent that a contribution is meaningful. The parties may seek to bring issues before the Court yet fail to address the best interests of this person. In such cases it may be appropriate for the incapacitated person to be made a party with a litigation friend and a legal representative (unless one professional such as the Official Solicitor can act in both capacities) [66]

---

[65]   Since taking responsibility for the Law Commission's consultation in her former identity as Professor Brenda Hoggett, Lady Hale of Richmond has rapidly risen through the High Court and the Court of Appeal to the House of Lords, carrying with her the new approach to these issues.

[66]   Such representation may be required in any event so as not to infringe the human rights of the incapacitated person, but the manner in which the proceedings are conducted must be proportionate to the matters in issue and funding may not be available for independent legal

Failing this an independent report will be required and a Court of Protection Visitor will often be best placed to provide this service.

4.90   A decision by the Court must be the last resort in contested cases and other forms of dispute resolution need to be made available as stepping stones. It could be part of the role of the Public Guardian to facilitate this. Piecemeal decision-making does not enable best interests to be comprehensively addressed and a care plan will generally be required as the cornerstone if not the foundation of the process. The Court cannot provide this but can be part of the process whereby it becomes established. It is suggested that, in cases that originate through implacable hostility on the part of family or others competing for influence, judges will insist that a care plan is negotiated through multi-disciplinary care management conferences and the Court will then resolve any stumbling blocks to enable this to be finalised. Decisions on specific issues can then be made within this framework.

4.91   Applications for 'adult care orders' are also becoming frequent where a child with learning disabilities has been placed in care under the Children Act 1989 and is approaching legal majority. The local authority may consider it necessary to continue to prevent or restrict a relationship with the parents and an application to the Court of Protection is then required. This may coincide with a transfer of responsibility from child services to adult services with a different approach from the social workers involved. The best interests approach under the MCA 2005 differs from the more paternalistic 'welfare of the child' approach under the Children Act 1989.

representation. See Court of Protection Rules 2007, SI 2007/1744, r 73, which gives the Court a discretion as to whether the incapacitated person is made a party.

Chapter 5

Welfare and Health Care, Advance Decisions and Research[1]

PRELIMINARY

5.1   A number of issues arise under the Mental Capacity Act 2005 (MCA 2005) in regard to welfare and health care. For example, as to health care, first, what medical treatment should be provided for an adult who cannot make choices; secondly, how can the adult before losing capacity influence decisions about subsequent treatment; and, thirdly, to what extent should medical research be permitted? Similar issues as the first two can arise in relation to such a person's more general welfare, for example, where they should live or with whom they should have contact. The welfare issue may be linked to a health care issue, but may be quite separate. These issues are considered in this chapter. Whilst health care and welfare in relation to an incapacitated adult are fully integrated into the statutory framework provided by the MCA 2005, the pre-existing common law remains relevant to an understanding of these provisions.

THE PRE-EXISTING COMMON LAW

The three bases for medical treatment

5.2   The starting point is that any 'invasive' or 'intrusive' medical treatment will constitute an unlawful act unless it is authorised by statute, or it is done under the doctrine of necessity (see below) or with the consent of the person concerned. A child's parents, or a child over 16,[2] can provide that consent. Adults who are competent can decide for themselves whether or not any treatment may be carried out on them and the court has no power to intervene, however unwise the decision may seem to others. An adult who is 'incompetent' cannot provide a valid consent to treatment and the common law had not recognised anyone else as having the legal power to give consent on another adult's behalf.

Court's power to authorise treatment

The demise of parens patriae

5.3   The common law, however, from an early time allowed the High Court to make medical treatment decisions for children and for adults without the mental capacity to decide for themselves. Originally the judges of the High Court exercised the Crown's prerogative power as parens patriae. This power still exists in relation to children. However, in relation to adults, a

---

[1]   The contribution of James Beck from the Official Solicitor's office to the material under this heading is gratefully acknowledged.
[2]   Family Law Reform Act 1969, s 8.

succession of Mental Health Acts have been enacted, starting with the Mental Health Act 1959, which provided a comprehensive statutory code for the treatment of patients for their mental disorder. These Acts left no scope for the continued exercise of parens patriae powers.

The declaratory jurisdiction

5.4 For a time the question remained open whether the courts retained any jurisdiction in relation to other treatment decisions which needed to be taken for adults who could not consent. This was decisively answered by the House of Lords in 1990 in the case of *Re F (Mental Patient: Sterilisation)*.[3] That case provided the foundation for much of the modern common law on this subject. The key ruling was that the High Court retained an inherent jurisdiction to make declarations as to what is lawful as being in the best interests of an incompetent adult.

5.5 Following this it became one of the many roles of the Family Division of the High Court of Justice in England and Wales to decide whether medical procedures should or should not be carried out on an adult who is unable to consent to the treatment in question; this tended to arise in three broad types of case, where medical opinion was that:

- a particular course of treatment will save life, for example, a blood transfusion or a Caesarean section;[4]
- a particular procedure should be carried out to enhance the patient's quality of life or prevent physical or mental deterioration, for example, a liver transplant or sterilisation;[5]
- life-prolonging treatment should either be withheld or withdrawn to allow the patient to die with dignity.[6]

Emerging principles

5.6 An equally important relatively early ruling (in terms of this developing jurisdiction) was also provided by the House of Lords in *Airedale NHS Trust v Bland*,[7] which involved a victim of the Hillsborough football tragedy who had been diagnosed as having entered a persistent vegetative state (PVS). In particular, this case is authority for the lawfulness of withholding or withdrawing nutrition and hydration supplied by artificial means (ANH) to a person in this condition.

5.7 Some basic principles relating to this whole jurisdiction emerging from these cases can be summarised as follows:

---

3   [1990] 2 AC 1.
4   *HE v A Hospital NHS Trust* [2003] 2 FLR 408 (blood transfusion); *St George's Healthcare NHS Trust v S* [1999] Fam 26 (Caesarean section).
5   *Re T (A Minor) (Wardship: Medical Treatment)* [1997] 1 WLR 242 (kidney transplant); *Re A (Male Sterilisation)* [2000] 1 FLR 549; and e g *Re S (Adult Patient: Sterilisation)* [2001] Fam 15.
6   *Airedale NHS Trust v Bland* [1993] AC 789.
7   [1993] AC 789.

(1) in the case of an incompetent adult, the principle of necessity renders lawful, despite the absence of consent, any treatment (which would otherwise be a tort at common law) a reasonable doctor would give in the best interests of the patient;

(2) the High Court has the power to declare whether a patient lacks competence and whether a particular treatment is lawful as being in his or her best interests;

(3) that jurisdiction is based upon a determination of best interests and is not (as has emerged in the US or in some Commonwealth jurisdictions) based on the doctrine of 'substituted choice' or 'substituted judgment' of what the patient would have wanted in the circumstances facing him or her.[8]

The development of the jurisdiction

Welfare

5.8 There is a similar starting point at common law as to the lawfulness of any non-consensual invasive or controlling act in relation to an adult's welfare, such as where they are to be accommodated. The inherent jurisdiction expanded so that it covered not only medical treatment but also other welfare-related issues.[9] Indeed, prior to the enactment of MCA 2005, one High Court judge had already commented:[10]

'... we have come a long way since the decision in *In Re F*. The courts have created and now exercise what is, in substance and reality, a jurisdiction in relation to incompetent adults which is for all practical purposes indistinguishable from its well-established *parens patriae* or wardship jurisdiction in relation to children.'

Power to grant injunctions

5.9 There was a distinction in principle between the adult jurisdiction to declare what is lawful and the power under the Children Act 1989 to make orders in children's cases. But this became more apparent than real as it was established that injunctive relief (where permissible) in support of a declaration could be granted.[11] However, the principle remained that doctors cannot be compelled personally to undertake a treatment they do not in their clinical judgment wish to provide, but in some circumstances the NHS Trust

---

8   *Airedale NHS Trust v Bland* [1993] AC 789, at pp 871–872.

9   See e g *Re F (Mental Patient: Sterilisation)* [1990] 2 AC 1; *Re C (Mental Patient: Contact)* [1993] 1 FLR 940; *Re F (Adult: Court's Jurisdiction)* [2000] Fam 38; and *A v A Health Authority, Re J (a child), R (on the application of S) v Secretary of State for the Home Department* [2002] Fam 213.

10   *E (By her litigation friend the Official Solicitor) v Channel Four; News International Ltd and St Helens Borough Council* [2005] 2 FLR 913, at [55], per Munby J.

11   See e g *A Local Authority v A* [2004] 2 WLR 926; and *Re SA (Vulnerable Adult With Capacity: Marriage)* [2005] EWHC 2942 (Fam), [2006] 1 FLR 867.

responsible for the treatment might be required to transfer the patient to the care of other doctors who will treat as the patient wants or in his or her best interests.[12]

Test of capacity

5.10   The common law test of capacity was issue-specific to the decision in question. It depended on whether the patient fully understands the nature of the proposed medical intervention, the reasons and the consequences of submitting or not submitting to it, and could weigh these in the balance and reach and communicate a decision.[13]

5.11   The fact that a patient has been sectioned under the Mental Health Act 1983 (as amended by the Mental Health Act 2007) and is subject to compulsory detention and treatment for his or her mental disorder is not determinative of whether he or she has the capacity to consent to treatment not related to that mental disorder. An example of this arose in a case that concerned a patient at Broadmoor with chronic paranoid schizophrenia and gangrene in his right foot. He was held by the Court of Appeal to have the capacity to refuse his consent to a proposed amputation of his leg and instead consent to more conservative treatment.[14]

Best interests

5.12   The common law approach was far wider than medical best interests so any assessment should not be restricted to the treating doctors. The Court attempted to reach an objective view of best interests in the light of all the relevant circumstances and evidence available to it. In addition to the medical factors, emotional and all other welfare issues have to be taken into account in deciding best interests. The Court of Appeal has said that the Court should draw up a checklist of the actual benefits and disadvantages and the potential gains and losses, including physical and psychological risks and consequences, and should reach a balanced conclusion as to what is right from the point of view of the individual concerned.[15]

Practice and procedure at common law

5.13   Adult cases under the inherent jurisdiction were and, where that jurisdiction still applies,[16] are brought in the Family Division of the High

---

[12]   *Re J (A Minor) (Child in Care: Medical Treatment)* [1993] Fam 15; *Re B (Consent to Treatment: Capacity)* [2002] 1 FLR 1090; and *R (Burke) v GMC and Others* [2005] QB 424, at [180]–[194], per Munby J.
[13]   *Re: MB (Medical Treatment)* [1997] 2 FLR 426.
[14]   *Re: C (Adult: Refusal of Treatment)* [1994] 1 WLR 290.
[15]   *Re: A (Male Sterilisation)* [2000] 1 FLR 549.
[16]   See **5.52**.

Court, but are proceedings to which the Civil Procedure Rules 1998[17] (CPR) apply. Applications are generally brought under CPR Part 8.[18]

5.14 The general practice under the inherent jurisdiction in relation to medical treatment cases was that the claimant should be the NHS Trust or other body responsible for the patient's care, although a claim could also be brought by a family member or other individual closely connected with the patient. The body with clinical or caring responsibility should in any event be made a party. The patient was always a party and usually a defendant. The Official Solicitor was generally invited to represent the incapacitated patient as litigation friend.[19] Cases could be dealt with, even 'out of hours' on an emergency basis; and when final evidence either as to capacity or best interests was not available the Court might be willing to grant an interim declaration.[20] As can be seen from the citations of the various authorities, the proceedings were often anonymised so that the identity of the patient did not reach the public domain.

Impact of the European Convention on Human Rights

Relevant Convention rights

5.15 The European Convention on Human Rights has been incorporated into our law by the Human Rights Act 1998 at a time when this jurisdiction has been developing. Articles with particular relevance to the substance of medical treatment cases are:

- Art 2 (right to life);
- Art 3 (not to suffer inhumane and degrading treatment); and
- Art 8 (right to a private life, including physical integrity).

5.16 An example of the interplay between the Art 2 and 3 rights is the case of *Trust A and Trust B v H (an Adult Patient)*.[21] H had a large ovarian tumour in her abdomen, which unless removed would cause her death even if benign. She suffered from schizophrenia and was severely delusional, believing she was married but had no children when she was divorced and was the mother of two children. The then-President, Sir Mark Potter, President held she lacked capacity to consent and that, having regard to the positive (but not absolute) duty under Art 2 to give life-sustaining treatment where responsible medical treatment was of the view that such treatment was in the patient's best interests, the proposed surgery was in her best interests and should be given. Although she was resisting such treatment it

---

[17] SI 1998/3132.
[18] The procedure in children's cases is different. Orders may be sought in relation to a child who is a ward of court, under the Children Act 1989, or by originating summons under the inherent jurisdiction (to which the Family Proceedings Rules 1991, SI 1991/1247 apply).
[19] See the President's Practice Direction *Declaratory Proceedings concerning Incapacitated Adults: Medical and Welfare Decisions* of 14 December 2001 and Practice Note *Official Solicitor: Declaratory Proceedings: Medical and Welfare Decisions for Adults Who Lack Capacity* [2006] 2 FLR 373.
[20] CPR, r 25.1(1)(b); and see *An NHS Trust v Miss T* [2004] EWHC 1279 (Fam).
[21] [2006] 2 FLR 958.

was lawful to overcome non-co-operation by sedation and a moderate and reasonable use of restraint, but that consideration had to be given to the patient's rights under Art 3 not to be subjected to degrading treatment.

The need for references to the High Court

5.17   In *Glass v UK*[22] the European Court of Human Rights at Strasbourg found the UK to be in breach of an 11-year-old's Art 8 rights in a case in which his parents were bitterly disputing the medical staff's diagnosis and proposal to provide palliative care, believing that more aggressive treatment to keep him alive should be undertaken. The hospital went ahead without referring the case to the High Court.[23] The breach was held to arise because UK law and practice, as described above, enabled a High Court application to be made and to protect the child's rights the NHS Trust should have applied for the Court's approval.

5.18   The withdrawal of ANH in PVS cases (where the patient has no awareness at all) requires 'as a matter of good practice' referral to the High Court but there was no clear authority on whether or when withholding or withdrawal in any other cases, including where the patient still has some awareness, should go to court. This fell to be considered in *R (Burke) v General Medical Council and Others*.[24] At first instance Munby J ruled that the effect of *Glass* was to convert the rule of good practice into a legal obligation and there are a range of circumstances in cases involving patients not in PVS where withholding/withdrawal of ANH should not take place without prior judicial authorisation. In a list matching Coleridge J's list for abortion cases he ruled that these were where:

(1)   there is any doubt or disagreement as to capacity;

(2)   there is lack of unanimity amongst the medical professionals as to prognosis, best interests or outcome or as to whether ANH should be withheld;

(3)   there is evidence that the patient when competent would have wanted ANH to continue;

(4)   there is evidence that the patient resists or disputes the proposed withdrawal;

(5)   persons having a reasonable claim to have their views taken into account assert that withdrawal is contrary to the patient's wishes or not in his or her best interests.

5.19   The Court of Appeal expressly overruled Munby J on his analysis of the effect of *Glass*, reaffirming, as was held to be the position in *Bland*, that the court does not authorise treatment which would otherwise be unlawful

---

22   [2004] 1 FLR 1019

23   The domestic case which took place was a judicial review brought by members of the family against the NHS Trust, which was dismissed as being too blunt an instrument – see *R v Portsmouth Hospitals NHS Trust ex parte Glass* [1999] 2 FLR 905.

24   [2005] EWCA 1003, [2005] QB 424 (at first instance); [2006] 1 QB 273 (Court of Appeal). Permission to appeal to the House of Lords was refused.

but makes a declaration as to whether or not the proposed treatment, or its withdrawal, will be lawful. The judgment of the court states:[25]

> 'Good practice may require medical practitioners to seek such a declaration where the legality of proposed treatment is in doubt. This is not, however, something that they are required to do as a matter of law.'

The background to reform

5.20 When the Law Commission first looked at reforming this area of law, the common law position was far less developed than it is now. At that time there was concern, especially among carers and service-providers, over the gaps and uncertainties in the law.[26] This particularly related to the wider welfare area, and there was much support for an overall rather than piecemeal approach to reform. Once the decision was taken that this should encompass lasting powers of attorney and deputies with health care and welfare powers, it was clear that the legislation should deal with health care and welfare more generally. Indeed, MCA 2005 would have been a much less powerful instrument if its general principles were limited so as not to cover this whole area. This gave Parliament the opportunity to lay down a statutory framework and develop the common law position in a number of respects (the principal features of which are noted below).

THE POSITION UNDER THE MENTAL CAPACITY ACT 2005

General

5.21 Adult cases relating to a welfare or health care issue concerning someone who cannot choose for him or herself are now dealt with by the Court of Protection under the jurisdiction granted it by MCA 2005.[27] No power under the Act may be exercised in relation to a child under 16, fully covered by the Children Act 1989. Cases concerning children of 16 or 17 may be started under either jurisdiction, and there is power for the Court to transfer a case to whichever jurisdiction in the particular circumstances is more appropriate.[28]

5.22 The general provisions of MCA 2005 relating to capacity, inability to make decisions, best interests and acts in connection with care or treatment[29] apply to medical treatment as to all other areas. Existing case-law decided under the common law retains considerable relevance, but must be read subject to the statutory definitions contained within the Act and

---

[25]   *R (Burke) v General Medical Council (Official Solicitor and others intervening)* [2006] 1 QB 273, at 308.

[26]   See *Mentally Incapacitated Adults and Decision-Making: A New Jurisdiction*, Law Com Consultation Paper No 128 (HMSO, 1993).

[27]   See Chapter 2.

[28]   Mental Capacity Act 2005 (Transfer of Proceedings) Order 2007, SI 2007/1899 made under MCA 2005, s 21. In relation to a child aged 16 or 17, the Children Act 1989 should in general only be invoked if the matter is capable of resolution prior to the child's 18th birthday.

[29]   These are to be found in MCA 2005, ss 2–5.

the (slowly but significantly increasing) body of case-law decided under MCA 2005. Such cases as have been decided under MCA 2005 have generally reached similar outcomes to those decided previously in relation to the key issues of capacity and best interests. This is perhaps unsurprising as the statutory tests represent a codification of the position that had developed at common law since (and drawing upon) the Law Commission's proposals.

Principles (s 1) and Codes of Practice (s 42)

5.23 MCA 2005's powerful key principles set out in s 1 and the Code of Practice under s 42 can be expected to have a growing influence on best practice. It is the duty of any person acting in relation to the welfare or health care of a person who lacks capacity to have regard to the relevant provisions of the Code. They apply both to those lay or professional people taking decisions for and on behalf of the person lacking capacity, and also in relation to the approach that the Court of Protection must take upon application to it for decisions and/or declarations on behalf of that person.[30]

Capacity (s 2)

5.24 Whether a person has or lacks capacity to take a welfare or health care decision will generally be a matter of medical evidence, often provided by a psychiatrist. In cases of learning disability a psychologist may be equally or better suited to give the opinion. There is no legal requirement under MCA 2005 that lack of capacity has to be established by medical evidence. The statutory test is similar, but not identical, to test as existed previously at common law – it avoids a cross-reference to suffering a mental illness or disorder within the meaning of the Mental Health Act 1983. As stated at **5.11**, it is possible that someone who is suffering from a mental illness and is being treated for that illness under compulsory powers may nonetheless have mental capacity to decide whether to undergo other medical treatment.[31]

5.25 The question must be decided on the balance of probabilities. It does not matter whether the impairment or disturbance is permanent or temporary. A lack of capacity cannot be established merely by reference to a person's age or appearance or an aspect of behaviour which might lead others to make unjustified assumptions about his or her capacity. Capacity is issue specific,[32] and the Courts have made it clear that it is necessary to be careful to frame with care both the issue and the information relevant to the

---

[30]   There is a currently unresolved debate as to whether this includes all matters upon which a Court may determine in relation to an incapacitated adult, or whether it only applies in respect of the discharge of powers that the incapacitated adult would otherwise have been able to exercise for themselves. It is beyond controversy that they apply whenever a Court is discharging such powers.

[31]   See *Re C (Adult: Refusal of Treatment)* [1994] 1 WLR 290 concerning whether a gangrenous foot should be amputated.

[32]   Section 2(1) of the MCA 2005.

consideration of the issue. A good example of this decided under MCA 2005 in the welfare context is *A Local Authority v Mrs A and Mr A*.[33] In this case, the Court had to consider whether a woman had capacity to consent to being administered contraception. The local authority advocated for a wide interpretation, on the basis that it was necessary for the person to be able to understand and weigh the reasonably foreseeable consequences of not using contraception, and that this extended to understanding what would be involved in having and caring for a child. The Official Solicitor submitted that this set the bar too high. The judge agreed, in large part because he considered that it was unrealistic to expect the woman in question to be able to foresee all the variables inherent in parenthood, especially during the course of a short GP appointment to discuss contraception. Furthermore, he held that the local authority's interpretation risked heading towards social engineering. Rather, contraception was a question in respect of which certain immediate medical issues had to be understood and weighed by the person in question.[34]

PART I

Inability to make decisions (s 3)

5.26 This is very similar to the position the common law had reached. MCA 2005, s 3 gives an emphasis both to the requirement that every effort is made to explain the information in a way appropriate to the person's circumstances, including using sign language or any other means (s 3(2)), and to the point that temporary retention of information relevant to the decision may be sufficient (s 3(3)).

Best interests (s 4)

5.27 This is a key provision of MCA 2005. Whilst it can be said to replicate the position reached under the common law, it is interesting to see the different points emphasised in the various subsections and whether in time they will lead to a different way of reaching a decision in any particular case. The overall test remains an objective one ('consider all relevant circumstances') and of best interests, not 'substituted choice' or 'judgment' as to what the person concerned would have decided. But emphasis is given to considering past and present wishes and feelings, and beliefs and values, and consulting relatives, carers and any attorney under a lasting power of attorney or deputy appointed by the Court. Helpful guidance as to the weight to be placed upon P's wishes and feelings can be found in the

---

33   [2010] EWHC 1549.
34   On the facts of the case, Mrs A did have capacity to understand these medical issues, but was unable to weigh them because of the undue influence placed on her by her husband. This finding was to some extent academic, since the court was unable to make any order as to best interests: if it declared that contraception was in Mrs A's best interests, either she would agree (in which case the declaration would not be necessary), or she would not (in which case there was no question of her being forcibly transported to hospital against her will, sedated, and provided with contraception and so the declaration would serve no purpose).

decision of Munby J (as he then was) in *ITW v Z & Ors*,[35] from which the following propositions can be derived:[36]

(a) P's wishes and feelings will always be a significant factor to which the court must pay close regard;

(b) The weight to be attached to P's wishes and feelings will always be case–specific and fact–specific. In some cases, in some situations, they may carry much, even, on occasions, preponderant, weight. In other cases, in other situations, and even where the circumstances may have some superficial similarity, they may carry very little weight;

(c) Even if one is dealing with a particular individual, the weight to be attached to their wishes and feelings must depend upon the particular context. In relation to one topic P's wishes and feelings may carry great weight whilst at the same time carrying much less weight in relation to another topic;

(d) In considering the weight and importance to be attached to P's wishes and feelings the court must of course, and as required by section 4(2) of the MCA 2005, have regard to all the relevant circumstances. The relevant circumstances will include, such matters as:

(i) the degree of P's incapacity: the nearer to the borderline the more weight must in principle be attached to P's wishes and feelings;

(ii) the strength and consistency of the views being expressed by P;

(iii) the possible impact on P of knowledge that his wishes and feelings are not being given effect to;

(iv) the extent to which P's wishes and feelings are, or are not, rational, sensible, responsible and pragmatically capable of sensible implementation in the particular circumstances; and

(v) the extent to which P's wishes and feelings, if given effect to, can properly be accommodated within the court's overall assessment of what is in his best interests.[37]

5.28 MCA 2005, s 4(5) requires that whenever a person has to make a determination relating to life-sustaining treatment he or she 'shall not be motivated by a desire to bring about death'. This was inserted in response to

---

[35]   [2009] EWHC 2525 (Fam). The case relates to a statutory will, but the discussion at paragraphs 32–36, (couched as observations upon preceding decisions in *Re S and S (ProtectedPersons)* [2009] WTLR 315 and *Re P (Statutory Will)* (2009) EWHC 163 (Ch), [2010] Ch 33) is of more general application. Munby J also made the point powerfully that there is no place left for substituted decision making in statutory wills (one place where the previous law had allowed for such an approach).

[36]   At paragraph 35. See further para **5.49** below.

[37]   The decision in *Dorset CC v EH* [2009] EWHC 784 (Fam) provides an example of consideration of this last circumstance within the context of the Court of Protection's welfare jurisdiction. Here, the local authority sought the Court's authorisation to move an elderly woman with dementia into a care home against her wishes. The Court concluded that the move should take place, notwithstanding expert evidence that she should continue to be cared for at home. In this case, the woman's wishes could not be given considerable weight because of her failure to understand the seriousness of her illness and the risks she faced in living alone in her own home.

concerns raised by the Catholic Church. It does not reverse the judicial finding of the House of Lords in *Airedale NHS Trust v Bland*[38] that it may be lawful to withdraw and withhold ANH to allow a person in PVS to die with dignity. The provision reflects a concern that a family member who is an attorney under a lasting power of attorney or a deputy appointed by the Court may have this improper motive.

'Acts in connection with care or treatment' (ss 5–6)

5.29 A person who does an act in connection with the care or treatment of another person will be put in the same position as if dealing with someone who had capacity to consent and had consented, and therefore will not incur any liability in doing the act, if:

- before doing the act he or she had taken reasonable steps to establish whether the person lacks capacity; and
- he or she reasonably believes the person lacks capacity and it is in that person's best interests for the act to be done (MCA 2005, s 5).

5.30 This replaces, in possibly somewhat wider terms, the common law doctrine of necessity. It provides the basis upon which the vast majority of medical treatment decisions in relation to an incapacitated person can be taken without seeking any court 'authorisation' (see the discussion on when cases need to go to court at **5.40–5.42**). The act must be connected to that person's care or treatment so, for instance, an invasive medical examination of an incapacitated victim of crime for the purpose of gathering evidence for a possible criminal prosecution would not be covered by this provision.

5.31 This will not protect from negligence. It will allow restraint of the incapacitated person, provided there is a reasonable belief that it is necessary to do the act to prevent harm and the act is a proportionate response. The means by which a deprivation of liberty may be authorised under the MCA 2005, as amended by the Mental Health Act 2007 are considered in Chapter 6.

5.32 The protection from liability does not allow acts contrary to a decision made within the scope of their authority of either an attorney under a lasting power of attorney or a deputy. However, MCA 2005 specifically provides that this is not to stop a person providing life-sustaining treatment or doing an act to prevent serious deterioration while a decision on any relevant issue is sought from the Court.

The powers of the Court of Protection

5.33 TheCourt of Protection is given power either to make declarations[39] (as the High Court can now do under its inherent jurisdiction), or to issue

---

[38]   [1993] AC 789, see **5.6**.
[39]   MCA 2005, s 15.

orders making the decision on the patient's behalf (including the power to give P's consent or refusal to medical treatment – see MCA 2005, s 17(1)(d)).[40] The court has the power to retrospectively declare an act to be lawful (s 15(1)(c)) It may also appoint a deputy with health care decision-making powers (subject to the requirements in MCA 2005, s 16(4) that it must additionally have regard to the principles that a decision by the Court is to be preferred and the powers conferred are to be as limited in scope and duration as reasonably practicable)[41] (and see the restrictions on the powers of any deputy contained in s 20 and described in Chapter 4 of this book). In one sense this Court starts with a clean sheet and its judges will be able to develop the law in new directions in the light of the statutory framework. However, it is likely that the existing case-law will be of persuasive authority in many areas, and it is clear that the Courts will continue to adopt the balance sheet approach outlined by Thorpe LJ in *Re A*.[42] It is open to the President of the Court of Protection to issue either Practice Directions or guidance as to the law.[43]

Practice and procedure under the Mental Capacity Act 2005

Court Rules and Practice Directions

5.34 The procedure is governed by the Court of Protection Rules 2007[44] and the President has issued a number of Practice Directions.[45] These establish the procedure to be adopted in welfare and medical treatment cases. Whilst they allow for practice and procedure similar in many ways to that previously adopted in the High Court, there are a number of important features to note.

Permission

5.35 MCA 2005 provides that, except in circumstances set out in the Act or the Rules, permission will need to be obtained to make an application to the Court. Most welfare and health care cases will require permission. The

---

[40] MCA 2005, s 16. Note that in the first reported case under MCA 2005 relating to healthcare (*DH NHS Foundation Trust v PS* [2010] EWHC 1217 (Fam)) the then President chose to authorise the treatment in question (for cancer) by way of declarations under s 15, rather than a decision under s 16. Although at least one of the Family Division judges who regularly hears health and welfare cases has strong views as to the distinction between ss 15 and 16, in the author's view it is unlikely that anything material will turn on which route the Court chooses to adopt.

[41] It is extremely rare, in practice, for deputies to be appointed with health care decision-making powers, in large part because of the presumption against such appointments in s 16(4) of the MCA 2005, and in part because the majority of cases that have come before the Courts have concerned either one-off or a discrete series of interventions, rather than a position where ongoing decisions would have to be made. See *G v E* [2010] EWHC 2512(COP) (Fam).

[42] *Re A (Mental Patient: Sterilisation)* [2000] 1 FLR 549.

[43] MCA 2005, s 52.

[44] SI 2007/1744.

[45] Court of Protection Rules 2007, Practice Directions 4A, 4B, 6A, 7A, 8A, 9A, 9B, 9C, 9E, 9G, 10A, 10B, 11A, 12A, 12B, 13A, 14A, 14B, 14C, 14D, 14E, 15A, 17A, 18A, 19A, 20A, 21A and 23B. As at the date of writing, these Practice Directions are the subject of review.

excepted circumstances set out in the Act are where the application is made by the person who lacks capacity, a parent, an attorney, a deputy or a person named in an existing court order. The Court of Protection Rules 2007, r 51 adds to these where the application is made by the Official Solicitor or Public Guardian, concerns a lasting power of attorney or is an application made within existing proceedings under Part 10 of the Rules. The requirement that permission needs to be obtained is an aspect of the policy that court proceedings are only brought as a matter of last resort – and one of the factors the Court of Protection must have in mind in deciding whether to grant permission is whether the benefit can be achieved in any other way (MCA 2005, s 50(3)). In practice, however, where the application is brought by a local authority or NHS body, permission is almost always granted at the paper stage without separate consideration by the Court.

Serious medical treatment cases

5.36 The President's Practice Direction 'Applications Relating to Serious Medical Treatment' makes special provision for these cases. 'Serious medical treatment' is defined for this purpose as treatment which involves providing, withdrawing or withholding treatment in circumstances where:

- (if a single treatment is proposed) there is a fine balance between its benefits and burdens and risks;
- (if there is a choice) a decision as to which treatment is finely balanced; or
- the treatment, procedure or investigation would be likely to involve serious consequences for the patient.

5.37 The Practice Direction first spells out that there are certain decisions which should be regarded as serious medical treatment decisions and should be brought to the Court. It also gives examples of other decisions which should be considered serious medical treatment (see **5.40–5.41**).[46] It provides that in these cases the person bringing the application will always be a party to the proceedings, as will a respondent named in the application form who files an acknowledgment of service, and the organisation providing clinical or caring services should usually be named as a respondent (if not the applicant). Whether or not 'P' is to be joined as a party is to be determined at the first directions hearing (as is the question whether the Official Solicitor or any other person should be appointed that person's litigation friend). In practice, however, the increasing trend (at least where time allows) is that such questions – along with any questions of permission – are determined on paper by the Court in advance of that hearing.

5.38 The Practice Direction also makes provision for the allocation of serious medical treatment cases. Where the application relates to the

---

[46] As at the date of writing, there is a proposal that this Practice Direction is to be modified so as to make it clear that serious medical treatment can encompass treatment which is not in and of itself serious, but where the consequence of administering/not administering it would be serious.

lawfulness of withholding or withdrawing ANH from a person in PVS or a minimally conscious state or it is a case involving an ethical dilemma in an untested area then the whole proceedings (including the permission stage) must be conducted by the President or a judge nominated by the President. All other serious medical treatment cases or cases in which a declaration of incompatibility is sought pursuant to the Human Rights Act 1998, s 4 must be conducted by the President, the Chancellor or a High Court judge (nominated to sit as a Court of Protection judge). Whether the Practice Direction covers a case is a matter for the Senior Judge of the Court of Protection or a judge nominated by him or her. In practice, this has meant that applications lodged at the Court which have not been made on an urgent basis are referred to a district judge to make a decision as to allocation (for urgent cases see **5.39**). In a case requiring to be allocated to a High Court Judge which is not urgent (in the sense that P's life or health is not at immediate risk) but which nonetheless needs a speedy process (such as where P needs to be given treatment for cancer and any significant delay is likely to prejudicial), it is advisable before issue to alert the Court's Listing and Appeals team to the application and the need for it to be processed and issued quickly.

5.39 The practice to be followed in urgent cases is set out in Practice Direction 10B. When it is not possible to apply within court hours contact should be made with the security officer at the Royal Courts of Justice, who will invariably refer the matter to the Family Division High Court judge covering urgent out-of-hours business (and will usually contact the Official Solicitor). The Practice Direction suggests that for urgent applications brought during office hours contact should be made with the Court of Protection. However, in serious medical treatment cases the current practice which has developed is to go direct to the Clerk of the Rules of the High Court Family Division to seek an urgent hearing before the first available Family Division judge and giving an undertaking to issue the proceedings at the Court of Protection within the next working day.[47] That judge will determine the allocation of the case.

When should cases be brought to Court?

5.40 The Practice Direction in large part reflects the position reached at common law as to when a serious medical treatment decision should be decided by the Court. The first category concerns decisions to withhold or

---

[47] Difficulties can be encountered when listing a return date for the application after the urgent hearing has occurred as the Clerk of the Rules usually requires a case number which has on occasions not been available from the Court of Protection for a week or more after an application has been lodged. It is advisable to phone the listings office at the Court of Protection to ensure that they are aware of the urgency of the application and the need for it to be promptly issued. As noted in the previous edition, the administration of the Court of Protection into HM Courts Service on 1 April 2009 there appearshas led to have been greatersome improvement in liaison between the Clerk of the Rules Office in the Royal Courts of Justice and the Listings and Appeals Team of the Court of Protection at Archway. However, it remains advisable for practitioners to communicate with both offices and to ensure that appropriate liaison is taking place.

withdraw ANH. This covers people in PVS or a minimally conscious state. As discussed above, in *Airedale NHS Trust v Bland* it had been established that, as a matter of good practice, all cases where it is proposed to withdraw ANH from a patient in PVS should go to court. This is partly a reflection of the importance of the decision for the individual and also provides a reassurance to the public as to how these decisions are taken. That it is a matter of 'good practice' and not a legal obligation was reaffirmed by the Court of Appeal in *R (Burke) v General Medical Council*.[48] This is now buttressed by the Practice Direction, which interestingly also covers withholding or withdrawal of ANH in cases where a person is in a minimally conscious state (which had not previously authoritatively been established by case-law).

5.41 The second category of case set out in the Practice Direction is organ or bone marrow donation by a person who lacks capacity to consent. The third is non-therapeutic sterilisation. Other examples of 'serious medical treatment' given in the Practice Direction which should be taken to the Court of Protection are:

- certain termination of pregnancy cases, where there is a dispute over capacity or the patient may regain capacity during her pregnancy, any lack of unanimity, where the procedures under the Abortion Act 1967, s 1 have not been followed, where the patient or members of her immediate family have opposed a termination, or where there are other exceptional circumstances (including that this may be the patient's last chance to bear a child);
- other medical treatment for the purpose of a donation to someone else;
- treatment which requires a degree of force to restrain the person concerned;[49]
- treatment which is experimental or innovative; and
- cases involving an ethical dilemma in an untested area.

5.42 These situations apart, there may be other procedures or treatments which can be regarded as serious medical treatment (because of the circumstances and consequences) and which, if so, may be brought to court. Where the decision as to the appropriate treatment is finely balanced either as to its benefit or the choice of treatment testing whether it is in the best interests of the person concerned through Court of Protection proceedings may well be appropriate. The general principle is that the Court's jurisdiction should be invoked whenever there is a serious justiciable issue requiring a decision by a court:[50]

---

48   [2006] 1 QB 273.
49   Examples of the levels of restraint permitted by the Court of Protection in 2010 include sedating P for a period of 6 days prior to her gynaecological operation (*Re D* [2010] EWHC 2535 (COP)), restraining P for 18 hours a day for 5 days to ensure she received an intravenous immunosuppressant drug (*Re SB*) and restraining P for 3 hours every fortnight for 6 months (*Re KA*). Both of these latter cases were only reported by way of press reports.
50   Coleridge J in *D v An NHS Trust (Medical Treatment: Consent)* [2004] 1 FLR 1110.

'In cases of controversy and cases involving momentous and irrevocable decisions, the courts have treated as justiciable any genuine question as to what the best interests of a patient require or justify.'

Welfare or less serious medical treatment cases

5.43 As indicated above, in most instances of medical treatment it will be perfectly proper to proceed upon the basis of the authority given by MCA 2005, s 5. It must be a decision to be taken in the circumstances of an individual case whether the protection of seeking a decision from the Court should be obtained. Similarly, more general welfare decisions may be taken in the best interests of the person concerned without going to court.[51] However, there may be a dispute which cannot be resolved by any other means, for example, between a close family member and the local authority's social services or between family members or between treating clinicians and/or other professionals involved in a person's care, as to what those best interests are: 'Ultimately, if all other attempts to resolve the dispute have failed, the court might need to decide what is in the person's best interests.'[52] When any of these cases need to be taken to the Court (and, if required, permission is granted) the Court decides who is to hear the case and gives directions as to the procedure to be followed. It determines who the parties are to be, and in particular whether the person concerned is to be made a party and, if so, who the litigation friend is to be, or whether it can reach a decision on the basis of the information made available to it and a report from the Public Guardian or Visitor or social or health services under MCA 2005, s 47. It also considers such matters as permission to obtain independent expert evidence, obtaining disclosure from third parties (eg medical records, social services' files, care home records, financial documents) and the filing of statements.

Withholding or withdrawing life-sustaining treatment

5.44 Given the importance accorded by both Houses of Parliament during the Parliamentary Debates on the MCA 2005 to issues related to withholding or withdrawing life-sustaining treatment, a short commentary drawing some of the threads together is appropriate. Two of the leading cases are *Bland* and *Burke*, to which reference has already been made.[53]

---

[51]   A point emphasised strongly in *G v E* [2010] EWHC 2512(COP) (Fam), in which Baker J made it clear that the regime of the MCA 2005 was intended to produce collaborative decision making between family members and professionals.

[52]   Code, para 5.68. As at the date of writing, it is likely that there will be promulgated a Practice Direction or Guidance which updates the Practice Direction which applied in relation to proceedings under the inherent jurisdiction: [2006] 2 FLR 373, attaching to it the Practice Note from the Official Solicitor: "Declaratory Proceedings: Medical and Welfare Decisions for Adults who Lack Capacity."

[53]   *Airedale NHS Trust v Bland* [1993] AC 789; *R (Burke) v General Medical Council (Official Solicitor and others intervening)* [2004] EWHC 1879 (Admin), [2005] QB 424 (at first instance); [2005] EWCA 1003, [2006] 1 QB 273 (Court of Appeal).

5.45 In *Bland* the House of Lords decided that, where there is no continuing duty on doctors to sustain life through medical treatment, including the provision of ANH, because of the futility of doing so in the case of a patient in PVS, it would be lawful to withhold or withdraw that treatment. It has subsequently been held that this decision is compatible with the incorporation of the European Convention on Human Rights in our law[54] and the decision has been re-affirmed in *Pretty v UK*.[55] It is the basis for the distinction in this jurisprudence between omissions and positive acts causing death.

5.46 The *Burke* case was a judicial review concerning the lawfulness of guidelines issued by the General Medical Council (GMC)[56] and was brought by a competent adult who feared that the guidance would not adequately protect him from doctors' withholding or withdrawing ANH at a time when, as a result of his wasting disease, he would need it to be kept alive. The case provided the opportunity, taken by Munby J, for a judgment covering a number of important issues, although the Court of Appeal in its judgment, allowing the GMC's appeal and setting aside the declarations made at first instance, has approached the case more narrowly, finding that Mr Burke's fears are addressed by the law as it stands. The judgment of the court given in the appeal recognises that whilst the duty to keep a patient alive by administering ANH or other life-prolonging treatment is not absolute, the only exceptions are either where a competent patient refuses to receive it or where it is not considered to be in the best interests of an incompetent patient artificially to be kept alive. This latter circumstance covers patients in PVS and where the patient's continued life involves an extreme degree of pain, discomfort or indignity and he or she has not shown a wish to be kept alive.[57]

5.47 In relation to Mr Burke's own situation, the Court of Appeal robustly declared:[58]

> 'Indeed, it seems to us that for a doctor deliberately to interrupt life-prolonging treatment in the face of a competent patient's expressed wish to be kept alive, with the intention of thereby terminating the patient's life, would leave the doctor with no answer to a charge of murder.'

and:[59]

> 'Where life depends upon the continued provision of ANH there can be no question of the supply of ANH not being clinically indicated unless a clinical decision has

---

[54]   *NHS Trust A v H* [2001] 2 FLR 501.
[55]   (2002) 35 EHRR 1.
[56]   *Withholding and Withdrawing Life-prolonging Treatments: Good Practice in Decision-making* (August 2002). With effect from 1 July 2010, this guidance has now been replaced by *Treatment and care towards the end of life: good practice in decision making*, which expressly incorporates reference to *Burke*.
[57]   This issue also arises in severely damaged baby cases: see eg *Re J (a Minor)(Wardship: Medical Treatment)* [1991] Fam 33.
[58]   *R (Burke) v General Medical Council (Official Solicitor and others intervening)* [2006] 1 QB 273 at 297.
[59]   Ibid, at 301.

been taken that the life in question should come to an end. That is not a decision that can lawfully be taken in the case of a competent patient who expresses the wish to remain alive.'

Intolerability

5.48 The Court of Appeal in *Burke* expressly disavowed Munby J's 'test' that, when considering best interests in relation to an incompetent patient and whether to sustain life, the importance of respecting life needed to be reflected by adopting as the 'touchstone' of best interests whether or not the continuing treatment was 'intolerable' from the patient's point of view. It held that the test of whether it is in the best interests of the patient to provide or continue ANH must depend on the particular circumstances. It also overturned Munby J's ruling that it is possible for a competent patient by an advance directive to require that any particular form of medical treatment, including life-sustaining treatment, be given.

Best interests under the Mental Capacity Act 2005

5.49 As noted above (at **5.27**), the test of best interests adopts an objective approach,[60] but also requires more subjective factors such as the past and present wishes and feelings of the person concerned (so far as ascertainable) to be considered.[61] It will be interesting to see whether a future case with similar features to those in *W Healthcare NHS Trust v KH*[62] will be decided in the same way. In this case, concerning whether ANH should be reinstated, objective best interests and the patient's ascertainable past views did not appear to coincide. It was the unanimous medical view that the PEG tube[63] should be reinserted, but the patient's family did not want this to happen since they believed that in the circumstances she would want to die. The Court at first instance and on appeal decided it was in her best interests to be kept alive; absent a binding advance decision (see **5.66** below), the authors consider it likely that the Court would reach the same judgment now, even though it would be required to adopt the more precise analytical route set down in statute.

5.50 MCA 2005, s 4(5)[64] specifically relates to life-sustaining treatment:

'Where the determination relates to life-sustaining treatment [the decision-maker] must not, in considering whether the treatment is in the best interests of the person concerned, be motivated by a desire to bring about his death.'

---

[60] MCA 2005, s 4(2).
[61] MCA 2005, s 4(6).
[62] [2005] 1 WLR 834.
[63] PEG stands for percutaneous (through the skin) endoscopic gastrotomy (stomach tube).
[64] MCA 2005, s 4(5) was introduced as a Government amendment in the House of Lords to meet concerns on behalf of the Catholic Church expressed by Archbishop Smith that the Bill would allow discontinuance of life-sustaining treatment prompted by this improper motive.

This does not override the decision or argument in the *Bland* case.[65] See also the general assurance given by MCA 2005, s 62 that nothing in MCA 2005 is to be taken as affecting the law relating to murder, manslaughter or assisted suicide

An exclusive jurisdiction

5.51 Although MCA 2005 does not expressly state this to be the case, the new Court of Protection jurisdiction has left no room for the continuing operation of a separate High Court inherent jurisdiction in relation to adults and cases covered by the Act. In practice this means that only judges nominated to be judges of the Court of Protection[66] are able to hear these cases. However, the inherent High Court jurisdiction remains available to protect vulnerable persons who require the Court's protection but do not fall within the categories of incapacitated persons covered by MCA 2005 or the circumstances of their cases are not within the Act.[67] The precise scope of the High Court's jurisdiction in this regard has yet fully to be defined, with most practitioners considering that it is more limited than that granted the Court of Protection will by MCA 2005. In particular, it would appear doubtful that the High Court has the power to do more than enable (by declaratory and/or injunctive relief) the vulnerable adult to take the relevant decision for themselves, freed from the pressures that have rendered them incapable of free choice.[68]

5.52 Furthermore, it is clear that that the Court of Protection has no jurisdiction in respect of disputes where the patient has the capacity to make his or her own treatment decisions. Experience has shown that this can result in significant problems where that person has fluctuating capacity. In practice serious cases will be are restricted to nominated judges from the Family Division of the High Court and where necessary such a judge will choose to sit in a dual jurisdiction; they have also shown themselves willing

---

[65] Reference to the parliamentary record supports this interpretation – see statement of Baroness Ashton of Upholland, House of Lords Committee Stage, *Hansard*, HL Deb, vol 668, ser 5, col 1175 (25 January 2005).

[66] See MCA 2005, s 46.

[67] *Re SK (Proposed Plaintiff) (An adult by her litigation friend)* [2005] 2 FLR 230; *Re SA (Vulnerable adult with capacity: marriage)* [2006] 1 FLR 867. In SA, Munby J held that the protective jurisdiction can be exercised in relation to a vulnerable adult who, even if not incapacitated by mental disorder or illness, is reasonably believed to be under constraint, subject to coercion or undue influence, or for some other reason deprived of the capacity to make the relevant decision. In *City of Westminster v IC, KC and NNC* [2007] EWHC 3096 (Fam), Roderic Wood J stated that: 'Save where it would be demonstrably inconsistent with the will of Parliament, the inherent jurisdiction remains alive, in appropriate cases, where it is necessary, lawful and proportionate, to meet circumstances unmet by the scope of the MCA.'

[68] In *A v DL, RL and ML* [2010] EWHC 2675 (Fam), the President confirmed that an order could in principle be made under the inherent jurisdiction (or under s 222 of the Local Government Act 1972) to protect an elderly couple (with capacity) considered to be at risk of physical, emotional and financial abuse from their son, who lived with them. Unfortunately, the precise terms of the proposed order were kept confidential, and hence the decision is not of as much assistance as it could be in determining the scope of the court's jurisdiction. For case summary, see Part IX of this work.

to be robust in their interpretation of their mandate under MCA 2005 so as to ensure that whenever the person in question's capacity has decreased sufficiently they are brought within the protective scope of the Act.

Overlap with judicial review

5.53 The procedure described works well when those responsible for the medical care of the patient (generally an NHS Trust) either bring the proceedings to seek a decision from the court or are a party to the proceedings and are willing to abide by the result.[69] There may be cases in which the public body responsible for the treatment has already taken a decision and the question then arises how that decision can appropriately be challenged. There is existing case-law on decided prior to the enactment of MCA 2005 when judicial review or a best interests application is the appropriate way to proceed.,[70] and there is no good reason to doubt that such case-law does not continue to apply. In the welfare field, there has yet to be a reported decision from the Court of Protection as to the overlap between the two jurisdictions, but the thrust of the unreported decisions tend to suggest that the powers of the Court of Protection is limited to choosing (on a best interests basis) between options that are actually available, and that it does not have the ability – for instance – to dictate to a public authority to make available a resource that is not, in fact, available. When the need to proceed under by way of both judicial review and under MCA 2005 arises it is necessary to ensure that a judge who can hear judicial review applications and is a judge of the Court of Protection will be available.

INDEPENDENT MENTAL CAPACITY ADVOCATES

Establishment

5.54 MCA 2005 imposes a duty on the Secretary of State (in practice the Secretary of State for Health) in England and the Welsh Assembly in Wales to make arrangements to enable independent mental capacity advocates (IMCAs) to be available to represent and support incapacitated persons in circumstances defined in the Act.[71] These arrangements must be designed to achieve the laudable principle that:[72]

> '... a person to whom a proposed act or decision relates should, so far as practicable, be represented and supported by a person who is independent of any person who will be responsible for the act or decision.'

5.55 This adopts the conclusion of the Joint Parliamentary Committee scrutinising the draft Bill which was accepted by the Government that:[73]

---

[69]   See *Simms v Simms* [2003] Fam 83 where at a late stage the NHS Trust at whose hospital it was thought that the medical procedure would take place indicated its opposition. This led to one of the cases being re-heard in Belfast and the operation taking place there.

[70]   *A v A Health Authority* [2002] Fam 213.

[71]   MCA 2005, s 35.

[72]   MCA 2005, s 35(4).

[73]   Joint Committee on the Draft Mental Incapacity Bill, Session 2002–2003, HL 189-1, HC 1083, para 297.

'We are convinced that independent advocacy services play an essential role in assisting people with capacity problems to make and communicate decisions; helping them to enforce their rights and guard against unwarranted intrusion into their lives; providing a focus on the views and wishes of an incapacitated person in the determination of their best interests; providing additional safeguards against abuse and exploitation; and assisting in the resolution of disputes.'

5.56 MCA 2005 empowers the Secretary of State (or Welsh Assembly) to discharge this duty by making Regulations providing for the circumstances and conditions under which such an advocate may act and as to his or her appointment. This he has done (in England) in the Mental Capacity Act 2005 (Independent Mental Capacity Advocates) (General) Regulations 2006.[74]

Appointment, functions and role

5.57 The IMCA service is locally based (commissioned by the relevant local authority). The qualifying conditions for a person to be an IMCA are that he or she is (or belongs to a class of persons) approved by the local authority, and that he or she has appropriate experience or training, is a person of integrity and good character and is able to act independently of any person who instructs him or her.

5.58 The Regulations provide for the functions of such advocates and the steps to be taken for the purposes of:[75]

- providing support so the person whom he or she has been instructed to represent may participate as fully as possible in any relevant decision;
- obtaining and evaluating relevant information;
- ascertaining what the person's wishes and feelings would be likely to be and the beliefs and values likely to influence that person;
- ascertaining what alternative courses of action are available; and
- obtaining a further medical opinion.

5.59 The IMCA's functions are to:

(1) verify that the instructions were issued by an authorised person;
(2) to the extent it is practicable and appropriate, interview the patient and examine relevant health, social services or care home records;
(3) to the extent practicable and appropriate, consult the professional carers and other persons in a position to comment on the patient's wishes, feelings, beliefs or values;
(4) take all practicable steps to obtain information about the patient, or the proposed act or decision;
(5) evaluate all the information he or she has obtained so as to ascertain the extent of the support provided to enable the patient to participate in the decision and what the patient's wishes and feelings would

---

[74] SI 2006/1832.
[75] MCA 2005, s 36.

likely be and the beliefs and values likely to influence the patient, what alternative courses of action are available and where medical treatment is proposed whether the patient would benefit from a further medical opinion; and

(6) prepare a report for the person who instructed him or her, to include such submissions as he or she considers appropriate.

An IMCA who has been instructed also has power to challenge the decision taken as if he or she were someone engaged in caring for the patient or interested in the patient's welfare.

The duty to instruct

NHS bodies

5.60   An NHS body is under a duty to instruct such an advocate and to take into account any information given or submissions made by that advocate before providing 'serious medical treatment' (as defined in the Regulations in a similar way to that subsequently adopted in the President's Practice Direction as described at **5.36**) when there is no one else for the provider of the treatment to discuss it with.[76] This will occur when there is neither a person in the specified list[77] who can speak for the person – namely, a person nominated by the person, an attorney under a lasting power of attorney or pre-existing enduring power of attorney, or a deputy – nor a non-professional carer or friend whom it is appropriate to consult.[78] If the treatment has to be provided as a matter of urgency it may be provided even though no advocate has been instructed.

5.61   A similar duty arises where it is proposed that an incapacitated person should be accommodated in long-stay accommodation in a hospital or care home, or should transfer to another hospital or care home, where this accommodation is provided or arranged by the NHS.[79] If the accommodation is to last more than 28 days in a hospital or 8 weeks in a care home an advocate is to be instructed when there is no other person to discuss it with. The role of the advocate is again to support and represent the person concerned and any information and submissions from the advocate must be taken into account. This does not apply if the accommodation arises

---

[76] Not being treatment regulated by the Mental Health Act 1983, Part 4: MCA 2005, s 37.
[77] This is set out in MCA 2005, s 40.
[78] Paragraph 10.69 of the Code of Practice refers to IMCAs being available to people who have no family or friends who are available and appropriate to support or represent them. There is currently no case law on what factors would prevent a family member or friend from being an "appropriate adult". Clearly concerns as to such a person having a conflict of interest or mental health problems would seem a reasonable basis to exclude their involvement as an appropriate adult but – for instance – would the fact that such a person may hold strong religious views sufficient to deem them to be not appropriate. The author has been informed of cases where IMCAs have been appointed where there are dissenting family members who simply have strong moral objections to the proposed provision or with holding of treatment. The IMCA should only accept appointment where satisfied that that person is not appropriate.
[79] MCA 2005, s 38.

as a result of an obligation under the Mental Health Act 1983 nor when it is being arranged as a matter of urgency.[80]

Local authorities

5.62 Matching provisions are made, and duty imposed, on a local authority in relation to long-stay accommodation arranged by that authority.[81] These apply to residential accommodation provided in accordance with the National Assistance Act 1948, s 21 or 29 or following discharge under the Mental Health Act 1983, s 117. The accommodation may be in a care home, nursing home, ordinary or sheltered housing, housing association or other registered social housing, or in private sector housing provided by a local authority or in hostel accommodation. Similar exceptions are made where the person concerned is required to live in the accommodation in question under the Mental Health Act 1983 or in relation to urgent placements.[82]

Expansion of role

5.63 Separate Regulations have also been made expanding the role, adjusting the obligation to make arrangements and prescribing different circumstances in which an advocate may be instructed to act. These are the Mental Capacity Act 2005 (Independent Mental Capacity Advocates) (Expansion of Role) Regulations 2006.[83] The NHS body or local authority may instruct an IMCA (if satisfied it would be beneficial to the person to be so represented) when reviewing accommodation arrangements or proposing to take protective measures to minimise the risk of abuse or neglect.

Powers of the advocate

5.64 An advocate under these provisions may, for the purpose of enabling him or her to carry out his or her functions:

- interview in private the person he or she has been instructed to represent; and
- examine and take copies of any health record, social services record or care home record which the person holding the record considers may be relevant to the advocate's investigation.[84]

---

[80]   Provision is made to ensure that an advocate is involved in relation to people whose residence is initially intended to be less than the 28 days or 8 weeks if the period is later extended beyond the applicable period (MCA 2005, s 38(4)).
[81]   MCA 2005, s 39.
[82]   MCA 2005, s 39(3) and (4).
[83]   SI 2006/2883.
[84]   MCA 2005, s 35(6).

Comment

5.65 These provisions were amongst the first to be brought into force (1 April 2007). Whilst it is to be expected that there are some local variations in practice as the service is very much locally based, with a number of different charitable organisations commissioned to fulfil the role in different parts of the country, IMCAs have now become an accepted and valuable part of the machinery provided by MCA 2005. Their primary role is to support someone where there are no family members or friends (except where protective measures are being considered) – particular examples include older people with dementia who have lost contact with all friends and family, or people with severe learning disabilities or long-term mental health problems who have been in residential institutions for long periods and lack outside contacts. The role of IMCAs has already been expanded. It is, perhaps, indicative of a vote of confidence in them that they are to be, for instance by being given a further role under the amendments to MCA 2005 made by the Mental Health Act 2007 (see Chapter 6).[85] It is, however, unfortunately likely that as budgetary pressures tighten, those providing IMCA services will encounter increasing difficulty in maintaining them, will consequently deleterious effects upon those incapacitated adults who most require their assistance.

THE COMPETENT ADULT – ADVANCE DECISIONS

Preliminary

5.66 In any case in which an adult is found to be competent[86] very different principles come into play. Whether as Munby J (as he then was) analysed it in *Burke*[87] that the adult is the arbiter of his or her own best interests or it is purely a matter of adult autonomy irrespective of best interests, the court has no basis or jurisdiction to investigate a competent adult's best interests. The principle of adult autonomy is determinative.

5.67 Particularly graphic examples of cases the High Court has considered under the inherent jurisdiction are furnished by *Re B (Consent to Treatment: Capacity*,[88] which related to refusal to consent to continued artificial ventilation, and *Re Z (An Adult: Capacity*,[89] where the individual had arranged to travel to Switzerland to be assisted to commit suicide in a manner that was lawful in that country. No such stark decisions have yet been reported under MCA 2005, but it is likely that it is only a matter of time before they are.

---

[85]   Note, however, that concern was expressed in the Department of Health's second annual report upon the IMCA service as to the continued low level of referrals for serious medical treatment decisions, and also about the low level of adult protection referrals. See www.dh.gov.uk/prod_consum_dh/groups/dh_digitalassets/@dh/@en/@ps/documents/digitalasset/dh_111846.pdf, accessed 19 July 2010, at para 4.

[86]   There is a presumption of competence in MCA 2005, s 1(2).

[87]   See **5.18**.

[88]   [2002] 1 FLR 1090.

[89]   [2005] 2 FCR 256.

ADVANCE DIRECTIVES AT COMMON LAW

Refusal of treatment

5.68 The common law has needed to consider the position of persons who are incompetent at the time a decision as to their medical treatment has to be taken but who have made an advance directive refusing that treatment. Not surprisingly, the issue soon emerged in the context of a Jehovah's witness refusing consent to a blood transfusion;[90] and it has also been litigated in the context of a patient seeking removal of his ventilator.[91]

PART I

Essential features

5.69 Advance refusals to consent to particular treatments are an aspect of a competent adult's autonomy.[92] An advance refusal of medical treatment is to be given binding effect if, but only if:

(1) made at a time when the adult had capacity to make a decision of such a nature;

(2) intended to apply when that person is incapable;

(3) it relates to the circumstances which have arisen;

(4) the maker understood the nature and consequences of his or her decision; and

(5) there was no undue influence or coercion by a third party.

5.70 No particular form is needed, and such a refusal may be revoked in any way[93] or as a result of a change in relevant circumstances. A court will need to be satisfied the advance refusal remains valid and applicable to the particular circumstances, and if there is doubt that doubt will be resolved in favour of the preservation of life and the best interests test applied.[94] The greatest difficulty in practice has been whether from the drafting of an advance directive it can be clearly inferred that such a refusal was intended to apply in the circumstances which have arisen[95], and it is clear that there is not always consistency of practice amongst medical professionals in their interpretation of the application of the facts to the directive before them.

The relationship with suicide

5.71 It is settled law that whilst no one has the right to ask for and be given treatment which constitutes a positive act (such as the administration of an

---

90   *Re T (Adult: Refusal of Treatment)* [1993] Fam 95; and more recently *HE v A Hospital NHS Trust* [2003] 2 FLR 408.

91   *Re AK (Medical Treatment: Consent)* [2001] 1 FLR 129.

92   Documents setting out wishes as to medical treatment were initially described as 'living wills'.

93   An advance refusal set out in a signed document may be revoked by a subsequent verbal expression of contrary wishes.

94   *HE v A Hospital NHS Trust* [2003] 2 FLR 408.

95   This may be one factor which has led to a body such as the Voluntary Euthanasia Society to offer a standard form for an advance directive refusing life-sustaining treatment, and it is possible to download a living will from www.livingwill.org.uk.

excessive dose of diamorphine) to assist in their suicide, they may refuse the provision or continuation of life-sustaining treatment such as ANH even when the inevitable consequence is death.[96]

Requests for treatment

5.72 An advance directive may request rather than seek to refuse treatment. But there is no general right for a person to require, either at the time or in an advance decision, that a particular form of medical treatment be given. This was reaffirmed in robust terms by the Court of Appeal in its judgment in *Burke*.[97]

ADVANCE DECISIONS UNDER THE MENTAL CAPACITY ACT 2005

Recognition

5.73 MCA 2005, ss 24–26 give statutory recognition to, and govern the applicability and effect of, advance decisions to refuse specified treatments made by an adult when competent which are to have effect when the adult becomes incompetent.

5.74 A number of conditions are laid down which must be met before such a decision is to be valid and applicable. These replicate the common law position in a number of respects in relation to refusals of treatment, and in some modify it by providing additional safeguards as indicated below.

Advance refusals of treatment

5.75 These provisions of MCA 2005 in their terms only apply to advance refusals of specified treatments. It is necessary to specify the treatment which is to be refused, although this does not have to be done in medical language and can be expressed in layman's terms.[98] The circumstances in which the refusal is to apply may also be specified. Such a decision may be subsequently withdrawn or altered when the maker of the decision has capacity to do so. This need not be in writing unless the altered decision is a decision to refuse life-sustaining treatment.[99]

---

[96] Reaffirmed in *Pretty v United Kingdom* (2002) 35 EHRR 1. In deciding whether effect must be given to an advance refusal of life-sustaining treatment it is not necessary to inquire into the motives of the person making it. The Catholic Bishops Conference of England and Wales submitted to the Court of Appeal in the *Burke* appeal that adult autonomy is limited by an inability to refuse treatment motivated by a suicidal intent. It is suggested that this not established in existing case-law as at that point, and remains the case at present.
[97] See **5.46**.
[98] MCA 2005, s 24(1)(a) and (2).
[99] MCA 2005, s 24(5).

Advance requests for treatment

5.76 Advance requests for treatment are dealt with differently under MCA 2005. They are treated as a relevant written statement which, if made when the person had capacity, must be considered by the decision-maker in determining best interests.[100]

Conditions for validity

5.77 To have the effect prescribed in MCA 2005 an advance decision to refuse a treatment must have been made by a person after he or she has reached the age of 18 and at a time when he or she had capacity to do so. It loses its validity if:[101]

- the person has withdrawn the decision (by any means) at a time when he or she had capacity to do so;
- he or she has created a lasting power of attorney after the decision was made in which he or she gives the donee of the power the authority to give or refuse consent to the treatment in question; or
- he or she has since the decision was made acted inconsistently with that being his or her fixed intention.[102]

Applicability

5.78 An advance decision is not applicable if:[103]

- at the time the provision of the treatment is in question the person has the capacity to give or refuse consent to it;
- the treatment falls outside the treatment specified in the decision;
- any circumstances specified in the decision are absent; or
- there are reasonable grounds for believing that circumstances exist which the maker of the advance decision did not anticipate at the time of its making and which would have affected his or her decision had he or she anticipated them.

Life-sustaining treatment

5.79 In addition to these conditions, there are statutory conditions for the applicability of advance decisions refusing life-sustaining treatment. These are that:[104]

- the decision includes a statement by the maker that it is to apply to the life-sustaining treatment even if his or her life is at risk;
- the decision is in writing; and

---

[100] MCA 2005, s 4(6). See also **5.27**.
[101] MCA 2005, s 25(2).
[102] See *HE v A Hospital NHS Trust* as a good example (a previous Jehovah's witness who had become betrothed to a Muslim and was professing she would live by the principles of that faith).
[103] MCA 2005, s 25(3) and (4).
[104] MCA 2005, s 25(5) and (6).

- it is signed by or under the direction and in the presence of its maker and that signature is made or acknowledged in the presence of a witness who signs or acknowledges his or her signature in the presence of the maker of the decision.

Implications of an advance decision

Effect

5.80 A valid and applicable advance decision has effect as if the maker had made it, and had the capacity to make it, at the time the question arises whether the treatment specified in it should be carried out or continued.

5.81 If the person providing treatment withholds or withdraws the treatment when he or she reasonably believes that an advance decision refusing the treatment exists which is valid and applicable to the treatment, he or she is protected from legal liability in doing so.[105] Conversely, a person does not incur liability for carrying out or continuing treatment unless or until he or she is satisfied that an advance decision exists which is valid and applicable to the treatment.[106]

Doubt or disagreement

5.82 If there is any doubt or disagreement over whether an advance decision exists, is valid or is applicable to a treatment, an application can be made to the Court of Protection for it to make a declaration.[107] In an unreported case in 2009 where P's family claimed that a valid written advanced directive was given to paramedics during air ambulance evacuation and subsequently lost, the court heard oral evidence and made a finding that a valid and applicable advance directive existed refusing the use of blood or blood products in P's treatment. While a decision is being sought, those treating the person concerned are entitled to take nothing in the advance decision as preventing them providing life-sustaining treatment or doing any act they reasonably believe to be necessary to prevent a serious deterioration in that person's condition.[108]

The Code of Practice

5.83 Chapter 9 of the Code of Practice contains valuable guidance and suggestions for best practice in this area. In particular, it suggests that, whilst there is no set form for written advance decisions, it is helpful to include the following information:[109]

---

[105]   MCA 2005, s 26(3).
[106]   MCA 2005, s 26(2).
[107]   MCA 2005, s 26(4).
[108]   MCA 2005, s 26(5).
[109]   Code of Practice, para 9.19.

- full details of its maker, including date of birth, home address and any distinguishing features (so that e g an unconscious person might be identified);
- the name and address of general practitioner and whether they have a copy;
- a statement that the document should be used if the maker lacks capacity to make treatment decisions;
- a clear statement of the decision, the treatment to be refused and the circumstances in which the decision will apply;
- the date the document was written (or reviewed); and
- the person's signature (or that of the person signing in their presence on their behalf) and the signature of a witness (if there is one).

5.84 In addition, if the decision relates to life-sustaining treatment, it must contain a clear statement that the decision is intended to apply even if the treatment in question is necessary to sustain life (and there must be a witness to the signature).

Comment

Striking a balance

5.85 The statutory provisions on advance decisions are designed to strike a balance between, on the one hand, recognition of a competent adult's autonomy and, on the other, the fears expressed during the parliamentary debates on the Bill[110] that a person could be locked into an advance refusal he or she would wish to change but can no longer do so.

The alternative of a lasting power of attorney

5.86 It is a matter of individual choice whether a person wishes to plan in advance for possible future lack of capacity by indicating a refusal of specified treatments. An alternative is to create a lasting power of attorney with the authority for the person chosen as donee to take health care decisions.

Decisions by health care professionals

5.87 In the absence of either an advance decision or a lasting power of attorney, decisions will be taken by the health care professionals in the person's best interests. A written statement which does not amount to an

---

[110]   See e g *Hansard*, HC Deb, vol 425, ser 6, cols 37–102 (11 October 2004); *Hansard*, HC Official Report, SC A (Mental Capacity Bill), 28 October 2004, vol 1, HL Paoer 79-1, HC Paper 95-1; and *Hansard*, HL Deb, vol 668, ser 5, cols 11–26 and 42–106 (10 January 2005), 1396–1432 and 1443–1512 (27 January 2005), vol 670, cols 1276–1324 (15 March 2005) and vol 671, cols 412–459 (24 March 2005).

advance decision will be taken into account,[111] but it will depend on the facts of the case at the time what the overall best interests are.[112] (see **5.27**).

5.88   Those taking treatment decisions when faced with an advance refusal of the treatment will need to take a view on the validity and applicability of the decision. For example, they will need to make an assumption as to the person's capacity at the time the decision was made (to which the statutory presumption of capacity will apply). In most instances there may be no doubt. The formalities around making an advance decision refusing life-sustaining treatment may make it easier to make this assumption in such a case. In some instances, however, where it is thought possible that the advance decision may be challenged in the future and there may be some doubt as to capacity, it may be helpful for the maker to obtain evidence confirming his or her capacity at the time.

5.89   Of greater difficulty may be (as now under the common law) whether the maker of the decision really had in mind the circumstances which have arisen and intended it to apply in those circumstances; or whether relevant circumstances have changed (eg the prospect of a new cure) so as to invalidate the decision. As the Code of Practice states, particular care will need to be taken for advance decisions which do not appear to have been reviewed or updated for some time.[113]

References to the Court of Protection

5.90   There are likely to be some issues and problems in applying these provisions in individual cases which will need to be referred to the Court of Protection. As at the date of publication, however, no reported decisions had been handed down addressing these provisions; it is likely that this an indication less of their complexity and more of the paucity of judgments that are reported.

MEDICAL RESEARCH

Common law position

The regulation of research

5.91   It is beyond the scope of this chapter to delve deeply into the different types of research – for example, therapeutic, non-therapeutic and observational – and the volume of current learning on what is or is not permissible in accordance with modern ethical principles. There is in place a system of Local Research Ethics Committees and Multi-Centre Research Ethics Committees to regulate research carried out in an NHS body. This

---

[111]   MCA 2005, s 4(6).

[112]   Further, as discussed at **5.49**, an example of a case under the existing common law in which the court accepted the evidence of family members that the patient had said she would not want to be kept alive in the circumstances but nonetheless held that her best interests were to reinstate ANH is *W Healthcare NHS Trust v KH and Others* [2005] 1 WLR 834, CA

[113]   Code of Practice, para 9.51.

came into existence to relate to research involving patients who are fully informed and freely give their consent.

General principles

5.92 As a general principle it can be stated that medical research which involves some invasion of bodily integrity on a person who is not able to consent to it is not permissible under the existing common law, as it cannot be justified under the doctrine of necessity. A court might declare therapeutic research lawful if done in that person's best interests, although this has not been tested in court and often the point of research is not to benefit the particular individual but others who might in the future be suffering from a similar condition.

5.93 The closest the common law has come to recognising benefits to others as a factor in the best interests equation arose in the cases in which the taking of samples from one sibling for the potential benefit of another were authorised as benefiting the child, or incapacitated adult, to contribute to the family's welfare in this way.[114] This is not a precedent justifying research. Nor is the decision in *Simms v Simms; A v A (a child)*[115] in which experimental and innovative treatment was authorised to victims of vCJD (Variant Creutzfeldt-Jakob disease), not by way of research, but as medical treatment in their best interests as in the circumstances being the only hope for them in slowing down the decline in their condition.

Clinical Trials Regulations

5.94 Therapeutic research in the form of clinical trials on medicinal products for human use is now authorised and regulated under and in accordance with the Medicines for Human Use (Clinical Trials) Regulations 2004[116] made under the authority given by the European Union Directive on Good Clinical Practice in Clinical Trials.[117] These govern such trials in relation to both those who can provide informed consent and those who cannot, and in the latter case include the additional protections required by the Directive.

5.95 The general principles underlying these Regulations are that:

- the clinical trial must have the approval of the relevant ethics committee and be authorised by the appropriate minister as licensing authority;
- the anticipated therapeutic and public health benefits must justify the risks; and
- informed consent must be given (which must be written, signed and dated) after an interview with a member of the investigating team.

---

[114]   *Re Y (Mental Patient: Bone Marrow Donation)* [1997] Fam 110.
[115]   [2003] Fam 83.
[116]   SI 2004/1031. These Regulations came into force on 1 May 2004.
[117]   Directive 2001/20/EC.

5.96 The involvement of an adult who lacks capacity to consent requires the informed consent of his or her 'legal representative' and is subject to the following additional conditions:

- the research is essential to validate data obtained in clinical trials on persons able to give consent and relates directly to a life-threatening or debilitating clinical condition from which the incapacitated adult suffers; and
- the trial has the potential to produce a benefit to the patient which outweighs the potential risks.

5.97 For the purposes of the Regulations, an incapacitated participant's legal representative is either:

(1) a person close to the patient (a 'personal legal representative'); or, where no one can act in that capacity,

(2) someone such as the doctor responsible for the care of the patient or other person nominated by the health care provider, being someone not involved in the conduct of the trial (a 'professional legal representative').

5.98 The legal representative may withdraw the subject from the trial at any time. If an adult prior to the onset of incapacity has refused to give his or her consent, he or she cannot be included as a subject.

Research authorised by the Mental Capacity Act 2005

Background

5.99 The draft Mental Incapacity Bill presented to Parliament in June 2003 did not contain any provisions on research. The Joint Scrutiny Committee on this Bill, in response to evidence it received from the British Medical Association, the Royal College of Psychiatrists, the British Psychological Society and The Law Society, concluded that if properly regulated research involving people who may lack capacity is not possible then treatment for incapacitating disorders will not be developed. It recommended, therefore, that clauses should be included to enable strictly controlled medical research to explore the causes and consequences of mental incapacity and to develop effective treatment for such conditions. Also that these clauses should set out the key principles governing such research and the protections against exploitation or harm.[118]

5.100 As a result, provisions were included in the Mental Capacity Bill as presented to Parliament, and these were refined through various amendments made during the course of the Bill's consideration. They now form MCA 2005, ss 30–34.[119]

---

[118] See recommendations 81–88, HL Paper 189-1 HC Paper 1083-1 (Session 2002-03).
[119] See Chapter 11 of the Code of Practice for a general explanation of and guide to these provisions.

Application of the Act

5.101   The new provisions apply to any intrusive research carried out on, or in relation to, a person who lacks capacity to consent to it other than a clinical trial subject to the Medicines for Human Use (Clinical Trials) Regulations 2004 (because they already make provision for trials involving participants who lack capacity). They are based upon long-standing international standards such as those laid down by the World Medical Association (originally in the Helsinki Declaration in 1964 and updated since) and in the Council of Europe Convention on Human Rights and Biomedicine.

Pre-condition to authorisation

5.102   The pre-condition to the authorisation of research under these provisions is that a committee established to advise on the ethics of intrusive research in relation to people who lack capacity to consent to it and recognised for this purpose by the Secretary of State for Health (in relation to research in England) or the Welsh Assembly (in relation to Wales) has approved the research project.[120]

5.103   That approval can only be given in relation to a person who lacks capacity to consent if:[121]

- the research is connected with the person's impairing condition or its treatment;
- there are reasonable grounds for believing that research of comparable effectiveness cannot be carried out if the project is confined to persons who can consent;
- the research has the potential to benefit the person without imposing a disproportionate burden or it is intended to provide knowledge of the causes or treatment of, or the care of persons affected by, the same or a similar condition;
- in the case of research which falls only in the latter category, there are reasonable grounds for believing that the risk to the individual in taking part is negligible and anything done to that person will not interfere with his or her freedom of action or privacy in any way or be unduly invasive or restrictive; and
- there are arrangements in place to ensure the particular conditions (referred to below) will be met.

Pre-conditions relating to the individual

5.104   Before a person who lacks capacity to consent can take part in an approved research project, particular conditions relating to his or her participation must be met.

---

[120]   MCA 2005, s 30.
[121]   MCA 2005, s 31.

5.105 These conditions relate first to the requirement for a researcher to consult a carer (someone not professionally interested in the person's welfare) or, if a carer who is prepared to be consulted cannot be identified, a person not connected with the research project whom, in accordance with guidance to be issued by the Secretary of State (or the Welsh Assembly), the researcher has nominated as the person prepared to be consulted (eg a general practitioner or specialist engaged in the person's treatment).[122]

5.106 The regime established here is the equivalent of that provided for under the Clinical Trials Regulations outlined above. It includes provision for the consultee advising that the person concerned would not have wanted to take part, in which event that person is not to be included, or if already taking part, must be withdrawn. It also includes provision relating to treatment being provided as a matter of urgency and carrying on necessary research associated with that treatment.

5.107 Secondly, additional safeguards are provided that:

- nothing may be done in the course of the research to which the person appears to object (except where what is being done is intended to protect the person or reduce his or her pain or discomfort) or would be contrary to any known advance decision of that person or current statement of wishes;
- the person's interests must be assumed to outweigh those of science and society; and
- if the person lacking capacity indicates in any way that he or she wishes to be withdrawn he or she must be withdrawn, as he or she must be if any of the conditions for the approval of the research project cease to be met (although any treatment being given to which the research is associated may continue if there is a significant risk to health if discontinued).[123]

5.108 Regulations may be made (by the Secretary of State or the Welsh Assembly) covering the continuation of a research project in relation to a person who had consented to take part in it before these provisions were brought into force and who loses capacity to consent to continuing to take part in it before the conclusion of the project.[124]

Comment

5.109 These provisions, which have yet to be the subject of any decisions (either reported, or, to the best of the authors' knowledge, unreported), cover the whole range of research activities which would require a person's

---

[122]   MCA 2005, s 32. The Secretary of State and Welsh Ministers have, in accordance with MCA 2005, s 32(3), issued 'Guidance on nominating a consultee for research involving adults who lack capacity to consent' (February 2008).

[123]   MCA 2005, s 33.

[124]   See Mental Capacity Act 2005 (Loss of Capacity During Research Project) (England) Regulations 2007, SI 2007/679 and equivalent Welsh regulations made under MCA 2005, s 34.

consent if that person had capacity, which includes research involving them, their tissue or their data.[125] The provisions steer a careful balance between allowing intrusive procedures when not necessarily of direct benefit to that person and facilitating research into an impairing condition. They are also designed to cater for situations where the research is but one aspect of the clinical or professional care of the person who lacks capacity (which will be governed by the best interests test).

PART I

---

[125] Research on anonymised medical data or tissue may be possible outside the terms of MCA 2005, although subject to controls under the Data Protection Act 1998 or the Human Tissue Act 2004 respectively.

Chapter 6

Deprivation of Liberty Safeguards

BACKGROUND

6.1 With effect from 1 April 2009, the Mental Capacity Act 2005 (MCA 2005) was substantively amended by the Mental Health Act 2007 (MHA 2007) to provide mechanisms for authorising, subject to safeguards, the deprivation of liberty of a person who cannot consent when that is necessary in their best interests for their care or treatment.[1] The Mental Health Act 1983 (MHA 1983), as amended by the MHA 2007 contains its own compulsory powers for the detention, assessment or treatment of patients for their mental disorder. Whilst it is beyond the scope of this book to set out any detailed description or analysis of the mental health legislation, there are some interesting parallels and comparisons with the MCA 2005, particularly in relation to some health care issues discussed in Chapter 5. These set the scene and provide the context for a more detailed explanation of the deprivation of liberty safeguards.

THE MENTAL HEALTH ACT 1983, AS AMENDED BY THE MENTAL HEALTH ACT 2007

Powers of admission, detention and treatment

6.2 The MHA 1983, as amended by the MHA 2007, is principally concerned with the admission of patients to hospital for assessment and treatment for their mental disorder. However, MHA 2007 extended powers of compulsion by introducing compulsory community treatment orders (also referred to as supervised community treatment) for patients previously detained in hospital who are now living in the community, but who continue to need treatment for their mental disorder. Mental disorder is defined as any disorder or disability of the mind (MHA 1983, s 1(2), as amended by MHA 2007). MHA 1983 enables compulsory powers of detention and treatment to be used when the statutory conditions for 'sectioning' the patient are met. In the case of admission for assessment, the patient must be suffering from mental disorder of a nature or degree which warrants the detention of the patient in a hospital for assessment, and:[2]

> '... he ought to be so detained in the interests of his own health or safety or with a view to the protection of other persons.'

---

[1] Prior to that date under the MCA 2005 as originally enacted a person acting in connection with the care or treatment in the best interests of an incapacitated person could restrain that person if it was to prevent harm to that person and was a proportionate response but could not deprive them of their liberty (ss 5 and 6 – see Chapter 2). The Court of Protection could make a welfare order which had the effect of depriving the person concerned of their liberty putting in place as many safeguards as are practicable, including provision for review (see *Re PS (Incapacitated or Vulnerable Adult)* [2007] EWHC 623 (Fam), [2007] 2 FLR 1083 and *Salford City Council v GJ, NJ and BJ (by their litigation friends)* [2008] EWHC 1097 (Fam), [2008] 2 FLR 1295).

[2] MHA 1983, s 2(2).

6.3 In the case of admission for treatment, the grounds need to be established that:[3]

'(a) he is suffering from mental disorder of a nature or degree which makes it appropriate for him to receive medical treatment in a hospital; and

...

(c) it is necessary for the health or safety of the patient or for the protection of other persons that he should receive such treatment and it cannot be provided unless he is detained under this section; and

(d) appropriate medical treatment is available for him.'

6.4 The relevant criteria for community treatment orders are that:[4]

'(a) the patient is suffering from mental disorder of a nature or degree which makes it appropriate for him to receive medical treatment;

(b) it is necessary for his health or safety or for the protection of other persons that he should receive such treatment;

(c) subject to his being liable to be recalled as mentioned in paragraph (d) below, such treatment can be provided without his continuing to be detained in a hospital;

(d) it is necessary that the responsible clinician should be able to exercise the power ... to recall the patient to hospital; and

(e) appropriate medical treatment is available for him.'

6.5 MHA 1983 sets out the conditions and procedures for use of these powers. These include that the application for admission (either for assessment or treatment) must be made on the recommendation in the prescribed form of two registered medical practitioners. The Act also provides for patients to be received into guardianship, giving the appointed guardian (usually a local authority) the power to require a patient in the community to reside at a specified place and attend for treatment. The 2007 Act broadened the powers of the guardian by introducing a new power to take and convey a person subject to guardianship to their required place of residence (MHA 2007, Sch 3, para 3(5)).

Review and appeals

6.6 MHA 1983 then provides the procedures for review and appeals to the Health, Education and Social Care Chamber of the First-tier Tribunal (prior to 3 November 2008 the independent mental health review tribunals (MHRT)) in relation to the use, or continued use, of the compulsory powers.[5] The MHRT for Wales remains as a separate devolved tribunal. There is a right of appeal on a point of law from both tribunals to the Upper Tribunal.

---

3   MHA 1983, s 3(2), as amended by MHA 2007.
4   MHA 1983, s 17A(5), as amended by MHA 2007.
5   Tribunals, Courts and Enforcement Act 2007, Part 1.

Purpose

6.7 The purpose of MHA 1983 is to provide the statutory framework for the compulsory care and treatment of people for their mental disorder when they are unable or unwilling to consent to that care and treatment, and when it is necessary for that care and treatment to be given to protect themselves or others from harm.

6.8 The key point for the exercise of these powers is the inability or unwillingness of the patient who suffers from a mental disorder to consent. This encompasses people who, notwithstanding their mental disorder, have capacity to do so – and we have already seen from cases such as *Re C (Adult: Refusal of Treatment)*[6] how it is possible for someone detained under MHA 1983 to have capacity in relation to a treatment decision. Inability to consent will also include people who do not have capacity, but the question whether an individual patient has or does not have decision-making capacity is not the key determinant of whether the powers conferred by MHA 1983 should be used.

COMPARISONS

6.9 The Mental Capacity Act 2005 (MCA 2005) is based wholly on a capacity test. Its provisions have no application to people who have the capacity to make their own decisions. Some, who lack capacity, will not come within the definition of those for whom compulsory powers under MHA 1983 can be exercised. People with learning difficulties, for example, who may thereby not be able to give their consent to treatment, will not generally be subject to the compulsory powers of MHA 1983, unless they are also abnormally aggressive or seriously irresponsible. Other examples are people in a persistent vegetative state or anyone suffering from 'locked-in' syndrome, which prevents them from communicating, persons with brain injuries or temporarily unconscious, drunk or under the influence of drugs.

Differences

6.10 It can be seen that the differences between these two approaches are that:

    (1) MCA 2005 relates to a person's functioning – incapacity to make a particular decision – whereas MHA 1983 relates to a person's status, as someone diagnosed as having a mental disorder within the meaning of the Act and subject to its powers;

    (2) MCA 2005 covers all decision-making, whereas MHA 1983 is, to a very large degree, limited to decisions about care in hospital and medical treatment for mental disorder;

---

[6]   [1994] 1 WLR 290; see **5.10–5.11**.

PART I

(3) MHA 1983 authorises detention, but this was specifically excluded under MCA 2005 as originally enacted;[7] and

(4) MCA 2005 specifically excludes[8] anyone giving a patient medical treatment for mental disorder, or consenting to a patient being given medical treatment for mental disorder, if the patient is, at the relevant time, already detained and subject to the compulsory treatment provisions of MHA 1983, Part 4.

Overlaps

6.11 There are areas of overlap. For example:

(1) people who are detained in hospital under MHA 1983 and who also lack capacity to make financial decisions may be subject to the provisions of MCA 2005; and, equally,

(2) an elderly person, for example, with Alzheimer's disease, whose day-to-day life is managed in accordance with the provisions of MCA 2005, may be made subject to MHA 1983 if it is no longer possible to care for such a person at home and he or she requires treatment for the mental disorder and is resisting being admitted to hospital.

THE DEPRIVATION OF LIBERTY SAFEGUARDS

The 'Bournewood Gap'

6.12 The great majority of people with a mental disorder are not treated under the MHA 1983. That Act specifically provides that nothing in that Act is to be treated as preventing the informal admission of a patient requiring treatment for mental disorder to any hospital or registered establishment.[9] Moreover, there are those people being treated or living in hospitals or care homes who suffer from a mental disorder but are not there to be treated for their mental disorder and are not within scope of the MHA 1983. They may not have resisted nor objected to their admission nor to their continued stay in the hospital or care home. This does not give rise to any issue of particular concern when they have capacity and it is their choice. However, it can be seen that questions can arise as to how such patients should be dealt with who may be compliant but who do not have the capacity to reach their own decisions about what is happening to them. This is particularly the case so far as they are deprived of their liberty.[10] That there were no safeguards in

---

7   See MCA 2005, s 6, which provides the conditions under which a person may 'restrain' a person whilst remaining within the protection given by s 5, but this protection is not available if there is a deprivation of liberty. However, new provisions inserted into MCA 2005 by MHA 2007 (implemented on 1 April 2009) allow deprivation of liberty in specific circumstances – see **6.17**ff.

8   See MCA 2005, s 28

9   MHA 1983, s 131.

10   This is not a new problem. The Mental Health Act Commission, established in 1983 to keep under review the care and treatment of patients detained under MHA 1983, identified in its *First Biennial Report (1983–1985)* (HMSO, 1985) the lack of safeguards for 'de facto' detained patients.

relation to the deprivation of their liberty was characterised as 'the Bournewood gap'. The 'Bournewood gap' takes its name from, and achieved prominence as a result of, the decision of the European Court of Human Rights in *HL v UK*.[11]

The decisions of the domestic courts

6.13 Mr HL, an autistic man, was readmitted to the Bournewood Hospital after a period in the community with paid carers, but the decision was taken not to section him under MHA 1983 as he had not resisted admission. The ensuing dispute between the carers and the hospital over his care and treatment was first litigated in judicial review proceedings in the domestic courts. The carers lost at first instance and ultimately in the House of Lords, in the latter case basically on the ground that the circumstances were covered by the common law doctrine of necessity. This reversed the decision of the Court of Appeal, which had upheld their claim that Mr HL had been unlawfully detained.[12]

European Court of Human Rights

6.14 The case was then taken to the European Court of Human Rights. The unanimous decision was:

(1) Mr HL had been deprived of his liberty contrary to Art 5(1) of the European Convention on Human Rights (ECHR);

(2) that detention was arbitrary and not in accordance with a procedure prescribed by law; and

(3) the procedures available to Mr HL did not comply with the requirements of Art 5(4) as there was no procedure under which he could seek a merits review of whether the conditions for his detention remained applicable.

6.15 The specific criticisms the European Court made, and the contrast it drew between the safeguards available to a person detained under MHA 1983 and an informal patient in Mr HL's position, related to the lack of any formal procedures as to:

- who could authorise an admission;
- the reasons needing to be given for that admission (whether it was for treatment or assessment);
- the need for continuing clinical assessment and review; and
- who could represent the patient and be able to seek a review in an independent tribunal as to the lawfulness of the continued detention.

---

[11] Application no 45508/99, judgment on the merits given on 5 October 2004 [2004] 1 FLR 1019.

[12] *R v Bournewood Community and Mental Health NHS Trust ex parte L* [1999] AC 458, HL; [1998] 2 WLR 764, CA.

6.16 The discussion in the court related to the position under the inherent jurisdiction as it was at the time these events occurred (1997). The enactment of MCA 2005 in some respects, notably the creation of the Independent Mental Capacity Advocacy Service, dealt with some of the points raised. However, the decision in the case came too late for the Government to deal with it fully in MCA 2005 as enacted and it was recognised that it did not fill the gap. Following a period of consultation, the Government brought forward a new scheme enacted in the MHA 2007, amending MCA 2005 so that it can be lawful to deprive a compliant patient of their liberty other than through activating the Mental Health Act powers if the conditions of the scheme are met.

THE MCA SOLUTION

6.17 MHA 2007, s 50 and Schs 7 and 8 amended MCA 2005 and render it lawful to deprive a person of their liberty either if it is a consequence of giving effect to an order of the Court of Protection on a personal welfare matter or, if the deprivation of liberty is in a hospital or care home, if a standard or urgent authorisation (under the provisions of MCA 2005, Sch A1) is in force.[13] The Court of Appeal confirmed in *G v E*[14] that the scheme enacted by these amendments is both compliant with Article 5(1) ECHR and plugs the 'Bournewood Gap.'

Meaning of deprivation of liberty

6.18 For the purposes of these provisions deprivation of liberty is defined as having the same meaning as in Art 5(1) of the ECHR.[15] As established both in the ECHR judgment in *HL v UK* and in the High Court in *JE v DE, Surrey CC and EW*,[16] the difference between restricting a person and depriving them of their liberty is one of degree or intensity rather than of nature or substance and in order to determine whether there is a deprivation of liberty there must be an assessment of the specific factors in each case, such as the type, duration, effects and manner of implementation of the measure in question and its impact on the person. Guidance on identifying deprivation of liberty, and on all other aspects of operating these provisions, is included in a supplement to the Code of Practice issued under MCA 2005,[17] although this guidance must be read subject to the subsequent decisions of the courts, not all of which is entirely consistent.

---

[13] The amendments came into force on 1 April 2009 (The Mental Health Act 2007 (Commencement No 10 and Transitional Provisions) Order 2009, SI 2009/139.
[14] [2010] EWCA Civ 822.
[15] The leading ECHR cases relating to deprivation of liberty are *Guzzardi v Italy* (1980) 3 EHRR 333; *Ashingdale v UK* (1985) 7 EHRR 528; *Nielson v Denmark* (1988) 11 EHRR 175; *HM v Switzerland* (2002) 38 EHRR 314; *HL v UK* (2004) 40 EHRR 761; and *Storck v Germany* (2005) 43 EHRR 96.
[16] [2006] EWHC 3459 (Fam).
[17] Ministry of Justice 'Mental Capacity Act: Deprivation of Liberty Safeguards – Code of Practice to supplement the main Mental Capacity Act 2005 Code of Practice' (TSO, 2008). The Deprivation of Liberty Code is also available online at www.dh.gov.uk/en/Publicationsandstatistics/Publications/PublicationsPolicyAndGuidance/DH_085476.

6.19   Particular factors identified by the European Court in *HL v UK* which contributed to a deprivation of liberty were:

- restraint was used, including sedation, to admit a person who was resisting;
- staff exercised complete and effective control over care and movement for a significant period;
- staff exercised control over assessments, treatment, contacts and residence;
- a decision had been taken that the person would be prevented from leaving if they made a meaningful attempt to do so;
- a request by carers for the person to be discharged to their care was refused;
- the person was unable to maintain social contacts because of restrictions placed on access by other people; and
- the person lost autonomy because they were under continuous supervision and control.

6.20   As the person in question is incapable of giving valid consent, logically this would suggest that 'consent' should not be a consideration. However, in the ECHR case of *HM v Switzerland*[18] the fact that HM ultimately did not object to her placement in the nursing home was regarded as relevant to the court's view that her situation was not of a degree or intensity to justify the conclusion she had been deprived of her liberty. In *Storck v Germany*[19] the court concluded that the applicant's behaviour in trying to leave the clinic (as a result of which she was on one occasion chained to a radiator and on another returned by the police) was inconsistent with any valid consent. In *JE v DE and Surrey CC*[20] the Court found that Surrey County Council was exercising complete and effective control over where DE could live, whether he could leave the home permanently and whether he could be with his wife, JE. These objective factors allied with the subjective that DE had not validly consented to the confinement in question constituted deprivation of liberty.

6.21   In *JE v DE and Surrey CC*[21] Munby J identified that that there were three elements necessary for there to be a deprivation of liberty falling within the scope of Art 5(1): an objective element of a person's confinement in a particular restricted space for a not negligible length of time; a subjective element, namely that the person has not validly consented to the confinement in question; and that the deprivation of liberty must be imputable to the State. This decision pre-dated the coming into force of the MCA 2005, but subsequent decisions have followed the same course in identifying these three elements.[22] They have also made it clear that the State owes obligations in respect of persons deprived of their liberty even

---

[18]   Note 17 above.
[19]   Ibid.
[20]   [2006] EWHC 3459 (Fam).
[21]   [2006] EWHC 3459 (Fam).
[22]   See, for instance, *G v E and others* [2010] EWHC 621 (Fam) at para [77]. For case summary, see Part IX of this work.

where it is not, itself, responsible for depriving them of their liberty: in *Re A (child) and Re C (adult)*,[23] Munby LJ (as he had then become) held that the State owes positive obligations under Article 5 to protect individuals from arbitrary interferences with their right to liberty, whether by state agents or by private individuals. He therefore held that local authorities must therefore take reasonable steps to prevent (or seek court authorisation for) a deprivation of liberty which they are aware of, or which they ought to be aware of.[24]

6.22 Not all restrictions on a person's liberty will constitute a deprivation of liberty. In particular, in assessing whether in their degree and intensity they cross the threshold there is some divergence of opinion in the existing case-law whether the purpose or benefits of the restrictions should be taken into account. Munby J in *JE v DE and Surrey County Council*[25] suggested it was an error to confuse the question of deprivation of liberty with whether it had been justified in the person's best interests, holding that the fundamental issue in that case was whether DE was free to leave the care home in the sense of being able to remove himself permanently to live where and with whom he chose. However, in Re MIG and MEG,[26] Parker J, whilst accepting that 'purpose' was not relevant, simultaneously accepted that it was relevant to consider the reason why the person in question was deprived of their liberty, applying in the process the decision in *Austin v Metropolitan Police Commissioner*,[27] in which the House of Lords held that crowd control measures adopted by the police would fall outside the application of Art 5 if they were resorted to in good faith, were proportionate and were enforced for no longer than was reasonably necessary. In Re A and Re C,[28] Munby LJ associated himself expressly with the conclusions of Parker J,[29] and appeared to draw back somewhat from the position set out in *JE v DE*.[30] It is not immediately obvious how one is to differentiate between the purpose for depriving a person of their liberty and the reason why this is the case, and it is submitted that very particular caution should be exercised before attributing more than very limited weight to any matters that might be seen as going to the justification for the deprivation of liberty in determining whether the circumstances amount to a deprivation of liberty.

6.23 The Code of Practice on the Deprivation of Liberty Safeguards provides a summary of some of the most relevant cases decided at the point of its drafting.[31] Based on the issues raised in those cases, the Code suggests

---

[23]   [2010] EWHC 978 (Fam).
[24]   Ibid paragraph 95.
[25]   Ibid.
[26]   [2010] EWHC 785 (Fam). This decision was appealed by the Official Solicitor to the Court of Appeal, whose judgment remains outstanding as at the date of publication. For case summary, see Part IX of this work.
[27]   [2009] UKHL 5, [2009] AC 564.
[28]   Above, footnote 22.
[29]   Paragraph 126.
[30]   Above, footnote 22.
[31]   Paragraphs 2.17–2.24.

a list of factors that should, in general, be considered by the decision-maker in considering whether or not deprivation of liberty is occurring.[32]

- All the circumstances of each and every case.
- What measures are being taken in relation to the individual? When are they required? For what period do they endure? What are the effects of any restraints or restrictions on the individual? Why are they necessary? What aim do they seek to meet?
- What are the views of the relevant person, their family or carers? Do any of them object to the measures?
- How are any restraints or restrictions implemented? Do any of the constraints on the individual's personal freedom go beyond 'restraint' or 'restriction' to the extent that they constitute a deprivation of liberty?
- Are there any less restrictive options for delivering care or treatment that avoid deprivation of liberty altogether?
- Does the cumulative effect of all the restrictions imposed on the person amount to a deprivation of liberty, even if individually they would not?[33]

6.24 Whilst the checklist of factors set out above remains entirely valid, it must be read subject to the increasing body of jurisprudence in this area. From this jurisprudence, and without alleviation the obligation to consider the specific facts of each case, it is possible to identify certain categories of case as more likely to fall on one side of the line than the other. On the cases decided as at the time of writing, the following circumstances **may** give rise to a situation where no deprivation of liberty would be found for purposes of Art 5(1) ECHR:

- Where a person suffering from a severe learning disability, incapable of independent living, is placed with a foster family in a domestic environment which they regard as home; where they are not restrained or locked in any way; where continuous control and supervision is exercised to meet their care needs and ensure their safety (and would have been exercised even at home); and where the relevant family members are supportive of the placement;[34]
- Where a person suffering from a learning disability and behavioural problems lives at home but is locked in their bedroom at night to prevent them from wandering around the house and injuring themselves, and where this causes them no concern;[35]
- Where a 16 or 17 year old is placed in a care home or in foster care under a s 20 Children Act 1989 agreement between the relevant

[32] Paragraph 2.6.
[33] In guidance issued by the Care Quality Commission in October 2010.
[34] Taken from the facts of MIG's case in *Re MIG and MEG*. It is submitted that the facts relating to MEG are so specific as not safely to allow any generalisation.
[35] *Re A (child) and Re C (adult)* [2010] EWHC 978 (Fam).

local authority and the parents, where the parents retain the right under s 20(8) to remove the child at any time from the accommodation.[36]

Court of Protection powers

6.25   Under MCA 2005, s 4A (inserted by MHA 2007, s 50) the Court of Protection has the power by making an order under MCA 2005, s16(2)(a) to make the decision for an incapacitated person which has the effect of depriving them of their liberty. It cannot, however, do so if the patient is ineligible to be deprived of their liberty under that Act as amended by MHA 2007 because they are or should be detained under the Mental Health Act powers.[37] A person may lawfully deprive someone of their liberty whilst a decision is sought from the Court if there is a question about whether that person may be lawfully deprived of their liberty and the deprivation is necessary to enable life-sustaining treatment to be given or any treatment believed necessary to prevent a serious deterioration in their condition.[38]

Deprivation of liberty in a hospital or care home

6.26   The managing authority of a hospital or care home is able lawfully to deprive a patient or resident of their liberty if they are detained for the purpose of being given care or treatment and a standard or urgent authorisation is in force which relates to the relevant person and to the hospital or care home in which they are detained. In this event the managing authority is put in the same position as if the resident had capacity to consent and had consented to their detention (no liability is incurred for the deprivation of liberty but there is no protection for any negligence).[39] The authorisation also extends to cover (1) any deprivation of liberty that occurs during transport of P to and from contact sessions;[40] and (2) the ability of the managing authority to return P to the establishment at which he resides upon any outing from there.[41] It is suggested that it cannot cover any deprivation of liberty which may occur during the course of P's initial journey to the hospital or care home mentioned in the authorisation (and hence a separate authorisation from the Court will be required[42]). The authorisation under these procedures does not extend to the treatment to which the patient cannot consent, to which MCA 2005, s 5 will continue to apply.

---

[36]   *YB v BCC & Ors* [2010] EWHC 3355 (COP)(Fam), per Mostyn J.

[37]   MCA 2005, s 16A, as inserted by MHA 2007, s 50(3); and see *W PCT v TB (an adult by her litigation friend the Official Solicitor)* [2009] EWHC 1737 (Fam) and *GJ v The Foundation Trust* [2009] EWHC 2972 (Fam) (for case summary, see Part IX of this work).

[38]   MCA 2005, s 4B, as inserted by MHA 2007, s 50(2).

[39]   MCA 2005, Sch A1, Part 1, inserted by MHA 2007, Sch 7.

[40]   *DCC v KH* (2009) CoP Case No 11729380.

[41]   Unreported decision of Mostyn J of June 2010 brought to the author's attention by the Official Solicitor's office.

[42]   See paragraph 2.15 of the Deprivation of Liberty Safeguards Code of Practice, although it is not the author's experience that deprivations of liberty in the initial transport is necessarily as exceptional as the Code of Practice envisages.

6.27 The authorisation procedure usually begins with a request by the managing authority (generally the managers of a hospital or care home where the person is, or may be, deprived of their liberty) to the supervisory body (see **6.32**). Before a standard authorisation can be obtained, the supervisory body arranges for assessments to be carried out to determine whether the following requirements are met in relation to the detained resident.[43]

The age requirement

6.28 The person must be 18 or over.

The mental health requirement

6.29 The person must be suffering from a mental disorder within the meaning of MHA 1983, as amended (which includes for these purposes a learning disability whether or not associated with abnormally aggressive or seriously irresponsible conduct).

The mental capacity requirement

6.30 The person must lack capacity in relation to the question whether or not they should be accommodated in the hospital or care home for the purpose of being given the care or treatment concerned. This must be in accordance with MCA 2005, ss 1–3.

The best interests requirement

6.31 It must be in the person's best interests to be a detained resident and the deprivation of liberty must be necessary to prevent harm and be a proportionate response to the likelihood and seriousness of that harm.

The eligibility requirement

6.32 A person is ineligible if already subject to MHA 1983 through being:

- detained in hospital under MHA 1983 powers or meeting the criteria for detention and objecting to being detained in the hospital or to some or all of the treatment (ie in those circumstances MHA 1983 powers should be used if the person is to be detained);[44]
- on leave of absence or subject to guardianship, a community treatment regime or conditional discharge and subject to a measure which would be inconsistent with an authorisation if granted; or

---

[43] MCA 2005, Sch A1, Part 3.

[44] This was considered by Roderick Wood J in *W PCT v TB (an adult by her litigation friend the Official Solicitor)* [2009] EWHC 1737 (Fam) and by Charles J in *GJ v The Foundation Trust* [2009] EWHC 2972 (Fam).

- on leave of absence or subject to a community treatment regime or conditional discharge and the authorisation if granted would be for deprivation of liberty in a hospital for the purpose of treatment for mental disorder.[45]

The no refusals requirement

6.33 There must not be a valid and effective advance decision by the detained resident refusing the treatment in question, nor a valid refusal of the proposed care or treatment by a deputy or donee of a lasting power of attorney (LPA) within the scope of their authority.

STANDARD AUTHORISATIONS

6.34 A standard authorisation is an authorisation given by the supervisory body after it has been requested to do so and once the procedure set out below has been followed.[46] The supervisory body is:

- in the case of a care home, the local authority where the person is ordinarily resident or where the care home is situated; or
- in the case of a hospital, the primary care trust in England which commissions the care or in Wales, the National Assembly of Wales or the local health board if the care is commissioned by it.

6.35 The managing authority must request a standard authorisation if it is accommodating a detained resident who appears to meet all the qualifying requirements or is likely to do so within the next 28 days or if it will be so accommodating or detaining the person up to 28 days in advance of its doing so. The relevant managing authority must also make a request if there is, or is to be, a change in the place of detention.

6.36 An authorisation cannot be given unless assessments have been commissioned by the supervisory body which conclude that all the qualifying requirements are met. Regulations[47] specify who can carry out assessments, covering the need for more than one assessor, the professional skills, training and competence required and independence from decisions about providing or commissioning care to the person concerned and the timeframe within which the assessments must be completed. The mental health and best interests assessments must be carried out by different assessors. It is the responsibility of the supervisory body to appoint eligible and suitable assessors. Anyone carrying out assessments (other than the age assessment) must have undergone specific training.

---

45   The details of 'Persons ineligible' are set out in MCA 2005, Sch 1A, as inserted by MHA 2007, Sch 8.

46   See generally MCA 2005, Sch A1, Part 4. Provisions relating to the suspension of a standard authorisation are in Part 6, a change in supervisory responsibility in Part 7, review in Part 8 and generally relating to assessments in Part 9. Part 10 provides for the relevant person's representative and Part 11 for the role of independent mental capacity advocates.

47   The Mental Capacity (Deprivation of Liberty: Standard Authorisations, Assessments and Ordinary Residence) Regulations 2008, SI 2008/1858, as amended by SI 2009/827.

6.37   The best interests assessor must first decide whether a deprivation of liberty is occurring or is likely to occur. The assessment must take account of any relevant needs assessment or care plan, and of the opinion of the mental health assessor on the impact of the proposed course of action on the person's mental health. The assessor must consult the managing authority and take into account the views of anyone named by the person, anyone engaged in caring for the person or interested in their welfare, any donee of a LPA granted by the person or deputy appointed by the Court. If the person does not have anyone to speak for them who is not paid to provide care an independent mental capacity advocate (IMCA) must be appointed to support and represent them during the assessment process.

6.38   The best interests assessor is required to record the name and address of every interested person consulted (as they will be entitled to information about the outcome). If that assessor concludes that deprivation of liberty is not in the person's best interests but becomes aware that they are already being deprived of their liberty, the assessor must draw this to the attention of the supervisory body. If the assessment recommends authorisation the assessor must state the maximum authorisation period, which may not be for more than a year,[48] and may recommend conditions to be attached to the authorisation. The best interests assessor must also identify someone to recommend for appointment as representative of the person being deprived of their liberty.

6.39   If existing equivalent assessments have been carried out within the past year they may be used if the supervisory body is satisfied there is no reason that they may no longer be accurate. If any of the assessments conclude that the person does not meet the criteria the supervisory body must turn down the request for authorisation and inform all persons with an interest. If all the assessments recommend it, the supervisory body must give the authorisation and:

- set the period of the authorisation, which may not be longer than the maximum period identified in the best interests assessment;
- issue the authorisation in writing, stating the period for which it is valid, the purpose for which it is given and the reason why each qualifying requirement is met;
- if appropriate, attach conditions;
- appoint someone to act as the person's representative during the term of the authorisation;
- provide a copy of the authorisation to the managing authority, the person being deprived of their liberty and their representative, any IMCA who has been involved and any other interested person

---

[48]   The period starting either at the exact time on the day when it was granted or on any later time specified in the document giving the authorisation: *Re MB* [2010] EWHC 2508 (COP) at paragraph 45 (for case summary, see Part IX of this work). The maximum period that can be included in the authorisation should be calculated by including the whole of the day on which the authorisation is given (or expressed to start) and on the basis that it ends at the end of the last day: paragraph 47.

consulted by the best interests assessor (in due course notifying them when the authorisation ceases to be in force); and
- keep written records.

6.40 If an authorisation is granted the supervisory body must appoint a person to be the detained resident's representative,[49] this being someone who the supervisory body considers will maintain contact with the resident and support and represent them in relation to the authorisation, including requesting review or appealing to the Court of Protection on their behalf. The representative has a right of access to the Court (any person other than the detained resident would require the permission of the Court to bring a case). The managing authority in acting on the authorisation must:

- ensure that any conditions are complied with;
- take all practicable steps to ensure that the detained resident understands the effect of the authorisation, their right of appeal to the Court of Protection and their right to request a review;
- give the same information to the person's representative; and
- keep the person's case under consideration and request a review if necessary.

6.41 The supervisory body may review a standard authorisation at any time and must do so if requested by the detained resident, their representative or the managing authority. The managing authority must request a review if it appears that there has been a change in the person's circumstances. The relevant person or their representative may make a request at any time. The supervisory body must decide whether any of the qualifying requirements appear to be reviewable and, if so, commission review assessments. A review may lead to the authorisation being terminated, a change in the recorded reasons or a change in the conditions attached to the authorisation. When the review is complete the supervisory body must inform the managing authority, the relevant person and their representative of the outcome.

6.42 A managing authority may apply for a further authorisation to begin when an authorisation expires. In this event, the full assessment process is repeated.

Urgent authorisations

6.43 Urgent authorisations[50] may be given by the managing authority of a care home or hospital to provide a lawful basis for a deprivation of liberty whilst a standard authorisation is being obtained when it is urgently required and the qualifying requirements appear to be met. The managing authority must record the urgent authorisation in writing, giving its reasons for giving the authorisation. The managing authority is to take all practicable steps

---

49   See the Mental Capacity (Deprivation of Liberty: Appointment of Relevant Person's Representative Regulations 2008 (SI 2008/1315), as amended by SI 2008/2368.
50   MCA 2005, Sch A1, Part 5.

(verbally and in writing) to ensure the person understands the effect of the authorisation and their right of appeal to the Court of Protection and to notify any IMCA who has been involved.

6.44   An urgent authorisation takes effect at the exact time that it was given on a particular day.[51] It can only last for a maximum of 7 days,[52] unless extended for up to a further 7 days by the supervisory body if there are exceptional reasons why it has not been possible to decide on a request for standard authorisation and it is essential that the detention continues. Absent such exceptional circumstances, an urgent authorisation can only be extended by a standard authorisation or a court order. In any event, it is only possible for one urgent authorisation to be given in respect of any one period of deprivation of liberty.[53]

The Standard Authorisations, Assessments and Ordinary Residence Regulations

6.45   The Mental Capacity (Deprivation of Liberty: Standard Authorisations, Assessments and Ordinary Residence) Regulations 2008[54] fill out the detail of obtaining standard authorisations and who the assessors are to be.

6.46   The eligibility requirements for people who are to carry out the assessments are that:

- all assessors are adequately insured[55] and the supervisory body (primary care trust or local authority) is satisfied that they have suitable skills and have undergone a Criminal Record Bureau check (reg 3);
- mental health assessments can only be carried out by medical practitioners who have been approved under MHA 1983, s 12[56] or are registered medical practitioners who have at least 3 years'

---

[51]   *Re MB* (above, footnote 48), at paragraph 35.
[52]   Calculated by including the whole of the day upon which the authorisation was granted. The maximum period for which the authorisation can run extends to the end of the relevant day upon which the authorisation expires: *Re MB* at paragraphs 43. The same goes for the calculation of any extended period: paragraph 41.
[53]   Ibid at paragraphs 59–77, construing paragraph 77 of Sch A1. Charles J also indicated that, where the best interests assessor upon an application for a standard authorisation following an urgent authorisation reaches the view that the best interests requirement was no longer met, it could in some circumstances nonetheless still be in the person's best interests for them to be subject to a short further period of deprivation of liberty pending changes to arrangements and/or the assistance of the Court. Such a period could only be authorised by the grant of a standard authorisation, rather than the grant of a second urgent authorisation.
[54]   SI 2008/1858, as amended by SI 2009/827.
[55]   This has been amended by SI 2009/827 to include assessors covered by an indemnity arrangement.
[56]   Medical practitioners eligible to recommend the admission of a patient to hospital under MHA 1983.

post-registration experience in the diagnosis or treatment of mental disorder and have completed the relevant training[57] (reg 4);

- best interests assessments can only be carried out by mental health practitioners approved under MHA 1983, s 114(1)[58] or certain health practitioners (nurses, occupational therapists or psychologists) with the relevant skills and specialism, or social workers, all of whom must have had at least 2 years' post-registration experience, and have completed the required training (reg 5);
- mental capacity assessments can only be carried out by people who are eligible to carry out a mental health or best interests assessment (reg 6);
- eligibility assessments can only be carried out by medical practitioners approved under MHA 1983, s 12 and eligible to carry out a mental health assessment or an approved mental health professional eligible to carry out a best interests assessment (reg 7); and
- age assessments and no refusals assessments can only be carried out by people who are eligible to carry out a best interests assessment (regs 8 and 9).

6.47 The Regulations provide some limitations on who a supervisory body may select as assessors (even if otherwise eligible) by preventing the selection of:

- a person who is a relative of the relevant person or a person or relative of someone who has a financial interest in that person's care (regs 10 and 11); and
- a person to carry out a best interests assessment who is involved in the care of the person to be assessed or who is employed by the supervisory body where the managing authority and supervisory body are the same (reg 12).

6.48 All assessments for a standard authorisation are to be completed within 21 days or where an urgent authorisation is in force during the period of that authorisation (reg 13) and assessments to decide whether or not there is an unauthorised deprivation of liberty within 7 days (reg 14). When the eligibility and best interests assessors are not the same person the former may require the latter to provide any relevant information as to eligibility they have (reg 15).

6.49 Regulation 16 specifies the information to be provided in a request for a standard authorisation (the text of this regulation is reproduced in Part IV of this book). The Regulations also provide the mechanism for resolving a dispute over which local authority is the supervisory body where there is a

---

[57] A Mental Health Assessors training programme made available by the Royal College of Psychiatrists.

[58] Approved mental health professionals appointed under MHA 1983 by a local social services authority.

question as to the relevant person's ordinary residence (the supervisory body in the case of a care home being the local authority in which the person is ordinarily resident[59]).

The Appointment of Relevant Person's Representative Regulations

6.50 MCA 2005, Sch A1, para 139 requires that the supervisory body appoints a representative, selected for that purpose, to represent a person in respect of whom a standard authorisation has been issued. That representative is to maintain contact and to support and represent the person in matters relating to their deprivation of liberty. The Mental Capacity (Deprivation of Liberty: Appointment of Relevant Person's Representative) Regulations 2008[60] provide for the selection and appointment of representatives by:

- detailing the eligibility requirements for appointment as a representative (reg 3[61]);
- enabling the best interests assessor to determine whether the relevant person has capacity to select a person to be their representative (reg 4);
- enabling the relevant person to select a family member, friend or carer to be their representative where they have capacity to make that decision (reg 5);
- enabling a donee of a LPA (granting welfare powers) or a deputy appointed by the Court of Protection to select themselves or a family member, friend or carer to be the representative where the scope of their authority permits it (reg 6);
- requiring the best interests assessor to confirm the eligibility of the person selected by the relevant person or donee or deputy, and if so to recommend that appointment but if not to invite a further selection (reg 7);
- where no selection has been made by the relevant person, donee or deputy, enabling the best interests assessor to select a relevant person's family member, friend or carer (reg 8);
- enabling the supervisory body to select and pay for a person in a professional capacity to be a representative (regs 9 and 15); and
- requiring that the process of appointing a representative begins as soon as a best interests assessor is selected upon a request for a standard authorisation or as soon as an existing representative's appointment is about to terminate (reg 10).

6.51 The formalities of appointment and termination of appointment of a representative are detailed in regs 12–14.[62]

---

[59] MCA 2005, Sch A1, para 182(2).
[60] SI 2008/1315, as amended by SI 2008/2368.
[61] Text reproduced in Part IV of this book.
[62] Text reproduced in Part IV of this book.

REVIEW BY THE COURT OF PROTECTION

6.52 A person who has been deprived of their liberty or their representative may apply to the Court of Protection for a review of the lawfulness of their detention.[63] Where a standard authorisation has been given, the Court of Protection may determine any question relating to:

(1) whether the person meets any of the qualifying requirements;

(2) the period for which the standard authorisation is to be in force;

(3) the purpose for which it has been given; or

(4) the conditions subject to which it has been given,

and may make an order terminating or varying the authorisation, or requiring the supervisory body to do so.

6.53 Where an urgent authorisation has been given, the Court may determine:

(1) whether the urgent authorisation should have been given;

(2) the period during which the urgent authorisation is to be in force; or

(3) the purpose for which it is given,

and may make an order terminating or varying the authorisation, or requiring the managing authority to do so.

6.54 When making orders under MCA 2005, s 21A, the Court may also consider a person's liability for any act done in connection with the standard or urgent authorisation before its variation or termination, including making an order excluding a person from liability.

MONITORING

6.55 The operation of these provisions is being monitored and will be reported on by the Care Quality Commission.[64] They are reviewing as and when they carry out an inspection how the hospitals and care homes they inspect are carrying out these safeguards and will publish annual statistics. To this end, both hospitals and care homes must notify the Commission about any application to deprive a person of their liberty and about the outcome of that application.[65] As at the date of writing, the Commission has not yet reported upon the operation of the provisions.

---

[63] MCA 2005, s 21A, as inserted by MHA 2007, Sch 8, para 2. See also Court of Protection (Amendment) Rules 2009 (SI 2009/582) which inserted Part 10A to the Court of Protection Rules 2007. Practice Direction – Deprivation of Liberty Applications (reproduced in Part IV) sets out the procedure to be followed in such cases, and contains the relevant court forms.

[64] See the Mental Capacity (Deprivation of Liberty: Monitoring and Reporting; and Assessments Amendment) Regulations 2009 (SI 2009/827). The Care Quality Commission has issued general guidance on the MCA 2005 and specific guidance on the DOLS safeguards, available at: www.cqc.org.uk/guidanceforprofessionals/adultsocialcare/complyingwiththeregulations/mentalcapacityact.cfm.

[65] Regulation 18(1) of the Care Quality Commission (Registration) Regulations 2009 (SI 2009/3112).

COMMENT

6.56 Information on how practice in operating the provisions has developed in their first year of operation has yet to be published. Hospitals or care homes (or those commissioning the treatment or accommodation) which house patients or residents who are (or upon admission will be) subject to restrictions upon their liberty need to reach a view on whether the restrictions may amount to a deprivation of liberty. As indicated above, this view will often have to be formed in the context of a lack of certainty as to whether the threshold has been or will be crossed. It may be possible to adopt policies and procedures minimising the restrictions imposed upon the person concerned and consequent risk that there could be a deprivation of liberty. On the other hand, it may become the practice to seek an authorisation under these provisions more often than strictly needed on the basis of a possibility that someone could argue that there is such a deprivation. However, their very complexity may act as a disincentive. In cases where there is the alternative of using the Mental Health Act powers, it may prove easier to use those powers with the safeguards they provide. There was a great deal of uncertainty when the provisions of Sch A1 came into effect as to how they would operate in practice. That uncertainty has now begun to lift to some extent, and the picture that has been painted is not an entirely reassuring one. As at 30 September 2010, 1,436 people were the subject of a standard authorisation,[66] a figure which is both strikingly low and chimes with the conclusions of a report upon the initial period of implementation was published by the Mental Health Alliance in July 2010,[67] which identified how much lower use of the provisions had been made than had been predicted. Two main reasons were highlighted for the low take up:

> "First of all, the introduction of DoLS was highlighting a very widespread lack of understanding of the main Mental Capacity Act, which meant that care staff did not know when they were exceeding the powers it gave them and therefore could not know when they needed to apply for a DoLS authorisation. One especially common misunderstanding – which appeared to be shared by some best-interests assessors as well as care providers, and which may derive from the tenor of some Government guidance – was that actions which were necessary in the person's best interests would not amount to deprivation of liberty, thereby confusing the person's objective situation with the justification for it.
>
> Secondly, in the absence of a proper legal definition or clear guidance there was great confusion about what "deprivation of liberty" actually meant in practical terms, as distinct from legal theory. The whole scheme depended on the managing authorities being able to recognise that it was happening or about to happen, but care homes and non-psychiatric hospitals in particular lacked the expertise to do this and generally took their cue from their supervisory body, being in many areas expected to seek advice from it before submitting an application. However, there appeared to be no consistency of policy between supervisory bodies, which might in itself explain much of the variation between them in application rates."[68]

---

[66] See: www.ic.nhs.uk/statistics-and-data-collections/mental-health/mental-health-act/quarterly-analysis-of-mental-capacity-act-2005-deprivation-of-liberty-safeguards-assessments-england-quarter-2-2010-11.

[67] Deprivation of Liberty Safeguards: An initial review of implementation available at: www.mentalhealthalliance.org.uk/resources/DoLS_report_July2010.pdf.

[68] Ibid, p 6.

The report further noted the impression that many supervisory bodies were treating the DOLS safeguards as:

> "... an administrative rather than a quasi-judicial process, and that they and their assessors are exercising more discretion than the statute actually gives them. In some instances this may simply be because the inflexibility of the scheme means that to follow it to the letter can sometimes lead to perverse or impractical outcomes, but in other cases it seems more likely to result from ignorance of the law."[69]

It went to identify specific shortcomings in the practical implementation of the scheme, and make numerous recommendations, in particular so as to increase the effectiveness of the safeguards contained within Sch A1.

Given the increasing body of jurisprudence outlined above as to both the procedural aspects of the Sch A1 scheme and as to the meaning of deprivation of liberty (and the judgments making it clear what happens when authorities get it wrong), it is perhaps to be hoped that the equivalent report by the Mental Health Alliance for 2011 will be more positive. At the very least, the excuses for non-compliance with the provisions of the scheme are diminishing with the passage of time.

---

[69]   Ibid, p 7.

Chapter 7

Court Practice and Procedure

PRELIMINARY

Role of the Lord Chancellor

7.1 In the Mental Capacity Act 2005 (MCA 2005) and hence the paragraphs that follow, references are made to the Lord Chancellor, who was given various powers. These references must be interpreted in the light of the constitutional reforms that overlapped with the Act before Parliament, so an overview of the impact of those reforms is needed.[1]

7.2 In June 2003 abolition of the office of Lord Chancellor was announced as part of a suite of constitutional reforms which also includes the establishment of an independent Judicial Appointments Commission and a new Supreme Court. The overall aim of these reforms is to put the relationship between the executive, legislature and judiciary on a modern footing, respecting the separation of powers between the three. On 26 January 2004 the Government announced proposals which included the transfer of the Lord Chancellor's judiciary-related functions, and these were effected within the reforms by the Constitutional Reform Act 2005.[2]

7.3 Following concerns expressed by the judiciary a Concordat was established between the Lord Chancellor and the Lord Chief Justice.[3] So far as is relevant to the new mental capacity jurisdiction the roles become as follows. The Lord Chancellor is:

- under a duty to ensure that there is an efficient and effective system to support the carrying on of the business of the courts in England and Wales, as set out in the Courts Act 2003, Part 1;[4]
- accountable to Parliament for the overall efficiency and effectiveness of the administration of the court system, including the proper use of public resources voted by Parliament;
- responsible for ensuring that the public interest is served in decisions taken on matters affecting the judiciary in relation to the administration of justice; and
- responsible for supporting the judiciary in enabling them to fulfil their functions for dispensing justice.

---

[1]   The consequential amendments have been made by statutory instrument under the Constitutional Reform Act 2005.

[2]   The title Lord Chancellor was to be abolished in favour of Secretary of State for Constitutional Affairs but the Bill was amended to retain that title although the role and functions of the office are substantively recast.

[3]   The Concordat is 'an essential tool for protecting the independence of the judiciary, as a blueprint governing the relations between the judiciary and the government for the long-term and as providing a much-needed, non-contentious way of appointing and disciplining the judiciary', per Lord Woolf CJ.

[4]   This includes the provision and allocation of resources which include financial, material and human resources.

7.4 The Lord Chief Justice is responsible for ensuring that appropriate structures are in place to ensure the well-being of and training and provision of guidance for the judiciary, and for the deployment of individual members of the judiciary and the allocation of work within the courts.

7.5 The Lord Chancellor, in consultation with the Lord Chief Justice, is responsible for the efficient and effective administration of the court system including setting the framework for the organisation of the courts system (such as geographical and functional jurisdictional boundaries). This includes determining the number of judges required for each jurisdiction and region and the number required at each level of the judiciary; also the provision of the courts, their location and sitting times and consequent administrative staffing to meet the expected business requirement.

Judiciary

7.6 The majority of judicial appointments fall within the remit of the Judicial Appointments Commission (JAC). The Lord Chief Justice is responsible, after consulting the Lord Chancellor, for determining which individual judge should be assigned to which court and the authorisation of individual members of the judiciary to sit in particular levels of court. Also for deciding the level of judge appropriate to hear particular classes of case (including the issuing of Practice Directions in that regard) and the nominations of judges to particular posts including those that provide judicial leadership not formal promotion.

7.7 The Lord Chief Justice is responsible for the provision and sponsorship of judicial training within the resources provided by the Lord Chancellor, but responsibility for assessing the need for and providing training of professional judicial office-holders remains with the Judicial Studies Board (JSB).

Rules and Practice Directions

7.8 In general, functions relating to the allowing of procedural Rules of Court remain with the Lord Chancellor. The making of such rules and Practice Directions will rest with the relevant rule committees where such a committee exists, and otherwise will be exercised by the Lord Chief Justice, with the concurrence of the Lord Chancellor.[5]

STATUS OF THE COURT OF PROTECTION

Preliminary

7.9 MCA 2005, Part 2, comprising ss 45–56, deals with the creation of the new Court of Protection and its powers.

---

[5]   MCA 2005 makes no provision for a Rules Committee.

The Court

Name and venue

7.10 MCA 2005 created a new superior court of record[6] with an official seal known as the Court of Protection and the former office of the Supreme Court (as it was then known) called the Court of Protection ceased to exist. The functions of the new Court are described in Chapter 4.

7.11 The Court has a central office and registry at a place appointed by the Lord Chancellor, which is presently at Archway Tower, Junction Road, London and may sit at any place in England and Wales, on any day and at any time. The Lord Chancellor may designate as additional registries of the Court any district registry of the High Court and any county court office.[7] The District Registries at Bristol, Cardiff, Birmingham, Manchester, Preston and Newcastle have initially been designated as Regional Hearing Centres.

Administration

7.12 Hitherto there has been a close relationship between the former Court of Protection and the Public Guardianship Office to the extent that it could be difficult to identify which was responding, but the establishment of the Public Guardian with an office and a statutory role makes this less appropriate. A policy decision was needed as to whether the Office of the Public Guardian or an independent body (eg HM Courts Service) provided the administration for the new Court of Protection. There were significant advantages and disadvantages with each option and a compromise was reached whereby there would be separate but shared administrative functions.[8] This did not prove satisfactory and in 2009 the administration of the Court was transferred from the Public Guardian to HM Courts Service.

Forms

7.13 The forms used by the former Court of Protection have been reviewed and entirely rewritten so as to be fit for purpose and align with other court forms. The new forms are reproduced in Part VI of this volume. As might be expected of a court of this nature, the applications and acknowledgment of service forms inquire whether the party needs any special assistance or facilities at an attended hearing. This information should be volunteered in advance for any other person who attends a hearing.

---

[6] Thus able to establish precedent unlike the former Court.

[7] In this context references to the Lord Chancellor should be interpreted as being with the concurrence of the Lord Chief Justice pursuant to the constitutional reforms.

[8] This topic is considered in Chapter 8, which deals with the role of the new Public Guardian.

Judges

7.14 MCA 2005 also provides that, subject to the Court of Protection rules, the jurisdiction of the new Court shall be exercisable by a number of judges nominated for that purpose by the Lord Chancellor.[9] The judges who may be nominated are the President of the Family Division, the Chancellor of the Chancery Division,[10] puisne judges of the High Court,[11] circuit judges and district judges.[12] There is no provision whereby Recorders or deputy district judges may sit in the Court of Protection. This denies the court the important resource of judges who can sit in place of full time judges who are on annual or sick leave and a pool of potential future appointees to the court.

7.15 In October 2007 the Lord Chancellor appointed President of the Family Division, Sir Mark Potter, as President of the Court of Protection. On his retirement in April 2010, Sir Nicholas Wall was appointed President of the Court of the Protection. The Chancellor is Vice-President.[13] The former Master of the old Court of Protection, Denzil Lush, was appointed to be Senior Judge having such administrative functions in relation to the Court as the Lord Chancellor may direct.[14] Three district judges were nominated to sit full-time at Archway and one part-time, but the terms of these appointments were time limited so that two of these district judges have already moved on with others being appointed. The potential lack of continuity is a matter of concern and it is unfortunate that practitioners experienced in the work of the Court of Protection cannot apply for direct appointment. Instead they must enter the generic district judge competition run by the Judicial Appointments Commission and, as their experience of the civil and family courts may be limited their chances of appointment are reduced.

Regional judges

7.16 Some 27 district judges (including in the Principal Registry of the Family Division) and 14 family and Chancery circuit judges were initially nominated to sit in the Court on a regional basis.[15] Not all of them are based at regional hearing centres so they may arrange to hear cases in their usual courts or elsewhere according to the convenience of the court system and the parties. There is scope for flexibility and parties should not hesitate to make their wishes known in case these can be accommodated.

---

[9] The references in this and the following paragraph to the Lord Chancellor may be interpreted as being to the Lord Chief Justice after consulting the Lord Chancellor – see **7.1**ff.
[10] The Senior Judge of the Chancery Division whose title was previously the Vice-Chancellor.
[11] This is no longer reserved to judges of the Family or Chancery Division although no judges of the Queen's Bench Division have yet been nominated.
[12] The Court of Protection Rules do not make provision for delegation to nominated officers who are not judges.
[13] MCA 2005, s 46.
[14] He is responsible for the day-to-day running of the Court.
[15] In Scotland the new jurisdiction was given to every Sheriff but this has not proved to be ideal because some have little experience or interest in the jurisdiction.

7.17 In view of the specialist and developing nature of this work it is essential that the nominated judges who sit in the regions are not left to their own devices but are supported individually and collectively, and that there develops a cadre of judges who communicate with one another.[16] One of the advantages of regionalisation is that more provincial solicitors and barristers will appear before the 'local' Court of Protection and thereby gain experience with which they may better advise their clients. It is to be hoped that the nominated judges will develop relationships with local firms who undertake this field of practice and make themselves available to give lectures to or attend seminars arranged by professional or representative organisations.[17]

Allocation of cases

7.18 MCA 2005 provides for three levels of the judiciary to be nominated to sit in the Court, thus following the practice in the civil and family courts where the Rules and Practice Directions allocate cases between these levels.[18] To date there have been no formal Allocation Directions. It is difficult to see how the new Court of Protection will function with three tiers, because previous experience shows that there is no identifiable middle tier for allocation to circuit judges. In practice serious medical treatment decisions continue to be heard by High Court judges, though sitting in the Court of Protection rather than as Family Division judges exercising the inherent jurisdiction. Other personal welfare decisions are allocated to circuit or district judges according to availability and suitability, so these roles may prove to be interchangeable. Financial management decisions tend to be heard at first instance by district judges although appeals from them lie to circuit judges.

Transfer of cases

7.19 In the case of a mentally incapacitated person under the age of 18 years the Lord Chancellor may by order make provision as to transfer of proceedings from the Court of Protection to a court with jurisdiction under the Children Act 1989, or vice versa.[19]

---

[16]   Collective communication is very effective within the judicial e-mail network.

[17]   For example, Age Concern, MENCAP, MIND and Headway (the brain injury association). Solicitors for the Elderly now has a large number of members and functions on a regional basis, as does STEP (the Society of Trust and Estate Practitioners) both of which cover this area of work.

[18]   Circuit judges (unlike district judges) do not sit in the High Court unless specifically authorised to do so on a case-by-case basis under Senior Courts Act 1981 (formerly Supreme Court Act 1981), s 9.

[19]   MCA 2005, s 21. See the Mental Capacity Act 2005 (Transfer of Proceedings) Order 2007, SI 2007/1899 reproduced in Part IV of this volume.

Powers

General

7.20 The Court has in connection with its jurisdiction the same powers, rights, privileges and authority as the High Court.[20] It must be emphasised that the powers may only be exercised within the Court's jurisdiction, so although it may resolve disputes or uncertainty concerning the personal welfare, health care or financial management of the mentally incapacitated person, the Court has no jurisdiction to resolve disputes between that person and other persons. Similarly it has no power to order a local authority to provide a particular care plan or to resolve a dispute between two authorities as to responsibility based upon ordinary residence. In such instances the Court of Protection may need to authorise the conduct of proceedings in another court which has the appropriate jurisdiction.

7.21 Office copies of orders made, directions given or other instruments issued by the Court and sealed with its official seal are admissible in all legal proceedings as evidence of the originals without further proof.[21]

Interim orders and directions

7.22 The Court may, pending the determination of an application to it in relation to a person, make an order or give directions in respect of any matter if:[22]

(1) there is reason to believe that this person lacks capacity in relation to the matter;

(2) the matter is one to which its powers under MCA 2005 extend; and

(3) it is in the person's best interests to make the order, or give the directions, without delay.

The proper test for the involvement of the Court in the first instance is whether there is evidence giving good cause for concern that P may lack capacity in some relevant regard. Once that is raised as a serious possibility, the Court then moves on to the second stage to decide what action, if any, it is in P's best interests to take before a final determination of his capacity can be made.[23]

---

[20] MCA 2005, s 47(1). The Law of Property Act 1925, s 204 (orders of High Court conclusive in favour of purchasers) will apply in relation to orders and directions of the court as it applies to orders of the High Court.

[21] MCA 2005, s 47(3).

[22] MCA 2005, s 48.

[23] *In the matter of H* (Court of Protection No 11649371), HHJ Hazel Marshall QC (see Case Summaries and **4.12**).

Reports

7.23 The Court may, where in proceedings brought in respect of a person it is considering a question relating to that person:[24]

    (1) require a report to be made to it by the Public Guardian or by a Court of Protection Visitor; or

    (2) require a local authority, or an NHS body,[25] to arrange for a report to be made by one of its officers or employees, or such other person as the authority, or the NHS body, considers appropriate.

7.24 The report must deal with such matters relating to the person, and be made in writing or orally, as the Court may direct.[26]

7.25 When preparing a report the Public Guardian or a Court of Protection Visitor[27] may, at all reasonable times, examine and take copies of any health record, any record of or held by, a local authority and compiled in connection with a social services function, and any record held by a person registered under the Care Standards Act 2000, Part 2 so far as the record relates to the person. When making a visit the Public Guardian or a Court of Protection Visitor may interview the person in private.

7.26 A Special Visitor when making a visit may, if the Court so directs, carry out in private a medical, psychiatric or psychological examination of the person's capacity and condition.

THE COURT RULES

Court of Protection Rules 2007[28] (COPR 2007)

7.27 The Lord Chancellor is empowered to make Rules of Court with respect to the practice and procedure of the Court,[29] and these may, in particular, make provision:

    (1) as to the manner and form in which proceedings are to be commenced;

    (2) as to the persons entitled to be notified of, and be made parties to, the proceedings;

    (3) for the allocation, in such circumstances as may be specified, of any specified description of proceedings to a specified judge or to specified descriptions of judges;

    (4) for the exercise of the jurisdiction of the Court, in such circumstances as may be specified, by its officers or other staff;

---

[24]   MCA 2005, s 49.

[25]   As defined in the Health and Social Care (Community Health and Standards) Act 2003, s 148.

[26]   Court of Protection Rules may specify matters which, unless the court directs otherwise, must also be dealt with in the report.

[27]   The status and role of the Public Guardian and the Visitors is considered in Chapter 8.

[28]   SI 2007/1744.

[29]   MCA 2005, s 51. The reference to the Lord Chancellor should be interpreted as being to the Lord Chief Justice with the concurrence of the Lord Chancellor. There is no provision for a Rules Committee.

(5) for enabling the Court to appoint a suitable person (who may, with his consent, be the Official Solicitor) to act in the name of, or on behalf of, or to represent the person to whom the proceedings relate;

(6) for enabling an application to the Court to be disposed of without a hearing;

(7) for enabling the Court to proceed with, or with any part of, a hearing in the absence of the person to whom the proceedings relate;

(8) for enabling or requiring the proceedings or any part of them to be conducted in private and for enabling the Court to determine who is to be admitted when the Court sits in private and to exclude specified persons when it sits in public;

(9) as to what may be received as evidence (whether or not admissible apart from the rules) and the manner in which it is to be presented; and

(10) for the enforcement of orders made and directions given in the proceedings.

COPR 2007 may, instead of providing for any matter, refer to provision made by directions.

7.28 The Court of Protection Rules 2001[30] and their predecessors were brief and left much to judicial discretion. This may be appropriate for a jurisdiction of this nature where the objective is to address the best interests of the incapacitated person rather than personal disputes between members of their families, carers and other concerned persons. But it is not easy for practitioners to know how they should prepare or conduct their cases. These uncertainties were displayed at almost every hearing and extended to identifying the persons who might attend and participate.

7.29 An Informal Rules Group was set up to consider the content of the first Rules of the new Court of Protection and these were made on 24 June 2007 and came into force on 1 October 2007.[31] They are reproduced in Part IV of this volume and referred to in the text as appropriate.

7.30 In December 2009, an Ad Hoc and informal rules committee was set up with a view to seeing how the rules worked and whether change was necessary. The committee held a number of meetings and published a report which recommended many changes in July 2010. The commentary to the rules in this volume highlights some of the proposals of this committee. Although the President of the Court of Protection accepted the committee's proposals, it remains to be seen whether the proposals will be implemented.

---

[30] SI 2001/824.
[31] The COPR 2007, SI 2007/1744. The 2001 Rules were revoked along with the Court of Protection (Enduring Powers of Attorney) Rules 2001, SI 2001/825.

Practice Directions

7.31 The President of the Court of Protection may, with the concurrence of the Lord Chancellor, give directions as to the practice and procedure of the Court. No such directions may be given by anyone else without the approval of the President and the Lord Chancellor, but this does not prevent the President from giving directions which contain guidance as to law or making judicial decisions.[32] The first Practice Directions were produced with the new Rules and are reproduced in Part IV of this volume and referred to in the text as appropriate.

7.32 Whenever considering COPR 2007 or the text that follows it is important to refer to the relevant Practice Direction for further up-to-date guidance of a practical nature.

The overriding objective

General

7.33 COPR 2007 commence in Part 2 with a statement of the 'overriding objective', borrowed from the Civil Procedure Rules 1998[33] (CPR) in which context it has proved extremely successful. The objective is to enable the Court to deal with cases justly, having regard to the principles contained in MCA 2005, and the Court will seek to give effect to the overriding objective when it exercises any power or interprets any rule or Practice Direction.

7.34 Dealing with a case justly includes, so far as is practicable, ensuring that it is dealt with expeditiously and fairly, that the parties are on an equal footing and that the incapacitated person's interests and position are properly considered. Also dealing with the case in ways which are proportionate to the nature, importance and complexity of the issues, saving expense and allotting to it an appropriate share of the Court's resources, while taking account of the need to allot resources to other cases.

Duties of the Court and parties

7.35 The Court is expected to further the overriding objective by actively managing cases, which means encouraging the parties to co-operate with each other in the conduct of the proceedings. It should identify the issues at an early stage, including who should be parties, and then decide which issues need a full investigation and hearing and which do not, and the procedure to be followed. In the process the Court will decide the order in which issues are to be resolved and fix timetables or otherwise control the progress of the case. The parties are required to help the Court to further the overriding objective.

---

[32] MCA 2005, s 52. The references to the Lord Chancellor may be interpreted as being to the Lord Chief Justice though with the concurrence of the Lord Chancellor.

[33] SI 1998/3132.

7.36 The parties will be encouraged to use an alternative dispute resolution procedure when appropriate. The Court will also consider whether the likely benefits of taking a particular step justify the cost, deal with as many aspects of the case as it can on the same occasion and where possible without the parties needing to attend. All of this involves giving directions to ensure that the case proceeds quickly and efficiently and making use of technology.

Interpretation

7.37 COPR 2007, Part 3 contains an interpretation clause and also makes provision for computation of time. In order to fill any gaps the CPR (and Practice Directions) are to be applied with any necessary modifications.[34]

Case management powers

General

7.38 COPR 2007, Part 5[35] deals with the Court's general powers of case management. The Court may take any step or give any direction for the purpose of managing the case and furthering the overriding objective, and in particular:

(1) extend or shorten the time for compliance with any rule, Practice Direction, or court order or direction (even if an application is made out of the time);
(2) adjourn or bring forward a hearing;
(3) require the incapacitated person or a party (including the legal representative or litigation friend) to attend Court;
(4) hold a hearing and receive evidence by telephone or any other method of direct oral communication;
(5) stay any proceedings or judgment generally or until a specified date or event;
(6) consolidate proceedings;
(7) hear two or more applications on the same occasion;
(8) direct a separate hearing of any issue;
(9) decide the order in which issues are to be heard;
(10) exclude an issue from consideration;
(11) dismiss or give judgment on an application after a preliminary decision; and
(12) direct a party to file and serve an estimate of costs.

7.39 The Court will take into account whether or not a party has complied with any rule or Practice Direction.

---

[34]   COPR 2007, rr 6–8.
[35]   COPR 2007, rr 25–28.

Security for costs

7.40   The Court may make provision for security for costs to the same extent as the civil courts.[36]

Court's own initiative

7.41   The Court may make (or vary or revoke) any order, even if a party has not sought that order, dispense with the requirement of any rule and generally exercise its powers on its own initiative without hearing the parties. But if it proposes to make an order on its own initiative it may give the parties and any person it thinks fit an opportunity to make representations and, where it does so, it will specify the time by which, and the manner in which, the representations must be made. If the Court proposes to hold a hearing it will give the parties and any other person likely to be affected by the order at least 3 days' notice.

7.42   An error of procedure will not invalidate any step taken unless the Court so orders and the Court may waive the error or require it to be remedied or make such other order as appears just.

Human rights

7.43   A party who seeks to rely upon any provision of or right arising under the Human Rights Act 1998 or who seeks a remedy available under that Act must inform the Court in the manner set out in the relevant Practice Direction specifying the Convention right which it is alleged has been infringed and details of the alleged infringement, and the remedy sought and whether this includes a declaration of incompatibility.[37] The Court may not make a declaration of incompatibility unless 21 days' notice, or such other period of notice as the Court directs, has been given to the Crown, and a minister or other permitted person will then be joined as a party on filing an application.[38]

PRACTICE AND PROCEDURE

Court documents

7.44   COPR 2007, Part 4 deals with Court documents.[39] The documents used in proceedings include permission forms and application forms, application notices and orders, and also other documents referred to in Practice Directions. An application form is used to commence proceedings, and an application notice will relate to an application within existing proceedings.[40] The usual slip rule enables the Court to correct any clerical

---

[36]   CPR, rr 25.12–25.15 are incorporated.
[37]   Ie under the Human Rights Act 1998, s 4.
[38]   COPR 2007, Part 11, r 83. A Practice Direction (PD 11A) deals with this.
[39]   A Practice Direction (PD 4A) deals with Court Documents.
[40]   COPR 2007, Pts 9 and 10 respectively.

mistakes in an order or direction or any error arising in an order or direction from any accidental slip or omission, but an endorsement shall show that this has been done.[41]

Statements of truth

7.45 When submitted by a party such documents, and also witness statements, may need to be verified by a 'statement of truth', which is the modern form of oath. This is a statement that the party putting forward the document (or litigation friend on that person's behalf) believes that the facts stated therein are true. The statement must be signed by the party or litigation friend (or legal representative on such person's behalf) or the witness. If this is not done the document may not be relied upon without the Court's permission, and it would be contempt of court to make a false statement.[42]

Personal details

7.46 Where a party does not wish to reveal a home address or telephone number, or other personal details, those particulars must be provided to the Court but will not be revealed to any other person unless the Court so directs. Nevertheless a party must provide an address for service within the jurisdiction.[43]

Access to documents

7.47 Unless the Court orders otherwise, a party may inspect or obtain a copy of any filed document and any communication with the Court in the proceedings. A non-party may generally inspect or obtain a copy of a judgment or order given or made in public, and the Court may authorise further disclosure (with or without editing). There are restrictions on the use of such documents in other proceedings.[44] Further provisions deal with the Public Guardian's access to Court documents.[45]

Service of documents

7.48 COPR 2007, Part 6[46] makes general provision for service which includes both the service of documents and notifying the issue of an application form, but other rules may make different provision or the Court may order otherwise.

---

[41] COPR 2007, rr 23–24.
[42] COPR 2007, rr 11–14. A Practice Direction (PD 4B) deals with Statements of Truth.
[43] COPR 2007, r 15.
[44] COPR 2007, rr 16–19.
[45] COPR 2007, rr 20–21.
[46] COPR 2007, rr 29–39. A Practice Direction (PD 6A) deals with Service of Documents.

Who serves?

7.49 An order or judgment, an acknowledgment of service or notification and a notice of hearing (other than for committal) will generally be served by the Court. Any other document is to be served by the party seeking to rely upon it, except where the Court directs or a rule or Practice Direction provides otherwise.

How is service effected?

7.50 Several methods of service are allowed. Unless a solicitor is acting the document may be delivered to the person personally or his or her last known home address. It may also be sent to that address by first class post (or by an alternative method of service which provides for delivery on the next working day). Otherwise documents will be served on a solicitor who has stated that he or she is authorised to accept service unless personal service is required. COPR 2007 confirms when a document is deemed to have been served, deals with service out of the jurisdiction and makes provision for a certificate of service (or non-service).

7.51 The Court may direct that service be effected by another method (including substituted service) where there is good reason for this and will then specify the method of service and the date when the document will be deemed to be served. It may also dispense with service. Special provision is made for service of documents on children and protected parties (which will include the incapacitated person to whom the proceedings relate), the aim being to reach a responsible person who will arrange representation for the child protected party.

Notifying the incapacitated person

7.52 Clearly the person alleged to be incapacitated and thereby the subject of the proceedings should be notified of the steps being taken and given an opportunity to intervene or contribute, unless clearly unable to do so. Even then it may be that this person should be notified in case someone in close contact needs to know and thereby have an opportunity to become involved. Care was therefore taken by the Rules Group to develop COPR 2007, Part 7, which makes appropriate provision.[47] If the incapacitated person is made a party (see below) other provisions then apply.

7.53 Notification must be given when an application form has been issued or withdrawn, and of the date of any hearing to dispose of the application. This will be done by the applicant or his or her agent, or such other person as the Court directs, and appropriate explanations must be given.[48] Final orders and appeals are similarly dealt with, and the Court may direct notification on other occasions. The manner of notification is prescribed in

---

[47]   COPR 2007, rr 40–49. A Practice Direction (PD 7A) deals with Notifying P.
[48]   These are specified in COPR 2007, r 42.

COPR 2007 and provision made for a certificate of notification to be filed, although the Court may dispense with or vary any of these requirements.

Permission to apply

Who may apply?

7.54   It has in the past been found necessary to control those who may bring applications to the Court of Protection. Genuine applications must not be discouraged but a screening process is needed to prevent those who seek to interfere without justification from causing inconvenience and expense to others. A procedure similar to that under the Children Act 1989 has been adopted whereby certain categories of person have a right to apply but others must obtain permission from the Court.[49] No permission is required for an application to the Court by the following:

(1)   a person who lacks, or is alleged to lack, capacity;

(2)   if such a person has not reached 18, anyone with parental responsibility[50] for him or her;

(3)   the donor or a donee of a lasting power of attorney to which the application relates;

(4)   a deputy appointed by the Court for a person to whom the application relates; or

(5)   a person named in an existing order of the Court, if the application relates to the order.

7.55   Subject to COPR 2007[51] permission is required for any other application to the Court. In deciding whether to grant permission the Court must, in particular, have regard to:

(1)   the applicant's connection with the person to whom the application relates;

(2)   the reasons for the application;

(3)   the benefit to the person to whom the application relates of a proposed order or directions; and

(4)   whether the benefit can be achieved in any other way.

7.56   COPR 2007, Part 8[52] provides that permission is not required where an application is made by the Official Solicitor or Public Guardian, or within existing proceedings or by a respondent to an application. Also where the application concerns a lasting power of attorney, an enduring power of attorney or property and affairs (other than certain applications relating to trust and trustees). However, an application relating to a gift, settlement, disposition of property or statutory will require permission unless made by a deputy or applicant to be appointed as a deputy, a registered attorney under an enduring power or donee under a lasting power of attorney, or a person

---

[49]   MCA 2005, s 50.
[50]   This has the same meaning as in the Children Act 1989.
[51]   Also to MCA 2005, Sch 3, para 20(2) (declarations relating to private international law).
[52]   COPR 2007, rr 50–53.

who may be a beneficiary under the incapacitated person's estate or is a person for whom he or she might be expected to provide.[53]

Applications for permission

7.57 A permission form must be filed with any information or documents specified in the relevant Practice Direction, a draft of the intended application form and an assessment of capacity form where this is required by the relevant Practice Direction. Within 14 days the Court will either grant the application (in whole or in part, or subject to conditions) or refuse it, or fix a date for the hearing in accordance with procedures that are laid down in COPR 2007. It is likely that most applications will be dealt with on paper (ie without an attended hearing), but there will be a right to be heard in the event that permission is refused or the conditions are not acceptable. If permission is granted directions will usually be given as to the application itself and other person involved will be notified.[54]

Starting proceedings

Initial steps

7.58 COPR 2007, Part 9[55] and no fewer than eight Practice Directions[56] cover the procedure for starting new proceedings. The appropriate forms must be used and may need to be varied, but not so as to omit any information or guidance which the form gives to the intended recipient. Proceedings are started when the Court issues an application form at the request of the applicant but this will not be done until any required permission is granted. The date will be entered on the application form by the Court. The rules and Practice Directions prescribe the information to be contained in the form and the documents to be filed with it.[57]

7.59 Within 21 days of issue the applicant must serve a copy of the application form on the named respondents, together with copies of any filed documents and a form for acknowledging service. A certificate of service must then be filed within 7 days. Specific requirements are then specified in respect of applications relating to lasting and enduring powers of attorney.[58]

---

[53]   COPR 2007, rr 52 and 53.
[54]   COPR 2007, Pt 8, rr 55–60. A Practice Direction (PD 8A) deals with Permission.
[55]   COPR 2007, rr 61–76.
[56]   These are reproduced in Part IV of this work and should be referred to for greater detail. In particular they cover the Application Form (PD 9A), Notifying other Persons (PD 9B), Responding to an Application (PD 9C), Applications by Deputies, Attorneys and Donees relating to Property and Affairs (PD 9D), Applications relating to Serious Medical Treatment (PD 9E), Applications relating to Statutory Wills and Gifts (PD 9F), Applications relating to Trustees (PD 9G) and Applications relating to Registration of Enduring Powers of Attorney (PD 9H).
[57]   PD 9A contains a Table setting out the documents that must be filed.
[58]   See generally Chapter 3.

PART I

7.60 As stated above, the incapacitated person must be notified in accordance with COPR 2007, Part 7 that an application form has been issued, unless the requirement to do so has been dispensed with. The applicant must also within 21 days of issue notify the persons specified in the relevant Practice Direction of the application whether it relates to property and affairs or personal welfare, or to both, and the orders sought. A form for acknowledging service should be attached and a certificate of service must then be filed within seven days of service.

Responding to an application

7.61 A person who is served with or notified of an application form and wishes to take part in proceedings must within 21 days file an acknowledgment of service or notification providing an address for service within the jurisdiction and stating the interest in the proceedings and whether he or she wishes to be joined as a party. The Court then serves this on the applicant and on anyone else who has filed an acknowledgment. The acknowledgment or notification must also state whether the person consents to or opposes the application, and if so the grounds for doing so, and if a different order is sought what that order is. A witness statement should in those events accompany the form containing any evidence upon which the person intends to rely. The Court will then consider whether to join this person as a party and make any appropriate order.

Parties

7.62 The Court addresses the best interests of vulnerable incapacitated individuals so will not be concerned to resolve disputes between members of the family which may have continued for years and resurface in the context of a struggle for control over the incapacitated member. This has implications as to who is, or may be, party to the proceedings. In this respect the Court differs from the civil courts whose purpose is to resolve disputes between parties who select themselves. The approach is more akin to the family courts when addressing the best interests of children.[59] In reality the Court is often called upon to make a decision following an application by a party and will only do so after giving other persons with a relevant interest the opportunity to state their case. Treating these persons as parties introduces an unnecessarily adversarial approach to the hearing, yet those persons may expect this.

7.63 There is an issue as to whether the incapacitated person to whom the proceedings relate should also be made a party; in that event a representative such as the litigation friend in civil proceedings is required. A procedure similar to that adopted in private law proceedings under the Children Act 1989 is appropriate. The Court is given power to make this person a

---

[59] The Family Proceedings Rules 1991, SI 1991/1247 specify who may bring proceedings and who shall be parties. Other persons must seek the permission of the Court to become involved.

party if this is thought necessary, usually when none of the other parties appear to be addressing the best interests of this person and the Court wishes to have further input. However, this raises the question as to how such representation is to be funded, especially in cases where the issue does not concern financial affairs. In regard to health care decisions the High Court previously ensures that this person was a party and the Official Solicitor was usually appointed as the representative. This procedure is likely to continue for serious health care decisions.

7.64   COPR 2007 provides that unless the Court otherwise directs, the parties are the applicant and any person who is named as a respondent in the application form and who files an acknowledgment of service. The Court may order other persons to be joined as parties if it considers that it is desirable to do so for the purpose of the application, and may remove a party. But unless the Court orders otherwise, the incapacitated person is not named as a respondent. A party is bound by any order or direction of the Court made in the course of the proceedings, and so also is the incapacitated person and any person who has been served with or notified of the application form.

7.65   Any person with sufficient interest may apply to be joined as a party and this is done by filing an application notice within the proceedings which will state the applicant's full name and address, his or her interest in the proceedings and the further information required when responding to an application including, where appropriate, a statement in support. The Court will serve this on all parties make an order joining the person if it decides to do so. A person who wishes to be removed as a party must apply for an order to that effect.

Applications within proceedings

7.66   The procedure in COPR 2007, Part 10 is used for these applications.[60] The Court may grant an interim remedy before an application form has been issued only if the matter is urgent or it is otherwise necessary to do so in the interests of justice. The applicant must file an application notice with the evidence upon which he relies (unless such evidence has already been filed) unless any rule or Practice Direction permits an application without or the Court dispenses with the requirement. If the applicant makes an application without giving notice, the evidence in support must state why notice has not been given.

7.67   An application notice must state the order or direction that the applicant is seeking, the brief grounds relied on and such other information as may be required by any rule or a Practice Direction. The Court will issue the application notice and, if there is to be a hearing, give notice of the date to the applicant. The applicant must within 21 days serve a copy of the

---

[60]   COPR 2007, rr 77–82. Practice Directions deal with such applications (PD 10A) and also Urgent and Interim Applications (PD 10B).

application notice together with the notice of hearing and evidence relied upon on anyone named as a respondent (if not otherwise a party to the proceedings), every party and any other person that the Court may direct. The applicant must then file a certificate of service within 7 days.

Applications without notice

7.68 Where the Court has dealt with an application made without notice and made an order, whether granting or dismissing the application, the applicant must, as soon as practicable or within such period as the Court may direct, serve the documents mentioned at **7.66** on the persons there identified. Provision is made for reconsideration of any such order.

Interim remedies

7.69 The Court may grant an interim injunction, declaration or any other interim order it considers appropriate. Unless the Court orders otherwise, a person on whom a new application is served or who is given notice of such an application may not apply for an interim remedy before filing an acknowledgment of service or notification.

Dealing with applications

7.70 COPR 2007, Part 12[61] explains how the Court deals with applications. As soon as practicable after any application has been issued the Court considers how to deal with it and may do so at a hearing or without a hearing. In considering whether it is necessary to hold a hearing, the Court has regard to:

(1) the nature of the proceedings and the orders sought;
(2) whether the application is opposed by a person who appears to the Court to have an interest in matters relating to the incapacitated person's best interests;
(3) whether the application involves a substantial dispute of fact;
(4) the complexity of the facts and the law;
(5) any wider public interest in the proceedings;
(6) the circumstances of the incapacitated person and of any party, in particular, as to whether their rights would be adequately protected if a hearing were not held;
(7) whether the parties agree that the Court should dispose of the application without a hearing; and
(8) any other matter specified in the relevant Practice Direction.

7.71 Where the Court considers that a hearing is necessary, it gives notice of the date to the parties and any other person it directs, and states whether the hearing is for disposing of the matter or for directions.

---

[61]   COPR 2007, rr 84–89. Practice Directions deal with the exercise of the jurisdiction by certain judges (PD 12A) and the procedure for disputing the Court's jurisdiction (PD 12B).

Directions

7.72   The Court may give directions in writing or set a date for a directions hearing and do anything else required by a Practice Direction. The rule sets out a long list of things the Court might do, including requiring a report, joining or removing parties, and setting a timetable (eg for disclosure of documents and witness statements). In fact the Court may give directions at any time on its own initiative or on the application of a party.

7.73   In general, the time specified by a rule or by the Court for a person to do any act may be varied by the written agreement of the parties, but not if this would make it necessary to vary the date of a hearing and an application must be made to the Court for this to be done.

Allocation

7.74   The Court will also consider whether the application is of a type that must under a Practice Direction be dealt with by a particular level of judge.

Disputing the Court's jurisdiction

7.75   A person who wishes to dispute the Court's jurisdiction or argue that the Court should not exercise its jurisdiction may apply to the Court at any time for an appropriate order. The appropriate form should be used and the application must be supported by evidence. The consequence may be the setting aside of the original application, the discharge of any order made and a stay of the proceedings.

Hearing the incapacitated person

7.76   The Court may hear the incapacitated person on the question of whether or not an order should be made and, whether or not he or she is a party to the proceedings and may proceed with a hearing in his or her absence if it considers that it would be appropriate to do so. Any other person who is served with or notified of the application may only take part in a hearing if he or she files an acknowledgment and is made a party or the Court permits.

Reconsideration

7.77   Where the Court makes an order without a hearing or without notice to any person who is affected by it, that order must contain a statement of the right to apply for a reconsideration. A party or person affected by the order (including the incapacitated person) may then apply, within 21 days of service or such other period as the Court may direct, for reconsideration of the order. The Court will reconsider the order without a hearing or arrange a hearing for this purpose, and may affirm, set aside or vary the order. Any judge of the Court may do this, including the judge who made the first decision, but any further challenge must be by appeal.

Hearings

7.78 The Court is anxious not to exclude any person with a legitimate interest but also conscious that personal information concerning the incapacitated individual is to be discussed and there should not be any unnecessary intrusion into this person's right to privacy. COPR 2007, Part 13[62] deals with hearings, which are to be in private unless the Court orders otherwise for the whole or part of the hearing, in which event it may exclude any person, or class of persons, from attending. A private hearing is a hearing which only the parties, their legal representatives, the incapacitated person, any litigation friend and court officers are entitled to attend, but the judge may authorise other persons to attend or exclude any person from attending in whole or in part.

7.79 The Court may also impose restrictions on the publication of any information or the identity of any party (including the incapacitated person even if not a party), witness or other person. Conversely, the Court may make an order authorising the publication of information. Such orders may be made only where it appears to the Court that there is good reason for doing so.

7.80 How formal should hearings be, and will this change under the new jurisdiction? Options include the formality of a courtroom trial, the relative informality of a chambers hearing or a round the table conference. The proceedings are now recorded so transcripts can be obtained where appropriate.[63] Telephone conferences and video links may be utilised as part of the hearing process.[64] Should evidence be taken on oath? Should the public be admitted and (anonymised) case reports be published, or will it be a contempt to publish information about the hearing?[65] These are all issues to be faced by the new Court.

Types of case

7.81 A degree of flexibility in the procedures is essential because the various categories of case that come before the Court require different treatment. There is a world of difference between contested hearings

---

[62] COPR 2007, rr 90–93. A Practice Direction (PD 4B) deals with the privacy of hearings and reporting restrictions.

[63] This also protects the judge from allegations of inappropriate behaviour by a disaffected party.

[64] There should be consistency so these facilities need to be available at all regional hearing centres.

[65] If all hearings continue to be held in private with no reporting there is little opportunity for practitioners to gain experience in the new jurisdiction and, perhaps of equal importance, for the public to be aware of how decisions are made by the Court on behalf of incapacitated adults.

involving a seriously dysfunctional family and fund management meetings intended to reassure hesitant deputies. The categories based on experience in the former Court of Protection can be identified in general terms as follows:

- *Specific authorities and issues* – Most applications for authority to make gifts and execute statutory wills and to resolve uncertainty (e g as to capacity) are non-contentious but a hearing may be needed and, unless there is a need for evidence to be taken in an adversarial climate, a procedure is required that imposes minimum stress and expense on those involved. It is sufficient that the essential background facts are identified and viewpoints exchanged and that everyone with a legitimate interest is afforded the opportunity of attending the hearing.

- *Contested applications* – Many attended hearings resolve disputes between members of the family or concerned persons as to the welfare of the incapacitated individual. The issue may be whether an enduring or lasting power of attorney should be registered, who should be appointed as deputy or whether a representative should be replaced. In a large proportion of these cases the contestants had fallen out with one another long before and the dispute over control is symptomatic of a dysfunctional family, although legal and factual issues may need to be determined. Some degree of case management is required so that the hearing is manageable, but it may be possible for the Court to steer the parties to a consensus or make a decision after a hearing lasting no more than 2 hours.

- *Serious allegations or complex issues* – Cases do arise where the Court must make significant findings of fact (e g as to the conduct of a party) and a full trial is then unavoidable. This requires active case management.

- *Fund management* – Hearings to make policy decisions in regard to the investment and application of substantial funds arising from compensation awards were a regular feature of the former Court of Protection. These took the form of a conference involving concerned members of the family and care professionals although financial advisers and solicitors sometimes attended. There was little need for prior directions and little uncertainty as to who should attend. These hearings are now less favoured because more power is devolved to deputies, but they may need to be revived for large damages awards because many deputies and families found them reassuring.

Evidence

7.82 COPR 2007, Part 14[66] and several Practice Directions deal with the delivery of evidence. In contrast to the regimes for civil and family proceedings, which have express statutory provisions concerning the

---

[66] COPR 2007, rr 94–118. The Practice Directions deal with Written Evidence (PD 14A), Depositions (PD 14B), Fees for Examiners (PD 14C), Witness Summons (PD 14D) and Section 49 Reports (PD 14E).

admissibility of hearsay evidence, neither the MCA 2005 nor the COPR 2007 directly refer to hearsay evidence. Nevertheless, it has been held that proceedings in the Court of Protection fall within the wide definition of 'civil proceedings' under the Civil Evidence Act 1995, s 11 and hearsay evidence will be admissible in accordance with the provisions of that Act.[67]

Admissions

7.83 A party may admit the truth of the whole or part of another party's case by giving notice in writing, and the Court may allow a party to amend or withdraw an admission.

Witnesses' evidence

7.84 The Court may control the evidence by giving directions as to the issues on which it is required, the nature of the evidence and the way in which the evidence is to be placed before the Court. In so doing it may exclude evidence that would otherwise be admissible, allow or limit cross-examination and admit such evidence, whether written or oral, as it thinks fit. Any fact which needs to be proved by evidence of a witness is normally proved by their oral evidence at a final hearing (although a witness statement may stand as evidence-in-chief), and otherwise by their evidence in writing. The Court may allow a witness to give evidence through a video link or by other communication technology.

7.85 A witness statement is a written statement of the evidence which that person would be allowed to give orally, and it must contain a statement of truth and be in proper form.[68] A party may not rely upon written evidence unless it has been duly filed, or this is expressly permitted by the Rules or a Practice Direction or the Court gives permission. The Court will give directions about the service of witness statements including the order in which they are to be served. A witness giving oral evidence at the final hearing may, if there is good reason for this and the Court permits, amplify his or her witness statement and give evidence in relation to new matters which have arisen since the witness statement was made.

7.86 The Court may allow or direct any party to issue a witness summons requiring the person named in it to attend before the Court and give oral evidence or produce any document to the Court. Provision is made in COPR 2007 for applications of this nature. Where a party has access to information which is not reasonably available to the other party, the Court may direct that party to prepare and file a document recording the information.

---

[67] See the decision of McFarlane J in *London Borough of Enfield v SA* [2010] EWHC 196 (Admin). For case summary, see Part IX of this work.
[68] In some instances an affidavit may be required. A witness summary may be permitted to be served where for some reason the statement is going to be late.

Depositions

7.87 A party may apply for an order for a person (the 'deponent') to be examined on oath before a judge or other person nominated by the Court prior to the hearing. Documents may be ordered to be produced at such examination. Provision is made in COPR 2007 for applications of this nature. The resulting deposition may be put in evidence at a hearing unless the Court orders otherwise. There are further provisions concerned with taking evidence outside the jurisdiction.[69]

Reports

7.88 Where the Court orders a report pursuant to MCA 2005, s 49 (see **7.23**), it is the duty of the person who is required to make the report to help the Court on the matters within his or her expertise. COPR 2007 spells out further the duty of this person to:

(1) contact or seek to interview such persons as he or she thinks appropriate or as the Court directs;

(2) ascertain what the incapacitated person's wishes and feelings are, and the beliefs and values that would be likely to influence him or her if he or she had the capacity to make a decision in relation to the matter to which the application relates;

(3) describe the incapacitated person's circumstances; and

(4) address such other matters as are required in a Practice Direction or as the Court may direct.

7.89 The Court may, on the application of any party, permit written questions to be put to the maker of the report and send a copy of the replies to the parties and to such other persons as the Court may direct. Unless the Court directs otherwise, the maker of the report may examine and take copies of any document in the Court records.[70]

Experts

7.90 COPR 2007, Part 15[71] deals with expert evidence. In this context an expert is one who has been instructed other than pursuant to MCA 2005, s 49 to give or prepare evidence for the purpose of proceedings. No person may file expert evidence unless the Court or a Practice Direction permits, or if it is filed with the permission or application form[72] and is evidence that the incapacitated person is a person who lacks capacity to make a decision in relation to the matter to which the application relates or as to his or her best interests. An applicant may only rely upon such evidence to the extent and for the purposes that the Court allows.

---

[69]   See generally PD 14B.

[70]   See generally PD 14E.

[71]   COPR 2007, rr 119–131. A Practice Direction (PD 15A) deals with Expert Evidence.

[72]   COPR 2007, r 64(a) requires the applicant to file any evidence upon which he or she wishes to rely with the application form and r 54 requires certain documents to be filed with the application for permission form.

7.91   Expert evidence is generally given in a written report. It is the duty of the expert to help the Court on the matters within his or her expertise, and expert evidence will be restricted to that which is reasonably required to resolve the proceedings. When a party applies for directions as to expert evidence he or she must identify the field and, where practicable, the expert and also provide any other material information about the expert with a draft letter of instruction. The Court when giving directions will confirm such matters and also deal with service of the report on the parties and on persons.

7.92   In a simple or non-controversial situation a single expert may be allowed or appointed. Where each party instructs their own expert there may be a direction for these experts to communicate with one another and produce a joint statement of issues on which they are agreed and issues on which they disagree, with reasons. There are also provisions for 'single joint experts' who will be instructed by the parties jointly. An expert may request directions from the Court to clarify his or her function, and the Court may allow the parties to put written questions to an expert on his or her report. Where a party has disclosed an expert's report, any party may use this as evidence at any hearing in the proceedings.

7.93   The expert's report must state the substance of all material instructions, whether written or oral, on the basis of which it was written and conclude with a statement that the expert understands his or her duty to the Court and has complied with that duty. Unless the Court otherwise directs, and subject to any final costs order, the instructing party is responsible for the payment of the expert's fees and expenses, including the cost of answering questions put by any other party.

Disclosure

7.94   Disclosure of documents means stating that documents exist or have existed, and is dealt with in COPR 2007, Part 16.[73] A party's duty to disclose documents by producing a list is limited to documents which are or have been in his or her control.[74] The list must indicate separately the documents in respect of which the party claims a right or duty to withhold inspection and those that are no longer in his or her control, stating what has happened to them. There is a need to balance the incapacitated persons right to privacy against the need for adequate disclosure to enable best interests to be addressed. For example, in property and affairs applications the Court must consider whether it is necessary to disclose the contents of the last Will.

7.95   The Court may either on its own initiative or on the application of a party make an order to give general or specific disclosure. Any party to whom the order applies is under a continuing duty to provide such

---

[73]   COPR 2007, rr 132–139.
[74]   This means that he or she has or has had physical possession of them or the right to inspect or take copies of them.

disclosure until the proceedings are concluded. General disclosure relates not only to documents that are to be relied upon but also to those that adversely affect the party's own case, or adversely affect or support another party's case. Specific disclosure relates to specified documents or classes of documents and may include carrying out a search to the extent stated in the order. There is no equivalent to the provision in the Civil Procedure Rules 1998 for pre-action disclosure.

Inspection

7.96 A party has a right to inspect any document disclosed to him or her except where it is no longer in the control of the party who disclosed it, or the party disclosing the document has a right or duty to withhold inspection of it. An opportunity must be given for inspection and a copy of the document may be requested on payment of reasonable copying costs. A timetable is usually laid down for this process. Where documents are withheld the party wishing to inspect may apply to the Court to decide whether this should be upheld. A party may not without the permission of the Court rely upon any document which he or she fails to disclose or in respect of which he or she fails to permit inspection.

Litigation friends

7.97 A party will need a litigation friend to conduct the proceedings on his or her behalf if he or she is a child[75] or a 'protected party' (ie lacks capacity to conduct the proceedings). COPR 2007, Part 17[76] and a Practice Direction make detailed provision for this. A person may act as a litigation friend if he or she satisfies two conditions, namely he or she can fairly and competently conduct proceedings on behalf of the incapacitated party and he or she has no interests adverse to those of that person.

7.98 The incapacitated person, if made a party, may also need a litigation friend but this will generally be the Official Solicitor because the persons who might otherwise provide such support are likely to be parties themselves or have an adverse interest. In other words, a person who should really be a party may not hijack the incapacitated person's case.

7.99 The Court has full control over the appointment and removal of litigation friends. It may make an order appointing the Official Solicitor or some other person to act as a litigation friend either on its own initiative or on the application of any person, but only with the consent of the person to be appointed. A deputy with the power to conduct legal proceedings on the protected party's behalf is entitled to be the litigation friend of that party, but otherwise if no one has been appointed by the Court, a person who wishes to

---

[75] The Court may allow a child to proceed without a litigation friend if of sufficient understanding.
[76] COPR 2007, rr 140–149 and Practice Direction PD 17A.

act as a litigation friend must file a certificate of suitability and serve this on the child or protected party. The certificate states that he or she satisfies the above two conditions.

7.100 Specific provision is made for the situation where the appointment of a litigation friend comes to an end and where the incapacitated person who is the subject of proceedings ceases to lack capacity.

Representation

7.101 The procedure to be followed when there is a change of solicitor is dealt with in COPR 2007, Part 18.[77] A notice of the change must be filed with the Court and served on all other parties, and the new address for service must be stated. A solicitor may apply for an order declaring that he or she has ceased to be the solicitor acting for a party.

Costs

7.102 The costs of and incidental to all proceedings are in the Court's discretion but the MCA 2005 requires the Rules to make detailed provision for regulating those costs.[78] The Court has full power to determine by whom and to what extent the costs of any proceedings are to be paid, and to disallow costs or order the legal or other representatives[79] concerned to meet the whole or part of any wasted costs. 'Wasted costs' means any costs incurred by a party:

   (1) as a result of any improper, unreasonable or negligent act or omission on the part of any legal or other representative or any employee of such a representative; or

   (2) which, in the light of any such act or omission occurring after they were incurred, the Court considers it is unreasonable to expect that party to pay.

This enables unreasonable conduct by representatives to be controlled by costs sanctions.

7.103 COPR 2007 may make provision:[80]

   (1) as to the way in which, and funds from which, fees and costs are to be paid;

   (2) for charging fees and costs upon the estate of the person to whom the proceedings relate; and

   (3) for the payment of fees and costs within a specified time of the death of the person to whom the proceedings relate or the conclusion of the proceedings.

---

[77]   COPR 2007, rr 150–154. A Practice Direction (PD 18A) deals with Change of Solicitor.
[78]   MCA 2005, s 55.
[79]   This expression means any person exercising a right of audience or right to conduct litigation on behalf of a party to proceedings.
[80]   MCA 2005, s 56.

7.104   A charge on the estate of a person created by this provision does not cause any interest of the person in any property to fail or determine or to be prevented from recommencing.

7.105   COPR 2007, Part 19[81] and a Practice Direction deal with costs and incorporate much of the regime for assessment of the CPR which is accordingly reproduced in Part IV of this volume (including the Practice Direction on costs).

The general rule

7.106   Where the proceedings concern the incapacitated person's property and affairs, the general rule is that the costs of the proceedings or of that part of the proceedings that concerns his or her property and affairs shall be paid by him or her or charged to his or her estate. Where the proceedings concern the incapacitated person's personal welfare, the general rule is that there will be no order as to the costs of the proceedings or of that part of the proceedings that concerns his or her personal welfare. Where the proceedings concern both property and affairs and personal welfare, the Court, insofar as practicable, will apportion the costs as between the respective issues.

7.107   The Court may depart from the general rule if the circumstances so justify, and in deciding whether departure is justified the Court will have regard to all the circumstances, including the conduct of the parties, whether a party has succeeded on part of his or her case, even if he or she has not been wholly successful, and the role of any public body involved in the proceedings. The conduct of the parties includes conduct before, as well as during, the proceedings and whether it was reasonable for a party to raise, pursue or contest a particular issue. Also the manner in which a party has made or responded to an application or a particular issue, and whether a party who has succeeded in his or her application or response to an application, in whole or in part, exaggerated any matter contained in his or her application or response. Costs can even be awarded against non-parties but appropriate procedures must be followed.

Assessment

7.108   The Court may order fixed costs or the payment of a contribution to the costs. It may also where appropriate carry out a summary assessment of the costs, but where the Court orders costs to be assessed by way of detailed assessment, this takes place in the High Court. Where the Court orders that a deputy, donee or attorney is entitled to remuneration out of the incapacitated person's estate for discharging his or her functions, the Court may make such order as it thinks fit, including an order that he or she be paid a fixed amount, he or she be paid at a specified rate or the amount of the

---

[81]   COPR 2007, rr 155–168. The Practice Directions deal with costs generally (PD 19A) and Fixed Costs (PD 19B).

remuneration shall be determined in accordance with the schedule of fees set out in the relevant Practice Direction. Alternatively, the Court may order a detailed assessment of such remuneration by a costs officer.

Public funding

7.109 Historically, public funding (Legal Aid) has never been available for applications to or hearings before the former Court of Protection. If the finances did not justify an application other solutions had to be found. In consequence there was no legal representation in a high proportion of cases. A new approach now has to be adopted with personal welfare cases, some of which were previously dealt with by the High Court but are now being absorbed within the Court of Protection's jurisdiction.[82] The Legal Services Commission has been authorised[83] to fund Legal Help, Help at Court and Legal Representation in relation to proceedings or potential proceedings before the Court of Protection in certain circumstances.[84]

7.110 Basically this is where the proceedings concern the person's life, liberty, physical safety, medical treatment (including psychological treatment), right to family life or the person's capacity to marry or enter into a civil partnership or to enter into sexual relations *and* the Court has ordered or is likely to order an oral hearing at which it will be necessary for the applicant for funding to be legally represented.[85] In addition the Commission may fund Legal Help in relation to the making of lasting powers of attorney and advance decisions where the client is either aged at least 70 or a disabled person within the meaning of the Disability Discrimination Act 1995, s 1. As to the general approach the Guidance states that:

> 'Where legal services are required for eligible clients in relation to issues under the 2005 Act, Legal Help will be the normal vehicle for funding such advice and assistance as the client requires ... For cases where an application to Court may be necessary, the relative accessibility of the Court of Protection, combined with the availability of an impartial Court Reporting Service report, will assist the court in reaching a decision in many cases. This will make a grant of Legal Representation unnecessary in many cases as support will be available when needed through Legal Help. Similarly Legal Help may be used to settle potential disputes through negotiation, mediation or other settlement.
>
> However there will be some cases before the Court of Protection which raise fundamental issues for the client which will require Legal Representation at a formal hearing. For example, important cases concerning decisions over the giving or withholding of medical treatment in respect of people who lack capacity to consent

---

[82] These are applications for declaratory relief, e g in medical treatment cases. See generally Chapter 5.

[83] Under the Access to Justice Act 1999, s 6(8). The full guidance is available online at www.legalservices.gov.uk/docs/civil_contracting/guidance_mental_capacity_0607.pdf.

[84] Applications for Legal Representation are made to the Mental Health Unit based in the Nottingham and Liverpool offices, and exceptional funding applications to the Special Cases Unit in London.

[85] If Legal Representation is required for an individual case before the Court of Protection which falls outside this authorisation, an application can be made for exceptional funding.

to that treatment, which prior to the 2005 Act [MCA 2005] would have been heard under the inherent jurisdiction of the High Court, and which will now be heard by the Court of Protection.'

7.111 The funding criteria are quite stringent. The usual financial eligibility rules for Community Legal Service (CLS) funding apply, and in addition to the nature of the proceedings it is necessary for the applicant for funding to need representation at an oral hearing. The Court has the discretion as to whether to hold an oral hearing. In the most urgent and important cases Legal Representation may be granted before the Court has made this determination, whilst in other cases it may be appropriate to await that decision.[86] Any directions or indications given by the Court will be taken into account as well as whether the proceedings are being heard by a High Court judge or brought by a local authority or NHS body. In general the Commission will only grant Legal Representation if the applicant wishes to put forward a new and significant argument which would not otherwise be advanced. As a rule there should not be more parties separately represented than there are either cases to put or desired outcomes.

7.112 Funding may be not just for the subject of the proceedings ('P') but sometimes for other parties, such as P's immediate family, provided all other relevant criteria are satisfied including additional factors such as the applicant's connection with P and hence their interest in the proceedings. Since the authorisation is intended to capture the serious health and welfare cases which would previously have been considered by the High Court under its inherent jurisdiction, the Commission will take into account case-law on that jurisdiction in deciding whether a case comes within the authorisation.[87] Accommodation cases will also be within scope where they concern P's family life. This is likely to be the case where either the issue is whether or not P should remain with his or her family or where a change of accommodation would have a serious impact on contact between P and his or her family. Cost-benefit criteria may also be an important consideration in such applications.

Fees

7.113 It has been Government policy that the existing Court of Protection be self-funding, raising its income from court fees, although some subsidy is necessary for those who cannot afford the fees. Such subsidy is likely to be enhanced and increased for the new enlarged jurisdiction because many applications relate to situations where there is no money available or involved.

---

[86] If Legal Representation were granted but the Court subsequently directed that an oral hearing was not required consideration would be given to discharge of the certificate.

[87] For example, *Re Airedale NHS Trust v Bland* [1993] AC 789; *R (Burke) v GMC and Others* [2005] EWCA 1003; *Re S (Sterilisation)* [2000] 2 FLR 389; and *D v An NHS Trust* [2003] EWHC 2793 (Fam).

7.114 The Lord Chancellor may with the consent of the Treasury by order prescribe fees payable in respect of anything dealt with by the Court.[88] Such order may (and does) contain provision as to scales or rates of fees, exemptions from and reductions in fees and remission of fees in whole or in part.[89] Before making an order the Lord Chancellor must consult the President and Vice-President and the Senior Judge of the Court of Protection. Such steps as are reasonably practicable must then be taken to bring information about fees to the attention of persons likely to have to pay them. The fees will be recoverable summarily as a civil debt.

Appeals

7.115 MCA 2005 provides some flexibility as to how appeals may be dealt with.[90] Having stated that an appeal lies to the Court of Appeal from any decision of the Court of Protection, it is further enacted that COPR 2007 may provide that an appeal from the decision of a court officer,[91] district judge or circuit judge lies to a prescribed higher judge of the Court of Protection. These higher judges are identified according to the status of the first instance judge. COPR 2007, Part 20[92] makes detailed provision and the appeal routes are:

(1) from a district judge to a circuit judge (but any second appeal will be to the Court of Appeal);

(2) from a circuit judge to a High Court judge who is nominated to sit in the Court of Protection (including the President of the Family Division or the Chancellor of the Chancery Division); and

(3) from a High Court Judge to the Court of Appeal.

7.116 The Court may deal with an appeal or any part of an appeal at a hearing or without a hearing, having regard to the same matters as on reconsideration of orders made without a hearing or without notice to a person.[93] An appeal will generally be limited to a review of the decision of the first instance judge although there is some discretion. The appeal judge has all the powers of the first instance judge whose decision is being appealed and may affirm, set aside or vary any order made by the first instance judge, refer any issue to that judge for determination or order a new hearing as well as making a costs order. But authorisation is not limited to cases concerning medical treatment and may extend to decisions which would have the effect of depriving a person who lacked capacity to consent of their liberty.

---

[88]   MCA 2005, s 54. Following the constitutional reforms this remains the responsibility of the Lord Chancellor.

[89]   See Court of Protection Fees Order 2007, SI 2007/1745.

[90]   MCA 2005, s 53.

[91]   An officer as provided for under MCA 2005, s 51(2)(d). This is the new term for what used to be called 'nominated officers', but in practice decisions are presently made by nominated judges.

[92]   COPR 2007, rr 169–182. A Practice Direction (PD 20A) deals with Appeals.

[93]   See COPR 2007, r 89.

Permission to appeal

7.117 COPR 2007 provides that permission is required to appeal against a decision of the Court (other than an order for committal to prison) and prescribes how this is obtained, the requirements to be satisfied and the considerations to be taken into account. An application for permission to appeal may be made by an 'appellant's notice' or a 'respondent's notice' to the first instance judge or the appeal judge, and where it is refused by the first instance judge, a further application for permission may be made to a specified higher judge. There are time-limits but these may be varied on application.

7.118 Permission to appeal will be granted only where the Court considers that the appeal would have a real prospect of success, or there is some other compelling reason why the appeal should be heard. Where a higher judge of the Court makes a decision on an appeal, no appeal may be made to the Court of Appeal from that decision unless the Court of Appeal considers that the appeal would raise an important point of principle or practice, or there is some other compelling reason for the Court of Appeal to hear it.

Enforcement

7.119 The Court's powers of enforcement are much more extensive than may at first appear. The Court has in connection with its jurisdiction the same powers, rights, privileges and authority as the High Court,[94] which means that it may fine or commit to prison for contempt, grant injunctions, summons witnesses and order production of evidence. COPR 2007, Part 21 makes further provision,[95] whilst the relevant Practice Direction (PD 21A) deals with Contempts of Court. Applications for enforcement may be made and the CPR relating to third party debt orders and charging orders apply as do the remaining Rules of the Supreme Court 1965 as to enforcement of judgments and orders and writs of execution and fieri facias. These are reproduced in Part IV of this volume. However, it must not be overlooked that the Court's jurisdiction is limited to 'the purposes of' the MCA 2005 and the appropriate order may be to direct the deputy (or some other person) to take proceedings in another court.

7.120 The Court may direct that a penal notice is to be attached to any order warning the person on whom the copy of the order is served that disobeying the order would be a contempt of court punishable by imprisonment or a fine. An application relating to the committal of a person for contempt of court can be made to a judge (which includes a district judge) by filing an application notice, stating the grounds of the application, and must be supported by an affidavit made in accordance with the relevant Practice Direction. COPR 2007 makes further provision. In addition the

---

[94] MCA 2005, s 47(1).
[95] COPR 2007, rr 183–194.

Court may make an order for committal on its own initiative against a person guilty of contempt of court, which may include misbehaviour in the face of the Court.

Transitional provisions

7.121   These are to be found in COPR 2007, Part 22.[96] They include the transition from receiver to deputy and the nomination of officers to deal with such matters thereby implementing MCA 2005, Sch 5, Part 1.

Miscellaneous provisions

7.122   Provision is made in COPR 2007, Part 23[97] for the giving of security by deputies, references to the Court by the Public Guardian following objections to the registration of an enduring power of attorney and disposal of property where an incapacitated person ceases to lack capacity. Practice Directions deal with certain objections to the registration of enduring powers of attorney (PD 23A) and the procedure where 'P' ceases to lack capacity or dies (PD 23B).

PRACTICAL POINTS

The workload

Volume of cases

7.123   There is now a wider range of cases under the new jurisdiction because this relates not only to financial management but also to social welfare and health care – in fact the entire range of personal decision-making for adults who lack capacity. In consequence there has been an increased volume of cases for the new Court of Protection to cope with. Estimates prior to the implementation of the MCA 2005 of the extent of this increase differed, but much depends upon how accessible the Court makes itself to parties who wish to pursue disputes or clarify their rights or those of an incapacitated person. The cost of proceedings is a severe discouragement to those who might otherwise apply to the Court and relatively few firms of solicitors have gained experience of the jurisdiction.

7.124   The previous unmet need for a decision-making body has emerged, especially in regard to the welfare of adults with severe learning disabilities and the place of residence of senile parents. The Court will no doubt develop techniques for dealing with these cases, for example, referring welfare and health care issues initially to multi-disciplinary case conferences, but even then some of the more intransigent cases will be referred back to the Court. The level of fees charged by the Court and the Public Guardian are likely to prove a disincentive to bringing cases before the Court.

---

[96]   COPR 2007, rr 195–199. Practice Directions deal with Transitional Provisions (PD 22A), Transitory Provisions (PD 22B) and Certain Specified Appeals (PD 22C).
[97]   COPR 2007, rr 200–202.

Cases under the new jurisdiction

7.125 The following are examples of situations that now are dealt with under the new jurisdiction but were not encountered by the former Court of Protection. They illustrate the need for local dispute resolution by a nominated district or circuit judge as to the best interests of the person lacking capacity.

- *Residential care dispute* – Dispute between a son and daughter who live some distance apart as to which residential care or nursing home their mother should move to. She has Alzheimer's disease and is incapable of participating in the decision but has adequate funds to meet the fees.

- *Contact disputes* – There may be a preliminary issue as to whether the adults in the following examples have capacity to decide whom they wish to have contact with. The Court may wish to decide this first and only proceed to an intrusive best interests inquiry if capacity to make the decision is lacking.

  (a) A daughter from an Asian background has married outside her ethnic origins and adopted a way of life that results in her being cut off by her family. She still wishes to visit her learning disabled brother but the family prevent this.

  (b) Older parents with a learning disabled son became involved in a bitter divorce which results in father being excluded from the matrimonial home where mother continues to care for this son. A daughter who has sided with father is then denied access to her brother.

- *Adult care dispute* – A child with learning disabilities has been placed in care under the Children Act 1989 and the social workers involved are concerned about the role of the parents upon the child attaining majority.[98]

- *Adult protection issues* – Social services respond to allegations of abuse by moving a senile elderly person into a care home and restricting access by family carers who then challenge this intervention.[99]

- *Activities* – A charity providing outdoor adventure holidays for adults with learning disabilities wishes to take an individual on a mountaineering course but mother (who may be over-protective) thinks it is too dangerous and objects. Care workers and a personal advocate support this opportunity for personal development. The charity seeks reassurance that this is in the best interests of the individual so that it would only be vulnerable to legal proceedings if negligent (and not irrespective of fault in the event of an accident).[100]

---

[98] Such cases have become quite common.

[99] Ideally the local authority should initiate proceedings to justify its intervention but there have been cases where the family members have had to apply to the Court.

[100] This type of activity may well be covered under MCA 2005, s 5 and not require Court of Protection authority.

- *Education* – Father wants his 19-year-old son with severe learning disabilities to attend a residential training college and has arranged funding. Mother prefers him to live with her but has made no arrangements for his daytime activities. The local authority has offered a place at the local training centre and is very concerned that mother will not allow him to attend. A local nominated judge could see the parties, consider welfare reports and make a decision (if an attempt at mediation did not result in the deadlock being resolved).
- *Minor medical decisions* – Parents wish to arrange for their 23-year-old daughter with Down's syndrome to have some dental treatment which will improve her appearance but is not otherwise necessary. She appears to want this treatment but there is doubt as to whether she can legally consent so the dentist is unwilling to proceed, perhaps because there is some element of risk. A local nominated judge could resolve this.
- *Sexual relationships* – Care workers are concerned as to whether a resident with learning disabilities being supported in a group living arrangement is competent to enter into a sexual relationship with another resident. They seek a declaration from the Court.[101]

Integration with other courts

Judicial support

7.126 Historically there has been little liaison between the former Court of Protection and the civil or family courts, although there were occasions when one must refer to the other. Now that a few generic judges spread throughout the country are nominated to sit in the new Court of Protection there is proving to be more integration of an informal nature, with judicial colleagues seeking support and guidance on capacity issues. Cases with a capacity element may be transferred to, or listed before, the local nominated judge because of their additional expertise. For example:

- *Ancillary relief* – Following a divorce between an elderly couple financial claims are made which include the future of the former matrimonial home. At a financial dispute resolution hearing the husband makes proposals under which the wife may remain in the home for life. The lawyers involved agree that these proposals are more beneficial to the wife than she is likely to achieve at a contested hearing. She cannot grasp the implications and refuses to accept. The district judge is in a dilemma because if she persists in refusing the offer she is in danger of paying all the costs and losing the home. The judge questions whether she lacks mental capacity and should be treated as a 'protected party' with a 'next friend' appointed to conduct the proceedings on her behalf (often the Official Solicitor), but she refuses to be medically examined. A

---

[101] The Court does not have power to consent on a person's behalf to a sexual relationship: MCA 2005, s 27(1)(b).

nominated judge to whom the case is transferred could tackle all the issues and resolve them locally with minimum delay and expense.

- *Possession* – A landlord or mortgagee brings a possession claim for non-payment of sums due and the elderly tenant or mortgagor attends but appears confused and unable to cope. Doubts arise as to mental capacity and the judge is in great difficulty knowing how to proceed. If this defendant is a protected party a litigation friend must be appointed but a separate application would have to be made to the Court of Protection for the appointment of a deputy. The case could be referred to a nominated judge who could deal with the capacity issue, the need for practical support and the merits of the possession claim all in the same series of hearings, invoking the jurisdiction of the Court of Protection if necessary.

- *Contract* – A local shopkeeper sues a customer with learning disabilities who has been placed 'in the community' for non-payment of bills for normal provisions. Support from social services (who set up this living arrangement) has evaporated with everyone passing the buck. A district judge dealing with the matter as a 'small claim' will be in difficulty, but could pass the case to a nominated judge who would have the powers (under a dual jurisdiction if necessary) and experience to deal with it.

Dual jurisdiction

7.127 There are situations where it might be helpful for a nominated judge to sit in a dual capacity, namely in the Court of Protection and also the civil or family court. The following examples illustrate both the need for local dispute resolution and an overlap with the existing role of the civil or family courts:

(1) Following a divorce between elderly parents there is a dispute as to which parent is to continue to care for their 40-year-old mentally disabled child and the future of the matrimonial home may depend on this. *A nominated district judge could simultaneously deal with the care issue under the new jurisdiction and the ancillary relief claims in the county court, these being interdependent.*[102]

(2) There is a dispute between parents relating to contact by father with their two children, the older of whom has learning disabilities but is by now an adult. *An application in the county court under the Children Act 1989 relating to the younger child could be linked with an application to the Court of Protection in respect of the older child and heard together by a nominated district judge.*

(3) Older parents with a learning disabled adult son became involved in a bitter divorce which results in father being excluded from the matrimonial home where mother continues to care for the son. A daughter who has sided with father is then denied access to her

---

[102] If the child had not yet attained majority the residence and ancillary relief claims would have been amalgamated in the county court.

brother and seeks to establish that it is in his best interests to see her on a regular basis. *A nominated district judge could resolve the issue under the new jurisdiction in the context of the divorce proceedings thereby having an overview of the whole family situation.*

(4) A local authority has made a decision about the placement of an incapacitated adult, and it may be necessary, if that decision is to be challenged, to proceed both by way of proceedings for judicial review and a best interests claim under the new Court of Protection jurisdiction. *A nominated High Court judge could deal with both matters together.*

7.128 A nominated judge will not be able to exercise the Court of Protection jurisdiction unless an application has been made to that court and the case referred to the nominated judge, but that can be facilitated where the issue first arises in the civil or family court. Some nominated district judges have taken the view that they can immediately exercise their Court of Protection jurisdiction, presumably upon an undertaking by a party to make an application to that Court. In this situation the nominated district judges who sit full-time at Archway and normally refer cases to regional judges where appropriate may be expected to be supportive.

Chapter 8

The Public Guardian and Supporting Services

BACKGROUND

The administration

8.1   The former Court of Protection depended heavily upon the support that it received from its administrative arm, the Public Guardianship Office, whose responsibilities extended across the whole of England and Wales.[1] That office supported the court in the same way that Her Majesty's Courts Service now supports all other courts,[2] but that was only a small part of its functions. The administration also provided services to promote the financial and social well-being of clients who were not able to manage their financial affairs because of mental incapacity (known as 'patients'). The incapacity might have been related to an illness suffered by some older people (eg dementia), or the result of an accident or negligence (eg brain injury) or of mental illness (eg schizophrenia). Some people with learning difficulties were clients depending on the nature or extent of their financial affairs. Most patients fell into the first of these categories, but by reason of their age the average duration of these files in the office was between 2 and 3 years. A significant 'core business' developed latterly of brain-injured patients with substantial awards who, because of improvements in health care, might live for a normal lifespan.

8.2   Support was provided for the families and advisers of the incapable person after someone had applied to the Court of Protection to manage that person's financial affairs. When the Court had considered the application, it appointed someone, called a Receiver, to manage and administer the person's financial affairs whilst they were unable to do so themselves. The administration thus assisted and supported the Receiver in completing his or her duties and worked with the Receiver to promote the best interests of the patient (the 'Protection function').

8.3   Sometimes the administration would act as Receiver through a designated official (the 'Receivership function'). This occurred only as a last resort when the Court of Protection could find no one else willing or suitable to become the Receiver. The staff would then be involved on a daily basis in the client's financial and legal affairs. As a result, the administrative arm developed and maintained very close working relationships with its clients, their families, carers and any other people or organisations involved in their welfare.

8.4   There have been several changes during recent years.

---

[1]   Separate arrangements existed for Scotland and Northern Ireland.

[2]   Until April 2005 the Court Service administered the High Court of Justice, the county courts and the Crown Courts whilst magistrates' courts were administered by 42 separate committees, but all have now been merged into HM Courts Service.

The Public Trust Office

Nature

8.5 On 2 January 1987 the Receivership and Protection Divisions of the Court became part of a new department known as the Public Trust Office (PTO).[3] There was also transferred to this department two other parts of the Lord Chancellor's Department concerned with private money, namely the Public Trustee Office and the Court Funds Office. The head of this department was an official known as both the Accountant General of the Supreme Court and the Public Trustee.

8.6 The PTO became an executive agency in July 1994 and in 2000 employed some 580 staff and had annual administrative running costs of £21m. The Court of Protection remained a separate body wholly dependent upon the PTO. The new PTO was thus an amalgam of four separate functions (only two of which related to mental incapacity), namely:

(1) the *Public Trustee*, whose office was established in 1906, acted as an executor or trustee and could be appointed by individuals, the court or trustees. By 2000 the current caseload of the Trust Division was 1,750 but diminishing and client funds amounted to £711m (the Official Solicitor also had a similar function);

(2) the *Receivership Division*, which managed the financial affairs of incapacitated people who had no one else suitable to do so, with the Public Trustee acting as receiver (there were some 2,800 cases in early 2000 and client funds of £252m);

(3) the *Protection Division*, which supervised receivers appointed by the Court of Protection (the caseload in 2000 was 22,000 with client funds of £1.78bn) and also registered enduring powers of attorney (the EPA Team registers about three times as many enduring powers as there are receivers appointed); and

(4) the *Court Funds Office* (first so named in 1975), which administered funds held in court for whatever purpose (about £2.47bn in 2000) and had accumulated substantial unclaimed balances (about £33m). It proved to be an unsatisfactory partnership. There was an expectation that the PTO would perform to certain standards, but it was also expected to be self-financing which stifled development and produced the injustice of cross-subsidy.

Quinquennial Review

8.7 In 1999 the PTO was criticised by both the National Audit Office and the Public Accounts Committee[4] for failing to ensure that a large proportion of receivers submitted annual accounts and failing to ensure, through its visits programme, that patients' funds were being used for their benefit. It was also criticised for serious weaknesses in financial and management

---

3   Public Trustee and Administration of Funds Act 1986.
4   Committee of Public Accounts *Thirty-Fifth Report, Session 1998–99* (1999).

information across its activities. An administrative *Quinquennial Review* in November 1999 then proposed that the Office should be dismantled and those services that were still required delivered through other organisations and private sector suppliers. In particular:

- enduring powers of attorney should be registered at the Official Solicitor's Office;
- the tasks of receiver and trustee should be delegated to local panel solicitors with problem cases being taken over by the Official Solicitor;
- there should be a 'partnership' with local authorities whereby someone from the authority be appointed for a patient in its care;
- the work of the Protection Division should be transferred to the Official Solicitor's Office;
- visiting of patients (and receivers) should be undertaken by the Benefits Agency, local authorities and charities under service level agreements;
- the Inland Revenue should interview receivers and monitor their accounts;
- the Court Funds Office services should be reduced and transferred to the Court Service.

8.8 A Director of Change was appointed in the absence of the Public Trustee, who resigned, and receivers and solicitors witnessed a downturn in the service provided as experienced staff became involved in the process of change and the remainder struggled on with the workload in a demoralised state. There were serious concerns amongst the professionals involved. It was unclear what, if anything, would replace the PTO and it was foreseen that when a new decision-making jurisdiction was introduced there would be the need for an administrative and supervisory body, which could have developed from the existing PTO. With its break up there would be the need to create a new organisation from scratch but it would be preferable to build on and develop the existing organisation. The outcome was a consultation paper *Making Changes: The Future of the Public Trust Office* (April 2000) followed by a Report *The Way Forward* (December 2000). This represented a major shift from the previous administrative proposals and heralded 'ongoing and extensive' consultation linked with the *Making Decisions* policy proposals which were then receiving serious consideration.[5] The Lord Chancellor stated the policy as follows:

> 'I am seeking to create a centre of excellence in service provision for the mentally incapacitated in this area. My prime concern is to protect the vulnerable while avoiding intrusive State intervention where it is not necessary.'

8.9 A centre of excellence was indeed what was needed. The problem remained how to achieve this, but at least the professionals involved could look beyond the long-neglected and marginalised PTO to a new administrative body that would concentrate on the needs of incapacitated adults. The Trust functions were to be co-located with the office of the

---

[5]   These followed Law Commission recommendations and are considered in Chapter 1.

Official Solicitor[6] and Court Funds transferred to the then Court Service. There was no reason why these should be retained by the new body. The remaining Protection and Receivership functions which directly related to adults who lack mental capacity[7] were to be performed by the new body,[8] which would include a unit for the registration of enduring powers of attorney (EPAs). This was to be reformed with an emphasis on:

(1) pre-appointment procedures to assist in appointing the right receiver;
(2) providing greater assistance to receivers;
(3) extending visiting services with more visits and better targeting;
(4) providing more support in the completion of accounts;
(5) finding suitable receivers to avoid last resort work; and
(6) eliminating the existing cross-subsidy of fees.[9]

Other planned changes included the setting up of a Strategic Investment Board to oversee all clients funds, a series of regional Open Days for receivers providing support and information and a newsletter for receivers, called *Reaching Out*.

The Public Guardianship Office

Launch of the PGO

8.10 Everything happened very quickly and from 1 April 2001 the PTO ceased to exist and its mental incapacity functions were transferred to the new Public Guardianship Office (PGO) which was an executive agency of the Department for Constitutional Affairs. The PGO thus became the administrative arm of the Court of Protection responsible for implementing the Court's decisions. Initially the PGO occupied the premises of the former PTO at Stewart House, Kingsway, London but a move soon took place to new premises at Archway Tower in North London.

8.11 The PGO's focus was on overseeing the work of receivers who were appointed by the Court to look after the financial affairs of people who had lost, or never had, mental capacity. These were either lay people, for example, a close relative, or a professional, usually a solicitor, or an officer from a local authority. The Chief Executive of the PGO was appointed as receiver in place of the former Public Trustee in a small number of cases,[10] and in a handful of cases was subsequently appointed as a receiver of last resort. The PGO also implemented the Court's function of registering EPAs, but the Court's oversight of an attorney differed from that of a receiver in that the client's choice of attorney was made when the client had capacity.

---

6   This became the Office of the Official Solicitor and Public Trustee.
7   This includes minors who are unlikely to have capacity when they attain their majority.
8   Provisionally named the Mental Incapacity Support Unit, but that name was much criticised.
9   The Office is expected to be self-financing and derives its income from the fees charged to clients, but remission of fees may take place on a discretionary basis so some public subsidy is required.
10   Less than 250.

Once registered, an attorney did not have to submit accounts to the Court unless expressly required and the donor was not usually visited by one of the Visitors so there was no continuing involvement unless a dispute arose.

Progress

8.12 The PGO had a difficult beginning and the standard of service declined further, with a proliferation of complaints mainly concerning delay or inattention. This was contributed to by the departure of experienced members of staff, the move to the new office outside Central London, an unsatisfactory telephone call system, the reorganisation of case officers into larger teams and inaccessible file storage. The office was in danger of imploding. A 'Change Programme' led to an implant of new management and ideas which began to bear fruit. The following changes were initially made:

(1) a new Customer Services Division was created;
(2) an Independent Complaints Examiner was appointed;
(3) a new senior management team was put in place;
(4) a Consultative Forum was established;
(5) Receiver's Forums were to take place;
(6) Open Days were planned when clients could meet their case workers;
(7) the cross-subsidy of fees was to be eliminated; and
(8) all cases with capital under £10,000 were to be reviewed.

The Mission statement

8.13 The PGO stated that its Mission was:

(a) to work with the families, friends, carers and others from the professional and not-for-profit sectors to promote the finances and well-being of people with mental incapacity; and
(2) to provide a responsive and accessible service, designed to meet the individual needs of our many different clients and their representatives,

and that its Vision was: 'Financial protection and a better life for all who need its services.' The Values which shaped the way the PGO did business and helped to achieve the vision of financial protection and a better life for all who needed these services, was expressed as follows:

Customer focus	–	Putting the needs of our clients and customers first.
Achievement	–	Results count. This means taking responsibility for resolving issues for our clients and customers.
Professionalism	–	Being effective and responsible, and ensuring we have the skills to do the job.
Collaboration	–	Working in partnership with each other, with stakeholders, and working with common purpose.
Valuing people	–	Recognising each person as a unique individual.

Forward looking   –   Being progressive, innovative and flexible.

The Consultative Forum

8.14 One of the new initiatives prior to the launch of the PGO was the formation of a Consultative Forum, a body comprising representatives of 'stakeholders' that had regular meetings and whose role was to advise on the Change Programme. Members included representatives of Action on Elder Abuse, Age Concern, Alzheimer's Disease Society, Carers National Association, Headway, MENCAP, MIND, The Royal College of Psychiatrists and The Law Society.[11] A representative of the General Visitors subsequently joined the Forum. The Forum met four times each year and the terms of Reference were:

'To maintain a forum for continuing dialogue with user representatives that reflects the PGO's diverse client base.

To work in partnership with the PGO – identifying problems and solutions.

To discuss key issues in mental incapacity and decision-making policy development with DCA representatives.

To assist the PGO in planning for likely future enhancements in the jurisdiction of the Court of Protection.

To ensure that important issues are addressed and are client focused.'

8.15 In the early years discussions concentrated upon the continued failings in performance of the PGO and the fire-fighting that was taking place to contain this. With the improvement in service delivery a change of climate became apparent and members contributed to new initiatives and plans for the implementation of the new jurisdiction. The breadth of experience and perspective within the Forum was a valuable resource to the senior executives at the PGO and the members were able to provide feedback to their organisations.

National Audit Office Report

8.16 There was a more positive Report on the PGO by the National Audit Office in June 2005.[12] This found that:

'Since its creation in 2001, the Public Guardianship Office has improved the quality of information it receives on the stewardship of the financial affairs of people who lose mental capacity. It has begun to target its scrutiny, reducing the regulatory burden on some receivers deemed to be a lower risk, and in some cases where the client has assets less than £16,000 in value. The Public Guardianship Office needs, however, to do more to target its resources, focusing on those cases where the risk of mismanagement or financial abuse are greatest. It should also make it easier for people to report concerns about potential exploitation.

---

11   District Judge Gordon Ashton, the Deputy Master, then represented the judiciary.
12   *Public Guardianship Office: protecting and promoting the financial affairs of people who lose mental capacity*: Report by the Comptroller and Auditor General, HC 27 (2005–06), ISBN 0102932786.

The Report recognised that, with over 24,000 receivership cases to supervise, the resources that could be devoted to scrutinising each case were necessarily limited, but recommended more effective targeting of resources and making better use of the information available to help direct scrutiny.

8.17 The PGO sought to improve its knowledge of the nature of the risks it was trying to regulate by commissioning research, and collected a variety of information on individual cases. The Office currently lacked an overall picture of the circumstances in which abuse or mismanagement most often occurred, how instances of mismanagement or abuse had been detected and whether its regulatory controls were effective in detecting and remedying these problems. The Report recommended that the PGO should build on its recent establishment of an investigation team by improving procedures for receiving, evaluating and following up potential concerns that come to its attention. An inability to access case information quickly when receivers and others called with queries and delays in dealing with some transactions were identified. The continuing lack of an electronic case management system[13] was stated to be inhibiting improvement and efficiency.

8.18 The PGO recognised that public awareness of the services it provided was limited and put a marketing strategy in place in April 2004 to raise its profile with other organisations and the public. In January 2005, it began to roll out a marketing programme across England and Wales. The Report recommended that the PGO should continue to raise its profile and make it easier for people to report concerns. Relatives, friends, social workers and other professionals are, in many instances, well placed to spot the first signs of potential mismanagement or financial abuse but were not sufficiently aware of the PGO's role in reporting concerns. When presenting this Report the Head of the National Audit Office commented:

> 'The Public Guardianship Office must do more ... to target its scrutiny at the cases presenting the greatest risks. It should also make sure that a larger proportion of the public and professionals know about its work and how to report concerns. The vulnerable people who rely on the Public Guardianship Office to protect their financial affairs deserve the best possible service.'

A critical analysis

8.19 In 2005 a project team within the PGO concluded a critical analysis of all office functions and its conclusions have influenced the delivery of services under the new jurisdiction. The test applied was to establish what 'added value' any particular function might provide for the client or his or her family/carers, and whether any other appropriate agency which was better placed to provide the service or afford the protection required. It was recognised that there must be better inter-departmental coordination and more effective co-operation in achieving the best outcomes for the incapacitated adults.

---

13   A planned system was cancelled in 2003 after difficulties in implementation.

8.20   After being settled for many years it was also considered that the relationship with receivers and families needed to be revised. The process in receivership cases had been seen as a source of dissatisfaction for customers which added little of value. The initial forms were complex and time-consuming to complete at what was generally a stressful time. Accessing the required financial information when there was no authority to do so could be a problem. There was then a long delay before an order was issued, causing a hiatus in financial management. A new procedure was introduced which:

(1) utilised simpler application forms;

(2) made provision for more 'up front' processing (a bond for a fixed amount and advance notice to the patient);

(3) speeded up the process of appointment;

(4) simplified the first order by focusing on the powers that were immediately needed including authority to investigate and report back to the Court; and

(5) introduced a management plan to provide the basis for more proactive engagement between the Court, PGO and receiver.

8.21   The management plan, which was to be prepared by the receiver, would be required 3 months after appointment and related to the forthcoming year. It set out what monies were needed and why, and (subject to an assets threshold) was accompanied by written advice from an independent financial adviser. When the management plan was lodged the receiver would indicate what further powers or authorities were desired. The case would then be considered on its own merits, with supervisory and regulatory provisions being applied according to a risk assessment. A 'one size fits all' approach would thus no longer be adopted. Professional receivers were further empowered and the one case lay receiver subjected to closer scrutiny whilst receiving more support.

Other jurisdictions

8.22   There was a difference of approach to the need for and the services provided by a Public Guardian in the separate jurisdictions of the UK and Ireland.

Scotland

8.23   The Adults with Incapacity (Scotland) Act 2000 introduced a new jurisdiction for Scotland. This established with effect from 2 April 2001 a Public Guardian based in Falkirk with supervisory and support functions. She has published a useful range of forms, precedents and guidance notes.[14] There is also a Mental Welfare Commission which was established in 1960 and has been given additional functions under the Act. A 2-year review of the operation of this legislation was commissioned by the Scottish Executive

---

14   These are available on the website: www.publicguardian-scotland.gov.uk.

in 2002 and the Report, *Learning from Experience*, was published in the Autumn of 2004. In broad terms the Adults with Incapacity (Scotland) Act 2000 was considered to be meeting its central aims, but there was concern about lack of publicity and knowledge as to how it may benefit incapacitated adults and their carers. This Report resulted in amendments to the Act by the Adult Support and Protection (Scotland) Act 2007. The jurisdiction in Scotland is briefly explained in Chapter 10.

Northern Ireland

8.24 There is at present no equivalent of a Public Guardian in Northern Ireland. All jurisdiction relating to incapacitated persons is vested in the High Court by virtue of s 28(1) of the Judicature (Northern Ireland) Act 1978 and carried out by the Office of Care and Protection, which is a part of the Family Division of the Court. Judicial responsibility lies with the Family Judge (or another Judge assigned by the Lord Chief Justice) and with the Master (Care and Protection). An assessment is presently being made of future needs and the additional functions which might be assigned to a Public Guardian. There is concern about a single organisation being both regulator and provider and a desire to relinquish last resort work. An advocacy service would be welcomed with a cadre of advocates to take on legal representation unless the Official Solicitor was engaged for this. The availability of funding is a crucial issue.

Ireland

8.25 There is no equivalent of the Public Guardian in the Republic of Ireland and any intervention by the courts is based on the Wardship jurisdiction exercised by the President of the High Court, who has Medical Visitors at his disposal. There is a need for modernising legislation although some lawyers consider that the present system works adequately and it is unlikely that a comprehensive new jurisdiction will be introduced in the foreseeable future. The Office of the General Solicitor for Minors and Wards of Court assists the court.

THE PUBLIC GUARDIAN

8.26 The Mental Capacity Act 2005[15] (MCA 2005) established a new a statutory office-holder appointed by the Lord Chancellor[16] and known as the Public Guardian.

---

[15] MCA 2005, s 57.
[16] For the meaning in this context see Chapter 7 at **7.1**ff.

PART 1

Office of the Public Guardian

8.27 The Lord Chancellor[17] may, after consulting the Public Guardian, provide him with such officers and staff, or enter into such contracts with other persons for the provision (by them or their subcontractors) of officers, staff or services, as the Lord Chancellor thinks necessary for the proper discharge of the Public Guardian's functions. Any functions of the Public Guardian may, to the extent authorised by him or her, be performed by any of his officers. So the Office of the Public Guardian ('OPG') is itself recognised by and funded under the authority of Parliament is an agency of the Ministry of Justice.[18]

Functions

8.28 The Public Guardian has the following basic functions:[19]

(1) establishing and maintaining a register of lasting powers of attorney;[20]

(2) establishing and maintaining a register of orders appointing deputies;

(3) supervising deputies appointed by the Court;

(4) directing a Court of Protection Visitor to visit (i) a donee of a lasting power of attorney, (ii) a deputy appointed by the Court, or (iii) the person granting the power of attorney or for whom the deputy is appointed, and to make a report to the Public Guardian on such matters as he or she may direct;

(5) receiving security which the Court requires a person to give for the discharge of his or her functions;

(6) receiving reports from donees of lasting powers of attorney and deputies appointed by the Court;

(7) reporting to the Court on such matters relating to proceedings under MCA 2005 as the Court requires;

(8) dealing with representations (including complaints) about the way in which a donee of a lasting power of attorney or a deputy appointed by the Court is exercising his or her powers;

(9) publishing, in any manner the Public Guardian thinks appropriate, any information he or she thinks appropriate about the discharge of his or her functions.

8.29 These functions thus fall into three categories: registration, supervision and investigation. With the exception of the first one they may be discharged in co-operation with any other person who has functions in relation to the care or treatment of the incapacitated person. It is intended that the Public Guardian will work closely with organisations such as local

---

[17]   For the meaning in this context see Chapter 7 at **7.1**ff.
[18]   MCA 2005, s 57(4), (5).
[19]   MCA 2005, s 58.
[20]   He must also continue the Register of enduring powers of attorney: MCA 2005, Sch 4, Pt 4, para 14.

authorities and NHS Trusts. The Lord Chancellor[21] may by regulations make provision conferring on the Public Guardian other functions in connection with MCA 2005 or in connection with the discharge by the Public Guardian of his or her functions. In particular, regulations may make provision as to:[22]

- the giving of security by deputies appointed by the Court and the enforcement and discharge of security so given;
- the fees which may be charged by the Public Guardian;
- the way in which, and funds from which, such fees are to be paid;
- exemptions from and reductions in such fees;
- remission of such fees in whole or in part;
- the making of reports to the Public Guardian by deputies appointed by the Court and others who are directed by the Court to carry out any transaction for a person who lacks capacity.

This provides considerable scope for development of the operation and services of the OPG as experience is gained under the new jurisdiction. In particular it is hoped that the Public Guardian will be able to address some of the abuse that takes place by attorneys and others.

8.30 The OPG may be contacted at:

Office of the Public Guardian
PO Box 15118
Birmingham B16 6GX
DX 744240 Birmingham 79
Tel: 0300 456 0300 (Phone lines are open Monday–Friday 9am–5pm (Except Wednesday 10am–5pm))
Fax: 020 7664 7551
Textphone: 020 7664 7755
Website: www.publicguardian.gov.uk/index.htm

Powers

8.31 For the purpose of enabling him to carry out his functions, the Public Guardian may, at all reasonable times, examine and take copies of any health record, any record of (or held by) a local authority and compiled in connection with a social services function and any record held by a person registered under the Care Standards Act 2000, Part 2 so far as the record relates to the client. He (or his officers) may also for that purpose interview the incapacitated person in private.[23] The Public Guardian is empowered to apply to the Court of Protection in connection with his functions under the Act in such circumstances as he considers it necessary or appropriate to do so.[24]

---

[21] For the meaning in this context see Chapter 7 at **7.1**ff.
[22] MCA 2005, s 58(3) and (4). See Lasting Powers of Attorney, Enduring Powers of Attorney and Public Guardian Regulations 2007, SI 2007/1253.
[23] MCA 2005, s 58(5) and (6).
[24] 2007 Regs, reg 43.

Fees

8.32   Annual fees are charged for the supervision of deputies payable annually in arrears on 31 March.[25] The current fees under Type I and II supervision are £800 and £350 (£175 at lower rate) respectively and there is a one-off fee of £100 on the appointment. The fees are revised at intervals and are to be found on the OPG website.[26] There is no fee for Type III supervision which is minimal and applies to the smallest estates. Each case will be reviewed regularly and the type of supervision allocated may change as circumstances change. Supervision fees will be calculated on a pro-rata basis if:

- there has been more than one type of supervision applied in a one-year period; or
- supervision has been in place for less than one year; or
- the person lacking capacity or the deputy dies. (Fees are payable up to the date of death).

Fees are also charged for the registration of enduring powers of attorney and lasting powers of attorney. In certain circumstances fee exemption or remission may apply.[27]

Annual Report

8.33   The Public Guardian must make an annual report to the Lord Chancellor[28] about the discharge of his or her functions.[29]

Public Guardian Board

8.34   There is a new body known as the Public Guardian Board whose duty is to scrutinise and review the way in which the Public Guardian discharges his or her functions and make such recommendations to the Lord Chancellor about that matter as it thinks appropriate.[30] The Lord Chancellor[31] must, in discharging his functions in regulating the Public Guardian, give due consideration to recommendations made by the Board.

8.35   The members of the Board are appointed by the Lord Chancellor and comprise at least one judge of the new Court of Protection and at least four members who are persons appearing to the Lord Chancellor to have appropriate knowledge or experience of the work of the Public Guardian. Members hold and vacate office in accordance with the terms of the

---

[25]   Public Guardian (Fees etc) Regulations 2007, SI 2007/2051 and Public Guardian (Fees etc) (Amendment) Regulations 2007, SI 2007/2616.
[26]   www.publicguardian.gov.uk/about/OPG-fees.htm
[27]   Refer to www.publicguardian.gov.uk/about/exemptions-remissions.htm
[28]   For the meaning in this context see Chapter 7 at **7.1**ff.
[29]   MCA 2005, s 60. The Annual Reports and Accounts are available at: www.publicguardian.gov.uk/about/statutory-documents.htm
[30]   MCA 2005, s 59.
[31]   For the meaning in this context see Chapter 7 at **7.1**ff.

instrument appointing them and receive such payments by way of reimbursement of expenses, allowances and remuneration as the Lord Chancellor may determine.[32] The Lord Chancellor[33] may by regulations make provision as to:[34]

- the appointment of members of the Board (and, in particular, the procedures to be followed in connection with appointments);
- the selection of one of the members to be the chairman;
- the term of office of the chairman and members;
- their resignation, suspension or removal;
- the procedure of the Board (including quorum); and
- the validation of proceedings in the event of a vacancy among the members or a defect in the appointment of a member.

Annual Report

8.36 The Board must make an annual report to the Lord Chancellor[35] about the discharge of its functions.[36]

Challenges ahead

8.37 The Office of the Public Guardian is fundamentally different in status and functions from its predecessor, the Public Guardianship Office, despite a similarity of name. It has a statutory existence with supervisory and regulatory functions.[37] It is hoped that the Public Guardian (through his or her senior staff to whom he or she can delegate his or her powers) will act fearlessly and independently, becoming a mediator and problem-solver as well as performing administrative functions and investigating abuse.

The new role

8.38 The Public Guardian has three distinct and sometimes conflicting roles: administrative, supervisory and policy-making. He or she must:

(1) be a supporter of patients and their families and carers;
(2) be an ally of good attorneys and managers;
(3) be an enemy of abusers and a channel for whistle-blowers;
(4) develop the right public image and educate the public by promoting his or her services;
(5) monitor standards in decision-making for vulnerable adults that everyone is expected to follow;

---

[32] In consequence of the Constitutional Reform Act 2005 the members of the Board will be appointed by the Lord Chief Justice.
[33] For the meaning in this context see Chapter 7 at **7.1**ff.
[34] MCA 2005, s 59(6).
[35] For the meaning in this context see Chapter 7 at **7.1**ff.
[36] MCA 2005, s 59(9). Information about the Board is available at: www.publicguardian.gov.uk/about/public-guardian-board.htm
[37] It also provided the administrative arm of the Court of Protection until this function was transferred to HMCS on 1 April 2009.

PART I

(6) establish procedures for investigating allegations of abuse; and

(7) work with local authorities and other agencies.

The new Office of the Public Guardian (OPG) places emphasis on promoting the concept of the assumption of capacity and being dedicated to ensure that appointed decision makers only become involved in decisions when necessary and always act in the best interests of the client. Partnerships must be developed with social services and health authorities and agencies and also those charitable organisations working in this area.

Dispute resolution

8.39   There is an additional role that may be actively developed, namely that of dispute resolution. This will run in tandem with the new emphasis on ADR[38] in the civil courts. The OPG is beginning to look at ways in which it can establish its own dispute resolution procedures. It must not be overlooked that the objective is to address the best interests of the incapacitated individual rather than resolve disputes between other persons, especially when these persons are not addressing this individual's welfare. In the case of many dysfunctional families the issue becomes control over rather than the welfare of the vulnerable member and involving an outsider may be the appropriate solution.

Investigating abuse

8.40   An Investigations Unit was established at the PGO and lessons were learnt as to how such a unit may best function. Internal procedures for referring cases have been developed and other procedures agreed for external referrals. A protocol has been agreed by the OPG with local authorities on how to work with them to safeguard vulnerable adults.[39] Publicity is necessary if this is to function effectively and a dedicated helpline is in place. Cases may be referred by adult protection officers in local authorities and the OPG has consulted with the Association of Directors of Social Services on a Working Protocol. Referrals may now extend beyond financial abuse and include other forms of abuse, but the OPG will only be able to carry out its own investigation where the individual lacks mental capacity. In some instances a new deputy will be appointed following an application to the Court and instructed to take appropriate action.

The Public Guardian's jurisdiction is to investigate representations and complaints about the way in which a donee of an LPA or a deputy appointed

---

[38] Alternative dispute resolution.

[39] The OPG website has a section entitled 'What to do if you think a vulnerable person is being abused'. This provides information on who to contact and includes details of the OPG's dedicated phone line.

by the Court is exercising his powers.[40] As LPAs can be registered before the donor loses capacity, the Public Guardian is obliged to consider representations about the actions of an LPA donee even if the donor has capacity. However, the practice adopted is to firstly investigate the donor's capacity and ability to address the concerns himself, and the Public Guardian will generally only take forward a full investigation if the donor lacks capacity or is otherwise unable to address the concerns.

Use of technology

8.41   The objectives will only be achieved if the OPG becomes a trailblazer in the use of technology. A willingness to do this has already been demonstrated. The PGO developed a website and was ahead of HM Courts Service in the development of electronic filing whilst the staff communicated with one another by secure e-mail. There was even a willingness to communicate with receivers, solicitors and others by e-mail although security issues had to be fully addressed. A policy for use of video links was developed with a published list of access venues. All these initiatives are being continued by the OPG.

Partnerships

8.42   Following up the progress made by the PGO, the OPG has continued the partnerships that were established with other organisations and bodies and developed further partnerships. These include working arrangements with voluntary organisations, The Law Society, the Department for Work and Pensions, the Department of Health, HM Revenue and Customs, the police, the Criminal Records Bureau, the Citizen's Advice Bureau and the British Banking Association.

Funding

8.43   Separate fees are now charged for the work of the OPG as distinct from the Court of Protection. Although the Public Guardian appears to have inherited the objective of full cost recovery in regard to all basic functions, this will be harder to achieve in a jurisdiction which extends beyond cases where there is money to be administered. The need for waiver of fees on hardship grounds in more cases will exacerbate the shortfall in fee income. This problem has yet to be addressed but it is hoped that lack of resources will not frustrate access to justice under the new jurisdiction.

Relationship with the Court of Protection

8.44   The new Court of Protection deals with disputes that require a hearing and may be the ultimate decision-maker when matters cannot be resolved by

---

[40]   Under MCA, s 58(1)(h). This is extended to attorneys acting under a registered EPA by Reg 48 of the LPA, EPA and PG Regs.

the Public Guardian. The Court also retains a considerable volume of paper-based decision-making which is no longer delegated to nominated officers, although input of this nature has been developed again with the nominated district judges considering and implementing their recommendations. Recourse to the Court for the resolution of disputes should be regarded as a last resort. The extent to which the Public Guardian may ultimately act on his own initiative will be dictated by decisions of the Court of Protection on references and appeals, and no doubt by the High Court in the event of judicial reviews. But the OPG will have a more authoritative role than the former PGO.

8.45 This enhanced role for the Public Guardian does lead to a change in the relationship with the Court of Protection. It was questioned in the first edition of this book whether, if the OPG is to act independently from the Court of Protection, it should also administer the Court in the same way as HM Courts Service administers the civil and criminal courts. There is a need to demonstrate the distinction between administrative and judicial functions and to maintain judicial independence, yet there are significant advantages in maintaining a link between the Court and the OPG. Even where there is no dispute an order of the Court is generally required, and this is the reality in the overwhelming majority of cases. Any nominated officers of the future who are given decision-making powers, or even the power to make recommendations, should be independent of the OPG.

8.46 It may be significant that the list of functions conferred by MCA 2005 does not expressly include the PGO's previous function of processing originating applications to the new Court of Protection, although the Lord Chancellor may by regulation confer this additional function on the Public Guardian. Initially there were two separate administrations, in separate offices within Archway but both under the control of the Public Guardian, with the Court having its own staff. Master Lush identified a need to 'disentangle the close relationship that currently exists between the Court of Protection and the PGO in a way that achieves a proper distinction between the two organisations, whilst retaining the positive aspects of the present close working arrangements' but the former Chief Executive of the PGO had concerns as to how that close relationship might be maintained. The concern that the Public Guardian, who may be a party to court proceedings and appeal orders of the judges, also administered the Court has now been resolved. During 2009 the administration of the Court was transferred to HM Courts Service and much of the work of the OPG has been moved to Birmingham and Nottingham.[41]

---

41   The postal address is now Office of the Public Guardian, PO Box 15118, Birmingham B16 6GX (DX 744240 Birmingham 79).

COURT OF PROTECTION VISITORS

Background[42]

Historical

8.47 The office of Visitor dates from the Lunatics' Visitors Act 1833, which authorised the Lord Chancellor to appoint two physicians and a barrister to visit patients at least once a year – more often, if necessary – and to superintend, inspect and report on their care and treatment.[43] Under the Lunacy Regulation Act 1853 the Masters in Lunacy became ex officio Visitors.[44] The first Visitors were paid an annual salary, but only worked part-time and were allowed to remain in private practice. The Lunacy Regulation Act 1862 required them to visit on a full-time basis and increased their salary to compensate. Consequently, the post became both lucrative and prestigious and attracted some of the leading psychiatrists of the day.

8.48 Until 1981 all visits to Court of Protection patients were carried out by the Medical and Legal Visitors. The majority of these visits required a combination of social work, public relations and plain common sense, and did not warrant the expense of being made by an eminent psychiatrist or leading counsel. So, with effect from 1 October 1981, the Lord Chancellor created a panel of lay General Visitors, membership of which was initially drawn from the welfare officers in his own department.[45] The Medical Visitors and Legal Visitors subsequently ceased to be full-time employees of the Lord Chancellor's Department, and made their visits on an ad hoc basis. In March 2000 there were six General Visitors, each covering a particular region of England and Wales.

8.49 If the Court considered that a patient should be visited for any reason, it sent one of the Lord Chancellor's Visitors and there was a strategy to ensure that visits were carried out in the most suitable cases. The visits were usually carried out at the patient's place of residence, but the Visitors did not have automatic rights of entry and inspection, although anyone who obstructed a visit might commit an offence.[46] There were ultimately three panels whose qualifications and functions were defined in the Mental Health Act 1983 (MHA 1983):[47]

- Medical Visitors;

---

[42] The material under this heading relies on articles written by Denzil Lush, Master of the Court of Protection, and is reproduced because it may guide future use of Court of Protection Visitors.

[43] 3 & 4 Will IV, c 36. The Act also introduced a system of percentage, whereby patients were required to pay a percentage of their clear annual income to the court, in order to fund the Visitors' salaries. This is the origin of the present fee structure in the Court of Protection.

[44] This provision can now be found in the Mental Health Act 1983, s 103(7). The Master occasionally visits patients in their own home.

[45] Supreme Court Act 1981, s 144 (now renamed the Senior Courts Act 1981).

[46] Mental Health Act 1983, s 129. This is also a contempt of court.

[47] In MHA 1983, ss 102 and 103 respectively.

- Legal Visitors (though usually there has only been one at any time); and
- General Visitors.

MHA 1983 also provided that:[48]

'... every visit ... shall be made by a General Visitor unless, in a case where it appears to the judge that it is in the circumstances essential for the visit to be made by a Visitor with medical or legal qualifications, the judge directs that the visit shall be made by a Medical or a Legal Visitor.'

and the Rules made further provision.[49]

Types of Visitor

Medical Visitors

8.50 A Medical Visitor had to be a 'registered medical practitioner who appears to the Lord Chancellor to have special knowledge and experience of cases of mental disorder'.[50] There were six and between them they conducted about one hundred visits each year. They were all senior consultant psychiatrists, mostly retired or semi-retired, and some also sat as medical members of Mental Health Review Tribunals. Each Medical Visitor covered a particular region of England and Wales, roughly approximating to the former court Circuits, but there were reserve Visitors who could be called upon when necessary. A report made in their official capacity could not be requested by anyone other than the Court of Protection[51] – not even the county court or High Court – and they were independent, unbiased experts with no personal interest (other than a purely professional interest) in the outcome of their reports.

8.51 The reports by Medical Visitors addressed the particular issues they had been asked to investigate. Their principal function was to assess an individual's:

- capacity to manage and administer their property and financial affairs, either on entry into the jurisdiction or exit from it;
- capacity to create or revoke an enduring power of attorney, which nearly always requires a retrospective assessment; and
- testamentary capacity.

8.52 These visits were only commissioned where other medical evidence was conflicting, unsatisfactory or non-existent. The Medical Visitors also reported on a variety of other matters which the Court might wish to consider before taking action, for example, a patient's life expectancy, which might be helpful for setting an investment strategy, or deciding whether an intended lifetime gift was likely to be effective for inheritance tax purposes.

---

[48]   MHA 1983, s 103(3). A Visitor might interview a patient in private: s 103(5).
[49]   Court of Protection Rules 2001, SI 2001/824, r 67.
[50]   MHA 1983, s 102(3)(a).
[51]   Ie a Master or nominated judge.

8.53 The Medical Visitors could carry out a medical examination of the patient in private and were entitled to the production of any medical records relating to the patient,[52] and in as much as there was one, the standard format of their report was:

(1) the reason for the visit;
(2) information and records studied;
(3) the patient's history;
(4) clinical examination; and
(5) opinion.

8.54 Occasionally a medical visit was abortive because the patient either refused to admit the Visitor into his or her home or was no longer available. Nevertheless, even though a visit was abortive, it might still be possible for the Court to accept jurisdiction on the basis of the Visitor's examination of the patient's medical records alone. The Court had an emergency jurisdiction which enabled it to intervene if it had *reason to believe* that a person may be incapable, by reason of mental disorder, of managing and administering his or her property and affairs, and it was of the opinion that it was *necessary* to make immediate provision in respect of that person's affairs.[53]

Legal Visitor

8.55 The Legal Visitor had to be a lawyer with a 10-year general qualification within the meaning of the Courts and Legal Services Act 1990, s 71.[54] His or her main function was to advise the Medical and General Visitors, and indeed the Court itself, on any questions of law, evidence and procedure arising out of the visits. It was unusual, though not unprecedented, for him or her to carry out a visit personally.

General Visitors

8.56 The General Visitors regarded themselves as 'the eyes and the ears of the court, and the voice of the patient'. The purpose of their visits was to enable the Court and the PGO to assess whether a patient's needs were being properly addressed and to alert them to any action needed to bring about improvements. Their reports might cover, for example, how money had actually been expended; the patient's or donor's present wishes and feelings, so far as they were ascertainable, as to who should manage their property and financial affairs during their incapacity; whether a proposed course of action was likely to be in a patient's best interests; the suitability of a patient's accommodation; whether a patient required residential care or specialist nursing care.

---

[52] MHA 1983, s 103(6).
[53] MHA 1983, s 98.
[54] MHA 1983, s 102(3)(b) (as amended).

8.57 Additionally, the Visitors could show patients, receivers and carers that the Court and the PGO were interested in their welfare and ready to discuss any particular difficulties or concerns. In most cases they represented the only face-to-face contact a patient or receiver had with the authorities. Their routine reports followed a set format:

(1) A brief summary of the case.

(2) Accommodation. The Visitor is required to give: (i) a description of the patient's accommodation including staff attitudes and/or comments on family arrangements; (ii) details on the costs of extras, or contributions to household finances; and (iii) the cost of particular requirements.

(3) Visitors. In other words, who comes to see the patient; what is their relationship to or connection with the patient; how frequently do they visit; and what interest do they show in the patient's welfare?

(4) The patient's needs at the time of the visit.

(5) Care: namely (i) the arrangements for care and attention; (ii) the degree of attention required; and (iii) the patient's progress over the last 6–12 months.

(6) Co-operation from the receiver. What degree of co-operation is received in payment of charges and provision of extras and what degree of general interest is shown?

(7) The patient's condition: (i) physical; (ii) mental; and (iii) material.

(8) Whether the case needs to be brought to anyone's attention. For example, the patient's GP or the local social services.

(9) Recommendations for further visits. Whether they should be annual or less frequent, or whether the patient's name can safely be removed from the Visitors' Permanent List.

(10) Whether a visit by a Medical Visitor is advisable.

(11) Further comments, such as: overall care; present and future problems for the Court of Protection; and possible action.

8.58 Occasionally, a General Visitor was asked to carry out a special visit when a particular problem arose. For example:

- where the relationship between a patient and his or her receiver, carers or family was strained or appeared to have broken down completely;
- where a receiver was behaving in a manner or proposing a course of action which the Court had reason to believe might not be in the patient's best interests; or
- to assist in resolving some particular difficulty with the Court or the PGO, for example, expenditure, accounts or investment strategy.

Enduring powers of attorney

8.59 Although there was provision[55] for the donors of enduring powers of attorney to be visited, in practice they were never visited by the General

---

[55]   Enduring Powers of Attorney Act 1985, s 10(1)(a) and (2).

Visitors.[56] This was principally because the philosophy underlying the Enduring Powers of Attorney Act 1985 is that there should be minimal public intervention in the operation of the enduring powers of attorney scheme. The Law Commission has suggested that:[57]

> '... apart from the registration procedure, we would regard court involvement in the running of any given EPA as very much more the exception than the rule. This would underline the essential distinction to be drawn between the court's functions under Part VII of the Mental Health Act 1983 on the one hand and those under the EPA scheme on the other. Under the former, the court has a continuing responsibility to supervise the receiver: under the latter the responsibility would be firmly vested in the attorney and the court would only be involved if a problem arose.'

Recommendations for change

Confidentiality of reports

8.60 Visitors' reports were confidential: their contents could not be disclosed to anyone unless authorised by the Court of Protection.[58] However, the Court might in its discretion allow the report, or part of it, to be disclosed and in that event there was provision for written questions to be submitted.[59] The General Visitors were reluctant to have their reports routinely disclosed because this could inhibit their comments, but one way round this was for them to include an addendum with confidential comments which would not be disclosed.

8.61 Some cases, though not all, held that the principles of natural justice must prevail over the Court of Protection's paternalistic jurisdiction.[60] In initial applications for the appointment of a receiver and in applications to determine proceedings, where the ultimate issue was whether an individual should either become or remain subject to the jurisdiction, the Court leant towards disclosing the Visitor's report, and the individual was permitted to test the report by putting questions to the Visitor. The Court only withheld disclosure where it felt that this would better serve the best interests of the alleged patient. In all other cases, the judge directed disclosure if there was a positive advantage in so doing, either in the interest of the patient generally, or because this would assist the judge in the exercise of his or her functions.

8.62 In 2001 the Master issued a direction, having in mind the freedom of information and data protection legislation, that the default position should be that copies of reports could be supplied to receivers and clients on

---

[56]   The donor of an enduring power of attorney may be visited by one of the Medical Visitors when there is a conflict of evidence as to whether the donor had the capacity to create or revoke an enduring power, or whether an application to register the power is premature.

[57]   *The Incapacitated Principal*, Law Com No 122, Cmnd 8977 (HMSO July 1983), at para 4.78.

[58]   MHA 1983, s 103(8). Any unauthorised disclosure is an offence. This goes further than the rules in relation to reports by CAFCASS (Children and Family Court Advisory and Support Service) Reporters in children cases which may only be disclosed to the parties and their legal advisers.

[59]   Court of Protection Rules 2001, SI 2001/824, r 29.

[60]   *Re WLW* [1972] Ch 456, Goff J.

request.[61] This direction never took effect. At the annual Conference of the General Visitors in September 2003 various concerns were articulated, including:

(1) if a client expressed dissatisfaction with a receiver who subsequently saw the report, the receiver might treat the client adversely as a result;

(2) disclosure should be managed sensitively because the routine copying of reports to receivers might damage relationships between those involved;

(3) disclosure might forewarn a receiver that corrective action was being planned; and

(4) clients regard their relationship with the Visitor as confidential and believe that only the Court will read the report.

8.63 It was recommended that the existing procedure be retained but revised so that where no action was required following a visit a pro forma letter be sent to the receiver confirming this. Where action was required the receiver would become aware in any event. Any request by the client or receiver for a copy of the report should be referred to the Court, which may direct that instead of an entire copy only a summary be provided, or a relevant extract. Visitors should mark reports where they felt that disclosure would not be in the best interests of the client and the Court should have due regard to this view when deciding whether to authorise disclosure. Disclosure of the entire report would be the norm except when it contained comments about a third party.

National Audit Office

8.64 The National Audit Office has been critical of the way that Visitors have in the past been deployed and the consequent recommendations have influenced the arrangements made under the new jurisdiction. A report in 1994 recommended 'strengthening the planning, frequency and conduct of visits to help ensure proper use of patients' monies and greater attention to their individual circumstances and needs'.[62] The Public Accounts Committee, which considered that report, concluded:[63]

'We believe that there are fundamental benefits in regular visits to patients, carried out by sympathetic and well-trained staff who are properly briefed on the patient's circumstances. We therefore consider it unacceptable that so few private receivership patients are visited each year, and that many will never be visited at all. We are surprised that visits which do take place are undertaken by officials whose main job

---

61   The Deputy Master has since expressed the view, consistent with the position with CAFCASS reports in children cases, that other than in exceptional circumstances he is reluctant to rely upon any Report that has not been disclosed to the parties and that to do so without justification may make any decision vulnerable to an appeal.

62   *Looking After the Financial Affairs of People with Mental Incapacity* (National Audit Office, 1994), at p 42, para 6.10.

63   HC 39 Session 1993–94, at para 40.

is to look after the welfare of employees of the Lord Chancellor's Department. We regard this as clearly unsatisfactory and do not believe these arrangements give this task sufficient priority.'

8.65 A second report in 1999[64] resulted in the following recommendations being made:

(1) publicly advertise Visitor work, so that applicants with wider experience of dealing with people with mental incapacity are able to apply;

(2) improve its monitoring of visits to Public Trustee receivership patients and ensure that visits are made to all patients each year unless, exceptionally, the patient's circumstances do not warrant a visit;

(3) improve its management information on patients to be visited, the required frequency of visits and actual visits made in order to provide assurance to management that visit requirements for individual patients are being met;

(4) assess whether, for patients removed from the visit list, adequate trigger points exist to keep the position under review so that they are returned promptly to the list where changes in personal circumstances are such that visits should be resumed;

(5) consider whether current arrangements for visiting are the most appropriate, or whether alternative arrangements, perhaps involving local organisations, with appropriate quality controls, or the appointment of additional Visitors would enable more local delivery of visits;

(6) monitor whether Visitors are applying the guidance on repeat visits consistently;

(7) improve and computerise its management information on visits to patients to ensure that visits are concentrated on patients with the greatest need and investigate the reasons for the wide differences in visiting rates across regions; and

(8) ensure that Visitors have up-to-date and adequate briefing on patients' circumstances to ensure that patients receive maximum benefit from visits.

Interim reform

8.66 The PGO made strenuous efforts to comply with these recommendations. The Visiting programme became delivered through a network of self-employed, regionally based Visitors. The number increased to 17 and recruitment was by open competition according to set criteria concentrating on candidates with social services, welfare and mental health backgrounds, followed by a training programme. In its second year of existence the PGO arranged some 7,000 visits compared with 1,800 in the penultimate year of the PTO. Yet even with this expansion in the number of

---

[64]   *Protecting the Welfare of People with Mental Incapacity* (National Audit Office, 1999) at p 3, para 9.

PART I

visits, clients up until 2004–05 had been visited on average only once every 5 years, unless more frequent visits were judged appropriate by the court, Visitor or caseworker. The visits that did take place were also better targeted under guidelines laid down as to the purpose of the visit. All cases where the PGO acted as receiver of last resort were visited, new cases were targeted, repeat visits were made where this had previously been recommended and special visits were made where the Court requested this. Urgent visits would also be arranged where annual accounts had been outstanding for some time or fraud was suspected.

Purpose of visits

8.67 Initially the Court and the PGO agreed that the purpose of a visit to a client was to:

- confirm that their affordable needs were being met and where they were not to recommend what expenditure might be considered;
- establish whether or not the client's circumstances reflected financial information supplied by the Receiver and to report any discrepancies;
- provide an opportunity for the client to communicate in person with a representative of the office and where appropriate pass on the client's views;
- advise on the client's views generally and inform case management; and
- comment on any issues raised in their briefing.

Subsequently the following new comprehensive purpose was defined:

'To provide an independent assessment of the client's circumstances and to help the PGO and the Court decide what further can be done to promote the client's well-being'.

8.68 An internal *Review on the effectiveness of visits carried out by the Lord Chancellor's Visitors* was completed in February 2004 and produced a series of recommendations intended to achieve the following benefits:

(1) transparent terms and conditions for the Visitors;
(2) agreed standards of performance for Visitors, expressed through a formal agreement with the PGO;
(3) a formalised system for monitoring Visitors' performance;
(4) a process for obtaining qualitative feedback on the value of visits to clients and for collecting and recording evidence to demonstrate the effectiveness of visits;
(5) clear policies and processes for arranging visits, disclosing reports and Visitor's safety; and
(6) a formal process for reviewing fees.

The way that the Visitors operated has influenced the Visitors Service under the new jurisdiction save that there is no longer such emphasis on the financial aspects and a more hands-off approach is adopted, with less supervision.

The new regime

Appointment

8.69 For the purpose of the new jurisdiction there are two panels of Court of Protection Visitors[65] appointed by the Lord Chancellor:[66] a panel of Special Visitors and a panel of General Visitors.[67] They are appointed to carry out visits and produce reports in much the same way as previously although the brief may be wider. There is not seen to be the need for a Legal Visitor under the new regime. It is the OPG practice to recruit by open competition rather than private invitation. Visitors are appointed for such term and subject to such conditions, and may be paid such remuneration and allowances, as the Lord Chancellor may determine. The OPG administers the panel of visitors but the Court can draw on this as a resource.

General Visitors

8.70 A General Visitor need not have a medical qualification. The older ones have social work, welfare or PGO backgrounds but more recently there has been recruitment from new areas such as local authority finance teams and those with legal and medical experience. It is unlikely that outsourcing to bodies such as other government agencies, local authorities or NHS organisations would be adopted because this would lack the transparent independence of the Visitors Service. In some cases the Court needs a report because of conflict between family and such bodies. There is a statutory power to request reports from these bodies when that is thought appropriate, but in most instances the judges will seek a report from their own reporting service just as they turn to CAFCASS in children cases. Outsourcing to the not-for-profit sector may not be desirable because consistent training might not be available and uniform standards would be difficult to impose and enforce. It is essential for the Public Guardian to maintain his or her own independent 'eyes and ears' and for this facility to be available to the Court. Mental capacity issues represent a discrete area where a body of experience needs to be developed, and the role of the Visitors is so important that a specialist service needs to be established and maintained.

8.71 There is now a core of a small number of General Visitors employed by the OPG supported by casuals, on the 'Hub and Spoke' principle. The employed full-timers are based at home and operate on a regional basis. In order to maintain a sufficient reserve of visiting services a panel of self-employed casual General Visitors are retained who can be commissioned to prepare reports. An employment basis for the General Visitors may be preferred because this allows for more central control and frees the way for more training, the provision of standard facilities (including laptop computers with appropriate pro formas) and access to

---

[65] This title replaces 'Lord Chancellor's Visitors'.
[66] All references to the Lord Chancellor should be read in the light of the constitutional reforms – see Chapter 7 at **7.1**ff.
[67] MCA 2005, s 61(1)–(4).

networked or secure e-mail communication. But this must not be at the expense of a loss of independence. The Visitors may be accountable to the Public Guardian as employees but are accountable to the Court when delivering reports requested directly by the Court. They may be required to attend hearings to give evidence and in that respect are vulnerable to cross-examination. So their approach to the reporting process and any constraints placed upon them will become apparent.

8.72 A high proportion of the visiting carried out for the OPG is still done by the enlarged body of self employed visitors supplementing the small employed group. This has enabled the Public Guardian to guarantee a rapid response if necessary but also to deploy some very experienced or more specialist Visitors within the wider group for particular visits. Reporting timescales have been greatly shortened to only five weeks or less from the time of visits being commissioned, and the Public Guardian can also get a visit done the same day if need be.

Frequency of visiting, including the decision whether there will be a visit at all, is now tied to supervision levels (from 1 to 3) allocated after the order is received from the Court. Only Type 1 cases are routinely visited and repeat visited. Type 2A has been introduced as an intermediate level for new lay deputies largely but also to address other short term situations and these also generally receive a visit. Prior to implementation and this 'risk based' approach to supervision and visiting, the OPG had aimed to have some level of visiting to almost all its clients although it never fully achieved this. Many clients will now not be visited at all in this model but they should have been assessed first as low risk/'light touch'.

8.73 The OPG no longer directs all its visiting to the client – in many cases the Visitor is instructed to interview the deputy only, or to ensure that the deputy is seen as well as the client. In some cases professional deputies are visited to discuss several clients at the same time rather than visit the clients individually. There is a new emphasis on regulation and ensuring that principles of the Act and the Code of Practice are complied with, for example that clients are seen by the deputy or their representative and that as far as possible efforts are made to consult with them.

Special Visitors

8.74 A Special Visitor must be a registered medical practitioner (or appear to the Lord Chancellor to have other suitable qualifications or training), and must also appear to the Lord Chancellor to have special knowledge of and experience in cases of impairment of or disturbance in the functioning of the mind or brain. This is the main distinction between the Special and General Visitors. The scale of remuneration is also different and the method of recruitment may differ as these are specialist appointments, but fundamentally the funding mechanism and the process of recruitment is the same with both groups of visitors.. A small number of suitably experienced psychiatrists (or in some instances psychologists) are appointed on a consultancy basis and called upon when the need arises.

8.75 The role of the Special Visitors may be restricted to reporting in two areas. First, they will by reason of their qualification and experience be well placed to provide reports expressing an opinion on capacity. Secondly, they will be able to assist in cases where there are communication difficulties and to report on the wishes and feelings of the incapacitated individual when others have difficulty in doing so. It may be that, other than in these two respects, the Court will not seek a report from a Special Visitor in health and welfare cases because where guidance is needed that will be the role of experts' evidence.

Reports by Visitors

8.76 Under MCA 2005 the Court of Protection may require a report to be made to it by a Visitor, in writing or orally, on such matters as may be specified.[68] The Public Guardian may also direct a Visitor to visit a donee of a lasting power of attorney, a deputy or the incapacitated person and make a report on such matters as may be directed.[69] The jurisdiction now extends to personal welfare and health care decisions affecting mentally incapacitated adults, in addition to the former jurisdiction over their property and financial affairs. Accordingly, the Visitors may now be required to report on matters relating to where a patient should live and whether a decision should be made to withhold or withdraw medical treatment.

8.77 The demand for reports is unlikely to reduce from the previous level for financial affairs, and to this are now added health and welfare reports of a more specific nature. There may of course be an overlap. However, the Official Solicitor is appointed to represent the incapacitated person in many personal welfare cases and a report is unlikely to be required then from a General Visitor. Where there is an issue as to mental capacity and the evidence from medical experts is felt by the Court to be insufficient, a report from a Special Visitor who has reviewed the existing evidence is often a process of great value.

Powers

8.78 For the purpose of carrying out their functions in relation to a person who lacks capacity, Court of Protection Visitors may, at all reasonable times, examine and take copies of:

(1) any health record;
(2) any record of, or held by, a local authority and compiled in connection with a social services function; and

---

68   MCA 2005, s 49.
69   MCA 2005, s 58(1)(d).

(3) any record held by a person registered under the Care Standards Act 2000, Part 2 so far as the record relates to the person who lacks capacity.

They may also for that purpose interview the person who lacks capacity in private.[70]

The changed climate

8.79 It has been recognised that changes are required in the relationship between the Public Guardian and the new panels of Visitors compared with that of the PGO, which dealt with the former Visitors as self-employed contractors. There is a need to ensure that Visitors are adequately protected financially and legally, with health and safety checks (especially in respect of lone visits), public liability insurance, and clearly defined job roles, skills sets and person specifications. The Public Guardian has established increased levels of accountability in terms of quality standards, reporting timescales, professional updating and training.

Association of Independent Visitors

8.80 After October 2007 clients of the Court were no longer certain to receive a periodic visit from a Court of Protection Visitor or their successors. Some solicitors and local authorities regretted the loss of the useful independent monitoring and advice this gave them about their clients. They saw the need to commission such visits themselves to fill this gap and to address Mental Capacity Act issues and the good practice requirements enshrined in the Code of Practice. One new resource which can assist in this area is the *Association of Independent Visitors* which was set up by a group of experienced former and current Court Visitors following the implementation of the Act. Its members emphasise that their private work is, as the name suggests, completely independent of the OPG or the Court.[71]

THE OFFICIAL SOLICITOR[72]

Status and function

8.81 The Official Solicitor was an officer of the Supreme Court appointed by the Lord Chancellor under the Supreme Court Act 1981, s 90. His main function is to represent parties to proceedings who are without capacity, deceased or unascertained when no other suitable person or agency is able and willing to do so. The purpose is to prevent a possible denial of justice and safeguard the welfare, property or status of the party. Such proceedings may be in the county court, High Court or Court of Protection. The Official

---

[70] MCA 2005, s 61(5)–(6).
[71] They can be contacted via their website *www.aivuk.org.uk* which enables the enquirer to find the visitor covering every area of the country according to postcode.
[72] The contribution of James Beck from the Official Solicitor's office to the material under this heading is gratefully acknowledged.

Solicitor usually becomes formally involved when appointed by the Court, and he may act as his own solicitor, or instruct a private firm of solicitors to act for him.

8.82 On 1 April 2007 the Offices of Court Funds, Official Solicitor and Public Trustee was created, when the Court Funds Office merged with the Official Solicitor and Public Trustee. Following the creation of a new Supreme Court to replace the House of Lords as the ultimate appeal court, from October 2009 the title became the Official Solicitor to the Senior Courts.[73]

8.83 The Official Solicitor can be contacted at:
> 81 Chancery Lane
> London WC2A 1DD
> DX 0012 London/Chancery Lane WC2
> Tel: 020 7911 7127
> Fax: 020 7911 7105
> E-mail: inquiries@offsol.gsi.gov.uk
> Website: www.officialsolicitor.gov.uk/os/offsol.htm

Background

8.84 The development of the functions of the Official Solicitor's office date back to the eighteenth century. The state has always recognised the need for representation of an incapacitated person when a benevolent relative or friend cannot be found to act on his or her behalf. This function was undertaken on behalf of the Crown as parens patriae in various ways. The office of the Official Solicitor to the Supreme Court of Judicature was created by an Order of the Lord Chancellor on 6 November 1875 under the power given to him by the Supreme Court of Judicature Act 1873, s 84 to appoint officers to serve the Supreme Court generally. It was not until 1981 that this became a statutory office and was renamed the Official Solicitor to the Supreme Court.

8.85 The distinct office of the Public Trustee was created under the Public Trustee Act 1906. Since then trustee services have become more readily available in the private sector so the Public Trustee has tended to become a trustee of last resort. In the early 1980s the Court of Protection was relocated within the Public Trustee Office, which later became known as the Public Trust Office. Subsequently the Public Trustee was given the additional responsibilities of acting as receiver of last resort, performing judicial functions as authorised by the Court of Protection Rules and dealing with the registration of enduring powers of attorney.

8.86 The offices of the Official Solicitor and the Public Trustee were co-located from 1 April 2001 when the trust division of the PTO was

---

[73] Constitutional Reform Act 2005, Sch 11, para 26. The Supreme Court Act 1981 was also renamed the Senior Courts Act 1981.

abolished and some of the Official Solicitor's work was transferred to CAFCASS.[74] Although both are now housed in one office building they continue to have separate corporate functions and the Public Trustee is not involved in mental capacity issues. Functionally the Official Solicitor is part of the judicial system of England and Wales (that is, excluding Scotland and Northern Ireland), while the Public Trustee is a separate and independent statutory body, and both are appointed by the Lord Chancellor.

The present office

8.87   The office is currently administered as part of the Ministry of Justice. At the time of writing the Official Solicitor to the Senior Courts is Alastair Pitblado and the Public Trustee is Eddie Bloomfield. There are currently around 110 permanent staff, of whom 20 are lawyers. The staff are civil servants who specialise in particular areas of the work.[75] About 50 of the staff are caseworkers, all of whom have access to in-house legal advice where appropriate, and some of whom have the conduct of cases under the direct supervision of the lawyers. In 2009–10 the Official Solicitor accepted 2,681 new cases (representing either a child or adult under disability but excluding contempt cases where the party may or may not have had capacity). Of these new cases, 813 were proceedings in the Court of Protection with 545 relating to property and affairs and 268 relating to healthcare and welfare. There has been a significant increase in healthcare and welfare work undertaken by the Official Solicitor in the Court of Protection, from 42 current cases in April 2008 to 352 ongoing cases in March 2010, with a 52% rise in new cases accepted between 2008/9 and 2009/10.[76]

8.88   Both the Official Solicitor and the Public Trustee have such powers and perform such duties as may be conferred on them by statute and by Rules of Court, and, in the case of the Official Solicitor, also at common law. The Official Solicitor's role in court proceedings is recognised by the Court Rules,[77] and the Court of Protection Rules 2007[78] and Practice Directions make specific provision for his involvement[79]. By way of guidance he issued Practice Notes dealing with medical and welfare decisions for incapacitated adults,[80] including sterilisation[81] and persistent

---

74   This followed the *Quinquennial Review of the Public Trust Office* in 1999 (see **8.7**ff).
75   Part of the work of the Official Solicitor is covered in Chapter 5.
76   See the Official Solicitor and Public Trustee Annual Report 2009-10.
77   See the Civil Procedure Rules 1998, SI 1998/3132, rr 21.4–21.7 and PD 21-002, para 3.6 and the Family Proceedings Rules 1991, SI 1991/1247, r 9.5(1)(a).
78   SI 2007/1744.
79   Rule 11 allows the Court to request him to make an application, r 13 enables the Court to request him to represent the patient, r 49(2) allows him to act in place of any solicitor when the Court of Protection is dissatisfied and rr 67 or 68 enable the Court to request him to make inquiries and report back.
80   Practice Note: *Medical and Welfare Decisions for Adults* [2001] 2 FLR 158 and Practice Note: *Family Division: Incapacitated Adults* (2002) *The Times*, 4 January.
81   Practice Note: *Sterilisation Cases* [2001] 2 FLR 155.

vegetative state (PVS) cases.[82] These are no longer of direct application following the implementation of the MCA 2005.

Vision Statement

8.89 The vision statement of the Official Solicitor's Office is:

> '... to be an organisation delivering high quality customer focused legal services for vulnerable persons, where those services need to be provided by the public sector ...'

or, in summary, to achieve justice for those who need its services.

Acceptance policy

8.90 The Official Solicitor requires evidence of incapacity (or a judicial determination of incapacity) before he can accept appointment to represent a party to court proceedings. He operates a 'last resort' acceptance policy, namely that he will only accept appointment when there is no other suitable and willing person who could be appointed (although in Court of Protection cases the Official Solicitor invariably consents to act as family members and friends are usually conflicted due to such proceedings tending to involve disputes within the family or between a family and a public authority).

8.91 Once appointed as litigation friend (or next friend/guardian ad litem in family proceedings) he will decide whether the solicitor's role is handled in-house or external solicitors are to be instructed. He operates to a fixed budget and has to consider how his costs in litigation to which he may become a party are to be funded. Depending on the circumstances, this may be out of the incapacitated party's own estate; where external solicitors are used their costs may be met through public funding where available; or he can seek an undertaking as to costs, or an order for all or some of his costs, from another party to the litigation.

The incapacity work of the Official Solicitor

Giving advice

8.92 Inquiries are frequently made by the judiciary and members of the legal profession, IMCAs, members of the medical profession and social workers. Other members of the general public are usually encouraged to obtain the advice of their own solicitor, or perhaps consult their local Citizens Advice Bureau.

Representing adults who lack capacity

8.93 An order of the Court, appointing the Official Solicitor to act as a representative in a civil court case for a person who lacks capacity, will

PART I

---

[82]   Practice Note: *PVS Cases* [2001] 2 FLR 155.

either be made with his prior consent or will only take effect if his consent is obtained. The Official Solicitor needs to be satisfied that his involvement in the case will be consistent with the *Vision Statement* of his office, and in appropriate cases he will also require security that his charges and expenses will be met before agreeing to act.

8.94 It is desirable that the Official Solicitor be consulted about any proposed application which seeks his involvement in any proceedings before a court in England and Wales. In proceedings before the Court of Protection, particularly with regard to personal welfare applications, the Official Solicitor will usually require certain provisions to be included in any order appointing him, which will allow his staff to obtain financial information from third parties and public bodies about the incapacitated party and allow for that party's costs to be obtained from public funding where eligible or from his or her estate if not eligible. The Official Solicitor's lawyers will usually provide precedent draft orders to facilitate his early involvement and speedy acceptance of appointment. The time required by the Official Solicitor to carry out such financial enquiries should not be underestimated, particularly if the incapacitated party's financial circumstances are complicated or where a relative or partner is managing those finances and are obstructive. Failure to consult the Official Solicitor prior to issuing proceedings or failing to provide any obtainable financial and personal information about the incapacitated party (such as their National Insurance Number) may result in avoidable delay.

The Official Solicitor is unable to act as solicitor to individual members of the general public as though he were a solicitor in private practice, nor will he respond to inquiries from individuals who are seeking free legal advice for their own benefit.

Assisting the civil and family courts

8.95 The Official Solicitor may also be called on to give confidential advice to judges, to instruct counsel to appear before a judge to assist the court as advocate to the court, or to investigate any matter on which the court needs a special report.[83] A common inquiry requested is to ascertain the mental capacity of a party to proceedings before the court. A special report may be requested by the court from the Official Solicitor when the judge feels he or she needs help to ascertain facts or information relevant to the case which would not otherwise be made available to the court. It is probably a contempt of court to interfere with an investigation by the Official Solicitor.

---

[83]   Known as a *Harbin v Masterman* inquiry [1896] 1 Ch 351.

Assisting the Court of Protection

8.96 Subject to his consent, the Official Solicitor may be asked to bring an application or represent an incapacitated party in any proceedings.[84] He is frequently asked to assist the Court in applications for statutory wills or authority to make gifts or other dispositions. He will usually be appointed to represent the incapacitated party because the deputy or attorney has a personal interest in the outcome. This work is undertaken in-house and costs are generally payable from the incapacitated party's estate. In serious medical treatment cases the Official Solicitor usually acts in-house both as litigation friend and solicitor. In such cases the Official Solicitor does not seek to fund his costs either from public funding or from the incapacitated party's own estate. Instead the current practice is that he seeks half his costs from the NHS body seeking the Court's decision and funds the balance from his own budget.[85]

Adult medical and welfare declarations

8.97 In the past the Official Solicitor has represented mentally disordered adults, and sometimes acted as adviser to the court, at the hearings of applications in the Family Division concerning, for example, the sterilisation of women suffering from severe learning disabilities, or the withdrawal of life-sustaining treatment (PVS cases). Other applications were made concerning a wide range of welfare disputes, usually in respect of residence and contact matters, when there was a serious justiciable issue requiring a decision by the High Court. Such matters will normally now come within the jurisdiction of the Court of Protection.

8.98 Where the Official Solicitor is appointed to act, he will wish to play a full role in the proceedings and to have an opportunity to properly investigate the case. The Official Solicitor will invariably wish to instruct, on a sole or joint basis, one or more experts to advise on capacity and or best interests. When drafting directions orders prior to the Official Solicitor accepting appointment, care should be taken to ensure that the timetable for his involvement is realistic and allows sufficient time for investigations, including the selection and instruction of independent experts.

Other jurisdictions

8.99 Although there should be a clear definition of the range of services to be provided by the Official Solicitor, there is a diversity of services available in the jurisdictions of the UK and Ireland.

---

[84] Court of Protection Rules 2001, rr 11 and 13.

[85] Recently blessed as a proper exercise of a court's discretion by Munby J in *X NHS Trust v J (by her litigation friend the Official Solicitor)* [2005] EWHC 1273 (Fam), [2006] Lloyd's Rep Med 151. See generally Chapter 5. The President is due to hear a case sometime in 2010 on whether this practice developed under the inherent jurisdiction should continue in cases under the MCA 2005.

Scotland

8.100   There is no equivalent of the Official Solicitor in Scotland and the Office of the Public Guardian has no recourse to a professional legal service other than in response to its own departmental administrative requirements. This is proving to be a significant disadvantage. However, in a case where the incapacitated party had been moved to Scotland it was possible through liaison with the relevant Scottish local authority to obtain a mirror order from the local Sheriff's Court under the Adults with Incapacity (Scotland) Act 2000 to confirm and implement an earlier decision of the Court of Protection relating to residence and contact.

Northern Ireland

8.101   The Official Solicitor based in Belfast has two legal officers and a staff of eight, which includes four caseworkers. She acts as Controller of last resort, amicus to the court where required, a general overseer and investigator and representative for persons under legal disability[86] in civil court proceedings. The workload is heavy and financial resources restricted. Costs are sought where feasible but there is no full costs recovery because this could obstruct access to justice for those who need the services. Proposals include contracting out certain work to an accredited panel of solicitors and transferring children work elsewhere, leaving financial oversight, representation of patients and court assistance as core functions.

Ireland

8.102   The equivalent in the Republic of Ireland is the Office of the General Solicitor for Minors and Wards of Court situated in Dublin. Its origins lie in Chancery practice but it was brought within the public service in 1969. There is no equivalent of the Public Guardian. The General Solicitor may assist the High Court to arrange medical examinations, act as guardian ad litem of a Ward (or a minor) and act as a Committee of the Estate (or of the Person) of last resort. In many ways this latter role appears similar to that of a social worker but with a legal or administrative bias and legal services may be provided. There is a very heavy caseload for the Office but a lack of support from a multi-disciplinary team, and although the institutions where Wards were placed have now been closed down there are no resources available for those now living in the community.

The future[87]

8.103   Funding of litigation in the Court of Protection has been a cause of concern for the Official Solicitor since the inception of the MCA 2005. Increasing numbers of incapacitated parties are ineligible for public funding

---

[86]   This includes both patients and children.
[87]   The material under this heading has been contributed by James Beck from the Official Solicitor's Office.

but lack sufficient financial resources to realistically fund their cases (which is most likely to occur when the party lacks significant capital but has private pension or other income which takes them marginally over eligibility levels). The Official Solicitor cannot fund such litigation from his own budget and as such in some serious personal welfare cases the Official Solicitor may find he is unable to accept appointment unless some third party is willing to fund the costs (such as another public body). Linked to this is the question of whether his costs of acting in certain cases should be met by other public bodies given the forthcoming reduction in budgets of local authorities and the limited increase in budgets for NHS Trusts following the Comprehensive Spending Review in 2010?

8.104 The inter-relationship between the Official Solicitor and the Independent Mental Capacity Advocate service continues to evolve and practice varies widely across England and Wales particularly in relation to the methods by which IMCAs seek to challenge the decision-maker regarding a proposed s 5 act. Connected with this issue is the question of the Official Solicitor's own role in initiating proceedings on behalf of the incapacitated party. The Official Solicitor has to date invariably limited his role in Court of Protection proceedings to acting for an incapacitated party when proceedings have been brought by others such as public authorities or family members. This may well alter not least because of the likely need for challenges to be brought in the Court of Protection in respect of actual or proposed deprivations of liberty under Deprivation of Liberty Safeguards (DOLS) procedures. It may also alter due to future funding pressure which may make public authorities reluctant to issue proceedings or which may reduce still further the availability of public funding to family members and friends.

8.105 Whilst the introduction of DOLS in 2007 has generated an increase in work for the Official Solicitor, it would appear from the statistics provided by the Department of Health that nationally it is not being implemented in a consistent manner by local authorities and primary care trusts.[88] More uniform application of DOLS coupled with greater public awareness may result in much higher volumes of cases.

In respect of deprivation of liberty falling outside DOLS and provided by a court order under MCA 2005, s 16(2)(a), the court appears to expect the Official Solicitor to play a long-term role, partaking indefinitely in annual reviews of such deprivations of liberty.[89] Partaking on such a long-term involvement in respect of a potentially significant number of cases will present new challenges to the Official Solicitor and his resources particularly if the number of such cases rise.

8.106 Another area of interest is the inter-relationship between clinical negligence or personal injury proceedings and adult welfare work. The

---

[88] Mental Capacity Act 2005 Deprivation of Liberty Safeguards Assessments (England) First Report on Annual Data 2009/10 Health & Social Care Information Centre July 2010.
[89] See Munby J in *Salford City Council v BJ* [2009] EWHC 3310 (Fam) at paras 23–25.

decisions of property and affairs deputies who are invariably appointed following significant interim or final damages payments have led to satellite litigation in the Court of Protection. This raises interesting questions and issues as to the respective roles of both the property and affairs deputy and the Official Solicitor in terms of determining the incapacitated claimant's best interests.

8.107 It was unclear following implementation of the MCA 2005 whether there was a role for a state body to be appointed as deputy of last resort, and, if so, which body that might be. The Official Solicitor or Public Trustee were potential candidates because the Public Guardian does not accept that role (unlike the Chief Executive of the former Public Guardianship Office). This is now resolved as Official Solicitor currently acts as deputy of last resort in 37 cases.

Chapter 9

Miscellaneous

ENDURING POWERS – TRANSITIONAL (MENTAL CAPACITY ACT 2005, SCH 4)

9.1 The Mental Capacity Act 2005 (MCA 2005) repealed the Enduring Powers of Attorney Act 1985 (EPAA 1985) so no new enduring powers of attorney (EPAs) can now be created.[1] There remain in place countless numbers of EPAs, some already registered but perhaps the majority unregistered and held in deed boxes and solicitors' offices across the country as 'insurance policies' in case of future incapacity. The registered EPAs cannot be replaced by new lasting powers of attorney (LPAs) because the donors will invariably lack capacity to grant a new power. Although it may be prudent for those who have already executed an enduring power to replace this with a new lasting power, many simply will not do so and it would be contrary to public policy to require donors – who have in good faith provided for the management of their property and affairs in the event of incapacity – to go to the effort and expense of making new LPAs. The status of these EPAs, registered and unregistered, has therefore been addressed.

9.2 MCA 2005, Sch 4 provides for the recognition and operation of EPAs made before the commencement of the Act. Although EPAA 1985 is repealed, all EPAs made prior to the commencement of MCA 2005 remain effective and operate as EPAs. The provisions of Sch 4 replicate the provisions of EPAA 1985. MCA 2005 therefore confirms that an EPA is a power of attorney, which has been executed in the prescribed form and which is not revoked on the onset of incapacity provided it is registered with the Public Guardian.[2] The attorney must, as soon as is practicable, make an application to register the EPA if he or she has reason to believe that the donor is or is becoming mentally incapable.[3] The attorney must, furthermore, notify a prescribed class of relatives before applying to register the LPA.

9.3 EPAs are dealt with in more detail in Chapter 3 and a detailed account of the rules and principles applicable to their operation is beyond the scope of this work.[4] However, practitioners will need to be able to advise on and

---

[1]   MCA 2005, Sch 7.

[2]   This preserves, for existing EPAs, a 'diagnostic threshold' which has to be attained before the power can be registered and as a result, a presumption that the donor is incapable of managing his or her property and affairs. MCA 2005, s 1 does not therefore apply (MCA 2005, Sch 4, para 1(1)).

[3]   MCA 2005, Sch 7, Part 2, para 4(1). MCA 2005, Sch 7, Part 8 defines 'mentally incapable' in the context of the management of the donor's property and affairs.

[4]   The topic is covered in greater and better detail in *Cretney & Lush on Enduring Powers of Attorney* (Jordans, 5th edn, 2001), which will remain the definitive work on the subject. The same law and procedure will apply to existing EPAs, only different statutory provisions will apply to their operation.

administer two distinct types of statutory power of attorney and apply different principles and procedures to each one. There will no doubt be endless debate over whether one is better than the other, but the inevitable result will be the complexity of two different jurisdictions applicable to persons in identical circumstances.

TRANSITIONAL PROVISIONS (MENTAL CAPACITY ACT 2005, SCH 5)

9.4 MCA 2005, Sch 5[5] deals with transitional provisions and savings in two Parts. Part 1 covers the repeal of the Mental Health Act 1983, Part VII (which established the jurisdiction of the previous Court of Protection) and Part 2 covers the repeal of EPAA 1985 (which established EPAs).

Mental Health Act 1983, Part VII

9.5 A receiver under the former regime is in effect converted into a deputy under the new jurisdiction from its commencement but with the same functions as he or she had as receiver. Application may be made to the Court to end the appointment, to make a decision not authorised or for the Court to exercise its powers. Any existing order or appointment, direction or authority will continue to have effect despite the repeal of the Mental Health Act 1983, Part VII.

9.6 Any pending application for the exercise of a power under the Mental Health Act 1983, Part VII was treated, insofar as a corresponding power is exercisable, as an application for the exercise of that power.[6] An appeal which had not been determined continued to be dealt with under the former regime. All fees and other payments which, having become due, had not been paid were to be paid to the new Court of Protection after the commencement day.

9.7 The records of the former Court of Protection are to be treated as records of the new Court of Protection and the Public Guardian for the purpose of exercising any of his or her functions has access thereto. The new Court of Protection Rules may provide that former receivers must continue to render accounts.

Enduring Powers of Attorney Act 1985

9.8 Any order or determination made, or other thing done, under EPAA 1985 continues to have effect under the new jurisdiction from its commencement and insofar as it could have been done under MCA 2005,

---

5   MCA 2005, s 66(4).
6   An application for the appointment of a receiver will be treated as an application for the appointment of a deputy.

Sch 4[7] is so treated. Any instrument registered under EPAA 1985 is to be treated as having been registered by the Public Guardian under Sch 4.

9.9 Any pending application for the exercise of a power under EPAA 1985 was treated, insofar as a corresponding power was exercisable under MCA 2005, Sch 4, as an application for the exercise of that power. Special provisions apply to powers given by trustees. An appeal which had not been determined continued to be dealt with under the former regime.

INTERNATIONAL PROTECTION OF ADULTS

The position in Non-Convention Countries

9.10 It remains difficult to determine jurisdiction and ascertain the relevant law in non-Convention countries yet with increased tourism and home ownership abroad (especially for retired people) capacity issues arise quite frequently. Accordingly an attempt has been made in Part X of this volume to lead a pathway through this jungle. It is intended that this Part will develop further in future editions as contacts within other jurisdictions are established.

Scotland

9.11 In the 2010 edition of this work the incapacity law of Scotland was summarised in a new Chapter 10. That material has now been moved to and incorporated in the new Part X of this edition.

CONSEQUENTIAL AMENDMENTS AND REPEALS (MENTAL CAPACITY ACT 2005, SCH 6)

9.12 It is inevitable that there is a long list of minor and consequential amendments to earlier legislation and these are to be found in MCA 2005, Sch 6. They date from the Fines and Recoveries Act 1833 and include amendments to the following legislation:

- Trustee Act 1925;
- Law of Property Act 1925;
- Administration of Estates Act 1925;
- National Assistance Act 1948, s 49;
- Intestates' Estates Act 1952;
- Variation of Trusts Act 1958;
- Administration of Justice Act 1960;
- Industrial and Provident Societies Act 1965;
- Compulsory Purchase Act 1965;
- Leasehold Reform Act 1967;
- Medicines Act 1968;
- Family Law Reform Act 1969;
- Local Authority Social Services Act 1970;

---

[7]   See above.

- Local Government Act 1972;
- Matrimonial Causes Act 1973;
- Consumer Credit Act 1974;
- Sale of Goods Act 1979;
- Limitation Act 1980, s 38;
- Mental Health Act 1983;
- Insolvency Act 1986;
- Public Trustee and Administration of Funds Act 1986;
- Child Support Act 1991;
- Social Security Administration Act 1992;
- Leasehold Reform, Housing and Urban Development Act 1993;
- Disability Discrimination Act 1995;
- Trusts of Land and Appointment of Trustees Act 1996;
- Adoption and Children Act 2002; and
- Licensing Act 2003.

9.13 In addition, specific repeals of earlier legislation are to be found in MCA 2005, Sch 7. The following wholesale repeals are noteworthy:

- Mental Health Act 1983, Part VII; and
- Enduring Powers of Attorney Act 1985.

9.14 With effect from 1 October 2009 numerous amendments were made by the Mental Capacity Act 2005 (Transitional and Consequential Provisions) Order 2007[8] to various Statutory Instruments. These are set out in Schedule 1 and include such diverse regulations and court rules as:

- National Savings Bank Regulations 1972;
- Premium Savings Bond Regulations 1972;
- National Savings Stock Register Regulations 1976;
- Motor Vehicles (Tests) Regulations 1981;
- Mental Health Review Tribunal Rules 1983;
- Road Vehicles (Construction and Use) Regulations 1986;
- Insolvency Rules 1986;
- Non-contentious Probate Rules 1987;
- Savings Certificates Regulations 1991.

In the present context the most significant amendment is that to the Insolvency Rules 1986 whereby the new definition of 'lacks capacity' is adopted for incapacitated persons. Similar changes were made by amendments to the Civil Procedure Rules 1998 and the Family Proceedings Rules 1991.

---

8   SI 2007/1898. See Part IV of this volume.

PART II

Procedural Guides

PART II: Procedural Guides

Contents

Procedural Guide 1: Application to Register an Enduring Power of Attorney — 365

Procedural Guide 2: Application to Register a Lasting Power of Attorney — 366

Procedural Guide 3: Application for Appointment of a Deputy Relating to Property and Financial Affairs — 367

Procedural Guide 4: Applications Relating to Personal Welfare — 369

Procedural Guide 5: Proceedings in the High Court or a County Court Involving a Protected Party — 370

Procedural Guide 6: Resolving doubt about capacity under the Civil Procedure Rules 1998 — 382

PART II

PROCEDURAL GUIDE 1: APPLICATION TO REGISTER AN ENDURING POWER OF ATTORNEY

The procedure for registering an enduring power of attorney is as follows.

(1) Notice of registration to be given – the legislation sets out to whom notice is given	MCA 2005, Sch 3, Part 3 2007 Regs, reg 23 and Sch 7	Form EP1PG
(2) Registration	MCA 2005, Sch 8	Form EP2PG
	2007 Regs, reg 24	Original or certified copy of the enduring power of attorney; Fee (see Form OPG506 for fees details and exemptions); no evidence of capacity is required
(3) If no objections are received, registration is completed with a target time of 35 days	MCA 2005, Sch 4	
(4) Objections		
(a) Objections must be made within 5 weeks on specified grounds	MCA 2005, Sch 4	
(b) The objection is made by application to the Court supported by evidence	MCA 2005, Sch 4. COPR 2007, Practice Direction H, Part 9, paras 6–10	Form COP8 or COP1 if the person objecting was not entitled to notice of registration; Form COP24; No fee
This must be served on the donor/attorney within 21 days and notice given to P in 7 days	2007 Regs, reg 26	
(c) Duties of Public Guardian	COPR 2007, r 68(4)	Form COP20
(d) Certificate of service to be filed within 7 days of service		
(e) Acknowledgment of service to be filed	COPR 2007, r 72	Form COP5
(f) Court gives directions or makes an order		

PART II

PROCEDURAL GUIDE 2: APPLICATION TO REGISTER A LASTING POWER OF ATTORNEY

The procedure in regard to application to register a lasting power of attorney is as follows.

(1) Notice of registration	2007 Regs, reg 10 and Sch 2	Form LPA001
(2) Application to register	2007 Regs, reg 11 and Sch 3	Form LPA002 The lasting power of attorney Fee
(3) OPG sends notice of receipt	2007 Regs, reg 13	Form LPA003A/003B
(4) OPG registers after 6 weeks	2007 Regs, regs 12 and 17	Form LPA004
(5) Objections		
(a) An objection should be made within 5 weeks: objections can be made to the Public Guardian on factual grounds or to the Court on prescribed grounds	2007 Regs, regs 14(2) and 15(3)	
(b) If an objection is made to the Public Guardian, he or she will give notification if the ground is established	2007 Regs, reg 14(4)	
(c) If the objection is made to the Court, an application is required (no permission is needed) and evidence must be filed	COPR 2007, rr 51(2)(b) and 64 and Part 9, Practice Direction A	Form COP7; Form COP24 No fee is payable If the person objecting is not a person who received Form LPA001 the application is made on Form COP1

PROCEDURAL GUIDE 3: APPLICATION FOR APPOINTMENT OF A DEPUTY RELATING TO PROPERTY AND FINANCIAL AFFAIRS

The procedure in regard to application for appointment of a deputy relating to property and financial affairs is as follows.

(1) Is permission needed?	MCA 2005, s 50; COPR 2007, Part 8	Form COP2 should be filed with the application
(2) The substantive application should be filed at the same time as permission is sought	COPR 2007, Part 9 Practice Direction A; COPR 2007, rr 62–64 and Practice Directions A, B and D	Form COP1 (application form); Form COP1A (Annex A being supporting information required); Form COP3 (assessment of capacity form); Form COP4 (deputy's declaration form); Copy enduring power of attorney or lasting power of attorney if applicable; Court fee
(3) Within 14 days, the Court will deal with the application for permission if this is required. The Court will either grant permission, refuse the application without a hearing or fix a hearing. If a hearing is fixed, the Court will give directions to notify any person of the hearing	COPR 2007, rr 55 and 56; COPR 2007, r 89 will apply where permission is refused without a hearing; COPR 2007, Part 20 deals with an appeal following a hearing; COPR 2007, r 56 and Practice Direction A, para 8 deal with notification of persons of a permission hearing; COPR 2007, r 57 deals with acknowledgement of the permission application	If a hearing is fixed, a person notified of the hearing must file Form COP5 within 21 days

(4) If permission is given for the application, the Court will issue the application	COPR 2007, r 65	The Court will give the applicant: Form COP5 (acknowledgement of service) Form COP14 (notice of proceedings to P) Form COP14A (guidance notes for Form COP14) Form COP15 (notice that an application has been issued) Form COP15A (guidance notes for Form COP15) Form COP20 (certificate of service and notification)
(5) Serve application form and accompanying documents on respondent(s) within 21 days	COPR 2007, r 66	Forms COP1, COP1A and any other accompanying documents to that form, COP5 and COP15
(6) Notify P of the application (NB: P may not be a party and hence not a respondent)	COPR 2007, r 69	P is served with Forms COP14 and COP5
Notify any other persons of the application.	COPR 2007, r 70	Forms COP15 and COP5
(7) Within 7 days of service and notification, the applicant must file a certificate of service	COPR 2007, rr 68(4) and 70(3)	Form COP20
(8) Any person who is served or notified of an application and who wishes to take part in the proceedings must file an acknowledgement of service within 21 days	COPR 2007, r 72	Form COP5
(9) Consideration of application by the Court. The Court will order a hearing, give directions or make a final order without a hearing	COPR 2007, rr 84 and 85	

PROCEDURAL GUIDE 4: APPLICATIONS RELATING TO PERSONAL WELFARE

The procedure in regard to applications relating to personal welfare is as follows.

(1) Is permission required?	MCA 2005, s 50; COPR 2007, Part 8	Form COP2
(2) The substantive application should be filed at the same time as permission is sought	COPR 2007 Part 9, Practice Direction A (what is filed when seeking permission); COPR 2007, rr 62–64 and Practice Directions A and E (if appropriate)	Form COP1 (application form); Form COP1B, Annex B (supporting information for personal welfare applications); Form COP2 (if permission is required); Form COP3 (assessment of capacity); Form COP4 (deputy's declaration form); Copy of enduring power of attorney or lasting power of attorney (if appropriate); Court fee
(3)–(9) Steps from seeking permission to the final hearing	See Procedural Guide 3: Application for Appointment of a Deputy Relating to Property and Financial Affairs	
(10) Miscellaneous points		
(a) Dealing with the application	COPR 2007, r 84: the Court must consider the application as soon as practicable after issue (NB: there may be important issues that require attention urgently)	
(b) Urgent applications	If an urgent hearing is required, an urgent application should be filed as soon as possible: see COPR 2007, Part 10 and Practice Directions A and B	Form COP9 and evidence in support and, if appropriate, a disc with a draft order
(c) Serious medical treatment applications	COPR 2007 Part 9, Practice Direction E sets out the Court's approach	

PART II

PROCEDURAL GUIDE 5: PROCEEDINGS IN THE HIGH COURT OR A COUNTY COURT INVOLVING A PROTECTED PARTY

Legal background

The Civil Procedural Rules 1998 Part 21 contains special provisions which apply to proceedings involving protected parties (as defined). These are supplemented by a Practice Direction. Unless the Court orders otherwise it is necessary for a protected party to be represented by a litigation friend.

Any proceedings commenced or conducted in breach of this requirement will be a nullity (unless the Court otherwise orders) and a solicitor who purports to act on the record for a protected party without a litigation friend may become personally liable for the costs of opposing parties.

Under the 2007 amendment to the CPR the old term 'patient' was replaced by the new term 'protected party' and a new definition applies. This became necessary because of the implementation on 1 October 2007 of the Mental Capacity Act 2005.

Procedure

The procedure in regard to 'protected parties' is as follows.

Who is a protected party?	A party, or an intended party, who lacks capacity (within the meaning of MCA 2005) to conduct the proceedings	CPR, r 21.1(2)(d)
Who 'lacks capacity'?	A person lacks capacity in relation to a matter if at the material time he or she is unable to make a decision for him or herself in relation to the matter because of an impairment of, or a disturbance in the functioning of, the mind or brain	MCA 2005, s 2(1)
When is a person unable to make a decision for him or herself?	If unable to: • understand the information relevant to the decision; • retain that information;	

	• use or weigh that information as part of the process of making the decision; or	
	• communicate his or her decision (whether by talking, using sign language or any other means)	MCA 2005, s 3(1)
Requirement for a litigation friend	A *protected party* must have a litigation friend to conduct proceedings on his or her behalf	CPR, r 21.2(1)
When must a litigation friend be appointed?	A person may not, without permission of the Court:	
	• make an application against a protected party before proceedings have started; or	
	• take any step in proceedings except:	
	• issuing and serving a claim form; or	
	• applying for the appointment of a litigation friend under CPR, r 21.6,	
	until the protected party has a litigation friend	CPR, r 21.3(2)
	If a party becomes a protected party during proceedings, no party may take any step in the proceedings without the permission of the Court until the protected party has a litigation friend	CPR, r 21.3(3)
	Any step taken before a protected party has a litigation friend shall be of no effect, unless the Court otherwise orders	CPR, r 21.3(4)

PART II

How do you decide if a party is a protected party?	As to assessment of mental capacity see generally the notes to CPR, r 21.1	
	In case of uncertainty, application should be made to the Court to resolve this	
Title to proceedings	The name of a protected party should be followed by '(a protected party by … his litigation friend)'	PD21, para 1.1
Who is appointed (without a court order)?	A deputy appointed by the Court of Protection under MCA 2005 with power to conduct proceedings on the protected party's behalf is entitled to be the litigation friend of the protected party in any proceedings to which his or her power extends	CPR, r 21.4(2)
	If nobody has been appointed by the Court (or appointed as a deputy as above) a person may act as a litigation friend if he or she: • can fairly and competently conduct proceedings on behalf of the protected party; and • has no interest adverse to that of the protected party; • (claim or counterclaim) undertakes to pay any costs which the protected party may be ordered to pay.	CPR, r 21.4(3)
Appointment without a court order	(If the Court has not appointed one) a person wishing to act as a litigation friend must:	

	• (if empowered by the Court of Protection) file an official copy of the order conferring the power;	
	• (otherwise) file a certificate of suitability:	
	• claimant) when making the claim;	
	• (defendant) when first taking a step in the proceedings	CPR, r 21.5
Certificate of suitability of litigation friend	States that the proposed litigation friend: • consents to act; • believes the person to be a protected party (with reasons and medical evidence); • can fairly and competently conduct proceedings on behalf of the person; • has no adverse interest; and • (claimant) undertakes to pay any costs which the claimant may be ordered to pay in the proceedings	
	A counterclaim is treated like a claim for the purpose of the costs undertaking	Form N235; CPR, r 21.4(3); PD21, para 2.2; CPR, r 20.3(1)
Service of certificate of suitability	The litigation friend must: • serve the certificate of suitability on every person on whom the claim form should be served; and	CPR, r 21.5(4)(a)

PART II

	• file a certificate of service when he or she files the certificate of suitability	CPR, r 21.5(4)(b); CPR, r 6.13
Certificate of service	States required details of method of service	CPR, r 6.17
Application for appointment by the Court	An application for an order appointing a litigation friend may be made by: • a person who wishes to be the litigation friend; or • a party The claimant must apply where: • a person makes a claim against a protected party; • the protected party has no litigation friend; and • either (i) someone who is not entitled files a defence or (ii) the claimant wishes to take some step in the proceedings	CPR, r 21.6; PD21, paras 3.1–3.4
	An application must be supported by evidence and the Court must be satisfied that the person appointed is 'suitable'	CPR, r 21.6(4); CPR, r 21.6(5); CPR, r 21.4(3)
Change of litigation friend	The Court may: • direct that a person may not act as a litigation friend; • terminate the appointment; and • appoint a new litigation friend in substitution for an existing one	

	An application for an order must be supported by evidence and the Court may not appoint a litigation friend unless satisfied that the person is suitable	CPR, r 21.7; CPR, r 21.4(3)
Who is appointed by the Court?	On an application the Court may appoint: • the person proposed; or • any other person who complies with the conditions in CPR, r 21.4(3)	CPR, r 21.8(4)
Appointment of the Official Solicitor	The Official Solicitor may be appointed as litigation friend provided: • he or she consents; and • provision is made for payment of his or her costs	PD21, para 3.4
Appointment ceasing – protected party	When a protected party acquires capacity, the litigation friend's appointment continues until ended by a court order:	CPR, r 21.9(2)
	application may be made by former protected party, litigation friend or a party; and	CPR, r 21.9(3); PD21, para 4.5
	the application must be supported by evidence	PD21, para 4.6
	The protected party must file and serve a notice: • that the appointment has ceased; • giving his or her address for service; and • stating whether or not he or she intends to carry on the proceedings	CPR, r 21.9(4) PD21, para 4.7

	If he or she does not do so within 28 days the Court may, on application, strike out any claim or defence brought by the protected party	CPR, r 21.9(5)
Service of claim form – protected party	Service of the claim form is upon: • the attorney under a registered enduring power of attorney; • the donee of a lasting power of attorney; • the deputy appointed by the Court of Protection; or • (if none) the person with whom the protected party resides or in whose care he or she is	CPR, r 6.13(2)
Service of claim form – general	The court may by order: • permit the claim form to be served on the ... protected party, or on a person other than as specified; • treat a document as if it had been properly served although it has been served on someone other than as specified.	CPR, r 6.13(4) CPR, r 6.13(6)
Service generally	Once a litigation friend has been appointed, service will be upon him or her as if the litigation friend was the party	CPR, r 6.25(2)

	The Court may by order:	
	• permit a document to be served on the protected party, or on a person other than as specified;	CPR, r 6.25(3)
	• treat a document as if it had been properly served although it has been served on someone other than as specified	CPR, r 6.25(5)
Service of application relating to a litigation friend	An application for an order appointing or changing a litigation friend must be served on:	CPR, r 21.8
	• every person on whom the claim form should be served; and	CPR, r 21.8(1)
	• (if appointing) the protected party unless the Court otherwise orders; or	CPR, r 21.8(2)
	• (if changing) the existing and proposed litigation friend	CPR, r 21.8(3)
Statement of truth	Where a statement of truth is required the litigation friend or his or her legal representative signs this to verify that the litigation friend believes the facts stated in the document are true	CPR, r 22.1(6) PD22, paras 3.1(1) and 3.7 CPR, r 22.1(5)
Default judgment	A claimant may only obtain a default judgment against a protected party:	
	• on an application supported by evidence that he or she is entitled to the judgment claimed;	CPR, r 12.10(a)(i) PD12, para 2.3(1)
	• after appointment of a litigation friend	CPR, r 12.11(3); PD12, para 4.2
	A counterclaim is treated like a claim.	CPR, r 20.3

PART II

Judgment on an admission	There are restrictions on obtaining a judgment by or against a protected party based on an admission.	CPR, r 14.1(4)
Hearing	A hearing may be in private if this is necessary to protect the interests of a protected party:	CPR, r 39.2(3)(d)
	• e g 'approval of a compromise or settlement, or application for payment of money out of court to such party'	PD39, para 1.6
Availability of witness statements	The Court may at a trial make a direction that a witness statement which stands as evidence in chief is not open to inspection due to the need to protect the interests of a protected party	CPR, r 32.13(3)(e)
Compromise or settlement	Where a claim or counterclaim is made:	
	• by or on behalf of a protected party; or	
	• against a protected party,	
	no settlement, compromise or payment and no acceptance of money paid into Court shall be valid, so far as it relates to such claim, without Court approval	CPR, r 21.10(1)
	Where before proceedings in which such a claim is made are begun:	
	• an agreement is reached for the settlement of the claim;	

	• and the sole purpose of proceedings is to obtain the approval of the Court to a settlement or compromise	
	the claim must be made using the CPR Part 8 procedure and include a request to the Court for approval	CPR, r 21.10(2) PD21, paras 5.1–5.3; Form N292
	If in the Chancery Division, it will be heard by the judge, rather than the master, if the amount involved exceeds £100,000	PD2B, para 5.1(a)
Structured settlements	A Practice Direction deals with the procedure where a structured settlement is contemplated	PD40C
Interim payments	The approval of the Court must be obtained before making a voluntary interim payment to a protected party	CPR, r 21.10(1)
Acceptance of offers and payments into court	An offer or payment may only be accepted on behalf of a protected party with the permission of the Court.	CPR, r 21.10(1)
	In such cases a payment out of court requires a court order	CPR, r 21.11(1)(b)
Who is a protected beneficiary?	A protected party who lacks capacity to manage and control any money recovered by him or her or on his or her behalf or for his or her benefit in the proceedings	CPR, r 21.1(2)(e)

Control of money recovered	Where in any proceedings: • money is recovered on behalf of or for the benefit of a protected party; or • money paid into court is accepted by or on behalf of a protected party, the Court will first consider whether the protected party is a protected beneficiary, and subject thereto: • the money is dealt with under directions of the Court and not otherwise	CPR, r 21.11 PD21, paras 8.1–8.5
	These may provide that the money shall be wholly or partly paid into court and: • invested; or • otherwise dealt with (e g paid to or for the benefit of the protected beneficiary); or • transferred to another court if more convenient	CPR, r 21.11(2) PD21, paras 9.1–9.8; PD21, paras 10.1–10.7; PD21, para 8.1(2) CPR, r 30.7; PD21, para 8.2(3)
Payment out of funds in court held for protected beneficiaries	Applications are to a master or district judge (a hearing may not be required): • for payment out to a protected beneficiary; • to vary an investment strategy	PD21, para 13
Deputy for a protected beneficiary	It will usually be necessary for the Court of Protection to appoint a financial deputy for the estate of a protected beneficiary:	PD21, paras 10.1–10.7

	• money of a protected beneficiary will be transferred;	Forms N292; CFO 200
	• applications for payment out of funds are to the Court of Protection	PD21, para 13.3
Costs	Costs payable to the solicitor for a protected party must be approved by the Court	CPR, r 48.5
	Neither:	
	• the fast-track costs provision; nor	CPR, r 46.1(2)(c)(ii)
	• the power of a court officer to assess costs (unless under CPR, r 48.5)	CPR, r 47.3(1)(b)
	apply to a hearing for the Court's approval of a settlement or compromise of a claim by a protected party	
	The liability of a litigation friend for costs continues until:	
	• the appointment ceases; and	
	• the former protected party serves notice on the other parties; or the litigation friend serves notice.	CPR, r 21.9(6) PD21, para 5.5
Forms	Certificate of suitability of litigation friend: Form N235	
	Order approving terms of a settlement or compromise (includes transfer of fund to Court of Protection): Form N292	
Court fees	No additional fee is prescribed	

PROCEDURAL GUIDE 6: RESOLVING DOUBT ABOUT CAPACITY UNDER THE CIVIL PROCEDURE RULES 1998

Issue

A problem arises when there is a significant doubt as to whether a party lacks capacity because the proceedings should not continue until this doubt has been resolved. There is no simple solution but this Procedural Guide sets out some of the options available to the parties and the court.

Procedure

The procedure in regard to 'protected parties' is as follows.

The Procedural Problem		
Why is 'capacity' relevant?	Special provisions apply to parties who lack capacity – **See generally PG5**	Rule 21 & PD21; MCA 2005 Part 1
What aspects of capacity are relevant?	Capacity: • … to conduct the proceedings • … to manage and control any monies recovered	See generally Rule 21 & PD21
What are the implications?	A party who lacks capacity to conduct the proceedings is a protected party	Rule 21.1(2)(d)
	A party who lacks capacity to manage and control any monies recovered is a *protected beneficiary*	Rule 21.1(2)(e)
What are the consequences?	A *protected party* will normally require a *litigation friend* to be appointed	Rule 21.2(1)
	A *protected beneficiary* will not be permitted to receive money	Rule 21.11(3)
Who may raise doubts as to the capacity of a party?	The solicitors to the party, another party or the court	Rule 3.3

	The court should investigate question of capacity whenever there is reason to suppose it may be absent	*Masterman-Lister case* [2002] EWCA Civ 1889
What should be done when doubts are raised?	The doubts must be resolved and any proceedings stayed until this has been done	Rule 21.3(2),(3); Rule 21.3(4)
What discretion does the court have?	The court may allow steps to be taken before the appointment of a litigation friend	Rule 21.3(2),(3)
How will the court exercise that discretion?	The court may allow steps to be taken which are needed at that stage provided that these will not prejudice the party who may lack capacity	
What if proceedings continue and a party is later found to lack capacity?	Any step taken before a protected party has a litigation friend has no effect *unless the court orders otherwise*	Rule 21.3(4)
When will the court order otherwise?	The court may waive the procedural irregularity and give consequential directions if this will not prejudice the party who lacked capacity and there has been no abuse of process	
How will the court know if there has been prejudice?	A litigation friend will have been appointed and can make submissions	

Resolving Doubt as to Capacity

What help do the CPR provide?	The Rules assume that it is known whether a party lacks capacity so any doubt must be addressed as an issue in the proceedings	Rule 1.1(2)(a); Rule 3.1(2)
What is required?	• Expert evidence • Factual evidence	

The expert evidence?	Medical evidence as to *an impairment of, or a disturbance in the functioning of, the mind or brain* [the diagnostic threshold].	MCA 2005, s 2(1)
The factual evidence	Evidence of expert and lay witnesses as to whether the party is *unable to make a decision in the matter for himself* according to the statutory criteria	MCA 2005, s 3(1)
Are both types of evidence required?	In practice the medical evidence may extend to ability to make and communicate decisions – in which event unless challenged it will be all that is required	
What is the standard of proof?	There is a presumption of capacity but lack of capacity may be proved on the balance of probability	MCA 2005, s 1(2); and s 2(4)
Claimant	Where significant doubt arises the court will expect the party to produce evidence to dispel that doubt Claim may be stayed until claimant submits to a medical examination	
Defendant	The court will expect the claimant to produce evidence if the defendant does not respond	

What if a Defendant will not Co-operate?
The following options may be available to the claimant

Certificate	A suitable adult may be prepared to complete the *Certificate of suitability of litigation friend* which states a belief that the person is a protected party	Form N235
Evidence	Medical evidence may already exist which establishes the diagnostic threshold	
	Evidence of conduct may be available (e g as to how the party has responded to the claim) – this may in itself create doubts as to capacity	
Lack of medical evidence	The court has no power to force the defendant to submit to a medical examination	
	A default order would not be appropriate because an actual finding of lack of capacity is required	
Involve social services?	A recital in a court order that there is an appearance of need for community care services coupled with a request for an indication as to whether such assessment has been or will be carried out may produce information. A social worker may be invited to attend the next directions hearing.	NHS and Community Care Act 1990, s 47
Official Solicitor	Cannot act for party in the absence of a finding of lack of capacity	*Harbin v Masterman* [1986] 1 Ch 351, CA

PART II

	The court can direct Official Solicitor to make inquiries and report	
Court of Protection	*See below*	
Who will be the Litigation Friend? *The following options may be available for a defendant*		
Person already involved	• *Attorney* (under registered enduring or lasting power) • *Deputy* appointed by Court of Protection • *Appointee* for social security benefits	Rule 21.4(2); MCA 2005
Concerned person	Relative, partner, friend, carer or personal advocate	Rule 21.4(3)
Solicitor to party	Not appropriate – conflict of roles	
Official Solicitor	Litigation friend of last resort if consents. Will require provision for costs	
Involving the Court of Protection		
What can this Court do?	• Make declaration as to capacity • Make decisions on behalf of a person who lacks capacity • Appoint a deputy to do so Nominate a person to conduct proceedings	MCA 2005, ss 15, 16
Why involve this Court?	• Resolve capacity issues • Find someone to be litigation friend	MCA 2005

	• Clarify whether the Court of Protection needs to be involved with any damages recovered	
Advantages	• Expertise in this area	MCA 2005, ss 48, 49
	• Power to give directions even before finding of incapacity	
	• Additional powers to obtain reports	
What reports can be obtained?	• Local authority (eg. social services)	MCA 2005, s 49
	• NHS body (health authority or Trust)	
	• Court of Protection general visitor	
	• Court of Protection special visitor	
	• Public Guardian	
Disadvantages	• Cost and delay	
	• Someone must apply to this Court	

PART II

PART III

Mental Capacity Act 2005

PART III: Mental Capacity Act 2005

Contents

Mental Capacity Act 2005   393

Mental Capacity Act 2005

ARRANGEMENT OF SECTIONS

PART 1
PERSONS WHO LACK CAPACITY

The principles

Section		Page
1	The principles	396

Preliminary

2	People who lack capacity	397
3	Inability to make decisions	398
4	Best interests	399
4A	Restriction on deprivation of liberty	402
4B	Deprivation of liberty necessary for life-sustaining treatment etc	403
5	Acts in connection with care or treatment	403
6	Section 5 acts: limitations	404
7	Payment for necessary goods and services	405
8	Expenditure	406

Lasting powers of attorney

9	Lasting powers of attorney	407
10	Appointment of donees	408
11	Lasting powers of attorney: restrictions	409
12	Scope of lasting powers of attorney: gifts	410
13	Revocation of lasting powers of attorney etc	411
14	Protection of donee and others if no power created or power revoked	412

General powers of the court and appointment of deputies

15	Power to make declarations	413
16	Powers to make decisions and appoint deputies: general	413
16A	Section 16 powers: Mental Health Act patients etc	414
17	Section 16 powers: personal welfare	415
18	Section 16 powers: property and affairs	415
19	Appointment of deputies	416
20	Restrictions on deputies	418
21	Transfer of proceedings relating to people under 18	419

Powers of the court in relation to Schedule A1

21A	Powers of court in relation to Schedule A1	419

Powers of the court in relation to lasting powers of attorney

22	Powers of court in relation to validity of lasting powers of attorney	420
23	Powers of court in relation to operation of lasting powers of attorney	421

Advance decisions to refuse treatment

24	Advance decisions to refuse treatment: general	422
25	Validity and applicability of advance decisions	423
26	Effect of advance decisions	423

Excluded decisions

27	Family relationships etc	424
28	Mental Health Act matters	425

PART III

29 Voting rights   426

Research

30 Research   426
31 Requirements for approval   427
32 Consulting carers etc   428
33 Additional safeguards   429
34 Loss of capacity during research project   430

Independent mental capacity advocate service

35 Appointment of independent mental capacity advocates   430
36 Functions of independent mental capacity advocates   431
37 Provision of serious medical treatment by NHS body   432
38 Provision of accommodation by NHS body   432
39 Provision of accommodation by local authority   434
39A Person becomes subject to Schedule A1   435
39B Section 39A: supplementary provision   436
39C Person unrepresented whilst subject to Schedule A1   436
39D Person subject to Schedule A1 without paid representative   437
39E Limitation on duty to instruct advocate under section 39D   438
40 Exceptions   439
41 Power to adjust role of independent mental capacity advocate   439

Miscellaneous and supplementary

42 Codes of practice   439
43 Codes of practice: procedure   441
44 Ill-treatment or neglect   442

PART 2
THE COURT OF PROTECTION AND THE PUBLIC GUARDIAN

The Court of Protection

45 The Court of Protection   443
46 The judges of the Court of Protection   443

Supplementary powers

47 General powers and effect of orders etc   444
48 Interim orders and directions   445
49 Power to call for reports   445

Practice and procedure

50 Applications to the Court of Protection   447
51 Court of Protection Rules   447
52 Practice directions   448
53 Rights of appeal   449

Fees and costs

54 Fees   449
55 Costs   450
56 Fees and costs: supplementary   451

The Public Guardian

57 The Public Guardian   451
58 Functions of the Public Guardian   451
59 Public Guardian Board   453
60 Annual report   454

Court of Protection Visitors
61   Court of Protection Visitors   454

PART 3
MISCELLANEOUS AND GENERAL
Declaratory provision
62   Scope of the Act   455

Private international law
63   International protection of adults   455

General
64   Interpretation   456
65   Rules, regulations and orders   457
66   Existing receivers and enduring powers of attorney etc   458
67   Minor and consequential amendments and repeals   458
68   Commencement and extent   459
69   Short title   459

SCHEDULES
Schedule A1 – Hospital and Care Home Residents: Deprivation of
   Liberty   460
   Part 1 – Authorisation to Deprive Residents of Liberty etc   460
   Part 2 – Interpretation: Main Terms   461
   Part 3 – The Qualifying Requirements   461
   Part 4 – Standard Authorisations   464
   Part 5 – Urgent Authorisations   478
   Part 6 – Eligibility Requirement not Met: Suspension of Standard
      Authorisation   482
   Part 7 – Standard Authorisations: Change in Supervisory
      Responsibility   483
   Part 8 – Standard Authorisations: Review   484
   Part 9 – Assessments under this Schedule   491
   Part 10 – Relevant Person's Representative   494
   Part 11 – IMCAs   498
   Part 12 – Miscellaneous   499
   Part 13 – Interpretation   501
Schedule 1 – Lasting Powers of Attorney: Formalities   507
   Part 1 – Making instruments   507
   Part 2 – Registration   509
   Part 3 – Cancellation of registration and notification of severance   513
   Part 4 – Records of alterations in registered powers   514
Schedule 1A – Persons Ineligible to be Deprived of Liberty by this Act   515
   Part 1 – Ineligible Persons   515
   Part 2 – Interpretation   517
Schedule 2 – Property and Affairs: Supplementary Provisions   520
Schedule 3 – International Protection of Adults   523
   Part 1 – Preliminary   523
   Part 2 – Jurisdiction of competent authority   525
   Part 3 – Applicable law   526
   Part 4 – Recognition and enforcement   528
   Part 5 – Co-operation   530
   Part 6 – General   530
Schedule 4 – Provisions Applying to Existing Enduring Powers of
   Attorney   532
   Part 1 – Enduring powers of attorney   532

PART III

Part 2 – Action on actual or impending incapacity of donor   535
Part 3 – Notification prior to registration   536
Part 4 – Registration   538
Part 5 – Legal position after registration   539
Part 6 – Protection of attorney and third parties   541
Part 7 – Joint and joint and several attorneys   543
Part 8 – Interpretation   544
Schedule 5 – Transitional Provisions and Savings   545
Part 1 – Repeal of Part 7 of the Mental Health Act 1983   545
Part 2 – Repeal of the Enduring Powers of Attorney Act 1985   548
Schedule 6 – Minor and Consequential Amendments   549
Schedule 7 – Repeals   563

PART 1
PERSONS WHO LACK CAPACITY

The principles

1 The principles

(1) The following principles apply for the purposes of this Act.

(2) A person must be assumed to have capacity unless it is established that he lacks capacity.

(3) A person is not to be treated as unable to make a decision unless all practicable steps to help him to do so have been taken without success.

(4) A person is not to be treated as unable to make a decision merely because he makes an unwise decision.

(5) An act done, or decision made, under this Act for or on behalf of a person who lacks capacity must be done, or made, in his best interests.

(6) Before the act is done, or the decision is made, regard must be had to whether the purpose for which it is needed can be as effectively achieved in a way that is less restrictive of the person's rights and freedom of action.

Scope of provision—This section sets out the principles on which the Mental Capacity Act 2005 (MCA 2005) is based. A clear statement of principles was recommended by the Joint Scrutiny Committee on the Draft Mental Incapacity Bill as 'an initial point of reference' to underpin the Act and guide its interpretation and operation. Anyone using the provisions of MCA 2005 is required to act in accordance with the principles, which serve as 'benchmarks' for decision-makers. The common law origins of each of the five principles and their operation in practice are described in Chapter 2 (**2.29–2.52**).

'assumed to have capacity' (s 1(2))—This principle is more generally known as the presumption of capacity – the starting point when assessing someone's capacity to make a particular decision. The presumption is rebuttable if it is established that the person concerned lacks the capacity to make the decision in question at the relevant time, using the test of capacity set out in ss 2–3. Where capacity is in doubt, a lower threshold is required for engagement of the powers of the Court of Protection under MCA2005, s 48 (*Re F* [2009] EWHC B30 (Fam) at 44).

'unable to make a decision' (s 1(3))—As defined in s 3.

'all practicable steps' (s 1(3))—The term 'practicable' is interpreted in the MCA 2005 Code of Practice as 'practical and appropriate', depending on 'personal circumstances, the kind of decision that has to be made and the time available to make the decision'. Resource constraints may also be relevant. Chapter 3 of the Code suggests a range of practicable steps to help someone make a decision for themselves. A distinction must be drawn between providing appropriate support and using excessive persuasion or 'undue influence'.

'an unwise decision' (s 1(4))—Based on the common law principle that the law does not insist that a person behaves 'in such a manner as to deserve approbation from the prudent, the wise or the good' (*Bird v Luckie* (1850) 8 Hare 301). When someone's capacity is being assessed, it is the ability to make the decision (not necessarily a sensible or wise decision) that is under scrutiny, not the outcome.

'best interests' (s 1(5))—This principle establishes 'best interests' as the criterion to govern all actions done for, and all decisions made on behalf of, someone who lacks capacity to make those decisions for themselves. The term 'best interests' is not defined in MCA 2005, but s 4 expands on the determination of best interests.

'regard must be had' (s 1(6))—While 'regard must be had' to the principle of acting in a less restrictive way, the 'best interests' principle takes priority – the option which is in the person's best interests must be chosen, which may not necessarily be the least restrictive alternative.

'the purpose for which it is needed' (s 1(6))—Other options need only be considered so long as the desired purpose of the action or decision can still be achieved.

'less restrictive' (s 1(6))—But not necessarily the least restrictive alternative (see above).

Preliminary

2 People who lack capacity

(1) For the purposes of this Act, a person lacks capacity in relation to a matter if at the material time he is unable to make a decision for himself in relation to the matter because of an impairment of, or a disturbance in the functioning of, the mind or brain.

(2) It does not matter whether the impairment or disturbance is permanent or temporary.

(3) A lack of capacity cannot be established merely by reference to –

    (a)   a person's age or appearance, or
    (b)   a condition of his, or an aspect of his behaviour, which might lead others to make unjustified assumptions about his capacity.

(4) In proceedings under this Act or any other enactment, any question whether a person lacks capacity within the meaning of this Act must be decided on the balance of probabilities.

(5) No power which a person ('D') may exercise under this Act –

    (a)   in relation to a person who lacks capacity, or
    (b)   where D reasonably thinks that a person lacks capacity,

is exercisable in relation to a person under 16.

(6) Subsection (5) is subject to section 18(3).

Scope of provision—This section sets out the Act's definition of a person who lacks capacity to make a decision. Section 3 sets out the test for assessing whether a person is unable to make a decision and therefore lacks capacity (see below). By applying these together, the Act adopts a functional approach to defining capacity, requiring capacity to be assessed in relation to a specific decision rather than the ability to make decisions generally. The definition and test of capacity are described in Chapter 2 (**2.53–2.67**).

'For the purposes of this Act' (s 2(1))—The definition applies 'For the purposes of this Act'. Schedule 6 makes consequential amendments to existing statutes in order to ensure that the definition is used in relation to other proceedings. Common law definitions of capacity (such as capacity to make a will (*Banks v Goodfellow* (1870) LR 5 QB 549) or to enter into marriage (*Sheffield City Council v E & S* [2005] 1 FLR 965)) are not affected, but assessments of capacity to make such decisions after the MCA 2005 came into effect should have regard to the MCA test of capacity (*Scammell and Scammell v Farmer* [2008] EWHC 1100 at 24–29). For an early decision on the test of capacity under the MCA 2005 jurisdiction in regard to a brain injured claimant see *Saulle v Nouvet* [2007] EWHC 2902 (QB) in which it was confirmed that the MCA test of capacity should be used to assess litigation capacity in proceedings to which the Civil Procedure Rules apply (for case summary see Part IX of this work).

'in relation to a matter' (s 2(1))—This confirms that capacity is decision-specific.

'at the material time' (s 2(1))—This confirms that capacity is time-specific.

'because of an impairment of, or a disturbance in the functioning of, the mind or brain' (s 2(1))—This sets a 'diagnostic threshold' for a lack of capacity to be established. If a person fails the diagnostic test, there can be no finding of lack of capacity under the Act. The diagnostic threshold covers a wide range of conditions and disorders, whether temporary or permanent (s 2(2)).

Equal consideration or non-discrimination—(s 2(3))—During parliamentary debates on the Bill, attempts were made to introduce some form of 'non-discrimination' or 'equal consideration' principle into the legislation. The Government's response was to insert s 2(3), aimed at preventing unjustified assumptions being made about a person's mental capacity. A similar provision was introduced in s 4(1) relating to the determination of best interests.

'balance of probabilities' (s 2(4))—That a lack of capacity is 'more likely than not' (*Re H (Minors) (Sexual Abuse—Standard of Proof)* [1996] AC 563, at p 586).

'a person under 16' (s 2(5)–(6))—The powers under this Act apply in general only to people lacking capacity who are aged 16 years or over. However, as was the case under the previous law, the Act's powers to deal with property and financial affairs might be exercised in relation to a child whose disabilities will cause a lack of capacity to manage those affairs to continue into adulthood (see s 18(3)). The different concepts of 'competence' in relation to children under 16 years and 'capacity' applying to young people aged 16–17 are discussed in Chapter 2 (**2.85–2.88**).

3 Inability to make decisions

(1) For the purposes of section 2, a person is unable to make a decision for himself if he is unable –

    (a)   to understand the information relevant to the decision,

    (b)   to retain that information,

    (c)   to use or weigh that information as part of the process of making the decision, or

    (d)   to communicate his decision (whether by talking, using sign language or any other means).

(2) A person is not to be regarded as unable to understand the information relevant to a decision if he is able to understand an explanation of it given to him in a way that is appropriate to his circumstances (using simple language, visual aids or any other means).

(3) The fact that a person is able to retain the information relevant to a decision for a short period only does not prevent him from being regarded as able to make the decision.

(4) The information relevant to a decision includes information about the reasonably foreseeable consequences of –

    (a)   deciding one way or another, or

    (b)   failing to make the decision.

Scope of provision—This section sets out the test for determining whether a person is unable to make a particular decision and therefore lacks capacity for the purposes of this Act (see s 2). This is a 'functional' test, focusing on the ability of the person concerned to make a particular decision and the processes followed by the person in arriving at the decision – not on the outcome.

'information relevant to the decision' (s 3(1)(a))—Includes the particular nature of the decision in question, the purpose for which the decision is needed and the likely effects of making the decision. It also includes the reasonably foreseeable consequences of deciding one way or another or of making no decision at all (s 3(4)). Identifying what is the specific decision in question, and the information relevant to the decision, is not always straightforward – see for example *Re S: D v R (Deputy of S) and S* [2010] EWHC 2405 (COP). For case summary, see Part IX of this work.

'retain the information' (s 3(1)(b))—For long enough to make an effective decision, depending on what is necessary for the decision in question. The ability to retain information for a short period only will not automatically disqualify the person from making the decision (s 3(3)).

'use or weigh that information' (s 3(1)(c))—Understanding the information is not sufficient – the person must be able to use the information as part of the process of making a decision. The courts have defined the process as the ability to weigh all relevant information in the balance and then use the information in order to arrive at a decision (*Re MB* [1997] 2 FLR 426; *R v Collins and Ashworth Hospital Authority ex parte Brady* [2001] 58 BMLR 173). Further guidance on applying this element of the capacity test is given in The *PCT v P, AH & The Local Authority* [2009] EW Misc 10 (EWCOP).

'[unable to] communicate his decision' (s 3(1)(d))—By any possible means. This residual category will affect a minority of people where 'the assessor does not know, one way or the other, whether the person is capable of deciding or not' (Law Com No 231, at para 3.20). Communicating by blinking one eye can be sufficient to indicate capacity (*Re AK (Adult Patient) (Medical Treatment—Consent)* [2001] 1 FLR 129).

'explanation ... appropriate to his circumstances' (s 3(2))—Appropriate to the particular circumstances of the person concerned, using the most effective means of communication ('simple language, visual aids or any other means') to assist his or her understanding and to enable the person to use the information as required by s 3(1)(c).

'reasonably foreseeable consequences' (s 3(4))—see *A Local Authority v Mrs A* [2010] EWHC 1549 for an example of the court's interpretation of the reasonably foreseeable consequences of making a personal welfare decision (in this case concerning consent to contraceptive treatment).

4 Best interests

(1) In determining for the purposes of this Act what is in a person's best interests, the person making the determination must not make it merely on the basis of –

    (a)   the person's age or appearance, or
    (b)   a condition of his, or an aspect of his behaviour, which might lead others to make unjustified assumptions about what might be in his best interests.

(2) The person making the determination must consider all the relevant circumstances and, in particular, take the following steps.

(3) He must consider –

    (a)   whether it is likely that the person will at some time have capacity in relation to the matter in question, and
    (b)   if it appears likely that he will, when that is likely to be.

(4) He must, so far as reasonably practicable, permit and encourage the person to participate, or to improve his ability to participate, as fully as possible in any act done for him and any decision affecting him.

(5) Where the determination relates to life-sustaining treatment he must not, in considering whether the treatment is in the best interests of the person concerned, be motivated by a desire to bring about his death.

(6) He must consider, so far as is reasonably ascertainable –

    (a)   the person's past and present wishes and feelings (and, in particular, any relevant written statement made by him when he had capacity),

    (b)   the beliefs and values that would be likely to influence his decision if he had capacity, and

    (c)   the other factors that he would be likely to consider if he were able to do so.

(7) He must take into account, if it is practicable and appropriate to consult them, the views of –

    (a)   anyone named by the person as someone to be consulted on the matter in question or on matters of that kind,

    (b)   anyone engaged in caring for the person or interested in his welfare,

    (c)   any donee of a lasting power of attorney granted by the person, and

    (d)   any deputy appointed for the person by the court,

as to what would be in the person's best interests and, in particular, as to the matters mentioned in subsection (6).

(8) The duties imposed by subsections (1) to (7) also apply in relation to the exercise of any powers which –

    (a)   are exercisable under a lasting power of attorney, or

    (b)   are exercisable by a person under this Act where he reasonably believes that another person lacks capacity.

(9) In the case of an act done, or a decision made, by a person other than the court, there is sufficient compliance with this section if (having complied with the requirements of subsections (1) to (7)) he reasonably believes that what he does or decides is in the best interests of the person concerned.

(10) 'Life-sustaining treatment' means treatment which in the view of a person providing health care for the person concerned is necessary to sustain life.

(11) 'Relevant circumstances' are those –

    (a)   of which the person making the determination is aware, and

    (b)   which it would be reasonable to regard as relevant.

Scope of provision—This section sets out a checklist of factors that must be always considered when determining whether a decision made on behalf of a person lacking capacity to make that decision for themselves, or an act carried out in connection with the person's care or treatment, is in that person's best interests. There is no statutory definition of best interests, since this will depend on the particular act or decision in question and the individual circumstances of the person concerned. The processes involved in determining best interests are described in Chapter 2 (**2.113–2.145**).

Equal consideration or non-discrimination (s 4(1))—See also s 2(3) above. This is to ensure that determinations of best interests are not based on preconceived ideas or negative assumptions, for example, about the value or quality of life experienced by older people or people with mental or physical disabilities who now lack capacity to make specific decisions for themselves.

'all relevant circumstances' (s 4(2))—The statutory checklist sets out the minimum necessary considerations but all other matters relevant in the particular situation must also be taken into account. Relevant circumstances are defined in s 4(11).

'in particular, take the following steps' s 4(2))—Not all the factors in the checklist will be relevant to all types of decisions or actions, but they must still be considered if only to be disregarded as irrelevant to that particular situation. None of the factors takes priority over any other consideration, although some may be of 'magnetic importance' an any particular case (Re M (*ITW v Z*) [2009]

EWHC 2525 (Fam) at 32), but all factors must be weighed against each other in order to identify the decision or course of action that is in the person's best interests.

Regaining capacity (s 4(3))—If the individual concerned is likely to regain capacity to make that particular decision in the future, it may be possible to delay the decision until the person can make it him or herself, if that is in the person's best interests. Clearly, urgent decisions should not be delayed.

'so far as reasonably practicable, permit and encourage the person to participate' (s 4(4))—This complements the principle in s 1(3). The guidance in Chapter 3 of the Code of Practice suggests a range of steps, particularly help with communication, which may permit and encourage someone lacking capacity to be involved and to participate as fully as possible in decision-making. What is 'reasonably practicable' will depend on the particular circumstances. The importance of involving the person in the decision-making process has been reinforced by the Court of Protection (*C v V, Re S and S (Protected Persons)* [2008] EWHC B16 (Fam) at 54–55).

'life-sustaining treatment' (s 4(5))—Defined in s 4(10).

'not be motivated by a desire to bring about his death' (s 4(5))—A great deal of the debate in both Houses of Parliament concerned life and death decisions affecting people who lack capacity to make those decisions for themselves. In order to provide clarity and reassurance on these very difficult issues, the Government agreed to a number of amendments introducing specific statements in the legislation (see also s 62). This provision does not change the law, but it puts beyond doubt that the decision-maker's motivation must be the objective determination of the person's best interests, not a desire to bring about the person's death, when the decision relates to the provision, withholding or withdrawal of life-sustaining treatment.

'reasonably ascertainable' (s 4(6))—Whether expressed orally, in writing or through behaviour, or reported by family members or others who know (or knew) the person concerned – see also s 4(7). This factor in the best interests checklist places the focus firmly on the person lacking capacity, taking into account the issues most important to him or her. However, the person's views will not automatically determine the outcome.

'past and present wishes and feelings' (s 4(6)(a))—It has been suggested that there is a presumption in favour of implementing the person's wishes unless they are irrational, impractical, or irresponsible (with reference to resources), or there is a sufficiently countervailing consideration (*C v V, Re S and S (Protected Persons)* [2008] EWHC B16 (Fam) at 57–58). The need to give great weight to the person's wishes was confirmed in *Re P* [2009] EWHC 163 (Ch) (for case summary, see Part IX of this work), although it was felt to be an overstatement to speak in terms of a 'presumption'. The 'closer' the person is to having capacity, greater weight should be given to their views (*Re GC* [2008] EWHC 3402 (Fam) at 23). Note however that past and present wishes may conflict (MCA 2005, Code of Practice, para 5.38). Further guidance is given in *Re M, ITW v Z, M and Ors* [2009] EWHC 2825 (Fam) and *Re G (TJ)* [2010] EWHC 3005 (COP) (for case summary see Part IX of this work).

'relevant written statements' (s 4(6)(a))—Including any written expressions of wishes or preferences about medical treatment. 'The more specific and well thought out the statement, the more likely it will be persuasive in determining best interests' (*Hansard*, HL Deb, vol 670, ser 5, cols 1441–1442 (17 March 2005)).

'beliefs and values' (s 4(6)(b))—Including any social or psychological factors, political affiliations, cultural background, spiritual and religious beliefs, subscriptions to charitable causes or known past behaviour.

'other factors' (s 4(6)(c))—Such as emotional ties, family obligations, altruistic motives or concern for others. 'The actual wishes of P, which are altruistic and not in any way, directly or indirectly self-interested, can be a relevant factor' (*Re G (TJ)* [2010] EWHC 3005 (COP) at 56).

'if it is practicable and appropriate to consult them' (s 4(7))—This ensures that carers, family members and other relevant people are consulted on decisions affecting the person lacking capacity to make those decisions for themselves, but only if it is 'practicable and appropriate' to do so, depending on the particular circumstances. It may be appropriate to consult with former carers and to take into account oral statements made to them by the person who lacks capacity (*Re M, ITW v Z and Ors* [2009] EWHC 2525 (Fam) at 36).The Senior Judge of the Court of Protection has held that where consultation is likely to be unduly onerous, contentious, futile or serve no useful purpose, it is not 'practicable or appropriate' (*Re Allen* [2009] (CoP No 11661992) (unreported)). The requirement for consultation must be balanced against the right to confidentiality of the person lacking capacity. The views of those consulted will not necessarily determine the outcome – the weight given to them will depend on their relationship and amount of contact with the person concerned and the extent of their knowledge of the matter in question.

'interested in his welfare' (s 4(7)(b))—The nature of and motivation for the interest will be relevant in deciding whether to consult persons in this category.

'The duties imposed' (s 4(8))—The principle set out in s 1(5) confirms that any act done, or any decision made, on behalf of a person lacking capacity must be done in his or her best interests. Section 4(8) confirms that the best interests principle, and the duties to be carried out in determining best interests, also apply in the specified circumstances where the person concerned may not in fact lack capacity in relation to the act or decision in question.

'reasonably believes' (s 4(9))—This is an objective test – the decision-maker must, so far as possible, apply the best interests checklist and therefore be able to point to objective reasons to justify why they 'reasonably believe' that what they are doing or deciding is in the person's best interests. In considering what is 'reasonable' in any particular case, higher expectations are likely to be placed on those appointed to act under formal powers (attorneys and deputies) and those acting in a professional capacity than on family members and friends who are caring for a person lacking capacity without any formal authority.

[4A Restriction on deprivation of liberty]

[(1) This Act does not authorise any person ('D') to deprive any other person ('P') of his liberty.

(2) But that is subject to —

    (a)   the following provisions of this section, and
    (b)   section 4B.

(3) D may deprive P of his liberty if, by doing so, D is giving effect to a relevant decision of the court.

(4) A relevant decision of the court is a decision made by an order under section 16(2)(a) in relation to a matter concerning P's personal welfare.

(5) D may deprive P of his liberty if the deprivation is authorised by Schedule A1 (hospital and care home residents: deprivation of liberty).]

Amendment—Section inserted by the Mental Health Act 2007, s 50(1), (2).

Scope of provision—This section is part of the Deprivation of Liberty safeguards enacted in the Mental Health Act 2007 (MHA 2007) and brought into force on 1 April 2009. The safeguards are explained in Chapter 6.

'Deprive any other person of his liberty'—See discussion in Chapter 6 at **6.19–6.23**.

'Relevant decision of the court' (s 4A(3))—The Court of Protection may by making an order under s 16(2)(a) decide on P's behalf that in their best interests they should be treated or accommodated in such a way that they are deprived of their liberty (subject to any conditions contained in the order).

'Authorised by Schedule A1' (s 4A(5))—This Schedule sets out the procedures to be followed, assessments to be made and safeguards to be in place for a managing authority of a hospital or care home to obtain authorisation from a primary care trust (or in Wales, Welsh ministers) or local authority to deprive a person in its care of their liberty.

[4B Deprivation of liberty necessary for life-sustaining treatment etc]

[(1) If the following conditions are met, D is authorised to deprive P of his liberty while a decision as respects any relevant issue is sought from the court.

(2) The first condition is that there is a question about whether D is authorised to deprive P of his liberty under section 4A.

(3) The second condition is that the deprivation of liberty —

    (a)   is wholly or partly for the purpose of—
        (i)   giving P life-sustaining treatment, or
        (ii) doing any vital act, or
    (b)   consists wholly or partly of—
        (i)   giving P life-sustaining treatment, or
        (ii) doing any vital act.

(4) The third condition is that the deprivation of liberty is necessary in order to —

    (a)   give the life-sustaining treatment, or
    (b)   do the vital act.

(5) A vital act is any act which the person doing it reasonably believes to be necessary to prevent a serious deterioration in P's condition.]

Amendment—Section inserted by the Mental Health Act 2007, s 50(1), (2).

Scope of provision—This section makes clear that, if the conditions are met, a person may be deprived of his liberty to save his life or prevent a serious deterioration in his condition whilst a decision is sought from the Court of Protection on any question as to whether he may lawfully be deprived of his liberty.

5 Acts in connection with care or treatment

(1) If a person ('D') does an act in connection with the care or treatment of another person ('P'), the act is one to which this section applies if –

    (a)   before doing the act, D takes reasonable steps to establish whether P lacks capacity in relation to the matter in question, and
    (b)   when doing the act, D reasonably believes –
        (i)   that P lacks capacity in relation to the matter, and
        (ii) that it will be in P's best interests for the act to be done.

(2) D does not incur any liability in relation to the act that he would not have incurred if P –

    (a)   had had capacity to consent in relation to the matter, and
    (b)   had consented to D's doing the act.

(3) Nothing in this section excludes a person's civil liability for loss or damage, or his criminal liability, resulting from his negligence in doing the act.

(4) Nothing in this section affects the operation of sections 24 to 26 (advance decisions to refuse treatment).

Scope of provision—This section provides protection from liability for anyone involved in providing care or treatment for a person who lacks capacity to consent to such care or treatment, provided they are acting in the person's best interests and without negligence. In this way, the Act clarifies in statute the former common law 'principle of necessity', setting out the circumstances in which caring actions and decisions can lawfully be taken on behalf of adults who lack capacity to consent to them.

PART III

'a person ('D')' (s 5(1))—The Act does not define who may act – it depends on what is reasonable and appropriate for the act in question. The provision therefore refers to anyone carrying out such an act and may relate to several people at any given time. It may also include a person who instructs another to act. Munby LJ has given guidance to local authorities as to the exercise of their powers in respect of the welfare of adults lacking capacity to consent, stressing that 'the local authority, is the servant of those in need of its support and assistance, not their master' (*A Local Authority v A (Re A (Adult) and Re C (Child))* [2010] EWHC 978 (Fam) at 52).

'in connection with the care or treatment of another person ('P')' (s 5 (1))—The Act does not define 'care' or 'treatment' other than to clarify that treatment includes 'a diagnostic or other procedure' (s 64(1)). The Code of Practice provides a non-exhaustive list of examples (para 6.5) of such acts which would otherwise require consent.

'reasonable steps to establish whether P lacks capacity' (s 5(1)(a))—applying the definition and test of capacity in ss 2–3, in accordance with the principles in s 1. What is 'reasonable' will depend on the particular circumstances. This does not necessarily require a formal assessment of capacity, although professional practice may require this (e g in relation to capacity to consent to medical treatment). The Code of Practice suggests some reasonable steps to provide objective evidence of lack of capacity (para 4.45).

'reasonably believes' (s 5(1)(b))—This is an objective test. See also s 4(9).

'best interests' (s 5(1)(b)(ii))—determined by following the checklist set out in s 4 and the 'less restrictive' principle in s 1(6).

'D does not incur any liability' (s 5(2))—Such acts can be performed as if the person concerned had capacity and had given consent. There is no need to obtain any formal powers or authority to act.

'negligence' (s 5(3))—Consent is not a defence to a claim of negligence. Similarly in relation to people who lack capacity to consent, this clarifies that protection from liability does not extend to situations where D has acted negligently, whether in carrying out the act or by failing to act in breach of duty.

'advance decisions to refuse treatment' (s 5(4))—A valid and applicable advance decision is not affected by s 5 which gives no protection from liability if the advance decision is not followed (see ss 24–26).

6 Section 5 acts: limitations

(1) If D does an act that is intended to restrain P, it is not an act to which section 5 applies unless two further conditions are satisfied.

(2) The first condition is that D reasonably believes that it is necessary to do the act in order to prevent harm to P.

(3) The second is that the act is a proportionate response to –

    (a) the likelihood of P's suffering harm, and

    (b) the seriousness of that harm.

(4) For the purposes of this section D restrains P if he –

    (a) uses, or threatens to use, force to secure the doing of an act which P resists, or

    (b) restricts P's liberty of movement, whether or not P resists.

(5) ...

(6) Section 5 does not authorise a person to do an act which conflicts with a decision made, within the scope of his authority and in accordance with this Part, by –

(a)   a donee of a lasting power of attorney granted by P, or

(b)   a deputy appointed for P by the court.

(7) But nothing in subsection (6) stops a person –

(a)   providing life-sustaining treatment, or

(b)   doing any act which he reasonably believes to be necessary to prevent a serious deterioration in P's condition,

while a decision as respects any relevant issue is sought from the court.

Amendment—Subsection (5) repealed by the Mental Health Act 2007, ss 50(1), (4)(a), 55, Sch 11, Pt 10. See Chapter 6 for a description of the Deprivation of Liberty Safeguards which made this subsection redundant.

Scope of provision—This section imposes two important limitations on the acts which can be carried out with protection from liability under s 5. The first relates to acts intended to restrain a person who lacks capacity and the second to situations where the act might conflict with a decision made by a donee of a lasting power of attorney or a deputy appointed by the court.

'restrain' (s 6(1))—Restraint is defined in s 6(4) and can take many forms. Restraint may be verbal or physical and may vary from shouting at someone, to holding them down, using mechanical devices such as seat belts or cot sides, to locking them in a room. It may also include the prescribing of a sedative or other chemical restraint which restricts liberty of movement. See for example *DH NHS Foundation Trust v PS* [2010] EWHC 1217 (Fam).

'necessary to do the act in order to prevent harm to P' (s 6(2))—The Act does not define 'harm', since this will vary according to individual circumstances. It is not confined to physical harm. The restraining act must be 'necessary' to avert harm – not simply to enable the carer or professional to do something more quickly or easily.

'a proportionate response' (s 6(3))—What is likely to be a 'proportionate response' to the likelihood and seriousness of harm, both in scale and nature, will depend on the particular circumstances and the desired outcome. Where there are objective reasons for believing that restraint is necessary to prevent the person from coming to any harm, only the minimum necessary force or intervention may be used and for the shortest possible duration.

'restricts P's liberty of movement' (s 6(4)(b))—But not where such restrictions on movement amount to a deprivation of liberty under the European Convention on Human Rights (ECHR), Art 5(1). This is dealt with in ss 4A–4B.

Decisions of donees or deputies (s 6(6))—This section confirms that the provisions of s 5 do not authorise a person to do any act which conflicts with a decision made by a donee of a lasting power of attorney previously granted by the person lacking capacity, or by a deputy appointed by the Court, so long as the donee or deputy is acting within the scope of their authority. The formal decision-making powers provided by the Act therefore take precedence. In cases of dispute, an application may be made for permission to apply to the Court of Protection to resolve the matter.

'life sustaining treatment' (s 6(7))—Defined in s 4(10). Life-sustaining treatment, or treatment necessary to prevent a serious deterioration in the person's condition, can be given pending a ruling from the court.

7 Payment for necessary goods and services

(1) If necessary goods or services are supplied to a person who lacks capacity to contract for the supply, he must pay a reasonable price for them.

(2) 'Necessary' means suitable to a person's condition in life and to his actual requirements at the time when the goods or services are supplied.

Scope of provision—This section combines the provision under the Sale of Goods Act 1979, s 3(2) concerning the enforceability of a contract to provide necessary goods with the matching common law rule about necessary services. It clarifies that the obligation to pay a reasonable price applies to both the supply of necessary goods and the provision of necessary services to a person without capacity to contract for them, and it is the person who lacks capacity who must pay.

'necessary' (s 7(1))—Defined in s 7(2), based on the definition set out in the Sale of Goods Act 1979, s 3(3).

'lacks capacity to contract for the supply' (s 7(1))—Applying the definition and test of capacity in ss 2–3, in accordance with the principles in s 1. The person is bound by the terms of the contract, even if it was unfair, unless it can be shown that the other party to the contract was aware of the person's lack of capacity or should have been aware of this (*Imperial Loan Company v Stone* [1892] 1 QB 599). If the other party knows, or must be taken to have known of the lack of capacity, the contract is voidable.

'he must pay' (s 7(1))—The legal responsibility for paying for necessary goods and services lies with the person for whom they are supplied even though that person lacks the capacity to contract for them. Where the person also lacks the capacity to arrange for payment to be made, the carer who has arranged for the supply of goods or services (as an act in connection with care or treatment carried out under s 5) may also arrange settlement of the bill. The carer will have protection from liability so long as the provision of goods or services was in the person's best interests.

'reasonable price' (s 7(1))—The obligation is to pay 'a reasonable price' so this provision cannot be used to enforce a contract which involves gross overcharging for goods or services.

'condition in life' (s 7(2))—This refers to the person's living conditions and place in society, rather than any mental or physical condition. 'The aim is to make sure that people can enjoy a similar standard of living and way of life to those they had before lacking capacity' (Code of Practice, para 6.58).

'actual requirements' (s 7(2))—Goods are not necessary if the person already has an adequate supply.

8 Expenditure

(1) If an act to which section 5 applies involves expenditure, it is lawful for D –

    (a)   to pledge P's credit for the purpose of the expenditure, and
    (b)   to apply money in P's possession for meeting the expenditure.

(2) If the expenditure is borne for P by D, it is lawful for D –

    (a)   to reimburse himself out of money in P's possession, or
    (b)   to be otherwise indemnified by P.

(3) Subsections (1) and (2) do not affect any power under which (apart from those subsections) a person –

    (a)   has lawful control of P's money or other property, and
    (b)   has power to spend money for P's benefit.

Scope of provision—Under this section, arrangements may be made to meet the expenditure involved in cases where necessary goods or services must be paid for. The intention is to make it possible for ordinary but necessary goods and services to be provided for people who lack the capacity to arrange and pay for them, but without requiring formal authority to meet any expenditure involved. However, s 8 does not authorise access to the incapacitated person's income or assets or to sell the person's property.

'to pledge P's credit' (s 8(1)(a))—If neither the carer (D) who arranged the supply of goods or services nor the person who lacks capacity (P) can produce the necessary funds, D may promise that P will pay.

'money in P's possession' (s 8(1)(b) and (2)(a))—A distinction is drawn between the use of available cash in the possession of the person lacking capacity, which can be used to pay for goods or services (s 8(1)(b)) or to repay D (s 8(2)(a)), and the removal of money from a bank account or selling valuable items of property, which is not permitted without formal authority (s 8(3)).

'to be otherwise indemnified by P' (s 8(2)(b))—Formal arrangements may need to be made (such as registering a relevant power of attorney or applying to the Court of Protection) before D can be reimbursed.

'any power' (s 8(3))—Someone may already have formal authority to deal with the person's property or financial affairs, for example, under an enduring or lasting power of attorney, as a deputy appointed by the Court of Protection or as a social security 'appointee'. Section 8(3) makes clear that these arrangements are not affected or changed by the above provisions. D cannot make arrangements for goods or services to be provided for P if this conflicts with a decision made by a donee or deputy (s 6(6)).

Lasting powers of attorney

9 Lasting powers of attorney

(1) A lasting power of attorney is a power of attorney under which the donor ('P') confers on the donee (or donees) authority to make decisions about all or any of the following –

    (a)   P's personal welfare or specified matters concerning P's personal welfare, and

    (b)   P's property and affairs or specified matters concerning P's property and affairs,

and which includes authority to make such decisions in circumstances where P no longer has capacity.

(2) A lasting power of attorney is not created unless –

    (a)   section 10 is complied with,

    (b)   an instrument conferring authority of the kind mentioned in subsection (1) is made and registered in accordance with Schedule 1, and

    (c)   at the time when P executes the instrument, P has reached 18 and has capacity to execute it.

(3) An instrument which –

    (a)   purports to create a lasting power of attorney, but

    (b)   does not comply with this section, section 10 or Schedule 1,

confers no authority.

(4) The authority conferred by a lasting power of attorney is subject to –

    (a)   the provisions of this Act and, in particular, sections 1 (the principles) and 4 (best interests), and

    (b)   any conditions or restrictions specified in the instrument.

Scope of provision—Sections 9–14 introduce the legal framework for lasting powers of attorney, whereby one person, the donor, can confer authority on a donee by a power of attorney to make decisions. The formalities for making a lasting power of attorney, which includes the registration process, are dealt with at Sch 1.

'power of attorney' (s 9(1))—It cannot be emphasised enough that a lasting power of attorney is a power of attorney and therefore the common law principles governing the relationship between a principal and his or her agent apply to a lasting power of attorney. See Part I, para **3.4**.

PART III

'donee (or donees)' (s 9(1))—The Act uses the term donee to define the attorney acting under a lasting power of attorney. This distinguishes the donee of a lasting power of attorney from an attorney acting under an enduring power of attorney where the term 'attorney' is used.

'specified matters' (s 9(1)(a) and (b))—Sections 2 and 3 define capacity in relation to a particular decision at a particular time. A donor of a power of attorney may therefore delegate specific decisions to an attorney as well as a more general authority to make decisions in relation to more broadly defined matters such as property and affairs or welfare.

'personal welfare' (s 9(1)(a))—This term is not defined by the Act. It does include giving or refusing consent to the carrying out or continuation of a treatment by a person providing health care for P. It can be interpreted in its widest sense and by reference to what it does not include. Thus it excludes acts of restraint unless authorised by the Act (s 11(1)–(6)), acts outside the scope of the Act (ss 27–29) and the giving or refusing of consent to life-sustaining treatment unless expressly authorised in the power.

'property and affairs' (s 9(1)(b))—This term is likewise not defined but can be construed in its literal sense. See Part I, para **3.30**.

'and which includes authority to make such decisions in circumstances where P lacks capacity' (s 9(1))—A lasting power of attorney can be used in respect of property and affairs where P has capacity; it can therefore also be used where P lacks capacity.

'is subject to' (s 9(4))—The authority conferred on the donee of a power is subject to the provisions of the Act and in particular the principles contained in s 1 and the best interests criteria in s 4, as well as any conditions or restrictions contained in the instrument. The power cannot therefore be expanded, only restricted.

10 Appointment of donees

(1) A donee of a lasting power of attorney must be –

    (a) an individual who has reached 18, or
    (b) if the power relates only to P's property and affairs, either such an individual or a trust corporation.

(2) An individual who is bankrupt may not be appointed as donee of a lasting power of attorney in relation to P's property and affairs.

(3) Subsections (4) to (7) apply in relation to an instrument under which two or more persons are to act as donees of a lasting power of attorney.

(4) The instrument may appoint them to act –

    (a) jointly,
    (b) jointly and severally, or
    (c) jointly in respect of some matters and jointly and severally in respect of others.

(5) To the extent to which it does not specify whether they are to act jointly or jointly and severally, the instrument is to be assumed to appoint them to act jointly.

(6) If they are to act jointly, a failure, as respects one of them, to comply with the requirements of subsection (1) or (2) or Part 1 or 2 of Schedule 1 prevents a lasting power of attorney from being created.

(7) If they are to act jointly and severally, a failure, as respects one of them, to comply with the requirements of subsection (1) or (2) or Part 1 or 2 of Schedule 1 –

    (a) prevents the appointment taking effect in his case, but
    (b) does not prevent a lasting power of attorney from being created in the case of the other or others.

(8) An instrument used to create a lasting power of attorney –

    (a) cannot give the donee (or, if more than one, any of them) power to appoint a substitute or successor, but

    (b) may itself appoint a person to replace the donee (or, if more than one, any of them) on the occurrence of an event mentioned in section 13(6)(a) to (d) which has the effect of terminating the donee's appointment.

Scope of provision—Who can be a donee of a lasting power of attorney.

'trust corporation' (s 10(1)(b))—A trust corporation cannot therefore act as a welfare attorney. The term is defined by s 64(1), which imports the definition supplied by the Trustee Act 1925, s 68(1)—'the Public Trustee or a corporation either appointed by the court in any particular case to be a trustee, or entitled by rules made under subsection (3) of section four of the Public Trustee Act 1906, to act as custodian trustee.'

'jointly and severally' (s 10(4)–(7))—The prescribed forms issued pursuant to Sch 1, para 1 alter the terminology and refer to two or more attorneys being appointed together and independently.

'the instrument is to be assumed to appoint them to act jointly' (s 10(5))—The prescribed forms provide for a clear choice in the way an attorney is appointed, but if this is not exercised or the appointment of more than one attorney is incompatible with a joint and several appointment then there is a presumption in favour of a joint appointment. This is to avoid such a clause making the appointment invalid which may have arisen where the appointment of attorneys under an enduring power of attorney was unclear. See Sch 4, para 20(1).

'a person to replace the donee' (s 10(8)(b))—While a donee cannot him or herself appoint a successor, the donor may appoint a replacement attorney. However, the replacement attorney can only be appointed on the occurrence of one of the events mentioned in s 13(6)(a)–(d), i e disclaimer, death, bankruptcy, dissolution of a marriage or incapacity. A donee whose authority is terminated, for instance, by an order of the Court of Protection, cannot be replaced under this provision.

11 Lasting powers of attorney: restrictions

(1) A lasting power of attorney does not authorise the donee (or, if more than one, any of them) to do an act that is intended to restrain P, unless three conditions are satisfied.

(2) The first condition is that P lacks, or the donee reasonably believes that P lacks, capacity in relation to the matter in question.

(3) The second is that the donee reasonably believes that it is necessary to do the act in order to prevent harm to P.

(4) The third is that the act is a proportionate response to –

    (a) the likelihood of P's suffering harm, and
    (b) the seriousness of that harm.

(5) For the purposes of this section, the donee restrains P if he –

    (a) uses, or threatens to use, force to secure the doing of an act which P resists, or
    (b) restricts P's liberty of movement, whether or not P resists,

or if he authorises another person to do any of those things.

(6) ...

(7) Where a lasting power of attorney authorises the donee (or, if more than one, any of them) to make decisions about P's personal welfare, the authority –

PART III

(a) does not extend to making such decisions in circumstances other than those where P lacks, or the donee reasonably believes that P lacks, capacity,

(b) is subject to sections 24 to 26 (advance decisions to refuse treatment), and

(c) extends to giving or refusing consent to the carrying out or continuation of a treatment by a person providing health care for P.

(8) But subsection (7)(c) –

(a) does not authorise the giving or refusing of consent to the carrying out or continuation of life-sustaining treatment, unless the instrument contains express provision to that effect, and

(b) is subject to any conditions or restrictions in the instrument.

Amendment—Subsection (6) repealed by the Mental Health Act 2007, ss 50(1), (4)(b), 55, Sch 11, Pt 10.

Scope of provision—Section 11(1)–(5) deal with a welfare attorney's limited authority to restrain the donor. Section 11(7) establishes the vital principle that a welfare power can only be used to make decisions which the donor lacks capacity to make and s 11(8) allows a welfare lasting power of attorney to extend to the giving or refusing of consent to life-sustaining treatment so long as an express provision to that effect is contained in the power.

'life-sustaining treatment' (s 11(8))—Section 4(10) defines this as 'treatment which in the view of a person providing health care for the person concerned is necessary to sustain life'.

12 Scope of lasting powers of attorney: gifts

(1) Where a lasting power of attorney confers authority to make decisions about P's property and affairs, it does not authorise a donee (or, if more than one, any of them) to dispose of the donor's property by making gifts except to the extent permitted by subsection (2).

(2) The donee may make gifts –

(a) on customary occasions to persons (including himself) who are related to or connected with the donor, or

(b) to any charity to whom the donor made or might have been expected to make gifts,

if the value of each such gift is not unreasonable having regard to all the circumstances and, in particular, the size of the donor's estate.

(3) 'Customary occasion' means –

(a) the occasion or anniversary of a birth, a marriage or the formation of a civil partnership, or

(b) any other occasion on which presents are customarily given within families or among friends or associates.

(4) Subsection (2) is subject to any conditions or restrictions in the instrument.

Scope of provision—This section allows a donee of a financial power to act to benefit him or herself or others to the extent permitted by the Act. This is to escape the normal rule that a donee of a power of attorney cannot act to benefit him or herself. The power to benefit him or herself or others must, however, be within the scope of this section. There is no authority within this section to maintain another person whom the donor might be expected to provide for. A donee who wishes to make a provision or gift not within the scope of this section must apply to the Court of Protection.

'the value of each such gift is not unreasonable having regard to all the circumstances and in particular, the size of the donor's estate' (s 12(2))—There is no limit or even guidance to what is reasonable. An attorney must use his or her judgment, balancing prudence with an assessment of the donor's best interests.

'subject to any conditions or restrictions in the instrument' (s 12(4))—A donor of a power of attorney can only act to restrict this power; he or she cannot expand it. See Part I, para **3.37**.

13 Revocation of lasting powers of attorney etc

(1) This section applies if –

    (a)   P has executed an instrument with a view to creating a lasting power of attorney, or

    (b)   a lasting power of attorney is registered as having been conferred by P,

and in this section references to revoking the power include revoking the instrument.

(2) P may, at any time when he has capacity to do so, revoke the power.

(3) P's bankruptcy revokes the power so far as it relates to P's property and affairs.

(4) But where P is bankrupt merely because an interim bankruptcy restrictions order has effect in respect of him, the power is suspended, so far as it relates to P's property and affairs, for so long as the order has effect.

(5) The occurrence in relation to a donee of an event mentioned in subsection (6) –

    (a)   terminates his appointment, and

    (b)   except in the cases given in subsection (7), revokes the power.

(6) The events are –

    (a)   the disclaimer of the appointment by the donee in accordance with such requirements as may be prescribed for the purposes of this section in regulations made by the Lord Chancellor,

    (b)   subject to subsections (8) and (9), the death or bankruptcy of the donee or, if the donee is a trust corporation, its winding-up or dissolution,

    (c)   subject to subsection (11), the dissolution or annulment of a marriage or civil partnership between the donor and the donee,

    (d)   the lack of capacity of the donee.

(7) The cases are –

    (a)   the donee is replaced under the terms of the instrument,

    (b)   he is one of two or more persons appointed to act as donees jointly and severally in respect of any matter and, after the event, there is at least one remaining donee.

(8) The bankruptcy of a donee does not terminate his appointment, or revoke the power, in so far as his authority relates to P's personal welfare.

(9) Where the donee is bankrupt merely because an interim bankruptcy restrictions order has effect in respect of him, his appointment and the power are suspended, so far as they relate to P's property and affairs, for so long as the order has effect.

(10) Where the donee is one of two or more appointed to act jointly and severally under the power in respect of any matter, the reference in subsection (9) to the suspension of the power is to its suspension in so far as it relates to that donee.

(11) The dissolution or annulment of a marriage or civil partnership does not terminate the appointment of a donee, or revoke the power, if the instrument provided that it was not to do so.

Scope of provision—Section 13 sets out the common law principle for revocation of a lasting power of attorney and expands the circumstances in which automatic revocation takes place. Revocation of the power does not of itself lead to cancellation of registration – that is subject to a separate process. For instance, the Lasting Power of Attorney, Enduring Power of Attorney and Public Guardian Regulations 2007, SI 2007/1253, reg 21 requires the Public Guardian to cancel registration of a power if he or she is satisfied that it has been properly revoked.

'revoke' (s 13(2))—There is no definition of revocation and common law principles apply to an act of revocation and the Act's principles will apply to whether the donor has capacity to revoke the power. There is, however, no formal process for revocation to lead to cancellation of registration. See Part I, para **3.117**.

'events' (s 13(6)) These events automatically terminate the appointment of the donee. If there is no replacement donee, then the power is revoked. However, cancellation of the registration still requires an application to the Public Guardian.

'the dissolution or annulment of a marriage or civil partnership' (s 13(6)(c))—This is an extension of the common law principle, which does not revoke an appointment on such an event. An enduring power of attorney, for instance, is not revoked on the divorce of the donee from the donor. This is a concept borrowed from the Wills Act 1837, which provides for the failure of the appointment of an executor or a gift in favour of a divorced spouse. Section 13(11) does, however, make such revocation subject to a contrary intention in the instrument appointing the donee.

14 Protection of donee and others if no power created or power revoked

(1) Subsections (2) and (3) apply if –

(a) an instrument has been registered under Schedule 1 as a lasting power of attorney, but
(b) a lasting power of attorney was not created,

whether or not the registration has been cancelled at the time of the act or transaction in question.

(2) A donee who acts in purported exercise of the power does not incur any liability (to P or any other person) because of the non-existence of the power unless at the time of acting he –

(a) knows that a lasting power of attorney was not created, or
(b) is aware of circumstances which, if a lasting power of attorney had been created, would have terminated his authority to act as a donee.

(3) Any transaction between the donee and another person is, in favour of that person, as valid as if the power had been in existence, unless at the time of the transaction that person has knowledge of a matter referred to in subsection (2).

(4) If the interest of a purchaser depends on whether a transaction between the donee and the other person was valid by virtue of subsection (3), it is conclusively presumed in favour of the purchaser that the transaction was valid if –

(a) the transaction was completed within 12 months of the date on which the instrument was registered, or
(b) the other person makes a statutory declaration, before or within 3 months after the completion of the purchase, that he had no reason at the time of

the transaction to doubt that the donee had authority to dispose of the property which was the subject of the transaction.

(5) In its application to a lasting power of attorney which relates to matters in addition to P's property and affairs, section 5 of the Powers of Attorney Act 1971 (protection where power is revoked) has effect as if references to revocation included the cessation of the power in relation to P's property and affairs.

(6) Where two or more donees are appointed under a lasting power of attorney, this section applies as if references to the donee were to all or any of them.

Scope of provision—This repeats similar provisions in the Powers of Attorney Act 1971, s 5 and the Enduring Powers of Attorney Act 1985, s 9 (now MCA 2005, Sch 4, para 16) to protect an attorney and a third party dealing in good faith without knowledge of the non-existence of the power at the relevant time.

General powers of the court and appointment of deputies

15 Power to make declarations

(1) The court may make declarations as to –

  (a) whether a person has or lacks capacity to make a decision specified in the declaration;
  (b) whether a person has or lacks capacity to make decisions on such matters as are described in the declaration;
  (c) the lawfulness or otherwise of any act done, or yet to be done, in relation to that person.

(2) 'Act' includes an omission and a course of conduct.

Scope of provision—This section confers on the Court the discretionary power to make declarations of the nature stated. This includes the initial decision as to whether there is a lack of capacity which will trigger the remaining jurisdiction of the Court. It may be anticipated that this new statutory jurisdiction will replace the inherent jurisdiction previously assumed by the Family Division of the High Court to make declarations in respect of mentally incapacitated adults in regard to medical treatment and personal welfare (see generally Chapter 5).

Further explanation—This topic is covered in Chapter 4.

'Lacks capacity'—For the purposes of the Act this is defined in s 2.

16 Powers to make decisions and appoint deputies: general

(1) This section applies if a person ('P') lacks capacity in relation to a matter or matters concerning –

  (a) P's personal welfare, or
  (b) P's property and affairs.

(2) The court may –

  (a) by making an order, make the decision or decisions on P's behalf in relation to the matter or matters, or
  (b) appoint a person (a 'deputy') to make decisions on P's behalf in relation to the matter or matters.

(3) The powers of the court under this section are subject to the provisions of this Act and, in particular, to sections 1 (the principles) and 4 (best interests).

PART III

(4) When deciding whether it is in P's best interests to appoint a deputy, the court must have regard (in addition to the matters mentioned in section 4) to the principles that –

    (a) a decision by the court is to be preferred to the appointment of a deputy to make a decision, and

    (b) the powers conferred on a deputy should be as limited in scope and duration as is reasonably practicable in the circumstances.

(5) The court may make such further orders or give such directions, and confer on a deputy such powers or impose on him such duties, as it thinks necessary or expedient for giving effect to, or otherwise in connection with, an order or appointment made by it under subsection (2).

(6) Without prejudice to section 4, the court may make the order, give the directions or make the appointment on such terms as it considers are in P's best interests, even though no application is before the court for an order, directions or an appointment on those terms.

(7) An order of the court may be varied or discharged by a subsequent order.

(8) The court may, in particular, revoke the appointment of a deputy or vary the powers conferred on him if it is satisfied that the deputy –

    (a) has behaved, or is behaving, in a way that contravenes the authority conferred on him by the court or is not in P's best interests, or

    (b) proposes to behave in a way that would contravene that authority or would not be in P's best interests.

Scope of provision—This section confers on the Court the power to make decisions on behalf of an incapacitated adult or to appoint a deputy in respect of personal welfare or financial affairs. It also confirms the principles that must be applied, and a decision of the Court is to be preferred. The power may be exercised of the Court's own initiative and does not depend upon the specific application being made. Any order may be varied or discharged subsequently.

Further explanation—This topic is covered in Chapter 4.

'decisions'—The Court or the deputy may only make the decisions that P could have made and may not, for example, dictate what care provision is to be made for P.

'best interests'—See s 4 and Chapter 2.

'personal welfare'—Includes health care (s 17). For the extent of the power see s 17.

'property and affairs'—For examples of the powers that are generally exercised see s 18.

Excluded decisions—For decisions that may not be made see ss 27–29. For decisions that may not be made by a deputy see s 20.

'deputy'—See ss 19–20.

[16A Section 16 powers: Mental Health Act patients etc]

[(1) If a person is ineligible to be deprived of liberty by this Act, the court may not include in a welfare order provision which authorises the person to be deprived of his liberty.

(2) If—

    (a) a welfare order includes provision which authorises a person to be deprived of his liberty, and

(b)   that person becomes ineligible to be deprived of liberty by this Act,
the provision ceases to have effect for as long as the person remains
ineligible.

(3) Nothing in subsection (2) affects the power of the court under section 16(7) to
vary or discharge the welfare order.

(4) For the purposes of this section —

(a)   Schedule 1A applies for determining whether or not P is ineligible to be
deprived of liberty by this Act;

(b)   'welfare order' means an order under section 16(2)(a).]

Amendment—Section inserted by the Mental Health Act 2007, s 50(1), (3).

Scope of provision—As part of the Deprivation of Liberty safeguards implemented on 1 April
2009, this section secures that a person ineligible to be deprived of their liberty under this Act
because they may be made subject to the compulsory powers for treatment of their mental disorder
under the Mental Health Act 1983 (MHA 1983) (as amended) cannot be deprived of their liberty by
a welfare order made by the Court of Protection. See s 4A above for the power of the Court to make
a welfare order which deprives someone of their liberty. See Sch 1A for when someone is ineligible
to be deprived of their liberty by this Act.

17 Section 16 powers: personal welfare

(1) The powers under section 16 as respects P's personal welfare extend in
particular to –

(a)   deciding where P is to live;

(b)   deciding what contact, if any, P is to have with any specified persons;

(c)   making an order prohibiting a named person from having contact with P;

(d)   giving or refusing consent to the carrying out or continuation of a treatment
by a person providing health care for P;

(e)   giving a direction that a person responsible for P's health care allow a
different person to take over that responsibility.

(2) Subsection (1) is subject to section 20 (restrictions on deputies).

Scope of provision—This section helpfully identifies the typical decisions that may be made in
respect of personal welfare, but the powers of the Court are not restricted to these.

'consent to … treatment'—The Court does not have power to order that treatment shall be carried
out.

Age—These powers only apply in respect of persons aged at least 16 years. Between ages 16 and 18
they overlap powers under the Children Act 1989.

Deputies—The powers of deputies are restricted under s 20.

18 Section 16 powers: property and affairs

(1) The powers under section 16 as respects P's property and affairs extend in
particular to –

(a)   the control and management of P's property;

(b)   the sale, exchange, charging, gift or other disposition of P's property;

(c)   the acquisition of property in P's name or on P's behalf;

(d)   the carrying on, on P's behalf, of any profession, trade or business;

(e)   the taking of a decision which will have the effect of dissolving a partnership of which P is a member;

(f)   the carrying out of any contract entered into by P;

(g)   the discharge of P's debts and of any of P's obligations, whether legally enforceable or not;

(h)   the settlement of any of P's property, whether for P's benefit or for the benefit of others;

(i)   the execution for P of a will;

(j)   the exercise of any power (including a power to consent) vested in P whether beneficially or as trustee or otherwise;

(k)   the conduct of legal proceedings in P's name or on P's behalf.

(2) No will may be made under subsection (1)(i) at a time when P has not reached 18.

(3) The powers under section 16 as respects any other matter relating to P's property and affairs may be exercised even though P has not reached 16, if the court considers it likely that P will still lack capacity to make decisions in respect of that matter when he reaches 18.

(4) Schedule 2 supplements the provisions of this section.

(5) Section 16(7) (variation and discharge of court orders) is subject to paragraph 6 of Schedule 2.

(6) Subsection (1) is subject to section 20 (restrictions on deputies).

Scope of provision—This section helpfully identifies the typical decisions that may be made in respect of property and affairs, and follows the powers of the former Court of Protection.

'property'—Includes any thing in action and any interest in real or personal property (s 64(1)).

'execution ... of a will' (s 18(1)(i))—This refers to the so-called 'statutory will' which can be authorised by the Court (and was also within the powers of the former Court of Protection). This includes a codicil (s 64(1)).

'conduct of legal proceedings'—For civil proceedings see Civil Procedure Rules 1998, SI 1998/3132, Part 21 and for family proceedings see Family Proceedings Rules 1991, SI 1991/1247, Part IX [from April 2011 Family Procedure Rules 2010, SI 2010/2955, Part 15].

Gift or settlement—This power may be exercised to enable an attorney to make a gift or settlement which is beyond the authority of a lasting or enduring power of attorney.

Age—These powers generally only apply in respect of persons aged at least 16 years, but may be exercised where the Court is satisfied that the individual will lack capacity on attaining majority (s 18(3)). Typically this would be a child with a substantial damages award following a serious brain injury. However, a will may not be made for a person under the age of 18.

Deputies—The powers of deputies are restricted under s 20.

Schedule 2—This deals in particular with wills, vesting orders, variation of settlements and the preservation of interests in property disposed of on behalf of persons lacking capacity.

19 Appointment of deputies

(1) A deputy appointed by the court must be –

(a)   an individual who has reached 18, or

(b)   as respects powers in relation to property and affairs, an individual who has reached 18 or a trust corporation.

(2) The court may appoint an individual by appointing the holder for the time being of a specified office or position.

(3) A person may not be appointed as a deputy without his consent.

(4) The court may appoint two or more deputies to act –

    (a)   jointly,

    (b)   jointly and severally, or

    (c)   jointly in respect of some matters and jointly and severally in respect of others.

(5) When appointing a deputy or deputies, the court may at the same time appoint one or more other persons to succeed the existing deputy or those deputies –

    (a)   in such circumstances, or on the happening of such events, as may be specified by the court;

    (b)   for such period as may be so specified.

(6) A deputy is to be treated as P's agent in relation to anything done or decided by him within the scope of his appointment and in accordance with this Part.

(7) The deputy is entitled –

    (a)   to be reimbursed out of P's property for his reasonable expenses in discharging his functions, and

    (b)   if the court so directs when appointing him, to remuneration out of P's property for discharging them.

(8) The court may confer on a deputy powers to –

    (a)   take possession or control of all or any specified part of P's property;

    (b)   exercise all or any specified powers in respect of it, including such powers of investment as the court may determine.

(9) The court may require a deputy –

    (a)   to give to the Public Guardian such security as the court thinks fit for the due discharge of his functions, and

    (b)   to submit to the Public Guardian such reports at such times or at such intervals as the court may direct.

Scope of provision—This section regulates the appointment of a deputy by the Court for an adult who lacks capacity. Such appointment will generally be made where property and affairs need to be managed, but is less likely in respect of personal welfare decisions that can be made by the Court on a one-off basis. Different deputies may be appointed for different functions.

Age—A deputy must be at least 18 years old.

Trust corporation (s 19(1)(b))—May be a deputy in regard to property and affairs but not personal welfare. But the holder for the time being of a specified office or position may be appointed. Trust corporation has the meaning given in the Trustee Act 1925, s 68(1) (s 64(1)).

Number—There is no restriction on the number of deputies that may be appointed for an incapacitated individual but in practice a single appointment is likely to be made for each type of decision unless there are circumstances justifying a joint appointment.

Succession (s 19(5))—This provision helpfully allows the Court to appoint successors whose powers arise in specified circumstances (e g on the death of the primary deputy).

Status (s 19(6))—The Act makes it clear that a deputy acts as agent rather than trustee.

Expenses—The deputy may be reimbursed for expenses and also charge remuneration when so authorised by the Court, but this depends upon the incapacitated person having financial resources and many personal welfare deputies will have to carry out their duties at their own expense.

Security (s 58(1)(e))—This is generally only required from a deputy for property and affairs. It is ordered by the Court and dealt with through the Office of the Public Guardian.

Reports (s 58(1)(f))—It is part of the functions of the Public Guardian to receive reports from deputies.

20 Restrictions on deputies

(1) A deputy does not have power to make a decision on behalf of P in relation to a matter if he knows or has reasonable grounds for believing that P has capacity in relation to the matter.

(2) Nothing in section 16(5) or 17 permits a deputy to be given power –

(a) to prohibit a named person from having contact with P;
(b) to direct a person responsible for P's health care to allow a different person to take over that responsibility.

(3) A deputy may not be given powers with respect to –

(a) the settlement of any of P's property, whether for P's benefit or for the benefit of others,
(b) the execution for P of a will, or
(c) the exercise of any power (including a power to consent) vested in P whether beneficially or as trustee or otherwise.

(4) A deputy may not be given power to make a decision on behalf of P which is inconsistent with a decision made, within the scope of his authority and in accordance with this Act, by the donee of a lasting power of attorney granted by P (or, if there is more than one donee, by any of them).

(5) A deputy may not refuse consent to the carrying out or continuation of life-sustaining treatment in relation to P.

(6) The authority conferred on a deputy is subject to the provisions of this Act and, in particular, sections 1 (the principles) and 4 (best interests).

(7) A deputy may not do an act that is intended to restrain P unless four conditions are satisfied.

(8) The first condition is that, in doing the act, the deputy is acting within the scope of an authority expressly conferred on him by the court.

(9) The second is that P lacks, or the deputy reasonably believes that P lacks, capacity in relation to the matter in question.

(10) The third is that the deputy reasonably believes that it is necessary to do the act in order to prevent harm to P.

(11) The fourth is that the act is a proportionate response to –

(a) the likelihood of P's suffering harm, [and]
(b) the seriousness of that harm.

(12) For the purposes of this section, a deputy restrains P if he –

(a) uses, or threatens to use, force to secure the doing of an act which P resists, or
(b) restricts P's liberty of movement, whether or not P resists,

or if he authorises another person to do any of those things.

(13) ...

Amendment—Mental Health Act 2007, ss 50(1), (4)(c), 51, 55, Sch 11, Pt 10.

Scope of provision—This section confirms the underlying principle that decisions may only be made for adults who are unable to make those decisions for themselves, and identifies a range of decisions that the Court cannot delegate to deputies but must make itself. It then imposes restrictions on the exercise of a deputy's powers.

Lasting power of attorney—A valid decision of a donee may not be overridden by a deputy.

Restraint—Four conditions precedent apply to the exercise of any powers of restraint by a deputy. These are required to make the Act human rights compliant.

Deprivation of liberty—See generally Chapter 6.

21 Transfer of proceedings relating to people under 18

[(1)] The [Lord Chief Justice, with the concurrence of the Lord Chancellor,] may by order make provision as to the transfer of proceedings relating to a person under 18, in such circumstances as are specified in the order –

(a) from the Court of Protection to a court having jurisdiction under the Children Act 1989, or

(b) from a court having jurisdiction under that Act to the Court of Protection.

[(2) The Lord Chief Justice may nominate any of the following to exercise his functions under this section –

(a) the President of the Court of Protection;

(b) a judicial office holder (as defined in section 109(4) of the Constitutional Reform Act 2005).]

Amendments—SI 2006/1016.

Provision—Mental Capacity Act 2005 (Transfer of Proceedings) Order 2007, SI 2007/1899.

[Powers of the court in relation to Schedule A1]

Amendment—Cross heading inserted by the Mental Health Act 2007, s 50(7), Sch 9, Pt 1, paras 1, 2.

[21A Powers of court in relation to Schedule A1]

[(1) This section applies if either of the following has been given under Schedule A1 —

(a) a standard authorisation;

(b) an urgent authorisation.

(2) Where a standard authorisation has been given, the court may determine any question relating to any of the following matters—

(a) whether the relevant person meets one or more of the qualifying requirements;

(b) the period during which the standard authorisation is to be in force;

(c) the purpose for which the standard authorisation is given;

(d)   the conditions subject to which the standard authorisation is given.

(3) If the court determines any question under subsection (2), the court may make an order —

(a)   varying or terminating the standard authorisation, or

(b)   directing the supervisory body to vary or terminate the standard authorisation.

(4) Where an urgent authorisation has been given, the court may determine any question relating to any of the following matters —

(a)   whether the urgent authorisation should have been given;

(b)   the period during which the urgent authorisation is to be in force;

(c)   the purpose for which the urgent authorisation is given.

(5) Where the court determines any question under subsection (4), the court may make an order—

(a)   varying or terminating the urgent authorisation, or

(b)   directing the managing authority of the relevant hospital or care home to vary or terminate the urgent authorisation.

(6) Where the court makes an order under subsection (3) or (5), the court may make an order about a person's liability for any act done in connection with the standard or urgent authorisation before its variation or termination.

(7) An order under subsection (6) may, in particular, exclude a person from liability.]

Amendment—Section inserted by the Mental Health Act 2007, s 50(7), Sch 9, Pt 1, paras 1, 2.

Scope of provision—As part of the Deprivation of Liberty safeguards, this section ensures compliance with Art 5(4) of the ECHR by giving the Court of Protection jurisdiction to review the lawfulness of the detention of anyone for whom authorisation has been granted to provide care or treatment in conditions which amount to a deprivation of their liberty. The Court of Appeal in *G v E* [2010] EWCA Civ 822 confirmed that the scheme implemented by this section and Sch A1 is compatible with Art 5 ECHR.

'Standard authorisation' (s 21A(1)(a))—An authorisation given under Part 4 of Sch A1 authorising deprivation of liberty for a period of up to 12 months. The procedures and qualifying requirements for a standard authorisation are described in Chapter 6 (at **6.32–6.44**).

'Urgent authorisation' (s 21A(1)(b))—An authorisation given under Part 5 of Sch A1 authorising deprivation of liberty in urgent circumstances for up to 7 days (renewable for a further 7 days) while a standard authorisation is obtained. The procedures to obtain an urgent authorisation are described in Chapter 6 (at **6.45–6.46**).

'supervisory body' (s 21A(3)(b))—See definitions at Sch A1, paras 180–182.

'managing authority' (s 21A(5)(b))—See definitions at Sch A1, paras 176,177 and 179.

Powers of the court in relation to lasting powers of attorney

22 Powers of court in relation to validity of lasting powers of attorney

(1) This section and section 23 apply if –

(a)   a person ('P') has executed or purported to execute an instrument with a view to creating a lasting power of attorney, or

(b)   an instrument has been registered as a lasting power of attorney conferred by P.

(2) The court may determine any question relating to –

    (a)   whether one or more of the requirements for the creation of a lasting power of attorney have been met;

    (b)   whether the power has been revoked or has otherwise come to an end.

(3) Subsection (4) applies if the court is satisfied –

    (a)   that fraud or undue pressure was used to induce P –

        (i)   to execute an instrument for the purpose of creating a lasting power of attorney, or

        (ii)   to create a lasting power of attorney, or

    (b)   that the donee (or, if more than one, any of them) of a lasting power of attorney –

        (i)   has behaved, or is behaving, in a way that contravenes his authority or is not in P's best interests, or

        (ii)   proposes to behave in a way that would contravene his authority or would not be in P's best interests.

(4) The court may –

    (a)   direct that an instrument purporting to create the lasting power of attorney is not to be registered, or

    (b)   if P lacks capacity to do so, revoke the instrument or the lasting power of attorney.

(5) If there is more than one donee, the court may under subsection (4)(b) revoke the instrument or the lasting power of attorney so far as it relates to any of them.

(6) 'Donee' includes an intended donee.

Scope of provision—The Court of Protection has jurisdiction for determining issues concerning the validity of a lasting power of attorney (as opposed to a formal defect which the Public Guardian can deal with).

'contravenes his authority or is not in P's best interests' (s 22(3)(b))—The Court may revoke the power if satisfied that the donee has behaved or proposes to behave in such a way. At the time of publication, no case has yet been brought before the Court on these grounds. An application to revoke a lasting power of attorney on such grounds requires a high standard of proof and this contrasts with the more flexible grounds of 'unsuitability' that apply to enduring powers of attorney – see Sch 4, para 16(4)(g).

'purported to execute an instrument' (s 22(1)(a))—The Court's powers are also exercisable before the instrument is registered, and before it is actually a lasting power of attorney.

23 Powers of court in relation to operation of lasting powers of attorney

(1) The court may determine any question as to the meaning or effect of a lasting power of attorney or an instrument purporting to create one.

(2) The court may –

    (a)   give directions with respect to decisions –

        (i)   which the donee of a lasting power of attorney has authority to make, and

        (ii)   which P lacks capacity to make;

    (b)   give any consent or authorisation to act which the donee would have to obtain from P if P had capacity to give it.

(3) The court may, if P lacks capacity to do so –

(a) give directions to the donee with respect to the rendering by him of reports or accounts and the production of records kept by him for that purpose;

(b) require the donee to supply information or produce documents or things in his possession as donee;

(c) give directions with respect to the remuneration or expenses of the donee;

(d) relieve the donee wholly or partly from any liability which he has or may have incurred on account of a breach of his duties as donee.

(4) The court may authorise the making of gifts which are not within section 12(2) (permitted gifts).

(5) Where two or more donees are appointed under a lasting power of attorney, this section applies as if references to the donee were to all or any of them.

Scope of provision—It is for the Court to provide authority for the attorney to carry out certain acts that are otherwise beyond the scope of his or her authority, or to require the attorney to carry out a particular act.

'the Court may authorise the making of gifts' (s 23(4))—The Court may authorise the attorney to make gifts on an application by the attorney. This is without prejudice to the Court's powers to authorise the making of gifts under s 16(1)(b).

Advance decisions to refuse treatment

24 Advance decisions to refuse treatment: general

(1) 'Advance decision' means a decision made by a person ('P'), after he has reached 18 and when he has capacity to do so, that if –

(a) at a later time and in such circumstances as he may specify, a specified treatment is proposed to be carried out or continued by a person providing health care for him, and

(b) at that time he lacks capacity to consent to the carrying out or continuation of the treatment,

the specified treatment is not to be carried out or continued.

(2) For the purposes of subsection (1)(a), a decision may be regarded as specifying a treatment or circumstances even though expressed in layman's terms.

(3) P may withdraw or alter an advance decision at any time when he has capacity to do so.

(4) A withdrawal (including a partial withdrawal) need not be in writing.

(5) An alteration of an advance decision need not be in writing (unless section 25(5) applies in relation to the decision resulting from the alteration).

Scope of provision—This and the following two sections provide the statutory framework within which advance decisions refusing specified medical treatment are to be given effect. They are discussed in Chapter 5 (at **5.65–5.70**).

'An alteration of an advance decision' (s 24(5))—Needs only be in writing if the effect of the alteration is a decision to refuse a life-sustaining treatment even though life is at risk.

25 Validity and applicability of advance decisions

(1) An advance decision does not affect the liability which a person may incur for carrying out or continuing a treatment in relation to P unless the decision is at the material time –

    (a)   valid, and
    (b)   applicable to the treatment.

(2) An advance decision is not valid if P –

    (a)   has withdrawn the decision at a time when he had capacity to do so,
    (b)   has, under a lasting power of attorney created after the advance decision was made, conferred authority on the donee (or, if more than one, any of them) to give or refuse consent to the treatment to which the advance decision relates, or
    (c)   has done anything else clearly inconsistent with the advance decision remaining his fixed decision.

(3) An advance decision is not applicable to the treatment in question if at the material time P has capacity to give or refuse consent to it.

(4) An advance decision is not applicable to the treatment in question if –

    (a)   that treatment is not the treatment specified in the advance decision,
    (b)   any circumstances specified in the advance decision are absent, or
    (c)   there are reasonable grounds for believing that circumstances exist which P did not anticipate at the time of the advance decision and which would have affected his decision had he anticipated them.

(5) An advance decision is not applicable to life-sustaining treatment unless –

    (a)   the decision is verified by a statement by P to the effect that it is to apply to that treatment even if life is at risk, and
    (b)   the decision and statement comply with subsection (6).

(6) A decision or statement complies with this subsection only if –

    (a)   it is in writing,
    (b)   it is signed by P or by another person in P's presence and by P's direction,
    (c)   the signature is made or acknowledged by P in the presence of a witness, and
    (d)   the witness signs it, or acknowledges his signature, in P's presence.

(7) The existence of any lasting power of attorney other than one of a description mentioned in subsection (2)(b) does not prevent the advance decision from being regarded as valid and applicable.

'Under a lasting power of attorney' (s 25(2)(b))—See ss 9–14.

26 Effect of advance decisions

(1) If P has made an advance decision which is –

    (a)   valid, and
    (b)   applicable to a treatment,

the decision has effect as if he had made it, and had had capacity to make it, at the time when the question arises whether the treatment should be carried out or continued.

(2) A person does not incur liability for carrying out or continuing the treatment unless, at the time, he is satisfied that an advance decision exists which is valid and applicable to the treatment.

(3) A person does not incur liability for the consequences of withholding or withdrawing a treatment from P if, at the time, he reasonably believes that an advance decision exists which is valid and applicable to the treatment.

(4) The court may make a declaration as to whether an advance decision –

(a)   exists;
(b)   is valid;
(c)   is applicable to a treatment.

(5) Nothing in an apparent advance decision stops a person –

(a)   providing life-sustaining treatment, or
(b)   doing any act he reasonably believes to be necessary to prevent a serious deterioration in P's condition,

while a decision as respects any relevant issue is sought from the court.

'Has effect ...' (s 26(1))—A valid and applicable advance refusal of treatment is to be respected as a binding decision by the person concerned.

'Any relevant issue' (s 26(5))—Examples are whether an advance decision has been made, whether it is valid and applicable as applying to the specified treatment or whether it has been revoked or the maker has acted inconsistently with this being his or her fixed intent.

Excluded decisions

27 Family relationships etc

(1) Nothing in this Act permits a decision on any of the following matters to be made on behalf of a person –

(a)   consenting to marriage or a civil partnership,
(b)   consenting to have sexual relations,
(c)   consenting to a decree of divorce being granted on the basis of two years' separation,
(d)   consenting to a dissolution order being made in relation to a civil partnership on the basis of two years' separation,
(e)   consenting to a child's being placed for adoption by an adoption agency,
(f)   consenting to the making of an adoption order,
(g)   discharging parental responsibilities in matters not relating to a child's property,
(h)   giving a consent under the Human Fertilisation and Embryology Act 1990,
[(i)   giving a consent under the Human Fertilisation and Embryology Act 2008.]

(2) 'Adoption order' means –

(a)   an adoption order within the meaning of the Adoption and Children Act 2002 (including a future adoption order), and
(b)   an order under section 84 of that Act (parental responsibility prior to adoption abroad).

Amendment—Paragraph (1)(i) inserted by Human Fertilisation and Embryology Act 2008, s 56, Sch 6, Pt 1, para 40.

Scope of provision—There are certain acts and decisions which can never be made under the Act on behalf of a person who lacks capacity to make such decisions for themselves, either because they are so personal to the individual concerned or because they are governed by other legislation. This section excludes specified decisions on family relationships from being taken on behalf of a person lacking capacity to make the decision in question.

'civil partnership' (s 27(1)(a))—As defined in the Civil Partnership Act 2004, s 1.

'sexual relations' (s 27(1)(b))—While the Act does not permit anyone to consent to sexual relations on behalf of a person lacking capacity to consent, this does not prevent action being taken under the common law to protect a vulnerable person from abuse or exploitation or under the criminal law (Sexual Offences Act 2003) if a sexual offence has been committed (see *R v C* [2009] UKHL 42).

'decree of divorce' (s 27(1)(c)); **'dissolution order'** (s 27(1)(d))—Where a person lacking capacity becomes involved in divorce or dissolution proceedings on any basis other than 2 years' separation, or where someone loses capacity during the course of such proceedings, a litigation friend will be appointed under the Family Proceedings Rules 1991, SI 1991/1247, Part IX to give instructions and otherwise act on their behalf in relation to the proceedings.

'adoption order' (s 27(1)(f))—Defined in s 27(2).

'parental responsibilities' (s 27(1)(g))—Matters concerned with the discharging of parental responsibilities not related to a child's property are dealt with under the Children Act 1989.

28 Mental Health Act matters

(1) Nothing in this Act authorises anyone –

   (a)   to give a patient medical treatment for mental disorder, or
   (b)   to consent to a patient's being given medical treatment for mental disorder,

if, at the time when it is proposed to treat the patient, his treatment is regulated by Part 4 of the Mental Health Act.

[(1A) Subsection (1) does not apply in relation to any form of treatment to which section 58A of that Act (electro-convulsive therapy, etc) applies if the patient comes within subsection (7) of that section (informal patient under 18 who cannot give consent).

(1B) Section 5 does not apply to an act to which section 64B of the Mental Health Act applies (treatment of community patients not recalled to hospital).]

(2) 'Medical treatment', 'mental disorder' and 'patient' have the same meaning as in that Act.

Amendments—Subsections (1A) and (1B) inserted by the Mental Health Act 2007, s 28(10), s 35(4), (5): SI 2008/1900.

Scope of provision—This confirms that the Act's decision-making powers cannot be used to give or to consent to treatment for mental disorder if the treatment is regulated by MHA 1983, Part 4. The powers available under Part 4 take precedence over the decision-making powers under MCA 2005 in relation to treatment for mental disorder of detained patients.

'regulated by Part 4 of the Mental Health Act' (s 28(1))—The purpose of Part 4 is to clarify the extent to which treatment for mental disorder can be imposed on detained patients in hospital and to provide specific statutory safeguards concerning the provision of treatment without consent (MHA 1983, ss 57–58).

'electro-convulsive therapy' (s 28(1A)) —New requirements for patients to consent to ECT are set out in MHA 1983, s 58A (inserted by MHA 2007, s 27). Section 28(1A) allows patients aged 16-17 who lack capacity to consent to ECT to be treated under MCA 2005, s 5, rather than using MHA powers, so long as the treatment is in their best interests, does not amount to a deprivation of their liberty and a Second Opinion Appointed Doctor considers ECT to be appropriate.

'**community patients**' (s 28(1B))—Means patients being treated compulsorily under a community treatment order made under MHA 1983, s 17A (inserted by MHA 2007, s 32). Section 28(1B) prohibits such patients being treated under s 5, requiring MHA powers to be used instead.

'**Medical treatment**'—Includes nursing and also psychological intervention and specialist mental health habilitation, rehabilitation and care; and is to be construed as a reference to medical treatment the purpose of which is to alleviate, or prevent a worsening of, the disorder or one or more of its symptoms or manifestations (MHA 1983, s 145, as amended by MHA 2007, s 7).

'**Mental disorder**'—Means any disorder or disability of the mind (MHA 1983, s 1(2), as amended and simplified by MHA 2007, s 1(2)).

'**Patient**'—Means a person suffering or appearing to be suffering from mental disorder (MHA 1983, s 145).

29 Voting rights

(1) Nothing in this Act permits a decision on voting at an election for any public office, or at a referendum, to be made on behalf of a person.

(2) 'Referendum' has the same meaning as in section 101 of the Political Parties, Elections and Referendums Act 2000.

Scope of provision—This confirms that no one can make a decision on voting or cast a vote at an election or a referendum on behalf of a person lacking capacity to vote.

Research

30 Research

(1) Intrusive research carried out on, or in relation to, a person who lacks capacity to consent to it is unlawful unless it is carried out –

(a) as part of a research project which is for the time being approved by the appropriate body for the purposes of this Act in accordance with section 31, and

(b) in accordance with sections 32 and 33.

(2) Research is intrusive if it is of a kind that would be unlawful if it was carried out –

(a) on or in relation to a person who had capacity to consent to it, but

(b) without his consent.

(3) A clinical trial which is subject to the provisions of clinical trials regulations is not to be treated as research for the purposes of this section.

[(3A) Research is not intrusive to the extent that it consists of the use of a person's human cells to bring about the creation in vitro of an embryo or human admixed embryo, or the subsequent storage or use of an embryo or human admixed embryo so created.

(3B) Expressions used in subsection (3A) and in Schedule 3 to the Human Fertilisation and Embryology Act 1990 (consents to use or storage of gametes, embryos or human admixed embryos etc.) have the same meaning in that subsection as in that Schedule.]

(4) 'Appropriate body', in relation to a research project, means the person, committee or other body specified in regulations made by the appropriate authority as the appropriate body in relation to a project of the kind in question.

(5) 'Clinical trials regulations' means –

  (a) the Medicines for Human Use (Clinical Trials) Regulations 2004 and any other regulations replacing those regulations or amending them, and
  (b) any other regulations relating to clinical trials and designated by the Secretary of State as clinical trials regulations for the purposes of this section.

(6) In this section, section 32 and section 34, 'appropriate authority' means –

  (a) in relation to the carrying out of research in England, the Secretary of State, and
  (b) in relation to the carrying out of research in Wales, the National Assembly for Wales.

Amendment—Subsections (3A) and (3B) inserted by Human Fertilisation and Embryology Act 2008, s 65, Sch 7, para 25.

Scope of provision—This section, ss 31–34 and the Regulations and Guidance referred to in the notes provide the legal framework within which beneficial research in relation to impairing conditions may be carried out on someone who is unable to consent, subject to the safeguards provided. These provisions are discussed in Chapter 5 (at **5.86–5.94**).

'Appropriate body' (s 30(1))—Prescribed in the Mental Capacity Act 2005 (Appropriate Body) (England) Regulations 2006, SI 2006/2810 as a committee established to advise on, or on matters which include, the ethics of intrusive research in relation to people who lack capacity to consent to it and recognised for that purpose by the Secretary of State. For Wales, see the equivalent 2007 Regulations approved by the Minister for Health and Social Services (SI 2007/833 (W 71)).

'Clinical trials regulations' (s 30(5))—See SI 2004/3224, SI 2005/2754, SI 2005/2759, SI 2006/562· SI 2006/1928, SI 2006/2984, SI 2007/289, SI 2007/3101, SR 2008/192, SI 2008/941 and SI 2009/1164 for amendments to the Medicines for Human Use (Clinical Trials) Regulations 2004.

'Secretary of State' (s 30(6))—For England the appropriate authority is the Secretary of State for Health.

31 Requirements for approval

(1) The appropriate body may not approve a research project for the purposes of this Act unless satisfied that the following requirements will be met in relation to research carried out as part of the project on, or in relation to, a person who lacks capacity to consent to taking part in the project ('P').

(2) The research must be connected with –

  (a) an impairing condition affecting P, or
  (b) its treatment.

(3) 'Impairing condition' means a condition which is (or may be) attributable to, or which causes or contributes to (or may cause or contribute to), the impairment of, or disturbance in the functioning of, the mind or brain.

(4) There must be reasonable grounds for believing that research of comparable effectiveness cannot be carried out if the project has to be confined to, or relate only to, persons who have capacity to consent to taking part in it.

(5) The research must –

  (a) have the potential to benefit P without imposing on P a burden that is disproportionate to the potential benefit to P, or

    (b)   be intended to provide knowledge of the causes or treatment of, or of the care of persons affected by, the same or a similar condition.

(6) If the research falls within paragraph (b) of subsection (5) but not within paragraph (a), there must be reasonable grounds for believing –

    (a)   that the risk to P from taking part in the project is likely to be negligible, and

    (b)   that anything done to, or in relation to, P will not –

        (i)   interfere with P's freedom of action or privacy in a significant way, or

        (ii) be unduly invasive or restrictive.

(7) There must be reasonable arrangements in place for ensuring that the requirements of sections 32 and 33 will be met.

Scope of provision—This section sets out the primary requirements which must be met before a research project which includes research on a person who cannot consent can be approved.

'Appropriate body' (s 31(1))—See note to s 30(1).

32 Consulting carers etc

(1) This section applies if a person ('R') –

    (a)   is conducting an approved research project, and

    (b)   wishes to carry out research, as part of the project, on or in relation to a person ('P') who lacks capacity to consent to taking part in the project.

(2) R must take reasonable steps to identify a person who –

    (a)   otherwise than in a professional capacity or for remuneration, is engaged in caring for P or is interested in P's welfare, and

    (b)   is prepared to be consulted by R under this section.

(3) If R is unable to identify such a person he must, in accordance with guidance issued by the appropriate authority, nominate a person who –

    (a)   is prepared to be consulted by R under this section, but

    (b)   has no connection with the project.

(4) R must provide the person identified under subsection (2), or nominated under subsection (3), with information about the project and ask him –

    (a)   for advice as to whether P should take part in the project, and

    (b)   what, in his opinion, P's wishes and feelings about taking part in the project would be likely to be if P had capacity in relation to the matter.

(5) If, at any time, the person consulted advises R that in his opinion P's wishes and feelings would be likely to lead him to decline to take part in the project (or to wish to withdraw from it) if he had capacity in relation to the matter, R must ensure –

    (a)   if P is not already taking part in the project, that he does not take part in it;

    (b)   if P is taking part in the project, that he is withdrawn from it.

(6) But subsection (5)(b) does not require treatment that P has been receiving as part of the project to be discontinued if R has reasonable grounds for believing that there would be a significant risk to P's health if it were discontinued.

(7) The fact that a person is the donee of a lasting power of attorney given by P, or is P's deputy, does not prevent him from being the person consulted under this section.

(8) Subsection (9) applies if treatment is being, or is about to be, provided for P as a matter of urgency and R considers that, having regard to the nature of the research and of the particular circumstances of the case –

    (a)   it is also necessary to take action for the purposes of the research as a matter of urgency, but

    (b)   it is not reasonably practicable to consult under the previous provisions of this section.

(9) R may take the action if –

    (a)   he has the agreement of a registered medical practitioner who is not involved in the organisation or conduct of the research project, or

    (b)   where it is not reasonably practicable in the time available to obtain that agreement, he acts in accordance with a procedure approved by the appropriate body at the time when the research project was approved under section 31.

(10) But R may not continue to act in reliance on subsection (9) if he has reasonable grounds for believing that it is no longer necessary to take the action as a matter of urgency.

'In accordance with guidance issued by the appropriate authority' (s 32(3))—Guidance has been issued by the Department of Health in partnership with the Welsh Assembly Government in February 2008 (see www.dh.gov.uk/publications).

33 Additional safeguards

(1) This section applies in relation to a person who is taking part in an approved research project even though he lacks capacity to consent to taking part.

(2) Nothing may be done to, or in relation to, him in the course of the research –

    (a)   to which he appears to object (whether by showing signs of resistance or otherwise) except where what is being done is intended to protect him from harm or to reduce or prevent pain or discomfort, or

    (b)   which would be contrary to –

        (i)   an advance decision of his which has effect, or

        (ii)   any other form of statement made by him and not subsequently withdrawn,

of which R is aware.

(3) The interests of the person must be assumed to outweigh those of science and society.

(4) If he indicates (in any way) that he wishes to be withdrawn from the project he must be withdrawn without delay.

(5) P must be withdrawn from the project, without delay, if at any time the person conducting the research has reasonable grounds for believing that one or more of the requirements set out in section 31(2) to (7) is no longer met in relation to research being carried out on, or in relation to, P.

(6) But neither subsection (4) nor subsection (5) requires treatment that P has been receiving as part of the project to be discontinued if R has reasonable grounds for believing that there would be a significant risk to P's health if it were discontinued.

'An advance decision ... which has effect' (s 33(2)(b))—See ss 24–26.

34 Loss of capacity during research project

(1) This section applies where a person ('P') –

    (a)   has consented to take part in a research project begun before the commencement of section 30, but

    (b)   before the conclusion of the project, loses capacity to consent to continue to take part in it.

(2) The appropriate authority may by regulations provide that, despite P's loss of capacity, research of a prescribed kind may be carried out on, or in relation to, P if –

    (a)   the project satisfies prescribed requirements,

    (b)   any information or material relating to P which is used in the research is of a prescribed description and was obtained before P's loss of capacity, and

    (c)   the person conducting the project takes in relation to P such steps as may be prescribed for the purpose of protecting him.

(3) The regulations may, in particular, –

    (a)   make provision about when, for the purposes of the regulations, a project is to be treated as having begun;

    (b)   include provision similar to any made by section 31, 32 or 33.

'Regulations' (s 34(2))—See the Mental Capacity Act 2005 (Loss of Capacity during Research Project) (England) Regulations 2007, SI 2007/679 and equivalent Welsh Regulations (SI 2007/837 (W 72)).

Independent mental capacity advocate service

35 Appointment of independent mental capacity advocates

(1) The appropriate authority must make such arrangements as it considers reasonable to enable persons ('independent mental capacity advocates') to be available to represent and support persons to whom acts or decisions proposed under sections 37, 38 and 39 relate [or persons who fall within section 39A, 39C or 39D].

(2) The appropriate authority may make regulations as to the appointment of independent mental capacity advocates.

(3) The regulations may, in particular, provide –

    (a)   that a person may act as an independent mental capacity advocate only in such circumstances, or only subject to such conditions, as may be prescribed;

    (b)   for the appointment of a person as an independent mental capacity advocate to be subject to approval in accordance with the regulations.

(4) In making arrangements under subsection (1), the appropriate authority must have regard to the principle that a person to whom a proposed act or decision relates should, so far as practicable, be represented and supported by a person who is independent of any person who will be responsible for the act or decision.

(5) The arrangements may include provision for payments to be made to, or in relation to, persons carrying out functions in accordance with the arrangements.

(6) For the purpose of enabling him to carry out his functions, an independent mental capacity advocate –

    (a)   may interview in private the person whom he has been instructed to represent, and

(b) may, at all reasonable times, examine and take copies of –
    (i) any health record,
    (ii) any record of, or held by, a local authority and compiled in connection with a social services function, and
    (iii) any record held by a person registered under Part 2 of the Care Standards Act 2000 [or Chapter 2 of Part I of the Health and Social Care Act 2008],

which the person holding the record considers may be relevant to the independent mental capacity advocate's investigation.

(7) In this section, section 36 and section 37, 'the appropriate authority' means –

(a) in relation to the provision of the services of independent mental capacity advocates in England, the Secretary of State, and

(b) in relation to the provision of the services of independent mental capacity advocates in Wales, the National Assembly for Wales.

Amendment—Words in subsection (1)inserted by the Mental Health Act 2007, s 50(7), Sch 9, Pt 1, paras 1, 3; words in subsection (6)(b)(iii) inserted by SI 2010/813.

Scope of provision—The Secretary of State for Health in England and National Assembly for Wales have discharged their duty to make arrangements (s 35(1)) to make available independent mental capacity advocates through the provision of local funding, circulars and the Regulations referred to in the notes to this and the following sections (see www.dh.gov.uk/en/SocialCare/Deliveringadultsocialcare/MentalCapacity/IMCA). IMCAs are a locally contracted service and there are a large number of different providers in different parts of the country. These provisions are described in Chapter 5 (at **5.50–5.59**).

'Regulations' (s 35(2))—For England see the Mental Capacity Act 2005 (Independent Mental Capacity Advocates) (General) Regulations 2006, SI 2006/1832 as amended by the Mental Health and Mental Capacity (Advocacy) Amendment (England) Regulations 2009, SI 2009/2376 and for Wales the Mental Capacity Act 2005 (Independent Mental Capacity Advocates) (Wales) Regulations 2007, SI 2007/852 (W 77) and the Mental Capacity (Deprivation of Liberty: Appointment of Relevant Person's Representative) (Wales) Regulations 2009, SI 2009/266 (W 29).

36 Functions of independent mental capacity advocates

(1) The appropriate authority may make regulations as to the functions of independent mental capacity advocates.

(2) The regulations may, in particular, make provision requiring an advocate to take such steps as may be prescribed for the purpose of –

(a) providing support to the person whom he has been instructed to represent ('P') so that P may participate as fully as possible in any relevant decision;
(b) obtaining and evaluating relevant information;
(c) ascertaining what P's wishes and feelings would be likely to be, and the beliefs and values that would be likely to influence P, if he had capacity;
(d) ascertaining what alternative courses of action are available in relation to P;
(e) obtaining a further medical opinion where treatment is proposed and the advocate thinks that one should be obtained.

(3) The regulations may also make provision as to circumstances in which the advocate may challenge, or provide assistance for the purpose of challenging, any relevant decision.

'Regulations'—See the Mental Capacity Act 2005 (Independent Mental Capacity Advocates) (General) Regulations 2006, SI 2006/1832 and for Wales SI 2007/852 (W 77).

37 Provision of serious medical treatment by NHS body

(1) This section applies if an NHS body –

    (a)   is proposing to provide, or secure the provision of, serious medical treatment for a person ('P') who lacks capacity to consent to the treatment, and

    (b)   is satisfied that there is no person, other than one engaged in providing care or treatment for P in a professional capacity or for remuneration, whom it would be appropriate to consult in determining what would be in P's best interests.

(2) But this section does not apply if P's treatment is regulated by Part 4 [or 4A] of the Mental Health Act.

(3) Before the treatment is provided, the NHS body must instruct an independent mental capacity advocate to represent P.

(4) If the treatment needs to be provided as a matter of urgency, it may be provided even though the NHS body has not been able to comply with subsection (3).

(5) The NHS body must, in providing or securing the provision of treatment for P, take into account any information given, or submissions made, by the independent mental capacity advocate.

(6) 'Serious medical treatment' means treatment which involves providing, withholding or withdrawing treatment of a kind prescribed by regulations made by the appropriate authority.

(7) 'NHS body' has such meaning as may be prescribed by regulations made for the purposes of this section by –

    (a)   the Secretary of State, in relation to bodies in England, or

    (b)   the National Assembly for Wales, in relation to bodies in Wales.

Amendment—Words in square brackets inserted by the Mental Health Act 2007, s 35(4), (6).

'Regulated by Part 4 or 4A of the Mental Health Act' (s 37(2))—Where a person is being treated under Mental Health Act powers and that treatment is regulated by Part 4, which lays down the extent to which treatment for mental disorder can be imposed on detained patients in hospital under MHA 1983 and the safeguards available concerning the provision of treatment without consent, or by Part 4A, which regulates the treatment of community patients in the community, an IMCA is not required in relation to that treatment.

'Prescribed by regulations' (s 37(6) and (7))—'Serious medical treatment' for the purposes of this section is treatment which involves providing, withdrawing or withholding treatment in circumstances where (a) in a case where a single treatment is being proposed, there is a fine balance between its benefits to the patient and the burdens and risks it is likely to entail for him or her, (b) in a case where there is a choice of treatments, a decision as to which one to use is finely balanced, or (c) what is proposed would be likely to involve serious consequences for the patient (Mental Capacity Act 2005 (Independent Mental Capacity Advocates) (General) Regulations 2006, SI 2006/1832, reg 4(2)). The Welsh Regulations (SI 2007/852 (W 77)) give the same definition. The meaning of NHS Body in England is (a) a strategic health authority, (b) an NHS foundation trust, (c) a primary care trust, (d) an NHS trust or (e) a care trust. In Wales the meaning is (a) a local health board, (b) an NHS trust all or most of whose hospitals, establishments and facilities are situated in Wales or (c) a Special Health Authority performing functions only or mainly in respect of Wales (reg 3 of the respective Regulations).

38 Provision of accommodation by NHS body

(1) This section applies if an NHS body proposes to make arrangements –

(a)   for the provision of accommodation in a hospital or care home for a person ('P') who lacks capacity to agree to the arrangements, or

(b)   for a change in P's accommodation to another hospital or care home,

and is satisfied that there is no person, other than one engaged in providing care or treatment for P in a professional capacity or for remuneration, whom it would be appropriate for it to consult in determining what would be in P's best interests.

(2)   But this section does not apply if P is accommodated as a result of an obligation imposed on him under the Mental Health Act.

[(2A)   And this section does not apply if –

(a)   an independent mental capacity advocate must be appointed under section 39A or 39C (whether or not by the NHS body) to represent P, and

(b)   the hospital or care home in which P is to be accommodated under the arrangements referred to in this section is the relevant hospital or care home under the authorisation referred to in that section.]

(3)   Before making the arrangements, the NHS body must instruct an independent mental capacity advocate to represent P unless it is satisfied that –

(a)   the accommodation is likely to be provided for a continuous period which is less than the applicable period, or

(b)   the arrangements need to be made as a matter of urgency.

(4)   If the NHS body –

(a)   did not instruct an independent mental capacity advocate to represent P before making the arrangements because it was satisfied that subsection (3)(a) or (b) applied, but

(b)   subsequently has reason to believe that the accommodation is likely to be provided for a continuous period –

(i)   beginning with the day on which accommodation was first provided in accordance with the arrangements, and

(ii)   ending on or after the expiry of the applicable period,

it must instruct an independent mental capacity advocate to represent P.

(5)   The NHS body must, in deciding what arrangements to make for P, take into account any information given, or submissions made, by the independent mental capacity advocate.

(6)   'Care home' has the meaning given in section 3 of the Care Standards Act 2000.

(7)   ['Hospital' means –

(a)   in relation to England, a hospital as defined by section 275 of the National Health Service Act 2006; and

(b)   in relation to Wales, a health service hospital as defined by section 206 of the National Health Service (Wales) Act 2006 or an independent hospital as defined by section 2 of the Care Standards Act 2000.]

(8)   'NHS body' has such meaning as may be prescribed by regulations made for the purposes of this section by –

(a)   the Secretary of State, in relation to bodies in England, or

(b)   the National Assembly for Wales, in relation to bodies in Wales.

(9)   'Applicable period' means –

(a)   in relation to accommodation in a hospital, 28 days, and

(b)   in relation to accommodation in a care home, 8 weeks.

PART III

[(10) For the purposes of subsection (1), a person appointed under Part 10 of Schedule A1 to be P's representative is not, by virtue of that appointment, engaged in providing care or treatment for P in a professional capacity or for remuneration.]

Amendments—Words in subs (7) inserted by the National Health Service (Consequential Provisions) Act 2006, s 2, Sch 1, paras 277, 278. Subsections (2A) and (10) inserted by the Mental Health Act 2007, s 50(7), Sch 9, Pt 1, paras 1, 4(1), (2), (3); words in subsection (7) substituted by SI 2010/813.

'Obligation imposed under the Mental Health Act' (s 38(2))—Where the person concerned is to be detained in hospital or otherwise required to live in particular accommodation under the compulsory powers in MHA 1983 an IMCA is not required.

'Care home' (s 38(6))—This covers any care home, not being a hospital, independent clinic or a children's home, which provides accommodation together with nursing or personal care.

'Hospital' (s 38(7))—This covers (a) any NHS hospital in which treatment is provided and (b) any non-NHS hospital the main purpose of which is to provide treatment or palliative care or treatment or nursing care for persons liable to be detained under the Mental Health Act.

'Regulations prescribing NHS body' (s 38(8))—See note to s 37(6) and (7).

39 Provision of accommodation by local authority

(1) This section applies if a local authority propose to make arrangements –

(a) for the provision of residential accommodation for a person ('P') who lacks capacity to agree to the arrangements, or
(b) for a change in P's residential accommodation,

and are satisfied that there is no person, other than one engaged in providing care or treatment for P in a professional capacity or for remuneration, whom it would be appropriate for them to consult in determining what would be in P's best interests.

(2) But this section applies only if the accommodation is to be provided in accordance with –

(a) section 21 or 29 of the National Assistance Act 1948, or
(b) section 117 of the Mental Health Act,

as the result of a decision taken by the local authority under section 47 of the National Health Service and Community Care Act 1990.

(3) This section does not apply if P is accommodated as a result of an obligation imposed on him under the Mental Health Act.

[(3A) And this section does not apply if —

(a) an independent mental capacity advocate must be appointed under section 39A or 39C (whether or not by the local authority) to represent P, and
(b) the place in which P is to be accommodated under the arrangements referred to in this section is the relevant hospital or care home under the authorisation referred to in that section.]

(4) Before making the arrangements, the local authority must instruct an independent mental capacity advocate to represent P unless they are satisfied that –

(a) the accommodation is likely to be provided for a continuous period of less than 8 weeks, or
(b) the arrangements need to be made as a matter of urgency.

(5) If the local authority –

    (a)   did not instruct an independent mental capacity advocate to represent P before making the arrangements because they were satisfied that subsection (4)(a) or (b) applied, but

    (b)   subsequently have reason to believe that the accommodation is likely to be provided for a continuous period that will end 8 weeks or more after the day on which accommodation was first provided in accordance with the arrangements,

they must instruct an independent mental capacity advocate to represent P.

(6) The local authority must, in deciding what arrangements to make for P, take into account any information given, or submissions made, by the independent mental capacity advocate.

[(7) For the purposes of subsection (1), a person appointed under Part 10 of Schedule A1 to be P's representative is not, by virtue of that appointment, engaged in providing care or treatment for P in a professional capacity or for remuneration.]

Amendments—Subsections (3A) and (7) inserted by the Mental Health Act 2007, s 50(7), Sch 9, Pt 1, paras 1, 5(1), (2), (3).

'If the accommodation is to be provided in accordance with ...' (s 39(2))—This may be accommodation in a care home, nursing home, ordinary and sheltered housing, housing association or other registered social housing, or in private sector housing provided by a local authority, or in hostel accommodation; and it includes people accommodated following discharge under MHA 1983, s 117. It applies where following a care needs assessment under the National Health Service and Community Care Act 1990, s 47 the local authority decides that the person's needs call for the provision of any such services.

'Obligation imposed under the Mental Health Act' (s 39(3))—See note to s 38(2).

[39A Person becomes subject to Schedule A1]

[(1) This section applies if —

    (a)   a person ('P') becomes subject to Schedule A1, and

    (b)   the managing authority of the relevant hospital or care home are satisfied that there is no person, other than one engaged in providing care or treatment for P in a professional capacity or for remuneration, whom it would be appropriate to consult in determining what would be in P's best interests.

(2) The managing authority must notify the supervisory body that this section applies.

(3) The supervisory body must instruct an independent mental capacity advocate to represent P.

(4) Schedule A1 makes provision about the role of an independent mental capacity advocate appointed under this section.

(5) This section is subject to paragraph 161 of Schedule A1.

(6) For the purposes of subsection (1), a person appointed under Part 10 of Schedule A1 to be P's representative is not, by virtue of that appointment, engaged in providing care or treatment for P in a professional capacity or for remuneration.]

Amendment—Section inserted by the Mental Health Act 2007, s 50(7), Sch 9, Pt 1, paras 1, 6.

Effect of provision—The effect of this section, part of the Deprivation of Liberty safeguards, is that when in any of the circumstances set out in the following section, an authorisation is sought by the managing authority of a hospital or care home to deprive a patient or resident of their liberty and there are no family, friends or non-professional carers to support that person, an independent mental capacity advocate (IMCA) must be instructed by the supervising primary care trust (or in Wales, the National Assembly or local health board) or local authority.

'Subject to paragraph 161 of Schedule A1' (s 39A(5))—An IMCA under this section does not retain the full powers of an IMCA after a representative for that person has been appointed under Sch A1, Part 10 once a standard authorisation has been given.

[39B Section 39A: supplementary provision]

[(1) This section applies for the purposes of section 39A.

(2) P becomes subject to Schedule A1 in any of the following cases.

(3) The first case is where an urgent authorisation is given in relation to P under paragraph 76(2) of Schedule A1 (urgent authorisation given before request made for standard authorisation).

(4) The second case is where the following conditions are met.

(5) The first condition is that a request is made under Schedule A1 for a standard authorisation to be given in relation to P ('the requested authorisation').

(6) The second condition is that no urgent authorisation was given under paragraph 76(2) of Schedule A1 before that request was made.

(7) The third condition is that the requested authorisation will not be in force on or before, or immediately after, the expiry of an existing standard authorisation.

(8) The expiry of a standard authorisation is the date when the authorisation is expected to cease to be in force.

(9) The third case is where, under paragraph 69 of Schedule A1, the supervisory body select a person to carry out an assessment of whether or not the relevant person is a detained resident.]

Amendment—Section inserted by the Mental Health Act 2007, s 50(7), Sch 9, Pt 1, paras 1, 6.

Effect of provision—See s 39A.

'Urgent authorisation/standard authorisation/assessment of whether or not a detained resident'—See notes to Sch A1.

[39C Person unrepresented whilst subject to Schedule A1]

[(1) This section applies if —

    (a) an authorisation under Schedule A1 is in force in relation to a person ('P'),
    (b) the appointment of a person as P's representative ends in accordance with regulations made under Part 10 of Schedule A1, and
    (c) the managing authority of the relevant hospital or care home are satisfied that there is no person, other than one engaged in providing care or treatment for P in a professional capacity or for remuneration, whom it would be appropriate to consult in determining what would be in P's best interests.

(2) The managing authority must notify the supervisory body that this section applies.

(3) The supervisory body must instruct an independent mental capacity advocate to represent P.

(4) Paragraph 159 of Schedule A1 makes provision about the role of an independent mental capacity advocate appointed under this section.

(5) The appointment of an independent mental capacity advocate under this section ends when a new appointment of a person as P's representative is made in accordance with Part 10 of Schedule A1.

(6) For the purposes of subsection (1), a person appointed under Part 10 of Schedule A1 to be P's representative is not, by virtue of that appointment, engaged in providing care or treatment for P in a professional capacity or for remuneration.]

Amendment—Section inserted by the Mental Health Act 2007, s 50(7), Sch 9, Pt 1, paras 1, 6.

Scope of provision—This section provides for an IMCA to be appointed to represent the person who is being deprived of their liberty while an authorisation is in force, during gaps in the appointment of a representative for the person (e g when a new representative is being sought) and there is no one other than a paid or professional carer who it is appropriate to consult about the person's best interests.

'The appointment of a person as P's representative ends in accordance with regulations made under Part 10 of Schedule A1' (s 39C(1)(b))—See the Mental Capacity (Deprivation of Liberty—Appointment of Relevant Person's Representative) Regulations 2008, SI 2008/1315, regs 13 and 14.

[39D Person subject to Schedule A1 without paid representative]

[(1) This section applies if —

    (a)   an authorisation under Schedule A1 is in force in relation to a person ('P'),

    (b)   P has a representative ('R') appointed under Part 10 of Schedule A1, and

    (c)   R is not being paid under regulations under Part 10 of Schedule A1 for acting as P's representative.

(2) The supervisory body must instruct an independent mental capacity advocate to represent P in any of the following cases.

(3) The first case is where P makes a request to the supervisory body to instruct an advocate.

(4) The second case is where R makes a request to the supervisory body to instruct an advocate.

(5) The third case is where the supervisory body have reason to believe one or more of the following—

    (a)   that, without the help of an advocate, P and R would be unable to exercise one or both of the relevant rights;

    (b)   that P and R have each failed to exercise a relevant right when it would have been reasonable to exercise it;

    (c)   that P and R are each unlikely to exercise a relevant right when it would be reasonable to exercise it.

(6) The duty in subsection (2) is subject to section 39E.

(7) If an advocate is appointed under this section, the advocate is, in particular, to take such steps as are practicable to help P and R to understand the following matters —

    (a)   the effect of the authorisation;

PART III

(b)   the purpose of the authorisation;

(c)   the duration of the authorisation;

(d)   any conditions to which the authorisation is subject;

(e)   the reasons why each assessor who carried out an assessment in connection with the request for the authorisation, or in connection with a review of the authorisation, decided that P met the qualifying requirement in question;

(f)   the relevant rights;

(g)   how to exercise the relevant rights.

(8) The advocate is, in particular, to take such steps as are practicable to help P or R —

(a)   to exercise the right to apply to court, if it appears to the advocate that P or R wishes to exercise that right, or

(b)   to exercise the right of review, if it appears to the advocate that P or R wishes to exercise that right.

(9) If the advocate helps P or R to exercise the right of review —

(a)   the advocate may make submissions to the supervisory body on the question of whether a qualifying requirement is reviewable;

(b)   the advocate may give information, or make submissions, to any assessor carrying out a review assessment.

(10) In this section —

'relevant rights' means —

(a)   the right to apply to court, and

(b)   the right of review;

'right to apply to court' means the right to make an application to the court to exercise its jurisdiction under section 21A;

'right of review' means the right under Part 8 of Schedule A1 to request a review.]

Amendment—Section inserted by the Mental Health Act 2007, s 50(7), Sch 9, Pt 1, paras 1, 6.

Scope of provision—Under this section, the supervisory body must instruct an IMCA if requested to do so by the person deprived of their liberty or their unpaid representative, in order to assist them to exercise their rights either to request a review or to apply to the Court of Protection for determination of any matter relating to the authorisation to deprive the person of their liberty. The supervisory body may also appoint an IMCA if this will help to ensure that the person's rights are protected.

'Is not being paid under Regulations under Part 10 of Schedule A1'—Under the Mental Capacity (Deprivation of Liberty—Appointment of Relevant Person's Representative) Regulations 2008, SI 2008/1315, reg 5 where a supervisory body selects the representative it may pay that representative.

[39E Limitation on duty to instruct advocate under section 39D]

[(1) This section applies if an advocate is already representing P in accordance with an instruction under section 39D.

(2) Section 39D(2) does not require another advocate to be instructed, unless the following conditions are met.

(3) The first condition is that the existing advocate was instructed —

(a)   because of a request by R, or

(b)   because the supervisory body had reason to believe one or more of the things in section 39D(5).

(4) The second condition is that the other advocate would be instructed because of a request by P.]

Amendment—Section inserted by the Mental Health Act 2007, s 50(7), Sch 9, Pt 1, paras 1, 6.

[40 Exceptions

[(1)] The duty imposed by section 37(3), 38(3) or (4)[, 39(4) or (5), 39A(3), 39C(3) or 39D(2)] does not apply where there is –

(a)   a person nominated by P (in whatever manner) as a person to be consulted on matters to which that duty relates,

(b)   a donee of a lasting power of attorney created by P who is authorised to make decisions in relation to those matters, or

(c)   a deputy appointed by the court for P with power to make decisions in relation to those matters.]

[(2) A person appointed under Part 10 of Schedule A1 to be P's representative is not, by virtue of that appointment, a person nominated by P as a person to be consulted in matters to which a duty mentioned in subsection (1) relates.]]

Amendment—Section substituted by the Mental Health Act 2007, s 49. Subsection (1) numbered as such, words in square brackets substituted and subsection (2) inserted by the Mental Health Act 2007, s 50(7), Sch 9, Pt 1, paras 1, 7(1)–(4).

41 Power to adjust role of independent mental capacity advocate

(1) The appropriate authority may make regulations –

(a)   expanding the role of independent mental capacity advocates in relation to persons who lack capacity, and

(b)   adjusting the obligation to make arrangements imposed by section 35.

(2) The regulations may, in particular –

(a)   prescribe circumstances (different to those set out in sections 37, 38 and 39) in which an independent mental capacity advocate must, or circumstances in which one may, be instructed by a person of a prescribed description to represent a person who lacks capacity, and

(b)   include provision similar to any made by section 37, 38, 39 or 40.

(3) 'Appropriate authority' has the same meaning as in section 35.

'Regulations' (s 41(1))—This power has been exercised in England in the Mental Capacity Act 2005 (Independent Mental Capacity Advocates) (Expansion of Role) Regulations 2006, SI 2006/2883 and in Wales in SI 2007/852 (W 77).

Miscellaneous and supplementary

42 Codes of practice

(1) The Lord Chancellor must prepare and issue one or more codes of practice –

(a)   for the guidance of persons assessing whether a person has capacity in relation to any matter,

(b)   for the guidance of persons acting in connection with the care or treatment of another person (see section 5),

(c)   for the guidance of donees of lasting powers of attorney,

(d)   for the guidance of deputies appointed by the court,

(e)   for the guidance of persons carrying out research in reliance on any provision made by or under this Act (and otherwise with respect to sections 30 to 34),

(f)   for the guidance of independent mental capacity advocates,

[(fa) for the guidance of persons exercising functions under Schedule A1,

(fb) for the guidance of representatives appointed under Part 10 of Schedule A1,]

(g)   with respect to the provisions of sections 24 to 26 (advance decisions and apparent advance decisions), and

(h)   with respect to such other matters concerned with this Act as he thinks fit.

(2) The Lord Chancellor may from time to time revise a code.

(3) The Lord Chancellor may delegate the preparation or revision of the whole or any part of a code so far as he considers expedient.

(4) It is the duty of a person to have regard to any relevant code if he is acting in relation to a person who lacks capacity and is doing so in one or more of the following ways –

(a)   as the donee of a lasting power of attorney,

(b)   as a deputy appointed by the court,

(c)   as a person carrying out research in reliance on any provision made by or under this Act (see sections 30 to 34),

(d)   as an independent mental capacity advocate,

[(da) in the exercise of functions under Schedule A1,

(db) as a representative appointed under Part 10 of Schedule A1,]

(e)   in a professional capacity,

(f)   for remuneration.

(5) If it appears to a court or tribunal conducting any criminal or civil proceedings that –

(a)   a provision of a code, or

(b)   a failure to comply with a code,

is relevant to a question arising in the proceedings, the provision or failure must be taken into account in deciding the question.

(6) A code under subsection (1)(d) may contain separate guidance for deputies appointed by virtue of paragraph 1(2) of Schedule 5 (functions of deputy conferred on receiver appointed under the Mental Health Act).

(7) In this section and in section 43, 'code' means a code prepared or revised under this section.

Amendments—Paragraphs in square brackets inserted by the Mental Health Act 2007, s 50(7), Sch 9, Pt 1, paras 1, 8(1)–(3).

Scope of provision—This makes provision for the Lord Chancellor to prepare and issue a statutory Code (or Codes) of Practice for the guidance of practitioners using the Act and those affected by its provisions, and also to assist with interpretation and implementation of the Act. The Government decided to issue one main Code of Practice to include guidance on the whole of the MCA 2005 as enacted. A supplement to main Code has since been issued, dealing with the Deprivation of Liberty Safeguards which came into effect on 1 April 2009. The Code and supplement are reproduced in Part V of this book.

'delegate the preparation or revision' (s 42(3))—Responsibility for the Code of Practice has now passed from the Ministry of Justice (formerly the Department for Constitutional Affairs, which published the Code) to the Office of the Public Guardian (OPG).

'have regard to' (s 42(4))—The statutory duty to 'have regard to' the Code applies to those exercising formal powers or duties under the Act, and to professionals and others acting for remuneration. Family members or informal carers not under such a duty 'should follow the guidance in the Code so far as they are aware of it' (Code of Practice, p 2).

'a court or tribunal conducting any criminal or civil proceedings' (s 42(5))—There is no liability for breach of the Code itself, but compliance or non-compliance may be an element in deciding the issue of liability for breach of some other statutory or common law duty. This applies not only to those categories of people who have a duty to have regard to the Code of Practice, but also to others involved in legal proceedings, since they may also have an obligation to act in accordance with the principles of the Act and in the best interests of a person lacking capacity.

43 Codes of practice: procedure

(1) Before preparing or revising a code, the Lord Chancellor must consult –

(a) the National Assembly for Wales, and
(b) such other persons as he considers appropriate.

(2) The Lord Chancellor may not issue a code unless –

(a) a draft of the code has been laid by him before both Houses of Parliament, and
(b) the 40 day period has elapsed without either House resolving not to approve the draft.

(3) The Lord Chancellor must arrange for any code that he has issued to be published in such a way as he considers appropriate for bringing it to the attention of persons likely to be concerned with its provisions.

(4) '40 day period', in relation to the draft of a proposed code, means –

(a) if the draft is laid before one House on a day later than the day on which it is laid before the other House, the period of 40 days beginning with the later of the two days;
(b) in any other case, the period of 40 days beginning with the day on which it is laid before each House.

(5) In calculating the period of 40 days, no account is to be taken of any period during which Parliament is dissolved or prorogued or during which both Houses are adjourned for more than 4 days.

Scope of provision—This section sets out the procedures required for the preparation or revision of the Code(s) and for parliamentary approval.

'National Assembly for Wales' (s 43(1)(a))—Since health and social care responsibilities are devolved in relation to Wales, the National Assembly for Wales must specifically be consulted and involved in the preparation of the Codes.

'such other persons' (s 43(1)(b))—There must be formal consultation with anyone whom the Lord Chancellor considers appropriate before a Code is prepared or revised.

'resolving not to approve the draft' (s 43(2)(b))—The Code takes effect after the 40-day period (as defined in s 43(4)–(5)) unless, within that time, either House has resolved not to approve it (known as the 'negative resolution' procedure).

'**published in such a way as he considers appropriate**' (s 43(3))—The Lord Chancellor is allowed considerable flexibility in arranging for the Codes to be produced in the most appropriate format and for bringing the guidance to the attention of everyone who needs to know about it.

44 Ill-treatment or neglect

(1) Subsection (2) applies if a person ('D') –

   (a)   has the care of a person ('P') who lacks, or whom D reasonably believes to lack, capacity,

   (b)   is the donee of a lasting power of attorney, or an enduring power of attorney (within the meaning of Schedule 4), created by P, or

   (c)   is a deputy appointed by the court for P.

(2) D is guilty of an offence if he ill-treats or wilfully neglects P.

(3) A person guilty of an offence under this section is liable –

   (a)   on summary conviction, to imprisonment for a term not exceeding 12 months or a fine not exceeding the statutory maximum or both;

   (b)   on conviction on indictment, to imprisonment for a term not exceeding 5 years or a fine or both.

Scope of provision—This section creates new criminal offences of ill-treatment or wilful neglect of a person lacking capacity, carrying penalties on conviction ranging from a fine to a term of imprisonment of up to 5 years. Ill-treatment and neglect are separate offences (*R v Newington* (1990) Cr App R 247, CA). No lower age limit is specified, so the offence will also apply to the ill-treatment or wilful neglect of children under 16 whose lack of capacity is caused by an impairment of, or disturbance in the functioning of, the mind or brain, not solely by the immaturity of youth.

'**has the care of a person ('P')**' (s 44(1)(a))—This includes not only family carers, but also health and social care staff in hospitals or care homes or providing domiciliary care.

'**who lacks ... capacity**' (s 44(1)(a)—Section 44 provides no further guidance on the particular decision (or decisions) P lacks capacity to make, so there is a 'disconnect between MCA 2005 s 44 (referring to 'persons without capacity') and the elaborate definition sections (MCA 2005 ss 2 and 3)' (*R v Dunn* (2010) All ER (D) 250 (Nov)). In this case of ill-treatment of residents by the manageress of a care home, it was held that it was open for the jury to conclude that the decisions regarding care (the 'matter') had been made because the victims lacked capacity, and there was no need to complicate matters by referring to MCA 2005 s 3.

'**reasonably believes**' (s 44(1)(a))—This is an objective test. See also ss 4(9) and 5(1).

'**ill-treats**' (s 44(2))—A single act is sufficient to show ill-treatment (*R v Holmes* [1979] Crim LR 52). For a conviction of ill-treatment, it is necessary to show deliberate conduct by the accused which could properly be described as ill-treatment, whether or not it had caused or was likely to cause harm. The accused must either realise that he or she is inexcusably ill-treating the other person or be reckless as to whether he or she is doing so (*R v Newington* (1990) Cr App R 247, CA).

'**wilfully neglects**' (s 44(2))—In the context of the offence of wilfully neglecting a child (Children and Young Persons Act 1933, s 1), it has been held that neglect cannot be described as *wilful* unless the person either had directed his or her mind to whether there was some risk (although it might fall far short of a probability) that the child's health might suffer from the neglect and had made a conscious decision to refrain from acting, or had so refrained because he or she did not care whether the child might be at risk or not (*R v Sheppard* [1981] AC 394, HL). Similar considerations are likely to apply in cases of wilful neglect of an adult lacking capacity.

'**imprisonment for a term not exceeding 5 years**' (s 44(3)(b))—This has the effect of making it an 'arrestable offence' under the Police and Criminal Evidence Act 1984, s 2. It also reflects the potential severity of the crime, with sentences in parallel with those for serious assaults on individuals, including the offences of inflicting grievous bodily harm and assault occasioning actual bodily harm under the Offences Against the Person Act 1861, which both carry maximum sentences of 5 years' imprisonment.

PART 2
THE COURT OF PROTECTION AND THE PUBLIC GUARDIAN

The Court of Protection

45 The Court of Protection

(1) There is to be a superior court of record known as the Court of Protection.

(2) The court is to have an official seal.

(3) The court may sit at any place in England and Wales, on any day and at any time.

(4) The court is to have a central office and registry at a place appointed by the Lord Chancellor[, after consulting the Lord Chief Justice].

(5) The Lord Chancellor may[, after consulting the Lord Chief Justice,] designate as additional registries of the court any district registry of the High Court and any county court office.

[(5A) The Lord Chief Justice may nominate any of the following to exercise his functions under this section –

    (a)   the President of the Court of Protection;

    (b)   a judicial office holder (as defined in section 109(4) of the Constitutional Reform Act 2005).]

(6) The office of the Supreme Court called the Court of Protection ceases to exist.

Amendments—SI 2006/1016.

Scope of provision—This section establishes the new Court of Protection which effectively replaces the former court of that name. This is not simply 'new wine in an old bottle' – it is an 'entirely new vintage' with a different status and structure and its own Rules.

Further explanation—This topic is covered in Chapter 7.

Central office and registry—Presently at Archway Tower, 2 Junction Road, London N19 5SZ. No additional registries have yet been designated.

'The court may sit ...'—Although the nominated Court centres are at Birmingham, Bristol, Cardiff, Manchester (and Preston) and Newcastle, in practice the nominated judges will sit at the most convenient venue and the parties may ask that their needs be taken into account.

Lord Chancellor—For consideration of the relative powers of the Lord Chancellor and the Lord Chief Justice (who in practice delegates his functions to the President of the Court) see Chapter 7.

Powers—For the powers of the Court see ss 15–23.

46 The judges of the Court of Protection

(1) Subject to Court of Protection Rules under section 51(2)(d), the jurisdiction of the court is exercisable by a judge nominated for that purpose by –

    (a)   the [Lord Chief Justice], or

[(b) where nominated by the Lord Chief Justice to act on his behalf under this subsection –

    (i) the President of the Court of Protection; or

    (ii) a judicial office holder (as defined in section 109(4) of the Constitutional Reform Act 2005)].

(2) To be nominated, a judge must be –

    (a) the President of the Family Division,

    (b) the Vice-Chancellor,

    (c) a puisne judge of the High Court,

    (d) a circuit judge, or

    (e) a district judge.

(3) The [Lord Chief Justice, after consulting the Lord Chancellor,] must –

    (a) appoint one of the judges nominated by virtue of subsection (2)(a) to (c) to be President of the Court of Protection, and

    (b) appoint another of those judges to be Vice-President of the Court of Protection.

(4) The [Lord Chief Justice, after consulting the Lord Chancellor,] must appoint one of the judges nominated by virtue of subsection (2)(d) or (e) to be Senior Judge of the Court of Protection, having such administrative functions in relation to the court as the Lord Chancellor[, after consulting the Lord Chief Justice,] may direct.

Amendments—SI 2006/1016.

Scope of provision—This section provides for existing civil and family judges to be nominated to sit in the Court of Protection.

Judges—Only individuals who have already been appointed as judges (of the nature specified) may be nominated to sit in the Court of Protection. Such appointments are now made by the Judicial Appointments Commission, and this means that solicitors and barristers with considerable experience of the Court of Protection may not be appointed unless they fulfil the requirements of a generic civil judge on a competitive basis. Only judges with relevant experience or an interest in the work of the Court will in practice be nominated.

'President'—Presently the President of the Family Division of the High Court (Sir Nicholas Wall).

'Vice-President'—Presently the Chancellor of the Chancery Division of the High Court (Sir Andrew Morritt).

'Senior Judge'—Presently Denzil Lush, the former Master of the old Court of Protection.

The nominated judges—Some 16 district judges have been nominated to sit on a regional basis and four to sit full-time at Archway. Most hearings will be before these district judges. In addition a number of family and chancery circuit judges have been nominated. All Family Division and Chancery Division High Court judges are nominated.

Supplementary powers

47 General powers and effect of orders etc

(1) The court has in connection with its jurisdiction the same powers, rights, privileges and authority as the High Court.

(2) Section 204 of the Law of Property Act 1925 (orders of High Court conclusive in favour of purchasers) applies in relation to orders and directions of the court as it applies to orders of the High Court.

(3) Office copies of orders made, directions given or other instruments issued by the court and sealed with its official seal are admissible in all legal proceedings as evidence of the originals without any further proof.

Scope of provision—This section confirms the powers of the nominated judges when sitting in the Court of Protection and how their orders may be proven in other courts and situations.

'the same powers ... as the High Court' (s 47(1))—This provision, which can easily be overlooked, is extremely important. It vests in judges of the Court of Protection when sitting in that jurisdiction all the powers, rights, privileges and authority of a judge sitting in the High Court. This will include the power to grant injunctions and enforcement powers, including the power to commit for contempt. Equally, any order will have the same status as an order made in the High Court.

48 Interim orders and directions

The court may, pending the determination of an application to it in relation to a person ('P'), make an order or give directions in respect of any matter if –

    (a)   there is reason to believe that P lacks capacity in relation to the matter,

    (b)   the matter is one to which its powers under this Act extend, and

    (c)   it is in P's best interests to make the order, or give the directions, without delay.

Scope of provision—This section enables the Court, following an application, to exercise its powers on an interim basis if satisfied that this is in P's best interests provided that the Court has reason to believe that P lacks capacity in relation to the matter. A finding of lack of capacity on the part of P will not be required. The Court must nevertheless apply the general principle in MCA 2005, s 1. See *Re F* CoP Case No: 11649371, 28 May 2009, HHJ Hazel Marshall QC (summary in Part IX).

'lacks capacity' (s 48(a))—See ss 2–3, and Chapter 2.

'Best interests' (s 48(c))—See s 4 and Chapter 2.

49 Power to call for reports

(1) This section applies where, in proceedings brought in respect of a person ('P') under Part 1, the court is considering a question relating to P.

(2) The court may require a report to be made to it by the Public Guardian or by a Court of Protection Visitor.

(3) The court may require a local authority, or an NHS body, to arrange for a report to be made –

    (a)   by one of its officers or employees, or

    (b)   by such other person (other than the Public Guardian or a Court of Protection Visitor) as the authority, or the NHS body, considers appropriate.

(4) The report must deal with such matters relating to P as the court may direct.

(5) Court of Protection Rules may specify matters which, unless the court directs otherwise, must also be dealt with in the report.

(6) The report may be made in writing or orally, as the court may direct.

(7) In complying with a requirement, the Public Guardian or a Court of Protection Visitor may, at all reasonable times, examine and take copies of –

    (a)   any health record,

(b)   any record of, or held by, a local authority and compiled in connection with a social services function, and

(c)   any record held by a person registered under Part 2 of the Care Standards Act 2000 [or Chapter 2 of Part 1 of the Health and Social Care Act 2008],

so far as the record relates to P.

(8) If the Public Guardian or a Court of Protection Visitor is making a visit in the course of complying with a requirement, he may interview P in private.

(9) If a Court of Protection Visitor who is a Special Visitor is making a visit in the course of complying with a requirement, he may if the court so directs carry out in private a medical, psychiatric or psychological examination of P's capacity and condition.

(10) 'NHS body' has the meaning given in section 148 of the Health and Social Care (Community Health and Standards) Act 2003.

(11) 'Requirement' means a requirement imposed under subsection (2) or (3).

Amendment—Words in subsection (7)(c) inserted by SI 2010/813.

Scope of provision—The Court may, in the exercise of its jurisdiction, obtain independent reports from several sources and this section sets out the authority for this.

'Report'—The Court decides which of the bodies specified shall provide the report, but a local authority or an NHS body may delegate the task (though not to the Public Guardian or by a Court of Protection Visitor).

Fees—There is no provision for fees to be charged for any report requested by the Court.

'Public Guardian'—See ss 57–58 and Chapter 8.

'Court of Protection Visitor'—See s 61 and Chapter 8.

'Court of Protection Rules'—See Court of Protection Rules 2007, SI 2007/1744, reproduced in Part IV of this book.

'local authority, or an NHS body'—This will typically be a social services department or NHS Trust.

'in writing or orally'—A report in writing will usually be produced but the Court can require the individual producing the report to give evidence at a hearing and this is likely in cases of urgency.

'Special Visitor'—This will be a medical visitor, usually a consultant psychiatrist, who is asked to report (inter alia) on capacity issues.

'social services function'—Defined in s 64(1) as having the meaning given in the Local Authority Social Services Act 1970, s 1A.

'local authority'—According to s 64(1) means:

(a)   the council of a county in England in which there are no district councils;
(b)   the council of a district in England;
(c)   the council of a county or county borough in Wales;
(d)   the council of a London borough;
(e)   the Common Council of the City of London; or
(f)   the Council of the Isles of Scilly.

'NHS body'—The statutory reference extends to a primary care trust, a strategic health authority, an NHS trust and an NHS foundation trust. Also in Wales a local health board and a special health authority.

Practice and procedure

50 Applications to the Court of Protection

(1) No permission is required for an application to the court for the exercise of any of its powers under this Act –

-   (a)   by a person who lacks, or is alleged to lack, capacity,
-   (b)   if such a person has not reached 18, by anyone with parental responsibility for him,
-   (c)   by the donor or a donee of a lasting power of attorney to which the application relates,
-   (d)   by a deputy appointed by the court for a person to whom the application relates, or
-   (e)   by a person named in an existing order of the court, if the application relates to the order.

[(1A) Nor is permission required for an application to the court under section 21A by the relevant per-son's representative.]

(2) But, subject to Court of Protection Rules and to paragraph 20(2) of Schedule 3 (declarations relating to private international law), permission is required for any other application to the court.

(3) In deciding whether to grant permission the court must, in particular, have regard to –

-   (a)   the applicant's connection with the person to whom the application relates,
-   (b)   the reasons for the application,
-   (c)   the benefit to the person to whom the application relates of a proposed order or directions, and
-   (d)   whether the benefit can be achieved in any other way.

(4) 'Parental responsibility' has the same meaning as in the Children Act 1989.

Amendment—Subsection (1A) inserted by the Mental Health Act 2007, s 50(7), Sch 9, Pt 1, paras 1, 9.

Scope of provision—Certain categories of person are entitled to apply to the Court, but others need permission and the Court in considering whether to grant such permission must have regard to specified factors.

Court of Protection Rules—Permission to apply is dealt with in Part 8 (rr 50–60) and Practice Direction 8A.

51 Court of Protection Rules

[(1) Rules of court with respect to the practice and procedure of the court (to be called 'Court of Protection Rules') may be made in accordance with Part 1 of Schedule 1 to the Constitutional Reform Act 2005.]

(2) Court of Protection Rules may, in particular, make provision –

-   (a)   as to the manner and form in which proceedings are to be commenced;
-   (b)   as to the persons entitled to be notified of, and be made parties to, the proceedings;
-   (c)   for the allocation, in such circumstances as may be specified, of any specified description of proceedings to a specified judge or to specified descriptions of judges;

(d)   for the exercise of the jurisdiction of the court, in such circumstances as may be specified, by its officers or other staff;

(e)   for enabling the court to appoint a suitable person (who may, with his consent, be the Official Solicitor) to act in the name of, or on behalf of, or to represent the person to whom the proceedings relate;

(f)   for enabling an application to the court to be disposed of without a hearing;

(g)   for enabling the court to proceed with, or with any part of, a hearing in the absence of the person to whom the proceedings relate;

(h)   for enabling or requiring the proceedings or any part of them to be conducted in private and for enabling the court to determine who is to be admitted when the court sits in private and to exclude specified persons when it sits in public;

(i)   as to what may be received as evidence (whether or not admissible apart from the rules) and the manner in which it is to be presented;

(j)   for the enforcement of orders made and directions given in the proceedings.

(3) Court of Protection Rules may, instead of providing for any matter, refer to provision made or to be made about that matter by directions.

(4) Court of Protection Rules may make different provision for different areas.

Amendments—SI 2006/1016.

Scope of provision—This section authorises the court rules and identifies some of the matters that should be dealt with in those rules.

'Court of Protection Rules'—See Court of Protection Rules 2007, SI 2007/1744, reproduced in Part IV of this book.

'directions' (s 51(3))—This refers to the Practice Directions authorised by s 52.

[52 Practice directions

(1) Directions as to the practice and procedure of the court may be given in accordance with Part 1 of Schedule 2 to the Constitutional Reform Act 2005.

(2) Practice directions given otherwise than under subsection (1) may not be given without the approval of –

(a)   the Lord Chancellor, and

(b)   the Lord Chief Justice.

(3) The Lord Chief Justice may nominate any of the following to exercise his functions under this section –

(a)   the President of the Court of Protection;

(b)   a judicial office holder (as defined in section 109(4) of the Constitutional Reform Act 2005).]

Amendments—Substituted by SI 2006/1016.

Scope of provision—This section enables Practice Directions (sometimes referred to as 'PDs') to be formulated for the guidance of the Court and practitioners (and those who appear before the Court). The current Practice Directions are reproduced in Part IV of this work.

53 Rights of appeal

(1) Subject to the provisions of this section, an appeal lies to the Court of Appeal from any decision of the court.

(2) Court of Protection Rules may provide that where a decision of the court is made by –

    (a)   a person exercising the jurisdiction of the court by virtue of rules made under section 51(2)(d),

    (b)   a district judge, or

    (c)   a circuit judge,

an appeal from that decision lies to a prescribed higher judge of the court and not to the Court of Appeal.

(3) For the purposes of this section the higher judges of the court are –

    (a)   in relation to a person mentioned in subsection (2)(a), a circuit judge or a district judge;

    (b)   in relation to a person mentioned in subsection (2)(b), a circuit judge;

    (c)   in relation to any person mentioned in subsection (2), one of the judges nominated by virtue of section 46(2)(a) to (c).

(4) Court of Protection Rules may make provision –

    (a)   that, in such cases as may be specified, an appeal from a decision of the court may not be made without permission;

    (b)   as to the person or persons entitled to grant permission to appeal;

    (c)   as to any requirements to be satisfied before permission is granted;

    (d)   that where a higher judge of the court makes a decision on an appeal, no appeal may be made to the Court of Appeal from that decision unless the Court of Appeal considers that –

        (i)   the appeal would raise an important point of principle or practice, or

        (ii)   there is some other compelling reason for the Court of Appeal to hear it;

    (e)   as to any considerations to be taken into account in relation to granting or refusing permission to appeal.

Scope of provision—This section authorises the Court of Protection Rules to make provision for appeals from first instance decisions, with a default provision that appeals lie to the Court of Appeal.

'Court of Protection Rules' (s 53(2) and (4))—See Court of Protection Rules 2007, SI 2007/1744, Part 20 (rr 169–182) and Practice Direction 20A.

Fees and costs

54 Fees

(1) The Lord Chancellor may with the consent of the Treasury by order prescribe fees payable in respect of anything dealt with by the court.

(2) An order under this section may in particular contain provision as to –

    (a)   scales or rates of fees;

    (b)   exemptions from and reductions in fees;

    (c)   remission of fees in whole or in part.

(3) Before making an order under this section, the Lord Chancellor must consult –

    (a)   the President of the Court of Protection,

(b) the Vice-President of the Court of Protection, and

(c) the Senior Judge of the Court of Protection.

(4) The Lord Chancellor must take such steps as are reasonably practicable to bring information about fees to the attention of persons likely to have to pay them.

(5) Fees payable under this section are recoverable summarily as a civil debt.

Scope of provision—This section enables fees to be prescribed (and recovered) for applications to the Court. The principle of full cost recovery applies to the Court but some subsidy from central government is inevitable in respect of those who are fees exempt or for whom a waiver is applied.

'prescribe fees' (s 54(1))—See Court of Protection Fees Order 2007, SI 2007/1745, as amended by Court of Protection Fees (Amendment) Order 2009, SI 2009/513.

55 Costs

(1) Subject to Court of Protection Rules, the costs of and incidental to all proceedings in the court are in its discretion.

(2) The rules may in particular make provision for regulating matters relating to the costs of those proceedings, including prescribing scales of costs to be paid to legal or other representatives.

(3) The court has full power to determine by whom and to what extent the costs are to be paid.

(4) The court may, in any proceedings –

(a) disallow, or

(b) order the legal or other representatives concerned to meet,

the whole of any wasted costs or such part of them as may be determined in accordance with the rules.

(5) 'Legal or other representative', in relation to a party to proceedings, means any person exercising a right of audience or right to conduct litigation on his behalf.

(6) 'Wasted costs' means any costs incurred by a party –

(a) as a result of any improper, unreasonable or negligent act or omission on the part of any legal or other representative or any employee of such a representative, or

(b) which, in the light of any such act or omission occurring after they were incurred, the court considers it is unreasonable to expect that party to pay.

Scope of provision—This section establishes the basic principle that the costs of and incidental to all proceedings are in the discretion of the Court and allows the rules to make provision for regulating the costs.

'Court of Protection Rules' (s 55(1))—See Court of Protection Rules 2007, SI 2007/1744, Part 19 (rr 155–168) and Practice Direction 19A.

'right of audience' (s 55(5))—General rights of audience are granted to duly qualified barristers or solicitors and a party may be represented at a trial or hearing in the courts by a person with these advocacy rights. Fellows of the Institute of Legal Executives and the Association of Law Costs Draftsmen also have limited advocacy rights. Employees of solicitors may appear at hearings 'in private'. The Court has a discretionary power to grant an unqualified person a right of audience in relation to particular proceedings before that court. See the Courts and Legal Services Act 1990, ss 27–28. The term 'lay representative' relates to a person who does not possess advocacy rights and may not even be a lawyer, but to whom the Court grants a right of audience on behalf of a party in relation to the proceedings before that Court. The party must apply at the outset of a hearing if he or she wishes an unqualified individual to be granted a right of audience – *Clarkson v Gilbert* [2000] 2 FLR 839, CA.

Decisions of the Court— see the case summaries in Part IX.

56 Fees and costs: supplementary

(1) Court of Protection Rules may make provision –

- (a)   as to the way in which, and funds from which, fees and costs are to be paid;
- (b)   for charging fees and costs upon the estate of the person to whom the proceedings relate;
- (c)   for the payment of fees and costs within a specified time of the death of the person to whom the proceedings relate or the conclusion of the proceedings.

(2) A charge on the estate of a person created by virtue of subsection (1)(b) does not cause any interest of the person in any property to fail or determine or to be prevented from recommencing.

The Public Guardian

57 The Public Guardian

(1) For the purposes of this Act, there is to be an officer, to be known as the Public Guardian.

(2) The Public Guardian is to be appointed by the Lord Chancellor.

(3) There is to be paid to the Public Guardian out of money provided by Parliament such salary as the Lord Chancellor may determine.

(4) The Lord Chancellor may, after consulting the Public Guardian –

- (a)   provide him with such officers and staff, or
- (b)   enter into such contracts with other persons for the provision (by them or their sub-contractors) of officers, staff or services,

as the Lord Chancellor thinks necessary for the proper discharge of the Public Guardian's functions.

(5) Any functions of the Public Guardian may, to the extent authorised by him, be performed by any of his officers.

Scope of provision—This section establishes a new a statutory office-holder known as the Public Guardian, with officers and staff to whom the functions of the office may be delegated. Hence the 'Office of the Public Guardian' which effectively replaces the former 'Public Guardianship Office'.

Further explanation—This topic is covered in Chapter 8.

58 Functions of the Public Guardian

(1) The Public Guardian has the following functions –

- (a)   establishing and maintaining a register of lasting powers of attorney,
- (b)   establishing and maintaining a register of orders appointing deputies,
- (c)   supervising deputies appointed by the court,
- (d)   directing a Court of Protection Visitor to visit –

PART III

> (i)   a donee of a lasting power of attorney,
> (ii) a deputy appointed by the court, or
> (iii) the person granting the power of attorney or for whom the deputy is appointed ('P'),
>
> and to make a report to the Public Guardian on such matters as he may direct,

(e) receiving security which the court requires a person to give for the discharge of his functions,

(f) receiving reports from donees of lasting powers of attorney and deputies appointed by the court,

(g) reporting to the court on such matters relating to proceedings under this Act as the court requires,

(h) dealing with representations (including complaints) about the way in which a donee of a lasting power of attorney or a deputy appointed by the court is exercising his powers,

(i) publishing, in any manner the Public Guardian thinks appropriate, any information he thinks appropriate about the discharge of his functions.

(2) The functions conferred by subsection (1)(c) and (h) may be discharged in co-operation with any other person who has functions in relation to the care or treatment of P.

(3) The Lord Chancellor may by regulations make provision –

(a) conferring on the Public Guardian other functions in connection with this Act;

(b) in connection with the discharge by the Public Guardian of his functions.

(4) Regulations made under subsection (3)(b) may in particular make provision as to –

(a) the giving of security by deputies appointed by the court and the enforcement and discharge of security so given;

(b) the fees which may be charged by the Public Guardian;

(c) the way in which, and funds from which, such fees are to be paid;

(d) exemptions from and reductions in such fees;

(e) remission of such fees in whole or in part;

(f) the making of reports to the Public Guardian by deputies appointed by the court and others who are directed by the court to carry out any transaction for a person who lacks capacity.

(5) For the purpose of enabling him to carry out his functions, the Public Guardian may, at all reasonable times, examine and take copies of –

(a) any health record,

(b) any record of, or held by, a local authority and compiled in connection with a social services function, and

(c) any record held by a person registered under Part 2 of the Care Standards Act 2000 [or Chapter 2 of Part 1 of the Health and Social Care Act 2008],

so far as the record relates to P.

(6) The Public Guardian may also for that purpose interview P in private.

Amendment—Words in subsection (5)(c) inserted by SI 2010/813.

Scope of provision—This section defines the basic functions and powers of the Public Guardian but more may be added by regulations made by the Lord Chancellor.

Further explanation—This topic is covered in Chapter 8.

'**supervising deputies**' (s 58(1)(c))—The Public Guardian's power or duty to 'supervise' extends only to deputies appointed by the Court. The Public Guardian has further powers in respect of donees of lasting powers of attorney or attorneys under enduring powers of attorney under the Lasting Power of Attorney, Enduring Power of Attorney and Public Guardian Regulations 2007, SI 2007/1253, regs 46 and 47.

'**directing a Court of Protection Visitor**' (s 58(1)(d))—The Public Guardian may himself or herself direct a visit if it is in connection with an investigation or report that the Public Guardian has been directed to carry out by the Court.

'**Report**' (s 58(1)(d))—The Public Guardian may require a report by a Court of Protection Visitor independently of the Court of Protection.

'**receiving reports**' (s 58(1)(f))—The Public Guardian may receive reports, but it is for the Court to order that a report be made to the Public Guardian – see s 23(3).

'**Regulations**' (s 58(3)(b))—See the Lasting Power of Attorney, Enduring Power of Attorney and Public Guardian Regulations 2007, SI 2007/1253; Lasting Powers of Attorney, Enduring Powers of Attorney and Public Guardian (Amendment) Regulations 2007, SI 2007/2161 and Lasting Powers of Attorney, Enduring Powers of Attorney and Public Guardian (Amendment) Regulations 2009, SI 2009/1884.

'**Regulations**' (s 58(4))—Public Guardian (Fees, etc) Regulations 2007, SI 2007/2051; Public Guardian (Fees, etc) (Amendment) Regulations 2007, SI 2007/2616; and Public Guardian (Fees, etc) (Amendment) Regulations 2009, SI 2009/514.

59 Public Guardian Board

(1) There is to be a body, to be known as the Public Guardian Board.

(2) The Board's duty is to scrutinise and review the way in which the Public Guardian discharges his functions and to make such recommendations to the Lord Chancellor about that matter as it thinks appropriate.

(3) The Lord Chancellor must, in discharging his functions under sections 57 and 58, give due consideration to recommendations made by the Board.

(4) ...

(5) The Board must have –

  (a) at least one member who is a judge of the court, and
  (b) at least four members who are persons appearing to the Lord Chancellor to have appropriate knowledge or experience of the work of the Public Guardian.

[(5A) Where a person to be appointed as a member of the Board is a judge of the court, the appointment is to be made by the Lord Chief Justice after consulting the Lord Chancellor.

(5B) In any other case, the appointment of a person as a member of the Board is to be made by the Lord Chancellor.]

(6) The Lord Chancellor may by regulations make provision as to –

  (a) the appointment of members of the Board (and, in particular, the procedures to be followed in connection with appointments);
  (b) the selection of one of the members to be the chairman;
  (c) the term of office of the chairman and members;
  (d) their resignation, suspension or removal;
  (e) the procedure of the Board (including quorum);

    (f)   the validation of proceedings in the event of a vacancy among the members or a defect in the appointment of a member.

(7) Subject to any provision made in reliance on subsection (6)(c) or (d), a person is to hold and vacate office as a member of the Board in accordance with the terms of the instrument appointing him.

(8) The Lord Chancellor may make such payments to or in respect of members of the Board by way of reimbursement of expenses, allowances and remuneration as he may determine.

(9) The Board must make an annual report to the Lord Chancellor about the discharge of its functions.

[(10) The Lord Chief Justice may nominate any of the following to exercise his functions under this section –

    (a)   the President of the Court of Protection;
    (b)   a judicial office holder (as defined in section 109(4) of the Constitutional Reform Act 2005).]

Amendments—SI 2006/1016.

Scope of provision—This section creates the Public Guardian Board whose duty is to scrutinise and review the way in which the Public Guardian discharges his or her functions.

Regulations (s 59(6))—Public Guardian Board Regulations 2007, SI 2007/1770.

Annual report—The Board must make an annual report. The first such report is available through the website—www.publicguardian.gov.uk.

60 Annual report

(1) The Public Guardian must make an annual report to the Lord Chancellor about the discharge of his functions.

(2) The Lord Chancellor must, within one month of receiving the report, lay a copy of it before Parliament.

Scope of provision—This section requires the Public Guardian to make an annual report.

Annual report—The first annual report is available through the website: www.publicguardian.gov.uk.

Court of Protection Visitors

61 Court of Protection Visitors

(1) A Court of Protection Visitor is a person who is appointed by the Lord Chancellor to –

    (a)   a panel of Special Visitors, or
    (b)   a panel of General Visitors.

(2) A person is not qualified to be a Special Visitor unless he –

    (a)   is a registered medical practitioner or appears to the Lord Chancellor to have other suitable qualifications or training, and

(b) appears to the Lord Chancellor to have special knowledge of and experience in cases of impairment of or disturbance in the functioning of the mind or brain.

(3) A General Visitor need not have a medical qualification.

(4) A Court of Protection Visitor –

(a) may be appointed for such term and subject to such conditions, and
(b) may be paid such remuneration and allowances,

as the Lord Chancellor may determine.

(5) For the purpose of carrying out his functions under this Act in relation to a person who lacks capacity ('P'), a Court of Protection Visitor may, at all reasonable times, examine and take copies of –

(a) any health record,
(b) any record of, or held by, a local authority and compiled in connection with a social services function, and
(c) any record held by a person registered under Part 2 of the Care Standards Act 2000 [or Chapter 2 of Part 1 of the Health and Social Care Act 2008],

so far as the record relates to P.

(6) A Court of Protection Visitor may also for that purpose interview P in private.

Amendment—Words in subsection (5)(c) inserted by SI 2010/813.

Scope of provision—The former Lord Chancellor's Visitors are recreated as Court of Protection Visitors though with some variation.

Further explanation—This topic is covered in Chapter 8.

'Special Visitor'—This will be a medical visitor, usually a consultant psychiatrist, who is asked to report (inter alia) on capacity issues.

Reports—The Visitors may be required to prepare reports for the Court of Protection (s 49(2)) or the Public Guardian (s 58(1)(d)).

PART 3
MISCELLANEOUS AND GENERAL

Declaratory provision

62 Scope of the Act

For the avoidance of doubt, it is hereby declared that nothing in this Act is to be taken to affect the law relating to murder or manslaughter or the operation of section 2 of the Suicide Act 1961 (assisting suicide).

'section 2 of the Suicide Act 1961'—It is an offence to aid, abet, counsel or procure the suicide, or attempted suicide, of another, but no prosecution may be brought without the consent of the Director of Public Prosecutions.

Private international law

63 International protection of adults

Schedule 3 –

(a)   gives effect in England and Wales to the Convention on the International
       Protection of Adults signed at the Hague on 13th January 2000 (Cm. 5881)
       (in so far as this Act does not otherwise do so), and

(b)   makes related provision as to the private international law of England and
       Wales.

Convention on the International Protection of Adults—Under the auspices of the Hague
Conference on Private International Law (which aims to establish international agreements to reduce
conflicts of law and to lay down rules to determine jurisdiction and related matters) this Convention
(No 35) was concluded on 13 January 2000. It came into force on 1 January 2009. So far six
countries have ratified – the UK (in relation to Scotland), Estonia (with effect from 1 November
2011), Finland,France, Germany and Switzerland. Its provisions are explained in Part X at **?**. For a
full text see www.hcch.net.

General

64 Interpretation

(1) In this Act –

'the 1985 Act' means the Enduring Powers of Attorney Act 1985,
'advance decision' has the meaning given in section 24(1),
['authorisation under Schedule A1' means either –
    (a)   a standard authorisation under that Schedule, or
    (b)   an urgent authorisation under that Schedule;]
'the court' means the Court of Protection established by section 45,
'Court of Protection Rules' has the meaning given in section 51(1),
'Court of Protection Visitor' has the meaning given in section 61,
'deputy' has the meaning given in section 16(2)(b),
'enactment' includes a provision of subordinate legislation (within the meaning
    of the Interpretation Act 1978),
'health record' has the meaning given in section 68 of the Data Protection
    Act 1998 (as read with section 69 of that Act),
'the Human Rights Convention' has the same meaning as 'the Convention' in the
    Human Rights Act 1998,
'independent mental capacity advocate' has the meaning given in section 35(1),
'lasting power of attorney' has the meaning given in section 9,
'life-sustaining treatment' has the meaning given in section 4(10),
'local authority'[, except in Schedule A1,] means –
    (a)   the council of a county in England in which there are no district
       councils,
    (b)   the council of a district in England,
    (c)   the council of a county or county borough in Wales,
    (d)   the council of a London borough,
    (e)   the Common Council of the City of London, or
    (f)   the Council of the Isles of Scilly,
'Mental Health Act' means the Mental Health Act 1983,
'prescribed', in relation to regulations made under this Act, means prescribed by
    those regulations,
'property' includes any thing in action and any interest in real or personal
    property,
'public authority' has the same meaning as in the Human Rights Act 1998,
'Public Guardian' has the meaning given in section 57,
'purchaser' and 'purchase' have the meaning given in section 205(1) of the Law
    of Property Act 1925,

'social services function' has the meaning given in section 1A of the Local
Authority Social Services Act 1970,

'treatment' includes a diagnostic or other procedure,

'trust corporation' has the meaning given in section 68(1) of the Trustee
Act 1925, and

'will' includes codicil.

(2) In this Act, references to making decisions, in relation to a donee of a lasting
power of attorney or a deputy appointed by the court, include, where appropriate,
acting on decisions made.

(3) In this Act, references to the bankruptcy of an individual include a case where a
bankruptcy restrictions order under the Insolvency Act 1986 has effect in respect of
him.

(4) 'Bankruptcy restrictions order' includes an interim bankruptcy restrictions order.

[(5) In this Act, references to deprivation of a person's liberty have the same
meaning as in Article 5(1) of the Human Rights Convention.

(6) For the purposes of such references, it does not matter whether a person is
deprived of his liberty by a public authority or not.]

Amendment—Words and paras in square brackets inserted by the Mental Health Act 2007, s 50(7),
Sch 9, Pt 1, paras 1, 10(1)-(4).

Scope of provision—This section provides an interpretation of some of the terms used in the Act.

65 Rules, regulations and orders

(1) Any power to make rules, regulations or orders under this Act[, other than the
power in section 21] –

    (a)   is exercisable by statutory instrument;

    (b)   includes power to make supplementary, incidental, consequential,
transitional or saving provision;

    (c)   includes power to make different provision for different cases.

(2) Any statutory instrument containing rules, regulations or orders made by the
Lord Chancellor or the Secretary of State under this Act, other than –

    (a)   regulations under section 34 (loss of capacity during research project),

    (b)   regulations under section 41 (adjusting role of independent mental capacity
advocacy service),

    (c)   regulations under paragraph 32(1)(b) of Schedule 3 (private international
law relating to the protection of adults),

    (d)   an order of the kind mentioned in section 67(6) (consequential
amendments of primary legislation), or

    (e)   an order under section 68 (commencement),

is subject to annulment in pursuance of a resolution of either House of Parliament.

(3) A statutory instrument containing an Order in Council under paragraph 31 of
Schedule 3 (provision to give further effect to Hague Convention) is subject to
annulment in pursuance of a resolution of either House of Parliament.

(4) A statutory instrument containing regulations made by the Secretary of State
under section 34 or 41 or by the Lord Chancellor under paragraph 32(1)(b) of
Schedule 3 may not be made unless a draft has been laid before and approved by
resolution of each House of Parliament.

[(4A) Subsection (2) does not apply to a statutory instrument containing regulations made by the Secretary of State under Schedule A1.

(4B) If such a statutory instrument contains regulations under paragraph 42(2)(b), 129, 162 or 164 of Schedule A1 (whether or not it also contains other regulations), the instrument may not be made unless a draft has been laid before and approved by resolution of each House of Parliament.

(4C) Subject to that, such a statutory instrument is subject to annulment in pursuance of a resolution of either House of Parliament.]

[(5) An order under section 21 –

    (a)   may include supplementary, incidental, consequential, transitional or saving provision;
    (b)   may make different provision for different cases;
    (c)   is to be made in the form of a statutory instrument to which the Statutory Instruments Act 1946 applies as if the order were made by a Minister of the Crown; and
    (d)   is subject to annulment in pursuance of a resolution of either House of Parliament.]

Amendments—SI 2006/1016. Subsections (4A)–(4C) inserted by the Mental Health Act 2007, s 50(7), Sch 9, Pt 1, paras 1, 11.

66 Existing receivers and enduring powers of attorney etc

(1) The following provisions cease to have effect –

    (a)   Part 7 of the Mental Health Act,
    (b)   the Enduring Powers of Attorney Act 1985.

(2) No enduring power of attorney within the meaning of the 1985 Act is to be created after the commencement of subsection (1)(b).

(3) Schedule 4 has effect in place of the 1985 Act in relation to any enduring power of attorney created before the commencement of subsection (1)(b).

(4) Schedule 5 contains transitional provisions and savings in relation to Part 7 of the Mental Health Act and the 1985 Act.

Scope of provision—The former jurisdiction in regard to the financial affairs of 'patients' under MHA 1983, Part 7 has been replaced by MCA 2005 subject to transitional provisions in Sch 5, and the Enduring Powers of Attorney Act 1985 has ceased to have effect save that its provisions have in effect been repeated in Sch 4 to the MCA 2005 in respect of those powers executed before 1 October 2007.

67 Minor and consequential amendments and repeals

(1) Schedule 6 contains minor and consequential amendments.

(2) Schedule 7 contains repeals.

(3) The Lord Chancellor may by order make supplementary, incidental, consequential, transitional or saving provision for the purposes of, in consequence of, or for giving full effect to a provision of this Act.

(4) An order under subsection (3) may, in particular –

    (a)   provide for a provision of this Act which comes into force before another provision of this Act has come into force to have effect, until the other provision has come into force, with specified modifications;

(b)   amend, repeal or revoke an enactment, other than one contained in an Act or Measure passed in a Session after the one in which this Act is passed.

(5) The amendments that may be made under subsection (4)(b) are in addition to those made by or under any other provision of this Act.

(6) An order under subsection (3) which amends or repeals a provision of an Act or Measure may not be made unless a draft has been laid before and approved by resolution of each House of Parliament.

68 Commencement and extent

(1) This Act, other than sections 30 to 41, comes into force in accordance with provision made by order by the Lord Chancellor.

(2) Sections 30 to 41 come into force in accordance with provision made by order by –

(a)   the Secretary of State, in relation to England, and

(b)   the National Assembly for Wales, in relation to Wales.

(3) An order under this section may appoint different days for different provisions and different purposes.

(4) Subject to subsections (5) and (6), this Act extends to England and Wales only.

(5) The following provisions extend to the United Kingdom –

(a)   paragraph 16(1) of Schedule 1 (evidence of instruments and of registration of lasting powers of attorney),

(b)   paragraph 15(3) of Schedule 4 (evidence of instruments and of registration of enduring powers of attorney).

(6) Subject to any provision made in Schedule 6, the amendments and repeals made by Schedules 6 and 7 have the same extent as the enactments to which they relate.

Scope of provision—Most of the provisions of the original Act came into effect for England and Wales on 1 October 2007 though some were implemented earlier.

Orders—Mental Capacity Act 2005 (Commencement No 1) Order 2006, SI 2006/2814 (as amended by SI 2006/3473); Mental Capacity Act 2005 (Commencement No 1)(England and Wales) Order 2007, SI 2007/563; Mental Capacity Act 2005 (Commencement) (Wales) Order 2007, SI 2007/856; and Mental Capacity Act 2005 (Commencement No 2) Order 2007, SI 2007/1897.

69 Short title

This Act may be cited as the Mental Capacity Act 2005.

SCHEDULES

[SCHEDULE A1
HOSPITAL AND CARE HOME RESIDENTS: DEPRIVATION OF LIBERTY

PART 1
AUTHORISATION TO DEPRIVE RESIDENTS OF LIBERTY ETC

Application of Part

1 (1) This Part applies if the following conditions are met.

(2) The first condition is that a person ('P') is detained in a hospital or care home –for the purpose of being given care or treatment –in circumstances which amount to deprivation of the person's liberty.

(3) The second condition is that a standard or urgent authorisation is in force.

(4) The third condition is that the standard or urgent authorisation relates –

  (a)   to P, and
  (b)   to the hospital or care home in which P is detained.

Amendment—Schedule A1 inserted by the Mental Health Act 2007, s 50(5), Sch 7. This schedule below and related provisions above, which amend the Act to provide deprivation of liberty safeguards, were commenced on 1 April 2009 (the Mental Health Act 2007 (Commencement No 10 and Transitional Provisions) Order 2009, SI 2009/139 (C.9)). They are outlined in Chapter 6 of the book. The nature and effect of the deprivation of liberty safeguards are discussed in Chapter 6 at **6.14–6.44**.

Authorisation to deprive P of liberty

2 The managing authority of the hospital or care home may deprive P of his liberty by detaining him as mentioned in paragraph 1(2).

'Deprive P of his liberty'—See discussion at **6.16–6.19**.

No liability for acts done for purpose of depriving P of liberty

3 (1) This paragraph applies to any act which a person ('D') does for the purpose of detaining P as mentioned in paragraph 1(2).

(2) D does not incur any liability in relation to the act that he would not have incurred if P –

  (a)   had had capacity to consent in relation to D's doing the act, and
  (b)   had consented to D's doing the act.

No protection for negligent acts etc

4 (1) Paragraphs 2 and 3 do not exclude a person's civil liability for loss or damage, or his criminal liability, resulting from his negligence in doing any thing.

(2) Paragraphs 2 and 3 do not authorise a person to do anything otherwise than for the purpose of the standard or urgent authorisation that is in force.

(3) In a case where a standard authorisation is in force, paragraphs 2 and 3 do not authorise a person to do anything which does not comply with the conditions (if any) included in the authorisation.

PART 2
INTERPRETATION: MAIN TERMS

Introduction

5 This Part applies for the purposes of this Schedule.

Detained resident

6 'Detained resident' means a person detained in a hospital or care home –for the purpose of being given care or treatment –in circumstances which amount to deprivation of the person's liberty.

Relevant person etc

7 In relation to a person who is, or is to be, a detained resident –

'relevant person' means the person in question;
'relevant hospital or care home' means the hospital or care home in question;
'relevant care or treatment' means the care or treatment in question.

Authorisations

8 'Standard authorisation' means an authorisation given under Part 4.

9 'Urgent authorisation' means an authorisation given under Part 5.

10 'Authorisation under this Schedule' means either of the following –

(a)   a standard authorisation;
(b)   an urgent authorisation.

11 (1) The purpose of a standard authorisation is the purpose which is stated in the authorisation in accordance with paragraph 55(1)(d).

(2) The purpose of an urgent authorisation is the purpose which is stated in the authorisation in accordance with paragraph 80(d).

PART 3
THE QUALIFYING REQUIREMENTS

The qualifying requirements

12 (1) These are the qualifying requirements referred to in this Schedule –

(a)   the age requirement;
(b)   the mental health requirement;

(c)   the mental capacity requirement;
(d)   the best interests requirement;
(e)   the eligibility requirement;
(f)   the no refusals requirement.

(2) Any question of whether a person who is, or is to be, a detained resident meets the qualifying requirements is to be determined in accordance with this Part.

(3) In a case where –

(a)   the question of whether a person meets a particular qualifying requirement arises in relation to the giving of a standard authorisation, and

(b)   any circumstances relevant to determining that question are expected to change between the time when the determination is made and the time when the authorisation is expected to come into force,

those circumstances are to be taken into account as they are expected to be at the later time.

The age requirement

13 The relevant person meets the age requirement if he has reached 18.

The mental health requirement

14 (1) The relevant person meets the mental health requirement if he is suffering from mental disorder (within the meaning of the Mental Health Act, but disregarding any exclusion for persons with learning disability).

(2) An exclusion for persons with learning disability is any provision of the Mental Health Act which provides for a person with learning disability not to be regarded as suffering from mental disorder for one or more purposes of that Act.

'mental disorder' (para 14(1))—Defined as 'any disorder or disability of the mind' (MHA 1983 (as amended), s 1(2)).

'learning disability' (para 14(1))—Defined as 'a state of arrested or incomplete development of the mind which includes significant impairment of intelligence and social functioning' (MHA 1983 (as amended), s 1(4)).

'exclusion for persons with learning disability' (para 14(2))—Under MHA 1983, a person with learning disability is not to be regarded as suffering from mental disorder unless that disability 'is associated with abnormally aggressive or seriously irresponsible conduct' (MHA 1983 (as amended), s 1(2A)). This exclusion should be disregarded for the purpose of applying the deprivation of liberty safeguards.

The mental capacity requirement

15 The relevant person meets the mental capacity requirement if he lacks capacity in relation to the question whether or not he should be accommodated in the relevant hospital or care home for the purpose of being given the relevant care or treatment.

'lacks capacity'   Defined in MCA 2005, ss 2–3.

The best interests requirement

16 (1) The relevant person meets the best interests requirement if all of the following conditions are met.

(2) The first condition is that the relevant person is, or is to be, a detained resident.

(3) The second condition is that it is in the best interests of the relevant person for him to be a detained resident.

(4) The third condition is that, in order to prevent harm to the relevant person, it is necessary for him to be a detained resident.

(5) The fourth condition is that it is a proportionate response to –

    (a)   the likelihood of the relevant person suffering harm, and
    (b)   the seriousness of that harm,

for him to be a detained resident.

'best interests' (para 16(1))—Defined in MCA 2005, s 4. See Chapter 2.

'harm' (para 16(5))—For a discussion on the meaning of 'harm' see Chapter 2 (at **2.138**).

The eligibility requirement

17 (1) The relevant person meets the eligibility requirement unless he is ineligible to be deprived of liberty by this Act.

(2) Schedule 1A applies for the purpose of determining whether or not P is ineligible to be deprived of liberty by this Act.

'eligibility' (para 17(1))—The eligibility requirement and the interface between MCA 2005 and MHA 1983 were considered by Roderick Wood J in *W PCT v TB (an adult by her litigation friend the Official Solicitor)* [2009] EWHC 1737 (Fam) and by Charles J in *GJ v The Foundation Trust* [2009] EWHC 2972 (Fam).

The no refusals requirement

18 The relevant person meets the no refusals requirement unless there is a refusal within the meaning of paragraph 19 or 20.

19 (1) There is a refusal if these conditions are met –

    (a)   the relevant person has made an advance decision;
    (b)   the advance decision is valid;
    (c)   the advance decision is applicable to some or all of the relevant treatment.

(2) Expressions used in this paragraph and any of sections 24, 25 or 26 have the same meaning in this paragraph as in that section.

'advance decision'—See Chapter 5.

20 (1) There is a refusal if it would be in conflict with a valid decision of a donee or deputy for the relevant person to be accommodated in the relevant hospital or care home for the purpose of receiving some or all of the relevant care or treatment –

    (a)   in circumstances which amount to deprivation of the person's liberty, or
    (b)   at all.

(2) A donee is a donee of a lasting power of attorney granted by the relevant person.

(3) A decision of a donee or deputy is valid if it is made –

    (a)   within the scope of his authority as donee or deputy, and

    (b)   in accordance with Part 1 of this Act.

'donee of a lasting power of attorney'—See Chapter 3.

'deputy'—See Chapter 4.

PART 4
STANDARD AUTHORISATIONS

Supervisory body to give authorisation

21 Only the supervisory body may give a standard authorisation.

'the supervisory body'—See definitions at paras 180–182 of this Schedule.

22 The supervisory body may not give a standard authorisation unless –

    (a)   the managing authority of the relevant hospital or care home have requested it, or

    (b)   paragraph 71 applies (right of third party to require consideration of whether authorisation needed).

'the managing authority'—See definitions at paras 176,177 and 179 of this Schedule.

23

The managing authority may not make a request for a standard authorisation unless –

    (a)   they are required to do so by paragraph 24 (as read with paragraphs 27 to 29),

    (b)   they are required to do so by paragraph 25 (as read with paragraph 28), or

    (c)   they are permitted to do so by paragraph 30.

Duty to request authorisation: basic cases

24 (1) The managing authority must request a standard authorisation in any of the following cases.

(2) The first case is where it appears to the managing authority that the relevant person –

    (a)   is not yet accommodated in the relevant hospital or care home,

    (b)   is likely –at some time within the next 28 days –to be a detained resident in the relevant hospital or care home, and

    (c)   is likely –

        (i)   at that time, or

        (ii) at some later time within the next 28 days,

        to meet all of the qualifying requirements.

(3) The second case is where it appears to the managing authority that the relevant person –

(a)   is already accommodated in the relevant hospital or care home,

(b)   is likely –at some time within the next 28 days –to be a detained resident in the relevant hospital or care home, and

(c)   is likely –
 (i)   at that time, or
 (ii)   at some later time within the next 28 days,
 to meet all of the qualifying requirements.

(4) The third case is where it appears to the managing authority that the relevant person –

(a)   is a detained resident in the relevant hospital or care home, and

(b)   meets all of the qualifying requirements, or is likely to do so at some time within the next 28 days.

(5) This paragraph is subject to paragraphs 27 to 29.

Duty to request authorisation: change in place of detention

25 (1) The relevant managing authority must request a standard authorisation if it appears to them that these conditions are met.

(2) The first condition is that a standard authorisation –

(a)   has been given, and

(b)   has not ceased to be in force.

(3) The second condition is that there is, or is to be, a change in the place of detention.

(4) This paragraph is subject to paragraph 28.

26 (1) This paragraph applies for the purposes of paragraph 25.

(2) There is a change in the place of detention if the relevant person –

(a)   ceases to be a detained resident in the stated hospital or care home, and

(b)   becomes a detained resident in a different hospital or care home ('the new hospital or care home').

(3) The stated hospital or care home is the hospital or care home to which the standard authorisation relates.

(4) The relevant managing authority are the managing authority of the new hospital or care home.

Other authority for detention: request for authorisation

27 (1) This paragraph applies if, by virtue of section 4A(3), a decision of the court authorises the relevant person to be a detained resident.

(2) Paragraph 24 does not require a request for a standard authorisation to be made in relation to that detention unless these conditions are met.

(3) The first condition is that the standard authorisation would be in force at a time immediately after the expiry of the other authority.

(4) The second condition is that the standard authorisation would not be in force at any time on or before the expiry of the other authority.

(5) The third condition is that it would, in the managing authority's view, be unreasonable to delay making the request until a time nearer the expiry of the other authority.

(6) In this paragraph –

    (a)   the other authority is –

        (i)   the decision mentioned in sub-paragraph (1), or

        (ii) any further decision of the court which, by virtue of section 4A(3), authorises, or is expected to authorise, the relevant person to be a detained resident;

    (b)   the expiry of the other authority is the time when the other authority is expected to cease to authorise the relevant person to be a detained resident.

Request refused: no further request unless change of circumstances

28 (1) This paragraph applies if –

    (a)   a managing authority request a standard authorisation under paragraph 24 or 25, and

    (b)   the supervisory body are prohibited by paragraph 50(2) from giving the authorisation.

(2) Paragraph 24 or 25 does not require that managing authority to make a new request for a standard authorisation unless it appears to the managing authority that –

    (a)   there has been a change in the relevant person's case, and

    (b)   because of that change, the supervisory body are likely to give a standard authorisation if requested.

Authorisation given: request for further authorisation

29 (1) This paragraph applies if a standard authorisation –

    (a)   has been given in relation to the detention of the relevant person, and

    (b)   that authorisation ('the existing authorisation') has not ceased to be in force.

(2) Paragraph 24 does not require a new request for a standard authorisation ('the new authorisation') to be made unless these conditions are met.

(3) The first condition is that the new authorisation would be in force at a time immediately after the expiry of the existing authorisation.

(4) The second condition is that the new authorisation would not be in force at any time on or before the expiry of the existing authorisation.

(5) The third condition is that it would, in the managing authority's view, be unreasonable to delay making the request until a time nearer the expiry of the existing authorisation.

(6) The expiry of the existing authorisation is the time when it is expected to cease to be in force.

Power to request authorisation

30 (1) This paragraph applies if –

(a) a standard authorisation has been given in relation to the detention of the relevant person,

(b) that authorisation ('the existing authorisation') has not ceased to be in force,

(c) the requirement under paragraph 24 to make a request for a new standard authorisation does not apply, because of paragraph 29, and

(d) a review of the existing authorisation has been requested, or is being carried out, in accordance with Part 8.

(2) The managing authority may request a new standard authorisation which would be in force on or before the expiry of the existing authorisation; but only if it would also be in force immediately after that expiry.

(3) The expiry of the existing authorisation is the time when it is expected to cease to be in force.

(4) Further provision relating to cases where a request is made under this paragraph can be found in –

(a) paragraph 62 (effect of decision about request), and

(b) paragraph 124 (effect of request on Part 8 review).

Information included in request

31 A request for a standard authorisation must include the information (if any) required by regulations.

'information ... required by regulations'—See the Mental Capacity (Deprivation of Liberty—Standard Authorisations, Assessments and Ordinary Residence) Regulations 2008, SI 2008/1858, reg 16 (text reproduced in Part V of this book) (and in relation to Wales, see SI 2009/266).

Records of requests

32 (1) The managing authority of a hospital or care home must keep a written record of –

(a) each request that they make for a standard authorisation, and

(b) the reasons for making each request.

(2) A supervisory body must keep a written record of each request for a standard authorisation that is made to them.

Relevant person must be assessed

33 (1) This paragraph applies if the supervisory body are requested to give a standard authorisation.

(2) The supervisory body must secure that all of these assessments are carried out in relation to the relevant person –

(a) an age assessment;

(b) a mental health assessment;

    (c)   a mental capacity assessment;

    (d)   a best interests assessment;

    (e)   an eligibility assessment;

    (f)   a no refusals assessment.

(3) The person who carries out any such assessment is referred to as the assessor.

(4) Regulations may be made about the period (or periods) within which assessors must carry out assessments.

(5) This paragraph is subject to paragraphs 49 and 133.

'Regulations' (para 33(4))—See the Mental Capacity (Deprivation of Liberty—Standard Authorisations, Assessments and Ordinary Residence) Regulations 2008, SI 2008/1858, regs 13 and 14 (text reproduced in Part V of this book).

Age assessment

34 An age assessment is an assessment of whether the relevant person meets the age requirement.

Mental health assessment

35 A mental health assessment is an assessment of whether the relevant person meets the mental health requirement.

36 When carrying out a mental health assessment, the assessor must also –

    (a)   consider how (if at all) the relevant person's mental health is likely to be affected by his being a detained resident, and

    (b)   notify the best interests assessor of his conclusions.

Mental capacity assessment

37 A mental capacity assessment is an assessment of whether the relevant person meets the mental capacity requirement.

Best interests assessment

38 A best interests assessment is an assessment of whether the relevant person meets the best interests requirement.

39 (1) In carrying out a best interests assessment, the assessor must comply with the duties in sub-paragraphs (2) and (3).

(2) The assessor must consult the managing authority of the relevant hospital or care home.

(3) The assessor must have regard to all of the following –

    (a)   the conclusions which the mental health assessor has notified to the best interests assessor in accordance with paragraph 36(b);

    (b)   any relevant needs assessment;

    (c)   any relevant care plan.

(4) A relevant needs assessment is an assessment of the relevant person's needs which –

    (a)   was carried out in connection with the relevant person being accommodated in the relevant hospital or care home, and

    (b)   was carried out by or on behalf of –

        (i)   the managing authority of the relevant hospital or care home, or

        (ii) the supervisory body.

(5) A relevant care plan is a care plan which –

    (a)   sets out how the relevant person's needs are to be met whilst he is accommodated in the relevant hospital or care home, and

    (b)   was drawn up by or on behalf of –

        (i)   the managing authority of the relevant hospital or care home, or

        (ii) the supervisory body.

(6) The managing authority must give the assessor a copy of –

    (a)   any relevant needs assessment carried out by them or on their behalf, or

    (b)   any relevant care plan drawn up by them or on their behalf.

(7) The supervisory body must give the assessor a copy of –

    (a)   any relevant needs assessment carried out by them or on their behalf, or

    (b)   any relevant care plan drawn up by them or on their behalf.

(8) The duties in sub-paragraphs (2) and (3) do not affect any other duty to consult or to take the views of others into account.

40 (1) This paragraph applies whatever conclusion the best interests assessment comes to.

(2) The assessor must state in the best interests assessment the name and address of every interested person whom he has consulted in carrying out the assessment.

41 Paragraphs 42 and 43 apply if the best interests assessment comes to the conclusion that the relevant person meets the best interests requirement.

42 (1) The assessor must state in the assessment the maximum authorisation period.

(2) The maximum authorisation period is the shorter of these periods –

    (a)   the period which, in the assessor's opinion, would be the appropriate maximum period for the relevant person to be a detained resident under the standard authorisation that has been requested;

    (b)   1 year, or such shorter period as may be prescribed in regulations.

(3) Regulations under sub-paragraph (2)(b) –

    (a)   need not provide for a shorter period to apply in relation to all standard authorisations;

    (b)   may provide for different periods to apply in relation to different kinds of standard authorisations.

(4) Before making regulations under sub-paragraph (2)(b) the Secretary of State must consult all of the following –

(a)   each body required by regulations under paragraph 162 to monitor and report on the operation of this Schedule in relation to England;

(b)   such other persons as the Secretary of State considers it appropriate to consult.

(5) Before making regulations under sub-paragraph (2)(b) the National Assembly for Wales must consult all of the following –

(a)   each person or body directed under paragraph 163(2) to carry out any function of the Assembly of monitoring and reporting on the operation of this Schedule in relation to Wales;

(b)   such other persons as the Assembly considers it appropriate to consult.

'prescribed in regulations' (para 42(2)(b))—The power has not yet been exercised.

43   The assessor may include in the assessment recommendations about conditions to which the standard authorisation is, or is not, to be subject in accordance with paragraph 53.

44   (1) This paragraph applies if the best interests assessment comes to the conclusion that the relevant person does not meet the best interests requirement.

(2) If, on the basis of the information taken into account in carrying out the assessment, it appears to the assessor that there is an unauthorised deprivation of liberty, he must include a statement to that effect in the assessment.

(3) There is an unauthorised deprivation of liberty if the managing authority of the relevant hospital or care home are already depriving the relevant person of his liberty without authority of the kind mentioned in section 4A.

45   The duties with which the best interests assessor must comply are subject to the provision included in appointment regulations under Part 10 (in particular, provision made under paragraph 146).

'appointment regulations'—Mental Capacity (Deprivation of Liberty—Appointment of Relevant Person's Representative) Regulations 2008, SI 2008/1315 (as amended by SI 2008/2368) (text reproduced in Part V of this book). For Wales, see the Mental Capacity (Deprivation of Liberty: Appointment of Relevant Person's Representative) (Wales) Regulations 2009, SI 2009/266. No provision has as yet been made under para 146.

Eligibility assessment

46   An eligibility assessment is an assessment of whether the relevant person meets the eligibility requirement.

47   (1) Regulations may –

(a)   require an eligibility assessor to request a best interests assessor to provide relevant eligibility information, and

(b)   require the best interests assessor, if such a request is made, to provide such relevant eligibility information as he may have.

(2) In this paragraph –

'best interests assessor' means any person who is carrying out, or has carried out, a best interests assessment in relation to the relevant person;

'eligibility assessor' means a person carrying out an eligibility assessment in relation to the relevant person;

'relevant eligibility information' is information relevant to assessing whether or not the relevant person is ineligible by virtue of paragraph 5 of Schedule 1A.

'Regulations may' (para 47(1))—See the Mental Capacity (Deprivation of Liberty—Standard Authorisations, Assessments and Ordinary Residence) Regulations 2008, SI 2008/1858, reg 15 (text reproduced in Part V of this book).

No refusals assessment

48 A no refusals assessment is an assessment of whether the relevant person meets the no refusals requirement.

Equivalent assessment already carried out

49 (1) The supervisory body are not required by paragraph 33 to secure that a particular kind of assessment ('the required assessment') is carried out in relation to the relevant person if the following conditions are met.

(2) The first condition is that the supervisory body have a written copy of an assessment of the relevant person ('the existing assessment') that has already been carried out.

(3) The second condition is that the existing assessment complies with all requirements under this Schedule with which the required assessment would have to comply (if it were carried out).

(4) The third condition is that the existing assessment was carried out within the previous 12 months; but this condition need not be met if the required assessment is an age assessment.

(5) The fourth condition is that the supervisory body are satisfied that there is no reason why the existing assessment may no longer be accurate.

(6) If the required assessment is a best interests assessment, in satisfying themselves as mentioned in sub-paragraph (5), the supervisory body must take into account any information given, or submissions made, by –

    (a)   the relevant person's representative,
    (b)   any section 39C IMCA, or
    (c)   any section 39D IMCA.

(7) It does not matter whether the existing assessment was carried out in connection with a request for a standard authorisation or for some other purpose.

(8) If, because of this paragraph, the supervisory body are not required by paragraph 33 to secure that the required assessment is carried out, the existing assessment is to be treated for the purposes of this Schedule –

    (a)   as an assessment of the same kind as the required assessment, and
    (b)   as having been carried out under paragraph 33 in connection with the request for the standard authorisation.

PART III

Duty to give authorisation

50 (1) The supervisory body must give a standard authorisation if –

(a)   all assessments are positive, and
(b)   the supervisory body have written copies of all those assessments.

(2) The supervisory body must not give a standard authorisation except in accordance with sub-paragraph (1).

(3) All assessments are positive if each assessment carried out under paragraph 33 has come to the conclusion that the relevant person meets the qualifying requirement to which the assessment relates.

Terms of authorisation

51 (1) If the supervisory body are required to give a standard authorisation, they must decide the period during which the authorisation is to be in force.

(2) That period must not exceed the maximum authorisation period stated in the best interests assessment.

52 A standard authorisation may provide for the authorisation to come into force at a time after it is given.

53 (1) A standard authorisation may be given subject to conditions.

(2) Before deciding whether to give the authorisation subject to conditions, the supervisory body must have regard to any recommendations in the best interests assessment about such conditions.

(3) The managing authority of the relevant hospital or care home must ensure that any conditions are complied with.

Form of authorisation

54 A standard authorisation must be in writing.

55 (1) A standard authorisation must state the following things –

(a)   the name of the relevant person;
(b)   the name of the relevant hospital or care home;
(c)   the period during which the authorisation is to be in force;
(d)   the purpose for which the authorisation is given;
(e)   any conditions subject to which the authorisation is given;
(f)   the reason why each qualifying requirement is met.

(2) The statement of the reason why the eligibility requirement is met must be framed by reference to the cases in the table in paragraph 2 of Schedule 1A.

56 (1) If the name of the relevant hospital or care home changes, the standard authorisation is to be read as if it stated the current name of the hospital or care home.

(2) But sub-paragraph (1) is subject to any provision relating to the change of name which is made in any enactment or in any instrument made under an enactment.

Duty to give information about decision

57 (1) This paragraph applies if –

    (a)   a request is made for a standard authorisation, and

    (b)   the supervisory body are required by paragraph 50(1) to give the standard authorisation.

(2) The supervisory body must give a copy of the authorisation to each of the following –

    (a)   the relevant person's representative;

    (b)   the managing authority of the relevant hospital or care home;

    (c)   the relevant person;

    (d)   any section 39A IMCA;

    (e)   every interested person consulted by the best interests assessor.

(3) The supervisory body must comply with this paragraph as soon as practicable after they give the standard authorisation.

58 (1) This paragraph applies if –

    (a)   a request is made for a standard authorisation, and

    (b)   the supervisory body are prohibited by paragraph 50(2) from giving the standard authorisation.

(2) The supervisory body must give notice, stating that they are prohibited from giving the authorisation, to each of the following –

    (a)   the managing authority of the relevant hospital or care home;

    (b)   the relevant person;

    (c)   any section 39A IMCA;

    (d)   every interested person consulted by the best interests assessor.

(3) The supervisory body must comply with this paragraph as soon as practicable after it becomes apparent to them that they are prohibited from giving the authorisation.

Duty to give information about effect of authorisation

59 (1) This paragraph applies if a standard authorisation is given.

(2) The managing authority of the relevant hospital or care home must take such steps as are practicable to ensure that the relevant person understands all of the following –

    (a)   the effect of the authorisation;

    (b)   the right to make an application to the court to exercise its jurisdiction under section 21A;

    (c)   the right under Part 8 to request a review;

    (d)   the right to have a section 39D IMCA appointed;

    (e)   how to have a section 39D IMCA appointed.

(3) Those steps must be taken as soon as is practicable after the authorisation is given.

(4) Those steps must include the giving of appropriate information both orally and in writing.

(5) Any written information given to the relevant person must also be given by the managing authority to the relevant person's representative.

(6) They must give the information to the representative as soon as is practicable after it is given to the relevant person.

(7) Sub-paragraph (8) applies if the managing authority is notified that a section 39D IMCA has been appointed.

(8) As soon as is practicable after being notified, the managing authority must give the section 39D IMCA a copy of the written information given in accordance with sub-paragraph (4).

Records of authorisations

60

A supervisory body must keep a written record of all of the following information –

    (a)   the standard authorisations that they have given;
    (b)   the requests for standard authorisations in response to which they have not given an authorisation;
    (c)   in relation to each standard authorisation given: the matters stated in the authorisation in accordance with paragraph 55.

Variation of an authorisation

61

(1) A standard authorisation may not be varied except in accordance with Part 7 or 8.

(2) This paragraph does not affect the powers of the Court of Protection or of any other court.

Effect of decision about request made under paragraph 25 or 30

62 (1) This paragraph applies where the managing authority request a new standard authorisation under either of the following –

    (a)   paragraph 25 (change in place of detention);
    (b)   paragraph 30 (existing authorisation subject to review).

(2) If the supervisory body are required by paragraph 50(1) to give the new authorisation, the existing authorisation terminates at the time when the new authorisation comes into force.

(3) If the supervisory body are prohibited by paragraph 50(2) from giving the new authorisation, there is no effect on the existing authorisation's continuation in force.

When an authorisation is in force

63 (1) A standard authorisation comes into force when it is given.

(2) But if the authorisation provides for it to come into force at a later time, it comes into force at that time.

'**Comes into force when it is given**'(para 63(1)—this means the exact time on the day when it is given: *Re MB* [2010] EWHC 2508 (COP) at paragraph 45, per Charles J.

64 (1) A standard authorisation ceases to be in force at the end of the period stated in the authorisation in accordance with paragraph 55(1)(c).

(2) But if the authorisation terminates before then in accordance with paragraph 62(2) or any other provision of this Schedule, it ceases to be in force when the termination takes effect.

(3) This paragraph does not affect the powers of the Court of Protection or of any other court.

65 (1) This paragraph applies if a standard authorisation ceases to be in force.

(2) The supervisory body must give notice that the authorisation has ceased to be in force.

(3) The supervisory body must give that notice to all of the following –

    (a)   the managing authority of the relevant hospital or care home;
    (b)   the relevant person;
    (c)   the relevant person's representative;
    (d)   every interested person consulted by the best interests assessor.

(4) The supervisory body must give that notice as soon as practicable after the authorisation ceases to be in force.

When a request for a standard authorisation is 'disposed of'

66 A request for a standard authorisation is to be regarded for the purposes of this Schedule as disposed of if the supervisory body have given –

    (a)   a copy of the authorisation in accordance with paragraph 57, or
    (b)   notice in accordance with paragraph 58.

Right of third party to require consideration of whether authorisation needed

67 For the purposes of paragraphs 68 to 73 there is an unauthorised deprivation of liberty if –

    (a)   a person is already a detained resident in a hospital or care home, and
    (b)   the detention of the person is not authorised as mentioned in section 4A.

68 (1) If the following conditions are met, an eligible person may request the supervisory body to decide whether or not there is an unauthorised deprivation of liberty.

(2) The first condition is that the eligible person has notified the managing authority of the relevant hospital or care home that it appears to the eligible person that there is an unauthorised deprivation of liberty.

(3) The second condition is that the eligible person has asked the managing authority to request a standard authorisation in relation to the detention of the relevant person.

(4) The third condition is that the managing authority has not requested a standard authorisation within a reasonable period after the eligible person asks it to do so.

(5) In this paragraph 'eligible person' means any person other than the managing authority of the relevant hospital or care home.

69 (1) This paragraph applies if an eligible person requests the supervisory body to decide whether or not there is an unauthorised deprivation of liberty.

(2) The supervisory body must select and appoint a person to carry out an assessment of whether or not the relevant person is a detained resident.

(3) But the supervisory body need not select and appoint a person to carry out such an assessment in either of these cases.

(4) The first case is where it appears to the supervisory body that the request by the eligible person is frivolous or vexatious.

(5) The second case is where it appears to the supervisory body that –

    (a)   the question of whether or not there is an unauthorised deprivation of liberty has already been decided, and
    (b)   since that decision, there has been no change of circumstances which would merit the question being decided again.

(6) The supervisory body must not select and appoint a person to carry out an assessment under this paragraph unless it appears to the supervisory body that the person would be –

    (a)   suitable to carry out a best interests assessment (if one were obtained in connection with a request for a standard authorisation relating to the relevant person), and
    (b)   eligible to carry out such a best interests assessment.

(7) The supervisory body must notify the persons specified in sub-paragraph (8) –

    (a)   that the supervisory body have been requested to decide whether or not there is an unauthorised deprivation of liberty;
    (b)   of their decision whether or not to select and appoint a person to carry out an assessment under this paragraph;
    (c)   if their decision is to select and appoint a person, of the person appointed.

(8) The persons referred to in sub-paragraph (7) are –

    (a)   the eligible person who made the request under paragraph 68;
    (b)   the person to whom the request relates;
    (c)   the managing authority of the relevant hospital or care home;
    (d)   any section 39A IMCA.

70 (1) Regulations may be made about the period within which an assessment under paragraph 69 must be carried out.

(2) Regulations made under paragraph 129(3) apply in relation to the selection and appointment of a person under paragraph 69 as they apply to the selection of a person under paragraph 129 to carry out a best interests assessment.

(3) The following provisions apply to an assessment under paragraph 69 as they apply to an assessment carried out in connection with a request for a standard authorisation –

- (a) paragraph 131 (examination and copying of records);
- (b) paragraph 132 (representations);
- (c) paragraphs 134 and 135(1) and (2) (duty to keep records and give copies).

(4) The copies of the assessment which the supervisory body are required to give under paragraph 135(2) must be given as soon as practicable after the supervisory body are themselves given a copy of the assessment.

'**Regulations**' (para 70(1))—See the Mental Capacity (Deprivation of Liberty—Standard Authorisations, Assessments and Ordinary Residence) Regulations 2008, SI 2008/1858, reg 14 (text reproduced in Part V of this book).

'**Regulations made under paragraph 129(3)**' (para 70(2))—Namely the Mental Capacity (Deprivation of Liberty—Standard Authorisations, Assessments and Ordinary Residence) Regulations 2008, SI 2008/1858, as amended by Mental Capacity (Deprivation of Liberty: Monitoring and Reporting; and Assessments – Amendment) Regulations 2009, SI 2009/827 apply and for Wales Mental Capacity (Deprivation of Liberty: Assessments, Standard Authorisations and Disputes about Residence) (Wales) Regulations 2009, SI 2009/783.

71 (1) This paragraph applies if –

- (a) the supervisory body obtain an assessment under paragraph 69,
- (b) the assessment comes to the conclusion that the relevant person is a detained resident, and
- (c) it appears to the supervisory body that the detention of the person is not authorised as mentioned in section 4A.

(2) This Schedule (including Part 5) applies as if the managing authority of the relevant hospital or care home had, in accordance with Part 4, requested the supervisory body to give a standard authorisation in relation to the relevant person.

(3) The managing authority of the relevant hospital or care home must supply the supervisory body with the information (if any) which the managing authority would, by virtue of paragraph 31, have had to include in a request for a standard authorisation.

(4) The supervisory body must notify the persons specified in paragraph 69(8) –

- (a) of the outcome of the assessment obtained under paragraph 69, and
- (b) that this Schedule applies as mentioned in sub-paragraph (2).

72 (1) This paragraph applies if –

- (a) the supervisory body obtain an assessment under paragraph 69, and
- (b) the assessment comes to the conclusion that the relevant person is not a detained resident.

(2) The supervisory body must notify the persons specified in paragraph 69(8) of the outcome of the assessment.

73 (1) This paragraph applies if –

(a)   the supervisory body obtain an assessment under paragraph 69,

(b)   the assessment comes to the conclusion that the relevant person is a detained resident, and

(c)   it appears to the supervisory body that the detention of the person is authorised as mentioned in section 4A.

(2) The supervisory body must notify the persons specified in paragraph 69(8) –

(a)   of the outcome of the assessment, and

(b)   that it appears to the supervisory body that the detention is authorised.

PART 5
URGENT AUTHORISATIONS

Managing authority to give authorisation

74 Only the managing authority of the relevant hospital or care home may give an urgent authorisation.

75 The managing authority may give an urgent authorisation only if they are required to do so by paragraph 76 (as read with paragraph 77).

Duty to give authorisation

76 (1) The managing authority must give an urgent authorisation in either of the following cases.

(2) The first case is where –

(a)   the managing authority are required to make a request under paragraph 24 or 25 for a standard authorisation, and

(b)   they believe that the need for the relevant person to be a detained resident is so urgent that it is appropriate for the detention to begin before they make the request.

(3) The second case is where –

(a)   the managing authority have made a request under paragraph 24 or 25 for a standard authorisation, and

(b)   they believe that the need for the relevant person to be a detained resident is so urgent that it is appropriate for the detention to begin before the request is disposed of.

(4) References in this paragraph to the detention of the relevant person are references to the detention to which paragraph 24 or 25 relates.

(5) This paragraph is subject to paragraph 77.

77 (1) This paragraph applies where the managing authority have given an urgent authorisation ('the original authorisation') in connection with a case where a person is, or is to be, a detained resident ('the existing detention').

(2) No new urgent authorisation is to be given under paragraph 76 in connection with the existing detention.

(3) But the managing authority may request the supervisory body to extend the duration of the original authorisation.

(4) Only one request under sub-paragraph (3) may be made in relation to the original authorisation.

(5) Paragraphs 84 to 86 apply to any request made under sub-paragraph (3).

Terms of authorisation

78 (1) If the managing authority decide to give an urgent authorisation, they must decide the period during which the authorisation is to be in force.

(2) That period must not exceed 7 days.

Form of authorisation

79 An urgent authorisation must be in writing.

80 An urgent authorisation must state the following things –

  (a)   the name of the relevant person;
  (b)   the name of the relevant hospital or care home;
  (c)   the period during which the authorisation is to be in force;
  (d)   the purpose for which the authorisation is given.

81 (1) If the name of the relevant hospital or care home changes, the urgent authorisation is to be read as if it stated the current name of the hospital or care home.

(2) But sub-paragraph (1) is subject to any provision relating to the change of name which is made in any enactment or in any instrument made under an enactment.

Duty to keep records and give copies

82 (1) This paragraph applies if an urgent authorisation is given.

(2) The managing authority must keep a written record of why they have given the urgent authorisation.

(3) As soon as practicable after giving the authorisation, the managing authority must give a copy of the authorisation to all of the following –

  (a)   the relevant person;
  (b)   any section 39A IMCA.

Duty to give information about authorisation

83 (1) This paragraph applies if an urgent authorisation is given.

(2) The managing authority of the relevant hospital or care home must take such steps as are practicable to ensure that the relevant person understands all of the following –

  (a)   the effect of the authorisation;
  (b)   the right to make an application to the court to exercise its jurisdiction under section 21A.

(3) Those steps must be taken as soon as is practicable after the authorisation is given.

(4) Those steps must include the giving of appropriate information both orally and in writing.

Request for extension of duration

84 (1) This paragraph applies if the managing authority make a request under paragraph 77 for the supervisory body to extend the duration of the original authorisation.

(2) The managing authority must keep a written record of why they have made the request.

(3) The managing authority must give the relevant person notice that they have made the request.

(4) The supervisory body may extend the duration of the original authorisation if it appears to them that –

(a)   the managing authority have made the required request for a standard authorisation,

(b)   there are exceptional reasons why it has not yet been possible for that request to be disposed of, and

(c)   it is essential for the existing detention to continue until the request is disposed of.

(5) The supervisory body must keep a written record that the request has been made to them.

(6) In this paragraph and paragraphs 85 and 86 –

(a)   'original authorisation' and 'existing detention' have the same meaning as in paragraph 77;

(b)   the required request for a standard authorisation is the request that is referred to in paragraph 76(2) or (3).

85 (1) This paragraph applies if, under paragraph 84, the supervisory body decide to extend the duration of the original authorisation.

(2) The supervisory body must decide the period of the extension.

(3) That period must not exceed 7 days.

(4) The supervisory body must give the managing authority notice stating the period of the extension.

(5) The managing authority must then vary the original authorisation so that it states the extended duration.

(6) Paragraphs 82(3) and 83 apply (with the necessary modifications) to the variation of the original authorisation as they apply to the giving of an urgent authorisation.

(7) The supervisory body must keep a written record of –

(a)   the outcome of the request, and

(b)   the period of the extension.

'must not exceed 7 days' (para 85(3))—The calculation of the maximum period of 7 days for an urgent authorisation and any extension of an urgent authorisation should be calculated by including the whole of the day on which the urgent authorisation was actually given: *Re MB* [2010] EWHC 2508 (COP) at paragraph 41, per Charles J. In calculating whether an urgent authorisation or its extension exceeds the maximum period allowed, the period ends at the end of the last day: *Re MB* at paragraph 43.

86 (1) This paragraph applies if, under paragraph 84, the supervisory body decide not to extend the duration of the original authorisation.

(2) The supervisory body must give the managing authority notice stating –

    (a)   the decision, and

    (b)   their reasons for making it.

(3) The managing authority must give a copy of that notice to all of the following –

    (a)   the relevant person;

    (b)   any section 39A IMCA.

(4) The supervisory body must keep a written record of the outcome of the request.

No variation

87 (1) An urgent authorisation may not be varied except in accordance with paragraph 85.

(2) This paragraph does not affect the powers of the Court of Protection or of any other court.

When an authorisation is in force

88 An urgent authorisation comes into force when it is given.

'Comes into force when it is given'—This means the exact time on the day when it is given: *Re MB* [2010] EWHC 2508 (COP) at paragraph 35, per Charles J. The calculation of the maximum period of 7 days for an urgent authorisation and any extension of an urgent authorisation should be calculated by including the whole of the day on which the urgent authorisation was actually given: *Re MB* at paragraph 41.

89

(1) An urgent authorisation ceases to be in force at the end of the period stated in the authorisation in accordance with paragraph 80(c) (subject to any variation in accordance with paragraph 85).

(2) But if the required request is disposed of before the end of that period, the urgent authorisation ceases to be in force as follows.

(3) If the supervisory body are required by paragraph 50(1) to give the requested authorisation, the urgent authorisation ceases to be in force when the requested authorisation comes into force.

(4) If the supervisory body are prohibited by paragraph 50(2) from giving the requested authorisation, the urgent authorisation ceases to be in force when the managing authority receive notice under paragraph 58.

(5) In this paragraph –

'required request' means the request referred to in paragraph 76(2) or (3);

'requested authorisation' means the standard authorisation to which the required request relates.

(6) This paragraph does not affect the powers of the Court of Protection or of any other court.

90 (1) This paragraph applies if an urgent authorisation ceases to be in force.

(2) The supervisory body must give notice that the authorisation has ceased to be in force.

(3) The supervisory body must give that notice to all of the following –

    (a)   the relevant person;

    (b)   any section 39A IMCA.

(4) The supervisory body must give that notice as soon as practicable after the authorisation ceases to be in force.

PART 6
ELIGIBILITY REQUIREMENT NOT MET: SUSPENSION OF STANDARD AUTHORISATION

91 (1) This Part applies if the following conditions are met.

(2) The first condition is that a standard authorisation –

    (a)   has been given, and

    (b)   has not ceased to be in force.

(3) The second condition is that the managing authority of the relevant hospital or care home are satisfied that the relevant person has ceased to meet the eligibility requirement.

(4) But this Part does not apply if the relevant person is ineligible by virtue of paragraph 5 of Schedule 1A (in which case see Part 8).

92 The managing authority of the relevant hospital or care home must give the supervisory body notice that the relevant person has ceased to meet the eligibility requirement.

93 (1) This paragraph applies if the managing authority give the supervisory body notice under paragraph 92.

(2) The standard authorisation is suspended from the time when the notice is given.

(3) The supervisory body must give notice that the standard authorisation has been suspended to the following persons –

    (a)   the relevant person;

    (b)   the relevant person's representative;

    (c)   the managing authority of the relevant hospital or care home.

94 (1) This paragraph applies if, whilst the standard authorisation is suspended, the managing authority are satisfied that the relevant person meets the eligibility requirement again.

(2) The managing authority must give the supervisory body notice that the relevant person meets the eligibility requirement again.

95 (1) This paragraph applies if the managing authority give the supervisory body notice under paragraph 94.

(2) The standard authorisation ceases to be suspended from the time when the notice is given.

(3) The supervisory body must give notice that the standard authorisation has ceased to be suspended to the following persons –

    (a)   the relevant person;
    (b)   the relevant person's representative;
    (c)   any section 39D IMCA;
    (d)   the managing authority of the relevant hospital or care home.

(4) The supervisory body must give notice under this paragraph as soon as practicable after they are given notice under paragraph 94.

96 (1) This paragraph applies if no notice is given under paragraph 94 before the end of the relevant 28 day period.

(2) The standard authorisation ceases to have effect at the end of the relevant 28 day period.

(3) The relevant 28 day period is the period of 28 days beginning with the day on which the standard authorisation is suspended under paragraph 93.

97 The effect of suspending the standard authorisation is that Part 1 ceases to apply for as long as the authorisation is suspended.

PART 7
STANDARD AUTHORISATIONS: CHANGE IN SUPERVISORY
RESPONSIBILITY

Application of this Part

98 (1) This Part applies if these conditions are met.

(2) The first condition is that a standard authorisation –

    (a)   has been given, and
    (b)   has not ceased to be in force.

(3) The second condition is that there is a change in supervisory responsibility.

(4) The third condition is that there is not a change in the place of detention (within the meaning of paragraph 25).

99 For the purposes of this Part there is a change in supervisory responsibility if –

    (a)   one body ('the old supervisory body') have ceased to be supervisory body in relation to the standard authorisation, and
    (b)   a different body ('the new supervisory body') have become supervisory body in relation to the standard authorisation.

Effect of change in supervisory responsibility

100 (1) The new supervisory body becomes the supervisory body in relation to the authorisation.

(2) Anything done by or in relation to the old supervisory body in connection with the authorisation has effect, so far as is necessary for continuing its effect after the change, as if done by or in relation to the new supervisory body.

(3) Anything which relates to the authorisation and which is in the process of being done by or in relation to the old supervisory body at the time of the change may be continued by or in relation to the new supervisory body.

(4) But –

    (a)   the old supervisory body do not, by virtue of this paragraph, cease to be liable for anything done by them in connection with the authorisation before the change; and

    (b)   the new supervisory body do not, by virtue of this paragraph, become liable for any such thing.

PART 8
STANDARD AUTHORISATIONS: REVIEW

Application of this Part

101 (1) This Part applies if a standard authorisation –

    (a)   has been given, and
    (b)   has not ceased to be in force.

(2) Paragraphs 102 to 122 are subject to paragraphs 123 to 125.

Review by supervisory body

102 (1) The supervisory body may at any time carry out a review of the standard authorisation in accordance with this Part.

(2) The supervisory body must carry out such a review if they are requested to do so by an eligible person.

(3) Each of the following is an eligible person –

    (a)   the relevant person;
    (b)   the relevant person's representative;
    (c)   the managing authority of the relevant hospital or care home.

Request for review

103 (1) An eligible person may, at any time, request the supervisory body to carry out a review of the standard authorisation in accordance with this Part.

(2) The managing authority of the relevant hospital or care home must make such a request if one or more of the qualifying requirements appear to them to be reviewable.

Grounds for review

104 (1) Paragraphs 105 to 107 set out the grounds on which the qualifying requirements are reviewable.

(2) A qualifying requirement is not reviewable on any other ground.

Non-qualification ground

105 (1) Any of the following qualifying requirements is reviewable on the ground that the relevant person does not meet the requirement –

    (a)   the age requirement;
    (b)   the mental health requirement;
    (c)   the mental capacity requirement;
    (d)   the best interests requirement;
    (e)   the no refusals requirement.

(2) The eligibility requirement is reviewable on the ground that the relevant person is ineligible by virtue of paragraph 5 of Schedule 1A.

(3) The ground in sub-paragraph (1) and the ground in sub-paragraph (2) are referred to as the non-qualification ground.

Change of reason ground

106 (1) Any of the following qualifying requirements is reviewable on the ground set out in sub-paragraph (2) –

    (a)   the mental health requirement;
    (b)   the mental capacity requirement;
    (c)   the best interests requirement;
    (d)   the eligibility requirement;
    (e)   the no refusals requirement.

(2) The ground is that the reason why the relevant person meets the requirement is not the reason stated in the standard authorisation.

(3) This ground is referred to as the change of reason ground.

Variation of conditions ground

107 (1) The best interests requirement is reviewable on the ground that –

    (a)   there has been a change in the relevant person's case, and
    (b)   because of that change, it would be appropriate to vary the conditions to which the standard authorisation is subject.

(2) This ground is referred to as the variation of conditions ground.

(3) A reference to varying the conditions to which the standard authorisation is subject is a reference to –

    (a)   amendment of an existing condition,
    (b)   omission of an existing condition, or
    (c)   inclusion of a new condition (whether or not there are already any existing conditions).

PART III

Notice that review to be carried out

108 (1) If the supervisory body are to carry out a review of the standard authorisation, they must give notice of the review to the following persons –

    (a)   the relevant person;

    (b)   the relevant person's representative;

    (c)   the managing authority of the relevant hospital or care home.

(2) The supervisory body must give the notice –

    (a)   before they begin the review, or

    (b)   if that is not practicable, as soon as practicable after they have begun it.

(3) This paragraph does not require the supervisory body to give notice to any person who has requested the review.

Starting a review

109 To start a review of the standard authorisation, the supervisory body must decide which, if any, of the qualifying requirements appear to be reviewable.

No reviewable qualifying requirements

110 (1) This paragraph applies if no qualifying requirements appear to be reviewable.

(2) This Part does not require the supervisory body to take any action in respect of the standard authorisation.

One or more reviewable qualifying requirements

111 (1) This paragraph applies if one or more qualifying requirements appear to be reviewable.

(2) The supervisory body must secure that a separate review assessment is carried out in relation to each qualifying requirement which appears to be reviewable.

(3) But sub-paragraph (2) does not require the supervisory body to secure that a best interests review assessment is carried out in a case where the best interests requirement appears to the supervisory body to be non-assessable.

(4) The best interests requirement is non-assessable if –

    (a)   the requirement is reviewable only on the variation of conditions ground, and

    (b)   the change in the relevant person's case is not significant.

(5) In making any decision whether the change in the relevant person's case is significant, regard must be had to –

    (a)   the nature of the change, and

    (b)   the period that the change is likely to last for.

Review assessments

112 (1) A review assessment is an assessment of whether the relevant person meets a qualifying requirement.

(2) In relation to a review assessment –

    (a) a negative conclusion is a conclusion that the relevant person does not meet the qualifying requirement to which the assessment relates;

    (b) a positive conclusion is a conclusion that the relevant person meets the qualifying requirement to which the assessment relates.

(3) An age review assessment is a review assessment carried out in relation to the age requirement.

(4) A mental health review assessment is a review assessment carried out in relation to the mental health requirement.

(5) A mental capacity review assessment is a review assessment carried out in relation to the mental capacity requirement.

(6) A best interests review assessment is a review assessment carried out in relation to the best interests requirement.

(7) An eligibility review assessment is a review assessment carried out in relation to the eligibility requirement.

(8) A no refusals review assessment is a review assessment carried out in relation to the no refusals requirement.

113 (1) In carrying out a review assessment, the assessor must comply with any duties which would be imposed upon him under Part 4 if the assessment were being carried out in connection with a request for a standard authorisation.

(2) But in the case of a best interests review assessment, paragraphs 43 and 44 do not apply.

(3) Instead of what is required by paragraph 43, the best interests review assessment must include recommendations about whether –and, if so, how –it would be appropriate to vary the conditions to which the standard authorisation is subject.

Best interests requirement reviewable but non-assessable

114 (1) This paragraph applies in a case where –

    (a) the best interests requirement appears to be reviewable, but

    (b) in accordance with paragraph 111(3), the supervisory body are not required to secure that a best interests review assessment is carried out.

(2) The supervisory body may vary the conditions to which the standard authorisation is subject in such ways (if any) as the supervisory body think are appropriate in the circumstances.

Best interests review assessment positive

115 (1) This paragraph applies in a case where –

    (a) a best interests review assessment is carried out, and

    (b) the assessment comes to a positive conclusion.

(2) The supervisory body must decide the following questions –

   (a)   whether or not the best interests requirement is reviewable on the change of reason ground;

   (b)   whether or not the best interests requirement is reviewable on the variation of conditions ground;

   (c)   if so, whether or not the change in the person's case is significant.

(3) If the supervisory body decide that the best interests requirement is reviewable on the change of reason ground, they must vary the standard authorisation so that it states the reason why the relevant person now meets that requirement.

(4) If the supervisory body decide that –

   (a)   the best interests requirement is reviewable on the variation of conditions ground, and

   (b)   the change in the relevant person's case is not significant,

they may vary the conditions to which the standard authorisation is subject in such ways (if any) as they think are appropriate in the circumstances.

(5) If the supervisory body decide that –

   (a)   the best interests requirement is reviewable on the variation of conditions ground, and

   (b)   the change in the relevant person's case is significant,

they must vary the conditions to which the standard authorisation is subject in such ways as they think are appropriate in the circumstances.

(6) If the supervisory body decide that the best interests requirement is not reviewable on –

   (a)   the change of reason ground, or

   (b)   the variation of conditions ground,

this Part does not require the supervisory body to take any action in respect of the standard authorisation so far as the best interests requirement relates to it.

Mental health, mental capacity, eligibility or no refusals review assessment positive

116 (1) This paragraph applies if the following conditions are met.

(2) The first condition is that one or more of the following are carried out –

   (a)   a mental health review assessment;

   (b)   a mental capacity review assessment;

   (c)   an eligibility review assessment;

   (d)   a no refusals review assessment.

(3) The second condition is that each assessment carried out comes to a positive conclusion.

(4) The supervisory body must decide whether or not each of the assessed qualifying requirements is reviewable on the change of reason ground.

(5) If the supervisory body decide that any of the assessed qualifying requirements is reviewable on the change of reason ground, they must vary the standard authorisation so that it states the reason why the relevant person now meets the requirement or requirements in question.

(6) If the supervisory body decide that none of the assessed qualifying requirements are reviewable on the change of reason ground, this Part does not require the supervisory body to take any action in respect of the standard authorisation so far as those requirements relate to it.

(7) An assessed qualifying requirement is a qualifying requirement in relation to which a review assessment is carried out.

One or more review assessments negative

117 (1) This paragraph applies if one or more of the review assessments carried out comes to a negative conclusion.

(2) The supervisory body must terminate the standard authorisation with immediate effect.

Completion of a review

118 (1) The review of the standard authorisation is complete in any of the following cases.

(2) The first case is where paragraph 110 applies.

(3) The second case is where –

    (a)   paragraph 111 applies, and
    (b)   paragraph 117 requires the supervisory body to terminate the standard authorisation.

(4) In such a case, the supervisory body need not comply with any of the other provisions of paragraphs 114 to 116 which would be applicable to the review (were it not for this sub-paragraph).

(5) The third case is where –

    (a)   paragraph 111 applies,
    (b)   paragraph 117 does not require the supervisory body to terminate the standard authorisation, and
    (c)   the supervisory body comply with all of the provisions of paragraphs 114 to 116 (so far as they are applicable to the review).

Variations under this Part

119 Any variation of the standard authorisation made under this Part must be in writing.

Notice of outcome of review

120 (1) When the review of the standard authorisation is complete, the supervisory body must give notice to all of the following –

    (a)   the managing authority of the relevant hospital or care home;
    (b)   the relevant person;
    (c)   the relevant person's representative;
    (d)   any section 39D IMCA.

PART III

(2) That notice must state –

    (a)   the outcome of the review, and

    (b)   what variation (if any) has been made to the authorisation under this Part.

Records

121 A supervisory body must keep a written record of the following information –

    (a)   each request for a review that is made to them;

    (b)   the outcome of each request;

    (c)   each review which they carry out;

    (d)   the outcome of each review which they carry out;

    (e)   any variation of an authorisation made in consequence of a review.

Relationship between review and suspension under Part 6

122 (1) This paragraph applies if a standard authorisation is suspended in accordance with Part 6.

(2) No review may be requested under this Part whilst the standard authorisation is suspended.

(3) If a review has already been requested, or is being carried out, when the standard authorisation is suspended, no steps are to be taken in connection with that review whilst the authorisation is suspended.

Relationship between review and request for new authorisation

123 (1) This paragraph applies if, in accordance with paragraph 24 (as read with paragraph 29), the managing authority of the relevant hospital or care home make a request for a new standard authorisation which would be in force after the expiry of the existing authorisation.

(2) No review may be requested under this Part until the request for the new standard authorisation has been disposed of.

(3) If a review has already been requested, or is being carried out, when the new standard authorisation is requested, no steps are to be taken in connection with that review until the request for the new standard authorisation has been disposed of.

124 (1) This paragraph applies if –

    (a)   a review under this Part has been requested, or is being carried out, and

    (b)   the managing authority of the relevant hospital or care home make a request under paragraph 30 for a new standard authorisation which would be in force on or before, and after, the expiry of the existing authorisation.

(2) No steps are to be taken in connection with the review under this Part until the request for the new standard authorisation has been disposed of.

125 In paragraphs 123 and 124 –

    (a)   the existing authorisation is the authorisation referred to in paragraph 101;

(b) the expiry of the existing authorisation is the time when it is expected to cease to be in force.

PART 9
ASSESSMENTS UNDER THIS SCHEDULE

Introduction

126 This Part contains provision about assessments under this Schedule.

127 An assessment under this Schedule is either of the following –

(a) an assessment carried out in connection with a request for a standard authorisation under Part 4;

(b) a review assessment carried out in connection with a review of a standard authorisation under Part 8.

128 In this Part, in relation to an assessment under this Schedule –

'assessor' means the person carrying out the assessment;

'relevant procedure' means –

(a) the request for the standard authorisation, or

(b) the review of the standard authorisation;

'supervisory body' means the supervisory body responsible for securing that the assessment is carried out.

Supervisory body to select assessor

129 (1) It is for the supervisory body to select a person to carry out an assessment under this Schedule.

(2) The supervisory body must not select a person to carry out an assessment unless the person –

(a) appears to the supervisory body to be suitable to carry out the assessment (having regard, in particular, to the type of assessment and the person to be assessed), and

(b) is eligible to carry out the assessment.

(3) Regulations may make provision about the selection, and eligibility, of persons to carry out assessments under this Schedule.

(4) Sub-paragraphs (5) and (6) apply if two or more assessments are to be obtained for the purposes of the relevant procedure.

(5) In a case where the assessments to be obtained include a mental health assessment and a best interests assessment, the supervisory body must not select the same person to carry out both assessments.

(6) Except as prohibited by sub-paragraph (5), the supervisory body may select the same person to carry out any number of the assessments which the person appears to be suitable, and is eligible, to carry out.

'**Regulations**' (para 129(3))—See the Mental Capacity (Deprivation of Liberty—Standard Authorisations, Assessments and Ordinary Residence) Regulations 2008, SI 2008/1858 (text reproduced in Part V of this book), as amended by the Mental Capacity (Deprivation of Liberty: Monitoring and Reporting; and Assessments – Amendment) Regulations 2009, SI 2009/827 and for

Wales the Mental Capacity (Deprivation of Liberty: Assessments, Standard Authorisations and Disputes about Residence) (Wales) Regulations 2009, SI 2009/783.

130 (1) This paragraph applies to regulations under paragraph 129(3).

(2) The regulations may make provision relating to a person's –

    (a)   qualifications,

    (b)   skills,

    (c)   training,

    (d)   experience,

    (e)   relationship to, or connection with, the relevant person or any other person,

    (f)   involvement in the care or treatment of the relevant person,

    (g)   connection with the supervisory body, or

    (h)   connection with the relevant hospital or care home, or with any other establishment or undertaking.

(3) The provision that the regulations may make in relation to a person's training may provide for particular training to be specified by the appropriate authority otherwise than in the regulations.

(4) In sub-paragraph (3) the 'appropriate authority' means –

    (a)   in relation to England: the Secretary of State;

    (b)   in relation to Wales: the National Assembly for Wales.

(5) The regulations may make provision requiring a person to be insured in respect of liabilities that may arise in connection with the carrying out of an assessment.

(6) In relation to cases where two or more assessments are to be obtained for the purposes of the relevant procedure, the regulations may limit the number, kind or combination of assessments which a particular person is eligible to carry out.

(7) Sub-paragraphs (2) to (6) do not limit the generality of the provision that may be made in the regulations.

'The regulations may' (para 130(2))—See the Mental Capacity (Deprivation of Liberty—Standard Authorisations, Assessments and Ordinary Residence) Regulations 2008, SI 2008/1858, Parts 2 and 3, as amended by SI 2009/827 (text reproduced in Part V of this book).

'The regulations may' (para 130(5))—This is provided for in the Mental Capacity (Deprivation of Liberty—Standard Authorisations, Assessments and Ordinary Residence) Regulations 2008, SI 2008/1858, reg 2 (the text of which is reproduced in Part V of this book).

'the regulations may' (para 130(6))—See the Mental Capacity (Deprivation of Liberty—Standard Authorisations, Assessments and Ordinary Residence) Regulations 2008, SI 2008/1858, Part 2, as amended by SI 2009/827 (text reproduced in Part V of this book).

Examination and copying of records

131 An assessor may, at all reasonable times, examine and take copies of –

    (a)   any health record,

    (b)   any record of, or held by, a local authority and compiled in accordance with a social services function, and

    (c)   any record held by a person registered under Part 2 of the Care Standards Act 2000 [or Chapter 2 of Part 1 of the Health and Social Care Act 2008],

which the assessor considers may be relevant to the assessment which is being carried out.

Amendment—Words in subsection (c) inserted by SI 2010/813.

Representations

132 In carrying out an assessment under this Schedule, the assessor must take into account any information given, or submissions made, by any of the following –

    (a)   the relevant person's representative;
    (b)   any section 39A IMCA;
    (c)   any section 39C IMCA;
    (d)   any section 39D IMCA.

Assessments to stop if any comes to negative conclusion

133 (1) This paragraph applies if an assessment under this Schedule comes to the conclusion that the relevant person does not meet one of the qualifying requirements.

(2) This Schedule does not require the supervisory body to secure that any other assessments under this Schedule are carried out in relation to the relevant procedure.

(3) The supervisory body must give notice to any assessor who is carrying out another assessment in connection with the relevant procedure that they are to cease carrying out that assessment.

(4) If an assessor receives such notice, this Schedule does not require the assessor to continue carrying out that assessment.

Duty to keep records and give copies

134 (1) This paragraph applies if an assessor has carried out an assessment under this Schedule (whatever conclusions the assessment has come to).

(2) The assessor must keep a written record of the assessment.

(3) As soon as practicable after carrying out the assessment, the assessor must give copies of the assessment to the supervisory body.

135 (1) This paragraph applies to the supervisory body if they are given a copy of an assessment under this Schedule.

(2) The supervisory body must give copies of the assessment to all of the following –

    (a)   the managing authority of the relevant hospital or care home;
    (b)   the relevant person;
    (c)   any section 39A IMCA;
    (d)   the relevant person's representative.

(3) If –

    (a)   the assessment is obtained in relation to a request for a standard authorisation, and
    (b)   the supervisory body are required by paragraph 50(1) to give the standard authorisation,

PART III

the supervisory body must give the copies of the assessment when they give copies of the authorisation in accordance with paragraph 57.

(4) If –

(a)   the assessment is obtained in relation to a request for a standard authorisation, and

(b)   the supervisory body are prohibited by paragraph 50(2) from giving the standard authorisation,

the supervisory body must give the copies of the assessment when they give notice in accordance with paragraph 58.

(5) If the assessment is obtained in connection with the review of a standard authorisation, the supervisory body must give the copies of the assessment when they give notice in accordance with paragraph 120.

136 (1) This paragraph applies to the supervisory body if –

(a)   they are given a copy of a best interests assessment, and

(b)   the assessment includes, in accordance with paragraph 44(2), a statement that it appears to the assessor that there is an unauthorised deprivation of liberty.

(2) The supervisory body must notify all of the persons listed in sub-paragraph (3) that the assessment includes such a statement.

(3) Those persons are –

(a)   the managing authority of the relevant hospital or care home;

(b)   the relevant person;

(c)   any section 39A IMCA;

(d)   any interested person consulted by the best interests assessor.

(4) The supervisory body must comply with this paragraph when (or at some time before) they comply with paragraph 135.

PART 10
RELEVANT PERSON'S REPRESENTATIVE

The representative

137 In this Schedule the relevant person's representative is the person appointed as such in accordance with this Part.

138 (1) Regulations may make provision about the selection and appointment of representatives.

(2) In this Part such regulations are referred to as 'appointment regulations'.

'appointment regulations'—See the Mental Capacity (Deprivation of Liberty—Appointment of Relevant Person's Representative) Regulations 2008, SI 2008/1315 (as amended by SI 2008/2368) (the text of which is reproduced in Part V of this book).

Supervisory body to appoint representative

139 (1) The supervisory body must appoint a person to be the relevant person's representative as soon as practicable after a standard authorisation is given.

(2) The supervisory body must appoint a person to be the relevant person's representative if a vacancy arises whilst a standard authorisation is in force.

(3) Where a vacancy arises, the appointment under sub-paragraph (2) is to be made as soon as practicable after the supervisory body becomes aware of the vacancy.

140 (1) The selection of a person for appointment under paragraph 139 must not be made unless it appears to the person making the selection that the prospective representative would, if appointed –

    (a)   maintain contact with the relevant person,

    (b)   represent the relevant person in matters relating to or connected with this Schedule, and

    (c)   support the relevant person in matters relating to or connected with this Schedule.

141 (1) Any appointment of a representative for a relevant person is in addition to, and does not affect, any appointment of a donee or deputy.

(2) The functions of any representative are in addition to, and do not affect –

    (a)   the authority of any donee,

    (b)   the powers of any deputy, or

    (c)   any powers of the court.

Appointment regulations

142 Appointment regulations may provide that the procedure for appointing a representative may begin at any time after a request for a standard authorisation is made (including a time before the request has been disposed of).

'Appointment regulations may'—See the Mental Capacity (Deprivation of Liberty—Appointment of Relevant Person's Representative) Regulations 2008, SI 2008/1315, reg 10 (the text of which is reproduced in Part V of this book).

143 (1) Appointment regulations may make provision about who is to select a person for appointment as a representative.

(2) But regulations under this paragraph may only provide for the following to make a selection –

    (a)   the relevant person, if he has capacity in relation to the question of which person should be his representative;

    (b)   a donee of a lasting power of attorney granted by the relevant person, if it is within the scope of his authority to select a person;

    (c)   a deputy, if it is within the scope of his authority to select a person;

    (d)   a best interests assessor;

    (e)   the supervisory body.

(3) Regulations under this paragraph may provide that a selection by the relevant person, a donee or a deputy is subject to approval by a best interests assessor or the supervisory body.

(4) Regulations under this paragraph may provide that, if more than one selection is necessary in connection with the appointment of a particular representative –

    (a)   the same person may make more than one selection;

PART III

(b)   different persons may make different selections.

(5) For the purposes of this paragraph a best interests assessor is a person carrying out a best interests assessment in connection with the standard authorisation in question (including the giving of that authorisation).

'**Appointment regulations may**'—See the Mental Capacity (Deprivation of Liberty—Appointment of Relevant Person's Representative) Regulations 2008, SI 2008/1315, Part 1 (as amended by SI 2008/2368) (the text of which is reproduced in Part IV of this book).

144 (1) Appointment regulations may make provision about who may, or may not, be –

(a)   selected for appointment as a representative, or
(b)   appointed as a representative.

(2) Regulations under this paragraph may relate to any of the following matters –

(a)   a person's age;
(b)   a person's suitability;
(c)   a person's independence;
(d)   a person's willingness;
(e)   a person's qualifications.

'**Appointment regulations may**'—See the Mental Capacity (Deprivation of Liberty—Appointment of Relevant Person's Representative) Regulations 2008, SI 2008/1315 (as amended by SI 2008/2368) (the text of which is reproduced in Part V of this book).

145 Appointment regulations may make provision about the formalities of appointing a person as a representative.

'**Appointment regulations may**'—See the Mental Capacity (Deprivation of Liberty—Appointment of Relevant Person's Representative) Regulations 2008, SI 2008/1315, reg 12 (the text of which is reproduced in Part IV of this book).

146 In a case where a best interests assessor is to select a person to be appointed as a representative, appointment regulations may provide for the variation of the assessor's duties in relation to the assessment which he is carrying out.

'**regulations may**'—This power has not yet been exercised.

Monitoring of representatives

147

Regulations may make provision requiring the managing authority of the relevant hospital or care home to –

(a)   monitor, and
(b)   report to the supervisory body on,

the extent to which a representative is maintaining contact with the relevant person.

'**Regulations may**'—For Wales, the Mental Capacity (Deprivation of Liberty: Appointment of Relevant Person's Representative) (Wales) Regulations 2009, SI 2009/266, reg 15.

Termination

148 Regulations may make provision about the circumstances in which the appointment of a person as the relevant person's representative ends or may be ended.

'**Regulations may**'—See the Mental Capacity (Deprivation of Liberty—Appointment of Relevant Person's Representative) Regulations 2008, SI 2008/1315, reg 13 (the text of which is reproduced in Part V of this book).

149 Regulations may make provision about the formalities of ending the appointment of a person as a representative.

'**Regulations may**'—See the Mental Capacity (Deprivation of Liberty—Appointment of Relevant Person's Representative) Regulations 2008, SI 2008/1315, reg 14 (the text of which is reproduced in Part V of this book).

Suspension of representative's functions

150 (1) Regulations may make provision about the circumstances in which functions exercisable by, or in relation to, the relevant person's representative (whether under this Schedule or not) may be –

    (a)   suspended, and

    (b)   if suspended, revived.

(2) The regulations may make provision about the formalities for giving effect to the suspension or revival of a function.

(3) The regulations may make provision about the effect of the suspension or revival of a function.

'**Regulations may**'—This power has not yet been exercised.

Payment of representative

151 Regulations may make provision for payments to be made to, or in relation to, persons exercising functions as the relevant person's representative.

'**Regulations may**'—See the Mental Capacity (Deprivation of Liberty—Appointment of Relevant Person's Representative) Regulations 2008, SI 2008/1315, reg 15 (the text of which is reproduced in Part V of this book), under which a supervisory body may pay a representative when selected by that body.

Regulations under this Part

152 The provisions of this Part which specify provision that may be made in regulations under this Part do not affect the generality of the power to make such regulations.

Effect of appointment of section 39C IMCA

153 Paragraphs 159 and 160 make provision about the exercise of functions by, or towards, the relevant person's representative during periods when –

(a) no person is appointed as the relevant person's representative, but

(b) a person is appointed as a section 39C IMCA.

PART 11
IMCAS

Application of Part

154 This Part applies for the purposes of this Schedule.

The IMCAs

155 A section 39A IMCA is an independent mental capacity advocate appointed under section 39A.

156 A section 39C IMCA is an independent mental capacity advocate appointed under section 39C

157 A section 39D IMCA is an independent mental capacity advocate appointed under section 39D.

158 An IMCA is a section 39A IMCA or a section 39C IMCA or a section 39D IMCA.

Section 39C IMCA: functions

159 (1) This paragraph applies if, and for as long as, there is a section 39C IMCA.

(2) In the application of the relevant provisions, references to the relevant person's representative are to be read as references to the section 39C IMCA.

(3) But sub-paragraph (2) does not apply to any function under the relevant provisions for as long as the function is suspended in accordance with provision made under Part 10.

(4) In this paragraph and paragraph 160 the relevant provisions are –

(a) paragraph 102(3)(b) (request for review under Part 8);
(b) paragraph 108(1)(b) (notice of review under Part 8);
(c) paragraph 120(1)(c) (notice of outcome of review under Part 8).

160 (1) This paragraph applies if –

(a) a person is appointed as the relevant person's representative, and
(b) a person accordingly ceases to hold an appointment as a section 39C IMCA.

(2) Where a function under a relevant provision has been exercised by, or towards, the section 39C IMCA, there is no requirement for that function to be exercised again by, or towards, the relevant person's representative.

Section 39A IMCA: restriction of functions

161 (1) This paragraph applies if –

- (a) there is a section 39A IMCA, and
- (b) a person is appointed under Part 10 to be the relevant person's representative (whether or not that person, or any person subsequently appointed, is currently the relevant person's representative).

(2) The duties imposed on, and the powers exercisable by, the section 39A IMCA do not apply.

(3) The duties imposed on, and the powers exercisable by, any other person do not apply, so far as they fall to be performed or exercised towards the section 39A IMCA.

(4) But sub-paragraph (2) does not apply to any power of challenge exercisable by the section 39A IMCA.

(5) And sub-paragraph (3) does not apply to any duty or power of any other person so far as it relates to any power of challenge exercisable by the section 39A IMCA.

(6) Before exercising any power of challenge, the section 39A IMCA must take the views of the relevant person's representative into account.

(7) A power of challenge is a power to make an application to the court to exercise its jurisdiction under section 21A in connection with the giving of the standard authorisation.

PART 12
MISCELLANEOUS

Monitoring of operation of Schedule

162 (1) Regulations may make provision for, and in connection with, requiring one or more prescribed bodies to monitor, and report on, the operation of this Schedule in relation to England.

(2) The regulations may, in particular, give a prescribed body authority to do one or more of the following things –

- (a) to visit hospitals and care homes;
- (b) to visit and interview persons accommodated in hospitals and care homes;
- (c) to require the production of, and to inspect, records relating to the care or treatment of persons.

(3) 'Prescribed' means prescribed in regulations under this paragraph.

'Regulations may'—See the Mental Capacity (Deprivation of Liberty: Monitoring and Reporting; and Assessments – Amendment) Regulations 2009, SI 2009/827.

163 (1) Regulations may make provision for, and in connection with, enabling the National Assembly for Wales to monitor, and report on, the operation of this Schedule in relation to Wales.

(2) The National Assembly may direct one or more persons or bodies to carry out the Assembly's functions under regulations under this paragraph.

'Regulations may'—This power has not yet been exercised.

Disclosure of information

164 (1) Regulations may require either or both of the following to disclose prescribed information to prescribed bodies –

    (a)   supervisory bodies;

    (b)   managing authorities of hospitals or care homes.

(2) 'Prescribed' means prescribed in regulations under this paragraph.

(3) Regulations under this paragraph may only prescribe information relating to matters with which this Schedule is concerned.

'Regulations may'—This power has not yet been exercised.

Directions by National Assembly in relation to supervisory functions

165 (1) The National Assembly for Wales may direct a Local Health Board to exercise in relation to its area any supervisory functions which are specified in the direction.

(2) Directions under this paragraph must not preclude the National Assembly from exercising the functions specified in the directions.

(3) In this paragraph 'supervisory functions' means functions which the National Assembly have as supervisory body, so far as they are exercisable in relation to hospitals (whether NHS or independent hospitals, and whether in Wales or England).

166 (1) This paragraph applies where, under paragraph 165, a Local Health Board ('the specified LHB') is directed to exercise supervisory functions ('delegated functions').

(2) The National Assembly for Wales may give directions to the specified LHB about the Board's exercise of delegated functions.

(3) The National Assembly may give directions for any delegated functions to be exercised, on behalf of the specified LHB, by a committee, sub-committee or officer of that Board.

(4) The National Assembly may give directions providing for any delegated functions to be exercised by the specified LHB jointly with one or more other Local Health Boards.

(5) Where, under sub-paragraph (4), delegated functions are exercisable jointly, the National Assembly may give directions providing for the functions to be exercised, on behalf of the Local Health Boards in question, by a joint committee or joint sub-committee.

167 (1) Directions under paragraph 165 must be given in regulations.

(2) Directions under paragraph 166 may be given –

    (a)   in regulations, or

    (b)   by instrument in writing.

168 The power under paragraph 165 or paragraph 166 to give directions includes power to vary or revoke directions given under that paragraph.

Notices

169 Any notice under this Schedule must be in writing.

Regulations

170 (1) This paragraph applies to all regulations under this Schedule, except regulations under paragraph 162, 163, 167 or 183.

(2) It is for the Secretary of State to make such regulations in relation to authorisations under this Schedule which relate to hospitals and care homes situated in England.

(3) It is for the National Assembly for Wales to make such regulations in relation to authorisations under this Schedule which relate to hospitals and care homes situated in Wales.

171 It is for the Secretary of State to make regulations under paragraph 162.

172 It is for the National Assembly for Wales to make regulations under paragraph 163 or 167.

173 (1) This paragraph applies to regulations under paragraph 183.

(2) It is for the Secretary of State to make such regulations in relation to cases where a question as to the ordinary residence of a person is to be determined by the Secretary of State.

(3) It is for the National Assembly for Wales to make such regulations in relation to cases where a question as to the ordinary residence of a person is to be determined by the National Assembly.

PART 13
INTERPRETATION

Introduction

174 This Part applies for the purposes of this Schedule.

Hospitals and their managing authorities

175 (1) 'Hospital' means –

    (a)   an NHS hospital, or
    (b)   an independent hospital.

(2) 'NHS hospital' means –

    (a)   a health service hospital as defined by section 275 of the National Health Service Act 2006 or section 206 of the National Health Service (Wales) Act 2006, or
    (b)   a hospital as defined by section 206 of the National Health Service (Wales) Act 2006 vested in a Local Health Board.

[(3) 'Independent hospital' –

PART III

(a)   in relation to England, means a hospital as defined by section 275 of the National Health Service Act 2006 that is not an NHS hospital; and

(b)   in relation to Wales, means a hospital as defined by section 2 of the Care Standards Act 2000 that is not an NHS hospital.]

Amendment—Subparagraph (3) substituted by SI 2010/813.

176 (1) 'Managing authority', in relation to an NHS hospital, means –

(a)   if the hospital –
(i)   is vested in the appropriate national authority for the purposes of its functions under the National Health Service Act 2006 or of the National Health Service (Wales) Act 2006, or
(ii)   consists of any accommodation provided by a local authority and used as a hospital by or on behalf of the appropriate national authority under either of those Acts,
the Primary Care Trust, Strategic Health Authority, Local Health Board or Special Health Authority responsible for the administration of the hospital;

(b)   if the hospital is vested in a Primary Care Trust, National Health Service trust or NHS foundation trust, that trust;

(c)   if the hospital is vested in a Local Health Board, that Board.

(2) For this purpose the appropriate national authority is –

(a)   in relation to England: the Secretary of State;

(b)   in relation to Wales: the National Assembly for Wales;

(c)   in relation to England and Wales: the Secretary of State and the National Assembly acting jointly.

[**177** 'Managing authority', in relation to an independent hospital, means –

(a)   in relation to England, the person registered, or required to be registered, under Chapter 2 of Part 1 of the Health and Social Care Act 2008 in respect of regulated activities (within the meaning of that Part) carried on in the hospital, and

(b)   in relation to Wales, the person registered, or required to be registered, under Part 2 of the Care Standards Act 2000 in respect of the hospital.]

Amendment—Paragraph substituted by SI 2010/813.

Care homes and their managing authorities

178 'Care home' has the meaning given by section 3 of the Care Standards Act 2000.

[**179** 'Managing authority, in relation to a care home, means –

(a)   in relation to England, the person registered, or required to be registered, under Chapter 2 of Part 1 of the Health and Social Care Act 2008 in respect of the provision of residential accommodation, together with nursing or personal care, in the care home, and

(b)   in relation to Wales, the person registered, or required to be registered, under Part 2 of the Care Standards Act 2000 in respect of the care home.]

Amendment—Paragraph substituted by SI 2010/813.

Supervisory bodies: hospitals

180 (1) The identity of the supervisory body is determined under this paragraph in cases where the relevant hospital is situated in England.

(2) If a Primary Care Trust commissions the relevant care or treatment, that Trust is the supervisory body.

(3) If the National Assembly for Wales or a Local Health Board commission the relevant care or treatment, the National Assembly are the supervisory body.

(4) In any other case, the supervisory body are the Primary Care Trust for the area in which the relevant hospital is situated.

(5) If a hospital is situated in the areas of two (or more) Primary Care Trusts, it is to be regarded for the purposes of sub-paragraph (4) as situated in whichever of the areas the greater (or greatest) part of the hospital is situated.

181 (1) The identity of the supervisory body is determined under this paragraph in cases where the relevant hospital is situated in Wales.

(2) The National Assembly for Wales are the supervisory body.

(3) But if a Primary Care Trust commissions the relevant care or treatment, that Trust is the supervisory body.

Supervisory bodies: care homes

182 (1) The identity of the supervisory body is determined under this paragraph in cases where the relevant care home is situated in England or in Wales.

(2) The supervisory body are the local authority for the area in which the relevant person is ordinarily resident.

(3) But if the relevant person is not ordinarily resident in the area of a local authority, the supervisory body are the local authority for the area in which the care home is situated.

(4) In relation to England 'local authority' means –

    (a)   the council of a county;
    (b)   the council of a district for which there is no county council;
    (c)   the council of a London borough;
    (d)   the Common Council of the City of London;
    (e)   the Council of the Isles of Scilly.

(5) In relation to Wales 'local authority' means the council of a county or county borough.

(6) If a care home is situated in the areas of two (or more) local authorities, it is to be regarded for the purposes of sub-paragraph (3) as situated in whichever of the areas the greater (or greatest) part of the care home is situated.

183 (1) Subsections (5) and (6) of section 24 of the National Assistance Act 1948 (deemed place of ordinary residence) apply to any determination of where a person is ordinarily resident for the purposes of paragraph 182 as those subsections apply to such a determination for the purposes specified in those subsections.

(2) In the application of section 24(6) of the 1948 Act by virtue of subsection (1), section 24(6) is to be read as if it referred to a hospital vested in a Local Health Board as well as to hospitals vested in the Secretary of State and the other bodies mentioned in section 24(6).

(3) Any question arising as to the ordinary residence of a person is to be determined by the Secretary of State or by the National Assembly for Wales.

(4) The Secretary of State and the National Assembly must make and publish arrangements for determining which cases are to be dealt with by the Secretary of State and which are to be dealt with by the National Assembly.

(5) Those arrangements may include provision for the Secretary of State and the National Assembly to agree, in relation to any question that has arisen, which of them is to deal with the case.

(6) Regulations may make provision about arrangements that are to have effect before, upon, or after the determination of any question as to the ordinary residence of a person.

(7) The regulations may, in particular, authorise or require a local authority to do any or all of the following things –

(a) to act as supervisory body even though it may wish to dispute that it is the supervisory body;

(b) to become the supervisory body in place of another local authority;

(c) to recover from another local authority expenditure incurred in exercising functions as the supervisory body.

'Regulations may' (para 183(6))—See the Mental Capacity (Deprivation of Liberty—Standard Authorisations, Assessments and Ordinary Residence) Regulations 2008, SI 2008/1858, Part 6, as amended by SI 2009/827 (the text of which is reproduced in Part V of this book).

Same body managing authority and supervisory body

184 (1) This paragraph applies if, in connection with a particular person's detention as a resident in a hospital or care home, the same body are both –

(a) the managing authority of the relevant hospital or care home, and

(b) the supervisory body.

(2) The fact that a single body are acting in both capacities does not prevent the body from carrying out functions under this Schedule in each capacity.

(3) But, in such a case, this Schedule has effect subject to any modifications contained in regulations that may be made for this purpose.

Interested persons

185 Each of the following is an interested person –

(a) the relevant person's spouse or civil partner;

(b) where the relevant person and another person of the opposite sex are not married to each other but are living together as husband and wife: the other person;

(c) where the relevant person and another person of the same sex are not civil partners of each other but are living together as if they were civil partners: the other person;

(d)   the relevant person's children and step-children;
(e)   the relevant person's parents and step-parents;
(f)   the relevant person's brothers and sisters, half-brothers and half-sisters, and stepbrothers and stepsisters;
(g)   the relevant person's grandparents;
(h)   a deputy appointed for the relevant person by the court;
(i)   a donee of a lasting power of attorney granted by the relevant person.

186 (1) An interested person consulted by the best interests assessor is any person whose name is stated in the relevant best interests assessment in accordance with paragraph 40 (interested persons whom the assessor consulted in carrying out the assessment).

(2) The relevant best interests assessment is the most recent best interests assessment carried out in connection with the standard authorisation in question (whether the assessment was carried out under Part 4 or Part 8).

187 Where this Schedule imposes on a person a duty towards an interested person, the duty does not apply if the person on whom the duty is imposed –

(a)   is not aware of the interested person's identity or of a way of contacting him, and
(b)   cannot reasonably ascertain it.

188 The following table contains an index of provisions defining or otherwise explaining expressions used in this Schedule –

age assessment	paragraph 34
age requirement	paragraph 13
age review assessment	paragraph 112(3)
appointment regulations	paragraph 138
assessment under this Schedule	paragraph 127
assessor (except in Part 8)	paragraph 33
assessor (in Part 8)	paragraphs 33 and 128
authorisation under this Schedule	paragraph 10
best interests (determination of)	section 4
best interests assessment	paragraph 38
best interests requirement	paragraph 16
best interests review assessment	paragraph 112(6)
care home	paragraph 178
change of reason ground	paragraph 106
complete (in relation to a review of a standard authorisation)	paragraph 118
deprivation of a person's liberty	section 64(5) and (6)
deputy	section 16(2)(b)
detained resident	paragraph 6
disposed of (in relation to a request for a standard authorisation)	paragraph 66
eligibility assessment	paragraph 46

PART III

eligibility requirement	paragraph 17
eligibility review assessment	paragraph 112(7)
eligible person (in relation to paragraphs 68 to 73)	paragraph 68
eligible person (in relation to Part 8)	paragraph 102(3)
expiry (in relation to an existing authorisation)	paragraph 125(b)
existing authorisation (in Part 8)	paragraph 125(a)
hospital	paragraph 175
IMCA	paragraph 158
in force (in relation to a standard authorisation)	paragraphs 63 and 64
in force (in relation to an urgent authorisation)	paragraphs 88 and 89
ineligible (in relation to the eligibility requirement)	Schedule 1A
interested person	paragraph 185
interested person consulted by the best interests assessor	paragraph 186
lack of capacity	section 2
lasting power of attorney	section 9
managing authority (in relation to a care home)	paragraph 179
managing authority (in relation to a hospital)	paragraph 176 or 177
maximum authorisation period	paragraph 42
mental capacity assessment	paragraph 37
mental capacity requirement	paragraph 15
mental capacity review assessment	paragraph 112(5)
mental health assessment	paragraph 35
mental health requirement	paragraph 14
mental health review assessment	paragraph 112(4)
negative conclusion	paragraph 112(2)(a)
new supervisory body	paragraph 99(b)
no refusals assessment	paragraph 48
no refusals requirement	paragraph 18
no refusals review assessment	paragraph 112(8)
non-qualification ground	paragraph 105
old supervisory body	paragraph 99(a)
positive conclusion	paragraph 112(2)(b)
purpose of a standard authorisation	paragraph 11(1)
purpose of an urgent authorisation	paragraph 11(2)
qualifying requirements	paragraph 12
refusal (for the purposes of the no refusals requirement)	paragraphs 19 and 20

relevant care or treatment	paragraph 7
relevant hospital or care home	paragraph 7
relevant managing authority	paragraph 26(4)
relevant person	paragraph 7
relevant person's representative	paragraph 137
relevant procedure	paragraph 128
review assessment	paragraph 112(1)
reviewable	paragraph 104
section 39A IMCA	paragraph 155
section 39C IMCA	paragraph 156
section 39D IMCA	paragraph 157
standard authorisation	paragraph 8
supervisory body (except in Part 8)	paragraph 180, 181 or 182
supervisory body (in Part 8)	paragraph 128 and paragraph 180, 181 or 182
unauthorised deprivation of liberty (in relation to paragraphs 68 to 73)	paragraph 67
urgent authorisation	paragraph 9
variation of conditions ground	paragraph 107]

PART III

Amendment—Schedule inserted by the Mental Health Act 2007, s 50(5), Sch 7. The MCA 2005, Schs A1 and 1A and related provisions above, which amend the Act to provide deprivation of liberty safeguards, commenced on 1 April 2009 (the Mental Health Act 2007 (Commencement No 10 and Transitional Provisions) Order 2009, SI 2009/139 (C.9)). The nature and effect of the deprivation of liberty safeguards are discussed in Chapter 6 at **6.17**ff.

SCHEDULE 1
LASTING POWERS OF ATTORNEY: FORMALITIES

Section 9

PART 1
MAKING INSTRUMENTS

General requirements as to making instruments

1 (1) An instrument is not made in accordance with this Schedule unless –

(a) it is in the prescribed form,
(b) it complies with paragraph 2, and
(c) any prescribed requirements in connection with its execution are satisfied.

(2) Regulations may make different provision according to whether –

(a) the instrument relates to personal welfare or to property and affairs (or to both);
(b) only one or more than one donee is to be appointed (and if more than one, whether jointly or jointly and severally).

(3) In this Schedule –

(a) 'prescribed' means prescribed by regulations, and

   (b)   'regulations' means regulations made for the purposes of this Schedule by the Lord Chancellor.

'Regulations' (paras 1(2) and (3))—See Lasting Power of Attorney, Enduring Power of Attorney and Public Guardian Regulations 2007, SI 2007/1253; Lasting Powers of Attorney, Enduring Powers of Attorney and Public Guardian (Amendment) Regulations 2009, SI 2009/1884.

Requirements as to content of instruments

2 (1) The instrument must include –

   (a)   the prescribed information about the purpose of the instrument and the effect of a lasting power of attorney,

   (b)   a statement by the donor to the effect that he –
      (i)   has read the prescribed information or a prescribed part of it (or has had it read to him), and
      (ii) intends the authority conferred under the instrument to include authority to make decisions on his behalf in circumstances where he no longer has capacity,

   (c)   a statement by the donor –
      (i)   naming a person or persons whom the donor wishes to be notified of any application for the registration of the instrument, or
      (ii) stating that there are no persons whom he wishes to be notified of any such application,

   (d)   a statement by the donee (or, if more than one, each of them) to the effect that he –
      (i)   has read the prescribed information or a prescribed part of it (or has had it read to him), and
      (ii) understands the duties imposed on a donee of a lasting power of attorney under sections 1 (the principles) and 4 (best interests), and

   (e)   a certificate by a person of a prescribed description that, in his opinion, at the time when the donor executes the instrument –
      (i)   the donor understands the purpose of the instrument and the scope of the authority conferred under it,
      (ii) no fraud or undue pressure is being used to induce the donor to create a lasting power of attorney, and
      (iii) there is nothing else which would prevent a lasting power of attorney from being created by the instrument.

(2) Regulations may –

   (a)   prescribe a maximum number of named persons;

   (b)   provide that, where the instrument includes a statement under sub-paragraph (1)(c)(ii), two persons of a prescribed description must each give a certificate under sub-paragraph (1)(e).

(3) The persons who may be named persons do not include a person who is appointed as donee under the instrument.

(4) In this Schedule, 'named person' means a person named under sub-paragraph (1)(c).

(5) A certificate under sub-paragraph (1)(e) –

   (a)   must be made in the prescribed form, and

   (b)   must include any prescribed information.

(6) The certificate may not be given by a person appointed as donee under the instrument.

'maximum number' (para 2(2)(a))—There is a maximum of five named persons – see the Lasting Power of Attorney, Enduring Power of Attorney and Public Guardian Regulations 2007, SI 2007/1253, reg 6.

'named persons' (para 2(2)(a))—The donor must refer to named individuals, rather than to a class of persons or a description. The status of the named persons is determined by reference to when the instrument is executed, not the application for registration.

'a donee' (para 2(3))—This includes a replacement donee.

Failure to comply with prescribed form

3 (1) If an instrument differs in an immaterial respect in form or mode of expression from the prescribed form, it is to be treated by the Public Guardian as sufficient in point of form and expression.

(2) The court may declare that an instrument which is not in the prescribed form is to be treated as if it were, if it is satisfied that the persons executing the instrument intended it to create a lasting power of attorney.

'treated by the Public Guardian' (para 3(1))—The Public Guardian has the sole discretion of determining whether the difference is immaterial or not. There is no redress against a decision of the Public Guardian other than by way of an application to the Court of Protection for a declaration under para 3(2).

PART 2
REGISTRATION

Applications and procedure for registration

4 (1) An application to the Public Guardian for the registration of an instrument intended to create a lasting power of attorney –

    (a)   must be made in the prescribed form, and
    (b)   must include any prescribed information.

(2) The application may be made –

    (a)   by the donor,
    (b)   by the donee or donees, or
    (c)   if the instrument appoints two or more donees to act jointly and severally in respect of any matter, by any of the donees.

(3) The application must be accompanied by –

    (a)   the instrument, and
    (b)   any fee provided for under section 58(4)(b).

(4) A person who, in an application for registration, makes a statement which he knows to be false in a material particular is guilty of an offence and is liable –

    (a)   on summary conviction, to imprisonment for a term not exceeding 12 months or a fine not exceeding the statutory maximum or both;
    (b)   on conviction on indictment, to imprisonment for a term not exceeding 2 years or a fine or both.

PART III

'**prescribed form**' (para 4(1)(a))—Form LPA001 – Lasting Power of Attorney, Enduring Power of Attorney and Public Guardian Regulations 2007, SI 2007/1253, Sch 2.

5 Subject to paragraphs 11 to 14, the Public Guardian must register the instrument as a lasting power of attorney at the end of the prescribed period.

'**the Public Guardian must**'—There is a positive obligation on the Public Guardian to register the instrument unless there is a defect in the form or process or there is an objection.

'**prescribed period**'—The period of 6 weeks beginning with the date on which the Public Guardian gave out the last notice under para 7 or 8 – Lasting Power of Attorney, Enduring Power of Attorney and Public Guardian Regulations 2007, SI 2007/1253, reg 12.

Notification requirements

6 (1) A donor about to make an application under paragraph 4(2)(a) must notify any named persons that he is about to do so.

(2) The donee (or donees) about to make an application under paragraph 4(2)(b) or (c) must notify any named persons that he is (or they are) about to do so.

7 As soon as is practicable after receiving an application by the donor under paragraph 4(2)(a), the Public Guardian must notify the donee (or donees) that the application has been received.

'**the Public Guardian must notify**'—The Public Guardian can provide notice by post using Form LPA003A – Lasting Power of Attorney, Enduring Power of Attorney and Public Guardian Regulations 2007, SI 2007/1253, Sch 4.

8 (1) As soon as is practicable after receiving an application by a donee (or donees) under paragraph 4(2)(b), the Public Guardian must notify the donor that the application has been received.

(2) As soon as is practicable after receiving an application by a donee under paragraph 4(2)(c), the Public Guardian must notify –

(a)   the donor, and
(b)   the donee or donees who did not join in making the application,

that the application has been received.

'**the Public Guardian must notify the donor**'—The Public Guardian can provide notice by post using Form LPA003B – Lasting Power of Attorney, Enduring Power of Attorney and Public Guardian Regulations 2007, SI 2007/1253, Sch 4.

9 (1) A notice under paragraph 6 must be made in the prescribed form.

(2) A notice under paragraph 6, 7 or 8 must include such information, if any, as may be prescribed.

'**prescribed form**'—Form LPA001 – Lasting Power of Attorney, Enduring Power of Attorney and Public Guardian Regulations 2007, SI 2007/1253, Sch 2.

Power to dispense with notification requirements

10 The court may –

(a) on the application of the donor, dispense with the requirement to notify under paragraph 6(1), or

(b) on the application of the donee or donees concerned, dispense with the requirement to notify under paragraph 6(2),

if satisfied that no useful purpose would be served by giving the notice.

'**The court may … on an application by**'—Only the Court (ie not the Public Guardian) can dispense with notice, pursuant to a formal application being made.

Instrument not made properly or containing ineffective provision

11 (1) If it appears to the Public Guardian that an instrument accompanying an application under paragraph 4 is not made in accordance with this Schedule, he must not register the instrument unless the court directs him to do so.

(2) Sub-paragraph (3) applies if it appears to the Public Guardian that the instrument contains a provision which –

(a) would be ineffective as part of a lasting power of attorney, or

(b) would prevent the instrument from operating as a valid lasting power of attorney.

(3) The Public Guardian –

(a) must apply to the court for it to determine the matter under section 23(1), and

(b) pending the determination by the court, must not register the instrument.

(4) Sub-paragraph (5) applies if the court determines under section 23(1) (whether or not on an application by the Public Guardian) that the instrument contains a provision which –

(a) would be ineffective as part of a lasting power of attorney, or

(b) would prevent the instrument from operating as a valid lasting power of attorney.

(5) The court must –

(a) notify the Public Guardian that it has severed the provision, or

(b) direct him not to register the instrument.

(6) Where the court notifies the Public Guardian that it has severed a provision, he must register the instrument with a note to that effect attached to it.

'**If it appears to the Public Guardian**' (para 11(1))—A failure to complete the form correctly may mean that it has not been completed in accordance with the Schedule. The Public Guardian has discretion as to whether or not he or she should refuse registration and there is no redress against this decision except by an application to the Court of Protection to direct the Public Guardian to register the instrument.

'**if it appears to the Public Guardian**' (para 11(2))—This provision covers a situation where the instrument contains a provision such as a condition or restriction which prevents the instrument from operating as lasting power. The Public Guardian must then apply to the Court of Protection for the provision to be severed.

Deputy already appointed

12 (1) Sub-paragraph (2) applies if it appears to the Public Guardian that –

PART III

(a) there is a deputy appointed by the court for the donor, and

(b) the powers conferred on the deputy would, if the instrument were registered, to any extent conflict with the powers conferred on the attorney.

(2) The Public Guardian must not register the instrument unless the court directs him to do so.

Objection by donee or named person

13 (1) Sub-paragraph (2) applies if a donee or a named person –

(a) receives a notice under paragraph 6, 7 or 8 of an application for the registration of an instrument, and

(b) before the end of the prescribed period, gives notice to the Public Guardian of an objection to the registration on the ground that an event mentioned in section 13(3) or (6)(a) to (d) has occurred which has revoked the instrument.

(2) If the Public Guardian is satisfied that the ground for making the objection is established, he must not register the instrument unless the court, on the application of the person applying for the registration –

(a) is satisfied that the ground is not established, and

(b) directs the Public Guardian to register the instrument.

(3) Sub-paragraph (4) applies if a donee or a named person –

(a) receives a notice under paragraph 6, 7 or 8 of an application for the registration of an instrument, and

(b) before the end of the prescribed period –

(i) makes an application to the court objecting to the registration on a prescribed ground, and

(ii) notifies the Public Guardian of the application.

(4) The Public Guardian must not register the instrument unless the court directs him to do so.

'**gives notice to**' (para 13(1)(b))—Using Form LPA007.

'**makes an application to the court**' (para 13(3)(b)(i))—Using Form COP7.

'**notifies the Public Guardian**' (para 13(3)(b)(ii))—Using Form LPA008.

Objection by donor

14 (1) This paragraph applies if the donor –

(a) receives a notice under paragraph 8 of an application for the registration of an instrument, and

(b) before the end of the prescribed period, gives notice to the Public Guardian of an objection to the registration.

(2) The Public Guardian must not register the instrument unless the court, on the application of the donee or, if more than one, any of them –

(a) is satisfied that the donor lacks capacity to object to the registration, and

(b) directs the Public Guardian to register the instrument.

'**gives notice**' (para 14(1)(b))—Using Form LPA006.

Notification of registration

15 Where an instrument is registered under this Schedule, the Public Guardian must give notice of the fact in the prescribed form to –

   (a)   the donor, and
   (b)   the donee or, if more than one, each of them.

'the Public Guardian must give notice'—Form LPA004 set out in the Lasting Power of Attorney, Enduring Power of Attorney and Public Guardian Regulations 2007, SI 2007/1253, Sch 5.

Evidence of registration

16 (1) A document purporting to be an office copy of an instrument registered under this Schedule is, in any part of the United Kingdom, evidence of –

   (a)   the contents of the instrument, and
   (b)   the fact that it has been registered.

(2) Sub-paragraph (1) is without prejudice to –

   (a)   section 3 of the Powers of Attorney Act 1971 (proof by certified copy), and
   (b)   any other method of proof authorised by law.

PART III

PART 3
CANCELLATION OF REGISTRATION AND NOTIFICATION OF SEVERANCE

17 (1) The Public Guardian must cancel the registration of an instrument as a lasting power of attorney on being satisfied that the power has been revoked –

   (a)   as a result of the donor's bankruptcy, or
   (b)   on the occurrence of an event mentioned in section 13(6)(a) to (d).

(2) If the Public Guardian cancels the registration of an instrument he must notify –

   (a)   the donor, and
   (b)   the donee or, if more than one, each of them.

'cancel the registration' (para 17(1))—This power is expanded by the Lasting Power of Attorney, Enduring Power of Attorney and Public Guardian Regulations 2007, SI 2007/1253, reg 21, which covers revocation by the donor.

18 The court must direct the Public Guardian to cancel the registration of an instrument as a lasting power of attorney if it –

   (a)   determines under section 22(2)(a) that a requirement for creating the power was not met,
   (b)   determines under section 22(2)(b) that the power has been revoked or has otherwise come to an end, or
   (c)   revokes the power under section 22(4)(b) (fraud etc).

19 (1) Sub-paragraph (2) applies if the court determines under section 23(1) that a lasting power of attorney contains a provision which –

   (a)   is ineffective as part of a lasting power of attorney, or
   (b)   prevents the instrument from operating as a valid lasting power of attorney.

(2) The court must –

- (a) notify the Public Guardian that it has severed the provision, or
- (b) direct him to cancel the registration of the instrument as a lasting power of attorney.

20 On the cancellation of the registration of an instrument, the instrument and any office copies of it must be delivered up to the Public Guardian to be cancelled.

PART 4
RECORDS OF ALTERATIONS IN REGISTERED POWERS

Partial revocation or suspension of power as a result of bankruptcy

21 If in the case of a registered instrument it appears to the Public Guardian that under section 13 a lasting power of attorney is revoked, or suspended, in relation to the donor's property and affairs (but not in relation to other matters), the Public Guardian must attach to the instrument a note to that effect.

Termination of appointment of donee which does not revoke power

22 If in the case of a registered instrument it appears to the Public Guardian that an event has occurred –

- (a) which has terminated the appointment of the donee, but
- (b) which has not revoked the instrument,

the Public Guardian must attach to the instrument a note to that effect.

Replacement of donee

23 If in the case of a registered instrument it appears to the Public Guardian that the donee has been replaced under the terms of the instrument the Public Guardian must attach to the instrument a note to that effect.

Severance of ineffective provisions

24 If in the case of a registered instrument the court notifies the Public Guardian under paragraph 19(2)(a) that it has severed a provision of the instrument, the Public Guardian must attach to it a note to that effect.

Notification of alterations

25 If the Public Guardian attaches a note to an instrument under paragraph 21, 22, 23 or 24 he must give notice of the note to the donee or donees of the power (or, as the case may be, to the other donee or donees of the power).

[SCHEDULE 1A

PERSONS INELIGIBLE TO BE DEPRIVED OF LIBERTY BY THIS ACT

PART 1
INELIGIBLE PERSONS

Application

1 This Schedule applies for the purposes of –

    (a)   section 16A, and

    (b)   paragraph 17 of Schedule A1.

Amendment—Schedule 1A inserted by MHA 2007, s 50(6), Sch 8.

Scope of the Schedule—Schedule 1A sets out who is ineligible to be lawfully deprived of their liberty under the provisions of MCA 2005 either through a welfare order made under MCA 2005, s 16(2)(a) or a standard authorisation pursuant to MCA 2005, Sch A1, para 17. For a discussion of the issues involved, see *W PCT v TB (an adult by her litigation friend the Official Solicitor)* [2009] EWHC 1737 (Fam) and *GJ v The Foundation Trust* [2009] EWHC 2972 (Fam).

Determining ineligibility

2 A person ('P') is ineligible to be deprived of liberty by this Act ('ineligible') if –

    (a)   P falls within one of the cases set out in the second column of the following table, and

    (b)   the corresponding entry in the third column of the table – or the provision, or one of the provisions, referred to in that entry – provides that he is ineligible.

	Status of P	*Determination of ineligibility*
Case A	P is – (a) subject to the hospital treatment regime, and (b) detained in a hospital under that regime.	P is ineligible.
Case B	P is – (a) subject to the hospital treatment regime, but (b) not detained in a hospital under that regime.	See paragraphs 3 and 4.
Case C	P is subject to the community treatment regime.	See paragraphs 3 and 4.
Case D	P is subject to the guardianship regime.	See paragraphs 3 and 5.

Case E	P is – (a) within the scope of the Mental Health Act, but (b) not subject to any of the mental health regimes.	See paragraph 5.

Authorised course of action not in accordance with regime

3 (1) This paragraph applies in cases B, C and D in the table in paragraph 2.

(2) P is ineligible if the authorised course of action is not in accordance with a requirement which the relevant regime imposes.

(3) That includes any requirement as to where P is, or is not, to reside.

(4) The relevant regime is the mental health regime to which P is subject.

Treatment for mental disorder in a hospital

4 (1) This paragraph applies in cases B and C in the table in paragraph 2.

(2) P is ineligible if the relevant care or treatment consists in whole or in part of medical treatment for mental disorder in a hospital.

P objects to being a mental health patient etc

5 (1) This paragraph applies in cases D and E in the table in paragraph 2.

(2) P is ineligible if the following conditions are met.

(3) The first condition is that the relevant instrument authorises P to be a mental health patient.

(4) The second condition is that P objects –

(a) to being a mental health patient, or
(b) to being given some or all of the mental health treatment.

(5) The third condition is that a donee or deputy has not made a valid decision to consent to each matter to which P objects.

(6) In determining whether or not P objects to something, regard must be had to all the circumstances (so far as they are reasonably ascertainable), including the following –

(a) P's behaviour;
(b) P's wishes and feelings;
(c) P's views, beliefs and values.

(7) But regard is to be had to circumstances from the past only so far as it is still appropriate to have regard to them.

PART 2
INTERPRETATION

Application

6 This Part applies for the purposes of this Schedule.

Mental health regimes

7 The mental health regimes are –

(a) the hospital treatment regime,
(b) the community treatment regime, and
(c) the guardianship regime.

Hospital treatment regime

8 (1) P is subject to the hospital treatment regime if he is subject to –

(a) a hospital treatment obligation under the relevant enactment, or
(b) an obligation under another England and Wales enactment which has the same effect as a hospital treatment obligation.

(2) But where P is subject to any such obligation, he is to be regarded as not subject to the hospital treatment regime during any period when he is subject to the community treatment regime.

(3) A hospital treatment obligation is an application, order or direction of a kind listed in the first column of the following table.

(4) In relation to a hospital treatment obligation, the relevant enactment is the enactment in the Mental Health Act which is referred to in the corresponding entry in the second column of the following table.

Hospital treatment obligation	*Relevant enactment*
Application for admission for assessment	Section 2
Application for admission for assessment	Section 4
Application for admission for treatment	Section 3
Order for remand to hospital	Section 35
Order for remand to hospital	Section 36
Hospital order	Section 37
Interim hospital order	Section 38
Order for detention in hospital	Section 44
Hospital direction	Section 45A
Transfer direction	Section 47
Transfer direction	Section 48
Hospital order	Section 51

Community treatment regime

9 P is subject to the community treatment regime if he is subject to –

    (a)   a community treatment order under section 17A of the Mental Health Act, or

    (b)   an obligation under another England and Wales enactment which has the same effect as a community treatment order.

Guardianship regime

10 P is subject to the guardianship regime if he is subject to –

    (a)   a guardianship application under section 7 of the Mental Health Act,

    (b)   a guardianship order under section 37 of the Mental Health Act, or

    (c)   an obligation under another England and Wales enactment which has the same effect as a guardianship application or guardianship order.

England and Wales enactments

11 (1) An England and Wales enactment is an enactment which extends to England and Wales (whether or not it also extends elsewhere).

(2) It does not matter if the enactment is in the Mental Health Act or not.

P within scope of Mental Health Act

12 (1) P is within the scope of the Mental Health Act if –

    (a)   an application in respect of P could be made under section 2 or 3 of the Mental Health Act, and

    (b)   P could be detained in a hospital in pursuance of such an application, were one made.

(2) The following provisions of this paragraph apply when determining whether an application in respect of P could be made under section 2 or 3 of the Mental Health Act.

(3) If the grounds in section 2(2) of the Mental Health Act are met in P's case, it is to be assumed that the recommendations referred to in section 2(3) of that Act have been given.

(4) If the grounds in section 3(2) of the Mental Health Act are met in P's case, it is to be assumed that the recommendations referred to in section 3(3) of that Act have been given.

(5) In determining whether the ground in section 3(2)(c) of the Mental Health Act is met in P's case, it is to be assumed that the treatment referred to in section 3(2)(c) cannot be provided under this Act.

Authorised course of action, relevant care or treatment & relevant instrument

13 In a case where this Schedule applies for the purposes of section 16A –

'authorised course of action' means any course of action amounting to deprivation of liberty which the order under section 16(2)(a) authorises;
'relevant care or treatment' means any care or treatment which –

(a)   comprises, or forms part of, the authorised course of action, or
(b)   is to be given in connection with the authorised course of action;

'relevant instrument' means the order under section 16(2)(a).

14 In a case where this Schedule applies for the purposes of paragraph 17 of Schedule A1 –

'authorised course of action' means the accommodation of the relevant person in the relevant hospital or care home for the purpose of being given the relevant care or treatment;
'relevant care or treatment' has the same meaning as in Schedule A1;
'relevant instrument' means the standard authorisation under Schedule A1.

15 (1) This paragraph applies where the question whether a person is ineligible to be deprived of liberty by this Act is relevant to either of these decisions –

(a)   whether or not to include particular provision ('the proposed provision') in an order under section 16(2)(a);
(b)   whether or not to give a standard authorisation under Schedule A1.

(2) A reference in this Schedule to the authorised course of action or the relevant care or treatment is to be read as a reference to that thing as it would be if –

(a)   the proposed provision were included in the order, or
(b)   the standard authorisation were given.

(3) A reference in this Schedule to the relevant instrument is to be read as follows –

(a)   where the relevant instrument is an order under section 16(2)(a): as a reference to the order as it would be if the proposed provision were included in it;
(b)   where the relevant instrument is a standard authorisation: as a reference to the standard authorisation as it would be if it were given.

Expressions used in paragraph 5

16 (1) These expressions have the meanings given –

'donee' means a donee of a lasting power of attorney granted by P;
'mental health patient' means a person accommodated in a hospital for the purpose of being given medical treatment for mental disorder;
'mental health treatment' means the medical treatment for mental disorder referred to in the definition of 'mental health patient'.

(2) A decision of a donee or deputy is valid if it is made –

(a)   within the scope of his authority as donee or deputy, and
(b)   in accordance with Part 1 of this Act.

Expressions with same meaning as in Mental Health Act

17 (1) 'Hospital' has the same meaning as in Part 2 of the Mental Health Act.

(2) 'Medical treatment' has the same meaning as in the Mental Health Act.

PART III

(3) 'Mental disorder' has the same meaning as in Schedule A1 (see paragraph 14).]

Amendment—Schedule inserted by the Mental Health Act 2007, s 50(6), Sch 8. MCA 2005, Schs A1 and 1A and related provisions above (ss 4A–4B), which provide Deprivation of Liberty Safeguards under MCA 2005, were commenced on 1 April 2009. They are outlined in Part I, Chapter 6 of this book.

SCHEDULE 2
PROPERTY AND AFFAIRS: SUPPLEMENTARY PROVISIONS

Section 18(4)

Wills: general

1 Paragraphs 2 to 4 apply in relation to the execution of a will, by virtue of section 18, on behalf of P.

Provision that may be made in will

2 The will may make any provision (whether by disposing of property or exercising a power or otherwise) which could be made by a will executed by P if he had capacity to make it.

Wills: requirements relating to execution

3 (1) Sub-paragraph (2) applies if under section 16 the court makes an order or gives directions requiring or authorising a person ('the authorised person') to execute a will on behalf of P.

(2) Any will executed in pursuance of the order or direction –

    (a)   must state that it is signed by P acting by the authorised person,

    (b)   must be signed by the authorised person with the name of P and his own name, in the presence of two or more witnesses present at the same time,

    (c)   must be attested and subscribed by those witnesses in the presence of the authorised person, and

    (d)   must be sealed with the official seal of the court.

Wills: effect of execution

4 (1) This paragraph applies where a will is executed in accordance with paragraph 3.

(2) The Wills Act 1837 has effect in relation to the will as if it were signed by P by his own hand, except that –

    (a)   section 9 of the 1837 Act (requirements as to signing and attestation) does not apply, and

    (b)   in the subsequent provisions of the 1837 Act any reference to execution in the manner required by the previous provisions is to be read as a reference to execution in accordance with paragraph 3.

(3) The will has the same effect for all purposes as if –

(a) P had had the capacity to make a valid will, and

(b) the will had been executed by him in the manner required by the 1837 Act.

(4) But sub-paragraph (3) does not have effect in relation to the will –

(a) in so far as it disposes of immovable property outside England and Wales, or

(b) in so far as it relates to any other property or matter if, when the will is executed –

    (i) P is domiciled outside England and Wales, and

    (ii) the condition in sub-paragraph (5) is met.

(5) The condition is that, under the law of P's domicile, any question of his testamentary capacity would fall to be determined in accordance with the law of a place outside England and Wales.

Vesting orders ancillary to settlement etc

5 (1) If provision is made by virtue of section 18 for –

(a) the settlement of any property of P, or

(b) the exercise of a power vested in him of appointing trustees or retiring from a trust,

the court may also make as respects the property settled or the trust property such consequential vesting or other orders as the case may require.

(2) The power under sub-paragraph (1) includes, in the case of the exercise of such a power, any order which could have been made in such a case under Part 4 of the Trustee Act 1925.

Variation of settlements

6 (1) If a settlement has been made by virtue of section 18, the court may by order vary or revoke the settlement if –

(a) the settlement makes provision for its variation or revocation,

(b) the court is satisfied that a material fact was not disclosed when the settlement was made, or

(c) the court is satisfied that there has been a substantial change of circumstances.

(2) Any such order may give such consequential directions as the court thinks fit.

Vesting of stock in curator appointed outside England and Wales

7 (1) Sub-paragraph (2) applies if the court is satisfied –

(a) that under the law prevailing in a place outside England and Wales a person ('M') has been appointed to exercise powers in respect of the property or affairs of P on the ground (however formulated) that P lacks capacity to make decisions with respect to the management and administration of his property and affairs, and

(b) that, having regard to the nature of the appointment and to the circumstances of the case, it is expedient that the court should exercise its powers under this paragraph.

(2) The court may direct –

    (a)   any stocks standing in the name of P, or

    (b)   the right to receive dividends from the stocks,

to be transferred into M's name or otherwise dealt with as required by M, and may give such directions as the court thinks fit for dealing with accrued dividends from the stocks.

(3) 'Stocks' includes –

    (a)   shares, and

    (b)   any funds, annuity or security transferable in the books kept by any body corporate or unincorporated company or society or by an instrument of transfer either alone or accompanied by other formalities,

and 'dividends' is to be construed accordingly.

Preservation of interests in property disposed of on behalf of person lacking capacity

8 (1) Sub-paragraphs (2) and (3) apply if –

    (a)   P's property has been disposed of by virtue of section 18,

    (b)   under P's will or intestacy, or by a gift perfected or nomination taking effect on his death, any other person would have taken an interest in the property but for the disposal, and

    (c)   on P's death, any property belonging to P's estate represents the property disposed of.

(2) The person takes the same interest, if and so far as circumstances allow, in the property representing the property disposed of.

(3) If the property disposed of was real property, any property representing it is to be treated, so long as it remains part of P's estate, as if it were real property.

(4) The court may direct that, on a disposal of P's property –

    (a)   which is made by virtue of section 18, and

    (b)   which would apart from this paragraph result in the conversion of personal property into real property,

property representing the property disposed of is to be treated, so long as it remains P's property or forms part of P's estate, as if it were personal property.

(5) References in sub-paragraphs (1) to (4) to the disposal of property are to –

    (a)   the sale, exchange, charging of or other dealing (otherwise than by will) with property other than money;

    (b)   the removal of property from one place to another;

    (c)   the application of money in acquiring property;

    (d)   the transfer of money from one account to another;

and references to property representing property disposed of are to be construed accordingly and as including the result of successive disposals.

(6) The court may give such directions as appear to it necessary or expedient for the purpose of facilitating the operation of sub-paragraphs (1) to (3), including the carrying of money to a separate account and the transfer of property other than money.

9 (1) Sub-paragraph (2) applies if the court has ordered or directed the expenditure of money –

  (a) for carrying out permanent improvements on any of P's property, or
  (b) otherwise for the permanent benefit of any of P's property.

(2) The court may order that –

  (a) the whole of the money expended or to be expended, or
  (b) any part of it,

is to be a charge on the property either without interest or with interest at a specified rate.

(3) An order under sub-paragraph (2) may provide for excluding or restricting the operation of paragraph 8(1) to (3).

(4) A charge under sub-paragraph (2) may be made in favour of such person as may be just and, in particular, where the money charged is paid out of P's general estate, may be made in favour of a person as trustee for P.

(5) No charge under sub-paragraph (2) may confer any right of sale or foreclosure during P's lifetime.

Powers as patron of benefice

10 (1) Any functions which P has as patron of a benefice may be discharged only by a person ('R') appointed by the court.

(2) R must be an individual capable of appointment under section 8(1)(b) of the 1986 Measure (which provides for an individual able to make a declaration of communicant status, a clerk in Holy Orders, etc to be appointed to discharge a registered patron's functions).

(3) The 1986 Measure applies to R as it applies to an individual appointed by the registered patron of the benefice under section 8(1)(b) or (3) of that Measure to discharge his functions as patron.

(4) 'The 1986 Measure' means the Patronage (Benefices) Measure 1986 (No 3).

SCHEDULE 3

INTERNATIONAL PROTECTION OF ADULTS

Section 63

PART 1
PRELIMINARY

Introduction

1 This Part applies for the purposes of this Schedule.

The Convention

2 (1) 'Convention' means the Convention referred to in section 63.

(2) 'Convention country' means a country in which the Convention is in force.

(3) A reference to an Article or Chapter is to an Article or Chapter of the Convention.

(4) An expression which appears in this Schedule and in the Convention is to be construed in accordance with the Convention.

'Convention'—This is the Convention on the International Protection of Adults concluded at the Hague on 13 January 2000 (No 35) (see www.hcch.net). It came into force on 1 January 2009.

'Convention country'—The Convention countries are currentlythe UK (in relation to Scotland), Estonia (with effect from 1 November 2011), Finland, France, Germanyand Switzerland.

Countries, territories and nationals

3 (1) 'Country' includes a territory which has its own system of law.

(2) Where a country has more than one territory with its own system of law, a reference to the country, in relation to one of its nationals, is to the territory with which the national has the closer, or the closest, connection.

Adults with incapacity

4 'Adult' means a person who –

    (a)   as a result of an impairment or insufficiency of his personal faculties, cannot protect his interests, and

    (b)   has reached 16.

'Adult'—This contrasts with the Convention which is limited to persons who have reached 18.

Protective measures

5 (1) 'Protective measure' means a measure directed to the protection of the person or property of an adult; and it may deal in particular with any of the following –

    (a)   the determination of incapacity and the institution of a protective regime,

    (b)   placing the adult under the protection of an appropriate authority,

    (c)   guardianship, curatorship or any corresponding system,

    (d)   the designation and functions of a person having charge of the adult's person or property, or representing or otherwise helping him,

    (e)   placing the adult in a place where protection can be provided,

    (f)   administering, conserving or disposing of the adult's property,

    (g)   authorising a specific intervention for the protection of the person or property of the adult.

(2) Where a measure of like effect to a protective measure has been taken in relation to a person before he reaches 16, this Schedule applies to the measure in so far as it has effect in relation to him once he has reached 16.

Central Authority

6 (1) Any function under the Convention of a Central Authority is exercisable in England and Wales by the Lord Chancellor.

(2) A communication may be sent to the Central Authority in relation to England and Wales by sending it to the Lord Chancellor.

'Central Authority in relation to England and Wales'—No authority has yet been designated.

PART 2
JURISDICTION OF COMPETENT AUTHORITY

Scope of jurisdiction

7 (1) The court may exercise its functions under this Act (in so far as it cannot otherwise do so) in relation to –

- (a) an adult habitually resident in England and Wales,
- (b) an adult's property in England and Wales,
- (c) an adult present in England and Wales or who has property there, if the matter is urgent, or
- (d) an adult present in England and Wales, if a protective measure which is temporary and limited in its effect to England and Wales is proposed in relation to him.

(2) An adult present in England and Wales is to be treated for the purposes of this paragraph as habitually resident there if –

- (a) his habitual residence cannot be ascertained,
- (b) he is a refugee, or
- (c) he has been displaced as a result of disturbance in the country of his habitual residence.

8 (1) The court may also exercise its functions under this Act (in so far as it cannot otherwise do so) in relation to an adult if sub-paragraph (2) or (3) applies in relation to him.

(2) This sub-paragraph applies in relation to an adult if –

- (a) he is a British citizen,
- (b) he has a closer connection with England and Wales than with Scotland or Northern Ireland, and
- (c) Article 7 has, in relation to the matter concerned, been complied with.

(3) This sub-paragraph applies in relation to an adult if the Lord Chancellor, having consulted such persons as he considers appropriate, agrees to a request under Article 8 in relation to the adult.

'Article 7 has ... been complied with'—Under this Article if it is considered that the state of nationality is in a better position to assess the interests of one of its nationals habitually resident elsewhere (or if habitual residence cannot be established elsewhere) it is to advise the authorities of the state of habitual residence (or presence) before assuming jurisdiction to take protective measures, and shall not do so if that state has either taken or declined to take protective measures.

'a request under Article 8'—The authorities of the state of habitual residence (or presence where habitual residence cannot be established) may request the authorities of another state with which the person has a connection (which includes the state of nationality) to take protective measures.

Exercise of jurisdiction

9 (1) This paragraph applies where jurisdiction is exercisable under this Schedule in connection with a matter which involves a Convention country other than England and Wales.

(2) Any Article on which the jurisdiction is based applies in relation to the matter in so far as it involves the other country (and the court must, accordingly, comply with any duty conferred on it as a result).

(3) Article 12 also applies, so far as its provisions allow, in relation to the matter in so far as it involves the other country.

'**Article 12 applies**'—Under this Article once a state with jurisdiction under the Convention has taken protective measures they remain in force even if the circumstances on which the jurisdiction was taken have changed (e g a change of habitual residence) unless the authorities of a state which has jurisdiction have modified, replaced or terminated them.

10 A reference in this Schedule to the exercise of jurisdiction under this Schedule is to the exercise of functions under this Act as a result of this Part of this Schedule.

PART 3
APPLICABLE LAW

Applicable law

11 In exercising jurisdiction under this Schedule, the court may, if it thinks that the matter has a substantial connection with a country other than England and Wales, apply the law of that other country.

12 Where a protective measure is taken in one country but implemented in another, the conditions of implementation are governed by the law of the other country.

Lasting powers of attorney, etc

13 (1) If the donor of a lasting power is habitually resident in England and Wales at the time of granting the power, the law applicable to the existence, extent, modification or extinction of the power is –

  (a) the law of England and Wales, or
  (b) if he specifies in writing the law of a connected country for the purpose, that law.

(2) If he is habitually resident in another country at that time, but England and Wales is a connected country, the law applicable in that respect is –

  (a) the law of the other country, or
  (b) if he specifies in writing the law of England and Wales for the purpose, that law.

(3) A country is connected, in relation to the donor, if it is a country –

  (a) of which he is a national,
  (b) in which he was habitually resident, or
  (c) in which he has property.

(4) Where this paragraph applies as a result of sub-paragraph (3)(c), it applies only in relation to the property which the donor has in the connected country.

(5) The law applicable to the manner of the exercise of a lasting power is the law of the country where it is exercised.

(6) In this Part of this Schedule, 'lasting power' means –

    (a)   a lasting power of attorney (see section 9),

    (b)   an enduring power of attorney within the meaning of Schedule 4, or

    (c)   any other power of like effect.

14 (1) Where a lasting power is not exercised in a manner sufficient to guarantee the protection of the person or property of the donor, the court, in exercising jurisdiction under this Schedule, may disapply or modify the power.

(2) Where, in accordance with this Part of this Schedule, the law applicable to the power is, in one or more respects, that of a country other than England and Wales, the court must, so far as possible, have regard to the law of the other country in that respect (or those respects).

'Donor'—It should be noted that the provisions of paragraph 14 are not limited to Adults as in the Convention. These provisions unlike the remainder of Sch 3 do therefore apply whether or not the Donor has an impairment or insufficiency of personal faculties.

15 Regulations may provide for Schedule 1 (lasting powers of attorney: formalities) to apply with modifications in relation to a lasting power which comes within paragraph 13(6)(c) above.

'Regulations'—No specific Regulations relating to this Schedule have yet been made.

Protection of third parties

16 (1) This paragraph applies where a person (a 'representative') in purported exercise of an authority to act on behalf of an adult enters into a transaction with a third party.

(2) The validity of the transaction may not be questioned in proceedings, nor may the third party be held liable, merely because –

    (a)   where the representative and third party are in England and Wales when entering into the transaction, sub-paragraph (3) applies;

    (b)   where they are in another country at that time, sub-paragraph (4) applies.

(3) This sub-paragraph applies if –

    (a)   the law applicable to the authority in one or more respects is, as a result of this Schedule, the law of a country other than England and Wales, and

    (b)   the representative is not entitled to exercise the authority in that respect (or those respects) under the law of that other country.

(4) This sub-paragraph applies if –

    (a)   the law applicable to the authority in one or more respects is, as a result of this Part of this Schedule, the law of England and Wales, and

    (b)   the representative is not entitled to exercise the authority in that respect (or those respects) under that law.

PART III

(5) This paragraph does not apply if the third party knew or ought to have known that the applicable law was –

    (a)   in a case within sub-paragraph (3), the law of the other country;

    (b)   in a case within sub-paragraph (4), the law of England and Wales.

Mandatory rules

17 Where the court is entitled to exercise jurisdiction under this Schedule, the mandatory provisions of the law of England and Wales apply, regardless of any system of law which would otherwise apply in relation to the matter.

Public policy

18 Nothing in this Part of this Schedule requires or enables the application in England and Wales of a provision of the law of another country if its application would be manifestly contrary to public policy.

'Public Policy'—The judgment in *Re MN* [2010] EWHC 1926 concludes that the best interests test and other principles of s1 are not matters of public policy.

PART 4
RECOGNITION AND ENFORCEMENT

Recognition

19 (1) A protective measure taken in relation to an adult under the law of a country other than England and Wales is to be recognised in England and Wales if it was taken on the ground that the adult is habitually resident in the other country.

(2) A protective measure taken in relation to an adult under the law of a Convention country other than England and Wales is to be recognised in England and Wales if it was taken on a ground mentioned in Chapter 2 (jurisdiction).

(3) But the court may disapply this paragraph in relation to a measure if it thinks that –

    (a)   the case in which the measure was taken was not urgent,

    (b)   the adult was not given an opportunity to be heard, and

    (c)   that omission amounted to a breach of natural justice.

(4) It may also disapply this paragraph in relation to a measure if it thinks that –

    (a)   recognition of the measure would be manifestly contrary to public policy,

    (b)   the measure would be inconsistent with a mandatory provision of the law of England and Wales, or

    (c)   the measure is inconsistent with one subsequently taken, or recognised, in England and Wales in relation to the adult.

(5) And the court may disapply this paragraph in relation to a measure taken under the law of a Convention country in a matter to which Article 33 applies, if the court thinks that that Article has not been complied with in connection with that matter.

'Mandatory provision'—The judgment in *Re MN* [2010] EWHC 1926 concludes that the best interests test and other principles of s1 are not mandatory provisions.

'**Article 33**'—Under this Article it is possible for the authorities in one contracting state to place someone in an establishment in another contracting state. The authorities in the requesting state must first consult the authorities in that contracting state and may not make the placement if that state has indicated opposition within a reasonable time. See note to Sch 3, para 35.

20 (1) An interested person may apply to the court for a declaration as to whether a protective measure taken under the law of a country other than England and Wales is to be recognised in England and Wales.

(2) No permission is required for an application to the court under this paragraph.

21 For the purposes of paragraphs 19 and 20, any finding of fact relied on when the measure was taken is conclusive.

Enforcement

22 (1) An interested person may apply to the court for a declaration as to whether a protective measure taken under the law of, and enforceable in, a country other than England and Wales is enforceable, or to be registered, in England and Wales in accordance with Court of Protection Rules.

(2) The court must make the declaration if –

  (a)   the measure comes within sub-paragraph (1) or (2) of paragraph 19, and
  (b)   the paragraph is not disapplied in relation to it as a result of sub-paragraph (3), (4) or (5).

(3) A measure to which a declaration under this paragraph relates is enforceable in England and Wales as if it were a measure of like effect taken by the court.

Measures taken in relation to those aged under 16

23 (1) This paragraph applies where –

  (a)   provision giving effect to, or otherwise deriving from, the Convention in a country other than England and Wales applies in relation to a person who has not reached 16, and
  (b)   a measure is taken in relation to that person in reliance on that provision.

(2) This Part of this Schedule applies in relation to that measure as it applies in relation to a protective measure taken in relation to an adult under the law of a Convention country other than England and Wales.

Supplementary

24 The court may not review the merits of a measure taken outside England and Wales except to establish whether the measure complies with this Schedule in so far as it is, as a result of this Schedule, required to do so.

25 Court of Protection Rules may make provision about an application under paragraph 20 or 22.

'**Court of Protection Rules**'—No special provisions have been made in the Court of Protection Rules 2007, SI 2007/1744.

PART III

PART 5
CO-OPERATION

Proposal for cross-border placement

26 (1) This paragraph applies where a public authority proposes to place an adult in an establishment in a Convention country other than England and Wales.

(2) The public authority must consult an appropriate authority in that other country about the proposed placement and, for that purpose, must send it –

    (a)   a report on the adult, and
    (b)   a statement of its reasons for the proposed placement.

(3) If the appropriate authority in the other country opposes the proposed placement within a reasonable time, the public authority may not proceed with it.

27 A proposal received by a public authority under Article 33 in relation to an adult is to proceed unless the authority opposes it within a reasonable time.

'**Article 33**'—See note under Sch 3, para 19.

Adult in danger etc

28 (1) This paragraph applies if a public authority is told that an adult –

    (a)   who is in serious danger, and
    (b)   in relation to whom the public authority has taken, or is considering taking, protective measures,

is, or has become resident, in a Convention country other than England and Wales.

(2) The public authority must tell an appropriate authority in that other country about –

    (a)   the danger, and
    (b)   the measures taken or under consideration.

29 A public authority may not request from, or send to, an appropriate authority in a Convention country information in accordance with Chapter 5 (co-operation) in relation to an adult if it thinks that doing so –

    (a)   would be likely to endanger the adult or his property, or
    (b)   would amount to a serious threat to the liberty or life of a member of the adult's family.

'**Chapter 5**'—See text of Convention (Arts 28–36) for the duties placed under the Convention of co-operation between contracting states to achieve the purposes of the Convention.

PART 6
GENERAL

Certificates

30 A certificate given under Article 38 by an authority in a Convention country other than England and Wales is, unless the contrary is shown, proof of the matters contained in it.

'**Article 38**'—This Article provides for the authorities of a contracting state where a measure of protection has been taken or a power of representation confirmed to issue to the person entrusted with the protection of the adult's person or property a certificate indicating the capacity in which that person is entitled to act and the powers conferred. Sadly Article 38 Certificates are not currently available in England & Wales.

Powers to make further provision as to private international law

31 Her Majesty may by Order in Council confer on the Lord Chancellor, the court or another public authority functions for enabling the Convention to be given effect in England and Wales.

'**Order in Council**'—No Order has yet been made.

32 (1) Regulations may make provision –

(a) giving further effect to the Convention, or
(b) otherwise about the private international law of England and Wales in relation to the protection of adults.

(2) The regulations may –

(a) confer functions on the court or another public authority;
(b) amend this Schedule;
(c) provide for this Schedule to apply with specified modifications;
(d) make provision about countries other than Convention countries.

'**Regulations**'—No Regulations have yet been made.

Exceptions

33 Nothing in this Schedule applies, and no provision made under paragraph 32 is to apply, to any matter to which the Convention, as a result of Article 4, does not apply.

'**Article 4**'—Article 4 sets out a list of matters to which the Convention does not apply, namely maintenance obligations, formation, annulment or dissolution of marriage (or similar relationship), property regimes in respect of marriage, trusts or succession, social security, public health measures, criminal sanctions, asylum or immigration or public safety. This is an extremely complex area of the law. Professor Lagarde's report is a helpful resource in understanding some of these complexities. www.hcch.

Regulations and orders

34 A reference in this Schedule to regulations or an order (other than an Order in Council) is to regulations or an order made for the purposes of this Schedule by the Lord Chancellor.

Commencement

35 The following provisions of this Schedule have effect only if the Convention is in force in accordance with Article 57 –

(a) paragraph 8,
(b) paragraph 9,

(c) paragraph 19(2) and (5),
(d) Part 5,
(e) paragraph 30.

If the Convention is in force in accordance with Article 57—Most experts agree that the Convention came into force in accordance with Article 57 on 1 January 2009 when the Convention came into force however some argue that the Convention has not come into force in England & Wales and accordingly that these paragraphs and Part 5 do not yet have effect.

Scope of provision—These paragraphs and Part of the Schedule listed came into force on 1 January 2009 when the Convention came into force and it is thoughtcan be used in a case arising in England or Wales with a Scottish or other Convention country element.

SCHEDULE 4

PROVISIONS APPLYING TO EXISTING ENDURING POWERS OF ATTORNEY

Section 66(3)

PART 1
ENDURING POWERS OF ATTORNEY

Enduring power of attorney to survive mental incapacity of donor

1 (1) Where an individual has created a power of attorney which is an enduring power within the meaning of this Schedule –

(a) the power is not revoked by any subsequent mental incapacity of his,
(b) upon such incapacity supervening, the donee of the power may not do anything under the authority of the power except as provided by sub-paragraph (2) unless or until the instrument creating the power is registered under paragraph 13, and
(c) if and so long as paragraph (b) operates to suspend the donee's authority to act under the power, section 5 of the Powers of Attorney Act 1971 (protection of donee and third persons), so far as applicable, applies as if the power had been revoked by the donor's mental incapacity,

and, accordingly, section 1 of this Act does not apply.

(2) Despite sub-paragraph (1)(b), where the attorney has made an application for registration of the instrument then, until it is registered, the attorney may take action under the power –

(a) to maintain the donor or prevent loss to his estate, or
(b) to maintain himself or other persons in so far as paragraph 3(2) permits him to do so.

(3) Where the attorney purports to act as provided by sub-paragraph (2) then, in favour of a person who deals with him without knowledge that the attorney is acting otherwise than in accordance with sub-paragraph (2)(a) or (b), the transaction between them is as valid as if the attorney were acting in accordance with sub-paragraph (2)(a) or (b).

Scope of provision—Schedule 4 incorporates the provisions of the Enduring Powers of Attorney Act 1985, which is repealed by s 66(1)(b) so that the same provisions apply to instruments made in accordance with that Act, but within the framework of the MCA 2005.

'**enduring power of attorney**' (para 1(1))—That is an enduring power of attorney as defined by para 2 of this Schedule and made prior to 1 October 2007.

'**an enduring power within the meaning of this Schedule**' (para 1(1))—That is an enduring power of attorney created under the Enduring Powers of Attorney Act 1985 prior to 1 October 2007 (and see Sch 4, para 2). This Schedule sets out the regime to apply to enduring powers of attorney made before this date in replacement of the provisions of the 1985 Act.

'**section 5 of the Powers of Attorney Act 1971**' (para 1(1)(c))—Provides that a donee who acts in pursuance of a power when it has been revoked shall not incur any liability by reason of the revocation if not aware of the revocation; and that a transaction with a third party dealing with the donee without knowledge of the revocation shall be as valid as if the power had been in existence. It also provides a mechanism for a purchaser to establish conclusive proof that he or she was unaware of a revocation.

'**section 1 of this Act does not apply**' (para 1(1))—That is the principles which otherwise apply for the purposes of the Act, such as in relation to lasting powers of attorney.

Characteristics of an enduring power of attorney

2 (1) Subject to sub-paragraphs (5) and (6) and paragraph 20, a power of attorney is an enduring power within the meaning of this Schedule if the instrument which creates the power –

(a)   is in the prescribed form,
(b)   was executed in the prescribed manner by the donor and the attorney, and
(c)   incorporated at the time of execution by the donor the prescribed explanatory information.

(2) In this paragraph, 'prescribed' means prescribed by such of the following regulations as applied when the instrument was executed –

(a)   the Enduring Powers of Attorney (Prescribed Form) Regulations 1986,
(b)   the Enduring Powers of Attorney (Prescribed Form) Regulations 1987,
(c)   the Enduring Powers of Attorney (Prescribed Form) Regulations 1990,
(d)   the Enduring Powers of Attorney (Welsh Language Prescribed Form) Regulations 2000.

(3) An instrument in the prescribed form purporting to have been executed in the prescribed manner is to be taken, in the absence of evidence to the contrary, to be a document which incorporated at the time of execution by the donor the prescribed explanatory information.

(4) If an instrument differs in an immaterial respect in form or mode of expression from the prescribed form it is to be treated as sufficient in point of form and expression.

(5) A power of attorney cannot be an enduring power unless, when he executes the instrument creating it, the attorney is –

(a)   an individual who has reached 18 and is not bankrupt, or
(b)   a trust corporation.

(6) A power of attorney which gives the attorney a right to appoint a substitute or successor cannot be an enduring power.

(7) An enduring power is revoked by the bankruptcy of the donor or attorney.

(8) But where the donor or attorney is bankrupt merely because an interim bankruptcy restrictions order has effect in respect of him, the power is suspended for so long as the order has effect.

(9) An enduring power is revoked if the court –

    (a)   exercises a power under sections 16 to 20 in relation to the donor, and

    (b)   directs that the enduring power is to be revoked.

(10) No disclaimer of an enduring power, whether by deed or otherwise, is valid unless and until the attorney gives notice of it to the donor or, where paragraph 4(6) or 15(1) applies, to the Public Guardian.

'**the prescribed explanatory information**' (para 2(3))—Mamely the explanatory information as prescribed in whichever of the above regulations apply.

'**a power under sections16 to 20**' (para 2(9))—That is the Court makes a decision for the incapacitated person or appoints a deputy.

'**where paragraph 4(6) or 15(1) applies**' (para 2(10))—That is once the attorney has reason to believe that the donor is or is becoming mentally incapable or after the power has been registered.

Scope of authority etc of attorney under enduring power

3 (1) If the instrument which creates an enduring power of attorney is expressed to confer general authority on the attorney, the instrument operates to confer, subject to –

    (a)   the restriction imposed by sub-paragraph (3), and

    (b)   any conditions or restrictions contained in the instrument,

authority to do on behalf of the donor anything which the donor could lawfully do by an attorney at the time when the donor executed the instrument.

(2) Subject to any conditions or restrictions contained in the instrument, an attorney under an enduring power, whether general or limited, may (without obtaining any consent) act under the power so as to benefit himself or other persons than the donor to the following extent but no further –

    (a)   he may so act in relation to himself or in relation to any other person if the donor might be expected to provide for his or that person's needs respectively, and

    (b)   he may do whatever the donor might be expected to do to meet those needs.

(3) Without prejudice to sub-paragraph (2) but subject to any conditions or restrictions contained in the instrument, an attorney under an enduring power, whether general or limited, may (without obtaining any consent) dispose of the property of the donor by way of gift to the following extent but no further –

    (a)   he may make gifts of a seasonal nature or at a time, or on an anniversary, of a birth, a marriage or the formation of a civil partnership, to persons (including himself) who are related to or connected with the donor, and

    (b)   he may make gifts to any charity to whom the donor made or might be expected to make gifts,

provided that the value of each such gift is not unreasonable having regard to all the circumstances and in particular the size of the donor's estate.

'**provide for … that person's needs**' (para 3(2)(a))—In contrast to the donee of a lasting power of attorney, an attorney acting under an enduring power of attorney has an express power to provide for the needs of the attorney or a third party that the donor might be expected to provide for. See Chapter 3 at **3.35** and **3.36**.

PART 2
ACTION ON ACTUAL OR IMPENDING INCAPACITY OF DONOR

Duties of attorney in event of actual or impending incapacity of donor

4 (1) Sub-paragraphs (2) to (6) apply if the attorney under an enduring power has reason to believe that the donor is or is becoming mentally incapable.

(2) The attorney must, as soon as practicable, make an application to the Public Guardian for the registration of the instrument creating the power.

(3) Before making an application for registration the attorney must comply with the provisions as to notice set out in Part 3 of this Schedule.

(4) An application for registration –

    (a) must be made in the prescribed form, and
    (b) must contain such statements as may be prescribed.

(5) The attorney –

    (a) may, before making an application for the registration of the instrument, refer to the court for its determination any question as to the validity of the power, and
    (b) must comply with any direction given to him by the court on that determination.

(6) No disclaimer of the power is valid unless and until the attorney gives notice of it to the Public Guardian; and the Public Guardian must notify the donor if he receives a notice under this sub-paragraph.

(7) A person who, in an application for registration, makes a statement which he knows to be false in a material particular is guilty of an offence and is liable –

    (a) on summary conviction, to imprisonment for a term not exceeding 12 months or a fine not exceeding the statutory maximum or both;
    (b) on conviction on indictment, to imprisonment for a term not exceeding 2 years or a fine or both.

(8) In this paragraph, 'prescribed' means prescribed by regulations made for the purposes of this Schedule by the Lord Chancellor.

'mentally incapable' (para 4(1))—Defined by para 23(1) as meaning 'in relation to any person, that he is incapable by reason of mental disorder ... of managing and administering his property and affairs and "mentally capable" and "mental capacity" are to be construed accordingly'. The definition of 'mental disorder' is still supplied by MHA 1983, s 1(2) (for these purposes without amendment by MHA 2007) as meaning 'mental illness, arrested or incomplete development of mind, psychopathic disorder and any other disorder or disability of mind'.

'prescribed form/statements as may be prescribed' (para 4(4))—See the Lasting Powers of Attorney, Enduring Powers of Attorney and Public Guardian Regulations 2007, SI 2007/1253, Sch 8.

'prescribed by regulations' (para 4(8))—See the Lasting Powers of Attorney, Enduring Powers of Attorney and Public Guardian Regulations 2007, SI 2007/1253, as amended by the Public Guardian (Fees, etc) Regulations 2007, SI 2007/2051; the Lasting Powers of Attorney, Enduring Powers of Attorney and Public Guardian (Amendment) Regulations 2007, SI 2007/2161 and the Lasting Powers of Attorney, Enduring Powers of Attorney and Public Guardian (Amendment) Regulations 2009, SI 2009/1884.

PART III

PART 3

NOTIFICATION PRIOR TO REGISTRATION

Duty to give notice to relatives

5 Subject to paragraph 7, before making an application for registration the attorney must give notice of his intention to do so to all those persons (if any) who are entitled to receive notice by virtue of paragraph 6.

6 (1) Subject to sub-paragraphs (2) to (4), persons of the following classes ('relatives') are entitled to receive notice under paragraph 5 –

    (a)   the donor's spouse or civil partner,

    (b)   the donor's children,

    (c)   the donor's parents,

    (d)   the donor's brothers and sisters, whether of the whole or half blood,

    (e)   the widow, widower or surviving civil partner of a child of the donor,

    (f)   the donor's grandchildren,

    (g)   the children of the donor's brothers and sisters of the whole blood,

    (h)   the children of the donor's brothers and sisters of the half blood,

    (i)   the donor's uncles and aunts of the whole blood,

    (j)   the children of the donor's uncles and aunts of the whole blood.

(2) A person is not entitled to receive notice under paragraph 5 if –

    (a)   his name or address is not known to the attorney and cannot be reasonably ascertained by him, or

    (b)   the attorney has reason to believe that he has not reached 18 or is mentally incapable.

(3) Except where sub-paragraph (4) applies –

    (a)   no more than 3 persons are entitled to receive notice under paragraph 5, and

    (b)   in determining the persons who are so entitled, persons falling within the class in sub-paragraph (1)(a) are to be preferred to persons falling within the class in sub-paragraph (1)(b), those falling within the class in sub-paragraph (1)(b) are to be preferred to those falling within the class in sub-paragraph (1)(c), and so on.

(4) Despite the limit of 3 specified in sub-paragraph (3), where –

    (a)   there is more than one person falling within any of classes (a) to (j) of sub-paragraph (1), and

    (b)   at least one of those persons would be entitled to receive notice under paragraph 5,

then, subject to sub-paragraph (2), all the persons falling within that class are entitled to receive notice under paragraph 5.

7 (1) An attorney is not required to give notice under paragraph 5 –

    (a)   to himself, or

    (b)   to any other attorney under the power who is joining in making the application,

even though he or, as the case may be, the other attorney is entitled to receive notice by virtue of paragraph 6.

(2) In the case of any person who is entitled to receive notice by virtue of paragraph 6, the attorney, before applying for registration, may make an application to the court to be dispensed from the requirement to give him notice; and the court must grant the application if it is satisfied –

(a) that it would be undesirable or impracticable for the attorney to give him notice, or

(b) that no useful purpose is likely to be served by giving him notice.

Duty to give notice to donor

8 (1) Subject to sub-paragraph (2), before making an application for registration the attorney must give notice of his intention to do so to the donor.

(2) Paragraph 7(2) applies in relation to the donor as it applies in relation to a person who is entitled to receive notice under paragraph 5.

Contents of notices

9 A notice to relatives under this Part of this Schedule must –

(a) be in the prescribed form,

(b) state that the attorney proposes to make an application to the Public Guardian for the registration of the instrument creating the enduring power in question,

(c) inform the person to whom it is given of his right to object to the registration under paragraph 13(4), and

(d) specify, as the grounds on which an objection to registration may be made, the grounds set out in paragraph 13(9).

'notice ... in the prescribed form'—See the Lasting Powers of Attorney, Enduring Powers of Attorney and Public Guardian Regulations 2007, SI 2007/1253, Sch 7, as amended by the Public Guardian (Fees, etc) Regulations 2007, SI 2007/2051.

10 A notice to the donor under this Part of this Schedule –

(a) must be in the prescribed form,

(b) must contain the statement mentioned in paragraph 9(b), and

(c) must inform the donor that, while the instrument remains registered, any revocation of the power by him will be ineffective unless and until the revocation is confirmed by the court.

'notice ... in the prescribed form'—See the Lasting Powers of Attorney, Enduring Powers of Attorney and Public Guardian Regulations 2007, SI 2007/1253, Sch 7, as amended by the Public Guardian (Fees, etc) Regulations 2007, SI 2007/2051.

Duty to give notice to other attorneys

11 (1) Subject to sub-paragraph (2), before making an application for registration an attorney under a joint and several power must give notice of his intention to do so to any other attorney under the power who is not joining in making the application; and paragraphs 7(2) and 9 apply in relation to attorneys entitled to receive notice by virtue of this paragraph as they apply in relation to persons entitled to receive notice by virtue of paragraph 6.

PART III

(2) An attorney is not entitled to receive notice by virtue of this paragraph if –

    (a)   his address is not known to the applying attorney and cannot reasonably be ascertained by him, or

    (b)   the applying attorney has reason to believe that he has not reached 18 or is mentally incapable.

Supplementary

12 Despite section 7 of the Interpretation Act 1978 (construction of references to service by post), for the purposes of this Part of this Schedule a notice given by post is to be regarded as given on the date on which it was posted.

'Despite section 7 of the Interpretation Act 1978'—That is the default position that a document served by post is deemed to have been effected at the time at which it would be delivered in the ordinary course of post is disapplied.

PART 4
REGISTRATION

Registration of instrument creating power

13 (1) If an application is made in accordance with paragraph 4(3) and (4) the Public Guardian must, subject to the provisions of this paragraph, register the instrument to which the application relates.

(2) If it appears to the Public Guardian that –

    (a)   there is a deputy appointed for the donor of the power created by the instrument, and

    (b)   the powers conferred on the deputy would, if the instrument were registered, to any extent conflict with the powers conferred on the attorney,

the Public Guardian must not register the instrument except in accordance with the court's directions.

(3) The court may, on the application of the attorney, direct the Public Guardian to register an instrument even though notice has not been given as required by paragraph 4(3) and Part 3 of this Schedule to a person entitled to receive it, if the court is satisfied –

    (a)   that it was undesirable or impracticable for the attorney to give notice to that person, or

    (b)   that no useful purpose is likely to be served by giving him notice.

(4) Sub-paragraph (5) applies if, before the end of the period of 5 weeks beginning with the date (or the latest date) on which the attorney gave notice under paragraph 5 of an application for registration, the Public Guardian receives a valid notice of objection to the registration from a person entitled to notice of the application.

(5) The Public Guardian must not register the instrument except in accordance with the court's directions.

(6) Sub-paragraph (7) applies if, in the case of an application for registration –

    (a)   it appears from the application that there is no one to whom notice has been given under paragraph 5, or

    (b)   the Public Guardian has reason to believe that appropriate inquiries might bring to light evidence on which he could be satisfied that one of the grounds of objection set out in sub-paragraph (9) was established.

(7) The Public Guardian –

(a) must not register the instrument, and

(b) must undertake such inquiries as he thinks appropriate in all the circumstances.

(8) If, having complied with sub-paragraph (7)(b), the Public Guardian is satisfied that one of the grounds of objection set out in sub-paragraph (9) is established –

(a) the attorney may apply to the court for directions, and

(b) the Public Guardian must not register the instrument except in accordance with the court's directions.

(9) A notice of objection under this paragraph is valid if made on one or more of the following grounds –

(a) that the power purported to have been created by the instrument was not valid as an enduring power of attorney,

(b) that the power created by the instrument no longer subsists,

(c) that the application is premature because the donor is not yet becoming mentally incapable,

(d) that fraud or undue pressure was used to induce the donor to create the power,

(e) that, having regard to all the circumstances and in particular the attorney's relationship to or connection with the donor, the attorney is unsuitable to be the donor's attorney.

(10) If any of those grounds is established to the satisfaction of the court it must direct the Public Guardian not to register the instrument, but if not so satisfied it must direct its registration.

(11) If the court directs the Public Guardian not to register an instrument because it is satisfied that the ground in sub-paragraph (9)(d) or (e) is established, it must by order revoke the power created by the instrument.

(12) If the court directs the Public Guardian not to register an instrument because it is satisfied that any ground in sub-paragraph (9) except that in paragraph (c) is established, the instrument must be delivered up to be cancelled unless the court otherwise directs.

Register of enduring powers

14 The Public Guardian has the function of establishing and maintaining a register of enduring powers for the purposes of this Schedule.

PART 5
LEGAL POSITION AFTER REGISTRATION

Effect and proof of registration

15 (1) The effect of the registration of an instrument under paragraph 13 is that –

(a) no revocation of the power by the donor is valid unless and until the court confirms the revocation under paragraph 16(3);

PART III

(b) no disclaimer of the power is valid unless and until the attorney gives notice of it to the Public Guardian;

(c) the donor may not extend or restrict the scope of the authority conferred by the instrument and no instruction or consent given by him after registration, in the case of a consent, confers any right and, in the case of an instruction, imposes or confers any obligation or right on or creates any liability of the attorney or other persons having notice of the instruction or consent.

(2) Sub-paragraph (1) applies for so long as the instrument is registered under paragraph 13 whether or not the donor is for the time being mentally incapable.

(3) A document purporting to be an office copy of an instrument registered under this Schedule is, in any part of the United Kingdom, evidence of –

(a) the contents of the instrument, and

(b) the fact that it has been so registered.

(4) Sub-paragraph (3) is without prejudice to section 3 of the Powers of Attorney Act 1971 (proof by certified copies) and to any other method of proof authorised by law.

'**section 3 of the Powers of Attorney Act 1971**' (para 15(4))—Provides that that the contents of an instrument creating a power of attorney may be proved by means of a copy which is certified by the donor, a solicitor, notary public or stockbroker that it is a true and complete copy of the original.

Functions of court with regard to registered power

16 (1) Where an instrument has been registered under paragraph 13, the court has the following functions with respect to the power and the donor of and the attorney appointed to act under the power.

(2) The court may –

(a) determine any question as to the meaning or effect of the instrument;

(b) give directions with respect to –
   (i) the management or disposal by the attorney of the property and affairs of the donor;
   (ii) the rendering of accounts by the attorney and the production of the records kept by him for the purpose;
   (iii) the remuneration or expenses of the attorney whether or not in default of or in accordance with any provision made by the instrument, including directions for the repayment of excessive or the payment of additional remuneration;

(c) require the attorney to supply information or produce documents or things in his possession as attorney;

(d) give any consent or authorisation to act which the attorney would have to obtain from a mentally capable donor;

(e) authorise the attorney to act so as to benefit himself or other persons than the donor otherwise than in accordance with paragraph 3(2) and (3) (but subject to any conditions or restrictions contained in the instrument);

(f) relieve the attorney wholly or partly from any liability which he has or may have incurred on account of a breach of his duties as attorney.

(3) On application made for the purpose by or on behalf of the donor, the court must confirm the revocation of the power if satisfied that the donor –

(a) has done whatever is necessary in law to effect an express revocation of the power, and

(b) was mentally capable of revoking a power of attorney when he did so (whether or not he is so when the court considers the application).

(4) The court must direct the Public Guardian to cancel the registration of an instrument registered under paragraph 13 in any of the following circumstances –

(a) on confirming the revocation of the power under sub-paragraph (3),
(b) on directing under paragraph 2(9)(b) that the power is to be revoked,
(c) on being satisfied that the donor is and is likely to remain mentally capable,
(d) on being satisfied that the power has expired or has been revoked by the mental incapacity of the attorney,
(e) on being satisfied that the power was not a valid and subsisting enduring power when registration was effected,
(f) on being satisfied that fraud or undue pressure was used to induce the donor to create the power,
(g) on being satisfied that, having regard to all the circumstances and in particular the attorney's relationship to or connection with the donor, the attorney is unsuitable to be the donor's attorney.

(5) If the court directs the Public Guardian to cancel the registration of an instrument on being satisfied of the matters specified in sub-paragraph (4)(f) or (g) it must by order revoke the power created by the instrument.

(6) If the court directs the cancellation of the registration of an instrument under sub-paragraph (4) except paragraph (c) the instrument must be delivered up to the Public Guardian to be cancelled, unless the court otherwise directs.

Cancellation of registration by Public Guardian

17 The Public Guardian must cancel the registration of an instrument creating an enduring power of attorney –

(a) on receipt of a disclaimer signed by the attorney;
(b) if satisfied that the power has been revoked by the death or bankruptcy of the donor or attorney or, if the attorney is a body corporate, by its winding up or dissolution;
(c) on receipt of notification from the court that the court has revoked the power;
(d) on confirmation from the court that the donor has revoked the power.

PART 6
PROTECTION OF ATTORNEY AND THIRD PARTIES

Protection of attorney and third persons where power is invalid or revoked

18 (1) Sub-paragraphs (2) and (3) apply where an instrument which did not create a valid power of attorney has been registered under paragraph 13 (whether or not the registration has been cancelled at the time of the act or transaction in question).

(2) An attorney who acts in pursuance of the power does not incur any liability (either to the donor or to any other person) because of the non-existence of the power unless at the time of acting he knows –

(a) that the instrument did not create a valid enduring power,
(b) that an event has occurred which, if the instrument had created a valid enduring power, would have had the effect of revoking the power, or

(c)   that, if the instrument had created a valid enduring power, the power would have expired before that time.

(3) Any transaction between the attorney and another person is, in favour of that person, as valid as if the power had then been in existence, unless at the time of the transaction that person has knowledge of any of the matters mentioned in sub-paragraph (2).

(4) If the interest of a purchaser depends on whether a transaction between the attorney and another person was valid by virtue of sub-paragraph (3), it is conclusively presumed in favour of the purchaser that the transaction was valid if –

(a)   the transaction between that person and the attorney was completed within 12 months of the date on which the instrument was registered, or
(b)   that person makes a statutory declaration, before or within 3 months after the completion of the purchase, that he had no reason at the time of the transaction to doubt that the attorney had authority to dispose of the property which was the subject of the transaction.

(5) For the purposes of section 5 of the Powers of Attorney Act 1971 (protection where power is revoked) in its application to an enduring power the revocation of which by the donor is by virtue of paragraph 15 invalid unless and until confirmed by the court under paragraph 16 –

(a)   knowledge of the confirmation of the revocation is knowledge of the revocation of the power, but
(b)   knowledge of the unconfirmed revocation is not.

'**section 5 of the Powers of Attorney Act 1971**' (para 18(5))—See note to Sch 4, para 1.

Further protection of attorney and third persons

19 (1) If –

(a)   an instrument framed in a form prescribed as mentioned in paragraph 2(2) creates a power which is not a valid enduring power, and
(b)   the power is revoked by the mental incapacity of the donor,

sub-paragraphs (2) and (3) apply, whether or not the instrument has been registered.

(2) An attorney who acts in pursuance of the power does not, by reason of the revocation, incur any liability (either to the donor or to any other person) unless at the time of acting he knows –

(a)   that the instrument did not create a valid enduring power, and
(b)   that the donor has become mentally incapable.

(3) Any transaction between the attorney and another person is, in favour of that person, as valid as if the power had then been in existence, unless at the time of the transaction that person knows –

(a)   that the instrument did not create a valid enduring power, and
(b)   that the donor has become mentally incapable.

(4) Paragraph 18(4) applies for the purpose of determining whether a transaction was valid by virtue of sub-paragraph (3) as it applies for the purpose or determining whether a transaction was valid by virtue of paragraph 18(3).

PART 7
JOINT AND JOINT AND SEVERAL ATTORNEYS

Application to joint and joint and several attorneys

20 (1) An instrument which appoints more than one person to be an attorney cannot create an enduring power unless the attorneys are appointed to act –

    (a)   jointly, or

    (b)   jointly and severally.

(2) This Schedule, in its application to joint attorneys, applies to them collectively as it applies to a single attorney but subject to the modifications specified in paragraph 21.

(3) This Schedule, in its application to joint and several attorneys, applies with the modifications specified in sub-paragraphs (4) to (7) and in paragraph 22.

(4) A failure, as respects any one attorney, to comply with the requirements for the creation of enduring powers –

    (a)   prevents the instrument from creating such a power in his case, but

    (b)   does not affect its efficacy for that purpose as respects the other or others or its efficacy in his case for the purpose of creating a power of attorney which is not an enduring power.

(5) If one or more but not both or all the attorneys makes or joins in making an application for registration of the instrument –

    (a)   an attorney who is not an applicant as well as one who is may act pending the registration of the instrument as provided in paragraph 1(2),

    (b)   notice of the application must also be given under Part 3 of this Schedule to the other attorney or attorneys, and

    (c)   objection may validly be taken to the registration on a ground relating to an attorney or to the power of an attorney who is not an applicant as well as to one or the power of one who is an applicant.

(6) The Public Guardian is not precluded by paragraph 13(5) or (8) from registering an instrument and the court must not direct him not to do so under paragraph 13(10) if an enduring power subsists as respects some attorney who is not affected by the ground or grounds of the objection in question; and where the Public Guardian registers an instrument in that case, he must make against the registration an entry in the prescribed form.

(7) Sub-paragraph (6) does not preclude the court from revoking a power in so far as it confers a power on any other attorney in respect of whom the ground in paragraph 13(9)(d) or (e) is established; and where any ground in paragraph 13(9) affecting any other attorney is established the court must direct the Public Guardian to make against the registration an entry in the prescribed form.

(8) In sub-paragraph (4), 'the requirements for the creation of enduring powers' means the provisions of –

    (a)   paragraph 2 other than sub-paragraphs (8) and (9), and

    (b)   the regulations mentioned in paragraph 2.

PART III

Joint attorneys

21 (1) In paragraph 2(5), the reference to the time when the attorney executes the instrument is to be read as a reference to the time when the second or last attorney executes the instrument.

(2) In paragraph 2(6) to (8), the reference to the attorney is to be read as a reference to any attorney under the power.

(3) Paragraph 13 has effect as if the ground of objection to the registration of the instrument specified in sub-paragraph (9)(e) applied to any attorney under the power.

(4) In paragraph 16(2), references to the attorney are to be read as including references to any attorney under the power.

(5) In paragraph 16(4), references to the attorney are to be read as including references to any attorney under the power.

(6) In paragraph 17, references to the attorney are to be read as including references to any attorney under the power.

Joint and several attorneys

22 (1) In paragraph 2(7), the reference to the bankruptcy of the attorney is to be read as a reference to the bankruptcy of the last remaining attorney under the power; and the bankruptcy of any other attorney under the power causes that person to cease to be an attorney under the power.

(2) In paragraph 2(8), the reference to the suspension of the power is to be read as a reference to its suspension in so far as it relates to the attorney in respect of whom the interim bankruptcy restrictions order has effect.

(3) The restriction upon disclaimer imposed by paragraph 4(6) applies only to those attorneys who have reason to believe that the donor is or is becoming mentally incapable.

PART 8
INTERPRETATION

23 (1) In this Schedule –
'enduring power' is to be construed in accordance with paragraph 2,
'mentally incapable' or 'mental incapacity', except where it refers to revocation at common law, means in relation to any person, that he is incapable by reason of mental disorder ... of managing and administering his property and affairs and 'mentally capable' and 'mental capacity' are to be construed accordingly,
'notice' means notice in writing, and
'prescribed', except for the purposes of paragraph 2, means prescribed by regulations made for the purposes of this Schedule by the Lord Chancellor.

[(1A) In sub-paragraph (1), 'mental disorder' has the same meaning as in the Mental Health Act but disregarding the amendments made to that Act by the Mental Health Act 2007.]

(2) Any question arising under or for the purposes of this Schedule as to what the donor of the power might at any time be expected to do is to be determined by assuming that he had full mental capacity at the time but otherwise by reference to the circumstances existing at that time.

Amendments—Words omitted in sub-para (1) and sub-para (1A) inserted by the Mental Health Act 2007, ss 1(4), 55, Sch 1, Pt 2, para 23(1)-(3), Sch 11, Pt 1.

'prescribed by regulations' (para 23(1))—See the Lasting Powers of Attorney, Enduring Powers of Attorney and Public Guardian Regulations 2007, SI 2007/1253, as amended by the Public Guardian (Fees, etc) Regulations 2007, SI 2007/2051; the Lasting Powers of Attorney, Enduring Powers of Attorney and Public Guardian (Amendment) Regulations 2007, SI 2007/2161; and the Lasting Powers of Attorney, Enduring Powers of Attorney and Public Guardian (Amendment) Regulations 2009, SI 2009/1884.

SCHEDULE 5
TRANSITIONAL PROVISIONS AND SAVINGS

Section 66(4)

PART III

PART 1
REPEAL OF PART 7 OF THE MENTAL HEALTH ACT 1983

Existing receivers

1 (1) This paragraph applies where, immediately before the commencement day, there is a receiver ('R') for a person ('P') appointed under section 99 of the Mental Health Act.

(2) On and after that day –

    (a) this Act applies as if R were a deputy appointed for P by the court, but with the functions that R had as receiver immediately before that day, and

    (b) a reference in any other enactment to a deputy appointed by the court includes a person appointed as a deputy as a result of paragraph (a).

(3) On any application to it by R, the court may end R's appointment as P's deputy.

(4) Where, as a result of section 20(1), R may not make a decision on behalf of P in relation to a relevant matter, R must apply to the court.

(5) If, on the application, the court is satisfied that P is capable of managing his property and affairs in relation to the relevant matter –

    (a) it must make an order ending R's appointment as P's deputy in relation to that matter, but

    (b) it may, in relation to any other matter, exercise in relation to P any of the powers which it has under sections 15 to 19.

(6) If it is not satisfied, the court may exercise in relation to P any of the powers which it has under sections 15 to 19.

(7) R's appointment as P's deputy ceases to have effect if P dies.

(8) 'Relevant matter' means a matter in relation to which, immediately before the commencement day, R was authorised to act as P's receiver.

(9) In sub-paragraph (1), the reference to a receiver appointed under section 99 of the Mental Health Act includes a reference to a person who by virtue of Schedule 5 to that Act was deemed to be a receiver appointed under that section.

Orders, appointments etc

2 (1) Any order or appointment made, direction or authority given or other thing done which has, or by virtue of Schedule 5 to the Mental Health Act was deemed to have, effect under Part 7 of the Act immediately before the commencement day is to continue to have effect despite the repeal of Part 7.

(2) In so far as any such order, appointment, direction, authority or thing could have been made, given or done under sections 15 to 20 if those sections had then been in force –

    (a)   it is to be treated as made, given or done under those sections, and

    (b)   the powers of variation and discharge conferred by section 16(7) apply accordingly.

(3) Sub-paragraph (1) –

    (a)   does not apply to nominations under section 93(1) or (4) of the Mental Health Act, and

    (b)   as respects receivers, has effect subject to paragraph 1.

(4) This Act does not affect the operation of section 109 of the Mental Health Act (effect and proof of orders etc) in relation to orders made and directions given under Part 7 of that Act.

(5) This paragraph is without prejudice to section 16 of the Interpretation Act 1978 (general savings on repeal).

Pending proceedings

3 (1) Any application for the exercise of a power under Part 7 of the Mental Health Act which is pending immediately before the commencement day is to be treated, in so far as a corresponding power is exercisable under sections 16 to 20, as an application for the exercise of that power.

(2) For the purposes of sub-paragraph (1) an application for the appointment of a receiver is to be treated as an application for the appointment of a deputy.

Appeals

4 (1) Part 7 of the Mental Health Act and the rules made under it are to continue to apply to any appeal brought by virtue of section 105 of that Act which has not been determined before the commencement day.

(2) If in the case of an appeal brought by virtue of section 105(1) (appeal to nominated judge) the judge nominated under section 93 of the Mental Health Act has begun to hear the appeal, he is to continue to do so but otherwise it is to be heard by a puisne judge of the High Court nominated under section 46.

Fees

5 All fees and other payments which, having become due, have not been paid to the former Court of Protection before the commencement day, are to be paid to the new Court of Protection.

Court records

6 (1) The records of the former Court of Protection are to be treated, on and after the commencement day, as records of the new Court of Protection and are to be dealt with accordingly under the Public Records Act 1958.

(2) On and after the commencement day, the Public Guardian is, for the purpose of exercising any of his functions, to be given such access as he may require to such of the records mentioned in sub-paragraph (1) as relate to the appointment of receivers under section 99 of the Mental Health Act.

Existing charges

7 This Act does not affect the operation in relation to a charge created before the commencement day of –

- (a) so much of section 101(6) of the Mental Health Act as precludes a charge created under section 101(5) from conferring a right of sale or foreclosure during the lifetime of the patient, or
- (b) section 106(6) of the Mental Health Act (charge created by virtue of section 106(5) not to cause interest to fail etc).

Preservation of interests on disposal of property

8 Paragraph 8(1) of Schedule 2 applies in relation to any disposal of property (within the meaning of that provision) by a person living on 1st November 1960, being a disposal effected under the Lunacy Act 1890 as it applies in relation to the disposal of property effected under sections 16 to 20.

Accounts

9 Court of Protection Rules may provide that, in a case where paragraph 1 applies, R is to have a duty to render accounts –

- (a) while he is receiver;
- (b) after he is discharged.

Interpretation

10 In this Part of this Schedule –

- (a) 'the commencement day' means the day on which section 66(1)(a) (repeal of Part 7 of the Mental Health Act) comes into force,
- (b) 'the former Court of Protection' means the office abolished by section 45, and
- (c) 'the new Court of Protection' means the court established by that section.

PART 2
REPEAL OF THE ENDURING POWERS OF ATTORNEY ACT 1985

Orders, determinations, etc

11 (1) Any order or determination made, or other thing done, under the 1985 Act which has effect immediately before the commencement day continues to have effect despite the repeal of that Act.

(2) In so far as any such order, determination or thing could have been made or done under Schedule 4 if it had then been in force –

  (a)   it is to be treated as made or done under that Schedule, and
  (b)   the powers of variation and discharge exercisable by the court apply accordingly.

(3) Any instrument registered under the 1985 Act is to be treated as having been registered by the Public Guardian under Schedule 4.

(4) This paragraph is without prejudice to section 16 of the Interpretation Act 1978 (general savings on repeal).

Pending proceedings

12 (1) An application for the exercise of a power under the 1985 Act which is pending immediately before the commencement day is to be treated, in so far as a corresponding power is exercisable under Schedule 4, as an application for the exercise of that power.

(2) For the purposes of sub-paragraph (1) –

  (a)   a pending application under section 4(2) of the 1985 Act for the registration of an instrument is to be treated as an application to the Public Guardian under paragraph 4 of Schedule 4 and any notice given in connection with that application under Schedule 1 to the 1985 Act is to be treated as given under Part 3 of Schedule 4,
  (b)   a notice of objection to the registration of an instrument is to be treated as a notice of objection under paragraph 13 of Schedule 4, and
  (c)   pending proceedings under section 5 of the 1985 Act are to be treated as proceedings on an application for the exercise by the court of a power which would become exercisable in relation to an instrument under paragraph 16(2) of Schedule 4 on its registration.

Appeals

13 (1) The 1985 Act and, so far as relevant, the provisions of Part 7 of the Mental Health Act and the rules made under it as applied by section 10 of the 1985 Act are to continue to have effect in relation to any appeal brought by virtue of section 10(1)(c) of the 1985 Act which has not been determined before the commencement day.

(2) If, in the case of an appeal brought by virtue of section 105(1) of the Mental Health Act as applied by section 10(1)(c) of the 1985 Act (appeal to nominated judge), the judge nominated under section 93 of the Mental Health Act has begun to hear the appeal, he is to continue to do so but otherwise the appeal is to be heard by a puisne judge of the High Court nominated under section 46.

Exercise of powers of donor as trustee

14 (1) Section 2(8) of the 1985 Act (which prevents a power of attorney under section 25 of the Trustee Act 1925 as enacted from being an enduring power) is to continue to apply to any enduring power –

(a)   created before 1st March 2000, and
(b)   having effect immediately before the commencement day.

(2) Section 3(3) of the 1985 Act (which entitles the donee of an enduring power to exercise the donor's powers as trustee) is to continue to apply to any enduring power to which, as a result of the provision mentioned in sub-paragraph (3), it applies immediately before the commencement day.

(3) The provision is section 4(3)(a) of the Trustee Delegation Act 1999 (which provides for section 3(3) of the 1985 Act to cease to apply to an enduring power when its registration is cancelled, if it was registered in response to an application made before 1st March 2001).

(4) Even though section 4 of the 1999 Act is repealed by this Act, that section is to continue to apply in relation to an enduring power –

(a)   to which section 3(3) of the 1985 Act applies as a result of sub-paragraph (2), or
(b)   to which, immediately before the repeal of section 4 of the 1999 Act, section 1 of that Act applies as a result of section 4 of it.

(5) The reference in section 1(9) of the 1999 Act to section 4(6) of that Act is to be read with sub-paragraphs (2) to (4).

Interpretation

15 In this Part of this Schedule, 'the commencement day' means the day on which section 66(1)(b) (repeal of the 1985 Act) comes into force.

SCHEDULE 6

MINOR AND CONSEQUENTIAL AMENDMENTS

Section 67(1)

Fines and Recoveries Act 1833

1 (1) The Fines and Recoveries Act 1833 is amended as follows.

(2) In section 33 (case where protector of settlement lacks capacity to act), for the words from 'shall be incapable' to 'is incapable as aforesaid' substitute 'lacks capacity (within the meaning of the Mental Capacity Act 2005) to manage his property and affairs, the Court of Protection is to take his place as protector of the settlement while he lacks capacity'.

(3) In sections 48 and 49 (mental health jurisdiction), for each reference to the judge having jurisdiction under Part 7 of the Mental Health Act substitute a reference to the Court of Protection.

PART III

Improvement of Land Act 1864

2 In section 68 of the Improvement of Land Act 1864 (apportionment of rentcharges) –

    (a)   for ', curator, or receiver of' substitute 'or curator of, or a deputy with powers in relation to property and affairs appointed by the Court of Protection for,', and

    (b)   for 'or patient within the meaning of Part VII of the Mental Health Act 1983' substitute 'person who lacks capacity (within the meaning of the Mental Capacity Act 2005) to receive the notice'.

Trustee Act 1925

3 (1) The Trustee Act 1925 is amended as follows.

(2) In section 36 (appointment of new trustee) –

    (a)   in subsection (6C), for the words from 'a power of attorney' to the end, substitute 'an enduring power of attorney or lasting power of attorney registered under the Mental Capacity Act 2005', and

    (b)   in subsection (9) –

        (i)   for the words from 'is incapable' to 'exercising' substitute 'lacks capacity to exercise', and

        (ii)   for the words from 'the authority' to the end substitute 'the Court of Protection'.

(3) In section 41(1) (power of court to appoint new trustee) for the words from 'is incapable' to 'exercising' substitute 'lacks capacity to exercise'.

(4) In section 54 (mental health jurisdiction) –

    (a)   for subsection (1) substitute –

        '(1) Subject to subsection (2), the Court of Protection may not make an order, or give a direction or authority, in relation to a person who lacks capacity to exercise his functions as trustee, if the High Court may make an order to that effect under this Act.',

    (b)   in subsection (2) –

        (i)   for the words from the beginning to 'of a receiver' substitute 'Where a person lacks capacity to exercise his functions as a trustee and a deputy is appointed for him by the Court of Protection or an application for the appointment of a deputy',

        (ii)   for 'the said authority', in each place, substitute 'the Court of Protection', and

        (iii)   for 'the patient', in each place, substitute 'the person concerned', and

    (c)   omit subsection (3).

(5) In section 55 (order made on particular allegation to be conclusive evidence of it) –

    (a)   for the words from 'Part VII' to 'Northern Ireland' substitute 'sections 15 to 20 of the Mental Capacity Act 2005 or any corresponding provisions having effect in Northern Ireland', and

    (b)   for paragraph (a) substitute –

        '(a) that a trustee or mortgagee lacks capacity in relation to the matter in question;'.

(6) In section 68 (definitions), at the end add –

'(3) Any reference in this Act to a person who lacks capacity in relation to a matter is to a person –

    (a) who lacks capacity within the meaning of the Mental Capacity Act 2005 in relation to that matter, or

    (b) in respect of whom the powers conferred by section 48 of that Act are exercisable and have been exercised in relation to that matter.'.

Law of Property Act 1925

4 (1) The Law of Property Act 1925 is amended as follows.

(2) In section 22 (conveyances on behalf of persons who lack capacity) –

    (a) in subsection (1) –

      (i) for the words from 'in a person suffering' to 'is acting' substitute ', either solely or jointly with any other person or persons, in a person lacking capacity (within the meaning of the Mental Capacity Act 2005) to convey or create a legal estate, a deputy appointed for him by the Court of Protection or (if no deputy is appointed', and

      (ii) for 'the authority having jurisdiction under Part VII of the Mental Health Act 1983' substitute 'the Court of Protection',

    (b) in subsection (2), for 'is incapable, by reason of mental disorder, of exercising' substitute 'lacks capacity (within the meaning of that Act) to exercise', and

    (c) in subsection (3), for the words from 'an enduring power' to the end substitute 'an enduring power of attorney or lasting power of attorney (within the meaning of the 2005 Act) is entitled to act for the trustee who lacks capacity in relation to the dealing.'.

(3) In section 205(1) (interpretation), omit paragraph (xiii).

Administration of Estates Act 1925

5 (1) The Administration of Estates Act 1925 is amended as follows.

(2) In section 41(1) (powers of personal representatives to appropriate), in the proviso –

    (a) in paragraph (ii) –

      (i) for the words from 'is incapable' to 'the consent' substitute 'lacks capacity (within the meaning of the Mental Capacity Act 2005) to give the consent, it', and

      (ii) for 'or receiver' substitute 'or a person appointed as deputy for him by the Court of Protection', and

    (b) in paragraph (iv), for 'no receiver is acting for a person suffering from mental disorder' substitute 'no deputy is appointed for a person who lacks capacity to consent'.

(3) Omit section 55(1)(viii) (definitions of 'person of unsound mind' and 'defective').

National Assistance Act 1948

6 In section 49 of the National Assistance Act 1948 (expenses of council officers acting for persons who lack capacity) –

    (a)   for the words from 'applies' to 'affairs of a patient' substitute 'applies for appointment by the Court of Protection as a deputy', and

    (b)   for 'such functions' substitute 'his functions as deputy'.

USA Veterans' Pensions (Administration) Act 1949

7 In section 1 of the USA Veterans' Pensions (Administration) Act 1949 (administration of pensions) –

    (a)   in subsection (4), omit the words from 'or for whom' to '1983', and

    (b)   after subsection (4), insert –

'(4A)An agreement under subsection (1) is not to be made in relation to a person who lacks capacity (within the meaning of the Mental Capacity Act 2005) for the purposes of this Act if –

    (a)   there is a donee of an enduring power of attorney or lasting power of attorney (within the meaning of the 2005 Act), or a deputy appointed for the person by the Court of Protection, and

    (b)   the donee or deputy has power in relation to the person for the purposes of this Act.

(4B) The proviso at the end of subsection (4) also applies in relation to subsection (4A).'.

Intestates' Estates Act 1952

8 In Schedule 2 to the Intestates' Estates Act 1952 (rights of surviving spouse or civil partner in relation to home), for paragraph 6(1) substitute –

'(1) Where the surviving spouse or civil partner lacks capacity (within the meaning of the Mental Capacity Act 2005) to make a requirement or give a consent under this Schedule, the requirement or consent may be made or given by a deputy appointed by the Court of Protection with power in that respect or, if no deputy has that power, by that court.'.

Variation of Trusts Act 1958

9 In section 1 of the Variation of Trusts Act 1958 (jurisdiction of courts to vary trusts) –

    (a)   in subsection (3), for the words from 'shall be determined' to the end substitute 'who lacks capacity (within the meaning of the Mental Capacity Act 2005) to give his assent is to be determined by the Court of Protection', and

    (b)   in subsection (6), for the words from 'the powers' to the end substitute 'the powers of the Court of Protection'.

Administration of Justice Act 1960

10 In section 12(1)(b) of the Administration of Justice Act 1960 (contempt of court to publish information about proceedings in private relating to persons with incapacity) for the words from 'under Part VIII' to 'that Act' substitute 'under the Mental Capacity Act 2005, or under any provision of the Mental Health Act 1983'.

Industrial and Provident Societies Act 1965

11 In section 26 of the Industrial and Provident Societies Act 1965 (payments for mentally incapable people), for subsection (2) substitute –

'(2) Subsection (1) does not apply where the member or person concerned lacks capacity (within the meaning of the Mental Capacity Act 2005) for the purposes of this Act and –

(a) there is a donee of an enduring power of attorney or lasting power of attorney (within the meaning of the 2005 Act), or a deputy appointed for the member or person by the Court of Protection, and

(b) the donee or deputy has power in relation to the member or person for the purposes of this Act.'.

Compulsory Purchase Act 1965

12 In Schedule 1 to the Compulsory Purchase Act 1965 (persons without power to sell their interests), for paragraph 1(2)(b) substitute –

'(b) do not have effect in relation to a person who lacks capacity (within the meaning of the Mental Capacity Act 2005) for the purposes of this Act if –

(i) there is a donee of an enduring power of attorney or lasting power of attorney (within the meaning of the 2005 Act), or a deputy appointed for the person by the Court of Protection, and

(ii) the donee or deputy has power in relation to the person for the purposes of this Act.'.

Leasehold Reform Act 1967

13 (1) For section 26(2) of the Leasehold Reform Act 1967 (landlord lacking capacity) substitute –

'(2) Where a landlord lacks capacity (within the meaning of the Mental Capacity Act 2005) to exercise his functions as a landlord, those functions are to be exercised –

(a) by a donee of an enduring power of attorney or lasting power of attorney (within the meaning of the 2005 Act), or a deputy appointed for him by the Court of Protection, with power to exercise those functions, or

(b) if no donee or deputy has that power, by a person authorised in that respect by that court.'.

PART III

(2) That amendment does not affect any proceedings pending at the commencement of this paragraph in which a receiver or a person authorised under Part 7 of the Mental Health Act is acting on behalf of the landlord.

Medicines Act 1968

14 In section 72 of the Medicines Act 1968 (pharmacist lacking capacity) –

(a) in subsection (1)(c), for the words from 'a receiver' to '1959' substitute 'he becomes a person who lacks capacity (within the meaning of the Mental Capacity Act 2005) to carry on the business',

(b) after subsection (1) insert –

'(1A)In subsection (1)(c), the reference to a person who lacks capacity to carry on the business is to a person –

(a) in respect of whom there is a donee of an enduring power of attorney or lasting power of attorney (within the meaning of the Mental Capacity Act 2005), or

(b) for whom a deputy is appointed by the Court of Protection,

and in relation to whom the donee or deputy has power for the purposes of this Act.',

(c) in subsection (3)(d) –

(i) for 'receiver' substitute 'deputy', and

(ii) after 'guardian' insert 'or from the date of registration of the instrument appointing the donee', and

(d) in subsection (4)(c), for 'receiver' substitute 'donee, deputy'.

Family Law Reform Act 1969

15 For section 21(4) of the Family Law Reform Act 1969 (consent required for taking of bodily sample from person lacking capacity), substitute –

'(4) A bodily sample may be taken from a person who lacks capacity (within the meaning of the Mental Capacity Act 2005) to give his consent, if consent is given by the court giving the direction under section 20 or by –

(a) a donee of an enduring power of attorney or lasting power of attorney (within the meaning of that Act), or

(b) a deputy appointed, or any other person authorised, by the Court of Protection,

with power in that respect.'.

Local Authority Social Services Act 1970

16 (1) Schedule 1 to the Local Authority Social Services Act 1970 (enactments conferring functions assigned to social services committee) is amended as follows.

(2) In the entry for section 49 of the National Assistance Act 1948 (expenses of local authority officer appointed for person who lacks capacity) for 'receiver' substitute 'deputy'.

(3) At the end, insert –

'Mental Capacity
Act 2005

Section 39   Instructing independent mental capacity advocate before
                             providing accommodation for person lacking capacity.

Section 49   Reports in proceedings.'.

Courts Act 1971

17 In Part 1A of Schedule 2 to the Courts Act 1971 (office-holders eligible for appointment as circuit judges), omit the reference to a Master of the Court of Protection.

Local Government Act 1972

18 (1) Omit section 118 of the Local Government Act 1972 (payment of pension etc where recipient lacks capacity).

(2) Sub-paragraph (3) applies where, before the commencement of this paragraph, a local authority has, in respect of a person referred to in that section as 'the patient', made payments under that section –

    (a)   to an institution or person having the care of the patient, or
    (b)   in accordance with subsection (1)(a) or (b) of that section.

(3) The local authority may, in respect of the patient, continue to make payments under that section to that institution or person, or in accordance with subsection (1)(a) or (b) of that section, despite the repeal made by sub-paragraph (1).

Matrimonial Causes Act 1973

19 In section 40 of the Matrimonial Causes Act 1973 (payments to person who lacks capacity) (which becomes subsection (1)) –

    (a)   for the words from 'is incapable' to 'affairs' substitute '('P') lacks capacity (within the meaning of the Mental Capacity Act 2005) in relation to the provisions of the order',
    (b)   for 'that person under Part VIII of that Act' substitute 'P under that Act',
    (c)   for the words from 'such persons' to the end substitute 'such person ('D') as it may direct', and
    (d)   at the end insert –
        '(2) In carrying out any functions of his in relation to an order made under subsection (1), D must act in P's best interests (within the meaning of that Act).'.

Juries Act 1974

20 In Schedule 1 to the Juries Act 1974 (disqualification for jury service), for paragraph 3 substitute –

    '3
    A person who lacks capacity, within the meaning of the Mental Capacity Act 2005, to serve as a juror.'.

PART III

Consumer Credit Act 1974

21 For section 37(1)(c) of the Consumer Credit Act 1974 (termination of consumer credit licence if holder lacks capacity) substitute –

'(c) becomes a person who lacks capacity (within the meaning of the Mental Capacity Act 2005) to carry on the activities covered by the licence.'.

Solicitors Act 1974

22 (1) The Solicitors Act 1974 is amended as follows.

(2) For section 12(1)(j) (application for practising certificate by solicitor lacking capacity) substitute –

'*(j)   while he lacks capacity (within the meaning of the Mental Capacity Act 2005) to act as a solicitor and powers under sections 15 to 20 or section 48 of that Act are exercisable in relation to him;'.*

(3) In section 62(4) (contentious business agreements made by clients) for paragraphs (c) and (d) substitute –

'(c) as a deputy for him appointed by the Court of Protection with powers in relation to his property and affairs, or

(d) as another person authorised under that Act to act on his behalf.'.

(4) In paragraph 1(1) of Schedule 1 (circumstances in which Law Society may intervene in solicitor's practice), for paragraph (f) substitute –

'(f) a solicitor lacks capacity (within the meaning of the Mental Capacity Act 2005) to act as a solicitor and powers under sections 15 to 20 or section 48 of that Act are exercisable in relation to him;'.

Local Government (Miscellaneous Provisions) Act 1976

23 In section 31 of the Local Government (Miscellaneous Provisions) Act 1976 (the title to which becomes 'Indemnities for local authority officers appointed as deputies or administrators'), for the words from 'as a receiver' to '1959' substitute 'as a deputy for a person by the Court of Protection'.

Sale of Goods Act 1979

24 In section 3(2) of the Sale of Goods Act 1979 (capacity to buy and sell) the words 'mental incapacity or' cease to have effect in England and Wales.

Limitation Act 1980

25 In section 38 of the Limitation Act 1980 (interpretation) substitute –

(a) in subsection (2) for 'of unsound mind' substitute 'lacks capacity (within the meaning of the Mental Capacity Act 2005) to conduct legal proceedings', and

(b) omit subsections (3) and (4).

Public Passenger Vehicles Act 1981

26 In section 57(2)(c) of the Public Passenger Vehicles Act 1981 (termination of public service vehicle licence if holder lacks capacity) for the words from 'becomes a patient' to 'or' substitute 'becomes a person who lacks capacity (within the meaning of the Mental Capacity Act 2005) to use a vehicle under the licence, or'.

Judicial Pensions Act 1981

27 In Schedule 1 to the Judicial Pensions Act 1981 (pensions of Supreme Court officers, etc), in paragraph 1, omit the reference to a Master of the Court of Protection except in the case of a person holding that office immediately before the commencement of this paragraph or who had previously retired from that office or died.

[Senior Courts Act 1981]

28 In Schedule 2 to the [Senior Courts Act 1981] (qualifications for appointment to office in Supreme Court), omit paragraph 11 (Master of the Court of Protection).

Mental Health Act 1983

29 (1) The Mental Health Act is amended as follows.

(2) In section 134(3) (cases where correspondence of detained patients may not be withheld) for paragraph (b) substitute –

> '(b) any judge or officer of the Court of Protection, any of the Court of Protection Visitors or any person asked by that Court for a report under section 49 of the Mental Capacity Act 2005 concerning the patient;'.

(3) In section 139 (protection for acts done in pursuance of 1983 Act), in subsection (1), omit from 'or in, or in pursuance' to 'Part VII of this Act,'.

(4) Section 142 (payment of pension etc where recipient lacks capacity) ceases to have effect in England and Wales.

(5) Sub-paragraph (6) applies where, before the commencement of sub-paragraph (4), an authority has, in respect of a person referred to in that section as 'the patient', made payments under that section –

(a) to an institution or person having the care of the patient, or
(b) in accordance with subsection (2)(a) or (b) of that section.

(6) The authority may, in respect of the patient, continue to make payments under that section to that institution or person, or in accordance with subsection (2)(a) or (b) of that section, despite the amendment made by sub-paragraph (4).

(7) In section 145(1) (interpretation), in the definition of 'patient', omit '(except in Part VII of this Act)'.

(8) In section 146 (provisions having effect in Scotland), omit from '104(4)' to 'section),'.

(9) In section 147 (provisions having effect in Northern Ireland), omit from '104(4)' to 'section),'.

PART III

Administration of Justice Act 1985

30 In section 18(3) of the Administration of Justice Act 1985 (licensed conveyancer who lacks capacity), for the words from 'that person' to the end substitute 'he becomes a person who lacks capacity (within the meaning of the Mental Capacity Act 2005) to practise as a licensed conveyancer.'.

Insolvency Act 1986

31 (1) The Insolvency Act 1986 is amended as follows.

(2) In section 389A (people not authorised to act as nominee or supervisor in voluntary arrangement), in subsection (3) –

    (a) omit the 'or' immediately after paragraph (b),
    (b) in paragraph (c), omit 'Part VII of the Mental Health Act 1983 or', and
    (c) after that paragraph, insert ', or
    (d) he lacks capacity (within the meaning of the Mental Capacity Act 2005) to act as nominee or supervisor'.

(3) In section 390 (people not qualified to be insolvency practitioners), in subsection (4) –

    (a) omit the 'or' immediately after paragraph (b),
    (b) in paragraph (c), omit 'Part VII of the Mental Health Act 1983 or', and
    (c) after that paragraph, insert ', or
    (d) he lacks capacity (within the meaning of the Mental Capacity Act 2005) to act as an insolvency practitioner.'.

Building Societies Act 1986

32 In section 102D(9) of the Building Societies Act 1986 (references to a person holding an account on trust for another) –

    (a) in paragraph (a), for 'Part VII of the Mental Health Act 1983' substitute 'the Mental Capacity Act 2005', and
    (b) for paragraph (b) substitute –
        '(b) to an attorney holding an account for another person under –
            (i) an enduring power of attorney or lasting power of attorney registered under the Mental Capacity Act 2005, or
            (ii) an enduring power registered under the Enduring Powers of Attorney (Northern Ireland) Order 1987;'.

Public Trustee and Administration of Funds Act 1986

33 In section 3 of the Public Trustee and Administration of Funds Act 1986 (functions of the Public Trustee) –

    (a) for subsections (1) to (5) substitute –
        '(1) The Public Trustee may exercise the functions of a deputy appointed by the Court of Protection.',
    (b) in subsection (6), for 'the 1906 Act' substitute 'the Public Trustee Act 1906', and
    (c) omit subsection (7).

Patronage (Benefices) Measure 1986 (No 3)

34 (1) The Patronage (Benefices) Measure 1986 (No 3) is amended as follows.

(2) In section 5 (rights of patronage exercisable otherwise than by registered patron), after subsection (3) insert –

> '(3A)The reference in subsection (3) to a power of attorney does not include an enduring power of attorney or lasting power of attorney (within the meaning of the Mental Capacity Act 2005).'

(3) In section 9 (information to be sent to designated officer when benefice becomes vacant), after subsection (5) insert –

> '(5A)Subsections (5B) and (5C) apply where the functions of a registered patron are, as a result of paragraph 10 of Schedule 2 to the Mental Capacity Act 2005 (patron's loss of capacity to discharge functions), to be discharged by an individual appointed by the Court of Protection.
>
> (5B) If the individual is a clerk in Holy Orders, subsection (5) applies to him as it applies to the registered patron.
>
> (5C) If the individual is not a clerk in Holy Orders, subsection (1) (other than paragraph (b)) applies to him as it applies to the registered patron.'

Courts and Legal Services Act 1990

35 (1) The Courts and Legal Services Act 1990 is amended as follows.

(2) In Schedule 11 (judges etc barred from legal practice), for the reference to a Master of the Court of Protection substitute a reference to each of the following –

(a) Senior Judge of the Court of Protection,
(b) President of the Court of Protection,
(c) Vice-President of the Court of Protection.

(3) In paragraph 5(3) of Schedule 14 (exercise of powers of intervention in registered foreign lawyer's practice), for paragraph (f) substitute –

> '(f) he lacks capacity (within the meaning of the Mental Capacity Act 2005) to act as a registered foreign lawyer and powers under sections 15 to 20 or section 48 are exercisable in relation to him;'.

Child Support Act 1991

36 In section 50 of the Child Support Act 1991 (unauthorised disclosure of information) –

(a) in subsection (8) –
  (i) immediately after paragraph (a), insert 'or',
  (ii) omit paragraphs (b) and (d) and the 'or' immediately after paragraph (c), and
  (iii) for ', receiver, custodian or appointee' substitute 'or custodian', and
(b) after that subsection, insert –
  '(9) Where the person to whom the information relates lacks capacity (within the meaning of the Mental Capacity Act 2005) to consent to its disclosure, the appropriate person is –

      (a)   a donce of an enduring power of attorney or lasting power of attorney (within the meaning of that Act), or

      (b)   a deputy appointed for him, or any other person authorised, by the Court of Protection,

with power in that respect.'.

Social Security Administration Act 1992

37 In section 123 of the Social Security Administration Act 1992 (unauthorised disclosure of information) –

  (a)   in subsection (10), omit –

      (i)   in paragraph (b), 'a receiver appointed under section 99 of the Mental Health Act 1983 or',

      (ii)   in paragraph (d)(i), 'sub-paragraph (a) of rule 41(1) of the Court of Protection Rules 1984 or',

      (iii)   in paragraph (d)(ii), 'a receiver ad interim appointed under sub-paragraph (b) of the said rule 41(1) or', and

      (iv)   'receiver,', and

  (b)   after that subsection, insert –

      '(11) Where the person to whom the information relates lacks capacity (within the meaning of the Mental Capacity Act 2005) to consent to its disclosure, the appropriate person is –

      (a)   a donee of an enduring power of attorney or lasting power of attorney (within the meaning of that Act), or

      (b)   a deputy appointed for him, or any other person authorised, by the Court of Protection,

with power in that respect.'.

Judicial Pensions and Retirement Act 1993

38 (1) The Judicial Pensions and Retirement Act 1993 is amended as follows.

(2) In Schedule 1 (qualifying judicial offices), in Part 2, under the cross-heading 'Court officers', omit the reference to a Master of the Court of Protection except in the case of a person holding that office immediately before the commencement of this sub-paragraph or who had previously retired from that office or died.

(3) In Schedule 5 (retirement: the relevant offices), omit the entries relating to the Master and Deputy or temporary Master of the Court of Protection, except in the case of a person holding any of those offices immediately before the commencement of this sub-paragraph.

(4) In Schedule 7 (retirement: transitional provisions), omit paragraph 5(5)(i)(g) except in the case of a person holding office as a deputy or temporary Master of the Court of Protection immediately before the commencement of this sub-paragraph.

Leasehold Reform, Housing and Urban Development Act 1993

39 (1) For paragraph 4 of Schedule 2 to the Leasehold Reform, Housing and Urban Development Act 1993 (landlord under a disability), substitute –

    '4

(1)   This paragraph applies where a Chapter I or Chapter II landlord lacks capacity (within the meaning of the Mental Capacity Act 2005) to exercise his functions as a landlord.

(2)   For the purposes of the Chapter concerned, the landlord's place is to be taken –

(a)   by a donee of an enduring power of attorney or lasting power of attorney (within the meaning of the 2005 Act), or a deputy appointed for him by the Court of Protection, with power to exercise those functions, or

(b)   if no deputy or donee has that power, by a person authorised in that respect by that court.'.

(2) That amendment does not affect any proceedings pending at the commencement of this paragraph in which a receiver or a person authorised under Part 7 of the Mental Health Act 1983 is acting on behalf of the landlord.

Goods Vehicles (Licensing of Operators) Act 1995

40 (1) The Goods Vehicles (Licensing of Operators) Act 1995 is amended as follows.

(2) In section 16(5) (termination of licence), for 'he becomes a patient within the meaning of Part VII of the Mental Health Act 1983' substitute 'he becomes a person who lacks capacity (within the meaning of the Mental Capacity Act 2005) to use a vehicle under the licence'.

(3) In section 48 (licence not to be transferable, etc) –

(a)   in subsection (2) –

(i)   for 'or become a patient within the meaning of Part VII of the Mental Health Act 1983' substitute ', or become a person who lacks capacity (within the meaning of the Mental Capacity Act 2005) to use a vehicle under the licence,', and

(ii)   in paragraph (a), for 'became a patient' substitute 'became a person who lacked capacity in that respect', and

(b)   in subsection (5), for 'a patient within the meaning of Part VII of the Mental Health Act 1983' substitute 'a person lacking capacity'.

Disability Discrimination Act 1995

41 In section 20(7) of the Disability Discrimination Act 1995 (regulations to disapply provisions about incapacity), in paragraph (b), for 'Part VII of the Mental Health Act 1983' substitute 'the Mental Capacity Act 2005'.

Trusts of Land and Appointment of Trustees Act 1996

42 (1) The Trusts of Land and Appointment of Trustees Act 1996 is amended as follows.

(2) In section 9 (delegation by trustees), in subsection (6), for the words from 'an enduring power' to the end substitute 'an enduring power of attorney or lasting power of attorney within the meaning of the Mental Capacity Act 2005'.

PART III

(3) In section 20 (the title to which becomes 'Appointment of substitute for trustee who lacks capacity') –

    (a)   in subsection (1)(a), for 'is incapable by reason of mental disorder of exercising' substitute 'lacks capacity (within the meaning of the Mental Capacity Act 2005) to exercise', and

    (b)   in subsection (2) –

        (i)   for paragraph (a) substitute –

           '(a) a deputy appointed for the trustee by the Court of Protection,',

        (ii)   in paragraph (b), for the words from 'a power of attorney' to the end substitute 'an enduring power of attorney or lasting power of attorney registered under the Mental Capacity Act 2005', and

        (iii)   in paragraph (c), for the words from 'the authority' to the end substitute 'the Court of Protection'.

Human Rights Act 1998

43 In section 4(5) of the Human Rights Act 1998 (courts which may make declarations of incompatibility), after paragraph (e) insert –

        '(f) the Court of Protection, in any matter being dealt with by the President of the Family Division, the Vice-Chancellor or a puisne judge of the High Court.'

Access to Justice Act 1999

44 In paragraph 1 of Schedule 2 to the Access to Justice Act 1999 (services excluded from the Community Legal Service), after paragraph (e) insert –

        '(ea) the creation of lasting powers of attorney under the Mental Capacity Act 2005,

        (eb) the making of advance decisions under that Act,'.

Adoption and Children Act 2002

45 In section 52(1)(a) of the Adoption and Children Act 2002 (parental consent to adoption), for 'is incapable of giving consent' substitute 'lacks capacity (within the meaning of the Mental Capacity Act 2005) to give consent'.

Licensing Act 2003

46 (1) The Licensing Act 2003 is amended as follows.

(2) In section 27(1) (lapse of premises licence), for paragraph (b) substitute –

        '(b) becomes a person who lacks capacity (within the meaning of the Mental Capacity Act 2005) to hold the licence,'.

(3) In section 47 (interim authority notice in relation to premises licence) –

    (a)   in subsection (5), for paragraph (b) substitute –

        '(b) the former holder lacks capacity (within the meaning of the Mental Capacity Act 2005) to hold the licence and that person acts for him under an enduring power of attorney or lasting power of attorney registered under that Act,', and

(b)   in subsection (10), omit the definition of 'mentally incapable'.

Courts Act 2003

47 (1) The Courts Act 2003 is amended as follows.

(2) In section 1(1) (the courts in relation to which the Lord Chancellor must discharge his general duty), after paragraph (a) insert –
'(aa) the Court of Protection,'.

(3) In section 64(2) (judicial titles which the Lord Chancellor may by order alter) –

(a)   omit the reference to a Master of the Court of Protection, and
(b)   at the appropriate place insert a reference to each of the following –
(i)   Senior Judge of the Court of Protection,
(ii) President of the Court of Protection,
(iii) Vice-president of the Court of Protection.

Amendment—In para 28 words in square brackets substituted by the Constitutional Reform Act 2005, s 59(5), Sch 11, Pt 1, para 1(2).

Prospective Amendment—In para 22 words prospectively repealed by the Legal Services Act 2007, s 210, Sch 23.

SCHEDULE 7
REPEALS

Section 67(2)

Short title and chapter	Extent of repeal
Trustee Act 1925	Section 54(3).
Law of Property Act 1925	Section 205(1)(xiii).
Administration of Estates Act 1925	Section 55(1)(viii)
U.S.A. Veterans' Pensions (Administration) Act 1949	In section 1(4), the words from 'or for whom' to '1983'.
Mental Health Act 1959	In Schedule 7, in Part 1, the entries relating to –
	section 33 of the Fines and Recoveries Act 1833,
	section 68 of the Improvement of Land Act 1864,
	section 55 of the Trustee Act 1925,
	section 205(1) of the Law of Property Act 1925,
	section 49 of the National Assistance Act 1948, and
	section 1 of the Variation of Trusts Act 1958.
Courts Act 1971	In Schedule 2, in Part 1A, the words 'Master of the Court of Protection'.

Local Government Act 1972	Section 118.
Limitation Act 1980	Section 38(3) and (4).
[Senior Courts Act 1981]	In Schedule 2, in Part 2, paragraph 11.
Mental Health Act 1983	Part 7.
	In section 139(1) the words from 'or in, or in pursuance' to 'Part VII of this Act,'.
	In section 145(1), in the definition of 'patient' the words '(except in Part VII of this Act)'.
	In sections 146 and 147 the words from '104(4)' to 'section),'.
	Schedule 3.
	In Schedule 4, paragraphs 1, 2, 4, 5, 7, 9, 14, 20, 22, 25, 32, 38, 55 and 56.
	In Schedule 5, paragraphs 26, 43, 44 and 45.
Enduring Powers of Attorney Act 1985	The whole Act.
Insolvency Act 1986	In section 389A(3) –
	the 'or' immediately after paragraph (b), and in paragraph (c), the words 'Part VII of the Mental Health Act 1983 or'.
	In section 390(4) –
	the 'or' immediately after paragraph (b), and in paragraph (c), the words 'Part VII of the Mental Health Act 1983 or'.
Public Trustee and Administration of Funds Act 1986	Section 2.
	Section 3(7).
Child Support Act 1991	In section 50(8) –
	paragraphs (b) and (d), and the 'or' immediately after paragraph (c).
Social Security Administration Act 1992	In section 123(10) –
	in paragraph (b), 'a receiver appointed under section 99 of the Mental Health Act 1983 or',
	in paragraph (d)(i), 'sub-paragraph (a) of rule 41(1) of the Court of Protection Rules Act 1984 or',
	in paragraph (d)(ii), 'a receiver ad interim appointed under sub-paragraph (b) of the said rule 41(1) or', and
	'receiver,'.
Trustee Delegation Act 1999	Section 4.
	Section 6.
	In section 7(3), the words 'in accordance with section 4 above'.

Care Standards Act 2000	In Schedule 4, paragraph 8.
Licensing Act 2003	In section 47(10), the definition of 'mentally incapable'.
Courts Act 2003	In section 64(2), the words 'Master of the Court of Protection'.

Amendment—Words substituted by the Constitutional Reform Act 2005, s 59(5), Sch 11, Pt 1, para 1(2).

PART IV

Court of Protection Rules 2007 and Practice Directions

PART IV: Court of Protection Rules 2007 and Practice Directions

Contents

Court of Protection Rules 2007	573
Practice Direction – General provisions	680
Practice Direction A – Court documents (PD4A)	680
Practice Direction B – Statements of truth (PD4B)	682
Practice Direction – Service of documents	685
Practice Direction A – Service (PD6A)	685
Practice Direction – Notifying P	688
Practice Direction A – Notifying P (PD7A)	688
Practice Direction – Permission	690
Practice Direction A – Permission (PD8A)	690
Practice Direction – How to start proceedings	692
Practice Direction A – The application form (PD9A)	692
Practice Direction B – Notification of other persons that an application form has been issued (PD9B)	695
Practice Direction C – Responding to an application (PD9C)	697
Practice Direction D – Applications by currently appointed deputies, attorneys and donees in relation to P's property and affairs (PD9D)	699
Practice Direction E – Applications relating to serious medical treatment (PD9E)	702
Practice Direction F – Applications relating to statutory wills, codicils, settlements and other dealings with P's property (PD9F)	706
Practice Direction G – Applications to appoint or discharge a trustee (PD9G)	709
Practice Direction H – Applications relating to the registration of enduring powers of attorney (PD9H)	712
Practice Direction – Applications within proceedings	714
Practice Direction A – Applications within proceedings (PD10A)	714
Practice Direction B – Urgent and interim applications (PD10B)	717
Practice Direction – Deprivation of liberty applications	720
Practice Direction – Human Rights	726

Practice Direction A – Human Rights Act 1998 (PD11A)   726

Practice Direction – Dealing with applications   728

Practice Direction A – Court's jurisdiction to be exercised by certain
    judges (PD12A)   728

Practice Direction B – Procedure for disputing the court's
    jurisdiction (PD12B)   730

Practice Direction – Hearings   731

Practice Direction A – Hearings (including reporting restrictions)
    (PD13A)   731

Practice Direction – Admissions, evidence and depositions   736

Practice Direction A – Written evidence (PD14A)   736

Practice Direction B – Depositions (PD14B)   746

Practice Direction C – Fees for examiners of the court (PD14C)   751

Practice Direction D – Witness summons (PD14D)   753

Practice Direction E – Section 49 reports (PD14E)   754

Practice Direction – Experts   759

Practice Direction A – Expert evidence (PD15A)   759

Practice Direction – Litigation friend   761

Practice Direction A – Litigation friend (PD17A)   761

Practice Direction – Change of solicitor   764

Practice Direction A – Change of solicitor (PD18A)   764

Practice Direction – Costs   765

Practice Direction A – Costs in the Court of Protection (PD19A)   765

Practice Direction – Fixed Costs   767

Practice Direction B – Fixed costs in the Court of Protection
    (PD19B)   767

Practice Direction – Solicitors' and other professionals' fixed costs 772

Practice Direction B – Fixed costs in the Court of Protection
    (PD19B)   772

Practice Direction – Appeals   776

Practice Direction A – Appeals (PD20A)   776

Practice Direction – Enforcement   782

Practice Direction A – Contempt of court (PD21A)   782

Practice Direction – Transitory and transitional provisions   784

Practice Direction A – Transitional provisions (PD22A)   784

Practice Direction B – Transitory provisions (PD22B)   786

Practice Direction C – Appeals against decisions made under Part 7 of the Mental Health Act 1983 or under the Enduring Powers of Attorney Act 1985 which are brought on or after commencement (PD22C)   789

Practice Direction – Miscellaneous   791

Practice Direction A – Request for directions where notice of objection prevents public guardian from registering enduring power of attorney (PD23A)   791

Practice Direction B – Where P ceases to lack capacity or dies (PD23B)   793

PART IV

Court of Protection Rules 2007, SI 2007/1744

ARRANGEMENT OF RULES

PART 1
PRELIMINARY

Rule   Page

1   Title and commencement   581
2   Revocations   582

PART 2
THE OVERRIDING OBJECTIVE

3   The overriding objective   583
4   The duty of the parties   585
5   Court's duty to manage cases   585

PART 3
INTERPRETATION AND GENERAL PROVISIONS

6   Interpretation   587
7   Court officers   589
8   Computation of time   589
9   Application of the Civil Procedure Rules   590

PART 4
COURT DOCUMENTS

10   Documents used in court proceedings   590
11   Documents required to be verified by a statement of truth   591
12   Failure to verify a document   592
13   Failure to verify a witness statement   592
14   False statements   592
15   Personal details   592
16   Supply of documents to a party from court records   593
17   Supply of documents to a non-party from court records   593
18   Subsequent use of court documents   594
19   Editing information in court documents   594
20   Public Guardian to be supplied with court documents relevant to supervision of deputies   594
21   Provision of court order to Public Guardian   595
22   Amendment of application   595
23   Clerical mistakes or slips   596
24   Endorsement of amendment   596

PART 5
GENERAL CASE MANAGEMENT POWERS

25   The court's general powers of case management   596
26   Court's power to dispense with requirement of any rule   598
27   Exercise of powers on the court's own initiative   598
28   General power of the court to rectify matters where there has been an error of procedure   599

PART 6
SERVICE OF DOCUMENTS

Service generally

29   Scope   599

PART IV

30 Who is to serve   599
31 Methods of service   600
32 Service of documents on children and protected parties   601
33 Service of documents on P if he becomes a party   602
34 Substituted service   602
35 Deemed service   602
36 Certificate of service   603
37 Certificate of non-service   603
38 Power of court to dispense with service   604

Service out of the jurisdiction
39 Application of Family Procedure (Adoption) Rules 2005   604

PART 7
NOTIFYING P

General requirement to notify P
40 General   604
41 Who is to notify P   605

Circumstances in which P must be notified
42 Application forms   605
43 Appeals   606
44 Final orders   606
45 Other matters   607

Manner of notification, and accompanying documents
46 Manner of notification   607
47 Acknowledgment of notification   608
48 Certificate of notification   608
49 Dispensing with requirement to notify, etc   608

PART 8
PERMISSION
50 General   608
51 Where the court's permission is not required   609
52 Exceptions to rule 51(2)(a)   610
53 Permission – supplementary   611
54 Application for permission   612
55 What the court will do when an application for permission to start
    proceedings is filed   612
56 Persons to be notified of the hearing of an application for permission   613
57 Acknowledgment of notification of permission application   613
58 Failure to file acknowledgment of notification   613
59 Service of an order giving or refusing permission   614
60 Appeal against a permission decision following a hearing   614

PART 9
HOW TO START PROCEEDINGS

Initial steps
61 General   614
62 When proceedings are started   615
63 Contents of the application form   615
64 Documents to be filed with the application form   615
65 What the court will do when an application form is filed   616

Steps following issue of application form
66 Applicant to serve the application form on named respondents   616
67 Applications relating to lasting powers of attorney   617
68 Applications relating to enduring powers of attorney   618
69 Applicant to notify P of an application   618
70 Applicant to notify other persons of an application   618
71 Requirements for certain applications   619

Responding to an application
72 Responding to an application   620

The parties to the proceedings
73 Parties to the proceedings   621
74 Persons to be bound as if parties   623
75 Application to be joined as a party   623
76 Applications for removal as a party to proceedings   624

PART 10
APPLICATIONS WITHIN PROCEEDINGS
77 Types of applications for which the Part 10 procedure may be used   624
78 Application notice to be filed   624
79 What an application notice must include   625
80 Service of an application notice   625
81 Applications without notice   626

Interim Remedies
82 Orders for interim remedies   626

PART 10A
DEPRIVATION OF LIBERTY
82A   627

PART 11
HUMAN RIGHTS
83 General   627

PART 12
DEALING WITH APPLICATIONS
84 Dealing with the application   628
85 Directions   629

Allocation of proceedings
86 Court's jurisdiction in certain kinds of case to be exercised by certain judges   630

Disputing the jurisdiction of the court
87 Procedure for disputing the court's jurisdiction   630

Participation in hearings
88 Participation in hearings   631

Reconsideration of court orders
89 Orders made without a hearing or without notice to any person   631

PART IV

PART 13
HEARINGS

Private hearings
90 General rule – hearing to be in private   632
91 Court's general power to authorise publication of information about
    proceedings   633

Power to order a public hearing
92 Court's power to order that a hearing be held in public   633

Supplementary
93 Supplementary provisions relating to public or private hearings   634

PART 14
ADMISSIONS, EVIDENCE AND DEPOSITIONS

Admissions
94 Making an admission   635

Evidence
95   Power of court to control evidence   635
96   Evidence of witnesses – general rule   636
97   Written evidence – general rule   637
98   Evidence by video link or other means   637
99   Service of witness statements for use at final hearing   637
100 Form of witness statement   637
101 Witness summaries   638
102 Affidavit evidence   638
103 Form of affidavit   638
104 Affidavit made outside the jurisdiction   638
105 Notarial acts and instruments   639
106 Summoning of witnesses   639
107 Power of court to direct a party to provide information   639

Depositions
108 Evidence by deposition   640
109 Conduct of examination   640
110 Fees and expenses of examiners of the court   641
111 Examiners of the court   641
112 Enforcing attendance of a witness   641
113 Use of deposition at a hearing   642

Taking evidence outside the jurisdiction
114 Interpretation   642
115 Where a person to be examined is in another Regulation State   642
116 Where a person to be examined is out of the jurisdiction – letter of
     request   643

Section 49 reports
117 Reports under section 49 of the Act   644
118 Written questions to person making a report under section 49   645

PART 15
EXPERTS

119 References to expert   645
120 Restriction on filing an expert's report   645
121 Duty to restrict expert evidence   646

122 Experts – overriding duty to the court   646
123 Court's power to restrict expert evidence   646
124 General requirement for expert evidence to be given in a written report   647
125 Written questions to experts   647
126 Contents of expert's report   648
127 Use by one party of expert's report disclosed by another   648
128 Discussions between experts   648
129 Expert's right to ask court for directions   649
130 Court's power to direct that evidence is to be given by a single joint
     expert   649
131 Instructions to a single joint expert   649

PART 16
DISCLOSURE

132 Meaning of disclosure   650
133 General or specific disclosure   650
134 Procedure for general or specific disclosure   651
135 Ongoing duty of disclosure   651
136 Right to inspect documents   652
137 Inspection and copying of documents   652
138 Claim to withhold inspection or disclosure of document   652
139 Consequence of failure to disclose documents or permit inspection   653

PART 17
LITIGATION FRIEND

140 Who may act as a litigation friend   653
141 Requirement for a litigation friend   654
142 Litigation friend without a court order   654
143 Litigation friend by court order   655
144 Court's power to prevent a person from acting as litigation friend or to
     order change   656
145 Appointment of litigation friend by court order – supplementary   657
146 Procedure where appointment of litigation friend comes to an end – for
     a child or protected party   657
147 Procedure where appointment of litigation friend comes to an end – for
     P   658
148 Procedure where P ceases to lack capacity   658
149 Practice direction in relation to litigation friends   659

PART 18
CHANGE OF SOLICITOR

150 Change of solicitor   659
151 LSC funded clients   660
152 Order that a solicitor has ceased to act   660
153 Removal of solicitor who has ceased to act on application of another
     party   660
154 Practice direction relating to change of solicitor   661

PART 19
COSTS

155 Interpretation   661
156 Property and affairs – the general rule   662
157 Personal welfare – the general rule   662
158 Apportioning costs – the general rule   663
159 Departing from the general rule   663
160 Rules about costs in the Civil Procedure Rules to apply   663
161 Detailed assessment of costs   664

PART IV

162 Employment of a solicitor by two or more persons   664
163 Costs of the Official Solicitor   665
164 Procedure for assessing costs   665
165 Costs following P's death   665
166 Costs orders in favour of or against non-parties   665
167 Remuneration of a deputy, donee or attorney   665
168 Practice direction as to costs   666

PART 20
APPEALS
169 Scope of this Part   666
170 Interpretation   666
171 Dealing with appeals   666
172 Permission to appeal   667
173 Matters to be taken into account when considering an application for
     permission   667
174 Parties to comply with the practice direction   667
175 Appellant's notice   668
176 Respondent's notice   668
177 Variation of time   669
178 Power of appeal judge on appeal   669
179 Determination of appeals   669
180 Allocation   670

Appeals to the Court of Appeal
181 Appeals against decision of a puisne judge of the High Court, etc   670
182 Second appeals   670

PART 21
ENFORCEMENT
183 Enforcement methods – general   671
184 Application of the Civil Procedure Rules 1998 and RSC Orders   671

Orders for committal
185 Contempt of court – generally   673
186 Application for order of committal   673
187 Oral evidence   673
188 Hearing for committal order   673
189 Power to suspend execution of committal order   674
190 Warrant for arrest   674
191 Discharge of person committed   674
192 Penal notices   674
193 Saving for other powers   675
194 Power of court to commit on its own initiative   675

PART 22
TRANSITORY AND TRANSITIONAL PROVISIONS
195 Transitory provision: applications by former receivers   675
196 Transitory provision: dealing with applications under rule 195 676
197 Appeal against a decision of a nominated officer   676
198 Application of Rules to proceedings within paragraphs 3 and 12 of
     Schedule 5 to the Act   676
199 Practice direction   676

PART 23
MISCELLANEOUS

200 Order or directions requiring a person to give security for discharge of
functions 677
201 Objections to registration of an enduring power of attorney: request for
directions 678
202 Disposal of property where P ceases to lack capacity 679

PRACTICE DIRECTION – GENERAL PROVISIONS 680

PRACTICE DIRECTION A – COURT DOCUMENTS (PD4A) 680

PRACTICE DIRECTION B – STATEMENTS OF TRUTH (PD4B) 682

PRACTICE DIRECTION – SERVICE OF DOCUMENTS 685

PRACTICE DIRECTION A – SERVICE (PD6A) 685

PRACTICE DIRECTION – NOTIFYING P 688

PRACTICE DIRECTION A – NOTIFYING P (PD7A) 688

PRACTICE DIRECTION – PERMISSION 690

PRACTICE DIRECTION A – PERMISSION (PD8A) 690

PRACTICE DIRECTION – HOW TO START PROCEEDINGS 692

PRACTICE DIRECTION A – THE APPLICATION FORM (PD9A) 692

PRACTICE DIRECTION B – NOTIFICATION OF OTHER PERSONS
THAT AN APPLICATION FORM HAS BEEN ISSUED (PD9B) 695

PRACTICE DIRECTION C – RESPONDING TO AN APPLICATION
(PD9C) 697

PRACTICE DIRECTION D – APPLICATIONS BY CURRENTLY
APPOINTED DEPUTIES, ATTORNEYS AND DONEES IN RELATION
TO P'S PROPERTY AND AFFAIRS (PD9D) 699

PRACTICE DIRECTION E – APPLICATIONS RELATING TO
SERIOUS MEDICAL TREATMENT (PD9E) 702

PRACTICE DIRECTION F – APPLICATIONS RELATING TO
STATUTORY WILLS, CODICILS, SETTLEMENTS AND OTHER
DEALINGS WITH P'S PROPERTY (PD9F) 706

PRACTICE DIRECTION G – APPLICATIONS TO APPOINT OR
DISCHARGE A TRUSTEE (PD9G) 709

PRACTICE DIRECTION H – APPLICATIONS RELATING TO THE
REGISTRATION OF ENDURING POWERS OF ATTORNEY (PD9H) 712

PRACTICE DIRECTION – APPLICATIONS WITHIN PROCEEDINGS 714

PRACTICE DIRECTION A – APPLICATIONS WITHIN
PROCEEDINGS (PD10A) 714

PART IV

PRACTICE DIRECTION B – URGENT AND INTERIM APPLICATIONS (PD10B)   717

PRACTICE DIRECTION – DEPRIVATION OF LIBERTY APPLICATIONS   720

PRACTICE DIRECTION – HUMAN RIGHTS   726

PRACTICE DIRECTION A – HUMAN RIGHTS ACT 1998 (PD11A)   726

PRACTICE DIRECTION – DEALING WITH APPLICATIONS   728

PRACTICE DIRECTION A – COURT'S JURISDICTION TO BE EXERCISED BY CERTAIN JUDGES (PD12A)   728

PRACTICE DIRECTION B – PROCEDURE FOR DISPUTING THE COURT'S JURISDICTION (PD12B)   730

PRACTICE DIRECTION – HEARINGS   731

PRACTICE DIRECTION A – HEARINGS (INCLUDING REPORTING RESTRICTIONS) (PD13A)   731

PRACTICE DIRECTION – ADMISSIONS, EVIDENCE AND DEPOSITIONS   736

PRACTICE DIRECTION A – WRITTEN EVIDENCE (PD14A)   736

PRACTICE DIRECTION B – DEPOSITIONS (PD14B)   746

PRACTICE DIRECTION C – FEES FOR EXAMINERS OF THE COURT (PD14C)   751

PRACTICE DIRECTION D – WITNESS SUMMONS (PD14D)   753

PRACTICE DIRECTION E – SECTION 49 REPORTS (PD14E)   754

PRACTICE DIRECTION – EXPERTS   759

PRACTICE DIRECTION A – EXPERT EVIDENCE (PD15A)   759

PRACTICE DIRECTION – LITIGATION FRIEND   761

PRACTICE DIRECTION A – LITIGATION FRIEND (PD17A)   761

PRACTICE DIRECTION – CHANGE OF SOLICITOR   764

PRACTICE DIRECTION A – CHANGE OF SOLICITOR (PD18A)   764

PRACTICE DIRECTION – COSTS   765

PRACTICE DIRECTION A – COSTS IN THE COURT OF PROTECTION (PD19A)   765

PRACTICE DIRECTION – FIXED COSTS   767

PRACTICE DIRECTION B – FIXED COSTS IN THE COURT OF
PROTECTION (PD19B)   767

PRACTICE DIRECTION – SOLICITORS' AND OTHER
PROFESSIONALS' FIXED COSTS   772

PRACTICE DIRECTION B – FIXED COSTS IN THE COURT OF
PROTECTION (PD19B)   772

PRACTICE DIRECTION – APPEALS   776

PRACTICE DIRECTION A – APPEALS (PD20A)   776

PRACTICE DIRECTION – ENFORCEMENT   782

PRACTICE DIRECTION A – CONTEMPT OF COURT (PD21A)   782

PRACTICE DIRECTION – TRANSITORY AND TRANSITIONAL
PROVISIONS   784

PRACTICE DIRECTION A – TRANSITIONAL PROVISIONS (PD22A)   784

PRACTICE DIRECTION B – TRANSITORY PROVISIONS (PD22B)   786

PRACTICE DIRECTION C – APPEALS AGAINST DECISIONS MADE
UNDER PART 7 OF THE MENTAL HEALTH ACT 1983 OR UNDER
THE ENDURING POWERS OF ATTORNEY ACT 1985 WHICH ARE
BROUGHT ON OR AFTER COMMENCEMENT (PD22C)   789

PRACTICE DIRECTION – MISCELLANEOUS   791

PRACTICE DIRECTION A – REQUEST FOR DIRECTIONS WHERE
NOTICE OF OBJECTION PREVENTS PUBLIC GUARDIAN FROM
REGISTERING ENDURING POWER OF ATTORNEY (PD23A)   791

PRACTICE DIRECTION B – WHERE P CEASES TO LACK
CAPACITY OR DIES (PD23B)   793

PART 1
PRELIMINARY

1 Title and commencement

These Rules may be cited as the Court of Protection Rules 2007 and come into force
on 1 October 2007.

Authority—The authority to make the rules is derived from the Mental Capacity Act 2005 (MCA
2005), ss 49(5), 51, 53(2) and (4), 65(1) and 67(4)(b).

Jurisdiction—The jurisdiction of the Court of Protection and hence of the rules is limited to
England and Wales. The rules are made by the Lord Chief Justice who can appoint a nominee with
the agreement of the Lord Chancellor. The President of the Family Division was therefore appointed
President of the Court of Protection and authorised to make these rules.

Commencement—The rules came into force on 1 October 2007. Part 22 of the Court of Protection
Rules 2007 (COPR 2007) contains transitional provisions in respect of applications received before

commencement of MCA 2005 but which have not been dealt with before 1 October 2007. It also sets out the procedure to follow in respect of an appeal from a pre-1 October 2007 decision. Part 22 is also supplemented by three Practice Directions.

MCA 2005—MCA 2005, Sch 5, paras 5 and 12 also contain provisions in respect of pending proceedings.

Future changes—In 2009, an Ad Hoc Rules Committee was set up by the President of the Family Division. Its stated aim was to "review the Court of Protection Rules 2007 which govern practice and procedure in the Court of Protection" and "to produce recommendations for new rules or amendments to existing rules, and supporting practice directions and forms, which set out a fair and efficient procedure in rules which are both simple and simply expressed". The Committee presented its final report in July 2010 and its recommendations were accepted by the President of the Family Division. However, there is no date set for the implementation of its recommendations yet. Where appropriate, its recommendations are incorporated into the commentary on the rules. For ease of reference, references to this report are to the Rules Committee Report.

2 Revocations

The following rules are revoked –

    (a)   the Court of Protection Rules 2001; and

    (b)   the Court of Protection (Enduring Powers of Attorney) Rules 2001.

Rule 2(a)—The Court of Protection Rules 2001, SI 2001/824 are replaced by these rules.

Policy aim—The stated policy aim of the new rules was described as providing a human-rights compliant process equally appropriate for cases relating to property and financial affairs which were heard in the 'old' Court of Protection and the personal welfare cases heard under the inherent jurisdiction of the High Court and which were governed by the Civil Procedure Rules 1998 (CPR), SI 1998/3132. The new rules were supposed seek to synthesise the previous regimes in the High Court and the old Court of Protection into one new set of rules able to cope with the new Court of Protection and its wide and extended jurisdiction.

The old Court of Protection was a more informal office of the Supreme Court. During the consultation process leading to the implementation of the rules, concerns were expressed by some that these rules would bring with them a loss of informality, ease of use, accessibility and speed that court users enjoyed with the old Court. However, a stated objective of the rules is to ensure that there is a greater understanding of procedures and to lend clarity to the court process.

Thus, the previous practice of making applications by informal letter or even by telephone to the Court is now replaced by a formal application being made on a specific form. The rules impose time-limits although they may not suit the circumstances or needs of every case. Formal directions are given in all cases. Formal hearings are also envisaged by the rules and judicial scrutiny replaces the use of civil servants known as nominated officers dealing with many routine matters.

On implementation of the MCA 2005, the clear challenge for the Court was to ensure that cases progressed in a way appropriate for each particular case and to ensure that procedural rules do not frustrate the real aims of the Court and the legislation that created it.

Whilst the court tries to take a pragmatic view in the orders it makes and its approach to case management, many criticise the rules as bringing too much formality to a jurisdiction that perhaps could have done without it. So too have the court forms been criticised. In its report, the Rules Committee stated that "the unanimous view" was that "the attempt to create a common practice and procedure for all types of application ... had failed and the practice and procedure should be application specific." The Rules Committee made various recommendations therefore to change the rules and the court forms.

Rule 2(b)—The Court of Protection (Enduring Powers of Attorney) Rules 2001, SI 2001/825 are replaced by the Lasting Powers of Attorney, Enduring Powers of Attorney and Public Guardian Regulations 2007, SI 2007/1253.

Scope—As the title suggests, these regulations deal with lasting powers of attorney, enduring powers of attorney and the functions of the Public Guardian. The Schedules to the regulations set out draft forms referred to in the Regulations.

PART 2
THE OVERRIDING OBJECTIVE

3 The overriding objective

(1) These Rules have the overriding objective of enabling the court to deal with a case justly, having regard to the principles contained in the Act.

(2) The court will seek to give effect to the overriding objective when it –

    (a)   exercises any power under these Rules; or

    (b)   interprets any rule or practice direction.

(3) Dealing with a case justly includes, so far as is practicable –

    (a)   ensuring that it is dealt with expeditiously and fairly;

    (b)   ensuring that P's interests and position are properly considered;

    (c)   dealing with the case in ways which are proportionate to the nature, importance and complexity of the issues;

    (d)   ensuring that the parties are on an equal footing;

    (e)   saving expense; and

    (f)   allotting to it an appropriate share of the court's resources, while taking account of the need to allot resources to other cases.

Rule 3(1)—The overriding objective of the rules is placed at the beginning to emphasise its importance and the need to support this objective when considering any matter under the other rules. The overriding objective, however, is not a new concept. Its genesis is in the CPR from where it has been imported with slight variations into the Family Proceedings Rules 1991, SI 1991/1247, r 51D (which applies it to ancillary relief proceedings), the Family Procedure (Adoption) Rules 2005, SI 2005/2795 and the Criminal Procedure Rules 2005, SI 2005/384. The overriding objective compels the court to deal with a case justly. These rules derive from MCA 2005 and the concept of dealing with a case justly must therefore be read in the context of the statutory principles set out at MCA 2005, s 1. In particular, one of the principles is that any act or decision must be in P's best interests. Accordingly, r 3(1) provides that regard must be had to the statutory principles.

Rule 3(2)(b)—The application of the overriding objective to Practice Directions is not included in the CPR. However, it is only proper that it should apply to Practice Directions within these rules. The overriding objective includes consideration of the statutory principles in MCA 2005 which apply to absolutely everything that derives from MCA 2005, which must include the Practice Directions.

'Justly'—When considering a course of action, the Court must consider if it is just for the person who lacks capacity as well as the parties. To do otherwise may not be in the best interests of P which would fall foul of r 3(3)(b).

Rule 3(3)(a): 'Expeditiously'—The Court will consider how best to conclude each case speedily but at the same time having P's best interests in mind.

There will clearly be some cases where a case must be concluded within a day, for example, an application for a statutory will where P is very ill and death is imminent. Some personal welfare applications may also need to be conducted at speed: for example where P is vulnerable and needs to be removed from a particular place or situation urgently or where P requires urgent medical treatment. There may also be some applications where delay can result in loss to P, for example, where permission is sought by a deputy to purchase a property and if the application is not heard quickly, the purchase will be lost.

However, it should not be overlooked that the nature of the Court's work is such that it is probably in P's interest in every case for the Court to ensure that the case progresses in an expeditious manner. Thus, the need for a case to progress quickly cannot be underestimated.

However, the court's resources are finite and stretched. The court must therefore realistically weigh the degree of expedition required in each a case which is not any easy task.

The Court will impose a timetable when making directions. In many cases, it may be appropriate for the court to shorten the time for certain steps to be taken. For example, when an application is issued and served on a respondent, the respondent has 21 days to acknowledge service (r 72). It may be appropriate to allow a shorter period so that the substantive application may progress. An example where this could apply is where an application is made for a deputy to be appointed to manage P's property and finances. P's finances may have been in complete disarray for many months before it was appreciated by P's family or social services that P needed assistance. Shortening the court process by reducing time periods in the rules will therefore be in P's best interests and just within the meaning of the overriding objective.

Rule 3(3)(b): 'P's interests and position are considered'—Consideration should be given as to whether P should be a party and whether the Official Solicitor should be asked to represent P. If P is not a party, it must not be forgotten that the case concerns P and the Court must therefore consider P's interests and position at every stage of the case. This rule should also be read in conjunction with r 3(1) which obligates reference to the principles contained in MCA 2005.

In the modern technological age, expedition in a case may include provision in an order for service of orders or other specified documents by e-mail.

Rule 3(3)(c): 'Proportionate to the nature, importance and complexity of the issues'—The nature of the Court's jurisdiction is that its work is diverse. One case may require a decision about serious medical treatment; another case may be an application to appoint the director of social services to be a deputy to allow the local authority to manage P's pension and state benefits. What this illustrates is that in every case, the Court's approach must be proportionate in terms of the directions it gives and case management generally.

Proportionality also extends to the final order. For example, when appointing a deputy, the Court should consider how wide the order should be drawn and balance the supervisory role of the Court against the freedom of a deputy or P's family to act on their own initiative on a day-to-day basis without having to constantly refer back to the Court.

In some cases, various allegations may be made, typically about the behaviour of a family member. When deciding whether or not a fact finding hearing is necessary, the court will need to consider if that is proportionate. See r 5(2)(c).

'nature'—The Court must have in mind when making any decision that it is working in a delicate and important jurisdiction where each case concerns a person who is vulnerable or at risk in one way or another. This criterion only appears in the Family Procedure (Adoption) Rules 2005, SI 2005/2795, which is also concerned with a delicate and important jurisdiction.

'Importance'—The Court's decision will affect P, a person who has no capacity and who is personally removed from the decision-making process. The decision could affect P for the remainder of his or her life; it may also affect P's family after P's death.

'Complexity'—The approach of the Court will also vary according to the type of case.

'Equal footing'—This refers to the parties only and P may not be a party. However, P's best interests still need to be considered.

'Saving expense'—Rules 156 and 157 contain general rules about who should pay the costs of a case. Although the Court may depart from the general rule if the circumstances so justify, the Court should have these rules in mind when considering the orders or directions it makes.

It is submitted that the Court should also consider if any final order it makes should avoid further costs being incurred. For example, by giving a deputy wide powers to avoid further applications being made which will incur costs including heavy court fees, dealing with a case on paper and avoiding hearings unless absolutely necessary.

'Court's resources'—Within the context of civil and family rules, this provision is often used to justify a conclusion that the court will not allow any more court time to be spent on a particular application or case. Thus, in *Albon v Naza Motor Trading* [2007] EWHC 2613 (Ch) Lightman J refused to adjourn a trial where a party had failed to act justly, reasonably and in accordance with the court's directions.

However, in the Court of Protection, use of the Court's resources takes on a more prominent role. It may include considering whether a hearing should take place in an old age home, whether a case deserves to be heard by a High Court judge or whether the case can be dealt with on paper. It may also colour the court's approach to an application by a family member who is obsessed with a particular issue and keeps trying to raise it or who seeks to derail a case which that family members believes will reach a conclusion unfavourable to his or her position.

4 The duty of the parties

The parties are required to help the court to further the overriding objective.

Scope—This includes providing full information as well as complying with orders and directions. Furtherance of the overriding objective is also achieved by the parties co-operating with each other to try to narrow or agree issues in dispute.

If a party refuses to co-operate with other parties or with the court, this may justify a costs sanction being applied. It is suggested that where a party faces an opponent who pays no regard to the obligation in this rule, the matter should be brought to the court's attention so that the court may consider warning that party about the potential for the court to make a costs order against him. See r 156 and the reference to *Re RC* (5 August 2010, unreported).

5 Court's duty to manage cases

(1) The court will further the overriding objective by actively managing cases.

(2) Active case management includes –

    (a) encouraging the parties to co-operate with each other in the conduct of the proceedings;

    (b) identifying at an early stage –

        (i) the issues; and

        (ii) who should be a party to the proceedings;

    (c) deciding promptly –

        (i) which issues need a full investigation and hearing and which do not; and

        (ii) the procedure to be followed in the case;

    (d) deciding the order in which issues are to be resolved;

    (e) encouraging the parties to use an alternative dispute resolution procedure if the court considers that appropriate;

    (f) fixing timetables or otherwise controlling the progress of the case;

    (g) considering whether the likely benefits of taking a particular step justify the cost of taking it;

    (h) dealing with as many aspects of the case as the court can on the same occasion;

    (i) dealing with the case without the parties needing to attend at court;

    (j) making use of technology; and

    (k) giving directions to ensure that the case proceeds quickly and efficiently.

Note—*Re AVS –v- A NHS Foundation Trust* (2010 EWHC 2746 (COP) is a judgment given by the Wall P after a directions hearing where he discusses his reasons for the directions he has made. It is a useful case to understand the court's approach.

Rule 5(1)—All case files are seen by a judge who will make appropriate orders or directions in every case (see r 89 and the rules concerning reconsideration of orders).

In some cases, the court's involvement may simply be the giving of directions on paper or at a single hearing. Other cases may require a number of directions or case management hearings to allow the court to monitor events and to make appropriate directions to progress the case to a final hearing.

Rule 5(2)(a)—It must be in P's best interests that a dispute is resolved as quickly as possible. Failure to co-operate must therefore not be in P's best interests. It may also be a factor that the court considers under r 159 when deciding whether to depart from the usual costs rules. In *Re RC* which is discussed in the commentary to rule 156, the court suggested that a warning needed to be given before departing from the no costs principle in rule 157 in health and welfare cases. Accordingly, non-co-operation by a party should be brought to the court's attention at the earliest possible time so

PART IV

that the court may warn that party of the costs consequences of non-compliance with the obligation in this rule. It will also allow the court to make further orders to remedy any problem that has arisen or to apply appropriate sanctions if necessary.

Rule 5(2)(b)(i)—The judge will read the court file, ascertain the issues and give appropriate directions. If the issues are not clear, the judge may seek clarification or list a directions hearing.

The Court is alive to the fact that some cases are an expression of family tensions and disagreements that can go back many years. It will therefore wish to ascertain whether or not there are genuine issues to be tried. A directions hearing will enable the court to achieve this aim.

In some cases, the court may need to decide if a fact finding hearing is necessary. This arises where allegations are made against a party which can affect the outcome of the case. A typical example is where allegations are made about the conduct or behaviour or a party, often a family member, by a local authority or family members.

The dilemma faced by the court is whether a fact finding hearing is proportionate either as a stand alone hearing or together with the final hearing.

There are clearly some cases where allegations that are made will be very serious and require a specific finding by the court to allow the main issue in the case to be decided. Such a case presents no problem as the court will recognise the need for the fact finding hearing and give appropriate directions. However, it is the case where there are a large number of minor allegations that can be difficult. If the court is required to make findings on each matter, it will lengthen the hearing and the time taken to dispose of the case often to the detriment of P. Accordingly, the court may consider that it will look at the various allegations in the round and form a view based on the more general evidence of the parties rather the embark on a disproportionate fact finding exercise. Obviously, each case is unique and the court will therefore need to consider the overriding objective, proportionality and its various case management duties as set out in this rule.

Rule 5(2)(b)(ii)—Given the general costs rules in rr 156 and 157, the Court will be loath to add parties to a case unless absolutely necessary.

When considering parties, however, the court is entitled to look further than those intimately involved in a dispute. It may consider that notice of the proceedings be given to a local authority, the Public Guardian or some other public body with a view to untimately joining them as a party.

Rule 5(2)(c)(i)—The comments about family disputes made under r 5(2)(b)(i) apply equally here. The Court will ensure that it is only trying the real issues in the case and not simply allowing disgruntled family members or others to use the court process for other unfair means.

Rule 5(2)(c)(ii)—Many applications may require uncomplicated directions for the parties to file evidence and a hearing date to be allocated. Others may require more involved directions. The Court will be anxious to ascertain what is best for each case.

For example, where objections to registration of an enduring power of attorney are received from a family member, the Court may simply order the attorney and the family member to file evidence so the case can proceed to a final hearing quickly. However, if the issues raised are more complicated, medical evidence may be required if capacity is an issue and the Official Solicitor may need to represent P.

The Rules Committee recommended that the practice and procedure of the court should reflect the differences in the nature of the court's work. It divided this work into three categories; non-contentious property and affairs applications, contentious property and affairs applications and health and welfare applications. Accordingly, any amendments to the rules may provide for a separate process for each of these work categories.

Rule 5(2)(d)—If, for example, amongst many issues in a case, it is alleged that P has capacity, the Court may deal with the issue of capacity first.

Rule 5(2)(e)—Litigants in any forum are expected to try to resolve their disputes and litigation is regarded as a last resort. Failure to engage in alternative dispute resolution (ADR) or mediation can result in unfavourable costs orders being made (see for example *Dunnett v Railtrack Plc* [2002] EWCA Civ 303)

Within the context of the Court of Protection, however, ADR and mediation can be problematic. This is because litigation in the court is different from the civil and family courts where there is simply an issue between two parties. In the Court of Protection, the court has to consider P's best interests in addition to considering the position of the parties in dispute. There may also be serious allegations such as fraud or abuse which require investigation and which cannot be negotiated away in ADR or mediation. Indeed, the overriding objective in rule 3 provides that a just disposal of the case must have regard to the principles in the Mental Capacity Act 2005. The result of ADR or mediation may not produce a settlement that complies with the Act which includes P's best interests.

However, ADR can be imposed by a judge giving a firm view at the case management hearing or by solicitors or the OPG giving guidance.

Nevertheless, the court should never be slow to demand of parties that they meet to discuss issues with a view to narrowing them or even settling them. Furthermore, a party who fails to try to resolve a dispute may find that the Court views him or her as unsuitable to be an attorney or deputy simply because he or she has shown him or herself unable to engage with others in a constructive way.

Rule 5(2)(f)—The Court will fix a timetable up to trial in most cases. The timetable will set out the steps to be taken by the parties and the dates for compliance. Those dates must be obeyed.

In more serious cases, the Court will consider imposing a self-reporting order in terms that if a party fails to comply with an order, that party must inform the Court so that the judge may give further directions to keep the case on track for its trial date. Indeed, failure to comply with an order is almost certainly not going to be in P's best interests.

Rule 5(2)(i)—Many of the Court's applications are dealt with on paper. However, the court can order a telephone hearing or video link

Rule 5(2)(j)—Part 14, Practice Direction A, para 21 and Practice Direction A, Annex 2 refer to video conferencing. Part 10, Practice Direction B, para 7 requires a disk containing a draft order when an urgent application is made. Part 10, Practice Direction A, paras 18–20 and Practice Direction B, para 12 deal with telephone hearings. Part 6, Practice Direction A, paras 4–8 deal with service by electronic means.

Rule 5(2)(k)—This may include shortening time for service of documents and taking other steps to ensure that the next or final hearing is not delayed. To achieve this objective, r 26 gives the court unparalleled flexibility.

PART 3
INTERPRETATION AND GENERAL PROVISIONS

6 Interpretation

In these Rules –

'the Act' means the Mental Capacity Act 2005;

'applicant' means a person who makes, or who seeks permission to make, an application to the court;

'application form' means the document that is to be used to begin proceedings in accordance with Part 9 of these Rules or any other provision of these Rules or the practice directions which requires the use of an application form;

'application notice' means the document that is to be used to make an application in accordance with Part 10 of these Rules or any other provision of these Rules or the practice directions which requires the use of an application notice;

'attorney' means the person appointed as such by an enduring power of attorney created, or purporting to have been created, in accordance with the regulations mentioned in paragraph 2 of Schedule 4 to the Act;

'business day' means a day other than –

(a) a Saturday, Sunday, Christmas Day or Good Friday; or

(b) a bank holiday in England and Wales, under the Banking and Financial Dealings Act 1971;

'child' means a person under 18;

'court' means the Court of Protection;

'deputy' means a deputy appointed under the Act;

'donee' means the donee of a lasting power of attorney;

'donor' means the donor of a lasting power of attorney, except where this expression is used in rule 68 or 201(5) (where it means the donor of an enduring power of attorney);

'enduring power of attorney' means an instrument created in accordance with such of the regulations mentioned in paragraph 2 of Schedule 4 to the Act as applied when it was executed;

'filing' in relation to a document means delivering it, by post or otherwise, to the court office;

'judge' means a judge nominated to be a judge of the court under the Act;

'lasting power of attorney' has the meaning given in section 9 of the Act;

['legal representative' means a –
  (a)   barrister,
  (b)   solicitor,
  (c)   solicitor's employee,
  (d)   manager of a body recognised under section 9 of the Administration of Justice Act 1985, or
  (e)   person who, for the purposes of the Legal Services Act 2007, is an authorised person in relation to an activity which constitutes the conduct of litigation (within the meaning of that Act),
  who has been instructed to act for a party in relation to any application;]

'LSC funded client' means an individual who receives services funded by the Legal Services Commission as part of the Community Legal Service within the meaning of Part I of the Access to Justice Act 1999;

'order' includes a declaration made by the court;

'P' means
  [(a)]   any person (other than a protected party) who lacks or, so far as consistent with the context, is alleged to lack capacity to make a decision or decisions in relation to any matter that is the subject of an application to the court[; and
  (b)   a relevant person as defined by paragraph 7 of Schedule A1 to the Act,]

and references to a person who lacks capacity are to be construed in accordance with the Act;

'party' is to be construed in accordance with rule 73;

'permission form' means the form that is to be used to make an application for permission to begin proceedings in accordance with Part 8 of these Rules;

'personal welfare' is to be construed in accordance with section 17 of the Act;

'President' and 'Vice-President' refer to those judges appointed as such under section 46(3)(a) and (b) of the Act;

'property and affairs' is to be construed in accordance with section 18 of the Act;

'protected party' means a party or an intended party (other than P or a child) who lacks capacity to conduct the proceedings;

'respondent' means a person who is named as a respondent in the application form or notice, as the case may be;

'Senior Judge' means the judge who has been nominated to be Senior Judge under section 46(4) of the Act, and references in these Rules to a circuit judge include the Senior Judge;

'Visitor' means a person appointed as such by the Lord Chancellor under section 61 of the Act.

Amendment—In definition 'P' words in square brackets inserted by Court of Protection (Amendment) Rules 2009, SI 2009/582; definition of 'legal representative' amended by SI 2009/3348.

"Child"—Note that section 18(3) of the Act allows the court to appoint a deputy for P where P is under 18 years. It is assumed that as the child is also P, the age restriction in this definition is not relevant.

'Filing'—Reference to is made to delivering a document by 'post or otherwise' to the Court office. Rule 10(3)(a) permits filing by fax and para 7 of Practice Direction A to Part 4 sets out the requirements for filing by fax. In particular, para 7(c) provides that the document is only considered filed when delivered by the Court's fax machine regardless of the time that is shown to have been transmitted from the party's machine.

There is no provision for e-mail filing.

'Judge'—High Court, circuit and district judges who have been nominated to hear Court of Protection cases.

'Senior Judge'—The present incumbent is Senior Judge Denzil Lush, Master of the old Court of Protection.

The Rules Committee made two recommendations for amendment to this rule. The first is to include a definition of 'hearing' to include hearings by telephone, video link or any other method permitted or directed by the rules. This would link this rule with r 25(2)(d). The second is to include definitions imported by the deprivation of liberty provisions in Part 10A.

7 Court officers

(1) Where these Rules permit or require the court to perform an act of a purely formal or administrative character, that act may be performed by a court officer.

(2) A requirement that a court officer carry out any act at the request of any person is subject to the payment of any fee required by a fees order for the carrying out of that act.

Rule 7(1)—Court officers should not be confused with nominated officers, who carried out much of the daily work of the old court, nor the nominated officers referred to in Part 22 who deal with transitional cases.

However, the Rules Committee has recommended that "strictly defined and limited non-contentious property and affairs applications" should be dealt with by court officers with an automatic right to refer any decision taken by the court officer to a judge. This recommendation is based on the reasoning that many issues placed before the court are administrative or straightforward and undisputed and allowing the work to be undertaken by a court officer will free up judge time and reduce delay.

8 Computation of time

(1) This rule shows how to calculate any period of time which is specified –

(a)   by these Rules;
(b)   by a practice direction; or
(c)   in an order or direction of the court.

(2) A period of time expressed as a number of days must be computed as clear days.

(3) In this rule 'clear days' means that in computing the number of days –

(a)   the day on which the period begins; and
(b)   if the end of the period is defined by reference to an event, the day on which that event occurs,

are not included.

(4) Where the specified period is 7 days or less, and would include a day which is not a business day, that day does not count.

PART IV

(5) When the specified period for doing any act at the court office ends on a day on which the office is closed, that act will be done in time if done on the next day on which the court office is open.

Court times—The court office closes at 4 pm.

"In an order or direction of the court"—In certain urgent matters, they could may need to abridge time and it may therefore be necessary to adapt the effect of this rule.

9 Application of the Civil Procedure Rules

In any case not expressly provided for by these Rules or the practice directions made under them, the Civil Procedure Rules 1998 (including any practice directions made under them) may be applied with any necessary modifications, insofar as is necessary to further the overriding objective.

Application of CPR—Application of CPR is not mandatory. The Court *may* apply it with any modifications.

Before applying CPR, the Court will not only consider the overriding objective but also whether it is in P's best interests. Indeed, P's best interests may preclude use of the CPR when it will bring about a more expensive and formal procedure which is not required in a particular case.

PART 4
COURT DOCUMENTS

10 Documents used in court proceedings

(1) The court will seal or otherwise authenticate with the stamp of the court the following documents on issue –

    (a)   a permission form;
    (b)   an application form;
    (c)   an application notice;
    (d)   an order; and
    (e)   any other document which a rule or practice direction requires to be sealed or stamped.

(2) Where these Rules or any practice direction require a document to be signed, that requirement is satisfied if the signature is printed by computer or other mechanical means.

(3) A practice direction may make provision for documents to be filed or sent to the court by –

    (a)   facsimile; or
    (b)   other means.

Rule 10(1)—The absence of a seal will mean that the document is not prima facie valid.

Rule 10(3)(a)—Practice Direction A, para 7 deals with filing documents at court by fax. Paragraph 7(c) provides that a document sent by fax is not considered delivered until it is delivered to the Court's fax machine. The fact that the sender has a record of its transmission is irrelevant.

Rule 10(3)(b)—There are no facilities to file by e-mail.

11 Documents required to be verified by a statement of truth

(1) The following documents must be verified by a statement of truth –

  (a)   a permission form, an application form or an application notice, where the applicant seeks to rely upon matters set out in the document as evidence;

  (b)   a witness statement;

  (c)   a certificate of –

    (i)   service or non-service; or

    (ii)   notification or non-notification;

  (d)   a deputy's declaration; and

  (e)   any other document required by a rule or practice direction to be so verified.

(2) Subject to paragraph (3), a statement of truth is a statement that –

  (a)   the party putting forward the document;

  (b)   in the case of a witness statement, the maker of the witness statement; or

  (c)   in the case of a certificate referred to in paragraph (1)(c), the person who signs the certificate,

believes that the facts stated in the document being verified are true.

(3) If a party is conducting proceedings with a litigation friend, the statement of truth in –

  (a)   a permission form;

  (b)   an application form; or

  (c)   an application notice,

is a statement that the litigation friend believes the facts stated in the document being verified are true.

(4) The statement of truth must be signed –

  (a)   in the case of a permission form, an application form or an application notice –

    (i)   by the party or litigation friend; or

    (ii)   by the legal representative on behalf of the party or litigation friend; and

  (b)   in the case of a witness statement, by the maker of the statement.

(5) A statement of truth which is not contained in the document which it verifies must clearly identify that document.

(6) A statement of truth in a permission form, an application form or an application notice may be made by –

  (a)   a person who is not a party; or

  (b)   two or more parties jointly,

where this is permitted by a relevant practice direction.

Rule 11(1)—Practice Direction B sets out the form and requirements of the statement of truth. The purpose of the statement of truth is set out at r 11(2).

Rule 11(4)—Paragraphs 7–16 of Practice Direction B explain who may sign the statement of truth. A legal representative who signs the statement of truth should have regard to para 16 of Practice Direction B, which sets out the basis upon which he or she is able to sign. Paragraphs 17–20 set out the procedure to follow where the person who should sign the statement of truth cannot read or sign the document.

PART IV

Position Statements—In some cases, a position statement will be filed by a party. The Rules Committee has recommended that this rule be amended to make it clear that the position statement does not need to have a statement of truth.

1(a): Court Forms—There are certain problems with the existing court forms. For example, the same information has to be repeated on various forms; some forms are verbose. The Rules Committee accepted the need to amend the forms and proposed various changes to the forms. If these changes are implemented, this rule may require amendment.

12 Failure to verify a document

If a permission form, application form or application notice is not verified by a statement of truth, the applicant may not rely upon the document as evidence of any of the matters set out in it unless the court permits.

13 Failure to verify a witness statement

If a witness statement is not verified by a statement of truth, it shall not be admissible in evidence unless the court permits.

14 False statements

(1) Proceedings for contempt of court may be brought against a person if he makes, or causes to be made, a false statement in a document verified by a statement of truth without an honest belief in its truth.

(2) Proceedings under this rule may be brought only –

    (a)   by the Attorney General; or
    (b)   with the permission of the court.

15 Personal details

(1) Where a party does not wish to reveal –

    (a)   his home address or telephone number;
    (b)   P's home address or telephone number;
    (c)   the name of the person with whom P is living (if that person is not the applicant); or
    (d)   the address or telephone number of his place of business, or the place of business of any of the persons mentioned in sub-paragraphs (b) or (c),

he must provide those particulars to the court.

(2) Where paragraph (1) applies, the particulars given will not be revealed to any person unless the court so directs.

(3) Where a party changes his home address during the course of the proceedings, he must give notice of the change to the court.

(4) Where a party does not reveal his home address, he must nonetheless provide an address for service which must be within the jurisdiction of the court.

Rule 15(1)—A similar provision is found in the Family Proceedings Rules 1991, SI 1991/1247, r 10(3).

This rule is based on a presumption that details will not be revealed unless the Court directs that it should.

However, r 15(4) provides that an address for service must be provided.

Rule 15(2)—When considering whether to reveal an address, the Court will have to consider P's best interests, the overall interests of justice and, within the context of the case, the overriding objective.

It is suggested that there should be a very good reason to maintain confidentiality. For example, identifying P's residence or care home could place him or her at risk.

16 Supply of documents to a party from court records

Unless the court orders otherwise, a party to proceedings may inspect or obtain from the records of the court a copy of –

    (a)   any document filed by a party to the proceedings; or

    (b)   any communication in the proceedings between the court and –

        (i)   a party to the proceedings; or

        (ii) another person.

'Unless the court orders otherwise'—For example, because it is not in P's best interests or where P or a party's rights of privacy would be compromised.

'Document'—This may include transcripts of hearings or of a judgment, skeleton arguments and opening and closing submissions. It does not include letters as r 16(b) refers to communications.

17 Supply of documents to a non-party from court records

(1) Subject to rules 20 and 92(2), a person who is not a party to proceedings may inspect or obtain from the court records a copy of any judgment or order given or made in public.

(2) The court may, on an application made to it, authorise a person who is not a party to proceedings to –

    (a)   inspect any other documents in the court records; or

    (b)   obtain a copy of any such documents, or extracts from such documents.

(3) A person making an application for an authorisation under paragraph (2) must do so in accordance with Part 10.

(4) Before giving an authorisation under paragraph (2), the court will consider whether any document is to be provided on an edited basis.

Rule 17(1): 'Court records'—Any new Court case has its own file entirely separate from the Public Guardian's file. However, files opened before 1 October 2007 will contain Court and Public Guardian documents; for example, court orders and correspondence relating to court proceedings together with Receiver's accounts and correspondence between the Receiver and the Public Guardian.

However, the fact that one file contains a mixture of documents does not mean that the whole file should be regarded as a Court file and subject to disclosure pursuant to this rule. The Court would need to consider where a document properly belongs before ordering its disclosure.

This issue could arise where, for example, a family member believes that a Receiver appointed some years ago has misappropriated monies. An application is made for disclosure of accounts and bank statements sent by the Receiver to the Public Guardian. These are not Court documents and do not form part of the formal records of the Court. It may therefore be necessary to join the Public Guardian as a party to the application so that he may make representations.

'Given or made in public'—Given that r 90 provides that proceedings are held in private, the opportunity to use r 17(1) may be limited. There may be cases where the judgment or final order was made at a public hearing. If so, there may be restrictions on publication of the names and other details.

Rule 17(2): 'extracts'—Any order permitting disclosure would have to set out exactly what part of a document is to be extracted and disclosed.

Rule 17(4): 'edited basis'—See rules 19 and 20(6) which allow a document to be edited prior to service or disclosure.

Similar provisions to rr 16 and 17 are contained at CPR Part 5. Cases decided in accordance with those provisions may provide useful guidance to the Court in considering an application under rr 16 and 17. However, those cases are commercial cases; any application under these rules will consider P's best interests and the nature of the case may lend itself to a different outcome.

Nevertheless, some useful principles can be taken from existing case-law:

- The applicant should identify what document he or she requires as far as possible (per Moore-Bick J in *Dian v Davis Frankel and Mead* [2004] EWHC 2662 Comm).
- An application should be made promptly (*Chan U Seek v Alvis Vehicles Ltd and Guardian Newspapers* [2004] EWHC 3092 Ch).
- An application by a newspaper for disclosure in an 'old and stale case' may be refused (per Parker J in *Chan*).
- What end is disclosure intended to serve (per Moore-Bick J in *Dian*).
- Where an applicant wanted disclosure of documents that would help it in related litigation, despite there being a private and evidence interest as opposed to a public interest, disclosure was granted (see *Dian*).
- Although a newspaper's motive in seeking disclosure went beyond its stated desire to prepare an accurate report of the case disclosure was still given (see *Chan*).
- The fact that only the judge read the document may not bar disclosure (*Chan* and *Dian*).
- The 'press are just part of the public' (per Parker J in *Chan*).
- A transcript may not be part of the records of the court (*Chan*).
- Disclosure may be refused where there are strong considerations of commercial confidentiality (*Lilly Icos Ltd v Pfizer (No 2)* [2002] EWCA Civ 2).

18 Subsequent use of court documents

(1) Where a document has been filed or disclosed, a party to whom it was provided may use the document only for the purpose of the proceedings in which it was filed or disclosed, except where –

    (a) the document has been read to or by the court or referred to at a public hearing; or

    (b) the court otherwise permits.

(2) Paragraph (1)(a) is subject to any order of the court made under rule 92(2).

19 Editing information in court documents

(1) A party may apply to the court for an order that a specified part of a document is to be edited prior to the document's service or disclosure.

(2) An order under paragraph (1) may be made at any time.

(3) Where the court makes an order under this rule any subsequent use of that document in the proceedings shall be of the document as edited, unless the court directs otherwise.

(4) An application under this rule must be made in accordance with Part 10.

20 Public Guardian to be supplied with court documents relevant to supervision of deputies

(1) This rule applies in any case where the court makes an order –

    (a)   appointing a person to act as a deputy; or

    (b)   varying an order under which a deputy has been appointed.

(2) Subject to paragraphs (3) and (6), the Public Guardian is entitled to be supplied with a copy of qualifying documents if he reasonably considers that it is necessary for him to have regard to them in connection with the discharge of his functions under section 58 of the Act in relation to the supervision of deputies.

(3) The court may direct that the right to be supplied with documents under paragraph (2) does not apply in relation to such one or more documents, or descriptions of documents, as the court may specify.

(4) A direction under paragraph (3) or (6) may be given –

    (a)   either on the court's own initiative or on an application made to it; and

    (b)   either –

        (i)   at the same time as the court makes the order which appoints the deputy, or which varies it; or

        (ii)   subsequently.

(5) 'Qualifying documents' means documents which –

    (a)   are filed in court in connection with the proceedings in which the court makes the order referred to in paragraph (1); and

    (b)   are relevant to –

        (i)   the decision to appoint the deputy;

        (ii)   any powers conferred on him;

        (iii) any duties imposed on him; or

        (iv) any other terms applying to those powers and duties which are contained in the order.

(6) The court may direct that any document is to be provided to the Public Guardian on an edited basis.

21 Provision of court order to Public Guardian

Any order of the court requiring the Public Guardian to do something, or not to do something, will be served by the court on the Public Guardian as soon as practicable and in any event not later than 7 days after the order was made.

Note—This rule only covers a situation where the court's order is directed to the Public Guardian. However, it may be sensible in some cases to order a deputy or other parties to inform the Public Guardian of a particular court order against them. Although the court has power to do this under the exisiting rules, it has been suggested that this rule should be amended to include such a provision if only to emphasise the possibility of such an order.

22 Amendment of application

(1) The court may allow or direct an applicant, at any stage of the proceedings, to amend his application form or notice.

(2) The amendment may be effected by making in writing the necessary alterations to the application form or notice, but if the amendments are so numerous or of such a nature or length that written alteration would make it difficult or inconvenient to read, a fresh document amended as allowed or directed may be issued.

PART IV

23 Clerical mistakes or slips

The court may at any time correct any clerical mistakes in an order or direction or any error arising in an order or direction from any accidental slip or omission.

The slip rule—This provision adopts what is commonly known as the slip rule.

24 Endorsement of amendment

Where an application form or notice, order or direction has been amended under this Part, a note shall be placed on it showing the date on which it was amended and the alteration shall be sealed.

PART 5
GENERAL CASE MANAGEMENT POWERS

25 The court's general powers of case management

(1) The list of powers in this rule is in addition to any powers given to the court by any other rule or practice direction or by any other enactment or any powers it may otherwise have.

(2) The court may –

    (a) extend or shorten the time for compliance with any rule, practice direction, or court order or direction (even if an application for extension is made after the time for compliance has expired);

    (b) adjourn or bring forward a hearing;

    (c) require P, a party, a party's legal representative or litigation friend, to attend court;

    (d) hold a hearing and receive evidence by telephone or any other method of direct oral communication;

    (e) stay the whole or part of any proceedings or judgment either generally or until a specified date or event;

    (f) consolidate proceedings;

    (g) hear two or more applications on the same occasion;

    (h) direct a separate hearing of any issue;

    (i) decide the order in which issues are to be heard;

    (j) exclude an issue from consideration;

    (k) dismiss or give judgment on an application after a decision is made on a preliminary basis;

    (l) direct any party to file and serve an estimate of costs; and

    (m) take any step or give any direction for the purpose of managing the case and furthering the overriding objective.

(3) A judge to whom a matter is allocated may, if he considers that the matter is one which ought properly to be dealt with by another judge, transfer the matter to such a judge.

(4) Where the court gives directions it may take into account whether or not a party has complied with any rule or practice direction.

(5) The court may make any order it considers appropriate even if a party has not sought that order.

(6) A power of the court under these Rules to make an order includes a power to vary or revoke the order;

(7) Rules 25.12 to 25.15 of the Civil Procedure Rules 1998 (which make provision about security for costs) apply in proceedings to which these Rules apply as if the references in those Rules to 'defendant' and 'claimant' were to 'respondent' and 'applicant' respectively.

Scope of rule—This rule deals with the Court's case management powers. Case management at the Court of Protection is undertaken by the Senior Judge and nominated district judges who sit at the court in Archway, London.

If a case is transferred to a Regional Court, for example, because it is more convenient for the parties for a case to be held there, the judges at Archway will endeavour manage the case until the final hearing although in some cases, this may not be practical.

All applications in existing cases and new case files will be seen by a judge. When approaching case management, the judges will ascertain the issues and decide the best path for the case.

When giving directions, the Court will always have P's best interests in mind.

The Court will manage cases in a proportionate way to try to avoid unnecessary costs being incurred. Many cases will be dealt with solely on paper. If an interim hearing is required, it is likely to be conducted on the telephone to save costs.

The Court is mindful of the fact that the costs of a case will often be met by recourse to P's funds.

The Court is alive to the fact that the nature of its work is very diverse. Accordingly, the Court will manage a case in a way that suits the needs of that case. The Court will endeavour to adopt a flexible approach rather than just utilise standard and unyielding procedures.

Some cases may involve parties who have no dispute between them but who require a court order for a specific purpose to validate their wishes; such a case can be fast tracked to reach a speedy conclusion. Other cases, however, may reveal implacable hostility between the parties which demand a full investigation or raise serious welfare issues; such cases will require careful case management.

Some practitioners found it difficult to adapt to the existence of a new Court with new procedures. The business of the old Court of Protection was often conducted by letters, informal hearings, telephone calls seeking advice and permission being given for certain steps to be taken over the telephone. Indeed, the Court still receives letters from practitioners asking for advice or requesting a telephone conversation with a judge to discuss a particular point. However, as time passes, this is less frequent as practitioners appreciate that the rules and procedures imposed on a case have to be respected.

Rule 25(2)(a)—This provision is important as, in places, the rules can be cumbersome; for example, 21 days is allowed to acknowledge service of proceedings (r 72). Thus, there may be a need even in a routine case to shorten time for certain basic steps to be taken so that the Court may proceed to make a final order quickly. The Court will almost certainly have to shorten certain time-limits in more serious cases as failure to do so would be against P's best interests and a breach of the overriding objective.

Rule 25(2)(b)—For example, an application for a statutory will where the Court is informed that P's health has deteriorated and there is a concern that P may not live until the hearing date.

Rule 25(2)(c)—As well as considering attendance at a hearing, the court should consider if it can dispense with attendance at a hearing. For example, whether the Official Solicitor needs to attend a directions hearing and if he can present his position in writing. See paragraph 7 of the President's Guidance dated December 2010.

Rule 25(2)(d): 'telephone'—See Part 10, Practice Direction A, paras 18–20 which deal with telephone hearings. A telephone hearing is very useful in the context of the work of the Court of Protection. Many applications are dealt with on paper and if the papers are not clear on a point, the judge may arrange for a telephone hearing to take place on short notice to allow the issue to be clarified and the matter finalised.

Rule 25(2)(d): 'other method of direct oral communication'—See Part 10, Practice Direction A, para 21 and Part 14, Practice Direction A, Annex 2 which deal with video conferencing. There are facilities for video conferencing at Archway.

PART IV

Rule 25(2)(e)—When ordering a stay, the court must ensure that it is in P's best interests and that any delay to the final outcome of a case is not contrary to P's interests.

Rule 25(2)(f)—For example, where objections to registration of an enduring power of attorney are received from different people, it is sensible to consolidate them to be heard together.

Rule 25(2)(h)—A common example is where it is contended that P does not lack capacity. It may be sensible to deal with this at a separate hearing. Another example is where a fact finding hearing is necessary. The court may decide to list this hearing in advance of the final hearing.

Rule 25(2)(j)—An example is where the Court feels that an issue is really an expression of bad feelings or ill-will within a family and that issue has no real bearing on the substantive dispute before the Court.

Rule 25(2)(m): 'any direction ... and furthering the overriding objective'—This rule gives a very wide power to the Court. It could include a costs capping order.

Rule 25(3)—Part 9, Practice Direction E, paras 11 and 12 contain guidelines for serious medical cases which should be heard by a High Court judge.

Rule 86 and Part 12, Practice Direction A, paras 2 and 3 also deal with allocation of certain cases to the President and others to a High Court judge.

Subject to those rules, it will be for the resident judge at Archway to consider which tier of judiciary is most appropriate to the case. The Court will also consider if the case should be transferred to a regional judge, for example, where the parties live outside London and it would be more convenient for them to attend court at a regional centre.

It would seem to be clear from the rules that only the most exceptional cases should be heard by a High Court judge.

Rule 25(7)—CPR, rr 25.12–25.15 concern security for costs.

The Rules Committee has suggested that this rule should be amended to include a provision that will expect the court to direct the heading of the case to be used in documents in the case to allow identification of the parties. Traditionally, a case was often referred to as *Re A*, *Re B* etc. However, this is not helpful as it does not identify the parties. In most health and welfare cases, the court will direct that there should be an applicant and respondent and it does make sense to include this in the court's case management powers.

26 Court's power to dispense with requirement of any rule

In addition to its general powers and the powers listed in rule 25, the court may dispense with the requirement of any rule.

Scope of rule—This rule is consistent with the nature of the Court's work and the need for flexibility.

27 Exercise of powers on the court's own initiative

(1) Except where these Rules or some other enactment make different provision, the court may exercise its powers on its own initiative.

(2) The court may make an order on its own initiative without hearing the parties or giving them the opportunity to make representations.

(3) Where the court proposes to make an order on its own initiative it may give the parties and any person it thinks fit an opportunity to make representations and, where it does so, it will specify the time by which, and the manner in which, the representations must be made.

(4) Where the court proposes –

    (a)   to make an order on its own initiative; and

    (b)   to hold a hearing to decide whether to make the order, it will give the parties and may give any other person it thinks likely to be affected by the order at least 3 days' notice of the hearing.

28 General power of the court to rectify matters where there has been an error of procedure

Where there has been an error of procedure, such as a failure to comply with a rule or practice direction –

    (a)   the error does not invalidate any step taken in the proceedings unless the court so orders; and

    (b)   the court may waive the error or require it to be remedied or may make such other order as appears to the court to be just.

PART 6
SERVICE OF DOCUMENTS

Service generally

29 Scope

(1) Subject to paragraph (2), the rules in this Part apply to –

    (a)   the service of documents; and

    (b)   to the requirement under rule 70 for a person to be notified of the issue of an application form,

and references to 'serve', 'service', 'notice' and 'notify', and kindred expressions shall be construed accordingly.

(2) The rules in this Part do not apply where –

    (a)   any other enactment, a rule in another Part or a practice direction makes different provision; or

    (b)   the court directs otherwise.

30 Who is to serve

(1) The general rule is that the following documents will be served by the court –

    (a)   an order or judgment of the court;

    (b)   an acknowledgment of service or notification; and

    (c)   except where the application is for an order for committal, a notice of hearing.

(2) Any other document is to be served by the party seeking to rely upon it, except where –

    (a)   a rule or practice direction provides otherwise; or

    (b)   the court directs otherwise.

(3) Where the court is to serve a document –

    (a)   it is for the court to decide which of the methods of service specified in rule 31 is to be used; and

    (b)   if the document is being served on behalf of a party, that party must provide sufficient copies.

Note—Proposals for reform: The Rules Committee considered the rules of service and notification. It stated that it was "clear that many people do no understand the difference between these concepts and the purpose of the present provisions, and that they introduce confusion and annoyance and the potential for turning a non-contentious application into one that is disputed".

The Rules Committee made a number of recommendations to Parts 6 and 7 including:

1   PD 6A should be amended to allow for service on a legal representative qualified to practice in England and Wales but working elsewhere in the EU (see EU Services Directive 2006/123/EC)

2   Guidance should be incorporated into a practice direction to set out how an applicant should give notice prior to proceedings including if appropriate obtaining consents to file with an application. This would allow an application that is non-contentious and unopposed to be filed with all necessary notifictions and consents such that it could proceed to the making of a final order without any delay

3   The time limits in the various rules needed to be changed. This recommendation is set against the criticism that delay in a routine application occurs naturally by dint of time limits imposed in the rules.

Rule 30(3)(a): 'It is for the court to decide ...'—Practice Direction A, para 13 provides that service by the Court will normally be by first class post although there is nothing to stop the Court using the document exchange or some other means of service if it wishes.

31 Methods of service

(1) A document may be served by any of the methods specified in this rule.

(2) Where it is not known whether a solicitor is acting on behalf of a person, the document may be served by –

(a)   delivering it to the person personally;

(b)   delivering it at his home address or last known home address; or

(c)   sending it to that address, or last known address, by first class post (or by an alternative method of service which provides for delivery on the next working day).

(3) Where a solicitor –

(a)   is authorised to accept service on behalf of a person; and

(b)   has informed the person serving the document in writing that he is so authorised,

the document must be served on the solicitor, unless personal service is required by an enactment, rule, practice direction or court order.

(4) Where it appears to the court that there is a good reason to authorise service by a method other than those specified in paragraphs (2) or (3), the court may direct that service is effected by that method.

(5) A direction that service is effected by an alternative method must specify –

(a)   the method of service; and

(b)   the date when the document will be deemed to be served.

(6) A practice direction may set out how documents are to be served by document exchange, electronic communication or other means.

Rule 31(3): 'unless personal service is required ...'—Good practice would suggest that the solicitor is told about any service direct on his or her client and provided with a copy of any relevant order unless this would not be appropriate.

Rule 31(4)—This rule and r 31(5) deal with service by an alternative method.

The procedure to follow when making the application is set out at Practice Direction A, para 15. The application must be made on Form COP9. This means that even if the application is made at the outset of proceedings on filing COP1, Form COP9 should still be used for this application. The witness statement in support of the application is on Form COP24.

An order under this rule could therefore allow service on P through the manager of a residential home or for oral service by a relative or solicitor explaining the application personally to P.

Rule 31(6)—Practice Direction A, paras 1–8 contain rules about electronic service and service by document exchange.

Paragraph 5(a) sets out conditions to allow service by electronic means.

32 Service of documents on children and protected parties

(1) The following table shows the person on whom a document must be served if it is a document which would otherwise be served on –

(a)   a child; or
(b)   a protected party.

Type of document	Nature of party	Person to be served
Application form	Child	A person who has parental responsibility for the child within the meaning of the Children Act 1989; or
		if there is no such person, a person with whom the child resides or in whose care the child is.
Application form	Protected party	The person who is authorised to conduct the proceedings in the protected party's name or on his behalf; or
		a person who is a duly appointed attorney, donee or deputy of the protected party; or
		if there is no such person, a person with whom the protected party lives or in whose care the latter is.
Application for an order appointing a litigation friend, where a child or protected party has no litigation friend	Child or protected party	See rule 145 (appointment of litigation friend by court order – supplementary).
Any other document	Child or protected party	The litigation friend or other duly authorised person who is conducting the proceedings on behalf of the child or protected party.

(2) The court may make an order for service on a child or a protected party by permitting the document to be served on some person other than the person specified in the table set out in paragraph (1) above (which may include service on the child or the protected party).

(3) An application for an order under paragraph (2) may be made without notice.

(4) The court may order that, although a document has been served on someone other than the person specified in the table, the document is to be treated as if it had been properly served.

(5) This rule does not apply in relation to the service of documents upon a child in any case where the court has made an order under rule 141(4) permitting the child to conduct proceedings without a litigation friend.

Rule 32(2)—The application should be made on Form COP9. Although the Practice Direction is silent as to the procedure to follow, it is suggested that a witness statement in Form COP24 should accompany the application explaining why the order is required.

33 Service of documents on P if he becomes a party

(1) If P becomes a party to the proceedings, all documents to be served on him must be served on his litigation friend or other person duly authorised to conduct proceedings on P's behalf.

(2) The court may make an order for service on P by permitting the document to be served on some person other than the person specified in paragraph (1) above (which may include service on P).

(3) An application for an order under paragraph (2) may be made without notice.

(4) The court may order that, although a document has been served on someone other than a person specified in paragraph (1), the document is to be treated as if it had been properly served.

(5) This rule does not apply in relation to the service of documents upon P in any case where the court has made an order under rule 147(2) (procedure where appointment of a litigation friend comes to an end – for P).

Rule 33(1)—A person duly authorised to conduct proceedings would include the Official Solicitor.

Rule 33(2)—This would cover service on a care worker or the manager of a care home if appropriate or anyone else whom the Court felt should be involved. Before allowing any document to be served personally on P, however, the Court should exercise care as P could be caused unnecessary distress.

34 Substituted service

Where it appears to the court that it is impracticable for any reason to serve a document in accordance with any of the methods provided under rule 31, the court may make an order for substituted service of the document by taking such steps as the court may direct to bring it to the notice of the person to be served.

Scope of rule—Substituted service of a document could include an order that it is served on the manager of a care home for him or her to serve on P.

35 Deemed service

(1) A document which is served in accordance with these Rules or any relevant practice direction shall be deemed to be served on the day shown in the following table –

Method of service	Deemed day of service
First class post (or other service for next-day delivery)	The second day after it was posted.

Document exchange	The second day after it was left at the document exchange.
Delivering the document to a permitted address	The day after it was delivered to that address.
Fax	If it is transmitted on a business day before 4 p.m., on that day; or
	in any other case, on the business day after the day on which it is transmitted.
Other electronic means	The second day after the day on which it is transmitted.

(2) If a document is served personally –

    (a)   after 5 p.m., on a business day; or

    (b)   at any time on a Saturday, Sunday or a Bank Holiday,

it will be treated as being served on the next business day.

36 Certificate of service

(1) Where a rule, practice direction or court order requires a certificate of service for the document, the certificate must state the details set out in the following table –

Method of service	*Details to be certified*
First class post (or any other service for next-day delivery)	Date of posting.
Personal service	Date of personal service
Document exchange	Date when the document was left at the document exchange.
Delivery of document to permitted address	Date when the document was delivered to that address.
Fax	Date of transmission.
Other electronic means	Date of transmission and the means used.
Alternative method permitted by the court	As required by the court.

(2) The certificate must be filed within 7 days after service of the document to which it relates.

Form—The certificate of service is Form COP20. The Rules Committee has recommended that the form be changed to allow service of a number of people to be included on one shorter form as opposed to the present requirement of filing one long form for each person served.

37 Certificate of non-service

(1) Where an applicant or other person is unable to serve any document under these Rules or as directed by the court, he must file a certificate of non-service stating the reasons why service has not been effected.

(2) The certificate of non-service must be filed within 7 days of the latest date on which service should have been effected.

Form—The certificate of non-service is Form COP20.

38 Power of court to dispense with service

(1) The court may dispense with any requirement to serve a document.

(2) An application for an order to dispense with service may be made without notice.

Practice Direction—Practice Direction A, para 17 provides that the application should be made on Form COP9. Although not mandatory, it may be prudent in some cases to file a witness statement in Form COP24 explaining why the order is required.

Service out of the jurisdiction

39 Application of Family Procedure (Adoption) Rules 2005

(1) The rules in Section 2 of Part 6 of the Family Procedure (Adoption) Rules 2005 ('the 2005 Rules') apply, with the modifications set out in this rule, to the service of documents out of the jurisdiction.

(2) References in the 2005 Rules to the Hague Convention shall be read in these Rules as references to the Convention on the International Protection of Adults signed at the Hague on 13th January 2000 (Cm. 5881).

(3) References in the 2005 Rules to the Senior Master of the Queen's Bench Division shall be read in these Rules as references to the Senior Judge.

Scope of rule—This rule incorporates the Family Procedure (Adoption) Rules 2005, SI 2005/2795, Part 6, Section 2 which is set out in Part IV of this book for convenience together with its Practice Direction.

However, on 1 April 2011, the Family Proceedings Rules 2010 will replace the Family Procedure (Adoption) Rules 2005. However, r 39 will not be amended which suggests that the 2005 rules will still be applied in the Court of Protection.

In the event that the court applies the new rules, reference should be made to r 6 of the FPR 2010 which contains the relevant corresponding provisions.

PART 7
NOTIFYING P

General requirement to notify P

40 General

(1) Subject to paragraphs (2) and (3), the rules in this Part apply where P is to be given notice of any matter or document, or is to be provided with any document, either under the Rules or in accordance with an order or direction of the court.

(2) If P becomes a party, the rules in this Part do not apply and service is to be effected in accordance with Part 6 or as directed by the court.

(3) In any case the court may, either on its own initiative or on application, direct that P must not be notified of any matter or document, or provided with any document, whether in accordance with this Part or at all.

Scope of rule—This rule sets out a general obligation to notify P of any matter or document. It is supplemented by Practice Direction A.See the commentary under r30 regarding recommendations for change to this rule made by the Rules Committee.

It should be noted that unlike r 32, there is no provision for service on a person who has parental responsibility under the Children Act 1989 where P is a child.

Rule 69 specifically provides that P must be notified in accordance with COPR 2007, Part 7 unless this requirement has been dispensed with under r 49 or where P is a party and P will be served in accordance with Part 6 (r 40(2)).

Rule 74 provides that P will be bound by any order made or directions given by the court in the same way that a party is bound.

For consideration as to whether it is appropriate for P to be a party to proceedings, see rr 3(3)(b), 5(2)(b)(ii), 50–53 and 85(c).

Rule 40(2)—Part 6 sets out the manner in which proceedings are served.

Rule 40(3)—For example, if notification will harm or distress P in some way. If at the outset of a case, it is believed that notice will harm P in any way, the medical practitioner who completes the assessment of capacity form (COP3) should include this information which should be brought to the Court's attention.

41 Who is to notify P

(1) Where P is to be notified under this Part, notification must be effected by –

    (a)   the applicant;
    (b)   the appellant (where the matter relates to an appeal);
    (c)   an agent duly appointed by the applicant or the appellant; or
    (d)   such other person as the court may direct.

(2) The person within paragraph (1) is referred to in this Part as 'the person effecting notification'.

Rule 41(1)(c): 'an agent'—This could include a doctor, care worker, social worker or a member of P's family. The question of notifying P is a delicate matter and the applicant must give careful consideration as to how this should be done.

Circumstances in which P must be notified

42 Application forms

(1) P must be notified-

    (a)   that an application form has been issued by the court;
    (b)   that an application form has been withdrawn; and
    (c)   of the date on which a hearing is to be held in relation to the matter, where that hearing is for disposing of the application.

(2) Where P is to be notified that an application form has been issued, the person effecting notification must explain to P –

    (a)   who the applicant is;
    (b)   that the application raises the question of whether P lacks capacity in relation to a matter or matters, and what that means;
    (c)   what will happen if the court makes the order or direction that has been applied for; and
    (d)   where the application contains a proposal for the appointment of a person to make decisions on P's behalf in relation to the matter to which the application relates, details of who that person is.

(3) Where P is to be notified that an application form has been withdrawn, the person effecting notification must explain to P –

(a) that the application form has been withdrawn; and

(b) the consequences of that withdrawal.

(4) The person effecting notification must also inform P that he may seek advice and assistance in relation to any matter of which he is notified.

Rule 42(1)(a)—Practice Direction A, para 3 provides that an application does not include an application notice that is made under Part 10, being an application made in the course of proceedings. However, P may be notified if the applicant believes this is appropriate. It should also be noted that the notification requirement is when the application is issued. This means that P cannot be informed before the application is made which is not practical.

Rule 42(2)—If an agent is instructed to effect service in accordance with r 41(1)(c), the agent should be informed as to the requirements of this rule so that notice is properly given. The agent should also be instructed that in many cases, P will not have any understanding as to what is being said but the rule's requirements still apply. Rule 42(4) states that P should be told that he or she may take advice. The obvious criticism of this rule is that it is an onerous or unnecessary task to explain something to a person who may have no ability to understand the information at all. See commentary on r43 below.

43 Appeals

(1) P must be notified –

(a) that an appellant's notice has been issued by the court;

(b) that an appellant's notice has been withdrawn; and

(c) of the date on which a hearing is to be held in relation to the matter, where that hearing is for disposing of the appellant's notice.

(2) Where P is to be notified that an appellant's notice has been issued, the person effecting notification must explain to P –

(a) who the appellant is;

(b) the issues raised by the appeal; and

(c) what will happen if the court makes the order or direction that has been applied for.

(3) Where P is to be notified that an appellant's notice has been withdrawn, the person effecting notification must explain to P –

(a) that the appellant's notice has been withdrawn; and

(b) the consequences of that withdrawal.

(4) The person effecting notification must also inform P that he may seek advice and assistance in relation to any matter of which he is notified.

Rule 43(2)—Care must be taken as with r 42(2) that the person giving notice is aware of the requirements of this rule and of r 43(4).

The Rules Committee has recognised that rr 42 and 43 are difficult to comply with when P has no ability to comprehend information. Instead of dispensing with notice, it has suggested that the person who effects service should instead comment on the extent to which P appeared to comprehend information and this should be included in the information given in the certificate filed in accordance with r 48.

44 Final orders

(1) P must be notified of a final order of the court.

(2) Where P is notified in accordance with this rule, the person effecting notification must explain to P the effect of the order.

(3) The person effecting notification must also inform P that he may seek advice and assistance in relation to any matter of which he is notified.

Rule 44(2)—The person should also be able to explain the order in simple language.

In practice, this means that P is notified twice in even the most straight-forward application; on making the application and of the final order which could be said to be unnecessary.

45 Other matters

(1) This rule applies where the court directs that P is to be notified of any other matter.

(2) The person effecting notification must explain to P such matters as may be directed by the court.

(3) The person effecting notification must also inform P that he may seek advice and assistance in relation to any matter of which he is notified.

Rule 45(3)—The comments made under r 44(2) apply equally here.

Manner of notification, and accompanying documents

46 Manner of notification

(1) Where P is to be notified under this Part, the person effecting notification must provide P with the information specified in rules 42 to 45 in a way that is appropriate to P's circumstances (for example, using simple language, visual aids or any other appropriate means).

(2) The information referred to in paragraph (1) must be provided to P personally.

(3) P must be provided with the information mentioned in paragraph (1) as soon as practicable and in any event within 21 days of the date on which –

    (a)   the application form or appellant's notice was issued or withdrawn;

    (b)   the order was made; or

    (c)   the person effecting notification received the notice of hearing from the court and in any event no later than 14 days before the date specified in the notice of the hearing,

as the case may be.

Scope of rule—In many cases, P will not be able to understand anything and the requirement of this rule may be discharged by simply telling P about the application or order in very simple terms.

A letter is unlikely to be acceptable as P may not understand its contents.

Every effort should be made to inform P in a way that he or she will understand. The rule gives examples such as using simple language or visual aids. It should also not be forgotten that MCA 2005 allows the Court to determine that P lacks capacity for one matter but not for another.

For example, P may not be able to look after his or her intricate financial affairs but may have capacity to understand basic matters. P is therefore entitled to know about any application or order and for that information to be imparted to him or her in a way which he or she will understand.

The manner of notification should be considered as soon as possible so that immediately it is required, P can be notified in a considered way.

Notification is given on Form COP14. Form COP14A gives guidance on how to complete Form COP14.

PART IV

47 Acknowledgment of notification

When P is notified that an application form or an appellant's notice has been issued, he must also be provided with a form for acknowledging notification.

Scope of rule—The acknowledgement is Form COP5. Very often P will be unable to do anything with the form. When the certificate of notification (Form COP20) is returned to the Court, good practice suggests that the Court is informed in an accompanying letter that it is unlikely that P will return the acknowledgement. For example, it could be noted that 'I left the acknowledgement on P's bedside table but as he had no understanding of what was happening, I believe that he will do nothing with it'.

48 Certificate of notification

The person effecting notification must, within 7 days beginning with the date on which notification in accordance with this Part was given, file a certificate of notification which certifies –

(a)   the date on which P was notified; and
(b)   that he was notified in accordance with this Part.

Scope of rule—The certificate is Form COP20. If notification has not been possible, r 37 provides that COP20 must be filed within 7 days of the latest date on which service should have been effected. It should be noted that until COP20 is filed, the Court often cannot take any further step in an application. It is very common for this step to be overlooked, which causes unnecessary delay.

49 Dispensing with requirement to notify, etc

(1) The applicant, the appellant or other person directed by the court to effect notification may apply to the court seeking an order –

(a)   dispensing with the requirement to comply with the provisions in this Part; or
(b)   requiring some other person to comply with the provisions in this Part.

(2) An application under this rule must be made in accordance with Part 10.

Scope of rule—The application is made on COP9. Practice Direction A, para 9 gives examples where an application may be appropriate, such as where P is in a persistent vegetative state or where notification will cause significant and disproportionate distress.

   The Court will consider if dispensing with notification is in P's best interests and consistent with the overriding objective contained in r 3 which compels the Court to consider P's interests and position.

PART 8
PERMISSION

50 General

Subject to these Rules and to section 50(1) of, and paragraph 20 of Schedule 3 to, the Act, the applicant must apply for permission to start proceedings under the Act.

(Section 50(1) of the Act specifies persons who do not need to apply for permission. Paragraph 20 of Schedule 3 to the Act specifies an application for which permission is not needed.)

Scope of rule—This rule deals with the requirement to seek permission before making an application. It is supplemented by Practice Direction A.

MCA 2005, s 50 sets out when permission is required.

MCA 2005, s 50(1) provides that permission is not required for an application by:

(a) a person who lacks capacity;

(b) a person who has parental responsibility for a person who lacks capacity who is under 18 years;

(c) the donor of a lasting power of attorney to which the application relates;

(d) a deputy appointed by the court for a person to whom the application relates; or

(e) a person named in an existing order of the court if the application relates to that order.

MCA 2005, Sch 3, para 20(2) provides that permission is not required when an interested person applies to the Court for a declaration as to whether a protective measure taken under the law of a country outside England and Wales is to be recognised in England and Wales.

MCA 2005, s 50(2) also allows the Court's rules to expand the above categories. Rule 51 therefore provides that the Official Solicitor and the Public Guardian do not require permission. Subject to certain restrictions, permission is also not required where the application concerns P's property and affairs, a lasting power of attorney, an enduring power of attorney, an application made in the course of proceedings and where an acknowledgement is filed which seeks an order which is different to the order sought in the main application.

All other applications require permission (MCA 2005, s 50(2)). This means that normally, health and welfare matters require permission. Such applications could include those where orders are sought for the withholding or giving of urgent medical treatment, cases where P may be subjected to physical or sexual abuse or where P may be deprived of his or her liberty.

Although it may seem harsh that many personal welfare decisions need permission, it should be noted that many such decisions will be taken without the need to apply to the Court. Those involved will follow the Code of Practice and the statutory guidelines. Accordingly, it was envisaged that such matters would only come to Court when they could not be resolved by any other means or where the matter is so serious that the Court needs to decide the matter. The permission provisions in the rules therefore act as a check to ensure that applications are necessary and well founded.

There is no doubt that Part 8 requires revision to make it easier to understand. The rules appear complicated and a lay person is unlikely to understand them and there is no reason why these rules cannot be simplified. Consideration also needs to be given as to whether permission should be required in cases involving serious medical treatment.

51 Where the court's permission is not required

The permission of the court is not required –

(1) where an application is made by –

  (a)   the Official Solicitor; or

  (b)   the Public Guardian;

(2) where the application concerns –

  (a)   P's property and affairs, unless the application is of a kind specified in rule 52;

  (b)   a lasting power of attorney which is, or purports to be, created under the Act; or

  (c)   an instrument which is, or purports to be, an enduring power of attorney;

[(2A) where an application is made under section 21A of the Act by the relevant person's representative;]

(3) where an application is made in accordance with Part 10; or

(4) where a person files an acknowledgment of service or notification in accordance with this Part or Part 9, for any order proposed that is different from that sought by the applicant.

Amendment—Paragraph (2A) inserted by Court of Protection (Amendment) Rules 2009, SI 2009/582.

52 Exceptions to rule 51(2)(a)

(1) For the purposes of rule 51(2)(a), the permission of the court is required to make any of the applications specified in this rule.

(2) An application for the exercise of the jurisdiction of the court under section 54(2) of the Trustee Act 1925, where the application is made by a person other than –

    (a)   a person who has made an application for the appointment of a deputy;

    (b)   a continuing trustee; or

    (c)   any other person who, according to the practice of the Chancery Division, would have been entitled to make the application if it had been made in the High Court.

(3) An application under section 36(9) of the Trustee Act 1925 for leave to appoint a new trustee in place of P, where the application is made by a person other than –

    (a)   a co-trustee; or

    (b)   another person with the power to appoint a new trustee.

(4) An application seeking the exercise of the court's jurisdiction under section 18(1)(b) (where the application relates to making a gift of P's property), (h) or (i) of the Act, where the application is made by a person other than –

    (a)   a person who has made an application for the appointment of a deputy;

    (b)   a person who, under any known will of P or under his intestacy, may become entitled to any property of P or any interest in it;

    (c)   a person who is an attorney appointed under an enduring power of attorney which has been registered in accordance with the Act or the regulations referred to in Schedule 4 to the Act;

    (d)   a person who is a donee of a lasting power of attorney which has been registered in accordance with the Act; or

    (e)   a person for whom P might be expected to provide if he had capacity to do so.

(5) An application under section 20 of the Trusts of Land and Appointment of Trustees Act 1996, where the application is made by a person other than a beneficiary under the trust or, if there is more than one, by both or all of them.

Rule 52(2)—The Trustee Act 1925, s 54 provides:

'54(1) Subject to subsection (2) the Court of Protection may not make an order, or give a direction or authority, in relation to a person who lacks capacity to exercise his functions as trustee, if the High Court may make an order to that effect under this Act.

(2) Where a person lacks capacity to exercise his functions as a trustee and a deputy is appointed for him by the Court of Protection or an application for the appointment of a deputy has been made but not determined, then, except as respects a trust which is subject to an order for administration made by the High Court [the Court of Protection] shall have concurrent jurisdiction with the High Court in relation to –

    (a)   mortgaged property of which the person concerned has become a trustee merely by reason of the mortgage having been paid off;

    (b)   matters consequent on the making of provision by the Court of Protection for the exercise of a power of appointing trustees or retiring from a trust;

    (c)   matters consequent on the making of provision by the Court of Protection for the carrying out of any contract entered into by the person concerned;

(d) property to some interest in which the person concerned is beneficially entitled but which, or some interest in which, is held by the person concerned under an express, implied or constructive trust.

(2A) Rules may be made in accordance with Part 1 of Schedule 1 to the Constitutional Reform Act 2005 with respect to the exercise of the jurisdiction referred to in subsection (2).'

The section has been amended by MCA 2005.

Rule 52(2) lists three categories of person who do not require permission to make an application; anyone else requires permission.

Rule 52(3)—The Trustee Act 1925, s 36(9) provides:

'(9) Where a trustee lacks capacity to exercise his functions as trustee and is also entitled in possession to some beneficial interest in the trust property, no appointment of a new trustee in his place shall be made by virtue of para (b) of subsection (1) of this section unless leave to make the appointment has been given by the Court of Protection.'

This section has been amended by MCA 2005.

Rule 52(3) lists those who do not require permission and all other persons will require permission to make an application.

Rule 52(4)—MCA 2005, s 18(1)(b), (h) and (i) provide:

'18(1) The powers under section 16 as respects P's property and affairs extend in particular to –

...

(b) the sale, exchange, charging, gift or other disposition of P's property;

...

(h) the settlement of any of P's property, whether for P's benefit or for the benefit of others;

...

(i) the execution for P of a will.'

Rule 52(4) lists those who do not require permission and all other persons will require permission.

Rule 52(5)—The Trusts of Land and Appointment of Trustee Act 1996, s 20 provides:

'20(1) This section applies where -
  (a) a trustee lacks capacity (within the meaning of the Mental Capacity Act 2005) to exercise his functions as trustee,
  (b) there is no person who is both entitled and willing and able to appoint a trustee in place of him under section 36(1) of the Trustee Act 1925, and
  (c) the beneficiaries under the trust are of full age and capacity and (taken together) are absolutely entitled to the property subject to the trust.

20(2) The beneficiaries may give to –
  (a) a deputy appointed for the trustee by the Court of Protection,
  (b) an attorney acting for him under the authority of an enduring power of attorney or lasting power of attorney registered under the Mental Capacity Act 2005, or
  (c) a person authorised for the purpose by the Court of Protection,

a written direction to appoint by writing the person or persons specified in the direction to be a trustee or trustees in place of the incapable trustee.'

The section has been amended by MCA 2005.

Rule 52(5) sets out who does not require permission and who must apply.

53 Permission – supplementary

(1) The provisions of rule 52(2) apply with such modifications as may be necessary to an application under section 18(1)(j) of the Act for an order for the exercise of any power vested in P of appointing trustees or retiring from a trust.

(2) Where part of the application concerns a matter which requires permission, and part of it does not, permission need only be sought for that part of it which requires permission.

Rule 53(1)—MCA 2005, s 16 refers to the Court's power to make decisions on behalf of P in relation to a matter or to appoint a deputy. MCA 2005, s 18 sets out the Court's powers under s 16. MCA 2005, s 18(1)(j) refers to the exercise of any power (including a power to consent) vested in P whether beneficially or as trustee or otherwise.

Rule 53(2)—See Practice Direction A, paras 2–4. Paragraph 3 provides that a single application form can deal with a matter that does require permission in addition to a matter that does not. However, para 4 allows two separate applications to be issued. However, two fees will become payable which may not make this a sensible course to follow.

54 Application for permission

The applicant must apply for permission by filing a permission form and must file with it –

(a) any information or documents specified in the relevant practice direction;
(b) a draft of the application form which he seeks permission to have issued; and
(c) an assessment of capacity form, where this is required by the relevant practice direction.

Scope of rule—The application for permission is on Form COP2. If this is not submitted, the Court will not be able to process the application until it is filed, thus causing delay.

In practice, most practitioners file all the papers required to make the application together with COP2 even though r 64 does not apply. This means that if permission is granted without a hearing, the application can then be issued immediately without any delay.

55 What the court will do when an application for permission to start proceedings is filed

Within 14 days of a permission form being filed, the court will issue it and –

(a) grant the application in whole or in part, or subject to conditions, without a hearing and may give directions in connection with the issue of the application form;
(b) refuse the application without a hearing; or
(c) fix a date for the hearing of the application.

Rule 55(a)—If permission is granted, r 65 provides that the Court will issue the application form. Rule 55(a) allows the Court to give directions concerning the issue of the application form. Practice Direction A, para 7 allows the applicant not to file any of the annexes to the application form or any of the documents required by r 64. On granting permission, the Court would therefore have to direct that the applicant file all relevant documents to comply with r 64. However, this will cause delay and the course suggested under r 54 may be preferable.

Rule 55(b)—If permission is refused on paper, reasons will be provided (r 59(b)). Rule 89 allows the applicant to apply for reconsideration within 21 days of the order being served (not made). The application is made on Form COP9 as it is considered a Part 10 application. The Court can order a hearing or reconsider the order on paper (r 89(4)). The Court may affirm, set aside or vary the order (r 89(5)). Any appeal from the order made on reconsideration is governed by Part 20 (r 89(8)).

Rule 55(c)—If a date is fixed for a hearing, r 56 will apply.

56 Persons to be notified of the hearing of an application for permission

(1) Where the court fixes a date for a hearing under rule 55(c), it will notify the applicant and such other persons as it thinks fit, and provide them with –

    (a)   subject to paragraph (2), the documents mentioned in rule 54; and

    (b)   a form for acknowledging notification.

(2) The court may direct that any document is to be provided on an edited basis.

Rule 56(1)(b)—See Form COP5.

57 Acknowledgment of notification of permission application

(1) Any person who is notified of an application for permission and who wishes to take part in the permission hearing must file an acknowledgment of notification in accordance with the following provisions of this rule.

(2) The acknowledgment of notification must be filed not more than 21 days after notice of the application was given.

(3) The court will serve the acknowledgment of notification on the applicant and on any other person who has filed such an acknowledgment.

(4) The acknowledgment of notification must –

    (a)   state whether the person acknowledging notification consents to the application for permission;

    (b)   state whether he opposes the application for permission, and if so, set out the grounds for doing so;

    (c)   state whether he proposes that permission should be granted to make an application for a different order, and if so, set out what that order is;

    (d)   provide an address for service, which must be within the jurisdiction of the court; and

    (e)   be signed by him or his legal representative.

(5) The acknowledgment of notification may include or be accompanied by an application for directions.

(6) Subject to rules 120 and 123 (restrictions on filing an expert's report and court's power to restrict expert evidence), where a person opposes the application for permission or proposes that permission is granted for a different order, the acknowledgment of notification must be accompanied by a witness statement containing any evidence upon which that person intends to rely.

Form—Form COP5 is the acknowledgement form which has to be filed within 21 days after notice is given unless the Court has ordered it to be filed in a shorter period. A witness statement should be filed together with COP5 if the application is opposed (r 57(6)). If no COP5 is filed, r 58 provides that the person who failed to file it may not take part in the hearing unless the Court gives permission.

58 Failure to file acknowledgment of notification

Where a person notified of the application for permission has not filed an acknowledgment of notification in accordance with rule 57, he may not take part in a hearing to decide whether permission should be given unless the court permits him to do so.

59 Service of an order giving or refusing permission

The court will serve –

(a) the order granting or refusing permission;

(b) if refusing permission without a hearing, the reasons for its decision in summary form; and

(c) any directions,

on the applicant and on any other person notified of the application who filed an acknowledgment of notification.

60 Appeal against a permission decision following a hearing

Where the court grants or refuses permission following a hearing, any appeal against the permission decision shall be dealt with in accordance with Part 20 (appeals).

PART 9
HOW TO START PROCEEDINGS

Initial steps

61 General

(1) Applications to the court to start proceedings shall be made in accordance with this Part and, as applicable, Part 8 and the relevant practice directions.

(2) The appropriate forms must be used in the cases to which they apply, with such variations as the case requires, but not so as to omit any information or guidance which any form gives to the intended recipient.

(3) If permission to make an application is required, the court shall not issue the application form until permission is granted.

Rule 61(1)—Part 8 sets out the procedure where permission is required to commence an application.

Rule 61(2)—Form COP1 is the basic application form. If the application relates to property and affairs, a supporting information Form COP1A has to be completed with COP1. If the application relates to personal welfare, the supporting application form is COP1B. The Rules Committee have recommended that a single COP 1 should be used for one application relating to a number of people.

If the application is to object to the registration of a lasting power of attorney, the application form is Form COP7. If the application is to object to an enduring power of attorney, Form COP8 should be used.

Registration of an enduring power of attorney is on Form EP2PG which is found in the Lasting Powers of Attorney, Enduring Powers of Attorney and Public Guardian Regulations 2007, SI 2007/1253, Sch 8.

Registration of a lasting power of attorney is on Form LPA002 which is found in the Lasting Powers of Attorney, Enduring Powers of Attorney and Public Guardian Regulations 2007, SI 2007/1253, Sch 3.

Rule 61(3)—If part of an application requires permission and part does not, the Court will not issue the application until permission has been granted for the part that requires it (Part 8, Practice Direction A, para 3).

If permission is refused for a part of an application for which permission is granted, the application form will only be issued for the part that does not require permission (Part 8, Practice Direction A, para 4).

If permission is granted, r 65 provides that the Court will issue the application.

62 When proceedings are started

(1) The general rule is that proceedings are started when the court issues an application form at the request of the applicant.

(2) An application form is issued on the date entered on the application form by the court.

63 Contents of the application form

The application form must –

    (a)   state the matter which the applicant wants the court to decide;

    (b)   state the order which the applicant is seeking;

    (c)   name –

        (i)   the applicant;

        (ii) P;

        (iii) as a respondent, any person (other than P) whom the applicant reasonably believes to have an interest which means that he ought to be heard in relation to the application (as opposed to being notified of it in accordance with rule 70); and

        (iv) any person whom the applicant intends to notify in accordance with rule 70; and

    (d)   if the applicant is applying in a representative capacity, state what that capacity is.

Rule 63(c)(iii)—See for example PD 9F paragraph 9. This rule also needs to be read in conjunction with PD 9A paragraph 2 which repeats the rule and PD 9B.

64 Documents to be filed with the application form

When an applicant files his application form with the court, he must also file –

    (a)   in accordance with the relevant practice direction, any evidence upon which he intends to rely;

    (b)   if permission was required to make the application, a copy of the court's order granting permission;

    (c)   an assessment of capacity form, where this is required by the relevant practice direction;

    (d)   any other documents referred to in the application form; and

    (e)   such other information and material as may be set out in a practice direction.

Rules 63/64: The application form—Care is required to ensure that the correct forms are filed at Court when making an application and also that the forms are completed properly. Much time can be lost by using an obsolete form as it will be rejected by the court.

Unfortunately, the relevant rules are not in one place. It is therefore helpful to explain where the core rules are found so that reference can be made to them.

Contents of the application form—Rule 63 sets out the basic requirements of the contents of the application form. Rule 64 sets out the documents that must be filed with the application form.

Practice Direction A, paras 2–8 contain further requirements as to the contents of the application form.

Certain applications also have their own specific requirements:

    (1)   Practice Direction D deals with certain applications by deputies, attorneys or donors which are listed at paras 4 and 5. Paragraph 8 deals with the contents of the application form.

    (2)   Practice Direction F deals with applications relating to statutory wills and codicils,

settlements and other dealings with P's property which are listed at paras 2–4. Paragraph 6 sets out the information that must be given when an application is made.

(3) Practice Direction G deals with applications to appoint or discharge a trustee as listed at paras 2 and 3. Paragraphs 5, 8 and 9 set out the required information when an application is made.

(4) Practice Direction H deals with applications relating to the registration of an enduring power of attorney as listed at para 2. Paragraphs 6–8 deal with the form of application.

The practitioner should also have the following in mind:

(1) Rule 10 provides that the Court must seal the application form.

(2) Rule 15 contains provisions where a party does not wish to reveal personal details.

(3) The provisions of rr 16 and 17 which allow others to seek copies of court documents.

(4) Rule 18 restricts the use of documents filed at Court outside of the proceedings.

The application form should be prepared with care. Although the Court understands that practitioners may still err in using the court's procedures in place of the old rules, the information required by the rules is important for the proper disposal of the application. The Court is likely to order that this information be provided before the application can proceed further. It is therefore important to read the relevant rules and Practice Direction and to check that the information required has been provided.

An application relating to deprivation of liberty is governed by its own rules and practice direction: see Part 10A and the DOLS practice direction. This sets out the requirements for such an application.

What is filed at Court—Practice Direction A, paras 9–12 set out what has to be filed with the application form.

Procedural Guides 1–4 set out which documents are filed when making an application which will vary depending on the application.

If it is not possible to file the assessment of capacity form (COP3), Practice Direction A, para 14 provides that a witness statement must be filed with the application explaining why it has not been possible to obtain an assessment of capacity, what attempts have been made to obtain the assessment and why the applicant knows or believes that P lacks capacity.

Rule 63(c)(iii)—See the commentary on r 70 regarding notification.

See also r 54 and its commentary.

65 What the court will do when an application form is filed

As soon as practicable after an application form is filed the court will issue the application form in any case where permission –

(a)   is not required; or

(b)   has been granted by the court; and

do anything else that may be set out in a practice direction.

Steps following issue of application form

66 Applicant to serve the application form on named respondents

(1) As soon as practicable and in any event within 21 days of the date on which the application form was issued, the applicant must serve a copy of the application form on any person who is named as a respondent in the application form, together with copies of any documents filed in accordance with rule 64 and a form for acknowledging service.

(2) The applicant must file a certificate of service within 7 days beginning with the date on which the documents were served.

Rule 66(1)—During the consultation process, concern was raised that the time-limits imposed by the service rules may cause delay. Assuming permission is required for an application, the Court must deal with the granting of permission within 14 days (r 55). Rule 66 allows a further 21 days after permission is granted and the application is issued for service of the application. Rule 72 allows 21 days after service for acknowledgement of the application. It must be assumed, therefore, that where the application is urgent or these time-limits are not practical, the Court will need to give specific directions to vary the time-limits. Rule 26 allows the Court to dispense with the requirements of any rule. When considering whether to reduce these time-limits, the Court will have regard to P's best interests and the overriding objective.

It is possible to say that in a large number of personal welfare applications, these time-limits may be wholly unrealistic and to a lesser extent in property and finance applications. The Court should be alive to the need to synthesise the need for the Court to follow clear and defined rules with the need to do justice and avoid delay.

A problem that some court users have identified with this rule is that it may be impossible to comply with the 21 day time limit because delays at the court mean that by the time the applicant receives the application, 21 days has already elapsed from the date the application was actually issued. It is suggested that the only way to deal with this is to explain this in a letter when filing COP 20.

See also the commentary on r 25(2)(a).

Rule 66(2)—The certificate of service is Form COP20.

67 Applications relating to lasting powers of attorney

(1) Where the application concerns the powers of the court under section 22 or 23 of the Act (powers of the court in relation to the validity and operation of lasting powers of attorney) the applicant must serve a copy of the application form, together with copies of any documents filed in accordance with rule 64 and a form for acknowledging service –

    (a)   unless the applicant is the donor or donee of the lasting power of attorney ('the power'), on the donor and every donee of the power;

    (b)   if he is the donor, on every donee of the power; and

    (c)   if he is a donee, on the donor and any other donee of the power,

but only if the above-mentioned persons have not been served or notified under any other rule.

(2) Where the application is solely in respect of an objection to the registration of a power, the requirements of rules 66 and 70 do not apply to an application made under this rule by –

    (a)   a donee of the power; or

    (b)   a person named in a statement made by the donor of the power in accordance with paragraph 2(1)(c)(i) of Schedule 1 to the Act.

(3) The applicant must comply with paragraph (1) as soon as practicable and in any event within 21 days of date on which the application form was issued.

(4) The applicant must file a certificate of service within 7 days beginning with the date on which the documents were served.

(5) Where the applicant knows or has reasonable grounds to believe that the donor of the power lacks capacity to make a decision in relation to any matter that is the subject of the application, he must notify the donor in accordance with Part 7.

Rule 67(1)—This rule contains specific provisions for service of the application when it relates to a lasting power of attorney.

MCA 2005, ss 22 and 23 allow the Court to determine questions relating to lasting powers of attorney.

Rule 67(4)—Form COP20,

68 Applications relating to enduring powers of attorney

(1) Where the application concerns the powers of the court under paragraphs 2(9), 4(5)(a) and (b), 7(2), 10(c), 13, or 16(2), (3), (4) and (6) of Schedule 4 to the Act, the applicant must serve a copy of the application form, together with copies of any documents filed in accordance with rule 64 and a form for acknowledging service –

  (a) unless the applicant is the donor or attorney under the enduring power of attorney ('the power'), on the donor and every attorney of the power;
  (b) if he is the donor, on every attorney under the power; or
  (c) if he is an attorney, on the donor and any other attorney under the power,

but only if the above-mentioned persons have not been served or notified under any other rule.

(2) Where the application is solely in respect of an objection to the registration of a power, the requirements of rules 66 and 70 do not apply to an application made under this rule by –

  (a) an attorney under the power; or
  (b) a person listed in paragraph 6(1) of Schedule 4 to the Act.

(3) The applicant must comply with paragraph (1) as soon as practicable and in any event within 21 days of the date on which the application form was issued.

(4) The applicant must file a certificate of service within 7 days beginning with the date on which the documents were served.

(5) Where the applicant knows or has reasonable grounds to believe that the donor of the power lacks capacity to make a decision in relation to any matter that is the subject of the application, he must notify the donor in accordance with Part 7.

Rule 68(1)—This rule applies to specific paragraphs in MCA 2005, Sch 4, namely:

  (1) para 2(9): revocation of an enduring power of attorney;
  (2) para 4(5)(a) and (b): referral to the Court any question as to the validity of the power;
  (3) para 7(2): application to dispense with notice of registration;
  (4) para 10(c): provisions relating to notice of registration to the donor;
  (5) para 13: registration by the Public Guardian and the Court's powers; and
  (6) para 16(2), (3), (4) and (6): determining questions relating to the enduring power of attorney and cancelling registration.

Rule 68(4)—Form COP20.

69 Applicant to notify P of an application

P must be notified in accordance with Part 7 that an application form has been issued, unless the requirement to do so has been dispensed with under rule 49.

Note—This rule is unclear as r40(2) in Part 7 says that if P becomes a party, Part 7 does not apply and service is effected in accordance with Part 6 or as directed by the court.

70 Applicant to notify other persons of an application

(1) As soon as practicable and in any event within 21 days of the date on which the application form was issued, the applicant must notify the persons specified in the relevant practice direction –

> (a) that an application form has been issued;
>
> (b) whether it relates to the exercise of the court's jurisdiction in relation to P's property and affairs, or his personal welfare, or to both; and
>
> (c) of the order or orders sought.

(2) Notification of the issue of the application form must be accompanied by a form for acknowledging notification.

(3) The applicant must file a certificate of notification within 7 days beginning with the date on which notification was given.

Rule 70(1)—Practice Direction B deals with notification. Notice is given by Form COP15. Notification should be given to:

(1) The respondent to the application.

(2) At least three people who have an interest in being notified.

(3) Members of P's family who are likely to have an interest (see in particular para 7 of the Practice Direction).

(4) Other persons set out in the Practice Direction, for example, an NHS Trust responsible for P's care (see para 10 of the Practice Direction).

The Practice Direction contains a presumption of notification (see paras 7 and 10) although para 6 sets out circumstances when the presumption may be displaced.

In cases where the applicant contends that notification should not be given, paras 9 and 11 provide that the application form must contain evidence to explain why the person or body is not notified.

'As soon as practicable'—In some cases, the Court may need to direct that notification takes place in a period shorter than 21 days.

Although not binding, there are some decisions under the old rules which may assist.

In *Re B (Court of Protection: Notice of Proceedings)* [1987] 2 All ER 475 Millett J (as he then was) considered an application by a Receiver for guidance as to who should be notified of an application.

The Receiver was concerned that certain relatives would indulge in what Millett J described as 'mutual mud-slinging and exacerbate the existing family divisions' such that the Receiver believed that notification of proceedings should be dispensed with to avoid bitterness and hostility. Millett J referred to this 'as the price which has to be paid if a dispute is to be resolved by judicial means'. He refused to dispense with notification on this ground alone.

Re Davey (Deceased) [1980] 3 All ER 342 concerned an application for a statutory will. P was 92 years old and in poor health. Unbeknown to P's family, P had recently married an employee of the care home where she resided. The marriage revoked an earlier will of P. The deputy master dispensed with notice of the application to P's husband and made an order in the same terms as the will that had been revoked by P's marriage. He did so on the basis that due to P's health and age, the matter was urgent; if P died before the court made a final order it would not be possible to challenge the validity of the will and the estate would devolve on intestacy to the husband; the marriage was suspicious and if P died, the husband could still challenge the will under the Inheritance (Provisions for Family and Dependents) Act 1975. Fox J upheld the deputy master's decision. Indeed, P died a few days after execution of the statutory will.

The Rules Committee has suggested that time limits in Part 9 require review.

Rule 70(2)—See Form COP5.

Rule 70(3)—See Form COP20.

71 Requirements for certain applications

A practice direction may make additional or different provision in relation to specified applications.

Scope of rules—Rules 66–70 essentially deal with service and notification of applications by the applicant to others.

Rule 71 allows a Practice Direction to make 'additional or different provision in relation to specified applications'. Since the court will often require more specific information to enable it to

PART IV

properly consider certain applications, this rule allows for a practice direction to ensure that particular documents or information are filed at the start of a case. Thus, Practice Directions D to H set out specific requirements for certain named applications. See also the Practice Direction for deprivation of liberty applications at Part 10A.

Responding to an application

72 Responding to an application

(1) A person who is served with or notified of an application form and who wishes to take part in proceedings must file an acknowledgment of service or notification in accordance with this rule.

(2) The acknowledgment of service or notification must be filed not more than 21 days after the application form was served or notification of the application was given.

(3) The court will serve the acknowledgment of service or notification on the applicant and on any other person who has filed such an acknowledgment.

(4) The acknowledgment of service or notification must –

   (a)   state whether the person acknowledging service or notification consents to the application;
   (b)   state whether he opposes the application and, if so, set out the grounds for doing so;
   (c)   state whether he seeks a different order from that set out in the application form and, if so, set out what that order is;
   (d)   provide an address for service, which must be within the jurisdiction of the court; and
   (e)   be signed by him or his legal representative.

(5) Subject to rules 120 and 123 (restriction on filing an expert's report and court's power to restrict expert evidence), where a person who has been served in accordance with rule 66, 67 or 68 opposes the application or seeks a different order, the acknowledgment of service must be accompanied by a witness statement containing any evidence upon which that person intends to rely.

(6) In addition to complying with the other requirements of this rule, an acknowledgment of notification filed by a person notified of the application in accordance with rule 67(5), 68(5), 69 or 70 must –

   (a)   indicate whether the person wishes to be joined as a party to the proceedings; and
   (b)   state the person's interest in the proceedings.

(7) Subject to rules 120 and 123 (restriction on filing an expert's report and court's power to restrict expert evidence), where a person has been notified in accordance with rule 67(5), 68(5), 69, 70, the acknowledgment of notification must be accompanied by a witness statement containing any evidence of his interest in the proceedings and, if he opposes the application or seeks a different order, any evidence upon which he intends to rely.

(8) The court will consider whether to join a person mentioned in paragraph (6) as a party to the proceedings and, if it decides to do so, will make an order to that effect.

(9) Where a person who is notified in accordance with rule 67(5), 68(5), 69 or 70 complies with the requirements of this rule, he need not comply with the requirements of rule 75 (application to be joined as a party).

(10) Where a person has filed an acknowledgment of notification in accordance with rule 57 (acknowledgment of notification of permission application) he must still acknowledge service or notification of an issued application form in accordance with this rule.

(11) A practice direction may make provision about responding to applications.

Rule 72(1)—Acknowledgement is on Form COP5.
The effect of filing COP5 is that if the person served was named as a respondent, he or she becomes a party (r 73(1)(b) and Practice Direction C, para 3).
If COP5 is filed to acknowledge notification, this can be considered as an application to be a party (r 72(6) and Practice Direction C, para 4).
If a person is not served with or notified of an application, he or she must apply to be a party by making an application under Part 10.
Practice Direction C contains rules at paras 6–13 about signing Form COP5 and the address for service on the form.
If the name of the person served or notified is incorrect, this should be noted on Form COP5. For example, if John Smith is referred to as John Brown, the form should state 'John Smith described as John Brown' (Practice Direction C, para 14).
The acknowledgment cannot be amended without a formal application under Part 10 seeking the Court's permission to do so.

Rule 72(2): 'not more than 21 days'—This suggests that if someone wishes to file COP 5 after the expiration of 21 days, an application on COP 9 is required and the court will need to make a specific order.

Rule 72(3)—Even though the person is not a party, by filing COP 5 he would be entitled to see COP 5's filed by others whether or not they are parties.

Rule 72(4)(c): 'seeks a different order'—Rule 51(4) provides that permission is not required if a different order is required.

Rule 72(5)—'witness statement'—This rule follows the general rule in r 97.
Rule 99(1) states that a witness statement is a written statement which contains the evidence which the person would be allowed to give orally.
It must contain a statement of truth (r 100). Without one, r 13 provides that it is not admissible in evidence unless the Court permits.
Part 14, Practice Direction A, paras 33–50 set out the main requirements of a witness statement.
The Rules Committee has recommended that time limits in this rule require review. If so, this rule will need to be amended as there may not be sufficient time to file evidence in the time allowed for acknowledgement of service. Accordingly, this rule will require amendment to include another date for filing evidence.

Rule 72(7)—See the comments on r 72(5) concerning witness statements.

Rule 72(8)—Rule 5(2)(b)(ii) contains the obligation of the Court when managing a case to consider who should be a party. See also the commentary to r 73. However, it is not clear how this rule sits with r73(1) which applies to grant automatic party status.

Rule 72(11)—This is the basis for Practice Direction C.

The parties to the proceedings

73 Parties to the proceedings

(1) Unless the court otherwise directs, the parties to any proceedings are –

    (a)   the applicant; and
    (b)   any person who is named as a respondent in the application form and who files an acknowledgment of service in respect of the application form.

(2) The court may order a person to be joined as a party if it considers that it is desirable to do so for the purpose of dealing with the application.

(3) The court may at any time direct that any person who is a party to the proceedings is to be removed as a party.

(4) Unless the court orders otherwise, P shall not be named as a respondent to any proceedings.

(5) A party to the proceedings is bound by any order or direction of the court made in the course of those proceedings.

Rule 73(1)—This would appear to be an automatic consequence of filing COP 5. See also r72(8) and r88(3).

Rule 73(2)—The Court will consider whether P is joined as a party. The effect of r 73(4) is that P is not named as a respondent unless the Court permits.

Deciding whether or not to make P a party is an important decision. There may be cases where notification to P of an application is sufficient and there is no need for P to become a party. Indeed, this may be distressing for P.

An example of such a case would be an application by a family member to be a deputy in respect of P's property and affairs where P lacks capacity to manage his routine financial affairs due to Alzheimer's disease. Joining P as a party would give P no added benefit and could distress P. It would also increase costs unnecessarily as P would need a litigation friend through a relative or the Official Solicitor.

On the other hand, there will be cases where P is at the centre of the issues before the Court and it is only correct that P is a party. For example, a personal welfare application which will personally affect P.

The Court will need to consider P's best interests, the overriding objective and the need to do justice and weigh the correct balance of protection that P requires. Proportionality should also be considered.

The Official Solicitor will normally be appointed to represent P. He will be able to visit P and provide information to the Court which is a factor the Court should have in mind.

There will also be some cases where there is a clear need for a high level of protection for P. However, there may be cases where the Court can order a report pursuant to MCA 2005, s 49 as an alternative to joining P. The report will be independent and will allow the Court to consider P's position.

In *Re H M F* [1975] 2 All ER 795, a case concerning a statutory will, Goulding J offered some guidance on the question of who should be a respondent, namely:

(1) consideration should be given to the best interests of P;
(2) the Court should consider what course will enable the Court to exercise its jurisdiction properly;
(3) where an application is made for a statutory will, it is better for the legatees under a previous will to be brought before the Court rather than be represented by the Attorney-General;
(4) the need to maintain confidentiality of P's affairs must cede to the necessity of the Court to act fairly in exercising its powers;
(5) the fact that individual charities joined as parties may result in a process of bargaining or unseemly contention was not a factor to justify the Attorney-General representing the charities who were legatees under a previous will of P; and
(6) there may be cases of emergency where the Court would feel that it ought to proceed without any representation of a previous interest at all.

Although decided under the old rules and not binding, the propositions are useful.

Rule 73(4)—It has been suggested that in serious medical treatment cases, P should be named as a Respondent from the outset and this rule should be amended. See also r50 and the comment that some believe that permission should not be required in serious medical treatment cases.

74 Persons to be bound as if parties

(1) The persons mentioned in paragraph (2) shall be bound by any order made or directions given by the court in the same way that a party to the proceedings is so bound.

(2) The persons referred to in paragraph (1) are –

    (a)   P; and

    (b)   any person who has been served with or notified of an application form in accordance with these Rules.

Rule 74(2)—The effect of this rule is that if a person is notified of an application but not joined as a party, he or she will be bound by the Court's order.

75 Application to be joined as a party

(1) Any person with sufficient interest may apply to the court to be joined as a party to the proceedings.

(2) An application to be joined as a party must be made by filing an application notice in accordance with Part 10 which must –

    (a)   state the full name and address of the person seeking to be joined as a party to the proceedings;

    (b)   state his interest in the proceedings;

    (c)   state whether he consents to the application;

    (d)   state whether he opposes the application and, if so, set out the grounds for doing so;

    (e)   state whether he proposes that an order different from that set out in the application form should be made and, if so, set out what that order is;

    (f)   provide an address for service, which must be within the jurisdiction of the court; and

    (g)   be signed by him or his legal representative.

(3) Subject to rules 120 and 123 (restriction on filing an expert's report and court's power to restrict expert evidence), an application to be joined must be accompanied by –

    (a)   a witness statement containing evidence of his interest in the proceedings and, if he proposes that an order different from that set out in the application form should be made, the evidence on which he intends to rely; and

    (b)   a sufficient number of copies of the application notice to enable service of the application on every other party to the proceedings.

(4) The court will serve the application notice and any accompanying documents on all parties to the proceedings.

(5) The court will consider whether to join a person applying under this rule as a party to the proceedings and, if it decides to do so, will make an order to that effect.

Rule 75 (1): 'with sufficient interest'—This could include an interested group where the Court is deciding an issue of interest to that group. For example, in a novel case where the Court will make significant pronouncements on end of life issues, there may be groups who believe they should be given a voice in the proceedings. It could also include a health trust or authority who will be treating or funding P and who wish to be heard in a case. The media may also come within this rule.

    When considering an application to be joined, the court will have to carefully consider whether or not P's best interests are served. There may well be cases where the public interest demands that an interested party be joined but this will cause delay to the case. On the one hand, delay could prima facie not be in P's best interests but on the other hand, the delay may result in a more informed debate on the issue affecting P which is in P's best interests. How the courts will deal with this remains to be seen.

Where this rule is more likely to apply in practice is to family members or others connected to P who were notified or have otherwise heard about the proceedings and who wish to become parties. For example, in a personal welfare application where issues are raised about P's ability to continue to reside in a care home, the directors of the care home may apply to become parties.

76 Applications for removal as a party to proceedings

A person who wishes to be removed as a party to the proceedings must apply to the court for an order to that effect in accordance with Part 10.

PART 10
APPLICATIONS WITHIN PROCEEDINGS

77 Types of applications for which the Part 10 procedure may be used

(1) The Part 10 procedure is the procedure set out in this Part.

(2) The Part 10 procedure may be used if the application is made by any person –

    (a)   in the course of existing proceedings; or

    (b)   as provided for in a rule or practice direction.

(3) The court may grant an interim remedy before an application form has been issued only if –

    (a)   the matter is urgent; or

    (b)   it is otherwise necessary to do so in the interests of justice.

(4) An application made during the course of existing proceedings includes an application made during appeal proceedings.

Scope of rule—This rule deals with applications made to the Court. It is supplemented by Practice Directions A and B.

Practice Directions—Practice Direction A deals with applications made within proceedings. Practice Direction B deals with urgent applications.

Application—An application can be by telephone or by video conference (Practice Direction A, paras 18–21).

Consent—If a consent order is filed for approval, the parties must ensure the Court has all the necessary material to allow it to approve the order. Consent to an order may be by letter. If a hearing is to be vacated as a consequence of the consent order, the Court should be informed as soon as the matter is compromised (Practice Direction A, paras 22 and 23).

The Rules Committee has made a number of recommendations to Part 10. It was felt that some of the provisions of the rules were not clear. For example, it has recommended the rewriting of r78 to improve the sequencing "which is confusing".

78 Application notice to be filed

(1) Subject to paragraph (5), the applicant must file an application notice to make an application under this Part.

(2) The applicant must, when he files the application notice, file the evidence upon which he relies (unless such evidence has already been filed).

(3) The court will issue the application notice and, if there is to be a hearing, give notice of the date on which the matter is to be heard by the court.

(4) Notice under paragraph (3) must be given to –

    (a)   the applicant;

    (b)   anyone who is named as a respondent in the application notice (if not otherwise a party to the proceedings);

    (c)   every party to the proceedings; and

    (d)   any other person, as the court may direct.

(5) An applicant may make an application under this Part without filing an application notice if –

    (a)   this is permitted by any rule or practice direction; or

    (b)   the court dispenses with the requirement for an application notice.

(6) If the applicant makes an application without giving notice, the evidence in support of the application must state why notice has not been given.

Rule 78(1)—The application is made on Form COP9.

Rule 78(2)—The evidence should be filed using Form COP24.

Rule 78(3)—If no hearing date is listed, the court will not notify the parties and the applicant must serve the application: see r80 .

Rule 78(5)(b)—For example, an application is made during the course of a hearing or by letter and the Court treats the letter as a formal application.

79 What an application notice must include

An application notice must state –

    (a)   what order or direction the applicant is seeking;

    (b)   briefly, the grounds on which the applicant is seeking the order or direction; and

    (c)   such other information as may be required by any rule or a practice direction.

Practice Direction—Practice Direction A sets out further requirements of the application notice.

    If the order required is unusually long or complex, a disk containing the draft order should be made available to the Court. The practitioner is also expected to ensure that the disk will be compatible with the Court's software (Practice Direction A, para 4).

    The evidence in support of the application must set out all the facts on which the applicant relies and of which the Court should be made aware (Practice Direction A, para 7).

80 Service of an application notice

(1) Subject to paragraphs (4) and (5), the applicant must serve a copy of the application notice on –

    (a)   anyone who is named as a respondent in the application notice (if not otherwise a party to the proceedings);

    (b)   every party to the proceedings; and

    (c)   any other person, as the court may direct,

as soon as practicable and in any event within 21 days of the date on which it was issued.

(2) The application notice must be accompanied by a copy of the evidence filed in support.

(3) The applicant must file a certificate of service within 7 days beginning with the date on which the documents were served.

(4) This rule does not require a copy of evidence to be served on a person upon whom it has already been served, but the applicant must in such a case give to that person notice of the evidence upon which he intends to rely.

(5) An application may be made without serving a copy of the application notice if this is permitted by –

    (a)   a rule;
    (b)   a practice direction; or
    (c)   the court.

Rule 80(1)—Practice Direction A, para 9 sets out the circumstances where an application may be made without service of the application notice.
    The evidence in support of the application must say why service was not effected (Practice Direction A, para 10).
    However, the Court retains the overall discretion to decide if service should be effected or not (see Practice Direction A, para 11).

Rule 80(3)—Form COP20.

81 Applications without notice

(1) This rule applies where the court has dealt with an application which was made without notice having been given to any person.

(2) Where the court makes an order, whether granting or dismissing the application, the applicant must, as soon as practicable or within such period as the court may direct, serve the documents mentioned in paragraph (3) on –

    (a)   anyone named as a respondent in the application notice (if not otherwise a party to the proceedings);
    (b)   every party to the proceedings; and
    (c)   any other person, as the court may direct.

(3) The documents referred to in paragraph (2) are –

    (a)   a copy of the application notice;
    (b)   the court's order; and
    (c)   any evidence filed in support of the application.

(Rule 89 provides for reconsideration of orders made without a hearing or without notice to a person.)

Rule 81(1)—The requirements for notice being given of an application are contained in Practice Direction A, para 13.
    There is no requirement to file a certificate of service in Form COP20.

Interim Remedies

82 Orders for interim remedies

(1) The court may grant the following interim remedies –

    (a)   an interim injunction;

    (b)   an interim declaration; or

    (c)   any other interim order it considers appropriate.

(2) Unless the court orders otherwise, a person on whom an application form is served under Part 9, or who is given notice of such an application, may not apply for an interim remedy before he has filed an acknowledgment of service or notification in accordance with Part 9.

(3) This rule does not limit any other power of the court to grant interim relief.

Practice Direction—Practice Direction B amplifies this rule. The following should be noted:

    (1)   The respondent should be informed unless justice would be defeated by so doing (para 5).
    (2)   A further hearing will be ordered to fully consider the matter (para 6).
    (3)   If the order sought is unusually long or complex, a disk should be provided for the Court's use (para 7).
    (4)   In exceptional cases, an oral application may be made without issue of an application notice (para 9).
    (5)   An urgent hearing may be by telephone (para 11).

An injunction may be varied by another judge (para 16).

PART 10A
DEPRIVATION OF LIBERTY

82A

The practice direction to this Part sets out procedure governing –

    (a)   applications to the court for orders relating to the deprivation, or proposed deprivation, of liberty of P; and
    (b)   proceedings (for example, relating to costs or appeals) connected with or consequent upon such applications.

Amendment—Part 10A inserted by Court of Protection (Amendment) Rules 2009, SI 2009/582.

'Practice Direction'—This rule is supplemented by Practice Direction – Deprivation of liberty applications.

PART 11
HUMAN RIGHTS

83 General

(1) A party who seeks to rely upon any provision of or right arising under the Human Rights Act 1998 ('the 1998 Act') or who seeks a remedy available under that Act must inform the court in the manner set out in the relevant practice direction specifying –

    (a)   the Convention right (within the meaning of the 1998 Act) which it is alleged has been infringed and details of the alleged infringement; and
    (b)   the remedy sought and whether this includes a declaration of incompatibility under section 4 of the 1998 Act.

(2) The court may not make a declaration of incompatibility unless 21 days' notice, or such other period of notice as the court directs, has been given to the Crown.

(3) Where notice has been given to the Crown, a Minister or other person permitted by the 1998 Act will be joined as a party on filing an application in accordance with rule 75 (application to be joined as a party).

'Practice Direction'—This rule is supplemented by Practice Direction A.

A claim under Part 11 will be heard by a High Court judge, the Chancellor or the President of the Family Division (Practice Direction A, para 9 and Part 12, Practice Direction A, para 3(b)).

In practice, if such a claim is issued, a resident judge at the Court of Protection will immediately transfer the case to a High Court judge who will give directions and deal with the case thereafter.

Rule 83(1)

Practice Direction A provides that the claim is made on:

(1) COP1 if it is part of an application;
(2) COP5 if the claim is made in response to an application;
(3) COP9 if the claim is made during the course of proceedings;
(4) COP35 or COP36 if raised on an appeal.

PART 12
DEALING WITH APPLICATIONS

84 Dealing with the application

(1) As soon as practicable after any application has been issued the court shall consider how to deal with it.

(2) The court may deal with an application or any part of an application at a hearing or without a hearing.

(3) In considering whether it is necessary to hold a hearing, the court shall, as appropriate, have regard to –

(a) the nature of the proceedings and the orders sought;
(b) whether the application is opposed by a person who appears to the court to have an interest in matters relating to P's best interests;
(c) whether the application involves a substantial dispute of fact;
(d) the complexity of the facts and the law;
(e) any wider public interest in the proceedings;
(f) the circumstances of P and of any party, in particular as to whether their rights would be adequately protected if a hearing were not held;
(g) whether the parties agree that the court should dispose of the application without a hearing; and
(h) any other matter specified in the relevant practice direction.

(4) Where the court considers that a hearing is necessary, it will –

(a) give notice of the hearing date to the parties and to any other person it directs; and
(b) state whether the hearing is for disposing of the matter or for directions.

(5) Where the court decides that it can deal with the matter without a hearing it will do so and serve a copy of its order on the parties and on any other person it directs.

Rule 84(1)—The application will be placed before a judge who will consider what directions or orders should be made. Sometimes, the application may not be given to the judge until time for notification or service has elapsed and Form COP20 is filed or time for acknowledging service has expired, on the basis that prior to these stages in the proceedings, no step can be taken. Given the volume of work being processed at the court, if an application needs to be processed quickly for good reason, the practitioner should inform the court by letter of the need for expedition or consider arranging a short hearing for the judge to deal with matters.

"As soon as practicable"—Note that this is not a fixed time period and is open-ended.

Rule 84(2)—The Court's practice is to aim to deal with an application solely on paper unless a hearing is necessary.

Rule 84(3)(a): 'nature of the proceedings and the orders sought'—See the note on r 3(3)(c). Some cases will certainly require a hearing, such as personal welfare cases where the Court will need to consider the aim of the proceedings and tailor-make orders to suit the individual case.

85 Directions

(1) The court may –

    (a)   give directions in writing; or

    (b)   set a date for a directions hearing; and

    (c)   do anything else that may be set out in a practice direction.

(2) When giving directions, the court may do any of the following –

    (a)   require a report under section 49 of the Act and give directions as to any such report;

    (b)   give directions as to any requirements contained in these Rules or a practice direction for the giving of notification to any person or for that person to do anything in response to a notification;

    (c)   if the court considers that P should be a party to the proceedings, give directions joining him as a party;

    (d)   if P is joined as a party to proceedings, give directions as to the appointment of a litigation friend;

    (e)   if the court considers that any other person or persons should be a party to the proceedings, give directions joining them as a party;

    (f)   if the court considers that any party to the proceedings should not be a party, give directions for that person's removal as a party;

    (g)   give directions for the management of the case and set a timetable for the steps to be taken between the giving of directions and the hearing;

    (h)   subject to rule 86, give directions as to the type of judge who is to hear the case;

    (i)   give directions as to whether the proceedings or any part of them are to be heard in public, or as to whether any particular person should be permitted to attend the hearing, or as to whether any publication of the proceedings is to be permitted;

    (j)   give directions as to the disclosure of documents, service of witness statements and any expert evidence;

    (k)   give directions as to the attendance of witnesses and as to whether, and the extent to which, cross-examination will be permitted at any hearing; and

    (l)   give such other directions as the court thinks fit.

(3) The court may give directions at any time –

    (a)   on its own initiative; or

    (b)   on the application of a party.

(4) Subject to paragraphs (5) and (6) and unless these Rules or a practice direction provide otherwise or the court directs otherwise, the time specified by a rule or by the court for a person to do any act may be varied by the written agreement of the parties.

(5) A party must apply to the court if he wishes to vary –

    (a) the date the court has fixed for the final hearing; or

    (b) the period within which the final hearing is to take place.

(6) The time specified by a rule or practice direction or by the court may not be varied by the parties if the variation would make it necessary to vary the date the court has fixed for any hearing or the period within which the final hearing is to take place.

Rule 85(1)—When deciding whether to order a hearing, the Court will consider the matters in r 84(3) together with rr 3(3) and 5(2).

    In respect of a matter involving serious medical treatment, Part 9, Practice Direction E, para 13 anticipates that there will be a first directions hearing. Paragraphs 14 and 15 set out the matters that will be considered.

Rule 85(2)(c)—See the commentary to r 73(2).

Rule 85(2)(d)—For example, the Official Solicitor.

Allocation of proceedings

86 Court's jurisdiction in certain kinds of case to be exercised by certain judges

(1) The court will consider whether the application is of a type specified in the relevant practice direction as being one which must be dealt with by –

    (a) the President;

    (b) the Vice-President; or

    (c) one of the other judges nominated by virtue of section 46(2)(a) to (c) of the Act.

(2) The practice direction made under this rule shall specify the categories of case which must be dealt with by a judge mentioned in paragraph (1).

(3) Applications in any matter other than those specified in the relevant practice direction may be dealt with by any judge.

'Practice Direction'—This rule is supplemented by Practice Direction A. This provides that certain cases must be heard by the President or a High Court judge (paras 2 and 3).

    See also Part 9, Practice Direction E and r 25(3).

Disputing the jurisdiction of the court

87 Procedure for disputing the court's jurisdiction

(1) A person who wishes to –

    (a) dispute the court's jurisdiction to hear an application; or

    (b) argue that the court should not exercise its jurisdiction,

may apply to the court at any time for an order declaring that it has no such jurisdiction or should not exercise any jurisdiction that it may have.

(2) An application under this rule must be –

    (a) made by using the form specified in the relevant practice direction; and

    (b) supported by evidence.

(3) An order containing a declaration that the court has no jurisdiction or will not exercise its jurisdiction may also make further provision, including –

    (a)   setting aside the application;

    (b)   discharging any order made; and

    (c)   staying the proceedings.

'Practice Direction'—This rule is supplemented by Practice Direction B. The application is made in accordance with Part 9 on Form COP9 or on the acknowledgement in Form COP5.

    This rule should also be read with r 148 which applies where P ceases to lack capacity. Strangely, Part 12, Practice Direction B deals with such an application which should be made on Form COP9 and be supported by evidence.

Participation in hearings

88 Participation in hearings

(1) The court may hear P on the question of whether or not an order should be made, whether or not he is a party to the proceedings.

(2) The court may proceed with a hearing in the absence of P if it considers that it would be appropriate to do so.

(3) A person other than P who is served with or notified of the application may only take part in a hearing if –

    (a)   he files an acknowledgment in accordance with the Rules and is made a party to the proceedings; or

    (b)   the court permits.

Reconsideration of court orders

89 Orders made without a hearing or without notice to any person

(1) This rule applies where the court makes an order –

    (a)   without a hearing; or

    (b)   without notice to any person who is affected by it.

(2) Where this rule applies –

    (a)   P;

    (b)   any party to the proceedings; or

    (c)   any other person affected by the order,

may apply to the court for reconsideration of the order made.

(3) An application under paragraph (2) must be made –

    (a)   within 21 days of the order being served or such other period as the court may direct; and

    (b)   in accordance with Part 10.

(4) The court will –

    (a)   reconsider the order without directing a hearing; or

    (b)   fix a date for the matter to be heard, and notify all parties to the proceedings and such other persons as the court may direct, of that date.

(5) Where an application is made in accordance with this rule, the court may affirm, set aside or vary any order made.

PART IV

(6) Reconsideration may be by any judge of the court –

    (a)   including the judge who made the decision in respect of which the reconsideration is sought; but

    (b)   may not be by a judge who is not a prescribed higher judge within the meaning of section 53(3) of the Act in relation to the first-mentioned judge.

(7) No application may be made seeking a reconsideration of a decision that has been made under paragraph (5).

(8) An appeal against a decision made under paragraph (5) may be made in accordance with Part 20 (appeals).

(9) Any order made without a hearing or without notice to any person, other than one made under paragraph (5), must contain a statement of the right to apply for a reconsideration of the decision in accordance with this rule.

(10) An application made under this rule may include a request that the court reconsider the matter at a hearing.

Rule 89(6)(a)—This provision allows the judge who made the original decision to review his decision. The Rules Committee has suggested that this rule should be changed to include a table showing the type of judge who may reconsider a decision. It has also recommended a practice direction which could explain matters, for example when a reconsideration should be referred to a different judge or when and how other parties should be notified of the application.

PART 13
HEARINGS

Private hearings

90 General rule – hearing to be in private

(1) The general rule is that a hearing is to be held in private.

(2) A private hearing is a hearing which only the following persons are entitled to attend –

    (a)   the parties;

    (b)   P (whether or not a party);

    (c)   any person acting in the proceedings as a litigation friend;

    (d)   any legal representative of a person specified in any of sub-paragraphs (a) to (c); and

    (e)   any court officer.

(3) In relation to a private hearing, the court may make an order –

    (a)   authorising any person, or class of persons, to attend the hearing or a part of it; or

    (b)   excluding any person, or class of persons, from attending the hearing or a part of it.

Rule 90(1)—A hearing will be in private. Rule 90(2) sets out who may attend.

Prior to the implementation of this rule, there was some debate as to whether the hearing should be in public or private, some favouring more openness. However, the rules committee finally settled on a presumption that a hearing will be in private unless it is ordered otherwise.

A private hearing does not contravene the European Convention for the Protection of Human Rights and Fundamental Freedoms 1950, Art 6, which is incorporated into law through the Human Rights Act 1998 (see *R v Bow County Court ex parte Pelling (No 2)* [2001] EWCA Civ 122).

Publication of information about proceedings in private could amount to contempt of court. Thus, without permission, there can be no lawful publication of information about a case (see Practice Direction A, paras 7 and 8).

Rules 90, 91 and 92 allow the Court to order to displace the rule of privacy.

Rule 90(3)(a) and (b)—For example, the press, certain relatives or interested groups.

The Rules Committee has suggested that a practice direction on the preparation of bundle should be added to Part 13.

91 Court's general power to authorise publication of information about proceedings

(1) For the purposes of the law relating to contempt of court, information relating to proceedings held in private may be published where the court makes an order under paragraph (2).

(2) The court may make an order authorising –

    (a) the publication of such information relating to the proceedings as it may specify; or

    (b) the publication of the text or a summary of the whole or part of a judgment or order made by the court.

(3) Where the court makes an order under paragraph (2) it may do so on such terms as it thinks fit, and in particular may –

    (a) impose restrictions on the publication of the identity of –
      (i) any party;
      (ii) P (whether or not a party);
      (iii) any witness; or
      (iv) any other person;

    (b) prohibit the publication of any information that may lead to any such person being identified;

    (c) prohibit the further publication of any information relating to the proceedings from such date as the court may specify; or

    (d) impose such other restrictions on the publication of information relating to the proceedings as the court may specify.

Scope of rule— This rule allows the court to impose conditions on the authorised publication of information in a case.

Power to order a public hearing

92 Court's power to order that a hearing be held in public

(1) The court may make an order –

    (a) for a hearing to be held in public;

    (b) for a part of a hearing to be held in public; or

    (c) excluding any person, or class of persons, from attending a public hearing or a part of it.

(2) Where the court makes an order under paragraph (1), it may in the same order or by a subsequent order –

    (a) impose restrictions on the publication of the identity of –
      (i) any party;
      (ii) P (whether or not a party);

PART IV

        (iii) any witness; or

        (iv) any other person;

  (b)   prohibit the publication of any information that may lead to any such person being identified;

  (c)   prohibit the further publication of any information relating to the proceedings from such date as the court may specify; or

  (d)   impose such other restrictions on the publication of information relating to the proceedings as the court may specify.

Scope of rule—This rule allows waiver of the rule that a hearing must be in private. It also allows the court to restrict the publication of information in respect of a case heard in public.

Supplementary

93 Supplementary provisions relating to public or private hearings

(1) An order under rule 90, 91 or 92 may be made –

  (a)   only where it appears to the court that there is good reason for making the order;

  (b)   at any time; and

  (c)   either on the court's own initiative or on an application made by any person in accordance with Part 10.

(2) A practice direction may make further provision in connection with –

  (a)   private hearings;

  (b)   public hearings; or

  (c)   the publication of information about any proceedings.

Scope of rule—This rule sets out the test for determining an application under rr 90, 91 and 92.

Rule 93(1)(a) provides that there has to be a good reason for making the order.

In *Independent News and Media Limited v A* [2009] EWHC 2858 (Fam) Hedley J considered this rule in connection with an application by the media under r 91. He held that the court needs to adopt a two-stage approach. The first stage is to consider whether 'good reason' can be established. He described this as a gatekeeping test and 'necessarily of a somewhat summary nature'. If no good reason can be found, that is the end of the matter. If good reason is found, this will not automatically entitle an applicant to an order. Instead, it obligates the court to undertake the exercise applied in *Re S (A Child) (Identification: Restrictions on Publication)* [2005] 1 AC 593.

In *Re S*, Lord Steyn considered the interplay between Arts 8 and 10 of the European Convention on Human Rights and set out four propositions.

The first is that neither article has precedence over the other. Second, where the values under the two articles are in conflict, an 'intense focus' on the comparative importance of the specific rights being claimed in the individual case is necessary. Third, the justification for interfering with or restricting each right must be taken into account. Fourth, the proportionality test must be applied to each. Lord Steyn called this the ultimate balancing test.

As there is no statutory commentary on the meaning of 'good reason', Hedley J held that it should be given its ordinary meaning. He also stated that 'real weight' had to be given to r 90(1) and the general rule that matters were dealt with in private and 'real value' must be given to the concept of good reason before the court acts otherwise than in accordance with the general rule.

In this case, Hedley J held that the applicant media organisations had demonstrated good reason; first, all of the issues in the case were within the public domain and the issues they addressed were readily apparent; second, the court was equipped with powers to preserve privacy whilst addressing the issues in the case and third, the court's decision would have major implications for the future welfare of A and it was in the public interest that there should be understanding of the jurisdiction and powers of the court and how they are exercised. Accordingly, Hedley J allowed the media to attend the proceedings but in all other respects, the proceedings would remain private. He also allowed some reporting of the case.

Hedley J's decision was appealed (2010 EWCA Civ 343) and save for the issue of when Article 10 of the European Convention of Human Rights was engaged, the decision was upheld.

With regard to "good reason" in r 93, they said that "… We do not propose to reqrite the words 'good reason'. They mean what, taken together, they say …" They also said that even when good reason appears, there may be better reason to refuse authorization of publicity. The Court of Appeal also endorsed the two stage approach to be undertaken before making an order. First, whether there is good reason and if so, whether the requisite balancing exercise justified the making of the order. When considering the issues raised by rr 90, 91 and 92, the following additional matters may also be relevant:

(1) The need to prevent disclosure of private and confidential information relating to P or others.
(2) Whether information relating to the mental or physical condition of P should be in the public domain.
(3) The effect of publicity on P's family and others connected with P.
(4) The effect and any distress suffered by P, his or her family or those connected with P due to a public hearing.
(5) The inability of P to respond to public debate or media comment due to his or her lack of capacity.
(6) Any loss of dignity to P.
(7) The effect of publicity on any medical or care team, residential unit or service.
(8) Whether the public interest be satisfied by anonymised court reporting of any judgment or of the proceedings
(9) Whether the need for a public hearing will cause delay to the proceedings
(10) Whether the matter or issue is already in the public domain.

When considering an application, the aim should be to protect P rather than to confer anonymity on other individuals and organisations (Practice Direction A, para 27).

An order may include restrictions on identifying specified family members, carers, doctors or organisations where the absence of such a restriction is likely to prejudice their ability to care for P or where their identification might lead to identifying P and defeat the purpose of the order.

An application under rr 90, 91 or 92 must be made on Form COP9 using the Part 10 procedure.

Rule 25(2)(h) allows the Court to deal with an application under this rule as a discrete issue and Part 13, Practice Direction A, para 6 calls on the Court to consider doing so. Delay in deciding the substantive issue in a case may call upon the court to consider not dealing with a media application as a discrete issue.

The order should last for no longer than is necessary to achieve the purpose for which it was made. However, in some cases, it may need to last until P's death or even a later date (see Practice Direction A, para 29).

Practice Direction—Practice Direction A, Part 2 sets out the circumstances where notice may need to be given to the national media and the procedural route to follow.

PART 14
ADMISSIONS, EVIDENCE AND DEPOSITIONS

Admissions

94 Making an admission

(1) Without prejudice to the ability to make an admission in any other way, a party may admit the truth of the whole or part of another party's case by giving notice in writing.

(2) The court may allow a party to amend or withdraw an admission.

Evidence

95 Power of court to control evidence

The court may –

    (a) control the evidence by giving directions as to –
        (i) the issues on which it requires evidence;

       (ii)   the nature of the evidence which it requires to decide those issues; and

       (iii) the way in which the evidence is to be placed before the court;

(b)   use its power under this rule to exclude evidence that would otherwise be admissible;

(c)   allow or limit cross-examination; and

(d)   admit such evidence, whether written or oral, as it thinks fit.

Rule 95(b)—This rule was criticised during the consultation process leading to the formulation of the rules. However, it is submitted that this rule simply allows the Court to have complete control over the evidence in a case. This is consistent with the Court's duty to properly manage cases. Indeed, where P's funds may ultimately pay the costs of litigation, it is only correct that the Court should retain a wide power to exclude evidence. Obviously, any decision to exclude evidence must take into account P's best interests and the overriding objective.

Rule 95(d)—This rule furthers the Court's control over evidence. For example, it may be quicker and simpler to allow a family member to give short oral evidence at a hearing rather than insist on a formal witness statement and cause an adjournment or extra costs because the family member is acting in person and may need to instruct a solicitor to assist with the preparation of a witness statement. Again, P's best interests will be considered.

The Court will be eager to approach the control of evidence in a way that is proportionate to the case and consistent with the overriding objective.

In civil proceedings governed by the CPR, cases are allocated to one of three tracks. A straightforward case which can be tried in a few hours will be allocated to the small claims track. Highly complex cases are allocated to the multi-track and cases which will last up to a day and are not unduly complicated are allocated to the fast track. Each track has its own variations of the standard litigation procedure set out in the rules and its own approach. A small claims case will often be approached in a less formal way than a multi-track case. The obvious advantage of the track system is that each case can find a home that is best suited to it; the track will also affect the costs in the case.

However, these rules apply to every case in the Court. The Court's workload is diverse. Thus, effective case management is vital and the Court must be given the option to control evidence. For example, in a case where objection is made to registering an enduring power of attorney by a family member, the Court may only need to order the attorney and the objector to file evidence and list a short hearing. In a more serious case, there may be a need to make detailed provisions for evidence.

96 Evidence of witnesses – general rule

(1) The general rule is that any fact which needs to be proved by evidence of a witness is to be proved –

(a)   where there is a final hearing, by their oral evidence; or

(b)   at any other hearing, or if there is no hearing, by their evidence in writing.

(2) Where a witness is called to give oral evidence under paragraph (1)(a), his witness statement shall stand as his evidence in chief unless the court directs otherwise.

(3) A witness giving oral evidence at the final hearing may, if the court permits –

(a)   amplify his witness statement; and

(b)   give evidence in relation to new matters which have arisen since the witness statement was made.

(4) The court may so permit only if it considers that there is good reason not to confine the evidence of the witness to the contents of his witness statement.

(5) This rule is subject to –

(a)   any provision to the contrary in these Rules or elsewhere; or

(b)   any order or direction of the court.

Rule 96(1)(a)—The general rule may vary in some cases. On the final hearing of a contested application for a statutory will, for example, it may suffice for the judge to read the witness statements of the parties followed by submissions.

Rule 96(4)—A good reason will include consideration of P's best interests and the overriding objective. Thus, in a dispute which centres around family members and their interaction with P, it could well be in P's best interests for the Court to allow a witness to speak beyond his or her statement if only to gain a flavour of the family dynamics in a case.

In a more serious case where there are allegations of abuse to P, witnesses may have been reluctant to put all of their story in writing due to family or other reasons. To not allow them to amplify their written evidence would therefore not be in P's best interests.

97 Written evidence – general rule

A party may not rely upon written evidence unless –

    (a)   it has been filed in accordance with these Rules or a practice direction;

    (b)   it is expressly permitted by these Rules or a practice direction; or

    (c)   the court gives permission.

Rule 97(c)—Rule 99 provides that the Court will order when witness statements have to be filed for the final hearing of a case. However, if a party wants to adduce further evidence, it will require permission under this rule.

When considering whether to give permission, the Court will consider P's best interests, the overriding objective and the general interests of justice. In all cases, the Court will need to have full information to allow it to reach a fair decision. It is not uncommon for practitioners to assume that the Court will accede to the request to adduce late evidence as a matter of course. This is not correct. The absence of proper reasons may result in evidence not being admitted.

P's interests will also include considering the costs consequences of any delay or adjournment to a hearing.

98 Evidence by video link or other means

The court may allow a witness to give evidence through a video link or by other communication technology.

'Practice Direction'—Practice Direction A, Annex 2 sets out rules for video conferences.

99 Service of witness statements for use at final hearing

(1) A witness statement is a written statement which contains the evidence which that person would be allowed to give orally.

(2) The court will give directions about the service of any witness statement that a party intends to rely upon at the final hearing.

(3) The court may give directions as to the order in which witness statements are to be served.

    (Rules 11 and 100 require witness statements to be verified by a statement of truth.)

100 Form of witness statement

A witness statement must contain a statement of truth and comply with the requirements set out in the relevant practice direction.

PART IV

'**Practice Direction**'— Practice Direction A, paras 33–45 set out the format of the witness statement.

The witness statement must be included in or attached to Form COP24 which is the witness statement designed for use in the Court of Protection.

The statement should be in the witness's own words and should ideally follow the chronological sequence of the events or matters dealt with, and each paragraph should be confined to a distinct portion of the subject (Practice Direction A, paras 35 and 42). This requirement is taken from the CPR.

An exhibit should be verified and identified by the witness and remain separate from the witness statement.

101 Witness summaries

(1) A party who wishes to file a witness statement for use at final hearing, but is unable to do so, may apply, without notice, to be permitted to file a witness summary instead.

(2) A witness summary is a summary of –

(a)   the evidence, if known, which would otherwise be included in a witness statement; or

(b)   if the evidence is not known, the matters about which the party filing the witness summary proposes to question the witness.

(3) Unless the court directs otherwise, a witness summary must include the name and address of the intended witness.

(4) Unless the court directs otherwise, a witness summary must be filed within the period in which a witness statement would have had to be filed.

(5) Where a party files a witness summary, so far as practicable, rules 96(3)(a) (amplifying witness statements) and 99 (service of witness statements for use at a final hearing) shall apply to the summary.

102 Affidavit evidence

Evidence must be given by affidavit instead of or in addition to a witness statement if this is required by the court, a provision contained in any rule, a practice direction or any other enactment.

103 Form of affidavit

An affidavit must comply with the requirements set out in the relevant practice direction.

'**Practice Direction**'—Practice Direction A, paras 1–19 contain the rules relating to the format of affidavits and other general matters. Paragraphs 20–31 set out the rules relating to exhibits. Paragraph 32 allows an affirmation instead of an affidavit.

104 Affidavit made outside the jurisdiction

A person may make an affidavit outside the jurisdiction in accordance with –

(a)   this Part; or

(b)   the law of the place where he makes the affidavit.

105 Notarial acts and instruments

A notarial act or instrument may, without further proof, be received in evidence as duly authenticated in accordance with the requirements of law unless the contrary is proved.

106 Summoning of witnesses

(1) The court may allow or direct any party to issue a witness summons requiring the person named in it to attend before the court and give oral evidence or produce any document to the court.

(2) An application by a party for the issue of a witness summons may be made by filing an application notice which includes –

- (a) the name and address of the applicant and of his solicitor, if any;
- (b) the name, address and occupation of the proposed witness;
- (c) particulars of any document which the proposed witness is to be required to produce; and
- (d) the grounds on which the application is made.

(3) The general rule is that a witness summons is binding if it is served at least 7 days before the date on which the witness is required to attend before the court, and the requirements of paragraph (6) have been complied with.

(4) The court may direct that a witness summons shall be binding although it will be served less than 7 days before the date on which the witness is required to attend before the court.

(5) Unless the court directs otherwise, a witness summons is to be served by the person making the application.

(6) At the time of service the witness must be offered or paid –

- (a) a sum reasonably sufficient to cover his expenses in travelling to and from the court; and
- (b) such sum by way of compensation for loss of time as may be specified in the relevant practice direction.

(7) The court may order that the witness is to be paid such general costs as it considers appropriate.

Rule 106(2)—Practice Direction D sets out the rules relating to witness summonses.
The application for a witness summons will be made on Form COP9 and Part 10 will apply.

Rule 106(6)—The sum paid is calculated by reference to the sums payable to witnesses attending the Crown Court which is the same basis as payment under the CPR (Practice Direction D, para 9). The sums payable are fixed pursuant to the Prosecution of Offenders Act 1985 and the Costs in Criminal Cases (General) Regulations 1986, SI 1986/1335. The amount for an ordinary witness (as opposed to an expert or professional witness) for a period not exceeding 4 hours is £29.75 and exceeding 4 hours is £59.50. Subsistence allowance starts at £2.25 for a period not exceeding 5 hours.

107 Power of court to direct a party to provide information

(1) Where a party has access to information which is not reasonably available to the other party, the court may direct that party to prepare and file a document recording the information.

(2) The court will give directions about serving a copy of that document on the other parties.

'Practice Direction'—This rule is supplemented by Practice Direction A, para 54.

Depositions

108 Evidence by deposition

(1) A party may apply for an order for a person to be examined before the hearing takes place.

(2) A person from whom evidence is to be obtained following an order under this rule is referred to as a 'deponent' and the evidence is referred to as a 'deposition'.

(3) An order under this rule shall be for a deponent to be examined on oath before –

   (a)   a circuit judge or a district judge, whether or not nominated as a judge of the court;
   (b)   an examiner of the court; or
   (c)   such other person as the court appoints.

(4) The order may require the production of any document which the court considers is necessary for the purposes of the examination.

(5) The order will state the date, time and place of the examination.

(6) At the time of service of the order, the deponent must be offered or paid –

   (a)   a sum reasonably sufficient to cover his expenses in travelling to and from the place of examination; and
   (b)   such sum by way of compensation for loss of time as may be specified in the relevant practice direction.

(7) Where the court makes an order for a deposition to be taken, it may also order the party who obtained the order to file a witness statement or witness summary in relation to the evidence to be given by the person to be examined.

Rule 108(1)—Practice Direction B contains further rules about depositions.
   The application is made on Form COP9 and may be made without notice.

109 Conduct of examination

(1) Subject to any directions contained in the order for examination, the examination must be conducted in the same way as if the witness were giving evidence at a final hearing.

(2) If all the parties are present, the examiner may conduct the examination of a person not named in the order for examination if all the parties and the person to be examined consent.

(3) The examiner must ensure that the evidence given by the witness is recorded in full.

(4) The examiner must send a copy of the deposition –

   (a)   to the person who obtained the order for the examination of the witness; and
   (b)   to the court.

(5) The court will give directions as to the service of a copy of the deposition on the other parties.

110 Fees and expenses of examiners of the court

(1) An examiner of the court may charge a fee for the examination and he need not send the deposition to the court until the fee is paid, unless the court directs otherwise.

(2) The examiner's fees and expenses must be paid by the party who obtained the order for examination.

(3) If the fees and expenses due to an examiner are not paid within a reasonable time, he may report that fact to the court.

(4) The court may order the party who obtained the order for examination to deposit in the court office a specified sum in respect of the examiner's fees and, where it does so, the examiner will not be asked to act until the sum has been deposited.

(5) An order under this rule does not affect any decision as to the person who is ultimately to bear the costs of the examination.

'**Practice Direction**'—Practice Direction C supplements this rule.

111 Examiners of the court

(1) The Lord Chancellor shall appoint persons to be examiners of the court.

(2) The persons appointed shall be barristers or solicitor-advocates who have been practising for a period of not less than 3 years.

(3) The Lord Chancellor may revoke an appointment at any time.

(4) In addition to appointing persons in accordance with this rule, examiners appointed under rule 34.15 of the Civil Procedure Rules 1998 may act as examiners in the court.

112 Enforcing attendance of a witness

(1) If a person served with an order to attend before an examiner –

   (a)   fails to attend; or
   (b)   refuses to be sworn for the purpose of the examination or to answer any lawful question or produce any document at the examination,

a certificate of his failure or refusal, signed by the examiner, must be filed by the party requiring the deposition.

(2) On the certificate being filed, the party requiring the deposition may apply to the court for an order requiring that person to attend or to be sworn or to answer any question or produce any document, as the case may be.

(3) An application for an order under this rule may be made without notice.

(4) The court may order the person against whom an order is sought or made under this rule to pay any costs resulting from his failure or refusal.

PART IV

113 Use of deposition at a hearing

(1) A deposition ordered under rule 108, 115 or 116 may be put in evidence at a hearing unless the court orders otherwise.

(2) A party intending to put a deposition in evidence at a hearing must file notice of his intention to do so on the court and serve the notice on every other party.

(3) Unless the court directs otherwise, he must file the notice at least 14 days before the day fixed for the hearing.

(4) The court may require a deponent to attend the hearing and give evidence orally.

Taking evidence outside the jurisdiction

114 Interpretation

In this Section –

    (a) 'Regulation State' has the same meaning as 'Member State' in the Taking of Evidence Regulation, that is all Member States except Denmark; and

    (b) 'the Taking of Evidence Regulation' means Council Regulation (EC) No. 1206/2001 of 28 May 2001 on co-operation between the courts of Member States in the taking of evidence in civil and commercial matters.

115 Where a person to be examined is in another Regulation State

(1) This rule applies where a party wishes to take a deposition from a person who is –

    (a) outside the jurisdiction; and

    (b) in a Regulation State.

(2) The court may order the issue of the request to a designated court ('the requested court') in the Regulation State in which the proposed deponent is.

(3) If the court makes an order for the issue of a request, the party who sought the order must file –

    (a) a draft Form A as set out in the annex to the Taking of Evidence Regulation (request for the taking of evidence);

    (b) except where paragraph (4) applies, a translation of the form;

    (c) an undertaking to be responsible for the costs sought by the requested court in relation to –

        (i) fees paid to experts and interpreters; and

        (ii) where requested by that party, the use of special procedure or communications technology; and

    (d) an undertaking to be responsible for the court's expenses.

(4) There is no need to file a translation if –

    (a) English is one of the official languages of the Regulation State where the examination is to take place; or

    (b) the Regulation State has indicated, in accordance with the Taking of Evidence Regulation, that English is a language which it will accept.

(5) Where article 17 of the Taking of Evidence Regulation (direct taking of evidence by the requested court) allows evidence to be taken directly in another Regulation State, the court may make an order for the submission of a request in accordance with that article.

(6) If the court makes an order for the submission of a request under paragraph (5), the party who sought the order must file –

    (a)   draft Form I as set out in the annex to the Taking of Evidence Regulation (request for direct taking of evidence);

    (b)   except where paragraph (4) applies, a translation of the form; and

    (c)   an undertaking to be responsible for the requested court's expenses.

'Practice Direction'—Practice Direction B contains further rules relevant to this rule and r 116.

'Form'—An application is made on Form COP9.

116 Where a person to be examined is out of the jurisdiction – letter of request

(1) This rule applies where a party wishes to take a deposition from a person who is –

    (a)   out of the jurisdiction; and

    (b)   not in a Regulation State within the meaning of rule 114.

(2) The court may order the issue of a letter of request to the judicial authorities of the country in which the proposed deponent is.

(3) A letter of request is a request to a judicial authority to take the evidence of that person, or arrange for it to be taken.

(4) If the government of a country permits a person appointed by the court to examine a person in that country, the court may make an order appointing a special examiner for that purpose.

(5) A person may be examined under this rule on oath or affirmation in accordance with any procedure permitted in the country in which the examination is to take place.

(6) If the court makes an order for the issue of a letter of request, the party who sought the order must file –

    (a)   the following documents and, except where paragraph (7) applies, a translation of them –

        (i)   a draft letter of request;

        (ii)   a statement of the issues relevant to the proceedings; and

        (iii)   a list of questions or the subject matter of questions to be put to the person to be examined; and

    (b)   an undertaking to be responsible for the Secretary of State's expenses.

(7) There is no need to file a translation if –

    (a)   English is one of the official languages of the country where the examination is to take place; or

    (b)   a practice direction has specified that country is a country where no translation is necessary.

Section 49 reports

117 Reports under section 49 of the Act

(1) This rule applies where the court requires a report to be made to it under section 49 of the Act.

(2) It is the duty of the person who is required to make the report to help the court on the matters within his expertise.

(3) Unless the court directs otherwise, the person making the report must –

    (a) contact or seek to interview such persons as he thinks appropriate or as the court directs;

    (b) to the extent that it is practicable and appropriate to do so, ascertain what P's wishes and feelings are, and the beliefs and values that would be likely to influence P if he had the capacity to make a decision in relation to the matter to which the application relates;

    (c) describe P's circumstances; and

    (d) address such other matters as are required in a practice direction or as the court may direct.

(4) The court will send a copy of the report to the parties and to such persons as the court may direct.

(5) Subject to paragraphs (6) and (7), the person who is required to make the report may examine and take copies of any document in the court records.

(6) The court may direct that the right to inspect documents under this rule does not apply in relation to such documents, or descriptions of documents, as the court may specify.

(7) The court may direct that any information is to be provided to the maker of the report on an edited basis.

Scope of rule—MCA 2005, s 49 allows the Court to call for reports.
    Rule 117 will apply where a request for a report has been made pursuant to MCA 2005, s 49. Practice Direction E supplements this rule.
    When giving directions in a case, r 85(2)(a) allows the Court to order a report.
    In deciding whether to order a report, the following may be useful to have in mind:

    (1) Where there is no particular legal or factual dispute, it is not appropriate to order a report.

    (2) Where P requires a high level of protection, it may be preferable for P to be joined as a party and legally represented instead of ordering a report.

    (3) An impartial report may be welcome for cases between (1) and (2) above to assist the Court in reaching a decision or to help the Court to solve a particular issue.

    (4) A report should be considered as an alternative to full, formal representation of P in a case.

    (5) The appropriateness of a stranger interviewing P.

    (6) Consideration should be given to proportionality.

    (7) The author of a report should be properly trained and qualified to carry out the task. For example, to asses a person who lacks capacity and who has serious communication difficulties requires an appropriately trained assessor.

    (8) It should not always follow that P should pay for the report whether or not he or she is a party.

    (9) The cost of a report should be proportionate.

'Practice Direction'—Practice Direction E, paras 11–16 set out the contents of a report. The Practice Direction also sets out what steps to take to notify the person or body making the report. The Annex to Practice Direction E contains a draft order which can be adapted in each case.
    If a report is ordered and the author of the report is required to attend court, the court will need to address who is to pay for the costs of attendance.

118 Written questions to person making a report under section 49

(1) Where a report is made under section 49 the court may, on the application of any party, permit written questions relevant to the issues before the court to be put to the person by whom the report was made.

(2) The questions sought to be put to the maker of the report shall be submitted to the court, and the court may put them to the maker of the report with such amendments (if any) as it thinks fit and the maker of the report shall give his replies in writing to the questions so put.

(3) The court will send a copy of the replies given by the maker of the report under this rule to the parties and to such other persons as the court may direct.

PART 15
EXPERTS

119 References to expert

A reference to an expert in this Part –

    (a)   is to an expert who has been instructed to give or prepare evidence for the purpose of court proceedings; but

    (b)   does not include any person instructed to make a report under section 49 of the Act.

Meaning of expert—An expert is not defined in the rules either in Part 15 or in r 6.

During the consultation process, it was suggested that no distinction should be made between a heath care professional (such as a doctor) acting as an expert and that of carers or family who are close to P. However, this idea is not reflected in these rules.

Those close to P cannot be independent or unbiased which is a requirement for an expert acting within Part 15 (see Practice Direction A, paras 3 and 4). Family members too cannot be said to have expertise within the meaning of this Part. Thus, the expert in these rules is to be understood in the traditional sense only.

The Rules Committee has recommended that a new practice direction should be added to Part 15 based on the President's Practice Direction in Family Proceedings which came into force in April 2008 and is entitled "Experts in Family Proceedings relating to Children".

120 Restriction on filing an expert's report

(1) No person may file expert evidence unless the court or a practice direction permits, or if it is filed with the permission form or application form and is evidence –

    (a)   that P is a person who lacks capacity to make a decision or decisions in relation to the matter or matters to which the application relates;

    (b)   as to P's best interests; or

    (c)   that is required by any rule or practice direction to be filed with the permission form or application form.

(2) An applicant may only rely upon any expert evidence so filed in support of the permission form or application form to the extent and for the purposes that the court allows.

    (Rule 64(a) requires the applicant to file any evidence upon which he wishes to rely with the application form and rule 54 requires certain documents to be filed with the application for permission form.)

Rule 120(1)—After the filing of the permission form or application form, no expert evidence may be filed without permission of the Court (Practice Direction A, para 1) or pursuant to a Practice Direction.

121 Duty to restrict expert evidence

Expert evidence shall be restricted to that which is reasonably required to resolve the proceedings.

'Practice Direction'—Practice Direction A, para 1 supposes that expert evidence will be given by a single joint expert. Rule 130 gives the Court power to order a joint expert. The Practice Direction makes it clear that the aim of this Part of the rules is to limit the use of expert evidence to that which is reasonably required (Practice Direction A, para 1).

Expert evidence—The Court will consider what added value expert evidence will give to the case. If expert evidence is allowed, it should be restricted to what is reasonably required to resolve the proceedings.

Reference should also be made to the President's guidance note dated December 2010 wherein it is made clear that it will be rare for the court to sanction the instruction of more than one expert. The guidance also warns the expert not to analyse or summarise the evidence and to be brief (see paragraphs 8 and 9).

122 Experts – overriding duty to the court

It is the duty of the expert to help the court on the matters within his expertise.

Practice Direction—Practice Direction A, paras 2–7 set out the general duties of an expert. For example, that the expert be objective and independent.

If a matter is beyond his or her expertise, the expert should say so (Practice Direction A, para 6(a)).

The duty of the expert is to help the Court; this duty overrides any obligation to the person from whom the expert has received instructions or by whom he or she is paid.

123 Court's power to restrict expert evidence

(1) Subject to rule 120, no party may file or adduce expert evidence unless the court or a practice direction permits.

(2) When a party applies for a direction under this rule he must –

   (a) identify the field in respect of which he wishes to rely upon expert evidence;
   (b) where practicable, identify the expert in that field upon whose evidence he wishes to rely;
   (c) provide any other material information about the expert; and
   (d) provide a draft letter of instruction to the expert.

(3) Where a direction is given under this rule, the court shall specify the field or fields in respect of which the expert evidence is to be provided.

(4) The court may specify the person who is to provide the evidence referred to in paragraph (3).

(5) Where a direction is given under this rule for a party to call an expert or put in evidence an expert's report, the court shall give directions for the service of the report on the parties and on such other persons as the court may direct.

(6) The court may limit the amount of the expert's fees and expenses that the party who wishes to rely upon the expert may recover from any other party.

Rule 123(2)—The Court should be given the fullest possible information. It is not acceptable to simply say that, for example, a psychiatrist is required.

The Court should be told the following:

(1) Why the expert evidence is required.
(2) Whether all parties agree that an expert is required and, if not, why there is disagreement.
(3) Whether a joint expert is appropriate.
(4) The name of the proposed expert.
(5) The expert's qualifications.
(6) The reason the expert is suitable.
(7) How much the expert will charge.
(8) Who is to pay initially for the report (but see r 125(7)).
(9) When the report can be served.
(10) Whether P needs to be seen or examined.
(11) Whether any order for disclosure is required to allow the expert to properly complete his or her report.

The Court will also have regard to the overriding objective: in particular, the need to deal with a case justly. See also r 5(2)(g).

A draft letter of instruction to the expert should also be available for the Court to consider (see r 123(2)(d)).

In serious cases where an urgent hearing is being convened and where time is of the essence, it may be necessary to arrange for an expert to be on standby to deal with matters arising from the hearing.

See also r 125(7) which deals with the costs of an expert's report.

124 General requirement for expert evidence to be given in a written report

Expert evidence is to be given in a written report unless the court directs otherwise.

Scope of rule—The purpose of this rule is to ensure that an expert attends only when it is necessary and in the interests of justice.

Content of the report—Rule 126 deals with the content of the report.

r 14—The expert should also be told about r 14, which sets out the consequences of making a false statement.

125 Written questions to experts

(1) A party may put written questions to –

(a) an expert instructed by another party; or
(b) a single joint expert appointed under rule 130,

about a report prepared by such person.

(2) Written questions under paragraph (1) –

(a) may be put once only;
(b) must be put within 28 days beginning with the date on which the expert's report was served; and
(c) must be for the purpose only of clarification of the report.

(3) Paragraph (2) does not apply in any case where –

(a) the court permits it to be done on a further occasion;
(b) the other party or parties agree; or
(c) any practice direction provides otherwise.

(4) An expert's answers to questions put in accordance with paragraph (1) shall be treated as part of the expert's report.

(5) Paragraph (6) applies where –

    (a)   a party has put a written question to an expert instructed by another party in accordance with this rule; and

    (b)   the expert does not answer that question.

(6) The court may make one or both of the following orders in relation to the party who instructed the expert –

    (a)   that the party may not rely upon the evidence of that expert; or

    (b)   that the party may not recover the fees and expenses of that expert, or part of them, from any other party.

(7) Unless the court otherwise directs, and subject to any final costs order that may be made, the instructing party is responsible for the payment of the expert's fees and expenses, including the expert's costs of answering questions put by any other party.

Rule 125(7)—This rule lays down a general principle that the party who instructs an expert is responsible for payment of the expert's fees, which include the cost of answering questions put by the other party. It must follow that where a joint expert is instructed, the parties initially pay an equal contribution to the cost. However, the Court may make another order for payment of the expert's costs both initially and after a final hearing.

126 Contents of expert's report

(1) The court may give directions as to the matters to be covered in an expert's report.

(2) An expert's report must comply with the requirements set out in the relevant practice direction.

(3) At the end of an expert's report there must be a statement that –

    (a)   the expert understands his duty to the court; and

    (b)   he has complied with that duty.

(4) The expert's report must state the substance of all material instructions, whether written or oral, on the basis of which the report was written.

(5) The instructions to the expert shall not be privileged against disclosure.

Form and content of the report—The expected form and content of the report are set out at Practice Direction A, paras 8–12.

127 Use by one party of expert's report disclosed by another

Where a party has disclosed an expert's report, any party may use that expert's report as evidence at any hearing in the proceedings.

128 Discussions between experts

(1) The court may, at any stage, direct a discussion between experts for the purpose of requiring the experts to –

    (a)   identify and discuss the expert issues in the proceedings; and

    (b)   where possible, reach an agreed opinion on those issues.

(2) The court may specify the issues which the experts must discuss.

(3) The court may direct that following a discussion between the experts they must prepare a statement for the court showing –

(a) those issues on which they agree; and

(b) those issues on which they disagree and a summary of their reasons for disagreeing.

(4) Unless the court otherwise directs, the content of the discussions between experts may be referred to at any hearing or at any stage in the proceedings.

Scope of rule —This rule furthers the overriding objective: see r 5(2)(a).

129 Expert's right to ask court for directions

(1) An expert may file a written request for directions to assist him in carrying out his function as an expert.

(2) An expert must, unless the court directs otherwise, provide a copy of any proposed request for directions under paragraph (1) –

(a) to the party instructing him, at least 7 days before he files the request; and

(b) to all other parties, at least 4 days before he files it.

(3) The court, when it gives directions, may also direct that a party be served with a copy of the directions.

Practice Direction—Practice Direction A, para 1 states that where possible a single expert is appropriate. However, there may be cases where the Court would be assisted by having two expert views on a matter to allow the Court to become acquainted with a range of views.

130 Court's power to direct that evidence is to be given by a single joint expert

(1) Where two or more parties wish to submit expert evidence on a particular issue, the court may direct that the evidence on that issue is to be given by one expert only.

(2) The parties wishing to submit the expert evidence are called 'the instructing parties'.

(3) Where the instructing parties cannot agree who should be the expert, the court may –

(a) select the expert from a list prepared or identified by the instructing parties; or

(b) direct the manner by which the expert is to be selected.

131 Instructions to a single joint expert

(1) Where the court gives a direction under rule 130 for a single joint expert to be used, each party may give instructions to the expert.

(2) Unless the court otherwise directs, when an instructing party gives instructions to the expert he must, at the same time, send a copy of the instructions to the other instructing parties.

(3) The court may give directions about –

(a) the payment of the expert's fees and expenses; and

(b) any inspection, examination or experiments which the expert wishes to
carry out.

(4) The court may, before an expert is instructed, limit the amount that can be paid
by way of fees and expenses to the expert.

(5) Unless the court otherwise directs, and subject to any final costs order that may
be made, the instructing parties are jointly and severally liable for the payment of
the expert's fees and expenses.

PART 16
DISCLOSURE

132 Meaning of disclosure

A party discloses a document by stating that the document exists or has existed.

Scope of rule—This rule deals with disclosure. There is no Practice Direction. The provisions are
based on the CPR 1998. The Rules Committee has said that the disclosure rules might more usefully
be based on family procedure with the emphasis on full and frank disclosure.

When dealing with disclosure, it is also useful to recall r 107. This provides that where a party has
access to information which is not reasonably available to the other party, the Court may direct that
party to prepare and file a document recording the information.

Unlike the CPR, document is not defined in the rules. It is defined in the CPR as 'anything in
which information of any description is recorded' (CPR, r 31(4)).

It is submitted that a document within the context of these rules should be given the widest
possible interpretation to include not only paper documents but also electronic documents, disks and
audio tapes.

When dealing with any issue relating to disclosure, it should not be overlooked that the Court will
always have P's best interests in mind.

133 General or specific disclosure

(1) The court may either on its own initiative or on the application of a party make
an order to give general or specific disclosure.

(2) General disclosure requires a party to disclose –

(a) the documents on which he relies; and

(b) the documents which –
(i)   adversely affect his own case;
(ii)   adversely affect another party's case; or
(iii) support another party's case.

(3) An order for specific disclosure is an order that a party must do one or more of
the following things –

(a) disclose documents or classes of documents specified in the order;
(b) carry out a search to the extent stated in the order; or
(c) disclose any document located as a result of that search.

(4) A party's duty to disclose documents is limited to documents which are or have
been in his control.

(5) For the purpose of paragraph (4) a party has or has had a document in his
control if –

    (a)   it is or was in his physical possession;

    (b)   he has or has had possession of it; or

    (c)   he has or has had a right to inspect or take copies of it.

Rule 133(2)—Sometimes a document may attract legal professional privilege. There are two categories of document: the first are communications which are privileged in all circumstances whether or not litigation is involved. This category would include letters between a solicitor and client or counsel. The second category are those which are privileged only if they came into existence in contemplation of litigation. If such correspondence or other documents are relevant to a dispute, care should be taken when dealing with disclosure and careful consideration given as to whether privilege needs to be waived.

Rule 133(3)—The following principles have been extracted from case-law under the old rules of the Court of Protection although they may be of use:

    (1)   Disclosure could be given of a confidential report to the Court by the Lord Chancellor's Visitor unless it is against the best interests of P (*Re W L W* [1972] 1 Ch 456).

    (2)   On an application by P for release of papers held by the Official Solicitor in litigation relating to P, the Court of Appeal in *Re E (Mental Health Patient)* [1985] 1 WLR 245 held:

        (a)   the paramount consideration was the interest and benefit of P;

        (b)   the Official Solicitor may have access to confidential papers to which an ordinary litigation friend may not have access and it is important to preserve the confidence of those who gave information; and

        (c)   the cases where the Court should exercise its discretion to withhold disclosure of a confidential report or other confidential documents from a party or parent must be rare and where the Court is fully satisfied judicially that real harm to the patient must ensue from disclosure.

134 Procedure for general or specific disclosure

(1) This rule applies where the court makes an order under rule 133 to give general or specific disclosure.

(2) Each party must make, and serve on every other party, a list of documents to be disclosed.

(3) A copy of each list must be filed within 7 days of the date on which it is served.

(4) The list must identify the documents in a convenient order and manner and as concisely as possible.

(5) The list must indicate –

    (a)   the documents in respect of which the party claims a right or duty to withhold inspection (see rule 138); and

    (b)   the documents that are no longer in his control, stating what has happened to them.

135 Ongoing duty of disclosure

(1) Where the court makes an order to give general or specific disclosure under rule 133, any party to whom the order applies is under a continuing duty to provide such disclosure as is required by the order until the proceedings are concluded.

(2) If a document to which the duty of disclosure imposed by paragraph (1) extends comes to a party's notice at any time during the proceedings, he must immediately notify every other party.

PART IV

136 Right to inspect documents

(1) A party to whom a document has been disclosed has a right to inspect any document disclosed to him except where –

    (a)   the document is no longer in the control of the party who disclosed it; or

    (b)   the party disclosing the document has a right or duty to withhold inspection of it.

(2) The right to inspect disclosed documents extends to any document mentioned in –

    (a)   a document filed or served in the course of the proceedings by any other party; or

    (b)   correspondence sent by any other party.

Scope of rule—This provision is taken from CPR, r 31(3) with one omission. The CPR allow a party to not give disclosure where that party believes it is disproportionate to the issues in the case. This provision is not included in this rule presumably because this would not be in P's interests.

137 Inspection and copying of documents

(1) Where a party has a right to inspect a document, he –

    (a)   must give the party who disclosed the document written notice of his wish to inspect it; and

    (b)   may request a copy of the document.

(2) Not more than 14 days after the date on which the party who disclosed the document received the notice under paragraph (1)(a), he must permit inspection of the document at a convenient place and time.

(3) Where a party has requested a copy of the document, the party who disclosed the document must supply him with a copy not more than 14 days after the date on which he received the request.

(4) For the purposes of paragraph (2), the party who disclosed the document must give reasonable notice of the time and place for inspection.

(5) For the purposes of paragraph (3), the party requesting a copy of the document is responsible for the payment of reasonable copying costs, subject to any final costs order that may be made.

138 Claim to withhold inspection or disclosure of document

(1) A party who wishes to claim that he has a right or duty to withhold inspection of a document, or part of a document, must state in writing –

    (a)   that he has such a right or duty; and

    (b)   the grounds on which he claims that right or duty.

(2) The statement must be made in the list in which the document is disclosed (see rule 134(2)).

(3) A party may, by filing an application notice in accordance with Part 10, apply to the court to decide whether the claim made under paragraph (1) should be upheld.

139 Consequence of failure to disclose documents or permit inspection

A party may not rely upon any document which he fails to disclose or in respect of which he fails to permit inspection unless the court permits.

PART 17
LITIGATION FRIEND

140 Who may act as a litigation friend

(1) A person may act as a litigation friend on behalf of a person mentioned in paragraph (2) if he –

   (a)   can fairly and competently conduct proceedings on behalf of that person; and

   (b)   has no interests adverse to those of that person.

(2) The persons for whom a litigation friend may act are –

   (a)   P;

   (b)   a child; or

   (c)   a protected party.

Practice Direction—See the Practice Direction – Litigation friend.

Background—Rules of Court generally make special provision for parties who are not capable of conducting their own litigation (eg Civil Procedure Rules 1998 Part 21; Family Proceedings Rules 1989, Part IX; Family Procedure Rules 2010, Parts 15 and 16). There are two categories, namely children and those who lack mental capacity (now termed 'protected party' but previously 'patient'). They must have a representative known as a 'litigation friend' (previously a 'next friend' or 'guardian ad litem' in family proceedings).

Litigation friend—This is the person who acts as representative for a child or protected party (or for 'P' in the Court of Protection). There is a difference between the role of the litigation friend and a solicitor and for this reason a solicitor will not usually be appointed as a litigation friend, although a litigation friend may instruct a solicitor.

Suitability—This rule makes it clear that a litigation friend must fairly and competently conduct the proceedings for the party and have no adverse interest. There is also the duty under the MCA 2005 to act in the 'best interests' of the protected party. It will be interesting to see whether there is any tension between these two provisions (eg where the duty to the court would be not to pursue a hopeless point but the party will wish to see this fully argued – see in the context of care proceedings *RP v Nottingham City Council & Official Solicitor* [2008] EWCA Civ 462).

Persons for whom a litigation friend may act—There is a significant difference between the needs of P (if made a party) and of a child or protected party. A relative or concerned person may act as litigation friend for a party other than P, but such person would be likely to have a conflict of interest in acting for P and if wishing to participate should become a party in their own right. The litigation friend for P will generally be the Official Solicitor unless an independent professional person (eg a social worker who is not otherwise involved) was available for appointment.

'P'—Means 'any person (other than a protected party) who lacks or, so far as is consistent with the context, is alleged to lack capacity to make a decision or decisions in relation to any matter that is the subject of an application to the court and references to a person who lacks capacity are to be construed in accordance with the Act' (r 6). Thus P is the person to whom the proceedings relate.

'child'—This refers to 'a person under 18' rather than a child of a party.

'protected party'—Means 'a party or an intended party (other than P or a child) who lacks capacity to conduct the proceedings' (r 6). Lack of capacity is defined in MCA 2005, s 2.

Status of litigation friend—As the appointment is to 'conduct proceedings on behalf of' the child or protected party, any act which in the ordinary conduct of any proceedings is required or authorised to be done by a party shall or may be done by the litigation friend. Unless the litigation friend is also a deputy appointed by the Court of Protection or an attorney under a lasting or registered enduring power of attorney, he or she will have no status in regard to the affairs of the protected party outside the proceedings in which he or she is appointed.

Need for a solicitor—There is no requirement in the Rules for a solicitor to act on behalf of a child or protected party whose proceedings are being conducted by a litigation friend. Nevertheless, in a complex or high value case the Court may consider that the litigation friend who acts without a solicitor is not 'suitable' within r 140(1) and appoint someone else under r 144(1).

141 Requirement for a litigation friend

(1) Subject to rule 147, P (if a party to proceedings) must have a litigation friend.

(2) A protected party (if a party to the proceedings) must have a litigation friend.

(3) A child (if a party to proceedings) must have a litigation friend to conduct those proceedings on his behalf unless the court makes an order under paragraph (4).

(4) The court may make an order permitting the child to conduct proceedings without a litigation friend.

(5) An application for an order under paragraph (4) –

    (a)   may be made by the child;

    (b)   if the child already has a litigation friend, must be made on notice to the litigation friend; and

    (c)   if the child has no litigation friend, may be made without notice.

(6) Where –

    (a)   the court has made an order under paragraph (4); and

    (b)   it subsequently appears to the court that it is desirable for a litigation friend to conduct the proceedings on behalf of the child,

the court may appoint a person to be the child's litigation friend.

Scope of rule—The general principle is that a child or protected party may only conduct proceedings by a litigation friend. P will only need a litigation friend if he or she is made a party (which is not always the case) and lacks capacity to conduct the proceedings.

'child'— An all or nothing approach to age is no longer adopted (*Gillick v West Norfolk & Wisbech Area Health Authority* [1985] 3 All ER 402, HL). There is provision for a child to act personally even before attaining 18, but approval of the court is required (r 141(4)) and may subsequently be withdrawn (r 141(6)). The Court will only authorise a child to conduct proceedings when satisfied that the child has the required capacity (i e is of sufficient maturity and understanding). It is both prudent and good practice for the litigation friend to consult the child once the child is able to make a meaningful contribution, and particularly as the child approaches 18 since on attaining that age the appointment of the litigation friend ceases and the child (now an adult) may take over conduct of the proceedings.

Exceptions—Unlike the CPR (r 21.3), the Court is not given an express discretion to permit specified steps to be taken before a litigation friend is appointed or retrospectively to approve any steps that have been taken without such appointment, but there is no specific provision that a step taken in the absence of a litigation friend for a party is of no effect so the Court probably retains a discretion.

142 Litigation friend without a court order

(1) This rule does not apply –

    (a)   in relation to P;

    (b)   where the court has appointed a person under rule 143 or 144; or

    (c)   where the Official Solicitor is to act as litigation friend.

(2) A deputy with the power to conduct legal proceedings in the name of the protected party or on the protected party's behalf is entitled to be a litigation friend of the protected party in any proceedings to which his power relates.

(3) If no one has been appointed by the court, or in the case of a protected party, there is no deputy with the power to conduct proceedings, a person who wishes to act as a litigation friend must –

    (a)   file a certificate of suitability stating that he satisfies the conditions specified in rule 140(1); and

    (b)   serve the certificate of suitability on –

        (i)   the person on whom an application form is to be served in accordance with rule 32 (service on children and protected parties); and

        (ii) every other person who is a party to the proceedings.

(4) If the person referred to in paragraph (2) wishes to act as a litigation friend for the protected party, he must file and serve a copy of the court order which appointed him on those persons mentioned in paragraph (3)(b).

Scope of rule—This rule sets out the procedural steps for the appointment of a litigation friend otherwise than by a court order. It will be relied upon in most cases. A deputy already authorised to conduct proceedings in the name of the protected party will be entitled to act in that capacity. If there is no such deputy an appointment can be made upon the appropriate documents being filed by the person desiring to be appointed a litigation friend.

Exceptions—This provision does not apply if the appointment is for P or it is to be of the Official Solicitor or if the Court has already made other provision.

'certificate of suitability' (r 142(3)(a))—This document confirms that the person to be appointed meets the criteria whereby a person may be regarded as suitable for appointment as litigation friend (r 140(1)). The certificate does not include an undertaking as to costs (unlike proceedings in the civil courts). It is not required where the person is a deputy authorised by the Court of Protection to conduct the proceedings.

Deputy appointed by the Court of Protection—An official copy of the order of the Court of Protection, which confers his or her power to act, must be filed and served.

Service—The certificate of suitability must be served on the child or person alleged to lack capacity (thus providing an opportunity for objections) and also on the other parties.

143 Litigation friend by court order

(1) The court may make an order appointing –

    (a)   the Official Solicitor; or

    (b)   some other person,

to act as a litigation friend.

(2) The court may act under paragraph (1) –

    (a)   either on its own initiative or on the application of any person; but

    (b)   only with the consent of the person to be appointed.

(3) An application for an order under paragraph (1) must be supported by evidence.

(4) The court may not appoint a litigation friend under this rule unless it is satisfied that the person to be appointed satisfies the conditions specified in rule 140(1).

(5) The court may at any stage of the proceedings give directions as to the appointment of a litigation friend.

Official Solicitor—The Official Solicitor will usually be appointed in respect of P. For other parties the Official Solicitor should be approached in case of difficulty and may be appointed if he or she consents, but in practice the Official Solicitor will only consent if there is no one else suitable and willing to act. It is not necessary to approach the Official Solicitor in all cases and the Court will not be concerned to ascertain whether he or she has declined to consent before appointing someone else. The Official Solicitor should not be appointed without his or her consent, which will not usually be forthcoming until provision is made for payment of his or her costs. Save in the most urgent of cases, it is unlikely that the Official Solicitor will be able to complete his or her inquiries in less than 3 months. Accordingly, a lengthy adjournment of the proceedings might become necessary and a substantive hearing should not be fixed within such period of the Official Solicitor's initial appointment without consulting him or her. Where the circumstances of the case justify the involvement of the Official Solicitor, a completed questionnaire and copy of the order appointing him or her (subject to his or her consent) together with a copy of the Court file should be sent to the Official Solicitor's office. The Official Solicitor may be contacted at 81 Chancery Lane, London WC2A 1DD; Tel 020 7911 7127; Fax 020 7911 7105.

'on its own initiative'—The Court does not have to await an application and can proceed to make an appointment of its own initiative. This may occur where the need for a litigation friend is first identified at a hearing.

Consent—A person will not be appointed without their consent.

Evidence—This will be in the form of a medical report (or certificate) or a witness statement, and possibly both. The Court will need to make a relevant finding of lack of capacity and cannot do so without evidence.

Directions—Where the Court does not have the evidence on the basis of which to make a decision it will give directions as to how matters are to proceed.

144 Court's power to prevent a person from acting as litigation friend or to order change

(1) The court may either on its own initiative or on the application of any person –

    (a)   direct that a person may not act as a litigation friend;

    (b)   terminate a litigation friend's appointment; or

    (c)   appoint a new litigation friend in place of an existing one.

(2) An application for an order under paragraph (1) must be supported by evidence.

(3) The court may not appoint a litigation friend under this rule unless it is satisfied that the person to be appointed satisfies the conditions specified in rule 140(1).

Scope of rule—The Court may prevent a person from being a litigation friend or replace a litigation friend during the course of proceedings, whether or not appointed by an order. See **'Suitability'** in r 140. Any dispute as to who should be the litigation friend would be dealt with under this provision.

Evidence—This will be in the form of a medical report (or certificate) and witness statement. The Court will need to make a relevant finding of lack of capacity and cannot do so without evidence.

Termination—The rules express no limit on the power to terminate the appointment and if the litigation friend manifestly acts contrary to the child's or protected party's best interests, the Court will remove him or her, even though neither his or her good faith nor his or her diligence is in issue (*Re A (Conjoined Twins: Medical Treatment) (No 2)* (2001) CCS 2, [2001] 1 FLR 267, CA). In respect of mentally incapable adults, what are this person's best interests has now been clarified by MCA 2005, s 4.

145 Appointment of litigation friend by court order – supplementary

The applicant must serve a copy of an application for an order under rule 143 or 144 on –

(a)   the person on whom an application form is to be served in accordance with rule 32 (service on children and protected parties);

(b)   every other person who is a party to the proceedings;

(c)   any person who is the litigation friend, or who is purporting to act as the litigation friend, when the application is made; and

(d)   unless he is the applicant, the person who it is proposed should be the litigation friend,

as soon as practicable and in any event within 21 days of the date on which it was issued.

Scope of rule—This rule makes provision for the service of applications for the appointment or removal of a litigation friend. Basically, everyone involved or with a relevant interest must be notified. This includes the child or person alleged to lack capacity.

146 Procedure where appointment of litigation friend comes to an end – for a child or protected party

(1) This rule applies –

(a)   when a child reaches 18, provided he is neither –

(i)   P; nor

(ii)   a protected party; and

(b)   where a protected party ceases to be a person who lacks capacity to conduct the proceedings himself.

(2) Where paragraph (1)(a) applies, the litigation friend's appointment ends.

(3) Where paragraph (1)(b) applies, the litigation friend's appointment continues until it is brought to an end by a court order

(4) An application for an order under paragraph (3) may be made by –

(a)   the former protected party;

(b)   his litigation friend; or

(c)   any other person who is a party to the proceedings.

(5) The applicant must serve a copy of the application notice seeking an order under this rule on all parties to the proceedings as soon as practicable and in any event within 21 days of the date on which it was issued.

(6) Where paragraph (2) applies the child must serve notice on every other party –

(a)   stating that he has reached full age;

(b)   stating that the appointment of the litigation friend has ended; and

(c)   providing his address for service.

(7) Where paragraph (3) applies, the former protected party must provide his address for service to all other parties to the proceedings.

Scope of rule—This rule makes provision for the appointment of a litigation friend to terminate in respect of a child (who is not also a protected party) or a protected party.

Child—When a child (who is not also a protected party) attains majority the appointment ceases but the child must serve notice on the other parties to this effect stating his or her address for service.

Protected party   An application on notice to all other parties must be made by the protected party or litigation friend (or another party) for an order terminating the appointment. It will be supported by evidence that this party has ceased to be a person who lacks capacity to conduct the proceedings. The former protected party must provide an address for service if the application is successful.

147 Procedure where appointment of litigation friend comes to an end – for P

(1) This rule applies where P ceases to be a person who lacks capacity to conduct the proceedings himself but continues to lack capacity in relation to the matter or matters to which the application relates.

(2) The litigation friend's appointment continues until it is brought to an end by a court order.

(3) An application for an order under paragraph (2) may be made by –

    (a)   P;

    (b)   his litigation friend; or

    (c)   any other person who is a party to the proceedings.

(4) The applicant must serve a copy of the application notice seeking an order under this rule on all other parties to the proceedings as soon as practicable and in any event within 21 days of the date on which it was issued.

(5) Where the court makes an order under this rule, P must provide his address for service to all other parties to the proceedings.

Scope of rule—This further rule makes provision for the termination of the appointment of a litigation friend for P in the event that capacity to conduct the proceedings (but not to decide the matters brought before the Court) is restored.

Procedure— An application on notice to all other parties must be made by P or the litigation friend (or another party) for an order terminating the appointment. It must be supported by evidence that P has ceased to be a person who lacks capacity to conduct the proceedings. P must provide an address for service if the application is successful.

148 Procedure where P ceases to lack capacity

(1) This rule applies where P ceases to lack capacity both to conduct the proceedings himself and in relation to the matter or matters to which the application relates.

(2) The litigation friend's appointment continues until it is brought to an end by a court order.

(3) An application may be made by –

    (a)   P;

    (b)   his litigation friend; or

    (c)   any other person who is a party to the proceedings,

for the proceedings to come to an end.

(4) The applicant must serve a copy of the application notice seeking an order under this rule on all parties to the proceedings as soon as practicable and in any event within 21 days of the date on which it was issued.

Scope of rule—This additional rule makes provision for the proceedings to be brought to an end in the event that capacity to conduct the proceedings *and* decide the matters brought before the Court is restored.

Procedure—An application on notice to all other parties must be made by P or the litigation friend (or another party) for an order bringing the proceedings to an end. It must be supported by evidence that P now has the required capacity.

149 Practice direction in relation to litigation friends

A practice direction may make additional or different provision in relation to litigation friends.

Practice Direction—This rule provides the authority for the Practice Direction – Litigation friend. It is strange that the rule allows the Practice Direction to make different provision because in the event of conflict between the Rules and a Practice Direction the former normally take precedence.

PART 18
CHANGE OF SOLICITOR

150 Change of solicitor

(1) This rule applies where a party to proceedings –

  (a)   for whom a solicitor is acting wants to change his solicitor or act in person; or

  (b)   after having conducted the proceedings in person, appoints a solicitor to act on his behalf (except where the solicitor is appointed only to act as an advocate for a hearing).

(2) The party proposing the change must –

  (a)   file a notice of the change with the court; and

  (b)   serve the notice of the change on every other party to the proceedings and, if there is one, on the solicitor who will cease to act.

(3) The notice must state the party's address for service.

(4) The notice filed at court must state that it has been served as required by paragraph (2)(b).

(5) Where there is a solicitor who will cease to act, he will continue to be considered the party's solicitor unless and until –

  (a)   the notice is filed and served in accordance with paragraphs (2), (3) and (4); or

  (b)   the court makes an order under rule 152 and the order is served in accordance with that rule.

Scope of rule—This rule sets out the procedure where there is a change of solicitor. It is supplemented by Practice Direction A.

  For the sake of completeness, reference should be made to Part 67 of the CPR. This deals with proceedings against solicitors where an order is sought for the solicitor to deliver a bill or cash account, where there are issues concerning solicitors' remuneration and matters arising from an intervention in a solicitors' practice. Such proceedings would need to be brought as Part 8 CPR proceedings and not in the Court of Protection.

Rule 150(2)(a)—Form COP30 should be used.

151 LSC funded clients

(1) Where the certificate of any person ('A') who is an LSC funded client is revoked or discharged –

    (a) the solicitor who acted for A will cease to be the solicitor acting in the case as soon as his retainer is determined under regulation 4 of the Community Legal Services (Costs) Regulations 2000; and

    (b) if A wishes to continue and appoints a solicitor to act on his behalf, rule 150(2), (3) and (4) will apply as if A had previously conducted the application in person.

(2) In this rule, 'certificate' means a certificate issued under the Funding Code (approved under section 9 of the Access to Justice Act 1999).

152 Order that a solicitor has ceased to act

(1) A solicitor may apply for an order declaring that he has ceased to be the solicitor acting for a party.

(2) Where an application is made under this rule –

    (a) the solicitor must serve the application notice on the party for whom the solicitor is acting, unless the court directs otherwise; and

    (b) the application must be supported by evidence.

(3) Where the court makes an order that a solicitor has ceased to act, the solicitor must –

    (a) serve a copy of the order on every other party to the proceedings; and

    (b) file a certificate of service.

Rule 152(1)—The application is made on Form COP9 and should be supported by evidence (r 152(2)(b)).

Rule 152(3)(b)—The certificate of service is Form COP20.

153 Removal of solicitor who has ceased to act on application of another party

(1) Where –

    (a) a solicitor who has acted for a party –
        (i)   has died;
        (ii) has become bankrupt;
        (iii) has ceased to practice; or
        (iv) cannot be found; and

    (b) the party has not served a notice of a change of solicitor or notice of intention to act in person as required by rule 150,

any other party may apply for an order declaring that the solicitor has ceased to be the solicitor acting for the other party in the case.

(2) Where an application is made under this rule, the applicant must serve the application on the party to whose solicitor the application relates, unless the court directs otherwise.

(3) Where the court makes an order under this rule –

(a) the court will give directions about serving a copy of the order on every other party to the proceedings; and

(b) where the order is served by a party, that party must file a certificate of service.

154 Practice direction relating to change of solicitor

A practice direction may make additional or different provision in relation to change of solicitor.

PART 19
COSTS

155 Interpretation

(1) In this Part –

(a) 'additional liability' means the percentage increase, the insurance premium, or the additional amount in respect of provision made by a membership organisation, as the case may be;

(b) 'authorised court officer' means any officer of the Supreme Court Costs Office, whom the Lord Chancellor has authorised to assess costs;

(c) 'costs' include fees, charges, disbursements, expenses, reimbursement permitted to a litigant in person, any additional liability incurred under a funding arrangement and any fee or reward charged by a lay representative for acting on behalf of a party in proceedings;

(d) 'costs judge' means a taxing Master of the Supreme Court;

(e) 'costs officer' means a costs judge or an authorised court officer;

(f) 'detailed assessment' means the procedure by which the amount of costs or remuneration is decided by a costs officer in accordance with Part 47 of the Civil Procedure Rules 1998 (which are applied to proceedings under these Rules, with modifications, by rule 160);

(g) 'fixed costs' are to be construed in accordance with the relevant practice direction;

(h) 'fund' includes any estate or property held for the benefit of any person or class of persons and any fund to which a trustee or personal representative is entitled in his capacity as such;

(i) 'funding arrangement' means an arrangement where a person has –

(i) entered into a conditional fee agreement or a collective conditional fee agreement which provides for a success fee within the meaning of section 58(2) of the Courts and Legal Services Act 1990;

(ii) taken out an insurance policy to which section 29 of the Access to Justice Act 1999 (recovery of insurance premiums by way of costs) applies; or

(iii) made an agreement with a membership organisation to meet his legal costs;

(j) 'insurance premium' means a sum of money paid or payable for insurance against the risk of incurring a costs liability in the proceedings, taken out after the event that is the subject matter of the claim;

(k) 'membership organisation' means a body prescribed for the purposes of section 30 of the Access to Justice Act 1999 (recovery where body undertakes to meet costs liabilities);

PART IV

(l)   'paying party' means a party liable to pay costs;

(m)   'percentage increase' means the percentage by which the amount of a legal representative's fee can be increased in accordance with a conditional fee agreement which provides for a success fee;

(n)   'receiving party' means a party entitled to be paid costs;

(o)   'summary assessment' means the procedure by which the court, when making an order about costs, orders payment of a sum of money instead of fixed costs or 'detailed assessment'.

(2) The costs to which the rules in this Part apply include –

(a)   where the costs may be assessed by the court, costs payable by a client to his solicitor; and

(b)   costs which are payable by one party to another party under the terms of a contract, where the court makes an order for an assessment of those costs.

(3) Where advocacy or litigation services are provided to a client under a conditional fee agreement, costs are recoverable under this Part notwithstanding that the client is liable to pay his legal representative's fees and expenses only to the extent that sums are recovered in respect of the proceedings, whether by way of costs or otherwise.

(4) In paragraph (3), the reference to a conditional fee agreement is to an agreement which satisfies all the conditions applicable to it by virtue of section 58 of the Courts and Legal Services Act 1990.

Scope of rule—This rule deals with costs. It is supplemented by Practice Direction A. However, r 160 incorporates the costs provisions of the CPR save that some provisions are excluded. The excluded provisions are set out in r 160 and in Practice Direction A.

The Rules Committee has said that the costs rules need to be "revisited" and it has therefore made a number of recommendations. In particular, it has suggested that guidance should be given in a practice direction as to when the court may depart from the general rule that costs relating to property and affairs are paid from P's estate .

156 Property and affairs – the general rule

Where the proceedings concern P's property and affairs the general rule is that the costs of the proceedings or of that part of the proceedings that concerns P's property and affairs, shall be paid by P or charged to his estate.

Scope of rule—This rule lays down a general presumption. However, r 159 allows the Court to depart from the general presumption.

157 Personal welfare – the general rule

Where the proceedings concern P's personal welfare the general rule is that there will be no order as to the costs of the proceedings or of that part of the proceedings that concerns P's personal welfare.

Scope of rule—This rule reflects a presumption that each party will pay its own costs. Hedley J in *A NHS Trust and B Trust –v- DU, AO, EB and AU* (2009) EWHC 3504 Fam referred to this as "the conventional approach". One advantage of such a presumption is that some cases may settle at an early stage due to the fear of financing a long case.

158 Apportioning costs – the general rule

Where the proceedings concern both property and affairs and personal welfare the court, insofar as practicable, will apportion the costs as between the respective issues.

159 Departing from the general rule

(1) The court may depart from rules 156 to 158 if the circumstances so justify, and in deciding whether departure is justified the court will have regard to all the circumstances, including –

- (a) the conduct of the parties;
- (b) whether a party has succeeded on part of his case, even if he has not been wholly successful; and
- (c) the role of any public body involved in the proceedings.

(2) The conduct of the parties includes –

- (a) conduct before, as well as during, the proceedings;
- (b) whether it was reasonable for a party to raise, pursue or contest a particular issue;
- (c) the manner in which a party has made or responded to an application or a particular issue; and
- (d) whether a party who has succeeded in his application or response to an application, in whole or in part, exaggerated any matter contained in his application or response.

(3) Without prejudice to rules 156 to 158 and the foregoing provisions of this rule, the court may permit a party to recover their fixed costs in accordance with the relevant practice direction.

Note—Guidance on the application of this rule was given by Senior Judge Lush in an appeal from a district judge in *Re RC* (2010) Case No 11639140, namely:

1 The incidence of costs in cases where there is a Lasting Power of Attorney for health and welfare should not necessarily differ from the general rule in property and affairs cases subject to rule 159
2 Before awarding costs, the ability of the party to pay those costs should be considered
3 A warning should be given to a party that a costs order could be made against him
4 The fact that the litigant against whom the judge awarded costs was infuriating should not sway the court into saying that the case was exceptional. In this case, the litigant was "not untypical of many of the litigants in person who appear on a regular basis in health and welfare proceedings in the Court of Protection…It could almost be said that this aspect of the court's jurisdiction was created to deal with situations of this kind where a local authority, NHS Trust or private care home is experiencing problems with a particularly difficult and vociferous relative."
5 The court should only depart from the general rule where the circumstances so justify. Such circumstances would include conduct where the person against whom it is proposed to award costs is clearly acting in bad faith.

In *A NHS Trust* referred to under r 157, Hedley J said that although the court retains the power to mark its displeasure of any behaviour by making adverse orders as to costs, "it is a power rarely exercised but one which the court retains."

160 Rules about costs in the Civil Procedure Rules to apply

(1) Subject to the provisions of these Rules, Parts 44, 47 and 48 of the Civil Procedure Rules 1998 ('the 1998 Rules') shall apply with the modifications in this

PART IV

rule and such other modifications as may be appropriate, to costs incurred in relation to proceedings under these Rules as they apply to costs incurred in relation to proceedings in the High Court.

(2) The provisions of Part 47 of the 1998 Rules shall apply with the modifications in this rule and such other modifications as may be appropriate, to a detailed assessment of the remuneration of a deputy under these Rules as they apply to a detailed assessment of costs in proceedings to which the 1998 Rules apply.

(3) Where the definitions in Part 43 (referred to in Parts 44, 47 and 48) of the 1998 Rules are different from the definitions in rule 155 of these Rules, the latter shall prevail.

(4) Rules 44.1, 44.3(1) to (5), 44.6, 44.7, 44.9, 44.10, 44.11. 44.12 and 44.12A of the 1998 Rules do not apply.

(5) In rule 44.17 of the 1998 Rules, the references to Parts 45 and 46 do not apply.

(6) In rule 47.3(1)(c) of the 1998 Rules, the words 'unless the costs are being assessed under rule 48.5 (costs where money is payable to a child or a patient)' are removed.

(7) In rule 47.3(2) of the 1998 Rules, the words 'or a district judge' are removed.

(8) Rule 47.4(3) and (4) of the 1998 Rules do not apply.

(9) Rules 47.9(4), 47.10 and 47.11 of the 1998 Rules do not apply where the costs are to be paid by P or charged to his estate.

(10) Rules 48.2, 48.3, 48.6A, and 48.10 of the 1998 Rules do not apply.

(11) Rule 48.1(1) of the 1998 Rules is removed and is replaced by the following: 'This paragraph applies where a person applies for an order for specific disclosure before the commencement of proceedings'.

161 Detailed assessment of costs

(1) Where the court orders costs to be assessed by way of detailed assessment, the detailed assessment proceedings shall take place in the High Court.

(2) A fee is payable in respect of the detailed assessment of costs and on an appeal against a decision made in a detailed assessment of costs.

(3) Where a detailed assessment of costs has taken place, the amount payable by P is the amount which the court certifies as payable.

Assessment—The assessment will be carried out at the Supreme Court Costs Office (see Practice Direction A, para 20).

162 Employment of a solicitor by two or more persons

Where two or more persons having the same interest in relation to a matter act in relation to the proceedings by separate legal representatives, they shall not be permitted more than one set of costs of the representation unless and to the extent that the court certifies that the circumstances justify separate representation.

163 Costs of the Official Solicitor

Any costs incurred by the Official Solicitor in relation to proceedings under these Rules or in carrying out any directions given by the court and not provided for by remuneration under rule 167 shall be paid by such persons or out of such funds as the court may direct.

164 Procedure for assessing costs

Where the court orders a party, or P, to pay costs to another party it may either –

    (a)   make a summary assessment of the costs; or

    (b)   order a detailed assessment of the costs by a costs officer,

unless any rule, practice direction or other enactment provides otherwise.

Rule 164(a)—A statement of costs should be filed before a hearing which is listed for up to one day. However, it has to be recognised that some matters may incur substantial costs even though they take one day to be heard and a detailed assessment may be more appropriate.

165 Costs following P's death

An order or direction that costs incurred during P's lifetime be paid out of or charged on his estate may be made within 6 years after P's death.

166 Costs orders in favour of or against non-parties

(1) Where the court is considering whether to make a costs order in favour of or against a person who is not a party to proceedings –

    (a)   that person must be added as a party to the proceedings for the purposes of costs only; and

    (b)   he must be given a reasonable opportunity to attend a hearing at which the court will consider the matter further.

(2) This rule does not apply where the court is considering whether to make an order against the Legal Services Commission.

167 Remuneration of a deputy, donee or attorney

(1) Where the court orders that a deputy, donee or attorney is entitled to remuneration out of P's estate for discharging his functions as such, the court may make such order as it thinks fit, including an order that –

    (a)   he be paid a fixed amount;

    (b)   he be paid at a specified rate; or

    (c)   the amount of the remuneration shall be determined in accordance with the schedule of fees set out in the relevant practice direction.

(2) Any amount permitted by the court under paragraph (1) shall constitute a debt due from P's estate.

(3) The court may order a detailed assessment of the remuneration by a costs officer, in accordance with rule 164(b).

PART IV

Practice Direction—See Practice Direction B which came into effect on 1 April 2008 and which deals with fixed costs in the Court of Protection.

168 Practice direction as to costs

A practice direction may make further provision in respect of costs in proceedings.

Practice Direction—See Practice Direction B which came into effect on 1 April 2008 and which deals with fixed costs in the Court of Protection.

PART 20
APPEALS

169 Scope of this Part

This Part applies to an appeal against any decision of the court except where, in relation to those cases that are to be dealt with in accordance with Part 22 (transitory and transitional provisions), Part 22 makes different provision.

Scope of part—MCA 2005, s 53 allows the rules to provide a mechanism for appeals. MCA 2005 also allows the rules to consider whether permission to appeal is required or not. Part 20 sets out these rules. It is supplemented by Practice Direction A.

Reference should also be made to r 89 which contains provision for the Court to reconsider orders made without a hearing or without notice to any person.

Part 22 contains rules dealing with appeals in cases to which the transitory provisions apply.

170 Interpretation

(1) In the following provisions of this Part –

   (a) 'appeal judge' means a judge of the court to whom an appeal is made;

   (b) 'first instance judge' means the judge of the court from whose decision an appeal is brought;

   (c) 'appellant' means the person who brings or seeks to bring an appeal;

   (d) 'respondent' means –

      (i) a person other than the appellant who was a party to the proceedings before the first instance judge and who is affected by the appeal; or

      (ii) a person who is permitted or directed by the first instance judge or the appeal judge to be a party to the appeal.

(2) In this Part, where the expression 'permission' is used it means 'permission to appeal' unless otherwise stated.

171 Dealing with appeals

(1) The court may deal with an appeal or any part of an appeal at a hearing or without a hearing.

(2) In considering whether it is necessary to hold a hearing, the court shall have regard to the matters set out in rule 84(3).

(Rule 89 provides for reconsideration of orders made without a hearing or without notice to a person.)

172 Permission to appeal

(1) Subject to paragraph (8), an appeal against a decision of the court may not be made without permission.

(2) Any person bound by an order of the court by virtue of rule 74 (persons to be bound as if parties) may seek permission to appeal under this Part.

(3) Permission is to be granted or refused in accordance with this Part.

(4) An application for permission to appeal may be made to the first instance judge or the appeal judge.

(5) Where an application for permission is refused by the first instance judge, a further application for permission may be made in accordance with paragraphs (6) and (7).

(6) Where the decision sought to be appealed is a decision of a district judge, permission may be granted or refused by –

    (a)   the President;
    (b)   the Vice-President;
    (c)   one of the other judges nominated by virtue of section 46(2)(a) to (c) of the Act; or
    (d)   a circuit judge.

(7) Where the decision sought to be appealed is a decision of a circuit judge, permission may only be granted or refused by one of the judges mentioned in paragraph (6)(a) to (c).

(8) Permission is not required to appeal against an order for committal to prison.

Rule 172(1)—The only case where permission is not required is an appeal against an order for committal to prison. During the consultation process, the suggestion was made that serious medical decisions should not require permission. This was not adopted.

173 Matters to be taken into account when considering an application for permission

(1) Permission to appeal shall be granted only where –

    (a)   the court considers that the appeal would have a real prospect of success; or
    (b)   there is some other compelling reason why the appeal should be heard.

(2) An order giving permission may –

    (a)   limit the issues to be heard; and
    (b)   be made subject to conditions.

'reasonable prospect of success'—See *Swain v Hillman* [2001] 1 All ER 91 where the Court of Appeal said that this phrase was self-explanatory.

'compelling reason'—In serious medical cases, this could be the fact that the consequences of the decision would be irreversible for P or that it could lead to P's death.

174 Parties to comply with the practice direction

All parties to an appeal must comply with any relevant practice direction.

175 Appellant's notice

(1) Where the appellant seeks permission from the appeal judge, it must be requested in the appellant's notice.

(2) The appellant must file an appellant's notice at the court within –

    (a)   such period as may be directed or specified in the order of the first instance judge; or

    (b)   where that judge makes no such direction or order, 21 days after the date of the decision being appealed.

(3) The court will issue the appellant's notice and unless it orders otherwise, the appellant must serve the appellant's notice on each respondent and on such other persons as the court may direct, as soon as practicable and in any event within 21 days of the date on which it was issued.

(4) The appellant must file a certificate of service within 7 days beginning with the date on which he served the appellant's notice.

Rule 175(1)—The appellant's notice is Form COP35.

Rule 175(4)—The certificate of service is Form COP20.

176 Respondent's notice

(1) A respondent who –

    (a)   is seeking permission from the appeal judge to appeal; or

    (b)   wishes to ask the appeal judge to uphold the order of the first instance judge for reasons different from or additional to those given by the first instance judge,

must file a respondent's notice.

(2) Where the respondent seeks permission from the appeal judge, permission must be requested in the respondent's notice.

(3) A respondent's notice must be filed within –

    (a)   such period as may be directed by the first instance judge; or

    (b)   where the first instance judge makes no such direction, 21 days beginning with the date referred to in paragraph (4).

(4) The date is the soonest of –

    (a)   the date on which the respondent is served with the appellant's notice where –

        (i)   permission to appeal was given by the first instance judge; or

        (ii)   permission to appeal is not required;

    (b)   the date on which the respondent is served with notification that the appeal judge has given the appellant permission to appeal; or

    (c)   the date on which the respondent is served with the notification that the application for permission to appeal and the appeal itself are to be heard together.

(5) The court will issue a respondent's notice and, unless it orders otherwise, the respondent must serve the respondent's notice on the appellant, any other respondent and on such other parties as the court may direct, as soon as practicable and in any event within 21 days of the date on which it was issued.

(6) The respondent must file a certificate of service within 7 days beginning with the date on which the copy of the respondent's notice was served.

Forms—The respondent's notice is Form COP36. Skeleton arguments should be on Form COP37.

177 Variation of time

(1) An application to vary the time limit for filing an appellant's or respondent's notice must be made to the appeal judge.

(2) The parties may not agree to extend any date or time limit for or in respect of an appeal set by –

    (a)   these Rules;

    (b)   the relevant practice direction; or

    (c)   an order of the appeal judge or the first instance judge.

178 Power of appeal judge on appeal

(1) In relation to an appeal, an appeal judge has all the powers of the first instance judge whose decision is being appealed.

(2) In particular, the appeal judge has the power to –

    (a)   affirm, set aside or vary any order made by the first instance judge;

    (b)   refer any claim or issue to that judge for determination;

    (c)   order a new hearing;

    (d)   make a costs order.

(3) The appeal judge may exercise his powers in relation to the whole or part of an order made by the first instance judge.

179 Determination of appeals

(1) An appeal will be limited to a review of the decision of the first instance judge unless –

    (a)   a practice direction makes different provision for a particular category of appeal; or

    (b)   the appeal judge considers that in the circumstances of the appeal it would be in the interests of justice to hold a re-hearing.

(2) Unless he orders otherwise, the appeal judge will not receive –

    (a)   oral evidence; or

    (b)   evidence that was not before the first instance judge.

(3) The appeal judge will allow an appeal where the decision of the first instance judge was –

    (a)   wrong; or

    (b)   unjust, because of a serious procedural or other irregularity in the proceedings before the first instance judge.

(4) The appeal judge may draw any inference of fact that he considers justified on the evidence.

(5) At the hearing of the appeal a party may not rely upon a matter not contained in his appellant's or respondent's notice unless the appeal judge gives permission.

PART IV

180 Allocation

Except in accordance with the relevant practice direction –

> (a) an appeal from a first instance decision of a circuit judge shall be heard by a judge of the court nominated by virtue of section 46(2)(a) to (c) of the Act; and
>
> (b) an appeal from a decision of a district judge shall be heard by a circuit judge.

Appeals—Appeals from a district judge are heard by a circuit judge (r 180(b)) although permission may be granted or refused by a circuit judge, High Court judge, the Chancellor or the President (r 172(6)).

Appeals from first instance decisions of a circuit judge are heard by a High Court judge, the Chancellor or the President (r 180(a)). Permission may be obtained from a High Court judge, the Chancellor or the President (r 172(7)).

Appeals to the Court of Appeal

181 Appeals against decision of a puisne judge of the High Court, etc

(1) Where the decision sought to be appealed is a decision of a judge nominated by virtue of section 46(2)(a) to (c) of the Act, an appeal will lie only to the Court of Appeal.

(2) The judge nominated by virtue of section 46(2)(a) to (c) of the Act may grant permission to appeal to the Court of Appeal in accordance with this Part, where the decision sought to be appealed was a decision made by a judge so nominated as a first instance judge.

Scope of rule—This rule provides that appeals from a High Court judge, the Chancellor or the President are to the Court of Appeal.

182 Second appeals

(1) A decision of a judge of the court which was itself made on appeal from a judge of the court may only be appealed further to the Court of Appeal.

(2) Permission is required from the Court of Appeal for such an appeal.

(3) The Court of Appeal will not give permission unless it considers that –

> (a) the appeal would raise an important point of principle or practice; or
>
> (b) there is some other compelling reason for the Court of Appeal to hear it.

(4) Nothing in this rule or in rule 181 applies to a second appeal from a decision of a nominated officer.

Scope of rule—Appeal from an appeal – a second appeal – is always to the Court of Appeal, which must grant permission. The test for permission to be granted (r 182(3)) is more restrictive than the test for the granting of permission for a first appeal.

PART 21
ENFORCEMENT

183 Enforcement methods – general

(1) The rules in this Part make provision for the enforcement of judgments and orders.

(2) The relevant practice direction may set out methods of enforcing judgments or orders.

(3) An application for an order for enforcement may be made on application by any person in accordance with Part 10.

Scope of rule—This rule deals with enforcement. It is supplemented by Practice Direction A.

Rule 183(3)—This rule provides that an application for enforcement is made in accordance with Part 10. The application is therefore made on Form COP9.

This presents a problem. In the civil courts, applications for orders to obtain information, third party debt orders and charging orders have their own dedicated application forms. This is because the application forms follow the relevant Practice Direction in the CPR which prescribes the information that has to be included on an application form.

Where an application is made in the Court of Protection, only Form COP9 is used. This form is a general application form. Accordingly, the practitioner must ensure that all the information required by the CPR for a particular method of enforcement is included in COP9. The alternative is to attach the appropriate civil court application form to COP9. This way, nothing will have been omitted. Furthermore, if the enforcement application is transferred to the High Court or the county court, it will avoid the problem of being asked to complete a proper application form there, which will only delay the process.

The civil court application forms are:

- Order to question an individual debtor: N316.
- Order to question an officer of a company or other corporation: N316A.
- Third Party Debt Orders: N349.
- Charging Orders: N379.

184 Application of the Civil Procedure Rules 1998 and RSC Orders

The following provisions apply, as far as they are relevant and with such modifications as may be necessary, to the enforcement of orders made in proceedings under these Rules –

(a) Parts 70 (General Rules about Enforcement of Judgments and Orders), 71 (Orders to Obtain Information from Judgment Debtors), 72 (Third Party Debt Orders) and 73 (Charging Orders, Stop Orders and Stop Notices) of the Civil Procedure Rules 1998; and

(b) Orders 45 (Enforcement of Judgments and Orders: General), 46 (Writs of Execution: General) and 47 (Writs of *Fieri Facias*) of the Rules of the Supreme Court.

Scope of rule—This rule incorporates provisions of other rules which deal with enforcement of judgments.

CPR Part 70—This rule contains general rules about enforcement.

It allows a judgment creditor to use any method of enforcement or even more than one method of enforcement. It allows transfer of a High Court case to the county court for enforcement purposes.

CPR Part 70 has a Practice Direction which supplements the rule.

CPR Part 71—This rule sets out the procedure for obtaining an order to obtain information from a judgment debtor.

The judgment creditor may wish to ascertain the full extent of the judgment debtor's assets, liabilities, income and expenditure and other information. He or she may therefore apply to the Court for an order that the judgment debtor attend the court on a specified day.

The purpose of this rule is to enable the judgment creditor to enforce a judgment or order which he or she will be able to do effectively if he or she has knowledge of the judgment debtor's financial position.

The Practice Direction to CPR Part 71 contains a sample of the form that the judgment debtor will complete when he or she attends court. However, there is nothing to stop the judgment creditor from asking further questions.

Normally, the examination is carried out by a court officer. The court officer will ask the judgment debtor to complete the form. On occasion, the judgment creditor will attend to put questions to the judgment debtor. If the judgment debtor refuses to answer questions, a judge (or master in the High Court) can rule on whether the question should be answered. In complicated cases, a judge is often asked by the judgment creditor to preside over the questioning.

If the judgment debtor fails to attend court, a committal order can be made and if he or she still fails to attend, a warrant can be issued by a judge for him or her to be arrested and brought to court.

It is suggested that if such a procedure is invoked following a judgment in the Court of Protection, the case should be transferred either to the High Court or the county court for enforcement. This is more sensible as those courts regularly deal with these matters.

The Practice Direction to CPR Part 71 sets out the information that must be included in the application form.

CPR Part 72—This rule allows the court to make a third party debt order. Prior to the CPR, this process used to be known as obtaining a garnishee order.

This rule allows the court to make an order requiring a third party to pay the judgment creditor a specified sum.

The application is made without notice to the judgment debtor. Assuming the application form contains the correct information and the debt is one that can be attached, an interim third party debt order will be made. This is served on the judgment debtor and the third party. The court will also list a date for the hearing when it will consider making the order final. Pending the final order, the third party will not release the attached funds to the judgment debtor.

There is a considerable body of case-law concerning what is and what is not an attachable debt and reference should be made to this before making the application.

The rules also contain provisions to allow a debtor who will suffer hardship by the order applying to the court for an order to release funds from his or her account.

CPR Part 73—This rule allows a judgment creditor to apply for a charging order which is an equitable mortgage over land or other property such as shares. It is a discretionary order.

The normal application has to contain specific information as provided for in the Practice Direction which supplements this rule. If a charging order over land is sought, up-to-date official copies of the entry at HM Land Registry should be attached to the application as proof that the judgment debtor owns the property.

The application is considered without notice by a judge on paper. An interim charging order is then granted if the application is approved. The interest created by the interim order can be immediately registered at HM Land Registry. The interim order will also contain a hearing date for the final hearing when the Court will determine if the interim order should be made final. Once a final order is granted, that is the end of the application. If the judgment creditor wants to obtain an order for sale of the property, this requires new proceedings in the civil courts. If the application is by a deputy, permission of the Court of Protection will be required.

This rule also allows the Court to make a stop order and stop notice to effectively stop certain steps in relation to securities and funds. The Charging Orders Act 1979, s 5 sets out the scope of the Court's power. Unlike charging orders, there is no specified application notice in the civil courts and Form COP9 will not present any problem.

Supreme Court Rules 1965 Orders 45, 46 and 47—Prior to the introduction of the CPR, the High Court and the county court each had their own set of rules. The former operated through the Supreme Court Rules 1965, the latter through the County Court Rules 1981.

The aim of the CPR was to codify and place together all rules in the High Court and the county court for ease of practice and reference. However, the task has not yet been fully completed which means that certain of the old rules remain as an annex to the CPR.

Rule 184 incorporates three of those rules which were referred to as Orders. These are Orders 45, 46 and 47. These rules govern certain enforcement methods such as the issue of a writ of sequestration, a writ of *fieri facias* (known as writ of fi fa) and a writ of possession against land.

Orders for committal

185 Contempt of court – generally

An application relating to the committal of a person for contempt of court shall be made to a judge and the power to punish for contempt may be exercised by an order of committal.

Definition of a judge—Judge is defined by r 6 as a judge nominated to be a judge of the Court of Protection under MCA 2005.

186 Application for order of committal

(1) An application for an order of committal must be made by filing an application notice, stating the grounds of the application, and must be supported by an affidavit made in accordance with the relevant practice direction.

(2) Subject to paragraph (3), the application notice, a copy of the affidavit in support thereof and notice of the date of the hearing of the application must be served personally on the person sought to be committed.

(3) Without prejudice to its powers under Part 6, the court may dispense with service under this rule if it thinks it just to do so.

Rule 186(1)—The application is made on Form COP9. The contents of the affidavit are set out at Practice Direction A, paras 4, 5 and 6.

187 Oral evidence

If on the hearing of the application the person sought to be committed expresses a wish to give oral evidence on his own behalf, he shall be entitled to do so.

Legal advice—The person should also be given an opportunity to obtain legal advice if he or she is not legally represented at the hearing. (See *Hammerton v Hammerton* [2007] EWCA Civ 248 and *Greensill v Greensill* [2007] EWCA Civ 680.)

Practice Direction A, para 9 clearly contemplates the situation where at the first hearing the Court cannot proceed for whatever reason.

188 Hearing for committal order

(1) Except where the court permits, no grounds shall be relied upon at the hearing except the grounds set out in the application notice.

(2) Notwithstanding rule 90(1) (general rule – hearing to be in private), when determining an application for committal the court will hold the hearing in public unless it directs otherwise.

(3) If the court hearing an application in private decides that a person has committed a contempt of court, it shall state publicly –

    (a) the name of that person;
    (b) in general terms the nature of the contempt in respect of which the order of committal is being made; and
    (c) any punishment imposed.

(4) If the person sought to be committed does not attend the hearing, the court may fix a date and time for the person to be brought before the court.

Standard of proof—The standard of proof is that a breach must be proved beyond reasonable doubt and the breach must normally be wilful and deliberate.

The nature of Court of Protection proceedings should be considered when approaching the imposition of a punishment for contempt.

Proceedings in the Court of Protection are varied: some cases may be identical or similar to regular civil proceedings, others may be more like family cases. The Court will therefore have to approach punishment with care and consideration of the various authorities (see e g *Hale v Tanner* [2000] 2 FLR 879).

The Court should also have in mind that the objective of committal is to mark disapproval of the breach of its order and to secure compliance.

It is also suggested that the effect on P or P's family of committal proceedings and any punishment imposed should be considered.

189 Power to suspend execution of committal order

(1) A judge who has made an order of committal may direct that the execution of the order of committal shall be suspended for such period or on such terms and conditions as may be specified.

(2) Where an order is suspended under paragraph (1), the applicant for the order of committal must, unless the court otherwise directs, serve on the person against whom it was made a notice informing him of the making and terms of the direction under that paragraph.

190 Warrant for arrest

A warrant for the arrest of a person against whom an order of committal has been made shall not, without further order of the court, be enforced more than 2 years after the date on which the warrant is issued.

191 Discharge of person committed

(1) The court may, on the application of any person committed to prison for contempt of court, discharge him.

(2) Where a person has been committed for failing to comply with a judgment or order requiring him to deliver any thing to some other person or to deposit it in court or elsewhere, and a writ of sequestration has also been issued to enforce that judgment or order, then, if the thing is in the custody or power of the person committed, the commissioners appointed by the writ of sequestration may take possession of it as if it were the property of that person and, without prejudice to the generality of paragraph (1), the court may discharge the person committed and may give such directions for dealing with the thing taken by the commissioners as it thinks fit.

192 Penal notices

(1) The court may direct that a penal notice is to be attached to any order warning the person on whom the copy of the order is served that disobeying the order would be a contempt of court punishable by imprisonment or a fine.

(2) Unless the court gives a direction under paragraph (1), a penal notice may not be attached to any order.

(3) A penal notice is to be in the following terms: 'You must obey this order. If you do not, you may be sent to prison for contempt of court.'.

193 Saving for other powers

The rules in this Part do not limit the power of the court to make an order requiring a person guilty of contempt to pay a fine or give security for his good behaviour and those rules, so far as applicable, shall apply in relation to an application for such an order as they apply in relation to an application for an order of committal.

194 Power of court to commit on its own initiative

The preceding provisions of these Rules shall not be taken as affecting the power of the court to make an order for committal on its own initiative against a person guilty of contempt of court.

PART 22
TRANSITORY AND TRANSITIONAL PROVISIONS

195 Transitory provision: applications by former receivers

(1) This rule and rule 196 –

    (a) apply in any case where a person becomes a deputy by virtue of paragraph 1(2) of Schedule 5 to the Act; but

    (b) shall cease to have effect at the end of the period specified in the relevant practice direction.

(2) The deputy may make an application to the court in connection with –

    (a) any decision in connection with the day-to-day management of P's property and affairs; or

    (b) any supplementary decision which is necessary to give full effect to any order made, or directions given, before 1st October 2007 under Part 7 of the Mental Health Act 1983.

(3) Decisions within paragraph (2) include those that may be specified in the relevant practice direction.

(4) An application –

    (a) may relate only to a particular decision or decisions to be made on P's behalf;

    (b) must specify details of the decision or decisions to be made; and

    (c) must be made using the application form set out in the relevant practice direction.

Scope of rule—Rules 195 to 197 and PD22B no longer apply. PD22C is obsolete.

196 Transitory provision: dealing with applications under rule 195

(1) The court may, in determining an application under rule 195, treat the application as if it were an application to vary the functions of the deputy which is made in accordance with the relevant practice direction made under rule 71, and dispose of it accordingly.

(2) In any other case, an application under rule 195 may be determined by an order made or directions given by –

    (a) the court; or
    (b) a person nominated under paragraph (3).

(3) The Senior Judge or the President may nominate an officer or officers of the court for the purpose of determining applications under rule 195.

(4) Where an officer has been nominated under paragraph (3) to determine an application, he may refer to a judge any proceedings or any question arising in any proceedings which ought, in the officer's opinion, to be considered by a judge.

197 Appeal against a decision of a nominated officer

(1) This rule applies in relation to decisions made under rules 195 and 196 by a nominated officer.

(2) An appeal from a decision to which this rule applies lies to a judge of the court nominated by virtue of section 46(2)(e) of the Act.

(3) No permission is required for an appeal under paragraph (2).

(4) A judge determining an appeal under paragraph (2) has all the powers that an appeal judge on appeal has by virtue of rule 178.

(5) An appeal from a decision made under paragraph (2) ('a second appeal') lies to a judge of the court nominated by virtue of section 46(2)(d) of the Act.

(6) A second appeal may be made from a decision of a nominated officer, and a judge to whom such an appeal is made may, if he considers the matter is one which ought to be heard by a judge of the court nominated by virtue of section 46(2)(a) to (c), transfer the matter to such a judge.

(7) An appeal from a decision made on a second appeal lies to the Court of Appeal.

198 Application of Rules to proceedings within paragraphs 3 and 12 of Schedule 5 to the Act

(1) In this rule, 'pending proceedings' means proceedings on an application within paragraph 3 or 12 of Schedule 5 to the Act.

(2) A practice direction shall make provision for the extent to which these Rules shall apply to pending proceedings.

199 Practice direction

A practice direction may make additional or different provision in relation to transitory and transitional matters.

PART 23
MISCELLANEOUS

200 Order or directions requiring a person to give security for discharge of functions

(1) This rule applies where the court makes an order or gives a direction –

(a)   conferring functions on any person (whether as deputy or otherwise); and
(b)   requiring him to give security for the discharge of those functions.

(2) The person on whom functions are conferred must give the security before he undertakes to discharge his functions, unless the court permits it to be given subsequently.

(3) Paragraphs (4) to (6) apply where the security is required to be given before any action can be taken.

(4) Subject to paragraph (5), the security must be given in accordance with the requirements of regulation 33(2)(a) of the Public Guardian Regulations (which makes provision about the giving of security by means of a bond that is endorsed by an authorised insurance company or deposit-taker).

(5) The court may impose such other requirements in relation to the giving of the security as it considers appropriate (whether in addition to, or instead of, those specified in paragraph (4)).

(6) In specifying the date from which the order or directions referred to in paragraph (1) are to take effect, the court will have regard to the need to postpone that date for such reasonable period as would enable the Public Guardian to be satisfied that –

(a)   if paragraph (4) applies, the requirements of regulation 34 of the Public Guardian Regulations have been met in relation to the security; and
(b)   any other requirements imposed by the court under paragraph (5) have been met.

(7) 'The Public Guardian Regulations' means the Lasting Powers of Attorney, Enduring Powers of Attorney and Public Guardian Regulations 2007.

Rule 200—*The Giving of Security.* Section 19(9) of the MCA 2005 provides that the court may require a deputy to provide such security as the court thinks fit for the discharge of his functions. Rule 200 contains details as to the time and manner of the giving of security. It is almost inevitable that a property and affairs deputy will be asked by the court to give security unless the deputy is a local authority.

The usual means of giving security is by way of a bond endorsed by an authorised insurance company or deposit taker although security can be provided in some other manner: see reg 33 of the Lasting Powers of Attorney, Enduring Powers of Attorney and Public Guardian Regulations 2007.

The amount of the security is decided by a judge when the order appointing the deputy is made. The decision is a judicial decision and not a mechanical one based on a formula or percentage of P's assets.

In *Niall Baker v H and the Official Solicitor* (unreported, 15 October 2009) HHJ Marshall QC provides helpful guidance on how the court should approach fixing the level of security. She emphasised that the purpose of the security is to protect P and his resources from the consequences of negligence or default. The court should therefore consider the real and realistic degree of the risk to P. If the cost of obtaining security imposes an unreasonable burden on P's estate, it may be possible to mitigate this by reconsidering the terms of the deputyship order and restricting the assets under the deputy's control.

PART IV

However, the court concluded that 'the whole issue of the appropriate level of security must therefore be considered in the round, if possible together with any aspects of the deputyship order which can sensibly be tailored to minimise the risks whilst not causing serious practical disadvantages.'

The judge did suggest some factors to have in mind when fixing a security, namely:

(1) The value and vulnerability of the assets which are under the control of the deputy.
(2) How long it might be before a default or loss is discovered.
(3) The availability and extent of any other remedy or resource available to P in the event of a default or loss.
(4) P's immediate needs in the event of a default or loss.
(5) The cost to P of ordering security and the possibilities and cost of increasing his protection in any other way.
(6) The gravity of the consequences of loss or default for P in his circumstances.
(7) The status, experience and record of the particular deputy.

A particular problem can arise with a solicitor deputy. He may argue (as was the case in *Baker*) that the combination of his professional indemnity insurance and experience as a deputy acting for others should obviate the need for a security.

When confronting this problem, the court should have in mind the following:

(1) The amount of experience of the solicitor deputy.
(2) The level of the solicitor's indemnity cover.
(3) The fact that a claim under the solicitor's policy will be based on alleged negligence of the deputy and the insurers will need to evaluate the claim and settlement may take a long time as opposed to a claim under a security which will provoke an immediate payment.
(4) Whether a delay due to a claim under the solicitor's indemnity insurance is in P's best interests having regard to the nature of P's funds and P's needs.
(5) Whether there should be some level of cover calculated by reference to P's annual expenditure as opposed to the total value of P's assets.

To ensure that the court fixes the security at a sensible level, when submitting an application to appoint a deputy the practitioner would be well advised to file a short note addressing the issue and providing as much information as possible to allow the court to arrive at a fair conclusion on the issue of security.

It is open to a deputy nevertheless to object to the level of security by seeking a reconsideration under r 89.

201 Objections to registration of an enduring power of attorney: request for directions

(1) This rule applies in any case where –

(a) the Public Guardian (having received a notice of objection to the registration of an instrument creating an enduring power of attorney) is prevented by paragraph 13(5) of Schedule 4 to the Act from registering the instrument except in accordance with the court's directions; and

(b) on or before the relevant day, no application for the court to give such directions has been made under Part 9 (how to start proceedings).

(2) In paragraph (1)(b) the relevant day is the later of –

(a) the final day of the period specified in paragraph 13(4) of Schedule 4 to the Act; or

(b) the final day of the period of 14 days beginning with the date on which the Public Guardian receives the notice of objection.

(3) The Public Guardian may seek the court's directions about registering the instrument by filing a request in accordance with the relevant practice direction.

(4) As soon as practicable and in any event within 21 days of the date on which the request was made, the court will notify –

(a) the person (or persons) who gave the notice of objection; and

(b) the attorney or, if more than one, each of them.

(5) As soon as practicable and in any event within 21 days of the date on which the request is filed, the Public Guardian must notify the donor of the power that the request has been so filed.

(6) The notice under paragraph (4) must –

(a) state that the Public Guardian has requested the court's directions about registration;

(b) state that the court will give directions in response to the request unless an application under Part 9 is made to it before the end of the period of 21 days commencing with the date on which the notice is issued; and

(c) set out the steps required to make such an application.

(7) 'Notice of objection' means a notice of objection which is made in accordance with paragraph 13(4) of Schedule 4 to the Act.

Scope of rule—This rule is supplemented by Practice Direction A. The rule deals with the situation where the Public Guardian has received an objection to registration of an enduring power of attorney but no application has been made to the Court. The Public Guardian may apply to the Court for directions.

The application by the Public Guardian is made on Form COP17. The Public Guardian will also notify the donor in accordance with Part 7 that he or she has applied for directions.

Once Form COP17 has been filed, the Court will give notice that an application has been made to the person who gave notice of the objection and to the attorneys under the enduring power of attorney.

Any person who wishes to participate in the proceedings has to file Form COP8 and comply with the requirements of Part 9, Practice Direction H.

If no application is received, the Court will proceed to deal with the matter.

It is likely that the Court will order that unless any application is made to object to registration of the enduring power of attorney within a given period of time, the enduring power of attorney can be registered.

202 Disposal of property where P ceases to lack capacity

(1) This rule applies where P ceases to lack capacity.

(2) In this rule, 'relevant property' means any property belonging to P and forming part of his estate, and which –

(a) remains under the control of anyone appointed by order of the court; or

(b) is held under the direction of the court.

(3) The court may at any time make an order for any relevant property to be transferred to P, or at P's direction, provided that it is satisfied that P has the capacity to make decisions in relation to that property.

(4) An application for an order under this rule is to be made in accordance with Part 10.

Practice Direction—Practice Direction B supplements this rule.

Procedure—Where P ceases to lack capacity, the application is brought using the procedure under Part 10 and therefore Form COP9 will be used.

If P has died, Form COP9 should be used when applying for any final directions hearing. The Public Guardian will require a final report from the deputy. Any security bond will not be discharged until the Court is satisfied that the Public Guardian does not require a final report or that he or she is satisfied with the final report.

Practice Direction – General provisions

Practice Direction A – Court documents (PD4A)

This practice direction supplements Part 4 of the Court of Protection Rules 2007

Signature of documents by mechanical means

1. Where, under rule 10(2), a replica signature is printed electronically or by other mechanical means on any document, the name of the person whose signature is printed must also be printed so that the person may be identified.

Form of documents

2. Documents drafted by a legal representative should bear his signature and if they are drafted by a legal representative as a member or employee of a firm, they should state the capacity in which he is signing, and the name of the firm by which he is employed.

3. Every document prepared by a party for filing or use at the court must:

    (a)   unless the nature of the document renders it impracticable, be on A4 paper of durable quality having a margin not less than 3.5 centimetres wide;

    (b)   be fully legible and should normally be typed;

    (c)   where possible be bound securely in a manner which would not hamper filing;

    (d)   have the pages numbered consecutively;

    (e)   be divided into numbered paragraphs; and

    (f)   have all numbers, including dates, expressed as figures.

4. A document which is a copy produced by a colour photostat machine or other similar device may be filed at the court office provided that the coloured date seal of the court is not reproduced on the copy.

Documents for filing at court

5. The date on which a document was filed at court must be recorded on the document. This may be done with a seal or a receipt stamp.

6. Particulars of the date of delivery at a court office of any document for filing and the title of the proceedings in which the document is filed shall be entered in court records, on the court file, or on a computer kept in the court office for that purpose. Except where a document has been delivered at the court office through the post, the time of delivery should also be recorded.

Filing by facsimile

7. In relation to the filing of documents by facsimile ('fax'):

    (a)   subject to subparagraphs (h) and (i), a party may file a document at court by sending it by fax;

    (b)   where a party files a document by fax, he must not send a hard copy in addition;

(c) a party filing a document by fax should be aware that the document is not filed at court until it is delivered by the court's fax machine, regardless of the time that is shown to have been transmitted from the party's machine;

(d) the time of delivery of the faxed document will be recorded on it in accordance with paragraph 6;

(e) it remains the responsibility of the party to ensure that the document is delivered to the court in time;

(f) if a fax is delivered after 4pm, it will be treated as filed on the next day the court office is open;

(g) if a fax relates to a hearing, the date and time of the hearing should be prominently displayed;

(h) fax should not be used to send letters or documents of a routine or non-urgent nature;

(i) fax should not be used, except in an unavoidable emergency, to deliver:
   (i) a document which attracts a fee;
   (ii) a document relating to a hearing less than 2 hours ahead of that hearing; or
   (iii) skeleton arguments;

(j) where paragraph 7(i)(i) applies, the fax should give an explanation for the emergency and include an undertaking that the fee or money has been dispatched that day by post or will be paid at the court office counter the following business day; and

(k) where the court has several fax machines, each allocated to an individual section, fax messages should only be sent to the machine of the section for which the message is intended.

Editing information from court documents

8. An application made pursuant to rule 19 for an order that a specified part of a document is to be edited must be made in accordance with the Part 10 procedure, using a COP9 application notice.

9. The person making the application must provide the court with a draft copy of the document which is sought to be edited, with the part or parts which are sought to be deleted clearly marked.

Copies

10. Unless:

(a) a rule or practice direction provides otherwise; or

(b) the court directs otherwise,

when a document is to be filed at the court, the person filing the document must provide the original and one copy of the document.

Practice Direction B – Statements of truth (PD4B)

This practice direction supplements Part 4 of the Court of Protection Rules 2007

General

1. Rule 11 makes provision for certain documents to be verified by a statement of truth. These documents are specified in rule 11(1).

Form of the statement of truth

2. The form of the statement of truth verifying an application form is as follows:

'[I believe] [The applicant believes] that the facts stated in this application form and its annex(es) are true.'[1]

3. The form of the statement of truth verifying a document for court proceedings is as follows:

'[I believe] [The (applicant or as may be) believes] that the facts stated in this [name of document being verified] [and attachments] are true.'

4. The form of the statement of truth verifying a witness statement is as follows:

'I believe that the facts stated in this witness statement are true.'

5. The form of the statement of truth verifying an expert's report or a report prepared pursuant to section 49 of the Act is as follows:

'I confirm that insofar as the facts stated in my report are within my own knowledge I have made clear which they are and I believe them to be true and that the opinions expressed represent my true and complete professional opinion.'

6. Where the statement of truth is contained in a separate document, the document being verified should be identified in the statement of truth by including in the statement of truth:

(a)   the name of the person to whom the proceedings relate (P) (unless an order to the contrary pursuant to rule 19 has been made);
(b)   the case number as entered on the application form, if available;
(c)   the date the application form was issued, if available; and
(d)   the title of the document being verified.

Who may sign the statement of truth

7. A statement of truth verifying a witness statement must be signed by the witness.

8. A statement of truth verifying an expert's report must be signed by the expert.

9. A statement of truth verifying a report prepared pursuant to section 49 of the Act must be signed by the person who prepared the report.

---

[1]   Rule 11(3) provides that where a party is conducting proceedings with a litigation friend, a statement of truth in a permission form, an application form or application notice is a statement that the litigation friend believes the facts stated in the document being verified are true.

10. The individual who signs a statement of truth must print his name clearly beneath his signature.

11. Where a document is to be verified on behalf of a company or other corporation the statement of truth must be signed by a person holding a senior position in the company or corporation. That person must state the office or position he holds.

12. For the purposes of paragraph 11, each of the following persons is a person holding a senior position:

(a)   in respect of a registered company or corporation, a director, the treasurer, secretary, chief executive, manager or other officer of the company or corporation; and

(b)   in respect of a corporation which is not registered, in addition to those persons set out in (a), the mayor, chairman, president, town clerk or similar officer of the corporation.

13. Where the document is to be verified on behalf of a partnership, those who may sign the statement of truth are:

(a)   any of the partners; and

(b)   a person having the control or management of the partnership business.

14. Where a party is legally represented, the legal representative may sign the statement of truth on behalf of the client. The statement signed by the legal representative will refer to the client's belief, not the belief of the legal representative. In signing he must state the capacity in which he signs and the name of his firm where appropriate.

15. A legal representative who signs a statement of truth must sign in his own name and not that of his firm or employer.

16. Where a legal representative has signed a statement of truth, his signature will be taken by the court as his statement:

(a)   that the client on whose behalf he has signed had authorised him to do so;

(b)   that before signing he had explained to the client that in signing the statement of truth he would be confirming the client's belief that the facts stated in the document were true; and

(c)   that before signing he had informed the client of the possible consequences to the client if it should subsequently appear that the client did not have an honest belief in the truth of those facts.

(Rule 14 sets out the consequences of verifying a document containing a false statement without an honest belief in its truth.)

Persons unable to read or sign documents to be verified by a statement of truth

17. Where a document containing a statement of truth is to be signed by a person who is unable to read or sign the document, it must contain a certificate made by an authorised person.

18. An authorised person is a person able to administer oaths and take affidavits but need not be independent of the parties or their representatives.

19. The authorised person must certify:

(a)   that the document has been read to the person signing it;

(b) that the person appeared to understand it and approved its content as accurate;

(c) that the declaration of truth has been read to that person;

(d) that the person appeared to understand the declaration and the consequences of making a false declaration (see rule 14); and

(e) that the person signed or made his mark in the presence of the authorised person.

Form of certificate of authorised person

20. 'I certify that I [name and address of authorised person] have read over the contents of this document and the declaration of truth to the person signing the document [if there are exhibits, add "and explained the nature and effect of the exhibits referred to in it"] who appeared to understand (a) the document and approved its content as accurate and (b) the declaration of truth and the consequences of making a false declaration, and made his mark in my presence.'

Practice Direction – Service of documents

Practice Direction A – Service (PD6A)

This practice direction supplements Part 6 of the Court of Protection Rules 2007

Service by document exchange

1. Rule 31(6) allows documents to be served by document exchange in accordance with a practice direction.

2. Service by document exchange (DX) may take place only where:

(a)   the party's address for service includes a numbered box at a DX; or

(b)   the writing paper of the party who is to be served or of his legal representative sets out the DX box number; and

(c)   the party or his legal representative has not indicated in writing that he is unwilling to accept service by DX.

3. Service by DX is effected by leaving the document addressed to the numbered box:

(a)   at the DX of the party who is to be served; or

(b)   at a DX which sends documents to the party's DX every business day.

Service by electronic means

4. Rule 31(6) allows documents to be served by electronic means in accordance with a practice direction.

5. Subject to the provisions of paragraph 7 below, where a document is to be served by electronic means:

(a)   the party who is to be served or his legal representative must have previously expressly indicated in writing to the party serving:

(i)   that he is willing to accept service by electronic means, and

(ii)   the fax number, e-mail address, or electronic identification to which it should be sent; and

(b)   the following shall be taken as sufficient written identification for the purposes of the preceding paragraph:

(i)   a fax number set out on the writing paper of the legal representative of the party who is to be served, or

(ii)   a fax number, e-mail address or electronic identification set out on an application form or a response to an application filed with the court.

6. Where a party seeks to serve a document by electronic means he should first seek to clarify with the party who is to be served whether there are any limitations to the recipient's agreement to accept service by such means, including in relation to the format in which documents are to be sent and the maximum size of attachments that may be received.

7. An address for service given by a party must be within the jurisdiction and any fax number must be at the address for service. Where an email address or electronic identification is given in conjunction with an address for service, the email address or electronic identification will be deemed to be at the address for service.

PART IV

8. Where a document is served by electronic means, the party serving the document need not in addition send a hard copy by post or document exchange.

Service on business partners

9. A document which is served by leaving it with a person at the principal or last known place of business of the partnership, must at the same time have served with it a notice as to whether the person is being served:

(a)   as a partner;

(b)   as a person having control or management of the partnership business; or

(c)   as both.

Service on a company or other corporation

10. Personal service on a registered company or corporation in accordance with rule 31 is effected by leaving a document with a person holding a senior position in the company or corporation.

11. Each of the following persons is a person holding a senior position:

(a)   in respect of a registered company or corporation, a director, the treasurer, secretary, chief executive, manager or other officer of the company or corporation; and

(b)   in respect of a corporation which is not registered, in addition to those persons set out in (a), the mayor, chairman, president, town clerk or similar officer of the corporation.

Change of address

12. A party or his legal representative who changes his address for service shall give notice in writing of the change as soon as it has taken place to the court and every other party.

Service by the court

13. Where the court effects service of a document, the method will normally be by first class post.

14. Where the court effects service of an acknowledgment of service, the court will also serve or deliver a copy of any notice of funding that has been filed provided:

(a)   it was filed at the same time as the acknowledgment of service; and

(b)   copies were provided for service.

Applications for service by an alternative method

15. An application for an order for service by an alternative method pursuant to rule 31(4) must be made by filing a COP9 application notice in accordance with Part 10, and supported by a witness statement containing evidence which states:

(a)   the reason an order for an alternative method of service is sought;

(b)   what steps have been taken to serve by other permitted means; and

(c) the alternative method of service that is proposed, and the reason/s why it is believed that service by such a method will come to the notice of the person to be served.

Certificate of service or non-service

16. Where a certificate of service or non-service is required to be filed, form COP20 should be used.

Application to dispense with service

17. An application for an order to dispense with service pursuant to rule 38 should be made by filing a COP9 application notice in accordance with Part 10.

Practice Direction – Notifying P

Practice Direction A – Notifying P (PD7A)

This practice direction supplements Part 7 of the Court of Protection Rules 2007

General

1. Part 7 sets out the procedure to be followed where P is to be given notice of any matter or document, or provided with any document.[2] Where P becomes a party, Part 7 does not apply and service is to be effected in accordance with Part 6 or as directed by the court.[3]

When P must be notified

2. P must be notified of the things specified in rules 42 to 45, unless the court directs otherwise. P must, therefore, be notified:

    (a)   that an application form has been issued by the court or withdrawn;[4]

    (b)   that an appellant's notice has been issued by the court or withdrawn;[5]

    (c)   that a final order has been made;[6] and

    (d)   of any other matter as the court may direct.[7]

When P may be notified of an application notice

3. The applicant is not required to, but may notify P of an application notice that is issued in accordance with Part 10. This should be done if the applicant considers it appropriate to do so, and must be done if the court makes a direction to that effect.

4. Where P is to be notified of an application notice, unless the court directs otherwise, the person notifying P must explain to him:

    (a)   who the applicant is;

    (b)   what the application is about;

    (c)   what will happen if the court makes the order or direction that has been applied for; and

    (d)   that P may seek advice and assistance in relation to any matter of which he is notified.

5. The person effecting notification must provide P with the information referred to in paragraph 4 in the manner set out in rule 46, and must comply with rules 47 and 48.

---

2   Rule 40.
3   Rule 40(2).
4   Rule 42.
5   Rule 43.
6   Rule 44.
7   Rule 45.

How and of what P is to be notified

6. Rule 46 sets out the manner in which P is to be notified, and rules 42 to 45 set out the matters of which P is to be notified. Rule 47 provides that P must be provided with a COP5 form for acknowledging notification. P must also be provided with a COP14 form which explains the matter for which notification is being provided.

Certificates of notification and non-notification

7. Rule 48 requires the person notifying P to file a certificate within 7 days of providing notification. Where a person fails to notify P (or is unable to do so), he must file a certificate of non-notification.[8] A certificate of notification, or non-notification (as appropriate), must be filed using a COP20 form.

Dispensing with notification

8. The person required to notify P may apply to the court for an order either:

    (a)   dispensing with the requirement to notify P; or
    (b)   requiring some other person to effect the notification,[9]

using a COP9 application notice in accordance with Part 10.

9. Such an application would be appropriate where, for example, P is in a permanent vegetative state or a minimally conscious state; or where notification by the applicant is likely to cause significant and disproportionate distress to P.

PART IV

---

8   Rule 37.
9   Rule 49.

Practice Direction – Permission

Practice Direction A – Permission (PD8A)

This practice direction supplements Part 8 of the Court of Protection Rules 2007

Where permission is required

1. An applicant must apply for permission to start proceedings under the Act, unless either section 50 of, paragraph 20(2) of Schedule 3 to, the Act or rule 51 applies. The application must be made using form COP2 ('the permission form').

2. If part of the application is a matter for which permission is required and part of it is not, permission must be sought for the part that requires it.[10]

3. In such circumstances, the applicant may file a single application form seeking both orders. The application form will not be issued until permission has been granted for the part that requires it. If permission is refused for that part, the application form will be issued only for the part of the application not requiring permission.

4. Alternatively, the applicant may file two separate application forms (and pay two application fees) so that the application not requiring permission can be commenced immediately. If permission is subsequently granted for the application requiring it, the court may consolidate the applications.

Documents to be filed with the permission form

5. The applicant must file the following documents with the permission form:

   (a) a draft of the application form using form COP1; and
   (b) an assessment of capacity form using form COP3.[11]

6. If the applicant is unable to complete an assessment of capacity form (as may be the case, for example, where P does not reside with the applicant and the applicant is unable to take P to a doctor, or where P refuses to undergo the assessment), the applicant should file a witness statement with the permission form explaining:

   (a) why he has not been able to obtain an assessment of capacity;
   (b) what attempts (if any) he has made to obtain an assessment of capacity; and
   (c) why he knows or believes that P lacks capacity to make a decision or decisions in relation to any matter that is the subject of the proposed application to the court.

7. The applicant is not required to file any of the annexes to the application form with the permission form,[12] or any of the other information referred to in rule 64, but may do so if he wishes.

---

[10]   Rule 53(2).
[11]   The COP3 for is not needed for applications concerning the court's power under ss 22 or 23 of, or Sch 4 to, the Act.
[12]   Annex A (Supporting information for property and affairs applications) and Annex B (Supporting information for personal welfare applications).

Notice of permission application

8. Where the court decides to hold a hearing in order to make a decision as to permission, it will notify the applicant and such other persons it requires to be notified.[13] If any such person wishes to participate in the permission hearing, he must file an acknowledgment of notification[14] using form COP5.

What the court will do if it grants permission

9. If the court grants permission, it may give directions in connection with the issue of the application form.[15]

---

[13] See r 56.
[14] In accordance with r 57.
[15] Rule 65 provides that the court will issue the application form where permission has been granted.

Practice Direction – How to start proceedings

Practice Direction A – The application form (PD9A)

This practice direction supplements Part 9 of the Court of Protection Rules 2007

The application form

1. To begin proceedings, the applicant must file an application form using form COP1.

2. The application form must:
   - (a) state the matter which the applicant wants the court to decide;
   - (b) state the order which the applicant is seeking;
   - (c) name (unless an order to the contrary pursuant to rule 19 has been made):
     - (i) the applicant,
     - (ii) P,
     - (iii) as a respondent, any person (other than P) whom the applicant reasonably believes to have an interest which means that he ought to be heard in relation to the application (as opposed to being notified of it), and
     - (iv) any person whom the applicant intends to notify in accordance with rule 70; and
   - (d) if the applicant is applying in a representative capacity, state what that capacity is.[16]

3. The application form must include (unless an order to the contrary pursuant to rule 19 has been made):
   - (a) an address at which the applicant resides or carries on business;
   - (b) an address at which P resides or carries on business;
   - (c) an address at which each person named as a respondent to the proceedings resides or carries on business, and details of how each respondent is connected to P; and
   - (d) an address at which any person (other than P) whom the applicant intends to notify of the application resides or carries on business, and details of how each person is connected to P.

4. Paragraph 3 applies even though a solicitor or litigation friend has agreed, as the case may be, to accept service.

5. The application form must be headed with the name of the person to whom the application relates (unless an order to the contrary pursuant to rule 19 has been made).

Statement of truth

6. Rule 11 requires an application form to be verified by a statement of truth where the applicant seeks to rely on matters set out in it as evidence.

7. The form of the statement of truth is as follows:

---

[16]   Rule 63.

'[I believe] [The applicant believes] that the facts stated in this application form and its annex(es) are true.'

8. Attention is drawn to rule 14 which sets out the consequences of verifying an application form containing a false statement without an honest belief in its truth.

(Practice direction B accompanying Part 4 sets out more detailed requirements for statements of truth.)

Documents to be filed with the application form

9. The application form must be supported by evidence set out in either:

(a)   a witness statement; or

(b)   the application form provided it is verified by a statement of truth.

10. A witness statement must be verified by a statement of truth in the following terms:

'I believe that the facts stated in this witness statement are true.'

11. The evidence must set out the facts on which the applicant relies, and all material facts known to the applicant of which the court should be made aware.

12. The documents or instruments, as the case may be, specified in the table below must be filed with the court along with the application form, unless this is impractical or the court has directed otherwise.

Type of document or instrument	When document is to be filed
Any order granting permission	If permission is required.
Assessment of capacity form (COP3)	Unless already filed with the permission form.[17]
Annex A: Supporting information for property and affairs applications (COP1A)	Where an order relating to P's property and affairs is sought.[18]
Annex B: Supporting information for personal welfare applications (COP1B)	Where an order relating to P's personal welfare is sought.[19]
Lasting power of attorney or enduring power of attorney	Where the application concerns the court's power under section 22 or 23 of, or Schedule 4 to, the Act (where available).
Deputy's declaration (COP4)	Where the application is for the appointment of a deputy.

PART IV

---

[17]   The COP3 form is not needed for applications concerning the court's power under ss 22 or 23 of, or Sch 4 to, the Act.

[18]   Annex A is not needed for applications concerning the court's power under ss 22 or 23 of, or Sch 4 to, the Act.

[19]   Annex B is not needed for applications concerning the court's power under ss 22 or 23 of, or Sch 4 to, the Act.

Type of document or instrument	When document is to be filed
Order appointing a deputy	Where the application relates to or is made by a deputy.
Order appointing a litigation friend	Where the application is made by, or where the application relates to the appointment of, a litigation friend.
Order of the Court of Protection	Where the application relates to the order.
Order of another court (and where the judgment is not in English, a translation of it into English:	Where the application relates to an order made by another court.
(i) certified by a notary public or other qualified person; or	
(ii) accompanied by written evidence confirming that the translation is accurate).	

13. Rule 10 and practice direction A accompanying Part 4 set out how documents are to be filed at court.

14. If the applicant is unable to complete an assessment of capacity form (as may be the case, for example, where P does not reside with the applicant and the applicant is unable to take P to a doctor, or where P refuses to undergo the assessment), the applicant should file a witness statement with the application form explaining:

(a) why he has not been able to obtain an assessment of capacity;

(b) what attempts (if any) he has made to obtain an assessment of capacity; and

(c) why he knows or believes that P lacks capacity to make a decision or decisions in relation to any matter that is subject of the proposed application.

Start of proceedings

15. The date on which the application form was received by the court will be recorded by a date stamp either on the application form held on the court file or on the letter that accompanied the application form when it was received by the court.

16. Any enquiry as to the date on which the court received an application form should be directed to a court officer.

Practice Direction B – Notification of other persons that an application form has been issued (PD9B)

This practice direction supplements Part 9 of the Court of Protection Rules 2007

General

1. Rule 70 requires the applicant to notify certain persons of the application in accordance with the relevant practice direction.[20]

Who is to be notified

2. The persons who should be notified will vary according to the nature of the application.

3. A person who has been named as respondent in the application form should not also be notified. Any reference in this practice direction to a person to be notified does not apply where the person has already been named as a respondent.

4. The applicant must seek to identify at least three persons who are likely to have an interest in being notified that an application form has been issued. The applicant should notify them:

    (a)   that an application form has been issued;

    (b)   whether it relates to the exercise of the court's jurisdiction in relation to P's property and affairs, or his personal welfare, or both; and

    (c)   of the order or orders sought.

5. Members of P's close family are, by virtue of their relationship to P, likely to have an interest in being notified that an application has been made to the court concerning P. It should be presumed, for example that a spouse or civil partner, any other partner, parents and children are likely to have an interest in the application.

6. This presumption may be displaced where the applicant is aware of circumstances which reasonably indicate that P's family should not be notified, but that others should be notified instead. For example, where the applicant knows that the relative in question has had little or no involvement in P's life and has shown no inclination to do so, he may reasonably conclude that that relative need not be notified. In some cases, P may be closer to persons who are not relatives and if so, it will be appropriate to notify them instead of family members.

7. The following list of people is ordered according to the presumed closeness in terms of relationship to P. They should be notified in descending order (as appropriate to P's circumstances):

    (a)   spouse or civil partner;

    (b)   person who is not a spouse or a civil partner but who has been living with P as if they were;

    (c)   parent or guardian;

    (d)   child;

PART IV

---

[20]   See r 67(2) for certain applications relating to lasting powers of attorney, and r 68(2) for certain applications relating to enduring powers of attorney, which do not require notification to be given in accordance with this practice direction.

    (e)   brother or sister;

    (f)   grandparent or grandchild;

    (g)   aunt or uncle;

    (h)   child of a person falling within subparagraph (e);

    (i)   step-parent; and

    (j)   half-brother or half-sister.

(If any of the people to be notified are children or protected parties, see rule 32.)

8. Where the applicant decides that a person listed in one of the categories in paragraph 7 ought to be notified, and there are other persons in that category (eg P has four siblings), the applicant should notify all persons falling within that category unless there is a good reason not to do so. For example, it may be a good reason not to notify every person in the category if one or more of them has had little or no involvement in P's life and has shown no inclination to do so.

9. Where the applicant chooses not to notify a person listed in paragraph 7 because the presumption has been displaced (see paragraphs 6 and 8 above) the evidence in support of the application form must also set out why that person was not notified.

10. In addition to the list in paragraph 7, the following persons must be notified where appropriate:

    (a)   where P is under 18, any person with parental responsibility for P within the meaning of the Children Act 1989;

    (b)   any legal or natural person who is likely to be affected by the outcome of any application. For example, where there is an organisation (including an NHS body) responsible for P's care (and the application is made by another person) the organisation should be notified where the application relates to the provision to, or withdrawal from, P of medical or other treatment or accommodation;

    (c)   any deputy appointed by the court, an attorney appointed under an enduring power of attorney or a donee of a lasting power of attorney (where that person has power to make decisions on behalf of P in regard to a matter to which the application relates). For example, where the application relates to P's property, and a deputy has been appointed to make decisions in relation to P's property, the deputy should be notified; and

    (d)   any other person not already mentioned whom the applicant reasonably considers has an interest in being notified that an application form has been issued. For example, P may have a close friend with an interest in being notified because he provides care to P on an informal basis.

11. Where the applicant chooses not to notify a person listed in paragraph 10 the evidence in support of the application form must also set out why that person was not notified.

Method of notification

12. Notification must be provided using a COP15 form.

13. The provisions of Part 6 and practice direction A accompanying Part 6 apply similarly to notification as they do to service.[21]

---

[21]   See r 29(1).

Practice Direction C – Responding to an application (PD9C)

This practice direction supplements Part 9 of the Court of Protection Rules 2007

General

1. Rule 72(11) enables a practice direction to make provision about responding to applications. Rule 72 sets out the procedure to be followed where a person who has been served with or notified of an application form wishes to become, or apply to become, a party to proceedings.

2. Rule 75 sets out the procedure to be followed where a person who has not been served with or notified of an application form in accordance with rules 66 to 70 wishes to apply to become a party to proceedings.

Responding to the application

Persons served with an application

3. Where a person is served with an application form pursuant to rule 66, 67 or 68 he must, if he wishes to be a party to the proceedings, file an acknowledgment of service using form COP5 in accordance with rule 72. By doing this, he becomes a party.[22]

Persons notified of an application

4. Where a person has been notified of an application pursuant to rule 67(5), 68(5), 69 or 70, he must, if he wishes to be a party to the proceedings, apply to the court to be joined as a party by filing an acknowledgment of notification using form COP5 in accordance with rule 72.

Persons not served with or notified of an application

5. Where a person was not served with or notified of an application form, he must, if he wishes to be a party to the proceedings, apply to the court to be joined as a party, by filing an application to be joined using form COP10 in accordance with rule 75.

Signing the acknowledgment

6. An acknowledgment must be signed by the person acknowledging service or notification, or by his legal representative or litigation friend.

7. Where the respondent is a company or other corporation, a person holding a senior position in the company or corporation may sign the acknowledgment on the respondent's behalf, but must state the position he holds.

8. Each of the following persons is a person holding a senior position:

---

[22]   Rule 73(1)(b).

   (a)   in respect of a registered company or corporation, a director, the treasurer, secretary, chief executive, manager or other officer of the company or corporation; and

   (b)   in respect of a corporation which is not a registered company, in addition to those persons set out at (a), the mayor, chairman, president, town clerk or similar officer of the corporation.

9. Where the respondent is a partnership, the acknowledgment may be signed by:

   (a)   any of the partners; or

   (b)   a person having the control or management of the partnership business.

10. The name of the person acknowledging service or notification should be set out in full on the acknowledgment.

11. If two or more persons acknowledge service or notification of an application through the same legal representative at the same time, only one acknowledgment of service need be used.

Address for service

12. The acknowledgment must include an address for the service of documents, which must be within the jurisdiction of the court.

13. When the person acknowledging service or notification is represented by a legal representative, and the legal representative has signed the acknowledgment, the address must be the legal representative's business address.

Corrections and amendments to the acknowledgment

14. Where the name of the person acknowledging service or notification has been set out incorrectly on the application form, it should be correctly set out in the acknowledgment followed by the words 'described as' and the incorrect name.

15. An acknowledgment of service or notification may be amended only with the permission of the court.

16. An application under paragraph 15 must be made by filing a COP9 application notice in accordance with Part 10 and supported by evidence.

Practice Direction D – Applications by currently appointed deputies, attorneys and donees in relation to P's property and affairs (PD9D)

This practice direction supplements Part 9 of the Court of Protection Rules 2007

General

1. Rule 71 enables a practice direction to make additional or different provision in relation to specified applications.

Applications to which this practice direction applies

2. This practice direction applies to applications:

  (a) which are made by a person who is appointed to act as a deputy for P, or by an attorney under a registered enduring power of attorney or a donee of a registered lasting power of attorney;

  (b) which relate to the applicant's powers and duties as a deputy, attorney or donee, in connection with making decisions as to P's property and affairs;

  (c) where the applicant reasonably considers that the order sought is not likely to be significant to P's estate or to any other of P's interests; and

  (d) where the applicant knows, or reasonably believes, that there are unlikely to be any objections to the application he proposes to make.

3. Applications may only be made using the procedure in this practice direction if the deputy, attorney or donee does not have the authority to make the decision or decisions in question.

Applications by deputies which may be suitable for the procedure set out in this practice direction

4. Examples of applications by deputies that may be suitable for the procedure in this practice direction include, but are not limited to:

  (a) applications for regular payments from P's assets to the deputy in respect of remuneration;

  (b) applications seeking minor variations only as to the expenses that can be paid from P's estate;

  (c) applications to change an accounting period;

  (d) applications to set or change the time by which an annual account may be submitted;

  (e) applications in relation to the sale of property owned by P, where the sale is non-contentious;

  (f) applications for authority to disclose information as to P's assets, state of health or other circumstances;

  (g) applications to make a gift or loan from P's assets, provided that the sum in question is not disproportionately large when compared to the size of P's estate as a whole;

  (h) applications to sell or otherwise deal with P's investments, provided that the sum in question is not disproportionately large when compared to the size of P's estate as a whole;

(i)   applications for the receipt or discharge of a sum due to or by P;

(j)   applications for authority to apply for a grant of probate or representation, where P would be the person entitled to the grant but for his lack of capacity;

(k)   applications relating to the lease or grant of a tenancy in relation to property owned by P;

(l)   applications for release of funds to repair or improve P's property;

(m)   applications to sell P's furniture or effects;

(n)   applications for release of capital to meet expenses required for the care of P;

(o)   applications to arrange an overdraft or bank loan on P's behalf;

(p)   applications to open a bank account on behalf of P or for the purpose of the deputyship at a private bank, a bank that is not located in England and Wales, or at a bank which has unusual conditions attached to the operation of the account; and

(q)   applications for the variation of an order for security made pursuant to rule 200.[23]

Applications by attorneys or donees which may be suitable for the procedure set out in this practice direction

5. Examples of applications by attorneys or donees that may be suitable for the procedure in this practice direction include, but are not limited to –

(a)   applications for regular payments from P's assets to the attorney or donee in respect of remuneration;

(b)   applications to make a gift from P's assets, provided that the sum in question is not disproportionately large when compared to the size of P's estate as a whole;

(c)   applications to authorise a sale of P's property to the attorney or donee, or a family member of P, the attorney or donee, at proper market value, and provided that the market value of the property in question is not disproportionately large when compared to the size of P's estate as a whole;

(d)   applications for authority to obtain a copy of P's will;

(e)   applications for the approval of equity releases; and

(f)   applications for orders for sale pursuant to paragraphs 8 and 9 of Schedule 2 to the Act.

Applications which are not suitable for the procedure set out in this practice direction

6. Examples of applications which are not suitable for the procedure in this practice direction include, but are not limited to:

(a)   applications for the removal of a deputy;

(b)   applications seeking authorisation to commence, continue or defend litigation on behalf of P;

(c)   applications for the settlement of P's property, whether for P's benefit or for the benefit of others;

---

[23]   Not withstanding para 9 of this practice direction, the Public Guardian must be notified of such an application.

    (d)   applications to vary the terms of a trust or estate in which P has an interest;

    (e)   applications for a statutory will or codicil; and

    (f)   applications to operate or cease to operate a business belonging to P, or to dissolve a partnership of which P is a member.

7. An application which is likely to be contested, or which involves large sums of money (when compared to the size of P's estate as a whole) is not suitable for the procedure set out in this practice direction.

Procedure for applications to which this practice direction applies

8. Applications must be made by filing a COP1 application form, together with any evidence in support of the application. However, Annexes A and B to the application form are not required to be filed, nor is an assessment of capacity form.

9. Notwithstanding rules 66 to 70, applications to which this practice direction applies may be made, in the first instance, without serving the application form on anyone and without notifying anyone that the application has been made.

10. The court may decide, upon considering the application, that other persons ought to be notified of the application and given the opportunity to respond. In such a case, the court will give directions as to who should be served with or notified of the application and the manner in which they are to be served or notified, as the case may be.

11. The court may deal with the application without a hearing and will give directions as to who should be served with any order that it makes.

Right of reconsideration

12. Where the application is determined without notice having been given to any person or without a hearing, P, any party or any person affected by the order may apply to the court, within 21 days of having been served with the court's order, to have the order reconsidered.[24] An application to have an order reconsidered must be made by filing a COP9 application notice in accordance with Part 10.

---

[24]   Rule 89 sets out the procedure for applications for reconsideration.

Practice Direction E – Applications relating to serious medical treatment (PD9E)

This practice direction supplements Part 9 of the Court of Protection Rules 2007

General

1. Rule 71 enables a practice direction to make additional or different provision in relation to specified applications.

Applications to which this practice direction applies

2. This practice direction sets out the procedure to be followed where the application concerns serious medical treatment in relation to P.

Meaning of 'serious medical treatment' in relation to the Rules and this practice direction

3. Serious medical treatment means treatment which involves providing, withdrawing or withholding treatment in circumstances where:

    (a)   in a case where a single treatment is being proposed, there is a fine balance between its benefits to P and the burdens and risks it is likely to entail for him;

    (b)   in a case where there is a choice of treatments, a decision as to which one to use is finely balanced; or

    (c)   the treatment, procedure or investigation proposed would be likely to involve serious consequences for P.

4. 'Serious consequences' are those which could have a serious impact on P, either from the effects of the treatment, procedure or investigation itself or its wider implications. This may include treatments, procedures or investigations which:

    (a)   cause, or may cause, serious and prolonged pain, distress or side effects;

    (b)   have potentially major consequences for P; or

    (c)   have a serious impact on P's future life choices.

Matters which should be brought to the court

5. Cases involving any of the following decisions should be regarded as serious medical treatment for the purpose of the Rules and this practice direction, and should be brought to the court:

    (a)   decisions about the proposed withholding or withdrawal of artificial nutrition and hydration from a person in a permanent vegetative state or a minimally conscious state;

    (b)   cases involving organ or bone marrow donation by a person who lacks capacity to consent; and

    (c)   cases involving non-therapeutic sterilisation of a person who lacks capacity to consent.

6. Examples of serious medical treatment may include:

(a) certain terminations of pregnancy in relation to a person who lacks capacity to consent to such a procedure;

(b) a medical procedure performed on a person who lacks capacity to consent to it, where the procedure is for the purpose of a donation to another person;

(c) a medical procedure or treatment to be carried out on a person who lacks capacity to consent to it, where that procedure or treatment must be carried out using a degree of force to restrain the person concerned;

(d) an experimental or innovative treatment for the benefit of a person who lacks capacity to consent to such treatment; and

(e) a case involving an ethical dilemma in an untested area.

7. There may be other procedures or treatments not contained in the list in paragraphs 5 and 6 above which can be regarded as serious medical treatment. Whether or not a procedure is regarded as serious medical treatment will depend on the circumstances and the consequences for the patient.

Consultation with the Official Solicitor

8. Members of the Official Solicitor's staff are prepared to discuss applications in relation to serious medical treatment before an application is made. Any enquiries about adult medical and welfare cases should be addressed to a family and medical litigation lawyer at the Office of the Official Solicitor, 81 Chancery Lane, London WC2A IDD, ph: 020 7911 7127, fax: 020 7911 7105, email: enquiries@offsol.gsi.gov.uk.

In fact, this position is now known as the healthcare and welfare lawyer at the Official Solicitor.

Parties to proceedings

9. The person bringing the application will always be a party to proceedings, as will a respondent named in the application form who files an acknowledgment of service.[25] In cases involving issues as to serious medical treatment, an organisation which is, or will be, responsible for providing clinical or caring services to P should usually be named as a respondent in the application form (where it is not already the applicant in the proceedings).

(Practice direction B accompanying Part 9 sets out the persons who are to be notified that an application form has been issued.)

10. The court will consider whether anyone not already a party should be joined as a party to the proceedings. Other persons with sufficient interest may apply to be joined as parties to the proceedings[26] and the court has a duty to identify at as early a stage as possible who the parties to the proceedings should be.[27]

Allocation of the case

11. Where an application is made to the court in relation to:

---

[25] Rule 73(1).
[26] Rule 75.
[27] Rule 5(2)(b)(ii).

   (a) the lawfulness of withholding or withdrawing artificial nutrition and hydration from a person in a permanent vegetative state, or a minimally conscious state; or

   (b) a case involving an ethical dilemma in an untested area,

the proceedings (including permission, the giving of any directions, and any hearing) must be conducted by the President of the Court of Protection or by another judge nominated by the President.

12. Where an application is made to the court in relation to serious medical treatment (other than that outlined in paragraph 11) the proceedings (including permission, the giving of any directions, and any hearing) must be conducted by a judge of the court who has been nominated as such by virtue of section 46(2)(a) to (c) of the Act (ie the President of the Family Division, the Chancellor or a puisne judge of the High Court).

Matters to be considered at the first directions hearing

13. Unless the matter is one which needs to be disposed of urgently, the court will list it for a first directions hearing.

(Practice direction B accompanying Part 10 sets out the procedure to be followed for urgent applications.)

14. The court may give such directions as it considers appropriate. If the court has not already done so, it should in particular consider whether to do any or all of the following at the first directions hearing:

   (a) decide whether P should be joined as party to the proceedings, and give directions to that effect;

   (b) if P is to be joined as a party to the proceedings, decide whether the Official Solicitor should be invited to act as a litigation friend or whether some other person should be appointed as a litigation friend;

   (c) identify anyone else who has been notified of the proceedings and who has filed an acknowledgment and applied to be joined as a party to proceedings, and consider that application; and

   (d) set a timetable for the proceedings including, where possible, a date for the final hearing.

15. The court should also consider whether to give any of the other directions listed in rule 85(2).

16. The court will ordinarily make an order pursuant to rule 92 that any hearing shall be held in public, with restrictions to be imposed in relation to publication of information about the proceedings.

Declarations

17. Where a declaration is needed, the order sought should be in the following or similar terms:

   • That P lacks capacity to make a decision in relation to the (proposed medical treatment or procedure).

      Eg "That P lacks capacity to make a decision in relation to sterilisation by vasectomy"; and

- That, having regard to the best interests of P, it is lawful for the (proposed medical treatment or procedure) to be carried out by (proposed healthcare provider).

18. Where the application is for the withdrawal of life-sustaining treatment, the order sought should be in the following or similar terms:

- That P lacks capacity to consent to continued life-sustaining treatment measures (and specify what these are); and
- That, having regard to the best interests of P, it is lawful for (name of healthcare provider) to withdraw the life-sustaining treatment from P.

Practice Direction F – Applications relating to statutory wills, codicils, settlements and other dealings with P's property (PD9F)

This practice direction supplements Part 9 of the Court of Protection Rules 2007

General

1. Rule 71 enables a practice direction to make additional or different provision in relation to specified applications.

Applications to which this practice direction applies

2. This practice direction makes provision for applications that relate to:

    (a)   the execution of a will or codicil of P;

    (b)   the settlement of any of P's property; and

    (c)   the sale, exchange, charging, gift or other disposition of P's property.

3. A deputy may not be given powers with respect to:

    (a)   the settlement of any of P's property;

    (b)   the execution of a will of P; or

    (c)   the exercise of any power (including a power to consent) vested in P whether beneficially or as a trustee or otherwise.[28]

4. Hence, an application must be made to the court for a decision in relation to such matters. This practice direction is concerned with matters mentioned at paragraphs 3(a) and (b) above. Practice direction G accompanying Part 9 contains provisions as to applications falling with paragraph 3(c).

Permission to make applications to the court

5. Section 50(1) of, paragraph 20(2) to Schedule 3 to, the Act and rules 51 and 52 set out the circumstances in which permission is or is not required to make an application to the court for the exercise of any of its powers under the Act.

Information to be provided with application form

6. In addition to the application form COP1 (and its annexes) and any information or documents required to be provided by the Rules or another practice direction, the following information must be provided (in the form of a witness statement, attaching documents as exhibits where necessary) for any application to which this practice direction applies:

    (a)   where the application is for the execution of a statutory will or codicil, a copy of the draft will or codicil,[29] plus one copy;

    (b)   a copy of any existing will or codicil;

    (c)   any consents to act by proposed executors;

---

28   Section 20(3) of the Act.

29   The Annex to this practice direction contains an example of a will.

(d)   details of P's family, preferably in the form of a family tree, including details of the full name and date of birth of each person included in the family tree;

(e)   a schedule showing details of P's current assets, with up to date valuations;

(f)   a schedule showing the estimated net yearly income and spending of P;

(g)   a statement showing P's needs, both current and future estimates, and his general circumstances;

(h)   if P is living in National Health Service accommodation, information on whether he may be discharged to local authority accommodation, to other fee-paying accommodation or to his own home;

(i)   if the applicant considers it relevant, full details of the resources of any proposed beneficiary, and details of any likely changes if the application is successful;

(j)   details of any capital gains tax, inheritance tax or income tax which may be chargeable in respect of the subject matter of the application;

(k)   an explanation of the effect, if any, that the proposed changes will have on P's circumstances, preferably in the form of a 'before and after' schedule of assets and income;

(l)   if appropriate, a statement of whether any land would be affected by the proposed will or settlement and if so, details of its location and title number, if applicable;

(m)   where the application is for a settlement of property or for the variation of an existing settlement or trust, a draft of the proposed deed, plus one copy;

(n)   a copy of any registered enduring power of attorney or lasting power of attorney;

(o)   confirmation that P is a resident of England or Wales; and

(p)   an up to date report of P's present medical condition, life expectancy, likelihood of requiring increased expenditure in the foreseeable future, and testamentary capacity.

7. The court may direct that other material is to be filed by the applicant, and if it does, the information will be set out in the form of a witness statement.

8. If any of the information mentioned above has been provided already (e g by way of inclusion in an annex to the application form) it need not be provided again.

Respondents and persons who must be notified of an application

9. The applicant must name as a respondent:

(a)   any beneficiary under an existing will or codicil who is likely to be materially or adversely affected by the application;

(b)   any beneficiary under a proposed will or codicil who is likely to be materially or adversely affected by the application; and

(c)   any prospective beneficiary under P's intestacy where P has no existing will.

(Practice direction B accompanying Part 9 sets out the procedure for notifying others of an application.)

10. The court will consider at the earliest opportunity whether P should be joined as a party to the proceedings and, if he is so joined, the court will consider whether the Official Solicitor should be invited to act as a litigation friend, or whether some other person should be appointed as a litigation friend.

PART IV

Procedure on execution of a will

11. Once a will of P has been executed, the applicant must send the original and two copies of the will to the court for sealing.

12. The court shall seal the original and the copy and return both documents to the applicant.

(Paragraph 3(2) of Schedule 2 to the Mental Capacity Act 2005 sets out the requirements for execution of a will on behalf of P, where the will is executed pursuant to an order or direction of the court.)

Annex

Example form of statutory will

(This only shows the manner in which the authorised person makes the will and executes the same.)

This is the last will of me AB [the person who lacks capacity] of _____ acting by CD the person authorised in that behalf by an order dated the _____ day of _____ 20____ made under the Mental Capacity Act 2005.

I revoke all my former wills and codicils and declare this to be my last will.

I appoint EF and GH to be executors and trustees of this my will.   1.

I give _____   2.

In witness of which this will is signed by me AB acting by CD under the order mentioned above on (date).

SIGNED by the said AB [the person who lacks capacity]

by the said CD [authorised person]

AB [person who lacks   and by the said CD with his (or her) own capacity

CD [authorised person]   name pursuant to the said order in our

presence and attested by us in the

presence of the said CD.

[Name and addresses of witness]

Sealed with the official seal of the Court of Protection the _____ day of _____ 20____

Practice Direction G – Applications to appoint or discharge a trustee (PD9G)

This practice direction supplements Part 9 of the Court of Protection Rules 2007

General

1. Rule 71 enables a practice direction to make additional or different provision in relation to specified applications.

Applications to which this practice direction applies

2. This practice direction makes provision for applications:

(a) for the exercise of any power (including a power to consent) vested in P whether as a trustee or otherwise (section 18(1)(j) of the Act);

(b) under section 36(9) of the Trustee Act 1925 for leave to appoint a new trustee in place of P;

(c) under section 54 of the Trustee Act 1925 as to the court's jurisdiction;

(d) under section 20 of the Trusts of Land and Appointment of Trustees Act 1996; or

(e) for the court's approval of the appointment of a trustee in accordance with the terms of a trust.

3. A deputy may not be appointed to exercise any power vested in P, whether as a trustee or otherwise.[30] Hence, an application must be made to the court for the court to make such a decision.

Permission to make applications to the court

4. Section 50(1) of, paragraph 20(2) to Schedule 3 to, the Act and rules 51 and 52 set out the circumstances in which permission is or is not required to make an application to the court for the exercise of any of its powers under the Act.

Information to be provided with the application form

5. In addition to the application form COP1 (and its annexes) and any information or documents required to be provided by the Rules or another practice direction, the following information must be provided (in the form of a witness statement, attaching documents as exhibits where necessary) for any application to which this practice direction applies:

(a) a copy of the existing trust document;

(b) where relevant, a copy of any original conveyance, transfer, lease, assignment, settlement trust or will trust;

(c) the names and addresses of any present trustees and details of any beneficial interest they have in the trust property. If the present trustees are

---

[30] Section 20(3) of the Act prevents a deputy being given power to exercise such powers on behalf of P.

not the original trustees, an explanation should be provided as to how they became trustees and copies of any deeds of appointment and retirement should be provided;

(d) the full name, address and date of birth of any person proposed to replace P as a trustee, and details of his relationship to P;

(e) confirmation that the trust is not under an order for administration in the Chancery Division;

(f) if there is only one continuing trustee, the applicant must confirm that both the trustee and the proposed new trustee have not made an enduring power of attorney or a lasting power of attorney in favour of the other party;

(g) if an enduring power of attorney or a lasting power of attorney has been executed by a continuing trustee, a certified copy of that document must be provided. If the power has not been registered, the applicant must confirm that the trustee is still capable of carrying out his duties as a trustee;

(h) the full name and address of any person who has an interest in any trust property as the beneficiary of a will, and whether any of them are children or persons who lack capacity;

(i) if the proposed new trustee is not a solicitor or a trust corporation (for example, a bank) and has not been appointed as a deputy for the trustee lacking capacity, the applicant must provide a witness statement from a person independent of the applicant, who has no interest in the trust property, attesting to the applicant's fitness to be appointed as trustee;

(j) if the application relates to a transfer of assets in a will trust or similar settlement into the names of new trustees, accurate details of the trust assets must be provided (including full details of any stocks and shares held);

(k) a copy of any notice of severance and evidence of service;

(l) a copy of the will and grant of probate to the deceased's estate (where relevant);

(m) confirmation of all relevant consents; and

(n) a copy of a signed trustee's special undertaking.

6. The court may direct that other material is to be filed by the applicant, and if it does, the information will be set out in the form of a witness statement.

7. If any of the information mentioned above has been provided already (e g by way of inclusion in an annex to the application form) it need not be provided again.

Additional information to be provided where the application relates to real property

8. In addition to the information specified in paragraph 5 above, where the application relates to real property, the information specified in paragraph 9 below must be provided. The information will be set out in the form of a witness statement.

9. The information which must be provided is:

(a) the address of the property concerned, and whether it is freehold or leasehold;

(b) the title number of the property and a copy of its entry in the Land Registry (if registered land). If the land is unregistered, the applicant should inform the court accordingly; and

(c) if the property is leasehold the applicant should advise the court as to whether he has a licence or consent to the assignment, and provide a copy of the same (or advise if a licence or consent is not necessary and the reason why it is not needed).

10. If any of the information mentioned above has been provided already (eg by way of inclusion in an annex to the application form) it need not be provided again.

Practice Direction H – Applications relating to the registration of enduring powers of attorney (PD9H)

This practice direction supplements Part 9 of the Court of Protection Rules 2007

General

1. Rule 71 enables a practice direction to make additional or different provision in relation to specified applications.

Applications to which this practice direction applies

2. This practice direction applies where:

(a) an application has been made to the Public Guardian to register an instrument creating an enduring power of attorney; and

(b) the Public Guardian has received a notice of objection to registration which prevents him from registering the instrument except in accordance with the court's directions.

Objections to registration

3. A notice of objection will prevent the Public Guardian from registering the instrument if the objection is made on one of the following grounds:[31]

(a) that the power purported to have been created by the instrument was not valid as an enduring power of attorney;

(b) that the power created by the instrument no longer subsists;

(c) that the application is premature because the donor is not yet becoming mentally incapable;

(d) that fraud or undue pressure was used to induce the donor to create the power; or

(e) that, having regard to all the circumstances and in particular the attorney's relationship to or connection with the donor, the attorney is unsuitable to be the donor's attorney.

4. This practice direction sets out the procedure to be followed by a person entitled to be given notice of the application to register the instrument who wishes to apply to the court for:

(a) directions that the instrument should be registered; or

(b) directions that the instrument should not be registered.

5. The persons who are entitled to receive notice of an application are the donor, certain of his relatives and any attorneys under the enduring power who are not making the application for registration.[32]

---

[31] The grounds are set out in para 13(9) of Sch 4 to the Act. The Public Guardian is prevented from registering the instrument by para 13(4) and (5) of that Schedule.

[32] Paragraphs 5 to 11 of Sch 4 to the Act set out who is entitled to receive notice.

Procedure for applications to which this practice direction applies

6. An application must be made using form COP8.

(Practice direction B accompanying Part 4 sets out more detailed requirements for statements of truth.)

7. The application form must state:

    (a)   what directions the applicant is seeking; and
    (b)   if the applicant objects to registration, the grounds on which he does so; or
    (c)   if the applicant is seeking registration, his reasons for doing so.

8. The application form must be supported by evidence set out in either:

    (a)   a witness statement; or
    (b)   if it is verified by a statement of truth, the application form.

9. As soon as practicable and in any event within 21 days of the application form being issued, the applicant must serve a copy of the application form, together with an acknowledgment of service using form COP5:

    (a)   unless the applicant is the donor or an attorney, on the donor of the power and every attorney under the power;
    (b)   if he is the donor, on every attorney under the power; or
    (c)   if he is an attorney, on the donor and any other attorney under the power.

10. Where the applicant knows or has reasonable grounds to believe that the donor of the power lacks capacity to make a decision in relation to any matter that is the subject of the application, he must notify the donor of the application in accordance with Part 7.

PART IV

Practice Direction – Applications within proceedings

Practice Direction A – Applications within proceedings (PD10A)

This practice direction supplements Part 10 of the Court of Protection Rules 2007

Application notice

1. Rule 77 provides that an applicant may use the Part 10 procedure if the application is made:

    (a)   in the course of existing proceedings; or

    (b)   as provided for in a rule or relevant practice direction.

2. An application under Part 10 must be made by filing an application notice using form COP9.

3. An application notice must, in addition to the matters set out in rule 79, be signed and include (unless an order to the contrary pursuant to rule 19 has been made):

    (a)   the name of the person to whom the application relates (P);

    (b)   the case number (if available);

    (c)   the full name of the applicant;

    (d)   where the applicant is not already a party, his address; and

    (e)   a draft of the order sought.

4. If the order sought is unusually long or complex, a disk containing the draft order sought should be made available to the court in a format compatible with the word processing software used by the court. (Queries in relation to software should be directed to a court officer.)

5. The application notice must be supported by evidence set out in either:

    (a)   a witness statement; or

    (b)   the application notice provided that it is verified by a statement of truth.

6. For the purposes of rules 90 to 92, a statement of truth in an application notice may be made by a person who is not a party.[33]

7. The evidence must set out the facts on which the applicant relies for the application, and all material facts known to the applicant of which the court should be made aware.

8. A copy of the application notice and evidence in support must be served by the person making the application as soon as practicable and in any event within 21 days of the application notice being issued.

9. An application may be made without service of an application notice only:

    (a)   where there is exceptional urgency;

    (b)   where the overriding objective is best furthered by doing so;

    (c)   by consent of all parties;

    (d)   with the permission of the court; or

---

[33]   See r 11(6)(a).

(e)   where a rule or other practice direction permits.

(Practice direction B accompanying Part 10 sets out more detailed requirements for urgent applications.)

10. Where an application is made without service on the respondent, the evidence in support of the application must also set out why service was not effected.

11. The court may decide, upon considering the application, that other persons ought to be served with or notified of it and have the opportunity of responding. In such a case, the court will give directions as to who should be served with or notified of the application.

12. On receipt of an application notice, the court will issue the application notice and, if there is to be a hearing, give notice of the date on which the matter is to be heard by the court.

13. Notice will be given to:

    (a)   the applicant;
    (b)   anyone who is named as a respondent in the application notice (if not otherwise a party to the proceedings);
    (c)   every other party to the proceedings; and
    (d)   any other person, as the court may direct.

14. Any directions given by the court may specify the form that the evidence is to take and when it is to be served.

15. Applications should wherever possible be made so that they can be considered at a directions hearing or other hearing for which a date has already been fixed or for which a date is about to be fixed.

16. Where a date for a hearing has been fixed and a party wishes to make an application at that hearing but does not have sufficient time to file an application notice, he should inform the court (if possible in writing) and, if possible, the other parties as soon as he can of the nature of the application and the reason for it. He should then make the application orally at the hearing.

Type of case may be indicated in the application notice

17. The applicant may indicated in the application notice that the application:

    (a)   is urgent;
    (b)   should be dealt with by a particular judge or level of judge within the court;
    (c)   requires a hearing; or
    (d)   any combination of the above.

Telephone hearings

18. The court may direct that an application or part of an application will be dealt with by a telephone hearing.

19. The applicant should indicate in his application notice if he seeks a direction pursuant to paragraph 17. Where he has not done so but nevertheless wishes to seek such a direction the request should be made as early as possible.

20. A direction under paragraph 17 will not normally be given unless every party entitled to be given notice of the application and to be heard at the hearing has consented to the direction.

Video conferencing

21. Where the parties to a matter wish to use video conferencing facilities, and those facilities are available, they should apply to the court for such a direction.

(Practice direction A accompanying Part 14 contains guidance on the use of video conferencing.)

Consent orders

22. The parties to an application for a consent order must ensure that they provide the court with any material it needs to be satisfied that it is appropriate to make the order. Subject to any rule or practice direction, a letter signed by all parties will generally be acceptable for this purpose.

23. Where an order has been agreed in relation to an application for which a hearing date has been fixed, the parties must inform the court immediately.

Practice Direction B – Urgent and interim applications (PD10B)

This practice direction supplements Part 10 of the Court of Protection Rules 2007

Urgent applications and applications without notice

1. These fall into two categories:

  (a)   applications where an application form has already been issued; and

  (b)   applications where an application form has not yet been issued,

and, in both cases, where notice of the application has not been given to the respondent(s).

2. Wherever possible, urgent applications should be made within court hours. These applications will normally be dealt with at court but cases of extreme urgency may be dealt with by telephone. Telephone contact may be made with the court during business hours on 084 5330 2900.

3. When it is not possible to apply within court hours, contact should be made with the security office at the Royal Courts of Justice on 020 7947 6000. The security officer should be informed of the nature of the case.

4. In some cases, urgent applications arise because applications to the court have not been pursued sufficiently promptly. This is undesirable, and should be avoided. A judge who has concerns that the facility for urgent applications may have been abused may require the applicant or the applicant's representative to attend at a subsequent hearing to provide an explanation for the delay.

Applications without notice

5. The applicant should take steps to advise the respondent(s) by telephone or in writing of the application, unless justice would be defeated if notice were given.

6. If an order is made without notice to any other party, the order will ordinarily contain:

  (a)   an undertaking by the applicant to the court to serve the application notice, evidence in support and any order made on the respondent and any other person the court may direct as soon as practicable or as ordered by the court; and

  (b)   a return date for a further hearing at which the other parties can be present.

Applications where an application form has already been issued

7. An application notice using form COP9, evidence in support and a draft order should be filed with the court in advance of the hearing wherever possible. If the order sought is unusually long or complex, a disk containing the draft order sought should be made available to the court in a format compatible with the word processing software used by the court. (Queries in relation to software should be directed to a court officer.)

(Practice direction A accompanying Part 10 sets out more detailed requirements in relation to an application notice.)

8. If an application is made before the application notice has been filed, a draft order should be provided at the hearing, and the application notice and evidence in support must be filed with the court on the next working day or as ordered by the court.

Applications made before the issue of an application form

9. Where the exceptional urgency of the matter requires, an application may be started without filing an application form if the court allows it (but where time permits an application should be made in writing). In such a case, an application may be made to the court orally. The court will require an undertaking that the application form in the terms of the oral application be filed on the next working day, or as required by the court.

10. An order made before the issue of the application form should state in the title after the names of the applicant and the respondent, 'the Applicant and Respondent in an Intended Application'.

Applications made by telephone

11. Where it is not possible to file an application form or notice, applications can be made by telephone in accordance with the contact details set out in paragraphs 2 and 3 of this practice direction.

Hearings conducted by telephone

12. When a hearing is to take place by telephone, if practical it should be conducted by tape-recorded conference call, and arranged (and paid for in the first instance) by the applicant. All parties and the judge should be informed that the call is being recorded by the service provider. The applicant should order a transcript of the hearing from the service provider.

Type of case may be indicated in the application notice

13. The applicant may indicate in the application notice that the application:

    (a)   is urgent;
    (b)   should be dealt with by a particular judge or level of judge within the court;
    (c)   requires a hearing; or
    (d)   any combination of the above.

Urgent cases in relation to serious medical treatment

14. Practice direction E accompanying Part 9 sets out the procedure in relation to applications relating to serious medical treatment. Practice direction A accompanying Part 12 sets out the manner in which those cases are to be allocated.

Interim injunction applications

15. Rule 82 enables the court to grant an interim injunction.

16. Any judge of the court may vary or discharge an interim injunction granted by any judge of the court.

17. Any order for an interim injunction must set out clearly what the respondent or any other person must or must not do. The order may contain an undertaking by the applicant to pay any damages which the respondent(s) sustains which the court considers the applicant should pay.

Practice Direction – Deprivation of liberty applications

This practice direction supplements Part 10A of the Court of Protection Rules 2007

Introduction

1.1 This practice direction sets out the procedure to be followed in deprivation of liberty ('DoL') applications. 'DoL applications', for these purposes, means applications to the court for orders under section 21A of the Mental Capacity Act 2005 relating to a standard or urgent authorisation under Schedule A1 of that Act to deprive a person of his or her liberty; or proceedings (for example, relating to costs or appeals) connected with or consequent upon such applications. By their nature, such applications are of special urgency and therefore will be dealt with by the court according to the special procedure described here. Other applications may, while not being DoL applications within the meaning of the term explained above, raise issues relating to deprivation of liberty and require similarly urgent attention; and while the special DoL procedure will not apply to such applications, they should as explained in paragraph 3.4 be raised with the DoL team at the earliest possible stage so that they can be handled appropriately. The key features of the special DoL procedure are:

(a)   special DoL court forms ensure that DoL court papers stand out as such and receive special handling by the court office;

(b)   the application is placed before a judge of the court as soon as possible – if necessary, before issue of the application – for judicial directions to be given as to the steps to be taken in the application, and who is to take each step and by when;

(c)   the usual Court of Protection Rules (for example, as to method and timing of service of the application) will apply only so far as consistent with the judicial directions given for the particular case;

(d)   a dedicated team in the court office ('the DoL team') will deal with DoL applications at all stages, including liaison with would-be applicants/other parties;

(e)   the progress of each DoL case will be monitored by a judge assigned to that case, assisted by the DoL team.

Before issuing an application

2.1 Potential applicants should contact the DoL team at the earliest possible stage before issuing a DoL application. Where this is not possible, the applicant should liaise with the DoL team at the same time as, or as soon as possible after, lodging the application. The DoL team can be contacted by telephone in the first instance and by fax.

2.2 The information that the DoL team needs, with as much advance warning as possible, is (1) that a DoL application is to be made; (2) how urgent the application is (ie, by when should the Court's decision, or interim decision, on the merits be given); and (3) when the Court will receive the application papers. In extremely urgent cases, the DoL team can arrange for a telephone application to be made to the judge for directions and/or an interim order even before the application has been issued. Further brief details should be given which may include:

–   the parties' details

- where the parties live
- the issue to be decided
- the date of urgent or standard authorisation
- the date of effective detention
- the parties' legal representatives
- any family members or others who are involved
- whether there have been any other court proceedings involving the parties and if so, where.

2.3 Contact details for the DoL team are:

Court of Protection

DoLs Application Branch

Archway Tower

2 Junction Road

London

N19 5FZ

DX 141150 Archway 2

Telephone: 0845 330 2900

Fax: 020 7664 7712

2.4 The court office is open for personal attendance between the hours of 10 a.m. to 4.00 p.m. on working days. The DoL team can receive telephone calls and faxes between the same hours. Faxes transmitted after 4.00 p.m. will be dealt with the next working day.

2.5 When in an emergency it is necessary to make a telephone application to a judge outside normal court hours, the security office at the Royal Courts of Justice should be contacted on 020 7947 6000. The security officer should be informed of the nature of the case. In the Family Division, the out-of-hours application procedure involves the judge being contacted through a Family Division duty officer, and the RCJ security officer will need to contact the duty officer and not the judge's clerk or the judge.

2.6 Intending applicants/other parties may find it helpful to refer to:

- the *Code of Practice Deprivation of Liberty Safeguards* (June 2008), ISBN 978-0113228157, supplementing the main *Mental Capacity Act 2005 Code of Practice*: in particular Chapter 10, *What is the Court of Protection and who can apply to it?*; and
- the judgment of Mr Justice Munby in *Salford City Council v GJ, NJ and BJ (Incapacitated Adults)* [2008] EWHC 1097 (Fam); [2008] 2 FLR 1295. Although this case was decided before the coming into force of the DoL amendments to the Mental Capacity Act 2005, it sets out helpful guidance on the appropriate court procedures for cases relating to the deprivation of liberty of adults.

2.7 The DoL team will be pleased to explain the court's procedures for handling DoL cases. Please note that the team (as with all court staff) is not permitted to give advice on matters of law. Please do not contact the DoL team unless your inquiry concerns a deprivation of liberty question (whether relating to a potential application, or a case which is already lodged with the Court).

DoL court forms

3.1 The special DoL court forms are as follows:

- *DLA: Deprivation of Liberty Application Form*: to be used for all DoL applications;

- *DLB: Deprivation of Liberty Request for Urgent Consideration*: this short form allows applicants to set out the reasons why the case is urgent, the timetable they wish the case to follow, and any interim relief sought. A draft of any order sought should be attached. Ideally, the DLB (plus any draft order) should be placed at the top of the draft application and both issued and served together;

- *DLC: Deprivation of Liberty Permission Form*: P (the person who is being, or may be, deprived of his/her liberty); and P's appointed representative, attorney or deputy do not need the court's permission to make a DoL application. Anyone else (including family members) needs permission. Where the applicant needs permission to make a DoL application, the DLC form should be lodged and served together with a draft of the DLA and, where appropriate, the DLB. The DLB should always be placed at the top of the papers and (where this is so) mention that permission is required and that a completed DLC is attached;

- *DLD: Deprivation of Liberty Certificate of Service/non-service and Certificate of notification/non-notification*;

- *DLE: Deprivation of Liberty Acknowledgement of service/notification.*

These forms can be obtained from the Court of Protection office or downloaded from the court's website www.hmcs.gov.uk.

3.2 To ensure that papers relating to DoL applications are promptly directed to the DoL team at the court, it is essential that the appropriate DoL court forms are used.

3.3 The DoL court forms should be used for, and only for, DoL applications. If in such a case it is anticipated that other issues may arise, the DoL forms should identify and describe briefly those issues and any relief which may be sought in respect of them: sections 3.5 and 5 of form DLA, the Deprivation of Liberty Application Form, offer an opportunity to do this. 'Other issues' are perhaps most likely to arise in the event that the court decides the DoL application in the applicant's favour. In such a case, if the applicant has already identified the 'other issues' in his/her form DLA, the court will be able to address these, either by dealing with them immediately or by giving directions for their future handling.

3.4 Accordingly, unless the court expressly directs, applicants should not issue a second and separate application (using the standard court forms) relating to any 'other issues'.

3.5 Where an application seeks relief concerning a deprivation of P's liberty other than under 21A section in respect of a standard or urgent authorisation (for example, where the application is for an order under 16(2)(a)), section the dedicated DoL court forms should not be used. Rather the standard court forms should be used for such an application, but it should be made clear on them that relief relating to a deprivation of P's liberty is being sought, and the proposed applicant should contact the DoL team to discuss handling at the earliest possible stage before issuing the application.

How to issue a DoL application

4.1 To issue a DoL application, the following forms should be filed at court:

- form DLA
- form DLB (plus draft order)
- form DLC if appropriate
- court fee of £400.00

Where a draft order is lodged with the court, it would be helpful – although not compulsory – if an electronic version of the order could also be lodged on disc, if possible.

4.2 In cases of extreme emergency or where it is not possible to attend at the court office, for example during weekends, the court will expect an applicant to undertake to file forms DLA and DLC and to pay the court fee unless an exemption applies.

Inviting the court to make judicial directions for the handling of the application

5.1 The following is a sample list of possible issues which the court is likely to wish to consider in judicial directions in a DoL case. It is intended as a prompt, not as a definitive list of the issues that may need to be covered:

- upon whom, by when and how service of the application should be effected;
- dispensing with acknowledgement of service of the application or allowing a short period of time for so doing, which in some cases may amount to a few hours only;
- whether further lay or expert evidence should be obtained;
- whether P/the detained person should be a party and represented by the Official Solicitor and whether any other person should be a party;
- whether any family members should be formally notified of the application and of any hearing and joined as parties;
- fixing a date for a First Hearing and giving a time estimate;
- fixing a trial window for any final hearing and giving a time estimate;
- the level of judge appropriate to hear the case;
- whether the case is such that it should be immediately transferred to the High Court for a High Court Judge to give directions;
- provision for a bundle for the judge at the First Hearing.

5.2 If you are an applicant without legal representation, and you are not sure exactly what directions you should ask for, you may prefer simply to invite the judge to make appropriate directions in light of the nature and urgency of the case as you have explained it on the DLB form. In exceptionally urgent cases, there may not be time to formulate draft directions: the court will understand if applicants in such cases (whether or not legally represented) simply ask the judge for appropriate directions.

After issue of the application

6.1 The DoL team will immediately take steps to ensure that the application is placed before a judge nominated to hear Court of Protection cases and DoL applications. During working hours, the application will be placed before a Judge at Archway Tower. Out of hours, at weekends and on public holidays, the application will be placed before the judge who is most immediately available.

6.2 As soon as the court office is put on notice of a DoL application, the DoL team will notify a judge to put the judge on stand-by to deal with the application. The judge will consider the application on the papers and make a first order.

Steps after the judge's first order

7.1 The DoL team will:

- action every point in the judge's note or instruction;
- refer any query that arises to the judge immediately or, if not available, to another judge;
- make all arrangements for any transfer of the case to another court and/or for a hearing.

7.2 The applicant or his/her legal representative should follow all steps in the judge's order and:

- form DLD should be filed with the court if appropriate; and
- form DLE should be included in any documents served unless ordered otherwise.

The First Hearing

8.1 The First Hearing will be listed for the court to fix a date for any subsequent hearing(s), give directions and/or to make an interim or final order if appropriate. The court will make such orders and give such directions as are appropriate in the case.

8.2 The court will aim to have the First Hearing before a judge of every DoL application within 5 working days of the date of issue of the application.

8.3 Applicants can indicate on the DLB form if they think that the application needs to be considered within a shorter timetable, and set out proposals for such a timetable. On the first paper consideration the court will consider when the First Hearing should be listed.

8.4 If time allows and no specific direction has been made by the court, an indexed and paginated bundle should be prepared for the judge and any skeleton arguments and draft orders given to the court as soon as they are available. A copy of the index should be provided to all parties and, where another party appears in person, a copy of the bundle should be provided.

Hearing in private

9.1 Part 13 of the Court of Protection Rules 2007 provides at rule 90, as supplemented by Practice Direction A to Part 13, that the general rule is that a hearing is held in private. Rule 92 allows the court to order that a hearing be in public if the criteria in rule 93 apply.

Costs

10.1 The general rule, in rule 157 of the Court of Protection Rules 2007, is that in a health and welfare case there will be no order as to costs of the proceedings. The general rule applies to DoL applications.

Appeals

11.1 Part 20 of the Court of Protection Rules 2007 applies to appeals. Permission is required to appeal (rule 172) and this will only be granted where the court considers that the appeal would have a real prospect of success or there is some other compelling reason why the appeal should be heard (rule 173).

Practice Direction – Human Rights

Practice Direction A – Human Rights Act 1998 (PD11A)

This practice direction supplements Part 11 of the Court of Protection Rules 2007

Procedure for making claim

1. A claim made pursuant to rule 83 in relation to the Human Rights Act 1998 ('the 1998 Act') should be included in the application form using form COP1. If the claim forms part of a response by a person served with or notified of the application, it should be included in the acknowledgment of service using form COP5.

2. If the claim in relation to the 1998 Act is made during the course of proceedings, it should be made by filing an application notice using form COP9.

3. If the claim is raised in an appeal, the claim should be filed with the appellant's or the respondent's notice as appropriate, using form COP35 or COP36.

Notice to the Crown

4. Where notice is served on the Crown in accordance with rule 83(2), notice of the claim must be served by the person making the claim on the person named in the list published under section 17 of the Crown Proceedings Act 1947.

5. The notice must be in the form directed by the court and will normally include the directions given by the court. The notice must also be served by the person making the claim on all the parties. The applicant must provide the Crown with a copy of the document in which the claim in relation to the 1998 Act is raised (for example, the application form).

6. The court may ask the parties to assist in the preparation of the notice.

Joining of the Crown

7. Unless the court orders otherwise, the Minister or other person permitted by the 1998 Act to be joined as a party must, if he wishes to be joined, file an application to be joined using form COP10. (Section 5(2) of the 1998 Act entitles the Crown to be joined to proceedings where the court is considering whether to make a declaration of incompatibility, provided notice is given in accordance with rules of court. The Minister or other person will be regarded as having sufficient interest for the purpose of rule 75(1).)

8. Where the Minister has nominated a person to be joined as a party (as permitted by section 5(2)(a) of the 1998 Act) that person must (unless the court orders otherwise) file an application to be joined using form COP10, which must also be accompanied by the Minister's written nomination.

Allocation

9. Where a claim is made to the court pursuant to rule 83 the proceedings (including permission, the giving of any directions, and any hearing) must be conducted by a

judge of the court who has been nominated as such by virtue of section 46(2)(a) to (c) of the Act (ie the President of the Family Division, the Chancellor or a puisne judge of the High Court).

Practice Direction – Dealing with applications

Practice Direction A – Court's jurisdiction to be exercised by certain judges (PD12A)

This practice direction supplements Part 12 of the Court of Protection Rules 2007

General

1. Rule 86 allows a practice direction to specify types of application which may be dealt with only by the President, the Vice-President or one of the other judges nominated by virtue of section 46(2)(a) to (c) of the Act.

Cases to be heard by the President or the President's nominee

2. Where an application is made to the court in relation to:

    (a)   the lawfulness of withholding or withdrawing artificial nutrition and hydration from a person in a permanent vegetative state, or a minimally conscious state; or

    (b)   a case involving an ethical dilemma in an untested area,

the proceedings (including permission, the giving of any directions, and any hearing) must be conducted by the President of the Court of Protection or by another judge nominated by the President.

Cases to be heard by a judge nominated by virtue of section 46(2)(a) to (c) of the Act

3. Where an application is made to the court:

    (a)   in relation to serious medical treatment (other than that outlined in paragraph 2); or

    (b)   pursuant to rule 83, in which a declaration of incompatibility pursuant to section 4 of the Human Rights Act 1998 is sought,

the proceedings (including permission, the giving of any directions, and any hearing) must be conducted a judge of the court who has been nominated as such by virtue of section 46(2)(a) to (c) of the Act (ie the President of the Family Division, the Chancellor or a puisne judge of the High Court).

Court's general discretion as to allocation

4. The Senior Judge or his nominee may determine whether a matter is one to which this practice direction applies.

5. The judge to whom a matter is allocated in accordance with this practice direction may determine that the matter is one which may properly be heard by a judge of the court other than one nominated by virtue of section 46(2)(a) to (c) of the Act; and he may reallocate the matter accordingly.

Applications relating to serious medical treatment

6. Applications which relate to serious medical treatment should also be conducted in accordance with practice direction E accompanying Part 9 of the Rules.

PART IV

Practice Direction B – Procedure for disputing the court's jurisdiction (PD12B)

This practice direction supplements Part 12 of the Court of Protection Rules 2007

Disputing the jurisdiction of the court – generally

1. A person who wishes to:

    (a)   dispute the court's jurisdiction to hear an application; or

    (b)   argue that the court should not exercise such jurisdiction as it may have,

may apply to the court for an order to that effect.[34]

2. If an application to dispute jurisdiction is made by a person who is given notice of an application for permission, this must be stated in the acknowledgment of notification, using form COP5 filed in accordance with rule 57.

3. Where a person who has been served with or notified of an application form wishes to dispute the court's jurisdiction, he must state this in the acknowledgment of service or notification (as the case may be), using form COP5 filed in accordance with rule 72.

4. In any other case (with the exception of those cases provided for in paragraphs 5 to 7), a person who wishes to dispute the court's jurisdiction must do so by filing an application notice using form COP9 in accordance with Part 10.

Disputing the jurisdiction of the court – where P ceases to lack capacity

5. Where P ceases to lack capacity in relation to the matter or matters to which the application relates, an application may be made to the court for the proceedings to come to an end.[35]

6. Applications in such circumstances may only be made by the following persons:

    (a)   P;

    (b)   his litigation friend; or

    (c)   any other person who is a party to the proceedings.[36]

7. The application must be made by filing an application notice using form COP9 in accordance with Part 10. The application must be served on all other parties to the proceedings.[37]

Evidence

8. An application made pursuant to rule 87 must be supported by evidence. Where it is alleged that P has capacity to make decisions in relation to the matter or matters to which the proceedings relate, the application should be supported by evidence to that effect.

---

[34]   Rule 87.
[35]   Rule 148.
[36]   Rule 148(3).
[37]   See r 148(4).

Practice Direction – Hearings

Practice Direction A – Hearings (including reporting restrictions) (PD13A)

This practice direction supplements Part 13 of the Court of Protection Rules 2007

General

1. Hearings before the court will generally be in private[38] but the court may order that the whole or part of any hearing is to be held in public.[39] The court also has power to:

    (a)   authorise the publication of information about a private hearing;[40]

    (b)   authorise persons to attend a private hearing;[41]

    (c)   exclude persons from attending either a private or public hearing;[42] or

    (d)   restrict or prohibit the publication of information about a private or public hearing.[43]

2. Part 1 of this practice direction applies to any application for an order under rules 90 to 92.

3. Part 2 of the practice direction makes additional provision in relation to orders founded on Convention rights which would restrict the publication of information.

(Section 1 of the Human Rights Act 1998 defines 'the Convention rights'.)

Part 1

Applications under rules 90, 91 or 92

4. An application for an order under rules 90, 91 or 92 must be commenced by filing an application notice form using COP9 in accordance with Part 10.

5. For the purposes of rules 90 to 92, a statement of truth in an application notice may be made by a person who is not a party.[44]

6. For an application commenced under rules 90, 91 or 92, the court should consider whether to direct that the application should be dealt with as a discrete issue.[45]

---

[38]   Rule 90.
[39]   Rule 92.
[40]   Rule 91.
[41]   Rule 90(3)(a).
[42]   Rules 90(3)(b) and 92(1)(c).
[43]   Rules 91(3) and 92(2).
[44]   See rule 11(6)(a).
[45]   Rule 25(2)(h) sets out the court's case management power to do so.

PART IV

Part 2

Powers of the court to impose reporting restrictions

Court sitting in private

7. Section 12(1) of the Administration of Justice Act 1960[46] provides that, in any proceedings brought under the Mental Capacity Act 2005 before a court which is sitting in private, publication of information about the proceedings will generally be contempt of court. However, rule 91(1) makes it clear that there will be no contempt where the court has authorised the publication of the information under rule 91. Where the court makes such an order, it may (at the same time or subsequently) restrict or prohibit the publication of information relating to a person's identity. Such restrictions may be imposed either on an application made by any person (usually a party to the proceedings) or of the court's own initiative.[47]

8. The general rule is that hearings will be in private and that there can be no lawful publication of information unless the court has authorised it. Where reporting restrictions are imposed as part of the order authorising publication, they will simply set out what can be published and there will be no need to comply with the requirements as to notice which are set out in Part 2 of this practice direction. But if the restrictions are subsequent to the order authorising publication, then the requirements of Part 2 should be complied with.

Court sitting in public

9. Where a hearing is to be held in public as a result of a court order under rule 92, the court may restrict or prohibit the publication of information about the proceedings.[48] Such restrictions may be imposed either on an application made by any person (usually a party to the proceedings) or of the court's own initiative.[49]

Notification in relation to reporting restrictions

10. In connection with the imposition of reporting restrictions, attention is drawn to section 12(2) of the Human Rights Act 1998. This means that where an application has been made for an order restricting the exercise of the right to freedom of expression, the order must not be made where the person against whom the application is made is neither present nor represented unless the court is satisfied:

    (a)   that the applicant has taken all practicable steps to notify the respondent; or
    (b)   that there are compelling reasons why the respondent should not be notified.

11. The need to ensure that P's Convention rights are protected may be at issue when the court is considering whether to make an order that a public hearing should be held. In particular, there is a general duty under section 1 of the Mental Capacity Act 2005 to ensure that things done for or on behalf of P are done in his best interests. Part 2 of this practice direction should therefore be complied with where the court is considering making an order under rule 92(2) of its own initiative.

---

[46]   Section 12(1)(b) was amended by para 10 of Sch 6 the Mental Capacity Act 2005.
[47]   Rule 93(1)(c).
[48]   Rule 92(2).
[49]   Rule 93(1)(c).

12. In summary, the requirements to notify in accordance with the requirements of Part 2 of this practice direction will apply in any case where:

    (a)   the court has made an order for the publication of information about proceedings which are conducted in private and, after the order has been made:

        (i)   an application founded on P's Convention rights is made to the court for an order under rule 91(3) which would impose restrictions (or further restrictions) on the information that may be published, or

        (ii)   of its own initiative, the court is considering whether to impose such restrictions on the basis of P's Convention rights; or

    (b)   the court has already made an order for a hearing to be held in public and:

        (i)   an application founded on Convention rights is made to the court for an order under rule 92(2) which would impose restrictions (or further restrictions) on the information that may be published, or

        (ii)   of its own initiative, the court is considering whether to vary or impose further such restrictions.

Notice of reporting restrictions to be given to national news media

13. Notice of the possibility that reporting restrictions may be imposed can be effected via the Press Association's CopyDirect service, to which national newspapers and broadcasters subscribe as a means of receiving notice of such applications. Such service should be the norm. The court retains the power to make orders without notice (whether in response to an application or of its own initiative) but such cases will be exceptional.

14. CopyDirect will be responsible for notifying the individual media organisations. Where the order would affect the world at large this is sufficient service for the purposes of advance notice. The website: http://www.medialawyer.press.net/ courtapplications gives details of the organisations represented and instructions for service of the application.

Notice of an application to be given by applicant

15. A person who has made an application founded on Convention rights should give advance notice of the application to the national media via the Press Association's CopyDirect service. He should first telephone CopyDirect (tel. no 0870 830 6429). Unless an order pursuant to rule 19 has been made, a copy of the following documents should be sent either by fax (fax no 0870 837 6429) or to the e-mail address provided by CopyDirect:

    (a)   the application form or application notice seeking the restriction order;

    (b)   the witness statement filed in support;

    (c)   any legal submissions in support; and

    (d)   an explanatory note setting out the nature of the proceedings in the form set out in the Annex to this practice direction.

16. It is helpful if applications are accompanied by an explanatory note from which persons served can readily understand the nature of the case (though care should be taken that the information does not breach any rule or order of the court in relation to the use or publication of information). In any case where notice of an application has not been given, the explanatory note should explain why.

PART IV

17. Unless there is a particular reason not to do so, copies of all the documents referred to above should be served. If there is a reason for not serving some or all of the documents (or parts of them), the applicant should ensure sufficient detail is given to enable the media to make an informed decision as to whether it wishes to attend a hearing or be legally represented.

18. The CopyDirect service does not extend to local or regional media or magazines. If service of the application on any specific organisation or person not covered is required, it should be effected directly.

19. The court may dispense with any of the requirements set out in paragraphs 15 to 18.

Notice of own-initiative order to be given by court

20. In any case where the court will gives advance notice of an own-initiative order to the national media, it will send such of the information listed in paragraph 15 as it considers necessary.

Responding to a notice

21. Where a media organisation or any other person has been notified of an application or own-initiative order, they may decide that they wish to participate in any hearing to determine whether reporting restrictions should be imposed. In order to take part, the person must file an acknowledgment of service ('the acknowledgment') using form COP5 within 21 days beginning with the date on which the notice of the reporting restrictions was given to him by CopyDirect.

22. The acknowledgment must be filed in accordance with rule 75.

23. A person who has filed an acknowledgment will not become a party to the substantive proceedings (ie. the proceedings in relation to which an application form was filed) except to such extent (if any) as the court may direct.

The hearing

24. Any application or own-initiative order which invokes. Convention rights will involve a balancing of rights under Article 8 (right to respect for private and family life) and Article 10 (freedom of expression). There is no automatic precedence as between these Articles, and both are subject to qualification where (among other considerations) the rights of others are engaged.

25. In the case of an application, section 12(4) of the Human Rights Act 1998 requires the court to have particular regard to the importance of freedom of expression. It must also have regard to the extent to which material has or is about to become available to the public, the extent of the public interest in such material being published and the terms of any relevant privacy code (such as those of the Press Complaints Commission).

26. The same approach will be taken where the court is considering an own-initiative order imposing reporting restrictions.

Scope of order

Persons protected

27. The aim should be to protect P rather than to confer anonymity on other individuals or organisations. However, the order may include restrictions on identifying or approaching specified family members, carers, doctors or organisations or other persons as the court directs in cases where the absence of such restriction is likely to prejudice their ability to care for P, or where identification of such persons might lead to identification of P and defeat the purpose of the order. In cases where the court receives expert evidence the identity of the experts (as opposed to treating clinicians) is not normally subject to restriction, unless evidence in support is provided for such a restriction.

Information already in the public domain

28. Orders will not usually be made prohibiting publication of material which is already in the public domain, other than in exceptional cases.

Duration of order

29. Orders should last for no longer than is necessary to achieve the purpose for which they are made. The order may need to last until P's death. In some cases a later date may be necessary to maintain the anonymity of doctors or carers after the death of a patient.

Annex

Application for a Reporting Restriction Order

EXPLANATORY NOTE

1 AB is in a permanent vegetative state. An application has been made by the NHS Hospital Trust responsible for his care for the Court of Protection to make a decision on the question of withdrawing artificial nutrition and hydration. This course is supported by AB's family.

2 On [date] the application will be heard by the Court of Protection [in public].

3 A Reporting Restriction Order has been [made/applied for] to protect AB's right to confidentiality in respect of his medical treatment. This does not restrict publication of information or discussion about the treatment of patients in a permanent vegetative state, provided that such publication is not likely to lead to the identification of AB, those caring for him, the NHS Trust concerned or the establishment at which he is being cared for.

Practice Direction – Admissions, evidence and depositions

Practice Direction A – Written evidence (PD14A)

This practice direction supplements Part 14 of the Court of Protection Rules 2007

Affidavits

Deponent

1. A deponent is a person who gives evidence by affidavit or affirmation.

Heading

2. The affidavit should be headed with the title of the proceedings, including the case number (if known) and the full name of the person to whom the proceedings relate (unless an order to the contrary pursuant to rule 19 has been made).

3. At the top right hand corner of the first page (and on the back-sheet) there should be clearly written:

    (a)   the party on whose behalf it is made (unless an order to the contrary pursuant to rule 19 has been made);
    (b)   the initials and surname of the deponent;
    (c)   the number of the affidavit in relation to that deponent; and
    (d)   the date sworn.

Body of affidavit

4. The affidavit must, if practicable, be in the deponent's own words. It should be expressed in the first person, and the deponent should:

    (a)   commence 'I (full name) of (address) state on oath …';
    (b)   if giving evidence in his professional, business or other occupational capacity, give the address at which he works in (a) above, the position he holds and the name of his firm or employer;
    (c)   give his occupation or, if he has none, his description; and
    (d)   state if he is a party to the proceedings or employed by a party to the proceedings.

5. An affidavit must indicate:

    (a)   which of the statements in it are made from the deponent's own knowledge and which are matters of information or belief; and
    (b)   the source for any matters of information or belief.

6. Where a deponent:

    (a)   refers to an exhibit or exhibits, he should state 'there is now produced and shown to me marked "…," the *(description of exhibit)*'; and
    (b)   makes more than one affidavit (to which there are exhibits) in the same proceedings, the numbering of the exhibits should run consecutively throughout and not start again with each affidavit.

Jurat

7. The jurat of an affidavit is a statement set out at the end of the document which authenticates the affidavit.

8. It must:

(a) be signed by all deponents;

(b) be completed and signed by the person before whom the affidavit was sworn whose name and qualifications must be printed beneath his signature;

(c) contain the full address of the person before whom the affidavit was sworn; and

(d) follow immediately on from the text and not be put on a separate page.

Format of affidavits

9. An affidavit should:

(a) be produced on durable quality A4 paper with a 3.5 centimetre margin;

(b) be fully legible and should normally be typed on one side of the paper only;

(c) where possible, be bound securely in a manner which would not hamper filing;

(d) have the pages numbered consecutively as a separate document;

(e) be divided into numbered paragraphs; and

(f) have all numbers, including dates, expressed in figures.

10. It is usually convenient for an affidavit to follow the chronological sequence of events or matters dealt with. Each paragraph of an affidavit should as far as possible be confined to a distinct portion of the subject.

11. An affidavit must be included in, or attached to, a COP25 form.

Inability of deponent to read or sign affidavit

12. Where an affidavit is sworn by a person who is unable to read or sign it, the person before whom the affidavit is sworn must certify in the jurat that:

(a) he read the affidavit to the deponent;

(b) the deponent appeared to understand it; and

(c) the deponent signed, or made his mark, in his presence.

13. If that certificate is not included in the jurat, the affidavit may not be used in evidence unless the court is satisfied that it was read to the deponent and that he appeared to understand it. Two versions of the form of the jurat with the certificate are set out in Annex 1 to this practice direction.

Alterations to affidavits

14. Any alteration to an affidavit must be initialled by both the deponent and the person before whom the affidavit was sworn.

15. An affidavit which contains an alteration that has not been initialled may be filed or used in evidence only with the permission of the court.

PART IV

Who may administer oaths

16. Only the following may administer oaths:

    (a)   Commissioners for Oaths;[50]
    (b)   practising solicitors;[51]
    (c)   other persons specified by statute;[52]
    (d)   certain officials of the Supreme Court;[53]
    (e)   a circuit judge or district judge;[54]
    (f)   any justice of the peace;[55] and
    (g)   certain officials of any county court appointed by the judge of that court for the purpose.[56]

17. An affidavit must be sworn before a person independent of the parties or their representatives.

Filing of affidavits

18. If the court directs that an affidavit is to be filed, it must be filed in the court office.

19. Where an affidavit is in a foreign language:

    (a)   the party wishing to rely on it:
        (i)   must have it translated, and
        (ii) must file the foreign language affidavit with the court; and
    (b)   the translator must make and file with the court an affidavit verifying the translation and exhibiting both the translation and a copy of the foreign language affidavit.

Exhibits

Manner of exhibiting documents

20. A document used in conjunction with an affidavit should be:

    (a)   produced to and verified by the deponent, and remain separate from the affidavit; and
    (b)   identified by a declaration of the person before whom the affidavit was sworn.

21. The declaration should be headed with the name of the proceedings in the same way as the affidavit.

22. The first page of each exhibit should be marked:

    (a)   as in paragraph 3 above; and
    (b)   with the exhibit mark referred to in the affidavit.

---

[50]   Commissioner for Oaths Act 1889 and 1891.
[51]   Section 81 of the Solicitors Act 1974.
[52]   Section 65 of the Administration of Justice Act 1985; s 113 of the Courts and Legal Services Act 1990 and the Commissioners for Oaths (Prescribed Bodies) Regulations 1994 and 1995.
[53]   Section 2 of the Commissioners for Oaths Act 1889.
[54]   Section 58 of the County Courts Act 1984.
[55]   Section 58 as above.
[56]   Section 58 as above.

Letters

23. Copies of individual letters should be collected together and exhibited in a bundle or bundles. The letters should be arranged in chronological order with the earliest at the top, and firmly secured.

24. When a bundle of correspondence is exhibited it should be arranged and secured as above and numbered consecutively.

Other documents

25. Photocopies instead of original documents may be exhibited provided the originals are made available for inspection by other parties before the hearing and by the judge at the hearing.

26. Court documents must not be exhibited (official copies of such documents prove themselves).

Exhibits other than documents

27. Items other than documents should be clearly marked with an exhibit number or letter in such a manner that the mark cannot become detached from the exhibit.

28. Small items may be placed in a container and the container appropriately marked.

General provisions

29. Where an exhibit contains more than one document:

    (a)   the bundle should not be stapled but should be securely fastened in a way that does not hinder the reading of the documents; and

    (b)   the pages should be numbered consecutively at the bottom centre.

30. Every page of an exhibit should be clearly legible. Typed copies of illegible documents should be included, paginated with 'a' etc numbers.

31. Where on account of their bulk the service of copies of exhibits on the other parties would be difficult or impracticable, the directions of the court should be sought as to the arrangements for bringing the exhibits to the attention of the other parties and as to their custody pending the final hearing.

Affirmations

32. All provisions in this or any other practice direction relating to affidavits apply to affirmations with the following exceptions:

    (a)   the deponent should commence 'I (*name*) of (*address*) do solemnly and sincerely affirm ...'; and

    (b)   in the jurat the word 'sworn' is replaced by the word 'affirmed'.

PART IV

Witness statements

Heading

33. The witness statements should be headed with the title of the proceedings; including the case number (if known) and the full name of the person to whom the proceedings relate (unless an order to the contrary pursuant to rule 19 has been made).

34. At the top right hand corner of the first page there should be clearly written:

    (a)   the party on whose behalf it is made (unless an order to the contrary pursuant to rule 19 has been made);

    (b)   the initials and surname of the witness;

    (c)   the number of the statement in relation to that witness; and

    (d)   the date the statement was made.

Body of witness statement

35. The witness statement must, if practicable, be in the intended witness's own words. The statement should be expressed in the first person and should also state:

    (a)   his place of residence or, if he is making the statement in his professional, business or other occupational capacity, the address at which he works, the position he holds and the name of his firm or employer;

    (b)   his occupation, or if he has none, his description; and

    (c)   if he is a party to the proceedings or employed by a party to the proceedings.

36. A witness statement must indicate:

    (a)   which of the statements in it are made from the witness's own knowledge and which are matters of information or belief; and

    (b)   the source for any matters of information or belief.

37. An exhibit used in conjunction with a witness statement should be verified and identified by the witness and remain separate from the witness statement.

38. Where a witness refers to an exhibit or exhibits, he should state: 'I refer to the (*description of exhibit*) marked "…" '.

39. The provisions of paragraphs 22 to 31 apply similarly to witness statements as they do to affidavits, where appropriate.

40. Where a witness makes more than one witness statement to which there are exhibits, the numbering of the exhibits should run consecutively throughout and not start again with each witness statement.

Format of witness statement

41. A witness statement should adhere to the format specified in paragraph 9 for affidavits.

42. It is usually convenient for a witness statement to follow the chronological sequence of the events or matters dealt with and each paragraph of a witness statement should, as far as possible, be confined to a distinct portion of the subject.

43. A witness statement must be included in, or attached to, a COP24 form.

Statement of truth

44. A witness statement is the equivalent of oral evidence which the witness would, if called, give in evidence. It must be verified by a statement of truth in the following terms:

'I believe that the facts stated in this witness statement are true.'

(Practice direction B accompanying Part 4 sets out more detailed requirements for statements of truth.)

45. Attention is drawn to rule 14 which sets out the consequences of verifying a witness statement containing a false statement without an honest belief in its truth.

Alterations to witness statements

46. Any alteration to a witness statement must be initialled by the person making the statement or by the authorised person where appropriate.

47. A witness statement which contains an alteration that has not been initialled may only be used in evidence with the permission of the court.

Filing of witness statements

48. Where a witness statement is in a foreign language:

   (a)   the party wishing to rely on it must:
      (i)   have it translated, and
      (ii)   file the foreign language witness statement with the court; and
   (b)   the translator must make and file with the court an affidavit verifying the translation and exhibiting both the translation and a copy of the foreign language witness statement.

Defects in affidavits, witness statements and exhibits

49. Where:

   (a)   an affidavit;
   (b)   a witness statement; or
   (c)   an exhibit to either an affidavit or a witness statement,

does not comply with Part 14 or this practice direction in relation to its form, the court may refuse to admit it as evidence and may refuse to allow the costs arising from its preparation.

50. However, the court may allow a person to file a defective affidavit or witness statement or to use a defective exhibit.

Agreed bundles for hearings

51. The court may give directions requiring the parties to use their best endeavours to agree a bundle or bundles of documents for use at any hearing.

52. All documents contained in bundles which have been agreed for use at a hearing shall be admissible at that hearing as evidence of their contents, unless –

   (a)   the court orders otherwise; or

(b)   a party gives written notice of objection to the admissibility of particular documents.

Evidence by video link

53. Guidance on the use of video conferencing is set out at Annex 2 to this practice direction.

Information

54. The court may direct a party with access to information which is not reasonably available to another party to serve on that other party a document which records the information.[57] The document served must include sufficient details of all the facts, tests, experiments and assumptions which underlie any part of the information to enable the party on whom it is served to make, or to obtain, a proper interpretation of the information and an assessment of its significance.

Annex 1

Certificate to be used where a deponent to an affidavit is unable to read or sign it

Sworn at …this …day of … Before me, I having first read over the contents of this affidavit to the deponent [if there are exhibits, add 'and explained the nature and effect of the exhibits referred to in it'] who appeared to understand it and approved its contents as accurate, and made his mark on the affidavit in my presence.

Or (after, Before me) the witness to the mark of the deponent having first sworn that he had read over etc. (as above) and that he saw him make his mark on the affidavit. (Witness must sign).

Certificate to be used where a deponent to an affirmation is unable to read or sign it

Affirmed at …this …day of … Before me, I having first read over the contents of this affirmation to the deponent [if there are exhibits, add 'and explained the nature and effect of the exhibits referred to in it'] who appeared to understand it and approved its content as accurate, and made his mark on the affirmation in my presence.

Or (after, Before me) the witness to the mark of the deponent having been first sworn that he had read over etc (as above) and that he saw him make his mark on the affirmation. (Witness must sign).

---

[57]   Rule 107.

Annex 2

Guidance on the use of video conferencing

1. This guidance is for the use of video conferencing (VC) to provide evidence in the Court of Protection. It is in part based upon the VC guidance contained in the practice direction that supplements Part 32 of the Civil Procedure Rules.

2. Rule 98 of the Court of Protection Rules provides that the court may allow a witness to give evidence through a video link or by other means. It is, however, inevitably not as ideal as having the witness physically present in court. Its convenience should not therefore be allowed to dictate its use. Consideration should be given in each case as to whether its use is likely to be beneficial to the efficient, fair and economic disposal of the proceedings.

3. For VC purposes, the location at which the judge sits is referred to as the 'local site'. The local site may be either a courtroom with VC equipment either permanently or temporarily installed, or another venue such as a studio or conference room set-up for VC. The other site or sites to and from which transmission is made are referred to as 'the remote site'.

Preliminary arrangements

4. The court's permission is required for any part of any proceedings to be dealt with by means of VC. Before seeking a direction, the applicant should notify the appropriate court officer of the intention to seek it, and should enquire as to the availability of the court's VC equipment for the duration of the proposed VC. The application for a direction should be made to the court by filing a COP9 application notice in accordance with the Part 10 procedure.

5. If a witness at a remote site is to give evidence by an interpreter, consideration should be given at this stage as to whether the interpreter should be at the local site or the remote site.

6. Where the VC process is to be used to take evidence from a person in a foreign jurisdiction, the parties should consider whether that is permissible under local law.

7. If a VC direction is given, arrangements for the transmission will then need to be made. The court will ordinarily direct that the party seeking permission to use VC is to be responsible for this. That party is hereafter referred to as 'the VC arranging party'.

VC arranging party's responsibilities

8. The VC arranging party must contact the appropriate court officer and make arrangements for the VC transmission.

9. The court has established procedures with Her Majesty's Court Service that enables the witness's nearest local court with VC facilities to be used as the remote site. The VC arranging party must advise the court whether the party wishes to make use of local court facilities for the remote site.

10. If the party is unable to make use of local court VC facilities, then the VC arranging party is responsible for arranging an alternative remote site. This may consist of a solicitor's office or a commercial VC facility, and in some circumstances may require portable VC equipment to be brought to the witness. Details of the

remote site, and of the equipment to be used, together with all necessary contact names and telephone numbers, will have to be provided to the court.

11. The VC arranging party must arrange for recording equipment to be provided by the court so that the evidence can be recorded. A court officer will normally be present to operate the recording equipment when the local site is a courtroom. The equipment should be set up and tested before the VC transmission.

12. In rare instances, it may be necessary for the local site to be somewhere other than the courtroom (or other VC facility onsite at the court). If this is the case, the VC arranging party should ensure:

    (a)   that arrangements are made, if practicable, for the royal coat of arms to be placed above the judge's seat at the alternate venue;

    (b)   that the number of microphones is adequate for the speakers;

    (c)   that the panning of the camera for the practitioners' table encompasses all legal representatives so that the viewer can see everyone seated there; and

    (d)   that a court officer is present to operate the recording equipment.

Court of Protection responsibilities

13. If the VC arranging party has advised that the party wishes to utilise local court facilities for the remote site, a court officer will contact the nearest local court (with VC facilities) to the witness and:

    (a)   agree and book a mutually convenient date and time for the attendance;

    (b)   advise the local court as to the number and details of those parties attending to give evidence by VC;

    (c)   confirm with the local court the reporting arrangements for the parties attending to give their evidence; and

    (d)   advise the parties by letter of the date, time and arrangements for attending the designated local court to give their evidence by VC.

14. Provided the local site is to be the courtroom (or other VC facility on-site at the court), a court officer will also:

    (a)   set-up the courtroom for the VC;

    (b)   establish the VC link with the remote site at the date and time that has been booked; and

    (c)   be available in order to deal with any technical problems during the transmission should they develop.

Local court responsibilities

15. The local court will advise the court staff (London or regional court as applicable) of the number to be called to establish the VC link with the remote site. Where the local court is utilising a third party networked VC service (such as the *Martin Dawes* service utilised by the closed nation-wide prison network), it will be responsible for arranging a bridging link for the date and time agreed.

16. The local court will make arrangements to meet the witness on their arrival at the court, escort them to the room where they are to give evidence by VC, switch on the VC equipment and ensure a link is established with the local site.

The hearing

17. Those involved with VC need to be aware that due to varying technology standards, there may be delays between the receipt of the picture and that of the accompanying sound. If due allowance is not made for this, there may be a tendency to 'speak over' the witness, whose voice will continue to be heard for a short period after he or she appears on the screen to have finished speaking.

18. Picture quality may also vary, and is generally enhanced if those appearing on VC monitors keep their movements to a minimum.

19. It is recommended that the practitioners and witness should arrive at their respective VC sites about 20 minutes prior to the scheduled commencement of the transmission.

20. Consideration will need to be given in advance to any documents to which the witness is likely to be referred. The parties should endeavour to agree on this. It will usually be most convenient for a bundle of the copy documents to be prepared in advance, which the VC arranging party should then send to the remote site.

21. Additional documents are sometimes quite properly introduced during the course of a witness's evidence. To cater for this, the VC arranging party should ensure that equipment is available to enable documents to be transmitted between sites during the course of the VC transmission. The procedure for conducting the transmission will be determined by the judge. The judge will also determine who is to control the cameras.

22. At the beginning of the transmission, the judge may wish to give directions as to the seating arrangements at the remote site so that those present are visible at the local site during the taking of the evidence.

23. The examination of the witness at the remote site should then follow as closely as possible the practice adopted when a witness is in the courtroom. During examination, cross-examination and re-examination, the witness must be able to see the legal representative asking the question and also any other person (whether another legal representative or the judge) making any statements in regard to the witness's evidence. It will in practice be most convenient if everyone remains seated throughout the transmission.

PART IV

Practice Direction B – Depositions (PD14B)

This practice direction supplements Part 14 of the Court of Protection Rules 2007

Depositions to be taken in England and Wales

1. A party may apply for an order for a person to be examined on oath before:

    (a)   a judge;

    (b)   an examiner of the court; or

    (c)   such other person as the court may appoint.[58]

2. The party who obtains an order for the examination of a deponent before an examiner of the court must:

    (a)   apply to the court for the allocation of an examiner;

    (b)   when allocated, provide the examiner with copies of all documents in the proceedings necessary to inform the examiner of the issues; and

    (c)   pay the deponent a sum to cover his travelling expenses to and from the examination and compensation for his loss of time.

3. In ensuring that the deponent's evidence is recorded in full, the court or the examiner may permit it to be recorded in full on audiotape or videotape, but the deposition must always be recorded in writing by the examiner or by a competent shorthand writer or stenographer.

4. If the deposition is not recorded word for word, it must contain, as nearly as may be, the statement of the deponent. The examiner may record word for word any particular questions or answers which appear to him to have special importance.

5. If a deponent objects to answering any question or where any objection is taken to any question, the examiner must:

    (a)   record in the deposition or a document attached to it:

        (i)   the question,

        (ii)   the nature of and grounds for the objection, and

        (iii)   any answer given; and

    (b)   give his opinion as to the validity of the objection and must record it in the deposition or a document attached to it.

6. Documents and exhibits must:

    (a)   have an identifying number or letter marked on them by the examiner; and

    (b)   be preserved by the party or his legal representative who obtained the order for the examination, or as the court or the examiner may direct.

7. The examiner may put any question to the deponent as to:

    (a)   the meaning of any of his answers; or

    (b)   any matter arising in the course of the examination.

8. Where a deponent:

    (a)   fails to attend the examination; or

    (b)   refuses to:

        (i)   be sworn, or

        (ii)   answer any lawful question, or

        (iii)   produce any document,

---

[58]   Rule 108.

the examiner will sign a certificate of such failure or refusal and may include in his certificate any comment as to the conduct of the deponent or of any person attending the examination.

9. The party who obtained the order for the examination must file the certificate with the court and may apply for an order that the deponent attend for examination or such other order as he considers appropriate.[59] The application must be made by filing a COP9 application notice, and may be made without notice.

10. The court will make such order on the application as it thinks fit including an order for the deponent to pay any costs resulting from his failure or refusal.

11. A deponent who wilfully refuses to obey an order made against him under Part 14 may be proceeded against for contempt of court.[60]

12. A deposition must:

    (a)   be signed by the examiner;

    (b)   have any amendments to it initialled by the examiner and the deponent; and

    (c)   be endorsed by the examiner with:

        (i)   a statement of the time occupied by the examination, and

        (ii) a record of any refusal by the deponent to sign the deposition and of his reasons for not doing so, and

        (iii) be sent by the examiner to the court where the proceedings are taking place for filing on the court file.

13. Rule 110 deals with the fees and expenses of the examiner.

Travelling expenses and compensation for loss of time

14. When a deponent is served with an order for examination he must be offered a sum to cover his travelling expenses to and from the examination and compensation for his loss of time.[61]

15. The sum referred to in paragraph 14 is to be based on the sums payable to witnesses attending the Crown Court.[62]

Depositions to be taken abroad for use as evidence in proceedings before courts in England and Wales (where the Taking of Evidence Regulation does not apply)

16. Where a party wishes to take a deposition from a person outside the jurisdiction, the court may order the issue of a letter of request to the judicial authorities of the country in which the proposed deponent is.[63]

17. An application for an order referred to in paragraph 16 should be made by filing a COP9 application notice in accordance with Part 10. The documents which a party applying for an order for the issue of a letter of request must file with his application notice are set out in rule 116.

---

[59]   Rule 112.

[60]   Rules 185–194.

[61]   Rule 108(6).

[62]   These sums are fixed pursuant to the Prosecution of Offenders Act 1985 and the Costs in Criminal Cases (General) Regulations 1986.

[63]   Rule 116.

18. In addition, the party applying for the order must file a draft order.

19. The application will be dealt with by the Senior Judge or his nominee who will, if appropriate, sign the letter of request.

20. If parties are in doubt as to whether a translation under rule 116(7) is required, they should seek guidance from the court office.

21. A special examiner appointed under rule 116(4) may be the British Consul or the Consul-General or his deputy in the country where the evidence is to be taken if:

    (a)   there is in respect of that country a Civil Procedure Convention providing for the taking of evidence in that country for the assistance of proceedings in the High Court or other court in this country; or

    (b)   with the consent of the Secretary of State.

22. The provisions of paragraphs 1 to 12 above apply to the depositions referred to in paragraphs 16 to 22.

Taking of evidence between EU Member States

Taking of Evidence Regulation

23. Where evidence is to be taken:

    (a)   from a person in another Member State of the European Union for use as evidence in proceedings before courts in England and Wales; or

    (b)   from a person in England and Wales for use as evidence in proceedings before a court in another Member State,

Council Regulation (EC) No 1206/2001 of 28 May 2001 on co-operation between the courts of the Member States in the taking of evidence in civil or commercial matters ('the Taking of Evidence Regulation') applies.

24. The website link to the Taking of Evidence Regulation is annexed to this practice direction as Annex B.

25. The Taking of Evidence Regulation does not apply to Denmark. In relation to Denmark, therefore, rule 116 will continue to apply.

(Article 21(1) of the Taking of Evidence Regulation provides that the Regulation prevails over other provisions contained in bilateral or multilateral agreements or arrangements concluded by the Member States and in particular the Hague Convention of 1 March 1954 on Civil Procedure and the Hague Convention of 18 March 1970 on the Taking of Evidence Abroad in Civil or Commercial Matters.)

Meaning of 'designated court'

26. In accordance with the Taking of Evidence Regulation, each Regulation State has prepared a list of courts competent to take evidence in accordance with the Regulation indicating the territorial and, where appropriate, special jurisdiction of those courts.

27. Where rule 115 refers to a 'designated court' in relation to another Regulation State, the reference is to the court, referred to in the list of competent courts of that State, which is appropriate to the application in hand.

Evidence to be taken in another Regulation State for use in England and Wales

28. Where a person wishes to take a deposition from a person in another Regulation State, the court where the proceedings are taking place may order the issue of a request as is prescribed as Form A in the Taking of Evidence Regulation.

29. An application to the court for an order under rule 115 should be made by filing a COP9 application notice in accordance with Part 10.

30. Rule 115 provides that the party applying for the order must file a draft form of request in the prescribed form. Where completion of the form requires attachments or documents to accompany the form, these must also be filed.

31. If the court grants an order under rule 115, it will send the form of request directly to the designated court.

32. Where the taking of evidence requires the use of an expert, the designated court may require a deposit in advance towards the costs of that expert. Subject to any final order in relation to costs, the party who obtained the order is responsible for the payment of any such deposit which should be deposited with the court for onward transmission. Under the provisions of the Taking of Evidence Regulation, the designated court is not required to execute the request until such payment is received.

33. Article 17 permits the court where proceedings are taking place to take evidence directly from a deponent in another Regulation State if the conditions of the article are satisfied. Direct taking of evidence can only take place if evidence is given voluntarily without the need for coercive measures. Rule 115 provides for the court to make an order for the submission of a request to take evidence directly. The form of request is Form I annexed to the Taking of Evidence Regulation and rule 115 makes provision for a draft of this form to be filed by the party seeking the order. An application for an order under rule 115 should be by filing a COP9 application notice in accordance with Part 10.

Annex A

Draft letter of request (where the Taking of Evidence Regulation does not apply)

To the Competent Judicial Authority of   in   the   of

I [*name*] Senior Judge of the Court of Protection of England and Wales respectfully request the assistance of your court with regard to the following matters.

1. An application is now pending in the   Court of Protection in England and Wales entitled as follows [*set out full title and case number*] in which [*name*] of [*address*] is the applicant and [*name*] of [*address*] is the respondent.

2. The names and addresses of the representatives or agents of [*set out names and addresses of representatives of the parties*].

3. The application by the applicant is for:
   (a)   [set out the nature of the application]
   (b)   [the order sought, and]
   (c)   [a summary of the facts.]

4. It is necessary for the purposes of justice and for the due determination of the matter in dispute between the parties that you cause the following witnesses, who are resident within your jurisdiction, to be examined. The names and addresses of the witnesses are as follows: [*set out names and addresses of witnesses*]

5. The witnesses should be examined on oath or if that is not possible within your laws or is impossible of performance by reason of the internal practice and procedure of your court or by reason of practical difficulties, they should be examined in accordance with whatever procedure your laws provide for in these matters.

6. Either

The witness should be examined in accordance with the list of questions annexed hereto.

Or

The witness should be examined regarding [*set out full details of evidence sought*].

N.B. Where the witness is required to produce documents, these should be clearly identified.

7. I would ask that you cause me, or the agents of the parties (if appointed), to be informed of the date and place where the examination is to take place.

8. Finally, I request that you will cause the evidence of the said witness to be reduced into writing and all documents produced on such examinations to be duly marked for identification and that you will further be pleased to authenticate such examinations by the seal of your court or in such other way as is in accordance with your procedure and return the written evidence and documents produced to me addressed as follows:

Senior Judge of the Court of Protection
Archway Tower
2 Junction Road
London N195SZ
England

Annex B

Council Regulation (EC) NO 1206/2001

This regulation can be found at: www.justice.gov.uk/civil/procrules_fin/contents/form_section_images/practice_directions/pd34_pdf_tif_gif/pd34_cr_1206_2001.pdf

Practice Direction C – Fees for examiners of the court (PD14C)

This practice direction supplements Part 14 of the Court of Protection Rules 2007

General

1. This practice direction sets out:

(a) how to calculate the fees an examiner of the court ('an examiner') may charge; and

(b) the expenses he may recover.

(Rule 108 provides that the court may make an order for evidence to be obtained by the examination of a witness before an examiner.)

2. Subject to any final order or direction of the court in relation to costs, the party who obtained the order for the examination must pay the fees and expenses of the examiner.

(Rule 110 permits an examiner to charge a fee for the examination and contains other provisions about his fees and expenses, and rule 111 provides who may be appointed as an examiner.)

The examination fee

3. An examiner may charge an hourly rate for each hour (or part of an hour) that he is engaged in examining the witness.

4. The hourly rate is to be calculated by reference to the formula set out in paragraph 6.

5. The examination fee will be the hourly rate multiplied by the number of hours the examination has taken. That is:

Examination fee = hourly rate x number of hours.

How to calculate the hourly rate – the formula

6. Divide the amount of the minimum annual salary of a post within Group 7 of the judicial salary structure as designated by the Review Body on Senior Salaries,[64] by 220 to give 'x'; and then divide 'x' by **6** to give **the hourly rate**.

That is:

$$\frac{\text{Minimum annual salary}}{220} = \text{x}$$

$$\frac{\text{x}}{6} = \text{hourly rate}$$

---

[64]   The Report of the Review Body on Senior Salaries is published annually by the Stationery Office.

PART IV

Single fee chargeable on making the appointment for examination

7. An examiner is also entitled to charge a single fee of twice the hourly rate (calculated in accordance with paragraph 6 above) as 'the appointment fee' when the appointment for the examination is made.

8. The examiner is entitled to retain the appointment fee where the witness fails to attend on the date and time arranged.

9. Where the examiner fails to attend on the date and time arranged he may not charge a further appointment fee for arranging a subsequent appointment.

(The examiner need not send the deposition to the court until his fees are paid, unless the court directs otherwise – see rule 110(1).)

Examiner's expenses

10. An examiner is also entitled to recover the following expenses –

  (a) all reasonable travelling expenses;
  (b) any other expenses reasonably incurred; and
  (c) subject to paragraph 11, any reasonable charge for the room where the examination takes place.

11. No expenses may be recovered under sub-paragraph 10(c) if the examination takes place at the examiner's usual business address.

(If the examiner's fees and expenses are not paid within a reasonable time he may report the fact to the court – see rule 110(3).)

Practice Direction D – Witness summons (PD14D)

This practice direction supplements Part 14 of the Court of Protection Rules 2007

Issue of a witness summons

1. Rule 106 makes provision as to the taking out of a witness summons.

2. A witness summons may require a witness to:

    (a)   attend court to give evidence;

    (b)   produce documents to the court; or

    (c)   both (a) and (b),

on either a date fixed for a hearing or such date as the court may direct.

3. An application for a witness summons should be made by filing a COP9 application notice in accordance with the Part 10 procedure.

4. In the event the court grants the application, the witness summons will be prepared by the court.

5. A mistake in the name or address of a person named in the witness summons may be corrected if the summons has not been served.

6. If the mistake is a result of an error in the original application notice, an application to correct the mistake should be made by filing a further COP9 application notice in accordance with the Part 10 procedure. The application notice should set out the corrections that need to be made to the witness summons.

7. If the mistake is a result of a clerical mistake, the person taking out the summons should write to the court advising them of the mistake and seeking an amendment under rule 23 (clerical mistakes or slips).

8. The corrected summons must be re-sealed by the court and marked 'Amended and Re-sealed'.

Travelling expenses and compensation for loss of time

9. When a witness is served with a witness summons he must be offered a sum to cover his travelling expenses to and from the court and compensation for his loss of time.[65]

10. The sum referred to in paragraph 9 is to be based on the sums payable to witnesses attending the Crown Court.[66]

11. In addition, the witness must be paid such general or other costs as the court may allow.[67]

---

[65]   Rule 106(6)(a) and (b).

[66]   These sums are fixed pursuant to the Prosecution of Offenders Act 1985 and the Costs in Criminal Cases (General) Regulations 1986.

[67]   Rule 106(7).

PART IV

Practice Direction E – Section 49 reports (PD14E)

This practice direction supplements Part 14 of the Court of Protection Rules 2007

General

1. Attention is drawn to:

   (a) section 49 of the Act – which makes provision for the court to require a report dealing with such matters relating to P as the court may direct;

   (b) rule 85(2)(a) – which provides that the court, when giving directions, may require a section 49 report and give directions about any such report;

   (c) rule 117 – which sets out the duties of a person required to prepare a section 49 report and specifies to whom the report may be sent; and

   (d) rule 118 – which makes provision for the court to permit written questions to be put to a person who has made a section 49 report.

The court's direction for a report

2. The Annex to this practice direction contains the form of an order requiring a report under section 49 of the Act and the forms of directions relating to the report. When requiring a section 49 report, the court will as far as possible base its order and directions on those forms.

Reports by Public Guardian or a Court of Protection Visitor

3. Where a report is to be prepared by either the Public Guardian or a Court of Protection Visitor,[68] a copy of the order and the directions will be sent to the Public Guardian.

4. In the case of a report which is to be made by a Court of Protection Visitor, the Public Guardian must ensure that:

   (a) a person is nominated from the panel of General Visitors or the panel of Special Visitors, as appropriate; and

   (b) the court is notified of his name and contact details as soon as practicable.

5. The nomination of a Court of Protection Visitor should be made before the end of the period of 7 days beginning with the date on which the Public Guardian received a copy of the order.

Reports under arrangements made by a local authority or an NHS body

6. Where a report is to be prepared under arrangements made by a local authority or an NHS body,[69] a copy of the order and the directions will be sent to a senior officer of that authority or body. That person must ensure that:

   (a) an appropriate person is nominated to make the report; and

   (b) the court is notified of his name and contact details as soon as practicable.

---

[68]   See s 49(2) of the Act.
[69]   See s 49(3) of the Act.

7. The nomination should be made before the end of the period of 7 days beginning with the date on which the senior office of that local authority or NHS body received a copy of the order.

Access to information

8. The court will generally provide to the person who is to produce a report:

   (a)   a copy of the application form and any annexes to it;
   (b)   the name and contact details of P;
   (c)   the name and contact details of the parties; and
   (d)   the name and contact details of any legal representative of a person specified in (b) or (c).

9. The court order requiring the report, the directions relating to it and the information described in paragraph 8 will generally be sent by first class mail or by facsimile. If the circumstances warrant a different form of communication, the documents and information will also be sent by first class mail or by facsimile at the first available opportunity.

10. Section 49(7) of the Act sets out other documents relating to P which the Public Guardian or a Court of Protection Visitor may examine or of which he may take copies for the purpose of making the report.

The contents of the report

11. The person required to prepare a section 49 report must:

   (a)   prepare it having regard to the provisions of rule 117;
   (b)   produce it in the manner specified in this practice direction (subject to any directions given by the court); and
   (c)   produce it in accordance with the timetable set out in the court's directions.

12. The report should contain four main sections. These are:

   (a)   the details of the person who prepared the report;
   (b)   the details of P;
   (c)   the matters and material considered in preparing the report; and
   (d)   the conclusions reached.

13. In the first section (details of the person who prepared the report), the report should:

   (a)   state the full name of the person who prepared the report;
   (b)   state whether he was appointed under section 49(2) or (3) of the Act;
   (c)   state whether he is:
         (i)   the Public Guardian,
         (ii)   a General Visitor,
         (iii) a Special Visitor,
         (iv)   an officer, employee or other person nominated by a local authority, or
         (v)   an officer, employee or other person nominated by an NHS body;
   (d)   state his occupation or employment (for example, social worker employed by a local authority or general practitioner in private practice); and
   (e)   list his qualifications and experience.

14. In the second section (P's details), the report should (unless an order to the contrary pursuant to rule 19 has been made):

(a)   state P's full name, date of birth and present place of residence;

(b)   state P's nationality, racial origin, cultural background and religious persuasion (if appropriate);

(c)   identify P's immediate family (specifying their relationship to P and contact details);

(d)   identify any other person who has a significant role in P's life (for example, a close friend or a carer) specifying their role and contact details; and

(e)   give a summary of P's medical history.

15. In the third section (matters and material considered), the report should:

(a)   list any interview conducted with P (specifying time and place);[70]

(b)   list any interview conducted with one or more persons other than P (specifying time and place);[71]

(c)   state:

   (i)   whether any examination of P was conducted by a Special Visitor under section 49(9) of the Act, and

   (ii)   the name and qualifications of any person who assisted with any such examination;

(d)   give a summary of any key events in P's life which appear to have a direct bearing on the matters to be dealt with in the report;

(e)   set out the details of any of the following material which was relied on in the preparation of the report:

   (i)   any literature or other material,

   (ii)   any records obtained under section 49(7) of the Act;

(f)   set out the details of facts and opinions relied on in the preparation of the report (ensuring that there is a clear distinction between the two);

(g)   where there is a range of opinion on an issue addressed in the report:

   (i)   summarise the range of opinion,

   (ii)   state the views held by the person who prepared the report and give reasons for them, and

   (iii) if those views are qualified in any way, state the nature of the qualification; and

(h)   indicate which of the facts are within the knowledge of the person who prepared the report.

16. In the fourth section (conclusions), the report should:

(a)   identify any issues or questions which were specified in the directions given by the court as being matters in which the court had a particular interest;

(b)   address clearly such issues or questions;

(c)   state clearly all conclusions reached by the person who prepared the report;

(d)   state clearly the recommendations made by the person who prepared the report; and

(e)   contain a statement of truth in the following terms:

---

[70]   The person preparing the report should ensure that he keeps any notes made during the interview with P, so that the notes are available for production to the court if necessary.

[71]   The person preparing the report should ensure that he keeps any notes made during the interview with an person other than P, so that the notes are available for production to the court if necessary.

'I confirm that insofar as the facts stated in my report are within my own knowledge I have made clear which they are, and I believe them to be true, and that the opinions I have expressed represent my true and complete professional opinion.'

Annex

Order for section 49 report

Requirement for section 49 report

1. That in relation to case number [*insert case number*] a report is required under section 49 of the Mental Capacity Act 2005 in relation to [*insert name of P*].

Person required to prepare the report

2. The report must be prepared by [the Public Guardian] [a Court of Protection Visitor who is a General Visitor] [a Court of Protection Visitor who is a Special Visitor] [a person nominated by a local authority] [a person nominated by an NHS body].

3. [In the case of a report to be prepared by a Special Visitor, the Visitor may carry out in private a [medical] [psychiatric] [psychological] examination of P's capacity or condition].

Producing the report

4. [The report must be made to the court in writing]. [The report must be made orally to the court].

5. The report must be produced on or before [*insert date*].

6. [Where the report is made in writing, it must be delivered to the court by [first class post] [facsimile] [.   ]]

Content of report

7. Subject to any directions given under the next paragraph, the report must contain all the material required by relevant practice direction and be prepared in the form there specified.

8. [The report need not address the following:

.   ]

9. [The court is particularly interested in the following issues or questions and these must also be addressed in the report:

.   ]

Persons to whom report is likely to be disclosed

10. At the time of ordering the report, it is the court's intention to disclose it under rule [117(4)] to [the parties only] [the parties and   ]

PART IV

Other directions
11. [   ].

Practice Direction – Experts

Practice Direction A – Expert evidence (PD15A)

This practice direction supplements Part 15 of the Court of Protection Rules 2007

General

1. Part 15 is intended to limit the use of expert evidence to that which is reasonably required. In addition, where possible, matters requiring expert evidence should be dealt with by a single expert. After a permission form or an application form is issued, no person may file expert evidence unless the court or a practice direction permits.[72]

Expert evidence – general requirements

2. It is the duty of an expert to help the court on matters within his own expertise.[73]

3. Expert evidence should be the independent product of the expert uninfluenced by the pressures of the proceedings.

4. An expert should assist the court by providing objective, unbiased opinion on matters within his expertise, and should not assume the role of an advocate.

5. An expert should consider all material facts, including those which might detract from his opinion.

6. An expert should make it clear:

    (a)   when a question or issue falls outside his expertise; and

    (b)   when he is not able to reach a definite opinion, for example because he has insufficient information.

7. If, after producing a report, an expert changes his view on any material matter, such change of view should be communicated to all the parties without delay, and when appropriate to the court.

Form and content of expert's report

8. An expert's report should be addressed to the court and not to the party from whom the expert has received his instructions.

9. An expert's report must:

    (a)   give details of the expert's qualifications;

    (b)   give details of any literature or other material which the expert has relied on in making the report;

    (c)   contain a statement setting out the substance of all facts and instructions given to the expert which are material to the opinions expressed in the report or upon which those opinions are based (or annex the instructions insofar as they are in writing);

---

[72]   Rule 120.
[73]   Rule 122.

    (d)   make clear which of the facts stated in the report are within the expert's own knowledge;

    (e)   say who carried out any examination, measurement, test or experiment which the expert has used for the report, give the qualifications of that person, and say whether or not the test or experiment has been carried out under the expert's supervision;

    (f)   where there is a range of opinion on the matters dealt with in the report–
        (i)   summarise the range of opinion, and
        (ii) give reasons for his own opinion;

    (g)   contain a summary of the conclusions reached;

    (h)   if the expert is not able to give his opinion without qualification, state the qualification; and

    (i)   contain a statement that the expert understands his duty to the court, and has complied and will continue to comply with that duty.

10. An expert's report must be verified by a statement of truth as well as containing the statements required in paragraph 9(h) and (i) above.

11. The form of the statement of truth is as follows:

> 'I confirm that insofar as the facts stated in my report are within my own knowledge I have made clear which they are and I believe them to be true and that the opinions I have expressed represent my true and complete professional opinion.'

12. Attention is drawn to rule 14 which sets out the consequences of verifying a document containing a false statement without an honest belief in its truth.

(Practice direction B accompanying Part 4 sets out more detailed requirements for statements of truth.)

Questions to experts

13. Questions asked for the purpose of clarifying the expert's report should be put, in writing, to the expert not later than 28 days after service of the expert's report.[74]

14. Where a party sends a written question or questions direct to an expert, a copy of the questions should, at the same time, be sent to the other party or parties.

Orders

15. Where an order requires an act to be done by an expert, or otherwise affects an expert, the party instructing that expert must serve a copy of the order on the expert instructed by him. In the case of a jointly instructed expert, the applicant must serve the order.

---

[74]   Rule 125.

Practice Direction – Litigation friend

Practice Direction A – Litigation friend (PD17A)

This practice direction supplements Part 17 of the Court of Protection Rules 2007

General

1. Part 17 contains rules about the appointment of a litigation friend to conduct proceedings on behalf of P, a child, or a protected party.[75] This practice direction is made under rule 149 and provides guidance in relation to the appointment and removal of a litigation friend pursuant to Part 17.

2. Rule 140 provides that a litigation friend may be appointed for:

    (a) P;

    (b) a child; or

    (c) a protected party.

3. Where:

    (a) P has a litigation friend, P should be referred to in the proceedings as 'P (by A.B., his litigation friend)';

    (b) the protected party has a litigation friend, he should be referred to in the proceedings as 'E.F. (by A.B., his litigation friend)';

    (c) a child has a litigation friend, the child should be referred to in the proceedings as 'C.D. (a child by A.B., his litigation friend)'; and

    (d) a child is conducting proceedings on his own behalf, the child should be referred to in the proceedings as 'A.B. (a child)'.

Litigation friend without a court order

4. Rule 142 makes provision for the appointment of a litigation friend without a court order. The rule does not apply:

    (a) in relation to P;

    (b) where the court has appointed a litigation friend; or

    (c) where the Official Solicitor is to act as litigation friend.

Deputy as a litigation friend

5. Rule 142(2) provides that where there is a deputy appointed with power to conduct legal proceedings in the name of the protected party or on the protected party's behalf, that deputy is entitled to be a litigation friend of the protected party in any proceedings to which the deputy's power relates. To be a litigation friend the deputy must file and serve a copy of the court order which appointed him on:

    (a) every person on whom an application form in relation to a protected party must be served in accordance with rule 32; and

    (b) every other person who is a party to the proceedings.

---

[75]   'Protected party' means a party, or an intended party (other than P or a child) who lacks capacity to conduct the proceedings.

Litigation friend where there is no deputy

6. A person who wishes to become a litigation friend without a court order pursuant to rule 142 must file a certificate of suitability using form COP22.

7. In addition to the matters listed in rule 140(1), the certificate of suitability referred to in rule 142(3) which the litigation friend files must also:

    (a)   state that he consents to act;

    (b)   state that he knows or believes that the child or the protected party lacks capacity to conduct the proceedings himself; and

    (c)   state the grounds of his belief and, if his belief is based upon medical opinion, or the opinion of another suitably qualified expert, attach any relevant document to the certificate.

8. The certificate of suitability must contain a statement of truth.

9. The litigation friend must serve the certificate of suitability on:

    (a)   every person on whom an application form must be served in accordance with rule 32; and

    (b)   every other person who is a party to the proceedings.

10. The litigation friend is not required to serve the document referred to in paragraph 7(c) when he serves a certificate of suitability under paragraph 9 (unless the court directs otherwise).

11. The litigation friend must file the certificate of suitability together with a certificate of service of it when he first takes a step in the proceedings.

Litigation friend by court order

12. Rule 143 sets out when and how the court may appoint a litigation friend, either on application or on its own initiative.

13. An application for an order appointing a litigation friend must be made by filing a COP9 application notice in accordance with the Part 10 procedure. The application must be supported by evidence, as required by rule 143(3).

14. The evidence in support must satisfy the court that the proposed litigation friend:

    (a)   consents to act;

    (b)   can fairly and competently conduct proceedings on behalf of P, the child, or the protected party; and

    (c)   has no interest adverse to that of P, the child, or the protected party.

Change of litigation friend and prevention of person acting as litigation friend

15. Rule 144(1) provides that the court may, on application or on its own initiative:

    (a)   direct that a person may not act as a litigation friend;

    (b)   terminate a litigation friend's appointment; or

    (c)   appoint a new litigation friend in place of an existing one.

16. An application made pursuant to rule 144 should be made by filing a COP9 application notice in accordance with the Part 10 procedure and must be supported by evidence.

17. If the order sought is the substitution of a new litigation friend for an existing one, the evidence must satisfy the court of the matters set out in paragraph 14.

Procedure where the need for a litigation friend has come to an end

18. Rules 146, 147 and 148 make provision for where the need for a litigation friend comes to an end during the proceedings.

19. Where a child having reached full age files a notice under rule 146(6) and the notice states that the child intends to carry on with or continue to participate in the proceedings he shall subsequently be described in the proceedings as:

'A.B. (formerly a child but now of full age).'

20. Where an application is made under rule 146 or 147 the application must be supported by evidence that P or the protected party now has capacity to conduct the proceedings in question.

21. Where an application is made under rule 148 the application must be supported by evidence that P now has capacity in relation to the matter or matters to which the proceedings relate.

Costs

22. Rule 166 allows the court to make an order against a person who is not a party to proceedings (including a litigation friend).

Practice Direction – Change of solicitor

Practice Direction A – Change of solicitor (PD18A)

This practice direction supplements Part 18 of the Court of Protection Rules 2007

General

1. Part 18 contains rules about a change of solicitor. This practice direction is made under rule 154 and specifies the forms and procedures to be used in relation to a change of solicitor in specified circumstances.

Where COP30 form should be used

2. A COP30 form should be used where a party to proceedings:

  (a) for whom a solicitor is acting, wishes to change his solicitor, or intends to act in person; or
  (b) having conducted the proceedings in person, appoints a solicitor to act on his behalf (this requirement does not apply where a solicitor is appointed only to act as an advocate for a hearing).

Where COP9 form should be used

3. A COP9 form should be used where:

  (a) a solicitor applies for an order declaring that he has ceased to be the solicitor acting for a party; or
  (b) another party applies for an order declaring that the solicitor has ceased to be the solicitor acting for another party in the proceedings.

Practice Direction – Costs

Practice Direction A – Costs in the Court of Protection (PD19A)

This practice direction supplements Part 19 of the Court of Protection Rules 2007

Modifications to the Civil Procedure Rules 1998

1. The practice direction supplementing Parts 43 to 48 of the Civil Procedure Rules 1998 ('the CPR Practice Direction') applies, insofar as those Parts apply to proceedings in the Court of Protection, with such modifications as are appropriate together with the modifications specified in this practice direction.

2. The following paragraphs of the CPR Practice Direction do not apply:

6.4(1); 8.1 to 8.4; 13.2(1); 13.3; 13.4; 13.7(2); 13.11; 13.13(a); 15 to 17; 23.2A; 24 to 27; 28.1(2); 31; 49A; 50; and 51.

3. In paragraphs 2.5 and 28.1(3) of the CPR Practice Direction, the words 'or the parties may agree in writing' are removed.

4. In paragraph 13.5(4) of the CPR Practice Direction, the words 'any party against whom an order for payment of those costs is intended to be sought' are replaced with 'all parties to the proceedings and any other person that the court may direct.'

5. In paragraph 19.2(1) of the CPR Practice Direction, the words 'application form,' are inserted after 'includes'.

6. In paragraph 19.2(3)(b) of the CPR Practice Direction, the second and third sentences are removed.

7. In paragraph 19.3(3) of the CPR Practice Direction, the words 'of the Court of Protection Rules 2007' are inserted after 'Part 6'.

8. In paragraph 21.19A of the CPR Practice Direction, the words 'High Court or Country Court' are removed and replaced with 'Court of Protection'.

9. The reference in paragraph 23.2 of the CPR Practice Direction to district registry or county court shall be read, in proceedings to which this Practice Direction applies, as a reference to the registry of the Court of Protection.

10. In paragraph 23.18 of the CPR Practice Direction, the words 'CPR Part 52 and CPR rule 47.20' are removed and replaced with 'Part 20 of the Court of Protection Rules'.

11. The following paragraphs of the CPR Practice Direction are to be read as if the references in those paragraphs to a district judge were removed. –

20.3(1); 21.19A; 22.1; 28.1(4)(a); 28.1(5); 30.1(3); 30.1(4); 36.3; 37.6(1); 38.1(2); and 38.3(2).

12. In paragraph 33.1 of the CPR Practice Direction the words 'under rule 2.11' are removed.

13. In paragraph 33.2 of the CPR Practice Direction, the words 'for an order under rule 3.1(2)(a)' are removed; and the words 'that time' are removed and the following words are substituted: 'the time specified by rule 47.7 for commencing the detailed assessment proceedings'.

PART IV

14. Paragraph 35.1 of the CPR Practice Direction is replaced with the following: 'A party may apply to the appropriate officer for an order to shorten or extend the time for service of points of dispute'.

15. In paragraph 37.4 of the CPR Practice Direction, the words 'Rules 40.3' to 'default costs certificate' are replaced with the words 'rule 30 of the Court of Protection Rules 2007, which applies to the service of court orders'.

16. In paragraph 38.1(1) of the CPR Practice Direction, the words 'court officer' are replaced with 'authorised court officer'.

17. In rule 38.3(1) of the CPR Practice Direction, the following words are removed: 'rule 3.1(3) (which enables the court when making an order to make it subject to conditions) and to'.

18. In paragraphs 30.1(4), 36.2, 41.1(1), 42.6, 53.3, 53.7 and 53.8 of the CPR Practice Direction, the words 'Part 23 (General Rules about Applications for Court Orders)' are removed and replaced with 'Part 10 (Applications within proceedings)'.

19. References in the CPR Practice Direction to 'claimant' and 'defendant' shall be read, in proceedings to which this Practice Direction applies, to 'applicant' and 'respondent' respectively.

Other provisions

20. The appropriate venue for detailed assessment of costs proceedings is the Supreme Court Costs Office, Clifford's Inn, Fetter Lane, London EC4A 1DQ.

Practice Direction – Fixed Costs

Practice Direction B – Fixed costs in the Court of Protection (PD19B)

This practice direction supplements Part 19 of the Court of Protection Rules 2007 (PD19B)

General

1. This practice direction sets out the fixed costs that may be claimed by solicitors and public authorities acting in Court of Protection proceedings and the fixed amounts of remuneration that may be claimed by solicitors and office holders in public authorities appointed to act as a deputy for P. Rule 167 enables a practice direction to set out a schedule of fees to determine the amount of remuneration payable to deputies. Rule 168 enables a practice direction to make provision in respect of costs in proceedings.

2. The practice direction applies principally to solicitors or office holders in public authorities appointed to act as deputy. However, the court may direct that its provisions shall also apply to other professionals acting as deputy including accountants, case managers and not-for-profit organisations

3. This Practice Direction applies where the period covered by the category of fixed costs or remuneration ends on or after 1 February 2011. The Practice Direction supersedes the earlier Practice Directions and Practice Notes relating to fixed costs issued by the Court of Protection. However solicitors and office holders in public authorities should continue to claim the rates applicable in the previous Practice Directions and Practice Notes, where the period covered by the category of fixed costs or remuneration ended before1 February 2011.

When does this practice direction apply?

4. Rule 156 provides that, where the proceedings concern P's property and affairs, the general rule is that costs of the proceedings shall be paid by P or charged to his estate. The provisions of this practice direction apply where the professional or deputy is entitled to be paid costs out of P's estate. They do not apply where the court order provides for one party to receive costs from another.

Claims generally

5. The court order or direction will state whether fixed costs or remuneration applies, or whether there is to be a detailed assessment by a costs officer. Where a court order or direction provides for a detailed assessment of costs, professionals may elect to take fixed costs or remuneration in lieu of a detailed assessment.

Payments on account

6. Where professional deputies elect for detailed assessment of annual management charges, they may take payments on account for the first three quarters of the year, which are proportionate and reasonable taking into account the size of the estate and

the functions they have performed. Interim quarterly Bills must not exceed 20% of the estimated annual management charges – that is up to 60% for the whole year. Interim bills of account must not be submitted to the Senior Courts Costs Office. At the end of the annual management year, the deputy must submit their annual bill to the Senior Courts Costs Office for detailed assessment and adjust the final total due to reflect payments on account already received Solicitors' costs in court proceedings

7. The fixed costs are as follows:

		An amount not exceeding
Category I	Work up to and including the date upon which the court makes an order appointing a deputy for property and affairs.	£850 (plus VAT)
Category II	Applications under sections 36 (9) or 54 of the Trustee Act 1925 or section 20 of the Trusts of Land and Appointment of Trustees Act 1996 for the appointment of a new trustee in the place of 'P' and applications under section 18(1)(j) of the Mental Capacity Act 2005 for authority to exercise any power vested in P, whether beneficially, or as trustee, or otherwise	£385 (plus VAT)

8. The categories of fixed costs, above will apply as follows:

- Category I to all orders appointing a deputy for property and affairs made on or after 1 February 2011.
- Category II to all applications for the appointment of a new trustee made on or after 1 February 2011.

Remuneration of solicitors appointed as deputy for P

9. The following fixed rates of remuneration will apply where the court appoints a solicitor to act as deputy:

		An amount not exceeding
Category III	Annual management fee where the court appoints a professional deputy for property and affairs, payable on the anniversary of the court order	
	(a) for the first year:	£1,500 (plus VAT)

	(b) for the second and subsequent years:	£1,185 (plus VAT)
	Where the net assets* of P are below £16,000, the professional deputy for property and affairs may take an annual management fee not exceeding 4.5% of P's net assets* on the anniversary of the court order appointing the professional as deputy.	
Category IV	Where the court appoints a professional deputy for personal welfare, the deputy may take an annual management fee not exceeding 2.5% of P's net assets* on the anniversary of the court order appointing the professional as deputy for personal up to a maximum of £500.	
Category V	Preparation and lodgement of the annual report or annual account to the Public Guardian	£235 (plus VAT)
Category VI	Preparation of an HMRC income tax return on behalf of P	£235 (plus VAT)

PART IV

10. The categories of remuneration, above will apply as follows:

- Category III and IV to all annual management fees for anniversaries falling on or after 1 February 2011.
- Category V to reports or accounts lodged on or after 1 February 2011.
- Category VI to all HMRC returns made on or after 1 February 2011.

11. In cases where fixed costs are not appropriate, professionals may, if preferred, apply to the Supreme Court Costs Office for a detailed assessment of costs. However, this does not apply if P's net assets are below are £16,000 where the option for detailed assessment will only arise if the court makes a specific order for detailed assessment in relation to an estate with net assets of a value of less than £16,000.

12. Where the period for which an annual management fee claimed is less than one year, for example where the deputyship comes to an end before the anniversary of appointment, then the amount claimed must be the same proportion of the applicable fee as the period bears to one year.

Conveyancing costs

13. Where a deputy or other person authorised by the court is selling or purchasing a property on behalf of P, the following fixed rates will apply except where the sale or purchase is by trustees in which case, the costs should be agreed with the trustees:

Category VII	A value element of 0.15% of the consideration with a minimum sum of £350 and a maximum sum of £1,500, plus disbursements.

14. Category VII applies to any conveyancing transaction where contracts are exchanged on or after 1 February 2011.

Remuneration of public authority deputies

15. The following fixed rates of remuneration will apply where the court appoints a holder of an office in a public authority to act as deputy:

		An amount not exceeding
Category I	Work up to and including the date upon which the court makes an order appointing a deputy for property and affairs.	£670
Category II	Annual management fee where the court appoints a local authority deputy for property and affairs, payable on the anniversary of the court order	
	(a) for the first year:	£700
	(b) for the second and subsequent years:	£585
	(c) Where the net assets* of P are below £16,000, the local authority deputy for property and affairs may take an annual management fee not exceeding 3% of P's net assets on the anniversary of the court order appointing the local authority as deputy	

	(d) Where the court appoints a local authority deputy for personal welfare, the local authority may take an annual management fee not exceeding 2.5% of P's net assets* on the anniversary of the court order appointing the local authority as deputy for personal welfare up to a maximum of £500.	
Category III	Annual property management fee to include work involved in preparing property for sale, instructing agents, conveyancers, etc or the ongoing maintenance of property including management and letting of a rental property.	£270
Category IV	Preparation and lodgement of an annual report or account to the Public Guardian	£195

PART IV

16. The categories of remuneration, above will apply as follows:

- Category I to all orders appointing a deputy for property and affairs made on or after 1 February 2011.
- Category II to all annual management fees for anniversaries falling on or after 1 February 2011.
- Category III on the anniversary of appointment as deputy where the anniversary falls on or after 1 February 2011; or upon completion of the sale of a property, where the transaction was concluded on or after 1 February 2011.
- Category V to reports or accounts lodged on or after 1 February 2011.

17. Where the period for which the annual management fee ends before an anniversary, for example where the deputyship comes to an end before the anniversary of appointment, then the amount claimed must be the same proportion of the applicable fee as the period bears to one year.

Practice Direction – Solicitors' and other professionals' fixed costs

Practice Direction B – Fixed costs in the Court of Protection (PD19B)

Important note—This Practice Direction has been superceeded by the a new PD19 (reproduced above)), however, the rates in this previous version will apply to costs incurred prior to 1 February 2011 so it is reproduced here in italics.

This practice direction supplements Part 19 of the Court of Protection Rules 2007 (PD19B)

- *Solicitors' costs in court proceedings*
- *Remuneration of solicitors appointed as deputy for P*
- *Remuneration of public authority deputies*

General

1. This practice direction sets out the fixed costs that may be claimed by solicitors and public authorities acting in Court of Protection proceedings and the fixed amounts of remuneration that may be claimed by solicitors and office holders in public authorities appointed to act as a deputy for P. Rule 167 enables a practice direction to set out a schedule of fees to determine the amount of remuneration payable to deputies.

Rule 168 enables a practice direction to make provision in respect of costs in proceedings.

2. This Practice Direction applies where the period covered by the category of fixed costs or remuneration ends on or after 1 May 2009. The Practice Direction supersedes the earlier Practice Directions and Practice Notes relating to fixed costs issued by the Court of Protection. However solicitors and office holders in public authorities should continue to claim the rates applicable in the previous Practice Directions and Practice Notes, where the period covered by the category of fixed costs or remuneration ended before1 May 2009.

When does this practice direction apply?

3. Rule 156 provides that, where the proceedings concern P's property and affairs, the general rule is that costs of the proceedings shall be paid by P or charged to his estate. The provisions of this practice direction apply where the solicitor or deputy is entitled to be paid costs out of P's estate. They do not apply where the court order provides for one party to receive costs from another.

Claims by solicitors – generally

4. The court order or direction will state whether fixed costs or remuneration applies, or whether there is to be a detailed assessment by a costs officer. Where a court order or direction provides for a detailed assessment of costs, solicitors may elect to take fixed costs or remuneration in lieu of a detailed assessment.

Solicitors' costs in court proceedings

5. The fixed costs are as follows:

Category I

Work up to and including the date upon which the court makes an order appointing a deputy for property and affairs.

Amount £825 (plus VAT)

Category II

Applications under sections 36(9) or 54 of the Trustee Act 1925 or section 20 of the Trusts of Land and Appointment of Trustees Act 1996 for the appointment of a new trustee in the place of 'P' and applications under section 18(1)(j) of the Mental Capacity Act 2005 for authority to exercise any power vested in P, whether beneficially, or as trustee, or otherwise.

Amount £370 (plus VAT)

6. The categories of fixed costs above will apply as follows:

- *Category I to all orders appointing a deputy for property and affairs made on or after 1 May 2009.*
- *Category II to all applications for the appointment of a new trustee made on or after 1 May 2009.*

Remuneration of solicitors appointed as deputy for P

7. The following fixed rates of remuneration will apply where the court appoints a solicitor to act as deputy:

Category III

Annual management fee where the court appoints a professional deputy for property and affairs, payable on the anniversary of the court order

- *(a) For the first year: Amount £1,440 (plus VAT)*
- *(b) For the second and subsequent years: Amount £1,140 (plus VAT)*
  Provided that, where the net assets of P are below £16,000, the professional deputy for property and affairs may take an annual management fee not exceeding 4.5% of P's net assets on the anniversary of the court order appointing the professional as deputy.

Category IV

Where the court appoints a professional deputy for health and welfare, the deputy may take an annual management fee not exceeding 2.5% of P's net assets on the anniversary of the court order appointing the professional as deputy for health and welfare up to a maximum of £500.

Category V

Preparation and lodgement of the annual report or annual account to the Public Guardian.

Amount £225 (plus VAT)

Category VI

Preparation of an HMRC income tax return on behalf of P.

Amount £225 (plus VAT)

8. The categories of remuneration, above will apply as follows:

- *Category III and IV to all annual management fees for anniversaries falling on or after 1 April 2009.*
- *Category V to reports or accounts lodged on or after 1 May 2009.*
- *Category VI to all HMRC returns made on or after 1 May 2009.*

9. Where the period for which an annual management fee claimed is less than one year, for example where the deputyship comes to an end before the anniversary of appointment, then the amount claimed must be the same proportion of the applicable fee as the period bears to one year.

Remuneration of public authority deputies

10. Where an office holder in a public authority is appointed to act as deputy for P, he may claim the following fixed costs:

Category I

Work up to and including the date upon which the court makes an order appointing a deputy for property and affairs.

Amount £645 (plus VAT)

Category II

Annual management fee where the court appoints a local authority deputy for property and affairs, payable on the anniversary of the court order:

- *(a) for the first year: Amount £670 (plus VAT)*
- *(b) for the second and subsequent years: Amount £565 (plus VAT)*
- *(c) Provided that, where the net assets of P are below £16,000, the local authority deputy for property and affairs may take an annual management fee not exceeding 3% of P's net assets on the anniversary of the court order appointing the local authority as deputy*
- *(d) Where the court appoints a local authority deputy for health and welfare, the local authority may take an annual management fee not exceeding 2.5% of P's net assets on the anniversary of the court order appointing the local authority as deputy for health and welfare up to a maximum of £500.*

Category III

Annual property management fee to include work involved in preparing property for sale, instructing agents, conveyancers, etc or the ongoing maintenance of property including management and letting of a rental property.

Amount £260 (plus VAT)

Category IV

Preparation and lodgement of an annual report or account to the Public Guardian

Amount £185 (plus VAT)

11. The categories of remuneration, above will apply as follows:

- *Category I to all orders appointing a deputy for property and affairs made on or after 1 May 2009.*
- *Category II to all annual management fees for anniversaries falling on or after 1 May 2009.*
- *Category III on the anniversary of appointment as deputy where the anniversary falls on or after 1 May 2009; or upon completion of the sale of a property, where the transaction was concluded on or after 1 May 2009.*
- *Category V to reports or accounts lodged on or after 1 May 2009.*

12. Where the period for which the annual management fee ends before an anniversary, for example where the deputyship comes to an end before the anniversary of appointment, then the amount claimed must be the same proportion of the applicable fee as the period bears to one year.

This Practice Direction is made by the President with the agreement of the Lord Chancellor, and will come into effect on 1 May 2009.

Sir Mark Potter

President

PART IV

Practice Direction – Appeals

Practice Direction A – Appeals (PD20A)

This practice direction supplements Part 20 of the Court of Protection Rules 2007

1. This practice direction applies to appeal proceedings within the Court of Protection pursuant to Part 20 (except where Part 22 makes different provision). Where an appeal lies to the Court of Appeal, the Civil Procedure Rules 1998 apply to such an appeal.

Permission

2. Rules 172 and 173 set out the procedure for seeking the court's permission to appeal.

3. Unless the appeal is against an order of committal to prison, the court's permission is required to appeal. An application for permission may be made either to the judge at the hearing at which the decision being appealed was made (the first instance judge), or to an appeal judge.[76]

Appellant

Appellant's Notice

4. Rule 175 sets out the procedure and time limits for filing and serving an appellant's notice. This is summarised in the following table:

Permission given by the first instance judge	Permission not given by a first instance judge	Permission not needed
Appellant's notice to be filed within the time directed by the first instance judge; OR Where no time directed, within 21 days of the decision being appealed/ permission decision.	Appellant's notice including application for permission to be filed within 21 days of the decision being appealed.	Appellant's notice to be filed within 21 days of the decision being appealed.
Appellant's notice to be served on all respondents as soon as practicable, and no later than 21 days after it is issued.	Appellant's notice to be served on all respondents as soon as practicable, and no later than 21 days after it is issued.	Appellant's notice to be served on all respondents as soon as practicable, and no later than 21 days after it is issued.

---

[76]   But see r 182, which sets out certain requirements in relation to second appeals.

5. Where the first instance judge announces his decision and reserves the reasons for his judgment until a later date, he should, in the exercise of his powers under rule 175(2)(a), fix a period for filing the appellant's notice that takes this into account.

6. Except where the appeal judge orders otherwise, a sealed copy of the appellant's notice must be served on all respondents in accordance with the time limits prescribed by rule 175(3). At this time the appellant should also serve a skeleton argument on all respondents if permission was granted by the first instance judge.

7. The appellant must, within 7 days beginning on the date on which the copy of the appellant's notice was served, file a certificate of service in relation to service of the appellant's notice.[77]

(Part 6 sets out the rules relating to service.)

Extension of time for filing appellant's notice

8. Where the time for filing an appellant's notice has expired, the appellant must:

    (a)   file an appellant's notice; and
    (b)   include in that appellant's notice an application for an extension of time.

9. The appellant's notice should state the reason(s) for the delay and the steps taken prior to the application being made.

10. Where the appellant's notice includes an application for an extension of time and permission to appeal has been given or is not required, the respondent has the right to be heard on that application.

Documents to be filed and served with appellant's notice

11. The appellant must file the following documents with his appellant's notice:

    (a)   one additional copy of the appellant's notice for the court;
    (b)   one copy of his skeleton argument;
    (c)   a sealed copy of the order being appealed;
    (d)   a copy of any order giving or refusing permission to appeal, together with a copy of the judge's reasons for allowing or refusing permission to appeal;
    (e)   any witness statements or affidavits in support of any application included in the appellant's notice;
    (f)   the application form and any application notice or response (where relevant to the subject of the appeal);
    (g)   any other documents which the appellant reasonably considers necessary to enable the court to reach its decision on the hearing of the application or appeal;
    (h)   a suitable record of the judgment of the first instance judge; and
    (i)   such other documents as the court may direct.

12. Where it is not possible to file all of the above documents with the appellant's notice, the appellant must indicate which documents have not yet been filed and the reasons why they are not currently available. The appellant must then provide a reasonable estimate of when the missing document or documents can be filed and file and serve them as soon as reasonably practicable.

---

[77]   Rule 175(4).

13. Notice of an application to be made to the court for a remedy incidental to the appeal (eg an interim remedy under rule 82) may be included in the appellant's notice, or in an application notice using form COP9 (which is to be attached to the appellant's notice).

14. The appellant should consider what other information the court will need. This may include a list of persons who feature in the case or glossaries of technical terms. A chronology of relevant events will be necessary in most appeals.

15. The information set out in paragraph 11 must be served on each respondent when the appellant's notice is served.

Skeleton arguments

16. The appellant's notice must, subject to paragraph 17, be accompanied by a skeleton argument using, or attached to, a skeleton argument COP37 form.

17. Where the appellant is unable to provide a skeleton argument to accompany the appellant's notice it must be filed and served on all respondents within 21 days of filing the notice.

18. A skeleton argument must contain a numbered list of the points which the party wishes to make. These should both define and confine the areas of controversy. Each point should be stated as concisely as the nature of the case allows.

19. A numbered point must be followed by a reference to any document on which the appellant wishes to rely.

20. A skeleton argument must state, in respect of each authority cited:

    (a)   the proposition of law that the authority demonstrates; and

    (b)   the parts of the authority (identified by page or paragraph references) that support the proposition.

21. If more than one authority is cited in support of a given proposition, the skeleton argument must briefly state the reason for taking that course. This statement should not materially add to the length of the skeleton argument but should be sufficient to demonstrate, in the context of the argument:

    (a)   the relevance of the authority or authorities to that argument; and

    (b)   that the citation is necessary for a proper presentation of that argument.

Suitable record of the judgment

22. Where the judgment to be appealed has been officially recorded by the court, an approved transcript of that record should accompany the appellant's notice. Photocopies will not be accepted for this purpose. However, where there is no officially recorded judgment, the following will be acceptable:

Written judgments

23. Where the judgment was given in writing, a copy of that judgment endorsed with the judge's signature.

Note of judgment

24. When the judgment was not officially recorded or given in writing, a note of the judgment (agreed between the appellant's and respondent's advocates) should be submitted for approval to the first instance judge. If the parties cannot agree on a single note of the judgment, both versions should be provided to that judge with an explanatory letter. For the purpose of an application for permission to appeal the note need not be approved by the respondent or the first instance judge.

Advocates' notes of judgments where appellant is unrepresented

25. When the appellant was unrepresented before the first instance judge it is the duty of any advocate for the respondent to make his note of the judgment promptly available, free of charge, to the appellant where there is no officially recorded judgment or if the court so directs. Where the appellant was represented before the first instance judge, it is the duty of his own former advocate to make his note available in these circumstances. The appellant should submit the note of the judgment to the appeal judge.

Transcripts or notes of evidence

26. When the evidence is relevant to the appeal an official transcript of the relevant evidence must be obtained. Transcripts or notes of evidence are generally not needed for the purpose of determining an application for permission to appeal.

27. If evidence relevant to the appeal was not officially recorded, a typed version of the judge's notes of evidence must be obtained.

28. Where the first instance judge or the appeal judge is satisfied that:

    (a)   an unrepresented appellant; or

    (b)   an appellant whose legal representation is provided free of charge to the appellant and not funded by the Community Legal Service,

is in such poor financial circumstances that the cost of a transcript would be an excessive burden the court may certify that the cost of obtaining one official transcript should be borne at public expense.

29. In the case of a request for an official transcript of evidence or proceedings to be paid for at public expense, the court must also be satisfied that there are reasonable grounds for appeal. Whenever possible a request for a transcript at public expense should be made to the first instance judge when asking for permission to appeal.

Respondent

30. A person who has been named as a respondent in appeal proceedings and who wishes only to request that the appeal judge upholds the judgment or order of the first instance judge, whether for the reasons given by the first instance judge or otherwise, does not make an appeal and does not therefore require permission to appeal in accordance with rule 172.

31. A person who has been named as a respondent in appeal proceedings, and who also wishes to seek permission to appeal must do so in accordance with rule 172.

32. Unless the court otherwise directs, a respondent need not take any action when served with an appellant's notice until such time as notification is given to him that permission to appeal has been granted (unless paragraph 31 applies).

Respondent's notice

33. A respondent who wishes to appeal or who wishes to ask the appeal judge to uphold the order of the first instance judge for reasons different from or additional to those given by the first instance judge must file a respondent's notice.

34. If the respondent does not file a respondent's notice, he will not be entitled, except with the permission of the court, to rely on any reasons for upholding the decision which are different from or additional to those relied on by the first instance judge.

35. Rule 176 sets out the procedure and time limits for filing and serving a respondent's notice.

36. Where the first instance judge announces his decision and reserves the reasons for his judgment until a later date, he should, in the exercise of his powers under rule 176(3)(a) fix a period for filing the respondent's notice that takes this into account.

37. Except where the appeal judge orders otherwise, a sealed copy of the respondent's notice must be served on all parties to the appeal proceedings in accordance with the time limits prescribed by rule 176(5), along with any other material required to be served in accordance with paragraphs 40 to 43 below.

38. The respondent must, within 7 days beginning with the date on which the copy of the respondent's notice was served, file a certificate of service in relation to service of the respondent's notice.

(Part 6 sets out the rules relating to service.)

39. Paragraphs 8 to 10 apply in respect of a respondent's notice as they apply to an appellant's notice.

Documents to be filed and served with respondent's notice

40. The respondent must file the following documents with his respondent's notice:

   (a)   one additional copy of the respondent's notice for the court;
   (b)   one copy of his skeleton argument;
   (c)   a sealed copy of the order being appealed;
   (d)   a copy of any order giving or refusing permission to appeal, together with a copy of the judge's reasons for allowing or refusing permission to appeal; and
   (e)   any witness statements or affidavits in support of any application included in the respondent's notice.
   (f)   any other documents which the respondent reasonably considers necessary to enable the court to reach its decision on the hearing of the application or appeal; and
   (g)   such other documents as the court may direct.

41. A respondent may include an application for a remedy incidental to the appeal as set out in paragraph 13.

42. The respondent should consider what other information the appeal judge will need. This may include a list of persons who feature in the case or glossaries of technical terms. A chronology of relevant events will be necessary in most appeals.

43. The information set out in paragraph 40 must be served on the appellant and any other respondent when the respondent's notice is served.

Skeleton argument

44. The respondent must file and serve a skeleton argument in all cases where he proposes to address arguments to the court.

45. The respondent's notice must, subject to paragraph 46, be accompanied by a skeleton argument using, or attached to, a skeleton argument COP37 form.

46. Where the respondent is unable to provide a skeleton argument to accompany the respondent's notice it must be filed and served on all respondents within 21 days of filing the notice.

47. A respondent who does not file a respondent's notice but who files a skeleton argument must file and serve that skeleton argument at least 7 days before the appeal hearing.

48. A respondent's skeleton argument must conform to the requirements at paragraphs 18 to 21 with any necessary modifications. It should, where appropriate, answer the arguments set out in the appellant's skeleton argument.

49. Where a respondent's skeleton argument is not served with the respondent's notice, the respondent must serve his skeleton argument on all parties to the proceedings at the same time as he files it at the court, and must file a certificate of service.

Appeal hearing

50. The court will send the parties notification of the date of the hearing of the appeal, together with any other directions given by the court.

Practice Direction – Enforcement

Practice Direction A – Contempt of court (PD21A)

This practice direction supplements Part 21 of the Court of Protection Rules 2007

General

1. This practice direction applies to any application for an order for committal of a person to prison for contempt of court ('the committal application').

Applications for committal after permission granted or where permission not needed

2. An application for an order of committal must be commenced by filing a COP9 application notice in accordance with Part 21.

3. The applicant must file the original and one copy of the application notice, together with the original and one copy of the affidavit that is required by rule 186(1).

4. The affidavit must contain:

    (a)   the name and description of the person making the application;
    (b)   the name, address and description of the person sought to be committed;
    (c)   the grounds on which committal is sought;
    (d)   a description of each alleged act of contempt, identifying:
        (i)   each act separately and numerically, and
        (ii) if known, the date of each act; and
    (e)   any additional information required by paragraphs 5 and 6.

5. Where the allegation of contempt relates to prior proceedings before the court, the affidavit must also state:

    (a)   the case number of those prior proceedings;
    (b)   the date of the proceedings; and
    (c)   the name of P.

6. The affidavit must also set out in full any order, judgment or undertaking which it is alleged has been disobeyed or broken by the person sought to be committed. This will apply where the allegation of contempt is made on the grounds that:

    (a)   a person is required by a judgment or order to do an act, and has refused or neglected to do it within the time fixed by the judgment or order or any subsequent order;
    (b)   a person has disobeyed a judgment or order requiring him to abstain from doing an act; or
    (c)   a person has breached the terms of an undertaking which he gave to the court.

(Practice direction A accompanying Part 14 sets out further details in relation to affidavits.)

Hearing of application

7. When filing the application notice, the applicant must obtain from the court a date for the hearing of the committal application.

8. The court may at any time give case management directions (including directions for the service of evidence by the person sought to be committed and evidence in reply by the applicant) or may hold a directions hearing.

9. The court may on the hearing date:

    (a)   give case management directions with a view to a hearing of the committal application on a future date; or

    (b)   if the committal application is ready to be heard, proceed forthwith to hear it.

10. Where the person sought to be committed gives oral evidence at the hearing (in accordance with rule 187), he may be cross-examined.

PART IV

Practice Direction – Transitory and transitional provisions

Practice Direction A – Transitional provisions (PD22A)

This practice direction supplements Part 22 of the Court of Protection Rules

Introductory

1. In this practice direction:

    (a) 'commencement' means 1 October 2007;

    (b) 'pending proceedings' means proceedings on an application within paragraph 3 or 12 of Schedule 5 to the Act; and

    (c) 'the Previous Rules' means the Court of Protection Rules 2001,[78] as in force immediately before commencement.

Applications received after commencement

2. If an application under the Previous Rules is received at the court on or after commencement, it will be returned.

Applications received before commencement

3. The general presumption will be that:

    (a) any step in pending proceedings which is to be taken on or after commencement is to be taken under the Rules; and

    (b) pending proceedings are to be decided having regard to the Rules.

4. However, the general presumption is subject to:

    (a) any contrary provision in paragraphs 5 to 8 of this practice direction; and

    (b) any directions given by the court (including directions which disapply one or more of those paragraphs).

5. Any step already taken in the proceedings before commencement in accordance with the Previous Rules will remain valid on or after commencement.

6. A party to the proceedings will not normally be required to take any action that would amount to taking that step again under the Rules. For example, if evidence has been given in accordance with Part 5 of the Previous Rules, a person will not normally be required to comply with the requirements in Part 14 of the Rules (admissions, evidence and depositions).

7. Any question as to whether permission is required for the making of the application which commenced the pending proceedings will normally be determined in accordance with the Previous Rules.

8. If after commencement a party to the proceedings has served a document, or given notification, in accordance with:

---

[78]   SI 2001/824.

(a) Part 4 of the Previous Rules (which makes provisions as to service of documents and giving of notice); or

(b) rule 10(4) of the Enduring Powers of Attorney Rules 2001 (notifications in connection with certain applications relating to enduring powers of attorney),[79]

the court may treat that as valid service or notification. If it does, it will give directions as to the extent to which it is appropriate to disapply rules 66 to 70 of the Rules or to modify the application of the Rules to the proceedings.

Case management

9. Part 2 of the Rules (the overriding objective) will apply to all pending proceedings and a court officer may at any time refer the proceedings to a judge so that case management decisions can be made about the proceedings and the conduct of any hearing.

10. A judge may at any time direct how the Rules are to apply to the proceedings.

Orders made before commencement

11. Where a court order has been made before commencement under the Previous Rules, the order must still be complied with on or after commencement.

Costs

12. Any assessment of costs that takes place on or after commencement will be in accordance with Part 19 of the Rules.

---

[79] SI 2001/825.

Practice Direction B – Transitory provisions (PD22B)

This practice direction supplements Part 22 of the Court of Protection Rules 2007

Applications to which this practice direction applies

1. Rules 195 and 196 make provision for an application by a person who becomes a deputy by virtue of paragraph 1(2) of Schedule 5 to the Act, i e a receiver appointed under the Mental Health Act 1983 at the time of commencement (referred to in this practice direction as 'a deputy').

2. Rules 195 and 196 and the provisions of this practice direction will cease to have effect on 30th June 2008. On and after 30th June 2008, a deputy who wishes to apply to the court for an order must use the procedure under either Part 9 or Part 10 of the Rules, as appropriate.

Applications which may be suitable for the procedure set out in this practice direction

3. Examples of applications that may be suitable for the procedure set out in this practice direction include, but are not limited to:

   (a) applications for regular payments from P's assets to the deputy in respect of remuneration;
   (b) applications seeking minor variations only to the expenses that can be paid from P's estate;
   (c) applications for the receipt or discharge of a sum due to or by P as a result of an entitlement in or obligation to an estate;
   (d) applications for release of funds to repair or improve P's property;
   (e) applications to sell P's furniture and effects;
   (f) applications for the release of capital to meet expenses required for the care of P;
   (g) applications for authority to access P's funds on P's behalf;
   (h) applications for directions with regard to the management of P's investments (including any held at the Court Funds Office);
   (i) applications to approve the sale price of a property, where the sale has previously been authorised;
   (j) applications to approve the purchase of a property, where the purchase has previously been authorised; and
   (k) applications for authority to manage and let a property belonging to P.

4. Applications listed in paragraph 3 above may be heard by an officer nominated by the Senior Judge or the President pursuant to rule 196.

Applications which must be dealt with by a judge

5. Examples of applications which are not suitable for the procedure set out in this practice direction include, but are not limited to:

   (a) applications to appoint a new deputy, or to discharge an existing deputy;
   (b) applications seeking authorisation to commence, continue or defend litigation on behalf of P;

(c)   applications for the settlement of P's property, whether for P's benefit or the benefit of others;

(d)   applications to vary the terms of a trust in which P has an interest;

(e)   applications for a statutory will or codicil;

(f)   applications to operate or to cease to operate a business belonging to P, or to dissolve a partnership of which P is a member;

(g)   applications for authority to purchase or sell real property;

(h)   applications to make a gift or loan from P's assets;

(i)   applications to end proceedings or discharge court orders, where it is alleged that P has ceased to lack capacity;

(j)   applications to set, vary or dispense with security in relation to a deputy;

(k)   applications to change an accounting period;

(l)   applications to set or change the time by which an annual account may be submitted;

(m)   applications in relation to the sale of property owned by P;

(n)   applications for authority to disclose information as to P's assets, state of health or other circumstances;

(o)   applications to sell or otherwise deal with P's investments;

(p)   applications for authority to apply for a grant of probate or representation, where P would be the person entitled to the grant but for his lack of capacity;

(q)   applications relating to the lease or grant of a tenancy in relation to a property owned by P;

(r)   applications to arrange an overdraft on the bank account operated for the purpose of the deputyship; and

(s)   applications to open a bank account on behalf of P or for the purpose of the deputyship at a private bank, a bank that is not located in England and Wales, or at a bank which has unusual conditions attached to the operation of the account.

6. An application which is likely to be contested, or which involves large sums of money (when compared with the size of P's estate as a whole) is not suitable for the procedure set out in this practice direction.

Procedure to be followed

7. Applications to which the procedure in this practice direction applies may be made by filing a COP9 application notice, together with any evidence in support of the application.

8. The application may be made without serving an application notice on anyone and without notifying anyone that the application has been made.

How applications will be dealt with under the transitory procedure

9. Subject to paragraph 10, the nominated officer will deal with an application made in accordance with this practice direction without a hearing.

10. The nominated officer may decide, upon considering the application, that other persons ought to be informed of the application and given the opportunity to respond. In such a case, the nominated officer will refer the application to a judge.

11. The nominated officer will give directions as to who is to be served with any order that he makes.

12. Following a nominated officer's decision, the nominated officer will refer the matter to a judge, who will consider what (if any) further orders may be required to ensure that the deputy is on the same footing as a person who became a deputy by virtue of section 19 of the Act.

Reconsideration of and appeals against decisions of nominated officers

13. Where the application is determined without a hearing or without notice having been given to anyone, P, any party to the proceedings or any person affected by the order may apply to the court, within 21 days of having been served with the court's order, to have the order reconsidered.[80] An application to have an order reconsidered must be made by filing a COP9 application notice in accordance with Part 10.

14. Rule 197 sets out the appeal route in relation to decisions of nominated officers.

---

[80]   Rule 89.

Practice Direction C – Appeals against decisions made under Part 7 of the Mental Health Act 1983 or under the Enduring Powers of Attorney Act 1985 which are brought on or after commencement (PD22C)

This practice direction supplements Part 22 of the Court of Protection Rules 2007

General

1. Rule 199 enables a practice direction to be made in relation to transitory and transitional matters.

2. This practice direction sets out the procedure to be followed in relation to appeals against decisions made under Part 7 of the Mental Health Act 1983 ('the 1983 Act') or under the Enduring Powers of Attorney Act 1985 ('the 1985 Act'), which are brought on or after commencement of the Mental Capacity Act 2005 ('the 2005 Act').

3. Appeals to which this practice direction applies are to be dealt with in accordance with Part 20 (appeals), unless this practice direction makes different provision.[81]

Appeals against decisions made by nominated officers

4. Where the appeal is from a first instance decision of an officer nominated by virtue of section 93(4) of the 1983 Act, the appeal will be heard by a district judge nominated to exercise the jurisdiction of the court under section 46(2)(e) of the 2005 Act.

5. Where the appeal is from a decision of a district judge made under paragraph 4 above, it will be heard by a circuit judge nominated to exercise the jurisdiction of the court under section 46(2)(d) of the 2005 Act.

6. The Court of Appeal will hear an appeal against a decision of a circuit judge made under paragraph 5 above. Rule 182(2) and (3) apply to such an appeal.

Appeals by decisions of the Master of the former Court of Protection

7. An appeal from a decision of the Master of the Court of Protection[82] will be heard by a judge of the court nominated by virtue of section 46(2)(a) to (c) of the 2005 Act (ie the President, the Chancellor, or a puisne judge of the High Court).

8. Where the appeal is from a decision that was made under paragraph 7 above, it must be dealt with in accordance with rule 181 (appeals against decisions of a puisne judge of the High Court etc).

---

[81]   See r 169.

[82]   The judicial officer appointed by the Lord Chancellor under s 89 of the Supreme Court Act 1981.

Appeals made under Part 7 of the 1983 Act or under the 1985 Act pending at the time of commencement

9. This practice direction does not apply to appeals made under Part 7 of the 1983 Act or under the 1985 Act which are pending on 1 October 2007.

10. Paragraph 4(1) of Schedule 5 to the 2005 Act provides that an appeal brought by virtue of section 105 of the 1983 Act and which has not been determined before the commencement day, shall be determined in accordance with Part 7 of the 1983 Act and the rules made under it.

11. Where an appeal has been brought by virtue of section 10(1)(c) of the 1985 Act and has not been determined before the commencement day, the provisions of the 1985 Act, Part 7 of the 1983 Act (so far as they are relevant) and the rules made under that Part as applied by section 10 of the 1985 Act, shall continue to apply to such an appeal.[83]

12. If the appeal has been brought under section 105(1) of the 1983 Act, or by virtue of section 10(1)(c) of the 1985 Act, and the judge nominated under section 93 of the 1983 Act has begun to hear the appeal, he will continue to do so; otherwise, the appeal is to be heard by a puisne judge of the High Court nominated under section 46 of the 2005 Act.[84]

---

[83] Paragraph 13(1) of Sch 5 to the 2005 Act.
[84] Paragraph 4(2) and para 13(2) of Sch 5 to the 2005 Act.

Practice Direction – Miscellaneous

Practice Direction A – Request for directions where notice of objection prevents public guardian from registering enduring power of attorney (PD23A)

This practice direction supplements Part 23 of the Court of Protection Rules 2007

1. Rule 201 provides for the Public Guardian to request the court's directions where a notice of objection prevents him from registering an instrument creating an enduring power of attorney. This practice direction makes provision about such requests.

(Practice direction H accompanying Part 9 deals with applications made by persons other than the Public Guardian who are seeking the court's directions about registration.)

2. Time limits apply before the Public Guardian can request directions.[85] These are measured from the date (or the latest date) on which the attorney gave notice[86] to the donor's relatives of the attorney's intention to make an application for the registration of the instrument creating the enduring power. The Public Guardian cannot request directions until 5 weeks have expired beginning with the date of notification.

3. However, this period is extended if it would otherwise expire less than 14 days after the Public Guardian receives the notice of objection which prevents him from registering the instrument. In this case, the Public Guardian may not request directions from the court until the end of the 14 day period which begins with the date on which he received the notice of objection.

4. The request for directions must be made using form COP17. The Public Guardian must file the form and any document he considers may assist the court to give directions about the registration of the instrument.

5. The Public Guardian will notify the donor in accordance with Part 7 that he has made a request within 21 days of the date on which he makes it. However, the Public Guardian is not required to serve the request on any other person or otherwise to notify them that a request has been made. He will participate in the proceedings only if the court requests him to do so.

6. As soon as practicable after a request has been filed, notice of that fact[87] will be given by a court officer to:

    (a)   the person (or persons) who gave the notice of objection; and
    (b)   the attorney under the enduring power or, if more than one, each of them.

7. If any person wishes to participate in the proceedings, he then has 21 days to file an application using form COP8. The application must be made in accordance with the detailed requirements for applications relating to the registration of enduring powers of attorney, which are set out in practice direction H accompanying Part 9. If no such application is received, the court will proceed to consider the matter in

---

[85]   These time limits are imposed by r 201(1)(b) and (2).
[86]   See para 5 of Sch 4 to the Act.
[87]   Rule 200(6) sets out what the notice must contain.

response to the Public Guardian's request and will give directions to the Public Guardian.

Practice Direction B – Where P ceases to lack capacity or dies (PD23B)

This practice direction supplements Part 23 of the Court of Protection Rules 2007

General

1. An order of the Court of Protection will continue until it is discharged or, if made for a specified period, will cease to have effect when that period comes to an end.

2. Where P ceases to lack capacity or dies, steps may need to be taken to finalise the court's involvement in P's affairs.

Application to end proceedings

3. Where P ceases to lack capacity in relation to the matter or matters to which the proceedings relate, an application may be made by any of the following people to the court to end the proceedings and discharge any orders made in respect of that person:[88]

    (a)   P;

    (b)   his litigation friend; or

    (c)   any other person who is a party to the proceedings.

4. An application under rule 148 or 202 should be made by filing a COP9 application notice in accordance with the Part 10 procedure, together with any evidence in support of the application. The application should in particular be supported by evidence that P no longer lacks capacity to make decisions in relation to the matter or matters to which the proceedings relate.

Applications where proceedings have concluded

5. Where P ceases to lack capacity after proceedings have concluded, an application may be made to the court to discharge any orders made (including an order appointing a deputy or an order in relation to a security bond) by filing a COP9 application notice in accordance with the Part 10 procedure, together with any evidence in support of the application. The application notice should set out details of the order or orders the applicant seeks to have discharged, and should in particular be supported by evidence that P no longer lacks capacity to make decisions in relation to the matter or matters to which the proceedings relate.

6. If the Court Funds Office is holding funds or assets on behalf of P, it will require an order of the court to the effect that P no longer lacks capacity to make decisions with regard to the use and disposition of those funds or assets before any funds or assets can be transferred to him.

Procedure to be followed when P dies

7. An application for any final directions needed following P's death (including to discharge an order appointing a deputy or to discharge a security bond) should be

---

[88]   Rule 148.

made by filing a COP9 application notice in accordance with the Part 10 procedure. An application should attach the original or a certified copy of P's death certificate.

8. Any security bond taken out by the deputy will remain in force until the end of the period of 7 years commencing with the date of P's death, or until it is discharged by the court.[89]

9. The Public Guardian may require a deputy to submit a final report upon P's death.[90] Before it will discharge a security bond, the court must be satisfied that the Public Guardian either:

(a)   does not require a final report; or

(b)   is satisfied with the final report provided by the deputy.

Personal representatives and administrators

10. Where there are solicitor's costs outstanding which would be due from P's estate, the personal representative or administrator may agree any of these costs without an order from the court. If these costs cannot be agreed, the personal representative, administrator or the solicitor may apply to the court for costs to be assessed,[91] using a COP9 application notice in accordance with the Part 10 procedure.

11. If there are funds or other assets held in the Court Funds Office on behalf of P, P's personal representative or administrator will need to contact the Court Funds Office directly regarding those funds.

---

[89]   Regulation 37 of the Lasting Powers of Attorney, Enduring Powers of Attorney and Public Guardian Regulations 2007.

[90]   Regulation 40 of the Lasting Powers of Attorney, Enduring Powers of Attorney and Public Guardian Regulations 2007.

[91]   Rule 166 provides that an order or directions that costs incurred during P's lifetime be paid out of or charged on his estate may be made within 6 years after P's death.

PART V

Other Statutory Instruments and Practice Directions

PART V: Other Statutory Instruments and Practice Directions

Contents

Lasting Powers of Attorney, Enduring Powers of Attorney and
Public Guardian Regulations 2007   799

Public Guardian (Fees, etc) Regulations 2007   822

Court of Protection Fees Order 2007   827

Mental Capacity Act 2005 (Transitional and Consequential
Provisions) Order 2007   831

Mental Capacity Act 2005 (Transfer of Proceedings) Order 2007   851

Mental Capacity (Deprivation of Liberty: Appointment of Relevant
Person's Representative) Regulations 2008   854

Mental Capacity (Deprivation of Liberty: Standard Authorisations,
Assessments and Ordinary Residence) Regulations 2008   859

Civil Procedure Rules 1998   868

Practice Direction – Children and Protected Parties (PD21)   891

Practice Direction – About Costs (PDCosts)   920

Family Procedure (Adoption) Rules 2005   1005

Practice Direction – Service out of the Jurisdiction   1009

Guidance in cases involving protected parties in which the Official
Solicitor is being invited to act as guardian ad litem or litigation
friend   1026

PART V

Lasting Powers of Attorney, Enduring Powers of Attorney and Public Guardian Regulations 2007, SI 2007/1253

ARRANGEMENT OF REGULATIONS

PART 1
PRELIMINARY

Regulation   Page

1	Citation and commencement	801
2	Interpretation	801
3	Minimal differences from forms prescribed in these Regulations	801
4	Computation of time	801

PART 2
LASTING POWERS OF ATTORNEY

Instruments intended to create a lasting power of attorney

5	Forms for lasting powers of attorney	802
6	Maximum number of named persons	802
7	Requirement for two LPA certificates where instrument has no named persons	802
8	Persons who may provide an LPA certificate	802
9	Execution of instrument	803

Registering the instrument

10	Notice to be given by a person about to apply for registration of lasting power of attorney	804
11	Application for registration	804
12		805
13	Notice of receipt of application for registration	805
14	Objection to registration: notice to Public Guardian to be given by the donee of the power or a named person	805
14A	Objection to registration: notice to Public Guardian to be given by the donor	806
15	Objection to registration: application to the court	807
16	Notifying applicants of non-registration of lasting power of attorney	807
17	Notice to be given on registration of lasting power of attorney	807

Post-registration

18	Changes to instrument registered as lasting power of attorney	808
19	Loss or destruction of instrument registered as lasting power of attorney	808
20	Disclaimer of appointment by a donee of lasting power of attorney	809
21	Revocation by donor of lasting power of attorney	809
22	Revocation of a lasting power of attorney on death of donor	809

PART 3
ENDURING POWERS OF ATTORNEY

23	Notice of intention to apply for registration of enduring power of attorney	810
24	Application for registration	810
25	Notice of objection to registration	810
26	Notifying applicants of non-registration of enduring power of attorney	811
27	Registration of instrument creating an enduring power of attorney	811

PART V

28 Objection or revocation not applying to all joint and several attorneys   811
29 Loss or destruction of instrument registered as enduring power of
   attorney   811

PART 4
FUNCTIONS OF THE PUBLIC GUARDIAN

The registers
30 Establishing and maintaining the registers   812
31 Disclosure of information on a register: search by the Public Guardian   812
32 Disclosure of additional information held by the Public Guardian   812

Security for discharge of functions
33 Persons required to give security for the discharge of their functions   813
34 Security given under regulation 33(2)(a): requirement for endorsement   814
35 Security given under regulation 33(2)(a): maintenance or replacement   814
36 Enforcement following court order of any endorsed security   815
37 Discharge of any endorsed security   815

Deputies
38 Application for additional time to submit a report   815
39 Content of reports   816
40 Power to require final report on termination of appointment   816
41 Power to require information from deputies   817
42 Right of deputy to require review of decisions made by the Public
   Guardian   817

Miscellaneous functions
43 Applications to the Court of Protection   818
44 Visits by the Public Guardian or by Court of Protection Visitors at his
   direction   818
45 Functions in relation to persons carrying out specific transactions   819
46 Power to require information from donees of lasting power of attorney   819
47 Power to require information from attorneys under enduring power of
   attorney   819
48 Other functions in relation to enduring powers of attorney   820

Schedule 1 – Form for Instrument Intended to Create a Lasting Power
   of Attorney (LPA PFA and LPA HW)   820
Schedule 2 – Notice of Intention to Apply for Registration of a Lasting
   Power of Attorney (LPA 001)   821
Schedule 3 – Application to Register a Lasting Power of Attorney (LPA
   002)   821
Schedule 4 – Notice of Receipt of an Application to Register a Lasting
   Power of Attorney (LPA 003A and LPA 003B)   821
Schedule 5 – Notice of Registration of a Lasting Power of Attorney
   (LPA 004)   821
Schedule 6 – Disclaimer by Donee of a Lasting Power of Attorney
   (LPA 005)   821
Schedule 7 – Notice of Intention to Apply for Registration of an
   Enduring Power of Attorney (EP1 PG)   821
Schedule 8 – Application to Register an Enduring Power of Attorney
   (EP2 PG)   822

PART 1
PRELIMINARY

1 Citation and commencement

(1) These Regulations may be cited as the Lasting Powers of Attorney, Enduring Powers of Attorney and Public Guardian Regulations 2007.

(2) These Regulations shall come into force on 1 October 2007.

2 Interpretation

(1) In these Regulations –

'the Act' means the Mental Capacity Act 2005;

'court' means the Court of Protection;

'LPA certificate', in relation to an instrument made with a view to creating a lasting power of attorney, means the certificate which is required to be included in the instrument by virtue of paragraph 2(1)(e) of Schedule 1 to the Act;

'named person', in relation to an instrument made with a view to creating a lasting power of attorney, means a person who is named in the instrument as being a person to be notified of any application for the registration of the instrument;

'prescribed information', in relation to any instrument intended to create a lasting power of attorney, means the information contained in the form used for the instrument which appears under the heading 'prescribed information'.

3 Minimal differences from forms prescribed in these Regulations

(1) In these Regulations, any reference to a form –

(a) in the case of a form set out in Schedules 1 to 7 to these Regulations, is to be regarded as including a Welsh version of that form; and

(b) in the case of a form set out in Schedules 2 to 7 to these Regulations, is to be regarded as also including –

(i) a form to the same effect but which differs in an immaterial respect in form or mode of expression;

(ii) a form to the same effect but with such variations as the circumstances may require or the court or the Public Guardian may approve; or

(iii) a Welsh version of a form within (i) or (ii).

4 Computation of time

(1) This regulation shows how to calculate any period of time which is specified in these Regulations.

(2) A period of time expressed as a number of days must be computed as clear days.

(3) Where the specified period is 7 days or less, and would include a day which is not a business day, that day does not count.

(4) When the specified period for doing any act at the office of the Public Guardian ends on a day on which the office is closed, that act will be done in time if done on the next day on which the office is open.

(5) In this regulation –

'business day' means a day other than –
    (a)   a Saturday, Sunday, Christmas Day or Good Friday; or
    (b)   a bank holiday under the Banking and Financial Dealings Act 1971, in England and Wales; and
'clear days' means that in computing the number of days –
    (a)   the day on which the period begins, and
    (b)   if the end of the period is defined by reference to an event, the day on which that event occurs,
are not included.

PART 2
LASTING POWERS OF ATTORNEY

Instruments intended to create a lasting power of attorney

5 Forms for lasting powers of attorney

The forms set out in Parts 1 and 2 of Schedule 1 to these Regulations are the forms which, in the circumstances to which they apply, are to be used for instruments intended to create a lasting power of attorney.

6 Maximum number of named persons

The maximum number of named persons that the donor of a lasting power of attorney may specify in the instrument intended to create the power is 5.

7 Requirement for two LPA certificates where instrument has no named persons

Where an instrument intended to create a lasting power of attorney includes a statement by the donor that there are no persons whom he wishes to be notified of any application for the registration of the instrument –

    (a)   the instrument must include two LPA certificates; and
    (b)   each certificate must be completed and signed by a different person.

8 Persons who may provide an LPA certificate

(1) Subject to paragraph (3), the following persons may give an LPA certificate –

    (a)   a person chosen by the donor as being someone who has known him personally for the period of at least two years which ends immediately before the date on which that person signs the LPA certificate;
    (b)   a person chosen by the donor who, on account of his professional skills and expertise, reasonably considers that he is competent to make the judgments necessary to certify the matters set out in paragraph (2)(1)(e) of Schedule 1 to the Act.

(2) The following are examples of persons within paragraph (1)(b) –

(a)   a registered health care professional;

(b)   a barrister, solicitor or advocate called or admitted in any part of the United Kingdom;

(c)   a registered social worker; or

(d)   an independent mental capacity advocate.

(3) A person is disqualified from giving an LPA certificate in respect of any instrument intended to create a lasting power of attorney if that person is –

(a)   a family member of the donor;

(b)   a donee of that power;

(c)   a donee of –

  (i)   any other lasting power of attorney, or

  (ii)   an enduring power of attorney,

  which has been executed by the donor (whether or not it has been revoked);

(d)   a family member of a donee within sub-paragraph (b);

(e)   a director or employee of a trust corporation acting as a donee within sub-paragraph (b);

(f)   a business partner or employee of –

  (i)   the donor, or

  (ii)   a donee within sub-paragraph (b);

(g)   an owner, director, manager or employee of any care home in which the donor is living when the instrument is executed; or

(h)   a family member of a person within sub-paragraph (g).

(4) In this regulation –

'care home' has the meaning given in section 3 of the Care Standards Act 2000;

'registered health care professional' means a person who is a member of a profession regulated by a body mentioned in section 25(3) of the National Health Service Reform and Health Care Professions Act 2002; and

'registered social worker' means a person registered as a social worker in a register maintained by –

(a)   the General Social Care Council;

(b)   the Care Council for Wales;

(c)   the Scottish Social Services Council; or

(d)   the Northern Ireland Social Care Council.

9 Execution of instrument

(1) An instrument intended to create a lasting power of attorney must be executed in accordance with this regulation.

(2) The donor must read (or have read to him) all the prescribed information.

(3) As soon as reasonably practicable after the steps required by paragraph (2) have been taken, the donor must –

(a)   complete the provisions of Part A of the instrument that apply to him (or direct another person to do so); and

(b)   subject to paragraph (7), sign Part A of the instrument in the presence of a witness.

(4) As soon as reasonably practicable after the steps required by paragraph (3) have been taken –

(a)   the person giving an LPA certificate, or

(b)   if regulation 7 applies (two LPA certificates required), each of the persons giving a certificate,

must complete the LPA certificate at Part B of the instrument and sign it.

(5) As soon as reasonably practicable after the steps required by paragraph (4) have been taken –

(a)   the donee, or
(b)   if more than one, each of the donees,

must read (or have read to him) all the prescribed information.

(6) As soon as reasonably practicable after the steps required by paragraph (5) have been taken, the donee or, if more than one, each of them –

(a)   must complete the provisions of Part C of the instrument that apply to him (or direct another person to do so); and
(b)   subject to paragraph (7), must sign Part C of the instrument in the presence of a witness.

(7) If the instrument is to be signed by any person at the direction of the donor, or at the direction of any donee, the signature must be done in the presence of two witnesses.

(8) For the purposes of this regulation –

(a)   the donor may not witness any signature required for the power;
(b)   a donee may not witness any signature required for the power apart from that of another donee.

(9) A person witnessing a signature must –

(a)   sign the instrument; and
(b)   give his full name and address.

(10) Any reference in this regulation to a person signing an instrument (however expressed) includes his signing it by means of a mark made on the instrument at the appropriate place.

Registering the instrument

10 Notice to be given by a person about to apply for registration of lasting power of attorney

Schedule 2 to these Regulations sets out the form of notice ('LPA 001') which must be given by a donor or donee who is about to make an application for the registration of an instrument intended to create a lasting power of attorney.

11 Application for registration

(1) Schedule 3 to these Regulations sets out the form ('LPA 002') which must be used for making an application to the Public Guardian for the registration of an instrument intended to create a lasting power of attorney.

(2) Where the instrument to be registered which is sent with the application is neither –

(a)   the original instrument intended to create the power, nor
(b)   a certified copy of it,

the Public Guardian must not register the instrument unless the court directs him to do so.

(3) In paragraph (2) 'a certified copy' means a photographic or other facsimile copy which is certified as an accurate copy by –

    (a)   the donor; or

    (b)   a solicitor or notary.

Period to elapse before registration in cases not involving objection or defect

12   The period at the end of which the Public Guardian must register an instrument in accordance with paragraph 5 of Schedule 1 to the Act is the period of 6 weeks beginning with –

    (a)   the date on which the Public Guardian gave the notice or notices under paragraph 7 or 8 of Schedule 1 to the Act of receipt of an application for registration; or

    (b)   if notices were given on more than one date, the latest of those dates.

13 Notice of receipt of application for registration

(1) Part 1 of Schedule 4 to these Regulations sets out the form of notice ('LPA 003A') which the Public Guardian must give to the donee (or donees) when the Public Guardian receives an application for the registration of a lasting power of attorney.

(2) Part 2 of Schedule 4 sets out the form of notice ('LPA 003B') which the Public Guardian must give to the donor when the Public Guardian receives such an application.

(3) Where it appears to the Public Guardian that there is good reason to do so, the Public Guardian must also provide (or arrange for the provision of) an explanation to the donor of –

    (a)   the notice referred to in paragraph (2) and what the effect of it is; and

    (b)   why it is being brought to his attention.

(4) Any information provided under paragraph (3) must be provided –

    (a)   to the donor personally; and

    (b)   in a way that is appropriate to the donor's circumstances (for example using simple language, visual aids or other appropriate means).

14 Objection to registration: notice to Public Guardian [to be given by the donee of the power or a named person]

(1) This regulation deals with any objection to the registration of an instrument as a lasting power of attorney which is to be made to the Public Guardian [by the donee of the power or a named person].

(2) Where [the donee of the power or a named person] –

    (a)   is entitled to receive notice under paragraph 6, 7 or 8 of Schedule 1 to the Act of an application for the registration of the instrument, and

    (b)   wishes to object to registration on a ground set out in paragraph 13(1) of Schedule 1 to the Act,

PART V

he must do so before the end of the period of 5 weeks beginning with the date on which the notice is given.

(3) A notice of objection must be given in writing, setting out –

    (a)   the name and address of the objector;
    (b)   ... the name and address of the donor of the power;
    (c)   if known, the name and address of the donee (or donees); and
    (d)   the ground for making the objection.

(4) The Public Guardian must notify the objector as to whether he is satisfied that the ground of the objection is established.

(5) At any time after receiving the notice of objection and before giving the notice required by paragraph (4), the Public Guardian may require the objector to provide such further information, or produce such documents, as the Public Guardian reasonably considers necessary to enable him to determine whether the ground for making the objection is established.

(6) Where –

    (a)   the Public Guardian is satisfied that the ground of the objection is established, but
    (b)   by virtue of section 13(7) of the Act, the instrument is not revoked,

the notice under paragraph (4) must contain a statement to that effect.

(7) Nothing in this regulation prevents an objector from making a further objection under paragraph 13 of Schedule 1 to the Act where –

    (a)   the notice under paragraph (4) indicates that the Public Guardian is not satisfied that the particular ground of objection to which that notice relates is established; and
    (b)   the period specified in paragraph (2) has not expired.

Amendments—Words inserted, substituted and omitted by Lasting Powers of Attorney, Enduring Powers of Attorney and Public Guardian (Amendment) Regulations 2007, SI 2007/2161.

14A Objection to registration: notice to Public Guardian to be given by the donor

(1) This regulation deals with any objection to the registration of an instrument as a lasting power of attorney which is to be made to the Public Guardian by the donor of the power.

(2) Where the donor of the power –

    (a)   is entitled to receive notice under paragraph 8 of Schedule 1 to the Act of an application for the registration of the instrument, and
    (b)   wishes to object to the registration

he must do so before the end of the period of 5 weeks beginning with the date on which the notice is given.

(3) The donor of the power must give notice of his objection in writing to the Public Guardian, setting out –

    (a)   the name and address of the donor of the power
    (b)   if known, the name and address of the donee (or donees); and
    (c)   the ground for making the objection.

Amendments—Inserted by Lasting Powers of Attorney, Enduring Powers of Attorney and Public Guardian (Amendment) Regulations 2007, SI 2007/2161.

15 Objection to registration: application to the court

(1) This regulation deals with any objection to the registration of an instrument as a lasting power of attorney which is to be made to the court.

(2) The grounds for making an application to the court are –

(a) that one or more of the requirements for the creation of a lasting power of attorney have not been met;

(b) that the power has been revoked, or has otherwise come to an end, on a ground other than the grounds set out in paragraph 13(1) of Schedule 1 to the Act;

(c) any of the grounds set out in paragraph (a) or (b) of section 22(3) of the Act.

(3) Where any person –

(a) is entitled to receive notice under paragraph 6, 7 or 8 of Schedule 1 to the Act of an application for the registration of the instrument, and

(b) wishes to object to registration on one or more of the grounds set out in paragraph (2),

he must make an application to the court before the end of the period of 5 weeks beginning with the date on which the notice is given.

(4) The notice of an application to the court, which a person making an objection to the court is required to give to the Public Guardian under paragraph 13(3)(b)(ii) of Schedule 1 to the Act, must be in writing.

16 Notifying applicants of non-registration of lasting power of attorney

Where the Public Guardian is prevented from registering an instrument as a lasting power of attorney by virtue of –

(a) paragraph 11(1) of Schedule 1 to the Act (instrument not made in accordance with Schedule),

(b) paragraph 12(2) of that Schedule (deputy already appointed),

(c) paragraph 13(2) of that Schedule (objection by donee or named person on grounds of bankruptcy, disclaimer, death etc),

(d) paragraph 14(2) of that Schedule (objection by donor), or

(e) regulation 11(2) of these Regulations (application for registration not accompanied by original instrument or certified copy),

he must notify the person (or persons) who applied for registration of that fact.

17 Notice to be given on registration of lasting power of attorney

(1) Where the Public Guardian registers an instrument as a lasting power of attorney, he must –

(a) retain a copy of the instrument; and

(b) return to the person (or persons) who applied for registration the original instrument, or the certified copy of it, which accompanied the application for registration.

PART V

(2) Schedule 5 to these Regulations sets out the form of notice ('LPA 004') which the Public Guardian must give to the donor and donee (or donees) when the Public Guardian registers an instrument.

(3) Where it appears to the Public Guardian that there is good reason to do so, the Public Guardian must also provide (or arrange for the provision of) an explanation to the donor of –

    (a)   the notice referred to in paragraph (2) and what the effect of it is; and

    (b)   why it is being brought to his attention.

(4) Any information provided under paragraph (3) must be provided –

    (a)   to the donor personally; and

    (b)   in a way that is appropriate to the donor's circumstances (for example using simple language, visual aids or other appropriate means).

(5) 'Certified copy' is to be construed in accordance with regulation 11(3).

Post-registration

18 Changes to instrument registered as lasting power of attorney

(1) This regulation applies in any case where any of paragraphs 21 to 24 of Schedule 1 to the Act requires the Public Guardian to attach a note to an instrument registered as a lasting power of attorney.

(2) The Public Guardian must give a notice to the donor and the donee (or, if more than one, each of them) requiring him to deliver to the Public Guardian –

    (a)   the original ...instrument which was sent to the Public Guardian for registration;

    (b)   any office copy of that registered instrument; and

    (c)   any certified copy of that registered instrument.

(3) On receipt of the document, the Public Guardian must –

    (a)   attach the required note; and

    (b)   return the document to the person from whom it was obtained.

Amendment—Word omitted by Lasting Powers of Attorney, Enduring Powers of Attorney and Public Guardian (Amendment) Regulations 2009, SI 2009/1884.

19 Loss or destruction of instrument registered as lasting power of attorney

(1) This regulation applies where –

    (a)   a person is required by or under the Act to deliver up to the Public Guardian any of the following documents –

        (i)   an instrument registered as a lasting power of attorney;

        (ii) an office copy of that registered instrument;

        (iii) a certified copy of that registered instrument; and

    (b)   the document has been lost or destroyed.

(2) The person required to deliver up the document must provide to the Public Guardian in writing –

(a) if known, the date of the loss or destruction and the circumstances in which it occurred;

(b) otherwise, a statement of when he last had the document in his possession.

20 Disclaimer of appointment by a donee of lasting power of attorney

(1) Schedule 6 to these Regulations sets out the form ('LPA 005') which a donee of an instrument registered as a lasting power of attorney must use to disclaim his appointment as donee.

(2) The donee must send –

(a) the completed form to the donor; and

(b) a copy of it to –

(i) the Public Guardian; and

(ii) any other donee who, for the time being, is appointed under the power.

21 Revocation by donor of lasting power of attorney

(1) A donor who revokes a lasting power to attorney must –

(a) notify the Public Guardian that he has done so; and

(b) notify the donee (or, if more than one, each of them) of the revocation.

(2) Where the Public Guardian receives a notice under paragraph (1)(a), he must cancel the registration of the instrument creating the power if he is satisfied that the donor has taken such steps as are necessary in law to revoke it.

(3) The Public Guardian may require the donor to provide such further information, or produce such documents, as the Public Guardian reasonably considers necessary to enable him to determine whether the steps necessary for revocation have been taken.

(4) Where the Public Guardian cancels the registration of the instrument he must notify –

(a) the donor; and

(b) the donee or, if more than one, each of them.

22 Revocation of a lasting power of attorney on death of donor

(1) The Public Guardian must cancel the registration of an instrument as a lasting power of attorney if he is satisfied that the power has been revoked as a result of the donor's death.

(2) Where the Public Guardian cancels the registration of an instrument he must notify the donee or, if more than one, each of them.

PART V

PART 3
ENDURING POWERS OF ATTORNEY

23 Notice of intention to apply for registration of enduring power of attorney

(1) Schedule 7 to these Regulations sets out the form of notice ('EP1PG') which an attorney (or attorneys) under an enduring power of attorney must give of his intention to make an application for the registration of the instrument creating the power.

(2) In the case of the notice to be given to the donor, the attorney must also provide (or arrange for the provision of) an explanation to the donor of –

    (a)   the notice and what the effect of it is; and
    (b)   why it is being brought to his attention.

(3) The information provided under paragraph (2) must be provided –

    (a)   to the donor personally; and
    (b)   in a way that is appropriate to the donor's circumstances (for example using simple language, visual aids or other appropriate means).

24 Application for registration

(1) Schedule 8 to these Regulations sets out the form ('EP2PG') which must be used for making an application to the Public Guardian for the registration of an instrument creating an enduring power of attorney.

(2) Where the instrument to be registered which is sent with the application is neither –

    (a)   the original instrument creating the power, nor
    (b)   a certified copy of it,

the Public Guardian must not register the instrument unless the court directs him to do so.

(3) 'Certified copy', in relation to an enduring power of attorney, means a copy certified in accordance with section 3 of the Powers of Attorney Act 1971.

25 Notice of objection to registration

(1) This regulation deals with any objection to the registration of an instrument creating an enduring power of attorney which is to be made to the Public Guardian under paragraph 13(4) of Schedule 4 to the Act.

(2) A notice of objection must be given in writing, setting out –

    (a)   the name and address of the objector;
    (b)   if different, the name and address of the donor of the power;
    (c)   if known, the name and address of the attorney (or attorneys); and
    (d)   the ground for making the objection.

26 Notifying applicants of non-registration of enduring power of attorney

Where the Public Guardian is prevented from registering an instrument creating an enduring power of attorney by virtue of –

(a) paragraph 13(2) of Schedule 4 to the Act (deputy already appointed),

(b) paragraph 13(5) of that Schedule (receipt by Public Guardian of valid notice of objection from person entitled to notice of application to register),

(c) paragraph 13(7) of that Schedule (Public Guardian required to undertake appropriate enquiries in certain circumstances), or

(d) regulation 24(2) of these Regulations (application for registration not accompanied by original instrument or certified copy),

he must notify the person (or persons) who applied for registration of that fact.

27 Registration of instrument creating an enduring power of attorney

(1) Where the Public Guardian registers an instrument creating an enduring power of attorney, he must –

(a) retain a copy of the instrument; and

(b) return to the person (or persons) who applied for registration the original instrument, or the certified copy of it, which accompanied the application.

(2) 'Certified copy' has the same meaning as in regulation 24(3).

28 Objection or revocation not applying to all joint and several attorneys

In a case within paragraph 20(6) or (7) of Schedule 4 to the Act, the form of the entry to be made in the register in respect of an instrument creating the enduring power of attorney is a stamp bearing the following words (inserting the information indicated, as appropriate) –

'THE REGISTRATION OF THIS ENDURING POWER OF ATTORNEY IS QUALIFIED AND EXTENDS TO THE APPOINTMENT OF ....(insert name of attorney(s) not affected by ground(s) of objection or revocation) ONLY AS THE ATTORNEY(S) OF .... (insert name of donor)'.

29 Loss or destruction of instrument registered as enduring power of attorney

(1) This regulation applies where –

(a) a person is required by or under the Act to deliver up to the Public Guardian any of the following documents –
(i) an instrument registered as an enduring power of attorney;
(ii) an office copy of that registered instrument; or
(iii) a certified copy of that registered instrument; and

(b) the document has been lost or destroyed.

(2) The person who is required to deliver up the document must provide to the Public Guardian in writing –

(a) if known, the date of the loss or destruction and the circumstances in which it occurred;

PART V

(b)   otherwise, a statement of when he last had the document in his possession.

PART 4
FUNCTIONS OF THE PUBLIC GUARDIAN

The registers

30 Establishing and maintaining the registers

(1) In this Part 'the registers' means –

- (a)   the register of lasting powers of attorney,
- (b)   the register of enduring powers of attorney, and
- (c)   the register of court orders appointing deputies,

which the Public Guardian must establish and maintain.

(2) On each register the Public Guardian may include –

- (a)   such descriptions of information about a registered instrument or a registered order as the Public Guardian considers appropriate; and
- (b)   entries which relate to an instrument or order for which registration has been cancelled.

31 Disclosure of information on a register: search by the Public Guardian

(1) Any person may, by an application made under paragraph (2), request the Public Guardian to carry out a search of one or more of the registers.

(2) An application must –

- (a)   state –
  - (i)   the register or registers to be searched;
  - (ii)   the name of the person to whom the application relates; and
  - (iii)   such other details about that person as the Public Guardian may require for the purpose of carrying out the search; and
- (b)   be accompanied by any fee provided for under section 58(4)(b) of the Act.

(3) The Public Guardian may require the applicant to provide such further information, or produce such documents, as the Public Guardian reasonably considers necessary to enable him to carry out the search.

(4) As soon as reasonably practicable after receiving the application –

- (a)   the Public Guardian must notify the applicant of the result of the search; and
- (b)   in the event that it reveals one or more entries on the register, the Public Guardian must disclose to the applicant all the information appearing on the register in respect of each entry.

32 Disclosure of additional information held by the Public Guardian

(1) This regulation applies in any case where, as a result of a search made under regulation 31, a person has obtained information relating to a registered instrument or a registered order which confers authority to make decisions about matters concerning a person ('P').

(2) On receipt of an application made in accordance with paragraph (4), the Public Guardian may, if he considers that there is good reason to do so, disclose to the applicant such additional information as he considers appropriate.

(3) 'Additional information' means any information relating to P –

(a) which the Public Guardian has obtained in exercising the functions conferred on him under the Act; but

(b) which does not appear on the register.

(4) An application must state –

(a) the name of P;

(b) the reasons for making the application; and

(c) what steps, if any, the applicant has taken to obtain the information from P.

(5) The Public Guardian may require the applicant to provide such further information, or produce such documents, as the Public Guardian reasonably considers necessary to enable him to determine the application.

(6) In determining whether to disclose any additional information [relating] to P, the Public Guardian must, in particular, have regard to –

(a) the connection between P and the applicant;

(b) the reasons for requesting the information (in particular, why the information cannot or should not be obtained directly from P);

(c) the benefit to P, or any detriment he may suffer, if a disclosure is made; and

(d) any detriment that another person may suffer if a disclosure is made.

Amendment—Word in reg 32(6)inserted by Lasting Powers of Attorney, Enduring Powers of Attorney and Public Guardian (Amendment) Regulations 2009, SI 2009/1884.

Security for discharge of functions

33 Persons required to give security for the discharge of their functions

(1) This regulation applies in any case where the court orders a person ('S') to give to the Public Guardian security for the discharge of his functions.

(2) The security must be given by S –

(a) by means of a bond which is entered into in accordance with regulation 34; or

(b) in such other manner as the court may direct.

(3) For the purposes of paragraph (2)(a), S complies with the requirement to give the security only if –

(a) the endorsement required by regulation 34(2) has been provided; and

(b) the person who provided it has notified the Public Guardian of that fact.

(4) For the purposes of paragraph (2)(b), S complies with the requirement to give the security –

(a) in any case where the court directs that any other endorsement must be provided, only if –

(i) that endorsement has been provided; and

(ii) the person who provided it has notified the Public Guardian of that fact;

(b) in any case where the court directs that any other requirements must be met

PART V

in relation to the giving of the security, only if the Public Guardian is satisfied that those other requirements have been met.

34 Security given under regulation 33(2)(a): requirement for endorsement

(1) This regulation has effect for the purposes of regulation 33(2)(a).

(2) A bond is entered into in accordance with this regulation only if it is endorsed by –

    (a) an authorised insurance company; or
    (b) an authorised deposit-taker.

(3) A person may enter into the bond under –

    (a) arrangements made by the Public Guardian; or
    (b) other arrangements which are made by the person entering into the bond or on his behalf.

(4) The Public Guardian may make arrangements with any person specified in paragraph (2) with a view to facilitating the provision by them of bonds which persons required to give security to the Public Guardian may enter into.

(5) In this regulation –

'authorised insurance company' means –
    (a) a person who has permission under Part 4 of the Financial Services and Markets Act 2000 to effect or carry out contracts of insurance;
    (b) an EEA firm of the kind mentioned in paragraph 5(d) of Schedule 3 to that Act, which has permission under paragraph 15 of that Schedule to effect or carry out contracts of insurance;
    (c) a person who carries on insurance market activity (within the meaning given in section 316(3) of that Act); and
'authorised deposit-taker' means –
    (a) a person who has permission under Part 4 of the Financial Services and Markets Act 2000 to accept deposits;
    (b) an EEA firm of the kind mentioned in paragraph 5(d) of Schedule 3 to that Act, which has permission under paragraph 15 of that Schedule to accept deposits.

(6) The definitions of 'authorised insurance company' and 'authorised deposit-taker' must be read with –

    (a) section 22 of the Financial Services and Markets Act 2000;
    (b) any relevant order under that section; and
    (c) Schedule 2 to that Act.

35 Security given under regulation 33(2)(a): maintenance or replacement

(1) This regulation applies to any security given under regulation 33(2)(a).

(2) At such times or at such intervals as the Public Guardian may direct by notice in writing, any person ('S') who has given the security must satisfy the Public Guardian that any premiums payable in respect of it have been paid.

(3) Where S proposes to replace a security already given by him, the new security is not to be regarded as having been given until the Public Guardian is satisfied that –

    (a)   the requirements set out in sub-paragraphs (a) and (b) of regulation 33(3) have been met in relation to it; and

    (b)   no payment is due from S in connection with the discharge of his functions.

36 Enforcement following court order of any endorsed security

(1) This regulation applies to any security given to the Public Guardian in respect of which an endorsement has been provided.

(2) Where the court orders the enforcement of the security, the Public Guardian must –

    (a)   notify any person who endorsed the security of the contents of the order; and

    (b)   notify the court when payment has been made of the amount secured.

37 Discharge of any endorsed security

(1) This regulation applies to any security given by a person ('S') to the Public Guardian in respect of which an endorsement has been provided.

(2) The security may be discharged if the court makes an order discharging it.

(3) In any other case, the security may not be discharged until the end of the period of 7 years commencing with whichever of the following dates first occurs –

    (a)   if the person on whose behalf S was appointed to act dies, the date of his death;

    (b)   if S dies, the date of his death;

    (c)   if the court makes an order which discharges S but which does not also discharge the security under paragraph (2), the date of the order;

    (d)   the date when S otherwise ceases to be under a duty to discharge the functions in respect of which he was ordered to give security.

(4) For the purposes of paragraph (3), if a person takes any step with a view to discharging the security before the end of the period specified in that paragraph, the security is to be treated for all purposes as if it were still in place.

Deputies

38 Application for additional time to submit a report

(1) This regulation applies where the court requires a deputy to submit a report to the Public Guardian and specifies a time or interval for it to be submitted.

(2) A deputy may apply to the Public Guardian requesting more time for submitting a particular report.

(3) An application must –

    (a)   state the reason for requesting more time; and

    (b)   contain or be accompanied by such information as the Public Guardian may reasonably require to determine the application.

PART V

(4) In response to an application, the Public Guardian may, if he considers it appropriate to do so, undertake that he will not take steps to secure performance of the deputy's duty to submit the report at the relevant time on the condition that the report is submitted on or before such later date as he may specify.

39 Content of reports

(1) Any report which the court requires a deputy to submit to the Public Guardian must include such material as the court may direct.

(2) The report must also contain or be accompanied by –

(a)   specified information or information of a specified description; or
(b)   specified documents or documents of a specified description.

(3) But paragraph (2) –

(a)   extends only to information or documents which are reasonably required in connection with the exercise by the Public Guardian of functions conferred on him under the Act; and
(b)   is subject to paragraph (1) and to any other directions given by the court.

(4) Where powers as respects a person's property and affairs are conferred on a deputy under section 16 of the Act, the information specified by the Public Guardian under paragraph (2) may include accounts which –

(a)   deal with specified matters; and
(b)   are provided in a specified form.

(5) The Public Guardian may require –

(a)   any information provided to be verified in such manner, or
(b)   any document produced to be authenticated in such manner,

as he may reasonably require.

(6) 'Specified' means specified in a notice in writing given to the deputy by the Public Guardian.

40 Power to require final report on termination of appointment

(1) This regulation applies where –

(a)   the person on whose behalf a deputy was appointed to act has died;
(b)   the deputy has died;
(c)   the court has made an order discharging the deputy; or
(d)   the deputy otherwise ceases to be under a duty to discharge the functions to which his appointment relates.

(2) The Public Guardian may require the deputy (or, in the case of the deputy's death, his personal representatives) to submit a final report on the discharge of his functions.

(3) A final report must be submitted –

(a)   before the end of such reasonable period as may be specified; and
(b)   at such place as may be specified.

(4) The Public Guardian must consider the final report, together with any other information that he may have relating to the discharge by the deputy of his functions.

(5) Where the Public Guardian is dissatisfied with any aspect of the final report he may apply to the court for an appropriate remedy (including enforcement of security given by the deputy).

(6) 'Specified' means specified in a notice in writing given to the deputy or his personal representatives by the Public Guardian.

41 Power to require information from deputies

(1) This regulation applies in any case where –

    (a)   the Public Guardian has received representations (including complaints) about –

        (i)   the way in which a deputy is exercising his powers; or

        (ii)   any failure to exercise them; or

    (b)   it appears to the Public Guardian that there are other circumstances which –

        (i)   give rise to concerns about, or dissatisfaction with, the conduct of the deputy (including any failure to act); or

        (ii)   otherwise constitute good reason to seek information about the deputy's discharge of his functions.

(2) The Public Guardian may require the deputy –

    (a)   to provide specified information or information of a specified description; or

    (b)   to produce specified documents or documents of a specified description.

(3) The information or documents must be provided or produced –

    (a)   before the end of such reasonable period as may be specified; and

    (b)   at such place as may be specified.

(4) The Public Guardian may require –

    (a)   any information provided to be verified in such manner, or

    (b)   any document produced to be authenticated in such manner,

as he may reasonably require.

(5) 'Specified' means specified in a notice in writing given to the deputy by the Public Guardian.

42 Right of deputy to require review of decisions made by the Public Guardian

(1) A deputy may require the Public Guardian to reconsider any decision he has made in relation to the deputy.

(2) The right under paragraph (1) is exercisable by giving notice of exercise of the right to the Public Guardian before the end of the period of 14 days beginning with the date on which notice of the decision is given to the deputy.

(3) The notice of exercise of the right must –

    (a)   state the grounds on which reconsideration is required; and

(b)   contain or be accompanied by any relevant information or documents.

(4) At any time after receiving the notice and before reconsidering the decision to which it relates, the Public Guardian may require the deputy to provide him with such further information, or to produce such documents, as he reasonably considers necessary to enable him to reconsider the matter.

(5) The Public Guardian must give to the deputy –

(a)   written notice of his decision on reconsideration, and
(b)   if he upholds the previous decision, a statement of his reasons.

Miscellaneous functions

43 Applications to the Court of Protection

The Public Guardian has the function of making applications to the court in connection with his functions under the Act in such circumstances as he considers it necessary or appropriate to do so.

44 Visits by the Public Guardian or by Court of Protection Visitors at his direction

(1) This regulation applies where the Public Guardian visits, or directs a Court of Protection Visitor to visit, any person under any provision of the Act or these Regulations.

(2) The Public Guardian must notify (or make arrangements to notify) the person to be visited of –

(a)   the date or dates on which it is proposed that the visit will take place;
(b)   to the extent that it is practicable to do so, any specific matters likely to be covered in the course of the visit; and
(c)   any proposal to inform any other person that the visit is to take place.

(3) Where the visit is to be carried out by a Court of Protection Visitor –

(a)   the Public Guardian may –
    (i)   give such directions to the Visitor, and
    (ii) provide him with such information concerning the person to be visited,

as the Public Guardian considers necessary for the purposes of enabling the visit to take place and the Visitor to prepare any report the Public Guardian may require; and

(b)   the Visitor must seek to carry out the visit and take all reasonable steps to obtain such other information as he considers necessary for the purpose of preparing a report.

(4) A Court of Protection Visitor must submit any report requested by the Public Guardian in accordance with any timetable specified by the Public Guardian.

(5) If he considers it appropriate to do so, the Public Guardian may, in relation to any person interviewed in the course of preparing a report –

(a)   disclose the report to him; and
(b)   invite him to comment on it.

45 Functions in relation to persons carrying out specific transactions

(1) This regulation applies where, in accordance with an order made under section 16(2)(a) of the Act, a person ('T') has been authorised to carry out any transaction for a person who lacks capacity.

(2) The Public Guardian has the functions of –

- (a) receiving any reports from T which the court may require;
- (b) dealing with representations (including complaints) about –
  - (i) the way in which the transaction has been or is being carried out; or
  - (ii) any failure to carry it out.

(3) Regulations 38 to 41 have effect in relation to T as they have effect in relation a deputy.

46 Power to require information from donees of lasting power of attorney

(1) This regulation applies where it appears to the Public Guardian that there are circumstances suggesting that the donee of a lasting power of attorney may –

- (a) have behaved, or may be behaving, in a way that contravenes his authority or is not in the best interests of the donor of the power,
- (b) be proposing to behave in a way that would contravene that authority or would not be in the donor's best interests, or
- (c) have failed to comply with the requirements of an order made, or directions given, by the court.

(2) The Public Guardian may require the donee –

- (a) to provide specified information or information of a specified description; or
- (b) to produce specified documents or documents of a specified description.

(3) The information or documents must be provided or produced –

- (a) before the end of such reasonable period as may be specified; and
- (b) at such place as may be specified.

(4) The Public Guardian may require –

- (a) any information provided to be verified in such manner, or
- (b) any document produced to be authenticated in such manner,

as he may reasonably require.

(5) 'Specified' means specified in a notice in writing given to the donee by the Public Guardian.

47 Power to require information from attorneys under enduring power of attorney

(1) This regulation applies where it appears to the Public Guardian that there are circumstances suggesting that, having regard to all the circumstances (and in particular the attorney's relationship to or connection with the donor) the attorney under a registered enduring power of attorney may be unsuitable to be the donor's attorney.

(2) The Public Guardian may require the attorney –

    (a)   to provide specified information or information of a specified description; or

    (b)   to produce specified documents or documents of a specified description.

(3) The information or documents must be provided or produced –

    (a)   before the end of such reasonable period as may be specified; and

    (b)   at such place as may be specified.

(4) The Public Guardian may require –

    (a)   any information provided to be verified in such manner, or

    (b)   any document produced to be authenticated in such manner,

as he may reasonably require.

(5) 'Specified' means specified in a notice in writing given to the attorney by the Public Guardian.

48 Other functions in relation to enduring powers of attorney

The Public Guardian has the following functions –

    (a)   directing a Court of Protection Visitor –
        (i)   to visit an attorney under a registered enduring power of attorney, or
        (ii) to visit the donor of a registered enduring power of attorney,

and to make a report to the Public Guardian on such matters as he may direct;

    (b)   dealing with representations (including complaints) about the way in which an attorney under a registered enduring power of attorney is exercising his powers.

[SCHEDULE 1

FORM FOR INSTRUMENT INTENDED TO CREATE A LASTING POWER OF ATTORNEY (LPA PFA AND LPA HW)

PART 1: FORM FOR INSTRUMENT INTENDED TO CREATE A PROPERTY AND FINANCIAL AFFAIRS LASTING POWER OF ATTORNEY

This form can be found in Part VII of this work.

PART 2: FORM FOR INSTRUMENT INTENDED TO CREATE A HEALTH AND WELFARE LASTING POWER OF ATTORNEY

This form can be found in Part VII of this work.]

Amendment—Schedule substituted by Lasting Powers of Attorney, Enduring Powers of Attorney and Public Guardian (Amendment) Regulations 2009, SI 2009/1884.

SCHEDULE 2
NOTICE OF INTENTION TO APPLY FOR REGISTRATION OF A LASTING POWER OF ATTORNEY (LPA 001)

This form can be found in Part VII of this work.

SCHEDULE 3
APPLICATION TO REGISTER A LASTING POWER OF ATTORNEY (LPA 002)

This form can be found in Part VII of this work.

SCHEDULE 4
NOTICE OF RECEIPT OF AN APPLICATION TO REGISTER A LASTING POWER OF ATTORNEY (LPA 003A AND LPA 003B)

PART 1: NOTICE TO AN ATTORNEY OF RECEIPT OF AN APPLICATION TO REGISTER A LASTING POWER OF ATTORNEY

This form can be found in Part VII of this work.

PART 2: NOTICE TO DONOR OF RECEIPT OF AN APPLICATION TO REGISTER A LASTING POWER OF ATTORNEY

This form can be found in Part VII of this work.

SCHEDULE 5
NOTICE OF REGISTRATION OF A LASTING POWER OF ATTORNEY (LPA 004)

This form can be found in Part VII of this work.

SCHEDULE 6
DISCLAIMER BY DONEE OF A LASTING POWER OF ATTORNEY (LPA 005)

This form can be found in Part VII of this work.

SCHEDULE 7
NOTICE OF INTENTION TO APPLY FOR REGISTRATION OF AN ENDURING POWER OF ATTORNEY (EP1 PG)

This form can be found in Part VII of this work.

PART V

Amendment—Form EP1 PG amended by Public Guardian (Fees, etc) Regulations 2007, SI 2007/2051.

SCHEDULE 8
APPLICATION TO REGISTER AN ENDURING POWER OF ATTORNEY
(EP2 PG)

This form can be found in Part VII of this work.

Public Guardian (Fees, etc) Regulations 2007,
SI 2007/2051

ARRANGEMENT OF REGULATIONS

Regulation		Page
1	Citation and commencement	822
2	Interpretation	822
3	Schedule of fees	823
4	Enduring power of attorney registration fee	823
4A	Enduring power of attorney office copy fee	823
5	Lasting power of attorney registration fee	823
5A	Lasting power of attorney office copy fee	824
6	Application to search the registers fee	824
7	Appointment of deputy fee	824
8	Appointment of deputy: supervision fees	824
9	Exemptions	825
10	Reductions and remissions in exceptional circumstances	826
11	Transitional provision	826
12	Amendment to Schedule 7 of the Lasting Powers of Attorney, Enduring Powers of Attorney and Public Guardian Regulations 2007	826
	Schedule – Fees to be taken	826

1 Citation and commencement

These Regulations may be cited as the Public Guardian (Fees, etc) Regulations 2007 and shall come into force on 1 October 2007.

2 Interpretation

In these Regulations—

'the Act' means the Mental Capacity Act 2005;

'court' means the Court of Protection;

['office copy' means a true copy of the original marked by the Public Guardian as being an office copy;]

'P' means the person in respect of whom a deputy has been appointed under section 16 of the Act; and

'Public Guardian' means the officer appointed in accordance with section 57 of
the Act;

'the registers' means—

    (a)   the register of lasting powers of attorney,

    (b)   the register of enduring powers of attorney, and

    (c)   the register of court orders appointing deputies,

established and maintained by the Public Guardian under section 58(1)(a) and (b) of
and paragraph 14 of Schedule 4 to the Act.

Amendment—Definition 'office copy' inserted by Public Guardian (Fees, etc) (Amendment)
Regulations 2009, SI 2009/514.

3 Schedule of fees

The fees set out in the Schedule to these Regulations shall apply in accordance with
the following provisions of these Regulations.

4 Enduring power of attorney registration fee

(1) A fee for the registration of an enduring power of attorney shall be payable by
the person seeking to register the enduring power of attorney under regulation 24 of
the Lasting Powers of Attorney, Enduring Powers of Attorney and Public Guardian
Regulations 2007(2) (application for registration).

(2) The fee prescribed by paragraph (1) shall be payable upon the application to
register the enduring power of attorney.

[4A Enduring power of attorney office copy fee

(1) A fee for an office copy of an enduring power of attorney registered under
paragraph 13 in Part 4 of Schedule 4 to the Mental Capacity Act 2005 shall be
payable by the person requesting the office copy.

(2) The fee prescribed by paragraph (1) shall be payable at the time the request for
an office copy is made.]

Amendment—Regulation inserted by Public Guardian (Fees, etc) (Amendment) Regulations 2009,
SI 2009/514.

5 Lasting power of attorney registration fee

(1) A fee for the registration of a lasting power of attorney shall be payable by the
person seeking to register the lasting power of attorney under regulation 11 of the
Lasting Powers of Attorney, Enduring Powers of Attorney and Public Guardian
Regulations 2007 (application for registration).

(2) The fee prescribed by paragraph (1) shall be payable upon the application to
register the lasting power of attorney.

PART V

[5A Lasting power of attorney office copy fee

(1) A fee for an office copy of a lasting power of attorney registered under Part 2 of Schedule 1 to the Mental Capacity Act 2005 shall be payable by the person requesting the office copy.

(2) The fee prescribed by paragraph (1) shall be payable at the time the request for an office copy is made.]

Amendment—Regulation inserted by Public Guardian (Fees, etc) (Amendment) Regulations 2009, SI 2009/514.

6 Application to search the registers fee

(1) A fee for an application to search the registers made under regulation 31 of the Lasting Powers of Attorney, Enduring Powers of Attorney and Public Guardian Regulations 2007 (disclosure of information on a register: search by the Public Guardian) shall be payable by the person making the application.

(2) The fee prescribed by paragraph (1) shall be payable upon the application to search the registers.

(3) The fee prescribed by paragraph (1) shall not be payable where the person making the application is a:

    (a)   registered health care professional; or
    (b)   a representative of a public authority.

(4) In paragraph (3) 'registered health care professional' means a person who is a member of a profession regulated by a body mentioned in section 25(3) of the National Health Service Reform and Health Care Professions Act 2002(3).

7 Appointment of deputy fee

(1) This regulation applies where—

    (a)   the court has appointed a deputy under section 16 of the Act (powers to make decisions and appoint deputies: general); ...
    (b)   ...

(2) Where paragraph (1) applies a fee shall be payable by P.

(3) The fee prescribed by paragraph (2) shall be payable by P within 30 days of the date of the invoice for the fee.

Amendment—Paragraph (b) and word preceding it omitted by Public Guardian (Fees, etc) (Amendment) Regulations 2009, SI 2009/514.

8 Appointment of deputy: supervision fees

(1) This regulation applies where—

    (a)   the court has appointed a deputy under section 16 of the Act (powers to make decisions and appoint deputies: general); ...
    (b)   ...

(2) Where paragraph (1) applies the Public Guardian shall determine the level of supervision required under section 58(1)(c) of the Act.

(3) The levels of supervision are—

   (a)   type I (highest);
   [(aa) type IIA (intermediate); and]
   (b)   type II (lower); and
   (c)   type III (minimal).

(4) Where the level of supervision determined by the Public Guardian in accordance with paragraph (2) is type I (highest)[, type IIA (intermediate)] or type II (lower) an annual supervision fee shall be payable by P until the appointment of the deputy is terminated.

(5) Subject to paragraphs (6) and (7), the appropriate supervision fee prescribed by paragraph (2) shall be due on 31 March each year and shall be payable by P within 30 days of the date of the invoice for the fee.

(6) Where the period for which the fee prescribed by paragraph (4) is payable is less than one year, the amount of the fee payable shall be such proportion of the full fee as that period bears to one year.

(7) Where the deputy's appointment terminates, the appropriate fee prescribed by paragraph (4) shall be due on the date of termination and shall be payable within 30 days of the date of the invoice for the fee.

(8) In the event of termination of the appointment due to P's death, the appropriate fee prescribed by paragraph (2) shall be payable by P's estate.

Amendments—Sub-paragraph (1)(b) omitted, sub-para (3)(aa) inserted and words in para (4) inserted by Public Guardian (Fees, etc) (Amendment) Regulations 2009, SI 2009/514.

9 Exemptions

(1) Subject to paragraph (2) no fee shall be payable under these regulations when, at the time when the fee would otherwise become payable, the relevant person is in receipt of any qualifying benefit.

(2) Paragraph (1) does not apply to a person who has an award of damages in excess of £16,000 which has been disregarded for the purposes of determining eligibility for that benefit.

(3) For the purposes of regulation 4 the relevant person is the donor of the enduring power of attorney.

(4) For the purposes of regulation 5 the relevant person is the donor of the lasting power of attorney.

(5) For the purposes of regulation 6 the relevant person is the person making the application.

(6) the purposes of regulations 7 and 8 the relevant person is P.

(7) The following are qualifying benefits for the purposes of paragraph (1)—

   (a)   income support under the Social Security Contributions and Benefits Act 1992(4);
   (b)   working tax credit, provided that—
         (i)   child tax credit is being paid to the relevant person, or to a couple (as defined in section 3(5)(A) of the Tax Credits Act 2002(5)) which includes the relevant person; or
         (ii)   there is a disability element or severe disability element (or both) to the child tax credit received by the relevant person;

PART V

- (c) income-based job-seeker's allowance under the Jobseekers Act 1995(6);
- (d) guarantee credit under the State Pensions Credit Act 2002(7);
- (e) council tax benefit under the Social Security Contributions and Benefits Act 1992; ...
- (f) housing benefit under the Social Security Contributions and Benefits Act 1992[; and
- (g) income-related employment and support allowance under Part 1 of the Welfare Reform Act 2007.]

Amendments—Word omitted in sub-para (7)(e) and sub-para (7)(g) and word 'and' preceding it inserted by Public Guardian (Fees, etc) (Amendment) Regulations 2009, SI 2009/514.

10 Reductions and remissions in exceptional circumstances

Where it appears to the Public Guardian that the payment of any fee prescribed by these Regulations would, owing to the exceptional circumstances of the particular case, involve undue hardship, he may reduce or remit the fee in that case.

11 Transitional provision

(1) In respect of the administration fee that would have been payable under rule 78 of the Court of Protection Rules 2001(8) on 31 March 2008, the appropriate proportion of that fee shall be due on 30 September 2007 and shall be payable within 30 days of the date of the invoice for the fee.

(2) Where the period for which the fee prescribed by paragraph (1) is payable is less than six months, the amount of the fee payable shall be such proportion of that fee as that period bears to six months.

12 Amendment to Schedule 7 of the Lasting Powers of Attorney, Enduring Powers of Attorney and Public Guardian Regulations 2007

(1) Schedule 7 of the Lasting Powers of Attorney, Enduring Powers of Attorney and Public Guardian Regulations 2007 is amended as follows.

(2) For paragraph 1 of Form EP1PG substitute 'You have the right to object to the proposed registration on one or more of the grounds set out below. You must notify the Office of the Public Guardian of your objection within five weeks from the day this notice was given to you. You may make an application to the Court of Protection under rule 68 of the Court of Protection Rules 2007(9) for a decision on the matter. No fee is payable for such an application. If you do not make such an application, the Public Guardian will ask for the court's directions about registration.'

Regulation 3

SCHEDULE
FEES TO BE TAKEN

Column 1	Column 2
Enduring power of attorney registration (regulation 4)	£120.00

[Enduring power of attorney office copy fee (regulation 4A)	£25]
Lasting power of attorney registration (regulation 5)	[£120.00]
[Lasting power of attorney office copy fee (regulation 5A)	£25]
Application to search the registers (regulation 6)	£25.00
Appointment of deputy (regulation 7)	[£100.00]
Type I (highest) supervision (regulation 8)	£800.00 per annum
[Type IIA (intermediate) supervision (regulation 8)	£350.00 per annum]
Type II (lower) supervision (regulation 8)	£175.00 per annum
Type III (minimal) supervision (regulation 8)	No fee

Amendments—Entries inserted and figures substituted by Public Guardian (Fees, etc) (Amendment) Regulations 2009, SI 2009/514.

Court of Protection Fees Order 2007, SI 2007/1745

1 Citation and commencement

This Order may be cited as the Court of Protection Fees Order 2007 and comes into force on 1 October 2007.

2 Interpretation

In this Order –

'the Act' means the Mental Capacity Act 2005;
'appellant' means the person who brings or seeks to bring an appeal;
'court' means the Court of Protection;
'P' means any person (other than a protected party) who lacks or, so far as consistent with the context, is alleged to lack capacity to make a decision or decisions in relation to any matter that is the subject of an application to the court and references to a person who lacks capacity are to be construed in accordance with the Act;
'protected party' means a party or an intended party (other than P or a child) who lacks capacity to conduct the proceedings;

'the Regulations' means the Lasting Powers of Attorney, Enduring Powers of
Attorney and Public Guardian Regulations 2007; and
'the Rules' means the Court of Protection Rules 2007.

3 Schedule of fees

The fees set out in the Schedule to this Order shall apply in accordance with the
following provisions of this Order.

4 Application fee

(1) An application fee shall be payable by the applicant on making an application
under Part 9 of the Rules (how to start proceedings) in accordance with the
following provisions of this article.

(2) Where permission to start proceedings is required under Part 8 of the Rules
(permission), the fee prescribed by paragraph (1) shall be payable on making an
application for permission.

(3) The fee prescribed by paragraph (1) shall not be payable where the application
is made under –

    (a) rule 67 of the Rules (applications relating to lasting powers of attorney)
by –
       (i)   the donee of a lasting power of attorney, or
      (ii) a person named in a statement made by the donor of a lasting power
of attorney in accordance with paragraph 2(1)(c)(i) of Part 1 of
Schedule 1 to the Act,

and is solely in respect of an objection to the registration of a lasting power of
attorney; or

    (b) rule 68 of the Rules (applications relating to enduring powers of attorney)
by –
       (i)   a donor of an enduring power of attorney,
      (ii) an attorney under an enduring power of attorney, or
     (iii) a person listed in paragraph 6(1) of Part 3 of Schedule 4 to the Act,
and is solely in respect of an objection to the registration of an
enduring power of attorney.

(4) The fee prescribed by paragraph (1) shall not be payable where the application
is made by the Public Guardian.

(5) Where a fee has been paid under paragraph (1) it shall be refunded where P dies
within five days of the application being filed.

5 Appeal fee

(1) An appeal fee shall be payable by the appellant on the filing of an appellant's
notice under Part 20 of the Rules (appeals) in accordance with the following
provisions of this article.

(2) The fee prescribed by paragraph (1) shall not be payable where the appeal is –

    (a) brought by the Public Guardian; or
    (b) an appeal against a decision of a nominated officer made under rule 197 of
the Rules (appeal against a decision of a nominated officer).

(3) The fee prescribed by paragraph (1) shall be refunded where P dies within five days of the appellant's notice being filed.

6 Hearing fees

(1) A hearing fee shall be payable by the applicant where the court has –

    (a)   held a hearing in order to determine the case; and
    (b)   made a final order, declaration or decision.

(2) A hearing fee shall be payable by the appellant in relation to an appeal where the court has –

    (a)   held a hearing in order to determine the appeal; and
    (b)   made a final order, declaration or decision in relation to the appeal.

(3) The fees prescribed by paragraphs (1) and (2) shall not be payable where the hearing is in respect of an application or appeal brought by the Public Guardian.

(4) The fee prescribed by paragraph (2) shall not be payable where the hearing is in respect of an appeal against a decision of a nominated officer made under rule 197 of the Rules (appeal against a decision of a nominated officer).

(5) The fee prescribed by paragraph (1) shall not be payable where the applicant was not required to pay an application fee under Article 4(1) by virtue of Article 4(3).

(6) The fees prescribed by paragraphs (1) and (2) shall be payable by the applicant or appellant as the case may be within 30 days of the date of the invoice for the fee.

PART V

7 Fee for request for copy of court document

(1) A fee for a copy of a court document shall be payable by the person requesting the copy of the document.

(2) (*revoked*)

(3) The fees prescribed by paragraph (1) shall be payable at the time the request for the copy is made to the court.

Amendments—SI 2009/513.

8 Exemptions

(1) Subject to paragraph (2) no fee shall be payable under this Order by a person who, at the time when a fee would otherwise become payable, is in receipt of any qualifying benefit.

(2) Paragraph (1) does not apply to a person who has an award of damages in excess of £16,000 which has been disregarded for the purposes of determining eligibility for that benefit.

(3) The following are qualifying benefits for the purposes of paragraph 1 above –

    (a)   income support under the Social Security Contributions and Benefits Act 1992;
    (b)   working tax credit, provided that –

(i) child tax credit is being paid to the person, or to a couple (as defined in section 3(5)(A) of the Tax Credits Act 2002) which includes the person; or

(ii) there is a disability element or severe disability element (or both) to the tax credit received by the person;

(c) income-based jobseeker's allowance under the Jobseekers Act 1995;

(d) guarantee credit under the State Pensions Credit Act 2002;

(e) council tax benefit under the Social Security Contributions and Benefits Act 1992;

(f) housing benefit under the Social Security Contributions and Benefits Act 1992; and

(g) income-related employment and support allowance under Part 1 of the Welfare Reform Act 2007.

Amendments—SI 2009/513.

9 Reductions and remissions in exceptional circumstances

Where it appears to the Lord Chancellor that the payment of any fee prescribed by this Order would, owing to the exceptional circumstances of the particular case, involve undue hardship, he may reduce or remit the fee in that case.

10 Transitional provision

(1) In this article 'Court of Protection' means the office of the Supreme Court called the Court of Protection which ceases to exist under section 45(6) of the Act.

(2) Where a hearing that takes place on or after 1 October 2007 was listed by the Court of Protection before 1 October 2007, no hearing fee shall be payable under Article 6.

SCHEDULE

FEES TO BE TAKEN

Article 3

Column 1	Column 2
Application fee (Article 4)	£400.00
Appeal fee (Article 5)	£400.00
Hearing fees (Article 6)	£500.00
Copy of a document fee (Article 7(1))	£5.00

Amendments—SI 2009/513.

Mental Capacity Act 2005 (Transitional and Consequential Provisions) Order 2007,
SI 2007/1898

1 Citation and commencement

This Order may be cited as the Mental Capacity Act 2005 (Transitional and Consequential Provisions) Order 2007, and comes into force on 1 October 2007.

2 Interpretation

In this Order –

    (a) 'the Act' means the Mental Capacity Act 2005; and

    (b) 'Court of Protection' refers

        (i) the first time the expression appears in article 4, to the office of the Supreme Court called the Court of Protection mentioned in section 45(6) of the Act, and

        (ii) where the expression appears in articles 3, 4(a) and (b), to the superior court of record established by section 45(1) of the Act.

3 Proceedings begun in the High Court before 1 October 2007

(1) This article applies to any proceedings about P's personal welfare begun in the High Court before 1 October 2007 in respect of which the Court of Protection would, but for this article, have jurisdiction on and after that date under section 16 of the Act.

(2) The proceedings may continue to be dealt with, until they are finally decided, in accordance with the arrangements existing immediately before 1 October 2007.

(3) For the purposes of paragraph (2), an application is finally decided when it is determined and there is no possibility of the determination being reversed or varied on an appeal.

(4) In dealing with proceedings under this article, the High Court retains all the powers and jurisdiction in relation to any matter that is the subject of the proceedings that it had immediately before the commencement of the Act.

(5) In this article –

    (a) 'P' means any person (other than a protected party) who lacks, or so far as consistent with the context is alleged to lack, capacity to make a decision or decisions in relation to any matter that is the subject of an application to the court and references to a person who lacks capacity are to be construed in accordance with the Act;

    (b) 'personal welfare' is to be construed in accordance with section 17 of the Act; and

    (c) 'protected party' means a party, or an intended party (other than P or a child), who lacks capacity to conduct the proceedings.

PART V

4 Senior Judge of the Court of Protection

The person who, immediately before the commencement of Part 2 of the Act, holds the office of Master of the Court of Protection, shall be treated as –

(a) being a circuit judge nominated under section 46(1) of the Act to exercise the jurisdiction of the Court of Protection; and

(b) having been appointed the Senior Judge of the Court of Protection under section 46(4) of the Act.

5 Advance decisions to refuse life-sustaining treatment

(1) An advance decision refusing life-sustaining treatment shall be treated as valid and applicable to a treatment and does not have to satisfy the requirements mentioned in paragraph (3) if the conditions in paragraph (2) are met.

(2) The conditions that must be met are that –

(a) a person providing health care for a person ('P') reasonably believes that –
  (i) P has made the advance decision refusing life-sustaining treatment before 1 October 2007, and
  (ii) P has lacked the capacity to comply with the provisions mentioned in paragraph (3) since 1 October 2007;

(b) the advance decision is in writing;

(c) P has not –
  (i) withdrawn the decision at a time when he had capacity to do so, or
  (ii) done anything else clearly inconsistent with the advance decision remaining his fixed decision;

(d) P does not have the capacity to give or refuse consent to the treatment in question at the material time;

(e) the treatment in question is the treatment specified in the advance decision;

(f) any circumstances specified in the advance decision are present; and

(g) there are no reasonable grounds for believing that circumstances exist which P did not anticipate at the time of the advance decision and which would have affected his decision had he anticipated them.

(3) The requirements that do not have to be satisfied are as follows –

(a) the requirement for the decision to be verified by a statement by P to the effect that the advance decision is to apply to that treatment even if life is at risk (section 25(5)(a) of the Act); and

(b) the requirement for a signed and witnessed advance decision (section 25(6)(b) to (d) of the Act).

(4) In this article, 'advance decision' has the meaning given in section 24(1) of the Act.

6 Minor and consequential amendments

Schedule 1 contains minor and consequential amendments.

SCHEDULE 1
MINOR AND CONSEQUENTIAL AMENDMENTS

Article 6

1 Trustee Savings Bank Life Annuity Regulations 1930

In regulation 16(2) of the Trustee Savings Bank Life Annuity Regulations 1930 –

  (a) for the words 'a person who is incapable, by reason of mental disorder within the meaning of the Mental Health Act 1959, of managing and administering his property and affairs' substitute 'a person who lacks mental capacity within the meaning of the Mental Capacity Act 2005 to administer and manage his property and affairs'; and

  (b) for the word 'receiver' substitute 'deputy'.

2 Savings Contract Regulations 1969

(1) The Savings Contract Regulations 1969 are amended in accordance with this paragraph.

(2) In regulation 2(1) (interpretation), omit the entries for 'mentally disordered person' and 'receiver' and, in the appropriate alphabetical position, insert –

  (a) ' "deputy" in the application of these Regulations to England and Wales, means, in relation to any decision made for a person who lacks capacity, a deputy appointed by the Court of Protection for that person with power to make decisions in relation to the matters in question;'; and

  (b) ' "person who lacks capacity" means a person who lacks capacity within the meaning of the Mental Capacity Act 2005;'.

(3) In regulation 7 (payment in case of mentally disordered persons) –

  (a) in the title, for 'mentally disordered persons' substitute 'persons who lack capacity'; and

  (b) in paragraphs (1) and (2) in each place –
    (i)   for 'mentally disordered person' substitute 'person who lacks capacity', and
    (ii) for 'receiver' substitute 'deputy'.

(4) In regulation 12 (persons under disability) –

  (a) for 'mentally disordered person' substitute 'person who lacks capacity'; and

  (b) for 'receiver' substitute 'deputy'.

(5) In regulation 27 (application to Scotland) –

  (a) in paragraph (a), for 'mentally disordered person' substitute 'person who lacks capacity'; and

  (b) in paragraph (b), for 'receiver in relation to a mentally disordered person' substitute 'deputy in relation to a person who lacks capacity'.

(6) In regulation 28(2) (application to Northern Ireland) –

  (a) in sub-paragraph (a), for 'mentally disordered person' substitute 'person who lacks capacity'; and

PART V

(b)   in sub-paragraph (b), for 'receiver in relation to a mentally disordered person' substitute 'deputy in relation to a person who lacks capacity'.

(7) In regulation 29(2)(a) (application to the Isle of Man), for 'receiver in relation to a mentally disordered person' substitute 'deputy in relation to a person who lacks capacity'.

(8) In regulation 30 (application to the Channel Islands) –

(a)   in paragraphs (2)(a) and (3)(a), for 'mentally disordered person' substitute 'person who lacks capacity'; and
(b)   in paragraphs (2)(b) and (3)(b), for 'receiver in relation to a mentally disordered person' substitute 'deputy in relation to a person who lacks capacity'.

3 Pensions Increase (Judicial Pensions) Regulations 1972

In paragraph 9 of the Schedule to the Pensions Increase (Judicial Pensions) Regulations 1972, omit the reference to a Master of the Court of Protection except in the case of a person holding that office immediately before the commencement of this paragraph or who had previously retired from that office or died.

4 National Savings Bank Regulations 1972

(1) The National Savings Bank Regulations 1972 are amended in accordance with this paragraph.

(2) In regulation 2(1) (interpretation), omit the entries for 'mentally disordered person' and 'receiver' and, in the appropriate alphabetical position, insert –

(a)   ' "deputy" in the application of these Regulations to England and Wales, means, in relation to any decision made for a person who lacks capacity, a deputy appointed by the Court of Protection for that person with power to make decisions in relation to the matters in question;'; and
(b)   ' "person who lacks capacity" means a person who lacks capacity within the meaning of the Mental Capacity Act 2005;'.

(3) In regulation 7 (mentally disordered persons) –

(a)   in the title, for 'Mentally disordered persons' substitute 'Persons who lack capacity';
(b)   in paragraph (1), for 'mentally disordered person, by his receiver' substitute 'person who lacks capacity, by his deputy';
(c)   in paragraphs (2), (3) and (4) in each place –
(i)   for 'mentally disordered person' substitute 'person who lacks capacity', and
(ii)   for 'receiver' substitute 'deputy';

(4) In regulation 8(4)(c) (joint accounts) –

(a)   for 'mentally disordered person' substitute 'person who lacks capacity'; and
(b)   for 'receiver' substitute 'deputy'.

(5) In regulation 9(4) (trust accounts) –

(a)   for both references to 'mentally disordered person' substitute 'person who lacks capacity'; and

(b) for 'receiver' substitute 'deputy'.

(6) In regulation 37(1)(b) (payment under nomination) –

(a) for 'mentally disordered person' substitute 'person who lacks capacity'; and

(b) for 'receiver' substitute 'deputy'.

(7) In regulation 45 (persons under disability) –

(a) for 'mentally disordered person' substitute 'person who lacks capacity'; and

(b) for 'receiver' substitute 'deputy'.

(8) In regulation 57(2)(a) (application to the Isle of Man), for 'receiver in relation to a mentally disordered person' substitute 'deputy in relation to a person who lacks capacity'.

(9) In regulation 58 (application to the Channel Islands) –

(a) in paragraphs (2)(a) and (3)(a), for 'mentally disordered person' substitute 'person who lacks capacity'; and

(b) in paragraphs (2)(b) and (3)(b), for 'receiver in relation to a mentally disordered person' substitute 'deputy in relation to a person who lacks capacity'.

5 Premium Savings Bond Regulations 1972

(1) The Premium Savings Bond Regulations 1972 are amended in accordance with this paragraph.

(2) In regulation 2(1) (interpretation), omit the entries for 'mentally disordered person' and 'receiver' and, in the appropriate alphabetical position, insert –

(a) ' "deputy" in the application of these Regulations to England and Wales, means, in relation to any decision made for a person who lacks capacity, a deputy appointed by the Court of Protection for that person with power to make decisions in relation to the matters in question;'; and

(b) ' "person who lacks capacity" means a person who lacks capacity within the meaning of the Mental Capacity Act 2005;'.

(3) In regulation 4 (persons entitled to purchase and hold bonds) –

(a) in paragraph (3)(b), for 'mentally disordered person, by his receiver' substitute 'a person who lacks capacity, by his deputy'; and

(b) in paragraph (5)(b), for 'mentally disordered person' substitute 'person who lacks capacity'.

(4) In regulation 10 (payment in case of mentally disordered persons) –

(a) in the title, for 'Mentally disordered persons' substitute 'Persons who lack capacity';

(b) in paragraph (1) –
  (i) for 'mentally disordered person' substitute 'person who lacks capacity', and
  (ii) for 'receiver' substitute 'deputy'; and

(c) in paragraph (2), for 'mentally disordered person for whose estate no receiver' substitute 'person who lacks capacity for whom no deputy has been appointed in relation to his property and affairs'.

PART V

(5)In regulation 16 (persons under disability) –

(a)   for 'mentally disordered person' substitute 'person who lacks capacity'; and

(b)   for 'receiver' substitute 'deputy'.

(6) In regulation 31 (application to Scotland) –

(a)   in paragraph (a), for 'mentally disordered person' substitute 'person who lacks capacity'; and

(b)   in paragraph (b), for 'receiver in relation to a mentally disordered person' substitute 'deputy in relation to a person who lacks capacity'.

(7) In regulation 32(2) (application to Northern Ireland) –

(a)   in paragraph (a), for 'mentally disordered person' substitute 'person who lacks capacity'; and

(b)   in paragraph (b), for 'receiver in relation to a mentally disordered person' substitute 'deputy in relation to a person who lacks capacity'.

(8) In regulation 33(2)(a) (application to the Isle of Man), for 'receiver in relation to a mentally disordered person' substitute 'deputy in relation to a person who lacks capacity'.

(9) In regulation 34 (application to the Channel Islands) –

(a)   in paragraphs (2)(a) and (3)(a), for 'mentally disordered person' substitute 'person who lacks capacity'; and

(b)   in paragraphs (2)(b) and (3)(b), for 'receiver in relation to a mentally disordered person' substitute 'deputy in relation to a person who lacks capacity'.

6 National Savings Stock Register Regulations 1976

(1) The National Savings Stock Register Regulations 1976 are amended in accordance with this paragraph.

(2) In regulation 2(1) (interpretation), omit the entries for 'mentally disordered person' and 'receiver' and, in the appropriate alphabetical position, insert –

(a)   ' "deputy" in the application of these Regulations to England and Wales, means, in relation to any decision made for a person who lacks capacity, a deputy appointed by the Court of Protection for that person with power to make decisions in relation to the matters in question;'; and

(b)   ' "person who lacks capacity" means a person who lacks capacity within the meaning of the Mental Capacity Act 2005;'.

(3) In regulation 31 (persons under disability) –

(a)   in paragraphs (1) and (2) in each place –
(i)   for 'mentally disordered person' substitute 'person who lacks capacity'; and
(ii)   for 'receiver' substitute 'deputy'; and

(b)   in paragraphs (3) and (4), for 'mentally disordered person' substitute 'person who lacks capacity'.

(4) In regulation 59 (application to Scotland) –

(a)   in paragraph (a), for 'mentally disordered person' substitute 'person who lacks capacity'; and

(b) in paragraph (b), for 'receiver in relation to a mentally disordered person' substitute 'deputy in relation to a person who lacks capacity'.

(5) In regulation 60(2) (application to Northern Ireland) –

(a) in paragraph (a), for 'mentally disordered person' substitute 'person who lacks capacity'; and

(b) in paragraph (b), for 'receiver in relation to a mentally disordered person' substitute 'deputy in relation to a person who lacks capacity'.

(6) In regulation 61(2)(a) (application to the Isle of Man), for 'receiver in relation to a mentally disordered person' substitute 'deputy in relation to a person who lacks capacity'.

(7) In regulation 62 (application to the Channel Islands) –

(a) in paragraphs (2)(a) and (3)(a), for 'mentally disordered person' substitute 'person who lacks capacity'; and

(b) in paragraphs (2)(b) and (3)(b), for 'receiver in relation to a mentally disordered person' substitute 'deputy in relation to a person who lacks capacity'.

7 Motor Vehicles (Tests) Regulations 1981

In regulation 9(1)(c) (cessations: general) of the Motor Vehicles (Tests) Regulations 1981, for the words from 'patient' to 'Mental Health Act 1983' substitute 'person who lacks capacity (within the meaning of the Mental Capacity Act 2005) to carry on the activities covered by the authorisation'.

8 The Mental Health Review Tribunal Rules 1983

For rule 7(c) (notice to other persons interested) of the Mental Health Review Tribunal Rules 1983, substitute –

'(c) where there is an extant order of either –

(i) the office of the Supreme Court called the Court of Protection mentioned in section 45(6) of the Mental Capacity Act 2005, or

(ii) the superior court of record established by section 45(1) of the Mental Capacity Act 2005, to the court referred to in sub-paragraph (ii) of this rule;'

9 Savings Certificates (Yearly Plan) Regulations 1984

(1) The Savings Certificates (Yearly Plan) Regulations 1984 are amended in accordance with this paragraph.

(2) In regulation 2 (interpretation), omit the entries for 'mentally disordered person' and 'receiver' and, in the appropriate alphabetical position, insert –

(a) ' "deputy" in the application of these Regulations to England and Wales, means, in relation to any decision made for a person who lacks capacity, a deputy appointed by the Court of Protection for that person with power to make decisions in relation to the matters in question;'; and

(b) ' "person who lacks capacity" means a person who lacks capacity within the meaning of the Mental Capacity Act 2005;'.

PART V

(3) In regulation 4(2)(b) (persons entitled to enter into agreements and to hold certificates), for 'mentally disordered person, by his receiver' substitute 'person who lacks capacity, by his deputy'.

(4) In regulation 5(2) (maximum payments), for 'mentally disordered person' substitute 'person who lacks capacity'.

(5) In regulation 8 (repayment in case of persons under 7 years of age and mentally disordered persons) –

    (a) in the title, for 'mentally disordered persons' substitute 'persons who lack capacity';

    (b) in paragraph (2), for 'mentally disordered person, by his receiver' substitute 'person who lacks capacity, by his deputy'; and

    (c) in paragraph (3), for 'mentally disordered person for whose estate no receiver' substitute 'person who lacks capacity for whom no deputy'.

(6) In regulation 9(1)(a) (repayment in case of joint trustees) –

    (a) for 'mentally disordered person' substitute 'person who lacks capacity'; and

    (b) for 'receiver' substitute 'deputy'.

(7) In regulation 10(1)(a) (repayment in case of certificate held by person jointly) –

    (a) for 'mentally disordered person' substitute 'person who lacks capacity'; and

    (b) for 'receiver' substitute 'deputy'.

(8) In regulation 18 (persons under disability) –

    (a) for 'mentally disordered person' substitute 'person who lacks capacity'; and

    (b) for 'receiver' substitute 'deputy'.

(9) In regulation 33 (application to Scotland) –

    (a) in paragraph (a), for 'mentally disordered person' substitute 'person who lacks capacity'; and

    (b) in paragraph (b), for 'receiver in relation to a mentally disordered person' substitute 'deputy in relation to a person who lacks capacity'.

(10) In regulation 34(2) (application to Northern Ireland) –

    (a) in paragraph (a), for 'mentally disordered person' substitute 'person who lacks capacity'; and

    (b) in paragraph (b), for 'receiver in relation to a mentally disordered person' substitute 'deputy in relation to a person who lacks capacity'.

(11) In regulation 35(2)(a) (application to the Isle of Man), for 'receiver in relation to a mentally disordered person' substitute 'deputy in relation to a person who lacks capacity'.

(12) In regulation 36 (application to the Channel Islands) –

    (a) in paragraphs (2)(a) and (3)(a), for 'mentally disordered person' substitute 'person who lacks capacity'; and

    (b) in paragraphs (2)(b) and (3)(b), for 'receiver in relation to a mentally disordered person' substitute 'deputy in relation to a person who lacks capacity'.

10 Road Vehicles (Construction and Use) Regulations 1986

In paragraph 5(1)(c) of Part 1 of Schedule 3B (authorised sealers) to the Road Vehicles (Construction and Use) Regulations 1986, for the words from 'patient' to 'Mental Health Act 1983, substitute 'person who lacks capacity (within the meaning of the Mental Capacity Act 2005) to carry on the activities covered by the authorisation'.

11 Operation of Public Service Vehicles (Partnership) Regulations 1986

On the entry as to section 57(2) of the Public Passenger Vehicles Act 1981, in column 2 of Part 1 of the Schedule to the Operation of Public Service Vehicles (Partnership) Regulations 1986, for the words from 'patient' to 'Mental Health Act 1983', substitute 'person who lacks capacity (within the meaning of the Mental Capacity Act 2005) to carry on the activities covered by the licence'.

12 Insolvency Rules 1986

(1) The Insolvency Rules 1986 are amended in accordance with this paragraph.

(2) In rule 4.214 (witness unfit for examination) –

  (a) in paragraph (1) –
    (i) omit the words 'mental disorder or', and
    (ii) before 'is suffering' insert 'is a person who lacks capacity within the meaning of the Mental Capacity Act 2005 or', and
  (b) in paragraph (3)(a), for the words 'patient within the meaning of the Mental Health Act 1983' substitute 'person who lacks capacity within the meaning of the Mental Capacity Act 2005'.

(3) In rule 6.174 (bankrupt unfit for examination) –

  (a) in paragraph (1) –
    (i) omit the words 'mental disorder or', and
    (ii) before 'is suffering' insert 'is a person who lacks capacity within the meaning of the Mental Capacity Act 2005 or', and
  (b) in paragraph (3)(a), for the words 'patient within the meaning of the Mental Health Act 1983', substitute 'person who lacks capacity within the meaning of the Mental Capacity Act 2005'.

(4) In the heading to Part 7 of Chapter 7, for 'Persons Incapable of Managing their Affairs', substitute 'Persons who Lack Capacity to Manage their Affairs'.

(5) In rule 7.43 (introductory) –

  (a) in paragraph (1), for 'is incapable of managing and administering his property and affairs', substitute 'lacks capacity within the meaning of the Mental Capacity Act 2005 to manage and administer his property and affairs'; and
  (b) in paragraph (1)(a), for 'mental disorder within the meaning of the Mental Health Act 1983', substitute 'lacking capacity within the meaning of the Mental Capacity Act 2005'.

(6) In paragraph 4.64 of Part 4 of Schedule 4, Forms Index (companies winding up) –

(a) after the words 'person who', insert 'lacks capacity to manage and administer his property and affairs or'; and

(b) for the words 'mental disorder or', substitute 'a'.

(7) In paragraph 6.57 of Part 6 of Schedule 4, Forms Index (bankruptcy) –

(a) after the words 'bankrupt who', insert 'lacks capacity to manage and administer his property and affairs or'; and

(b) for the words 'mental disorder or', substitute 'a'.

(8) For form 4.64 in Schedule 4 (forms), substitute the form in Schedule 2 (Part 1).

(9) For form 6.57 in Schedule 4 (forms), substitute the form in Schedule 2 (Part 2).

13 Non-contentious Probate Rules 1987

(1) Rule 31 (grant to attorneys) and 35 (grants in case of mental incapacity) of the Non-contentious Probate Rules 1987 are amended in accordance with this paragraph.

(2) For rule 31(3) substitute –

'(3) Where the donor referred to in paragraph (1) above lacks capacity within the meaning of the Mental Capacity Act 2005 and the attorney is acting under an enduring power of attorney or lasting power of attorney, the application shall be made in accordance with rule 35.'

(3) For rule 35, in the title, for the words 'mental incapacity' substitute 'lack of mental capacity'.

(4) In rule 35(1), for the words 'incapable person' substitute 'person who lacks capacity within the meaning of the Mental Capacity Act 2005'.

(5) In rule 35(2) –

(a) for the words 'is by reason of mental incapacity incapable of managing', substitute 'lacks capacity within the meaning of the Mental Capacity Act 2005 to manage';

(b) for each reference to an incapable person substitute a reference to a person who lacks capacity within the meaning of the Mental Capacity Act 2005; and

(c) at the end of sub-paragraph (b), insert 'or lasting power of attorney'.

(6) In rule 35(4), for the words 'incapable person', substitute 'person who lacks capacity within the meaning of the Mental Capacity Act 2005'.

14 Judicial Pension (Preservation of Benefits) Order 1988

In Schedule 2 to the Judicial Pension (Preservation of Benefits) Order 1988, omit the reference to a Master of the Court of Protection except in the case of a person holding that office immediately before the commencement of this paragraph or who had previously retired from that office or died.

15 Judicial Pensions (Requisite Benefits) Order 1988

In Schedule 2 (office) to the Judicial Pensions (Requisite Benefits) Order 1988, omit the reference to a Master of the Court of Protection except in the case of a person holding that office immediately before the commencement of this paragraph or who had previously retired from that office or died.

16 Church of England Pensions Regulations 1988

(1) Regulation 30 (payment of pensions in respect of persons suffering from mental disorder) of the Church of England Pensions Regulations 1988 is amended in accordance with this paragraph.

(2) In paragraph (1) –

    (a) for the words 'is incapable by reason of mental disorder within the meaning of the Mental Health Act, 1983, of managing and administering', substitute 'lacks capacity (within the meaning of the Mental Capacity Act 2005) to manage and administer'; and

    (b) in sub-paragraph (a), for the words 'suffering from mental disorder', substitute 'a person lacking capacity (within the meaning of the Mental Capacity Act 2005) to manage and administer his property and affairs'.

(3) In paragraph (2) –

    (a) for the words 'authority having jurisdiction under Part VII of the Mental Health Act, 1983', substitute 'Court of Protection'; and

    (b) for each reference to 'that authority' substitute a reference to 'the Court of Protection'.

(4) In paragraph (3) –

    (a) for the words 'the authority having jurisdiction under Part VII of the Mental Health Act, 1983 give', substitute 'the Court of Protection gives'; and

    (b) for the words 'that authority', substitute 'the Court of Protection'.

17 Savings Certificates Regulations 1991

(1) The Savings Certificates Regulations 1991 are amended in accordance with this paragraph.

(2) In regulation 2(1) (interpretation), omit the entries for 'mentally disordered person' and 'receiver' and, in the appropriate alphabetical position, insert –

    (a) ' "deputy" in the application of these Regulations to England and Wales, means, in relation to any decision made for a person who lacks capacity, a deputy appointed by the Court of Protection for that person with power to make decisions in relation to the matters in question;'; and

    (b) ' "person who lacks capacity" means a person who lacks capacity within the meaning of the Mental Capacity Act 2005;'.

(3) In regulation 4(2)(c) (persons entitled to purchase and hold certificates), for 'mentally disordered person, by his receiver' substitute 'person who lacks capacity, by his deputy'.

(4) In regulation 9 (repayment in case of persons under 7 years of age and mentally disordered persons) –

    (a) in the title, for 'mentally disordered persons' substitute 'persons who lack capacity';

PART V

(b)   in paragraph (2), for 'mentally disordered person shall be made by his receiver' substitute 'person who lacks capacity shall be made by his deputy'; and

(c)   in paragraph (4), for the words from 'mentally disordered person for' to 'of the mentally disordered person' substitute 'person who lacks capacity in respect of whom no deputy has been appointed, the Director of Savings may, if he thinks fit, pay the whole or any part of the amount repayable in respect of the certificate to any person who satisfies him that he will apply the payment for the maintenance or otherwise for the benefit of the person who lacks capacity'.

(5) In regulation 10(1)(a) (repayment in case of certificate held by persons jointly) –

(a)   for 'mentally disordered person' substitute 'person who lacks capacity'; and

(b)   for 'receiver' substitute 'person who lacks capacity'.

(6) In regulation 18 (persons under disability) –

(a)   for 'mentally disordered person' substitute 'person who lacks capacity'; and

(b)   for 'receiver' substitute 'deputy'.

(7) In regulation 33 (application to Scotland) –

(a)   in paragraph (a), for 'mentally disordered person' substitute 'person who lacks capacity'; and

(b)   in paragraph (b), for 'receiver in relation to a mentally disordered person' substitute 'deputy in relation to a person who lacks capacity'.

(8) In regulation 34 (application to Northern Ireland) –

(a)   in paragraph (b), for 'mentally disordered person' substitute 'person who lacks capacity'; and

(b)   in paragraph (c), for 'receiver in relation to a mentally disordered person' substitute 'deputy in relation to a person who lacks capacity'.

(9) In regulation 35(2) (application to the Isle of Man) –

(a)   in paragraph (a), for 'mentally disordered person' substitute 'person who lacks capacity'; and

(b)   in paragraph (b), for 'receiver in relation to any act or thing done in respect of a mentally disordered person shall be construed as a reference to a receiver' substitute 'deputy in relation to any decision made for a person who lacks capacity shall be construed as a reference to a deputy'.

(10) In regulation 36 (application to the Channel Islands) –

(a)   in paragraphs (2)(a) and (3)(a), for 'mentally disordered person' substitute 'person who lacks capacity'; and

(b)   in paragraphs (2)(b) and (3)(b), for 'receiver in relation to a mentally disordered person' substitute 'deputy in relation to a person who lacks capacity'.

(11) In paragraph 2 of Part 1 of Schedule 1 (persons entitled to hold index-linked certificates to be purchased before 7th September 1981), for 'receiver on behalf of and in the name of a mentally disordered person' substitute 'deputy on behalf of and in the name of a person who lacks capacity'.

18 Savings Certificates (Children's Bonus Bonds) Regulations 1991

(1) The Savings Certificates (Children's Bonus Bonds) Regulations 1991 are amended in accordance with this paragraph.

(2) In regulation 2(1) (interpretation), omit the entries for 'mentally disordered person' and 'receiver' and, in the appropriate alphabetical position, insert –

> (a) ' "deputy" in the application of these Regulations to England and Wales, means, in relation to any decision made for a person who lacks capacity, a deputy appointed by the Court of Protection for that person with power to make decisions in relation to the matters in question;'; and

> (b) ' "person who lacks capacity" means a person who lacks capacity within the meaning of the Mental Capacity Act 2005;'.

(3) In regulation 8(2) (repayment in case of persons under 16 years of age), for 'mentally disordered person' substitute 'person who lacks capacity'.

(4) In regulation 9 (repayment in case of mentally disordered persons) –

> (a) in the title, for 'mentally disordered persons' substitute 'persons who lack capacity';

> (b) in paragraph (1), for 'mentally disordered person shall be made by his receiver' substitute 'person who lacks capacity shall be made by his deputy'; and

> (c) in paragraph (2), for 'mentally disordered person for whose estate no receiver' substitute 'person who lacks capacity for whom no deputy'.

(5) In regulation 15 (persons under disability) –

> (a) for 'mentally disordered person' substitute 'person who lacks capacity'; and

> (b) for 'receiver' substitute 'deputy'.

(6) In regulation 29 (application to Scotland) –

> (a) in paragraph (a), for 'mentally disordered person' substitute 'person who lacks capacity'; and

> (b) in paragraph (b), for 'receiver in relation to a mentally disordered person' substitute 'deputy in relation to a person who lacks capacity'.

(7) In regulation 30 (application to Northern Ireland) –

> (a) n paragraph (a), for 'mentally disordered person' substitute 'person who lacks capacity'; and

> (b) in paragraph (b), for 'receiver in relation to a mentally disordered person' substitute 'deputy in relation to a person who lacks capacity'.

(8) In regulation 31(2) (application to the Isle of Man) –

> (a) in paragraph (a), for 'mentally disordered person' substitute 'person who lacks capacity'; and

> (b) in paragraph (b), for 'receiver in relation to any act or thing done in respect of a mentally disordered person shall be construed as a reference to a receiver' substitute 'deputy in relation to any decision made for a person who lacks capacity shall be construed as a reference to a deputy'.

(9) In regulation 32 (application to the Channel Islands) –

> (a) in paragraphs (2)(a) and (3)(a), for 'mentally disordered person' substitute 'person who lacks capacity'; and

PART V

(b)   in paragraphs (2)(b) and (3)(b), for 'receiver in relation to a mentally disordered person' substitute 'deputy in relation to a person who lacks capacity'.

19 Judicial Pensions (Transfer Between Judicial Pension Schemes) Regulations 1995

In Schedule 2 (existing judicial scheme judicial offices included in each arrangement) to the Judicial Pensions (Transfer Between Judicial Pension Schemes) Regulations 1995, under the cross-heading 'District Judiciary Scheme', omit the reference to a Master of the Court of Protection except in the case of a person holding that office immediately before the commencement of this paragraph or who had previously retired from that office or died.

20 Judicial Pensions (Additional Voluntary Contributions) Regulations 1995

In Schedule 4 (existing judicial scheme judicial offices included in each arrangement) to the Judicial Pensions (Additional Voluntary Contributions) Regulations 1995, under the cross-heading 'District Judiciary Scheme', omit the reference to a Master of the Court of Protection except in the case of a person holding that office immediately before the commencement of this paragraph or who had previously retired from that office or died.

21 Goods Vehicles (Licensing of Operators) Regulations 1995

(1) Regulations 29 (partnerships) and 31 (continuance of licence on death, bankruptcy etc) of the Goods Vehicles (Licensing of Operators) Regulations 1995 are amended in accordance with this paragraph.

(2) In regulation 29(11)(b), for the words from 'patient' to 'Mental Health Act 1983', substitute 'person who lacks capacity (within the meaning of the Mental Capacity Act 2005) to carry on the activities covered by the licence'.

(3) In regulation 31 –

(a)   in paragraph (2), for the words from 'patient' to 'Mental Health Act 1983', substitute 'person who lacks capacity (within the meaning of the Mental Capacity Act 2005) to carry on the activities covered by the licence'; and
(b)   in paragraph (3), for the words from 'patient' to 'Mental Health Act 1983', substitute 'person who lacks capacity (within the meaning of the Mental Capacity Act 2005) to carry on the activities covered by the licence'.

22 Landfill Tax Regulations 1996

For regulation 33(1C)(a) (bodies eligible for approval) of the Landfill Tax Regulations 1996, substitute –

'(a)   in England and Wales, the person lacks capacity within the meaning of the Mental Capacity Act 2005 to administer and manage his property and affairs;'.

23 (*revoked*)

Amendment—Paragraph revoked by SI 2008/2836.

24 General Chiropractic Council (Constitution and Procedure) Rules Order 1999

In rule 2 (grounds of removal) of the General Chiropractic Council (Constitution and Procedure) Rules Order of Council 1999, in paragraph (1)(d) for 'or is otherwise incapable, by reason of mental disorder, of properly managing his property or affairs', substitute 'or lacks capacity within the meaning of the Mental Capacity Act 2005, to properly manage his property or affairs'.

25 Health Service Medicines (Price Control Appeals) Regulations 2000

In regulation 7 (appointment of tribunal) of the Health Service Medicines (Price Control Appeals) Regulations 2000, in paragraph (3)(b), for 'incapacity' substitute 'lack of capacity (within the meaning of the Mental Capacity Act 2005)'.

26 Ionising Radiation (Medical Exposure) Regulations 2000

In regulation 7 (optimisation) of the Ionising Radiation (Medical Exposure) Regulations 2000 –

    (a)   in paragraph (5)(b), after 'capacity' insert '(within the meaning of the Mental Capacity Act 2005 in the case of a child aged sixteen or seventeen)'; and

    (b)   in paragraph (5)(c), after 'capacity' insert '(within the meaning of the Mental Capacity Act 2005)'.

27 Carers (Services) and Direct Payments (Amendment) (England) Regulations 2001

For regulation 2(2) (services of an intimate nature and prescribed circumstances) of the Carers (Services) and Direct Payments (Amendment) (England) Regulations 2001, substitute –

    '(2) Where a service (A) is being delivered to the person cared for, a service of an intimate nature may be provided if –

    (a)   during the delivery of service A, the person cared for asks the person delivering that service to provide a service of an intimate nature;

    (b)   the person lacks capacity (within the meaning of the Mental Capacity Act 2005) to consent to the provision of a service of an intimate nature and it is provided in accordance with the principles of that Act; or

    (c)   except where sub-paragraph (b) applies, the person cared for is in a situation in which he is likely to suffer serious personal harm unless a service of an intimate nature is provided to him and the person providing service A reasonably believes that it is necessary to provide a service of an intimate nature because the likelihood of serious personal harm to the person cared for is imminent.'.

28 Care Homes Regulations 2001

(1) The Care Homes Regulations 2001 are amended in accordance with this paragraph.

(2) In regulation 2 (interpretation), in paragraph (1), in the appropriate alphabetical position, insert –

  (a) ' "the 2005 Act" means the Mental Capacity Act 2005;' and
  (b) ' "lacks capacity" means lacks capacity within the meaning of the 2005 Act;'.

(3) In regulation 13 (further requirements as to health and welfare), for paragraph (7) substitute –

  '(7) The registered person shall ensure that no service user is subject to physical restraint unless –

  (a) restraint of the kind employed is the only practicable means of securing the welfare of that or any other service user and there are exceptional circumstances; or
  (b) in the case of a person who lacks capacity in relation to the matter in question, the act meets the conditions of section 6 of the 2005 Act.'.

29 Private and Voluntary Health Care (England) Regulations 2001

(1) The Private and Voluntary Health Care (England) Regulations 2001 are amended in accordance with this paragraph.

(2) In regulation 2 (interpretation) –

  (a) in paragraph (1), at the beginning insert –
       ' "the 2005 Act" means the Mental Capacity Act 2005;'; and
  (b) at the end, add –

  '(4) For the purpose of any decision required to be made under these Regulations as to a person's capacity, lack of capacity shall be interpreted in accordance with the 2005 Act and any reference to a person who lacks capacity shall be construed accordingly.'.

(3) In regulation 9 (policies and procedures), in paragraph (3) –

  (a) in sub-paragraph (a), for 'competence' substitute 'capacity';
  (b) in sub-paragraph (b), for 'competent patient' substitute 'patient who has capacity'; and
  (c) for sub-paragraph (c), substitute –
       '(c) in the case of patient who lacks capacity the requirements of the 2005 Act are complied with before any treatment proposed for him is administered; and'.

(4) In regulation 16 (care and welfare of patients), in paragraphs (1) and (3), after 'so far as practicable,' insert '(and, where the person lacks capacity, in accordance with the principles of the 2005 Act)'.

(5) In regulation 35 (resuscitation), in paragraph (2) –

  (a) in sub-paragraph (a), for 'are competent' substitute 'have the capacity'; and
  (b) after sub-paragraph (a), insert –
       '(aa) take proper account of valid and applicable advance decisions made by patients under the 2005 Act;'.

(6) In regulation 37 (surgical procedures) –

    (a)   in paragraph (2), after 'a patient' insert 'who has the capacity to do so';

    (b)   in paragraph (3), for 'is not competent' substitute 'lacks the capacity'; and

    (c)   after paragraph (3), insert –

'(4) In the case of a patient who lacks capacity to consent to surgery, the registered person shall take proper account of any valid and applicable advance decisions made by the patient under the 2005 Act.'.

30 Domiciliary Care Agencies Regulations 2002

(1) The Domiciliary Care Agencies Regulations 2002 are amended in accordance with this paragraph.

(2) In regulation 2 (interpretation), in paragraph (1), in the appropriate alphabetical position, insert –

    ' "the 2005 Act" means the Mental Capacity Act 2005;

    "lacks capacity" means lacks capacity within the meaning of the 2005 Act;'.

(3) In regulation 14 (arrangements for the provision of personal care), for paragraph (10) substitute –

'(10) The registered person shall ensure that no service user is subject to physical restraint unless –

    (a)   restraint of the kind employed is the only practicable means of securing the welfare of that or any other service user and there are exceptional circumstances; or

    (b)   in the case of a person who lacks capacity in relation to the matter in question, the act meets the conditions of section 6 of the 2005 Act.'.

31 Land Registration Rules 2003

(1) Rule 61 (documents executed by attorney) of, and Schedule 3 (forms referred to in rule 206) to, the Land Registration Rules 2003 are amended in accordance with this paragraph.

(2) In rule 61 –

    (a)   for paragraph (1)(c) substitute –
        '(c)   a document which under section 4 of the Evidence and Powers of Attorney Act 1940, paragraph 16 of Part 2 of Schedule 1, or paragraph 15(3) of Part 5 of Schedule 4 to the Mental Capacity Act 2005 is sufficient evidence of the contents of the power, or'; and

    (b)   for paragraph (2) substitute –

'(2) If an order or direction under section 22 or 23 of, or paragraph 16 of Part 5 of Schedule 4 to, the Mental Capacity Act 2005 has been made with respect to a power or the donor of the power or the attorney appointed under it, the order or direction must be produced to the registrar.'.

(3) In Schedule 3 –

    (a)   in Form 1 (certificate as to execution of power of attorney (rule 61)) –
        (i)   for the first bullet point substitute –

PART V

'the power of attorney ('the power') is in existence [and is made and, where required, has been registered under *(state statutory provisions under which the power is made and, where required, has been registered, if applicable)]*,', and

(ii) in the fourth bullet point, for the words 'or section 7(3) of the Enduring Powers of Attorney Act 1985', substitute –

', paragraph 16 of Part 2 of Schedule 1, or paragraph 15(3) of Part 5 of Schedule 4 to the Mental Capacity Act 2005'; and

(b) in Form 2 (statutory declaration/certificate as to non-revocation for powers more than 12 months old at the date of the disposition for which they are used (rule 62) –

(i) in the third bullet point, for the words 'valid enduring power', substitute 'valid lasting or enduring power of attorney',

(ii) after the third bullet point, insert –

'Where the power is in the form prescribed for a lasting power of attorney –

that a lasting power of attorney was not created, or

of circumstances which, if the lasting power of attorney had been created, would have terminated the attorney's authority to act as an attorney, or', and

(iii) in the heading immediately before the fourth bullet point, after the words 'enduring power', insert 'of attorney'.

32 National Health Service (Travel Expenses and Remission of Charges) Regulations 2003

In regulation 7 (claims to entitlement) of the National Health Service (Travel Expenses and Remission of Charges) Regulations 2003, for paragraph (3), substitute –

'(3) A claim may be made on behalf of another person where that person –

(a) is unable by reason of physical incapacity; or

(b) lacks capacity within the meaning of the Mental Capacity Act 2005,

to make the claim himself.'.

33 Child Trust Funds Regulations 2004

In regulation 33A(2) (the official solicitor or accountant of court to be the person who has the authority to manage an account) of the Child Trust Funds Regulations 2004, in Condition 4 –

(a) in sub-paragraph (a), for the word 'receiver' substitute 'deputy';

(b) for sub-paragraph (b), substitute '(b) determined that such a person lacks capacity within the meaning of the Mental Capacity Act 2005 to manage the child's property and affairs'; and

(c) in the modifications of condition 4 for Scotland –

(i) in sub-paragraph (b), for the word 'receiver' substitute 'deputy'; and

(ii) in sub-paragraph (c), for the word 'patient' substitute 'person lacking capacity'.

34 National Health Service (Complaints) Regulations 2004

In regulation 8 (person who may make complaints) of the National Health Service (Complaints) Regulations 2004 –

- (a) in paragraph (2)(c), omit 'or mental' and 'or';
- (b) after paragraph(2)(c), insert –
    '(cc) is unable because he lacks capacity within the meaning of the Mental Capacity Act 2005 to make the complaint himself; or';
- (c) in paragraph (3), after 'who is' insert 'physically'; and
- (d) after paragraph (3) insert –

'**(3A)** In the case of a patient or person affected who lacks capacity within the meaning of the Mental Capacity Act 2005 the representative must be either a person appointed or authorised to act on his behalf under the 2005 Act or another person who, in the opinion of the complaints manager, had or has a sufficient interest in his welfare and is a suitable person to act as representative'.

35 Commonhold Regulations 2004

(1) In the table of contents in Schedule 2 (articles of association) to the Commonhold Regulations 2004, under the heading 'Votes of Members', for the words 'Entitlement to vote –Mental Capacity' substitute 'Entitlement to vote –lack of mental capacity'.

(2) In the title to article 29 of Schedule 2 (articles of association) to the Commonhold Regulations 2004, for the words 'mental incapacity' substitute 'lack of mental capacity'.

(3) In article 29 of Schedule 2 (articles of association) to the Commonhold Regulations 2004, for each reference to 'receiver' substitute a reference to 'deputy'.

36 Adult Placement Schemes (England) Regulations 2004

(1) The Adult Placement Schemes (England) Regulations 2004 are amended in accordance with this paragraph.

(2) In regulation 2 (interpretation), in the appropriate alphabetical position, insert –

- (a) ' "the 2005 Act" means the Mental Capacity Act 2005;'; and
- (b) ' "lacks capacity" means lacks capacity within the meaning of the 2005 Act;'.

(3) In regulation 17 (carer agreements), for paragraph (2)(e) substitute –

- '(e) specifies that a service user is not to be subject to physical restraint unless –
    - (i) restraint of the kind employed is the only practicable means of securing the welfare of that, or another, service user; or
    - (ii) in the case of a person who lacks capacity in relation to the matter in question, the act meets the conditions of section 6 of the 2005 Act;'

(4) In regulation 19 (adult placement carer handbook), for paragraph (3)(c) substitute –

'(c) specifies that a service user is not to be subject to physical restraint unless –
  (i) restraint of the kind employed is the only practicable means of securing the welfare of that, or another, service user, or
  (ii) in the case of a person who lacks capacity in relation to the matter in question, the act meets the conditions of section 6 of the 2005 Act;'.

37 Damages (Variation of Periodical Payments) Order 2005

For article 3(d) (defendant's financial resources) of the Damages (Variation of Periodical Payments) Order 2005, substitute –

'(d) the order is made by consent and the claimant is neither a child, nor a person who lacks capacity within the meaning of the Mental Capacity Act 2005 to administer and manage his property and affairs nor a patient within the meaning of Part VII of the Mental Health (Northern Ireland) Order 1986,'.

38 Disability Discrimination (Service Providers and Public Authorities Carrying Out Functions) Regulations 2005

In regulation 3(b) (circumstances in which mental incapacity justification does not apply) of the Disability Discrimination (Service Providers and Public Authorities Carrying Out Functions) Regulations 2005, for the words 'functions conferred by or under Part 7 of the Mental Health Act 1983', substitute 'being a deputy appointed by the Court of Protection'.

39 Disability Discrimination (Private Clubs etc) Regulations 2005

(1) In regulation 3(b) (circumstances in which mental incapacity justification does not apply) of the Disability Discrimination (Private Clubs etc) Regulations 2005, for the words 'functions conferred by or under Part 7 of the Mental Health Act 1983', substitute 'being a deputy appointed by the Court of Protection'.

(2) In regulation 13(3)(b) (duty of associations to make adjustments: justification) of these regulations, for the words 'functions conferred by or under Part 7 of the Mental Health Act 1983', substitute 'being a deputy appointed by the Court of Protection'.

40 Disability Discrimination (Premises) Regulations 2006

In regulation 2(b) (circumstances in which mental incapacity justification does not apply) of the Disability Discrimination (Premises) Regulations 2006, for the words 'functions conferred by or under Part 7 of the Mental Health Act 1983', substitute 'being a deputy appointed by the Court of Protection'.

SCHEDULE 2
AMENDMENTS TO FORMS IN SCHEDULE 4 (FORMS) OF THE
INSOLVENCY RULES 1986: FORM 4.64 AND FORM 6.57

PART 1
NEW FORM 4.64

****

PART 2
NEW FORM 6.57

****

Mental Capacity Act 2005 (Transfer of Proceedings) Order 2007, SI 2007/1899

ARRANGEMENT OF ARTICLES

Article		Page
1	Citation and commencement	850
2	Transfers from the Court of Protection to a court having jurisdiction under the Children Act	852
3	Transfers from a court having jurisdiction under the Children Act to the Court of Protection	853
4	Avoidance of double liability for fees	853

1 Citation and commencement

(1) This Order may be cited as the Mental Capacity Act 2005 (Transfer of Proceedings) Order 2007.

(2) This Order shall come into force on 1st October 2007.

(3) In this Order 'the Children Act' means the Children Act 1989.

Scope of provision—The Children Act 1989 allows the court to make decisions in relation to people under 18 years. The typical application under the Act will concern where the child should reside and the terms of contact between a parent and the child. However, the Act does allow the court to make other decisions relating to a child.

The new Court of Protection will normally be called upon to exercise its powers in relation to a person over 16 years. However, the Mental Capacity Act 2005 (MCA 2005), s 18(3) allows the Court to exercise its powers in relation to property and finance matters over a person under 16.

The purpose of this Order is to allow a case to be dealt by the court best placed to deal with the issues relating to a young person. There may also be instances where a child is of an age where the Children Act 1989 will no longer apply in the near future but the court still needs to be involved with that person's life in one way or another.

Many of the judges nominated to sit in the Court of Protection also exercise jurisdiction in children's cases. This will either allow a case to be followed through by the same judge or by another judge who will readily appreciate the issues.

2 Transfers from the Court of Protection to a court having jurisdiction under the Children Act

(1) This article applies to any proceedings in the Court of Protection which relate to a person under 18.

(2) The Court of Protection may direct the transfer of the whole or part of the proceedings to a court having jurisdiction under the Children Act where it considers that in all the circumstances, it is just and convenient to transfer the proceedings.

(3) In making a determination, the Court of Protection must have regard to –

    (a)   whether the proceedings should be heard together with other proceedings that are pending in a court having jurisdiction under the Children Act;

    (b)   whether any order that may be made by a court having jurisdiction under that Act is likely to be a more appropriate way of dealing with the proceedings;

    (c)   the need to meet any requirements that would apply if the proceedings had been started in a court having jurisdiction under the Children Act; and

    (d)   any other matter that the court considers relevant.

(4) The Court of Protection –

    (a)   may exercise the power to make an order under paragraph (2) on an application or on its own initiative; and

    (b)   where it orders a transfer, must give reasons for its decision.

(5) Any proceedings transferred under this article –

    (a)   are to be treated for all purposes as if they were proceedings under the Children Act which had been started in a court having jurisdiction under that Act; and

    (b)   are to be dealt with after the transfer in accordance with directions given by a court having jurisdiction under that Act.

Scope of provision—This article deals with a case in the Court of Protection. It sets out the matters to which the Court must have regard when considering the transfer of a case to a children's court.
The children's court could be the High Court, the county court or the Family Proceedings Court.
Article 2(3) sets out the matters to which the Court of Protection must have regard.

'whether the proceedings should be heard together with [other proceedings in the children's court]' (art 2(3)(a) —If there are other linked or connected proceedings, it may be more sensible for them to be dealt with in one court.
For example:
There are two children, X and Y. X suffered brain damage at birth, the father is his deputy and X's affairs are the subject of the Court of Protection. Y is healthy and not subject to the Court.
The parents are to divorce. There are ancillary relief proceedings and a dispute about residence and contact concerning both children.
One of the assets is the matrimonial home which was partially purchased with funds from X's fund in court after permission was given by the Court of Protection. X has an interest in the property. Issues have arisen concerning this property.
Both parents want residence of X and Y and there are also problems with contact.
It is clearly desirable in this case for all the family litigation to be heard in one court. The Court of Protection has no jurisdiction to deal with ancillary relief or matters concerning Y so matters concerning X could be transferred to be heard in the children's court by a family judge who is also nominated to hear Court of Protection matters.

'whether any order [made by the children's court] is likely to be a more appropriate way of dealing with the proceedings' (art 2(3)(b))—It is important to examine the powers and remedies available in both jurisdictions to see whether the children's court would be a better forum for a matter to be adjudicated. For example, the Court of Protection cannot order a CAFCASS report or order the parents to attend a conciliation hearing which many courts offer.

Overall, it may be felt that a children's dispute should be dealt with in a court which regularly deals with such disputes rather than the Court of Protection.

Under the Children Act 1989, the welfare principle will apply and the child's interests are paramount. The court would have to consider if this principle is more appropriate than simply applying the best interests test under MCA 2005.

'the need to meet any requirements that would apply if the proceedings had been started in [the children's court]' (art 2(3)(c))—For example, a child has a deputy who is a solicitor; an issue has arisen as to where the child should live. The deputy could not make an application in the family court without the permission of the Court of Protection and of the family court.

'any other matter that the court considers relevant' (art 2(3)(d))—This will depend on the circumstances and the facts of each case. When considering the issue of transfer, the court must have regard to P's best interests.

3 Transfers from a court having jurisdiction under the Children Act to the Court of Protection

(1) This article applies to any proceedings in a court having jurisdiction under the Children Act which relate to a person under 18.

(2) A court having jurisdiction under the Children Act may direct the transfer of the whole or part of the proceedings to the Court of Protection where it considers that in all circumstances, it is just and convenient to transfer the proceedings.

(3) In making a determination, the court having jurisdiction under the Children Act must have regard to –

> (a)   whether the proceedings should be heard together with other proceedings that are pending in the Court of Protection;
> (b)   whether any order that may be made by the Court of Protection is likely to be a more appropriate way of dealing with the proceedings;
> (c)   the extent to which any order made as respects a person who lacks capacity is likely to continue to have effect when that person reaches 18; and
> (d)   any other matter that the court considers relevant.

(4) A court having jurisdiction under the Children Act –

> (a)   may exercise the power to make an order under paragraph (2) on an application or on its own initiative; and
> (b)   where it orders a transfer, must give reasons for its decision.

(5) Any proceedings transferred under this article –

> (a)   are to be treated for all purposes as if they were proceedings under the Mental Capacity Act 2005 which had been started in the Court of Protection; and
> (b)   are to be dealt with after the transfer in accordance with directions given by the Court of Protection.

Scope of provision—This article deals with transfer from the children's court to the Court of Protection.

The same criteria are applied as in art 2.

4 Avoidance of double liability for fees

Any fee paid for the purpose of starting any proceedings that are transferred under article 2 or 3 is to be treated as if it were the fee that would have been payable if the proceedings had started in the court to which the transfer is made.

Mental Capacity (Deprivation of Liberty: Appointment of Relevant Person's Representative) Regulations 2008, SI 2008/1315

ARRANGEMENT OF REGULATIONS

Regulation   Page
1 Citation, commencement and application   854
2 Interpretation   854

PART 1
SELECTION OF REPRESENTATIVES
3 Selection of a person to be a representative – general   855
4 Determination of capacity   856
5 Selection by the relevant person   856
6 Selection by a donee or deputy   856
7 Confirmation of eligibility of family member, friend or carer and
   recommendation to the supervisory body   856
8 Selection by the best interests assessor   856
9 Selection by the supervisory body   857

PART 2
APPOINTMENT OF REPRESENTATIVES
10 Commencement of appointment procedure   857
11 Appointment of representative   858
12 Formalities of appointing a representative   858
13 Termination of representative's appointment   858
14 Formalities of termination of representative's appointment   859
15 Payment to a representative   859

1 Citation, commencement and application

(1) These Regulations may be cited as the Mental Capacity (Deprivation of Liberty: Appointment of Relevant Person's Representative) Regulations 2008 and shall come into force on 3rd November 2008.

(2) These Regulations apply in relation to England only.

2 Interpretation

In these Regulations –

'best interests assessor' means a person selected to carry out a best interests assessment under paragraph 38 of Schedule A1 to the Act;

'donee' is a person who has a lasting power of attorney conferred on them by the relevant person, giving that donee the authority to make decisions about the relevant person's personal welfare;

'the Act' means the Mental Capacity Act 2005; and

'the relevant person's managing authority' means the managing authority that has made the application for a standard authorisation in respect of the relevant person.

PART 1
SELECTION OF REPRESENTATIVES

3 Selection of a person to be a representative – general

(1) In addition to any requirements in regulations 6 to 9 and 11, a person can only be selected to be a representative if they are –

    (a)   18 years of age or over;

    (b)   able to keep in contact with the relevant person;

    (c)   willing to be the relevant person's representative;

    (d)   not financially interested in the relevant person's managing authority;

    (e)   not a relative of a person who is financially interested in the managing authority;

    (f)   not employed by, or providing services to, the relevant person's managing authority, where the relevant person's managing authority is a care home;

    (g)   not employed to work in the relevant person's managing authority in a role that is, or could be, related to the relevant person's case, where the relevant person's managing authority is a hospital; and

    (h)   not employed to work in the supervisory body that is appointing the representative in a role that is, or could be, related to the relevant person's case.

(2) For the purposes of this regulation a 'relative' means –

    (a)   a spouse, ex-spouse, civil partner or ex-civil partner;

    (b)   a person living with the relevant person as if they were a spouse or a civil partner;

    (c)   a parent or child;

    (d)   a brother or sister;

    (e)   a child of a person falling within sub-paragraphs (a), (b) or (d);

    (f)   a grandparent or grandchild;

    (g)   a grandparent-in-law or grandchild-in-law;

    (h)   an uncle or aunt;

    (i)   a brother-in-law or sister-in-law;

    (j)   a son-in-law or daughter-in-law;

    (k)   a first cousin; or

    (l)   a half-brother or half-sister.

(3) For the purposes of this regulation –

    (a)   the relationships in paragraph (2)(c) to (k) include step relationships;

    (b)   references to step relationships and in-laws in paragraph (2) are to be read in accordance with section 246 of the Civil Partnership Act 2004;

    (c)   a person has a financial interest in a managing authority where –

        (i)   that person is a partner, director, other office-holder or major shareholder of the managing authority that has made the application for a standard authorisation, and

        (ii)   the managing authority is a care home or independent hospital; and

    (d)   a major shareholder means –

        (i)   any person holding one tenth or more of the issued shares in the managing authority, where the managing authority is a company limited by shares, and

        (ii)   in all other cases, any of the owners of the managing authority.

4 Determination of capacity

The best interests assessor must determine whether the relevant person has capacity to select a representative.

5 Selection by the relevant person

(1) Where the best interests assessor determines that the relevant person has capacity, the relevant person may select a family member, friend or carer.

(2) Where the relevant person does not wish to make a selection under paragraph (1), regulation 8 applies.

6 Selection by a donee or deputy

(1) Where –

    (a)   the best interests assessor determines that the relevant person lacks capacity to select a representative; and

    (b)   the relevant person has a donee or deputy and the donee's or deputy's scope of authority permits the selection of a family member, friend or carer of the relevant person,

the donee or deputy may select such a person.

(2) A donee or deputy may select himself or herself to be the relevant person's representative.

(3) Where a donee or deputy does not wish to make a selection under paragraph (1) or (2), regulation 8 applies.

7 Confirmation of eligibility of family member, friend or carer and recommendation to the supervisory body

(1) The best interests assessor must confirm that a person selected under regulation 5(1) or 6(1) or (2) is eligible to be a representative.

(2) Where the best interests assessor confirms the selected person's eligibility under paragraph (1), the assessor must recommend the appointment of that person as a representative to the supervisory body.

(3) Where the best interests assessor is unable to confirm the selected person's eligibility under paragraph (1), the assessor must –

    (a)   advise the person who made the selection of that decision and give the reasons for it; and

    (b)   invite them to make a further selection.

8 Selection by the best interests assessor

(1) The best interests assessor may select a family member, friend or carer as a representative where paragraph (2) applies.

(2) The best interests assessor may make a selection where –

    (a)   the relevant person has the capacity to make a selection under regulation 5(1) but does not wish to do so;

(b)   the relevant person's donee or deputy does not wish to make a selection under regulation 6(1) or (2); or

(c)   the relevant person lacks the capacity to make a selection and –

(i)   does not have a donee or deputy, or

(ii)   has a donee or deputy but the donee's or deputy's scope of authority does not permit the selection of a representative.

(3) Where the best interests assessor selects a person in accordance with paragraph (2), the assessor must recommend that person for appointment as a representative to the supervisory body.

(4) But the best interests assessor must not select a person under paragraph (2) where the relevant person, donee or deputy objects to that selection.

(5) The best interests assessor must notify the supervisory body if they do not select a person who is eligible to be a representative.

9 Selection by the supervisory body

(1) Where a supervisory body is given notice under regulation 8(5), it may select a person to be the representative, who –

(a)   would be performing the role in a professional capacity;

(b)   has satisfactory skills and experience to perform the role;

(c)   is not a family member, friend or carer of the relevant person;

(d)   is not employed by, or providing services to, the relevant person's managing authority, where the relevant person's managing authority is a care home;

(e)   is not employed to work in the relevant person's managing authority in a role that is, or could be, related to the relevant person's case, where the relevant person's managing authority is a hospital; and

(f)   is not employed by the supervisory body.

(2) The supervisory body must be satisfied that there is in respect of the person –

(a)   an enhanced criminal record certificate issued pursuant to section 113B of the Police Act 1997(enhanced criminal record certificates);or

(b)   if the purpose for which the certificate is required is not one prescribed under subsection (2) of that section, a criminal record certificate issued pursuant to section 113A of that Act (criminal record certificates).

Amendments—SI 2008/2368.

PART 2
APPOINTMENT OF REPRESENTATIVES

10 Commencement of appointment procedure

The procedure for appointing a representative must begin as soon as –

(a)   a best interests assessor is selected by the supervisory body for the purposes of a request for a standard authorisation; or

(b)   a relevant person's representative's appointment terminates, or is to be terminated, under regulation 14 and the relevant person remains subject to a standard authorisation.

11 Appointment of representative

Except where regulation 9 applies, a supervisory body may not appoint a representative unless the person is recommended to it under regulations 7 or 8.

12 Formalities of appointing a representative

(1) The offer of an appointment to a representative must be made in writing and state –

(a)   the duties of a representative to –
  (i)   maintain contact with the relevant person,
  (ii) represent the relevant person in matters relating to, or connected with, the deprivation of liberty, and
  (iii) support the relevant person in matters relating to, or connected with, the deprivation of liberty; and
(b)   the length of the period of the appointment.

(2) The representative must inform the supervisory body in writing that they are willing to accept the appointment and that they have understood the duties set out in sub-paragraph (1)(a).

(3) The appointment must be made for the period of the standard authorisation.

(4) The supervisory body must send copies of the written appointment to –

(a)   the appointed person;
(b)   the relevant person;
(c)   the relevant person's managing authority;
(d)   any donee or deputy of the relevant person;
(e)   any independent mental capacity advocate appointed in accordance with sections 37 to 39D of the Act, involved in the relevant person's case; and
(f)   every interested person named by the best interests assessor in their report as somebody the assessor has consulted in carrying out the assessment.

13 Termination of representative's appointment

A person ceases to be a representative if –

(a)   the person dies;
(b)   the person informs the supervisory body that they are no longer willing to continue as representative;
(c)   the period of the appointment ends;
(d)   a relevant person who has selected a family member, friend or carer under regulation 5(1) who has been appointed as their representative informs the supervisory body that they object to the person continuing to be a representative;
(e)   a donee or deputy who has selected a family member, friend or carer of the relevant person under regulation 6(1) who has been appointed as a representative informs the supervisory body that they object to the person continuing to be a representative;
(f)   the supervisory body terminates the appointment because it is satisfied that the representative is not maintaining sufficient contact with the relevant person in order to support and represent them;

(g)   the supervisory body terminates the appointment because it is satisfied that the representative is not acting in the best interests of the relevant person; or

(h)   the supervisory body terminates the appointment because it is satisfied that the person is no longer eligible or was not eligible at the time of appointment, to be a representative.

14   Formalities of termination of representative's appointment

(1) Where a representative's appointment is to be terminated for a reason specified in paragraphs (c) to (h) of regulation 13, the supervisory body must inform the representative of –

(a)   the pending termination of the appointment;

(b)   the reasons for the termination of the appointment; and

(c)   the date on which the appointment terminates.

(2) The supervisory body must send copies of the termination of the appointment to –

(a)   the relevant person;

(b)   the relevant person's managing authority;

(c)   any donee or deputy of the relevant person;

(d)   any independent mental capacity advocate appointed in accordance with sections 37 to 39D of the Act, involved in the relevant person's case; and

(e)   every interested person named by the best interests assessor in their report as somebody the assessor has consulted in carrying out the assessment.

15   Payment to a representative

A supervisory body may make payments to a representative appointed following a selection under regulation 9.

Mental Capacity (Deprivation of Liberty: Standard Authorisations, Assessments and Ordinary Residence) Regulations 2008, SI 2008/1858

ARRANGEMENT OF REGULATIONS

PART 1
PRELIMINARY

Regulation	Page
1 Citation, commencement and application	860
2 Interpretation	860

PART 2
ELIGIBILITY TO CARRY OUT ASSESSMENTS

3 Eligibility – general	861

PART V

4 Eligibility to carry out a mental health assessment   861
5 Eligibility to carry out a best interests assessment   862
6 Eligibility to carry out a mental capacity assessment   862
7 Eligibility to carry out an eligibility assessment   863
8 Eligibility to carry out an age assessment   863
9 Eligibility to carry out a no refusals assessment   863

PART 3
SELECTION OF ASSESSORS
10 Selection of assessors – relatives   863
11 Selection of assessors – financial interest   864
12 Selection of best interests assessors   864

PART 4
ASSESSMENTS
13 Time frame for assessments   864
14 Time limit for carrying out an assessment to decide whether or not there
    is an unauthorised deprivation of liberty   864
15 Relevant eligibility information   865

PART 5
REQUESTS FOR A STANDARD AUTHORISATION
16 Information to be provided in a request for a standard authorisation 865

PART 6
SUPERVISORY BODIES: CARE HOMES
17 Application and Interpretation of Part 6   866
18 Arrangements where there is a question as to the ordinary residence 867
19 Effect of change in supervisory body following determination of any
    question about ordinary residence   867

PART 1
PRELIMINARY

1 Citation, commencement and application

(1) These Regulations may be cited as the Mental Capacity (Deprivation of Liberty: Standard Authorisations, Assessments and Ordinary Residence) Regulations 2008 and shall come into force on 3rd November 2008.

(2) These Regulations apply in relation to England only.

2 Interpretation

In these Regulations –

'approved mental health professional' means a person approved under section 114(1) of the Mental Health Act 1983 to act as an approved mental health professional for the purposes of that Act;

'best interests assessor' means a person selected to carry out a best interests assessment under paragraph 38 of Schedule A1 to the Act;

'General Social Care Council' has the meaning given by section 54(1) of the Care Standards Act 2000; and

'the Act' means the Mental Capacity Act 2005.

PART 2
ELIGIBILITY TO CARRY OUT ASSESSMENTS

3 Eligibility – general

(1) In addition to any requirement in regulations 4 to 9, a person is eligible to carry out an assessment where paragraphs (2) to (4) are met.

[(2) The person must satisfy the supervisory body that there is in force in relation to that person an adequate and appropriate indemnity arrangement which provides cover in respect of any liabilities that might arise in connection with carrying out the assessment.

(2A) For the purposes of this regulation, an 'indemnity arrangement' may comprise –

  (a) a policy of insurance;
  (b) an arrangement made for the purposes of indemnifying a person; or
  (c) a combination of a policy of insurance and an arrangement made for the purposes of indemnifying a person.]

(3) The supervisory body must be satisfied that the person has the skills and experience appropriate to the assessment to be carried out which must include, but are not limited to, the following –

  (a) an applied knowledge of the Mental Capacity Act 2005 and related Code of Practice; and
  (b) the ability to keep appropriate records and to provide clear and reasoned reports in accordance with legal requirements and good practice.

(4) The supervisory body must be satisfied that there is in respect of the person –

  (a) an enhanced criminal record certificate issued under section 113B of the Police Act 1997 (enhanced criminal record certificates); or
  (b) if the purpose for which the certificate is required is not one prescribed under subsection (2) of that section, a criminal record certificate issued pursuant to section 113A of that Act (criminal record certificates).

Amendment—Paragraph (2) substituted by paras (2), (2A) by Mental Capacity (Deprivation of Liberty: Monitoring and Reporting; and Assessments – Amendment) Regulations 2009, SI 2009/827.

4 Eligibility to carry out a mental health assessment

(1) A person is eligible to carry out a mental health assessment if paragraphs (2) and (3) are met.

(2) The person must be –

  (a) approved under section 12 of the Mental Health Act 1983; or
  (b) a registered medical practitioner who the supervisory body is satisfied has at least three years post registration experience in the diagnosis or treatment of mental disorder.

(3) The supervisory body must be satisfied that the person has successfully completed the Deprivation of Liberty Safeguards Mental Health Assessors training programme made available by the Royal College of Psychiatrists.

(4) Except in the 12 month period beginning with the date the person has successfully completed the programme referred to in paragraph (3), the supervisory body must be satisfied that the person has, in the 12 months prior to selection, completed further training relevant to their role as a mental health assessor.

5 Eligibility to carry out a best interests assessment

(1) A person is eligible to carry out a best interests assessment if paragraphs (2) and (3) are met.

(2) The person must be one of the following –

    (a) an approved mental health professional;

    (b) a social worker registered with the General Social Care Council;

    (c) a first level nurse, registered in Sub-Part 1 of the Nurses' Part of the Register maintained under article 5 of the Nursing and Midwifery Order 2001;

    (d) an occupational therapist registered in Part 6 of the register maintained under article 5 of the Health Professions Order 2001; or

    (e) a chartered psychologist who is listed in the British Psychological Society's Register of Chartered Psychologists and who holds a relevant practising certificate issued by that Society.

(3) The supervisory body must be satisfied that the person –

    (a) is not suspended from the register or list relevant to the person's profession mentioned in paragraph (2);

    (b) has at least two years post registration experience in one of the professions mentioned in paragraph (2);

    (c) has successfully completed training that has been approved by the Secretary of State to be a best interests assessor;

    (d) except in the 12 month period beginning with the date the person has successfully completed the training referred to in sub-paragraph (c), the supervisory body must be satisfied that the person has, in the 12 months prior to selection, completed further training relevant to their role as a best interests assessor; and

    (e) has the skills necessary to obtain, evaluate and analyse complex evidence and differing views and to weigh them appropriately in decision making.

'Chartered Psychologist'—By virtue of the Health Care and Associated Professions (Miscellaneous Amendments and Practitioner Psychologists) Order 2009 (Commencement No 1 and Transitional Provisions) Order of Council 2009, SI 2009/1357, until the end of 30th June 2012, reference to a chartered psychologist is to be treated as a reference to a chartered psychologist or a psychologist registered in Part 14 of the register maintained by the Health Professions Council.

6 Eligibility to carry out a mental capacity assessment

A person is eligible to carry out a mental capacity assessment if that person is eligible to carry out –

    (a) a mental health assessment; or

    (b) a best interests assessment.

7 Eligibility to carry out an eligibility assessment

A person is eligible to carry out an eligibility assessment if that person is –

- (a) approved under section 12 of the Mental Health Act 1983 and is eligible to carry out a mental health assessment; or
- (b) an approved mental health professional and is eligible to carry out a best interests assessment.

8 Eligibility to carry out an age assessment

A person is eligible to carry out an age assessment if that person is eligible to carry out a best interests assessment.

9 Eligibility to carry out a no refusals assessment

A person is eligible to carry out a no refusals assessment if that person is eligible to carry out a best interests assessment.

PART 3
SELECTION OF ASSESSORS

10 Selection of assessors – relatives

(1) A supervisory body must not select a person to carry out an assessment if the person is –

- (a) a relative of the relevant person; or
- (b) a relative of a person who is financially interested in the care of the relevant person.

(2) For the purposes of this regulation a 'relative' means –

- (a) a spouse, ex-spouse, civil partner or ex-civil partner;
- (b) a person living with the relevant person as if they were a spouse or a civil partner;
- (c) a parent or child;
- (d) a brother or sister;
- (e) a child of a person falling within sub-paragraphs (a), (b) or (d);
- (f) a grandparent or grandchild;
- (g) a grandparent-in-law or grandchild-in-law;
- (h) an uncle or aunt;
- (i) a brother-in-law or sister-in-law;
- (j) a son-in-law or daughter-in-law;
- (k) a first cousin; or
- (l) a half-brother or half-sister.

(3) For the purposes of this regulation –

- (a) the relationships in paragraph (2)(c) to (k) include step relationships;
- (b) references to step relationships and in-laws in paragraph (2) are to be read in accordance with section 246 of the Civil Partnership Act 2004; and
- (c) financial interest has the meaning given in regulation 11.

PART V

11 Selection of assessors – financial interest

(1) A supervisory body must not select a person to carry out an assessment where the person has a financial interest in the case.

(2) A person has a financial interest in a case where –

    (a)   that person is a partner, director, other office-holder or major shareholder of the managing authority that has made the application for a standard authorisation; and

    (b)   the managing authority is a care home or independent hospital.

(3) A major shareholder means –

    (a)   any person holding one tenth or more of the issued shares in the managing authority, where the managing authority is a company limited by shares; and

    (b)   in all other cases, any of the owners of the managing authority.

12 Selection of best interests assessors

(1) A supervisory body must not select a person to carry out a best interests assessment if that person is involved in the care, or making decisions about the care, of the relevant person.

(2) Where the managing authority and supervisory body are both the same body, the supervisory body must not select a person to carry out a best interests assessment who is employed by it or who is providing services to it.

PART 4
ASSESSMENTS

13 Time frame for assessments

(1) Except as provided in paragraph (2), all assessments required for a standard authorisation must be completed within the period of 21 days beginning with the date that the supervisory body receives a request for such an authorisation.

(2) Where a supervisory body receives a request for a standard authorisation and the managing authority has given an urgent authorisation under paragraph 76 of Schedule A1 to the Act, the assessments required for that standard authorisation must be completed within the period during which the urgent authorisation is in force.

14 Time limit for carrying out an assessment to decide whether or not there is an unauthorised deprivation of liberty

Subject to paragraph 69(3) to (5) of Schedule A1 to the Act, an assessment required under that paragraph must be completed within the period of 7 days beginning with the date that the supervisory body receives the request from an eligible person.

15 Relevant eligibility information

(1) This regulation applies where an individual is being assessed and the eligibility assessor and the best interests assessor are not the same person.

(2) The eligibility assessor must request that the best interests assessor provides any relevant eligibility information that the best interests assessor may have.

(3) The best interests assessor must comply with any request made under this regulation.

(4) In this regulation 'eligibility assessor' means a person selected to carry out the eligibility assessment under paragraph 46 of Schedule A1 to the Act.

PART 5
REQUESTS FOR A STANDARD AUTHORISATION

16 Information to be provided in a request for a standard authorisation

(1) A request for a standard authorisation must include the following information –

- (a)   the name and gender of the relevant person;
- (b)   the age of the relevant person or, where this is not known, whether the managing authority believes that the relevant person is aged 18 years or older;
- (c)   the address and telephone number where the relevant person is currently located;
- (d)   the name, address and telephone number of the managing authority and the name of the person within the managing authority who is dealing with the request;
- (e)   the purpose for which the authorisation is requested;
- (f)   the date from which the standard authorisation is sought; and
- (g)   whether the managing authority has given an urgent authorisation under paragraph 76 of Schedule A1 to the Act and, if so, the date on which it expires.

(2) Except as provided for in paragraph (3), a request for a standard authorisation must include the following information if it is available or could reasonably be obtained by the managing authority –

- (a)   any medical information relating to the relevant person's health that the managing authority considers to be relevant to the proposed restrictions to the relevant person's liberty;
- (b)   the diagnosis of the mental disorder (within the meaning of the Mental Health Act 1983 but disregarding any exclusion for persons with learning disability) that the relevant person is suffering from;
- (c)   any relevant care plans and relevant needs assessments;
- (d)   the racial, ethnic or national origins of the relevant person;
- (e)   whether the relevant person has any special communication needs;
- (f)   details of the proposed restrictions on the relevant person's liberty;
- (g)   whether section 39A of the Act (person becomes subject to Schedule A1) applies;
- (h)   where the purpose of the proposed restrictions to the relevant person's

PART V

liberty is to give treatment, whether the relevant person has made an advance decision that may be valid and applicable to some or all of that treatment;

(i) whether the relevant person is subject to –

(i)   the hospital treatment regime,

(ii) the community treatment regime, or

(iii) the guardianship regime;

(j) the name, address and telephone number of –

(i)   anyone named by the relevant person as someone to be consulted about his welfare,

(ii) anyone engaged in caring for the person or interested in his welfare,

(iii) any donee of a lasting power of attorney granted by the person,

(iv) any deputy appointed for the person by the court, and

(v) any independent mental capacity advocate appointed in accordance with sections 37 to 39D of the Act; and

(k) whether there is an existing authorisation in relation to the detention of the relevant person and, if so, the date of the expiry of that authorisation.

(3) Where –

(a) there is an existing authorisation in force in relation to the detention of the relevant person; and

(b) the managing authority makes a request in accordance with paragraph 30 of Schedule A1 to the Act for a further standard authorisation in relation to the same relevant person,

the request need not include any of the information mentioned in paragraph (2)(a) to (j) if that information remains the same as that supplied in relation to the request for the existing authorisation.

(4) In this regulation 'existing authorisation' has the same meaning as in paragraph 29 of Schedule A1 to the Act.

PART 6
SUPERVISORY BODIES: CARE HOMES

Disputes about the Place of Ordinary Residence

17 Application and Interpretation of Part 6

(1) This Part applies where –

(a) a local authority ('local authority A') receives a request from –

(i)   a care home for a standard authorisation under paragraph 24, 25 or 30 of Schedule A1 to the Act, or

(ii) an eligible person to decide whether or not there is an unauthorised deprivation of liberty in a care home under paragraph 68 of Schedule A1 to the Act;

(b) local authority A wishes to dispute that it is the supervisory body; and

(c) a question as to the ordinary residence of the relevant person is to be determined by the Secretary of State under paragraph 183 of Schedule A1 to the Act.

(2) In this Part –

(a) 'local authority A' has the meaning given in paragraph (1); and

(b)   'local authority C' has the meaning given in regulation 18(2).

18 Arrangements where there is a question as to the ordinary residence

(1) Local authority A must act as supervisory body in relation to a request mentioned in regulation 17(1)(a) until the determination of the question as to the ordinary residence of the relevant person.

(2) But where another local authority ('local authority C') agrees to act as the supervisory body in place of local authority A, that local authority shall become the supervisory body until the determination of the question as to the ordinary residence of the relevant person.

(3) When the question about the ordinary residence of the relevant person has been determined, the local authority which has been identified as the supervisory body shall become the supervisory body.

19 Effect of change in supervisory body following determination of any question about ordinary residence

(1) Where the question of ordinary residence of the relevant person is determined in accordance with paragraph 183(3) of Schedule A1 to the Act, and another local authority ('local authority B') becomes the supervisory body in place of local authority A or local authority C, as the case may be, [paragraphs (3) to (6A)] shall apply.

(2) Where the question of ordinary residence of the relevant person is determined in accordance with paragraph 183(3) of Schedule A1 to the Act and local authority C remains the supervisory body, [paragraphs (7) to (10)] shall apply.

(3) Local authority B shall be treated as the supervisory body that received the request mentioned in regulation 17(1)(a) and must comply with the time limits specified in –

(a)   regulation 13 for carrying out the assessments required for a standard authorisation; or

(b)   regulation 14 for carrying out an assessment required under paragraph 69 of Schedule A1 to the Act,

as the case may be, where the assessments have still to be completed.

(4) Anything done by or in relation to local authority A or local authority C in connection with the authorisation or request, as the case may be, has effect, so far as is necessary for continuing its effect after the change, as if done by or in relation to local authority B.

(5) Anything which relates to the authorisation or request and which is in the process of being done by or in relation to local authority A or local authority C at the time of the change may be continued by or in relation to local authority B.

(6) But –

(a)   local authority A or local authority C does not, by virtue of this regulation, cease to be liable for anything done by it in connection with the authorisation or request before the change; and

(b)   local authority B does not, by virtue of this regulation, become liable for any such thing.

PART V

[(6A) Local authority A or local authority C shall be entitled to recover from local authority B expenditure incurred in exercising functions as the supervisory body.]

(7) Local authority C shall be treated as the supervisory body that received the request mentioned in regulation 17(1)(a) and must comply with the time limits specified in –

    (a) regulation 13 for carrying out the assessments required for a standard authorisation; or

    (b) regulation 14 for carrying out an assessment required under paragraph 69 of Schedule A1 to the Act,

as the case may be, where the assessments have still to be completed.

(8) Anything done by or in relation to local authority A in connection with the authorisation or request, as the case may be, has effect, so far as is necessary for continuing its effect after the change, as if done by or in relation to local authority C.(9) Anything which relates to the authorisation or request and which is in the process of being done by or in relation to local authority A at the time of the change may be continued by or in relation to local authority C.

(10) But –

    (a) local authority A does not, by virtue of this regulation, cease to be liable for anything done by it in connection with the authorisation or request before the change; and

    (b) local authority C does not, by virtue of this regulation, become liable for any such thing.

Amendments—Words in paras (1) and (2) substituted and para (6A) inserted by Mental Capacity (Deprivation of Liberty: Monitoring and Reporting; and Assessments – Amendment) Regulations 2009, SI 2009/827.

Civil Procedure Rules 1998, SI 1998/3132

ARRANGEMENT OF RULES

PART 21
CHILDREN AND PROTECTED PARTIES

Rule		Page
21.1	Scope of this Part	872
21.2	Requirement for a litigation friend in proceedings by or against children and protected parties	877
21.3	Stage of proceedings at which a litigation friend becomes necessary	879
21.4	Who may be a litigation friend without a court order	879
21.5	How a person becomes a litigation friend without a court order	881
21.6	How a person becomes a litigation friend by court order	882
21.7	Court's power to change a litigation friend and to prevent person acting as a litigation friend	883
21.8	Appointment of a litigation friend by court order – supplementary	884
21.9	Procedure where appointment of a litigation friend ceases	885
21.10	Compromise etc. by or on behalf of a child or protected party	886

21.11 Control of money recovered by or on behalf of a child or protected
       party   888
21.12 Expenses incurred by a litigation friend   890

       PRACTICE DIRECTION – CHILDREN AND PROTECTED PARTIES
                             (PD21)   891

                            PART 43
              SCOPE OF COST RULES AND DEFINITIONS
43.1   Scope of this Part   898
43.2   Definitions and application   898
43.3   Meaning of summary assessment   900
43.4   Meaning of detailed assessment   900

                            PART 44
                GENERAL RULES ABOUT COSTS
44.2   Solicitor's duty to notify client   900
44.3   Court's discretion and circumstances to be taken into account when
       exercising its discretion as to costs   900
44.3A Costs orders relating to funding arrangements   901
44.3B Limits on recovery under funding arrangements   901
44.3C Orders in respect of pro bono representation   902
44.4   Basis of assessment   902
44.5   Factors to be taken into account in deciding the amount of costs   903
44.8   Time for complying with an order for costs   904
44.13 Special situations   904
44.14 Court's powers in relation to misconduct   905
44.15 Providing information about funding arrangements   905
44.16   906
44.17 Application of costs rules   906

                            PART 47
     PROCEDURE FOR DETAILED ASSESSMENT OF COSTS AND DEFAULT
                          PROVISIONS

       Section I – General Rules about Detailed Assessment
47.1   Time when detailed assessment may be carried out   907
47.2   No stay of detailed assessment where there is an appeal   907
47.3   Powers of an authorised court officer   907
47.4   Venue for detailed assessment proceedings   907

    *Section II – Costs Payable by One Party to Another – Commencement of Detailed
                            Assessment Proceedings*
47.5   Application of this section   908
47.6   Commencement of detailed assessment proceedings   908
47.7   Period for commencing detailed assessment proceedings   908
47.8   Sanction for delay in commencing detailed assessment proceedings   909
47.9   Points of dispute and consequence of not serving   909
47.10 Procedure where costs are agreed   910

    Section III – Costs Payable by One Party to Another – Default Provisions
47.11 Default costs certificate   910
47.12 Setting aside default costs certificate   911

    *Section IV – Costs Payable by One Party to Another – Procedure where Points of
                            Dispute are Served*
47.13 Optional reply   911

47.14 Detailed assessment hearing   911

Section V – Interim Costs Certificate and Final Costs Certificate
47.15 Power to issue an interim certificate   912
47.16 Final costs certificate   913

Section VI – Detailed Assessment Procedure for Costs of a LSC Funded Client or an Assisted Person where Costs are Payable out of the Community Legal Service Fund
47.17 Detailed assessment procedure for costs of a LSC funded client or an assisted person where costs are payable out of the Community Legal Service Fund   913
47.17A Detailed assessment procedure where costs are payable out of a fund other than the Community Legal Service Fund   914

Section VII – Costs of Detailed Assessment Proceedings
47.18 Liability for costs of detailed assessment proceedings   914
47.19 Offers to settle without prejudice save as to costs of the detailed assessment proceedings   915

Section VIII – Appeals from Authorised Court Officers in Detailed Assessment Proceedings
47.20 Right to appeal   915
47.21 Court to hear appeal   915
47.22 Appeal procedure   916
47.23 Powers of the court on appeal   916

PART 48
COSTS – SPECIAL CASES

Section I – Costs Payable by or to Particular Persons
48.1 Pre-commencement disclosure and orders for disclosure against a person who is not a party   916
48.4 Limitations on court's power to award costs in favour of trustee or personal representative   917
48.5 Costs where money is payable by or to a child or protected party   917
48.6 Litigants in person   918

Section II – Costs Relating to Solicitors and Other Legal Representatives
48.7 Personal liability of legal representative for costs – wasted costs orders   918
48.8 Basis of detailed assessment of solicitor and client costs   919
48.9   919

PRACTICE DIRECTION – ABOUT COSTS (PDCOSTS)   920

PART 70
GENERAL RULES ABOUT ENFORCEMENT OF JUDGMENTS AND ORDERS
70.1 Scope of this Part and interpretation   978
70.2 Methods of enforcing judgments or orders   978
70.3 Transfer of proceedings for enforcement   978
70.4 Enforcement of judgment or order by or against non-party   979
70.5 Enforcement of decisions of bodies other than the High Court and county courts and compromises enforceable by enactment   979
70.6 Effect of setting aside judgment or order   980

PART 71
ORDERS TO OBTAIN INFORMATION FROM JUDGMENT DEBTORS
71.1 Scope of this Part   980

71.2 Order to attend court   980
71.3 Service of order   981
71.4 Travelling expenses   981
71.5 Judgment creditor's affidavit   981
71.6 Conduct of the hearing   982
71.7 Adjournment of the hearing   982
71.8 Failure to comply with order   982

PART 72
THIRD PARTY DEBT ORDERS
72.1 Scope of this Part and interpretation   983
72.2 Third party debt order   983
72.3 Application for third party debt order   983
72.4 Interim third party debt order   984
72.5 Service of interim order   984
72.6 Obligations of third parties served with interim order   984
72.7 Arrangements for debtors in hardship   985
72.8 Further consideration of the application   986
72.9 Effect of final third party order   986
72.10 Money in court   987
72.11 Costs   987

PART 73
CHARGING ORDERS, STOP ORDERS AND STOP NOTICES
73.1 Scope of this Part and interpretation   987

Section I – Charging Orders
73.2 Scope of this Section   988
73.3 Application for charging order   988
73.4 Interim charging order   988
73.5 Service of interim order   989
73.6 Effect of interim order in relation to securities   989
73.7 Effect of interim order in relation to funds in court   990
73.8 Further consideration of the application   990
73.9 Discharge or variation of order   990
73.10 Enforcement of charging order by sale   991

Section II – Stop Orders
73.11 Interpretation   991
73.12 Application for stop order   991
73.13 Stop order relating to funds in court   992
73.14 Stop order relating to securities   992
73.15 Variation or discharge of order   992

Section III – Stop Notices
73.16 General   993
73.17 Request for stop notice   993
73.18 Effect of stop notice   993
73.19 Amendment of stop notice   994
73.20 Withdrawal of stop notice   994
73.21 Discharge or variation of stop notice   994
73.22   994

Schedule 1
RSC Order 45 – Enforcement of Judgments and Orders: General   995
RSC Order 46 – Writs of Execution: General   995
RSC Order 47 – Writs of Fieri Facias   999

PART V

PART 21
CHILDREN AND PROTECTED PARTIES

21.1 Scope of this Part

(1) This Part –

    (a)   contains special provisions which apply in proceedings involving children and protected parties;

    (b)   sets out how a person becomes a litigation friend; and

    (c)   does not apply to proceedings under Part 75 where one of the parties to the proceedings is a child.

(2) In this Part –

    (a)   'the 2005 Act' means the Mental Capacity Act 2005;

    (b)   'child' means a person under 18;

    (c)   'lacks capacity' means lacks capacity within the meaning of the 2005 Act;

    (d)   'protected party' means a party, or an intended party, who lacks capacity to conduct the proceedings;

    (e)   'protected beneficiary' means a protected party who lacks capacity to manage and control any money recovered by him or on his behalf or for his benefit in the proceedings.

    (Rules 6.13 and 6.25 contain provisions about the service of documents on children and protected parties.)

    (Rule 48.5 deals with costs where money is payable by or to a child or protected party.)

Amendments—SI 2003/3361; SI 2007/2204; SI 2008/2178.

Practice Direction—See generally Practice Direction 21.

'Part 75' (r 21.1(1)(c))—This deals with traffic enforcement.

Background—The Civil Procedure Rules 1998 (CPR) Part 21 made special provision for two categories of litigant:

    (1)   'children' who are, by reason of age, deemed incapable of acting personally unless permitted by the court; and

    (2)   'patients' who were treated as being incapable of conducting the proceedings.

For the purpose of the then CPR, 'patient' meant 'a person who, by reason of mental disorder within the meaning of the Mental Health Act 1983 is incapable of managing and administering his property and affairs'. This test was also used to establish the jurisdiction of the former Court of Protection to administer the property and affairs of patients under the Mental Health Act 1983 (MHA 1983), Part VII (ss 93–11). 'Mental disorder' was defined by MHA 1983, s 1(2) as 'mental illness, arrested or incomplete development of mind, psychopathic disorder and any other disorder or disability of mind'. Nothing in the definition was to be construed as implying that a person may be dealt with as suffering from mental disorder by reason only of 'promiscuity or other immoral conduct, sexual deviancy or dependence on alcohol or drugs' (MHA 1983, s 1(3)).

Following the 2007 rule amendments the term 'patient' is replaced by 'protected party' and a new definition applies. This became necessary because of the implementation of the Mental Capacity Act 2005 (MCA 2005).

Mental Capacity Act 2005—This legislation established from 1 October 2007 a comprehensive statutory framework for decisions to be made by and on behalf of those whose capacity to make their own decisions is in doubt. A new regional Court of Protection has jurisdiction to make declarations or decisions or to appoint a deputy to make decisions on the person's behalf. A small number of district judges and circuit judges are appointed to sit in the new Court and difficult capacity issues may be referred to them.

The general principles that apply within the new mental capacity jurisdiction are to be found in the MCA 2005, ss 1–4. They include a new test of 'incapacity' and a 'best interests' approach to any delegated decision-making according to a checklist of factors, thus now incorporated into Part 21. (For an overview of the Act see Section 3 of this book.)

Persons who lack capacity—There are basically three categories of person who may come within the definition of a protected party, namely those with:

(1) a mental illness – the largest group comprises elderly people who become mentally impaired (e g by senile dementia or Alzheimer's disease);

(2) learning disabilities – the previous term was 'mental handicap'; and

(3) brain damage – the courts generally encounter persons with an acquired brain injury. If the damage was caused during the developmental years (e g in childbirth) this will be classed as learning disabilities.

Scope of provision—A representative known as a 'litigation friend' must generally be appointed to conduct the proceedings in the name and on behalf of a child or protected party, and any settlement or compromise must be approved by the Court.

'child' (r 21.1(2)(a))—Defined as 'a person under 18' by r 21.1(2)(a). There is provision for the child to act personally even before attaining that age (r 21.2(3)) but approval of the Court is required and may subsequently be withdrawn (r 21.2(5)).

'protected party' (r 21.1(2)(d))—Means 'a party, or an intended party, who lacks capacity [within the meaning of MCA 2005] to conduct the proceedings'. Lack of capacity is also defined (see below).

'protected beneficiary' (r 21.1(2)(e))—Means 'a protected party who lacks capacity to manage and control any money recovered by him or on his behalf or for his benefit in the proceedings'. It was necessary to introduce this additional definition because of the decision-specific nature of tests of capacity. A party may lack capacity to conduct the proceedings but nevertheless have the capacity to manage and control his or her money. However, this definition is insufficient for two reasons. First, there is an assumption that only a person who is a protected party may be incapable of financial management. The rule fails to make allowance for the converse, namely that a litigant who has capacity to conduct court proceedings may not have capacity to manage his or her financial affairs. This situation might arise, for example, where a wealthy man with complex financial affairs wished to bring a small claim.

Secondly, if the approach of the civil court is to be compatible with that of the Court of Protection it becomes necessary to aggregate the damages recovered with the existing wealth of the protected party and then to decide whether there is capacity to manage the entirety. The rules committee has only looked at this from the perspective of a brain injured litigant who recovers a substantial sum and did not previously have any personal savings or income of significance.

'child' or 'protected party'—It is possible for a child also to be a protected party and this may be relevant if that condition will continue to subsist on ceasing to be a child (e g with regard to the disposal of money awarded to the child). Thus a child who has severe learning disabilities will continue to be a protected party even after attaining the age of 18.

'litigation friend' (r 21.1(1)(b))—This expression is used for the representative, whether the party is a claimant or defendant, and replaces both 'next friend' and 'guardian ad litem' used in previous rules. Those terms are still used in family proceedings governed by Family Proceedings Rules 1991, SI 1991/1247, Part IX.

'lacks capacity'—This term is expressly defined as being 'within the meaning of the Mental Capacity Act 2005' so as to incorporate the principles that apply within that legislation and the jurisprudence that will develop in the new mental capacity jurisdiction. Nevertheless, many of the principles that have evolved under previous case-law are still relevant. MCA 2005, s 2(1) sets out the definition:

'A person lacks capacity in relation to a matter if at the material time he is unable to make a decision for himself in relation to the matter because of an impairment of, or a disturbance in the functioning of, the mind or brain.'

This is a two-stage test, because it must be established, first, that there is an impairment of, or disturbance in the functioning of, the person's mind or brain (the diagnostic threshold); and, secondly, that the impairment or disturbance is sufficient to render the person incapable of making that particular decision. The impairment or disturbance may be permanent or temporary and no reference is made to the degree of impairment or disturbance. This provides a useful screening process – merely being eccentric is not a basis for being deprived of one's right to conduct litigation.

MCA 2005, s 3(1) provides that a person is unable to make a decision if unable to:

- understand the information relevant to the decision;
- retain that information;
- use or weigh that information as part of the process of making the decision; or
- communicate his or her decision (whether by talking, using sign language or any other means).

Explanations must be provided in ways appropriate to the person's circumstances (using simple language, visual aids or any other means). This is not a significant change of approach because it was previously held (in regard to medical treatment though the test was no doubt universal) that the individual must be able to (a) understand and retain information, and (b) weigh that information in the balance to arrive at a choice (per Butler-Sloss LJ in *Re MB* [1997] 2 FLR 426, CA).

'conduct the proceedings'—Tests of capacity are now seen as being decision-specific, so it is the capacity of the party to conduct the particular proceedings that is relevant rather than capacity to manage and administer his or her property and affairs in general (as defined under the former test). Thus a person might be a protected party for complex personal injury proceedings yet not for a simultaneous small claim.

Even under the former rule, the Court of Appeal concentrated on the issue-specific nature of tests of capacity and decided that the test related to the individual and his immediate problems. Thus Chadwick LJ in *Masterman-Lister v Brutton & Co and Jewell & anor* [2002] EWCA Civ 1889, [2003] 1 WLR 1511 stated:

> '[T]he test to be applied … is whether the party to legal proceedings is capable of understanding, with the assistance of such proper explanation from legal advisers and experts in other disciplines as the case may require, the issues on which his consent or decision is likely to be necessary in the course of those proceedings. If he has capacity to understand that which he needs to understand in order to pursue or defend a claim, I can see no reason why the law – whether substantive or procedural – should require the interposition of a next friend or guardian ad litem (or, as such a person is now described in the Civil Procedure Rules, a litigation friend).'

Presumptions as to capacity—Adults are presumed competent until the contrary is proved. This is relevant to the burden of proof. In general the person who alleges that an individual lacks capacity must prove this (upon the balance of probabilities rather than beyond reasonable doubt). Capacity, because it can vary, must be assessed at the time that the decision is to be taken. If an individual has previously been found to lack capacity, there is no presumption of continuance, but if there is clear evidence of incapacity for a considerable period, then the burden of proof may be more easily discharged even though it remains on whoever asserts incapacity.

Doubts about capacity may arise for several reasons but these should not be confused with tests of capacity. Thus the status of the individual (being elderly and living in a nursing home), the outcome of a decision (one that no person in his or her right mind would be expected to reach) or appearance, behaviour or conversation may cause capacity to be questioned, but these factors do not determine capacity. It is not unusual for outward appearances to create a false impression of lack of capacity (eg physical disabilities may obstruct the power of speech or movement) even where mental capacity is not affected. Conversely, a person may appear capable through social training and experience when in reality he or she lacks the understanding needed to make decisions. In all these situations a proper assessment of capacity should be made.

Mental disorder—The existence of a mental disorder is no longer a criterion for a person being treated as incapable of conducting proceedings. The new diagnostic threshold of 'an impairment of, or a disturbance in the functioning of, the mind or brain' was introduced because the term 'mental disorder' has acquired distinct interpretations in the context of treatment under the Mental Health legislation. Being mentally disordered does not necessarily result in a person being a protected party, and an assessment of capacity must still be made. Thus:

- (a) an individual may be sectioned under the provisions of MHA 1983 yet not be a protected party as regards court proceedings because the criteria are different (consider *Re C (Adult: Refusal of Medical Treatment)* [1994] 1 All ER 819); and
- (b) an individual with learning disabilities may still have the capacity to conduct litigation depending on the complexity and the support available.

Communication difficulties—Other methods of communication should always be attempted when necessary and an interpreter may be provided for those with communication difficulties in the same way as for those who do not understand the language used in court.

Physical disabilities—Where the ability of an individual to conduct or participate in proceedings is impaired due to physical disabilities, steps can be taken by the court to overcome these. Thus the loop system may be provided for those who are hard of hearing and enlarged print may be used in all documents for those whose sight is impaired. If necessary, hearings should be conducted in a courtroom or chambers with disabled access but they may now be conducted elsewhere should the need arise (r 2.7).

Tests of capacity—There is no universal test of capacity. Legal capacity depends on understanding rather than wisdom; the quality of the decision is irrelevant as long as the person understands what he or she is deciding. Legal tests vary according to the particular transaction or act involved but are generally issue-specific, ie they relate to the matters which the individual is required to understand. As capacity depends on time and context, a decision as to capacity in one context does not bind a court that has to consider the same issue in a different context.

A person found to be a protected party may nevertheless be capable of getting married, signing an enduring power of attorney (*Re K; Re F* [1988] 1 All ER 358) or consenting to medical treatment (*Re MB* [1997] 2 FLR 426, CA), because the matters to be taken into account are different. For a full explanation of the various tests that apply for different purposes reference should be made to the joint Law Society and BMA publication *Assessment of Mental Capacity: Guidance for doctors and lawyers* (2nd edn, 2004).

Assessment of capacity—Mental capacity is a question of fact so any issue of capacity can only be determined by a judge in legal proceedings acting not as a medical expert, but as a lay person influenced by personal observation and on the basis of evidence not only from doctors, but also those who know the individual. For comprehensive guidance as to the manner in which capacity should be assessed reference should be made to *Assessment of Mental Capacity: Guidance for doctors and lawyers* (above).

The mental abilities required to conduct litigation have been identified as comprising the ability to recognise a problem, obtain and receive, understand and retain relevant information, including advice; the ability to weigh the information (including that derived from advice) in the balance in reaching a decision; and the ability to communicate that decision (*Masterman-Lister*, see above).

The approach adopted by Boreham J in *White v Fell* (1987) (unreported) was referred to by the Court of Appeal with approval and may still be of assistance:

> 'The expression "incapable of managing her own affairs and property" must be construed in a common sense way as a whole. It does not call for proof of complete incapacity. On the other hand it is not enough to prove that the Plaintiff is now substantially less capable of managing her own affairs and property than she would have been had the accident not occurred.'

But 'understanding' needs to be examined in depth. Thus in *Mitchell v Alasia* [2005] EWHC 11(QB), Cox J relied on qualities such as impulsiveness and volatility when deciding that the claimant was by reason of his mental disorder incapable of managing and administering his own affairs. And in *Lindsay v Wood* [2006] EWHC 2895 (QB), Stanley Burnton J observed that:

> 'When considering the question of capacity, psychiatrists and psychologists will normally wish to take into account all aspects of the personality and behaviour of the person in question, including vulnerability to exploitation.'

For an early decision on the test of capacity in regard to a brain-injured claimant see *Saulle v Nouvet* [2007] EWHC 2902 (QB).

Guidance on the approach to capacity issues (in child care proceedings but of more general application) is to be found in *RP v Nottingham City Council & Official Solicitor* [2008] EWCA Civ 462.

Time-specific assessment—In *Saulle v Nouvet* [2007] EWHC 2902 (QB), Mr Andrew Edis QC sitting as a Deputy Judge of the High Court dealt with the fact that circumstances might change and made the following observations:

> '... the Court must focus on the matters which arise for decision now, and on the Claimant's capacity to deal with them now. I am required not to attempt to foretell the future and provide for situations which may arise when he may have to take some other decision at some other time when his mental state may be different ... I consider that [Dr X] may well be right when he suggests that there may be times in the future when the Claimant will lack capacity to make

PART V

particular decisions, and note his concern that if that happens when he does not have the support of his family for any reason, he may not come to the attention of the Court of Protection until it is too late. This is a risk against which the old test for capacity used by the Court of Protection under Part VII of the 1983 Act used to guard. The modern law is different.'

Ability to rely upon advice—The extent to which an individual with impaired capacity may rely upon the advice of others was considered by Boreham J in *White v Fell* (1987) (unreported but quoted by Wright J in *Masterman-Lister*, see above, at first instance):

'Few people have the capacity to manage all their affairs unaided. In matters of law, particularly litigation, medicine, and given sufficient resources, finance professional advice is almost universally needed and sought ... [S]he may not understand all the intricacies of litigation, or of a settlement, or of a wise investment policy ... But if that were the appropriate test then quite a substantial proportion of the adult population might be regarded as under disability.'

Medical evidence—Legal practitioners and judges should not jump to conclusions about whether there is an impairment of, or a disturbance in the functioning of, the mind or brain without appropriate evidence, especially in the case of litigants who may merely be stubborn or eccentric. The evidence of a suitably qualified person is required as to the diagnosis, and this evidence will generally extend to the issue of capacity. In *Masterman-Lister* (see above) Kennedy LJ said that 'even where the issue does not seem to be contentious, a district judge who is responsible for case management will almost certainly require the assistance of a medical report before being able to be satisfied that incapacity exists'.

Usually this expert will be a person with medical qualifications and ideally a psychiatrist. However, a psychologist, especially if of an appropriate speciality, may be better qualified in respect of a person with learning disabilities. Such opinion is merely part of the evidence and the factual evidence of a carer or social worker may also be relevant and even more persuasive. The typical general medical practitioner has little knowledge of mental capacity and the various legal tests that apply, so the appropriate test should be spelt out, and it should be explained that different tests apply to different types of decision.

Any doctor or other medical witness asked to assist in relation to capacity needs to know the area of the alleged protected party's activities in relation to which his or her advice is sought (*Masterman-Lister*, see above). All relevant information should be provided, so when the test is whether the individual is incapable of conducting civil proceedings the doctor must be given some idea of the nature and complexity of those proceedings. The doctor will need to know what decisions the individual will be called upon to make for the conduct of that litigation. Only then can the doctor express an opinion whether the individual is capable of giving instructions.

Issues as to capacity—There is unlikely to be any issue as to whether a party is a child. The rules make no express provision as to issues regarding whether a party is a protected party. Such an issue may be raised by the court or one of the parties, or by a litigation friend if there is doubt about whether a party has recovered capacity. It will then be necessary for the proceedings to be stayed until the issue is resolved, and the court may order an inquiry to be made in the proceedings to determine the issue. Notice should be given to the party alleged to be a protected party in case he or she wishes to contest this or arrange representation. This inquiry would normally be heard before a district judge who can compel the attendance of witnesses (including medical attendants and the claimant or defendant him or herself) and the production of documents. Where there are practical difficulties in obtaining medical evidence the Official Solicitor may be consulted. The court can also direct the Official Solicitor to make inquiries and to report about such matters as the court thinks fit (*Harbin v Masterman* [1896] 1 Ch 351, CA).

Courts should always, as a matter of practice, at the first convenient opportunity investigate the question of capacity whenever there is any reason to suspect that it may be absent (e g significant head injury) other than in cases where the Court of Protection has already accepted jurisdiction. Although medical evidence will be required (see above), the judge may consider that he would be assisted by seeing the person alleged to lack capacity (*Masterman-Lister*, see above).

Where, understandably, a claimant's legal team is unable to present a positive case as to whether their client is a protected party, consideration should be given to seeking an order of the court directing the Official Solicitor to review the evidence, to appoint his or her own medical expert, and to appear and make such submissions as he considers appropriate (*Lindsay v Wood* [2006] EWHC 2895 (QB)). The *Masterman-Lister* decision has been explored by the Court of Appeal in a subsequent case where a 50/50 settlement was agreed and proceedings later commenced with a litigation friend to assess quantum (*Bailey v Warren* [2006] EWCA Civ 51, [2006] All ER (D) 78).

While evidence is required to support an application for the appointment of a litigation friend, it does not follow that the other party to the litigation is then entitled to put in evidence disputing the basis for the appointment. It cannot properly be contended that a defendant is at risk of suffering prejudice from the appointment of a litigation friend for the claimant (*Folks v Faizey* [2006] EWCA Civ 381) although in a claim for damages following a brain injury where the quantum of damages will also be affected by a finding that the claimant is a protected beneficiary the court may permit the defendant to present evidence and submissions.

Human rights—When a person is treated as a protected party, whether or not as a result of an order of the court, he or she is thereby deprived of important rights, long cherished by English law and now safeguarded by the European Convention on Human Rights (ECHR). Although the CPR do not contain any requirement for a judicial determination of the question, courts should always, as a matter of practice, at the first convenient opportunity investigate the question of capacity whenever there is any reason to suspect that it may be absent, other than in cases where the Court of Protection is already involved (*Masterman-Lister*, see above).

21.2 Requirement for a litigation friend in proceedings by or against children and protected parties

(1) A protected party must have a litigation friend to conduct proceedings on his behalf.

(2) A child must have a litigation friend to conduct proceedings on his behalf unless the court makes an order under paragraph (3).

(3) The court may make an order permitting a child to conduct proceedings without a litigation friend.

(4) An application for an order under paragraph (3) –

    (a)   may be made by the child;

    (b)   if the child already has a litigation friend, must be made on notice to the litigation friend; and

    (c)   if the child has no litigation friend, may be made without notice.

(5) Where –

    (a)   the court has made an order under paragraph (3); and

    (b)   it subsequently appears to the court that it is desirable for a litigation friend to conduct the proceedings on behalf of the child,

the court may appoint a person to be the child's litigation friend.

Amendment—SI 2007/2204.

Practice Direction—See generally Practice Direction 21.

Scope of provision—The general rule is that a child or protected party may only conduct proceedings, whether as claimant or defendant, by a litigation friend. This applies equally to counterclaims and additional claims under Part 20 (r 20.3(1)). The rule only refers to 'a litigation friend' so a child or protected party may not have more than one in any particular proceedings. There is nothing to prevent that party having a different litigation friend in other proceedings of a different nature, unless a deputy (formerly a receiver) has been appointed in which event he or she should generally be the only litigation friend for the protected party unless the Court of Protection otherwise orders.

Verification that a party is a child or protected party—Practice Direction 21, para 2.3 requires the litigation friend to state in the 'certificate of suitability' that he or she consents to act and knows or believes the party to be a child or protected party. The grounds for this belief must be stated and if based upon medical opinion this document must be attached. It is unlikely to be difficult to ascertain the age of a party, but there may be doubt as to whether a party is a protected party (see the notes to r 21.1 for the procedure then to be adopted).

Even where the issue does not seem to be contentious, a district judge who is responsible for case management will generally require the assistance of a medical report before being able to be satisfied that incapacity exists. An admission by a person alleged to lack capacity will carry little weight. It may assist for the judge to see the person alleged to lack capacity (*Masterman-Lister*, see discussion at notes to r 21.1).

Notification to the child or protected party—Neither the CPR nor the Practice Directions actually provide that a child or protected party must be given notice of the proceedings, unless (in the case of a protected party) the court is involved in the appointment of the litigation friend, so it is possible for proceedings in the name of a child or protected party to be commenced or defended without the personal knowledge of that party. Reliance is placed on the certificate of suitability (see above) and upon service on the parent or guardian of the child, or the person with whom the protected party resides or in whose care he or she is (see also Practice Direction 21, para 2.4). It cannot be assumed that this person will inform the protected party in every situation where this would be prudent.

The child as a party (r 21.2(3))—An all or nothing approach to age is no longer adopted (*Gillick v West Norfolk & Wisbech Area Health Authority* [1985] 3 All ER 402, HL). The court may now authorise a child to conduct proceedings, but will only do so when satisfied that the child has the required capacity (ie is of sufficient maturity and understanding). It is both prudent and good practice for the litigation friend to consult the child once able to make a meaningful contribution and particularly as the child approaches 18, since on attaining that age the appointment of the litigation friend ceases and the child (now an adult) may take over conduct of the proceedings (r 21.9(1)).

The protected party as a party—An adult who has the necessary capacity will not be a protected party even if mentally disordered so there is no need for a comparable provision whereby the court may authorise a protected party to conduct proceedings. However, the court may permit proceedings to continue (to a limited extent) even though a litigation friend has not been appointed and may validate proceedings that have continued in breach of the requirements (r 21.3). If the protected party recovers capacity, the appointment of the litigation friend may be terminated by the court order under r 21.9(2), (3).

Duty of litigation friend—The duty of a litigation friend was set out in Practice Direction 21, para 2.1 as being 'fairly and competently to conduct proceedings on behalf of a child or protected party. He must have no interest in the proceedings adverse to that of the child or protected party and all steps and decisions he takes in the proceedings must be taken for the benefit of the child or protected party'. This statement was omitted when amendments were made following the implementation of the MCA 2005 which imposes a duty to act in the 'best interests' of the protected party as defined in MCA 2005.

Status of litigation friend—As the appointment is to 'conduct proceedings ... on behalf' of the child or protected party, subject to the provisions of the rules, any act which in the ordinary conduct of any proceedings is required or authorised to be done by a party shall or may be done by the litigation friend. Unless the litigation friend is also a deputy (formerly a receiver) appointed by the Court of Protection or an attorney under a lasting or registered enduring power of attorney, he or she will have no status in regard to the affairs of the protected party outside the proceedings in which he or she is appointed. It follows that if money is awarded to a child or protected party the litigation friend has no authority to receive or expend that money. The money may only be dealt with pursuant to the directions of the court and in this respect reference must be made to r 21.11. Similarly, any settlement or compromise will have to be approved by the court under r 21.10.

Statement of truth—CPR Part 22 makes provision for certain documents to be verified by a 'statement of truth'. If a party is a child or a protected party it will be the litigation friend (or legal representative on his or her behalf) who makes and signs this statement (r 22.1(5), (6)).

Need for a solicitor—There is no requirement in the CPR for a solicitor to act on behalf of a child or protected party whose proceedings are being conducted by a litigation friend. Nevertheless, in a complex or high value case the court may consider that the litigation friend who acts without a solicitor is not 'suitable' within r 21.4(3) and appoint someone else under r 21.7(1)(c).

21.3 Stage of proceedings at which a litigation friend becomes necessary

(1) This rule does not apply where the court has made an order under rule 21.2(3).

(2) A person may not, without the permission of the court –

    (a) make an application against a child or protected party before proceedings have started; or

    (b) take any step in proceedings except –

        (i) issuing and serving a claim form; or

        (ii) applying for the appointment of a litigation friend under rule 21.6,

until the child or protected party has a litigation friend.

(3) If during proceedings a party lacks capacity to continue to conduct proceedings, no party may take any further step in the proceedings without the permission of the court until the protected party has a litigation friend.

(4) Any step taken before a child or protected party has a litigation friend has no effect unless the court orders otherwise.

Amendment—SI 2007/2204.

Scope of provision—The general principle is that a litigation friend must be appointed before any step is taken in proceedings involving a protected party.

Exceptions—The court has a discretion to permit specified steps to be taken before a litigation friend is appointed ('without the permission of the court' (r 21.3(2), (3)) or retrospectively to approve any steps that have been taken without such appointment ('unless the court otherwise orders' (r 21.3(4)). This alleviates the problem under former rules that, where the disability was not identified by the parties or their solicitors or arose during the proceedings without their knowledge, steps taken had no effect and liabilities could arise in respect of abortive costs.

Implications—It is now possible to make urgent orders in proceedings involving a child or protected party before the appointment of a litigation friend, but the court should be made fully aware of all relevant circumstances. Where it is realised during the course of proceedings that a party is (and has been) a child or a protected party, then, provided everyone has acted in good faith and there has been no manifest disadvantage to the party subsequently found to have been a protected party, it is likely that the court will regularise the position retrospectively (*Masterman-Lister*, see discussion at notes to r 21.1). This might be the case where the proceedings have effectively been guided throughout by the person now being appointed as litigation friend. Proceedings inappropriately conducted by the child or protected party or an unsuitable person on his or her behalf will be treated as being of no effect and further proceedings may then be commenced in proper form (the Limitation Acts are unlikely to apply). Query whether steps should be retrospectively approved when this would cause prejudice to a party not at fault.

Effect on timetable—Until there is a litigation friend no party may take any step in the proceedings so it is assumed that any timetable is suspended. When the court appoints the litigation friend it may be prudent to consider further directions as to the future conduct of the proceedings.

21.4 Who may be a litigation friend without a court order

(1) This rule does not apply if the court has appointed a person to be a litigation friend.

(2) A deputy appointed by the Court of Protection under the 2005 Act with power to conduct proceedings on the protected party's behalf is entitled to be the litigation friend of the protected party in any proceedings to which his power extends.

PART V

(3) If nobody has been appointed by the court or, in the case of a protected party, has been appointed as a deputy as set out in paragraph (2), a person may act as a litigation friend if he –

    (a)   can fairly and competently conduct proceedings on behalf of the child or protected party;

    (b)   has no interest adverse to that of the child or protected party; and

    (c)   where the child or protected party is a claimant, undertakes to pay any costs which the child or protected party may be ordered to pay in relation to the proceedings, subject to any right he may have to be repaid from the assets of the child or protected party.

Amendment—SI 2007/2204.

Scope of provision—This rule identifies who may act as a litigation friend without an order appointing him.

Authorised person—Any person authorised under MCA 2005 (ie as a deputy appointed by the Court of Protection) to conduct legal proceedings in the name or on behalf of a protected party is entitled to become the litigation friend in accordance with such authority. An office copy of the order or other authorisation sealed with the official seal of the Court of Protection should be filed. Care should be taken to examine this document because simply being appointed a deputy does not by itself give authority to conduct proceedings. It is not clear if the Court has power to appoint someone else (as under the former rules), but this situation is unlikely to arise and conflict between the court dealing with the litigation and the Court of Protection should be avoided.

Attorneys—An attorney under a registered enduring power of attorney (EPA) or a lasting power of attorney (LPA) is not specifically mentioned but would be an obvious person to act as litigation friend because he or she will control the financial affairs of the protected party (see MCA 2005) and there will, in consequence, be no need for a deputy. An ordinary power of attorney is of no significance because it ceases to have effect upon the incapacity of the donor, but of course the person acting may otherwise be suitable as litigation friend. If an EPA is registered this would normally indicate that the donor is a protected party, but that is not the case for an LPA because registration may take place at an earlier stage.

    The court controls its own procedures and principles of agency do not apply. So a power of attorney cannot confer a right to conduct litigation or of audience (*Gregory v Turner, R (on the application of Morris) v North Somerset Council* [2003] EWCA Civ 183). Doubt was cast as to whether a litigation friend has the right of audience of the party although the court retains a discretion to allow this.

Suitability—There can be no doubt as to the suitability of a person authorised by the Court of Protection (if doubt arises the matter should be referred back to that Court). The rule helpfully sets out the criteria whereby other persons may be regarded as suitable to act as litigation friend (r 21.4(3)), but the court may not waive any of these criteria which the proposed person is unable to satisfy (*R (on the application of Hussain) v Birmingham City Council* (2002) CO/3487/01 CaseTrack, [2002] CP Rep 54, QBD (Admin)). These criteria feature throughout Part 21, as amplified by Practice Direction 21, para 2.1, and the court must be satisfied that they are complied with before appointing a litigation friend. They may be relied upon where there is a dispute as to who should be appointed. Apart from this there is no restriction on who may be a litigation friend save that the person appointed must not be a child or a protected party and (in practice) should normally be within the jurisdiction. If the court becomes aware of the person's unsuitability it may remove him or her under r 21.7 and substitute another person as litigation friend, but there is no express duty to monitor the situation.

Undertaking as to costs (r 21.4(3)(c))—This undertaking is required from the litigation friend of a claimant (unless appointed by the Court of Protection) but not a defendant, and this is confirmed in Practice Direction 21, para 2.2(e) and 2.3(4). It will also be required when a counterclaim or additional claim is made by a protected party because this is to be treated as if it were a claim for the purpose of the Rules (r 20.3(1) as interpreted by r 20.2(2)(a)). The undertaking is contained in Form N235, Certificate of Suitability of Litigation Friend. A mother's undertaking to meet any liability in costs 'if her circumstances were to change, enabling her to afford them' did not satisfy the requirement of r 21.4(3)(c) and she was, accordingly, ineligible for appointment as a litigation friend (*R (on the application of Hussain) v Birmingham City Council*, above).

The requirement imposes a severe limitation upon the ability of a child or protected party to bring a claim. Query whether it amounts to discrimination against a person with a mental disability contrary to the Disability Discrimination Act 1995 or will otherwise be in breach of the Human Rights Act 1998. The Court of Protection Rules 2007, SI 2007/1744 (the latest court rules to be produced) do not require this undertaking. The litigation friend is, in effect, expected to provide an indemnity so may wish to be protected by a Public Funding certificate or an after-the-event (ATE) insurance indemnity policy, or otherwise be in control of adequate funds held by the child or protected party. One way of circumventing the undertaking in the case of a protected party is to obtain the authority of the Court of Protection to bring the proceedings. The Court has a general discretion as to costs and will take into account the role of the litigation friend but may have power to impose a personal costs liability in case of misconduct quite apart from the undertaking. Further difficulties arise in regard to conditional fee arrangements.

Costs order against litigation friend—An order for costs should not be made against a litigation friend personally without giving him or her a chance to be heard. This probably means adopting the r 48.2 procedure since the litigation friend is not otherwise a party. Such approach will only be appropriate when the litigation friend has misbehaved in the proceedings. The undertaking to pay the child or protected party's costs (if given) is quite different from a personal costs order.

Personal liability of solicitor for costs—A solicitor who acts in any proceedings for or on behalf of a child or protected party without a litigation friend may be held personally liable to pay any wasted costs of the proceedings incurred by the other party, even though the solicitor may not have been aware that the person for whom he or she has been acting is in fact a child or a protected party (*Yonge v Toynbee* [1910] 1 KB 215, CA). However, provided everyone has acted in good faith and there has been no manifest disadvantage to the party subsequently found to have been a child or protected party, it is likely that the court will regularise the position retrospectively (*Masterman-Lister*, see discussion at notes to r 21.1).

21.5 How a person becomes a litigation friend without a court order

(1) If the court has not appointed a litigation friend, a person who wishes to act as a litigation friend must follow the procedure set out in this rule.

(2) A deputy appointed by the Court of Protection under the 2005 Act with power to conduct proceedings on the protected party's behalf must file an official copy(GL) of the order of the Court of Protection which confers his power to act either –

   (a) where the deputy is to act as a litigation friend for a claimant, at the time the claim is made; or

   (b) where the deputy is to act as a litigation friend for a defendant, at the time when he first takes a step in the proceedings on behalf of the defendant.

(3) Any other person must file a certificate of suitability stating that he satisfies the conditions specified in rule 21.4(3) either –

   (a) where the person is to act as a litigation friend for a claimant, at the time when the claim is made; or

   (b) where the person is to act as a litigation friend for a defendant, at the time when he first takes a step in the proceedings on behalf of the defendant.

(4) The litigation friend must –

   (a) serve the certificate of suitability on every person on whom, in accordance with rule 6.13 (service on a parent, guardian etc.), the claim form should be served; and

   (b) file a certificate of service when filing the certificate of suitability.

   (Rules 6.17 and 6.29 set out the details to be contained in a certificate of service.)

PART V

Amendments— SI 2007/2204; SI 2008/2178.

Practice Direction—See generally Practice Direction 21.

Scope of provision—This rule sets out the procedural steps for the appointment of a litigation friend otherwise than by a court order. It will be relied upon in most cases.

No need for court appointment of litigation friend—A litigation friend may be appointed simply by filing the relevant documents. The certificate is a prerequisite for appointment without a court order, but will not be conclusive in the event of a dispute as to suitability. It is strange that there is no requirement for the child or protected party to be personally notified that proceedings are being brought or defended in his or her name because he or she may wish to make representations as to who the litigation friend should be or dispute that he or she is a protected party (see generally the provisions as to service in CPR Part 6). It is now good practice for anyone intending to become a litigation friend to serve upon or draw to the attention of the intended protected party the notice of his or her intention to act as litigation friend and certificate of suitability unless there is no prospect of a relevant responseand the court may require confirmation of this. The Court of Appeal has recommended a change in the rules so that a person cannot become a protected party without knowing what is going on (see *Masterman-Lister* at notes to r 21.1).

'certificate of suitability' (r 21.5(3))—This document confirms that the person to be appointed meets the criteria whereby a person may be regarded as suitable for appointment as litigation friend (r 21.4(3)). As to suitability, see note to r 21.4. The certificate is not required where the person is a deputy authorised by the Court of Protection to conduct the proceedings (see note to r 21.4).

Deputy appointed by the Court of Protection—An official copy of the order of the Court of Protection, which confers the person's power to act, must be filed. The rules do not contemplate the Court of Protection authorising a person to conduct proceedings without appointing him or her to be a deputy, but this could happen. Presumably the Court would ensure that this person was appointed and exclude any competing application.

'certificate of service' (r 21.5(6)(b))—Practice Direction 21, para 2.4 clarifies the persons on whom the certificate of suitability (when required) must be served in accordance with this rule. The alleged protected party is not included (but see note *'No need for court appointment of litigation friend'* above).

Forms—Form N235 (Certificate of suitability of litigation friend).

21.6 How a person becomes a litigation friend by court order

(1) The court may make an order appointing a litigation friend.

(2) An application for an order appointing a litigation friend may be made by –

    (a)   a person who wishes to be the litigation friend; or
    (b)   a party.

(3) Where –

    (a)   a person makes a claim against a child or protected party;
    (b)   the child or protected party has no litigation friend;
    (c)   the court has not made an order under rule 21.2(3) (order that a child can conduct proceedings without a litigation friend); and
    (d)   either –
        (i)   someone who is not entitled to be a litigation friend files a defence; or
        (ii) the claimant wishes to take some step in the proceedings,

the claimant must apply to the court for an order appointing a litigation friend for the child or protected party.

(4) An application for an order appointing a litigation friend must be supported by evidence.

(5) The court may not appoint a litigation friend under this rule unless it is satisfied that the person to be appointed satisfies the conditions in rule 21.4(3).

Amendment—SI 2007/2204.

Practice Direction—See generally Practice Direction 21.

Scope of provision—This rule sets out the procedural steps for the appointment of a litigation friend by a court order, that is, where it has not been possible to appoint a litigation friend under r 21.5. The court must be satisfied that the person to be appointed is suitable for appointment in accordance with the criteria set out in r 21.4(3). Although the rules do not so provide, the application should be served upon or at least brought to the notice of the party unless there is no prospect of a relevant response (see note '*No need for court appointment of litigation friend*' under r 21.5).

Official Solicitor—The Official Solicitor should be approached in case of difficulty and may be appointed if he or she consents, but in practice he or she will only consent if there is no one else suitable and willing to act. It is not necessary to approach the Official Solicitor in all cases and the court will not be concerned to ascertain whether he or she has declined to consent before appointing someone else. The Official Solicitor should not be appointed without his or her consent, which will not usually be forthcoming until provision is made for payment of his or her costs (Practice Direction 21, para 3.6). Save in the most urgent of cases, it is unlikely that the Official Solicitor will be able to complete his or her inquiries in less than 3 months. Accordingly, a lengthy adjournment of the proceedings might become necessary and a substantive hearing should not be fixed within such period of the Official Solicitor's initial appointment without consulting him or her. Where the circumstances of the case justify the involvement of the Official Solicitor, a completed questionnaire and copy of the order appointing him or her (subject to his or her consent) together with a copy of the court file should be sent to the Official Solicitor's office. The Official Solicitor may be contacted at 81 Chancery Lane, London WC2A 1DD; Tel: 020 7911 7127; Fax: 020 7911 7105.

Service—See r 21.8(1) and (2) for the special rules that apply to an application for appointment by the court of a litigation friend. The (alleged) protected party must be served on a first application to appoint a litigation friend unless the court orders otherwise, but there is still no requirement for a child to be notified of proceedings to be conducted in his or her name and on his or her behalf even though the child may be approaching 18 (see note to r 21.2).

Evidence—Practice Direction 21, para 3.4 clarifies the evidence required. This will presumably include evidence that the party is a child or protected party although this is not expressly stated.

Suitability—See note to r 21.4. The court may appoint the person proposed or any other person who complies with the conditions specified in r 21.4(3) (r 21.8(4)). Thus, the criteria of suitability in r 21.4(3) must be satisfied even though r 21.4(1) expressly states that the rule does not apply if the court has appointed a person to be a litigation friend.

21.7 Court's power to change a litigation friend and to prevent person acting as a litigation friend

(1) The court may –

    (a)   direct that a person may not act as a litigation friend;
    (b)   terminate a litigation friend's appointment; or
    (c)   appoint a new litigation friend in substitution for an existing one.

(2) An application for an order under paragraph (1) must be supported by evidence.

(3) The court may not appoint a litigation friend under this rule unless it is satisfied that the person to be appointed satisfies the conditions in rule 21.4(3).

Amendments—SI 2007/2204.

Scope of provision—The court may prevent a person from being a litigation friend or replace a litigation friend during the course of proceedings whether or not appointed by an order. See '*Suitability*' below. Any dispute as to who should be the litigation friend would be dealt with under this provision.

Service—See r 21.8(1) and (3). See generally note to r 21.6 as to service. Although this does not include the protected party, it is good practice to consult this person as capacity is not an 'all or nothing' concept.

Suitability—See note to r 21.4. The court may appoint the person proposed or any other person who complies with the conditions specified in r 21.4(3) (r 21.8(4)). Thus, the criteria of suitability in r 21.4(3) must be satisfied even though r 21.4(1) expressly states that the rule does not apply if the court has appointed a person to be a litigation friend.

Applications—This rule contemplates an application by a party or presumably a non-party such as an alternative representative for the child or protected party. The court may, as part of its case management powers, initiate the process (r 3.3) – concern as to an actual or potential litigation friend does not necessarily mean that there is someone with an interest in making the application.

Termination—The rules express no limit on the power to terminate the appointment and if the litigation friend manifestly acts contrary to the child's or the protected party's best interests, the court will remove him or her, even though neither his or her good faith nor diligence is in issue (*Re A (Conjoined Twins: Medical Treatment) (No 2)* (2001) CCS 2, [2001] 1 FLR 267, CA). In respect of mentally incapable adults, what are this person's best interests has now been clarified by MCA 2005, s 4. (For an overview of the Act see Section 3 of this book.)

21.8 Appointment of a litigation friend by court order – supplementary

(1) An application for an order under rule 21.6 or 21.7 must be served on every person on whom, in accordance with rule 6.13 (service on parent, guardian etc.), the claim form must be served.

(2) Where an application for an order under rule 21.6 is in respect of a protected party, the application must also be served on the protected party unless the court orders otherwise.

(3) An application for an order under rule 21.7 must also be served on –

   (a) the person who is the litigation friend, or who is purporting to act as the litigation friend, when the application is made; and

   (b) the person who it is proposed should be the litigation friend, if he is not the applicant.

(4) On an application for an order under rule 21.6 or 21.7, the court may appoint the person proposed or any other person who satisfies the conditions specified in rule 21.4(3).

Amendments—SI 2007/2204; SI 2008/2178.

Scope of provision—This rule supplements r 6.13 (which deals with service of the proceedings) and also provides that the court is not obliged to appoint the person proposed but may appoint any other person who complies with the conditions specified in r 21.4(3). Although the rules do not so provide, the application should be served upon or at least brought to the notice of the party unless there is no prospect of a relevant response (see note '*No need for court appointment of litigation friend*' under r 21.5).

Service—Service of the application on the parent or guardian of the child, or the person with whom the protected party resides or in whose care he is, is required in all cases. The application under r 21.6 to appoint a litigation friend must actually be served on the protected party (unless the court orders otherwise) but this is not a universal provision. Where it is proposed to change the litigation friend both the existing and intended litigation friend must be served (but not apparently the protected party). There is no requirement to serve a child in any of these situations, but see the note to r 21.2.

Who is appointed—The court may decide to appoint any other person who meets the criteria set out in r 21.4(3) and is willing to act.

21.9 Procedure where appointment of a litigation friend ceases

(1) When a child who is not a protected party reaches the age of 18, the litigation friend's appointment ceases.

(2) Where a protected party regains or acquires capacity to conduct the proceedings, the litigation friend's appointment continues until it is ended by court order.

(3) An application for an order under paragraph (2) may be made by –

    (a)   the former protected party;

    (b)   the litigation friend; or

    (c)   a party.

(4) The child or protected party in respect of whom the appointment to act has ceased must serve notice on the other parties –

    (a)   stating that the appointment of his litigation friend to act has ceased;

    (b)   giving his address for service; and

    (c)   stating whether or not he intends to carry on the proceedings.

(5) If the child or protected party does not serve the notice required by paragraph (4) within 28 days after the day on which the appointment of the litigation friend ceases the court may, on application, strike out any claim brought by or defence raised by the child or protected party.

(6) The liability of a litigation friend for costs continues until –

    (a)   the person in respect of whom his appointment to act has ceased serves the notice referred to in paragraph (4); or

    (b)   the litigation friend serves notice on the parties that his appointment to act has ceased.

Amendments—SI 2007/2204.

Practice Direction—See generally Practice Direction 21.

Scope of provision—This rule makes provision for a party ceasing to be a child or protected party.

Child—There will be no need for a litigation friend when the child attains 18 (unless the child is also a protected party) so the appointment then ceases automatically. If this party does not by notice under r 21.9(4) continue the proceedings they may be struck out. There is no express requirement for the child to be notified of the existence of the proceedings up to that point, but notice of an application to strike out under r 21.9(5) must presumably be given to the party formerly a child. The litigation friend will remain liable for costs unless the child gives notice as aforesaid or the litigation friend gives notice under r 21.9(6)(b) which must also be given to the party formerly a child.

Protected party—The position is different in respect of a protected party who recovers capacity. The litigation friend will only be removed by court order following an application under r 21.9(3) and evidence will be required as to capacity. Notice must still be served by the former protected party under r 21.9(4) or the proceedings may be struck out, and the litigation friend will remain liable for costs until that notice is served or he or she serves his or her own notice under r 21.9(6)(b).

Liability of litigation friend for costs—The litigation friend of a claimant may have had to give an undertaking as to costs pursuant to r 21.4(3)(c). This liability continues until notice is served on the other parties either by the claimant or the former litigation friend as mentioned above. Presumably the reference in r 21.9(6) to 'The liability of a litigation friend for costs ...' refers to such undertaking and is not sufficient to create any additional liability. It is not clear whether, when discharged, the litigation friend is released from all liability for costs or only costs incurred from that date, although it is probably the latter.

Relationship between the civil court and the Court of Protection—Doubt may arise in a brain injury claim as to whether the claimant lacks or continues to lack capacity either to litigate or to manage property and affairs. This may be relevant as to the need for a litigation friend and also the quantum of damages to be awarded. In *Saulle v Nouvet* [2007] EWHC 2902 (QB), Mr Andrew Edis QC sitting as a deputy judge of the High Court assumed that the civil court must deal with both assessments of capacity but although that court can make a definitive decision as to capacity to litigate it cannot make a decision as to capacity to manage financial affairs that will be binding on the Court of Protection. Conversely, the Court of Protection has a statutory power to make declarations as to present (but not past) capacity which may relate to both litigation and management of financial affairs and any such declarations are likely to be followed by a civil court. In substantial personal injury claims where the quantum of damages may be affected by the involvement of the Court of Protection there are therefore advantages in the civil court referring both issues of capacity to the Court of Protection for determination. However, where the amount of money involved would not normally trigger the intervention of the Court of Protection it is proportionate and desirable for the civil court to adjudicate on both aspects of capacity (i e to decide whether the litigant is a protected party and if so whether he or she is also a protected beneficiary).

Where there is a reference to the Court of Protection in regard to capacity issues the proceedings should be stayed pending the outcome. It is likely that the defendant will be made a party to the Court of Protection proceedings in view of the financial interest and the advocates in the civil proceedings will thus have a right of audience.

21.10 Compromise etc. by or on behalf of a child or protected party

(1) Where a claim is made –

    (a)   by or on behalf of a child or protected party; or

    (b)   against a child or protected party,

no settlement, compromise or payment (including any voluntary interim payment) and no acceptance of money paid into court shall be valid, so far as it relates to the claim by, on behalf of or against the child or protected party, without the approval of the court.

(2) Where –

    (a)   before proceedings in which a claim is made by or on behalf of, or against, a child or protected party (whether alone or with any other person) are begun, an agreement is reached for the settlement of the claim; and

    (b)   the sole purpose of proceedings is to obtain the approval of the court to a settlement or compromise of the claim,

the claim must –

    (i)   be made using the procedure set out in Part 8 (alternative procedure for claims); and

    (ii)   include a request to the court for approval of the settlement or compromise.

(3) In proceedings to which Section II [or Section VI] of Part 45 applies, the court will not make an order for detailed assessment of the costs payable to the child or protected party but will assess the costs in the manner set out in that Section.

    (Rule 48.5 contains provisions about costs where money is payable to a child or protected party.)

Amendments—SI 2004/3419; SI 2007/2204; SI 2010/621.

Practice Direction—See generally Practice Direction 21.

Scope of provision—This provision ensures that the approval of the court is obtained to any settlement or compromise on behalf of a child or protected party, and extends to accepting any Part 36 offer. It applies to claims other than for money and where the claim is made against the child or protected party. Without this approval the settlement, compromise or payment of any claim is wholly invalid and unenforceable, and is made entirely at the risk of the parties and their solicitors. An unexpected consequence is that the acceptance by a defendant of a Part 36 offer to settle made by a litigation friend (including a partial settlement relating to liability) may be withdrawn before court approval is obtained (*Drinkall v Whitwood* (2002) CCS 103, [2003] EWCA Civ 1547, [2004] 1 WLR 462, CA).

Purpose—There are three distinct reasons for this provision:

(1) to enable defendants to obtain a valid discharge from the claim;
(2) to protect children and protected parties from any lack of skill and experience on the part of their advisers which might lead to a settlement of a money claim for less than it is worth (*Black v Yates* [1991] 4 All ER 722); and
(3) to ensure that solicitors and counsel are paid their proper costs and fees, and no more (this extends to both overcharging and recommending an unfavourable settlement influenced by an attractive costs offer).

Early settlements—Where a compromise or settlement is reached before proceedings are begun the Part 8 procedure is used to seek approval of the court (r 21.10(2)). This does not prevent the settlement of small claims (e g under £1,000) by payment to parents or carers prior to any proceedings on the basis of their indemnity and that may be appropriate to avoid disproportionate costs, but there are risks especially if the true value of the claim was not recognised.

Late settlements—Where the compromise or settlement is reached after the proceedings have been commenced, approval is sought by way of an application in the course of those proceedings. It would be an abuse of the process of the court for the parties and their solicitors in any subsisting proceedings to make or act on any such settlement, compromise or payment without the court's approval.

Hearing—The hearing will usually be before the Master or district judge in claims involving a child but before a Master, designated civil judge or his or her nominee in the case of a protected party (Practice Direction 21, paras 5.6 and 6.5). In practice, subject to financial limits, most district judges have been nominated to hear these applications. Very large claims in the High Court may be dealt with by High Court judges.

The hearing (except for very small sums when a hearing may be dispensed with) should generally be attended by the litigation friend and child or protected party unless there is good reason to the contrary. The court will wish to be satisfied that the settlement or compromise is one that should be approved and may wish to ascertain the views of the litigation friend (and the child if of sufficient maturity and understanding) and inspect any scars which feature in a personal injuries claim. A written opinion from counsel or a suitably experienced solicitor as to liability and quantum will be helpful and may be required.

Costs—The requirement for court approval extends to costs (r 48.5). There will be a detailed assessment (r 48.5(2)), but in certain circumstances this may be dispensed with (Practice Direction Costs, para 50.2). The claimant's solicitor does not usually seek any costs over and above those recovered from the defendant, so that the child or protected party receives the full damages without any deduction for costs (this may not be so where conditional fees apply). If such further costs are expressly waived approval of costs may not be required where there has been summary assessment or costs can be agreed or are to be paid by an insurer (Practice Direction Costs, para 51.1). It is not clear how this impinges on obligations under a public funding certificate, but the former practice may continue of the court being invited to record its approval of an agreement as to costs and dispense with assessment.

Need for a public hearing—Although any hearing should normally be held in public to comply with the ECHR, Art 6(1), there are exceptions and hearings involving the interests of a child or protected party may be in private (see r 39.2(3)(d) and Practice Direction 39, para 1.4A). It has been held that the hearing of an application for the approval of a proposed settlement of a personal injury or Fatal Accident Act claim and the basic reasons therefore should be given in open court, although any part of the hearing intended to acquaint the court with the negotiations culminating in the

PART V

proposed settlement and other details of the claim and the status and medical condition of the claimant should remain private (*Beatham v Carlisle Hospitals NHS Trust* (1999) CCS 4, (1999) *The Times*, May 20, QBD, Buckley J).

Varying the settlement—Once the settlement has been approved it is final and cannot be varied or revoked on the ground that an unforeseen event has destroyed the assumption on which it was made pursuant to the case management power of the court under r 3.1(7) (*Roult (by his mother and litigation friend) v North West Strategic Health Authority* [2009] EWCA Civ 444, [2009] PIQR P18).

Appeals—A decision not to appeal, where permission has been obtained on the express understanding that the possible appellant needs time to consider the matter, and with no consideration moving from the possible respondents, is not a 'compromise' and does not require the approval of the court (*Re A (Conjoined Twins: Medical Treatment) (No 2)* (2001) CCS 2, [2001] 1 FLR 267, CA).

Role of the Court of Protection—These provisions apply even where the proceedings are being conducted by the protected party's deputy as litigation friend under the authority of the Court of Protection. In that event the approval of the Master of the former Court of Protection had to be first obtained to proceed with the settlement. This requirement does not apply under the new jurisdiction.

Structured settlement—Where a structured settlement is contemplated reference should be made to Practice Direction 40C.

Provisional damages—See Practice Direction 41, Provisional Damages.

Part 45, Section II—This relates to fixed recoverable costs for road traffic accidents.

Forms—Form N292 (Order on settlement on behalf of a child or protected party).

21.11 Control of money recovered by or on behalf of a child or protected party

(1) Where in any proceedings –

    (a)   money is recovered by or on behalf of or for the benefit of a child or protected party; or

    (b)   money paid into court is accepted by or on behalf of a child or protected party,

the money will be dealt with in accordance with directions given by the court under this rule and not otherwise.

(2) Directions given under this rule may provide that the money shall be wholly or partly paid into court and invested or otherwise dealt with.

(3) Where money is recovered by or on behalf of a protected party or money paid into court is accepted by or on behalf of a protected party, before giving directions in accordance with this rule, the court will first consider whether the protected party is a protected beneficiary.

Amendments—SI 2007/2204.

Practice Direction—See generally Practice Direction 21, paras 8–10 and 13.

Scope of provision—This rule ensures that there is supervision by the appropriate court of money awarded to or recovered by a child or protected beneficiary. This fund (or the balance after allowing for any money authorised to be released for the immediate benefit of the child or protected beneficiary) will be transferred to the Court Funds Office and applied for the benefit of the claimant in such manner as the court thinks fit (see notes below). Small sums may be released to the parents or carers of a child or protected beneficiary if the court is satisfied that they will invest or use the money for the benefit of the child or protected beneficiary, and this may increasingly become the policy now that lower than market interest rates are obtained on 'special account' making it unattractive to retain the fund in court.

The restriction on the judges who can approve settlements for protected parties (Practice Direction 21, paras 5.6 and 6.5) does not appear to extend to this later stage although in practice the directions will be given in most cases at the same hearing as the approval.

'protected beneficiary' (r 21.1(2)(e))—A separate definition is provided because a party may lack capacity to conduct the proceedings and thus be a protected party but, nevertheless, have the capacity to manage money. The protected beneficiary is a protected party who also lacks the capacity to manage and control any money recovered by him or her or on his or her behalf or for his or her benefit in the proceedings. The court must consider the question of mental capacity before it purports to control the money recovered for a protected party.

The definition of a protected beneficiary is insufficient for two reasons. First, there is an assumption (which may not be justified) that only a person who is a protected party may be a protected beneficiary. Secondly, if the approach of the civil court is to be compatible with that of the Court of Protection it becomes necessary to aggregate the damages recovered with the existing wealth of the protected party and then to decide whether there is capacity to manage the entirety.

Procedure—See Practice Direction 21, paras 8–12. The hearing may be in private under r 39.2(3)(d), but initial indications (at least in the High Court) are that approval should be given in public (*Beatham v Carlisle Hospitals NHS Trust* (1999) CCS 4, (1999) *The Times*, May 20, QBD).

Order—See Form N292.

Investment and other directions—The court should give directions relating to the fund on the new Form CFO 320 (introduced March 2009) as soon as possible after the award is made or settlement approved. This may be at the hearing before a district judge or master approving the settlement, but if the award is made at a trial these directions are likely to be adjourned to a district judge or master in chambers at a later date. Investment directions basically comprise a choice between high interest or equity investment, or a combination of the two. This will be influenced by the use to be made of the fund (e g if periodic payments are to be made) and the period of time that the fund is likely to remain invested (capital growth may be appropriate if the child is young, but accumulation of interest will be the only safe course for a child approaching 18). There is provision to direct that interest or instalments of capital be paid out at regular intervals for the support or maintenance of the child or protected beneficiary. In the case of a child, if a birth certificate is produced 'majority directions' can be given to the effect that the fund be paid out on attaining majority (this will not be appropriate if the child is also or may prove to be a protected beneficiary). The court staff then complete CFO Form 212 which is sent to the Court Funds Office and a local file is created for the fund.

Transfer to another court—Unless reserved to a particular district judge who has knowledge of the family background, it may be helpful for the file in respect of a continuing fund to be transferred to the county court in the area where the child or protected beneficiary lives so that attendance at hearings relating to the application of the fund will be more convenient.

Powers of litigation friend—The role of the litigation friend is restricted to the conduct of the proceedings and his or her powers do not extend to dealing with the financial affairs of the protected beneficiary (*Leather v Kirby* [1965] 3 All ER 927). He or she should, however, ensure that the fund is properly invested by the court and may have a sufficient continuing interest (e g as a parent or carer) to remain involved in the application of the fund by the court on behalf of the child or protected beneficiary. The person who is the litigation friend may, of course, also be the protected beneficiary's deputy (formerly receiver) or attorney and continue to administer the fund in that capacity.

Control of money: protected beneficiary—If the fund is substantial (over £30,000), or the protected beneficiary already has income or assets which need to be administered, the Court of Protection should administer the entire affairs. Subject to any public funding costs provision, the fund will be transferred to the Court of Protection to the credit of the protected beneficiary to be dealt with as the Court of Protection in its discretion thinks fit. The protected beneficiary's solicitor should approach the Court of Protection at an earlier stage so that there is no delay when the fund becomes available. Where, however, the fund is under £20,000 and there is no other reason to involve the Court of Protection (state benefits can be dealt with by an appointee), it can remain in

PART V

court and be dealt with as if the protected beneficiary were a child (Practice Direction 21, para 10.2). Between these two figures, the Senior Judge of the Court of Protection should be consulted.

If there is a registered enduring or lasting power of attorney (in which event there will not be a deputy appointed by the Court of Protection), it would normally be appropriate for the attorney or donee who is managing the affairs to receive the fund. There may be concern about this if the fund is very large in relation to the estate that such attorney was appointed to administer, and in that event reference should be made to the Senior Judge of the Court of Protection who may wish to superimpose the appointment of a financial deputy.

Need for Court of Protection involvement—Someone who is treated as a protected party and has a litigation friend does not necessarily need to come under the jurisdiction of the Court of Protection. Conversely, a person within the jurisdiction of the Court of Protection is likely to require a litigation friend for civil proceedings. However, decision-specific tests of capacity must be applied.

21.12 Expenses incurred by a litigation friend

(1) In proceedings to which rule 21.11 applies, a litigation friend who incurs expenses on behalf of a child or protected party in any proceedings is entitled on application to recover the amount paid or payable out of any money recovered or paid into court to the extent that it –

(a) has been reasonably incurred; and

(b) is reasonable in amount.

(2) Expenses may include all or part of –

(a) an insurance premium, as defined by rule 43.2(1)(m); or

(b) interest on a loan taken out to pay an insurance premium or other recoverable disbursement.

(3) No application may be made under the rule for expenses that –

(a) are of a type that may be recoverable on an assessment of costs payable by or out of money belonging to a child or protected party; but

(b) are disallowed in whole or in part on such an assessment.

(Expenses which are also 'costs' as defined in rule 43.2(1)(a) are dealt with under rule 48.5(2).)

(4) In deciding whether the expenses were reasonably incurred and reasonable in amount, the court will have regard to all the circumstances of the case including the factors set out in rule 44.5(3).

(5) When the court is considering the factors to be taken into account in assessing the reasonableness of the expenses, it will have regard to the facts and circumstances as they reasonably appeared to the litigation friend or to the child's or protected party's legal representative when the expense was incurred.

(6) Where the claim is settled or compromised, or judgment is given, on terms that an amount not exceeding £5,000 is paid to the child or protected party, the total amount the litigation friend may recover under paragraph (1) must not exceed 25% of the sum so agreed or awarded, unless the court directs otherwise. Such total amount must not exceed 50% of the sum so agreed or awarded.

Amendments—SI 2007/2204.

Practice Direction—See generally Practice Direction 21, para 11.

Scope of provision—This rule clarifies the approach to be adopted by the court when a litigation friend seeks approval to deduct from the damages any expenses that are not recoverable from the defendant. These may comprise the whole or part of a success fee or insurance premium and interest on a loan to fund the premium. There has in the past been a difference of approach by district judges when approving settlements, but there is no reason why a child or protected party should be in a better position than any other claimant in such respect. If the expenses were reasonably incurred at the inception of the claim and are reasonable in amount then the litigation friend should be indemnified. However, if the amounts were unreasonable this may reflect on the advice initially given by the solicitors involved. There is no procedure whereby such expenses may be approved in advance.

There is a limit of 25 per cent on the amount that may be deducted from damages not exceeding £5,000, although the court has a discretion to increase this up to 50 per cent.

Any costs that are not recovered from the defendant should be assessed as between solicitor and client under r 48.5(2) before they may be deducted from the damages, although in claims of low value it is usual for a solicitor acting for a child or protected party to waive any further costs.

For a case dealing with the validity of a CFA where the claimant was found to be a protected party see *Findlay v Barrington Jones & MIB* [2009] EWHC 90130.

Practice Direction – Children and Protected Parties (PD21)

This Practice Direction supplements CPR Part 21 (PD21)

General

1.1 In proceedings where one of the parties is a protected party, the protected party should be referred to in the title to the proceedings as 'A.B. (a protected party by C.D. his litigation friend)'.

1.2 In proceedings where one of the parties is a child, where –

(1)   the child has a litigation friend, the child should be referred to in the title to the proceedings as 'A.B. (a child by C.D. his litigation friend)'; or

(2)   the child is conducting the proceedings on his own behalf, the child should be referred to in the title as 'A.B. (a child)'.

1.3 A settlement of a claim by a child includes an agreement on a sum to be apportioned to a dependent child under the Fatal Accidents Act 1976.

The Litigation Friend

2.1 A person may become a litigation friend –

(a)   without a court order under rule 21.5, or

(b)   by a court order under rule 21.6.

2.2 A person who wishes to become a litigation friend without a court order pursuant to rule 21.5(3) must file a certificate of suitability in Practice Form N235 –

(a)   stating that he consents to act,

(b)   stating that he knows or believes that the [claimant] [defendant] [is a child][lacks capacity to conduct the proceedings],

(c)   in the case of a protected party, stating the grounds of his belief and, if his belief is based upon medical opinion or the opinion of another suitably qualified expert, attaching any relevant document to the certificate,

(d)   stating that he can fairly and competently conduct proceedings on behalf of the child or protected party and has no interest adverse to that of the child or protected party, and

(e)   where the child or protected party is a claimant, undertaking to pay any costs which the child or protected party may be ordered to pay in relation to the proceedings, subject to any right he may have to be repaid from the assets of the child or protected party.

2.3 The certificate of suitability must be verified by a statement of truth.

(Part 22 contains provisions about statements of truth.)

2.4 The litigation friend is not required to serve the document referred to in paragraph 2.2(*c*) when he serves a certificate of suitability on the person to be served under rule 21.5(4)(*a*).

Application for a Court Order Appointing a Litigation Friend

3.1 Rule 21.6 sets out who may apply for an order appointing a litigation friend.

3.2 An application must be made in accordance with Part 23 and must be supported by evidence.

3.3 The evidence in support must satisfy the court that the proposed litigation friend –

(1) consents to act,
(2) can fairly and competently conduct proceedings on behalf of the child or protected party,
(3) has no interest adverse to that of the child or protected party, and
(4) where the child or protected party is a claimant, undertakes to pay any costs which the child or protected party may be ordered to pay in relation to the proceedings, subject to any right he may have to be repaid from the assets of the child or protected party.

3.4 Where it is sought to appoint the Official Solicitor as the litigation friend, provision must be made for payment of his charges.

Procedure where the Need for a Litigation Friend Has Come to an End

4.1 Rule 21.9 deals with the situation where the need for a litigation friend comes to an end during the proceedings because either –

(1) a child who is not also a protected party reaches the age of 18 (full age) during the proceedings, or
(2) a protected party regains or acquires capacity to conduct the proceedings.

4.2 A child on reaching full age must serve on the other parties to the proceedings and file with the court a notice –

(1) stating that he has reached full age,
(2) stating that his litigation friend's appointment has ceased,
(3) giving an address for service, and
(4) stating whether or not he intends to carry on with or continue to defend the proceedings.

4.3 If the notice states that the child intends to carry on with or continue to defend the proceedings he must subsequently be described in the proceedings as 'A.B. (formerly a child but now of full age)'.

4.4 Whether or not a child having reached full age serves a notice in accordance with rule 21.9(4) and paragraph 4.2 above, a litigation friend may, at any time after the child has reached full age, serve a notice on the other parties that his appointment has ceased.

4.5 Where a protected party regains or acquires capacity to conduct the proceedings, an application under rule 21.9(3) must be made for an order under rule 21.9(2) that the litigation friend's appointment has ceased.

4.6 The application must be supported by the following evidence –

    (1)   a medical report or other suitably qualified expert's report indicating that the protected party has regained or acquired capacity to conduct the proceedings,

    (2)   a copy of any relevant order or declaration of the Court of Protection, and

    (3)   if the application is made by the protected party, a statement whether or not he intends to carry on with or continue to defend the proceedings.

4.7 An order under rule 21.9(2) must be served on the other parties to the proceedings. The former protected party must file with the court a notice –

    (1)   stating that his litigation friend's appointment has ceased,

    (2)   giving an address for service, and

    (3)   stating whether or not he intends to carry on with or continue to defend the proceedings.

Settlement or Compromise by or on behalf of a Child or Protected Party Before the Issue of Proceedings

5.1 Where a claim by or on behalf of a child or protected party has been dealt with by agreement before the issue of proceedings and only the approval of the court to the agreement is sought, the claim must, in addition to containing the details of the claim and satisfying the requirements of rule 21.10(2), include the following –

    (1)   subject to paragraph 5.3, the terms of the settlement or compromise or have attached to it a draft consent order in Practice Form N292;

    (2)   details of whether and to what extent the defendant admits liability;

    (3)   the age and occupation (if any) of the child or protected party;

    (4)   the litigation friend's approval of the proposed settlement or compromise,

    (5)   a copy of any financial advice relating to the proposed settlement; and

    (6)   in a personal injury case arising from an accident –

        (a)   details of the circumstances of the accident,

        (b)   any medical reports,

        (c)   where appropriate, a schedule of any past and future expenses and losses claimed and any other relevant information relating to the personal injury as set out in the practice direction which supplements Part 16 (statements of case), and

        (d)   where considerations of liability are raised –

            (i)   any evidence or reports in any criminal proceedings or in an inquest, and

            (ii)   details of any prosecution brought.

5.2

    (1)   An opinion on the merits of the settlement or compromise given by counsel or solicitor acting for the child or protected party must, except in very clear cases, be obtained.

(2) A copy of the opinion and, unless the instructions on which it was given are sufficiently set out in it, a copy of the instructions, must be supplied to the court.

5.3 Where in any personal injury case a claim for damages for future pecuniary loss is settled, the provisions in paragraphs 5.4 and 5.5 must in addition be complied with.

5.4 The court must be satisfied that the parties have considered whether the damages should wholly or partly take the form of periodical payments.

5.5 Where the settlement includes provision for periodical payments, the claim must –

(1) set out the terms of the settlement or compromise; or
(2) have attached to it a draft consent order,

which must satisfy the requirements of rules 41.8 and 41.9 as appropriate.

5.6 Applications for the approval of a settlement or compromise will normally be heard by –

(1) a Master or a district judge in proceedings involving a child; and
(2) a Master, designated civil judge or his nominee in proceedings involving a protected party.

(For information about provisional damages claims see Part 41 and the practice direction which supplements it.)

Settlement or Compromise by or on behalf of a Child or Protected Party After Proceedings Have Been Issued

6.1 Where in any personal injury case a claim for damages for future pecuniary loss, by or on behalf of a child or protected party, is dealt with by agreement after proceedings have been issued, an application must be made for the court's approval of the agreement.

6.2 The court must be satisfied that the parties have considered whether the damages should wholly or partly take the form of periodical payments.

6.3 Where the settlement includes provision for periodical payments, an application under paragraph 6.1 must –

(1) set out the terms of the settlement or compromise; or
(2) have attached to it a draft consent order,

which must satisfy the requirements of rules 41.8 and 41.9 as appropriate.

6.4 The court must be supplied with –

(1) an opinion on the merits of the settlement or compromise given by counsel or solicitor acting for the child or protected party, except in very clear cases; and
(2) a copy of any financial advice.

6.5 Applications for the approval of a settlement or compromise, except at the trial, will normally be heard by –

(1) a Master or a district judge in proceedings involving a child; and
(2) a Master, designated civil judge or his nominee in proceedings involving a protected party.

Apportionment under the Fatal Accidents Act 1976

7.1 A judgment on or settlement in respect of a claim under the Fatal Accidents Act 1976 must be apportioned between the persons by or on whose behalf the claim has been brought.

7.2 Where a claim is brought on behalf of a dependent child or children, any settlement (including an agreement on a sum to be apportioned to a dependent child under the Fatal Accidents Act 1976) must be approved by the court.

7.3 The money apportioned to any dependent child must be invested on the child's behalf in accordance with rules 21.10 and 21.11 and paragraphs 8 and 9 below.

7.4 In order to approve an apportionment of money to a dependent child, the court will require the following information:

    (1)   the matters set out in paragraphs 5.1(2) and (3), and
    (2)   in respect of the deceased –
        (a)   where death was caused by an accident, the matters set out in paragraphs 5.1(6)(a), (b) and (c), and
        (b)   his future loss of earnings, and
    (3)   the extent and nature of the dependency.

Control of Money Recovered By or On Behalf of a Child or Protected Party

8.1 When giving directions under rule 21.11, the court –

    (1)   may direct the money to be paid into court for investment,
    (2)   may direct that certain sums be paid direct to the child or protected beneficiary, his litigation friend or his legal representative for the immediate benefit of the child or protected beneficiary or for expenses incurred on his behalf, and
    (3)   may direct that the application in respect of the investment of the money be transferred to a local district registry.

8.2 The court will consider the general aims to be achieved for the money in court (the fund) by investment and will give directions as to the type of investment.

8.3 Where a child also lacks capacity to manage and control any money recovered by him or on his behalf in the proceedings, and is likely to remain so on reaching full age, his fund should be administered as a protected beneficiary's fund.

8.4 Where a child or protected beneficiary is in receipt of publicly funded legal services the fund will be subject to a first charge under section 10 of the Access to Justice Act 1999 (statutory charge) and an order for the investment of money on the child's or protected beneficiary's behalf must contain a direction to that effect.

Investment On Behalf of a Child

9.1 At the hearing of an application for the approval of a settlement or compromise the litigation friend or his legal representative must provide, in addition to the information required by paragraphs 5 and 6 –

    (1)   a CFO form 320 (initial application for investment of damages) for completion by the judge hearing the application; and
    (2)   any evidence or information which the litigation friend wishes the court to consider in relation to the investment of the award for damages.

PART V

9.2 Following the hearing in paragraph 9.1, the court will forward to the Court Funds Office a request for investment decision (form 212) and the Public Trustee's investment managers will make the appropriate investment.

9.3 Where an award for damages for a child is made at trial, unless paragraph 9.7 applies, the trial judge will –

(1)   direct the money to be paid into court and placed into the special investment account until further investment directions have been given by the court;

(2)   direct the litigation friend to make an application to a Master or district judge for further investment directions; and

(3)   give such other directions as the trial judge thinks fit, including a direction that the hearing of the application for further investment directions will be fixed for a date within 28 days from the date of the trial.

9.4 The application under paragraph 9.3(2) must be made by filing with the court –

(1)   a completed CFO form 320; and

(2)   any evidence or information which the litigation friend wishes the court to consider in relation to the investment of the award for damages.

9.5 The application must be sent in proceedings in the Royal Courts of Justice to the Masters' Support Unit (Room E16) at the Royal Courts of Justice.

9.6 If the application required by paragraph 9.3(2) is not made to the court, the money paid into court in accordance with paragraph 9.3(1) will remain in the special investment account subject to any further order of the court or paragraph 9.8.

9.7 If the money to be invested is very small the court may order it to be paid direct to the litigation friend to be put into a building society account (or similar) for the child's use.

9.8 If the money is invested in court, it must be paid out to the child on application when he reaches full age.

Investment On Behalf of a Protected Beneficiary

10.1 The Court of Protection has jurisdiction to make decisions in the best interests of a protected beneficiary. Fees may be charged for the administration of funds and these must be provided for in any settlement.

10.2 Where the sum to be administered for the benefit of the protected beneficiary is –

(1)   £30,000 or more, unless a person with authority as –

(a)   the attorney under a registered enduring power of attorney;

(b)   the donee of a lasting power of attorney; or

(c)   the deputy appointed by the Court of Protection,

to administer or manage the protected beneficiary's financial affairs has been appointed, the order approving the settlement will contain a direction to the litigation friend to apply to the Court of Protection for the appointment of a deputy, after which the fund will be dealt with as directed by the Court of Protection; or

(2)   under £30,000, it may be retained in court and invested in the same way as the fund of a child.

10.3 A form of order transferring the fund to the Court of Protection is set out in practice form N292.

10.4 In order for the Court Funds Office to release a fund which is subject to the statutory charge, the litigation friend or his legal representative or the person with authority referred to in paragraph 10.2(1) must provide the appropriate regional office of the Legal Services Commission with an undertaking in respect of a sum to cover their costs, following which the regional office will advise the Court Funds Office in writing of that sum, enabling them to transfer the balance to the Court of Protection on receipt of a CFO form 200 payment schedule authorised by the court.

10.5 The CFO form 200 should be completed and presented to the court where the settlement or trial took place for authorisation, subject to paragraphs 10.6 and 10.7.

10.6 Where the settlement took place in the Royal Courts of Justice the CFO form 200 must be completed and presented for authorisation –

    (1)   on behalf of a child, in the Masters' Support Unit, Room E105, and

    (2)   on behalf of a protected beneficiary, in the Judgment and Orders Section in the Action Department, Room E17.

10.7 Where the trial took place in the Royal Courts of Justice, the CFO form 200 is completed and authorised by the court officer.

Expenses Incurred by a Litigation Friend

11.1 A litigation friend may make a claim for expenses under rule 21.12(1) –

    (1)   where the court has ordered an assessment of costs under rule 48.5(2), at the detailed assessment hearing;

    (2)   where the litigation friend's expenses are not of a type which would be recoverable as costs on an assessment of costs between the parties, to the Master or district judge at the hearing to approve the settlement or compromise under Part 21 (the Master or district judge may adjourn the matter to the costs judge); or

    (3)   where an assessment of costs under Part 48.5(2) is not required, and no approval under Part 21 is necessary, by a Part 23 application supported by a witness statement to a costs judge or district judge as appropriate.

11.2 In all circumstances, the litigation friend must support a claim for expenses by filing a witness statement setting out –

    (1)   the nature and amount of the expense; and

    (2)   the reason the expense was incurred.

Guardian's Accounts

12 Paragraph 8 of the practice direction supplementing Part 40 (Judgments and Orders) deals with the approval of the accounts of a guardian of assets of a child.

Payment out of Funds in Court

13.1 Applications to a Master or district judge –

    (1)   for payment out of money from the fund for the benefit of the child, or

    (2)   to vary an investment strategy,

may be dealt with without a hearing unless the court directs otherwise.

13.2 When the child reaches full age –

PART V

(1) where his fund in court is a sum of money, it will be paid out to him on application; or

(2) where his fund is in the form of investments other than money (for example shares or unit trusts), the investments will on application be –

(a) sold and the proceeds of sale paid out to him; or

(b) transferred into his name.

13.3 Where the fund is administered by the Court of Protection, any payment out of money from that fund must be in accordance with any decision or order of the Court of Protection.

13.4 If an application is required for the payment out of money from a fund administered by the Court of Protection, that application must be made to the Court of Protection.

(For further information on payments out of court, see the practice direction supplementing Part 37.)

****

PART 43
SCOPE OF COST RULES AND DEFINITIONS

43.1 Scope of this Part

This Part contains definitions and interpretation of certain matters set out in the rules about costs contained in Parts 44 to 48.

(Part 44 contains general rules about costs; Part 45 deals with fixed costs; Part 46 deals with fast track trial costs; Part 47 deals with the detailed assessment of costs and related appeals and Part 48 deals with costs payable in special cases)

43.2 Definitions and application

(1) In Parts 44 to 48, unless the context otherwise requires –

(a) 'costs' includes fees, charges, disbursements, expenses, remuneration, reimbursement allowed to a litigant in person under rule 48.6, any additional liability incurred under a funding arrangement and any fee or reward charged by a lay representative for acting on behalf of a party in proceedings allocated to the small claims track;

(b) 'costs judge' means a taxing master of the [Senior Courts];

[(ba) 'Costs Office' means the Senior Courts Costs Office];

(c) 'costs officer' means –

(i) a costs judge;

(ii) a district judge; and

(iii) an authorised court officer;

(d) 'authorised court officer' means any officer of –

(i) a county court;

(ii) a district registry;

(iii) the Principal Registry of the Family Division; or

(iv) the [Costs Office];

whom the Lord Chancellor has authorised to assess costs;

(e) 'fund' includes any estate or property held for the benefit of any person or class of person and any fund to which a trustee or personal representative is entitled in that capacity;

(f) 'receiving party' means a party entitled to be paid costs;

(g) 'paying party' means a party liable to pay costs;

(h) 'assisted person' means an assisted person within the statutory provisions relating to legal aid;

(i) 'LSC funded client' means an individual who receives services funded by the Legal Services Commission as part of the Community Legal Service within the meaning of Part I of the Access to Justice Act 1999;

(j) 'fixed costs' means the amounts which are to be allowed in respect of solicitors' charges in the circumstances set out in Section I of Part 45;

(k) 'funding arrangement' means an arrangement where a person has –

  (i) entered into a conditional fee agreement or a collective conditional fee agreement which provides for a success fee within the meaning of section 58(2) of the Courts and Legal Services Act 1990;

  (ii) taken out an insurance policy to which section 29 of the Access to Justice Act 1999 (recovery of insurance premiums by way of costs) applies; or

  (iii) made an agreement with a membership organisation to meet that person's legal costs;

(l) 'percentage increase' means the percentage by which the amount of a legal representative's fee can be increased in accordance with a conditional fee agreement which provides for a success fee;

(m) 'insurance premiums' means a sum of money paid or payable for insurance against the risk of incurring a costs liability in the proceedings, taken out after the event that is the subject matter of the claim;

(n) 'membership organisation' means a body prescribed for the purposes of section 30 of the Access to Justice Act 1999 (recovery where body undertakes to meet costs liabilities);

(o) 'additional liability' means the percentage increase, the insurance premium, or the additional amount in respect of provision made by a membership organisation, as the case may be;

(p) 'free of charge' has the same meaning as in section 194(10) of the Legal Services Act 2007;

(q) 'pro bono representation' means legal representation provided free of charge; and

(r) 'the prescribed charity' has the same meaning as in section 194(8) of the Legal Services Act 2007.

(2) The costs to which Parts 44 to 48 apply include –

  (a) the following costs where those costs may be assessed by the court –
    (i) costs of proceedings before an arbitrator or umpire;
    (ii) costs of proceedings before a tribunal or other statutory body; and
    (iii) costs payable by a client to his solicitor; and

  (b) costs which are payable by one party to another party under the terms of a contract, where the court makes an order for an assessment of those costs.

(3) Where advocacy or litigation services are provided to a client under a conditional fee agreement, costs are recoverable under Parts 44 to 48 notwithstanding that the client is liable to pay his legal representative's fees and expenses only to the extent that sums are recovered in respect of the proceedings, whether by way of costs or otherwise.

PART V

(4) In paragraph (3), the reference to a conditional fee agreement is to an agreement which satisfies all the conditions applicable to it by virtue of section 58 of the Courts and Legal Services Act 1990.

Amendments—SI 2000/1317; SI 2001/256; SI 2003/1242; SI 2003/1329; SI 2003/2113;SI 2008/ 2178; SI 2009/2092.

43.3 Meaning of summary assessment

'Summary assessment' means the procedure by which the court, when making an order about costs, orders payment of a sum of money instead of fixed costs or 'detailed assessment'.

43.4 Meaning of detailed assessment

'Detailed assessment' means the procedure by which the amount of costs is decided by a costs officer in accordance with Part 47.

PART 44
GENERAL RULES ABOUT COSTS

44.2 Solicitor's duty to notify client

Where –

    (a)   the court makes a costs order against a legally represented party; and
    (b)   the party is not present when the order is made,

the party's solicitor must notify his client in writing of the costs order no later than 7 days after the solicitor receives notice of the order.

44.3 Court's discretion and circumstances to be taken into account when exercising its discretion as to costs

(6) The orders which the court may make under this rule include an order that a party must pay –

    (a)   a proportion of another party's costs;
    (b)   a stated amount in respect of another party's costs;
    (c)   costs from or until a certain date only;
    (d)   costs incurred before proceedings have begun;
    (e)   costs relating to particular steps taken in the proceedings;
    (f)   costs relating only to a distinct part of the proceedings; and
    (g)   interest on costs from or until a certain date, including a date before judgment.

(7) Where the court would otherwise consider making an order under paragraph (6)(f), it must instead, if practicable, make an order under paragraph (6)(a) or (c).

(8) Where the court has ordered a party to pay costs, it may order an amount to be paid on account before the costs are assessed.

(9) Where a party entitled to costs is also liable to pay costs the court may assess the costs which that party is liable to pay and either –

(a) set off the amount assessed against the amount the party is entitled to be paid and direct him to pay any balance; or

(b) delay the issue of a certificate for the costs to which the party is entitled until he has paid the amount which he is liable to pay.

Amendments—SI 2006/3435.

44.3A Costs orders relating to funding arrangements

(1) The court will not assess any additional liability until the conclusion of the proceedings, or the part of the proceedings, to which the funding arrangement relates.

('Funding arrangement' and 'additional liability' are defined in rule 43.2)

(2) At the conclusion of the proceedings, or the part of the proceedings, to which the funding arrangement relates the court may –

(a) make a summary assessment of all the costs, including any additional liability;

(b) make an order for detailed assessment of the additional liability but make a summary assessment of the other costs; or

(c) make an order for detailed assessment of all the costs.

(Part 47 sets out the procedure for the detailed assessment of costs)

Amendments—Inserted by SI 2000/1317.

44.3B Limits on recovery under funding arrangements

(1) Unless the court orders otherwise, a party may not recover as an additional liability –

(a) any proportion of the percentage increase relating to the cost to the legal representative of the postponement of the payment of his fees and expenses;

(b) any provision made by a membership organisation which exceeds the likely cost to that party of the premium of an insurance policy against the risk of incurring a liability to pay the costs of other parties to the proceedings;

(c) any additional liability for any period during which that party failed to provide information about a funding arrangement in accordance with a rule, practice direction or court order;

(d) any percentage increase where that party has failed to comply with –
(i) a requirement in the [Costs Practice Direction]; or
(ii) a court order,
to disclose in any assessment proceedings, the reasons for setting the percentage increase at the level stated in the conditional fee agreement;

(e) any insurance premium where that party has failed to provide information about the insurance policy in question by the time required by a rule, practice direction or court order.

(Paragraph 9.3 of the Practice Direction (Pre-Action Conduct) provides that a party must inform any other party as soon as possible about a funding arrangement entered into before the start of proceedings.)

(2) This rule does not apply in any assessment under rule 48.9 (assessment of a solicitor's bill to his client).

(Rule 3.9 sets out the circumstances the court will consider on an application for the relief from a sanction for the failure to comply with any rule, practice direction or court order)

Amendments—Inserted by SI 2000/1317; SI 2009/2092; amended by SI 2009/3390.

44.3C Orders in respect of pro bono representation

(1) In this rule, 'the 2007 Act' means the Legal Services Act 2007.

(2) Where the court makes an order under section 194(3) of the 2007 Act –

    (a)   the court may order the payment to the prescribed charity of a sum no greater than the costs specified in Part 45 to which the party with pro bono representation would have been entitled in accordance with that Part and in respect of that representation had it not been provided free of charge; or

    (b)   where Part 45 does not apply, the court may determine the amount of the payment (other than a sum equivalent to fixed costs) to be made by the paying party to the prescribed charity by –

        (i)   making a summary assessment; or

        (ii) making an order for detailed assessment,

    of a sum equivalent to all or part of the costs the paying party would have been ordered to pay to the party with pro bono representation in respect of that representation had it not been provided free of charge.

(3) Where the court makes an order under section 194(3) of the 2007 Act, the order must specify that the payment by the paying party must be made to the prescribed charity.

(4) The receiving party must send a copy of the order to the prescribed charity within 7 days of receipt of the order.

(5) Where the court considers making or makes an order under section 194(3) of the 2007 Act, Parts 43 to 48 apply, where appropriate, with the following modifications –

    (a)   references to 'costs orders', 'orders about costs' or 'orders for the payment of costs' are to be read, unless otherwise stated, as if they refer to an order under section 194(3);

    (b)   references to 'costs' are to be read, as if they referred to a sum equivalent to the costs that would have been claimed by, incurred by or awarded to the party with pro bono representation in respect of that representation had it not been provided free of charge; and

    (c)   references to 'receiving party' are to be read, as meaning a party who has pro bono representation and who would have been entitled to be paid costs in respect of that representation had it not been provided free of charge.

Amendment—Inserted by SI 2008/2178.

44.4 Basis of assessment

(1) Where the court is to assess the amount of costs (whether by summary or detailed assessment) it will assess those costs –

    (a)   on the standard basis; or

    (b)   on the indemnity basis,

but the court will not in either case allow costs which have been unreasonably incurred or are unreasonable in amount.

> (Rule 48.3 sets out how the court decides the amount of costs payable under a contract)

(2) Where the amount of costs is to be assessed on the standard basis, the court will –

(a)   only allow costs which are proportionate to the matters in issue; and

(b)   resolve any doubt which it may have as to whether costs were reasonably incurred or reasonable and proportionate in amount in favour of the paying party.

> (Factors which the court may take into account are set out in rule 44.5)

(3) Where the amount of costs is to be assessed on the indemnity basis, the court will resolve any doubt which it may have as to whether costs were reasonably incurred or were reasonable in amount in favour of the receiving party.

(4) Where –

(a)   the court makes an order about costs without indicating the basis on which the costs are to be assessed; or

(b)   the court makes an order for costs to be assessed on a basis other than the standard basis or the indemnity basis,

the costs will be assessed on the standard basis.

(5) ...

(6) Where the amount of a solicitor's remuneration in respect of non-contentious business is regulated by any general orders made under the Solicitors Act 1974, the amount of the costs to be allowed in respect of any such business which falls to be assessed by the court will be decided in accordance with those general orders rather than this rule and rule 44.5.

Amendments—SI 2000/1317.

44.5 Factors to be taken into account in deciding the amount of costs

(1) The court is to have regard to all the circumstances in deciding whether costs were –

(a)   if it is assessing costs on the standard basis –
 (i)   proportionately and reasonably incurred; or
 (ii) were proportionate and reasonable in amount, or

(b)   if it is assessing costs on the indemnity basis –
 (i)   unreasonably incurred; or
 (ii) unreasonable in amount.

(2) In particular the court must give effect to any orders which have already been made.

(3) The court must also have regard to –

(a)   the conduct of all the parties, including in particular –
 (i)   conduct before, as well as during, the proceedings; and
 (ii) the efforts made, if any, before and during the proceedings in order to try to resolve the dispute;

(b)   the amount or value of any money or property involved;

(c) the importance of the matter to all the parties;
(d) the particular complexity of the matter or the difficulty or novelty of the questions raised;
(e) the skill, effort, specialised knowledge and responsibility involved;
(f) the time spent on the case; and
(g) the place where and the circumstances in which work or any part of it was done.

(Rule 35.4(4) gives the court power to limit the amount that a party may recover with regard to the fees and expenses of an expert)

***

44.8 Time for complying with an order for costs

A party must comply with an order for the payment of costs within 14 days of –

(a) the date of the judgment or order if it states the amount of those costs;
(b) if the amount of those costs (or part of them) is decided later in accordance with Part 47, the date of the certificate which states the amount; or
(c) in either case, such later date as the court may specify.

(Part 47 sets out the procedure for detailed assessment of costs)

Amendments—SI 2000/1317.

***

44.13 Special situations

(1) Where the court makes an order which does not mention costs –

(a) subject to paragraphs (1A) and (1B), the general rule is that no party is entitled –
(i)   to costs; or
(ii) to seek an order under section 194(3) of the Legal Services Act 2007, in relation to that order; but
(b) this does not affect any entitlement of a party to recover costs out of a fund held by that party as trustee or personal representative, or pursuant to any lease, mortgage or other security.

(1A) Where the court makes –

(a) an order granting permission to appeal;
(b) an order granting permission to apply for judicial review; or
(c) any other order or direction sought by a party on an application without notice,

and its order does not mention costs, it will be deemed to include an order for applicant's costs in the case.

(1B) Any party affected by a deemed order for costs under paragraph (1A) may apply at any time to vary the order.

(2) The court hearing an appeal may, unless it dismisses the appeal, make orders about the costs of the proceedings giving rise to the appeal as well as the costs of the appeal.

(3) Where proceedings are transferred from one court to another, the court to which they are transferred may deal with all the costs, including the costs before the transfer.

(4) Paragraph (3) is subject to any order of the court which ordered the transfer.

Amendments—SI 2001/4015; SI 2005/2292; SI 2008/2178.

44.14 Court's powers in relation to misconduct

(1) The court may make an order under this rule where –

    (a)   a party or his legal representative, in connection with a summary or detailed assessment, fails to comply with a rule, practice direction or court order; or

    (b)   it appears to the court that the conduct of a party or his legal representative, before or during the proceedings which gave rise to the assessment proceedings, was unreasonable or improper.

(2) Where paragraph (1) applies, the court may –

    (a)   disallow all or part of the costs which are being assessed; or

    (b)   order the party at fault or his legal representative to pay costs which he has caused any other party to incur.

(3) Where –

    (a)   the court makes an order under paragraph (2) against a legally represented party; and

    (b)   the party is not present when the order is made,

the party's solicitor must notify his client in writing of the order no later than 7 days after the solicitor receives notice of the order.

Amendments—SI 2000/1317.

44.15 Providing information about funding arrangements

(1) A party who seeks to recover an additional liability must provide information about the funding arrangement to the court and to other parties as required by a rule, practice direction or court order.

(2) Where the funding arrangement has changed, and the information a party has previously provided in accordance with paragraph (1) is no longer accurate, that party must file notice of the change and serve it on all other parties within 7 days.

(3) Where paragraph (2) applies, and a party has already filed –

    (a)   an allocation questionnaire; or

    (b)   a pre-trial check list (listing questionnaire),

he must file and serve a new estimate of the costs with the notice.

(The [Costs Practice Direction] sets out –

    –   the information to be provided when a party issues or responds to a claim form, files an allocation questionnaire, a pre-trial check list, and a claim for costs;

    –   the meaning of estimate of costs and the information required in it)

PART V

(Rule 44.3B sets out situations where the party will not recover a sum representing any additional liability)

Amendments—Inserted by SI 2000/1317; amended by SI 2002/2058; amended by SI 2009/3390.

44.16 (1) This rule applies where the Conditional Fee Agreements Regulations 2000 or the Collective Conditional Fee Agreements Regulations 2000 continues to apply to an agreement which provides for a success fee.

(2) Where –

(a) the court disallows any amount of a legal representative's percentage increase in summary or detailed assessment proceedings; and

(b) the legal representative applies for an order that the disallowed amount should continue to be payable by his client,

the court may adjourn the hearing to allow the client to be –

(i) notified of the order sought; and

(ii) separately represented.

(Regulation 3(2)(b) of the Conditional Fee Agreements Regulations 2000, which applies to Conditional Fee Agreements entered into before 1 November 2005, provides that a conditional fee agreement which provides for a success fee must state that any amount of a percentage increase disallowed on assessment ceases to be payable unless the court is satisfied that it should continue to be so payable. Regulation 5(2)(b) of the Collective Conditional Fee Agreements Regulations 2000, which applies to Collective Conditional Fee Agreements entered into before 1 November 2005, makes similar provision in relation to collective conditional fee agreements)

Amendments—Inserted by SI 2000/1317; amended by SI 2001/256; SI 2002/2058; substituted by SI 2005/3515.

44.17 Application of costs rules

This Part and ... Part 47 (procedure for detailed assessment of costs and default provisions) and Part 48 (special cases), do not apply to the assessment of costs in proceedings to the extent that –

(a) section 11 of the Access to Justice Act 1999, and the provisions made under that Act; or

(b) regulations made under the Legal Aid Act 1988;

make different provision.

(The [Costs Practice Direction] sets out the procedure to be followed where a party was wholly or partially funded by the Legal Services Commission)

Amendments—Inserted by SI 2000/1317; amended by SI 2009/3390.

***

PART 47
PROCEDURE FOR DETAILED ASSESSMENT OF COSTS AND DEFAULT PROVISIONS

(The definitions contained in Part 43 are relevant to this Part)

Section I – General Rules about Detailed Assessment

47.1 Time when detailed assessment may be carried out

The general rule is that the costs of any proceedings or any part of the proceedings are not to be assessed by the detailed procedure until the conclusion of the proceedings but the court may order them to be assessed immediately.

> (The [Costs Practice Direction] gives further guidance about when proceedings are concluded for the purpose of this rule)

Amendment—SI 2009/3390.

47.2 No stay of detailed assessment where there is an appeal

Detailed assessment is not stayed pending an appeal unless the court so orders.

47.3 Powers of an authorised court officer

(1) An authorised court officer has all the powers of the court when making a detailed assessment, except –

    (a)   power to make a wasted costs order as defined in rule 48.7;
    (b)   power to make an order under –
        (i)   rule 44.14 (powers in relation to misconduct);
        (ii) rule 47.8 (sanction for delay in commencing detailed assessment proceedings);
        (iii) paragraph (2) (objection to detailed assessment by authorised court officer); and
    (c)   power to make a detailed assessment of costs payable to a solicitor by his client unless the costs are being assessed under rule 48.5 (costs where money is payable to a child or protected party).

(2) Where a party objects to the detailed assessment of costs being made by an authorised court officer, the court may order it to be made by a costs judge.

> (The [Costs Practice Direction] sets out the relevant procedure)

Amendment—SI 2009/3390.

Senior Executive Officers	£30,000 (excluding VAT)
Principal Officers	£75,000 (excluding VAT)

Amendment—SI 2007/2204.

47.4 Venue for detailed assessment proceedings

(1) All applications and requests in detailed assessment proceedings must be made to or filed at the appropriate office.

> (The [Costs Practice Direction] sets out the meaning of 'appropriate office' in any particular case)

(2) The court may direct that the appropriate office is to be the Costs Office.

Amendment—SI 2009/2092; SI 2009/3390.

Section II – Costs Payable by One Party to Another – Commencement of
Detailed Assessment Proceedings

47.5 Application of this section

This Section of Part 47 applies where a cost officer is to make a detailed assessment
of –

  (a) costs which are payable by one party to another; or
  (b) the sum which is payable by one party to the prescribed charity pursuant to
       an order under section 194(3) of the Legal Services Act 2007.

Amendment—Substituted by SI 2008/2178.

47.6 Commencement of detailed assessment proceedings

(1) Detailed assessment proceedings are commenced by the receiving party serving
on the paying party –

  (a) notice of commencement in the relevant practice form; and
  (b) a copy of the bill of costs.

      (Rule 47.7 sets out the period for commencing detailed assessment proceedings)

(2) The receiving party must also serve a copy of the notice of commencement and
the bill on any other relevant persons specified in the [Costs Practice Direction].

(3) A person on whom a copy of the notice of commencement is served under
paragraph (2) is a party to the detailed assessment proceedings (in addition to the
paying party and the receiving party).

      (The [Costs Practice Direction] deals with –
  –   other documents which the party must file when he requests detailed
      assessment;
  –   the court's powers where it considers that a hearing may be necessary;
  –   the form of a bill;
  –   the length of notice which will be given if a hearing date is fixed).

Amendment—SI 2009/3390.

47.7 Period for commencing detailed assessment proceedings

The following table shows the period for commencing detailed assessment
proceedings.

Source of right to detailed assessment	Time by which detailed assessment proceedings must be commenced
Judgment, direction, order, award or other determination	3 months after the date of the judgment etc Where detailed assessment is stayed pending an appeal, 3 months after the date of the order lifting the stay.

Discontinuance under Part 38	3 months after the date of service of notice of discontinuance under rule 38.3; or 3 months after the date of the dismissal of application to set the notice of discontinuance aside under rule 38.4
Acceptance of an offer to settle under Part 36	3 months after the date when the right to costs arose.

Amendments—SI 2006/3435.

47.8 Sanction for delay in commencing detailed assessment proceedings

(1) Where the receiving party fails to commence detailed assessment proceedings within the period specified –

    (a)   in rule 47.7; or

    (b)   by any direction of the court,

the paying party may apply for an order requiring the receiving party to commence detailed assessment proceedings within such time as the court may specify.

(2) On an application under paragraph (1), the court may direct that, unless the receiving party commences detailed assessment proceedings within the time specified by the court, all or part of the costs to which the receiving party would otherwise be entitled will be disallowed.

(3) If –

    (a)   the paying party has not made an application in accordance with paragraph (1); and

    (b)   the receiving party commences the proceedings later than the period specified in rule 47.7,

the court may disallow all or part of the interest otherwise payable to the receiving party under –

    (i)   section 17 of the Judgments Act 1838; or

    (ii)   section 74 of the County Courts Act 1984,

but must not impose any other sanction except in accordance with rule 44.14 (powers in relation to misconduct).

(4) Where the costs to be assessed in a detailed assessment are payable out of the Community Legal Service Fund, this rule applies as if the receiving party were the solicitor to whom the costs are payable and the paying party were the Legal Services Commission.

Amendments—SI 2000/1317.

47.9 Points of dispute and consequence of not serving

(1) The paying party and any other party to the detailed assessment proceedings may dispute any item in the bill of costs by serving points of dispute on –

    (a)   the receiving party; and

    (b)   every other party to the detailed assessment proceedings.

PART V

(2) The period for serving points of dispute is 21 days after the date of service of the notice of commencement.

(3) If a party serves points of dispute after the period set out in paragraph (2), he may not be heard further in the detailed assessment proceedings, unless the court gives permission.

> (The [Costs Practice Direction] sets out requirements about the form of points of dispute)

(4) The receiving party may file a request for a default costs certificate if –

    (a)   the period set out in rule 47.9(2) for serving points of dispute has expired; and

    (b)   he has not been served with any points of dispute.

(5) If any party (including the paying party) serves points of dispute before the issue of a default costs certificate the court may not issue the default costs certificate.

> (Section IV of this Part sets out the procedure to be followed after points of dispute have been filed)

Amendment—SI 2009/3390.

47.10 Procedure where costs are agreed

(1) If the paying party and the receiving party agree the amount of costs, either party may apply for a costs certificate (either interim or final) in the amount agreed.

> (Rule 47.15 and rule 47.16 contain further provisions about interim and final costs certificates respectively)

(2) An application for a certificate under paragraph (1) must be made to the court which would be the venue for detailed assessment proceedings under rule 47.4.

Amendments—SI 2000/1317.

Section III – Costs Payable by One Party to Another – Default Provisions

47.11 Default costs certificate

(1) Where the receiving party is permitted by rule 47.9 to obtain a default costs certificate, that party does so by filing a request in the relevant practice form.

> (The [Costs Practice Direction] deals with the procedure by which the receiving party may obtain a default costs certificate)

(2) A default costs certificate will include an order to pay the costs to which it relates.

(3) Where a receiving party obtains a default costs certificate, the costs payable to that party for the commencement of detailed assessment proceedings will be the sum set out in the [Costs Practice Direction].

(4) A receiving party who obtains a default costs certificate in detailed assessment proceedings pursuant to an order under section 194(3) of the Legal Services Act 2007 must send a copy of the default costs certificate to the prescribed charity.

Amendments—SI 1999/1008; SI 2009/2092; SI 2009/3390.

47.12 Setting aside default costs certificate

(1) The court must set aside a default costs certificate if the receiving party was not entitled to it.

(2) In any other case, the court may set aside or vary a default costs certificate if it appears to the court that there is some good reason why the detailed assessment proceedings should continue.

(3) Where –

   (a) the receiving party has purported to serve the notice of commencement on the paying party;

   (b) a default costs certificate has been issued; and

   (c) the receiving party subsequently discovers that the notice of commencement did not reach the paying party at least 21 days before the default costs certificate was issued;

the receiving party must –

   (i)   file a request for the default costs certificate to be set aside; or

   (ii) apply to the court for directions.

(4) Where paragraph (3) applies, the receiving party may take no further step in –

   (a) the detailed assessment proceedings; or

   (b) the enforcement of the default costs certificate,

until the certificate has been set aside or the court has given directions.

   (The [Costs Practice Direction] contains further details about the procedure for setting aside a default costs certificate and the matters which the court must take into account)

(5) Where the court sets aside or varies a default costs certificate in detailed assessment proceedings pursuant to an order under section 194(3) of the Legal Services Act 2007, the receiving party must send a copy of the order setting aside or varying the default costs certificate to the prescribed charity.

Amendment—SI 2008/2178; SI 2009/3390.

Section IV – Costs Payable by One Party to Another – Procedure where Points of Dispute are Served

47.13 Optional reply

(1) Where any party to the detailed assessment proceedings serves points of dispute, the receiving party may serve a reply on the other parties to the assessment proceedings.

(2) He may do so within 21 days after service on him of the points of dispute to which his reply relates.

   (The [Costs Practice Direction] sets out the meaning of reply)

Amendments—SI 2000/1317; SI 2009/3390.

47.14 Detailed assessment hearing

(1) Where points of dispute are served in accordance with this Part, the receiving party must file a request for a detailed assessment hearing.

(2) He must file the request within 3 months of the expiry of the period for commencing detailed assessment proceedings as specified –

   (a)   in rule 47.7; or

   (b)   by any direction of the court.

(3) Where the receiving party fails to file a request in accordance with paragraph (2), the paying party may apply for an order requiring the receiving party to file the request within such time as the court may specify.

(4) On an application under paragraph (3), the court may direct that, unless the receiving party requests a detailed assessment hearing within the time specified by the court, all or part of the costs to which the receiving party would otherwise be entitled will be disallowed.

(5) If –

   (a)   the paying party has not made an application in accordance with paragraph (3); and

   (b)   the receiving party files a request for a detailed assessment hearing later than the period specified in paragraph (2),

the court may disallow all or part of the interest otherwise payable to the receiving party under –

   (i)   section 17 of the Judgments Act 1838; or

   (ii)   section 74 of the County Courts Act 1984,

but must not impose any other sanction except in accordance with rule 44.14 (powers in relation to misconduct).

(6) No party other than –

   (a)   the receiving party;

   (b)   the paying party; and

   (c)   any party who has served points of dispute under rule 47.9,

may be heard at the detailed assessment hearing unless the court gives permission.

(7) Only items specified in the points of dispute may be raised at the hearing, unless the court gives permission.

   (The [Costs Practice Direction] specifies other documents which must be filed with the request for hearing and the length of notice which the court will give when it fixes a hearing date)

Amendments—SI 1999/1008; SI 2002/2058; SI 2009/3390.

Section V – Interim Costs Certificate and Final Costs Certificate

47.15 Power to issue an interim certificate

(1) The court may at any time after the receiving party has filed a request for a detailed assessment hearing –

   (a)   issue an interim costs certificate for such sum as it considers appropriate;

   (b)   amend or cancel an interim certificate.

(2) An interim certificate will include an order to pay the costs to which it relates, unless the court orders otherwise.

(3) The court may order the costs certified in an interim certificate to be paid into court.

(4) Where the court –

    (a)   issues an interim costs certificate; or

    (b)   amends or cancels an interim certificate,

in detailed assessment proceedings pursuant to an order under section 194(3) of the Legal Services Act 2007, the receiving party must send a copy of the interim costs certificate or the order amending or cancelling the interim costs certificate to the prescribed charity.

Amendment—SI 2008/2178.

47.16 Final costs certificate

(1) In this rule a completed bill means a bill calculated to show the amount due following the detailed assessment of the costs.

(2) The period for filing the completed bill is 14 days after the end of the detailed assessment hearing.

(3) When a completed bill is filed the court will issue a final costs certificate and serve it on the parties to the detailed assessment proceedings.

(4) Paragraph (3) is subject to any order made by the court that a certificate is not to be issued until other costs have been paid.

(5) A final costs certificate will include an order to pay the costs to which it relates, unless the court orders otherwise.

    (The [Costs Practice Direction] deals with the form of a final costs certificate)

(6) Where the court issues a final costs certificate in detailed assessment proceedings pursuant to an order under section 194(3) of the Legal Services Act 2007, the receiving party must send a copy of the final costs certificate to the prescribed charity.

Amendments—SI 1999/1008; SI 2008/2178; SI 2009/3390.

Section VI – Detailed Assessment Procedure for Costs of a LSC Funded Client or an Assisted Person where Costs are Payable out of the Community Legal Service Fund

47.17 Detailed assessment procedure for costs of a LSC funded client or an assisted person where costs are payable out of the Community Legal Service Fund

(1) Where the court is to assess costs of a LSC funded client or an assisted person which are payable out of the Community Legal Service Fund, that person's solicitor may commence detailed assessment proceedings by filing a request in the relevant practice form.

(2) A request under paragraph (1) must be filed within 3 months after the date when the right to detailed assessment arose.

(3) The solicitor must also serve a copy of the request for detailed assessment on the LSC funded client or the assisted person, if notice of that person's interest has been given to the court in accordance with community legal service or legal aid regulations.

(4) Where the solicitor has certified that the LSC funded client or the assisted person wishes to attend an assessment hearing, the court will, on receipt of the request for assessment, fix a date for the assessment hearing.

(5) Where paragraph (3) does not apply, the court will, on receipt of the request for assessment provisionally assess the costs without the attendance of the solicitor, unless it considers that a hearing is necessary.

(6) After the court has provisionally assessed the bill, it will return the bill to the solicitor.

(7) The court will fix a date for an assessment hearing if the solicitor informs the court, within 14 days after he receives the provisionally assessed bill, that he wants the court to hold such a hearing.

Amendments—SI 2000/1317; SI 2000/2092.

47.17A Detailed assessment procedure where costs are payable out of a fund other than the Community Legal Service Fund

(1) Where the court is to assess costs which are payable out of a fund other than the Community Legal Service Fund, the receiving party may commence detailed assessment proceedings by filing a request in the relevant practice form.

(2) A request under paragraph (1) must be filed within 3 months after the date when the right to detailed assessment arose.

(3) The court may direct that the party seeking assessment serve a copy of the request on any person who has a financial interest in the outcome of the assessment.

(4) The court will, on receipt of the request for assessment, provisionally assess the costs without the attendance of the receiving party, unless it considers that a hearing is necessary.

(5) After the court has provisionally assessed the bill, it will return the bill to the receiving party.

(6) The court will fix a date for an assessment hearing if the party informs the court, within 14 days after he receives the provisionally assessed bill, that he wants the court to hold such a hearing.

Amendments—Inserted by SI 2000/1317.

Section VII – Costs of Detailed Assessment Proceedings

47.18 Liability for costs of detailed assessment proceedings

(1) The receiving party is entitled to the costs of the detailed assessment proceedings except where –

    (a)   the provisions of any Act, any of these Rules or any relevant practice direction provide otherwise; or

    (b)   the court makes some other order in relation to all or part of the costs of the detailed assessment proceedings.

(1A) Paragraph (1) does not apply where the receiving party has pro bono representation in the detailed assessment proceedings but that party may apply for an order in respect of that representation under section 194(3) of the Legal Services Act 2007.

(2) In deciding whether to make some other order, the court must have regard to all the circumstances, including –

    (a)   the conduct of all the parties;

    (b)   the amount, if any, by which the bill of costs has been reduced; and

    (c)   whether it was reasonable for a party to claim the costs of a particular item or to dispute that item.

Amendments—SI 2008/2178.

47.19 Offers to settle without prejudice save as to costs of the detailed assessment proceedings

(1) Where –

    (a)   a party (whether the paying party or the receiving party) makes a written offer to settle the costs of the proceedings which gave rise to the assessment proceedings; and

    (b)   the offer is expressed to be without prejudice(GL) save as to the costs of the detailed assessment proceedings,

the court will take the offer into account in deciding who should pay the costs of those proceedings.

(2) The fact of the offer must not be communicated to the costs officer until the question of costs of the detailed assessment proceedings falls to be decided.

    (The [Costs Practice Direction] provides that rule 47.19 does not apply where the receiving party is a LSC funded client or an assisted person, unless the court orders otherwise)

Amendments—SI 2000/1317; SI 2002/2058; SI 2009/3390.

Section VIII – Appeals from Authorised Court Officers in Detailed Assessment Proceedings

47.20 Right to appeal

(1) Any party to detailed assessment proceedings may appeal against a decision of an authorised court officer in those proceedings.

(2) For the purposes of this Section, a LSC funded client or an assisted person is not a party to detailed assessment proceedings.

    (Part 52 sets out general rules about appeals)

Amendments—SI 2000/940; SI 2000/1317.

47.21 Court to hear appeal

An appeal against a decision of an authorised court officer is to a costs judge or a district judge of the High Court.

Amendments—SI 2000/940.

47.22 Appeal procedure

(1) The appellant must file an appeal notice within 21 days after the date of the decision he wishes to appeal against.

(2) On receipt of the appeal notice, the court will –

    (a)   serve a copy of the notice on the parties to the detailed assessment proceedings; and

    (b)   give notice of the appeal hearing to those parties.

Amendments—SI 2000/940; SI 2000/1317; SI 2007/2204.

47.23 Powers of the court on appeal

On an appeal from an authorised court officer the court will –

    (a)   re-hear the proceedings which gave rise to the decision appealed against; and

    (b)   make any order and give any directions as it considers appropriate.

Amendments—SI 2000/940.

PART 48
COSTS – SPECIAL CASES

(The definitions contained in Part 43 are relevant to this Part)

Section I – Costs Payable by or to Particular Persons

48.1 Pre-commencement disclosure and orders for disclosure against a person who is not a party

(1) This paragraph applies where a person applies –

    (a)   for an order under –
        (i)   section 33 of the Senior Courts Act 1981; or
        (ii) section 52 of the County Courts Act 1984,
        (which give the court powers exercisable before commencement of proceedings); or

    (b)   for an order under –
        (i)   section 34 of the Senior Courts Act 1981; or
        (ii) section 53 of the County Courts Act 1984,
        (which give the court power to make an order against a non-party for disclosure of documents, inspection of property etc.).

(2) The general rule is that the court will award the person against whom the order is sought his costs –

    (a)   of the application; and

    (b)   of complying with any order made on the application.

(3) The court may however make a different order, having regard to all the circumstances, including –

    (a)   the extent to which it was reasonable for the person against whom the order was sought to oppose the application; and (b)　whether the parties to the application have complied with any relevant pre-action protocol.

Amendments—Constitutional Reform Act 2005, s 59(5), Sch 11, Pt 1, para 1(2).

***

48.4　Limitations on court's power to award costs in favour of trustee or personal representative

(1)　This rule applies where –

(a)　a person is or has been a party to any proceedings in the capacity of trustee or personal representative; and

(b)　rule 48.3 does not apply.

(2)　The general rule is that he is entitled to be paid the costs of those proceedings, insofar as they are not recovered from or paid by any other person, out of the relevant trust fund or estate.

(3)　Where he is entitled to be paid any of those costs out of the fund or estate, those costs will be assessed on the indemnity basis.

Amendments—SI 1999/1008; SI 2001/4015.

48.5　Costs where money is payable by or to a child or protected party

(1)　This rule applies to any proceedings where a party is a child or protected party and –

(a)　money is ordered or agreed to be paid to, or for the benefit of, that party; or

(b)　money is ordered to be paid by him or on his behalf.

('Child' and 'protected party' have the same meaning as in rule 21.1(2))

(2)　The general rule is that –

(a)　the court must order a detailed assessment of the costs payable by, or out of money belonging to, any party who is a child or protected party; and

(b)　on an assessment under paragraph (a), the court must also assess any costs payable to that party in the proceedings, unless –

(i)　the court has issued a default costs certificate in relation to those costs under rule 47.11; or

(ii)　the costs are payable in proceedings to which Section II of Part 45 applies.

(3)　The court need not order detailed assessment of costs in the circumstances set out in the [Costs Practice Direction].

(4)　Where –

(a)　a claimant is a child or protected party; and

(b)　a detailed assessment has taken place under paragraph (2)(a),

the only amount payable by the child or protected party is the amount which the court certifies as payable.

(This rule applies to a counterclaim by or on behalf of a child or protected party by virtue of rule 20.3)

Amendments—SI 2004/3419; SI 2005/2292; SI 2007/2204; SI 2009/3390.

PART V

48.6 Litigants in person

(1) This rule applies where the court orders (whether by summary assessment or detailed assessment) that the costs of a litigant in person are to be paid by any other person.

(2) The costs allowed under this rule must not exceed, except in the case of a disbursement, two-thirds of the amount which would have been allowed if the litigant in person had been represented by a legal representative.

(3) The litigant in person shall be allowed –

- (a)   costs for the same categories of –
     (i)   work; and
     (ii)   disbursements,
     which would have been allowed if the work had been done or the disbursements had been made by a legal representative on the litigant in person's behalf;
- (b)   the payments reasonably made by him for legal services relating to the conduct of the proceedings; and
- (c)   the costs of obtaining expert assistance in assessing the costs claim.

(4) The amount of costs to be allowed to the litigant in person for any item of work claimed shall be –

- (a)   where the litigant can prove financial loss, the amount that he can prove he has lost for time reasonably spent on doing the work; or
- (b)   where the litigant cannot prove financial loss, an amount for the time reasonably spent on doing the work at the rate set out in the [Costs Practice Direction].

(5) A litigant who is allowed costs for attending at court to conduct his case is not entitled to a witness allowance in respect of such attendance in addition to those costs.

(6) For the purposes of this rule, a litigant in person includes –

- (a)   a company or other corporation which is acting without a legal representative; and
- (b)   a barrister, solicitor, solicitor's employee [, manager of a body recognised under section 9 of the Administration of Justice Act 1985 or a person who, for the purposes of the Legal Services Act 2007, is an authorised person in relation to an activity which constitutes the conduct of litigation (within the meaning of that Act)] who is acting for himself.

Amendments—SI 2002/2058; SI 2009/3390.

Section II – Costs Relating to Solicitors and Other Legal Representatives

48.7 Personal liability of legal representative for costs – wasted costs orders

(1) This rule applies where the court is considering whether to make an order under section 51(6) of the Senior Courts Act 1981 (court's power to disallow or (as the case may be) order a legal representative to meet, 'wasted costs').

(2) The court must give the legal representative a reasonable opportunity to attend a hearing to give reasons why it should not make such an order.

(3) ...

(4) When the court makes a wasted costs order, it must –

    (a)   specify the amount to be disallowed or paid; or

    (b)   direct a costs judge or a district judge to decide the amount of costs to be disallowed or paid.

(5) The court may direct that notice must be given to the legal representative's client, in such manner as the court may direct –

    (a)   of any proceedings under this rule; or

    (b)   of any order made under it against his legal representative.

(6) Before making a wasted costs order, the court may direct a costs judge or a district judge to inquire into the matter and report to the court.

(7) The court may refer the question of wasted costs to a costs judge or a district judge, instead of making a wasted costs order.

Amendments—SI 2000/1317; SI 2002/2058; Constitutional Reform Act 2005, s 59(5), Sch 11, Pt 1, para 1(2).

48.8 Basis of detailed assessment of solicitor and client costs

(1) This rule applies to every assessment of a solicitor's bill to his client except a bill which is to be paid out of the Community Legal Service Fund under the Legal Aid Act 1988 or the Access to Justice Act 1999.

(1A) Section 74(3) of the Solicitors Act 1974 applies unless the solicitor and client have entered into a written agreement which expressly permits payment to the solicitor of an amount of costs greater than that which the client could have recovered from another party to the proceedings.

(2) Subject to paragraph (1A), costs are to be assessed on the indemnity basis but are to be presumed –

    (a)   to have been reasonably incurred if they were incurred with the express or implied approval of the client;

    (b)   to be reasonable in amount if their amount was expressly or impliedly approved by the client;

    (c)   to have been unreasonably incurred if –

        (i)   they are of an unusual nature or amount; and

        (ii)   the solicitor did not tell his client that as a result he might not recover all of them from the other party.

(3) Where the court is considering a percentage increase, whether on the application of the legal representative under rule 44.16 or on the application of the client, the court will have regard to all the relevant factors as they reasonably appeared to the solicitor or counsel when the conditional fee agreement was entered into or varied.

((4) In paragraph (3), 'conditional fee agreement' means an agreement enforceable under section 58 of the Courts and Legal Services Act 1990 at the date on which that agreement was entered into or varied.

Amendments—SI 1999/1008; SI 2000/1317; SI 2001/256.

48.9 *(revoked)*

Practice Direction – About Costs (PDCosts)

This Practice Direction supplements CPR Parts 43–48 (PDCosts)

Section 1 – Introduction

1.1 This practice direction supplements Parts 43 to 48 of the Civil Procedure Rules. It applies to all proceedings to which those Parts apply.

1.2 Paragraphs 57.1 to 57.9 of this practice direction deal with various transitional provisions affecting proceedings about costs.

1.3 Attention is drawn to the powers to make orders about costs conferred on the Senior Courts and any county court by Section 51 of the Senior Courts Act 1981.

1.4 In these Directions –

'counsel' means a barrister or other person with a right of audience in relation to all proceedings in the High Court or in the county courts in which he is instructed to act.

'LSC' means Legal Services Commission.

'solicitor' means a solicitor of the Senior Courts or other person with a right of audience in relation to proceedings, who is conducting the claim or defence (as the case may be) on behalf of a party to the proceedings and, where the context admits, includes a patent agent.

1.5 In respect of any document which is required by these Directions to be signed by a party or his legal representative the practice direction supplementing Part 22 will apply as if the document in question was a statement of truth. (The practice direction supplementing Part 22 makes provision for cases in which a party is a child, a protected party or a company or other corporation and cases in which a document is signed on behalf of a partnership).

Section 2 – Scope of Costs Rules and Definitions

RULE 43.2 DEFINITIONS AND APPLICATION

2.1 Where the court makes an order for costs and the receiving party has entered into a funding arrangement as defined in rule 43.2, the costs payable by the paying party include any additional liability (also defined in rule 43.2) unless the court orders otherwise.

2.2 In the following paragraphs –

'funding arrangement', 'percentage increase', 'insurance premium', 'membership organisation' and 'additional liability' have the meanings given to them by rule 43.2.

A 'conditional fee agreement' is an agreement with a person providing advocacy or litigation services which provides for his fees and expenses, or part of them, to be payable only in specified circumstances, whether or not it provides for a success fee as mentioned in section 58(2)(b) of the Courts and Legal Services Act 1990.

'base costs' means costs other than the amount of any additional liability.

2.3 Rule 44.3A(1) provides that the court will not assess any additional liability until the conclusion of the proceedings or the part of the proceedings to which the funding arrangement relates. (As to the time when detailed assessment may be carried out see paragraph 27.1 below).

2.4 For the purposes of the following paragraphs of this practice direction and rule 44.3A proceedings are concluded when the court has finally determined the matters in issue in the claim, whether or not there is an appeal. The making of an award of provisional damages under Part 41 will also be treated as a final determination of the matters in issue.

2.5 The court may order or the parties may agree in writing that, although the proceedings are continuing, they will nevertheless be treated as concluded.

Section 3 – Model Forms for Claims for Costs

RULE 43.3 MEANING OF SUMMARY ASSESSMENT

3.1 Rule 43.3 defines summary assessment. When carrying out a summary assessment of costs where there is an additional liability the court may assess the base costs alone, or the base costs and the additional liability.

3.2 Form N260 is a model form of Statement of Costs to be used for summary assessments.

3.3 Further details about Statements of Costs are given in paragraph 13.5 below.

RULE 43.4 MEANING OF DETAILED ASSESSMENT

3.4 Rule 43.4 defines detailed assessment. When carrying out a detailed assessment of costs where there is an additional liability the court will assess both the base costs and the additional liability, or, if the base costs have already been assessed, the additional liability alone.

3.5 Precedents A, B, C and D in the Schedule of Costs Precedents annexed to this practice direction are model forms of bills of costs to be used for detailed assessments.

3.6 Further details about bills of costs are given in the next section of these Directions and in paragraphs 28.1 to 49.1, below.

3.7 Precedents A, B, C and D in the Schedule of Costs Precedents and the next section of this practice direction all refer to a model form of bill of costs. The use of a model form is not compulsory, but is encouraged. A party wishing to rely upon a bill which departs from the model forms should include in the background information of the bill an explanation for that departure.

3.8 In any order of the court (whether made before or after 26 April 1999) the word 'taxation' will be taken to mean 'detailed assessment' and the words 'to be taxed' will be taken to mean 'to be decided by detailed assessment' unless in either case the context otherwise requires.

Section 4 – Form and Contents of Bills of Costs

4.1 A bill of costs may consist of such of the following sections as may be appropriate –

    (1)   title page;
    (2)   background information;
    (3)   items of costs claimed under the headings specified in paragraph 4.6;
    (4)   summary showing the total costs claimed on each page of the bill;
    (5)   schedules of time spent on non-routine attendances; and
    (6)   the certificates referred to in paragraph 4.15.

4.2 Where it is necessary or convenient to do so, a bill of costs may be divided into two or more parts, each part containing sections (2), (3) and (4) above. Circumstances in which it will be necessary or convenient to divide a bill into parts include –

    (1)   Where the receiving party acted in person during the course of the proceedings (whether or not that party also had a legal representative at that time) the bill must be divided into different parts so as to distinguish between;
        (a)   the costs claimed for work done by the legal representative; and
        (b)   the costs claimed for work done by the receiving party in person.
    (1A) Where the receiving party had pro bono representation for part of the proceedings and an order under section 194(3) of the Legal Services Act 2007 has been made, the bill must be divided into different parts so as to distinguish between:
        (a)   the sum equivalent to the costs claimed for work done by the legal representative acting free of charge; and
        (b)   the costs claimed for work done by the legal representative not acting free of charge.
    (2)   Where the receiving party was represented by different solicitors during the course of the proceedings, the bill must be divided into different parts so as to distinguish between the costs payable in respect of each solicitor.
    (3)   Where the receiving party obtained legal aid or LSC funding in respect of all or part of the proceedings the bill must be divided into separate parts so as to distinguish between;
        (a)   costs claimed before legal aid or LSC funding was granted;
        (b)   costs claimed after legal aid or LSC funding was granted; and
        (c)   any costs claimed after legal aid or LSC funding ceased.
    (4)   Where value added tax (VAT) is claimed and there was a change in the rate of VAT during the course of the proceedings, the bill must be divided into separate parts so as to distinguish between;
        (a)   costs claimed at the old rate of VAT; and
        (b)   costs claimed at the new rate of VAT.
    (5)   Where the bill covers costs payable under an order or orders under which there are different paying parties the bill must be divided into parts so as to deal separately with the costs payable by each paying party.
    (6)   Where the bill covers costs payable under an order or orders, in respect of which the receiving party wishes to claim interest from different dates, the bill must be divided to enable such interest to be calculated.

4.3 Where a party claims costs against another party and also claims costs against the LSC only for work done in the same period, the costs claimed against the LSC only can be claimed either in a separate part of the bill or in additional columns in the same part of the bill. Precedents C and D in the Schedule of Costs Precedents annexed to this Practice Direction show how bills should be drafted when costs are claimed against the LSC only.

4.4 The title page of the bill of costs must set out –

    (1)   the full title of the proceedings;

    (2)   the name of the party whose bill it is and a description of the document showing the right to assessment (as to which see paragraph 40.4, below);

    (3)   if VAT is included as part of the claim for costs, the VAT number of the legal representative or other person in respect of whom VAT is claimed;

    (4)   details of all legal aid certificates, LSC certificates and relevant amendment certificates in respect of which claims for costs are included in the bill.

4.5 The background information included in the bill of costs should set out –

    (1)   a brief description of the proceedings up to the date of the notice of commencement;

    (2)   a statement of the status of the solicitor or solicitor's employee in respect of whom costs are claimed and (if those costs are calculated on the basis of hourly rates) the hourly rates claimed for each such person.

It should be noted that 'legal executive' means a Fellow of the Institute of Legal Executives.

Other clerks, who are fee earners of equivalent experience, may be entitled to similar rates. It should be borne in mind that Fellows of the Institute of Legal Executives will have spent approximately 6 years in practice, and taken both general and specialist examinations. The Fellows have therefore acquired considerable practical and academic experience. Clerks without the equivalent experience of legal executives will normally be treated as being the equivalent of trainee solicitors and para-legals.

    (3)   a brief explanation of any agreement or arrangement between the receiving party and his solicitors which affects the costs claimed in the bill.

4.6 The bill of costs may consist of items under such of the following heads as may be appropriate –

    (1)   attendances on the court and counsel up to the date of the notice of commencement;

    (2)   attendances on and communications with the receiving party;

    (3)   attendances on and communications with witnesses including any expert witness;

    (4)   attendances to inspect any property or place for the purposes of the proceedings;

    (5)   attendances on and communications with other persons, including offices of public records;

    (6)   communications with the court and with counsel;

    (7)   work done on documents: preparing and considering documentation, including documentation necessary to comply with Practice Direction (Pre-Action Conduct) or any relevant pre-action protocols where appropriate, work done in connection with arithmetical calculations of compensation and/or interest and time spent collating documents;

    (8)   work done in connection with negotiations with a view to settlement if not already covered in the heads listed above;

    (9)   attendances on and communications with London and other agents and work done by them;

    (10) other work done which was of or incidental to the proceedings and which is not already covered in the heads listed above.

4.7 In respect of each of the heads of costs –

    (1)   'communications' means letters out and telephone calls;

    (2)   communications, which are not routine communications, must be set out in chronological order;

PART V

(3) routine communications should be set out as a single item at the end of each head.

4.8 Routine communications are letters out, e-mails out and telephone calls which because of their simplicity should not be regarded as letters or e-mails of substance or telephone calls which properly amount to an attendance.

4.9 Each item claimed in the bill of costs must be consecutively numbered.

4.10 In each part of the bill of costs which claims items under head (1) (attendances on court and counsel) a note should be made of –

(1) all relevant events, including events which do not constitute chargeable items;

(2) any orders for costs which the court made (whether or not a claim is made in respect of those costs in this bill of costs).

4.11 The numbered items of costs may be set out on paper divided into columns. Precedents A, B, C and D in the Schedule of Costs Precedents annexed to this practice direction illustrate various model forms of bills of costs.

4.12 In respect of heads (2) to (10) in paragraph 4.6 above, if the number of attendances and communications other than routine communications is twenty or more, the claim for the costs of those items in that section of the bill of costs should be for the total only and should refer to a schedule in which the full record of dates and details is set out. If the bill of costs contains more than one schedule each schedule should be numbered consecutively.

4.13 The bill of costs must not contain any claims in respect of costs or court fees which relate solely to the detailed assessment proceedings other than costs claimed for preparing and checking the bill.

4.14 The summary must show the total profit costs and disbursements claimed separately from the total VAT claimed. Where the bill of costs is divided into parts the summary must also give totals for each part. If each page of the bill gives a page total the summary must also set out the page totals for each page.

4.15 The bill of costs must contain such of the certificates, the texts of which are set out in Precedent F of the Schedule of Costs Precedents annexed to this practice direction, as are appropriate.

4.16 The following provisions relate to work done by solicitors –

(1) Routine letters out and routine telephone calls will in general be allowed on a unit basis of 6 minutes each, the charge being calculated by reference to the appropriate hourly rate. The unit charge for letters out will include perusing and considering the relevant letters in and no separate charge should be made for in-coming letters.

(2) E-mails received by solicitors will not normally be allowed. The court may, in its discretion, allow an actual time charge for preparation of e-mails sent by solicitors, which properly amount to attendances provided that the time taken has been recorded. The court may also, in its discretion, allow a sum in respect of routine e-mails sent to the client or others on a unit basis of 6 minutes each, the charge being calculated by reference to the appropriate hourly rate.

(3) Local travelling expenses incurred by solicitors will not be allowed. The definition of 'local' is a matter for the discretion of the court. While no absolute rule can be laid down, as a matter of guidance, 'local' will, in general, be taken to mean within a radius of 10 miles from the court dealing with the case at the relevant time. Where travelling and waiting

time is claimed, this should be allowed at the rate agreed with the client unless this is more than the hourly rate on the assessment.

(4) The cost of postage, couriers, out-going telephone calls, fax and telex messages will in general not be allowed but the court may exceptionally in its discretion allow such expenses in unusual circumstances or where the cost is unusually heavy.

(5) The cost of making copies of documents will not in general be allowed but the court may exceptionally in its discretion make an allowance for copying in unusual circumstances or where the documents copied are unusually numerous in relation to the nature of the case. Where this discretion is invoked the number of copies made, their purpose and the costs claimed for them must be set out in the bill.

(6) Agency charges as between a principal solicitor and his agent will be dealt with on the principle that such charges, where appropriate, form part of the principal solicitor's charges. Where these charges relate to head (1) in paragraph 4.6 (attendances at court and on counsel) they should be included in their chronological order in that head. In other cases they should be included in head (9) (attendances on London and other agents).

4.17

(1) Where a claim is made for a percentage increase in addition to an hourly rate or base fee, the amount of the increase must be shown separately, either in the appropriate arithmetic column or in the narrative column. (For an example see Precedent A or Precedent B.)

(2) Where a claim is made against the LSC only and includes enhancement and where a claim is made in family proceedings and includes a claim for uplift or general care and conduct, the amount of enhancement, uplift and general care and conduct must be shown, in respect of each item upon which it is claimed, as a separate amount either in the appropriate arithmetic column or in the narrative column. (For an example, see Precedent C.)

'Enhancement' means the increase in prescribed rates which may be allowed by a costs officer in accordance with the Legal Aid in Civil Proceedings (Remuneration) Regulations 1994 or the Legal Aid in Family Proceedings Regulations 1991.

COSTS OF PREPARING THE BILL

4.18 A claim may be made for the reasonable costs of preparing and checking the bill of costs.

Section 5 – Special Provisions Relating to VAT

5.1 This section deals with claims for value added tax (VAT) which are made in respect of costs being dealt with by way of summary assessment or detailed assessment.

VAT REGISTRATION NUMBER

5.2 The number allocated by HM Revenue and Customs to every person registered under the Value Added Tax Act 1983 (except a Government Department) must appear in a prominent place at the head of every statement, bill of costs, fee sheet, account or voucher on which VAT is being included as part of a claim for costs.

PART V

ENTITLEMENT TO VAT ON COSTS

5.3 VAT should not be included in a claim for costs if the receiving party is able to recover the VAT as input tax. Where the receiving party is able to obtain credit from HM Revenue and Customs for a proportion of the VAT as input tax, only that proportion which is not eligible for credit should be included in the claim for costs.

5.4 The receiving party has responsibility for ensuring that VAT is claimed only when the receiving party is unable to recover the VAT or a proportion thereof as input tax.

5.5 Where there is a dispute as to whether VAT is properly claimed the receiving party must provide a certificate signed by the solicitors or the auditors of the receiving party substantially in the form illustrated in Precedent F in the Schedule of Costs Precedents annexed to this practice direction. Where the receiving party is a litigant in person who is claiming VAT, reference should be made by him to HM Revenue and Customs and wherever possible a Statement to similar effect produced at the hearing at which the costs are assessed.

5.6 Where there is a dispute as to whether any service in respect of which a charge is proposed to be made in the bill is zero rated or exempt, reference should be made to HM Revenue and Customs and wherever possible the view of HM Revenue and Customs obtained and made known at the hearing at which the costs are assessed. Such application should be made by the receiving party. In the case of a bill from a solicitor to his own client, such application should be made by the client.

FORM OF BILL OF COSTS WHERE VAT RATE CHANGES

5.7 Where there is a change in the rate of VAT, suppliers of goods and services are entitled by ss 88(1) and 88(2) of the VAT Act 1994 in most circumstances to elect whether the new or the old rate of VAT should apply to a supply where the basic and actual tax points span a period during which there has been a change in VAT rates.

5.8 It will be assumed, unless a contrary indication is given in writing, that an election to take advantage of the provisions mentioned in paragraph 5.7 above and to charge VAT at the lower rate has been made. In any case in which an election to charge at the lower rate is not made, such a decision must be justified to the court assessing the costs.

APPORTIONMENT

5.9 All bills of costs, fees and disbursements on which VAT is included must be divided into separate parts so as to show work done before, on and after the date or dates from which any change in the rate of VAT takes effect. Where, however, a lump sum charge is made for work which spans a period during which there has been a change in VAT rates, and paragraphs 5.7 and 5.8 above do not apply, reference should be made to paragraphs 8 and 9 of Appendix F of Customs' Notice 700 (or any revised edition of that Notice), a copy of which should be in the possession of every registered trader. If necessary, the lump sum should be apportioned. The totals of profit costs and disbursements in each part must be carried separately to the summary.

5.10 Should there be a change in the rate between the conclusion of a detailed assessment and the issue of the final costs certificate, any interested party may apply for the detailed assessment to be varied so as to take account of any increase or reduction in the amount of tax payable. Once the final costs certificate has been issued, no variation under this paragraph will be permitted.

DISBURSEMENTS NOT CLASSIFIED AS SUCH FOR VAT PURPOSES

5.11

(1) Legal representatives often make payments to third parties for the supply of goods or services where no VAT was chargeable on the supply by the third party: for example, the cost of meals taken and travel costs. The question whether legal representatives should include VAT in respect of these payments when invoicing their clients or in claims for costs between litigants should be decided in accordance with this Direction and with the criteria set out in the VAT Guide (Notice 700) published by HM Revenue and Customs.

(2) Payments to third parties which are normally treated as part of the legal representative's overheads (for example, postage costs and telephone costs) will not be treated as disbursements. The third party supply should be included as part of the costs of the legal representatives' legal services and VAT must be added to the total bill charged to the client.

(3) Disputes may arise in respect of payments made to a third party which the legal representative shows as disbursements in the invoice delivered to the receiving party. Some payments, although correctly described as disbursements for some purposes, are not classified as disbursements for VAT purposes. Items not classified as disbursements for VAT purposes must be shown as part of the services provided by the legal representative and, therefore, VAT must be added in respect of them whether or not VAT was chargeable on the supply by the third party.

(4) Guidance as to the circumstances in which disbursements may or may not be classified as disbursements for VAT purposes is given in the VAT Guide (Notice 700, paragraph 25.1). One of the key issues is whether the third party supply (i) was made to the legal representative (and therefore subsumed in the onward supply of legal services), or (ii) was made direct to the receiving party (the third party having no right to demand payment from the legal representative, who makes the payment only as agent for the receiving party).

(5) Examples of payments under (i) are: travelling expenses, such as an airline ticket, and subsistence expenses, such as the cost of meals, where the person travelling and receiving the meals is the legal representative. The supplies by the airline and the restaurant are supplies to the legal representative, not to the client.

(6) Payments under (ii) are classified as disbursements for VAT purposes and, therefore, the legal representative need not add VAT in respect of them. Simple examples are payments by a legal representative of court fees and payment of fees to an expert witness.

5.12 *Omitted.*

LEGAL AID/LSC FUNDING

5.13 (1)VAT will be payable in respect of every supply made pursuant to a legal aid/LSC certificate where –

(a) the person making the supply is a taxable person; and
(b) the assisted person/LSC funded client –
    (i) belongs in the United Kingdom or another member State of the European Union; and
    (ii) is a private individual or receives the supply for non-business purposes.

PART V

(2) Where the assisted person/LSC funded client belongs outside the European Union, VAT is generally not payable unless the supply relates to land in the United Kingdom.

(3) For the purpose of sub-paragraphs (1) and (2), the place where a person belongs is determined by section 9 of the Value Added Tax Act 1994.

(4) Where the assisted person/LSC funded client is registered for VAT and the legal services paid for by the LSC are in connection with that person's business, the VAT on those services will be payable by the LSC only.

5.14 Any summary of costs payable by the LSC must be drawn so as to show the total VAT on counsel's fees as a separate item from the VAT on other disbursements and the VAT on profit costs.

TAX INVOICE

5.15 A bill of costs filed for detailed assessment is always retained by the Court. Accordingly if a solicitor waives his solicitor and client costs and accepts the costs certified by the court as payable by the unsuccessful party in settlement, it will be necessary for a short statement as to the amount of the certified costs and the VAT thereon to be prepared for use as the tax invoice.

VOUCHERS

5.16 Where receipted accounts for disbursements made by the solicitor or his client are retained as tax invoices a photostat copy of any such receipted account may be produced and will be accepted as sufficient evidence of payment when disbursements are vouched.

CERTIFICATES

5.17 In a costs certificate payable by the LSC, the VAT on solicitor's costs, counsel's fees and disbursements will be shown separately.

LITIGANTS ACTING IN PERSON

5.18 Where a litigant acts in litigation on his own behalf he is not treated for the purposes of VAT as having supplied services and therefore no VAT is chargeable in respect of work done by that litigant (even where, for example, that litigant is a solicitor or other legal representative).

5.19 Consequently in the circumstances described in the preceding paragraph, a bill of costs presented for agreement or assessment should not claim any VAT which will not be allowed on assessment.

GOVERNMENT DEPARTMENTS

5.20 On an assessment between parties, where costs are being paid to a Government Department in respect of services rendered by its legal staff, VAT should not be added.

PAYMENT PURSUANT TO AN ORDER UNDER SECTION 194(3) OF THE LEGAL SERVICES ACT 2007

5.21 Where an order is made under section 194(3) of the Legal Services Act 2007 any bill presented for agreement or assessment pursuant to that order must not include a claim for VAT.

Section 6 – Estimates of Costs

6.1 This section sets out certain steps which parties and their legal representatives must take in order to keep the parties informed about their potential liability in respect of costs and in order to assist the court to decide what, if any, order to make about costs and about case management.

6.2

(1) In this section an 'estimate of costs' means –
    (a) an estimate of costs of –
        (i) base costs (including disbursements) already incurred; and
        (ii) base costs (including disbursements) to be incurred,
    which a party, if successful in the proceedings, intends to seek to recover from any other party under an order for costs; or
    (b) in proceedings where the party has pro bono representation and intends, if successful in the proceedings, to seek an order under section 194(3) of the Legal Services Act 2007, an estimate of the sum equivalent to –
        (i) the base costs (including disbursements) that the party would have already incurred had the legal representation provided to that party not been free of charge; and
        (ii) the base costs (including disbursements) that the party would incur if the legal representation to be provided to that party were not free of charge.

('Base costs' are defined in paragraph 2.2 of this Practice Direction.)

(2) A party who intends to recover an additional liability (defined in rule 43.2) need not reveal the amount of that liability in the estimate.

6.3 The court may at any stage in a case order any party to file an estimate of costs and to serve copies of the estimate on all other parties. The court may direct that the estimate be prepared in such a way as to demonstrate the likely effects of giving or not giving a particular case management direction which the court is considering, for example a direction for a split trial or for the trial of a preliminary issue. The court may specify a time limit for filing and serving the estimate. However, if no time limit is specified the estimate should be filed and served within 28 days of the date of the order.

6.4

(1) When –
    (a) a party to a claim which is outside the financial scope of the small claims track files an allocation questionnaire; or
    (b) a party to a claim which is being dealt with on the fast track or the multi track, or under Part 8, files a pre-trial check list (listing questionnaire),

PART V

he must also file an estimate of costs and serve a copy of it on every other party, unless the court otherwise directs. Where a party is represented, the legal representative must in addition serve an estimate on the party he represents.

(2) Where a party is required to file and serve a new estimate of costs in accordance with Rule 44.15(3), if that party is represented the legal representative must in addition serve the new estimate on the party he represents.

(3) This paragraph does not apply to litigants in person.

6.5 An estimate of costs should be substantially in the form illustrated in Precedent H in the Schedule of Costs Precedents annexed to the Practice Direction.

6.5A

(1) If there is a difference of 20% or more between the base costs claimed by a receiving party on detailed assessment and the costs shown in an estimate of costs filed by that party, the receiving party must provide a statement of the reasons for the difference with his bill of costs.

(2) If a paying party –
  (a) claims that he reasonably relied on an estimate of costs filed by a receiving party; or
  (b) wishes to rely upon the costs shown in the estimate in order to dispute the reasonableness or proportionality of the costs claimed,
  the paying party must serve a statement setting out his case in this regard in his points of dispute.

('Relevant person' is defined in paragraph 32.10(1) of the Costs Practice Direction)

6.6

(1) On an assessment of the costs of a party, the court may have regard to any estimate previously filed by that party, or by any other party in the same proceedings. Such an estimate may be taken into account as a factor among others, when assessing the reasonableness and proportionality of any costs claimed.

(2) In particular, where –
  (a) there is a difference of 20% or more between the base costs claimed by a receiving party and the costs shown in an estimate of costs filed by that party; and
  (b) it appears to the court that –
    (i) the receiving party has not provided a satisfactory explanation for that difference; or
    (ii) the paying party reasonably relied on the estimate of costs;
  the court may regard the difference between the costs claimed and the costs shown in the estimate as evidence that the costs claimed are unreasonable or disproportionate.

Directions Relating to Part 44 – General Rules About Costs

Section 7 – Solicitor's Duty to Notify Client: Rule 44.2

7.1 For the purposes of rule 44.2 'client' includes a party for whom a solicitor is acting and any other person (for example, an insurer, a trade union or the LSC) who has instructed the solicitor to act or who is liable to pay his fees.

7.2 Where a solicitor notifies a client of an order under that rule, he must also explain why the order came to be made.

7.3 Although rule 44.2 does not specify any sanction for breach of the rule the court may, either in the order for costs itself or in a subsequent order, require the solicitor to produce to the court evidence showing that he took reasonable steps to comply with the rule.

Section 8 – Court's Discretion and Circumstances to Be Taken into Account When Exercising its Discretion as to Costs: Rule 44.3

8.4 In deciding what order to make about costs the court is required to have regard to all the circumstances including any payment into court or admissible offer to settle made by a party which is drawn to the court's attention, and which is not an offer to which costs consequences under Part 36 apply.

8.5 There are certain costs orders which the court will commonly make in proceedings before trial. The following table sets out the general effect of these orders. The table is not an exhaustive list of the orders which the court may make.

Term	Effect
Costs Costs in any event	The party in whose favour the order is made is entitled to the costs in respect of the part of the proceedings to which the order relates, whatever other costs orders are made in the proceedings.
Costs in the case Costs in the application	The party in whose favour the court makes an order for costs at the end of the proceedings is entitled to his costs of the part of the proceedings to which the order relates.
Costs reserved	The decision about costs is deferred to a later occasion, but if no later order is made the costs will be costs in the case.
Claimant's/defendant's costs in case/application	If the party in whose favour the costs order is made is awarded costs at the end of the proceedings, that party is entitled to his costs of the part of the proceedings to which the order relates. If any other party is awarded costs at the end of the proceedings, the party in whose favour the final costs order is made is not liable to pay the costs of any other party in respect of the part of the proceedings to which the order relates.
Costs thrown away	Where, for example, a judgment or order is set aside, the party in whose favour the costs order is made is entitled to the costs which have been incurred as a consequence. This includes the costs of –

Term	Effect
	(a) preparing for and attending any hearing at which the judgment or order which has been set aside was made;
	(b) preparing for and attending any hearing to set aside the judgment or order in question;
	(c) preparing for and attending any hearing at which the court orders the proceedings or the part in question to be adjourned;
	(d) any steps taken to enforce a judgment or order which has subsequently been set aside.
Costs of and caused by	Where, for example, the court makes this order on an application to amend a statement of case, the party in whose favour the costs order is made is entitled to the costs of preparing for and attending the application and the costs of any consequential amendment to his own statement of case.
Costs here and below	The party in whose favour the costs order is made is entitled not only to his costs in respect of the proceedings in which the court makes the order but also to his costs of the proceedings in any lower court. In the case of an appeal from a Divisional Court the party is not entitled to any costs incurred in any court below the Divisional Court.
No order as to costs Each party to pay his own costs	Each party is to bear his own costs of the part of the proceedings to which the order relates whatever costs order the court makes at the end of the proceedings.

8.6 Where, under rule 44.3(8), the court orders an amount to be paid before costs are assessed –

(1)   the order will state that amount, and
(2)   if no other date for payment is specified in the order rule 44.8 (Time for complying with an order for costs) will apply.

FEES OF COUNSEL

8.7

(1)   This paragraph applies where the court orders the detailed assessment of the costs of a hearing at which one or more counsel appeared for a party.
(2)   Where an order for costs states the opinion of the court as to whether or not the hearing was fit for the attendance of one or more counsel, a costs officer conducting a detailed assessment of costs to which that order relates will have regard to the opinion stated.
(3)   The court will generally express an opinion only where –
(a)   the paying party asks it to do so;

(b) more than one counsel appeared for a party or,

(c) the court wishes to record its opinion that the case was not fit for the attendance of counsel.

FEES PAYABLE TO CONVEYANCING COUNSEL APPOINTED BY THE COURT TO ASSIST IT

8.8

(1) Where the court refers any matter to the conveyancing counsel of the court the fees payable to counsel in respect of the work done or to be done will be assessed by the court in accordance with rule 44.3.

(2) An appeal from a decision of the court in respect of the fees of such counsel will be dealt with under the general rules as to appeals set out in Part 52. If the appeal is against the decision of an authorised court officer, it will be dealt with in accordance with rules 47.20 to 47.23.

Section 9 – Costs Orders Relating to Funding Arrangements: Rule 44.3A

9.1 Under an order for payment of 'costs', the costs payable will include an additional liability incurred under a funding arrangement.

9.2

(1) If before the conclusion of the proceedings the court carries out a summary assessment of the base costs it may identify separately the amount allowed in respect of: solicitors' charges; counsels' fees; other disbursements; and any value added tax (VAT). (Sections 13 and 14 of this practice direction deal with summary assessment.)

(2) If an order for the base costs of a previous application or hearing did not identify separately the amounts allowed for solicitor's charges, counsel's fees and other disbursements, a court which later makes an assessment of an additional liability may apportion the base costs previously ordered.

Section 10 – Limits on Recovery Under Funding Arrangements: Rule 44.3B

10.1 In a case to which rule 44.3B(1)(c) or (d) applies the party in default may apply for relief from the sanction. He should do so as quickly as possible after he becomes aware of the default. An application, supported by evidence, should be made under Part 23 to a costs judge or district judge of the court which is dealing with the case. (Attention is drawn to rules 3.8 and 3.9 which deal with sanctions and relief from sanctions).

10.2 Where the amount of any percentage increase recoverable by counsel may be affected by the outcome of the application, the solicitor issuing the application must serve on counsel a copy of the application notice and notice of the hearing as soon as practicable and in any event at least 2 days before the hearing. Counsel may make written submissions or may attend and make oral submissions at the hearing. (Paragraph 1.4 contains definitions of the terms 'counsel' and 'solicitor'.)

PART V

Section 10A – Orders in Respect of Pro Bono Representation: Rule 44.3C

10A.1 Rule 44.3C(2) sets out how the court may determine the amount of payment when making an order under section 194(3) of the Legal Services Act 2007. Paragraph 13.2 of this Practice Direction provides that the general rule is that the court will make a summary assessment of costs in the circumstances outlined in that paragraph unless there is good reason not to do so. This will apply to rule 44.3C(2)(b) with the modification that the summary assessment of the costs is to be read as meaning the summary assessment of the sum equivalent to the costs that would have been claimed by the party with pro bono representation in respect of that representation had it not been provided free of charge.

10A.2 Where an order under section 194(3) of the Legal Services Act 2007 is sought, to assist the court in making a summary assessment of the amount payable to the prescribed charity, the party who has pro bono representation must prepare, file and serve in accordance with paragraph 13.5(2) a written statement of the sum equivalent to the costs that party would have claimed for that legal representation had it not been provided free of charge.

Section 11 – Factors to be Taken into Account in Deciding the Amount of Costs: Rule 44.5

11.1 In applying the test of proportionality the court will have regard to rule 1.1(2)(c). The relationship between the total of the costs incurred and the financial value of the claim may not be a reliable guide. A fixed percentage cannot be applied in all cases to the value of the claim in order to ascertain whether or not the costs are proportionate.

11.2 In any proceedings there will be costs which will inevitably be incurred and which are necessary for the successful conduct of the case. Solicitors are not required to conduct litigation at rates which are uneconomic. Thus in a modest claim the proportion of costs is likely to be higher than in a large claim, and may even equal or possibly exceed the amount in dispute.

11.3 Where a trial takes place, the time taken by the court in dealing with a particular issue may not be an accurate guide to the amount of time properly spent by the legal or other representatives in preparation for the trial of that issue.

11.4 Where a party has entered into a funding arrangement the costs claimed may, subject to rule 44.3B include an additional liability.

11.5 In deciding whether the costs claimed are reasonable and (on a standard basis assessment) proportionate, the court will consider the amount of any additional liability separately from the base costs.

11.6 In deciding whether the base costs are reasonable and (if relevant) proportionate the court will consider the factors set out in rule 44.5.

11.7 Subject to paragraph 17.8(2), when the court is considering the factors to be taken into account in assessing an additional liability, it will have regard to the facts and circumstances as they reasonably appeared to the solicitor or counsel when the funding arrangement was entered into and at the time of any variation of the arrangement.

11.8

    (1)   In deciding whether a percentage increase is reasonable relevant factors to be taken into account may include –

(a) the risk that the circumstances in which the costs, fees or expenses would be payable might or might not occur;

(b) the legal representative's liability for any disbursements;

(c) what other methods of financing the costs were available to the receiving party.

11.9 A percentage increase will not be reduced simply on the ground that, when added to base costs which are reasonable and (where relevant) proportionate, the total appears disproportionate.

11.10 In deciding whether the cost of insurance cover is reasonable, relevant factors to be taken into account include:

(1) where the insurance cover is not purchased in support of a conditional fee agreement with a success fee, how its cost compares with the likely cost of funding the case with a conditional fee agreement with a success fee and supporting insurance cover;

(2) the level and extent of the cover provided;

(3) the availability of any pre-existing insurance cover;

(4) whether any part of the premium would be rebated in the event of early settlement;

(5) the amount of commission payable to the receiving party or his legal representatives or other agents.

11.11 Where the court is considering a provision made by a membership organisation, rule 44.3B(1)(b) provides that any such provision which exceeds the likely cost to the receiving party of the premium of an insurance policy against the risk of incurring a liability to pay the costs of other parties to the proceedings is not recoverable. In such circumstances the court will, when assessing the additional liability, have regard to the factors set out in paragraph 11.10 above, in addition to the factors set out in rule 44.5.

Section 12 – Procedure for Assessing Costs: Rule 44.7

12.1 Where the court does not order fixed costs (or no fixed costs are provided for) the amount of costs payable will be assessed by the court. This rule allows the court making an order about costs either –

(a) to make a summary assessment of the amount of the costs, or

(b) to order the amount to be decided in accordance with Part 47 (a detailed assessment).

12.2 An order for costs will be treated as an order for the amount of costs to be decided by a detailed assessment unless the order otherwise provides.

12.3 Whenever the court awards costs to be assessed by way of detailed assessment it should consider whether to exercise the power in rule 44.3(8) (Courts Discretion as to Costs) to order the paying party to pay such sum of money as it thinks just on account of those costs.

Section 13 – Summary Assessment: General Provisions

13.1 Whenever a court makes an order about costs which does not provide for fixed costs to be paid the court should consider whether to make a summary assessment of costs.

PART V

13.2 The general rule is that the court should make a summary assessment of the costs –

   (1)   at the conclusion of the trial of a case which has been dealt with on the fast track, in which case the order will deal with the costs of the whole claim, and

   (2)   at the conclusion of any other hearing, which has lasted not more than one day, in which case the order will deal with the costs of the application or matter to which the hearing related. If this hearing disposes of the claim, the order may deal with the costs of the whole claim;

   (3)   in hearings in the Court of Appeal to which Paragraph 14 of the Practice Direction supplementing Part 52 (Appeals) applies;

unless there is good reason not to do so, e g where the paying party shows substantial grounds for disputing the sum claimed for costs that cannot be dealt with summarily or there is insufficient time to carry out a summary assessment.

13.3 The general rule in paragraph 13.2 does not apply to a mortgagee's costs incurred in mortgage possession proceedings or other proceedings relating to a mortgage unless the mortgagee asks the court to make an order for his costs to be paid by another party. Paragraphs 50.3 and 50.4 deal in more detail with costs relating to mortgages.

13.4 Where an application has been made and the parties to the application agree an order by consent without any party attending, the parties should agree a figure for costs to be inserted in the consent order or agree that there should be no order for costs. If the parties cannot agree the costs position, attendance on the appointment will be necessary but, unless good reason can be shown for the failure to deal with costs as set out above, no costs will be allowed for that attendance.

13.5

   (1)   It is the duty of the parties and their legal representatives to assist the judge in making a summary assessment of costs in any case to which paragraph 13.2 above applies, in accordance with the following paragraphs.

   (2)   Each party who intends to claim costs must prepare a written statement of the costs he intends to claim showing separately in the form of a schedule –

       (a)   the number of hours to be claimed,

       (b)   the hourly rate to be claimed,

       (c)   the grade of fee earner;

       (d)   the amount and nature of any disbursement to be claimed, other than counsel's fee for appearing at the hearing,

       (e)   the amount of solicitor's costs to be claimed for attending or appearing at the hearing,

       (f)   the fees of counsel to be claimed in respect of the hearing, and

       (g)   any value added tax (VAT) to be claimed on these amounts.

   (3)   The statement of costs should follow as closely as possible Form N260 and must be signed by the party or his legal representative. Where a litigant is an assisted person or is a LSC funded client or is represented by a solicitor in the litigant's employment the statement of costs need not include the certificate appended at the end of Form N260.

   (4)   The statement of costs must be filed at court and copies of it must be served on any party against whom an order for payment of those costs is intended to be sought. The statement of costs should be filed and the copies of it should be served as soon as possible and in any event not less than 24 hours before the date fixed for the hearing.

(5) Where the litigant is or may be entitled to claim an additional liability the statement filed and served need not reveal the amount of that liability.

13.6 The failure by a party, without reasonable excuse, to comply with the foregoing paragraphs will be taken into account by the court in deciding what order to make about the costs of the claim, hearing or application, and about the costs of any further hearing or detailed assessment hearing that may be necessary as a result of that failure.

13.7 If the court makes a summary assessment of costs at the conclusion of proceedings the court will specify separately –

(1) the base costs, and if appropriate, the additional liability allowed as solicitor's charges, counsel's fees, other disbursements and any VAT; and

(2) the amount which is awarded under Part 46 (Fast Track Trial Costs).

13.8 The court awarding costs cannot make an order for a summary assessment of costs by a costs officer. If a summary assessment of costs is appropriate but the court awarding costs is unable to do so on the day, the court must give directions as to a further hearing before the same judge.

13.9 The court will not make a summary assessment of the costs of a receiving party who is an assisted person or LSC funded client.

13.10 A summary assessment of costs payable by an assisted person or LSC funded client is not by itself a determination of that person's liability to pay those costs (as to which see rule 44.17 and paragraphs 21.1 to 23.17 of this practice direction).

13.11

(1) The court will not make a summary assessment of the costs of a receiving party who is a child or protected party within the meaning of Part 21 unless the solicitor acting for the child or protected party has waived the right to further costs (see paragraph 51.1 below).

(2) The court may make a summary assessment of costs payable by a child or protected party

13.12

(1) Attention is drawn to rule 44.3A which prevents the court from making a summary assessment of an additional liability before the conclusion of the proceedings or the part of the proceedings to which the funding arrangement relates. Where this applies, the court should nonetheless make a summary assessment of the base costs of the hearing or application unless there is a good reason not to do so.

(2) Where the court makes a summary assessment of the base costs all statements of costs and costs estimates put before the judge will be retained on the court file.

13.13 The court will not give its approval to disproportionate and unreasonable costs. Accordingly –

(a) When the amount of the costs to be paid has been agreed between the parties the order for costs must state that the order is by consent.

(b) If the judge is to make an order which is not by consent, the judge will, so far as possible, ensure that the final figure is not disproportionate and/or unreasonable having regard to Part 1 of the CPR. The judge will retain this responsibility notwithstanding the absence of challenge to individual items in the make-up of the figure sought. The fact that the paying party is not disputing the amount of costs can however be taken as some indication that the amount is proportionate and reasonable. The judge will therefore intervene only if satisfied that the costs are so disproportionate that it is right to do so.

Section 14 – Summary Assessment Where Costs Claimed Include an Additional Liability

ORDERS MADE BEFORE THE CONCLUSION OF THE PROCEEDINGS

14.1 The existence of a conditional fee agreement or other funding arrangement within the meaning of rule 43.2 is not by itself a sufficient reason for not carrying out a summary assessment.

14.2 Where a legal representative acting for the receiving party has entered into a conditional fee agreement the court may summarily assess all the costs (other than any additional liability).

14.3 Where costs have been summarily assessed an order for payment will not be made unless the court has been satisfied that in respect of the costs claimed, the receiving party is at the time liable to pay to his legal representative an amount equal to or greater than the costs claimed. A statement in the form of the certificate appended at the end of Form N260 may be sufficient proof of liability. The giving of information under rule 44.15 (where that rule applies) is not sufficient.

14.4 The court may direct that any costs, for which the receiving party may not in the event be liable, shall be paid into court to await the outcome of the case, or shall not be enforceable until further order, or it may postpone the receiving party's right to receive payment in some other way.

ORDERS MADE AT THE CONCLUSION OF THE PROCEEDINGS

14.5 Where there has been a trial of one or more issues separately from other issues, the court will not normally order detailed assessment of the additional liability until all issues have been tried unless the parties agree.

14.6 Rule 44.3A(2) sets out the ways in which the court may deal with the assessment of the costs where there is a funding arrangement. Where the court makes a summary assessment of the base costs –

(1) The order may state separately the base costs allowed as (a) solicitor's charges, (b) counsel's fees, (c) any other disbursements and (d) any VAT.
(2) the statements of costs upon which the judge based his summary assessment will be retained on the court file.

14.7 Where the court makes a summary assessment of an additional liability at the conclusion of proceedings, that assessment must relate to the whole of the proceedings; this will include any additional liability relating to base costs allowed by the court when making a summary assessment on a previous application or hearing.

14.8 Paragraph 13.13 applies where the parties are agreed about the total amount to be paid by way of costs, or are agreed about the amount of the base costs that will be paid. Where they disagree about the additional liability the court may summarily assess that liability or make an order for a detailed assessment.

14.9 In order to facilitate the court in making a summary assessment of any additional liability at the conclusion of the proceedings the party seeking such costs must prepare and have available for the court a bundle of documents which must include –

(1) a copy of every notice of funding arrangement (Form N251) which has been filed by him;
(2) a copy of every estimate and statement of costs filed by him;
(3) a copy of the risk assessment prepared at the time any relevant funding arrangement was entered into and on the basis of which the amount of the additional liability was fixed.

Section 18 – Court's Powers in Relation to Misconduct: Rule 44.14

18.1 Before making an order under rule 44.14 the court must give the party or legal representative in question a reasonable opportunity to attend a hearing to give reasons why it should not make such an order.

18.2 Conduct before or during the proceedings which gave rise to the assessment which is unreasonable or improper includes steps which are calculated to prevent or inhibit the court from furthering the overriding objective.

18.3 Although rule 44.14(3) does not specify any sanction for breach of the obligation imposed by the rule the court may, either in the order under paragraph (2) or in a subsequent order, require the solicitor to produce to the court evidence that he took reasonable steps to comply with the obligation.

Section 19 – Providing Information about Funding Arrangements: Rule 44.15

19.1

(1) A party who wishes to claim an additional liability in respect of a funding arrangement must give any other party information about that claim if he is to recover the additional liability. There is no requirement to specify the amount of the additional liability separately nor to state how it is calculated until it falls to be assessed. That principle is reflected in rules 44.3A and rule 44.15, in the following paragraphs and in Sections 6, 13, 14 and 31 of this Practice Direction. Section 6 deals with estimates of costs, Sections 13 and 14 deal with summary assessment and Section 31 deals with detailed assessment.
(2) In the following paragraphs a party who has entered into a funding arrangement is treated as a person who intends to recover a sum representing an additional liability by way of costs.
(3) Attention is drawn to paragraph 57.9 of this Practice Direction which sets out time limits for the provision of information where a funding arrangement is entered into between 31 March and 2 July 2000 and proceedings relevant to that arrangement are commenced before 3 July 2000.

PART V

METHOD OF GIVING INFORMATION

19.2

(1) In this paragraph, 'claim form' includes petition and application notice, and the notice of funding to be filed or served is a notice containing the information set out in Form N251.

(2) (a) A claimant who has entered into a funding arrangement before starting the proceedings to which it relates must provide information to the court by filing the notice when he issues the claim form.

   (b) He must provide information to every other party by serving the notice. If he serves the claim form himself he must serve the notice with the claim form. If the court is to serve the claim form, the court will also serve the notice if the claimant provides it with sufficient copies for service.

(3) A defendant who has entered into a funding arrangement before filing any document

   (a) must provide information to the court by filing notice with his first document. A 'first document' may be an acknowledgment of service, a defence, or any other document, such as an application to set aside a default judgment.

   (b) must provide information to every party by serving notice. If he serves his first document himself he must serve the notice with that document. If the court is to serve his first document the court will also serve the notice if the defendant provides it with sufficient copies for service

(4) In all other circumstances a party must file and serve notice within 7 days of entering into the funding arrangement concerned.

(Practice Direction (Pre-Action Conduct) provides that a party [must] inform any other party as soon as possible about a funding arrangement entered into prior to the start of proceedings.)

Transitional Provisions—Note, parenthesis below Paragraph 19.2 subject to transitional provisions where the funding arrangement was entered into before 1 October 2009.

NOTICE OF CHANGE OF INFORMATION

19.3

(1) Rule 44.15 imposes a duty on a party to give notice of change if the information he has previously provided is no longer accurate. To comply he must file and serve notice containing the information set out in Form N251. Rule 44.15(3) may impose other duties in relation to new estimates of costs.

(2) Further notification need not be provided where a party has already given notice:

   (a) that he has entered into a conditional fee agreement with a legal representative and during the currency of that agreement either of them enters into another such agreement with an additional legal representative; or

   (b) of some insurance cover, unless that cover is cancelled or unless new cover is taken out with a different insurer.

(3) Part 6 applies to the service of notices.

(4) The notice must be signed by the party or by his legal representative.

INFORMATION WHICH MUST BE PROVIDED

19.4

(1)   Unless the court otherwise orders, a party who is required to supply information about a funding arrangement must state whether he has –
      entered into a conditional fee agreement which provides for a success fee within the meaning of section 58(2) of the Courts and Legal Services Act 1990;
      taken out an insurance policy to which section 29 of the Access to Justice Act 1999 applies;
      made an arrangement with a body which is prescribed for the purpose of section 30 of that Act;
      or more than one of these.

(2)   Where the funding arrangement is a conditional fee agreement, the party must state the date of the agreement and identify the claim or claims to which it relates (including Part 20 claims if any).

(3)   Where the funding arrangement is an insurance policy, the party must –
      (a)   state the name and address of the insurer, the policy number and the date of the policy, and identify the claim or claims to which it relates (including Part 20 claims if any);
      (b)   state the level of cover provided by the insurance; and
      (c)   state whether the insurance premiums are staged and, if so, the points at which an increased premium is payable.

(4)   Where the funding arrangement is by way of an arrangement with a relevant body the party must state the name of the body and set out the date and terms of the undertaking it has given and must identify the claim or claims to which it relates (including Part 20 claims if any).

(5)   Where a party has entered into more than one funding arrangement in respect of a claim, for example a conditional fee agreement and an insurance policy, a single notice containing the information set out in Form N251 may contain the required information about both or all of them.

19.5   Where the court makes a Group Litigation Order, the court may give directions as to the extent to which individual parties should provide information in accordance with rule 44.15. (Part 19 deals with Group Litigation Orders.)

Transitional Provisions—Note, Paragraph 19.4(3) subject to transitional provisions where the funding arrangement was entered into before 1 October 2009.

Section 20 – Procedure Where Legal Representative Wishes to Recover from his Client an Agreed Percentage Increase Which has been Disallowed or Reduced on Assessment: Rule 44.16

20.1(1)Attention is drawn to regulation 3(2)(b) of the Conditional Fee Agreements Regulations 2000 and to regulation 5(2)(b) of the Collective Conditional Fee Agreements Regulations 2000, which provide that some or all of a success fee ceases to be payable in certain circumstances (Both sets of regulations were revoked by the Conditional Fee Agreements (Revocation) Regulations 2005 but continue to have effect in relation to conditional fee agreements and collective conditional fee agreements entered into before 1 November 2005).

(2)   Rule 44.16 allows the court to adjourn a hearing at which the legal representative acting for the receiving party applies for an order that a disallowed amount should continue to be payable under the agreement.

PART V

20.2 In the following paragraphs 'counsel' means counsel who has acted in the case under a conditional fee agreement which provides for a success fee. A reference to counsel includes a reference to any person who appeared as an advocate in the case and who is not a partner or employee of the solicitor or firm which is conducting the claim or defence (as the case may be) on behalf of the receiving party.

PROCEDURE FOLLOWING SUMMARY ASSESSMENT

20.3

(1) If the court disallows any amount of a legal representative's percentage increase, the court will, unless sub-paragraph (2) applies, give directions to enable an application to be made by the legal representative for the disallowed amount to be payable by his client, including, if appropriate, a direction that the application will be determined by a costs judge or district judge of the court dealing with the case.

(2) The court that has made the summary assessment may then and there decide the issue whether the disallowed amount should continue to be payable, if:

(a) the receiving party and all parties to the relevant agreement consent to the court doing so;

(b) the receiving party (or, if corporate, an officer) is present in court; and

(c) the court is satisfied that the issue can be fairly decided then and there.

PROCEDURE FOLLOWING DETAILED ASSESSMENT

20.4

(1) Where detailed assessment proceedings have been commenced, and the paying party serves points of dispute (as to which see Section 34 of this Practice Direction), which show that he is seeking a reduction in any percentage increase charged by counsel on his fees, the solicitor acting for the receiving party must within 3 days of service deliver to counsel a copy of the relevant points of dispute and the bill of costs or the relevant parts of the bill.

(2) Counsel must within 10 days thereafter inform the solicitor in writing whether or not he will accept the reduction sought or some other reduction. Counsel may state any points he wishes to have made in a reply to the points of dispute, and the solicitor must serve them on the paying party as or as part of a reply.

(3) Counsel who fails to inform the solicitor within the time limits set out above will be taken to accept the reduction unless the court otherwise orders.

20.5 Where the paying party serves points of dispute seeking a reduction in any percentage increase charged by a legal representative acting for the receiving party, and that legal representative intends, if necessary, to apply for an order that any amount of the percentage disallowed as against the paying party shall continue to be payable by his client, the solicitor acting for the receiving party must, within 14 days of service of the points of dispute, give to his client a clear written explanation of the nature of the relevant point of dispute and the effect it will have if it is upheld in whole or in part by the court, and of the client's right to attend any subsequent hearings at court when the matter is raised.

20.6 Where the solicitor acting for a receiving party files a request for a detailed assessment hearing it must if appropriate, be accompanied by a certificate signed by him stating:

    (1) that the amount of the percentage increase in respect of counsel's fees or solicitor's charges is disputed;

    (2) whether an application will be made for an order that any amount of that increase which is disallowed should continue to be payable by his client;

    (3) that he has given his client an explanation in accordance with paragraph 20.5; and,

    (4) whether his client wishes to attend court when the amount of any relevant percentage increase may be decided.

20.7

    (1) The solicitor acting for the receiving party must within 7 days of receiving from the court notice of the date of the assessment hearing, notify his client, and if appropriate, counsel in writing of the date, time and place of the hearing.

    (2) Counsel may attend or be represented at the detailed assessment hearing and may make oral or written submissions.

20.8

    (1) At the detailed assessment hearing, the court will deal with the assessment of the costs payable by one party to another, including the amount of the percentage increase, and give a certificate accordingly.

    (2) The court may decide the issue whether the disallowed amount should continue to be payable under the relevant conditional fee agreement without an adjournment if:

        (a) the receiving party and all parties to the relevant agreement consent to the court deciding the issue without an adjournment,

        (b) the receiving party (or, if corporate, an officer or employee who has authority to consent on behalf of the receiving party) is present in court, and

        (c) the court is satisfied that the issue can be fairly decided without an adjournment.

    (3) In any other case the court will give directions and fix a date for the hearing of the application.

Section 21 – Application of Costs Rules: Rule 44.17

21.1 Rule 44.17(b) excludes the costs rules to the extent that regulations under the Legal Aid Act 1988 make different provision. The primary examples of such regulations are the regulations providing prescribed rates (with or without enhancement).

21.2 Rule 44.17(a) provides that the procedure for detailed assessment does not apply to the extent that section 11 of the Access to Justice Act 1999 and provisions made under that Act make different provision.

21.3 Section 11 of the Access to Justice Act 1999 provides special protection against liability for costs for litigants who receive funding by the LSC (Legal Services Commission) as part of the Community Legal Service. Any costs ordered to be paid by a LSC funded client must not exceed the amount which is reasonable for him to pay having regard to all the circumstances including –

PART V

    (a)   the financial resources of all the parties to the proceedings, and

    (b)   their conduct in connection with the dispute to which the proceedings relate.

21.4 In this Practice Direction

    'cost protection' means the limit on costs awarded against a LSC funded client set out in Section 11(1) of the Access to Justice Act 1999.

    'partner' has the meaning given by the Community Legal Service (Costs) Regulations 2000.

21.5 Whether or not cost protection applies depends upon the 'level of service' for which funding was provided by the LSC in accordance with the Funding Code approved under section 9 of the Access to Justice Act 1999. The levels of service referred to are:

    (1)   Legal Help – advice and assistance about a legal problem, not including representation or advocacy in proceedings.

    (2)   Help at Court – advocacy at a specific hearing, where the advocate is not formally representing the client in the proceedings.

    (3)   Family Mediation.

    (4)   Legal Representation – representation in actual or contemplated proceedings. Legal Representation can take the form of Investigative Help (limited to investigating the merits of a potential claim) or Full Representation.

    (5)   General Family Help and Help with Mediation.

21.6 Levels of service (4) and (5) are provided under a certificate (similar to a legal aid certificate). The certificate will state which level of service is covered. Where there are proceedings, a copy of the certificate will be lodged with the court.

21.7 Cost protection does not apply where –

    (1)   The LSC funded client receives Help at Court;

    (2)   The LSC funded client receives Legal Help only, ie where the solicitor is advising, but not representing a litigant in person. However, where the LSC funded client receives Legal Help, eg to write a letter before action, but later receives Legal Representation or General Family Help or Help with Mediation in respect of the same dispute, other than in family proceedings, cost protection does apply to all costs incurred by the receiving party in the funded proceedings or prospective proceedings;

    (3)   The LSC funded client receives General Family help or Help with Mediation in family proceedings;

    (4)   The LSC funded client receives Legal Representation in family proceedings.

21.8 Where cost protection does not apply, the court may award costs in the normal way.

21.9 Where work is done before the issue of a certificate, cost protection does not apply to those costs, except where –

    (1)   pre-action Legal Help is given and the LSC funded client subsequently receives Legal Representation or General Family Help or Help with Mediation in respect of the same dispute, other than in family proceedings; or

    (2)   where urgent work is undertaken immediately before the grant of an emergency certificate, other than in family proceedings, when no emergency application could be made as the LSC's offices were closed,

provided that the solicitor seeks an emergency certificate at the first available opportunity and the certificate is granted.

21.10 If a LSC funded client's certificate is revoked, costs protection does not apply to work done before or after revocation.

21.11 If a LSC funded client's certificate is discharged, costs protection only applies to costs incurred before the date on which funded services ceased to be provided under the certificate. This may be a date before the date on which the certificate is formally discharged by the LSC (*Burridge v Stafford: Khan v Ali* [2000] 1 WLR 927, [1999] 4 All ER 660, CA).

21.11A Where an LSC funded client has cost protection, the procedure described in Sections 22 and 23 of this Practice Direction applies. However that procedure does not apply in relation to costs claimed during any periods in the proceedings when the LSC funded client did not have cost protection, and the procedure set out in CPR Parts 45 to 47 will apply (as appropriate) in relation to those periods.

ASSESSING A LSC FUNDED CLIENT'S RESOURCES

21.12 The first £100,000 of the value of the LSC funded client's interest in the main or only home is disregarded when assessing his or her financial resources for the purposes of S.11 and cannot be the subject of any enforcement process by the receiving party. The receiving party cannot apply for an order to sell the LSC funded client's home, but could secure the debt against any value exceeding £100,000 by way of a charging order.

21.13 The court may only take into account the value of the LSC funded client's clothes, household furniture, tools and implements of trade to the extent that it considers that having regard to the quantity or value of the items, the circumstances are exceptional.

21.14 The LSC funded client's resources include the resources of his partner, unless the partner has a contrary interest in the dispute in respect of which funded services are provided.

PARTY ACTING IN A REPRESENTATIVE, FIDUCIARY OR OFFICIAL CAPACITY

21.15

(1) Where a LSC funded client is acting in a representative, fiduciary or official capacity, the court shall not take the personal resources of the party into account for the purposes of either a Section 11 order or costs against the Commission, but shall have regard to the value of any property or estate or the amount of any fund out of which the party is entitled to be indemnified, and may also have regard to the resources of any persons who are beneficially interested in the property, estate or fund.

(2) Similarly, where a party is acting as a litigation friend to a client who is a child or a protected party, the court shall not take the personal resources of the litigation friend into account in assessing the resources of the client.

(3) The purpose of this provision is to ensure that any liability is determined with reference to the value of the property or fund being used to pay for the litigation, and the financial position of those who may benefit from or rely on it.

PART V

COSTS AGAINST THE LSC

21.16 Regulation 5 of the Community Legal Service (Cost Protection) Regulations 2000 governs when costs can be awarded against the LSC. This provision only applies where cost protection applies and the costs ordered to be paid by the LSC funded client do not fully meet the costs that would have been ordered to be paid by him if cost protection did not apply.

21.17 In this section and the following two sections of this practice direction 'non-funded party' means a party to proceedings who has not received LSC funded services in relation to these proceedings under a legal aid certificate or a certificate issued under the LSC Funding Code other than a certificate which has been revoked.

21.18 The following criteria set out in Regulation 5 must be satisfied before the LSC can be ordered to pay the whole or any part of the costs incurred by a non-funded party –

    (1) the proceedings are finally decided in favour of a non-funded party;

    (2) unless there is good reason for delay the non-funded party provides written notice of intention to seek an order against the LSC within 3 months of the making of the Section 11(1) costs order;

    (3) the court is satisfied that it is just and equitable in the circumstances that provision for the costs should be made out of public funds; and

    (4) where costs are incurred in a court of first instance, the following additional criteria must also be met –

        (i) the proceedings were instituted by the LSC funded client;

        (ii) the non-funded party is an individual; and

        (iii) the non-funded party will suffer financial hardship unless the order is made.

    ('Section 11(1) costs order' is defined in paragraph 22.1, below)

21.19 In determining whether conditions (3) and (4) are satisfied, the court shall take into account the resources of the non-funded party and his partner (unless the partner has a contrary interest).

21.19A An order made under Regulation 5 may be made in relation to proceedings in the Court of Appeal, Court of Protection by a costs judge or a district judge.

EFFECT OF APPEALS

21.20

    (1) An order for costs can only be made against the LSC when the proceedings (including any appeal) are finally decided. Therefore, where a court of first instance decides in favour of a non-funded party and an appeal lies, any order made against the LSC shall not take effect unless –

        (a) where permission to appeal is required, the time limit for permission to appeal expires, without permission being granted;

        (b) where permission to appeal is granted or is not required, the time limit for appeal expires without an appeal being brought.

    (2) Accordingly, if the LSC funded client appeals, any earlier order against the LSC can never take effect. If the appeal is unsuccessful, an application can be made to the appeal court for a fresh order.

Section 22 – Orders for Costs to which Section 11 of the Access to Justice Act 1999 Applies

22.1 In this Practice Direction:

'order for costs to be determined' means an order for costs to which Section 11 of the Access to Justice Act 1999 applies under which the amount of costs payable by the LSC funded client is to be determined by a costs judge or district judge under Section 23 of this Practice Direction.

'order specifying the costs payable' means an order for costs to which Section 11 of the Act applies and which specifies the amount which the LSC funded client is to pay.

'full costs' means, where an order to which Section 11 of the Act applies is made against a LSC funded client, the amount of costs which that person would, had cost protection not applied, have been ordered to pay.

'determination proceedings' means proceedings to which paragraphs 22.1 to 22.10 apply.

'Section 11(1) costs order' means an order for costs to be determined or an order specifying the costs payable other than an order specifying the costs payable which was made in determination proceedings.

'statement of resources' means

(1) a statement, verified by a statement of truth, made by a party to proceedings setting out:

(a) his income and capital and financial commitments during the previous year and, if applicable, those of his partner;

(b) his estimated future financial resources and expectations and, if applicable, those of his partner ('partner' is defined in paragraph 21.4, above);

(c) a declaration that he and, if applicable, his partner, has not deliberately foregone or deprived himself of any resources or expectations;

(d) particulars of any application for funding made by him in connection with the proceedings; and,

(e) any other facts relevant to the determination of his resources; or

(2) a statement, verified by a statement of truth, made by a client receiving funded services, setting out the information provided by the client under Regulation 6 of the Community Legal Service (Financial) Regulations 2000, and stating that there has been no significant change in the client's financial circumstances since the date on which the information was provided or, as the case may be, details of any such change.

'Regional Director' means any Regional Director appointed by the LSC and any member of his staff authorised to act on his behalf.

22.2 Regulations 8 to 13 of the Community Legal Service (Costs) Regulations 2000 as amended set out the procedure for seeking costs against a funded client and the LSC. The effect of these Regulations is set out in this section and the next section of this Practice Direction.

22.3 As from 5 June 2000, Regulations 9 to 13 of the Community Legal Service (Costs) Regulations 2000 as amended also apply to certificates issued under the Legal Aid Act 1988 where costs against the assisted person fall to be assessed under Regulation 124 of the Civil Legal Aid (General) Regulations 1989. In this section and the next section of this Practice Direction the expression 'LSC funded client' includes an assisted person (defined in rule 43.2).

22.4 Regulation 8 of the Community Legal Service (Costs) Regulations 2000 as amended provides that a party intending to seek an order for costs against a LSC funded client may at any time file and serve on the LSC funded client a statement of resources. If that statement is served 7 or more days before a date fixed for a hearing at which an order for costs may be made, the LSC funded client must also make a statement of resources and produce it at the hearing.

22.5 If the court decides to make an order for costs against a LSC funded client to whom cost protection applies it may either:

(1)   make an order for costs to be determined, or
(2)   make an order specifying the costs payable.

22.6 If the court makes an order for costs to be determined it may also

(1)   state the amount of full costs, or
(2)   make findings of facts, eg, concerning the conduct of all the parties which are to be taken into account by the court in the subsequent determination proceedings.

22.7 The court will not make an order specifying the costs payable unless:

(1)   it considers that it has sufficient information before it to decide what amount is a reasonable amount for the LSC funded client to pay in accordance with Section 11 of the Act, and
(2)   either
      (a)   the order also states the amount of full costs, or
      (b)   the court considers that it has sufficient information before it to decide what amount is a reasonable amount for the LSC funded client to pay in accordance with Section 11 of the Act and is satisfied that, if it were to determine the full costs at that time, they would exceed the amounts specified in the order.

22.8 Where an order specifying the costs payable is made and the LSC funded client does not have cost protection in respect of all of the costs awarded in that order, the order must identify the sum payable (if any) in respect of which the LSC funded client has cost protection and the sum payable (if any) in respect of which he does not have cost protection.

22.9 The court cannot make an order under Regulations 8 to 13 of the Community Legal Service (Costs) Regulations 2000 as amended except in proceedings to which the next section of this Practice Direction applies.

Section 23 – Determination Proceedings and Similar Proceedings under the Community Legal Service (Costs) Regulations 2000

23.1 This section of this Practice Direction deals with:

(1)   proceedings subsequent to the making of an order for costs to be determined,
(2)   variations in the amount stated in an order specifying the amount of costs payable and
(3)   the late determination of costs under an order for costs to be determined;
(4)   appeals in respect of determination.

23.2 In this section of this Practice Direction 'appropriate court office' means:

(1)   the district registry or county court in which the case was being dealt with when the Section 11(1) order was made, or to which it has subsequently been transferred; or

(2)   in all other cases, the Costs Office.

23.2A

(1)   This paragraph applies where the appropriate office is any of the following county courts:

Barnet, Bow, Brentford, Bromley, Central London, Clerkenwell, Croydon, Edmonton, Ilford, Kingston, Lambeth, Mayors and City of London, Romford, Shoreditch, Uxbridge, Wandsworth, West London, Willesden and Woolwich.

(2)   Where this paragraph applies –

(i)   a receiving party seeking an order specifying costs payable by an LSC funded client and/or by the Legal Services Commission under this section must file his application in the Costs Office and, for all purposes relating to that application, the Costs Office will be treated as the appropriate office in that case; and

(ii)   unless an order is made transferring the application to the Costs Office as part of the High Court, an appeal from any decision made by a costs judge shall lie to the Designated Civil Judge for the London Group of County Courts or such judge as he shall nominate. The appeal notice and any other relevant papers should be lodged at the Central London Civil Justice Centre.

23.3

(1)   A receiving party seeking an order specifying costs payable by an LSC funded client and/or by the LSC may within 3 months of an order for costs to be determined, file in the appropriate court office an application in Form N244 accompanied by

(a)   the receiving party's bill of costs (unless the full costs have already been determined);

(b)   the receiving party's statement of resources (unless the court is determining an application against a costs order against the LSC and the costs were not incurred in the court of first instance); and

(c)   if the receiving party intends to seek costs against the LSC, written notice to that effect.

(2)   If the LSC funded client's liability has already been determined and is less than the full costs, the application will be for costs against the LSC only. If the LSC funded client's liability has not yet been determined, the receiving party must indicate if costs will be sought against the LSC if the funded client's liability is determined as less than the full costs.

(The LSC funded client's certificate will contain the addresses of the LSC funded client, his solicitor, and the relevant Regional Office of the LSC)

23.4 The receiving party must file the above documents in the appropriate court office and (where relevant) serve copies on the LSC funded client and the Regional Director. In respect of applications for funded services made before 3 December 2001 a failure to file a request within the 3 months time limit specified in Regulation 10(2) is an absolute bar to the making of a costs order against the LSC. Where the application for funded services was made on or after 3 December 2001 the court does have power to extend the 3 months time limit, but only if the applicant can show good reason for the delay.

23.5 On being served with the application, the LSC funded client must respond by filing a statement of resources and serving a copy of it on the receiving party (and the Regional Director where relevant) within 21 days. The LSC funded client may also file and serve written points disputing the bill within the same time limit. (Under rule 3.1 the court may extend or shorten this time limit.)

23.6 If the LSC funded client fails to file a statement of resources without good reason, the court will determine his liability (and the amount of full costs if relevant) and need not hold an oral hearing for such determination.

23.7 When the LSC funded client files a statement or the 21 day period for doing so expires, the court will fix a hearing date and give the relevant parties at least 14 days notice. The court may fix a hearing without waiting for the expiry of the 21 day period if the application is made only against the LSC.

23.8 Determination proceedings will be listed for hearing before a costs judge or district judge. The determination of the liability on the LSC funded client will be listed as a private hearing.

23.9 Where the LSC funded client does not have cost protection in respect of all of the costs awarded, the order made by the costs judge or district judge must in addition to specifying the costs payable, identify the full costs in respect of which cost protection applies and the full costs in respect of which cost protection does not apply.

23.10 The Regional Director may appear at any hearing at which a costs order may be made against the LSC. Instead of appearing, he may file a written statement at court and serve a copy on the receiving party. The written statement should be filed and a copy served, not less than 7 days before the hearing.

VARIATION OF AN ORDER SPECIFYING THE COSTS PAYABLE

23.11

(1) This paragraph applies where the amount stated in an order specifying the costs payable plus the amount ordered to be paid by the LSC is less than the full costs to which cost protection applies.

(2) The receiving party may apply to the court for a variation of the amount which the LSC funded client is required to pay on the ground that there has been a significant change in the client's circumstances since the date of the order.

23.12 On an application under paragraph 23.11, where the order specifying the costs payable does not state the full costs.

(1) the receiving party must file with his application the receiving party's statement of resources and bill of costs and copies of these documents should be served with the application.

(2) The LSC funded client must respond to the application by making a statement of resources which must be filed at court and served on the receiving party within 21 days thereafter. The LSC funded client may also file and serve written points disputing the bill within the same time limit.

(3) The court will, when determining the application assess the full costs identifying any part of them to which cost protection does apply and any part of them to which cost protection does not apply.

23.13 On an application under paragraph 23.11 the order specifying the costs payable may be varied as the court thinks fit. That variation must not increase:

(1) the amount of any costs ordered to be paid by the LSC, and

(2) the amount payable by the LSC funded client,

to a sum which is greater than the amount of the full costs plus the costs of the application.

23.14

(1) Where an order for costs to be determined has been made but the receiving party has not applied, within the three month time limit under paragraph 23.2, the receiving party may apply on any of the following grounds for a determination of the amount which the funded client is required to pay:

(a) there has been a significant change in the funded client's circumstances since the date of the order for costs to be determined; or

(b) material additional information about the funded client's financial resources is available which could not with reasonable diligence have been obtained by the receiving party at the relevant time; or

(c) there were other good reasons for the failure by the receiving party to make an application within the time limit.

(2) An application for costs payable by the LSC cannot be made under this paragraph.

23.15

(1) Where the receiving party has received funded services in relation to the proceedings, the LSC may make an application under paragraphs 23.11 and 23.14 above.

(2) In respect of an application under paragraph 23.11 made by the LSC, the LSC must file and serve copies of the documents described in paragraph 23.12(1).

23.16 An application under paragraph 23.11, 23.14 and 23.15 must be commenced before the expiration of 6 years from the date on which the court made the order specifying the costs payable, or (as the case may be) the order for costs to be determined.

23.17 Applications under paragraphs 23.11, 23.14 and 23.15 should be made in the appropriate court office and should be made in Form N244 to be listed for a hearing before a costs judge or district judge.

APPEALS

23.18

(1) Save as mentioned above any determination made under Regulation 9 or 10 of the Costs Regulations is final (Regulation 11(1)). Any party with a financial interest in the assessment of the full costs, other than a funded party, may appeal against that assessment in accordance with CPR Part 52 (Regulation 11(2) and CPR rule 47.20).

(2) The receiving party or the Commission may appeal on a point of law against the making of a costs order against the Commission, against the amount of costs the Commission is required to pay or against the court's refusal to make such an order (Regulation 11(4)).

PART V

Section 23A – Costs Capping Orders

WHEN TO MAKE AN APPLICATION

23A.1 The court will make a costs capping order only in exceptional circumstances.

23A.2 An application for a costs capping order must be made as soon as possible, preferably before or at the first case management hearing or shortly afterwards. The stage which the proceedings have reached at the time of the application will be one of the factors the court will consider when deciding whether to make a costs capping order.

ESTIMATE OF COSTS

23A.3 The estimate of costs required by rule 44.19 must be in the form illustrated in Precedent H in the Schedule of Costs Precedents annexed to this Practice Direction.

SCHEDULE OF COSTS

23A.4 The schedule of costs referred to in rule 44.19(3) –

    (a)   must set out –
        (i)   each sub-heading as it appears in the applicant's estimate of costs (column 1);
        (ii) alongside each sub-heading, the amount claimed by the applicant in the applicant's estimate of costs (column 2); and
        (iii) alongside the figures referred to in sub-paragraph (ii) the amount that the respondent proposes should be allowed under each sub-heading (column 3); and
    (b)   must be supported by a statement of truth.

ASSESSING THE QUANTUM OF THE COSTS CAP

23A.5 When assessing the quantum of a costs cap, the court will take into account the factors detailed in rule 44.5 and the relevant provisions supporting that rule in this Practice Direction. The court may also take into account when considering a party's estimate of the costs they are likely to incur in the future conduct of the proceedings a reasonable allowance on costs for contingencies.

Directions Relating to Part 47 – Procedure for Detailed Assessment of Costs and Default Provisions

Section 28 – Time when Assessment may be Carried Out: Rule 47.1

28.1

    (1)   For the purposes of rule 47.1, proceedings are concluded when the court has finally determined the matters in issue in the claim, whether or not there is an appeal.
    (2)   For the purposes of this rule, the making of an award of provisional damages under Part 41 will be treated as a final determination of the matters in issue.
    (3)   The court may order or the parties may agree in writing that, although the proceedings are continuing, they will nevertheless be treated as concluded.
    (4)   (a) A party who is served with a notice of commencement (see

paragraph 32.3 below) may apply to a costs judge or a district judge to determine whether the party who served it is entitled to commence detailed assessment proceedings.

(b) On hearing such an application the orders which the court may make include: an order allowing the detailed assessment proceedings to continue, or an order setting aside the notice of commencement.

(5) A costs judge or a district judge may make an order allowing detailed assessment proceedings to be commenced where there is no realistic prospect of the claim continuing.

Section 29 – No Stay of Detailed Assessment where there is an Appeal: Rule 47.2

29.1

(1) Rule 47.2 provides that detailed assessment is not stayed pending an appeal unless the court so orders.

(2) An application to stay the detailed assessment of costs pending an appeal may be made to the court whose order is being appealed or to the court who will hear the appeal.

Section 30 – Powers of an Authorised Court Officer: Rule 47.3

30.1

(1) The court officers authorised by the Lord Chancellor to assess costs in the Costs Office and the Principal Registry of the Family Division are authorised to deal with claims for costs not exceeding £30,000 (excluding VAT) in the case of senior executive officers, or their equivalent, and £75,000 (excluding VAT) in the case of principal officers.

(2) In calculating whether or not a bill of costs is within the authorised amounts, the figure to be taken into account is the total claim for costs including any additional liability.

(3) Where the receiving party, paying party and any other party to the detailed assessment proceedings who has served points of dispute are agreed that the assessment should not be made by an authorised court officer, the receiving party should so inform the court when requesting a hearing date. The court will then list the hearing before a costs judge or a district judge.

(4) In any other case a party who objects to the assessment being made by an authorised court officer must make an application to the costs judge or district judge under Part 23 (General Rules about Applications for Court Orders) setting out the reasons for the objection and if sufficient reason is shown the court will direct that the bill be assessed by a costs judge or district judge.

Section 31 – Venue for Detailed Assessment Proceedings: Rule 47.4

31.1 For the purposes of rule 47.4(1) the 'appropriate office' means –

(1) the district registry or county court in which the case was being dealt with when the judgment or order was made or the event occurred which gave rise to the right to assessment, or to which it has subsequently been transferred;

PART V

(1A) where a tribunal, person or other body makes an order for the detailed assessment of costs, a county court (subject to paragraph 31.1A(1)); or

(2) in all other cases, including Court of Appeal cases, the Costs Office.

31.1A

(1) This paragraph applies where the appropriate office is any of the following county courts:

Barnet, Bow, Brentford, Bromley, Central London, Clerkenwell, Croydon, Edmonton, Ilford, Kingston, Lambeth, Mayors and City of London, Romford, Shoreditch, Uxbridge, Wandsworth, West London, Willesden and Woolwich.

(2) Where this paragraph applies: –

  (i) the receiving party must file any request for a detailed assessment hearing in the Costs Office and, for all purposes relating to that detailed assessment, the Costs Office will be treated as the appropriate office in that case; and

  (ii) unless an order is made under rule 47.4(2) directing that the Costs Office as part of the High Court shall be the appropriate office, an appeal from any decision made by a costs judge shall lie to the Designated Civil Judge for the London Group of County Courts or such judge as he shall nominate. The appeal notice and any other relevant papers should be lodged at the Central London Civil Justice Centre.

31.2

(1) A direction under rule 47.4(2) or (3) specifying a particular court, registry or office as the appropriate office may be given on application or on the court's own initiative.

(2) Before making such a direction on its own initiative the court will give the parties the opportunity to make representations.

(3) Unless the Costs Office is the appropriate office for the purposes of Rule 47.4(1) an order directing that an assessment is to take place at the Costs Office will be made only if it is appropriate to do so having regard to the size of the bill of costs, the difficulty of the issues involved, the likely length of the hearing, the cost to the parties and any other relevant matter.

Section 32 – Commencement of Detailed Assessment Proceedings: Rule 47.6

32.1 Precedents A, B, C and D in the Schedule of Costs Precedents annexed to this practice direction are model forms of bills of costs for detailed assessment. Further information about bills of costs is set out in Section 4.

32.2 A detailed assessment may be in respect of:

(1) base costs, where a claim for additional liability has not been made or has been agreed;

(2) a claim for additional liability only, base costs having been summarily assessed or agreed;

  or

(3) both base costs and additional liability.

32.3 If the detailed assessment is in respect of costs without any additional liability, the receiving party must serve on the paying party and all the other relevant persons the following documents:

    (a)   a notice of commencement;

    (b)   a copy of the bill of costs;

    (c)   copies of the fee notes of counsel and of any expert in respect of fees claimed in the bill;

    (d)   written evidence as to any other disbursement which is claimed and which exceeds £250;

    (e)   a statement giving the name and address for service of any person upon whom the receiving party intends to serve the notice of commencement.

32.4 If the detailed assessment is in respect of an additional liability only, the receiving party must serve on the paying party and all other relevant persons the following documents:

    (a)   a notice of commencement;

    (b)   a copy of the bill of costs;

    (c)   the relevant details of the additional liability;

    (d)   a statement giving the name and address of any person upon whom the receiving party intends to serve the notice of commencement.

32.5 The relevant details of an additional liability are as follows:

    (1)   In the case of a conditional fee agreement with a success fee:

        (a)   a statement showing the amount of costs which have been summarily assessed or agreed, and the percentage increase which has been claimed in respect of those costs;

        (b)   a statement of the reasons for the percentage increase given in accordance with regulation 3(1)(a) of the Conditional Fee Agreements Regulations or regulation 5(1)(c) of the Collective Conditional Fee Agreements Regulations 2000 (Both sets of regulations were revoked by the Conditional Fee Agreements (Revocation) Regulations 2005 but continue to have effect in relation to conditional fee agreements and collective conditional fee agreements entered into before 1 November 2005).

    (2)   If the additional liability is an insurance premium: a copy of the insurance certificate showing whether the policy covers the receiving party's own costs; his opponents costs; or his own costs and his opponent's costs; and the maximum extent of that cover, and the amount of the premium paid or payable.

    (3)   If the receiving party claims an additional amount under Section 30 of the Access of Justice Act 1999: a statement setting out the basis upon which the receiving party's liability for the additional amount is calculated.

32.6 Attention is drawn to the fact that the additional amount recoverable pursuant to section 30 of the Access to Justice Act 1999 in respect of a membership organisation must not exceed the likely cost of the premium of an insurance policy against the risk of incurring a liability to pay the costs of other parties to the proceedings as provided by the Access to Justice (Membership Organisation) Regulations 2000 Regulation 4 (for the purposes of arrangements entered into before 1 November 2005) and The Access to Justice (Membership Organisation) Regulations 2005 Regulation 5 (for the purposes of arrangements entered into on or after 1 November 2005).

32.7 If a detailed assessment is in respect of both base costs and an additional liability, the receiving party must serve on the paying party and all other relevant persons the documents listed in paragraph 32.3 and the documents giving relevant details of an additional liability listed in paragraph 32.5.

PART V

32.8

(1) The notice of commencement should be in Form N252.
(2) Before it is served, it must be completed to show as separate items:
   (a) the total amount of the costs claimed in the bill;
   (b) the extra sum which will be payable by way of fixed costs and court fees if a default costs certificate is obtained.

32.9

(1) This paragraph applies where the notice of commencement is to be served outside England and Wales.
(2) The date to be inserted in the notice of commencement for the paying party to send points of dispute is a date (not less than 21 days from the date of service of the notice) which must be calculated by reference to Section IV of Part 6 as if the notice were a claim form and as if the date to be inserted was the date for the filing of a defence.

32.10

(1) For the purposes of rule 47.6(2) a 'relevant person' means:
   (a) any person who has taken part in the proceedings which gave rise to the assessment and who is directly liable under an order for costs made against him;
   (b) any person who has given to the receiving party notice in writing that he has a financial interest in the outcome of the assessment and wishes to be a party accordingly;
   (c) any other person whom the court orders to be treated as such.
(2) Where a party is unsure whether a person is or is not a relevant person, that party may apply to the appropriate office for directions.
(3) The court will generally not make an order that the person in respect of whom the application is made will be treated as a relevant person, unless within a specified time he applies to the court to be joined as a party to the assessment proceedings in accordance with Part 19 (Parties and Group Litigation).

32.11

(1) This paragraph applies in cases in which the bill of costs is capable of being copied onto a computer disk.
(2) If, before the detailed assessment hearing, a paying party requests a disk copy of a bill to which this paragraph applies, the receiving party must supply him with a copy free of charge not more than 7 days after the date on which he received the request.

Section 33 – Period for Commencing Detailed Assessment Proceedings: Rule 47.7

33.1 The parties may agree under rule 2.11 (Time limits may be varied by parties) to extend or shorten the time specified by rule 47.7 for commencing the detailed assessment proceedings.

33.2 A party may apply to the appropriate office for an order under rule 3.1(2)(a) to extend or shorten that time.

33.3 Attention is drawn to rule 47.6(1). The detailed assessment proceedings are commenced by service of the documents referred to.

33.4 Permission to commence assessment proceedings out of time is not required.

Section 34 – Sanction for Delay in Commencing Detailed Assessment Proceedings: Rule 47.8

34.1

(1) An application for an order under rule 47.8 must be made in writing and be issued in the appropriate office.

(2) The application notice must be served at least 7 days before the hearing.

Section 35 – Points of Dispute and Consequences of not Serving: Rule 47.9

35.1 The parties may agree under rule 2.11 (Time limits may be varied by parties) to extend or shorten the time specified by rule 47.9 for service of points of dispute. A party may apply to the appropriate office for an order under rule 3.1(2)(a) to extend or shorten that time.

35.2 Points of dispute should be short and to the point and should follow as closely as possible Precedent G of the Schedule of Costs Precedents annexed to this practice direction.

35.3 Points of dispute must –

(1) identify each item in the bill of costs which is disputed,

(2) in each case state concisely the nature and grounds of dispute,

(3) where practicable suggest a figure to be allowed for each item in respect of which a reduction is sought, and

(4) be signed by the party serving them or his solicitor.

35.4

(1) The normal period for serving points of dispute is 21 days after the date of service of the notice of commencement.

(2) Where a notice of commencement is served on a party outside England and Wales the period within which that party should serve points of dispute is to be calculated by reference to Section IV of Part 6 as if the notice of commencement was a claim form and as if the period for serving points of dispute were the period for filing a defence.

35.5 A party who serves points of dispute on the receiving party must at the same time serve a copy on every other party to the detailed assessment proceedings, whose name and address for service appears on the statement served by the receiving party in accordance with paragraph 32.3 or 32.4 above.

35.6

(1) This paragraph applies in cases in which points of dispute are capable of being copied onto a computer disk.

(2) If, within 14 days of the receipt of the points of dispute, the receiving party requests a disk copy of them, the paying party must supply him with a copy free of charge not more than 7 days after the date on which he received the request.

35.7

(1) Where the receiving party claims an additional liability, a party who serves

points of dispute on the receiving party may include a request for information about other methods of financing costs which were available to the receiving party.

(2) Part 18 (further information) and the Practice Direction Supplementing that part apply to such a request.

Section 36 – Procedure where Costs are Agreed: Rule 47.10

36.1 Where the parties have agreed terms as to the issue of a costs certificate (either interim or final) they should apply under rule 40.6 (Consent judgments and orders) for an order that a certificate be issued in terms set out in the application. Such an application may be dealt with by a court officer, who may issue the certificate.

36.2 Where in the course of proceedings the receiving party claims that the paying party has agreed to pay costs but that he will neither pay those costs nor join in a consent application under paragraph 36.1, the receiving party may apply under Part 23 (General Rules about Applications for Court Orders) for a certificate either interim or final to be issued.

36.3 An application under paragraph 36.2 must be supported by evidence and will be heard by a costs judge or a district judge. The respondent to the application must file and serve any evidence he relies on at least 2 days before the hearing date.

36.4 Nothing in rule 47.10 prevents parties who seek a judgment or order by consent from including in the draft a term that a party shall pay to another party a specified sum in respect of costs.

36.5

(1) The receiving party may discontinue the detailed assessment proceedings in accordance with Part 38 (Discontinuance).

(2) Where the receiving party discontinues the detailed assessment proceedings before a detailed assessment hearing has been requested, the paying party may apply to the appropriate office for an order about the costs of the detailed assessment proceedings.

(3) Where a detailed assessment hearing has been requested the receiving party may not discontinue unless the court gives permission.

(4) A bill of costs may be withdrawn by consent whether or not a detailed assessment hearing has been requested.

Section 37 – Default Costs Certificate: Rule 47.11

37.1(1) A request for the issue of a default costs certificate must be made in Form N254 and must be signed by the receiving party or his solicitor.

(2) The request must be accompanied by a copy of the document giving the right to detailed assessment. (Section 40.4 of the Costs Practice Direction identifies the appropriate documents.)

37.2 The request must be filed at the appropriate office.

37.3 A default costs certificate will be in Form N255.

37.4 Attention is drawn to Rules 40.3 (Drawing up and Filing of Judgments and Orders) and 40.4 (Service of Judgments and Orders) which apply to the preparation and service of a default costs certificate. The receiving party will be treated as having permission to draw up a default costs certificate by virtue of this practice direction.

37.5 The issue of a default costs certificate does not prohibit, govern or affect any detailed assessment of the same costs which are payable out of the Community Legal Service Fund.

37.6 An application for an order staying enforcement of a default costs certificate may be made either –

(1) to a costs judge or district judge of the court office which issued the certificate; or

(2) to the court (if different) which has general jurisdiction to enforce the certificate.

37.7 Proceedings for enforcement of default costs certificates may not be issued in the Costs Office.

37.8 The fixed costs payable in respect of solicitor's charges on the issue of the default costs certificate are £80.

Section 38 – Setting Aside Default Costs Certificate: Rule 47.12

38.1

(1) A court officer may set aside a default costs certificate at the request of the receiving party under rule 47.12(3).

(2) A costs judge or a district judge will make any other order or give any directions under this rule.

38.2

(1) An application for an order under rule 47.12(2) to set aside or vary a default costs certificate must be supported by evidence.

(2) In deciding whether to set aside or vary a certificate under rule 47.12(2) the matters to which the court must have regard include whether the party seeking the order made the application promptly.

(3) As a general rule a default costs certificate will be set aside under rule 47.12(2) only if the applicant shows a good reason for the court to do so and if he files with his application a copy of the bill and a copy of the default costs certificate, and a draft of the points of dispute he proposes to serve if his application is granted.

38.3

(1) Attention is drawn to rule 3.1(3) (which enables the court when making an order to make it subject to conditions) and to rule 44.3(8) (which enables the court to order a party whom it has ordered to pay costs to pay an amount on account before the costs are assessed).

(2) A costs judge or a district judge may exercise the power of the court to make an order under rule 44.3(8) although he did not make the order about costs which led to the issue of the default costs certificate.

38.4 If a default costs certificate is set aside the court will give directions for the management of the detailed assessment proceedings.

Section 39 – Optional Reply: Rule 47.13

39.1

    (1)   Where the receiving party wishes to serve a reply, he must also serve a copy on every other party to the detailed assessment proceedings. The time for doing so is within 21 days after service of the points of dispute.

    (2)   A reply means –
        (i)   a separate document prepared by the receiving party; or
        (ii)   his written comments added to the points of dispute.

    (3)   A reply must be signed by the party serving it or his solicitor.

Section 40 – Detailed Assessment Hearing: Rule 47.14

40.1 The time for requesting a detailed assessment hearing is within 3 months of the expiry of the period for commencing detailed assessment proceedings.

40.2 The request for a detailed assessment hearing must be in Form N258. The request must be accompanied by –

    (a)   a copy of the notice of commencement of detailed assessment proceedings;

    (b)   a copy of the bill of costs,

    (c)   the document giving the right to detailed assessment (see paragraph 40.4 below);

    (d)   a copy of the points of dispute, annotated as necessary in order to show which items have been agreed and their value and to show which items remain in dispute and their value;

    (e)   as many copies of the points of dispute so annotated as there are persons who have served points of dispute;

    (f)   a copy of any replies served;

    (g)   a copy of all orders made by the court relating to the costs which are to be assessed;

    (h)   copies of the fee notes and other written evidence as served on the paying party in accordance with paragraph 32.3 above;

    (i)   where there is a dispute as to the receiving party's liability to pay costs to the solicitors who acted for the receiving party, any agreement, letter or other written information provided by the solicitor to his client explaining how the solicitor's charges are to be calculated;

    (j)   a statement signed by the receiving party or his solicitor giving the name, address for service, reference and telephone number and fax number, if any, of –
        (i)   the receiving party;
        (ii)   the paying party;
        (iii) any other person who has served points of dispute or who has given notice to the receiving party under paragraph 32.10(1)(b) above;
        and giving an estimate of the length of time the detailed assessment hearing will take;

    (k)   where the application for a detailed assessment hearing is made by a party other than the receiving party, such of the documents set out in this paragraph as are in the possession of that party;

    (l)   where the court is to assess the costs of an assisted person or LSC funded client –
        (i)   the legal aid certificate, LSC certificate and relevant amendment certificates, any authorities and any certificates of discharge or revocation.

    (ii) a certificate, in Precedent F(3) of the Schedule of Costs Precedents;

    (iii) if the assisted person has a financial interest in the detailed assessment hearing and wishes to attend, the postal address of that person to which the court will send notice of any hearing;

    (iv) if the rates payable out of the LSC fund are prescribed rates, a schedule to the bill of costs setting out all the items in the bill which are claimed against other parties calculated at the legal aid prescribed rates with or without any claim for enhancement: (further information as to this schedule is set out in Section 48 of this practice direction);

    (v) a copy of any default costs certificate in respect of costs claimed in the bill of costs.

40.3

(1) This paragraph applies to any document described in paragraph 40.2(i) above which the receiving party has filed in the appropriate office. The document must be the latest relevant version and in any event have been filed not more than 2 years before filing the request for a detailed assessment hearing.

(2) In respect of any documents to which this paragraph applies, the receiving party may, instead of filing a copy of it, specify in the request for a detailed assessment hearing the case number under which a copy of the document was previously filed.

40.4 'The document giving the right to detailed assessment' means such one or more of the following documents as are appropriate to the detailed assessment proceedings –

(a) a copy of the judgment or order of the court giving the right to detailed assessment;

(b) a copy of the notice served under rule 3.7 (sanctions for non-payment of certain fees) where a claim is struck out under that rule;

(c) a copy of the notice of acceptance where an offer to settle is accepted under Part 36 (Offers to settle);

(d) a copy of the notice of discontinuance in a case which is discontinued under Part 38 (Discontinuance);

(e) a copy of the award made on an arbitration under any Act or pursuant to an agreement, where no court has made an order for the enforcement of the award;

(f) a copy of the order, award or determination of a statutorily constituted tribunal or body;

(g) in a case under the Sheriffs Act 1887, the sheriff's bill of fees and charges, unless a court order giving the right to detailed assessment has been made;

(h) a notice of revocation or discharge under Regulation 82 of the Civil Legal Aid (General) Regulations 1989.

(j) In the county courts certain Acts and Regulations provide for costs incurred in proceedings under those Acts and Regulations to be assessed in the county court if so ordered on application. Where such an application is made, a copy of the order.

40.5 On receipt of the request for a detailed assessment hearing the court will fix a date for the hearing, or, if the costs officer so decides, will give directions or fix a date for a preliminary appointment.

40.6

(1) The court will give at least 14 days' notice of the time and place of the

PART V

detailed assessment hearing to every person named in the statement referred to in paragraph 40.2(j) above.

(2)   The court will when giving notice, give each person who has served points of dispute a copy of the points of dispute annotated by the receiving party in compliance with paragraph 40.2(d) above.

(3)   Attention is drawn to rule 47.14(6) & (7): apart from the receiving party, only those who have served points of dispute may be heard on the detailed assessment unless the court gives permission, and only items specified in the points of dispute may be raised unless the court gives permission.

40.7

(1)   If the receiving party does not file a request for a detailed assessment hearing within the prescribed time, the paying party may apply to the court to fix a time within which the receiving party must do so. The sanction, for failure to commence detailed assessment proceedings within the time specified by the court, is that all or part of the costs may be disallowed (see rule 47.8(2)).

(2)   Where the receiving party commences detailed assessment proceedings after the time specified in the rules but before the paying party has made an application to the court to specify a time, the only sanction which the court may impose is to disallow all or part of the interest which would otherwise be payable for the period of delay, unless the court exercises its powers under rule 44.14 (court's powers in relation to misconduct).

40.8 If either party wishes to make an application in the detailed assessment proceedings the provisions of Part 23 (General Rules about Applications for Court Orders) apply.

40.9

(1)   This paragraph deals with the procedure to be adopted where a date has been given by the court for a detailed assessment hearing and –
(a)   the detailed assessment proceedings are settled; or
(b)   a party to the detailed assessment proceedings wishes to apply to vary the date which the court has fixed; or
(c)   the parties to the detailed assessment proceedings agree about changes they wish to make to any direction given for the management of the detailed assessment proceedings.

(2)   If detailed assessment proceedings are settled, the receiving party must give notice of that fact to the court immediately, preferably by fax.

(3)   A party who wishes to apply to vary a direction must do so in accordance with Part 23 (General Rules about Applications for Court Orders).

(4)   If the parties agree about changes they wish to make to any direction given for the management of the detailed assessment proceedings –
(a)   they must apply to the court for an order by consent; and
(b)   they must file a draft of the directions sought and an agreed statement of the reasons why the variation is sought; and
(c)   the court may make an order in the agreed terms or in other terms without a hearing, but it may direct that a hearing is to be listed.

40.10

(1)   If a party wishes to vary his bill of costs, points of dispute or a reply, an amended or supplementary document must be filed with the court and copies of it must be served on all other relevant parties.

(2)   Permission is not required to vary a bill of costs, points of dispute or a

reply but the court may disallow the variation or permit it only upon conditions, including conditions as to the payment of any costs caused or wasted by the variation.

40.11 Unless the court directs otherwise the receiving party must file with the court the papers in support of the bill not less than 7 days before the date for the detailed assessment hearing and not more than 14 days before that date.

40.12 The following provisions apply in respect of the papers to be filed in support of the bill;

    (a) if the claim is for costs only without any additional liability the papers to be filed, and the order in which they are to be arranged are as follows:

        (i) instructions and briefs to counsel arranged in chronological order together with all advices, opinions and drafts received and response to such instructions;

        (ii) reports and opinions of medical and other experts;

        (iii) any other relevant papers;

        (iv) a full set of any relevant pleadings to the extent that they have not already been filed in court;

        (v) correspondence, files and attendance notes;

    (b) where the claim is in respect of an additional liability only, such of the papers listed at (a) above, as are relevant to the issues raised by the claim for additional liability;

    (c) where the claim is for both base costs and an additional liability, the papers listed at (a) above, together with any papers relevant to the issues raised by the claim for additional liability.

40.13 The provisions set out in Section 20 of the practice direction apply where the court disallows any amount of a legal representative's percentage increase, and the legal representative applies for an order that the disallowed amount should continue to be payable by the client in accordance with Rule 44.16.

40.14 The court may direct the receiving party to produce any document which in the opinion of the court is necessary to enable it to reach its decision. These documents will in the first instance be produced to the court, but the court may ask the receiving party to elect whether to disclose the particular document to the paying party in order to rely on the contents of the document, or whether to decline disclosure and instead rely on other evidence.

40.15 Costs assessed at a detailed assessment at the conclusion of proceedings may include an assessment of any additional liability in respect of the costs of a previous application or hearing.

40.16 Once the detailed assessment hearing has ended it is the responsibility of the legal representative appearing for the receiving party or, as the case may be, the receiving party in person to remove the papers filed in support of the bill.

Section 41 – Power to Issue an Interim Certificate: Rule 47.15

41.1

    (1) A party wishing to apply for an interim certificate may do so by making an application in accordance with Part 23 (General Rules about Applications for Court Orders).

PART V

(2)   Attention is drawn to the fact that the court's power to issue an interim certificate arises only after the receiving party has filed a request for a detailed assessment hearing.

Section 42 – Final Costs Certificate: Rule 47.16

42.1 At the detailed assessment hearing the court will indicate any disallowance or reduction in the sums claimed in the bill of costs by making an appropriate note on the bill.

42.2 The receiving party must, in order to complete the bill after the detailed assessment hearing make clear the correct figures agreed or allowed in respect of each item and must re-calculate the summary of the bill appropriately.

42.3 The completed bill of costs must be filed with the court no later than 14 days after the detailed assessment hearing.

42.4 At the same time as filing the completed bill of costs, the party whose bill it is must also produce receipted fee notes and receipted accounts in respect of all disbursements except those covered by a certificate in Precedent F(5) in the Schedule of Costs Precedents annexed to this practice direction.

42.5 No final costs certificate will be issued until all relevant court fees payable on the assessment of costs have been paid.

42.6 If the receiving party fails to file a completed bill in accordance with rule 47.16 the paying party may make an application under Part 23 (General Rules about Applications for Court Orders) seeking an appropriate order under rule 3.1 (The court's general powers of management).

42.7 A final costs certificate will show –

(a)   the amount of any costs which have been agreed between the parties or which have been allowed on detailed assessment;
(b)   where applicable the amount agreed or allowed in respect of VAT on the costs agreed or allowed.

This provision is subject to any contrary provision made by the statutory provisions relating to costs payable out of the Community Legal Service Fund.

42.8 A final costs certificate will include disbursements in respect of the fees of counsel only if receipted fee notes or accounts in respect of those disbursements have been produced to the court and only to the extent indicated by those receipts.

42.9 Where the certificate relates to costs payable between parties a separate certificate will be issued for each party entitled to costs.

42.10 Form N257 is a model form of interim costs certificate and Form N256 is a model form of final costs certificate.

42.11 An application for an order staying enforcement of an interim costs certificate or final costs certificate may be made either –

(1)   to a costs judge or district judge of the court office which issued the certificate; or
(2)   to the court (if different) which has general jurisdiction to enforce the certificate.

42.12 Proceedings for enforcement of interim costs certificates or final costs certificates may not be issued in the Costs Office.

Section 43 – Detailed Assessment Procedure where Costs are Payable out of the Community Legal Service Fund: Rule 47.17

43.1 The provisions of this section apply where the court is to assess costs which are payable only out of the community legal service fund. Paragraphs 39.1 to 40.16 and 49.1 to 49.8 apply in cases involving costs payable by another person as well as costs payable only out of the Community Legal Service Fund.

43.2 The time for requesting a detailed assessment under rule 47.17 is within 3 months after the date when the right to detailed assessment arose.

43.3 The request for a detailed assessment of costs must be in Form N258A. The request must be accompanied by –

- (a) a copy of the bill of costs;
- (b) the document giving the right to detailed assessment (for further information as to this document, see paragraph 40.4 above);
- (c) a copy of all orders made by the court relating to the costs which are to be assessed;
- (d) copies of any fee notes of counsel and any expert in respect of fees claimed in the bill;
- (e) written evidence as to any other disbursement which is claimed and which exceeds £250;
- (f) the legal aid certificates, LSC certificates, any relevant amendment certificates, any authorities and any certificates of discharge or revocation;
- (g) in the Costs Office the relevant papers in support of the bill as described in paragraph 40.12 above; in cases proceeding in district registries and county courts this provision does not apply and the papers should only be lodged if requested by the costs officer;
- (h) a statement signed by the solicitor giving his name, address for service, reference, telephone number, fax number and, if the assisted person has a financial interest in the detailed assessment and wishes to attend, giving the postal address of that person, to which the court will send notice of any hearing.

43.4 Rule 47.17 provides that the court will hold a detailed assessment hearing if the assisted person has a financial interest in the detailed assessment and wishes to attend. The court may also hold a detailed assessment hearing in any other case, instead of provisionally assessing a bill of costs, where it considers that a hearing is necessary. Before deciding whether a hearing is necessary under this rule, the court may require the solicitor whose bill it is, to provide further information relating to the bill.

43.5 Where the court has provisionally assessed a bill of costs it will send to the solicitor a notice, in Form N253 annexed to this practice direction, of the amount of costs which the court proposes to allow together with the bill itself. The legal representative should, if the provisional assessment is to be accepted, then complete the bill.

43.6 The court will fix a date for a detailed assessment hearing if the solicitor informs the court within 14 days after he receives the notice of the amount allowed on the provisional assessment that he wants the court to hold such a hearing.

43.7 The court will give at least 14 days notice of the time and place of the detailed assessment hearing to the solicitor and, if the assisted person has a financial interest in the detailed assessment and wishes to attend, to the assisted person.

43.8 If the solicitor whose bill it is, or any other party wishes to make an application in the detailed assessment proceedings, the provisions of Part 23 (General Rules about Applications for Court Orders) applies.

43.9 It is the responsibility of the legal representative to complete the bill by entering in the bill the correct figures allowed in respect of each item, recalculating the summary of the bill appropriately and completing the Community Legal Service assessment certificate (Form EX80A).

Section 44 – Costs of Detailed Assessment Proceedings

WHERE COSTS ARE PAYABLE OUT OF A FUND OTHER THAN THE COMMUNITY LEGAL SERVICE FUND: RULE 47.17A

44.1 Rule 47.17A provides that the court will make a provisional assessment of a bill of costs payable out of a fund (other than the Community Legal Service Fund) unless it considers that a hearing is necessary. It also enables the court to direct under rule 47.17A(3) that the receiving party must serve a copy of the request for assessment and copies of the documents which accompany it, on any person who has a financial interest in the outcome of the assessment.

44.2

(a) A person has a financial interest in the outcome of the assessment if the assessment will or may affect the amount of money or property to which he is or may become entitled out of the fund.

(b) Where an interest in the fund is itself held by a trustee for the benefit of some other person, that trustee will be treated as the person having such a financial interest.

(c) 'Trustee' includes a personal representative, receiver or any other person acting in a fiduciary capacity.

44.3 The request for a detailed assessment of costs out of the fund should be in Form N258B, be accompanied by the documents set out at paragraph 43.3(a) to (e) and (g) above and the following;

(a) a statement signed by the receiving party giving his name, address for service, reference, telephone number, fax number and,

(b) a statement of the postal address of any person who has a financial interest in the outcome of the assessment, to which the court may send notice of any hearing; and

(c) in respect of each person stated to have such an interest if such person is a child or protected party, a statement to that effect.

44.4 The court will decide, having regard to the amount of the bill, the size of the fund and the number of persons who have a financial interest, which of those persons should be served. The court may dispense with service on all or some of them.

44.5 Where the court makes an order dispensing with service on all such persons it may proceed at once to make a provisional assessment, or, if it decides that a hearing is necessary, give appropriate directions. Before deciding whether a hearing is necessary under this rule, the court may require the receiving party to provide further information relating to the bill.

44.6
   (1)   Where the court has provisionally assessed a bill of costs, it will send to the receiving party, a notice in Form N253 of the amount of costs which the court proposes to allow together with the bill itself. If the receiving party is legally represented the legal representative should, if the provisional assessment is to be accepted, then complete the bill.
   (2)   The court will fix a date for a detailed assessment hearing, if the receiving party informs the court within 14 days after he receives the notice in Form N253 of the amount allowed on the provisional assessment, that he wants the court to hold such a hearing.

44.7 Where the court makes an order that a person who has a financial interest is to be served with a copy of the request for assessment, it may give directions about service and about the hearing.

44.8 The court will give at least 14 days notice of the time and place of the detailed assessment hearing to the receiving party and, to any person who has a financial interest in the outcome of the assessment and has been served with a copy of the request for assessment.

44.9 If the receiving party, or any other party or any person who has a financial interest in the outcome of assessment, wishes to make an application in the detailed assessment proceedings, the provisions of Part 23 (General Rules about Applications for Court Orders) applies.

44.10 If the receiving party is legally represented the legal representative must in order to complete the bill after the assessment make clear the correct figures allowed in respect of each item and must recalculate the summary of the bill if appropriate.

Section 45 – Liability for Costs of Detailed Assessment Proceedings: Rule 47.18

45.1 As a general rule the court will assess the receiving party's costs of the detailed assessment proceedings and add them to the bill of costs.

45.2 If the costs of the detailed assessment proceedings are awarded to the paying party, the court will either assess those costs by summary assessment or make an order for them to be decided by detailed assessment.

45.3 No party should file or serve a statement of costs of the detailed assessment proceedings unless the court orders him to do so.

45.4 Attention is drawn to the fact that in deciding what order to make about the costs of detailed assessment proceedings the court must have regard to the conduct of all parties, the amount by which the bill of costs has been reduced and whether it was reasonable for a party to claim the costs of a particular item or to dispute that item.

45.5(1)In respect of interest on the costs of detailed assessment proceedings, the interest shall begin to run from the date of the default, interim or final costs certificate as the case may be.

   (2)   This provision applies only to the costs of the detailed assessment proceedings themselves. The costs of the substantive proceedings are governed by rule 40.8(1).

Section 46 – Offers to Settle Without Prejudice Save as to the Costs of the Detailed Assessment Proceedings: Rule 47.19

46.1 Rule 47.19 allows the court to take into account offers to settle, without prejudice save as to the costs of detailed assessment proceedings, when deciding who is liable for the costs of those proceedings. The rule does not specify a time within which such an offer should be made. An offer made by the paying party should usually be made within 14 days after service of the notice of commencement on that party. If the offer is made by the receiving party, it should normally be made within 14 days after the service of points of dispute by the paying party. Offers made after these periods are likely to be given less weight by the court in deciding what order as to costs to make unless there is good reason for the offer not being made until the later time.

46.2 Where an offer to settle is made it should specify whether or not it is intended to be inclusive of the cost of preparation of the bill, interest and value added tax (VAT). The offer may include or exclude some or all of these items but the position must be made clear on the face of the offer so that the offeree is clear about the terms of the offer when it is being considered. Unless the offer states otherwise, the offer will be treated as being inclusive of all these items.

46.3 Where an offer to settle is accepted, an application may be made for a certificate in agreed terms, or the bill of costs may be withdrawn, in accordance with rule 47.10 (Procedure where costs are agreed).

46.4 Where the receiving party is an assisted person or an LSC funded client, an offer to settle without prejudice save as to the costs of the detailed assessment proceedings will not have the consequences specified under rule 47.19 unless the court so orders.

Section 47 – Appeals from Authorised Court Officers in Detailed Assessment Proceedings: Right to Appeal: Rule 47.20

47.1 This Section and the next Section of this practice direction relate only to appeals from authorised court officers in detailed assessment proceedings. All other appeals arising out of detailed assessment proceedings (and arising out of summary assessments) are dealt with in accordance with Part 52 and the practice direction which supplements that Part. The destination of appeals is dealt with in accordance with the Access to Justice Act 1999 (Destination of Appeals) Order 2000.

47.2 In respect of appeals from authorised court officers, there is no requirement to obtain permission, or to seek written reasons.

Section 48 – Procedure on Appeal from Authorised Court Officers: Rule 47.22

48.1 The appellant must file a notice which should be in Form N161 (an appellant's notice).

48.2 The appeal will be heard by a costs judge or a district judge of the High Court, and is a re-hearing.

48.3 The appellant's notice should, if possible, be accompanied by a suitable record of the judgment appealed against. Where reasons given for the decision have been officially recorded by the court an approved transcript of that record should accompany the notice. Photocopies will not be accepted for this purpose. Where there is no official record the following documents will be acceptable:

(1)   The officer's comments written on the bill.
(2)   Advocates' notes of the reasons agreed by the respondent if possible and approved by the authorised court officer.

When the appellant was unrepresented before the authorised court officer, it is the duty of any advocate for the respondent to make his own note of the reasons promptly available, free of charge to the appellant where there is no official record or if the court so directs. Where the appellant was represented before the authorised court officer, it is the duty of his/her own former advocate to make his/her notes available. The appellant should submit the note of the reasons to the costs judge or district judge hearing the appeal.

48.4 The appellant may not be able to obtain a suitable record of the authorised court officer's decision within the time in which the appellant's notice must be filed. In such cases, the appellant's notice must still be completed to the best of the appellant's ability. It may however be amended subsequently with the permission of the costs judge or district judge hearing the appeal.

Section 49 – Costs Payable by the LSC at Prescribed Rates:

49.1 This section applies to a bill of costs of an assisted person or LSC funded client which is payable by another person where the costs which can be claimed against the LSC are restricted to prescribed rates (with or without enhancement).

49.2 Where this section applies, the solicitor of the assisted person or LSC funded client must file a legal aid/LSC schedule in accordance with paragraph 40.2(l) above. The schedule should follow as closely as possible Precedent E of the Schedule of Costs Precedents annexed to this practice direction.

49.3 The schedule must set out by reference to the item numbers in the bill of costs, all the costs claimed as payable by another person, but the arithmetic in the schedule should claim those items at prescribed rates only (with or without any claim for enhancement).

49.4 Where there has been a change in the prescribed rates during the period covered by the bill of costs, the schedule (as opposed to the bill) should be divided into separate parts, so as to deal separately with each change of rate. The schedule must also be divided so as to correspond with any divisions in the bill of costs.

49.5 If the bill of costs contains additional columns setting out costs claimed against the LSC only, the schedule may be set out in a separate document or, alternatively, may be included in the additional columns of the bill.

49.6 The detailed assessment of the legal aid/LSC schedule will take place immediately after the detailed assessment of the bill of costs.

49.7 Attention is drawn to the possibility that, on occasions, the court may decide to conduct the detailed assessment of the legal aid/LSC schedule separately from any detailed assessment of the bill of costs. This will occur, for example, where a default costs certificate is obtained as between the parties but that certificate is not set aside at the time of the detailed assessment pursuant to the Legal Aid Act 1988 or regulations thereunder.

PART V

49.8 Where costs have been assessed at prescribed rates it is the responsibility of the legal representative to enter the correct figures allowed in respect of each item and to recalculate the summary of the legal aid/LSC schedule.

Directions Relating to Part 48 – Costs – Special Cases

Section 52 – Litigants in Person: Rule 48.6

52.1 In order to qualify as an expert for the purpose of rule 48.6(3)(c) (expert assistance in connection with assessing the claim for costs), the person in question must be a –

    (1)   barrister,
    (2)   solicitor,
    (3)   Fellow of the Institute of Legal Executives,
    (4)   Fellow of the Association of Law Costs Draftsmen,
    (5)   law costs draftsman who is a member of the Academy of Experts,
    (6)   law costs draftsman who is a member of the Expert Witness Institute.

52.2 Where a litigant in person wishes to prove that he has suffered financial loss he should produce to the court any written evidence he relies on to support that claim, and serve a copy of that evidence on any party against whom he seeks costs at least 24 hours before the hearing at which the question may be decided.

52.3 Where a litigant in person commences detailed assessment proceedings under rule 47.6 he should serve copies of that written evidence with the notice of commencement.

52.4 The amount which may be allowed to a litigant in person under rule 46.3(5)(b) and rule 48.6(4) is £9.25 per hour.

52.5 Attention is drawn to rule 48.6(6)(b). A solicitor who, instead of acting for himself, is represented in the proceedings by his firm or by himself in his firm name, is not, for the purpose of the Civil Procedure Rules, a litigant in person.

Section 53 – Personal Liability of Legal Representative for Costs – Wasted Costs Orders: Rule 48.7

53.1 Rule 48.7 deals with wasted costs orders against legal representatives. Such orders can be made at any stage in the proceedings up to and including the proceedings relating to the detailed assessment of costs. In general, applications for wasted costs are best left until after the end of the trial.

53.2 The court may make a wasted costs order against a legal representative on its own initiative.

53.3 A party may apply for a wasted costs order –

    (1)   by filing an application notice in accordance with Part 23; or
    (2)   by making an application orally in the course of any hearing.

53.4 It is appropriate for the court to make a wasted costs order against a legal representative, only if –

    (1)   the legal representative has acted improperly, unreasonably or negligently;
    (2)   his conduct has caused a party to incur unnecessary costs; and
    (3)   it is just in all the circumstances to order him to compensate that party for the whole or part of those costs.

53.5 The court will give directions about the procedure that will be followed in each case in order to ensure that the issues are dealt with in a way which is fair and as simple and summary as the circumstances permit.

53.6 As a general rule the court will consider whether to make a wasted costs order in two stages –

   (1) in the first stage, the court must be satisfied –
      (a) that it has before it evidence or other material which, if unanswered, would be likely to lead to a wasted costs order being made; and
      (b) the wasted costs proceedings are justified notwithstanding the likely costs involved.
   (2) at the second stage (even if the court is satisfied under paragraph (1)) the court will consider, after giving the legal representative an opportunity to give reasons why the court should not make a wasted costs order, whether it is appropriate to make a wasted costs order in accordance with paragraph 53.4 above.

53.7 On an application for a wasted costs order under Part 23 the court may proceed to the second stage described in paragraph 53.6 without first adjourning the hearing if it is satisfied that the legal representative has already had a reasonable opportunity to give reasons why the court should not make a wasted costs order. In other cases the court will adjourn the hearing before proceeding to the second stage.

53.8 On an application for a wasted costs order under Part 23 the application notice and any evidence in support must identify –

   (1) what the legal representative is alleged to have done or failed to do; and
   (2) the costs that he may be ordered to pay or which are sought against him.

53.9 A wasted costs order is an order –

   (1) that the legal representative pay a specified sum in respect of costs to a party; or
   (2) for costs relating to a specified sum or items of work to be disallowed.

53.10 Attention is drawn to rule 44.3A(1) and (2) which respectively prevent the court from assessing any additional liability until the conclusion of the proceedings (or the part of the proceedings) to which the funding arrangement relates, and set out the orders the court may make at the conclusion of the proceedings.

Section 54 – Basis of Detailed Assessment of Solicitor and Client Costs: Rule 48.8

54.1 A client and his solicitor may agree whatever terms they consider appropriate about the payment of the solicitor's charges for his services. If however, the costs are of an unusual nature (either in amount or in the type of costs incurred) those costs will be presumed to have been unreasonably incurred unless the solicitor satisfies the court that he informed the client that they were unusual and, where the costs relate to litigation, that he informed the client they might not be allowed on an assessment of costs between the parties. That information must have been given to the client before the costs were incurred.

54.2

   (1) Costs as between a solicitor and client are assessed on the indemnity basis as defined by rule 44.4.

PART V

(2) Attention is drawn to the presumptions set out in rule 48.8(2). These presumptions may be rebutted by evidence to the contrary.

54.3 Rule 48.10 and Section 56 of this practice direction deal with the procedure to be followed for obtaining the assessment of a solicitor's bill pursuant to an order under Part III of the Solicitors Act 1974.

54.4 If a party fails to comply with the requirements of rule 48.10 concerning the service of a breakdown of costs or points of dispute, any other party may apply to the court in which the detailed assessment hearing should take place for an order requiring compliance with rule 48.10. If the court makes such an order, it may –

(a) make it subject to conditions including a condition to pay a sum of money into court; and

(b) specify the consequence of failure to comply with the order or a condition.

54.5

(1) A client who has entered into a conditional fee agreement with a solicitor may apply for assessment of the base costs (which is carried out in accordance with rule 48.8(2) as if there were no conditional fee agreement) or for assessment of the percentage increase (success fee) or both.

(2) Where the court is to assess the percentage increase the court will have regard to all the relevant factors as they appeared to the solicitor or counsel when the conditional fee agreement was entered into.

54.6 Where the client applies to the court to reduce the percentage increase which the solicitor has charged the client under the conditional fee agreement, the client must set out in his application notice –

(a) the reasons why the percentage increase should be reduced; and

(b) what the percentage increase should be.

54.7 The factors relevant to assessing the percentage increase include –

(a) the risk that the circumstances in which the fees or expenses would be payable might not occur;

(b) the disadvantages relating to the absence of payment on account;

(c) whether there is a conditional fee agreement between the solicitor and counsel;

(d) the solicitor's liability for any disbursements.

54.8 When the court is considering the factors to be taken into account, it will have regard to the circumstances as they reasonably appeared to the solicitor or counsel when the conditional fee agreement was entered into.

Section 56 – Procedure on Assessment of Solicitor and Client Costs: Rule 48.10

56.1 The paragraphs in this section apply to orders made under Part III of the Solicitors Act 1974 for the assessment of costs. In these paragraphs 'client' includes any person entitled to make an application under Part III of that Act.

56.2 The procedure for obtaining an order under Part III of the Solicitors Act 1974 is by the alternative procedure for claims under Part 8, as modified by rule 67.3 and the Practice Direction supplementing Part 67. Precedent J of the Schedule of Costs Precedents annexed to this practice direction is a model form of claim form. The application must be accompanied by the bill or bills in respect of which assessment is sought, and, if the claim concerns a conditional fee agreement, a copy of that agreement. If the original bill is not available a copy will suffice.

56.3 Model forms of order, which the court may make, are set out in Precedents K, L and M of the Schedule of Costs Precedents annexed to this practice direction.

56.4 Attention is drawn to the time limits within which the required steps must be taken: ie the solicitor must serve a breakdown of costs within 28 days of the order for costs to be assessed, the client must serve points of dispute within 14 days after service on him of the breakdown, and any reply must be served within 14 days of service of the points of dispute.

56.5 The breakdown of costs referred to in rule 48.10 is a document which contains the following information –

   (a)   details of the work done under each of the bills sent for assessment; and
   (b)   in applications under Section 70 of the Solicitors Act 1974, an account showing money received by the solicitor to the credit of the client and sums paid out of that money on behalf of the client but not payments out which were made in satisfaction of the bill or of any items which are claimed in the bill.

56.6 Precedent P of the Schedule of Costs Precedents annexed to this practice direction is a model form of breakdown of costs. A party who is required to serve a breakdown of costs must also serve –

   (1)   copies of the fee notes of counsel and of any expert in respect of fees claimed in the breakdown, and
   (2)   written evidence as to any other disbursement which is claimed in the breakdown and which exceeds £250.

56.7 The provisions relating to default costs certificates (rule 47.11) do not apply to cases to which rule 48.10 applies.

56.8 Points of dispute should, as far as practicable, be in the form complying with paragraphs 35.1–35.7.

56.9 The time for requesting a detailed assessment hearing is within 3 months after the date of the order for the costs to be assessed.

56.10 The form of request for a hearing date must be in Form N258C. The request must be accompanied by copies of –

   (a)   the order sending the bill or bills for assessment;
   (b)   the bill or bills sent for assessment;
   (c)   the solicitor's breakdown of costs and any invoices or accounts served with that breakdown;
   (d)   a copy of the points of dispute, annotated as necessary in order to show which items have been agreed and their value and to show which items remain in dispute;
   (e)   as many copies of the points of dispute so annotated as there are other parties to the proceedings to whom the court should give details of the assessment hearing requested;
   (f)   a copy of any replies served;
   (g)   a statement signed by the party filing the request or his legal representative giving the names and addresses for service of all parties to the proceedings.

56.11 The request must include an estimate of the length of time the detailed assessment hearing will take.

PART V

56.12 On receipt of the request for a detailed assessment hearing the court will fix a date for the hearing or if the costs judge or district judge so decides, will give directions or fix a date for a preliminary appointment.

56.13

    (1)   The court will give at least 14 days notice of the time and place of the detailed assessment hearing to every person named in the statement referred to in paragraph 56.10(g) above.

    (2)   The court will when giving notice, give all parties other than the party who requested the hearing a copy of the points of dispute annotated by the party requesting the hearing in compliance with paragraph 56.10(e) above.

    (3)   Attention is drawn to rule 47.14(6) and (7): apart from the solicitor whose bill it is, only those parties who have served points of dispute may be heard on the detailed assessment unless the court gives permission, and only items specified in the points of dispute may be raised unless the court gives permission.

56.14

    (1)   If a party wishes to vary his breakdown of costs, points of dispute or reply, an amended or supplementary document must be filed with the court and copies of it must be served on all other relevant parties.

    (2)   Permission is not required to vary a breakdown of costs, points of dispute or a reply but the court may disallow the variation or permit it only upon conditions, including conditions as to the payment of any costs caused or wasted by the variation.

56.15 Unless the court directs otherwise the solicitor must file with the court the papers in support of the bill not less than 7 days before the date for the detailed assessment hearing and not more than 14 days before that date.

56.16 Once the detailed assessment hearing has ended it is the responsibility of the legal representative appearing for the solicitor or, as the case may be, the solicitor in person to remove the papers filed in support of the bill.

56.17

    (1)   Attention is drawn to rule 47.15 (power to issue an interim certificate).

    (2)   If, in the course of a detailed assessment hearing of a solicitor's bill to his client, it appears to the costs judge or district judge that in any event the solicitor will be liable in connection with that bill to pay money to the client, he may issue an interim certificate specifying an amount which in his opinion is payable by the solicitor to his client. Such a certificate will include an order to pay the sum it certifies unless the court orders otherwise.

56.18

    (1)   Attention is drawn to rule 47.16 which requires the solicitor to file a completed bill within 14 days after the end of the detailed assessment hearing. The court may dispense with the requirement to file a completed bill.

    (2)   After the detailed assessment hearing is concluded the court will –

        (a)   complete the court copy of the bill so as to show the amount allowed;

        (b)   determine the result of the cash account;

        (c)   award the costs of the detailed assessment hearing in accordance with Section 70(8) of the Solicitors Act 1974; and

(d) issue a final costs certificate showing the amount due following the detailed assessment hearing.

56.19 A final costs certificate will include an order to pay the sum it certifies unless the court orders otherwise.

Section 57 – Transitional Arrangements:

57.1 In this section 'the previous rules' means the Rules of the Supreme Court 1965 ('RSC') or County Court Rules 1981 ('CCR'), as appropriate.

GENERAL SCHEME OF TRANSITIONAL ARRANGEMENTS CONCERNING COSTS PROCEEDINGS

57.2

(1) Paragraph 18 of the practice direction which supplements Part 51 (Transitional Arrangements) provides that the CPR govern any assessments of costs which take place on or after 26 April 1999 and states a presumption to be applied in respect of costs for work undertaken before 26 April 1999.

(2) The following paragraphs provide five further transitional arrangements –

(a) to provide an additional presumption to be applied when assessing costs which were awarded by an order made in a county court before 26 April 1999 which allowed costs 'on Scale 1' to be determined in accordance with CCR Appendix A, or 'on the lower scale' to be determined in accordance with CCR Appendix C;

(b) to preserve the effect of CCR Appendix B Part III, paragraph 2;

(c) to clarify the approach to be taken where a bill of costs was provisionally taxed before 26 April 1999 and the receiving party is unwilling to accept the result of the provisional taxation;

(d) to preserve the right to carry in objections or apply for a reconsideration in all taxation proceedings commenced before 26 April 1999;

(e) to deal with funding arrangements made before 3 July 2000.

SCALE 1 OR LOWER SCALE COSTS

57.3 Where an order was made in county court proceedings before 26 April 1999 under which the costs were allowed on Scale 1 or the lower scale, the general presumption is that no costs will be allowed under that order which would not have been allowed in a taxation before 26 April 1999.

FIXED COSTS ON THE LOWER SCALE

57.4 The amount to be allowed as fixed costs for making or opposing an application for a rehearing to set aside a judgment given before 26 April 1999 where the costs are on lower scale is £11.25.

BILLS PROVISIONALLY TAXED BEFORE 26 APRIL 1999

57.5 In respect of bills of costs provisionally taxed before 26 April 1999 –

(1) The previous rules apply on the question who can request a hearing and the time limits for doing so; and

(2)   The CPR govern any subsequent hearing in that case.

BILLS TAXED BEFORE 26 APRIL 1999

57.6 Where a bill of costs was taxed before 26 April 1999, the previous rules govern the steps which can be taken to challenge that taxation.

OTHER TAXATION PROCEEDINGS

57.7

(1)   This paragraph applies to taxation proceedings which were commenced before 26 April 1999, were assigned for taxation to a taxing master or district judge, and which were still pending on 26 April 1999.

(2)   Any assessment of costs that takes place in cases to which this paragraph applies which is conducted on or after 26 April 1999, will be conducted in accordance with the CPR.

(3)   In addition to the possibility of appeal under rules 47.20 to 47.23 and Part 52 any party to a detailed assessment who is dissatisfied with any decision on a detailed assessment made by a costs judge or district judge may apply to that costs judge or district judge for a review of the decision. The review shall, for procedural purposes, be treated as if it were an appeal from an authorised court officer.

(4)   The right of review provided by paragraph (3) above, will not apply in cases in which, at least 28 days before the date of the assessment hearing, all parties were served with notice that the rights of appeal in respect of that hearing would be governed by Part 47 Section VIII (Appeals from Authorised Court Officers in Detailed Assessment Proceedings) and Part 52 (Appeals).

(5)   An order for the service of notice under sub-paragraph (4) above may be made on the application of any party to the detailed assessment proceedings or may be made by the court of its own initiative.

TRANSITIONAL PROVISIONS CONCERNING THE ACCESS TO JUSTICE ACT 1999 SECTIONS 28 TO 31

57.8

(1)   Sections 28 to 31 of the Access to Justice Act 1999, the Conditional Fee Agreements Regulations 2000, the Access to Justice (Membership Organisations) Regulations 2000 and the Access to Justice Act 1999 (Transitional Provisions) Order 2000 came into force on 1 April 2000. The Civil Procedure (Amendment No 3) Rules came into force on 3 July 2000 (The Conditional Fee Agreements Regulations 2000 were revoked by the Conditional Fee Agreements (Revocation) Regulations 2005 but continue to have effect in relation to conditional fee agreements entered into before 1 November 2005. The Access to Justice (Membership Organisation) Regulations 2000 were revoked by the Access to Justice (Membership Organisation) Regulations 2005 but continue to have effect in relation to arrangements entered into before 1 November 2005).

(2)   The Access to Justice Act 1999 (Transitional Provisions) Order 2000 provides that no conditional fee agreement or other arrangement about costs entered into before 1 April 2000 can be a funding arrangement, as defined in rule 43.2. The order also has the effect that where an conditional fee agreement or other funding arrangement has been entered into before 1

April 2000 and a second or subsequent funding arrangement of the same type is entered into on or after 1 April 2000, the second or subsequent funding arrangement does not give rise to a liability which is recoverable from a paying party.

(3) The Collective Conditional Fee Agreements Regulations 2000 came into force on 30 November 2000. The Regulations apply to agreements entered into between 30 November 2000 and 31 October 2005. Agreements entered into before 30 November 2000 are treated as if the Regulations had not come into force. The Regulations do not apply to collective conditional fee agreements entered into on or after 1 November 2005.

57.9

(1) Rule 39 of the Civil Procedure (Amendment No 3) Rules 2000 applies where between 1 April and 2 July 2000 (including both dates) –
 – a funding arrangement is entered into, and
 – proceedings are started in respect of a claim which is the subject of that agreement.

(2) Attention is drawn to the need to act promptly so as to comply with the requirements of the Rules and the practice directions by 31 July 2000 (ie within the 28 days from 3 July 2000 permitted by Rule 39) if that compliance is to be treated as compliance with the relevant provision. Attention is drawn in particular to Rule 44.15 (Providing Information about Funding Arrangements) and Section 19 of this practice direction.

(3) Nothing in the legislation referred to above makes provision for a party who has entered into a funding arrangement to recover from another party any amount of an additional liability which relates to anything done or any costs incurred before the arrangement was entered into.

Schedule of Costs Precedents

A: Model form of bill of costs (receiving party's solicitor and counsel on CFA terms)

B: Model form of bill of costs (detailed assessment of additional liability only)

C: Model form of bill of costs (payable by Defendant and the LSC)

D: Model form of bill of costs (alternative form, single column for amounts claimed, separate parts for costs payable by the LSC only)

E: Legal Aid/LSC Schedule of Costs

F: Certificates for inclusion in bill of costs

G: Points of dispute

H: Estimate of costs served on other parties

J: Solicitors Act 1974: Part 8 claim form under Part III of the Act

K: Solicitors Act 1974: order for delivery of bill

L: Solicitors Act 1974: order for detailed assessment (client)

M: Solicitors Act 1974: order for detailed assessment (solicitors)

P: Solicitors Act 1974: breakdown of costs

****

PART 70
GENERAL RULES ABOUT ENFORCEMENT OF JUDGMENTS AND ORDERS

70.1 Scope of this Part and interpretation

(1) This Part contains general rules about enforcement of judgments and orders.

> (Rules about specific methods of enforcement are contained in Parts 71 to 73, Schedule 1 RSC Orders 45 to 47 …and 52 and Schedule 2 CCR Orders 25 to 29)

(2) In this Part and in Parts 71 to 73 –

(a) 'judgment creditor' means a person who has obtained or is entitled to enforce a judgment or order;

(b) 'judgment debtor' means a person against whom a judgment or order was given or made;

(c) 'judgment or order' includes an award which the court has –
   (i) registered for enforcement;
   (ii) ordered to be enforced; or
   (iii) given permission to enforce
   as if it were a judgment or order of the court, and in relation to such an award, 'the court which made the judgment or order' means the court which registered the award or made such an order; and

(d) 'judgment or order for the payment of money' includes a judgment or order for the payment of costs, but does not include a judgment or order for the payment of money into court.

Amendments—Inserted by SI 2001/2792; amended by SI 2002/2058.

70.2 Methods of enforcing judgments or orders

(1) [Practice Direction 70] sets out methods of enforcing judgments or orders for the payment of money.

(2) A judgment creditor may, except where an enactment, rule or practice direction provides otherwise –

(a) use any method of enforcement which is available; and

(b) use more than one method of enforcement, either at the same time or one after another.

Amendments—Inserted by SI 2001/2792; SI 2009/3390.

70.3 Transfer of proceedings for enforcement

(1) A judgment creditor wishing to enforce a High Court judgment or order in a county court must apply to the High Court for an order transferring the proceedings to that county court.

(2) A practice direction may make provisions about the transfer of proceedings for enforcement.

> (CCR Order 25 rule 13 contains provisions about the transfer of county court proceedings to the High Court for enforcement)

Amendments—Inserted by SI 2001/2792.

70.4 Enforcement of judgment or order by or against non-party

If a judgment or order is given or made in favour of or against a person who is not a party to proceedings, it may be enforced by or against that person by the same methods as if he were a party.

Amendments—Inserted by SI 2001/2792.

70.5 Enforcement of decisions of bodies other than the High Court and county courts and compromises enforceable by enactment

(1) This rule applies, subject to paragraph (2), where an enactment provides that –

  (a) a decision of a court, tribunal, body or person other than the High Court or a county court; or
  (b) a compromise,

may be enforced as if it were a court order or that any sum of money payable under that decision or compromise may be recoverable as if payable under a court order.

(2) This rule does not apply to –

  (a) any judgment to which Part 74 applies;
  (b) arbitration awards;
  (c) any order to which RSC Order 115 applies; or
  (d) proceedings to which Part 75 (traffic enforcement) applies.

(2A) Unless paragraph (3) applies, a party may enforce the decision or compromise by applying for a specific method of enforcement under Parts 71 to 73, Schedule 1 RSC Orders 45 to 47 and 52 and Schedule 2 CCR Orders 25 to 29 and must –

  (a) file with the court a copy of the decision or compromise being enforced; and
  (b) provide the court with the information required by [Practice Direction 70].

(3) If an enactment provides that a decision or compromise is enforceable or a sum of money is recoverable if a court so orders, an application for such an order must be made in accordance with paragraphs (4) to (7A) of this rule.

(4) The application –

  (a) may, unless paragraph (4A) applies, be made without notice; and
  (b) must be made to the court for the district where the person against whom the order is sought, resides or carries on business, unless the court otherwise orders.

(4A) Where a compromise requires a person to whom a sum of money is payable under the compromise to do anything in addition to discontinuing or not starting proceedings ('a conditional compromise'), an application under paragraph (4) must be made on notice.

(5) The application notice must –

  (a) be in the form; and
  (b) contain the information

required by [Practice Direction 70].

(6) A copy of the decision or compromise must be filed with the application notice.

(7) An application other than in relation to a conditional compromise may be dealt with by a court officer without a hearing.

PART V

(7A) Where an application relates to a conditional compromise, the respondent may oppose it by filing a response within 14 days of service of the application notice and if the respondent –

(a) does not file a response within the time allowed, the court will make the order; or

(b) files a response within the time allowed, the court will make such order as appears appropriate.

(8) If an enactment provides that a decision or compromise may be enforced in the same manner as an order of the High Court if it is registered, any application to the High Court for registration must be made in accordance with [Practice Direction 70].

Amendments—Inserted by SI 2001/2792; amended by SI 2001/4015; SI 2002/2058; SI 2003/2113; substituted by SI 2008/3327; SI 2009/3390.

70.6 Effect of setting aside judgment or order

If a judgment or order is set aside, any enforcement of the judgment or order shall cease to have effect unless the court otherwise orders.

Amendments—Inserted by SI 2001/2792.

PART 71
ORDERS TO OBTAIN INFORMATION FROM JUDGMENT DEBTORS

71.1 Scope of this Part

This Part contains rules which provide for a judgment debtor to be required to attend court to provide information, for the purpose of enabling a judgment creditor to enforce a judgment or order against him.

Amendments—Inserted by SI 2001/2792.

71.2 Order to attend court

(1) A judgment creditor may apply for an order requiring –

(a) a judgment debtor; or

(b) if a judgment debtor is a company or other corporation, an officer of that body;

to attend court to provide information about –

(i) the judgment debtor's means; or

(ii) any other matter about which information is needed to enforce a judgment or order.

(2) An application under paragraph (1) –

(a) may be made without notice; and

(b) (i) must be issued in the court which made the judgment or order which it is sought to enforce, except that

(ii) if the proceedings have since been transferred to a different court, it must be issued in that court.

(3) The application notice must –

    (a)   be in the form; and

    (b)   contain the information

required by [Practice Direction 71].

(4) An application under paragraph (1) may be dealt with by a court officer without a hearing.

(5) If the application notice complies with paragraph (3), an order to attend court will be issued in the terms of paragraph (6).

(6) A person served with an order issued under this rule must –

    (a)   attend court at the time and place specified in the order;

    (b)   when he does so, produce at court documents in his control which are described in the order; and

    (c)   answer on oath such questions as the court may require.

(7) An order under this rule will contain a notice in the following terms –

    'You must obey this order. If you do not, you may be sent to prison for contempt of court.'

Amendments—Inserted by SI 2001/2792; SI 2009/3390.

71.3 Service of order

(1) An order to attend court must, unless the court otherwise orders, be served personally on the person ordered to attend court not less than 14 days before the hearing.

(2) If the order is to be served by the judgment creditor, he must inform the court not less than 7 days before the date of the hearing if he has been unable to serve it.

Amendments—Inserted by SI 2001/2792.

71.4 Travelling expenses

(1) A person ordered to attend court may, within 7 days of being served with the order, ask the judgment creditor to pay him a sum reasonably sufficient to cover his travelling expenses to and from court.

(2) The judgment creditor must pay such a sum if requested.

Amendments—Inserted by SI 2001/2792.

71.5 Judgment creditor's affidavit

(1) The judgment creditor must file an affidavit(GL) or affidavits –

    (a)   by the person who served the order (unless it was served by the court) giving details of how and when it was served;

    (b)   stating either that –

        (i)   the person ordered to attend court has not requested payment of his travelling expenses; or

        (ii)   the judgment creditor has paid a sum in accordance with such a request; and

(c)   stating how much of the judgment debt remains unpaid.

(2) The judgment creditor must either –

(a)   file the affidavit$^{(GL)}$ or affidavits not less than 2 days before the hearing; or

(b)   produce it or them at the hearing.

Amendments—Inserted by SI 2001/2792.

71.6 Conduct of the hearing

(1) The person ordered to attend court will be questioned on oath.

(2) The questioning will be carried out by a court officer unless the court has ordered that the hearing shall be before a judge.

(3) The judgment creditor or his representative –

(a)   may attend and ask questions where the questioning takes place before a court officer; and

(b)   must attend and conduct the questioning if the hearing is before a judge.

Amendments—Inserted by SI 2001/2792.

71.7 Adjournment of the hearing

If the hearing is adjourned, the court will give directions as to the manner in which notice of the new hearing is to be served on the judgment debtor.

Amendments—Inserted by SI 2001/2792.

71.8 Failure to comply with order

(1) If a person against whom an order has been made under rule 71.2 –

(a)   fails to attend court;

(b)   refuses at the hearing to take the oath or to answer any question; or

(c)   otherwise fails to comply with the order;

the court will refer the matter to a High Court judge or circuit judge.

(2) That judge may, subject to paragraphs (3) and (4), make a committal order against the person.

(3) A committal order for failing to attend court may not be made unless the judgment creditor has complied with rules 71.4 and 71.5.

(4) If a committal order is made, the judge will direct that –

(a)   the order shall be suspended provided that the person –

(i)   attends court at a time and place specified in the order; and

(ii)   complies with all the terms of that order and the original order; and

(b)   if the person fails to comply with any term on which the committal order is suspended, he shall be brought before a judge to consider whether the committal order should be discharged.

Amendments—Inserted by SI 2001/2792; amended by SI 2001/4015.

PART 72
THIRD PARTY DEBT ORDERS

72.1 Scope of this Part and interpretation

(1) This Part contains rules which provide for a judgment creditor to obtain an order for the payment to him of money which a third party who is within the jurisdiction owes to the judgment debtor.

(2) In this Part, 'bank or building society' includes any person carrying on a business in the course of which he lawfully accepts deposits in the United Kingdom.

Amendments—Inserted by SI 2001/2792; amended by SI 2001/4015.

72.2 Third party debt order

(1) Upon the application of a judgment creditor, the court may make an order (a 'final third party debt order') requiring a third party to pay to the judgment creditor –

  (a) the amount of any debt due or accruing due to the judgment debtor from the third party; or
  (b) so much of that debt as is sufficient to satisfy the judgment debt and the judgment creditor's costs of the application.

(2) The court will not make an order under paragraph 1 without first making an order (an 'interim third party debt order') as provided by rule 72.4(2).

(3) In deciding whether money standing to the credit of the judgment debtor in an account to which section 40 of the Senior Courts Act 1981 or section 108 of the County Courts Act 1984 relates may be made the subject of a third party debt order, any condition applying to the account that a receipt for money deposited in the account must be produced before any money is withdrawn will be disregarded.

> (Section 40(3) of the Senior Courts Act 1981 and section 108(3) of the County Courts Act 1984 contain a list of other conditions applying to accounts that will also be disregarded)

Amendments—Inserted by SI 2001/2792; Constitutional Reform Act 2005, s 59(5), Sch 11, Pt 1, para 1(2).

72.3 Application for third party debt order

(1) An application for a third party debt order –

  (a) may be made without notice; and
  (b) (i) must be issued in the court which made the judgment or order which it is sought to enforce; except that
       (ii) if the proceedings have since been transferred to a different court, it must be issued in that court.

(2) The application notice must –

  (a) (i) be in the form; and
       (ii) contain the information
       required by [Practice Direction 72]; and
  (b) be verified by a statement of truth.

Amendments—Inserted by SI 2001/2792; SI 2009/3390.

72.4 Interim third party debt order

(1) An application for a third party debt order will initially be dealt with by a judge without a hearing.

(2) The judge may make an interim third party debt order –

    (a)   fixing a hearing to consider whether to make a final third party debt order; and

    (b)   directing that until that hearing the third party must not make any payment which reduces the amount he owes the judgment debtor to less than the amount specified in the order.

(3) An interim third party debt order will specify the amount of money which the third party must retain, which will be the total of –

    (a)   the amount of money remaining due to the judgment creditor under the judgment or order; and

    (b)   an amount for the judgment creditor's fixed costs of the application, as specified in [Practice Direction 72].

(4) An interim third party debt order becomes binding on a third party when it is served on him.

(5) The date of the hearing to consider the application shall be not less than 28 days after the interim third party debt order is made.

Amendments—Inserted by SI 2001/2792; SI 2009/3390.

72.5 Service of interim order

(1) Copies of an interim third party debt order, the application notice and any documents filed in support of it must be served –

    (a)   on the third party, not less than 21 days before the date fixed for the hearing; and

    (b)   on the judgment debtor not less than –

        (i)   7 days after a copy has been served on the third party; and

        (ii) 7 days before the date fixed for the hearing.

(2) If the judgment creditor serves the order, he must either –

    (a)   file a certificate of service not less than 2 days before the hearing; or

    (b)   produce a certificate of service at the hearing.

Amendments—Inserted by SI 2001/2792.

72.6 Obligations of third parties served with interim order

(1) A bank or building society served with an interim third party debt order must carry out a search to identify all accounts held with it by the judgment debtor.

(2) The bank or building society must disclose to the court and the creditor within 7 days of being served with the order, in respect of each account held by the judgment debtor –

    (a)   the number of the account;

(b) whether the account is in credit; and

(c) if the account is in credit –

  (i)   whether the balance of the account is sufficient to cover the amount specified in the order;

  (ii) the amount of the balance at the date it was served with the order, if it is less than the amount specified in the order; and

  (iii) whether the bank or building society asserts any right to the money in the account, whether pursuant to a right of set-off or otherwise, and if so giving details of the grounds for that assertion.

(3) If –

(a) the judgment debtor does not hold an account with the bank or building society; or

(b) the bank or building society is unable to comply with the order for any other reason (for example, because it has more than one account holder whose details match the information contained in the order, and cannot identify which account the order applies to),

the bank or building society must inform the court and the judgment creditor of that fact within 7 days of being served with the order.

(4) Any third party other than a bank or building society served with an interim third party debt order must notify the court and the judgment creditor in writing within 7 days of being served with the order, if he claims –

(a) not to owe any money to the judgment debtor; or

(b) to owe less than the amount specified in the order.

Amendments—Inserted by SI 2001/2792; amended by SI 2001/4015.

72.7 Arrangements for debtors in hardship

(1) If –

(a) a judgment debtor is an individual;

(b) he is prevented from withdrawing money from his account with a bank or building society as a result of an interim third party debt order; and

(c) he or his family is suffering hardship in meeting ordinary living expenses as a result,

the court may, on an application by the judgment debtor, make an order permitting the bank or building society to make a payment or payments out of the account ('a hardship payment order').

(2) An application for a hardship payment order may be made –

(a) in High Court proceedings, at the Royal Courts of Justice or to any district registry; and

(b) in county court proceedings, to any county court.

(3) A judgment debtor may only apply to one court for a hardship payment order.

(4) An application notice seeking a hardship payment order must –

(a) include detailed evidence explaining why the judgment debtor needs a payment of the amount requested; and

(b) be verified by a statement of truth.

(5) Unless the court orders otherwise, the application notice –

(a) must be served on the judgment creditor at least 2 days before the hearing; but

(b) does not need to be served on the third party.

(6) A hardship payment order may –

(a) permit the third party to make one or more payments out of the account; and

(b) specify to whom the payments may be made.

Amendments—Inserted by SI 2001/2792.

72.8 Further consideration of the application

(1) If the judgment debtor or the third party objects to the court making a final third party debt order, he must file and serve written evidence stating the grounds for his objections.

(2) If the judgment debtor or the third party knows or believes that a person other than the judgment debtor has any claim to the money specified in the interim order, he must file and serve written evidence stating his knowledge of that matter.

(3) If –

(a) the third party has given notice under rule 72.6 that he does not owe any money to the judgment debtor, or that the amount which he owes is less than the amount specified in the interim order; and

(b) the judgment creditor wishes to dispute this,

the judgment creditor must file and serve written evidence setting out the grounds on which he disputes the third party's case.

(4) Written evidence under paragraphs (1), (2) or (3) must be filed and served on each other party as soon as possible, and in any event not less than 3 days before the hearing.

(5) If the court is notified that some person other than the judgment debtor may have a claim to the money specified in the interim order, it will serve on that person notice of the application and the hearing.

(6) At the hearing the court may –

(a) make a final third party debt order;

(b) discharge the interim third party debt order and dismiss the application;

(c) decide any issues in dispute between the parties, or between any of the parties and any other person who has a claim to the money specified in the interim order; or

(d) direct a trial of any such issues, and if necessary give directions.

Amendments—Inserted by SI 2001/2792.

72.9 Effect of final third party order

(1) A final third party debt order shall be enforceable as an order to pay money.

(2) If –

(a) the third party pays money to the judgment creditor in compliance with a third party debt order; or

(b) the order is enforced against him,

the third party shall, to the extent of the amount paid by him or realised by enforcement against him, be discharged from his debt to the judgment debtor.

(3) Paragraph (2) applies even if the third party debt order, or the original judgment or order against the judgment debtor, is later set aside.

Amendments—Inserted by SI 2001/2792.

72.10 Money in court

(1) If money is standing to the credit of the judgment debtor in court –

   (a)   the judgment creditor may not apply for a third party debt order in respect of that money; but

   (b)   he may apply for an order that the money in court, or so much of it as is sufficient to satisfy the judgment or order and the costs of the application, be paid to him.

(2) An application notice seeking an order under this rule must be served on –

   (a)   the judgment debtor; and

   (b)   the Accountant General at the Court Funds Office.

(3) If an application notice has been issued under this rule, the money in court must not be paid out until the application has been disposed of.

Amendments—Inserted by SI 2001/2792.

72.11 Costs

If the judgment creditor is awarded costs on an application for an order under rule 72.2 or 72.10 –

   (a)   he shall, unless the court otherwise directs, retain those costs out of the money recovered by him under the order; and

   (b)   the costs shall be deemed to be paid first out of the money he recovers, in priority to the judgment debt.

Amendments—Inserted by SI 2001/2792.

PART 73
CHARGING ORDERS, STOP ORDERS AND STOP NOTICES

73.1 Scope of this Part and interpretation

(1) This Part contains rules which provide for a judgment creditor to enforce a judgment by obtaining –

   (a)   a charging order (Section I);

   (b)   a stop order (Section II); or

   (c)   a stop notice (Section III),

over or against the judgment debtor's interest in an asset.

(2) In this Part –

   (a)   'the 1979 Act' means the Charging Orders Act 1979;

(b) 'the 1992 Regulations' means the Council Tax (Administration and Enforcement) Regulations 1992;

(c) 'funds in court' includes securities held in court;

(d) 'securities' means securities of any of the kinds specified in section 2(2)(b) of the 1979 Act.

Amendments—Inserted by SI 2001/2792.

Section I – Charging Orders

73.2 Scope of this Section

This Section applies to an application by a judgment creditor for a charging order under –

(a) section 1 of the 1979 Act; or

(b) regulation 50 of the 1992 Regulations.

Amendments—Inserted by SI 2001/2792.

73.3 Application for charging order

(1) An application for a charging order may be made without notice.

(2) An application for a charging order must be issued in the court which made the judgment or order which it is sought to enforce, unless –

(a) the proceedings have since been transferred to a different court, in which case the application must be issued in that court;

(b) the application is made under the 1992 Regulations, in which case it must be issued in the county court for the district in which the relevant dwelling (as defined in regulation 50(3)(b) of those Regulations) is situated;

(c) the application is for a charging order over an interest in a fund in court, in which case it must be issued in the court in which the claim relating to that fund is or was proceeding; or

(d) the application is to enforce a judgment or order of the High Court and it is required by section 1(2) of the 1979 Act to be made to a county court.

(3) Subject to paragraph (2), a judgment creditor may apply for a single charging order in respect of more than one judgment or order against the same debtor.

(4) The application notice must –

(a) (i)   be in the form; and
     (ii) contain the information,
     required by [Practice Direction 73]; and

(b) be verified by a statement of truth.

Amendments—Inserted by SI 2001/2792; SI 2009/3390.

73.4 Interim charging order

(1) An application for a charging order will initially be dealt with by a judge without a hearing.

(2) The judge may make an order (an 'interim charging order') –

(a)   imposing a charge over the judgment debtor's interest in the asset to which the application relates; and

(b)   fixing a hearing to consider whether to make a final charging order as provided by rule 73.8(2)(a).

Amendments—Inserted by SI 2001/2792.

73.5 Service of interim order

(1) Copies of the interim charging order, the application notice and any documents filed in support of it must, not less than 21 days before the hearing, be served on the following persons –

(a)   the judgment debtor;

(b)   such other creditors as the court directs;

(c)   if the order relates to an interest under a trust, on such of the trustees as the court directs;

(d)   if the interest charged is in securities other than securities held in court, then –

    (i)   in the case of stock for which the Bank of England keeps the register, the Bank of England;

    (ii)   in the case of government stock to which (i) does not apply, the keeper of the register;

    (iii)   in the case of stock of any body incorporated within England and Wales, that body;

    (iv)   in the case of stock of any body incorporated outside England and Wales or of any state or territory outside the United Kingdom, which is registered in a register kept in England and Wales, the keeper of that register;

    (v)   in the case of units of any unit trust in respect of which a register of the unit holders is kept in England and Wales, the keeper of that register; and

(e)   if the interest charged is in funds in court, the Accountant General at the Court Funds Office.

(2) If the judgment creditor serves the order, he must either –

(a)   file a certificate of service not less than 2 days before the hearing; or

(b)   produce a certificate of service at the hearing.

Amendments—Inserted by SI 2001/2792.

73.6 Effect of interim order in relation to securities

(1) If a judgment debtor disposes of his interest in any securities, while they are subject to an interim charging order which has been served on him, that disposition shall not, so long as that order remains in force, be valid as against the judgment creditor.

(2) A person served under rule 73.5(1)(d) with an interim charging order relating to securities must not, unless the court gives permission –

(a)   permit any transfer of any of the securities; or

(b)   pay any dividend, interest or redemption payment relating to them.

(3) If a person acts in breach of paragraph (2), he will be liable to pay to the judgment creditor –

    (a)   the value of the securities transferred or the amount of the payment made (as the case may be); or

    (b)   if less, the amount necessary to satisfy the debt in relation to which the interim charging order was made.

Amendments—Inserted by SI 2001/2792.

73.7 Effect of interim order in relation to funds in court

If a judgment debtor disposes of his interest in funds in court while they are subject to an interim charging order which has been served on him and on the Accountant General in accordance with rule 73.5(1), that disposition shall not, so long as that order remains in force, be valid as against the judgment creditor.

Amendments—Inserted by SI 2001/2792.

73.8 Further consideration of the application

(1) If any person objects to the court making a final charging order, he must –

    (a)   file; and

    (b)   serve on the applicant,

written evidence stating the grounds of his objections, not less than 7 days before the hearing.

(2) At the hearing the court may –

    (a)   make a final charging order confirming that the charge imposed by the interim charging order shall continue, with or without modification;

    (b)   discharge the interim charging order and dismiss the application;

    (c)   decide any issues in dispute between the parties, or between any of the parties and any other person who objects to the court making a final charging order; or

    (d)   direct a trial of any such issues, and if necessary give directions.

(3) If the court makes a final charging order which charges securities other than securities held in court, the order will include a stop notice unless the court otherwise orders.

    (Section III of this Part contains provisions about stop notices)

(4) Any order made at the hearing must be served on all the persons on whom the interim charging order was required to be served.

Amendments—Inserted by SI 2001/2792.

73.9 Discharge or variation of order

(1) Any application to discharge or vary a charging order must be made to the court which made the charging order.

    (Section 3(5) of the 1979 Act and regulation 51(4) of the 1992 Regulations provide that the court may at any time, on the application of the debtor, or of any person interested in any property to which the order relates, or (where the 1992 Regulations apply) of the authority, make an order discharging or varying the charging order)

(2) The court may direct that –

(a) any interested person should be joined as a party to such an application; or
(b) the application should be served on any such person.

(3) An order discharging or varying a charging order must be served on all the persons on whom the charging order was required to be served.

Amendments—Inserted by SI 2001/2792.

73.10 Enforcement of charging order by sale

(1) Subject to the provisions of any enactment, the court may, upon a claim by a person who has obtained a charging order over an interest in property, order the sale of the property to enforce the charging order.

(2) A claim for an order for sale under this rule should be made to the court which made the charging order, unless that court does not have jurisdiction to make an order for sale.

(A claim under this rule is a proceeding for the enforcement of a charge, and section 23(c) of the County Courts Act 1984 provides the extent of the county court's jurisdiction to hear and determine such proceedings)

(3) The claimant must use the Part 8 procedure.

(4) A copy of the charging order must be filed with the claim form.

(5) The claimant's written evidence must include the information required by [Practice Direction 73].

Amendments—Inserted by SI 2001/2792; SI 2009/3390.

Section II – Stop Orders

73.11 Interpretation

In this Section, 'stop order' means an order of the High Court not to take, in relation to funds in court or securities specified in the order, any of the steps listed in section 5(5) of the 1979 Act.

Amendments—Inserted by SI 2001/2792.

73.12 Application for stop order

(1) The High Court may make –

(a) a stop order relating to funds in court, on the application of any person –
 (i) who has a mortgage or charge on the interest of any person in the funds; or
 (ii) to whom that interest has been assigned; or
 (iii) who is a judgment creditor of the person entitled to that interest; or

PART V

(h)   a stop order relating to securities other than securities held in court, on the application of any person claiming to be beneficially entitled to an interest in the securities.

(2) An application for a stop order must be made –

(a)   by application notice in existing proceedings; or
(b)   by Part 8 claim form if there are no existing proceedings in the High Court.

(3) The application notice or claim form must be served on –

(a)   every person whose interest may be affected by the order applied for; and
(b)   either –
   (i)   the Accountant General at the Court Funds Office, if the application relates to funds in court; or
   (ii)   the person specified in rule 73.5(1)(d), if the application relates to securities other than securities held in court.

Amendments—Inserted by SI 2001/2792.

73.13 Stop order relating to funds in court

A stop order relating to funds in court shall prohibit the transfer, sale, delivery out, payment or other dealing with –

(a)   the funds or any part of them; or
(b)   any income on the funds.

Amendments—Inserted by SI 2001/2792.

73.14 Stop order relating to securities

(1) A stop order relating to securities other than securities held in court may prohibit all or any of the following steps –

(a)   the registration of any transfer of the securities;
(b)   the making of any payment by way of dividend, interest or otherwise in respect of the securities; and
(c)   in the case of units of a unit trust, any acquisition of or other dealing with the units by any person or body exercising functions under the trust.

(2) The order shall specify –

(a)   the securities to which it relates;
(b)   the name in which the securities stand;
(c)   the steps which may not be taken; and
(d)   whether the prohibition applies to the securities only or to the dividends or interest as well.

Amendments—Inserted by SI 2001/2792.

73.15 Variation or discharge of order

(1) The court may, on the application of any person claiming to have a beneficial interest in the funds or securities to which a stop order relates, make an order discharging or varying the order.

(2) An application notice seeking the variation or discharge of a stop order must be served on the person who obtained the order.

Amendments—Inserted by SI 2001/2792.

Section III – Stop Notices

73.16 General

In this Section –

(a) 'stop notice' means a notice issued by the court which requires a person or body not to take, in relation to securities specified in the notice, any of the steps listed in section 5(5) of the 1979 Act, without first giving notice to the person who obtained the notice; and

(b) 'securities' does not include securities held in court.

Amendments—Inserted by SI 2001/2792.

73.17 Request for stop notice

(1) The High Court may, on the request of any person claiming to be beneficially entitled to an interest in securities, issue a stop notice.

> (A stop notice may also be included in a final charging order, by either the High Court or a county court, under rule 73.8(3))

(2) A request for a stop notice must be made by filing –

(a) a draft stop notice; and

(b) written evidence which –

(i) identifies the securities in question;

(ii) describes the applicant's interest in the securities; and

(iii) gives an address for service for the applicant.

> (A sample form of stop notice is annexed to [Practice Direction 73])

(3) If a court officer considers that the request complies with paragraph (2), he will issue a stop notice.

(4) The applicant must serve copies of the stop notice and his written evidence on the person to whom the stop notice is addressed.

Amendments—Inserted by SI 2001/2792; SI 2009/3390.

73.18 Effect of stop notice

(1) A stop notice –

(a) takes effect when it is served in accordance with rule 73.17(4); and

(b) remains in force unless it is withdrawn or discharged in accordance with rule 73.20 or 73.21.

(2) While a stop notice is in force, the person on whom it is served –

(a) must not –

(i) register a transfer of the securities described in the notice; or

(ii) take any other step restrained by the notice,

PART V

without first giving 14 days' notice to the person who obtained the stop notice; but

(b)   must not, by reason only of the notice, refuse to register a transfer or to take any other step, after he has given 14 days' notice under paragraph (2)(a) and that period has expired.

Amendments—Inserted by SI 2001/2792.

73.19 Amendment of stop notice

(1) If any securities are incorrectly described in a stop notice which has been obtained and served in accordance with rule 73.17, the applicant may request an amended stop notice in accordance with that rule.

(2) The amended stop notice takes effect when it is served.

Amendments—Inserted by SI 2001/2792.

73.20 Withdrawal of stop notice

(1) A person who has obtained a stop notice may withdraw it by serving a request for its withdrawal on –

(a)   the person or body on whom the stop notice was served; and
(b)   the court which issued the stop notice.

(2) The request must be signed by the person who obtained the stop notice, and his signature must be witnessed by a practising solicitor.

Amendments—Inserted by SI 2001/2792.

73.21 Discharge or variation of stop notice

(1) The court may, on the application of any person claiming to be beneficially entitled to an interest in the securities to which a stop notice relates, make an order discharging or varying the notice.

(2) An application to discharge or vary a stop notice must be made to the court which issued the notice.

(3) The application notice must be served on the person who obtained the stop notice.

Amendments—Inserted by SI 2001/2792.

73.22 [Practice Direction 73] makes provision for the procedure to be followed when applying for an order under section 23 of the Partnership Act 1890.

Amendments—Inserted by SI 2006/1689; SI 2009/3390.

****

SCHEDULE 1

RSC ORDER 45
ENFORCEMENT OF JUDGMENTS AND ORDERS: GENERAL

1A Interpretation

In this Order, and in RSC Orders 46 and 47 –

    (a)   'enforcement officer' means an individual who is authorised to act as an enforcement officer under the Courts Act 2003; and

    (b)   'relevant enforcement officer' means –

        (i)   in relation to a writ of execution which is directed to an single enforcement officer, that officer;

        (ii)   in relation to a writ of execution which is directed to two or more enforcement officers, the officer to whom the writ is allocated.

Amendments—Inserted by SI 2003/3361.

1 Enforcement of judgment, etc, for payment of money

(1)–(3) …

(4) In this Order references to any writ shall be construed as including references to any further writ in aid of the first mentioned writ.

Amendments—SI 2001/2792.

2 Notice of seizure

When first executing a writ of *fieri facias*, the Sheriff or his officer or the relevant enforcement officer shall deliver to the debtor or leave at each place where execution is levied a notice in Form No 55 in [Practice Direction 4] informing the debtor of the execution.

Amendments—SI 2003/3361; SI 2009/3390.

3 Enforcement of judgment for possession of land

(1) Subject to the provisions of these rules, a judgment or order for the giving of possession of land may be enforced by one or more of the following means, that is to say –

    (a)   writ of possession;

    (b)   in a case in which rule 5 applies, an order of committal;

    (c)   in such a case, writ of sequestration.

(2) A writ of possession to enforce a judgment or order for the giving of possession of any land shall not be issued without the permission of the court except where the judgment or order was given or made in proceedings by a mortgagee or mortgagor or by any person having the right to foreclose or redeem any mortgage, being proceedings in which there is a claim for –

    (a)   payment of moneys secured by the mortgage;

PART V

(b) sale of the mortgaged property;

(c) foreclosure;

(d) delivery of possession (whether before or after foreclosure or without foreclosure) to the mortgagee by the mortgagor or by any other person who is alleged to be in possession of the property;

(e) redemption;

(f) reconveyance of the land or its release from the security; or

(g) delivery of possession by the mortgagee.

(2A) In paragraph (2) 'mortgage' includes a legal or equitable mortgage and a legal or equitable charge, and reference to a mortgagor, a mortgagee and mortgaged land is to be interpreted accordingly.

(3) Such permission as is referred to in paragraph (2) shall not be granted unless it is shown –

(a) that every person in actual possession of the whole or any part of the land has received such notice of the proceedings as appears to the court sufficient to enable him to apply to the court for any relief to which he may be entitled; and

(b) if the operation of the judgment or order is suspended by subsection (2) of section 16 of the Landlord and Tenant Act 1954, that the applicant has not received notice in writing from the tenant that he desires that the provisions of paragraphs (a) and (b) of that subsection shall have effect.

(4) A writ of possession may include provision for enforcing the payment of any money adjudged or ordered to be paid by the judgment or order which is to be enforced by the writ.

Amendments—SI 2001/256.

4 Enforcement of judgment for delivery of goods

(1) Subject to the provisions of these rules, a judgment or order for the delivery of any goods which does not give a person against whom the judgment is given or order made the alternative of paying the assessed value of the goods may be enforced by one or more of the following means, that is to say –

(a) writ of delivery to recover the goods without alternative provision for recovery of the assessed value thereof (hereafter in this rule referred to as a 'writ of specific delivery');

(b) in a case in which rule 5 applies, an order of committal;

(c) in such a case, writ of sequestration.

(2) Subject to the provisions of these rules, a judgment or order for the delivery of any goods or payment of their assessed value may be enforced by one or more of the following means, that is to say –

(a) writ of delivery to recover the goods or their assessed value;

(b) by order of the court, writ of specific delivery;

(c) in a case in which rule 5 applies, writ of sequestration.

An application for an order under sub-paragraph (b) shall be made in accordance with CPR Part 23, which must be served on the defendant against whom the judgment or order sought to be enforced was given or made.

(3) A writ of specific delivery, and a writ of delivery to recover any goods or their assessed value, may include provision for enforcing the payment of any money adjudged or ordered to be paid by the judgment or order which is to be enforced by the writ.

(4) A judgment or order for the payment of the assessed value of any goods may be enforced by the same means as any other judgment or order for the payment of money.

5 Enforcement of judgment to do or abstain from doing any act

(1) Where –

- (a) a person required by a judgment or order to do an act within a time specified in the judgment or order refuses or neglects to do it within that time or, as the case may be, within that time as extended or abridged under a court order or CPR rule 2.11; or
- (b) a person disobeys a judgment or order requiring him to abstain from doing an act,

then, subject to the provisions of these rules, the judgment or order may be enforced by one or more of the following means, that is to say –

- (i) with the permission of the court, a writ of sequestration against the property of that person;
- (ii) where that person is a body corporate, with the permission of the court, a writ of sequestration against the property of any director or other officer of the body;
- (iii) subject to the provisions of the Debtors Act 1869 and 1878, an order of committal against that person or, where that person is a body corporate, against any such officer.

(2) Where a judgment or order requires a person to do an act within a time therein specified and an order is subsequently made under rule 6 requiring the act to be done within some other time, references in paragraph (1) of this rule to a judgment or order shall be construed as references to the order made under rule 6.

(3) Where under any judgment or order requiring the delivery of any goods the person liable to execution has the alternative of paying the assessed value of the goods, the judgment or order shall not be enforceable by order of committal under paragraph (1), but the court may, on the application of the person entitled to enforce the judgment or order, make an order requiring the first mentioned person to deliver the goods to the applicant within a time specified in the order, and that order may be so enforced.

6 Judgment, etc requiring act to be done: order fixing time for doing it

(1) Notwithstanding that a judgment or order requiring a person to do an act specifies a time within which the act is to be done, the court shall, have power to make an order requiring the act to be done within another time, being such time after service of that order, or such other time, as may be specified therein.

(2) Where a judgment or order requiring a person to do an act does not specify a time within which the act is to be done, the court shall have power subsequently to make an order requiring the act to be done within such time after service of that order, or such other time, as may be specified therein.

PART V

(3) An application for an order under this rule must be made in accordance with CPR Part 23 and the application notice must, be served on the person required to do the act in question.

7 Service of copy of judgment, etc, prerequisite to enforcement under rule 5

(1) In this rule references to an order shall be construed as including references to a judgment.

(2) Subject to paragraphs (6) and (7) of this rule, an order shall not be enforced under rule 5 unless –

(a) a copy of the order has been served personally on the person required to do or abstain from doing the act in question; and

(b) in the case of an order requiring a person to do an act, the copy has been so served before the expiration of the time within which he was required to do the act.

(3) Subject as aforesaid, an order requiring a body corporate to do or abstain from doing an act shall not be enforced as mentioned in rule 5(1)(b)(ii) or (iii) unless –

(a) a copy of the order has also been served personally on the officer against whose property permission is sought to issue a writ of sequestration or against whom an order of committal is sought; and

(b) in the case of an order requiring the body corporate to do an act, the copy has been so served before the expiration of the time within which the body was required to do the act.

(4) There must be prominently displayed on the front of the copy of an order served under this rule a warning to the person on whom the copy is served that disobedience to the order would be a contempt of court punishable by imprisonment, or (in the case of an order requiring a body corporate to do or abstain from doing an act) punishable by sequestration of the assets of the body corporate and by imprisonment of any individual responsible.

(5) With the copy of an order required to be served under this rule, being an order requiring a person to do an act, there must also be served a copy of any order or agreement under CPR rule 2.11 extending or abridging the time for doing the act and, where the first-mentioned order was made under rule 5(3) or 6 of this Order, a copy of the previous order requiring the act to be done.

(6) An order requiring a person to abstain from doing an act may be enforced under rule 5 notwithstanding that service of a copy of the order has not been effected in accordance with this rule if the court is satisfied that pending such service, the person against whom or against whose property is sought to enforce the order has had notice thereof either –

(a) by being present when the order was made; or

(b) by being notified of the terms of the order, whether by telephone, telegram or otherwise.

(7) The court may dispense with service of a copy of an order under this rule if it thinks it just to do so.

8 Court may order act to be done at expense of disobedient party

If ...a mandatory order, an injunction or a judgment or order for the specific performance of a contract is not complied with, then, without prejudice to its powers under section 39 of the Act and its powers to punish the disobedient party for contempt, the court may direct that the act required to be done may, so far as practicable, be done by the party by whom the order or judgment was obtained or some other person appointed by the court, at the cost of the disobedient party, and upon the act being done the expenses incurred may be ascertained in such manner as the court may direct and execution may issue against the disobedient party for the amount so ascertained and for costs.

Amendments—SI 2003/3361.

11 Matters occurring after judgment: stay of execution, etc

Without prejudice to Order 47, rule 1, a party against whom a judgment has been given or an order made may apply to the court for a stay of execution of the judgment or order or other relief on the ground of matters which have occurred since the date of the judgment or order, and the court may by order grant such relief, and on such terms, as it thinks just.

12 Forms of writs

(1) A writ of *fieri facias* must be in such of the Forms Nos 53 to 63 in [Practice Direction 4] as is appropriate in the particular case.

(2) A writ of delivery must be in Form No 64 or 65 in [Practice Direction 4], whichever is appropriate.

(3) A writ of possession must be in Form No 66 or 66A in [Practice Direction 4], whichever is appropriate.

(4) A writ of sequestration must be in Form No 67 in [Practice Direction 4].

Amendment—SI 2009/3390.

RSC ORDER 46
WRITS OF EXECUTION: GENERAL

1 Definition

In this Order, unless the context otherwise requires, 'writ of execution' includes a writ of *fieri facias*, a writ of possession, a writ of delivery, a writ of sequestration and any further writ in aid of any of the aforementioned writs.

2 When permission to issue any writ of execution is necessary

(1) A writ of execution to enforce a judgment or order may not issue without the permission of the court in the following cases, that is to say –

    (a) where 6 years or more have elapsed since the date of the judgment or order;

PART V

   (b)   where any change has taken place, whether by death or otherwise, in the parties entitled or liable to execution under the judgment or order;

   (c)   where the judgment or order is against the assets of a deceased person coming to the hands of his executors or administrators after the date of the judgment or order, and it is sought to issue execution against such assets;

   (d)   where under the judgment or order any person is entitled to a remedy subject to the fulfilment of any condition which it is alleged has been fulfilled;

   (e)   where any goods sought to be seized under a writ of execution are in the hands of a receiver appointed by the court or a sequestrator.

(2) Paragraph (1) is without prejudice to section 2 of the Reserve and Auxiliary Forces (Protection of Civil Interests) Act 1951, or any other enactment or rule by virtue of which a person is required to obtain the permission of the court for the issue of a writ of execution or to proceed to execution on or otherwise to the enforcement of a judgment or order.

(3) Where the court grants permission, whether under this rule or otherwise, for the issue of a writ of execution and the writ is not issued within one year after the date of the order granting such permission, the order shall cease to have effect, without prejudice, however, to the making of a fresh order.

3 Permission required for issue of writ in aid of other writ

A writ of execution in aid of any other writ of execution shall not issue without the permission of the court.

4 Application for permission to issue writ

(1) An application for permission to issue a writ of execution may be made in accordance with CPR Part 23 but the application notice need not be served on the respondent unless the court directs.

(2) Such an application must be supported by a witness statement or affidavit –

   (a)   identifying the judgment or order to which the application relates and, if the judgment or order is for the payment of money, stating the amount originally due thereunder and the amount due thereunder at the date the application notice is filed;

   (b)   stating, where the case falls within rule 2(1)(a), the reasons for the delay in enforcing the judgment or order;

   (c)   stating where the case falls within rule 2(1)(b), the change which has taken place in the parties entitled or liable to execution since the date of the judgment or order;

   (d)   stating, where the case falls within rule 2(1)(c) or (d), that a demand to satisfy the judgment or order was made on the person liable to satisfy it and that he has refused or failed to do so;

   (e)   giving such other information as is necessary to satisfy the court that the applicant is entitled to proceed to execution on the judgment or order in question and that the person against whom it is sought to issue execution is liable to execution on it.

(3) The court hearing such application may grant permission in accordance with the application or may order that any issue or question, a decision on which is necessary to determine the rights of the parties, be tried in any manner in which any question

of fact or law arising in proceedings may be tried and, in either case, may impose such terms as to costs or otherwise as it thinks just.

5 Application for permission to issue writ of sequestration

(1) Notwithstanding anything in rules 2 and 4, an application for permission to issue a writ of sequestration must be made in accordance with CPR Part 23 and be heard by a judge.

(2) Subject to paragraph (3), the application notice, stating the grounds of the application and accompanied by a copy of the witness statement or affidavit in support of the application, must be served personally on the person against whose property it is sought to issue the writ.

(3) The court may dispense with service of the application notice under this rule if it thinks it just to do so.

(4) The judge hearing an application for permission to issue a writ of sequestration may sit in private in any case in which, if the application were for an order of committal, he would be entitled to do so by virtue of Order 52, rule 6 but, except in such a case, the application shall be heard in public.

6 Issue of writ of execution

(1) Issue of a writ of execution takes place on its being sealed by a court officer of the appropriate office.

(2) Before such a writ is issued, a praecipe for its issue must be filed.

(3) The praecipe must be signed by or on behalf of the solicitor of the person entitled to execution or, if that person is acting in person, by him.

(4) No such writ shall be sealed unless at the time of the tender thereof for sealing –

    (a) the person tendering it produces –
        (i) the judgment or order on which the writ is to issue, or an office copy thereof;
        (ii) where the writ may not issue without the permission of the court, the order granting such permission or evidence of the granting of it;
        (iii) where judgment on failure to acknowledge service has been entered against a State, as defined in section 14 of the State Immunity Act 1978, evidence that the State has been served in accordance with CPR rule 40.10 and that the judgment has taken effect; and
    (b) the court officer authorised to seal it is satisfied that the period, if any, specified in the judgment or order for the payment of any money or the doing of any other act thereunder has expired.

(5) Every writ of execution shall bear the date of the day on which it is issued.

(6) In this rule 'the appropriate office' means –

    (a) where the proceedings in which execution is to issue are in a district registry, that registry;
    (b) where the proceedings are in the Principal Registry of the Family Division, that registry;
    (c) where the proceedings are Admiralty proceedings or commercial proceedings which are not in a district registry, the Admiralty and Commercial Registry;

PART V

(ca) where the proceedings are in the Chancery Division, Chancery Chambers;

(d)   in any other case, the Central Office of the Senior Courts.

Amendment—SI 2009/2092.

8 Duration and renewal of writ of execution

(1) For the purpose of execution, a writ of execution is valid in the first instance for 12 months beginning with the date of its issue.

(2) Where a writ has not been wholly executed the court may by order extend the validity of the writ from time to time for a period of 12 months at any one time beginning with the day on which the order is made, if an application for extension is made to the court before the day next following that on which the writ would otherwise expire or such later day, if any, as the court may allow.

(3) Before a writ the validity of which had been extended under paragraph (2) is executed either the writ must be sealed with the seal of the office out of which it was issued showing the date on which the order extending its validity was made or the applicant for the order must serve a notice (in Form No 71 in [Practice Direction 4]) sealed as aforesaid, on the sheriff to whom the writ is directed or the relevant enforcement officer informing him of the making of the order and the date thereof.

(4) The priority of a writ, the validity of which has been extended under this rule, shall be determined by reference to the date on which it was originally delivered to the sheriff or relevant enforcement officer.

(5) The production of a writ of execution, or of such a notice as is mentioned in paragraph (3) purporting in either case to be sealed as mentioned in that paragraph, shall be evidence that the validity of that writ, or, as the case may be, of the writ referred to in that notice, has been extended under paragraph (2).

(6) If, during the validity of a writ of execution, an interpleader summons is issued in relation to an execution under that writ, the validity of the writ shall be extended until the expiry of 12 months from the conclusion of the interpleader proceedings.

Amendments—SI 2003/3361; SI 2009/3390.

9 Return to writ of execution

(1) Any party at whose instance or against whom a writ of execution was issued may serve a notice on the sheriff to whom the writ was directed or the relevant enforcement officer requiring him, within such time as may be specified in the notice, to indorse on the writ a statement of the manner in which he has executed it and to send to that party a copy of the statement.

(2) If a sheriff or enforcement officer on whom such a notice is served fails to comply with it the party by whom it was served may apply to the court for an order directing the sheriff or enforcement officer to comply with the notice.

Amendments—SI 2003/3361.

RSC ORDER 47
WRITS OF FIERI FACIAS

1 Power to stay execution by writ of *fieri facias*

(1) Where a judgment is given or an order made for the payment by any person of money, and the court is satisfied, on an application made at the time of the judgment or order, or at any time thereafter, by the judgment debtor or other party liable to execution –

(a) that there are special circumstances which render it inexpedient to enforce the judgment or order; or

(b) that the applicant is unable from any cause to pay the money,

then, notwithstanding anything in rule 2 or 3, the court may by order stay the execution of the judgment or order by writ of *fieri facias* either absolutely or for such period and subject to such conditions as the court thinks fit.

(2) An application under this rule, if not made at the time the judgment is given or order made, must be made in accordance with CPR Part 23 and may be so made notwithstanding that the party liable to execution did not acknowledge service of the claim form or serve a defence or take any previous part in the proceedings.

(3) The grounds on which an application under this rule is made must be set out in the application notice and be supported by a witness statement or affidavit made by or on behalf of the applicant substantiating the said grounds and, in particular, where such application is made on the grounds of the applicant's inability to pay, disclosing his income, the nature and value of any property of his and the amount of any other liabilities of his.

(4) The application notice and a copy of the supporting witness statement or affidavit must, not less than 4 clear days before the hearing, be served on the party entitled to enforce the judgment or order.

(5) An order staying execution under this rule may be varied or revoked by a subsequent order.

3 Separate writs to enforce payment of costs, etc

(1) Where only the payment of money, together with costs to be assessed in accordance with CPR Part 47 (detailed costs assessment), is adjudged or ordered, then, if when the money becomes payable under the judgment or order the costs have not been assessed, the party entitled to enforce that judgment or order may issue a writ of *fieri facias* to enforce payment of the sum (other than for costs) adjudged or ordered and, not less than 8 days after the issue of that writ, he may issue a second writ to enforce payment of the assessed costs.

(2) A party entitled to enforce a judgment or order for the delivery of possession of any property (other than money) may, if he so elects, issue a separate writ of *fieri facias* to enforce payment of any damages or costs awarded to him by that judgment or order.

4 No expenses of execution in certain cases

Where a judgment or order is for less than £600 and does not entitle the claimant to costs against the person against whom the writ of *fieri facias* to enforce the judgment or order is issued, the writ may not authorise the sheriff or enforcement officer to whom it is directed to levy any fees, poundage or other costs of execution.

Amendments—SI 2003/3361.

5 Writ of *fieri facias* de bonis ecclesiasticis, etc

(1) Where it appears upon the return of any writ of *fieri facias* that the person against whom the writ was issued has no goods or chattels in the county of the sheriffs to whom the writ was directed or the district of the relevant enforcement officer but that he is the incumbent of a benefice named in the return, then, after the writ and return have been filed, the party by whom the writ of *fieri facias* was issued may issue a writ of *fieri facias* de bonis ecclesiasticis or a writ of sequestrari de bonis ecclesiasticis directed to the bishop of the diocese within which that benefice is.

(2) Any such writ must be delivered to the bishop to be executed by him.

(3) Only such fees for the execution of any such writ shall be taken by or allowed to the bishop or any diocesan officer as are for the time being authorised by or under any enactment, including any measure of the General Synod.

Amendments—SI 2003/3361.

6 Order for sale otherwise than by auction

(1) An order of the court under paragraph 10 of Schedule 7 to the Courts Act 2003 that a sale of goods seized under an execution may be made otherwise than by public auction may be made on the application of –

    (a)   the person at whose instance the writ of execution under which the sale is to be made was issued;

    (b)   the person against whom that writ was issued (in this rule referred to as 'the judgment debtor');

    (c)   if the writ was directed to a sheriff, that sheriff; and

    (d)   if the writ was directed to one or more enforcement officers, the relevant enforcement officer.

(2) Such an application must be made in accordance with CPR Part 23 and the application notice must contain a short statement of the grounds of the application.

(3) Where the applicant for an order under this rule is not the sheriff or enforcement officer, the sheriff or enforcement officer must, on the demand of the applicant, send to the applicant a list stating –

    (a)   whether he has notice of the issue of another writ or writs of execution against the goods of the judgment debtor; and

    (b)   so far as is known to him, the name and address of every creditor who has obtained the issue of another such writ of execution,

and where the sheriff or enforcement officer is the applicant, he must prepare such a list.

(4) Not less than 4 clear days before the hearing the applicant must serve the application notice on each of the other persons by whom the application might have been made and on every person named in the list under paragraph (3).

(5) Service of the application notice on a person named in the list under paragraph (3) is notice to him for the purpose of paragraph 10(3) of Schedule 7 to the Courts Act 2003.

> (Paragraph 10(3) provides that if the person who seized the goods has notice of another execution or other executions, the court must not consider an application for leave to sell privately until the notice prescribed by Civil Procedure Rules has been given to the other execution creditor or creditors)

(6) The applicant must produce the list under paragraph (3) to the court on the hearing of the application.

(7) Every person on whom the application notice was served may attend and be heard on the hearing of the application.

Amendments—SI 2003/3361.

Family Procedure (Adoption) Rules 2005, SI 2005/2795

ARRANGEMENT OF RULES

Section 2
Service Out of the Jurisdiction

Rule		Page
42	Scope and definitions	1005
43	Service of documents	1006
44	Method of service – general provisions	1006
45	Service through foreign governments, judicial authorities and British Consular authorities	1006
46	Procedure where service is to be through foreign governments, judicial authorities and British Consular authorities	1007
47	Service in accordance with the Service Regulation	1008
48	Undertaking to be responsible for expenses of the Foreign and Commonwealth Office	1008
	PRACTICE DIRECTION – SERVICE OUT OF THE JURISDICTION	1009

****

Section 2

Service Out of the Jurisdiction

42 Scope and definitions

(1) This Section contains rules about –

    (*a*)   service out of the jurisdiction; and

    (*b*)   the procedure for serving out of the jurisdiction.

      (Rule 6 defines 'jurisdiction'.)

PART V

(2) In this Section –

'application form' includes application notice; and

'the Hague Convention' means the Convention on the service abroad of judicial and extra-judicial documents in civil or commercial matters signed at the Hague on November 15, 1965.

43 Service of documents

(1) Any document to be served for the purposes of these Rules may be served out of the jurisdiction without the permission of the court.

(2) Subject to paragraph (4) or (5), any document served out of the jurisdiction in a country in which English is not the official language must be accompanied by a translation of the document –

(a) in the official language of the country in which the document is to be served; or

(b) if there is more than one official language of the country, in any one of those languages which is appropriate to the place in that country in which the document is to be served.

(3) Every translation filed under this rule must be signed by the translator to certify that the translation is accurate.

(4) Any document served out of the jurisdiction in a country in which English is not the official language need not be accompanied by a translation of the document where –

(a) the person on whom the document is to be served is able to read and understand English; and

(b) service of the document is to be effected directly on that person.

(5) Paragraphs (2) and (3) do not apply where service is to be effected in accordance with the Service Regulation.

44 Method of service – general provisions

(1) Where an application form is to be served out of the jurisdiction, it may be served by any method –

(a) permitted by the law of the country in which it is to be served; or

(b) provided for by –

    (i) rule 45 (service through foreign governments, judicial authorities and British Consular authorities); or

    (ii) rule 47 (service in accordance with the Service Regulation).

(2) Nothing in this rule or in any court order will authorise or require any person to do anything in the country where the application form is to be served which is against the law of that country.

45 Service through foreign governments, judicial authorities and British Consular authorities

(1) Where an application form is to be served on a respondent in any country which is a party to the Hague Convention, the application form may be served –

    (*a*)   through the authority designated under the Hague Convention in respect of that country; or

    (*b*)   if the law of that country permits –

        (i)   through the judicial authorities of that country; or

        (ii)   through a British Consular authority in that country.

(2) Where an application form is to be served on a respondent in any country which is not a party to the Hague Convention, the application form may be served, if the law of that country so permits –

    (*a*)   through the government of that country, where that government is willing to serve it; or

    (*b*)   through a British Consular authority in that country.

(3) Paragraph (2) does not apply where the application form is to be served in –

    (*a*)   Scotland, Northern Ireland, the Isle of Man or the Channel Islands;

    (*b*)   any Commonwealth State; or

    (*c*)   any United Kingdom Overseas Territory listed in the relevant practice direction.

(4) This rule does not apply where service is to be effected in accordance with the Service Regulation.

46 Procedure where service is to be through foreign governments, judicial authorities and British Consular authorities

(1) This rule applies where the applicant wishes to serve the application form through –

    (*a*)   the judicial authorities of the country where the application form is to be served;

    (*b*)   a British Consular authority in that country;

    (*c*)   the authority designated under the Hague Convention in respect of that country; or

    (*d*)   the government of that country.

(2) Where this rule applies, the applicant must file –

    (*a*)   a request for service of the application form by the method in paragraph (1) that he has chosen;

    (*b*)   a copy of the application form;

    (*c*)   any translation required under rule 43; and

    (*d*)   any other documents, copies of documents or translations required by the relevant practice direction.

(3) When the applicant files the documents specified in paragraph (2), a court officer will –

    (*a*)   seal, or otherwise authenticate with the stamp of the court, the copy of the application form; and

    (*b*)   forward the documents to the Senior Master of the Queen's Bench Division.

(4) The Senior Master will send documents forwarded under this rule –

    (*a*)   where the application form is being served through the authority designated under the Hague Convention, to that authority; or

    (*b*)   in any other case, to the Foreign and Commonwealth Office with a request

PART V

that it arranges for the application to be served by the method indicated in the request for service filed under paragraph (2) or, where that request indicates alternative methods, by the most convenient method.

(5) An official certificate will be evidence of the facts stated in the certificate if it –

(*a*) states that the application form has been served in accordance with this rule either personally, or in accordance with the law of the country in which service was effected;

(*b*) specifies the date on which the application form was served; and

(*c*) is made by –

   (i) a British Consular authority in the country where the application form was served;

   (ii) the government or judicial authorities in that country; or

   (iii) any other authority designated in respect of that country under the Hague Convention.

(6) A document purporting to be an official certificate under paragraph (5) will be treated as such a certificate, unless it is proved not to be.

(7) This rule does not apply where service is to be effected in accordance with the Service Regulation.

47 Service in accordance with the Service Regulation

(1) This rule applies where an application form is to be served in accordance with the Service Regulation.

(2) The applicant must file the application form and any translations or other documents required by the Service Regulation.

(3) When the applicant files the documents referred to in paragraph (2), a court officer will –

(*a*) seal, or otherwise authenticate with the stamp of the court, the copy of the application form; and

(*b*) forward the documents to the Senior Master of the Queen's Bench Division.

(The Service Regulation is annexed to the relevant practice direction.)

48 Undertaking to be responsible for expenses of the Foreign and Commonwealth Office

Every request for service filed under rule 46 (service through foreign governments, judicial authorities etc) must contain an undertaking by the person making the request –

(*a*) to be responsible for all expenses incurred by the Foreign and Commonwealth Office or foreign judicial authority; and

(*b*) to pay those expenses to the Foreign and Commonwealth Office or foreign judicial authority on being informed of the amount.

****

Practice Direction – Service out of the Jurisdiction

This Practice Direction supplements Part 6, Section 2 of the Family Procedure (Adoption) Rules 2005

Service in other Member States of the European Union

1.1 Where service is to be effected in another Member of State of the European Union, Council Regulation (EC) No. 1348/2000 of 29 May 2000 on the service in the Member States of judicial and extrajudicial documents in civil or commercial matters ('the Service Regulation') applies.

1.2 The Service Regulation is annexed to this Practice Direction.

(Article 20(1) of the Service Regulation provides that the Regulation prevails over other provisions contained in bilateral or multilateral agreements or arrangements concluded by the Member of States and in particular Article IV of the protocol to the Brussels Convention of 1968 and the Hague Convention of 15 November 1965)

Originally published in the official languages of the European Community in the Official Journal of the European Communities by the Office for Official Publications of the European Communities

Documents to be filed under rule 46(2)(d)

2.1 A duplicate of the application form and of any translation required by rule 43 must be provided for each party to be served out of the jurisdiction.

2.2 The documents to be served in certain countries require legalisation and the Foreign Process Section (Room E02), Royal Courts of Justice will advise on request. Some countries require legalisation and some require a formal letter of request.

Service in Scotland, Northern Ireland, the Channel Islands, the Isle of Man, Commonwealth countries and United Kingdom Overseas Territories.

3.1 Where rule 45(3) applies, service should be effected by the applicant or his agent direct except in the case of a Commonwealth State where the judicial authorities have required service to be in accordance with rule 44(1)(b)(i). These are presently Malta and Singapore.

3.2 For the purposes of rule 45(3)(c), the following countries are United Kingdom Overseas Territories:

- (a) Anguilla;
- (b) Bermuda;
- (c) British Antarctic Territory;
- (d) British Indian Ocean Territory;
- (e) Cayman Islands;
- (f) Falkland Islands;
- (g) Gibraltar;
- (h) Montserrat;

PART V

(*i*)   Pitcairn, Henderson, Ducie and Oeno;
(*j*)   St. Helena and Dependencies;
(*k*)   South Georgia and the South Sandwich Islands;
(*l*)   Sovereign Base Areas of Akrotiri and Dhekelia;
(*m*) Turks and Caicos Islands; and
(*n*)   Virgin Islands.

Service of application notices and orders

4.1 The provisions of Section 2 of Part 6 (special provisions about service out of the jurisdiction) also apply to service out of the jurisdiction of an application notice or order.

4.2 Where an application notice is to be served out of the jurisdiction in accordance with Section 2 of Part 6 the court must have regard to the country in which the application notice is to be served in setting the date for the hearing of the application and giving any direction about service of the respondent's evidence.

Period for responding to an application

5 Where a Part 10 application needs to be served out of the jurisdiction, the period for responding to service is 7 days less than the number of days listed in the Table.

TABLE

Place or country	number of days
Abu Dhabi	22
Afghanistan	23
Albania	25
Algeria	22
Angola	22
Anguilla	31
Antigua	23
Antilles (Netherlands)	31
Argentina	22
Armenia	21
Ascension	31
Australia	25
Austria	21
Azores	23
Bahamas	22
Bahrain	22
Balearic Islands	21
Bangladesh	23
Barbados	23
Belarus	21
Belgium	21

Place or country	number of days
Belize	23
Benin	25
Bermuda	31
Bhutan	28
Bolivia	23
Bosnia-Hercegovina	21
Botswana	23
Brazil	22
Brunei	25
Bulgaria	23
Burkina Faso	23
Burma	23
Burundi	22
Cameroon	22
Canada	22
Canary Islands	22
Cape Verde Islands	25
Caroline Islands	31
Cayman Islands	31
Central African Republic	25
Chad	25
Chile	22
China	24
Christmas Island	27
Cocos (Keeling) Islands	41
Colombia	22
Comoros	23
Congo (People's Republic)	25
Corsica	21
Costa Rica	23
Croatia	21
Cuba	24
Cyprus	31
Cyrenaica (see Libya)	21
Czech Republic	21
Denmark	21
Djibouti	22
Dominica	23
Dominican Republic	23
Dubai	22
Ecuador	22

PART V

Place or country	number of days
Egypt (Arab Republic)	22
El Salvador (Republic of)	25
Equatorial Guinea	23
Estonia	21
Ethiopia	22
Falkland Islands and Dependencies	31
Faroe Islands	31
Fiji	23
Finland	24
France	21
French Guiana	31
French Polynesia	31
French West Indies	31
Gabon	25
Gambia	22
Georgia	21
Germany	21
Ghana	22
Gibraltar	31
Greece	21
Greenland	31
Grenada	24
Guatemala	24
Guernsey	18
Guyana	22
Haiti	23
Holland (Netherlands)	21
Honduras	24
Hong Kong	31
Hungary	22
Iceland	22
India	23
Indonesia	22
Iran	22
Iraq	22
Ireland (Republic of)	21
Ireland (Northern)	21
Isle of Man	18
Israel	22
Italy	21
Ivory Coast	22

Place or country	number of days
Jamaica	22
Japan	23
Jersey	18
Jordan	23
Kampuchea	38
Kazakhstan	21
Kenya	22
Kirgizstan	21
Korea (North)	28
Korea (South)	24
Kuwait	22
Laos	30
Latvia	21
Lebanon	22
Lesotho	23
Liberia	22
Libya	21
Liechtenstein	21
Lithuania	21
Luxembourg	21
Macau	31
Macedonia	21
Madagascar	23
Madeira	31
Malawi	23
Malaya	24
Maldive Islands	26
Mali	25
Malta	21
Mariana Islands	26
Marshall Islands	32
Mauritania	23
Mauritius	22
Mexico	23
Moldova	21
Monaco	21
Montserrat	31
Morocco	22
Mozambique	23
Nauru Island	36
Nepal	23

PART V

Place or country	number of days
Netherlands	21
Nevis	24
New Caledonia	31
New Hebrides (now Vanuatu)	29
New Zealand	26
New Zealand Island Territories	50
Nicaragua	24
Niger (Republic of)	25
Nigeria	22
Norfolk Island	31
Norway	21
Oman (Sultanate of)	22
Pakistan	23
Panama (Republic of)	26
Papua New Guinea	26
Paraguay	22
Peru	22
Philippines	23
Pitcairn Island	31
Poland	21
Portugal	21
Portuguese Timor	31
Puerto Rico	23
Qatar	23
Reunion	31
Romania	22
Russia	21
Rwanda	23
Sabah	23
St. Helena	31
St. Kitts–Nevis	24
St. Lucia	24
St. Pierre and Miquelon	31
St. Vincent and the Grenadines	24
Samoa (U.S.A. Territory) (See also Western Samoa)	30
Sarawak	28
Saudi Arabia	24
Scotland	21
Senegal	22
Seychelles	22
Sharjah	24

Place or country	number of days
Sierra Leone	22
Singapore	22
Slovakia	21
Slovenia	21
Society Islands (French Polynesia)	31
Solomon Islands	29
Somali Democratic Republic	22
South Africa (Republic of)	22
South Georgia (Falkland Island Dependencies)	31
South Orkneys	21
South Shetlands	21
Spain	21
Spanish Territories of North Africa	31
Sri Lanka	23
Sudan	22
Suriname	22
Swaziland	22
Sweden	21
Switzerland	21
Syria	23
Taiwan	23
Tajikistan	21
Tanzania	22
Thailand	23
Tibet	34
Tobago	23
Togo	22
Tonga	30
Tortola	31
Trinidad & Tobago	23
Tristan Da Cunha	31
Tunisia	22
Turkey	21
Turkmenistan	21
Turks & Caicos Islands	31
Uganda	22
Ukraine	21
United States of America	22
Uruguay	22
Uzbekistan	21
Vanuatu	29

PART V

Place or country	number of days
Vatican City State	21
Venezuela	22
Vietnam	28
Virgin Islands – British (Tortola)	31
Virgin Islands – U.S.A	24
Wake Island	25
Western Samoa	34
Yemen (Republic of)	30
Yugoslavia (except for Bosnia-Hercegovina Croatia Macedonia and Slovenia)	21
Zaire	25
Zambia	23
Zimbabwe	22

Further information

6 Further information concerning service out of the jurisdiction can be obtained from the Foreign Process Section, Room E02, Royal Courts of Justice, Strand, London WC2A 2LL (telephone 020 7947 6691).

Annex

Council regulation (EC) No 1348/2000 of 29 May 2000 on the service in the Member States of judicial and extrajudicial documents in civil or commercial matters

THE COUNCIL OF THE EUROPEAN UNION,

Having regard to the Treaty establishing the European Community, and in particular Article 61(c) and Article 67(1) thereof,

Having regard to the proposal from the Commission,

Having regard to the opinion of the European Parliament,

Having regard to the opinion of the Economic and Social Committee,

Whereas:

(1) The Union has set itself the objective of maintaining and developing the Union as an area of freedom, security and justice, in which the free movement of persons is assured. To establish such an area, the Community is to adopt, among others, the measures relating to judicial cooperation in civil matters needed for the proper functioning of the internal market.

(2) The proper functioning of the internal market entails the need to improve and expedite the transmission of judicial and extrajudicial documents in civil or commercial matters for service between the Member States.

(3) This is a subject now falling within the ambit of Article 65 of the Treaty.

(4) In accordance with the principles of subsidiarity and proportionality as set out in Article 5 of the Treaty, the objectives of this Regulation cannot be sufficiently

achieved by the Member States and can therefore be better achieved by the Community. This Regulation does not go beyond what is necessary to achieve those objectives.

(5) The Council, by an Act dated 26 May 1997, drew up a Convention on the service in the Member States of the European Union of judicial and extrajudicial documents in civil or commercial matters and recommended it for adoption by the Member States in accordance with their respective constitutional rules. That Convention has not entered into force. Continuity in the results of the negotiations for conclusion of the Convention should be ensured. The main content of this Regulation is substantially taken over from it.

(6) Efficiency and speed in judicial procedures in civil matters means that the transmission of judicial and extrajudicial documents is to be made direct and by rapid means between local bodies designated by the Member States. However, the Member States may indicate their intention of designating only one transmitting or receiving agency or one agency to perform both functions for a period of five years. This designation may, however, be renewed every five years.

(7) Speed in transmission warrants the use of all appropriate means, provided that certain conditions as to the legibility and reliability of the document received are observed. Security in transmission requires that the document to be transmitted be accompanied by a pre-printed form, to be completed in the language of the place where service is to be effected, or in another language accepted by the Member State in question.

(8) To secure the effectiveness of this Regulation, the possibility of refusing service of documents is confined to exceptional situations.

(9) Speed of transmission warrants documents being served within days of reception of the document. However, if service has not been effected after one month has elapsed, the receiving agency should inform the transmitting agency. The expiry of this period should not imply that the request be returned to the transmitting agency where it is clear that service is feasible within a reasonable period.

(10) For the protection of the addressee's interests, service should be effected in the official language or one of the official languages of the place where it is to be effected or in another language of the originating Member State which the addressee understands.

(11) Given the differences between the Member States as regards their rules of procedure, the material date for the purposes of service varies from one Member State to another. Having regard to such situations and the possible difficulties that may arise, this Regulation should provide for a system where it is the law of the receiving Member State which determines the date of service. However, if the relevant documents in the context of proceedings to be brought or pending in the Member State of origin are to be served within a specified period, the date to be taken into consideration with respect to the applicant shall be that determined according to the law of the Member State of origin. A Member State is, however, authorised to derogate from the aforementioned provisions for a transitional period of five years, for appropriate reasons. Such a derogation may be renewed by a Member State at five-year intervals due to reasons related to its legal system.

(12) This Regulation prevails over the provisions contained in bilateral or multilateral agreements or arrangements having the same scope, concluded by the Member States, and in particular the Protocol annexed to the Brussels Convention of 27 September 1968 and the Hague Convention of 15 November 1965 in relations between the Member States party thereto. This Regulation does not preclude

Member States from maintaining or concluding agreements or arrangements to expedite or simplify the transmission of documents, provided that they are compatible with the Regulation.

(13) The information transmitted pursuant to this Regulation should enjoy suitable protection. This matter falls within the scope of Directive 95/46/EC of the European Parliament and of the Council of 24 October 1995 on the protection of individuals with regard to the processing of personal data and on the free movement of such data, and of Directive 97/66/EC of the European Parliament and of the Council of 15 December 1997 concerning the processing of personal data and the protection of privacy in the telecommunications sector.

(14) The measures necessary for the implementation of this Regulation should be adopted in accordance with Council Decision 1999/468/EC of 28 June 1999 laying down the procedures for the exercise of implementing powers conferred on the Commission.

(15) These measures also include drawing up and updating the manual using appropriate modern means.

(16) No later than three years after the date of entry into force of this Regulation, the Commission should review its application and propose such amendments as may appear necessary.

(17) The United Kingdom and Ireland, in accordance with Article 3 of the Protocol on the position of the United Kingdom and Ireland annexed to the Treaty on European Union and the Treaty establishing the European Community, have given notice of their wish to take part in the adoption and application of this Regulation.

(18) Denmark, in accordance with Articles 1 and 2 of the Protocol on the position of Denmark annexed to the Treaty on European Union and the Treaty establishing the European Community, is not participating in the adoption of this Regulation, and is therefore not bound by it nor subject to its application,

HAS ADOPTED THIS REGULATION:

CHAPTER I
GENERAL PROVISIONS

Article 1
Scope

1 This Regulation shall apply in civil and commercial matters where a judicial or extrajudicial document has to be transmitted from one Member State to another for service there.

2 This Regulation shall not apply where the address of the person to be served with the document is not known.

Article 2
Transmitting and receiving agencies

1 Each Member State shall designate the public officers, authorities or other persons, hereinafter referred to as 'transmitting agencies', competent for the transmission of judicial or extrajudicial documents to be served in another Member State.

2 Each Member State shall designate the public officers, authorities or other persons, hereinafter referred to as 'receiving agencies', competent for the receipt of judicial or extrajudicial documents from another Member State.

3 A Member State may designate one transmitting agency and one receiving agency or one agency to perform both functions. A federal State, a State in which several legal systems apply or a State with autonomous territorial units shall be free to designate more than one such agency. The designation shall have effect for a period of five years and may be renewed at five-year intervals.

4 Each Member State shall provide the Commission with the following information:

  (a) the names and addresses of the receiving agencies referred to in paragraphs 2 and 3;
  (b) the geographical areas in which they have jurisdiction;
  (c) the means of receipt of documents available to them; and
  (d) the languages that may be used for the completion of the standard form in the Annex.

Member States shall notify the Commission of any subsequent modification of such information.

Article 3
Central body

Each Member State shall designate a central body responsible for:

  (a) supplying information to the transmitting agencies;
  (b) seeking solutions to any difficulties which may arise during transmission of documents for service;
  (c) forwarding, in exceptional cases, at the request of a transmitting agency, a request for service to the competent receiving agency.

A federal State, a State in which several legal systems apply or a State with autonomous territorial units shall be free to designate more than one central body.

CHAPTER II
JUDICIAL DOCUMENTS

Section 1
Transmission and service of judicial documents

Article 4
Transmission of documents

1 Judicial documents shall be transmitted directly and as soon as possible between the agencies designated on the basis of Article 2.

2 The transmission of documents, requests, confirmations, receipts, certificates and any other papers between transmitting agencies and receiving agencies may be carried out by any appropriate means, provided that the content of the document received is true and faithful to that of the document forwarded and that all information in it is easily legible.

3 The document to be transmitted shall be accompanied by a request drawn up using the standard form in the Annex. The form shall be completed in the official language of the Member State addressed or, if there are several official languages in that Member State, the official language or one of the official languages of the place where service is to be effected, or in another language which that Member State has indicated it can accept. Each Member State shall indicate the official language or languages of the European Union other than its own which is or are acceptable to it for completion of the form.

4 The documents and all papers that are transmitted shall be exempted from legalisation or any equivalent formality.

5 When the transmitting agency wishes a copy of the document to be returned together with the certificate referred to in Article 10, it shall send the document in duplicate.

Article 5
Translation of documents

1 The applicant shall be advised by the transmitting agency to which he or she forwards the document for transmission that the addressee may refuse to accept it if it is not in one of the languages provided for in Article 8.

2 The applicant shall bear any costs of translation prior to the transmission of the document, without prejudice to any possible subsequent decision by the court or competent authority on liability for such costs.

Article 6
Receipt of documents by receiving agency

1 On receipt of a document, a receiving agency shall, as soon as possible and in any event within seven days of receipt, send a receipt to the transmitting agency by the swiftest possible means of transmission using the standard form in the Annex.

2 Where the request for service cannot be fulfilled on the basis of the information or documents transmitted, the receiving agency shall contact the transmitting agency by the swiftest possible means in order to secure the missing information or documents.

3 If the request for service is manifestly outside the scope of this Regulation or if non-compliance with the formal conditions required makes service impossible, the request and the documents transmitted shall be returned, on receipt, to the transmitting agency, together with the notice of return in the standard form in the Annex.

4 A receiving agency receiving a document for service but not having territorial jurisdiction to serve it shall forward it, as well as the request, to the receiving agency having territorial jurisdiction in the same Member State if the request complies with the conditions laid down in Article 4(3) and shall inform the transmitting agency accordingly, using the standard form in the Annex. That receiving agency shall inform the transmitting agency when it receives the document, in the manner provided for in paragraph 1.

Article 7
Service of documents

1 The receiving agency shall itself serve the document or have it served, either in accordance with the law of the Member State addressed or by a particular form requested by the transmitting agency, unless such a method is incompatible with the law of that Member State.

2 All steps required for service of the document shall be effected as soon as possible. In any event, if it has not been possible to effect service within one month of receipt, the receiving agency shall inform the transmitting agency by means of the certificate in the standard form in the Annex, which shall be drawn up under the conditions referred to in Article 10(2). The period shall be calculated in accordance with the law of the Member State addressed.

Article 8
Refusal to accept a document

1 The receiving agency shall inform the addressee that he or she may refuse to accept the document to be served if it is in a language other than either of the following languages:

(a) the official language of the Member State addressed or, if there are several official languages in that Member State, the official language or one of the official languages of the place where service is to be effected; or

(b) a language of the Member State of transmission which the addressee understands.

2 Where the receiving agency is informed that the addressee refuses to accept the document in accordance with paragraph 1, it shall immediately inform the transmitting agency by means of the certificate provided for in Article 10 and return the request and the documents of which a translation is requested.

Article 9
Date of service

1 Without prejudice to Article 8, the date of service of a document pursuant to Article 7 shall be the date on which it is served in accordance with the law of the Member State addressed.

2 However, where a document shall be served within a particular period in the context of proceedings to be brought or pending in the Member State of origin, the date to be taken into account with respect to the applicant shall be that fixed by the law of that Member State.

3 A Member State shall be authorised to derogate from the provisions of paragraphs 1 and 2 for a transitional period of five years, for appropriate reasons. This transitional period may be renewed by a Member State at five-yearly intervals due to reasons related to its legal system. That Member State shall inform the Commission of the content of such a derogation and the circumstances of the case.

Article 10
Certificate of service and copy of the document served

1 When the formalities concerning the service of the document have been completed, a certificate of completion of those formalities shall be drawn up in the standard form in the Annex and addressed to the transmitting agency, together with, where Article 4(5) applies, a copy of the document served.

2 The certificate shall be completed in the official language or one of the official languages of the Member State of origin or in another language which the Member State of origin has indicated that it can accept. Each Member State shall indicate the official language or languages of the European Union other than its own which is or are acceptable to it for completion of the form.

Article 11
Costs of service

1 The service of judicial documents coming from a Member State shall not give rise to any payment or reimbursement of taxes or costs for services rendered by the Member State addressed.

2 The applicant shall pay or reimburse the costs occasioned by:

   (a) the employment of a judicial officer or of a person competent under the law of the Member State addressed;
   (b) the use of a particular method of service.

Section 2
Other means of transmission and service of judicial documents

Article 12
Transmission by consular or diplomatic channels

Each Member State shall be free, in exceptional circumstances, to use consular or diplomatic channels to forward judicial documents, for the purpose of service, to those agencies of another Member State which are designated pursuant to Article 2 or 3.

Article 13
Service by diplomatic or consular agents

1 Each Member State shall be free to effect service of judicial documents on persons residing in another Member State, without application of any compulsion, directly through its diplomatic or consular agents.

2 Any Member State may make it known, in accordance with Article 23(1), that it is opposed to such service within its territory, unless the documents are to be served on nationals of the Member State in which the documents originate.

Article 14
Service by post

1 Each Member State shall be free to effect service of judicial documents directly by post to persons residing in another Member State.

2 Any Member State may specify, in accordance with Article 23(1), the conditions under which it will accept service of judicial documents by post.

Article 15
Direct service

1 This Regulation shall not interfere with the freedom of any person interested in a judicial proceeding to effect service of judicial documents directly through the judicial officers, officials or other competent persons of the Member State addressed.

2 Any Member State may make it known, in accordance with Article 23(1), that it is opposed to the service of judicial documents in its territory pursuant to paragraph 1.

CHAPTER III
EXTRAJUDICIAL DOCUMENTS

Article 16
Transmission

Extrajudicial documents may be transmitted for service in another Member State in accordance with the provisions of this Regulation.

CHAPTER IV
FINAL PROVISIONS

Article 17
Implementing rules

The measures necessary for the implementation of this Regulation relating to the matters referred to below shall be adopted in accordance with the advisory procedure referred to in Article 18(2):

   (a)   drawing up and annually updating a manual containing the information provided by Member States in accordance with Article 2(4);

   (b)   drawing up a glossary in the official languages of the European Union of documents which may be served under this Regulation;

   (c)   updating or making technical amendments to the standard form set out in the Annex.

Article 18
Committee

1 The Commission shall be assisted by a committee.

2 Where reference is made to this paragraph, Articles 3 and 7 of Decision 1999/468/EC shall apply.

3 The Committee shall adopt its rules of procedure.

PART V

Article 19
Defendant not entering an appearance

1 Where a writ of summons or an equivalent document has had to be transmitted to another Member State for the purpose of service, under the provisions of this Regulation, and the defendant has not appeared, judgment shall not be given until it is established that:

(a) the document was served by a method prescribed by the internal law of the Member State addressed for the service of documents in domestic actions upon persons who are within its territory; or

(b) the document was actually delivered to the defendant or to his residence by another method provided for by this Regulation;

and that in either of these cases the service or the delivery was effected in sufficient time to enable the defendant to defend.

2 Each Member State shall be free to make it known, in accordance with Article 23(1), that the judge, notwithstanding the provisions of paragraph 1, may give judgment even if no certificate of service or delivery has been received, if all the following conditions are fulfilled:

(a) the document was transmitted by one of the methods provided for in this Regulation;

(b) a period of time of not less than six months, considered adequate by the judge in the particular case, has elapsed since the date of the transmission of the document;

(c) no certificate of any kind has been received, even though every reasonable effort has been made to obtain it through the competent authorities or bodies of the Member State addressed.

3 Notwithstanding paragraphs 1 and 2, the judge may order, in case of urgency, any provisional or protective measures.

4 When a writ of summons or an equivalent document has had to be transmitted to another Member State for the purpose of service, under the provisions of this Regulation, and a judgment has been entered against a defendant who has not appeared, the judge shall have the power to relieve the defendant from the effects of the expiration of the time for appeal from the judgment if the following conditions are fulfilled:

(a) the defendant, without any fault on his part, did not have knowledge of the document in sufficient time to defend, or knowledge of the judgment in sufficient time to appeal; and

(b) the defendant has disclosed a prima facie defence to the action on the merits.

An application for relief may be filed only within a reasonable time after the defendant has knowledge of the judgment.

Each Member State may make it known, in accordance with Article 23(1), that such application will not be entertained if it is filed after the expiration of a time to be stated by it in that communication, but which shall in no case be less than one year following the date of the judgment.

5 Paragraph 4 shall not apply to judgments concerning status or capacity of persons.

Article 20
Relationship with agreements or arrangements to which Member States are Parties

1 This Regulation shall, in relation to matters to which it applies, prevail over other provisions contained in bilateral or multilateral agreements or arrangements concluded by the Member States, and in particular Article IV of the Protocol to the Brussels Convention of 1968 and the Hague Convention of 15 November 1965.

2 This Regulation shall not preclude individual Member States from maintaining or concluding agreements or arrangements to expedite further or simplify the transmission of documents, provided that they are compatible with this Regulation.

3 Member States shall send to the Commission:

    (a) a copy of the agreements or arrangements referred to in paragraph 2 concluded between the Member States as well as drafts of such agreements or arrangements which they intend to adopt; and

    (b) any denunciation of, or amendments to, these agreements or arrangements.

Article 21
Legal aid

This Regulation shall not affect the application of Article 23 of the Convention on Civil Procedure of 17 July 1905, Article 24 of the Convention on Civil Procedure of 1 March 1954 or Article 13 of the Convention on International Access to Justice of 25 October 1980 between the Member States Parties to these Conventions.

Article 22
Protection of information transmitted

1 Information, including in particular personal data, transmitted under this Regulation shall be used by the receiving agency only for the purpose for which it was transmitted.

2 Receiving agencies shall ensure the confidentiality of such information, in accordance with their national law.

3 Paragraphs 1 and 2 shall not affect national laws enabling data subjects to be informed of the use made of information transmitted under this Regulation.

4 This Regulation shall be without prejudice to Directives 95/46/EC and 97/66/EC.

Article 23
Communication and publication

1 Member States shall communicate to the Commission the information referred to in Articles 2, 3, 4, 9, 10, 13, 14, 15, 17(a) and 19.

2 The Commission shall publish in the Official Journal of the European Communities the information referred to in paragraph 1.

Article 24
Review

No later than 1 June 2004, and every five years thereafter, the Commission shall present to the European Parliament, the Council and the Economic and Social Committee a report on the application of this Regulation, paying special attention to the effectiveness of the bodies designated pursuant to Article 2 and to the practical application of point (c) of Article 3 and Article 9. The report shall be accompanied if need be by proposals for adaptations of this Regulation in line with the evolution of notification systems.

Article 25
Entry into force

This Regulation shall enter into force on 31 May 2001.

This Regulation shall be binding in its entirety and directly applicable in the Member States in accordance with the Treaty establishing the European Community.

Done at Brussels, 29 May 2000.

For the Council

The President

A. Costa

Guidance in cases involving protected parties in which the Official Solicitor is being invited to act as guardian ad litem or litigation friend

Public and private law children's cases

1 Many practitioners and judges will know of the Official Solicitor's recent difficulties in accepting requests to act as guardian ad litem / litigation friend for protected parties in proceedings relating to children. Although, currently, there are unallocated cases, the backlog has reduced significantly in recent months.

2 The Official Solicitor is subject to severe budgetary constraints – a situation which is unlikely to ameliorate in the medium term.

3 In all cases, the Official Solicitor will need to be satisfied of the following criteria before accepting a case, and parties may need reminding of the need to provide confirmation of these matters immediately on approaching the Official Solicitor's office:

- satisfactory evidence or a finding by the court that the party lacks capacity to conduct the proceedings and is therefore a protected party;
- confirmation that there is security for the costs of legal representation;
- there is no other person who is suitable and willing to act as guardian ad litem/litigation friend.

4 In order to assist the Official Solicitor in the decisions he makes about allocating case workers, in certain cases, judges should consider whether it may be appropriate to indicate with as much particularity as possible the relative urgency of the

proceedings and the likely effect upon the child (and family) of delay. The Official Solicitor will very carefully consider giving priority to such cases.

5 It is and remains the judge's duty in children's cases, so far as he is able, to eradicate delay.

Court of Protection welfare cases (including medical cases)

6 The number of welfare cases brought under the provisions of the Mental Capacity Act 2005 is rising exponentially with concomitant resource implications for the Official Solicitor.

7 Judges should be alert to the problems the Official Solicitor may have in attending at each and every preliminary hearing. Consideration should be given, in appropriate cases, to dispensing with the requirement that he should be present at a time when he is unable to contribute meaningfully to the process. In circumstances where his position has been / will be communicated in writing it may be particularly appropriate for the judge to indicate that the Official Solicitor's attendance at the next directions' hearing is unnecessary.

8 The Court of Protection Rules make clear that the judge is under a duty to restrict expert evidence to that which is reasonably required to resolve the proceedings. The explanatory note to r 121 states that the court will consider what 'added value' expert evidence will give to the case. Unnecessary expert assessments must be avoided. It will be rare indeed for the court to sanction the instruction of more than one expert to advise in relation to the same issue.

9 The Practice Direction – Experts (PD15A) specifies that the expert should assist by "providing objective, unbiased opinion on matters within his expertise, and should not assume the role of advocate". The form and content of the expert's report are prescribed, in detail, by paragraph 9 of the Practice Direction. It is no part of the expert's function to analyse or summarise the evidence. Focussed brevity in report writing is to be preferred over discussion.

Mrs Justice Pauffley

December 2010.

PART V

PART VI

Codes of Practice

PART VI: Codes of Practice

Contents

Mental Capacity Act 2005: Code of Practice   1033

Mental Capacity Act 2005: Deprivation of Liberty Safeguards Code
of Practice   1272

PART VI

Mental Capacity Act 2005: Code of Practice

Issued by the Lord Chancellor on 23 April 2007 in accordance with sections 42 and 43 of the Act

FOREWORD BY LORD FALCONER

The Mental Capacity Act 2005 is a vitally important piece of legislation, and one that will make a real difference to the lives of people who may lack mental capacity. It will empower people to make decisions for themselves wherever possible, and protect people who lack capacity by providing a flexible framework that places individuals at the very heart of the decision-making process. It will ensure that they participate as much as possible in any decisions made on their behalf, and that these are made in their best interests. It also allows people to plan ahead for a time in the future when they might lack the capacity, for any number of reasons, to make decisions for themselves.

The Act covers a wide range of decisions and circumstances, but legislation alone is not the whole story. We have always recognised that the Act needs to be supported by practical guidance, and the Code of Practice is a key part of this. It explains how the Act will operate on a day-to-day basis and offers examples of best practice to carers and practitioners.

Many individuals and organisations have read and commented upon earlier drafts of the Code of Practice and I am very grateful to all those who contributed to this process. This Code of Practice is a better document as a result of this input.

A number of people will be under a formal duty to have regard to the Code: professionals and paid carers for example, or people acting as attorneys or as deputies appointed by the Court of Protection. But for many people, the most important relationships will be with the wide range of less formal carers, the close family and friends who know the person best, some of whom will have been caring for them for many years. The Code is also here to provide help and guidance for them. It will be crucial to the Code's success that all those relying upon it have a document that is clear and that they can understand. I have been particularly keen that we do all we can to achieve this.

The Code of Practice will be important in shaping the way the Mental Capacity Act 2005 is put into practice and I strongly encourage you to take the time to read and digest it.

PART VI

INTRODUCTION

The Mental Capacity Act 2005, covering England and Wales, provides a statutory framework for people who lack capacity to make decisions for themselves, or who have capacity and want to make preparations for a time when they may lack capacity in the future. It sets out who can take decisions, in which situations, and how they should go about this. The Act received Royal Assent on 7 April 2005 and will come into force during 2007.

The legal framework provided by the Mental Capacity Act 2005 is supported by this Code of Practice (the Code), which provides guidance and information about how the Act works in practice. Section 42 of the Act requires the Lord Chancellor to produce a Code of Practice for the guidance of a range of people with different duties and functions under the Act. Before the Code is prepared, section 43 requires that the Lord Chancellor must have consulted the National Assembly for Wales and such other persons as he considers appropriate. The Code is also subject to the approval of Parliament and must have been placed before both Houses of Parliament for a 40-day period without either House voting against it. This Code of Practice has been produced in accordance with these requirements.

The Code has statutory force, which means that certain categories of people have a legal duty to have regard to it when working with or caring for adults who may lack capacity to make decisions for themselves. These categories of people are listed below.

How should the Code of Practice be used?

The Code of Practice provides guidance to anyone who is working with and/ or caring for adults who may lack capacity to make particular decisions. It describes their responsibilities when acting or making decisions on behalf of individuals who lack the capacity to act or make these decisions for themselves. In particular, the Code of Practice focuses on those who have a duty of care to someone who lacks the capacity to agree to the care that is being provided.

Who is the Code of Practice for?

The Act does not impose a legal duty on anyone to 'comply' with the Code – it should be viewed as guidance rather than instruction. But if they have not followed relevant guidance contained in the Code then they will be expected to give good reasons why they have departed from it.

Certain categories of people are legally required to 'have regard to' relevant guidance in the Code of Practice. That means they must be aware of the Code of Practice when acting or making decisions on behalf of someone who lacks capacity to make a decision for themselves, and they should be able to explain how they have had regard to the Code when acting or making decisions.

The categories of people that are required to have regard to the Code of Practice include anyone who is:

- an attorney under a Lasting Power of Attorney (LPA) (see chapter 7)
- a deputy appointed by the new Court of Protection (see chapter 8)
- acting as an Independent Mental Capacity Advocate (see chapter 10)
- carrying out research approved in accordance with the Act (see chapter 11)
- acting in a professional capacity for, or in relation to, a person who lacks capacity working
- being paid for acts for or in relation to a person who lacks capacity.
- The last two categories cover a wide range of people. People acting in a professional capacity may include:
- a variety of healthcare staff (doctors, dentists, nurses, therapists, radiologists, paramedics etc)
- social care staff (social workers, care managers, etc)
- others who may occasionally be involved in the care of people who lack capacity to make the decision in question, such as ambulance crew, housing workers, or police officers.

People who are being paid for acts for or in relation to a person who lacks capacity may include:

- care assistants in a care home
- care workers providing domiciliary care services, and
- others who have been contracted to provide a service to people who lack capacity to consent to that service.

However, the Act applies more generally to everyone who looks after, or cares for, someone who lacks capacity to make particular decisions for themselves. This includes family carers or other carers. Although these carers are not legally required to have regard to the Code of Practice, the guidance given in the Code will help them to understand the Act and apply it. They should follow the guidance in the Code as far as they are aware of it.

What does 'lacks capacity' mean?

One of the most important terms in the Code is 'a person who lacks capacity'.

Whenever the term 'a person who lacks capacity' is used, it means **a person who lacks capacity to make a particular decision or take a particular action for themselves at the time the decision or action needs to be taken.**

This reflects the fact that people may lack capacity to make some decisions for themselves, but will have capacity to make other decisions. For example, they may have capacity to make small decisions about everyday issues such as what to wear or what to eat, but lack capacity to make more complex decisions about financial matters.

It also reflects the fact that a person who lacks capacity to make a decision for themselves at a certain time may be able to make that decision at a later date. This may be because they have an illness or condition that means their capacity changes. Alternatively, it may be because at the time the decision needs to be made, they are unconscious or barely conscious whether due to an accident or being under anaesthetic or their ability to make a decision may be affected by the influence of alcohol or drugs.

Finally, it reflects the fact that while some people may always lack capacity to make some types of decisions – for example, due to a condition or severe learning disability that has affected them from birth – others may learn new skills that enable them to gain capacity and make decisions for themselves.

Chapter 4 provides a full definition of what is meant by 'lacks capacity'.

What does the Code of Practice actually cover?

The Code explains the Act and its key provisions.
- Chapter 1 introduces the Mental Capacity Act 2005.
- Chapter 2 sets out the five statutory principles behind the Act and the way they affect how it is put in practice.
- Chapter 3 explains how the Act makes sure that people are given the right help and support to make their own decisions.
- Chapter 4 explains how the Act defines 'a person who lacks capacity to make a decision' and sets out a single clear test for assessing whether a person lacks capacity to make a particular decision at a particular time.
- Chapter 5 explains what the Act means by acting in the best interests of someone lacking capacity to make a decision for themselves, and describes the checklist set out in the Act for working out what is in someone's best interests.
- Chapter 6 explains how the Act protects people providing care or treatment for someone who lacks the capacity to consent to the action being taken.
- Chapter 7 shows how people who wish to plan ahead for the possibility that they might lack the capacity to make particular decisions for themselves in the future are able to grant Lasting Powers of Attorney (LPAs) to named individuals to make certain decisions on their behalf, and how attorneys appointed under an LPA should act.
- Chapter 8 describes the role of the new Court of Protection, established under the Act, to make a decision or to appoint a

decision-maker on someone's behalf in cases where there is no other way of resolving a matter affecting a person who lacks capacity to make the decision in question.

- Chapter 9 explains the procedures that must be followed if someone wishes to make an advance decision to refuse medical treatment to come into effect when they lack capacity to refuse the specified treatment.
- Chapter 10 describes the role of Independent Mental Capacity Advocates appointed under the Act to help and represent particularly vulnerable people who lack capacity to make certain significant decisions. It also sets out when they should be instructed.
- Chapter 11 provides guidance on how the Act sets out specific safeguards and controls for research involving, or in relation to, people lacking capacity to consent to their participation.
- Chapter 12 explains those parts of the Act which can apply to children and young people and how these relate to other laws affecting them.
- Chapter 13 explains how the Act relates to the Mental Health Act 1983.
- Chapter 14 sets out the role of the Public Guardian, a new public office established by the Act to oversee attorneys and deputies and to act as a single point of contact for referring allegations of abuse in relation to attorneys and deputies to other relevant agencies.
- Chapter 15 examines the various ways that disputes over decisions made under the Act or otherwise affecting people lacking capacity to make relevant decisions can be resolved.
- Chapter 16 summarises how the laws about data protection and freedom of information relate to the provisions of the Act.

PART VI

What is the legal status of the Code?

Where does it apply?

The Act and therefore this Code applies to everyone it concerns who is habitually resident or present in England and Wales. However, it will also be possible for the Court of Protection to consider cases which involve persons who have assets or property outside this jurisdiction, or who live abroad but have assets or property in England or Wales.

What happens if people don't comply with it?

There are no specific sanctions for failure to comply with the Code. But a failure to comply with the Code can be used in evidence before a court or tribunal in any civil or criminal proceedings, if the court or tribunal considers it to be relevant to those proceedings. For example, if a court or tribunal believes that anyone making decisions for someone who lacks capacity has not acted in the best interests of the person they care for, the court can use the person's failure to comply with the Code as evidence.

That's why it's important that anyone working with or caring for a person who lacks capacity to make specific decisions should become familiar with the Code.

Where can I find out more?

The Code of Practice is not an exhaustive guide or complete statement of the law. Other materials have been produced by the Department for Constitutional Affairs, the Department of Health and the Office of the Public Guardian to help explain aspects of the Act from different perspectives and for people in different situations. These include guides for family carers and other carers and basic information of interest to the general public. Professional organisations may also produce specialist information and guidance for their members.

The Code also provides information on where to get more detailed guidance from other sources. A list of contact details is provided in Annex A and further information appears in the footnotes to each chapter. References made and any links provided to material or organisations do not form part of the Code and do not attract the same legal status. Signposts to further information are provided for assistance only and references made should not suggest that the Department for Constitutional Affairs endorses such material.

Using the code

References in the Code of Practice

Throughout the Code of Practice, the Mental Capacity Act 2005 is referred to as 'the Act' and any sections quoted refer to this Act unless otherwise stated. References are shown as follows: section 4(1). This refers to the section of the Act. The subsection number is in brackets.

Where reference is made to provisions from other legislation, the full title of the relevant Act will be set out, for example 'the Mental Health Act 1983', unless otherwise stated. (For example, in chapter 13, the Mental Health Act 1983 is referred to as MHA and the Mental Capacity Act as MCA.) The Code of Practice is sometimes referred to as the Code.

Scenarios used in the Code of Practice

The Code includes many boxes within the text in which there are scenarios, using imaginary characters and situations. These are intended to help illustrate what is meant in the main text. The scenarios should not in any way be taken as templates for decisions that need to be made in similar situations.

Alternative formats and further information

The Code is also available in Welsh and can be made available in other formats on request.

****

1 WHAT IS THE MENTAL CAPACITY ACT 2005?

1.1 The Mental Capacity Act 2005 (the Act) provides the legal framework for acting and making decisions on behalf of individuals who lack the mental capacity to make particular decisions for themselves. Everyone working with and/or caring for an adult who may lack capacity to make specific decisions must comply with this Act when making decisions or acting for that person, when the person lacks the capacity to make a particular decision for themselves. The same rules apply whether the decisions are life-changing events or everyday matters.

1.2 The Act's starting point is to confirm in legislation that it should be assumed that an adult (aged 16 or over) has full legal capacity to make decisions for themselves (the right to autonomy) unless it can be shown that they lack capacity to make a decision for themselves at the time the decision needs to be made. This is known as the presumption of capacity. The Act also states that people must be given all appropriate help and support to enable them to make their own decisions or to maximise their participation in any decision-making process.

1.3 The underlying philosophy of the Act is to ensure that any decision made, or action taken, on behalf of someone who lacks the capacity to make the decision or act for themselves is made in their best interests.

1.4 The Act is intended to assist and support people who may lack capacity and to discourage anyone who is involved in caring for someone who lacks capacity from being overly restrictive or controlling. But the Act also aims to balance an individual's right to make decisions for themselves with their right to be protected from harm if they lack capacity to make decisions to protect themselves.

1.5 The Act sets out a legal framework of how to act and make decisions on behalf of people who lack capacity to make specific decisions for themselves. It sets out some core principles and methods for making decisions and carrying out actions in relation to personal welfare, healthcare and financial matters affecting people who may lack capacity to make specific decisions about these issues for themselves.

1.6 Many of the provisions in the Act are based upon existing common law principles (i.e. principles that have been established through decisions made by courts in individual cases). The Act clarifies and improves upon these principles and builds on current good practice which is based on the principles.

PART VI

1.7 The Act introduces several new roles, bodies and powers, all of which will support the Act's provisions. These include:

- Attorneys appointed under Lasting Powers of Attorney (see chapter 7)
- The new Court of Protection, and court-appointed deputies (see chapter 8)
- Independent Mental Capacity Advocates (see chapter 10).

The roles, bodies and powers are all explained in more depth in the specific chapters of the Code highlighted above.

What decisions are covered by the Act, and what decisions are excluded?

1.8 The Act covers a wide range of decisions made, or actions taken, on behalf of people who may lack capacity to make specific decisions for themselves. These can be decisions about day-to-day matters – like what to wear, or what to buy when doing the weekly shopping – or decisions about major life-changing events, such as whether the person should move into a care home or undergo a major surgical operation.

1.9 There are certain decisions which can never be made on behalf of a person who lacks capacity to make those specific decisions. This is because they are either so personal to the individual concerned, or governed by other legislation.

1.10 Sections 27–29 and 62 of the Act set out the specific decisions which can never be made or actions which can never be carried out under the Act, whether by family members, carers, professionals, attorneys or the Court of Protection. These are summarised below.

Decisions concerning family relationships (section 27)

Nothing in the Act permits a decision to be made on someone else's behalf on any of the following matters:

- consenting to marriage or a civil partnership
- consenting to have sexual relations
- consenting to a decree of divorce on the basis of two years' separation
- consenting to the dissolution of a civil partnership
- consenting to a child being placed for adoption or the making of an adoption order
- discharging parental responsibility for a child in matters not relating to the child's property, or
- giving consent under the Human Fertilisation and Embryology Act 1990.

Mental Health Act matters (section 28)

Where a person who lacks capacity to consent is currently detained and being treated under Part 4 of the Mental Health Act 1983, nothing in the Act authorises anyone to:

- give the person treatment for mental disorder, or
- consent to the person being given treatment for mental disorder.

Further guidance is given in chapter 13 of the Code.

Voting rights (section 29)

Nothing in the Act permits a decision on voting, at an election for any public office or at a referendum, to be made on behalf of a person who lacks capacity to vote.

Unlawful killing or assisting suicide (section 62)

For the avoidance of doubt, nothing in the Act is to be taken to affect the law relating to murder, manslaughter or assisting suicide.

    1.11 Although the Act does not allow anyone to make a decision about these matters on behalf of someone who lacks capacity to make such a decision for themselves (for example, consenting to have sexual relations), this does not prevent action being taken to protect a vulnerable person from abuse or exploitation.

How does the Act relate to other legislation?

    1.12 The Mental Capacity Act 2005 will apply in conjunction with other legislation affecting people who may lack capacity in relation to specific matters. This means that healthcare and social care staff acting under the Act should also be aware of their obligations under other legislation, including (but not limited to) the:

- Care Standards Act 2000
- Data Protection Act 1998
- Disability Discrimination Act 1995
- Human Rights Act 1998
- Mental Health Act 1983
- National Health Service and Community Care Act 1990
- Human Tissue Act 2004.

What does the Act say about the Code of Practice?

    1.13 Section 42 of the Act sets out the purpose of the Code of Practice, which is to provide guidance for specific people in specific circumstances. Section 43 explains the procedures that had to be

PART VI

followed in preparing the Code and consulting on its contents, and
for its consideration by Parliament.

Section 42, subsections (4) and (5), set out the categories of people
who are placed under a legal duty to 'have regard to' the Code and
gives further information about the status of the Code. More details
can be found in the Introduction, which explains the legal status of
the Code.

2   WHAT ARE THE STATUTORY PRINCIPLES AND HOW SHOULD THEY BE APPLIED?

Section 1 of the Act sets out the five 'statutory principles' – the values that
underpin the legal requirements in the Act. The Act is intended to be
enabling and supportive of people who lack capacity, not restricting or
controlling of their lives. It aims to protect people who lack capacity to
make particular decisions, but also to maximise their ability to make
decisions, or to participate in decision-making, as far as they are able to do
so.

The five statutory principles are:

1. A person must be assumed to have capacity unless it is established
    that they lack capacity.
2. A person is not to be treated as unable to make a decision unless all
    practicable steps to help him to do so have been taken without
    success.
3. A person is not to be treated as unable to make a decision merely
    because he makes an unwise decision.
4. An act done, or decision made, under this Act for or on behalf of a
    person who lacks capacity must be done, or made, in his best
    interests.
5. Before the act is done, or the decision is made, regard must be had
    to whether the purpose for which it is needed can be as effectively
    achieved in a way that is less restrictive of the person's rights and
    freedom of action.

This chapter provides guidance on how people should interpret and apply
the statutory principles when using the Act. Following the principles and
applying them to the Act's framework for decision-making will help to
ensure not only that appropriate action is taken in individual cases, but also
to point the way to solutions in difficult or uncertain situations.

In this chapter, as throughout the Code, a person's capacity (or lack of
capacity) refers specifically to their capacity to make a particular
decision at the time it needs to be made.

Quick summary

- Every adult has the right to make their own decisions if they have the capacity to do so. Family carers and healthcare or social care staff must assume that a person has the capacity to make decisions, unless it can be established that the person does not have capacity.
- People should receive support to help them make their own decisions. Before concluding that individuals lack capacity to make a particular decision, it is important to take all possible steps to try to help them reach a decision themselves.
- People have the right to make decisions that others might think are unwise. A person who makes a decision that others think is unwise should not automatically be labelled as lacking the capacity to make a decision.
- Any act done for, or any decision made on behalf of, someone who lacks capacity must be in their best interests.
- Any act done for, or any decision made on behalf of, someone who lacks capacity should be an option that is less restrictive of their basic rights and freedoms – as long as it is still in their best interests.

What is the role of the statutory principles?

2.1 The statutory principles aim to:
- protect people who lack capacity and
- help them take part, as much as possible, in decisions that affect them.

They aim to assist and support people who may lack capacity to make particular decisions, not to restrict or control their lives.

2.2 The statutory principles apply to any act done or decision made under the Act. When followed and applied to the Act's decision-making framework, they will help people take appropriate action in individual cases. They will also help people find solutions in difficult or uncertain situations.

How should the statutory principles be applied?

Principle 1: '*A person must be assumed to have capacity unless it is established that he lacks capacity.*' *(section 1(2))*

2.3 This principle states that every adult has the right to make their own decisions – unless there is proof that they lack the capacity to make a particular decision when it needs to be made. This has been a fundamental principle of the common law for many years and it is now set out in the Act.

2.4 It is important to balance people's right to make a decision with their right to safety and protection when they can't make decisions to protect themselves. But the starting assumption must always be that an individual has the capacity, until there is proof that they do not. Chapter 4 explains the Act's definition of 'lack of capacity' and the processes involved in assessing capacity.

Scenario: Assessing a person's capacity to make decisions

When planning her retirement, Mrs Arnold made and registered a Lasting Power of Attorney (LPA) – a legal process that would allow her son to manage her property and financial affairs if she ever lacked capacity to manage them herself. She has now been diagnosed with dementia, and her son is worried that she is becoming confused about money.

Her son must assume that his mother has capacity to manage her affairs. Then he must consider each of Mrs Arnold's financial decisions as she makes them, giving her any help and support she needs to make these decisions herself.

Mrs Arnold's son goes shopping with her, and he sees she is quite capable of finding goods and making sure she gets the correct change. But when she needs to make decisions about her investments, Mrs Arnold gets confused – even though she has made such decisions in the past. She still doesn't understand after her son explains the different options.

Her son concludes that she has capacity to deal with everyday financial matters but not more difficult affairs at this time. Therefore, he is able to use the LPA for the difficult financial decisions his mother can't make. But Mrs Arnold can continue to deal with her other affairs for as long as she has capacity to do so.

2.5   Some people may need help to be able to make a decision or to communicate their decision. However, this does not necessarily mean that they cannot make that decision – unless there is proof that they do lack capacity to do so. Anyone who believes that a person lacks capacity should be able to prove their case. Chapter 4 explains the standard of proof required.

Principle 2: *'A person is not to be treated as unable to make a decision unless all practicable steps to help him to do so have been taken without success.' (section 1(3))*

2.6   It is important to do everything practical (the Act uses the term 'practicable') to help a person make a decision for themselves before concluding that they lack capacity to do so. People with an illness or disability affecting their ability to make a decision should receive support to help them make as many decisions as they can. This principle aims to stop people being automatically labelled as lacking capacity to make particular decisions. Because it encourages individuals to play as big a role as possible in decision-making, it also helps prevent unnecessary interventions in their lives.

2.7 The kind of support people might need to help them make a decision varies. It depends on personal circumstances, the kind of decision that has to be made and the time available to make the decision. It might include:

- using a different form of communication (for example, non-verbal communication)
- providing information in a more accessible form (for example, photographs, drawings, or tapes)
- treating a medical condition which may be affecting the person's capacity or
- having a structured programme to improve a person's capacity to make particular decisions (for example, helping a person with learning disabilities to learn new skills).

Chapter 3 gives more information on ways to help people make decisions for themselves.

Scenario: *Taking steps to help people make decisions for themselves*

Mr Jackson is brought into hospital following a traffic accident. He is conscious but in shock. He cannot speak and is clearly in distress, making noises and gestures.

From his behaviour, hospital staff conclude that Mr Jackson currently lacks capacity to make decisions about treatment for his injuries, and they give him urgent treatment. They hope that after he has recovered from the shock they can use an advocate to help explain things to him.

However, one of the nurses thinks she recognises some of his gestures as sign language, and tries signing to him. Mr Jackson immediately becomes calmer, and the doctors realise that he can communicate in sign language. He can also answer some written questions about his injuries.

The hospital brings in a qualified sign-language interpreter and concludes that Mr Jackson has the capacity to make decisions about any further treatment.

PART VI

2.8 Anyone supporting a person who may lack capacity should not use excessive persuasion or 'undue pressure'.[1] This might include behaving in a manner which is overbearing or dominating, or seeking to influence the person's decision, and could push a person

---

[1] Undue influence in relation to consent to medical treatment was considered in *Re T (Adult: Refusal of Treatment)* [1992] 4 All E R 649, 662 and in financial matters in *Royal Bank of Scotland v Etridge* [2001] UKHL 44.

into making a decision they might not otherwise have made. However, it is important to provide appropriate advice and information.

Scenario: Giving appropriate advice and support

Sara, a young woman with severe depression, is getting treatment from mental health services. Her psychiatrist determines that she has capacity to make decisions about treatment, if she gets advice and support.

Her mother is trying to persuade Sara to agree to electro-convulsive therapy (ECT), which helped her mother when she had clinical depression in the past. However, a friend has told Sara that ECT is 'barbaric'.

The psychiatrist provides factual information about the different types of treatment available and explains their advantages and disadvantages. She also describes how different people experience different reactions or side effects. Sara is then able to consider what treatment is right for her, based on factual information rather than the personal opinions of her mother and friend.

2.9 In some situations treatment cannot be delayed while a person gets support to make a decision. This can happen in emergency situations or when an urgent decision is required (for example, immediate medical treatment). In these situations, the only practical and appropriate steps might be to keep a person informed of what is happening and why.

Principle 3: *'A person is not to be treated as unable to make a decision merely because he makes an unwise decision.' (section 1(4))*

2.10 Everybody has their own values, beliefs, preferences and attitudes. A person should not be assumed to lack the capacity to make a decision just because other people think their decision is unwise. This applies even if family members, friends or healthcare or social care staff are unhappy with a decision.

Scenario: Allowing people to make decisions that others think are unwise

Mr Garvey is a 40-year-old man with a history of mental health problems. He sees a Community Psychiatric Nurse (CPN) regularly. Mr Garvey decides to spend £2,000 of his savings on a camper van to travel around Scotland for six months. His CPN is concerned that it

---

will be difficult to give Mr Garvey continuous support and treatment while travelling, and that his mental health might deteriorate as a result.

However, having talked it through with his CPN, it is clear that Mr Garvey is fully aware of these concerns and has the capacity to make this particular decision. He has decided he would like to have a break and thinks this will be good for him.

Just because, in the CPN's opinion, continuity of care might be a wiser option, it should not be assumed that Mr Garvey lacks the capacity to make this decision for himself.

2.11 There may be cause for concern if somebody:
- repeatedly makes unwise decisions that put them at significant risk of harm or exploitation or
- makes a particular unwise decision that is obviously irrational or out of character.

These things do not necessarily mean that somebody lacks capacity. But there might be need for further investigation, taking into account the person's past decisions and choices. For example, have they developed a medical condition or disorder that is affecting their capacity to make particular decisions? Are they easily influenced by undue pressure? Or do they need more information to help them understand the consequences of the decision they are making?

PART VI

Scenario: Decisions that cause concern

Cyril, an elderly man with early signs of dementia, spends nearly £300 on fresh fish from a door-to-door salesman. He has always been fond of fish and has previously bought small amounts in this way. Before his dementia, Cyril was always very careful with his money and would never have spent so much on fish in one go.

This decision alone may not automatically mean Cyril lacks capacity to manage all aspects of his property and affairs. But his daughter makes further enquiries and discovers Cyril has overpaid his cleaner on several occasions – something he has never done in the past. He has also made payments from his savings that he cannot account for.

His daughter decides it is time to use the registered Lasting Power of Attorney her father made in the past. This gives her the authority to manage Cyril's property and affairs whenever he lacks the capacity to manage them himself. She takes control of Cyril's chequebook to protect him from possible exploitation, but she can still ensure he has enough money to spend on his everyday needs.

Principle 4: *'An act done, or decision made, under this Act for or on behalf of a person who lacks capacity must be done, or made, in his best interests.'* *(section 1(5))*

    2.12 The principle of acting or making a decision in the best interests of a person who lacks capacity to make the decision in question is a well-established principle in the common law.[2] This principle is now set out in the Act, so that a person's best interests must be the basis for all decisions made and actions carried out on their behalf in situations where they lack capacity to make those particular decisions for themselves. The only exceptions to this are around research (see chapter 11) and advance decisions to refuse treatment (see chapter 9) where other safeguards apply.

    2.13 It is impossible to give a single description of what 'best interests' are, because they depend on individual circumstances. However, section 4 of the Act sets out a checklist of steps to follow in order to determine what is in the best interests of a person who lacks capacity to make the decision in question each time someone acts or makes a decision on that person's behalf. See chapter 5 for detailed guidance and examples.

Principle 5: *'Before the act is done, or the decision is made, regard must be had to whether the purpose for which it is needed can be as effectively achieved in a way that is less restrictive of the person's rights and freedom of action.'* *(section 1(6))*

    2.14 Before somebody makes a decision or acts on behalf of a person who lacks capacity to make that decision or consent to the act, they must always question if they can do something else that would interfere less with the person's basic rights and freedoms. This is called finding the 'less restrictive alternative'. It includes considering whether there is a need to act or make a decision at all.

    2.15 Where there is more than one option, it is important to explore ways that would be less restrictive or allow the most freedom for a person who lacks capacity to make the decision in question. However, the final decision must always allow the original purpose of the decision or act to be achieved.

    2.16 Any decision or action must still be in the best interests of the person who lacks capacity. So sometimes it may be necessary to choose an option that is not the least restrictive alternative if that option is in the person's best interests. In practice, the process of choosing a less restrictive option and deciding what is in the person's best interests will be combined. But both principles must be applied each time a decision or action may be taken on behalf of a person who lacks capacity to make the relevant decision.

---

[2]   See for example *Re MB (Medical Treatment)* [1997] 2 FLR 426, CA; *Re A (Male Sterilisation)* [2000] 1 FLR 549; *Re S (Sterilisation: Patient's Best Interests)* [2000] 2 FLR 389; *Re F (Adult Patient: Sterilisation)* [2001] Fam 15.

Scenario: Finding a less restrictive option

Sunil, a young man with severe learning disabilities, also has a very severe and unpredictable form of epilepsy that is associated with drop attacks. This can result in serious injury. A neurologist has advised that, to limit the harm that might come from these attacks, Sunil should either be under constant close observation, or wear a protective helmet.

After assessment, it is decided that Sunil lacks capacity to decide on the most appropriate course of action for himself. But through his actions and behaviour, Sunil makes it clear he doesn't like to be too closely observed – even though he likes having company.

The staff of the home where he lives consider various options, such as providing a special room for him with soft furnishings, finding ways to keep him under close observation or getting him to wear a helmet. In discussion with Sunil's parents, they agree that the option that is in his best interests, and is less restrictive, will be the helmet – as it will enable him to go out, and prevent further harm.

---

3 HOW SHOULD PEOPLE BE HELPED TO MAKE THEIR OWN DECISIONS?

Before deciding that someone lacks capacity to make a particular decision, it is important to take all practical and appropriate steps to enable them to make that decision themselves (statutory principle 2, see chapter 2). In addition, as section 3(2) of the Act underlines, these steps (such as helping individuals to communicate) must be taken in a way which reflects the person's individual circumstances and meets their particular needs. This chapter provides practical guidance on how to support people to make decisions for themselves, or play as big a role as possible in decision-making.

PART VI

In this chapter, as throughout the Code, a person's capacity (or lack of capacity) refers specifically to their capacity to make a particular decision at the time it needs to be made.

Quick summary

To help someone make a decision for themselves, check the following points:

Providing relevant information
- Does the person have all the relevant information they need to make a particular decision?
- If they have a choice, have they been given information on all the alternatives?

Communicating in an appropriate way
- Could information be explained or presented in a way that is easier for the person to understand (for example, by using simple language or visual aids)?
- Have different methods of communication been explored if required, including non-verbal communication?
- Could anyone else help with communication (for example, a family member, support worker, interpreter, speech and language therapist or advocate)?

Making the person feel at ease
- Are there particular times of day when the person's understanding is better?
- Are there particular locations where they may feel more at ease?
- Could the decision be put off to see whether the person can make the decision at a later time when circumstances are right for them?

Supporting the person
- Can anyone else help or support the person to make choices or express a view?

How can someone be helped to make a decision?

3.1 There are several ways in which people can be helped and supported to enable them to make a decision for themselves. These will vary depending on the decision to be made, the time-scale for making the decision and the individual circumstances of the person making it.

3.2 The Act applies to a wide range of people with different conditions that may affect their capacity to make particular decisions. So, the appropriate steps to take will depend on:
- a person's individual circumstances (for example, somebody with learning difficulties may need a different approach to somebody with dementia)
- the decision the person has to make and
- the length of time they have to make it.

3.3 Significant, one-off decisions (such as moving house) will require different considerations from day-to-day decisions about a person's care and welfare. However, the same general processes should apply to each decision.

3.4 In most cases, only some of the steps described in this chapter will be relevant or appropriate, and the list included here is not exhaustive. It is up to the people (whether family carers, paid carers, healthcare staff or anyone else) caring for or supporting an individual to consider what is possible and appropriate in individual cases. In all cases it is extremely important to find the most effective way of communicating with the person concerned. Good communication is essential for explaining relevant information in an appropriate way and for ensuring that the steps being taken meet an individual's needs.

3.5 Providing appropriate help with decision-making should form part of care planning processes for people receiving health or social care services. Examples include:

- Person Centred Planning for people with learning disabilities
- the Care Programme Approach for people with mental disorders
- the Single Assessment Process for older people in England, and
- the Unified Assessment Process in Wales.

What happens in emergency situations?

3.6 Clearly, in emergency medical situations (for example, where a person collapses with a heart attack or for some unknown reason and is brought unconscious into a hospital), urgent decisions will have to be made and immediate action taken in the person's best interests. In these situations, it may not be practical or appropriate to delay the treatment while trying to help the person make their own decisions, or to consult with any known attorneys or deputies. However, even in emergency situations, healthcare staff should try to communicate with the person and keep them informed of what is happening.

What information should be provided to people and how should it be provided?

3.7 Providing relevant information is essential in all decision-making. For example, to make a choice about what they want for breakfast, people need to know what food is available. If the decision concerns medical treatment, the doctor must explain the purpose and effect of the course of treatment and the likely consequences of accepting or refusing treatment.

3.8 All practical and appropriate steps must be taken to help people to make a decision for themselves. Information must be tailored to an individual's needs and abilities. It must also be in the easiest and most appropriate form of communication for the person concerned.

PART VI

What information is relevant?

3.9 The Act cannot state exactly what information will be relevant in each case. Anyone helping someone to make a decision for themselves should therefore follow these steps.

- Take time to explain anything that might help the person make a decision. It is important that they have access to all the information they need to make an informed decision.
- Try not to give more detail than the person needs – this might confuse them. In some cases, a simple, broad explanation will be enough. But it must not miss out important information.
- What are the risks and benefits? Describe any foreseeable consequences of making the decision, and of not making any decision at all.
- Explain the effects the decision might have on the person and those close to them – including the people involved in their care.
- If they have a choice, give them the same information in a balanced way for all the options.
- For some types of decisions, it may be important to give access to advice from elsewhere. This may be independent or specialist advice (for example, from a medical practitioner or a financial or legal adviser). But it might simply be advice from trusted friends or relatives.

Communication – general guidance

3.10 To help someone make a decision for themselves, all possible and appropriate means of communication should be tried.

- Ask people who know the person well about the best form of communication (try speaking to family members, carers, day centre staff or support workers). They may also know somebody the person can communicate with easily, or the time when it is best to communicate with them.
- Use simple language. Where appropriate, use pictures, objects or illustrations to demonstrate ideas.
- Speak at the right volume and speed, with appropriate words and sentence structure. It may be helpful to pause to check understanding or show that a choice is available.
- Break down difficult information into smaller points that are easy to understand. Allow the person time to consider and understand each point before continuing.
- It may be necessary to repeat information or go back over a point several times.
- Is help available from people the person trusts (relatives, friends, GP, social worker, religious or community leaders)? If so, make sure the person's right to confidentiality is respected.
- Be aware of cultural, ethnic or religious factors that shape a person's way of thinking, behaviour or communication. For

example, in some cultures it is important to involve the community in decision-making. Some religious beliefs (for example, those of Jehovah's Witnesses or Christian Scientists) may influence the person's approach to medical treatment and information about treatment decisions.

- If necessary, consider using a professional language interpreter. Even if a person communicated in English or Welsh in the past, they may have lost some verbal skills (for example, because of dementia). They may now prefer to communicate in their first language. It is often more appropriate to use a professional interpreter rather than to use family members.

- If using pictures to help communication, make sure they are relevant and the person can understand them easily. For example, a red bus may represent a form of transport to one person but a day trip to another.

- Would an advocate (someone who can support and represent the person) improve communication in the current situation? (See chapters 10 and 15 for more information about advocates.)

Scenario: Providing relevant information

Mrs Thomas has Alzheimer's disease and lives n a care home. She enjoys taking part in the activities provided at the home. Today there is a choice between going to a flower show, attending her usual pottery class or watching a DVD. Although she has the capacity to choose, having to decide is making her anxious.

The care assistant carefully explains the different options. She tells Mrs Thomas about the DVD she could watch, but Mrs Thomas doesn't like the sound of it. The care assistant shows her a leaflet about the flower show. She explains the plans for the day, where the show is being held and how long it will take to get there in the mini-van. She has to repeat this information several times, as Mrs Thomas keeps asking whether they will be back in time for supper. She also tells Mrs Thomas that one of her friends is going on the trip.

At first, Mrs Thomas is reluctant to disturb her usual routine. But the care assistant reassures her she will not lose her place at pottery if she misses a class. With this information, Mrs Thomas can therefore choose whether or not to go on the day trip.

PART VI

Helping people with specific communication or cognitive problems

3.11 Where people have specific communication or cognitive problems, the following steps can help:
- Find out how the person is used to communicating. Do they use picture boards or Makaton (signs and symbols for people with

communication or learning difficulties)? Or do they have a way of communicating that is only known to those close to them?

- If the person has hearing difficulties, use their preferred method of communication (for example, visual aids, written messages or sign language). Where possible, use a qualified interpreter.
- Are mechanical devices such as voice synthesisers, keyboards or other computer equipment available to help?
- If the person does not use verbal communication skills, allow more time to learn how to communicate effectively.
- For people who use non-verbal methods of communication, their behaviour (in particular, changes in behaviour) can provide indications of their feelings.
- Some people may prefer to use non-verbal means of communication and can communicate most effectively in written form using computers or other communication technologies. This is particularly true for those with autistic spectrum disorders.
- For people with specific communication difficulties, consider other types of professional help (for example, a speech and language therapist or an expert in clinical neuropsychology).

Scenario: Helping people with specific communication difficulties

David is a deafblind man with learning disabilities who has no formal communication. He lives in a specialist home. He begins to bang his head against the wall and repeats this behaviour throughout the day. He has not done this before.

The staff in the home are worried and discuss ways to reduce the risk of injury. They come up with a range of possible interventions, aimed at engaging him with activities and keeping him away from objects that could injure him. They assess these as less restrictive ways to ensure he is safe. But David lacks the capacity to make a decision about which would be the best option.

The staff call in a specialist in challenging behaviour, who says that David's behaviour is communicative. After investigating this further, staff discover he is in pain because of tooth decay. They consult a dentist about how to resolve this, and the dentist decides it is in David's best interests to get treatment for the tooth decay. After treatment, David's head-banging stops.

What steps should be taken to put a person at ease?

3.12 To help put someone at ease and so improve their ability to make a decision, careful consideration should be given to both location and timing.

Location

3.13 In terms of location, consider the following:
- Where possible, choose a location where the person feels most at ease. For example, people are usually more comfortable in their own home than at a doctor's surgery.
- Would the person find it easier to make their decision in a relevant location? For example, could you help them decide about medical treatment by taking them to hospital to see what is involved?
- Choose a quiet location where the discussion can't be easily interrupted.
- Try to eliminate any background noise or distractions (for example, the television or radio, or people talking).
- Choose a location where the person's privacy and dignity can be properly respected.

Timing

3.14 In terms of timing, consider the following:
- Try to choose the time of day when the person is most alert – some people are better in the mornings, others are more lively in the afternoon or early evening. It may be necessary to try several times before a decision can be made.
- If the person's capacity is likely to improve in the foreseeable future, wait until it has done so – if practical and appropriate. For example, this might be the case after treatment for depression or a psychotic episode. Obviously, this may not be practical and appropriate if the decision is urgent.
- Some medication could affect a person's capacity (for example, medication which causes drowsiness or affects memory). Can the decision be delayed until side effects have subsided?
- Take one decision at a time – be careful to avoid making the person tired or confused.
- Don't rush – allow the person time to think things over or ask for clarification, where that is possible and appropriate.
- Avoid or challenge time limits that are unnecessary if the decision is not urgent. Delaying the decision may enable further steps to be taken to assist people to make the decision for themselves.

PART VI

Scenario: Getting the location and timing right

Luke, a young man, was seriously injured in a road traffic accident and suffered permanent brain damage. He has been in hospital several months, and has made good progress, but he gets very frustrated at his inability to concentrate or do things for himself.

Luke now needs surgical treatment on his leg. During the early morning ward round, the surgeon tries to explain what is involved in the operation. She asks Luke to sign a consent form, but he gets angry and says he doesn't want to talk about it.

His key nurse knows that Luke becomes more alert and capable later in the day. After lunch, she asks him if he would like to discuss the operation again. She also knows that he responds better one-to-one than in a group. So she takes Luke into a private room and repeats the information that the surgeon gave him earlier. He understands why the treatment is needed, what is involved and the likely consequences. Therefore, Luke has the capacity to make a decision about the operation.

Support from other people

3.15 In some circumstances, individuals will be more comfortable making decisions when someone else is there to support them.
  • Might the person benefit from having another person present? Sometimes having a relative or friend nearby can provide helpful support and reduce anxiety. However, some people might find this intrusive, and it could increase their anxiety or affect their ability to make a free choice. Find ways of getting the person's views on this, for example, by watching their behaviour towards other people.
  • Always respect a person's right to confidentiality.

Scenario: Getting help from other people

Jane has a learning disability. She expresses herself using some words, facial expressions and body language. She has lived in her current community home all her life, but now needs to move to a new group home. She finds it difficult to discuss abstract ideas or things she hasn't experienced. Staff conclude that she lacks the capacity to decide for herself which new group home she should move to.

The staff involve an advocate to help Jane express her views. Jane's advocate spends time with her in different environments. The advocate uses pictures, symbols and Makaton to find out the things that are important to Jane, and speaks to people who know Jane to find out what they think she likes. She then supports Jane to show their work to her care manager, and checks that the new homes suggested for her are able to meet Jane's needs and preferences.

When the care manager has found some suitable places, Jane's advocate visits the homes with Jane. They take photos of the houses to help her distinguish between them. The advocate then uses the photos to help Jane work out which home she prefers. Jane's own feelings can now play an important part in deciding what is in her best interests – and so in the final decision about where she will live.

What other ways are there to enable decision-making?

3.16 There are other ways to help someone make a decision for themselves.

- Many people find it helpful to talk things over with people they trust – or people who have been in a similar situation or faced similar dilemmas. For example, people with learning difficulties may benefit from the help of a designated support worker or being part of a support network.
- If someone is very distressed (for example, following a death of someone close) or where there are long-standing problems that affect someone's ability to understand an issue, it may be possible to delay a decision so that the person can have psychological therapy, if needed.
- Some organisations have produced materials to help people who need support to make decisions and for those who support them. Some of this material is designed to help people with specific conditions, such as Alzheimer's disease or profound learning disability.
- It may be important to provide access to technology. For example, some people who appear not to communicate well verbally can do so very well using computers.

PART VI

Scenario: Making the most of technology

Ms Patel has an autistic spectrum disorder. Her family and care staff find it difficult to communicate with her. She refuses to make eye contact, and gets very upset and angry when her carers try to encourage her to speak.

One member of staff notices that Ms Patel is interested in the computer equipment. He shows her how to use the keyboard, and they are able to have a conversation using the computer. An IT specialist works with her to make sure she can make the most of her computing skills to communicate her feelings and decisions.

4   HOW DOES THE ACT DEFINE A PERSON'S CAPACITY TO MAKE A DECISION AND HOW SHOULD CAPACITY BE ASSESSED?

This chapter explains what the Act means by 'capacity' and 'lack of capacity'. It provides guidance on how to assess whether someone has the capacity to make a decision, and suggests when professionals should be involved in the assessment.

> In this chapter, as throughout the Code, a person's capacity (or lack of capacity) refers specifically to their capacity to make a particular decision at the time it needs to be made

Quick summary

This checklist is a summary of points to consider when assessing a person's capacity to make a specific decision. Readers should also refer to the more detailed guidance in this chapter and chapters 2 and 3.

Presuming someone has capacity
- The starting assumption must always be that a person has the capacity to make a decision, unless it can be established that they lack capacity.

Understanding what is meant by capacity and lack of capacity
- A person's capacity must be assessed specifically in terms of their capacity to make a particular decision at the time it needs to be made.

Treating everyone equally
- A person's capacity must not be judged simply on the basis of their age, appearance, condition or an aspect of their behaviour.

Supporting the person to make the decision for themselves
- It is important to take all possible steps to try to help people make a decision for themselves (see chapter 2, principle 2, and chapter 3).

Assessing capacity

Anyone assessing someone's capacity to make a decision for themselves should use the two-stage test of capacity.
- Does the person have an impairment of the mind or brain, or is there some sort of disturbance affecting the way their mind or brain works? (It doesn't matter whether the impairment or disturbance is temporary or permanent.)

- If so, does that impairment or disturbance mean that the person is unable to make the decision in question at the time it needs to be made?

Assessing ability to make a decision

- Does the person have a general understanding of what decision they need to make and why they need to make it?
- Does the person have a general understanding of the likely consequences of making, or not making, this decision?
- Is the person able to understand, retain, use and weigh up the information relevant to this decision?
- Can the person communicate their decision (by talking, using sign language or any other means)? Would the services of a professional (such as a speech and language therapist) be helpful?

Assessing capacity to make more complex or serious decisions

- Is there a need for a more thorough assessment (perhaps by involving a doctor or other professional expert)?

What is mental capacity?

4.1 Mental capacity is the ability to make a decision.
- This includes the ability to make a decision that affects daily life – such as when to get up, what to wear or whether to go to the doctor when feeling ill – as well as more serious or significant decisions.
- It also refers to a person's ability to make a decision that may have legal consequences – for them or others. Examples include agreeing to have medical treatment, buying goods or making a will.

4.2 The starting point must always be to assume that a person has the capacity to make a specific decision (see chapter 2, principle 1). Some people may need help to be able to make or communicate a decision (see chapter 3). But this does not necessarily mean that they lack capacity to do so. What matters is their ability to carry out the processes involved in making the decision – and not the outcome.

What does the Act mean by 'lack of capacity'?

4.3 Section 2(1) of the Act states:

> 'For the purposes of this Act, a person lacks capacity in relation to a matter if at the material time he is unable to make a decision for himself in relation to the matter because of an impairment of, or a disturbance in the functioning of, the mind or brain.'

This means that a person lacks capacity if:

PART VI

- they have an impairment or disturbance (for example, a disability, condition or trauma) that affects the way their mind or brain works, and
- the impairment or disturbance means that they are unable to make a specific decision at the time it needs to be made.

4.4   An assessment of a person's capacity must be based on their ability to make a specific decision at the time it needs to be made, and not their ability to make decisions in general. Section 3 of the Act defines what it means to be unable to make a decision (this is explained in paragraph 4.14 below).

4.5   Section 2(2) states that the impairment or disturbance does not have to be permanent. A person can lack capacity to make a decision at the time it needs to be made even if:
- the loss of capacity is partial
- the loss of capacity is temporary
- their capacity changes over time.

A person may also lack capacity to make a decision about one issue but not about others.

4.6   The Act generally applies to people who are aged 16 or older. Chapter 12 explains how the Act affects children and young people – in particular those aged 16 and 17 years.

What safeguards does the Act provide around assessing someone's capacity?

4.7   An assessment that a person lacks capacity to make a decision must never be based simply on:
- their age
- their appearance
- assumptions about their condition, or
- any aspect of their behaviour. (section 2(3))

4.8   The Act deliberately uses the word 'appearance', because it covers all aspects of the way people look. So for example, it includes the physical characteristics of certain conditions (for example, scars, features linked to Down's syndrome or muscle spasms caused by cerebral palsy) as well as aspects of appearance like skin colour, tattoos and body piercings, or the way people dress (including religious dress).

4.9   The word 'condition' is also wide-ranging. It includes physical disabilities, learning difficulties and disabilities, illness related to age, and temporary conditions (for example, drunkenness or unconsciousness). Aspects of behaviour might include extrovert (for example, shouting or gesticulating) and withdrawn behaviour (for example, talking to yourself or avoiding eye contact).

Scenario: Treating everybody equally

Tom, a man with cerebral palsy, has slurred speech. Sometimes he also falls over for no obvious reason

One day Tom falls in the supermarket. Staff call an ambulance, even though he says he is fine. They think he may need treatment after his fall.

When the ambulance comes, the ambulance crew know they must not make assumptions about Tom's capacity to decide about treatment, based simply on his condition and the effects of his disability. They talk to him and find that he is capable of making healthcare decisions for himself.

What proof of lack of capacity does the Act require?

4.10 Anybody who claims that an individual lacks capacity should be able to provide proof. They need to be able to show, *on the balance of probabilities*, that the individual lacks capacity to make a particular decision, at the time it needs to be made (section 2(4)). This means being able to show that it is more likely than not that the person lacks capacity to make the decision in question.

What is the test of capacity?

To help determine if a person lacks capacity to make particular decisions, the Act sets out a two-stage test of capacity.

Stage 1: Does the person have an impairment of, or a disturbance in the functioning of, their mind or brain?

4.11 Stage 1 requires proof that the person has an impairment of the mind or brain, or some sort of or disturbance that affects the way their mind or brain works. If a person does not have such an impairment or disturbance of the mind or brain, they will not lack capacity under the Act.

4.12 Examples of an impairment or disturbance in the functioning of the mind or brain may include the following:
- conditions associated with some forms of mental illness
- dementia
- significant learning disabilities
- the long-term effects of brain damage
- physical or medical conditions that cause confusion, drowsiness or loss of consciousness
- delirium
- concussion following a head injury, and

- the symptoms of alcohol or drug use.

Scenario: Assessing whether an impairment or disturbance is affecting someone's ability to make a decision

Mrs Collins is 82 and has had a stroke. This has weakened the left-hand side of her body. She is living in a house that has been the family home for years. Her son wants her to sell the house and live with him.

Mrs Collins likes the idea, but her daughter does not. She thinks her mother will lose independence and her condition will get worse. She talks to her mother's consultant to get information that will help stop the sale. But he says that although Mrs Collins is anxious about the physical effects the stroke has had on her body, it has not caused any mental impairment or affected her brain, so she still has capacity to make her own decision about selling her house.

Stage 2: Does the impairment or disturbance mean that the person is unable to make a specific decision when they need to?

4.13   For a person to lack capacity to make a decision, the Act says their impairment or disturbance must affect their ability to make the specific decision when they need to. But first people must be given all practical and appropriate support to help them make the decision for themselves (see chapter 2, principle 2). Stage 2 can only apply if all practical and appropriate support to help the person make the decision has failed. See chapter 3 for guidance on ways of helping people to make their own decisions.

What does the Act mean by 'inability to make a decision'?

4.14   A person is unable to make a decision if they cannot:
1.   understand information about the decision to be made (the Act calls this 'relevant information')
2.   retain that information in their mind
3.   use or weigh that information as part of the decision-making process, or
4.   communicate their decision (by talking, using sign language or any other means). See section 3(1).

4.15   These four points are explained in more detail below. The first three should be applied together. If a person cannot do any of these three things, they will be treated as unable to make the decision. The fourth only applies in situations where people cannot communicate their decision in any way.

Understanding information about the decision to be made

4.16 It is important not to assess someone's understanding before they have been given relevant information about a decision. Every effort must be made to provide information in a way that is most appropriate to help the person to understand. Quick or inadequate explanations are not acceptable unless the situation is urgent (see chapter 3 for some practical steps). Relevant information includes:

- the nature of the decision
- the reason why the decision is needed, and
- the likely effects of deciding one way or another, or making no decision at all.

4.17 Section 3(2) outlines the need to present information in a way that is appropriate to meet the individual's needs and circumstances. It also stresses the importance of explaining information using the most effective form of communication for that person (such as simple language, sign language, visual representations, computer support or any other means).

4.18 For example:

- a person with a learning disability may need somebody to read information to them. They might also need illustrations to help them to understand what is happening. Or they might stop the reader to ask what things mean. It might also be helpful for them to discuss information with an advocate.
- a person with anxiety or depression may find it difficult to reach a decision about treatment in a group meeting with professionals. They may prefer to read the relevant documents in private. This way they can come to a conclusion alone, and ask for help if necessary.
- someone who has a brain injury might need to be given information several times. It will be necessary to check that the person understands the information. If they have difficulty understanding, it might be useful to present information in a different way (for example, different forms of words, pictures or diagrams). Written information, audiotapes, videos and posters can help people remember important facts.

4.19 Relevant information must include what the likely consequences of a decision would be (the possible effects of deciding one way or another) – and also the likely consequences of making no decision at all (section 3(4)). In some cases, it may be enough to give a broad explanation using simple language. But a person might need more detailed information or access to advice, depending on the decision that needs to be made. If a decision could have serious or grave consequences, it is even more important that a person understands the information relevant to that decision.

PART VI

Scenario: Providing relevant information in an appropriate format

Mr Leslie has learning disabilities and has developed an irregular heartbeat. He has been prescribed medication for this, but is anxious about having regular blood tests to check his medication levels. His doctor gives him a leaflet to explain:

- the reason for the tests
- what a blood test involves
- the risks in having or not having the tests, and
- that he has the right to decide whether or not to have the test.

The leaflet uses simple language and photographs to explain these things. Mr Leslie's carer helps him read the leaflet over the next few days, and checks that he understands it.

Mr Leslie goes back to tell the doctor that, even though he is scared of needles, he will agree to the blood tests so that he can get the right medication. He is able to pick out the equipment needed to do the blood test. So the doctor concludes that Mr Leslie can understand, retain and use the relevant information and therefore has the capacity to make the decision to have the test.

Retaining information

4.20 The person must be able to hold the information in their mind long enough to use it to make an effective decision. But section 3(3) states that people who can only retain information for a short while must not automatically be assumed to lack the capacity to decide – it depends on what is necessary for the decision in question. Items such as notebooks, photographs, posters, videos and voice recorders can help people record and retain information.

Scenario: Assessing a person's ability to retain information

Walter, an elderly man, is diagnosed with dementia and has problems remembering things in the short term. He can't always remember his great-grandchildren's names, but he recognises them when they come to visit. He can also pick them out on photographs.

Walter would like to buy premium bonds (a type of financial investment) for each of his great-grandchildren. He asks his solicitor to make the arrangements. After assessing his capacity to make financial decisions, the solicitor is satisfied that Walter has capacity to make this decision, despite his short-term memory problems.

Using or weighing information as part of the decision-making process

4.21 For someone to have capacity, they must have the ability to weigh up information and use it to arrive at a decision. Sometimes people can understand information but an impairment or disturbance stops them using it. In other cases, the impairment or disturbance leads to a person making a specific decision without understanding or using the information they have been given.[3]

4.22 For example, a person with the eating disorder anorexia nervosa may understand information about the consequences of not eating. But their compulsion not to eat might be too strong for them to ignore. Some people who have serious brain damage might make impulsive decisions regardless of information they have been given or their understanding of it.

Inability to communicate a decision in any way

4.23 Sometimes there is no way for a person to communicate. This will apply to very few people, but it does include:
- people who are unconscious or in a coma, or
- those with the very rare condition sometimes known as 'locked-in syndrome', who are conscious but cannot speak or move at all.

If a person cannot communicate their decision in any way at all, the Act says they should be treated as if they are unable to make that decision.

4.24 Before deciding that someone falls into this category, it is important to make all practical and appropriate efforts to help them communicate. This might call for the involvement of speech and language therapists, specialists in non-verbal communication or other professionals. Chapter 3 gives advice for communicating with people who have specific disabilities or cognitive problems.

4.25 Communication by simple muscle movements can show that somebody can communicate and may have capacity to make a decision.[4] For example, a person might blink an eye or squeeze a hand to say 'yes' or 'no'. In these cases, assessment must use the first three points listed in paragraph 4.14, which are explained in more depth in paragraphs 4.16–4.22.

What other issues might affect capacity?

People with fluctuating or temporary capacity

4.26 Some people have fluctuating capacity – they have a problem or condition that gets worse occasionally and affects their ability to

PART VI

---

[3] This issue has been considered in a number of court cases, including *Re MB* [1997] 2 FLR 426; *R v Collins and Ashworth Hospital Authority ex parte Brady* [2001] 58 BMLR 173.

[4] This was demonstrated in the case *Re AK (Adult Patient) (Medical Treatment: Consent)* [2001] 1 FLR 129.

make decisions. For example, someone who has manic depression may have a temporary manic phase which causes them to lack capacity to make financial decisions, leading them to get into debt even though at other times they are perfectly able to manage their money. A person with a psychotic illness may have delusions that affect their capacity to make decisions at certain times but disappear at others. Temporary factors may also affect someone's ability to make decisions. Examples include acute illness, severe pain, the effect of medication, or distress after a death or shock. More guidance on how to support someone with fluctuating or temporary capacity to make a decision can be found in chapter 3, particularly paragraphs 3.12–3.16. More information about factors that may indicate that a person may regain or develop capacity in the future can be found at paragraph 5.28.

4.27 As in any other situation, an assessment must only examine a person's capacity to make a particular decision when it needs to be made. It may be possible to put off the decision until the person has the capacity to make it (see also guidance on best interests in chapter 5).

Ongoing conditions that may affect capacity

4.28 Generally, capacity assessments should be related to a specific decision. But there may be people with an ongoing condition that affects their ability to make certain decisions or that may affect other decisions in their life. One decision on its own may make sense, but may give cause for concern when considered alongside others.

4.29 Again, it is important to review capacity from time to time, as people can improve their decision-making capabilities. In particular, someone with an ongoing condition may become able to make some, if not all, decisions. Some people (for example, people with learning disabilities) will learn new skills throughout their life, improving their capacity to make certain decisions. So assessments should be reviewed from time to time. Capacity should always be reviewed:

- whenever a care plan is being developed or reviewed
- at other relevant stages of the care planning process, and
- as particular decisions need to be made.

4.30 It is important to acknowledge the difference between:

- unwise decisions, which a person has the right to make (chapter 2, principle 3), and
- decisions based on a lack of understanding of risks or inability to weigh up the information about a decision.

Information about decisions the person has made based on a lack of understanding of risks or inability to weigh up the information can form part of a capacity assessment – particularly if someone repeatedly makes decisions that put them at risk or result in harm to them or someone else.

> ### Scenario: Ongoing conditions
>
> Paul had an accident at work and suffered severe head injuries. He was awarded compensation to pay for care he will need throughout his life as a result of his head injury. An application was made to the Court of Protection to consider how the award of compensation should be managed, including whether to appoint a deputy to manage Paul's financial affairs. Paul objected as he believed he could manage his life and should be able to spend his money however he liked.
>
> He wrote a list of what he intended to spend his money on. This included fully-staffed luxury properties and holiday villas, cars with chauffeurs, jewellery and various other items for himself and his family. But spending money on all these luxury items would not leave enough money to cover the costs of his care in future years.
>
> The court judged that Paul had capacity to make day-to-day financial decisions, but he did not understand why he had received compensation and what the money was supposed to be used for. Nor did he understand how buying luxuries now could affect his future care. The court therefore decided Paul lacked capacity to manage large amounts of money and appointed a deputy to make ongoing financial decisions relating to his care. But it gave him access to enough funds to cover everyday needs and occasional treats.

What other legal tests of capacity are there?

4.31 The Act makes clear that the definition of 'lack of capacity' and the two-stage test for capacity set out in the Act are 'for the purposes of this Act'. This means that the definition and test are to be used in situations covered by this Act. Schedule 6 of the Act also amends existing laws to ensure that the definition and test are used in other areas of law not covered directly by this Act.

For example, Schedule 6, paragraph 20 allows a person to be disqualified from jury service if they lack the capacity (using this Act's definition) to carry out a juror's tasks.

4.32 There are several tests of capacity that have been produced following judgments in court cases (known as common law tests).[5] These cover:

- capacity to make a will[6]
- capacity to make a gift[7]
- capacity to enter into a contract[8]

---

[5] For details, see British Medical Association & Law Society, *Assessment of Mental Capacity: Guidance for Doctors and Lawyers* (BMA, 1995; BMJ Books, 2nd edn, 2004; Law Society Publishing, 3rd edn, 2009).

[6] *Banks v Goodfellow* (1870) LR 5 QB 549.

[7] *Re Beaney (deceased)* [1978] 2 All ER 595.

[8] *Boughton v Knight* (1873) LR 3 PD 64.

- capacity to litigate (take part in legal cases),[9] and
- capacity to enter into marriage.[10]

4.33 The Act's new definition of capacity is in line with the existing common law tests, and the Act does not replace them. When cases come before the court on the above issues, judges can adopt the new definition if they think it is appropriate. The Act will apply to all other cases relating to financial, healthcare or welfare decisions.

When should capacity be assessed?

4.34 Assessing capacity correctly is vitally important to everyone affected by the Act. Someone who is assessed as lacking capacity may be denied their right to make a specific decision – particularly if others think that the decision would not be in their best interests or could cause harm. Also, if a person lacks capacity to make specific decisions, that person might make decisions they do not really understand. Again, this could cause harm or put the person at risk. So it is important to carry out an assessment when a person's capacity is in doubt. It is also important that the person who does an assessment can justify their conclusions. Many organisations will provide specific professional guidance for members of their profession.[11]

4.35 There are a number of reasons why people may question a person's capacity to make a specific decision:
- the person's behaviour or circumstances cause doubt as to whether they have the capacity to make a decision
- somebody else says they are concerned about the person's capacity, or
- the person has previously been diagnosed with an impairment or disturbance that affects the way their mind or brain works (see paragraphs 4.11–4.12 above), and it has already been shown they lack capacity to make other decisions in their life.

4.36 The starting assumption must be that the person has the capacity to make the specific decision. If, however, anyone thinks a person lacks capacity, it is important to then ask the following questions:
- Does the person have all the relevant information they need to make the decision?
- If they are making a decision that involves choosing between alternatives, do they have information on all the different options?

---

9 *Masterman-Lister v Brutton & Co and Jewell & Home Counties Dairies* [2003] 3 All ER 162, CA.
10 *E (an Alleged Patient), Re; Sheffield City Council v E & S* [2005] 1 FLR 965.
11 See for example, British Medical Association & Law Society, *Assessment of Mental Capacity: Guidance for Doctors and Lawyers* (BMA, 1995; BMJ Books, 2nd edn, 2004; Law Society Publishing, 3rd edn, 2009); the Joint Royal Colleges Ambulance Service Liaison Committee Clinical Practice Guidelines (JRCALC, available online at www2.warwick.ac.uk/fac/med/research/hsri/ emergencycare/jrcalc_2006/ clinical_guidelines_2006.pdf) and British Psychological Society, *Guidelines on assessing capacity* (BPS, 2006 available online at www.bps.org.uk)

- Would the person have a better understanding if information was explained or presented in another way?
- Are there times of day when the person's understanding is better?
- Are there locations where they may feel more at ease?
- Can the decision be put off until the circumstances are different and the person concerned may be able to make the decision?
- Can anyone else help the person to make choices or express a view (for example, a family member or carer, an advocate or someone to help with communication)?

4.37 Chapter 3 describes ways to deal with these questions and suggest steps which may help people make their own decisions. If all practical and appropriate steps fail, an assessment will then be needed of the person's capacity to make the decision that now needs to be made.

Who should assess capacity?

4.38 The person who assesses an individual's capacity to make a decision will usually be the person who is directly concerned with the individual at the time the decision needs to be made. This means that different people will be involved in assessing someone's capacity to make different decisions at different times.

For most day-to-day decisions, this will be the person caring for them at the time a decision must be made. For example, a care worker might need to assess if the person can agree to being bathed. Then a district nurse might assess if the person can consent to have a dressing changed.

4.39 For acts of care or treatment (see chapter 6), the assessor must have a 'reasonable belief' that the person lacks capacity to agree to the action or decision to be taken (see paragraphs 4.44–4.45 for a description of reasonable belief).

4.40 If a doctor or healthcare professional proposes treatment or an examination, they must assess the person's capacity to consent. In settings such as a hospital, this can involve the multi-disciplinary team (a team of people from different professional backgrounds who share responsibility for a patient). But ultimately, it is up to the professional responsible for the person's treatment to make sure that capacity has been assessed.

4.41 For a legal transaction (for example, making a will), a solicitor or legal practitioner must assess the client's capacity to instruct them. They must assess whether the client has the capacity to satisfy any relevant legal test. In cases of doubt, they should get an opinion from a doctor or other professional expert.

4.42 More complex decisions are likely to need more formal assessments (see paragraph 4.54 below). A professional opinion on the person's capacity might be necessary. This could be, for example, from a psychiatrist, psychologist, a speech and language therapist, occupational therapist or social worker. But the final

PART VI

decision about a person's capacity must be made by the person intending to make the decision or carry out the action on behalf of the person who lacks capacity – not the professional, who is there to advise.

4.43 Any assessor should have the skills and ability to communicate effectively with the person (see chapter 3). If necessary, they should get professional help to communicate with the person.

Scenario: Getting help with assessing capacity

Ms Dodd suffered brain damage in a road accident and is unable to speak. At first, her family thought she was not able to make decisions. But they soon discovered that she could choose by pointing at things, such as the clothes she wants to wear or the food she prefers. Her behaviour also indicates that she enjoys attending a day centre, but she refuses to go swimming. Her carers have assessed her as having capacity to make these decisions.

Ms Dodd needs hospital treatment but she gets distressed when away from home. Her mother feels that Ms Dodd is refusing treatment by her behaviour, but her father thinks she lacks capacity to say no to treatment that could improve her condition.

The clinician who is proposing the treatment will have to assess Ms Dodd's capacity to consent. He gets help from a member of staff at the day centre who knows Ms Dodd's communication well and also discusses things with her parents. Over several meetings the clinician explains the treatment options to Ms Dodd with the help of the staff member. The final decision about Ms Dodd's capacity rests with the clinician, but he will need to use information from the staff member and others who know Ms Dodd well to make this assessment.

What is 'reasonable belief' of lack of capacity?

4.44 Carers (whether family carers or other carers) and care workers do not have to be experts in assessing capacity. But to have protection from liability when providing care or treatment (see chapter 6), they must have a 'reasonable belief' that the person they care for lacks capacity to make relevant decisions about their care or treatment (section 5(1)). To have this reasonable belief, they must have taken 'reasonable' steps to establish that that the person lacks capacity to make a decision or consent to an act at the time the decision or consent is needed. They must also establish that the act or decision is in the person's best interests (see chapter 5).

They do not usually need to follow formal processes, such as involving a professional to make an assessment. However, if somebody challenges their assessment (see paragraph 4.63 below), they must be able to describe the steps they have taken. They must also have objective reasons for believing the person lacks capacity to make the decision in question.

4.45 The steps that are accepted as 'reasonable' will depend on individual circumstances and the urgency of the decision. Professionals, who are qualified in their particular field, are normally expected to undertake a fuller assessment, reflecting their higher degree of knowledge and experience, than family members or other carers who have no formal qualifications. See paragraph 4.36 for a list of points to consider when assessing someone's capacity. The following may also be helpful:

- Start by assuming the person has capacity to make the specific decision. Is there anything to prove otherwise?
- Does the person have a previous diagnosis of disability or mental disorder? Does that condition now affect their capacity to make this decision? If there has been no previous diagnosis, it may be best to get a medical opinion.
- Make every effort to communicate with the person to explain what is happening.
- Make every effort to try to help the person make the decision in question.
- See if there is a way to explain or present information about the decision in a way that makes it easier to understand. If the person has a choice, do they have information about all the options?
- Can the decision be delayed to take time to help the person make the decision, or to give the person time to regain the capacity to make the decision for themselves?
- Does the person understand what decision they need to make and why they need to make it?
- Can they understand information about the decision? Can they retain it, use it and weigh it to make the decision?
- Be aware that the fact that a person agrees with you or assents to what is proposed does not necessarily mean that they have capacity to make the decision.

What other factors might affect an assessment of capacity?

4.46 It is important to assess people when they are in the best state to make the decision, if possible. Whether this is possible will depend on the nature and urgency of the decision to be made. Many of the practical steps suggested in chapter 3 will help to create the best environment for assessing capacity. The assessor must then carry out the two stages of the test of capacity (see paragraphs 4.11–4.25 above).

4.47 In many cases, it may be clear that the person has an impairment or disturbance in the functioning of their mind or brain which could affect their ability to make a decision. For example, there might be a past diagnosis of a disability or mental disorder, or there may be signs that an illness is returning. Old assumptions about an illness or condition should be reviewed. Sometimes an illness develops gradually (for example, dementia), and it is hard to know when it starts to affect capacity. Anyone assessing someone's capacity may need to ask for a medical opinion as to whether a person has an illness or condition that could affect their capacity to make a decision in this specific case.

Scenario: Getting a professional opinion

Mr Elliott is 87 years old and lives alone. He has poor short-term memory, and he often forgets to eat. He also sometimes neglects his personal hygiene. His daughter talks to him about the possibility of moving into residential care. She decides that he understands the reasons for her concerns as well as the risks of continuing to live alone and, having weighed these up, he has the capacity to decide to stay at home and accept the consequences.

Two months later, Mr Elliott has a fall and breaks his leg. While being treated in hospital, he becomes confused and depressed. He says he wants to go home, but the staff think that the deterioration in his mental health has affected his capacity to make this decision at this time. They think he cannot understand the consequences or weigh up the risks he faces if he goes home. They refer him to a specialist in old age psychiatry, who assesses whether his mental health is affecting his capacity to make this decision. The staff will then use the specialist's opinion to help their assessment of Mr Elliott's capacity.

4.48 Anyone assessing someone's capacity must not assume that a person lacks capacity simply because they have a particular diagnosis or condition. There must be proof that the diagnosed illness or condition affects the ability to make a decision when it needs to be made. The person assessing capacity should ask the following questions:
- Does the person have a general understanding of what decision they need to make and why they need to make it?
- Do they understand the likely consequences of making, or not making, this decision?
- Can they understand and process information about the decision? And can they use it to help them make a decision?

In borderline cases, or where there is doubt, the assessor must be able to show that it is more likely than not that the answer to these questions is 'no'.

What practical steps should be taken when assessing capacity?

4.49 Anyone assessing someone's capacity will need to decide which of these steps are relevant to their situation.

- They should make sure that they understand the nature and effect of the decision to be made themselves. They may need access to relevant documents and background information (for example, details of the person's finances if assessing capacity to manage affairs). See chapter 16 for details on access to information.

- They may need other relevant information to support the assessment (for example, healthcare records or the views of staff involved in the person's care).

- Family members and close friends may be able to provide valuable background information (for example, the person's past behaviour and abilities and the types of decisions they can currently make). But their personal views and wishes about what they would want for the person must not influence the assessment.

- They should again explain to the person all the information relevant to the decision. The explanation must be in the most appropriate and effective form of communication for that person.

- Check the person's understanding after a few minutes. The person should be able to give a rough explanation of the information that was explained. There are different methods for people who use nonverbal means of communication (for example, observing behaviour or their ability to recognise objects or pictures).

- Avoid questions that need only a 'yes' or 'no' answer (for example, did you understand what I just said?). They are not enough to assess the person's capacity to make a decision. But there may be no alternative in cases where there are major communication difficulties. In these cases, check the response by asking questions again in a different way.

- Skills and behaviour do not necessarily reflect the person's capacity to make specific decisions. The fact that someone has good social or language skills, polite behaviour or good manners doesn't necessarily mean they understand the information or are able to weigh it up.

- Repeating these steps can help confirm the result.

4.50 For certain kinds of complex decisions (for example, making a will), there are specific legal tests (see paragraph 4.32 above) in addition to the two-stage test for capacity. In some cases, medical or psychometric tests may also be helpful tools (for example, for assessing cognitive skills) in assessing a person's capacity to make particular decisions, but the relevant legal test of capacity must still be fulfilled.

When should professionals be involved?

4.51 Anyone assessing someone's capacity may need to get a professional opinion when assessing a person's capacity to make complex or major decisions. In some cases this will simply involve contacting the person's general practitioner (GP) or family doctor. If the person has a particular condition or disorder, it may be appropriate to contact a specialist (for example, consultant psychiatrist, psychologist or other professional with experience of caring for patients with that condition). A speech and language therapist might be able to help if there are communication difficulties. In some cases, a multi-disciplinary approach is best. This means combining the skills and expertise of different professionals.

4.52 Professionals should never express an opinion without carrying out a proper examination and assessment of the person's capacity to make the decision. They must apply the appropriate test of capacity. In some cases, they will need to meet the person more than once – particularly if the person has communication difficulties. Professionals can get background information from a person's family and carers. But the personal views of these people about what they want for the person who lacks capacity must not influence the outcome of that assessment.

4.53 Professional involvement might be needed if:

- the decision that needs to be made is complicated or has serious consequences
- an assessor concludes a person lacks capacity, and the person challenges the finding
- family members, carers and/or professionals disagree about a person's capacity
- there is a conflict of interest between the assessor and the person being assessed
- the person being assessed is expressing different views to different people – they may be trying to please everyone or telling people what they think they want to hear
- somebody might challenge the person's capacity to make the decision – either at the time of the decision or later (for example, a family member might challenge a will after a person has died on the basis that the person lacked capacity when they made the will)
- somebody has been accused of abusing a vulnerable adult who may lack capacity to make decisions that protect them
- a person repeatedly makes decisions that put them at risk or could result in suffering or damage.

Scenario: Involving professional opinion

Ms Ledger is a young woman with learning disabilities and some autistic spectrum disorders. Recently she began a sexual relationship

---

with a much older man, who is trying to persuade her to move in with him and come off the pill. There are rumours that he has been violent towards her and has taken her bankbook.

Ms Ledger boasts about the relationship to her friends. But she has admitted to her key worker that she is sometimes afraid of the man. Staff at her sheltered accommodation decide to make a referral under the local adult protection procedures. They arrange for a clinical psychologist to assess Ms Ledger's understanding of the relationship and her capacity to consent to it.

4.54 In some cases, it may be a legal requirement, or good professional practice, to undertake a formal assessment of capacity. These cases include:

- where a person's capacity to sign a legal document (for example, a will), could later be challenged, in which case an expert should be asked for an opinion[12]
- to establish whether a person who might be involved in a legal case needs the assistance of the Official Solicitor or other litigation friend (somebody to represent their views to a court and give instructions to their legal representative) and there is doubt about the person's capacity to instruct a solicitor or take part in the case[13]
- whenever the Court of Protection has to decide if a person lacks capacity in a certain matter
- if the courts are required to make a decision about a person's capacity in other legal proceedings[14]
- if there may be legal consequences of a finding of capacity (for example, deciding on financial compensation following a claim for personal injury).

PART VI

Are assessment processes confidential?

4.55 People involved in assessing capacity will need to share information about a person's circumstances. But there are ethical codes and laws that require professionals to keep personal information confidential. As a general rule, professionals must ask their patients or clients if they can reveal information to somebody else – even close relatives. But sometimes information may be

[12] *Kenward v Adams* (1975) *The Times*, 29 November.
[13] Civil Procedure Rules 1998, r 21.1
[14] *Masterman-Lister v Brutton & Co and Jewell & Home Counties Dairies* [2002] EWCA Civ 1889, CA at 54.

disclosed without the consent of the person who the information concerns (for example, to protect the person or prevent harm to other people).[15]

4.56 Anyone assessing someone's capacity needs accurate information concerning the person being assessed that is relevant to the decision the person has to make. So professionals should, where possible, make relevant information available. They should make every effort to get the person's permission to reveal relevant information. They should give a full explanation of why this is necessary, and they should tell the person about the risks and consequences of revealing, and not revealing information. If the person is unable to give permission, the professional might still be allowed to provide information that will help make an accurate assessment of the person's capacity to make the specific decision. Chapter 16 has more detail on how to access information.

What if someone refuses to be assessed?

4.57 There may be circumstances in which a person whose capacity is in doubt refuses to undergo an assessment of capacity or refuses to be examined by a doctor or other professional. In these circumstances, it might help to explain to someone refusing an assessment why it is needed and what the consequences of refusal are. But threats or attempts to force the person to agree to an assessment are not acceptable.

4.58 If the person lacks capacity to agree or refuse, the assessment can normally go ahead, as long as the person does not object to the assessment, and it is in their best interests (see chapter 5).

4.59 Nobody can be forced to undergo an assessment of capacity. If someone refuses to open the door to their home, it cannot be forced. If there are serious worries about the person's mental health, it may be possible to get a warrant to force entry and assess the person for treatment in hospital – but the situation must meet the requirements of the Mental Health Act 1983 (section 135). But simply refusing an assessment of capacity is in no way sufficient grounds for an assessment under the Mental Health Act 1983 (see chapter 13).

Who should keep a record of assessments?

4.60 Assessments of capacity to take day-to-day decisions or consent to care require no formal assessment procedures or recorded documentation. Paragraphs 4.44–4.45 above explain the steps to take to reach a 'reasonable belief' that someone lacks capacity to

---

[15]   For example, in the circumstances discussed in *W v Egdell and others* [1990] 1 All ER 835 at 848; *R (S) v Plymouth City Council and C* [2002] EWCA Civ 388 at 49.

make a particular decision. It is good practice for paid care workers to keep a record of the steps they take when caring for the person concerned.

Professional records

4.61 It is good practice for professionals to carry out a proper assessment of a person's capacity to make particular decisions and to record the findings in the relevant professional records.

- A doctor or healthcare professional proposing treatment should carry out an assessment of the person's capacity to consent (with a multi-disciplinary team, if appropriate) and record it in the patient's clinical notes.
- Solicitors should assess a client's capacity to give instructions or carry out a legal transaction (obtaining a medical or other professional opinion, if necessary) and record it on the client's file.
- An assessment of a person's capacity to consent or agree to the provision of services will be part of the care planning processes for health and social care needs, and should be recorded in the relevant documentation. This includes:
- Person Centred Planning for people with learning disabilities
- the Care Programme Approach for people with mental illness
- the Single Assessment Process for older people in England, and
- the Unified Assessment Process in Wales.

Formal reports or certificates of capacity

4.62 In some cases, a more detailed report or certificate of capacity may be required, for example,

- for use in court or other legal processes
- as required by Regulations, Rules or Orders made under the Act.

How can someone challenge a finding of lack of capacity?

4.63 There are likely to be occasions when someone may wish to challenge the results of an assessment of capacity. The first step is to raise the matter with the person who carried out the assessment. If the challenge comes from the individual who is said to lack capacity, they might need support from family, friends or an advocate. Ask the assessor to:

- give reasons why they believe the person lacks capacity to make the decision, and
- provide objective evidence to support that belief.

PART VI

4.64 The assessor must show they have applied the principles of the Mental Capacity Act (see chapter 2). Attorneys, deputies and professionals will need to show that they have also followed guidance in this chapter.

4.65 It might be possible to get a second opinion from an independent professional or another expert in assessing capacity. Chapter 15 has other suggestions for dealing with disagreements. But if a disagreement cannot be resolved, the person who is challenging the assessment may be able to apply to the Court of Protection. The Court of Protection can rule on whether a person has capacity to make the decision covered by the assessment (see chapter 8).

5   WHAT DOES THE ACT MEAN WHEN IT TALKS ABOUT 'BEST INTERESTS'?

One of the key principles of the Act is that any act done for, or any decision made on behalf of a person who lacks capacity must be done, or made, in that person's *best interests*. That is the same whether the person making the decision or acting is a family carer, a paid care worker, an attorney, a court-appointed deputy, or a healthcare professional, and whether the decision is a minor issue – like what to wear – or a major issue, like whether to provide particular healthcare.

As long as these acts or decisions are in the best interests of the person who lacks capacity to make the decision for themselves, or to consent to acts concerned with their care or treatment, then the decision-maker or carer will be protected from liability.

There are exceptions to this, including circumstances where a person has made an advance decision to refuse treatment (see chapter 9) and, in specific circumstances, the involvement of a person who lacks capacity in research (see chapter 11). But otherwise the underpinning principle of the Act is that all acts and decisions should be made in the best interests of the person without capacity.

Working out what is in someone else's best interests may be difficult, and the Act requires people to follow certain steps to help them work out whether a particular act or decision is in a person's best interests. In some cases, there may be disagreement about what someone's best interests really are. As long as the person who acts or makes the decision has followed the steps to establish whether a person has capacity, and done everything they reasonably can to work out what someone's best interests are, the law should protect them.

This chapter explains what the Act means by 'best interests' and what things should be considered when trying to work out what is in someone's best interests. It also highlights some of the difficulties that might come up in working out what the best interests of a person who lacks capacity to make the decision actually are.

> In this chapter, as throughout the Code, a person's capacity (or lack of capacity) refers specifically to their capacity to make a particular decision at the time it needs to be made.

Quick summary

A person trying to work out the best interests of a person who lacks capacity to make a particular decision ('lacks capacity') should:

Encourage participation

- do whatever is possible to permit and encourage the person to take part, or to improve their ability to take part, in making the decision

Identify all relevant circumstances

- try to identify all the things that the person who lacks capacity would take into account if they were making the decision or acting for themselves

Find out the person's views

- try to find out the views of the person who lacks capacity, including:
  - the person's past and present wishes and feelings – these may have been expressed verbally, in writing or through behaviour or habits.
  - any beliefs and values (e.g. religious, cultural, moral or political) that would be likely to influence the decision in question.
  - any other factors the person themselves would be likely to consider if they were making the decision or acting for themselves.

Avoid discrimination

- not make assumptions about someone's best interests simply on the basis of the person's age, appearance, condition or behaviour.

Assess whether the person might regain capacity

- consider whether the person is likely to regain capacity (e.g. after receiving medical treatment). If so, can the decision wait until then?

If the decision concerns life-sustaining treatment

- not be motivated in any way by a desire to bring about the person's death. They should not make assumptions about the person's quality of life.

Consult others

- if it is practical and appropriate to do so, consult other people for their views about the person's best interests and to see if they have

PART VI

any information about the person's wishes and feelings, beliefs and values. In particular, try to consult:

- anyone previously named by the person as someone to be consulted on either the decision in question or on similar issues
- anyone engaged in caring for the person
- close relatives, friends or others who take an interest in the person's welfare
- any attorney appointed under a Lasting Power of Attorney or Enduring Power of Attorney made by the person
- any deputy appointed by the Court of Protection to make decisions for the person.

- For decisions about major medical treatment or where the person should live and where there is no-one who fits into any of the above categories, an Independent Mental Capacity Advocate (IMCA) must be consulted. (See chapter 10 for more information about IMCAs.)
- When consulting, remember that the person who lacks the capacity to make the decision or act for themselves still has a right to keep their affairs private – so it would not be right to share every piece of information with everyone.

Avoid restricting the person's rights

- see if there are other options that may be less restrictive of the person's rights.

Take all of this into account

- weigh up all of these factors in order to work out what is in the person's best interests.

What is the best interests principle and who does it apply to?

5.1 The best interests principle underpins the Mental Capacity Act. It is set out in section 1(5) of the Act.

> 'An act done, or decision made, under this Act for or on behalf of a person who lacks capacity must be done, or made, in his best interests.'

The concept has been developed by the courts in cases relating to people who lack capacity to make specific decisions for themselves, mainly decisions concerned with the provision of medical treatment or social care.

5.2 This principle covers all aspects of financial, personal welfare and healthcare decision-making and actions. It applies to anyone making decisions or acting under the provisions of the Act, including:

- family carers, other carers and care workers
- healthcare and social care staff
- attorneys appointed under a Lasting Power of Attorney or registered Enduring Power of Attorney
- deputies appointed by the court to make decisions on behalf of someone who lacks capacity, and

- the Court of Protection.

5.3 However, as chapter 2 explained, the Act's first key principle is that people must be assumed to have capacity to make a decision or act for themselves unless it is established that they lack it. That means that working out a person's best interests is only relevant when that person has been assessed as lacking, or is reasonably believed to lack, capacity to make the decision in question or give consent to an act being done.

People with capacity are able to decide for themselves what they want to do. When they do this, they might choose an option that other people don't think is in their best interests. That is their choice and does not, in itself, mean that they lack capacity to make those decisions.

Exceptions to the best interests principle

5.4 There are two circumstances when the best interests principle will not apply. The first is where someone has previously made an advance decision to refuse medical treatment while they had the capacity to do so. Their advance decision should be respected when they lack capacity, even if others think that the decision to refuse treatment is not in their best interests (guidance on advance decisions is given in chapter 9).

The second concerns the involvement in research, in certain circumstances, of someone lacking capacity to consent (see chapter 11).

What does the Act mean by best interests?

5.5 The term 'best interests' is not actually defined in the Act. This is because so many different types of decisions and actions are covered by the Act, and so many different people and circumstances are affected by it.

5.6 Section 4 of the Act explains how to work out the best interests of a person who lacks capacity to make a decision at the time it needs to be made. This section sets out a checklist of common factors that must always be considered by anyone who needs to decide what is in the best interests of a person who lacks capacity in any particular situation. This checklist is only the starting point: in many cases, extra factors will need to be considered.

5.7 When working out what is in the best interests of the person who lacks capacity to make a decision or act for themselves, decision-makers must take into account all relevant factors that it would be reasonable to consider, not just those that they think are important. They must not act or make a decision based on what they would want to do if they were the person who lacked capacity.

Scenario: Whose best interests?

Pedro, a young man with a severe learning disability, lives in a care home. He has dental problems which cause him a lot of pain, but refuses to open his mouth for his teeth to be cleaned.

The staff suggest that it would be a good idea to give Pedro an occasional general anaesthetic so that a dentist can clean his teeth and fill any cavities. His mother is worried about the effects of an anaesthetic, but she hates to see him distressed and suggests instead that he should be given strong painkillers when needed.

While the views of Pedro's mother and carers are important in working out what course of action would be in his best interests, the decision must *not* be based on what would be less stressful for them. Instead, it must focus on Pedro's best interests.

Having talked to others, the dentist tries to find ways of involving Pedro in the decision, with the help of his key worker and an advocate, to try to find out the cause and location of the problem and to explain to him that they are trying to stop the pain. The dentist tries to find out if any other forms of dental care would be better, such as a mouthwash or dental gum.

The dentist concludes that it would be in Pedro's best interests for:
- proper investigation to be carried out under anaesthetic so that immediate treatment can be provided
- options for his future dental care to be reviewed by the care team, involving Pedro as far as possible.

Who can be a decision-maker?

5.8 Under the Act, many different people may be required to make decisions or act on behalf of someone who lacks capacity to make decisions for themselves. The person making the decision is referred to throughout this chapter, and in other parts of the Code, as the 'decision-maker', and it is the decision-maker's responsibility to work out what would be in the best interests of the person who lacks capacity.
- For most day-to-day actions or decisions, the decision-maker will be the carer most directly involved with the person at the time.
- Where the decision involves the provision of medical treatment, the doctor or other member of healthcare staff responsible for carrying out the particular treatment or procedure is the decision-maker.
- Where nursing or paid care is provided, the nurse or paid carer will be the decision-maker.

- If a Lasting Power of Attorney (or Enduring Power of Attorney) has been made and registered, or a deputy has been appointed under a court order, the attorney or deputy will be the decision-maker, for decisions within the scope of their authority.

5.9 What this means is that a range of different decision-makers may be involved with a person who lacks capacity to make different decisions.

5.10 In some cases, the same person may make different types of decision for someone who lacks capacity to make decisions for themselves. For instance, a family carer may carry out certain acts in caring for the person on a day-to-day basis, but if they are also an attorney, appointed under a Lasting Power of Attorney (LPA), they may also make specific decisions concerning the person's property and affairs or their personal welfare (depending on what decisions the LPA has been set up to cover).

5.11 There are also times when a joint decision might be made by a number of people. For example, when a care plan for a person who lacks capacity to make relevant decisions is being put together, different healthcare or social care staff might be involved in making decisions or recommendations about the person's care package. Sometimes these decisions will be made by a team of healthcare or social care staff as a whole. At other times, the decision will be made by a specific individual within the team. A different member of the team may then implement that decision, based on what the team has worked out to be the person's best interests.

5.12 No matter who is making the decision, the most important thing is that the decision-maker tries to work out what would be in the best interests of the person who lacks capacity.

PART VI

Scenario: Coming to a joint decision

Jack, a young man with a brain injury, lacks capacity to agree to a rehabilitation programme designed to improve his condition. But the healthcare and social care staff who are looking after him believe that he clearly needs the programme, and have obtained the necessary funding from the Primary Care Trust.

However, Jack's family want to take him home from hospital as they believe they can provide better care for him at home.

A 'best interests' case conference is held, involving Jack, his parents and other family members and the relevant professionals, in order to decide what course of action would be in the Jack's best interests.

A plan is developed to enable Jack to live at home, but attend the day hospital every weekday. Jack seems happy with the proposals and both the family carers and the healthcare and social care staff are satisfied that the plan is in his best interests.

What must be taken into account when trying to work out someone's best interests?

5.13 Because every case – and every decision – is different, the law can't set out all the factors that will need to be taken into account in working out someone's best interests. But section 4 of the Act sets out some common factors that must always be considered when trying to work out someone's best interests. These factors are summarised in the checklist here:

- Working out what is in someone's best interests cannot be based simply on someone's age, appearance, condition or behaviour. (see paragraphs 5.16–5.17).
- All relevant circumstances should be considered when working out someone's best interests (paragraphs 5.18–5.20).
- Every effort should be made to encourage and enable the person who lacks capacity to take part in making the decision (paragraphs 5.21–5.24).
- If there is a chance that the person will regain the capacity to make a particular decision, then it may be possible to put off the decision until later if it is not urgent (paragraphs 5.25–5.28).
- Special considerations apply to decisions about life-sustaining treatment (paragraphs 5.29–5.36).
- The person's past and present wishes and feelings, beliefs and values should be taken into account (paragraphs 5.37–5.48).
- The views of other people who are close to the person who lacks capacity should be considered, as well as the views of an attorney or deputy (paragraphs 5.49–5.55).

It's important not to take shortcuts in working out best interests, and a proper and objective assessment must be carried out on every occasion. If the decision is urgent, there may not be time to examine all possible factors, but the decision must still be made in the best interests of the person who lacks capacity. Not all the factors in the checklist will be relevant to all types of decisions or actions, and in many cases other factors will have to be considered as well, even though some of them may then not be found to be relevant.

5.14 What is in a person's best interests may well change over time. This means that even where similar actions need to be taken repeatedly in connection with the person's care or treatment, the person's best interests should be regularly reviewed.

5.15 Any staff involved in the care of a person who lacks capacity should make sure a record is kept of the process of working out the best interests of that person for each relevant decision, setting out:

- how the decision about the person's best interests was reached
- what the reasons for reaching the decision were
- who was consulted to help work out best interests, and
- what particular factors were taken into account.

This record should remain on the person's file.

For major decisions based on the best interests of a person who lacks capacity, it may also be useful for family and other carers to keep a similar kind of record.

What safeguards does the Act provide around working out someone's best interests?

5.16 Section 4(1) states that anyone working out someone's best interests must not make unjustified assumptions about what their best interests might be simply on the basis of the person's age, appearance, condition or any aspect of their behaviour. In this way, the Act ensures that people who lack capacity to make decisions for themselves are not subject to discrimination or treated any less favourably than anyone else.

5.17 'Appearance' is a broad term and refers to all aspects of physical appearance, including skin colour, mode of dress and any visible medical problems, disfiguring scars or other disabilities. A person's 'condition' also covers a range of factors including physical disabilities, learning difficulties or disabilities, age-related illness or temporary conditions (such as drunkenness or unconsciousness). 'Behaviour' refers to behaviour that might seem unusual to others, such as talking too loudly or laughing inappropriately.

PART VI

Scenario: Following the checklist

Martina, an elderly woman with dementia, is beginning to neglect her appearance and personal hygiene and has several times been found wandering in the street unable to find her way home. Her care workers are concerned that Martina no longer has capacity to make appropriate decisions relating to her daily care. Her daughter is her personal welfare attorney and believes the time has come to act under the Lasting Power of Attorney (LPA).

She assumes it would be best for Martina to move into a care home, since the staff would be able to help her wash and dress smartly and prevent her from wandering.

However, it cannot be assumed *simply on the basis of her age, condition, appearance or behaviour* either that Martina lacks capacity to make such a decision or that such a move would be in her best interests.

Instead, steps must be taken to assess her capacity. If it is then agreed that Martina lacks the capacity to make this decision, all the relevant factors in the best interests' checklist must be considered to try to work out what her best interests would be.

Her daughter must therefore consider:

- Martina's past and present wishes and feelings
- the views of the people involved in her care
- any alternative ways of meeting her care needs effectively which might be less restrictive of Martina's rights and freedoms, such as increased provision of home care or attendance at a day centre.

By following this process, Martina's daughter can then take decisions on behalf of her mother and in her best interests, when her mother lacks the capacity to make them herself, on any matters that fall under the authority of the LPA.

How does a decision-maker work out what 'all relevant circumstances' are?

5.18 When trying to work out someone's best interests, the decision-maker should try to identify all the issues that would be most relevant to the individual who lacks capacity and to the particular decision, as well as those in the 'checklist'. Clearly, it is not always possible or practical to investigate in depth every issue which may have some relevance to the person who lacks capacity or the decision in question. So relevant circumstances are defined in section 4(11) of the Act as those:

'(a) of which the person making the determination is aware, and (b) which it would be reasonable to regard as relevant.'

5.19 The relevant circumstances will of course vary from case to case. For example, when making a decision about major medical treatment, a doctor would need to consider the clinical needs of the patient, the potential benefits and burdens of the treatment on the person's health and life expectancy and any other factors relevant to making a professional judgement.[16] But it would not be reasonable to consider issues such as life expectancy when working out whether it would be in someone's best interests to be given medication for a minor problem.

5.20 Financial decisions are another area where the relevant circumstances will vary. For example, if a person had received a substantial sum of money as compensation for an accident resulting in brain injury, the decision-maker would have to consider a wide range of circumstances when making decisions about how the money is spent or invested, such as:

---

[16]   *An NHS Trust v S* [2003] EWHC 365 (Fam) at 47.

- whether the person's condition is likely to change
- whether the person needs professional care, and
- whether the person needs to live somewhere else to make it easier
  for them.

These kinds of issues can only be decided on a case-by-case basis.

How should the person who lacks capacity be involved in working out their best interests?

5.21 Wherever possible, the person who lacks capacity to make a decision should still be involved in the decision-making process (section 4(4)).

5.22 Even if the person lacks capacity to make the decision, they may have views on matters affecting the decision, and on what outcome would be preferred. Their involvement can help work out what would be in their best interests.

5.23 The decision-maker should make sure that all practical means are used to enable and encourage the person to participate as fully as possible in the decision-making process and any action taken as a result, or to help the person improve their ability to participate.

5.24 Consulting the person who lacks capacity will involve taking time to explain what is happening and why a decision needs to be made. Chapter 3 includes a number of practical steps to assist and enable decision-making which may be also be helpful in encouraging greater participation. These include:

- using simple language and/or illustrations or photographs to help the person understand the options
- asking them about the decision at a time and location where the person feels most relaxed and at ease
- breaking the information down into easy-to-understand points
- using specialist interpreters or signers to communicate with the person.

This may mean that other people are required to communicate with the person to establish their views. For example, a trusted relative or friend, a full-time carer or an advocate may be able to help the person to express wishes or aspirations or to indicate a preference between different options.

More information on all of these steps can be found in chapter 3.

PART VI

Scenario: Involving someone in working out their best interests

The parents of Amy, a young woman with learning difficulties, are going through a divorce and are arguing about who should continue to care for their daughter. Though she cannot understand what is happening, attempts are made to see if Amy can give some indication of where she would prefer to live.

An advocate is appointed to work with Amy to help her understand the situation and to find out her likes and dislikes and matters which are important to her. With the advocate's help, Amy is able to participate in decisions about her future care.

How do the chances of someone regaining and developing capacity affect working out what is in their best interests?

5.25 There are some situations where decisions may be deferred, if someone who currently lacks capacity may regain the capacity to make the decision for themselves. Section 4(3) of the Act requires the decision-maker to consider:
- whether the individual concerned is likely to regain the capacity to make that particular decision in the future, and
- if so, when that is likely to be.

It may then be possible to put off the decision until the person can make it for themselves.

5.26 In emergency situations – such as when urgent medical treatment is needed – it may not be possible to wait to see if the person may regain capacity so they can decide for themselves whether or not to have the urgent treatment.

5.27 Where a person currently lacks capacity to make a decision relating to their day-to-day care, the person may – over time and with the right support – be able to develop the skills to do so. Though others may need to make the decision on the person's behalf at the moment, all possible support should be given to that person to enable them to develop the skills so that they can make the decision for themselves in the future.

Scenario: Taking a short-term decision for someone who may regain capacity

Mr Fowler has suffered a stroke leaving him severely disabled and unable to speak. Within days, he has shown signs of improvement, so with intensive treatment there is hope he will recover over time. But at present both his wife and the hospital staff find it difficult to communicate with him and have been unable to find out his wishes.

He has always looked after the family finances, so Mrs Fowler suddenly discovers she has no access to his personal bank account to provide the family with money to live on or pay the bills. Because the decision can't be put off while efforts are made to find effective means of communicating with Mr Fowler, an application is made to the Court of Protection for an order that allows Mrs Fowler to access Mr Fowler's money.

> The decision about longer-term arrangements, on the other hand, can be delayed until alternative methods of communication have been tried and the extent of Mr Fowler's recovery is known.

5.28 Some factors which may indicate that a person may regain or develop capacity in the future are:
- the cause of the lack of capacity can be treated, either by medication or some other form of treatment or therapy
- the lack of capacity is likely to decrease in time (for example, where it is caused by the effects of medication or alcohol, or following a sudden shock)
- a person with learning disabilities may learn new skills or be subject to new experiences which increase their understanding and ability to make certain decisions
- the person may have a condition which causes capacity to come and go at various times (such as some forms of mental illness) so it may be possible to arrange for the decision to be made during a time when they do have capacity
- a person previously unable to communicate may learn a new form of communication (see chapter 3).

How should someone's best interests be worked out when making decisions about life-sustaining treatment?

5.29 A special factor in the checklist applies to decisions about treatment which is necessary to keep the person alive ('life-sustaining treatment') and this is set out in section 4(5) of the Act. The fundamental rule is that anyone who is deciding whether or not life-sustaining treatment is in the best interests of someone who lacks capacity to consent to or refuse such treatment must not be motivated by a desire to bring about the person's death.

5.30 Whether a treatment is 'life-sustaining' depends not only on the type of treatment, but also on the particular circumstances in which it may be prescribed. For example, in some situations giving antibiotics may be life-sustaining, whereas in other circumstances antibiotics are used to treat a non-life-threatening condition. It is up to the doctor or healthcare professional providing treatment to assess whether the treatment is life-sustaining in each particular situation.

5.31 All reasonable steps which are in the person's best interests should be taken to prolong their life. There will be a limited number of cases where treatment is futile, overly burdensome to the patient or where there is no prospect of recovery. In circumstances such as these, it may be that an assessment of best interests leads to the conclusion that it would be in the best interests of the patient to withdraw or withhold life-sustaining treatment, even if this may result in the person's death. The decision-maker must make a decision based on the best interests of the person who lacks

PART VI

capacity. They must not be motivated by a desire to bring about the person's death for whatever reason, even if this is from a sense of compassion. Healthcare and social care staff should also refer to relevant professional guidance when making decisions regarding life-sustaining treatment.

5.32 As with all decisions, before deciding to withdraw or withhold life-sustaining treatment, the decision-maker must consider the range of treatment options available to work out what would be in the person's best interests. All the factors in the best interests checklist should be considered, and in particular, the decision-maker should consider any statements that the person has previously made about their wishes and feelings about life-sustaining treatment.

5.33 Importantly, section 4(5) cannot be interpreted to mean that doctors are under an obligation to provide, or to continue to provide, life-sustaining treatment where that treatment is not in the best interests of the person, even where the person's death is foreseen. Doctors must apply the best interests' checklist and use their professional skills to decide whether life-sustaining treatment is in the person's best interests. If the doctor's assessment is disputed, and there is no other way of resolving the dispute, ultimately the Court of Protection may be asked to decide what is in the person's best interests.

5.34 Where a person has made a written statement in advance that requests particular medical treatments, such as artificial nutrition and hydration (ANH), these requests should be taken into account by the treating doctor in the same way as requests made by a patient who has the capacity to make such decisions. Like anyone else involved in making this decision, the doctor must weigh written statements alongside all other relevant factors to decide whether it is in the best interests of the patient to provide or continue life-sustaining treatment.

5.35 If someone has made an advance decision to refuse life-sustaining treatment, specific rules apply. More information about these can be found in chapter 9 and in paragraph 5.45 below.

5.36 As mentioned in paragraph 5.33 above, where there is any doubt about the patient's best interests, an application should be made to the Court of Protection for a decision as to whether withholding or withdrawing life-sustaining treatment is in the patient's best interests.

How do a person's wishes and feelings, beliefs and values affect working out what is in their best interests?

5.37 Section 4(6) of the Act requires the decision-maker to consider, as far as they are 'reasonably ascertainable':

> '(a) the person's past and present wishes and feelings (and in particular, any relevant written statements made by him when he had capacity),

(b) the beliefs and values that would be likely to influence his decision if he had capacity, and

(c) the other factors that he would be likely to consider if he were able to do so.'

Paragraphs 5.38–5.48 below give further guidance on each of these factors.

5.38 In setting out the requirements for working out a person's 'best interests', section 4 of the Act puts the person who lacks capacity at the centre of the decision to be made. Even if they cannot make the decision, their wishes and feelings, beliefs and values should be taken fully into account – whether expressed in the past or now. But their wishes and feelings, beliefs and values will not necessarily be the deciding factor in working out their best interests. Any such assessment must consider past and current wishes and feelings, beliefs and values alongside all other factors, but the final decision must be based entirely on what is in the person's best interests.

Scenario: *Considering wishes and feelings as part of best interests*

Andre, a young man with severe learning disabilities who does not use any formal system of communication, cuts his leg while outdoors. There is some earth in the wound. A doctor wants to give him a tetanus jab, but Andre appears scared of the needle and pushes it away. Assessments have shown that he is unable to understand the risk of infection following his injury, or the consequences of rejecting the injection.

The doctor decides that it is in the Andre's best interests to give the vaccination. She asks a nurse to comfort Andre, and if necessary, restrain him while she gives the injection. She has objective reasons for believing she is acting in Andre's best interests, and for believing that Andre lacks capacity to make the decision for himself. So she should be protected from liability under section 5 of the Act (see chapter 6).

PART VI

What is 'reasonably ascertainable'?

5.39 How much someone can learn about a person's past and present views will depend on circumstances and the time available. 'Reasonably ascertainable' means considering all possible information in the time available. What is available in an emergency will be different to what is available in a non-emergency. But even in an emergency, there may still be an opportunity to try to communicate with the person or his friends, family or carers (see chapter 3 for guidance on helping communication).

What role do a person's past and present wishes and feelings play?

5.40 People who cannot express their current wishes and feelings in words may express themselves through their behaviour. Expressions of pleasure or distress and emotional responses will also be relevant in working out what is in their best interests. It is also important to be sure that other people have not influenced a person's views. An advocate could help the person make choices and express their views.

5.41 The person may have held strong views in the past which could have a bearing on the decision now to be made. All reasonable efforts must be made to find out whether the person has expressed views in the past that will shape the decision to be made. This could have been through verbal communication, writing, behaviour or habits, or recorded in any other way (for example, home videos or audiotapes).

5.42 Section 4(6)(a) places special emphasis on written statements the person might have made before losing capacity. These could provide a lot of information about a person's wishes. For example, these statements could include information about the type of medical treatment they would want in the case of future illness, where they would prefer to live, or how they wish to be cared for.

5.43 The decision-maker should consider written statements carefully. If their decision does not follow something a person has put in writing, they must record the reasons why. They should be able to justify their reasons if someone challenges their decision.

5.44 A doctor should take written statements made by a person before losing capacity which request specific treatments as seriously as those made by people who currently have capacity to make treatment decisions. But they would not have to follow a written request if they think the specific treatment would be clinically unnecessary or not appropriate for the person's condition, so not in the person's best interests.

5.45 It is important to note the distinction between a written statement expressing treatment preferences and a statement which constitutes an advance decision to refuse treatment. This is covered by section 24 of the Act, and it has a different status in law. Doctors cannot ignore a written statement that is a valid advance decision to refuse treatment. An advance decision to refuse treatment must be followed if it meets the Act's requirements and applies to the person's circumstances. In these cases, the treatment must not be given (see chapter 9 for more information). If there is not a valid and applicable advance decision, treatment should be provided based on the person's best interests.

What role do beliefs and values play?

5.46 Everybody's values and beliefs influence the decisions they make. They may become especially important for someone who lacks capacity to make a decision because of a progressive illness such as dementia, for example. Evidence of a person's beliefs and values can be found in things like their:

- cultural background
- religious beliefs
- political convictions, or
- past behaviour or habits.

Some people set out their values and beliefs in a written statement while they still have capacity.

Scenario: Considering beliefs and values

Anita, a young woman, suffers serious brain damage during a car accident. The court appoints her father as deputy to invest the compensation she received. As the decision-maker he must think about her wishes, beliefs and values before deciding how to invest the money.

Anita had worked for an overseas charity. Her father talks to her former colleagues. They tell him how Anita's political beliefs shaped her work and personal beliefs, so he decides not to invest in the bonds that a financial adviser had recommended, because they are from companies Anita would not have approved of. Instead, he employs an ethical investment adviser to choose appropriate companies in line with her beliefs.

PART VI

What other factors should a decision-maker consider?

5.47 Section 4(6)(c) of the Act requires decision-makers to consider any other factors the person who lacks capacity would consider if they were able to do so. This might include the effect of the decision on other people, obligations to dependants or the duties of a responsible citizen.

5.48 The Act allows actions that benefit other people, as long as they are in the best interests of the person who lacks capacity to make the decision. For example, having considered all the circumstances of the particular case, a decision might be made to take a blood sample from a person who lacks capacity to consent, to check for a genetic link to cancer within the family, because this might benefit someone else in the family. But it might still be in the best interests of the person who lacks capacity. 'Best interests' goes beyond the person's medical interests.

For example, courts have previously ruled that possible wider benefits to a person who lacks capacity to consent, such as providing or gaining emotional support from close relationships, are important factors in working out the person's own best interests.[17] If it is likely that the person who lacks capacity would have considered these factors themselves, they can be seen as part of the person's best interests.

Who should be consulted when working out someone's best interests?

5.49 The Act places a duty on the decision-maker to consult other people close to a person who lacks capacity, where practical and appropriate, on decisions affecting the person and what might be in the person's best interests. This also applies to those involved in caring for the person and interested in the person's welfare. Under section 4(7), the decision-maker has a duty to take into account the views of the following people, where it is practical and appropriate to do so:

- anyone the person has previously named as someone they want to be consulted
- anyone involved in caring for the person
- anyone interested in their welfare (for example, family carers, other close relatives, or an advocate already working with the person)
- an attorney appointed by the person under a Lasting Power of Attorney, and
- a deputy appointed for that person by the Court of Protection.

5.50 If there is no-one to speak to about the person's best interests, in some circumstances the person may qualify for an Independent Mental Capacity Advocate (IMCA). For more information on IMCAs, see chapter 10.

5.51 Decision-makers must show they have thought carefully about who to speak to. If it is practical and appropriate to speak to the above people, they must do so and must take their views into account. They must be able to explain why they did not speak to a particular person – it is good practice to have a clear record of their reasons. It is also good practice to give careful consideration to the views of family carers, if it is possible to do so.

5.52 It is also good practice for healthcare and social care staff to record at the end of the process why they think a specific decision is in the person's best interests. This is particularly important if healthcare and social care staff go against the views of somebody who has been consulted while working out the person's best interests.

5.53 The decision-maker should try to find out:

- what the people consulted think is in the person's best interests in this matter, and
- if they can give information on the person's wishes and feelings, beliefs and values.

---

[17]   See for example *Re Y (Mental Incapacity: Bone marrow transplant)* [1996] 2 FLR 787; *Re A (Male Sterilisation)* [2000] 1 FLR 549.

5.54 This information may be available from somebody the person named before they lost capacity as someone they wish to be consulted. People who are close to the person who lacks capacity, such as close family members, are likely to know them best. They may also be able to help with communication or interpret signs that show the person's present wishes and feelings. Everybody's views are equally important – even if they do not agree with each other. They must be considered alongside the views of the person who lacks capacity and other factors. See paragraphs 5.62–5.69 below for guidance on dealing with conflicting views.

Scenario: *Considering other people's views*

Lucia, a young woman with severe brain damage, is cared for at home by her parents and attends a day centre a couple of days each week. The day centre staff would like to take some of the service users on holiday. They speak to Lucia's parents as part of the process of assessing whether the holiday would be in her best interests.

The parents think that the holiday would be good for her, but they are worried that Lucia gets very anxious if she is surrounded by strangers who don't know how to communicate with her. Having tried to seek Lucia's views and involve her in the decision, the staff and parents agree that a holiday would be in her best interests, as long as her care assistant can go with her to help with communication.

5.55 Where an attorney has been appointed under a Lasting Power of Attorney or Enduring Power of Attorney, or a deputy has been appointed by a court, they must make the decisions on any matters they have been appointed to deal with. Attorneys and deputies should also be consulted, if practical and appropriate, on other issues affecting the person who lacks capacity.

For instance, an attorney who is appointed only to look after the person's property and affairs may have information about the person's beliefs and values, wishes and feelings, that could help work out what would be in the person's best interests regarding healthcare or treatment decisions. (See chapters 7 and 8 for more information about the roles of attorneys and deputies.)

How can decision-makers respect confidentiality?

5.56 Decision-makers must balance the duty to consult other people with the right to confidentiality of the person who lacks capacity. So if confidential information is to be discussed, they should only seek the views of people who it is appropriate to consult, where their views are relevant to the decision to be made and the particular circumstances.

PART VI

5.57 There may be occasions where it is in the person's best interests for personal information (for example, about their medical condition, if the decision concerns the provision of medical treatment) to be revealed to the people consulted as part of the process of working out their best interests (further guidance on this is given in chapter 16). Healthcare and social care staff who are trying to determine a person's best interests must follow their professional guidance, as well as other relevant guidance, about confidentiality.

When does the best interests principle apply?

5.58 Section 1(5) of the Act confirms that the principle applies to any act done, or any decision made, on behalf of someone where there is reasonable belief that the person lacks capacity under the Act. This covers informal day-to-day decisions and actions as well as decisions made by the courts.

Reasonable belief about a person's best interests

5.59 Section 4(9) confirms that if someone acts or makes a decision in the reasonable belief that what they are doing is in the best interests of the person who lacks capacity, then – provided they have followed the checklist in section 4 – they will have complied with the best interests principle set out in the Act. Coming to an incorrect conclusion about a person's capacity or best interests does not necessarily mean that the decision-maker would not get protection from liability (this is explained in chapter 6). But they must be able to show that it was reasonable for them to think that the person lacked capacity and that they were acting in the person's best interests at the time they made their decision or took action.

5.60 Where there is a need for a court decision, the court is likely to require formal evidence of what might be in the person's best interests. This will include evidence from relevant professionals (for example, psychiatrists or social workers). But in most day-to-day situations, there is no need for such formality. In emergency situations, it may not be practical or possible to gather formal evidence.

5.61 Where the court is not involved, people are still expected to have reasonable grounds for believing that they are acting in somebody's best interests. This does not mean that decision-makers can simply impose their own views. They must have objective reasons for their decisions – and they must be able to demonstrate them. They must be able to show they have considered all relevant circumstances and applied all elements of the best interests checklist.

Scenario: Demonstrating reasonable belief

Mrs Prior is mugged and knocked unconscious. She is brought to hospital without any means of identification. She has head injuries and a stab wound, and has lost a lot of blood. In casualty, a doctor arranges an urgent blood transfusion. Because this is necessary to save her life, the doctor believes this is in her best interests.

When her relatives are contacted, they say that Mrs Prior's beliefs meant that she would have refused all blood products. But since Mrs Prior's handbag had been stolen, the doctor had no idea who the woman was nor what her beliefs her. He needed to make an immediate decision and Mrs Prior lacked capacity to make the decision for herself. Therefore he had reasonable grounds for believing that his action was in his patient's best interests – and so was protected from liability.

Now that the doctor knows Mrs Prior's beliefs, he can take them into account in future decisions about her medical treatment if she lacks capacity to make them for herself. He can also consult her family, now that he knows where they are.

What problems could arise when working out someone's best interests?

5.62 It is important that the best interests principle and the statutory checklist are flexible. Without flexibility, it would be impossible to prioritise factors in different cases – and it would be difficult to ensure that the outcome is the best possible for the person who lacks capacity to make the particular decision. Some cases will be straightforward. Others will require decision-makers to balance the pros and cons of all relevant factors.[18] But this flexibility could lead to problems in reaching a conclusion about a person's best interests.

What happens when there are conflicting concerns?

5.63 A decision-maker may be faced with people who disagree about a person's best interests. Family members, partners and carers may disagree between themselves. Or they might have different memories about what views the person expressed in the past. Carers and family might disagree with a professional's view about the person's care or treatment needs.

5.64 The decision-maker will need to find a way of balancing these concerns or deciding between them. The first approach should be to review all elements of the best interests checklist with everyone involved. They should include the person who lacks capacity (as

---

[18]   *Re A (Male Sterilisation)* [2000] 1 FLR 549.

much as they are able to take part) and anyone who has been involved in earlier discussions. It may be possible to reach an agreement at a meeting to air everyone's concerns. But an agreement in itself might not be in the person's best interests. Ultimate responsibility for working out best interests lies with the decision-maker.

Scenario: Dealing with disagreement

Some time ago, Mr Graham made a Lasting Power of Attorney (LPA) appointing his son and daughter as joint attorneys to manage his finances and property. He now has Alzheimer's disease and has moved into private residential care. The son and daughter have to decide what to do with Mr Graham's house.

His son thinks it is in their father's best interests to sell it and invest the money for Mr Graham's future care. But his daughter thinks it is in Mr Graham's best interests to keep the property, because he enjoys visiting and spending time in his old home.

After making every effort to get Mr Graham's views, the family meets to discuss all the issues involved. After hearing other family views, the attorneys agree that it would be in their father's best interests to keep the property for so long as he is able to enjoy visiting it.

Family, partners and carers who are consulted

5.65 If disagreement continues, the decision-maker will need to weigh up the views of different parties. This will depend entirely upon the circumstances of each case, the people involved and their relationship with the person who lacks capacity. Sometimes the decision-maker will find that carers have an insight into how to interpret a person's wishes and feelings that can help them reach a decision.

5.66 At the same time, paid care workers and voluntary sector support workers may have specialist knowledge about up-to-date care options or treatments. Some may also have known the person for many years.

5.67 People with conflicting interests should not be cut out of the process (for example, those who stand to inherit from the person's will may still have a right to be consulted about the person's care or medical treatment). But decision-makers must always ensure that the interests of those consulted do not overly influence the process of working out a person's best interests. In weighing up different contributions, the decision-maker should consider:

- how long an individual has known the person who lacks capacity, and
- what their relationship is.

Scenario: Settling disagreements

Robert is 19 and has learning disabilities and autism. He is about to leave his residential special school. His parents want Robert to go to a specialist unit run by a charitable organisation, but he has been offered a place in a local supported living scheme. The parents don't think Robert will get appropriate care there.

The school sets up a 'best interests' meeting. People who attend include Robert, his parents, teachers from his school and professionals involved in preparing Robert's care plan. Robert's parents and teachers know him best. They set out their views and help Robert to communicate where he would like to live.

Social care staff identify some different placements within the county. Robert visits these with his parents. After further discussion, everyone agrees that a community placement near his family home would be in Robert's best interests.

Settling disputes about best interests

5.68 If someone wants to challenge a decision-maker's conclusions, there are several options:
- Involve an advocate to act on behalf of the person who lacks capacity to make the decision (see paragraph 5.69 below).
- Get a second opinion.
- Hold a formal or informal 'best interests' case conference.
- Attempt some form of mediation (see chapter 15).
- Pursue a complaint through the organisation's formal procedures.

Ultimately, if all other attempts to resolve the dispute have failed, the court might need to decide what is in the person's best interests. Chapter 8 provides more information about the Court of Protection.

Advocacy

5.69 An advocate might be useful in providing support for the person who lacks capacity to make a decision in the process of working out their best interests, if:
- the person who lacks capacity has no close family or friends to take an interest in their welfare, and they do not qualify for an Independent Mental Capacity Advocate (see chapter 10)
- family members disagree about the person's best interests
- family members and professionals disagree about the person's best interests
- there is a conflict of interest for people who have been consulted in the best interests assessment (for example, the sale of a family property where the person lives)

PART VI

- the person who lacks capacity is already in contact with an advocate
- the proposed course of action may lead to the use of restraint or other restrictions on the person who lacks capacity
- there is a concern about the protection of a vulnerable adult.

6   WHAT PROTECTION DOES THE ACT OFFER FOR PEOPLE PROVIDING CARE OR TREATMENT?

Section 5 of the Act allows carers, healthcare and social care staff to carry out certain tasks without fear of liability. These tasks involve the personal care, healthcare or treatment of people who lack capacity to consent to them. The aim is to give legal backing for acts that need to be carried out in the best interests of the person who lacks capacity to consent.[19]

This chapter explains:

- how the Act provides protection from liability
- how that protection works in practice
- where protection is restricted or limited, and
- when a carer can use a person's money to buy goods or services without formal permission.

> In this chapter, as throughout the Code, a person's capacity (or lack of capacity) refers specifically to their capacity to make a particular decision at the time it needs to be made.

Quick summary

The following steps list all the things that people providing care or treatment should bear in mind to ensure they are protected by the Act.

Acting in connection with the care or treatment of someone who lacks capacity to consent

- Is the action to be carried out in connection with the care or treatment of a person who lacks capacity to give consent to that act?
- Does it involve major life changes for the person concerned? If so, it will need special consideration.
- Who is carrying out the action? Is it appropriate for that person to do so at the relevant time?

Checking whether the person has capacity to consent

- Have all possible steps been taken to try to help the person make a decision for themselves about the action?

---

[19]   The provisions of section 5 are based on the common law 'doctrine of necessity' as set out in *Re F (Mental Patient: Sterilisation)* [1990] 2 AC 1.

- Has the two-stage test of capacity been applied?
- Are there reasonable grounds for believing the person lacks capacity to give permission?

Acting in the person's best interests

- Has the best interests checklist been applied and all relevant circumstances considered?
- Is a less restrictive option available?
- Is it reasonable to believe that the proposed act is in the person's best interests?

Understanding possible limitations on protection from liability

- If restraint is being considered, is it necessary to prevent harm to the person who lacks capacity, and is it a proportionate response to the likelihood of the person suffering harm – and to the seriousness of that harm?
- Could the restraint be classed as a 'deprivation of the person's liberty'?
- Does the action conflict with a decision that has been made by an attorney or deputy under their powers?

Paying for necessary goods and services

- If someone wishes to use the person's money to buy goods or pay for services for someone who lacks capacity to do so themselves, are those goods or services necessary and in the person's best interests?
- Is it necessary to take money from the person's bank or building society account or to sell the person's property to pay for goods or services? If so, formal authority will be required.

What protection do people have when caring for those who lack capacity to consent?

6.1 Every day, millions of acts are done to and for people who lack capacity either to:
  - take decisions about their own care or treatment, or
  - consent to someone else caring for them.

Such acts range from everyday tasks of caring (for example, helping someone to wash) to life-changing events (for example, serious medical treatment or arranging for someone to go into a care home). In theory, many of these actions could be against the law. Legally, people have the right to stop others from interfering with their body or property unless they give permission. But what happens if someone lacks capacity to give permission? Carers who dress people who cannot dress themselves are potentially interfering with someone's body without their consent, so could theoretically be

PART VI

prosecuted for assault. A neighbour who enters and cleans the house of a person who lacks capacity could be trespassing on the person's property.

6.2   Section 5 of the Act provides 'protection from liability'. In other words, it protects people who carry out these actions. It stops them being prosecuted for acts that could otherwise be classed as civil wrongs or crimes. By protecting family and other carers from liability, the Act allows necessary caring acts or treatment to take place as if a person who lacks capacity to consent had consented to them. People providing care of this sort do not therefore need to get formal authority to act.

6.3   Importantly, section 5 does not give people caring for or treating someone the power to make any other decisions on behalf of those who lack capacity to make their own decisions. Instead, it offers protection from liability so that they can act in connection with the person's care or treatment. The power to make decisions on behalf of someone who lacks capacity can be granted through other parts of the Act (such as the powers granted to attorneys and deputies, which are explained in chapters 7 and 8).

What type of actions might have protection from liability?

6.4   Section 5(1) provides possible protection for actions carried out *in connection with care or treatment*. The action may be carried out on behalf of someone who is believed to lack capacity to give permission for the action, so long as it is in that person's best interests (see chapter 5). The Act does not define 'care' or 'treatment'. They should be given their normal meaning. However, section 64(1) makes clear that treatment includes diagnostic or other procedures.

6.5   Actions that might be covered by section 5 include:

Personal care

- helping with washing, dressing or personal hygiene
- helping with eating and drinking
- helping with communication
- helping with mobility (moving around)
- helping someone take part in education, social or leisure activities
- going into a person's home to drop off shopping or to see if they are alright
- doing the shopping or buying necessary goods with the person's money
- arranging household services (for example, arranging repairs or maintenance for gas and electricity supplies)
- providing services that help around the home (such as homecare or meals on wheels)

- undertaking actions related to community care services (for example, day care, residential accommodation or nursing care) – but see also paragraphs 6.7–6.14 below
- helping someone to move home (including moving property and clearing the former home).

Healthcare and treatment

- carrying out diagnostic examinations and tests (to identify an illness, condition or other problem)
- providing professional medical, dental and similar treatment
- giving medication
- taking someone to hospital for assessment or treatment
- providing nursing care (whether in hospital or in the community)
- carrying out any other necessary medical procedures (for example, taking a blood sample) or therapies (for example, physiotherapy or chiropody)
- providing care in an emergency.

6.6 These actions only receive protection from liability if the person is reasonably believed to lack capacity to give permission for the action. The action must also be in the person's best interests and follow the Act's principles (see paragraph 6.26 onwards).

6.7 Some acts in connection with care or treatment may cause major life changes with significant consequences for the person concerned. Those requiring particularly careful consideration include a change of residence, perhaps into a care home or nursing home, or major decisions about healthcare and medical treatment. These are described in the following paragraphs.

A change of residence

6.8 Sometimes a person cannot get sufficient or appropriate care in their own home, and they may have to move – perhaps to live with relatives or to go into a care home or nursing home. If the person lacks capacity to consent to a move, the decision-maker(s) must consider whether the move is in the person's best interests (by referring to the best interests checklist in chapter 5 and in particular the person's past and present wishes and feelings, as well as the views of other relevant people). The decision-maker(s) must also consider whether there is a less restrictive option (see chapter 2, principle 5).

This may involve speaking to:

- anyone currently involved in the person's care
- family carers and other family members close to the person and interested in their welfare
- others who have an interest in the person's welfare
- anyone the person has previously named as someone to be consulted, and

PART VI

- an attorney or deputy who has been legally appointed to make particular decisions on their behalf.

6.9   Some cases will require an Independent Mental Capacity Advocate (IMCA). The IMCA represents and supports the person who lacks capacity and they will provide information to make sure the final decision is in the person's best interests (see chapter 10). An IMCA is needed when there is no-one close to the person who lacks capacity to give an opinion about what is best for them, and:

- an NHS body is proposing to provide serious medical treatment or
- an NHS body or local authority is proposing to arrange accommodation in hospital or a care home or other longer-term accommodation and
  - the person will stay in hospital longer than 28 days, or
  - they will stay in a care home for more than eight weeks.

There are also some circumstances where an IMCA may be appointed
on a discretionary basis. More guidance is available in chapter 10.

6.10   Sometimes the final outcome may not be what the person who lacks capacity wanted. For example, they might want to stay at home, but those caring for them might decide a move is in their best interests. In all cases, those making the decision must first consider other options that might restrict the person's rights and freedom of action less (see chapter 2, principle 5).

6.11   In some cases, there may be no alternative but to move the person. Such a move would normally require the person's formal consent if they had capacity to give, or refuse, it. In cases where a person lacks capacity to consent, section 5 of the Act allows carers to carry out actions relating to the move – as long as the Act's principles and the requirements for working out best interests have been followed. This applies even if the person continues to object to the move.

However, section 6 places clear limits on the use of force or restraint by only permitting restraint to be used (for example, to transport the person to their new home) where this is necessary to protect the person from harm and is a proportionate response to the risk of harm (see paragraphs 6.40–6.53). Any action taken to move the person concerned or their property could incur liability unless protected under section 5.

6.12   If there is a serious disagreement about the need to move the person that cannot be settled in any other way, the Court of Protection can be asked to decide what the person's best interests are and where they should live. For example, this could happen if members of a family disagree over what is best for a relative who lacks capacity to give or deny permission for a move.

6.13   In some circumstances, being placed in a hospital or care home may deprive the person of their liberty (see paragraphs 6.49–6.53). If this is the case, there is no protection from liability – even if the placement was considered to be in the best interests of the person (section 6(5)). It is up to the decision-maker to first look at a range of alternative and less restrictive options to see if there is any way of avoiding taking away the person's liberty.

6.14 If there is no alternative way of caring for the person, specific authority will be required to keep the person in a situation which deprives them of their liberty. For instance, sometimes the Court of Protection might be prepared to grant an order of which a consequence is the deprivation of a person's liberty – if it is satisfied that this is in the person's best interests. In other cases, if the person needs treatment for a mental disorder and meets the criteria for detention under the Mental Health Act 1983, this may be used to admit or keep the person in hospital (see chapter 13).

Healthcare and treatment decisions

6.15 Section 5 also allows actions to be taken to ensure a person who lacks capacity to consent receives necessary medical treatment. This could involve taking the person to hospital for out-patient treatment or arranging for admission to hospital. Even if a person who lacks capacity to consent objects to the proposed treatment or admission to hospital, the action might still be allowed under section 5 (but see paragraphs 6.20 and 6.22 below). But there are limits about whether force or restraint can be used to impose treatment (see paragraphs 6.40–6.53).

6.16 Major healthcare and treatment decisions – for example, major surgery or a decision that no attempt is to be made to resuscitate the patient (known as 'DNR' decisions) – will also need special consideration. Unless there is a valid and applicable advance decision to refuse the specific treatment, healthcare staff must carefully work out what would be in the person's best interests (see chapter 5). As part of the process of working this out, they will need to consider (where practical and appropriate):

- the past and present wishes and feelings, beliefs and values of the person who lacks capacity to make the treatment decision, including any advance statement the person wrote setting out their wishes when they had capacity
- the views of anyone previously named by the person as someone to be consulted
- the views of anyone engaged in caring for the person
- the views of anyone interested in their welfare, and
- the views of any attorney or deputy appointed for the person.

In specific cases where there is no-one else available to consult about the person's best interests, an IMCA must be appointed to support and represent the person (see paragraph 6.9 above and chapter 10).

Healthcare staff must also consider whether there are alternative treatment options that might be less intrusive or restrictive (see chapter 2, principle 5). When deciding about the provision or withdrawal of life-sustaining treatment, anyone working out what is

in the best interests of a person who lacks capacity must not be
motivated by a desire to bring about the person's death (see chapter
5).

6.17 Multi-disciplinary meetings are often the best way to decide on a
person's best interests. They bring together healthcare and social
care staff with different skills to discuss the person's options and
may involve those who are closest to the person concerned. But
final responsibility for deciding what is in a person's best interest
lies with the member of healthcare staff responsible for the person's
treatment. They should record their decision, how they reached it
and the reasons for it in the person's clinical notes. As long as they
have recorded objective reasons to show that the decision is in the
person's best interests, and the other requirements of section 5 of
the Act are met, all healthcare staff taking actions in connection
with the particular treatment will be protected from liability.

6.18 Some treatment decisions are so serious that the court has to make
them – unless the person has previously made a Lasting Power of
Attorney appointing an attorney to make such healthcare decisions
for them (see chapter 7) or they have made a valid advance decision
to refuse the proposed treatment (see chapter 9). The Court of
Protection must be asked to make decisions relating to:[20]

- the proposed withholding or withdrawal of artificial nutrition
  and
  hydration (ANH) from a patient in a permanent vegetative state
  (PVS)
- cases where it is proposed that a person who lacks capacity to
  consent should donate an organ or bone marrow to another
  person
- the proposed non-therapeutic sterilisation of a person who
  lacks
  capacity to consent (for example, for contraceptive purposes)
- cases where there is a dispute about whether a particular
  treatment
  will be in a person's best interests.

See paragraphs 8.18–8.24 for more details on these types of cases.

6.19 This last category may include cases that introduce ethical
dilemmas concerning untested or innovative treatments (for
example, new treatments for variant Creutzfeldt-Jakob Disease
(CDJ)) where it is not known if the treatment will be effective, or
certain cases involving a termination of pregnancy. It may also
include cases where there is conflict between professionals or
between professionals and family members which cannot be
resolved in any other way.

Where there is conflict, it is advisable for parties to get legal advice,
though they may not necessarily be able to get legal aid to pay for

---

[20]   The procedures resulting from those court judgements are set out in a Practice Note from the
Official Solicitor (available at www.officialsolicitor.gov.uk) and will be set out in a Practice
Direction from the new Court of Protection.

this advice. Chapter 8 gives more information about the need to refer cases to court for a decision.

Who is protected from liability by section 5?

6.20 Section 5 of the Act is most likely to affect:

- family carers and other kinds of carers
- care workers
- healthcare and social care staff, and
- others who may occasionally be involved in the care or treatment of a person who lacks capacity to consent (for example, ambulance staff, housing workers, police officers and volunteer support workers).

6.21 At any time, it is likely that several people will be carrying out tasks that are covered by section 5 of the Act. Section 5 does not:

- give one person more rights than another to carry out tasks
- specify who has the authority to act in a specific instance
- allow somebody to make decisions relating to subjects other than the care or treatment of the person who lacks capacity, or
- allow somebody to give consent on behalf of a person who lacks capacity to do so.

6.22 To receive protection from liability under section 5, all actions must be related to the care or treatment of the person who lacks capacity to consent. Before taking action, carers must first reasonably believe that:

- the person lacks the capacity to make that particular decision at the time it needs to be made, and
- the action is in the person's best interests.

This is explained further in paragraphs 6.26–6.34 below.

Scenario: *Protecting multiple carers*

Mr Rose, an older man with dementia, gets help from several people. His sister sometimes cooks meals for him. A district nurse visits him to change the dressing on a pressure sore, and a friend often takes Mr Rose to the park, guiding him when they cross the road. Each of these individuals would be protected from liability under section 5 of the Act – but only if they take reasonable steps to check that he lacks capacity to consent to the actions they take and hold a reasonable belief that the actions are in Mr Rose's best interests.

6.23 Section 5 may also protect carers who need to use the person's money to pay for goods or services that the person needs but lacks the capacity to purchase for themselves. However, there are strict controls over who may have access to another person's money. See paragraphs 6.56–6.66 for more information.

PART VI

6.24 Carers who provide personal care services must not carry out specialist procedures that are normally done by trained healthcare staff. If the action involves medical treatment, the doctor or other member of healthcare staff with responsibility for the patient will be the decision-maker who has to decide whether the proposed treatment is in the person's best interests (see chapter 5). A doctor can delegate responsibility for giving the treatment to other people in the clinical team who have the appropriate skills or expertise. People who do more than their experience or qualifications allow may not be protected from liability.

Care planning

6.25 Decisions about a person's care or treatment are often made by a multi-disciplinary team (a team of professionals with different skills that contribute to a person's care), by drawing up a care plan for the person. The preparation of a care plan should always include an assessment of the person's capacity to consent to the actions covered by the care plan, and confirm that those actions are agreed to be in the person's best interests. Healthcare and social care staff may then be able to assume that any actions they take under the care plan are in the person's best interests, and therefore receive protection from liability under section 5. But a person's capacity and best interests must still be reviewed regularly.

What steps should people take to be protected from liability?

6.26 As well as taking the following steps, somebody who wants to be protected from liability should bear in mind the statutory principles set out in section 1 of the Act (see chapter 2).

6.27 First, reasonable steps must be taken to find out whether a person has the capacity to make a decision about the proposed action (section 5(1)(a)). If the person has capacity, they must give their consent for anyone to take an action on their behalf, so that the person taking the action is protected from liability. For guidance on what is classed as 'reasonable steps', see paragraphs 6.29–6.34. But reasonable steps must always include:

• taking all practical and appropriate steps to help people to make a decision about an action themselves, and

• applying the two-stage test of capacity (see chapter 4).

The person who is going to take the action must have a 'reasonable belief' that the individual lacks capacity to give consent for the action at the time it needs to be taken.

6.28 Secondly, the person proposing to take action must have reasonable grounds for believing that the action is in the best interests of the person who lacks capacity. They should apply all elements of the best interests checklist (see chapter 5), and in particular

- consider whether the person is likely to regain capacity to make this decision in the future. Can the action wait until then?
- consider whether a less restrictive option is available (chapter 2, principle 5), and
- have objective reasons for thinking an action is in the best interests of the person who lacks capacity to consent to it.

What is 'reasonable'?

6.29 As explained in chapter 4, anyone assessing a person's capacity to make decisions for themselves or give consent must focus wholly on whether the person has capacity to make a specific decision at the time it needs to be made and not the person's capacity to make decisions generally. For example, a carer helping a person to dress can assess a person's capacity to agree to their help by explaining the different options (getting dressed or staying in nightclothes), and the consequences (being able to go out, or staying in all day).

6.30 Carers do not have to be experts in assessing capacity. But they must be able to show that they have taken *reasonable steps* to find out if the person has the capacity to make the specific decision. Only then will they have *reasonable grounds for believing* the person lacks capacity in relation to that particular matter. See paragraphs 4.44–4.45 for guidance on what is classed as 'reasonable' – although this will vary, depending on circumstances.

6.31 For the majority of decisions, formal assessment processes are unlikely to be required. But in some circumstances, professional practice requires some formal procedures to be carried out (for example, where consent to medical treatment is required, the doctor will need to assess – and record the person's capacity to consent). Under section 5, carers and professionals will be protected from liability as long as they arc ablc to provide some objective reasons that explain why they believe that the person lacks capacity to consent to the action. If somebody challenges their belief, both carers and professionals will be protected from liability as long as they can show that they took steps to find out whether the person has capacity and that they have a reasonable belief that the person lacks capacity.

6.32 Similarly, carers, relatives and others involved in caring for someone who lacks capacity must have *reasonable grounds for believing* that their action is in the person's best interests. They must not simply impose their own views. They must be able to show that they considered all relevant circumstances and applied the best interests checklist. This includes showing that they have tried to involve the person who lacks capacity, and find out their wishes and feelings, beliefs and values. They must also have asked other people's opinions, where practical and appropriate. If somebody challenges their decision, they will be protected from liability if they can show that it was reasonable for them to believe that their action was in the person's best interests – in all the circumstances of that particular case.

6.33 If healthcare and social care staff are involved, their skills and knowledge will affect what is classed as 'reasonable'. For example, a doctor assessing somebody's capacity to consent to treatment must demonstrate more skill than someone without medical training. They should also record in the person's healthcare record the steps they took and the reasons for the finding. Healthcare and social care staff should apply normal clinical and professional standards when deciding what treatments to offer. They must then decide whether the proposed treatment is in the best interests of the person who lacks capacity to consent. This includes considering all relevant circumstances and applying the best interests checklist (see chapter 5).

6.34 Healthcare and social care staff can be said to have 'reasonable grounds for believing' that a person lacks capacity if:
- they are working to a person's care plan, and
- the care planning process involved an assessment of the person's capacity to make a decision about actions in the care plan.

It is also reasonable for them to assume that the care planning process assessed a person's best interests. But they should still make every effort to communicate with the person to find out if they still lack capacity and the action is still in their best interests.

Scenario: *Working with a care plan*

Margaret, an elderly woman, has serious mental health and physical problems. She lives in a nursing home and a care plan has been prepared by the multi-disciplinary team, in consultation with her relatives in deciding what course of action would be in Margaret's best interests. The care plan covers the medication she has been prescribed, the physiotherapy she needs, help with her personal care and other therapeutic activities such as art therapy.

Although attempts were made to involve Margaret in the care planning process, she has been assessed by the doctor responsible for her care as lacking capacity to consent to most aspects of her care plan. The care plan can be relied on by the nurse or care assistant who administers the medication, by the physiotherapist and art therapist, and also by the care assistant who helps with Margaret's personal care, providing them with reasonable grounds for believing that they are acting in her best interests.

However, as each act is performed, they must all take reasonable steps to communicate with Margaret to explain what they are doing and to

> ascertain whether she has the capacity to consent to the act in question. If they think she does, they must stop the treatment unless or until Margaret agrees that it should continue.

What happens in emergency situations?

6.35 Sometimes people who lack capacity to consent will require emergency medical treatment to save their life or prevent them from serious harm. In these situations, what steps are 'reasonable' will differ to those in non-urgent cases. In emergencies, it will almost always be in the person's best interests to give urgent treatment without delay. One exception to this is when the healthcare staff giving treatment are satisfied that an advance decision to refuse treatment exists (see paragraph 6.37).

What happens in cases of negligence?

6.36 Section 5 does not provide a defence in cases of negligence – either in carrying out a particular act or by failing to act where necessary. For example, a doctor may be protected against a claim of battery for carrying out an operation that is in a person's best interests. But if they perform the operation negligently, they are not protected from a charge of negligence. So the person who lacks capacity has the same rights in cases of negligence as someone who has consented to the operation.

What is the effect of an advance decision to refuse treatment?

6.37 Sometimes people will make an advance decision to refuse treatment while they still have capacity to do so and before they need that particular treatment. Healthcare staff must respect this decision if it is valid and applies to the proposed treatment.

6.38 If healthcare staff are satisfied that an advance decision is valid and applies to the proposed treatment, they are not protected from liability if they give any treatment that goes against it. But they are protected from liability if they did not know about an advance decision or they are not satisfied that the advance decision is valid and applies in the current circumstances (section 26(2)). See chapter 9 for further guidance.

What limits are there on protection from liability?

6.39 Section 6 imposes some important limitations on acts which can be carried out with protection from liability under section 5 (as described in the first part of this chapter). The key areas where acts

PART VI

might not be protected from liability are where there is
inappropriate use of restraint or where a person who lacks capacity
is deprived of their liberty.

Using restraint

6.40 Section 6(4) of the Act states that someone is using restraint if
they:
- use force – or threaten to use force – to make someone do
  something that they are resisting, or
- restrict a person's freedom of movement, whether they are
  resisting or not.

6.41 Any action intended to restrain a person who lacks capacity will
not attract protection from liability unless the following two
conditions are met:
- the person taking action must reasonably believe that restraint
  is *necessary* to prevent *harm* to the person who lacks capacity,
  and
- the amount or type of restraint used and the amount of time it
  lasts must be a *proportionate response* to the likelihood and
  seriousness of harm.

See paragraphs 6.44–6.48 for more explanation of the terms
necessary, harm and a *proportionate response.*

6.42 Healthcare and social care staff should also refer to:
- professional and other guidance on restraint or physical
  intervention, such as that issued by the Department of Health[21]
  or Welsh Assembly Government,[22] and
- limitations imposed by regulations and standards, such as the
  national minimum standards for care services (see chapter 14).

6.43 In addition to the requirements of the Act, the common law
imposes a duty of care on healthcare and social care staff in respect
of all people to whom they provide services. Therefore if a person
who lacks capacity to consent has challenging behaviour, or is in the
acute stages of illness causing them to act in way which may cause
harm to others, staff may, under the common law, take appropriate
and necessary action to restrain or remove the person, in order to
prevent harm, both to the person concerned and to anyone else.
However, within this context, the common law would not provide
sufficient grounds for an action that would have the effect of
depriving someone of their liberty (see paragraphs 6.49–6.53).

---

[21]   For guidance on using restraint with people with learning disabilities and autistic spectrum
       disorder, see *Guidance for restrictive physical interventions* (published by the Department of
       Health and Department for Education and Skills and available at www.dh.gov.uk/assetRoot/
       04/06/84/61/04068461.pdf).
[22]   In Wales, the relevant guidance is the Welsh Assembly Government's *Framework for
       restrictive physical intervention policy and practice* (available at www.childrenfirst.wales.
       gov.uk/content/framework/phys-int-e.pdf).

When might restraint be 'necessary'?

6.44 Anybody considering using restraint must have objective reasons to justify that restraint is necessary. They must be able to show that the person being cared for is likely to suffer harm unless proportionate restraint is used. A carer or professional must not use restraint just so that they can do something more easily. If restraint is necessary to prevent harm to the person who lacks capacity, it must be the minimum amount of force for the shortest time possible.

Scenario: Appropriate use of restraint

Derek, a man with learning disabilities, has begun to behave in a challenging way. Staff at his care home think he might have a medical condition that is causing him distress. They take him to the doctor, who thinks that Derek might have a hormone imbalance. But the doctor needs to take a blood test to confirm this, and when he tries to take the test Derek attempts to fight him off.

The results might be negative – so the test might not be necessary. But the doctor decides that a test is in Derek's best interests, because failing to treat a problem like a hormone imbalance might make it worse. It is therefore in Derek's best interests to restrain him to take the blood test. The temporary restraint is in proportion to the likely harm caused by failing to treat a possible medical condition.

PART VI

What is 'harm'?

6.45 The Act does not define 'harm', because it will vary depending on the situation. For example,
- a person with learning disabilities might run into a busy road without warning, if they do not understand the dangers of cars
- a person with dementia may wander away from home and get lost, if they cannot remember where they live
- a person with manic depression might engage in excessive spending during a manic phase, causing them to get into debt
- a person may also be at risk of harm if they behave in a way that encourages others to assault or exploit them (for example, by behaving in a dangerously provocative way).

6.46 Common sense measures can often help remove the risk of harm (for example, by locking away poisonous chemicals or removing obstacles). Also, care planning should include risk assessments and set out appropriate actions to try to prevent possible risks. But it is impossible to remove all risk, and a proportionate response is needed when the risk of harm does arise.

What is a 'proportionate response'?

6.47   A 'proportionate response' means using the least intrusive type and minimum amount of restraint to achieve a specific outcome in the best interests of the person who lacks capacity. On occasions when the use of force may be necessary, carers and healthcare and social care staff should use the minimum amount of force for the shortest possible time.

For example, a carer may need to hold a person's arm while they cross the road, if the person does not understand the dangers of roads. But it would not be a proportionate response to stop the person going outdoors at all. It may be appropriate to have a secure lock on a door that faces a busy road, but it would not be a proportionate response to lock someone in a bedroom all the time to prevent them from attempting to cross the road.

6.48   Carers and healthcare and social care staff should consider less restrictive options before using restraint. Where possible, they should ask other people involved in the person's care what action they think is necessary to protect the person from harm. For example, it may be appropriate to get an advocate to work with the person to see if they can avoid or minimise the need for restraint to be used.

Scenario: Avoiding restraint

Oscar has learning disabilities. People at the college he attends sometimes cannot understand him, and he gets frustrated. Sometimes he hits the wall and hurts himself.

Staff don't want to take Oscar out of class, because he says he enjoys college and is learning new skills. They have allowed his support worker to sit with him, but he still gets upset. The support worker could try to hold Oscar back. But she thinks this is too forceful, even though it would stop him hurting himself.

Instead, she gets expert advice from members of the local community team. Observation helps them understand Oscar's behaviour better. They come up with a support strategy that reduces the risk of harmful behaviour and is less restrictive of his freedom.

When are acts seen as depriving a person of their liberty?

6.49   Although section 5 of the Act permits the use of restraint where it is necessary under the above conditions, section 6(5) confirms that there is no protection under the Act for actions that result in someone being deprived of their liberty (as defined by Article 5(1) of the European Convention on Human Rights). This applies not only to public authorities covered by the Human Rights Act 1998 but to everyone who might otherwise get protection under section 5 of the Act. It also applies to attorneys or deputies – they cannot give permission for an action that takes away a person's liberty.

6.50 Sometimes there is no alternative way to provide care or treatment other than depriving the person of their liberty. In this situation, some people may be detained in hospital under the Mental Health Act 1983– but this only applies to people who require hospital treatment for a mental disorder (see chapter 13). Otherwise, actions that amount to a deprivation of liberty will not be lawful unless formal authorisation is obtained.

6.51 In some cases, the Court of Protection might grant an order that permits the deprivation of a person's liberty, if it is satisfied that this is in a person's best interests.

6.52 It is difficult to define the difference between actions that amount to a restriction of someone's liberty and those that result in a deprivation of liberty. In recent legal cases, the European Court of Human Rights said that the difference was 'one of degree or intensity, not one of nature or substance'.[23] There must therefore be particular factors in the specific situation of the person concerned which provide the 'degree' or 'intensity' to result in a deprivation of liberty. In practice, this can relate to:

- the type of care being provided
- how long the situation lasts
- its effects, or
- the way in a particular situation came about.[24]

The European Court of Human Rights has identified the following as factors contributing to deprivation of liberty in its judgments on cases to date:

- restraint was used, including sedation, to admit a person who is resisting
- professionals exercised complete and effective control over care and movement for a significant period
- professionals exercised control over assessments, treatment, contacts and residence
- the person would be prevented from leaving if they made a meaningful attempt to do so
- a request by carers for the person to be discharged to their care was refused
- the person was unable to maintain social contacts because of restrictions placed on access to other people

PART VI

---

[23] *HL v The United Kingdom* (Application no, 45508/99). Judgment 5 October 2004, para 89.

[24] In *HL v UK* (also known as the 'Bournewood' case), the European Court said that 'the key factor in the present case [is] that the health care professionals treating and managing the applicant exercised complete and effective control over his care and movements'. They found 'the concrete situation was that the applicant was under continuous supervision and control and was not free to leave.'

- the person lost autonomy because they were under continuous supervision and control.[25]

6.53 The Government has announced that it intends to amend the Act to introduce new procedures and provisions for people who lack capacity to make relevant decisions but who need to be deprived of their liberty, in their best interests, otherwise than under the Mental Health Act 1983 (the so-called 'Bournewood provisions'). This chapter will be fully revised in due course to reflect those changes. Information about the Government's current proposals in respect of the Bournewood safeguards is available on the Department of Health website. This information includes draft illustrative Code of Practice guidance about the proposed safeguards. See paragraphs 13.52–13.55 for more details.

How does section 5 apply to attorneys and deputies?

6.54 Section 5 does not provide protection for actions that go against the decision of someone who has been authorised to make decisions for a person who lacks capacity to make such decision for themselves. For instance, if someone goes against the decision of an attorney acting under a Lasting Power of Attorney (LPA) (see chapter 7) or a deputy appointed by the Court of Protection (see chapter 8), they will not be protected under section 5.

6.55 Attorneys and deputies must only make decisions within the scope of the authority of the LPA or court order. Sometimes carers or healthcare and social care staff might feel that an attorney or deputy is making decisions they should not be making, or that are not in a person's best interests. If this is the case, and the disagreement cannot be settled any other way, either the carers, the staff or the attorney or deputy can apply to the Court of Protection. If the dispute concerns the provision of medical treatment, medical staff can still give life-sustaining treatment, or treatment which stops a person's condition getting seriously worse, while the court is coming to a decision (section 6(6)).

Who can pay for goods or services?

6.56 Carers may have to spend money on behalf of someone who lacks capacity to purchase necessary goods or services. For example, they may need to pay for a milk delivery or for a chiropodist to provide a service at the person's home. In some cases, they might have to pay for more costly arrangements such as house repairs or organising a holiday. Carers are likely to be protected from liability if their actions are properly taken under section 5, and in the best interests of the person who lacks capacity.

---

[25]   These are listed in the Department of Health's draft illustrative Code of Practice guidance about the proposed safeguards. www.dh.gov.uk/assetRoot/04/14/17/64/04141764.pdf

6.57 In general, a contract entered into by a person who lacks capacity to make the contract cannot be enforced if the other person knows, or must be taken to have known, of the lack of capacity. Section 7 of the Act modifies this rule and states that where the contract is for 'necessary' goods or services for a person who lacks capacity to make the arrangements for themselves, that person must pay a reasonable price for them.

What are necessary goods and services?

6.58 'Necessary' means something that is suitable to the person's condition in life (their place in society, rather than any mental or physical condition) and their actual requirements when the goods or services are provided (section 7(2)). The aim is to make sure that people can enjoy a similar standard of living and way of life to those they had before lacking capacity. For example, if a person who now lacks capacity previously chose to buy expensive designer clothes, these are still necessary goods – as long as they can still afford them. But they would not be necessary for a person who always wore cheap clothes, no matter how wealthy they were.

6.59 Goods are not necessary if the person already has a sufficient supply of them. For example, buying one or two new pairs of shoes for a person who lacks capacity could be necessary. But a dozen pairs would probably not be necessary.

How should payments be arranged?

6.60 If a person lacks capacity to arrange for payment for necessary goods and services, sections 5 and 8 allow a carer to arrange payment on their behalf.

6.61 The carer must first take reasonable steps to check whether a person can arrange for payment themselves, or has the capacity to consent to the carer doing it for them. If the person lacks the capacity to consent or pay themselves, the carer must decide what goods or services would be necessary for the person and in their best interests. The carer can then lawfully deal with payment for those goods and services in one of three ways:

- If neither the carer nor the person who lacks capacity can produce the necessary funds, the carer may promise that the person who lacks capacity will pay. A supplier may not be happy with this, or the carer may be worried that they will be held responsible for any debt. In such cases, the carer must follow the formal steps in paragraphs 6.62–6.66 below.
- If the person who lacks capacity has cash, the carer may use that money to pay for goods or services (for example, to pay the milkman or the hairdresser).
- The carer may choose to pay for the goods or services with their own money. The person who lacks capacity must pay

PART VI

them back. This may involve using cash in the person's possession or running up an IOU. (This is not appropriate for paid care workers, whose contracts might stop them handling their clients' money.) The carer must follow formal steps to get money held in a bank or building society account (see paragraphs 6.63–6.66 below).

6.62 Carers should keep bills, receipts and other proof of payment when paying for goods and services. They will need these documents when asking to get money back. Keeping appropriate financial records and documentation is a requirement of the national minimum standards for care homes or domiciliary care agencies.

Access to a person's assets

6.63 The Act does not give a carer or care worker access to a person's income or assets. Nor does it allow them to sell the person's property.

6.64 Anyone wanting access to money in a person's bank or building society will need formal legal authority. They will also need legal authority to sell a person's property. Such authority could be given in a Lasting Power of Attorney (LPA) appointing an attorney to deal with property and affairs, or in an order of the Court of Protection (either a single decision of the court or an order appointing a deputy to make financial decisions for the person who lacks capacity to make such decisions).

Scenario: Being granted access to a person's assets

A storm blew some tiles off the roof of a house owned by Gordon, a man with Alzheimer's disease. He lacks capacity to arrange for repairs and claim on his insurance. The repairs are likely to be costly.

Gordon's son decides to organise the repairs, and he agrees to pay because his father doesn't have enough cash available. The son could then apply to the Court of Protection for authority to claim insurance on his father's behalf and for him to be reimbursed from his father's bank account to cover the cost of the repairs once the insurance payment had been received.

6.65 Sometimes another person will already have legal control of the finances and property of a person who lacks capacity to manage their own affairs. This could be an attorney acting under a registered EPA or an appropriate LPA (see chapter 7) or a deputy appointed by the Court of Protection (see chapter 8). Or it could be someone (usually a carer) that has the right to act as an 'appointee' (under Social Security Regulations) and claim benefits for a person who lacks capacity to make their own claim and use the money on the person's behalf. But an appointee cannot deal with other assets or savings from sources other than benefits.

6.66 Section 6(6) makes clear that a family carer or other carer cannot make arrangements for goods or services to be supplied to a person who lacks capacity if this conflicts with a decision made by someone who has formal powers over the person's money and property, such as an attorney or deputy acting within the scope of their authority. Where there is no conflict and the carer has paid for necessary goods and services the carer may ask for money back from an attorney, a deputy or where relevant, an appointee.

7 WHAT DOES THE ACT SAY ABOUT LASTING POWERS OF ATTORNEY?

This chapter explains what Lasting Powers of Attorney (LPAs) are and how they should be used. It also sets out:

- how LPAs differ from Enduring Powers of Attorney (EPAs)
- the types of decisions that people can appoint attorneys to make (attorneys are also called 'donees' in the Act)
- situations in which an LPA can and cannot be used
- the duties and responsibilities of attorneys
- the standards required of attorneys, and
- measures for dealing with attorneys who don't meet appropriate standards.

This chapter also explains what should happen to EPAs that were made before the Act comes into force.

> In this chapter, as throughout the Code, a person's capacity (or lack of capacity) refers specifically to their capacity to make a particular decision at the time it needs to be made.

Quick summary

Anyone asked to be an attorney should:

- consider whether they have the skills and ability to act as an attorney (especially if it is for a property and affairs LPA)
- ask themselves whether they actually want to be an attorney and take on the duties and responsibilities of the role.

Before acting under an LPA, attorneys must:

- make sure the LPA has been registered with the Public Guardian
- take all practical and appropriate steps to help the donor make the particular decision for themselves.

PART VI

When acting under an LPA:

- make sure that the Act's statutory principles are followed
- check whether the person has the capacity to make that particular decision for themselves. If they do:
  - a personal welfare LPA cannot be used – the person must make the decision
  - a property and affairs LPA can be used even if the person has capacity to make the decision, unless they have stated in the LPA that they should make decisions for themselves when they have capacity to do so.

At all times, remember:

- anything done under the authority of the LPA must be in the person's best interests
- anyone acting as an attorney must have regard to guidance in this Code of Practice that is relevant to the decision that is to be made
- attorneys must fulfil their responsibilities and duties to the person who lacks capacity.

What is a Lasting Power of Attorney (LPA)?

7.1 Sometimes one person will want to give another person authority to make a decision on their behalf. A power of attorney is a legal document that allows them to do so. Under a power of attorney, the chosen person (the attorney or donee) can make decisions that are as valid as one made by the person (the donor).

7.2 Before the Enduring Powers of Attorney Act 1985, every power of attorney automatically became invalid as soon as the donor lacked the capacity to make their own decision. But that Act introduced the Enduring Power of Attorney (EPA). An EPA allows an attorney to make decisions about property and financial affairs even if the donor lacks capacity to manage their own affairs.

7.3 The Mental Capacity Act replaces the EPA with the Lasting Power of Attorney (LPA). It also increases the range of different types of decisions that people can authorise others to make on their behalf. As well as property and affairs (including financial matters), LPAs can also cover personal welfare (including healthcare and consent to medical treatment) for people who lack capacity to make such decisions for themselves.

7.4 The donor can choose one person or several to make different kinds of decisions. See paragraphs 7.21–7.31 for more information about personal welfare LPAs. See paragraphs 7.32–7.42 for more information about LPAs on property and affairs.

How do LPAs compare to EPAs?

7.5 There are a number of differences between LPAs and EPAs. These are summarised as follows:

- EPAs only cover property and affairs. LPAs can also cover personal welfare.
- Donors must use the relevant specific form (prescribed in regulations) to make EPAs and LPAs. There are different forms for EPAs, personal welfare LPAs and property and affairs LPAs.
- EPAs must be registered with the Public Guardian when the donor can no longer manage their own affairs (or when they start to lose capacity). But LPAs can be registered at any time before they are used – before or after the donor lacks capacity to make particular decisions that the LPA covers. If the LPA is not registered, it can't be used.
- EPAs can be used while the donor still has capacity to manage their own property and affairs, as can property and affairs LPAs, so long as the donor does not say otherwise in the LPA. But personal welfare LPAs can only be used once the donor lacks capacity to make the welfare decision in question.
- Once the Act comes into force, only LPAs can be made but existing EPAs will continue to be valid. There will be different laws and procedures for EPAs and LPAs.
- Attorneys making decisions under a registered EPA or LPA must follow the Act's principles and act in the best interests of the donor.
- The duties under the law of agency apply to attorneys of both EPAs and LPAs (see paragraphs 7.58–7.68 below).
- Decisions that the courts have made about EPAs may also affect how people use LPAs.
- Attorneys acting under an LPA have a legal duty to have regard to the guidance in this Code of Practice. EPA attorneys do not. But the Code's guidance will still be helpful to them.

How does a donor create an LPA?

7.6 The donor must also follow the right procedures for creating and registering an LPA, as set out below. Otherwise the LPA might not be valid. It is not always necessary to get legal advice. But it is a good idea for certain cases (for example, if the donor's circumstances are complicated).

7.7 Only adults aged 18 or over can make an LPA, and they can only make an LPA if they have the capacity to do so. For an LPA to be valid:
- the LPA must be a written document set out in the statutory form prescribed by regulations[26]
- the document must include prescribed information about the nature and effect of the LPA (as set out in the regulations)

---

[26] The prescribed forms will be available from the Office of the Public Guardian (OPG) or from legal stationers.

- the donor must sign a statement saying that they have read the prescribed information (or somebody has read it to them) and that they want the LPA to apply when they no longer have capacity
- the document must name people (not any of the attorneys) who should be told about an application to register the LPA, or it should say that there is no-one they wish to be told
- the attorneys must sign a statement saying that they have read the prescribed information and that they understand their duties – in particular the duty to act in the donor's best interests
- the document must include a certificate completed by an independent third party,[27] confirming that:
  - in their opinion, the donor understands the LPA's purpose
  - nobody used fraud or undue pressure to trick or force the donor into making the LPA and
  - there is nothing to stop the LPA being created.

Who can be an attorney?

7.8 A donor should think carefully before choosing someone to be their attorney. An attorney should be someone who is trustworthy, competent and reliable. They should have the skills and ability to carry out the necessary tasks.

7.9 Attorneys must be at least 18 years of age. For property and affairs LPAs, the attorney could be either:
- an individual (as long as they are not bankrupt at the time the LPA is made), or
- a trust corporation (often parts of banks or other financial institutions).

If an attorney nominated under a property and affairs LPA becomes bankrupt at any point, they will no longer be allowed to act as an attorney for property and affairs. People who are bankrupt can still act as an attorney for personal welfare LPAs.

7.10 The donor must name an individual rather than a job title in a company or organisation, (for example, 'The Director of Adult Services' or 'my solicitor' would not be sufficient). A paid care worker (such as a care home manager) should not agree to act as an attorney, apart from in unusual circumstances (for example, if they are the only close relative of the donor).

7.11 Section 10(4) of the Act allows the donor to appoint two or more attorneys and to specify whether they should act 'jointly', 'jointly and severally', or 'jointly in respect of some matters and jointly and severally in respect of others'.
- Joint attorneys must always act together. All attorneys must agree decisions and sign any relevant documents.

---

[27] Details of who may and who may not be a certificate provider will be available in regulations. The OPG will produce guidance for certificate providers on their role.

- Joint and several attorneys can act together but may also act independently if they wish. Any action taken by any attorney alone is as valid as if they were the only attorney.

7.12 The donor may want to appoint attorneys to act jointly in some matters but jointly and severally in others. For example, a donor could choose to appoint two or more financial attorneys jointly and severally. But they might say then when selling the donor's house, the attorneys must act jointly. The donor may appoint welfare attorneys to act jointly and severally but specify that they must act jointly in relation to giving consent to surgery. If a donor who has appointed two or more attorneys does not specify how they should act, they must always act jointly (section 10(5)).

7.13 Section 10(8) says that donors may choose to name replacement attorneys to take over the duties in certain circumstances (for example, in the event of an attorney's death). The donor may name a specific attorney to be replaced, or the replacements can take over from any attorney, if necessary. Donors cannot give their attorneys the right to appoint a substitute or successor.

How should somebody register and use an LPA?

7.14 An LPA must be registered with the Office of the Public Guardian (OPG) before it can be used. An unregistered LPA will not give the attorney any legal powers to make a decision for the donor. The donor can register the LPA while they are still capable, or the attorney can apply to register the LPA at any time.

7.15 There are advantages in registering the LPA soon after the donor makes it (for example, to ensure that there is no delay when the LPA needs to be used). But if this has not been done, an LPA can be registered after the donor lacks the capacity to make a decision covered by the LPA.

7.16 If an LPA is unregistered, attorneys must register it before making any decisions under the LPA. If the LPA has been registered but not used for some time, the attorney should tell the OPG when they begin to act under it – so that the attorney can be sent relevant, up-to-date information about the rules governing LPAs.

7.17 While they still have capacity, donors should let the OPG know of permanent changes of address for the donor or the attorney or any other changes in circumstances. If the donor no longer has capacity to do this, attorneys should report any such changes to the OPG. Examples include an attorney of a property and affairs LPA becoming bankrupt or the ending of a marriage between the donor and their attorney. This will help keep OPG records up to date, and will make sure that attorneys do not make decisions that they no longer have the authority to make.

PART VI

What guidance should an attorney follow?

7.18 Section 9(4) states that attorneys must meet the requirements set out in the Act. Most importantly, they have to follow the statutory principles (section 1) and make decisions in the best interests of the person who lacks capacity (section 4). They must also respect any conditions or restrictions that the LPA document contains. See chapter 2 for guidance on how to apply the Act's principles.

7.19 Chapter 3 gives suggestions of ways to help people make their own decisions in accordance with the Act's second principle. Attorneys should also refer to the guidance in chapter 4 when assessing the donor's capacity to make particular decisions, and in particular, should follow the steps suggested for establishing a 'reasonable belief' that the donor lacks capacity (see paragraphs 4.44–4.45). Assessments of capacity or best interests must not be based merely on:

• a donor's age or appearance, or
• unjustified assumptions about any condition they might have or their behaviour.

7.20 When deciding what is in the donor's best interests, attorneys should refer to the guidance in chapter 5. In particular, they must consider the donor's past and present wishes and feelings, beliefs and values. Where practical and appropriate, they should consult with:

• anyone involved in caring for the donor
• close relatives and anyone else with an interest in their welfare
• other attorneys appointed by the donor.

See paragraphs 7.52–7.68 for a description of an attorney's duties.

Scenario: Making decisions in a donor's best interests

Mr Young has been a member of the Green Party for a long time. He has appointed his solicitor as his attorney under a property and affairs LPA. But Mr Young did not state in the LPA that investments made on his behalf must be ethical investments. When the attorney assesses his client's best interests, however, the attorney considers the donor's past wishes, values and beliefs. He makes sure that he only invests in companies that are socially and environmentally responsible.

What decisions can an LPA attorney make?

Personal welfare LPAs

7.21 LPAs can be used to appoint attorneys to make decisions about personal welfare, which can include healthcare and medical treatment decisions. Personal welfare LPAs might include decisions about:

• where the donor should live and who they should live with
• the donor's day-to-day care, including diet and dress

- who the donor may have contact with
- consenting to or refusing medical examination and treatment on the donor's behalf
- arrangements needed for the donor to be given medical, dental or optical treatment
- assessments for and provision of community care services
- whether the donor should take part in social activities, leisure activities, education or training
- the donor's personal correspondence and papers
- rights of access to personal information about the donor, or
- complaints about the donor's care or treatment.

7.22 The standard form for personal welfare LPAs allows attorneys to make decisions about anything that relates to the donor's personal welfare. But donors can add restrictions or conditions to areas where they would not wish the attorney to have the power to act. For example, a donor might only want an attorney to make decisions about their social care and not their healthcare. There are particular rules for LPAs authorising an attorney to make decisions about life-sustaining treatment (see paragraphs 7.30–7.31 below).

7.23 A general personal welfare LPA gives the attorney the right to make all of the decisions set out above although this is not a full list of the actions they can take or decisions they can make. However, a personal welfare LPA can only be used at a time when the donor lacks capacity to make a specific welfare decision.

PART VI

Scenario: Denying attorneys the right to make certain decisions

Mrs Hutchison is in the early stages of Alzheimer's disease. She is anxious to get all her affairs in order while she still has capacity to do so. She makes a personal welfare LPA, appointing her daughter as attorney. But Mrs Hutchison knows that her daughter doesn't always get on with some members of the family – and she wouldn't want her daughter to stop those relatives from seeing her.

She states in the LPA that her attorney does not have the authority to decide who can contact her or visit her. If her daughter wants to prevent anyone having contact with Mrs Hutchison, she must ask the Court of Protection to decide.

7.24 Before making a decision under a personal welfare LPA, the attorney must be sure that:
- the LPA has been registered with the OPG
- the donor lacks the capacity to make the particular decision or the attorney reasonably believes that the donor lacks capacity to take the decisions covered by the LPA (having applied the Act's principles), and
- they are making the decision in the donor's best interests.

7.25 When healthcare or social care staff are involved in preparing a care plan for someone who has appointed a personal welfare attorney, they must first assess whether the donor has capacity to agree to the care plan or to parts of it. If the donor lacks capacity, professionals must then consult the attorney and get their agreement to the care plan. They will also need to consult the attorney when considering what action is in the person's best interests.

Personal welfare LPAs that authorise an attorney to make healthcare decisions

7.26 A personal welfare LPA allows attorneys to make decisions to accept or refuse healthcare or treatment unless the donor has stated clearly in the LPA that they do not want the attorney to make these decisions.

7.27 Even where the LPA includes healthcare decisions, attorneys do not have the right to consent to or refuse treatment in situations where:

- **the donor has capacity to make the particular healthcare decision (section 11(7)(a))**
  An attorney has no decision-making power if the donor can make their own treatment decisions.

- **the donor has made an advance decision to refuse the proposed treatment (section 11(7)(b))**
  An attorney cannot consent to treatment if the donor has made a valid and applicable advance decision to refuse a specific treatment (see chapter 9). But if the donor made an LPA after the advance decision, and gave the attorney the right to consent to or refuse the treatment, the attorney can choose not to follow the advance decision.

- **a decision relates to life-sustaining treatment (section 11(7)(c))**
  An attorney has no power to consent to or refuse life-sustaining treatment, unless the LPA document expressly authorises this (See paragraphs 7.30–7.31 below.)

- **the donor is detained under the Mental Health Act (section 28)**
  An attorney cannot consent to or refuse treatment for a mental disorder for a patient detained under the Mental Health Act 1983 (see also chapter 13).

7.28 LPAs cannot give attorneys the power to demand specific forms of medical treatment that healthcare staff do not believe are necessary or appropriate for the donor's particular condition.

7.29 Attorneys must always follow the Act's principles and make decisions in the donor's best interests. If healthcare staff disagree with the attorney's assessment of best interests, they should discuss the case with other medical experts and/or get a formal second opinion. Then they should discuss the matter further with the attorney. If they cannot settle the disagreement, they can apply to the Court of Protection (see paragraphs 7.45–7.49 below). While the court is coming to a decision, healthcare staff can give life-sustaining treatment to prolong the donor's life or stop their condition getting worse.

Personal welfare LPAs that authorise an attorney to make decisions about life-sustaining treatment

7.30 An attorney can only consent to or refuse life-sustaining treatment on behalf of the donor if, when making the LPA, the donor has specifically stated in the LPA document that they want the attorney to have this authority.

7.31 As with all decisions, an attorney must act in the donor's best interests when making decisions about such treatment. This will involve applying the best interests checklist (see chapter 5) and consulting with carers, family members and others interested in the donor's welfare. In particular, the attorney must not be motivated in any way by the desire to bring about the donor's death (see paragraphs 5.29–5.36). Anyone who doubts that the attorney is acting in the donor's best interests can apply to the Court of Protection for a decision.

Scenario: Making decisions about life-sustaining treatment

Mrs Joshi has never trusted doctors. She prefers to rely on alternative therapies. Because she saw her father suffer after invasive treatment for cancer, she is clear that she would refuse such treatment herself.

She is diagnosed with cancer and discusses her wishes with her husband. Mrs Joshi knows that he would respect her wishes if he ever had to make a decision about her treatment. She makes a personal welfare LPA appointing him as her attorney with authority to make all her welfare and healthcare decisions. She includes a specific statement authorising him to consent to or refuse life-sustaining treatment.

He will then be able to consider her views and make decisions about treatment in her best interests if she later lacks capacity to make those decisions herself.

Property and affairs LPAs

7.32 A donor can make an LPA giving an attorney the right to make decisions about property and affairs (including financial matters). Unless the donor states otherwise, once the LPA is registered, the attorney is allowed to make all decisions about the donor's property and affairs even if the donor still has capacity to make the decisions for themselves. In this situation, the LPA will continue to apply when the donor no longer has capacity.

7.33 Alternatively a donor can state in the LPA document that the LPA should only apply when they lack capacity to make a relevant decision. It is the donor's responsibility to decide how their capacity should then be assessed. For example, the donor may trust the attorney to carry out an assessment, or they may say that the LPA only applies if their GP or another doctor confirms in writing that they lack capacity to make specific decisions about property or finances. Financial institutions may wish to see the written confirmation before recognising the attorney's authority to act under the LPA.

7.34 The fact that someone has made a property and affairs LPA does not mean that they cannot continue to carry out financial transactions for themselves. The donor may have full capacity, but perhaps anticipates that they may lack capacity at some future time. Or they may have fluctuating or partial capacity and therefore be able to make some decisions (or at some times), but need an attorney to make others (or at other times). The attorney should allow and encourage the donor to do as much as possible, and should only act when the donor asks them to or to make those decisions the donor lacks capacity to make. However, in other cases, the donor may wish to hand over responsibility for all decisions to the attorney, even those they still have capacity to make.

7.35 If the donor restricts the decisions an attorney can make, banks may ask the attorney to sign a declaration that protects the bank from liability if the attorney misuses the account.[28]

7.36 If a donor does not restrict decisions the attorney can make, the attorney will be able to decide on any or all of the person's property and financial affairs. This might include:
- buying or selling property
- opening, closing or operating any bank, building society or other account
- giving access to the donor's financial information
- claiming, receiving and using (on the donor's behalf) all benefits, pensions, allowances and rebates (unless the Department for Work and Pensions has already appointed someone and everyone is happy for this to continue)
- receiving any income, inheritance or other entitlement on behalf of the donor
- dealing with the donor's tax affairs
- paying the donor's mortgage, rent and household expenses
- insuring, maintaining and repairing the donor's property
- investing the donor's savings
- making limited gifts on the donor's behalf (but see paragraphs 7.40–7.42 below)
- paying for private medical care and residential care or nursing home fees

---

[28]   See British Banking Association's guidance for bank staff on 'Banking for mentally incapacitated and learning disabled customers'.

- applying for any entitlement to funding for NHS care, social care or adaptations
- using the donor's money to buy a vehicle or any equipment or other help they need
- repaying interest and capital on any loan taken out by the donor.

7.37 A general property and affairs LPA will allow the attorney to carry out any or all of the actions above (although this is not a full list of the actions they can take). However, the donor may want to specify the types of powers they wish the attorney to have, or to exclude particular types of decisions. If the donor holds any assets as trustee, they should get legal advice about how the LPA may affect this.

7.38 The attorney must make these decisions personally and cannot generally give someone else authority to carry out their duties (see paragraphs 7.61–7.62 below). But if the donor wants the attorney to be able to give authority to a specialist to make specific decisions, they need to state this clearly in the LPA document (for example, appointing an investment manager to make particular investment decisions).

7.39 Donors may like to appoint someone (perhaps a family member or a professional) to go through their accounts with the attorney from time to time. This might help to reassure donors that somebody will check their financial affairs when they lack capacity to do so. It may also be helpful for attorneys to arrange a regular check that everything is being done properly. The donor should ensure that the person is willing to carry out this role and is prepared to ask for the accounts if the attorney does not provide them. They should include this arrangement in the signed LPA document. The LPA should also say whether the person can charge a fee for this service.

What gifts can an attorney make under a property and affairs LPA?

7.40 An attorney can only make gifts of the donor's money or belongings to people who are related to or connected with the donor (including the attorney) on specific occasions, including:
- births or birthdays
- weddings or wedding anniversaries
- civil partnership ceremonies or anniversaries, or
- any other occasion when families, friends or associates usually give presents (section 12(3)(b)).

7.41 If the donor previously made donations to any charity regularly or from time to time, the attorney can make donations from the person's funds. This also applies if the donor could have been expected to make such payments (section 12(2)(b)). But the value of any gift or donation must be reasonable and take into account the size of the donor's estate. For example, it would not be reasonable to buy expensive gifts at Christmas if the donor was living on modest means and had to do without essential items in order to pay for them.

7.42 The donor cannot use the LPA to make more extensive gifts than those allowed under section 12 of the Act. But they can impose stricter conditions or restrictions on the attorney's powers to make gifts. They should state these restrictions clearly in the LPA document when they are creating it. When deciding on appropriate gifts, the attorney should consider the donor's wishes and feelings to work out what would be in the donor's best interests. The attorney can apply to the Court of Protection for permission to make gifts that are not included in the LPA (for example, for tax planning purposes).

Are there any other restrictions on attorneys' powers?

7.43 Attorneys are not protected from liability if they do something that is intended to restrain the donor, unless:
- the attorney reasonably believes that the donor lacks capacity to make the decision in question, and
- the attorney reasonably believes that restraint is necessary to prevent harm to the donor, and
- the type of restraint used is in proportion to the likelihood and the seriousness of the harm.

If an attorney needs to make a decision or take action which may involve the use of restraint, they should take account of the guidance set out in chapter 6.

7.44 Attorneys have no authority to take actions that result in the donor being deprived of their liberty. Any deprivation of liberty will only be lawful if this has been properly authorised and there is other protection available for the person who lacks capacity. An example would be the protection around detention under the Mental Health Act 1983 (see chapter 13) or a court ruling. Chapter 6 gives more guidance on working out whether an action is restraint or a deprivation of liberty.

What powers does the Court of Protection have over LPAs?

7.45 The Court of Protection has a range of powers to:
- determine whether an LPA is valid
- give directions about using the LPA, and
- to remove an attorney (for example, if the attorney does not act in the best interests of the donor).

Chapter 8 gives more information about the Court of Protection's powers.

7.46 If somebody has doubts over whether an LPA is valid, they can ask the court to decide whether the LPA:
- meets the Act's requirements

- has been revoked (cancelled) by the donor, or
- has come to an end for any other reason.

7.47 The court can also stop somebody registering an LPA or rule that an LPA is invalid if:

- the donor made the LPA as a result of undue pressure or fraud, or
- the attorney behaves, has behaved or is planning to behave in a way that goes against their duties or is not in the donor's best interests.

7.48 The court can also clarify an LPA's meaning, if it is not clear, and it can tell attorneys how they should use an LPA. If an attorney thinks that an LPA does not give them enough powers, they can ask the court to extend their powers – if the donor no longer has capacity to authorise this. The court can also authorise an attorney to give a gift that the Act does not normally allow (section 12(2)), if it is in the donor's best interests.

7.49 All attorneys should keep records of their dealings with the donor's affairs (see also paragraph 7.67 below). The court can order attorneys to produce records (for example, financial accounts) and to provide specific reports, information or documentation. If somebody has concerns about an attorney's payment or expenses, the court could resolve the matter.

What responsibilities do attorneys have?

7.50 A donor cannot insist on somebody agreeing to become an attorney. It is down to the proposed attorney to decide whether to take on this responsibility. When an attorney accepts the role by signing the LPA document, this is confirmation that they are willing to act under the LPA once it is registered. An attorney can withdraw from the appointment if they ever become unable or unwilling to act, but if the LPA has been registered they must follow the correct procedures for withdrawing. (see paragraph 7.66 below).

7.51 Once the attorney starts to act under an LPA, they must meet certain standards. If they don't carry out the duties below, they could be removed from the role. In some circumstances they could face charges of fraud or negligence.

What duties does the Act impose?

7.52 Attorneys acting under an LPA have a duty to:

- follow the Act's statutory principles (see chapter 2)
- make decisions in the donor's best interests
- have regard to the guidance in the Code of Practice
- only make those decisions the LPA gives them authority to make.

PART VI

Principles and best interests

7.53 Attorneys must act in accordance with the Act's statutory principles (section 1) and in the best interests of the donor (the steps for working out best interests are set out in section 4). In particular, attorneys must consider whether the donor has capacity to make the decision for themselves. If not, they should consider whether the donor is likely to regain capacity to make the decision in the future. If so, it may be possible to delay the decision until the donor can make it.

The Code of Practice

7.54 As well as this chapter, attorneys should pay special attention to the following guidance set out in the Code:
- chapter 2, which sets out how the Act's principles should be applied
- chapter 3, which describes the steps which can be taken to try to
  help the person make decisions for themselves
- chapter 4, which describes the Act's definition of lack of capacity
  and gives guidance on assessing capacity, and
- chapter 5, which gives guidance on working out the donor's best interests.

7.55 In some circumstances, attorneys might also find it useful to refer to guidance in:
- chapter 6, which explains when attorneys who have caring responsibilities may have protection from liability and gives guidance on the few circumstances when the Act allows restraint in connection with care and treatment
- chapter 8, which gives a summary of the Court of Protection's powers relating to LPAs
- chapter 9, which explains how LPAs may be affected if the donor has made an advance decision to refuse treatment, and
- chapter 15, which describes ways to settle disagreements.

Only making decisions covered by an LPA

7.56 A personal welfare attorney has no authority to make decisions about a donor's property and affairs (such as their finances). A property and affairs attorney has no authority in decisions about a donor's personal care. (But the same person could be appointed in separate LPAs to carry out both these roles.) Under any LPA, the attorney will have authority in a wide range of decisions. But if a donor includes restrictions in the LPA document, this will limit the attorney's authority (section 9(4)(b)). If the attorney thinks that they need greater powers, they can apply to the Court of Protection which may decide to give the attorney the authority required or alternatively to appoint the attorney as a deputy with the necessary powers (see chapter 8).

7.57 It is good practice for decision-makers to consult attorneys about any decision or action, whether or not it is covered by the LPA. This is because an attorney is likely to have known the donor for some time and may have important information about their wishes and feelings. Researchers can also consult attorneys if they are thinking about involving the donor in research (see chapter 11).

Scenario: Consulting attorneys

Mr Varadi makes a personal welfare LPA appointing his son and daughter as his joint attorneys. He also makes a property and affairs LPA, appointing his son and his solicitor to act jointly and severally. He registers the property and affairs LPA straight away, so his attorneys can help with financial decisions.

Two years later, Mr Varadi has a stroke, is unable to speak and has difficulty communicating his wishes. He also lacks the capacity to make decisions about treatment. The attorneys apply to register the personal welfare LPA. Both feel that they should delay decisions about Mr Varadi's future care, because he might regain capacity to make the decisions himself. But they agree that some decisions cannot wait.

Although the solicitor has no authority to make welfare decisions, the welfare attorneys consult him about their father's best interests. They speak to him about immediate treatment decisions and their suggestion to delay making decisions about his future care. Similarly, the property and affairs attorneys consult the daughter about the financial decisions that Mr Varadi does not have the capacity to make himself.

PART VI

What are an attorney's other duties?

7.58 An attorney appointed under an LPA is acting as the chosen agent of the donor and therefore, under the law of agency, the attorney has certain duties towards the donor. An attorney takes on a role which carries a great deal of power, which they must use carefully and responsibly. They have a duty to:

- apply certain standards of care and skill (duty of care) when making decisions
- carry out the donor's instructions
- not take advantage of their position and not benefit themselves, but benefit the donor (fiduciary duty)
- not delegate decisions, unless authorised to do so
- act in good faith
- respect confidentiality
- comply with the directions of the Court of Protection

- not give up the role without telling the donor and the court.

In relation to property and affairs LPAs, they have a duty to:
- keep accounts
- keep the donor's money and property separate from their own.

Duty of care

7.59 'Duty of care' means applying a certain standard of care and skill – depending on whether the attorney is paid for their services or holds relevant professional qualifications.
- Attorneys who are not being paid must apply the same care, skill and diligence they would use to make decisions about their own life. An attorney who claims to have particular skills or qualifications must show greater skill in those particular areas than someone who does not make such claims.
- If attorneys are being paid for their services, they should demonstrate a higher degree of care and skill.
- Attorneys who undertake their duties in the course of their professional work (such as solicitors or corporate trustees) must display professional competence and follow their profession's rules and standards.

Fiduciary duty

7.60 A fiduciary duty means attorneys must not take advantage of their position. Nor should they put themselves in a position where their personal interests conflict with their duties. They also must not allow any other influences to affect the way in which they act as an attorney. Decisions should always benefit the donor, and not the attorney. Attorneys must not profit or get any personal benefit from their position, apart from receiving gifts where the Act allows it, whether or not it is at the donor's expense.

Duty not to delegate

7.61 Attorneys cannot usually delegate their authority to someone else. They must carry out their duties personally. The attorney may seek professional or expert advice (for example, investment advice from a financial adviser or advice on medical treatment from a doctor). But they cannot, as a general rule, allow someone else to make a decision that they have been appointed to make, unless this has been specifically authorised by the donor in the LPA.

7.62 In certain circumstances, attorneys may have limited powers to delegate (for example, through necessity or unforeseen circumstances, or for specific tasks which the donor would not have expected the attorney to attend to personally). But attorneys cannot usually delegate any decisions that rely on their discretion.

Duty of good faith

7.63 Acting in good faith means acting with honesty and integrity. For example, an attorney must try to make sure that their decisions do not go against a decision the donor made while they still had capacity (unless it would be in the donor's best interests to do so).

Duty of confidentiality

7.64 Attorneys have a duty to keep the donor's affairs confidential, unless:

- before they lost capacity to do so, the donor agreed that some personal or financial information may be revealed for a particular purpose (for example, they have named someone they want to check their financial accounts), or
- there is some other good reason to release it (for example, it is in the public interest or the best interests of the person who lacks capacity, or there is a risk of harm to the donor or others).

In the latter circumstances, it may be advisable for the attorney to get legal advice. Chapter 16 gives more information about confidentiality.

Duty to comply with the directions of the Court of Protection

7.65 Under sections 22 and 23 of the Act, the Court of Protection has wide-ranging powers to decide on issues relating to the operation or validity of an LPA. It can also:

- give extra authority to attorneys
- order them to produce records (for example, financial accounts), or
- order them to provide specific information or documentation to the court.

Attorneys must comply with any decision or order that the court makes.

Duty not to disclaim without notifying the donor and the OPG

7.66 Once someone becomes an attorney, they cannot give up that role without notifying the donor and the OPG. If they decide to give up their role, they must follow the relevant guidance available from the OPG.

Duty to keep accounts

7.67 Property and affairs attorneys must keep accounts of transactions carried out on the donor's behalf. Sometimes the Court of Protection will ask to see accounts. If the attorney is not a financial expert and the donor's affairs are relatively straightforward, a record

of the donor's income and expenditure (for example, through bank
statements) may be enough. The more complicated the donor's
affairs, the more detailed the accounts may need to be.

Duty to keep the donor's money and property separate

7.68 Property and affairs attorneys should usually keep the donor's
money and property separate from their own or anyone else's. There
may be occasions where donors and attorneys have agreed in the
past to keep their money in a joint bank account (for example, if a
husband is acting as his wife's attorney). It might be possible to
continue this under the LPA. But in most circumstances, attorneys
must keep finances separate to avoid any possibility of mistakes or
confusion.

How does the Act protect donors from abuse?

What should someone do if they think an attorney is abusing their position?

7.69 Attorneys are in a position of trust, so there is always a risk of
them abusing their position. Donors can help prevent abuse by
carefully choosing a suitable and trustworthy attorney. But others
have a role to play in looking out for possible signs of abuse or
exploitation, and reporting any concerns to the OPG. The OPG will
then follow this up in co-operation with relevant agencies.

7.70 Signs that an attorney may be exploiting the donor (or failing to act
in the donor's best interests) include:
- stopping relatives or friends contacting the donor – for
example, the attorney may prevent contact or the donor may
suddenly refuse visits or telephone calls from family and
friends for no reason
- sudden unexplained changes in living arrangements (for
example, someone moves in to care for a donor they've had
little contact with)
- not allowing healthcare or social care staff to see the donor
- taking the donor out of hospital against medical advice, while
the donor is having necessary medical treatment
- unpaid bills (for example, residential care or nursing home
fees)
- an attorney opening a credit card account for the donor
- spending money on things that are not obviously related to the
donor's needs
- the attorney spending money in an unusual or extravagant way
- transferring financial assets to another country.

7.71 Somebody who suspects abuse should contact the OPG
immediately. The OPG may direct a Court of Protection Visitor to
visit an attorney to investigate. In cases of suspected physical or

sexual abuse, theft or serious fraud, the person should contact the police. They might also be able to refer the matter to the relevant local adult protection authorities.

7.72 In serious cases, the OPG will refer the matter to the Court of Protection. The court may revoke (cancel) the LPA or (through the OPG) prevent it being registered, if it decides that:

- the LPA does not meet the legal requirements for creating an LPA
- the LPA has been revoked or come to an end for any other reason
- somebody used fraud or undue pressure to get the donor to make
  the LPA
- the attorney has done something that they do not have authority to do, or
- the attorney has behaved or is planning to behave in a way that is not in the donor's best interests.

The court might then consider whether the authority previously given to an attorney can be managed by:

- the court making a single decision, or
- appointing a deputy.

What should an attorney do if they think someone else is abusing the donor?

7.73 An attorney who thinks someone else is abusing or exploiting the donor should report it to the OPG and ask for advice on what action they should take. They should contact the police if they suspect physical or sexual abuse, theft or serious fraud. They might also be able to refer the matter to local adult protection authorities.

7.74 Chapter 13 gives more information about protecting vulnerable people from abuse, ill treatment or neglect. It also discusses the duties and responsibilities of the various agencies involved, including the OPG and local authorities. In particular, it is a criminal offence (with a maximum penalty of five years' imprisonment, a fine, or both) for anyone (including attorneys) to wilfully neglect or ill-treat a person in their care who lacks capacity to make decisions for themselves (section 44).

What happens to existing EPAs once the Act comes into force?

7.75 Once the Act comes into force, it will not be possible to make new EPAs. Only LPAs can then be made.

7.76 Some donors will have created EPAs before the Act came into force with the expectation that their chosen attorneys will manage their property and affairs in the future, whether or not they have capacity to do so themselves.

PART VI

7.77 If donors still have capacity after the Act comes into force, they can cancel the EPA and make an LPA covering their property and affairs. They should also notify attorneys and anyone else aware of the EPA (for example, a bank) that they have cancelled it.

7.78 Some donors will choose not to cancel their EPA or they may already lack the capacity to do so. In such cases, the Act allows existing EPAs, whether registered or not, to continue to be valid so that attorneys can meet the donor's expectations (Schedule 4). An EPA must be registered with the OPG when the attorney thinks the donor lacks capacity to manage their own affairs, or is beginning to lack capacity to do so.

7.79 EPA attorneys may find guidance in this chapter helpful. In particular, all attorneys must comply with the duties described in paragraphs 7.58–7.68 above. EPA attorneys can also be found liable under section 44 of the new Act, which sets out the new criminal offences of ill treatment and wilful neglect. The OPG has produced guidance on EPAs (see Annex A for details of publications and contact information).

8   WHAT IS THE ROLE OF THE COURT OF PROTECTION AND COURT-APPOINTED DEPUTIES?

This chapter describes the role of the Court of Protection and the role of court-appointed deputies. It explains the powers that the court has and how to make an application to the court. It also looks at how the court appoints a deputy to act and make decisions on behalf of someone who lacks capacity to make those decisions. In particular, it gives guidance on a deputy's duties and the consequences of not carrying them out responsibly.

The Office of the Public Guardian (OPG) produces detailed guidance for deputies. See the Annex for more details of the publications and how to get them. Further details on the court's procedures are given in the Court of Protection Rules and Practice Directions issued by the court.

In this chapter, as throughout the Code, a person's capacity (or lack of capacity) refers specifically to their capacity to make a particular decision at the time it needs to be made.

Quick summary

The Court of Protection has powers to:

- decide whether a person has capacity to make a particular decision for themselves
- make declarations, decisions or orders on financial or welfare matters affecting people who lack capacity to make such decisions

- appoint deputies to make decisions for people lacking capacity to make those decisions
- decide whether an LPA or EPA is valid, and
- remove deputies or attorneys who fail to carry out their duties.

Before accepting an appointment as a deputy, a person the court nominates should consider whether:

- they have the skills and ability to carry out a deputy's duties (especially in relation to property and affairs)
- they actually want to take on the duties and responsibilities.

Anyone acting as a deputy must:

- make sure that they only make those decisions that they are authorised to make by the order of the court
- make sure that they follow the Act's statutory principles, including:
  - considering whether the person has capacity to make a particular decision for themselves. If they do, the deputy should allow them to do so unless the person agrees that the deputy should make the decision
  - taking all possible steps to try to help a person make the particular decision
- always make decisions in the person's best interests
- have regard to guidance in the Code of Practice that is relevant to the situation
- fulfil their duties towards the person concerned (in particular the duty of care and fiduciary duties to respect the degree of trust placed in them by the court).

What is the Court of Protection?

8.1 Section 45 of the Act sets up a specialist court, the Court of Protection, to deal with decision-making for adults (and children in a few cases) who may lack capacity to make specific decisions for themselves. The new Court of Protection replaces the old court of the same name, which only dealt with decisions about the property and financial affairs of people lacking capacity to manage their own affairs. As well as property and affairs, the new court also deals with serious decisions affecting healthcare and personal welfare matters. These were previously dealt with by the High Court under its inherent jurisdiction.

8.2 The new Court of Protection is a superior court of record and is able to establish precedent (it can set examples for future cases) and build up expertise in all issues related to lack of capacity. It has the same powers, rights, privileges and authority as the High Court. When reaching any decision, the court must apply all the statutory principles set out in section 1 of the Act. In particular, it must make

PART VI

a decision in the best interests of the person who lacks capacity to make the specific decision. There will usually be a fee for applications to the court.[29]

How can somebody make an application to the Court of Protection?

8.3 In most cases concerning personal welfare matters, the core principles of the Act and the processes set out in chapters 5 and 6 will be enough to:
- help people take action or make decisions in the best interests of someone who lacks capacity to make decisions about their own care or treatment, or
- find ways of settling disagreements about such actions or decisions.

But an application to the Court of Protection may be necessary for:
- particularly difficult decisions
- disagreements that cannot be resolved in any other way (see chapter 15), or
- situations where ongoing decisions may need to be made about the personal welfare of a person who lacks capacity to make decisions for themselves.

8.4 An order of the court will usually be necessary for matters relating to the property and affairs (including financial matters) of people who lack capacity to make specific financial decisions for themselves, unless:
- their only income is state benefits (see paragraph 8.36 below), or
- they have previously made an Enduring Power of Attorney (EPA) or a Lasting Power of Attorney (LPA) to give somebody authority to manage their property and affairs (see chapter 7).

8.5 Receivers appointed by the court before the Act commences will be treated as deputies. But they will keep their existing powers and duties. They must meet the requirements set out in the Act and, in particular, follow the statutory principles and act in the best interests of the person for whom they have been appointed. They must also have regard to guidance in this chapter and other parts of the Code of Practice. Further guidance for receivers is available from the OPG.

Cases involving young people aged 16 or 17

8.6 Either a court dealing with family proceedings or the Court of Protection can hear cases involving people aged 16 or 17 who lack capacity. In some cases, the Court of Protection can hear cases involving people younger than 16 (for example, when somebody

---

[29]   Details of the fees charged by the court, and the circumstances in which the fees may be waived or remitted, are available from the Office of the Public Guardian (OPG).

needs to be appointed to make longer-term decisions about their financial affairs). Under section 21 of the Mental Capacity Act, the Court of Protection can transfer cases concerning children to a court that has powers under the Children Act 1989. Such a court can also transfer cases to the Court of Protection, if necessary. Chapter 12 gives more detail on cases where this might apply.

Who should make the application?

8.7 The person making the application will vary, depending on the circumstances. For example, a person wishing to challenge a finding that they lack capacity may apply to the court, supported by others where necessary. Where there is a disagreement among family members, for example, a family member may wish to apply to the court to settle the disagreement – bearing in mind the need, in most cases, to get permission beforehand (see paragraphs 8.11–8.12 below).

8.8 For cases about serious or major decisions concerning medical treatment (see paragraphs 8.18–8.24 below), the NHS Trust or other organisation responsible for the patient's care will usually make the application. If social care staff are concerned about a decision that affects the welfare of a person who lacks capacity, the relevant local authority should make the application.

8.9 For decisions about the property and affairs of someone who lacks capacity to manage their own affairs, the applicant will usually be the person (for example, family carer) who needs specific authority from the court to deal with the individual's money or property.

8.10 If the applicant is the person who is alleged to lack capacity, they will always be a party to the court proceedings. In all other cases, the court will decide whether the person who lacks, or is alleged to lack, capacity should be involved as a party to the case. Where the person is a party to the case, the court may appoint the Official Solicitor to act for them.

PART VI

Who must ask the court for permission to make an application?

8.11 As a general rule, potential applicants must get the permission of the Court of Protection before making an application (section 50). People who the Act says do not need to ask for permission include:

- a person who lacks, or is alleged to lack, capacity in relation to a specific decision or action (or anyone with parental responsibility, if the person is under 18 years)
- the donor of the LPA an application relates to – or their attorney
- a deputy who has been appointed by the court to act for the person
  concerned, and

- a person named in an existing court order relating to the application.

The Court of Protection Rules also set out specific types of cases where permission is not required.

8.12 When deciding whether to give permission for an application, the court must consider:
- the applicant's connection to the person the application is about
- the reasons for the application
- whether a proposed order or direction of the court will benefit the person the application is about, and
- whether it is possible to get that benefit another way.

Scenario: Considering whether to give permission for an application

Sunita, a young Asian woman, has always been close to her older brother, who has severe learning disabilities and lives in a care home. Two years ago, Sunita married a non-Asian man, and her family cut off contact with her. She still wants to visit her brother and to be consulted about his care and what is in his best interests. But the family is not letting her. The Court of Protection gives Sunita permission to apply to the court for an order allowing her contact with her brother.

What powers does the Court of Protection have?

8.13 The Court of Protection may:
- make declarations, decisions and orders on financial and welfare matters affecting people who lack, or are alleged to lack, capacity (the lack of capacity must relate to the particular issue being presented to the court)
- appoint deputies to make decisions for people who lack capacity to make those decisions
- remove deputies or attorneys who act inappropriately.

The Court can also hear cases about LPAs and EPAs. The court's powers concerning EPAs are set out in Schedule 4 of the Act.

8.14 The court must always follow the statutory principles set out in section 1 of the Act (see chapter 2) and make the decision in the best interests of the person concerned (see chapter 5).

What declarations can the court make?

8.15 Section 15 of the Act provides the court with powers to make a declaration (a ruling) on specific issues. For example, it can make a declaration as to whether a person has capacity to make a particular decision or give consent for or take a particular action. The court will require evidence of any assessment of the person's capacity and may wish to see relevant written evidence (for example, a diary, letters or other papers). If the court decides the person has capacity to make that decision, they will not take the case further. The person can now make the decision for themselves.

8.16 Applications concerning a person's capacity are likely to be rare – people can usually settle doubts and disagreements informally (see chapters 4 and 15). But an application may be relevant if:

- a person wants to challenge a decision that they lack capacity
- professionals disagree about a person's capacity to make a specific (usually serious) decision
- there is a dispute over whether the person has capacity (for example, between family members).

8.17 The court can also make a declaration as to whether a specific act relating to a person's care or treatment is lawful (either where somebody has carried out the action or is proposing to). Under section 15, this can include an omission or failure to provide care or treatment that the person needs.

This power to decide on the lawfulness of an act is particularly relevant for major medical treatment cases where there is doubt or disagreement over whether the treatment would be in the person's best interests. Healthcare staff can still give life-sustaining treatment, or treatment which stops a person's condition getting seriously worse, while the court is coming to a decision.

Serious healthcare and treatment decisions

8.18 Prior to the Act coming into force, the courts decided that some decisions relating to the provision of medical treatment were so serious that in each case, an application should be made to the court for a declaration that the proposed action was lawful before that action was taken. Cases involving any of the following decisions should therefore be brought before a court:

- decisions about the proposed withholding or withdrawal of artificial nutrition and hydration (ANH) from patients in a permanent vegetative state (PVS)
- cases involving organ or bone marrow donation by a person who lacks capacity to consent
- cases involving the proposed non-therapeutic sterilisation of a person who lacks capacity to consent to this (e.g. for contraceptive purposes) and
- all other cases where there is a doubt or dispute about whether a particular treatment will be in a person's best interests.

8.19 The case law requirement to seek a declaration in cases involving the withholding or withdrawing of artificial nutrition and hydration to people in a permanent vegetative state is unaffected by the Act[30] and as a matter of practice, these cases should be put to the Court of Protection for approval.

PART VI

---

[30] *Airedale NHS Trust v Bland* [1993] AC 789.

8.20 Cases involving organ or bone marrow donation by a person who lacks capacity to consent should also be referred to the Court of Protection. Such cases involve medical procedures being performed on a person who lacks capacity to consent but which would benefit a third party (though would not necessarily directly or physically benefit the person who lacks capacity). However, sometimes such procedures may be in the person's overall best interests (see chapter 5). For example, the person might receive emotional, social and psychological benefits as a result of the help they have given, and in some cases the person may experience only minimal physical discomfort.

8.21 A prime example of this is the case of *Re Y*[31] where it was found to be in Y's best interests for her to donate bone marrow to her sister. The court decided that it was in Y's best interests to continue to receive strong emotional support from her mother, which might be diminished if her sister's health were to deteriorate further, or she were to die.

Further details on this area are available in Department of Health or Welsh Assembly guidance.[32]

8.22 Non-therapeutic sterilisation is the sterilisation for contraceptive purposes of a person who cannot consent. Such cases will require a careful assessment of whether such sterilisation would be in the best interests of the person who lacks capacity and such cases should continue to be referred to the court.[33] The court has also given guidance on when certain termination of pregnancy cases should be brought before the court.[34]

8.23 Other cases likely to be referred to the court include those involving ethical dilemmas in untested areas (such as innovative treatments for variant CJD), or where there are otherwise irresolvable conflicts between healthcare staff, or between staff and family members.

8.24 There are also a few types of cases that should generally be dealt with by the court, since other dispute resolution methods are unlikely to be appropriate (see chapter 15). This includes, for example, cases where it is unclear whether proposed serious and/or invasive medical treatment is likely to be in the best interests of the person who lacks capacity to consent.

---

[31] *Re Y (Mental incapacity: Bone marrow transplant)* [1996] 2 FLR 787.

[32] Reference Guide to Consent for Examination or Treatment, Department of Health, March 2001:   www.dh.gov.uk/PublicationsAndStatistics/Publications/PublicationsPolicyAnd Guidance/PublicationsPolicyAndGuidanceArticle/fs/en?CONTENT_ID=4006757&chk= snmdw8

[33] See e.g. *Re A (medical treatment: male sterilisation)* (1999) 53 BMLR 66 where a mother applied for a declaration that a vasectomy was in the best interests of A, her son, (who had Down's syndrome and was borderline between significant and severe impairment of intelligence), in the absence of his consent. After balancing the burdens and benefits of the proposed vasectomy to A, the Court of Appeal held that the vasectomy would not be in A's best interests.

[34] *D v An NHS Trust (Medical Treatment: Consent: Termination)* [2004] 1 FLR 1110.

What powers does the court have to make decisions and appoint deputies?

8.25 In cases of serious dispute, where there is no other way of finding a solution or when the authority of the court is needed in order to make a particular decision or take a particular action, the court can be asked to make a decision to settle the matter using its powers under section 16.

However, if there is a need for ongoing decision-making powers and there is no relevant EPA or LPA, the court may appoint a deputy to make future decisions. It will also state what decisions the deputy has the authority to make on the person's behalf.

8.26 In deciding what type of order to make, the court must apply the Act's principles and the best interests checklist. In addition, it must follow two further principles, intended to make any intervention as limited as possible:

- Where possible, the court should make the decision itself in preference to appointing a deputy.
- If a deputy needs to be appointed, their appointment should be as limited in scope and for as short a time as possible.

What decisions can the court make?

8.27 In some cases, the court must make a decision, because someone needs specific authority to act and there is no other route for getting it. These include cases where:

- there is no EPA or property and affairs LPA in place and someone needs to make a financial decision for a person who lacks capacity to make that decision (for example, the decision to terminate a tenancy agreement), or
- it is necessary to make a will, or to amend an existing will, on behalf of a person who lacks capacity to do so.

8.28 Examples of other types of cases where a court decision might be appropriate include cases where:

- there is genuine doubt or disagreement about the existence, validity or applicability of an advance decision to refuse treatment (see chapter 9)
- there is a major disagreement regarding a serious decision (for example, about where a person who lacks capacity to decide for themselves should live)
- a family carer or a solicitor asks for personal information about someone who lacks capacity to consent to that information being revealed (for example, where there have been allegations of abuse of a person living in a care home)
- someone suspects that a person who lacks capacity to make decisions to protect themselves is at risk of harm or abuse from a named individual (the court could stop that individual contacting the person who lacks capacity).

8.29 Anyone carrying out actions under a decision or order of the court must still also follow the Act's principles.

Scenario: Making a decision to settle disagreements

Mrs Worrell has Alzheimer's disease. Her son and daughter argue over which care home their mother should move to. Although Mrs Worrell lacks the capacity to make this decision herself, she has enough money to pay the fees of a care home.

Her solicitor acts as attorney in relation to her financial affairs under a registered EPA. But he has no power to get involved in this family dispute – nor does he want to get involved.

The Court of Protection makes a decision in Mrs Worrell's best interests, and decides which care home can best meet her needs. Once this matter is resolved, there is no need to appoint a deputy.

What powers does the court have in relation to LPAs?

8.30 The Court of Protection can determine the validity of an LPA or EPA and can give directions as to how an attorney should use their powers under an LPA (see chapter 7). In particular, the court can cancel an LPA and end the attorney's appointment. The court might do this if the attorney was not carrying out their duties properly or acting in the best interests of the donor. The court must then decide whether it is necessary to appoint a deputy to take over the attorney's role.

What are the rules for appointing deputies?

8.31 Sometimes it is not practical or appropriate for the court to make a single declaration or decision. In such cases, if the court thinks that somebody needs to make future or ongoing decisions for someone whose condition makes it likely they will lack capacity to make some further decisions in the future, it can appoint a deputy to act for and make decisions for that person. A deputy's authority should be as limited in scope and duration as possible (see paragraphs 8.35–8.39 below).

How does the court appoint deputies?

8.32 It is for the court to decide who to appoint as a deputy. Different skills may be required depending on whether the deputy's decisions will be about a person's welfare (including healthcare), their finances or both. The court will decide whether the proposed deputy is reliable and trustworthy and has an appropriate level of skill and competence to carry out the necessary tasks.

8.33 In the majority of cases, the deputy is likely to be a family member or someone who knows the person well. But in some cases the court may decide to appoint a deputy who is independent of the family (for example, where the person's affairs or care needs are particularly complicated). This could be, for example, the Director of Adult Services in the relevant local authority (but see paragraph 8.60 below) or a professional deputy. The OPG has a panel of professional deputies (mainly solicitors who specialise in this area of law) who may be appointed to deal with property and affairs if the court decides that would be in the person's best interests.

When might a deputy need to be appointed?

8.34 Whether a person who lacks capacity to make specific decisions needs a deputy will depend on:
- the individual circumstances of the person concerned
- whether future or ongoing decisions are likely to be necessary, and
- whether the appointment is for decisions about property and affairs or personal welfare.

Property and affairs

8.35 The court will appoint a deputy to manage a person's property and affairs (including financial matters) in similar circumstances to those in which they would have appointed a receiver in the past. If a person who lacks capacity to make decisions about property and affairs has not made an EPA or LPA, applications to the court are necessary:
- for dealing with cash assets over a specified amount that remain after any debts have been paid
- for selling a person's property, or
- where the person has a level of income or capital that the court thinks a deputy needs to manage.

8.36 If the only income of a person who lacks capacity is social security benefits and they have no property or savings, there will usually be no need for a deputy to be appointed. This is because the person's benefits can be managed by an appointee, appointed by the Department for Work and Pensions to receive and deal with the benefits of a person who lacks capacity to do this for themselves. Although appointees are not covered by the Act, they will be expected to act in the person's best interests and must do so if they are involved in caring for the person. If the court does appoint a property and affairs deputy for someone who has an appointee, it is likely that the deputy would take over the appointee's role.

8.37 Anybody considered for appointment as a property and affairs deputy will need to sign a declaration giving details of their circumstances and ability to manage financial affairs. The declaration will include details of the tasks and duties the deputy

PART VI

must carry out. The deputy must assure the court that they have the skills, knowledge and commitment to carry them out.

Personal welfare (including healthcare)

8.38 Deputies for personal welfare decisions will only be required in the most difficult cases where:
- important and necessary actions cannot be carried out without the court's authority, or
- there is no other way of settling the matter in the best interests of the person who lacks capacity to make particular welfare decisions.

8.39 Examples include when:
- someone needs to make a series of linked welfare decisions over time and it would not be beneficial or appropriate to require all of those decisions to be made by the court. For example, someone (such as a family carer) who is close to a person with profound and multiple learning disabilities might apply to be appointed as a deputy with authority to make such decisions
- the most appropriate way to act in the person's best interests is to have a deputy, who will consult relevant people but have the final authority to make decisions
- there is a history of serious family disputes that could have a detrimental effect on the person's future care unless a deputy is appointed to make necessary decisions
- the person who lacks capacity is felt to be at risk of serious harm if left in the care of family members. In these rare cases, welfare decisions may need to be made by someone independent of the family, such as a local authority officer. There may even be a need for an additional court order prohibiting those family members from having contact with the person.

Who can be a deputy?

8.40 Section 19(1) states that deputies must be at least 18 years of age. Deputies with responsibility for property and affairs can be either an individual or a trust corporation (often parts of banks or other financial institutions). No-one can be appointed as a deputy without their consent.

8.41 Paid care workers (for example, care home managers) should not agree to act as a deputy because of the possible conflict of interest – unless there are exceptional circumstances (for example, if the care worker is the only close relative of the person who lacks capacity). But the court can appoint someone who is an office-holder or in a specified position (for example, the Director of Adult Services of the relevant local authority). In this situation, the court will need to be satisfied that there is no conflict of interest before making such an appointment (see paragraphs 8.58–8.60).

8.42 The court can appoint two or more deputies and state whether they should act 'jointly', 'jointly and severally' or 'jointly in respect of some matters and jointly and severally in respect of others' (section 19 (4)(c)).

- Joint deputies must always act together. They must all agree decisions or actions, and all sign any relevant documents.
- Joint and several deputies can act together, but they may also act independently if they wish. Any action taken by any deputy alone is as valid as if that person were the only deputy.

8.43 Deputies may be appointed jointly for some issues and jointly and severally for others. For example, two deputies could be appointed jointly and severally for most decisions, but the court might rule that they act jointly when selling property.

Scenario: *Acting jointly and severally*

Toby had a road accident and suffered brain damage and other disabilities. He gets financial compensation but lacks capacity to manage this amount of money or make decisions about his future care. His divorced parents are arguing about where their son should live and how his compensation money should be used. Toby has always been close to his sister, who is keen to be involved but is anxious about dealing with such a large amount of money.

The court decides where Toby will live. It also appoints his sister and a solicitor as joint and several deputies to manage his property and affairs. His sister can deal with any day-to-day decisions that Toby lacks capacity to make, and the solicitor can deal with more complicated matters.

PART VI

What happens if a deputy can no longer carry out their duties?

8.44 When appointing a deputy, the court can also appoint someone to be a successor deputy (someone who can take over the deputy's duties in certain situations). The court will state the circumstances under which this could occur. In some cases it will also state a period of time in which the successor deputy can act. Appointment of a successor deputy might be useful if the person appointed as deputy is already elderly and wants to be sure that somebody will take over their duties in the future, if necessary.

Scenario: *Appointing a successor deputy*

Neil, a man with Down's syndrome, inherits a lot of money and property. His parents were already retired when the court appointed

---

them as joint deputies to manage Neil's property and affairs. They are worried about what will happen to Neil when they cannot carry out their duties as deputies any more. The court agrees to appoint other relatives as successor deputies. They will then be able to take over as deputies after the parents' death or if his parents are no longer able to carry out the deputy's role.

Can the court protect people lacking capacity from financial loss?

8.45 Under section 19(9)(a) of the Act the court can ask a property and affairs deputy to provide some form of security (for example, a guarantee bond) to the Public Guardian to cover any loss as a result of the deputy's behaviour in carrying out their role. The court can also ask a deputy to provide reports and accounts to the Public Guardian, as it sees fit.

Are there any restrictions on a deputy's powers?

8.46 Section 20 sets out some specific restrictions on a deputy's powers. In particular, a deputy has no authority to make decisions or take action:

- if they do something that is intended to restrain the person who lacks capacity – apart from under certain circumstances (guidance on the circumstances when restraint might be permitted is given in chapter 6)[35]
- if they think that the person concerned has capacity to make the particular decision for themselves
- if their decision goes against a decision made by an attorney acting under a Lasting Power of Attorney granted by the person before they lost capacity, or
- to refuse the provision or continuation of life-sustaining treatment for a person who lacks capacity to consent – such decisions must be taken by the court.

If a deputy thinks their powers are not enough for them to carry out their duties effectively, they can apply to the court to change their powers. See paragraph 8.54 below.

What responsibilities do deputies have?

8.47 Once a deputy has been appointed by the court, the order of appointment will set out their specific powers and the scope of their authority. On taking up the appointment, the deputy will assume a number of duties and responsibilities and will be required to act in

---

[35] It is worth noting that there is a drafting error in section 20 of the Act. The word 'or' in section 20(11)(a) should have been 'and' in order to be consistent with sections 6(3)(a) and 11(4)(a). The Government will make the necessary amendment to correct this error at the earliest available legislative opportunity.

accordance with certain standards. Failure to comply with the duties set out below could result in the Court of Protection revoking the order appointing the deputy and, in some circumstances, the deputy could be personally liable to claims for negligence or criminal charges of fraud.

8.48 Deputies should always inform any third party they are dealing with that the court has appointed them as deputy. The court will give the deputy official documents to prove their appointment and the extent of their authority.

8.49 A deputy must act whenever a decision or action is needed and it falls within their duties as set out in the court order appointing them. A deputy who fails to act at all in such situations could be in breach of duty.

What duties does the Act impose?

8.50 Deputies must:
- follow the Act's statutory principles (see chapter 2)
- make decisions or act in the best interests of the person who lacks capacity
- have regard to the guidance in this Code of Practice
- only make decisions the Court has given them authority to make.

Principles and best interests

8.51 Deputies must act in accordance with the Act's statutory principles (section 1) and in particular the best interests of the person who lacks capacity (the steps for working out best interests are set out in section 4). In particular, deputies must consider whether the person has capacity to make the decision for themselves. If not, they should consider whether the person is likely to regain capacity to make the decision in the future. If so, it may be possible to delay the decision until the person can make it.

The Code of Practice

8.52 As well as this chapter, deputies should pay special attention to the following guidance set out in the Code:
- chapter 2, which sets out how the Act's principles should be applied
- chapter 3, which describes the steps which can be taken to try to help the person make decisions for themselves
- chapter 4, which describes the Act's definition of lack of capacity
  and gives guidance on assessing capacity, and
- chapter 5, which gives guidance on working out someone's best

PART VI

interests.

8.53 In some situations, deputies might also find it useful to refer to guidance in:

- chapter 6, which explains when deputies who have caring responsibilities may have protection from liability and gives guidance on the few circumstances when the Act allows restraint in connection with care and treatment, and
- chapter 15, which describes ways to settle disagreements.

Only making decisions the court authorises a deputy to make

8.54 A deputy has a duty to act only within the scope of the actual powers given by the court, which are set out in the order of appointment. It is possible that a deputy will think their powers are not enough for them to carry out their duties effectively. In this situation, they must apply to the court either to:

- ask the court to make the decision in question, or
- ask the court to change the deputy's powers.

What are a deputy's other duties?

8.55 Section 19(6) states that a deputy is to be treated as 'the agent' of the person who lacks capacity when they act on their behalf. Being an agent means that the deputy has legal duties (under the law of agency) to the person they are representing. It also means that when they carry out tasks within their powers, they are not personally liable to third parties.

8.56 Deputies must carry out their duties carefully and responsibly. They have a duty to:

- act with due care and skill (duty of care)
- not take advantage of their situation (fiduciary duty)
- indemnify the person against liability to third parties caused by the deputy's negligence
- not delegate duties unless authorised to do so
- act in good faith
- respect the person's confidentiality, and
- comply with the directions of the Court of Protection.

Property and affairs deputies also have a duty to:

- keep accounts, and
- keep the person's money and property separate from own finances.

Duty of care

8.57 'Duty of care' means applying a certain standard of care and skill – depending on whether the deputy is paid for their services or holds relevant professional qualifications.

- Deputies who are not being paid must use the same care, skill and diligence they would use when making decisions for themselves or managing their own affairs. If they do not, they could be held liable for acting negligently. A deputy who claims to have particular skills or qualifications must show greater skill in those particular areas than a person who does not make such claims.
- If deputies are being paid for their services, they are expected to demonstrate a higher degree of care or skill when carrying out their duties.
- Deputies whose duties form part of their professional work (for example, solicitors or accountants) must display normal professional competence and follow their profession's rules and standards.

Fiduciary duty

8.58 A fiduciary duty means deputies must not take advantage of their position. Nor should they put themselves in a position where their personal interests conflict with their duties. For example, deputies should not buy property that they are selling for the person they have been appointed to represent. They should also not accept a third party commission in any transactions. Deputies must not allow anything else to influence their duties. They cannot use their position for any personal benefit, whether or not it is at the person's expense.

8.59 In many cases, the deputy will be a family member. In rare situations, this could lead to potential conflicts of interests. When making decisions, deputies should follow the Act's statutory principles and apply the best interests checklist and not allow their own personal interests to influence the decision.

8.60 Sometimes the court will consider appointing the Director of Adult Services in England or Director of Social Services in Wales of the relevant local authority as a deputy. The court will need to be satisfied that the authority has arrangements to avoid possible conflicts of interest. For example where the person for whom a financial deputy is required receives community care services from the local authority, the court will wish to be satisfied that decisions about the person's finances will be made in the best interests of that person, regardless of any implications for the services provided.

Duty not to delegate

8.61 A deputy may seek professional or expert advice (for example, investment advice from a financial adviser or a second medical opinion from a doctor). But they cannot give their decision-making responsibilities to someone else. In certain circumstances, the court

PART VI

will authorise the delegation of specific tasks (for example, appointing a discretionary investment manager for the conduct of investment business).

8.62 In certain circumstances, deputies may have limited powers to delegate (for example, through necessity or unforeseen circumstances, or for specific tasks which the court would not have expected the deputy to attend to personally). But deputies cannot usually delegate any decisions that rely on their discretion. If the deputy is the Director of Adult Services in England or Director of Social Services in Wales, or a solicitor, they can delegate specific tasks to other staff. But the deputy is still responsible for any actions or decisions taken, and can therefore be held accountable for any errors that are made.

Duty of good faith

8.63 Acting in good faith means acting with honesty and integrity. For example, a deputy must try to make sure that their decisions do not go against a decision the person made while they still had capacity (unless it would be in the person's best interests to do so).

Duty of confidentiality

8.64 Deputies have a duty to keep the person's affairs confidential, unless:
- before they lost capacity to do so, the person agreed that information could be revealed where necessary
- there is some other good reason to release information (for example, it is in the public interest or in the best interests of the person who lacks capacity, or where there is a risk of harm to the person concerned or to other people).

In the latter circumstances, it is advisable for the deputy to contact the OPG for guidance or get legal advice. See chapter 16 for more information about revealing personal information.

Duty to comply with the directions of the Court of Protection

8.65 The Court of Protection may give specific directions to deputies about how they should use their powers. It can also order deputies to provide reports (for example, financial accounts or reports on the welfare of the person who lacks capacity) to the Public Guardian at any time or at such intervals as the court directs. Deputies must comply with any direction of the court or request from the Public Guardian.

Duty to keep accounts

8.66 A deputy appointed to manage property and affairs is expected to keep, and periodically submit to the Public Guardian, correct accounts of all their dealings and transactions on the person's behalf.

Duty to keep the person's money and property separate

8.67 Property and affairs deputies should usually keep the person's money and property separate from their own or anyone else's. This is to avoid any possibility of mistakes or confusion in handling the person's affairs. Sometimes there may be good reason not to do so (for example, a husband might be his wife's deputy and they might have had a joint account for many years).

Changes of contact details

8.68 A deputy should inform the OPG of any changes of contact details or circumstances (for the deputy or the person they are acting for). This will help make sure that the OPG has up-to-date records. It will also allow the court to discharge people who are no longer eligible to act as deputies.

Who is responsible for supervising deputies?

8.69 Deputies are accountable to the Court of Protection. The court can cancel a deputy's appointment at any time if it decides the appointment is no longer in the best interests of the person who lacks capacity.

8.70 The OPG is responsible for supervising and supporting deputies. But it must also protect people lacking capacity from possible abuse or exploitation. Anybody who suspects that a deputy is abusing their position should contact the OPG immediately. The OPG may instruct a Court of Protection Visitor to visit a deputy to investigate any matter of concern. It can also apply to the court to cancel a deputy's appointment.

8.71 The OPG will consider carefully any concerns or complaints against deputies. But if somebody suspects physical or sexual abuse or serious fraud, they should contact the police and/or social services immediately, as well as informing the OPG. Chapter 14 gives more information about the role of the OPG. It also discusses the protection of vulnerable people from abuse, ill treatment or wilful neglect and the responsibilities of various relevant agencies.

PART VI

9   WHAT DOES THE ACT SAY ABOUT ADVANCE DECISIONS TO REFUSE TREATMENT?

This chapter explains what to do when somebody has made an advance decision to refuse treatment. It sets out:

- what the Act means by an 'advance decision'
- guidance on making, updating and cancelling advance decisions
- how to check whether an advance decision exists
- how to check that an advance decision is valid and that it applies to current circumstances
- the responsibilities of healthcare professionals when an advance decision exists
- how to handle disagreements about advance decisions.

> In this chapter, as throughout the Code, a person's capacity (or lack of capacity) refers specifically to their capacity to make a particular decision at the time it needs to be made.

Quick summary

- An advance decision enables someone aged 18 and over, while still capable, to refuse specified medical treatment for a time in the future when they may lack the capacity to consent to or refuse that treatment.
- An advance decision to refuse treatment must be valid and applicable to current circumstances. If it is, it has the same effect as a decision that is made by a person with capacity: healthcare professionals must follow the decision.
- Healthcare professionals will be protected from liability if they:
  - stop or withhold treatment because they reasonably believe that an advance decision exists, and that it is valid and applicable
  - treat a person because, having taken all practical and appropriate steps to find out if the person has made an advance decision to refuse treatment, they do not know or are not satisfied that a valid and applicable advance decision exists.
- People can only make an advance decision under the Act if they are 18 or over and have the capacity to make the decision. They must say what treatment they want to refuse, and they can cancel their decision – or part of it – at any time.
- If the advance decision refuses life-sustaining treatment, it must:
  - be in writing (it can be written by a someone else or recorded in healthcare notes)
  - be signed and witnessed, and
  - state clearly that the decision applies even if life is at risk.
- To establish whether an advance decision is valid and applicable, healthcare professionals must try to find out if the person:

- has done anything that clearly goes against their advance decision
- has withdrawn their decision
- has subsequently conferred the power to make that decision on an attorney, or
- would have changed their decision if they had known more about the current circumstances.

- Sometimes healthcare professionals will conclude that an advance decision does not exist, is not valid and/or applicable – but that it is an expression of the person's wishes. The healthcare professional must then consider what is set out in the advance decision as an expression of previous wishes when working out the person's best interests (see chapter 5).
- Some healthcare professionals may disagree in principle with patients' decisions to refuse life-sustaining treatment. They do not have to act against their beliefs. But they must not simply abandon patients or act in a way that that affects their care.
- Advance decisions to refuse treatment for mental disorder may not apply if the person who made the advance decision is or is liable to be detained under the Mental Health Act 1983.

How can someone make an advance decision to refuse treatment?

What is an advance decision to refuse treatment?

9.1 It is a general principle of law and medical practice that people have a right to consent to or refuse treatment. The courts have recognised that adults have the right to say in advance that they want to refuse treatment if they lose capacity in the future – even if this results in their death. A valid and applicable advance decision to refuse treatment has the same force as a contemporaneous decision. This has been a fundamental principle of the common law for many years and it is now set out in the Act. Sections 24–26 of the Act set out the when a person can make an advance decision to refuse treatment. This applies if:
- the person is 18 or older, and
- they have the capacity to make an advance decision about treatment.

Information on advance decisions to refuse treatment made by young people (under the age of 18) will be available at www.dh.gov.uk/consent

9.2 Healthcare professionals must follow an advance decision if it is valid and applies to the particular circumstances. If they do not, they could face criminal prosecution (they could be charged for committing a crime) or civil liability (somebody could sue them).

9.3 Advance decisions can have serious consequences for the people who make them. They can also have an important impact on family

PART VI

and friends, and professionals involved in their care. Before healthcare professionals can apply an advance decision, there must be proof that the decision:

- exists
- is valid, and
- is applicable in the current circumstances.

These tests are legal requirements under section 25(1). Paragraphs 9.38–9.44 explain the standard of proof the Act requires.

Who can make an advance decision to refuse treatment?

9.4 It is up to individuals to decide whether they want to refuse treatment in advance. They are entitled to do so if they want, but there is no obligation to do so. Some people choose to make advance decisions while they are still healthy, even if there is no prospect of illness. This might be because they want to keep some control over what might happen to them in the future. Others may think of an advance decision as part of their preparations for growing older (similar to making a will). Or they might make an advance decision after they have been told they have a specific disease or condition.

Many people prefer not to make an advance decision, and instead leave healthcare professionals to make decisions in their best interests at the time a decision needs to be made. Another option is to make a Lasting Power of Attorney. This allows a trusted family member or friend to make personal welfare decisions, such as those around treatment, on someone's behalf, and in their best interests if they ever lose capacity to make those decisions themselves (see paragraph 9.33 below and chapter 7).

9.5 People can only make advance decisions to refuse treatment. Nobody has the legal right to demand specific treatment, either at the time or in advance. So no-one can insist (either at the time or in advance) on being given treatments that healthcare professionals consider to be clinically unnecessary, futile or inappropriate. But people can make a request or state their wishes and preferences in advance. Healthcare professionals should then consider the request when deciding what is in a patient's best interests (see chapter 5) if the patient lacks capacity.

9.6 Nobody can ask for and receive procedures that are against the law (for example, help with committing suicide). As section 62 sets out, the Act does not change any of the laws relating to murder, manslaughter or helping someone to commit suicide.

Capacity to make an advance decision

9.7 For most people, there will be no doubt about their capacity to make an advance decision. Even those who lack capacity to make some decisions may have the capacity to make an advance decision. In some cases it may be helpful to get evidence of a person's capacity to make the advance decision (for example, if there is a possibility that the advance decision may be challenged in the future). It is also important to remember that capacity can change over time, and a person who lacks capacity to make a decision now might be able to make it in the future.

Chapter 3 explains how to assess a person's capacity to make a decision.

Scenario: *Respecting capacity to make an advance decision*

Mrs Long's family has a history of polycystic ovary syndrome. She has made a written advance decision refusing any treatment or procedures that might affect her fertility. The document states that her ovaries and uterus must not be removed. She is having surgery to treat a blocked fallopian tube and, during the consent process, she told her doctor about her advance decision.

During surgery the doctor discovers a solid mass that he thinks might be cancerous. In his clinical judgement, he thinks it would be in Mrs Long's best interests for him to remove the ovary. But he knows that Mrs Long had capacity when she made her valid and applicable advance decision, so he must respect her rights and follow her decision. After surgery, he can discuss the matter with Mrs Long and advise her about treatment options.

9.8 In line with principle 1 of the Act, that 'a person must be assumed to have capacity unless it is established that he lacks capacity', healthcare professionals should always start from the assumption that a person who has made an advance decision had capacity to make it, unless they are aware of reasonable grounds to doubt the person had the capacity to make the advance decision at the time they made it. If a healthcare professional is not satisfied that the person had capacity at the time they made the advance decision, or if there are doubts about its existence, validity or applicability, they can treat the person without fear of liability. It is good practice to record their decisions and the reasons for them. The Act does not require them to record their assessment of the person's capacity at the time the decision was made, but it would be good practice to do so.

9.9 Healthcare professionals may have particular concerns about the capacity of someone with a history of suicide attempts or suicidal thoughts who has made an advance decision. It is important to remember that making an advance decision which, if followed, may result in death does not necessarily mean a person is or feels suicidal. Nor does it necessarily mean the person lacks capacity to make the advance decision. If the person is clearly suicidal, this may raise questions about their capacity to make an advance decision at the time they made it.

What should people include in an advance decision?

9.10 There are no particular formalities about the format of an advance decision. It can be written or verbal, unless it deals with life-sustaining treatment, in which case it must be written and specific rules apply (see paragraphs 9.24–9.28 below).

9.11 An advance decision to refuse treatment:

- must state precisely what treatment is to be refused – a statement giving a general desire not to be treated is not enough
- may set out the circumstances when the refusal should apply – it is helpful to include as much detail as possible
- will only apply at a time when the person lacks capacity to consent to or refuse the specific treatment.

Specific rules apply to life-sustaining treatment.

9.12 People can use medical language or everyday language in their advance decision. But they must make clear what their wishes are and what treatment they would like to refuse.

9.13 An advance decision refusing all treatment in any situation (for example, where a person explains that their decision is based on their religion or personal beliefs) may be valid and applicable.

9.14 It is recommended that people who are thinking about making an advance decision get advice from:

- healthcare professionals (for example, their GP or the person most closely involved with current healthcare or treatment), or
- an organisation that can provide advice on specific conditions or situations (they might have their own format for recording an advance decision).

But it is up to the person whether they want to do this or not. Healthcare professionals should record details of any discussion on healthcare records.

9.15 Some people may also want to get legal advice. This will help them make sure that they express their decision clearly and accurately. It will also help to make sure that people understand their advance decision in the future.

9.16 It is a good idea to try to include possible future circumstances in the advance decision. For example, a woman may want to state in the advance decision whether or not it should still apply if she later becomes pregnant. If the document does not anticipate a change in circumstance, healthcare professionals may decide that it is not applicable if those particular circumstances arise.

9.17 If an advance decision is recorded on a patient's healthcare records, it is confidential. Some patients will tell others about their advance decision (for example, they might tell healthcare professionals, friends or family). Others will not. People who do not ask for their advance decision to be recorded on their healthcare record will need to think about where it should be kept and how they are going to let people know about their decision.

Written advance decisions

9.18 A written document can be evidence of an advance decision. It is helpful to tell others that the document exists and where it is. A person may want to carry it with them in case of emergency, or carry a card, bracelet or other indication that they have made an advance decision and explaining where it is kept.

9.19 There is no set form for written advance decisions, because contents will vary depending on a person's wishes and situation. But it is helpful to include the following information:

- full details of the person making the advance decision, including date of birth, home address and any distinguishing features (in case healthcare professionals need to identify an unconscious person, for example)
- the name and address of the person's GP and whether they have a copy of the document
- a statement that the document should be used if the person ever lacks capacity to make treatment decisions
- a clear statement of the decision, the treatment to be refused and the circumstances in which the decision will apply
- the date the document was written (or reviewed)
- the person's signature (or the signature of someone the person has asked to sign on their behalf and in their presence)
- the signature of the person witnessing the signature, if there is one (or a statement directing somebody to sign on the person's behalf).

See paragraphs 9.24–9.28 below if the advance decision deals with life-sustaining treatment.

9.20 Witnessing the person's signature is not essential, except in cases where the person is making an advance decision to refuse life-sustaining treatment. But if there is a witness, they are witnessing the signature and the fact that it confirms the wishes set out in the advance decision. It may be helpful to give a description of the relationship between the witness and person making the advance decision. The role of the witness is to witness the person's signature, it is not to certify that the person has the capacity to make the advance decision – even if the witness is a healthcare professional or knows the person.

9.21 It is possible that a professional acting as a witness will also be the person who assesses the person's capacity. If so, the professional should also make a record of the assessment, because acting as a witness does not prove that there has been an assessment.

PART VI

Verbal advance decisions

9.22 There is no set format for verbal advance decisions. This is because they will vary depending on a person's wishes and situation. Healthcare professionals will need to consider whether a verbal advance decision exists and whether it is valid and applicable (see paragraphs 9.38– 9.44).

9.23 Where possible, healthcare professionals should record a verbal advance decision to refuse treatment in a person's healthcare record. This will produce a written record that could prevent confusion about the decision in the future. The record should include:

- a note that the decision should apply if the person lacks capacity to make treatment decisions in the future
- a clear note of the decision, the treatment to be refused and the circumstances in which the decision will apply
- details of someone who was present when the oral advance decision was recorded and the role in which they were present (for example, healthcare professional or family member), and
- whether they heard the decision, took part in it or are just aware that it exists.

What rules apply to advance decisions to refuse life-sustaining treatment?

9.24 The Act imposes particular legal requirements and safeguards on the making of advance decisions to refuse life-sustaining treatment. Advance decisions to refuse life-sustaining treatment must meet specific requirements:

- They must be put in writing. If the person is unable to write, someone else should write it down for them. For example, a family member can write down the decision on their behalf, or a healthcare professional can record it in the person's healthcare notes.
- The person must sign the advance decision. If they are unable to sign, they can direct someone to sign on their behalf in their presence.
- The person making the decision must sign in the presence of a witness to the signature. The witness must then sign the document in the presence of the person making the advance decision. If the person making the advance decision is unable to sign, the witness can witness them directing someone else to sign on their behalf. The witness must then sign to indicate that they have witnessed the nominated person signing the document in front of the person making the advance decision.
- The advance decision must include a clear, specific written statement from the person making the advance decision that the advance decision is to apply to the specific treatment even if life is at risk.

- If this statement is made at a different time or in a separate document to the advance decision, the person making the advance decision (or someone they have directed to sign) must sign it in the presence of a witness, who must also sign it.

9.25 Section 4(10) states that life-sustaining treatment is treatment which a healthcare professional who is providing care to the person regards as necessary to sustain life. This decision will not just depend on the type of treatment. It will also depend on the circumstances in which the healthcare professional is giving it. For example, in some situations antibiotics may be life-sustaining, but in others they can be used to treat conditions that do not threaten life.

9.26 Artificial nutrition and hydration (ANH) has been recognised as a form of medical treatment. ANH involves using tubes to provide nutrition and fluids to someone who cannot take them by mouth. It bypasses the natural mechanisms that control hunger and thirst and requires clinical monitoring. An advance decision can refuse ANH. Refusing ANH in an advance decision is likely to result in the person's death, if the advance decision is followed.

9.27 It is very important to discuss advance decisions to refuse life-sustaining treatment with a healthcare professional. But it is not compulsory. A healthcare professional will be able to explain:

- what types of treatment may be life-sustaining treatment, and in what circumstances
- the implications and consequences of refusing such treatment (see also paragraph 9.14).

9.28 An advance decision cannot refuse actions that are needed to keep a person comfortable (sometimes called basic or essential care). Examples include warmth, shelter, actions to keep a person clean and the offer of food and water by mouth. Section 5 of the Act allows healthcare professionals to carry out these actions in the best interests of a person who lacks capacity to consent (see chapter 6). An advance decision can refuse artificial nutrition and hydration.

When should someone review or update an advance decision?

9.29 Anyone who has made an advance decision is advised to regularly review and update it as necessary. Decisions made a long time in advance are not automatically invalid or inapplicable, but they may raise doubts when deciding whether they are valid and applicable. A written decision that is regularly reviewed is more likely to be valid and applicable to current circumstances – particularly for progressive illnesses. This is because it is more likely to have taken on board changes that have occurred in a person's life since they made their decision.

9.30 Views and circumstances may change over time. A new stage in a person's illness, the development of new treatments or a major change in personal circumstances may be appropriate times to review and update an advance decision.

PART VI

How can someone withdraw an advance decision?

9.31 Section 24(3) allows people to cancel or alter an advance decision at any time while they still have capacity to do so. There are no formal processes to follow. People can cancel their decision verbally or in writing, and they can destroy any original written document. Where possible, the person who made the advance decision should tell anybody who knew about their advance decision that it has been cancelled. They can do this at any time. For example, they can do this on their way to the operating theatre or immediately before being given an anaesthetic. Healthcare professionals should record a verbal cancellation in healthcare records. This then forms a written record for future reference.

How can someone make changes to an advance decision?

9.32 People can makes changes to an advance decision verbally or in writing (section 24(3)) whether or not the advance decision was made in writing. It is good practice for healthcare professionals to record a change of decision in the person's healthcare notes. But if the person wants to change an advance decision to include a refusal of life-sustaining treatment, they must follow the procedures described in paragraphs 9.24–9.28.

How do advance decisions relate to other rules about decision-making?

9.33 A valid and applicable advance decision to refuse treatment is as effective as a refusal made when a person has capacity. Therefore, an advance decision overrules:
- the decision of any personal welfare Lasting Power of Attorney (LPA) made before the advance decision was made. So an attorney cannot give consent to treatment that has been refused in an advance decision made after the LPA was signed
- the decision of any court-appointed deputy (so a deputy cannot give consent to treatment that has been refused in an advance decision which is valid and applicable)
- the provisions of section 5 of the Act, which would otherwise allow healthcare professionals to give treatment that they believe is in a person's best interests.

9.34 An LPA made after an advance decision will make the advance decision invalid, if the LPA gives the attorney the authority to make decisions about the same treatment (see paragraph 9.40).

9.35 The Court of Protection may make declarations as to the existence, validity and applicability of an advance decision, but it has no power to overrule a valid and applicable advance decision to refuse treatment.

9.36 Where an advance decision is being followed, the best interests principle (see chapter 5) does not apply. This is because an advance decision reflects the decision of an adult with capacity who has made the decision for themselves. Healthcare professionals must follow a valid and applicable advance decision, even if they think it goes against a person's best interests.

Advance decisions regarding treatment for mental disorder

9.37 Advance decisions can refuse any kind of treatment, whether for a physical or mental disorder. But generally an advance decision to refuse treatment for mental disorder can be overruled if the person is detained in hospital under the Mental Health Act 1983, when treatment could be given compulsorily under Part 4 of that Act. Advance decisions to refuse treatment for other illnesses or conditions are not affected by the fact that the person is detained in hospital under the Mental Health Act. For further information see chapter 13.

How can somebody decide on the existence, validity and applicability of advance decisions?

Deciding whether an advance decision exists

9.38 It is the responsibility of the person making the advance decision to make sure their decision will be drawn to the attention of healthcare professionals when it is needed. Some people will want their decision to be recorded on their healthcare records. Those who do not will need to find other ways of alerting people that they have made an advance decision and where somebody will find any written document and supporting evidence. Some people carry a card or wear a bracelet. It is also useful to share this information with family and friends, who may alert healthcare professionals to the existence of an advance decision. But it is not compulsory. Providing their GP with a copy of the written document will allow them to record the decision in the person's healthcare records.

9.39 It is important to be able to establish that the person making the advance decision was 18 or over when they made their decision, and that they had the capacity to make that decision when they made it, in line with the two-stage test for capacity set out in chapter 3. But as explained in paragraphs 9.7–9.9 above, healthcare professionals should always start from the assumption that the person had the capacity to make the advance decision.

Deciding whether an advance decision is valid

9.40 An existing advance decision must still be valid at the time it needs to be put into effect. Healthcare professionals must consider the factors in section 25 of the Act before concluding that an advance decision is valid. Events that would make an advance decision invalid include those where:

PART VI

- the person withdrew the decision while they still had capacity to do so
- after making the advance decision, the person made a Lasting Power of Attorney (LPA) giving an attorney authority to make treatment decisions that are the same as those covered by the advance decision (see also paragraph 9.33)
- the person has done something that clearly goes against the advance decision which suggests that they have changed their mind.

Scenario: Assessing whether an advance decision is valid

A young man, Angus, sees a friend die after prolonged hospital treatment. Angus makes a signed and witnessed advance decision to refuse treatment to keep him alive if he is ever injured in this way. The advance decision includes a statement that this will apply even if his life is at risk.

A few years later, Angus is seriously injured in a road traffic accident. He is paralysed from the neck down and cannot breathe without the help of a machine. At first he stays conscious and gives permission to be treated. He takes part in a rehabilitation programme. Some months later he loses consciousness.

At this point somebody finds his written advance decision, even though Angus has not mentioned it during his treatment. His actions before his lack of capacity obviously go against the advance decision. Anyone assessing the advance decision needs to consider very carefully the doubt this has created about the validity of the advance decision, and whether the advance decision is valid and applicable as a result.

Deciding whether an advance decision is applicable

9.41 To be applicable, an advance decision must apply to the situation in question and in the current circumstances. Healthcare professionals must first determine if the person still has capacity to accept or refuse treatment at the relevant time (section 25(3)). If the person has capacity, they can refuse treatment there and then. Or they can change their decision and accept treatment. The advance decision is not applicable in such situations.

9.42 The advance decision must also apply to the proposed treatment. It is not applicable to the treatment in question if (section 25(4)):

- the proposed treatment is not the treatment specified in the advance decision
- the circumstances are different from those that may have been set out in the advance decision, or

- there are reasonable grounds for believing that there have been changes in circumstance, which would have affected the decision if the person had known about them at the time they made the advance decision.

9.43 So when deciding whether an advance decision applies to the proposed treatment, healthcare professionals must consider:
- how long ago the advance decision was made, and
- whether there have been changes in the patient's personal life (for example, the person is pregnant, and this was not anticipated when they made the advance decision) that might affect the validity of the advance decision, and
- whether there have been developments in medical treatment that the person did not foresee (for example, new medications, treatment or therapies).

9.44 For an advance decision to apply to life-sustaining treatment, it must meet the requirements set out in paragraphs 9.24–9.28.

Scenario: Assessing if an advance decision is applicable

Mr Moss is HIV positive. Several years ago he began to have AIDS-related symptoms. He has accepted general treatment, but made an advance decision to refuse specific retro-viral treatments, saying he didn't want to be a 'guinea pig' for the medical profession. Five years later, he is admitted to hospital seriously ill and keeps falling unconscious.

The doctors treating Mr Moss examine his advance decision. They are aware that there have been major developments in retro-viral treatment recently. They discuss this with Mr Moss's partner and both agree that there are reasonable grounds to believe that Mr Moss may have changed his advance decision if he had known about newer treatment options. So the doctors decide the advance decision does not apply to the new retro-virals and give him treatment.

If Mr Moss regains his capacity, he can change his advance decision and accept or refuse future treatment.

PART VI

What should healthcare professionals do if an advance decision is not valid or applicable?

9.45 If an advance decision is not valid or applicable to current circumstances:
- healthcare professionals must consider the advance decision as part of their assessment of the person's best interests (see chapter 5) if they have reasonable grounds to think it is a true expression of the person's wishes, and
- they must not assume that because an advance decision is either invalid or not applicable, they should always provide the

specified treatment (including life-sustaining treatment) – they must base this decision on what is in the person's best interests.

What happens to decisions made before the Act comes into force?

9.46 Advance decisions made before the Act comes into force may still be valid and applicable. Healthcare professionals should apply the rules in the Act to advance decisions made before the Act comes into force, subject to the transitional protections that will apply to advance decisions that refuse life-sustaining treatment. Further guidance will be available at www.dh.gov.uk/consent.

What implications do advance decisions have for healthcare professionals?

What are healthcare professionals' responsibilities?

9.47 Healthcare professionals should be aware that:
- a patient they propose to treat may have refused treatment in advance, and
- valid and applicable advance decisions to refuse treatment have the same legal status as decisions made by people with capacity at the time of treatment.

9.48 Where appropriate, when discussing treatment options with people who have capacity, healthcare professionals should ask if there are any specific types of treatment they do not wish to receive if they ever lack capacity to consent in the future.

9.49 If somebody tells a healthcare professional that an advance decision exists for a patient who now lacks capacity to consent, they should make reasonable efforts to find out what the decision is. Reasonable efforts might include having discussions with relatives of the patient, looking in the patient's clinical notes held in the hospital or contacting the patient's GP.

9.50 Once they know a verbal or written advance decision exists, healthcare professionals must determine whether:
- it is valid (see paragraph 9.40), and
- it is applicable to the proposed treatment (see paragraphs 9.41–9.44).

9.51 When establishing whether an advance decision applies to current circumstances, healthcare professionals should take special care if the decision does not seem to have been reviewed or updated for some time. If the person's current circumstances are significantly different from those when the decision was made, the advance decision may not be applicable. People close to the person concerned, or anyone named in the advance decision, may be able to help explain the person's prior wishes.

9.52 If healthcare professionals are satisfied that an advance decision to refuse treatment exists, is valid and is applicable, they must follow it and not provide the treatment refused in the advance decision.

9.53 If healthcare professionals are not satisfied that an advance decision exists that is both valid and applicable, they can treat the person without fear of liability. But treatment must be in the person's best interests (see chapter 5). They should make clear notes explaining why they have not followed an advance decision which they consider to be invalid or not applicable.

9.54 Sometimes professionals can give or continue treatment while they resolve doubts over an advance decision. It may be useful to get information from someone who can provide information about the person's capacity when they made the advance decision. The Court of Protection can settle disagreements about the existence, validity or applicability of an advance decision. Section 26 of the Act allows healthcare professionals to give necessary treatment, including life-sustaining treatment, to stop a person's condition getting seriously worse while the court decides.

Do advance decisions apply in emergencies?

9.55 A healthcare professional must provide treatment in the patient's best interests, unless they are satisfied that there is a advance decision that is:
- valid, and
- applicable in the circumstances.

9.56 Healthcare professionals should not delay emergency treatment to look for an advance decision if there is no clear indication that one exists. But if it is clear that a person has made an advance decision that is likely to be relevant, healthcare professionals should assess its validity and applicability as soon as possible. Sometimes the urgency of treatment decisions will make this difficult.

When can healthcare professionals be found liable?

9.57 Healthcare professionals must follow an advance decision if they are satisfied that it exists, is valid and is applicable to their circumstances. Failure to follow an advance decision in this situation could lead to a claim for damages for battery or a criminal charge of assault.

9.58 But they are protected from liability if they are not:
- aware of an advance decision, or
- satisfied that an advance decision exists, is valid and is applicable to the particular treatment and the current circumstances (section 26(2)).

If healthcare professionals have genuine doubts, and are therefore not 'satisfied', about the existence, validity or applicability of the advance decision, treatment can be provided without incurring liability.

9.59 Healthcare professionals will be protected from liability for failing to provide treatment if they 'reasonably believe' that a valid and

PART VI

applicable advance decision to refuse that treatment exists. But they must be able to demonstrate that their belief was reasonable (section 26(3)) and point to reasonable grounds showing why they believe this. Healthcare professionals can only base their decision on the evidence that is available at the time they need consider an advance decision.

9.60 Some situations might be enough in themselves to raise concern about the existence, validity or applicability of an advance decision to refuse treatment. These could include situations when:

- a disagreement between relatives and healthcare professionals about whether verbal comments were really an advance decision
- evidence about the person's state of mind raises questions about their capacity at the time they made the decision (see paragraphs 9.7–9.9)
- evidence of important changes in the person's behaviour before they lost capacity that might suggest a change of mind.

In cases where serious doubt remains and cannot be resolved in any other way, it will be possible to seek a declaration from the court.

What if a healthcare professional has a conscientious objection to stopping or providing life-sustaining treatment?

9.61 Some healthcare professionals may disagree in principle with patients' rights to refuse life-sustaining treatment. The Act does not change the current legal situation. They do not have to do something that goes against their beliefs. But they must not simply abandon patients or cause their care to suffer.

9.62 Healthcare professionals should make their views clear to the patient and the healthcare team as soon as someone raises the subject of withholding, stopping or providing life-sustaining treatment. Patients who still have capacity should then have the option of transferring their care to another healthcare professional, if it is possible to do this without affecting their care.

9.63 In cases where the patient now lacks capacity but has made a valid and applicable advance decision to refuse treatment which a doctor or health professional cannot, for reasons of conscience, comply with, arrangements should be made for the management of the patient's care to be transferred to another healthcare professional.[36] Where a transfer cannot be agreed, the Court of Protection can direct those responsible for the person's healthcare (for example, a Trust, doctor or other health professional) to make arrangements to take over responsibility for the person's healthcare (section 17(1)(e)).

---

[36]   *Re B (Adult: Refusal of Medical Treatment)* [2002] EWHC 429 (Fam) at para 100(viii).

What happens if there is a disagreement about an advance decision?

9.64 It is ultimately the responsibility of the healthcare professional who is in charge of the person's care when the treatment is required to decide whether there is an advance decision which is valid and applicable in the circumstances. In the event of disagreement about an advance decision between healthcare professionals, or between healthcare professionals and family members or others close to the person, the senior clinician must consider all the available evidence. This is likely to be a hospital consultant or the GP where the person is being treated in the community.

9.65 The senior clinician may need to consult with relevant colleagues and others who are close to or familiar with the patient. All staff involved in the person's care should be given the opportunity to express their views. If the person is in hospital, their GP may also have relevant information.

9.66 The point of such discussions should not be to try to overrule the person's advance decision but rather to seek evidence concerning its validity and to confirm its scope and its applicability to the current circumstances. Details of these discussions should be recorded in the person's healthcare records. Where the senior clinician has a reasonable belief that an advance decision to refuse medical treatment is both valid and applicable, the person's advance decision should be complied with.

When can somebody apply to the Court of Protection?

9.67 The Court of Protection can make a decision where there is genuine doubt or disagreement about an advance decision's existence, validity or applicability. But the court does not have the power to overturn a valid and applicable advance decision.

9.68 The court has a range of powers (sections 16–17) to resolve disputes concerning the personal care and medical treatment of a person who lacks capacity (see chapter 8). It can decide whether:

- a person has capacity to accept or refuse treatment at the time it is proposed
- an advance decision to refuse treatment is valid
- an advance decision is applicable to the proposed treatment in the current circumstances.

9.69 While the court decides, healthcare professionals can provide life-sustaining treatment or treatment to stop a serious deterioration in their condition. The court has emergency procedures which operate 24 hours a day to deal with urgent cases quickly. See chapter 8 for guidance on applying to the court.

PART VI

10   WHAT IS THE NEW INDEPENDENT MENTAL CAPACITY ADVOCATE SERVICE AND HOW DOES IT WORK?

This chapter describes the new Independent Mental Capacity Advocate (IMCA) service created under the Act. The purpose of the IMCA service is to help particularly vulnerable people who lack the capacity to make important decisions about serious medical treatment and changes of accommodation, and who have no family or friends that it would be appropriate to consult about those decisions. IMCAs will work with and support people who lack capacity, and represent their views to those who are working out their best interests.

The chapter provides guidance both for IMCAs and for everyone who may need to instruct an IMCA. It explains how IMCAs should be appointed. It also explains the IMCA's duties and the situations when an IMCA should be instructed. Both IMCAs and decision-makers are required to have regard to the Code of Practice.

> In this chapter, as throughout the Code, a person's capacity (or lack of capacity) refers specifically to their capacity to make a particular decision at the time it needs to be made.

Quick summary

Understanding the role of the IMCA service

- The aim of the IMCA service is to provide independent safeguards for people who lack capacity to make certain important decisions and, at the time such decisions need to be made, have no-one else (other than paid staff) to support or represent them or be consulted.
- IMCAs must be independent.

Instructing and consulting an IMCA

- An IMCA must be instructed, and then consulted, for people lacking capacity who have no-one else to support them (other than paid staff), whenever:
  - an NHS body is proposing to provide serious medical treatment, or
  - an NHS body or local authority is proposing to arrange accommodation (or a change of accommodation) in hospital or a care home, and
  - the person will stay in hospital longer than 28 days, or
  - they will stay in the care home for more than eight weeks.
- An IMCA may be instructed to support someone who lacks capacity to make decisions concerning:
  - care reviews, where no-one else is available to be consulted

- adult protection cases, whether or not family, friends or others are involved

Ensuring an IMCA's views are taken into consideration

- The IMCA's role is to support and represent the person who lacks capacity. Because of this, IMCAs have the right to see relevant healthcare and social care records.
- Any information or reports provided by an IMCA must be taken into account as part of the process of working out whether a proposed decision is in the person's best interests.

What is the IMCA service?

10.1 Sections 35–41 of the Act set up a new IMCA service that provides safeguards for people who:
- lack capacity to make a specified decision at the time it needs to be made
- are facing a decision on a long-term move or about serious medical treatment and
- have nobody else who is willing and able to represent them or be consulted in the process of working out their best interests.

10.2 Regulations made under the Act also state that IMCAs may be involved in other decisions, concerning:
- a care review, or
- an adult protection case.

In adult protection cases, an IMCA may be appointed even where family members or others are available to be consulted.

10.3 Most people who lack capacity to make a specific decision will have people to support them (for example, family members or friends who take an interest in their welfare). Anybody working out a person's best interests must consult these people, where possible, and take their views into account (see chapter 5). But if a person who lacks capacity has nobody to represent them or no-one who it is appropriate to consult, an IMCA must be instructed in prescribed circumstances. The prescribed circumstances are:
- providing, withholding or stopping serious medical treatment
- moving a person into long-term care in hospital or a care home (see 10.11 for definition), or
- moving the person to a different hospital or care home.

The only exception to this can be in situations where an urgent decision is needed. Further details on the situations where there is a duty to instruct an IMCA are given in paragraphs 10.40–10.58.

In other circumstances, an IMCA *may* be appointed for the person (see paragraphs 10.59–10.68). These include:
- care reviews or
- adult protection cases.

10.4 The IMCA will:
- be independent of the person making the decision
- provide support for the person who lacks capacity

PART VI

- represent the person without capacity in discussions to work out whether the proposed decision is in the person's best interests
- provide information to help work out what is in the person's best interests (see chapter 5), and
- raise questions or challenge decisions which appear not to be in the best interests of the person.

The information the IMCA provides must be taken into account by decision-makers whenever they are working out what is in a person's best interests. See paragraphs 10.20–10.39 for more information on an IMCA's role. For more information on who is a decision-maker, see chapter 5.

10.5 The IMCA service will build on good practice in the independent advocacy sector. But IMCAs have a different role from many other advocates. They:

- provide statutory advocacy
- are instructed to support and represent people who lack capacity to make decisions on specific issues
- have a right to meet in private the person they are supporting
- are allowed access to relevant healthcare records and social care records
- provide support and representation specifically while the decision is being made, and
- act quickly so their report can form part of decision-making.

Who is responsible for delivering the service?

10.6 The IMCA service is available in England and Wales. Both countries have regulations for setting up and managing the service.

- England's regulations[37] are available at www.opsi.gov.uk/si/si200618.htm and www.opsi.gov.uk/si/dsis2006.htm.
- The regulations for Wales[38] are available at www.new.wales.gov.uk/consultations/closed/healandsoccarecloscons/.

---

[37]   *The Mental Capacity Act 2005 (Independent Mental Capacity Advocate) (General) Regulations 2006* (SI 2006/1832). The 'General Regulations'. These regulations set out the details on how the IMCA will be appointed, the functions of the IMCA, including their role in challenging the decision-maker and include definitions of 'serious medical treatment' and 'NHS body'.
The Mental Capacity Act 2005 (Independent Mental Capacity Advocate) (Expansion of Role) Regulations 2006 (SI 2006/2883). The 'Expansion Regulations'. These regulations specify the circumstances in which local authorities and NHS bodies may provide the IMCA service on a discretionary basis. These include involving the IMCA in a care review and in adult protection cases.

[38]   *The Mental Capacity Act 2005 (Independent Mental Capacity Advocate) (Wales) Regulations 2007* (SI 2007/852 (W.77)). These regulations will remain in draft form until they are made by the National Assembly for Wales. The target coming into force date is 1 October 2007. Unlike the two sets of English regulations there will be one set only for Wales. Although the Welsh regulations will remain in draft form until the coming into force date, these have been drafted to give effect to similar and corresponding provisions to the regulations in England.

Guidance has been issued to local health boards and local authorities involved in commissioning IMCA services for their area.

10.7 In England the Secretary of State for Health delivers the service through local authorities, who work in partnership with NHS organisations. Local authorities have financial responsibility for the service. In Wales the National Assembly for Wales delivers the service through local health boards, who have financial responsibility for the service and work in partnership with local authority social services departments and other NHS organisations. The service is commissioned from independent organisations, usually advocacy organisations.

10.8 Local authorities or NHS organisations are responsible for instructing an IMCA to represent a person who lacks capacity. In these circumstances they are called the 'responsible body'.

10.9 For decisions about serious medical treatment, the responsible body will be the NHS organisation providing the person's healthcare or treatment. But if the person is in an independent or voluntary sector hospital, the responsible body will be the NHS organisation arranging and funding the person's care, which should have arrangements in place with the independent or voluntary sector hospital to ensure an IMCA is appointed promptly.

10.10 For decisions about admission to accommodation in hospital for 28 days or more, the responsible body will be the NHS body that manages the hospital. For admission to an independent or voluntary sector hospital for 28 days or more, the responsible body will be the NHS organisation arranging and funding the person's care. The independent or voluntary hospital must have arrangements in place with the NHS organisation to ensure that an IMCA can be appointed without delay.

10.11 For decisions about moves into long-term accommodation[39] (for eight weeks or longer), or about a change of accommodation, the responsible body will be either:

- the NHS body that proposes the move or change of accommodation (e.g. a nursing home), or
- the local authority that has carried out an assessment of the person under the NHS and Community Care Act 1990 and decided the move may be necessary.

10.12 Sometimes NHS organisations and local authorities will make decisions together about moving a person into long-term care. In these cases, the organisation that must instruct the IMCA is the one that is ultimately responsible for the decision to move the person. The IMCA to be instructed is the one who works wherever the person is at the time that the person needs support and representation.

PART VI

---

[39] This may be accommodation in a care home, nursing home, ordinary and sheltered housing, housing association or other registered social housing or in private sector housing provided by a local authority or in hostel accommodation.

What are the responsible body's duties?

10.13 The responsible body:

- *must* instruct an IMCA to support and represent a person in the situations set out in paragraphs 10.40–10.58
- *may* decide to instruct an IMCA in situations described in paragraphs 10.59–10.68
- *must*, in all circumstances when an IMCA is instructed, take properly into account the information that the IMCA provides when working out whether the particular decision (such as giving, withholding or stopping treatment, changing a person's accommodation, or carrying out a recommendation following a care review or an allegation requiring adult protection) is in the best interests of the person who lacks capacity.

10.14 The responsible body should also have procedures, training and awareness programmes to make sure that:

- all relevant staff know when they need to instruct an IMCA and are able to do so promptly
- all relevant staff know how to get in touch with the IMCA service and know the procedure for instructing an IMCA
- they record an IMCA's involvement in a case and any information the IMCA provides to help decision-making
- they also record how a decision-maker has taken into account the IMCA's report and information as part of the process of working out the person's best interests (this should include reasons for disagreeing with that advice, if relevant)
- they give access to relevant records when requested by an IMCA under section 35(6)(b) of the Act
- the IMCA gets information about changes that may affect the support and representation the IMCA provides
- decision-makers let all relevant people know when an IMCA is working on a person's case, and
- decision-makers inform the IMCA of the final decision taken and the reason for it.

10.15 Sometimes an IMCA and staff working for the responsible body might disagree. If this happens, they should try to settle the disagreement through discussion and negotiation as soon as possible. If they cannot do this, they should then follow the responsible body's formal procedures for settling disputes or complaints (see paragraphs 10.34 to 10.39 below).

10.16 In some situations the IMCA may challenge a responsible body's decision, or they may help somebody who is challenging a decision. The General Regulations in England and the Regulations in Wales set out when this may happen (see also chapter 15). If there is no other way of resolving the disagreement, the decision may be challenged in the Court of Protection.

Who can be an IMCA?

10.17 In England, a person can only be an IMCA if the local authority approves their appointment. In Wales, the local health board will provide approval. Qualified employees of an approved organisation can act as IMCAs. Local authorities and health boards will usually commission independent advocacy organisations to provide the IMCA service. These organisations will work to appropriate organisational standards set through the contracting/commissioning process.

10.18 Individual IMCAs must:
- have specific experience
- have IMCA training
- have integrity and a good character, and
- be able to act independently.

All IMCAs must complete the IMCA training in order that they can work as an independent mental capacity advocate. A national advocacy qualification is also being developed, which will include the IMCA training.

Before a local authority or health board appoints an IMCA, they must carry out checks with the Criminal Records Bureau (CRB) to get a criminal record certificate or enhanced criminal record certificate for that individual.[40]

10.19 IMCAs must be independent. People cannot act as IMCAs if they:
- care for or treat (in a paid or professional capacity) the person they will be representing (this does not apply if they are an existing advocate acting for that person), or
- have links to the person instructing them, to the decision-maker or to other individuals involved in the person's care or treatment that may affect their independence.

What is an IMCA's role?

10.20 An IMCA must decide how best to represent and support the person who lacks capacity that they are helping. They:
- must confirm that the person instructing them has the authority to do so
- should interview or meet in private the person who lacks capacity, if possible
- must act in accordance with the principles of the Act (as set out in section 1 of the Act and chapter 2 of the Code) and take account of relevant guidance in the Code
- may examine any relevant records that section 35(6) of the Act gives them access to

---

[40] IMCAs were named as a group that is subject to mandatory checking under the new vetting and barring system in the Safeguarding Vulnerable Groups Act 2006. Roll-out of the bulk of the scheme will take place in 2008.

- should get the views of professionals and paid workers providing care or treatment for the person who lacks capacity
- should get the views of anybody else who can give information about the wishes and feelings, beliefs or values of the person who lacks capacity
- should get hold of any other information they think will be necessary
- must find out what support a person who lacks capacity has had to help them make the specific decision
- must try to find out what the person's wishes and feelings, beliefs and values would be likely to be if the person had capacity
- should find out what alternative options there are
- should consider whether getting another medical opinion would help the person who lacks capacity, and
- must write a report on their findings for the local authority or NHS body.

10.21 Where possible, decision-makers should make decisions based on a full understanding of a person's past and present wishes. The IMCA should provide the decision-maker with as much of this information as possible – and anything else they think is relevant. The report they give the decision-maker may include questions about the proposed action or may include suggested alternatives, if they think that these would be better suited to the person's wishes and feelings.

10.22 Another important part of the IMCA's role is communicating their findings. Decision-makers should find the most effective way to enable them to do this. In some of the IMCA pilot areas,[41] hospital discharge teams added a 'Need to instruct an IMCA?' question on their patient or service user forms. This allowed staff to identify the need for an IMCA as early as possible, and to discuss the timetable for the decision to be made. Some decisions need a very quick IMCA response, others will allow more time. In the pilot areas, IMCA involvement led to better informed discharge planning, with a clearer focus on the best interests of a person who lacked capacity. It did not cause additional delays in the hospital discharge.

Representing and supporting the person who lacks capacity

10.23 IMCAs should take account of the guidance in chapter 5.
- IMCAs should find out whether the decision-maker has given all practical and appropriate support to help the person who lacks capacity to be involved as much as possible in decision-making. If the person has communication difficulties,

---

[41]   For further information see www.dh.gov.uk/imca

the IMCA should also find out if the decision-maker has obtained any specialist help (for example, from a speech and language therapist).

- Sometimes an IMCA may find information to suggest a person might regain capacity in the future, either so they can make the decision themselves or be more involved in decision-making. In such a situation, the IMCA can ask the decision-maker to delay the decision, if it is not urgent.

- The IMCA will need to get as much information as possible about the person's wishes, feelings, beliefs and values – both past and present. They should also consider the person's religion and any cultural factors that may influence the decision.

10.24 Sometimes a responsible body will not have time to instruct an IMCA (for example in an emergency or if a decision is urgent). If this is the case, this should be recorded, with the reason an IMCA has not been instructed. Where the decision concerns a move of accommodation, the local authority must appoint an IMCA as soon as possible afterwards. Sometimes the IMCA will not have time to carry out full investigations. In these situations, the IMCA must make a judgement about what they can achieve in the time available to support and represent the person who lacks capacity.

10.25 Sometimes an IMCA might not be able to get a good picture of what the person might want. They should still try to make sure the decision-maker considers all relevant information by:

- raising relevant issues and questions, and
- providing additional, relevant information to help the final decision.

Finding and evaluating information

10.26 Section 35(6) provides IMCAs with certain powers to enable them to carry out their duties. These include:

- the right to have an interview in private with the person who lacks capacity, and
- the right to examine, and take copies of, any records that the person holding the record thinks are relevant to the investigation (for example, clinical records, care plans, social care assessment documents or care home records).

10.27 The IMCA may also need to meet professionals or paid carers providing care or treatment for the person who lacks capacity. These people can help assess the information in case records or other sources. They can also comment on possible alternative courses of action. Ultimately, it is the decision-maker's responsibility to decide whether a proposed course of action is in the person's best interests. However, the Act requires the decision-maker to take account of the reports made and information given by the IMCA. In most cases a decision on the person's best interests will be made through

PART VI

discussion involving all the relevant people who are providing care or treatment, as well as the IMCA.

Finding out the person's wishes and feelings, beliefs and values

10.28 The IMCA needs to try and find out what the person's wishes and feelings might be, and what their underlying beliefs and values might also be. The IMCA should try to communicate both verbally and non-verbally with the person who may lack capacity, as appropriate. For example, this might mean using pictures or photographs. But there will be cases where the person cannot communicate at all (for example, if they are unconscious). The IMCA may also talk to other professionals or paid carers directly involved in providing present or past care or treatment. The IMCA might also need to examine health and social care records and any written statements of preferences the person may have made while they still had capacity to do so.

Chapter 5 contains further guidance on finding out the views of people who lack capacity. Chapter 3 contains further guidance on helping someone to make their own decision.

Considering alternative courses of action

10.29 The IMCA will need to check whether the decision-maker has considered all possible options. They should also ask whether the proposed option is less restrictive of the person's rights or future choices or would allow them more freedom (chapter 2, principle 5).

10.30 The IMCA may wish to discuss possible options with other professionals or paid carers directly involved in providing care or treatment for the person. But they must respect the confidentiality of the person they are representing.

Scenario: Using an IMCA

Mrs Nolan has dementia. She is being discharged from hospital. She has no close family or friends. She also lacks the capacity to decide whether she should return home or move to a care home. The local authority instructs an IMCA.

Mrs Nolan tells the IMCA that she wants to go back to her own home, which she can remember and describe. But the hospital care team thinks she needs additional support, which can only be provided in a care home.

The IMCA reviewed all the assessments of Mrs Nolan's needs, spoke to people involved in her care and wrote a report stating that Mrs Nolan had strong and clear wishes. The IMCA also suggested that a care package could be provided to support Mrs Nolan if she were

---

allowed to return home. The care manager now has to decide what is in Mrs Nolan's best interests. He must consider the views of the hospital care team and the IMCA's report.

Getting a second medical opinion

10.31 For decisions about serious medical treatment, the IMCA may consider seeking a second medical opinion from a doctor with appropriate expertise. This puts a person who lacks the capacity to make a specific decision in the same position as a person who has capacity, who has the right to request a second opinion.

What happens if the IMCA disagrees with the decision-maker?

10.32 The IMCA's role is to support and represent their client. They may do this through asking questions, raising issues, offering information and writing a report. They will often take part in a meeting involving different healthcare and social care staff to work out what is in the person's best interests. There may sometimes be cases when an IMCA thinks that a decision-maker has not paid enough attention to their report and other relevant information and is particularly concerned about the decision made. They may then need to challenge the decision.

10.33 An IMCA has the same rights to challenge a decision as any other person caring for the person or interested in his welfare. The right of challenge applies both to decisions about lack of capacity and a person's best interests.

10.34 Chapter 15 sets out how disagreements can be settled. The approach will vary, depending on the type and urgency of the disagreement. It could be a formal or informal approach.

Disagreements about health care or treatment
- Consult the Patient Advice and Liaison Service (England)
- Consult the Community Health Council (Wales)
- Use the NHS Complaints Procedure
- Refer the matter to the local continuing care review panel
- Engage the services of the Independent Complaints Advocacy Service (England) or another advocate.

Disagreements about social care
- Use the care home's complaints procedure (if the person is in a care home)
- Use the local authority complaints procedure.

10.35 Before using these formal methods, the IMCA and the decision-maker should discuss the areas they disagree about – particularly those that might have a serious impact on the person the IMCA is representing. The IMCA and decision-maker should make time to listen to each other's views and to understand the reason for the differences. Sometimes these discussions can help settle a disagreement.

PART VI

10.36 Sometimes an IMCA service will have a steering group, with representatives from the local NHS organisations and the local authority. These representatives can sometimes negotiate between two differing views. Or they can clarify policy on a certain issue. They should also be involved if an IMCA believes they have discovered poor practice on an important issue.

10.37 IMCAs may use complaints procedures as necessary to try to settle a disagreement – and they can pursue a complaint as far as the relevant ombudsman if needed. In particularly serious or urgent cases, an IMCA may seek permission to refer a case to the Court of Protection for a decision. The Court will make a decision in the best interests of the person who lacks capacity.

10.38 The first step in making a formal challenge is to approach the Official Solicitor (OS) with the facts of the case. The OS can decide to apply to the court as a litigation friend (acting on behalf of the person the IMCA is representing). If the OS decides not to apply himself, the IMCA can ask for permission to apply to the Court of Protection. The OS can still be asked to act as a litigation friend for the person who lacks capacity.

10.39 In extremely serious cases, the IMCA might want to consider an application for judicial review in the High Court. This might happen if the IMCA thinks there are very serious consequences to a decision that has been made by a public authority. There are time limits for making an application, and the IMCA would have to instruct solicitors – and may be liable for the costs of the case going to court. So IMCAs should get legal advice before choosing this approach. The IMCA can also ask the OS to consider making the claim.

What decisions require an IMCA?

10.40 There are three types of decisions which require an IMCA to be instructed for people who lack capacity. These are:
- decisions about providing, withholding or stopping serious medical treatment
- decisions about whether to place people into accommodation (for example a care home or a long stay hospital), and
- decisions about whether to move people to different long stay accommodation.

For these decisions all local authorities and all health bodies must refer the same kinds of decisions to an IMCA for anyone who lacks capacity and qualifies for the IMCA service.

10.41 There are two further types of decisions where the responsible body has the power to instruct an IMCA for a person who lacks capacity. These are decisions relating to:
- care reviews and
- adult protection cases.

In such cases, the relevant local authority or NHS body must decide in each individual case whether it would be of particular benefit to the person who lacks capacity to have an IMCA to support them. The factors which should be considered are explained in paragraphs 10.59–10.68.[42]

Decisions about serious medical treatment

10.42 Where a serious medical treatment decision is being considered for a person who lacks the capacity to consent, and who qualifies for additional safeguards, section 37 of the Act imposes a duty on the NHS body to instruct an IMCA. NHS bodies must instruct an IMCA whenever they are proposing to take a decision about 'serious medical treatment', or proposing that another organisation (such as a private hospital) carry out the treatment on their behalf, if:

- the person concerned does not have the capacity to make a decision about the treatment, and
- there is no-one appropriate to consult about whether the decision is in the person's best interests, other than paid care staff.

10.43 Regulations for England and Wales set out the definition of 'serious medical treatment' for decisions that require an IMCA. It includes treatments for both mental and physical conditions.

Serious medical treatment is defined as treatment which involves giving new treatment, stopping treatment that has already started or withholding treatment that could be offered in circumstances where:

- if a single treatment is proposed there is a fine balance between the likely benefits and the burdens to the patient and the risks involved
- a decision between a choice of treatments is finely balanced, or
- what is proposed is likely to have serious consequences for the patient.

10.44 'Serious consequences' are those which could have a serious impact on the patient, either from the effects of the treatment itself or its wider implications. This may include treatments which:

- cause serious and prolonged pain, distress or side effects
- have potentially major consequences for the patient (for example, stopping life-sustaining treatment or having major surgery such as heart surgery), or
- have a serious impact on the patient's future life choices (for example, interventions for ovarian cancer).

10.45 It is impossible to set out all types of procedures that may amount to 'serious medical treatment', although some examples of medical treatments that might be considered serious include:

- chemotherapy and surgery for cancer

PART VI

---

[42]   See chapter 11 for information about the role of 'consultees' when research is proposed involving a person who lacks capacity to make a decision about whether to agree to take part in research. In certain situations IMCAs may be involved as consultees for research purposes.

- electro-convulsive therapy
- therapeutic sterilisation
- major surgery (such as open-heart surgery or brain/neuro-surgery)
- major amputations (for example, loss of an arm or leg)
- treatments which will result in permanent loss of hearing or sight
- withholding or stopping artificial nutrition and hydration, and
- termination of pregnancy.

These are illustrative examples only, and whether these or other procedures are considered serious medical treatment in any given case, will depend on the circumstances and the consequences for the patient. There are also many more treatments which will be defined as serious medical treatments under the Act's regulations. Decision-makers who are not sure whether they need to instruct an IMCA should consult their colleagues.

10.46 The only situation in which the duty to instruct an IMCA need not be followed, is when an urgent decision is needed (for example, to save the person's life). This decision must be recorded with the reason for the non-referral. Responsible bodies will however still need to instruct an IMCA for any serious treatment that follows the emergency treatment.

10.47 While a decision-maker is waiting for the IMCA's report, they must still act in the person's best interests (for example, to give treatment that stops the person's condition getting worse).

Scenario: Using an IMCA for serious medical treatment

Mr Jones had a fall and suffered serious head injuries. Hospital staff could not find any family or friends. He needed urgent surgery, but afterwards still lacked capacity to accept or refuse medical treatment.

The hospital did not involve an IMCA in the decision to operate, because it needed to make an emergency decision. But it did instruct an IMCA when it needed to carry out further serious medical treatment.

The IMCA met with Mr Jones looked at his case notes and reviewed the options with the consultant. The decision-maker then made the clinical decision about Mr Jones' best interests taking into account the IMCA's report.

10.48 Some decisions about medical treatment are so serious that the courts need to make them (see chapter 8). But responsible bodies should still instruct an IMCA in these cases. The OS may be involved as a litigation friend of the person who lacks capacity.

10.49 Responsible bodies do not have to instruct an IMCA for patients detained under the Mental Health Act 1983, if:

- the treatment is for mental disorder, and
- they can give it without the patient's consent under that Act.

10.50 If serious medical treatment proposed for the detained patient is not for their mental disorder, the patient then has a right to an IMCA – as long as they meet the Mental Capacity Act's requirements. So a detained patient without capacity to consent to cancer treatment, for example, should qualify for an IMCA if there are no family or friends whom it would be appropriate to consult.

Decisions about accommodation or changes of residence

10.51 The Act imposes similar duties on NHS bodies and local authorities who are responsible for long-term accommodation decisions for a person who lacks the capacity to agree to the placement and who qualifies for the additional safeguard of an IMCA. The right to an IMCA applies to decisions about long-term accommodation in a hospital or care home if it is:

- provided or arranged by the NHS, or
- residential care that is provided or arranged by the local authority or provided under section 117 of the Mental Health Act 1983, or
- a move between such accommodation.

10.52 Responsible bodies have a duty to instruct an IMCA if:

- an NHS organisation proposes to place a person who lacks capacity in a hospital – or to move them to another hospital – for longer than 28 days, or
- an NHS organisation proposes to place a person who lacks capacity in a care home – or to move them to a different care home – for what is likely to be longer than eight weeks.

In either situation the other qualifying conditions apply. So, if the accommodation is for less than 28 days in a hospital or less than 8 weeks in a care home, then an IMCA need not be appointed.

10.53 The duty also applies if a local authority carries out an assessment under section 47 of the NHS and Community Care Act 1990, and it decides to:

- provide care services for a person who lacks capacity in the form of residential accommodation in a care home or its equivalent (see paragraph 10.11) which is likely to be longer than eight weeks, or
- move a person who lacks capacity to another care home or its equivalent for a period likely to exceed eight weeks.

10.54 In some cases, a care home may decide to de-register so that they can provide accommodation and care in a different way. If a local authority makes the new arrangements, then an IMCA should still be instructed if a patient lacks capacity and meets the other qualifying conditions.

10.55 Sometimes a person's placement will be longer than expected. The responsible body should involve an IMCA as soon as they realise the stay will be longer than 28 days or eight weeks, as appropriate.

10.56 People who fund themselves in long-term accommodation have the same rights to an IMCA as others, if the local authority:

- carries out an assessment under section 47 of the NHS and Community Care Act 1990, and
- decides it has a duty to the person (under either section 21 or 29 of the National Assistance Act 1947 or section 117 of the Mental Health Act 1983).

10.57 Responsible bodies can only put aside the duty to involve an IMCA if the placement or move is urgent (for example, an emergency admission to hospital or possible homelessness). The decision-maker must involve an IMCA as soon as possible after making an emergency decision, if:

- the person is likely to stay in hospital for longer than 28 days, or
- they will stay in other accommodation for longer than eight weeks.

10.58 Responsible bodies do not have to involve IMCAs if the person in question is going to be required to stay in the accommodation under the Mental Health Act 1983. But if a person is discharged from detention, they have a right to an IMCA in future accommodation decisions (if they meet the usual conditions set out in the Act).

When can a local authority or NHS body decide to instruct an IMCA?

10.59 The Expansion Regulations have given local authorities and NHS bodies the power to apply the IMCA role to two further types of decisions:

- a care review, and
- adult protection cases that involve vulnerable people.

10.60 In these situations, the responsible body must consider in each individual case whether to instruct an IMCA. Where an IMCA is instructed:

- the decision-maker must be satisfied that having an IMCA will be of particular benefit to the person who lacks capacity
- the decision-maker must also follow the best interests checklist, including getting the views of anyone engaged in caring for a person when assessing their best interests, and
- the decision-maker must consider the IMCA's report and related information when making a decision.

10.61 Responsible bodies are expected to take a strategic approach in deciding when they will use IMCAs in these two additional situations. They should establish a policy locally for determining these decisions, setting out the criteria for appointing an IMCA including the issues to be taken into account when deciding if an IMCA will be of particular benefit to the person concerned.

However, decision-makers will need to consider each case separately to see if the criteria are met. Local authorities or NHS bodies may want to publish their approach for ease of access, setting out the ways they intend to use these additional powers and review it periodically.

Involving an IMCA in care reviews

10.62 A responsible body can instruct an IMCA to support and represent a person who lacks capacity when:
- they have arranged accommodation for that person
- they aim to review the arrangements (as part of a care plan or otherwise), and
- there are no family or friends who it would be appropriate to consult.

10.63 Section 7 of the Local Authority Social Services Act 1970 sets out current requirements for care reviews. It states that there should be a review 'within three months of help being provided or major changes made to services'. There should then be a review every year – or more often, if needed.

10.64 Reviews should relate to decisions about accommodation:
- for someone who lacks capacity to make a decision about accommodation
- that will be provided for a continuous period of more than 12 weeks
- that are not the result of an obligation under the Mental Health Act 1983, and
- that do not relate to circumstances where sections 37 to 39 of the Act would apply.

10.65 Where the person is to be detained or required to live in accommodation under the Mental Health Act 1983, an IMCA will not be needed since the safeguards available under that Act will apply.

Involving IMCAs in adult protection cases

10.66 Responsible bodies have powers to instruct an IMCA to support and represent a person who lacks capacity where it is alleged that:
- the person is or has been abused or neglected by another person, or
- the person is abusing or has abused another person.

The responsible bodies can only instruct an IMCA if they propose to take, or have already taken, protective measures. This is in accordance with adult protection procedures set up under statutory guidance.[43]

---

[43] Published guidance: No secrets: Guidance on developing and implementing multi-agency policies and procedures to protect vulnerable adults from abuse for England (on the Department of Health website) and In safe hands in Wales.

PART VI

10.67 In adult protection cases (and no other cases), access to IMCAs is not restricted to people who have no-one else to support or represent them. People who lack capacity who have family and friends can still have an IMCA to support them in the adult protection procedures.

10.68 In some situations, a case may start out as an adult protection case where a local authority may consider whether or not to involve an IMCA under the criteria they have set – but may then become a case where the allegations or evidence give rise to the question of whether the person should be moved in their best interests. In these situations the case has become one where an IMCA must be involved if there is no-one else appropriate to support and represent the person in this decision.

Who qualifies for an IMCA?

10.69 Apart from the adult protection cases discussed above, IMCAs are only available to people who:
- lack capacity to make a specific decision about serious medical treatment or long-term accommodation, *and*
- have no family or friends who are available and appropriate to support or represent them apart from professionals or paid workers providing care or treatment, *and*
- have not previously named someone who could help with a decision, *and*
- have not made a Lasting Power of Attorney or Enduring Power of Attorney (see paragraph 10.70 below).

10.70 The Act says that IMCAs cannot be instructed if:
- a person who now lacks capacity previously named a person that should be consulted about decisions that affect them, and that person is available and willing to help
- the person who lacks capacity has appointed an attorney, either under a Lasting Power of Attorney or an Enduring Power of Attorney, and the attorney continues to manage the person's affairs
- the Court of Protection has appointed a deputy, who continues to act on the person's behalf.

10.71 However, where a person has no family or friends to represent them, but does have an attorney or deputy who has been appointed solely to deal with their property and affairs, they should not be denied access to an IMCA. The Government is seeking to amend the Act at the earliest opportunity to ensure that, in such circumstances, an IMCA should always be appointed to represent

---

No secrets applies to adults aged 18 or over. The Children Act 1989 applies to 16 and 17 year olds who may be facing abuse. Part V of the Act covers the Protection of Children, which includes at section 47 the duty to investigate by a local authority in order to decide whether they should take any action to safeguard or promote a child's welfare where he or she requires protection or may suffer harm. See also chapter 12 of this Code.

the person's views when they lack the capacity to make decisions relating to serious medical treatment or long-term accommodation moves.

10.72 A responsible body can still instruct an IMCA if the Court of Protection is deciding on a deputy, but none is in place when a decision needs to be made.

Scenario: Qualifying for an IMCA

Ms Lewis, a woman with a history of mental health problems has lived in a care home for several years. Her home will soon close, and she has no-one who could help her. She has become very anxious and now lacks capacity to make a decision about future accommodation. The local authority instructs an IMCA to support her. The IMCA visits Ms Lewis, talks to staff who have been involved in her care and reviews her case notes.

In his report, the IMCA includes the information that Ms Lewis is very close to another client in the care home. The IMCA notes that they could move together – if it is also in the interests of the other client. The local authority now has to decide on the best interests of the client, considering the information that the IMCA has provided.

Will IMCAs be available to people in prisons?

10.73 IMCAs should be available to people who are in prison and lack capacity to make decisions about serious medical treatment or long-term accommodation.

Who is it 'appropriate to consult'?

10.74 The IMCA is a safeguard for those people who lack capacity, who have no-one close to them who 'it would be appropriate to consult'. (This is apart from adult protection cases where this criterion does not apply.) The safeguard is intended to apply to those people who have little or no network of support, such as close family or friends, who take an interest in their welfare or no-one willing or able to be formally consulted in decision-making processes.

10.75 The Act does not define those 'whom it would be appropriate to consult' and the evaluation of the IMCA pilots reported that decision-makers in the local authority and in the NHS, whose decision it is to determine this, sometimes found it difficult to establish when an IMCA was required.[44] Section 4(7) provides that consultation about a person's best interests shall include among others, anyone:

- named by the person as someone to be consulted on a relevant decision
- engaged in caring for them, or
- interested in their welfare (see chapter 4).

10.76 The decision-maker must determine if it is possible and practical to speak to these people, and those described in paragraph 10.70 when working out whether the proposed decision is in the person's best interests. If it is not possible, practical and appropriate to consult anyone, an IMCA should be instructed.

10.77 There may be situations where a person who lacks capacity has family or friends, but it is not practical or appropriate to consult them. For example, an elderly person with dementia may have an adult child who now lives in Australia, or an older person may have relatives who very rarely visit. Or, a family member may simply refuse to be consulted. In such cases, decision-makers must instruct an IMCA – for serious medical treatment and care moves and record the reason for the decision.

10.78 The person who lacks capacity may have friends or neighbours who know their wishes and feelings but are not willing or able to help with the specific decision to be made. They may think it is too much of a responsibility. If they are elderly and frail themselves, it may be too difficult for them to attend case conferences and participate formally. In this situation, the responsible body should instruct an IMCA, and the IMCA may visit them and enable them to be involved more informally.

10.79 If a family disagrees with a decision-maker's proposed action, this is not grounds for concluding that there is nobody whose views are relevant to the decision.

10.80 A person who lacks capacity and already has an advocate may still be entitled to an IMCA. The IMCA would consult with the advocate. Where that advocate meets the appointment criteria for the IMCA service, they may be appointed to fulfil the IMCA role for this person in addition to their other duties.

11 HOW DOES THE ACT AFFECT RESEARCH PROJECTS INVOLVING A PERSON WHO LACKS CAPACITY?

It is important that research involving people who lack capacity can be carried out, and that is carried out properly. Without it, we would not improve our knowledge of what causes a person to lack or lose capacity, and the diagnosis, treatment, care and needs of people who lack capacity.

---

[44]   see www.dh.gov.uk/PolicyAndGuidance/HealthAndSocialCareTopics/SocialCare/IMCA/fs/
en

This chapter gives guidance on involving people who lack capacity to consent to take part in research. It sets out:

- what the Act means by 'research'
- the requirements that people must meet if their research project involves somebody who lacks capacity
- the specific responsibilities of researchers, and
- how the Act applies to research that started before the Act came into force.

This chapter only deals with research in relation to adults. Further guidance will be provided on how the Act applies in relation to research involving those under the age of 18.

> In this chapter, as throughout the Code, a person's capacity (or lack of capacity) refers specifically to their capacity to make a particular decision at the time it needs to be made.

Quick summary

The Act's rules for research that includes people who lack capacity to consent to their involvement cover:

- when research can be carried out
- the ethical approval process
- respecting the wishes and feelings of people who lack capacity
- other safeguards to protect people who lack capacity
- how to engage with a person who lacks capacity
- how to engage with carers and other relevant people.

This chapter also explains:

- the specific rules that apply to research involving human tissue and
- what to do if research projects have already been given the go-ahead.

The Act applies to all research that is intrusive. 'Intrusive' means research that would be unlawful if it involved a person who had capacity but had not consented to take part. The Act does not apply to research involving clinical trials (testing new drugs).

Why does the Act cover research?

11.1 Because the Act is intended to assist and support people who may lack capacity, the Act protects people who take part in research projects but lack capacity to make decisions about their involvement. It makes sure that researchers respect their wishes and feelings. The Act does not apply to research that involves clinical trials of medicines –because these are covered by other rules.[45]

How can research involving people who lack capacity help?

A high percentage of patients with Down's syndrome lack capacity to agree or refuse to take part in research. Research involving patients with Down's syndrome has shown that they are more likely than other people to get pre-senile dementia. Research has also shown that when this happens the pathological changes that occur in a person with Down's syndrome (changes affecting their body and brain) are similar to those that occur in someone with Alzheimer's disease. This means that we now know that treatment similar to that used for memory disorders in patients with Alzheimer's is appropriate to treat dementia in those with Down's syndrome.

What is 'research'?

11.2 The Act does not have a specific definition for 'research'. The Department of Health and National Assembly for Wales publications *Research governance framework for health and social care* both state:

'research can be defined as the attempt to derive generalisable new knowledge by addressing clearly defined questions with systematic and rigorous methods.'[46]

Research may:

- provide information that can be applied generally to an illness, disorder or condition
- demonstrate how effective and safe a new treatment is
- add to evidence that one form of treatment works better than another
- add to evidence that one form of treatment is safer than another, or
- examine wider issues (for example, the factors that affect someone's capacity to make a decision).

11.3 Researchers must state clearly if an activity is part of someone's care and not part of the research. Sometimes experimental medicine or treatment may be performed for the person's benefit and be the best option for their care. But in these cases, it may be difficult to decide whether treatment is research or care. Where there is doubt, the researcher should seek legal advice.

---

[45] The Medicines for Human Use (Clinical Trials) Regulations 2004.
[46] www.dh.gov.uk/PublicationsAndStatistics/Publications/PublicationsPolicyAndGuidance/
      PublicationsPolicyAndGuidanceArticle/fx/en?CONTENT_ID=4008777&chk=dMRd/5   and
      www.word.wales.gov.uk/content/governance/governance-e.htm

What assumptions can a researcher make about capacity?

11.4 Researchers should assume that a person has capacity, unless there is proof that they lack capacity to make a specific decision (see chapter 3). The person must also receive support to try to help them make their own decision (see chapter 2). The person whose capacity is in question has the right to make decisions that others might not agree with, and they have the right not to take part in research.

What research does the Act cover?

11.5 It is expected that most of the researchers who ask for their research to be approved under the Act will be medical or social care researchers. However, the Act can cover more than just medical and social care research. Intrusive research which does not meet the requirements of the Act cannot be carried out lawfully in relation to people who lack capacity.

11.6 The Act applies to research that:

- is 'intrusive' (if a person taking part had capacity, the researcher would need to get their consent to involve them)
- involves people who have an impairment of, or a disturbance in the functioning of, their mind or brain which makes them unable to decide whether or not to agree to take part in the research (ie they lack capacity to consent), and
- is not a clinical trial covered under the Medicines for Human Use (Clinical Trials) Regulations 2004.

11.7 There are circumstances where no consent is needed to lawfully involve a person in research. These apply to all persons, whether they have capacity or not:

- Sometimes research only involves data that has been anonymised (it cannot be traced back to individuals). Confidentiality and data protection laws do not apply in this case.
- Under the Human Tissue Act 2004, research that deals only with human tissue that has been anonymised does not require consent (see paragraphs 11.37–11.40). This applies to both those who have capacity and those who do not. But the research must have ethical approval, and the tissue must come from a living person.[47]
- If researchers collected human tissue samples before 31 August 2006, they do not need a person's consent to work on them. But they will normally have to get ethical approval.
- Regulations[48] made under section 251 of the NHS Act 2006 (formerly known as section 60 of the Health and Social Care Act 2001[49]) allow people to use confidential patient

PART VI

---

[47] Human Tissue Act 2004, s 1(9).
[48] Health Service (Control of Patient Information) Regulations 2002 Section I. 2002/1438.
[49] Section 60 of the Health and Social Care Act 2001 was included in the NHS Act 2006 which consolidated all the previous health legislation still in force.

information without breaking the law on confidentiality by applying to the Patient Information Advisory Group for approval on behalf of the Secretary of State.[50]

Who is responsible for making sure research meets the Act's requirements?

11.8 Responsibility for meeting the Act's requirements lies with:
- the 'appropriate body', as defined in regulations made by the Secretary of State (for regulations applying in England) or the National Assembly for Wales (for regulations applying in Wales) (see paragraph 11.10), and
- the researchers carrying out the research (see paragraphs 11.20–11.40).

How can research get approval?

11.9 Research covered by the Act cannot include people who lack capacity to consent to the research unless:
- it has the approval of 'the appropriate body', and
- it follows other requirements in the Act to:
  - consider the views of carers and other relevant people
  - treat the person's interests as more important than those of science and society, and
  - respect any objections a person who lacks capacity makes during research.

11.10 An 'appropriate body' is an organisation that can approve research projects. In England, the 'appropriate body' must be a research ethics committee recognised by the Secretary of State.[51] In Wales, the 'appropriate body' must be a research ethics committee recognised by the Welsh Assembly Government.

11.11 The appropriate body can only approve a research project if the research is linked to:
- an impairing condition that affects the person who lacks capacity, or
- the treatment of that condition (see paragraph 11.17)

and:
- there are reasonable grounds for believing that the research would be less effective if only people with capacity are involved, and
- the research project has made arrangements to consult carers and to follow the other requirements of the Act.

11.12 Research must also meet one of two requirements:

---

[50]   The Patient Information Advisory Group considers applications on behalf of the Secretary of State to allow the common law duty of confidentiality to be aside. It was established under section 61of the Health and Social Care Act 2006 (now known as section 252 of the NHS Act 2006). Further information can be found at www.advisorybodies.doh.gov.uk/PIAG.

[51]   Mental Capacity Act 2005 (Appropriate Body) (England) Regulations 2006.

1. The research must have some chance of benefiting the person who lacks capacity, as set out in paragraph 11.14 below. The benefit must be in proportion to any burden caused by taking part, or

2. The aim of the research must be to provide knowledge about the cause of, or treatment or care of people with, the same impairing condition – or a similar condition.

If researchers are relying on the second requirement, the Act sets out further requirements that must be met:

- the risk to the person who lacks capacity must be negligible
- there must be no significant interference with the freedom of action or privacy of the person who lacks capacity, and
- nothing must be done to or in relation to the person who lacks capacity which is unduly invasive or restrictive (see paragraphs 11.16–11.19 below).

11.13 An impairing condition:

- is caused by (or may be caused by) an impairment of, or disturbance in the functioning of, the person's mind or brain
- causes (or may cause) an impairment or disturbance of the mind or brain, or
- contributes to (or may contribute to) an impairment or disturbance of the mind or brain.

Balancing the benefit and burden of research

11.14 Potential benefits of research for a person who lacks capacity could include:

- developing more effective ways of treating a person or managing their condition
- improving the quality of healthcare, social care or other services that they have access to
- discovering the cause of their condition, if they would benefit from that knowledge, or
- reducing the risk of the person being harmed, excluded or disadvantaged.

11.15 Benefits may be direct or indirect (for example, the person might benefit at a later date if policies or care packages affecting them are changed because of the research). It might be that participation in the research itself will be of benefit to the person in particular circumstances. For example, if the research involves interviews and the person has the opportunity to express their views, this could be considered of real benefit to a particular individual.

Providing knowledge about causes, treatment or care of people with the same impairing condition or a similar condition

11.16 It is possible for research to be carried out which doesn't actually benefit the person taking part, as long as it aims to provide knowledge about the causes, treatment or care of people with the same impairing condition, or a similar condition. *'Care'* and *'treatment'* are not limited to medical care and treatment. For example, research could examine how day-to-day life in prison affects prisoners with mental health conditions.

11.17 It is the person's actual condition that must be the same or similar in research, not the underlying cause. A *'similar condition'* may therefore have a different cause to that suffered by the participant. For example, research into ways of supporting people with learning disabilities to live more independently might involve a person with a learning disability caused by a head trauma. But its findings might help people with similar learning disabilities that have different causes.

Scenario: Research that helps find a cause or treatment

Mr Neal has Down's syndrome. For many years he has lived in supported housing and worked in a local supermarket. But several months ago, he became aggressive, forgetful and he started to make mistakes at work. His consultant believes that this may indicate the start of Alzheimer's disease.

Mr Neal's condition is now so bad that he does not have capacity to consent to treatment or make other decisions about his care. A research team is researching the cause of dementia in people with Down's syndrome. They would like to involve Mr Neal. The research satisfies the Act's requirement that it is intended to provide knowledge of the causes or treatment of that condition, even though it may not directly benefit Mr Neal. So the approving body might give permission – if the research meets other requirements.

11.18 Any risk to people involved in this category of research must be 'negligible' (minimal). This means that a person should suffer no harm or distress by taking part. Researchers must consider risks to psychological wellbeing as well as physical wellbeing. This is particularly relevant for research related to observations or interviews.

11.19 Research in this category also must not affect a person's freedom of action or privacy in a significant way, and it should not be unduly invasive or restrictive. What will be considered as unduly invasive will be different for different people and different types of research. For example, in psychological research some people may think a specific question is intrusive, but others would not. Actions will not usually be classed as unduly invasive if they do not go beyond the experience of daily life, a routine medical examination or a psychological examination.

Scenario: Assessing the risk to research participants

A research project is studying:

- how well people with a learning disability make financial decisions, and
- communication techniques that may improve their decision-making capacity.

Some of the participants lack capacity to agree to take part. The Research Ethics Committee is satisfied that some of these participants may benefit from the study because their capacity to make financial decisions may be improved. For those who will not gain any personal benefit, the Committee is satisfied that:

- the research meets the other conditions of the Act
- the research methods (psychological testing and different communication techniques) involve no risk to participants, and
- the research could not have been carried out as effectively with people who have capacity.

What responsibilities do researchers have?

11.20 Before starting the research, the research team must make arrangements to:
- obtain approval for the research from the 'appropriate body'
- get the views of any carers and other relevant people before involving a person who lacks capacity in research (see paragraphs 11.22–11.28). There is an exception to this consultation requirement in situations where urgent treatment needs to be given or is about to be given
- respect the objections, wishes and feelings of the person, and
- place more importance on the person's interests than on those of science and society.

11.21 The research proposal must give enough information about what the team will do if a person who lacks capacity needs urgent treatment during research and it is not possible to speak to the person's carer or someone else who acts or makes decisions on behalf of the person (see paragraphs 11.32–11.36).

Consulting carers

11.22 Once it has been established that a person lacks capacity to agree to participate, then before they are included in research the researcher must consult with specified people in accordance with section 32 of the Act to determine whether the person should be included in the research.

PART VI

Who can researchers consult?

11.23 The researcher should as a matter of good practice take reasonable steps to identify someone to consult. That person (the consultee) must be involved in the person's care, interested in their welfare and must be willing to help. They must not be a professional or paid care worker. They will probably be a family member, but could be another person.

11.24 The researcher must take into account previous wishes and feelings that the person might have expressed about who they would, or would not, like involved in future decisions.

11.25 A person is not prevented from being consulted if they are an attorney authorised under a registered Lasting Power of Attorney or are a deputy appointed by the Court of Protection. But that person must not be acting in a professional or paid capacity (for example, person's solicitor).

11.26 Where there is no-one who meets the conditions mentioned at paragraphs 11.23 and 11.25, the researcher must nominate a person to be the consulted. In this situation, they must follow guidance from the Secretary of State for Health in England or the National Assembly for Wales (the guidance will be available from mid-2007). The person who is nominated must have no connection with the research project.

11.27 The researcher must provide the consultee with information about the research project and ask them:
- for advice about whether the person who lacks capacity should take part in the project, and
- what they think the person's feelings and wishes would be, if they had capacity to decide whether to take part.

11.28 Sometimes the consultee will say that the person would probably not take part in the project or that they would ask to be withdrawn. In this situation, the researcher must not include the person in the project, or they should withdraw them from it. But if the project has started, and the person is getting treatment as part of the research, the researcher may decide that the person should not be withdrawn if the researcher reasonably believes that this would cause a significant risk to the person's health. The researcher may decide that the person should continue with the research while the risk exists. But they should stop any parts of the study that are not related to the risk to the person's health.

What other safeguards does the Act require?

11.29 Even when a consultee agrees that a person can take part in research, the researcher must still consider the person's wishes and feelings.

11.30 Researchers must not do anything the person who lacks capacity objects to. They must not do anything to go against any advance decision to refuse treatment or other statement the person has previously made expressing preferences about their care or treatment. They must assume that the person's interests in this matter are more important than those of science and society.

11.31 A researcher must withdraw someone from a project if:

- they indicate in any way that they want to be withdrawn from the project (for example, if they become upset or distressed), or
- any of the Act's requirements are no longer met.

What happens if urgent decisions are required during the research project?

11.32 Anyone responsible for caring for a person must give them urgent treatment if they need it. In some circumstances, it may not be possible to separate the research from the urgent treatment.

11.33 A research proposal should explain to the appropriate body how researchers will deal with urgent decisions which may occur during the project, when there may not be time to carry out the consultations required under the Act. For example, after a patient has arrived in intensive care, the doctor may want to chart the course of an injury by taking samples or measurements immediately and then taking further samples after some type of treatment to compare with the first set.

11.34 Special rules apply where a person who lacks capacity is getting, or about to get, urgent treatment and researchers want to include them in a research project. If in these circumstances a researcher thinks that it is necessary to take urgent action for the purposes of the research, and they think it is not practical to consult someone about it, the researcher can take that action if:

- they get agreement from a registered medical practitioner not involved with the research, or
- they follow a procedure that the appropriate body agreed to at approval stage.

11.35 The medical practitioner may have a connection to the person who lacks capacity (for example, they might be their doctor). But they must not be involved in the research project in any way. This is to avoid conflicts of interest.

11.36 This exception to the duty to consult only applies:

- for as long as the person needs urgent treatment, and
- when the researcher needs to take action urgently for research to be valid.

It is likely to be limited to research into procedures or treatments used in emergencies. It does not apply where the researcher simply wants to act quickly.

What happens for research involving human tissue?

11.37 A person with capacity has to give their permission for someone to remove tissue from their body (for example, taking a biopsy (a sample) for diagnosis or removal of tissue in surgery). The Act allows the removal of tissue from the body of a person who lacks capacity, if it is in their best interests (see chapter 5).

11.38 People with capacity must also give permission for the storage or use of tissue for certain purposes, set out in the Human Tissue Act 2004, (for example, transplants and research). But there are situations in which permission is not required by law:
- research where the samples are anonymised and the research has ethical approval[52]
- clinical audit
- education or training relating to human health
- performance assessment
- public health monitoring, and
- quality assurance.

11.39 If an adult lacks capacity to consent, the Human Tissue Act 2004 says that tissue can be stored or used without seeking permission if the storage or use is:
- to get information relevant to the health of another individual (for example, before conducting a transplant), as long as the researcher or healthcare professional storing or using the human tissue believes they are doing it in the best interests of the person who lacks capacity to consent
- for a clinical trial approved and carried out under the Medicines for Human Use (Clinical Trials) Regulations 2004, or
- for intrusive research:
    - after the Mental Capacity Act comes into force
    - that meets the Act's requirements, and
    - that has ethical approval.

11.40 Tissue samples that were obtained before 31 August 2006 are existing holdings under the Human Tissue Act. Researchers can work with these tissues without seeking permission. But they will still need to get ethical approval. Guidance is available in the Human Tissue Authority Code of Practice on consent.[53]

What should happen to research that started before the Act came into force?

What if a person has capacity when research starts but loses capacity?

11.41 Some people with capacity will agree to take part in research but may then lose capacity before the end of the project. In this situation, researchers will be able to continue research as long as they comply with the conditions set out in the Mental Capacity Act 2005 (Loss of Capacity During Research Project) (England) Regulations 2007 or equivalent Welsh regulations.

---

[52]   Section 1(9) of the Human Tissue Act 2004.
[53]   www.hta.gov.uk

The regulations only apply to tissue and data collected before the loss of capacity from a person who gave consent before 31 March 2008 to join a project that starts before 1 October 2007.

11.42 The regulations do not cover research involving direct intervention (for example, taking of further blood pressure readings) or the taking of further tissue after loss of capacity. Such research must comply with sections 30 to 33 of the Act to be lawful.

11.43 Where the regulations do apply, research can only continue if the project already has procedures to deal with people who lose capacity during the project. An appropriate body must have approved the procedures. The researcher must follow the procedures that have been approved.

11.44 The researcher must also:
- seek out the views of someone involved in the person's care or interested in their welfare and if a carer can't be found they must nominate a consultee (see paragraphs 11.22–11.28)
- respect advance decisions and expressed preferences, wishes or objections that the person has made in the past, and
- treat the person's interests as more important than those of science and society.

The appropriate body must be satisfied that the research project has reasonable arrangements to meet these requirements.

11.45 If at any time the researcher believes that procedures are no longer in place or the appropriate body no longer approves the research, they must stop research on the person immediately.

11.46 Where regulations do apply, research does not have to:
- be linked to an impairing condition of the person
- have the potential to benefit that person, or
- aim to provide knowledge relevant to others with the same or a similar condition.

What happens to existing projects that a person never had capacity to agree to?

11.47 There are no regulations for projects that:
- started before the Act comes into force, and
- a person never had the capacity to agree to.

Projects that already have ethical approval will need to obtain approval from an appropriate body under sections 30 and 31 of the Mental Capacity Act and to comply with the requirements of sections 32 and 33 of that Act by 1 October 2008. Research that does not have ethical approval must get approval from an appropriate body by 1 October 2007 to continue lawfully. This is the case in England and it is expected that similar arrangements will apply in Wales.

PART VI

12   HOW DOES THE ACT APPLY TO CHILDREN AND YOUNG PEOPLE?

This chapter looks at the few parts of the Act that may affect children under 16 years of age. It also explains the position of young people aged 16 and 17 years and the overlapping laws that affect them.

This chapter does not deal with research. Further guidance will be provided on how the Act applies in relation to research involving those under the age of 18.

Within this Code of Practice, 'children' refers to people aged below 16. 'Young people' refers to people aged 16–17. This differs from the Children Act 1989 and the law more generally, where the term 'child' is used to refer to people aged under 18.

> In this chapter, as throughout the Code, a person's capacity (or lack of capacity) refers specifically to their capacity to make a particular decision at the time it needs to be made.

Quick summary

Children under 16
- The Act does not generally apply to people under the age of 16.
- There are two exceptions:
  - The Court of Protection can make decisions about a child's property or finances (or appoint a deputy to make these decisions) if the child lacks capacity to make such decisions within section 2(1) of the Act and is likely to still lack capacity to make financial decisions when they reach the age of 18 (section 18(3)).
  - Offences of ill treatment or wilful neglect of a person who lacks capacity within section 2(1) can also apply to victims younger than 16 (section 44).

Young people aged 16–17 years
- Most of the Act applies to young people aged 16–17 years, who may lack capacity within section 2(1) to make specific decisions.
- There are three exceptions:
  - Only people aged 18 and over can make a Lasting Power of Attorney (LPA).
  - Only people aged 18 and over can make an advance decision to refuse
    medical treatment.
  - The Court of Protection may only make a statutory will for a person aged
    18 and over.

Care or treatment for young people aged 16–17

- People carrying out acts in connection with the care or treatment of a young person aged 16–17 who lacks capacity to consent within section 2(1) will generally have protection from liability (section 5), as long as the person carrying out the act:
  - has taken reasonable steps to establish that the young person lacks capacity
  - reasonably believes that the young person lacks capacity and that the act is in the young person's best interests, and
  - follows the Act's principles.
- When assessing the young person's best interests (see chapter 5), the person providing care or treatment must consult those involved in the young person's care and anyone interested in their welfare – if it is practical and appropriate to do so. This may include the young person's parents. Care should be taken not to unlawfully breach the young person's right to confidentiality (see chapter 16).
- Nothing in section 5 excludes a person's civil liability for loss or damage, or his criminal liability, resulting from his negligence in carrying out the act.

Legal proceedings involving young people aged 16-17

- Sometimes there will be disagreements about the care, treatment or welfare of a young person aged 16 or 17 who lacks capacity to make relevant decisions. Depending on the circumstances, the case may be heard in the family courts or the Court of Protection.
- The Court of Protection may transfer a case to the family courts, and vice versa.

Does the Act apply to children?

12.1 Section 2(5) of the Act states that, with the exception of section 2(6), as explained below, no powers under the Act may be exercised in relation to a child under 16.

12.2 Care and treatment of children under the age of 16 is generally governed by common law principles. Further information is provide at www.dh.gov.uk/consent.

Can the Act help with decisions about a child's property or finances?

12.3 Section 2(6) makes an exception for some decisions about a child's property and financial affairs. The Court of Protection can make decisions about property and affairs of those under 16 in cases where the person is likely to still lack capacity to make financial decisions after reaching the age of 18. The court's ruling will still apply when the person reaches the age of 18, which means there will not be a need for further court proceedings once the person reaches the age of 18.

12.4 The Court of Protection can:

PART VI

- make an order (for example, concerning the investment of an award of compensation for the child), and/or
- appoint a deputy to manage the child's property and affairs and to make ongoing financial decisions on the child's behalf.

In making a decision, the court must follow the Act's principles and decide in the child's best interests as set out in chapter 5 of the Code.

Scenario: Applying the Act to children

Tom was nine when a drunk driver knocked him off his bicycle. He suffered severe head injuries and permanent brain damage. He received a large amount of money in compensation. He is unlikely to recover enough to be able to make financial decisions when he is 18. So the Court of Protection appoints Tom's father as deputy to manage his financial affairs in order to pay for the care Tom will need in the future.

What if somebody mistreats or neglects a child who lacks capacity?

12.5 Section 44 covers the offences of ill treatment or wilful neglect of a person who lacks capacity to make relevant decisions (see chapter 14). This section also applies to children under 16 and young people aged 16 or 17. But it only applies if the child's lack of capacity to make a decision for themselves is caused by an impairment or disturbance that affects how their mind or brain works (see chapter 4). If the lack of capacity is solely the result of the child's youth or immaturity, then the ill treatment or wilful neglect would be dealt with under the separate offences of child cruelty or neglect.

Does the Act apply to young people aged 16–17?

12.6 Most of the Act applies to people aged 16 years and over. There is an overlap with the Children Act 1989. For the Act to apply to a young person, they must lack capacity to make a particular decision (in line with the Act's definition of lack of capacity described in chapter 4). In such situations either this Act or the Children Act 1989 may apply, depending upon the particular circumstances. However, there may also be situations where neither of these Acts provides an appropriate solution. In such cases, it may be necessary to look to the powers available under the Mental Health Act 1983 or the High Court's inherent powers to deal with cases involving young people.

12.7 There are currently no specific rules for deciding when to use either the Children Act 1989 or the Mental Capacity Act 2005 or when to apply to the High Court. But, the examples below show circumstances where this Act may be the most appropriate (see also paragraphs 12.21–12.23 below).

- In unusual circumstances it might be in a young person's best interests for the Court of Protection to make an order and/or appoint a property and affairs deputy. For example, this might occur when a young person receives financial compensation and the court appoints a parent or a solicitor as a property and affairs deputy.
- It may be appropriate for the Court of Protection to make a welfare decision concerning a young person who lacks capacity to decide for themselves (for example, about where the young person should live) if the court decides that the parents are not acting in the young person's best interests.
- It might be appropriate to refer a case to the Court of Protection where there is disagreement between a person interested in the care and welfare of a young person and the young person's medical team about the young person's best interests or capacity.

Do any parts of the Act not apply to young people aged 16 or 17?

LPAs

12.8 Only people aged 18 or over can make a Lasting Power of Attorney (LPA) (section 9(2)(c)).

Advance decisions to refuse treatment

12.9 Information on decisions to refuse treatment made in advance by young people under the age of 18 will be available at www.dh.gov.uk/consent.

Making a will

12.10 The law generally does not allow anyone below the age of 18 to make a will. So section 18(2) confirms that the Court of Protection can only make a statutory will on behalf of those aged 18 and over.

What does the Act say about care or treatment of young people aged 16 or 17?

Background information concerning competent young people

12.11 The Family Law Reform Act 1969 presumes that young people have the legal capacity to agree to surgical, medical or dental treatment.[54] This also applies to any associated procedures (for example, investigations, anaesthesia or nursing care).

12.12 It does not apply to some rarer types of procedure (for example, organ donation or other procedures which are not therapeutic for the young person) or research. In those cases, anyone under 18 is presumed to lack legal capacity, subject to the test of 'Gillick competence' (testing whether they are mature and intelligent enough to understand a proposed treatment or procedure).[55]

12.13 Even where a young person is presumed to have legal capacity to consent to treatment, they may not necessarily be able to make the relevant decision. As with adults, decision-makers should assess the young person's capacity to consent to the proposed care or treatment (see chapter 4). If a young person lacks capacity to consent within section 2(1) of the Act because of an impairment of, or a disturbance in the functioning of, the mind or brain then the Mental Capacity Act will apply in the same way as it does to those who are 18 and over. If however they are unable to make the decision for some other reason, for example because they are overwhelmed by the implications of the decision, the Act will not apply to them and the legality of any treatment should be assessed under common law principles.

12.14 If a young person has capacity to agree to treatment, their decision to consent must be respected. Difficult issues can arise if a young person has legal and mental capacity and refuses consent – especially if a person with parental responsibility wishes to give consent on the young person's behalf. The Family Division of the High Court can hear cases where there is disagreement. The Court of Protection has no power to settle a dispute about a young person who is said to have the mental capacity to make the specific decision.

12.15 It may be unclear whether a young person lacks capacity within section 2(1) of the Act. In those circumstances, it would be prudent for the person providing care or treatment for the young person to seek a declaration from the court.

If the young person lacks capacity to make care or treatment decisions

12.16 Under the common law, a person with parental responsibility for a young person is generally able to consent to the young person receiving care or medical treatment where they lack capacity under section 2(1) of the Act. They should act in the young person's best interests.

---

54   Family Law Reform Act 1969, s 8(1).
55   In the case of *Gillick v West Norfolk and Wisbech Area Health Authority* [1986] 1 AC 112 the court found that a child below 16 years of age will be competent to consent to medical treatment if they have sufficient intelligence and understanding to understand what is proposed. This test applies in relation to all people under 18 where there is no presumption of competence in relation to the procedure – for example where the procedure is not one referred to in section 8 of the Family Law Reform Act 1969, e g organ donation.

12.17 However if a young person lacks the mental capacity to make a specific care or treatment decision within section 2(1) of the Act, healthcare staff providing treatment, or a person providing care to the young person, can carry out treatment or care with protection from liability (section 5) whether or not a person with parental responsibility consents.[56] They must follow the Act's principles and make sure that the actions they carry out are in the young person's best interests. They must make every effort to work out and consider the young person's wishes, feelings, beliefs and values – both past and present – and consider all other factors in the best interests checklist (see chapter 5).

12.18 When assessing a young person's best interests, healthcare staff must take into account the views of anyone involved in caring for the young person and anyone interested in their welfare, where it is practical and appropriate to do so. This may include the young person's parents and others with parental responsibility for the young person. Care should be taken not to unlawfully breach the young person's right to confidentiality (see chapter 16).

12.19 If a young person has said they do not want their parents to be consulted, it may not be appropriate to involve them (for example, where there have been allegations of abuse).

12.20 If there is a disagreement about whether the proposed care or treatment is in the best interests of a young person, or there is disagreement about whether the young person lacks capacity and there is no other way of resolving the matter, it would be prudent for those in disagreement to seek a declaration or other order from the appropriate court (see paragraphs 12.23–12.25 below).

PART VI

Scenario: Working out a young person's best interests

Mary is 16 and has Down's syndrome. Her mother wants Mary to have dental treatment that will improve her appearance but is not otherwise necessary.

To be protected under section 5 of the Act, the dentist must consider whether Mary has capacity to agree to the treatment and what would be in her best interests. He decides that she is unable to understand what is involved or the possible consequences of the proposed treatment and so lacks capacity to make the decision.

But Mary seems to want the treatment, so he takes her views into account in deciding whether the treatment is in her best interests. He also consults with both her parents and with her teacher and GP to see if there are other relevant factors to take into account.

---

[56] Nothing in section 5 excludes a person's civil liability for loss or damage, or his criminal liability, resulting from his negligence in doing the Act.

> He decides that the treatment is likely to improve Mary's confidence
> and self-esteem and is in her best interests.

12.21 There may be particular difficulties where young people with mental health problems require in-patient psychiatric treatment, and are treated informally rather than detained under the Mental Health Act 1983. The Mental Capacity Act and its principles apply to decisions related to the care and treatment of young people who lack mental capacity to consent, including treatment for mental disorder. As with any other form of treatment, somebody assessing a young person's best interests should consult anyone involved in caring for the young person or anyone interested in their welfare, as far as is practical and appropriate. This may include the young person's parents or those with parental responsibility for the young person.

But the Act does not allow any actions that result in a young person being deprived of their liberty (see chapter 6). In such circumstances, detention under the Mental Health Act 1983 and the safeguards provided under that Act might be appropriate (see also chapter 13).

12.22 People may disagree about a young person's capacity to make the specific decision or about their best interests, or it may not be clear whether they lack capacity within section 2(1) or for some other reason. In this situation, legal proceedings may be necessary if there is no other way of settling the disagreement (see chapters 8 and 15). If those involved in caring for the young person or who are interested in the young person's welfare do not agree with the proposed treatment, it may be necessary for an interested party to make an application to the appropriate court.

What powers do the courts have in cases involving young people?

12.23 A case involving a young person who lacks mental capacity to make a specific decision could be heard in the family courts (probably in the Family Division of the High Court) or in the Court of Protection.

12.24 If a case might require an ongoing order (because the young person is likely to still lack capacity when they are 18), it may be more appropriate for the Court of Protection to hear the case. For one-off cases not involving property or finances, the Family Division may be more appropriate.

12.25 So that the appropriate court hears a case, the Court of Protection can transfer cases to the family courts, and vice versa (section 21).

Scenario: Hearing cases in the appropriate court

Shola is 17. She has serious learning disabilities and lacks the capacity to decide where she should live. Her parents are involved in a bitter divorce. They cannot agree on several issues concerning Shola's care – including where she should live. Her mother wants to continue to look after Shola at home. But her father wants Shola to move into a care home.

In this case, it may be more appropriate for the Court of Protection to deal with the case. This is because an order made in the Court of Protection could continue into Shola's adulthood. However an order made by the family court under the Children Act 1989 would end on Shola's eighteenth birthday.

---

13   WHAT IS THE RELATIONSHIP BETWEEN THE MENTAL CAPACITY ACT AND THE MENTAL HEALTH ACT 1983?

This chapter explains the relationship between the Mental Capacity Act 2005 (MCA) and the Mental Health Act 1983 (MHA). It:

- sets out when it may be appropriate to detain someone under the MHA rather than to rely on the MCA
- describes how the MCA affects people lacking capacity who are also subject to the MHA
- explains when doctors cannot give certain treatments for a mental disorder (in particular, psychosurgery) to someone who lacks capacity to consent to it, and
- sets out changes that the Government is planning to make to both Acts.

It does not provide a full description of the MHA. The MHA has its own Memorandum to explain the Act and its own Code of Practice to guide people about how to use it.[57]

In this chapter, as throughout the Code, a person's capacity (or lack of capacity) refers specifically to their capacity to make a particular decision at the time it needs to be made.

Quick summary

- Professionals may need to think about using the MHA to detain and treat somebody who lacks capacity to consent to treatment (rather than use the MCA), if:

---

[57]   Department of Health & Welsh Office, *Mental Health Act 1983 Code of Practice* (TSO, 1999), www.dh.gov.uk/assetRoot/04/07/49/61/04074961.pdf

- it is not possible to give the person the care or treatment they need without doing something that might deprive them of their liberty
- the person needs treatment that cannot be given under the MCA (for example, because the person has made a valid and applicable advance decision to refuse an essential part of treatment)
- the person may need to be restrained in a way that is not allowed under the MCA
- it is not possible to assess or treat the person safely or effectively without treatment being compulsory (perhaps because the person is expected to regain capacity to consent, but might then refuse to give consent)
- the person lacks capacity to decide on some elements of the treatment but has capacity to refuse a vital part of it – and they have done so, or
- there is some other reason why the person might not get treatment, and they or somebody else might suffer harm as a result.

- Before making an application under the MHA, decision-makers should consider whether they could achieve their aims safely and effectively by using the MCA instead.
- Compulsory treatment under the MHA is not an option if:
  - the patient's mental disorder does not justify detention in hospital, or
  - the patient needs treatment only for a physical illness or disability.
- The MCA applies to people subject to the MHA in the same way as it applies to anyone else, with four exceptions:
  - if someone is detained under the MHA, decision-makers cannot normally rely on the MCA to give treatment for mental disorder or make decisions about that treatment on that person's behalf
  - if somebody can be treated for their mental disorder without their consent because they are detained under the MHA, healthcare staff can treat them even if it goes against an advance decision to refuse that treatment
  - if a person is subject to guardianship, the guardian has the exclusive right to take certain decisions, including where the person is to live, and
  - Independent Mental Capacity Advocates do not have to be involved in decisions about serious medical treatment or accommodation, if those decisions are made under the MHA.
- Healthcare staff cannot give psychosurgery (i.e. neurosurgery for mental disorder) to a person who lacks capacity to agree to it. This applies whether or not the person is otherwise subject to the MHA.

Who does the MHA apply to?

13.1 The MHA provides ways of assessing, treating and caring for people who have a serious mental disorder that puts them or other people at risk. It sets out when:

- people with mental disorders can be detained in hospital for assessment or treatment
- people who are detained can be given treatment for their mental disorder without their consent (it also sets out the safeguards people must get in this situation), and
- people with mental disorders can be made subject to guardianship or after-care under supervision to protect them or other people.

13.2 Most of the MHA does not distinguish between people who have the capacity to make decisions and those who do not. Many people covered by the MHA have the capacity to make decisions for themselves. Most people who lack capacity to make decisions about their treatment will never be affected by the MHA, even if they need treatment for a mental disorder.

13.3 But there are cases where decision-makers will need to decide whether to use the MHA or MCA, or both, to meet the needs of people with mental health problems who lack capacity to make decisions about their own treatment.

What are the MCA's limits?

13.4 Section 5 of the MCA provides legal protection for people who care for or treat someone who lacks capacity (see chapter 6). But they must follow the Act's principles and may only take action that is in a person's best interests (see chapter 5). This applies to care or treatment for physical and mental conditions. So it can apply to treatment for people with mental disorders, however serious those disorders are.

13.5 But section 5 does have its limits. For example, somebody using restraint only has protection if the restraint is:

- necessary to protect the person who lacks capacity from harm, and
- in proportion to the likelihood and seriousness of that harm.

13.6 There is no protection under section 5 for actions that deprive a person of their liberty (see chapter 6 for guidance). Similarly, the MCA does not allow giving treatment that goes against a valid and applicable advance decision to refuse treatment (see chapter 9).

13.7 None of these restrictions apply to treatment for mental disorder given under the MHA – but other restrictions do.

When can a person be detained under the MHA?

13.8 A person may be taken into hospital and detained for assessment under section 2 of the MHA for up to 28 days if:

PART VI

- they have a mental disorder that is serious enough for them to be detained in a hospital for assessment (or for assessment followed by treatment) for at least a limited period, and
- they need to be detained to protect their health or safety, or to protect others.

13.9 A patient may be admitted to hospital and detained for treatment under section 3 of the MHA if:

- they have a mental illness, severe mental impairment, psychopathic disorder or mental impairment (the MHA sets out definitions for these last three terms)
- their mental disorder is serious enough to need treatment in hospital
- treatment is needed for the person's health or safety, or for the protection of other people – and it cannot be provided without detention under this section, and
- (if the person has a mental impairment or psychopathic disorder) treatment is likely to improve their condition or stop it getting worse.

13.10 Decision-makers should consider using the MHA if, in their professional judgment, they are not sure it will be possible, or sufficient, to rely on the MCA. They do not have to ask the Court of Protection to rule that the MCA does not apply before using the MHA.

13.11 If a clinician believes that they can safely assess or treat a person under the MCA, they do not need to consider using the MHA. In this situation, it would be difficult to meet the requirements of the MHA anyway.

13.12 It might be necessary to consider using the MHA rather than the MCA if:

- it is not possible to give the person the care or treatment they need without carrying out an action that might deprive them of their liberty
- the person needs treatment that cannot be given under the MCA (for example, because the person has made a valid and applicable advance decision to refuse all or part of that treatment)
- the person may need to be restrained in a way that is not allowed under the MCA
- it is not possible to assess or treat the person safely or effectively without treatment being compulsory (perhaps because the person is expected to regain capacity to consent, but might then refuse to give consent)
- the person lacks capacity to decide on some elements of the treatment but has capacity to refuse a vital part of it – and they have done so, or
- there is some other reason why the person might not get the treatment they need, and they or somebody else might suffer harm as a result.

13.13 But it is important to remember that a person cannot be treated under the MHA unless they meet the relevant criteria for being detained. Unless they are sent to hospital under Part 3 of the MHA in connection with a criminal offence, people can only be detained where:

- the conditions summarised in paragraph 13.8 or 13.9 are met
- the relevant people agree that an application is necessary (normally two doctors and an approved social worker), and
- (in the case of section 3) the patient's nearest relative has not objected to the application.

'Nearest relative' is defined in section 26 of the MHA. It is usually, but not always, a family member.

Scenario: Using the MHA

Mr Oliver has a learning disability. For the last four years, he has had depression from time to time, and has twice had treatment for it at a psychiatric hospital. He is now seriously depressed and his care workers are worried about him.

Mr Oliver's consultant has given him medication and is considering electro-convulsive therapy. The consultant thinks this care plan will only work if Mr Oliver is detained in hospital. This will allow close observation and Mr Oliver will be stopped if he tries to leave. The consultant thinks an application should be made under section 3 of the MHA.

The consultant also speaks to Mr Oliver's nearest relative, his mother. She asks why Mr Oliver needs to be detained when he has not needed to be in the past. But after she hears the consultant's reasons, she does not object to the application. An approved social worker makes the application and obtains a second medical recommendation. Mr Oliver is then detained and taken to hospital for his treatment for depression to begin.

PART VI

13.14 Compulsory treatment under the MHA is not an option if:

- the patient's mental disorder does not justify detention in hospital, or
- the patient needs treatment only for a physical illness or disability.

13.15 There will be some cases where a person who lacks capacity cannot be treated either under the MHA or the MCA – even if the treatment is for mental disorder.

Scenario: Deciding whether to use the MHA or MCA

Mrs Carter is in her 80s and has dementia. Somebody finds her wandering in the street, very confused and angry. A neighbour takes her home and calls her doctor. At home, it looks like she has been deliberately smashing things. There are cuts on her hands and arms, but she won't let the doctor touch them, and she hasn't been taking her medication.

Her doctor wants to admit her to hospital for assessment. Mrs Carter gets angry and says that they'll never keep her in hospital. So the doctor thinks that it might be necessary to use the MHA. He arranges for an approved social worker to visit. The social worker discovers that Mrs Carter was expecting her son this morning, but he has not turned up. They find out that he has been delayed, but could not call because Mrs Carter's telephone has become unplugged.

When she is told that her son is on his way, Mrs Carter brightens up. She lets the doctor treat her cuts – which the doctor thinks it is in her best interests to do as soon as possible. When Mrs Carter's son arrives, the social worker explains the doctor is very worried, especially that Mrs Carter is not taking her medication. The son explains that he will help his mother take it in future. It is agreed that the MCA will allow him to do that. The social worker arranges to return a week later and calls the doctor to say that she thinks Mrs Carter can get the care she needs without being detained under the MHA. The doctor agrees.

How does the MCA apply to a patient subject to guardianship under the MHA?

13.16 Guardianship gives someone (usually a local authority social services department) the exclusive right to decide where a person should live – but in doing this they cannot deprive the person of their liberty. The guardian can also require the person to attend for treatment, work, training or education at specific times and places, and they can demand that a doctor, approved social worker or another relevant person have access to the person wherever they live. Guardianship can apply whether or not the person has the capacity to make decisions about care and treatment. It does not give anyone the right to treat the person without their permission or to consent to treatment on their behalf.

13.17 An application can be made for a person who has a mental disorder to be received into guardianship under section 7 of the MHA when:

  • the situation meets the conditions summarised in paragraph 13.18

- the relevant people agree an application for guardianship should be made (normally two doctors and an approved social worker), and
- the person's nearest relative does not object.

13.18 An application can be made in relation to any person who is 16 years or over if:

- they have a mental illness, severe mental impairment, psychopathic disorder or mental impairment that is serious enough to justify guardianship (see paragraph 13.20 below), and
- guardianship is necessary in the interests of the welfare of the patient or to protect other people.

13.19 Applicants (usually approved social workers) and doctors supporting the application will need to determine whether they could achieve their aims without guardianship. For patients who lack capacity, the obvious alternative will be action under the MCA.

13.20 But the fact that the person lacks capacity to make relevant decision is not the only factor that applicants need to consider. They need to consider all the circumstances of the case. They may conclude that guardianship is the best option for a person with a mental disorder who lacks capacity to make those decisions if, for example:

- they think it is important that one person or authority should be in charge of making decisions about where the person should live (for example, where there have been long-running or difficult disagreements about where the person should live)
- they think the person will probably respond well to the authority and attention of a guardian, and so be more prepared to accept treatment for the mental disorder (whether they are able to consent to it or it is being provided for them under the MCA), or
- they need authority to return the person to the place they are to live (for example, a care home) if they were to go absent.

Decision-makers must never consider guardianship as a way to avoid applying the MCA.

13.21 A guardian has the exclusive right to decide where a person lives, so nobody else can use the MCA to arrange for the person to live elsewhere. Somebody who knowingly helps a person leave the place a guardian requires them to stay may be committing a criminal offence under the MHA. A guardian also has the exclusive power to require the person to attend set times and places for treatment, occupation, education or training. This does not stop other people using the MCA to make similar arrangements or to treat the person in their best interests. But people cannot use the MCA in any way that conflicts with decisions which a guardian has a legal right to make under the MHA. See paragraph 13.16 above for general information about a guardian's powers.

PART VI

How does the MCA apply to a patient subject to after-care under supervision under the MHA?

13.22 When people are discharged from detention for medical treatment under the MHA, their responsible medical officer may decide to place them on after-care under supervision. The responsible medical officer is usually the person's consultant psychiatrist. Another doctor and an approved social worker must support their application.

13.23 After-care under supervision means:

- the person can be required to live at a specified place (where they can be taken to and returned, if necessary)
- the person can be required to attend for treatment, occupation, education or training at a specific time and place (where they can be taken, if necessary), and
- their supervisor, any doctor or approved social worker or any other relevant person must be given access to them wherever they live.

13.24 Responsible medical officers can apply for after-care under supervision under section 25A of the MHA if:

- the person is 16 or older and is liable to be detained in a hospital for treatment under section 3 (and certain other sections) of the MHA
- the person has a mental illness, severe mental impairment, psychopathic disorder or mental impairment
- without after-care under supervision the person's health or safety would be at risk of serious harm, they would be at risk of serious exploitation, or other people's safety would be at risk of serious harm, and
- after-care under supervision is likely to help make sure the person gets the after-care services they need.

'Liable to be detained' means that a hospital is allowed to detain them. Patients who are liable to be detained are not always actually in hospital, because they may have been given permission to leave hospital for a time.

13.25 After-care under supervision can be used whether or not the person lacks capacity to make relevant decisions. But if a person lacks capacity, decision-makers will need to decide whether action under the MCA could achieve their aims before making an application. The kinds of cases in which after-care under supervision might be considered for patients who lack capacity to take decisions about their own care and treatment are similar to those for guardianship.

How does the Mental Capacity Act affect people covered by the Mental Health Act?

13.26 There is no reason to assume a person lacks capacity to make their own decisions just because they are subject (under the MHA) to:

- detention
- guardianship, or
- after-care under supervision.

13.27 People who lack capacity to make specific decisions are still protected by the MCA even if they are subject to the MHA (this includes people who are subject to the MHA as a result of court proceedings). But there are four important exceptions:

- if someone is liable to be detained under the MHA, decision-makers cannot normally rely on the MCA to give mental health treatment or make decisions about that treatment on someone's behalf
- if somebody can be given mental health treatment without their consent because they are liable to be detained under the MHA, they can also be given mental health treatment that goes against an advance decision to refuse treatment
- if a person is subject to guardianship, the guardian has the exclusive right to take certain decisions, including where the person is to live, and
- Independent Mental Capacity Advocates do not have to be involved in decisions about serious medical treatment or accommodation, if those decisions are made under the MHA.

What are the implications for people who need treatment for a mental disorder?

13.28 Subject to certain conditions, Part 4 of the MHA allows doctors to give patients who are liable to be detained treatment for mental disorders without their consent – whether or not they have the capacity to give that consent. Paragraph 13.31 below lists a few important exceptions.

13.29 Where Part 4 of the MHA applies, the MCA cannot be used to give medical treatment for a mental disorder to patients who lack capacity to consent. Nor can anyone else, like an attorney or a deputy, use the MCA to give consent for that treatment. This is because Part 4 of the MHA already allows clinicians, if they comply with the relevant rules, to give patients medical treatment for mental disorder even though they lack the capacity to consent. In this context, medical treatment includes nursing and care, habilitation and rehabilitation under medical supervision.

13.30 But clinicians treating people for mental disorder under the MHA cannot simply ignore a person's capacity to consent to treatment. As a matter of good practice (and in some cases in order to comply with the MHA) they will always need to assess and record:

- whether patients have capacity to consent to treatment, and

PART VI

- if so, whether they have consented to or refused that treatment. For more information, see the MHA Code of Practice.

13.31 Part 4 of the MHA does not apply to patients:
- admitted in an emergency under section 4(4)(a) of the MHA, following a single medical recommendation and awaiting a second recommendation
- temporarily detained (held in hospital) under section 5 of the MHA while awaiting an application for detention under section 2 or section 3
- remanded by a court to hospital for a report on their medical condition under section 35 of the MHA
- detained under section 37(4), 135 or 136 of the MHA in a place of safety, or
- who have been conditionally discharged by the Mental Health Review Tribunal (and not recalled to hospital).

13.32 Since the MHA does not allow treatment for these patients without their consent, the MCA applies in the normal way, even if the treatment is for mental disorder.

13.33 Even when the MHA allows patients to be treated for mental disorders, the MCA applies in the normal way to treatment for physical disorders. But sometimes healthcare staff may decide to focus first on treating a detained patient's mental disorder in the hope that they will get back the capacity to make a decision about treatment for the physical disorder.

13.34 Where people are subject to guardianship or after-care under supervision under the MHA, the MCA applies as normal to all treatment. Guardianship and after-care under supervision do not give people the right to treat patients without consent.

Scenario: Using the MCA to treat a patient who is detained under the MHA

Mr Peters is detained in hospital under section 3 of the MHA and is receiving treatment under Part 4 of the MHA. Mr Peters has paranoid schizophrenia, delusions, hallucinations and thought disorder. He refuses all medical treatment. Mr Peters has recently developed blood in his urine and staff persuaded him to have an ultrasound scan. The scan revealed suspected renal carcinoma.

His consultant believes that he needs a CT scan and treatment for the carcinoma. But Mr Peters refuses a general anaesthetic and other medical procedures. The consultant assesses Mr Peters as lacking capacity to consent to treatment under the MCA's test of capacity. The MHA is not relevant here, because the CT scan is not part of Mr Peters' treatment for mental disorder.

> Under section 5 of the MCA, doctors can provide treatment without consent. But they must follow the principles of the Act and believe that treatment is in Mr Peters' best interests.

How does the Mental Health Act affect advance decisions to refuse treatment?

13.35 The MHA does not affect a person's advance decision to refuse treatment, unless Part 4 of the MHA means the person can be treated for mental disorder without their consent. In this situation healthcare staff can treat patients for their mental disorder, even if they have made an advance decision to refuse such treatment.

13.36 But even then healthcare staff must treat a valid and applicable advance decision as they would a decision made by a person with capacity at the time they are asked to consent to treatment. For example, they should consider whether they could use a different type of treatment which the patient has not refused in advance. If healthcare staff do not follow an advance decision, they should record in the patient's notes why they have chosen not to follow it.

13.37 Even if a patient is being treated without their consent under Part 4 of the MHA, an advance decision to refuse other forms of treatment is still valid. Being subject to guardianship or after-care under supervision does not affect an advance decision in any way. See chapter 9 for further guidance on advance decisions to refuse treatment.

PART VI

> *Scenario: Deciding on whether to follow an advance decision to refuse treatment*
>
> Miss Khan gets depression from time to time and has old physical injuries that cause her pain. She does not like the side effects of medication, and manages her health through diet and exercise. She knows that healthcare staff might doubt her decision-making capacity when she is depressed. So she makes an advance decision to refuse all medication for her physical pain and depression.
>
> A year later, she gets major depression and is detained under the MHA. Her GP (family doctor) tells her responsible medical officer (RMO) at the hospital about her advance decision. But Miss Khan's condition gets so bad that she will not discuss treatment. So the RMO decides to prescribe medication for her depression, despite her advance decision. This is possible because Miss Khan is detained under the MHA.
>
> The RMO also believes that Miss Khan now lacks capacity to consent to medication for her physical pain. He assesses the validity of the advance decision to refuse medication for the physical pain. Her GP says that Miss Khan seemed perfectly well when she made the

decision and seemed to understand what it meant. In the GP's view, Miss Khan had the capacity to make the advance decision. The RMO decides that the advance decision is valid and applicable, and does not prescribe medication for Miss Khan's pain – even though he thinks it would be in her best interests. When Miss Khan's condition improves, the consultant will be able to discuss whether she would like to change her mind about treatment for her physical pain.

Does the MHA affect the duties of attorneys and deputies?

13.38 In general, the MHA does not affect the powers of attorneys and deputies. But there are two exceptions:
- they will not be able to give consent on a patient's behalf for treatment under Part 4 of the MHA, where the patient is liable to be detained under the MHA (see 13.28–13.34 above), and
- they will not be able to take decisions:
  - about where a person subject to guardianship should live, or
  - that conflict with decisions that a guardian has a legal right to make.

13.39 Being subject to the MHA does not stop patients creating new Lasting Powers of Attorney (if they have the capacity to do so). Nor does it stop the Court of Protection from appointing a deputy for them.

13.40 In certain cases, people subject to the MHA may be required to meet specific conditions relating to:
- leave of absence from hospital
- after-care under supervision, or
- conditional discharge.

Conditions vary from case to case, but could include a requirement to:
- live in a particular place
- maintain contact with health services, or
- avoid a particular area.

13.41 If an attorney or deputy takes a decision that goes against one of these conditions, the patient will be taken to have gone against the condition. The MHA sets out the actions that could be taken in such circumstances. In the case of leave of absence or conditional discharge, this might involve the patient being recalled to hospital.

13.42 Attorneys and deputies are able to exercise patients' rights under the MHA on their behalf, if they have the relevant authority. In particular, some personal welfare attorneys and deputies may be able to apply to the Mental Health Review Tribunal (MHRT) for the patient's discharge from detention, guardianship or after-care under supervision.

13.43 The MHA also gives various rights to a patient's nearest relative. These include the right to:

- insist that a local authority social services department instructs an approved social worker to consider whether the patient should be made subject to the MHA
- apply for the patient to be admitted to hospital or guardianship
- object to an application for admission for treatment
- order the patient's discharge from hospital (subject to certain conditions) and
- order the patient's discharge from guardianship.

13.44 Attorneys and deputies may not exercise these rights, unless they are themselves the nearest relative. If the nearest relative and an attorney or deputy disagree, it may be helpful for them to discuss the issue, perhaps with the assistance of the patient's clinicians or social worker. But ultimately they have different roles and both must act as they think best. An attorney or deputy must act in the patient's best interests.

13.45 It is good practice for clinicians and others involved in the assessment or treatment of patients under the MHA to try to find out if the person has an attorney or deputy. But this may not always be possible. So attorneys and deputies should contact either:

- the healthcare professional responsible for the patient's treatment (generally known as the patient's RMO)
- the managers of the hospital where the patient is detained
- the person's guardian (normally the local authority social services department), or
- the person's supervisor (if the patient is subject to after-care under supervision).

Hospitals that treat detained patients normally have a Mental Health Act Administrator's office, which may be a useful first point of contact.

Does the MHA affect when Independent Mental Capacity Advocates must be instructed?

13.46 As explained in chapter 10, there is no duty to instruct an Independent Mental Capacity Advocate (IMCA) for decisions about serious medical treatment which is to be given under Part 4 of the MHA. Nor is there a duty to do so in respect of a move into accommodation, or a change of accommodation, if the person in question is to be required to live in it because of an obligation under the MHA. That obligation might be a condition of leave of absence or conditional discharge from hospital or a requirement imposed by a guardian or a supervisor.

13.47 However, the rules for instructing an IMCA for patients subject to the MHA who might undergo serious medical treatment not related to their mental disorder are the same as for any other patient.

13.48 The duty to instruct an IMCA would also apply as normal if accommodation is being planned as part of the after-care under section 117 of the MHA following the person's discharge from detention (and the person is not going to be required to live in it as

PART VI

a condition of after-care under supervision). This is because the person does not have to accept that accommodation.

What is the effect of section 57 of the Mental Health Act on the MCA?

13.49 Section 57 of the MHA states that psychosurgery (neurosurgery for mental disorder) requires:
- the consent of the patient, and
- the approval of an independent doctor and two other people appointed by the Mental Health Act Commission.

Psychosurgery is any surgical operation that destroys brain tissue or the function of brain tissue.

13.50 The same rules apply to other treatments specified in regulations under section 57. Currently, the only treatment included in regulations is the surgical implantation of hormones to reduce a man's sex drive.

13.51 The combined effect of section 57 of the MHA and section 28 of the MCA is, effectively, that a person who lacks the capacity to consent to one of these treatments for mental disorder may never be given it. Healthcare staff cannot use the MCA as an alternative way of giving these kinds of treatment. Nor can an attorney or deputy give permission for them on a person's behalf.

What changes does the Government plan to make to the MHA and the MCA?

13.52 The Government has introduced a Mental Health Bill into Parliament in order to modernise the MHA. Among the changes it proposes to make are:
- some amendments to the criteria for detention, including a new requirement that appropriate medical treatment be available for patients before they can be detained for treatment
- the introduction of supervised treatment in the community for suitable patients following a period of detention and treatment in hospital. This will help make sure that patients get the treatment they need and help stop them relapsing and returning to hospital
- the replacement of the approved social worker with the approved mental health professional. This will open up the possibility of approved mental healthcare professionals being drawn from other disciplines as well as social work. Other changes will open up the possibility of clinicians who are not doctors being approved to take on the role of the responsible medical officer. This role will be renamed the responsible clinician.
- provisions to make it possible for patients to apply to the county court for an unsuitable nearest relative to be replaced, and

- the abolition of after-care under supervision.

13.53 The Bill will also amend the MCA to introduce new procedures and provisions to make relevant decisions but who need to be deprived of their liberty, in their best interests, otherwise than under the Mental Health Act 1983 (the so-called 'Bournewood provisions').[58]

13.54 This chapter, as well as chapter 6, will be fully revised in due course to reflect those changes. Information about the Government's current proposals in respect of the Bournewood safeguards is available on the Department of Health website. This information includes draft illustrative Code of Practice guidance about the proposed safeguards.[59]

13.55 In the meantime, people taking decisions under both the MCA and the MHA must base those decisions on the Acts as they stand now.

14 WHAT MEANS OF PROTECTION EXIST FOR PEOPLE WHO LACK CAPACITY TO MAKE DECISIONS FOR THEMSELVES?

This chapter describes the different agencies that exist to help make sure that adults who lack capacity to make decisions for themselves are protected from abuse. It also explains the services those agencies provide and how they supervise people who provide care for or make decisions on behalf of people who lack capacity. Finally, it explains what somebody should do if they suspect that somebody is abusing a vulnerable adult who lacks capacity.

PART VI

> In this chapter, as throughout the Code, a person's capacity (or lack of capacity) refers specifically to their capacity to make a particular decision at the time it needs to be made.

Quick summary

- Always report suspicions of abuse of a person who lacks capacity to the relevant agency.

Concerns about an appointee

- When someone is concerned about the collection or use of social security benefits by an appointee on behalf a person who lacks capacity, they should contact the local Jobcentre Plus. If the appointee is for someone who is over the age of 60, contact The Pension Service.

---

[58] This refers to the European Court of Human Rights judgment (5 October 2004) in the case of *HL v The United Kingdom* (Application no, 45508/99).

[59] See www.dh.gov.uk/PublicationsAndStatistics/Publications/PublicationsPolicy AndGuidance/PublicationsPolicyAndGuidanceArticle/fs/en?CONTENT_ID= 4141656&chk=jlw07L

Concerns about an attorney or deputy

- If someone is concerned about the actions of an attorney or deputy, they should contact the Office of the Public Guardian.

Concerns about a possible criminal offence

- If there is a good reason to suspect that someone has committed a crime against a vulnerable person, such as theft or physical or sexual assault, contact the police.
- In addition, social services should also be contacted, so that they can support the vulnerable person during the investigation.

Concerns about possible ill-treatment or wilful neglect

- The Act introduces new criminal offences of ill treatment or wilful neglect of a person who lacks capacity to make relevant decisions (section 44).
- If someone is not being looked after properly, contact social services.
- In serious cases, contact the police.

Concerns about care standards

- In cases of concern about the standard of care in a care home or an adult placement scheme, or about the care provided by a home care worker, contact social services.
- It may also be appropriate to contact the Commission for Social Care Inspection (in England) or the Care and Social Services Inspectorate for Wales.

Concerns about healthcare or treatment

- If someone is concerned about the care or treatment given to the person in any NHS setting (such as an NHS hospital or clinic) contact the managers of the service.
- It may also be appropriate to make a formal complaint through the NHS complaints procedure (see chapter 15).

What is abuse?

14.1 The word 'abuse' covers a wide range of actions. In some cases, abuse is clearly deliberate and intentionally unkind. But sometimes abuse happens because somebody does not know how to act correctly – or they haven't got appropriate help and support. It is important to prevent abuse, wherever possible. If somebody is abused, it is important to investigate the abuse and take steps to stop it happening.

14.2 Abuse is anything that goes against a person's human and civil rights. This includes sexual, physical, verbal, financial and emotional abuse. Abuse can be:

- a single act
- a series of repeated acts

- a failure to provide necessary care, or
- neglect.

Abuse can take place anywhere (for example, in a person's own home, a care home or a hospital).

14.3 The main types of abuse are:

Type of abuse	Examples
Financial	<ul><li>theft</li><li>fraud</li><li>undue pressure</li><li>misuse of property, possessions or benefits</li><li>dishonest gain of property, possessions or benefits.</li></ul>
Physical	<ul><li>slapping, pushing, kicking or other forms of violence</li><li>misuse of medication (for example, increasing dosage to make someone drowsy)</li><li>inappropriate punishments (for example, not giving someone a meal because they have been 'bad').</li></ul>
Sexual	<ul><li>rape</li><li>sexual assault</li><li>sexual acts without consent (this includes if a person is not able to give consent or the abuser used pressure).</li></ul>
Psychologi-cal	<ul><li>emotional abuse</li><li>threats of harm, restraint or abandonment</li><li>refusing contact with other people</li><li>intimidation</li><li>threats to restrict someone's liberty.</li></ul>
Neglect and acts of omission	<ul><li>ignoring the person's medical or physical care needs</li><li>failing to get healthcare or social care</li><li>withholding medication, food or heating.</li></ul>

14.4 The Department of Health and the National Assembly for Wales have produced separate guidance on protecting vulnerable adults from abuse. *No secrets*[60] (England) and *In safe hands*[61] (Wales) both define vulnerable adults as people aged 18 and over who:

PART VI

---

[60] Department of Health and Home Office, *No secrets: Guidance on developing and implementing multi-agency policies and procedures to protect vulnerable adults from abuse*, (2000) www.dh.gov.uk/assetRoot/04/07/45/40/04074540.pdf

[61] National Assembly for Wales, *In safe hands: Implementing adult protection procedures in Wales* (2000), http://new.wales.gov.uk.about.departments/dhss/publications/social_services_publications/reports/insafehands?lang=en

- need community care services due to a mental disability, other disability, age or illness, and
- may be unable to take care of themselves or protect themselves against serious harm or exploitation.

This description applies to many people who lack capacity to make decisions for themselves.

14.5 Anyone who thinks that someone might be abusing a vulnerable adult who lacks capacity should:

- contact the local social services (see paragraphs 14.27–14.28 below)
- contact the Office of the Public Guardian (see paragraph 14.8 below), or
- seek advice from a relevant telephone helpline[62] or through the Community Legal Service.[63]

Full contact details are provided in Annex A.

14.6 In most cases, local adult protection procedures will say who should take action (see paragraphs 14.28–14.29 below). But some abuse will be a criminal offence, such as physical assault, sexual assault or rape, theft, fraud and some other forms of financial exploitation. In these cases, the person who suspects abuse should contact the police urgently. The criminal investigation may take priority over all other forms of investigation. So all agencies will have to work together to plan the best way to investigate possible abuse.

14.7 The Fraud Act 2006 (due to come into force in 2007) creates a new offence of 'fraud by abuse of position'. This new offence may apply to a range of people, including:

- attorneys under a Lasting Power of Attorney (LPA) or an Enduring Power of Attorney (EPA), or
- deputies appointed by the Court of Protection to make financial decisions on behalf of a person who lacks capacity.

Attorneys and deputies may be guilty of fraud if they dishonestly abuse their position, intend to benefit themselves or others, and cause loss or expose a person to the risk of loss. People who suspect fraud should report the case to the police.

How does the Act protect people from abuse?

The Office of the Public Guardian

14.8 Section 57 of the Act creates a new Public Guardian, supported by staff of the Office of the Public Guardian (OPG). The Public Guardian helps protect people who lack capacity by:

- setting up and managing a register of LPAs
- setting up and managing a register of EPAs

---

[62]   For example, the Action on Elder Abuse (0808 808 8141), Age Concern (0800 009966) or CarersLine (0808 808 7777).

[63]   Community Legal Service Direct www.clsdirect.org.uk

- setting up and managing a register of court orders that appoint deputies
- supervising deputies, working with other relevant organisations (for example, social services, if the person who lacks capacity is receiving social care)
- sending Court of Protection Visitors to visit people who may lack capacity to make particular decisions and those who have formal powers to act on their behalf (see paragraphs 14.10–14.11 below)
- receiving reports from attorneys acting under LPAs and from deputies
- providing reports to the Court of Protection, as requested, and
- dealing with representations (including complaints) about the way in which attorneys or deputies carry out their duties.

14.9 Section 59 of the Act creates a Public Guardian Board to oversee and review how the Public Guardian carries out these duties.

Court of Protection Visitors

14.10 The role of a Court of Protection Visitor is to provide independent advice to the court and the Public Guardian. They advise on how anyone given power under the Act should be, and is, carrying out their duties and responsibilities. There are two types of visitor: General Visitors and Special Visitors. Special visitors are registered medical practitioners with relevant expertise. The court or Public Guardian can send whichever type of visitor is most appropriate to visit and interview a person who may lack capacity. Visitors can also interview attorneys or deputies and inspect any relevant healthcare or social care records. Attorneys and deputies must co-operate with the visitors and provide them with all relevant information. If attorneys or deputies do not co-operate, the court can cancel their appointment, where it thinks that they have not acted in the person's best interests.

PART VI

Scenario: Using a General Visitor

Mrs Quinn made an LPA appointing her nephew, Ian, as her financial attorney. She recently lost capacity to make her own financial decisions, and Ian has registered the LPA. He has taken control of Mrs Quinn's financial affairs.

But Mrs Quinn's niece suspects that Ian is using Mrs Quinn's money to pay off his own debts. She contacts the OPG, which sends a General Visitor to visit Mrs Quinn and Ian. The visitor's report will assess the facts. It might suggest the case go to court to consider whether Ian has behaved in a way which:

- goes against his authority under the LPA, or
- is not in Mrs Quinn's best interests.

> The Public Guardian will decide whether the court should be involved
> in the matter. The court will then decide if it requires further evidence.
> If it thinks that Ian is abusing his position, the court may cancel the
> LPA.

14.11 Court of Protection Visitors have an important part to play in
investigating possible abuse. But their role is much wider than this.
They can also check on the general wellbeing of the person who
lacks capacity, and they can give support to attorneys and deputies
who need help to carry out their duties.

How does the Public Guardian oversee LPAs?

14.12 An LPA is a private arrangement between the donor and the
attorney (see chapter 7). Donors should only choose attorneys that
they can trust. The OPG provides information to help potential
donors understand:
- the impact of making an LPA
- what they can give an attorney authority to do
- what to consider when choosing an attorney.

14.13 The Public Guardian must make sure that an LPA meets the Act's
requirements. Before registering an LPA, the OPG will check
documentation. For property and affairs LPAs, it will check whether
an attorney appointed under the LPA is bankrupt since this would
revoke the authority.

14.14 The Public Guardian will not usually get involved once
somebody has registered an LPA – unless someone is worried about
how an attorney is carrying out their duties. If concerns are raised
about an attorney, the OPG works closely with organisations such as
local authorities and NHS Trusts to carry out investigations.

How does the Public Guardian supervise deputies?

14.15 Individuals do not choose who will act as a deputy for them. The
court will make the decision. There are measures to make sure that
the court appoints an appropriate deputy. The OPG will then
supervise deputies and support them in carrying out their duties,
while also making sure they do not abuse their position.

14.16 When a case comes before the Court of Protection, the Act states
that the court should make a decision to settle the matter rather than
appoint a deputy, if possible. Deputies are most likely to be needed
for financial matters where someone needs continued authority to
make decisions about the person's money or other assets. It will be
easier for the courts to make decisions in cases where a one-off
decision is needed about a person's welfare, so there are likely to be
fewer personal welfare deputies. But there will be occasions where

ongoing decisions about a person's welfare will be required, and so the court will appoint a personal welfare deputy (see chapter 8).

Scenario: Appointing deputies

Peter was in a motorbike accident that left him permanently and seriously brain-damaged. He has minimal awareness of his surroundings and an assessment has shown that he lacks capacity to make most decisions for himself.

Somebody needs to make several decisions about what treatment Peter needs and where he should be treated. His parents feel that healthcare staff do not always consider their views in decisions about what treatment is in Peter's best interests. So they make an application to the court to be appointed as joint personal welfare deputies.

There will be many care or treatment decisions for Peter in the future. The court decides it would not be practical to make a separate decision on each of them. It also thinks Peter needs some continuity in decision-making. So it appoints Peter's parents as joint personal welfare deputies.

14.17 The OPG may run checks on potential deputies if requested to by the court. It will carry out a risk assessment to determine what kind of supervision a deputy will need once they are appointed.

14.18 Deputies are accountable to the court. The OPG supervises the deputy's actions on the court's behalf, and the court may want the deputy to provide financial accounts or other reports to the OPG. The Public Guardian deals with complaints about the way deputies carry out their duties. It works with other relevant agencies to investigate them. Chapter 8 gives detailed information about the responsibilities of deputies.

What happens if someone says they are worried about an attorney or deputy?

14.19 Many people who lack capacity are likely to get care or support from a range of agencies. Even when an attorney or deputy is acting on behalf of a person who lacks capacity, the other carers still have a responsibility to the person to provide care and act in the person's best interests. Anybody who is caring for a person who lacks capacity, whether in a paid or unpaid role, who is worried about how attorneys or deputies carry out their duties should contact the Public Guardian.

14.20 The OPG will not always be the most appropriate organisation to investigate all complaints. It may investigate a case jointly with:
- healthcare or social care professionals

- social services
- NHS bodies
- the Commission for Social Care Inspection in England or the Care and Social Services Inspectorate for Wales (CSSIW)[64]
- the Healthcare Commission in England or the Healthcare Inspectorate for Wales, and
- in some cases, the police.

14.21 The OPG will usually refer concerns about personal welfare LPAs or personal welfare deputies to the relevant agency. In certain circumstances it will alert the police about a case. When it makes a referral, the OPG will make sure that the relevant agency keeps it informed of the action it takes. It will also make sure that the court has all the information it needs to take possible action against the attorney or deputy.

14.22 Examples of situations in which a referral might be necessary include where:

- someone has complained that a welfare attorney is physically abusing a donor – the OPG would refer this case to the relevant local authority adult protection procedures and possibly the police
- the OPG has found that a solicitor appointed as a financial deputy for an elderly woman has defrauded her estate – the OPG would refer this case to the police and the Law Society Consumer Complaints Service.

How does the Act deal with ill treatment and wilful neglect?

14.23 The Act introduces two new criminal offences: ill treatment and wilful neglect of a person who lacks capacity to make relevant decisions (section 44). The offences may apply to:

- anyone caring for a person who lacks capacity – this includes family carers, healthcare and social care staff in hospital or care homes and those providing care in a person's home
- an attorney appointed under an LPA or an EPA, or
- a deputy appointed for the person by the court.

14.24 These people may be guilty of an offence if they ill-treat or wilfully neglect the person they care for or represent. Penalties will range from a fine to a sentence of imprisonment of up to five years – or both.

14.25 Ill treatment and neglect are separate offences.[65] For a person to be found guilty of ill treatment, they must either:

- have deliberately ill-treated the person, or
- be reckless in the way they were ill-treating the person or not.

---

[64] In April 2007, the Care Standards Inspectorate for Wales (CSIW) and the Social Services Inspectorate for Wales (SSIW) came together to form the Care and Social Services Inspectorate for Wales.

[65] *R v Newington* (1990) 91 Cr App R 247, CA.

It does not matter whether the behaviour was likely to cause, or actually caused, harm or damage to the victim's health.

14.26 The meaning of 'wilful neglect' varies depending on the circumstances. But it usually means that a person has deliberately failed to carry out an act they knew they had a duty to do.

Scenario: Reporting abuse

Norma is 95 and has Alzheimer's disease. Her son, Brendan, is her personal welfare attorney under an LPA. A district nurse has noticed that Norma has bruises and other injuries. She suspects Brendan may be assaulting his mother when he is drunk. She alerts the police and the local Adult Protection Committee.

Following a criminal investigation, Brendan is charged with ill-treating his mother. The Public Guardian applies to the court to cancel the LPA. Social services start to make alternative arrangements for Norma's care.

What other measures protect people from abuse?

14.27 Local agencies have procedures that allow them to work together (called multi-agency working) to protect vulnerable adults – in care settings and elsewhere. Most areas have Adult Protection Committees. These committees:

- create policy (including reporting procedures)
- oversee investigations and other activity between agencies
- carry out joint training, and
- monitor and review progress.

Other local authorities have developed multi-agency Adult Protection Procedures, which are managed by a dedicated Adult Protection Co-ordinator.

14.28 Adult Protection Committees and Procedures (APCP) involve representatives from the NHS, social services, housing, the police and other relevant agencies. In England, they are essential points of contact for anyone who suspects abuse or ill treatment of a vulnerable adult. They can also give advice to the OPG if it is uncertain whether an intervention is necessary in a case of suspected abuse. In Wales, APCPs are not necessarily points of contact themselves, but they publish details of points of contact.

Who should check that staff are safe to work with vulnerable adults?

14.29 Under the Safeguarding Vulnerable Groups Act 2006, criminal record checks are now compulsory for staff who:

- have contact with service users in registered care homes
- provide personal care services in someone's home, and

PART VI

- are involved in providing adult placement schemes.

14.30 Potential employers must carry out a pre-employment criminal record check with the Criminal Records Bureau (CRB) for all potential new healthcare and social care staff. This includes nursing agency staff and home care agency staff.

See Annex A for sources of more detailed information.

14.31 The Protection of Vulnerable Adults (POVA) list has the names of people who have been barred from working with vulnerable adults (in England and Wales). Employers providing care in a residential setting or a person's own home must check whether potential employees are on the list.[66] If they are on the list, they must:

- refuse to employ them, or
- employ them in a position that does not give them regular contact with vulnerable adults.

It is an offence for anyone on the list to apply for a care position. In such cases, the employer should report the person making the application.

Who is responsible for monitoring the standard of care providers?

14.32 All care providers covered by the Care Standards Act 2000 must register with the Commission for Social Care Inspection in England (CSCI) or the Care and Social Services Inspectorate for Wales (CSSIW).[67] These agencies make sure that care providers meet certain standards. They require care providers to have procedures to protect people from harm or abuse. These agencies can take action if they discover dangerous or unsafe practices that could place people at risk.

14.33 Care providers must also have effective complaints procedures. If providers cannot settle complaints, CSCI or CSSIW can look into them.

14.34 CSCI or CSSIW assesses the effectiveness of local adult protection procedures. They will also monitor the arrangements local councils make in response to the Care Standards Act.

What is an appointee, and who monitors them?

14.35 The Department for Work and Pensions (DWP) can appoint someone (an appointee) to claim and spend benefits on a person's behalf[68] if that person:

- gets social security benefits or pensions
- lacks the capacity to act for themselves
- has not made a property and affairs LPA or an EPA, and

---

[66] www.dh.gov.uk/PublicationsAndStatistics/Publications/PublicationsPolicyAndGuidance/PublicationsPolicyAndGuidanceArticle/fs/en?CONTENT_ID=4085855&chk=p0kQeS
[67] See note 64 above regarding the merger of the Care Standards Inspectorate for Wales and the Social Services Inspectorate for Wales.
[68] www.dwp.gov.uk/publications/dwp/2005/gl21_apr.pdf

- the court has not appointed a property and affairs deputy.

14.36 The DWP checks that an appointee is trustworthy. It also investigates any allegations that an appointee is not acting appropriately or in the person's interests. It can remove an appointee who abuses their position. Concerns about appointees should be raised with the relevant DWP agency (the local Jobcentre Plus, or if the person is aged 60 or over, The Pension Service).

Are there any other means of protection that people should be aware of?

14.37 There are a number of additional means that exist to protect people who lack capacity to make decisions for themselves. Healthcare and social care staff, attorneys and deputies should be aware of:

- National Minimum Standards (for example, for healthcare, care homes, and home care agencies) which apply to both England and Wales (see paragraph 14.38)
- National Service Frameworks, which set out national standards for specific health and care services for particular groups (for example, for mental health services[69] or services for older people[70])
- complaints procedures for all NHS bodies and local councils (see chapter 15)
- Stop Now Orders (also known as Enforcement Orders) that allow consumer protection bodies to apply for court orders to stop poor trading practices (for example, unfair door-step selling or rogue traders).[71]
- The Public Interest Disclosure Act 1998, which encourages people to report malpractice in the workplace and protects people who report malpractice from being sacked or victimised.

14.38 Information about all national minimum standards are available on the CSCI[72] and Healthcare Commission websites[73] and the Welsh Assembly Government website. Chapter 15 gives guidance on complaints procedures. Individual local authorities will have their own complaints system in place.

[69] www.dh.gov.uk/assetRoot/04/07/72/09/04077209.pdf and www.wales.nhs.uk/sites3/page.cfm?orgid=438&pid=11071
[70] www.dh.gov.uk/assetRoot/04/07/12/83/04071283.pdf and www.wales.nhs.uk/sites3/home.cfm?orgid=439&redirect=yes&CFID=298511&CFTOKEN=6985382
[71] www.oft.gov.uk/Business/Legal/Stop+Now+Regulations.htm
[72] www.csci.org.uk/information_for_service_providers/national_minimum_standards/default.htm
[73] www.healthcarecommission.org.uk/_db/_documents/The_annual_health_check_in_2006_2007_assessing_and_rating_the_NHS_200609225143.pdf

PART VI

15   WHAT ARE THE BEST WAYS TO SETTLE DISAGREEMENTS AND DISPUTES ABOUT ISSUES COVERED IN THE ACT?

Sometimes people will disagree about:

- a person's capacity to make a decision
- their best interests
- a decision someone is making on their behalf, or
- an action someone is taking on their behalf.

It is in everybody's interests to settle disagreements and disputes quickly and effectively, with minimal stress and cost. This chapter sets out the different options available for settling disagreements. It also suggests ways to avoid letting a disagreement become a serious dispute. Finally, it sets out when it might be necessary to apply to the Court of Protection and when somebody can get legal funding.

> In this chapter, as throughout the Code, a person's capacity (or lack of capacity) refers specifically to their capacity to make a particular decision at the time it needs to be made.

Quick summary

- When disagreements occur about issues that are covered in the Act, it is usually best to try and settle them before they become serious.
- Advocates can help someone who finds it difficult to communicate their point of view. (This may be someone who has been assessed as lacking capacity.)
- Some disagreements can be effectively resolved by mediation.
- Where there is a concern about healthcare or social care provided to a person who lacks capacity, there are formal and informal ways of complaining about the care or treatment.
- The Health Service Ombudsman or the Local Government Ombudsman (in England) or the Public Services Ombudsman (in Wales) can be asked to investigate some problems that have not been resolved through formal complaints procedures.
- Disputes about the finances of a person who lacks capacity should usually be referred to the Office of the Public Guardian (OPG).
- When other methods of resolving disagreements are not appropriate, the matter can be referred to the Court of Protection.
- There are some decisions that are so serious that the Court of Protection should always make them.

What options are there for settling disagreements?

15.1 Disagreements about healthcare, social or other welfare services may be between:

- people who have assessed a person as lacking capacity to make a decision and the person they have assessed (see chapter 4 for how to challenge an assessment of lack of capacity)
- family members or other people concerned with the care and welfare of a person who lacks capacity
- family members and healthcare or social care staff involved in providing care or treatment
- healthcare and social care staff who have different views about what is in the best interests of a person who lacks capacity.

15.2 In general, disagreements can be resolved by either formal or informal procedures, and there is more information on both in this chapter. However, there are some disagreements and some subjects that are so serious they can only be resolved by the Court of Protection.

15.3 It is usually best to try and settle disagreements before they become serious disputes. Many people settle them by communicating effectively and taking the time to listen and to address worries. Disagreements between family members are often best settled informally, or sometimes through mediation. When professionals are in disagreement with a person's family, it is a good idea to start by:

- setting out the different options in a way that is easy to understand
- inviting a colleague to talk to the family and offer a second opinion
- offering to get independent expert advice
- using an advocate to support and represent the person who lacks capacity
- arranging a case conference or meeting to discuss matters in detail
- listening to, acknowledging and addressing worries, and
- where the situation is not urgent, allowing the family time to think it over.

Further guidance on how to deal with problems without going to court may also be found in the Community Legal Services Information Leaflet 'Alternatives to Court'.[74]

When is an advocate useful?

15.4 An advocate helps communicate the feelings and views of someone who has communication difficulties. The definition of advocacy set out in the Advocacy Charter adopted by most advocacy schemes is as follows: 'Advocacy is taking action to help people say what they want, secure their rights, represent their interests and obtain services they need. Advocates and advocacy

---

[74]   CLS (Community Legal Services) Direct Information Leaflet Number 23, www.clsdirect.org.uk/legalhelp/leaflet23.jsp?lang=en

schemes work in partnership with the people they support and take their side. Advocacy promotes social inclusion, equality and social justice.'[75]

An advocate may be able to help settle a disagreement simply by presenting a person's feelings to their family, carers or professionals. Most advocacy services are provided by the voluntary sector and are arranged at a local level. They have no link to any agency involved with the person.

15.5 Using advocates can help people who find it difficult to communicate (including those who have been assessed as lacking capacity) to:

- say what they want
- claim their rights
- represent their interests, and
- get the services they need.

15.6 Advocates may also be involved in supporting the person during mediation (see paragraphs 15.7–15.13 below) or helping with complaints procedures. Sometimes people who lack capacity or have been assessed as lacking capacity have a legal right to an advocate, for example:

- when making a formal complaint against the NHS (see paragraph 15.18), and
- where the Act requires the involvement of an Independent Mental Capacity Advocate (IMCA) (see chapter 10).

When is mediation useful?

15.7 A mediator helps people to come to an agreement that is acceptable to all parties. Mediation can help solve a problem at an early stage. It offers a wider range of solutions than the court can – and it may be less stressful for all parties, more cost-effective and quicker. People who come to an agreement through mediation are more likely to keep to it, because they have taken part in decision-making.

15.8 Mediators are independent. They have no personal interest in the outcome of a case. They do not make decisions or impose solutions. The mediator will decide whether the case is suitable for mediation. They will consider the likely chances of success and the need to protect the interests of the person who lacks capacity.

15.9 Any case that can be settled through negotiation is likely to benefit from mediation. It is most suitable when people are not communicating well or not understanding each other's point of view. It can improve relationships and stop future disputes, so it is a good option when it is in the person's interests for people to have a good relationship in the future.

---

[75]   Advocacy across London, *Advocacy Charter* (2002)

Scenario: Using mediation

Mrs Roberts has dementia and lacks capacity to decide where she should live. She currently lives with her son. But her daughter has found a care home where she thinks her mother will get better care. Her brother disagrees.

Mrs Roberts is upset by this family dispute, and so her son and daughter decide to try mediation. The mediator believes that Mrs Roberts is able to communicate her feelings and agrees to take on the case. During the sessions, the mediator helps them to focus on their mother's best interests rather than imposing their own views. In the end, everybody agrees that Mrs Roberts should continue to live with her son. But they agree to review the situation again in six months to see if the care home might then be better for her.

15.10 In mediation, everybody needs to take part as equally as possible so that a mediator can help everyone involved to focus on the person's best interests. It might also be appropriate to involve an advocate to help communicate the wishes of the person who lacks capacity.

15.11 The National Mediation Helpline[76] helps callers to identify an effective means of resolving their difficulty without going to court. It will arrange an appointment with a trained and accredited mediator. The Family Mediation Helpline[77] can provide information on family mediation and referrals to local family mediation services. Family mediators are trained to deal with the emotional, practical and financial needs of those going through relationship breakdown.

15.12 Healthcare and social care staff may also take part in mediation processes. But it may be more appropriate to follow the relevant healthcare or social care complaints procedures (see paragraphs 15.14–15.32).

15.13 In certain situations (mainly family mediation), legal aid may be available to fund mediation for people who meet the qualifying criteria (see paragraphs 15.38–15.44).

How can someone complain about healthcare?

15.14 There are formal and informal ways of complaining about a patient's healthcare or treatment. Healthcare staff and others need to know which methods are suitable in which situations.

15.15 In England, the Patient Advice and Liaison Service (PALS) provides an informal way of dealing with problems before they

---

[76] National Mediation Helpline, Tel: 0845 60 30 809, www.nationalmediationhelpline.com
[77] Family Mediation Helpline, Tel: 0845 60 26 627, www.familymediationhelpline.co.uk

reach the complaints stage. PALS operate in every NHS and Primary Care Trust in England. They provide advice and information to patients (or their relatives or carers) to try to solve problems quickly. They can direct people to specialist support services (for example, advocates, mental health support teams, social services or interpreting services). PALS do not investigate complaints. Their role is to explain complaints procedures and direct people to the formal NHS complaints process, if necessary. NHS complaints procedures deal with complaints about something that happened in the past that requires an apology or explanation. A court cannot help in this situation, but court proceedings may be necessary in some clinical negligence cases (see paragraph 15.22).

15.16 In Wales, complaints advocates based at Community Health Councils provide advice and support to anyone with concerns about treatment they have had.

Disagreements about proposed treatments

15.17 If a case is not urgent, the supportive atmosphere of the PALS may help settle it. In Wales, the local Community Health Council may be able to help. But urgent cases about proposed serious treatment may need to go to the Court of Protection (see paragraphs 15.35–15.36).

Scenario: Disagreeing about treatment or an assessment

Mrs Thompson has Alzheimer's and does not want a flu jab. Her daughter thinks she should have the injection. The doctor does not want to go against the wishes of his patient, because he believes she has capacity to refuse treatment.

Mrs Thompson's daughter goes to PALS. A member of staff gives her information and advice about what is meant by capacity to consent to or refuse treatment, and tells her how to find out about the flu jab. The PALS staff speak to the doctor, and then they explain his clinical assessment to Mrs Thompson's daughter.

The daughter is still unhappy. PALS staff advise her that the Independent Complaints Advocacy Service can help if she wishes to make a formal complaint.

The formal NHS complaints procedure

15.18 The formal NHS complaints procedure deals with complaints about NHS services provided by NHS organisations or primary care practitioners. As a first step, people should try to settle a disagreement through an informal discussion between:
- the healthcare staff involved

- the person who may lack capacity to make the decision in question (with support if necessary)
- their carers, and
- any appropriate relatives.

If the person who is complaining is not satisfied, the Independent Complaints Advocacy Service (ICAS) may help. In Wales, the complaints advocates based at Community Health Councils will support and advise anyone who wants to make a complaint.

15.19 In England, if the person is still unhappy after a local investigation, they can ask for an independent review by the Healthcare Commission. If the patient involved in the complaint was or is detained under the Mental Health Act 1983, the Mental Health Act Commission can be asked to look into the complaint. If people are still unhappy after this stage, they can go to the Health Service Ombudsman. More information on how to make a complaint in England is available from the Department of Health.

15.20 In Wales, if patients are still unhappy after a local investigation, they can ask for an independent review of their complaint by independent lay reviewers. After this, they can take their case to the Public Services Ombudsman for Wales. People can take their complaint direct to the Ombudsman if:

- the complaint is about care or treatment that took place after 1 April 2006, and
- they have tried to settle the problem locally first.

The Mental Health Act Commission may also investigate complaints about the care or treatment of detained patients in Wales, if attempts have been made to settle the complaint locally without success.

15.21 Regulations about first trying to settle complaints locally do not apply to NHS Foundation Trusts. But these Trusts are covered by the independent review stage operated by the Healthcare Commission and by the Health Service Ombudsman. People who have a complaint about an NHS Foundation Trust should contact the Trust for advice on how to make a complaint.

Cases of clinical negligence

15.22 The NHS Litigation Authority oversees all clinical negligence cases brought against the NHS in England. It actively encourages people to try other forms of settling complaints before going to court. The National Assembly for Wales also encourages people to try other forms of settling complaints before going to court.

How can somebody complain about social care?

15.23 The social services complaints procedure has been reformed. The reformed procedure came into effect on 1 September 2006 in England and on 1 April 2006 in Wales.

PART VI

15.24 A service provider's own complaints procedure should deal with complaints about:
- the way in which care services are delivered
- the type of services provided, or
- a failure to provide services.

15.25 Care agencies contracted by local authorities or registered with the Commission for Social Care Inspection (CSCI) in England or Care and Social Services Inspectorate for Wales (CSSIW) are legally obliged to have their own written complaints procedures. This includes residential homes, agencies providing care in people's homes, nursing agencies and adult placement schemes. The procedures should set out how to make a complaint and what to do with a complaint that cannot be settled locally.

Local authority complaints procedures

15.26 For services contracted by a local authority, it may be more appropriate to use the local authority's complaints procedure. A simple example would be a situation where a local authority places a person in a care home and the person's family are not happy with the placement. If their complaint is not about the services the home provides (for example, it might be about the local authority's assessment of the person's needs), it might be more appropriate to use the local authority's complaints procedure.

15.27 As a first step, people should try to settle a disagreement through an informal discussion, involving:
- the professionals involved
- the person who may lack capacity to make the decision in question (with support if necessary)
- their carers, and
- any appropriate relatives.

15.28 If the person making the complaint is not satisfied, the local authority will carry out a formal investigation using its complaints procedure. In England, after this stage, a social service Complaints Review Panel can hear the case. In Wales complaints can be referred to the National Assembly for Wales for hearing by an independent panel.

Other complaints about social care

15.29 People can take their complaint to the CSCI in England or the CSSIW in Wales, if:
- the complaint is about regulations or national minimum standards not being met, and
- the complainants are not happy with the provider's own complaints procedure or the response to their complaint.

15.30 If a complaint is about a local authority's administration, it may be referred to the Commission for Local Administration in England (the Local Government Ombudsman) or the Public Services Ombudsman for Wales.

What if a complaint covers healthcare and social care?

15.31 Taking a complaint through NHS or local authority complaints procedures can be a complicated process – especially if the complaint covers a number of service providers or both healthcare and social care. In such situations, local authorities and the NHS must work together and agree which organisation will lead in handling the complaint. If a person is not happy with the outcome, they can take their case to the Health Service Ombudsman or to the Local Government Ombudsman (in England). There is guidance which sets out how organisations should work together to handle complaints that cover healthcare and social care (in England *Learning from Complaints* and in Wales *Listening and learning*). The Public Services Ombudsman for Wales handles complaints that cover both healthcare and social care.

Who can handle complaints about other welfare issues?

15.32 The Independent Housing Ombudsman deals with complaints about registered social landlords in England. This applies mostly to housing associations. But it also applies to many landlords who manage homes that were formerly run by local authorities and some private landlords. In Wales, the Public Services Ombudsman for Wales deals with complaints about registered social landlords. Complaints about local authorities may be referred to the Local Government Ombudsman in England or the Public Services Ombudsman for Wales. They look at complaints about decisions on council housing, social services, Housing Benefit and planning applications. More information about complaints to an Ombudsman is available on the relevant websites (see Annex A).

What is the best way to handle disagreement about a person's finances?

15.33 Some examples of disagreements about a person's finances are:
- disputes over the amount of money a person who lacks capacity should pay their carer
- disputes over whether a person who lacks capacity should sell their house
- somebody questioning the actions of a carer, who may be using the money of a person who lacks capacity inappropriately or without proper authority

PART VI

- somebody questioning the actions of an attorney appointed under a Lasting Power of Attorney or an Enduring Power of Attorney or a deputy appointed by the court.

15.34 In all of the above circumstances, the most appropriate action would usually be to contact the Office of the Public Guardian (OPG) for guidance and advice. See chapter 14 for further details on the role of the OPG.

How can the Court of Protection help?

15.35 The Court of Protection deals with all areas of decision-making for adults who lack capacity to make particular decisions for themselves (see chapter 8 for more information about its roles and responsibilities). But the court is not always the right place to settle problems involving people who lack capacity. Other forms of settling disagreements may be more appropriate and less distressing.

15.36 There are some decisions that are so serious that the court should always make them. There are also other types of cases that the court should deal with when another method would generally not be suitable. See chapter 8 for more information about both kinds of cases.

Right of Appeal

15.37 Section 53 of the Act describes the rights of appeal against any decision taken by the Court of Protection. There are further details in the Court of Protection Rules. It may be advisable for anyone who wishes to appeal a decision made by the court to seek legal advice.

Will public legal funding be available?

15.38 Depending on their financial situation, once the Act comes into force people may be entitled to:
- publicly funded legal advice from accredited solicitors or advice agencies
- legal representation before the new Court of Protection (in the most serious cases).

Information about solicitors and organisations who give advice on different areas of law is available from Community Legal Services Direct (CLS Direct).[78] Further information about legal aid and public funding can be obtained from the Legal Services Commission.[79] See Annex A for full contact details.

---

[78] CLS Direct, Tel: 0845 345 4 345, www.clsdirect.org.uk
[79] www.legalservices.gov.uk

15.39 People who lack capacity to instruct a solicitor or conduct their own case will need a litigation friend. This person could be a relative, friend, attorney or the Official Solicitor (when no-one else is available). The litigation friend is able to instruct the solicitor and conduct the case on behalf of a person who lacks capacity to give instructions. If the person qualifies for public legal funding, the litigation friend can claim funding on their behalf.

When can someone get legal help?

15.40 Legal help is a type of legal aid (public funding) that pays for advice and assistance on legal issues, including those affecting a person who lacks capacity. But it does not provide representation for a full court hearing, although there is a related form of funding called 'help at court' under which a legal representative can speak in court on a client's behalf on an informal basis. To qualify for legal help, applicants must show that:
- they get specific social security benefits, or they earn less than a specific amount and do not have savings or other financial assets in excess of a specific amount
- they would benefit sufficiently from legal advice to justify the amount it costs, and
- they cannot get another form of funding.

15.41 Legal help can include:
- help from a solicitor or other representative in writing letters
- in exceptional circumstances, getting a barrister's opinion, and
- assistance in preparing for Court of Protection hearings.

15.42 People cannot get legal help for making a Lasting Power of Attorney or an advance decision to refuse treatment. But they can get general help and information from the OPG. The OPG cannot give legal or specialist advice. For example, they will not be able to advise someone on what powers they should delegate to their attorney under an LPA.

When can someone get legal representation?

15.43 Public funding for legal representation in the Court of Protection will be available from solicitors with a relevant contract – but only for the most serious cases. To qualify, applicants will normally face the same test as for legal help to qualify financially (paragraph 15.40). They will generally have to satisfy more detailed criteria than applicants for legal help, relating, for instance, to their prospects of being successful, to whether legal representation is necessary and to the cost benefit of being represented. They will also have to establish that the case could not be brought or funded in another way and that there are not alternatives to court proceedings that should be explored first.

PART VI

15.44 Serious personal welfare cases that were previously heard by the High Court will continue to have public funding for legal representation when they are transferred to the Court of Protection. These cases will normally be related to personal liberty, serious welfare decisions or medical treatment for a person who lacks capacity. But legal representation may also be available in other types of cases, depending on the particular circumstances.

16   WHAT RULES GOVERN ACCESS TO INFORMATION ABOUT A PERSON WHO LACKS CAPACITY?

This chapter gives guidance on:

- what personal information about someone who lacks capacity people involved in their care have the right to see, and
- how they can get hold of that information.

This chapter is only a general guide. It does not give detailed information about the law. Nor does it replace professional guidance or the guidance of the Information Commissioner's Office on the Data Protection Act 1998 (this guidance is available on its website, see Annex A). Where necessary, people should take legal advice.

This chapter is mainly for people such as family carers and other carers, deputies and attorneys, who care for or represent someone who lacks capacity to make specific decisions and in particular, lacks capacity to allow information about them to be disclosed. Professionals have their own codes of conduct, and they may have the support of experts in their organisations.

In this chapter, as throughout the Code, a person's capacity (or lack of capacity) refers specifically to their capacity to make a particular decision at the time it needs to be made.

Quick summary

Questions to ask when requesting personal information about someone who may lack capacity

- Am I acting under a Lasting Power of Attorney or as a deputy with specific authority?
- Does the person have capacity to agree that information can be disclosed? Have they previously agreed to disclose the information?
- What information do I need?
- Why do I need it?
- Who has the information?
- Can I show that:
  - I need the information to make a decision that is in the best interests of the person I am acting for, and

- the person does not have the capacity to act for themselves?
- Do I need to share the information with anyone else to make a decision that is in the best interests of the person who lacks capacity?
- Should I keep a record of my decision or action?
- How long should I keep the information for?
- Do I have the right to request the information under section 7 of the Data Protection Act 1998?

Questions to ask when considering whether to disclose information

- Is the request covered by section 7 of the Data Protection Act 1998? Is the request being made by a formally authorised representative?

If not:
- Is the disclosure legal?
- Is the disclosure justified, having balanced the person's best interests and the public interest against the person's right to privacy?

Questions to ask to decide whether the disclosure is legal or justified

- Do I (or does my organisation) have the information?
- Am I satisfied that the person concerned lacks capacity to agree to disclosure?
- Does the person requesting the information have any formal authority to act on behalf of the person who lacks capacity?
- Am I satisfied that the person making the request:
  - is acting in the best interests of the person concerned?
  - needs the information to act properly?
  - will respect confidentiality?
  - will keep the information for no longer than necessary?
- Should I get written confirmation of these things?

What laws and regulations affect access to information?

16.1 People caring for, or managing the finances of, someone who lacks capacity may need information to:
- assess the person's capacity to make a specific decision
- determine the person's best interests, and
- make appropriate decisions on the person's behalf.

16.2 The information they need varies depending on the circumstances. For example:
- a daughter providing full-time care for an elderly parent will make decisions based on her own experience and knowledge of her parent
- a deputy may need information from other people. For instance, if they were deciding whether a person needs to move into a care home or whether they should sell the person's home, they might need information from family members, the

PART VI

family doctor, the person's bank and their solicitor to make
sure they are making the decision in the person's best interests.

16.3 Much of the information needed to make decisions under the Act is
sensitive or confidential. It is regulated by:

- the Data Protection Act 1998
- the common law duty of confidentiality
- professional codes of conduct on confidentiality, and
- the Human Rights Act 1998 and European Convention on
  Human Rights, in particular Article 8 (the right to respect for
  private and family life), which means that it is only lawful to
  reveal someone's personal information if:
  - there is a legitimate aim in doing so
  - a democratic society would think it necessary to do so,
    and
  - the kind and amount of information disclosed is in relation
    to the need.

What information do people generally have a right to see?

16.4 Section 7 of the Data Protection Act 1998 gives everyone the right
to see personal information that an organisation holds about them.
They may also authorise someone else to access their information
on their behalf. The person holding the information has a legal duty
to release it. So, where possible, it is important to try to get a
person's consent before requesting to see information about them.

16.5 A person may have the capacity to agree to someone seeing their
personal information, even if they do not have the capacity to make
other decisions. In some situations, a person may have previously
given consent (while they still had capacity) for someone to see
their personal information in the future.

16.6 Doctors and lawyers cannot share information about their clients,
or that clients have given them, without the client's consent.
Sometimes it is fair to assume that a doctor or lawyer already has
someone's consent (for example, patients do not usually expect
healthcare staff or legal professionals to get consent every time they
share information with a colleague – but staff may choose to get
clients' consent in writing when they begin treating or acting for
that person). But in other circumstances, doctors and lawyers must
get specific consent to 'disclose' information (share it with someone
else).

16.7 If someone's capacity changes from time to time, the person
needing the information may want to wait until that person can give
their consent. Or they may decide that it is not necessary to get
access to information at all, if the person will be able to make a
decision on their own in the future.

16.8 If someone lacks the capacity to give consent, someone else might
still be able to see their personal information. This will depend on:

- whether the person requesting the information is acting as an agent (a representative recognised by the law, such as a deputy or attorney) for the person who lacks capacity
- whether disclosure is in the best interests of the person who lacks capacity, and
- what type of information has been requested.

When can attorneys and deputies ask to see personal information?

16.9 An attorney acting under a valid LPA or EPA (and sometimes a deputy) can ask to see information concerning the person they are representing, as long as the information applies to decisions the attorney has the legal right to make.

16.10 In practice, an attorney or deputy may only require limited information and may not need to make a formal request. In such circumstances, they can approach the information holder informally. Once satisfied that the request comes from an attorney or deputy (having seen appropriate authority), the person holding information should be able to release it. The attorney or deputy can still make a formal request for information in the future.

16.11 The attorney or deputy must treat the information confidentially. They should be extremely careful to protect it. If they fail to do so, the court can cancel the LPA or deputyship.

16.12 Before the Act came into effect, only a few receivers were appointed with the general authority to manage a person's property and affairs. So they needed specific authority from the Court of Protection to ask for access to the person's personal information. Similarly, a deputy who only has authority to act in specific areas only has the right to ask for information relating to decisions in those specific areas. For information relating to other areas, the deputy will need to apply to the Court of Protection.

16.13 Requests for personal information must be in writing, and there might be a fee. Information holders should release it promptly (always within 40 calendar days). Fees may be particularly high for getting copies of healthcare records – particularly where information may be in unusual formats (for example, x-rays). The maximum fee is currently £50. Complaints about a failure to comply with the Data Protection Act 1998 should be directed to the Information Commissioner's Office (see Annex A for contact details).

PART VI

What limitations are there?

16.14 Attorneys and deputies should only ask for information that will help them make a decision they need to make on behalf of the person who lacks capacity. For example, if the attorney needs to know when the person should take medication, they should not ask to see the entire healthcare record. The person who releases information must make sure that an attorney or deputy has official authority (they may ask for proof of identity and appointment). When asking to see personal information, attorneys and deputies should bear in mind that their decision must always be in the best interests of the person who lacks capacity to make that decision.

16.15 The attorney or deputy may not know the kind of information that someone holds about the person they are representing. So sometimes it might be difficult for them to make a specific request. They might even need to see all the information to make a decision. But again, the 'best interests' principle applies.

Scenario: Giving attorneys access to personal information

Mr Yapp is in the later stages of Alzheimer's disease. His son is responsible for Mr Yapp's personal welfare under a Lasting Power of Attorney. Mr Yapp has been in residential care for a number of years. But his son does not think that the home is able to meet his father's current needs as his condition has recently deteriorated.

The son asks to see his father's records. He wants specific information about his father's care, so that he can make a decision about his father's best interests. But the manager of the care home refuses, saying that the Data Protection Act stops him releasing personal information.

Mr Yapp's son points out that he can see his father's records, because he is his personal welfare attorney and needs the information to make a decision. The Data Protection Act 1998 requires the care home manager to provide access to personal data held on Mr Yapp.

16.16 The deputy or attorney may find that some information is held back (for example, when this contains references to people other than the person who lacks capacity). This might be to protect another person's privacy, if that person is mentioned in the records. It is unlikely that information relating to another person would help an attorney make a decision on behalf of the person who lacks capacity. The information holder might also be obliged to keep information about the other person confidential. There might be another reason why the person does not want information about them to be released. Under these circumstances, the attorney does not have the right to see that information.

16.17 An information holder should not release information if doing so would cause serious physical or mental harm to anyone – including the person the information is about. This applies to information on health, social care and education records.

16.18 The Information Commissioner's Office can give further details on:
  • how to request personal information

- restrictions on accessing information, and
- how to appeal against a decision not to release information.

When can someone see information about healthcare or social care?

16.19 Healthcare and social care staff may disclose information about somebody who lacks capacity only when it is in the best interests of the person concerned to do so, or when there is some other, lawful reason for them to do so.

16.20 The Act's requirement to consult relevant people when working out the best interests of a person who lacks capacity will encourage people to share the information that makes a consultation meaningful. But people who release information should be sure that they are acting lawfully and that they can justify releasing the information. They need to balance the person's right to privacy with what is in their best interests or the wider public interest (see paragraphs 16.24–16.25 below).

16.21 Sometimes it will be fairly obvious that staff should disclose information. For example, a doctor would need to tell a new care worker about what drugs a person needs or what allergies the person has. This is clearly in the person's best interests.

16.22 Other information may need to be disclosed as part of the process of working out someone's best interests. A social worker might decide to reveal information about someone's past when discussing their best interests with a close family member. But staff should always bear in mind that the Act requires them to consider the wishes and feelings of the person who lacks capacity.

16.23 In both these cases, staff should only disclose as much information as is relevant to the decision to be made.

PART VI

Scenario: Sharing appropriate information

Mr Jeremy has learning disabilities. His care home is about to close down. His care team carries out a careful assessment of his needs. They involve him as much as possible, and use the support of an Independent Mental Capacity Advocate. Following the assessment, he is placed with carers under an adult placement scheme.

The carers ask to see Mr Jeremy's case file, so that they can provide him with appropriate care in his best interests. The care manager seeks Mr Jeremy's consent to disclosure of his notes, but believes that Mr Jeremy lacks capacity to make this decision. She recognises that it is appropriate to provide the carers with sufficient information to enable them to act in Mr Jeremy's best interests. But it is not appropriate for them to see all the information on the case file. Much of it is not relevant to his current care needs. The care manager therefore only passes on relevant information from the file.

16.24 Sometimes a person's right to confidentiality will conflict with broader public concerns. Information can be released if it is in the public interest, even if it is not in the best interests of the person who lacks capacity. It can be difficult to decide in these cases, and information holders should consider each case on its merits. The NHS Code on Confidentiality gives examples of when disclosure is in the public interest. These include situations where disclosing information could prevent, or aid investigation of, serious crimes, or to prevent serious harm, such as spread of an infectious disease. It is then necessary to judge whether the public good that would be achieved by the disclosure outweighs both the obligation of confidentiality to the individual concerned and the broader public interest in the provision of a confidential service.

16.25 For disclosure to be in the public interest, it must be proportionate and limited to the relevant details. Healthcare or social care staff faced with this decision should seek advice from their legal advisers. It is not just things for 'the public's benefit' that are in the public interest – disclosure for the benefit of the person who lacks capacity can also be in the public interest (for example, to stop a person who lacks capacity suffering physical or mental harm).

What financial information can carers ask to see?

16.26 It is often more difficult to get financial information than it is to get information on a person's welfare. A bank manager, for example, is less likely to:
- know the individual concerned
- be able to make an assessment of the person's capacity to consent to disclosure, and
- be aware of the carer's relationship to the person.

So they are less likely than a doctor or social worker to be able to judge what is in a person's best interests and are bound by duties to keep clients' affairs confidential. It is likely that someone wanting financial information will need to apply to the Court of Protection for access to that information. This clearly does not apply to an attorney or a deputy appointed to manage the person's property and affairs, who will generally have the authority (because of their appointment) to obtain all relevant information about the person's property and affairs.

Is information still confidential after someone shares it?

16.27 Whenever a carer gets information, they should treat the information in confidence, and they should not share it with anyone else (unless there is a lawful basis for doing so). In some circumstances, the information holder might ask the carer to give a formal confirmation that they will keep information confidential.

16.28 Where the information is in written form, carers should store it carefully and not keep it for longer than necessary. In many cases, the need to keep the information will be temporary. So the carer should be able to reassure the information holder that they will not keep a permanent record of the information.

What is the best way to settle a disagreement about personal information?

16.29 A carer should always start by trying to get consent from the person whose information they are trying to access. If the person lacks capacity to consent, the carer should ask the information holder for the relevant information and explain why they need it. They may need to remind the information holder that they have to make a decision in the person's best interests and cannot do so without the relevant information.

16.30 This can be a sensitive area and disputes will inevitably arise. Healthcare and social care staff have a difficult judgement to make. They might feel strongly that disclosing the information would not be in the best interests of the person who lacks capacity and would amount to an invasion of their privacy. This may be upsetting for the carer who will probably have good motives for wanting the information. In all cases, an assessment of the interests and needs of the person who lacks capacity should determine whether staff should disclose information.

16.31 If a discussion fails to settle the matter, and the carer still is not happy, there are other ways to settle the disagreement (see chapter 15). The carer may need to use the appropriate complaints procedure. Since the complaint involves elements of data protection and confidentiality, as well as best interests, relevant experts should help deal with the complaint.

16.32 In cases where carers and staff cannot settle their disagreement, the carer can apply to the Court of Protection for the right to access to the specific information. The court would then need to decide if this was in the best interests of the person who lacks capacity to consent. In urgent cases, it might be necessary for the carer to apply directly to the court without going through the earlier stages.

KEY WORDS AND PHRASES USED IN THE CODE

The table below is not a full index or glossary. Instead, it is a list of key terms used in the Code or the Act, and the main references to them. References in bold indicate particularly valuable content for that term.

PART VI

Acts in connection with care or treatment	Tasks carried out by carers, healthcare or social care staff which involve the personal care, healthcare or medical treatment of people who lack capacity to consent to them – referred to in the Act as 'section 5 acts'.	**Chapter 6** 2.13–2.14, 4.39 Best interests and _ 5.10, 5,39 Deprivation of liberty and_ 6.39. 6.49–6.52
Advance decision to refuse treatment	A decision to refuse specified treatment made in advance by a person who has capacity to do so. This decision will then apply at a future time when that person lacks capacity to consent to, or refuse, the specified treatment. This is set out in Section 24(1) of the Act. Specific rules apply to advance decisions to refuse life-sustaining treatment.	**Chapter 9 (all)** Best interests and _ 5.5, 5.35, 5.45 Protection from liability and _ 6.37–6.38 LPAs and _ 7.55 Deputies and _ 8.28 Research and _ 11.30 Young people and _ 12.9 Mental Health Act 13.35–13.37
Adult protection procedures	Procedures devised by local authorities, in conjunction with other relevant agencies, to investigate and deal with allegations of abuse or ill treatment of vulnerable adults, and to put in place safeguards to provide protection from abuse.	**Chapter 14** 14.6, 14.22, 14.27–28, 14.34 IMCAs and _ 10.66–10.67
After-care under supervision	Arrangements for supervision in the community following discharge from hospital of certain patients previously detained under the Mental Health Act 1983.	**Chapter 13** **13.22–13.25**, 13.34, 13.37, 13.40, 13.42, 13.45, 13.48, 13.52
Agent	A person authorised to act on behalf of another person under the law of agency. Attorneys appointed under an LPA or EPA are agents and court-appointed deputies are deemed to be agents and must undertake certain duties as agents.	LPAs and _ 7.58–7.68 Deputies and _ 8.55–8.68
Appointee	Someone appointed under Social Security Regulations to claim and collect social security benefits or pensions on behalf of a person who lacks capacity to manage their own benefits. An appointee is permitted to use the money claimed to meet the person's needs.	Role of _ 6:65–6.66 Deputies and _ 8.56 Concerns about _ 14:35–14.36

Appropriate body	A committee which is established to advise on, or on matters which include, the ethics of intrusive research in relation to people who lack capacity to consent to it, and is recognised for those purposes by the Secretary of State (in England) or the National Assembly for Wales (in Wales).	**Chapter 11** 11.8–11.11, 11.20, 11.33–11.34, 11.43–11.47.
Approved Social Worker (ASW)	A specially trained social worker with responsibility for assessing a person's needs for care and treatment under the Mental Health Act 1983. In particular, an ASW assesses whether the person should be admitted to hospital for assessment and/or treatment.	**Chapter 13** 13.16, 13.22–13.23, 13.43, 13.52
Artificial Nutrition and Hydration (ANH)	Artificial nutrition and hydration (ANH) has been recognised as a form of medical treatment. ANH involves using tubes to provide nutrition and fluids to someone who cannot take them by mouth. It bypasses the natural mechanisms that control hunger and thirst and requires clinical monitoring.	**9.26** 5.34 6.18 8.18
Attorney	Someone appointed under either a Lasting Power of Attorney (LPA) or an Enduring Power of Attorney (EPA), who has the legal right to make decisions within the scope of their authority on behalf of the person (the donor) who made the Power of Attorney.	**Chapter 7** Best interests principle and _ 5.2, 5.13, 5.49, 5.55 Protection from liability as _ 6.54–6.55 Court of Protection and _ 8.30 Advance decisions and _ 9.33 Mental Health Act and _ 13.38–13.45 Public Guardian and _ 14.7–14.14 Legal help and _ 15.39–15.42 Accessing personal information as _ 16.9–16.16

PART VI

Best interests	Any decisions made, or anything done for a person who lacks capacity to make specific decisions, must be in the person's best interests. There are standard minimum steps to follow when working out someone's best interests. These are set out in section 4 of the Act, and in the non-exhaustive checklist in 5.13.	**Chapter 2 (Principle 4) Chapter 5** Protection from liability and _ 6.4–6.18 Reasonable belief and _ 6.32–6.36 Deprivation of liberty and _ 6.51–6.53 Acting as an attorney and _ 7.19–7.20, 7.29, 7.53 Court of Protection and _ 8.14–8.26 Acting as a deputy and _ 8.50–8.52 Advance decisions and _ 9.4–9.5
Bournewood provisions	A name given to some proposed new procedures and safeguards for people who lack capacity to make relevant decisions but who need to be deprived of their liberty, in their best interests, otherwise than under the Mental Health Act 1983. The name refers to a case which was eventually decided by the European Court of Human Rights.	6.53–6.54 13.53–13.54
Capacity	The ability to make a decision about a particular matter at the time the decision needs to be made. The legal definition of a person who lacks capacity is set out in section 2 of the Act.	**Chapter 4**

Carer	Someone who provides *unpaid* care by looking after a friend or neighbour who needs support because of sickness, age or disability. In this document, the role of the carer is different from the role of a professional care worker.	**Acting as decision-maker 5.8–5.10 Protection from liability 6.20–6.24** Assessing capacity as _ 4.44–4.45 Acting with reasonable belief 6.29–6.34 Paying for goods and services 6.56–6.66 Accessing information 16.26–16.32
Care worker	Someone employed to provide personal care for people who need help because of sickness, age or disability. They could be employed by the person themselves, by someone acting on the person's behalf or by a care agency.	Assessing capacity as _4.38, 4.44–4.45 Protection from liability 6.20 Paying for goods and services 6.56–6.66 Acting as an attorney 7.10 Acting as a deputy 8.41
Children Act 1989	A law relating to children and those with parental responsibility for children.	**Chapter 12**
Complaints Review Panel	A panel of people set up to review and reconsider complaints about health or social care services which have not been resolved under the first stage of the relevant complaints procedure.	15.28
Consultee	A person who is consulted, for example about the involvement in a research project of a person who lacks capacity to consent to their participation in the research.	11.23, 11.28–29, 11.44

PART VI

Court of Protection	The specialist Court for all issues relating to people who lack capacity to make specific decisions. The Court of Protection is established under section 45 of the Act.	**Chapter 8** _ must always make decisions about these issues 6.18 Decisions about life- sustaining treatment 5.33–5.36 LPAs and _ 7.45–7.49 Advance decisions and _ 9.35, 9.54, 9.67–9.69 Decisions regarding children and young people 12.3–12.4, 12.7, 12.10, 12.23–12.25 Access to legal help 15.40–15.44
Court of Protection Visitor	Someone who is appointed to report to the Court of Protection on how attorneys or deputies are carrying out their duties. Court of Protection Visitors are established under section 61 of the Act. They can also be directed by the Public Guardian to visit donors, attorney and deputies under section 58 (1) (d).	**14.10–14.11** Attorneys and _ 7.71 Deputies and _ 8.71
Criminal Records Bureau (CRB)	An Executive Agency of the Home Office which provides access to criminal record information. Organisations in the public, private and voluntary sectors can ask for the CRB to check candidates for jobs to see if they have any criminal records which would make them unsuitable for certain work, especially that involves children or vulnerable adults. For some jobs, a CRB check is mandatory.	Checking healthcare and social care staff 14.29–14.30 Checking IMCAs 10.18
Data Protection Act 1998	A law controlling the handling of, and access to, personal information, such as medical records, files held by public bodies and financial information held by credit reference agencies.	**Chapter 16**

Decision-maker	Under the Act, many different people may be required to make decisions or act on behalf of someone who lacks capacity to make decisions for themselves. The person making the decision is referred to throughout the Code, as the 'decision-maker', and it is the decision-maker's responsibility to work out what would be in the best interests of the person who lacks capacity.	**Chapter 5** Working with IMCAs 10.4, 10.21–10.29 Applying the MHA 13.3, 13.10, 13.27
Declaration	A kind of order made by the Court of Protection. For example, a declaration could say whether a person has or lacks capacity to make a particular decision, or declaring that a particular act would or would not be lawful. The Court's power to make declarations is set out in section 15 of the Act	**8.13–8.19** Advance decisions and _ 9.35
Deprivation of liberty	Deprivation of liberty is a term used in the European Convention on Human Rights about circumstances when a person's freedom is taken away. Its meaning in practice is being defined through case law.	**6.49–6.54** Protection from liability 6.13–6.14 Attorneys and _ 7.44 Mental Health Act and _ 13.12, 13.16

PART VI

Deputy	Someone appointed by the Court of Protection with ongoing legal authority as prescribed by the Court to make decisions on behalf of a person who lacks capacity to make particular decisions as set out in Section 16(2) of the Act.	**Chapter 8** Best interests principle and _ 5.2, 5.13, 5.49, 5.55 Protection from liability as _ 6.54–6.55 Attorneys becoming _ 7.56 Advance decisions and _ 9.33 IMCAs and _ 10.70–72 Acting for children and young people 12.4, 12.7 Public Guardian and _ 14.15–14.18 Complaints about 14.19–14.25 Accessing personal information as _ 16.9–16.16
Donor	A person who makes a Lasting Power of Attorney or Enduring Power of Attorney	**Chapter 7**
Enduring Power of Attorney (EPA)	A Power of Attorney created under the Enduring Powers of Attorney Act 1985 appointing an attorney to deal with the donor's property and financial affairs. Existing EPAs will continue to operate under Schedule 4 of the Act, which replaces the EPA Act 1985.	**Chapter 7** See also LPA
Family carer	A family member who looks after a relative who needs support because of sickness, age or disability. It does not mean a professional care-worker employed by a disabled person or a care assistant in a nursing home, for example.	**See carer**
Family Division of the High Court	The Division of the High Court that has the jurisdiction to deal with all matrimonial and civil partnership matters, family disputes, matters relating to children and some disputes about medical treatment.	12.14, 12.23

Fiduciary duty	Anyone acting under the law of agency will have this duty. In essence, it means that any decision taken or act done as an agent (such as an attorney or deputy) must not benefit themselves, but must benefit the person for whom they are acting.	_ for attorneys 7.58 _ for deputies 8.58
Guardianship	Arrangements, made under the Mental Health Act 1983, for a guardian to be appointed for a person with mental disorder to help ensure that the person gets the care they need in the community.	**13.16–13.21** 13.1, 13.25–13.27, 13.54
Health Service Ombudsman	An independent person whose organisation investigates complaints about National Health Service (NHS) care or treatment in England which have not been resolved through the NHS complaints procedure.	15.19, 15.21, 15.31
Human Rights Act 1998	A law largely incorporating into UK law the substantive rights set out in the European Convention on Human Rights.	6.49 16.3
Human Tissue Act 2004	A law to regulate issues relating to whole body donation and the taking, storage and use of human organs and tissue.	11.7 11.38–11.39
Ill treatment	Section 44 of the Act introduces a new offence of ill treatment of a person who lacks capacity by someone who is caring for them, or acting as a deputy or attorney for them. That person can be guilty of ill treatment if they have deliberately ill-treated a person who lacks capacity, or been reckless as to whether they were ill-treating the person or not. It does not matter whether the behaviour was likely to cause, or actually caused, harm or damage to the victim's health.	14.23–14.26
Independent Complaints Advocacy Service (ICAS)	In England, a service to support patients and their carers who wish to pursue a complaint about their NHS treatment or care.	15.18

PART VI

Independent Mental Capacity Advocate (IMCA)	Someone who provides support and representation for a person who lacks capacity to make specific decisions, where the person has no-one else to support them. The IMCA service is established under section 35 of the Act and the functions of IMCAs are set out in section 36. It is not the same as an ordinary advocacy service.	**Chapter 10** Consulting to work out best interests 5.51 Involvement in changes of residence 6.9 Involvement in serious medical decisions 6.16 MHA and _ 13.46–13.48
Information Commission- er's Office	An independent authority set up to promote access to official information and to protect personal information. It has powers to ensure that the laws about information, such as the Data Protection Act 1998, are followed.	16.13 16.18
Lasting Power of Attorney (LPA)	A Power of Attorney created under the Act (see Section 9(1)) appointing an attorney (or attorneys) to make decisions about the donor's personal welfare (including healthcare) and/or deal with the donor's property and affairs.	**Chapter 7** Best interests principle and _ 5.2, 5.13, 5.49, 5.55 Protection from liability as _ 6.54–6.55 Court of Protection and _ 8.30 Advance decisions and _ 9.33 Mental Health Act and _ 13.38–13.45 Public Guardian and _ 14.7–14.14 Legal help and _ 15.39–15.42 Accessing personal information as _ 16.9–16.16

Life-sustaining treatment	Treatment that, in the view of the person providing healthcare, is necessary to keep a person alive See Section 4(10) of the Act.	**Providing or stopping _ in best interests 5.29–5.36 Advance decisions to refuse _ 9.10–9.11, 9.19–9.20, 9.24–9.28** Protection from liability when providing _ 6.16, 6.55 Attorneys and _ 7.22, 7.27, 7.29-7.30 Deputies and _ 8.17, 8.46 Conscientious objection to stopping _ 9.61–9.63 IMCAs and _ 10.44
Litigation friend	A person appointed by the court to conduct legal proceedings on behalf of, and in the name of, someone who lacks capacity to conduct the litigation or to instruct a lawyer themselves.	4.54 10.38 15.39
Local Government Ombudsman	In England, an independent organisation that investigates complaints about councils and local authorities on most council matters including housing, planning, education and social services.	15.30–15.32
Makaton	A language programme using signs and symbols, for the teaching of communication, language and literacy skills for people with communication and learning difficulties.	3.11
Mediation	A process for resolving disagreements in which an impartial third party (the mediator) helps people in dispute to find a mutually acceptable resolution.	15.7–15.13
Mental capacity	See capacity	

PART VI

Mental Health Act 1983	A law mainly about the compulsory care and treatment of patients with mental health problems. In particular, it covers detention in hospital for mental health treatment.	**Chapter 13** Deprivation of liberty other than in line with _ 6.50–6.53, 7.44 Attorneys and _ 7.27 Advance decisions and _9.37 IMCAs and 10.44, 10.51, 10.56–10.58 Children and young people and _ 12.6, 12.21 Complaints regarding _ 15.19
Mental Health Review Tribunal	An independent judicial body with powers to direct the discharge of patients who are detained under the Mental Health Act 1983.	13.31 13.42
NHS Litigation Authority	A Special Health Authority (part of the NHS), responsible for handling negligence claims made against NHS bodies in England.	15.22
Office of the Public Guardian (OPG)	The Public Guardian is an officer established under Section 57 of the Act. The Public Guardian will be supported by the Office of the Public Guardian, which will supervise deputies, keep a register of deputies, Lasting Powers of Attorney and Enduring Powers of Attorney, check on what attorneys are doing, and investigate any complaints about attorneys or deputies. The OPG replaces the Public Guardianship Office (PGO) that has been in existence for many years.	**14.8–14.22** Registering LPAs with _ 7.14–7.17 Supervision of attorneys by _ 7.69–7.74 Registering EPAs with _ 7.78 Guidance for EPAs _ 7.79 Guidance for receivers_ 8.5 Panel of deputies of _ 8.35 Supervision of deputies by _ 8.69–8,77

Official Solicitor	Provides legal services for vulnerable persons, or in the interests of achieving justice. The Official Solicitor represents adults who lack capacity to conduct litigation in county court or High Court proceedings in England and Wales, and in the Court of Protection.	Helping with formal assessment of capacity 4.54 Acting in applications to the Court of Protection 8.10 Acting as litigation friend 10.38, 15.39
Patient Advice and Liaison Service (PALS)	In England, a service providing information, advice and support to help NHS patients, their families and carers. PALS act on behalf of service users when handling patient and family concerns and can liaise with staff, managers and, where appropriate, other relevant organisations, to find solutions.	15.15–15.17
Permanent vegetative state (PVS)	A condition caused by catastrophic brain damage whereby patients in PVS have a permanent and irreversible lack of awareness of their surroundings and no ability to interact at any level with those around them.	6.18 8.18
Personal welfare	Personal welfare decisions are any decisions about person's healthcare, where they live, what clothes they wear, what they eat and anything needed for their general care and well-being. Attorneys and deputies can be appointed to make decisions about personal welfare on behalf of a person who lacks capacity. Many acts of care are to do with personal welfare.	_ LPAs **7.21–7.31** _ **deputies** **8.38–8.39** Advance decisions about _ 9.4, 9.35 Role of High Court in decisions about _ 15.44

PART VI

Property and affairs	Any possessions owned by a person (such as a house or flat, jewellery or other possessions), the money they have in income, savings or investments and any expenditure. Attorneys and deputies can be appointed to make decisions about property and affairs on behalf of a person who lacks capacity.	_ **LPAs** **7.32–7.42** _ **deputies** **8.34–8.37** Restrictions on _ LPA 7.56 Duties of _ attorney 7.58, 7.67–7.68 _ EPAs 7.76–7.77 OPG panel of _ deputies 8.35 Duties of _ deputy 8.56, 8.67–8.68 _ of children and young people 12.3–12.4, 12.7
Protection from liability	Legal protection, granted to anyone who has acted or made decisions in line with the Act's principles.	**Chapter 6**
Protection of Vulnerable Adults (POVA) list	A register of individuals who have abused, neglected or otherwise harmed vulnerable adults in their care or placed vulnerable adults at risk of harm. Providers of care must not offer such individuals employment in care positions.	14.31
Public Services Ombudsman for Wales	An independent body that investigates complaints about local government and NHS organisations in Wales, and the National Assembly for Wales, concerning matters such as housing, planning, education, social services and health services.	15.20 15.30–15.32
Receiver	Someone appointed by the former Court of Protection to manage the property and affairs of a person lacking capacity to manage their own affairs. Existing receivers continue as deputies with legal authority to deal with the person's property and affairs.	8.5 8.35

Restraint	See Section 6(4) of the Act. The use or threat of force to help do an act which the person resists, or the restriction of the person's liberty of movement, whether or not they resist. Restraint may only be used where it is necessary to protect the person from harm and is proportionate to the risk of harm.	**6.39–6.44, 6.47–53** Use of _ in moves between accommodation 6.11 Use of _ in healthcare and treatment decisions 6.15 Attorneys and _ 7.43-7.44 Deputies and _ 8.46 MHA and _ 13.5
Statutory principles	The five key principles are set out in Section 1 of the Act. They are designed to emphasise the fundamental concepts and core values of the Act and to provide a benchmark to guide decision-makers, professionals and carers acting under the Act's provisions. The principles generally apply to all actions and decisions taken under the Act.	**Chapter 2**
Two-stage test of capacity	Using sections 2 and 3 of the Act to assess whether or not a person has capacity to make a decision for themselves at that time.	**4.10–4.13** Protection from liability 6.27 Applying _ to advance decisions 9.39
Wilful neglect	An intentional or deliberate omission or failure to carry out an act of care by someone who has care of a person who lacks (or whom the person reasonably believes lacks) capacity to care for themselves. Section 44 introduces a new offence of wilful neglect of a person who lacks capacity.	14.23–14.26
Written statements of wishes and feelings	Written statements the person might have made before losing capacity about their wishes and feelings regarding issues such as the type of medical treatment they would want in the case of future illness, where they would prefer to live, or how they wish to be cared for. They should be used to help find out what someone's wishes and feelings might be, as part of working out their best interests. They are not the same as advance decisions to refuse treatment and are not binding.	5.34 5.37 5.42–5.44

ANNEX A

The following list provides contact details for some organisations that provide information, guidance or materials related to the Code of Practice and the Mental Capacity Act. The list is not exhaustive: many other organisations may also produce their own materials.

British Banking Association

Provides guidance for bank staff on *'Banking for mentally incapacitated and learning disabled customers'*.
Available from www.bba.org.uk/bba/jsp/polopoly.jsp?d=146&a=5757, price £10 (members) /£12 (non-members). Not inclusive of VAT.

web: www.bba.org.uk

telephone: 020 7216 8800

British Medical Association

Co-authors (with the Law Society) of *Assessment of Mental Capacity: Guidance for Doctors and Lawyers* (Second edition) (London: BMJ Books, 2004). See www.bma.org.uk/ap.nsf/
Content/Assessmentmental?OpenDocument& Highlight=2,mental, capacity

Available from BMJ Books (www.bmjbookshop.com), price £20.99

web: www.bma.org.uk

telephone: 020 7387 4499

British Psychological Society

Publishers of *Guidelines on assessing capacity* – professional guidance available online to members.

web: www.bps.org.uk

telephone: (0)116 254 9568

Commission for Social Care Inspection

The Commission for Social Care Inspection (CSCI) registers, inspects and reports on social care services in England.

web: www.csci.org.uk

telephone: 0845 015 0120 / 0191 233 3323
textphone: 0845 015 2255 / 0191 233 3588

Community Legal Services Direct

Provides free legal information to people living in England and Wales to help them deal with legal problems.

web: www.clsdirect.org.uk

telephone (helpline):   0845 345 4 345

Criminal Records Bureau (CRB)

The CRB runs criminal records checks on people who apply for jobs working with children and vulnerable adults.

web: www.crb.org.uk

telephone: 0870 90 90 811

Department for Constitutional Affairs

The government department with responsibility for the Mental Capacity Act and the Code of Practice. Also publishes guidance for specific audiences www.dca.gov.uk/legal-policy/mental-capacity/guidance.htm

Department of Health

Publishes guidance for healthcare and social care staff in England. Key publications referenced in the Code include:

- on using restraint with people with learning disabilities and autistic spectrum disorder, see *Guidance for restrictive physical interventions* www.dh.gov.uk/assetRoot/04/06/84/61/04068461.pdf
- on adult protection procedures, see *No secrets: Guidance on developing and implementing multi-agency policies and procedures to protect vulnerable adults from abuse* www.dh.gov.uk/assetRoot/04/07/45/44/04074544.pdf
- on consent to examination and treatment, including advance decisions to refuse treatment www.dh/gov.uk/consent
- on the proposed Bournewood safeguards, a draft illustrative Code of Practice www.dh.gov.uk/assetRoot/04/14/17/64/04141764.pdf
- on IMCAs and the IMCA pilots www.dh.gov.uk/imca
- DH also is responsible for the *Mental Health Act 1983 Code of Practice* (TSO 1999) www.dh.gov.uk/assetRoot/04/07/49/61/04074961.pdf

PART VI

Family Mediation Helpline

Provides general information on family mediation and contact details for mediation services in your local area.

Web: www.familymediationhelpline.co.uk

telephone: 0845 60 26 627

Healthcare Commission

The health watchdog in England, undertaking reviews and investigations into the provision of NHS and private healthcare services.

Web: www.healthcarecommission.org.uk

telephone: 0845 601 3012
switchboard: 020 7448 9200

Healthcare Inspectorate for Wales

Undertakes reviews and investigations into the provision of NHS funded care, either by or for Welsh NHS organisations.

Web: www.hiw.org.uk
email: hiw@wales.gsi.gov.uk

telephone: 029 2092 8850

Housing Ombudsman Service

The Housing Ombudsman Service considers complaints against member organisations, and deals with other housing disputes.

Web: www.ihos.org.uk
email: info@housing-ombudsman.org.uk

telephone: 020 7421 3800

Information Commissioner's Office

The Information Commissioner's Office is the UK's independent authority set up to promote access to official information and to protect personal information.

Web: www.ico.gov.uk

telephone   08456 30 60 60
helpline:

Legal Services Commission

Looks after legal aid in England and Wales, and provides information, advice and legal representation.

Web: www.legalservices.gov.uk

See also Community Legal Services Direct.

Local Government Ombudsman

The Local Government Ombudsmen investigate complaints about councils and certain other bodies.

Web: www.lgo.org.uk

telephone: 0845 602 1983

National Mediation Helpline

Provides access to a simple, low cost method of resolving a wide range of disputes.

The National Mediation Helpline is operated on behalf of the Department for Constitutional Affairs (DCA) in conjunction with the Civil Mediation Council (CMC).

Web: www.nationalmediationhelpline.com

telephone: 0845 60 30 809

Office of the Public Guardian

The new Public Guardian is established under the Act and will be supported by the Office of the Public Guardian, which will replace the current Public Guardianship Office (PGO). The OPG will be an executive agency of the Department for Constitutional Affairs. Amongst its other roles, it provides forms for LPAs and EPAs.

Web: From October 2007, a new website will be created at
                   www.publicguardian.gov.uk

Official Solicitor

Provides legal services for vulnerable people and is able to represent people who lack capacity and act as a litigation friend.

Web: www.officialsolicitor.gov.uk

telephone: 020 7911 7127

Patient Advice and Liaison Service (PALS)

Provides information about the NHS and help resolve concerns or problems with the NHS, including support when making complaints.

Web: www.pals.nhs.uk

> The site includes contact details for local PALS offices around the country.

Patient Information Advisory Group

Considers applications on behalf of the Secretary of State to allow the common law duty of confidentiality to be aside.

Web: www.advisorybodies.doh.gov.uk/PIAG

Public Service Ombudsman for Wales

Investigates complaints about local authorities and NHS organisations in Wales, and about the National Assembly Government for Wales.

Web: www.ombudsman-wales.org.uk

telephone: 01656 641 150

Welsh Assembly Government

Produces key pieces of guidance for healthcare and social care staff, including:

- *In safe hands – Implementing Adult Protection Procedures in Wales* (July 2000) http://new.wales.gov.uk/about/departments/dhss/publications/social_services_publications/reports/insafehands?lang=en
- *Framework for restrictive physical intervention policy and practice* (available at www.childrenfirst.wales.gov.uk/content/framework/phys-int-e.pdf)

Copies of this publication can be downloaded from www.guardianship.gsi.gov.uk

Hard copies of this publication are available from TSO

For more information on the Mental Capacity Act contact the Public Guardianship Office:

9am – 5pm, Mon – Fri

Telephone:	0845 330 2900 (local call rate)
or	+44 207 664 7000 (for callers outside UK)
Text Phone:	020 7664 7755
Fax:	0870 739 5780 (UK callers)
Email:	custserv@guardianship.gsi.gov.uk
Website:	www.guardianship.gsi.gov.uk
Post:	Public Guardianship Office
	Archway Tower
	2 Junction Road
	London N19 5SZ

PART VI

Mental Capacity Act 2005: Deprivation of Liberty Safeguards Code of Practice

SUPPLEMENTING THE MAIN MENTAL CAPACITY ACT 2005 CODE OF PRACTICE

Issued by the Lord Chancellor on 26 August 2008 in accordance with sections 42 and 43 of the Act

FOREWORD BY IVAN LEWIS AND EDWINA HART MBE

The Mental Capacity Act 2005 ('the Act') provides a statutory framework for acting and making decisions on behalf of individuals who lack the mental capacity to do so for themselves. It introduced a number of laws to protect these individuals and ensure that they are given every chance to make decisions for themselves. The Act came into force in October 2007.

The Government has added new provisions to the Act: the deprivation of liberty safeguards. The safeguards focus on some of the most vulnerable people in our society: those who for their own safety and in their own best interests need to be accommodated under care and treatment regimes that may have the effect of depriving them of their liberty, but who lack the capacity to consent.

The deprivation of a person's liberty is a very serious matter and should not happen unless it is absolutely necessary, and in the best interests of the person concerned. That is why the safeguards have been created: to ensure that any decision to deprive someone of their liberty is made following defined processes and in consultation with specific authorities.

The new provisions in the Act set out the legal framework of the deprivation of liberty safeguards. This Code of Practice is formally issued by the Lord Chancellor as a Code of Practice under the Mental Capacity Act 2005. It provides guidance and information for those implementing the deprivation of liberty safeguards legislation on a daily basis. In some cases, this will be paid staff, in others those who have been appointed in law to represent individuals who lack capacity to make decisions for themselves (such as deputies or donees of a Lasting Power of Attorney).

Because of this broad audience, the Code of Practice has been written so as to make it as user-friendly as possible – like the main Mental Capacity Act 2005 Code of Practice, issued in April 2007. We are grateful to all those who commented on earlier drafts of the Code to help it achieve that goal.

Ivan Lewis

Edwina Hart

INTRODUCTION

The Mental Capacity Act 2005 ('the Act'), covering England and Wales, provides a statutory framework for acting and making decisions on behalf of people who lack the capacity to make those decisions for themselves. These can be small decisions – such as what clothes to wear – or major decisions, such as where to live.

In some cases, people lack the capacity to consent to particular treatment or care that is recognised by others as being in their best interests, or which will protect them from harm. Where this care might involve depriving vulnerable people of their liberty in either a hospital or a care home, extra safeguards have been introduced, in law, to protect their rights and ensure that the care or treatment they receive is in their best interests.

This Code of Practice helps explain how to identify when a person is, or is at risk of, being deprived of their liberty and how deprivation of liberty may be avoided. It also explains the safeguards that have been put in place to ensure that deprivation of liberty, where it does need to occur, has a lawful basis. In addition, it provides guidance on what someone should do if they suspect that a person who lacks capacity is being deprived of their liberty unlawfully.

These safeguards are an important way of protecting the rights of many vulnerable people and should not be viewed negatively. Depriving someone of their liberty can be a necessary requirement in order to provide effective care or treatment. By following the criteria set out in the safeguards, and explained in this Code of Practice, the decision to deprive someone of their liberty can be made lawfully and properly.

How does this Code of Practice relate to the main Mental Capacity Act 2005 Code of Practice?

This document adds to the guidance in the main Mental Capacity Act 2005 Code of Practice ('the main Code'), which was issued in April 2007, and should be used in conjunction with the main Code. It focuses specifically on the deprivation of liberty safeguards added to the Act. These can be found in sections 4A and 4B of, and Schedules A1 and 1A to, the Act.

Though these safeguards were mentioned in the main Code (particularly in chapters 6 and 13), they were not covered in any detail. That was because, at the time the main Code was published, the deprivation of liberty safeguards were still going through the Parliamentary process as part of the Mental Health Bill.[80]

PART VI

---

[80]   The Mental Health Bill was used as a vehicle to amend the Mental Capacity Act 2005 in order to introduce the deprivation of liberty safeguards. The Bill became the Mental Health Act 2007 following completion of its Parliamentary passage.

Although the main Code does not cover the deprivation of liberty safeguards, the principles of that Code, and much of its content, are directly relevant to the deprivation of liberty safeguards. It is important that both the Act and the main Code are adhered to whenever capacity and best interests issues, and the deprivation of liberty safeguards, are being considered. The deprivation of liberty safeguards are in addition to, and do not replace, other safeguards in the Act.

How should this Code of Practice be used?

This Code of Practice provides guidance to anyone working with and/or caring for adults who lack capacity, but it particularly focuses on those who have a 'duty of care' to a person who lacks the capacity to consent to the care or treatment that is being provided, where that care or treatment may include the need to deprive the person of their liberty. This Code of Practice is also intended to provide information for people who are, or could become, subject to the deprivation of liberty safeguards, and for their families, friends and carers, as well as for anyone who believes that someone is being deprived of their liberty unlawfully.

In this Code of Practice, as throughout the main Code, references to 'lack of capacity' refer to the capacity to make a particular decision at the time it needs to be made. In the context of the deprivation of liberty safeguards, the capacity is specifically the capacity to decide whether or not to consent to care or treatment which involves being kept in a hospital or care home in circumstances that amount to a deprivation of liberty, at the time that decision needs to be made.

What is the legal status of this Code of Practice?

As with the main Code, this Code of Practice is published by the Lord Chancellor, under sections 42 and 43 of the Mental Capacity Act 2005. The purpose of the main Code is to provide guidance and information about how the Act works in practice.

Both this Code and the main Code have statutory force, which means that certain people are under a legal duty to have regard to them. More details can be found in the Introduction to the main Code, which explains the legal status of the Code and who should have regard to it.

In addition to those for whom the main Code is intended, this Code of Practice specifically focuses on providing guidance for:

- people exercising functions relating to the deprivation of liberty safeguards, and

- people acting as a relevant person's representative[81] under the deprivation of liberty safeguards (see chapter 7).

Scenarios used in this Code of Practice

This Code of Practice includes boxes within the main text containing scenarios, using imaginary characters and situations. These are intended to help illustrate what is meant in the main text. They should not in any way be taken as templates for decisions that need to be made in similar situations. Decisions must always be made on the facts of each individual case.

Alternative formats and further information

This Code of Practice is also available in Welsh and can be made available in other formats on request.

1 WHAT ARE THE DEPRIVATION OF LIBERTY SAFEGUARDS AND WHY WERE THEY INTRODUCED?

The deprivation of liberty safeguards were introduced to provide a legal framework around the deprivation of liberty. Specifically, they were introduced to prevent breaches of the European Convention on Human Rights (ECHR) such as the one identified by the judgment of the European Court of Human Rights (ECtHR) in the case of *HL v the United Kingdom*[82] (commonly referred to as the 'Bournewood' judgment). The case concerned an autistic man (HL) with a learning disability, who lacked the capacity to decide whether he should be admitted to hospital for specific treatment. He was admitted on an informal basis under common law in his best interests, but this decision was challenged by HL's carers. In its judgment, the ECtHR held that this admission constituted a deprivation of HL's liberty and, further, that:

- the deprivation of liberty had not been in accordance with 'a procedure prescribed by law' and was, therefore, in breach of Article 5(1) of the ECHR, and
- there had been a contravention of Article 5(4) of the ECHR because HL had no means of applying quickly to a court to see if the deprivation of liberty was lawful.

To prevent further similar breaches of the ECHR, the Mental Capacity Act 2005 has been amended to provide safeguards for people who lack capacity specifically to consent to treatment or care in either a hospital or a

---

[81] A 'relevant person' is a person who is, or may become, deprived of their liberty in accordance with the deprivation of liberty safeguards.

[82] (2004) Application No: 00045508/99.

care home[83] that, in their own best interests, can only be provided in circumstances that amount to a deprivation of liberty, and where detention under the Mental Health Act 1983 is not appropriate for the person at that time. These safeguards are referred to in this Code of Practice as 'deprivation of liberty safeguards'.

What are the deprivation of liberty safeguards?

1.1 The deprivation of liberty safeguards provide legal protection for those vulnerable people who are, or may become, deprived of their liberty within the meaning of Article 5 of the ECHR in a hospital or care home, whether placed under public or private arrangements. They do not apply to people detained under the Mental Health Act 1983. The safeguards exist to provide a proper legal process and suitable protection in those circumstances where deprivation of liberty appears to be unavoidable, in a person's own best interests.

1.2 Every effort should be made, in both commissioning and providing care or treatment, to prevent deprivation of liberty. If deprivation of liberty cannot be avoided, it should be for no longer than is necessary.

1.3 The safeguards provide for deprivation of liberty to be made lawful through 'standard' or 'urgent' authorisation processes. These processes are designed to prevent arbitrary decisions to deprive a person of liberty and give a right to challenge deprivation of liberty authorisations.

1.4 The deprivation of liberty safeguards mean that a 'managing authority' (i.e. the relevant hospital or care home – see paragraph 3.1) must seek authorisation from a 'supervisory body' in order to be able lawfully to deprive someone of their liberty. Before giving such an authorisation, the supervisory body must be satisfied that the person has a mental disorder[84] and lacks capacity to decide about their residence or treatment. The supervisory body could be a primary care trust, a local authority, Welsh Ministers or a local health board (LHB) (see paragraph 3.3).

1.5 A decision as to whether or not deprivation of liberty arises will depend on all the circumstances of the case (as explained more fully in chapter 2). It is neither necessary nor appropriate to apply for a deprivation of liberty authorisation for everyone who is in hospital or a care home simply because the person concerned lacks capacity to decide whether or not they should be there. In deciding whether or not an application is necessary, a managing authority should carefully consider whether any restrictions that are, or will be,

---

[83]   Throughout this document, the term 'care home' means a care home registered under the Care Standards Act 2000.

[84]   As defined in section 1 of the Mental Health Act 1983, a mental disorder is any disorder or disability of the mind, apart from dependence on alcohol and drugs. This includes all learning disabilities. The distinction in the Mental Health Act 1983 between learning disabilities depending on whether or not they are associated with abnormally aggressive or seriously irresponsible behaviour is not relevant.

needed to provide ongoing care or treatment amount to a deprivation of liberty when looked at together.

1.6 The deprivation of liberty safeguards cover:
- how an application for authorisation should be applied for
- how an application for authorisation should be assessed
- the requirements that must be fulfilled for an authorisation to be given
- how an authorisation should be reviewed
- what support and representation must be provided for people who are subject to an authorisation, and
- how people can challenge authorisations.

Who is covered by these safeguards?

1.7 The safeguards apply to people in England and Wales who have a mental disorder and lack capacity to consent to the arrangements made for their care or treatment, but for whom receiving care or treatment in circumstances that amount to a deprivation of liberty may be necessary to protect them from harm and appears to be in their best interests. A large number of these people will be those with significant learning disabilities, or older people who have dementia or some similar disability, but they can also include those who have certain other neurological conditions (for example as a result of a brain injury).

1.8 In order to come within the scope of a deprivation of liberty authorisation, a person must be detained in a hospital or care home, for the purpose of being given care or treatment in circumstances that amount to a deprivation of liberty. The authorisation must relate to the individual concerned and to the hospital or care home in which they are detained.

1.9 For the purposes of Article 5 of the ECHR, there is no distinction in principle between depriving a person who lacks capacity of their liberty for the purpose of treating them for a physical condition, and depriving them of their liberty for treatment of a mental disorder. There will therefore be occasions when people who lack capacity to consent to admission are taken to hospital for treatment of physical illnesses or injuries, and then need to be cared for in circumstances that amount to a deprivation of liberty. In these circumstances, a deprivation of liberty authorisation must be applied for. Consequently, this Code of Practice must be followed and applied in acute hospital settings as well as care homes and mental health units.

1.10 It is important to bear in mind that, while the deprivation of liberty might be for the purpose of giving a person treatment, a deprivation of liberty authorisation does not itself authorise treatment. Treatment that is proposed following authorisation of deprivation of liberty may only be given with the person's consent (if they have capacity to make the decision) or in accordance with the wider

PART VI

provisions of the Mental Capacity Act 2005. More details of this are contained in paragraphs 5.10 to 5.13 of this Code.

1.11 The safeguards cannot apply to people while they are detained in hospital under the Mental Health Act 1983. The safeguards can, however, apply to a person who has previously been detained in hospital under the Mental Health Act 1983. There are other cases in which people who are – or could be – subject to the Mental Health Act 1983 will not meet the eligibility requirement for the safeguards. Chapter 13 of the main Code contains guidance on the relationship between the Mental Capacity Act 2005 and the Mental Health Act 1983 generally, as does the Code of Practice to the Mental Health Act 1983 itself. Paragraphs 4.40 to 4.57 of the present Code explain the relationship of the deprivation of liberty safeguards to the Mental Health Act 1983, and in particular how to assess if a person is eligible to be deprived of their liberty under the safeguards.

1.12 The safeguards relate only to people aged 18 and over. If the issue of depriving a person under the age of 18 of their liberty arises, other safeguards must be considered – such as the existing powers of the court, particularly those under section 25 of the Children Act 1989, or use of the Mental Health Act 1983.

When can someone be deprived of their liberty?

1.13 Depriving someone who lacks the capacity to consent to the arrangements made for their care or treatment of their liberty is a serious matter, and the decision to do so should not be taken lightly. The deprivation of liberty safeguards make it clear that a person may only be deprived of their liberty:
- in their own best interests to protect them from harm
- if it is a proportionate response to the likelihood and seriousness of the harm, and
- if there is no less restrictive alternative.

1.14 Under no circumstances must deprivation of liberty be used as a form of punishment, or for the convenience of professionals, carers or anyone else. Deprivation of liberty should not be extended due to delays in moving people between care or treatment settings, for example when somebody awaits discharge after completing a period of hospital treatment.

Are there any cultural considerations in implementing the safeguards?

1.15 The deprivation of liberty safeguards should not impact in any different way on different racial or ethnic groups, and care should be taken to ensure that the provisions are not operated in a manner that discriminates against particular racial or ethnic groups. It is up to managing authorities and supervisory bodies to ensure that their staff are aware of their responsibilities in this regard and of the need to ensure that the safeguards are operated fairly and equitably.

1.16 Assessors who carry out deprivation of liberty assessments to help decide whether a person should be deprived of their liberty (see chapter 4) should have the necessary skills and experience to take account of people's diverse backgrounds. Accordingly, they will need to have an understanding of, and respect for, the background of the relevant person. Supervisory bodies must take these factors into account when appointing assessors and must seek to appoint the most suitable available person for each case.

1.17 Interpreters should be available, where necessary, to help assessors to communicate not only with the relevant person but also with people with an interest in their care and treatment. An interpreter should be suitably qualified and experienced to enable them to provide effective language and communication support in the particular case concerned, and to offer appropriate assistance to the assessors involved. Information should be made available in other languages where relevant.

1.18 Any decision about the instruction of Independent Mental Capacity Advocates (see paragraphs 3.22 to 3.28) or relevant person's representatives (see chapter 7) should take account of the cultural, national, racial or ethnic background of the relevant person.

Where do the safeguards apply?

1.19 Although the Bournewood judgment was specifically about a patient who lacked capacity to consent to admission to hospital for mental health treatment, the judgment has wider implications that extend to people who lack capacity and who might be deprived of their liberty either in a hospital or in a care home.

1.20 It will only be lawful to deprive somebody of their liberty elsewhere (for example, in their own home, in supported living arrangements other than in a care home, or in a day centre) when following an order of the Court of Protection on a personal welfare matter. In such a case, the Court of Protection order itself provides a legal basis for the deprivation of liberty. This means that a separate deprivation of liberty authorisation under the processes set out in this Code of Practice is not required. More information about applying to the Court of Protection regarding personal welfare matters is given in chapter 10.

How do the safeguards apply to privately arranged care or treatment?

1.21 Under the Human Rights Act 1998, the duty to act in accordance with the ECHR applies only to public authorities. However, all states that have signed up to the ECHR are obliged to make sure that the rights set out in the ECHR apply to all of their citizens. The Mental Capacity Act 2005 therefore makes it clear that the

PART VI

deprivation of liberty safeguards apply to both publicly and privately arranged care or treatment.

How do the safeguards relate to the rest of the Mental Capacity Act 2005?

1.22 The deprivation of liberty safeguards are in addition to, and do not replace, other safeguards in the Mental Capacity Act 2005. This means that decisions made, and actions taken, for a person who is subject to a deprivation of liberty authorisation must fulfil the requirements of the Act in the same way as for any other person. In particular, any action taken under the deprivation of liberty safeguards must be in line with the principles of the Act:

- A person must be assumed to have capacity to make a decision unless it is established that they lack the capacity to make that decision.
- A person is not to be treated as unable to make a decision unless all practicable steps to help them to do so have been taken without success.
- A person is not to be treated as unable to make a decision merely because they make an unwise decision.
- An act done, or decision made, under the Act for or on behalf of a person who lacks capacity must be done, or made, in their best interests.
- Before the act is done, or the decision is made, regard must be had to whether the purpose for which it is needed can be as effectively achieved in a way that is less restrictive of the person's rights and freedom of action.

These principles are set out in chapter 2 of the main Code and explained in more detail in chapters 3 to 6 of the same document. Paragraph 5.13 of the main Code contains a checklist of factors that need to be taken into account in determining a person's best interests.

2   WHAT IS DEPRIVATION OF LIBERTY?

There is no simple definition of deprivation of liberty. The question of whether the steps taken by staff or institutions in relation to a person amount to a deprivation of that person's liberty is ultimately a legal question, and only the courts can determine the law. This guidance seeks to assist staff and institutions in considering whether or not the steps they are taking, or proposing to take, amount to a deprivation of a person's liberty. The deprivation of liberty safeguards give best interests assessors the authority to make recommendations about proposed deprivations of liberty, and supervisory bodies the power to give authorisations that deprive people of their liberty.

This chapter provides guidance for staff and institutions on how to assess whether particular steps they are taking, or proposing to take, might amount to a deprivation of liberty, based on existing case law. It also considers what other factors may be taken into account when considering the issue of deprivation of liberty, including, importantly, what is permissible under the Mental Capacity Act 2005 in relation to restraint or restriction. Finally, it provides a summary of some of the most important cases to date.

Further legal developments may occur after this guidance has been issued, and healthcare and social care staff need to keep themselves informed of legal developments that may have a bearing on their practice.

What does case law say to date?

2.1 The European Court of Human Rights (ECtHR) has drawn a distinction between the deprivation of liberty of an individual (which is unlawful, unless authorised) and restrictions on the liberty of movement of an individual.

2.2 The ECtHR made it clear that the question of whether someone has been deprived of liberty depends on the particular circumstances of the case. Specifically, the ECtHR said in its October 2004 judgment in *HL v the United Kingdom*:

> 'to determine whether there has been a deprivation of liberty, the starting-point must be the specific situation of the individual concerned and account must be taken of a whole range of factors arising in a particular case such as the type, duration, effects and manner of implementation of the measure in question. The distinction between a deprivation of, and restriction upon, liberty is merely one of degree or intensity and not one of nature or substance.'

2.3 The difference between deprivation of liberty and restriction upon liberty is one of degree or intensity. It may therefore be helpful to envisage a scale, which moves from 'restraint' or 'restriction' to 'deprivation of liberty'. Where an individual is on the scale will depend on the concrete circumstances of the individual and may change over time. For more information on how the Act defines restraint, see paragraphs 2.8–2.12.

2.4 Although the guidance in this chapter includes descriptions of past decisions of the courts, which should be used to help evaluate whether deprivation of liberty may be occurring, each individual case must be assessed on its own circumstances. No two cases are likely to be identical, so it is important to be aware of previous court judgments and the factors that the courts have identified as important.

2.5 The ECtHR and UK courts have determined a number of cases about deprivation of liberty. Their judgments indicate that the following factors can be relevant to identifying whether steps taken involve more than restraint and amount to a deprivation of liberty. It is important to remember that this list is not exclusive; other factors may arise in future in particular cases.

PART VI

- Restraint is used, including sedation, to admit a person to an institution where that person is resisting admission.
- Staff exercise complete and effective control over the care and movement of a person for a significant period.
- Staff exercise control over assessments, treatment, contacts and residence.
- A decision has been taken by the institution that the person will not be released into the care of others, or permitted to live elsewhere, unless the staff in the institution consider it appropriate.
- A request by carers for a person to be discharged to their care is refused.
- The person is unable to maintain social contacts because of restrictions placed on their access to other people.
- The person loses autonomy because they are under continuous supervision and control.

There is more information on some relevant cases at the end of this chapter (paragraphs 2.17–2.23).

How can deprivation of liberty be identified?

2.6 In determining whether deprivation of liberty has occurred, or is likely to occur, decision-makers need to consider all the facts in a particular case. There is unlikely to be any simple definition that can be applied in every case, and it is probable that no single factor will, in itself, determine whether the overall set of steps being taken in relation to the relevant person amount to a deprivation of liberty. In general, the decision-maker should always consider the following:

- All the circumstances of each and every case
- What measures are being taken in relation to the individual? When are they required? For what period do they endure? What are the effects of any restraints or restrictions on the individual? Why are they necessary? What aim do they seek to meet?
- What are the views of the relevant person, their family or carers? Do any of them object to the measures?
- How are any restraints or restrictions implemented? Do any of the constraints on the individual's personal freedom go beyond 'restraint' or 'restriction' to the extent that they constitute a deprivation of liberty?
- Are there any less restrictive options for delivering care or treatment that avoid deprivation of liberty altogether?
- Does the cumulative effect of all the restrictions imposed on the person amount to a deprivation of liberty, even if individually they would not?

What practical steps can be taken to reduce the risk of deprivation of liberty occurring?

2.7 There are many ways in which providers and commissioners of care can reduce the risk of taking steps that amount to a deprivation of liberty, by minimising the restrictions imposed and ensuring that decisions are taken with the involvement of the relevant person and their family, friends and carers. The processes for staff to follow are:

- Make sure that all decisions are taken (and reviewed) in a structured way, and reasons for decisions recorded.
- Follow established good practice for care planning.
- Make a proper assessment of whether the person lacks capacity to decide whether or not to accept the care or treatment proposed, in line with the principles of the Act (see chapter 3 of the main Code for further guidance).
- Before admitting a person to hospital or residential care in circumstances that may amount to a deprivation of liberty, consider whether the person's needs could be met in a less restrictive way. Any restrictions placed on the person while in hospital or in a care home must be kept to the minimum necessary, and should be in place for the shortest possible period.
- Take proper steps to help the relevant person retain contact with family, friends and carers. Where local advocacy services are available, their involvement should be encouraged to support the person and their family, friends and carers.
- Review the care plan on an ongoing basis. It may well be helpful to include an independent element, possibly via an advocacy service, in the review.

What does the Act mean by 'restraint'?

2.8 Section 6(4) of the Act states that someone is using restraint if they:

- use force – or threaten to use force – to make someone do something that they are resisting, or
- restrict a person's freedom of movement, whether they are resisting or not.

2.9 Paragraphs 6.40 to 6.48 of the main Code contain guidance about the appropriate use of restraint. Restraint is appropriate when it is used to prevent harm to the person who lacks capacity and it is a proportionate response to the likelihood and seriousness of harm. Appropriate use of restraint falls short of deprivation of liberty.

2.10 Preventing a person from leaving a care home or hospital unaccompanied because there is a risk that they would try to cross a road in a dangerous way, for example, is likely to be seen as a proportionate restriction or restraint to prevent the person from coming to harm. That would be unlikely, in itself, to constitute a

PART VI

deprivation of liberty. Similarly, locking a door to guard against immediate harm is unlikely, in itself, to amount to a deprivation of liberty.

2.11 The ECtHR has also indicated that the duration of any restrictions is a relevant factor when considering whether or not a person is deprived of their liberty. This suggests that actions that are immediately necessary to prevent harm may not, in themselves, constitute a deprivation of liberty.

2.12 However, where the restriction or restraint is frequent, cumulative and ongoing, or if there are other factors present, then care providers should consider whether this has gone beyond permissible restraint, as defined in the Act. If so, then they must either apply for authorisation under the deprivation of liberty safeguards (as explained in chapter 3) or change their care provision to reduce the level of restraint.

How does the use of restraint apply within a hospital or when taking someone to a hospital or a care home?

Within a hospital

2.13 If a person in hospital for mental health treatment, or being considered for admission to a hospital for mental health treatment, needs to be restrained, this is likely to indicate that they are objecting to treatment or to being in hospital. The care providers should consider whether the need for restraint means the person is objecting (see paragraph 4.46 of this Code for guidance on how to decide whether a person is objecting for this purpose). A person who objects to mental health treatment, and who meets the criteria for detention under the Mental Health Act 1983, is normally ineligible for an authorisation under the deprivation of liberty safeguards. If the care providers believe it is necessary to detain the person, they may wish to consider use of the Mental Health Act 1983.

Taking someone to a hospital or a care home

2.14 Transporting a person who lacks capacity from their home, or another location, to a hospital or care home will not usually amount to a deprivation of liberty (for example, to take them to hospital by ambulance in an emergency.) Even where there is an expectation that the person will be deprived of liberty within the care home or hospital, it is unlikely that the journey itself will constitute a deprivation of liberty so that an authorisation is needed before the journey commences. In almost all cases, it is likely that a person can be lawfully taken to a hospital or a care home under the wider provisions of the Act, as long as it is considered that being in the hospital or care home will be in their best interests.

2.15 In a very few cases, there may be exceptional circumstances where taking a person to a hospital or a care home amounts to a deprivation of liberty, for example where it is necessary to do more than persuade or restrain the person for the purpose of transportation, or where the journey is exceptionally long. In such cases, it may be necessary to seek an order from the Court of Protection to ensure that the journey is taken on a lawful basis.

How should managing authorities avoid unnecessary applications for standard authorisations?

2.16 While it is unlawful to deprive a person of their liberty without authorisation, managing authorities should take into consideration that unnecessary applications for standard authorisations in cases that do not in fact involve depriving a person of liberty may place undue stress upon the person being assessed and on their families or carers. Moreover, consideration must always be given to the possibility of less restrictive options for delivering care or treatment that avoid deprivation of liberty altogether.

Examples of case law

2.17 To provide further guidance, the following paragraphs contain short descriptions of what appear to be the significant features of recent or important cases in England and Wales and the ECtHR dealing with deprivation of liberty. Remember that:
*   these descriptions are for guidance only
*   only the courts can authoritatively determine the law; and
*   the courts are likely to give judgments in cases after this guidance is issued. Staff will need to keep up to date and take account of further relevant legal developments.

Cases where the courts found that the steps taken did not involve a deprivation of liberty

2.18 *LLBC v TG* (judgment of High Court of 14 November 2007)
TG was a 78-year-old man with dementia and cognitive impairment. TG was resident in a care home, but was admitted to hospital with pneumonia and septicaemia. While he was in hospital, there was a dispute between the local authority and TG's daughter and granddaughter about TG's future. The daughter and granddaughter wanted TG to live with them, but the local authority believed that TG needed 24-hour care in a residential care home. The council obtained an order from the court, directing that TG be delivered to the care home identified as appropriate by the council. Neither the daughter nor granddaughter was informed that a court hearing was taking place. That order was subsequently changed and TG was able to live with his daughter and granddaughter.

PART VI

TG's daughter and granddaughter claimed that the period of time he had spent at the care home amounted to a deprivation of his liberty. The judge considered that there was no deprivation of liberty, but the case was borderline. The key factors in his decision included:

- The care home was an ordinary care home where only ordinary restrictions of liberty applied.
- The family were able to visit TG on a largely unrestricted basis and were entitled to take him out from the home for outings.
- TG was personally compliant and expressed himself as happy in the care home. He had lived in a local authority care home for over three years and was objectively content with his situation there.
- There was no occasion where TG was objectively deprived of his liberty.

The judge said:

> 'Whilst I agree that the circumstances of the present case may be near the borderline between mere restrictions of liberty and Article 5 detention, I have come to the conclusion that, looked at as a whole and having regard to all the relevant circumstances, the placement of TG in Towerbridge falls short of engaging Article 5.'

2.19 *Nielsen v Denmark (ECtHR; (1988) 11 EHRR 175)*

The mother of a 12-year-old boy arranged for his admission to the state hospital's psychiatric ward. The boy had a nervous disorder and required treatment in the form of regular talks and environmental therapy. The treatment given, and the conditions under which it was administered, was appropriate. The duration of treatment was 5½ months. The boy, however, applied to the ECtHR, feeling that he had been deprived of his liberty.

The restrictions placed on the applicant's freedom of movement and contacts with the outside world were not much different from restrictions that might be imposed on a child in an ordinary hospital. The door of the ward was locked to prevent children exposing themselves to danger or running around disturbing other patients. The applicant was free to leave the ward with permission and to go out if accompanied by a member of staff. He was able to visit his family and friends, and towards the end of his stay to go to school. The Court held:

> 'The restrictions imposed on the applicant were not of a nature or degree similar to the cases of deprivation of liberty specified in paragraph (1) of Article 5. In particular, he was not detained as a person of unsound mind. .... Indeed, the restrictions to which the applicant was subject were no more than the normal requirements for the care of a child of 12 years of age receiving treatment in hospital. The conditions in which the applicant stayed thus did not, in principle, differ from those obtaining in many hospital wards where children with physical disorders are treated.'

It concluded:

> 'the hospitalisation of the applicant did not amount to a deprivation of liberty within the meaning of Article 5, but was a responsible exercise by his mother of her custodial rights in the interests of the child.'

2.20 *HM v Switzerland (ECtHR; (2002) 38 EHRR 314)*

An 84-year-old woman was placed indefinitely in a nursing home by state authorities. She had had the possibility of staying at home and being cared for there, but she and her son had refused to co-operate with the relevant care association, and her living conditions had subsequently deteriorated. The state authorities placed her in the home in order to provide her with necessary medical care and satisfactory living conditions and hygiene.

The woman was not placed in the secure ward of the home but was free to move within the home and to have social contacts with the outside world. She was initially undecided as to what solution she preferred and, after moving into the home, the applicant had agreed to stay there. However, she subsequently applied to the courts saying that she had been deprived of her liberty.

The Court held that she had not been deprived of her liberty:

> 'Bearing these elements in mind, in particular the fact that [the authorities] had ordered the applicant's placement in the nursing home in her own interests in order to provide her with the necessary medical care and satisfactory living conditions and standards of hygiene, and also taking into consideration the comparable circumstances of *Nielsen v Denmark* [see case summary above], the Court concludes that in the circumstances of the present case the applicant's placement in the nursing home did not amount to a deprivation of liberty within the meaning of Article 5(1), but was a responsible measure taken by the competent authorities in the applicant's best interests'

Cases where the courts have found that the steps taken involve a deprivation of liberty

2.21 *DE and JE v Surrey County Council (SCC)* (High Court judgment of 29 December 2006)

DE was a 76-year-old man who, following a major stroke, had become blind and had significant short-term memory impairment. He also had dementia and lacked capacity to decide where he should live, but was still often able to express his wishes with some clarity and force.

DE was married to JE. In August 2003, DE was living at home with JE. There was an occasion when JE felt that she could not care for DE, and placed him on a chair on the pavement in front of the house and called the police. The local authority then placed him in two care homes, referred to in the judgment of the court as the X home and the Y home.

Within the care homes, DE had a very substantial degree of freedom and lots of contact with the outside world. He was never subject to physical or chemical restraint.

DE repeatedly expressed the wish to live with JE, and JE also wanted DE to live with her. SCC would not agree to DE returning to live with, or visit, JE and made it clear that if JE were to persist in an attempt to remove DE, SCC would contact the police. DE and JE applied to the courts that this was a deprivation of his liberty.

In his judgment, Justice Munby said:

'The fundamental issue in this case ... is whether DE has been and is deprived of his liberty to leave the X home and whether DE has been and is deprived of his liberty to leave the Y home. And when I refer to leaving the X home and the Y home, I do not mean leaving for the purpose of some trip or outing approved by SCC or by those managing the institution; I mean leaving in the sense of removing himself permanently in order to live where and with whom he chooses, specifically removing himself to live at home with JE.'

He then said:

'DE was not and is not "free to leave", and was and is, in that sense, completely under the control of [the local authority], because, as [counsel for DE] put it, it was and is [the local authority] who decides the essential matters of where DE can live, whether he can leave and whether he can be with JE.'

He concluded:

'The simple reality is that DE will be permitted to leave the institution in which [the local authority] has placed him and be released to the care of JE only as and when, – if ever; probably never, – [the local authority] considers it appropriate. [The local authority's] motives may be the purest, but in my judgment, [it] has been and is continuing to deprive DE of his liberty.'

2.22 *HL v United Kingdom (ECtHR;* (2004) 40 EHRR 761)

A 48-year-old man who had had autism since birth was unable to speak and his level of understanding was limited. He was frequently agitated and had a history of self-harming behaviour. He lacked the capacity to consent to treatment.

For over 30 years, he was cared for in Bournewood Hospital. In 1994, he was entrusted to carers and for three years he lived successfully with his carers. Following an incident of self-harm at a day centre on 22 July 1997, the applicant was taken to Bournewood Hospital where he was re-admitted informally (not under the Mental Health Act 1983).

The carers wished to have the applicant released to their care, which the hospital refused. The carers were unable to visit him.

In its judgment in *HL v the United Kingdom*, the ECtHR said that:

'the key factor in the present case [is] that the health care professionals treating and managing the applicant exercised complete and effective control over his care and movements from the moment he presented acute behavioural problems on July 22, 1997 to the date when he was compulsorily detained on October 29, 1997.

'His responsible medical officer (Dr M) was clear that, had the applicant resisted admission or tried to leave thereafter, she would have prevented him from doing so and would have considered his involuntary committal under s. 3 of the 1983 Act; indeed, as soon as the Court of Appeal indicated that his appeal would be allowed, he was compulsorily detained under the 1983 Act. The correspondence between the applicant's carers and Dr M reflects both the carer's wish to have the applicant immediately released to their care and, equally, the clear intention of Dr M and the other relevant health care professionals to exercise strict control over his assessment, treatment, contacts and, notably, movement and residence; the applicant would only be released from hospital to the care of Mr and Mrs E as and when those professionals considered it appropriate. ... it was clear from the above noted correspondence that the applicant's contact with his carers was directed and controlled by the hospital, his carers visiting him for the first time after his admission on 2 November 1997.

'Accordingly, the concrete situation was that the applicant was under continuous supervision and control and was not free to leave.'

2.23 *Storck v Germany (ECtHR;* (2005) 43 EHRR 96)

A young woman was placed by her father in a psychiatric institution on occasions in 1974 and 1975. In July 1977, at the age of 18, she was placed again in a psychiatric institution. She was kept in a locked ward and was under the continuous supervision and control of the clinic personnel and was not free to leave the clinic during her entire stay of 20 months. When she attempted to flee, she was shackled. When she succeeded one time, she was brought back by the police. She was unable to maintain regular contact with the outside world.

She applied to the courts on the basis that she had been deprived of her liberty. There was a dispute about whether she consented to her confinement.

The Court noted:

'the applicant, on several occasions, had tried to flee from the clinic. She had to be shackled in order to prevent her from absconding and had to be brought back to the clinic by the police when she managed to escape on one occasion. Under these circumstances, the Court is unable to discern any factual basis for the assumption that the applicant – presuming that she had the capacity to consent – agreed to her continued stay in the clinic. In the alternative, assuming that the applicant was no longer capable of consenting following her treatment with strong medication, she cannot, in any event, be considered to have validly agreed to her stay in the clinic.'

2.24 These cases reinforce the need to carefully consider all the specific circumstances of the relevant individual before deciding whether or not a person is being deprived of their liberty. They also underline the vital importance of involving family, friends and carers in this decision-making process: a significant feature of a number of the cases that have come before the courts is a difference of opinion or communication issue between the commissioners or providers of care and family members and carers.

PART VI

3   HOW AND WHEN CAN DEPRIVATION OF LIBERTY BE APPLIED FOR AND AUTHORISED?

There are some circumstances in which depriving a person, who lacks capacity to consent to the arrangements made for their care or treatment, of their liberty is necessary to protect them from harm, and is in their best interests.

Deprivation of liberty can be authorised by supervisory bodies (primary care trusts (PCTs), local authorities, Welsh Ministers or local health boards (LHBs). To obtain authorisation to deprive someone of their liberty, managing authorities have to apply for an authorisation following the processes set out in this chapter.[85] Once an application has been received, the supervisory body must then follow the assessment processes set out in chapter 4 before it can authorise deprivation of liberty. It should be borne in mind that a deprivation of liberty authorisation does not, in itself, give authority to treat someone. This issue is covered in paragraphs 5.10 to 5.13.

In the vast majority of cases, it should be possible to plan in advance so that a standard authorisation can be obtained before the deprivation of liberty begins. There may, however, be some exceptional cases where the need for the deprivation of liberty is so urgent that it is in the best interests of the person for it to begin while the application is being considered. In that case, the care home or hospital may give an urgent authorisation for up to seven days (see chapter 6).

How, in summary, can deprivation of liberty be authorised?

3.1 A **managing authority** has responsibility for applying for authorisation of deprivation of liberty for any person who may come within the scope of the deprivation of liberty safeguards:

- In the case of an NHS hospital, the managing authority is the NHS body responsible for the running of the hospital in which the relevant person is, or is to be, a resident.

- In the case of a care home or a private hospital, the managing authority will be the person registered, or required to be registered, under part 2 of the Care Standards Act 2000 in respect of the hospital or care home.

3.2 If a healthcare or social care professional thinks that an authorisation is needed, they should inform the managing authority. This might be as a result of a care review or needs assessment but could happen at any other time too. (See chapter 9 for guidance on action to take if there is a concern that a person is already being deprived of their liberty, without authorisation.)

3.3 A **supervisory body** is responsible for considering requests for authorisations, commissioning the required assessments (see chapter 4) and, where all the assessments agree, authorising the deprivation of liberty:

- Where the deprivation of liberty safeguards are applied to a person in a hospital situated in England, the supervisory body will be:

    - if a PCT commissions[86] the relevant care or treatment (or it is commissioned on the PCT's behalf), that PCT

---

[85]   If a person is lawfully deprived of liberty in a care home or hospital as **a consequence of an order of the Court of Protection**, there is no need to apply for an authorisation. However, once the order of the Court of Protection has expired, for lawful deprivation of liberty to continue authorisation must be obtained by following the processes set out in this chapter.

[86]   Guidance on establishing the responsible commissioner can be found at http://www.dh.gov.uk/en/Publicationsandstatistics/Publications/ PublicationsPolicyAndGuidance/DH_078466

- – if the Welsh Ministers or an LHB commissions the relevant care and treatment in England, the Welsh Ministers, or
- – in any other case, the PCT for the area in which the hospital is situated.

- Where the deprivation of liberty safeguards are applied to a person in a hospital situated in Wales, the supervisory body will be the Welsh Ministers or an LHB **unless** a PCT commissions the relevant care and treatment in Wales, in which case the PCT will be the supervisory body.

- Where the deprivation of liberty safeguards are applied to a person in a care home, whether situated in England or Wales, the supervisory body will be the local authority for the area in which the person is ordinarily resident. However, if the person is not ordinarily resident in the area of any local authority (for example a person of no fixed abode), the supervisory body will be the local authority for the area in which the care home is situated.[87]

3.4 There are two types of authorisation: standard and urgent. A managing authority must request a standard authorisation when it appears likely that, at some time during the next 28 days, someone will be accommodated in its hospital or care home in circumstances that amount to a deprivation of liberty within the meaning of Article 5 of the European Convention on Human Rights. The request must be made to the supervisory body. Whenever possible, authorisation should be obtained in advance. Where this is not possible, and the managing authority believes it is necessary to deprive someone of their liberty in their best interests **before** the standard authorisation process can be completed, the managing authority must itself give an urgent authorisation and then obtain standard authorisation within seven calendar days (see chapter 6).

3.5 The flowchart at Annex 1 gives an overview of how the deprivation of liberty safeguards process should operate.

PART VI

---

[87] To work out the place of ordinary residence, the usual mechanisms under the National Assistance Act 1948 apply (see http://www.dh.gov.uk/en/SocialCare/Deliveringadultsocialcare/Ordinaryresidence/DH_079346). Any unresolved questions about the ordinary residence of a person will be handled by the Secretary of State or by the Welsh Ministers. Until a decision is made, the local authority that received the application must act as the supervisory body. After the decision is made, the local authority of ordinary residence must become the supervisory body. Regulations 17 to 19 of the Mental Capacity (Deprivation of Liberty: Standard Authorisations, Assessments and Ordinary Residence) Regulations 2008 set out, for England, arrangements that are to have effect while any question as to the ordinary residence of a person is determined in a case in which a local authority has received a request for a standard authorisation or a request to decide whether there is an unauthorised deprivation of liberty.

How should managing authorities decide whether to apply for an authorisation?

3.6 Managing authorities should have a procedure in place that identifies:

- whether deprivation of liberty is or may be necessary in a particular case
- what steps they should take to assess whether to seek authorisation
- whether they have taken all practical and reasonable steps to avoid a deprivation of liberty
- what action they should take if they do need to request an authorisation
- how they should review cases where authorisation is or may be necessary, and
- who should take the necessary action.

A flowchart that can be used to help develop such a procedure is at Annex 2.

What is the application process?

3.7 A managing authority must apply for a standard authorisation. The application should be made in writing to the supervisory body. A standard form is available for this purpose.

3.8 In England, the request from a managing authority for a standard authorisation must include:

- the name and gender of the relevant person
- the age of the relevant person or, where this is not known, whether the managing authority reasonably believes that the relevant person is aged 18 years or older
- the address at which the relevant person is currently located, and the telephone number at the address
- the name, address and telephone number of the managing authority and the name of the person within the managing authority who is dealing with the request
- the purpose for which the authorisation is requested
- the date from which the authorisation is sought, and
- whether the managing authority has given an urgent authorisation and, if so, the date on which it expires.

3.9 A request for a standard authorisation must also include, if it is available or could reasonably be obtained by the managing authority:

- any medical information relating to the relevant person's health that the managing authority reasonably considers to be relevant to the proposed restrictions to their liberty
- the diagnosis of the mental disorder (within the meaning of the Mental Health Act 1983 but disregarding any exclusion for persons with learning disability) from which the relevant person is suffering

- any relevant care plans and needs assessments
- the racial, ethnic or national origins of the relevant person
- whether the relevant person has any special communication needs
- details of the proposed restrictions on the relevant person's liberty
- whether it is necessary for an Independent Mental Capacity Advocate (IMCA) to be instructed
- where the purpose of the proposed restrictions to the relevant person's liberty is to give treatment, whether the relevant person has made an advance decision that may be valid and applicable to some or all of that treatment
- whether there is an existing standard authorisation in relation to the detention of the relevant person and, if so, the date of the expiry of that authorisation
- whether the relevant person is subject to any requirements of the Mental Health Act 1983, and
- the name, address and telephone number of:
  - anyone named by the relevant person as someone to be consulted about their welfare
  - anyone engaged in caring for the person or interested in their welfare
  - any donee of a Lasting Power of Attorney ('donee') granted by the person
  - any deputy appointed for the person by the court, and
  - any IMCA who has already been instructed.

If there is an existing authorisation, information that has not changed does not have to be resupplied.

3.10 In Wales, the request from a managing authority for a standard authorisation must include:

- the name of the relevant person
- the name, address and telephone number of the managing authority
- the reasons why the managing authority considers that the relevant person is being or will be detained in circumstances which amount to a deprivation of liberty
- the reasons why the managing authority considers that the relevant person satisfies the qualifying requirements
- details of any urgent authorisation
- information or documents in support of why the relevant person satisfies the qualifying requirements
- the name, address and telephone number of any person who has an interest in the welfare of the relevant person, and
- details of any relevant valid and applicable advance decision.

Where should applications be sent?

3.11 If the application is being made by a care home, the application must be sent to the local authority for the area in which the relevant

PART VI

person is ordinarily resident. If the relevant person is not ordinarily resident in the area of any local authority (for example, is of no fixed abode), if the care home does not know where the person currently lives, or if the person does not live in England or Wales, the application should be sent to the local authority in whose area the care home is located.

3.12 When the application is being made by a hospital:

- if the care is commissioned by a PCT, the application should be sent to that PCT
- if the care is commissioned by the Welsh Ministers, the application should be sent to the LHB for the area in which the relevant person is ordinarily resident
- if the care is commissioned by an LHB, the application should be sent to that LHB, and
- in any other case (for example, care that is commissioned privately), the application should be sent to the PCT for the area in which the relevant hospital is situated.

3.13 An application sent to the wrong supervisory body can be passed on to the correct supervisory body without the managing authority needing to reapply. But the managing authority should make every effort to establish which is the correct supervisory body to minimise delays in handling the application. (Footnote 8 explains how place of ordinary residence is determined and how disputes about the place of ordinary residence will be resolved.)

3.14 The managing authority must keep a written record of each request made for a standard authorisation and the reasons for making the request.

Who should be informed that an application has been made?

3.15 The managing authority should tell the relevant person's family, friends and carers, and any IMCA already involved in the relevant person's case, that it has applied for an authorisation of deprivation of liberty, unless it is impractical or impossible to do so, or undesirable in terms of the interests of the relevant person's health or safety. Anyone who is engaged in caring for the relevant person or interested in their welfare, or who has been named by them as a person to consult, must be given the opportunity to input their views on whether deprivation of liberty is in the best interests of the relevant person, as part of the best interests assessment (see paragraphs 4.58 to 4.76), as far as is practical and appropriate. The views of the relevant person about who to inform and consult should be taken into account.

3.16 The managing authority must notify the supervisory body if it is satisfied that there is no one who should be consulted in determining the relevant person's best interests, except those providing care and treatment for the relevant person in a professional capacity or for remuneration. In such a case, the supervisory body must instruct an IMCA to represent and support the relevant person before any assessments take place (see paragraphs 3.22 to 3.27 regarding the rights and role of an IMCA instructed in these circumstances).

What action does the supervisory body need to take when it receives an application for authorisation?

3.17 When it receives an application for authorisation of deprivation of liberty, the supervisory body must, as soon as is practical and possible:
- consider whether the request is appropriate and should be pursued, and
- seek any further information that it requires from the managing authority to help it with the decision.

If the supervisory body has any doubts about proceeding with the request, it should seek to resolve them with the managing authority.

3.18 Supervisory bodies should have a procedure in place that identifies the action they should take, who should take it and within what timescale. As far as practical and possible, they should communicate the procedure to managing authorities and give them the relevant contact details for making an application. The flowchart at Annex 3 summarises the process that a supervisory body should follow on receipt of a request from a managing authority for a standard deprivation of liberty authorisation.

Can an application for authorisation be made in advance?

3.19 A standard authorisation comes into force when it is given, or at any later time specified in the authorisation. Paragraph 3.4 refers to the timescales for initially applying for authorisations: 28 days are allowed so that authorisations can usually be sought as part of care planning (such as planning of discharge from hospital). There is no statutory limit on how far in advance of the expiry of one authorisation a fresh authorisation can be sought. Clearly, however, an authorisation should not be applied for too far in advance as this may prevent an assessor from making an accurate assessment of what the person's circumstances will be at the time the authorisation will come into force.

3.20 If a supervisory body considers that an application for an authorisation has been made too far in advance, it should raise the matter with the managing authority. The outcome may be an agreement with the managing authority that the application should be withdrawn, to be resubmitted at a more appropriate time.

PART VI

What happens when the managing authority and the supervisory body are the same organisation?

3.21 In some cases, a single organisation will be both supervisory body and managing authority – for example, where a local authority itself provides a residential care home, rather than purchasing the service from another organisation. This does not prevent it from acting in both capacities. However, in England the regulations specify that in such a situation the best interests assessor cannot be an employee of the supervisory body/managing authority, or providing services to it. For example, in a case involving a local authority care home, the best interests assessor could be an NHS employee or an independent practitioner. (See paragraphs 4.13 and 4.60 for full details of who can be a best interests assessor.) There are similar provisions for Wales.

When should an IMCA be instructed?

3.22 If there is nobody appropriate to consult, other than people engaged in providing care or treatment for the relevant person in a professional capacity[88] or for remuneration, the managing authority must notify the supervisory body when it submits the application for the deprivation of liberty authorisation. The supervisory body must then instruct an IMCA straight away to represent the person. It is particularly important that the IMCA is instructed quickly if an urgent authorisation has been given, so that they can make a meaningful input at a very early stage in the process. (See paragraph 3.28 for other stages in the deprivation of liberty safeguards process when an IMCA must or may be instructed.)

3.23 Chapter 10 of the main Code ('What is the new Independent Mental Capacity Advocate service and how does it work?') describes the wider rights and role of an IMCA. Supervisory bodies should follow the guidance in that chapter in identifying an IMCA who is suitably qualified to represent the relevant person. However, it is also important to note that an IMCA instructed at this initial stage of the deprivation of liberty safeguards process has additional rights and responsibilities compared to an IMCA more generally instructed under the Mental Capacity Act 2005. IMCAs in this context have the right to:

- as they consider appropriate, give information or make submissions to assessors, which assessors must take into account in carrying out their assessments
- receive copies of any assessments from the supervisory body
- receive a copy of any standard authorisation given by the supervisory body

---

[88] A friend or family member is **not** considered to be acting in a professional capacity simply because they have been appointed as the person's representative for a previous authorisation.

- be notified by the supervisory body if they are unable to give a standard authorisation because one or more of the deprivation of liberty assessments did not meet the qualifying requirements
- receive a copy of any urgent authorisation from the managing authority
- receive from the managing authority a copy of any notice declining to extend the duration of an urgent authorisation
- receive from the supervisory body a copy of any notice that an urgent authorisation has ceased to be in force, and
- apply to the Court of Protection for permission to take the relevant person's case to the Court in connection with a matter relating to the giving or refusal of a standard or urgent authorisation (in the same way as any other third party can).

The assessment and authorisation processes are described in chapters 4 and 5.

3.24 IMCAs will need to familiarise themselves with the relevant person's circumstances and to consider what they may need to tell any of the assessors during the course of the assessment process. They will also need to consider whether they have any concerns about the outcome of the assessment process.

3.25 Differences of opinion between an IMCA and an assessor should ideally be resolved while the assessment is still in progress. Where there are significant disagreements between an IMCA and one or more of the assessors that cannot be resolved between them, the supervisory body should be informed before the assessment is finalised. The supervisory body should then consider what action might be appropriate, including perhaps convening a meeting to discuss the matter. Wherever possible, differences of opinion should be resolved informally in order to minimise the need for an IMCA to make an application to the Court of Protection. However, an IMCA should not be discouraged from making an application to the Court of Protection should they consider it necessary. (Chapter 15 of the main Code ('What are the best ways to settle disagreements and disputes about issues covered in the Act?') contains general guidance about the resolution of disputes arising under the Act.)

3.26 An IMCA will also need to consider whether they have any concerns about the giving of an urgent authorisation (see chapter 6), and whether it would be appropriate to challenge the giving of such an authorisation via the Court of Protection.

3.27 Once a relevant person's representative is appointed (see chapter 7), the duties imposed on the IMCA cease to apply. The IMCA may, however, still apply to the Court of Protection for permission to take the relevant person's case to the Court in connection with the giving of a standard authorisation; but, in doing so, the IMCA must take account of the views of the relevant person's representative.

PART VI

Other circumstances in which an IMCA must or may be instructed

3.28 An IMCA must also be instructed during gaps in the appointment of a relevant person's representative (for instance, if a new representative is being sought – see paragraphs 7.34 to 7.36). In addition, an IMCA may be instructed at any time where:

- the relevant person does not have a paid 'professional' representative
- the relevant person or their representative requests that an IMCA is instructed to help them, or
- a supervisory body believes that instructing an IMCA will help to ensure that the person's rights are protected (see paragraphs 7.37 to 7.41).

4   WHAT IS THE ASSESSMENT PROCESS FOR A STANDARD AUTHORISATION OF DEPRIVATION OF LIBERTY?

When a supervisory body gives a standard authorisation of deprivation of liberty, the managing authority may lawfully deprive the relevant person of their liberty in the hospital or care home named in the authorisation.

This chapter describes the assessments that have to be undertaken in order for a standard authorisation to be given. It also sets out who is eligible to undertake the assessments.

What assessments are required before giving a standard authorisation?

4.1 As soon as the supervisory body has confirmed that the request for a standard authorisation should be pursued, it must obtain the relevant assessments to ascertain whether the qualifying requirements of the deprivation of liberty safeguards are met. The supervisory body has a legal responsibility to select assessors who are both suitable and eligible. Assessments must be completed within 21 days for a standard deprivation of liberty authorisation, or, where an urgent authorisation has been given, before the urgent authorisation expires.

4.2 The assessments (described in paragraphs 4.23 to 4.76) are:
- age assessment (paragraphs 4.23 and 4.24)
- no refusals assessment (paragraphs 4.25 to 4.28).
- mental capacity assessment (paragraphs 4.29 to 4.32)
- mental health assessment (paragraphs 4.33 to 4.39)
- eligibility assessment (paragraphs 4.40 to 4.57), and
- best interests assessment (paragraphs 4.58 to 4.76).

Standard forms are available for completion by each of the assessors.

4.3 If the person being assessed is not currently in the supervisory body's area, the supervisory body should seek, as far as is practical and possible, to arrange to use assessors based near where the person currently is.

Using equivalent assessments

4.4 The Act states that where an 'equivalent assessment' to any of these assessments has already been obtained, it may be relied upon instead of obtaining a fresh assessment.

4.5 An equivalent assessment is an assessment:

- that has been carried out in the last 12 months, not necessarily for the purpose of a deprivation of liberty authorisation (where the required assessment is an age assessment, there is no time limit on the use of an equivalent assessment)
- that meets all the requirements of the deprivation of liberty assessment,
- of which the supervisory body is satisfied that there is no reason to believe that it is no longer accurate, and
- of which the supervisory body has a written copy.

An example would be a recent assessment carried out for the purposes of the Mental Health Act 1983, which could serve as an equivalent to a mental health assessment.

4.6 Great care should be taken in deciding to use an equivalent assessment and this should not be done routinely. The older the assessment is, even if it took place within the last 12 months, the less likely it is to represent a valid equivalent assessment (unless it is an age assessment). For example, only a very recent mental capacity assessment would be appropriate where capacity is known to fluctuate, since one of the principles of the Act is that a person must be assumed to have capacity unless it is established that they lack capacity.

4.7 If an equivalent best interests assessment is used, the supervisory body must also take into account any information given, or submissions made, by the relevant person's representative or an Independent Mental Capacity Advocate (IMCA) instructed under the deprivation of liberty safeguards.

4.8 Supervisory bodies should record the reasons why they have used any equivalent assessment. A standard form is available for this purpose.

When must assessments take place?

4.9 The regulations for England[89] specify that all assessments required for a standard authorisation must be completed within 21 calendar days from the date on which the supervisory body receives a request from a managing authority. The regulations for Wales specify that all assessments required for a standard authorisation must be completed within 21 days from the date the assessors were instructed by the supervisory body.

PART VI

---

[89]   The Mental Capacity (Deprivation of Liberty: Standard Authorisations, Assessments and Ordinary Residence) Regulations 2008.

4.10 However, if an urgent authorisation is already in force, the assessments must be completed before the urgent authorisation expires. The regulations for Wales specify that, where the managing authority has given itself an urgent authorisation and applies for a standard authorisation, the assessors must complete the assessments within five days of the date of instruction.

4.11 Urgent authorisations may be given by managing authorities for an initial period not exceeding seven days. If there are exceptional reasons why it has not been possible to deal with the request for a standard authorisation within the period of the urgent authorisation, they may be extended **by the supervisory body** for up to a further seven days. It is for the supervisory body to decide what constitutes an 'exceptional reason', taking into account all the circumstances of an individual case.

4.12 Supervisory bodies must keep a record of all requests for standard authorisations that they receive and should acknowledge the receipt of requests from managing authorities for standard authorisations.

How should assessors be selected?

4.13 The six assessments do not have to be completed by different assessors. In fact, it is highly unlikely that there will be six separate assessors – not least because it is desirable to minimise the burden on the person being assessed. However, each assessor must make their own decisions, and to ensure that an appropriate degree of objectivity is brought to the assessment process:
- there **must** be a minimum of two assessors
- the mental health and best interests assessors **must** be different people
- the best interests assessor can be an employee of the supervisory body or managing authority, but **must not** be involved in the care or treatment of the person they are assessing nor in decisions about their care
- a potential best interests assessor should not be used if they are in a line management relationship with the professional proposing the deprivation of liberty or the mental health assessor
- none of the assessors may have a financial interest in the case of the person they are assessing (a person is considered to have a financial interest in a case where that person is a partner, director, other office-holder or major shareholder of the managing authority that has made the application for a standard authorisation)
- an assessor **must not** be a relative of the person being assessed, nor of a person with a financial interest in the person's care. For this purpose, a 'relative' is:
  a. a spouse, ex-spouse, civil partner or ex-civil partner
  b. a person living with the relevant person as if they were a spouse or a civil partner

c. a parent or child
d. a brother or sister
e. a child of a person falling within definitions a, b or d
f. a grandparent or grandchild
g. a grandparent-in-law or grandchild-in-law
h. an aunt or uncle
i. a sister-in-law or brother-in-law
j. a son-in-law or daughter-in-law
k. a first cousin, or
l. a half-brother or half-sister.
These relationships include step-relationships

- where the managing authority and supervisory body are both the same body (see paragraph 3.21), the supervisory body may not select to carry out a best interests assessment a person who is employed by the body, or providing services to it, and
- the supervisory body should seek to avoid appointing assessors in any other possible conflict of interests situations that might bring into question the objectivity of an assessment.

4.14 Other relevant factors for supervisory bodies to consider when appointing assessors include:

- the reason for the proposed deprivation of liberty
- whether the potential assessor has experience of working with the service user group from which the person being assessed comes (for example, older people, people with learning disabilities, people with autism, or people with brain injury)
- whether the potential assessor has experience of working with people from the cultural background of the person being assessed, and
- any other specific needs of the person being assessed, for example communication needs.

4.15 Supervisory bodies should ensure that sufficient assessors are available to meet their needs, and must be satisfied in each case that the assessors have the skills, experience, qualifications and training required by regulations to perform the function effectively. The regulations also require supervisory bodies to be satisfied that there is an appropriate criminal record certificate issued in respect of an assessor. It will be useful to keep a record of qualified assessors and their experience and availability. Supervisory bodies should consider making arrangements to ensure that assessors have the necessary opportunities to maintain their skills and knowledge (of legal developments, for example) and share, audit and review their practice.

4.16 Assessors act as individual professionals and are personally accountable for their decisions. Managing authorities and supervisory bodies must not dictate or seek to influence their decisions.

4.17 There is no reason in principle why interviews, examinations and fact-finding required as part of any deprivation of liberty safeguards assessment cannot serve more than one purpose, in order to avoid unnecessary burdens both on the person being assessed and on staff. However, if this does happen, all purposes of the interview or examination should be made clear to the relevant person, and to any family members, friends, carers or advocates supporting them.

Protection against liability

4.18 Nobody can or should carry out an assessment unless they are protected against any liabilities that might arise in connection with carrying out the assessment. Individual assessors will need to satisfy themselves, and any supervisory body that selects them as an assessor, that they are appropriately covered by either employers' or personal insurance.

What is the assessment process?

4.19 As indicated in paragraph 4.2, there are six assessments that must be conducted before a supervisory body can give an authorisation.

4.20 The assessments are set out in the order in which it will normally be most appropriate to complete them. In particular, it is recommended that the best interests assessment, which is likely to be the most time-consuming, is not started until there is a reasonable expectation that the other five qualifying requirements will be met.

4.21 But, ultimately, it is for the supervisory body to decide on the order in which the assessments should be undertaken and, in the light of the time available to complete the overall assessment process, the extent to which they should be undertaken to separate or simultaneous timescales. The supervisory body's decision about how many assessors will undertake the assessments (see paragraph 4.13) will also be a relevant factor.

4.22 The following paragraphs explain the assessment process.

Age assessment

4.23 The purpose of the age assessment is simply to confirm whether the relevant person is aged 18 or over. This is because, as paragraph 1.12 explains, the deprivation of liberty safeguards apply only to people aged 18 or over. For people under the age of 18, a different safeguards process applies. In most cases, this is likely to be a fairly straightforward assessment. If there is any doubt, age should be established by a birth certificate or other evidence that the assessor considers reliable. Where it is not possible to verify with any certainty whether a person is aged 18 or over, the assessor should base the assessment on the best of their knowledge and belief.

4.24 This assessment can be undertaken by anybody whom the supervisory body is satisfied is eligible to be a best interests assessor.

No refusals assessment

4.25 The purpose of the no refusals assessment is to establish whether an authorisation to deprive the relevant person of their liberty would conflict with other existing authority for decision-making for that person.

4.26 The following are instances of a conflict that would mean that a standard authorisation could not be given:

- If the relevant person has made **an advance decision to refuse treatment** that remains valid and is applicable to some or all of the treatment that is the purpose for which the authorisation is requested, then a standard authorisation cannot be given. See sections 24 to 26 of the Mental Capacity Act 2005 and chapter 9 of the main Code ('What does the Act say about advance decisions to refuse treatment?') for more information about advance decisions and when they are valid and applicable. Remember too that the deprivation of liberty authorisation does not, in itself, provide authority to treat the person (see paragraphs 5.10 to 5.13 of this Code).

- If any part of the proposal to deprive the person of their liberty (including any element of the care plan) would be in conflict with a **valid decision of a donee or a deputy** made within the scope of their authority, then a standard authorisation cannot be given. For example, if a donee or deputy decides that it would not be in the best interests of the relevant person to be in a particular care home, and that decision is within the scope of their authority, then the care plan will need to be reviewed with the donee or deputy.

4.27 If there is any such conflict, the no refusals assessment qualifying requirement will not be met and a standard authorisation for deprivation of liberty cannot be given.

4.28 The no refusals assessment can be undertaken by anybody that the supervisory body is satisfied is eligible to be a best interests assessor.

Mental capacity assessment

4.29 The purpose of the mental capacity assessment is to establish whether the relevant person lacks capacity to decide whether or not they should be accommodated in the relevant hospital or care home to be given care or treatment. The assessment refers specifically to the relevant person's capacity to make this decision at the time it needs to be made. The starting assumption should always be that a person has the capacity to make the decision.

PART VI

4.30 Sections 1 to 3 of the Act set out how a person's capacity to make decisions should be determined. Chapter 4 of the main Code ('How does the Act define a person's capacity to make a decision and how should capacity be assessed?') gives further guidance on ways to assess capacity. When assessing the capacity of a person being considered for the deprivation of liberty safeguards, these guidelines should be followed.

4.31 The regulations for England specify that the mental capacity assessment can be undertaken by anyone who is eligible to act as a mental health or best interests assessor. In deciding who to appoint for this assessment, the supervisory body should take account of the need for understanding and practical experience of the nature of the person's condition and its impact on decision-making.

4.32 Supervisory bodies may wish to consider using an eligible assessor who already knows the relevant person to undertake this assessment, if they think it would be of benefit. This will primarily arise if somebody involved in the person's care is considered best placed to carry out a reliable assessment, using their knowledge of the person over a period of time. It may also help in reducing any distress that might be caused to the person if they were assessed by somebody they did not know.

Mental health assessment

4.33 The purpose of the mental health assessment is to establish whether the relevant person has a mental disorder within the meaning of the Mental Health Act 1983. That means any disorder or disability of mind, apart from dependence on alcohol or drugs. It includes all learning disabilities. This is not an assessment to determine whether the person requires mental health treatment.

4.34 A distinction can be drawn between the mental health assessment and the mental capacity assessment:
- Although a person must have an impairment or disturbance of the functioning of the mind or brain in order to lack capacity, it does not follow that they automatically have a mental disorder within the meaning of the Mental Health Act 1983.
- The objective of the mental health assessment is to ensure that the person is medically diagnosed as being of 'unsound mind' and so comes within the scope of Article 5 of the European Convention on Human Rights.

4.35 In both England and Wales, the regulations specify that:
- the mental health assessment must be carried out by a doctor, and
- the assessing doctor has to either be approved under section 12 of the Mental Health Act 1983, or be a registered medical practitioner with at least three years' post-registration experience in the diagnosis or treatment of mental disorder, such as a GP with a special interest. This includes doctors who

are automatically treated as being section 12 approved because they are approved clinicians under the Mental Health Act 1983.

4.36 To be eligible to undertake assessments, in England a doctor will need to have completed the standard training for deprivation of liberty mental health assessors. Except in the 12 month period beginning with the date the doctor has successfully completed the standard training, the regulations for England also require the supervisory body to be satisfied that the doctor has, in the 12 months prior to selection, completed further training relevant to their role as a mental health assessor. In Wales, a doctor will need to have completed appropriate training and have appropriate skills and experience.

4.37 Supervisory bodies must consider the suitability of the assessor for the particular case (for example, whether they have experience relevant to the person's condition).

4.38 As with the mental capacity assessment, supervisory bodies may wish to consider using an eligible assessor who already knows the relevant person to undertake this assessment, if they think it would be of benefit.

4.39 The mental health assessor is required to consider how the mental health of the person being assessed is likely to be affected by being deprived of their liberty, and to report their conclusions to the best interests assessor. The mental health and best interests assessments cannot be carried out by the same person.

Eligibility assessment

4.40 This assessment relates specifically to the relevant person's status, or potential status, under the Mental Health Act 1983.

4.41 A person is not eligible for a deprivation of liberty authorisation if:
- they are detained as a hospital in-patient under the Mental Health Act 1983, or
- the authorisation, if given, would be inconsistent with an obligation placed on them under the Mental Health Act 1983, such as a requirement to live somewhere else. This will only affect people who are on leave of absence from detention under the Mental Health Act 1983 or who are subject to guardianship, supervised community treatment or conditional discharge.

4.42 Where the proposed authorisation relates to a care home, or to deprivation of liberty in a hospital for non-mental health treatment, the eligibility assessment will simply be a matter of checking that authorisation would not be inconsistent with an obligation placed on the person under the Mental Health Act 1983.

4.43 When a person is subject to guardianship under the Mental Health Act 1983, their guardian can decide where they are to live, but cannot authorise deprivation of liberty and cannot require them to live somewhere where they are deprived of liberty unless that deprivation of liberty is authorised.

PART VI

4.44 Occasionally, a person who is subject to guardianship and who lacks capacity to make the relevant decisions may need specific care or treatment in a care home or hospital that cannot be delivered without deprivation of liberty. This may be in a care home in which they are already living or in which the guardian thinks they ought to live, or it may be in a hospital where they need to be for physical health care. It may also apply if they need to be in hospital for mental health care. The process for obtaining a deprivation of liberty authorisation and the criteria to be applied are the same as for any other person.

4.45 If the proposed authorisation relates to deprivation of liberty in a hospital **wholly or partly for the purpose of treatment of mental disorder**, then the relevant person will not be eligible if:

- they object to being admitted to hospital, or to some or all the treatment they will receive there for mental disorder, **and**
- they meet the criteria for an application for admission under section 2 or section 3 of the Mental Health Act 1983 (unless an attorney or deputy, acting within their powers, had consented to the things to which the person is objecting).

4.46 In many cases, the relevant person will be able to state an objection. However, where the person is unable to communicate, or can only communicate to a limited extent, assessors will need to consider the person's behaviour, wishes, feelings, views, beliefs and values, both present and past, so far as they can be ascertained (see paragraphs 5.37 to 5.48 of the main Code for guidance on how to do this). If there is reason to think that a person would object if able to do so, then the person should be assumed to be objecting. Occasionally, it may be that the person's behaviour initially suggests an objection, but that this objection is in fact not directed at the treatment at all. In that case, the person should **not** be taken to be objecting.

4.47 Assessors should always bear in mind that their job is simply to establish whether the person objects to treatment or to being in hospital: whether that objection is reasonable or not is not the issue.

4.48 Even where a person does not object and a deprivation of liberty authorisation is possible, it should not be assumed that such an authorisation is invariably the correct course. There may be other factors that suggest that the Mental Health Act 1983 should be used (for example, where it is thought likely that the person will recover relevant capacity and will then refuse to consent to treatment, or where it is important for the hospital managers to have a formal power to retake a person who goes absent without leave). Further guidance on this is given in the Mental Health Act 1983 Code of Practice.

4.49 The eligibility assessor is not required to decide (or even consider) whether an application under the Mental Health Act 1983 would be in the person's best interests.

4.50 If the proposed authorisation relates to deprivation of liberty in a hospital **wholly or partly for the purpose of treatment of mental disorder**, then the person will also not be eligible if they are:

- currently on leave of absence from detention under the Mental Health Act 1983
- subject to supervised community treatment, or
- subject to conditional discharge,

in which case powers of recall under the Mental Health Act 1983 should be used.

4.51 People on leave of absence from detention under the Mental Health Act 1983 or subject to supervised community treatment or conditional discharge are, however, eligible for the deprivation of liberty safeguards if they require treatment in hospital for a physical disorder.

Who can conduct an eligibility assessment?

4.52 The regulations for England specify that the eligibility assessment must be completed by:

- a mental health assessor who is also a section 12 doctor, or
- a best interests assessor who is also an approved mental health professional (AMHP).

4.53 The assessment cannot be carried out by a non-section 12 doctor, even if they are qualified to be a mental health assessor, nor by a non-AMHP, even if they are qualified to be a best interests assessor. This will ensure that the eligibility assessor is sufficiently familiar with the Mental Health Act 1983, which will be particularly important in cases in which it appears that the powers available under the Mental Health Act 1983 may be more appropriate than the deprivation of liberty safeguards.

4.54 The eligibility assessment will often be carried out by the best interests assessor but, where this is not the case, the eligibility assessor must request the best interests assessor to provide any relevant eligibility information that the best interests assessor may have, and the best interests assessor must comply with this request.

What happens when people are assessed as ineligible?

4.55 If the eligibility assessor believes that the relevant person is not eligible, but (on the basis of the report of the best interests assessor) that they should nevertheless be deprived of liberty in their best interests, the eligibility assessor should immediately inform the supervisory body.

4.56 In the case of someone already subject to the Mental Health Act 1983, the eligibility assessor should inform the supervisory body with a view to contact being made with the relevant responsible clinician (i.e. the clinician in overall charge of the person's treatment) or, if the person is subject to guardianship, the relevant local social services authority. Otherwise, the assessor or supervisory body should take steps to arrange for the person to be assessed further with a view to an application being made for admission to hospital under the Mental Health Act 1983. Assessors will need to be familiar with local arrangements for doing this.

4.57 In some cases, even before the eligibility assessment is undertaken, it may be known that there is a chance that the person will have to be assessed with a view to an application under the Mental Health Act 1983 because the eligibility assessment might conclude that they are ineligible for a deprivation of liberty authorisation. In such cases, steps should be taken, where practical and possible, to arrange assessments in a way that minimises the number of separate interviews or examinations the person has to undergo.

Best interests assessment

4.58 The purpose of the best interests assessment is to establish, firstly, whether deprivation of liberty is occurring or is going to occur and, if so, whether:

- it is in the best interests of the relevant person to be deprived of liberty
- it is necessary for them to be deprived of liberty in order to prevent harm to themselves, and
- deprivation of liberty is a proportionate response to the likelihood of the relevant person suffering harm and the seriousness of that harm.

4.59 The best interests assessor is the person who is responsible for assessing what is in the best interests of a relevant person.

4.60 In both England and Wales, the best interests assessment must be undertaken by an AMHP, social worker, nurse, occupational therapist or chartered psychologist with the skills and experience specified in the regulations. In England, this includes at least two years' post-registration experience. In England, the supervisory body must also be satisfied that the assessor:

- is not suspended from the register or list relevant to the person's profession
- has successfully completed training that has been approved[90] by the Secretary of State to be a best interests assessor
- except in the 12 month period beginning with the date the person has successfully completed the approved training, has, in the 12 months prior to selection, completed further training relevant to their role as a best interests assessor, and
- has the skills necessary to obtain, evaluate and analyse complex evidence and differing views and to weigh them appropriately in decision-making.

---

[90]   Approved courses can be found at: http://www.dh.gov.uk/en/SocialCare/
Deliveringadultsocialcare/MentalCapacity/
MentalCapacityActDeprivationofLibertySafeguards/index.htm

4.61 Section 4 of the Mental Capacity Act 2005 sets out the best interests principles that apply for the purpose of the Act. Chapter 5 of the main Code ('What does the Act mean when it talks about "best interests"?') explains this in more detail, and, in particular, paragraph 5.13 of the main Code includes a checklist of factors that need to be taken into account in working out what is in a person's best interests. These principles and guidance apply equally to working out a person's best interests for the purpose of the deprivation of liberty safeguards. However, when it comes to best interests around deprivation of liberty, additional factors apply, including:

- whether any harm to the person could arise if the deprivation of liberty does not take place
- what that harm would be
- how likely that harm is to arise (i.e. is the level of risk sufficient to justify a step as serious as depriving a person of liberty?)
- what other care options there are which could avoid deprivation of liberty, and
- if deprivation of liberty is currently unavoidable, what action could be taken to avoid it in future.

Establishing whether deprivation of liberty is occurring

4.62 The first task of a best interests assessor is to establish whether deprivation of liberty is occurring, or is likely to occur, since there is no point in the assessment process proceeding further if deprivation of liberty is not at issue. If the best interests assessor concludes that deprivation of liberty is **not** occurring and is not likely to occur, they should state in their assessment report to the supervisory body that deprivation of liberty is not in the person's best interests because there is obviously a less restrictive option available. The best interests requirement will therefore not be met in such a case.

4.63 To establish whether deprivation of liberty is occurring, or is likely to occur, the best interests assessor must consult the managing authority of the hospital or care home where the person is, or will be, accommodated and examine any relevant needs assessments and care plans prepared for the person. The best interests assessor must consider whether the care plan and the manner in which it is being, or will be, implemented constitutes a deprivation of liberty. If not, then no deprivation of liberty authorisation is required for that care plan.

4.64 The managing authority and supervisory body must provide the best interests assessor with any needs assessments or care plans that they have undertaken or which have been undertaken on their behalf.

The best interests assessment process

4.65 If the best interests assessor considers that deprivation of liberty is occurring, or is likely to occur, they should start a full best interests assessment. In line with section 4(7) of the Act this involves seeking the views of a range of people connected to the relevant person to find out whether they believe that depriving the relevant person of their liberty is, or would be, in the person's best interests to protect them from harm or to enable them to follow the care plan proposed. The best interests assessor should, as far as is practical and possible, seek the views of:

- anyone the person has previously named as someone they want to be consulted
- anyone involved in caring for the person
- anyone interested in the person's welfare (for example, family carers, other close relatives, or an advocate already working with the person), and
- any donee or deputy who represents the person.

4.66 This may mean that the best interests assessor needs to explain key aspects of the care plan and what it aims to do to the people being consulted. The best interests assessor should then take the views received into account as far as is practical and appropriate. It is essential that the best interests assessor provides an independent and objective view of whether or not there is a genuine justification for deprivation of liberty, taking account of all the relevant views and factors.

4.67 The best interests assessor must state in their assessment the name and address of every interested person whom they have consulted in carrying out the assessment.

4.68 Family and friends may not be confident about expressing their views: it is the responsibility of the best interests assessor to enable them to do so – using support to meet communication or language needs as necessary.

Scenario: Consulting around best interests

Mr Simpson is 60 and has dementia with particularly poor short-term memory, which clinicians agree is most likely to be related to chronic excessive alcohol intake. After initial treatment in hospital, he has been admitted to a care home – a decision which he consented to.

However, though he had the mental capacity to consent to hospital admission, he has no insight into his dementia. He is unable to understand the health and safety implications of continuing to drink, and will do so heavily whenever he has access to alcohol and the money to buy it.

Although Mr Simpson had no access to alcohol in hospital, there is a pub within walking distance of the care home, which he visits and

---

drinks in. When he returns to the home intoxicated, his behaviour can be very distressing and potentially dangerous to other residents. The care home staff believe that if this continues, there may be no other option than to return him to hospital under the Mental Health Act 1983.

The care home staff have asked Mr Simpson to drink only in moderation, but this has not proved successful; and the landlord has been asked not to serve him more than one drink but has refused to do so. The manager of the home is now considering a care plan to prevent Mr Simpson from leaving the home without an escort, and to prevent visits from friends who bring alcohol. He believes this would be in Mr Simpson's best interests.

As the pub is open all day, if this new care plan was adopted, Mr Simpson would be stopped from going out at all without an escort, even though he often goes to the shops and the park as well as the pub. Staffing levels are such that an escort would only be available on some days and for limited periods.

Mr Simpson's daughter, his closest relative, is concerned that these restrictions are excessive and would amount to a deprivation of liberty. She believes that having a drink and socialising in the pub is her father's 'only remaining pleasure', and is sure that, if he still had capacity, he would choose to carry on drinking, regardless of the health risks.

She requests a best interests meeting to consider whether a less restrictive care plan could still meet his needs.

At this meeting, Mr Simpson's community mental health nurse confirms that Mr Simpson is likely to lack capacity in relation to this particular issue, and advises that if he continues to drink to excess his dementia is likely to advance rapidly and his life expectancy will be reduced. However, small amounts of alcohol will not be significantly harmful.

The consensus is that the proposed restrictions would severely limit Mr Simpson's ability to maintain social contact and to carry on the life he has been used to, and that this would amount to deprivation of liberty. Bearing in mind his daughter's view, it is felt that it would not be in Mr Simpson's best interests to prevent him from having any alcohol at all. However, in view of the health risks and the likelihood that he would otherwise have to be detained in hospital, it would be in Mr Simpson's best interests to ensure that he does not get intoxicated. (The possibility of limiting his access to his money would be unacceptable since he retains the capacity to decide how to spend it in other ways.)

PART VI

Discussion then focuses on ways of minimising restrictions so that he is still able to visit the pub, but drinks in moderation. The care home key worker says that when she has gone to the pub with Mr Simpson he has been fully co-operative and has had just one drink before coming back with her. It is therefore agreed that the home will provide an escort for him to visit the pub at least three times a week, and the shops and the park at other times, and that his daughter will be able to take him out at any time.

It is agreed that care home staff (in consultation with his daughter) will review Mr Simpson's care plan in two months' time and, if it is felt that increased restrictions are required, consider whether it is then necessary to request an authorisation for deprivation of liberty.

4.69 The best interests assessor must involve the relevant person in the assessment process as much as is possible and practical, and help them to participate in decision-making. The relevant person should be given the support needed to participate, using non-verbal means of communication where needed (see paragraphs 3.10 and 3.11 of the main Code) or the support of speech and language therapists. It may also help to involve others whom the relevant person already trusts and who are used to communicating with the relevant person.

4.70 The best interests assessor will need to consider the conclusions of the mental health assessor about how the person being assessed is likely to be affected by being deprived of their liberty. If the proposed care would involve the person being moved, then the assessor should consider the impact of the upheaval and of the journey itself on the person.

4.71 If the best interests assessment supports deprivation of liberty in the care home or hospital in question, the assessor must state what the maximum authorisation period should be in the case concerned. This must not exceed 12 months. The assessor should set out the reasons for selecting the period stated. This decision will be based on the information obtained during the consultation process – but should also reflect information from the person's care plan about how long any treatment or care will be required in circumstances that amount to a deprivation of liberty. It should also take into account any available indication of how likely it is that the relevant person's circumstances will change, including the expected progression of the illness or disability. The underlying principle is that deprivation of liberty should be for the minimum period necessary so, for the maximum 12-month period to apply, the assessor will need to be confident that there is unlikely to be a change in the person's circumstances that would affect the authorisation within that timescale.

The report of the best interests assessor

4.72 The best interests assessor must provide a report that explains their conclusion and their reasons for it. If they do not support deprivation of liberty, then their report should aim to be as useful as possible to the commissioners and providers of care in deciding on future action (for example, recommending an alternative approach to treatment or care in which deprivation of liberty could be avoided). It may be helpful for the best interests assessor to discuss the possibility of any such alternatives with the providers of care **during the assessment process**.

4.73 If the best interests assessor does not support deprivation of liberty, it would be good practice for their report to be included in the relevant person's care plan or case notes, to ensure that any views about how deprivation of liberty can be avoided are made clear to the providers of care and all relevant staff on an ongoing basis.

4.74 The best interests assessor may recommend that conditions should be attached to the authorisation. For example, they may make recommendations around contact issues, issues relevant to the person's culture or other major issues related to the deprivation of liberty, which – if not dealt with – would mean that the deprivation of liberty would cease to be in the person's best interests. The best interests assessor may also recommend conditions in order to work towards avoiding deprivation of liberty in future. But it is not the best interests assessor's role to specify conditions that do not directly relate to the issue of deprivation of liberty.

4.75 Conditions should not be a substitute for a properly constructed care plan (see paragraph 2.7 on good practice for care planning). In recommending conditions, best interests assessors should aim to impose the minimum necessary constraints, so that they do not unnecessarily prevent or inhibit the staff of the hospital or care home from responding appropriately to the person's needs, whether they remain the same or vary over time. It would be good practice for the best interests assessor to discuss any proposed conditions with the relevant personnel at the home or hospital before finalising the assessment, and to make clear in their report whether the rejection or variation of recommended conditions by the supervisory body would significantly affect the other conclusions they have reached.

4.76 Where possible, the best interests assessor should recommend someone to be appointed as the relevant person's representative (see chapter 7). The assessor should be well placed, as a result of the consultation process, to identify whether there is anybody suitable to take on this role. The appointment of the relevant person's representative cannot take place unless and until an authorisation is given. However, by identifying someone to take on this role at an early stage, the best interests assessor can help to ensure that a representative is appointed as soon as possible.

PART VI

Scenario: Application for standard authorisation

Mrs Jackson is 87 years old and lives by herself in an isolated bungalow in a rural area. Over the past few years, staff at her local health centre have become increasingly concerned about her wellbeing and ability to look after herself. Her appearance has become unkempt, she does not appear to be eating properly and her house is dirty.

The community mental health team have attempted to gain her trust, but she is unwilling to engage with them. She has refused care workers entry to her home and declined their help with personal hygiene and household chores.

Because it is believed that she is a potential risk to herself, she is admitted to psychiatric hospital under section 2 of the Mental Health Act 1983 for assessment of her mental disorder.

Following the assessment, it is felt that Mrs Jackson requires further treatment for mental disorder. An application is made for her detention to be continued under section 3 of the Mental Health Act 1983. She is prescribed antipsychotic medication, but this seems to have little effect on her behaviour. She remains extremely suspicious of people to the point of being delusional. She is assessed as potentially having mild dementia, most probably of the Alzheimer type, but because there is no obvious benefit from anti-dementia medication, further treatment for mental disorder is felt unnecessary.

Mrs Jackson insists that she wishes to return to her own home, but given past failed attempts to gain her acceptance of support at home and her likely future mental deterioration, transfer to a care home is believed to be most appropriate.

A best interests meeting is held by the mental health team to consider her future care and placement, and the team's approved social worker and the instructed IMCA are invited. The meeting concludes that Mrs Jackson does not have sufficient mental capacity to make an informed decision on her stated wish to return home. There is no advance decision in existence, no Lasting Power of Attorney or court deputy appointed and no practical way of contacting her immediate family.

An appropriate care home is identified. A care plan is developed to give Mrs Jackson as much choice and control over her daily living as possible. However, it is felt that the restrictions still necessary to ensure Mrs Jackson's wellbeing will be so intense and of such duration that a request for a standard deprivation of liberty authorisation should be made by the care home manager (the relevant managing authority).

> The best interests assessor agrees that the proposed course of action is in Mrs Jackson's best interests and recommends a standard authorisation for six months in the first instance.

What guidelines are there relating to the work of assessors?

Access to records

4.77 All assessors may, at any reasonable time, examine and take copies of:
- any health record
- any record of, or held by, a local authority that was compiled in accordance with a social services function, and
- any record held by a care home

which they consider may be relevant to their assessment. Assessors should list in their assessment report what records they examined.

Recording and reporting assessments

4.78 As soon as possible after carrying out their assessments, assessors must keep a written record of the assessment and must give copies of their assessment report(s) to the supervisory body. The supervisory body must in turn give copies of the assessment report(s) to:
- the managing authority
- the relevant person and their representative, and
- any IMCA instructed

at the same time that it gives them copies of the deprivation of liberty authorisation or notification that an authorisation is not to be given (see paragraphs 5.7 and 5.18 respectively).

5 WHAT SHOULD HAPPEN ONCE THE ASSESSMENTS ARE COMPLETE?

If all the assessments in the standard authorisation assessment process indicate that the relevant person meets all the qualifying requirements, then the supervisory body will give a deprivation of liberty authorisation. If any of the qualifying requirements are not met, however, different actions will need to be taken, depending on the circumstances of the individual case.

This chapter identifies potential outcomes of the assessment process and offers guidance on what should happen next.

What action should the supervisory body take if the assessments conclude that the person meets the requirements for authorisation?

5.1 If all the assessments conclude that the relevant person meets the requirements for authorisation, and the supervisory body has

PART VI

written copies of all the assessments, it must give a standard authorisation. A standard form is available for this purpose.

5.2 The supervisory body cannot give a standard authorisation if any of the requirements are not fulfilled.

5.3 The supervisory body must set the period of the authorisation, which may not be longer than that recommended by the best interests assessor (see paragraph 4.71).

5.4 When the supervisory body gives a standard authorisation, it must do so in writing and must state the following:

- the name of the relevant person
- the name of the relevant hospital or care home
- the period during which the authorisation is to be in force (which may not exceed the period recommended by the best interests assessor)
- the purpose for which the authorisation is given (i.e. why the person needs to be deprived of their liberty)
- any conditions subject to which the authorisation is given (see paragraph 5.5), and
- the reason why each qualifying requirement is met.

5.5 The supervisory body may attach conditions to the authorisation. Before deciding whether to give the authorisation subject to conditions, the supervisory body must consider any recommendations made by the best interests assessor (see paragraph 4.74). Where the supervisory body does not attach conditions as recommended by the best interests assessor, it should discuss the matter with the best interests assessor in case the rejection or variation of the conditions would significantly affect the other conclusions the best interests assessor reached in their report.

5.6 It is the responsibility of the supervisory body to appoint a representative for the relevant person (see chapter 7).

5.7 As soon as possible after giving the authorisation, the supervisory body must give a copy of the authorisation to:

- the managing authority
- the relevant person
- the relevant person's representative
- any Independent Mental Capacity Advocate (IMCA) involved, and
- every interested person named by the best interests assessor in their report as somebody they have consulted in carrying out their assessment.

The supervisory body must also keep a written record of any standard authorisation that it gives and of the matters referred to in paragraph 5.4.

5.8 The managing authority must take all practical and possible steps to ensure that the relevant person understands the effect of the authorisation and their rights around it. These include their right to challenge the authorisation via the Court of Protection, their right to request a review, and their right to have an IMCA instructed, along with the process for doing so (see paragraphs 7.37 to 7.41).

Appropriate information must be given to the relevant person both orally and in writing. Any written information must also be given to the relevant person's representative. This must happen as soon as possible and practical after the authorisation is given.

How long can an authorisation last?

5.9 A deprivation of liberty should last for the shortest period possible. The best interests assessor should only recommend authorisation for as long as the relevant person is likely to meet all the qualifying requirements. The authorisation may be for quite a short period. A short period may, for example, be appropriate if:

- the reason that the deprivation of liberty is in the person's best interests is because their usual care arrangements have temporarily broken down, or
- there are likely to be changes in the person's mental disorder in the relatively near future (for example, if the person is in rehabilitation following brain injury).

What restrictions exist on authorisations?

5.10 A deprivation of liberty authorisation – whether urgent or standard – relates solely to the issue of deprivation of liberty. It does not give authority to treat people, nor to do anything else that would normally require their consent. The arrangements for providing care and treatment to people in respect of whom a deprivation of liberty authorisation is in force are subject to the wider provisions of the Mental Capacity Act 2005.

5.11 This means that any treatment can only be given to a person who has not given their consent if:

- it is established that the person lacks capacity to make the decision concerned
- it is agreed that the treatment will be in their best interests, having taken account of the views of the person and of people close to them, and, where relevant in the case of serious medical treatment, of any IMCA involved
- the treatment does not conflict with a valid and applicable advance decision to refuse treatment, and
- the treatment does not conflict with a decision made by a donee of Lasting Power of Attorney or a deputy acting within the scope of their powers.

5.12 In deciding what is in a person's best interests, section 4 of the Act applies in the same way as it would if the person was not deprived of liberty. The guidance in chapter 5 of the main Code on assessing best interests is also relevant.

5.13 Life-sustaining treatment, or treatment to prevent a serious deterioration in the person's condition, may be provided while a decision in respect of any relevant issue is sought from the Court of

PART VI

Protection. The need to act in the best interests of the person concerned will continue to apply in the meantime.

Can a person be moved to a different location under a standard authorisation?

5.14 If a person who is subject to a standard authorisation moves to a different hospital or care home, the managing authority of the new hospital or care home must request a new standard authorisation. The application should be made **before** the move takes place.

5.15 If the move has to take place so urgently that this is impossible, the managing authority of the new hospital or care home will need to give an urgent authorisation (scc chapter 6).

5.16 The only exception is if the care regime in the new facility will not involve deprivation of liberty.

5.17 These arrangements are not an alternative to applying the provisions of sections 38 and 39 of the Act regarding change of residence.

What happens if an assessment concludes that one of the requirements is not met?

5.18 If any of the assessments conclude that one of the requirements is not met, then the assessment process should stop immediately and authorisation may not be given. The supervisory body should:

- inform anyone still engaged in carrying out an assessment that they are not required to complete it
- notify the managing authority, the relevant person, any IMCA involved and every interested person consulted by the best interests assessor that authorisation has not been given (a standard form is available for this purpose), and
- provide the managing authority, the relevant person and any IMCA involved with copies of those assessments that have been carried out. This must be done as soon as possible, because in some cases different arrangements will need to be made for the person's care.

5.19 If the reason the standard authorisation cannot be given is because the eligibility requirement is not met, it may be necessary to consider making the person subject to the Mental Health Act 1983. If this is the case, it may be possible to use the same assessors to make that decision, thereby minimising the assessment processes.

What are the responsibilities of the managing authority and the commissioners of care if a request for an authorisation is turned down?

5.20 The managing authority is responsible for ensuring that it does not deprive a person of their liberty without an authorisation. The managing authority must comply with the law in this respect: where a request for an authorisation is turned down, it will need to review the relevant person's actual or proposed care arrangements to ensure that a deprivation of liberty is not allowed to either continue or commence.

5.21 Supervisory bodies and other commissioners of care will need to purchase care packages in a way that makes it possible for managing authorities to comply with the outcome of the deprivation of liberty safeguards assessment process when a request for a standard authorisation is turned down.

5.22 The actions that both managing authorities and commissioners of care should consider if a request for an authorisation is turned down will depend on the reason why the authorisation has not been given:

- If the best interests assessor concluded that the relevant person was not in fact being, or likely to be, deprived of liberty, no action is likely to be necessary.
- If the best interests assessor concluded that the proposed or actual deprivation of liberty was not in the relevant person's best interests, the managing authority, in conjunction with the commissioner of the care, will need to consider how the care plan could be changed to avoid deprivation of liberty. (See, for example, the guidance on practical ways to reduce the risk of deprivation of liberty in paragraph 2.7.) They should examine carefully the reasons given in the best interests assessor's report, and may find it helpful to discuss the matter with the best interests assessor. Where appropriate, they should also discuss the matter with family and carers. If the person is not yet a resident in the care home or hospital, the revised care plan may not involve admission to that facility unless the conditions of care are adapted to be less restrictive and deprivation of liberty will not occur.
- If the mental capacity assessor concluded that the relevant person **has** capacity to make decisions about their care, the care home or hospital will need to consider, in conjunction with the commissioner of the care, how to support the person to make such decisions.
- If the relevant person was identified as not eligible to be subject to a deprivation of liberty authorisation, it may be appropriate to assess whether an application should be made to detain the person under the Mental Health Act 1983.
- If the relevant person does not have a mental disorder as defined in the Mental Health Act 1983, the care plan will need to be modified to avoid a deprivation of liberty, since there would be no lawful basis for depriving a person of liberty in those circumstances.
- Where there is a valid refusal by a donee or deputy, or an applicable and valid advance decision (see paragraphs 4.25 to 4.28), alternative care arrangements will need to be made. If there is a question about the refusal, a decision may be sought from the Court of Protection.

PART VI

- If the person is under 18, use of the Children Act 1989 may be considered.

5.23 Working out what action should be taken where a request for a standard deprivation of liberty authorisation is turned down in respect of a 'self-funder' may present particular problems, because the managing authority may not be able to make alternative care arrangements without discussing them with those controlling the funding, whether relatives of the person concerned or others. The desired outcome should be the provision of a care regime that does not constitute deprivation of liberty.

5.24 Where the best interests assessor comes to the conclusion that the best interests requirement is not met, but it appears to the assessor that the person being assessed is already being deprived of their liberty, the assessor must inform the supervisory body and explain in their report why they have reached that conclusion. The supervisory body must then inform the managing authority to review the relevant person's care plan immediately so that unauthorised deprivation of liberty does not continue. Any necessary changes must be made urgently to stop what would be an unlawful deprivation of liberty. The steps taken to stop the deprivation of liberty should be recorded in the care plan. Where possible, family, friends and carers should be involved in deciding how to prevent the unauthorised deprivation of liberty from continuing. If the supervisory body has any doubts about whether the matter is being satisfactorily resolved within an appropriately urgent timescale, it should alert the inspection body (see chapter 11).

6   WHEN CAN URGENT AUTHORISATIONS OF DEPRIVATION OF LIBERTY BE GIVEN?

Wherever possible, applications for deprivation of liberty authorisations should be made before the deprivation of liberty commences. However, where deprivation of liberty unavoidably needs to commence before a standard authorisation can be obtained, an urgent authorisation can be given which will make the deprivation of liberty lawful for a short period of time.

This chapter contains guidance on the rules around urgent authorisations.

When can an urgent authorisation be given?

6.1 A managing authority can itself give an urgent authorisation for deprivation of liberty where:
- it is required to make a request to the supervisory body for a standard authorisation, but believes that the need for the person to be deprived of their liberty is so urgent that deprivation needs to begin before the request is made, or

- it has made a request for a standard authorisation, but believes that the need for a person to be deprived of liberty has now become so urgent that deprivation of liberty needs to begin before the request is dealt with by the supervisory body.

This means that an urgent authorisation can never be given without a request for a standard authorisation being made simultaneously. Therefore, before giving an urgent authorisation, a managing authority will need to have a reasonable expectation that the six qualifying requirements for a standard authorisation are likely to be met.

6.2 Urgent authorisations should normally only be used in response to sudden unforeseen needs. However, they can also be used in care planning (for example, to avoid delays in transfer for rehabilitation, where delay would reduce the likely benefit of the rehabilitation).

6.3 However, an urgent authorisation should not be used where there is no expectation that a standard deprivation of liberty authorisation will be needed. Where, for example:

- a person who lacks capacity to make decisions about their care and treatment has developed a mental disorder as a result of a physical illness, and
- the physical illness requires treatment in hospital in circumstances that amount to a deprivation of liberty, and
- the treatment of that physical illness is expected to lead to rapid resolution of the mental disorder such that a standard deprivation of liberty authorisation would not be required,

it would not be appropriate to give an urgent authorisation simply to legitimise the short-term deprivation of liberty.

6.4 Similarly, an urgent deprivation of liberty authorisation should not be given when a person is, for example, in an accident and emergency unit or a care home, and it is anticipated that within a matter of a few hours or a few days the person will no longer be in that environment.

6.5 Any decision to give an urgent authorisation and take action that deprives a person of liberty must be in the person's best interests, as set out in section 4 of the Mental Capacity Act 2005. Where restraint is involved, all actions must comply with the additional conditions in section 6 of the Act (see chapter 6 of the main Code).

6.6 The managing authority must decide the period for which the urgent authorisation is given, but this must not exceed seven days (see paragraphs 6.20 to 6.28 regarding the possible extension of the seven-day period). The authorisation must be in writing and must state:

- the name of the relevant person
- the name of the relevant hospital or care home
- the period for which the authorisation is to be in force, and
- the purpose for which the authorisation is given.

A standard form is available for a managing authority to use to notify a supervisory body that it has given an urgent authorisation.

PART VI

6.7 Supervisory bodies and managing authorities should have a procedure in place that identifies:
- what actions should be taken when an urgent authorisation needs to be made
- who should take each action, and
- within what timescale.

What records should be kept about urgent authorisations?

6.8 The managing authority must keep a written record of any urgent authorisations given, including details of why it decided to give an urgent authorisation. They must give a copy of the authorisation to the relevant person and any IMCA instructed, and place a copy in the relevant person's records. The managing authority must also seek to ensure that, as far as possible, the relevant person understands the effect of the authorisation and the right to challenge the authorisation via the Court of Protection. Appropriate information must be given both orally and in writing.

6.9 The managing authority should, as far as possible and appropriate, notify the relevant person's family, friends and carers when an urgent authorisation is given in order to enable them to offer informed support to the person.

6.10 The processes surrounding the giving and receiving of urgent authorisations should be clearly recorded, and regularly monitored and audited, as part of a managing authority's or supervisory body's governance structure.

Who should be consulted before giving an urgent authorisation?

6.11 If the managing authority is considering depriving a person of liberty in an emergency and giving an urgent authorisation, they must, as far as is practical and possible, take account of the views of anyone engaged in caring for the relevant person or interested in their welfare. The aim should be to consult carers and family members at as early a stage as possible so that their views can be properly taken into account before a decision to give an urgent authorisation is taken.

6.12 The steps taken to involve family, friends or carers should be recorded in the relevant person's records, along with their views. The views of the carers will be important because their knowledge of the person will put them in a good position to gauge how the person will react to the deprivation of their liberty, and the effect it will have on their mental state. It may also be appropriate to consult any staff who may have some involvement in the person's case.

6.13 The ultimate decision, though, will need to be based on a judgement of what is in the relevant person's best interests. The decision-maker from the managing authority will need to be able to show that they have made a reasonable decision based on their professional judgement and taking account of all the relevant factors. This is an important decision, because it could mean the deprivation of a person's liberty without, at this stage, the full deprivation of liberty safeguards assessment process having taken place. The decision should therefore be taken at a senior level within the managing authority.

Scenario: Urgent authorisation followed by short-term standard authorisation

Mr Baker is 75, widowed and lives near his only family – his daughter. He is admitted to hospital having been found by his daughter on his kitchen floor. He is uncharacteristically confused and is not able to give a reliable history of what has happened. He has a routine physical examination, as well as blood and urine investigations, and is diagnosed as having a urinary tract infection. He is given antibiotics, but his nursing care is complicated by his fluctuating confusion. Once or twice he removes his clothes and walks through the ward naked, and at times he tries to leave the ward, unaware that he is in hospital, and believing that he is late for an important work meeting. During more lucid moments, however, he knows where he is and accepts the need for investigation and treatment in hospital.

The responsible consultant, in consultation with ward nursing staff and Mr Baker's daughter, feels that it would be in his best interests to place him in a side room to protect his dignity, and restrict his movements to ensure he remains on the ward.

However, after two days, his confusion appears to worsen: he starts having hallucinations and has to be restrained more often by staff to prevent him leaving the ward. After assessment by a doctor from the liaison psychiatry team, Mr Baker is prescribed antipsychotic medication for his own and other patients' safety. He does not resist taking this medication. The likely benefits and possible side effects are discussed with his daughter and, on balance, the medication is felt to be in his best interests in order to continue his medical investigations.

Staff become concerned about the level of restriction of liberty Mr Baker is now subject to. In particular, they are concerned about the duration of the restrictions; the fact that Mr Baker no longer has lucid intervals when he can give his consent to ongoing care and treatment in hospital; and the physical restraint that is still being required on occasion.

After discussion between the ward manager and Mr Baker's daughter, the managing authority gives an urgent authorisation and submits a request for a standard authorisation to the supervisory body (PCT). A best interests assessor is appointed, and the liaison psychiatrist provides the mental health and mental capacity assessments. In

> making all the deprivation of liberty safeguards assessments to see whether the qualifying requirements are met, it is considered that although restraint is being used, this does not mean he is objecting having regard to all the circumstances, so he is not ineligible and a standard authorisation is given.

Can a person be moved into care under an urgent authorisation?

6.14 There may be cases in which managing authorities are considering giving an urgent authorisation to enable them to move the relevant person to a new type of care. This may occur, for example, when considering whether to admit a person living at home or with relatives into a hospital care regime that would deprive them of their liberty, and when the need for admission appears to be so urgent that there would not be enough time to follow the standard authorisation process.

6.15 For some people, such a change of location may have a detrimental effect on their mental health, which might significantly distort the way they come across during any assessment process. In such a case, managing authorities should consider whether giving the urgent authorisation and admitting the person to hospital would outweigh the benefits of leaving the person in their existing location, where any assessment of their needs might be more accurate. This will involve looking carefully at the existing care arrangements and consulting with any carers involved, to establish whether or not the person could safely and beneficially be cared for in their home environment while the assessment process takes place. Where the relevant person is already known to statutory care providers, for example the community mental health team or social services, it will be important to involve them in this decision-making process. The relevant person's GP may also be an important source of knowledge about the person's situation, and may be able to offer a valuable opinion when the appropriateness of moving the person into a different care setting is under consideration.

What happens at the end of an urgent authorisation period?

6.16 An urgent authorisation will terminate at the end of the period for which it is given. As noted above, this is normally a maximum of seven days, but in exceptional circumstances an urgent authorisation can be extended to a maximum of 14 days **by the supervisory body**, as explained in paragraphs 6.20 to 6.28.

6.17 An urgent authorisation will terminate before this time if the standard authorisation applied for is given.

6.18 An urgent authorisation will also terminate if a managing authority receives notice from the supervisory body that the standard authorisation will not be given. It will not then be lawful to continue to deprive the relevant person of their liberty.

6.19 The supervisory body must inform the relevant person and any IMCA instructed that the urgent authorisation has ended. This notification can be combined with the notification to them of the outcome of the application for standard authorisation.

Scenario: Considering an urgent authorisation

Mr Watson is 35. He has autism and learning disabilities. He lives in the family home with his parents. Although he is well settled and generally calm at home, Mr Watson sometimes becomes disturbed when in an unfamiliar and crowded environment.

While his parents are away for a couple of days, and Mr Watson is in the care of a paid carer, he has an accident at home. His carer is concerned that he may have broken his arm and takes him to the A&E department at the local hospital, where it is decided that his arm needs to be X-rayed to check for a break. The outcome is that there is no break, just bad bruising, so there is no medical need to admit him.

However, because of the pain he is in and the crowded environment, Mr Watson has become very agitated to the extent that hospital security personnel feel a need to control him physically. The carer tries to restrain him and lead him outside where she says he is likely to be more settled and calm down.

Because restraint is being used, the A&E doctor wonders whether it his duty to use an urgent authorisation or other measure to detain Mr Watson in hospital if he believes it is in his best interests.

He consults a liaison psychiatry nurse, who reassures him that such restraint is permitted under the Mental Capacity Act 2005 where it is necessary to prevent harm to the person himself and so long as it is a proportionate response. The nurse assists the carer with gentle restraint to take Mr Watson to a quieter area. She suggests the doctor phone Mr Watson's parents for further information, and obtains painkillers for Mr Watson.

The doctor speaks to Mr Watson's parents, who believe that Mr Watson does not have the mental capacity to decide on his care and treatment in the current circumstances. They have experienced similar situations many times, and are confident that Mr Watson will calm down once he is back in his home environment. They state that if any more detailed assessment of his mental state is required it should take place there, in the company of the carer whom they know and trust. They reassure the doctor that Mr Watson is highly unlikely to present a danger to himself, his carer or the general public.

PART VI

> The doctor decides that it will be in Mr Watson's best interests to return home with his carer.

How and when can an urgent authorisation be extended?

6.20 If there are exceptional reasons why the request for a standard authorisation cannot be dealt with within the period of the original urgent authorisation, the managing authority may ask the supervisory body to extend the duration of the urgent authorisation for a maximum of a further seven days. The managing authority must keep a written record of the reason for making the request and must notify the relevant person, in writing, that they have made the request. Standard forms are available for managing authorities to request the extension of an urgent authorisation from a supervisory body and for supervisory bodies to record their decision in response to such a request.

6.21 Unless the duration of the urgent authorisation is extended by the supervisory body, or a standard authorisation is given before the urgent authorisation expires, the authority to deprive the person of liberty will cease once the urgent authorisation period has expired. It is therefore essential that any request for an extension of an urgent authorisation is made promptly. This will necessitate good communication between the managing authority and the supervisory body regarding the progress of the standard authorisation assessment process. Particular care may need to be taken where an urgent authorisation is due to expire over the weekend or on a bank holiday, when appropriate people at the managing authority and supervisory body may not be immediately available.

6.22 The supervisory body may only extend the duration of the urgent authorisation if:
- the managing authority has made a request for a standard authorisation
- there are exceptional reasons why it has not yet been possible to make a standard authorisation, and
- it is essential for the deprivation of liberty to continue while the supervisory body makes its decision.

6.23 Extensions can only be granted for exceptional reasons. An example of when an extension would be justified might be where:
- it was not possible to contact a person whom the best interests assessor needed to contact
- the assessment could not be relied upon without their input, and
- extension for the specified period would enable them to be contacted.

6.24 It is for the supervisory body to decide what constitutes an 'exceptional reason', but because of the seriousness of the issues involved, the supervisory body's decision must be soundly based and defensible. It would not, for example, be appropriate to use staffing shortages as a reason to extend an urgent authorisation.

6.25 An urgent authorisation can only be extended once.

6.26 The supervisory body must notify the managing authority of the length of any extension granted and must vary the original urgent authorisation so that it states the extended duration. The supervisory body must also keep a written record of the outcome of the request and the period of the extension.

6.27 The managing authority must give a copy of the varied urgent authorisation to the relevant person and any IMCA instructed, and must seek to ensure that, as far as possible, the relevant person understands the effect of the varied authorisation and the right to challenge the authorisation via the Court of Protection. The appropriate information must be given both orally and in writing.

6.28 If the supervisory body decides not to extend the urgent authorisation, it must inform the managing authority of its decision and the reasons for it. The managing authority must give a copy of the notice to the relevant person and any IMCA involved.

7   WHAT IS THE ROLE OF THE RELEVANT PERSON'S REPRESENTATIVE?

Once a standard deprivation of liberty authorisation has been given, supervisory bodies must appoint the relevant person's representative as soon as possible and practical to represent the person who has been deprived of their liberty.

This chapter explains the role of the relevant person's representative and gives guidance on their selection and appointment.

What is the role of the relevant person's representative?

7.1 The supervisory body must appoint a relevant person's representative for every person to whom they give a standard authorisation for deprivation of liberty. It is important that the representative is appointed at the time the authorisation is given or as soon as possible and practical thereafter.

7.2 The role of the relevant person's representative, once appointed, is:
- to maintain contact with the relevant person, and
- to represent and support the relevant person in all matters relating to the deprivation of liberty safeguards, including, if appropriate, triggering a review, using an organisation's complaints procedure on the person's behalf or making an application to the Court of Protection.

This is a crucial role in the deprivation of liberty process, providing the relevant person with representation and support that is independent of the commissioners and providers of the services they are receiving.

PART VI

7.3 The best interests principle of the Act applies to the relevant person's representative in the same way that it applies to other people acting or making decisions for people who lack capacity.

How should managing authorities work with the relevant person's representative?

7.4 As soon as possible and practical after a standard deprivation of liberty authorisation is given, the managing authority must seek to ensure that the relevant person and their representative understand:

- the effect of the authorisation
- their right to request a review (see chapter 8)
- the formal and informal complaints procedures that are available to them
- their right to make an application to the Court of Protection to seek variation or termination of the authorisation (see chapter 10), and
- their right, where the relevant person does not have a paid 'professional' representative, to request the support of an Independent Mental Capacity Advocate (IMCA) (see paragraphs 7.37 to 7.41).

7.5 When providing information to the person and their representative, the managing authority should take account of the communication and language needs of both the person and their representative. Provision of information should be seen as an ongoing responsibility, rather than a one-off activity.

Who can be the relevant person's representative?[91]

7.6 To be eligible to be the relevant person's representative, a person must be:

- 18 years of age or over
- able to keep in contact with the relevant person, and
- willing to be appointed.

The person must not be:

- financially interested in the relevant person's managing authority (a person is considered to be financially interested where that person is a partner, director, other office-holder or major shareholder of the managing authority)
- a relative of a person who has a financial interest in the relevant person's managing authority (paragraph 4.13 explains what is meant by 'relative')

---

[91] Requirements relating to the eligibility, selection and appointment of relevant person's representatives are covered in regulations. The regulations for England are The Mental Capacity (Deprivation of Liberty: Appointment of Relevant Person's Representative) Regulations 2008. The regulations for Wales are The Mental Capacity (Deprivation of Liberty: Appointment of Relevant Person's Representative) (Wales) Regulations 2008.

- employed by, or providing services to, the care home in which the person relevant person is residing
- employed by the hospital in a role that is, or could be, related to the treatment or care of the relevant person, or
- employed to work in the relevant person's supervisory body in a role that is, or could be, related to the relevant person's case.

7.7 The appointment of the relevant person's representative is in addition to, and does not affect, any appointment of a donee or deputy. Similarly, the functions of the representative are in addition to, and do not affect, the authority of any donee, the powers of any deputy or any powers of the court. A donee or deputy may themselves be appointed as the relevant person's representative if they meet the eligibility criteria set out in paragraph 7.6.

7.8 There is no presumption that the relevant person's representative should be the same as the person who is their nearest relative for the purposes of the Mental Health Act 1983, even where the relevant person is likely to be subject simultaneously to an authorisation under these safeguards and a provision of the Mental Health Act 1983. This is because the relevant person's representative is not selected in the same way as the nearest relative under the Mental Health Act 1983, nor do they perform the same role. However, there is nothing to stop the relevant person's representative being the same as their nearest relative under the Mental Health Act 1983.

When should the relevant person's representative be identified?

7.9 The process of identifying a representative must begin as soon as possible.

7.10 Normally, this should be when the best interests assessor is appointed – even if one or more of the other assessments has not yet been completed. This is because the best interests assessor must, as part of the assessment process, identify if there is anyone they would recommend to become the relevant person's representative. The best interests assessor should discuss the representative role with the people interviewed as part of the assessment.

7.11 This does leave a risk that the process to identify a representative might begin in cases where authorisation is not given. Nevertheless, it is important that the process begins, so that the representative can be appointed immediately the authorisation is given or as soon as possible and practical thereafter.

How should the relevant person's representative be selected?

7.12 The best interests assessor should first establish whether the relevant person has the capacity to select their own representative and, if so, invite them to do so. If the relevant person has capacity and selects an eligible person (according to the criteria set out in paragraph 7.6), the best interests assessor must recommend that person to the supervisory body for appointment.

7.13 Alternatively, if the relevant person lacks capacity and there is a donee or deputy with the appropriate authority, the donee or deputy may select the person to be recommended as the relevant person's representative, again subject to the criteria set out in paragraph 7.6. If a donee or deputy selects an eligible person, then the best interests assessor must recommend that person to the supervisory body for appointment.

7.14 It is up to the best interests assessor to confirm whether any representative proposed by the relevant person, a donee or a deputy is eligible. If the best interests assessor decides that a proposed representative is not eligible, they must advise the person who made the selection and invite them to make a further selection.

7.15 If neither the relevant person, nor a donee or deputy, selects an eligible person, then the best interests assessor must consider whether they are able to identify someone eligible who could act as the relevant person's representative.

7.16 In making a recommendation, the assessor should consider, and balance, factors such as:
- Does the relevant person have a preference?
- If they do not have the capacity to express a preference now, is there any written statement made by the relevant person when they had capacity that indicates who they may now want to be their representative?
- Will the proposed representative be able to keep in contact with the relevant person?
- Does the relevant person appear to trust and feel comfortable with the proposed representative?
- Would the proposed representative be able to represent the relevant person effectively?
- Is the proposed representative likely to represent the relevant person's best interests?

In most cases, the best interests assessor will be able to check at the same time that the proposed representative is willing to take on the role.

7.17 It should not be assumed that the representative needs to be someone who supports the deprivation of liberty.

7.18 The best interests assessor must not select a representative where the relevant person, if they have the capacity to do so, or a donee or a deputy acting within the scope of their authority, states they are not content with that selection.

7.19 If the best interests assessor is unable to recommend anybody to be the relevant person's representative, they must notify the supervisory body accordingly. The supervisory body must then itself identify an eligible person to be appointed as the representative. In doing so, the supervisory body may select a person who:
- would be performing the role in a professional capacity

- has satisfactory skills and experience to perform the role
- is not a family member, friend or carer of the relevant person
- is not employed by, or providing services to, the relevant person's managing authority, where the relevant person's managing authority is a care home
- is not employed to work in the relevant person's managing authority in a role that is, or could be, related to the relevant person's case, where the relevant person's managing authority is a hospital
- is not employed to work in the supervisory body that is appointing the representative in a role that is, or could be, related to the relevant person's case, and
- the supervisory body is satisfied that an appropriate criminal record certificate has been issued in respect of.

7.20 The supervisory body may pay a person they select to be the relevant person's representative in the circumstances set out in paragraph 7.19. This service could be commissioned, for example, through an advocacy services provider, ensuring that the service provides effective independent representation for the relevant person.

7.21 When selecting a suitable representative for the relevant person, the best interests assessor or supervisory body should pay particular attention to the communication and cultural needs of the relevant person.

How should the relevant person's representative be appointed?

7.22 The supervisory body must invite, in writing, the person recommended by the best interests assessor to become the relevant person's representative. If the best interests assessor does not recommend anyone, then the supervisory body should identify and appoint someone to undertake the role. If the person is willing to become the representative, the supervisory body must formally appoint them. If the person refuses, a further eligible person must be identified and invited to become the representative. This process must continue until an eligible person is appointed.

7.23 The appointment of the relevant person's representative by the supervisory body must be in writing and set out the role and responsibilities of the relevant person's representative. The letter of appointment should also state the name of the appointed person and the date of expiry of the appointment, which must be for the period of the standard authorisation that has been given. The supervisory body must send copies of the written appointment to:

- the appointed person
- the relevant person
- any donee or deputy of the relevant person
- any IMCA involved

- every interested person named by the best interests assessor in their report as somebody they have consulted in carrying out their assessment, and
- the managing authority of the relevant hospital or care home.

7.24 The relevant person's representative must confirm to the supervisory body in writing that they are willing to accept the appointment and have understood their roles and responsibilities in respect of the relevant person.

How should the work of the relevant person's representative be supported and monitored?

7.25 It is important that the representative has sufficient contact with the relevant person to ensure that the relevant person's best interests are being safeguarded. In order to fulfil their role, therefore, the representative will need to be able to have face-to-face contact with the relevant person. That means that the care home or hospital should accommodate visits by the representative at reasonable times. The name of the person's representative should be recorded in the person's health and social care records.

7.26 Managing authorities and supervisory bodies should inform the relevant person's representative about sources of support and information available to help them in the role, including how to access the support of an IMCA (see paragraphs 7.37 to 7.41).

7.27 If the representative has insufficient contact with the relevant person, for whatever reason, the person may effectively be unable to access important review and appeal rights. For this reason, if the representative does not maintain an appropriate level of contact with the person, the managing authority will need to consider informing the supervisory body. When the managing authority is reviewing the person's care plan, it should consider whether the representative is in sufficient contact with the relevant person to offer effective support. Records kept by managing authorities about frequency of contact will support this consideration.

7.28 Because the appropriate levels and methods of contact between a relevant person and their representative will vary from case to case, this is a matter about which the managing authority will need to exercise discretion. If the managing authority has any concerns, it may be best to raise the matter with the representative initially to see whether any perceived problems can be resolved informally. If after this the representative still does not maintain what the managing authority considers to be an appropriate level of contact with the relevant person, then the managing authority should notify the supervisory body.

When can the appointment of the relevant person's representative be terminated?

7.29 The appointment of the relevant person's representative will be terminated in any of the following circumstances:

- The standard authorisation comes to an end and a new authorisation is not applied for or, if applied for, is not given.
- The relevant person, if they have capacity to do so, objects to the representative continuing in their role and a different person is selected to be their representative instead.
- A donee or deputy, if it is within their authority to do so and the relevant person lacks the capacity to decide, objects to the representative continuing in their role and a different person is selected to be the representative instead.
- The supervisory body becomes aware that the representative is no longer willing or eligible to continue in the role.
- The supervisory body becomes aware that the relevant person's representative is not keeping in touch with the person, is not representing and supporting them effectively or is not acting in the person's best interests.
- The relevant person's representative dies.

7.30 If the supervisory body becomes aware that the representative may not be keeping in touch with the person, is not acting in the relevant person's best interests, or is no longer eligible, it should contact the representative to clarify the position before deciding whether to terminate the appointment.

7.31 When the appointment of the relevant person's representative ends, the supervisory body must give notice to all those listed in paragraph 7.23. This notice should be given as soon as possible, stating when the appointment ended and the reason why.

7.32 When the appointment of a relevant person's representative ends but the lawful deprivation of liberty continues, the supervisory body must appoint a suitable replacement to be the relevant person's representative as soon as possible and practical after they become aware of the vacancy. As before, a person qualified to be a best interests assessor should make a recommendation to the supervisory body and the supervisory body should take account of any such recommendations.

7.33 If the reason for the termination of the former representative's appointment is that they are no longer eligible, the views of the former representative on who might replace them should be sought. The person identified as most suitable should then be invited to accept the appointment. This process should continue until an eligible person is willing to accept appointment.

PART VI

What happens when there is no relevant person's representative available?

7.34 A person who is being deprived of their liberty will be in a particularly vulnerable position during any gaps in the appointment of the relevant person's representative, since there may be nobody to represent their interests or to apply for a review on their behalf. In these circumstances, if there is nobody who can support and represent the person (other than a person engaged in providing care and treatment for the relevant person in a professional capacity or for remuneration), the managing authority must notify the supervisory body, who must instruct an IMCA to represent the relevant person until a new representative is appointed.

7.35 The role of an IMCA instructed in these circumstances is essentially the same as that of the relevant person's representative. The role of the IMCA in this situation ends when the new relevant person's representative is appointed.

7.36 At any time when the relevant person does not have a representative, it will be particularly important for supervisory bodies to consider exercising their discretion to carry out a review if there is any significant change in the person's circumstances.

When should an IMCA be instructed?

7.37 Both the person who is deprived of liberty under a standard authorisation and their representative have a statutory right of access to an IMCA. It is the responsibility of the supervisory body to instruct an IMCA if the relevant person or their representative requests one. The intention is to provide extra support to the relevant person or a family member or friend acting as their representative if they need it, and to help them make use of the review process or access the Court of Protection safeguards. Where the relevant person has a paid 'professional' representative (see paragraphs 7.19 and 7.20), the need for additional advocacy support should not arise and so there is no requirement for an IMCA to be provided in those circumstances.

7.38 The role of the IMCA is to help represent the relevant person and, in particular, to assist the relevant person and their representative to understand the effect of the authorisation, what it means, why it has been given, why the relevant person meets the criteria for authorisation, how long it will last, any conditions to which the authorisation is subject and how to trigger a review or challenge in the Court of Protection. The IMCA can also provide support with a review (see chapter 8) or with an application to the Court of Protection (see chapter 10), for example to help the person to communicate their views.

7.39 The IMCA will have the right to make submissions to the supervisory body on the question of whether a qualifying requirement should be reviewed, or to give information, or make submissions, to any assessor carrying out a review assessment. Both the person and their representative must be told about the IMCA service and how to request an IMCA.

7.40 An IMCA must be instructed whenever requested by the relevant person or their representative. A request may be made more than once during the period of the authorisation. For example, help may be sought at the start of the authorisation and then again later in order to request a review.

7.41 In addition, if the supervisory body has reason to believe that the review and Court of Protection safeguards might not be used without the support of an IMCA, then they must instruct an IMCA. For example, if the supervisory body is aware that the person has selected a representative who needs support with communication, it should consider whether an IMCA is needed.

8   WHEN SHOULD AN AUTHORISATION BE REVIEWED AND WHAT HAPPENS WHEN IT ENDS?

When a person is deprived of their liberty, the managing authority has a duty to monitor the case on an ongoing basis to see if the person's circumstances change – which may mean they no longer need to be deprived of their liberty.

The managing authority must set out in the care plan clear roles and responsibilities for monitoring and confirm under what circumstances a review is necessary. For example, if a person's condition is changing frequently, then their situation should be reviewed more frequently.

This chapter explains the duties of managing authorities and supervisory bodies in relation to reviewing cases, and what happens when an authorisation ends. The review process is set out in flowchart form at Annex 4.

When should a standard authorisation be reviewed?

8.1 A standard authorisation can be reviewed at any time. The review is carried out by the supervisory body.

8.2 There are certain statutory grounds for carrying out a review. If the statutory grounds for a review are met, the supervisory body must carry out a review. If a review is requested by the relevant person, their representative or the managing authority, the supervisory body must carry out a review. Standard letters are available for the relevant person or their representative to request a review. There is also a standard form available for the managing authority to request a review. A supervisory body can also decide to carry out a review at its own discretion.

8.3 The statutory grounds for a review are:

PART VI

- The relevant person no longer meets the age, no refusals, mental capacity, mental health or best interests requirements.
- The relevant person no longer meets the eligibility requirement because they now object to receiving mental health treatment in hospital and they meet the criteria for an application for admission under section 2 or section 3 of the Mental Health Act 1983 (see paragraphs 4.45 to 4.48).
- There has been a change in the relevant person's situation and, because of the change, it would be appropriate to amend an existing condition to which the authorisation is subject, delete an existing condition or add a new condition.
- The reason(s) the person now meets the qualifying requirement(s) is(are) different from the reason(s) given at the time the standard authorisation was given.

8.4 Different arrangements apply if the person no longer meets the eligibility requirement because they have been detained under the Mental Health Act, or become subject to a requirement under that Act that conflicts with the authorisation. (See paragraphs 8.19 to 8.21 regarding the short-term suspension of a standard authorisation.)

8.5 A managing authority must request a review if it appears to it that one or more of the qualifying requirements is no longer met, or may no longer be met.

What happens when a review is going to take place?

8.6 The supervisory body must tell the relevant person, their representative and the managing authority if they are going to carry out a review. This must be done either before the review begins or as soon as possible and practical after it has begun. A standard form is available for this purpose.

8.7 The relevant person's records must include information about any formal reviews that have been requested, when they were considered, and the outcome. These records must be retained by the supervisory body.

8.8 Deprivation of liberty can be ended before a formal review. An authorisation only **permits** deprivation of liberty: it does not mean that a person **must be** deprived of liberty where circumstances no longer necessitate it. If a care home or hospital decides that deprivation of liberty is no longer necessary then they must end it immediately, by adjusting the care regime or implementing whatever other change is appropriate. The managing authority should then apply to the supervisory body to review and, if appropriate, formally terminate the authorisation.

How should standard authorisations be reviewed?

8.9 When a supervisory body receives a request for a review, it must first decide which, if any, of the qualifying requirements need to be reviewed. A standard form is available for recording this decision.

8.10 If the supervisory body concludes that none of the qualifying requirements need to be reviewed, no further action is necessary. For example, if there has been a very recent assessment or review and no new evidence has been submitted to show that the relevant person does not meet the criteria, or that circumstances have changed, no review is required.

8.11 If it appears that one or more of the qualifying requirements should be reviewed, the supervisory body must arrange for a separate review assessment to be carried out for each of these requirements.

8.12 The supervisory body must record when a review is requested, what it decides to do (whether it decides to carry out a review or not) and the reasons for its decision.

8.13 In general, review processes should follow the standard authorisation processes – so supervisory bodies should conduct the assessments outlined in chapter 4 of this Code of Practice for each of the qualifying requirements that need to be reviewed.

8.14 Where the supervisory body decides that the best interests requirement should be reviewed solely because details of the **conditions** attached to the authorisation need to be changed, and the review request does not include evidence that there is a significant change in the relevant person's overall circumstances, there is no need for a full reassessment of best interests. The supervisory body can simply vary the conditions attached to the authorisation as appropriate. In deciding whether a full reassessment is necessary, the supervisory body should consider whether the grounds for the authorisation, or the nature of the conditions, are being contested by anyone as part of the review request.

8.15 If the review relates to any of the other requirements, or to a significant change in the person's situation under the best interests requirement, the supervisory body must obtain a new assessment.

8.16 If the assessment shows that the requirement is still met, the supervisory body must check whether the reason that it is met has changed from the reason originally stated on the authorisation. If it has, the supervisory body should make any appropriate amendments to the authorisation. In addition, if the review relates to the best interests requirement, the supervisory body must consider whether any conditions should be changed following the new assessment.

PART VI

Scenario: The review process

Jo is 29 and sustained severe brain damage in a road traffic collision that killed her parents. She has great difficulty in verbal and written communication. Jo can get very frustrated and has been known to lash out at other people in the nursing care home where she now lives. At

---

first, she regularly attempted to leave the home, but the view of the organisation providing Jo's care was that such a move would place her at serious risk, so she should be prevented from leaving.

Jo was assessed under the deprivation of liberty safeguards and an authorisation was made for six months. That authorisation is not due to end for another three months. However, Jo has made huge progress at the home and her representative is no longer sure that the restrictions are necessary. Care home staff, however, do not think that her improvement reduces the best interests requirement of the deprivation of liberty authorisation.

Jo is assisted by her representative to request a review, in the form of a letter with pictures. The pictures appear to describe Jo's frustration with the legal processes that she perceives are preventing her from moving into her own accommodation.

The supervisory body appoints a best interests assessor to coordinate the review. The best interests assessor considers which of the qualifying requirements needs to be reviewed and by whom. It appears that the best interests assessment, as well as possibly the mental health and mental capacity assessments, should be reviewed.

To assess Jo's mental capacity and her own wishes for the best interests assessment, the best interests assessor feels that specialist help would be beneficial. A speech and language therapist meets with Jo and uses a visual communication system with her. Using this system, the therapist is able to say that in her view Jo is unlikely to have capacity to make the decision to leave the care home. The mental health assessment also confirmed that Jo was still considered to have a mental disorder.

The best interests assessor was uncertain, however, whether it was still in Jo's best interests to remain under the deprivation of liberty authorisation. It was not possible to coordinate full updated assessments from the rehabilitation team, who knew her well, in the time limits required. So, because the care home believed that the standard authorisation was still required, and it was a complex case, the best interests assessor recommended to the supervisory body that two conditions should be applied to the standard authorisation:

- assessments must be carried out by rehabilitation specialists on Jo's clinical progress, and
- a full case review should be held within one month.

At this review meeting, to which Jo's representative and the best interests assessor were invited, it was agreed that Jo had made such good progress that deprivation of liberty was no longer necessary, because the risks of her having increased freedom had reduced. The standard authorisation was therefore terminated, and a new care plan was prepared which focused on working towards more independent living.

What happens if any of the requirements are not met?

8.17 If any of the requirements are not met, then the authorisation must be terminated immediately.

8.18 The supervisory body must give written notice of the outcome of a review and any changes that have been made to the deprivation of liberty authorisation to:

- the managing authority and the care home or hospital itself
- the relevant person
- the relevant person's representative, and
- any Independent Mental Capacity Advocate (IMCA) involved.

Short-term suspension of authorisation

8.19 There are separate review arrangements for cases in which the eligibility requirement ceases to be met for a short period of time for reasons other than that the person is objecting to receiving mental health treatment in hospital. For example, if the relevant person is detained as a hospital in-patient under the Mental Health Act 1983, the managing authority must notify the supervisory body, who will suspend the authorisation.

8.20 If the relevant person then becomes eligible again within 28 days, the managing authority must notify the supervisory body who will remove the suspension. If no such notice is given within 28 days, then the authorisation will be terminated. Standard forms are available for managing authorities to notify supervisory bodies about the need for suspension of an authorisation, or that a suspension should be lifted.

8.21 If the person ceases to meet the eligibility requirement because they begin to object to receiving mental health treatment in hospital and they meet the criteria for an application for admission under section 2 or section 3 of the Mental Health Act 1983, a review should be started immediately (see paragraph 8.3).

Is a review necessary when the relevant person's capacity fluctuates?

8.22 Guidance about people with fluctuating or temporary capacity is contained in paragraphs 4.26 and 4.27 of the main Code. In the context of deprivation of liberty safeguards, where a relevant person's capacity to make decisions about the arrangements made for their care and treatment fluctuates on a short-term basis, a balance needs to be struck between:

PART VI

- the need to review and terminate an authorisation if a person regains capacity, and
- spending time and resources constantly reviewing, terminating and then seeking fresh deprivation of liberty authorisations as the relevant person's capacity changes.

8.23 Each case must be treated on its merits. Managing authorities should keep all cases under review: where a person subject to an authorisation is deemed to have regained the capacity to decide about the arrangements made for their care and treatment, the managing authority must assess whether there is consistent evidence of the regaining of capacity on a longer-term basis. This is a clinical judgement that will need to be made by a suitably qualified person.

8.24 Where there is consistent evidence of regaining capacity on this longer-term basis, deprivation of liberty should be lifted immediately, and a formal review and termination of the authorisation sought. However, it should be borne in mind that a deprivation of liberty authorisation carries with it certain safeguards that the relevant person will lose if the authorisation is terminated. Where the regaining of capacity is likely to be temporary, and the authorisation will be required again within a short period of time, the authorisation should be left in place, but with the situation kept under ongoing review.

Scenario: Fluctuating capacity

Walter, an older man with severe depression, is admitted to hospital from a care home. He seems confused and bewildered, but does not object. His family are unable to look after him at home, but they would prefer him to go into a different care home rather than stay in hospital. However, there is no alternative placement available, so when the assessment concludes that Walter lacks capacity to make decisions about his care and treatment, the only option seems to be that he should stay on the ward,

Because the care regime in the ward is extremely restrictive – Walter is not allowed to leave the hospital and his movement within the hospital is restricted for his own safety – ward staff think that they need to apply for a deprivation of liberty authorisation which is subsequently given.

However, over time Walter starts to experience lucid passages, during which he expresses relief at being on the ward rather than in the care home. A review meeting is convened and the participants agree that Walter now sometimes has capacity to make decisions about the arrangements made for his care and treatment. As this capacity fluctuates, it is decided, in consultation with his family, that the deprivation of liberty authorisation should remain in place for the time being.

> Walter remains on the ward and his progress is such that his family feel they could look after him at home. Walter seems happy with this proposal and the consultant psychiatrist with responsibility for his care agrees to this. The deprivation of liberty authorisation is reviewed and terminated.

What happens when an authorisation ends?

8.25 When an authorisation ends, the managing authority cannot lawfully continue to deprive a person of their liberty.

8.26 If the managing authority considers that a person will still need to be deprived of liberty after the authorisation ends, they need to request a further standard authorisation to begin immediately after the expiry of the existing authorisation.

8.27 There is no statutory time limit on how far in advance of the expiry of one authorisation the managing authority can apply for a renewal authorisation. It will need to be far enough in advance for the renewal authorisation to be given before the existing authorisation ends (but see paragraphs 3.19 and 3.20 about not applying for authorisations too far in advance).

8.28 Once underway, the process for renewing a standard authorisation is the same as that for obtaining an original authorisation, and the same assessment processes must take place. However, the need to instruct an IMCA will not usually arise because the relevant person should at this stage have a representative appointed.

8.29 When the standard authorisation ends, the supervisory body must inform in writing:

- the relevant person
- the relevant person's representative
- the managing authority, and
- every interested person named by the best interests assessor in their report as somebody they have consulted in carrying out their assessment.

9 WHAT HAPPENS IF SOMEONE THINKS A PERSON IS BEING DEPRIVED OF THEIR LIBERTY WITHOUT AUTHORISATION?

It is a serious issue to deprive someone of their liberty without authorisation if they lack the capacity to consent. If anyone believes that a person is being deprived of their liberty without authorisation, they should raise this with the relevant authorities.

If the conclusion is that the person is being deprived of their liberty unlawfully, this will normally result in a change in their care arrangements, or in an application for a deprivation of liberty authorisation being made.

This chapter explains the process for reporting concerns and for assessing whether unauthorised deprivation of liberty is occurring. The flowchart at

PART VI

Annex 3 summarises the process that a supervisory body should follow when it receives a request from somebody other than the managing authority to examine whether or not there is a current unauthorised deprivation of liberty.

What action should someone take if they think a person is being deprived of their liberty without authorisation?

9.1 If the relevant person themselves, any relative, friend or carer or any other third party (such as a person carrying out an inspection visit or a member of an advocacy organisation) believes that a person is being deprived of liberty without the managing authority having applied for an authorisation, they should draw this to the attention of the managing authority. A standard letter is available for this purpose. In the first instance, they should ask the managing authority to apply for an authorisation if it wants to continue with the care regime, or to change the care regime immediately. Given the seriousness of deprivation of liberty, a managing authority must respond within a reasonable time to the request. This would normally mean within 24 hours.

9.2 It may be possible for the managing authority to resolve the matter informally with the concerned person. For example, the managing authority could discuss the case with the concerned person, and perhaps make some adjustment to the care arrangements so that concerns that a deprivation of liberty may be occurring are removed. However, if the managing authority is unable to resolve the issue with the concerned person quickly, they should submit a request for a standard authorisation to the supervisory body.

9.3 If the concerned person has raised the matter with the managing authority, and the managing authority does not apply for an authorisation within a reasonable period, the concerned person can ask the supervisory body to decide whether there is an unauthorised deprivation of liberty. They should:
- tell the supervisory body the name of the person they are concerned about and the name of the hospital or care home, and
- as far as they are able, explain why they think that the person is deprived of their liberty.

A standard letter is available for this purpose.

9.4 In such circumstances, the supervisory body must select and appoint a person who is suitable and eligible to carry out a best interests assessment to consider whether the person is deprived of liberty.

9.5 The supervisory body does not, however, need to arrange such an assessment where it appears to the supervisory body that:
- the request they have received is frivolous or vexatious (for example, where the person is very obviously not deprived of their liberty) or where a very recent assessment has been carried out and repeated requests are received, or

- the question of whether or not there is an unauthorised deprivation of liberty has already been decided, and since that decision, there has been no change of circumstances that would merit the question being considered again.

The supervisory body should record the reasons for their decisions. A standard form is available for this purpose.

9.6 The supervisory body must notify the person who raised the concern, the relevant person, the managing authority of the relevant hospital or care home and any IMCA involved:

- that it has been to asked to assess whether or not there is an unauthorised deprivation of liberty
- whether or not it has decided to commission an assessment, and
- where relevant, who has been appointed as assessor.

What happens if somebody informs the supervisory body directly that they think a person is being deprived of their liberty without authorisation?

9.7 If a person raises concerns about a potential unauthorised deprivation of liberty directly with the supervisory body, the supervisory body should immediately arrange a preliminary assessment to determine whether a deprivation of liberty is occurring. The supervisory body should then immediately notify the managing authority, rather than asking the concerned person to contact the managing authority themselves, to ask them to request a standard authorisation in respect of the person who is possibly deprived of liberty. The supervisory body should agree with the managing authority what is a reasonable period within which a standard authorisation should be requested (unless the managing authority is able to resolve the matter informally with the concerned person as described in paragraph 9.2). If the managing authority does not submit an application within the agreed period, and the matter has not been resolved informally, the supervisory body should follow the process set out in paragraphs 9.3 to 9.6 to assess whether unlawful deprivation of liberty is occurring. Even if the concerned person prefers to deal directly with the managing authority, the supervisory body should monitor what happens very closely to ensure that no unlawful deprivation of liberty may be occurring without proper action being taken.

How will the assessment of unlawful deprivation of liberty be conducted?

9.8 An assessment of whether an unlawful deprivation of liberty is occurring must be carried out within seven calendar days. Although the assessment must be completed by somebody who is suitable and eligible to carry out a best interests assessment, it is not a best interests assessment as such. The purpose of the assessment is simply to establish whether unlawful deprivation of liberty is occurring.

9.9 The person nominated to undertake the assessment must consult the managing authority of the relevant hospital or care home, and examine any relevant needs assessments and care plans to consider whether they constitute a deprivation of liberty. They should also speak to the person who raised the concern about why they believe that the relevant person is being deprived of their liberty and consult, as far as is possible, with the relevant person's family and friends. If there is nobody appropriate to consult among family and friends, they should inform the supervisory body who must arrange for an IMCA to be instructed to support and represent the person. A standard form is available for the assessor to record the outcome of their assessment.

What happens once the assessment has been conducted?

9.10 There are three possible outcomes of this assessment. The assessor may conclude that:
- the person is not being deprived of their liberty
- the person is being lawfully deprived of their liberty because authorisation exists (this, though, is an unlikely outcome since the supervisory body should already be aware if any authorisation exists, thus rendering any assessment in response to a third party request unnecessary), or
- the person is being deprived of their liberty unlawfully.

9.11 The supervisory body must notify the following people of the outcome of the assessment:
- the concerned third party who made the request
- the relevant person
- the managing authority of the relevant hospital or care home, and
- any IMCA involved.

A standard form is available for this purpose.

9.12 If the outcome of the assessment is that there is an unauthorised deprivation of liberty, then the full assessment process should be completed as if a standard authorisation for deprivation of liberty had been applied for – unless the managing authority changes the care arrangements so that it is clear that there is no longer any deprivation of liberty.

9.13 If, having considered what could be done to avoid deprivation of liberty, the managing authority decides that the need to continue the deprivation of liberty is so urgent that the care regime should continue while the assessments are carried out, it must give an urgent authorisation and seek a standard authorisation within seven days. The managing authority must supply the supervisory body with the same information it would have had to include in a request for a standard authorisation.

9.14 If the concerned person does not accept the outcome of their request for assessment, they can apply to the Court of Protection to hear their case. See chapter 10 for more details of the role of the Court of Protection.

10 WHAT IS THE COURT OF PROTECTION AND WHEN CAN PEOPLE APPLY TO IT?

To comply with Article 5(4) of the European Convention on Human Rights, anybody deprived of their liberty in accordance with the safeguards described in this Code of Practice is entitled to the right of speedy access to a court that can review the lawfulness of their deprivation of liberty. The Court of Protection, established by the Mental Capacity Act 2005, is the court for this purpose. Chapter 8 of the main Code provides more details on its role, powers and responsibilities.

When can people apply to the Court of Protection about the deprivation of liberty safeguards and who can apply?

Applying before an authorisation is given

10.1 The relevant person, or someone acting on their behalf, may make an application to the Court of Protection **before** a decision has been reached on an application for authorisation to deprive a person of their liberty. This might be to ask the court to declare whether the relevant person has capacity, or whether an act done or proposed to be done in relation to that person is lawful (this may include whether or not the act is or would be in the best interests of the relevant person). It is up to the Court of Protection to decide whether or not to consider such an application in advance of the decision on authorisation.

Applying after an authorisation has been given

10.2 Once a standard authorisation has been given, the relevant person or their representative has the right to apply to the Court of Protection to determine any question relating to the following matters:
- whether the relevant person meets one or more of the qualifying requirements for deprivation of liberty
- the period for which the standard authorisation is to be in force
- the purpose for which the standard authorisation is given, or
- the conditions subject to which the standard authorisation is given.

10.3 Where an urgent authorisation has been given, the relevant person or certain persons acting on their behalf, such as a donee or deputy, has the right to apply to the Court of Protection to determine any question relating to the following matters:
- whether the urgent authorisation should have been given

PART VI

- the period for which the urgent authorisation is to be in force, or
- the purpose for which the urgent authorisation has been given.

10.4 Where a standard or urgent authorisation has been given, any other person may also apply to the Court of Protection for permission to take the relevant person's case to court to determine whether an authorisation should have been given. However, the Court of Protection has discretion to decide whether or not to consider an application from these people.

10.5 Wherever possible, concerns about the deprivation of liberty should be resolved informally or through the relevant supervisory body's or managing authority's complaints procedure, rather than through the Court of Protection. Chapter 15 of the main Code ('What are the best ways to settle disagreements and disputes about issues covered in the Act?') contains general guidance on how to settle disputes about issues covered in the Mental Capacity Act 2005. The review processes covered in chapter 8 of this Code also provide a way of resolving disputes or concerns, as explained in that chapter.

10.6 The aim should be to limit applications to the Court of Protection to cases that genuinely need to be referred to the court. However, with deprivation of liberty at stake, people should not be discouraged from making an application to the Court of Protection if it proves impossible to resolve concerns satisfactorily through other routes in a timely manner.

How should people apply to the Court of Protection?

10.7 Guidance on the court's procedures, including how to make an application, is given in the Court of Protection Rules and Practice Directions issued by the court.[92]

10.8 The following people have an automatic right of access to the Court of Protection and do not have to obtain permission from the court to make an application:

- a person who lacks, or is alleged to lack, capacity in relation to a specific decision or action
- the donor of a Lasting Power of Attorney to whom an application relates, or their donee
- a deputy who has been appointed by the court to act for the person concerned
- a person named in an existing court order[93] to which the application relates, and

---

[92] There will usually be a fee for applications to the court. Details of the fees charged by the court and the circumstances in which fees may be waived or remitted are available from the Office of the Public Guardian (http://www.publicguardian.gov.uk/).

[93] Examples of existing court orders include orders appointing a deputy or declarations made by the court in relation to treatment issues.

- the person appointed by the supervisory body as the relevant person's representative.

10.9 All other applicants must obtain the permission of the court before making an application. (See section 50 of the Mental Capacity Act 2005, as amended.) This can be done by completing the appropriate application form.

What orders can the Court of Protection make?

10.10 The court may make an order:
- varying or terminating a standard or urgent authorisation, or
- directing the supervisory body (in the case of a standard authorisation) or the managing authority (in the case of an urgent authorisation) to vary or terminate the authorisation.

What is the role of the Court of Protection in respect of people lacking capacity who are deprived of their liberty in settings other than hospitals or care homes?

10.11 The deprivation of liberty safeguards relate only to circumstances where a person is deprived of their liberty in a hospital or care home. Depriving a person who lacks capacity to consent to the arrangements made for their care or treatment of their liberty in other settings (for example in a person's own home, in supported living arrangements other than in care homes or in a day centre) will only be lawful following an order of the Court of Protection on a best interests personal welfare matter (see paragraph 6.51 of the main Code).

10.12 In such a case, application to the Court of Protection should be made before deprivation of liberty begins. A Court of Protection order will then itself provide a legal basis for the deprivation of liberty. A separate deprivation of liberty authorisation under the processes set out in this Code will not be required.

Is legal aid available to support applications to the Court of Protection in deprivation of liberty safeguards cases?

10.13 Legal aid will be available both for advice and representation before the Court of Protection.

11 HOW WILL THE SAFEGUARDS BE MONITORED?

The deprivation of a person's liberty is a significant issue. The deprivation of liberty safeguards are designed to ensure that a person who lacks capacity to consent to the arrangements made for their care or treatment is suitably protected against arbitrary detention. In order to provide reassurance that the

PART VI

safeguards processes are being correctly operated, it is important for there to
be an effective mechanism for monitoring the implementation of the
safeguards.

Who will monitor the safeguards?

11.1 Regulations[94] will confer the responsibility for the inspection
process of the operation of the deprivation of liberty safeguards in
England on a new regulator, the Care Quality Commission, bringing
together functions from the existing Commission for Social Care
Inspection, the Healthcare Commission and the Mental Health Act
Commission. The new body will be established during 2008,
subject to the passage of the relevant legislation through Parliament,
and is expected to be fully operational by 2009/10 in line with the
deprivation of liberty safeguards coming into force.

11.2 In Wales, the functions of monitoring the operation of the
deprivation of liberty safeguards will fall to Welsh Ministers. These
functions will be performed on their behalf by Healthcare
Inspectorate Wales and the Care and Social Services Inspectorate
Wales.

What will the inspection bodies do and what powers will they have?

11.3 The inspection bodies for care homes and hospitals will be
expected to:
- monitor the manner in which the deprivation of liberty
safeguards are being operated by:
  - visiting hospitals and care homes in accordance with their
  existing visiting programme
  - interviewing people accommodated in hospitals and care
  homes to the extent that they consider it necessary to do
  so, and
  - requiring the production of, and inspecting, relevant
  records relating to the care or treatment of people
  accommodated in hospitals and care homes
- report annually, summarising their activity and their findings
about the operation of the deprivation of liberty safeguards. In
England this report will be made to the Secretary of State for
Health, and in Wales the report will be made to the Welsh
Ministers. It will be for each monitoring body to decide
whether there should be a deprivation of liberty safeguards
specific report or whether the report should form part of a
wider report on the monitoring body's activities.

---

[94]   Draft regulations for England will be consulted upon later. Welsh Ministers are currently
considering how they will use their regulation-making powers for Wales.

11.4 The inspection bodies will have the power to require supervisory bodies and managing authorities of hospitals or care homes to disclose information to them.

11.5 The inspection process will not cover the revisiting of individual assessments (other than by way of a limited amount of sampling).

11.6 The inspection process will not constitute an alternative review or appeal process. However, if the inspection body comes across a case where they believe deprivation of liberty may be occurring without an authorisation, they should inform the supervisory body in the same way as any other third party may do.

11.7 The inspection bodies will look at the deprivation of liberty protocols and procedures in place within managing authorities and supervisory bodies. The aim is to use a small amount of sampling to evaluate the effect of these protocols and procedures on individual cases. Monitoring should take place at a time when the monitoring body is visiting the care home or in-patient setting as part of routine operations, not as an exception.

11.8 Supervisory bodies and managing authorities should keep their protocols and procedures under review and supervisory bodies should assess the nature of the authorisations they are giving in light of their local population. This information may be relevant to policy decisions about commissioning care and support services.

CHECKLISTS

Key points for care homes and hospitals (managing authorities)

- Managing authorities need to adapt their care planning processes to incorporate consideration of whether a person has capacity to consent to the services which are to be provided and whether their actions are likely to result in a deprivation of liberty.

- A managing authority must not, except in an urgent situation, deprive a person of liberty unless a standard authorisation has been given by the supervisory body for that specific situation, and remains in force.

- It is up to the managing authority to request such authorisation and implement the outcomes.

- Authorisation should be obtained from the supervisory body in advance of the deprivation of liberty, except in circumstances considered to be so urgent that the deprivation of liberty needs to begin immediately. In such cases, authorisation must be obtained within seven calendar days of the start of the deprivation of liberty.

- A managing authority must ensure that they comply with any conditions attached to the authorisation.

- A managing authority should monitor whether the relevant person's representative maintains regular contact with the person.

- Authorisation of deprivation of liberty should only be sought if it is genuinely necessary for a person to be deprived of liberty in their best interests in order to keep them safe. It is not necessary to apply

PART VI

for authorisations for all admissions to hospitals and care homes simply because the person concerned lacks capacity to decide whether to be admitted.

Key points for local authorities and NHS bodies (supervisory bodies)

- Supervisory bodies will receive applications from managing authorities for standard authorisations of deprivation of liberty. Deprivation of liberty cannot lawfully begin until the supervisory body has given authorisation, or the managing authority has itself given an urgent authorisation.
- Before an authorisation for deprivation of liberty may be given, the supervisory body must have obtained written assessments of the relevant person in order to ensure that they meet the qualifying requirements (including that the deprivation of liberty is necessary to protect them from harm and will be in their best interests).
- Supervisory bodies will need to ensure that sufficient assessors are available to meet the needs of their area and that these assessors have the skills, qualifications, experience and training to perform the function.
- Authorisation may not be given unless all the qualifying requirements are met.
- In giving authorisation, the supervisory body must specify its duration, which may not exceed 12 months and may not be for longer than recommended by the best interests assessor. Deprivation of liberty should not continue for longer than is necessary.
- The supervisory body may attach conditions to the authorisation if it considers it appropriate to do so.
- The supervisory body must give notice of its decision in writing to specified people, and notify others.
- The supervisory body must appoint a relevant person's representative to represent the interests of every person for whom they give a standard authorisation for deprivation of liberty.
- When an authorisation is in force, the relevant person, the relevant person's representative and any IMCA representing the individual have a right at any time to request that the supervisory body reviews the authorisation.

Key points for managing authorities and supervisory bodies

In addition to the above, both managing authorities and supervisory bodies should be aware of the following key points:

- An authorisation may last for a maximum period of 12 months.
- Anyone engaged in caring for the person, anyone named by them as a person to consult, and anyone with an interest in the person's welfare must be consulted in decision-making.
- Before the current authorisation expires, the managing authority may seek a fresh authorisation for up to another 12 months,

provided it is established, on the basis of further assessment, that the requirements continue to be met.

- The authorisation should be reviewed, and if appropriate revoked, before it expires if there has been a significant change in the person's circumstances. To this end, the managing authority will be required to ensure that the continued deprivation of liberty of a person remains necessary in the best interests of the person.
- A decision to deprive a person of liberty may be challenged by the relevant person, or by the relevant person's representative, by an application to the Court of Protection. However, managing authorities and supervisory bodies should always be prepared to try to resolve disputes locally and informally. No one should be forced to apply to the court because of failure or unwillingness on the part of a managing authority or supervisory body to engage in constructive discussion.
- If the court is asked to decide on a case where there is a question about whether deprivation of liberty is lawful or should continue to be authorised, the managing authority can continue with its current care regime where it is necessary:
  - for the purpose of giving the person life-sustaining treatment, or
  - to prevent a serious deterioration in their condition while the court makes its decision.
- The complete process of assessing and authorising deprivation of liberty should be clearly recorded, and regularly monitored and audited, as part of an organisation's governance structure.
- Management information should be recorded and retained, and used to measure the effectiveness of the deprivation of liberty processes. This information will also need to be shared with the inspection bodies.

PART VI

ANNEXES

Annex 1

Overview of the deprivation of liberty safeguards process

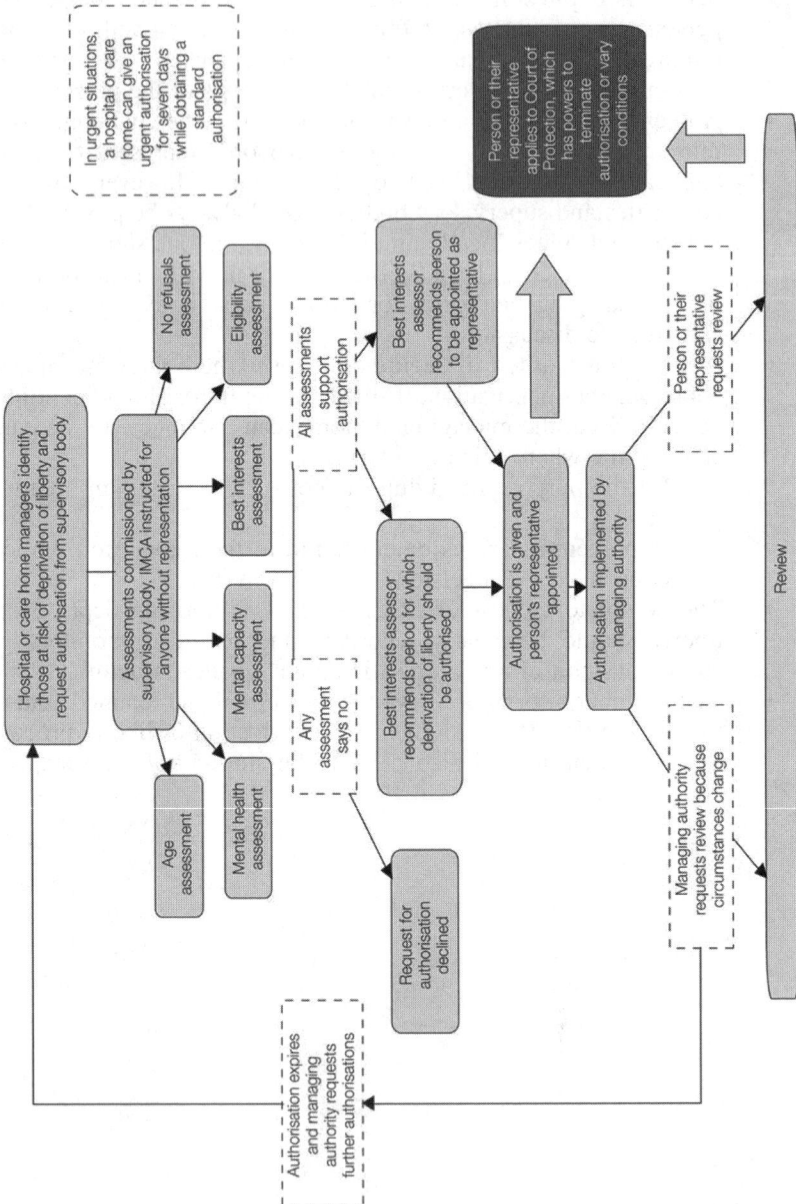

Annex 2

What should a managing authority consider before applying for authorisation of deprivation of liberty?

These questions are relevant **both** at admission **and** when reviewing the care of patients and residents. Bconsidering the following questions in the following or der, a managing authority will be helped to know whether an application for authorisation is required.

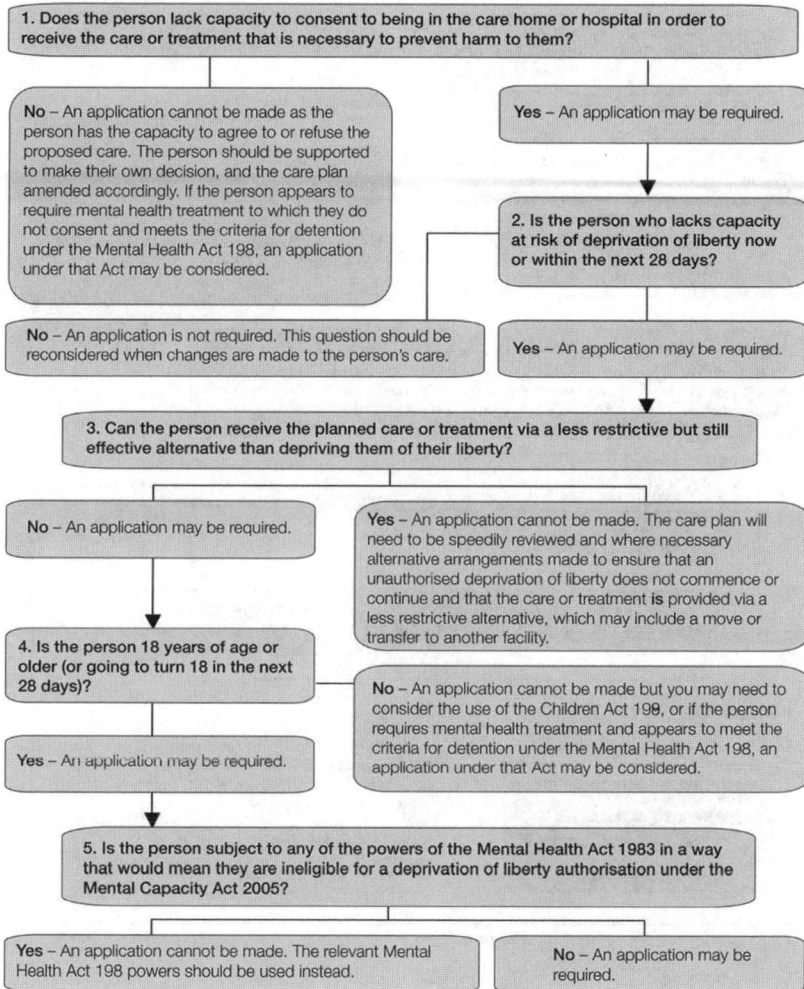

1. Does the person lack capacity to consent to being in the care home or hospital in order to receive the care or treatment that is necessary to prevent harm to them?

No – An application cannot be made as the person has the capacity to agree to or refuse the proposed care. The person should be supported to make their own decision, and the care plan amended accordingly. If the person appears to require mental health treatment to which they do not consent and meets the criteria for detention under the Mental Health Act 198, an application under that Act may be considered.

Yes – An application may be required.

2. Is the person who lacks capacity at risk of deprivation of liberty now or within the next 28 days?

No – An application is not required. This question should be reconsidered when changes are made to the person's care.

Yes – An application may be required.

3. Can the person receive the planned care or treatment via a less restrictive but still effective alternative than depriving them of their liberty?

No – An application may be required.

Yes – An application cannot be made. The care plan will need to be speedily reviewed and where necessary alternative arrangements made to ensure that an unauthorised deprivation of liberty does not commence or continue and that the care or treatment **is** provided via a less restrictive alternative, which may include a move or transfer to another facility.

4. Is the person 18 years of age or older (or going to turn 18 in the next 28 days)?

No – An application cannot be made but you may need to consider the use of the Children Act 198, or if the person requires mental health treatment and appears to meet the criteria for detention under the Mental Health Act 198, an application under that Act may be considered.

Yes – An application may be required.

5. Is the person subject to any of the powers of the Mental Health Act 1983 in a way that would mean they are ineligible for a deprivation of liberty authorisation under the Mental Capacity Act 2005?

Yes – An application cannot be made. The relevant Mental Health Act 198 powers should be used instead.

No – An application may be required.

PART VI

1353

Yes – The managing authority should give an urgent authorisation itself and apply to the supervisory body for a standard authorisation – in the case of a care home to a local authority and in the case of a hospital to a PT .

9. Is the need for the person to be deprived of their liberty so urgent that it has to start immediately?

No – The managing authority needs to apply to the supervisory body for a standard authorisation – in the case of a care home to a local authority and in the case of a hospital to a PT .

No – An application is required.

Yes – An application cannot be made. The care plan will need to be speedily reviewed and where necessary alternative arrangements made to ensure that an unauthorised deprivation of liberty does not commence or continue. If the person appears to meet the criteria for detention under the Mental Health Act 198, an application under that Act may be considered.

8. Has an attorney or deputy, with the authority to do so, indicated that they will object to the person entering (or staying in) the hospital or care home or that they will refuse any or all of the proposed treatment or care on their behalf?

7. Is the proposed deprivation of liberty for the purpose of mental health treatment in hospital and does the person object to going to (or staying in) hospital or to the proposed treatment? Does the person meet the criteria to be detained under section 2 or 3 of the Mental Health Act 1983 instead?

Yes (to both questions) – An application cannot be made (unless an attorney or deputy has consented on the person's behalf to the things to which the person objects).

No (to either question) – An application may be required.

6. Is the proposed deprivation of liberty in order to provide treatment in a case in which the person has made a valid and applicable advance decision to refuse that treatment?

No – An application may be required.

Definition of capacity: the ability to make a decision about a particular matter at the time the decision needs to be made.

Yes – An application cannot be made. The care plan will need to be speedily reviewed and where necessary alternative arrangements made to ensure that an unauthorised deprivation of liberty does not commence or continue. If the person appears to meet the criteria for detention under the Mental Health Act 198, an application under that Act may be considered.

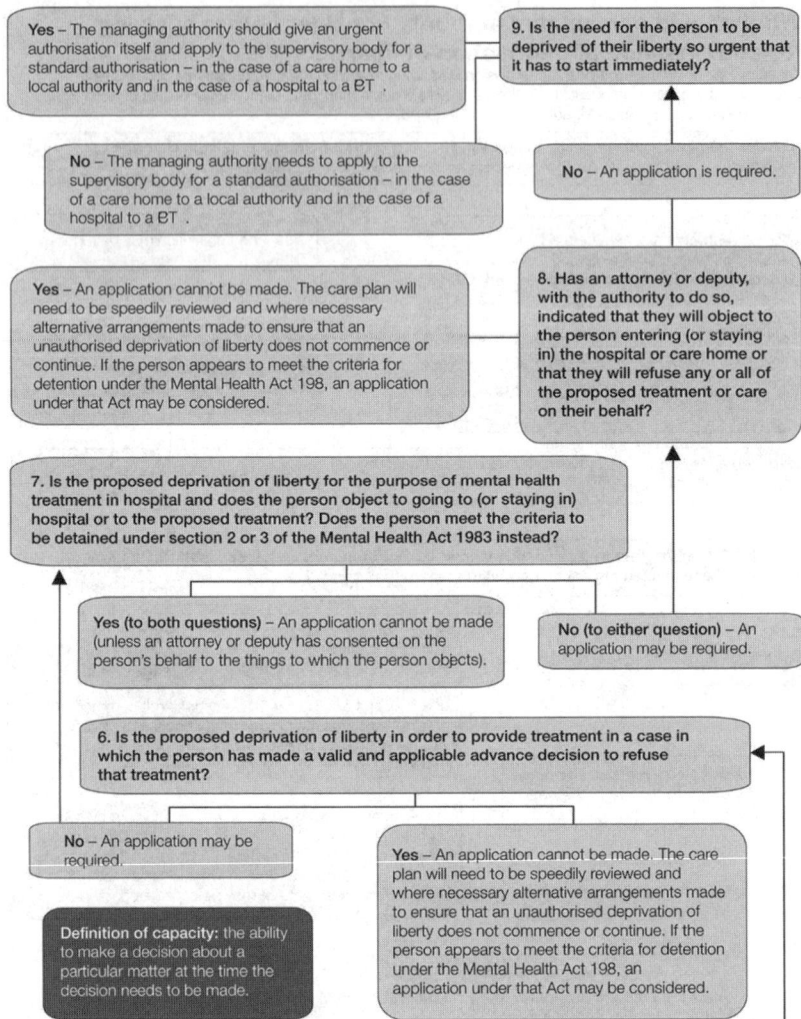

NB: An authorisation only relates to deprivation of liberty and does not give authority for any course of treatment.

Annex 3

Supervisory body action on receipt of a request from:
a) a managing authority for a standard deprivation of liberty authorisation
b) somebody other than a managing authority (an eligible person) to determine whether or not there is a current unauthorised deprivation of liberty

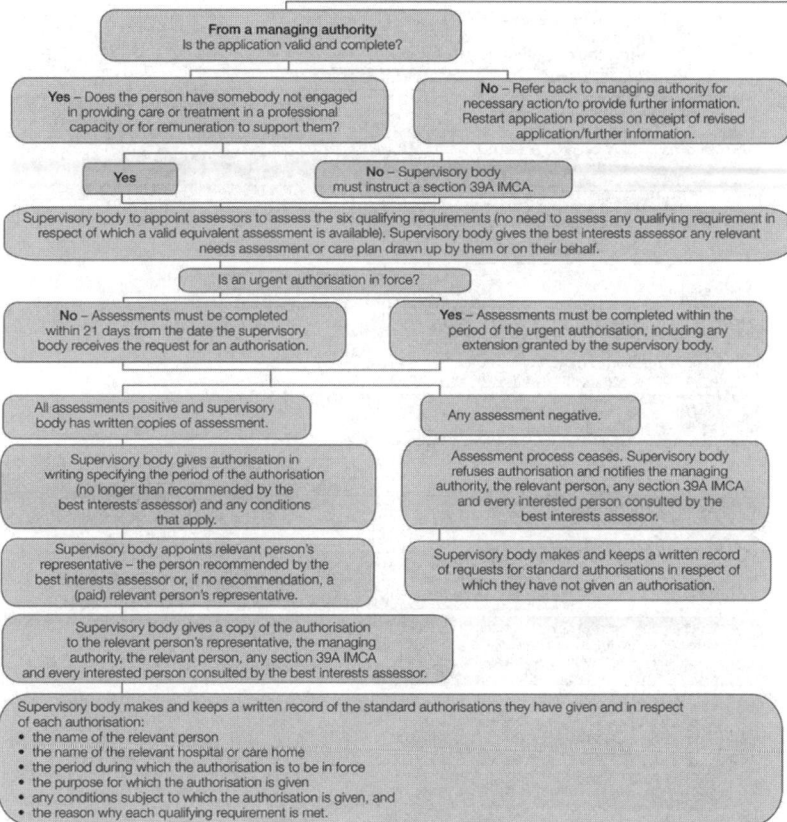

From a managing authority
Is the application valid and complete?

Yes – Does the person have somebody not engaged in providing care or treatment in a professional capacity or for remuneration to support them?

No – Refer back to managing authority for necessary action/to provide further information. Restart application process on receipt of revised application/further information.

Yes

No – Supervisory body must instruct a section 39A IMCA.

Supervisory body to appoint assessors to assess the six qualifying requirements (no need to assess any qualifying requirement in respect of which a valid equivalent assessment is available). Supervisory body gives the best interests assessor any relevant needs assessment or care plan drawn up by them or on their behalf.

Is an urgent authorisation in force?

No – Assessments must be completed within 21 days from the date the supervisory body receives the request for an authorisation.

Yes – Assessments must be completed within the period of the urgent authorisation, including any extension granted by the supervisory body.

All assessments positive and supervisory body has written copies of assessment.

Any assessment negative.

Supervisory body gives authorisation in writing specifying the period of the authorisation (no longer than recommended by the best interests assessor) and any conditions that apply.

Assessment process ceases. Supervisory body refuses authorisation and notifies the managing authority, the relevant person, any section 39A IMCA and every interested person consulted by the best interests assessor.

Supervisory body appoints relevant person's representative – the person recommended by the best interests assessor or, if no recommendation, a (paid) relevant person's representative.

Supervisory body makes and keeps a written record of requests for standard authorisations in respect of which they have not given an authorisation.

Supervisory body gives a copy of the authorisation to the relevant person's representative, the managing authority, the relevant person, any section 39A IMCA and every interested person consulted by the best interests assessor.

Supervisory body makes and keeps a written record of the standard authorisations they have given and in respect of each authorisation:
• the name of the relevant person
• the name of the relevant hospital or care home
• the period during which the authorisation is to be in force
• the purpose for which the authorisation is given
• any conditions subject to which the authorisation is given, and
• the reason why each qualifying requirement is met.

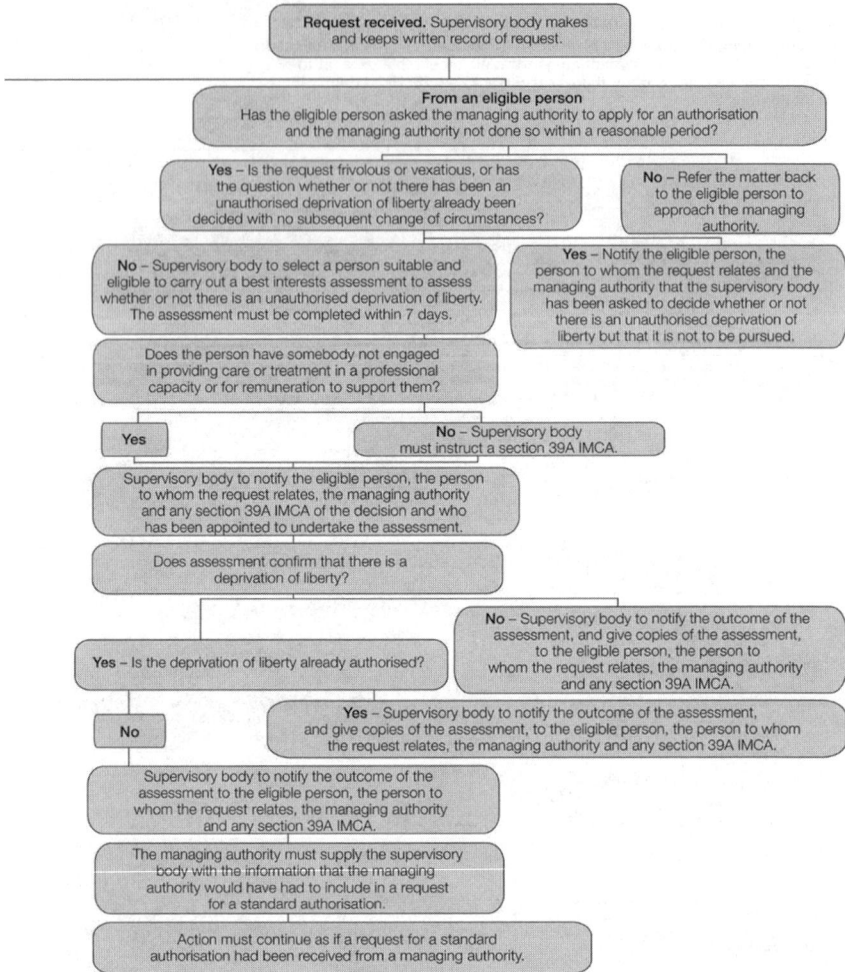

Annex 4

Standard authorisation review process

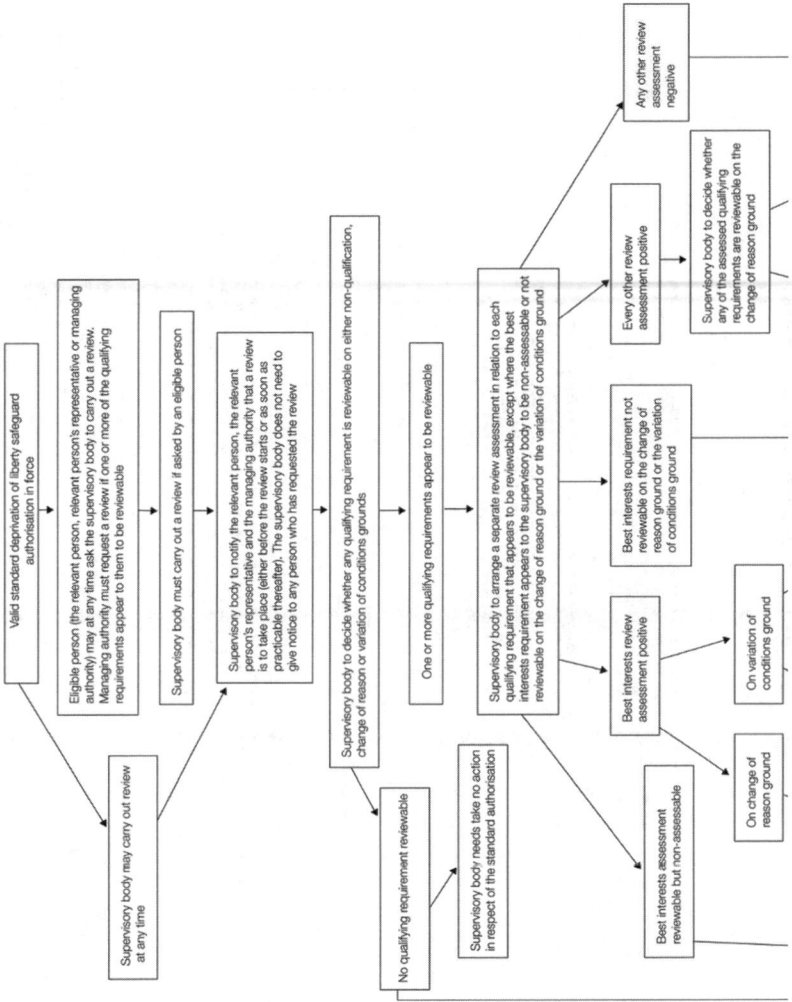

Valid standard deprivation of liberty safeguard authorisation in force

Supervisory body may carry out review at any time

Eligible person (the relevant person, relevant person's representative or managing authority) may at any time ask the supervisory body to carry out a review. Managing authority must request a review if one or more of the qualifying requirements appear to them to be reviewable

Supervisory body must carry out a review if asked by an eligible person

Supervisory body to notify the relevant person, the relevant person's representative and the managing authority that a review is to take place (either before the review starts or as soon as practicable thereafter). The supervisory body does not need to give notice to any person who has requested the review

Supervisory body to decide whether any qualifying requirement is reviewable on either non-qualification, change of reason or variation of conditions grounds

No qualifying requirement reviewable

One or more qualifying requirements appear to be reviewable

Supervisory body needs take no action in respect of the standard authorisation

Supervisory body to arrange a separate review assessment in relation to each qualifying requirement that appears to be reviewable, except where the best interests requirement appears to the supervisory body to be non-assessable or not reviewable on the change of reason ground or the variation of conditions ground

Best interests review assessment positive

Best interests requirement not reviewable on the change of reason ground or the variation of conditions ground

Every other review assessment positive

Any other review assessment negative

Best interests assessment reviewable but non-assessable

On change of reason ground

On variation of conditions ground

Supervisory body to decide whether any of the assessed qualifying requirements are reviewable on the change of reason ground

PART VI

1357

Standard authorisation review process

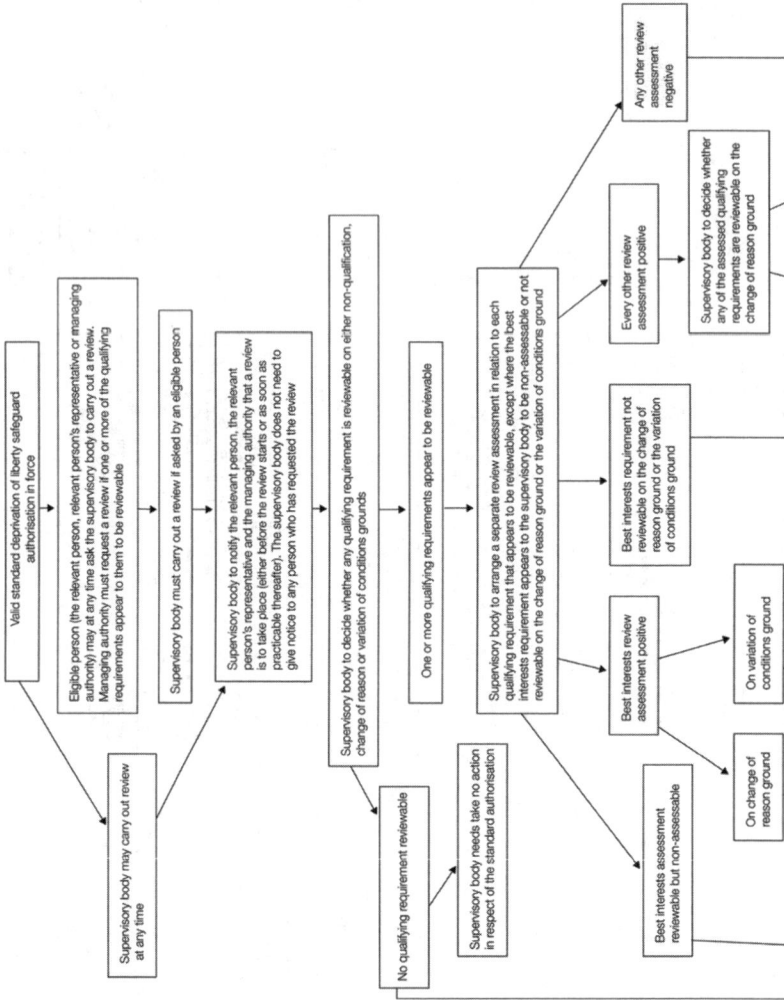

KEY WORDS AND PHRASES USED IN THE CODE OF PRACTICE

The table below is not a full index or glossary. Instead, it is a list of key terms used in this Code of Practice. References in bold indicate particularly valuable content for that term.

Advance decision to refuse treatment	A decision to refuse specified treatment made in advance by a person who has capacity to do so. This decision will then apply at a future time when that person lacks capacity to consent to, or refuse, the specified treatment. Specific rules apply to advance decisions to refuse life sustaining treatment.	4.26
Advocacy	Independent help and support with understanding issues and putting forward a person's own views, feelings and ideas.	2.7
Age assessment	An assessment, for the purpose of the deprivation of liberty safeguards, of whether the relevant person has reached age 18.	**4.23–4.24**
Approved mental health professional	A social worker or other professional approved by a local social services authority to act on behalf of a local social services authority in carrying out a variety of functions.	4.52, 4.53, 4.60
Assessor	A person who carries out a deprivation of liberty safeguards assessment.	**Chapter 4 (all)** 1.16–1.17, 3.21, 5.22, 9.10 Best interests, and appointing a relevant person's representative: 7.10–7.23
Best interests assessment	An assessment, for the purpose of the deprivation of liberty safeguards, of whether deprivation of liberty is in a detained person's best interests, is necessary to prevent harm to the person and is a proportionate response to the likelihood and seriousness of that harm.	**4.58–4.76** Best interests, and appointing a relevant person's representative: 7.10–7.23
Bournewood judgment	The commonly used term for the October 2004 judgment by the European Court of Human Rights in the case of *HL v the United Kingdom* that led to the introduction of the deprivation of liberty safeguards.	**Introduction to chapter 1** 1.19, 2.2, 2.22
Capacity	Short for mental capacity. The ability to make a decision about a particular matter at the time the decision needs to be made. A legal definition is contained in section 2 of the Mental Capacity Act 2005.	Throughout

Care home	A care facility registered under the Care Standards Act 2000.	Throughout
Care Quality Commission	The new integrated regulator for health and adult social care that, subject to the passage of legislation, will take over regulation of health and adult social care from 1 April 2009.	Chapter 11
Carer	Someone who provides unpaid care by looking after a friend or neighbour who needs support because of sickness, age or disability. In this document, the term carer does not mean a paid care worker.	Throughout
Children Act 1989	A law relating to children and those with parental responsibility for children.	1.12, 5.22
Conditions	Requirements that a supervisory body may impose when giving a standard deprivation of liberty authorisation, after taking account of any recommendations made by the best interests assessor.	**4.74–4.75** 5.5 Review of: 8.14, 8.16
Consent	Agreeing to a course of action – specifically in this document, to a care plan or treatment regime. For consent to be legally valid, the person giving it must have the capacity to take the decision, have been given sufficient information to make the decision, and not have been under any duress or inappropriate pressure.	Throughout
Court of Protection	The specialist court for all issues relating to people who lack capacity to make specific decisions.	**Chapter 10**
Deprivation of liberty	Deprivation of liberty is a term used in the European Convention on Human Rights about circumstances when a person's freedom is taken away. Its meaning in practice is being defined through case law.	**Chapter 2** Throughout
Deprivation of liberty safeguards	The framework of safeguards under the Mental Capacity Act 2005 for people who need to be deprived of their liberty in a hospital or care home in their best interests for care or treatment and who lack the capacity to consent to the arrangements made for their care or treatment.	Throughout
Deprivation of liberty safeguards assessment	Any one of the six assessments that need to be undertaken as part of the standard deprivation of liberty authorisation process.	**Chapter 4**

Deputy	Someone appointed by the Court of Protection with ongoing legal authority, as prescribed by the Court, to make decisions on behalf of a person who lacks capacity to make particular decisions.	4.26, 4.65, 5.11, 5.22, 7.7, 7.13–7.15, 7.18, 7.23, 7.29, 10.3, 10.8
Donee	Someone appointed under a Lasting Power of Attorney who has the legal right to make decisions within the scope of their authority on behalf of the person (the donor) who made the Lasting Power of Attorney.	3.9, 4.26, 4.65, 5.11, 5.22, 7.7, 7.13–7.15, 7.18, 7.23, 7.29, 10.3, 10.8
Eligibility assessment	An assessment, for the purpose of the deprivation of liberty safeguards, of whether or not a person is rendered ineligible for a standard deprivation of liberty authorisation because the authorisation would conflict with requirements that are, or could be, placed on the person under the Mental Health Act 1983.	**4.40–4.57**
European Convention on Human Rights	A convention drawn up within the Council of Europe setting out a number of civil and political rights and freedoms, and setting up a mechanism for the enforcement of the obligations entered into by contracting states.	Chapter 1, Chapter 2
European Court of Human Rights	The court to which any contracting state or individual can apply when they believe that there has been a violation of the European Convention on Human Rights.	Introduction to Chapter 1, 2.1–2.2
Guardianship under the Mental Health Act 1983	The appointment of a guardian to help and supervise patients in the community for their own welfare or to protect other people. The guardian may be either a local authority or a private individual approved by the local authority.	4.43, 4.44
Independent Mental Capacity Advocate (IMCA)	Someone who provides support and representation for a person who lacks capacity to make specific decisions, where the person has no-one else to support them. The IMCA service was established by the Mental Capacity Act 2005 and is not the same as an ordinary advocacy service.	**3.22–3.28, 7.34–7.41** 3.16, 4.7, 5.7–5.8, 5.18, 6.8, 6.19, 6.27–6.28, 7.4, 7.23, 7.26, 8.18, 8.28, 9.6, 9.9
Lasting Power of Attorney	A Power of Attorney created under the Mental Capacity Act 2005 appointing an attorney (donee), or attorneys, to make decisions about the donor's personal welfare, including health care, and/or deal with the donor's property and affairs.	10.8

PART VI

Life-sustaining treatment	Treatment that, in the view of the person providing health care, is necessary to keep a person alive.	5.13
Local authority	In the deprivation of liberty safeguards context, the local council responsible for social services in any particular area of the country.	1.4, 2.18, 2.21, 3.3, 3.11, 3.21, 4.77
Local health board (LHB)	Local health boards cover the same geographic areas as local authorities in Wales. They work alongside their respective local authorities in planning long-term strategies for dealing with issues of health and wellbeing in their areas.	1.4, 3.3
Main Code	The Code of Practice for the Mental Capacity Act 2005.	Throughout
Managing authority	The person or body with management responsibility for the hospital or care home in which a person is, or may become, deprived of their liberty.	**1.4–1.5, 3.1** Throughout
Maximum authorisation period	The maximum period for which a supervisory body may give a standard deprivation of liberty authorisation, which must not exceed the period recommended by the best interests assessor, and which cannot be for more than 12 months.	4.71
Mental Capacity Act 2005	Legislation that governs decision-making for people who lack capacity to make decisions for themselves or who have capacity and want to make preparations for a time when they may lack capacity in the future. It sets out who can take decisions, in which situations, and how they should go about this.	Throughout
Mental capacity assessment	An assessment, for the purpose of the deprivation of liberty safeguards, of whether a person lacks capacity in relation to the question of whether or not they should be accommodated in the relevant hospital or care home for the purpose of being given care or treatment.	4.29–4.32
Mental disorder	Any disorder or disability of the mind, apart from dependence on alcohol or drugs. This includes all learning disabilities.	1.4, 1.7, 1.9, 3.9, 4.33–4.35, 4.45, 4.50, 5.9, 5.22, 6.3
Mental Health Act 1983	Legislation mainly about the compulsory care and treatment of patients with mental health problems. It covers detention in hospital for mental health treatment, supervised community treatment and guardianship.	**4.33–4.57** 1.1, 1.11–1.12, 2.13, 4.5, 5.19, 5.22, 7.8, 8.3, 8.19–8.21

Mental health assessment	An assessment, for the purpose of the deprivation of liberty safeguards, of whether a person has a mental disorder.	**4.33–4.39**
No refusals assessment	An assessment, for the purpose of the deprivation of liberty safeguards, of whether there is any other existing authority for decision-making for the relevant person that would prevent the giving of a standard deprivation of liberty authorisation. This might include any valid advance decision, or valid decision by a deputy or donee appointed under a Lasting Power of Attorney.	**4.25–4.28**
Qualifying requirement	Any one of the six qualifying requirements (age, mental health, mental capacity, best interests, eligibility and no refusals) that need to be assessed and met in order for a standard deprivation of liberty authorisation to be given.	4.1
Relevant hospital or care home	The hospital or care home in which the person is, or may become, deprived of their liberty.	Throughout
Relevant person	A person who is, or may become, deprived of their liberty in a hospital or care home.	Throughout
Relevant person's representative	A person, independent of the relevant hospital or care home, appointed to maintain contact with the relevant person, and to represent and support the relevant person in all matters relating to the operation of the deprivation of liberty safeguards.	**Chapter 7**
Restraint	The use or threat of force to help carry out an act that the person resists. Restraint may only be used where it is necessary to protect the person from harm and is proportionate to the risk of harm.	2.8–2.15
Restriction of liberty	An act imposed on a person that is not of such a degree or intensity as to amount to a deprivation of liberty.	Chapter 2
Review	A formal, fresh look at a relevant person's situation when there has been, or may have been, a change of circumstances that may necessitate an amendment to, or termination of, a standard deprivation of liberty authorisation.	**Chapter 8**
Standard authorisation	An authorisation given by a supervisory body, after completion of the statutory assessment process, giving lawful authority to deprive a relevant person of their liberty in the relevant hospital or care home.	**Chapter 4** Throughout

PART VI

Supervised community treatment	Arrangements under which people can be discharged from detention in hospital under the Mental Health Act 1983, but remain subject to the Act in the community rather than in hospital. Patients on supervised community treatment can be recalled to hospital if treatment in hospital is necessary again.	4.41, 4.50, 4.51
Supervisory body	A primary care trust, local authority, Welsh Ministers or a local health board that is responsible for considering a deprivation of liberty request received from a managing authority, commissioning the statutory assessments and, where all the assessments agree, authorising deprivation of liberty.	**1.4, 3.3** Throughout
Unauthorised deprivation of liberty	A situation in which a person is deprived of their liberty in a hospital or care home without the deprivation being authorised by either a standard or urgent deprivation of liberty authorisation.	Chapter 9
Urgent authorisation	An authorisation given by a managing authority for a maximum of seven days, which may subsequently be extended by a maximum of a further seven days by a supervisory body, that gives the managing authority lawful authority to deprive a person of their liberty in a hospital or care home while the standard deprivation of liberty authorisation process is undertaken.	**Chapter 6** Throughout

PART VII

Forms

PART VII: Forms

Contents

Court of Protection Forms 1369
  Form COP1 – Application 1369
  COP1A – Annex A: Supporting information for property and
    affairs applications 1382
  COP1B – Annex B: Supporting information for personal welfare
    applications 1400
  Form COP2 – Permission 1407
  Form COP3 – Assessment of capacity 1411
  Form COP4 – Deputy's declaration 1423
  Form COP5 – Acknowledgment of service/notification 1431
  Form COP7 – Application to object to the registration of a Lasting
    Power of Attorney 1437
  Form COP8 – Application relating to the registration of an
    Enduring Power of Attorney 1443
  Form COP9 – Application notice 1449
  Form COP10 – Application notice for applications to be joined as
    a party 1454
  Form COP12 – Special undertaking by trustees 1459
  Form COP14 – Proceedings about you in the Court of Protection 1463
  Form COP15 – Notice that an application form has been issued 1465
  Form COP20A – Certificate of notification/non-notification of the
    person to whom proceedings relate 1467
  COP 21A – Guidance notes on completing form COP20A 1471
  Form COP20B – Certificate of service/non-service
    notification/non-notification 1472
  COP 21B – Guidance notes on completing form COP20B 1476
  Form COP22 – Certificate of suitability of litigation friend 1477
  Form COP23 – Certificate of failure or refusal of witness to attend
    before an examiner 1481
  Form COP24 – Witness statement 1485
  Form COP25 – Affidavit 1489
  Form COP29 – Notice of hearing for committal order 1493
  Form COP30 – Notice of change of solicitor 1494
  Form COP31 – Notice of intention to file evidence by deposition 1497
  Form COP35 – Appellant's notice 1499
  Form COP36 – Respondent's notice 1510
  Form COP37 – Skeleton argument 1520
  COP37 – Guidance notes 1522

Lasting Powers of Attorney Forms 1523
  Form LPA PFA and LPA HW – Form for Instrument Intended to
    Create a Lasting Power of Attorney 1524
  Form LPA 001 – Notice of Intention to Apply for Registration of a
    Lasting Power of Attorney 1559

Form LPA 002 – Application to Register a Lasting Power of
    Attorney   1563
Forms LPA 003A and LPA 003B – Notice of Receipt of an
    Application to Register a Lasting Power of Attorney   1577
Form LPA 004 – Notice of Registration of a Lasting Power of
    Attorney   1580
Form LPA 005 – Disclaimer by Donee of a Lasting Power of
    Attorney   1581

Enduring Power of Attorney Forms   1583
    Form EPI PG – Notice of Intention to Apply for Registration of an
        Enduring Power of Attorney   1583
    Form EP2 PG – Application to Register an Enduring Power of
        Attorney   1585

Deprivation of Liberty Forms   1597
    DLA – Deprivation of Liberty Application Form   1597
    DLB – Deprivation of Liberty Declaration of Exceptional Urgency   1606
    DLC – Deprivation of Liberty Permission Form   1608
    DLD – Deprivation of Liberty Certificate of Service/Non-service;
        Certificate of Notification/Non-notification   1610
    DLE – Deprivation of Liberty Acknowledgment of
        Service/Notification   1612

COURT OF PROTECTION FORMS

Form COP1 – Application

COP
1
03.10 Court of Protection
Application form

For office use only
Date received
Case no.
Date issued

SEAL

Full name of person to whom the application relates
(this is the name of the person who lacks, or is alleged to lack, capacity)

Please read first

- If you wish to apply to start proceedings in the Court of Protection you must complete this form and file it with the court.

- If your application is made in the course of existing proceedings then you need to complete a different form – the COP9 application notice for applications within proceedings.

- If you are appealing a Court of Protection decision then you need to complete the COP35 appellant's notice.

- You must pay a fee when you file an application. Please refer to the fees leaflet for details.

- You may need to pay for any costs you incur during proceedings. If the court considers that you have acted unreasonably you can be ordered to pay the costs incurred by other parties.

- Please continue on a separate sheet of paper if you need more space to answer a question. Write your name, the name and date of birth of the person to whom the application relates, and number of the question you are answering on each separate sheet.

- There are additional guidance notes at the end of this form.

- If you need help completing this form please check the website, www.hmcourts-service.gov.uk or www.direct.gov.uk, for further guidance or information, or contact Court Enquiry Service on 0300 456 4600 or courtofprotectionenquiries@hmcourts-service.gsi.gov.uk

- Court of Protection staff cannot give legal advice. If you need legal advice please contact a solicitor.

PART VII

Section 1 - Your details (the applicant)

1.1 Your details ☐ Mr.   ☐ Mrs.   ☐ Miss   ☐ Ms.   ☐ Other _____

First name [   ]

Middle name(s) [   ]

Last name [   ]

1.2 Address
(including
postcode)
[   ]

Telephone no.

Daytime	
Evening	
Mobile	

E-mail address [   ]

1.3 Is a solicitor representing you?   ☐ Yes   ☐ No

If Yes, please give the solicitor's details.

Name [   ]

Address
(including
postcode)
[   ]

Telephone no.		Fax no.	

DX no. [   ]

E-mail address [   ]

1.4 Which address should official documentation be sent to?

☐ Your address

☐ Solicitor's address

☐ Other address (please provide details)
[   ]

2

1.5   Are you the person to whom this application relates?   ☐Yes   ☐No

        If No, what is your relationship or connection to the person to
        whom the application relates?

        [   ]

1.6   If you are applying in a respresentative capacity, please state what that capacity is.

        [   ]

Section 2 - The person to whom this application relates

2.1   ☐ Mr.   ☐ Mrs.   ☐ Miss   ☐ Ms.   ☐ Other _____

        First name   [   ]

        Middle name(s) [   ]

        Last name   [   ]

2.2   Address
        (including
        postcode)   [   ]

        Telephone no. | Daytime | |
                        | Evening | |
                        | Mobile | |

        E-mail address [   ]

2.3   Date of birth   [D | D | M | M | Y | Y | Y | Y]   ☐ Male   ☐ Female

Section 3 - Permission to apply

3.1   Do you need the court's permission to make this application? **(See note 1)**   ☐Yes   ☐No

        If Yes, you also need to complete a COP2 permission form.

3

Section 4 - People to be served with/notified of this application

4.1   Please give details of all respondents. **(See note 2)**

Full name including title	Full address including postcode	Connection to the person to whom the application relates

4.2   Please give details of other people whom you will be notifying. **(See note 3)**

Full name including title	Full address including postcode	Connection to the person to whom the application relates

4

Section 5 - Order you are asking the court to make

5.1   Please state the matter you want the court to decide? **(See note 4)**

5.2   Please state the order you are asking the court to make? **(See note 5)**

5.3   How would the order benefit the person to whom the application relates? **(See note 6)**

PART VII

5

5.4   Are you aware of any previous application(s) to the Court of Protection regarding   ☐Yes   ☐No
       the person to whom this application relates?

               If Yes, please give as much of the following information as you can. If there has
               been more than one previous application please attach the information about
               other previous applications on a separate sheet of paper.

               The name of the applicant

               _____

               The date of the order

               | D | D | M | M | Y | Y | Y | Y |

               Case number

               _____

               Please attach a copy of the order(s), if available.

                        ☐ Copy attached   ☐ Not available

Section 6 - Attending court hearings

6.1   If the court requires you to attend a hearing do you need any special   ☐Yes   ☐No
       assistance or facilities? (See note 7)

               If Yes, please say what your requirements are. If necessary,
               court staff may contact you about your requirements.

               _____
               | |
               | |
               | |
               | |
               _____

6

Section 7 - Statement of truth

The statement of truth is to be signed by you, your solicitor or your litigation friend.

*(I believe) (The applicant believes) that the facts stated in this application form and its annex(es) are true.

Signed

*Applicant('s litigation friend)('s solicitor)

Name

Date

Name of firm

Position or office held

* Please delete the options in brackets that do not apply.

Now read note 8 about what you need to do next.

7

PART VII

Guidance notes

Note   1

Permission to apply

In some cases you will need the court's permission to make an application.

a) You **do not** need the court's permission if the application:

- is made by a person who lacks or is alleged to lack capacity (or, if the person is under 18 years, by anyone with parental responsibility);

- is made by the Official Solicitor, the Public Guardian, or a court appointed deputy;

- concerns a lasting power of attorney or an enduring power of attorney; or

- is about an existing court order and is made by a person named in that order.

b) You **may not** need the court's permission if the application concerns the property and affairs of the person to whom the application relates.

In most cases you will not need permission. There are some exceptions – you **do** need permission where:

- your application relates to the exercise of the jurisdiction of the court under section 54(2) of the Trustee Act 1925, and you are not:

  - person who has made an application for the appointment of a deputy;

  - a continuing trustee; or

  - any other person who, according to the practice of the Chancery Division, would have been entitled to make the application if it has been made in the High Court.

- your application is under section 36(9) of the Trustee Act 1925 for leave to appoint a new trustee in place of the person to whom the application relates, and you are not

  - a co-trustee; or

  - another person with the power to appoint a new trustee.

- your application is seeking the exercise of the court's jurisdiction under section 18(1)(b) (where this relates to the making a gift of the property of the person to whom the application relates), (h) or (i) of the Mental Capacity Act 2005 (the Act), and you are not:

  - a person who has made an application for the appointment of a deputy;

  - a person who, under any known will of the person to whom the application relates or under their intestacy, may become entitled to any property or any interest in it;

  - a person who is an attorney appointed under an enduring power of attorney which has been registered in accordance with the Act or the regulations referred to in Schedule 4 to the Act;

  - a person who is a donee of a lasting power of attorney which has been registered in accordance with the Act; or

  - a person for whom the person to whom the application relates might be expected to provide if they had capacity to do so.

- your application is under section 20 of the Trusts of Land and Appointment of Trustees Act 1996, and you are not a beneficiary under the trust or if there is more than one, by both or all of them.

c) You **do** need the court's permission for all other applications.

Where part of the application concerns a matter that requires permission, and part of it does not, you need the court's permission only for that part of it which requires permission.

Note   2

Respondents

You must provide the details of any person who you reasonably believe has an interest which means they ought to be heard by the court in relation to the application. Respondents have the opportunity to be joined as parties to the proceedings if they wish to participate in the hearing.

You must serve respondents with copies of all documents relating to your application when the court has issued your application form, in order to allow them the opportunity to support or oppose your application.

Other people to be notified

You must provide the details of other people who are likely to have an interest in being notified of your application. You must notify these people when the court has issued your application form. They have the opportunity to apply to the court to be joined as parties to the proceedings if they wish to participate.

You should seek to identify at least three people to be notified of your application. If you have not already named the following close family members as respondents, they should be notified in descending order as appropriate to the circumstances of the person to whom the application relates:

a) spouse or civil partner

b) person who is not a spouse or a civil partner but who has been living with the person to whom the application relates as if they were

c) parent or guardian

d) child

e) brother or sister

f) grandparent or grandchild

g) aunt or uncle

h) niece or nephew

i) step-parent

j) half-brother or half-sister

Where you think that a person listed in one of the categories ought to be notified, and there are other people in that category (e.g. the person has four siblings) you should provide the details of all of the people falling within that category – unless there is good reason not to do so

You do not need to provide the details for a close family member who has little or no involvement with the person to whom the application relates, or if there is another good reason why they should not be notified.

In some cases, the person to whom the application relates may be closer to people who are not relatives and if so, it will be appropriate to provide their details instead of close family members.

In addition to the above list, you should also provide the details (if applicable) of:

- any person with parental responsibility, if the person to whom the application relates is under 18;

- any legal or natural person who is likely to be affected by the outcome of the application (e.g. a local authority or primary care trust);

- any person who has the authority to act as an attorney or deputy in relation to the matter to which the application relates;

- any other person you consider to have an interest in being notified (e.g. a close friend who provides care on an informal basis).

Note 4

Matter you want the court to decide

In each case, the court needs to decide whether or not the person to whom the application relates is capable of making a decision about the matter to which the application relates. You therefore need to state the matter you are asking the court to decide (i.e. the matter that you feel the person to whom the application relates cannot decide for himself or herself).

For example, if your application relates to personal welfare you may want the court to decide if the person to whom the application relates is capable of deciding where they live. If your application relates to property and financial affairs, you may want the court to decide whether the person is able to make decisions about the management of their investments.

Note 5

Order you are asking the court to make

You need to state the order you are asking the court to make. Please be specific about what you are asking the court to do.

For example, you may want the court to order that the person to whom the application relates moves to a particular residence, or that a particular investment is made. In each of the examples you would need to provide the particular details of the residence or investment.

PART VII

Note   6

Benefit to the person to whom the application relates

You need to explain how the order you are asking for will benefit the person to whom the application relates. If you are asking the court to appoint a deputy, please explain why you think this is necessary and why the court should not make the decision on behalf of the person to whom the application relates.

Note   7

Attending court hearings

If you need special assistance or special facilities for a disability or impairment, please set out your requirements in full. It is important that you make the court aware of your needs to avoid causing any delays.

The court staff will need to know, for example, whether you want documents to be supplied in an alternative format, such as Braille or large print. They will also
need to know about any specific requirements should there be a hearing, such as wheelchair access, a hearing loop or a sign language interpreter.

Note   8

What you need to do next

When you have completed this application form you need to consider which other forms you need to complete. If you are in doubt please contact customer services.

Type of application	Forms to be completed
You need permission **and** Your application relates to property and affairs	You must complete the following forms now: • **COP2 Permission form** • **COP3 Assessment of capacity** You must complete the following form, but you can choose to do it now, or wait until permission is granted: • **COP1A Supporting information for property and affairs applications** If you are applying to be appointed as a deputy, then you must complete the following form, but you can choose to do it now or wait until permission is granted: • **COP4 Deputy's declaration**
You need permission **and** Your application relates to personal welfare	You must complete the following forms now: • **COP2 Permission form** • **COP3 Assessment of capacity** You must complete the following form, but you can choose to do it now, or wait until permission is granted: • **COP1B Supporting information for personal welfare applications** If you are applying to be appointed as a deputy then you must complete the following form, but you can choose to do it now or wait until permission is granted: • **COP4 Deputy's declaration**
You need permission **and** Your application relates to property and affairs and personal welfare	You must complete the following forms now: • **COP2 Permission form** • **COP3 Assessment of capacity** You must complete the following forms, but you can choose to do it now, or wait until permission is granted: • **COP1A Supporting information for property and affairs applications** • **COP1B Supporting information for personal welfare applications** If you are applying to be appointed as a deputy then you must complete the following form, but you can choose to do it now or wait until permission is granted: • **COP4 Deputy's declaration**

PART VII

Type of application	Forms to be completed
You do not need permission **and** Your application relates to property and affairs	You must complete the following forms now: • **COP3 Assessment of capacity** • **COP1A Supporting information for property and affairs applications** If you are applying to be appointed as a deputy then you must also complete the following form now: • **COP4 Deputy's declaration**
You do not need permission **and** Your application relates to personal welfare	You must complete the following forms now: • **COP3 Assessment of capacity** • **COP1B Supporting information for personal welfare applications** If you are applying to be appointed as a deputy then you must also complete the following form now: • **COP4 Deputy's declaration**
You do not need permission **and** Your application relates to property and affairs and personal welfare	You must complete the following forms now: • **COP3 Assessment of capacity** • **COP1A Supporting information for property and affairs applications** • **COP1B Supporting information for personal welfare applications** If you are applying to be appointed as a deputy then you must also complete the following form now: • **COP4 Deputy's declaration**

If you are unable to provide the COP3 assessment of capacity form

If you are unable to provide the COP3 assessment of capacity (for example, because the person to whom the application relates refuses to undergo an assessment) then you need to complete and file a COP24 witness statement with the application form explaining:

• why you are not able to provide an assessment of capacity;
• what attempts (if any) you have made to obtain an assessment of capacity; and
• why you know or believe that the person to whom the application relates lacks capacity to make a decision in relation to the matter you want the court to decide.

Other documents to be filed

The following documents must also be filed with the application form, if applicable:

- if permission has already been granted, a copy of the court order granting permission;

- the order appointing a deputy, where the application relates to or is made by a deputy;

- the order appointing a litigation friend, where the application is made by, or where the application relates to the appointment of a litigation friend;

- the order of the Court of Protection, where the application relates to the order;

- the order of another court, where the application relates to the order;

- any written evidence on which you intend to rely (in accordance with the relevant practice direction) using the COP24 witness statement form;

- any other documents you refer to in the application form; and

- any other information and material as may be set out in a practice direction that supplements the Court of Protection Rules 2007.

The court requires two copies (i.e. the original plus one copy) of each form and document you file.

Please return the original completed forms, documents and copies to:

Court of Protection
Archway Tower
2 Junction Road
London N19 5SZ

Note 8

What happens next?

If you need permission to apply

The court will notify you when permission is granted, refused or if a date has been fixed for a hearing of the application for permission.

If permission is granted then you will need to file any other forms you need to complete, if you have chosen not to file these with the permission form.

If permission is granted and the court has received the correct completed forms, the court will issue your application form and legal proceedings will start. The court will notify you when your application form has been issued and will return a sealed copy of the application form. You will need to serve a copy on each respondent and notify the person to whom the application relates and the other people you have named in section 4.2 of this form.

If you do not need permission to apply

When the court has received the correct completed forms, it will issue your application form and legal proceedings will start. The court will notify you when your application form has been issued and will return a sealed copy of the application form. You will need to serve a copy on each respondent and notify the person to whom the application relates and the other people you have named in section 4.2 of this form.

COP1A – Annex A: Supporting information for property and affairs applications

Court of Protection

Annex A
Supporting information for
property and affairs applications

For office use only
Date received
Case no.

Full name of person to whom the application relates
(this is the person who lacks, or is alleged to lack, capacity)

Please read first

- You need to complete and file this form if your application relates to property and affairs (which includes financial matters).

- If your application relates to personal welfare (which includes health matters) then you need to complete COP1B.

- Please continue on a separate sheet of paper if you need more space to answer a question. Write your name, the name and date of birth of the person to whom the application relates, and the number of the question you are answering on each separate sheet.

- If you need help completing this form please check the website, www.hmcourts-service.gov.uk or www.direct.gov.uk, for further guidance or information, or contact Court Enquiry Service on 0300 456 4600 or courtofprotectionenquiries@ hmcourts-service.gsi.gov.uk

- Court of Protection staff cannot give legal advice. If you need legal advice please contact a solicitor.

1

Section 1 - Your details (the applicant)

1.1   Full name

        Address (including postcode)

        Telephone no.

Section 2 - Information about the person to whom the application relates

2.1   What is the address of the person to whom the application relates?

2.2   What is their date of birth?

D D M M Y Y Y Y

2.3   What type of accommodation is the person to whom the application relates living in?

☐ Own home
☐ Family member/friend's home (including spouse/civil partner)
☐ Private rented home
☐ Council rented home
☐ Housing Association rented home
☐ Supported housing e.g. provided by organisation such as YMCA
☐ Local Authority nursing home or residential home
☐ Private nursing home or residential home
☐ NHS accommodation e.g. hospital, hostel
☐ Private hospital
☐ Other (please give details)

2.4   When did he or she move to this accommodation (if known)?

PART VII

2

2.5   If he or she lives in private accommodation, do they share accommodation with anyone else?   ☐ Yes   ☐ No

If Yes, please give the name of the other person(s) and state their connection to the person to whom the application relates.

2.6   Is the person to whom the application relates:

           ☐ Married or in a civil partnership

           ☐ In a relationship with a person who is not a spouse or civil partner, but living together as if they were

           ☐ Separated

           ☐ Divorced or their civil partnership has dissolved

                   Date of divorce/dissolution

           ☐ Widowed or a surviving civil partner

                   Date of death of spouse/civil partner

           ☐ Single

2.7   Do you personally visit the person to whom the application relates?   ☐ Yes   ☐ No

If Yes, how frequently?

2.8   Does anyone else visit the person to whom the application relates?   ☐ Yes   ☐ No

If Yes, please provide details of the most frequent visitors.

Name	Connection to the person to whom the application relates	Frequency of visits

3

2.9   Where the person to whom the application relates lives in his or her own home, please provide brief details of the arrangements made for domestic assistance and care and details of any proposed changes.

2.10   Is a social worker or care manager involved with the person to whom the application relates?   ☐ Yes   ☐ No

If Yes, please give details (if known).

Full name

Address
(including
postcode)

Telephone no.

2.11   Please provide the name and contact details for any GP or practitioner of the person to whom the application relates.

Full name

Address
(including
postcode)

Telephone no.

4

Section 3 – Powers granted/arrangements already made

Guardianship

3.1   Have powers of guardianship under the Mental Health Act 1983 been conferred   ☐ Yes   ☐ No
       on the Social Services Department of the Local Authority or some other approved
       person in relation to the welfare of the person to whom the application relates?

       If Yes, please give the full name, address and telephone number of the guardian or
       name of the Local Authority.

Name of guardian or Local Authority	
Address (including postcode)	
Telephone no.	

Will

3.2   Has the person to whom the application relates made a will?   ☐ Yes

                                                                               ☐ No **(Go to Section 3.5)**

                                                                               ☐ Not known **(Go to Section 3.5)**

                      If Yes, have you attached a copy of the will?   ☐ Yes   ☐ No

3.3   If you cannot obtain a copy of the will but you know who holds a copy, please give
       their name and contact details.

3.4   If known, please provide the names of the executor(s) of the will.

5

Power of attorney, enduring power of attorney and lasting power of attorney

3.5 Has the person to whom the application relates granted a power of attorney, enduring power of attorney or lasting power of attorney?
☐Yes ☐No ☐Don't know

If Yes, please state which type(s) and the date granted (if known).

☐ Power of attorney

☐ Enduring power of attorney

☐ Lasting power of attorney for property and affairs

☐ Lasting power of attorney for personal welfare

3.6 Has any enduring power of attorney or lasting power of attorney been registered with the Public Guardian?
☐Yes ☐No ☐Don't know

If Yes, please state the date(s) of registration

Enduring power of attorney

Lasting power of attorney

3.7 Has there been any unsuccessful applications to register an enduring power or attorney or a lasting power of attorney with the Public Guardian?
☐Yes ☐No ☐Don't know

3.8 Please state the name(s) and address(es) of the attorney(s) who act (or have acted) for the person to whom the application relates.

PART VII

6

1387

Section 4 – Income, assets and expenditure

Social security benefits

4.1   Does the person to whom the application relates receive any social security benefits?

☐ Yes

☐ No **(Go to Section 4.4)**

4.2   What is the national insurance number of the person to whom the application relates?

☐☐ ☐☐ ☐☐ ☐☐ ☐

4.3   Please give details below of all social security benefits the person to whom the application relates is entitled and state who is currently receiving these. Please also list any benefits that have been claimed for the person to whom the application relates but are not yet being received.

Social security benefit	Weekly amount	Received by
State retirement pension		
Attendance allowance		
Severe disablement allowance		
Disability living allowance		
Incapacity benefit		
Income support		
Council tax benefit		
Child benefit		
Other type of benefit (please give details)		

7

Occupational/company pensions and annuities

4.4 Does the person to whom the application relates receive any occupational/company pensions or annuities?

☐ Yes

☐ No **(Go to Section 4.5)**

If Yes, please give the following details for each occupational/company pension or annuity:

Name, address and reference of the company/payer	Amount received (indicate whether gross or net)	Frequency of payments

Trusts

4.5 Is the person to whom the application relates entitled to any income, property or capital from a trust?

☐ Yes

☐ No **(Go to Section 4.6)**

If Yes, please give details of any interest in a trust or similar to which the person to whom the application relates is entitled or to which they may become entitled. Please give the circumstances under which he/she will become entitled, together with details of the property and particulars of the will or settlement and the names of the present trustees.

8

Interest in a deceased's estate

4.6   Does the person to whom the application relates have any interest in   ☐ Yes
        the estate of someone who has died (or is he/she likely to become
        entitled to such an interest shortly)?   ☐ No **(Go to Section 4.7)**

        Please give full details of any interests to which the person to whom the application relates has become
        entitled (or may become entitled) under a will or intestacy.

        [blank box]

        Please provide the name, address and telephone number of the person dealing with the administration of
        the estate.

        [blank box]

Damages and criminal injuries compensation

4.7   Has the person to whom the application relates recently received a damages   ☐Yes   ☐No
        award (for example, following a road accident or medical negligence) or is he/
        she expected to receive a damages award?

        If Yes, please give details, including the name and address of solicitors involved
        in the case and the present position with regard to the litigation. Is a settlement/
        trial imminent?

        [blank box]

9

4.8   Has the person to whom the application relates made a claim to the Criminal   ☐ Yes   ☐ No
       Injuries Compensation Authority?

       If Yes, please give the name and address of solicitors involved in the case
       and details of any awards or interim payments, including the amount.

Income from employment

4.9   Please give details of any income the person to whom the application relates receives from employment.

Miscellaneous income

4.10   Please list any income to which the person to whom the application relates is (or may become)
       entitled which has not been mentioned elsewhere in this form. If there is none, please say so.

PART VII

10

1391

Money held in bank accounts

4.11   Does the person to whom the application relates have any money   ☐ Yes
held in bank or building society accounts (or similar)?

                                           ☐ No **(Go to Section 4.12)**

If Yes, please give the following details:

	Account 1	Account 2	Account 3
Name and full postal address of the bank/ building society branch where the account is held			
Name of the account			
Sort code			
Account number			
Type of account (e.g. current, deposit, high interest)			
How much is in the account?			
If the account is a joint account, please give the name and address of the co-holder			
If the account is a joint account, please give a brief explanation of the circumstances in which the monies came to be held in a joint account			

Please provide the above information for any additional accounts on a separate sheet of paper.

11

4.12 Does any other person or organisation (other than those already mentioned) hold money for the person to whom the application relates? ☐Yes ☐No

If Yes, please give full details including the name and address of those involved, the amount held and the reason for holding the money.

Investments

4.13 Does the person to whom the application relates own or have an interest in any investments such as stocks and shares, unit trusts, bonds etc? ☐Yes ☐No

If Yes, please give a full list of the investments of the person to whom the application relates. Alternatively, please provide a valuation from the fund manager. ☐Valuation attached

12

PART VII

Life assurance policies

4.14   Does the person to whom the application relates have any life assurance policies?   ☐ Yes   ☐ No

If Yes, please give full details of any policies, the premiums payable and whether you wish to continue to keep the policies going.

[ ]

Land and property

4.15   Does the person to whom the application relates own any land or property?

☐ Yes

☐ No **(Go to Section 4.21)**

If Yes, please enter the address(es) and state whether the land or property is freehold, leasehold or commonhold property.

[ ]

4.16   If leasehold, please give details (if known) of the length of the lease, any rent or service charges payable and any restriction on the sale of the property.

[ ]

13

4.17   Please state the approximate value of each property.

4.18   If any land or property is owned jointly, please give details of the other joint owner(s) and state what share of the property is held by the person to whom the application relates.

4.19   If any property has a mortgage owing, please give details including the names of the people who have taken out the mortgage, the mortgage provider and the outstanding balance.

4.20   Please give information on any recent or proposed sale of parts of the client's property or possessions (e.g. their home).

PART VII

14

Personal possessions

4.21   Please provide here an estimate of the overall value of the belongings of the person to whom the application relates.

4.22   Please list any items which are thought to be particularly valuable and give an indication of the value.

Business

4.23   Does the person to whom the application relates own or have any interest in a business?   ☐ Yes   ☐ No

If Yes, please provide the name and details of the business, who is running the business, and the role/interest of the person to whom the application relates.

15

Debts and money owed

4.24   Does the person to whom the application relates have any outstanding debts?   ☐Yes   ☐No

If Yes, please give details of any debts of the person to whom the application
relates including the name(s) of any creditors and the amount of the debt.

4.25   Does anyone owe the person to whom the application relates money?   ☐Yes   ☐No

If Yes, please give details including who owes the money and the amount.

Miscellaneous assets and investments

4.26   Please use this section to list any other property or other assets which the person to whom the application
relates may own or have an interest in which have not been mentioned elsewhere in this form. If there are
none, please say so.

16

PART VII

1397

Expenditure

4.27   If the person to whom the application relates is in a nursing or residential home or some other type of accommodation that is charged for, please state the cost of the accommodation and whether the amount is the annual, quarterly, monthly or weekly cost.

4.28   Has the person to whom the application relates been assessed by the Local Authority to pay a contribution towards their accommodation costs?   ☐ Yes   ☐ No

4.29   Please give information about any regular gifts and regular charitable donations made by the person to whom the application relates.

4.30   Please give information on any recent significant expenditure made on behalf of the person to whom the application relates, either using his/her funds or funds provided by someone else.

17

Section 5 – Other information

5.1   Please provide any additional background information about the person to whom the application relates
that is relevant to your application (such as key dates and facts).

Signed	

Name	

Date	

Name of firm	

Position or office held	

Now read note 8 of the COP1 application form about what you need to do next.

PART VII

COP1B – Annex B: Supporting information for personal welfare applications

**COP
1B**
03.10

Court of Protection

Annex B
Supporting information for personal welfare applications

For office use only
Date received
Case no.

Full name of person to whom the application relates
(this is the person who lacks, or is alleged to lack, capacity)

Please read first

- You need to complete and file this form if your application relates to personal welfare (which includes health matters).

- If your application relates to property and affairs (which includes financial matters) then you need to complete COP1A.

- Please continue on a separate sheet of paper if you need more space to answer a question. Write your name, the name and date of birth of the person to whom the application relates, and the number of the question you are answering on each separate sheet.

- If you need help completing this form please check the website, www.hmcourts-service.gov.uk or www.direct.gov.uk, for further guidance or information, or contact Court Enquiry Service on 0300 456 4600 or courtofprotectionenquiries@hmcourts-service.gsi.gov.uk.

- Court of Protection staff cannot give legal advice. If you need legal advice please contact a solicitor.

© Crown Copyright 2010

1

Section 1 - Your details (the applicant)

1.1   Full name

       Address (including postcode)

       Telephone no.

Section 2 - Information about the person to whom the application relates

2.1   What is the address of the person to whom the application relates?

2.2   What is their date of birth?

       D   D   M   M   Y   Y   Y   Y

2.3   What type of accommodation is the person to whom the application relates living in?

- [ ] Own home
- [ ] Family member/friend's home (including spouse/civil partner)
- [ ] Private rented home
- [ ] Council rented home
- [ ] Housing Association rented home
- [ ] Supported housing e.g. provided by organisation such as YMCA
- [ ] Local Authority nursing home or residential home
- [ ] Private nursing home or residential home
- [ ] NHS accommodation e.g. hospital, hostel
- [ ] Private hospital
- [ ] Other (please give details)

2.4   When did he or she move to this accommodation (if known)?

2

PART VII

2.5   If he or she lives in private accommodation, do they share accommodation with   ☐ Yes   ☐ No
anyone else?

If Yes, please give the name of the other person(s) and state their connection to the person to whom the application relates

2.6   Is the person to whom the application relates:

                ☐ Married or in a civil partnership

                ☐ In a relationship with a person who is not a spouse or civil partner, but living together as if they were

                ☐ Separated

                ☐ Divorced or their civil partnership has dissolved

                                Date of divorce/dissolution

                ☐ Widowed or a surviving civil partner

                                Date of death of spouse/civil partner

                ☐ Single

2.7   Do you personally visit the person to whom the application relates?   ☐ Yes   ☐ No

    If Yes, how frequently?

2.8   Does anyone else visit the person to whom the application relates?   ☐ Yes   ☐ No

If Yes, please provide details of the most frequent visitors.

Name	Connection to the person to whom the application relates	Frequency of visits

3

2.9　Where the person to whom the application relates lives in his or her own home, please provide brief details of the arrangements made for domestic assistance and care, and details of any proposed changes.

2.10　Is a social worker or care manager involved with the person to whom the application relates.　☐Yes　☐No

If Yes, please give details (if known).

Full name

Address (including postcode)

Telephone no.

2.11　Please provide the name and contact details for any GP or practitioner of the person to whom the application relates.

Full name

Address (including postcode)

Telephone no.

PART VII

4

Section 3 – Powers granted/arrangements already made

Guardianship

3.1   Have powers of guardianship under the Mental Health Act 1983 been conferred   ☐ Yes   ☐ No
       on the Social Services Department of the Local Authority or some other approved
       person in relation to the welfare of the person to whom the application relates?

       If Yes, please give the full name, address and telephone number of the guardian or
       name of the Local Authority.

Name of
guardian or
Local Authority

Address
(including
postcode)

Telephone no.

Will

3.2   Has the person to whom the application relates made a will?   ☐ Yes

                                                                              ☐ No **(Go to Section 3.5)**

                                                                              ☐ Not known **(Go to Section 3.5)**

           If Yes, have you attached a copy of the will?   ☐ Yes   ☐ No

3.3   If you cannot obtain a copy of the will but you know who holds a copy, please give
       their name and contact details.

3.4   If known, please provide the names of the executor(s) of the will.

5

Power of attorney, enduring power of attorney and lasting power of attorney

3.5   Has the person to whom the application relates granted a power of attorney, enduring power of attorney or lasting power of attorney?   ☐ Yes   ☐ No
    ☐ Don't know

          If Yes, please state which type(s) and the date granted (if known)

          ☐ Power of attorney

          ☐ Enduring power of attorney

          ☐ Lasting power of attorney for property and affairs

          ☐ Lasting power of attorney for personal welfare

3.6   Has any enduring power of attorney or lasting power of attorney been registered with the Public Guardian?   ☐ Yes   ☐ No
    ☐ Don't know

          If Yes, please state the date(s) of registration

          Enduring power of attorney

          Lasting power of attorney

3.7   Has there been any unsuccessful applications to register an enduring power or attorney or a lasting power of attorney with the Public Guardian?   ☐ Yes   ☐ No
    ☐ Don't know

3.8   Please state the name(s) and address(es) of the attorney(s) who act (or have acted) for the person to whom the application relates.

PART VII

6

1405

Section 4 – Other information

4.1   Please provide any additional background information about the person to whom the application relates
       that is relevant to your application (such as key dates and facts).

Section 5 – Signature

Signed

Name

Date

**Name
of firm**

**Position or
office held**

Now read note 8 of the COP1 application form about what you need to do next.

Form COP2 – Permission

COP 2 03.10 Court of Protection
Permission form

For office use only
Date received
Case no.
Date issued

SEAL

Full name of person to whom the application relates
(this is the name of the person who lacks, or is alleged to lack, capacity)

Please read first

- You must complete and file this form if you need permission to make an application to start proceedings.

- Some of the questions in section 3 of this form are the same as questions in section 5 of the COP1 application form. You need to answer the questions on both forms. Where the questions are the same you should copy the answers you provide on the application form.

- In deciding whether to grant permission to start proceedings the court will consider:

    – your connection with the person to whom the application relates;

    – the reasons for the application;

    – the benefit to the person to whom the application relates; and

    – whether the benefit can be achieved any other way.

- Please continue on a separate sheet of paper if you need more space to answer a question. Write your name, the name and date of birth of the person to whom the application relates, and the number of the question you are answering on each separate sheet.

- If you need help completing this form please check the website, www.hmcourts-service.gov.uk or www.direct.gov.uk, for further guidance or information, or contact Court Enquiry Service on 0300 456 4600 or courtofprotectionenquiries@ hmcourts-service.gsi.gov.uk.

- Court of Protection staff cannot give legal advice. If you need legal advice please contact a solicitor.

PART VII

Section 1 - Your details (the applicant)

1.1   Your details

☐ Mr.   ☐ Mrs.   ☐ Miss   ☐ Ms.   ☐ Other _____

First name

Middle name(s)

Last name

Section 2 - Your application for permission

2.1   What is your relationship or connection to the person to whom this application relates?

2.2   What are your reasons for making the application?

2.3   How would the order you have set out in Section 5 of the COP1 application form benefit the person to whom the application relates?

2.4   Is there any other way this benefit could be achieved?

2.5   Are you seeking any directions from the court at the permission hearing?   ☐Yes   ☐No

If Yes, please give details.

PART VII

3

Section 3 - Statement of truth

The statement of truth is to be signed by you, your solicitor or your litigation friend.

*(I believe) (The applicant believes) that the facts stated in this permission form and are true.

Signed

*Applicant('s litigation friend)('s solicitor)

Name

Date

**Name
of firm**

**Position or
office held**

* Please delete the options in
brackets that do not apply.

Now read note 8 of the COP1 application form about what you need to do next.

4

Form COP3 – Assessment of capacity

COP 3 03.10 Court of Protection

Assessment of capacity

For office use only
Date received
Case no.

Full name of person to whom the application relates
(this is the name of the person who lacks, or is alleged to lack, capacity)

Please read first

- If you are applying to start proceedings with the court you must file this form with your COP1 application form. The assessment must contain current information.

- You must complete Part A of this form.

- You then need to provide the form to the practitioner who will complete Part B.
  The practitioner will return the form to you or your solicitor for filing with the court.

- The practitioner may charge a fee for completing the form. Please ask the practitioner about the amount they will charge.

- The practitioner may be a registered medical practitioner, psychologist or psychiatrist who has examined and assessed the capacity of the person to whom the application relates. In some circumstances it might be appropriate for a registered therapist, such as a speech therapist or occupational therapist, to complete the form.

- When the form has been completed, its contents will be confidential to the court and those authorised by the court to see it, such as parties to the proceedings.

- Please continue on a separate sheet of paper if you need more space to answer a question. Write your name, the name and date of birth of the person to whom the application relates, and number of the question you are answering on each separate sheet.

- There are additional guidance notes at the end of this form.

- If you need help completing this form please check the website, www.hmcourts-service.gov.uk or www.direct.gov.uk, for further guidance or information, or contact Court Enquiry Service on 0300 456 4600 or courtofprotectionenquiries@hmcourts-service.gsi.gov.uk

- Court of Protection staff cannot give legal advice. If you need legal advice please contact a solicitor.

- This form has been prepared in consultation with the British Medical Association, the Royal College of Physicians and the Royal College of Psychiatrists.

PART VII

1

Part A - To be completed by the applicant

Section 1 - Your details (the applicant)

1.1   Your details   ☐ Mr.   ☐ Mrs.   ☐ Miss   ☐ Ms.   ☐ Other _____

First name

Middle name(s)

Last name

1.2   Address
(including
postcode)

Telephone no. | Daytime |
                 | Evening |
                 | Mobile |

E-mail address

1.3   Is a solicitor representing you?   ☐ Yes   ☐ No

If Yes, please give the solicitor's details.

Name

Address
(including
postcode)

Telephone no. | | Fax no. | |
DX no.
E-mail address

1.4   To which address should the practitioner return the form when they have completed Section 2?

☐ Your address

☐ Solicitor's address

☐ Other address (please provide details)

Section 2 - The person to whom the application relates (the person to be assessed by the practitioner)

2.1   ☐ Mr.   ☐ Mrs.   ☐ Miss   ☐ Ms.   ☐ Other _____

First name

Middle name(s)

Last name

Address (including postcode)

Telephone no.

Date of birth   ☐ Male   ☐ Female

Section 3 - About the application

3.1   Please state the matter you are asking the court to decide. **(see note 1)**

3.2   What order are you asking the court to make?

3.3   How would the order benefit the person to whom the application relates?

3.4   What is your relationship or connection to the person to whom the application relates?

PART VII

3

Section 4 - Further information

Please provide any further information about the circumstances of the person to whom the application relates that would be useful to the practitioner in assessing his or her capacity to make any decision(s) that is the subject of your application. **(see note 2)**

Now read note 3 about what you need to do next.

4

Part B - To be completed by the practitioner

Section 5 - Your details (the practitioner)

5.1 ☐ Mr. ☐ Mrs. ☐ Miss ☐ Ms. ☐ Dr. ☐ Other _____

First name

Middle name(s)

Last name

Address
(including
postcode)

Telephone no.

E-mail address

5.2 Nature of your professional relationship with the person to whom the application relates
(e.g. general practitioner, psychiatrist or other)

5.3 Professional qualifications

5

PART VII

Section 6 – Sensitive information

If there is information that you do not wish to provide in this form because of its sensitive nature you can provide the information directly to the court.

6.1   Are you providing any sensitive information separately to the court?   ☐ Yes   ☐ No

Please provide it in writing to:
Court of Protection
Archway Tower
2 Junction Road
London N19 5SZ

Please include your name and contact details, and the name, address and date of birth of the person to whom the application relates on any information you provide separately to the court.

Section 7 - Assessment of capacity

7.1   The person to whom the application relates has the following impairment of, or disturbance in the functioning of, the mind or brain: **(see note 4)**

This has lasted since:

As a result, the person is unable to make a decision for themselves in relation to the following matter(s) in question:

6

7.2   The person to whom the application relates is unable to make a decision in relation to the relevant matter because: **(see note 5)**

☐ he or she is unable to understand the following relevant information (please give details);

[blank text box]

and/or

☐ he or she is unable to retain the following relevant information (please give details);

[blank text box]

and/or

☐ he or she is unable to use or weigh the following relevant information as part of the process of making the decision(s) (please give details);

[blank text box]

or

☐ for cases where he or she can in fact understand, retain and use/weigh the information but is unable to communicate his or her decision(s) by any means at all (please give details).

[blank text box]

PART VII

7

7.3   My opinion is based on the following evidence of a lack of capacity:

7.4   Please answer either (a) **or** (b).

        (a) I have acted as a practitioner for the person to whom the application

        relates since ☐☐☐☐☐☐☐☐ and last assessed

        him or her on ☐☐☐☐☐☐☐☐

        (b) I assessed the person to whom the application

        relates on ☐☐☐☐☐☐☐☐

        following a referral from:

8

7.5 Has the person to whom this application relates made you aware of any views they have in relation to the relevant matter? ☐ Yes ☐ No

If Yes, please give details.

7.6 Do you consider there is a prospect that the person to whom the application relates might regain or acquire capacity in the future in respect of the decision to which the application relates? **(see note 6)**

☐ Yes – please state why and give an indication of when this might happen.

☐ No – please state why.

7.7 Are you aware of anyone who holds a different view regarding the capacity of the person to whom the application relates? ☐ Yes ☐ No

If Yes, please give details.

7.8   Do you, your family or friends have any interest (financial or otherwise) in any   ☐ Yes   ☐ No
       matter concerning the person to whom the application relates?

       If Yes, please give details.

7.9   Do you have any general comments or any other recommendations for future care? **(see note 7)**

Signed

Name   **Date**

Now read note 8 about what you need to do next.

Guidance notes

Note 1

About the application

These questions are repeated on the COP1 application form. Please copy your answers from the COP1 form so that the information on both forms is the same.

Note 2

Further information

Please provide any further information about the circumstances of the person to whom the application relates that would be relevant in assessing their capacity. For example, if your application relates to property and financial affairs, it would be useful for the practitioner to know the general financial circumstances of the person concerned. This information will help the practitioner evaluate the decision-making responsibility of the person to whom the application relates and may help to inform the practitioner's view on whether that person can make the decision(s) in question.

Note 3

What you need to do next

Please provide this form to the practitioner who will complete Part B.

The practitioner will return the form to you or your solicitor when they have completed Part B. You will then need to file the form with the court together with the COP1 application form and any other information the court requires. See note 8 on the COP1 form for further information.

Note 4

Assessing capacity

For the purpose of the Mental Capacity Act 2005 a person lacks capacity if, at the time a decision needs to be made, he or she is unable to make or communicate the decision because of an impairment of, or a disturbance in the functioning of, the mind or brain.

The Act contains a two-stage test of capacity:

1. Is there an impairment of, or disturbance in the functioning of, the person's mind or brain?

2. If so, is the impairment or disturbance sufficient that the person lacks the capacity to make a decision in relation to the matter in question?

Please refer to Part A of this form where the applicant has set out details of the application and relevant information about the circumstances of the person to whom the application relates. In particular, section 3.1 sets out the matter the applicant is asking the court to decide.

The assessment of capacity must be based on the person's ability to make a decision in relation to the relevant matter, and not their ability to make decisions in general. It does not matter therefore if the lack of capacity is temporary, if the person retains the capacity to make other decisions, or if the person's capacity fluctuates.

Under the Act, a person is regarded as being unable to make a decision if they cannot:

- understand information about the decision to be made;

- retain that information;

- use or weigh the information as part of the decision-making process; or

- communicate the decision (by any means).

A lack of capacity cannot be established merely by reference to a person's age or appearance or to a particular condition or an aspect of behaviour. A person is not to be treated as being unable to make a decision merely because they have made an unwise decision.

The test of capacity is not the same as the test for detention and treatment under the Mental Health Act 1983. Many people covered by the Mental Health Act have the capacity to make decisions for themselves. On the other hand, most people who lack capacity to make decisions will never be affected by the Mental Health Act.

Practitioners are required to have regard to the Mental Capacity Act 2005 Code of Practice. The Code of Practice is available online at www.publicguardian.gov. uk. Hard copies are available from The Stationery Office (TSO), for a fee, by:

- phoning 0870 600 5522;

- emailing customerservices@tso.co.uk; or

- ordering online at www.tsoshop.co.uk.

For further advice please see (for example):

- Making Decisions: A guide for people who work in health and social care (2nd edition), Mental Capacity Implementation Programme, 2007.

- Assessment of Mental Capacity: Guidance for Doctors and Lawyers (2nd edition), British Medical Association and Law Society (London: BMJ Books, 2004)

PART VII

11

Note 5

Capacity to make the decision in question

Please give your opinion of the nature of the lack of
capacity and the grounds on which this is based.
This requires a diagnosis and a statement giving clear
evidence that the person to whom the application
relates lacks capacity to make the decision(s) relevant
to the application. It is important that the evidence of
lack of capacity shows how this prevents the person
concerned from being able to take decision(s).

Note 6

Prospect of regaining or acquiring capacity

When reaching any decision the court must apply the
principles set out in the Act and in particular must
make a determination that is in the best interests of
the person to whom the application relates. It would
therefore assist the court if you could indicate whether
the person to whom the application relates is likely
to regain or acquire capacity sufficiently to be able to
make decisions in relation to the relevant matter.

Note 7

General comments

The court may make any order it considers appropriate
even if that order is not specified in the application
form. Where possible, the court will make a one-off
decision rather than appointing a deputy with on-going
decision making power. If you think that an order other
than the one being sought by the applicant would
be in the best interests of the person to whom the
application relates, please give details including your
reasons.

Note 8

What you need to do next

Please return the completed form to the applicant
or their solicitor, as specified in section 1.4. You are
advised to keep a copy for your records.

12

Form COP4 – Deputy's declaration

COP 4 03.10 Court of Protection

Deputy's declaration

For office use only
Date received
Case no.

Full name of person to whom the application relates
(this is the name of the person who lacks, or is alleged to lack, capacity)

Please read first

- If you are applying to be appointed as a deputy then you need to complete this form and file it with the court.

- The court will use the information you provide in the declaration to assess your suitability to be a deputy.

- If you are appointed as a deputy you must have regard to the Mental Capacity Act 2005 Code of Practice. The Code of Practice has information about the duties and responsibilities that you have to take on as a deputy.

- The Code of Practice is available online at www.publicguardian.gov.uk. Hardcopies are available from The Stationery Office (TSO), for a fee, by:

  – phoning 0870 600 5522;

  – emailing customerservices@tso.co.uk; or

  – ordering online at www.tso.shop.co.uk.

- Please continue on a separate sheet of paper if you need more space to answer a question. Write your name, the name and date of birth of person to whom the application relates, and number of the question you are answering on each separate sheet.

- If you need help completing this form please check the website, www.hmcourts-service.gov.uk or www.direct.gov.uk, for further guidance or information, or contact Court Enquiry Service on 0300 456 4600 or courtofprotectionenquiries@hmcourts-service.gsi.gov.uk.

- Court of Protection staff cannot give legal advice. If you need legal advice please contact a solicitor.

PART VII

1

Section 1 - Your details (the person applying to be appointed as a deputy)

1.1 Your details   ☐ Mr.   ☐ Mrs.   ☐ Miss   ☐ Ms.   ☐ Other _____

First name

Middle name(s)

Last name

1.2 Address
(including
postcode)

Telephone no. | Daytime |
               | Evening |
               | Mobile |

E-mail address

1.3 What is your connection to the person to whom the application relates?

Details of the person to whom the application relates

1.4 Full name

Address
(including
postcode)

Date of birth | D | D | M | M | Y | Y | Y | Y |

2

Section 2 - Your personal circumstances

2.1 What is your current occupation?
If you are not in paid employment, please give details of your current circumstances.

2.2 How long have you worked in your current occupation?

☐ Years   ☐ Months

2.3 Have you ever been appointed to act as a deputy or attorney for anyone else?　☐Yes　☐No

If Yes, please give the name(s) of the person(s) and (if known) the court reference(s).

2.4 Have you ever been convicted of a criminal offence?　☐Yes　☐No
(Do not include convictions spent under the Rehabilitation of Offenders Act 1974).

If Yes, please provide details of the offence, including the date of conviction.

2.5 Are there any circumstances (personal or otherwise) which would interfere with your ability to carry out the duties of a deputy effectively? (e.g. ill health or business/family commitments).　☐Yes　☐No

If Yes, please provide details.

2.6 If you are not appointed as a deputy or become unable to take up an appointment, are you aware of any other person (or officer holder) who might wish to be considered as a deputy?　☐Yes　☐No

If Yes, please provide details.

PART VII

Section 3 - Your financial circumstances

Please complete this section if you are applying to be appointed as a property and affairs deputy.

3.1   Do you have a personal bank or building society current/deposit account?   ☐Yes   ☐No

3.2   Have you ever been refused credit? (e.g. having a personal loan application refused)   ☐Yes   ☐No

If Yes, please provide details.

3.3   Do you have any outstanding judgment debts?   ☐Yes   ☐No

If Yes, please provide details.

3.4   Have you personally ever been declared bankrupt or the debtor under an   ☐Yes   ☐No
Individual Voluntary Arrangement under Part VIII of the Insolvency Act 1986?

If Yes, please provide details.

3.5   Are you currently an undischarged bankrupt or the debtor under an Individual   ☐Yes   ☐No
Voluntary Arrangement?

If Yes, please give provide details.

3.6   Has any business that you have been involved with (whether a company,   ☐Yes   ☐No
partnership or otherwise) been subject to a recognised insolvency regime
(e.g. voluntary arrangement, winding-up, administration, receivership,
administrative receivership)?

If Yes, please provide details.

4

3.7 Have you been the subject of a declaration under section 213 (fraudulent trading) ☐ Yes ☐ No
     or section 214 (wrongful trading) of the Insolvency Act 1986?

     If Yes, please provide details.

     _____

3.8 Have you been the subject of a bankruptcy restrictions order under section 281A ☐ Yes ☐ No
     or Schedule 4A of the Insolvency Act 1986, or a disqualification order under
     section 1 of the Company Directors (Disqualification) Act 1986?

     If Yes, please provide details.

     _____

3.9 Are you aware of any matter in which your financial interests may conflict with those ☐ Yes ☐ No
     of the person to whom the application relates? (e.g. occupation of a property which
     the person owns, any interest under the terms of their will)

     If Yes, please provide details.

     _____

PART VII

5

1427

Section 4 - Your personal undertakings to the person to whom the application relates

Becoming a deputy means that you have to take on a number of duties and responsibilities and have to act in accordance with certain standards. If you are appointed as a deputy, the court order will set out the exact powers conferred on you.

The main duties and responsibilities you may have to take on are set out below. Please review each one and tick 'Yes' if you give your undertaking to act in accordance with the duty or responsibility. You can use the 'Comments' section to support your undertakings. Please mention if you have a particular professional skill, life experience, public duty or role that you think is relevant.

If you do not give your undertaking and tick 'No', please use the 'Comments' section to explain your reasons. It may be because you do not yet have experience in the particular duty, or think you might not have the skills needed. It will not necessarily prevent your appointment as deputy.

Not all of the undertakings set out below will be relevant to every deputy. If you think this is the case, tick 'No' and explain in the 'Comments' section that the undertaking would be irrelevant to your appointment.

	Undertaking	Yes or No	Comments
1	I will have regard to the Mental Capacity Act 2005 Code of Practice and I will apply the principles of the Act when making a decision. In particular I will act in the best interests of the person to whom the application relates and I will only make those decisions that the person cannot make themselves.	☐ Yes ☐ No	
2	I will act within the scope of the powers conferred on me by the court as set out in the order of appointment and will apply to the court if I feel additional powers are needed.	☐ Yes ☐ No	
3	I will act with due care, skill and diligence, as I would do in making my own decisions and conducting my own affairs. Where I undertake my duties as a deputy in the course of my professional work (if relevant), I will abide by professional rules and standards.	☐ Yes ☐ No	
4	I will make decisions on behalf of the person to whom the application relates as required under the court order appointing me. I will not delegate any of my powers as a deputy unless this is expressly permitted in the court order appointing me.	☐ Yes ☐ No	
5	I will ensure that my personal interests do not conflict with my duties as a deputy, and I will not use my position for any personal benefit.	☐ Yes ☐ No	
6	I will act with honesty and integrity, and will take any decisions made by the person to whom the application relates while they still had capacity, into account when determing their best interests.	☐ Yes ☐ No	
7	I will keep the person's financial and personal information confidential (unless there is a good reason that requires me to disclose it).	☐ Yes ☐ No	

6

8	I will comply with any directions of the court or reasonable requests made by the Public Guardian, including requests for reports to be submitted.	☐ Yes ☐ No	
9	I will visit the person to whom the application relates as regularly as is appropriate and take an interest in their welfare.	☐ Yes ☐ No	
10	I will work with the person to whom the application relates and any carer(s) to achieve the best quality of life for him or her within the funds available.	☐ Yes ☐ No	
11	I will co-operate with any representative of the court or the Public Guardian who might wish to meet me or the person to whom the application relates to check that the deputyship arrangements are working.	☐ Yes ☐ No	
12	I will immediately inform the court and the Public Guardian if I have any reason to believe that the person to whom the application relates no longer lacks capacity and may be able to manage his or her own affairs.	☐ Yes ☐ No	

	Further undertakings if you are applying to be appointed as a property and affairs deputy	**Yes or No**	**Comments**
13	I understand that I may be required to provide security for my actions as deputy. If I am required to purchase insurance, such as a guarantee bond, I undertake to pay premiums promptly from the funds of the person to whom the application relates.	☐ Yes ☐ No	
14	I will keep accounts of dealings and transactions taken on behalf of the person to whom the application relates.	☐ Yes ☐ No	
15	I will keep the money and property of the person to whom the application relates separate from my own.	☐ Yes ☐ No	
16	I will ensure so far as is reasonable that the person to whom the application relates receives all benefits and other income to which they are entitled, that their bills are paid and that a tax return for them is completed annually.	☐ Yes ☐ No	
17	I will take reasonable steps to maintain the property of the person to whom the application relates (if applicable), for example arranging for insurance, repairs or improvements. If necessary I will arrange and oversee a sale or letting of property with appropriate legal advice.	☐ Yes ☐ No	

PART VII

7

1429

Section 5 - Personal statement to the court

Please state why you wish to be the deputy of the person to whom the application relates.

Section 6 - Statement of truth

The statement of truth is to be signed by the person applying to be appointed as a deputy.

I believe that the facts stated in this declaration are true.

Signed

Name   **Date**

Now read note 8 of the COP1 application form about what you need to do next.

8

Form COP5 – Acknowledgment of service/notification

COP 5 03.10 Court of Protection

Acknowledgment of service/notification

For office use only

Case no.

Full name of person to whom the application relates
(this is the name of the person who lacks, or is alleged to lack, capacity)

Please read first

- You need to complete this form and file it with the court if you:

  – have been given notice of an application for permission and you wish to take part in the permission hearing;

  – have been served with a COP1, COP7 or COP8 application form and you wish to take part in the proceedings;

  – have received a COP14 notice about proceedings about you in Court of Protection and you wish to be joined as a party to the proceedings;

  – have received a COP15 notice that an application form has been issued by the court and you wish to be joined as a party to the proceedings.

- As a party you will be able to participate in the proceedings. You may need to pay for any costs you incur during proceedings. If the court considers that you have acted unreasonably you can be ordered to pay the costs incurred by other parties.

- You have 21 days from the day you are served/ provided with notice to complete this form and file it with the court.

- You do not need to complete and file this form if you do not wish to be joined as a party to proceedings. You can still apply for a copy of any order of the court in respect of the proceedings by filing a COP9 application notice.

- Please continue on a separate sheet of paper if you need more space to answer a question. Write the case number, your name, the name of the person to whom the application relates, and the number of the question you are answering on each separate sheet.

- There are additional guidance notes at the end of this form.

- If you need help completing this form please check the website, www.hmcourts-service.gov.uk or www.direct.gov.uk, for further guidance or information, or contact Court Enquiry Service on 0300 456 4600 or courtofprotectionenquiries@ hmcourts-service.gsi.gov.uk

- Court of Protection staff cannot give legal advice. If you need legal advice please contact a solicitor.

PART VII

Section 1 - Your details (the person served/notified)

1.1   Your details   ☐ Mr.   ☐ Mrs.   ☐ Miss   ☐ Ms.   ☐ Other _____

First name

Middle name(s)

Last name

1.2   Address (including postcode)

Telephone no.	Daytime	
	Evening	
	Mobile	

E-mail address

1.3   Is a solicitor representing you?   ☐ Yes   ☐ No

If Yes, please give the solicitor's details.

Name

Address (including postcode)

| Telephone no. | | Fax no. | |

DX no.

E-mail address

1.4   Which address should official documentation be sent to?

☐ Your address

☐ Solicitor's address

☐ Other address (please provide details)

1.5   What is your role in these proceedings?

☐ Person to whom the application/appeal relates

☐ Respondent*

☐ Person notified that the application form has been issued

☐ Person notified that the permission form has been issued

*You are a respondent if you have been served with a copy of the COP1 application form.

Section 2 – Application to be joined as a party

Please do not complete this section if:

- you have been given notice of an application for permission; or
- you are a respondent.

You will be able to take part in the permission hearing/proceedings upon return of this acknowledgment form. **Please go to section 3.**

You must complete this section if you are the person to whom the application relates or a person notified that the application form has been issued and you wish to apply to be joined as a party.

2.1   Do you wish to be joined as a party to proceedings? **(see note 1)**   ☐Yes   ☐No

2.2   If Yes, Please state your interest in the proceedings. **(see note 2)**

PART VII

2.3   Evidence of your interest in the proceedings must be filed with this   ☐ Evidence
        acknowledgment. If you are attaching any written evidence please use the   attached
        COP24 witness statement form.

Section 3 – Acknowledgment of service/notification

3.1   Do you consent to the application?   ☐ Yes   ☐ No

         If Yes, **go to Section 3.5**

3.2   Do you oppose the application?   ☐ Yes   ☐ No

         If Yes, please set out your grounds for doing so.

         ┌───┐
         │   │
         │   │
         │   │
         │   │
         │   │
         │   │
         └───┘

3.3   Do you propose that a different order should be made?   ☐ Yes   ☐ No

         If Yes, please set out what that order is.

         ┌───┐
         │   │
         │   │
         │   │
         │   │
         │   │
         └───┘

3.4   If you oppose the order, or purpose a different order, any evidence on which you   ☐ Evidence
         intend to rely must be filed with this acknowledgment. If you are attaching any   attached
         written evidence please use the COP24 witness statement form.

3.5   Are you seeking any directions from the court?   ☐ Yes   ☐ No

         If Yes, please give details.

         ┌───┐
         │   │
         │   │
         │   │
         │   │
         └───┘

4

Section 4 – Attending court hearings

4.1   If the court requires you to attend a hearing do you need any special
      assistance or facilities? **(see note 3)**   ☐Yes   ☐No

      If Yes, please say what your requirements are. If necessary, court staff may
      contact you about your requirements.

Section 5 – Signature

Signed

*Person served/notified('s solicitor)('s litigation friend)

Name

Date

**Name
of firm**

**Position or
office held**   * Please delete the options in
                                                              brackets that do not apply.

Now read note 4 about what you need to do next.

PART VII

Guidance notes

Note 1

Application to be joined as a party

If you have been notified that an application has been issued and you wish to participate in the proceedings then you need to apply to be joined as a party.

If you have applied to be joined as a party the court will consider your application to be joined and if it decides to do so, will make an order to that effect.

Note 2

Your interest in the proceedings

You need to provide the court with information that will be useful in considering your application to be joined as a party. This could include what your connection is to the person to whom the application relates, how long you have known them and any other information that explains why you have an interest in the proceedings.

Note 3

Attending the court

If you need special assistance or special facilities for a disability or impairment, please set out your requirements in full. It is important that you make the court aware of your needs to avoid causing delays.

The court will need to know for example, whether you want documents to be supplied in any alternative format, such as Braille or large print. They will also need to know about any specific requirements should there be a hearing, such as wheelchair access, a hearing loop, or a sign language interpreter.

Note 4

What you need to do next

Please return the completed acknowledgment to:

> Court of Protection
> Archway Tower
> 2 Junction Road
> London N19 5SZ

Note 5

What happens next?

The court will serve the acknowledgment and any other documents you file with it on the applicant and other parties to the proceedings.

6

Form COP7 – Application to object to the registration of a Lasting Power of Attorney

COP 7 Court of Protection
03.10

Application to object to the registration of a lasting power of attorney (LPA)

For office use only
Date received
Case no.
Date issued

Name of the donor of the LPA (this is the person who made the LPA)

SEAL

Please read first

- You can only object using this form if you are an intended attorney or a named person who received an LPA001 notice of intention to apply for registration of a lasting power of attorney.

- There is no fee for filing this form with the court.

- An application to object must be made within five weeks from the day on which you received the LPA001 notice.

- If you are not one of the people who received the LPA001 notice but you wish to object, you can still do so but you need to file a COP1 application form and pay the specified fee. You need to notify the Public Guardian of your application. See note 1 at the end of this form for information on notifying the Public Guardian.

- An objection should be made to the Public Guardian (instead of the court) in the following circumstances:

  – if you are the donor, by using the form LPA006 objection by the donor to the registration of a lasting power of attorney;

  or

  – if you object on certain specified factual grounds, by using the form LPA007 objection to the Office of the Public Guardian of a proposed registration of a lasting power of attorney on factual grounds.

- You may need to pay for any costs you incur during the proceedings. If the court considers that you have acted unreasonably you can be ordered to pay the costs incurred by other parties.

- Please continue on a separate sheet of paper if you need more space to answer a question. Write your name, the name and date of birth of the person to whom the application relates, and the number of the question you are answering on each separate sheet.

- If you need help completing this form please check the website, www.hmcourts-service.gov.uk or www.direct.gov.uk, for further guidance or information, or contact Court Enquiry Service on 0300 456 4600 or courtofprotectionenquiries@hmcourts-service.gsi.gov.uk.

- Court of Protection staff cannot give legal advice. If you need legal advice please contact a solicitor.

PART VII

1

Section 1 - Your details (the applicant)

1.1   Your details   ☐ Mr.   ☐ Mrs.   ☐ Miss   ☐ Ms.   ☐ Other _____

      First name

      Middle name(s)

      Last name

1.2   Address
      (including
      postcode)

      Telephone no.

Daytime	
Evening	
Mobile	

      E-mail address

1.3   Is a solicitor representing you?   ☐ Yes   ☐ No

      If Yes, please give the solicitor's details.

      Name

      Address
      (including
      postcode)

Telephone no.		Fax no.	

      DX no.

      E-mail address

2

1.4   To which address should all official documentation be sent?

☐ Your address

☐ Solicitor's address

☐ Other address (please provide details)

1.5   Your description

☐ Attorney

☐ Other person entitled to be notified of the application to register the LPA

Section 2 - Objection to the registration of an LPA

2.1   Full name of the donor

☐ Mr.   ☐ Mrs.   ☐ Miss   ☐ Ms.   ☐ Other _____

First name

Middle name(s)

Last name

2.2   Full name of intended attorney(s)

☐ Mr.   ☐ Mrs.   ☐ Ms.   ☐ Miss   ☐ Other _____

First name

Last name

☐ Mr.   ☐ Mrs.   ☐ Ms.   ☐ Miss   ☐ Other _____

First name

Last name

PART VII

3

2.3   Date donor signed the LPA

D	D	M	M	Y	Y	Y	Y

2.4   Date you were given notice of the application to register the LPA

D	D	M	M	Y	Y	Y	Y

2.5   You can only object to the court against the registration of the LPA on grounds which are prescribed in regulations under the Mental Capacity Act 2005.

Please indicate your grounds for objecting to the proposed registration:

☐ The power purported to be created by the instrument* is not valid as a LPA.
(e.g. the donor did not have capacity to make an LPA).

☐ The power created by the instrument no longer exists
(e.g. the donor revoked it at a time when he or she had capacity to do so)

☐ Fraud or undue pressure was used to induce the donor to make the power.

☐ The attorney proposes to behave in a way that would contravene his authority or would not be in the donor's best interests.

*The instrument means the LPA made by the donor.

2.6   Any evidence in support of your application must be filed with this application   ☐ Evidence attached
form. If you are attaching any written evidence please use the COP24 witness
statement form.

2.7   You must have notified the Public Guardian of your intention to apply to the   ☐ I confirm that I have
court to object to the registration of the LPA. **(See note 1)**   notified the Public
                                                                                        Guardian

Section 3 - Attending court hearings

3.1   If the court requires you to attend a hearing do you need any special   ☐ Yes   ☐ No
assistance or facilities? **(See note 2)**

If Yes, please say what your requirements are. If necessary, court staff may contact
you about your requirements.

4

Section 4 – Statement of truth

The statement of truth is to be signed by you, your solicitor or your litigation friend.

*(I believe) (The applicant believes) that the facts stated in this application form are true.

Signed

*Applicant('s litigation friend)('s solicitor)

Name

Date

Name of firm

Position or office held

* Please delete the option in brackets that do not apply.

Now read note 3 about what you need to do next.

PART VII

5

Guidance notes

Note 1

Notifying the Public Guardian

You need to notify the Public Guardian, using the LPA008 form, without delay of your application to object. Upon notification the Office of the Public Guardian will suspend the registration until the court provides further directions. If the Public Guardian is not notified there is a risk that the LPA will be registered.

You can get copies of Office of the Public Guardian forms by calling 020 7664 7000, by downloading them from the Public Guardian website, www.publicguardian.gov.uk, or by writing to:

PO BOX 15118
Birmingham B16 6GX
or
DX744240
Birmingham 79

Note 2

Attending court hearings

If you need special assistance or special facilities for a disability or impairment, please set out your requirements in full. It is important that you make the court aware of your needs to avoid causing any delays.

The court staff will need to know, for example, whether you want documents to be supplied in an alternative format, such as Braille or large print. They will also need to know about any specific requirements should there be a hearing, such as wheelchair access, a hearing loop or a sign language interpreter.

Note 3

What you need to do next

The court requires two copies (i.e. the original plus one copy) of each form and document you file.

Please return the original completed forms, documents and copies to:

Court of Protection
Archway Tower
2 Junction Road
London N19 5SZ

Note 4

What happens next?

The court will notify you when your application form has been issued and will return a sealed copy of the application form. You will need to serve a copy on the donor and each attorney of the LPA.

6

Form COP8 – Application relating to the registration of an Enduring Power of Attorney

COP 8 03.10   Court of Protection

Application relating to the registration of an enduring power of attorney (EPA)

For office use only
Date received
Case no.
Date issued

Name of the donor of the EPA (this is the person who made the EPA)

SEAL

Please read first

- You need to complete and file this application form if you are the donor, an intended attorney or a relative of the donor entitled by Schedule 4 of the Mental Capacity Act 2005 (the Act) to be notified of the application to register the EPA and:

  - you wish to object to the registration of the EPA; or

  - you wish to seek the registration of the EPA where you have been notified that the registration has been suspended.

- If you are entitled to be notified then either you will have received an EP1PG notice of intention to apply for registration, or the Public Guardian will have notified you that the registration has been suspended.

- There is no fee for filing this form with the court.

- Schedule 4 of the Act provides for the court to dispense with the requirement to give notice. If you are one of the people entitled by the Act to be notified then you can object to the court using this form even if you have not received an EP1PG notice but you find out about the application through other means.

- If you wish to apply to object to the registration of the EPA then you should do so as soon as reasonably possible after receiving the EP1PG notice. You should notify the Public Guardian of your application. If you do not make an application, the Public Guardian will ask for the court's directions on registration. See note 1 at the end of this form for information on notifying the Public Guardian.

- You may need to pay for any costs you incur during the proceedings. If the court considers that you have acted unreasonably you can be ordered to pay the costs incurred by other parties.

- If you are not one of the people entitled by the Act to be notified of the application to register the EPA but you wish to object you can still do so but you need to file a COP1 application form and pay the specified fee. You should notify the Public Guardian of your application. See note 1 in the separate guidance for information on notifying the Public Guardian.

- Please continue on a separate sheet of paper if you need more space to answer a question. Write your name, the name and date of birth of the donor, and the number of the question you are answering on each separate sheet.

- If you need help completing this form please check the website, www.hmcourts-service.gov.uk or www.direct.gov.uk, for further guidance or information, or contact Court Enquiry Service on 0300 456 4600 or courtofprotectionenquiries@hmcourts-service.gsi.gov.uk.

- Court of Protection staff cannot give legal advice. If you need legal advice please contact a solicitor.

PART VII

1

Section 1 - Your details (the applicant)

1.1 Your details ☐ Mr. ☐ Mrs. ☐ Miss ☐ Ms. ☐ Other _____

First name

Middle name(s)

Last name

1.2 Address (including postcode)

Telephone no.	Daytime	
	Evening	
	Mobile	

E-mail address

1.3 Is a solicitor representing you? ☐ Yes ☐ No

If Yes, please give the solicitor's details.

Name

Address (including postcode)

Telephone no.		Fax no.	

DX no.

E-mail address

1.4 Which address should official documentation be sent to?

☐ Your address

☐ Solicitor's address

☐ Other address (please provide details)

1.5   Your description

☐ Donor (person making the EPA)

☐ Attorney

☐ Other person entitled to be notified of the application to register the EPA

Section 2 - Details of the EPA

2.1   Full name of the donor (if you are not the donor)

☐ Mr.   ☐ Mrs.   ☐ Miss   ☐ Ms.   ☐ Other _____

First name

Middle name(s)

Last name

2.2   Donor's address and telephone number (if you are not the donor)

Address
(including
postcode)

Telephone no.	Daytime	
	Evening	
	Mobile	

E-mail address

2.3   Donor's date of birth | D | D | M | M | Y | Y | Y | Y |

PART VII

2.4   Full name of intended attorney(s)

☐ Mr.   ☐ Mrs.   ☐ Ms.   ☐ Miss   ☐ Other _____

First name

Last name

☐ Mr.   ☐ Mrs.   ☐ Ms.   ☐ Miss   ☐ Other _____

First name

Last name

☐ Mr.   ☐ Mrs.   ☐ Ms.   ☐ Miss   ☐ Other _____

First name

Last name

2.5   Date donor signed the EPA

| D | D | M | M | Y | Y | Y | Y |

2.6   Date you were given notice of the application to register the EPA

| D | D | M | M | Y | Y | Y | Y |

Section 3 - Your application

3.1   Please state the directions you are seeking.

4

3.2   If you object to the registration of the EPA you can only do so on grounds which are prescribed in the Mental Capacity Act 2005.

Please indicate your grounds for objecting to the proposed registration:

☐ The power purported to be created by the instrument* is not valid as an enduring power of attorney

☐ The power created by the instrument no longer subsists

☐ The application is premature because the donor is not yet becoming mentally incapable

☐ Fraud or undue pressure was used to induce the donor to make the power

☐ The attorney is unsuitable to be the donor's attorney (having regard to all the circumstances and in particular the attorney's relationship to or connection with the donor).

The instrument means the EPA made by the donor.

Please tick to confirm

3.3   I have notified the Public Guardian of my intention to apply to the court in relation to the registration of the EPA. **(See note 1)**   ☐ I confirm I have notified the Public Guardian

3.4   If you seek registration please state your reasons for doing so.

3.5   Any evidence in support of your application must be filed with this application form. If you are attaching any written evidence please use the COP24 witness statement form.   ☐ Evidence attached

Section 4 - Attending court hearings

4.1   If the court requires you to attend a hearing do you need any special assistance or facilities? **(See note 2)**   ☐ Yes   ☐ No

If Yes, please say what your requirements are. If necessary, court staff may contact you about your requirements

PART VII

5

1447

Section 5 – Statement of truth

The statement of truth is to be signed by you, your solicitor or your litigation friend.

*(I believe) (The applicant believes) that the facts stated in this application form are true.

Signed

[   ]

*Applicant('s solicitor)('s litigation friend)

Name

[   ]

Date

[   ]

**Name
of firm**

[   ]

**Position or
office held**

[   ]   * Please delete the option in
                                                                            brackets that do not apply.

Now read note 3 about what you need to do next.

Guidance notes

Note 1

Notifying the Public Guardian

If you have not already done so, you should notify the Public Guardian of your objection within five weeks of receiving the EP1PG notice. Upon notification the Office of the Public Guardian will suspend the registration until the court provides further directions. If the Public Guardian is not notified there is a risk that the EPA will be registered.

You should also notify the Public Guardian of your application to the court.

You can notify the Public Guardian by writing to:

   PO BOX 15118
   Birmingham B16 6GX
   or
   DX744240
   Birmingham 79

Note 2

Attending court hearings

If you need special assistance or special facilities for a disability or impairment, please set out your requirements in full. It is important that you make the court aware of your needs to avoid causing any delays.

The court staff will need to know, for example, whether you want documents to be supplied in an alternative format, such as Braille or large print.

They will also need to know about any specific requirements should there be a hearing, such as wheelchair access, a hearing loop or a sign language interpreter.

Note 3

What you need to do next

The court requires two copies (i.e. the original plus one copy) of the each form and document you file.

Please return the original completed forms, documents and copies to:

   Court of Protection
   Archway Tower
   2 Junction Road
   London N19 5SZ

Note 4

What happens next?

The court will notify you when your application form has been issued and the court will return a sealed copy of the application form. You will need to serve a copy on the donor and each attorney of the EPA.

6

Form COP9 – Application notice

COP 9 **03.10** Court of Protection

Application notice

For office use only
Date received
Date issued

Case no.

Full name of person to whom the application relates
(this is the person who lacks, or is alleged, to lack capacity)

SEAL

Please read first

- This form can be used in a variety of circumstances and must be used for applications within proceedings. For further guidance on when this form is to be used please see the Court of Protection Rules 2007 and the Practice Directions accompanying the Rules or contact Customer Services at the number below.

- If you wish to apply to start proceedings please complete the COP1 application form.

- If you wish to apply to be joined as a party to the proceedings please complete the COP10 application notice for applications to be joined as a party.

- You may need to pay for any costs you incur during the proceedings. If the court considers that you have acted unreasonably you can be ordered to pay the costs incurred by other parties.

- Please continue on a separate sheet of paper if you need more space to answer a question. Write the case number, your name, the name of the person to whom the application relates, and number of the question you are answering on each separate sheet.

- If you need help completing this form please check the website, www.hmcourts-service.gov.uk or www.direct.gov.uk, for further guidance or information, or contact Court Enquiry Service on 0300 456 4600 or courtofprotectionenquiries@hmcourts-service.gsi.gov.uk

- Court of Protection staff cannot give legal advice. If you need legal advice please contact a solicitor.

PART VII

Section 1 - Your details

1.1   Your details   ☐ Mr.   ☐ Mrs.   ☐ Miss   ☐ Ms.   ☐ Other _____

       First name   [   ]

       Middle name(s) [   ]

       Last name   [   ]

1.2   Address
       (including   [   ]
       postcode)

       Telephone no. | Daytime | |
                       | Evening | |
                       | Mobile | |

       E-mail address [   ]

1.3   Is a solicitor representing you?   ☐ Yes   ☐ No

       If Yes, please give the solicitor's details.

       Name   [   ]

       Address
       (including   [   ]
       postcode)

       Telephone no.   [   ] Fax no. [   ]
       DX no.   [   ]
       E-mail address [   ]

1.4   Which address should official documentation be sent to?

                       ☐ Your address

                       ☐ Solicitor's address

                       ☐ Other address (please provide details)

                       [   ]

2

1.5   What is your role in the proceedings?

☐ Applicant (the person who filed the COP1 application form)

☐ Person to whom the application relates

☐ Other party to the proceedings

☐ Other (please give details)

Section 2 - Your application

2.1   What order or direction are you seeking from the court?

2.2   Please set out the grounds on which you are seeking the order or direction?

2.3   Any evidence in support of your application must be filed with this application notice. If you are attaching any written evidence please use the COP24 witness statement form.

☐ Evidence attached

If the court requires that evidence be given by affidavit then you need to use the COP25 affidavit form.

3

PART VII

2.4   Please provide the details of any person who you reasonably believe has an interest which means they ought to be heard by the court in relation to this application notice and who is not already a party to the proceedings.

Full name including title	Full address including postcode	Connection to the person to whom the proceedings relate

Section 3 – Statement of truth

The statement of truth is to be signed by you, your solicitor or your litigation friend.

*(I believe) (The applicant believes) that the facts stated in this application notice are true.

Signed

*Applicant('s litigation friend)('s solicitor)

Name

Date

Name of firm

Position or office held

* Please delete the options in brackets that do not apply.

Now read note 1 about what you need to do next.

4

Guidance notes

Note 1

What you need to do next

The court requires two copies (i.e. the original plus one copy) of each form and document you file.

Please return the original completed forms, documents and copies to:

> Court of Protection
> Archway Tower
> 2 Junction Road
> London N19 5SZ

Note 2

What happens next?

The court will notify you when your application notice has been issued. The court will return a sealed copy of the application notice. You may need to serve copies on:

- every other party to the proceedings;
- anyone who is named as a respondent in the application notice; and
- any other person as the court may direct.

5

Form COP10 – Application notice for applications to be joined as a party

COP 10 **03.10** Court of Protection

Application notice for applications to be joined as a party

For office use only
Date received
Date issued

Case no.

Full name of person to whom the application relates
(this is the name of the person who lacks, or is alleged to lack, capacity)

SEAL

Please read first

- If you wish to apply to be joined as a party to the proceedings then you need to complete this application notice. You must be joined as a party to oppose an application or seek a different order.

- Do not complete this form if you have been served with a copy of COP1 application form or have received a COP15 notice that an application form has been issued. Instead you need to complete and file a COP5 acknowledgment of service/notification in order to be joined as a party.

- If your application relates to another matter and is made in the course of existing proceedings then you need to complete the COP9 application notice.

- You may need to pay for any costs you incur during the proceedings. If the court considers that you have acted unreasonably you can be ordered to pay the costs incurred by other parties.

- Please continue on a separate sheet of paper if you need more space to answer a question. Write the case number, your name and the name of the person to whom the application relates, and the number of the question you are answering on each separate sheet.

- If you need help completing this form please check the website, www.hmcourts-service.gov.uk or www.direct.gov.uk, for further guidance or information, or contact Court Enquiry Service on 0300 456 4600 or courtofprotectionenquiries@hmcourts-service.gsi.gov.uk

- Court of Protection staff cannot give legal advice. If you need legal advice please contact a solicitor.

1

© Crown Copyright 2010

Section 1 - Your details (the person applying to be joined as a party)

1.1	Your details	☐ Mr.	☐ Mrs.	☐ Miss	☐ Ms.	☐ Other _____

First name

Middle name(s)

Last name

1.2 Address (including postcode)

Telephone no.	Daytime	
	Evening	
	Mobile	

E-mail address

1.3 Is a solicitor representing you? ☐ Yes ☐ No

If Yes, please give the solicitor's details.

Name

Address (including postcode)

Telephone no.		Fax no.	

DX no.

E-mail address

1.4 Which address should official documentation be sent to?

☐ Your address

☐ Solicitor's address

☐ Other address (please provide details)

2

PART VII

Section 2 - Your application

2.1   What is your connection to the person to whom the application relates?

2.2   What is your interest in the proceedings?

2.3   Do you consent to the application?   ☐ Yes   ☐ No

2.4   Do you oppose the application?   ☐ Yes   ☐ No

        If Yes, please set out your grounds for doing so.

2.5   Do you propose that a different order should be made?   ☐ Yes   ☐ No
        If Yes, please set out what the order is.

3

2.6   Any evidence in support of your application must be filed with this application   ☐ Evidence
       notice. If you are attaching any written evidence please use the COP24   attached
       witness statement form

Section 3 – Attending court hearings

3.1   If the court requires you to attend a hearing do you need any special   ☐ Yes   ☐ No
       assistance or facilities? **(see note 1)**

       If Yes, please say what your requirements are. If necessary, court staff may
       contact you about your requirements.

Section 4 - Statement of truth

       The statement of truth is to be signed by you, or your solicitor or your litigation friend.

       *(I believe) (The applicant believes) the facts stated in this application notice are true.

Signed

       *Applicant('s litigation friend)('s solicitor)

Name

Date

**Name
of firm**

**Position or
office held**   * Please delete the options in
                                                                    brackets that do not apply.

Now read note 2 about what you need to do next.

4

Note 1

Attending court hearings

If you need special assistance or special facilities for a disability or impairment, please set out your requirements in full. It is important that you make the court aware of your needs to avoid causing any delays.

The court staff will need to know, for example, whether you want documents to be supplied in an alternative format, such as Braille or large print. They will also need to know about any specific requirements should there be a hearing, such as wheelchair access, a hearing loop or a sign language interpreter.

Note 2

What you need to do next

The court requires a sufficient number of copies of this form to provide a copy to every party to the proceedings. Please contact Court Enquiry Service on 0300 456 4600 to find out how many copies you need to provide.

Please return the original completed form and copies to:
    Court of Protection
    Archway Tower
    2 Junction Road
    London N19 5SZ

Note 3

What happens next?

The court will serve the application notice and any accompanying documents on every party to the proceedings.

The court will consider your application to be joined and if it decides to do so, will make an order to that effect.

5

Form COP12 – Special undertaking by trustees

COP 12 03.10 Court of Protection

Special undertaking by trustees

For office use only
Date received
Case no.

Full name of person to whom the application relates
(this is the name of the person who lacks, or is alleged to lack, capacity)

Please read first

- If your application relates to the appointment of a trustee then you need to complete this undertaking and file it with the court together with a COP1 application form and any other required forms and documents. All new and continuing trustees must sign the undertaking (not just the person making the application).

- For further information on applications relating to trustees please see Practice Direction G that supplements Part 9 of the Court of Protection Rules 2007.

- Please continue on a separate sheet of paper if you need more space to answer a question. Write your name, the name and date of birth of the person to whom the application relates, and the number of the question you are answering on each separate sheet.

- If you need help completing this form please check the website, www.hmcourts-service.gov.uk or www.direct.gov.uk, for further guidance or information, or contact Court Enquiry Service on 0300 456 4600 or courtofprotectionenquiries@hmcourts-service.gsi.gov.uk

- Court of Protection staff cannot give legal advice. If you need legal advice please contact a solicitor.

PART VII

1

© Crown Copyright 2010

Section 1 - Details of the person to whom the application relates

1.1   Full name

Address
(including
postcode)

Date of birth | D | D | M | M | Y | Y | Y | Y |

Section 2 - Special undertaking by trustees

2.1   Name of continuing trustee

Address
(including
postcode)

Name of second continuing trustee (if applicable)

Address
(including
postcode)

Name of new trustee (if applicable)

Address
(including
postcode)

2

Name of second new trustee (if applicable)

Address
(including
postcode)

2.2   Name of
property, will,
settlement, etc.

2.3   I/WE HEREBY UNDERTAKE that in the event of such appointment being approved and made, where the above named person lacks capacity in relation to the trust, to sell any land or property to the whole of any part of which the person is absolutely entitled in equity at such fair and reasonable price as can be obtained through a sale on the open market.

AND THAT in the event of the sale being effected where the above named person lacks capacity in relation to the trust we will deal with the proceeds of sale or with the person's undivided share thereof, as the case may be, in such manner as the court may direct but so that where the person is a joint tenant we will deal with the proceeds in such manner as the court (on behalf of the person) and the other joint tenant shall jointly direct and on severance of the joint tenancy we will deal with the person's share of the proceeds in such manner as the court may direct.

PART VII

3

Section 5 – Signature

Signed

Name

Date

Signed

Name

Date

Signed

Name

Date

Signed

Name

Date

Now read note 8 of the COP1 application form about what you need to do next.

4

Form COP14 – Proceedings about you in the Court of Protection

COP 14 Court of Protection

03.10 **Proceedings about you in the Court of Protection**

For office use only

To (enter name and address of person to whom the application relates)

Name

Address

This notice is to tell you of proceedings about you in the Court of Protection.

The court has powers to make decisions about the property and affairs and personal welfare of people who lack capacity to make such decisions.

If you have any questions or need further information about this notice you can:

- ring Court Enquiry Service on 0300 456 4600;
- write to the Court of Protection, Archway Tower, 2 Junction Road, London N19 5SZ; or
- check the website, www.hmcourts-service.gov.uk or www.direct.gov.uk.

The Court of Protection staff cannot give legal advice. If you need legal advice please contact a solicitor.

Details of the proceedings

Case number

Date the *(application)(appeal) was issued

D	D	M	M	Y	Y	Y	Y

Name of the *(applicant)(appellant)

The *(application)(appeal) relates to your:

☐ property and affairs

☐ personal welfare

☐ property and affairs and personal welfare.

* Please delete the options in brackets that do not apply.

© Crown Copyright 2010

PART VII

1

1463

This notice is to tell you that

Signed	
Name	
Date	
Name of firm	
Position or office held	

2

Form COP15 – Notice that an application form has been issued

COP 15
03.10 Court of Protection

Notice that an application form has been issued

For office use only

To (enter name and address of person to be notified)

Name

Address

This notice is to tell you that an application form has been issued by the Court of Protection.

The court has powers to make decisions regarding the property and affairs and personal welfare of people who lack capacity to make such decisions.

If you wish to be involved in the proceedings, then you need to complete and file the COP5 acknowledgment of notification with the court and apply to be joined as a party.

If you have any questions or need further information about the application you can:
- ring Court Enquiry Service on 0300 456 4600;
- write to the Court of Protection, Archway Tower, 2 Junction Road, London N19 5SZ; or
- check the website, www.hmcourts-service.gov.uk or www.direct.gov.uk

Court of Protection staff cannot give legal advice. If you need legal advice please contact a solicitor.

Details of the application

Case number

Date the application was issued

D	D	M	M	Y	Y	Y	Y

Name of the applicant

Name of the person to whom the application relates (this is the person who lacks, or is alleged to lack, capacity)

Applicant's connection to the person to whom the application relates

The application relates to the exercise of the court's jurisdiction in relation to the person's:

☐ property and affairs

☐ personal welfare

☐ property and affairs and personal welfare.

1

© Crown Copyright 2010

PART VII

The matter the court has been asked to decide:

Order(s) the court has been asked to make:

Signed

Name

Date

Name of firm

Position or office held

2

Form COP20A – Certificate of notification/non-notification of the person to whom proceedings relate

Court of Protection

Certificate of notification/ non-notification of the person to whom the proceedings relate

Case no.

Please refer to the guidance note COP21A before completing this form

Full name of person to whom the application/appeal relates
(this is the person who lacks, or is alleged to lack, capacity)

Section 1 - Person notified

1.1 Address

☐ persons residence ☐ Other *(Please give details)*

1.2 Date of notification

| D | D | M | M | Y | Y | Y | Y |

Section 2 - Details of the person who provided notification

2.1 Your name:

2.2 In what capacity are you providing notice?

As the:

☐ Applicant ☐ Appellant

☐ Applicant's solicitor ☐ Appellant's solicitor

☐ Applicant's litigation friend ☐ Agent

☐ Other *(Please give details)*

1

PART VII

Section 3 – Notification (For non-notification please go to section 4)

Please tick one of the following statements:

(Please read: If you attempted to notify but were unable to carry out a full explanation as referred to in the bullet points of the relevant statement below you must give your reasons in section 4 as to why you could not carry out full notification)

3.1 ☐ **Application form has been issued**

I have notified the person to whom the application relates that an application form has been issued and I explained to the person:

- Who the applicant is;
- That the application raises the question of whether they lack capacity in relation to a matter or matters, and what that means;
- What will happen if the court makes the order or direction that has been applied for;
- Where the application contains a proposal for the appointment of a person to make decisions on their behalf in relation to the matter to which the application relates, details of who that person is; and
- That they may seek advice and assistance in relation to the application.

3.2 ☐ **Application has been withdrawn**

I have notified the person to whom the application relates that an application has been withdrawn and I explained to the person:

- That the application forms has been withdrawn;
- The consequence of the withdrawal; and
- That they may seek advice and assistance in relation to the application.

3.3 ☐ **Appellant's notice has been issued**

I have notified the person to whom the application relates that an appellant's notice has been issued and I explained to the person:

- Who the appellant is;
- The issues raised by the appeal;
- What will happen if the court makes the order or direction applied for; and
- That they may seek advice and assistance in relation to the appeal.

3.4 ☐ **Appellant's notice has been withdrawn**

I have notified the person to whom the application relates that an appellant's notice has been withdrawn and I explained to the person:

- That the notice has been withdrawn;
- The consequence of the withdrawal; and
- That they may seek advice and assistance in relation to the appeal.

3.5 ☐ **Final order has been made by the court**

I have notified the person to whom the application relates that a final order has been made by the court and I explained to the person:

- The effect of the order; and
- That they may seek advice and assistance in relation to the order.

3.6 ☐ **Another matter as directed by the court**

I have notified the person to whom the application relates of another matter as directed by the court and I explained to the person:

- The matters directed by the court; and
- That they may seek advice and assistance in relation to the matter.

Section 4 – Non-notification

If you could not provide notification, please describe your attempt to do so, and explain the reasons why notification was not provided.

PART VII

Section 5 – Statement of truth

The statement of truth must be signed by the person who provided notification.

I believe that the facts stated in this certificate are true.

| Signed | | Date | D D M M Y Y Y Y |

| Name | |

| Name of firm | | Position or office held | |

Please return the completed certificate to:

Court of Protection, Archway Tower, 2 Junction Road, London N19 5SZ

Note:

No other forms need to be attached with this form. However, it may assist the court if your completed **COP20A** and **COP20B** could be returned at the same time.

COP 21A – Guidance notes on completing form COP20A

Court of Protection: Guidance notes on completing form COP20A

Please read the following notes before completing form COP20A

The person to whom the application/appeal relates must be notified **personally** of the commencement/ withdrawal of any proceedings, a final order of the court or other matters as required by the court.

You must provide the person to whom the application/appeal relates with a COP14 notice which includes details of why the notification is being given to him/her. **Please read this note in conjunction with guidance note COP14A.**

You need to complete and file form COP20A with the court when you provide notification that an application/appeal has been issued/withdrawn or any other matter as the court directs.

Where the person is notified that an application form or appellant's notice has been issued, you **must** provide them with a COP5 acknowledgement of notification form.

You **must** complete and return the COP20A to the court **within seven days of notification taking place.**

In the case of non-notification, the COP20A **must** be returned to the court **within seven days of the latest date on which notification should have been made.**

Only the court can dispense with the requirement for notification. The requirement for notification cannot be dispensed with solely because of the person's alleged incapacity, unless the court has directed otherwise.

An application to dispense with notification or service may be made using a COP9 application form, with evidence in support on form COP24. Such an application would be appropriate where, for example, the person concerned is in a permanent vegetative state or a minimally conscious state; or where notification by the applicant is likely to cause significant and disproportionate distress to that person.

Failure to answer any of the sections on form COP20A may result in consideration of the application/appeal being delayed.

Completing form COP20A

1. Person notified (Section 1)

The certificate provided to the court must include the full name and address of the person notified and the date of notification.

2. Details of the person who provided notification (Section 2)

Definitions:

- **Agent** – a person carrying out the notification on another's behalf, e.g. nursing home proprietor.

- **Applicant** – the person applying to the court for a court order.

- **Appellant** – the person who is appealing against a decision made in court.

- **Final order** – the court order that brings the application or appeal to an end, e.g. the order appointing a deputy.

- **Litigation friend** – a person acting in legal proceedings on behalf of a person who lacks capacity (or on behalf of a child).

- **Other** – a person not covered by any of the above categories, e.g. a neighbour.

3. Notification (Section 3)

The certificate provided to the court must have the relevant tick-box answered, e.g. if you are notifying the person that an application has been issued, you tick the box in section 3.1: if you are notifying the person that an application has been withdrawn, you tick the box in section 3.2.

4. Non-notification (Section 4)

Where the applicant/appellant or his/her agent is unable to provide notification, he/she must explain as fully as possible why notification was not provided.

5. Statement of truth (Section 5)

The certificate provided to the court must include a signed and dated statement by the applicant/ appellant or his/her appointed agents.

Disclaimer

Your attention is drawn to the provisions of Part 7 of the Court of Protection Rules 2007 and Practice Direction 7A, which can be found on HMCS website, details below.

Court of Protection staff cannot give legal advice. If you need legal advice please contact a solicitor or your local Citizens Advice Bureau. Information in this guidance is believed to be correct at the time of publication; however we do not accept any liability for any error it may contain.

If you need further help completing form COP20A, please check the website www.hmcourts-service. gov.uk For additional guidance or information please contact our Court Enquiry Service on 0300 456 4600 or courtofprotectionenquiries@hmcourts-service.gsi. gov.uk

PART VII

Form COP20B – Certificate of service/non-service notification/non-notification

COP 20B 12.10 Court of Protection

Court of Protection

Certificate of service/non-service notification/non-notification

Case no.

Please refer to the guidance note COP21B before completing this form

Full name of person to whom the application relates
(this is the person who lacks, or is alleged to lack, capacity)

Section 1 - Details of the person who provided service/notification

1.1   Full name:

1.2   In what capacity are you serving/providing notice? *(Please see guidance)*

As the:

☐ Applicant   ☐ Respondent

☐ Applicant's solicitor   ☐ Respondent's solicitor

☐ Applicant's litigation friend ☐ Respondent's litigation friend

☐ Agent

☐ Other *(Please give details)*

Section 2 – People served *(See Section 3 for people notified)*

2.1   Title or description of the document *(tick only one box)*

☐ Application form (plus supporting evidence)

☐ Appellant's notice

☐ Respondent's notice

☐ Other *(Please give details)*

1   © Crown Copyright 2010

Please photocopy this sheet before use if additional people need to be served

2.2   In respect of all served

1. Respondent's name

Date of service

D	D	M	M	Y	Y	Y	Y

Address of service

Method of service

☐ 1st class post   ☐ fax

☐ in person   ☐ other electronic means

☐ DX   ☐ permitted address

☐ alternative method as directed by court order

2. Respondent's name

Date of service

D	D	M	M	Y	Y	Y	Y

Address of service

Method of service

☐ 1st class post   ☐ fax

☐ in person   ☐ other electronic means

☐ DX   ☐ permitted address

☐ alternative method as directed by court order

3. Respondent's name

Date of service

D	D	M	M	Y	Y	Y	Y

Address of service

Method of service

☐ 1st class post   ☐ fax

☐ in person   ☐ other electronic means

☐ DX   ☐ permitted address

☐ alternative method as directed by court order

4. Respondent's name

Date of service

D	D	M	M	Y	Y	Y	Y

Address of service

Method of service

☐ 1st class post   ☐ fax

☐ in person   ☐ other electronic means

☐ DX   ☐ permitted address

☐ alternative method as directed by court order

PART VII

2

Section 3 – People notified *Please photocopy this sheet before use if additional people need to be notified*

I have given notice of issue of application form (COP15) to the following:

1. **Name of person notified**

Address of notification

Date of notification

| D | D | M | M | Y | Y | Y | Y |

Method of notification

☐ 1st class post   ☐ fax

☐ in person   ☐ other electronic means

☐ DX   ☐ permitted address

☐ alternative method as directed by court order

---

2. **Name of person notified**

Address of notification

Date of notification

| D | D | M | M | Y | Y | Y | Y |

Method of notification

☐ 1st class post   ☐ fax

☐ in person   ☐ other electronic means

☐ DX   ☐ permitted address

☐ alternative method as directed by court order

---

3. **Name of person notified**

Address of notification

Date of notification

| D | D | M | M | Y | Y | Y | Y |

Method of notification

☐ 1st class post   ☐ fax

☐ in person   ☐ other electronic means

☐ DX   ☐ permitted address

☐ alternative method as directed by court order

---

4. **Name of person notified**

Address of notification

Date of notification

| D | D | M | M | Y | Y | Y | Y |

Method of notification

☐ 1st class post   ☐ fax

☐ in person   ☐ other electronic means

☐ DX   ☐ permitted address

☐ alternative method as directed by court order

3

Section 4 – Non-service/Non-notification

I could not serve/give notice to:

1. Name

   Reason:

2. Name

   Reason:

3. Name

   Reason:

Section 5 – Statement of truth

The statement of truth must be signed by the person who served/provided notification.

I believe that the facts stated in this certificate are true.

Signed   **Date** | D | D | M | M | Y | Y | Y | Y |

Name

Name of firm   **Position or office held**

Please return the completed certificate to:
Court of Protection, Archway Tower, 2 Junction Road, London N19 5SZ

Note:
No other forms need to be attached with this form. However, it may assist the court if your completed **COP20A** and **COP20B** could be returned at the same time.

PART VII

COP 21B – Guidance notes on completing form COP20B

Court of Protection: Guidance notes on completing form COP20B

Please read the following notes before completing form COP20B

Form COP20B must be completed when you have served/notified those people mentioned in the application/appeal form that an application/appeal has been issued/withdrawn or any other matter as the court directs.

You must provide the person being served/notified with a COP15 notice which includes details of why the notification/service is being given to him/her. **Please read this note in conjunction with guidance note COP15A.**

The court requires that persons who have an interest in the application/appeal must either be **notified** by giving them form COP15 or **served by** giving them a copy of the issued application and supporting evidence.

Where the person is served or notified that an application form or appellant's notice has been issued, you **must** provide them with a COP5 acknowledgement of notification form.

You **must** complete and return the COP20B to the court **within seven days of service or notification taking place.**

In the case of non-service or non-notification, the COP20B **must** be returned to the court within **seven days of the latest date on which notification or service should have been made.**

Failure to answer any of the sections on form COP20B may result in consideration of the application/appeal being delayed.

Completing form COP20B

1. Details of the person who provided service/notification (Section 1)

Definitions:
- **Agent** – a person carrying out the notification on another's behalf, e.g. nursing home proprietor.
- **Applicant** – the person applying to the court for a court order.
- **Appellant** – the person who is appealing against a decision made in court.
- **Final order** – the court order that brings the application to an end, e.g. the order appointing a deputy.
- **Litigation friend** – a person acting in legal proceedings on behalf of a person who lacks capacity (or on behalf of a child).
- **Respondent** – a party to the proceedings (other than the Applicant or Appellant).
- **Other** – a person not covered by any of the above categories, e.g. a neighbour.

2. Persons served or notified (Sections 2 and 3)

Service/notification must be made on those people listed on Sections 4.1 and 4.2 of the Application form COP1; Section 2.6 of the Appellant's notice COP35; or other persons as the court may direct.

The date of service/notification depends on the method of delivery used:
- First class post (or other service for next-day delivery): date of posting.
- Personal: date of personal service
- Document exchange: Date when the document was left at the document exchange.
- Delivery of document to permitted address: Date when document was delivered to the permitted address.
- Fax: Date of transmission.
- Other electronic means: Date of transmission and the means used.
- Alternative method permitted by the court: If the court has permitted an alternative method of delivery it will specify the date or other details to be stated on the certificate of service.

You must confirm the method of service/notification by completing the relevant tick box.

3. Non-service/Non-notification (Section 4)
Where the applicant/appellant or his/her agent is unable to serve a document or to provide notification, he/she must provide details of the person(s) not served or notified and state the reason(s) why service/notification could not be made.

4. Statement of truth (Section 5)
The certificate provided to the court must include a signed and dated statement by the applicant/appellant or his/her appointed agents.

Disclaimer

Your attention is drawn to the provisions of Part 7 of the Court of Protection Rules 2007, Practice Direction 6A and Practice Directions 9B and 9C. Copies of the Practice Directions can be found on HMCS website, details below.

Court of Protection staff cannot give legal advice. If you need legal advice please contact a solicitor or your local Citizens Advice Bureau. Information in this guidance is believed to be correct at the time of publication; however we do not accept any liability for any error it may contain.

If you need further help completing form COP20B, please check the website www.hmcourts-service.gov.uk For additional guidance or information please contact our Court Enquiry Service on 0300 456 4600 or courtofprotectionenquiries@hmcourts-service.gsi.gov.uk

Form COP22 – Certificate of suitability of litigation friend

COP 22 **03.10** Court of Protection

Certificate of suitability of litigation friend

For office use only

Case no.

Full name of person to whom the application relates
(this is the person who lacks, or is alleged to lack, capacity)

Please read first

- If you wish to act as a litigation friend for a party to the proceedings then you must complete this certificate and file it with the court.

- This does not apply if you wish to act as a litigation friend for the person to whom the application relates. You can apply for an order to be appointed as the litigation friend for the person to whom the application relates (where they are party to the proceedings) by filing a COP9 application notice.

- Please continue on a separate sheet of paper if you need more space to answer a question. Write the case number, your name, the name of the person to whom the application relates, and the number of the question you are answering on each separate sheet.

- If you need help completing this form please check the website, www.hmcourts-service.gov.uk or www.direct.gov.uk, for further guidance or information, or contact Court Enquiry Service on 0300 456 4600 or courtofprotectionenquiries@hmcourts-service.gsi.gov.uk

- Court of Protection staff cannot give legal advice. If you need legal advice please contact a solicitor.

PART VII

1

Section 1 - Your details (the litigation friend)

1.1   Your full name   ☐ Mr.   ☐ Mrs.   ☐ Miss   ☐ Ms.   ☐ Other _____

First name

Middle name(s)

Last name

1.2   Address
(including
postcode)

Telephone no. | Daytime |
                 | Evening |
                 | Mobile |

1.3   What is your relationship or connection to the person on whose behalf you wish
to act as a litigation friend?

Section 2 - Details of the person on whose behalf you wish to act as a litigation friend

2.1   I consent to act as a litigation friend for:

Name

Address
(including
postcode)

Telephone no.

2

2.2   Please tick to confirm:

☐ I know or believe that the person named in section 2.1 lacks capacity to conduct the proceedings on his or her own behalf.

The grounds for my belief are as follows:

If your belief is based upon medical opinion, please attach any relevant document and file it with the court. You are not required to serve the document on every other party to the proceedings (unless the court directs otherwise).   ☐ Document(s) attached

Section 3 - Suitability to be a litigation friend

3.1   Please tick to confirm:

☐ I am able to conduct proceedings on behalf of the person named in section 2.1 competently and fairly;

☐ I have no interests adverse to those of the person; and

☐ I have served a copy of this certificate on the relevant person specified in the table below and on every other person who is a party to the proceedings.

Nature of party	Person to be served
Child	• A person who has parental responsibility for the child within the meaning of the Children Act 1989; or • if there is no such person, a person with whom the child lives with or in whose care the child is.
Protected party (a person who lacks capacity to conduct proceedings, other than a child or the person to whom the application relates)	• The person who is authorised to conduct the proceedings in the protected party's name or on his or her behalf; • a person who is a duly appointed attorney or deputy of the protected party; or • if there is no such person, a person with whom the protected party lives or in whose care the latter is.

You must complete and file a COP20 certificate of service/non-service for every person served with a copy of this certificate.

3

Section 4 – Statement of truth

This statement of truth is to be signed by the person who wishes to become the litigation friend or their solicitor.

*(I believe)(The litigation friend believes) that the facts stated in this certificate are true.

Signed

*Litigation friend('s solicitor)

Name

Date

Name of firm

Position or office held

* Please delete the options in brackets that do not apply.

Please return the completed certificate to:
Court of Protection, Archway Tower, 2 Junction Road, London N19 5SZ

4

Form COP23 – Certificate of failure or refusal of witness to attend before an examiner

COP 23 Court of Protection
03.10 **Certificate of failure or refusal of witness to attend before an examiner**

For office use only

Case no.

Full name of person to whom the application relates
(this is the person who lacks, or is alleged to lack, capacity)

Please read first

- If you required a deposition and the person ordered to attend before the examiner failed to attend or refused to be sworn, answer a question or produce a document, then you need to complete this certificate and file it with the court.

- You need to arrange for the examiner to complete and sign section 1 of this certificate.

- You may apply to the court for a further order in respect of the witness after this certificate has been filed.

- Please continue on a separate sheet of paper if you need more space to answer a question. Write the case number, your name, the name of the person to whom the application relates, and the number of the question you are answering on each separate sheet.

- If you need help completing this form please check the website, www.hmcourts-service.gov.uk or www.direct.gov.uk, for further guidance or information, or contact Court Enquiry Service on 0300 456 4600 or courtofprotectionenquiries@ hmcourts-service.gsi.gov.uk

- Court of Protection staff cannot give legal advice. If you need legal advice please contact a solicitor.

PART VII

© Crown Copyright 2010

Section 1 - Failure or refusal of witness to attend before an examiner

This section is to be completed and signed by the examiner

1.1   What is the name of the witness?

1.2   What was the date of the order directing the examination?

D	D	M	M	Y	Y	Y	Y

1.3   On what day and at what time was the examination due to take place?

D	D	M	M	Y	Y	Y	Y

Time

1.4   Where was the examination due to take place?

1.5   The above named witness:

☐ failed to attend the examination

☐ refused to be sworn for the purpose of the examination

☐ refused to answer the following lawful question(s) at the examination (please specify)

☐ refused to produce the following document(s) at the examination (please specify)

2

1.6   Please provide any comments as to the conduct of the deponent or of any person attending the examination.

Signed _____

Name _____

Position or office held _____

Date _____

3

Section 2 - Your details (party requiring the deposition)

This section is to be completed and signed by the party requiring the deposition

2.1   ☐ Mr.   ☐ Mrs.   ☐ Miss   ☐ Ms.   ☐ Other _____

First name

Middle name(s)

Last name

2.2   Address
      (including
      postcode)

Telephone no.

2.3   What is your role in these proceedings?

☐ Applicant (the person who filed the COP1 application form)

☐ Respondent

☐ Other (please provide details)

Section 3 – Signature

Signed

*(Applicant)(Respondent)('s litigation friend)('s solicitor)

Name

Date

* Please delete the options in
brackets that do not apply.

**Name
of firm**

**Position or
office held**

**Please return the completed
certificate to:**
Court of Protection, Archway
Tower, 2 Junction Road,
London N19 5SZ

4

Form COP24 – Witness statement

COP 24 03.10 Court of Protection
Witness statement

Statement given by (name of witness)
Statement
☐ 1st ☐ 2nd ☐ 3rd ☐ Other _____
Filed on behalf of (name of party)
Date statement was made

Case no.

[ ]

Full name of person to whom the application relates
(this is the person who lacks, or is alleged to lack capacity)

[ ]

Please read first

- If you are filing written evidence with the court then it should be included in or attached to this form.

- If the court requires that evidence be given by affidavit then you need to use the COP25 affidavit form.

- You must initial any alterations to the witness statement.

- A document referred to in a witness statement and provided to the court is known as an exhibit. Each exhibit must be identified in some way (e.g. 'Exhibit A'). The first page of the exhibit must contain all of the information provided in the box in the top-right corner of this page.

- Practice Direction A accompanying Part 14 of the Court of Protection Rules 2007 sets out more detailed requirements in relation to witness statements.

- Please continue on a separate sheet of paper if you need more space to provide your witness statement. Please mark each separate sheet with all of the information provided in the box in the top-right corner of this page.

- If you need help completing this form please check the website, www.hmcourts-service.gov.uk or www.direct.gov.uk, for further guidance or information, or contact Court Enquiry Service on 0300 456 4600 or courtofprotectionenquiries@ hmcourts-service.gsi.gov.uk

- Court of Protection staff cannot give legal advice. If you need legal advice please contact a solicitor.

PART VII

Witness statement

1 Enter your full name

I, **1**

2 Enter your occupation or description

2

3 Enter your full address including postcode or, if making the statement in your professional, business or other occupational capacity, the position you hold, the name of your firm or employer and the address at which you work

of **3**

☐ am a party to the proceedings

☐ am employed by a party to the proceedings

and state that:

4 Set out in numbered paragraphs indicating:

- which of the statements are from your own knowledge and which are matters of information or belief, and

- the source for any matters of information or belief.

Where you refer to an exhibit, you should state the identifier you have used. For example, 'I refer to the (description of document) marked Exhibit A...'

4

continued over

2

4

continued over

PART VII

3

1487

4

Statement of truth

The statement of truth is to be signed by the witness.

I believe that the facts stated in this witness statement are true.

Signed

Name   **Date**

Please return the completed witness statement to:
Court of Protection, Archway Tower, 2 Junction Road, London N19 5SZ

4

Form COP25 – Affidavit

COP 25 **03.10** Court of Protection **Affidavit**	Sworn by (name of deponent)
	Affidavit ☐ 1st ☐ 2nd ☐ 3rd ☐ Other _____
	Filed on behalf of (name of party)
	Date sworn

Case no.

Full name of person to whom the application relates
(this is the person who lacks, or is alleged to lack, capacity)

Please read first

- If the court requires that evidence be given by affidavit then it must be included in or attached to this form.
- Only the following may administer oaths:
  - Commissioners for Oaths;
  - practising solicitors;
  - other persons specified by statute;
  - certain officials of the Supreme Court;
  - a circuit judge or district judge;
  - any justice of the peace;
  - certain officials of the county court.
- Practice Direction A accompanying Part 14 of the Court of Protection Rules 2007 sets out more detailed requirements in relation to affidavits.

- Please continue on a separate sheet of paper if you need more space to provide the affidavit. Please mark each separate sheet with all of the information provided in the box in the top-right corner of this page.
- If you need help completing this form please check the website, www.hmcourts-service.gov.uk or www.direct.gov.uk, for further guidance or information, or contact Court Enquiry Service on 0300 456 4600 or courtofprotectionenquiries@hmcourts-service.gsi.gov.uk
- Court of Protection staff cannot give legal advice. If you need legal advice please contact a solicitor.

PART VII

Affidavit

1 Enter full name of deponent	I, **1**
2 Enter occupation or description	**2**
3 Enter your full address including postcode or, if making the affidavit in your professional, business or other occupational capacity, the position you hold, the name of your firm or employer and the address at which you work	of **3**

☐ am a party to the proceedings

☐ am employed by a party to the proceedings

and ☐ state on oath **or** ☐ do solemnly and sincerely affirm

4 Set out in numbered paragraphs indicating:

- which of the statements are from your own knowledge and which are matters of information or belief, and

- the source for any matters of information or belief.

Where you refer to an exhibit, you should state the identifier you have used. For example, 'I refer to the (description of document) marked Exhibit A...'

4

continued over

2

4

continued over

PART VII

3

4

Sworn/affirmed by (signature)

before me (signature)

Full name

Qualifications

at (address)

On (date)

Please return the completed affidavit to:
Court of Protection, Archway Tower, 2 Junction Road, London N19 5SZ

4

Form COP29 – Notice of hearing for committal order

COP 29 03.10

Court of Protection

Notice of hearing for committal order

For office use only

To (enter name and address of person to be notified)

Name

Address

This notice is to tell you that the hearing date for the following case has been fixed.

Details of the case

Case no.

Applicant

Details of the hearing

Date   Time

Location

Important notice

The court has the power to send you to prison and to fine you if it finds that any of the allegations made against you are true and amount to a contempt of court.

You must attend court on the date shown on this form. It is in your own interest to do so. You should bring with you any witnesses and documents which you think will help you put your side of the case.

If you consider the allegations are not true you must tell the court why. If it is established that they are true, you must tell the court of any good reason why they do not amount to a contempt of court, or, if they do, why you should not be punished.

If you have any questions or need further information about the hearing please check the website, www.hmcourts-service.gov.uk or www.direct.gov.uk or contact Court Enquiry Service on 0300 456 4600. Court of Protection staff cannot give legal advice. If you need legal advice please contact a solicitor.

If you need any special assistance or facilities to attend the hearing please contact Court Enquiry Service on the number above immediately so that arrangements can be made (if you have not done so already).

© Crown Copyright 2010

PART VII

Form COP30 – Notice of change of solicitor

COP
30
03.10

Court of Protection

Notice of change of solicitor

For office use only

Case no.

Full name of person to whom the application relates
(this is the person who lacks, or is alleged to lack, capacity)

Please read first

- You must complete this notice and file it with the court if you:

    – are changing the solicitor who is acting for you;

    – have been conducting the proceedings in person and are now appointing a solicitor to act on your behalf; or

    – have had a solicitor acting on your behalf and now intend to act in person.

- If you are applying for an order declaring that the solicitor acting for another party has ceased to act, then you need to use the COP9 application notice.

- You must provide a copy of this notice to every other party to the proceedings. If applicable, you must also provide a copy to the solicitor who is ceasing to act for you.

- The court will not consider that a change has occurred until you have filed this notice.

- Please continue on a separate sheet of paper if you need more space to answer a question. Write the case number, your name, the name of the person to whom the application relates, and the number of the question you are answering on each separate sheet.

- If you need help completing this form please check the website, www.hmcourts-service.gov.uk or www.direct.gov.uk, for further guidance or information, or contact Court Enquiry Service on 0300 456 4600 or courtofprotectionenquiries@ hmcourts-service.gsi.gov.uk.

- Court of Protection staff cannot give legal advice. If you need legal advice please contact a solicitor.

1

© Crown Copyright 2010

Section 1 - Your details (party changing solicitor)

1.1   ☐ Mr.   ☐ Mrs.   ☐ Miss   ☐ Ms.   ☐ Other _____

First name

Middle name(s)

Last name

Address
(including
postcode)

Telephone no.

1.2   What is your role in these proceedings?

☐ Applicant (the person who filed the COP1 application form)

☐ Respondent

☐ Other (please provide details)

Section 2 - Change of solicitor

2.1   I give notice that:

☐ I am changing the solicitor who is acting for me.

☐ I have been conducting the proceedings in person but am now appointing a solicitor to act on my behalf.

☐ I have had a solicitor acting on my behalf but now intend to act in person.

2

PART VII

2.2   Details of solicitor being appointed (if applicable)

Name of solicitor

Name of firm

Address
(including postcode)

Telephone no.   Fax no.

DX no.

E-mail address

2.3   Details of solicitor who will cease to act (if applicable)

2.4   Which address should official documentation be sent to?

☐ Your address

☐ Solicitor's address

☐ Other address (please provide details)

2.5   Please tick to confirm:

☐ I have provided a copy of this notice to every other party to the proceedings and to my former solicitor (if applicable).

Section 3 – Signature

Signed   Name
                                              of firm

Name   Position or
                                              office held

Date

Please return the completed certificate to:
Court of Protection, Archway Tower, 2 Junction Road, London N19 5SZ

3

Form COP31 – Notice of intention to file evidence by deposition

COP 31 03.10 Court of Protection

Notice of intention to file evidence by deposition

For office use only

Case no.

Full name of person to whom the application relates
(this is the person who lacks, or is alleged to lack, capacity)

Please read first

- If you intend to use a deposition as evidence at a hearing then you must complete this notice to inform the court.

- You must file this notice at least 14 days before the date fixed for the hearing.

- You must provide a copy of this notice to every other party to the proceedings.

- The court may require the deponent (the person who was examined) to attend the hearing and give evidence in person.

- Please continue on a separate sheet of paper if you need more space to answer a question. Write the case number, your name, the name of the person to whom the application relates, and the number of the question you are answering on each separate sheet.

- If you need help completing this form please check the website, www.hmcourts-service.gov.uk or www.direct.gov.uk, for further guidance or information, or contact Court Enquiry Service on 0300 456 4600 or courtofprotectionenquiries@hmcourts-service.gsi.gov.uk

- Court of Protection staff cannot give legal advice. If you need legal advice please contact a solicitor.

PART VII

1

© Crown Copyright 2010

Section 1 - Your details (party intending to file evidence by deposition)

1.1   ☐ Mr.   ☐ Mrs.   ☐ Miss   ☐ Ms.   ☐ Other

Full name

1.2   Address
       (including
       postcode)

       Telephone no.

1.3   What is your role in these proceedings?

       ☐ Applicant (the person who filed the COP1 application form)

       ☐ Respondent

       ☐ Other (please provide details)

Section 2 - Evidence by deposition

2.1   I intend to put a deposition in evidence at the hearing fixed to | D | D | M | M | Y | Y | Y | Y |
       take place on

2.2   Full name of deponent (person who gave evidence by deposition)

Section 3 – Signature

Signed   Name
                                                    of firm

Name   Position or
                                                    office held

Date

Please return the completed certificate to:
Court of Protection, Archway Tower, 2 Junction Road, London N19 5SZ

2

Form COP35 – Appellant's notice

COP 35 Court of Protection
03.10 **Appellant's notice**

For office use only
Date received
Appeal case no.
Date issued

Full name of person to whom the proceedings relate
(this is the person who lacks, or is alleged to lack, capacity)

SEAL

Please read first

- If you wish to appeal against a decision of the Court of Protection then you must complete this form and file it with the court.

- Do not use this form if you are appealing to the Court of Appeal. You need to follow the Court of Appeal procedures.

- The first person to appeal against any decision of the court is called the appellant. Any other party to the appeal is called a respondent.

- Respondents can apply for permission if they wish to make an additional, different appeal, or can apply to have the order of the first instance judge upheld on different or additional grounds by filing a COP36 respondent's notice.

- You have limited time to file your appellant's notice with the court. You must file it:
  - within the time limit set by the first instance judge; or
  - where the first instance judge did not set a time limit, within 21 days of the date of the decision you wish to appeal against.

- You must pay a fee when you file an appellant's notice. Please refer to the fees leaflet for details.

- You may need to pay for any costs you incur during proceedings. If the court considers that you have acted unreasonably you can be ordered to pay the costs incurred by other parties.

- Please continue on a separate sheet of paper if you need more space to answer a question. Write your name, the name and date of birth of the person to whom the application relates, and the number of the question you are answering on each separate sheet.

- There are additional guidance notes at the end of this form.

- If you need help completing this form please check the website, www.hmcourts-service.gov.uk or www.direct.gov.uk, for further guidance or information, or contact Court Enquiry Service on 0300 456 4600 or courtofprotectionenquiries@hmcourts-service.gsi.gov.uk

- Court of Protection staff cannot give legal advice. If you need legal advice please contact a solicitor.

PART VII

Section 1 – Details of the decision you are appealing against

1.1   Case number

[   ]

1.2   The name of the first instance judge (the judge whose decision you want to appeal)

[   ]

1.3   Status of the first instance judge, if known

☐ Circuit judge

☐ District judge

1.4   Date of the decision you wish to appeal

D	D	M	M	Y	Y	Y	Y

1.5   Address of the person to whom the proceedings relate

[   ]

1.5   Date of birth of the person to whom the proceedings relate

D	D	M	M	Y	Y	Y	Y

2

Section 2 – Details of appellant and respondent(s)

Your details (the appellant)

2.1   Your details   ☐ Mr.   ☐ Mrs.   ☐ Miss   ☐ Ms.   ☐ Other _____

First name

Middle name(s)

Last name

2.2   Address
(including
postcode)

Telephone no. | Daytime |
                 | Evening |
                 | Mobile |

E-mail address

2.3   Is a solicitor representing you?   ☐ Yes   ☐ No

If Yes, please give the solicitor's details.

Name

Address
(including
postcode)

Telephone no.   Fax no.

DX no.

E-mail address

PART VII

2.5   Which address should official documentation be sent to?

☐ Your address

☐ Solicitor's address

☐ Other address (please provide details)

Details of respondent(s) to the appeal (see note 1)

2.6

Full name including title	Full address including postcode

Section 3 – Application for permission to appeal

3.1   Do you need permission from the court to appeal? **(see note 2)**

☐ Yes

☐ No, I am appealing against an order for committal to prison

3.2   If Yes, has permission to appeal been granted?

☐ Yes

☐ No, I now seek permission to appeal

4

Section 4 - Details of appeal

4.1   Nature of decision you wish to appeal **(see note 3)**

☐ Case management decision

☐ Grant or refusal of an interim application

☐ Final decision

☐ Other (please give details)

4.2   What are you asking the appeal judge to do? **(see note 4)**

4.3   If you are asking the appeal judge to affirm, set aside or vary part of the order please specify which part

5

Section 5 – Grounds for appeal and skeleton argument

5.1   Please set out your grounds for appeal. **(see note 5)**

5.2   Please use the COP37 skeleton argument form for your arguments in support of your grounds for appeal.

A skeleton argument: (tick only one box)

☐ is filed with this notice; or

☐ will follow within 21 days of filing this notice.

6

Section 6 – Other applications

Please complete this section if you are asking for orders in addition to the order asked for in section 4.2. If you make other applications with your appellant's notice the court can either deal with these at any hearing which deals with your application for permission to appeal, or at another separate hearing before the hearing of your appeal.

6.1   Are you applying for a stay of execution of any order against you?   ☐Yes   ☐No

If Yes, please state why you are applying for a stay of execution.

6.2   Are you applying for an extension of time for filing the appellant's notice? **(see note 6)**   ☐Yes   ☐No

If Yes, please state the reasons for the delay.

6.3   Are you making any other applications to the court? **(see note 7)**   ☐Yes   ☐No

If Yes, please state what order you are asking the court to make and state the reasons for your application.

PART VII

Evidence in support

6.4   Any evidence in support of other applications must be filed with this appellant's notice. If you are attaching any written evidence please use the COP24 witness statement form.   ☐Evidence attached

Section 7 – Supporting documents

7.1   To support your appeal you should file all relevant documents listed below with this notice. To show which documents you are filing, please tick the appropriate boxes.

☐ Two copies of your appellant's notice for the court (i.e. the original plus one copy);

☐ One copy of your skeleton argument;

☐ A sealed (stamped by the court) copy of the order being appealed;

☐ A suitable record of the judgment of the first instance judge;

☐ A copy of any order giving or refusing permission to appeal, together with a copy of the judge's reasons for allowing or refusing permission to appeal;

☐ Any witness statements or affidavits in support of any other applications included in your appellant's notice;

☐ The application form and any application notice or response (where relevant to the subject of the appeal);

☐ In cases where the decision itself was made on appeal, the order of the first instance judge, the reasons given and the appellant's notice used to appeal from that order;

☐ Any other documents which you reasonably consider necessary to enable the court to reach its decision on the hearing of the application or appeal; and

☐ Such other documents as the court may direct.

7.2   If you have not been able to obtain any of the documents listed in 7.1 within the time allowed to file the appellant's notice please list the documents in the table and explain why you cannot provide them. You will still need to file the documents with the court – please give the date you expect to be able to do so.

Title of document	Reason not supplied	Date when it will be supplied

8

Section 8 - Statement of truth

The statement of truth is to be signed by you, your solicitor or your litigation friend.

*(I believe) (The appellant believes) that the facts stated in this appellant's notice are true.

Signed

*Appellant('s solicitor)('s litigation friend)

Name

Date

Name of firm

Position or office held

* Please delete the options in brackets that do not apply.

Now read note 8 about what you need to do next.

9

Guidance notes

Note 1

Details of respondent(s) to the appeal

You must provide the details of the parties to the proceedings before the first instance judge who are affected by the appeal. You must serve respondents with copies of all documents relating to your appeal when the court has issued your appellant's notice in order to allow them the opportunity to respond.

Note 2

Application for permission to appeal

You do not need permission from the court to appeal if the order you are appealing against is an order for committal to prison.

You do need permission to appeal against any other order. Permission to appeal will be granted only where:

- the court considers that the appeal would have a real prospect of success; or
- there is some other compelling reason why the appeal should be heard.

Note 3

Details of appeal

Case management decisions include orders relating to:

- the timetable for hearing;
- the filing and exchange of information (of witnesses and experts);
- disclosure of documents; or
- adding a party to proceedings.

A grant or refusal of an interim application might include an injunction to prevent you from doing something or a declaration confirming an action is lawful.

Note 4

What are you asking the appeal judge to do?

You need to explain in section 4.3 what order you are asking the court to make. Please be specific about what you are asking the appeal judge to do. The appeal judge has the power to:

- affirm, set aside or vary any order made by the first instance judge;
- refer any claim or issue to that judge for determination;
- order a new hearing; or
- make a costs order.

Note 5

Grounds for appeal and arguments in support

An appeal must be based on relevant grounds (i.e. reasons for appealing). An appeal judge will only allow an appeal against a decision that is either wrong or unjust because of a serious procedural or other irregularity in the proceedings before the first instance judge.

Please set out briefly why you are appealing the judge's decision. Remember that you must not include any grounds for appeal that rely on new evidence (that is evidence that has become available since the order was made). You may not produce new evidence in your appeal unless the court allows you to do so (see section 6).

Note 6

Extension of time for filing the appellant's notice

If the time for filing your appellant's notice has expired then you need to file this notice and include an application for an extension of time. You need to state the reason(s) for the delay and the steps you have taken in attempting to avoid the delay.

Note 7

Other applications

If you wish to produce new evidence in your appeal you need to apply to the court to do so. You need to tell the court why the evidence was not available to the first instance judge and explain why you think it is necessary for the appeal.

10

Note 8

What you need to do next

Please return the appellant's notice and supporting documents to:

> Court of Protection
> Archway Tower
> 2 Junction Road
> London N19 5SZ

If your skeleton argument will follow your appellant's notice, it must be filed within 21 days of the appellant's notice.

Any supporting documents that you cannot obtain in time to file with your appellant's notice must be filed with the court in such time as the court may direct, and in any case as soon as possible.

Note 9

What happens next?

If you need permission to appeal

The court will tell you if permission is granted, refused or if a date has been fixed for a hearing of the application for permission.

If permission is granted the court will issue your appellant's notice and will return a sealed copy. You will need to serve a copy on each respondent and notify the person to whom the proceedings relate.

If you already have permission, or do not need permission to appeal

The court will issue your appellant's notice and will return a sealed copy. You will need to serve a copy on each respondent and notify the person to whom the proceedings relate.

PART VII

11

Form COP36 – Respondent's notice

COP
36
03.10
Court of Protection
Respondent's notice

For office use only
Date received
Date issued

Appeal case no.

Full name of person to whom the proceedings relate
(this is the person who lacks, or is alleged to lack, capacity)

SEAL

Please read first

- You must file this respondent's notice if you are served with a COP35 appellant's notice and you wish to:
  - appeal on different grounds against the same order; or
  - ask the court to uphold the order of the first instance judge for reasons different from, or additional to, those given by the first instance judge.
- You do not need to file a respondent's notice if you:
  - agree with the original order and reasons given by the first instance judge; or
  - agree with the appellant and support the appeal.
- The first person to appeal against any decision of the court is called the appellant. Any other party to the appeal is a respondent.
- You must file your respondent's notice:
  - within the time limit set by the first instance judge; or
  - where the first instance judge has set no time limit, within 21 days beginning with the date you were served with:
    - the appellant's notice, where permission to appeal has been given or is not required; or
    - notification that permission has been granted; or
    - notification that the application for permission and the appeal are to be heard together.

- You may need to pay for any costs you incur during proceedings. If the court considers that you have acted unreasonably you can be ordered to pay the costs incurred by other parties.
- Please continue on a separate sheet of paper if you need more space to answer a question. Write the appeal case number, your name, the name of the person to whom the application relates, and the number of the question you are answering on each separate sheet.
- There are additional guidance notes at the end of this form.
- If you need help completing this form please check the website, www.hmcourts-service.gov.uk or www.direct.gov.uk, for further guidance or information, or contact Court Enquiry Service on 0300 456 4600 or courtofprotectionenquiries@hmcourts-service.gsi.gov.uk
- Court of Protection staff cannot give legal advice. If you need legal advice please contact a solicitor.

1

© Crown Copyright 2010

Section 1 – Details of the case being appealed

1.1   Case number

Section 2 – Your details (the respondent)

2.1   ☐ Mr.   ☐ Mrs.   ☐ Miss   ☐ Ms.   ☐ Other _____

First name

Middle name

Last name

2.2   Address (including postcode)

Telephone no.

Daytime	
Evening	
Mobile	

E-mail address

2.3   Is a solicitor representing you?   ☐ Yes   ☐ No

If Yes, please give the solicitor's details.

Name

Address (including postcode)

Telephone no.   Fax no.

DX no.

E-mail address

PART VII

2.4   To which address should all official documentation be sent?

☐ Your address

☐ Solicitor's address

☐ Other address (please provide details)

```
┌─────────────────────────────────────────────────────────┐
│                                                           │
│                                                           │
│                                                           │
│                                                           │
│                                                           │
└─────────────────────────────────────────────────────────┘
```

Section 3 – Application for permission to make a different appeal

If you wish only to ask that the appeal judge upholds the judgment or order of the first instance judge you do not require permission - please go to section 4.

3.1   Do you need permission from the court to appeal? **(see note 1)**

☐ Yes

☐ No, I am appealing an order for committal to prison

3.2   If Yes, has permission to appeal been granted?

☐ Yes

☐ No, I now seek permission to appeal

Section 4 - Details of response to appeal

4.1   Nature of decision you wish to appeal **(see note 2)**

☐ Case management decision

☐ Grant or refusal of an interim application

☐ Final decision

☐ Other (please give details)

```
┌─────────────────────────────────────────────────────────┐
│                                                           │
│                                                           │
│                                                           │
│                                                           │
│                                                           │
│                                                           │
└─────────────────────────────────────────────────────────┘
```

3

4.2   What are you asking the appeal judge to do? **(see note 3)**

4.3   If you are asking the appeal judge to affirm, set aside or vary part of the order please specify which part.

4.4   If you are asking the appeal judge to uphold an order on different or additional grounds please specify those grounds.

PART VII

4

Section 5 – Grounds for response to an appeal and skeleton argument

5.1   Please set out your grounds for appeal. **(see note 4)**

5.2   Please use the COP37 skeleton argument form for your arguments in support of your grounds for appeal.

A skeleton argument: (tick only one box)

☐ is filed with this notice; or

☐ will follow within 21 days of filing this notice.

5

Section 6 – Other applications

Please complete this section if you are asking for orders in addition to the order asked for in section 4.2. If you make other applications with your respondent's notice the court can either deal with these at any hearing which deals with your application for permission to appeal, or at another separate hearing before the hearing of your appeal.

6.1   Are you applying for a stay of execution of any order against you?   ☐ Yes   ☐ No

If Yes, please state why you are applying for a stay of execution.

6.2   Are you applying for an extension of time for filing the respondent's notice? **(see note 5)**   ☐ Yes   ☐ No

If Yes, please state the reasons for the delay.

6.3   Are you making any other applications to the court? **(see note 6)**   ☐ Yes   ☐ No

If Yes, please state what order you are asking the court to make and state the reasons for your application.

PART VII

Evidence in support

6.4   Any evidence in support of other applications must be filed with this respondent's notice. If you are attaching any written evidence please use the COP24 witness statement form.   ☐ Evidence attached

6

Section 7 – Supporting documents

7.1   To support your appeal you should file all relevant documents listed below with this notice. To show which documents you are filing, please tick the appropriate boxes.

        ☐ Two copies of your respondent's notice for the court (i.e. the original and one copy);

        ☐ One copy of your skeleton argument;

        ☐ A sealed copy of the order being appealed;

        ☐ A copy of any order giving or refusing permission to appeal, together with a copy of the judge's reasons for allowing or refusing permission to appeal;

        ☐ Any witness statements or affidavits in support of any other applications included in your respondent's notice;

        ☐ Any other documents which you reasonably consider necessary to enable the court to reach its decision on the hearing of your application or appeal; and

        ☐ Such other documents as the court may direct.

7.2   If you have not been able to obtain any of the documents listed in 7.1 within the time allowed to file the respondent's notice please list the documents in the table and explain why you cannot provide them. You will still need to file the documents with the court. Please give the date you expect to be able to do so.

Title of document	Reason not supplied	Date when it will be supplied

7

Section 8 - Statement of truth

The statement of truth is to be signed by you, your solicitor or your litigation friend.

*(I believe) (The respondent believes) that the facts stated in this respondent's notice are true.

Signed

*Respondent('s solicitor)('s litigation friend)

Name

Date

Name of firm

Position or office held

* Please delete the options in brackets that do not apply.

Now read note 7 about what you need to do next.

8

Guidance notes

Application for permission to make a different appeal

You do not need permission from the court to appeal if the order you are appealing against is an order for committal to prison.

You do need permission to appeal against any other order. Permission to appeal will be granted only where:

- the court considers that the appeal would have a real prospect of success; or
- there is some other compelling reason why the appeal should be heard.

Note 2

Nature of the decision you want to appeal

Case management decisions include orders relating to:

- the timetable for hearing;
- the filing and exchange of information (of witnesses and experts);
- disclosure of documents; or
- adding a party to proceedings.

A grant or refusal of an interim application might include an injunction to prevent you from doing something or a declaration confirming an action is lawful.

Note 3

What are you asking the appeal judge to do?

You need to explain in section 4.2 what order you are asking the court to make. Please be specific about what you are asking the appeal judge to do. The appeal judge has the power to:

- affirm, set aside or vary any order made by the first instance judge;
- refer any claim or issue to that judge for determination;
- order a new hearing; or
- make a costs order.

Note 4

Grounds for response to appeal

Your response to an appeal must be based on relevant grounds. This applies if you wish to appeal the order, or if you wish the appeal judge to uphold the order on different or additional grounds. An appeal judge will only allow an appeal against a decision that is either wrong or unjust because of a serious procedural or other irregularity in the proceedings before the first instance judge.

Please set out briefly your grounds for appeal or for seeking to uphold the order. Remember that you must not include any grounds for appeal or for upholding the order that rely on new evidence (that is evidence that has become available since the order was made). You may not produce new evidence in your appeal unless the court allows you to do so (see section 6).

Note 5

Extension of time for filing the respondent's notice

Where the time for filing your respondent's notice has expired, you need to file this notice and include an application for an extension of time. You need to state the reason(s) for the delay and the steps you have taken in attempting to avoid the delay.

Note 6

Other applications

If you wish to produce new evidence in your appeal you need to apply to the court to do so. You need to tell the court why the evidence was not available to the first instance judge and explain why you think it is necessary for the appeal.

Note 7

What you need to do next

Please return the respondent's notice and supporting documents to:

Court of Protection
Archway Tower
2 Junction Road
London N19 5SZ

If your skeleton argument will follow your respondent's notice, it must be filed within 21 days of the respondent's notice.

Any supporting documents that you cannot obtain in time to file with your respondent's notice must be filed with the court in such time as the court may direct, and in any case as soon as possible.

9

Note 8

What happens next?

If you need permission to appeal

The court will tell you if permission is granted, refused or if a date has been fixed for a hearing of the application for permission.

If permission is granted, the court will issue your respondent's notice and will return a sealed copy. You will need to serve a copy on the appellant and any other respondents.

If you already have permission, or do not need permission to appeal

The court will issue your respondent's notice and will return a sealed copy. You will need to serve a copy on the appellant and any other respondents.

10

PART VII

Form COP37 – Skeleton argument

COP 37 10.07	Court of Protection **Skeleton argument**

Section 1 – Details of the case being appealed

Appeal case no.

Case no.

Full name of person to whom the application relates
(this is the name of the person who lacks, or is alleged to lack, capacity)

Section 2 – Your details

In the appeal, are you the:

☐ Appellant
☐ Respondent

☐ Mr.   ☐ Mrs.   ☐ Miss   ☐ Ms.   ☐ Other _____

First name

Last name

Address
(including
postcode)

Telephone no.

Daytime	
Mobile	

Section 3 – Skeleton argument

I *(the appellant)(the respondent) will rely on the following arguments at the hearing of the appeal.

Section 3 – Signature

Signed		**Name of firm**
Name		**Position or office held**
Date		

Now read note 2 about what you need to do next.

PART VII

COP37 – Guidance notes

Guidance notes

Note 1

Skeleton argument

A skeleton argument must contain a numbered list of the points which you wish to make. These should both define and confine the areas of controversy. Each point should be stated as concisely as the nature of the case allows.

A numbered point must be followed by a reference to any document on which you wish to rely.

A skeleton argument must state, in respect of each authority cited:

a) the proposition of law that the authority demonstrates; and

b) the parts of the authority (identified by page or paragraph references) that support the proposition.

If more than one authority is cited in support of a given proposition, the skeleton argument must briefly state the reason for taking that course. This statement should not materially add to the length of the skeleton argument but should be sufficient to demonstrate, in the context of the argument:

a) the relevance of the authority or authorities to that argument; and

b) that the citation is necessary for a proper presentation of that argument.

Please continue on a separate sheet of paper if you need more space to provide your skeleton argument. Write your name, the name of the person to whom the proceedings relate and the case number of the case you are appealing against on each separate sheet.

Note 2

What you need to do next

The skeleton argument is to be filed with your appellant's/respondent's notice. Where you are unable to provide it with your appellant's / respondent's notice you must file it and serve it on all parties to the proceedings within 21 days of filing your appellant's / respondent's notice.

The court requires two copies (i.e. the original plus one copy) of the skeleton argument.

Please return the original completed form and copy to:

> Court of Protection
> Archway Tower
> 2 Junction Road
> London N19 5SZ

LASTING POWERS OF ATTORNEY FORMS

These forms are taken from the Lasting Powers of Attorney, Enduring Powers of Attorney and Public Guardian Regulations 2007 (SI 2007/1253), as amended by the Lasting Powers of Attorney, Enduring Powers of Attorney and Public Guardian (Amendment) Regulations 2009 (SI 2009/1884).

Form LPA PFA and LPA HW – Form for Instrument Intended to Create a Lasting Power of Attorney

Part 1: Form for Instrument Intended to Create a Property and Financial Affairs Lasting Power of Attorney

Page 1 of 11 – **Keep all pages of this form together**

For OPG office use only

LPA PA
registered on

OPG reference
number

Office of the Public Guardian

Lasting power of attorney – property and financial affairs

About this lasting power of attorney

This lasting power of attorney allows you to choose people to act on your behalf (as an attorney) and make decisions about your **property and financial affairs**, when you are unable to make decisions for yourself.

If you also want someone to make decisions about your **health and welfare**, you will need a separate form (downloadable from our website or call 0300 456 0300).

Who can fill it in?

Anyone aged 18 or over, who has the mental capacity to do so.

Before you fill in the lasting power of attorney:

1. Please read the guidance available at **publicguardian.gov.uk** or by calling **0300 456 0300**. See, for example, the *Lasting power of attorney creation pack* or other relevant guidance booklets which are all available online or by post.

2. Make sure you understand the purpose of this lasting power of attorney and the extent of the authority you are giving your attorneys.

3. Read the separate **Information sheet** to understand all the people involved, and how the three parts of the form should be filled in.

4. Make sure you, your certificate provider(s), and your attorney(s) have read the section on page 2 called **Information you must read** before filling in their relevant part.

> **!** This lasting power of attorney could be rejected at registration if it contains any errors.

Checklist

See the information sheet for guidance on all the people involved

Part A: about you, the attorneys you are appointing, and people to be told

How many **attorneys** are you appointing? *Write in words.*

How many **replacement attorneys** are you appointing? *Write in words or write 'None' if this does not apply.*

How many **people to be told** are you choosing? *Write in words from 'None' to 'five'. If 'None' you must have two certificate providers in part B.*

Part B: about your certificate providers

How many **certificate providers do you have?** *(Tick one box)*

☐ One   OR   ☐ Two

If you have used any continuation sheets each one must be signed and dated.

Attached to the back of this lasting power of attorney are:
(Write the number of each)

continuation sheet A1	0
continuation sheet A2	0
continuation sheet A3:PFA	0
continuation sheet B	0
continuation sheet C	0
Total number of continuation sheets	0

LPA PA 10 09   © Crown copyright 2009

Information you must read ❗

This lasting power of attorney is a legal document.
Each person who signs parts A, B and C must read this information before signing.

Purpose of this lasting power of attorney

This lasting power of attorney gives your attorneys authority to make decisions about your property and financial affairs when you cannot make your own decisions. This can include running your bank accounts and savings accounts, decisions about making or selling investments and selling property, and spending your money.

When your attorneys can act for you

Your attorneys can use this lasting power of attorney only after it has been registered and stamped on every page by the Office of the Public Guardian. Your attorneys can make decisions for you as soon as this lasting power of attorney is registered – both when you have mental capacity and when you lack mental capacity, unless you put a restriction in this lasting power of attorney.

The Mental Capacity Act

Your attorneys cannot do whatever they like. They **must** follow the principles of the Mental Capacity Act 2005.

Guidance about these principles is in the Mental Capacity Act Code of Practice. Your attorneys must have regard to the Code of Practice. They can get a copy from The Stationery Office at **tso. co.uk** or read it online at **publicguardian.gov.uk**

Principles of the Act that your attorneys must follow

1 Your attorneys must assume that you can make your own decisions unless they establish that you cannot do so.

2 Your attorneys must help you to make as many of your own decisions as you can. They cannot treat you as unable to make the decision in question unless all practicable steps to help you to do so have been made without success.

3 Your attorneys must not treat you as unable to make the decision in question simply because you make an unwise decision.

4 Your attorneys must make decisions and act in your best interests when you are unable to make the decision in question.

5 Before your attorneys make the decision in question or act for you, they must consider whether they can make the decision or act in a way that is less restrictive of your rights and freedom but still achieves the purpose.

Your best interests

Your attorneys must act in your best interests in making decisions for you when you are unable to make the decision yourself. They must take into account all the relevant circumstances. This includes, if appropriate, consulting you and others who are interested in your welfare. Any guidance you add may assist your attorneys in identifying your views.

Cancelling this lasting power of attorney

You can cancel this lasting power of attorney at any time before or after it is registered as long as you have mental capacity to cancel it. Please read the guidance available at **publicguardian.gov.uk**

How to fill in this form

• Tick the boxes that apply like this ✔

• Use black or blue ink and write clearly

• Cross through any boxes or sections that don't apply to you, like this:

> Any other names you are known by in financial documents or accounts
>
> ▬▬▬▬▬▬▬▬▬▬▬▬▬▬▬▬

• Don't use correction fluid – please cross out any mistakes and rewrite nearby. All corrections must be initialled by the person completing that section of the form (and their witness) like this:

> Any other names you are known by in financial documents or accounts
>
> *WILLIAM EDWARD ~~SMITH~~*
> *A.S.B / W.E.S.   SMYTH*

• Your application could be rejected if your intentions are not clear and explicit. If you are in any doubt, please start again on a new copy of the form.

What happens after you've filled it in?

The next step is to **register** it. You or your attorneys can do this at any time. The person applying will need to fill in a registration form and may need to pay a fee at that time. They will also need to send notices to the 'people to be told' named at part A when the application to register this lasting power of attorney is made. You can find out more and download the registration form at **publicguardian.gov.uk**

The 'people to be told' are given time to raise any concerns or objections. This means the earliest the Office of Public Guardian can register this lasting power of attorney is 6 weeks after they notify the donor or attorneys that an application to register has been received.

Your lasting power of attorney will **end** if it can no longer be used. For example, if a sole attorney dies or can no longer act for you and no replacement attorney has been named in this lasting power of attorney. Please read the guidance available at **publicguardian.gov.uk**

PART VII

Valid only with Office of the Public Guardian stamp

Part A Declaration by the person who is giving this lasting power of attorney

Please write clearly using black or blue ink.

1   About the person who is giving this lasting power of attorney

Mr   Mrs   Ms   Miss   Other title

First names

Last name

Date of birth

D D M M Y Y Y Y

Address and postcode

Postcode

Any other names you are known by in financial documents or accounts

2   About the attorneys you are appointing

If you are appointing a trust corporation alone, cross through this section and go to 2A →

Thinking about your attorneys

- You can appoint more than one attorney if you want to. You do not have to appoint more than one attorney.
- Each attorney must be aged 18 or over. Choose people you know and trust to make decisions for you. You are recommended to read the separate guidance for people who want to make a lasting power of attorney for property and financial affairs.
- Your attorney must not be bankrupt.

Your first or only attorney

Mr   Mrs   Ms   Miss   Other title

First names of your first or only attorney

Last name of your first or only attorney

Date of birth of your first or only attorney

D D M M Y Y Y Y

Address and postcode of your first or only attorney

Postcode

Your second attorney
Please cross through this section if it does not apply.

Mr   Mrs   Ms   Miss   Other title

First names of your second attorney

Last name of your second attorney

Date of birth of your second attorney

D D M M Y Y Y Y

Address and postcode of your second attorney

Postcode

If you are appointing more than two attorneys, use continuation sheet A1 to tell us about your other attorneys.

Other attorneys you are appointing

Number of attorneys named in continuation sheet **A1** attached to this lasting power of attorney

Cross through this box if this does not apply

Helpline
☎ **0300 456 0300**
🖱 publicguardian.gov.uk

Valid only with Office of the Public Guardian stamp

Lasting power of attorney for property and financial affairs

2A About appointing a trust corporation as attorney or replacement attorney

About the trust corporation you are appointing *Please cross through this section if it does not apply.*

• A trust corporation cannot be going through winding-up proceedings.

Company name

Address

Are you appointing this trust corporation to act as an

☐ attorney, or

☐ replacement attorney?

Postcode

3 About appointing replacements if an attorney can no longer act

If you are appointing a trust corporation as replacement attorney, cross through this section.
Your trust corporation should then fill in continuation sheet C →

Thinking about replacement attorneys

• Replacement attorneys will only act once your attorney can no longer act for you.

• You can appoint replacements to replace an attorney who does not want to act for you or who is permanently no longer able to act because they are dead, bankrupt, have disclaimed, lack mental capacity or if they were married to you or were your civil partner, and have now had the marriage or civil partnership annulled or dissolved.

• You do not have to appoint any replacements.

• If you appoint only one attorney and no replacements, this lasting power of attorney will end when your attorney can no longer act.

Your first or only replacement attorney *Please cross through this section if it does not apply.*

Mr   Mrs   Ms   Miss   Other title
☐   ☐   ☐   ☐

Date of birth of your first or only replacement

D D M M Y Y Y Y

First names of your first or only replacement

Address and postcode of your first or only replacement

Last name of your first or only replacement

Postcode

If you are appointing more than one replacement, use continuation sheet A1 to tell us about your other replacement attorneys.

Other replacement attorneys you are appointing

Number of replacement attorneys named in continuation sheet **A1** attached to this lasting power of attorney

Cross through this box if this does not apply

Valid only with Office of the Public Guardian stamp

4   How you want your attorneys to make decisions

Thinking about how you want your attorneys to make decisions

⚠ If you leave this section blank, your attorneys will be appointed to make all decisions jointly.

- **Jointly**: this means that the attorneys must **make all decisions together**. → *For further information on appointing your attorneys jointly, see the separate guidance.*

- **Jointly and severally**: this means that attorneys can **make decisions together and separately**. This might be useful, for example, if one attorney is not available to make a decision at a certain time. If one attorney cannot act the remaining attorney is able to continue to make decisions.

- **Jointly for some decisions, and jointly and severally for other decisions**: this means that your attorneys **must make certain decisions together** and may make **certain decisions separately**. You will need to set out below how you want this to work in practice.

Choosing which decisions must be made together and which decisions may be made separately – how this will work in practice

- Please make your intentions clear about how your attorneys are to make decisions about running bank accounts and savings accounts, making or selling investments and selling property, and spending your money.

- Please check that your intentions will work in practice – it may not be possible to register or use this lasting power of attorney if, for example, a bank or building society account cannot be operated as you wish.

How you want your attorneys to make decisions

If you are appointing only one attorney and no replacement attorneys, now go to section 5 →

Jointly	☐	→ *Go to section 5 and cross through the box below*
Jointly and severally	☐	→ *Go to section 5 and cross through the box below*
Jointly for some decisions, and jointly and severally for other decisions	☐	

Only if you have ticked the last box above, now tell us in the space below which decisions your attorneys must make jointly and which decisions may be made jointly and severally

📄 *If you need more space, use continuation sheet A2*

Lasting power of attorney for property and financial affairs

5 About restrictions and conditions

Putting restrictions and conditions into words

- You should read the separate guidance for examples of conditions and restrictions that will not work in practice.
- Your attorneys **must** follow any restrictions or conditions you put in place. But it may not be possible to register or use this lasting power of attorney if a condition is not workable.
- **Either**: give any restrictions and conditions about property and financial affairs here
- **Or**: if you would like your attorneys to make decisions with no restrictions or conditions, you should cross through this box.

Restrictions and conditions about property and financial affairs

If you need more space, use continuation sheet A2

6 About guidance to your attorneys

Putting guidance into words

- Any guidance you add may help your attorneys to identify your views. You do not have to add any.
- Your attorneys do not have to follow your guidance but it will help them to understand your wishes when they make decisions for you.
- **Either**: Give any guidance about property and financial affairs here
- **Or:** if you have no guidance to add, please cross through this box.

Guidance to your attorneys about property and financial affairs

If you need more space, use continuation sheet A2

7 About paying your attorneys

Professional charges

- Professional attorneys, such as solicitors and accountants, charge for their services. You can also choose to pay a non-professional person for their services. You **should** discuss payment with your attorneys and record any agreement made here to avoid any confusion later.
- You can choose to pay non-professional attorneys for their services, but if you do not record any agreement here they will only be able to recover reasonable out-of-pocket expenses

Charges for services

If you need more space, use continuation sheet A2

→ *For further information on paying attorneys, please see the separate guidance.*

Helpline
☎ **0300 456 0300**
🖱 publicguardian.gov.uk

Valid only with Office of the Public Guardian stamp

PART VII

8 About people to be told when the application to register this lasting power of attorney is made

Thinking about people to be told

- For your protection you can choose up to **five people to be told** when your lasting power of attorney is being registered. This gives people who know you well an opportunity to raise any concerns or objections **before** this lasting power of attorney is registered and can be used.

> ❶ • You do not have to choose anyone. But if you leave this section blank, you must choose two people to sign the certificate to confirm understanding at part B.

- The people to be told cannot be your attorney or replacement named at part A or in continuation sheets to part A.

The first or only person to be told *Please cross through this section if it does not apply.*	**The second person to be told** *Please cross through this section if it does not apply.*
Mr Mrs Ms Miss Other title	Mr Mrs Ms Miss Other title
First names of first or only person to be told	First names of second person to be told
Last name of first or only person to be told	Last name of second person to be told
Address and postcode of first or only person to be told	Address and postcode of second person to be told
Postcode	Postcode

Other people to be told

Please cross through this section if it does not apply

📄 *Tell us about other people to be told on continuation sheet A1.*

Number of other people to be told named in continuation sheet **A1** attached to this lasting power of attorney

9 Declaration by the person who is giving this lasting power of attorney

Before signing please check that you have:

- filled in every answer that applies to you
- crossed through blank boxes that do not apply to you
- filled in any continuation sheets
- crossed through any mistakes you have made
- initialled any changes you have made.

No changes may be made to this lasting power of attorney and no continuation sheets may be added after part A has been filled in and signed. If any change appears to have been made, this lasting power of attorney will not be valid and will be rejected when an application is made to register it.

By signing (or marking) on this page, or by directing someone to sign continuation sheet A3:PFA, I confirm all of the following:

Statement of understanding

I have read or had read to me:

- the section called 'Information you must read' on page 2
- all information contained in part A and any continuation sheets to part A of this lasting power of attorney.

I appoint and give my attorneys authority to make decisions about my property and financial affairs, including when I cannot act for myself because I lack mental capacity, subject to the terms of this lasting power of attorney and to the provisions of the Mental Capacity Act 2005.

People to be told when the application to register this lasting power of attorney is made

I have chosen the people to be told, and have chosen **one** person to sign the certificate of understanding at part B.

OR

I do not want anyone to be told, and have chosen **two** people to sign certificates of understanding at part B.

If you cannot sign this lasting power of attorney you can make a mark instead.

📋 *If you cannot sign or make a mark use continuation sheet A3:PFA →*

Signed (or marked) by the person giving this lasting power of attorney and delivered as a deed

Sign with usual signature

Date signed or marked

D D M M Y Y Y Y

❗ Sign (or mark) and date each continuation sheet at the same time as you sign (or mark) part A.

You must sign (or mark) and date part A here *before* parts B and C are signed and dated.

The witness should be independent of you and:

- Must be 18 or over.
- **Cannot** be an attorney or replacement attorney named at part A or any continuation sheets to this lasting power of attorney or the employee of any trust corporation named as an attorney or replacement attorney.
- Can be a certificate provider at part B.
- Can be a person to be told when the application to register this lasting power of attorney is made.
- Must initial any changes made in Part A.

Witnessed by

Signature of witness

Full names of witness

Address and postcode of witness

Postcode

PART VII

Helpline
📞 **0300 456 0300**
🖱 publicguardian.gov.uk

Valid only with Office of the Public Guardian stamp

Part B

Declaration by your first or only certificate provider: certificate to confirm understanding

Your certificate provider fills in, signs and dates this part.

Declaration by the person who is signing this certificate

Please refer to separate guidance for certificate providers. If the guidance is not followed, this lasting power of attorney may not be valid and could be rejected when an application is made to register it.

In part A (section 8) has the person giving this lasting power of attorney chosen at least one person to be told when the application to register this lasting power of attorney is made?

If yes = **one** certificate provider fills in this part

If no = the **first** certificate provider fills in this part and the **second** certificate provider must fill in continuation sheet **B** .

The **donor** is the person who is giving this lasting power of attorney.

By signing below, I confirm:

My understanding of the role and responsibilities

I have read part A of this lasting power of attorney, including any continuation sheets.

I have read the section called **'Information you must read'** on page 2 of this lasting power of attorney.

I understand my role and responsibilities as a certificate provider.

Statement of acting independently

I confirm that I act independently of the attorneys and of the donor and I am aged 18 or over.

I am **not**:

- an attorney or replacement attorney named in this lasting power of attorney or any other lasting power of attorney or enduring power of attorney for the donor
- a family member related to the donor or any of their attorneys or replacements
- a business partner or paid employee of the donor or any of their attorneys or replacements
- the owner, director, manager or employee of a care home that the donor lives in, or a member of their family
- a director or employee of a trust corporation appointed as an attorney or replacement attorney in this lasting power of attorney.

How you formed your opinion

Before signing this certificate you must establish that the donor understands what it is, the authority they are giving their attorneys, and is not being pressurised into making it.

If someone challenges this lasting power of attorney, you may need to explain how you formed your opinion.

Statement of personal knowledge or relevant professional skills

Please cross through the box that does not apply.

EITHER

I have **known** the donor for at least **two years** and as more than an acquaintance. My personal knowledge of the donor is:

OR

I have **relevant professional skills**. (Please state your profession – for example, a GP or solicitor – and then the particular skills that are relevant to you forming your opinion – for example, a consultant specialising in geriatric care.)

My profession and particular skills are:

Continues over →

Lasting power of attorney for property and financial affairs

Part B – Declaration by the person who is signing this certificate (continued)

Things you certify

I certify that, in my opinion, at the time of signing part A:

- the donor understands the purpose of this lasting power of attorney and the scope of the authority conferred under it
- no fraud or undue pressure is being used to induce the donor to create this lasting power of attorney
- there is nothing else which would prevent this lasting power of attorney from being created by the completion of this form.

Your signature

❗ **Do not sign until part A of this lasting power of attorney has been filled in and signed.**

Sign **as soon as possible** after part A is signed. If this part is signed before part A is signed, this lasting power of attorney will not be valid and will be rejected when an application is made to register it.

Signature of certificate provider

Date signed

D D M M Y Y Y Y

Name and address of the person who is signing this certificate

Mr   Mrs   Ms   Miss   Other title

First names of certificate provider

Last name of certificate provider

Address and postcode of certificate provider

Postcode

Valid only with Office of the Public Guardian stamp

PART VII

1533

Part C   Declaration by each attorney or replacement attorney
Your attorney(s) and replacement attorney(s) sign and date this part.

📋 *If you are appointing more than one attorney, including replacement attorneys: photocopy this sheet before it is filled in so that each attorney has a copy to fill in and sign.*

Statement by the attorney or replacement attorney who is signing this declaration

- The attorney or replacement attorney must not be bankrupt.
- Before a replacement can act for you, they must get in touch with the Office of the Public Guardian and return the original lasting power of attorney form. They will get guidance at that time about what needs to happen next.

By signing below, I confirm all of the following:

Understanding of role and responsibilities

I have read the section called **'Information you must read'** on page 2 of this lasting power of attorney.

I understand my role and responsibilities under this lasting power of attorney, in particular:

- I have a duty to act based on the principles of the Mental Capacity Act 2005 and have regard to the Mental Capacity Act Code of Practice
- I can make decisions and act only when this lasting power of attorney has been registered
- I must make decisions and act in the best interests of the person who is giving this lasting power of attorney
- I can spend money to make gifts but only to charities or on customary occasions and for reasonable amounts
- I have a duty to keep accounts and financial records and produce them to the Office of the Public Guardian and/or to the Court of Protection on request.

Further statement of replacement attorney

If an original attorney's appointment is terminated, I will replace the original attorney if I am still eligible to act as an attorney.

I have the authority to act under this lasting power of attorney only after an original attorney's appointment is terminated and I have notified the Public Guardian of the event.

❗ For this lasting power of attorney to be valid and registered this part should not be signed before Part A or part B have been completed, signed and dated. Sign Part C **as soon as possible** after part B is signed.

Signed or marked by the attorney or replacement attorney as a deed and delivered (or if to be signed at their direction refer to separate guidance)

Full name of [attorney] or [replacement attorney]
delete as appropriate

Date signed or marked

The witness must be over 18 and can be:

- another attorney or replacement attorney named at part A or in continuation sheet A to this lasting power of attorney
- a certificate provider at part B of this lasting power of attorney.
- a person to be told when the application to register this lasting power of attorney is made.

The donor cannot be a witness.

The witness must see the attorney or replacement attorney sign or make a mark.

Signature of witness

Full name of witness

Address and postcode of witness

Postcode

Valid only with Office of the Public Guardian stamp

Lasting power of attorney

A1 Continuation sheet A1 – Additional people

Use this continuation sheet for details of all additional attorneys, replacement attorneys, or people to be told. Make copies of this sheet before filling it in if you need more than one sheet.

About the additional people

For each additional person, provide the following details

- Whether you want them to act as an attorney, replacement attorney or person to be told

> ⓘ **If you don't make your requirements for each person clear this lasting power of attorney could be rejected at registration**

- Their title, full name, address (including postcode)
- Their date of birth

For example:
- Third attorney
- Mr John Smith,
- 38 London Street, Posttown, PC6 9ZZ
- 19 January 1960

or:
- Second replacement attorney
- Mrs Susan Jones
- 27 Lincoln Road, Posttown, PC7 9XX
- 12 December 1962

About you

Name of person who is giving this lasting power of attorney

Date signed or marked

D D M M Y Y Y Y

Signed or marked by (or signed by the direction of) the person giving this lasting power of attorney

Please **attach** this sheet to the **back** of your lasting power of attorney **before** you sign and date the declaration in part A.

And number your continuation sheets consecutively.

This is continuation sheet number

Total number of continuation sheets

Helpline
☎ **0300 456 0300**
🖰 publicguardian.gov.uk

Valid only with Office of the Public Guardian stamp

PART VII

1535

A2 Continuation sheet A2 – how your attorneys make decisions jointly and severally, restrictions & conditions, guidance, payment

Only use this continuation sheet to provide further additional information about how you want your attorneys to act.
Make copies of this sheet before filling it in if you need more than one sheet.

About the additional information

For each additional piece of information you are providing, state whether it relates to:

- Which decisions your attorneys should make jointly and which decisions they should make jointly and severally (only if this applies)
- Restrictions and conditions
- Guidance to your attorneys
- Paying your attorneys

About you

Name of person who is giving this lasting power of attorney

Signed or marked by (or signed by the direction of) the person giving this lasting power of attorney

Date signed or marked

D D M M Y Y Y Y

Please **attach** this sheet to the **back** of your lasting power of attorney **before** you sign and date the declaration in part A.
And number your continuation sheets consecutively.

This is continuation sheet number

Total number of continuation sheets

Helpline
0300 456 0300
publicguardian.gov.uk

Valid only with Office of the Public Guardian stamp

Lasting power of attorney for property and financial affairs

A3:PFA Continuation sheet A3 (property and financial affairs) – if you cannot sign or make a mark

Use this continuation sheet if you cannot sign at part A of your lasting power of attorney.

Signature of someone signing on behalf of the person giving this lasting power of attorney

The person signing on behalf of the person giving this lasting power of attorney must

- sign in the person's presence **and** in the presence of **two witnesses.**
- sign in their own name
- not also be a witness.

Full name of the person signing

Signed as a deed and delivered in the presence of and at the direction of the person giving this lasting power of attorney and in the presence of two witnesses

❶ **Sign and date each continuation sheet at the same time as you sign part A here**

You must sign and date part A here *before* parts B and C are signed and dated.

Date signed

D D M M Y Y Y Y

Each witness

- Must be 18 or over
- **Cannot** be an attorney or replacement attorney named at part A or any continuation sheet A to this lasting power of attorney

- Can be a certificate provider at part B
- Can be a person to be told when the application to register this lasting power of attorney is made
- Must initial any changes made in Part A

Witnessed by
Signature of **first** witness

Also witnessed by
Signature of **second** witness

Date signed

D D M M Y Y Y Y

Date signed

D D M M Y Y Y Y

Full names of first witness

Full names of second witness

Address and postcode of first witness

Address and postcode of second witness

Postcode

Postcode

About you

Name of person who is giving this lasting power of attorney

Please **attach** to the **back** of your lasting power of attorney after this sheet has been signed and dated.
And number your continuation sheets consecutively.

This is continuation sheet number

Total number of continuation sheets

Helpline
☏ **0300 456 0300**
🖱 **publicguardian.gov.uk**

Valid only with Office of the Public Guardian stamp

PART VII

B Continuation sheet B – declaration by your second certificate provider: certificate to confirm understanding

Your second certificate provider signs and dates this continuation sheet

Declaration by the person who is signing this certificate

Please refer to separate guidance for certificate providers. If the guidance is not followed, this lasting power of attorney may not be valid and could be rejected when an application is made to register it.

In part A (property and financial affairs section 8, or health and welfare section 9) has the person giving this lasting power of attorney chosen at least one person to be told when the application to register this lasting power of attorney is made?

If yes = you only need **one** certificate provider so you do **not** need to fill in this continuation sheet

If no = the **second** certificate provider must fill in this continuation sheet

The **donor** is the person who is giving this lasting power of attorney.

By signing below, I confirm:

My understanding of the role and responsibilities

I have read part A of this lasting power of attorney, including any continuation sheets.

I have read the section called **'Information you must read'** on page 2 of this lasting power of attorney.

I understand my role and responsibilities as a certificate provider.

Statement of acting independently

I confirm that I act independently of the attorneys and of the donor and I am aged 18 or over.

I am **not**:

- an attorney or replacement attorney named in this lasting power of attorney or any other lasting power of attorney or enduring power of attorney for the donor
- a family member related to the donor or any of their attorneys or replacements
- a business partner or paid employee of the donor or any of their attorneys or replacements
- the owner, director, manager or employee of a care home that the donor lives in, or a member of their family
- a director or employee of a trust corporation appointed as an attorney or replacement attorney in this lasting power of attorney (for property and financial affairs only).

How you formed your opinion

Before signing this certificate you must establish that the donor understands what it is, the authority they are giving their attorneys, and is not being pressurised into making it.
If someone challenges this lasting power of attorney, you may need to explain how you formed your opinion.

Statement of personal knowledge or relevant professional skills

Please cross through the box that does not apply.

EITHER

I have **known** the donor for at least **two years** and as more than an acquaintance. My personal knowledge of the donor is:

OR

I have **relevant professional skills**. (Please state your profession – for example, a GP or solicitor – and then the particular skills that are relevant to you forming your opinion – for example, a consultant specialising in geriatric care'.)

My profession and particular skills are:

Number each page individually and attach both continuation sheet B pages to the back of your lasting power of attorney **after** you sign and date the declaration in part A.

This is continuation sheet number ☐

Total number of continuation sheets ☐

Continues over →

Valid only with Office of the Public Guardian stamp

B Continuation sheet B (continued) – declaration by your second certificate provider: certificate to confirm understanding

Declaration by the person who is signing this certificate (continued)

Things you certify

I certify that, in my opinion, at the time of signing part A:

- the donor understands the purpose of this lasting power of attorney and the scope of the authority conferred under it
- no fraud or undue pressure is being used to induce the donor to create this lasting power of attorney
- there is nothing else which would prevent this lasting power of attorney from being created by the completion of this form.

Your signature

🚫 **Do not sign until part A of this lasting power of attorney has been filled in and signed.**

Sign **as soon as possible** after part A is signed. If this part is signed before part A is signed, this lasting power of attorney will not be valid and will be rejected when an application is made to register it.

Signature of certificate provider

Date signed

D D M M Y Y Y Y

Name and address of the person who is signing this certificate

Mr   Mrs   Ms   Miss   Other title

First names of certificate provider

Last name of certificate provider

Address and postcode of certificate provider

Postcode

Number each page individually and attach both pages of continuation sheet B to the back of your lasting power of attorney **after** you sign and date the declaration in part A.

This is continuation sheet number

Total number of continuation sheets

PART VII

Valid only with Office of the Public Guardian stamp

C Continuation sheet C – appointing a trust corporation as attorney or replacement attorney

Use this continuation sheet if you are appointing a trust corporation as attorney or replacement attorney.

A trust corporation cannot be going through winding-up proceedings.

Statement by the trust corporation acting as attorney or replacement attorney – person(s) signing on behalf of the trust corporation sign and date this statement

By execution of this deed the trust corporation confirms all of the following:

Understanding of role and responsibilities

It has read the section called **'Information you must read'** on page 2 of this lasting power of attorney.

It understands its role and responsibilities under this lasting power of attorney, in particular it:

- has a duty to act based on the legal principles of the Mental Capacity Act 2005 and have regard to the Mental Capacity Act Code of Practice
- can make decisions and act only when this lasting power of attorney has been registered
- must make decisions and act in the best interests of the person who is giving this lasting power of attorney
- can spend money to make gifts but only to charities or on customary occasions and for reasonable amounts
- has a duty to keep accounts and financial records and produce them to the Office of the Public Guardian or the Court of Protection on request.

Tick the option which applies:

Either:

☐ Seal of trust corporation stamped below

Or:

☐ At least one authorised person has signed and dated in the right-hand column

❗ For this lasting power of attorney to be valid and registered this part should not be signed before Part A or part B have been completed, signed and dated. Sign part C as soon as possible after part B is signed.

I/We are authorised to sign on behalf of the trust corporation acting as attorney whose details are given in this continuation sheet to this lasting power of attorney.

Signed as a deed and delivered by

Signature of first authorised person

Full name of first person signing

Date signed

D D M M Y Y Y Y

Signature of second authorised person (*cross through if only one authorised person is required*)

Full name of second person signing

Date signed

D D M M Y Y Y Y

Company registration number

Please **attach** this sheet to the **back** of your lasting power of attorney **after** parts A and B are signed.

And number your continuation sheets consecutively.

This is continuation sheet number ☐

Total number of continuation sheets ☐

Helpline
0300 456 0300
publicguardian.gov.uk

Valid only with Office of the Public Guardian stamp

Part 2: Form for Instrument Intended to Create a Health and Welfare Lasting Power of Attorney

Page 1 of 12 – **Keep all pages of this form together**

For OPG office use only
LPA HW registered on
OPG reference number

Office of the Public Guardian

Lasting power of attorney for health and welfare

About this lasting power of attorney

This lasting power of attorney allows you to choose people to act on your behalf (as an attorney) and make decisions about your **health and personal welfare**, when you are unable to make decisions for yourself. This can include decisions about your healthcare and medical treatment, decisions about where you live and day-to-day decisions about your personal welfare, such as your diet, dress or daily routine.

If you also want someone to make decisions about your **property and financial affairs**, you will need a separate form (downloadable from our website or call 0300 456 0300).

Who can fill it in?

Anyone aged 18 or over, who has the mental capacity to do so.

Before you fill in the lasting power of attorney:

1. Please read the guidance available at **publicguardian.gov.uk** or by calling **0300 456 0300**. See, for example, the *Lasting power of attorney creation pack* or other relevant guidance booklets which are all available online or by post.
2. Make sure you understand the purpose of this lasting power of attorney and the extent of the authority you are giving your attorneys.
3. Read the separate **Information sheet** to understand all the people involved, and how the three parts of the form should be filled in.
4. Make sure you, your certificate provider(s), and your attorney(s) have read the section on page 2 called **Information you must read** before filling in their relevant part.

> **!** **This lasting power of attorney could be rejected at registration if it contains any errors.**

Checklist

See the information sheet for guidance on all the people involved

Part A: about you, the attorneys you are appointing, and people to be told

How many **attorneys** are you appointing? *Write in words.*

How many **replacement attorneys** are you appointing? *Write in words or write 'None' if this does not apply.*

How many **people to be told** are you choosing? *Write in words from 'None' to 'five'. If 'None' you must have two certificate providers in part B.*

Part B: about your certificate providers

How many **certificate providers do you have?** *(Tick one box)*

[ ] One   OR [ ] Two

If you have used any continuation sheets each one must be signed and dated.

Attached to the back of this lasting power of attorney are:
(Write the number of each)

continuation sheet A1	0
continuation sheet A2	0
continuation sheet A3:HW *2 pages*	0
continuation sheet B	0
Total number of continuation sheets	0

PART VII

LPA HW 10 09   © Crown copyright 2009

Helpline
0300 456 0300
publicguardian.gov.uk

Valid only with Office of the Public Guardian stamp

1541

Information you must read

This lasting power of attorney is a legal document.

Each person who signs parts A, B and C must read this information before signing.

Purpose of this lasting power of attorney

This lasting power of attorney gives your attorneys authority to make decisions about your health and welfare when you cannot make your own decisions. This can include where you live, who visits you and the type of care you receive.

When your attorneys can act for you

Your attorneys can use this lasting power of attorney only after it has been registered and stamped on every page by the Office of the Public Guardian. **Your attorneys can only act when you lack the capacity to make the decision in question.** You may have capacity to make some decisions about your personal health and welfare but not others.

The Mental Capacity Act

Your attorneys cannot do whatever they like. They **must** follow the principles of the Mental Capacity Act 2005.

Guidance about these principles is in the Mental Capacity Act Code of Practice. Your attorneys must have regard to the Code of Practice. They can get a copy from The Stationery Office at **tso. co.uk** or read it online at **publicguardian.gov.uk**

Principles of the Act that your attorneys must follow

1 Your attorneys must assume that you can make your own decisions unless they establish that you cannot do so.

2 Your attorneys must help you to make as many of your own decisions as you can. They cannot treat you as unable to make the decision in question unless all practicable steps to help you to do so have been made without success.

3 Your attorneys must not treat you as unable to make the decision in question simply because you make an unwise decision.

4 Your attorneys must make decisions and act in your best interests when you are unable to make the decision in question.

5 Before your attorneys make the decision in question or act for you, they must consider whether they can make the decision or act in a way that is less restrictive of your rights and freedom but still achieves the purpose.

Your best interests

Your attorneys must act in your best interests in making decisions for you when you are unable to make the decision in question yourself. They must take into account all the relevant circumstances. This includes, if appropriate, consulting you and others who are interested in your health and welfare. Any guidance you add may assist your attorneys in identifying your views.

Cancelling this lasting power of attorney

You can cancel this lasting power of attorney at any time before or after it is registered as long as you have mental capacity to cancel it. Please read the guidance available at **publicguardian.gov.uk**

How to fill in this form

- Tick the boxes that apply like this ✔

- Use black or blue ink and write clearly

- Cross through any boxes or sections that don't apply to you, like this:

> Any other names you are known by in financial documents or accounts

- Don't use correction fluid – please cross out any mistakes and rewrite nearby. All corrections must be initialled by the person completing that section of the form (and their witness) like this:

> Any other names you are known by in financial documents or accounts
> *WILLIAM EDWARD* ~~SMITH~~
> A.S.B / W.E.S.   *SMYTH*

- Your application could be rejected if your intentions are not clear and explicit. If you are in any doubt, please start again on a new copy of the form.

What happens after you've filled it in?

The next step is to **register** it. You or your attorneys can do this at any time. The person applying will need to fill in a registration form and may need to pay a fee at that time. They will also need to send notices to the 'people to be told' named at part A when the application to register this lasting power of attorney is made. You can find out more and download the registration form at **publicguardian.gov.uk**

The 'people to be told' are given time to raise any concerns or objections. This means the earliest the Office of Public Guardian can register this lasting power of attorney is 6 weeks after they notify the donor or attorneys that an application to register has been received.

Your lasting power of attorney will **end** if it can no longer be used. For example, if a sole attorney dies or can no longer act for you and no replacement attorney has been named in this lasting power of attorney. Please read the guidance available at **publicguardian.gov.uk**

Valid only with Office of the Public Guardian stamp

Part A Declaration by the person who is giving this lasting power of attorney

Please write clearly using black or blue ink.

1 About the person who is giving this lasting power of attorney

Mr ☐ Mrs ☐ Ms ☐ Miss ☐ Other title ☐

First names

Last name

Date of birth
`D D M M Y Y Y Y`

Address and postcode

Postcode ☐

Any other names you are known by in medical records or welfare records

2 About the attorneys you are appointing

Thinking about your attorneys

- You can appoint more than one attorney if you want to. You do not have to appoint more than one attorney.
- Each attorney must be aged 18 or over. Choose people you know and trust to make decisions for you. You are recommended to read the separate guidance for people who want to make a lasting power of attorney for health and welfare.

Your first or only attorney

Mr ☐ Mrs ☐ Ms ☐ Miss ☐ Other title ☐

First names of your first or only attorney

Last name of your first or only attorney

Date of birth of your first or only attorney
`D D M M Y Y Y Y`

Address and postcode of your first or only attorney

Postcode ☐

Your second attorney
Please cross through this section if it does not apply.

Mr ☐ Mrs ☐ Ms ☐ Miss ☐ Other title ☐

First names of your second attorney

Last name of your second attorney

Date of birth of your second attorney
`D D M M Y Y Y Y`

Address and postcode of your second attorney

Postcode ☐

If you are appointing more than two attorneys, use continuation sheet A1 to tell us about your other attorneys.

Other attorneys you are appointing

Number of attorneys named in continuation sheet **A1** attached to this lasting power of attorney

☐ *Cross through this box if this does not apply*

Helpline
0300 456 0300
publicguardian.gov.uk

Valid only with Office of the Public Guardian stamp

PART VII

3   About appointing replacements if an attorney can no longer act

Thinking about replacement attorneys

- Replacement attorneys will only act once your attorney can no longer act for you.
- You can appoint replacements to replace an attorney who does not want to act for you or who is permanently no longer able to act because they are dead, have disclaimed, lack mental capacity or if they were married to you or were your civil partner, and have now had the marriage or civil partnership annulled or dissolved.
- You do not have to appoint any replacements.
- If you appoint only one attorney and no replacements, this lasting power of attorney will end when your attorney can no longer act.

Your first or only replacement attorney   *Please cross through this section if it does not apply.*

Mr   Mrs   Ms   Miss   Other title

Date of birth of your first or only replacement

D D M M Y Y Y Y

First names of your first or only replacement

Address and postcode of your first or only replacement

Last name of your first or only replacement

Postcode

If you are appointing more than one replacement, use continuation sheet A1 to tell us about your other replacement attorneys.

Other replacement attorneys you are appointing

Number of replacement attorneys named in continuation sheet **A1** attached to this lasting power of attorney

Cross through this box if this does not apply

Valid only with Office of the Public Guardian stamp

4 How you want your attorneys to make decisions

Thinking about how you want your attorneys to make decisions

> If you leave this section blank, your attorneys will be appointed to make all decisions jointly.

- **Jointly**: this means that the attorneys must **make all decisions together**. → *For further information on appointing your attorneys jointly, see the separate guidance.*

- **Jointly and severally**: this means that attorneys can **make decisions together and separately**. This might be useful, for example, if one attorney is not available to make a decision at a certain time. If one attorney cannot act the remaining attorney is able to continue to make decisions.

- **Jointly for some decisions, and jointly and severally for other decisions**: this means that your attorneys **must make certain decisions together** and may make **certain decisions separately**. You will need to set out below how you want this to work in practice.

Choosing which decisions must be made together and which decisions may be made separately – how this will work in practice

- Please make your intentions clear about how your attorneys are to make the decision in question, for example about where you live, who visits you and the type of care you receive.

- Please check that your intentions will work in practice – it may not be possible to register or use this lasting power of attorney if they are not workable. Please read the separate guidance for examples that will not work in practice.

How you want your attorneys to make decisions

If you are appointing only one attorney and no replacement attorneys, now go to section 5 →

Jointly	☐	→ *Go to section 5 and cross through the box below*
Jointly and severally	☐	→ *Go to section 5 and cross through the box below*
Jointly for some decisions, and jointly and severally for other decisions	☐	

Only if you have ticked the last box above, now tell us in the space below which decisions your attorneys must make jointly and which decisions may be made jointly and severally

If you need more space, use continuation sheet A2

Helpline
0300 456 0300
publicguardian.gov.uk

Valid only with Office of the Public Guardian stamp

PART VII

1545

5 About life-sustaining treatment

Life-sustaining treatment means any treatment that a doctor considers necessary to keep you alive. Whether or not a treatment is life-sustaining will depend on the specific situation. Some treatments will be life-sustaining in some situations but not in others.

The decisions you authorise your attorneys to make for you in this lasting power of attorney take the place of any advance decision you have already made on the same subject.

You must be clear whether or not you want to give your attorneys this authority. This is very important so please be clear about the choice you are making. You might want to discuss this first with your attorneys or doctors and health professionals.

You must choose Option A OR Option B.

Your attorneys can **only** make decisions about life-sustaining treatment if you choose Option A. If you choose Option B, your doctors will take into account where it is practicable and appropriate the views of your attorneys and people who are interested in your welfare as well as any written statement you may have made.

When you make your choice and sign this section you **must** have a witness. If you cannot sign you can make a mark instead.

> *If you cannot sign or make a mark use continuation sheet A3:HW →*
> * someone else **must** sign for you at your direction.
> * they must sign in your presence **and** in the presence of **two witnesses.**

Option A — Do not sign both boxes

I want to give my attorneys authority to give or refuse consent to life-sustaining treatment on my behalf.

Signed in the presence of a witness by the person who is giving this lasting power of attorney

Your signature or mark

Date signed or marked

D D M M Y Y Y Y

The date you sign (or mark) here must be the same as the date you sign or mark section 10 Declaration.

Option B — Do not sign both boxes

I do not want to give my attorneys authority to give or refuse consent to life-sustaining treatment on my behalf.

Signed in the presence of a witness by the person who is giving this lasting power of attorney

Your signature or mark

Date signed or marked

D D M M Y Y Y Y

The date you sign (or mark) here must be the same as the date you sign or mark section 10 Declaration.

Who can be a witness

* You must be 18 or over.
* You **cannot** be an attorney or replacement attorney named at part A or any continuation sheets A to this lasting power of attorney.
* If you have been asked to be the certificate provider at part B, you can be a witness at part A.
* A person to be told when the application to register this lasting power of attorney is made can be a witness.

Witnessed by

Signature of witness

Full names of witness

Address and postcode of witness

Postcode

Valid only with Office of the Public Guardian stamp

Form LPA PFA and LPA HW – Form for Instrument Intended to Create a Lasting Power of Attorney

6 About restrictions and conditions

Putting restrictions and conditions into words

- You should read the separate guidance for examples of conditions and restrictions that will not work in practice.
- Your attorneys **must** follow any restrictions or conditions you put in place. But it may not be possible to register or use this lasting power of attorney if a condition is not workable.
- **Either**: give any restrictions and conditions about health and welfare here
- **Or**: if you would like your attorneys to make decisions with no restrictions or conditions, you should cross through this box.

Restrictions and conditions about health and welfare

If you need more space, use continuation sheet A2

7 About guidance to your attorneys

Putting guidance into words

- Any guidance you add may help your attorneys to identify your views. You do not have to add any.
- Your attorneys do not have to follow your guidance but it will help them to understand your wishes when they make decisions for you.
- **Either**: Give any guidance about health and welfare here
- **Or**: if you have no guidance to add, please cross through this box.

Guidance to your attorneys about health and welfare

If you need more space, use continuation sheet A2

8 About paying your attorneys

Professional charges

- Professional attorneys, such as solicitors and accountants, charge for their services. You can also choose to pay a non-professional person for their services. You **should** discuss payment with your attorneys and record any agreement made here to avoid any confusion later.
- You can choose to pay non-professional attorneys for their services, but if you do not record any agreement here they will only be able to recover reasonable out-of-pocket expenses

Charges for services

If you need more space, use continuation sheet A2

→ *For further information on paying attorneys, please see the separate guidance.*

Helpline
℘ **0300 456 0300**
publicguardian.gov.uk

Valid only with Office of the Public Guardian stamp

PART VII

1547

9   About people to be told when the application to register this lasting power of attorney is made

Thinking about people to be told

- For your protection you can choose up to **five people to be told** when your lasting power of attorney is being registered. This gives people who know you well an opportunity to raise any concerns or objections **before** this lasting power of attorney is registered and can be used.

> ❶ • **You do not have to choose anyone. But if you leave this section blank, you must choose two people to sign the certificate to confirm understanding at part B.**

- The people to be told cannot be your attorney or replacement named at part A or in continuation sheets to part A.

The first or only person to be told	**The second person to be told**
Please cross through this section if it does not apply.	*Please cross through this section if it does not apply.*

The first or only person to be told
Please cross through this section if it does not apply.

Mr   Mrs   Ms   Miss   Other title

First names of first or only person to be told

Last name of first or only person to be told

Address and postcode of first or only person to be told

Postcode

The second person to be told
Please cross through this section if it does not apply.

Mr   Mrs   Ms   Miss   Other title

First names of second person to be told

Last name of second person to be told

Address and postcode of second person to be told

Postcode

Other people to be told

Please cross through this section if it does not apply

📄 *Tell us about other people to be told on continuation sheet A1.*

Number of other people to be told named in continuation sheet **A1** attached to this lasting power of attorney

10 Declaration by the person who is giving this lasting power of attorney

Before signing please check that you have:

- filled in every answer that applies to you
- crossed through blank boxes that do not apply to you
- filled in any continuation sheets
- crossed through any mistakes you have made
- initialled any changes you have made.

No changes may be made to this lasting power of attorney and no continuation sheets may be added after part A has been filled in and signed. If any change appears to have been made, this lasting power of attorney will not be valid and will be rejected when an application is made to register it.

By signing (or marking) on this page, or by directing someone to sign continuation sheet A3:HW, I confirm all of the following:

Statement of understanding

I have read or had read to me:

- **the section called 'Information you must read' on page 2**
- **all information contained in part A and any continuation sheets to part A of this lasting power of attorney.**

I appoint and give my attorneys authority to make decisions about my health and welfare, when I cannot act for myself because I lack mental capacity, subject to the terms of this lasting power of attorney and to the provisions of the Mental Capacity Act 2005.

Statement about life-sustaining treatment

I have chosen option A or option B about life-sustaining treatment in section 5 of this lasting power of attorney.

People to be told when the application to register this lasting power of attorney is made

I have chosen the people to be told, and have chosen **one** person to sign the certificate of understanding at part B.

OR

I do not want anyone to be told, and have chosen **two** people to sign certificates of understanding at part B.

If you cannot sign this lasting power of attorney you can make a mark instead.

📋 *If you cannot sign or make a mark use continuation sheet A3:HW →*

Signed (or marked) by the person giving this lasting power of attorney and delivered as a deed

Date signed or marked

D	D	M	M	Y	Y	Y	Y

❗ **Sign (or mark) and date**
- **section 5 (Option A or Option B), and**
- **each continuation sheet**
at the same time as you sign (or mark) part A here.

You must sign (or mark) and date part A here *before* parts B and C are signed and dated.

The witness should be independent of you and:

- Must be 18 or over.
- **Cannot** be an attorney or replacement attorney named at part A or any continuation sheets to this lasting power of attorney.
- Can be a certificate provider at part B.
- Can be a person to be told when the application to register this lasting power of attorney is made.
- Must initial any changes made in Part A.

❗ **Sign section 5 (witnessing Option A or Option B) at the same time as you sign part A here.**

Witnessed by

Signature of witness

Full names of witness

Address and postcode of witness

Postcode

PART VII

Part B

Declaration by your first or only certificate provider: certificate to confirm understanding

Your certificate provider fills in, signs and dates this part.

Declaration by the person who is signing this certificate

Please refer to separate guidance for certificate providers. If the guidance is not followed, this lasting power of attorney may not be valid and could be rejected when an application is made to register it.

In part A (section 9) has the person giving this lasting power of attorney chosen at least one person to be told when the application to register this lasting power of attorney is made?

If yes = **one** certificate provider fills in this part

If no = the **first** certificate provider fills in this part and the **second** certificate provider must fill in continuation sheet **B** 📄.

The **donor** is the person who is giving this lasting power of attorney.

By signing below, I confirm:

My understanding of the role and responsibilities

I have read part A of this lasting power of attorney, including any continuation sheets.

I have read the section called '**Information you must read**' on page 2 of this lasting power of attorney.

I understand my role and responsibilities as a certificate provider.

Statement of acting independently

I confirm that I act independently of the attorneys and of the donor and I am aged 18 or over.

I am **not**:

- an attorney or replacement attorney named in this lasting power of attorney or any other lasting power of attorney or enduring power of attorney for the donor

- a family member related to the donor or any of their attorneys or replacements

- a business partner or paid employee of the donor or any of their attorneys or replacements

- the owner, director, manager or employee of a care home that the donor lives in, or a member of their family.

How you formed your opinion

Before signing this certificate you must establish that the donor understands what it is, the authority they are giving their attorneys, and is not being pressurised into making it.

If someone challenges this lasting power of attorney, you may need to explain how you formed your opinion.

Statement of personal knowledge or relevant professional skills

Please cross through the box that does not apply.

EITHER

I have **known** the donor for at least **two years** and as more than an acquaintance. My personal knowledge of the donor is:

OR

I have **relevant professional skills**. (Please state your profession – for example, a GP or solicitor – and then the particular skills that are relevant to you forming your opinion – for example, a consultant specialising in geriatric care.)

My profession and particular skills are:

Continues over →

Lasting power of attorney for health and welfare

Part B – Declaration by the person who is signing this certificate (continued)

Things you certify

I certify that, in my opinion, at the time of signing part A:

- the donor understands the purpose of this lasting power of attorney and the scope of the authority conferred under it
- no fraud or undue pressure is being used to induce the donor to create this lasting power of attorney
- there is nothing else which would prevent this lasting power of attorney from being created by the completion of this form.

Your signature

🛇 **Do not sign until part A of this lasting power of attorney has been filled in and signed.**

Sign **as soon as possible** after part A is signed. If this part is signed before part A is signed, this lasting power of attorney will not be valid and will be rejected when an application is made to register it.

Signature of certificate provider

Date signed

D D M M Y Y Y Y

Name and address of the person who is signing this certificate

Mr   Mrs   Ms   Miss   Other title

First names of certificate provider

Last name of certificate provider

Address and postcode of certificate provider

Postcode

PART VII

Valid only with Office of the Public Guardian stamp

Part C   Declaration by each attorney or replacement attorney
Your attorney(s) and replacement attorney(s) sign and date this part.

📋 *If you are appointing more than one attorney, including replacement attorneys: photocopy this sheet before it is filled in so that each attorney has a copy to fill in and sign.*

Statement by the attorney or replacement attorney who is signing this declaration

- Before a replacement can act for you, they must get in touch with the Office of the Public Guardian and return the original lasting power of attorney form. They will get guidance at that time about what needs to happen next.

By signing below, I confirm all of the following:

Understanding of role and responsibilities

I have read the section called **'Information you must read'** on page 2 of this lasting power of attorney.

I understand my role and responsibilities under this lasting power of attorney, in particular:

- I have a duty to act based on the principles of the Mental Capacity Act 2005 and have regard to the Mental Capacity Act Code of Practice
- I can make decisions and act only when this lasting power of attorney has been registered and when the person who is giving this lasting power of attorney lacks mental capacity
- I must make decisions and act in the best interests of the person who is giving this lasting power of attorney

Further statement of replacement attorney

If an original attorney's appointment is terminated, I will replace the original attorney if I am still eligible to act as an attorney.

I have the authority to act under this lasting power of attorney only after an original attorney's appointment is terminated and I have notified the Public Guardian of the event.

The witness must be over 18 and can be:

- another attorney or replacement attorney named at part A or in continuation sheet A to this lasting power of attorney
- a certificate provider at part B of this lasting power of attorney.
- a person to be told when the application to register this lasting power of attorney is made.

The donor cannot be a witness.

The witness must see the attorney or replacement attorney sign or make a mark.

❗ For this lasting power of attorney to be valid and registered this part should not be signed before Part A or part B have been completed, signed and dated. Sign part C **as soon as possible** after part B is signed.

Signed or marked by the attorney or replacement attorney as a deed and delivered (or if to be signed at their direction refer to separate guidance)

Full name of [attorney] or [replacement attorney] (delete as appropriate)

Date signed or marked

Signature of witness

Full name of witness

Address and postcode of witness to the attorney's or replacement attorney's signature

Postcode

Lasting power of attorney

A1 Continuation sheet A1 – Additional people

Use this continuation sheet for details of all additional attorneys, replacement attorneys, or people to be told.
Make copies of this sheet before filling it in if you need more than one sheet.

About the additional people

For each additional person, provide the following details

- Whether you want them to act as an attorney, replacement attorney or person to be told

  ❶ **If you don't make your requirements for each person clear this lasting power of attorney could be rejected at registration**

- Their title, full name, address (including postcode)
- Their date of birth

For example:
- Third attorney
- Mr John Smith,
- 38 London Street, Posttown, PC6 9ZZ
- 19 January 1960

or:
- Second replacement attorney
- Mrs Susan Jones
- 27 Lincoln Road, Posttown, PC7 9XX
- 12 December 1962

About you

Name of person who is giving this lasting power of attorney

Signed or marked by (or signed by the direction of) the person giving this lasting power of attorney

Date signed or marked

D D M M Y Y Y Y

Please **attach** this sheet to the **back** of your lasting power of attorney **before** you sign and date the declaration in part A.
And number your continuation sheets consecutively.

This is continuation sheet number

Total number of continuation sheets

Helpline
☎ **0300 456 0300**
🖰 publicguardian.gov.uk

Valid only with Office of the Public Guardian stamp

PART VII

1553

A2 Continuation sheet A2 – how your attorneys make decisions jointly and severally, restrictions & conditions, guidance, payment

Only use this continuation sheet to provide further additional information about how you want your attorneys to act. Make copies of this sheet before filling it in if you need more than one sheet.

About the additional information

For each additional piece of information you are providing, state whether it relates to:

- Which decisions your attorneys should make jointly and which decisions they should make jointly and severally (only if this applies)
- Restrictions and conditions
- Guidance to your attorneys
- Paying your attorneys

About you

Name of person who is giving this lasting power of attorney

Signed or marked by (or signed by the direction of) the person giving this lasting power of attorney

Date signed or marked

D D M M Y Y Y Y

Please **attach** this sheet to the **back** of your lasting power of attorney **before** you sign and date the declaration in part A.

And number your continuation sheets consecutively.

This is continuation sheet number

Total number of continuation sheets

Helpline
0300 456 0300
publicguardian.gov.uk

Valid only with Office of the Public Guardian stamp

A3:HW

Continuation sheet A3 (health and welfare) – if you cannot sign or make a mark

Use this continuation sheet if you cannot sign or make a mark at part A of your lasting power of attorney.

The person signing on behalf of the person giving this lasting power of attorney must

- sign in the person's presence **and** in the presence of **two witnesses**.
- sign in their own name
- not also be a witness.

Full name of the person signing

_____

Option A

Do not sign both boxes

I want to give my attorneys authority to give or refuse consent to life-sustaining treatment on my behalf.

Signature of someone signing for the person who is giving this lasting power of attorney

Date signed

| D | D | M | M | Y | Y | Y | Y |

The date you sign here must be the same as the date you sign below.

Option B

Do not sign both boxes

I do not want to give my attorneys authority to give or refuse consent to life-sustaining treatment on my behalf.

Signature of someone signing for the person who is giving this lasting power of attorney

Date signed

| D | D | M | M | Y | Y | Y | Y |

The date you sign here must be the same as the date you sign below.

Signature of someone signing on behalf of the person giving this lasting power of attorney

I confirm that I have signed at Option A or Option B in the presence of and directed by the person giving this lasting power of attorney and in the presence of two witnesses

Date signed

| D | D | M | M | Y | Y | Y | Y |

Sign and date Option A or Option B above, and each continuation sheet, at the same time as you sign part A here.

You must sign and date part A here *before* parts B and C are signed and dated.

Signed as a deed and delivered in the presence of and directed by the person giving this lasting power of attorney and in the presence of two witnesses

This continuation sheet has two pages.
Two witnesses must sign on the next page →

Number each page individually and attach both pages of continuation sheet A3:HW to the **back** of your lasting power of attorney after they have been signed and dated.

This is continuation sheet number

Total number of continuation sheets

Continues over →

Helpline
📞 **0300 456 0300**
🖱 publicguardian.gov.uk

Valid only with Office of the Public Guardian stamp

PART VII

1555

A3:HW — Continuation sheet A3 (health and welfare) – if you cannot sign or make a mark (continued)

Each witness

- Must be 18 or over.
- **Cannot** be an attorney or replacement attorney named at part A or any continuation sheets A to this lasting power of attorney.

- Can be a certificate provider at part B, .
- Can be a person to be told when the application to register this lasting power of attorney is made.
- Must initial any changes made in Part A.

Witnessed by
Signature of **first** witness

Date signed
D D M M Y Y Y Y

Full names of first witness

Address and postcode of first witness

Postcode

Also witnessed by
Signature of **second** witness

Date signed
D D M M Y Y Y Y

Full names of second witness

Address and postcode of second witness

Postcode

About you

Name of person who is giving this lasting power of attorney

This continuation sheet has two pages.

Number each page individually and attach both pages of continuation sheet A3:HW to the **back** of your lasting power of attorney after they have been signed and dated.

This is continuation sheet number

Total number of continuation sheets

Helpline
0300 456 0300
publicguardian.gov.uk

Valid only with Office of the Public Guardian stamp

B Continuation sheet B – declaration by your second certificate provider: certificate to confirm understanding

Your second certificate provider signs and dates this continuation sheet

Declaration by the person who is signing this certificate

Please refer to separate guidance for certificate providers. If the guidance is not followed, this lasting power of attorney may not be valid and could be rejected when an application is made to register it.

In part A (property and financial affairs section 8, or health and welfare section 9) has the person giving this lasting power of attorney chosen at least one person to be told when the application to register this lasting power of attorney is made?

If yes = you only need **one** certificate provider so you do **not** need to fill in this continuation sheet

If no = the **second** certificate provider must fill in this continuation sheet

The **donor** is the person who is giving this lasting power of attorney.

By signing below, I confirm:

My understanding of the role and responsibilities

I have read part A of this lasting power of attorney, including any continuation sheets.

I have read the section called **'Information you must read'** on page 2 of this lasting power of attorney.

I understand my role and responsibilities as a certificate provider.

Statement of acting independently

I confirm that I act independently of the attorneys and of the donor and I am aged 18 or over.

I am **not**:

- an attorney or replacement attorney named in this lasting power of attorney or any other lasting power of attorney or enduring power of attorney for the donor
- a family member related to the donor or any of their attorneys or replacements
- a business partner or paid employee of the donor or any of their attorneys or replacements
- the owner, director, manager or employee of a care home that the donor lives in, or a member of their family
- a director or employee of a trust corporation appointed as an attorney or replacement attorney in this lasting power of attorney (for property and financial affairs only).

How you formed your opinion

Before signing this certificate you must establish that the donor understands what it is, the authority they are giving their attorneys, and is not being pressurised into making it.

If someone challenges this lasting power of attorney, you may need to explain how you formed your opinion.

Statement of personal knowledge or relevant professional skills

Please cross through the box that does not apply.

EITHER

I have **known** the donor for at least **two years** and as more than an acquaintance. My personal knowledge of the donor is:

OR

I have **relevant professional skills**. (Please state your profession – for example, a GP or solicitor – and then the particular skills that are relevant to you forming your opinion – for example, a consultant specialising in geriatric care'.)

My profession and particular skills are:

Number each page individually and attach both continuation sheet B pages to the back of your lasting power of attorney **after** you sign and date the declaration in part A.

This is continuation sheet number [ ]

Total number of continuation sheets [ ]

Continues over →

Helpline
📞 **0300 456 0300**
🖱 **publicguardian.gov.uk**

Valid only with Office of the Public Guardian stamp

PART VII

B Continuation sheet B (continued) – declaration by your second certificate provider: certificate to confirm understanding

Declaration by the person who is signing this certificate (continued)

Things you certify

I **certify** that, in my opinion, at the time of signing part A:

- the donor understands the purpose of this lasting power of attorney and the scope of the authority conferred under it
- no fraud or undue pressure is being used to induce the donor to create this lasting power of attorney
- there is nothing else which would prevent this lasting power of attorney from being created by the completion of this form.

Your signature

🛈 **Do not sign until part A of this lasting power of attorney has been filled in and signed.**

Sign **as soon as possible** after part A is signed. If this part is signed before part A is signed, this lasting power of attorney will not be valid and will be rejected when an application is made to register it.

Signature of certificate provider

Date signed

D D M M Y Y Y Y

Name and address of the person who is signing this certificate

Mr   Mrs   Ms   Miss   Other title

First names of certificate provider

Last name of certificate provider

Address and postcode of certificate provider

Postcode

Number each page individually and attach both pages of continuation sheet B to the back of your lasting power of attorney **after** you sign and date the declaration in part A.

This is continuation sheet number

Total number of continuation sheets

Valid only with Office of the Public Guardian stamp

Form LPA 001 – Notice of Intention to Apply for Registration of a Lasting Power of Attorney

LPA 001 10.07

Notice of intention to apply for registration of a Lasting Power of Attorney

This notice must be sent to everyone named by the donor in the Lasting Power of Attorney as a person who should be notified of an application to register. Relatives are not entitled to notice unless named in the Lasting Power of Attorney.

The application to register may be made by the donor or the attorney(s).

Where attorneys are appointed to act together they **all** must apply to register.

Details of the named person

Name

Address

Telephone no.

Postcode

To the named person - You have the right to object to the proposed registration of the Lasting Power of Attorney. You have **five weeks** from the day on which this notice is given to object. Details of how to object and the grounds for doing so are on the back page.

Details of the Lasting Power of Attorney (LPA)

Who is applying to register the LPA? ☐ the donor ☐ the attorney(s)

Which type of LPA is being registered? ☐ Property and Affairs ☐ Personal Welfare

(You must complete separate applications for each LPA you wish to register.)

On what date did the donor sign the LPA?   D D M M Y Y Y Y

Details of the donor

Full name

Address

Telephone no.

Postcode

© Crown copyright 2007

PART VII

1559

Details of the attorney(s)

Name of 1ˢᵗ attorney

Address

Telephone no.

Postcode ☐☐☐☐☐☐☐

☐ solely   ☐ together and independently
☐ together   ☐ together in some matters and together and independently in others

Name of 2ⁿᵈ attorney

Address

Telephone no.

Postcode ☐☐☐☐☐☐☐

☐ together   ☐ together and independently
☐ together in some matters and together and independently in others

Name of 3ʳᵈ attorney

Address

Telephone no.

Postcode ☐☐☐☐☐☐☐

☐ together   ☐ together and independently
☐ together in some matters and together and independently in others

Name of 4ᵗʰ attorney

Address

Telephone no.

Postcode ☐☐☐☐☐☐☐

☐ together   ☐ together and independently
☐ together in some matters and together and independently in others

Signature and date ———————————————————————————————

This notice must be signed by all parties applying to register the lasting power of attorney.

Signed

Print name

Dated

D	D	M	M	Y	Y	Y	Y

PART VII

How to object to the registering of a Lasting Power of Attorney (LPA)

You can ask the Office of the Public Guardian (OPG) to stop the LPA from being registered if one of the factual grounds at (A) below has occurred. You need to tell us by completing Form LPA7 which is available from the OPG and by providing evidence to accompany it. You must send us the completed LPA7 form **within five weeks** from the date this notice was given. Failure to tell us could result in the LPA being registered.

(A) Factual grounds – you can ask the Office of the Public Guardian to stop registration if:

- The Donor is bankrupt or interim bankrupt (for property and affairs LPAs only)
- The Attorney is bankrupt or interim bankrupt (for property and affairs LPAs only)
- The Attorney is a trust corporation and is wound up or dissolved (for property and affairs LPAs only)
- The Donor is dead
- The Attorney is dead
- That there has been dissolution or annulment of a marriage or civil partnership between the Donor and Attorney (except if the LPA provided that such an event should not affect the instrument)
- The Attorney(s) lack the capacity to be an attorney under the LPA
- The Attorney(s) have disclaimed their appointment

Form LPA7 is available from the OPG on 0845 330 2900 or www.publicguardian.gov.uk

You have the right to object to the Court of Protection about the registration of the LPA, but only on the grounds mentioned at (B) below. To do this you must contact the Court and complete the application to object form they will send you. Using that form, you must set out your reasons for objecting. They must receive the objection within five weeks from the date this notice was given. You must also notify the OPG when you object to the Court by using the separate form LPA8 that the Court will send you. Failure to notify the OPG of an objection may result in registration of the LPA.

Note: If you are objecting to the appointment of a specific attorney, it will not prevent registration if other attorneys or a substitute attorney have been appointed.

(B) Prescribed grounds – you can only object to the Court of Protection against registration of the LPA on the following grounds:

- That the power purported to be created by the instrument* is not valid as a LPA. e.g. the person objecting does not believe the donor had capacity to make an LPA.
- That the power created by the instrument no longer exists e.g. the donor revoked it at a time when he/she had capacity to do so.
- That fraud or undue pressure was used to induce the donor to make the power.
- The attorney proposes to behave in a way that would contravene his authority or would not be in the donor's best interests.

Note: * The instrument means the LPA made by the donor.

The Court will only consider objections made if they are made on the above grounds. To obtain a Court objection form please contact the Court of Protection at Archway Tower, 2 Junction Road, London N19 5SZ or Telephone 0845 330 2900.

Form LPA 002 – Application to Register a Lasting Power of Attorney

LPA002 `10.07` Office of the Public Guardian

Application to register a Lasting Power of Attorney

Return your completed form to:
Office of the Public Guardian
Archway Tower
2 Junction Road
London N19 5SZ

Part 1 - The donor

Place a cross (x) against one option

Mr. ☐   Mrs. ☐   Ms. ☐   Miss ☐   Other ☐

If other, please specify ☐☐☐☐☐☐☐☐☐☐☐☐☐☐☐☐☐

Last name ☐☐☐☐☐☐☐☐☐☐☐☐☐☐☐☐☐☐☐☐☐☐☐☐

First name ☐☐☐☐☐☐☐☐☐☐☐☐☐☐☐☐☐☐☐☐☐☐☐☐

Middle name ☐☐☐☐☐☐☐☐☐☐☐☐☐☐☐☐☐☐☐☐☐☐☐☐

Address 1 ☐☐☐☐☐☐☐☐☐☐☐☐☐☐☐☐☐☐☐☐☐☐☐☐

Address 2 ☐☐☐☐☐☐☐☐☐☐☐☐☐☐☐☐☐☐☐☐☐☐☐☐

Address 3 ☐☐☐☐☐☐☐☐☐☐☐☐☐☐☐☐☐☐☐☐☐☐☐☐

Town/City ☐☐☐☐☐☐☐☐☐☐☐☐☐☐☐☐☐☐☐☐☐☐☐☐

County ☐☐☐☐☐☐☐☐☐☐☐☐☐☐☐☐☐☐☐☐☐☐☐☐

Postcode ☐☐☐☐☐☐☐   Daytime Tel. no. ☐☐☐☐☐☐ ☐☐☐☐☐☐

Date of birth ☐☐☐☐☐☐☐☐   If the exact date is unknown please state the year of birth
D D M M Y Y Y Y

e-mail address ☐☐☐☐☐☐☐☐☐☐☐☐☐☐☐☐☐☐☐☐☐☐☐☐

Please do not write below this line - For office use only

PART VII

Part 2 - The persons making the application

Note: We need to know who is applying and how the attorney(s) have been appointed, please answer the questions in parts two and three carefully.

Place a cross (x) against one option

Is the donor applying to register the Lasting Power of Attorney?   ☐ Yes

Is the attorney(s) applying to register the Lasting Power of Attorney?   ☐ Yes

Part 3 - How have the attorney(s) been appointed?

The LPA states whether the attorney is to act soley, together or together and independently

Place a cross (x) against one option

There is only one attorney appointed   ☐

There are attorneys appointed together and independently   ☐

There are attorneys appointed together   ☐

There are attorneys appointed together in some matters and together and independently in others   ☐

Note: We need to know which, if any of the attorney(s) are making this application to register the LPA. You can tell us this by putting a cross in the box at the start of each attorney(s) details in section 4.

2

Part 4 - Attorney one

Place a cross (x) in this box if attorney one is applying to register ☐

Place a cross (x) against one option

Mr. ☐ Mrs. ☐ Ms. ☐ Miss ☐ Other ☐

If other, please specify ☐☐☐☐☐☐☐☐☐☐☐☐☐☐☐☐☐

Last name ☐☐☐☐☐☐☐☐☐☐☐☐☐☐☐☐☐☐☐☐☐☐☐☐☐☐☐☐

First name ☐☐☐☐☐☐☐☐☐☐☐☐☐☐☐☐☐☐☐☐☐☐☐☐☐☐☐☐

Middle name ☐☐☐☐☐☐☐☐☐☐☐☐☐☐☐☐☐☐☐☐☐☐☐☐☐☐☐☐

Company name *(if relevant)* ☐☐☐☐☐☐☐☐☐☐☐☐☐☐☐☐☐☐☐☐☐☐☐☐☐☐☐☐

Address 1 ☐☐☐☐☐☐☐☐☐☐☐☐☐☐☐☐☐☐☐☐☐☐☐☐☐☐☐☐

Address 2 ☐☐☐☐☐☐☐☐☐☐☐☐☐☐☐☐☐☐☐☐☐☐☐☐☐☐☐☐

Address 3 ☐☐☐☐☐☐☐☐☐☐☐☐☐☐☐☐☐☐☐☐☐☐☐☐☐☐☐☐

Town/City ☐☐☐☐☐☐☐☐☐☐☐☐☐☐☐☐☐☐☐☐☐☐☐☐☐☐☐☐

County ☐☐☐☐☐☐☐☐☐☐☐☐☐☐☐☐☐☐☐☐☐☐☐☐☐☐☐☐

Postcode ☐☐☐☐☐☐☐ DX number ☐☐☐☐☐☐☐☐☐☐☐☐☐

Date of birth ☐☐☐☐☐☐☐☐ DX Exchange ☐☐☐☐☐☐☐☐☐☐☐☐☐
D D M M Y Y Y Y

Daytime Tel. no. ☐☐☐☐☐☐☐ ☐☐☐☐☐☐☐☐☐

Occupation ☐☐☐☐☐☐☐☐☐☐☐☐☐☐☐☐☐☐☐☐☐☐☐☐☐☐☐☐

e-mail address ☐☐☐☐☐☐☐☐☐☐☐☐☐☐☐☐☐☐☐☐☐☐☐☐☐☐☐☐

Place a cross (x) against one option that best describes your relationship to the donor

Civil partner / Spouse ☐ Child ☐ Solicitor ☐ Other ☐ Other professional ☐

If 'Other' or 'Other professional', please specify ☐☐☐☐☐☐☐☐☐☐☐☐☐☐☐☐

3

PART VII

Part 4 - Attorney two

Place a cross (x) in this box if attorney two is applying to register ☐

Place a cross (x) against one option

Mr. ☐   Mrs. ☐   Ms. ☐   Miss ☐   Other ☐

If other, please specify ☐☐☐☐☐☐☐☐☐☐☐☐☐☐☐☐☐

Last name ☐☐☐☐☐☐☐☐☐☐☐☐☐☐☐☐☐☐☐☐☐☐☐☐☐☐☐

First name ☐☐☐☐☐☐☐☐☐☐☐☐☐☐☐☐☐☐☐☐☐☐☐☐☐☐☐

Middle name ☐☐☐☐☐☐☐☐☐☐☐☐☐☐☐☐☐☐☐☐☐☐☐☐☐☐☐

Company name *(if relevant)* ☐☐☐☐☐☐☐☐☐☐☐☐☐☐☐☐☐☐☐☐☐☐☐☐☐☐☐

Address 1 ☐☐☐☐☐☐☐☐☐☐☐☐☐☐☐☐☐☐☐☐☐☐☐☐☐☐☐

Address 2 ☐☐☐☐☐☐☐☐☐☐☐☐☐☐☐☐☐☐☐☐☐☐☐☐☐☐☐

Address 3 ☐☐☐☐☐☐☐☐☐☐☐☐☐☐☐☐☐☐☐☐☐☐☐☐☐☐☐

Town/City ☐☐☐☐☐☐☐☐☐☐☐☐☐☐☐☐☐☐☐☐☐☐☐☐☐☐☐

County ☐☐☐☐☐☐☐☐☐☐☐☐☐☐☐☐☐☐☐☐☐☐☐☐☐☐☐

Postcode ☐☐☐☐☐☐☐   DX number ☐☐☐☐☐☐☐☐☐☐☐

Date of birth ☐☐☐☐☐☐☐☐   DX Exchange ☐☐☐☐☐☐☐☐☐☐☐☐
D D M M Y Y Y Y

Daytime Tel. no. ☐☐☐☐☐☐☐ ☐☐☐☐☐☐☐☐☐

Occupation ☐☐☐☐☐☐☐☐☐☐☐☐☐☐☐☐☐☐☐☐☐☐☐☐☐☐☐

e-mail address ☐☐☐☐☐☐☐☐☐☐☐☐☐☐☐☐☐☐☐☐☐☐☐☐☐☐☐

Place a cross (x) against one option that best describes your relationship to the donor

Civil partner / Spouse ☐   Child ☐   Solicitor ☐   Other ☐   Other professional ☐

If 'Other' or 'Other professional', please specify ☐☐☐☐☐☐☐☐☐☐☐☐☐☐☐☐☐

4

Part 4 - Attorney three

Place a cross (x) in this box if attorney three is applying to register ☐

Place a cross (x) against one option

Mr. ☐   Mrs. ☐   Ms. ☐   Miss ☐   Other ☐

If other, please specify ☐☐☐☐☐☐☐☐☐☐☐☐☐☐☐☐☐

Last name ☐☐☐☐☐☐☐☐☐☐☐☐☐☐☐☐☐☐☐☐☐☐☐☐☐☐

First name ☐☐☐☐☐☐☐☐☐☐☐☐☐☐☐☐☐☐☐☐☐☐☐☐☐☐

Middle name ☐☐☐☐☐☐☐☐☐☐☐☐☐☐☐☐☐☐☐☐☐☐☐☐☐☐

Company name *(if relevant)* ☐☐☐☐☐☐☐☐☐☐☐☐☐☐☐☐☐☐☐☐☐☐☐☐☐☐

Address 1 ☐☐☐☐☐☐☐☐☐☐☐☐☐☐☐☐☐☐☐☐☐☐☐☐☐☐

Address 2 ☐☐☐☐☐☐☐☐☐☐☐☐☐☐☐☐☐☐☐☐☐☐☐☐☐☐

Address 3 ☐☐☐☐☐☐☐☐☐☐☐☐☐☐☐☐☐☐☐☐☐☐☐☐☐☐

Town/City ☐☐☐☐☐☐☐☐☐☐☐☐☐☐☐☐☐☐☐☐☐☐☐☐☐☐

County ☐☐☐☐☐☐☐☐☐☐☐☐☐☐☐☐☐☐☐☐☐☐☐☐☐☐

Postcode ☐☐☐☐☐☐☐   DX number ☐☐☐☐☐☐☐☐☐

Date of birth ☐☐☐☐☐☐☐☐
D D M M Y Y Y Y   DX Exchange ☐☐☐☐☐☐☐☐☐☐☐☐☐☐

Daytime Tel. no. ☐☐☐☐☐☐☐ ☐☐☐☐☐☐☐☐☐

Occupation ☐☐☐☐☐☐☐☐☐☐☐☐☐☐☐☐☐☐☐☐☐☐☐☐☐☐

e-mail address ☐☐☐☐☐☐☐☐☐☐☐☐☐☐☐☐☐☐☐☐☐☐☐☐☐☐

Place a cross (x) against one option that best describes your relationship to the donor

Civil partner / Spouse ☐   Child ☐   Solicitor ☐   Other ☐   Other professional ☐

If 'Other' or 'Other professional', please specify ☐☐☐☐☐☐☐☐☐☐☐☐☐☐☐☐☐

PART VII

Part 4 - Attorney four

Place a cross (x) in this box if attorney four is applying to register ☐

If there are additional attorneys, please provide the following details in the 'Additional information' section at the end of this form.

Place a cross (x) against one option

Mr. ☐   Mrs. ☐   Ms. ☐   Miss ☐   Other ☐

If other, please specify ☐☐☐☐☐☐☐☐☐☐☐☐☐☐☐☐

Last name ☐☐☐☐☐☐☐☐☐☐☐☐☐☐☐☐☐☐☐☐☐☐☐☐☐

First name ☐☐☐☐☐☐☐☐☐☐☐☐☐☐☐☐☐☐☐☐☐☐☐☐☐

Middle name ☐☐☐☐☐☐☐☐☐☐☐☐☐☐☐☐☐☐☐☐☐☐☐☐☐

Company name (if relevant) ☐☐☐☐☐☐☐☐☐☐☐☐☐☐☐☐☐☐☐☐☐☐☐☐☐

Address 1 ☐☐☐☐☐☐☐☐☐☐☐☐☐☐☐☐☐☐☐☐☐☐☐☐☐

Address 2 ☐☐☐☐☐☐☐☐☐☐☐☐☐☐☐☐☐☐☐☐☐☐☐☐☐

Address 3 ☐☐☐☐☐☐☐☐☐☐☐☐☐☐☐☐☐☐☐☐☐☐☐☐☐

Town/City ☐☐☐☐☐☐☐☐☐☐☐☐☐☐☐☐☐☐☐☐☐☐☐☐☐

County ☐☐☐☐☐☐☐☐☐☐☐☐☐☐☐☐☐☐☐☐☐☐☐☐☐

Postcode ☐☐☐☐☐☐☐   DX number ☐☐☐☐☐☐☐☐☐☐

Date of birth ☐☐☐☐☐☐☐☐   DX Exchange ☐☐☐☐☐☐☐☐☐☐☐☐☐
D D M M Y Y Y Y

Daytime Tel. no. ☐☐☐☐☐☐☐ ☐☐☐☐☐☐☐☐

Occupation ☐☐☐☐☐☐☐☐☐☐☐☐☐☐☐☐☐☐☐☐☐☐☐☐☐

e-mail address ☐☐☐☐☐☐☐☐☐☐☐☐☐☐☐☐☐☐☐☐☐☐☐☐☐

Place a cross (x) against one option that best describes your relationship to the donor

Civil partner / Spouse ☐   Child ☐   Solicitor ☐   Other ☐   Other professional ☐

If 'Other' or 'Other professional', please specify ☐☐☐☐☐☐☐☐☐☐☐☐☐☐☐

6

Part 5 - Notification of named persons

The donor or attorney(s) making the application must give notice to the named persons nominated by the donor in the section of the LPA marked 'Notifying others when an application to register your LPA is made'. The date on which the notice was given **must** be completed (which is the date it was posted or given to the named person). If the donor decided not to notify any named persons, please place a cross in the box provided.

The donor did not specify any named individuals in the LPA ☐

Place a cross (x) against one option

☐ I   ☐ We

have given notice to register in the prescribed form (LP1) to the following person(s):

Date notice given
D D M M Y Y Y Y

Last name

First name

Address 1

Address 2

Address 3

Town/City

County

Postcode

PART VII

1569

Part 5 - continued

Date notice given
☐☐ ☐☐ ☐☐☐☐
D D M M Y Y Y Y

Last name
☐☐☐☐☐☐☐☐☐☐☐☐☐☐☐☐☐☐☐☐☐☐☐☐☐☐☐☐☐☐

First name
☐☐☐☐☐☐☐☐☐☐☐☐☐☐☐☐☐☐☐☐☐☐☐☐☐☐☐☐☐☐

Address 1
☐☐☐☐☐☐☐☐☐☐☐☐☐☐☐☐☐☐☐☐☐☐☐☐☐☐☐☐☐☐

Address 2
☐☐☐☐☐☐☐☐☐☐☐☐☐☐☐☐☐☐☐☐☐☐☐☐☐☐☐☐☐☐

Address 3
☐☐☐☐☐☐☐☐☐☐☐☐☐☐☐☐☐☐☐☐☐☐☐☐☐☐☐☐☐☐

Town/City
☐☐☐☐☐☐☐☐☐☐☐☐☐☐☐☐☐☐☐☐☐☐☐☐☐☐☐☐☐☐

County
☐☐☐☐☐☐☐☐☐☐☐☐☐☐☐☐☐☐☐☐☐☐☐☐☐☐☐☐☐☐

Postcode
☐☐☐☐☐☐☐

Date notice given
☐☐ ☐☐ ☐☐☐☐
D D M M Y Y Y Y

Last name
☐☐☐☐☐☐☐☐☐☐☐☐☐☐☐☐☐☐☐☐☐☐☐☐☐☐☐☐☐☐

First name
☐☐☐☐☐☐☐☐☐☐☐☐☐☐☐☐☐☐☐☐☐☐☐☐☐☐☐☐☐☐

Address 1
☐☐☐☐☐☐☐☐☐☐☐☐☐☐☐☐☐☐☐☐☐☐☐☐☐☐☐☐☐☐

Address 2
☐☐☐☐☐☐☐☐☐☐☐☐☐☐☐☐☐☐☐☐☐☐☐☐☐☐☐☐☐☐

Address 3
☐☐☐☐☐☐☐☐☐☐☐☐☐☐☐☐☐☐☐☐☐☐☐☐☐☐☐☐☐☐

Town/City
☐☐☐☐☐☐☐☐☐☐☐☐☐☐☐☐☐☐☐☐☐☐☐☐☐☐☐☐☐☐

County
☐☐☐☐☐☐☐☐☐☐☐☐☐☐☐☐☐☐☐☐☐☐☐☐☐☐☐☐☐☐

Postcode
☐☐☐☐☐☐☐

8

Part 5 - continued

Date notice given

D D M M Y Y Y Y

Last name

First name

Address 1

Address 2

Address 3

Town/City

County

Postcode

Date notice given

D D M M Y Y Y Y

Last name

First name

Address 1

Address 2

Address 3

Town/City

County

Postcode

PART VII

Part 6 - Fees

Guidelines on fee exemption and remission can be obtained from the Office of the Public Guardian.

Have you enclosed a cheque for the registration fee for this application?	☐ Yes	☐ No
Do you wish to apply for remission of the fee?	☐ Yes	☐ No
Do you wish to apply for exemption of the fee?	☐ Yes	☐ No
Do you wish to apply for postponement of the fee?	☐ Yes	☐ No

If you wish to apply for exemption, remission or postponement of all or part of the fee. You must complete the separate application form available from the Office of the Public Guardian.

Part 7 - Type of power

☐ I　　☐ We

apply to register the LPA (the original of which accompanies this application) made by the donor under the provisions of the Mental Capacity Act 2005.

What type of Lasting Power of Attorney are you applying to register?

☐ Property and affairs　　**OR**　　☐ Personal welfare

Date that the **donor** signed the Lasting Power of Attorney

☐☐☐☐☐☐☐☐
D　D　M　M　Y　Y　Y　Y

To your knowledge, has the donor made any other Enduring Powers of Attorney or Lasting Power of Attorney?　　☐ Yes　　☐ No

If Yes, please give details below including registration date if applicable

10

Part 8 - Donor declaration

Note: This section should only be completed by the donor if they are applying for the registration of the Lasting Power of Attorney.

I apply to register the Lasting Power of Attorney (the original of which accompanies this application).

I certify that the above information is correct and that to the best of my knowledge and belief, I have completed the application in accordance with the provisions of the Mental Capacity Act 2005 and all statutory instruments made under it.

Signed

Date

D D M M Y Y Y Y

Last name

First name

Part 9 - Attorney(s) declaration

Note: This section should only be completed by the attorney(s) if they are applying for the registration of the Lasting Power of Attorney.

☐ I ☐ We apply to register the Lasting Power of Attorney (the original of which accompanies this application).

☐ I ☐ We certify that the above information is correct to the best of my knowledge and belief.

☐ I ☐ We have completed the application within the provisions of the Mental Capacity Act 2005 and all statutory instruments made under it.

Signed

Date

D D M M Y Y Y Y

Last name

First name

Signed

Date

D D M M Y Y Y Y

Last name

First name

PART VII

11

1573

Part 9 - continued

Signed [   ]   Date [ ][ ][ ][ ][ ][ ][ ][ ]
                                       D D M M Y Y Y Y

Last name [ ]

First name [ ]

Signed [   ]   Date [ ][ ][ ][ ][ ][ ][ ][ ]
                                       D D M M Y Y Y Y

Last name [ ]

First name [ ]

Signed [   ]   Date [ ][ ][ ][ ][ ][ ][ ][ ]
                                       D D M M Y Y Y Y

Last name [ ]

First name [ ]

Part 10 - Declaration by a trust corporation

If you are a trust corporation making this application please complete this declaration.

[ ] I   [ ] We

certify that the above information is correct and that to the best of my knowledge and belief, I have completed the application in accordance with the provisions of the Mental Capacity Act 2005 and all statutory instruments made under it.

Company name [ ]

Signature of authorised person(s) [   ]   Company seal (If applicable)
                                  [   ]

Last name [ ]

First name [ ]

12

⌐Part 11 - Correspondence address

Place a cross (**x**) against one option

Mr. ☐   Mrs. ☐   Ms. ☐   Miss ☐   Other ☐

If other, please specify ☐☐☐☐☐☐☐☐☐☐☐☐☐☐

Last name ☐☐☐☐☐☐☐☐☐☐☐☐☐☐☐☐☐☐☐☐☐☐☐☐☐☐☐

First name ☐☐☐☐☐☐☐☐☐☐☐☐☐☐☐☐☐☐☐☐☐☐☐☐☐☐☐

Middle name ☐☐☐☐☐☐☐☐☐☐☐☐☐☐☐☐☐☐☐☐☐☐☐☐☐☐☐

Company name ☐☐☐☐☐☐☐☐☐☐☐☐☐☐☐☐☐☐☐☐☐☐☐☐☐☐☐

Company reference ☐☐☐☐☐☐☐☐☐☐☐☐☐☐☐☐☐☐☐☐☐☐☐☐☐☐☐

Address 1 ☐☐☐☐☐☐☐☐☐☐☐☐☐☐☐☐☐☐☐☐☐☐☐☐☐☐☐

Address 2 ☐☐☐☐☐☐☐☐☐☐☐☐☐☐☐☐☐☐☐☐☐☐☐☐☐☐☐

Address 3 ☐☐☐☐☐☐☐☐☐☐☐☐☐☐☐☐☐☐☐☐☐☐☐☐☐☐☐

Town/City ☐☐☐☐☐☐☐☐☐☐☐☐☐☐☐☐☐☐☐☐☐☐☐☐☐☐☐

County ☐☐☐☐☐☐☐☐☐☐☐☐☐☐☐☐☐☐☐☐☐☐☐☐☐☐☐

Postcode ☐☐☐☐☐☐☐   DX number ☐☐☐☐☐☐☐☐☐☐

DX Exchange ☐☐☐☐☐☐☐☐☐☐☐☐☐

Daytime Tel. no. ☐☐☐☐☐☐   ☐☐☐☐☐☐☐☐☐

e-mail address ☐☐☐☐☐☐☐☐☐☐☐☐☐☐☐☐☐☐☐☐☐☐☐☐☐☐☐

PART VII

Part 12 - Additional information

Please write down any additional information to support this application in the space below. If necessary attach additional sheets.

14

Forms LPA 003A and LPA 003B – Notice of Receipt of an Application to Register a Lasting Power of Attorney

Part 1: Notice to an Attorney of Receipt of an Application to Register a Lasting Power of Attorney

LPA 003A 10.07

Notice to an attorney of receipt of an application to register a Lasting Power of Attorney

Name of attorney

Take notice

An application to register a Lasting Power of Attorney (LPA) has been received by the Office of the Public Guardian.

We are sending you this notice because you are named as an attorney in the LPA and were not involved in the application to register.

You are hereby given notice of the proposed registration. **You have the right to object to the registration.** Details of how to do so are set out on page 2 of this notice. You have five weeks in which to object from the date this notice was given. (We will treat this notice as having been given two days after the date below.)

The names of the donor and the attorney(s) are set out below:

Donor's full name

The following attorney(s) have applied to register an LPA in the name of the above donor.

Attorney's full name

Attorney's full name

Attorney's full name

From
The Office of the Public Guardian
Archway Tower, 2 Junction Road
London N19 5SZ

Telephone 0845 330 2900

Dated

© Crown copyright 2007

How to object to the registering of a Lasting Power of Attorney (LPA)

You can ask the Office of the Public Guardian (OPG) to stop the LPA from being registered if one of the factual grounds at (A) below has occurred. You need to tell us by completing Form LPA7 which is available from the OPG and by providing evidence to accompany it. You must send us the completed LPA7 form **within five weeks** from the date this notice was given. Failure to tell us could result in the LPA being registered.

(A) Factual grounds – you can ask the Office of the Public Guardian to stop registration if:

- The Donor is bankrupt or interim bankrupt (for property and affairs LPAs only)
- The Attorney is bankrupt or interim bankrupt (for property and affairs LPAs only)
- The Attorney is a trust corporation and is wound up or dissolved (for property and affairs LPAs only)
- The Donor is dead
- The Attorney is dead
- That there has been dissolution or annulment of a marriage or civil partnership between the Donor and Attorney (except if the LPA provided that such an event should not affect the instrument)
- The Attorney lacks the capacity to be an attorney under the LPA
- The Attorney disclaimed their appointment

Form LPA7 is available from the OPG on 0845 330 2900 or www.publicguardian.gov.uk

You have the right to object to the Court of Protection about the registration of the LPA, but only on the grounds mentioned at (B) below. To do this you must contact the Court and complete the application to object form they will send you. Using that form, you must set out your reasons for objecting. They must receive the objection within five weeks from the date this notice was given. You must also notify the OPG when you object to the Court by using the separate form LPA8 that the Court will send you. Failure to notify the OPG of an objection may result in registration of the LPA.

Note: If you are objecting to the appointment of a specific attorney, it will not prevent registration if other attorneys or substitute attorneys have been appointed.

(B) Prescribed grounds – you can only object to the Court of Protection against registration of the LPA on the following grounds:

- That the power purported to be created by the instrument* is not valid as a LPA. e.g. the person objecting does not believe the donor had capacity to make an LPA.
- That the power created by the instrument no longer exists e.g. the donor revoked it at a time when he/she had capacity to do so.
- That fraud or undue pressure was used to induce the donor to make the power.
- The attorney proposes to behave in a way that would contravene his authority or would not be in the donor's best interests.

Note: * The instrument means the LPA made by the donor.

The Court will only consider objections made if they are made on the above grounds. To obtain a Court objection form please contact the Court of Protection at Archway Tower, 2 Junction Road, London N19 5SZ or telephone 0845 330 2900.

Part 2: Notice to Donor of Receipt of an Application to Register a Lasting Power of Attorney

LPA 003B 10 07

Notice to donor of receipt of an application to register a Lasting Power of Attorney

Name of donor

Take notice

An application to register your Lasting Power of Attorney (LPA) has been received by the Office of the Public Guardian (OPG).

We are sending you this notice because your attorney(s) in the LPA has asked the OPG to register your LPA, so that it can be used.

You are hereby given notice of the proposed registration. **You have a right to object to the registration.** You have five weeks in which to object from the date this notice was given. (We will treat this notice as having been given two days after the date below). You can object by using form LPA6, which you can get from the OPG.

The names of your attorney(s) are set out below:

Attorney's full name

Attorney's full name

Attorney's full name

Attorney's full name

Dated

From
The Office of the Public Guardian
Archway Tower, 2 Junction Road
London N19 5SZ

Telephone 0845 330 2900

PART VII

Form LPA 004 – Notice of Registration of a Lasting Power of Attorney

LPA 004 04 07

Notice of registration of a Lasting Power of Attorney

This notice is to confirm registration of a Lasting Power of Attorney.

Case no.

The donor

The attorney(s)

The Lasting Power of Attorney was entered into the register on

Notification of registration of the LPA is given as required in Schedule 1 Part 2 Paragraph 15 of the Mental Capacity Act 2005.

Form LPA 005 – Disclaimer by Donee of a Lasting Power of Attorney

LPA 005 10.07

Disclaimer by a proposed or acting attorney under a Lasting Power of Attorney

Take notice that

☐ a proposed attorney

☐ an attorney acting under a Lasting Power of Attorney

has disclaimed appointment.

Details of attorney disclaiming appointment

Name

Address

Telephone no.

Postcode

Date of the Lasting Power of Attorney

On what date was the Lasting Power of Attorney made? D D M M Y Y Y Y

Signature and date

I disclaim my appointment as attorney under the Lasting Power of Attorney made by the donor.

Signed

Dated   D D M M Y Y Y Y

Note: Where the LPA has been registered then a copy of this notice must be sent to the Office of the Public Guardian at: Archway Tower, 2 Junction Road, London N19 5SZ

Call OPG on 0845 330 2900 with any questions.

© Crown copyright 2007

PART VII

Details of the donor ——————————————————————————

Name

Address

Telephone no.

Postcode

Details of the other attorney(s) ——————————————————

Name

Address

Telephone no.

Postcode

Name

Address

Telephone no.

Postcode

Name

Address

Telephone no.

Postcode

ENDURING POWER OF ATTORNEY FORMS

Form EPI PG – Notice of Intention to Apply for Registration of an Enduring Power of Attorney

Form EP1PG

Mental Capacity Act 2005
Enduring Power of Attorney

Notice of intention to apply for registration of an Enduring Power of Attorney

To...

Of...

This form may be adapted for use by three or more attorneys. Any attorney who is appointed to act jointly and severally, but who does not join in the application, must also be named.	**TAKE NOTICE THAT** I .... of .... and I .... of .... The attorney(s) of .... of .... intend to apply to the Public Guardian for registration of the enduring power of attorney appointing me (us) attorney(s) and made by the donor on the ....
Give the name and address of the donor	
The grounds upon which you can object are limited and are shown at 2 overleaf	1. You have the right to object to the proposed registration on one or more of the grounds set out below. If you object, you must notify the Office of the Public Guardian and state which of the grounds you are relying on within five weeks from the day this notice was given to you. You may make an application to the Court of Protection under rule [68] of the Court of Protection Rules 2007 for a decision on the matter. No fee is payable for such an application. If you do not make such an application, the Public Guardian may ask for the court's directions about registration.

PART VII

Note: The instrument means the document used to make the enduring power of attorney made by the donor, which it is sought to register

The attorney(s) does not have to be a relative. Relatives are not entitled to know of the existence of the enduring power of attorney prior to being given this notice

Our staff will be able to assist with any questions you have regarding the objection (s). However, they cannot provide advice about your particular objection.

Note: Part 4 is addressed only to the donor

Note: This notice should be signed by every one of the attorneys who are applying to register the enduring power of attorney

Note: The attorney(s) must keep a record of the date on which notice was given to the donor and to relatives. This information will be required from the attorney(s) when an application to register the EPA is made

2. The grounds on which you may object to the proposed registration are:

- That the power purported to be created by the instrument is not valid as an enduring power of attorney
- That the power created by the instrument no longer subsists
- That the application is premature because the donor is not yet becoming mentally incapable
- That fraud or undue pressure was used to induce the donor to make the power
- That the attorney is unsuitable to be the donor's attorney (having regard to all the circumstances and in particular the attorney's relationship to or connection with the donor).

3. You can obtain the necessary forms to object by.
- Writing to us at the address on the foot of this form
- Calling us on 0845 330 2900
- Downloading the forms from our website at www.publicguardian.gov.uk

4. You are informed that while the enduring power of attorney remains registered, you will not be able to revoke it until the Court of Protection confirms the revocation.

Signed: .... Dated: ....

Signed: .... Dated: ....

Please write to:
Office of the Public Guardian
PO Box 15118
Birmingham
B16 6GX

www.publicguardian.gov.uk

EPHPG – 02.10

Form EP2 PG – Application to Register an Enduring Power of Attorney

Office of the Public Guardian
Mental Capacity Act 2005
Form EP2PG
Application for Registration of an Enduring
Power of Attorney

IMPORTANT: Please complete the form in **BLOCK CAPITALS** using a **black ball-point pen**. Place a clear cross 'X' mark inside square option boxes ☒ - do not circle the option.

Part One - The Donor

Please state the full name and present address of the donor. State the donor's first name in 'Forename 1' and the donor's other forenames in full in 'Other Forenames'. Company Name should be completed with the name of the nursing/care home or hospital where applicable.

Mr ☐ Mrs ☐ Ms ☐ Miss ☐ Other ☐
Place a cross against one option ☒

If Other, please specify here: [ ]

Last Name: [ ]

Forename 1: [ ]

Other Forenames: [ ]

Company Name: [ ]

Address 1: [ ]

Address 2: [ ]

Address 3: [ ]

Town/City: [ ]

County: [ ]

Postcode: [ ]

Donor Date of Birth: [ ] D D M M Y Y Y Y

If the exact date is unknown please state the year of birth

Please do not write below this line - For Office Use Only

PART VII

Part Two - Attorney One

Please state the full name and present address of the attorney. Professionals e,g, Solicitors or Accountants, should complete the Company Name field.

Mr   Mrs   Ms   Miss   Other
☐   ☐   ☐   ☐   ☐   If Other, please
Place a cross against one option ☒   specify here:

Last Name:

Forename 1:

Other Forenames:

Company Name:

Address 1:

Address 2:

Address 3:

Town/City:

County:

Postcode: DX No.
                                   (solicitors only):

DX Exchange (solicitors only):

Attorney Date of Birth: Daytime Tel No.:

D D M M Y Y Y Y   (STD Code):

Email Address:

Occupation:

Relationship to donor:

Civil Partner / Spouse   Child   Other Relation   No Relation   Solicitor   Other Professional   If 'Other Relation' or 'Other Professional', specify relationship:
☐   ☐   ☐   ☐   ☐   ☐
Place a cross against one option ☒

Part B of the Enduring Power of Attorney states whether the attorney is to act jointly, jointly and severally, or alone.

Appointment (*Place a cross against one option* ☒):   Jointly   ☐

                                                              Jointly and Severally   ☐

                                                              Alone   ☐

Part Three - Attorney Two

Please state the full name and present address of the attorney. Professionals e.g. Solicitors or Accountants, should complete the Company Name field.

Mr   Mrs   Ms   Miss   Other
☐   ☐   ☐   ☐   ☐
Place a cross against one option ☒

If Other, please specify here:

Last Name:

Forename 1:

Other Forenames:

Company Name:

Address 1:

Address 2:

Address 3:

Town/City:

County:

Postcode:

DX No. (solicitors only):

DX Exchange (solicitors only):

Attorney Date of Birth:

D D M M Y Y Y Y

Daytime Tel No.:

(STD Code):

Email Address:

Occupation:

Relationship to donor:

Civil Partner / Spouse   Child   Other Relation   No Relation   Solicitor   Other Professional
☐   ☐   ☐   ☐   ☐   ☐
Place a cross against one option ☒

If 'Other Relation' or 'Other Professional', specify relationship:

Part Four - Attorney Three

Please state the full name and present address of the attorney. Professionals e,g, Solicitors or Accountants, should complete the Company Name field.

Mr   Mrs   Ms   Miss   Other
☐   ☐   ☐   ☐   ☐
Place a cross against one option ☒

If Other, please specify here:

Last Name:

Forename 1:

PART VII

Part Four - Attorney Three cont'd

Other Forenames:	
Company Name:	
Address 1:	
Address 2:	
Address 3:	
Town/City:	
County:	
Postcode:	DX No. (solicitors only):
DX Exchange (solicitors only):	
Attorney Date of Birth:	Daytime Tel No.:
	D D M M Y Y Y Y (STD Code):
Email Address:	
Occupation:	

Relationship to donor:

Civil Partner / Spouse	Child	Other Relation	No Relation	Solicitor	Other Professional	If 'Other Relation' or 'Other Professional', specify relationship:
☐	☐	☐	☐	☐	☐	

Place a cross against one option ☒

If there are additional attorneys, please complete the above details in the 'Additional Information' section (at the end of this form).

Part Five - The Enduring Power of Attorney

I (We) the attorney(s) apply to register the Enduring Power of Attorney made by the donor under the Enduring Powers of Attorney Act 1985, the original, or if the original is lost or destroyed, a certified copy of which accompanies this application.

I (We) have reason to believe that the donor is or is becoming mentally incapable.

Date that the **Donor** signed the Enduring Power of Attorney.
You can find this in Part B of the Enduring Power of Attorney.

D D M M Y Y Y Y

To your knowledge, has the Donor made any other Enduring
Powers of Attorney?:   ☐   ☐
                                              Yes No
Place a cross against one option ☒

If 'Yes', please give details below including registration date if applicable:
....
....
....

Page 4 of 7

Part Six - Notice of Application to Donor

Notice must be given personally to the donor. It should be made clear if someone other than the attorney(s) gives the notice. The date on which the notice was given MUST be completed.

I (We) have given notice of the application to register in the prescribed form (EP1PG) to the donor personally,

on this date:

D D M M Y Y Y Y

If someone other than the attorney gives notice to the donor please complete the name and address details below. Please also complete the date above:

Full Name:
Address 1:
Address 2:
Address 3:
Town/City:
County: Postcode:

Part Seven - Notice of Application to Relatives

Please complete details of all relatives entitled to notice.

Please place a cross in the box ☒ if no relatives are entitled to notice: ☐

I (We) have given notice to register in the prescribed form (EP1PG) to the following relatives of the donor:

Full Name: Relationship to Donor:
Address: Date notice given:
D D M M Y Y Y Y

Full Name: Relationship to Donor:
Address: Date notice given:
D D M M Y Y Y Y

Full Name: Relationship to Donor:
Address: Date notice given:
D D M M Y Y Y Y

Full Name: Relationship to Donor:
Address: Date notice given:
D D M M Y Y Y Y

Full Name: Relationship to Donor:
Address: Date notice given:
D D M M Y Y Y Y

If there are additional relatives please complete the Relative Name, Relationship, Address and Date details in the 'Additional Information' section (at the end of this form).

PART VII

Part Eight - Notice of Application to Co-Attorney(s)

Do not complete this section if it does not apply. If there are additional co-attorneys please complete the Attorney Name, Relationship, Address and Date details in the 'Additional Information' section (at the end of this form).

Are all the attorneys applying to register? Yes ☐ No ☐ *Place a cross against one option* ☒

If no, I (We) have given notice to my (our) co-attorney(s) as follows:

Full Name: _____ Relationship to Donor: _____

Address: _____

Date notice given:

[ ][ ][ ][ ][ ][ ][ ][ ]
D D M M Y Y Y Y

Full Name: _____ Relationship to Donor: _____

Address: _____

Date notice given:

[ ][ ][ ][ ][ ][ ][ ][ ]
D D M M Y Y Y Y

Part Nine - Fees

Guidelines on remission and postponement of fees can be obtained from the Office of the Public Guardian.

Have you enclosed a cheque for the registration fee for this application? Yes ☐ No ☐ *Place a cross against one option* ☒

Do you wish to apply for postponement, exemption or remission of the fee? Yes ☐ No ☐ *Place a cross against one option* ☒

If yes, please complete the application for exemption or remission form.

Part Ten - Declaration

Note: The application should be signed by all attorneys who are making the application. This must not pre-date the date(s) when the notices were given.

I (We) certify that the above information is correct and that to the best of my (our) knowledge and belief I (We) have complied with the provisions of the Mental Capacity Act 2005.

Signed: _____ Dated: [ ][ ][ ][ ][ ][ ][ ][ ]
D D M M Y Y Y Y

Signed: _____ Dated: [ ][ ][ ][ ][ ][ ][ ][ ]
D D M M Y Y Y Y

Signed: _____ Dated: [ ][ ][ ][ ][ ][ ][ ][ ]
D D M M Y Y Y Y

Part Eleven - Correspondence Address

Solicitors please note: The address to which the correspondence should be sent **MUST** be entered here if this is different to the address of Attorney One. State the full name and present address. Insert the name of the Solicitor's Firm in the Company Name field, if appropriate, and the correspondence reference in the Company Reference field.

Mr Mrs Ms Miss Other
☐ ☐ ☐ ☐ ☐

Place a cross against one option ☒

If Other, please specify here:

Last Name:

Forename 1:

Other Forenames:

Company Name:

Company Reference:

Address 1:

Address 2:

Address 3:

Town/City:

County:

Postcode:

DX No. (solicitors only):

DX Exchange (solicitors only):

Daytime Tel No.:

(STD Code)

Email Address:

Part Twelve - Additional Information

Please write down any additional information to support this application in the space below. If necessary attach additional paper to the end of this form.

PART VII

Guidance notes for completing form EP2PG: Application to register an Enduring Power of Attorney

Please complete every section of the form clearly in BLOCK CAPITALS using BLACK ink.

Part One – The Donor

- This section of the form covers the information we need to know about the Donor of the Enduring Power of Attorney (EPA). The Donor is the person who appointed the Attorney or Attorneys when the EPA was set up.

- Place a cross in the box that relates to the Donor's title or write it in the space provided.

- Last Name: The Donor's last name is their surname.

- Forename 1 and Other Forenames: Put the Donor's first name next to Forename 1, and put their second name and any other middle names next to Other Forenames.

- Company Name: If the Donor is living in, for example, a hospital or care home, write the name of that place in this section. If not, write 'not applicable'.

- Address 1- Address 3: When filling in the Donor's address, ensure that you don't write the town/city, county or postcode in this section.

- Town/City, County, Postcode: Ensure you only write the relevant information on each line.

- If the Donor's address on the EPA is different to the one you wrote on the EP2PG form, explain why this is the case under Part Twelve – Additional Information – the final section of the form.

- Donor Date of Birth: Complete the boxes requesting the Donor's date of birth, including the day, month and year. If you do not know this, you can find it in the EPA itself, under the Donor's name and address. If the date of birth you enter here is different from that on the EPA itself, explain the reason for the difference in Part Twelve – Additional Information and provide a copy of the birth certificate as evidence.

Part Five – The Enduring Power of Attorney

- Part Five is to record the date the Donor signed the original EPA. Please enter the day, month and year in the relevant boxes.

- If you know that the Donor has made other EPAs, put a cross in the relevant square.

Part Six – Notice of Application to Donor

- Part Six of the form covers the requirement to personally notify the Donor that you are registering the EPA. It asks you to record the details of when this happened, using the notice in form EP1PG.

- If someone other than the Attorney personally notifies the Donor, enter that person's full name and address. Input the actual date (using the day, month and year boxes) that the Donor was given the notice in person.

- Please note that in certain circumstances the Court of Protection (the 'Court') may consider dispensing with the requirement to notify the Donor. This will normally only happen if a doctor certifies that it will cause the Donor harm or distress. You would then need to contact the Court to make an application to dispense with notice and pay the Court application fee.

- Part Six of the form must be completed unless the Court has agreed that you are not required to notify the Donor. If this is the case you must explain this in Part 12 – Additional Information.

Part Seven – Notice of Application to Relatives

- Part Seven of the form covers the details of the relatives that you must notify that you intend to register the EPA.

- Input their Full Names, Relationship to Donor and their Addresses in the spaces provided.

- Next to each person's contact details, input the actual date that notice was given to that person, including the day, month and year.

- If more relatives need to be notified than you can fit in this section, attach additional sheets of papers to the form with their details.

- In certain circumstances the Court may consider dispensing with the requirement to notify relatives. You would need to contact the Court to make an application and pay the Court application fee.

IMPORTANT: You must send us the EP2PG application to register the EPA within 10 working days of serving the last notice on the Donor and relatives.

PART VII

Part Five – The Enduring Power of Attorney

- Part Five is to record the date the Donor signed the original EPA. Please enter the day, month and year in the relevant boxes.

- If you know that the Donor has made other EPAs, put a cross in the relevant square.

Part Six – Notice of Application to Donor

- Part Six of the form covers the requirement to personally notify the Donor that you are registering the EPA. It asks you to record the details of when this happened, using the notice in form EP1PG.

- If someone other than the Attorney personally notifies the Donor, enter that person's full name and address. Input the actual date (using the day, month and year boxes) that the Donor was given the notice in person.

- Please note that in certain circumstances the Court of Protection (the 'Court') may consider dispensing with the requirement to notify the Donor. This will normally only happen if a doctor certifies that it will cause the Donor harm or distress. You would then need to contact the Court to make an application to dispense with notice and pay the Court application fee.

- Part Six of the form must be completed unless the Court has agreed that you are not required to notify the Donor. If this is the case you must explain this in Part 12 – Additional Information.

Part Seven – Notice of Application to Relatives

- Part Seven of the form covers the details of the relatives that you must notify that you intend to register the EPA.

- Input their Full Names, Relationship to Donor and their Addresses in the spaces provided.

- Next to each person's contact details, input the actual date that notice was given to that person, including the day, month and year.

- If more relatives need to be notified than you can fit in this section, attach additional sheets of papers to the form with their details.

- In certain circumstances the Court may consider dispensing with the requirement to notify relatives. You would need to contact the Court to make an application and pay the Court application fee.

IMPORTANT: You must send us the EP2PG application to register the EPA within 10 working days of serving the last notice on the Donor and relatives.

Part Eight – Notice of Application to Co-Attorney(s)

- Part Eight of the form is to be used only if there is more than one Attorney and the other Attorney(s) are not making this application with you. The details of those Attorney(s) are to be entered in this section.

- This section does not apply if the Attorneys are appointed jointly – as this would mean that they would both (or all) have had to make the application with you because the Donor appointed you to act together.

Part Nine – Fees

- This section of the form covers fee information. There is separate guidance available from the Office of the Public Guardian (OPG) on fees, exemptions and remissions. If you wish to apply for a postponement, exemption or remission of the fee, you should fill in the appropriate box. You will also need to complete the relevant application form.

- If the OPG provided you with the EP2PG registration application form, you should have received our fees guidance at the same time. You can also download it from our website.

Part Ten – Declaration

- Part Ten is the Attorney(s) declaration. This is where you or the Attorney(s) certify that you have complied with the provisions of the Mental Capacity Act 2005 and all the relevant statutory instruments made under it. Please note that false declarations may make the signatory liable to criminal prosecution.

- Input the date that you signed the application, including day, month and year.

Part Eleven – Correspondence Address

- Part Eleven of the form requests the address for all correspondence. This information is vital to your application and care should be taken to ensure accuracy.

- The registered EPA will be returned to this address. If this section is left blank, all correspondence will be sent to Attorney One.

- The boxes entitled DX Exchange are for those wishing to use Document Exchange as an alternative to the postal service.

- The telephone number and email address should be completed if applicable.

Part Twelve – Additional Information

- Part Twelve is for any additional information. For instance if there are more than three Attorneys, the details of the additional Attorney(s) should be entered here.

PART VII

Further Assistance

- The OPG publishes guidance about EPAs, Lasting Powers of Attorney (LPA) and the role of the Attorney. These are available to download from our website or you can call us for a hard copy.

- If you need further help in completing the EP2PG form please contact us.

Contact Us

Office of the Public Guardian
PO Box 15118
Birmingham B16 6GX

Phone Number: 0300 456 0300

Fax Number: 020 7664 7705

Email: customerservices@publicguardian.gsi.gov.uk

Website: www.publicguardian.gov.uk

DX: 744240 Birmingham 79

Textphone: 020 7664 7755 (If you have speech or hearing difficulties and have access to a textphone, you can call the OPG textphone for assistance.)

International Calls: +44 20 7664 7000

International Faxes: +44 20 7664 7705

Disclaimer

OPG and Court staff can provide advice about OPG and Court processes only and cannot provide legal advice or services. We recommend that you seek independent legal advice where appropriate. Information in this publication is believed to be correct at the time of printing, however we do not accept liability for any error it may contain.

DEPRIVATION OF LIBERTY FORMS

DLA – Deprivation of Liberty Application Form

COP DLA 04.09 Court of Protection

Deprivation of liberty
Application form
For urgent consideration

Case no.	
Date of application	
Date of issue	

SEAL

To the applicant(s) and interested party(ies). Representations as to the urgency of the claim may be made by applicant or interested parties to the Deprivation of Liberty Officer by fax: 020 7664 7712

If a standard/urgent authorisation has been given please fill in this two boxes.

Date of urgent/ standard authorisation [ ][ ]/[ ][ ]/[ ][ ][ ]   Date of effective detention [ ][ ]/[ ][ ]/[ ][ ][ ]

Section 1 – Contact details

Applicant

Name

Address   Telephone no.

          Mobile no.

Postcode [ ][ ][ ] [ ][ ][ ]

Email

What is the appliant's relationship to the relevant person? (This is the person that the application is about)

Applicant's solicitor or representatives

Name

Address   Telephone no.

          Mobile no.

          Fax no.

Postcode [ ][ ][ ] [ ][ ][ ]

Email

1

Counsel *(if known)*

Name

Address   Telephone no.

Mobile no.

Fax no.

Postcode

Email

Relevant person's details if not applicant

Name

Address   Telephone no.

Mobile no.

Fax no.

Postcode

Email

Supervisory body PCT/LA

Name

Address   Telephone no.

Mobile no.

Fax no.

Postcode

Email

2

Managing Authority/Hospital/Care Home

Name

Address

Telephone no.

Mobile no.

Fax no.

Postcode

Email

IMCA

Name

Address

Telephone no.

Mobile no.

Fax no.

Postcode

Email

Relevant person's representative

Name

Address

Telephone no.

Mobile no.

Fax no.

Postcode

Email

PART VII

3

Section 2 – Details of other interested parties

Name

Address   Telephone no.

                                           Fax no.

                                           DX no.

Postcode

Email

Name

Address   Telephone no.

                                           Fax no.

                                           DX no.

Postcode

Email

Section 3 – Details of issue to be challenged

3.1   Date of decision

3.2   Where an **urgent** authorisation has been given, the court may determine any question relating to any of the following matters:

☐ whether the urgent authorisation should have been given

☐ the period during which the urgent authorisation is to be in force

☐ the purpose for which the urgent authorisation is given

☐ other

4

3.3 Where a **standard** authorisation has been given, the court may determine any question relating to any of the following matters:

☐ whether the relevant person meets one or more of the qualifying requirements

☐ the period during which the standard authorisation is to be in force

☐ the purpose for which the standard authorisation is given

☐ the conditions subject to which the standard authorisation is given

☐ other

3.4 Do you require permission?   ☐ Yes   ☐ No

If Yes, complete form **COP DLC Permission Form**

3.5 Other issues that may arise

Are you making an interim application?   ☐ Yes   ☐ No

Do you intend to bring other applications if this application succeeds in whole or in part?   ☐ Yes   ☐ No

Do you intend to bring other applications if this application fails?   ☐ Yes   ☐ No

Section 4 – Detailed statement of grounds

☐ Set out below   ☐ Attached

5

PART VII

Section 5 – Other issues of the case

5.1   Are there other issues that will arise for determination in respect of the relevant
      person and any applications that you have made or intend to make in respect of   ☐ Yes   ☐ No
      them?

      If Yes, please give details below

6

Section 6 – Other applications

6.1 Are you aware of any previous application(s) to the Court of Protection regarding the person to whom this application relates? ☐ Yes ☐ No

> If Yes, please give as much of the following information as you can. If there has been more than one previous application please attach the information about other previous applications on a separate sheet of paper.
>
> The name of the applicant
>
> [   ]
>
> The date of the order
>
> [ ][ ] / [ ][ ] / [ ][ ][ ][ ]
>
> Case number
>
> [   ]
>
> Please attach a copy of the order(s), if available.
>
> ☐ Copy attached   ☐ Not available

Section 7 - Attending court hearings

7.1 If the court requires you to attend a hearing do you need any special assistance or facilities? ☐ Yes ☐ No

> If Yes, please say what your requirements are. If necessary, court staff may contact you about your requirements.
>
> [   ]

PART VII

7

Section 8 – Statement of facts relied on

Section 9 - Statement of truth

The statement of truth is to be signed by you, your solicitor or your litigation friend.

*(I believe) (The applicant believes) that the facts stated in this application form and its annex(es) are true.

Signed

Date   ☐☐/☐☐/☐☐☐☐

Name

Name of firm

Position or office held

8

Section 10 - Supporting documents

10.1 Which of the following documents are you filing with this application and any you will be filing later?

☐ Standard authorisation ☐ Best interests assessment

☐ Urgent authorisation ☐ Form COP DLB Declaration of exceptional urgency

☐ Age assessment ☐ Form COP DLC Permission Form (if applicable)

☐ No refusals assessment ☐ Form COP 24 Witness Statement

☐ Mental capacity assessment ☐ A copy of the Legal Aid or CSLF certificate (if legally represented)

☐ Mental health assessment ☐ Copies of any relevant statutory material

☐ Eligibility assessment ☐ Draft Order or Directions

10.2 The following documents not being in my possession. I request the Supervisory Body/ Managing Authority, to file copies of the following documents with their acknowledgment of service

☐ Standard authorisation ☐ Mental health assessment

☐ Urgent authorisation ☐ Eligibility assessment

☐ Age assessment ☐ Best interests assessment

☐ No refusals assessment ☐ Care plan

☐ Mental capacity assessment

10.3 Please explain why you have not supplied a document and a date when you expect it to be available:

Signed .... Applicant's Solicitor ....

PART VII

9

DLB – Deprivation of Liberty Declaration of Exceptional Urgency

COP DLB 04.09 Court of Protection
Deprivation of liberty
Declaration of
exceptional urgency

Case no.	
Date of application	
Date of issue	

To the applicant(s) and interested party(ies). Representations as to the urgency of the claim may be made by applicant or interested parties to the Deprivation of Liberty Officer by fax: 020 7664 7712

Full name of person to whom the application relates
(this is the name of the person who is deprived/will be deprived of their liberty)

Date of urgent/
standard authorisation ☐☐/☐☐/☐☐☐☐   Date of effective detention ☐☐/☐☐/☐☐☐☐

Section 1 - Reasons for urgency

1.1   Please give reasons for the urgency

1.2   Please state what interim relief is sought and why?

Signed   Dated ☐☐/☐☐/☐☐☐☐

Section 2 - Proposed timetable

2.1   Please tick the boxes that apply

☐ The application for interim relief should be considered within   ☐ hours ☐ days

☐ The form DLC Application for permission should be considered within   ☐ hours ☐ days

☐ Abridgement of time is sought for the lodging of acknowledgments of service

☐ If permission granted, a substantive hearing is sought by   ☐☐/☐☐/☐☐☐☐

1

© Crown Copyright 2009

Section 3 – Service

3.1   On whom have you served a copy of this form?

Relevant person

Date served

☐ ☐ / ☐ ☐ / ☐ ☐ ☐ ☐

☐ by fax machine

Fax no.

Time sent

☐ by e-mail (please give address below)

☐ by handing it to or leaving it with

Name

Managing Authority

Date served

☐ ☐ / ☐ ☐ / ☐ ☐ ☐ ☐

☐ by fax machine

Fax no.

Time sent

☐ by e-mail (please give address below)

☐ by handing it to or leaving it with

Name

Supervisory Body

Date served

☐ ☐ / ☐ ☐ / ☐ ☐ ☐ ☐

☐ by fax machine

Fax no.

Time sent

☐ by e-mail (please give address below)

☐ by handing it to or leaving it with

Name

IMCA

Date served

☐ ☐ / ☐ ☐ / ☐ ☐ ☐ ☐

☐ by fax machine

Fax no.

Time sent

☐ by e-mail (please give address below)

☐ by handing it to or leaving it with

Name

Relevant persons representative

Date served

☐ ☐ / ☐ ☐ / ☐ ☐ ☐ ☐

☐ by fax machine

Fax no.

Time sent

☐ by e-mail (please give address below)

☐ by handing it to or leaving it with

Name

Interested parties

Date served

☐ ☐ / ☐ ☐ / ☐ ☐ ☐ ☐

☐ by fax machine

Fax no.

Time sent

☐ by e-mail (please give address below)

☐ by handing it to or leaving it with

Name

PART VII

2

DLC – Deprivation of Liberty Permission Form

COP
DLC
04.09

Court of Protection

Deprivation of liberty

Permission form

For office use only
Date received
Case no.
Date issued

Full name of person to whom the application relates
(this is the name of the person who is deprived/will be deprived of their liberty)

SEAL

Section 1 - Your details (the applicant)

Applicant's full name

Address   Telephone no.

Postcode

Email

1.1   I seek permission for the following reason(s)

continued over the page ⇨

© Crown Copyright 2009

1

1.1   continued

Statement of truth

The statement of truth is to be signed by you, your solicitor or your litigation friend.

(I believe) (The applicant believes) that the facts stated in this permission form are true.

Signed

Date [ ][ ]/[ ][ ]/[ ][ ][ ]

Applicant('s litigation friend)('s solicitor)

Name

Name
of firm

Position or
office held

PART VII

DLD – Deprivation of Liberty Certificate of Service/Non-service; Certificate of Notification/Non-notification

COP DLD 04.09 Court of Protection **Deprivation of liberty** **Certificate of service/ non-service** **Certificate of notification/ non-notification**	Case no.
	Name of applicant
	Name of respondent
	Filed by
	Date

Full name of person to whom the application relates
(this is the person who is deprived/will be deprived of their liberty)

Section 1 – Details of the person served/notified

1.1   Name of the person(s) served/notified:

Name _____   Date served/notified
                                          ☐☐/☐☐/☐☐☐☐

Name _____   Date served/notified
                                          ☐☐/☐☐/☐☐☐☐

Name _____   Date served/notified
                                          ☐☐/☐☐/☐☐☐☐

Name _____   Date served/notified
                                          ☐☐/☐☐/☐☐☐☐

Section 2 – Document served

2.1   Title or description of the document (tick only **one** box)

☐ application form

☐ other (please give details)

© Crown Copyright 2009

1

Section 3 – Person(s) not served or notified

3.1   Name of the person(s) who have not been served/notified:

Name

Reason

Name

Reason

Name

Reason

Name

Reason

Section 4 – Statement of truth

The statement of truth must be signed by the person who served/provided notification.

I believe that the facts stated in this certificate are true.

Signed

Date

Name

Name of firm

Position or office held

PART VII

2

DLE – Deprivation of Liberty Acknowledgment of Service/Notification

COP DLE 04.09 Court of Protection	**Case no.**
Deprivation of liberty	**Name of applicant**
Acknowledgment of	**Name of respondent**
service/notification	**Name of party acknowledging**
	Date

Full name of person to whom the application relates
(this is the name of the person who is deprived/will be deprived of their liberty)

Section 1 - The person served/notified

1.1   Your details   ☐ Mr.   ☐ Mrs.   ☐ Miss   ☐ Ms.   ☐ Other _____

       First name

       Last name

1.2   Address (including postcode)   Telephone no.

       E-mail address

1.3   Is a solicitor representing you?   ☐ Yes   ☐ No

       If Yes, please give the solicitor's details.

       Name

       Address (including postcode)   Telephone no.

                                           Fax no.

                                           DX no.

       E-mail address

© Crown Copyright 2009

1

1.4   Which address should official documentation be sent to?

☐ Your address

☐ Solicitor's address

☐ Other address (please provide details)

>

Section 2 – Attending court hearings

2.1   If the court requires you to attend a hearing do you need any special
assistance or facilities?   ☐ Yes   ☐ No

If Yes, please say what your requirements are. If necessary, court staff may
contact you about your requirements.

>

Section 3 – Signature

Signed

Date served/ ☐☐/☐☐/☐☐☐☐
notified

Person served/notified ('s solicitor) ('s litigation friend)

Name

Name
of firm

Position or
office held

Section 4 – Supervisory Body or Managing Authority only

4.1   I am serving and filing the following documents:

1.

2.

3.

4.

Signed

Date   ☐☐/☐☐/☐☐☐☐

PART VII

PART VIII

Precedent Orders

PART VIII: Precedent Orders

Contents

Section A: Standard Orders   **1619**

A 1 – GENERAL TITLE   1619

A 2 – ORDER appointing a deputy for property and affairs   1619

A 3 – ORDER appointing local authority as deputy for property and
affairs   1622

A 4 – INTERIM ORDER for sale of property   1624

A 5 – INTERIM ORDER to investigate and report   1625

A 6 – ORDER discharging a property and affairs deputy where
capacity is regained   1625

A 7 – ORDER refusing permission to be appointed as deputy for
personal welfare   1626

A 8 – ORDER appointing a deputy for personal welfare   1627

Section B: Directions Orders   **1630**

B 1 – CASE MANAGEMENT CHECKLIST   1630

B 2 – MULTI-PURPOSE DIRECTIONS ORDER   1632

B 3 – FIRST DIRECTIONS ORDER family dispute as to residence
and contact   1637

B 4 – DIRECTIONS ORDER 'adult care' case   1640

B 5 – DIRECTIONS ORDER local authority personal welfare
application   1644

Section C: Final Orders   **1649**

C 1 – ORDER Capacity: financial affairs   1649

C 2 – ORDER EPA or Deputy   1650

C 3 – ORDER Discharge from the jurisdiction   1651

C 4 – ORDER Change of financial Deputy   1653

C 5 – ORDER Cancellation of EPA and appointment of financial
Deputy   1654

C 6 – ORDER Appointment of financial Deputy in respect of large
brain injury award   1657

PART VIII

Section A: Standard Orders

A selection of the most frequently used orders of the Court of Protection is reproduced below. These orders are generally made 'on paper' at Archway following uncontested applications and the content should be varied as appropriate to suit the circumstances of the particular case.

A more comprehensive range of Orders is available in *Atkin's Encyclopaedia of COURT FORMS in Civil Proceedings* (Second Edition), Vol 26(4) *Mental Health and Incapacity: Court of Protection* (2009 Issue, LexisNexis). Permission to reproduce the following extracts is acknowledged.

A 1
GENERAL TITLE

(Used for uncontested Orders)

THIS ORDER IS NOT VALID UNLESS IT BEARS THE IMPRESSED SEAL OF THE COURT OF PROTECTION IN THE BOTTOM RIGHT HAND CORNER ON ALL PAGES

COURT OF PROTECTION

MENTAL CAPACITY ACT 2005

Case No: 000000

In the Matter of [*A B*]

ORDER

[*state nature of Order as in headings below*]

MADE by District Judge [*name*]

AT Archway Tower, 2 Junction Road, London N19 5SZ [*or regional court address*]

ON [*date*]

* * * * * * *

A 2
ORDER appointing a deputy for property and affairs

[*GENERAL TITLE*]

Whereas

1. An application has been made for an order under the Mental Capacity Act 2005

2. The Court is satisfied that:

(a)   *A B* is unable to make various decisions for himself in relation to a matter or matters concerning his property and affairs because of an impairment of or a disturbance in the functioning of his mind or brain

(b)   the purpose for which the order is needed cannot be as effectively achieved in a way that is less restrictive of his rights and freedom of action

IT IS ORDERED THAT

1. Appointment of deputy

(a)   [*Name*] of [*address*] is appointed as deputy ('the deputy') to make decisions on behalf of *A B* that he is unable to make for himself in relation to his property and affairs subject to any conditions or restrictions set out in this order

(b)   The appointment will last until [three years from the date of the order] *or where there are no significant assets* [further order]

(c)   The deputy must apply the principles set out in Section 1 of the Mental Capacity Act 2005 and have regard to the guidance in the Code of Practice to the Act

2. Authority of deputy

(a)   The Court confers general authority on the deputy to take possession or control of the property and affairs of *A B* and to exercise the same powers of management and investment as he has as beneficial owner, subject to the terms and conditions set out in this order

(b)   The deputy may make provision for the needs of anyone who is related or connected with *A B*, if he provided for or might be expected to provide for that person's needs, by doing whatever he did or might reasonably be expected to do to meet those needs

(c)   The deputy may (without obtaining any further authority from the Court) dispose of *A B*'s money or property by way of gift to any charity to which he made or might have been expected to make gifts and on customary occasions to persons who are related to or connected with him, provided that the value of each such gift is not unreasonable having regard to all the circumstances and, in particular, the size of his estate

[(d)   The deputy may withdraw a sum not exceeding £... a year from the funds belonging to *A B* without needing to obtain the prior approval to the Court of Protection] – *or where there are no significant assets*

[(d)   The deputy is authorised to sell the property of *A B* known as [*name of property and address*] on the best possible terms and after payment of legal fees and other professional charges to invest the net proceeds for his benefit]

(e) For the purpose of giving effect to any decision the deputy may execute or sign any necessary deeds or documents

[3. Investments – *this clause is not required where there are no significant assets*

(a) The deputy must exercise such care and skill as is reasonable in the circumstances when investing the assets of *A B*

(b) The deputy may make any kind of investment that the person absolutely entitled to those assets could make

(c) This general power of investment includes investment in land and investment in assets outside England and Wales

(d) In exercising the power of investment, the deputy must have regard to the standard investment criteria namely the suitability of the investments and the need for diversification in so far as is appropriate to the circumstances of *A B*

(e) The deputy must from time to time review the investments, and consider whether, having regard to the standard investment criteria, they should be varied

(f) Unless the deputy reasonably concludes that in all the circumstances it is unnecessary or inappropriate to do so, before exercising any power of investment, the deputy must obtain and consider proper advice about the way in which, having regard to the standard investment criteria, the power should be exercised

> 'Proper advice' is the advice of a person who the deputy reasonably believes to be qualified to give it by his ability in and practical experience of financial and other matters relating to the proposed investment]

4. Reports

(a) The deputy is required to keep statements, vouchers, receipts and other financial records

(b) The deputy must submit an annual report to the Public Guardian

5. Costs and expenses

(a) The deputy is entitled to be reimbursed for reasonable expenses incurred provided they are in proportion to the size of the estate of *A B* and to the actual functions performed by the deputy

[(b) The deputy is authorised to pay [*name of solicitors*] fixed costs for this application and if the amount sought exceeds the fixed costs allowed the deputy is authorised to agree their costs and pay them from the funds belonging to *A B*

In default of agreement, or if the deputy or solicitors would prefer the costs to be assessed, this order is to be treated as authority to the Senior Court Costs Office to carry out a detailed assessment on the standard basis]

or if the deputy is a solicitor

[(b) The deputy is entitled to receive fixed costs in relation to this application and to receive fixed costs for the general management of the affairs of *A B*

If the deputy would prefer the costs to be assessed, this order is to be treated as authority to the Senior Court Costs Office to carry out a detailed assessment on the standard basis]

6.   Security

(a)   The deputy is required forthwith to obtain and maintain security in the sum of £... in accordance with the standard requirements as to the giving of security

(b)   To enable the deputy to give security, this order will come into force one calendar month after the date on which it was made

(c)   The deputy must not discharge any functions until the security is in place

*   *   *   *   *   *   *

A 3

ORDER appointing local authority as deputy for property and affairs

[*GENERAL TITLE*]

Whereas

1.   An application has been made for an order under the Mental Capacity Act 2005

2.   The Court is satisfied that:

(a)   *A B* is unable to make various decisions for himself in relation to a matter or matters concerning his property and affairs because of an impairment of or a disturbance in the functioning of his mind or brain

(b)   the purpose for which the order is needed cannot be as effectively achieved in a way that is less restrictive of his rights and freedom of action

IT IS ORDERED THAT

1. Appointment of deputy

(a) The holder of the office of .... of [*name of council and address*] is appointed as deputy ('the deputy') to make decisions on behalf of *A B* that he is unable to make for himself in relation to his property and affairs subject to any conditions or restrictions set out in this order

(b) The appointment will last until further order

(c) The deputy must apply the principles set out in Section 1 of the Mental Capacity Act 2005 and have regard to the guidance in the Code of Practice to the Act

2. Authority of deputy

(a) The Court confers general authority on the deputy to take possession or control of the property and affairs of *A B* and to exercise the same powers of management and investment as he has as beneficial owner, subject to the terms and conditions set out in this order

(b) The deputy may make provision for the needs of anyone who is related or connected with *A B*, if he provided for or might be expected to provide for that person's needs, by doing whatever he did or might reasonably be expected to do to meet those needs

(c) The deputy may (without obtaining any further authority from the Court) dispose of *A B*'s money or property by way of gift to any charity to which he made or might have been expected to make gifts and on customary occasions to persons who are related to or connected with him, provided that the value of each such gift is not unreasonable having regard to all the circumstances and, in particular, the size of his estate

(d) The deputy is authorised to sell the property of *A B* known as [*name of property and address*] on the best possible terms and after payment of legal fees and other professional charges to invest the net proceeds for his benefit

(e) For the purpose of giving effect to any decision the deputy may execute or sign any necessary deeds or documents

4. Reports

(a) The deputy is required to keep statements, vouchers, receipts and other financial records

(b) The deputy must submit an annual report to the Public Guardian

PART VIII

5.   Costs and expenses

(a)   The deputy is entitled to be reimbursed for reasonable expenses incurred provided they are in proportion to the size of the estate of *A B* and to the actual functions performed by the deputy

(b)   The deputy is entitled to receive fixed costs in relation to this application and to receive fixed costs for the general management of the affairs of *A B*

*   *   *   *   *   *   *

A 4
INTERIM ORDER for sale of property
[*GENERAL TITLE*]

Whereas

1.   [*Name of applicant*] ('the Applicant') has applied for an order under the Mental Capacity Act 2005

2.   From evidence that accompanied the application the Court is satisfied that:

(a)   *A B* is unable to make various decisions for himself in relation to a matter or matters concerning his property and affairs because of an impairment of or a disturbance in the functioning of his mind or brain

(b)   the purpose for which the order is needed cannot be as effectively achieved in a way that is less restrictive of his rights and freedom of action

IT IS ORDERED THAT

1.   The Applicant is authorised to sell the property of *A B* known as [*name of property and address*] on the best possible terms and after payment of legal fees and other professional charges to invest the net proceeds for the benefit of *A B* pending final determination of the application for appointment of a deputy for his property and affairs

2.   For the purpose of giving effect to this order the Applicant may execute or sign any necessary deeds or documents

*   *   *   *   *   *   *

A 5
INTERIM ORDER to investigate and report
[*GENERAL TITLE*]

Whereas

1. [*Name of applicant*] ('the Applicant') has applied for an order under the Mental Capacity Act 2005

2. The Court has reason to believe that *A B* lacks capacity in relation to matters concerning his property and affairs because of an impairment of or a disturbance in the functioning of his mind or brain and considers it in his best interests to make this interim order without delay

IT IS ORDERED THAT

1. The Applicant is directed to investigate and report to the Court of Protection as to the assets liabilities and property of *A B* and any dealings therewith and is to report back to the Court by 4.00 pm on .... 20 ...

2. For the purposes of giving effect to this order the Applicant may execute or sign any necessary deeds or documents

* * * * * * *

A 6
ORDER discharging a property and affairs deputy where capacity is regained
[GENERAL TITLE]

Whereas

[Either:

1. By order dated .... 20 ... X Y was appointed as receiver under Section 99 of the Mental Health Act 1983

2. On 1 October 2007 the receiver ('the deputy') became a deputy for property and affairs by virtue of Paragraph 1(2)(a) of Schedule 5 to the Mental Capacity Act 2005

Or:

1. By order dated .... 20 ... X Y was appointed deputy for property and affairs]

2/3. [*Name of applicant*] has applied for an order under Rule 202 of the Court of Protection Rules 2007 (supplemented by Practice Direction B to Part 23), which applies where a person ceases to lack capacity

3/4. From evidence that accompanied the application, the Court is satisfied that *A B* is able to make decisions in relation to his property and affairs

1625

4/5. Notice of the application has been given to the deputy

IT IS ORDERED THAT

1. The deputy is discharged and his powers are terminated

2. A final account by the deputy is dispensed with

[3. The deputy's security is to be discharged] – *where appropriate*

3/4. All property belonging to *A B* which remains under the control of the deputy is to be transferred forthwith to *A B* or as he directs

4/5. The funds in Court are to be transferred to *A B* as directed in the payment schedule, which is attached to and forms part of the order

5/6. The deputy's cost relating to this application and any outstanding costs of general management are to be assessed on the standard basis and when certified paid by *A B*

Payment Schedule

(Insert details of any funds held in court to be transferred to A B)

* * * * * * *

A 7

ORDER refusing permission to be appointed as deputy for personal welfare

[*GENERAL TITLE*]

Whereas

1. [*Name of the applicant*] ('the Applicant') has sought permission to apply to the Court to be appointed as a deputy to make personal welfare decisions for *A B*

2. Section 5 of the Mental Capacity Act 2005 confers a general authority to act without the need for any formal authorisation by the Court if a person does an act in connection with the care or treatment of a person who lacks capacity and acts in that person's best interests

3. Section 16(4) of the Mental Capacity Act 2005 provides that, when deciding whether it is in a person's best interests to appoint a deputy the Court must have regard to the principles that:

   (a) a decision of the Court is to be preferred to the appointment of a deputy and

   (b) the powers conferred on a deputy should be as limited in scope and duration as is reasonably practicable in the circumstances

4. In the permission form the Applicant failed to identify with sufficient particularity the reasons why it is necessary in this case to appoint a

deputy to make personal welfare decisions and what specific personal welfare powers the Applicant was seeking

IT IS ORDERED THAT

1. The application for such permission is refused pursuant to Section 50(3)(b) and (c) of the Mental Capacity Act 2005

2. For the avoidance of doubt, if an issue arises upon which a personal welfare decision or direction of the Court is sought this decision does not preclude the Applicant from re-applying at the material time [nor does it prejudice the Applicant's application to be appointed deputy to make decisions regarding *A B*'s property and financial affairs (which application is continuing)] – *as appropriate*

3. This order was made of the Court's own initiative without a hearing and without notice pursuant to Rule 27 of the Court of Protection Rules 2007

Any person affected by it may apply, pursuant to Rule 89 of the Court of Protection Rules 2007 within 21 days of the date on which the order was served to have it set aside

* * * * * * *

A 8

ORDER appointing a deputy for personal welfare

[*GENERAL TITLE*]

Whereas

1. An application has been made for an order under the Mental Capacity Act 2005

2. The Court is satisfied that:

    (a) *A B* is unable to make various decisions for himself in relation to a matter or matters concerning his personal welfare because of an impairment of or a disturbance in the functioning of his mind or brain

    (b) the purpose for which the order is needed cannot be as effectively achieved in a way that is less restrictive of his rights and freedom of action

IT IS ORDERED THAT

1. Appointment of deputy

(a) [*Deputy's forename and surname*] of]*address*] is appointed as deputy ('the deputy') to make personal welfare decisions on behalf of *A B* that he is unable to make for himself subject to the conditions and restrictions set out in the Mental Capacity Act 2005 and in this order

(b) The appointment will last until [three years from the date of the order] *or where appropriate* [further order]

(c) The deputy must apply the principles set out in Section 1 of the Mental Capacity Act 2005 and have regard to the guidance in the Code of Practice to the Mental Capacity Act 2005

2.   Authority of deputy

(a) The Court authorises the deputy to make the following decisions on behalf of *A B* that he is unable to make for himself when the decision needs to be made in relation to:

    (i)   where he should live

    (ii)   with whom he should live

    (iii)   decisions on day-to-day care including diet and dress

    (iv)   consenting to medical or dental examination and treatment on his behalf

    (v)   making arrangements for the provision of care services

    (vi)   whether he should take part in particular leisure or social activities and

    (vii)   complaints about his care or treatment

(b) For the purpose of giving effect to any of these decisions the deputy may execute or sign any necessary deeds or documents

(c) The deputy does not have authority to make a decision on behalf of *A B* in relation to a matter if the deputy knows or has reasonable grounds for believing that he has capacity in relation to the matter

(d) The deputy does not have the authority to make the following decisions or do the following things in relation to *A B*:

    (i)   to prohibit any person from having contact with him

    (ii)   to direct a person responsible for his health care to allow a different person to take over that responsibility

    (iii)   to make a decision that is inconsistent with a decision made, within the scope of his authority and in accordance with the Mental Capacity Act 2005 by the donee of a lasting power of attorney granted by him (or if there is more than one donee by any of them)

    (iv)   to consent to specific treatment if he has made a valid and applicable advance decision to refuse that specific treatment

    (v)   to refuse consent to the carrying out or continuation of life sustaining treatment in relation to him

(vi)   to do an act that is intended to restrain him otherwise than in accordance with the conditions specified in the Mental Capacity Act 2005

3. Reports

(a)   The deputy is required to keep a record of any decisions made or acts done pursuant to this order and the reasons for making or doing them

(b)   The deputy must submit an annual report to the Public Guardian

Section B: Directions Orders

There is a perception that one of the weaknesses of the new Court of Protection is that there are no precedents for case management Orders. In consequence the nominated district judges constantly find themselves needing to 're-invent the wheel' leading to a lack of consistency. Also practitioners are denied the opportunity to submit a draft of the order in advance of a directions hearing based on their knowledge of the case thereby assisting the judges with their work.

In this Part a few suggested pro-formas Orders are set out, based on the orders that some judges have been making, in the hope that this may promote the development of more useful precedents.

* * * * * * *

B 1

CASE MANAGEMENT CHECKLIST

This checklist is reproduced first to help with the content and structure of any case management order.

PRELIMINARY

JURISDICTION

Does the Court have jurisdiction based on

☐	Residence	see Hague Conference
☐	Domicile	Chapter 9
☐	Property	CoPR r 87

PERMISSION

Does the applicant need permission to apply

☐	property and affairs	CoPR Pt 8
☐	personal welfare	CoPR Pt 8

LACK OF CAPACITY

Does 'P' lack capacity in regard to

☐	property and affairs	MCA s 2
☐	personal welfare	MCA s 2
☐	conduct of proceedings	MCA s 2 & CoPR Pt 17

APPLICATION

Is the application:

☐	a new application	CoPR Pt 9
☐	within existing proceedings	CoPR Pt 10
☐	in proper form	CoPR Pt 4 and Pt 9 or 10

TRANSFER

Should the application be transferred to:

☐	a Regional Hearing Centre	CoPR Pt 2

☐   a particular Nominated Judge   CoPR Pt 2

PERSONS INVOLVED

NOTICE

Has notice been given to:

☐   'P'   CoPR Pt 7

☐   Y   CoPR Pt 9

☐   anyone else who should be given an opportunity
to participate

PARTIES

Have the following been identified:

☐   the Applicant(s)   CoPR r 73 and 85

☐   the Respondents   CoPR r 73 and 85

Should:

☐   'P' be a party   CoPR r 73

☐   any other persons be invited to become parties   CoPR r 73 and 85

LITIGATION FRIENDS

Does:

☐   'P' need a litigation friend   CoPR Pt 17

☐   any other party need a litigation friend   CoPR Pt 17

DIRECTIONS

DISCLOSURE

Are directions needed for: CoPR Pt 16

☐   disclosure of documents

☐   inspection of documents

EVIDENCE   CoPR Pt 14

Are directions needed for:

☐   exchange of witness statements

☐   examination of witness

EXPERTS   CoPR Pt 15

Is there a need for expert evidence:

☐   what discipline

☐   produced by party

☐   jointly instructed

REPORTS

Will the Court be assisted by a report from: CoPR Pt 14 – PD14E

☐   a General Visitor

☐   a Special Visitor

☐   the Public Guardian

☐   social services

☐   a health authority

PART VIII

HEARING

REQUIREMENT

At this stage: CoPR Pt 13

☐   can a final order be made

☐   can a provisional order be made

☐   should a telephone directions hearing be listed

☐   should an attended directions hearing be listed

☐   can a final hearing be listed

ADMINISTRATIVE

FILING OF DOCUMENTS

Should these be sent:

☐   to Archway

☐   to a Regional Hearing Centre

☐   to a nominated Judge by email

* * * * * * *

B 2

MULTI-PURPOSE DIRECTIONS ORDER

This pro-forma Order contains many provisions that may be adopted when initial Directions are given by a nominated District Judge. It should be modified to meet the particular circumstances.

THIS ORDER IS NOT VALID UNLESS IT BEARS THE IMPRESSED SEAL OF THE COURT OF PROTECTION IN THE BOTTOM RIGHT HAND CORNER ON ALL PAGES

COURT OF PROTECTION

MENTAL CAPACITY ACT 2005

Case No: 000000

IN THE MATTER OF [*FULL NAME*]

(referred to in this Order as '*A B*')

DIRECTIONS ORDER

MADE by District Judge [*name*]

AT Archway Tower, 2 Junction Road, London N19 5SZ [*or regional court address*]

ON [*date*]

UPON THE APPLICATION OF [*name*] – or

UPON HEARING counsel / solicitors for [*name*] and – *complete as appropriate*

WHEREAS

1. An application has been made by [*name and any relationship to A B*] for an order under the Mental Capacity Act 2005 in relation to *A B*

2. The application concerns *A B*s personal welfare *and/or* property and affairs.

3. [The Court has granted permission for the application to be brought] – *where required*

4. [The application has been referred to a nominated District Judge at this regional Court]

5. Acknowledgments have been received from [*names and relationship to A B (if any)*]

[*Personal welfare application*]

6. The personal welfare decisions that may need to be considered by the Court appear to be: - *complete as appropriate*

   (a) where and with whom *A B* is to live

   (b) with whom *A B* is to have contact

   (c) whether [*name*] is to be prohibited from having contact with to *A B*

   (d) whether *A B* should *give/refuse* consent to the carrying out or continuation of treatment by a person providing health care for *A B*

   (e) whether *A B* should take part in particular leisure or social activities

   (f) [*identify any other decision*]

7. It appears that there is a dispute *and/or* uncertainty as to the decisions that should be made.

8. The application was accompanied by evidence that *A B* is personally unable to make these decisions because of an impairment of, or a disturbance in the functioning of, the mind or brain

[*Property and affairs application*]

9. The application was accompanied by evidence that *A B* is personally unable to make various decisions regarding the management of property and financial affairs because of an impairment of, or a disturbance in the functioning of, the mind or brain.

10. The application was also accompanied by an inventory of the assets and liabilities and the income and expenditure of *A B*

[*All applications*]

11. The Court is satisfied on the evidence already presented that *A B* does not have capacity to make a decision on these matter *or*

PART VIII

There is a **preliminary issue** as to whether *A B* has capacity to make decisions on these matters

12. Notice of the application has been given to A B and to relatives and other persons to be notified in accordance with the Court of Protection Rules 2007

THE COURT NOW ORDERS THAT:

The parties

1. The parties to these proceedings are:

    1.1.   the Applicant(s), being [*names*]

    1.2.   [*name any other person identified at this stage*]

    1.3.   *A B* – *if appropriate at this stage*

    [The Official Solicitor is to be served by the Court with a copy of the application and this Order and to notify the Court within 8 weeks of service as to whether he consents to being appointed as litigation friend of *A B*]

2. Any other person (whether or not served with notice of the application) who wishes to be joined as a party must apply to the Court at the earliest opportunity

3. *A B* need not be joined as a party to these proceedings

    A copy of this Order is to be served by the Court on *A B* and any request that *he/she* be joined as a party (which may be made by *A B* or someone on *his/her* behalf) is to be made in writing to the Court within 14 days of service *or*

Involvement of the person to whom the application relates - *if not a party*

4. *A B* even though not a party should be involved in these proceedings to the extent that *he/she* is able to contribute and wishes to do so:

    4.1   a party who does not serve statements or documents on *A B* must be in a position to justify this at the hearing

    4.2   *A B* is to be enabled to attend any hearing if such attendance would not be too distressing or detrimental to health

Preliminary issue - *if appropriate*

5. The proceedings are stayed pending the determination of the preliminary issue and the following directions relate to that issue only *or*

    At the commencement of the [directions] hearing the Court will address the preliminary issue

6. The parties are to send to the Court and copy to each other no later than [*date*] any evidence that is to be relied upon as to the capacity of *A B*:

    6.1. medical evidence shall preferably be in the form of a report

    6.2. other evidence shall preferably be in the form of a statement exhibiting any documents relied upon

7. The Public Guardian is to arrange for one of the Court of Protection Special Visitors to attend upon and assess the capacity of *A B* at the present time in regard to decisions of the nature identified in this Order:

    7.1. A report is to be produced to the Court before [*date*]

    7.2. The Court will send a copy of the report to the parties and such other persons as the Court may direct

Statements

8. All statements to be relied upon in these proceedings shall:

    8.1. be headed with the title to these proceedings as set out in this Order;

    8.2. be in legible form (preferably typed) and with numbered paragraphs;

    8.3. commence with the name and address of the person making the statement;

    8.4. have attached any documents referred to;

    8.5. be dated and signed at the end;

    8.6. be copied with any attached documents to all other parties (or their solicitors) at the same time as they are sent to the Court.

9. The Applicant(s) shall no later than [*date*] send to the Court a statement (or separate statements) in support of their application which shall:

    9.1. identify the declarations or orders that the Court is requested to make

    9.2. concisely set out the facts and evidence to be relied upon

10. The other parties shall no later than [*date*] send to the Court their statements in response to the statement(s) received from the Applicant(s)

Documentary and other evidence

11. Each party shall send to the Court and the other parties no later than [*date*] a copy of any other documents to be relied upon.

12. The evidence of any other person that is to be relied upon is to be submitted in the form of a statement or a signed and dated letter to the Court [by *date*] *or* [at least 14 days before the hearing] and copied to the other parties.

PART VIII

Reports – *when required*

13. The Public Guardian is requested to arrange or produce the following report no later than [*date*]:

    13.1. a report as to the contents of any file maintained by the Office of the Public Guardian [or the former Public Guardianship Office]

    13.2. a report by the [*name*] social services department or [*name*] health authority as to [*identify the nature of the report*]

    13.3. a report by one of the Court of Protection General/Special Visitors as to [*identify the nature of the report*]

14. The Court will send a copy of the report to the parties and such other persons as the Court may direct or The Court will decide the extent to which this report is to be disclosed

Directions hearing – *when required*

15. There will be a directions hearing before District Judge [*name*] at [*name and address of court*] on [*date*] at [*time*] with a time estimate of [*duration of hearing*]:

    15.1. the parties should attend either personally or by their legal representatives;

    15.2. this hearing may be by telephone and the solicitors for the [*party*] shall arrange the telephone conference in the manner provided for in the Civil Procedure Rules 1998 (PD 23 para 6).

Hearing – *if required at this stage*

16. There will be a full hearing before District Judge [*name*] at [*name and address of court*] on [*date*] at [*time*] with a time estimate of [*duration of hearing*]:

    16.1. the parties are encouraged to attend (with or without their legal representatives)

    16.2. the hearing may continue in the absence of a party who does not attend or is not represented

    16.3. the Court has a discretion to decide who may be present for the whole or a part of the hearing

17. The Court may refuse to consider any statements or documents that have not been disclosed to the other parties prior to the hearing

18. The parties should be prepared to produce any financial records that are available (or a summary of the financial position of the *A B*) when they attend the hearing – *financial cases only*

19. If the hearing cannot be concluded further directions may be given to ensure that outstanding matters are properly dealt with at an adjourned hearing

Costs

20. A party who seeks to recover costs or expenses shall bring a summary or estimate of those costs to the hearing on the basis that:

    20.1. the Court may wish to consider a summary assessment or payment of a specified contribution

    20.2. where justified costs may be ordered to be paid out of *A B's* estate;

    20.3. a party who has acted unreasonably may be refused costs and ordered to pay the costs of another party in whole or in part

Further directions – *where Order made without a hearing*

21. This Order was made of the Court's own initiative without a hearing and without notice pursuant to Rule 27 of the Court of Protection Rules 2007 and any person affected by it may apply pursuant to Rule 89 within 21 days of the date on which the Order was served to have it varied or set aside

22. Any request to postpone the hearing or for further or other directions should be made with reasons to the Court in writing within 21 days of service of this Order

23. All communications with the Court in response to this order shall state the above Case Number and be sent to:

> **Court of Protection,**
> **Archway Tower,**
> **2 Junction Road,**
> **London N19 5SZ**

and if urgent or otherwise appropriate may be copied to District Judge [*name*] by email at the following address: [*email address of judge*] – *not all judges are willing to communicate in this way*

*   *   *   *   *   *   *

B 3

FIRST DIRECTIONS ORDER
family dispute as to residence and contact

This is an example of a first Directions Order made by a Regional District Judge in a case where there is a dispute between family members as to where an elderly parent should live and whether contact to certain members should be restricted.

THIS ORDER IS NOT VALID UNLESS IT BEARS THE IMPRESSED SEAL OF THE
COURT OF PROTECTION IN THE BOTTOM RIGHT HAND CORNER ON ALL PAGES

COURT OF PROTECTION

MENTAL CAPACITY ACT 2005

Case No: 000000

IN THE MATTER OF [*FULL NAME*]

(referred to in this Order as 'Mrs B')

DIRECTIONS ORDER

MADE by District Judge [*name*]

AT [*name*] Court of [*address*]

ON [*date*]

UPON THE APPLICATION OF [*name*]

WHEREAS

1. An application has been made by [*name*] through solicitors for an order
    under the Mental Capacity Act 2005 in relation to her mother Mrs B

2. The application concerns the personal welfare of Mrs B

3. The decisions that may need to be considered by the Court appear to
    be:

    (a) whether a personal welfare Deputy should be appointed for
         Mrs B

    (b) whether Mrs B is to live and be cared for in the vicinity of
         [*town 1*] or [*town 2*]

    (c) whether any person is to be prohibited from having contact with
         Mrs B

4. There is a dispute and/or uncertainty as to the decisions that should be
    made

5. The application was accompanied by evidence that Mrs B is personally
    unable to make these decisions because of an impairment of, or a
    disturbance in the functioning of, the mind or brain

6. The Court is satisfied on the evidence already presented that Mrs B
    does not have capacity to make a decision on these matter

7. Notice of the application has been given to Mrs B and to relatives and
    other persons to be notified in accordance with the Court of Protection
    Rules 2007

8. The Court has power to record the wishes of Mrs B and any decisions
    that she would make but not to direct that any specific care provision be
    provided for her

THE COURT NOW ORDERS THAT:

1. Permission is granted for this application to be brought

2. The appointment of a personal welfare Deputy is refused on the basis that it is sufficient for the Court to make decisions on the matters in issue

The parties

3. The parties to these proceedings are:

    3.1. the Applicant, being [*name*] of [*address*].

    3.2. [*name*] (son) of [*address*].

    3.3. [*name*] (daughter) of [*address*].

4. Any other person including a local authority (whether or not served with notice of the application) who wishes to be joined as a party must apply to the Court at the earliest opportunity

5. Mrs B need not be joined as a party to these proceedings

Involvement of the local authorities

6. The Applicant shall send a copy of this Order to the social services authorities for [*town 1*] and [*town 2*] having present or prospective responsibility for the care of Mrs B

7. If those authorities do not wish to become parties they may nevertheless send to the Court a statement addressing the best interests of Mrs B and exhibiting any relevant documents by [*date*]

8. Any such statements shall be copied by the Court to the parties

Statements

9. All statements to be relied upon in these proceedings shall: [set out as in B2 Multi-Purpose Directions Order]

10. The Applicant's statement dated [*date*] is admitted in support of her application but she shall no later than [*date*] send to the Court an updated statement which shall:

    10.1. identify the declarations or orders that the Court is requested to make, and in particular specifying any care home to which Mrs B could be moved (including whether there is a vacancy and funding can be available)

    10.2. concisely set out any further facts and evidence to be relied upon

11. The other parties shall no later than [*date*] send to the Court their statements in response to the statements received from the Applicant

PART VIII

Documentary and other evidence

12. Each party shall send to the Court and the other parties no later than [*date*] a copy of any other documents to be relied upon

13. The evidence of any other person that is to be relied upon is to be submitted in the form of a statement or a signed and dated letter to the Court at least 14 days before the hearing and copied to the other parties

Hearing

14. There will be a hearing before District Judge [*name*] at [*court address*] on [*date*] at [*time*] with a time estimate of [*duration*]:

  14.1. the parties are encouraged to attend (with or without their legal representatives)

  14.2. the hearing may continue in the absence of a party who does not attend or is not represented

  14.3. the Court has a discretion to decide who may be present for the whole or a part of the hearing

15. The Court may refuse to consider any statements or documents that have not been disclosed to the other parties prior to the hearing

16. The parties should be prepared to produce any financial records that are available (or a summary of the financial position of Mrs B) when they attend the hearing

17. If the hearing cannot be concluded further directions may be given to ensure that outstanding matters are properly dealt with at an adjourned hearing

Further directions

18. Any party may apply within 14 days of receipt of this Order for its terms to be varied or reconsidered

19. All communications with the Court in response to this order shall state the above Case Number and be sent to: [*as in B2 Multi-Purpose Directions Order*]

*   *   *   *   *   *   *

B 4

DIRECTIONS ORDER
'adult care' case

This is an example of a first Directions Order made in a case where there had been previous care proceedings relating to an abused child with severe learning disabilities. The child has now attained, or is shortly to attain, legal majority whereupon the care order under the Children Act 1989 is no longer effective but the parents seek to intervene.

THIS ORDER IS NOT VALID UNLESS IT BEARS THE IMPRESSED SEAL OF THE COURT OF PROTECTION IN THE BOTTOM RIGHT HAND CORNER ON ALL PAGES

COURT OF PROTECTION

MENTAL CAPACITY ACT 2005

Case No: 000000

IN THE MATTER OF [*FULL NAME*]

(referred to in this Order as '*R M*')

BETWEEN:

X COUNTY COUNCIL

Applicant

and

R M [*full name*]
**by her litigation friend The
Official Solicitor**

**The person to whom
the application relates**

M M [*full name – father*]

First Respondent

and

D M [*full name*]

Second Respondent

DIRECTIONS ORDER

BEFORE District Judge [*name*] sitting at Archway Tower, 2 Junction Road, London N19 5SZ [*or regional court address*]

On [*date*]

UPON reading all documents filed and in particular [*list relevant documents*]

AND UPON HEARING by way of a telephone conference the solicitor for the Applicant local authority, counsel for *R M* and the solicitor for the First and Second Respondents [*or as appropriate*]

BY CONSENT IT IS ORDERED THAT:

Parties

1.   D M (step-mother of *R M*) be named as Second Respondent in these proceedings

2.   Having consented the Official Solicitor is appointed to act as *R M*'s litigation friend

PART VIII

3.   In the interests of fairness [*name*] is given 14 days from the date of this order to apply to be made a party to these proceedings

4.   The Applicant is to use its best endeavours to locate [*name*] (*R M*'s natural mother) on the basis that:

   (a)   the Respondents have agreed to provide such contact details as they possess

   (b)   if the Applicant locates her it is to serve her with all papers from these proceedings and the Official Solicitor is to be informed of her address

5.   *R M*'s current address is not to be disclosed to the Respondents or any other person without the permission of the Official Solicitor or further order of the Court

Statements

6.   The Applicant by [*date*] file and serve on all parties and instructed experts a statement setting out the history of its involvement with *R M*, details of her current care arrangements and its view on future arrangements

7.   The Respondents by [*date*] file and serve on all parties and instructed experts their statements in response to the Applicant's statement and containing all further information upon which they wish to rely

Expert reports

8.   The Applicant, the Official Solicitor and the Respondents shall instruct an independent consultant psychiatrist in learning disabilities with particular expertise in the area of Autistic Spectrum Disorder, to investigate and report as to:

   (a)   *R M*'s capacity and best interests regarding future contact arrangements with the Respondents and others, including her sibling/half-siblings

   (b)   where *R M* should reside and the care she should receive

9.   The Applicant, the Official Solicitor and the Respondent shall instruct an independent social worker with a specialism in working with young adults and autistic spectrum disorders and learning difficulties, to investigate and report as to:

   (a)   *R M*'s best interests regarding future contact arrangements with the Respondents and others, including her sibling/half siblings

   (b)   where *R M* should reside and the care she should receive

10. The identities of the consultant psychiatrist and independent social worker are to be notified to the Court by [*date*]:

   (a)   These experts are to be instructed by way of joint letters of instruction to be drafted by the Official Solicitor by [*date*]

(b)   The cost of instructing these experts be shared equally between the parties and be deemed a reasonable cost for the purposes of any public funding certificates

(c)   To the extent that they consider it necessary these experts have permission to interview *R M* and any other person they consider to be necessary

11. These experts have permission to read *R M*'s social services' files and medical records, including any general practitioner records which are to be produced by her G.P. on the written request of the Official Solicitor who shall make such request within 14 days from the date of this order

Disclosure

12. The Official Solicitor and his representative have permission to read R. M's social services files and to draw any material they consider relevant to the attention of the Court and the parties

13. The Applicant do disclose to the Official Solicitor all papers from the judicial review proceedings brought against it by the Second Respondent, under claim number [*number*] within 7 days from the date of this order

14. The Chief Constable of [*place*] is directed to disclose to the Official Solicitor by [*date*] all information held relating to the investigation into *R M*'s allegation made on [*date*] of assault against the First Respondent:

(a)   such information shall on receipt be disclosed by the Official Solicitor to the other parties and any experts instructed within these proceedings

(b)   there be permission to apply as to the need for and implementation of this order

15. The Applicant is to seek permission of [*name*] County Court to disclose papers from the care proceedings brought by the Applicant pursuant to section 31 of the Children Act 1989, under case number [*number*], relating to *R M* The papers are to then be disclosed to the other parties and any experts instructed within these proceedings

Interim Orders

16. In the interim it will not be unlawful for *R M* to continue to reside in her current accommodation or for the Applicant to restrict her contact with her family at its discretion

Hearing

17. The matter be listed for a further directions hearing before District Judge [*name*] at [*name*] Court [*address*] with a time estimate of [*time*] on the first available date after [*date*] to consider:

(a)   the reports of the independent experts

(b)   any further directions

(c)   timetabling of a final hearing

18.   Costs reserved save for detailed assessment of any publicly funded parties' costs

*   *   *   *   *   *   *

B 5

DIRECTIONS ORDER
local authority personal welfare application

This is an example of an Order made when there was a threat by a mother to remove an incapacitated adult child from health authority care. It contains many provisions that may be requested by the Official Solicitor when acting as litigation friend of the person to whom the application relates. Not all clauses will be required and it should be modified to meet the particular circumstances.

THIS ORDER IS NOT VALID UNLESS IT BEARS THE IMPRESSED SEAL OF THE COURT OF PROTECTION IN THE BOTTOM RIGHT HAND CORNER ON ALL PAGES

COURT OF PROTECTION

MENTAL CAPACITY ACT 2005

Case No: 000000

IN THE MATTER OF [*FULL NAME*]

(referred to in this Order as '*AM*')

BETWEEN

[NAME] COUNTY COUNCIL ('The Council')

Applicant

-and-

[NAME] ('AM')
by his litigation friend, the Official Solicitor

**First Respondent
and the person to whom the application relates**

[NAME] ('PM')

Second Respondent

[NAME] NHS FOUNDATION TRUST ('The Trust')

Third Respondent

-and-

[NAME] PRIMARY CARE TRUST ('The PCT')

Fourth Respondent

BEFORE District Judge [*name*] sitting at Archway Tower, 2 Junction Road, London N19 5SZ [*or regional court address*]

On [*date*]

UPON HEARING the solicitor for the Applicant, counsel for the First Respondent and the Second Respondent in person [and the social worker involved in care provision] (there being no attendance on behalf of Third and Fourth Respondents) [*or as appropriate*]

AND UPON reading the bundle of documents lodged by the Applicant *or* all documents filed and in particular [*list relevant documents*]

AND UPON it being recorded that the Fourth Respondent is the supervisory authority in respect of the relevant DoLS authorisation and the Third Respondent is the relevant managing authority.

AND UPON the bases that:

(a)   the parties are those recorded in the Heading to this Order

(b)   the parties shall henceforth be referred in all orders and documents in these proceedings by the abbreviations appearing in brackets after their names (which shall for clarity be included in future Headings)

(c)   the mother of AM shall be referred to as 'NJ'

(d)   the responsible treating medical practitioners, social workers and any witness (other than an expert witness who gives evidence in these proceedings whether by statement or otherwise in writing or orally) shall be referred to by their initials

IN THE INTERIM and until further order IT IS ORDERED AND DECLARED that:

1.   AM lacks capacity to litigate in these proceedings and to make decisions:

    (a)   as to his residence

    (b)   as to the contact he should have with others

    (c)   as to the care package that he should receive

    (d)   about treatment in relation to both his general health and his medical needs

2.   It is lawful and in AM's best interests that he continues to:

    (a)   reside at the [*name*] Home ('the nursing home') in the care of The PCT

    (b)   have contact with his family by agreement between individual members and the Council

    (c)   receive a care package provided by The PCT in accordance with his assessed needs

IT IS FURTHER ORDERED AND DIRECTED that:

Parties

3.   The Official Solicitor having accepted the invitation of the Court to act as litigation friend of AM:

    (a)   is appointed as litigation friend

    (b)   is authorised in the name and on behalf of AM to apply for and accept any offer of public funding made to him by the Legal Services Commission and to sign the offer of public funding on AM's behalf

4.   The Trust and The PCT are made parties to these proceedings

5.   PM (the father of AM) is also made a party at his request

6.   Although NJ (the mother of AM) has not engaged with the Court and is not presently a party she is to receive from the Council a copy of this Order and may be shown and (at her request) given copies of all documents in the proceedings subject to the requirements of confidentiality recorded at the end of this Order

Disclosure

7.   The Council file and serve on all parties no later than [*date*] a copy of the Order dated [*date*] appointing its nominee to be a receiver for AM (becoming a deputy for financial affairs from 1st October 2007)

8.   Any third party is hereby directed and authorised to release to the Official Solicitor such information and documents as he may require on behalf of AM in the course of his investigations

Documents

9.   The Council, the Trust and the PCT prepare and serve upon the Official Solicitor no later than [*date*] a paginated bundle of any medical, social work or other care records (including those relating to safeguarding adults meetings and deprivation of liberty issues) held by them in relation to AM:

    (a)   from [*date*] to date

    (b)   pre-dating [*date*] if relevant

Experts

10.   The parties instruct on a joint basis:

    (a)   a consultant psychiatrist or psychologist to prepare a report on AM's capacity to make decisions of the nature specified in paragraph 1 of this Order and if AM lacks capacity, what is in his best interests in respect of residence, care and contact

(b)   an independent social worker to prepare a report as to AM's best interests in respect of residence, care and contact

11. The identity of such experts be agreed between the instructing parties by [*date*]

12. The Official Solicitor draft letters of instruction to the experts, to be circulated to the instructing parties for comment by 4pm on [*date*] and sent to the experts no later than 4pm on [*date*]. In the event of any disagreement, the parties may send side letters to the experts

13. These experts have permission to interview AM and read all and any records in respect of AM

14. The experts file and serve their reports by [*date*]

15. The costs of the instruction of the experts and their attendance at court to give evidence be met in the following shares and the same be a reasonable expense for the purposes of any party's LSC public funding certificate:

(a)   The Council – one third

(b)   The Official Solicitor – one third

(c)   The Trust and The PCT – one third (to be shared between them in such proportions as they may agree)

Further Evidence

16. The statement of [*name*] (social worker) dated [*date*] and the Minutes of the multi-disciplinary meeting on [*date*] be admitted in evidence and copies made available to the parties

17. By 4pm on [*date*] The Council (and The PCT and The Trust if so advised) file and serve all statements upon which they intend to rely as to AM's best interests and his eligibility for detention under Schedule 1A of the Mental Capacity Act 2005

18. By 4pm on [*date*] The Official Solicitor file and serve any statements upon which he intends to rely as to AM's best interests

Procedure

19. The Council by 4pm on [*date*] produce an index for a bundle of all documents to be used at the next hearing, and serve it on the other parties

(a)   The bundle be prepared in accordance with the President's Direction in respect of the format of bundles in the Family Division

(b)   The index be updated and circulated as appropriate when further documents are filed in these proceedings

PART VIII

20. This directions hearing is adjourned to [*time*] on [*date*] before District Judge [*name*] at [*name*] Court [*address*] with a time estimate of [*duration*]

21. The Council provide a copy of this Order (unsealed if a sealed copy is not then available) to The PCT and The Trust by 4pm on [*date*]:

    (a)   The PCT and/or The Trust may apply to set aside or vary this Order on 72 hours notice to the other parties

    (b)   Any such application is to be made by 4pm on [*date*] and referred to District Judge [*name*] who will consider further directions

22. Any party has permission to apply to District Judge [*name*] for further directions or orders before the adjourned hearing

23. All communications with the Court in response to this order shall state the above Case Number and be sent to: [*as in B2 Multi-Purpose Directions Order*]

Costs

24. The costs of this hearing are reserved to the final hearing save that there be detailed assessment of any publicly funded parties' costs at the conclusion of the proceedings

*   *   *   *   *   *   *

Section C: Final Orders

As the Court of Protection develops precedents for final Orders will become accepted and available. A few are set out here, based on the orders that some judges have been making, in the hope that this may promote the development of more useful precedents

* * * * * * *

C 1
ORDER
Capacity: financial affairs

This is an example of an Order made at a Regional hearing following a dispute as to whether the person to whom the application relates has capacity in regard to his financial affairs.

THIS ORDER IS NOT VALID UNLESS IT BEARS THE IMPRESSED SEAL OF THE COURT OF PROTECTION IN THE BOTTOM RIGHT HAND CORNER ON ALL PAGES

COURT OF PROTECTION

MENTAL CAPACITY ACT 2005

Case No: 000000

IN THE MATTER OF [*FULL NAME*]

(referred to in this Order as '*J T*')

FINAL ORDER

BEFORE District Judge [*name*] sitting at [*regional court address*] on [*date*]

UPON HEARING the solicitors for *J T* in his presence (there being no attendance by the Applicant)

WHEREAS

1. An application has been made by [*name and any relationship to J T*] for an order under the Mental Capacity Act 2005 in relation to *J T*

2. Notice of the application has been given to *J T* and to relatives and other persons to be notified in accordance with the Court of Protection Rules 2007

3. The application concerns *J T's* property and affairs

4. The Court has considered medical and other evidence as to whether *J T* is personally unable to make various decisions regarding the management of property and financial affairs because of an impairment of, or a disturbance in the functioning of, the mind or brain

PART VIII

5.   The Court has been assisted by a Report of the Medical Visitor [*name*]
     dated [*date*] following perusal of all previous medical evidence

THE COURT NOW ORDERS THAT:

1.   It be declared that *J T* has capacity to manage his property and financial
     affairs

2.   The costs of the solicitors who represented *J T* in this application shall
     be paid by *J T* and assessed on the standard basis if not agreed by him

                         *   *   *   *   *   *   *

C 2
ORDER
EPA or Deputy

This Order was made at a Regional hearing following a dispute as to
whether an enduring powers of attorney should be registered or a deputy be
appointed for financial affairs.

THIS ORDER IS NOT VALID UNLESS IT BEARS THE IMPRESSED SEAL OF THE
COURT OF PROTECTION IN THE BOTTOM RIGHT HAND CORNER ON ALL PAGES

COURT OF PROTECTION

MENTAL CAPACITY ACT 2005

                                                    Case No: 000000

IN THE MATTER OF [*FULL NAME*]

(referred to in this Order as '*M M*')

FINAL ORDER

BEFORE District Judge [*name*] sitting at [*regional court address*] on [*date*]

UPON considering the application of [*name*] County Council for
appointment as a financial deputy and the further application for registration
of an enduring power of attorney

AND UPON noting the consent of all parties involved to a compromise
whereby *E J* (a solicitor and one of the proposed attorneys) be appointed as
a finance deputy

AND UPON the Court being satisfied that:

(a)   *MM* is personally unable to make various decisions regarding the
      management of property and financial affairs because of an impairment
      of, or a disturbance in the functioning of, the mind or brain

(b)   the compromise is in the best interests of *M M*

THE COURT NOW ORDERS THAT:

1. The application for registration of the document purporting to be an enduring power of attorney dated [*date*] be refused and that document be revoked

2. E J of [*name of firm*], solicitors, [*address*] be appointed as a financial deputy for *M M* with comprehensive powers in the terms of an Order to be settled by a resident District Judge sitting at Archway – *for the terms of an Order see A 2 above*

3. The deputy is to agree and pay from the funds of *M M* the reasonable costs of [*name*] County Council in respect of the Council's application with permission to apply to District Judge [*name*] in the event of agreement not being reached

4. The costs of [*name*], solicitors are also to be paid from the funds of M M after approval by District Judge [*name*]. For the purpose of such approval a summary of the costs is to be submitted to District Judge [*name*] [by email *or* at [*name*] Court]

5. Any party may apply within 7 days of receipt of this Order for its terms to be varied or reconsidered

6. All written communications with the Court in response to this order shall be sent to Archway Tower, 2 Junction Road, London N19 5SZ

* * * * * * *

C 3
ORDER
Discharge from the jurisdiction

This 'imaginative' Order was made following a decision that the Applicant was capable of handling her financial affairs which included substantial damages recovered in a personal injury claim. Capacity depended upon taking professional advice and there were fears that due to her brain injury the Applicant may act without advice despite her assurances to the contrary.

THIS ORDER IS NOT VALID UNLESS IT BEARS THE IMPRESSED SEAL OF THE COURT OF PROTECTION IN THE BOTTOM RIGHT HAND CORNER ON ALL PAGES

COURT OF PROTECTION

MENTAL CAPACITY ACT 2005

Case No: 000000

IN THE MATTER OF [*FULL NAME*]

(referred to in this Order as '*J B*')

FINAL ORDER

BEFORE District Judge [*name*] sitting at [*regional court address*] on [*date*]

UPON the application of *J B* for an Order discharging her from the jurisdiction of the Court of Protection on the ground that she ceases to lack capacity to make decisions in relation to the matters to which these proceedings relate

AND UPON reading:

1.   the said application and accompanying Report of Dr [*name*], consultant clinical neuropsychologist dated [*date*]

2.   the statement of the Deputy, [*name*], dated [*name*]

3.   the Report of the Special Visitor, [*name*], consultant in adult psychiatry dated [*date*]

4.   the further documents submitted by *J B* pursuant to the directions Order dated [*name*]

AND UPON hearing *J B* and her financial deputy [*name*] and her daughter [*name*]

AND WHEREAS it appears to the Court that:

(a)   by an Order dated [*date*], [*name*] was appointed as receiver under section 99 of the Mental Health Act 1983

(b)   on [*date*] the receiver became a deputy by virtue of paragraph 1(2)(a) of Schedule 5 to the Mental Capacity Act 2005

(c)   *J B* is now able to make decisions for herself in relation to her property and affairs

(d)   this is dependent upon her continuing to seek and rely upon advice and guidance of the nature and quality that has hitherto been available to her

(e)   without such advice she may not understand the implications of any significant decisions and be vulnerable to abuse if she failed to avail herself of such support

THE COURT NOW ORDERS THAT:

1.   *J B* be discharged from the jurisdiction of this Court and the appointment of [*name*] as Deputy do cease with effect from [*date*] unless before that date an application is made pursuant to the following paragraph of this Order

2.   Either the said [*name*] or the daughter [*name*] may apply at any time for this decision to be reconsidered or for the Court again to assume jurisdiction based upon evidence of a deterioration in the health or serious inappropriate conduct on the part of *J B* arising after the date of this Order

3.   An application may be made to the Court for the purpose of implementing this Order and in particular for:

    3.1.   a final account to be delivered or dispensed with

3.2. the discharge of any security

3.3. funds and property to be released to *J B*

4. Following or immediately prior to the termination of her appointment the reasonable costs of [*name*] as Deputy and in connection with this application be paid by *J B* or from her estate, such costs to be assessed if not agreed

*   *   *   *   *   *   *

C 4
ORDER
Change of financial Deputy

The following two Orders were made in response to persistent applications to be discharged from the jurisdiction and, failing this, to change the professional deputy. The Applicant had sustained brain injuries in an accident and proved irresponsible when given some discretion in regard to the management of the damages award. He was given permission to instruct his own solicitor to pursue the application.

THIS ORDER IS NOT VALID UNLESS IT BEARS THE IMPRESSED SEAL OF THE COURT OF PROTECTION IN THE BOTTOM RIGHT HAND CORNER ON ALL PAGES

COURT OF PROTECTION

MENTAL CAPACITY ACT 2005

Case No: 000000

IN THE MATTER OF [*FULL NAME*]

(referred to in this Order as '*J M*')

ORDER 1

UPON READING the Court file

AND UPON considering a Report dated [*date*] by [*name*], consultant psychiatrist which was submitted by the solicitors acting for *J M*

IT IS ORDERED THAT:

1. The application by *J M* to be discharged from the jurisdiction of this Court is dismissed

2. The appointment of the Deputy is to continue on the existing terms pending further order

3. *J M* (through his solicitor) is to send to the Court at Archway, London and copy to the Deputy no later than [*date*] a statement explaining why he wishes to have a change of deputy and indicating who he wishes to be appointed

4. In default the application to change the deputy is dismissed

5. The Deputy is to send to the Court at Archway, London and copy to *J M* (through his solicitor) a statement in response and updating the Court as to the present position within 28 days of receiving the statement from *J M*

6. Any further reference to the Court is to be reserved to District Judge [*name*] or, in his absence, Senior Judge Lush

7. The Deputy is to agree and pay the costs of *J M*'s solicitors in connection with this application (with reference to District Judge [*name*] if not agreed)

ORDER 2

UPON READING the Court file

AND UPON considering:

(a) the Directions Order made on [*date*]

(b) a statement by *J M* dated [*date*]

(c) a statement by the Deputy, [*name*] dated [*date*] (a copy of which will have been made available to *J M*

IT IS ORDERED THAT:

1. The application by *J M* to change the Deputy is dismissed and the appointment of [*name*] is to continue on the existing terms until further order

2. The Deputy is to pay the costs of [*name*] solicitors in connection with this application in the sum of £[*amount*] plus VAT

3. If *J M* is dissatisfied with this decision he may within 21 days of receipt request that it be reviewed at a hearing before District Judge [*name*] sitting at [*Court*]

4. Any further reference to the Court is to be reserved to District Judge [*name*] or, in his absence, Senior Judge Lush

* * * * * * *

C 5

ORDER
Cancellation of EPA and appointment of financial Deputy

This is an example of an Order made when, following a reserved Judgment, registration of an EPA was refused and a financial Deputy was appointed.

THIS ORDER IS NOT VALID UNLESS IT BEARS THE IMPRESSED SEAL OF THE
COURT OF PROTECTION IN THE BOTTOM RIGHT HAND CORNER ON ALL PAGES

COURT OF PROTECTION

MENTAL CAPACITY ACT 2005

Case No: 000000

IN THE MATTER OF [*FULL NAME*]

(referred to in this Order as '*M S*')

FINAL ORDER

BEFORE District Judge [*name*] sitting at [*regional court address*] on [*date*]
pursuant to a reserved Judgment dated [*date*]

WHEREAS

1. An application has been made for an order under the Mental Capacity
    Act 2005

2. The court is satisfied that *M S* is unable to make various decisions for
    herself in relation to a matter or matters concerning her property and
    affairs because of an impairment of, or a disturbance in the functioning
    of, her mind or brain

3. The court is satisfied that the purpose for which the order is needed
    cannot be as effectively achieved in a way that is less restrictive of her
    rights and freedom of action

IT IS ORDERED THAT:

Cancellation of enduring power of attorney

1. In relation to the enduring power of attorney dated [*date*] of *M S*:

    1.1.   registration be cancelled

    1.2.   the document be revoked as a power of attorney

Appointment of deputy

2. [*name*] of [*address*] is appointed as deputy ('the deputy') to make
    decisions on behalf of *M S* that she is unable to make for herself in
    relation to her property and affairs subject to any conditions or
    restrictions set out in this order

3. The appointment will last until further order

4. The deputy must apply the principles set out in section 1 of the Mental
    Capacity Act 2005 and have regard to the guidance in the Code of
    Practice to the Act

PART VIII

Authority of deputy

5.   The court confers general authority on the deputy to take possession or control of the property and affairs of *M S* and to exercise the same powers of management and investment as she has as beneficial owner, subject to the terms and conditions set out in this order

6.   The deputy may make provision for the needs of anyone who is related to or connected with *M S*, if she provided for or might be expected to provide for that person's needs, by doing whatever she did or might reasonably be expected to do to meet those needs

7.   The deputy may (without obtaining any further authority from the court) dispose of money and property of *M S* by way of gift to any charity to which she made or might have been expected to make gifts and on customary occasions to persons who are related to or connected with her, provided that the value of each such gift is not unreasonable having regard to all the circumstances and, in particular, the size of her estate

8.   The deputy is authorised to sell the property of *M S* known as [*address*] on the best possible terms and after payment of legal fees and other professional charges to invest the net proceeds for her benefit

9.   For the purpose of giving effect to any decision the deputy may execute or sign any necessary deeds or documents

Reports

10. The deputy is required to keep statements, vouchers, receipts and other financial records

11. The deputy must submit an annual report to the Public Guardian

12. The deputy must submit a financial summary to the three children of *M S* on 1st June and 1st December each year commencing 1st December 2009

Costs and expenses

13. The deputy is entitled to be reimbursed for reasonable expenses incurred provided they are in proportion to the size of the estate of *M S* and the functions performed by the deputy

14. The deputy is authorised to pay a contribution of £[*amount*] to the costs of [*name*], solicitors for this application, from the funds belonging to *M S*

Security

15. The deputy is required forthwith to obtain and maintain security in the sum of £[*amount*] in accordance with the standard requirements as to the giving of security

16. To enable the deputy to give security, this order becomes effective one calendar month from the date it was made

17. The deputy must not discharge any functions until the security is in place

* * * * * * *

C 6

ORDER

Appointment of financial Deputy in respect of large brain injury award

This is an example of a purpose made Order following a fund management hearing where a parent was appointed as a financial Deputy in respect of a high value damages award for a young son. Additional supervision and safeguards were considered necessary as the parent although a dedicated carer was inexperienced in financial matters.

THIS ORDER IS NOT VALID UNLESS IT BEARS THE IMPRESSED SEAL OF THE COURT OF PROTECTION IN THE BOTTOM RIGHT HAND CORNER ON ALL PAGES

COURT OF PROTECTION

MENTAL CAPACITY ACT 2005

Case No: 000000

IN THE MATTER OF JOHN XX

(referred to in this Order as '*John*')

FINAL ORDER

BEFORE District Judge [*name*] sitting at [*regional court address*] on [*date*]

WHEREAS

1. An application has been made for an order under the Mental Capacity Act 2005

2. The Court is satisfied that:

    (I)   John is unable to make various decisions for himself in relation to a matter or matters concerning his property and affairs because of an impairment of or a disturbance in the functioning of his mind or brain

    (II)   the purpose for which the order is needed cannot be as effectively achieved in a way that is less restrictive of his rights and freedom of action

PART VIII

IT IS ORDERED THAT:

1. **Appointment of deputy**

(a) XY of ADDRESS is appointed as deputy ('the deputy') to make decisions on behalf of John that he is unable to make for himself in relation to his property and affairs subject to any conditions or restrictions set out in this order

(b) The appointment will last until DATE

(c) The deputy must apply the principles set out in Section 1 of the Mental Capacity Act 2005 and have regard to the guidance in the Code of Practice to the Act

2. **Authority of deputy**

(a) The Court confers general authority on the deputy to take possession or control of the property and affairs of John and to exercise the same powers of management and investment as he has as beneficial owner, subject to the terms and conditions set out in this order

(b) The deputy may make provision for the needs of anyone who is related or connected with John, if he might be expected to provide for that person's needs, by doing whatever he might reasonably be expected to do to meet those needs

(c) The deputy may expend the income of John for his benefit without needing to obtain the prior approval of the Court

(d) The deputy may now withdraw a sum not exceeding £100,000 from the funds belonging to John for the purpose of funding modifications to the home at ADDRESS, a suitable motor vehicle and (if desired) a residential caravan (this sum being in addition to the sum already released)

(e) The deputy may withdraw a sum not exceeding £30,000 a year from the funds belonging to John without needing to obtain the prior approval of the Court

(f) The deputy may withdraw further sums from the funds belonging to John without needing to obtain the prior approval of the Court for the purpose of investment as authorized by this order

(g) For the purpose of giving effect to any decision the deputy may execute or sign any necessary deeds or documents

3. **Restrictions on deputy**

The following restrictions are imposed upon the powers of the deputy.

(a) The initial investment scheme shall be approved by the Court before it is implemented, provided that the recommendations made by NAME of ADDRESS in their letter dated DATE are approved for this purpose.

(b)   Save as provided by this order the investment adviser must not release capital for any purpose other than for investment and capital from investments cannot be remitted to the deputy without the prior approval of the Court

(c)   Unspent income (including payments under the structured settlement) exceeding £2,500 in any year shall be accumulated and treated as capital

(d)   The deputy shall obtain the permission of the Court for expenditure of capital exceeding £30,000 in any 12 month period or for any single investment outside the United Kingdom exceeding £25,000 in value

4.   Investments

(a)   The deputy must exercise such care and skill as is reasonable in the circumstances when investing the assets of John

(b)   The deputy may make any kind of investment that the person absolutely entitled to those assets could make, subject to the terms and conditions set out in this order

(c)   This general power of investment includes investment in land and investment in assets outside England and Wales

(d)   In exercising the power of investment, the deputy must have regard to the standard investment criteria namely the suitability of the investments and the need for diversification in so far as is appropriate to the circumstances of John

(e)   The deputy must from time to time review the investments, and consider whether, having regard to the standard investment criteria, they should be varied

(f)   Unless the deputy reasonably concludes that in all the circumstances it is unnecessary or inappropriate to do so, before exercising any power of investment, the deputy must obtain and consider proper advice about the way in which, having regard to the standard investment criteria, the power should be exercised

'Proper advice' is the advice of an Independent Financial Adviser who the deputy reasonably believes to be appropriately qualified and experienced

5.   Reports

(a)   The deputy is required to keep statements, vouchers, receipts and other financial records

(b)   The deputy must submit an annual report to the Public Guardian

6.   Costs and expenses

(a)   The deputy is entitled to be reimbursed for reasonable expenses incurred provided they are in proportion to the size of the estate and to the actual functions performed by the deputy

PART VIII

(b) The deputy is authorised to pay YY, solicitors fixed costs for this application and if the amount sought exceeds the fixed costs allowed the deputy is authorised to agree their costs and pay them from the funds belonging to John. In default of agreement, or if the deputy or solicitors would prefer the costs to be assessed, this order is to be treated as authority to the Senior Court Costs Office to carry out a detailed assessment on the standard basis.

7. Security

(a) The deputy is required forthwith to obtain and maintain security in the sum of £700,000 in accordance with the standard requirements as to the giving of security

(b) To enable the deputy to give security, this order will come into force one calendar month after the date on which it was made

(c) The deputy must not discharge any functions until the security is in place and if the deputy acts without security the court may revoke this order and the deputy may be personally liable for any loss to the estate

6. Further applications

(a) This hearing is adjourned generally on terms that the deputy may within 12 months of the date of this Order request by letter addressed to Archway without a further court fee that:

(i) further capital sums be released or

(ii) the hearing be restored

(b) Any such request shall be referred to District Judge NAME for further directions or (if he is not available) to a resident district judge at Archway.

PART IX

Case Summaries

PART IX: Case Summaries

Assessment of capacity 1667
Enduring power of attorney 1667
Duty of solicitor when carrying out an assessment of capacity
to execute an EPA 1667
Re AS and DS 1667
Re HW 1668

Best interests 1670
Deputy 1670
Appointment – choice – wishes of 'P' – whether joint attorney
should be appointed 1670
Re: S and S (Protected Persons) 1670
Statutory will 1673
Approach to be adopted under MCA – interpretation of 'best
Interests' 1673
In the Matter of P 1673
Lifetime gifts 1674
Approach to be adopted under MCA – interpretation of 'best
interests' 1674
Re G (TJ) 1674

Capacity to litigate 1677
Civil proceedings – assessment of capacity 1677
Did a party to a settlement lack capacity? – implications 1677
*Martin Masterman-Lister v Brutton & Co and Jewell &
Home Counties Dairies* 1677
Civil proceedings – implications of lack of capacity 1679
Did a party to a settlement lack capacity? – implications 1679
Bailey v Warren 1679
Civil proceedings – assessment of capacity 1680
Capacity to litigate – factors of relevance for MCA 1680
D v R (Deputy of S) and S 1680
Civil proceedings – protected party – protected beneficiary 1682
CPR Pt 21 – how a civil court may resolve uncertainty as to
capacity 1682
In the matter of AKP 1682
Approach of the court to assessment of capacity – CPR Pt 21 –
implications of MCA 1683
Saulle v Nouvet 1683
CPR Pt 21 – how a civil court may resolve uncertainty as to
capacity 1685
In the matter of GS 1685

Court of Protection 1687
Jurisdiction – test of capacity – powers of the court 1687
Test of capacity to be satisfied for the court to assume
jurisdiction under s 48 MCA to make Interim orders and
directions 1687
Re F 1687

PART IX

Principles to be adopted in health and welfare applications   1688
  Justification for the interference in the private family life of P   1688
    Re GC   1688
Costs   1689
  Guidance for award of costs following cancellation of health
    and welfare LPA   1689
    Re RC   1689
Costs   1691
  Guidance for award of costs – circumstances under which
    professional should not advance themselves as deputy   1691
    EG v RS, JS and BEN PCT   1691
Evidence   1692
  Admissibility of hearsay evidence – Disclosure of police
    interviews   1692
    London Borough of Enfield v SA   1692
Public hearings   1695
  Basis upon which the Court of Protection should hear matters
    in public or private   1695
    A v Independent News and Media Limited   1695
Public hearings   1696
  Reporting of the names of parties   1696
    G v E & Ors   1696
Schedule 3 – international jurisdiction of the Court   1697
  Basis upon which Court of Protection is to exercise jurisdiction
    under Schedule 3 – whether required to consider s.1(5) in
    so doing   1697
    Re MN   1697

Deprivation of liberty safeguards   1700
  Meaning of deprivation of liberty   1700
    Circumstances under which there will be a deprivation of
      liberty – placement in residential home and foster
      placement   1700
    Re MIG and MEG   1700
  Meaning of deprivation of liberty   1701
    Circumstances under which there will be a deprivation of
      liberty – obligations upon local authority   1701
    Re A (child) and Re C (adult)   1701
  Meaning of deprivation of liberty   1702
    Circumstances under which there will be a deprivation of
      liberty – 16 and 17 year olds   1702
    Re RK   1702
  Eligibility to be deprived of liberty when the purpose of the
    treatment to be provided relates to mental disorder   1704

Placement in a residential home not registered as an
    independent hospital – to be assessed for treatment
    relating to mental disorder – authority under s 4A MCA –
    whether Case E, para 2, Sch 1A rendering person
    ineligible to be deprived of liberty under MCA applies to
    detention in a care home   1704
*W PCT v (1) TB (2) V (3) S MBC (4) C&W Partnership NHS
    Trust and (5) W MBC*   1704
Ineligible to be deprived of liberty by MCA as being subject to the
    Mental Health Act 1983   1705
Jurisdictional basis of a person being not ineligible to be
    deprived of liberty under MCA – tests or gateways for
    when ineligible under Sch 1A – general points and points
    of statutory construction.   1705
*GJ v (1) The Foundation Trust (2) The PCT and (3) The
    Secretary of State for Health*   1705
Schedule A1   1707
Interaction of urgent and standard authorisations – whether
    second urgent authorisation can be used   1707
Re MB   1707
Schedule A1   1709
Compatibility of DOLS safeguards with Article 5 ECHR   1709
G v E   1709

Deputies   1710
Civil proceedings – damages   1710
Need for a professional deputy to administer a brain injury
    award   1710
Eagle v Chambers   1710
Deputy for property and affairs – Security Bond   1711
Professional deputy – size of security bond   1711
In the Matter of H (a minor and an incapacitated person)   1711
When required   1713
When the Court should appoint a deputy for P – construction of
    s 16(4) MCA   1713
Re P   1713
When required   1714
When the Court should appoint a deputy for P – construction of
    s 16(4) MCA   1714
G v E   1714

Enduring Powers of Attorney   1715
Enduring power of attorney – validity   1715
Lack of capacity – standard of proof   1715
Re K, Re F   1715
Lack of capacity – burden of proof   1716
Re W (Enduring Power of Attorney)   1716
Lack of capacity – burden of proof – costs   1717
In the Matter of C   1717

PART IX

Appointment of substitute attorney – whether valid   1718
   In the Matter of J (Enduring Power of Attorney)   1718

Inherent jurisdiction   1720
  Survival of jurisdiction following the MCA   1720
   Scope of declaratory jurisdiction of the High Court   1720
    LBL v RYJ and VJ   1720

Inherent jurisdiction   1721
  Survival of jurisdiction following the MCA   1721
   Scope of declaratory jurisdiction of the High Court   1721
    A v DL, RL and ML   1721

Wills   1723
  Statutory will   1723
   Approach to be adopted under MCA   1723
    In the Matter of P   1723
   Approach to be adopted under MCA – exclusion of individual –
    benefitting charity   1725
    In the Matter of M   1725
  Statutory will   1726
   Approach to be adopted under MCA – interpretation of 'best
    Interests'   1726
    Re D (Statutory Will)   1726

Case Summaries[1]

The following case summaries and extracts from judgments of relevance to mental capacity issues may be of assistance to those referring to this volume.[2]

ASSESSMENT OF CAPACITY

ENDURING POWER OF ATTORNEY

Duty of solicitor when carrying out an assessment of capacity to execute an EPA

Re AS and DS

(2004) Court of Protection (*former*) Case No: 2120091/2
Deputy Master Ashton

Summary
Objections to the registration of an EPA on the basis that the donor did not have capacity to execute the document.

Decision
Registration refused and instruments revoked. In his judgment the Deputy Master stated:

'... although the burden of proof is initially upon the objectors they have produced sufficient evidence for the Court to be concerned and to seek an explanation as to how the documents came into existence. In effect the burden of proof is reversed. ...

On the face of it the right steps were taken to secure [an] enduring power of attorney. [The donor] attended an independent solicitor who was sufficiently satisfied to prepare the document and witness the signatures. The assessment of an experienced solicitor must be taken very seriously by the Court provided that adequate enquiry has been made and all appropriate information obtained. But a personal opinion based solely on a single interview, especially if other persons of influence were present, is less likely to carry weight than that of a consultant psychiatrist provided that the correct legal test has been applied. In this case the solicitor's assessment does not stand up to scrutiny for the following reasons:

1. the interview note is very brief and the solicitor was only able to give evidence as to what she would have done because she could not remember;

---

[1] The assistance of Victoria Butler-Cole of 39 Essex Street with providing updates to the 2011 edition is acknowledged with gratitude.

[2] In particular because of the historical lack of any reliable mechanism for disseminating judgments, the case summaries section of this book remains a work in progress, and suggestions for inclusions in future editions are very much welcomed. They can be made to the publishers or directly to alex.ruckkeene@39essex.com.

PART IX

2. there was no indication that the solicitor had enquired if these clients newly introduced by the daughter who expected to be their attorney already had solicitors in their own town whom they usually consulted;

3. the interview only lasted 30 minutes which included getting to know the new clients, explaining the wisdom of signing enduring powers of attorney, making a choice of attorney, considering any limitations or conditions, preparing and going through the documentation (which would be a slow process as [the donor] was hard of hearing) and arranging for the safe custody of the documents. There was thus little time for an effective mental health assessment;

4. despite the age of the client there is no indication that enquiry was made as to [his] mental health or a letter sought from [his] own GP. The solicitor was not informed of mental health problems and did not suspect these because of the demeanour of the client who was being 'led' by the daughter. Had the solicitor been more circumspect and insisted on the most basic enquiry, or insisted upon a second interview at a later date with the client on his own, the true position would almost certainly have emerged;

5. there could not be independent advice and proper consideration of an independent choice of attorney because the person to be named was present throughout.'

Comment

See comment following the next case.

Re HW

(2005) Court of Protection (*former*) Case No: 2122208
Deputy Master Ashton

Summary

Objections to the registration of an EPA on the basis that the donor did not have capacity to execute the document.

Decision

Registration refused and instruments revoked. In his judgment the Deputy Master stated:

'I feel bound to conclude at this stage that the solicitor did not carry out a proper assessment of mental capacity of the client (the Donor) for the following reasons:

1. instructions were taken from the daughter and son-in-law who wished to be appointed as attorneys and there was no independent corroboration of any of the information that they provided (e g as to the existence of other members of the family or the nature of the task involved);

2. the client was not seen alone by the solicitor so as to afford an opportunity to express any reservations privately and receive

impartial advice on his wider legal needs (the explanations given for this omission demonstrated a lack of appreciation of the reasons for this precaution);

3. the interview was conducted on the basis of explanations by the solicitor of the particular document involved with remarkably little communication by the client other than apparent nods of assent. There should have been an initial 'getting to know the client' discussion at which he was encouraged to do most of the talking, with a few questions designed to test his knowledge and the depth of his understanding;

4. there was no preliminary assessment of capacity as such – the understanding of the client was perceived rather than tested. There was merely a basic interview lasting half-an-hour which appears to have progressed on the assumption that there was capacity. This assumption was based upon the client's responses as the interview progressed to the explanations being given whereas these may merely have been manifestations of a learnt behaviour pattern;

5. despite the fact that the intended donor was elderly and in hospital no prior approach was made to the medical staff as to his diagnosis and present condition. This would have revealed that he had advanced Alzheimer's dementia and was under the care of a psychiatrist who considered that he did not have capacity to sign any documents.

I find that the half hour interview would not (and did not) reveal the true state of understanding of the client. It was not searching at all and relied solely upon the impression gained by a solicitor with little experience in this area whilst explaining a legal document. The solicitor appears to have been more concerned to meet the wishes of the daughter and son-in-law than provide impartial legal advice and services to a client who was new to her. … The solicitor has a duty to protect as well as empower the client yet despite having no independent knowledge as to the suitability of the proposed attorneys she would not admit to doubts as to capacity even when these were staring her in the face. It is difficult to conceive of more fundamental reasons for doubts than the unanimous opinion of the treating medical team.

In consequence the solicitor's tenaciously held view that the Donor was competent to execute the enduring power of attorney cannot override the medical evidence which is firmly to the contrary.'

Comment

The above two cases highlight the pitfalls for solicitors when asked by an expectant attorney to take instructions for the preparation of an EPA from a donor who was not previously a client.

PART IX

BEST INTERESTS

Appointment – choice – wishes of 'P' – whether joint attorney should be appointed

Re: S and S (Protected Persons)

CoP Case Nos: 11475121 &11475138 [2009] WTLR 315
25 November 2008
HHJ Hazel Marshall QC sitting as a nominated Judge

Facts
Mr & Mrs S appointed their daughters C and V as joint attorneys under an EPA. C opposed an application by V to register the EPA so it became clear that a deputy (then a receiver) would have to be appointed. The estate was substantial. V applied but C and her sons objected. A report from a doctor indicated that although Mr & Mrs S lacked capacity to make the decision they would prefer a professional deputy in view of the hostility between the daughters. The District Judge appointed V.

Decision
After referring to ss 1–4 and 16 of the MCA 2005 and the Code of Practice the judge stated:

> '51. ... there has been a whole sea change in the attitude of the law to persons whose mental capacity is impaired. The former approach was based on a stark division between those who had capacity to manage their own affairs, and those who did not. The former took their own decisions for better or worse, and the latter fell under a regime in which decisions were made for them, perhaps with a generous, and in some cases patronising, token nod to their feelings by asking them what they wanted, and then deciding what nonetheless was objectively "best" for them.

> 52. This is no longer appropriate. The statute now embodies the recognition that it is the basic right of any adult to be free to take and implement decisions affecting his own life and living, and that a person who lacks mental capacity should not be deprived of that right except insofar as is absolutely necessary in his best interests.

> 53. Two major changes are therefore embodied in the statute. The first is official recognition that capacity is not a blunt "all or nothing" condition, but is more complex, and is to be treated as being issue specific. A person may not have sufficient capacity to be able to make complex, refined or major decisions but may still have the capacity to make simpler or less momentous ones, or to hold genuine views as to what he wants to be the outcome of more complex decisions or situations.

> 54. The second change is the emphasis throughout the Act on the ascertainment of the actual or likely wishes, views and preferences of the person lacking full capacity, and on involving him in the decision making process. This approach underlies s.1(2) (presumption of

capacity), s 1(3) (duty to help P to make his own decision if he can), 1(4) (recognition that a person's capacity, and therefore right, to make decisions does not depend on how objectively "wise" those decisions are), s1(6) (P's rights and freedom of action should be restricted as little as practicable), and s 4(4) (duty on decision maker to involve P in decisions), and it is the only conceivable reason for imposing the duty to consider P's wishes or likely wishes (s 4.(6)) and to take trouble to ascertain them s 4.(7)).

55.   In my judgment it is the inescapable conclusion from the stress laid on these matters in the Act that the views and wishes of P in regard to decisions made on his behalf are to carry great weight. What, after all, is the point of taking great trouble to ascertain or deduce P's views, and to encourage P to be involved in the decision making process, unless the objective is to try to achieve the outcome which P wants or prefers, even if he does not have the capacity to achieve it for himself?

56.   The Act does not, of course, say that Ps' wishes are to be paramount, nor does it lay down any express presumption in favour of implementing them if they can be ascertained. Indeed the paramount objective is that of P's "best interests". However, by giving such prominence to the above matters, the Act does, in my judgment recognise that having his views and wishes taken into account and respected is a very significant aspect of P's best interests. Due regard should therefore be paid to this recognition when doing the weighing exercise of determining what is in P's best interests in all the relevant circumstances, including those wishes.

57.   As to how this will work in practice, in my judgment, where P can and does express a wish or view which is not irrational (in the sense of being a wish which a person with full capacity might reasonably have), is not impracticable as far as its physical implementation is concerned, and is not irresponsible having regard to the extent of P's resources (ie whether a responsible person of full capacity who had such resources might reasonably consider it worth using the necessary resources to implement his wish) then that situation carries great weight, and effectively gives rise to a presumption in favour of implementing those wishes, unless there is some potential sufficiently detrimental effect for P of doing so which outweighs this.

58.   That might be some extraneous consequence, or some other unforeseen, unknown or unappreciated factor. Whether this further consideration actually should justify overriding P's wishes might then be tested by asking whether, had he known of this further consideration, it appears (from what is known of P) that he would have changed his wishes. It might be further tested by asking whether the seriousness of this countervailing factor in terms of detriment to P is such that it must outweigh the detriment to an adult of having one's wishes overruled, and the sense of impotence, and the frustration and anger, which living with that awareness (insofar as P appreciates it) will cause to P. Given the policy of the Act to empower people to make their own decisions wherever possible, justification for overruling P and "saving him from himself" must, in

PART IX

my judgment be strong and cogent. Otherwise, taking a different course from that which P wishes would be likely to infringe the statutory direction in s.1(7) of the Act, that one must achieve any desired objective by the route which least restricts P's own rights and freedom of actions.

59. ... the learned judge ... fell into error in failing to give due weight to the wishes of Mr and Mrs S, both as a matter of evidence and in principle, and ... gave undue weight to the supposed disadvantages to them attendant on having an independent Deputy appointed, as being sufficient to override those wishes. He was led into this error by ... his attitude to the dispute between V and C.

* * * * * *

67. ... the learned judge was wrong to dismiss as non-existent the implications from the EPAs' having been joint appointments of the two daughters and not joint and several appointments. ... it was an almost inescapable inference that [Mr and Mrs S], as donors of the powers, wanted relevant decisions either to be joint, or to be made by neither appointee, and did not want their affairs to be dealt with by the sole decision of one appointee alone.

68. I am not to be taken to be suggesting that this factor weighs conclusively against ever making an appointment of one only of jointly appointed Attorneys to be a Deputy, in all circumstances. For example, one donee of the power may have died or emigrated, or there may be other unusual considerations. However, in my judgment it does raise a presumption, of greater or lesser weight, in favour of appointing a third party rather than one of the original joint appointees. The presumption that sole decisions would be unacceptable to the donor of the power may be less strong in situations where the donees are not linked, such as where they are, perhaps, suitable professional acquaintances. However, where the appointees are two relatives of similar relationship to P, the inference is rather stronger.

69. Mr and Mrs S knew their daughters' personalities far better than the court ever could, or should presume to investigate. They may well have had very good reasons for taking the view that the dynamics of their family overall were best served, in their own best interests, by ensuring that either both daughters should take decisions jointly for them, or that their views should merely carry equal weight in the decision making process of a third party, and that neither should have ascendancy, actual or perceived, over the other. To dismiss their deliberate choice of a joint appointment rather than a joint and several appointment as signifying nothing was therefore, in my judgment, illegitimate.'

Comment
The status of the wishes of the donor may have been overstated – see next case.

Approach to be adopted under MCA – interpretation of 'best Interests'

In the Matter of P

[2009] EWHC 163 (Ch) [2010] Ch 33
Lewison J

Summary

This case dealt with the approval of statutory wills under the MCA [*see below*] but the Judge also commented as follows on the approach to best interest in *Re: S and S (Protected Persons)* [*see above*]:

> '43 I agree with the broad thrust of this, although I think that HH Judge Marshall QC may have slightly overstated the importance to be given to P's wishes. First, section 1(6) is not a statutory direction that one "must achieve" any desired objective by the least restrictive route. Section 1(6) only requires that before a decision is made "regard must be had" to that question. It is an important question, to be sure, but it is not determinative. The only imperative is that the decision must be made in P's best interests. Second, although P's wishes must be given weight, if, as I think, Parliament has endorsed the "balance sheet" approach, they are only one part of the balance. I agree that those wishes are to be given great weight, but I would prefer not to speak in terms of presumptions. Third, any attempt to test a decision by reference to what P would hypothetically have done or wanted runs the risk of amounting to a "substituted judgment" rather than a decision of what would be in P's best interests. But despite this risk, the Act itself requires some hypothesising. The decision maker must consider the beliefs and values that would be likely to influence P's decision if he had capacity and also the other factors that P would be likely to consider if he were able to do so. This does not, I think, necessarily require those to be given effect. As the Code of Practice explains:
>
> > "In setting out the requirements for working out a person's 'best interests', section 4 of the Act puts the person who lacks capacity at the centre of the decision to be made. Even if they cannot make the decision, their wishes and feelings, beliefs and values should be taken fully into account – whether expressed in the past or now. But their wishes and feelings, beliefs and values will not necessarily be the deciding factor in working out their best interests. Any such assessment must consider past and current wishes and feelings, beliefs and values alongside all other factors, but the final decision must be based entirely on what is in the person's best interests." '

Comment

This decision helps to explain the relative importance of the wishes of the incapacitated person. It should be read subject to the approach adopted by Munby J in *Re M* [below] and also the judgment of Henderson J in *D v R* [below].

LIFETIME GIFTS

Approach to be adopted under MCA – interpretation of 'best interests'

Re G (TJ)

[2010] EWHC 3005 (COP)

Morgan J

Summary
The question for the Court was whether the Deputy could be required to make payments from the funds administered on behalf of a Mrs G to her adult daughter, C, by way of maintenance of C. It was common ground between the parties that the judge could only make an order in those terms if he was satisfied in accordance with the MCA that such an order was in the best interests of Mrs G. Morgan J invited submissions as to the approach to be taken, and gave a detailed judgment on the meaning of the phrase 'best interests' in the context of the facts before him.

Decision
At paragraphs 34 ff, Morgan J held as follows:

'34 The phrase "best interests" is not defined. That might suggest that it was intended that the application of the phrase would be responsive to the particular issue which arises and the facts of the individual case.

35 The context in which issues as to "best interests" arise in the present case concerns the property and affairs of Mrs G, rather than her welfare and healthcare. As I have explained, the court is given power to make a lifetime gift of P's property and to make a lifetime settlement of P's property for the benefit of others: see section 18(1)(b) and (h). The court can also make a will for P: see section 18(1)(i). Further, I note that under section 12, the donee of a lasting power of attorney may make certain gifts and by section 9(4), the authority conferred by a lasting power of attorney is subject to the requirement that the donee acts in the best interests of the donor of the power. These various references to gifts, lifetime and testamentary, and settlements for the benefit of others, suggest to me that the word "interests" in the phrase "best interests" is not confined to matters of self interest or, putting it another way, a court could conclude in an appropriate case that it is in the interests of P for P to act altruistically. It seems unlikely that the legislature thought that the power to make gifts should be confined to gifts which were not altruistic or where the gift would confer a benefit on P (or the donor of the lasting power of attorney) by reason of that person's emotional response to knowing of the gift.

36 Further help as to what is meant by "best interests" can be derived from section 4(6). Section 4(6)(a) refers to the past and present wishes and feelings of P. That suggests that giving effect to P's actual wishes can be relevant to assessing P's best interests. Section 4(6)(b) refers to the beliefs and values which would be likely to influence P's decision if he had capacity. I regard section 4(6)(b) as considerably

widening the matters which fall to be considered. The width of the relevant matters is further extended by section 4(6)(c) which refers to the other factors which P would be likely to consider if he were able to do so.

37 The provisions of section 4(6)(b) and (c) extend beyond the actual wishes of P. They refer to the matters which P would be likely to consider if he were able to make the relevant decision. P would be likely to consider any relevant beliefs and values and all other relevant factors. Therefore, the matters which the court must consider under these paragraphs of section 4(6) involve the court in drawing up the balance sheet of factors which P would be likely to draw up if he were able to do so. Of course, the ultimate question for the court is: what is in the best interests of P? The court will necessarily draw up its own balance sheet of factors and that may differ from P's notional balance sheet. The court is not obliged to give effect to the decision which P would have arrived at, if he had capacity to make the decision for himself. Indeed, section 4(6) does not expressly require the court to reconstruct the decision which P, acting reasonably or otherwise, would have reached. Nonetheless, if the court considers the balance sheet of factors which would be likely to influence P, if P had capacity, the court is likely to be able to say what decision P would be likely to have reached. The court is not obliged to give effect to the decision which P, acting reasonably, would have made (the test of "substituted judgment") but section 4(6) appears to require the court to consider what P would have decided (or, at least, the balance sheet of factors which P would be likely to have considered). My provisional view is that, in an appropriate case, a court could conclude that it is in the best interests of P for the court to give effect to the wishes which P would have formed on the relevant point, if he had capacity.'

Morgan J then considered the law as it stood prior to the enactment of the MCA, and also the decisions in are *In re S (Protected Persons)* [2009] WTLR 315, *In re P (Statutory Will)* [2010] Ch 33 and *In re M* [2010] 3 All ER 682 (aka *ITW v Z*). He held (at paragraph 52) that:

'... the discussion in these three cases is of great help to me in identifying the general approach which I should adopt in the present case. However, those cases did not need to focus upon a matter which is of importance in the present case, namely, whether in the absence of any other competing consideration, a court could decide that it is in the best interests of P to give effect to the wishes which P would have formed (but had not in fact formed) on the relevant topic.'

He then concluded:

'55 The best interests test involves identifying a number of relevant factors. The actual wishes of P can be a relevant factor: section 4(6)(a) says so. The beliefs and values which would be likely to influence P's decision, if he had capacity to make the relevant decision, are a relevant factor: section 4(6)(b) says so. The other factors which P would be likely to consider, if he had the capacity to consider them, are a relevant factor: section 4(6)(c) says so. Accordingly, the balance sheet of factors which P would draw up, if

PART IX

he had capacity to make the decision, is a relevant factor for the court's decision. Further, in most cases the court will be able to determine what decision it is likely that P would have made, if he had capacity. In such a case, in my judgment, P's balance sheet of factors and P's likely decision can be taken into account by the court. This involves an element of substituted judgment being taken into account, together with anything else which is relevant. However, it is absolutely clear that the ultimate test for the court is the test of best interests and not the test of substituted judgment. Nonetheless, the substituted judgment can be relevant and is not excluded from consideration. As Hoffmann LJ said in the Bland case, the substituted judgment can be subsumed within the concept of best interests. That appeared to be the view of the Law Commission also.

56   Further, the word "interest" in the best interests test does not confine the court to considering the self interest of P. The actual wishes of P, which are altruistic and not in any way, directly or indirectly self-interested, can be a relevant factor. Further, the wishes which P would have formed, if P had capacity, which may be altruistic wishes, can be a relevant factor. It is not necessary to establish that P would have been aware of the fact that P's wishes were carried into effect. Respect for P's wishes, actual or putative, can be a relevant factor even where P has no awareness of, and no reaction to, the fact that such wishes are being respected.'

Having gone through the various items set down in the checklist at s 4 of the MCA, Morgan J concluded on the facts of this case at paragraph 65 that:

'Having identified the factors as best I can, it emerges that the principal justification, so far as Mrs G is concerned, for making the order for maintenance payments in favour of C, is that those payments would be what Mrs G would have wanted if she had capacity to make the decision for herself. I recognise that this consideration is essentially a 'substituted judgment' for Mrs G. I am also very aware that the test laid down by the 2005 Act is the test of best interests and not of substituted judgment. However, for the reasons which I have tried to set out earlier, the test of best interests does not exclude respect for what would have been the wishes of Mrs G. A substituted judgment can be subsumed into the consideration of best interests. Accordingly, in this case, respect for what would have been Mrs G's wishes will define what is in her best interests, in the absence of any countervailing factors. There are no such countervailing factors here. I therefore conclude that an order which provides for the continuation of maintenance payments to C is in the best interests of Mrs G.'

Comment

This significant decision is one that must be read with very considerable care. It is not authority for a return to the substituted judgment test (ruled out by Lewison J in *Re P* [above]). Rather, on a proper analysis, it is authority for the following propositions: (1) an element of substituted judgment can be subsumed into the consideration of best interests; and (2) that, absent any countervailing factors, respect for what the Court can identify to have been P's wishes can define what would be in her best interests.

CAPACITY TO LITIGATE

CIVIL PROCEEDINGS – ASSESSMENT OF CAPACITY

Did a party to a settlement lack capacity? – implications

Martin Masterman-Lister v Brutton & Co and Jewell & Home Counties Dairies

[2002] EWCA Civ 1889
Court of Appeal

Summary

A claimant sought to re-open personal injury litigation many years later on the basis that he ought to have been classified as a 'patient' (ie incapable of conducting the litigation – now a 'protected party') under the former court rules (then RSC Ord 80 r 10 but now CPR Pt 21).

Decision
The following guidance was contained in the appeal judgments:

> **Kennedy LJ:** 'There is no reported English decision directly concerned with the capacity to litigate and compromise but the courts have considered capacity in other contexts ... the mental abilities required include the ability to recognise a problem, obtain and receive, understand and retain relevant information, including advice; the ability to weigh the information (including that derived from advice) in the balance in reaching a decision, and the ability to communicate that decision. ... of some importance is the issue-specific nature of the test; that is to say the requirement to consider the question of capacity in relation to the particular transaction (its nature and complexity) in respect of which the decisions as to capacity fall to be made. It is not difficult to envisage claimants in personal injury actions with capacity to deal with all matters and take all "lay client" decisions related to their actions up to and including a decision whether or not to settle, but lacking capacity to decide (even with advice) how to administer a large award. In such a case I see no justification for the assertion that the claimant is to be regarded as a "patient" from the commencement of proceedings. ... The conclusion that in law capacity depends on time and context means that inevitably a decision as to capacity in one context does not bind a court which has to consider the same issue in a different context. ... any medical witness asked to assist in relation to capacity therefore needs to know the area of the alleged "patient's" activities in relation to which his advice is sought. The final decision as to capacity ... rests with the court but, in almost every case, the court will need medical evidence to guide it.
>
> Normally no problem arises as to when the issue of capacity should be raised. It raises itself. But what if ... the claimant did lack capacity but, without any fault on anyone's part, no one recognised that fact? ... a court can regularise the position retrospectively. Provided everyone has acted in good faith and there has been no manifest disadvantage to the party subsequently found to have been a patient at the relevant time I cannot envisage any court refusing to regularise the position. ... finality in

PART IX

litigation is also important, and the Rules as to capacity are not designed to provide a vehicle for re-opening litigation which having apparently been properly conducted (whatever the wisdom of the individual decisions in relation to it) has for long been understood to be at an end.'

Chadwick LJ: 'The question of difficulty in any particular case is likely to be whether the party does have the mental capacity, with the assistance of such explanation as he may be given, to understand the nature and effect of the particular transaction. ... The test is issue specific; and, when applied to different issues, it may yield different answers. ... three features ... First, the need for the claimant to have "insight and understanding of the fact that she has a problem in respect of which she needs advice". Second, the need to be able to instruct an appropriate adviser "with sufficient clarity to enable him to understand the problem and advise her appropriately". Third, the need "to understand and make decisions based upon, or otherwise give effect to, such advice as she may receive". ... The courts have ample powers to protect those who are vulnerable to exploitation from being exploited; it is unnecessary to deny them the opportunity to take their own decisions if they are not being exploited. It is not the task of the courts to prevent those who have the mental capacity to make rational decisions from making decisions which others may regard as rash or irresponsible.

... the question whether he had capacity to take those decisions was not to be answered solely by reference to outcomes. I accept that as conceptually correct. ... he is not to be regarded as having capacity merely because the decision appears rational. But ... outcomes are likely to be important (although not conclusive) indicators of the existence, or lack, of understanding. ... I reject the submission that a person who would be incapable of taking investment decisions in relation to a large sum received as compensation is to be held, for that reason, to be incapable of pursuing a claim for that compensation. I accept that capacity to pursue a claim requires capacity to take a decision to compromise that claim; and that capacity to compromise requires an understanding of what the effects of a compromise will be – in particular, an understanding that it will be necessary to deal with the compensation monies in a way which will provide for the future. But that does not, as it seems to me, require an understanding as to how that will be done. ... there is no logical reason why a person who understands that something needs to be done, but who does not have the requisite understanding to do it for himself, should not confer on another the power to do what needs to be done.

... I find it of particular significance that, in this case, two experienced solicitors did not recognise the need for the appointment of a next friend; and that no criticism is made of either in that respect.'

Comment
This decision pre-dated the MCA and the change to CPR Pt 21 consequent thereon but the above extracts from the appeal judgments still represent valuable guidance.

CIVIL PROCEEDINGS – IMPLICATIONS OF LACK OF CAPACITY

Did a party to a settlement lack capacity? – implications

Bailey v Warren

[2006] EWCA Civ 51
Court of Appeal

Decision
The following general guidance was contained in the appeal judgments:

> **Hallett LJ:** 'Even if an individual had capacity to the extent of being able to cope with all the litigation, it did not mean he necessarily had the necessary capacity to administer a large award of damages. ... Similarly, I can see no justification for the assertion that if the evidence supports a conclusion that a claimant lacks the capacity to deal with matters of quantum that it necessarily follows that he lacks the capacity to decide whether or not he is prepared to accept he was equally to blame for a road traffic accident. All will depend on the facts of the case, the capacity of the individual and the nature and complexity of the issue to be decided. ... It is becoming increasingly common for the issues of liability and quantum to be split and separate trials ordered.
>
> ... however much judges may wish to protect an individual from the ill advised consequences of his or her own actions, courts should tread very carefully and only interfere with an individual's rights when absolutely necessary. The right to take decisions on a claim for damages is an important one and not to be taken away lightly. ... legal advisers [should] approach the question of mental capacity in a common sense way and without incurring unnecessary expense either by instructing experts for no good reason or by involving the Court of Protection on matters well within the lay client's understanding.
>
> Within CPR 21.3(4) there are no restrictions whatsoever on the court's discretion to validate steps taken in proceedings before a litigation friend is appointed. A court can regularise the position retrospectively provided, as Kennedy LJ observed in para 31 of Masterman-Lister 'everyone has acted in good faith and there has been no manifest disadvantage to the party subsequently found to have been a patient at the time'.
>
> **Arden LJ:** 'CPR 21.10(1) specifically provides that a compromise of a claim belonging to a patient without the approval of the court is of no effect. ... There is no saving for the case where the person is not known to be a patient at the time of the compromise. ... There is no requirement in CPR 21.10(1) that proceedings should have been issued. Thus approval is also required even if proceedings have not been issued ... CPR 21.10 applies even where the compromise is of only part of a claim ... The court may, however, approve a compromise to which a patient agrees although he has no litigation friend. The court's power is contained in CPR 21.3(4). If the court is asked to approve retrospectively the compromise of a claim belonging to a patient ... the court should be inclined to give its approval unless the compromise is clearly not beneficial to the patient. If the

compromise is not in the interests of the patient, the court cannot, despite the passage of time for which the other party is not responsible, approve it.'

Ward LJ: 'When a claim is being made by a person who is now a patient and the settlement relates to that claim, then the compromise needs the court's approval. It would make no sense to restrict the ambit of the rule to post-commencement compromises.'

Comment

This decision also pre-dated the MCA and the change to CPR Pt 21 consequent thereon but helps to clarify the court's powers.

CIVIL PROCEEDINGS – ASSESSMENT OF CAPACITY

Capacity to litigate – factors of relevance for MCA

D v R (Deputy of S) and S

[2010] EWHC 2405 (COP)

Henderson J

Summary

The Court had to decide whether a Mr S had capacity to decide whether Chancery proceedings started in his name and on his behalf by his daughter and deputy, R, should be discontinued or compromised. By the proceedings, R sought declarations that gifts of money made by Mr S to a Mrs D (previously a legal secretary employed by his solicitors) in 2006 and 2007 totalling over £500,000 were procured by undue influence and should be set aside.

Decision

Henderson J adopted the analysis of and approach to the MCA set down by Lewison J in *Re P (Statutory Will)* [2010] Ch 33 [above], but added a useful gloss on the terms of s 1(4) as follows:

'39 ... The fact that the decision is an unwise one does not, of itself, justify a conclusion of lack of capacity: see section 1(4). Just as a testator has always had the freedom (subject now to the constraints of the Inheritance (Provision for Family and Dependants) Act 1975) to make testamentary dispositions which are unreasonable, foolish or contrary to generally accepted standards of morality, so too a person in his lifetime has the freedom to act in a manner which is (for example) unwise, capricious, or designed to spite his relations. The pages of English fiction and of the law reports alike bear ample testimony to the exercise of this basic human right, even if it is not one enshrined in so many words in the European Convention on Human Rights (although Articles 8, 9 and 10 are, of course, all relevant in this context).

40   The significance of section 1(4) must not, however, be exaggerated. The fact that a decision is unwise or foolish may not, without more, be treated as conclusive, but it remains in my judgment a relevant consideration for the court to take into account in considering

whether the criteria of inability to make a decision for oneself in section 3(1) are satisfied. This will particularly be the case where there is a marked contrast between the unwise nature of the impugned decision and the person's former attitude to the conduct of his affairs at a time when his capacity was not in question.'

In respect of the particular litigation, the judge continued:

'43 At a superficial level, the nature of the decision may be simply stated. As I have already said more than once, it is whether to discontinue, or to continue to prosecute, the Chancery proceedings. But that decision cannot be taken, it seems to me, without at least a basic understanding of the nature of the claim, of the legal issues involved, and of the circumstances which have given rise to the claim. It would be an over-simplification to say that the claim is just a claim to set aside or reverse the gifts which Mr S made to Mrs D, because in the ordinary way a gift is irrevocable once it has been made and perfected by delivery or transfer of the relevant assets. If a gift is to be set aside or recovered, some vitiating factor such as fraud, misrepresentation or undue influence has to be established; and if the donor is to decide whether or not to pursue a claim, he needs to understand, at least in general terms, the nature of the vitiating factor upon which he may be able to rely, and to weigh up the arguments for and against pursuing the claim. Provided that the donor is equipped with this information, and provided that he understands it and takes it into account in reaching his decision, it will not matter if his decision is an imprudent one, or one which would fail to satisfy the "best interests" test in section 4. But if the donor is unable to assimilate, retain and evaluate the relevant information, he lacks the capacity to make the decision, however clearly he may articulate it.

44 The need for an understanding of the nature of the claim is particularly pronounced, in my view, where the claim is founded on a rebuttable presumption of undue influence, and where the relationship which arguably gave rise to the claim is still in existence. One would naturally not expect a lay person to have the same understanding as a lawyer of the principles expounded by the Court of Appeal in *Allcard v Skinner* (1887) 36 Ch D 145 and by the House of Lords in *Royal Bank of Scotland Plc v Etridge (No.2)* [2001] UKHL 44, [2002] 2 AC 773. But if a donor is to decide whether or not to pursue such a claim, he must in my view understand (at least in the simple terms envisaged by section 3(2)):

(a) the nature and extent of the relationship of trust and confidence arguably reposed by him in the donee;

(b) the extent to which it may be said that the gifts cannot readily be accounted for by the ordinary motives of ordinary people in such a relationship; and

(c) the nature of the evidential burden resting on the donee to rebut any presumption of undue influence (traditionally described as proof that the gifts were made only after full, free and informed thought about their nature and consequences: see *Hammond v*

Osborn [2002] EWCA Civ 885, [2002] WTLR 1125, at paragraphs [26] to [27] per Sir Martin Nourse).

45   It is only with the benefit of this minimum level of information that a donor in the position of Mr S can begin to reach a decision whether or not to pursue the claim, or (just as important) whether to attempt to settle it, and (if so) on what terms. Furthermore, where (as in the present case) the relationship with the donee which gave rise to the potential claim is apparently still subsisting, the court will in my judgment need to scrutinise with particular care whether the donor can stand back from the impugned transactions with sufficient detachment truly to understand the nature of the claim. By way of contrast, the necessary degree of understanding is likely to be far easier to establish where the donor was under an influence at the time of the gift (e.g. by a religious sect or guru) which has subsequently come to an end.'

Comment

This decision is of importance both for the comments of Henderson J upon s.1(4) MCA and also for the exposition of factors relevant to claims arising out of allegations of undue influence (of particular relevance for many vulnerable adults possessed of means). The judgment also serves as a case-study of the importance of the proper instruction of experts: in a lengthy section (not reproduced here), the judge set out detailed criticism of the basis upon which one party's expert had been instructed, which very substantially undermined the weight which could be placed upon the views of an otherwise extremely eminent practitioner in the field.

CIVIL PROCEEDINGS – PROTECTED PARTY – PROTECTED BENEFICIARY

CPR Pt 21 – how a civil court may resolve uncertainty as to capacity

In the matter of AKP

CoP Case No: 10185666
1 November 2007
District Judge Ashton sitting as a nominated Judge

Summary

A high value brain injury claim was brought by a solicitor receiver as litigation friend. Uncertainty arose as to whether the claimant was still a protected party (CPR r 21.1(d)) and also a protected beneficiary (CPR r 21.1(e)) after the MCA. The issue was referred to the (new) Court of Protection.

Decision

The judge offered the following guidance for cases such as this:

'This is the first application to be referred to me as a nominated District Judge of the new Court of Protection pursuant to the [MCA]. It was provoked by a capacity issue arising in the High Court of Justice, Queen's Bench Division, Bury District Registry (Claim No. 96P00137) in proceedings relating to a brain injury. The co-operation between the case managing district judge, the Senior Judge of the Court of Protection and myself as a regional judge in achieving an early hearing ... is a good example of how the two courts should work together. I allowed the defendant in the civil proceedings to be joined as a party because of a financial interest in the outcome.

The circumstances and evidence pre-date implementation of the new regime on 1st October 2007. ... The present issue, which affects the calculation of the compensation, is whether his financial affairs should remain under the jurisdiction of the new Court of Protection. There is also the related issue as to whether he still needs a litigation friend to conduct his proceedings or can give instructions himself. ...

It is not surprising that a reference has been made to the Court of Protection for decisions about capacity, given the proliferation of medical evidence and conflict between these expert opinions, some of which have changed recently. The former Court [of Protection] had assumed jurisdiction based upon the early reports and retained that jurisdiction in reliance on later reports by the medical Visitor whose view is unwavering, so the new Court must evaluate the opinions expressed and reach a considered conclusion. The advantage of this course is that declarations can be made that not only determine whether this Court should continue to exercise its jurisdiction but also that bind the High Court as to the need for a litigation friend. That has become possible pursuant to the Mental Capacity Act 2005. The High Court has no jurisdiction to decide whether the Court of Protection has jurisdiction over an individual but it needs to know.'

The court decided that AKP was not capable of conducting his own proceedings or managing his property and affairs but directed that the appointment of the present finance deputy should only continue for a period of 18 months after the damages claim was settled and that thereafter, unless this deputy (or someone else permitted by the Court) made an application to the contrary the jurisdiction of the Court of Protection over his financial affairs shall automatically cease.

Comment

This decision was before *Saulle v Nouvet – below*. The outcome was unusual but reflected the court's view that although by reason of the brain injury he could not make decisions about the conduct of the proceedings, after settlement and once the care plan was set up and his award invested he would with the support of his wife be capable of managing his own life.

Approach of the court to assessment of capacity – CPR Pt 21 – implications of MCA

Saulle v Nouvet

[2007] EWHC 2902 (QB)
Andrew Edis QC sitting as a deputy Judge

Summary

There was uncertainty as to whether the brain damaged claimant in a high value personal injury claim was a protected party (CPR r 21.1(d)) and, if so, was also a protected beneficiary (CPR r 21.1(e)). Consideration was given to the approach to these issues and the implications of the MCA which resulted in a change to the rules.

Decision

The judge decided that, as there was considerable medical evidence already obtained by the parties and counsel for the claimant was prepared to address the issue of capacity it was not necessary in the circumstances and on grounds of proportionality to involve the Official Solicitor. He stated:

'... the question I have to decide is whether:

(i)   The Claimant is a protected party within the meaning of CPR 21.1(d) which defines a "protected party" as a party "who lacks capacity to conduct the proceeding"

(ii) If I decide that the Claimant is a protected party, then I must go on to decide whether he is a "protected beneficiary" as defined by CPR 21.1(e), namely a protected party who "lacks capacity to manage and control any money recovered by him or on his behalf or for his benefit in the proceedings."

If I conclude that he is not a protected party, then ... it will not be necessary for me to consider whether the Claimant is a protected beneficiary, since he cannot have that status unless he is a protected party.

...the [MCA] concerns decisions which the Court of Protection has jurisdiction to make, and not decisions of the High Court Queens Bench Division in civil proceedings. The Court is not therefore required by the Act to adopt the definition and approach there set out at all. The [MCA] came into force on the 1st October 2007, as did the new CPR Part 21 and Practice Direction. The definition of "capacity" in section 2(1) is a definition "for the purposes of this Act". It is not one of the purposes of the Act to regulate or in any way address the way in which the Court approaches the question of capacity to litigate. The Act does not purport to regulate the conduct of any other "court".

Therefore, I conclude that the court conducting the proceedings, in this case the Queens Bench Division of the High Court, is required to decide two new questions which are created by the CPR and not by the 2005 Act. These are the questions I posed in para 1 of this judgment. In approaching them I adopt the definition of the 2005 Act, not because I am required to do so by the Act, but because I am required to do so by the CPR.

... The finding that a party is a protected beneficiary has consequences which are quite limited in that the substantive decisions which determine how the funds will be administered will be taken by the Court of Protection on the basis of its own determinations of capacity at times when they are necessary and in respect of particular decisions. The High Court merely makes a finding which enables that process to occur.

... The question I have to answer is whether the Claimant now lacks capacity in relation to those decisions because he is unable to make them for himself because of an impairment of, or disturbance in the functioning of his mind or brain. ... It follows from this test that the Court must focus on the matters which arise for decision now, and on the Claimant's capacity to deal with them now. I am required not to attempt to foretell the future and provide for situations which may arise when he may have to take some other decision at some other time when his mental state may be different. ... I consider that [Dr Rose] may well be right when he suggests that there may be times in the future when the Claimant will lack capacity to make particular decisions, and note his concern that if that happens when he does not have the support of his family for any reason, he may not come to the attention of the Court of Protection until it is too late. This is a risk against which the old test for capacity used by the Court of Protection under Part VII of the 1983 Act used to guard. The modern law is different.'

Comment

Tests of capacity are decision specific but the rules do not allow for the converse, namely that a party may be a 'protected beneficiary' even though not a 'protected party' (eg where the proceedings are simple but the party has a considerable estate which he lacks the capacity to manage [see the following case].

CPR Pt 21 – how a civil court may resolve uncertainty as to capacity

In the matter of GS

CoP Case No: 11582024
10 July 2008
District Judge Ashton sitting as a nominated Judge

Summary

In this modest value brain injury claim doubt arose prior to settlement as to whether the claimant was a protected party (CPR r 21.1(d)) and would also become a protected beneficiary (CPR r 21.1(e)). The claimant's experts believed he lacked capacity but the defendant's experts held the contrary view. The issue was referred to the (new) Court of Protection in the same manner as *In the matter of AKP – above*.

Decision

The judge offered the following guidance for cases such as this:

'This is an application to the new Court of Protection for a declaration pursuant to the Mental Capacity Act 2005, section 15 as to Graham Stone's capacity:

(a) to conduct his civil claim (which is now well advanced); and

(b) to manage his property and affairs (which will include damages of up to £400,000).

If he lacks capacity to do the former a litigation friend will need to be appointed for him in the civil proceedings although this would normally be any deputy already appointed. If he lacks capacity to do the latter his financial affairs will come under the jurisdiction of this Court and a financial deputy will need to be appointed for him. The calculation of compensation in the personal injury proceedings may in consequence be affected by the need to appoint such a deputy. The circumstances and

PART IX

much of the evidence pre-date implementation of the new mental capacity regime on 1st October 2007 but these matters must be determined under that regime.

... It is thus contemplated that a litigant who is a protected party may nevertheless not be a protected beneficiary, or in other words, a litigant may not have capacity to conduct litigation but may nevertheless have capacity to manage his financial affairs. But Rule 21 of the CPR fails to make allowance for the converse, namely that a litigant who has capacity to conduct court proceedings may not have capacity to manage his financial. This situation might arise, for example, where a wealthy man with complex financial affairs wished to bring a small claim.

[The decision in *Saulle v Nouvet*] identifies a weakness of dealing with the issue of capacity in the civil court. That court can make a definitive decision as to capacity to litigate but it cannot make a decision as to capacity to manage financial affairs that will be binding on the Court of Protection. Conversely, the Court of Protection has a statutory power to make declarations as to capacity which may relate to both litigation and management of financial affairs and any such declarations are likely to be followed by a civil court. In substantial personal injury claims where the quantum of damages may be affected by the involvement of the Court of Protection there are therefore advantages in the civil court referring both issues of capacity to the Court of Protection for determination. However, where the amount of money involved would not normally trigger the intervention of the Court of Protection it is proportionate and desirable for the civil court to adjudicate on both aspects of capacity (ie to decide whether the litigant is a protected party and if so then whether he or she is also a protected beneficiary).'

The court decided that:

'There is a presumption of capacity that applies to all of us. A balance must then be maintained between empowerment and protection and, unlike the previous regime under the Mental Health Act 1983, this has now swung towards empowerment under the Mental Capacity Act 2005. There is simply insufficient evidence for the Court to make a finding that GS lacks the capacity to make his own decisions either in the conduct of this litigation or thereafter in regard to his enhanced financial affairs. Hitherto he has been managing his more basic finances in a satisfactory manner and it is likely that he will, with guidance, cope with his damages award. If he does not do so, and his impairments lead to vulnerability, then the matter could be referred to the Court of Protection again and the matter would have to be reconsidered in the light of the evidence then available. On the evidence presently available I am not prepared to make any declaration as to incapacity.'

Comment
This decision followed *Saulle v Nouvet* – *above* and seeks to further explain the potential role of the Court of Protection.

COURT OF PROTECTION

JURISDICTION – TEST OF CAPACITY – POWERS OF THE COURT

Test of capacity to be satisfied for the court to assume jurisdiction under s 48 MCA to make Interim orders and directions

Re F

CoP Case No: 11649371
28 May 2009
HHJ Hazel Marshall QC sitting as a nominated Judge

Summary

The District Judge took the view that since the Act laid down that mental capacity was to be presumed, she had no jurisdiction to make an order unless and until this presumption was rebutted – and as to this, the evidence before her was insufficient. So she declined to make any order, whether joining in the relevant authorities or directing a psychiatric assessment and report under s 49 MCA. She was willing only to adjourn the case to enable further medical evidence to be provided.

Decision

The proper test for the engagement of s 48 in the first instance is whether there is evidence giving good cause for concern that P may lack capacity in some relevant regard. Once that is raised as a serious possibility, the court then moves on to the second stage to decide what action, if any, it is in P's best interests to take before a final determination of his capacity can be made. Such action can include not only taking immediate safeguarding steps (which may be positive or negative) with regard to P's affairs or life decisions, but it can also include giving directions to enable evidence to resolve the issue of capacity to be obtained quickly.

Exactly what direction may be appropriate will depend on the individual facts of the case, the circumstances of P, and the momentousness of the urgent decisions in question, balanced against the principle that P's right to autonomy of decision-making for himself is to be restricted as little as is consistent with his best interests. Thus, where capacity itself is in issue, it may well be the case that the only proper direction in the first place should be as to obtaining appropriate specialist evidence to enable.

The Judge stated:

> 'The "presumption of capacity" reinforces the general approach of the Act, that "P's" basic right to have the power to make decisions for himself is to be respected and protected, and can therefore only be displaced by sufficient evidence establishing that he does not have capacity in the relevant respect. However, such a finding is what ultimately grounds a formal declaration under s 15 of the Act, and s 48 expressly confers powers on the court to take steps "pending" the determination of that question. It follows that the evidence required to found the court's interim jurisdiction under this section must be something less than that required to justify the ultimate declaration.

PART IX

What is required, in my judgment, is simply sufficient evidence to justify a reasonable belief that P may lack capacity in the relevant regard. There are various phrases which might be used to describe this, such as "good" or "serious cause for concern" or "a real possibility" that P lacks capacity, but the concept behind each of them is the same, and is really quite easily recognised.

A lower threshold for engagement of the court's powers under s 48 is not at all inconsistent with the emphatic approach of the Mental Capacity Act 2005 that every adult is to be treated as entitled to make his own decisions, and is not to be interfered with in that regard without good reason to suppose that he is vulnerable through lack of capacity. ...'

Comment
It is clearly necessary, in doubtful cases, for the Court to be able to decide whether the individual lacks capacity. This decision ensures that the statutory presumption of capacity is not an obstacle and offers guidance as to the interim orders that may be made.

PRINCIPLES TO BE ADOPTED IN HEALTH AND WELFARE APPLICATIONS

Justification for the interference in the private family life of P

Re GC

[2008] EWHC 3402 (Fam)

Hedley J

Summary
GC, aged 82, had lived with his nephew, KS, for 28 years. KS was thought to have schizophrenia. On 7 April 2008 GC's pendant alarm went off accidentally. The police arrived at the house, and discovered that the two men were living in exceptionally squalid conditions. Both of them were admitted to Homerton Hospital. The hospital brought proceedings in the Court of Protection as to whether GC should be returned home on discharge from hospital. There was a disagreement between the two jointly instructed independent experts. The forensic psychiatrist considered that a return home was not in GC's best interests, whereas the social worker, favoured a trial period at home. The Court had to determine whether such a trial period should take place; in so doing, Hedley J gave general guidance as to the effect of ss.1 and 4 MCA in the context of applications of this nature.

Decision
Hedley J held at paragraph 14 and 15:

'[Sections 1 and 4] really provides the statutory framework within which the court approaches this case. It seems to me that when one applies the statutory provisions the impact of them is that the State does not intervene in the private family life of an individual, unless the continuance of that private family life is clearly inconsistent with the welfare of the person, whose best interests the court is required to determine. That is the same principle that governs State intervention under the Children Act 1989, and whilst the Children Act and the Mental Capacity Act deal with quite different problems and must be treated quite separately, in my judgment it is right that the fundamental principle governing the welfare agencies of the State's interventions in private life should be the same.'

Comment
The principles set down in the paragraph cited above are of cardinal importance; they have also been repeated by Hedley in another case (*The PCT v P, AH and a Local Authority* [2009] EW Misc 10 (EWCOP)), where he held that a placement of P away from the person with whom he enjoyed family life for purposes of Article 8 ECHR could only represent a proportionate interference with those rights where his best interests "compellingly" required such a placement (paragraph 58). Note also that, in at least one case, damages have been awarded to the family member for a breach of their Article 8 right to family life following a sustained denial of contact between P and the family member: *City of Sunderland v MM & Ors* (CoP Case No: 1155573T-01).

COSTS

Guidance for award of costs following cancellation of health and welfare LPA

Re RC

CoP Case No: 11639140

Senior Judge Lush

Summary
SC, the niece of the adult the subject matter of the proceedings (RC) appealed against a costs order made in favour of the London Borough of Hackney following proceedings, very shortly after which RC died. As Senior Judge Lush made clear in his judgment, he heard the appeal by RC's niece in significant part because he wished to give guidance as to whether the general rule in personal welfare proceedings necessarily applies to proceedings in which the applicant is asking the Court to direct the Public Guardian to cancel the registration of an LPA for health and welfare.

In broad terms, the proceedings, before DJ Marin, were on two tracks: one for cancellation of the registration of a health and welfare LPA in favour of SC, and the second for declarations and orders regarding RC's future placement. An order was made in these terms following a hearing extending over three days in May 2009. LBH sought an order that SC pay its costs of the second and third days of the hearing; the charity Jewish Care (JC) (in whose care home RC resided) sought an order that SC pay the entirety of its costs. DJ Marin approached the question of costs on the basis that the proceedings relating to the cancellation of the LPA should be considered as if they were health and welfare proceedings, and hence that the general rule for such proceedings (rule 157) applied. Having regard as to SC's conduct, DJ Marin ordered that she pay the costs of LBH of the second and third days of the hearing, and 50% of the costs of JC from the date that it was served with notice of the proceedings.

PART IX

Decision

Having conducted a review of the authorities, Senior Judge Lush confirmed that he had a residual jurisdiction to consider SC's appeal on costs, notwithstanding the death of her aunt, but that her other appeals against orders made by DJ Marin fell away because the jurisdiction of the Court of Protection lapsed upon the death of RC.

Senior Judge Lush concluded that DJ Marin was wrong to conclude that, because the LPA was a personal welfare LPA, consideration of issues of costs in proceedings relating to it should be approached by reference to Rule 157 (i.e. the general rule in welfare proceedings, namely that there be no order as to costs). Senior Judge Lush held that:

> '... because the format, the procedures for both execution and registration, and the grounds of objection are identical in relation to both types of instrument, as a general rule, the incidence of costs in cases where there is an LPA for health and welfare should not necessarily differ from the general rule in property and affairs cases, subject of course to the provisions of rule 159, which allows the court to depart from the general rule if the circumstances so justify.'

Senior Judge Lush then went to explain why he thought the original decision on costs was unjust. He expressed concerns as to: (1) the fact that Hackney had not given any warning to SC that it might seek its costs; (2) the fact that the judge below had not considered SC's ability to pay the costs awarded against her; (3) the fact that he was not satisfied that, when awarding costs against SC, the judge fully considered the nature of the relationship between her and her aunt, and whether she was acting in RC's best interests; and (4) the fact that it appeared that the District Judge might have allowed the fact that SC was a litigant in person whose conduct was infuriating to sway him into considering that the case before him was exceptional when the reality was "SC is not untypical of many of the litigants in person who appear on a regular basis in health and welfare proceedings in the Court of Protection."

Senior Judge Lush concluded that the general rule (Rule 157) should apply, and that the court should only depart from the general rule where the circumstances so justify. 'Without being prescriptive,' he continued:

> '... such circumstances would include conduct where the person against whom it is proposed to award costs is clearly acting in bad faith. Even then, there should be a carefully worded warning that costs could be awarded against them, and a consideration of their ability to pay. If one were to depart from rule 157 in all the cases involving litigants whom [the social worker expert] has described as 'extreme product champions,' the court would be overwhelmed by satellite litigation on costs, enforcement orders, and committal proceedings.'

Comment

The general guidance given by Senior Judge Lush is of assistance in clarifying the costs position regarding disputes concerning personal welfare LPAs, and also in making clear the circumstances under which the general rule in personal welfare proceedings other than those concerning LPAs will be displaced. The need for giving a clear costs warning is one that is particularly significant, as is the consideration that needs to be given both to the ability of the person in question to pay and to their motives in so acting: it is clear that the latitude that will be given to litigants in person (at least) is likely to continue to be significantly greater in Court of Protection proceedings than before the remainder of the civil courts.

COSTS

Guidance for award of costs – circumstances under which professional should not advance themselves as deputy

EG v RS, JS and BEN PCT

CoP Case No: 10237109

HHJ Cardinal sitting as a nominated Judge

Summary
An unsuccessful appeal by a solicitor (EG) against an order made that she pay the costs of her failed application for permission to apply to be appointed the health and welfare deputy of RS.

Facts
The case arose out a complex and acrimonious dispute regarding the welfare and finances of RS, a man severely injured in a road traffic accident and brain damaged as a result.

CH, the brother in law of RS and estranged husband of JS (RS' sister) was the property and affairs deputy of RS. At the material time, EG was CH's solicitor. She had sought to be appointed health and welfare deputy for RS, but was refused permission. In refusing permission, the District Judge ordered her to pay the costs of JS, the Official Solicitor (RS's litigation friend) and BEN PCT (the relevant PCT with responsibility EG appealed the decision.

Decision
HHJ Cardinal noted that EG had been (at the least) naïve to apply to be made the deputy, because it was or should have been obvious 'that she simply could not be seen by the family of RS as an impartial Deputy in the light of past events and of the current litigation' noted (at paragraph 28). His concerns as to her ability to act impartially were only further heightened by a letter that she had sent (as CH's solicitor) in which she set out contact arrangements between JS and RS that would be acceptable to CH. Indeed, he noted (at paragraph 35) that he could not think of a case 'where the involvement of the solicitor had hitherto been more clearly on one side only.'

HHJ Cardinal accepted (at paragraph 38(iv)) that as a matter of public policy the Courts should not discourage professionals from seeking appointments as Deputies by way of costs sanctions, but noted that there should be a limit to such applications:

> '... where there is clear opposition and acrimony given the role of the would-be Deputy hitherto. It seems to be that such an applicant ought to ask him or herself am I in any way compromised by my intervention to date? Is there any evidence of my taking sides too strongly? Can I be sure that all parties will indeed regard me as a neutral arbitrator? Am I really

PART IX

suitable given the history of conflict with my client and my support of him? Would my appointment mean more conflict?'

Comment

As HHJ Cardinal noted at the outset of his judgment, the appeal was 'a cautionary tale for all those who put themselves forward as professional deputies when too closely associated with one party in a dispute before the Court of Protection.' The facts of the case illustrate clearly how careful professionals must be in ensuring that they both are and seen to be independent and impartial when advancing themselves as deputies. It is not beyond the bounds of possibility that a solicitor who has provided advice to one party could then advance themselves as a professional deputy; however, this judgment makes it very clear that they do so at their peril where there could be any suggestion that they were 'tainted' by their prior association, especially where (as so often) they put themselves forward in the context of a dispute between family members. Merely being a professional is not, in such a circumstance, enough.

EVIDENCE

Admissibility of hearsay evidence – Disclosure of police interviews

London Borough of Enfield v SA

[2010] EWHC 196 (Admin)
McFarlane J

Summary

In a fact-finding hearing to determine whether allegations of abusive parenting were established, the following issues were addressed in respect of Court of Protection proceedings:

1. whether hearsay evidence is admissible?

2. if so, is hearsay evidence emanating from a witness who is, by reason of mental disability, not competent as a witness admissible?

3. where the subject of proceedings has been interviewed by police in an 'Achieving Best Evidence' interview are the fact of that interview and a copy of the DVD recording of it matters to be disclosed to the parties and the court?

4. where police propose to interview a person who is the subject of pending incapacity/best interest proceedings ('P'), are the police and/or applicant local authority under a duty to disclose the proposal to the court and parties and how is the issue of P's capacity to consent to the interview to be addressed?

Decision

In the course of his judgment the judge stated as to points 1 and 2 above:

'24. The express provision regarding hearsay that is made within the statutory scheme for both civil and family proceedings is in stark contrast to the MCA 2005 and the COPR 2007, which make absolutely no express reference to hearsay. MCA 2005, s 51(1) gives power to make "Court of Protection Rules" and s 51(2) provides that the rules may make provision, inter alia, "as to what may be received as evidence (whether or not admissible apart from the rules) and the manner in which it is to be presented" (s 51(2)(i)). The relevant rules are in COPR 2007, Part 14 and rule 95

25. It is of note that COPR 2007, r 95(a)–(c) are in almost exactly the same terms as CPR 1998, r 32.1(1)–(3). There is, however, no comparable provision in the CPR to r 95(d). ...

26 ... I conclude, first of all, that proceedings in the Court of Protection under the MCA 2005 must fall within the wide definition of "civil proceedings" under the Civil Evidence Act 1995, s 11 ...; they are civil proceedings before a tribunal to which the strict rules of evidence apply. The application of the strict rules of evidence is demonstrated by COPR 2007, Part 14 which makes detailed provision as to evidential matters within the context of, and by reference to, the ordinary law of evidence (for example the power to "exclude evidence that would otherwise be admissible" r 95(b)).

27. On that basis the CEA 1995 applies to proceedings in the Court of Protection and hearsay evidence will be admissible in accordance with the provisions of that Act. ...

32. ... I hold that COPR 2007, r 95(d) gives the Court of Protection power to admit hearsay evidence which originates from a person who is not competent as a witness and which would otherwise be inadmissible under CEA 1995, s 5. Admissibility is one thing, and the weight to be attached to any particular piece of hearsay evidence will be a matter for specific evaluation in each individual case. Within that evaluation, the fact that the individual from who the evidence originates is not a competent witness will no doubt be an important factor, just as it is, in a different context, when the family court has to evaluate what has been said by a very young child.'

The judge also stated as to points 3 and 4 above:

'36 SA had been interviewed in the "sensory room" at the day centre by a woman police officer with one of the centre workers also present. Counsel confirmed that the local authority legal department had a copy of a DVD recording of the interview which, if the court directed, could be disclosed. ...

What authority did the police have to interview SA?

41. The current edition of "Achieving Best Evidence" contains a substantial section (Part 3) dealing specifically with interviewing vulnerable adult witnesses. Paragraphs 3.42 to 3.53 set out in detail issues relating to obtaining the consent of such an interviewee. ...

46. In the absence of an absolutely pressing emergency (and given the availability of a High Court judge every single day of the year to deal urgently at any time of the day or night with an application, I use the phrase "absolutely pressing" in an extreme sense) where there are extant Court of Protection proceedings relating to an individual's capacity and best interests, any question of whether or not that individual is to be the subject of an ABE interview must be raised

with the court and be subject to direction from a judge. Where the substance of the interview may relate, as here, to allegations that another party to the proceedings (or someone closely connected to a party) has harmed the interviewee then there will be good grounds for the matter being raised, at least initially, without notice to that party. In every case, however, notice should be given to the Official Solicitor or any other person who acts as P's litigation friend. ...

Was the local authority under a duty to disclose the existence of the ABE interview?

48.   In this case the local authority were involved in the working with the police in planning the ABE interview that took place on 23rd June 2009 and they were provided with a copy of the DVD record of it soon thereafter. The local authority decided not to rely upon the content of the ABE interview and therefore considered that they were under no duty either to disclose the fact that the interview had taken place or the fact that they had a copy of the resulting DVD. The existence of the interview only came to the knowledge of the parents and the court in consequence of a question from the court during closing submissions. The local authority continue to submit that they have acted in accordance with the rules governing Court of Protection proceedings and that they were under no duty to disclose this information/material. Are they correct in that submission? ...

52.   ... it would seem that in this case [the local authority] have provided the disclosure that was required of them, yet the result, from the perspective of a judge who is embedded in the procedure and culture of child protection proceedings under the Children Act 1989, is totally unacceptable. In a fact-finding process, where the case is largely based upon what a vulnerable adult has said and the aim of the court in due course is to make orders to meet P's best interests, how can it be appropriate, fair to the interests of all parties (but particularly P) or in any way acceptable for the applicant local authority to take part in arranging a formal ABE interview of P and subsequently take possession of a DVD recording of the interview yet be under no duty to inform the other parties or the court that that is the case?

57.   The apparent difference in the approach to disclosure as between the family courts and the Court of Protection may well arise from the fact that the rules for the latter are based upon ordinary civil litigation with the expectation that disclosure will be based on whether documents "adversely affect [a party's] own case" or "support another party's case" (COPR, r 133(2)(b)) whereas the approach of the family court is that there is a duty to give the court all relevant material.

58.   There can, in my view, be no justification for there being a difference of this degree on the issue of disclosure between the family court and the Court of Protection in fact finding cases of this type where really the process and the issues are essentially identical whether the vulnerable complainant is a young child or an incapacitated adult. For the future in such cases in the Court of Protection it would seem to be justified for the court to make an order for "specific disclosure"

under COPR 2007, r 133(3) requiring all parties to give "full and frank disclosure" of all relevant material.'

Comment

This important decision addresses matters that were not anticipated when the CoP Rules were written. The Committee established to review the CoP rules recommended that they be amended to reflect the decision, a recommendation which was accepted by the President of the Family Division but which has not (at the time of writing) been advanced further.

PUBLIC HEARINGS

Basis upon which the Court of Protection should hear matters in public or private

A v Independent News and Media Limited

[2010] EWCA Civ 343

Court of Appeal

Summary

The case concerned a severely disabled adult, A, who was, in spite of his disabilities, a musical prodigy. The Official Solicitor contended that the proceedings, which involved applications for the appointment of welfare and financial deputies, should be heard in private, in accordance with the general rule. The Defendants sought access to the proceedings in order that they could then apply for such information as they thought appropriate to be made public, arguing that much of A's personal life was already in the public domain. The High Court made an order the effect of which was to enable designated representatives of the media to attend the hearing in the Court of Protection, and thereafter to apply to the judge for his authorisation to enable them to publish information disclosed in the proceedings.

Decision

The Court of Appeal upheld the decision of the High Court, noting that it would not be appropriate to accede to the Official Solicitor's suggestion that instead of allowing access by the media, parts of the Court of Protection's judgment could be published, since it would be wrong for a judge to tailor his judgment to the needs or concerns of the media. Further, the Court of Appeal considered that it was valuable for the public to know about what happens in the Court of Protection, where most hearings will be held in private, and that it was difficult to think of a more appropriate case to fulfil that function, in view of the public's existing familiarity with A's story.

Comment

The reporting of cases in the Court of Protection considers to be a vexed question, albeit that the trend is certainly towards increased openness, driven, especially, by the current President of the Family Division.

PART IX

Reporting of the names of parties

G v E & Ors

[2010] EWHC 2042 (Fam)

Baker J

Summary
Whether it was appropriate to make public the name of the local authority involved in ongoing health and welfare proceedings before the Court of Protection, where that local authority had been criticised in an earlier judgment.

Decision
Baker J concluded (at paragraph 16) that he should name Manchester City Council in the spirit of openness and accountability, and because there was no significant risk that E or members of his family might be identified as a result, Manchester being a large city. He said 'it is important that the residents and council tax payers of the city of Manchester know what has happened so that the local authority can be held responsible. And it is to be hoped that the publicity given to this case will highlight the very significant reforms of the law implemented by the MCA and in particular the DOLS in schedule A1, and the consequent very considerable obligations imposed on local authorities and others by the complex procedures set out in those reforms'.

The judge refused to make public the names of individual social workers because the criticisms he had made referred to failures higher up the chain of command, and refused to identify the company responsible for running the placement at which E had resided, since the company and its director had not been present at the hearing which resulted in criticisms being made, and since the concerns identified could properly be raised by the Official Solicitor with the Care Quality Commission instead.

Comment
This case (both this decision and as a whole, it having generated a number of decisions) represents something of a cautionary tale for local authorities, as the circumstances giving rise to the proceedings were, sadly, not entirely unusual.

SCHEDULE 3 – INTERNATIONAL JURISDICTION OF THE COURT

Basis upon which Court of Protection is to exercise jurisdiction under Schedule 3 – whether required to consider s.1(5) in so doing

Re MN

[2010] EWHC 1926 (Fam)

Hedley J

Summary

Whether and, if so, according to what criteria, should the Court of Protection recognise and enforce an order of a court of competent jurisdiction in California requiring the return of an elderly lady with dementia, MN, to that State. MN had been removed from California by her niece, PLH, to whom certain authority had been granted under the terms of an Advance Healthcare Directive. MN lacked capacity to make all relevant decisions and the Californian court had control of her property.

Decision

Whilst the facts of the particular case meant that the order of the California court was not, in fact, capable of enforcement as at the date it came before him, Hedley J took the opportunity to consider the issues and given a reasoned judgment so that both the parties and the Californian courts would be aware of the approach which would be adopted by the Court of Protection.

Hedley J reviewed the provisions of Schedule 3. He found that the starting point was to ask where MN was habitually resident, as it was only if she was habitually resident in England and Wales or that the Court would exercise its 'full original jurisdiction' under the Act (paragraph 20 – finding there also that this was not a case where her habitual residence could not be determined, an alternative route to the exercise of such full jurisdiction under paragraph 7(2)(a)). He then considered how the question of habitual residence was to be determined, holding as follows:

> '22 Habitual residence is an undefined term and in English authorities it is regarded as a question of fact to be determined in the individual circumstances of the case. It is well recognised in English law that the removal of a child from one jurisdiction to another by one parent without the consent of the other is wrongful and is not effective to change habitual residence – see e g *Re PJ* [2009] 2 FLR 1051 (CA). It seems to me that the wrongful removal (in this case without authority under the Directive whether because Part 3 is not engaged or the decision was not made in good faith) of an incapacitated adult should have the same consequence and should leave the courts of the country from which she was taken free to take protective measures. Thus in this case were the removal 'wrongful', I would hold that MN was habitually resident in California at the date of [the Californian] orders.
>
> 23 If, however the removal were a proper and lawful exercise of authority under the Directive, different considerations arise. The position in April 2010 was that MN had been living with her niece in

PART IX

England and Wales on the basis that the niece was providing her with
a permanent home. There is no evidence other than that MN is
content and well cared for there and indeed may lose or even have
lost any clear recollection of living on her own in California. In those
circumstances it seems to me most probable that MN will have
become habitually resident in England and Wales and this court will
be required to accept and exercise a full welfare jurisdiction under
the Act pursuant to paragraph 7(l)(a) of Schedule 3. Hence my view
that authority to remove is the key consideration.'

In light of the approach outlined above, Hedley J was unable to proceed further
without the issues of the construction of the Directive and the extent of the
authority conferred and indeed the validity of its exercise (all matters to be
determined under Californian) law either being determined in the California
proceedings, or upon the basis of a single joint expert being instructed to advise
the Court on the point.

In large part so as to assist the California court, Hedley J nonetheless went on to
consider the position in the event that MN was found to be habitually resident in
California, such that he was required to consider whether to recognise and
enforce the protective measures taken in California. He noted that the starting
point was that Paragraph 19(1) made recognition mandatory unless that
paragraph was disapplied in cases (other than those falling under the 2000
Hague Convention on the International Protection of Adults) by either
Paragraphs 19(3) or (4). He identified that the only relevant sub-paragraphs
could be Paragraph 19(4)(a) (i.e. that recognition of the measure would be
manifestly contrary to public policy) or Paragraph 19(4)(b) (b) (i.e, that the
measure would be inconsistent with a mandatory provision of the law of
England and Wales). At paragraph 26 of his judgment he had little hesitation in
dismissing Paragraph 19(4)(a) as being a relevant consideration on the facts of
this case, noting that:

"[a] decision of an experienced court with a sophisticated family and
capacity system would be most unlikely ever to give rise to a
consideration of 4(a); the use of the word 'manifestly' suggests
circumstances in which recognition of an order would be repellent to the
judicial conscience of the court."

That left sub-paragraph 19(4)(b), which, as Hedley J, recognised, raised a matter
both of importance and difficulty, namely the extent to which the court should
takes best interests into account in recognition and enforcement proceedings.
The submission of PLH, MN's niece, was that if recognition of an order was not
in the best interests of MN then to recognise (and enforce) such an order would
be contrary to a mandatory provision of the law namely Section 1(5) of the Act.
Thus a best interests exercise must always be undertaken to ensure that
Section 1(5) is not contravened.

However, as Hedley J recognised, if such an argument were right, it would drive
'a coach and four through the summary and mandatory nature of Part 4 of
Schedule 3,' because, in essence, it would require a full consideration of whether
the recognition and enforcement of the protective measure would be in the best
interests of P. As he noted at paragraph 29, the problem was particularly stark on
the facts of the case before him, because he would be required (by Paragraph 12
of Schedule 3) to consider MN's best interests in implementing any protective

measure recognised and enforced by the Court of Protection. In so doing, he noted he had evidence before him that 'might well persuade' him that a journey back to California could be undertaken consistent with MN's best interests. However, he then asked himself, rhetorically, how far ahead should he then look in determining whether a journey was in her best interests? To look too far would, in his view, come very close to a full best interests inquiry.

Hedley J therefore asked himself whether s.1(5) in fact applied. Section 1 provides in material part that '(l) The following principles apply for the purposes of this Act (5) An act done, or a decision made, under this Act for or on behalf of a person who lacks capacity must be done, or made, in his best interests...' In his view, the words of s.1(5) gave rise to the question of whether a decision to recognise and/or enforce an order was a decision made for or on behalf of MN.

In the end, Hedley J concluded at paragraph 31 that:

> '... a decision to recognise under paragraph 19(1) or to enforce under paragraph 22(2) is not a decision governed by the best interests of MN and that those paragraphs are not disapplied thereby by paragraph I 9(4)(b) and Section 1(5) of the Act. My reasons are really threefold. First, I do not think that a decision to recognise or enforce can be properly described as a decision for and on behalf of MN. She is clearly affected by the decision but it is a decision in respect of an order and not a person. Secondly, this rather technical reason is justified as reflecting the policy of the Schedule and of Part 4 namely ensuring that persons who lack capacity have their best interests and their affairs dealt with in the country of habitual residence; to decide otherwise would be to defeat that purpose. Thirdly, best interests in the implementation of an order clearly are relevant and are dealt with by paragraph 12 which would otherwise not really be necessary.'

Comment

Hedley J's judgment answers a number of important questions relating to Schedule 3, perhaps the most important of which is whether – inadvertently – a situation had arisen in which, in any application for recognition and enforcement was before the Court, the Court would be required to conduct a full best interests inquiry. Such a result would have been palpably at odds with the purpose of the Schedule that it is perhaps unsurprising that Hedley came to the conclusion that he did, but his decision in this regard is of considerable assistance. Nonetheless, as he recognised, difficult questions will continue to arise as to the depth and width of any best interests analysis engaged in for purposes of implementation of a protective measure to recognised and enforced.

DEPRIVATION OF LIBERTY SAFEGUARDS

MEANING OF DEPRIVATION OF LIBERTY

Circumstances under which there will be a deprivation of liberty – placement in residential home and foster placement

Re MIG and MEG

[2010] EWHC 785 (Fam)

Parker J

Summary

Whether placement in a foster family and a residential unit amounted to a deprivation of liberty for purposes of Article 5 ECHR.

Decision

The decision concerned two sisters, MIG and MEG. The decision is entirely fact-specific, but is of importance for certain statements of wider application made by the judge. At paragraph 198, she held that a person can be deprived of their liberty in a domestic setting. At paragraph 230 she accepted that it was impermissible for her to consider whether, if a person is objectively detained or confined, this was with good or benign intentions, or in their best interests. However, having considered the case of *Austin (FC) & another v Commissioner of Police of the Metropolis* [2009] UKHL 5 (paragraphs 164 and 230), she took the view it is permissible to look at the reasons why the person is living where they are, noting (at paragraph 164) that, in the instant case:

> '... it does seem to me to be realistic to put into the equation...that both girls were placed in their respective placements are children in need, because they need homes, rather than because they require restraint or treatment. It is also relevant in my view to consider the reasons why they are under continuous supervision and control.

Comment

The extent to which the Court is entitled to look to the purpose for the deprivation of P's liberty is a controversial cases. In many previous cases where a deprivation of liberty has been found, the reason for the detention was similarly that P needed care and/or treatment. On the facts of the case, it appeared that Parker J was particularly swayed by the fact that (1) no-one was objecting to the sisters' placements. They were not 'free to leave', but no-one was seeking to move them; and (2) because of their cognitive limitations, they would have been subject to similar constraints in any placement and even if they were living with their own family. The latter point applies with equal force to many cases in which a deprivation of liberty has been found, which tends to suggest that perhaps the most important factor is whether there is a dispute about where P should live, and in particular, whether P herself is expressing a desire to leave.

MEANING OF DEPRIVATION OF LIBERTY

Circumstances under which there will be a deprivation of liberty – obligations upon local authority

Re A (child) and Re C (adult)

[2010] EWHC 978 (Fam)

Munby LJ (Munby J having been appointed to the Court of Appeal between hearing the case and delivering judgment)

Summary

In both cases, the individuals concerned suffered from a syndrome characterised by learning disability, behavioural problems and disturbed sleep patterns. A and C each lived with their respective families and were cared for at home. Both were locked in their bedrooms at night to prevent them from wandering around the house and injuring themselves. There was no practical alternative to locking the bedroom doors, since having carers present would be likely to exacerbate the disturbed sleep. Neither A nor C was concerned about having the bedroom door locked at night. In both cases, the local authority was aware of the situation and were supportive of the families' approach. The issues on the case were whether (and if so, how), Article 5(1) ECHR imposed any obligations upon the local authorities to bring the matter to Court and whether the situation of A and C amounted to a deprivation of their liberty.

Decision

Munby LJ considered in some detail how Article 5(1) ECHR is engaged where the person responsible for the alleged deprivation of liberty is a private person not a public authority. At paragraph 84, he found, relying on Strasbourg case-law, that the State owes positive obligations under Article 5(1) to protect individuals from arbitrary interferences with their right to liberty, whether by state agents or by private individuals. At paragraph 95, he concluded that local authorities must therefore take reasonable steps to prevent (or seek court authorisation for) a deprivation of liberty which they are aware of, or which they ought to be aware of. This includes investigating whether there is a deprivation of liberty, monitoring the situation if appropriate, and taking steps to end the deprivation of liberty (for example by providing additional support services) or, if that is not possible, bringing the matter to court. However, on the facts of the case, the local authorities were not so directly involved with the alleged deprivation of liberty for Article 5 to be engaged. The local authorities had carried out assessments and had prepared care plans which involved limited domiciliary care and the provision of respite, but they were not directly or substantially involved in providing care, in particular at night time.

At paragraphs 110–62, Munby LJ found, on the facts of the cases before him, that there was no deprivation of liberty, relying on the analysis of the law contained in the decision of Parker J in *Re MIG and MEG* [2010] EWHC 785 (Fam) [above]. Critically, Munby LJ accepted (at paragraph 164) that the purpose of the restrictions imposed was relevant in ascertaining whether there is a deprivation of liberty. Thus, in circumstances where A and C were being locked in their bedrooms for their own safety only at night time when they would otherwise have been asleep but for the effects of their condition, were

PART IX

checked on by their families, and were happy with their care, there was no deprivation of liberty, only a restriction of liberty. The fact that they had no say over where they lived and how they were cared for, was outweighed by these considerations.

Munby LJ took the opportunity in this case to give some guidance to local authorities as to the exercise of their powers in respect of incapacitated adults. At paragraph 55, he made critical comments about a perceived local authority 'mindset' that treated individuals as being under the control of the local authority and as having to comply with its decisions as to their care. At paragraph 77, he stated that, where objections are made or where an absence of objection does not equate to consent, the local authority must seek the assistance of the court 'before it embarks upon any attempt to regulate, control, compel, restrain, confine or coerce a vulnerable adult.' At paragraph 99, he noted that applications should generally only be made without notice 'in the kind of circumstances which in the case of a child would justify a without notice application for an emergency protection order' (i.e. a genuine emergency or other great urgency and where there is compelling evidence that if notice is given, the individual's welfare will be seriously compromised). Finally, the judge noted (at paragraph 67) that although under s.47 of the National Assistance Act 1948 an order can be sought from a magistrates' court for the removal of a person from his residence for the purpose of receiving care and attention, the Law Commission has described this power as 'regarded largely as obsolete' and 'not necessarily compatible with Article 5.'

Comment
This case of importance, in particular, because of its analysis of the limits of local authority responsibilities for deprivations of liberty occurring in circumstances outside their direct control, as well as of the guidance offered for local authorities in the exercise of their powers in relation to incapacitated adults.

MEANING OF DEPRIVATION OF LIBERTY

Circumstances under which there will be a deprivation of liberty – 16 and 17 year olds

Re RK

[2010] EWHC 3355(COP) (Fam)

Mostyn J

Summary
Whether a 17 year old placed in residential accommodation by a local authority under a s.20 Children Act 1989 could be said to be deprived of their liberty at that placement

Decision
RK suffered a serious range of disabilities, including learning disabilities and communication difficulties. She lacked the capacity to make a range of decisions including, inter alia, where to live, and had the mental age of a very

young child. With her parents' consent, she had been moved from her parents' home under an arrangement made under s 20 of the Children Act 1989 between her parents and BCC, the relevant local authority. She was ultimately transferred to a care home, under the same agreement. The question was whether she was deprived of her liberty at that home.

Having reviewed the case law, he agreed with the three-fold analysis developed by Munby LJ and summarised most recently in *Re A and Re C* [above], namely that there needed to be (1) an objective element of 'a person's confinement to a certain limited place for a not negligible length of time'; (2) a subjective element, namely that the person has not 'validly consented to the confinement in question'; and (3) the deprivation of liberty must be one for which the State is responsible.

Mostyn J took the view that the essential function for the Court was to determine whether the measure in question amounted to a deprivation of liberty (paragraph 26). He noted that it seemed to him:

'... that a very obvious facet or attribute of an alleged deprivation of liberty is the existence of a formal empowerment to do it. It seems to me counter-intuitive for it to be argued that the state is depriving a person of his liberty where it has no formal powers to do so in the situation in hand' (paragraph 27).

With that consideration in mind, Mostyn J analysed the provisions of s 20 of the Children Act 1989, and came to the conclusion that, given the terms of s 20(8) (which provides that:

'[a]ny person who has parental responsibility for a child may at any time remove the child from accommodation provided by or on behalf of the local authority under this section ... the provision of accommodation to a child, whether aged 17 or 7, under s20(1), (3), (4) or (5) will not ever give rise to a deprivation of liberty within the terms of Art 5 of the European Convention on Human Rights' (paragraph 33).

The ratio for this aspect of his decision was, it appears, that, as the legal basis for her presence at the care home was 'truly voluntary' (paragraph 32), then it was impossible to see that there was an actual confinement at the hands of the state, i.e. that the third criterion set out by Munby LJ had been satisfied.

Mostyn J analysed the situation in the alternative, concluding that the facts did not demonstrate that there was an objective deprivation of liberty. He also found that there could not be said to be a subjective deprivation of liberty because RK's parents had consented on her behalf to her presence (paragraph 42). He noted, though, that if he were wrong in his analysis, then BCC would have no option but to bring proceedings for authorisation of the deprivation of liberty under s 16 of the MCA and/or a declaration of lawfulness under s 15, there being 'absolutely no way round that' (paragraph 44).

PART IX

Comment
This case is a troubling one for two reasons. Mostyn J's conclusions on the third criterion are difficult to square with principle and with the clear statements in *Re A and Re C* regarding the positive obligations imposed upon a local authority by Article 5(1) ECHR wherever it is aware of a deprivation of liberty occurring, whether that deprivation is at the hands of the State or a private individual. His

conclusions upon the ability of parents to consent on behalf of 16 and 17 year olds raises difficult questions, too, given the fact such individuals fall both within the Children Act 1989 and the MCA, the latter act containing no provision for such parental consent.

ELIGIBILITY TO BE DEPRIVED OF LIBERTY WHEN THE PURPOSE OF THE TREATMENT TO BE PROVIDED RELATES TO MENTAL DISORDER

Placement in a residential home not registered as an independent hospital – to be assessed for treatment relating to mental disorder – authority under s 4A MCA – whether Case E, para 2, Sch 1A rendering person ineligible to be deprived of liberty under MCA applies to detention in a care home

W PCT v (1) TB (2) V (3) S MBC (4) C&W Partnership NHS Trust and (5) W MBC

[2009] EWHC 1737 (Fam)
Roderick Wood J

Summary
A patient required treatment for her psychiatric disorder in a secure environment and for this purpose she was placed in a residential care home. She objected to this and in order to clarify the potential lawfulness of what was proposed the PCT applied for a declaration that she would be eligible to be deprived of her liberty under s 4A of the MCA.

Introduction
This case is an early example of judges having to work their way through the DOLS provisions in the MCA inserted by the Mental Health Act 2007 to establish guidelines on when someone is eligible to be deprived of their liberty under MCA or is ineligible as being subject to the Mental Health Act 1983 (MHA).

Facts
TB, aged 41, suffered from an acquired brain injury with an associated psychiatric disorder. She had a fixed belief that her symptoms had a physical cause and that a physical medical solution should be offered to her. A range of psychiatric treatments had in the past been provided but had largely failed. Following deterioration in her psychiatric state she was admitted to a residential care home run by V and then transferred to a new facility run by them (and also registered as a care home). TB objected, wishing instead to be taken to and treated in a hospital. A declaration from the CoP was sought by the PCT, supported by the Official Solicitor acting on behalf of TB, that she was eligible to be deprived of her liberty at V pursuant to an authority under s 4A of the MCA. She lacked capacity to decide for herself. At the time of the hearing the nature of the treatment regime and whether it could be carried out whilst she was at a home run by V remained in issue, although it was agreed that on balance placement at V was the appropriate provision whilst further enquiries and assessments were made. Sadly, as it is recorded in the judgment, subsequent to the hearing and before judgment TB died.

Decision

The Court made the declaration sought that she was eligible for a welfare order under s 16 or a standard authorisation under Sch A1 depriving her of her liberty whilst accommodated at a care home run by V.

The Judge, in considering whether she was ineligible to be deprived of her liberty under the MCA as being within Case E, para 2, Sch 1A, found that she was not a 'mental health patient' within the meaning of MHA as she was not being accommodated in a hospital for the purposes of being given medical treatment for a mental disorder.

Comment

This is an early case under the DOL safeguards added to the MCA which concerns the relationship between those safeguards and the MHA. It was not necessary in this case to go into the detail in the next following case as there was a relatively easy pathway to finding that the MHA could not apply as the home was a care home and not a hospital.

INELIGIBLE TO BE DEPRIVED OF LIBERTY BY MCA AS BEING SUBJECT TO THE MENTAL HEALTH ACT 1983

Jurisdictional basis of a person being not ineligible to be deprived of liberty under MCA – tests or gateways for when ineligible under Sch 1A – general points and points of statutory construction.

GJ v (1) The Foundation Trust (2) The PCT and (3) The Secretary of State for Health

[2009] EWHC 2972 (Fam)
Charles J

Summary

The applicant challenged a standard authorisation for the deprivation of his liberty in a hospital on the basis that he was ineligible as being within the scope of the Mental Health Act 1983 (MHA) but not subject to any of the mental health regimes and he objected to being a mental health patient (Case E, para 2, Sch A1). In rejecting this challenge, the Court took the opportunity to make general points of statutory construction on the relationship between the powers of detention under the MHA and MCA and applied the relevant provisions to this case.

Introduction

It was necessary for the Court to consider in more detail the DOLS provisions with a view to establishing whether it was right to have granted a standard authorisation under the MCA authorising deprivation of liberty in a hospital or whether the relevant person was ineligible on the basis that any compulsory powers used should have been those provided by the MHA. As this was an early case in the CoP's jurisdiction the Judge provided guidance of more general application.

PART IX

Facts

GJ, a man of 65, suffered from vascular dementia and Korsakoff's syndrome. He also had diabetes. He lacked capacity to decide questions about his treatment. He had on at least two occasions prior to his admission to hospital in December 2008 suffered a hypoglycaemic attack as a result of his neglecting his insulin injections and at least once he had administered insulin to himself twice within a ten minute period. On 11 December 2008 he was detained at a clinic under s 2 of the MHA (for assessment) and this was converted into detention under s 3 (for treatment) in January 2009 (in February an MHRT found that the criteria for continued detention under s 3 were met). On 10 June 2009 he was discharged to a residential care home (on trial leave under s 17 of the MHA). The authority for his detention under s 3 (and hence his s 17 leave) expired on 5 July and was not renewed. He was readmitted to the clinic on 31 July (having escaped from the care home on four occasions). On 6 August the clinic issued an urgent authorisation under the MCA for DOLS detention and on 13 August a standard authorisation was granted (lasting until 10 September). This standard authorisation appeared on its face to be flawed as recording him as being detained for treatment for his mental disorder and hence ineligible. On 4 September GJ applied to the CoP challenging that authorisation. On 12 September a further standard authorisation was granted (lasting until 16 November). This time on the eligibility form the doctor recorded that in his opinion GJ was not detainable under ss 2 or 3 of the MHA and was hence eligible for a DOLS detention. The CoP hearing into the validity of this second standard authorisation was held on 2 November. Subsequent to the hearing on 6 November GJ was detained under s 2 of the MHA.

Decision

Charles J, in upholding the standard authorisation, whilst describing it as a 'borderline' case, found that the purpose of the treatment was to provide GJ with physical treatment for his insulin dependent diabetes, he was not being provided with treatment for his mental disorder and at the relevant point in time he did not meet the criteria for detention under ss 2 or 3 of the MHA. The only effective reason for his detention at the clinic was the need for him to be treated for diabetes. Hence he was not an ineligible person within Case E, para 2, Sch 1A to the MCA.

Guidance was given on the construction and application of the relevant provisions:

- The MHA has primacy in that the decision makers under both the MHA and MCA should approach the questions they have to answer relating to the application of the MHA on the basis of an assumption that an alternative solution is not available under the MCA.

- An authorisation in accordance with the procedures in Sch A1 or an order of the CoP under s 16(2)(a) of the MCA for a deprivation of liberty can only be given or made if the person is not ineligible to be deprived of his liberty by the MCA, so if the authorisation cannot be given on that jurisdictional basis the court has no statutory power to authorise a deprivation of liberty.

- That jurisdictional basis is to be considered by reference to the reality of its purpose and result rather than the wording of an authorisation.

- The decision maker should approach the status test concerning eligibility in para 12(1)(a) and (b) of Sch A1 by asking himself whether in his view the criteria set by ss 2 or 3 of the MHA are met, and if an application was made under them a hospital would detain P.

- In applying para 5(3) of Sch 1A the decision maker should focus on the reason P should be deprived of his liberty by applying a 'but for' approach – is the only effective reason why P should be detained in hospital the need for physical treatment unconnected to the treatment for his mental disorder?

- If, however, having identified the package of care required for the mental disorder (including any physical disorder or illness connected to the mental disorder) the decision maker considers that the criteria set by ss 2 or 3 of the MHA are met, he could not then conclude that the only effective reason for the detention in hospital was the package of physical treatment.

- The decision maker should approach the test in para 5(4) of Sch 1A without taking any fine distinctions between the potential reasons for P's objection to treatment of different types or to simply being in hospital.

- The new DOLS provisions do not cover taking a person to a care home or a hospital (but an authorisation can be given before arrival to take effect on arrival).

- Case E in para 2 of Sch 1A as to when a person is ineligible does not cover an authorisation which results in P being deprived of his liberty in any place other than a hospital.

Comment

The Judge observed that each case would be fact specific and this case certainly shows how detailed a scrutiny of the facts might be needed in a case where there is a question whether the MHA should be used and not the MCA. There is probably not the same difficulty when the relevant person is subject to a mental health regime under the MHA (Cases A–D in para 2, Sch 1A) but it is Case E in which this issue is at its highest. There are likely to be a number of these cases, and this judgment should provide helpful guidance in tackling them.

SCHEDULE A1

Interaction of urgent and standard authorisations – whether second urgent authorisation can be used

Re MB

[2010] EWHC 2508 (COP)

Charles J

Summary

Mrs B had been admitted to a care home following concerns about physical assaults by her husband. An urgent authorisation was granted and then a standard authorisation lasting for one month. Prior to the expiry of the standard authorisation, a further standard authorisation was sought, but the best interests assessor concluded that the best interests requirement was no longer met. This was because Mrs B had displayed emotional and physical signs of distress at having been removed from her home. The local authority sought advice as to what they should do, and following some confusion due to difficulty in contacting the Court of Protection urgently, they issued a second urgent authorisation.

Decision

Charles J found that the procedure adopted by the local authority was not lawful (and hence represented a breach of Article 5(1) ECHR), and that, once an urgent authorisation has been given (and, if appropriate extended), detention can only lawfully be extended by a standard authorisation or by court order. In other words, one cannot use a second urgent authorisation in respect of the same deprivation of liberty. Charles J went on to give useful guidance about the duties of managing and supervisory authorities. Where a problem arose such as had occurred with Mrs B, the best interests assessor should carefully consider whether even if the continued deprivation of liberty is not ideal, there are viable alternatives for P's short term residence. If not, it may be appropriate to continue a standard authorisation for a short period while changes to the arrangements are made, or in order to seek the court's assistance. Where the issue is that a further authorisation cannot be given under DOLS then it will not be correct to issue an application under s.21A of the MCA (challenge to an authorisation) as the relief that can be granted by the court will not be adequate. 'Standard' COP proceedings will be required. If necessary, pending application to the court, it may be possible to rely on s 4B of the MCA (defence to a deprivation of liberty where it is necessary to perform a vital act or give life-sustaining treatment) but only if a decision is made with express reference to s.4 and recorded with full reasons in writing.

Charles J granted a declaration that Mrs B had been unlawfully deprived of her liberty from the expiry of the standard authorisation until the court declared the deprivation of liberty lawful at a subsequent hearing. This declaration was granted notwithstanding the fact that there was no criticism of the local authority or the best interests assessor, although the judge did say that he thought it was right that the Official Solicitor had not also sought damages for the breach of Article 5. It was also granted even though it appears that the judge considered the deprivation of liberty had been in Mrs B's best interests, as there was no suitable alternative accommodation that it would have been appropriate for her to move to at short notice that would have been a better option.

Comment

This judgment is essential reading for all best interests assessors and those involved in administering DOLS, and includes other pieces of advice, such as recording the time that authorisations start and end, in order that there is no risk of a gap or any confusion about the position.

SCHEDULE A1

Compatibility of DOLS safeguards with Article 5 ECHR

G v E

[2010] EWCA Civ 822

Sir Nicholas Wall (President), Thorpe LJ, Hedley J

Summary
An application was brought by the sister, E, of a young adult who had been removed from his foster placement and placed in a residential unit in response to safeguarding concerns. It was agreed that there was a deprivation of liberty, since there was complete control over his care, his movements, his assessments, treatment, social contacts and residence. Baker J held that there was no threshold condition in relation to deprivation of liberty: i.e. that the court may not entertain an application for an order under s 16 of the MCA 2005 that would have the effect of depriving a person of his liberty unless satisfied that his condition warrants compulsory confinement. He held that the proposed deprivation of liberty would fall to be assessed as part of the best interests analysis. E appealed.

Decision
The Court of Appeal (in a joint judgment from a panel including the President) had little hesitation in rejecting the appellant's arguments, holding (at para57) that:

> 'First and foremost, we are of the opinion that MCA 2005 generally, and DOLS in particular: (1) do indeed plug the Bournewood gap; and (2) are ECHR Article 5 compliant. No question of incompatibility arises. We accept Mr Gordon's submission – indeed, we understand it to be common ground – that the safeguards against arbitrary detention contained in ECHR Article 5 apply to persons lacking capacity. It is our view that MCA 2005 provides a "procedure prescribed by law" for depriving such persons of their liberty.'

The Court of Appeal noted that E's arguments relied very heavily on Strasbourg jurisprudence that was concerned exclusively with alleged mental illness and detention in a psychiatric hospital. The Court of Appeal was particularly concerned to highlight the fact that there is a substantial class of persons who are of 'unsound mind' for purposes of Article 5, but are not mentally ill. For such people (and unlike those falling under MHA 1983), the Court of Appeal emphasised that requiring psychiatric evidence of the necessity of their deprivation would be 'simply be unreal … [and] … would in some cases, be irrelevant. To require such evidence would, in our judgment, make MCA 2005 unworkable' (para 62). The Court of Appeal made it clear that it considered that the justification of detention under MCA 2005 is not a medical decision, but a decision for the court to be made in the best interests of the person whom it is sought to detain.

The Court of Appeal made it clear (paragraphs 65–70) that an interim declaration (even contained in an order made by consent, without independent

PART IX

consideration by the court of the evidence or findings of fact) can suffice to stop the clock running for purposes of regularizing a deprivation of liberty by reference to Article 5(1) ECHR.

Responding to a plea made by Baker J for further resources to be dedicated to CoP cases in the Family Division, the Court of Appeal indicated that this would not be possible, but that such applications (which would presumably include complex cases involving DoLs) be listed urgently before the President who: '... will be able to deal swiftly with any aspects of it which do not brook delay and who, if he is unable to retain it himself, will be able to allocate it appropriately' (para76). The Court of Appeal indicated that there may simply be occasions when it is not possible for hearings to be listed which take into account oral and/or expert evidence, noting that '[i]nto issues of fairness and proportionality has to be factored the impact which the intervention of the case may have on other ongoing or waiting cases in the judge's list.'

Comment
This decision is of some significance, not least because it is the first in which the Court of Appeal had cause to consider MCA 2005, and also because of the confirmation that the – elaborate – structure of Schedule A1 to the Act had in fact achieved the goal of closing the 'Bournewood gap,' something about which there had been a degree of doubt. It is also of significance for a different, less positive reason, namely the confirmation that the resources to deal with complex health and welfare cases under MCA 2005 are not always going to be available.

DEPUTIES

CIVIL PROCEEDINGS – DAMAGES

Need for a professional deputy to administer a brain injury award

Eagle v Chambers

[2004] EWCA Civ 1033
Court of Appeal

Summary
In a brain injury claim it was accepted that the defendant was liable to pay the costs of the receiver, but the issue was whether a professional was needed and the costs of this. The litigation solicitor responsible for handling the claim had been appointed receiver and the claimed head of damage was £288,593 in professional fees. The trial judge was critical of the fact that this was not a solicitor 'whose field is that of private client work, trusts and the like' and of the hourly charging rate. He considered that a member of the family could carry out the tasks of receiver seeking professional assistance where necessary and allowed £30,000.

Decision
On the appeal submissions were received from Master Lush of the (former) Court of Protection as follows:

'In my view it is not appropriate to say that the court will only appoint professional receivers in damages cases, nor that, if a professional receiver has been initially appointed, a lay receiver should not subsequently be appointed. I consider that the proper approach in general is that a professional receiver is desirable in acquired brain injury cases at least until the first or second year after the award. Such cases are likely to be more complex in the early stages. After this initial period, much will depend on whether there is a family member (or friend) who is both willing and suitable to act. If there is such a person able and suitable to act, he or she may employ a solicitor or accountant to deal with matters reasonably requiring professional assistance. If there is no such person willing to act, then no doubt it will be necessary for a professional receiver to remain in post (in the present case, either the current receiver or a new receiver appointed from the panel).

Should a panel receiver be appointed in the future, the ongoing costs would depend on the complexity of the case. A professional receiver's costs are subject to detailed assessment (if not agreed), and are likely to exceed £3,500 a year (plus VAT). The costs of a professional receiver vary widely from case to case, and it would be difficult to predict what they might be in the present case. An alternative to a receivership would be the creation of a trust. The Court of Protection usually insists on one of the trustees being a professional, whose costs for acting as trustee may not be significantly less than the costs of acting as receiver.'

It was held that this did not undermine the judge's findings and the award was upheld.

DEPUTY FOR PROPERTY AND AFFAIRS – SECURITY BOND

Professional deputy – size of security bond

In the Matter of H (a minor and an incapacitated person)

CoP Case No: 11461874
15 October 2009
HHJ Hazel Marshall QC sitting as a nominated Judge

Summary
A solicitor deputy applied to the Court for a reconsideration of the level of security which he was ordered to post in respect of a seriously brain injured child who had received a substantial damages award. The amount was £750,000 and he contended that security of this level was unnecessary and excessive in the circumstances of the case, and caused unnecessary costs to be borne by H's estate.

Decision
The Judge first looked at the law and past practice in this field, so as to show how the present situation had come about. She then provided general guidance:

'[The following] can be taken as a useful executive summary guide, whilst bearing in mind that it is only a guide and the individual circumstances of each case may well suggest other material points.

(1) If the Court has real doubts about whether a deputy can be trusted with P's assets, then it must consider not appointing him as a deputy. Alternatively (if this will largely allay such doubts) the court can and should consider imposing limits on the funds under the deputy's control and, in particular, should consider whether the general words of the order appointing the deputy should be narrowed to prevent his having any authority to deal with any property occupied by P as his home, (or any interest of P therein) without further order of the court.

(2) The court should then consider the amount of funds that are to be placed in the deputy's hands or under his control, and envisage the costs and/or loss to P if there were to be a total default by the deputy.

(3) The court should then consider whether the deputy carries professional indemnity insurance which would be effective to replace P's assets in his hands in the event of such a total default. This will include reviewing such matters as the level of aggregation of assets in the hands of a single deputy relative to his insurance.

(4) In the absence of adequate insurance cover then the starting point will be the value of the assets in or passing through the deputy's hands. This consideration may lead back to a review of the terms of the deputyship order with a view to limiting the value of the vulnerable assets.

(5) Where the deputy apparently has adequate and effective professional indemnity insurance, then the court

    (i) should require him to deposit a copy of this with the OPG and inform the OPG/the court immediately if its level is reduced, and

    (ii) should aim to set a level of security which will provide adequate resources to meet P's immediate expenditure needs for a period related to the time it may take to settle the insurance claim (perhaps up to 2–3 years), the costs of making such a claim, and an allowance in case immediate debts of P may have been left unpaid, applying a suitable margin for error.

(6) Having formed the above provisional view as to the appropriate level of security, the court should finally consider the level of premium and whether this would cause P undue financial hardship, or would otherwise in all the circumstances (including the apparent status of the deputy) appear to be an unjustifiable or wasteful use of P's resources, when balanced against the benefit of having that security. Special circumstances (e g husband/wife deputyships, or lay deputies of obvious stature, or situations in which the real risk would appear to be merely negligence rather than total default) may mitigate this, but must provide some real justification for taking the view that such a level of security is not reasonably necessary. The court will then decide whether it is in P's best interests to maintain the level of security originally assessed, or to reduce it to any extent.'

On the facts of this particular case the security was fixed at £175,000.

Comment

This guidance will be of assistance to the Court and practitioners in fixing security levels. It is interesting to note that the Official Solicitor acted as both litigation friend for the incapacitated person and as *Amicus Curiae* having concluded that there was no conflict for him in these two roles.

WHEN REQUIRED

When the Court should appoint a deputy for P – construction of s 16(4) MCA

Re P

[2010] EWHC 1592 (Fam)

Hedley J

Summary

The court has before it an application by the parents and sister of DP (a world-famous pianist) to be appointed his deputies in respect of all welfare and financial matters. Hedley J gave a judgment in which he appeared to give general guidance as to the interpretation of s 16(4) MCA.

Decision

The judge noted that s 16(4) of the MCA might at first glance suggest that the appointment of deputies was a rarity, since the provision states that a decision of the court is to be preferred. But, the judge found that this would be inconsistent with the aim of the MCA and said that, insofar as applications by family members are concerned, the courts should be sympathetic to their requests provided the family members are not embroiled in disputes with one another and appear able to carry out the functions of a deputy appropriately.

Hedley J stated (paragraph 8) that:

'... it must be appreciated that Section 16(4) has to be read in the context of the fact that, ordinarily, the court will appoint deputies where it feels confident that it can. It is perhaps important to take one step further back even than that, and for the court to remind itself that in a society structured as is ours, it is not the State, whether through the agency of an authority or the court, which is primarily responsible for individuals who are subjects or citizens of the State. It is for those who naturally have their care and wellbeing at heart, that is to say, members of the family, where they are willing and able to do so, to take first place in the care and upbringing, not only of children, but of those whose needs, because of disability, extend far into adulthood.'

Comment

This decision must be read subject to that of *Baker J G v E* [2010] EWHC 2512(COP) (Fam) [below].

When the Court should appoint a deputy for P – construction of s 16(4) MCA

G v E

[2010] EWHC 2512(COP) (Fam)

Baker J

Summary
Whether the carer of E (the person without capacity) should be appointed welfare or property and affairs deputy.

Decision
Baker J agreed with an unreported decision of HHJ Turner QC (sitting as a Judge of the High Court) in *LBC v LD and KD* (unreported, 25.6.10) that the scheme of the MCA 2005 was such that decisions should ordinarily be taken by those looking after and responsible for incapacitated adults, with particularly grave decisions or issues which are the subject of dispute being resolved by the courts. The appointment of a deputy, which entailed giving one person a protected position regarding decision-making, was not appropriate except in limited circumstances, notably those identified in the MCA Code of Practice. These include cases where P is at risk of harm from family members or there is a long history of disputes, or where P has substantial financial assets which require regular management.

In coming to his decision, Baker J made it clear that he considered that Hedley J had not in *Re P* been intending to give general guidance as to the meaning of s 16(4) of the MCA because, on the facts of that former case, the question was not whether deputies should be appointed, but the identity of those deputies.

Comment
It is suggested that, in light of this decision (and that in *LBC v LD and KD*), the appointment of welfare deputies is likely to be very rare, and local authorities or family members who wish to seek such an appointment will have to consider their positions very carefully. One of the central reasons a welfare deputy was not required in *G v E* was that the judge considered that E's carers could make routine decisions about such matters as holidays and respite care. Often the motivation for an application to be welfare deputy, whether by a local authority or a family member, is the belief that the other is obstructive or is likely to make the wrong decision. It is only when the court clarifies the identity of the 'lead' decision maker, as Baker J did in this case, that such concerns can be dealt with. It is suggested that it can be drawn from the judgment of Baker J that where P is not at risk of harm from his family members, the assumption is that his family will take the lead in routine decision-making, albeit collaboratively with relevant professionals. Where there is a risk of harm because of the decisions made by P's carers or family, it may be that the local authority has to take the lead to protect P. In this case, the court's approval of particular decisions will be required and is likely to be preferred to the granting of a welfare deputyship.

ENDURING POWERS OF ATTORNEY

ENDURING POWER OF ATTORNEY – VALIDITY

Lack of capacity – standard of proof

Re K, Re F

[1988] Ch 310
Hoffmann J

Summary
The issue was 'whether the power created by the instrument was valid if the donor understood the nature and effect of an enduring power of attorney notwithstanding that she was at the time of its execution incapable by reason of mental disorder of managing her property and affairs'.

Decision
In his judgment the judge stated:

'In practice it is likely that many enduring powers will be executed when symptoms of mental incapacity have begun to manifest themselves. These symptoms may result in the donor being mentally incapable in the statutory sense that she is unable on a regular basis to manage her property and affairs. But ... she may execute the power with full understanding and with the intention of taking advantage of the Act to have her affairs managed by an attorney of her choice rather than having them put in the hands of the Court of Protection. I can think of no reason of policy why this intention should be frustrated.

Plainly one cannot expect that the donor should have been able to pass an examination on the provisions of the Act. At the other extreme, I do not think that it would be sufficient if he realised only that it gave [someone] power to look after his property. [Counsel] helpfully summarised the matters which the donor should have understood in order that he can be said to have understood the nature and effect of the power. First, (if such be the terms of the power) that the attorney will be able to assume complete authority over the donor's affairs. Secondly, (if such be the terms of the power) that the attorney will in general be able to do anything with the donor's property which he himself could have done. Thirdly, that the authority will continue if the donor should be or become mentally incapable. Fourthly, that if he should be or become mentally incapable, the power will be irrevocable without confirmation by the court. I do not wish to prescribe another form of words in competition with the explanatory notes prescribed by the Lord Chancellor, but I accept [this] summary as a statement of the matters which should ordinarily be explained to the donor (whatever the precise language which may be used) and which the evidence should show he has understood.'

Comment
This was an early appeal following the introduction of EPAs and led to a practical approach to situations where these were executed once fears as to lack of capacity arose. It addressed the issue of applications for registration following soon after execution.

PART IX

Lack of capacity – burden of proof

Re W (Enduring Power of Attorney)

[2000] Ch 343
Jules Sher QC
and on appeal (upholding the judge) [2001] 1 FLR 832

Summary
The issue was where the burden of proof lay, on registration of an EPA, in relation to its validity. Enduring Powers of Attorney Act 1985 s 6(6) provided that where a ground of objection is established to the satisfaction of the court, the court shall refuse the application to register; but if the court is not so satisfied, the court shall register the instrument. The master had refused to register a power on the ground that he was not satisfied that the donor had understood its nature and effect.

Decision
It was held that at first instance (and upheld on appeal) that:

'... the onus of establishing any of the grounds set out in subsection (5) is firmly laid on the shoulders of the objectors. Under subsection (6) it is only if the ground concerned is established to the satisfaction of the court that the court can refuse to register the power. Indeed, if the ground is so established the court must refuse. The contrary position is expressly made equally emphatic: if the court is not so satisfied it 'shall register the instrument to which the application relates.'

Very few cases in these days turn on the onus of proof. In ordinary civil litigation the judge is nearly always able to form a view on a balance of probabilities as to whether an event did or did not happen. But the state of a woman's mind some three years before the court hearing is inherently an issue in respect of which it is quite likely that the judge may not be satisfied either way.

I am not satisfied on the evidence that Mrs. W did not have this understanding. This does not mean that I am satisfied that she did have it. The point of this judgment is that this last issue is not the question before me. If, as is the case, I am not satisfied that she lacked the necessary understanding, it seems to me that I am bid by the Act to register the power ...'

Comment
This decision made it much more difficult to pursue objections to the registration of EPAs.

Lack of capacity – burden of proof – costs

In the Matter of C

[2008] EWHC 1869 (Ch)
Warren J

Summary

There was an objection to the registration of an EPA on the footing that the donor lacked the mental capacity to make it. This appeal was against a finding of capacity.

Decision

In the course of his judgment the judge stated:

> '... the task of a judge at first instance is to form his own assessment, on all of the evidence before him, as to whether the donor of an enduring power understood the nature and effect of the power. What Hoffmann J said [in *Re K. Re F.*] is not legislation but it is sound guidance and should, in most cases, be an adequate touchstone to enable the judge to make his decision.

> This is not to say ... that Hoffmann J's statement of matters which ought ordinarily to be explained to a donor and which the evidence should show he has understood was effectively rendered of no relevance. First, as a matter of good practice, such explanations ought to be given and evidence retained to show, in the future, that the explanation had in fact been given and understood. Secondly, and relevantly for the present case, the judge has to assess the totality of the evidence. If he has before him seemingly compelling expert evidence (even if it is not contemporaneous) of mental incapacity, the evidential burden may shift to those seeking to register the EPA to show that the donor had capacity, or at least to produce enough doubt so that the Court is not satisfied that he did not have capacity. In the absence of clear evidence of compliance with Hoffmann J's recommendations, it may be difficult to displace the compelling nature of the expert evidence, so as to lead the judge to conclude that he is not satisfied that the ground of objection is made out ... Accordingly, in the absence of the further evidence adduced by Dr C, I do not consider that the decision of SJ Lush can be disturbed.'

A re-trial was ordered on the basis of new evidence but the judge had this to say as to costs:

> 'As to costs, I will deal with these at a hearing (at a date to be fixed). I will want to hear from Dr C why she should not bear the costs of this application so far given (a) that on the basis of the evidence before SJ Lush, I have held that her appeal would fail and (b) that in relation to the appeal itself, it has succeeded to the limited extent of procuring a rehearing only on the basis of evidence produced at a very late stage and which, so far as I can see, could – with the exception of the nursing home notes – have been produced long ago.'

Comment

This is one of very few appeals relating to registration of EPAs. It provides further guidance as to how these cases should be handled.

Appointment of substitute attorney – whether valid

In the Matter of J (Enduring Power of Attorney)

[2009] EWHC 436 (Ch)
Lewison J

Summary

The Donor executed a document which appointed his wife to be the attorney with his sons as substitute. Was it a valid EPA?

Facts

The form was based on Form 147 in vol. 31 of the Encyclopaedia of Forms and Precedents and stated:

> 'I ... appoint my wife [W] to be my Attorney for the purposes [of the] Enduring Powers of Attorney Act 1985 but if she shall have predeceased me or shall be unable to act or to continue to act as my Attorney whether registered or unregistered then in the alternative I appoint my son [A] and my son [B] and my son [C] jointly and severally to be my attorney(s) for the purpose of the Enduring Powers of Attorney Act 1985 with general authority to act on my behalf in relation to all my property and affairs.'

Decision

The Judge concluded that this was a valid EPA and must be registered without qualification. He declined to consider whether there is a power of severance and, if so, what limits (if any) there are upon its exercise. He stated:

> '16. It is fair to say that opinions have differed over the years about whether this is the correct construction of the section. I was shown articles in legal publications by the Assistant Public Trustee which suggested that it was not; booklets issued for public guidance by the Public Trust Office and the Public Guardianship Office which also suggested that it was not. On the other hand, I was also shown extracts from textbooks which suggested that it was. None of these publications gave reasons for their conclusions so they were of limited assistance. I was also shown examples of powers of attorney in the form of that in the present case which the Court of Protection had registered as valid enduring powers of attorney. In those cases the registration was qualified by stamping the power of attorney with words to the effect that it took effect only as regards particular named attorneys.

> * * * * * *

> 21. ... No other reason of policy was suggested for reaching the conclusion that what you can do by two pieces of paper you cannot also do by one. Such policy reasons as there are seem to me to point to the conclusion that it does not matter whether you use one piece of paper or two.

(i)   The principal policy objective of the 1985 Act was to abolish the common law rule that a power of attorney was revoked by the subsequent mental incapacity of the donor. The construction for which W contends does not undermine that policy.

(ii)   At common law, the appointment of successive attorneys is valid, and where the meaning of an Act is doubtful, Parliament is taken to have intended the least alteration of the common law.

(iii)   The Mental Capacity Act 2005, in which the current provisions are to be found, has as one of its policy objectives the encouragement of autonomy of protected persons. The Law Commission's report, on which the 1985 Act was based, also stressed the importance of the principle that people should be able to make such arrangements for the management of their affairs as they please.

(iv)   The Schedule should not be construed so as to leave technical traps for donors of powers, where the effect of falling into the trap may be irremediable once the problem has been identified.

(v)   There can be no doubt that a will appointing alternative or successive trustees would be valid to deal with the management of the affairs of a deceased person after his death. Why should it be any different for the management of his affairs during his lifetime?

22.   So it seems to me that the question is whether para 20 can be construed so as to permit the execution of an enduring power of attorney in the form of the one in this case.

* * * * * *

25.   The persons named in the instrument as actual or contingent attorneys are, I think, within the meaning of the word "attorney" as used in para 20 of the Schedule. So para20 is engaged where an enduring power purports to appoint successive attorneys. Ms Sandells, for W, submitted that para 20 should be construed as meaning that a valid enduring power of attorney must state whether, in the event that they exercise the power, the attorneys must exercise it jointly or jointly and severally. That, she said, was the correct meaning to be given to the phrase "appointed to act". Provided that an instrument makes this clear it complies with para20 ... In my judgment this is a permissible reading of para 20, and I hold that it is the correct one. I further consider that this construction applies whether the power of attorney purports to appoint attorneys in the alternative or in succession. What is important is that the power makes clear whether, while they are acting, the attorneys are to act jointly, or jointly and severally.'

Comment

The decision contains a useful summary of the development of the law relating to EPAs and resolves the uncertainty as to whether appointments by substitution can be made in a single document. This creates some complexity in the registration process and the Public Guardian argued against validity. Many

PART IX

donors have achieved the effect of successive attorneyships by executing two or more separate enduring powers of attorney.

INHERENT JURISDICTION

SURVIVAL OF JURISDICTION FOLLOWING THE MCA

Scope of declaratory jurisdiction of the High Court

LBL v RYJ and VJ

[2010] EWHC 2665 (COP)

Macur J

Summary

Applications were before Macur J by the local authority, LBL, seeking declarations that RYJ lacked capacity to make day-to-day decisions concerning her daily life and to appoint an appropriate officer of the local authority to be made Health and Welfare and Finance Deputy. In the alternative, if RYJ was determined to have capacity, LBL sought to invoke the inherent jurisdiction of the court, seeking those orders commonly following decisions as to "best interests" of an incapacitated person and amounting to empowering the local authority to direct where she should reside, be educated and with whom she had contact.

Decision

Noting the decisions in *Re SA (A Vulnerable Adult)* [2006] 1 FLR 867 and *A Local Authority and Mrs A* [2010] EWHC 1549, Macur J accepted (at paragraph 62) that the inherent jurisdiction continued to exist "to supplement the protection afforded by the Mental Capacity Act 2005 for those who, whilst 'capacitous' for the purposes of the Act, are 'incapacitated' by external forces – whatever they may be – outside their control from reaching a decision. However, she rejected what she understood to have been the initial contention of the local authority that the inherent jurisdiction of the court may be used in the case of a capacitous adult to impose a decision upon him/her whether as to welfare or finance. Rather, she took the view that the relevant case law established the ability of the court, via its inherent jurisdiction, to facilitate the process of unencumbered decision-making by those who they have determined have capacity free of external pressure or physical restraint in making those decisions.

On the facts of the case, Macur J found that RYJ's vulnerability was that which was associated with her age and limited intellectual functioning, but that she was able to recognise and withstand external pressure to an appropriate degree and that she was not and was unlikely to be subject to physical constraint or behaviour that would impact upon her free will and ability and capacity to reach decisions concerning residence, care and contact. At paragraph 64, she noted that, were she to have found that:

'... her vulnerability was exceptional/greater by reason of her limited intellectual functioning and age, these factors would need to have been considered in reaching my decision concerning capacity. If she is unable to withstand external pressure of 'normal/everyday' degree, whether emotional or physical, it seems to me that it would necessarily inform the answer to the question posed at section 3(1)(c) of the Act.'

In light of her conclusions on the facts, Macur J noted (at paragraph 65 that:

'... [i]n that I have not found that she is so exceptionally vulnerable for the purpose of my consideration under the Mental Capacity Act 2005, it seems to me that there is little that LBL can rely upon in hoping to invoke the inherent jurisdiction of the court. What is necessary in this case, quite clearly, is that the established network already available to RYJ is consolidated with co-operation of LBL, VJ and other family members.'

Comment

Macur J's comments at paragraph 64 of her judgment are of particular significance, and no little difficulty. On one view, they come close to denying any real space for the inherent jurisdiction at all, because they imply that the factors that would point towards a person falling within the inherent jurisdiction are, on a proper analysis, factors that fall for consideration in answering the question as to whether they lack the relevant capacity. Macur J's comments also make it clear that – at least from her perspective – the inherent jurisdiction of the Court is considerably more limited than some have advocated and that it can only properly be exercised so as to secure unencumbered decision-making (rather than, for instance, allowing decisions to be taken on behalf of the vulnerable adult). Her view should also be read alongside the perhaps more expansive one of the President in the case of *A v DL, RL and ML* [2010] EWHC 2675 (Fam) [below] (in which Macur J's judgment appears not to have been cited).

INHERENT JURISDICTION

SURVIVAL OF JURISDICTION FOLLOWING THE MCA

Scope of declaratory jurisdiction of the High Court

A v DL, RL and ML

[2010] EWHC 2675 (Fam)

Sir Nicholas Wall (President of the Family Division)

Summary

The case concerned an elderly couple who the local authority considered to be at risk of physical, emotional and financial abuse from their son, who lived with them. The local authority took the view that the couple did not lack capacity. The local authority had therefore rejected making an application under the MCA. It had also considered and rejected the possibility of an ASBO, or an order under s153A of the Housing Act 1996. That left two possibilities for obtaining the court's assistance to protect the parents: an order under the inherent jurisdiction, or an order under s 222 of the Local Government Act 1972. An ex parte application was therefore made to the Court.

Decision

The President noted that the question before him was whether there was a lacuna in circumstances where (it was asserted) the couple required protection and the only mechanism to engage it was action on the part of the local authority. The President (1) accepted that there was a lacuna; and (2) concluded, on the basis of the definition of the inherent jurisdiction of the Court given by Munby J in *Re SA (Vulnerable Adult with capacity: Marriage)* [2006] 1 FLR 867 that there was jurisdictional basis for the exercise of the inherent jurisdiction on the facts of the case before him (para 20).

On the evidence provided by the local authority, it was appropriate to make an order requiring the Official Solicitor to carry out an investigation to inform the court about the situation and whether the protective orders sought by the local authority were for the benefit of the parents, a procedure first created in *Harbin v Masterman* [1896] 1 Ch. 351. Interim injunctions were granted restraining DL from (1) assaulting or threatening to assault GRL or ML; (2) preventing GRL or ML from having contact with friends and family members; (3) seeking to persuade or coerce GRL into transferring ownership of the family home; (4) seeking to persuade or coerce ML into moving into a care home or nursing home; (5) engaging in behaviour towards GRL or ML that was otherwise degrading or coercive. A further injunction was granted on an interim basis granted restraining DL from: (1) giving orders to care staff; (2) interfering in the provision of care and support to ML; (3) refusing access to health and social care professionals; or (4) behaving in an aggressive and/or confrontational manner to care staff and care managers.

Comment

At the outset of his judgment, the President noted that the case was 'highly unusual,' which is perhaps a surprising comment. There are many safeguarding cases involving adults with capacity in which local authorities wish they had the power to take further steps to protect people, and confirmation that the decision in *Re SA* and the LGA 1972 can be relied on may well lead to further applications of this sought in the near future. The (difficult) question which the case left unanswered at the time of writing was the extent and nature of the relief the Court would ultimately be prepared to grant assuming (1) the Harbin v Masterman inquiry suggested that the proceedings were for the couple's benefit; and (2) the son had been given the opportunity to present his case. Although it would appear on one view that the approach taken by the President was somewhat wider than that adopted by Macur J in *LBL v RYJ and VJ* [2010] EWHC 2665 (COP) [above], it is suggested that the Courts will tread very carefully in making orders that go beyond securing the ability of the vulnerable adults to make decisions of their own free will.

WILLS

STATUTORY WILL

Approach to be adopted under MCA

In the Matter of P

[2009] EWHC 163 (Ch)
Lewison J

Summary
The Judge set out a useful summary of the jurisdiction in regard to statutory wills under the Mental Health Acts 1959 and 1983 and in particular the general principles laid down by Megarry V-C in *Re D (J)* [1982] Ch 237. He then explained the new legislative framework under the MCA and considered whether similar principles now applied in regard to statutory wills under the new jurisdiction.

Decision
The Judge concluded that:

'38 ... the guidance given under the Mental Health Acts 1959 and 1983 about the making of settlements or wills can no longer be directly applied to a decision being made under the 2005 Act. I say this for a number of reasons:

(i) The 2005 Act does not require the counter-factual assumption that P is not mentally disordered. The facts must be taken as they are. It is not therefore necessary to go through the mental gymnastics of imagining that P has a brief lucid interval and then relapses into his former state.

(ii) The goal of the enquiry is not what P "might be expected" to have done; but what is in P's best interests. This is more akin to the "balance sheet" approach than to the "substituted judgment" approach. The code of practice makes this clear in that it points out that the test of best interests was one that was worked out by the courts mainly in decisions relating to the provision of medical care (para 5.1);

(iii) The previous guidance was concerned with deciding what P would have wanted if he were not mentally disordered. But the 2005 Act requires the decision maker to consider P's present wishes and feelings, which ex hypothesi are wishes and feelings entertained by a person who lacks mental capacity in relation to the decision being made on his behalf;

(iv) The same structured decision making process applies to all decisions to be made on P's behalf, whether great or small, whereas the previous guidance was specific to the making of a will, gift or settlement. Moreover, it is a decision making process which must be followed, not only by the court, but by anyone who takes decisions on P's behalf.

(v)   In making his decision the decision maker must consider "all relevant circumstances".

(vi) The Act expressly directs the decision maker to take a number of steps before reaching a decision. These include encouraging P to participate in the decision. He must also "consider" P's past and present wishes, and his beliefs and values and must "take into account" the views of third parties as to what would be in P's best interests.

39.   Having gone through these steps, the decision maker must then form a value judgment of his own giving effect to the paramount statutory instruction that any decision must be made in P's best interests. In my judgment this process is quite different to that which applied under the former Mental Health Acts.

40.   That is not to say that P's expressed wishes should be lightly overridden. On the contrary, the Act expressly requires them to be considered; and for particular consideration to be given to wishes expressed by P when he had capacity. In *Re S and S (Protected Persons)* [*summarised above*] HH Judge Marshall QC considered the Act in a most impressive and sensitive judgment. She pointed out the stress that the Act lays on the ascertainment of P's wishes and feelings and on involving him in the decision making process ... [*see further extract under best interests above*].

* * * * * *

43.   In reaching a decision a third party decision maker will, if appropriate, take legal or other advice. The other advice may be medical, financial, or advice of any other kind. The court will, of course, act according to the law, and be assumed to have sufficient knowledge of the law (either before or after assistance from advocates) to make whatever decision it is called upon to make. But there is, in my judgment, no need (as envisaged by D (J)) to assume (a) that P has taken legal advice (which he has not) and then (b) to attempt to decide what P would have done with that advice if he had had capacity (which he does not). If P's wishes have been formed without having taken legal advice in circumstances where a person with capacity would have taken legal advice, that may be a reason for giving them less weight than might otherwise have been the case.

44.   There is one other aspect of the "best interests" test that I must consider. In deciding what provision should be made in a will to be executed on P's behalf and which, ex hypothesi, will only have effect after he is dead, what are P's best interests? Counsel stressed the principle of adult autonomy; and said that P's best interests would be served simply by giving effect to his wishes. That is, I think, part of the overall picture, and an important one at that. But what will live on after P's death is his memory; and for many people it is in their best interests that they be remembered with affection by their family and as having done "the right thing" by their will. In my judgment the decision maker is entitled to take into account, in assessing what is in P's best interests, how he will be remembered after his death.

45.   For these reasons I do not consider that the guidance given by D (J)

can be directly applied to the structured decision making process required by the 2005 Act, although it contains a good deal of wisdom, and wisdom can always be applied.'

Comment

This decision makes it clear that the statutory 'best interests' checklist must be applied when considering a statutory will, and it is no longer simply a question of deducing what the testator would have done in the event of a lucid interval.

Approach to be adopted under MCA – exclusion of individual – benefitting charity

In the Matter of M

[2009] EWHC 2525 (Fam)
Munby J

Summary

This application by M's Deputy for an order authorising him to execute a statutory will for M was opposed by Z who was a former carer and the sole beneficiary under a previous will. It was common ground that M lacked testamentary capacity. In previous proceedings the Judge had been very critical of Z's behaviour and stated that he had 'forfeited the trust and confidence of the court'.

Decision

After setting out the legal framework the Judge agreed with the decision of Lewison J in *In the Matter of P* [*see above*] and made three further points at para 32:

'(i) ... the statute lays down no hierarchy as between the various factors which have to be borne in mind, beyond the overarching principle that what is determinative is the judicial evaluation of what is in P's "best interests".

(ii) ... the weight to be attached to the various factors will, inevitably, differ depending upon the individual circumstances of the particular case. A feature or factor which in one case may carry great, possibly even preponderant, weight may in another, superficially similar, case carry much less, or even very little, weight.

(iii) ... there may, in the particular case, be one or more features or factors which, as Thorpe LJ has frequently put it, are of "magnetic importance" in influencing or even determining the outcome: see, for example, *Crossley v Crossley* [2007] EWCA Civ 1491, [2008] 1 FLR 1467, at para [15] (contrasting "the peripheral factors in the case" with the "factor of magnetic importance") and *White v White* [1999] Fam 304 (affirmed, [2001] 1 AC 596) where at page 314 he said "Although there is no ranking of the criteria to be found in the statute, there is as it were a magnetism that draws the individual case to attach to one, two, or several factors as having decisive influence on its determination." Now that was said in the context of section 25 of the Matrimonial Causes Act 1973 but the principle, as it seems to me, is of more general application.'

On the facts of the case M was excluded from benefit and the bulk of the estate was left to charities.

Comment

This decision offers further guidance as to how the statutory 'best interests' checklist must be applied when considering a statutory will, and draws an interesting analogy with cases under s 1 of the Children Act 1989, s 1 of the Adoption and Children Act 2002 and s 25 of the Matrimonial Causes Act 1973 (also the inherent jurisdiction of the Family Division in relation to incapacitated or vulnerable adults). It is to be doubted, however, whether it is appropriate for the Court to read directly across from proceedings relating to children to those related to incapacitated adults. The approach adopted by Munby J in this case has also been followed in subsequent cases outside the context of statutory wills (see, for instance, *Re G (TJ)* [above]).

STATUTORY WILL

Approach to be adopted under MCA – interpretation of 'best Interests'

Re D (Statutory Will)

[2010] EWHC 2159 (Ch)

HHJ Hodge QC sitting as a nominated Judge

Summary

The matter came before HHJ Hodge QC so that he could consider whether it would be appropriate for the Court of Protection to authorise a statutory Will for an incapacitated adult on the ground that this is in his or her best interests where there is a dispute or uncertainty as to the validity of a recent Will which departs from the terms of an earlier Will. DJ Ashton had earlier refused permission to the JAD's deputy apply for a statutory will, but upon reconsideration transferred the matter to one of Chancery Circuit Judges in Manchester (sitting as a nominated judge of the Court of Protection) for consideration of this point. In so doing, he had indicated that to exercise the jurisdiction in these circumstances:

'... would encourage many applications where the substantive issue is the validity of a new will made when there was doubt as to testamentary capacity or concern as to undue influence and this Court would be ill-equipped to resolve these disputes.'

Decision

After a careful examination of *Re P (Statutory Will)* [2010] Ch 33, and *Re M* [2009] EWHC 2525 (Fam), HHJ Hodge QC determined as follows upon the issues of principle:

'15 As recorded [...] above, DJ Ashton was concerned that one consequence of exercising the jurisdiction to direct the execution of a statutory will in any case where there was a dispute or uncertainty as to the validity of a recent will due to concerns about a possible lack of testamentary capacity (or want of knowledge and approval) or the possible exercise of undue influence might be to encourage many applications to the Court of Protection raising issues which that

Court would be ill-equipped to resolve. Given DJ Ashton OBE's unrivalled experience of the work of the Court of Protection outside London, that is a concern that cannot lightly be dismissed. Indeed, one of the points made by Munby J in Re M (cited above) at [50] was that the Court of Protection has no jurisdiction to rule on the validity of any will. It may well be impractical, and inappropriate, for that Court to embark upon a detailed investigation of all the evidence necessary to resolve a dispute as to the validity of a will made by a protected person. Nevertheless, as with the exercise of any jurisdiction under the 2005 Act, the overarching consideration, when deciding whether to direct the execution of a statutory will, must be a judicial evaluation of what is in the protected person's "best interests", having considered "all the relevant circumstances".

16   It would seem to me that the concerns outlined by the district judge are factors which the Court may take into account when deciding whether to order the execution of a statutory will; and they might, in an appropriate case, lead the Court to conclude that it should not exercise its power to do so. But, in my judgment, there can be no presumption, still less any principle of general application, that the Court should not direct the execution of a statutory will in any case where there is a dispute or uncertainty about the validity of a recent will, the terms of which depart from those of an earlier, apparently valid, will. The adoption of such an approach would tend to elevate one factor over all others, contrary to the structured decision-making process required by the 2005 Act. Like Lewison J in Re P (at [41]), I would prefer not to speak in terms of presumptions. Under section 4 (6) (a), one of the relevant factors to be considered by the Court in determining the protected person's best interests are that person's past and present wishes and feelings (and, in particular, any relevant written statement made by him when he had capacity). A previous will is obviously a relevant written statement which falls to be taken into account by the Court. But the weight to be given to it will depend upon the circumstances under which it was prepared; and if it were clearly to be demonstrated that it was made at a time when the protected person lacked capacity, no weight at all should be accorded to it. Moreover, Parliament has rejected the "substituted judgment" test in favour of the objective test as to what would be in the protected person's best interests. Given the importance attached by the Court to the protected person being remembered for having done the "right thing' by his will, it is open to the Court, in an appropriate case, to decide that the "right thing" to do, in the protected person's best interests, is to order the execution of a statutory will, rather than to leave him to be remembered for having bequeathed a contentious probate dispute to his relatives and the beneficiaries named in a disputed will. I therefore hold that the Court of Protection should not refrain, as a matter of principle, from directing the execution of a statutory will in any case where the validity of an earlier will is in dispute. However, the existence and nature of the dispute, and the ability of the Court of Protection to investigate the issues which underlie it, are clearly relevant factors to be taken into account when

deciding whether, overall, it is in the protected person's best interests to order the execution of a statutory will.'

On the facts of the case, HHJ Hodge QC decided to make a statutory will in a draft form agreed by Mrs D's deputy, the Official Solicitor and all three of Mrs D's children.

Comment

This case provides further evidence, if such is needed, of the sea change that has been brought about in the approach to property and affairs by the MCA 2005, and, in particular, of the primacy that is required to be given to the best interests of P in all acts done or decisions made for on P's behalf. It is to be hoped that the very real concerns expressed by DJ Ashton as to the potential expansion in scope of the role of the CoP in the realm of statutory wills (which, it is suggested, remain real notwithstanding the correctness of the principled decision taken by HHJ Hodge QC) are not borne out by an expansion in the number of applications for statutory wills.

PART X

International Protection of Adults

PART X: International Protection of Adults

CHAPTER 1
Introduction and Overview **1733**

Introduction 1733

Private International Law 1734

CHAPTER 2
The Convention on the International Protection of Adults **1735**

Introduction 1735

Mental Capacity Act 2005, Sch 3 1736

Jurisdiction and Habitual residence 1737

Applicable Law 1737

Recognition and Enforcement 1738

Protective Measures 1738

Within the United Kingdom 1738

The position in Non-Convention Countries 1739

CHAPTER 3
Northern Ireland **1741**

CHAPTER 4
Scotland **1743**

Background 1743

Adults with Incapacity (Scotland) Act 2000 1747

Measures outwith the Incapacity Act 1764

APPENDIX 1
Adults with incapacity **1765**

International questionnaire on cross border recognition and
enforcement 1765

APPENDIX 2
Completed questionnaires **1773**

Australia: NSW 1773

Australia: Victoria 1781

Belgium 1786

Canada: Alberta 1793

Canada: Manitoba	1800
Canada: Nova Scotia	1806
Canada: Ontario	1811
Canada: Saskatchewan	1816
Denmark	1821
Finland	1826
France	1831
Germany	1837
Iceland	1849
Japan	1854
Serbia	1859
Slovenia	1869
Spain	1878
Switzerland	1884
USA: Florida	1890

Chapter 1

Introduction and Overview

INTRODUCTION

1.1 'Only three people understood the Schleswig-Holstein Question. The first was Albert, the Prince consort and he is dead; the second is a German professor, and he is in an asylum: and the third was myself – and I have forgotten it.'[1]

1.2 Cross border capacity questions are equated to three-dimensional chess, rather than the Schleswig-Holstein Question, but there are definite parallels.

Finding anyone without some cross-border issue is becoming increasingly difficult. Does a spouse or partner have a different nationality or domicile? A little digging often reveals a foreign domicile of which the person was unaware. Do the children or other proposed deputy or attorney live in a different state? In a world which is globally interlinked, it is now not unusual for people of even quite moderate means to have assets situated in another state. The traditional response to any foreign issue was that you must consult a lawyer in the other jurisdiction. Why is this not sufficient?

Other states have completely different private international law rules. Many states with law based on a civil code hold that issues to do with questions of capacity are governed by the personal law of the person. This is often governed by the law of either nationality or by domicile in a civil law sense more akin to habitual residence. Ask the Outer Mongolian (OM) lawyer as to capacity questions for OM assets and he is likely to send the matter straight back, saying that British law must apply and that the British law should deal with the questions of capacity for a UK citizen. Clients are often puzzled to learn that the laws in Scotland are different to those in England & Wales and different again to those in Northern Ireland.

Cross-border issues arise whenever someone holds assets in more than one jurisdiction or has a factor, such as domicile, habitual residence or nationality linking them with another jurisdiction.

1.3 It is increasingly rare to find a person, who does not have such connections:

(1) property abroad, whether a holiday home or stock options,
(2) a child who is now living and working in a different jurisdiction,
(3) a parent, spouse, partner or cohabitee who was born overseas or who has a different nationality.

Any of these facts can raise cross-border issues. We all need to understand the consequences.

---

[1]   Lord Palmerston.

In relation to any capacity or other legal issue, the first questions should always be:

(1) do the courts of England and Wales have jurisdiction?

(2) which law will they apply? Will it be that of England & Wales or another state?

Although the Hague Convention has simplified some issues, it remains difficult to determine jurisdiction and ascertain the relevant applicable law in non-Convention countries and yet with increased tourism and home ownership abroad (especially for retired people) capacity issues arise quite frequently. Accordingly an attempt has been made in this section to lead a pathway through this jungle. It is intended that this Part will develop further in future editions as contacts within other jurisdictions are established.

PRIVATE INTERNATIONAL LAW

1.4 'Private international law is that part of law which comes into play when the issue before the court is so closely connected with a foreign system of law as to necessitate recourse to that system'[2]

Private international law (PIL) deals primarily with the application of laws in space and time. The local jurisdiction at a particular time is sovereign and can define as it wishes, and place a boundary at that or any other time as it thinks appropriate. Unlike garden fences, the boundaries created by separate jurisdictions are rarely co-terminous, and can be in different places at different times. Each jurisdiction has its own separate and distinct Private International Law rules which do not necessarily mesh with that of another state.

It is common in all private international law, to consider separately, issues of:

(1) Jurisdiction – do the Courts of a state consider that they have jurisdiction in the first place?

(2) Applicable Law – if they do, which state's laws will be applied?

(3) Recognition and Enforcement – if the Courts of a state make a particular order, will that order be recognised in the Courts of a different state?

In questions of capacity there is the additional issue of whether a form of Enduring, Lasting, Durable or other form of Power of Attorney or Representation intended to have effect after the onset of mental incapacity will also be valid and recognised in another state.

English PIL in the area of capacity of adults has in the past been very uncertain. Mental capacity is really a particular requirement for many separate and different legal acts, each with their own test and different connecting factor.

---

[2]   Private International Law – Cheshire, North and Fawcett 14th Edition.

Chapter 2

The Convention on the International Protection of Adults

INTRODUCTION

2.1 The Hague Conference on Private International Law seeks to establish international agreements to reduce conflicts of law and to lay down rules to determine jurisdiction and related matters. Under its auspices the Convention on the International Protection of Adults ('the Convention') was concluded on 13 January 2000. It applies to the protection in international situations of 'adults who, by reason of an impairment or insufficiency of their personal faculties, are not in a position to protect their interests'.[1]

2.2 The Convention came into force on 1 January 2009, the requisite three countries: the UK (in relation to Scotland[2]), Germany and France having ratified it. It has subsequently been ratified by Switzerland, Finland and Estonia.[3] By making provision for it in MCA 2005, Sch 3,[4] the UK gives effect to the Convention internally in relation to England and Wales, so far as it can, even though England & Wales has not yet ratified. The provisions of the Schedule are intended to be compatible with the Adults with Incapacity (Scotland) Act 2000, Sch 3, which gave effect to the Convention in Scotland. It sets out new uniform private international law rules for Convention states to establish questions of jurisdiction, applicable law, recognition and enforcement of measures for the protection of adults and powers of representation.

This does simplify the position for Convention states.

2.3 MCA 2005, Sch 3 is, since 1 January 2009, fully in force.[5] Before then it was in force except to the extent set out in para 35 of the Schedule and provided private international law rules to govern jurisdictional issues both within the United Kingdom between Scotland and England and Wales and Northern Ireland and in relation to all other jurisdictions.

---

[1]   For the text of the Convention see www.hcch.net/index_en.php?
      act=conventions.pdf&cid=71.
[2]   Instrument of ratification of 1 April 2003.
[3]   With effect from 1 November 2011.
[4]   See MCA 2005, s 63 and Sch 3.
[5]   Some experts express the view that para 35 of Sch 3 means that the excepted sections only
      have effect when the Convention comes into force in England & Wales. Others believe that
      since the Convention has come into force in other jurisdictions, the excepted sections are
      now in force in England & Wales.

It provides PIL rules for England & Wales with all other jurisdictions, and is not limited to England & Wales rules in relation to those jurisdictions that have ratified the conventions: Estonia, Finland, France, Germany, Scotland or Switzerland.[6]

2.4   These provisions cater for cross-border issues. Here are two potential examples:

(1)   A senior citizen resident in England acquires a second home in, say, France. If he became incapacitated and a receiver or deputy was appointed here, that representative might have had to gain a separate authority in France before he or she could dispose of the property in France.[7] Under the Convention that would not be necessary.

(2)   A person from, say, British Colombia, has under applicable provincial law made a health care representation agreement appointing a health care proxy. If that citizen is injured in Wales and unable to consent to medical treatment, under the Convention the Canadian proxy would have the legal authority to give substitute consent in Wales.

2.5   The provisions are a useful clarification of the private international law rules which are to apply, by countries which ratify the Convention, and within the UK by England and Wales and Scotland, but not by Northern Ireland.

MENTAL CAPACITY ACT 2005, SCH 3

2.6   Schedule 3 to the MCA 2005 extends the Convention in two ways. Firstly, the Convention applies to adults over the age of 18 whereas the MCA 2005 applies to persons over the age of 16. Secondly, the Convention only applies to adults who, by reason of an impairment or insufficiency of their personal faculties, are not in a position to protect their interests, whilst the MCA 2005 also applies to the donors of powers of attorney even if not impaired or insufficient.

It should be remembered that the Sch 3, para 33 specifically disapplies the Convention in relation to the matters set out in Art 4 of the Convention including trusts and succession. The jurisdiction of the Court of Protection in relation to these matters may therefore be limited.

---

[6]   However, unless or until the UK Government ratifies the Convention in relation to England and Wales, there cannot be full reciprocity in these countries – the UK Government has not yet, for example, designated the Central Authority for England and Wales under the Convention. Article 38 Certificates cannot yet be produced. Articles 7 and 8 cannot be invoked.

[7]   This would be so unless domestic private international law in France allowed foreign appointments to be recognised without further procedure (much as if the Convention already applied). This book cannot be taken as authority on the domestic law of France.

JURISDICTION AND HABITUAL RESIDENCE

2.7 In place of the traditional connecting factor of domicile, the Convention and Sch 3 now use habitual residence as the relevant connecting factor. Thus Sch 3 paras 7 and 8 give the Court jurisdiction to exercise its powers in respect of:

(1) an adult habitually resident in England and Wales in relation to him and his worldwide property;

(2) an adult's property in England and Wales;

(3) an adult present in England and Wales or who has property there, if the matter is urgent;

(4) an adult present in England and Wales, if a protective measure which is temporary and limited in its effect to England and Wales is proposed in relation to him.

In addition the Court can have jurisdiction for:

(1) the worldwide property and the person of an adult present in England and Wales whose habitual residence cannot be ascertained, is a refugee, or has been displaced as a result of disturbance in the country of his habitual residence;

(2) a British citizen and his worldwide property, who has a closer connection with England and Wales than with Scotland or Northern Ireland, and Art 7 of the Convention has, in relation to the matter concerned, been complied with;

(3) a person and his worldwide property, for whom the jurisdiction of habitual residence and the UK Minister of Justice agree that the matter is better dealt with in England as the state of nationality, of former residence or where property is situated, and Art 8 of the Convention has, in relation to the matter concerned, been complied with.

2.8 The case of *Marinos v Marinos*[8] is a helpful summary as to the definition of Habitual Residence for the purposes of European legislation. It is not clear as to whether the definition for Hague Convention purposes might in some circumstances be different.

APPLICABLE LAW

2.9 Generally each court is to apply its own law unless it it considers that there is a substantial connection with another state, in which case it may apply the internal law of that other state.[9]

2.10 In relation to "Lasting Powers" defined as Lasting Powers of Attorney, Enduring Powers of Attorney and other powers having a like effect, the law applicable is:

(1) that of the country of the Donor's habitual residence

---

[8] *Marinos v Marinos* [2007] EWHC 2047 and see also *Ikim v Ikimi* [2001] EWCA Civ 873 upheld in *Mark v Mark* [2005] UKHL 42.

[9] MCA 2005, Sch.3, para 11.

(2) that of a country of which he is a national, or in which he has formerly been habitually resident or in which he has property (but only in respect of that property), if the Donor specifies that law in writing,[10] (even if that applicable law does not itself recognise such powers).

Clearly there can be problems here if the applicable law is that of another state which does not recognise such a power or it was created in English form, when it should have been created in the form of another state.

RECOGNITION AND ENFORCEMENT

2.11   England & Wales will now recognise protective measures[11] taken in another state provided that the relevant adult is habitually resident in that other state.[12]

Recognition can be refused on limited grounds if the English Court finds that:

(1) the case in which the measure was taken was not urgent and the adult was not given an opportunity to be heard and the omission was in breach of the rules of natural justice; or

(2) recognition would be contrary to public policy; or

(3) the measure would be inconsistent with a mandatory provision in England & Wales; or

(4) the measure is inconsistent with a protective measure in England & Wales; or[13]

(5) article 33 has not been complied with in relation to cross-border placement.[14]

There are provisions under paras 20 and 22 for interested persons to apply to the Court for a declaration as to whether a protective measure taken under the law of another state is to be recognised or enforced.

PROTECTIVE MEASURES

2.12   Protective measures have a very wide definition both under the Convention and under para 5.1 of Sch 3 and may also include an order for a Statutory Will, subject to the special rules of Sch 2.

WITHIN THE UNITED KINGDOM

2.13   Schedule 3 applies these private international law rules to dealings with Scotland and Northern Ireland in the same way as to other states. An

---

10   MCA 2005, Sch.3, para 13.
11   Defined by MCA 2005, Sch 3, para 5.
12   MCA 2005, Sch 3, para 19(1) and *Re MN* [2010] EWHC 1926 (Fam).
13   MCA 2005 Sch 3, para 19(3) & (4).
14   MCA 2005 Sch 3, para 19(5).

order of the Court of Protection will therefore be recognised in Scotland unless a Scottish guardian has been appointed.

The position in Northern Ireland is somewhat more complex until it too introduces private international law rules similar to the Convention.

THE POSITION IN NON-CONVENTION COUNTRIES

2.14   Although the Court of Protection may have jurisdiction under Sch 3 of the MCA 2005, traditionally it would not make an order directly affecting property in another state if such an order would not be recognised in that other state or if it would infringe another court's jurisdiction

If the Convention does not apply there are no universal rules if a person who lacks capacity is resident in a Non-Convention state or has assets which are situated in such a State. Many states do, however, have authorities for the management of the property and affairs of people who lack capacity, similar to those in the UK.

In the same way that the Court of Protection will take jurisdiction in relation to assets in England and Wales belonging to a person resident in another state, the courts of other states may recognise the authority of their counterparts. This is consistent with the principles of many private international laws which provide that the capacity of a person is determined by the person's personal law. Some jurisdictions may therefore apply similar principles to those contained in the Convention.

2.15   If a person who lacks capacity and who is habitually resident in England and Wales has assets in another state, the requirements of that state will be different in each case and an agent in that state will need to be instructed. Many states will require a formal application to the local court.

The possible requirements may include:

(1)   a sealed and certified copy of the order appointing the deputy and also authorising the action in the other state. An explanation of the deputy's authority to act and the arrangements made for the protection of the property and affairs in England and Wales;

(2)   a sealed and certified copy of the relevant enduring, lasting, durable or continuing power of attorney. This has been problematic, since there was no mechanism for the OPG to produce such a copy, but it is understood that this issue is currently being addressed;

(3)   details of the assets for which authority is required and whether they are movable or immovable;

(4)   confirmation that no person has been appointed to administer those assets in the state where they are situated.

PART X

The court in the other state is likely either to confirm the deputy's authority, provide the deputy with authority to act or appoint a local guardian with authority to remit assets back to the deputy or the Court of Protection. In the event of dispute, the assets are likely to be retained in the other state until the dispute is resolved.

2.16   In the last section of this Part replies to relevant questions in various states are set out. These replies were obtained from a local expert by asking for replies to the form of questionnaire set out. Some local experts asked that their details should not be published. Some were happy for their e-mail contact to be available and in these cases the e-mail contact is published. This section will continue to expand and change in future editions.

The existence of answers to the questionnaire will not obviate the need to co-operate with local practitioners in the other state, but it is hoped that some signposts will assist mutual understanding of this complex subject.

It remains difficult to determine jurisdiction and ascertain the relevant law in non-Convention countries and yet with increased tourism and home ownership abroad (especially for retired people) capacity issues arise quite frequently. Accordingly an attempt has been made in this Part of this volume to lead a pathway through this jungle. It is intended that this Part will develop further in future editions as contacts within other jurisdictions are established.

Chapter 3

Northern Ireland

3.1 The law relating to adults without capacity in Northern Ireland is governed by the Mental Health (Northern Ireland) Order 1986 (SI 1986/595). Part Vlll deals with the property and affairs of a person ('the patient') who is 'incapable, by reason of mental disorder, of managing and administering his property and affairs'. Part VIII of the 1986 Order are similar to Part Vll of the England & Wales Mental Health Act 1983, save that its powers are exercised by the Office of Care and Protection, part of the Northern Ireland Courts and Tribunal Service.

3.2

> The Office of Care and Protection
> Room 2.2A, Second Floor
> Royal Courts of Justice
> Chichester Street
> Belfast
> BT1 3JF
> Telephone (028) 9072 4733
> Fax (028) 9032 2782
> www.courtsni.gov.uk

3.3 A person appointed in Northern Ireland to make decisions in respect of a patient's property and affairs is a Controller.

3.4 The Enduring Powers of Attorney (Northern Ireland) Order 1987 [SI 1987 No. 1627 (N.I. 16)] still subsists, so that Northern Ireland Enduring Powers of Attorney remain valid and can still be made.

3.5 The review of Northern Irish legislation has lagged behind that in Scotland and England and Wales. The Bamford Review, published in November 2007, suggested a new comprehensive legislative model. The Mental Capacity (Health, Welfare and Finance) Bill is likely to be dealt with by the Northern Ireland Assembly in the second half of 2011.

Until then, Northern Irish private international law remains similar to that of England & Wales before the MCA 2005.

PART X

Chapter 4

Scotland

BACKGROUND

4.1 Legal practice reflects the society which it serves. At any one time, an estimated 100,000 Scots have impairments of capacity of potential significance in law.[1] Private client practice accordingly encompasses adult incapacity work. Inevitably, that work can involve significant links outside Scotland, reflecting the multiplicity of connections between Scottish society and the present and past countries of the Commonwealth, the United States of America, Europe and elsewhere; and above all the other jurisdictions of the British Isles.

4.2 Inward and outward mobility is traditional. Many well-established Scottish families have interests elsewhere. An interim order in Scottish guardianship proceedings allowed spouse's consent to be given to the sale of property in Italy.[2] Modern travel and communications now counteract many of the previous consequences of distance. The attorney in London can in most practical ways be close to her elderly aunt in Edinburgh. The only son in California, whose job takes him worldwide, visited his father in Scotland with sufficient regularity to satisfy statutory criteria for appointment as his guardian.[3]

4.3 Also new is the mobility of people with impairments of capacity, sometimes to access specialist provision, sometimes to follow their families, or otherwise for convenience. An elderly lady returned to her native Northern Ireland for nursing home care: a Scottish guardian was appointed to deal with her property in Scotland.[4]

4.4 The relevant private international law of England and Wales, including from that perspective the Hague Convention on the International Protection of Adults, is described in Chapters 1, 2 and 3 of this part. This chapter outlines provisions of Scots law from the viewpoint of practitioners in England and Wales, commencing with this warning: Scots law is different. It is different in its fundamentals and structures, in the more recent experience leading to the introduction of modern incapacity provision, and in the content of that provision. Do not assume that similar terminology has the same meaning, or that relevant provisions of Scots law can be understood simply by translating terminology.[5] Note also that this chapter contains outlines of salient points, not full descriptions, and is referenced only selectively.

---

[1] Based on estimates by the Alliance which campaigned for passage of the Adults with Incapacity (Scotland) Act 2000, and referred to during the parliamentary proceedings.

[2] *C*, 23 Sept, 2009, Kilmarnock Sh Ct.

[3] *H*, 6 May, 2008, Dunoon Sh Ct.

[4] *H, Applicant*, 2007 SLT (Sh Ct) 5; 2006 GWD 21–447.

[5] Where concepts are substantially the same, terminology sometimes differs to indicate

Scots law

4.5   Scots law is based on Roman law,[6] emphasising principles rather than precedents, and thus in its fundamentals is akin to European rather than Anglo-American systems. The influence of English law has been so great that Scots law is now often described as a hybrid system. However, the development of Scottish adult incapacity law continues to be driven mainly by the application of principles, hence the central importance of the principles stated in s 1 of Adults with Incapacity (Scotland) Act 2000[7] as exemplified by the development, without any express statutory provision, of a power to make and alter Wills,[8] and the methodology adopted by the courts in resolving matters of fundamental importance.[9]

4.6   From 1707 to 2000 Scotland lacked its own separate legislature. The perpetual tendency for the needs of vulnerable people to slip down the order of priorities was compounded by the failure of the UK Parliament to meet the needs of law reform in Scotland. For many Scots lawyers, the establishment by the Scotland Act 1998 of a devolved Parliament for Scotland was valued more as a means to address a serious backlog of essential law reform, rather than for any nationalistic or party political significance. In less than a decade the Parliament[10] has comprehensively reformed land tenure and related matters in Scotland. Even before that, as its first and highest priority, it produced the Adults with Incapacity (Scotland) Act 2000 ('AWI(S)A 2000'). Legislation to cover the three overlapping areas of adult incapacity, mental health and vulnerable adults continued with the Mental Health (Care and Treatment) (Scotland) Act 2003 ('MH(CT)(S)A 2003') and the Adult Support and Protection (Scotland) Act 2007 ('ASP(S)A 2007'), both of which included amendments to AWI(S)A 2000, in the latter case following review of experience of the working of AWI(S)A 2000 as originally enacted.[11]

Englishness or Scottishness, such as 'social services' in England and 'social work' in Scotland – hence the Social Work (Scotland) Act 1968 ('SW(S)A 1968'); a 'substitute attorney' is the same as a 'replacement attorney'; and the Judicial Studies Committee fulfils the same function as the Judicial Studies Board, to give a few random examples.

[6]   For a review of the modern influence of Roman law, see Cairns and du Plessis 'Ten years of Roman Law in Scottish Courts' 2008 SLT News 191: 'while foreign law lacks legitimacy as a formal source of law, Roman law is always potentially or actually Scots law'.

[7]   See **4.32**.

[8]   See **4.66**.

[9]   See for example *Muldoon, Applicant*, 2005 SLT (Sh Ct) 52; 2005 SCLR 611; 2005 GWD 5-57; and *North Ayrshire Council v JM*, 2004 SCLR 956, Sh Ct.

[10]   'Parliament' refers to the UK Parliament at Westminster, 'the Parliament' to the Scottish Parliament at Holyrood. The legislative competence of the Scottish Parliament is limited to matters devolved to it by the Scotland Act. Legislation incompatible with ECHR is ultra vires. Acts of the pre-1707 Parliament of Scotland are designated APS (Act of the Parliament of Scotland) and those of 'the Parliament' asp (Acts of the Scottish Parliament). Note the distinction between SI (Statutory Instrument, which includes Instruments of solely Scottish application made under Westminster legislation) and SSI (Scottish Statutory Instrument, made under devolved powers).

[11]   AWI(S)A 2000 has also been amended by the Regulation of Care (Scotland) Act 2001, the Smoking, Health and Social Care (Scotland) Act 2005 and various SI's and SSI's.

The Scottish courts

4.7 In civil matters Scotland has two tiers of courts of first instance, the Court of Session, which sits only in Edinburgh, and the Sheriff Court. Lords Ordinary sit singly in the Outer House of the Court of Session. Appeal lies from them to the Inner House, which usually sits in divisions comprising at least three judges, though a larger court may be convened for matters of particular importance. In a few matters the Inner House hears cases at first instance, examples being exercise of the nobile officium[12] and the parens patriae jurisdiction.[13] Appeal lies from the Inner House to the Supreme Court (previously the House of Lords).

4.8 Sheriffs frequently hear cases of substantial value and great importance. Relatively few matters are excluded from their jurisdiction.[14] There are six Sheriffdoms, each led by a Sheriff Principal. Apart from Glasgow, the Sheriffdoms are divided into Sheriff Court Districts, each with its own Sheriff Court of which there are 50 altogether, six of them on islands. Courthouses range from small buildings in locations such as Lochmaddy to massive ones in the main cities. With a few exceptions, appeal lies from the Sheriff to the Sheriff Principal of that Sheriffdom, thence to the Inner House of the Court of Session, and thence to the Supreme Court (formerly House of Lords). Sheriffs are bound by precedents set by their own Sheriff Principal, but not by those of other Sheriffs Principal or other Sheriffs. Sheriffs Principal are not bound by the precedents of their own predecessors. All are bound by precedents set by the Inner House of the Court of Session and the Supreme Court.

4.9 Scotland has no Court of Protection, or equivalent separate court, nor an Official Solicitor (though since 2007 the Public Guardian may now initiate or enter proceedings as described in **4.26**).[15] Much information is available at www.scotcourts.gov.uk. For decisions under AWI(S)A 2000 go to 'Library', then 'Court Judgments', then 'Sheriff Courts Search' and search for 'Adults with Incapacity'.

Development of adult incapacity law prior to 2000

4.10 Fifteen years prior to AWI(S)A 2000 it was generally believed (though not universally accepted) that Powers of Attorney ceased to have effect upon the incapacity of the granter; the only general form of financial management for adults lacking relevant capacity was to appoint a curator bonis, whereupon the adult was deprived of all management capacity, even

---

12   An inherent jurisdiction to address matters not previously provided for in Scots law.
13   Though in *Morris, Petitioner*, 1986 the Inner House declared that future applications for appointment of tutors could be presented in the Outer House, and in *Law Hospital NHS Trust v Lord Advocate*, 1996 SC 301; 1996 SLT 848; [1996] 2 FLR 407; (1998) 39 BMLR 166; [1996] Fam Law 670, IH, the Inner House declared similarly in relation to applications to authorise withdrawal of treatment.
14   There is no general upper financial limit to their civil jurisdiction. They have exclusive jurisdiction in low-value cases.
15   AWI(S)A 2000, s 6(2)(da).

to decide and manage matters of which the adult was in fact capable; and the only available form of welfare guardianship was Mental Health Act guardianship, with fixed and limited powers.[16]

4.11 To the demand for Powers of Attorney that would indisputably be operable following the granter's incapacity, Westminster responded simplistically in the Law Reform (Miscellaneous Provisions) (Scotland) Act 1990, s 71, under which – for a decade – Powers of Attorney automatically remained in force in the event of subsequent incapacity of the granter, unless the document explicitly provided otherwise. Scotland thus experienced continuing Powers of Attorney with no effective regulation or control. The majority met a clear need and worked well, due to the sense and integrity of appointed attorneys rather than anything in relevant legislation; but inevitably there were many horror stories.[17]

4.12 The most positive progress was achieved by going back to the tutors to adults originating in Roman law, reviving first the tutor-dative[18] and then the tutor-at-law.[19] Tutors-dative, as revived, were appointed as guardians with specific welfare powers, tailored to need in each individual case, and usually for a limited period. Joint appointments were permitted, and common. Tutors-dative were also appointed for limited purposes in relation to property and financial affairs, such as approving and executing a deed of family arrangement (for example, to establish a family discretionary trust following the death of a parent). Tutors-at-law had plenary financial and welfare powers, and were generally appointed to displace a curator bonis.[20]

4.13 As noted above, in 1996[21] a test case established procedure for dealing with applications under the parens patriae jurisdiction to deal with proposed discontinuance of treatment in cases of persistent vegetative state.

Particular characteristics of Scots law

4.14 In addition to experience of the developments in the years leading up to AWI(S)A 2000, described in the previous section, two well-established characteristics of Scots law, unchanged by AWI(S)A 2000, are relevant to the understanding of Scottish incapacity law. Firstly, in Scotland if an adult lacks adequate capacity for a particular act or transaction, it will be void, regardless of whether any other party was at the time aware of the

---

16 Under the Mental Health (Scotland) Act 1984, guardianship powers being similar to those under Mental Health Act 1983.

17 The hospital patient who purportedly granted three Powers of Attorney in rapid succession to three different relatives; large numbers of Powers of Attorney granted by residents in a care home to the proprietor and operated dubiously; and so forth.

18 *Morris, Petitioner*, 1986; see Ward 'Revival of Tutors-Dative' 1987 SLT News 69.

19 *Britton v Britton's curator bonis*, 1992 SCLR 947.

20 In the first modern case, the curator bonis was a professional who had never met his ward and allowed her an income – from a substantial award of damages – less than if she had been dependent solely upon state benefits.

21 *Law Hospital NHS Trust v Lord Advocate*, 1996 SC 301; 1996 SLT 848; [1996] 2 FLR 407; (1998) 39 BMLR 166; [1996] Fam Law 670, IH.

incapacity. With a few exceptions such as purchase of 'necessaries', the position in law is the same as if the purported act or transaction had not taken place. Secondly, for most practical purposes adulthood in Scotland begins at 16. For example, it has always been possible, without parental consent, to marry at 16. Some special provisions apply to young people aged 16-18, but for adult incapacity legislation to commence at 16 fits easily with other statutes such as the Age of Legal Capacity (Scotland) Act 1991.

Literature

4.15 On adult incapacity law in Scotland, see Ward *Adult Incapacity* (2003) and *Adults with Incapacity Legislation* (2008), which updates *Adult Incapacity* and contains the updated text of AWI(S)A 2000. Together, the two volumes reproduce all relevant Statutory Instruments. On mental health law, see Franks and Cobb *Mental Health (Care and Treatment) (Scotland) Act 2003* – the text of the Act with annotations. On ASP(S)A 2007 and related topics, see Patrick and Smith *Adult Protection and the Law in Scotland* (2010). For a wider-ranging text on relevant subjects, see Patrick *Mental Health, Incapacity and the Law in Scotland* (2006). Several Codes of Practice have been issued under AWI(S)A 2000. For useful websites see **4.9** and **4.26**.

ADULTS WITH INCAPACITY (SCOTLAND) ACT 2000

General

4.16 AWI(S)A 2000 (also referred to as 'the Act' in this section) is a co-ordinated and integrated, but non-exclusive, code of provision for adults with incapacity in Scotland. The topics covered differ from those in MCA 2005. As noted above, adults are persons over 16.[22] During the law reform process, 'Incapable Adults' was used, but only as a working title. The title eventually adopted can appropriately be seen as a contraction of 'adults with impairments of capacity', or similar. In practice, 'the adult' has been almost universally adopted to refer to the person whose capacity is, or may be, impaired. The Act follows a similar overall pattern to most reformed jurisdictions. Gateway definitions of adult and incapacity give access to the Act's provisions. Guided by principles, procedures enable solutions to be selected from a flexible range of possibilities, and tailored to individual need. Implementation of those solutions is also guided by principles, and is subject (generally but not always) to supervision, accountability and re-assessment.

Jurisdiction and roles

4.17 Practitioners in England and Wales may choose not to instruct a city solicitor in a matter in which Lerwick Sheriff Court has jurisdiction; or to

---

[22] A guardianship application may be lodged up to three months prior to the 16th birthday, but the guardianship comes into force no earlier than that birthday (s 79A).

instruct a Stornoway solicitor when the Court of Session in Edinburgh has jurisdiction; or to instruct any Scottish solicitor where the judicial and administrative authorities of some other country have jurisdiction, or more appropriately have jurisdiction; and they may choose to attend themselves to matters dealt with by the Public Guardian upon submission of appropriate forms, without court process.

4.18 The jurisdiction and private international law provisions of AWI(S)A 2000 are set out in Sch 3, based on the Hague Convention on the International Protection of Adults of 13 January 2000 (see Part X, para **2.1** et seq). The Convention applies among jurisdictions in respect of which it has been ratified, currently Scotland, Germany, France and Switzerland. It also applies as between Scotland and England, by virtue of MCA 2005, Sch 3,[23] notwithstanding that the Convention has not yet been ratified in respect of England. The Central Authority for Scotland under the Hague Convention is the Scottish Government's Constitution, Law and Courts Directorate, EU and International Law Branch, Civil Law Division, The Scottish Government, 2 West, St Andrew's House, Regent Road, Edinburgh EH1 3DG, Tel: 0131 244 2417.

The Courts

The Sheriff Court

4.19 The main jurisdiction under AWI(S)A 2000 rests with the Sheriff Court, and allocation to Sheriffdom is governed by similar rules to those in the Convention. Accordingly, the Sheriff having jurisdiction is the Sheriff in whose Sheriffdom:

(a) the adult is habitually resident;
(b) relevant property is situated;
(c) the adult, or property belonging to the adult, is present in urgent cases where the adult is not habitually resident in Scotland;
(d) the adult is present, when the intervention sought is temporary and its effect limited to Scotland; and
(e) the adult is present, where the Sheriff considers it necessary in the adult's interests to take the proposed measure immediately.[24]

The Sheriff also has jurisdiction to vary or recall intervention and guardianship orders[25] made by that Sheriff if no contracting state under the Convention (other than the United Kingdom) has jurisdiction and either:

(a) no other court or authority has jurisdiction; or
(b) another court or authority has jurisdiction but (i) it would be unreasonable to expect an applicant to invoke that jurisdiction or (ii) that court or authority has declined to exercise jurisdiction.[26]

---

[23] See Part X, para **2.3**.
[24] AWI(S)A 2000, Sch 3, paras 2(1) and (3).
[25] See **4.65**.
[26] AWI(S)A 2000, Sch 3, para 2(2).

4.20 Note that the qualification 'other than the United Kingdom' means that recall or variation will be by the French courts where they have jurisdiction, but not automatically by the English courts even after ratification in respect of England. If the Scottish courts have jurisdiction, but no particular Sheriffdom is identified by the relevant rules, the fall-back Sheriff is the Sheriff at Edinburgh.

4.21 The Sheriff has jurisdiction to grant intervention and guardianship orders, to give directions to persons exercising functions under the Act,[27] to hear appeals against decisions as to incapacity and appeals against any decision under the Act as to the medical treatment of an adult[28] (but not under the procedure described at **4.56**), and a wide range of remits and appeals under the Act. Jurisdiction under the Act does not include declaratory powers (cf Part I, **4.5**) but the powers to give directions and to determine appeals against decisions as to incapacity may in some cases have similar effect. For the sheriff's powers in relation to Powers of Attorney, including non-Scottish Powers of Attorney, see **4.45**; and for powers in relation to non-Scottish equivalents of guardians see **4.65**.

4.22 'Which forum?' was a major issue during the law reform process. The Law Society of Scotland recommended that the primary jurisdiction should rest with the Sheriff Court, but that individual Sheriffs should be designated to deal with adult incapacity matters. That suggestion was adopted by the Scottish Law Commission in the draft Bill annexed to its *Report on Incapable Adults*.[29] Sadly, that proposal was not included in the Act, with inconsistent and uncoordinated results. In Glasgow Sheriff Court the designated sheriff concept has been informally adopted. Cases under the Act are most often dealt with by Sheriff John Baird. Many of the leading judgments which have developed this jurisdiction are his. In many other Sheriff Courts, several Sheriffs exercise this jurisdiction in a consistent and appropriate way. Overall, however, there is often a lack of the case management which such a jurisdiction requires (cf Part 1, para **7.34**), and there are inconsistencies which would have been less likely with designated sheriffs. In difficult cases where there is a possible choice of jurisdiction, it might be wise to seek advice about the particular Sheriff Court.[30] Review of the forum for this jurisdiction may enter the agenda during the currency of this volume. It may be concluded that dropping the 'designated sheriff' proposal was a reversible error. The Court of Protection provides an interesting model: specialised, structured in a manner conducive to consistency and co-ordinated development, yet accessible to judicial colleagues (eg see **Part I, para 4.10**).

---

[27]   Under AWI(S)A 2000, s 3(3): for examples see: *Application by Public Guardian for Directions* (Glasgow Sh. Ct. 30 June 2010), *Morton, Minuter for Directions* (Edinburgh Sh. Ct. 21 July 2010) and, as an ancillary matter, *Y W v Office of the Public Guardian* (Peterhead Sh. Ct. 25 June 2010).

[28]   With further appeal to the Court of Session, bypassing the Sheriff Principal.

[29]   Report No 151, published September 1995.

[30]   Also disappointing is the reluctance of the Sheriff Court Rules Council to address the requirements and consequences of this jurisdiction adequately.

The Court of Session

4.23 The role of the Court of Session as the first court to which a matter under the Act may be taken is limited to certain medical matters. See **4.56**.

Other functions under the Act

Public Guardian[31]

4.24 Scotland has its own entirely separate Public Guardian. The Office of the Public Guardian has extensive registration functions (including notification of registration), administers the scheme of Access to Funds (see **4.47** et seq), supervises guardians and appointees under intervention orders with financial powers, has investigative powers in relation to property and financial matters, and other powers and functions; but does not act as guardian, or have any other management functions, for any individual adults.

4.25 The Public Guardian's investigative functions include investigating, in relation to property and financial matters, complaints against continuing attorneys and non-Scottish equivalents, against guardians and non-Scottish equivalents, against appointees under intervention orders, and concerning the Access to Funds provisions of Part 3 of the Act. Certificates issued by the Public Guardian are conclusive evidence of their contents. They include certificates of registration of continuing and welfare Powers of Attorney ((CPA's) and (WPA's) respectively), various certificates under the Access to Funds scheme, and certificates of appointment under intervention and guardianship orders.

4.26 The Public Guardian has statutory duties to provide information and advice in property and financial matters, on request, to guardians, appointees under intervention orders, continuing attorneys and withdrawers under the Access to Funds scheme; and will generally provide helpful advice and guidance in response to reasonable requests from others, though the considerable information available on the Public Guardian's website should be checked before making an enquiry. The Public Guardian must investigate where she becomes aware of circumstances in which the property or financial affairs of an adult seem to be at risk. The Public Guardian may initiate or enter 'any proceedings before a court' where she considers that necessary to safeguard the property or financial affairs of an adult who lacks relevant capacity. Fees chargeable by the Public Guardian are prescribed by regulations and have been increased substantially.[32] Much useful information is available on her website (www.publicguardian-scotland.gov.uk) and the links which it provides.

---

[31]   AWI(S)A 2000, ss 6 and 7.
[32]   See Ward 'Out of the wrong pocket' 2008 JLSS 9.

Mental Welfare Commission[33]

4.27 The Mental Welfare Commission for Scotland exercises independent protective functions in relation to the rights, welfare and interests of adults with mental disorders in Scotland, including those with impairments of capacity. Many of the Commission's functions and powers are contained in MH(CT)(S)A 2003. Under AWI(S)A 2000 the Commission's functions include providing information and advice in personal welfare matters to guardians, welfare attorneys and appointees under intervention orders; and investigating complaints where either a local authority has failed to investigate, or the Commission is not satisfied with a local authority investigation. The Commission's investigative functions include investigating, in relation to personal welfare matters, complaints against welfare attorneys and non-Scottish equivalents, guardians and non-Scottish equivalents, and appointees under intervention orders.

Local authorities[34]

4.28 The functions of local authorities under the Act include supervising guardians in relation to welfare functions, investigating circumstances where the personal welfare of an adult appears to be at risk, and initiating applications for intervention or guardianship orders (in both personal welfare and property and financial matters) where this appears to be required and no-one else is taking action. The local authority supervises welfare guardians; supervises persons authorised under intervention orders and welfare attorneys where that has been ordered by the court; and has a duty to provide information and advice in welfare matters, when asked, to all of the foregoing.

Other Incapacity Act roles

4.29 The Act confers significant roles on an adult's primary carer[35] and nearest relative.[36] Others with roles include any named person[37] and any person providing independent advocacy services.[38]

Limitation of liability

4.30 The Act exempts certain persons exercising roles under the Act from liability for any breach of any duty of care or fiduciary duty owed to the adult. The exemption applies only if the person has acted reasonably and in good faith, and in accordance with the Act's general principles (see **4.32**), or has failed to act and the failure was reasonable and in good faith, and in

PART X

---

[33]   AWI(S)A 2000, s 9.
[34]   AWI(S)A 2000, ss 10, 53(3) and 57(2).
[35]   AWI(S)A 2000, s 87(1).
[36]   MH(CT)(S)A 2003, s 254; AWI(S)A 2000, s 4.
[37]   MH(CT)(S)A 2003, s 329.
[38]   AWI(S)A 2000, s 3(5A) and (5B); MH(CT)(S)A 2003, s 259(1).

accordance with the general principles. The persons protected by this provision are guardians, including non-Scottish equivalents, continuing and welfare attorneys and non-Scottish equivalents, appointees under intervention orders, withdrawers under the Access to Funds scheme, and managers of establishments acting under Part 4 of the Act.[39]

Illtreatment and wilful neglect

4.31 It is an offence under the Act for any person exercising powers under the Act in relation to an adult's personal welfare to ill-treat or wilfully neglect that adult. The maximum penalties are two years' imprisonment or a fine, or both.[40]

The principles

4.32 The Act commences with a statement of principles[41] which have proved to be invaluable, and which have been subject to minor consequential amendment but no calls for significant alteration. This Scottish experience led to the strong recommendation, described in Part I, para **2.26**, that legislation for England and Wales should likewise be governed by general principles. Scotland rejected a 'best interests' test for the reasons explained by the Scottish Law Commission in the passage quoted in Part I,para **2.46**. The Scottish principles, with brief comments in footnotes, are as follows:

'1.(1) The principles set out in subss (2) and (4) shall be given effect to in relation to any intervention in the affairs of an adult under or in pursuance of this Act, including any order made in or for the purpose of any proceedings under this Act for or in connection with an adult.[42]

(2) There shall be no intervention in the affairs of an adult unless the person responsible for authorising or effecting the intervention is satisfied that the intervention will benefit the adult and that such benefit cannot reasonably be achieved without the intervention.[43]

(3) Where it is determined that an intervention as mentioned in subs(1) is to be made, such intervention shall be the least restrictive option in relation to the freedom of the adult, consistent with the purpose of the intervention.[44]

(4) In determining if an intervention is to be made and, if so, what intervention is to be made, account shall be taken of–

---

[39] AWI(S)A 2000, s 82.
[40] AWI(S)A 2000, s 83.
[41] AWI(S)A 2000, s 1(1)–(5).
[42] 'Intervention' has a wide meaning, and encompasses a decision not to do something.
[43] 'Benefit' can include anything which the adult would have done if capable, including something gratuitous, such as making gifts or participating in non-therapeutic medical research – both of which are expressly provided for in the Act: AWI(S)A 2000, ss 66 and 51 respectively.
[44] Not the simplest or cheapest option, nor even – without qualification – the least restrictive option, but 'the least restrictive option in relation to the freedom of the adult, consisting with the purpose of the intervention'. The exercise of quasi-guardianship powers without assessment, judicial procedure or procedure subject to judicial control, or appropriate supervision and accountability, can never be the least restrictive option under this definition.

(a) the present and past wishes and feelings of the adult so far as they can be ascertained by any means of communication, whether human or by mechanical aid (whether of an interpretative nature or otherwise) appropriate to the adult;[45]

(b) the views of the nearest relative, named person and the primary carer of the adult, in so far as it is reasonable and practicable to do so;

(c) the views of –
    (i) any guardian, continuing attorney or welfare attorney of the adult who has powers relating to the proposed intervention;[46] and
    (ii) any person whom the sheriff has directed to be consulted,
    in so far as it is reasonable and practicable to do so; and

(d) the views of any other person appearing to the person responsible for authorising or effecting the intervention to have an interest in the welfare of the adult or in the proposed intervention, where these views have been made known to the person responsible, in so far as it is reasonable and practicable to do so.

(5) Any guardian, continuing attorney, welfare attorney or manager of an establishment exercising functions under this Act or under any order of the sheriff in relation to an adult shall, in so far as it is reasonable and practicable to do so, encourage the adult to exercise whatever skills he has concerning his property, financial affairs or personal welfare, as the case may be, and to develop new such skills.'

Definitions of adult, incapable and incapacity

4.33 These definitions are contained in s 1(6), which is in the following terms, again with comments in footnotes:

'(6) For the purposes of this Act,[47] and unless the context otherwise requires –
    "adult" means a person who has attained the age of 16 years;
    "incapable" means incapable of –
    (a) acting; or
    (b) making decisions; or
    (c) communicating decisions; or
    (d) understanding decisions; or
    (e) retaining the memory of decisions,[48]
    as mentioned in any provision of this Act, by reason of mental disorder[49] or of inability to communicate because of physical disability; but a person shall not fall within this definition by reason only of a lack or

---

[45] Unlike the following paragraphs, this paragraph is not limited to 'in so far as it is reasonable and practicable to do so'. The obligation is unqualified. The sheriff (only) must take account of the adult's wishes and feelings so far as expressed by a person providing independent advocacy services: AWI(S)A 2000, s 3(5A).

[46] Including similar appointments under the law of any country, but in the case of guardianship only if the guardianship is recognised by the Law of Scotland: AWI(S)A 2000, s 1(7).

[47] But not necessarily for other purposes, where other tests of incapacity may apply.

[48] Usually interpreted as meaning to a degree, and for a duration, appropriate to the matter in question.

[49] See **4.34**.

deficiency in a faculty of communication if that lack or deficiency can be made good by human or mechanical aid (whether of an interpretative nature or otherwise);[50] and

"incapacity" shall be construed accordingly.'

4.34 The relevant definition of mental disorder is contained in s 328 of MH(CT)(S)A 2003, and is as follows:

'(1) Subject to subs (2) below, in this Act "mental disorder" means any – (a) mental illness; (b) personality disorder; or (c) learning disability, however caused or manifested; and cognate expressions shall be construed accordingly.

(2) A person is not mentally disordered by reason only of any of the following – (a) sexual orientation; (b) sexual deviancy; (c) transsexualism; (d) transvestism; (e) dependence on, or use of, alcohol or drugs; (f) behaviour that causes, or is likely to cause, harassment, alarm or distress to any other person; (g) acting as no prudent person would act.'

Powers of Attorney (Part 2)

Terminology

4.35 Continuing and welfare Powers of Attorney are governed principally by the s 1 principles, and by Part 2, of AWI(S)A 2000. A continuing Power of Attorney ('CPA') is a Power of Attorney ('POA') in respect of the financial and property affairs of the granter (not 'donor') capable of operation after loss of relevant capacity. A welfare Power of Attorney ('WPA') confers powers in relation to personal welfare, which term includes healthcare matters, operable during relevant incapacity.

Overview

4.36 No POA other than a CPA or WPA granted in accordance with the Act's provisions, and registered by the Public Guardian, may be operated after loss of relevant capacity of the granter. A human rights based system of incapacity law emphasises the importance of autonomy and self-determination, and thus encourages the granting of such POA's while granters have the capacity to do so, or by people with some impairments of capacity who are nevertheless capable of granting POA's.[51] In Scotland large, and increasing, numbers of such POA's have been granted.[52] Granting of such POA's has become as much recommended, as a matter of prudence, as making a Will.

4.37 Procedural requirements contain necessary safeguards but avoid such difficulty and complexity as might be a deterrent to prospective granters or

---

[50] As with s 1(4)(a) (see **4.32**), this is not subject to the qualification 'in so far as it is reasonable and practicable to do so'.

[51] See Council of Europe *Recommendation on Principles concerning Powers of Attorney and Advance Directives for Incapacity* and relative explanatory memorandum R (2009) 11.

[52] Rising from 5,592 registrations in the first year after Part 2 came into force to 38,707 in the year to 31 March 2010.

attorneys. Under the principles of autonomy and self-determination, it is for the granter to decide whom to appoint, with what powers, when the POA should be registered, and in what circumstances the powers which are conferred may be exercised. However, welfare powers may only be exercised during relevant incapacity (or while the attorney reasonably believes that there is relevant incapacity), and a welfare attorney may not place the granter in hospital for treatment of a mental disorder against the granter's will, consent on behalf of the granter to forms of treatment specified by regulations, or take other specified steps generally in relation to healthcare matters.[53] These are minimum statutory limitations. The granter may – and often will – further limit the powers conferred, and further limit the circumstances in which they may be operated (such as by requiring written medical certification as a prerequisite for operation).

Underlying law, the POA document

4.38 As in England and Wales (see Part I, para **3.21**) the general law of POA's applies, subject only to the particular provisions of the Act if the POA is to be operable following loss of relevant capacity. A basic rule, applicable also to CPA's and WPA's, is that the attorney has no powers other than those conferred in the document. None are implied. No standard form is provided by or under the Act. A common form of POA document will contain a general power to do everything which may be competently done by such an attorney, followed by a list – often a long list – of specific powers conferred without prejudice to the general power. Some POA documents contain only specific powers, and no general power: in these cases the specific powers are strictly construed, and may be held not to have covered actions actually taken by the attorney.[54]

Formalities

4.39 This and the following paragraph apply only to CPA's and WPA's granted on or after 2 April 2001.[55] For POA's granted before that date, see **4.42**. CPA's and WPA's must be in writing and subscribed by the granter. They need not be witnessed, but usually are, such witnessing making them 'self-proving'. They must expressly state the granter's intention that they shall be a CPA or WPA (or both). Where a CPA is to be exerciseable only during relevant incapacity of the granter, the document must state that the granter has considered how such incapacity is to be determined, and all WPA's must contain such a statement.[56] The document must incorporate a certificate in prescribed form by a practising solicitor (which means a

---

[53] See AWI(S)A 2000, s 16(6).
[54] As in *McDowall's Executors v IRC* [2004] STC (SCD) 22, see also *M, Applicant* 2007 SLT (Sh Ct) 24; 2006 GWD 19–418.
[55] When Part 3 of AWI(S)A 2000 was brought into force.
[56] Curiously, the granter must state that he has considered this, but is not expressly required to include the outcome of such consideration!

practising Scottish solicitor), practising advocate or registered medical practitioner. The certificates confirms that:

    (a) the certifier has interviewed the granter immediately before the granter subscribed the POA,

    (b) the certifier is satisfied that the granter understood the nature and extent of the POA document, either from the certifier's own knowledge of the granter or because the certifier has consulted a person, named in the certificate, who has knowledge of the granter, and

    (c) the certifier has no reason to believe that the granter is acting under undue influence or that the granting of the POA is otherwise vitiated.

4.40 CPA's and WPA's may only be operated after registration. The form of application for registration is prescribed, and is available from the Public Guardian's website.[57] If they are registered before loss of relevant capacity, there is no provision for further registration upon loss of relevant capacity. However, the granter may state in the document a prerequisite for registration, such as medical certification of loss of capacity, though in practice it appears that relatively few granters do so.[58] The POA document should be checked for prerequisites for operation, as opposed to prerequisites for registration. If a CPA or WPA is produced for use in England and Wales, it is essential to see a certificate of registration and an official copy, issued by the Public Guardian, of the POA document: if it is unregistered, it is not (yet) operable, regardless of what it may say, and even if it has been registered the attorney may only exercise powers conferred by the document, and may only exercise those powers subject to any provisions in the document as to the circumstances in which they may be exercised.

Revocation and termination

4.41 The formalities for revocation are similar to those for granting, and include similar certification and registration of a revocation notice. No liability is incurred by persons acting in good faith in ignorance of the revocation. However, in matters of any significance it is prudent to check with the Office of the Public Guardian that the POA has not been revoked, and that no other termination of the POA or of the attorney's authority has been registered.

POA's executed before 2 April 2001

4.42 Doubts remain as to whether any Scottish POA executed before 1 January 1991 may be operated following the granter's loss of capacity. See **4.10**. It would be wise to take Scottish advice before acting in reliance on

---

[57]   See **4.26**.

[58]   Probably because of fear that it would then be too late to rectify if some defect caused the Public Guardian to refuse to register.

such a POA if the granter lacks capacity. In the case of Scottish POA's granted from 1 January 1991 to 1 April 2001, the position is the opposite, as explained in **4.11**. Unless the document specifies that it shall not be operable during the granter's incapacity, it may be relied upon (subject to its actual terms, and except in welfare matters) without enquiry as to whether the granter still has capacity or not. The formalities described in **4.39** do not apply, though the same rules of interpretation do apply. Under the transitional provisions of AWI(S)A 2000 such POA's are however now described as CPA's or WPA's or both, and several of the provisions of AWI(S)A 2000, including the powers of the sheriff described in **4.45**, apply to them. Commonly, what will be presented will be an official extract from the Books of Council and Session of the POA document, which extract may be relied on as evidence of the terms and content of the document.

Non-Scottish Powers of Attorney

4.43 Subject to the next paragraph, the law governing the existence, extent, modification and extinction of CPA's, WPA's and non-Scottish equivalents is the law of the habitual residence of the granter at time of granting, unless the granter specified in writing the law of a jurisdiction in which the granter had previously been habitually resident; or the law of the jurisdiction where property is situated, but only as regards that property; or, in the case of a non-British granter, the law of the state of the granter's nationality. Where a non-Scottish POA or equivalent is exercised in Scotland, the manner of exercise is governed by Scots law. A transaction entered in Scotland between an attorney or equivalent and a third party is not challengeable on the grounds that the attorney was not entitled to enter it by the law of some other country, unless the third party knew or ought to have known that the attorney's entitlement to act was governed by the law of that other country.[59]

4.44 The provisions described in the previous paragraph are subject to the powers of the sheriff described in **4.45**. Also, they do not displace any enactment or rule of law which has mandatory effect for the protection of an adult with incapacity in Scotland, whatever law would otherwise be applicable; and no provision of the law of any country other than Scotland may be applied so as to produce a result manifestly contrary to public policy.

Powers of the sheriff

4.45 The powers of the sheriff described in this paragraph may be exercised under AWI(S)A 2000, s 20 in relation to CPA's, WPA's and non-Scottish equivalents. The law applicable to exercise of these powers is Scots law, but the sheriff must to the extent possible take into account the law which governs the POA under the rules described in **4.43** and **4.44**.[60]

PART X

---

[59] AWI(S)A 2000, Sch 3, para 4.
[60] AWI(S)A 2000, Sch 3, para 3(3).

The sheriff's powers may be exercised upon application by anyone claiming an interest in the property, financial affairs or personal welfare of the granter. The prerequisites for granting an order under s 20 are that the sheriff is satisfied that the granter is incapable in relation to relevant matters and that the order is necessary to safeguard or promote the granter's interests in those matters. Under CPA's, the sheriff may order supervision by the Public Guardian, and/or may order the attorney to submit accounts for any specified period for audit by the Public Guardian. In relation to WPA's, the sheriff may order supervision by the local authority, and/or may order the welfare attorney to give a report to the sheriff as to the manner in which the attorney has exercised the attorney's powers during any specified period. In relation to both CPA's and WPA's, the sheriff may revoke any of the powers granted by the CPA or WPA, or may revoke the appointment of an attorney.[61] Revocation may be appealed, but the other orders under s 20 are final. Orders under s 20 are subject to provisions for registration with, and intimation by, the Public Guardian.

Accounts and funds (Part 3)

Joint accounts

4.46 AWI(S)A 2000, s 32 is the only provision of Part 3 of the Act which has remained unaltered since original enactment. It effected the simple but important reform that where one holder of a joint account loses relevant capacity, any other joint holder may continue to operate the account, unless the terms of the account provide otherwise or the court has barred the joint holder from operating it. Many accounts are now operated under this provision, which often renders any other intervention unnecessary.

'Access to funds'

4.47 The remainder of Part 3, replaced in its entirety with effect from 1 April 2008,[62] provides a scheme of limited financial guardianship under the jurisdiction of the Public Guardian rather than the sheriff (except where the Public Guardian refers a Part 3 application to the sheriff for determination[63]). Where applicable, Part 3 administration must be utilised rather than financial guardianship under Part 6.[64] Under the core provisions of Part 3, 'authority to intromit' is given to a 'withdrawer' who opens an operating account called the 'designated account', which receives funds of

---

61   Where there are joint attorneys, the sheriff may thus revoke the appointment of one of them.
62   The original Part 3 was the only Part of the Act which was not a success, and under-utilised. Usage has almost doubled since it was replaced: 378 in the year commencing 1 April 2008, compared with 195 and 197 in the two preceding years, rising further to 444 in the year to 31 March 2010.
63   AWI(S)A 2000, s 27F.
64   AWI(S)A 2000, s 58(1)(b).

the adult held by 'fundholders', and from which the withdrawer makes payments for the adult's benefit[65] in accordance with a budget approved by the Public Guardian.

4.48 The scheme allows for individual or joint withdrawers, reserve (ie replacement) withdrawers, and organisations as withdrawers.[66] The scheme is operated by various types of application on prescribed forms to the Public Guardian,[67] who issues certificates of authority. Preliminary application may be made to obtain information from fundholders about the adult's assets, and to authorise release of information by the fundholder for that purpose. Authority may be obtained to open an 'adult's current account' to receive the adult's income to 'feed' the withdrawer's 'designated account', if the adult does not have an existing account suitable for that purpose.

4.49 Authority may also be obtained to open an 'adult's second account', normally a savings-type account to hold surplus funds at a better rate of interest than the current account.[68] Other possibilities include authority to transfer funds between different accounts in the adult's name, to terminate existing standing orders and direct debits, to close existing accounts, and to authorise payment of lump sums in addition to the regular budgeted expenditure. The budget may be amended.

Procedure

4.50 Applications for authority to provide information about the adult's funds, to open accounts, and to intromit with the adult's funds must be accompanied by a medical certificate of incapacity in prescribed form by any medical practitioner. All or any of these applications may be made on a single combined form with a single medical certificate. Those applications, and also applications to add a joint withdrawer, except where the applicant is an organisation rather than one or more individuals, must also be countersigned by someone who has known the adult for at least a year,[69] and who confirms that he or she believes (a) that the information in the application form is true; and (b) that the applicant is a fit and proper person to intromit with the adult's funds. Intimation requirements are dealt with by the Public Guardian upon receipt of the application.[70] Where there are joint withdrawers, or a withdrawer and a reserve, a countersignatory's certificate is required for each. At time of going to press the application form has not yet been adjusted to accommodate this, so that the relevant pages require to

PART X

---

[65] See AWI(S)A 2000, s 24A for the purposes for which the withdrawer may intromit with the adult's funds.
[66] Organisations cannot be financial guardians under Part 6.
[67] The various forms are designated ATF (Access to Funds), which may be downloaded from the Public Guardian's website: see **4.26**.
[68] That at least was the intention, before interest rates plummeted.
[69] See AWI(S)A 2000, s 27A(1)(b) for persons not permitted to countersign.
[70] See AWI(S)A 2000, s 27C.

be printed off twice. Authority to intromit is usually granted for three years, but the Public Guardian may reduce or extend the period of validity of the withdrawal certificate.

Transition from guardianship

4.51   The procedural requirements are simplified for transition to Part 3 administration from financial guardianship under Part 6. If the Part 3 applicant is the financial guardian, countersignature is not required. The Public Guardian has discretion to dispense with the requirement for a medical certificate.

Part 3 scheme inapplicable or inappropriate

4.52   An application may not be made under Part 3 where, in relation to the funds in question, a guardian or continuing attorney has powers, or an intervention order has been granted. Circumstances in which Part 3 administration is inappropriate include 'where the adult has financial assets of a complex nature, for example, stocks and shares, investment bonds, etc. to be managed';[71] where heritable property[72] requires to be dealt with, or where a tenancy is to be given up; where a claim for compensation or other remedies require to be pursued, or there is other litigation; where a business is to be dealt with; and where tax-planning arrangements are contemplated.

Management of residents' finances (Part 4)

4.53   Part 4 of AWI(S)A 2000 provides a procedure for the management of the finances of an adult resident in an 'authorised establishment' by the managers of that establishment. Authorised establishments are NHS hospitals, for which the supervisory body for the purposes of Part 4 is the relevant health board, and independent hospitals, care homes and other services registered with the Scottish Commission for the Regulation of Care, for which that Commission ('the Care Commission') is the supervisory body. The procedure requires consideration of options by the managers of the establishment, medical examination, issue of a medical certificate of incapacity, and various intimation and notification requirements.

4.54   The consent of the supervisory body is required to manage funds in excess of £10,000. Subject to limitations, the managers may for the resident's benefit claim, receive, hold and spend funds, may hold moveable[73] property, and may dispose of moveable property (but only up to a cumulative value of £100 except with consent of the supervisory body). The supervisory body may authorise a named manager to withdraw funds from an existing account of the resident. An establishment registered with

---

[71]   Access to Funds Revised Code of Practice.
[72]   Land and buildings.
[73]   Property which is not land and buildings.

the Care Commission may opt out of the Part 4 scheme, and the supervisory body may revoke the power of a particular establishment to operate the scheme. The Part 4 scheme is not available when relevant powers are in force under a CPA, or a guardianship or intervention order.

Medical treatment and research (Part 5)

4.55 Medical treatment, with some limited exceptions, may be authorised by a certificate of incapacity by a medical practitioner, dental practitioner, ophthalmic optician or registered nurse.[74] Certificates may be issued for up to three years where incapacity is unlikely to improve because of severe or profound learning disability, dementia or a severe neurological disorder. Otherwise the maximum duration is one year. Authorisation is limited to treatment to preserve life or prevent serious deterioration when the certifier is aware of a pending application for a guardianship or intervention order with relevant powers.

4.56 The certification procedure may be followed when an appointee under a WPA, guardianship order or intervention order has relevant powers, but treatment is only authorised if the appointee consents or by reference of disagreement to a practitioner nominated by the Mental Welfare Commission, subject to appeal to the Court of Session. Some other disputes about medical treatment may also be appealed to the Court of Session; otherwise they may be appealed to the sheriff, and thence, with leave of the sheriff, to the Court of Session.

4.57 Persons with impaired capacity may also be treated on grounds of necessity; and they may be treated under relevant provisions of MH(CT)(S)A 2003. There is statutory provision for advance statements in MH(CT)(S)A 2003, but not in AWI(S)A 2000, nor is there statutory provision for withholding and withdrawing treatment.[75]

Guardianship and intervention orders (Part 6)

4.58 A guardian is the approximate equivalent of a deputy in England and Wales. The procedure for both guardianship and intervention orders is substantially the same. They are granted by the sheriff upon an application supported by three reports, two of them medical reports. One medical report must be produced by a 'relevant medical practitioner', usually a practitioner approved by a (Scottish) health board as having special experience in the diagnosis and treatment of mental disorder, though where the adult is not present in Scotland the term covers a medical practitioner with similar qualifications and experience who has consulted the Mental Welfare Commission about the report.[76] The other medical report may be provided by any medical practitioner, who need not be a Scottish medical

---

[74] Regulations may specify other categories of certifiers.
[75] Still regulated under the nobile officium: see **4.13**.
[76] Other categories of 'relevant medical practitioners' may be specified by regulations.

practitioner.[77] The third report is provided by a mental health officer[78] where the powers sought are or include welfare powers, and by a 'person who has sufficient knowledge' where only property and financial powers are sought.

4.59 Procedure includes requirements for intimation and a hearing. The sheriff may only dispense with intimation to the adult if satisfied that this would be likely to pose a serious risk to the adult's health. Where property and financial powers are given, the sheriff may order that caution[79] be obtained or other security given. Once the order has been made and any requirement for caution met, the Public Guardian issues a certificate of appointment.[80] The certificate is the document which should be inspected to ascertain details of the appointment, including the powers conferred.[81] Where the order confers powers in relation to heritable property,[82] it must be recorded or registered in the appropriate property register.[83] The local authority must apply for an order if it appears to be necessary and no-one else is applying or likely to apply.

Intervention orders

4.60 An intervention order may either authorise action specified in the order, or authorise a person to take action or make decisions as may be specified. The order may cover a single act such as signing a document, or a series of acts and decisions, such as giving up the lease of the adult's home and arranging all aspects of a transition to residential care. With limited exceptions, an intervention order can authorise anything which the adult, if capable, could have done in relation to the adult's personal welfare and/or property and financial affairs. An intervention order is the appropriate (though not the only) way to pursue or defend civil proceedings on behalf of an adult with impaired capacity, unless ongoing guardianship powers are likely to be required.

4.61 A guardianship order may not be granted where an intervention order will suffice, and the sheriff may grant an intervention order where guardianship has been applied for (but not vice versa). However, there is no

---

[77] *H, Applicant*, 2007 SLT (Sh Ct) 5; 2006 GWD 21-447.

[78] A specialised social worker.

[79] Pronounced 'kay-shun', a guarantee bond covering loss through default which the appointee fails to make good.

[80] Guardianship orders have increased in each successive year since Part 6 came into force, from 288 in 2002/03 to 1,536 in 2009/10. Intervention orders did likewise until 2007/08 (271) then dropped. In 2009/10 the total was 261.

[81] Until recently some guardians had no certificate of appointment, because they were originally appointed as curators bonis, tutors-dative or tutors-at-law under previous law and became guardians under the transitional provisions of AWI(S)A 2000. All such appointments still in force have now been renewed under the Act. The deadline for lodgement of renewal applications – for appointments otherwise still in force – was 5 October 2009. There could however be a small number of remaining transitional guardians originally appointed to children who have still not yet reached age 18.

[82] Land and buildings.

[83] The Land Register of Scotland, or for properties not yet registered in the Land Register, the General Register of Sasines.

rigid dividing line. Generally, an intervention order will be preferred for a self-limiting matter or series of matters, and guardianship where ongoing management may be required. However, while an intervention order was previously preferred for transactions such as selling a house when the proceeds were to be managed under Part 3, guardianship may now be preferred in such cases because the simplified transition to Part 3 administration described in **4.51** applies only to guardianship, and not to intervention orders.

Guardianship

4.62 Guardianship may be plenary or partial. The categories of powers which may be conferred are set out in s 64(1) as follows:

'(a) power to deal with such particular matters in relation to the property, financial affairs or personal welfare of the adult as may be specified in the order;

(b) power to deal with all aspects of the personal welfare of the adult, or with such aspects as may be specified in the order;

(c) power to pursue or defend an action of declarator of nullity of marriage, or of divorce or separation in the name of the adult;

(d) power to manage the property or financial affairs of the adult, or such parts of them as may be specified in the order;

(e) power to authorise the adult to carry out such transactions or categories of transactions as the guardian may specify.'

Unless otherwise ordered by the sheriff, the guardian is the adult's legal representative within the scope of the powers conferred. See s 64(2) for matters excluded from a guardian's powers.

4.63 The sheriff may appoint an individual guardian, joint guardians (guardians jointly exercising the same powers), dual guardians (such as one guardian exercising welfare powers and another exercising financial powers, though the term 'dual guardian' is not used in the Act), one or more substitute (ie replacement) guardians, permutations of the foregoing, and the chief social work officer as welfare guardian. No other office holder may be appointed as such, nor may any trust, corporation or other entity (cf Part I, para **4.29**). Financial guardians are under the supervision of the Public Guardian, to whom they must normally submit an inventory of estate and management plan following appointment, and annual accounts thereafter. Welfare guardians are supervised by local authorities. There are no specific provisions for deprivation of liberty cases, but the Scottish Law Commission has commenced a review of that topic.

Provisions applicable to guardians and non-Scottish equivalents

4.64 The provisions of Part 6 described in this paragraph apply both to Scottish guardians and to non-Scottish equivalents. Guardians and equivalents with welfare powers may exercise their powers whether or not the adult is in Scotland at the time.[84] Guardians and equivalents are personally liable under any transaction which they enter outwith the scope of their authority; and when they act without disclosing that they do so as guardians, they are also personally liable but (if not otherwise in breach of the Act) are entitled to be reimbursed from the adult's estate.[85]

4.65 Guardians and equivalents with welfare powers may obtain an order from the sheriff in the event of non-compliance with their decisions: orders can ordain the adult to comply; authorise a constable to enter premises, apprehend and remove the adult to a place specified by the guardian (or equivalent); and order compliance in the event of a person other than the adult failing to comply with a decision which 'that person might reasonably be expected to comply with'.[86] The sheriff has powers, upon application, to replace or remove a guardian or equivalent, or to recall a guardianship order or equivalent.[87] Guardianship and equivalent orders cease on the adult's death, though there is protection for persons acting in good faith and unaware of the adult's death.[88]

Wills and related matters

4.66 Scots law has always lacked any specific statutory procedure for making a Will for an incapable adult. However, a line of precedents has applied the s 1 principles in appropriate cases to confirm the competence of using intervention orders, and in the most recent reported case a guardianship order, to renounce inheritance rights, execute a codicil amending an existing Will, or execute a new Will.[89]

MEASURES OUTWITH THE INCAPACITY ACT

4.67 While Scottish law of trusts is distinct from that of England and Wales, trusts are frequently used in relation to incapacity in similar ways. Rules for administration of state benefits, vaccine damage payments and criminal injuries compensation payments are similar. Provisions for administration of sums awarded by the courts exist but have not been properly updated since the passing of AWI(S)A 2000. There is no Scottish equivalent to s 5 of MCA 2005, but the principle of necessity remains available to authorise some interventions.

---

[84] AWI(S)A 2000, s 67(3).
[85] AWI(S)A 2000, s 67(4).
[86] AWI(S)A 2000, s 70.
[87] AWI(S)A 2000, s 71, which contains the criteria for recall, considered in *City of Edinburgh Council v D*, 30 September 2010 (scotcourts website).
[88] AWI(S)A 2000, s 77.
[89] *B, Applicant*, 2005 SLT (Sh Ct) 95; 2005 GWD 19-334; *T, Applicant*, 2005 SLT (Sh Ct) 97; 2005 GWD 26-501; *M, Applicant*, 2007 SLT (Sh Ct) 24; 2006 GWD 19-418; *G, Applicant*, 2009 SLT (Sh Ct) 122.

Appendix 1

Adults with incapacity

INTERNATIONAL QUESTIONNAIRE
ON CROSS BORDER RECOGNITION AND ENFORCEMENT

Prepared for:	**COURT OF PROTECTION PRACTICE 2011**

Purpose

This Questionnaire is about the way your legal system deals with adults who by reason of an impairment or insufficiency of their personal faculties are not in a position to protect their interests ("**Adults**").

If you complete it we shall publish the information in our book about the law in England & Wales and it will help our lawyers to deal with the affairs of Adults who live or have property in, or have other connections with your State.

(The *Court of Protection* is that part of the Courts of England & Wales with jurisdiction to deal with matters concerning Adults)

Your Country, State or Law District ("State")

Name of State					
Is your State part of a larger Federal country?	☐	Yes	☐	No
If so, are any of the laws affecting Adults made at the level of the Federal Government?	☐	Yes	☐	No
Specify the areas of the law dealt with at State level and at Federal level.					

1. Convention on the International Protection of Adults (Hague 2000)

Has this Convention been ratified by your State?	☐	Yes	☐	No
Is ratification subject to any reservations, declarations or notifications?	☐	Yes	☐	No

Does your State intend to ratify the Convention?	☐	Yes	☐	No
Even if not ratified is it generally applied in any event?	☐	Yes	☐	No

Explanation

Please Detail any Reservations, Declarations or Notifications.
When may ratification be expected?

2. Jurisdiction

A. Does jurisdiction of your Courts usually depend upon the Personal Law of the Adult?

	☐	Yes	☐	No
If so, which is usually the relevant connecting factor?				
Habitual residence	☐	Yes	☐	No
Domicile	☐	Yes	☐	No
Nationality	☐	Yes	☐	No

B. Can jurisdiction of the Courts in your State also depend upon:

Habitual residence	☐	Yes	☐	No
Domicile	☐	Yes	☐	No
Nationality	☐	Yes	☐	No
Situs of property	☐	Yes	☐	No
Presence in the State	☐	Yes	☐	No

Explanation

> *If Domicile is used as a connecting factor, please give a short definition.*
>
>
> *In relation to each connecting factor to which you have answered "Yes", please indicate the purposes, classifications or categories that are linked by it.*

C. If the Courts of your State have jurisdiction, which internal law is applicable? That of:

Your State	☐	Yes	☐	No
Habitual residence	☐	Yes	☐	No
Domicile	☐	Yes	☐	No
Nationality	☐	Yes	☐	No
Situs of property	☐	Yes	☐	No

Explanation

> *In relation to each connecting factor to which you have answered "Yes", please indicate the purposes, classifications or categories that are linked by it.*

D. Does the internal law of your State have provision for Powers of Representation (also known as Continuing, Lasting or Durable Powers of Attorney) for the following:

Economic and financial matters	☐	Yes	☐	No
Personal welfare	☐	Yes	☐	No
Health care and medical treatment	☐	Yes	☐	No

Explanation

Please detail any restrictions or requirements (such as registration).

Does an ordinary Power cease to be effective in the event of a lack of capacity?

E. Does your State include power for the Courts to make orders or decisions about:

Impairment or insufficiency of personal faculties (lack of capacity)	☐	Yes	☐	No
Economic and financial matters	☐	Yes	☐	No
Personal welfare	☐	Yes	☐	No
Health care and medical treatment	☐	Yes	☐	No
A new Will or Testament	☐	Yes	☐	No

If you have answered 'yes' to any of the above, please confirm whether the Courts may authorize another person (such as a guardian, curator, receiver or deputy) to make decisions on behalf of the Adult on the following matters:

Economic and financial matters	☐	Yes	☐	No
Personal welfare	☐	Yes	☐	No
Health care and medical treatment	☐	Yes	☐	No
A new Will or Testament	☐	Yes	☐	No

If you have answered 'yes' to any of the above, and a person is authorized to make decisions on behalf of the Adult, please summarise the extent of that person's responsibility. For example, is there a duty to produce accounts to the Courts or other supervisory body? Does anyone oversee or monitor conduct? Are there any restrictions on what can or cannot be done in the name of the person who is incapable?

Please list the procedures

3. Recognition of Powers of Representation / Continuing or Lasting Powers of Attorney and protective measures for Adults from England & Wales

NOTE: these are ways that decisions may be dealt with under jurisdiction of the Courts of England & Wales in relation to Adults. They are recognised in some countries but not others.

A. Are the following Powers of Representation and delegations under the law of England & Wales recognised and enforceable:

Continuing Powers of Attorney for economic and financial matters	☐	Yes	☐	No
Continuing Powers of Attorney for personal welfare	☐	Yes	☐	No
Continuing Powers of Attorney for healthcare and medical treatment	☐	Yes	☐	No
Advance Directives	☐	Yes	☐	No

Are there any additional formalities required such as an Exequatur?

B. Are the following Protective Measures of the courts of England &
Wales recognised and enforceable in your State?

Decision as to impairment or insufficiency of personal faculties	☐ Yes	☐	No
Appointment of a Representative to deal with economic and financial matters	☐ Yes	☐	No
Appointment of a Representative to deal with personal welfare	☐ Yes	☐	No
Appointment of a Representative to deal with health care and medical treatment	☐ Yes	☐	No
Decision authorising the making of a new Will or Testament	☐ Yes	☐	No

Explanation

Please specify any limitations.

4. Procedures in your State

A. How may the following situations be dealt with for a person with
connections to England & Wales who by reason of an impairment or
insufficiency of their personal faculties is not in a position to protect their
interests.

Withdrawal of money from a bank account situated in your State

Sale of a home or other property in your State

> *If any particular consent is required please specify*

Family dispute as to care of the person currently resident in your State (eg. whether to return to England & Wales)

Decision about medical treatment in your State

B. Would the answers to A. above vary if person was not a national of the United Kingdom but had been habitually resident in England and Wales prior to their impairment or insufficiency?

C. Is there an emergency procedure?

PART X

5. Sources of information

Are there Websites that provide in respect of your State:

A list of solicitors/notaries/ advocates or lawyers able and willing to provide services of this nature	☐	Yes	☐	No
Guidance on the law and procedure that applies to Adults who by reason of an impairment or insufficiency of their personal faculties are not in a position to protect their interests	☐	Yes	☐	No

Please list the web addresses

Completed by:

Name	
eMail	

Are you a solicitor/notary/advocate or lawyer who provides legal advice and services for nationals of the United Kingdom in your State?	☐	Yes	☐	No
May we publish your email address so that lawyers in England & Wales can contact you for advice?	☐	Yes	☐	No

October 2010

Appendix 2

Completed questionnaires

Australia: NSW	1773
Australia: Victoria	1781
Belgium	1786
Canada: Alberta	1793
Canada: Manitoba	1800
Canada: Nova Scotia	1806
Canada: Ontario	1811
Canada: Saskatchewan	1816
Denmark	1821
Finland	1826
France	1831
Germany	1837
Iceland	1849
Japan	1854
Serbia	1859
Slovenia	1869
Spain	1878
Switzerland	1884
USA: Florida	1890

There has been reproduced in Appendix 1 above the *International Questionnaire* that has been sent to lawyers in many other countries. In this Appendix there appear extracts from the many responses received including, in some instances, the email addresses of the lawyers in case readers wish to seek further assistance. Completion of this *Questionnaire* was an onerous task and this has limited the number of responses, but it is hoped that the number of countries or jurisdictions covered will be increased in future editions. The authors would welcome suggestions as to how this service to readers may be improved and requests to add further countries or jurisdictions (perhaps with legal contacts who may be approached).

AUSTRALIA: NSW

Name of State	Australia, New South Wales				
Is your State part of a larger Federal country?		X	Yes		
If so, are any of the laws affecting Adults made at the level of the Federal Government?		X	Yes		

Explanation

> *Specify the areas of the law dealt with at State level and at Federal level.*
>
> Capacity – in terms of EPAs (Financial), Guardianship (Personal) and Statutory Wills are State level as are State appointed Financial Managers (equivalent of Court of Protection appointed Deputies)
>
> Other areas of law, such as Family Law, Bankruptcy and Corporations are Federal Law issues.

1. Convention on the International Protection of Adults (Hague 2000)

Has this Convention been ratified by your State?			✔	No
Does your State intend to ratify the Convention?	☐	Yes	☐	No
Even if not ratified is it generally applied in any event?			X	No

Explanation

> There is no current information as to any intention for Australia to ratify the Convention.

2. Jurisdiction

A. Does jurisdiction of your Courts usually depend upon the Personal Law of the Adult?

	X	Yes		
If so, which is usually the relevant connecting factor?				
Habitual residence	X	Yes		
Domicile	X	Yes		
Nationality			X	No

B. Can jurisdiction of the Courts in your State also depend upon:

Situs of property	✔	Yes	☐	No
Presence in the State	☐	Yes	☐	No

Explanation

> Domicile is approach in a manner very similar to England & Wales.
>
> Domicile Act 1979 (NSW) s 9 – The intention that a person must have in order to acquire a domicile of choice in a country is the intention to make his or her home indefinitely in that country
>
> There is no revival of domicile of origin and domicile of married women is not dependant on husband's domicile.
>
> Domicile is the usual connecting factor in matters concerning Estate matters. When it comes to Enduring Powers of Attorney and financial management orders the issue is one of situs of the property – it must be located in NSW.
>
> When it comes to Guardianship it is an issue of residency in NSW.

C. If the Courts of your State have jurisdiction, which internal law is applicable? That of:

Your State	X	Yes		

Explanation

> Generally in matters concerning capacity the law of NSW will apply either on a statutory basis (as with mutual recognition of EPAs and AEGs) or at common law given the situs of property or residency of the individual.

D. Does the internal law of your State have provision for Powers of Representation (also known as Continuing, Lasting or Durable Powers of Attorney) for the following:

Economic and financial matters	X	Yes		
Personal welfare	X	Yes		
Health care and medical treatment	X	Yes		

Explanation

> Enduring Powers of Attorney (financial).
>
> Powers of Attorney Act 2003 (NSW) – deals with enduring powers of attorney.
>
> Must be registered for any dealing in land (i.e. to register a deed of transfer or sign a mortgage deed but not to sign the contract of sale) otherwise does not need to be registered.
>
> EPA must be 'in or to the effect of' the prescribed form contained in Schedule 2 of the Act which includes provision for the donor's signature to be certified.

PART X

No powers for Attorneys to (a) make gifts, (b) benefit themselves or (c) benefit third parties unless expressly stated in the document.

There is provision for recognition of other State/Territory EPAs but only to the same extent that they comply with the law of NSW. Not revoked by either marriage or divorce.

Appointments of Enduring Guardian (personal, medical and dental)

Guardianship Act 1987 (NSW) – deals with enduring guardians (AEG) and also financial management orders. AEG does not need to be registered.

Appoints a substitute decision maker who can decide where the donor lives, what healthcare they receive, what personal services they receive and can consent to medical and dental treatment in accordance with the Act. Certain treatment such as sterilisation and experimental treatment requires the consent of the Guardianship Tribunal.

There is provision for recognition of other State/Territory AEGs but only to the same extent that they comply with the law of NSW.

Revoked by marriage (unless marriage is to the donee) but not revoked by divorce.

Death, resignation or incapacity of a joint donee terminates appointment unless express provision is made in the appointment allowing the surviving joint donee(s) to carry on acting.

Does an ordinary Power cease to be effective in the event of a lack of capacity?

Yes, general powers of attorney are still recognised but cease to be effective in the event of a lack of capacity.

E. Does your State include power for the Courts to make orders or decisions about:

Impairment or insufficiency of personal faculties (lack of capacity)	X	Yes	
Economic and financial matters	X	Yes	
Personal welfare	X	Yes	
Health care and medical treatment	X	Yes	
A new Will or Testament	X	Yes	

If you have answered 'yes' to any of the above, please confirm whether the Courts may authorize another person (such as a guardian, curator, receiver or deputy) to make decisions on behalf of the Adult on the following matters:

Economic and financial matters	X	Yes	
Personal welfare	X	Yes	
Health care and medical treatment	X	Yes	
A new Will or Testament	X	Yes	

If you have answered 'yes' to any of the above, and a person is authorized to make decisions on behalf of the Adult, please summarise the extent of that person's responsibility. For example, is there a duty to produce accounts to the Courts or other supervisory body? Does anyone oversee or monitor conduct? Are there any restrictions on what can or cannot be done in the name of the person who is incapable? Please list the procedures.

Please list the procedures

Financial

The Guardianship Tribunal can appoint 'financial managers' (either private individuals or the NSW Trustee and Guardian) to manage a person's financial affairs. The Tribunal will only make an order if:

- The person is not capable of managing their affairs.

- There is a need for someone else to manage their affairs for them.

- It is in the person's best interests to have a financial management order.

- The person has assets in NSW.

A financial management order will usually set out detailed terms as the scope and limits of the powers of the manager. If the manager wants to deal with the person's finances in ways not authorised or directed, they must get the NSW Trustee and Guardian's approval. Usual orders include:

- The manager must usually lodge security with the NSW Trustee and Guardian, for example the title deed of the protected person's house.

- The manager must usually lodge accounts each year with the NSW Trustee and Guardian to show that the person's finances are being properly managed.

- The NSW Trustee and Guardian may arrange for an authorised visitor to visit the protected person. The authorised visitor can make suggestions about spending money to benefit the person.

Personal welfare

The Guardianship Tribunal can also appoint 'guardians' to make lifestyle or personal decisions for someone who is incapable of making these decisions for themselves. Again, these can either be private individuals or the Public Guardian (although the administration is carried out by the NSW Trustee and Guardian).

The Tribunal can only consider guardianship applications about people who are resident in NSW and over the age of 16.

Applications to appoint a Manager or a Guardian can also be made in the Equity Division Protective of the Supreme Court but are more usually made via the Guardianship Tribunal.

Statutory wills

Under the Succession Act 2006 (NSW) the Supreme Court of NSW may authorise a will to be made, altered or revoked for a person without testamentary capacity.

If it appears to the Court that the person who lacks testamentary capacity should be separately represented in proceedings, the Court may order that the person be separately represented.

PART X

3. Recognition of Powers of Representation/Continuing or Lasting Powers of Attorney and protective measures for Adults from England & Wales

A. Are the following Powers of Representation and delegations under the law of England & Wales recognised and enforceable:

Continuing Powers of Attorney for economic and financial matters			X	No
Continuing Powers of Attorney for personal welfare			X	No
Continuing Powers of Attorney for healthcare and medical treatment			X	No
Advance Directives	X	Yes		

Are there any additional formalities required such as an Exequatur?

Advance Care Directives have no statutory basis in NSW and are not legally binding. However, NSW Health has published guidance which states that 'A failure to comply with an advance care directive that meets the standards discussed in this document and refuses treatment may be considered an assault and battery under common law. Civil liability may also ensue' so that tend to be practically enforceable.'
General rules are that an Advance Care Directive should be clear, unambiguous and reasonably current (no older than 2 years ideally) and witnessed by an independent adult.

B. Are the following Protective Measures of the courts of England & Wales recognised and enforceable in your State?

Decision as to impairment or insufficiency of personal faculties			X	No
Appointment of a Representative to deal with economic and financial matters			X	No
Appointment of a Representative to deal with personal welfare			X	No
Appointment of a Representative to deal with health care and medical treatment			X	No
Decision authorising the making of a new Will or Testament	X	Yes		

Explanation

> No provisions allowing for mutual recognition of English orders being enforceable in NSW without reference to the NSW Courts. This would be a practical issue as well in terms of enforcement as Banks and healthcare providers will insist on NSW documentation.
>
> A Will is likely to be different due to statutory mutual recognition provisions.
>
> Section 17 of the Succession Act 2006 (NSW) – A will of a deceased person that is a court authorised will for a minor is a valid will.
>
> Section 26 of the Succession Act 2006 (NSW) – A statutory will made according to the law of the place where the deceased was resident at the time of the execution of the will is to be regarded as a valid will of the deceased.
>
> (*Statutory will* means a will executed by virtue of a provision of an Act of New South Wales or other place on behalf of a person who, at the time of execution, lacked testamentary capacity.

4. Procedures in your State

A. How may the following situations be dealt with for a person with connections to England & Wales who by reason of an impairment or insufficiency of their personal faculties is not in a position to protect their interests.

Withdrawal of money from a bank account situated in your State

> In the absence of a duly appointed substitute decision maker this would require order of the Guardianship Tribunal (or the Supreme Court of NSW).

Sale of a home or other property in your State

> In the absence of a duly appointed substitute decision maker this would require order of the Guardianship Tribunal (or the Supreme Court of NSW).

Family dispute as to care of the person currently resident in your State (eg. whether to return to England & Wales)

> In the absence of a duly appointed substitute decision maker this would require order of the Guardianship Tribunal (or the Supreme Court of NSW).

Decision about medical treatment in your State

> In the absence of a duly appointed substitute decision maker this would require order of the Guardianship Tribunal (or the Supreme Court of NSW).

PART X

B. Would the answers to A. above vary if person was not a national of the United Kingdom but had been habitually resident in England and Wales prior to their impairment or insufficiency?

No.

C. Is there an emergency procedure?

Priority applications can be made to the Guardianship Tribunal.

5. Sources of information

STEP
Law Society of NSW has details of accredited specialists in the area of Wills and Estates http://www.lawsociety.com.au/
The Guardianship Tribunal http://www.gt.nsw.gov.au/
The NSW Trustee and Guardian http://www.tag.nsw.gov.au/

Completed by:

Name	Christopher Young
eMail	cyoung@wte.com.au

October 2010

AUSTRALIA: VICTORIA

Name of State	Australia, Victoria			
Is your State part of a larger Federal country?		X	Yes	
If so, are any of the laws affecting Adults made at the level of the Federal Government?		X	Yes	

Specify the areas of the law dealt with at State level and at Federal level.

Capacity – in terms of EPAs (Financial), Guardianship (Personal) and Statutory Wills are State level as are State appointed Financial Managers (equivalent of Court of Protection appointed Deputies)

Other areas of law, such as Family Law, Bankruptcy and Corporations are Federal Law issues.

1. Convention on the International Protection of Adults (Hague 2000)

Has this Convention been ratified by your State?			✔	No
Does your State intend to ratify the Convention?		☐ Yes	☐	No
Even if not ratified is it generally applied in any event?			X	No

Explanation

There is no current information as to any intention for Australia to ratify the Convention.

2. Jurisdiction

A. *Does jurisdiction of your Courts usually depend upon the Personal Law of the Adult?*

	X	Yes		
If so, which is usually the relevant connecting factor?				
Habitual residence	X	Yes		
Domicile				
Nationality				

B. *Can jurisdiction of the Courts in your State also depend upon:*

Presence in the State	X	Yes		

Explanation

> Domicile is approach in a manner very similar to England & Wales.

C. If the Courts of your State have jurisdiction, which internal law is applicable? That of:

Your State	X	Yes		

D. Does the internal law of your State have provision for Powers of Representation (also known as Continuing, Lasting or Durable Powers of Attorney) for the following:

Economic and financial matters	X	Yes		
Personal welfare	X	Yes		
Health care and medical treatment	X	Yes		

Explanation

> Enduring Powers of Attorney (Financial, Medical and Guardianship) must be witnessed by a person authorised to witness statutory declarations and must confirm that the donor appeared to have capacity.
>
> No registration is required.
>
> *Does an ordinary Power cease to be effective in the event of a lack of capacity?*
>
> Yes.

E. Does your State include power for the Courts to make orders or decisions about:

Impairment or insufficiency of personal faculties (lack of capacity)	X	Yes		
Economic and financial matters	X	Yes		
Personal welfare	X	Yes		
Health care and medical treatment	X	Yes		
A new Will or Testament	X	Yes		

If you have answered 'yes' to any of the above, please confirm whether the Courts may authorize another person (such as a guardian, curator, receiver or deputy) to make decisions on behalf of the Adult on the following matters:

Economic and financial matters	X	Yes		
Personal welfare	X	Yes		
Health care and medical treatment	X	Yes		
A new Will or Testament			X	No

If you have answered 'yes' to any of the above, and a person is authorized to make decisions on behalf of the Adult, please summarise the extent of that person's responsibility. For example, is there a duty to produce accounts to the Courts or other supervisory body? Does anyone oversee or monitor conduct? Are there any restrictions on what can or cannot be done in the name of the person who is incapable?

Please list the procedures

In financial administration – appointees must lodge annual accounts with the tribunal.

Appointed persons are required to act in the best interests of the represented person.

Orders are for a maximum of three years.

3. Recognition of Powers of Representation / Continuing or Lasting Powers of Attorney and protective measures for Adults from England & Wales

A. Are the following Powers of Representation and delegations under the law of England & Wales recognised and enforceable:

Continuing Powers of Attorney for economic and financial matters			X	No
Continuing Powers of Attorney for personal welfare			X	No
Continuing Powers of Attorney for healthcare and medical treatment			X	No
Advance Directives				

B. Are the following Protective Measures of the courts of England & Wales recognised and enforceable in your State?

Decision as to impairment or insufficiency of personal faculties			X	No
Appointment of a Representative to deal with economic and financial matters			X	No

PART X

Appointment of a Representative to deal with personal welfare		X	No
Appointment of a Representative to deal with health care and medical treatment		X	No
Decision authorising the making of a new Will or Testament		X	No

4. Procedures in your State

A. How may the following situations be dealt with:

Withdrawal of money from a bank account situated in your State

Use of a Power of Attorney.

Sale of a home or other property in your State

VCAT order required. (Victorian Civil Administrative Tribunal).

Family dispute as to care of the person currently resident in your State (eg. whether to return to England & Wales)

VCAT order required.

Decision about medical treatment in your State

VCAT order required.

B. Would the answers to A. above vary if person was not a national of the United Kingdom but had been habitually resident in England and Wales prior to their impairment or insufficiency?

No.

C. Is there an emergency procedure?

Yes.

5. Sources of information

http://www.publicadvocate.vic.gov.au/

Completed by:

Name	Mary Sealy

October 2010

PART X

BELGIUM

Name of State	Belgium				
Is your State part of a larger Federal country?				X	No

1. Convention on the International Protection of Adults (Hague 2000)

Has this Convention been ratified by your State?			X	No
Is ratification subject to any reservations, declarations or notifications?			X	No
Does your State intend to ratify the Convention?			X	No
Even if not ratified is it generally applied in any event?			X	No

2. Jurisdiction

A. *Does jurisdiction of your Courts usually depend upon the Personal Law of the Adult?*

		X	Yes		
If so, which is usually the relevant connecting factor?					
Habitual residence		X	Yes		

B. *Can jurisdiction of the Courts in your State also depend upon:*

		X	Yes		
Domicile		X	Yes		
Nationality		X	Yes		
Situs of property		X	Yes		
Presence in the State		X	Yes		

Explanation

Domicile means the place where a natural person has his main residence in Belgium according to the population registers, the aliens registers or the waiting register (art. 4, § 1, 1° Code on Private International Law – 16 juli 2004).

C. If the Courts of your State have jurisdiction, which internal law is applicable? That of:

Your State	X	Yes		
Habitual residence	X	Yes		
Domicile			X	No
Nationality	X	Yes		
Situs of property			X	No

D. Does the internal law of your State have provision for Powers of Representation (also known as Continuing, Lasting or Durable Powers of Attorney) for the following:

Economic and financial matters	X	Yes		
Personal welfare	X	Yes		
Health care and medical treatment	X	Yes		

Explanation

> Economic and financial matters & Personal welfare
>
> There is no specific protection statute including provisions for Powers of Representation. The general law on mandate (*lastgeving / mandat*) applies
>
> Health care and medical treatment:
>
> A person who is able to protect his personal interests and who does not fall within the scope of the protection statutes of extended minority (*verlengde minderjarigheid / minorité prolongée*) or provisional guardianship (*voorlopig bewind / administration provisoire*), has the right to appoint a representative in a living will. A specific written mandate that reflects the consent of the person, signed by the person and by the representative and dated, is required. (art. 14, § 1 *juncto* art. 13, §1 Law concerning the Rights of Patients – 22 august 2002).
>
> *Does an ordinary Power cease to be effective in the event of a lack of capacity?*
>
> A distinction has to be made between factual and judicial incapacity.
>
> 1) When the granter becomes factually incapable, an ordinary Power (*lastgeving / mandat*) stays effective.
>
> 2) When the granter becomes judicially incapable, an ordinary Power (*lastgeving / mandat*) becomes ineffective to the extent of the judicial incapacity of the granter. A full lack of judicial capacity causes the mandate to end, a partial lack of judicial capacity only causes the mandate to end for those legal acts that belong to the competence of the representative.

PART X

E. Does your State include power for the Courts to make orders or decisions about:

Impairment or insufficiency of personal faculties (lack of capacity)	X	Yes		
Economic and financial matters	X	Yes		
Personal welfare	X	Yes		
Health care and medical treatment	X	Yes		
A new Will or Testament	X	Yes		

If you have answered 'yes' to any of the above, please confirm whether the Courts may authorize another person (such as a guardian, curator, receiver or deputy) to make decisions on behalf of the Adult on the following matters:

Economic and financial matters	X	Yes		
Personal welfare	X	Yes		
Health care and medical treatment	X	Yes		
A new Will or Testament			X	No

If you have answered 'yes' to any of the above, and a person is authorized to make decisions on behalf of the Adult, please summarise the extent of that person's responsibility. For example, is there a duty to produce accounts to the Courts or other supervisory body? Does anyone oversee or monitor conduct? Are there any restrictions on what can or cannot be done in the name of the person who is incapable?

Please list the procedures

> Economic and financial matters
>
> The protection statute of provisional guardianship (*voorlopig bewind / administration provisoire*), art. 488*bis*, Civil Code;
>
> f), § 1: only economic and financial matters, not personal welfare.
>
> f), § 2: the Justice of the Peace determines the nature and the extent of the competences of the provisional guardian (*voorlopig bewindvoerder / administrateur provisoire*).
>
> d), first part: the Justice of the Peace can change the competences of the provisional guardian, can replace him and can end his mandate.
>
> c), § 2 and § 3: at the latest one month after the start of the provisional guardianship, every year and at the end of his judicial mandate, the provisional guardian has to make a report concerning the assets and the income of the protected person.
>
> b), § 4: a confidential counsellor (*vertrouwenspersoon / personne de confiance*) can assist the protected person and control the provisional guardian.

h), § 2: the provisional guardian can not make a grant or a will.

Personal welfare, health care and medical treatment

The Justice of the Peace can authorize the representative to go to the Court of First Instance. The Court of First Instance can authorize the representative to make a specific decision on behalf of the protected person.

3. Recognition of Powers of Representation / Continuing or Lasting Powers of Attorney and protective measures for Adults from England & Wales

A. Are the following Powers of Representation and delegations under the law of England & Wales recognised and enforceable:

Continuing Powers of Attorney for economic and financial matters	X	Yes		
Continuing Powers of Attorney for personal welfare	X	Yes		
Continuing Powers of Attorney for healthcare and medical treatment	X	Yes		
Advance Directives	X	Yes		

Are there any additional formalities required such as an Exequatur?

No (art. 27 Code on Private International Law – 16 juli 2004)

B. Are the following Protective Measures of the courts of England & Wales recognised and enforceable in your State?

Decision as to impairment or insufficiency of personal faculties	X	Yes		
Appointment of a Representative to deal with economic and financial matters	X	Yes		
Appointment of a Representative to deal with personal welfare	X	Yes		
Appointment of a Representative to deal with health care and medical treatment	X	Yes		
Decision authorising the making of a new Will or Testament			X	No

PART X

Explanation

---

art. 22 Code on Private International Law – 16 juli 2004

For foreign judicial decisions authorizing the making of a new Will or Testament, problems could arise due to the applicability of art. 25, §1, 1° Code on Private International Law – 16 juli 2004.

Art. 25, § 1 Code on Private International Law – 16 juli 2004 provides: Foreign legal decisions are not recognised or enforceable when:

- 1° in conflict with public policy;
- 2° violation of the rights of the defence;
- 3° only provoked to avoid the law applicable according to the Code on Private International Law;
- 4° open to a legal remedy;
- 5° in conflict with a Belgian decision or with a foreign decision recognisable in Belgium;
- 6° the claim was filed abroad after a claim, that is still pending between the same parties about the same subject, was filed in Belgium;
- 7° Belgian judges were exclusively competent to handle the claim;
- 8° the competence of foreign judges was exclusively based on the presence of the defendant or goods;
- 9° the recognition or the enforceability would be in conflict with the reasons for refusal in art. 39, 57, 72, 95, 115 and 121 Civil Code.

---

4. Procedures in your State

A. How may the following situations be dealt with for a person with connections to England & Wales who by reason of an impairment or insufficiency of their personal faculties is not in a position to protect their interests.

Withdrawal of money from a bank account situated in your State

---

The withdrawal of money from a bank is a legal act concerning financial matters, and consequently falls within the scope of the provisional guardianship (*voorlopig bewind / administration provisoire*) (see Court of Appeal Brussels 21 march 2007, *T.B.B.R.* 2008, afl.2, p. 79). Depending on the nature and the extent of his competence, the provisional guardian (*voorlopig bewindvoerder / administrateur provisoire*) will assist the protected person with or represent him for the withdrawal (art. 488*bis*, f), §§ 1-3 Civil Code).

Sale of a home or other property in your State

The sale of a home or other property is a legal act concerning economic matters, and consequently falls within the scope of the provisional guardianship (*voorlopig bewind / administration provisoire*). Depending on the nature and the extent of his competence, the provisional guardian (*voorlopig bewindvoerder / administrateur provisoire*) will assist the protected person with or represent him for the sale (art. 488*bis*, f), §§ 1-3 Civil Code).

When the provisional guardian has the competence to represent the protected person, he needs a special authorization from the Justice of the Peace to sell moveable property or real estate of the protected person (art. 488*bis*, f), § 3, b Civil Code). When the moveable property are the household goods or when the real estate is the house of the protected person, the provisional guardian needs a second special authorization from the Justice of the Peace (art. 488*bis*, f), § 4, b Civil Code).

Family dispute as to care of the person currently resident in your State (eg. whether to return to England & Wales)

Interim injunction proceeding before the president of the Court of First Instance (art. 584 Judicial Code).

Decision about medical treatment in your State

A distinction has to be made between factual capacity and factual incapacity.

1) A person who is factually capable of protecting his personal interests, has the right to preliminary and informed consent or reject to any medical treatment and to write this down in a living will. When this person is no longer able to protect his personal interests, the living will must be followed concerning medical treatments (art. 8, §§ 1 and 4 Law concerning the Rights of Patients – 22 august 2002).

The fact that a person falls within the scope of the provisional guardianship (*voorlopig bewind / administration provisoire*) does not unable him to make a living will. The provisional guardian (*voorlopig bewindvoerder / administrateur provisoire*) can not make a living will, since the provisional guardianship only applies to economic and financial matters (art. 488*bis*, f), § 1 Civil Code).

2) A person who is factually incapable of making a living will, who has not appointed a representative in a living will or when the representative appointed in a living will does not act, will be represented by a cascade of persons.

Primarily by the cohabiting spouse (*samenwonende echtgenoot / époux cohabitant*), the legal cohabitator (*wettelijk samenwonende partner / partenaire cohabitant légal*) or the factual cohabitator (*feitelijk samenwonende partner / partenaire cohabitant de fait*).

When this person does not want to represent him or is absent, in decreasing order by a child who has attained the age of majority, by a parent or by a brother or sister who has attained the age of majority. When these persons don't want to respresent him or are absent, by the involved medical practitioner.

When a conflict arises between two or more of these persons, by the involved medical practitioner (art. 14, § 2 Law concerning the Rights of Patients – 22 august 2002).

B. Would the answers to A. above vary if person was not a national of the United Kingdom but had been habitually resident in England and Wales prior to their impairment or insufficiency?

No

C. Is there an emergency procedure?

Interim injunction proceeding before the president of the Court of First Instance (art. 584 Judicial Code).

5. Sources of information

www.law.kuleuven.be/fvr

www.notaris.be or www.notaire.be

www.advocaat.be

Completed by:

Name	Wouter Janssens
eMail	wouter.janssens@law.kuleuven.be

Are you a solicitor/notary/advocate or lawyer who provides legal advice and services for nationals of the United Kingdom in your State?			X	No

October 2010

CANADA: ALBERTA

Name of State	Canada: Alberta				
Is your State part of a larger Federal country?		X	Yes		
If so, are any of the laws affecting Adults made at the level of the Federal Government?				X	No

Under the federal Constitution Act, s. 92 (13), "property and civil rights" are matters solely within the legislative jurisdiction of the provinces and territories of Canada.

Provincial Level:

The following are the main enactments:

Adult Guardianship and Trusteeship Act (**AGTA**) – provides for court appointment of substitute decision makers for persons determined by the court to lack capacity in personal matters (guardianship) or financial matters (trusteeship).

Powers of Attorney Act (**PAA**) – enables enduring powers of attorney, i.e. powers of attorney relating to financial matters of the "donor" that are not terminated by the subsequent mental incapacity of the donor;

Personal Directives Act (**PDA**) – enables personal directives, instruments that come into effect upon the incapacity of their maker, that give directions regarding personal matters (including health care decisions), and that may appoint an agent or provide written instructions to make decisions in personal matters.

All Alberta legislation accessible at http://www.canlii.org/en/ab/laws/.

1. Convention on the International Protection of Adults (Hague 2000)

Has this Convention been ratified by your State?				X	No
Does your State intend to ratify the Convention?		X	Yes		
Even if not ratified is it generally applied in any event?		X	Yes		

Explanation

No date has been set for ratification.

2. Jurisdiction

A. *Does jurisdiction of your Courts usually depend upon the Personal Law of the Adult?*

				X	No

B. Can jurisdiction of the Courts in your State also depend upon:

Habitual residence	X	Yes		
Domicile			X	No
Nationality			X	No
Situs of property	X	Yes		
Presence in the State	X	Yes		

Explanation

In relation to each connecting factor to which you have answered "Yes", please indicate the purposes, classifications or categories that are linked by it.

The AGTA generally limits the court's jurisdiction to appoint a trustee to situations where the Adult is ordinarily resident in Alberta. However if the Adult is not ordinarily resident in Alberta, the court could make a trusteeship order that applies exclusively to real property located in Alberta or if the court is satisfied that exceptional circumstances make it appropriate to grant a trusteeship order.

C. If the Courts of your State have jurisdiction, which internal law is applicable? That of:

Your State	X	Yes		

D. Does the internal law of your State have provision for Powers of Representation (also known as Continuing, Lasting or Durable Powers of Attorney) for the following:

Economic and financial matters	X	Yes		
Personal welfare	X	Yes		
Health care and medical treatment	X	Yes		

Explanation

Please detail any restrictions or requirements (such as registration).
An enduring power of attorney (for financial matters) must be in writing; it must be dated; it must be signed by the "donor" (or at the direction of a physically incapable donor) in the presence of a witness; it must be signed by the witness in the presence of the donor; and it must contain a statement indicating either (1) that it is to continue notwithstanding any mental incapacity or infirmity of the donor arising after execution of the power or (2) that it is to come into effect on the donor's mental incapacity or infirmity. The donors' spouse, the designated attorney, or the spouse or partner of the attorney cannot act as a witness.
A personal directive must meet similar formal requirements.
There is a registry for personal directives, but registration is not mandatory.
Does an ordinary Power cease to be effective in the event of a lack of capacity?
An ordinary power of attorney not complying with the formalities of the PAA ceases to be effective upon the incapacity of the donor.

E. Does your State include power for the Courts to make orders or decisions about:

Impairment or insufficiency of personal faculties (lack of capacity)	X	Yes		
Economic and financial matters	X	Yes		
Personal welfare	X	Yes		
Health care and medical treatment	X	Yes		
A new Will or Testament			X	No

If you have answered 'yes' to any of the above, please confirm whether the Courts may authorize another person (such as a guardian, curator, receiver or deputy) to make decisions on behalf of the Adult on the following matters:

Economic and financial matters	X	Yes		
Personal welfare	X	Yes		
Health care and medical treatment	X	Yes		
A new Will or Testament			X	No

If you have answered 'yes' to any of the above, and a person is authorized to make decisions on behalf of the Adult, please summarise the extent of that person's responsibility. For example, is there a duty to produce accounts to

PART X

the Courts or other supervisory body? Does anyone oversee or monitor conduct? Are there any restrictions on what can or cannot be done in the name of the person who is incapable?

Please list the procedures

> The Court has better information upon which to base their decisions for guardianship. The proposed represented or assisted adult is interviewed by the Office of the Public Guardian and has the opportunity to appear in Court if they object to application. An applicant must submit a plan for how they intend to manage the adult's personal affairs. The Guardianship Plan is a form that outlines the major decisions that the guardian thinks will be required for the represented adult for the next year and for the next five years. The plan also asks the guardian to outline how they will include the represented adult in the decision-making and how the represented adult will be informed of decisions when they are not able to participate.
>
> New applications for guardianship will also require that proposed guardians consent to collect a criminal record check and a personal reference check, where a new guardianship and trusteeship application then also a credit check is done. This is to ensure that there are appropriate safeguards in place to protect the proposed represented adult. Accountability would be exercised by reviewing the guardianship as stated by the Court. Anyone, including the represented adult, may ask the Court to review guardianship at any time.
>
> Court-appointed trustees have a duty to maintain accounts and submit accounts for examination and approval of the court if so required. Courts generally require accounts to be submitted for approval periodically.
>
> Any interested person who believes that a guardian or trustee is not complying with the terms of the guardianship or trusteeship order may make a written complaint to a designated official, who must initiate an investigation unless satisfied that the complaint is frivolous or vexatious.
>
> Court-appointed trustees can be given the power to do anything in relation to the Adult's financial matters that the latter could do if capable, except make a testamentary document. Trustees other than the Public Trustee can only sell real property if specifically authorized to do so by the court.

3. Recognition of Powers of Representation / Continuing or Lasting Powers of Attorney and protective measures for Adults from England & Wales

A. Are the following Powers of Representation and delegations under the law of England & Wales recognised and enforceable:

Continuing Powers of Attorney for economic and financial matters	X	Yes		
Continuing Powers of Attorney for personal welfare	X	Yes		
Continuing Powers of Attorney for healthcare and medical treatment	X	Yes		
Advance Directives	X	Yes		

Are there any additional formalities required such as an Exequatur?

> The PAA says that a power of attorney is an enduring power of attorney if, according to the law of the place where it is executed, (1) it is a valid power of attorney and (2) the attorney's authority is not terminated by any mental incapacity or infirmity of the donor occurring after its execution.
>
> The PDA's approach is somewhat different. It says that a directive made outside of Alberta that complies with the formal requirements for making a personal directive as set out in the Act has the same effect as if it had been made under the Act.
>
> No additional formalities are required.

B. Are the following Protective Measures of the courts of England & Wales recognized and enforceable in your State?

Decision as to impairment or insufficiency of personal faculties	X	Yes		
Appointment of a Representative to deal with economic and financial matters	X	Yes		
Appointment of a Representative to deal with personal welfare	X	Yes		
Appointment of a Representative to deal with health care and medical treatment	X	Yes		
Decision authorizing the making of a new Will or Testament			X	No

Explanation

> Please specify any limitations.
>
> An order of a non-Alberta court must be resealed under AGTA section 73 before it has effect in Alberta.

4. Procedures in your State

A. How may the following situations be dealt with.

Withdrawal of money from a bank account situated in your State

> A financial institution would require satisfactory evidence of a representative's authority to act on the Adult's behalf for the purpose of withdrawing the funds: e.g. a trusteeship order granted by an Alberta court; an equivalent order of a foreign court that has been resealed in Alberta; or an enduring power of attorney. In each case it would be necessary to satisfy the bank that the relevant instrument purports to give the representative the authority to withdraw the funds.

PART X

Sale of a home or other property in your State

> If any particular consent is required please specify
> This would require a trusteeship order granted by an Alberta court; an equivalent
> order of a foreign court that has been resealed in Alberta; or an enduring power of
> attorney. It would be necessary to establish that the relevant order or power of
> attorney purports to confer authority to sell the real property.

*Family dispute as to care of the person currently resident in your State (eg.
whether to return to England & Wales)*

> Through Guardianship or personal directive

Decision about medical treatment in your State

> Personal Directives Act that allows individuals to name a person(s) to make
> decisions on their behalf after they no longer have the capacity to make decisions,
> including written instructions. These instructions can include medical treatments one
> would or would not want and where they would like to live.
>
> If no personal directive then,
>
> A guardian, appointed by the Court, has the legal responsibility to make decisions
> for an adult who lacks the capacity to make personal decisions on health care.
>
> The Adult Guardianship and Trusteeship Act, defines Health care to includes:
>
> - any examination, diagnosis, procedure, or treatment undertaken to prevent or
>   manage any disease, illness, ailment or health condition;
>
> - any procedure undertaken for the purpose of an examination or diagnosis;
>
> - any medical, surgical, obstetrical or dental treatment;
>
> - anything done that is ancillary to any examination, diagnosis, procedure or
>   treatment;
>
> - any procedure undertake to prevent pregnancy, except sterilization that is not
>   medically necessary;
>
> - palliative care; and
>
> - A treatment plan.
>
> If a guardian has the authority to make health care decisions, he or she has full
> authority; equal to that of the adult if they were capable.

**B. Would the answers to A. above vary if person was not a national of the
United Kingdom but had been habitually resident in England and Wales
prior to their impairment or insufficiency?**

> No.

C. Is there an emergency procedure?

Yes, through emergency decision making (AGTA and PDA).

Under the AGTA, in cases of urgency the court may dispense with or modify any procedural requirements (e.g. documents to be filed or persons to be served) that would otherwise apply to an application under the Act. A guardianship or trusteeship order granted on such an urgent application must be reviewed within 90 days.

5. Sources of information

The Law Society of Alberta operates a lawyer referral service, but it does not include an online listing of lawyers by practice area. For more information about the referral service, see: http://www.lawsociety.ab.ca/public/lawyer_referral.aspx

General information about the law and procedure relating to incapable adults may be found at:

http://www.seniors.alberta.ca/opg/

http://justice.alberta.ca/programs_services/public_trustee/Pages/default.aspx

October 2010

CANADA: MANITOBA

Name of State	Canada: Manitoba			
Is your State part of a larger Federal country?		X	Yes	
If so, are any of the laws affecting Adults made at the level of the Federal Government?			X	No

The Mental Health Act; The Vulnerable Persons Living with a Mental Disability Act; The Health Care Directives Act; The Powers of Attorney Act.

Electronically available at

http://web2.gov.mb.ca/laws/index.php

Pursuant to s. 92(13) of the federal *Constitution Act* property and civil rights are solely within the jurisdiction of the provinces and territories of Canada.

1. Convention on the International Protection of Adults (Hague 2000)

Has this Convention been ratified by your State?			X	No
Is ratification subject to any reservations, declarations or notifications?	☐	Yes	☐	No
Does your State intend to ratify the Convention?	☐	Yes	☐	No
Even if not ratified is it generally applied in any event?	☐	Yes	☐	No

2. Jurisdiction

A. *Does jurisdiction of your Courts usually depend upon the Personal Law of the Adult?*

		X	No

B. *Can jurisdiction of the Courts in your State also depend upon:*

Habitual residence		X	Yes	
Domicile		X	Yes	
Nationality			X	No
Situs of property		X	Yes	
Presence in the State		X	Yes	

Explanation

Domicile is defined by The Domicile and Habitual Residence Act, ccsm c. D96

C. If the Courts of your State have jurisdiction, which internal law is applicable? That of:

Your State	X	Yes		

D. Does the internal law of your State have provision for Powers of Representation (also known as Continuing, Lasting or Durable Powers of Attorney) for the following:

Economic and financial matters	X	Yes		
Personal welfare			X	No
Health care and medical treatment	X	Yes		

The Powers of Attorney Act provides for enduring powers of attorney dealing with financial affairs only.

The Health Care Directives Act provides for the creation of a health care directive concerning medical treatment, and/or appointment of a proxy. Registration is not required.

The Powers of Attorney Act deals only with management of financial affairs. *The Health Care Directives Act* deals only with medical/treatment decisions. Manitoba does not have legislation that allows an attorney, proxy or other representative to make other personal decisions, unless he/she is appointed as committee or substitute decision maker in accordance with *The Mental Health Act* or *The Vulnerable Persons Living with a Mental Disability Act.*

Does an ordinary Power cease to be effective in the event of a lack of capacity?

Yes. In order for a power of attorney to be enduring, it must contain an "enduring clause" and be executed in accordance with the formalities set out in the Act.

E. Does your State include power for the Courts to make orders or decisions about:

Impairment or insufficiency of personal faculties (lack of capacity)	X	Yes		
Economic and financial matters	X	Yes		
Personal welfare	X	Yes		
Health care and medical treatment	X	Yes		
A new Will or Testament			X	No

PART X

If you have answered 'yes' to any of the above, please confirm whether the Courts may authorize another person (such as a guardian, curator, receiver or deputy) to make decisions on behalf of the Adult on the following matters:

Economic and financial matters	X	Yes		
Personal welfare	X	Yes		
Health care and medical treatment	X	Yes		
A new Will or Testament			X	No

If you have answered 'yes' to any of the above, and a person is authorized to make decisions on behalf of the Adult, please summarise the extent of that person's responsibility. For example, is there a duty to produce accounts to the Courts or other supervisory body? Does anyone oversee or monitor conduct? Are there any restrictions on what can or cannot be done in the name of the person who is incapable?

> *The Mental Health Act* and *Vulnerable Persons Living with a Mental Disability Act* both provide for administrative processes for the appointment of a committee or substitute decision maker for an adult. The Court of Queen's Bench may also appoint a committee for property or personal care of an adult. The appointment may be for property only, or both property and personal care. There is no provision in Manitoba for anyone other than an individual testator to make or amend a will.
>
> Private committees are required to pass accounts before the court, but there is no enforcement and it often does not happen.
>
> Private individuals appointed as Substitute Decision Maker (SDM) must provide a regular accounting to The Vulnerable Persons Commissioner, an official of The Department of Family Services and Consumer Affairs for Manitoba. The commissioner monitors receipt of the accounting.

3. Recognition of Powers of Representation / Continuing or Lasting Powers of Attorney and protective measures for Adults from England & Wales

A. Are the following Powers of Representation and delegations under the law of England & Wales recognised and enforceable:

Continuing Powers of Attorney for economic and financial matters	X	Yes		
Continuing Powers of Attorney for personal welfare			X	No
Continuing Powers of Attorney for healthcare and medical treatment	X	Yes		
Advance Directives	☐	Yes	☐	No

Are there any additional formalities required such as an Exequatur?

> s. 25 of *The Powers of Attorney Act* provides that a foreign enduring power of attorney is valid in Manitoba if:
>
> It is valid in accordance with the law of that place; and
>
> It provides that it is to continue despite the mental incompetence of the donor after execution.
>
> s. 10 of *The Health Care Directives Act* provides that a directive made outside Manitoba that complies with the requirements of the Act is deemed to be a directive made under the Act.

B. Are the following Protective Measures of the courts of England & Wales recognised and enforceable in your State?

Decision as to impairment or insufficiency of personal faculties	X	Yes		
Appointment of a Representative to deal with economic and financial matters	X	Yes		
Appointment of a Representative to deal with personal welfare			X	No
Appointment of a Representative to deal with health care and medical treatment	X	Yes		
Decision authorising the making of a new Will or Testament			X	No

Explanation

> Legislation in Manitoba does not recognize foreign appointments of committees or substitute decision makers. However, a committee, substitute decision maker or equivalent could apply to Court of Queen's Bench for an order recognizing the authority to deal with property or medical treatment.

4. Procedures in your State

A. How may the following situations be dealt with for a person with connections to England & Wales who by reason of an impairment or insufficiency of their personal faculties is not in a position to protect their interests.

Withdrawal of money from a bank account situated in your State

> A financial institution would develop its own policy as to whether to accept a 3rd party's authority to withdraw money from a bank account. Alternatively, the 3rd party may be required to obtain a court order.

PART X

Sale of a home or other property in your State

> A foreign enduring power of attorney would be accepted if it meets the requirements of *The Powers of Attorney Act. If there is no enduring power of attorney, a* 3rd party may apply to court to deal with real property.

Family dispute as to care of the person currently resident in your State (eg. whether to return to England & Wales)

> As a matter of practice, a decision of a close family member would be accepted, except in the case of a dispute or controversial issue. In that case, a committee or substitute decision maker would have to be appointed in Manitoba

Decision about medical treatment in your State

> As a matter of practice, most hospitals/physicians will accept the consent to treatment from a close relative, regardless of where he/she lives. However, in the case of a dispute or controversial decision, and if there is no valid health care directive, either a substitute decision maker/ committee would have to be appointed in Manitoba, or a court application would be required.

B. Would the answers to A. above vary if person was not a national of the United Kingdom but had been habitually resident in England and Wales prior to their impairment or insufficiency?

> No.

C. Is there an emergency procedure?

> The Mental Health Act and The Vulnerable Persons Living with a Mental Disability Act both contain emergency procedures.

5. Sources of information

> There is no website to provide names of lawyers. However, there is a Lawyer Referral Service that can be accessed by telephone or email. The website for further information about this service is:
>
> http://www.communitylegal.mb.ca/programs/
> law-phone-in-and-lawyer-referral-program/
>
> For information on the law and procedures see:
>
> Laws of Manitoba http://web2.gov.mb.ca/laws/index.php
>
> Public Trustee of Manitoba www.gov.mb.ca/publictrustee/

Completed by:

Name	JOANNA K. KNOWLTON

October 2010

CANADA: NOVA SCOTIA

Name of State	Canada: Nova Scotia				
Is your State part of a larger Federal country?		X	Yes		
If so, are any of the laws affecting Adults made at the level of the Federal Government?				X	No

1. Convention on the International Protection of Adults (Hague 2000)

Has this Convention been ratified by your State?				X	No
Does your State intend to ratify the Convention?		☐	Yes	☐	No
Even if not ratified is it generally applied in any event?		☐	Yes	☐	No

2. Jurisdiction

A. *Does jurisdiction of your Courts usually depend upon the Personal Law of the Adult?*

			X	No

B. *Can jurisdiction of the Courts in your State also depend upon:*

Habitual residence	X	Yes		
Domicile			X	No
Nationality			X	No
Situs of property	X	Yes		
Presence in the State	X	Yes		

C. *If the Courts of your State have jurisdiction, which internal law is applicable? That of:*

Your State	X	Yes		

D. Does the internal law of your State have provision for Powers of Representation (also known as Continuing, Lasting or Durable Powers of Attorney) for the following:

Economic and financial matters	x	Yes		
Personal welfare	x	Yes		
Health care and medical treatment	x	Yes		

Explanation

Does an ordinary Power cease to be effective in the event of a lack of capacity?
A Power of Attorney does cease to be effective during incapacity unless the document specifically states that it should not.

E. Does your State include power for the Courts to make orders or decisions about:

Impairment or insufficiency of personal faculties (lack of capacity)	X	Yes		
Economic and financial matters	X	Yes		
Personal welfare	X	Yes		
Health care and medical treatment	X	Yes		
A new Will or Testament			X	No

If you have answered 'yes' to any of the above, please confirm whether the Courts may authorize another person (such as a guardian, curator, receiver or deputy) to make decisions on behalf of the Adult on the following matters:

Economic and financial matters	X	Yes		
Personal welfare	X	Yes		
Health care and medical treatment	X	Yes		
A new Will or Testament			X	No

If you have answered 'yes' to any of the above, and a person is authorized to make decisions on behalf of the Adult, please summarise the extent of that person's responsibility. For example, is there a duty to produce accounts to the Courts or other supervisory body? Does anyone oversee or monitor conduct? Are there any restrictions on what can or cannot be done in the name of the person who is incapable?

PART X

- There is the duty to maintain accounts and to stand ready to account when requested or ordered by the Court;

- The Court monitors/supervises the accounts. The Public Trustee does not.

- The Guardian / trustee / attorney is not to benefit from the trust other than the normal trustee fees and disbursements necessary to manage the trust;

- The Guardian / trustee / attorney cannot be in a conflict of interest;

3. Recognition of Powers of Representation / Continuing or Lasting Powers of Attorney and protective measures for Adults from England & Wales

A. Are the following Powers of Representation and delegations under the law of England & Wales recognised and enforceable:

Continuing Powers of Attorney for economic and financial matters	X	Yes		
Continuing Powers of Attorney for personal welfare	X	Yes		
Continuing Powers of Attorney for healthcare and medical treatment	X	Yes		
Advance Directives	X	Yes		

Are there any additional formalities required such as an Exequatur?

Note: In order to deal with real property the Power of Attorney must comply with the laws of our jurisdiction as far as execution; affidavit in proof of execution in order to be recorded in the Registry of Deeds.

B. Are the following Protective Measures of the courts of England & Wales recognised and enforceable in your State?

Decision as to impairment or insufficiency of personal faculties	X	Yes		
Appointment of a Representative to deal with economic and financial matters	X	Yes		
Appointment of a Representative to deal with personal welfare	X	Yes		
Appointment of a Representative to deal with health care and medical treatment	X	Yes		
Decision authorising the making of a new Will or Testament			X	No

The order from the courts of England & Wales would have to be re-sealed in Nova Scotia by order of our Supreme Court. It is important to note that Guardians of financial affairs must be <u>bonded</u> in Nova Scotia.

4. Procedures in your State

A. *How may the following situations be dealt with.*

Withdrawal of money from a bank account situated in your State

Banks would require at minimum a certified copy of the enduring power of attorney or a certified copy of a Supreme Court order. The bank may or may not require it to be resealed.

Sale of a home or other property in your State

The Power of Attorney must meet Nova Scotia's statutory requirements. Any foreign Guardianship order would have to be re-sealed by the Supreme Court of Nova Scotia and bonding is required.

Family dispute as to care of the person currently resident in your State (eg. whether to return to England & Wales)

If there is a court appointed guardian of the person or a delegate named in a Personal Directive (An advance planning document for health and personal care) the guardian or the delegate would have the decision making power. An application may also be made to the Supreme Court of Nova Scotia under the Personal Directives Act or the Incompetent Persons Act to seek the court's direction.

Decision about medical treatment in your State

A court appointed Guardian of a person and delegate named in a Personal Directive has priority to make health care decisions. If neither exist, there is a statutory priority list.

B. *Would the answers to A. above vary if person was not a national of the United Kingdom but had been habitually resident in England and Wales prior to their impairment or insufficiency?*

No.

PART X

C. Is there an emergency procedure?

Application could be made to the Supreme Court on an emergency basis.

October 2010

CANADA: ONTARIO

Name of State	Canada: Ontario				
Is your State part of a larger Federal country?		X	Yes		
If so, are any of the laws affecting Adults made at the level of the Federal Government?				X	No
State/Provincial Level: Substitute Decisions Act; Health Care Consent Act, Mental Health Act, all available electronically at: http://www.e-laws.gov.on.ca/index.html. Under the federal Constitution Act, s. 92 (13), "property and civil rights" are matters solely within the legislative jurisdiction of the provinces and territories of Canada.					

1. Convention on the International Protection of Adults (Hague 2000)

Has this Convention been ratified by your State?			X	No
Does your State intend to ratify the Convention?	☐	Yes	☐	No
Even if not ratified is it generally applied in any event?	☐	Yes	☐	No

2. Jurisdiction

A. *Does jurisdiction of your Courts usually depend upon the Personal Law of the Adult?*

			X	No

B. *Can jurisdiction of the Courts in your State also depend upon:*

Habitual residence	X	Yes		
Domicile			X	No
Nationality			X	No
Situs of property	X	Yes		
Presence in the State	X	Yes		
A person must have a habitual residence, be physically situate or own property in the Province.				

C. If the Courts of your State have jurisdiction, which internal law is applicable? That of:

Your State	X	Yes		

D. Does the internal law of your State have provision for Powers of Representation (also known as Continuing, Lasting or Durable Powers of Attorney) for the following:

Economic and financial matters	x	Yes		
Personal welfare	x	Yes		
Health care and medical treatment	x	Yes		

Explanation

Does an ordinary Power cease to be effective in the event of a lack of capacity?
Powers of Attorney Act governs ordinary (fixed term or specific event) powers of attorney, which, if not stated to survive incapacity, would terminate on incapacity.

E. Does your State include power for the Courts to make orders or decisions about:

Impairment or insufficiency of personal faculties (lack of capacity)	X	Yes		
Economic and financial matters	X	Yes		
Personal welfare	X	Yes		
Health care and medical treatment	X	Yes		
A new Will or Testament			X	No

If you have answered 'yes' to any of the above, please confirm whether the Courts may authorize another person (such as a guardian, curator, receiver or deputy) to make decisions on behalf of the Adult on the following matters:

Economic and financial matters	X	Yes		
Personal welfare	X	Yes		
Health care and medical treatment	X	Yes		
A new Will or Testament			X	No

If you have answered 'yes' to any of the above, and a person is authorized to make decisions on behalf of the Adult, please summarise the extent of that person's responsibility. For example, is there a duty to produce accounts to the Courts or other supervisory body? Does anyone oversee or monitor conduct? Are there any restrictions on what can or cannot be done in the name of the person who is incapable?

•	Duty to maintain accounts and "pass accounts" with Court if so ordered;
•	Guardian or attorney for property cannot make a Will or testamentary document;
•	Guardian or trustee is a fiduciary so cannot act in a conflict of interest;
•	Public Guardian and Trustee can investigate allegations of risk of serious adverse effects if guardian or attorney is mismanaging or acting fraudulently;
•	No ongoing active monitoring unless regular periodic accountings are ordered by the Court.

3. Recognition of Powers of Representation / Continuing or Lasting Powers of Attorney and protective measures for Adults from England & Wales

A. Are the following Powers of Representation and delegations under the law of England & Wales recognised and enforceable:

Continuing Powers of Attorney for economic and financial matters	X	Yes		
Continuing Powers of Attorney for personal welfare	X	Yes		
Continuing Powers of Attorney for healthcare and medical treatment	X	Yes		
Advance Directives	X	Yes		

Are there any additional formalities required such as an Exequatur?

Ontario has no required form of a continuing power of attorney. If a document created in England and Wales meets the formal statutory requirements of the Ontario *Substitute Decisions Act,* it could be recognized in Ontario without further formality.

PART X

B. Are the following Protective Measures of the courts of England & Wales recognised and enforceable in your State?

Decision as to impairment or insufficiency of personal faculties	X	Yes		
Appointment of a Representative to deal with economic and financial matters	X	Yes		
Appointment of a Representative to deal with personal welfare	X	Yes		
Appointment of a Representative to deal with health care and medical treatment	X	Yes		
Decision authorising the making of a new Will or Testament			X	No

An order of a foreign Court (outside the province of Ontario) must be re-sealed in Ontario by the Ontario Superior Court of Justice under s. 86 of the *Substitute Decisions Act*, before it can have effect in Ontario.

4. Procedures in your State

A. How may the following situations be dealt with.

Withdrawal of money from a bank account situated in your State

Bank or financial institution would require a court order appointing a guardian of property (either made in Ontario or re-sealed in Ontario) or continuing power of attorney. Once satisfied of the authority, money is generally considered to be "moveables" under conflicts of laws provisions and could be transferred out of Ontario with the bank's permission.

Sale of a home or other property in your State

Sale of real estate requires a guardianship order (either made in Ontario or re-sealed in Ontario) or continuing power of attorney for property which meets Ontario's statutory requirements.

Family dispute as to care of the person currently resident in your State (eg. whether to return to England & Wales)

Would be governed by a court order appointing a guardian for personal care (with authority to decide living arrangements and shelter) under s.59(1) of the *Substitute Decisions Act*; or an advance direction signed when the person was capable; or a continuing power of attorney for personal care specifying a direction regarding living arrangements.

Decision about medical treatment in your State

> Governed by the *Health Care Consent Act, 1996, s. 20(1)*. Guardians & attorneys
> have priority to make decisions for incapable adults. If neither, there is a statutory
> priority of relatives (spouse, parents, siblings, children, etc.).

**B. Would the answers to A. above vary if person was not a national of the
United Kingdom but had been habitually resident in England and Wales
prior to their impairment or insufficiency?**

> No; jurisdiction in Ontario is based on physical presence in Ontario or owning land
> or having property in Ontario.

C. Is there an emergency procedure?

> Could obtain an expedited hearing date from the Ontario Superior Court of Justice if
> a court order was required (if no power of attorney or guardianship in place yet).

5. Sources of information

> List of lawyers would be available from the Law Society of Upper Canada, Lawyer
> Referral Service, http://www.lsuc.on.ca/faq.aspx?id=1146 (but lawyers not listed on
> site).
>
> Information on law and procedure relating to incapable adults:
> http://www.attorneygeneral.jus.gov.on.ca/english/family/pgt/incapacity/default.asp

October 21, 2010

PART X

CANADA: SASKATCHEWAN

Name of State	Canada: Saskatchewan				
Is your State part of a larger Federal country?		X	Yes		
If so, are any of the laws affecting Adults made at the level of the Federal Government?				X	No

State/Provincial Level: Public Guardian and Trustee Act, Adult Guardianship and Co-decision-making Act, Health Care Directives and Substitute Health Care Decision Makers Act, all available electronically at: http://www.justice.gov.sk.ca/PGT-leg

Under the Federal Constitution Act, s. 92 (13), "property and civil rights" are matters solely within the legislative jurisdiction of the provinces and territories of Canada.

1. Convention on the International Protection of Adults (Hague 2000)

Has this Convention been ratified by your State?				X	No
Is ratification subject to any reservations, declarations or notifications?	☐	Yes	☐	No	
Does your State intend to ratify the Convention?	☐	Yes	☐	No	
Even if not ratified is it generally applied in any event?	☐	Yes	☐	No	

2. Jurisdiction

A. *Does jurisdiction of your Courts usually depend upon the Personal Law of the Adult?*

		X	No

B. *Can jurisdiction of the Courts in your State also depend upon:*

Habitual residence	X	Yes		
Domicile			X	No
Nationality			X	No
Situs of property	X	Yes		
Presence in the State	X	Yes		

A person must have a habitual residence, be physically situated or own property in the Province.

C. If the Courts of your State have jurisdiction, which internal law is applicable? That of:

Your State	x	Yes		

D. Does the internal law of your State have provision for Powers of Representation (also known as Continuing, Lasting or Durable Powers of Attorney) for the following:

Economic and financial matters	x	Yes		
Personal welfare	x	Yes		
Health care and medical treatment	x	Yes		

Does an ordinary Power cease to be effective in the event of a lack of capacity? Powers of Attorney Act governs ordinary (fixed term or specific event) powers of attorney, which, if not stated to survive incapacity, would terminate on incapacity.

E. Does your State include power for the Courts to make orders or decisions about:

Impairment or insufficiency of personal faculties (lack of capacity)	X	Yes		
Economic and financial matters	X	Yes		
Personal welfare	X	Yes		
Health care and medical treatment	X	Yes		
A new Will or Testament			X	No

If you have answered 'yes' to any of the above, please confirm whether the Courts may authorize another person (such as a guardian, curator, receiver or deputy) to make decisions on behalf of the Adult on the following matters:

Economic and financial matters	X	Yes		
Personal welfare	X	Yes		
Health care and medical treatment	X	Yes		
A new Will or Testament			X	No

If you have answered 'yes' to any of the above, and a person is authorized to make decisions on behalf of the Adult, please summarise the extent of that person's responsibility. For example, is there a duty to produce accounts to the Courts or other supervisory body? Does anyone oversee or monitor conduct? Are there any restrictions on what can or cannot be done in the name of the person who is incapable?

•	Duty to maintain accounts and file annual accountings with the Court and PGT;
•	Guardian or attorney for property cannot make a Will or testamentary document;
•	Guardian or trustee is a fiduciary so cannot act in a conflict of interest;
•	Public Guardian and Trustee can investigate allegations of serious financial abuse;
•	No ongoing active monitoring unless the Court orders regular periodic accountings. PGT reviews property guardian accountings and applies for removal if improperly done.

3. Recognition of Powers of Representation / Continuing or Lasting Powers of Attorney and protective measures for Adults from England & Wales

A. Are the following Powers of Representation and delegations under the law of England & Wales recognised and enforceable:

Continuing Powers of Attorney for economic and financial matters	X	Yes		
Continuing Powers of Attorney for personal welfare	X	Yes		
Continuing Powers of Attorney for healthcare and medical treatment	X	Yes		
Advance Directives	X	Yes		

Are there any additional formalities required such as an Exequatur?

An advanced directive must also be made in accordance with *The Health Care Directives and Health Care Substitute Decision Makers Act.*

B. Are the following Protective Measures of the courts of England & Wales recognized and enforceable in your State?

Decision as to impairment or insufficiency of personal faculties			X	No
Appointment of a Representative to deal with economic and financial matters			X	No

Appointment of a Representative to deal with personal welfare			X	No
Appointment of a Representative to deal with health care and medical treatment			X	No
Decision authorizing the making of a new Will or Testament			X	No

Explanation

Please specify any limitations.

The province is considering a leasing of foreign orders provision but it is not yet in the legislative process.

4. Procedures in your State

A. *How may the following situations be dealt with.*

Withdrawal of money from a bank account situated in your State

Bank or financial institution would require a court order appointing a guardian of property (an order made in Canada) or enduring power of attorney. Once satisfied of the authority, money is generally considered to be "movables".

Sale of a home or other property in your State

Sale of real estate requires a guardianship order (either made in Saskatchewan or re-sealed in Saskatchewan) or enduring power of attorney for property which meets Saskatchewan s statutory requirements.

Family dispute as to care of the person currently resident in your State (eg. whether to return to England & Wales)

Would be governed by a court order appointing a guardian for personal care (with authority to decide living arrangements and shelter) or an enduring personal power of attorney.

Decision about medical treatment in your State

The Health Care Directives and Health Care Substitute Decision Makers Act has a statutory priority of relatives (spouse, parents, siblings, children, etc.).

PART X

B. Would the answers to A. above vary if person was not a national of the United Kingdom but had been habitually resident in England and Wales prior to their impairment or insufficiency?

> No; jurisdiction in Saskatchewan is based on physical presence in Saskatchewan or owning land or having property in Saskatchewan.

C. Is there an emergency procedure?

> If no power of attorney or guardianship was in place, a temporary personal or property guardianship order could be obtained.

5. Sources of information

> Information can be found at the Public Guardian and Trustee web site at http://www.justice.gov.sk.ca/pgt

Completed by:

Name	Ronald J. Kruzeniski, Q.C.
eMail	Ron.Kruzeniski@gov.sk.ca

Are you a solicitor/notary/advocate or lawyer who provides legal advice and services for nationals of the United Kingdom in your State?			X	No

October 21, 2010

DENMARK

Name of State	Denmark				
Is your State part of a larger Federal country?				X	No

Specify the areas of the law dealt with at State level and at Federal level.

The communities of the Faroe Islands and Greenland have their own rules to a certain extent.

1. Convention on the International Protection of Adults (Hague 2000)

Has this Convention been ratified by your State?				X	No

2. Jurisdiction

A. *Does jurisdiction of your Courts usually depend upon the Personal Law of the Adult?*

	X	Yes	
If so, which is usually the relevant connecting factor?			
Habitual residence	X	Yes	

B. *Can jurisdiction of the Courts in your State also depend upon:*

Presence in the State	X	Yes	

Presence is accepted as a ground of jurisdiction if the adult does not have his or her habitual residence in Denmark

C. *If the Courts of your State have jurisdiction, which internal law is applicable? That of:*

Your State	X	Yes	

Danish Courts and administrative authorities always apply Danish law as the *lex fori*.

PART X

D. Does the internal law of your State have provision for Powers of Representation (also known as Continuing, Lasting or Durable Powers of Attorney) for the following:

Economic and financial matters			X	No
Personal welfare			X	No
Health care and medical treatment			X	No

Explanation

There is no Danish legislation about powers of attorney. There is some evidence, – appeal court cases – that they are recognized in practice, but to what extent is uncertain.
Does an ordinary Power cease to be effective in the event of a lack of capacity?
No

E. Does your State include power for the Courts to make orders or decisions about:

Impairment or insufficiency of personal faculties (lack of capacity)	X	Yes		
Economic and financial matters	X	Yes		
Personal welfare	X	Yes		
Health care and medical treatment	X	Yes		
A new Will or Testament			X	No

If you have answered 'yes' to any of the above, please confirm whether the Courts may authorize another person (such as a guardian, curator, receiver or deputy) to make decisions on behalf of the Adult on the following matters:

Economic and financial matters	X			
Personal welfare	X			
Health care and medical treatment	X			
A new Will or Testament			X	No

If you have answered 'yes' to any of the above, and a person is authorized to make decisions on behalf of the Adult, please summarise the extent of that person's responsibility. For example, is there a duty to produce accounts to the Courts or other supervisory body? Does anyone oversee or monitor conduct? Are there any restrictions on what can or cannot be done in the name of the person who is incapable?

Please list the procedures

> The decisions are made by statsforvaltningen, five administrative bodies in Denmark, if the decision only is to appoint a representative and there are no objections. The decision may be brought before a court for a complete new process. A decision to remove the legal capacity is always made by the court.

> There is a duty for the guardian to produce accounts. Usual decisions, including some listed as selling or buying real estate, has to be approved by statsforvaltningen. A guardian cannot make decisions that imply use of force or detention.

3. Recognition of Powers of Representation / Continuing or Lasting Powers of Attorney and protective measures for Adults from England & Wales

A. Are the following Powers of Representation and delegations under the law of England & Wales recognised and enforceable:

Continuing Powers of Attorney for economic and financial matters	☐	Yes	☐	No
Continuing Powers of Attorney for personal welfare	☐	Yes	☐	No
Continuing Powers of Attorney for healthcare and medical treatment	☐	Yes	☐	No
Advance Directives	☐	Yes	☐	No

Are there any additional formalities required such as an Exequatur?

> Foreign powers are recognized provided the foreign authority or court had indirect, international jurisdiction (that is to say very similar rules of jurisdiction as the Danish rules); and the power are not against Danish public policy.

> Foreign powers are also accepted even if the foreign authority did not have indirect, international jurisdiction, provided the foreign powers is issued by a court or authority from the person's State of nationality and provided the power is recognized in the State where the person has his habitual residence.

PART X

B. Are the following Protective Measures of the courts of England & Wales recognised and enforceable in your State?

Decision as to impairment or insufficiency of personal faculties	☐ Yes	☐ No
Appointment of a Representative to deal with economic and financial matters	☐ Yes	☐ No
Appointment of a Representative to deal with personal welfare	☐ Yes	☐ No
Appointment of a Representative to deal with health care and medical treatment	☐ Yes	☐ No
Decision authorising the making of a new Will or Testament	☐ Yes	☐ No

Explanation

In the literature it is simply stated that foreign court decisions on guardianship are recognized. Accordingly they may be enforced, although it is difficult to imagine when that might be the case.

4. Procedures in your State

A. How may the following situations be dealt with:

Withdrawal of money from a bank account situated in your State

The situation is uncertain – no practice.

Sale of a home or other property in your State

If the person under guardianship has domicile in Denmark, approval of statsforvaltningen is needed.

Decision about medical treatment in your State

Danish doctors will apply the Danish legislation on patients rights.

B. Would the answers to A. above vary if person was not a national of the United Kingdom but had been habitually resident in England and Wales prior to their impairment or insufficiency?

?

C. Is there an emergency procedure?

Yes

Completed by:

Name	compiled from a number of responses

October 2010

FINLAND

Name of State	Finland				
Is your State part of a larger Federal country?				x	No

1. Convention on the International Protection of Adults (Hague 2000)

Has this Convention been ratified by your State?		x	Yes		
Is ratification subject to any reservations, declarations or notifications?				x	No

Explanation

The Convention enters into force for Finland 1.3.2011. The following description on Finnish private international law regarding protection of adults refers to the situation that occurs from that date.

2. Jurisdiction

A. Does jurisdiction of your Courts usually depend upon the Personal Law of the Adult?

		X	Yes		
If so, which is usually the relevant connecting factor?					
Habitual residence		X	Yes		

B. Can jurisdiction of the Courts in your State also depend upon:

Domicile				X	No
Nationality		X	Yes		
Situs of property		X	Yes		
Presence in the State		X	Yes		

Explanation

With minor exceptions Finland applies the grounds of jurisdiction existing in the Hague Convention of 2000 generally i.e. also in cases, where the Convention is not applicable.

C. If the Courts of your State have jurisdiction, which internal law is applicable? That of:

Your State	X	Yes		

Explanation

As regards applicable law, Finland applies the provisions in Chapter III of the Hague Convention.

D. Does the internal law of your State have provision for Powers of Representation (also known as Continuing, Lasting or Durable Powers of Attorney) for the following:

Economic and financial matters	X	Yes		
Personal welfare	X	Yes		
Health care and medical treatment	X	Yes		

Explanation

According to Finnish Act on continuing powers of attorney (Laki edunvalvontavaltuutuksesta (648/2007)) the powers become effective only after registration in the Local Register Office (maistraatti). Registration is possible, when the adult has for the most part become unable to take care of the matters covered by the powers of attorney.
An ordinary power based on "normal" letter of credentials ceases to be effective, when the grantor is declared incapable. If the grantor is declared incapable only in certain matters, which is possible according to Finnish Guardianship Act (442/1999), the letter ceases to be effective in these matters. A mere de facto loss of capacity does not have this effect.

E. Does your State include power for the Courts to make orders or decisions about:

Impairment or insufficiency of personal faculties (lack of capacity)	X	Yes		
Economic and financial matters	X	Yes		
Personal welfare	X	Yes		
Health care and medical treatment	X	Yes		
A new Will or Testament			X	No

PART X

If you have answered 'yes' to any of the above, please confirm whether the Courts may authorize another person (such as a guardian, curator, receiver or deputy) to make decisions on behalf of the Adult on the following matters:

Economic and financial matters	X	Yes		
Personal welfare	X	Yes		
Health care and medical treatment	X	Yes		
A new Will or Testament			X	No

Please list the procedures

The Local Register Office monitors the conduct of the representative. If the right of representation covers economic and financial matters, the representative must submit an inventory on the property of the adult to the Office and keep it updated. He also have to give an account on the administration of the property every year, if the Office has not prolonged the interval or given other relief.

The representative (curator) may not represent the adult in matters which are highly personal such as giving consent to marriage, giving consent to adoption of the child of the adult or making a will on behalf of the adult. The representative may not give donations from the property of the adult.

3. Recognition of Powers of Representation / Continuing or Lasting Powers of Attorney and protective measures for Adults from England & Wales

A. Are the following Powers of Representation and delegations under the law of England & Wales recognised and enforceable:

Continuing Powers of Attorney for economic and financial matters	☐	Yes	☐	No
Continuing Powers of Attorney for personal welfare	☐	Yes	☐	No
Continuing Powers of Attorney for healthcare and medical treatment	☐	Yes	☐	No
Advance Directives	☐	Yes	☐	No

Are there any additional formalities required such as an Exequatur?

We do not see this as a question of recognition but as a question of applicable law. If the powers of representation are existing under the law which, according to Article 15 of the Hague Convention is applied to such powers, then they are valid also in Finland provided that the application of that law is not against public policy or mandatory provisions in Finnish law.

B. Are the following Protective Measures of the courts of England & Wales recognised and enforceable in your State?

Decision as to impairment or insufficiency of personal faculties	X	Yes		
Appointment of a Representative to deal with economic and financial matters	X	Yes		
Appointment of a Representative to deal with personal welfare	X	Yes		
Appointment of a Representative to deal with health care and medical treatment	X	Yes		
Decision authorising the making of a new Will or Testament	☐	Yes	☐	No

Explanation

The measures are recognized and enforceable, unless there are grounds of refusal. With respect to health care and medical treatment there are mandatory provisions in Finnish patient law, which may lead to non-recognition of a foreign measure.

It is unclear, whether a measure authorizing the making of a will would be recognized. It is not excluded that such measure were considered to be against public policy. The question of characterization is also relevant here. It is unclear, whether that question is governed by the *lex protectionis* or by *lex successionis*.

4. Procedures in your State

A. How may the following situations be dealt with

Withdrawal of money from a bank account situated in your State

The representative may make the withdrawals if the measure is recognized in Finland or the powers of attorney are existing under the applicable law.

Sale of a home or other property in your State

If the Finnish guardianship legislation is applicable, the consent of Local Register Office is needed for the sale of real property or home of the adult. There are also other legal transactions which are considered to involve such risks that consent of the Office is needed. The main rule, however, is that the representative may freely dispose of the property of the adult.

PART X

Family dispute as to care of the person currently resident in your State (eg. whether to return to England & Wales)

> If the person has attained the age of 18 years, there is no procedure for such family dispute.

Decision about medical treatment in your State

> The doctor makes the decision. The consent of the patient is needed. If the patient is not able to give an informed consent, the legal representative or close relative of the patient may give the consent.

B. Would the answers to A. above vary if person was not a national of the United Kingdom but had been habitually resident in England and Wales prior to their impairment or insufficiency?

> No.

C. Is there an emergency procedure?

> Yes. See Article 10 of the Hague Convention.

5. Sources of information

> As to Finnish legislation concerning protection of adults (in Finnish and Swedish) see the database www.finlex.fi.
>
> Between the States that are parties to the Hague Convention of 2000 the Finnish Central Authority may be able to give advise on legislation and procedures and available lawyers. With regard to contact details, see the web pages of the Hague Conference.

Completed by:

Name	Markku Helin

October 2010

FRANCE

Name of State	France				
Is your State part of a larger Federal country?			Yes	X	No

1. Convention on the International Protection of Adults (Hague 2000)

Has this Convention been ratified by your State?	X	Yes		
Is ratification subject to any reservations, declarations or notifications?	X	Yes		

France has made three Declarations in relation to paragraph 1 article 28, paragraph 2 article 32 and article 42 of the Hague Convention.

Paragraph 1 article 28- the State has defined the meaning of "central authority"

Paragraph 2 article 32- the State has declared that a request for information should be directed to the "central French authority"

Article 42- the State has declared that a request made under article 8 and 33 should be addressed to the *Procureur de la République* of the Court which is competent to determine which measure of protection should be put in place.

2. Jurisdiction

A. *Does jurisdiction of your Courts usually depend upon the Personal Law of the Adult?*

	X	Yes		
If so, which is usually the relevant connecting factor?				
Nationality	X	Yes		

B. *Can jurisdiction of the Courts in your State also depend upon:*

Habitual residence	X	Yes		

C. *If the Courts of your State have jurisdiction, which internal law is applicable? That of:*

Your State			X	No
Habitual residence	X	Yes		
Domicile			X	No

PART X

| Nationality | | X | Yes | | |
| Situs of property | | | | X | No |

Explanation

The French court will apply the law of the adult's nationality. Article 3 of the French Civil Code provides that issues of capacity are governed by the law of the adult's nationality.

However, the application of the law of the nationality can cause some practical problems and therefore, the rules applicable can be adapted. For example, the Court can decide that if the French rules of the "*curatelle*" have similar effects with the German rules of "*curatelle*", the French rules of incapacity can be applied to a German national. The same would apply to a French national living in Germany. The application of "renvoi" in respect of a Canadian national domiciled in France has had the effect of applying French law to a Canadian national.

It is also possible to apply French law in the event of a renvoi.

D. Does the internal law of your State have provision for Powers of Representation (also known as Continuing, Lasting or Durable Powers of Attorney) for the following:

Economic and financial matters		X	Yes		
Personal welfare		X	Yes		
Health care and medical treatment		X	Yes		

Explanation

The French equivalent of Powers of Representation is known as *mandat de protection future ("MPF")*. This came into force on 1st January 2009.

The provisions that an individual can make in respect of Health care and medical treatment are limited by the rules contained in the French Code of Public Health. Similarly, provisions made in respect of financial matters are limited to those that a "*tuteur*" can accomplish.

Does an ordinary Power cease to be effective in the event of a lack of capacity?

Yes.

E. Does your State include power for the Courts to make orders or decisions about:

Impairment or insufficiency of personal faculties (lack of capacity)	X	Yes		
Economic and financial matters	X	Yes		
Personal welfare	X	Yes		
Health care and medical treatment	X	Yes		
A new Will or Testament			X	No

If you have answered 'yes' to any of the above, please confirm whether the Courts may authorize another person (such as a guardian, curator, receiver or deputy) to make decisions on behalf of the Adult on the following matters:

Economic and financial matters	X	Yes		
Personal welfare	X	Yes		
Health care and medical treatment	X	Yes		
A new Will or Testament		Yes	X	No

If you have answered 'yes' to any of the above, and a person is authorized to make decisions on behalf of the Adult, please summarise the extent of that person's responsibility. For example, is there a duty to produce accounts to the Courts or other supervisory body? Does anyone oversee or monitor conduct? Are there any restrictions on what can or cannot be done in the name of the person who is incapable?

Please list the procedures

The powers of the *tuteur* depend upon the type of act to be carried out i.e. he can act independently, or must obtain the agreement of the *subrogé tuteur*, or must obtain the consent of the family committee or must comply with specific formalities

He can make conservatory acts or administration acts (e.g. consent to a lease, carry out an inventory) which are necessary for the management of the adult's assets. He is not authorized to dispose of the adult's assets without obtaining the agreement of the Judge. (articles 503- 509 of the French Civil code). The Tuteur must produce accounts annually and provide receipts. His accounts are submitted to the Court, reviewed and approved if applicable (article 510).

PART X

3. Recognition of Powers of Representation / Continuing or Lasting Powers of Attorney and protective measures for Adults from England & Wales

A. Are the following Powers of Representation and delegations under the law of England & Wales recognised and enforceable:

Continuing Powers of Attorney for economic and financial matters	X	Yes		
Continuing Powers of Attorney for personal welfare	X	Yes		
Continuing Powers of Attorney for healthcare and medical treatment	X	Yes		
Advance Directives	☐	Yes	☐	No

Are there any additional formalities required such as an Exequatur?

No.

B. Are the following Protective Measures of the courts of England & Wales recognised and enforceable in your State?

Decision as to impairment or insufficiency of personal faculties	X	Yes		
Appointment of a Representative to deal with economic and financial matters	X	Yes		
Appointment of a Representative to deal with personal welfare	X	Yes		
Appointment of a Representative to deal with health care and medical treatment	X	Yes		
Decision authorising the making of a new Will or Testament			X	No

Explanation

The Protective Measures of the Courts do not require the obtaining of Exequatur as this relates to capacity.
Please specify any limitations.
However, the decision must take into account the applicable law in accordance with the rules of French private international law dealing with adult incapacity.

4. Procedures in your State

A. *How may the following situations be dealt with:*

Withdrawal of money from a bank account situated in your State

> Order from the court of England & Wales if habitually resident there.

Sale of a home or other property in your State

> The personal law of the adult who lacks capacity will apply in the event of a sale of immoveable properties situated in France. The Notaire will require sight of the LPA (sealed copy and translation) to ensure that the person selling the property on behalf of the adult is entitled to do so under the adult personal law. If no EPA or LPA, then an order of the English court will be required.

Family dispute as to care of the person currently resident in your State (eg. whether to return to England & Wales)

> Order from the court of England & Wales if habitually resident there.

Decision about medical treatment in your State

> The medical protection of the adult is organized by the *Juge des Tutelles* who takes into consideration the doctor's opinion. The Judge will consider the provisions of the Code of Public Health, which provides that the consent of the adult must always be sought if he is capable of expressing his will and can take part in the decision (article L.1111-4, 7e).
>
> When the consent of the adult cannot be obtained his "*tuteur*" can agree to the medical treatment on his behalf to the extent that it does not violate the integrity of the adult. A simple check up can be agreed by the "*tuteur*", however a surgery which could have a major impact on the life of the adult will be agreed by the Judge with reference to the doctor's opinion.
>
> The Public Health code provides that in the event of a "*tuteur*" refusing the adult to be treated and when such decision could have some vital consequences on the life of the adult, the doctor will treat the adult as necessary.

B. *Would the answers to A. above vary if person was not a national of the United Kingdom but had been habitually resident in England and Wales prior to their impairment or insufficiency?*

> No.

PART X

C. Is there an emergency procedure?

The *sauvegarde de justice* is an emergency measure which provides for a temporary need of protection. The measure is valid for a maximum of one year and renewable once.

Completed by:

Name	**Dawn Alderson & Emilie Totic**
eMail	**helpdesk@russell-cooke.co.uk**

October 2010

GERMANY

Name of State	Federal Republic of Germany			
Is your State part of a larger Federal country?		X	Yes	
If so, are any of the laws affecting Adults made at the level of the Federal Government?		X	Yes	

In Germany, **substantive law questions of capacity and incapacity, guardianship and custodianship** are regarded as belonging to private law, so that it is subject to concurrent legislation according to article 74, paragraph 1, number 1 GG (Grundgesetz – the German Constitution). Since the Federal Legislator has made use of his legislative rights by creating sections 1, 104, number 2, 105a, 1896-1908k BGB (Bürgerliches Gesetzbuch – the German Civil Code – free English version available at www.gesetze-im-internet.de/englisch_bgb/index.html), these questions are part of the Federal law.

The only exception consists of the substantive law concerning **involuntary commitment**, as this is governed by state laws such as the Bavarian "Gesetz über die Unterbringung psychisch Kranker und deren Betreuung" (Act on the Involuntary Commitment of Mentally Ill Persons and their Treatment) of April 5th, 1992, or the Lower Saxonian "Gesetz über Hilfen und Schutzmaßnahmen für psychisch Kranke" (Act on Help and Protective Measures for Mentally Ill Persons) of June 16th, 1997, because it is regarded as being part of police law. These acts, however, do not become relevant in cases of an accommodation based on the decision of a custodian and approved by the custodianship court (section 1906 BGB).

The **law of procedure** is also subject to concurrent legislation according to article 74, paragraph 1, number 1 GG. Insofar, the issues in question are dealt with at Federal level exclusively. As of September 1st, 2009, sections 271-311 FamFG (Gesetz über das Verfahren in Familiensachen und in den Angelegenheiten der freiwilligen Gerichtsbarkeit – Act on the Procedure in Family Matters and in Matters of Non-Contentious Jurisdiction) of December, 17th, 2008, contain the procedural provisions on the appointment of a custodian. Sections 312-341 FamFG concern the procedure on accommodation and involuntary commitment on both Federal and State level.

As far as **private international law** is concerned, the provisions applicable are to be found in the **Hague Convention on the International Protection of Adults** (see below) and – in cases where the Convention is not applicable – in **articles 7 EGBGB** (Einführungsgesetz zum Bürgerlichen Gesetzbuch – Introductory Act to the Civil Code; article 7 concerns capacity itself), **12 EGBGB** (on the protection of the other part of the contract in cases of incapacity – similar to article 13 of the Regulation Rome I), and **24 EGBGB** (on guardianship, custodianship, and curatorship). Private International Law is exclusively part of the Federal Law. Recognition and enforcement of foreign decisions in the area in question are to be found in sections 108 and 109 FamFG, where the Convention is not applicable.

PART X

1. Convention on the International Protection of Adults (Hague 2000)

Has this Convention been ratified by your State?		X	Yes	

Explanation

> The **Convention on the International Protection of Adults** has been ratified by
> Germany through the "Gesetz zu dem Haager Übereinkommen über den
> internationalen Schutz von Erwachsenen" of March 17th, 2007 (BGBl.
> [Bundesgesetzblatt = the German Federal Law Gazette] 2007 II, p. 323). It came into
> force on January 1st, 2009, and is accompanied by the "Gesetz zur Umsetzung des
> Haager Übereinkommens vom 13. Januar 2000 über den internationalen Schutz von
> Erwachsenen" (Act on the **Implementation** of the Hague Convention on the
> International Protection of Adults) of March 17th, 2007 (BGBl. 2007 I, p. 314, last
> changed by articles 46 and 110a of the "Gesetz zur Reform des Verfahrens in
> Familiensachen und in den Angelegenheiten der freiwilligen Gerichtsbarkeit
> (FGG-Reformgesetz)" of December, 17th, 2008), which designates the "Bundesamt
> für Justiz" as the Central Authority according to article 28 of the convention,
> provides provisions on local and subject matter jurisdiction of the
> "Betreuungsgerichte" (custodianship courts), and regulates the procedure of
> recognition according to articles 23 and 25 of the Convention.

2. Jurisdiction

A. *Does jurisdiction of your Courts usually depend upon the Personal Law of the Adult?*

	X	Yes		
If so, which is usually the relevant connecting factor?				
Habitual residence	X	Yes		
Domicile			X	No
Nationality	X	Yes		

B. *Can jurisdiction of the Courts in your State also depend upon:*

Habitual residence	X	Yes		
Domicile			X	No
Nationality	X	Yes		
Situs of property	X	Yes		
Presence in the State	X	Yes		

Explanation

As far as capacity, incapacity, and custodianship are concerned, **domicile** as a connecting factor is of no relevance. As to the connecting factors playing a role in the area of capacity, incapacity and custodianship, one must differentiate between the cases in which the Convention on the International Protection of Adults is applicable and the cases in which it is not:

Within the scope of the Convention, jurisdiction is primarily based on **habitual residence**, article 5, paragraphs 1 and 2 of the Convention. Where a habitual residence does not exist or cannot be ascertained, jurisdiction can be secondarily based on the simple presence of the adult in the state according to article 6 of the Convention. The presence in the state is also relevant with regard to urgent or temporary measures in terms of articles 10 and 11 of the Convention. The situs of property constitutes a connecting factor for measures of protection of the adult's property, article 9 of the Convention, as well as for urgent cases according to its article 10.

Where the Convention is not applicable, international jurisdiction is based on section 104 FamFG. In these cases **nationality** and **habitual residence** serve as co-ordinate alternative connecting factors, section 104, paragraph 1, sentence 1, numbers 1 and 2 FamFG. Apart from that, German courts are competent insofar as the adult is **in need of their assistance** according to section 104, paragraph 1, sentence 2 FamFG. This regulation intends to consider cases where the adult does not fulfill the requirements of nationality or habitual residence, but is only present in the state. Therefore, this connecting factor is regarded as providing jurisdiction for urgent and temporary measures only. However, this view is not unchallenged because section 104, paragraph 1, sentence 2 FamFG does not provide any explicit restriction.

As to the scope of this regulation, it is argued that the adult has to be regarded as being in need of the assistance of German courts already in situations where German substantive law is applicable. Since there are no decisions regarding this problem at the moment, the situation is relatively unclear insofar.

C. If the Courts of your State have jurisdiction, which internal law is applicable? That of:

Your State	X	Yes		
Habitual residence	X	Yes		
Domicile			X	No
Nationality	X	Yes		
Situs of property	X	Yes		

Explanation

If international jurisdiction lies with German courts, a **differentiation** must be made between the situations in which the Convention on the International Protection of Adults is applicable on the one hand and the cases where it is not on the other.

Within the scope of applicability of the Convention, the law applicable is the lex fori according to article 13, paragraph 1 of the Convention. Beyond that, article 13, paragraph 2 of the Convention provides the opportunity of exceptionally applying or taking into consideration the law of another State with which a substantial connection exists in certain cases. Insofar, the connecting factor is not specified, so that any kind of substantial connection may suffice.

Regarding the **powers of representation**, the habitual residence of the adult provides the connecting factor according to article 15, paragraph 1 of the Convention, if there has been no express written designation of the law applicable by the adult. The choice of law insofar may only refer to the law of the State of nationality, the law of the State of a former habitual residence of the adult, or the law of the State, in which property of the adult is located, the latter only insofar as the property itself is concerned.

Internal German private international law provides nationality as the primary connecting factor for measures concerning guardianship and custodianship according to article 24, paragraph 1, sentence 1 EGBGB. If the adult is a foreign citizen with his or her habitual residence – or, incase a habitual residence does not exist, his or her simple presence – in Germany, article 24, paragraph 1, sentence 2 EGBGB provides that a custodian can be appointed according to German law (sections 1896-1908i BGB). Temporary measures are subject to the lex fori of the State that ordered them, article 24, paragraph 3 EGBGB.

D. Does the internal law of your State have provision for Powers of Representation (also known as Continuing, Lasting or Durable Powers of Attorney) for the following:

Economic and financial matters	X	Yes		
Personal welfare	X	Yes		
Health care and medical treatment	X	Yes		

Explanation

In German substantive law, powers of representation or powers of attorney generally **do not cease to be effective** in the event of a lack of capacity or even in the event of the death of the person represented, section 168, sentence 1, and section 672, sentence 1 BGB. Instead, these powers can be revoked by the heirs of the deceased at any time according to section 168, sentence 3, section 1922, paragraph 1 BGB. Therefore, regulations such as the Enduring Powers of Attorney Act or the Mental Capacity Act were not necessary in Germany.

On principle, the validity of power of representation does not depend on a certain **form**. The written form is highly recommendable for reasons of evidence, of course. However, there are some cases in which a certain form is indeed necessary: Firstly, powers of attorney for a law suit must be in written form, section 80, sentence 1 ZPO (Zivilprozessordnung – the German Code of Procedure) and section 11, sentence 1 FamFG. Secondly, as far as dangerous medical measures are involved, section 1904, paragraph 5, sentence 2 BGB demands written power of attorney expressly including the measures in question. Similarly, section 1906, paragraph 5, sentence 2 BGB requires a power of attorney in the mentioned form for measures of accommodation. Thirdly, in cases where the purchase or sale of real estate is in question, power of attorney must meet the requirements of section 29, paragraph 1 GBO (Grundbuchordnung – the German Land Register Code), so that at least certification by a notary – or by a commissioner of oaths at the public authority responsible for the coordination of custodies, section 6, paragraph 2 BtBG (Betreuungsbehördengesetz – Act on the Public Authority Responsible for the Coordination of Custodies) – is necessary. Finally, living wills regarding certain medical measures also require a written document, section 1901a, paragraph 1, sentence 1 BGB.

A **registration** of the powers of representation is not necessary. However, an electronic central register for powers of attorney and for living wills exists in order to prevent unnecessary court orders. A registration is recommended.

Restrictions with regard to the content of the powers of representation concern affirmations in lieu of an oath, which may become necessary when applying for a certificate of inheritance. Moreover, a representative cannot submit tax declarations for the adult. As far as marriage or wills and testaments are concerned, they are of a strictly personal character, so that representation is not possible at all.

According to section 1896, paragraph 2, sentence 2 BGB, powers of representation may not be conferred upon persons who could not legally become custodians of the adult. These are persons who are in a situation of dependence or in another close connection to an institution, a home or another establishment to which the adult has been committed or in which he lives, section 1897, paragraph 3 BGB.

As far as **valid powers of representation** exist, custodianship is not required on principle, section 1896, paragraph 2, sentence 2 BGB. However, courts may nonetheless appoint a custodian, if custodianship appears to be necessary after an individual examination of the case. In case of a reservation of consent, the appointment of a custodian is always necessary, section 1903, paragraph 1, sentence 1 BGB.

The adult can influence the appointment decision of the custodianship court by **suggesting a person as custodian** before the situation of incapacity occurs. According to section 1897, paragraph 4, sentence 1 BGB, the custodianship court must follow this suggestion unless it is inconsistent with the adult's best interests. Conversely, the adult may also make a binding negative suggestion insofar, section 1897, paragraph 4, sentence 2 BGB.

E. Does your State include power for the Courts to make orders or decisions about:

Impairment or insufficiency of personal faculties (lack of capacity)	X	Yes		
Economic and financial matters	X	Yes		

Personal welfare	X	Yes		
Health care and medical treatment	X	Yes		
A new Will or Testament			X	No

If you have answered 'yes' to any of the above, please confirm whether the Courts may authorize another person (such as a guardian, curator, receiver or deputy) to make decisions on behalf of the Adult on the following matters:

Economic and financial matters	X	Yes		
Personal welfare	X	Yes		
Health care and medical treatment	X	Yes		
A new Will or Testament			X	No

If you have answered 'yes' to any of the above, and a person is authorized to make decisions on behalf of the Adult, please summarise the extent of that person's responsibility. For example, is there a duty to produce accounts to the Courts or other supervisory body? Does anyone oversee or monitor conduct? Are there any restrictions on what can or cannot be done in the name of the person who is incapable?

In Germany, courts can **appoint a custodian** in cases in which an adult is not in a position to protect his or her interests by reason of an impairment or insufficiency of his or her personal faculties.

The **scope of custodianship** is determined by the custodianship court in its appointment decision, section 286, paragraph 1, number 1 FamFG, and is based on a medical expert opinion, section 280, paragraph 3, number 4 FamFG. Custodianship alone does not lead to the adult's incapacity to contract. However, as far as it appears necessary to prevent a substantial danger for the person or the person's property, reservation of consent according to section 1903 BGB must be taken into account.

Since custodianship is only permissible insofar as it is necessary, and since a custodian may only be appointed temporarily, cf. section 1908d, paragraph 1 BGB, the court must determine a date on which it decides on the termination or prolongation of the custodianship in its decision, section 286, paragraph 3 FamFG. Custodianship may not be ordered against the free will of the adult, which means on the contrary that custodianship against the adult's will can be ordered, if he or she is fully incapable of entering into legal translations in terms of section 104, number 2 BGB.

The most extensive form of custodianship comprehends all forms of economic and financial matters, personal welfare, and health care and medical treatment. It is supposed to be the absolute exceptional case and must be expressly ordered by the custodianship court.

Even in this situation, there are, however, **statutory restrictions**: First of all, a custodian must always orientate his actions on the requests and the welfare of the adult, section 1901, paragraph 3, sentences 1-3 BGB. In order to do so, the custodian has to discuss important matters with the adult, section 1901, paragraph 3, sentence 3 BGB.

If the custodianship is conducted professionally, the custodian can be ordered by the court to draft a custodianship plan at the beginning of the custodianship, section 1901, paragraph 4, sentences 2 and 3 BGB. A priori, the custodian **cannot represent** the adult in terms of certain legal transactions, for example with the custodian's spouse or relatives by blood in direct line, if the legal transaction is not only the performance of a contract, a legal transaction regarding the transfer of a claim secured by certain security rights, and individual transactions and matters for which power of attorney has been revoked by the custodianship court in advance, section 1908i, paragraph 1, sentence 1 BGB in combination with sections 1795 and 1796 BGB. The same is the case with respect to legal acts of a strictly personal character, such as the determination of the religious confession, marriage, as well as making wills and testaments. Moreover, insofar as dangerous medical measures, sterilization, measures of accommodation, the abandonment of a rented home, or an advancement from the adult's property are concerned, the custodian needs the **approval** of the custodianship court, section 1904, paragraph 1, sentences 1 and 2, section 1905, paragraph 2, sentence 1, section 1906, paragraph 2, sentence 1, section 1907, paragraph 1, sentence 1, and section 1908 BGB. Custodianship court approval is also necessary in cases of certain statutorily defined legal transactions with inherent danger for the adult's fortune, section 1908i, paragraph 1, section 1 BGB in combination with sections 1810, 1812, 1819, 1820, 1821, 1822, numbers 1 to 4 and 6 to 13, 1823 BGB. Finally, the custodianship court must **cooperate** with the guardian as far as an investment of money in trust for the adult is concerned.

Even where an approval or a cooperation are not required, the custodian is nonetheless **advised and supervised** by the custodianship court which can intervene against violations of the duty of care by orders and prohibitions, section 1908i, paragraph 1, sentence 1 BGB in combination with section 1837, paragraphs 1 and 2 BGB. The court may also impose coercive fines, if necessary, section 1908i, paragraph 1, sentence 1 BGB in combination with section 1837, paragraph 3 BGB. Section 1908b, section 1 BGB enables the custodianship court to remove the custodian, if his suitability to care for the matters of the adult is no longer guaranteed, or if another good cause is given. This may be the case, if, for example, the custodian repeatedly ignores the express and reasonable requests of the adult. Apart from that, the adult can always request the court to review the appointment of the custodian, section 291, sentence 1 FamFG.

According to section 1901, paragraph 5 BGB, the custodian is obliged to inform the custodianship court of certain facts about the custodianship: Firstly, he must report circumstances which appear to render possible a cancellation of the custodianship. The same is the case, if the custodian gains knowledge about circumstances enabling a restriction of the scope of custodianship in the individual case. Conversely, he must also report circumstances allowing the expansion of the custodianship or requiring the appointment of a second custodian or the order of a reservation of consent. At the beginning of custodianship, the custodian must create an inventory of the adult's property. The court determines an accounting period. The custodian must act economically for the benefit of the adult's property and produce accounts to the court.

As far as the custodian violates his duties by acting in **excess of his or her authority** regarding certain legal transactions, he is liable as a falsus procurator vis-à-vis third parties, which means that he is liable for performance himself where applicable. Apart from that, claims for damages in the internal relationship between the custodian and the adult are to be taken into consideration in cases in which the custodian intentionally or negligently violates his duty of care, section 1908i, paragraph 1, sentence 1 BGB in combination with section 1833, paragraph 1, sentence 1 BGB.

PART X

3. Recognition of Powers of Representation / Continuing or Lasting Powers of Attorney and protective measures for Adults from England & Wales

A. Are the following Powers of Representation and delegations under the law of England & Wales recognised and enforceable:

Continuing Powers of Attorney for economic and financial matters	X	Yes	
Continuing Powers of Attorney for personal welfare	X	Yes	
Continuing Powers of Attorney for healthcare and medical treatment	X	Yes	
Advance Directives	X	Yes	

As to Powers of Representation and delegations created under the law of England and Wales, the **Convention on the International Protection of Adults is applicable**. Therefore, according to its article 15, the existence, extent, modification and extinction of such powers is governed by the law of the adult's habitual residence, if no express designation of the law applicable – limited to those in paragraph 2 – has been made, article 15, paragraphs 1 and 2 of the Convention. Recently, German scholars have begun a discussion of the question as to whether or not the Convention should be applicable only when the adult is already in a position where he or she cannot protect his or her own interests because of an impairment in terms of article 1 of the Convention. Before the occurrence of this situation, internal private international law should determine the law applicable. Since this would lead to the problem that the powers of representation could underlie two different substantive laws – according to the prevailing opinion in Germany, the connecting factor for general powers of attorney in internal private international law is constituted by legal residence –, this view is challenged strongly. However, as there are no court decisions regarding this problem yet, the situation is still unclear.

Additional formalities as allowed by article 15, paragraph 3 of the Convention are not required under German law.

The only **restrictions** result from article 20 of the Convention and refer to the substantive law restrictions mentioned under 2.E. Therefore, as far as, for example, certain medical treatments are in question, a custodianship court approval is necessary.

B. Are the following Protective Measures of the courts of England & Wales recognised and enforceable in your State?

Decision as to impairment or insufficiency of personal faculties	X	Yes	
Appointment of a Representative to deal with economic and financial matters	X	Yes	
Appointment of a Representative to deal with personal welfare	X	Yes	

Appointment of a Representative to deal with health care and medical treatment	X	Yes		
Decision authorising the making of a new Will or Testament			X	No

Explanation

Recognition and enforcement of measures taken by the courts of England and Wales are governed by **articles 22 and 25 of the Convention on the International Protection of Adults**. Therefore, on principle, all of the measures taken are to be recognised. However, recognition may be refused on grounds of article 22, paragraph 2 of the Convention. Especially article 22, paragraph 2, lit. c) of the Convention may be problematic insofar as **Wills and Testaments** are concerned, since they are regarded as strictly personal legal acts by German law.

As to **enforcement, article 25 of the Convention** provides that measures be declared enforceable by the State in which enforcement is supposed to be taking place. Measures must be enforced as if they had been taken by authorities of that State, article 27 of the Convention. Local jurisdiction lies with the custodianship courts in whose area of jurisdiction the adult has his habitual residence, section 6, paragraph 3, sentence 1 of the "Gesetz zur Umsetzung des Haager Übereinkommens vom 13. Januar 2000 über den internationalen Schutz von Erwachsenen" (Act on the Implementation of the Hague Convention on the International Protection of Adults). If no habitual residence exists, the competence lies with the custodianship court in whose area of jurisdiction the need of assistance arises, section 6, paragraph 3, sentence 2 of the aforementioned Act. Finally, subsidiary local jurisdiction lies with the Amtsgericht Schöneberg as custodianship court in Berlin, section 6, paragraph 3, sentence 3, and paragraph 2 of the Act.

4. Procedures in your State

A. *How may the following situations be dealt with.*

Withdrawal of money from a bank account situated in your State

In all of these cases, a **differentiation** must be made between the situations in which power of attorney exists, and where this is not the case.

Withdrawing money from a bank account in Germany by **continuing power of attorney** – even such created under German law – can be very problematic. German banks tend to refuse such transactions with the argument that bank employees cannot recognise the scope of the power of attorney, that they cannot examine whether the power of attorney had been created in a situation where the adult was still having legal capacity, and that they do not know as to whether or not the power of attorney had not been revoked in the meantime. The reason for this is to force the customers into using bank-intern forms for power of attorney.

However, these problems do not occur with representatives using **documents authenticated** by a notary because notaries must examine the legal capacity of the principal.

As far as a document regarding power of attorney is registered, banks will most probably recognise it.

PART X

If continuing power of attorney does not exist or is not recognised, a **custodian must be appointed** who acts as the adult's representative according to section 1902 BGB. As of September 1st, 2009, an approval by the custodianship court for banking transactions is not needed anymore.

The custodianship court appoints a custodian either on the application of the adult, who is regarded as having capacity for this procedure, section 275 FamFG, or of its own motion, section 1896, paragraph 1, sentence 1 BGB. Insofar, it might be helpful, if the document – if possible – contained a suggestion as to the person who should become custodian similar to section 1897, paragraph 4, sentence 1 BGB in favour of the representative. Thus, problems with German banks could easily be avoided in advance.

If appearing necessary, the custodianship court can appoint a curator for the adult concerning the appointment procedure, section 276 FamFG.

Sale of a home or other property in your State

Whereas the **sale of movables** through a representative with lasting power of attorney does not provide any specific problems, the **sale of real estate** in Germany can become problematic. That is because according to section 311b, paragraph 1 BGB, the contract must be authenticated by a notary. On principle, section 167, paragraph 2 BGB states that authority does not need to be in the form of the legal transaction to which it is related. However, irrevocable authority must nonetheless be authenticated by a notary. Since foreign powers of attorney are not authenticated by a German notary, the problem of substitution arises. Authentication through a German notary can be substituted by authentication through foreign authorities, if equality as to the juridical standards is guaranteed. Therefore, lasting powers of attorney registered by an English court should suffice.

The other problem is connected with the requirement of changing the **land register** in order to successfully transfer real estate. Section 29 GBO demands that all requirements for the change of the land register – and, therefore, authority in the case of representation – must be proven through public documents or documents attested by a notary. According to a recent decision by the OLG (Higher Regional Court) Schleswig of December 21st, 2009, this requirement also encompasses the occurrence of incapacity, incase the power of attorney depends on this situation. As far as lasting powers of attorney are unconditional, this will not provide any problems to lasting power of attorney registered by courts in England or Wales.

If lasting power of attorney does not exist, again a **custodian** must be appointed. Insofar as the sale of real estate is concerned, he must obtain the approval of the custodianship court according to section 1908i, paragraph 1, sentence 1 BGB in combination with section 1821, paragraph 1, numbers 1 and 2 BGB. (As to the appointment procedure see above).

Family dispute as to care of the person currently resident in your State (eg. whether to return to England & Wales)

As far as **lasting power of attorney expressly encompasses** the right to decide upon the place of the adult's residence lies with the representative. Although this is generally regarded as a strictly personal legal act, its delegation is exceptionally permissible in the form of lasting power of attorney according to German law. Therefore, foreign lasting power of attorney with regard to this are recognised without any problems.

If lasting power of attorney does not exist or does not comprehend the right mentioned above, a **custodian** must be appointed whose rights also encompass the decision on the place of the adult's residence. (As to the procedure at the custodianship court, see above).

Decision about medical treatment in your State

Even though decisions about medical treatment are regarded as strictly personal in German law, **power of attorney** can also cover this area in Germany. Section 1904, paragraph 5, sentences 1 and 2 in combination with paragraphs 1 and 2 BGB, however, firstly requires power of attorney to be written and expressly referring to the measures in question, if there is justified danger that the adult could die or suffer serious injury to his or her health by the measure. Secondly, the representative must obtain the approval of the custodianship court, the only exception being situations in which delay entails danger, section 1904, paragraph 5 in combination with paragraph 1, sentence 2 BGB. In this case an approval – even a subsequent one – is not necessary.

As far as power of attorney does not exist or does not encompass the measure in question, a **custodian** must be appointed. In the case of custodianship, court approval is also necessary according to section 1904, paragraph 1, sentence 1 BGB, except where delay entails danger, section 1904, paragraph 1, sentence 2 BGB. (As to the appointment procedure see above).

If a **living will** in writing with respect to certain medical measures, created at a time when the adult was still able to consent, exists, the custodian must examine whether or not the respective determinations still correspond to the current living and treatment situation, section 1901a, paragraph 1, sentence 1 BGB. If this is the case, the custodian must see to it that the adult's will is done, section 1901a, paragraph 1, sentence 2 BGB. Otherwise he must examine the presumed will of the adult and act accordingly, section 1901a, paragraph 2 BGB.

PART X

B. Would the answers to A. above vary if person was not a national of the United Kingdom but had been habitually resident in England and Wales prior to their impairment or insufficiency?

If the adult's **habitual residence remained** in England and Wales, international jurisdiction of German courts – and the application of German substantive law as lex fori in terms of article 13, paragraph 1 of the Convention on the International Protection of Adults – could not be based on article 5, paragraph 1 of the Convention. Therefore, as far as lasting power of attorney does not exist or does not encompass the matters in question, English or Welsh courts would have to decide on measures directed to the adult's protection. These measures would be recognised and made enforceable in Germany, as already described above. The limitations of a custodian's authority resulting from German law can be based on article 22, paragraph 2 in combination with article 25, paragraph 3 of the Convention, so that – as a result – the scope of measures possible would remain similar.

C. Is there an emergency procedure?

Apart from article 8, paragraph 2, lit. d) and f) of the Convention, which enables authorities competent according to articles 5 and 6 of the Convention to request a Contracting State to take measures for the adult or his or her property, so that in the case described above English or Welsh authorities could direct such a request to German authorities, emergency jurisdiction for urgent cases is provided in article 10, paragraph 1 of the Convention. This would allow German courts to take necessary measures directed to the adult's protection in an emergency case.

5. Sources of information

http://www.anwalt-suchservice.de/ass/rar/rechtsanwalt_betreuungsrecht.html (Search engine for attorneys, listed by area of law, region, and specialisation)

http://www.bmj.bund.de/enid/0,b771e6305f7472636964092d0935333130/ Publikationen/Betreuungsrecht_kh.html (Guidance on the law and procedure provided by the Federal Minstry of Justice – in German only)

http://wiki.btprax.de/Hauptseite (Guidance on the law and procedure provided as a wiki-source by the leading custodianship law journal – mainly in German)

http://bundesrecht.juris.de/englisch_bgb/englisch_bgb.html (English translation of the German Civil Code)

http://www.irene.de (Homepage of the "Institut de Recherches et d'Etudes Notarielles en Europe: provides the opportunity of purchasing translated power of attorney forms in different languages meeting the requirements of the respective laws)

Completed by:

Name	Dr. Maximilian Seibl, Georg-August-University, Göttingen

December 2010

ICELAND

Name of State	Iceland			
Is your State part of a larger Federal country?			X	No

1. Convention on the International Protection of Adults (Hague 2000)

Has this Convention been ratified by your State?			X	No
Does your State intend to ratify the Convention?			X	No
Even if not ratified is it generally applied in any event?			X	No

2. Jurisdiction

A. Does jurisdiction of your Courts usually depend upon the Personal Law of the Adult?

	X	Yes		
If so, which is usually the relevant connecting factor?				
Habitual residence	X	Yes		
Domicile	X	Yes		

B. Can jurisdiction of the Courts in your State also depend upon:

Habitual residence	X	Yes		
Domicile	X	Yes		
Nationality			X	No
Situs of property	X	Yes		
Presence in the State	X	Yes		

Explanation

If Domicile is used as a connecting factor, please give a short definition.

Domicile is where you have a legal residence or where you have a permanent home.

It is possible to choose between domicile or habitual residence. Physical presence is accepted as a ground of jurisdiction if the adult does not have his or her domicile or habitual residence in Iceland.

PART X

C. If the Courts of your State have jurisdiction, which internal law is applicable? That of:

Your State	X	Yes		

Explanation

D. Does the internal law of your State have provision for Powers of Representation (also known as Continuing, Lasting or Durable Powers of Attorney) for the following:

Economic and financial matters	X	Yes		
Personal welfare	X	Yes		
Health care and medical treatment	X	Yes		

Explanation

Please detail any restrictions or requirements (such as registration).
The attorney shall be in full possession of legal competence, financially solvent, reliable and prudent and otherwise fit for the task. The Registry is held in the Minstry of the Interior.
Does an ordinary Power cease to be effective in the event of a lack of capacity?
Yes

E. Does your State include power for the Courts to make orders or decisions about:

Impairment or insufficiency of personal faculties (lack of capacity)	X	Yes		
Economic and financial matters			X	No
Personal welfare			X	No
Health care and medical treatment			X	No
A new Will or Testament			X	No

If you have answered 'yes' to any of the above, please confirm whether the Courts may authorize another person (such as a guardian, curator, receiver or deputy) to make decisions on behalf of the Adult on the following matters:

Economic and financial matters	X	Yes		
Personal welfare	X	Yes		
Health care and medical treatment	X	Yes		
A new Will or Testament			X	No

If you have answered 'yes' to any of the above, and a person is authorized to make decisions on behalf of the Adult, please summarise the extent of that person's responsibility. For example, is there a duty to produce accounts to the Courts or other supervisory body? Does anyone oversee or monitor conduct? Are there any restrictions on what can or cannot be done in the name of the person who is incapable?

Please list the procedures

> The guardian shall have the power to take any necessary decisions concerning the personal affairs of the person concerned. A guardian has the duty to act in accordance with any instructions given by the supervisor of guardians of the Ministry of the Interior. Except for matters of a minor nature a guardian shall consult the person on any affairs in the charge of the guardian.

3. Recognition of Powers of Representation / Continuing or Lasting Powers of Attorney and protective measures for Adults from England & Wales

A. Are the following Powers of Representation and delegations under the law of England & Wales recognised and enforceable:

Continuing Powers of Attorney for economic and financial matters			X	No
Continuing Powers of Attorney for personal welfare			X	No
Continuing Powers of Attorney for healthcare and medical treatment			X	No
Advance Directives			X	No

B. Are the following Protective Measures of the courts of England & Wales recognised and enforceable in your State?

| Decision as to impairment or insufficiency of personal faculties | | | X | No |
| Appointment of a Representative to deal with economic and financial matters | | | X | No |

PART X

Appointment of a Representative to deal with personal welfare		X	No
Appointment of a Representative to deal with health care and medical treatment		X	No
Decision authorising the making of a new Will or Testament		X	No

4. Procedures in your State

A. How may the following situations be dealt.

Withdrawal of money from a bank account situated in your State

A person can request the appointment of an administrator to the supervisor of guardians. He can also be represented by a guardian.

Sale of a home or other property in your State

The administrator can be entrusted with administration of the property or by the guardian.

Family dispute as to care of the person currently resident in your State (eg. whether to return to England & Wales)

By the guardian.

Decision about medical treatment in your State

By the guardian.

B. Would the answers to A. above vary if person was not a national of the United Kingdom but had been habitually resident in England and Wales prior to their impairment or insufficiency?

No.

C. Is there an emergency procedure?

No.

5. Sources of information

www.lmfi.is
www.innanrikisraduneyti.is

Completed by:

Name	Kristin Benediktsdóttir

October 2010

JAPAN

Name of State	Japan			
Is your State part of a larger Federal country?			X	No

1. Convention on the International Protection of Adults (Hague 2000)

Has this Convention been ratified by your State?			X	No
Does your State intend to ratify the Convention?			X	No
Even if not ratified is it generally applied in any event?			X	No

2. Jurisdiction

A. *Does jurisdiction of your Courts usually depend upon the Personal Law of the Adult?*

	X	Yes		
If so, which is usually the relevant connecting factor?				
Habitual residence	X	Yes		
Domicile	X	Yes		
Nationality	X	Yes		

B. *Can jurisdiction of the Courts in your State also depend upon:*

Habitual residence	☒	Yes		No
Domicile	☒	Yes		No
Nationality	☒	Yes		No
Situs of property	☒	Yes		No
Presence in the State	☒	Yes		No

Explanation

Domicile is the city or town where the person has registered their residence, that is, the certificate of residence is issued.

Declaration on mental incapacity and *Making the Order* for adult guardianship are to be dealt with according to the Japanese Civil Law in a case where a person, regardless of his/her nationality, has been living in Japan (habitual residence, and domicile).

On the other hand, *choosing and appointing guardians/curators/assistants* (there are 3 types depending on the extent of his remaining capacity) are to be considered according to the Law of his/her nationality. However, there are two exceptions which apply the Japanese Law in these contexts, too.

For example for a person who has a Korean Nationality but has been living in Japan, the Japanese Court can *declare his/her mental insufficiency* (level 2) according to the Japanese Civil Law, and also can *appoint a curator* (level 2) by applying the Japanese Civil Law, if the Court *made* the Curatorship Order for him/her, even though, according to the Korean Civil Law he/she should be placed under full guardianship because of the lack of law of curatorship (there are only 2 types in the Korean Law) .

C. If the Courts of your State have jurisdiction, which internal law is applicable? That of:

Your State	X	Yes		

D. Does the internal law of your State have provision for Powers of Representation (also known as Continuing, Lasting or Durable Powers of Attorney) for the following:

Economic and financial matters	X	Yes		
Personal welfare	X	Yes		
Health care and medical treatment			X	No

Explanation

Registration is necessary to be made as soon as the instrument is created by notaries (only).

Does an ordinary Power cease to be effective in the event of a lack of capacity?

No.

E. Does your State include power for the Courts to make orders or decisions about:

Impairment or insufficiency of personal faculties (lack of capacity)	X	Yes		
Economic and financial matters			X	No

Personal welfare			X	No
Health care and medical treatment			X	No
A new Will or Testament			X	No

If you have answered 'yes' to any of the above, please confirm whether the Courts may authorize another person (such as a guardian, curator, receiver or deputy) to make decisions on behalf of the Adult on the following matters:

Economic and financial matters	X	Yes		
Personal welfare	X	Yes		
Health care and medical treatment			X	No
A new Will or Testament			X	No

If you have answered 'yes' to any of the above, and a person is authorized to make decisions on behalf of the Adult, please summarise the extent of that person's responsibility. For example, is there a duty to produce accounts to the Courts or other supervisory body? Does anyone oversee or monitor conduct? Are there any restrictions on what can or cannot be done in the name of the person who is incapable?

Please list the procedures

> The Court can order guardians to produce accounts to the Court annually, and can even appoint "guardian supervisors " to oversee or monitor guardians' conduct if the Courts considers it necessary in that particular case.

3. Recognition of Powers of Representation / Continuing or Lasting Powers of Attorney and protective measures for Adults from England & Wales

A. Are the following Powers of Representation and delegations under the law of England & Wales recognised and enforceable:

Continuing Powers of Attorney for economic and financial matters	☐	Yes	☐	No
Continuing Powers of Attorney for personal welfare	☐	Yes	☐	No
Continuing Powers of Attorney for healthcare and medical treatment			X	No
Advance Directives			X	No

Are there any additional formalities required such as an Exequatur?

> I am not so sure but in my opinion, the CPA/LPA/EPA for economic & financial matters and also personal welfare can be recognized in Japan too, if they were registered in England and Wales, but not for healthcare & medical treatment nor advance directives anyway (we do not have such law).

B. Are the following Protective Measures of the courts of England & Wales recognised and enforceable in your State?

Decision as to impairment or insufficiency of personal faculties	☐	Yes	☐	No
Appointment of a Representative to deal with economic and financial matters	☐	Yes	☐	No
Appointment of a Representative to deal with personal welfare	☐	Yes	☐	No
Appointment of a Representative to deal with health care and medical treatment			X	No
Decision authorising the making of a new Will or Testament	X	Yes		

Explanation

> The issues raised here are still open for interpretation (no provision in our laws).

4. Procedures in your State

A. How may the following situations be dealt with.

Withdrawal of money from a bank account situated in your State

> Appointment of guardians is necessary.

Sale of a home or other property in your State

> Application to the Court is necessary.

Family dispute as to care of the person currently resident in your State (eg. whether to return to England & Wales)

> No jurisdiction about these sorts of issues (e g care, medical treat etc) even for Japanese nationals, as mentioned above.

Decision about medical treatment in your State

No jurisdiction (as mentioned above).

B. Would the answers to A. above vary if person was not a national of the United Kingdom but had been habitually resident in England and Wales prior to their impairment or insufficiency?

No difference.

C. Is there an emergency procedure?

Negotiorum Gestio in the Civil Code

5. Sources of information

http://www.ls-tokyo.jp/intro.html http://www.jacsw.or.jp/contents/kenri/panf.htm http://www.courts.go.jp/mito/saiban/tetuzuki/mositate.html http://www.moj.go.jp/MINJI/minji17.html

Completed by:

Name	Dr Fumie Suga
eMail	f_suga@hosei.ac.jp

Are you a solicitor/notary/advocate or lawyer who provides legal advice and services for nationals of the United Kingdom in your State?			X	No

October 2010

SERBIA

Name of State	Serbia				
Is your State part of a larger Federal country?				X	No

1. Convention on the International Protection of Adults (Hague 2000)

Has this Convention been ratified by your State?				X	No
Does your State intend to ratify the Convention?				X	No
Even if not ratified is it generally applied in any event?				X	No

There are currently no indications that Serbian authorities are considering ratification of the Convention

2. Jurisdiction

A. *Does jurisdiction of your Courts usually depend upon the Personal Law of the Adult?*

				X	No
If so, which is usually the relevant connecting factor?					
Domicile		X	Yes		

B. *Can jurisdiction of the Courts in your State also depend upon:*

Habitual residence				X	No
Nationality		X	Yes		
Situs of property		X	Yes		
Presence in the State		X	Yes		

Explanation

There are two definitions of domicile in Serbia – one for citizens and the other one for foreigners – although they are fairly alike:
The Law of the Republic of Serbia on Citizens' Domicile and Residence (Official Journal of the Republic of Serbia, no. 42/1977 as amended) Art. 4(1):
'Domicile is the place in which a citizen has settled with the intention to permanently live in this place.'

The Act on Foreigners (Official Journal of the Republic of Serbia, no. 97/2008), Art. 74(2)

'The domicile, in the sense of this law, is the place in which a foreigner who was granted a permit for permanent settlement intendes to live permanently on a specific address.'

In order to be domiciled in Serbia, a foreigner has to obtain a permanent settlement permit.

Decision-making in the field of protection of adults in Serbia is shared between courts and administrative authorities. The court decides on depriving or limiting of a natural person's capacity to act. Once the decision on depriving or limiting capacity to act has been rendered, jurisdiction passes over to the administrative authority – the Social Care Centre that decides on appointment of a guardian, and approves guardian's decisions that go beyond ordinary everyday matters.

Pursuant to the PIL Code (Official Journal of the Republic of Serbia no. 43/1982) Art. 46(5), jurisdiction of courts in Serbia for depriving or limiting a natural person's capacity to act are based on his or her domicile.

Jurisdiction of competent administrative authority in Serbia for guardianship in cases with an international element is regulated by the PIL Code Arts. 75-77. The Code was enacted in the former Yugoslavia, but still remains in force in Serbia. All provisions of the Code that mention Yugoslav citizens are interpreted to refer to Serbian citizens. Jurisdiction for guardianship matters may be based on (Serbian) nationality (Art. 75 – but see exception in Art 76 based on foreign domicile of a Serbian national). If a foreign citizen is concerned, jurisdiction may be based on domicile provided that the State of his or her nationality has not taken the necessary measures (Art. 77(2)). Jurisdiction for provisional measures exists if the foreign citizen is present or has property in Serbia (Art. 77(1)).

The full text of the relevant provisions follows:

PIL Code (1982)

Chapter III. Jurisdiction and Procedure

1. Jurisdiction of the Courts and Other Authorities of the Federal

Republic of Yugoslavia in Matters with an International Element

Article 46

.......(first four paragraphs omitted)

Unless provided otherwise, if a legal relation is decided upon in non-litigious proceedings, the court of the Federal Republic of Yugoslavia shall have jurisdiction if the person in relation to whom the application has been submitted is domiciled, or has its seat in the Federal Republic of Yugoslavia, and when there is only one person participating in the proceedings – if that person is domiciled, or has its seat in the Federal Republic of Yugoslavia.

Article 75

The authority of the Federal Republic of Yugoslavia shall have exclusive jurisdiction in matters of guardianship of Yugoslav citizens, irrespective of where they are domiciled, unless provided otherwise by this Law.

Article 76

The authority of the Federal Republic of Yugoslavia shall not take decisions or measures in matters of guardianship of a Yugoslav citizen who is domiciled abroad if it establishes that the authority that has jurisdiction pursuant to the law of the foreign State has taken a decision or a measure by which the protection of the personality, rights and interest of the Yugoslav citizen have been secured.

Article 77

The authority of the Federal Republic of Yugoslavia shall take the necessary provisional measures for the protection of personality, rights and interests of a foreign citizen who is present or has property in the Federal Republic of Yugoslavia, and it shall inform thereof the authority of the State whose citizen that person is. The authority of the Federal Republic of Yugoslavia shall take the decision or measure in matters of guardianship of a foreign citizen who is domiciled in the Federal Republic of Yugoslavia if the protection of his personality, rights and interest has not been secured by the authority of the State whose citizen he is.

C. If the Courts of your State have jurisdiction, which internal law is applicable? That of:

Your State	☒	Yes	☐	No
Habitual residence	☐	Yes	☒	No
Domicile	☐	Yes	☒	No
Nationality	☒	Yes	☐	No
Situs of property	☒	Yes	x	No

Explanation

The applicable law to matters of protection of Adults is determined by provisions of the PIL Code.

Natural person's capacity may be taken away or limited only by decision of the court applying the law of that person's nationality (Art. 14(4) of the Serbian PIL Code).

As for the issue of appointing a guardian, according to Art. 15(1) of the Serbian PIL Code (1983), the law governing placing under guardianship, the end of guardianship, and relations between the guardian and the person who is placed under guardianship (the ward) is also the law of nationality of the person who is placed under guardianship. Provisional protective measures are determined according to Serbian law towards a foreign citizen who is present in the territory of Serbia or whose property is situated in Serbia.

PART X

PIL Code

Chapter II. Applicable Law

Article 14

The law governing legal capacity of a natural person and his capacity to act is the law of the State whose citizen he is. A natural person who would have no capacity to act under the law of the State whose citizen he is, shall have capacity to act if he has that capacity under the law of the place where the obligation arose. The law governing the removal or restriction of a natural person's capacity to act shall be the law referred to in paragraph 1 above. The provision of paragraph 2 above shall not be applied to family and succession relations.

Article 15

The law governing the placing under guardianship, the end of guardianship, and relations between the guardian and the person who is placed under guardianship (the ward), is the law of the State whose citizen is the person who is placed under guardianship. Provisional protective measures towards a foreign citizen or a stateless person who is present in the Federal Republic of Yugoslavia are determined according to the law of the Federal Republic of Yugoslavia and remain in force until the competent State makes the decision or undertakes the necessary measures. The provision of paragraph 2 above shall be applied also with respect to the protection of property of an absent foreign citizen or a stateless person which is situated in the territory of the Federal Republic of Yugoslavia.

D. Does the internal law of your State have provision for Powers of Representation (also known as Continuing, Lasting or Durable Powers of Attorney) for the following:

Economic and financial matters	☐	Yes	☒	No
Personal welfare	☐	Yes	☒	No
Health care and medical treatment	☐	Yes	☒	No

Explanation

Does an ordinary Power cease to be effective in the event of a lack of capacity? Yes.

E. Does your State include power for the Courts to make orders or decisions about:

Impairment or insufficiency of personal faculties (lack of capacity)	X	Yes		
Economic and financial matters	X	Yes		
Personal welfare	X	Yes		

Health care and medical treatment	X	Yes		
A new Will or Testament	X	Yes		

If you have answered 'yes' to any of the above, please confirm whether the Courts may authorize another person (such as a guardian, curator, receiver or deputy) to make decisions on behalf of the Adult on the following matters:

Economic and financial matters	X	Yes		
Personal welfare	X	Yes		
Health care and medical treatment	X	Yes		
A new Will or Testament			X	No

If you have answered 'yes' to any of the above, and a person is authorized to make decisions on behalf of the Adult, please summarise the extent of that person's responsibility. For example, is there a duty to produce accounts to the Courts or other supervisory body? Does anyone oversee or monitor conduct? Are there any restrictions on what can or cannot be done in the name of the person who is incapable?

Please list the procedures

As stated above, once a person's capacity has been taken away or limited, the administrative authority (Social Care Center) shall appoint him or her a guardian. The guardian takes care of the property of the ward (decides upon management and disposition of property), of his or her personal welfare and health. However, the guardian must obtain approval of the Social Care Center for any decision that concerns disposal of the ward's property that is beyond regular management of the ward's property, that concerns ward's education or any medical treatment. A guardian has a duty to file regular annual reports to the Social Care Center.

According to the Succession Act (Official Journal of the Republic of Serbia, no. 46/1995 as amended, Art. 80) a will is not affected by a subsequent loss of the power of insight and judgment. Exceptionally, if there is a fundamental change of circumstances that were decisive motive for drawing up a will, the court may cancel the will or certain provisions of the will at the request of an interested person. Such a request may be filed by the interested person within three years of the date of opening (declaration) of the will.

PART X

3. Recognition of Powers of Representation / Continuing or Lasting Powers of Attorney and protective measures for Adults from England & Wales

A. Are the following Powers of Representation and delegations under the law of England & Wales recognised and enforceable:

Continuing Powers of Attorney for economic and financial matters	☐	Yes	☐	No
Continuing Powers of Attorney for personal welfare	☐	Yes	☐	No
Continuing Powers of Attorney for healthcare and medical treatment	☐	Yes	☐	No
Advance Directives	☐	Yes	☐	No

Are there any additional formalities required such as an Exequatur?

There is no practice with continuing powers of attorney or advance directives in this country. It is therefore difficult to say whether they would be recognized in Serbia if issued abroad.
There is a provision in the Code of Obligations (Official Journal of the Socialist Federal Republic of Yugoslavia, no. 29/78, as amended), Art. 94(3) that allows for a power of attorney to remain valid even after death of a person, if its validity after the death was in accordance with the grantor's wishes or with the nature of the transaction.
This could be used as a point of reference, but the outcome is at this moment uncertain.
However, the power of attorney would cease to take effect in any legal proceedings before the court after the grantor loses capacity, pursuant to Art. 94 of the Code of Civil Procedure (Official Journal of the Republic of Serbia 125/2004 as amended).

B. Are the following Protective Measures of the courts of England & Wales recognised and enforceable in your State?

Decision as to impairment or insufficiency of personal faculties	X	Yes		
Appointment of a Representative to deal with economic and financial matters	X	Yes		
Appointment of a Representative to deal with personal welfare	X	Yes		
Appointment of a Representative to deal with health care and medical treatment	X	Yes		
Decision authorising the making of a new Will or Testament	X	Yes		

Explanation

A foreign judgment can be equated with the judgment of a domestic court and produce legal effect in Serbia only if recognized by a Serbian court (the PrivateInternational Law (PIL) Code, Article 86, paragraph 1). A foreignjudgment is any decision of a foreign court or other authority, if such decision isequated with a decision of the court in the country of origin (the PIL Code, Article 86, paragraphs 2 and 3). In orderto be recognized, the foreign judgment has to be brought in civil and commercialmatters. The characterization of a foreign judgment in that respect is done pursuantto domestic law. Matters of protection of adults are considered to be a civil matter.

Recognition and enforcement of a foreign judgment may be the main subject of a proceeding, or may be resolved as a preliminary question in a proceeding involving another matter (the PIL Code, Article 101, paragraph 5). If the judgment concerns a civil matter, the ruling on recognition and enforcement will be rendered in a non-litigious procedure by a competent district court. The court deciding on the recognition of a foreign judgment has to limit itself to examination of the formal conditions for recognition provided in Articles 86-96 (Article 101, paragraph 2). The court has no power to modify the judgment in any respect. As to persons authorized to request recognition, the law provides that recognition of foreign judgments relating to status of a natural person may be requested by anyone who has a legal interest in recognition (Article 101, paragraph 6). The court has no authority to review the foreign judgment as to facts that were established or the law that was applied.

The conditions for recognition and enforcement are laid out in the PIL Code and they are mostly of a procedural character. These conditions include the following:

(a) Finality (Article 87) – the party has to submit a confirmation by a foreign court or other competent authority that the judgment has become final pursuant to the law of the country of origin (i.e., that no appeal can be taken from this judgment and that it conclusively resolves the matter at issue).

(b) Jurisdiction – the foreign judgment will not be recognized if the Serbian court or other authority has exclusive jurisdiction for the matter that was decided by the judgment (Article 89, paragraph 1). For the exclusive jurisdiction to exist, there has to be an express provision in a statute (the PIL Code, Article 47). Exclusive jurisdiction of domestic administrative authorities exists for guardianship matters of a citizen of Serbia (the PIL Code, Art. 75), but the provision is subject to the following condition: "unless provided otherwise by this Law". In Art. 76 there is an exception from exclusive jurisdiction if a Serbian citizen is domiciled abroad and the foreign authority has taken a decision or measure by which protection of his or her personality, rights and interests have been secured (see provisions of the PIL Code cited above under item 2). Jurisdiction is not tested at all if recognition is sought for a status judgment that concerns only the nationals of the country of origin (the PIL Code, Article 94, paragraph 1).

(c) Reciprocity (Article 92, paragraph 1) – this condition does not necessitate the existence of a treaty on mutual recognition of judgments. It is enough that Serbian judgments are recognized in the practice of the country of origin. Reciprocity is presumed until a contrary proposition is established (Article 92, paragraph 3). In order to establish lack of reciprocity, one has to show that domestic judgments of the same kind as the judgment for which recognition is sought are not recognized in the country of origin. Reciprocity is not required if a domestic national seeks recognition, or if recognition of a status judgment concerning only the nationals of the country of origin is required (Article 92, paragraph 2 and Article 94, paragraph 1).

PART X

(d) Absence of procedural violation that prevented the party to participate in the proceedings (Article 88, paragraph 1), in particular inadequate service of process. The court will not review the fulfilment of this condition on its own motion, but only at the parties' request. If the party in any way participated in the hearing on the merits, that party cannot invoke the inadequacy of service in the recognition proceedings (Article 88, paragraph 2).

(e) Absence of violation of public policy (Article 91) – generally speaking, domestic courts rarely rely on the exception of public policy to deny recognition to foreign judgments. This condition does not apply at all to status judgments relative only to the status of a national of the country of origin. In contrast, foreign status judgments deciding on the status of domestic nationals are subjected to a stricter review than other judgments. If the foreign court applied foreign law deciding on the status of a citizen of Serbia, although Serbian law would be applicable pursuant to the domestic conflict of laws rules, the judgment will be recognized only if the foreign substantive solution does not essentially differ from the manner in which the domestic substantive law regulates the same issue (the principle of equivalence, Article 93).

(f) Absence of a final domestic judgment or of a foreign judgment that was already recognized in the same matter (Article 90).

4. Procedures in your State

A. *How may the following situations be dealt with.*

Withdrawal of money from a bank account situated in your State

If the person is a foreign national domiciled in Serbia, and the Serbian court has rendered the decision on the determination of incapacity pursuant to that person's national law, the Social Care Center would appoint a guardian to that person also on the basis of application of his national law. If the national law would allow the guardian to withdraw the money from the account without approval of a supervisory body, he could probably do it in Serbia (please, refer to provisions of the PIL Code on the applicable law, under item 3 above). However, it should be kept in mind that the Serbian law in such cases requires approval of the Social Care Center for disposal with the ward's property (Family Code, Art. 140(2)). The influence of the *lex fori* might be strong in such cases, i.e. the bank might require approval for withdrawal by the Socal Care Centre on the basis of its usual practice, without really checking the applicable law.

If a guardian has been appointed to that person by a foreign court or other competent authority (e.g. in the country of his origin or domicile), the judgment or decision on appointing a guardian would first have to be recognized, and the appointed guardian could then withdraw the money from the account, presumably without approval of the Social Care Center, since that person would not be within the jurisdiction of this authority (please, refer to provisions of the PIL Code on recognition of foreign judgments, under item 3 above). If approval of a foreign court or other authority is required under the applicable national law, the guardian would have to submit such approval, furnished with an apostille by notary or other competent authority.

Sale of a home or other property in your State

The same as in the previous question.

Family dispute as to care of the person currently resident in your State (eg. whether to return to England & Wales)

There are no provisions on this in the statutes. Presumably the same rules would apply – the guardian appointed under Serbian law might have to seek approval of the Social Care Centre, while the guardian appointed under foreign law, whose authority has been recognized by exequatur of the judgment granting authority, could make such a decision without approval of the Serbian Social Care Centre. If approval of a foreign court or other authority is required under the applicable national law, the guardian would have to submit such approval, furnished with an apostille by a notary or other competent authority.

Decision about medical treatment in your State

The same answer as to the first question under this item.

B. Would the answers to A. above vary if person was not a national of the United Kingdom but had been habitually resident in England and Wales prior to their impairment or insufficiency?

If a person was a Serbian national habitually resident in England and Wales prior to his or her impairment or insufficiency, but not domiciled there (according to the Serbian notion of domicile), the judgment or decision on appointment of a guardian would probably not be recognized, i.e. proceedings for appointment of a guardian would have initiated in Serbia, and the Social Care Centre would exercise its authorities of approval and control pursuant to Serbian law as the applicable national law.

C. Is there an emergency procedure?

As stated above (under item 2), Art. 77 of the PIL Code grants the Serbian competent authority (the Social Care Centre) power to take the necessary provisional measures for the protection of personality, rights and interests of a foreign citizen who is present or has property in Serbia. It shall inform the authority of the State whose citizen is concerned of any such measures. The usual procedure would be to appoint a temporary guardian under Art. 132 of the Family Act (Official Journal of the Republic of Serbia no. 18/2005). Pursuant to Art. 132(2), the Social Care Center shall appoint a temporary guardian to a foreign citizen who is present in Serbia or who has property in the territory of Serbia. Pursuant to Art. 132(3), the decision on appointment of a temporary guardian determines the legal transaction or type of legal transactions that the temporary guardian may engage in, depending on the circumstances of each particular case.

PART X

5. Sources of information

A list of lawyers practising in the province of Vojvodina can be obtained from the
Bar Association of Vojvodina http://www.akv.org.rs/ and a list of lawyers practising
in Serbia can be obtained from the Bar Association of Serbia
http://www.advokatska-komora.co.rs/.

Completed by:

Name	**Professor Dr Maja Stanivuković**
eMail	stanivuk@pf.uns.ac.rs

Are you a solicitor/notary/advocate or lawyer who provides legal advice and services for nationals of the United Kingdom in your State?	☒	Yes	☐	No

October 2010

SLOVENIA

Name of State	Slovenia				
Is your State part of a larger Federal country?				X	No

1. Convention on the International Protection of Adults (Hague 2000)

Has this Convention been ratified by your State?				X	No
Does your State intend to ratify the Convention?		☐	Yes	☐	No
Even if not ratified is it generally applied in any event?				X	No

Explanation

> The Convention on the International Protection of Adults was signed by the Republic of Slovenia on the 18th September 2008, but it has not yet been ratified.
>
> We have no information as to a likely date for ratification.

2. Jurisdiction

A. *Does jurisdiction of your Courts usually depend upon the Personal Law of the Adult?*

		X	Yes		
If so, which is usually the relevant connecting factor?					
Nationality		X	Yes		

B. *Can jurisdiction of the Courts in your State also depend upon:*

Habitual residence		☐	Yes	☐	No
Domicile		X	Yes		
Situs of property		X	Yes		
Presence in the State		X	Yes		

Explanation

Nationality:

The judicial authority of the Republic of Slovenia has exclusive jurisdiction in care cases of Slovene citizens, irrespective of where they have permanent residence (Article 84 of the Private International Law and Procedure Act, Uradni list (Official Gazette) RS, no. 56/1999, 45/2008). Nevertheless, the authority of the Republic of Slovenia does not issue decisions and does not take measures in care cases of a Slovene citizen if he or she has permanent residence abroad and if it establishes that the authority that has jurisdiction under the law of the foreign State has already issued a decision or adopted measures whereby it has ensured the personality, rights and interests of the Slovene citizen (Article 85 of the Private International Law and Procedure Act).

Presence in the State and situs of property:

The authority of the Republic of Slovenia protects the personality, rights and interests of a foreign citizen who is located in the Republic of Slovenia or has property here and informs the authority of that person's State about this (first paragraph of Article 86 of the Private International Law and Procedure Act).

Domicile:

The authority of the Republic of Slovenia issues decisions and adopts measures in care cases concerning a foreign citizen who has permanent residence in the Republic of Slovenia if the authority of his or her own State has not provided protection of her or his personality, rights and interests (second paragraph of Article 86 of the Private International Law and Procedure Act).

C. If the Courts of your State have jurisdiction, which internal law is applicable? That of:

Your State	X	Yes		
Habitual residence	☐	Yes	☐	No
Domicile	☐	Yes	☐	No
Nationality	X	Yes		
Situs of property	☐	Yes	☐	No

Explanation

Nationality:

In Slovenian law personal status is traditionally based on the national principle (*lex nationalis*). National law is decisive:

1) For assessing legal and contractual capacity of a natural person; for legal incapacitation and limitation of contractual capacity. For the sake of the security of legal transactions, the existence of contractual capacity may also exceptionally be assessed under the law of the place in which a liability arose, if the natural person has contractual capacity under the law of the State of which she or he is a citizen – it is not generally used for family and inheritance relations (Article 13 of the Private International Law and Procedure Act);

2) For the determination or change of the personal name of an individual (Article 14 of the Private International Law and Procedure Act), for declaring a missing person deceased (Article 16 of the Private International Law and Procedure Act);

3) For placing someone under the care of a guardian, for the ending of guardianship and for relationships between the guardian and her or his ward (the law of the ward's nationality is used – first paragraph of Article 15 of the Private International Law and Procedure Act).

Law of our State (lex fori):

Temporary protective measures are ordered for a foreign citizen or person without citizenship under the law of the Republic of Slovenia and they last until the State of jurisdiction decides on these and takes the necessary measures. The law of the Republic of Slovenia is also used in relation to the protection of property of an absent foreign citizen or person without citizenship, which is located on the territory of the Republic of Slovenia (second and third paragraphs of Article 15 of the Private International Law and Procedure Act).

D. Does the internal law of your State have provision for Powers of Representation (also known as Continuing, Lasting or Durable Powers of Attorney) for the following:

Economic and financial matters			X	No
Personal welfare			X	No
Health care and medical treatment	X	Yes		

Explanation

In Slovenia, only in the field of medicine is the personality of an adult patient in cases in which she or he is no longer capable of deciding for herself or himself specifically protected by the institution of an authorised health representative. A patient over 18 years of age may designate an authorised health representative in a written and notarised document (Article 32 of the Patients' Rights Act, Official Gazette RS, no. 15/2008). In the event of a patient being unable to decide for himself or herself, the authorised representative decides about his or her healthcare and other rights in the medical field. The patient can thus be sure that, in the event of being incapable of making a decision, an authorised health representative will do so instead of a guardian designated by the centre for social work.

An ordinary Power ceases with the loss of contractual capacity of the authorizing person or the authorized representative (Article 785 of the Obligations Act, Official Gazette RS, no. 97/2007 – consolidated text).

E. Does your State include power for the Courts to make orders or decisions about:

Impairment or insufficiency of personal faculties (lack of capacity)	X	Yes		
Economic and financial matters	X	Yes		
Personal welfare	X	Yes		
Health care and medical treatment	X	Yes		
A new Will or Testament	X	Yes		

If you have answered 'yes' to any of the above, please confirm whether the Courts may authorize another person (such as a guardian, curator, receiver or deputy) to make decisions on behalf of the Adult on the following matters:

Economic and financial matters	X	Yes		
Personal welfare	X	Yes		
Health care and medical treatment	X	Yes		
A new Will or Testament			X	No

If you have answered 'yes' to any of the above, and a person is authorized to make decisions on behalf of the Adult, please summarise the extent of that person's responsibility. For example, is there a duty to produce accounts to the Courts or other supervisory body? Does anyone oversee or monitor conduct? Are there any restrictions on what can or cannot be done in the name of the person who is incapable?

Slovene law protects adult persons who have permanently lost the capacity to decide independently for themselves, by means of deprivation of contractual capacity in a judicial proceeding, which follows placing the person under guardianship in a proceeding before a centre for social work.

A court may deprive a person of contractual capacity who, because of mental illness, mental retardation, dependence on alcohol or drugs, or other causes that affect their psycho-physical state, is incapable of taking care of themselves, their rights and benefits. The procedure may be started ex officio or on a motion.

Deprivation of contractual capacity may be full or partial. A person fully deprived of contractual capacity may no longer conclude legal transactions. All legal transactions that they conclude themselves are void. A guardian must therefore decide for such persons.

If a court partially deprives a person of contractual capacity, the approval of a guardian is required for the validity of all legal transactions, or the legal transaction may be challenged. A centre for social work may supplement a judicial decision on partial deprivation of contractual capacity in a proceeding of placing a person in care, by specifying, as necessary, legal transactions that a person partially deprived of contractual capacity may nevertheless conclude independently.

A guardian appointed by a centre for social work looks after the personality of the ward and her or his property rights in entirety (Article 187 of the Marriage and Family Relations Act, Official Gazette RS, no. 69/2004, 101/2007 – consolidated text). The property of the person under guardianship is handed over to the guardian for management only after it has been inventoried and valued. The guardian is independent in her or his work. Only in the case of more important legal transactions, which go beyond regular management, does she or he need the approval of the centre for social work (e.g., for alienation or encumbrance of real estate of major value, for renunciation of an inheritance or bequest – Articles 189 and 191 of the Marriage and Family Relations Act).

The deficiency of the Marriage and Family Relations Act is that it does not require the approval of the centre for social work for more important decisions by the guardian concerning the person of the ward (for example, placement in a home for the elderly). Such a requirement is only envisaged outside the Marriage and Family Relations Act, and only in the case of sterilization of a ward for medical reasons (Article 11 of the Act Regulating Health Measures in Exercising Freedom of Choice in Childbearing). A guardian must report annually on her or his work to the centre for social work and deliver a balance of account on her or his work. A guardian must also do this at the specific demand of the centre for social work. The guardian's care of the ward (in particular care for the ward's health) must be evident from the guardian's report. The report must also provide data on the management of the ward's property and disposal of it, on the ward's income and expenditure and on the final state of her or his property (Article 194 of the Marriage and Family Relations Act). The centre for social work must conscientiously examine the guardian's report and, as required, take all necessary measures to protect the ward's interests (Article 195 of the Marriage and Family Relations Act). If it finds that the guardian has been negligent in performing the duties of guardian, that she or he has abused her or his rights or that her or his work threatens the ward's interests or that it would be more beneficial for the ward to have a different guardian, it discharges the guardian (Article 198 of the Marriage and Family Relations Act of the Marriage and Family Relations Act).

A ward capable of so doing, her or his relations, competent authorities and professional institutions may object to the work of the guardian and centre for social work. The ministry responsible for the family decides on an objection (Article 200 of the Marriage and Family Relations Act).

Deprivation of contractual capacity or the extension of parental rights does not automatically affect the decision-making capacity of an individual about strictly personal matters. Capacity of judgement at the moment at which an individual makes such a decision is generally sufficient. A person deprived of contractual capacity may thus, for example, still validly decide about medical interventions. Only if, in the procedure of medical treatment it appears that the person is not capable of deciding and cannot thus independently decide about a medical intervention is a decision accepted by a guardian appointed by the centre for social work at the time of deprivation of contractual capacity. If in the procedure of medical treatment it appears that a person who is not of sound mind and thus not capable themselves of deciding on medical interventions, has not been deprived of contractual capacity, the centre for social work appoints a guardian for such a person only for this case. Such a guardian is also responsible to the centre for social work for their work.

PART X

If in a probate procedure the question is raised of the validity of a will because of the testator's unsoundness of mind at the time of making the will, the probate court directs the person whose right is least likely (normally the person contesting the validity of the will) to civil suit (point one of second paragraph of Article 210 of the Inheritance Act, Official Gazette SRS, no. 15/1976, 23/1978, Official Gazette RS, no. 17/1991-I, 13/1994, 117/2000, 67/2001, 83/2001, 73/2004). The probate court only declares the heirs when the validity of the will has been decided in civil proceedings.

3. Recognition of Powers of Representation / Continuing or Lasting Powers of Attorney and protective measures for Adults from England & Wales

A. Are the following Powers of Representation and delegations under the law of England & Wales recognised and enforceable:

Continuing Powers of Attorney for economic and financial matters	X	Yes		
Continuing Powers of Attorney for personal welfare	X	Yes		
Continuing Powers of Attorney for healthcare and medical treatment	X	Yes		
Advance Directives	X	Yes		

In addition to an Exequatur under the law of the state in which the court decision was issued, an applicant must enclose with the motion for recognition of a foreign court decision also the foreign court decision, or a notarized copy of it, together with attestation of the foreign court of jurisdiction or other authority that the court decision is res judicata under the law of the state in which it was issued. If the foreign court decision or a notarized copy of it are not in a language in official use at the court, the party that is applying for recognition must also submit a notarized translation of the foreign court decision in a language in official use by the court (Article 95 of the Private International Law and Procedure Act). A court shall nevertheless refuse recognition of a foreign court decision:

– if it finds to the objection of a person against whom it was issued that this person was unable to participate in the procedure because of an irregularity in the procedure (Articles 96 and 103 of the Private International Law and Procedure Act);

– if it finds to the objection of a person against whom it was issued that the jurisdiction of the foreign court was based exclusively on one of the following circumstances: the citizenship of the plaintiff; the property of the defendant in the State of issue of the decision; the defendant's personal service of the document by which the procedure was commenced; or if the court that issued the decision did not respect an agreement on jurisdiction of the Republic of Slovenia (Article 98 of the Private International Law and Procedure Act);

– if the court or other authority of the Republic of Slovenia has issued a decision res judicata in the same case or if in the Republic of Slovenia another foreign court decision issued in the same case has been recognized. The court delays recognition of a foreign court decision if before a court of the Republic of Slovenia, previously started civil proceedings are taking place in the same civil case and between the same parties, until such a case is completed res judicata (Article 99 of the Private International Law and Procedure Act).

B. Are the following Protective Measures of the courts of England & Wales recognised and enforceable in your State?

Decision as to impairment or insufficiency of personal faculties	X	Yes		
Appointment of a Representative to deal with economic and financial matters	X	Yes		
Appointment of a Representative to deal with personal welfare	X	Yes		
Appointment of a Representative to deal with health care and medical treatment	X	Yes		
Decision authorising the making of a new Will or Testament	X	Yes		

Explanation

For all foreign court decisions relating to personal status (in this case, decision as to impairment or insufficiency of personal faculties, appointment of a Representative to deal with economic and financial matters, appointment of a Representative to deal with personal welfare, appointment of a Representative to deal with health care and medical treatment) of a citizen of the State in which the decision was issued, all the limitations mentioned above in this section apply. In these cases, circumstances such as exclusive jurisdiction of a Slovene court, public order and the non-existence of reciprocity are not impediments to recognition of enforcement of a foreign court decision. These three circumstances, in addition to those enumerated above, would only be important if it was a matter of recognition and enforcement of a foreign court decision relating to the personal status of a Slovene citizen (for jurisdiction in guardianship cases, see section 2 of this questionnaire). Similarly, it is necessary to respect all the stated circumstances in recognition and enforcement of a decision authorising the making of a Testament, since in such a case it is no longer a matter of deciding on personal status.

PART X

4. Procedures in your State

A. *How may the following situations be dealt with.*

Withdrawal of money from a bank account situated in your State

The authority of the Republic of Slovenia is competent on the basis of the following statutory rules:

1) The authority of the Republic of Slovenia, by means of **urgent temporary measures,** protects the personality, rights and interests of a **foreign citizen who is located in the Republic of Slovenia or has property in this country,** and informs the authority of his State about this (first paragraph of Article 86 of the Private International Law and Procedure Act).

2) The authority of the Republic of Slovenia issues a decision and adopts measures in guardianship cases **of a foreign citizen who has permanent resident in the Republic of Slovenia, if the authority of her or his own state has not looked after the protection of her or his personality, rights and interests** (second paragraph of Article 86 of the Private International Law and Procedure Act).

Rules on the use of law:

For placing someone under the care of a guardian, for the ending of guardianship and for relationships between the guardian and his ward, the **law of the State of which the ward is a citizen is used** (first paragraph of Article 15 of the Private International Law and Procedure Act).

Temporary measures of care are ordered under the law of the Republic of Slovenia against a foreign citizen or person without citizenship, who is located in the Republic of Slovenia, and they last until the State of jurisdiction decides on this and adopts the necessary measures. The law of the Republic of Slovenia is also used in relation to the protection of property of an absent foreign citizen and person without citizenship which is located on the territory of the Republic of Slovenia (second and third paragraphs of Article 15 of the Private International Law and Procedure Act).

If the interests and benefits of a person, who does not her or himself have the capacity for withdrawal of money from a bank account situated in Slovenia, are protected by the appointment of a guardian for the withdrawal of money, the guardian must obtain the consent of the centre for social work when the withdrawal of a major amount of money is concerned.

Sale of a home or other property in your State

See the rules on jurisdiction and the use of law in the first box of this section. If the interests and benefits of a person, who has not her or himself capacity for the sale of a home or other property in Slovenia, are protected by the appointment of a guardian, the guardian requires the consent of the centre for social work for the sale of real estate and moveable property of major value.

Family dispute as to care of the person currently resident in your State (eg. whether to return to England & Wales)

In relation to guardianship of an adult person, see the rules on jurisdiction and use of law in the first box of this section.

Decision about medical treatment in your State

> See the rules on jurisdiction and use of law in the first box of this section.

B. Would the answers to A. above vary if person was not a national of the United Kingdom but had been habitually resident in England and Wales prior to their impairment or insufficiency?

> In care cases concerning an adult, citizenship and location of the ward or her or his property on the territory of the RS are crucial. The circumstance of where a person resided prior to the loss of capacity is not decisive. For details, see sub-section A of this section.

C. Is there an emergency procedure?

> The courts resolve all cases of family law (including the appointment of a guardian) as priority (Article 10a of the Marriage and Family Relations Act).

Completed by:

Name	Prof. Dr. Barbara Novak, University of Ljubljana

October 2010

SPAIN

Name of State	Spain					
Is your State part of a larger Federal country?		☐	Yes	☐	No	
If so, are any of the laws affecting Adults made at the level of the Federal Government?		X	Yes			

Spain is not a Federal country, but the Autonomous Communities have legislative and administrative powers in many areas.

Spanish general law regulates the procedure for incapacitation, the regimes of protection for incapable adults and the provisions of private international law. Some Autonomous Communities (but not all of them) have powers to legislate in the area of private law. The Communities of Aragón (Act 13/2006, 27th December), and Catalonia (Act 25/2010, 29th July) have enacted exhaustive statutory rules on the protection of incapables.

Both Spanish general law (Act 41/2002, covering the basic principles) and most Autonomous Communities have regulated the document of advance directives for medical treatment.

1. Convention on the International Protection of Adults (Hague 2000)

Has this Convention been ratified by your State?			X	No	
Does your State intend to ratify the Convention?	☐	Yes	☐	No	
Even if not ratified is it generally applied in any event?			X	No	

Explanation

It is uncertain at the moment whether Spain intends to ratify the Convention.

2. Jurisdiction

A. *Does jurisdiction of your Courts usually depend upon the Personal Law of the Adult?*

	X	Yes		
If so, which is usually the relevant connecting factor?				
Habitual residence	X	Yes		

B. Can jurisdiction of the Courts in your State also depend upon:

Domicile			X	No
Nationality			X	No
Situs of property	X	Yes		
Presence in the State	X	Yes		

Explanation

Situs of property and presence in the State are relevant for adopting interim and urgenct measures.

C. If the Courts of your State have jurisdiction, which internal law is applicable? That of:

Your State			x	No
Habitual residence			x	No
Domicile			x	No
Nationality	X	Yes		
Situs of property			x	No

Explanation

Nationality law is relevant to all purposes: assessment of incapacity, legal consequences of incapacity, regimes of protection, validity of powers. The law of residence and situs of property may be relevant for interim and emergency measures.

D. Does the internal law of your State have provision for Powers of Representation (also known as Continuing, Lasting or Durable Powers of Attorney) for the following:

Economic and financial matters	X	Yes		
Personal welfare	X	Yes		
Health care and medical treatment	X	Yes		

PART X

Explanation

> Durable powers of attorney are allowed under Spanish and Catalan law.
>
> In Spanish general law there are no specific restrictions. For practical purposes powers for economic and financial matters are given in a notarial deed. The notary has to notify the Civil Register, which provides publicity. In Catalan law, durable powers must be registered in an administrative Register (Registre de Nomenaments Tutelars no Testamentaris).
>
> The giving of powers for health care is subject to formal requirements which may vary depending on the Autonomous Community. A common requirement is that the power be given in a notarial deed or, alternatively, before three witnesses.
>
> *Does an ordinary Power cease to be effective in the event of a lack of capacity?*
>
> Yes.

E. Does your State include power for the Courts to make orders or decisions about:

Impairment or insufficiency of personal faculties (lack of capacity)	X	Yes		
Economic and financial matters	X	Yes		
Personal welfare	X	Yes		
Health care and medical treatment	X	Yes		
A new Will or Testament			X	No

If you have answered 'yes' to any of the above, please confirm whether the Courts may authorize another person (such as a guardian, curator, receiver or deputy) to make decisions on behalf of the Adult on the following matters:

Economic and financial matters	X	Yes		
Personal welfare	X	Yes		
Health care and medical treatment	X	Yes		
A new Will or Testament			X	No

If you have answered 'yes' to any of the above, and a person is authorized to make decisions on behalf of the Adult, please summarise the extent of that person's responsibility. For example, is there a duty to produce accounts to the Courts or other supervisory body? Does anyone oversee or monitor conduct? Are there any restrictions on what can or cannot be done in the name of the person who is incapable?

Please list the procedures

> A guardian or tutor needs judicial authorisation to alienate real estate and make other relevant financial transactions on behalf of the incapable.
>
> As regards personal welfare, a guardian needs judicial authorisation to commit the incapable person to a psychiatric hospital or institution.
>
> A guardian is under a duty to produce annual accounts and a final account on termination of the guardianship to the Court.
>
> The judge has the power to order additional control or supervision measures at the request of incapable person's close relatives, if he/she considers there is a need for it.
>
> A guardian is liable for negligence or misconduct in the fulfillment of his/her duties and can be removed by the judge at the request of the incapable person's close relatives or the public attorney.

3. Recognition of Powers of Representation / Continuing or Lasting Powers of Attorney and protective measures for Adults from England & Wales

A. Are the following Powers of Representation and delegations under the law of England & Wales recognised and enforceable:

Continuing Powers of Attorney for economic and financial matters	X	Yes		
Continuing Powers of Attorney for personal welfare	X	Yes		
Continuing Powers of Attorney for healthcare and medical treatment	X	Yes		
Advance Directives	X	Yes		

Are there any additional formalities required such as an Exequatur?

No.

B. Are the following Protective Measures of the courts of England & Wales recognised and enforceable in your State?

Decision as to impairment or insufficiency of personal faculties	X	Yes		
Appointment of a Representative to deal with economic and financial matters	X	Yes		
Appointment of a Representative to deal with personal welfare	X	Yes		

Appointment of a Representative to deal with health care and medical treatment	X	Yes	
Decision authorising the making of a new Will or Testament			X	No

Explanation

Decisions on incapacitation, extent of capacity, and the appointment of representatives are governed by the law of the nationality.

If a will is made before a Spanish notary, the notary may refuse to authorize the document if he considers that the person before him/her has insufficient capacity to express his/her will, regardless of the existence of a judicial decision authorizing the making of a new will.

4. Procedures in your State

A. *How may the following situations be dealt with.*

Withdrawal of money from a bank account situated in your State

Capacity of the account holder and authority to withdraw the money are governed by the law of the account holder's nationality.

Sale of a home or other property in your State

Capacity of the seller and authority to sell are governed by the law of the seller's nationality. If the sale has to be authorized by a public notary in Spain and the seller intervenes personally, the notary will assess the seller's capacity at the time of the transaction and may refuse to authorize the contract if he/she considers that the seller is not in the position to give consent.

Family dispute as to care of the person currently resident in your State (eg. whether to return to England & Wales)

The regimes of protection and the authority to make personal care decisions on behalf of an incapable are governed by the law of the incapable person's nationality.

Interim and emergency measures are governed by the law of the habitual residence.

Decision about medical treatment in your State

There are no specific rules governing medical treatment with regard to foreigners. As a matter of principle, the making of decisions should be governed by the law of the patient's nationality, and by Spanish law as a default law.

B. Would the answers to A. above vary if person was not a national of the United Kingdom but had been habitually resident in England and Wales prior to their impairment or insufficiency?

Yes, because the relevant law is the law of nationality, not the law of habitual residence.

Completed by:

Name	**Josep Ferrer Riba**
eMail	josep.ferrer@upf.edu

Are you a solicitor/notary/advocate or lawyer who provides legal advice and services for nationals of the United Kingdom in your State?			X	No

October 2010

SWITZERLAND

Name of State	Switzerland			
Is your State part of a larger Federal country?		X	Yes	
If so, are any of the laws affecting Adults made at the level of the Federal Government?		X	Yes	
The whole family law, including protection of adults with incapacity ("Vormundschaftsrecht"), is dealt with at the Federal level. Only some procedural rules are allowed at State or Canton level.				

1. Convention on the International Protection of Adults (Hague 2000)

Has this Convention been ratified by your State?	X	Yes		

Explanation

The Convention is valid law since 1 July 2009 without any reservations, declarations or notifications, and it has legal force for the whole Federation of Switzerland.

2. Jurisdiction

A. Does jurisdiction of your Courts usually depend upon the Personal Law of the Adult?

	X	Yes		
If so, which is usually the relevant connecting factor?				
Domicile	X	Yes		

B. Can jurisdiction of the Courts in your State also depend upon:

Habitual residence	X	Yes		
Nationality	X	Yes		
Situs of property	X	Yes		
Presence in the State	X	Yes		

Explanation

> The **jurisdiction concerning the protection of adults** is defined by the Hague Convention on the International Protection of Adults mentioned above.
>
> In circumstances where this convention does not apply, jurisdiction is the subject of quite complex regulations under Swiss private international law. Domicile, habitual residence and nationality are defined under Article 20 and following of the Swiss CPIL. An English (although not completely up to date) version of the CPIL is available at: http://www.umbricht.ch/pdf/SwissPIL.pdf
>
> A person's domicile is the place in which he resides with the intention of settling. It is also said to be the "centre of the existence" of a person.

C. If the Courts of your State have jurisdiction, which internal law is applicable? That of:

Your State	☐	Yes	☐	No
Habitual residence	☐	Yes	☐	No
Domicile	☐	Yes	☐	No
Nationality	☐	Yes	☐	No
Situs of property	☐	Yes	☐	No

Explanation

> Swiss private international law concerning the protection of adults refers to the Hague Convention.
>
> For other areas of private law, the question of applicable law is in detail regulated by Swiss private international law – CPIL.

D. Does the internal law of your State have provision for Powers of Representation (also known as Continuing, Lasting or Durable Powers of Attorney) for the following:

Economic and financial matters	X	Yes		
Personal welfare	X	Yes		
Health care and medical treatment	X	Yes		

PART X

Explanation

A new law concerning the protection of adults and also containing detailed provisions for Continuing Powers of Attorney will become legally effective in 2013 or 2014. Under the current law, only Powers of Attorney for economic and financial matters are regulated by Federal law. Concerning Health care and medical treatment, the law of the concerned state applies ("kantonales Gesundheitsgesetz").

An ordinary Power usually ceases to be effective in the event of a lack of capacity, unless the Power states otherwise.

E. Does your State include power for the Courts to make orders or decisions about:

Impairment or insufficiency of personal faculties (lack of capacity)	X	Yes		
Economic and financial matters	X	Yes		
Personal welfare	X	Yes		
Health care and medical treatment	X	Yes		
A new Will or Testament			X	No

Please confirm whether the Courts may authorize another person (such as a guardian, curator, receiver or deputy) to make decisions on behalf of the Adult on the following matters:

Economic and financial matters	X	Yes		
Personal welfare	X	Yes		
Health care and medical treatment	X	Yes		
A new Will or Testament			X	No

Under current law, the guardianship authority can either appoint a guardian ("Vormund"), who is responsible for all decisions on behalf of the Adult ("The guardian represents the ward in all legal matters"), or it can appoint a guardian only for specific matters, e.g. a welfare advocate ("Vermögensbeistand") who only takes care of economic matters of the person for whom he is appointed.

The guardianship authority ("Vormundschaftsbehörde") has to supervise the guardian. There is also a duty to produce accounts to the authority and to produce an annual report. There are a few restrictions concerning the possible decisions of the guardian. For example, if he wants to sell real estate of the person lacking mental capacity, he has to get the consent of the authority in advance.

Under new law (legally effective 2013 or 2014) the guardianship authority will
always designate a guardian ("Beistand") and in its order the authority will have to
describe the matters the guardian is responsible for and the coverage of his decision
making powers. The guardian is personally responsible for his acts and he has to
deliver annual reports to the guardianship authority. Similar to current law, there are
certain decisions he can only make if the guardianship authority gives his consent.

Concerning medical treatment, the decisions of the guardian always have to be in
line with the presumed will of the patient. If there is any doubt about the presumed
will, the guardian has to follow the objective interest of the patient.

3. Recognition of Powers of Representation / Continuing or Lasting Powers of Attorney and protective measures for Adults from England & Wales

A. Are the following Powers of Representation and delegations under the law of England & Wales recognised and enforceable:

Continuing Powers of Attorney for economic and financial matters	X	Yes		
Continuing Powers of Attorney for personal welfare	X	Yes		
Continuing Powers of Attorney for healthcare and medical treatment	X	Yes		
Advance Directives	☐	Yes	☐	No

As for the voluntary appointment of a representative, the law of England & Wales
would be applicable. This means that the power of attorney will remain valid and
enforceable.

As Switzerland so far did not have a regulation concerning Advance Directives (the
federal law will become legally effective in 2013 or 2014, as mentioned above), it
cannot be said generally that such directives are recognized. They would most
probably be taken into account for any medical treatment. If the treatment takes
place in a state hospital, the law of the concerned state will apply.

B. Are the following Protective Measures of the courts of England & Wales recognised and enforceable in your State?

Decision as to impairment or insufficiency of personal faculties	X	Yes		
Appointment of a Representative to deal with economic and financial matters	X	Yes		
Appointment of a Representative to deal with personal welfare	X	Yes		
Appointment of a Representative to deal with health care and medical treatment	☐	Yes	☐	No

PART X

Decision authorising the making of a new Will or Testament			X	No

Explanation

As for the recognition of court decisions concerning Protective Measures and the like, the Hague Convention does apply. It is not certain but most likely that the Hague Convention also applies to health care and medical treatment decisions.

Concerning the making of a Last Will by a resident of a foreign country, Swiss private international law says that testamentary capacity is determined by the respective regulations of this country. However, in Swiss law, the making of a testament is said to be absolutely personal and can under no circumstances be transferred to another person, not even by a court decision. If a legal representative produces a testament he has made for another person, Swiss authorities therefore might not recognize the testament. If the testament is valid under the law of England and Wales *and* this is certified by the competent English authorities, such a decision, if it needs to be enforced in Switzerland (e.g. if it concerns real estate in Switzerland) will probably be accepted.

4. Procedures in your State

A. *How may the following situations be dealt with.*

Withdrawal of money from a bank account situated in your State

If there is an appointment of a representative by a Court, the Hague Convention does apply: the decision is recognized in Switzerland. The representative has to present the legally valid decision of the English court including a description of his rights.

In case of a private power of attorney, a document containing the power of attorney needs to be deposited at the bank.

Sale of a home or other property in your State

Again, if there is a valid court decision concerning the appointment of a representative, it is recognized in Switzerland.

Although the sale of land needs public certification, the voluntary appointment of a representative does not. However, the notary needs a written document concerning the power of attorney and he has to verify its authenticity as well as the identity of the representative.

Family dispute as to care of the person currently resident in your State (eg. whether to return to England & Wales)

Again, this question is ruled by the Hague Convention. If there is an official representative of the person concerned, it will be up to him to decide.

Decision about medical treatment in your State

> This is a very difficult question to answer because current Swiss law does not provide a possibility to appoint a representative for medical treatment. If there is an English court decision concerning the appointment of a representative saying that decisions about medical matters are included, this decision would probably be recognized in Switzerland.

B. Would the answers to A. above vary if person was not a national of the United Kingdom but had been habitually resident in England and Wales prior to their impairment or insufficiency?

> No, as the Hague Convention is based on the habitual residence of a person, not (primarily) on their nationality. The result would be the same under Swiss private international law.

C. Is there an emergency procedure?

> Yes, as laid down in Article 10 of the convention and also in the Swiss international private law.
>
> In cases of emergency, the local guardianship authority ("Vormundschaftsbehörde") will (as it is laid down in Article 392 of the Swiss Civil Code) designate a representative who then will act for the adult who is unable to act for himself. This will also be the case if the legal representative of the person concerned is for any reason prevented from representing the person.

5. Sources of information

> http://www.swisslawyers.com/
>
> As for legal guidance, there is no information in English.

Completed by:

Name	Prof. Dr. Regina Aebi-Müller
eMail	Regina.Aebi@unilu.ch

Are you a solicitor/notary/advocate or lawyer who provides legal advice and services for nationals of the United Kingdom in your State?			X	No

October 2010

USA: FLORIDA

Name of State	USA: Florida			
Is your State part of a larger Federal country?		X	Yes	
If so, are any of the laws affecting Adults made at the level of the Federal Government?			X	No
Guardian procedures are dealt with at the state level in the state court system.				

1. Convention on the International Protection of Adults (Hague 2000)

Has this Convention been ratified by your State?			X	No
Does your State intend to ratify the Convention?	☐	Yes	☐	No
Even if not ratified is it generally applied in any event?			X	No

2. Jurisdiction

A. *Does jurisdiction of your Courts usually depend upon the Personal Law of the Adult?*

		X	Yes	
If so, which is usually the relevant connecting factor?				
Habitual residence		X	Yes	
Domicile		X	Yes	

B. *Can jurisdiction of the Courts in your State also depend upon:*

Nationality			X	No
Situs of property		X	Yes	
Presence in the State		X	Yes	

Explanation

The courts in the State of Florida have jurisdiction over people residing in the state or property located in the state. In Florida there are many residents with second homes. If one of them becomes incompetent while in the state, the state court would have jurisdiction.

C. If the Courts of your State have jurisdiction, which internal law is applicable? That of:

Your State	X	Yes		
Habitual residence			X	No
Domicile			X	No
Nationality			X	No
Situs of property	X	Yes		

Explanation

The courts can appoint a guardian of the person residing the state or of the property located with in the state. In litigation the courts can appoint a guardian-ad-litem for the purposes of the litigation only. In the case of adults this is done when the adult is located in another state and is incompetent but needs to have his or her interest protected in litigation.

D. Does the internal law of your State have provision for Powers of Representation (also known as Continuing, Lasting or Durable Powers of Attorney) for the following:

Economic and financial matters	X	Yes	
Personal welfare	X	Yes	
Health care and medical treatment	X	Yes	

Explanation

We call these Advance Directives and they consist of Durable Powers of Attorney, Living Wills and Health Care Surrogates. They do not have to be registered or filed with the courts. Also, in Living Trusts a provision is usually inserted that if the Trustee (usually the Settlor) becomes incompetent in the opinion of two doctors, he is removed as Trustee and an alternate trustee is appointed in the Trust Document to serve as trustee until the original trustee becomes competent again.

A Durable Power of Attorney will survive lack of capacity (that is why it is called a Durable Power of Attorney, but expires upon a court adjudication of incompetency and appointment of a legal guardian. We usually suggest a Durable Power of Attorney when a person is competent so as to avoid a later court proceeding for incompetency and appointment of a guardian.

PART X

E. Does your State include power for the Courts to make orders or decisions about:

Impairment or insufficiency of personal faculties (lack of capacity)	X	Yes		
Economic and financial matters	X	Yes		
Personal welfare	X	Yes		
Health care and medical treatment	X	Yes		
A new Will or Testament			X	No

If you have answered 'yes' to any of the above, please confirm whether the Courts may authorize another person (such as a guardian, curator, receiver or deputy) to make decisions on behalf of the Adult on the following matters:

Economic and financial matters	X	Yes		
Personal welfare	X	Yes		
Health care and medical treatment	X	Yes		
A new Will or Testament			x	No

If you have answered 'yes' to any of the above, and a person is authorized to make decisions on behalf of the Adult, please summarise the extent of that person's responsibility. For example, is there a duty to produce accounts to the Courts or other supervisory body? Does anyone oversee or monitor conduct? Are there any restrictions on what can or cannot be done in the name of the person who is incapable?

Please list the procedures

When a petition is filed in the court by an interested person, the court orders a medical and mental examination of the subject of the petition to ensure that the person is actually incompetent. Based on the medical report the judge can adjudicate a person incompetent and appoint a guardian for the person, the property or both. The guardian has to keep detailed records and make regular periodic filings of accounts to the court. Sometimes, the court may also ask for status reports. The court oversees or monitors the guardianship. The guardian and the lawyer for the guardian have to make application to the court for payment of their fees by detailing the services performed. The lawyer has to have an affidavit or live testimony from another lawyer that the services performed were usual and necessary and the fees charged are usual, necessary and fair.

3. Recognition of Powers of Representation / Continuing or Lasting Powers of Attorney and protective measures for Adults from England & Wales .

A. Are the following Powers of Representation and delegations under the law of England & Wales recognised and enforceable:

Continuing Powers of Attorney for economic and financial matters			X	No
Continuing Powers of Attorney for personal welfare			X	No
Continuing Powers of Attorney for healthcare and medical treatment			X	No
Advance Directives			X	No

Are there any additional formalities required such as an Exequatur?

Only Florida Statutes are applicable.

B. Are the following Protective Measures of the courts of England & Wales recognised and enforceable in your State?

Decision as to impairment or insufficiency of personal faculties			X	No
Appointment of a Representative to deal with economic and financial matters			X	No
Appointment of a Representative to deal with personal welfare			X	No
Appointment of a Representative to deal with health care and medical treatment			X	No
Decision authorising the making of a new Will or Testament			X	No

Explanation

Only Florida Statutes are applicable.

PART X

4. Procedures in your State

A. How may the following situations be dealt with for a person with connections to England & Wales who by reason of an impairment or insufficiency of their personal faculties is not in a position to protect their interests.

Withdrawal of money from a bank account situated in your State

> Yes, if the person is a resident of the state or the money is located in a bank in the state.

Sale of a home or other property in your State

> Sale of a home is not the usual course of action for a judge. A judge can order sale of property if the owner is incompetent.

Family dispute as to care of the person currently resident in your State (eg. whether to return to England & Wales)

> A Florida judge can resolve family disputes as to the care of a person located in the state.

Decision about medical treatment in your State

> A Florida judge can make decisions about medical treatment of persons located in the state. Some of the more famous cases from Florida dealt with the removal of a person from life support especially when the person was in a coma.

B. Would the answers to A. above vary if person was not a national of the United Kingdom but had been habitually resident in England and Wales prior to their impairment or insufficiency?

> There has to be some nexus to the state such as the person located in the state or has property located in the state.

C. Is there an emergency procedure?

> An interested person would have to file a petition with the court and ask for an emergency procedure. There is always a duty judge to hear emergencies until the person who petitions the court can appear before a regular probate judge.

5. Sources of information

> Local bar associations such as the Broward County Bar Association has a list of practitioners to whom such as case can be referred.

Completed by:

Name	Larry V. Bishins
eMail	lbishins@bellsouth.net

Are you a solicitor/notary/advocate or lawyer who provides legal advice and services for nationals of the United Kingdom in your State?	X	Yes		

October 2010

PART XI

Directories

PART XI: Directories

Organisations   1901

Websites   1914

Useful publications   1922

PART XI

Organisations

CARERS AND NURSING SERVICES

Name of organisation	Address
British Nursing Association	The Colonnades Beaconsfield Close Hatfield Herts AL10 5BL Tel: 0871 873 3324 Email: info@bna.org
Carers UK	20 Great Dover Street London SE1 4LX Tel: 020 7378 4999 Email: info@carersuk.org
Crossroads Care Association	10 Regent Place Rugby Warwickshire Tel: 0845 450 0350
National Council for Palliative Care	The Fitzpatrick Building 188–194 York Way London N7 9AS Tel: 020 7697 1520 Email: enquiries@ncpc.org.uk
The Relatives and Residents Association	1 The Ivories 6–18 Northampton Street London N1 2HY Tel: 020 7359 8148
National Care Association	45–49 Leather Lane London EC1N 7TJ Tel: 020 7831 7090
The Princess Royal Trust for Carers	Unit 14, Bourne Court Southend Road Woodford Green Essex IG8 8HD Tel: 0844 800 4361142 Email: info@carers.org

PART XI

ELDERLY

Name of organisation	Address
Age UK	207-221 Pentonville Road London N1 9UZ. Tel: 0800 107 8977 Email: contact@ageuk.org.uk
Age Cymru	Tŷ John Pathy 13/14 Neptune Court Vanguard Way Cardiff CF24 5PJ Tel: 029 2043 1555 Email: enquiries@agecymru.org.uk
Age NI	3 Lower Crescent Belfast BT7 1NR. Tel: 028 9024 5729 Email: info@ageni.org
Age Scotland	Causewayside House 160 Causewayside Edinburgh EH9 1PR. Tel: 0845 833 0200 Email: enquiries@ageconcernandhelptheagedscotland.org.uk
Action on Elder Abuse	PO Box 60001 Streatham SW16 9BY Tel: 020 8835 9280 Email: enquiries@elderabuse.org.uk
Aid for the Aged in Distress	Epworth House, 25 City Road London EC1Y 1AA Tel: 0870 803 1950
Alzheimer's Disease Society	Devon House 58 St Katharine's Way London E1W 1LB Tel: 020 20 7423 3500 Email: enquiries@alzheimers.org.uk
Charities Aid Foundation	25 Kings Hill Avenue West Malling Kent ME19 4TA Tel: 03000 123 000 Email: enquiries@cafonline.org

Name of organisation	Address
Charity Search	25 Portview Road Avonmouth Bristol BS11 9LD Tel: 0117 982 4060 Email: info@charitysearch.org.uk
Contact the Elderly	15 Henrietta Street London WC2E 8QG Tel: 020 7240 0630 Email: info@contact-the-elderly.org.uk
Counsel and Care for the Elderly	Twyman House 16 Bonny Street London NW1 9PG Tel: 020 7485 1550 Email: advice@counselandcare.org.uk
Dementia UK	6 Camden High Street London NW1 0JH Tel: 020 7874 7200 E-mail: info@dementiauk.org
National Benevolent Fund for the Aged, Elderly and Older People	1 Leslie Grove Place Croydon Surrey CR0 6TJ Tel: 020 8688 6655 Email: info@nbfa.org.uk

FINANCIAL

Name of organisation	Address
Financial Services Authority	25 The North Collonade Canary Wharf London E14 5HS Tel: 020 7676 1000
National Association of Pension Funds	Cheapside House 138 Cheapside London EC2V 6AE Tel: 020 7601 1700

PART XI

Name of organisation	Address
Nursing Homes Fees Agency	Floor 2, Midland House, West Way, Botley, Oxon OX2 0PL Tel: 01865 733000 Email: enquiries@nhfa.co.uk
Pensions Advisory Service	11 Belgrave Road London SW1V 1RB Tel: 0845 601 2923 Email: enquiries@pensionsadvisoryservice.org.uk
Society of Pension Consultants	St Bartholomew House 92 Fleet Street London EC4Y 1DG Tel: 020 7353 1688 Email: info@spc.uk.com
Independent Age	6 Avonmore Road London W14 8RL Tel: 020 7605 4200 Email: charity@independentage.org.uk

GENERAL

Name of organisation	Address
National Association of Citizens Advice Bureaux	Myddelton House 115–123 Pentonville Road London N1 9LZ
National Council of Voluntary Organisations (NCVO)	Regent's Wharf 8 All Saints' Street London N1 9RL Tel: 020 7713 6161
The Samaritans	The Upper Mill Kingston Road Ewell KT17 2AF Tel: 08457 90 90 90

HEALTH AND DISABILITY

Name of organisation	Address
Action against Victims of Medical Accidents (AVMA)	44 High Street Croydon Surrey CR0 1YB Tel: 0845 123 23 52
Arthritis Care	18 Stephenson Way London NW1 2HD Tel: 020 7380 6500 Email: info@arthritiscare.org.uk
Arthritis Research Campaign	Copeman House St Mary's Court, St Mary's Gate Chesterfield Derbyshire S41 7TD Tel: 0300 790 0400 Email: enquiries@arthritisresearchuk.org
British Heart Foundation	Greater London House, 180 Hampstead road, London NW1 7AW Email: supporterservices@bhf.org.uk Tel: 020 7554 0000
British Red Cross	44 Moorfields London EC2Y 9AL Tel: 0844 871 11 11 Email: information@redcross.org.uk
Cancer Research UK	Angel Building 407 St John Street London EC1V 4AD Tel: 020 7242 0200 Email: info@cancerresearchuk.org
Diabetes Research and Wellness Foundation	Northney Marina Hayling Island Hampshire PO11 0NH Tel: 02392 637 808 Email: drwf@diabeteswellnessnet.org.uk

PART XI

Name of organisation	Address
Diabetes UK	10 Parkway London NW1 7AA Tel: 020 7424 1000 Email: info@diabetes.org.uk
Disability Alliance	Universal House 88–94 Wentworth Street London E1 7SA Tel: 020 7247 8776 Email: office@disabilityalliance.org
Disabled Living Foundation	380–384 Harrow Road London W9 2HU Tel: 020 7289 6111 Email: info@dlf.org.uk
Disablement Information and Advice Lines (Dial UK)	Park Lodge St Catherine's Hospital Tickhill Road Doncaster DN4 8QN Tel: 01302 310 123 Email: informationenquiries@dialuk.org.uk
Macmillan Cancer Relief	89 Albert Embankment London SW3 7UD Tel: 0800 107 4448
Marie Curie Cancer Care	89 Albert Embankment London SE1 7TP Tel: 0800 716146 Email: info@mariecurie.org.uk
MIND	Granta House 15–19 Broadway Stratford London E15 4BQ Tel: 020 8519 2122 Email: contact@mind.org.uk
Motability	City Gate House 22 Southwark Bridge Road London SE1 9HB Tel: 0845 456 4566

Name of organisation	Address
Multiple Sclerosis Society	MS National Centre 372 Edgeware Road London NW2 6ND Tel: 020 8438 0700
MS Trust	Spirella Building Letchworth Herts SG6 4ET Tel: 01462 476700 Email: info@mstrust.org,uk
Parkinson's Disease Society	215 Vauxhall Bridge Road London SW1V 1EJ Tel: 020 7931 8080 Email: hello@parkinsons.org.uk
Patients Association	PO Box 935 Harrow Middlesex HA1 3YJ Tel: 020 8423 9111 Email: mailbox@patients-association.com
Royal Association for Disability and Rehabilitation (RADAR)	12 City Forum 250 City Road London EC1V 8AF Tel: 020 7250 3222 Email: radar@radar.org.uk
The Royal College of Surgeons	35–43 Lincoln's Inn Fields London WC2A 3PE Tel: 020 7405 3474
Royal National Institute of the Blind (RNIB)	105 Judd Street London W1H 9NE Tel: 020 7388 1266 Email: helpline@rnib.org.uk
Royal National Institute for Deaf People (RNID)	19–23 Featherstone Street London EC1Y 8SL Tel: 020 7296 8000 Email: helpline@rnid.org.uk
Stroke Association	Stroke House 240 City Road London EC1V 2PR Tel: 0845 3033100 Email: info@stroke.org.uk

PART XI

Name of organisation	Address
Housing and Care Homes	Abbeyfield Society Abbeyfield House 53 Victoria Street St Albans Hertfordshire AL1 3UW Tel: 01727 857536 Email: enquiries@abbeyfield.com
Elderly Accommodation Counsel	3rd Floor 89 Albert Embankment London SE1 7TP
National Association of Park Home Residents	PO Box 1067 Blandford Forum Dorset DT11 9YA jim@naphr.org
Registered Nursing Home Association	Calthorpe House Hagley Road Edgbaston Birmingham B16 8QY Tel: 0121 451 1088 frankursell@rnha.co.uk
Shelter	88 Old Street London EC1V 9HU 0808 800 4444 Email: info@shelter.org.uk
Tenant Service Authority and Housing Corporation	Maple House 149 Tottenham Court Road London W1P OBN 0845 230 7000 Email- ing enquiries@tsa.gsx.gov.uk,

HUMAN RIGHTS

Name of organisation	Address
Amnesty	99-119 Rosebery Avenue London EC1R 4RE Tel: 020 7814 6200 Email: info@amnesty.org.uk

Name of organisation	Address
JUSTICE	59 Carter Lane London EC4V 5AQ Tel: 020 7329 5100 Email admin@justice.org.uk
Liberty	21 Tabard Street London SE1 4LA Tel: 020 7403 3888 Email: info@liberty-human-rights.org.uk

LEGAL

Name of organisation	Address
Association of Personal Injury Lawyers	3 Alder Court Rennie Hogg Road Nottingham NG2 1RX Tel: 0115 9580585
Bar Council	289-293 High Holborn London WC1V 7HZ Tel: 020 7242 0082
The Law Society	113 Chancery Lane London WC2A 1PL Tel: 020 7242 1222
Legal Aid Practitioners' Group	242 Pentonville Road London N1 9UN United Kingdom Tel: 020 7833 7431 Email: carol.storer@lapg.co.uk
Society for Trust and Estate Practitioners	Artillery House (South) 11 – 19 Artillery Row London SW1P 1RT Tel: 020 7340 0500 Email: step@step.org
Solicitors for the Elderly	Suite 17, Conbar House Mead Lane Hertford Hertfordshire SG13 7AP.

PART XI

Name of organisation	Address
Solicitors Regulation Authority	Ipsley Court Berrington Close Redditch B98 0TD Tel: 0870 606 2555

OFFICIAL ADDRESSES

Name of organisation	Address
Care Quality Commission	Citygate Gallowgate Newcastle upon Tyne NE1 4PA Tel: 03000 616161
Charity Commission PO Box	1227 Liverpool L69 3UG Tel: 0845 300 0218
Court Service	Southside 105 Victoria Street London SW1E 6QT Tel: 020 7210 2266
Department of Health	Richmond House 79 Whitehall London SW1A 2NS Tel: 020 7210 4850
Department for Works and Pensions	Caxton House Tothill Street London SW1H 9DA
Equal & Human Rights Commission	3 More London Riverside Tooley Street London SE1 2RG Tel 020 3117 0235 Email: info@equalityhumanrights.com
Judicial Office for England and Wales	11th floor, Thomas More Building Royal Courts of Justice Strand London WC2A 2LL Email: general.enquiries@judiciary gsi.gov.uk>

Name of organisation	Address
Judicial Studies Board	Steel House 11 Tothill Street London SW1H 9LJ Email: jsb.web@jsb.gsi.gov.uk
Law Commission	Steel House 11 Tothill Street London SW1H 9LJ Tel: 020 3334 0200
Legal Services Commission	4 Abbey Orchard Street London SW1P 2BS Tel: 0207 783 7000
Ministry of Justice	102 Petty France London SW1H 9AJ Tel: 020 33343555 Email: general.queries@justice.gsi.gov.uk
Office of the Public Guardian (Court of Protection)	PO Box 15118 Birmingham B16 6GX Tel: 0300 456 0300 Email: customerservices@publicguardian.gsi.gov.uk
Official Solicitor	81 Kingsway London WC2A 1DD Tel: 020 7911 7127 Email: enquiries@offsol.gsi.gov.uk
Public Trustee	81 Chancery Lane, London WC2A 1DD Tel: 020 7911 7127 Email: enquiries@offsol.gsi.gov.uk
Royal Courts of Justice	The Strand London WC2R 1PL Tel: 020 7936 6000
Treasury Solicitor's Department	One Kemble Street London WC2B 4TS Tel: 0207 2103000

PART XI

OMBUDSMEN

Name of organisation	Address
Financial Ombudsman	South Quay Plaza 183 Marsh Wall Tel: 020 7964 1000 Email: complaint.info@financial-ombudsman.org.uk
Housing Ombudsman Service	81 Aldwych London WC2B 4HN Tel: 0300 111 3000 Email: info@housing-ombudsman.org.uk
Legal Services Ombudsman	22 Oxford Court Oxford Street Manchester M2 3WQ Tel: 0161 236 9532 Email: lso@olso.gsi.gov.uk
Local Government Ombudsman	PO Box 4771 Coventry CV4 0EH Email: advice@lgo.org.uk
Parliamentary and Health Service Ombudsman	Millbank Tower Millbank London SW1P 4QP Tel: 0345 015 4033 Email: phso.enquiries@ombudsman.org.uk
Pensions Ombudsman	11 Belgrave Road London SW1V 1RB Tel: 020 7630 2200 Email: enquiries@pensions-ombudsman.org.uk

PUBLISHERS

Name of organisation	Address
Age UK publications	Unit 6 Industrial Estate Brecon Powys LD3 8LA Tel: 0870 4422120

Name of organisation	Address
Bloomsbury Professional	41-43 Boltro Road Haywards Heath West Sussex RH16 1BJ+44 01235 465500 Email: customerservices@bloomsburyprofessional.com
Child Poverty Action Group publications	94 White Lion Street London N1 9PF Email: bookorders@cpag.org.uk
Jessica Kingsley	116 Pentonville Road London N1 9JB Tel: +44 (020) 7833 2307 Email: post@jkp.com
Jordan Publishing	21 St.Thomas Street Bristol BS1 6JS Tel: 0117 9230600 Email: customerservice@jordanpublishing.co.uk
Lexis-Nexis	Halsbury House 35 Chancery Lane London WC2A 1EL Tel: 020 7400 2500 Email: customer.services@lexisnexis.co.uk
Oxford University Press	Great Clarendon Street Oxford OX2 6DP Tel: 01865 556767 Email: bookorders.UK@oup.com
Sweet & Maxwell	100 Avenue Road London NW3 3PF Tel: 020 7393 7000
Welfare benefits	Child Poverty Action Group 94 White Lion Street London N1 9PF Tel: 020 7837 7979 Email: staff@cpag.org.uk

Websites

FINANCIAL

Website	Name
www.fsa.gov.uk	Financial Services Authority
www.ft.com	Electronic Share Information
www.hmrc.gov.uk	Tax Rates and Allowances
www.landreg.gov.uk/housepriceindex	House Prices
www.napf.co.uk	National Association of Pension Funds
www.nhfa.co.uk	Nursing Homes
www.opas.org.uk	Pensions Advisory Service
www.opra.co.uk	Occupational Pensions Regulatory Authority
www.pensionguide.gov.uk	Pensions Advice Resource
www.ship-ltd.org	Safe Home Income Plans (SHIP)
www.statistics.gov.uk	Retail Price Index and other statistics

GOVERNMENT

Website	Name
www.appeals-service.gov.uk	The Appeals Service – Social Security
www.cabinetoffice.gov.uk	Cabinet Office
www.charity-commission.gov.uk	Charity Commission
www.communities.gov.uk	Department for Communities and Local Government
www.dft.gov.uk	Department of Transport
www.dh.gov.uk	Department of Health
www.direct.gov.uk	UK Government

Website	Name
www.dwp.gov.uk	Department for Work and Pensions
www.equalities.gov.uk	Government Equalities Office
www.hmrc.gov.uk	HM Customs & Excise
www.hm-treasury.gov.uk	HM Treasury
www.homeoffice.gov.uk	Home Office
www.justice.gov.uk	Ministry of Justice
www.nationalarchives.gov.uk	The National Archives
www.number-10.gov.uk	No 10 Downing Street
www.parliament.uk	Houses of Parliament

HOUSING

Website	Name
www.housingcorp.gov.uk	Housing Corporation
www.nhbc.co.uk	National House Building Council

HUMAN RIGHTS

Website	Name
www.amnesty.org.uk	Amnesty International
www.bihr.org.uk	British Institute of Human Rights
www.echr.coe.int	European Court of Human Rights
www.equalityhumanrights.com	Equalities and Human Rights Commission
www.hrw.org.uk	Human Rights Watch
www.justice.org.uk	Justice

PART XI

Website	Name
www. liberty-human-rights. org.uk	Liberty

LEGAL

Website	Name
www.civiljusticecouncil. gov.uk	Civil Justice Council
www.courtfunds.gov.uk	Official Solicitor/Public Trustee/Court Funds Office
www.hmcourts-service. gov.uk	HM Courts Service
www.jsboard.co.uk	The Judicial Studies Board
www.judiciary.gov.uk	Judiciary of England &Wales
www.lawcom.gov.uk	The Law Commission
www.legalservices.gov. uk	Legal Services Commission
www.opsi.gov.uk	Office of Public Sector Information
www.publicguardian. gov.uk	Public Guardian Office

LEGAL INFORMATION RESOURCES

Website	Name
www.bailii.org/	British and Irish Legal Information Institute
www.casetrack.com	Smith Bernal case reports
www.everyform.net	General legal forms
www.harassment-law.co. uk	Harassment law
www.infolaw.co.uk	Information for Lawyers Limited
www.justis.com	Full text legal database
www.lawdirect.co.uk	Solicitors Directory

Website	Name
www.lawgazette.co.uk	Legal Resource
www.lawontheweb.co.uk	General legal site
www.lawreports.co.uk	Incorporated Council of Law Reporting
www.lawtel.co.uk	Legal resource
www.legalhub.co.uk	Legal resource
www.makeawill.org.uk	Law Society's will site
www.ncl.ac.uk	Web Journal of Current Legal Issues
www.online-law.co.uk	Online Law
www.monticello.org.uk	Law Resource
www.rightsnet.org.uk	Welfare Law Resource
www.thetimes.co.uk/tto/law/reports	The Times Law Reports
www.venables.co.uk	Legal Resources

LEGAL PROFESSIONAL

Website	Name
www.apil.org.uk	Association of Personal Injury Lawyers
www.apl.org.uk	Association of Pensions Lawyers
www.barcouncil.org.uk	Bar Council
www.lapg.co.uk	Legal Aid Practitioners Group
www.lawsociety.org.uk	The Law Society
www.lawyersonline.co.uk	Lawyers Online
www.lpld.org.uk	Lawyers for People with a Learning Disability
www.scl.org	Society for Computers & Law
www.solicitors-online.com	Society Directory of Solicitors

PART XI

Website	Name
www.solicitorsfortheelderly.com	Solicitors for the Elderly
www.spg.uk.com	Sole Practitioners Group
www.sra.org.uk	Solicitors Regulation Authority
www.step.org	Law Society of Trust and Estate Practitioners

LEGAL PUBLISHERS

Website	Name
www.ark-group.com	Ark Group Publishing
www.bloomsburyprofessional.com	Bloomsbury Professional
www.cpag.org.uk	CPAG Publications
www.familylaw.co.uk	Family Law
www.FT.com	Financial Times
www.hammickslegal.co.uk	Hammicks Legal Bookshop
www.jkp.com	Jessica Kingsley Publishers
www.jordanpublishing.co.uk	Jordan Publishing
www.lag.org.uk	Legal Action Group
www.lexisnexis.co.uk	Lexis Nexis
www.opsi.gov.uk	The Stationary Office
www.oup.co.uk	Oxford University Press
www.sweetandmaxwell.co.uk	Sweet & Maxwell
www.the-lawyer.co.uk	The Lawyer
www.the-times.co.uk	The Times
www.tso.gov.uk	HM Stationery Office

OMBUDSMEN

Website	Name
www.fos.org.uk	The Financial Services Ombudsman
www.housing-ombudsman.org.uk	The Housing Ombudsman
www.lgo.org.uk	Local Government Ombudsman
www.olso.org.uk	The Legal Services Ombudsman
www.ombudsman.org.uk	Parliamentary and Health Service Ombudsman
www.pensions-ombudsman.org.uk	Pensions Ombudsman

ORGANISATIONS – CARERS

Website	Name
www.aica.org.uk	Association of Independent Care Advisors
www.bettercaring.com	Better Caring resource
www.carers.org.uk	Crossroads Care
www.carersuk.org	Carers UK
www.cqc.org.uk	Care Quality Commission
www.hospiceinformation.org.uk	Hospice Information Service
www.nursing-home-directory.co.uk	The Care Directory

ORGANISATIONS – ELDERLY

Website	Name
www.abbeyfield.com	The Abbeyfield Society
www.aftaid.org.uk	Aid for the Aged in Distress

PART XI

Website	Name
www.ageuk.org.uk	Age UK
www.alzheimers.org.uk	Alzheimer's Society
www.charitysearch.org.uk	Charity Search for Older People
www.communitycare.co.uk	Community Care resource
www.contact-the-elderly.org.uk	Contact the Elderly
www.eac.org.uk	Elderly Accommodation Counsel
www.elderabuse.org.uk	Action on Elder Abuse
www.independentage.org.uk	Independent Age

ORGANISATIONS – GENERAL

Website	Name
www.adviceguide.org.uk	Citizen's Advice Bureau
www.avma.co.uk	Action for Victims of Medical Accidents (AVMA)
www.salrc.org.uk	Society for the Assistance of Ladies in Reduced Circumstances
www.salvationarmy.org.uk	The Salvation Army
www.samaritans.org	The Samaritans
www.ncvo-vol.org.uk	National Council for Voluntary Organisations

ORGANISATIONS – HEALTH AND DISABILITY

Website	Name
www.arc.org.uk	The Arthritis Research Campaign
www.arthritiscare.org.uk	Arthritis Care
www.bhf.org.uk	British Heart Foundation

Website	Name
www.bristolcancerhelp.org	Cancer Help Centre
www.cancerBACUP.org.uk	BACUP
www.cancerlink.org	Cancer Link
www.cancerresearchuk.org	Cancer Research UK
www.dct.org.uk	Dementia Care Trust
www.dementiauk.org	Dementia UK
www.diabetes.org.uk	Diabetes UK
www.disabilityalliance.org.uk	Disability Alliance
www.dlf.org.uk	Disabled Living Foundation
www.dialuk.info	Disablement Information & Advice Lines
www.hpa.org.uk	Health Protection Agency
www.hospicedirectory.org.uk	Hospice Directory
www.lcm.org.uk	London City Mission
www.macmillan.org.uk	Macmillan Cancer Relief
www.mariecurie.org.uk	Marie Curie Cancer
www.mencap.org.uk	MENCAP
www.mind.org.uk	MIND
www.motability.co.uk	Motability
www.mssociety.org.uk	MS Society
www.mstrust.org.uk	MS Trust
www.parkinsons.org.uk	Parkinson's UK
www.nhs.uk	The National Health Service
www.nhsdirect.nhs.uk	NHS Direct
www.nice.org.uk	National Institute for Health and Clinical Excellence

PART XI

Website	Name
www.radar.org.uk	Royal Association for Disability and Rehabilitation
www.redcross.org.uk	British Red Cross Society
www.rnib.org.uk	Royal National Institute for the Blind
www.rnid.org.uk	Royal National Institute for Deaf People
www.shelter.org.uk	Shelter
www.stroke.org.uk	The Stroke Association

ORGANISATIONS – PROFESSIONALS

Website	Name
www.adss.org.uk	Association of Directors of Social Services
www.bma.org.uk	British Medical Association
www.bna.co.uk	British Nursing Association
www.saif.org.uk	Society of Allied and Independent Funeral Directors
www.spc.uk.com	Society of Pension Consultants
www.tax.org.uk	Chartered Institute of Taxation

Useful publications

CORONERS

Blackstone's Guide to the Coroners and Justice Act 2009 (2010) Glassom & Knowles, OUP
Coroners: A Guide to the New Law (2010) Urpeth, Law Society
Coroners' Courts: A Guide to Law & Practice (2011) Dorries, OUP
Inquests: A Practitioner's Guide (2008) Thomas et al, LAG
Jervis on Coroners (2011) Matthews, Sweet & Maxwell

COURTS AND PROCEDURE

A Practitioner's Guide to the Court of Protection (2009) Terrell, Bloomsbury Professional
Court of Protection Practice 2011 Ashton, Jordan Publishing
Family Lawyer and the Court of Protection (2010) Marin, Family Law

Heywood & Massey: Court of Protection (loose-leaf) Rees, Sweet & Maxwell

Solicitors' Duties and Liabilities (2009) Billins, Law Society

The Companion to the Solicitor's Code of Conduct (2007), Law Society

Urgent Applications in the Court of Protection (2011) Pearce and Jackson, Jordan Publishing

DISCRIMINATION

Age Discrimination (2007) Davies, Bloomsbury Professional

Age Discrimination Handbook (2006) O'Dempsey et al, LAG

Age Discrimination – The New Law (2006) Cheetham, Jordan Publishing

Blackstone's Guide to the Disability Discrimination Legislation (2005) Monaghan, OUP

Blackstone's Guide to the Equality Act 2010 Wadham, OUP

Disability Discrimination (2008) Doyle, Jordan Publishing

Disability Rights Handbook (2007) Disability Alliance

Discrimination Law Handbook (2007) Palmer et al, LAG

Discrimination Law Service (loose-leaf), Bloomsbury Professional

Equality and Discrimination (2010) Doyle, Jordan Publishing

Equality Act 2010: A Guide to the New Law (2010) Duggan, Law Society

ELDERLY CLIENTS

Elderly Client Handbook (2010) Bielanska, Terrell, Ashton, Law Society

Elderly Clients – A Precedent Manual (2010), Lush, Jordan Publishing

Elderly Client Adviser (journal) Ark Group Publishers

Elderly People and the Law (1995) Ashton, Jordan Publishing

ESTATE AND FINANCIAL MANAGEMENT

A Practitioner's Guide to Beneficiaries' Actions (2003) Saker, Bloomsbury Professional

A Practitioner's Guide to Executorship and Administration (2009) Thurston, Bloomsbury Professional

A Practitioner's Guide to Powers of Attorney (2010) Thurston, Bloomsbury Professional

Blackstone Guide to the Pensions Act 2004 (2005) Jenkins and Poore, OUP

Cretney & Lush on Lasting and Enduring Powers of Attorney (2009), Jordan Publishing

Finance and Law for the Older Client (loose-leaf), Lexis Nexis

Lasting Powers of Attorney: A Practical Guide (2008) Ward, Law Society

Law Relating to Trustees (2010) Underhill & Hayton, Lexis-Nexis

Pensions Law and Practice with Precedents (loose-leaf), Sweet & Maxwell

Pensions Law Handbook (2010), Nabarro, Bloomsbury Professional

Powers of Attorney (2007) Aldridge, Sweet & Maxwell

PART XI

Practical Trust Precedents (loose-leaf), Sweet & Maxwell

Tolley's Pensions Administration and Trustees Service (loose-leaf), Lexis Nexis

Trust Drafting and Precedents (loose-leaf), Sweet & Maxwell

Trust Practitioner's Handbook (2008) Steel, Law Society

HEALTH AND MEDICAL CARE

Health and Social Care Handbook (2006) Bielanska, Scolding

Health Care Law (2011) Montgomery, OUP

Mason and McCall Smith's Law and Medical Ethics (2010), Mason and Laurie, OUP

Medical Law (2011) Herring, OUP

Medical Law and Ethics (2010) Herring, OUP

Medical Negligence (2008) Jones, Sweet & Maxwell

Medical Treatment Decisions and the Law (2010) Johnston, Bloomsbury Professional

HUMAN RIGHTS

Blackstone's Guide to the Human Rights Act 1998 (2009), OUP

Human Rights Alerter, Sweet & Maxwell

Human Rights Law & Practice (2009) Lester and Pannick, Lexis Nexis

Human Rights Practice (looseleaf), Sweet & Maxwell

Human Rights Updater, Lexis Nexis

MENTAL HEALTH

Assessment of Mental Capacity: A Practical Guide for Doctors and Lawyers (2009) BMA, Letts, Law Society

Blackstone's Guide to the Mental Capacity Act 2006 (2008) Bartlett, OUP

Blackstone's Guide to the Mental Health Act 2007 (2008) Bowen, OUP

Butterworths' New Law Guide to the Mental Health Act 2005 (2008), Lexis Nexis

Mental Capacity Act Manual (2009) Jones, Sweet & Maxwell

Mental Capacity – A Guide to the New Law (2008) Gleaney, Law Society

Mental Health – The New Law (2007) Fennell, Jordan Publishing

Mental Capacity – The New Law (2006) Ashton, Jordan Publishing

Mental Health Act Manual (2010) Jones, Sweet & Maxwell

Mental Health Law (2010) Hale, Sweet & Maxwell

Mental Health Law & Practice (2011) Fennell, Jordan Publishing

Mental Health Tribunals (2009) Butler and Wilson, Jordan Publishing

WELFARE

Care Standards: A Practical Guide (2009) Ridout, Jordan Publishing

Care Standards Legislation Handbook (2009) Pearl, Jordan Publishing

Community Care and the Law (2007) Clements, LAG

Community Care Law Reports, LAG

Community Care Practice and the Law (2008) Mandelstam, Jessica Kingsley

Council Tax Handbook (2009), CPAG

Debt Advice Handbook (2010), CPAG

Fuel Rights Handbook (2010), CPAG

Housing Benefit and Council Tax Benefit Legislation (2010/11), CPAG

Paying for Care Handbook (2009), CPAG

Personal Finance Handbook (2009), CPAG

Social Security and State Benefits: A Practical Guide, (2006), Bloomsbury Professional

Welfare Benefits and Tax Credits Handbook (2010/11), CPAG

Welfare Law (loose-leaf), Bloomsbury Professional

WILLS AND PROBATE

A Practitioner's Guide to Wills (2010) King et al, Wildys

Butterworths Wills, Probate and Administration Service (loose-leaf), Lexis Nexis

Contentious Probate Claims (2010) Francis, Sweet & Maxwell

Inheritance Act Claims Law Practice and Procedures (loose-leaf) Francis and Lord Walker, Jordan Publishing

Modern Approach to Wills, Administration and Estate Planning with Precedents (2011) King and Whitehouse, Jordan Publishing

Parker's Modern Wills Precedents (2011) Waterworth, Bloomsbury Professional

Practical Will Precedents (loose-leaf), Sweet & Maxwell

Probate Disputes and Remedies (2008) Withers, Jordan Publishing

Probate Practice Manual (loose-leaf), Sweet & Maxwell

Probate Practitioner's Handbook (2010) King, Law Society

Theobald on Wills (2010) Martin, Bridge and Oldham, Sweet & Maxwell

Tristram and Coote's Probate Practice (2011) D'Costa et al, Lexis Nexis

Will Draftsman's Handbook (2004) Riddett, Law Society

Williams, Mortimer & Sunnucks – Executors, Administrators and Probate (2007) Sunnucks, Sweet & Maxwell

Williams on Wills (2008), Lexis Nexis

PART XI

Index

References are to page numbers.

Absence of incapacitated party
  Court proceeding in   631
Abuse
  investigation of   334
Access to justice   54
Accommodation *see also* Care home;
  Hospital
Accommodation, long stay
  IMCA instruction prior to   250
  IMCA, circumstances for instruction
    of   251, 434
Acknowledgment of service   300, 620
  filing   620
  form   1431
  Practice Direction   697
  signing   697
Administration
  former arrangement for   321
  judicial functions, distinct but
    linked   336
  Public Guardian's role   333
Admission   306, 635
Adoption
  excluded decision   139, 424
Adult
  competent, advance decision   252
  lacking capacity, groups   23, 224
'Adult care'
  directions order   1640
  order   227
Adult contact
  Court jurisdiction   226
    hearing, nature of   226
Advance decision *see* Advance statement
Advance statement   252
  alteration   422
  Code of Practice   256
  common law, at   253
  effect   256, 423
  life sustaining treatment, as to   246, 423
  LPA alternative   257
  meaning   422
  refusal of medical treatment   253
  validity   253, 258
  refusing treatment   254
    applicability   255
    life sustaining treatment   255
    validity, conditions   255
  requesting treatment   254, 255
  statutory recognition   254
    balance sought in   257
  transitional (made before 1 Oct
    2007)   832

Advance statement—*continued*
  unclear, Court application   256
    treatment pending decision   256
  validity   423
  wishes, as to   120
  withdrawal   422
Advice
  Official Solicitor   351
Advocate
  independent mental capacity *see*
    Independent mental capacity
    advocate
Affidavit
  form   1489
Affidavit evidence   638, 736
  form   737
  made outside jurisdiction   638
Age   97
  authorised detention in hospital or care
    home, minimum for   275
  children *see* Child
  Court jurisdiction   209
    property and affairs   210
  discrimination   43, 46
  elderly people lacking capacity   224
  electro-convulsive therapy, and   141
Alcohol or drug misuse
  mental impairment from   95
Allocation of cases   289, 303, 630
  appeal hearing   670
Alternative dispute resolution
  encouragement of use of   294
Appeal   314, 449
  allocation   670
  Court of Appeal   670
  fee   828
  forms   1499
  hearing, court decision on   666
  permission   315, 667
    appellant's notice   668
    factors for grant   315, 667
    respondent's notice   668
    time-limit variation   669
  power of appeal judge   669
  Practice Direction   776
  review or re-hearing   669
  rules   666
Appellant's notice
  form   1499
Applicant   621
Application   447
  amendment   595

Application—*continued*
DoL application
 Practice Direction 627
fee 828
filing 615
form 582, 1369
 contents 615
 court authentication 590
 documents to be filed with 615
 notice of issue 695, 1465
 statement of truth 591
hearing 628
 considerations for holding 302
 none 628
interim 626, 717
notification 300
 incapacitated person 297
notification of issue 618
 Practice Direction 695
Official Solicitor bringing 353
permission to apply 240, 298, 608
 grant, factors for 298
 no permission required 609
 permission form 299
 Practice Direction 690
 serious medical treatment 241
 when not required 298
procedure
 after issue 628
 specified applications 619
 starting proceedings 614
responding to (Practice Direction) 697
serious medical treatment, parties 241
service 616
 lasting power of attorney, relating
  to 617
urgent (Practice Direction) 717
within proceedings 301, 624
 application notice 301, 624
 application without notice 302, 626
 Practice Direction 714, 717
Application notice 590, 591
amendment 595
forms 1449
Appropriate adult 36
Asian communities 35
Assessment
authorisation of deprivation of liberty, for
 list of required assessments 467
capacity, of *see also* Capacity; Doctor
detention authorisation, for 276
 best interests assessor 277, 862
 eligibility
  requirements for assessors 279,
   861
 information for standard
  authorisation 865
 mental health 861
 selection of assessors 863
 time-limits 864

Association
discrimination prohibition 47
Association of Independent Visitors 348
Attorney
application by (Practice Direction) 699
 list of suitable applications 700
decision of, acts contrary to 239
enduring power *see* Power of attorney
lasting power *see* Lasting power of
 attorney
no right of audience 57
remuneration of 665
Authorisation
detention in hospital/care home *see*
 Hospital

Best interests
appointment of Deputy,
 considerations for Court 212
assessor 277, 856, 862, 864
checklist 115
 application of 129
 no hierarchy 116
Code of Practice 121
concept 25, 114
 statutory enshrinement 78, 399
consultation requirement 123
 scope of 123
 when not 'practicable
  or appropriate' 123
detention authorisation, assessment 276,
  277, 279, 468, 862
determination 114, 399
 all relevant circumstances 117
 capacity to make decision in
  future 117
Joint Committee view 92
judicial review, interaction with 248
Law Commission proposal 91
life sustaining treatment 118, 238, 246
lifetime gifts 1674
LPA, and 159
medical treatment 237
 Court approach 232
principle 92
 duty to apply, scope 124
religious beliefs 120
religious or spiritual beliefs 120
statutory will *see* Will
'substituted judgment' element 121
 scope 121
wills 210
wishes and feelings 120
 case 1670
 weight to 122
Bone marrow donation 243
Bournewood Gap 269
amendments plugging 270

Brain injury
  settlement
    financial deputy,
      order for appointment
        of   1657
Bundles
  Practice Direction   741

Capacity   19
  assessment of   22, 106
    approach of court (case)   1682, 1683, 1685
    Code of Practice   87
    confidentiality   112
    EPA execution (case)   1667, 1668
    form and guidance notes   1411
    formal   107, 108, 109, 113
    legal requirement   109
    mental health legislation, use of   113
    method   111
    person for   107
    professional involvement,
      circumstances for   110
    record of   113, 114
    refusal   113
    time for   106
  burden of proof   86
  certificate of, for LPA   184, 186
    certificate provider   185
    contents   184
    persons excluded from providing   186
    persons who may provide   185
  common law test   232
    interaction with   102, 103
  declaration as to   207
  doubt about, procedure for resolving   382
    CPR, and   383
  financial affairs, final order as to   1649
  fluctuating   247
  lack of
    concept of   78
    definition   94, 397
    settlement, party to (case)   1679
  litigation, for
    case   102, 1677, 1680
  mental impairment   94
    scope of   95
  partial   19, 23, 95
  person lacking   94, 224
    brain injured   211, 224
    capacity   397
    elderly   224
    learning disabled   224
    meaning   143, 588
    mentally ill   224
    notification requirement   604
    party, as   602
  presumption   21, 22, 86, 95
    principle of   87
    rebuttal   87

Capacity—*continued*
  presumption—*continued*
    statutory enshrinement of   77
  reasonable belief that person
    lacks capacity   103
    best interests principle   124
    reasonable steps   104
  regaining
    best interests determination   117
    Code of Practice guidance   118
    discharge of property and
      affairs deputy   1625
  temporary lack of   20, 95
  test for lack of   95
    appearance   96
    condition or behaviour   96
    further guidance   101
    health care decision   236
    issue specific   236
Capacity presumption
  LPA, and   155
Care home
  accommodation in
    deprivation of liberty case   1702
    ill-treatment or neglect offence   143
    ill-treatment or neglect offences   143
    IMCA instruction prior to   250, 251
  detention in, authorisation *see also*
    Hospital   274
    assessments for   467
    interaction of urgent and
      standard   1707
    residence dispute by local
      authority   866
    standard procedure   275, 464, 860
    urgent procedure   278, 478
    supervisory body   503
Care home, accommodation in
  IMCA instruction prior to   432
Care or treatment, acts in connection with
  see Medical treatment; Permitted acts
Care plan
  assessment of capacity
    record of   114
Care Quality Commission
  Code of Practice compliance
    monitoring   82
  deprivation of
    liberty authorisation monitoring   282
Care services *see* Social care
Carer
  assessment of capacity by   107
  best interests consultation   123
  general powers and duties
    background to law   125
  ill-treatment or neglect offence   143
  negligence   132
  payment for goods and
    services for incapacitated
    person   137
  permitted acts   128, 131

Case management 293, 585
  active case management 585
  checklist 1630
  Court powers 294, 596
Case summaries 1667
Certificate provider
  LPA, for
    excluded persons 186
    list of possible 185
    professional 186
Channel Islands
  service in 1009
Child *see also* Young person 23, 97
  approaching majority, 'adult care
    order' 227, 317
  compromise or settlement, approval
    of 886
  control of money recovered for 888
  Court jurisdiction, property and
    affairs 210
  definition 872
  excluded decisions relating to 140, 424
  Gillick competence 104
  investment on behalf of 895
  litigation friend, requirement for *see also*
    Litigation friend 877
    order permitting child to conduct
      proceeding without 877
  medical treatment decision 235
  money recovered for, control of 895
  party, as 877
  personal care decision, Court
    jurisdiction 226
  service on 601
  settlement or compromise for 893
  transfer of proceedings, provision
    for 289, 419
Civil partnership 52
  excluded decision 139, 424
  incapacity, implications 53
  legislation 52
  status of civil partner 53
Civil Procedure Rules 872
  application 590
  doubt about capacity, procedure
    where 383
Clinical trials *see* Medical research
Code of Practice 79, 439
  acts in connection with care or treatment
    examples 128
    guidance 129
  advance decisions 256
  approval procedure 83
  assessment of capacity 87
  compliance issues 82
  consultation 83
  contents 80
  criminal or civil proceedings, relevance
    to 82

Code of Practice—*continued*
  decision-making, practical steps to
    enable 88
  dissemination 80
  informal carer, position of 81, 82
  issue 79
  legal status 81
  non-compliance sanctions 82
  persons with duty to 'have regard to' 81
  procedure 441
  publication 84
  review and improvement of 81
    Memorandum on 81
  revision 80, 83
  supplement 79, 80
    deprivation of liberty guidance 270
  text 1033
Commencement of proceedings 299, 615
Committal order
  notice of hearing for 1493
  rules 673
Commonwealth country
  service in 1009
Communication
  aids/interpreter 21, 57
  impairment of, and capacity 20
  inability to communicate 98, 102
Community care 32
  background
    concept 39
    reviews 39
  changes, recent 40, 41
  legislation 40
    guidance and
      circulars supplementing 42
    recent 41
Community treatment order 266
Compromise *see* Settlement
**Compulsory community treatment
  order (CTO)** 140
Conditional fee agreement 899
  additional liability 938
  costs order 901
Conditional fee arrangement
  success fee 941
Conduct
  costs, and 311
Confidentiality
  disclosure relating to person lacking
    capacity 112
  duty of 26, 112
  publicity restrictions, identity etc 304
Consent
  medical treatment, to *see* Medical
    treatment
Consultation
  best interests, as to 123
Contact
  'adult contact' disputes 226
  maturing child, issues 227

Contempt of Court
  rules 673
Contraception
  capacity to consent to 237
Contract
  goods or services
    enforcement 136
    'necessary' 136
Costs 310, 450, 451, 661
  appeal 915, 951
  apportioning 663
  bill of costs, form and contents 921
  capping order 952
  Civil Procedure Rules 898
    application of 663
  conditional fee agreement, orders relating
    to 901
  court discretion 900
  death of incapacitated party, charge on
    estate 665
  default costs certificate 910, 958
  deputy, failed application
    for appointment as 1691
  detailed assessment 664, 665
    appeals 915
    costs of, liability for 914, 966
    costs payable by one party to
      another 908
    general rules 907
    LSC funded client/assisted
      person 913
    meaning 900
    venue for 953
  discouragement to applicants, as 316
  estimate 596, 929
  final costs certificate 913, 964
  fixed (Practice Direction) 772
  general rule 311, 900
    departure from 311, 663
    personal welfare 662
    property and affairs 662
  interim costs certificate 912, 963
  litigant in person 918
  LPA registration cancellation 1689
  misconduct, court powers 905, 939
  non-party, for or against 665, 916
  Official Solicitor 665
  Practice Direction 765, 920
  pro bono representation 934
  procedure for assessment 665
  remuneration of deputy or attorney 665
  separate representation 664
  summary assessment 311, 665
    meaning 900, 921
    model form 921
  VAT provisions 925
  wasted costs order 905, 918
    right to be heard 939
Court of Appeal
  appeal to 670

Court of Protection
  access to justice 54
  administration 287
    separation of 336
  alternative dispute resolution 294
  appeal from 449
  application to *see* Application
  case management 293
    powers 294
  case types 305
    new jurisdiction, under 317
  case volume 316
  commencement of proceedings 295, 614
  cost of proceedings and funding
    problems 316, 354
  costs *see* Costs
  creation by MCA 2005 79, 286, 443
  decision-making powers 208, 212, 215
    conferring powers on Deputy 212
    lack of capacity pre-requisite for 208
  declaration 207
  deprivation of liberty, powers 274
    review of lawfulness 282
  Deputy, appointment etc *see* Deputy
  disclosure of documents 308
  documents *see also* Documents,
    Court 295, 590
    editing information in 594
    inspection and copies 593
    Public Guardian, copies 594
  enforcement powers 315
    penal notice 315
  error of procedure 295
  evaluation of current 64
  evidence *see also* Evidence
    assessment of capacity, of 108
  fees 827
  former Court, cessation of 287
  forms 287
  hearing *see also* Hearing
    judge for 728
    Practice Direction 731
    private general rule 304
    public, court power 633
    publicity, court power 633
    reporting restrictions 732
  historical 31, 58
    decision without hearing 61
    evaluation 64
    evidence 60
    fees and costs 61
    hearings, attended 65
    hearings, conduct of 61
    regional 63
    rules and procedure 58, 64
    venue 62
  human rights declaration of
    incompatibility 295
  incapacitated person, hearing 303
    human rights aspects 71

Court of Protection—*continued*
interim orders and directions   290, 302
judges   288, 443, 589
   continuity   288
   nominated   247, 320
   Practice Direction   728
   regional   288
jurisdiction   77, 224, 290, 581
   assumption of, test for   208
   case   1687
   discharge from   1651
   disputing   303, 630, 730
   empowerment, to enable   225
   enforcement   315
   health and welfare issues   235
   origins   58
   personal welfare decisions   225
   questions remaining on   75
   recognition and enforcement of
      foreign order   1697
   wide scope of   224
LPA
   application for exercise of
      powers   222
   intervention grounds   201
   intervention powers   217
   objection to registration   203
   registration objection, powers   199
office copies of orders etc, admissibility
      in proceedings   290
order *see also* Order   208, 290, 413
   miscellaneous   212
   own initiative   295
   precedent standard orders   1619
   variation or discharge   208
overriding objective   293
permission application   240, 298
   considerations for grant   93
   excepted circumstances   241
   factors for grant   241, 298
   permission form   299
   when not required   298
personal welfare decision   224
powers   205, 239, 290, 386
   exercise of, case on   205
President and Vice-President   288
procedural rules *see* Rules of Court
property and affairs, powers as to   209
reconsideration of order   303
reform   66
relationship with Public Guardian   335
report, power to require   291, 445
rules *see* Rules of Court
security for costs   295
serious medical treatment
      application   241
   circumstances for   242
   urgent case   242
status   287

Court of Protection—*continued*
threshold for engagement of powers   87,
      290
transitional   316
venue   287
   regional   63
visitor *see* Visitor
Court officer   589
Cross-border issues *see* International;
   Scotland

Decision
ability to make, practicable steps to
      help   88, 117, 237
   Code of Practice   88
   examples   88
   principle of   88
advance *see* Advance statement
conflict between decision-makers   214
Court order   208, 413
Deputy appointed to make *see also*
      Deputy   208, 213
excluded decisions   139, 424
inability to make   94, 398
   further guidance   101
   inability to communicate   102
   reasonably forseeable
      consequences   98, 99
   relevant time   98
   retaining information   100
   specific decision   98, 99
   test of   95, 98
   understanding the relevant
      information   98
   using and weighing the
      information   101
interrelated or sequential   90
participation of person lacking
      capacity   118
statutory framework under MCA
      2005   77
types *see also* Financial decision; Health
      decision; Personal welfare
      decision; Property and affairs,
      decision on   20, 23, 225
unwise   89
   principle as to   89
Decision-maker
advance choice of   25
best interests consultation, Code
      guidance   123
decisions excluded by law   139, 424
disputed decision   20
roles   24
scope of decisions   20
Decision-making *see* Decision
Decision-making procedure
introduction of   25
Declaration   206
capacity, as to   207

Declaration—*continued*
Court powers 207, 413
  capacity, as to 207
  lawfulness of act, as to 207
  medical treatment 130
deputy, by
  form 1423
High Court 29
  inherent jurisdiction 206, 230
  lawfulness of treatment 235
  vulnerable adults 30
interim 627
Dementia, senile
person with 224
Dentist/dental treatment *see* Medical
treatment
Department for Work and Pensions 36
Deposition 640
conduct of examination 640
examiner of the court 641
examiner's fees and expenses 641
hearing, use at 642
Practice Direction 746
Deprivation of liberty *see* Liberty,
deprivation of
Deputy
application by (Practice Direction) 699
  list of suitable applications 699
appointment
  Court of Protection powers 212
  failed application, guuidance on
    costs 1691
appointment of 208, 413, 416
  application procedure 367
  'best interests'
    considerations for Court 212
  cancellation of EPA, after 1654
  change of 1653
  Code of Practice guidance 212
  eligibility 213
  EPA registration as alternative, final
    order on 1650
  local authority (property and
    affairs) 1622
  order precedents (property and
    affairs) 1619
  refusal of permission 1626
  register of orders 330
  revocation 215
  supervision fee 824
  two or more 213
complaint about, Public Guardian
  powers 817
decision of
  acts contrary to 239
  conflict with
    other decision-maker 135,
    214, 404
decision-making powers 212
declaration
  form 1423

Deputy—*continued*
discharge where capacity
  is regained 1625
expenses 213
financial
  appointment after cancellation of
    EPA 1654
  appointment for large brain injury
    award, order for 1657
  change of deputy 1653
investment powers 213, 217
joint deputies 213
personal welfare, for
  order refusing permission 1626
powers, restriction of 212, 213, 418
  capacity, where P has 214
  excluded powers 214
  life sustaining treatment, as to 214
property, powers as to 213
public authority, remuneration 774
receiver, replacing 216, 358
remuneration of 665
reports 213
  content 816
  extension of time 815
  final report 816
representations and complaints on 330
restraint, conditions for 214
safeguards
  appointment of
    circumstances for, cases 1713
  security 213, 677
  security bond (property and affairs), case
    on size of 1711
  solicitor as, remuneration 773
  supervision fees 332
Detention *see* Mental disorder; Liberty,
deprivation of
Directions 303, 629
checklist 1631
pro-forma orders 1632
  'adult care' case 1640
  first directions order (family dispute
    as to residence and
    contact) 1637
  local authority personal welfare
    application 1644
  multi-purpose order 1632
Disability
adjustments duty 45
attitudes to, change to 33
judicial training 54
protected characteristic 43
terminology, use of appropriate 34
Disability discrimination prohibition
associations 47
court within scope 47
harassment 46
new legislation 44
victimisation 46

Disclosure 308, 500, 650
  failure, consequences of 653
  general 650, 651
  general and specific 308
  inspection right 652
  meaning 650
  non-party, by, costs 916
  non-party, to, order for 593
  ongoing duty 651
  privacy right, balance with 308
  specific 650, 651
Discrimination
  direct 44
  Equality Act 42
  Equality Act 2010
    overview 43
  forms of 32
  harmonisation 43, 46
  indirect 45
  legal services 54
  protected characteristics 43
  protection 46
Disposal of property
  cessation of lack of capacity, on 679
Dispute resolution *see also* Alternative
    dispute resolution
  Public Guardian, role 334
Doctor
  assessment of capacity by 107, 108
    record of 113
    witness to will 109
  certificate provider for LPA 186
  Special Visitor, as 346
Document
  court 295, 590
    editing information in 594
    electronic 590, 680
    fee for copy 829
    general provisions 680
    inspection and copies 296, 593
    inspection and copies, non-party 593
    personal details, omission of 296
    Public Guardian, copy to 594
    service address 296
    slip rule 295
    verification by statement of truth 296
  disclosure 308
  exhibiting 738
  filing *see* Filing
  inspection 309
  service *see also* Service 599
  verification by statement of truth 591

Elderly person
  mental health legislation, relevance
    to 268
  senile dementia, with 224
Electro-convulsive therapy (ECT) 140,
    141
Electronic document 590, 680

Electronic service 685
Empowerment, need for 37
  balance with protection 37
Enduring power of attorney (EPA) *see*
    Power of attorney
Enforcement
  writ of execution 999
Enforcement powers 315, 978
  Practice Direction 782
  rules 671
Equal consideration principle 96, 116
Error
  order, in 596
  procedural, Court power to waive 599
Ethnic communities
  attitudes in 35
  judicial training 54
European Union
  evidence provision 748
  service in, Practice Direction 1009
Evidence 305
  affidavit 638
  Court control 306, 635
  Court power to direct information
    provision 639
  deposition 640
    conduct of examination 640
    examiner of the court 641
    examiner's fees and expenses 641
    hearing, use at 642
    notice of intention to file 1497
  European Union member states,
    between 748
  expert *see* Expert
  hearsay, admissibility 305
    case 1692
  medical *see also* Assessment; Doctor;
    Expert
  medical, as to incapacity 385
  notarial act or instrument 639
  Official Solicitor, for, of incapacity 351
  outside the jurisdiction 642
  Practice Direction 736
  video link 637
    guidance (PD) 743
  witness *see also* Witness 636
  witness statement 306, 637
Examiner
  fees 751
Excluded decisions 139, 424
Execution
  stay of 1003
  writ of 999
Exhibits 738
Expenditure
  necessary goods and services, on 138,
    406
Expert *see also* Doctor; Lawyer 307
  assessment of capacity by 108, 110
  directions from Court 649

Expert—*continued*
discussions between 648
evidence
    Court power to restrict 646
    duty to restrict 646
    general requirement as to form 647
meaning 645
Official Solicitor instructing 353
overriding duty to court 646
Practice Direction 759
report 645, 647, 648
    disclosure, use after 648
single joint
    Court power as to 649
    instructions 649
written questions to 647

Family member(s)
carer, as *see* Carer
Family relationship
decision on 139, 424
    LPA, under 166
Fees 310, 313, 449, 451, 822
Court of Protection 827
exemptions 829
exemptions and reductions 314
list 830
Public Guardian, for work of 335
registration of power of attorney 332
supervision of deputies 332
Filing 590
checklist 1632
date 680
fax, by 680
Final orders
precedents 1649
Financial decision *see also* Property and
affairs, decision on 77
change of deputy for 1653
final order as to capacity in regard
    to 1649
Forms 295
Court of Protection 287
permission form 299
Fostering placement
deprivation of liberty issues 1700
Fraud
LPA
    objection to registration ground 201
    protection of donee from 184, 219
Funding arrangement
additional liability, information for 939
costs order relating to 901
meaning 899

Gift
application relating to, permission
    for 298
lifetime, 'best interests' case 1674

Gift—*continued*
LPA, power to make under 160, 410
    Court authority for 222
Goods and services *see* Payment
for goods and services
Guardianship order
powers broadened 266
Guidance 240

Hague Convention *see* International
Harassment 46
Health care 225
acts in connection with 128, 239
    excluded acts 139
Health care decision 77, 225
application
    form 1369
    information in support 1400
Court jurisdiction 225
LPA, and 164
Healthcare *see also* Medical treatment
Hearing 302, 628, 631
absence of incapacitated party 631
checklist 1632
fees 829
judge for 728
Practice Direction 731
private general rule 304, 632, 1695
    waiver 633
public, Court order for 633
public, order for
    case 1695
reporting restrictions 732
supplementary 634
taking part in 631
Help at Court
personal welfare decision 312
High Court
declaration as to lawfulness of
    treatment 235
inherent juridiction
    statutory jurisdiction, interaction
        with 30, 1720
inherent jurisdiction
    medical treatment 230, 231, 232, 234
    interaction with MCA
        jurisdiction 247
transitional (proceedings commenced
    before 1 Oct 2007) 831
Hospital
detention in, authorisation 274, 460
    assessments for 467
    best interests requirement 275
    form of 472
    ineligible persons 275, 515
    lack of capacity requirement 275
    negligent acts 460
    powers of Court 419, 460
    representative for patient 281, 854
    restrictions requiring 271

Hospital—*continued*
   detention in, authorisation—*continued*
     standard procedure   275, 276, 279,
                    464, 860
     urgent procedure   278, 478
     valid refusal prevents   276
   long-stay accommodation in, IMCA
     instruction prior to   250, 432
   mental disorder admission *see also*
     Mental disorder   265
   supervisory body   503
Human rights   48
   breach
     proceedings against public
      authority   50
     remedies for   50
   compatibility of MCA 2005   70
   Convention rights   48
   court as public authority   50
   Court of Protection, application to   51
   declaration of incompatibility   295
   deprivation of liberty   269
     compatibility of DOLS
      safeguards with Art 5   1709
     MCA amendment
      for compliance   270
     meaning   271
   discrimination prohibition   42
   interpretation of Convention   51
   margin of appreciation   50
   medical treatment, relevance to   233
   person lacking capacity   51
     involvement in court proceedings   71
   private and family life, justification
     for interference   1688
   procedure under rules   627
   proportionality principle   50
   public body determining civil
     rights or obligations   51
   Public Guardian, application to   51

Ill-treatment or neglect   442
   background   142
   ill-treatment   144
   neglect, wilful   144
   offences
     creation of   142
     scope   143
IMCA *see* Independent mental capacity
   advocate
Impairment, mental   94
   diagnostic hurdle   95
   establishing   95
   scope of   95
Inability to make decision *see* Decision
Incapacitated person
   meaning   588
   protection of identity of   633
Incapacity
   test for *see* Capacity

**Independent mental capacity
   advocate**   498
   accommodation provision by local
     authority   434
   accommodation provision by NHS
     body   432
   appointment   430, 435, 437
     circumstances for   130
     eligibility   249
     exceptions   439
     limitation on duty   438
   certificate provider for LPA   186
   duty to instruct,
     circumstances for expansion
      of   439
   establishment   248
   functions   249, 431, 498
     restriction of   499
   Official Solicitor, inter-relationship
     with   355
   powers   251
   role, expansion of   252
   serious medical treatment   432
Information provision
   Court power to direct   639
Inherent jurisdiction *see* High Court
Injunction
   interim   626
Inspection
   court records   593
   disclosed document   652
Interim remedy   290, 302, 626
International   455
   habitual residence, and recognition of US
     order   1697
   Hague Convention on Protection of
     Adults   523, 1735
     applicable law   526
     certificates   530
     commencement and ratification   1735
     cross-border co-operation   530
     example issues within scope of   1736
     mutual recognition and
      enforcement   528, 1697
     non-Convention countries, position
      in   359
     protective measures   524
     UK, within   1736
     private international law rules   1736
Interpreter   21, 57
Investigation and report
   interim order for   1625
Investigations Unit   334
Ireland   329
   General Solicitor for Minors and
     Wards of Court   354

Jewish community   35
Joinder
   party, as   623

Judge
  declaration as to capacity, regional judge
      making 207
  dual jurisdiction, sitting in 72, 208, 247
Judges 589
  Court of Protection 288, 443
      Practice Direction 728
  nominated 247, 320
  training through Judicial
      Studies Board 54
Judgment *see also* Order
  enforcement 995
Judicial Appointments Commission 286
Judicial review
  interaction with MCA jurisdiction 248
Judicial Studies Board 286
Judiciary
  allocation of cases 289
  appointments 286
  nomination for Court of Protection 288,
      289
  responsibility for training, guidance and
      deployment 286
Jurisdiction
  competent authority under Hague
      Convention on Protection of
      Adults 525
  Court *see* Court of Protection
  disputing 630
      Practice Direction 730

Lack of capacity *see* Capacity
Lasting power of attorney
  registration
      objection procedure
          form 1437
  accounts and records 221
  application to Court 222
      exercise of powers, as to 222
      Practice Direction 699
      service requirements 617
  appointment of donee 174, 408
  authority under
      scope and restrictions 157, 160, 164,
          409
  best interests 158, 159, 165
  capacity
      certificate of 184, 185
      donor lacking 155, 158, 223
      execution, at time of 188, 219
      presumption 155
      welfare decision, and 165
  complaints 224, 330
  content 173
  Court powers 217, 420, 421
      circumstances for 217
      exercise of own volition 222
      scope 217
      specific 218
  creation 154, 190
      first stage 190

Lasting power of attorney—*continued*
  creation—*continued*
      form 820
      second stage 192
  defective form 170, 218, 509
  definition 154, 407
  directions to donee 221, 421
  donee's behaviour, challenge ground 201,
          220
      discretion of Court 220
  drafting and execution 167
  fees 822
  fiduciary duty 158
  form, prescribed 169, 170, 507, 820
      attorney's statement 188
      certificate provider's statement 184
      donor's statement 174
      failure to comply 170, 509
      immaterial difference 218
      parts 173
  fraud or undue influence
      objection to registration ground 201
      protection of donee from 184, 219
  functions 155
  gifts 160, 410
      Court authority for 222
      power to make 161
  health care decision 164
  intervention by Court of Protection 201
  joint attorneys 174
      'jointly and severally' 175
      professional attorney, one is 175
  legal proceedings 163
  life sustaining treatment 165, 166
      specific provision for 180
  maintenance of others 160
  meaning and effect determination 220
  more than one attorney 174
  parties 154
  practical difficulties 156
  property and affairs, decisions on 155,
          158
  protection of donee 412
  protection of donor
      flexible drafting for 156
      levels of 181
  Public Guardian, role of 223, 514
  records of alterations 514
  register of 330
  registration 192
      application 804
      attorney's status prior to 195
      cancellation 193, 513
      cancellation costs 1689
      Court powers where objection to 199
      criterion 155
      evidence 513
      fee 823
      notices 196

Lasting power of attorney—*continued*
  registration—*continued*
    notification of application to
      register   182
    objection procedure   198, 203, 221,
       512, 678
    procedure   194, 197, 366, 509
    refusal   219
    withdrawal of objection   221
  relief of donee from liability   221
  remuneration of donee   665
  representations   330
  restraint   165
  restrictions   164, 409
  revocation   200, 219, 411
    misbehaviour of donee   220
    partial   514
  safeguards   181
  search of register, fee   824
  signature, witness to   181
  trust of land   163
  two donees   169
    revocation of one power   219
  validity, determination by Court   200,
     218, 420
  visit to donee   347
  welfare decisions   155, 156, 164
    limitations   164, 409
    problem areas   166
    separate LPA for   169
Law Commission
  best interests proposal   91
  capacity presumption and proof
    recommendations   87
  consultation papers and Report   66
  decision-making, proposals   88
  unwise decisions, recommendations   89
Lawyer
  assessment of capacity
    record of   114
  certificate provider for LPA   186
  change of solicitor   310
  conflict of interests problems   38
  elderly client practices, development
    of   39
  expertise in law on disabled people   38
  role of   37
Learning disability   224
  assessment of capacity   111
  mental health legislation, relevance
    to   267
  regaining capacity   118
Legal background
  declaratory jurisdiction of High Court   29
  incapacity, imprecision of terms   31
  parens patriae jurisdiction   29, 229
Legal competence *see* Capacity   21
Legal help
  personal welfare decision   312
Legal publishing initiatives   38

Legal Representation
  personal welfare decision   312
Legal services
  discrimination prohibition   54
Legal Services Commission
  costs against   946
  costs of LSC funded client   913, 948
  revocation or discharge of funding
    certificate   660
Legislation
  amendments (minor and
    consequential)   833
  background   31
  community care   40
  consequential amendments and
    repeals   359
  draft Bill   69
  Mental Capacity Act 2005   69
    amendments   360
    assessment of   72
    essential provisions   78
    human rights compatibility   70
    MHA 1983 compared   267
    principles, statement in   85
    review of implementation   80
    scope of   77
  Scotland   68, 328
    comparison   85
Less restrictive alternative   92
  principle of   93
Liability
  protection from, permitted acts   239, 403
Liberty, deprivation of
  application (DoL)
    Practice Direction   627
  authorisation   239, 265, 274, 460
    effect and duration of urgent   279
    monitoring of provisions   282
    negligent acts   460
    standard   270, 276, 279
    urgent   270, 278
  best interests issues   272
  'Bournewood Gap' case   269
  checklist   272
    jurisprudence, subject to   273
  Code of Practice guidance   270, 272
  Court power   274
    pending order, when lawful   274
  hospital or care home
    guidance to local authorities   129
  hospital or care home, detention in   274,
     435, 436
    assessment for standard
      authorisation   491
    practicalities   283
    representative for patient   281, 854
    review by Court   282
    review of standard authorisation   484
    safeguards   284

Liberty, deprivation of—*continued*
hospital or care home, detention
in—*continued*
standard authorisation 275, 276, 279,
464
standard procedure 860
suspension of standard
authorisation 482
transport to 274
urgent authorisation 278, 478
urgent procedure 278
ineligibility, where MHA applies 274,
414
lawful, circumstances 270
life sustaining treatment, for 274, 403
meaning and identification of 270, 1701,
1702
cumulative effect of restrictions 273
degree and intensity of
restrictions 272
elements 271
factors 271
placement in domestic setting 1700
position under MCA 2005
MHA 2007 amendments 270
restraint *see* Restraint
restriction on 274, 402
review by Court 419, 460
safeguards 419, 435, 436, 460, 515
compatibility of DOLS with Art
5 1709
Life sustaining treatment *see also* Medical
treatment
advance directive 246, 423
best interests 118, 238, 246
decision-maker, motivation of 119
deprivation of liberty pending Court
order 274
Deputy's powers restricted 214
liberty deprivation for 403
meaning 400
PVS patient 130
refusal 254
advance decision 254, 255
withholding or withdrawing 244
Litigant in person 55
assistance for (McKenzie friend) 56
costs 918
disadvantages faced by 55
lay representative 56
Litigation
capacity for 102, 1677, 1680
Litigation friend 309, 653
appointment as 386
certificate of suitability 385, 1477
cessation of appointment 657, 658, 885
change in 656, 883
court order appointing 655, 877, 882
application for 892
supplementary 657, 884

Litigation friend—*continued*
expenses 890, 897
incapacity of party ceases, procedure
on 658
Official Solicitor as 351, 353
Practice Direction 761, 891
prevention from acting as 656
requirement for 654, 877
service on 602
stage of proceedings for 879
statement of truth 591
without court order 654
procedure 881
Litigation friend, requirement for 382
effect of not having 383
Local authority *see also* Social
services departments
accommodation by, IMCA instruction
prior to 251, 434
appointment as deputy (property and
affairs) 1622
contact issues, maturing child 227
deprivation of liberty, duty to protect
individual from 1701
party, naming as 1696
personal welfare application,
directions order 1644
report, Court power to require 291
residence disputed, detention in care
home 866
residential care, guidance on removal
to 129
Lord Chancellor
administration of courts system 286
Codes of Practice *see* Code of Practice
Concordat with Lord Chief Justice 285
constitutional reforms affecting,
overview 285
duties relevant to capacity
jurisdiction 285
Public Guardian Board appointments,
powers 332
Public Guardian's officers and staff,
provision of 330
recasting of office of 285
Rules of Court, power to make 291
Lord Chief Justice 285
responsibilities 286
LPA *see* Lasting power of attorney

Marriage/divorce
excluded decision 139, 424
McKenzie friend 56
Medical practitioner *see* Doctor;
Psychiatrist
Medical research 258
approval 427
carer, consultation of 428
clinical trials 259, 426
adult lacking capacity, consent
for 260

Medical research—*continued*
general principle at common law 259
intrusive 426
loss of capacity during 430
MCA provisions 260, 426
pre-conditions and safeguards (adult
   lacking capacity) 261, 426, 427,
428, 429
Medical treatment
acts in connection with, authority
   for 127, 239, 244, 403
advance decision refusing, effect of 132,
168, 422, 423
authorisation by High Court 233, 234,
235
   legal background 229
   principles 230
best interests 232, 244
common law cases, relevance of 235
consent to 229
   advance refusal 253, 258
   assessment of capacity for 107, 113
   Court, by 240
   LPA, under 164
   mental disorder 425
Court application, non-serious cases 244
Court jurisdiction 225, 240, 241
   Practice Direction 242
declaration as to lawfulness 130, 208
deprivation of liberty pending Court
   order 274
dispute as to 244
experimental or innovative 243
force required 243
inherent jurisdiction 230, 231, 232
   interaction with MCA
      jurisdiction 247
injunctive relief 231
issues arising 229
liability protection 127, 403
life sustaining treatment 118
organ or bone marrow donation 243
pregnancy termination 243
principle of necessity and 125, 239
serious medical treatment 129
   categories 243
   Court application 241, 242, 702
   declaration 206
   IMCA, instruction of 250, 432
   Official Solicitor as litigation
      friend 353
   Practice Direction 241, 242, 702
   urgent case 242
statutory framework for capacity
   issues 235
withdrawal or withholding of 234, 242,
244
   declaration required 130
young person 105

Mental capacity *see also* Capacity
assessment of 22
   confidentiality issues 26
evidence of 22
meaning 22
**Mental Capacity Implementation
  Programme (MCIP)**
booklets 84
Mental disability *see* Capacity; Impairment,
mental
Mental disorder
admission to hospital
   assessment, for 265
   'compliant' patient 270
   compulsory 265
   reviews and appeal 266
   treatment, for 266
community treatment order 266
compulsory detention of patient 265
   authorisation procedure 275
   medical treatment excluded
      under MCA 2005 268
consent issues, person with 267
definition, as amended 265
definition, previous law 24
treatment decision 140
   discharge 140
Mental health treatment
decisions related to 140, 425
detention authorisation, assessment
   for 276, 279
person lacking capacity, for 267
Mental illness, person with 224
compulsory detention under MHA 232

National Audit Office Report
Public Guardianship Office, on 326
Visitor deployment, on 342
National Health Service 36
IMCA, instruction of 250
report, Court power to require 291
Nearest relative 36
Needle phobia
Court authorisation of treatment in case
   of 130
Neglect *see* Ill-treatment or neglect
Negligence
protection of s 5, and 132, 239
Negligent acts
managing authority of hospital or care
   home 460
Next friend
Official Solicitor as 351
Non-party
costs orders 665, 916
document inspection and copies 593
Northern Ireland 329
Official Solicitor 354
service in 1009
Notification
acknowledgment of 620

Notification—*continued*
application form issue 618, 695
checklist 1631
form 1431
incapacitated person, of 297, 300, 604
application form issue 618
certificate of 608
circumstances 605

Offences
background 142
Office of Public Guardian (OPG) *see*
Public Guardian
Official Solicitor
address 349
administration 350
appointment for incapacitated
person 347
evidence of incapacity needed 351
instruction of experts 353
'last resort' policy 351
background 349
case load 355
statistics 350
costs 355, 665
deprivation of liberty, annual reviews and
role in 355
deputy of last resort 356
incapacity services
advice 351
assistance in civil and family
cases 352
consultation prior to
involvement 352
Court of Protection work 353
representation 351
welfare cases 353
merger of Offices with 349
other jurisdictions 353
personal welfare decisions, involvement
with 225
present encumbent 350
public funding issues 354
role 350
personal welfare applications 352
scope in Court of Protection 353
status 348
vision statement 351
Order
clerical error, correction of 596
court authentication 590
Court powers 596
own initiative 598
directions *see* Directions
enforcement 978, 995
final 1649
capacity in regard to financial
affairs 1649
discharge from jurisdiction 1651
EPA or deputy, decision as to 1650

Order—*continued*
final—*continued*
financial deputy, change of 1653
inspection and copies 593
interim 627
investigation and report 1625
sale of property 1624
meaning 588
precedent standard orders 1619
reconsideration of, circumstances 631
service on Public Guardian 595
urgent, draft on disk required 587
Organ donation 243
Overriding objective 293, 583
active management to further 293, 585
duty of parties 585
Overseas territories
service in 1009

Parens patriae jurisdiction 29
children, exists in relation to 229
Parties 300, 621
identification of
checklist 1631
local authority, case on 1696
incapacitated person 300
joinder 301, 623
form 1454
local authority, case on naming of 1696
person lacking capacity becoming 602
persons bound as 623
removal application 624
serious medical treatment
application 241
Patient
previous term 321
Payment for goods and services 136, 405,
406
expenditure, methods of 138, 406
legal responsibility 137
settlement of bill by carer 137
'necessary' 136, 405
Penal notice 315
Permission *see also* Appeal; Application
application to court for 612
notification 613
application to court, for 240
form 1407
circumstances for 608, 616
no permission required 609
decision
appeal against 614
service of order 614
form
court authentication 590
statement of truth 591
Practice Direction 690
Permitted acts 127, 239
exclusions 139
limitations 132, 404

Persistent vegetative state
patient in, Court reference for withdrawal
   of treatment   130, 234, 242
Personal care
acts in connection with   128
excluded acts   139
Personal injury
Official Solicitor involvement   355
settlement
   choice of jurisdiction for   217
   Court powers   211
Personal welfare decision   77
application
   form   1369
   information in support   1400
application procedure   369
best interests   244
costs, general rule   311, 662
Court jurisdiction   224, 225
   'personal care'   226
   scope   225
Court power to make   208, 414, 415,
     419, 460
declaration   206
deputy for
   appointment, order for   1627
   refusal of permission
     for appointment   1626
inherent jurisdiction of High Court   231
jurisdiction
   scope   415
local authority application,
   directions order   1644
LPA, and   156, 164
   alternatives to LPA   168
Official Solicitor's involvement   352
public funding availability   312
types arising   229
Power of attorney
assessment of capacity for   107
background   145
best interests principle   124
decision made by, precedence of   135,
     404
enduring   31, 147, 532
   abolition   153
   application to Court   618, 699
   cancellation and appointment of
     financial deputy   1654
   cancellation of registration   541
   capacity for execution (case)   1667,
     1668
   deputy appointment as alternative,
     final order on   1650
   drawbacks and failings   150
   existing remain effective   153, 203,
     357, 358
   invalid/revoked power, protection
     provisions   541
   maintenance of others   160

Power of attorney—*continued*
enduring—*continued*
   registration   149, 150, 357, 365, 810
     form   1443
     objection to   712
   Regulations   810
   safeguards   148
   search of register, fee   824
   transitional   357, 358
   validity (case)   1715, 1716, 1718
   visit to donor, historical   340
fees   822
incapacity of donor   145, 147
lasting *see* Lasting power of attorney
limitations   145
meaning   145
two jurisdictions co-existing, complexity
   of   358
Practice Direction   240, 293, 316, 448, 692
bodies responsible for   286
first Practice Directions   293
welfare and medical cases   240
Pregnancy termination   243
Premises
discrimination prohibition
   adjustments duty for disabled
     people   45
   disposal and management   47
Presumption *see* Capacity
Principle of necessity   125
Principles   84, 396
fifth   93
first   87
fourth   92
health and welfare issues, influence
   on   236
second   88
statement in MCA 2005   85
third   89
Private and family life
justification for interference with   1688
Pro bono representation   934
Proceedings *see also* Application
commencement of   299, 614
Professional *see also* Expert
record of assessment of capacity   113
Property and affairs, decision on   225
application
   form   1369
   information in support   1382
costs, general rule   311, 662
Court jurisdiction   225
Court powers   208, 209, 415
LPA, under   155, 158
supplementary provisions   520
Protected beneficiary   163, 382
Protected party   163, 206
compromise or settlement, approval
   of   886
control of money recovered for   888

Protected party—*continued*
High Court procedure 370
investment on behalf of 896
litigation friend, requirement for *see also*
Litigation friend 382, 877, 879
effect of not having 383
meaning 588
CPR 872
money recovered for, control of 895
procedural guide 370
service on 601
settlement or compromise for 893
Protection, sources of 36
Psychiatrist
Special Visitor, appointment as 347
Public bodies
discrimination, duty to eliminate etc 44
Public funding *see also* Legal
Services Commission 37, 312
family member 313
financial eligibility 313
Official Solicitor's involvement 354
Public Guardian
Annual Report 332, 454
consultation paper on OPG's work 80
contact address 331
court document, copy of 594
court order, service on 595
dispute resolution 334
enduring power of attorney register 812
fees 335, 822
functions 330, 451
application processing, regulatory
power 336
categories of 330
court application in connection
with 331
Regulations 812
regulatory power of Lord
Chancellor 331
interview with incapacitated person 331
Investigations Unit 334
location of offices 336
LPA
administrative functions 223
complaint on donee's conduct to 222,
224
notification duty 196
objection to registration 197, 203
registration of 197, 812
role in relation to 223
office
address 331
office of
creation by MCA 2005 79, 329, 451
former office compared 333
recognition and funding 330
role 334
officers and staff, provision of 330

Public Guardian—*continued*
partnerships with
other organisations 335
powers 331
publication of information 330
records, examination and copies of 331
registers
duties 812
relationship with Court of
Protection 335
report, Court power to require 291
Practice Direction 754
representations and complaints to 330
investigation of 334
role 333
elements 333
enhanced 336
scrutiny and review of 332
technology initiatives 335
Visitor accountability to 348
Public Guardian Board 332
Annual Report 333
creation by MCA 2005 453
members 332
Public Guardianship Office
Change Programme 325
advisers 326
creation of 324
critical analysis of functions 327
difficulties encountered by 325
former administrative arm 321
management plan introduced 328
Mission Statement 325
National Audit Office Report 326
new procedure introduced 328
Visitors, reform of 343
Public Trust Office 322
criticisms 322
demise of 324
functions 322
reform options 323
Public Trustee
background 349
merger with Official Solicitor 349
present encumbent 350
Publication
Code of Practice 84
'easy read' booklet of MCA 2005 84
Publicity
Court power to authorise 633
local authority, case on naming of 1696
media involvement, case with 1695
restrictions 304, 593
identity of incapacitated person 633

Receiver
appointment 147
Deputy replacing 216, 358
new regime 216
old regime 216

Receiver—*continued*
transitional provisions   358, 545, 675
  Practice Direction   784
records and accounts   358
Reconsideration of order   303
Record
assessment of capacity   113
  formal report or certificate   114
professional records   113
examination and copy for preparation of
  report   291
Records
Public Guardian power to copy   331
Visitor's inspection and copy
  powers   347
Reform   66
health and welfare powers of High
  Court   235
Lord Chancellor, to office of   285
Refusal
assessment of capacity, to undergo   113
Registration
enduring power of attorney *see also*
  Power of attorney   365
lasting power of attorney *see* Lasting
  power of attorney
Relative
dispute among family members, Court
  role   227
nearest *see* Nearest relative
Religious beliefs
best interests checklist   120
Report   307
Court power to require   291, 445, 644
  order for   757
  Practice Direction   754
  sources   345
expert   645, 647
  contents   648
  disclosure, use after   648
records, examination and copy
  for preparation of   291
written questions   645
Reporting restrictions *see also*
Publicity   732
Representation
change of solicitor   310
Official Solicitor, by   351
public funding   312
Representative
detention in hospital or care home,
  for   281, 494, 854
Research
medical *see* Medical research
Residence dispute
detention in care home   866
Residence, change of
safeguard   130
Residence, habitual
case on   1697
Residential home *see* Care home

Residential unit
deprivation of liberty issues   1700
Respondent   621
Respondent's notice
form   1510
Responding to application   620
Practice Direction   697
Restraint   132, 404
circumstances for lawful   239
deprivation of liberty,
  whether amounts to   134, 271, 273
Deputy, conditions for restraining
  act   214
Review
implementation of MCA 2005   80
  Memorandum   81
Rules of Court   291, 447, 581
bodies responsible for   286
definitions   587
dispensing with, Court power   598
first rules made   292, 581
former Court rules, uncertainties of   292
interpretation   294
overriding objective   583
policy aim   582
Rules Committee
  establishment   74
  recommendations   74

Sale of property
Court power   210
interim order   1624
Same sex partner *see also* Civil
partnership   53
Scotland
accounts and funds   1758
adult incapacity law   1745
  characteristics of   1746
  literature   1747
adult's primary carer   1751
best interests concept in   91
Court of Session   1745
  role   1750
courts (civil)   1745
  website   1745
definitions   1753
financial guardianship   1758
guardianship   1761, 1763
  appointment of guardians   1763
  provisions applicable to Scottish and
    non-Scottish guardians   1763
ill-treatment and neglect offences   1752
incapacitated person moving to   354
intervention order   1761, 1762
  guardianship, inter-action with   1762
jurisdictional issues   1747
jurisdictional issues with England and
  Wales, law for   1735, 1736

Scotland—*continued*
legislation in   68, 328
    background   1744
    comparison   85
limitation of liability   1751
local authority functions   1751
management of finances (residents in
    'authorised
    establishments')   1760
medical treatment, authorisation of   1761
Mental Welfare Commission   1751
nearest relative   1751
'no intervention' and 'least restrictive
    option' provisions   93
no Official Solicitor in   354
overview   1743
powers of attorney
    1 Jan 1991–1 April 2001
       execution   1756
    applicable law   1757
    formalities   1755
    general law   1755
    overview   1754
    revocation   1756
    safeguards   1754
    terminology   1754
principles, statement in Act   1752
Public Guardian   1750
    investigative functions   1750
service in   1009
Sheriff Court   1745
    jurisdiction and role   1748
sheriff, powers   1757
trust law, use for incapacity
    matters   1764
wills, issues on   1764
Search of register   812
application fee   824
Security
Deputy giving   677
Public Guardian receipt of   330, 813
rules   677
Security bond
deputy for property and affairs, case on
    size of   1711
Serious medical treatment *see* Medical
    treatment
Service   599
acknowledgment of   620
address   296
child or protected party, on   601
company or corporation, on   686
court, by   686
deemed   602
dispensing with   604
electronic   685
litigation friend, on   602
methods   297, 600
out of jurisdiction   604
    Practice Direction   1009

Service—*continued*
out of jurisdiction—*continued*
    Rules   1005
    Service Regulation   1008, 1016
provisions for   296
substituted   602
who serves   297
Settlement
capacity of party (case)   1679
child or protected party, for   893
Court power to make orders   211
    investments   211
Practice Direction   706
Sexual relations
excluded decision   139, 424
Skeleton argument
form   1520
Slip rule   295
Social care
acts in connection with, authority
    for   127, 403
consent to provision of services   107
monitoring of   82
Social services departments   36
Social worker
certificate provider for LPA   186
Solicitor *see also* Lawyer
change
    notice of   1494
change of   659, 660, 661
    order that has ceased to act   660
    Practice Direction   764
    public funding certificate revocation
       or discharge, on   660
deputy, as, remuneration   773
duty as to assessment of capacity to
    execute EPA (case)   1668
fixed costs   772
removal   660
service on   600
Standard authorisation for deprivation of
    liberty *see also* Hospital   464
Statement of truth   296, 591
form of   682
signing   682
Sterilisation
non-therapeutic, Court reference for   130
Stop notice   993
Stop order   991
Strategic Investment Board   324
Success fee   899
costs order   901
Supervised community treatment   140
Supervisory body   503
Support services   36
basing of buck between   37

Telephone hearing   587
Testamentary capacity
test of   103, 107

Time
  computation rules   589
Time–limit   617
Time-limit
  appeal permission application filing   669
  Court power to vary   596, 617
Transfer of proceedings
  family courts, to and from   97, 235, 289,
                                           851
Transitional   316, 545, 831
  Practice Direction   784
  rules   675
Tribunal
  First-tier   266
    appeal to Upper Tribunal   266
Trust corporation
  donee of lasting power of attorney   174,
                                           408
Trust for land
  lasting power of attorney,
        powers under   163
Trustee
  application to appoint or discharge
        (Practice Direction)   709
  special undertaking   1459

Undertaking
  trustees, by   1459
Undue influence   27
  LPA, protection of donee from   184, 188,
                                           219
  presumption   28
Unrepresented party *see* Litigant in person
Urgent application   717
Urgent authorisation for deprivation of
        liberty   478
Urgent authoristaion for deprivation of
        liberty *see also* Hospital

Verification of documents   591
Victimisation   46
Video link evidence   637
  guidance (PD)   743
Visitor   454
  accountability   348
  appointment   345
  Association of Independent   348
  General   345, 455
    accountability   346
    employment status   345
    risk-based visits   346
    self-employed   346
  historical background   337
    confidentiality of
          Visitor's reports   341
    General Visitor   337, 338, 339
    General Visitor's reports   340
    Legal Visitor   337, 339
    medical examinations   339
    medical reports   338

Visitor—*continued*
  historical background—*continued*
    Medical Visitor   337, 338
    visits   338
  National Audit Office Report   342
  powers   347
  protection, financial and legal   348
  Public Guardian direction   330
  records, inspection and copies   347
  reform   341
    interim   343
    purpose of visits considered and
          reviewed   344
  Regulations   818
  report
    increased jurisdiction for   347
  report, Court power to require   291, 347
  Special   346, 454
    examination of patient, power   291
    report, circumstances for   347
    role   347
Voting
  decision on   426
Vulnerable adult
  declaration, High Court power   30, 247
  safeguarding, protocol   334

Wales
  directions by National Assembly   500
Wasted costs   450, 918
  right to be heard   939
Welfare decision *see* Personal welfare
        decision
Will
  assessment of capacity for   103, 107
    golden rule   109
  best interests   210
  Court order for execution   210
    best interests formula   210
  Practice Direction   706
  statutory
    'best interests', case   1673, 1726
    example   708
    jurisdiction, case   1720, 1721, 1723
Wishes and feelings
  account of   122, 159
  appointment of joint
        attorneys (case)   1670
  best interests checklist   120
  weight to be given to   122
    guidance   237
  written statement, medical treatment *see*
        also Advance statement   257
Witness
  certificate of failure/refusal to attend
        before examiner   1481
  deposition   640
    conduct of examination   640
    examiner of the court   641
    examiner's fees and expenses   641

Witness—*continued*
  deposition—*continued*
    use at hearing   642
    enforcing attendance   641
    evidence   636
      video link, by   637
      written   637
Witness statement   306, 591, 637
  form   637, 1485
  Practice Direction   740
Witness summary   638
Witness summons   306, 639
  Practice Direction   753

Written statement *see also* Advance
  statement
Young person   97
  aged 16 or 17   105
    presumption of capacity   105
  care home placement, deprivation of
    liberty case   1702
  competence and capacity   104
    interaction   105
  Court jurisdiction   209
  electro-convulsive therapy   141
  medical and dental treatment   105
    best interests   105
  medical treatment decision   235

FIXED COSTS IN THE COURT OF PROTECTION

Date in effect: 1 May 2009

Category I	Amount £825 (plus VAT)
Category II	Amount £370 (plus VAT)
Category III	Annual management fee where the court appoints a professional deputy for property and affairs, payable on the anniversary of the court order For the first year: Amount £1,440 (plus VAT) For the second and subsequent years: Amount £1,140 (plus VAT) Provided that, where the net assets of P are below £16,000, the professional deputy for property and affairs may take an annual management fee not exceeding 4.5% of P's net assets on the anniversary of the court order appointing the professional as deputy.
Category IV	Where the court appoints a professional deputy for health and welfare, the deputy may take an annual management fee not exceeding 2.5% of P's net assets on the anniversary of the court order appointing the professional as deputy for health and welfare up to a maximum of £500.
Category V	Amount £225 (plus VAT)
Category VI	Preparation of an HMRC income tax return on behalf of P. Amount £225 (plus VAT)

Remuneration of public authority deputies

Category I	Amount £645 (plus VAT)
Category II	For the first year: Amount £670 (plus VAT) For the second and subsequent years: Amount £565 (plus VAT) Provided that, where the net assets of P are below £16,000, the local authority deputy for property and affairs may take an annual management fee not exceeding 3% of P's net assets on the anniversary of the court order appointing the local authority as deputy Where the court appoints a local authority deputy for health and welfare, the local authority may take an annual management fee not exceeding 2.5% of P's net assets on the anniversary of the court order appointing the local authority as deputy for health and welfare up to a maximum of £500.
Category III	Amount £260 (plus VAT)
Category IV	Amount £185 (plus VAT)

FIXED COSTS IN THE COURT OF PROTECTION

Date in effect: 1 February 2011

	An amount not exceeding
Category I	£850 (plus VAT)
Category II	£385 (plus VAT)

Remuneration of solicitors appointed as deputy for P

	An amount not exceeding
Category III	For the first year: £1,500 (plus VAT) For the second and subsequent years: £1,185 (plus VAT) Where the net assets. of P are below £16,000, the professional deputy for property and affairs may take an annual management fee not exceeding 4.5% of P's net assets. on the anniversary of the court order appointing the professional as deputy.
Category IV	Where the court appoints a professional deputy for personal welfare, the deputy may take an annual management fee not exceeding 2.5% of P's net assets. on the anniversary of the court order appointing the professional as deputy for personal up to a maximum of £500.
Category V	£235 (plus VAT)
Category VI	£235 (plus VAT)

Conveyancing costs

Category VII	A value element of 0.15% of the consideration with a minimum sum of £350 and a maximum sum of £1,500, plus disbursements.

Remuneration of public authority deputies

	An amount not exceeding
Category I	£670
Category II	For the first year: £700
	For the second and subsequent years: £585
	Where the net assets* of P are below £16,000, the local authority deputy for property and affairs may take an annual management fee not exceeding 3% of P's net assets on the anniversary of the court order appointing the local authority as deputy
	Where the court appoints a local authority deputy for personal welfare, the local authority may take an annual management fee not exceeding 2.5% of P's net assets* on the anniversary of the court order appointing the local authority as deputy for personal welfare up to a maximum of £500.
Category III	£270
Category IV	£195